Circular Fare. If you're planning a round trip to Latin America, you're better off booking a

CIRCULAR FARES

Maximise your time and budget with the Iberia Group's flexible Circular Fares.

These unique tailor-made, multi-destination air passes enable you to travel (in a circular direction) from the UK to any number of 36 destinations in North, South and Central America.

For example, you could fly from London - Santiago de Chile - Buenos Aires - Rio de Janeiro - London – from £792.

Basically, you go further and your budget does too!

To find out more, call the Iberia Group on 0171-830 0011 or see your travel agent.

You'll soon realise that our Circular Fares run rings round what other airlines offer.

South
American
Handbook

Ben Box

Footprint Handbooks

The whole Brazilian plain seemed to lie beneath us,
extending away and away until it ended in dim blue
mists upon the farthest sky-line ...
I was still drinking in this wonderful panorama when
the heavy hand of the Professor fell upon my shoulder.
"This way, my young friend," said he; "vestigia nulla
retrorsum. Never look rearwards, but always to our
glorious goal."

Sir Arthur Conan Doyle

2

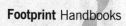

Footprint Handbooks

6 Riverside Court, Lower Bristol Road
Bath BA2 3DZ England
T 01225 469141 F 01225 469461
E mail handbooks@footprint.compulink.co.uk

ISBN 0 900751 74 6 ISSN 0309-4529
CIP DATA: A catalogue record for this book is
available from the British Library

In North America, published by

PASSPORT BOOKS
a division of *NTC Publishing Group*

4255 West Touhy Avenue, Lincolnwood
(Chicago), Illinois 60646-1975, USA
T 847 679 5500 F 847 679 24941
E mail NTCPUB2@AOL.COM

ISBN 0-8442-4904-1
Library of Congress Catalog Card
Number 96-69595
Passport Books and colophon are registered
trademarks of NTC Publishing group

©Footprint Handbooks Limited
73rd Edition
September 1996

First published in 1924 by South American
Publications Ltd

**Every effort has been made to ensure that
the facts in this Handbook are accurate.
However travellers should still obtain
advice from consulates, airlines etc about
current travel and visa requirements and
conditions before travelling. The editors
and publishers cannot accept responsibilty
for any loss, injury or inconvenience,
however caused.**

**Maps - neither the coloured nor the black
and white text maps are intended to have
any political significance.**

Title page quotation taken from Sir Arthur
Conan Doyle, *The Lost World* (taken from
*Traveller's Literary Companion South and
Central America*)

Cover design by Newell and Sorrell;
photography by Tony Stone Images and Dave
Saunders

Production: Design by Mytton Williams;
Secretarial assistance Jane Battell and Sara
Smith; Typesetting by Jo Morgan, Ann
Griffiths and Melanie Mason-Fayon; Maps by
Sebastian Ballard, Alasdair Dawson and Kevin
Feeney; Proofread by Rod Gray.

Printed and bound in Great Britain by
Clays Ltd., Bungay, Suffolk

Contents

DAGHNI RAJASINGAM + SACHIN KAPILA

JAN 1997

4 Rounding up

Acknowledgements, charts, climatic tables, standard time zones, advertisers,
index, maps

The Editor

Ben Box

A doctorate in medieval Spanish and Portugese studies provided very few job prospects for Ben Box, but a fascination for all things Latin. While studying for his degree, Ben travelled extensively in Spain and Portugal. He turned his attention to contemporary Iberian and Latin American affairs in 1980, beginning a career as a freelance writer at that time. He contributed regularly to national newspapers and learned tomes, and after increasing involvement with the *South American Handbook*, became its editor in 1989. Although he has travelled from the US/Mexico border to southern Chile (not all in one go) and in the Caribbean, Ben recognises that there are always more places to explore. He also edits the *Mexico and Central American Handbook* and jointly edits the *Caribbean Islands Handbook* with Sarah Cameron. To seek diversion from a household immersed in Latin America, he plays village cricket in summer and cycles the lanes of Suffolk.

Editorial team

Special thanks go to our regular subeditors Cherry Austin (Brazil), Charlie Nurse (Argentina, Chile, Paraguay, Uruguay), Alan Murphy (Bolivia, Ecuador, Peru), Peter Pollard (Colombia), Amanda Purves (Venezuela) and Rachel Rogers (The Guianas).

Specialist contributors: Sarah Cameron for economics sections; Nigel Gallop for music and dance; Paul Davies of Journey Latin America for details of air transport; John Alton of Strand Cruise and Travel Centre for details of sea transport; John Lewis for information on business travel; Binka and Robin le Breton for motoring; Ashley Rawlings for motorcycling; Hallam Murray for cycling; Hilary Bradt for hiking and trekking; Richard Robinson for world wide radio information; Mark Eckstein of David Bellamy Associates for responsible tourism and Dr David Snashall for health.

Correspondents: We are most grateful to our correspondents in the region, who are thanked at the end of the relevant chapters.

Acknowledgements
Much additional help has been received during the preparation of this edition. All contributions have been tremendously helpful and are duly acknowledged on page 1649.

Preface

IN July 1996, scientists claimed to have discovered the true source of the Amazon. Exactly which glacier or lake high in the Peruvian Andes becomes the world's greatest river has fascinated explorers and experts for many years and no doubt the latest claim will not be the last. Even if an undisputed source were to be found, it would not diminish the marvel of the transition of the Andean stream as it joins so many others on its journey from West to East. The goal of this book is to convey that and other enchantments as it encompasses not only the regions through which the Amazon and its tributaries flow, but also all the other landscapes of South America, the people and their environment.

This year, the format of the text has been redesigned, using two columns and an array of headings to make the information more accessible. The *South American Handbook* is now in the same style as all the Handbooks in the Footprint series and we are confident that this improvement will be appreciated by all our readers. We value highly the comments of users of the Handbook and, as ever, we look forward to receiving news from the road to add to that of our correspondents and the editorial team. All the travellers who have written in the past year are thanked at the end of the book.

At the *Fiesta del Níspero* in Lunahuaná, Peru, in September 1995, the editor was welcomed as an honoured guest by the mayor. The reason for this generosity was that the civic authorities hoped that, through the *Handbook*, more people would come to know Lunahuaná and its attractions. These include white water rafting,

Inca ruins and pisco distilleries in a fertile valley surrounded by barren mountains. That desire reflects the attitude throughout most of Peru to embrace tourism after several difficult years. A similar sentiment was also found in Chubut, in Argentine Patagonia, after the visit of Princess Diana of Wales. Many (but, it has to be said, not all) hoped that she will have raised the profile of the area. Certainly the photographs and television pictures of the Princess in close encounter with whales will have had an impact. (Would that the weather had permitted the editor to get as close to the whales the day after Diana's boat trip.)

It is apparent that several new angles are being offered for tourism in South America at present, among them are *estancia* and mystical tourism. Neither is new in itself. Farms in Uruguay, for instance, have been offering accommodation and tours for several years now, while mystical tourism has been in vogue to some degree ever since the Beatles went to India to explore transcendental meditation. The concept of *estancia* tourism is extending to all parts of the continent, adapted to local conditions and attractions. Perhaps because the millenium is approaching, or as a natural extension of New Age thinking, mystical tourism is growing, with one of its most obvious examples being the rediscovery of Andean Philosophy, especially at Sacsayhuamán outside Cusco and on the shores of Lake Titicaca. Editorial trips to Peru, Argentina and Uruguay in the latter part of 1995, showed the increasing popularity of both types of vacation. During his travels, the editor enjoyed the hospitality of many old and new friends, who are thanked at the end of the relevant chapters.

The Editor

Responsible Tourism

Much has been written about the adverse impacts of tourism on the environment and local communities. It is usually assumed that this only applies to the more excessive end of the travel industry such as the Spanish Costas and Bali. However it now seems that travellers can have an impact at almost any density and this is especially true in areas "off the beaten track" where local people may not be used to western conventions and lifestyles, and natural environments may be very sensitive.

Of course, tourism can have a beneficial impact and this is something to which every traveller can contribute. Many National Parks are part funded by receipts from people who travel to see exotic plants and animals, the Galápagos (Ecuador) and Manu (Peru) National Parks are good examples of such sites. Similarly, travellers can promote patronage and protection of valuable archaeological sites and heritages through their interest and entrance fees.

However, where visitor pressure is high and/or poorly regulated, damage can occur. It is also unfortunately true that many of the most popular destinations are in ecologically sensitive areas easily disturbed by extra human pressures. This is particularly significant because the desire to visit sites and communities that are off the beaten track is a driving force for many travellers. Eventually the very features that tourists travel so far to see may become degraded and so we seek out new sites, discarding the old, and leaving someone else to deal with the plight of local communities and the damaged environment.

Fortunately, there are signs of a new awareness of the responsibilities that the travel industry and its clients need to endorse. For example, some tour operators fund local conservation projects and travellers are now more aware of the impact they may have on host cultures and environments. We can all contribute to the success of what is variously described as responsible, green or alternative tourism. All that is required is a little forethought and consideration.

It would be impossible to identify all the possible impacts that might need to be addressed by travellers, but it is worthwhile noting the major areas in which we can all take a more responsible attitude in the countries we visit. These include, changes to natural ecosystems (air, water, land, ecology and wildlife), cultural values (beliefs and behaviour) and the built environment (sites of antiquity and archaeological significance). At an individual level, travellers can reduce their impact if greater consideration is given to their activities. Canoe trips up the headwaters of obscure rivers make for great stories, but how do local communities cope with the sudden invasive interest in their lives? Will the availability of easy tourist money and gauche behaviour affect them for the worse, possibly diluting and trivialising the significance of culture and customs? Similarly, have the environmental implications of increased visitor pressure been considered? Where does the fresh fish that feeds the trip come from? Hand caught by line is fine, but is dynamite fishing really necessary, given the scale of damage and waste that results?

Some of these impacts are caused by factors beyond the direct control of travellers, such as the management and operation of a hotel chain. However, even here it is possible to voice concern about damaging activities and an increasing number of hotels and travel operators are taking "green concerns" seriously, even if it is only to protect their share of the market.

Environmental Legislation Legislation is increasingly being enacted to control damage to the environment, and in some cases this can have a bearing on travellers. The establishment of National Parks may involve rules and guidelines for visitors and these should always be followed. In addition there may be local or national laws controlling behaviour and use of natural resources (especially wildlife) that are being increasingly enforced. If in doubt, ask. Finally, international legislation, principally the Convention on International Trade in Endangered Species of Wild Fauna and Flora (CITES), may affect travellers.

CITES aims to control the trade in live specimens of endangered plants and animals and also "recognizable parts or derivatives" of protected species. Sale of Black Coral, Turtle shells, protected Orchids and other wildlife is strictly controlled by signatories of the convention. The full list of protected wildlife varies, so if you feel the need to purchase souvenirs and trinkets derived from wildlife, it would be prudent to check whether they are protected. Every country included in this Handbook is a signatory of CITES. In addition, most European countries, the USA and Canada are all signatories. Importation of CITES protected species into these countries can lead to heavy fines, confiscation of goods and even imprisonment. Information on the status of legislation and protective measures can be obtained from Traffic International, UK office T (01223) 277427, e-mail traffic@wcmc.org.uk.

Green Travel Companies and Information The increasing awareness of the environmental impact of travel and tourism has led to a range of advice and information services as well as spawning specialist travel companies who claim to provide "responsible travel" for clients. This is an expanding field and the veracity of claims needs to be substantiated in some cases. The following organizations and publications can provide useful information for those with an interest in pursuing responsible travel opportunities.

Organizations Green Flag International Aims to work with travel industry and conservation bodies to improve environments at travel destinations and also to promote conservation programmes at resort destinations. Provides a travellers' guide for "green" tourism as well as advice on destinations, T (UK 01223) 890250. Tourism Concern Aims to promote a greater understanding of the impact of tourism on host communities and environments; Southlands College, Wimbledon Parkside, London SW19 5NN, T (UK 0181) 944-0464, e-mail tourconcern@gn.apc.org). Centre for Responsible Tourism CRT coordinates a North American network and advises on N American sources of information on responsible tourism. CRT, PO Box 827, San Anselmo, California 94979, USA. Centre for the Advancement of Responsive Travel CART has a range of publications available as well as information on alternative holiday destinations. T (UK – 01732) 352757.

Publications *The Good Tourist* by Katie Wood and Syd House (1991) published by Mandarin Paperbacks; addresses issues surrounding environmental impacts of tourism, suggests ways in which damage can be minimised, suggests a range of environmentally sensitive holidays and projects.

Introduction and hints

GETTING THERE

AIR

All the main airlines plying to each country are given in the "Information for travellers" sections. Airlines will only allow a certain weight of luggage without a surcharge; this is normally 30 kg for first class and 20 kg for business and economy classes, but these limits are often not strictly enforced when it is known that the plane is not going to be full. On some flights from the UK via Paris special outbound concessions are offered (by Iberia, Viasa, Air France, Avianca) of a 2-piece allowance up to 32 kg, but you may need to request this. Passengers seeking a larger baggage allowance can route via USA, but with certain exceptions, the fares are slightly higher using this route. On the other hand, weight limits for internal flights are often lower; best to enquire beforehand.

Prices and discounts

1 It is generally cheaper to fly from London rather than a point in Europe to Latin American destinations; fares vary from airline to airline, destination to destination and according to time of year. Check with an agency for the best deal for when you wish to travel.

2 Most airlines offer discounted fares of one sort or another on scheduled flights. These are not offered by the airlines directly to the public, but through agencies who specialize in this type of fare. In UK, these include Journey Latin America, 16 Devonshire Road, Chiswick, London W4 2HD (T 0181-747 3108); Trailfinders, 48 Earl's Court Road, London W8 6EJ (T 0171-938 3366); South American Experience, 47 Causton Street, Pimlico, London SW1P 4AT (T 0171-976 5511); Last Frontiers, Swan House, High Street, Long Crendon, Buckinghamshire, HP18 9AF (T 01844 208405); Passage to South America, 113 Shepherds Bush Road, London, W6 7LP (T 0171-602 9889); STA Travel, Priory House, 6 Wrights Lane, London W8 6TA (T 0171-938 4711), Cox & Kings Travel, St James Court, 45 Buckingham Gate, London (T 0171-873 5001).

The very busy seasons are 7 Dec – 15 Jan and 10 July – 10 Sept. If you intend travelling during those times, book as far ahead as possible. Between Feb-May and Sept-Nov special offers may be available.

3 Other fares fall into three groups, and are all on scheduled services:

● **Excursion (return) fares** with restricted validity eg 5-90 days. Carriers are introducing flexibility into these tickets, permitting a change of dates on payment of a fee.

● **Yearly fares**: these may be bought on a one-way or return basis. Some airlines require a specified return date, changeable upon payment of a fee. To leave the return completely open is possible for an extra fee. You must, fix the route (some of the cheapest flexible fares now have 6 months validity).

● **Student (or Under 26) fares**. (Do not assume that student tickets are the cheapest; though they are often very flexible, they are usually more expensive than A or B above). Some airlines are flexible on the age limit, others strict. One way and returns available, or "Open Jaws" (see below). **NB** If you foresee returning home at a busy time (eg Christmas, Aug), a booking is advisable on any type of open-return ticket.

4 For people intending to travel a linear route and return from a different point from that which they entered, there are "Open Jaws" fares, which are available on student, yearly, or excursion fares.

5 Many of these fares require a change of plane at an intermediate point, and a stopover may be permitted, or even obligatory, depending on schedules. Simply because a flight stops at a given airport does not mean you can break your journey there – the airline must have traffic rights to pick up or set down passengers between points A and B before it will be permitted. This is where dealing with a specialized agency (like Journey Latin America!) will really pay dividends. There are dozens of agencies that offer the simple returns to Rio or Lima at roughly the same (discounted) fare. On multi-stop itineraries, the specialized agencies can often save clients hundreds of pounds.

6 Although it's a little more complicated, it's possible to sell tickets in London for travel originating in Latin America at substantially cheaper fares than those available locally. This is useful for the traveller who doesn't know where he will end up, or who plans to travel for more than a year. Because of high local taxes (see paragraph 7) a one-way ticket from Latin America is more expensive than a one-way in the other direction, so it's always best to buy a return. Taxes are calculated as a percentage of the full IATA fare; on a discounted fare the tax can therefore make up as much as 30-50%

of the price.

7 Certain Latin American countries impose local tax on flights originating there. Among these are Ecuador, Peru, Bolivia, Uruguay, Colombia and Mexico. This often applies if you happen to have bought a ticket, say, London-Rio-Santiago-Lima-Los Angeles and then on to Australia.

8 There are several cheap French charters to Colombia, Ecuador, Peru, Bolivia and the southern countries, but no-one in the UK sells them (although AOM tickets are available through Journey Latin America).

Travellers starting their journey in continental Europe may try: Uniclam-Voyages, 63 rue Monsieur-le Prince, 75006 Paris for charters. The Swiss company, Balair (owned by Swissair) has regular charter flights to South America (every second week to Recife and Rio). For cheap flights in Switzerland, Globetrotter Travel Service, Renweg, 8001 Zürich, has been recommended. Also try Nouvelles Frontières, Paris, T (1) 41-41-58-58; Hajo Siewer Jet Tours, Martinstr 39, 57462 Olpe, Germany, T (02761) 924120. The German magazine *Reisefieber* is useful.

9 If you buy discounted air tickets *always* check the reservation with the airline concerned to make sure the flight still exists. Also remember the IATA airlines' schedules change in March and October each year, so if you're going to be away a long time it's best to leave return flight coupons open.

In addition, check whether you are entitled to any refund or re-issued ticket if you lose, or have stolen, a discounted air ticket. Some airlines require the repurchase of a ticket before you can apply for a refund, which will not be given until after the validity of the original ticket has expired. The Iberia group and Air France, for example, operate this costly system. Travel insurance in some cases covers lost tickets.

10 Note that some South American carriers change departure times of short-haul or domestic flights at short notice and, in some instances, schedules shown in the computers of transatlantic carriers differ

from those actually flown by smaller, local carriers. If you book, and reconfirm, both your transatlantic and onward sectors through your transatlantic carrier you may find that your travel plans have been based on out of date information. The surest solution is to reconfirm your outward flight in an office of the onward carrier itself.

Air passes

AeroPerú operates Sudameripass, a 60-day return ticket which is one of the cheapest ways of flying around the continent. If starting a journey in Miami, Mexico City or Cancún, it costs US$1,099 for up to 6 coupons on AeroPerú's network; if starting in Buenos Aires or Los Angeles it costs US$1,299. Extra coupons can be bought for US$100 each. There are seasonal permutations. Check with JLA for up-to-date details. Iberia and its partners, Viasa and Aerolíneas Argentinas, offer Latin American Circular Fares: available from the UK only, the fares are for circular routes (no back-tracking) in North, Central and South America. There are two zones, mid-Atlantic and South Atlantic, and a flat fare applies to each: mid-Atlantic £847 high season, £680 low; South Atlantic £968 high, £793 low. Two free stopovers are allowed, plus Caracas on mid-Atlantic routes, or Buenos Aires on South Atlantic routes. Additional stops are £35 each. Fares are valid for 3 months (extensions and business class available). Also worth noting here is the Mercosur Airpass which applies to Brazil, Argentina, Uruguay and Paraguay, using 9 local carriers, available to any passenger with a return ticket to a Mercosur country. It must be bought in conjunction with an international flight; minimum stay is 7 days, maximum 30, at least 2 countries must be visited. Maximum number of coupons is eight. Fares are calculated on a mileage basis and range from US$225 to US$870.

Miami is a good place for connections between South and Central America and Europe. Non-US citizens should note that it is very difficult to check air tickets purchased outside the USA through an agent in Miami and that it is unlikely that you will be allowed by US Immigration to enter the USA without an onward ticket already in your possession. Continental Airlines' hub, Houston, is another good place for connections.

If you buy internal airline tickets in Latin American countries you may find cash refunds difficult to get if you change your plans: better to change your ticket for a different one. On the other hand you can save money by buying tickets in a country with a black exchange market, for local currency, for flights on its national airline. Overbooking by Latin American airlines is very common (largely due to repeated block bookings by travel agents, which everyone knows will not be used), so always reconfirm the next stage of your flight within 72 hrs of your intended departure. And it does no harm to reconfirm yet again in the last 24 hrs, just to show them you mean it, and turn up for the flight in good time (at least 2 hrs before departure).

We advise people who travel the cheap way in Latin America to pay for all transport as they go along, and not in advance. This advice does not apply to people on a tight schedule: paying as you go along may save money, but it is likely to waste your time somewhat. The one exception to this general principle is in transatlantic flights; here money is saved by booking as far as possible in one operation. International air tickets are very expensive if purchased in Latin America. If buying airline tickets routed through the USA, check that US taxes are included in the price.

The national airlines of Argentina, Bolivia, Brazil, Chile, Colombia, Peru and Venezuela operate airpass schemes within those countries at a set price. See the respective country sections.

The Amerbuspass covers the whole of Latin America, from Mexico City to Ushuaia, and entitles the holder to 15-20% discounts on tickets with participating operators; bookable in all Latin American capitals, Europe, Asia, Africa, Oceania, it is valid for 9,999 miles, up to 180 days. Unlimited stopovers, travel with either a confirmed or open itinerary. Contact TISA Internacional, B Irigoyen 1370, Oficina 25/26, 1138 Buenos Aires, Argentina, T 307-1956/631-1108, F 300-5591, PO Box 40 Suc 1 (B), 1401 Buenos Aires.

TRAVEL TO THE USA

Until July 1988 all foreigners (except Canadians) needed visas to enter the USA. Despite subsequent relaxations of visa requirements for British air travellers with round-trip tickets to the USA, it is advisable to have a visa to allow entry by land, or on airlines from South and Central America which are not "participating carriers" on the Visa Waiver scheme. If you are thinking of travelling via the USA, or of visiting the USA after Latin America, you are strongly advised to get your visa from a US Consulate in your own country, not while travelling.

The US Department of Agriculture places restrictions on agricultural items brought to the United States from foreign countries as well as those brought to the mainland from Hawaii, Puerto Rico, and the US Virgin Islands. Prohibited items can harbour foreign animal and plant pests and diseases that could seriously damage America's crops, livestock, pets and the environment.

Because of this threat, travellers are required to list on the Customs' declaration form any meats, fruits, vegetables, plants, animals, and plant and animal products they are bringing into the country. The declaration must list all agricultural items carried in baggage, hand luggage and in vehicles coming across the border.

USDA inspectors will confiscate illegal items for destruction. Travellers who fail to declare items can be fined up to US$100 on the spot, and their exit from the airport will be delayed. Some items are permitted. Call 301-436-5908 for a copy of the helpful pamphlet, "Travelers Tips". The best advice is to check before purchasing an agricultural item and trying to bring it back to the United States.

SEA

Voyages on passenger-carrying cargo vessels between South America and Europe, the USA, or elsewhere, are listed here: the Blue Star line sails from Tilbury to Hamburg, Bremen, Antwerp, thence to Montevideo via the Brazilian ports of Salvador, Santos and Rio de Janeiro, returning via Rio Grande, Santos, Salvador and Recife, and Rotterdam. 12 passengers are carried; fare to Montevideo, £1,610, round trip £3,010 pp. The Grimaldi Line sails from Tilbury to Brazil (Vitória, Buenos Aires, Santos, Paranaguá, Rio), via Hamburg, Amsterdam and Antwerp, Le Harve, round trip about 51 days, US$3,040-5,400, also from Genoa to Paranaguá, Santos and Rio for US$1,100-1,400. The *Nordwoge* Shipping Company carries 7 passengers on a 70-day round trip Felixstowe, Bilbao, Panama Canal, Buenaventura, Guayaquil, Callao, Arica (or Iquique), San Antonio, Valparaíso, Talcahuano, Antofagasta, Guayaquil, Buenaventura, Panama Canal, Bilbao, various N European ports, Felixstowe, £5,300 pp. Fyffes has regular sailings Portsmouth-Suriname, 6 passengers on a banana boat, 35-38 day round trip, £1,980 pp.

Various German companies sail to the E coast of South America: either Tilbury, Bremen, Hamburg, Rotterdam, Antwerp, Le Havre, Bilbao, Santos, Buenos Aires, Montevideo, Rio Grande do Sul, Santos, Tilbury (on the *Augusta*), or Felixstowe, Hamburg, Antwerp, Bilbao, Santos, Buenos Aires, Montevideo, Rio Grande do Sul, Itajaí, Santos, Rio de Janeiro, Rotterdam, Felixstowe (*Hansa Clipper*). There are also German sailings from Livorno (Italy) to Valencia, San Juan (Puerto Rico), Cartagena, Panama Canal, Puerto Bolívar (Ecuador), Panama Canal, Cartagena, Santa Marta, San Juan, Valencia, Livorno, 35-day round trip, £2,500 pp. Projex Line's *EWL Venezuela* sails Felixstowe, Paramaribo, Georgetown, Port of Spain, La Guaira, Puerto Cabello, Willemstad, Oranjestad, Cartagena, Santa Marta, Bremen, Rotterdam, Felixstowe, 44-day round trip, £2,600 pp. Flensburger Befrachtungskontor UC

Hansen of Germany has a 50-day round trip on *Rickmers Brazil* and *Hapag Lloyd Amazonas*, Antwerp, Manaus, Itacoatiara, Belém, Rouen/Honfleur, Bremen, costing £3,500.

From the USA, Ivaran Lines serve East Coast USA, Brazilian ports, Montevideo and Buenos Aires; the *Americana* container ship carries 80 passengers in luxury accommodation (New Orleans, Houston, Puerto Cabello, La Guaira, Rio, Santos, Buenos Aires, Montevideo, Rio Grande do Sul, Itajaí, Paranaguá, Santos, Salvador, Fortaleza, Bridgetown, San Juan, Veracruz, Tampico, New Orleans, £6,645-11,340 pp round trip, fares depend on season, one-way N or S possible). Ivaran also have the *San Antonio*, carrying 12 passengers on the route Port Elizabeth (New Jersey), Baltimore, Norfolk, Savannah, Miami, Puerto Cabello, La Guaira, Rio, Santos, Buenos Aires, Montevideo, Rio Grande do Sul, Itajaí, Santos, Rio (possibly Salvador and Fortaleza), Port Elizabeth; 44-day round trip £4,085-4,825 pp, one-way subject to availability. *Sven Ottmann*, 2-week round trip Fort Lauderdale, Oranjestad, Willemstad, Puerto Cabello, La Guaira, Fort Lauderdale £1,300 pp; Chilean Line's *Laja* and *Lircay*, New Orleans, Houston, Tampico, Cristóbal, Panama Canal, Guayaquil, Callao, Antofagasta, San Antonio, Arica, Callao, Buenaventura, Panama Canal, Cristóbal, New Orleans, 48-day round trip, US$4,800-5,280 pp. Egon Oldendorff carries passengers on its USA or Canada/South America routes.

Enquiries regarding passages should be made through agencies in your own country, or through John Alton of Strand Cruise and Travel Centre, Charing Cross Shopping Concourse, The Strand, London WC2N 4HZ, T 0171-836 6363, F 0171-497 0078. In the USA, contact Freighter World Cruises, 180 South Lake Ave, Pasadena, CA 91101, T (818) 449-3106, or Travltips Cruise and Freighter Travel Association, 163-07 Depot Road, PO Box 188, Flushing, NY 11358, T (800) 872-8584. Do not try to get a passage on a non-passenger carrying cargo ship to South America from a European port; it is not possible.

Details on shipping cars are given in **Motoring**, below, and in the relevant country sections.

NB Some countries in Latin America officially require travellers who enter their territory to have an onward or return ticket. (Look under 'Information for travellers' sections for the countries you intend to visit.) In 1995-96 this regulation was rarely enforced by any country. (It does not apply to travellers with their own vehicles.) In lieu of an onward ticket out of the country you are entering, any ticket out of another Latin American country (or a ticket home) may suffice, or proof that you have sufficient funds to buy a ticket (a credit card will do).

ON ARRIVAL

APPEARANCE

There is a natural prejudice in all countries against travellers who ignore personal hygiene and have a generally dirty and unkempt appearance. Most Latin Americans, if they can afford it, devote great care to their clothes and appearance; it is appreciated if visitors do likewise. How you dress is mostly how people will judge you. Buying clothing locally can help you to look less like a tourist. The general prejudice previously reported against backpacks has virtually disappeared, unless carried by those whom officials identify as "hippies". It may be advantageous to carry a letter from someone in an official position testifying to one's good character, on official-looking notepaper.

Some countries have laws or prejudices against the wearing by civilians of army-surplus clothing. Men wearing earrings are liable to be ridiculed in more "macho" communities (eg parts of Argentina). A medium weight shawl with some wool content is recommended for women: it can double as pillow, light blanket, bathrobe or sunscreen as required. For men, a smart jacket can be very useful.

COURTESY

Remember that politeness – even a little ceremoniousness – is much appreciated. In this connection professional or business cards are useful. Men should always remove any headgear and say "con permiso" ("com licença" in Brazil) when entering offices, and be prepared to shake hands (this is much commoner in Latin America than in Europe or North America); always say "Buenos días" (until midday) or "Buenas tardes" ("Bom dia" or "Boa tarde" in Brazil) and wait for a reply before proceeding further; in a word, don't rush them! Always remember that the traveller from abroad has enjoyed greater advantages in life than most Latin American minor officials, and should be friendly and courteous in consequence. Never be impatient; do not criticize situations in public: the officials may know more English than you think and they can certainly interpret gestures and facial expressions. Be judicious about discussing politics with strangers. Politeness can be a liability, however, in some situations; most Latin Americans are disorderly queuers. In commercial transactions (buying a meal, goods in a shop, etc) politeness should be accompanied by firmness, and always ask the price first.

Politeness should also be extended to street traders; saying "No, gracias/Não, obrigado" with a smile is better than an arrogant dismissal. Whether you give money to beggars is a personal matter, but your decision should be influenced by whether a person is begging out of need or trying to cash in on the tourist trail. In the former case, local people giving may provide an indication. Giving money to children is a separate issue, upon which most agree: don't do it. There are occasions where giving food in a restaurant may be appropriate, but first inform yourself of local practice.

Moira Chubb, from New Zealand, suggests that if you are a guest and are offered food that arouses your suspicions, the only courteous way out is to feign an allergy or a stomach ailment. If worried about the purity of ice for drinks, ask for a beer.

CULTURE

Literature

This Handbook does not at present have space to contain sections on Latin American literature. Interested readers are recommended to see Jason Wilson, *Traveller's Literary Companion, South and Central America* (Brighton, UK: In Print, 1993), which has extracts from works by Latin American writers and by non-Latin Americans about the various countries and has very useful bibliographies.

Music and dance

The aim of the Music and Dance sections (specially written for us by Nigel Gallop) has been to give an overview of the traditional and popular music and dances of each country. Considerations of space and the desire to avoid a tedious inventory has meant that by no means every song style, dance or instrument has been noted. As to the performers mentioned, the choice has also been selective, giving preference to those who have achieved local fame over those who, for commercial or political reasons, have based themselves in Europe or North America and are probably already familiar to the overseas visitor. Readers may also notice that space has not been devoted to the forest indians, who are nevertheless present in most of the countries covered and whose music and dancing tends to exist only in its isolated cosmos, rarely relating to, or connecting with, national or regional musical cultures. Also not discussed, at present, is the classical music of the region.

DOCUMENTS

Passports

Remember that Latin Americans, especially officials, are very document-minded. You should always carry your passport in a safe place about your person, or if not going far, leave it in the hotel safe. If staying in a country for several weeks, it is worthwhile registering at your Embassy or Consulate. Then, if your passport is stolen, the process of replacing it is simplified and speeded up. Keeping photocopies of essential documents, including your flight ticket, and some additional passport-sized photographs, is recommended

Remember that it is your responsibility to ensure that your passport is stamped in and out when you cross frontiers. The absence of entry and exit stamps can cause serious difficulties: seek out the proper migration offices if the stamping process is not carried out as you cross. Also, do not lose your entry card; replacing one causes a lot of trouble, and possibly expense. Citizens of countries which oblige visitors to have a visa (eg France) can expect more delays and problems at border crossings.

If planning to study in Latin America for a long period, make every effort to get a student visa in advance.

Identity and Membership Cards

Membership cards of British, European and US motoring organizations have been found useful for discounts off hotel charges, car rentals, maps, towing charges, etc. Student cards must carry a photograph if they are to be of any use in Latin America for discounts. (If you describe yourself as a student on your tourist card you may be able to get discounts, even if you haven't a student card). Business people should carry a good supply of visiting cards, which are essential for good business relations in Latin America. Identity, membership or business cards in Spanish or Portuguese (or a translation) and an official letter of introduction in Spanish or Portuguese are also useful.

If you are in full-time education you will be entitled to an International Student Identity Card, which is distributed by student travel offices and travel agencies in 77 countries. The ISIC gives you special prices on all forms of transport (air, sea, rail etc), and access to a variety of other concessions and services. If you need to find the location of your nearest ISIC office contact: The ISIC Association, Box 9048, 1000 Copenhagen, Denmark T (+45) 33 93 93 03.

It is possible to get jobs in some countries of South America, *Jobs Abroad* will arrange work permits, visas and immigration, send 2 x 25p stamps for information to Worldwide House, Broad St, Port Ramsgate, Kent, CT11 8NQ.

KEEPING IN TOUCH
Mail
Postal services in most countries are not very efficient, and pilfering is frequent. All mail, especially packages, should be registered. Some travellers recommend that mail should be sent to one's Embassy (or, if a cardholder, American Express agent) rather than to the Poste Restante/General Delivery (*Lista de Correos*) department of a country's Post Office. Some Embassies and post offices, however, do not keep mail for more than a month. If there seems to be no mail at the Lista under the initial letter of your surname, ask them to look under the initial of your forename or your middle name. Remember that there is no W in Spanish; look under V, or ask. For the smallest risk of misunderstanding, use title, initial and surname only. (If you're a British male, and all else fails, ask them to look under "E" for "Esquire"! – Geoffrey van Dulken.) If having items sent to you by courier (eg DHL), do not use poste restante, but an address such as a hotel: a signature is required on receipt.

Phones
US travellers should know about AT&T's "USA Direct", by which you can connect with an AT & T operator without going through a local one. It is much cheaper than operator-assisted calls and is widely available. Sprint and MCI are also available; details given under individual countries. Other countries have similar systems, eg UK, Canada; obtain details before leaving home.

Communicating by fax is a convenient way of sending messages home. Many places with public fax machines (post offices, telephone companies or shops) will receive messages as well as send. Fax machines are often switched off; you may have to phone to confirm receipt.

World Band Radio
South America has more local and community radio stations than practically anywhere else in the world; a shortwave (world band) radio offers a practical means to brush up on the language, sample popular culture and absorb some of the richly varied regional music. International broadcasters such as the BBC World Service, the Voice of America, Boston (Mass)-based Monitor Radio International (operated by *Christian Science Monitor*) and the Quito-based Evangelical station, HCJB, keep the traveller abreast of news and events, in both English and Spanish.

Compact or miniature portables are recommended, with digital tuning and a full range of shortwave bands, as well as FM, long and medium wave. Detailed advice on radio models (£150 for a decent one) and wavelengths can be found in the annual publication, *Passport to World Band Radio* (Box 300, Penn's Park, PA 18943, USA). Details of local stations is listed in *World TV and Radio Handbook* (WTRH), PO Box 9027, 1006 AA Amsterdam, The Netherlands, US$19.95. Both of these, free wavelength guides and selected radio sets are available from the BBC World Service Bookshop, Bush House Arcade, Bush House, Strand, London WC2B 4PH, UK, T 0171-257 2576.

LANGUAGE
Without some knowledge of Spanish you can become very frustrated and feel helpless in many situations. English, or any other language, is absolutely useless off the beaten track. Some initial study, to get you up to a basic Spanish vocabulary of 500 words or so, and a pocket dictionary and phrase-book, are most strongly recommended: your pleasure will be doubled if you can talk to the locals. Not all the locals speak Spanish, of course; apart from Brazil's Portuguese, you will find that some Indians in the more remote highland parts of Bolivia and Peru, and lowland Indians in Amazonia, speak only their indigenous languages, though there will usually be at least one person in each village who can speak Spanish (or Portuguese).

Exchange Rates		
COUNTRY	**Unit of currency**	**Exchange rate/US$**
ARGENTINA	Peso	1.00
BOLIVIA	Boliviano	5.09
BRAZIL	Real	1.00
CHILE	Chilean peso	411.38
COLOMBIA	Colombian peso	1,059.30
GUYANA	Guyanese dollar	138.90
GUYANE	French franc	5.15
ECUADOR	Sucre	3,147.50
PARAGUAY	Guaraní	2,055.00
PERU	New sol	2.44
SURINAME	Suriname guilder	410.00
URUGUAY	Peso Uruguayo	8.10
VENEZUELA	Bolívar	470.25
Correct at 29 July 1996		

The basic Spanish of Hispanic America is that of south-western Spain, with soft "c's" and "z's" pronounced as "s", and not as "th" as in the other parts of Spain. Castilian Spanish is readily understood, but is not appreciated when spoken by non-Spaniards; try and learn the basic Latin American pronunciation. There are several regional variations in pronunciation, particularly in the River Plate countries, which are noted in the Argentine section **Information for travellers**. Differences in vocabulary also exist, both between peninsular Spanish and Latin American Spanish, and between the usages of the different countries.

If you are going to Brazil, you should learn some Portuguese. Spanish is not adequate: you may be understood but you will probably not be able to understand the answers. Language classes are available at low cost in a number of centres in South America, for instance Quito. See the text for details, under **Language Courses**.

MONEY

The three main ways of keeping in funds while travelling are with US dollars cash, US dollars travellers' cheques (TCs), or plastic.

Cash

Sterling and other currencies are not recommended. Though the risk of loss is greater, the chief benefit of US dollar notes is that better rates and lower commissions can usually be obtained for them. In many countries, US dollar notes are only accepted if they are in excellent, if not perfect condition (likewise, do not accept local currency notes in poor condition). Low-value US dollar bills should be carried for changing into local currency if arriving in a country when banks or *casas de cambio* are closed (US$5 or US$10 bills). They are very useful for shopping: shopkeepers and exchange shops (*casas de cambio*) tend to give better exchange rates than hotels or banks (but see below). The better hotels will normally change travellers' cheques for their guests (often at a rather poor rate), but if you are travelling on the cheap it is essential to keep in funds; watch weekends and public holidays carefully and never run out of local currency. Take plenty of local currency, in small denominations, when making trips into the interior.

Travellers' cheques

These are convenient but they attract thieves (though refunds can of course be arranged) and you will find that they are more difficult than dollar bills to change in small towns (denominations of US$50 and US$100 are preferable, though one does need a few of US$20). American Express, Visa or Thomas Cook US$ TCs are recommended, but less commission is often charged on Citibank or Bank of America TCs, if they are cashed at Latin American branches of those banks. These TCs are always accepted by banks, even though they may not be as well known outside banks as those of American Express, Visa or Thomas Cook. (It is also easier to obtain refunds for stolen TCs with the last three than with Citicorp cheques.) It is a good idea to take 2 kinds of cheque: if large numbers of one kind have recently been forged or stolen, making people suspicious, it is unlikely to have happened simultaneously with the other kind. Several banks charge a high fixed commission for changing TCs – some-times as much as US$5-10 a cheque – because they don't really want to be bothered. Exchange houses (*casas de cambio*) are usually much better for this service. Some establishments may ask to see the customer's record of purchase before accepting.

Plastic

It is straightfoward to obtain a cash advance against a credit card and, in the text, we give the names of banks that do this.

There are two international **ATM** (automatic telling machine) acceptance systems, Plus and Cirrus. Many issuers of debit and credit cards are linked to one, or both (eg Visa is Plus, Mastercard is Cirrus). Look for the relevant symbol on an ATM and draw cash using your PIN. Frequently, the rates of exchange on ATM withdrawals are the best available. Find out before you leave what ATM coverage there is in the countries you will visit and what international 'functionality' your card has. Check if your bank or credit card company imposes handling charges.

Obviously you must ensure that the account to which your debit card refers contains sufficient funds. With a credit card, obtain a credit limit sufficient for your needs, or pay money in to put the account in credit. If travelling for a long time, consider a direct debit to clear your account regularly. Do not rely on one card, in case of loss. If you do lose a card, immediately contact the 24-hr helpline of the issuer in your home country (keep this number in a safe place). (With thanks to Nigel Baker, Debit Card Manager, Nat-west Bank plc, London.)

For purchases, credit cards of the Visa and Mastercard (Eurocard, Access) groups, American Express (Amex), Carte Blanche and Diners Club can be used. Make sure you know the correct procedure if they are lost or stolen. Credit card transactions are normally at an officially recognized rate of exchange; they are often subject to tax. Many establishments in Latin America charge a fee of about 5% on credit card transactions; although forbidden by credit card company rules there is not a lot you can do about this, except get the charge itemized on the receipt and complain to the card company. For credit card security, insist that imprints are made in your presence and that any imprints incorrectly completed should be torn into tiny pieces. Also destroy the carbon papers after the form is completed (signatures can be copied from them).

NB In many countries, one can get at least US$500 in Amex travellers' cheques on the American Express card (US$1,000 on the gold card). One can also obtain cash at American Express via personal cheques, eg Eurocheque. If you are having additional sums of money sent out during a tour of Latin America, try to have it sent to one of the countries where you can easily exchange dollar travellers' cheques for dollars cash; see under the individual countries below for the current situation.

Money can be transferred between banks. A recommended method is, before leaving, to find out which local bank is correspondent to your bank at home, then when you need funds, telex your own bank and ask them to telex the money to the local bank (confirming by fax). Give exact information to your bank of the routing number of the receiving bank. Cash in dollars, local currency depending on the country can be received within 48 banking hours.

Exchange

Most of the countries described in this book have freedom of exchange between US dollars and the local currency. A few have a parallel rate of exchange which is not always better than the official rate. Local conditions are described in the relevant chapters. Changing money on the street: if possible, do not do so alone. If unsure of the currency of the country you are about to enter, check rates with more than one changer at the border, or ask locals or departing travellers.

Whenever you leave a country, sell any local currency before leaving, because the further away you get, the less the value of a country's money. **Note** If departing by air, do not leave yourself too little money to pay the airport departure tax, which is never waived.

Americans should know that if they run out of funds they can usually expect no help from the US Embassy or Consul other than a referral to some welfare organization. Find out before you go precisely what services and assistance your embassy or consulate can provide if you find yourself in difficulties.

PHOTOGRAPHY

Always ask permission before photographing people. The price of film varies from country to country, being cheapest in Chile (in the Iquique and Punta Arenas Tax Free Zones), Bolivia (in markets of major cities and in all free zones – Zofri) and Paraguay (always check the expiry date). Pre-paid Kodak slide film cannot be developed in South America; it is also very hard to find. Kodachrome is almost impossible to buy. Some travellers (but not all) have advised against mailing exposed films home; either take them with you, or have them developed, but not printed, once you have checked the laboratory's quality. Note that postal authorities may use less sensitive equipment for X-ray screening than the airports do. Modern controlled X-ray machines are supposed to be safe for any speed of film, but it is worth trying to avoid X-ray as the doses are cumulative. Many airport officials will allow film to be passed outside X-ray arches; they may also hand-check a suitcase with a large quantity of film if asked politely.

Dan Buck and Anne Meadows write: A note on developing film in South America. Black and white is a problem. Often it is shoddily machine-processed and the negatives are ruined. Ask the store if you can see an example of their laboratory's work and if they hand-develop.

Jeremy Till and Sarah Wigglesworth suggest that exposed film can be protected in humid areas by putting it in a balloon and tying a knot. Similarly keeping your camera in a plastic bag may reduce the effects of humidity.

SAFETY
Drugs

Users of drugs, even of soft ones, without medical prescription should be particularly careful, as some countries impose heavy penalties – up to 10 years' imprisonment – for even the simple possession of such substances. In this connection, the planting of drugs on travellers, by traffickers or the police, is not unknown. If offered drugs on the street, make no response at all and keep walking. Note that people who roll their own cigarettes are often suspected of carrying drugs and subjected to intensive searches. Advisable to stick to commercial brands of cigarettes – but better still not to smoke at all.

Keeping safe

Generally speaking, most places in Latin America are no more dangerous than any major city in Europe or North America. In provincial towns, main places of interest, on day time buses and in ordinary restaurants the visitor should be quite safe. Nevertheless, in large cities particularly, crime exists, most of which is opportunistic. If you are aware of the dangers, act confidently and use your common

sense you will lessen many of the risks. The following tips, all endorsed by travellers, are meant to forewarn, but not alarm, you. Keep all documents secure; hide your main cash supply in different places or under your clothes: extra pockets sewn inside shirts and trousers, pockets closed with a zip or safety pin, moneybelts (best worn below the waist rather than outside or at it or around the neck), neck or leg pouches, a thin chain for attaching a purse to your bag or under your clothes and elasticated support bandages for keeping money and cheques above the elbow or below the knee have been repeatedly recommended (the last by John Hatt in *The Tropical Traveller*). Keep cameras in bags (preferably with a chain or wire in the strap to defeat the slasher) or briefcases; take spare spectacles (eyeglasses); don't wear wrist-watches or jewellery. If you wear a shoulder-bag in a market, carry it in front of you. Backpacks are vulnerable to slashers: a good idea is to cover the pack with a sack (a plastic one will also keep out rain and dust) with maybe a layer of wire netting between, or make an inner frame of chicken wire. Use a pack which is lockable at its base.

Ignore mustard smearers and paint or shampoo sprayers, and strangers' remarks like "what's that on your shoulder?" or "have you seen that dirt on your shoe?" Furthermore, don't bend over to pick up money or other items in the street. These are all ruses intended to distract your attention and make you easy for an accomplice to steal from. If someone follows you when you're in the street, let him catch up with you and "give him the eye". While you should take local advice about being out at night, do not assume that daytime is safer than nighttime. If walking after dark, walk in the road, not on the pavement/sidewalk.

Be wary of "plainclothes policemen"; insist on seeing identification and on going to the police station by main roads. Do not hand over your identification (or money – which he should not need to see anyway) until you are at the station. On no account take them directly back to your lodgings. Be even more suspicious if he seeks confirmation of his status from a passer-by. If someone tries to bribe you, insist on a receipt. If attacked, remember your assailants may well be armed, and try not to resist.

It is best, if you can trust your hotel, to leave any valuables you don't need in safe-deposit there, when sightseeing locally. Always keep an inventory of what you have deposited. If you don't trust the hotel, lock everything in your pack and secure that in your room (some people take eyelet-screws for padlocking cupboards or drawers). If you lose valuables, always report to the police and note details of the report – for insurance purposes.

When you have all your luggage with you at a bus or railway station, be especially careful: don't get into arguments with any locals if you can help it, and lock all the items together with a chain or cable if you are waiting for some time. Take a taxi between airport/bus station/railway station and hotel, if you can possibly afford it. Keep your bags with you in the taxi and pay only when you and your luggage are safely out of the vehicle. Make sure the taxi has inner door handles, in case a quick exit is needed. Avoid night buses; never arrive at night; and watch your belongings whether they are stowed inside or outside the cabin (roof top luggage racks create extra problems, which are sometimes unavoidable – make sure your bag is waterproof). Major bus lines often issue a luggage ticket when bags are stored in the bus' hold, generally a safe system. When getting on a bus, keep your ticket handy; someone sitting in your seat may be a distraction for an accomplice to rob you while you are sorting out the problem. Finally, never accept food, drink, sweets or cigarettes from unknown fellow-travellers on buses or trains. They may be drugged, and you would wake up hours later without your belongings. In this connection, never accept a bar drink from an opened bottle (unless you can see that that bottle is in general use): always have it uncapped in front of you.

For specific local problems, see under the individual countries in the text.

Police

Whereas in Europe and North America we are accustomed to law enforcement on a systematic basis, in general, enforcement in Latin America is achieved by periodic campaigns. The most typical is a round-up of criminals in the cities just before Christmas. In December, therefore, you may well be asked for identification at any time, and if you cannot produce it, you will be jailed. If a visitor is jailed his/her friends should provide food every day. This is especially important for people on a diet, such as diabetics. In the event of a vehicle accident in which anyone is injured, all drivers involved are automatically detained until blame has been established, and this does not usually take less than 2 weeks.

Never offer a bribe unless you are fully conversant with the customs of the country. (In Chile, for instance, it would land you in serious trouble if you tried to bribe a *carabinero*.) Wait until the official makes the suggestion, or offer money in some form which is apparently not bribery, eg "In our country we have a system of on-the-spot fines (*multas de immediato*). Is there a similar system here?" Do not assume that an official who accepts a bribe is prepared to do anything else that is illegal. You bribe him to persuade him to do his job, or to persuade him not to do it, or to do it more quickly, or more slowly. You do not bribe him to do something which is against the law. The mere suggestion would make him very upset. If an official suggests that a bribe must be paid before you can proceed on your way, be patient (assuming you have the time) and he may relent.

SOUVENIRS

Remember that these can almost invariably be bought more cheaply away from the capital, though the choice may be less wide. Bargaining seems to be the general rule in most countries' street markets, but don't make a fool of yourself by bargaining over what, to you, is a small amount of money.

If British travellers have no space in their luggage, they might like to remember

Tumi, the Latin American Craft Centre, who specialize in Mexican and Andean products and who produce cultural and educational videos for schools: at 23/2A Chalk Farm Road, London NW1 8AG (F 0171-485 4152), 8/9 New Bond Street Place, Bath BA1 1BH (T 01225 462367, F 01225 444870), 1/2 Little Clarendon St, Oxford OX1 2HJ (T/F 01865-512307), 82 Park St, Bristol BS1 5LA (T/F 0117 929 0391). Tumi (Music) Ltd specializes in different rhythms of Latin America. See *Arts and Crafts of South America*, by Lucy Davies and Mo Fini, published by Tumi (1994), for a fine introduction to the subject. There are similar shops in the USA; one good one is on the ground floor of Citicorp Center, Lexington Avenue and 53rd Street, New York.

TRAVELLING ALONE

Many points of security, dress and language have been covered already. First time exposure to countries where sections of the population live in extreme poverty or squalor and may even be starving can cause odd psychological reactions in visitors. So can the exceptional curiosity extended to visitors, especially women. Simply be prepared for this and try not to over-react. These additional hints have mainly been supplied by women, but most apply to any single traveller. When you set out, err on the side of caution until your instincts have adjusted to the customs of a new culture. If, as a single woman, you can befriend a local woman, you will learn much more about the country you are visiting. Unless actively avoiding foreigners like yourself, don't go too far from the beaten track; there is a very definite "gringo trail" which you can join, or follow, if seeking company. This can be helpful when looking for safe accommodation, especially if arriving after dark (which is best avoided). Remember that for a single woman a taxi at night can be as dangerous as wandering around on her own. At borders dress as smartly as possible. Travelling by train is a good way to meet locals, but buses are much easier for a person alone; on major routes your seat is often reserved and your luggage can usually be locked in the hold.

It is easier for men to take the friendliness of locals at face value; women may be subject to much unwanted attention. To help minimize this, do not wear suggestive clothing and, advises Alex Rossi of Jawa Timur, Indonesia, do not flirt. By wearing a wedding ring, carrying a photograph of your "husband" and "children", and saying that your "husband" is close at hand, you may dissuade an aspiring suitor. If politeness fails, do not feel bad about showing offence and departing. When accepting a social invitation, make sure that someone knows the address and the time you left. Ask if you can bring a friend (even if you do not intend to do so). A good rule is always to act with confidence, as though you know where you are going, even if you do not. Someone who looks lost is more likely to attract unwanted attention. Do not disclose to strangers where you are staying. (Much of this information was supplied by Alex Rossi, and by Deirdre Mortell of Carrigaline, Co Cork).

WHAT TO TAKE

Everybody has his/her own list. In addition to items already suggested above, those most often mentioned include air cushions for slatted seats, inflatable travel pillow for neck support, strong shoes (and remember that footwear over 9½ English size, or 42 European size, is difficult to obtain in Latin America except Argentina and Brazil); a small first-aid kit and handbook, fully waterproof top clothing, waterproof treatment for leather footwear, wax earplugs (which are almost impossible to find outside large cities) and airline-type eye mask to help you sleep in noisy and poorly curtained hotel rooms, sandals (rubber-thong Japanese-type or other – can be worn in showers to avoid athlete's foot), a polyethylene sheet 2 x 1 metres to cover possibly infested beds and shelter your luggage, polyethylene bags of varying sizes (up to heavy duty rubbish bag size) with ties, a toilet bag you can tie round your waist, if you use an electric shaver, take a rechargeable type, a sheet sleeping-bag and pillow-case or separate pillow-case – in some countries they are not changed often in cheap hotels; a 1½-

2m piece of 100% cotton can be used as a towel, a bedsheet, beach towel, makeshift curtain and wrap; a mosquito net (or a hammock with a fitted net), a straw hat which can be rolled or flattened and reconstituted after 15 mins soaking in water, a clothes line, a nailbrush (useful for scrubbing dirt off clothes as well as off oneself), a vacuum flask, a water bottle, a small dual-voltage immersion heater, a small dual-voltage (or battery-driven) electric fan, a light nylon waterproof shopping bag, a universal bath- and basin-plug of the flanged type that will fit any wastepipe (or improvise one from a sheet of thick rubber); string, velcro, electrical insulating tape, large penknife preferably with tin and bottle openers, scissors and corkscrew – the famous Swiss Army range has been repeatedly recommended (for knife sharpening, go to a butcher's shop), a flour sack and roll of wire mesh for luggage protection, alarm clock or watch, candle, torch (flashlight) – especially one that will clip on to a pocket or belt, pocket mirror, pocket calculator, an adaptor and flex to enable you to take power from an electric-light socket (the Edison screw type is the most commonly used), a padlock (combination lock is best) for the doors of the cheapest and most casual hotels (or for tent zip if camping), spare chain-lengths and padlock for securing luggage to bed or bus/train seat. Remember not to throw away spent batteries containing mercury or cadmium; take them home to be disposed of, or recycled properly.

Useful medicaments are given at the end of the "Health" section (page 50); to these might be added some lip salve with sun protection, and pre-moistened wipes (such as "Wet Ones"). Always carry toilet paper. Natural fabric sticking plasters, as well as being long-lasting, are much appreciated as gifts. Dental floss can be used for backpack repairs, in addition to its original purpose. **Never** carry firearms. Their possession could land you in serious trouble.

A note for **contact lens wearers**: most countries have a wide selection of products for the care of lenses, so you don't need to take kilos of lotions. Lens solution can be difficult to find in Peru and Bolivia and outside major cities. Ask for it in a chemist/pharmacy, rather than an optician's.

Be careful when asking directions. Women probably know more about the neighbourhood; men about more distant locations. Policemen are often helpful. However, many Latin Americans will give you the wrong answer rather than admit they do not know; this may be partly because they fear losing face, but is also because they like to please. You are more likely to get reliable information if you carefully refrain from asking leading questions.

Lastly, a good principle is to take half the clothes (trousers with plenty of pockets are very useful), and twice the money, that you think you will need.

WHERE TO STAY

HOTELS
For about US$10, a cheap but not bad

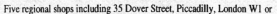

hotel room can be found in most countries, although in some of the Andean countries you may not have to pay that much. For the indigent, it is a good idea to ask for a boarding house – *casa de huéspedes, hospedaje, pensión, casa familial* or *residencial*, according to country; they are normally to be found in abundance near bus and railway stations and markets. Good value hotels can also be found near truckers' stops/service stations; they are usually secure. There are often great seasonal variations in hotel prices in resorts. Note that in the text "with bath" usually means "with shower and toilet", not "with bath tub". Remember, cheaper hotels don't always supply soap, towels and toilet paper; in colder (higher) regions they may not supply enough blankets, so take your own or a sleeping bag. Useful tips: book even cheap hotels in advance by registered mail, if you receive no reply don't worry; ask the car rental agency employees at the airport for advice when you arrive, as long as they are not busy they may have better value recommendations than airport tourist offices. In any class, hotel rooms facing the street may be noisy; always ask for the best, quietest room. To avoid price hikes for gringos, ask if there is a cheaper room.

Experiment in International Living Ltd, 287 Worcester Road, Malvern, Worcestershire, WR14 1AB, T 01684-562577, F 562212, or Ubierstrasse 30, 5300 Bonn 2, T 0228-95-7220, F 0228-35-8282, can arrange stays with families from 1 to 4 weeks in Chile, Ecuador and Brazil; EIL has offices in 38 countries. This has been recommended as an excellent way to meet people and learn the language.

NB The electric showers used in innumerable hotels should be checked for obvious flaws in the wiring; try not to touch the rose while it is producing hot water.

Cockroaches

These are ubiquitous and unpleasant, but not dangerous. Take some insecticide powder if staying in cheap hotels; Baygon (Bayer) has been recommended. Stuff toilet paper in any holes in walls that you may suspect of being parts of cockroach runs.

Toilets

Many hotels, restaurants and bars have inadequate water supplies. **Almost without exception used toilet paper should not be flushed down the pan, but placed in the receptacle provided**. This applies even in quite expensive hotels. Failing to observe this custom will block the pan or drain, a considerable health risk. It is quite common for people to stand on the toilet seat (facing the wall – easier to balance), as they do in Asia. If you are concerned about the hygiene of the facility, put paper on the seat.

CAMPING

There is a growing network of organized campsites, to which reference is made in the text immediately below hotel lists, under each town. If there is no organized site in town, a football pitch or gravel pit might serve. Obey the following rules for "wild" camping: (1) arrive in daylight and pitch your tent as it gets dark; (2) ask permission to camp from the parish priest, or the fire chief, or the police, or a farmer regarding his own property; (3) never ask

---

Hotel prices

Our hotel price ranges, including taxes and service charges but without meals unless stated, are as follows:

L1	Over US$200	**L2**	US$151-200	**L3**	US$101-150
A1	US$81-100	**A2**	US$61-80	**A3**	US$46-60
B	US$31-45	**C**	US$21-30	**D**	US$12-20
E	US$7-11	**F**	US$4-6	**G**	Up to US$3

NB Prices are for double rooms, except in **F** and **G** ranges where the price is almost always per person.

Other abbreviations used in the book (apart from pp = per person; a/c = air conditioned; rec = recommended; T = telephone; TCs = travellers' cheques; s/n = "sin número", no street number; p = piso – floor, in Spanish-speaking countries) should be self-explanatory.

a group of people – especially young people; (4) never camp on a beach (because of sandflies and thieves). If you can't get information from anyone, camp in a spot where you can't be seen from the nearest inhabited place, or road, and make sure no one saw you go there. In Argentina and Brazil, it is common to camp at gas/petrol stations. As Béatrice Völkle of Gampelen, Switzerland, adds, camping wild may be preferable to those organized sites which are treated as discotheques, with only the afternoon reserved for sleeping.

If taking a cooker, the most frequent recommendation is a multifuel stove (eg MSR International, Coleman Peak 1), which will burn unleaded petrol or, if that is not available, kerosene, *benzina blanca*, etc. Alcohol-burning stoves are simple, reliable, but slow and you have to carry a lot of fuel: for a methylated spirit-burning stove, the following fuels apply, *alcohol desnaturalizado, alcohol metílico, alcohol puro (de caña)* or *alcohol para quemar*. Ask for 95%, but 70% will suffice. In all countries fuel can usually be found in chemists/pharmacies. Gas cylinders and bottles are usually exchangeable, but if not can be recharged; specify whether you use butane or propane. Gas canisters are not always available. The Camping Clube do Brasil gives 50% discounts to holders of international campers' cards.

YOUTH HOSTELS

Organizations affiliated to the Youth Hostels movement exist in Argentina, Brazil, Colombia, Chile, Peru and Uruguay. There is an associate organization in Ecuador. Further information in the country sections and from the IYHA.

FOOD

In all countries except Brazil and Chile (where cold meats, cheese, eggs, fruit etc generally figure) breakfast usually means coffee or tea with rolls and butter, and anything more is charged extra. In Colombia and Ecuador breakfast usually means eggs, a roll, fruit juice and a mug of milk with coffee; say "breakfast without eggs" if you do not want that much. There is a paragraph on each nation's food under "Information for travellers". Vegetarians should be able to list all the foods they cannot eat; saying "Soy vegetariano/a" (I'm a vegetarian) or "no como carne" (I don't eat meat) is often not enough. Most restaurants serve a daily special meal, usually at lunchtime, which is cheap and good. Other than that you can expect to pay between US$10-15 on breakfast and dinner per day.

GETTING AROUND

NB See above for details of air transport including air passes.

Before you start, remember that distances are great and journeys by land are long: plan accordingly and do not try to do too much in the time available.

BUSES AND TRAINS

The continent has an extensive road system for motor traffic, with frequent bus services. The buses are often comfortable; Brazil and Chile are the best; Colombia is quite good, Ecuador not far behind; Bolivia and Peru have good and bad; the difficulties of Andean terrain affect the quality of vehicles. In mountainous country do not expect buses to get to their destination after long journeys anywhere near on time. Do not turn up for a bus at the last minute; if it is full it may depart early. Tall travellers are advised to take aisle rather than window seats on long journeys as this allows more leg room. When the journey takes more than 3 or 4 hrs, meal stops at country inns or bars, good and bad, are the rule. Usually, no announcement is made on the duration of a stop: follow the driver, if he eats, eat. See what the locals are eating – and buy likewise, or make sure you're stocked up well on food and drink at the start. For drinks, stick to bottled water or soft drinks or coffee (black). The food sold by vendors at bus stops may be all right: watch if locals are buying, though unpeeled fruit is of course reliable. (See above on **Security** in buses.)

Where they still run, trains are slower than buses. They tend to provide finer scenery and you can normally see much more wildlife than from the road – it is less disturbed by one or two trains a day than by the more frequent road traffic. Moreover, so many buses now show video films that you can't see the countryside because the curtains are drawn. Complaining to the conductor that you cannot see the beautiful landscape may persuade him to give you his seat at the front.

MOTORING

The machine

What kind of motoring you do will depend on what kind of car you set out with. Four-wheel drive is not necessary, but it does give you greater flexibility in mountain and jungle territory, although you may not get far in Amazonas, where roads are frequently impassable. In Patagonia, main roads are gravel rather than paved: perfectly passable without four-wheel drive, just rough and dusty. Consider fitting wire guards for headlamps, and for windscreens too, if you don't mind peering out through a grill like a caged chimpanzee. Wherever you travel you should expect from time to time to find roads that are badly maintained, damaged or closed during the wet season, and delays because of floods, landslides and huge potholes. Don't plan your schedules too tightly.

Diesel cars are much cheaper to run than petrol ones, and the fuel is easily available; in Venezuela you may have to look hard for it outside Caracas. Most towns can supply a mechanic of sorts, and probably parts for Bosch fuel injection equipment. Watch the mechanics like a hawk, since there's always a brisk market in spares, and some of yours may be highly desirable. That apart, they enjoy a challenge, and can fix most things, eventually.

For prolonged motoring over 3000 metres, you may need to fit high altitude jets on your carburettors. Some fuel injection engines need adjusting too, and ignition settings may have to be changed: check the manufacturer's recommendations. The electronic ignition and fuel metering systems on modern emission controlled cars are allergic to humidity, heat and dust, and cannot be repaired by bush mechanics. Standard European and

Japanese cars run on fuel with a higher octane rating than is commonly available in North, South or Central America, and in Brazil petrol (gasolina) is in fact gasohol, with a 12% admixture of alcohol. A high compression fuel injection engine will not like this. Unleaded fuel is available in Chile, Colombia and Ecuador, and to an increasing extent in Argentina and coastal Peru. The most easily maintained petrol engined cars, then, are the types manufactured in Latin American countries, ie pre-emission control models such as the VW Kombi with carburettors and conventional (non-electronic) ignition, or the old type Toyota Landcruisers common in Central America. Older model American cars, especially Ford or GM pickups, are easily maintained, but high fuel consumption offsets this advantage. (Note that Colombia does not have a network for spares and repairs of VW, while Ecuador, Venezuela and Brazil do. Argentina is very expensive for maintenance of any make of car.)

Preparation

Preparing the car for the journey is largely a matter of common sense: obviously any part that is not in first class condition should be replaced. It's well worth installing extra heavy-duty shock-absorbers (such as Spax or Koni) before starting out, because a long trip on rough roads in a heavily laden car will give heavy wear. Fit tubes on "tubeless" tyres, since air plugs for tubeless tyres are hard to find, and if you bend the rim on a pothole, the tyre will not hold air. Take spare tubes, and an extra spare tyre. Also take spare plugs, fan-belts, radiator hoses and headlamp bulbs; even though local equivalents can easily be found in cities, it is wise to take spares for those occasions late at night or in remote areas when you might need them. You can also change the fanbelt after a stretch of long, hot driving to prevent wear (eg after 15,000 km/10,000 miles). If your vehicle has more than one fanbelt, always replace them all at the same time (make sure you have the necessary tools if doing it yourself). If your car has sophisticated electrics, spare "black boxes" for the ignition and fuel injection are advisable, plus a spare voltage regulator or the appropriate diodes for the alternator, and elements for the fuel, air and oil filters if these are not a common type. (Some drivers take a spare alternator of the correct amperage, especially if the regulator is incorporated into the alternator.) Dirty fuel is a frequent problem, so be prepared to change filters more often than you would at home: in a diesel car you will need to check the sediment bowl often, too. An extra in-line fuel filter is a good idea if feasible (although harder to find, metal canister type is preferable to plastic), and for travel on dusty roads an oil bath air filter is best for a diesel car. It is wise to carry a spade, jumper cables, tow rope and an air pump. Fit tow hooks to both sides of the vehicle frame. A 12 volt neon light for camping and repairs will be invaluable. Spare fuel containers should be steel and not plastic, and a siphon pipe is essential for those places where fuel is sold out of the drum. Take a 10 litre water container for self and vehicle. Note that in some areas gas stations are few and far between. Fill up when you see one: the next one may be out of fuel. Some countries have periodic fuel conservation strategies which means you can't get any after a certain hour in the evening, and often not at weekends either.

Security

Apart from the mechanical aspects, spare no ingenuity in making your car secure. Your model should be the Brink's armoured van: anything less secure can be broken into by the determined and skilled thief. Use heavy chain and padlocks to chain doors shut, fit security catches on windows, remove interior window winders (so that a hand reaching in from a forced vent cannot open the window). All these will help, but none is foolproof. Anything on the outside – wing mirrors, spot lamps, motifs etc – is likely to be stolen too. So are wheels if not secured by locking nuts. Try never to leave the car unattended except in a locked garage or guarded parking space. Remove all belongings and leave the empty glove compartment open when the car is unattended. Also lock the clutch or accelerator to the steering wheel with a heavy, obvious chain or lock. Street children will generally protect your car fiercely in exchange for a tip. Be sure to note down key numbers and carry spares of the most important ones (but don't keep all spares inside the vehicle).

Documents

A *carnet de passage* is no longer necessary in any country (but please see **Additional notes** below). Land entry procedures for all countries – with the exception of Colombia – are simple, though time-consuming, as the car has to be checked by customs, police and agriculture officials. All you need is the registration document in the name of the driver, or, in the case of a car registered in someone else's name, a notarized letter of authorization. Most countries give a limited period of stay, but allow an extension if requested in advance. Of course, do be very careful to keep **all** the papers you are given when you enter, to produce when you leave. Bringing a car in by sea or air is much more complicated and expensive: generally you will have to hire an agent to clear it through customs, expensive and slow. Insurance for the vehicle against accident, damage or theft is best arranged in the country of origin, but it is getting increasingly difficult to find agencies who offer this service. In Latin American countries it is very expensive to insure against accident and theft, especially as you should take into account the value of the car increased by duties calculated in real (ie non devaluing) terms. If the car is stolen or written off you will be required to pay very high import duty on its value. A few countries insist on compulsory third party insurance, to be bought at the border: in other countries it's technically required, but not checked up on (Venezuela seems to be the only country where it is easy to obtain – Ed). Get the legally required minimum cover, not expensive, as soon as you can, because if you should be involved in an accident and are uninsured, your car could be confiscated. If anyone is hurt, do not pick them up (you may become liable). Seek assistance from the nearest police station or hospital if you are able to do so. You may find yourself facing a hostile crowd, even if you are not to blame.

Journey's End

When you finally reach your destination, what happens to the car? Shipping it back is one alternative. From Brazil, Grimaldi line to Genoa is the cheapest: there are also frequent sailings from Montevideo and Buenos Aires to most other destinations. The other alternative is to sell the car. Until now, this has been virtually impossible except in Paraguay, but the economic liberalization in Argentina, Chile and Brazil makes it legal – if not simple – to import cars into those countries. Probably safer not to count on it though, unless you have the sort of car in great demand, like a Mercedes saloon. You can sell anything in Paraguay if you have the time. Legalizing the permanent import of a temporarily imported car costs about 30% of its street value. If you leave it to the buyer to "take care of" obtaining the correct documentation, you should not expect to receive a very favourable price. Dealers are adept at taking advantage of the fact that they can wait, and you cannot, so be prepared for "on – off – on again" dealing.

Car Hire

The main international car hire companies operate in all countries, but they do tend to be very expensive, reflecting the high costs and accident rates. Hotels and tourist agencies will tell you where to find cheaper rates, but you will need to check that you have such basics as spare wheel, toolkit and functioning lights etc. You'll probably have more

fun if you drive yourself, although it's always possible to hire a car with driver. If you plan to do a lot of driving and will have time at the end to dispose of it, investigate the possibility of buying a second hand car locally: since hiring is so expensive it may well work out cheaper and will probably do you just as well.

Car Hire Insurance Check exactly what the hirer's insurance policy covers. In many cases it will only protect you against minor bumps and scrapes, not major accidents, nor "natural" damage (eg flooding). Ask if extra cover is available. Also find out, if using a credit card, whether the card automatically includes insurance. Beware of being billed for scratches which were on the vehicle before you hired it.

Additional notes on motoring

A great deal of conflicting information surrounds what documents are required in addition to the vehicle's registration. According to the RAC in the UK there are three recognized documents for taking a vehicle into South America: a *carnet de passages* issued by the Fedération Internationale de l'Automobile (FIA – Paris), a *carnet de passages* issued by the Alliance Internationale de Tourisme (AIT-Geneva), and the *Libreta de Pasos por Aduana* issued by the Federación Interamericana de Touring y Automóvil Clubs (FITAC). The following list gives official requirements, with comments about actual practice: Argentina requires a written undertaking that the car will be exported after a given period, either of the *carnets*, or the *libreta* (in practice, nothing is asked for beyond the title document, except at remote border crossings which may demand a *libreta*); Bolivia, *libreta* only; Brazil, a written undertaking only (nothing asked for); Chile, either *carnet*, or the *libreta* (in practice nothing asked for), insurance is obligatory; Colombia, either *carnet* or, according to a law of 31.12.1992, you have to purchase a bond on entry to the value of 10% of your vehicle (in practice, nothing asked for), insurance is necessary; Ecuador, until 1995 either *carnet*, or the *libreta* was essential, but latest reports indicate that neither is now required (ask at an embassy in advance); Paraguay, either *carnet*, or the *libreta*; Peru, either *carnet*, the *libreta* and, for caravans and trailers, an inventory (the consulate in London says that a *libreta* is necessary, but if you cannot obtain one a written declaration that the car will leave Peru, authorized at a Peruvian consulate before leaving your home country, will do instead, in addition a traveller reports that *Formulario 015*, which can be requested at the border, entitles visitors to bring a vehicle into Peru duty free for 3 months, it is not extendable, it is free, but our correspondent was charged US$35 anyway); Uruguay, the *libreta* or the FIA *carnet* only (in practice nothing asked for); Venezuela, either *carnet* or the *libreta* (the consulate in London says a *Certificado de uso por turismo* must be completed at a Venezuelan embassy before arrival, no other documents required; in the USA the vehicle's title document must be legalized by a Venezuelan consul, US$100, this, plus title and a letter of intent from your shipper's agent must be taken to US customs at least 2 days before sailing, no *libreta* or *carnet* needed). In view of this confusion, contact the automobile clubs of the countries you intend to drive in and get their advice. In general, motorists in South America seem to fare better with a *carnet de passages* than without it.

The *libreta*, a 10-page book of three-part passes for customs, should be available from any South American automobile club member of FITAC; cost seems to be US$200, half refundable. The *carnet de passages* is issued only in the country where the vehicle is registered (in

the UK it costs £65 for 25 pages, £55 for 10 pages, valid 12 months, either bank indemnity or insurance indemnity, half of the premium refundable value of the vehicle and countries to be visited required), available from the RAC or the AA. In the USA the AAA seems not to issue the *carnet*, although the HQ in Washington DC may give advice. It is available from the Canadian Automobile Association (1775 Courtwood Crescent, Ottawa, K2C 3JZ, T 613-226-7631, F 613-225-7383) for Canadian and US citizens, cost C$450; full details obtainable from the CAA. For this information thanks go to Paul Gowen, RAC Touring Information Manager, Binka Le Breton and other motorists.

While a normal car will reach most places of interest, high ground clearance is useful for badly surfaced or unsurfaced roads and for fording rivers: 4-wheel drive is recommended for mountain terrain and unmade roads off the beaten track.

If you want to buy a second-hand car, check for corrosion if making the deal in a coastal city and always check, if not change, the full set of tyres.

Shipping a vehicle

From Europe or the USA you can either go to Panama and take the new *Crucero Express* ferry from Colón to Cartagena (Colombia), or shop around for the best value sailing to whichever port best suits your travelling plans. Try Boyd Steamship Corporation (T Balboa 636311), Buenaventura or Guayaquil; Sudamericana de Vapores (T Cristóbal 293844), Buenaventura; Central American Lines (T Colón 412880, Panama City 361036), Cartagena; Vencaribe (T Cristóbal 450461, Panama City 521258) or Cía Transatlántica España (T 696300) for Venezuela. Alternatively you can ship a vehicle from Europe to Brazil, Uruguay or Argentina. Recommended as good value are Polish Ocean Lines, 10 Lutego, Gdynia, Poland: one-month voyage Gydnia-Buenos Aires US$1,000 for passenger (inc food), US$300 for motorcycle, US$1,300 for a VW Kombi. Motorcycles do not have to be stripped down. *Carnet* is necessary;

POL agent deals with customs. Departure dates are not scheduled in advance. Vehicles can also be shipped from the USA. You have to get a special exemption in order to be allowed to be carried to Colombia in a non Colombian vessel, which takes time to obtain. Anything left inside the car while it is being shipped will be stolen. As long as your vehicle is not over 2.28m high, it can go in a container, but permission must be obtained for any belongings to remain in the car, and separate insurance for effects purchased. If the car is going ro-ro (drive on), it should be empty of all belongings, unless they are thoroughly secured.

A book containing much practical information on South American motoring conditions and requirements, as well as being a travelogue, is *Driving to Heaven*, by Derek Stansfield (available from the author, Ropley, Broad Oak, Sturminster Newton, Dorset DT10 2HG, T/F 01258-472534, £8.85 plus postage, if outside the UK).

MOTORCYCLING

People are generally very amicable to motorcyclists and you can make many friends by returning friendship to those who show an interest in you.

The Machine

It should be off road capable: my choice would be the BMW R80/100/GS for its rugged and simple design and reliable shaft drive, but a Kawasaki KLR 650s, Honda Transalp/Dominator, or the ubiquitous Yamaha XT600 Tenere would also be suitable. Buying a bike in the States and driving down works out cheaper than buying one in the UK. A road bike can go most places an off road bike can go at the cost of greater effort.

Preparations

Many roads in Latin America are rough. Fit heavy duty front fork springs and the best quality rebuildable shock absorber you can afford (Ohlins, White Power). Fit lockable luggage such as Krausers (reinforce luggage frames) or make some detachable aluminium panniers. Fit a tank bag and tank panniers for better weight distribution. A large capacity fuel tank (Acerbis), +300 mile/480 km range is essential if going off the beaten track. A washable air filter is a good idea (K&N), also fuel filters, fueltap rubber seals and smaller jets for high altitude Andean motoring. A good set of trails-type tyres as well as a high mudguard are useful. Get to know the bike before you go, ask the dealers in your country what goes wrong with it and arrange a link whereby you can get parts flown out to you. If riding a chain driven bike, a fully enclosed chaincase is useful. A hefty bash plate/sump guard is invaluable.

Spares

Reduce service intervals by half if driving in severe conditions. A spare rear tyre is useful but you can buy modern tyres in most capital cities. Take oil filters, fork and shock seals, tubes, a good manual, spare cables (taped into position), a plug cap and spare plug lead. A spare electronic ignition is a good idea, try and buy a second hand one and make arrangements to have parts sent out to you. A first class tool kit is a must and if riding a bike with a chain then a spare set of sprockets and an 'o' ring chain should be carried. Spare brake and clutch levers should also be taken as these break easily in a fall. Parts are few and far between, but mechanics are skilled at making do and can usually repair things. Castrol oil can be bought everywhere and relied upon.

Take a puncture repair kit and tyre levers. Find out about any weak spots on the bike and improve them. Get the book for international dealer coverage from your manufacturer, but don't rely on it. They frequently have few or no parts for modern, large machinery.

Clothes and Equipment

A tough waterproof jacket, comfortable strong boots, gloves and a helmet with which you can use glass goggles (Halycon) which will not scratch and wear out like a plastic visor. The best quality tent and camping gear that you can afford and a petrol stove which runs on bike fuel is helpful.

Security
Not a problem in most countries. Try not to leave a fully laden bike on its own. An Abus D or chain will keep the bike secure. A cheap alarm gives you peace of mind if you leave the bike outside a hotel at night. Most hotels will allow you to bring the bike inside. Look for hotels that have a courtyard or more secure parking and never leave luggage on the bike overnight or whilst unattended.

Documents
Passport, International Driving Licence, bike registration document are necessary. Riders fare much better with a *carnet de passages* than without it. Get your licence endorsed by police in Bolivia.

Shipping
Bikes may be sent from Panama to Colombia by cargo flight (eg CAC). You must drain the fuel, oil and battery acid, or remove the battery, but it is easier to disconnect and seal the overflow tube. Tape cardboard over fragile bits and insist on loading the bike yourself. The Darién Gap is impossible unless you carry the bike. See the Colombia chapter for the *Crucero Express* which carries motorbikes between Panama and Colombia.

Border Crossings
Do not try to cross borders on a Sunday or a holiday anywhere as a charge is levied on the usually free borders in South America. South American customs and immigration inspectors are mostly friendly, polite and efficient. If in doubt ask to see the boss and/or the rule book.

CYCLING
Hallam Murray writes (with recent additions from other cyclists): since the early 1980s, bicycle technology has improved in leaps and bounds. With the advent of Kevlar tyres and puncture-resistant inner tubes it is now theoretically possible to cycle from Alaska to Tierra del Fuego without so much as a single puncture. For the traveller with a zest for adventure and a limited budget there is unlikely to be a finer way to explore. At first glance a bicycle may not appear to be the most obvious vehicle for a major journey, but given ample time and reasonable energy it most certainly is the best. It can be ridden, carried by almost every form of transport from an aeroplane to a canoe, and can even be lifted across one's shoulders over short distances. Cyclists can be the envy of travellers using more orthodox transport, since they can travel at their own pace, explore more remote regions and meet people who are not normally in contact with tourists.

Choosing a Bicycle
The choice of bicycle depends on the type and length of expedition being undertaken and on the terrain and road surfaces likely to be encountered. Unless you are planning a journey almost exclusively on paved roads – when a high quality touring bike such as a Dawes Super Galaxy would probably suffice – a mountain bike is strongly recommended. The good quality ones (and the cast iron rule is **never** to skimp on quality) are incredibly tough and rugged, with low gear ratios for difficult terrain, wide tyres with plenty of tread for good road-holding, cantilever brakes, and a low centre of gravity for improved stability. Although touring bikes, and to a lesser extent mountain bikes, and spares are available in the larger Latin American cities, remember that in the developing world most indigenous manufactured goods are shoddy and rarely last. In some countries, such as Mexico, Chile and Uruguay, imported components can be found but they tend to be extremely expensive. (Shimano parts are generally the easiest to find.) Buy everything you possibly can before you leave home.

Bicycle Equipment
A small but comprehensive tool kit (to include chain rivet and crank removers, a spoke key and possibly a block remover), a spare tyre and inner tubes, a puncture repair kit with plenty of extra patches and glue, a set of brake blocks, brake and gear cables and all types of nuts and bolts, at least 12 spokes (best taped to the chain stay), a light oil for the chain (eg Finish-Line Teflon Dry-Lube), tube of waterproof

grease, a pump secured by a pump lock, a Blackburn parking block (a most invaluable accessory, cheap and virtually weightless), a cyclometer, a loud bell, and a secure lock and chain. *Richard's Bicycle Book* makes useful reading for even the most mechanically minded.

Luggage and equipment

Strong and waterproof front and back panniers are a must. When packed these are likely to be heavy and should be carried on the strongest racks available. Poor quality racks have ruined many a journey for they take incredible strain on unpaved roads. A top bag cum rucksack (eg Carradice) makes a good addition for use on and off the bike. A Cannondale front bag is good for maps, camera, compass, altimeter, notebook and small tape-recorder. (Other rec panniers are Ortlieb – front and back – which is waterpoof and almost "sandproof", Mac-Pac, Madden and Karimoor.) "Gaffa" tape is excellent for protecting vulnerable parts of panniers and for carrying out all manner of repairs. My most vital equipment included a light and waterproof tent, a 3 season sleeping bag, an Optimus petrol stove (recommended as it is light and efficient and petrol can be found almost everywhere, but see page 29, **Camping**), a plastic survival bag for storing luggage at night when camping, 4 elastic straps, 4 one-litre water bottles, Swiss Army knife, torch, candle, comprehensive medical kit, money belts, a hat and sunglasses to protect against hours of ferocious tropical sun and small presents such as postcards of home, balloons and plastic badges. A rubber mouse can do wonders for making contact with children in isolated villages.

All equipment and clothes should be packed in plastic bags to give extra protection against dust and rain. (Also protect all documents, etc carried close to the body from sweat.) Always take the minimum clothing. It's better to buy extra items en route when you find you need them. Naturally the choice will depend on whether you are planning a journey through tropical lowlands, deserts, high mountains or a combination, and

whether rain is to be expected. Generally it is best to carry several layers of thin light clothes than fewer heavy, bulky ones. Always keep one set of dry clothes, including long trousers, to put on at the end of the day. The incredibly light, strong, waterproof and wind resistant goretex jacket and overtrousers are invaluable. Training shoes can be used for both cycling and walking.

Useful Tips

Wind, not hills is the enemy of the cyclist. Try to make the best use of the times of day when there is little; mornings tend to be best but there is no steadfast rule. In parts of Patagonia there can be gusting winds of 80 kph around the clock at some times of year, whereas in other areas there can be none. Take care to avoid dehydration, by drinking regularly. In hot, dry areas with limited supplies of water, be sure to carry an ample supply. For food, carry the staples (sugar, salt, dried milk, tea, coffee, porridge oats, raisins, dried soups, etc) and supplemented these with whatever local foods can be found in the markets. Give your bicycle a thorough daily check for loose nuts or bolts or bearings. See that all parts run smoothly. A good chain should last 2,000 miles, 3,200 km or more but be sure to keep it as clean as possible – an old toothbrush is good for this – and to oil it lightly from time to time. Always camp out of sight of a road. Remember that thieves are attracted to towns and cities, so when sight-seeing, try to leave your bicycle with someone such as a café owner or a priest. Country people tend to be more honest and are usually friendly and very inquisitive. However, don't take unnecessary risks; always see that your bicycle is secure (most hotels will allow bikes to be kept in rooms). In more remote regions dogs can be vicious; carry a stick or some small stones to frighten them off. Traffic on main roads can be a nightmare; it is usually far more rewarding to keep to the smaller roads or to paths if they exist. Most towns have a bicycle shop of some description, but it is best to do your own repairs and adjustments whenever possible. In an emergency it is amazing how one can improvise with wire, string, dental floss, nuts and bolts, odd pieces of tin or "Gaffa" tape!

The Expedition Advisory Centre, administered by the Royal Geographical Society, 1, Kensington Gore, London SW7 2AR has published a useful monograph entitled *Bicycle Expeditions*, by Paul Vickers. Published in March 1990, it is available direct from the Centre, price £6.50 (postage extra if outside the UK). (In the UK there is also the Cyclist's Touring Club, CTC, Cotterell House, 69 Meadrow, Godalming, Surrey, GU7 3HS, T 01483-417217, e-mail cycling@ctc.org.uk, for touring, and technical information.)

Most cyclists agree that the main danger comes from other traffic. A rearview mirror has been frequently recommended to forewarn you of vehicles which are too close behind. You also need to watch for oncoming, overtaking vehicles, unstable loads on trucks, protruding loads etc. Make yourself conspicuous by wearing bright clothing and a helmet.

Ryan Flegal of Los Angeles, California, says that, instead of taking your own expensive bicycle from home with the attendant need for specialized tools and high risks of loss, one can buy a bike in Latin America. "Affix a sturdy rear rack, improvise securing luggage to the bicycle, and go. Carry only a patch kit and wrench to remove the wheel, and rely on the many bike mechanics in the area to do the rest". A steel frame is more durable when heavily laden and can be welded if damaged, unlike aluminium. If undertaking your own maintenance, make sure you know how to do it, and research what tyres you will need, before you go.

RIVER TRANSPORT

Because expanding air services have captured the lucrative end of the passenger market, passenger services on the rivers are in decline. Worst hit have been the upper reaches; rivers like the Ucayali in Peru, but the trend is apparent throughout the region. The situation has been aggravated for the casual traveller by a new generation of purpose-built tugs (all engine-room and bridge) that can handle up to a dozen freight barges but have no passenger accommodation. In Peru passenger boats must now supplement incomes by carrying cargo, and this lengthens their journey cycle. In the face of long delays, travellers might consider shorter "legs" involving more frequent changes of boat; though the more local the service, the slower and more uncomfortable it will be.

Hammocks, mosquito nets (not always good quality), plastic containers for water storage, kettles and cooking utensils can be purchased in any sizeable riverside town, as well as tinned food such as sardines, meat loaf, frankfurters, ham and fruit. Fresh bread, cake, eggs, fruit – papayas, bananas, pineapples, oranges etc – are available in most villages. Cabin bunks are provided with thin mattresses but these are often foul. Replacements can be bought locally but rolls of plastic foam that can be cut to size are also available and much cheaper. Eye-screws for securing washing lines and mosquito nets are useful, and tall passengers who are not taking a hammock and who may find insufficient headroom on some boats should consider a camp-chair. The writer yearned for a cushion.

HM Wams (Amsterdam) endorses the recommendation of taking hammock, mosquito net and food, adding that in Venezuelan Amazonas hitching rides on boats is possible if you camp at the harbour or police post where all boats must register. Take any boat going in your direction as long as it reaches the next police post. See the special section on the Brazilian Amazon, page 581.

HIKING AND TREKKING

A network of paths and tracks covers much of South America and is in constant use by the local people. In countries with a large Indian population – Ecuador, Peru and Bolivia, for instance – you can walk just about anywhere, but in the more European countries, such as Venezuela, Chile, and Argentina, you must usually limit yourself to the many excellent national parks with hiking trails. Most South American countries have an Instituto Geográfico Militar which sells topographical maps, scale 1:100,000 or 1:50,000. The physical features shown on these are usually accurate; the trails and place names less so. National Parks offices also sell maps.

Hiking and backpacking should not be approached casually. Even if you only plan to be out a couple of hours you should have comfortable, safe footwear (which can cope with the wet) and a daypack to carry your sweater and waterproof (which must be more than showerproof). At high altitudes the difference in temperature between sun and shade is remarkable. The longer trips mentioned in this book require basic backpacking equipment. Essential items are: backpack with frame, sleeping bag, closed cell foam mat for insulation, stove, tent or tarpaulin, dried food (not tins), water bottle, compass. Some but not all of these things are available locally.

When planning treks in the Andes you should be aware of the effects and dangers of acute mountain sickness, and cerebral and pulmonary oedema (see Health, page 36). These can be avoided by spending a few days acclimatizing to the altitude before starting your walk, and by climbing slowly. Otherwise there are fewer dangers than in most cities. Hikers have little to fear from the animal kingdom apart from insects (although it's best to avoid actually stepping on a snake), and robbery and assault are very rare. You are much more of a threat to the environment than vice versa. Leave no evidence of your passing; don't litter and don't give gratuitous presents of sweets or money to rural villagers. Respect their system of reciprocity; if they give you hospitality or food, then is the time to reciprocate with presents.

For trekking in mountain areas, where the weather can deteriorate rapidly (eg in Torres del Paine), trekkers should consider taking the following equipment (list supplied by Andrew Dobbie of Swansea, who adds that it "is in no way finite"): Clothing: warm hat (wool or man-made fibre), thermal underwear, T-shirts/shirts, trousers (quick-drying and preferably windproof, never jeans), warm (wool or fleece) jumper/jacket (preferably two), gloves, waterproof jacket and over trousers (preferably Gore-Tex), shorts, walking boots and socks, change of footwear or flip-flops. Camping Gear: tent (capable of withstanding high winds), sleeping mat (closed cell – Karrimat – or inflatable – Thermarest), sleeping bag (3-season minimum rating), sleeping bag liner, stove and spare parts, fuel, matches and lighter, cooking and eating utensils, pan scrubber, survival bag. Food: very much personal preference but at least two days more supplies than you plan to use; tea, coffee, sugar, dried milk; porridge, dried fruit, honey; soup, pasta, rice, soya (TVP); fresh fruit and vegetables; bread, cheese, crackers; biscuits, chocolate; salt, pepper, other herbs and spices, cooking oil. Miscellaneous: map and compass, torch and spare batteries, pen and notebook, Swiss army knife, sunglasses, sun cream, lip salve and insect repellent, first aid kit, water bottle, toiletries and towel.

Maps and Guide Books

Those from the Institutos Geográficos Militares in the capitals (see above) are often the only good maps available in Latin America. It is therefore wise to get as many as possible in your home country before leaving, especially if travelling by land. A recommended series of general maps is that published by International Travel Map Productions (ITM), 345 West Broadway, Vancouver BC, V5Y 1P8, Canada, T (604) 879-3621, F (604) 879-4521, compiled with historical notes, by the late Kevin Healey. Available are South America South, North East and North West (1:4M), Amazon Basin (1:4M), Ecuador (1:1M), The Galapagos Islands (1:500,000), Easter Island (1:30,000), Argentina (1:4M), Rio de Janeiro (1:20,000), Venezuela (1:1.75M), Central America (1:1.8M), Panama (1:800,000), Guatemala and El Salvador (1:500,000), El Salvador (1:375,000), Nicaragua (1:750,000), Honduras (1:750,000), Costa Rica (1:500,000),

Belize (1:350,000), Mexico (1:3.3M), Mexico City (1:10,000), Mexico South (1:1M), the Yucatán (1:1M) and Baja California (1:1M). Another map series that has been mentioned is that of New World Edition, Bertelsmann, Neumarkter Strasse 18, 81673 München, Germany, *Mittelamerika, Südamerika Nord, Südamerika Sud, Brasilien* (all 1:4M). For information on Bradt Publications' Backpacking Guide Series (covering Chile and Argentina, Peru and Bolivia, Ecuador, Venezuela), other titles and imported maps and guides, contact 41 Nortoft Road, Chalfont St Peter, Bucks, SL9 0LA, UK, T/F 01494 873478.

A very useful book, highly recommended, aimed specifically at the budget traveller is *The Tropical Traveller*, by John Hatt (Penguin Books, 3rd edition, 1993).

The South American Explorers' Club is at Avenida Portugal 146 (Casilla 3714), Lima, Peru (T 425-0142), Jorge Washington y Leonidas Plaza, Apartado 17-21-431, Eloy Alfaro, Quito, Ecuador (T 225-228), and 126 Indian Creek Road, Ithaca, NY 14850, USA T (607) 277-0488, e-mail explorer@samexplo.org. (For further details see under Lima and Quito.) Books, maps and travel planning services are available at the US office. The South American Explorers Club is represented in the UK by Bradt Publications.

The Latin American Travel Advisor is a quarterly news bulletin with up-to-date detailed and reliable information on countries throughout South and Central America. The publication focuses on public safety, health, weather and natural phenomena, travel costs, the economy and politics in each country. Annual airmail subscriptions US$39, a single current issue US$15, information transmitted by fax or e-mail US$10 per country. Payment by US$ cheque, Mastercard or Visa (no money orders, credit card payments by mail or fax with card number, expiry date, cardholder's name and signature). Contact PO Box 17-17-908, Quito, Ecuador, F 593-2-562-566. Internet LATA@pi.pro.ec, World Wide

Web http://www.amerispan.com/latc or http://www.greenarrow.com/latc.htm.

TRAVELLING WITH CHILDREN

People contemplating overland travel in South America with children should remember that a lot of time can be spent waiting for buses, trains, and especially for aeroplanes. On bus journeys, if the children are good at amusing themselves, or can readily sleep while travelling, the problems can be considerably lessened. If your child is of an early reading age, take reading material with you as it is difficult, and expensive to find. A bag of, say 30 pieces, of Duplo or Lego can keep young children occupied for hours. Travel on trains, while not as fast or at times as comfortable as buses, allows more scope for moving about. Some trains provide tables between seats, so that games can be played. Beware of doors left open for ventilation especially if air-conditioning is not working.

Food

Food can be a problem if the children are not adaptable. It is easier to take biscuits, drinks, bread etc with you on longer trips than to rely on meal stops where the food may not be to taste. Avocados are safe, easy to eat and nutritious; they can be fed to babies as young as 6 months and most older children like them. A small immersion heater and jug for making hot drinks is invaluable, but remember that electric current varies. Try and get a dual-voltage one (110v and 220v).

Fares

On all long-distance buses you pay for each seat, and there are no half-fares if the children occupy a seat each. For shorter trips it is cheaper, if less comfortable, to seat small children on your knee. Often there are spare seats which children can occupy after tickets have been collected. In city and local excursion buses, small children generally do not pay a fare, but are not entitled to a seat when paying customers are standing. On sightseeing tours you should *always* bargain for a family rate – often children can go free. (In trains, reductions for children are general, but not universal.)

All civil airlines charge half for children under 12, but some military services don't have half-fares, or have younger age limits. Children's fares on Lloyd Aéreo Boliviano are considerably more than half, and there is only a 7kg baggage allowance. (LAB also checks children's ages on passports.) Note that a child travelling free on a long excursion is not always covered by the operator's travel insurance; it is adviseable to pay a small premium to arrange cover.

Hotels

In all hotels, try to negotiate family rates. If charges are per person, always insist that two children will occupy one bed only, therefore counting as one tariff. If rates are per bed, the same applies. In either case you can almost always get a reduced rate at cheaper hotels. Occasionally when travelling with a child you will be refused a room in a hotel that is "unsuitable". On river boat trips, unless you have very large hammocks, it may be more comfortable and cost effective to hire a 2-berth cabin for 2 adults and a child. (In restaurants, you can normally buy children's helpings, or divide one full-size helping between two children.)

Travel with children can bring you into closer contact with Latin American families and, generally, presents no special problems – in fact the path is often smoother for family groups. Officials tend to be more amenable where children are concerned and they are pleased if your child knows a little Spanish or Portuguese. Moreover, even thieves and pickpockets seem to have some of the traditional respect for families, and may leave you alone because of it!

Health

WITH THE FOLLOWING advice and precautions, you should keep as healthy as you do at home. In Latin America the health risks are different from those encountered in Europe or the USA, especially in the tropical regions, but the region's medical practitioners have particular experience in dealing with locally occurring diseases.

Medical care

Epidemic diseases have been largely brought under control by vaccination programmes and public sanitation but, in rural areas, the latter is rudimentary and the chances of contracting infections of various sorts are higher than at home. There are English-speaking doctors in most major cities. If you fall ill the best plan may be to attend the out-patient department of a local hospital or contact your Embassy representative for the name of a reputable doctor. (We give the names of hospitals and some recommended doctors in the main city sections. – Ed.)

Medicines

Self-medication is undesirable except for minor complaints but may be forced on you by circumstances. Whatever the circumstances, be wary of medicines prescribed for you by pharmacists; many are poorly trained and unscrupulous enough to sell you potentially dangerous drugs or old stock they want to get rid of. The large number of pharmacies throughout Latin America is a considerable surprise to most people, as is the range of medicines you can purchase over the counter. There is a tendency towards over-prescription of

drug mixtures and in general this should be resisted. Many drugs are manufactured under licence from American or European companies so the trade names may be familiar to you. This means that you do not need to carry a whole chest of medicines, but remember that the shelf-life of some items, especially vaccines and antibiotics, is markedly reduced in tropical conditions. Buy your supplies at the better outlets where they have refrigerators, even though it is more expensive. Check the expiry date of all preparations you buy.

Immigration officials sometimes confiscate scheduled drugs (Lomotil is an example) if they are not accompanied by a doctor's prescription.

Make local enquiries about health risks if you are apprehensive and take the general advice of European or North American families who have lived or are living in the country.

Before travelling

Take out medical insurance. You should have a dental check-up, obtain a spare glasses prescription, a spare oral contraceptive prescription and, if you suffer from a chronic illness (such as diabetes,

high blood pressure, ear or sinus troubles, cardiopulmonary disease or a nervous disorder) arrange for a check-up with your doctor, who can at the same time provide you with a letter explaining the details of your disability, if possible in English and Spanish (or Portuguese for Brazil). Check current practice in malaria prophylaxis (prevention).

Vaccination and immunisation

Smallpox vaccination is no longer required anywhere in the world. A major outbreak of cholera occurred, unusually, in Peru in 1990-91 and most other Latin American countries were affected subsequently. The epidemic continues, spread by travellers and fuelled by insanitary living conditions, untreated sewage and polluted water supplies. A vaccine against cholera is available but is not very effective and is not recognized as necessary for international travel by the World Health Organization. Nevertheless some immigration officials are demanding it in Latin America, so this should be borne in mind. Cholera is largely a water borne disease, either in drinking water, or via food which has been washed in contaminated water, or seafood which has been living in such water. The usual food hygiene precautions should protect the traveller from cholera; if they don't, the treatment is rapid rehydration with water and salts and sometimes the use of antibiotics.

The following vaccinations are recommended:

Yellow fever: this is a live vaccine not to be given to children under 9 months of age or persons allergic to eggs. Immunity lasts 10 years. An international certificate of yellow fever vaccination will be given and should be kept because it is sometimes asked for.

Typhoid (monovalent): one dose followed by a booster in a month's time. Immunity from this course lasts 2 to 3 years. An oral preparation is now available and a newer, more expensive vaccination against typhoid, Typhim Vi, less likely to cause post-injection symptoms.

Poliomyelitis: this is a live vaccine generally given orally and a full course consists of three doses with a booster in tropical regions every 3 to 5 years.

Tetanus: one dose should be given with a booster (vital) at 6 weeks and another at 6 months, and 10-yearly boosters thereafter are recommended.

Children should, in addition, be properly protected against diphtheria, and against pertussis (whooping cough), measles and HIB, which tend to be more serious infections than at home. Measles, mumps and rubella vaccine is now widely available but those teenage girls who have not had rubella (German measles) should be tested and vaccinated. Consult your doctor for advice on tuberculosis inoculation: the disease is still widespread.

Infectious Hepatitis (jaundice) is endemic throughout Latin America and seems to be frequently caught by travellers. The main symptoms are pains in the stomach, lack of appetite, lassitude, and the typical yellow colour of the skin. Medically speaking there are two different types, the less serious but more common is hepatitis A, for which the best protection is the careful preparation of food, the avoidance of contaminated drinking water and scrupulous attention to toilet hygiene. Human normal immunoglobulin (gamma globulin) confers considerable protection against the disease and is particularly useful in epidemics; it should be obtained from a reputable source and is certainly useful for travellers who intend to live rough: they should have a shot before leaving and have it repeated every 6 months. The dose of gamma globulin depends on the concentration of the particular preparation used, so the manufacturer's advice should be taken. A smaller dose than usual can be given if exposure is for one or 2 months only. At last a vaccine is now in production and generally available against hepatitis A. Trials have shown it to be safe and effective. It is more expensive than gamma globulin, but the protection is better and lasts longer. Three doses over 6 months would appear to give immunity lasting up to 10 years; then boosters would be required. Havrix monodose is now available, and Junior Havrix.

The other, more serious, version is hepatitis B which is acquired usually by injections with unclean needles, blood transfusions, as a sexually transmitted disease and possibly by insect bites. This disease can be effectively prevented by a specific vaccination requiring three shots over 6 months before travelling but this is quite expensive. If you have had jaundice in the past it would be worthwhile having a blood test to see if you are immune to either of the two types because this might avoid the necessity for vaccination or gamma globulin.

Other vaccinations might be considered in the case of epidemics, eg meningitis. There is an effective vaccination against **rabies** which should be considered by all travellers, especially those going to remote areas and if there is a particular occupational risk, ie zoologists or veterinarians.

AIDS

In South America AIDS is increasing in its prevalence, as in most countries, but is not wholly confined to the well known high risk sections of the population, ie homosexual men, intravenous drug abusers, prostitutes and children of infected mothers. Heterosexual transmission is now the dominant mode and so the main risk to travellers is from casual sex. The same precautions should be taken as when encountering any sexually transmitted disease. The AIDS virus (HIV) can be passed via unsterilized needles which have been previously used to inject an HIV positive patient, but the risk of this is very small indeed. It would however be sensible to check that needles have been properly sterilised or disposable needles used. If you wish to take your own disposable needles, be prepared to explain what they are for. The risk of receiving a blood transfusion with blood infected with the HIV virus is greater than from dirty needles because of the amount of fluid exchanged. Supplies of blood for transfusion should now be screened for HIV in all reputable hospitals so again the risk must be very small indeed. Catching the AIDS virus does not usually produce an illness in itself; the only way to be sure if you feel you have been put at risk is to have a blood test for HIV antibodies on your return to a place where there are reliable laboratory facilities. The test does not become positive for many weeks. Presently the higher risks are probably in Brazil and the West Indies.

MALARIA

In South America malaria is theoretically confined to coastal and jungle zones but is now on the increase again. Mosquitoes do not thrive above 2,500 metres so you are safe at altitude. There are different varieties of malaria, some resistant to the normal drugs. Make local enquiries if you intend to visit possibly infected zones and use a prophylactic regime. Start taking the tablets a few days before exposure and continue to take them for 6 weeks after leaving the malarial zone. Remember to give the drugs to babies and children also. Opinion varies on the precise drugs and dosage to be used for protection; all the drugs may have some side effects, and it is important to balance the risk of catching the disease against the albeit rare side effects. The increasing complexity of the subject as the malarial parasite becomes immune to the new generation of drugs has made concentration on the physical prevention of being bitten by mosquitoes more important, ie the use of long-sleeved shirts/blouses and long trousers, repellents and nets. Clothes can now available impregnated with the insecticide Permethrin or Deltamethrin, or it is possible to impregnate the clothes yourself. Wide meshed nets impregnated with Permethrin are also becoming available, are lighter to carry and less claustrophobic to sleep in.

Prophylaxis and treatment

If your itinerary takes you into a malarial area, seek expert advice before you go on a suitable prophylactic regime. This is especially true for pregnant women who are particularly prone to malaria.

You can catch malaria even when sticking to the regime's rules, although it is unlikely. If you do develop symptoms (high fever, shivering, headache, sometimes diarrhoea) seek medical advice immediately. If this is not possible, and there is a great likelihood of malaria, the *treatment* is:

Normal types Chloroquine, a single dose of 4 tablets (600 mg) followed by 2 tablets (300 mg) in 6 hrs and 300 mg each day following.

Falciparum type or type in doubt: take local advice: various combinations of drugs are being used, eg quinine, tetracycline, or Halofantrine.

If Falciparum type malaria is definitely diagnosed, it is wise to get to a good hospital as the treatment can be complex and the illness very serious.

Dengue

Dengue fever is increasing worldwide, including in South and Central American countries. The more severe haemorrhagic dengue is much more of a problem for local people who have been exposed to the disease more than once. The treatment for simple dengue is painkillers and rest. For haemorrhagic dengue hospital treatment is necessary. There is no vaccine against the Aedes mosquito that carries the virus: you must just avoid mosquito bites.

ALTITUDE

Acute mountain sickness or *soroche* can strike from about 3,000 metres upwards. It is more likely to affect those who ascend rapidly (eg by plane) and those who overexert themselves. Teenagers are particularly prone. Past experience is not always a good guide: the author, having spent years in Peru travelling constantly between sea level and very high altitude, never suffered the slightest symptoms, then was severely affected climbing Kilimanjaro in Tanzania.

On reaching heights above 3,000 metres, heart pounding and shortness of breath, especially on exertion, are almost universal and a normal response to the lack of oxygen in the air. *Soroche* takes a few hours or days to come on and presents with headache, lassitude, dizziness, loss of appetite, nausea and vomiting. Insomnia is common and often associated with a suffocating feeling when lying in bed. Keen observers may note their breathing tends to wax and wane at night and their face tends to be puffy in the

mornings – this is all part of the syndrome. The treatment is rest, pain killers (preferably not aspirin-based) for the headache and anti-sickness pills for vomiting. Oxygen may help at very high altitudes. Various local panaceas ("Coramina glucosada", "Effortil", "Micoren") have their advocates and *mate* (or *te*) *de coca* (an infusion of coca leaves, widely available) certainly alleviates some of the symptoms.

On arrival at places over 3,000 metres, a few hours' rest in a chair and avoidance of alcohol, cigarettes and heavy food will go a long way towards preventing *soroche*. Should the symptoms be severe and prolonged it is best to descend to lower altitude and re-ascend slowly or in stages. If this is impossible because of shortage of time or if the likelihood of acute mountain sickness is high then the drug Acetazolamide (Diamox) can be used as a preventative and continued during the ascent. There is good evidence of the value of this drug in the prevention of *soroche* but some people do experience funny side effects. The usual dose is 500 mg of the slow-release preparation each night, starting the night before ascending above 3,000 metres. (Detailed information is available from the Mountain Medicine Centre, c/o Dr Charles Clarke, Dept of Neurological Sciences, St Bartholomew's Hospital, 38 Little Britain, London EC1A 7BE – Ed.)

Other problems experienced at high altitude are sunburn, excessively dry air causing skin cracking, sore eyes (it may be wise to leave your contact lenses out) and stuffy noses. It is unwise to ascend to high altitude if you are pregnant, especially in the first 3 months, or if you have any history of heart, lung or blood disease, including sickle-cell.

There is a further, albeit rare, hazard due to rapid ascent to high altitude called acute pulmonary oedema. The condition can affect mountaineers; but also occurs in Andean natives returning from a period at the coast. The condition comes on quite rapidly with breathlessness, noisy breathing, cough, blueness of the lips and frothing at the mouth. Anybody developing this must be brought down as soon as possible, given oxygen and taken to hospital.

Rapid descent from high places will aggravate sinus and middle ear infections, and make bad teeth ache painfully. The same problems are sometimes experienced during descent at the end of a flight.

Despite these various hazards (mostly preventable) of high-altitude travel, many people find the environment healthier and more invigorating than at sea-level.

OTHER COMMON PROBLEMS

CHAGAS' DISEASE

(South American Trypanosomiasis) is a chronic disease, very rarely caught by travellers, but very difficult to treat. It is transmitted by the simultaneous biting and excreting of the Reduvid bug (Triatoma or Rhodnius), also known as the *vinchuca*, or *barbeiro*. Somewhat resembling a small cockroach (coloured black and red, or black and yellow), this nocturnal "kissing bug" lives in poor adobe houses with dirt floors often frequented by oppossums. If you cannot avoid such accommodation, sleep off the floor with a candle lit, use a mosquito net, keep as much of your skin covered as possible and wash any bites thoroughly with soap and water, or a disinfectant (do not scratch the bites).

HEAT AND COLD

Full acclimatization to high temperatures takes about 2 weeks and during this period it is normal to feel relatively apathetic, especially if the relative humidity is high. Drink plenty of water (up to 15 litres a day are required when working physically hard in the tropics), use salt on your food and avoid extreme exertion. Tepid showers are more cooling than hot or cold ones. Large hats do not cool you down, but do prevent sunburn. Remember that, especially in the highlands, there can be a large and sudden drop in temperature between sun and shade and between night and day, so dress accordingly. Warm jackets and woollens are essential after dark at high altitude.

INSECTS

These can be a great nuisance, especially in the tropics, and some, of course, are carriers of serious diseases. The best way of keeping them away at night is to sleep off the ground with a mosquito net and to burn mosquito coils containing pyrethrum. The best way to use insecticide aerosol sprays is to spray the room thoroughly in all areas and then shut the door for a while, re-entering when the smell has dispersed. Tablets of insecticide are also available which, when placed on a heated mat plugged into a wall socket, fill the room with insecticide fumes in the same way. The best repellents contain di-ethyl-meta-toluamide (DET) or di-methyl phthalate – sold as "Deet", "Six-Twelve Plus", "Off", "Boots' Liquid Insect Repellent", "Autan", "Flypel". Liquid is best for arms and face (care around eyes) and aerosol spray for clothes and ankles to deter chiggers, mites and ticks. Liquid DEET suspended in water can be used to impregnate cotton clothes and mosquito nets.

If you are bitten, itching may be relieved by baking-soda baths, anti-histamine tablets (care with alcohol or driving), corticosteroid creams (great care – never use if any hint of sepsis) or by judicious scratching. Calamine lotion and cream have limited effectiveness and antihistamine creams (eg Antihisan, May & Baker) have a tendency to cause skin allergies and are, therefore, not generally recommended.

Bites which become infected (commonly in the tropics) should be treated with a local antiseptic or antibiotic cream, such as Cetrimide BP (Savlon) as should infected scratches.

Skin infestations with body lice (crabs) and scabies are, unfortunately, easy to pick up. Use whatever local commercial preparation is recommended for lice and scabies. Crotamiton cream (Eurax, Geigy) alleviates itching and also kills a number of skin parasites. Malathion lotion 5% (Prioderm) kills lice effectively, but do not use the toxic agricultural insecticide Malathion.

Ticks attach themselves usually to the

lower part of the body often after walking in areas where cattle have grazed. They take a while to attach themselves strongly but do swell up as they suck your blood. The important thing is to remove them gently so that they do not inject any disease into your body and if the head part of the tick is left inside the skin it may cause a nasty allergic reaction some days later, and become infected. Don't use petrol, vaseline, lighted cigarettes etc, to remove the tick but, with a pair of tweezers, remove the beast gently by gripping it at the attached (head) end and rock it out very much the way that a tooth is extracted.

Certain **tropical flies** which lay their eggs under the skin of sheep and cattle also occasionally do the same thing to humans with the unpleasant result that a maggot grows under the skin and this presents as a boil or pimple. The best way of removing these is to cover the boil with oil, vaseline or nail varnish so as to stop the maggot breathing, then to squeeze it out gently the next day.

INTESTINAL UPSETS

Practically nobody escapes this one, so be prepared for it. Most of the time it is due to the insanitary preparation of food. Don't eat uncooked fish or vegetables, fruit with the skin on (always peel your fruit yourself), food that is exposed to flies, or salads.

Drinking water

Tap water is rarely safe outside the major cities, especially in the rainy season, and stream water is often contaminated by communities living surprisingly high in the mountains. Filtered or bottled (make sure it is opened in your presence – Ed) water is usually available and safe. If your hotel has a central hot-water supply, this is safe to drink after cooling. Ice for drinks should be made from boiled water but rarely is, so stand your glass on the ice cubes rather than putting them in the drink.

Fresh, unpasteurized milk is a source of food poisoning germs, tuberculosis and brucellosis. This applies equally to ice-cream, yoghurt and cheese made from unpasteurized milk. Fresh milk can be rendered safe by heating it to 62°C for 30 mins followed by rapid cooling, or by boiling it. Matured or processed cheeses are safer than fresh varieties. Heat-treated (UHT), pasteurized or sterilized milk is becoming more available. Fruit juice should be pure, not diluted with water.

At certain times of the year, some fish and shellfish concentrate non-infectious toxins from their environment and cause a kind of food poisoning. If the local authorities notify the public not to eat these foods, do not ignore the warning.

Diarrhoea

Diarrhoea is usually caused by eating food which is contaminated by food poisoning germs. Drinking water is rarely the culprit. Seawater or river water is more likely to be contaminated by sewage and so swimming in such dilute effluent can also be a cause. Infection with various organisms can give rise to diarrhoea, eg viruses, bacteria (eg Escherichia coli, probably the most common cause), protozoa (amoeba), salmonella and cholera. The diarrhoea may come on suddenly or rather slowly. It may or may not be accompanied by vomiting or by severe abdominal pain and the passage of blood or mucus when it is called dysentery. How do you know which type you have and how to treat it?

If you can time the onset of the diarrhoea to the minute (acute) then it is probably due to a virus or a bacterium and/or the onset of dysentery. The treatment, in addition to rehydration is Ciprofloxacin 500 mgs every 12 hrs. The drug is now widely available as are various similar ones.

If the diarrhoea comes on slowly or intermittently (sub-acute) then it is more likely to be protozoal, ie caused by an amoeba or giardia and antibiotics will have little effect. These cases are best treated by a doctor, as is any outbreak of diarrhoea continuing for more than 3 days. Sometimes blood is passed in sub-acute amoebic dysentery and for this you should certainly seek medical help. If this is not available then the best treatment is probably Tinidazole (Fasigyn) 1 tablet 4 times a day for 3 days. If there are severe stomach cramps, the following drugs may help but are not very useful in the management of acute diarrhoea: Loperamide (Imodium, Arret) and Diphenoxylate with Atropine (Lomotil). They should not be given to children.

Any kind of diarrhoea whether or not accompanied by vomiting responds well to the replacement of water and salts taken as frequent small sips of some kind of rehydration solution. There are preparatory preparations consisting of sachets of powder which you dissolve in boiled water, or you can make you own by adding half a teaspoonful of salt (3.5 grams) and 4 tablespoonfuls of sugar (40 grams) to a litre of boiled water.

Thus the lynchpins of treatment for diarrhoea are rest, fluid and salt replacement, antibiotics such as Ciprofloxacin for the bacterial types and special diagnostic tests and medical treatment for the amoeba and giardia infections. Salmonella infections and cholera can be devastating diseases and it would be wise to get to a hospital as soon as possible if these were suspected. Fasting, peculiar diets and the consumption of large quantities of yoghurt have not been found useful in calming travellers diarrhoea or in rehabilitating inflamed bowels. Oral rehydration has on the other hand, especially in children, been a lifesaving technique and it should always be practised whatever other treatment you use. As there is some evidence that alcohol and milk might prolong diarrhoea they should probably be avoided during and immediately after an attack. Diarrhoea occurring day after day for long periods of time (chronic diarrhoea) is notoriously resistant to amateur attempts at treatment and again warrants proper diagnostic tests (most towns with reasonable-sized hospitals have laboratories for stool samples). There are ways of preventing travellers diarrhoea for short periods of time by taking antibiotics, but this is not a foolproof technique and should not be used other than in exceptional circumstances. Doxycycline is possibly the best drug. Some preventatives such as Enterovioform can

have serious side effects if taken for long periods.

Paradoxically, constipation is also common, probably induced by dietary change, inadequate fluid intake in hot places and long bus journeys. Simple laxatives are useful in the short term and bulky foods such as maize, beans and plenty of fruit are also useful.

SUNBURN

The burning power of the tropical sun, especially at high altitude, is phenomenal. Always wear a wide-brimmed hat and use some form of suncream lotion on untanned skin. Normal temperate-zone suntan lotions (protection factor up to 7) are not much good; you need to use the types designed specifically for the tropics, or for mountaineers or skiers, with protection factors up to 15. These are often not available in South America; a reasonable substitute is zinc oxide ointment. Glare from the sun can cause conjunctivitis, so wear sunglasses. especially on tropical beaches, where high protection-factor sunscreen cream should also be used.

SNAKEBITE

If you are unlucky enough to be bitten by a venomous snake, spider, scorpion or sea creature, try (within limits) to catch the animal for identification. The reactions to be expected are: fright, swelling, pain and bruising around the bite, soreness of the regional lymph glands, nausea, vomiting and fever. If any of the following symptoms supervene, get the victim to a doctor without delay: numbness and tingling of the face, muscular spasms, convulsion, shortness of breath and haemorrhage. The tiny coral snake, with red, black and white bands, is the most dangerous, but is very timid.

Commercial snakebite and scorpion kits are available, but only useful for the specific type of snake or scorpion for which they are designed. The serum has to be given intravenously so is not much good unless you have had some practice at making injections into veins. If the bite is on a limb, immobilize the limb and apply a tight bandage between the bite

Water purification

There are a number of methods for purifying water in order to make it safe to drink. Dirty water should first be strained through a filter bag, and then boiled or treated. Bringing water to a rolling **boil** at sea level is sufficient to make water safe for drinking, but at higher altitudes you have to boil the water for longer to ensure that all the microbes are killed.

Various sterilizing methods can be used, and there are proprietary preparations containing **chlorine** (eg *'Puritabs'*) or **iodine** (eg *'Pota Aqua'*) compounds. Chlorine compounds generally do not kill protozoa (eg giardia). It is rare for iodine compounds to lead to thyroid problems, if used for less than a year.

There are a number of **water filters** now on the market, available both in personal and expedition size. There are broadly two types of water filter, **mechanical** and **chemical**. Mechanical filters are usually a combination of carbon, ceramic and paper, although they can be difficult to use. Ceramic filters tend to last longer in terms of volume of water purified. The best brand is possibly the Swiss-made *Katadyn*. Although cheaper, the disadvantage of mechanical filters is that they do not always kill viruses or protozoa: treat with iodine before being passed through the filter.

Chemical filters usually use a combination of an iodine resin filter and a mechanical filter. The advantage of this system is that, according to the manufacturers' claims, everything in the water will be killed. The disadvantage is that the filters need replacing, adding a third to the price. Probably the best chemical filter is manufactured by *Pur*.

and the body, releasing it for 90 seconds every 15 mins. Reassurance of the bitten person is very important because death from snakebite is very rare. Do not slash the bite area and try to suck out the poison because this sort of heroism does more harm than good. Hospitals usually hold stocks of snake bite serum. Best precaution: don't walk in snake territory with bare feet or sandals – wear proper shoes or boots.

Spiders and Scorpions These may be found in the more basic hotels in the Andean countries. If bitten by *Latrodectus* or *Loxosceles* spiders, or stung by scorpions, rest and take plenty of fluids, and call a doctor. Precaution: keep beds away from the walls, and look inside shoes in morning.

OTHER RISKS

Remember that **rabies** is endemic throughout Latin America so avoid dogs that are behaving strangely, and cover your toes at night to foil the vampire bats, which also carry the disease. If you are bitten by a domestic or wild animal, don't leave things to chance. Scrub the wound with soap and water and/or disinfectant, try to have the animal captured (within limits) or at least determine its ownership where possible and seek medical assistance at once. The course of treatment depends on whether you have already been satisfactorily vaccinated against rabies. If you have (and this is worthwhile if you are spending lengths of time in developing countries) then some further doses of vaccine are all that is required. Human diploid cell vaccine is the best, but expensive: other, older kinds of vaccine such as that derived from duck embryos may be the only types available. These are effective, much cheaper and interchangeable generally with the human derived types. If not already vaccinated then anti-rabies serum (immunoglobulin) may be required in addition. It is wise to finish the course of treatment whether the animal survives or not.

Typhus can still occur, carried by ticks. There is usually a reaction at the site of the bite and a fever: seek medical advice.

Intestinal worms are common, and the more serious ones such as **hookworm** can be contracted from walking barefoot on infested earth or beaches. Various other tropical diseases can be caught in jungle areas, usually transmitted by biting insects; they are often related to African diseases and were probably introduced by the slave trade from Africa. **Onchocerciasis** (river-blindness), carried by blackflies, is found in parts of Mexico and Venezuela. Cutaneous **leishmaniasis** (Espundia) is carried by sandflies and causes a sore that won't heal; wearing long trousers and long-sleeved shirts in infectious areas helps to avoid the fly. Epidemics of meningitis occur from time to time. Be careful about swimming in piranha- (or caribe-) infested rivers. It is a good idea not to swim naked: the candiru fish can follow urine currents and become lodged in body orifices; swimwear offers some protection.

Dangerous animals Apart from mosquitoes, the most dangerous animals are men, be they bandits or behind steering wheels. Think carefully about violent confrontations and wear a seatbelt, if you are lucky enough to have one available to you.

Leptospirosis: Various forms of leptospirosis occur in most of the Caribbean islands, transmitted by a bacterium which is excreted in rodent urine. Fresh water and moist soil harbour the organisms which enter the body through cuts and scratches. If you suffer from any form of prolonged fever, consult a doctor.

Prickly heat, a very common, intensely itchy rash, is avoided by frequent washing and by wearing loose clothing. Cured by allowing skin to dry off through use of powder, and spending 2 nights in an air-conditioned hotel! **Athlete's foot** and other fungal skin infections are best treated with Tinaderm or Canestan.

WHEN YOU RETURN HOME

Remember to take your anti-malarial tablets for 6 weeks. If you have had attacks of diarrhoea, it is worth having a stool specimen tested in case you have picked up amoebic dysentery. If you have been living rough, a blood test may be worthwhile to detect worms and other parasites. If you

have been exposed to bilharzia by swimming in lakes, etc, check by means of a blood test when you get home, but leave it for 6 weeks because the test is slow to become positive. Report any untoward symptoms to your doctor and tell the doctor exactly where you have been and, if you know, what is the likelihood of diseases to which you were exposed.

BASIC SUPPLIES

The following items you may find useful to take with you from home: sunglasses (if you use clip-on sunglasses, take a spare pair – Ed), ear plugs, suntan cream, insect repellent, flea powder, mosquito net, coils or tablets, tampons, condoms, contraceptives, water sterilizing tablets, anti-malaria tablets, anti-infective ointment, dusting powder for feet, travel sickness pills, antacid tablets, anti-diarrhoea tablets, sachets of rehydration salts and a first aid kit.

Health packs containing sterile syringes, needles, gloves, etc, are available for travellers from various sources (eg Schiphol airport, Amsterdam); one such is made by Safa of Liverpool, UK. Emergency dental kits are available at leading retail outlets and dentists, made by Dental Save, 144 High St, Nailsea, Avon, BS19 1AP, UK, T 01275-810291, F 01275-858112, also available from Fiona Mahon Associates, PO Box 204, Hayes, Middx, UB4 9HN, UK, T 0181-842 3141, F 0181-845 7370.

FURTHER INFORMATION

Further information on health risks abroad, vaccinations, etc, may be available from a local travel clinic. If you wish to take specific drugs with you such as antibiotics, these are best prescribed by your own doctor. Beware, however, that not all doctors can be experts on the health problems of tropical countries. More detailed or more up-to-date information than local doctors can provide are available from various sources.

In the UK there are hospital departments specializing in tropical diseases in London, Liverpool, Birmingham and

Glasgow and the Malaria Reference Laboratory at the London School of Hygiene and Tropical Medicine provides free advice about malaria, T 0891-600-350. In the USA the local public health services can give such information and information is available centrally from the Centres for Disease Control in Atlanta, T (404) 332 4559.

There are in addition computerized databases which can be accessed for a specific destination, up to the minute information. In the UK there is MASTA (Medical Advisory Service to Travellers Abroad), T 0171-631 4408, Tx 895 3474, F 0171-436 5389 and Travax (Glasgow, T 0141-946 7120, extension 247).

Further information on medical problems overseas can be obtained from the book by Richard Dawood (Editor) – *Travellers Health, How to Stay Healthy Abroad*, Oxford University Press, 1992, £7.99. We strongly recommend this revised and updated edition, especially to the intrepid traveller heading for the more out of the way places. General advice is also available in the UK in "Health Advice for Travellers" published jointly by the Department of Health and the Central Office of Information available free from your UK Travel Agent.

The above information has been compiled for us by Dr David Snashall, who is presently Senior Lecturer in Occupational Health at the United Medical Schools of Guys and St Thomas' Hospitals in London and Chief Medical Advisor of the British Foreign and Commonwealth Office. He has travelled extensively in Central and South America, worked in Peru and in East Africa and keeps in close touch with developments in preventative and tropical medicine. We incorporate also some welcome observations on the text by Dr C J Schofield, editor of Parasitology Today.

Argentina

HORIZONS

THE LAND

Argentina is the second largest country in area in South America, equivalent to 29% of that of Europe. It stretches 3,460 km from N to S and 1,580 km from E to W. Apart from the estuary of the Río de la Plata its coast line is 2,575 km long. Its W frontier runs along the crest of the high Andes, a formidable barrier between it and Chile. Its neighbours to the N are Bolivia and Paraguay and (in the NE) Brazil. To the E is Uruguay. Its far S limit is the Beagle Channel. The area figures exclude the sector of Antarctica claimed by Argentina.

Argentina is enormously varied both in its types of land and its climates. Geographers usually recognize four main physical areas: the Andes, the North and Mesopotamia, the Pampas, and Patagonia.

The first division, the Andes, includes the whole length of the Cordilleras, low and deeply glaciated in the Patagonian S, high and dry in the prolongation into NW Argentina of the Bolivian Altiplano, the high plateau. South of this is the very parched desert and mountain region S of Tucumán and W of Córdoba. The oases strung along the eastern foot of the Andes

– Jujuy, Salta, Tucumán, Catamarca, La Rioja, San Juan, Mendoza and the small town of San Rafael – were the first places to be colonized by the Spaniards.

The second division, the North and Mesopotamia, contains the vast forested plains of the Chaco, and the floodplain and gently rolling land known as the Argentine Mesopotamia lying between the rivers Paraná and Uruguay. The Province of Misiones in the NE is actually on the great Paraná plateau. These plains cover 582,750 sq km.

The third division, the pampa, takes up the heart of the land. These vast, rich plains lie S of the Chaco, E of the Andes, W of the Atlantic and the Río Paraná and N of the Río Colorado. The eastern part, which receives more rain, is usually called the Humid Pampa, and the western part the Dry Pampa. The Pampas stretch for hundreds of kilometres in almost unrelieved flatness, covering some 650,000 sq km.

The final division is Patagonia, the area S of the Río Colorado – a land of arid, wind-swept plateaux cut across by ravines. In the deep S the wind is wilder and more continuous. There is no real summer, but to compensate for this the winters are rarely severe. Patagonia covers about 780,000 sq km.

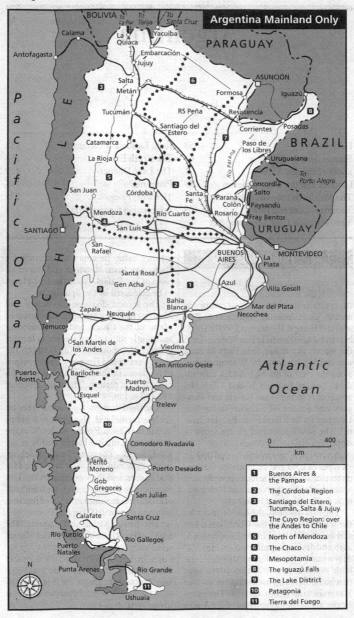

Argentina Mainland Only

BOLIVIA
To La Paz
To Tarija
To Santa Cruz

Calama
Antofagasta

La Quiaca
Yacuiba
PARAGUAY

Embarcación
Jujuy
Salta
Metán
Tucumán
Catamarca
La Rioja
San Juan
Córdoba
Mendoza
San Luis
San Rafael

ASUNCIÓN
Formosa
RS Peña
Santiago del Estero
Santa Fe
Río Cuarto
Rosario

Iguazú
Resistencia
Corrientes
Posadas
BRAZIL
Paso de los Libres
Uruguaiana
To Porto Alegre
Concordia
Salto
Paysandú
Fray Bentos
URUGUAY
Paraná
Colón

Río Paraná

SANTIAGO
C H I L E
Pacific Ocean

Santa Rosa
Gen Acha
BUENOS AIRES
La Plata
MONTEVIDEO

Zapala
Neuquén
Bahía Blanca
Azul
Villa Gesell
Mar del Plata
Necochea

Temuco
San Martín de los Andes
Viedma
San Antonio Oeste

Atlantic Ocean

Puerto Montt
Bariloche
Esquel
Puerto Madryn
Trelew

Comodoro Rivadavia

Perito Moreno
Puerto Deseado
Gob Gregores
San Julián

Calafate
Santa Cruz
Río Turbio
Puerto Natales
Río Gallegos

Punta Arenas
Río Grande

N

Ushuaia

0   400
km

1	Buenos Aires & the Pampas
2	The Córdoba Region
3	Santiago del Estero, Tucumán, Salta & Jujuy
4	The Cuyo Region: over the Andes to Chile
5	North of Mendoza
6	The Chaco
7	Mesopotamia
8	The Iguazú Falls
9	The Lake District
10	Patagonia
11	Tierra del Fuego

CLIMATE

Climate ranges from sub-tropical in the N to cold temperate in Tierra del Fuego, but is temperate and quite healthy in the densely populated central zone. From mid-Dec to the end of Feb Buenos Aires can be oppressively hot and humid, with temperatures ranging from 27°C (80°F) to 35°C (95°F) and an average humidity of 70%. Beware of the high pollen count in the pollinating season if you have allergy problems. The winter months of June, July and Aug are best for a business visit, though spring weather in Buenos Aires is often very pleasant indeed. The skiing season in Bariloche ends by 30 August. Corrientes and Misiones provinces are wet in Aug and especially September.

HISTORY

When, in the early 16th century, the first Europeans came to Argentina, the native Indians had already halted the Inca drive S from Peru through Bolivia into N Argentina. The Spaniard Juan de Solís landed on the shores of the Plata estuary in 1516, but the expedition failed and he was killed. Magellan touched at the estuary 4 years later, but turned S to make his way into the Pacific. In 1527 both Sebastian Cabot and his rival Diego García sailed into the estuary and up the Paraná and the Paraguay. They formed a small settlement, Sancti Spiritus, at the junction of the Caraña and Coronda rivers near their confluence with the Paraná, but it was wiped out by the Indians about 2 years later and Cabot and García returned to Spain. 8 years later, in 1535, Pedro de Mendoza, with a large force well supplied with equipment and horses, founded a settlement at Buenos Aires. The natives soon made it too difficult for him; the settlement was abandoned and Mendoza returned home, but not before sending Juan de Ayolas with a small force up the Paraná. Ayolas set off for Peru, already conquered by Pizarro, leaving Irala in charge. It is not known for certain what happened to Ayolas, but in 1537 Irala and his men settled at Asunción, in Paraguay, where the natives were friendly. There were no further expeditions from Spain to colonize what is now called Argentina, and it was not until 1573 that the settlement at Asunción sent forces S to establish Santa Fe and not until 11 June 1580 that Juan de Garay refounded the settlement at Buenos Aires. It was only under his successor, Hernando Arias de Saavedra (1592-1614), that the new colony became secure.

In the meantime there had been successful expeditions into Argentina both from Peru and Chile – the first, from Peru, as early as 1543. These expeditions led, in the latter half of the 16th century, to the foundation at the eastern foot of the Andes of the oldest towns in Argentina: Santiago del Estero, Tucumán, Córdoba, Salta, La Rioja and Jujuy by Spaniards from Peru following the old Inca road, and San Juan, Mendoza, and San Luis by those from Chile, across the Andes.

For 270 years after its foundation Buenos Aires was of little importance. From 1543 all the Spanish territories in South America were governed from Lima, the Vice-Regal capital. Spanish trade was via Lima, Panama and the Caribbean and Spain did not allow Buenos Aires to take part in any overseas trade until 1778; its population then was only 24,203. It was merely a military outpost for Spain to confront the Portuguese outpost at Colonia, across the estuary, and lived, in the main, by smuggling. Even when in 1776 the Viceroyalty of Río de la Plata was formed, it made little difference to Buenos Aires as a capital, for its control of the *cabildos* (town councils) in distant towns was very tenuous. When the British, following Spain's alliance with Napoleon, attacked Buenos Aires in 1806 and again in 1807 before being repulsed by local levies, there was no inkling of its future potential. But the defeat of these attacks, known as the Reconquista, had one important result: a great increase in the confidence of the *porteños* (the name given to those born in Buenos Aires) to deal with all comers, including the mothercountry, whose restrictions were increasingly unpopular. On 25 May 1810, the *cabildo* of Buenos Aires deposed the viceroy and announced that it was governing henceforth on behalf of King Ferdinand VII, then a captive of Napoleon. 6 years later, when Buenos Aires was threatened by invasion from Peru and blockaded by a Spanish fleet in the Río de la Plata, a national congress held at Tucumán declared independence on 9 July 1816. The declaration was given reality by the genius and devotion of José de San Martín, who boldly marched an Argentine army across the Andes to free Chile, and (with the help of Lord Cochrane, commander of the Chilean Navy), embarked his forces for Peru, where he captured Lima, the first step in the liberation of Peru.

When San Martín returned home, it was to find the country rent by conflict between the central government and the provinces. Disillusioned, he retired to France. The internal conflict was to last a long time. On the one hand stood the Unitarist party, bent on central control; on the other the Federalist party, insisting on local autonomy. The latter had for members the great *caudillos* (the large landowners backed by the *gauchos*) suspicious of the cities. One of their leaders, Juan Manuel de Rosas, took control of the country in 1829. During his second term as Governor of Buenos Aires he asked for and was given extraordinary powers. The result was a 17-year reign of terror. His rule was an international scandal, and when he began a blockade of Asunción in 1845, Britain and France promptly countered with a 3-year blockade of Buenos Aires. In 1851 Justo José de Urquiza, Governor of Entre Ríos, one of his old henchmen, organized a triple alliance of Brazil, Uruguay, and the Argentine opposition to overthrow him. He was defeated in 1852 at Caseros, a few kilometres from Buenos Aires, and fled to England, where he farmed quietly for 25 years, dying at Southampton.

Rosas had started his career as a Federalist; once in power he was a Unitarist. His downfall meant the triumph of federalism. In 1853 a federal system was finally incorporated in the constitution, but the old quarrel had not been solved. Buenos Aires refused to join the new federation, which had its capital at

Paraná. In 1859 Buenos Aires, under Bartolomé Mitre, was defeated by the federal forces under Urquiza, but 2 years later Buenos Aires defeated the federal forces. Once again it became the seat of the federal government, with Bartolomé Mitre as its first constitutional president. (It was during his term that the Triple Alliance of Argentina, Brazil, and Uruguay defeated Francisco Solano López of Paraguay.) There was another political flareup of the old quarrel in 1880, ending in the humiliation of Buenos Aires, which then ceased to be the capital of its province; a new provincial capital was founded at La Plata, 56 km to the SE. The conquest at about the same time of all the Indian tribes of the pampas and the S by a young colonel, Julio A Roca was to make possible the final supremacy of Buenos Aires over all rivals.

Politically Argentina was a constitutional republic with a very restricted suffrage up to the passage in 1912 of the Sáenz Peña law, which established universal manhood suffrage. From 1916 to 1930 the Unión Cívica Radical (founded in 1890) held power, under the leadership of Hipólito Yrigoyen and Marcelo T de Alvear, but lost it to the military uprising of 1930. Though seriously affected by the world depression of the 1930s, Argentina's rich soil and educated population had made it one of the 10 wealthiest countries in the world, but this wealth was most unevenly distributed, and the political methods followed by the conservatives and their military associates in the 1930s denied the middle and working classes any effective share in their own country's wealth and government. In 1943 came another military coup, which had a distinctly fascist tinge. By 1946, Gen Juan Domingo Perón, emerged as President, basing his power on an alliance between the army and labour; his contacts with labour were greatly assisted by his charismatic wife Eva (since commemorated in the rock-opera and film 'Evita') and the living conditions of the workers were greatly improved – but at the expense of the economic state of the country. By the time a military coup unseated Perón in

1955 serious harm had been done; ever since, Argentina has been a politically divided society and has been struggling to recover its lost economic health.

An uneasy alternation of three military and two constitutional regimes followed between 1955 and 1973. The military group which seized power in 1966 was discredited by a deteriorating economy and the emergence of several guerrilla groups in a climate of tension and violence. Perón returned from exile in Madrid to resume as President in Oct 1973, but died on 1 July 1974, leaving the Presidency to his widow, Vice-President María Estela Martínez de Perón. The subsequent chaotic political situation, including guerrilla warfare, led to the point in Mar 1976 where another military was almost welcomed. Sra de Perón was deposed from the Presidency by a military junta, led by Gen Jorge Videla, and guerrilla warfare and the other features of dissidence were repressed with great brutality: about 9,000 people (according to official statistics; human rights organizations believe the total is at least double this) disappeared without trace during the so-called 'dirty war'. Gen Videla was appointed President in 1978 by the military; his nominated successor, Gen Roberto Viola took over for 3 years in Mar 1981 but was replaced by Gen Leopoldo Galtieri in Dec 1981. The latter was in turn replaced in June 1982 by Gen (ret) Reynaldo Bignone.

Confidence in the military ebbed when their economic policies began to go sour in 1980. In 1982-83 pressure for a democratic restoration grew particularly after the South Atlantic conflict with Great Britain in 1982. General elections on 30 October 1983 were won by the Unión Cívica Radical (UCR), with Dr Raúl Alfonsín as president. During 1985 Gens Videla, Viola and Galtieri were sentenced to long terms of imprisonment for their parts in the 'dirty war'. President Alfonsín's popularity gradually waned as his Government failed to solve economic problems. When Alfonsín was defeated by Dr Carlos Saúl Menem of the Partido Justicialista (Peronists) in May 1989, Al-

fonsín stepped down early because of economic instability. Strained relations between the Peronist Government and the military led to several rebellions, which Pres Menem attempted to appease by pardoning the imprisoned Generals. His popularity among civilians declined, but in 1991-92 the Economy Minister, Domingo Cavallo, succeeded in restoring confidence in the economy and the Government as a whole. After triumphing in Oct 1993 congressional elections at the expense of the UCR, the Peronists themselves lost some ground in April 1994 elections to a constituent assembly. The party to gain most, especially in Buenos Aires, was Frente Grande, a broad coalition of left wing groups and disaffected Peronists. Behind some Peronists' loss of confidence were unrestrained corruption and a pact in Dec 1993 between Menem and Alfonsín pledging UCR support for constitutional changes which included re-election of the president for a second term of 4 years.

By the 1995 elections, the majority of the electorate favoured stability over constitutional concerns and returned Pres Menem, without recourse to a second ballot. The Peronists also increased their majority in congress and gained a majority in the Senate. The early months of the new administration were characterized by the political repercussions of 1995's recession, notably unemployment and unrest in those provinces which were unable to pay their public servants. Menem made his priorities the reduction of joblessness, the scrapping of overlapping state and provincial authorities and the reduction of corruption. His plans, including the assumption of emergency powers to ensure fiscal stability in 1996 and the formation of a government/business/union council to address labour issues, were often at odds with those of Cavallo. The latter's authority, challenged frequently by congress, by Menem making personnel changes and by the recession itself, stayed credible enough for him to remain in charge of the economic ministry.

THE TRANSFORMATION OF THE PAMPAS

The pampas, the economic heart of the country, extend fanwise from Buenos Aires for a distance of between 550 and 650 km. Apart from three groups of *sierras* or low hills near Córdoba, Tandil and Bahía Blanca, the surface seems an endless flat monotony, relieved occasionally, in the SW, by sand dunes. There are few rivers. Drinking water is pumped to the surface from a depth of from 30 to 150m by the windpumps which are such a prominent feature of the landscape. There are no trees other than those that have been planted, except in the *monte* of the W. There is, in most years however, ample rainfall. It is greatest at Rosario, where it is about 1,020 mm, and evenly distributed throughout the year. The further S from Rosario, the less the rain. Menem's chief priority was to reduce unemployment, although this would be difficult given the government's insistence that the provinces restructure their finances and reduce inefficiencies. Despite the country's overall economic improvement, most provinces have not enjoyed prosperity. In early 1995, a series of revelations by army personnel concerning the disappearance of thousands of Argentines in the 1970s and 1980s reopened the wounds of the 'dirty war', despite official attempts to suppress discussion of the subject. At Buenos Aires it is about 940 mm; it drops to 535 at Bahía Blanca, and is only 400 along the boundary of the Humid Pampa. The further from Rosario, too, the more the rainfall is concentrated during the summer. Over the whole of the pampa the summers are hot, the winters mild, but there is a large climatic difference between various regions: at Rosario the growing season between frosts is about 300 days; at Bahía Blanca it falls to 145 days.

When the Spaniards arrived in Argentina the pampas were an area of tall coarse grasses. The cattle and horses they brought with them were soon to roam wild and in time transformed the Indian's way of life. The only part of the pampa occupied by the settlers was the so-called Rim, between the Río Salado, S of the capital, and the Paraná-Plata rivers. Here, in large *estancias*, cattle, horses and mules in great herds roamed the open range. There was a line of forts along the Río Salado: a not very effective protection against marauding Indians. The Spaniards had also brought European grasses with them; these soon supplanted the coarse native grasses, and formed a green carpet which stopped abruptly at the Río Salado.

The *estancia* owners and their dependent *gauchos* were in no sense an agricultural people, but towards the end of the 18th century, tenants – to the great contempt of both *estanciero* and *gaucho* – began to plant wheat in the valleys along the Paraná-Plata shore. The fall of Rosas in 1852, and the constitution of 1853, made it possible for Argentina to take a leap forward, but it must be remembered that its white population at that time was only 1,200,000.

The rapidly rising population of Europe during the latter half of the 19th century and the consequent demand for cheap food was the spur that impelled Argentina (as it did the United States and Canada) to occupy its grasslands and take to agriculture. This was made possible by the new techniques already developed: agricultural machinery, barbed wire, well-drilling machines and windpumps, roads and railways, and ocean-going steamships. Roads were, and are, a difficulty in the pampa; the soil lacks gravel or stones to surface the roads, and dirt roads become a quagmire in wet weather and a fume of dust in the dry. Railways, on the other hand, were simple and cheap to build. The system grew as need arose and capital (mostly from Britain) became available. The lines in the pampa radiated out fanwise (with intricate intercommunication) from the ports of Buenos Aires, Rosario, Santa Fe and Bahía Blanca. Argentina, unlike most other countries, had extensive railways before a road system was built.

The occupation of the pampa was finally achieved by a war against the Indians in 1878-83 which virtually exterminated them. Many of the officers were given gifts of land of more than 40,000 ha each. The pampa had passed into private hands on the old traditional pattern of large estates.

Cattle products – hides, tallow, and salt beef – had been the mainstay of Argentine overseas trade during the whole of the colonial period. In the early 19th century wool challenged the supremacy of cattle. The occupation of the grasslands did not, at first, alter the complexion of the foreign trade; it merely increased its volume. In 1877, however, the first ship with refrigeration chambers made it possible to send frozen beef to England, but the meat of the scrub cattle was too strong for English taste. As a result, pedigree bulls were imported from England and the upgrading of the herds began. The same process was applied to sheep. But the improved herds could only flourish where there were no ticks – prevalent in the N – and where forage crops were available. Argentina adopted as its main forage crop alfalfa (lucerne), a plant like clover which proved extremely suitable on the pampa. It has since been supplemented with barley, oats, rye, maize, sorghum and oilseeds.

A striking thing about the Pampas is the bird life. Flamingoes rise in a pink and white cloud, heron egrets gleam white against the blue sky, pink spoonbills dig in the mud and rheas stalk in the distance. Most fascinating are the oven birds, the *horneros*, which build oven-shaped nests six times as big as themselves on the top of telegraph and fence posts.

The transformation of the pampa has had two profound effects. Because its newly-created riches flowed out and its needs flowed in mainly through Buenos Aires, that port grew from comparative insignificance into one of the great cities in the world. Also, the transformation of the Humid Pampa led, through immigration, to a vast predominance of the European strain. The first immigrants settled NW of Santa Fe in 1856. Between 1857 and 1930 total immigration was over 6 million, almost all from Europe. The process has continued; Italians have been by far the most numerous, followed by Spaniards, and then, far behind, groups of other Europeans and Latin Americans. British and North Americans normally came as stockbreeders, technicians and business executives.

CULTURE

PEOPLE

In the Federal Capital and Province of Buenos Aires, where almost 40% of the population lives, the people are almost exclusively of European origin. In the far northern provinces, colonized from neighbouring countries, at least half the people are *mestizos* though they form about 15% of the population of the whole country. It is estimated that 12.8% are foreign born and generally of European origin, though there are also important communities of Syrians, Lebanese, Armenians, Japanese and, most recently, Koreans.

Not surprisingly, the traditional image of the Argentine is that of the *gaucho*; *gauchismo* has been a powerful influence in literature, sociology and folklore, and is celebrated each year in the week before the 'Day of Tradition', 10 November.

In the highlands of the NW, in the Chaco, Misiones and in the SW, there are still some indigenous groups. The exact total of the Indian population is unknown; estimates vary from 100,000 to 300,000. As was noted above, the pampas Indians were virtually exterminated in the 19th century; the Indians of Tierra del Fuego are extinct. Surviving peoples include the Wichi and others in Salta and Jujuy provinces (see page 117), various Chaco Indians (see page 177) and tribes related to the Mapuche and Tehuelche nations in the SW. A number of organizations represent indigenous interests, but any legislation, under federal law, has to be enacted separately by each province.

MUSIC AND DANCE

Buenos Aires contains a third of the country's population and its music is the Tango. Indeed to the outside world there is no other Argentine music. Although also sung and played, the Tango was born as a dance just before the turn of the 20th century. The exact moment of the birth was not recorded by any contemporary observer and continues to be a matter of debate, though the roots can be traced. The name 'Tango' predates the dance and was given to the carnivals (and dances) of the black inhabitants of the Río de la Plata in the early 19th century. Elements of the black tradition were taken over by whites, as the black population declined into insignificance. However, the name 'Tango Americano' was also given to the Habanera (a Cuban descendent of the English Country Dance) which became the rage in Spain and bounced back into the Río de la Plata in the middle of the 19th centry, not only as a fashionable dance, together with the polka, mazurka, waltz and cuadrille, but also as a song form in the very popular 'Zarzuelas', or Spanish operettas. However the Habanera led not a double, but a triple life, by also infiltrating the lowest levels of society directly from Cuba via sailors who arrived in the ports of Montevideo and Buenos Aires. Here it encountered the Milonga, originally a Gaucho song style, but by 1880 a dance, especially popular with the so-called 'Compadritos' and 'Orilleros', who frequented the port area and its brothels, whence the Argentine Tango emerged around the turn of the century to dazzle the populace with its brilliant, personalized footwork, which could not be accomplished without the partners staying glued together. As a dance it became the rage and, as the infant recording industry grew by leaps and bounds, it also became popular as a song and an instrumental genre, with the original violins and floorutes being eclipsed by the *bandoneón* button accordion, then being imported from Germany. In 1911 the new dance took Paris by storm and returned triumphant to Buenos Aires. It achieved both respectability and notoriety, becoming a global phenomenon after the First World War. The golden voice of the renowned Carlos Gardel soon gave a wholly new dimension to the music of the Tango until his death in 1935. After losing some popularity in Argentina, it came to the forefront again in the 1940s (1920-50 is considered the real golden age). Its resurgence was assisted by Perón's decree that 50% of all music played on the radio must be Argentine, only to suffer a second, much more serious decline in the face of rock music over the past 2 decades. To see the Tango and Milonga danced in Buenos Aires today, you need to visit one of the clubs or *confiterías* where it is specially featured, see Buenos Aires **Nightclubs and folklore**. Apart from Carlos Gardel, other great names connected with the Tango are Francisco Canaro (Uruguayan), Osvaldo Pugliese and Astor Piazzolla, who has modernized it by fusion with jazz styles (*nuevo tango*). Whilst the majority of Argentine young people will agree that the Tango represents the soul of Buenos Aires, don't expect them to dance it or listen to it. They are more likely to be interested in the country's indigenous rock music.

If the Tango represents the soul of Buenos Aires, this is not the case in the rest of the country. The provinces have a very rich and attractive heritage of folk dances, mainly for couples, with arms held out and fingers clicked or handkerchiefs waved, with the 'Paso Valseado' as the basic step. Descended from the Zamacueca, and therefore a cousin of the Chilean Cueca and Peruvian Marinera, is the slow and stately Zamba, where the handkerchief is used to greatest effect. Equally popular throughout most of the country are the faster Gato, Chacarera and Escondido. These were the dances of the Gaucho and their rhythm evokes that of a cantering horse. Guitar and the *bombo* drum provide the accompaniment. Particularly spectacular is the Malambo, where the Gaucho shows off his dextrous footwork, the spurs of his boots adding a steely note to the rhythm.

Different regions of the country have their own specialities. The music of Cuyo in the W is sentimental and very similar to that of neighbouring Chile, with its Cuecas for dance and Tonadas for song. The NW on the other hand is Andean, with its musical culture closer to that of Bolivia, particularly on the Puna, where the Indians play the *quena* and *charango* and sound mournful notes on the great long *erke*. Here the dances are Bailecitos and Carnavalitos, while the songs are Vidalitas and the extraordinary high pitched Bagualas, the very essence of primeval pain. In the NE provinces of Corrientes and Misiones, the music shares cultural similarities with Paraguay. The Polca and Galopa are danced and the local Chamamé is sung, to the accordion or the harp, the style being sentimental. Santiago del Estero is the heartland of the Chacarera and the lyrics are often part Spanish and part Quichua, a local dialect of the Andean Quechua language. Down in the Province of Buenos Aires you are more likely to hear the Gauchos singing their Milongas, Estilos and Cifras and challenging each other to a Payada or rhymed duel. Argentina experienced a great folk revival in the 50's and 60's and some of the most celebrated groups are still drawing enthusiastic audiences today. These groups include Los Chalchaleros and Los Frontcrizos, the perennial virtuoso singer and guitarist, Eduardo Falú and, more recently, León Gieco from Santa Fe.

THE ECONOMY

Structure of production Argentina is one of the more highly developed countries of the region. It has the third largest gdp in Latin America, but by far the highest per capita income. Wealth traditionally came from farming although agriculture, forestry and fishing now account for only 6% of gdp. Nevertheless, over half of export earnings are generated by farming and food processing. There has been a shift from livestock to crop production since the 1960s. The area sown to oilseeds has risen steeply, now exceeding that of wheat. The fertility of the pampas is so high that fertilizers are unnecessary, but farmers have been hit by rising costs, falling commodity prices and lack of cheap credit to invest in modernization. In the 1990s, 150,000-200,000 small and medium sized farms were under severe financial pressure and many faced bankruptcy, leading to a consolidation of land holdings. Cresud, the only landholding company traded on the stock market, increased its holdings from 20,000 to 348,000 ha in 1994-96. Cattle and sheep herds have been reduced because of stiff competition abroad, low wool prices and outbreaks of foot and mouth disease. A vaccination drive started in 1989 has been successful and no further outbreaks have been recorded since 1994, leading farmers to hope that beef import bans imposed by the USA, Japan and Southeast Asian countries might be lifted. Exports of about 450,000 tonnes a year, earning some US$900mn, could double if

YPF – from State Company to Oil Magnate

The oil industry was deregulated in 1991 and the state oil company, Yacimientos Petrolíferos Fiscales (YPF) was privatized in 1993, although the Government retains 20%, the employees 10% and provincial governments 11%. YPF is the largest company in Argentina with a market capitalization of US$9bn, and it controls half the domestic oil industry with production, refining and retailing. Exports have risen since the opening in 1994 of an oil pipeline from Neuquén to Concepción in Chile, built by YPF and the Chilean oil company, ENAP, with a capacity of 107,000b/d. YPF and Petrobrás, of Brazil, have a strategic alliance with offshore drilling in the Gulf of Mexico and South Atlantic and are moving into joint downstream activities. In 1995 YPF bought a US-based oil and gas company, Maxus, which has stakes in Venezuela, Bolivia, Ecuador and Indonesia. An agreement with Britain in 1995 opened up the possibility of joint ventures to explore and exploit hydrocarbons in the disputed waters around the Falklands/Malvinas Islands. British Gas and YPF announced their interest in jointly exploring for gas and oil with a 51%/49% stake respectively. The two companies are already partners in the Transgas project to build one of two proposed pipelines to supply Argentine natural gas to Chile.

the bans are lifted. Fishing received a boost in 1993 from an agreement with Britain to share fish resources in the South Atlantic, thereby increasing by 70% Argentina's share of the illex squid catch.

Manufacturing was developed behind high import protection barriers, but these have now been swept aside. The sector accounts for 26% of gdp and is closely linked with agricultural activity, with food processing and beverages accounting for a quarter of manufacturing output. The regional customs union, Mercosur, opened up a huge market for companies established in Argentina and many food companies have been bought by multinationals. Trade with Brazil has traditionally been biased towards foodstuffs but enterprises in other areas are now growing. Several multinational motor vehicle companies are investing in new plant, many around Córdoba. All plan to sell vehicles to other Mercosur countries as well as within Argentina.

Argentina is self-sufficient in energy and has an exportable surplus of oil, natural gas and hydroelectricity. Hydroelectric potential lies on 10 main rivers: the rivers Paraná and Uruguay in the N where huge joint projects have been built with Paraguay (Yacyretá, Corpus) and Uruguay (Salto Grande), and on rivers in Río Negro and Neuquén provinces. The Government is divesting its stake in electricity generating and will offer its participation to private investors once ratification is secured from the Paraguayan and Uruguayan parliaments. More hydroelectricity generating plants are planned which will be built under concession by private contractors. Argentina has had nuclear power since 1974 when the first stage of the Atucha power station was opened using German technology. Atucha I and II were both privatized in 1994. Crude oil output is around 450,000 b/d and reserves are to be kept at 10 years' production with more exploration in a US$3bn, 10-year investment programme. By the mid-1990s only five of Argentina's 19 identified oil-bearing basins had been brought into production. The country has more natural gas than

oil and reserves are about 560 billion cu m, equivalent to about 30 years' consumption at present rates.

Mining was discouraged by previous administrations, who declared the border region a security zone and closed to foreign investment, but there are substantial mineral deposits in the foothills of the Andes. Only 17% of the country has been adequately surveyed but investment is now being encouraged by new investment and taxation legislation introduced in 1993. The first major project will be the Bajo de la Alumbrera porphyry copper and gold deposit in Catamarca which is believed to have 752 million tonnes of ore. Mining operations will start in 1997 and production should reach 180,000 tonnes of copper and 640,000 ozs of gold a year. Another copper-gold deposit in Catamarca is Agua Rica, which could be developed into an open pit mine to rival Alumbrera. Both are being developed by Australian and Canadian companies. Lithium deposits at the Salar del Hombre Muerto dry lake bed also in Catamarca are believed to be sufficient for 70 years' production.

Recent trends In the 1980s large fiscal deficits, monetary expansion and a high velocity of circulation caused very high inflation, which was difficult to curb because of structural imbalances in the economy, inadequate levels of investment and inefficiencies and corruption in both the public and private sectors. The Government introduced several stabilization programmes, the first of which was the Austral Plan, named after the currency it introduced, but none was successful. Output and investment contracted as confidence was eroded and the economy became increasingly dollarized. The external debt rose sharply but rescheduling agreements with commercial bank creditors backed by IMF financing facilities all collapsed as policy commitments were not met and payment arrears mounted.

The Menem administration tackled structural economic reform, which initially brought further recession and unemployment. In 1991 it passed a

Convertibility Law, fixing the peso at par with the US dollar and permitting the Central Bank to print local currency only if it is fully backed by gold or hard currency. This was the key to achieving price stability; the annual average growth of consumer prices fell from 3,080% in 1989 to 3.9% in 1994 and remained in single figures thereafter. Dozens of state companies were privatized, many using debt reduction techniques. Fiscal surpluses were recorded in 1992-93 and gdp growth rates averaging 7.7% a year were recorded in 1991-94. After a current account surplus in 1990, increasing deficits were recorded in following years, reaching nearly US$10bn in 1994, but these were amply financed by capital inflows and international reserves increased. Imports soared from US$3.7bn in 1990 to US$19.9bn in 1994, while gross domestic investment in the same years rose by 22% to 23% of gdp. In 1993 an agreement was signed with international banks to restructure bank debt by securitizing it into bonds, following the Mexican model of debt or debt service reduction.

Cracks began to appear in the model in the second half of 1994 when a fiscal deficit became apparent. Tax collections fell and current spending rose. The tax structure concentrates on consumption with a high rate of VAT, but the demand side of the economy had been growing only slowly, partly because of rising unemployment as a result of privatizations and streamlined payrolls. The devaluation of the Mexican peso in December 1994 created what became known as the 'tequila effect'. Loss of confidence in Mexico spread to other Latin American countries and Argentina suffered a sharp liquidity squeeze as US$8bn in bank deposits, 15% of the total, fled the country. Many banks were merged, yet at 130, there were still too many for the country's deposit base. Unemployment soared to over 18% by May 1995, consumer demand fell sharply, tax collections dwindled and a recession loomed. Riots broke out in parts of the country as provincial governments failed to pay wages for several months.

Argentina : Fact File

Geographic

Land area	2,780,400 sq km
forested	18.6%
pastures	51.9%
cultivated	9.9%

Demographic

Population (1995)	34,587,000
annual growth rate (1990-95)	1.2%
urban	86.9%
rural	13.1%
density	12.4 per sq km
Religious affiliation	
Roman Catholic	91.6%
Birth rate per 1,000 (1995)	19.5
	(world av 25.0)

Education and Health

Life expectancy at birth,	
male	68 years
female	72 years
Infant mortality rate	
per 1,000 live births (1992)	34.0
Physicians (1992)	1 per 376 persons
Hospital beds	1 per 227 persons
Calorie intake as %	
of FAO requirement	109%
Population age 25 and over	
with no formal schooling	5.7%
Literate males (over 15)	96.2%
Literate females (over 15)	96.2%

Economic

GNP (1993)	US$244,013mn
GNP per capita	US$7,290
Public external debt (1993)	
	US$61,534mn
Tourism receipts (1993)	US$3,614mn
Inflation (annual av 1991-94)	96.3%
Radio	1 per 1.6 persons
Television	1 per 4.8 persons
Telephone	1 per 8.2 persons

Employment

Population economically active (1990)	
	12,305,346
Unemployment rate (1989)	7.3%
% of labour force in	
agriculture	12.0
mining	0.5
manufacturing	19.9
construction	10.1
Military forces	67,300

Source *Encyclopaedia Britannica*

The Government turned to the IMF, which negotiated a US$7bn rescue package with multilateral lenders. In 1995 exports rose by 33%, as goods were diverted from the weak domestic market, encouraged by high commodity prices and a consumer boom in Brazil, but gdp declined by 2.5%. The recession appeared to be over by the end of the year, though, with industrial production, imports and demand picking up, and unemployment declining, while 90% of bank deposits had returned. A private pension scheme was launched to ease pressure on the bankrupt state scheme as well as raise the savings ratio, reduce dependence on foreign capital and increase investment funds for industry. Investor confidence was seen to have returned when the Merval index of blue-chip stocks recovered and ended the year slightly higher than it had begun, but consumer demand was likely to pick up only slowly with Argentines concerned about job security.

GOVERNMENT

The country's official name is La República Argentina (RA), the Argentine Republic. The form of government has traditionally been a representative, republican federal system. Of the two legislative houses, the Senate has 72 seats, and the Chamber of Deputies 257. By the 1853 Constitution (amended most recently in 1994) the country is divided into a Federal Capital (the city of Buenos Aires) and 23 Provinces. Each Province has its own Governor, Senate and Chamber of Deputies. The municipal government of the Federal Capital is exercised by a Mayor who is directly elected. The Constitution grants the city autonomous rule.

COMMUNICATIONS

Argentina has only four good seaports: Buenos Aires, La Plata, Rosario and Bahía Blanca. Necochea/Quequén is also a good port, but the swell can sometimes prevent ships entering or sailing for days. The two great rivers flowing southward into the Plata, the Paraná and the Uruguay, are not very reliable shipping routes. The Colorado and the Negro rivers in northern Patagonia are navigable by small vessels only. Internal air services are highly developed.

Most of Argentina is served by about 215,578 km of road, but only 29% are paved and a further 17% improved. The 30,059 km (1992) of railway line, owned mostly by British companies until they were taken over by the State in 1948, used to carry less than 10% of passengers and freight, until privatization in the early 1990s caused an even greater reduction in rail's share of national transportation.

Buenos Aires

A part from the capital itself, with its museums, theatres, public buildings, parks and shopping, this region contains the Tigre Delta (waterways, lunch spots).

The Río de la Plata, or River Plate, on which Buenos Aires lies, is not a river but an estuary or great basin, 160 km long and from 37 to 90 km wide, into which flow the Ríos Paraná and Uruguay and their tributaries. It is muddy and shallow and the passage of ocean vessels is only made possible by continuous dredging. The tides are of little importance, for there is only a 1.2m rise and fall at spring tides. The depth of water is determined by the direction of the wind and the flow of the Paraná and Uruguay rivers.

The capital has been virtually rebuilt since the beginning of this century and very few of the old buildings are left. In the centre, which has maintained the original lay-out since its foundation, the streets are often very narrow and are mostly one-way. Its original name, 'Santa María del Buen Ayre' was a recognition of the good winds which brought sailors across the ocean.

BASICS *Area*, the capital spreads over some 200 sq km; together with Gran Buenos Aires (including the suburbs in the province of Buenos Aires), the area is 4,326 sq km. The *population* of the Federal Capital itself is about 2.92 million, but the population of greater Buenos Aires is 10.87 million. *Phone code* 01.

NB Extreme humidity and unusual pollen conditions may affect asthma sufferers.

Street numeration: numbers start from the dock side rising from E to W, but N/S streets are numbered from Av Rivadavia, one block N of Av de Mayo rising in both directions. Calle Juan D Perón used to be called Cangallo and MT de Alvear is still referred to by its old name, Charcas.

PLACES OF INTEREST

The heart of the city, now as in colonial days, is the Plaza de Mayo, with the historic Cabildo, the Town Hall, where the movement for independence from Spain was first planned; the pink Casa Rosada (Presidential Palace); the Municipalidad (City Hall); and the Cathedral, where San Martín is buried. (For a note on the Mothers of the Plaza de Mayo, see page 72). Within a few blocks are the fashionable church of Nuestra Señora de la Merced and the main banks and business houses.

Running W from the Plaza, the Av de Mayo leads 1½ km to the Congress building in the Plaza del Congreso. Halfway it crosses the wide Av (Nueve) de Julio. The Av de Julio itself, one of the widest in the world, consists of three major carriageways, with heavy traffic, separated in some parts by wide grass borders. In the N the Av de Julio meets the Av del Libertador, the principal way out of the city to the N and W.

North of the Plaza de Mayo is the shopping, theatre and commercial area. The city's traditional shopping centre, C Florida (with excellent newsstands), is in this district. This is the popular down-

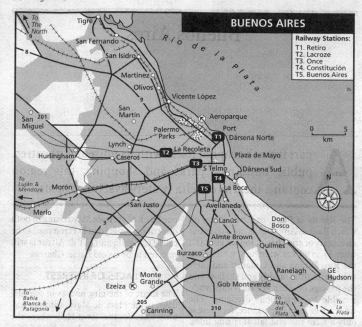

BUENOS AIRES

Railway Stations:
T1. Retiro
T2. Lacroze
T3. Once
T4. Constitución
T5. Buenos Aires

town meeting place, particularly in the late afternoon; it is reserved for pedestrians only and the buskers in the 500 block are worth visiting. Another shopping street is Av Santa Fe, which crosses Florida at the Plaza San Martín; it has become as touristy and as expensive as Florida. Av Corrientes is the entertainment centre, a street of theatres, restaurants, cafés and night life. Close by, in C Lavalle (part reserved to pedestrians) and in nearby streets, there are numerous cinemas and many good and reasonable restaurants.

East of the Plaza de Mayo, behind the Casa Rosada, a broad avenue, Paseo Colón, runs S towards San Telmo and the picturesque old port district known as the Boca, where the Riachuelo floorows into the Plata. The Boca is reached by bus 152 from Av LN Alem, or bus 29 from Plaza de Mayo, in the centre, US$0.50. For a tour of the Boca, start at Plaza Vuelta de Rocha, near Av Pedro de Mendoza and Dr Del Valle Iberucea, then walk up Caminito, the little

pedestrian street used as a theatre and an art market. Visit the Museo de Bellas Artes de la Boca (see page 70). The Boca, mostly Italian, has its own distinctive life and parts of it are becoming touristy, but the area, with the adjacent industrial and meat-packing suburb of Avellaneda across the high Avellaneda bridge, is generally dirty and run down.

One of the few places which still have late colonial and Rosista buildings is the *barrio* of San Telmo, S of Plaza de Mayo, centred on Plaza Dorrego along the slope which marks the old beach of the Río de la Plata. It is a recognized artistic centre, with plenty of cafés, antique shops and a pleasant atmosphere; and there is a regular Sat and Sun morning antiques market at the Plaza Dorrego (see page 82). The 29 bus connects the Boca with San Telmo, and passes the end of C Florida, the pedestrianized shopping street. East of San Telmo on the far side of the docks, the spacious Av Costanera runs along the

Plata estuary. The Puerto Madero dock area has been renovated, the 19th century warehouses being turned into restaurants and bars, a popular nightspot. A stretch of marshland (claimed from the river by a system similar to the one used in the construction of the Dutch polders) forms the interesting **Costanera Sur Wildlife Reserve**, which has many *coypu* (large rodents) and many types of birds, including the rare black-headed duck and the curve-billed reed hunter. The entrance is at Av Tristán Achabal Rodríguez 1550 (reached by buses 4 and 2); it opens daily from 0700-2000 (free, guided tours available), but much can be seen from the road before then (binoculars useful). There are three trails ranging from 2 km to 6 km long. In summer it is very hot with little shade. For details, contact *Fundación Vida Silvestre*, Defensa 245, p 6, 1075 Buenos Aires, T 331-4864/343-3778.

Principal Public Buildings

Casa de Gobierno on the E side of the Plaza de Mayo, and called the *Casa Rosada* because it is pink, contains the offices of the President of the Republic. It is notable for its statuary, the rich furnishing of its halls and for its libraries. The Museo de los Presidentes is on the lower floors (see under **Museums**). Behind the building, in the semicircular Parque Colón, is a large statue of Columbus.

The **Cabildo** on the W side of the same Plaza, the old town hall, was put up in 1711 but has been rebuilt several times. Its original structure, fittings and furniture were replaced in 1940 and it was declared a national monument. See under **Museums**.

Antiguo Congreso Nacional (Old Congress Hall) on the S of the Square, built 1864, is a National Monument. It has been encircled and built over by the Banco Hipotecario. Guided tours Thur, 1500-1700, free.

Palacio del Congreso (Congress Hall) to the SW at the far end of Av de Mayo, of great size and in Greco-Roman architecture, is the seat of the legislature. It contains the Senate and the Chamber of Deputies. There is limited access for the

public at sittings announced a week in advance. Passes are given in the Anexo 10 mins before sessions; there they take your passport and give you a ticket for your seat and a pink slip to reclaim your passport. You may stay as long as you wish, but must remain seated. A guided tour (in English) can be taken on Mon, Tues and Fri at 1100 and 1700 when Congress is not sitting.

Teatro Colón, one of the world's great opera houses, overlooks Av 9 de Julio, with its main entrance on Libertad, between Tucumán and Viamonte. The Colón's interior is resplendent with red plush and gilt; the stage is huge, and salons, dressing rooms and banquet halls are equally sumptuous. The season runs from April to early Dec, and there are concert performances most days. Open daily to visitors (not Sun), guided tours Mon-Fri hourly 0900-1600, Sat 0900-1200, in Spanish, French and English, US$5 (children US$2), from entrance at Viamonte 1180, recommended. Closed Jan-Feb, T 382-6632. Tickets, sold several days before performance, on the C Tucumán side of the theatre. The cheapest seat is US$6 (available even on the same day), and there are free performances most days (Tues-Fri) at 1730 in the Salón Dorado – check programme in the visitors' entrance.

The **Bolsa de Comercio**, built in 1916 is a handsome building containing the stock exchange (entrance 25 de Mayo y Sarmiento).

Churches

Most historic churches apart from the Cathedral are open 0730-1230, 1600-2000.

The **Cathedral**, Rivadavia 437, on the N of Plaza de Mayo is flanked by the former residence of the Archbishop. On this site was built the first church in Buenos Aires, which after reconstruction in 1677 collapsed in 1753 and the rebuilding was not completed until 1823. The 18th century towers were never rebuilt, so that the architectural proportions have suffered. A frieze upon the Greek façade represents Joseph and his brethren. The tomb (1878) of the Liberator, Gen José de

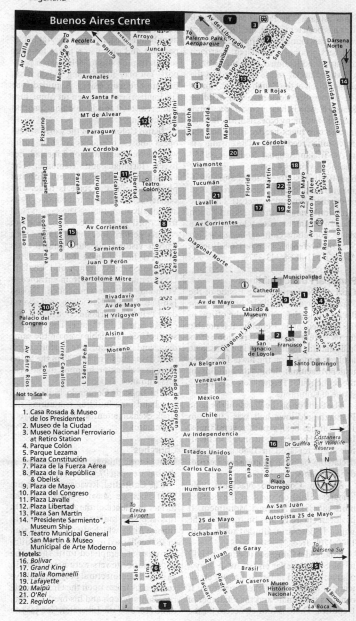

Buenos Aires Centre

1. Casa Rosada & Museo de los Presidentes
2. Museo de la Ciudad
3. Museo Nacional Ferroviario at Retiro Station
4. Parque Colón
5. Parque Lezama
6. Plaza Constitución
7. Plaza de la Fuerza Aérea
8. Plaza de la República & Obelisk
9. Plaza de Mayo
10. Plaza del Congreso
11. Plaza Lavalle
12. Plaza Libertad
13. Plaza San Martín
14. "Presidente Sarmiento", Museum Ship
15. Teatro Municipal General San Martín & Museo Municipal de Arte Moderno

Hotels:
16. *Bolívar*
17. *Grand King*
18. *Italia Romanelli*
19. *Lafayette*
20. *Maipú*
21. *O'Rei*
22. *Regidor*

San Martín, is imposing. Masses: Mon-Fri 0900,1100,1230, Sat 1730, Sun 1100,1200,1300. Visiting hours Mon-Fri 0800-1830, Sat 0900-1230, 1700-1930, Sun 0900-1400, 1600-1930.

San Ignacio de Loyola, Alsina y Bolívar 225, inaugurated in 1675, consecrated in 1734, is the oldest Colonial building in Buenos Aires. It has two lofty towers. Open weekends 1700 (guided tours only). **San Francisco**, Alsina y Defensa, controlled by the Franciscan Order, was begun in 1726 and given a new façade in 1808.

La Merced, C J D Perón and Reconquista 207, was founded 1604 and rebuilt in the early 18th century. One of the altars has a wooden figure of Nuestro Señor, carved during the 18th century by an Indian in Misiones. It has one of the few fine carillons of bells in Buenos Aires.

Santo Domingo, Defensa y Belgrano, was founded in 1751. During the British attack on Buenos Aires in 1806 some of Whitelocke's soldiers took refuge in the church. The local forces bombarded it (some of the hits can still be seen on one of the towers); the British capitulated and their regimental colours were preserved in the church. A flame burns over the gate in memory of Gen Belgrano who died nearby. There are summer evening concerts in the church; check times.

El Pilar, Junín 1904, is a jewel of colonial architecture dating from 1732, facing onto the public gardens of the Plaza Recoleta. A fine wooden image of San Pedro de Alcántara, attributed to the famous 17th century Spanish sculptor Alonso Cano, is preserved in a side chapel on the left.

Next to it is the **Cemetery of the Recoleta**, entrance at Junín 1822, not far from Museo de Bellas Artes (see below). It is one of the sights of Buenos Aires (open 0700-1800). "A Doric portico gives on to the main, paved, cypress-lined avenue of a little city of the dead. At the end of the avenue there is a great bronze statue of the resurrected Saviour; on either side, hard up against each other, like houses in a street, there are the family vaults of the Argentine patricians. Every

possible style of architecture is represented." GS Fraser, in *News from Latin America*. Evita Perón is buried here; her tomb is now marked beside the inscription, Familia Duarte: from the entrance go to the main plaza; turn left and where this avenue meets a main avenue (about 13 'blocks'), turn right; take the 2nd or 3rd passage on the left. On Sat and Sun there is a good craft market near the entrance (1100-1800). The Centro Cultural Ciudad de Buenos Aires alongside the Recoleta cemetery specializes in contemporary local art with many free exhibitions by young artists. Several colectivos: 110, 17; 60 (walk from corner of Las Heras y Junín, 2 blocks); from downtown, eg Correo Central, 61/62, 93, to Pueyrredón casi Av del Libertador, or 130 to Facultad de Derecho.

Another well known cemetery is that of La Chacarita, reached by Subte to the Federico Lacroze station, which has the much-visited, lovingly-tended tombs of Juan Perón and Carlos Gardel, the tango singer.

Museums, libraries and art exhibitions

NB State museums and parks are free on Wed. Check opening hours with Tourist Office; many close in Jan or Feb.

Museo de los Presidentes (basement of Casa Rosada), Hipólito Yrigoyen 219. Historical memorabilia, particularly of Former Presidents, 19th century tunnels (open Tues, Wed, Thur 0900-1400, Fri, Sun 1400-1800).

Museo de Bellas Artes (National Gallery), Av del Libertador 1473, T 803-0802. In addition to a fine collection of European works, particularly strong in the 19th century French school, there are 16th and 17th century paintings representing the conquest of Mexico, many good Argentine works including new 19th and 20th century exhibits, and wooden carvings from the Argentine hinterland. Open Tues-Sun 1230-1930, Sat 0930-1930 (closes Jan-Feb). Entrance US$1 (Thur free), ISIC holders free. Warmly recommended.

The Museo Nacional de Arte Deco-

rativo is at Av del Libertador 1902, collecions of painting, furniture, porcelain, crystal, sculpture; classical music concerts Wed and Thur, open daily except Tues 1400-1900, T 802-6606, US$2, half-price to ISIC holders, closed January. The building is shared with the **Museo Nacional de Arte Oriental**; permanent exhibition of Chinese, Japanese, Hindu and Islamic art, open daily 1500-1900.

Biblioteca Nacional (The National Library), founded in 1810. About 500,000 volumes and 10,000 manuscripts, now housed in futuristic new building at Av del Libertador 1600 y Agüero 2502, T 806-6155, where only a fraction of the stock is available. Cultural events and festivals held here.

Museo Nacional de Historia, Defensa 1600, T 307-4457, in San Telmo, Parque Lezama. Trophies and mementoes of historical events, divided into halls depicting stages of Argentine history. Here are San Martín's uniforms, a replica of his sabre, and the original furniture and door of the house in which he died at Boulogne. Closed for renovation late 1995.

Museo de la Ciudad, Alsina 412, T 343-2123. Permanent exhibition covering social history and popular culture, special exhibitions on daily life in Buenos Aires changed every 2 months, and a reference library open to the public. open Mon-Fri, 1100-1900, Sun, 1500-1900. Open all year, US$0.50.

Museo y Biblioteca Mitre, San Martín 336, preserves intact the household of President Bartolomé Mitre; has coin and map collection and historical archives. Open Mon-Fri 1330-1830, US$1, T 394-8240.

Museo de Ciencias Naturales Av Angel Gallardo 470, facing Parque Centenario. It houses palaeontological, zoological, mineralogical, botanical, archaeological and marine sections. Meteorites from Campo del Cielo on display. Open all year, daily, 1400-1730 (closed holidays), US$0.20. Library, Mon-Fri, 1100-1700; T 982-5243.

Museo de la Dirección Nacional del Antártico, Angel Gallardo 470, in the Museo de Ciencias Naturales, Tues, Thur and Sun, 1400-1800. Specimens of flora, fauna and fossils and a library of taped birdsong, T 44-7327.

Museo Municipal de Arte Moderno, San Juan 350, with a salon at Av Corrientes 1530, 9th floor: international exhibitions and a permanent collection of 20th century art; open Mon-Fri 1000-2000, Sat and Sun 1200-2000, US$1.50 (US$1 at the salon, Wed free), T 374-9426.

Museo Municipal de Artes Plásticas Eduardo Sivori, Junín 1930 (in Cultural Centre, La Recoleta) and Hostal del Ceivo, Infanta Isabel 555, T 778-3855, emphasis on 19th and 20th century Argentine art, entry US$1, open daily 1200-2000.

Museo de Bellas Artes de la Boca, Pedro de Mendoza 1835, Boca, has many works on local life, contemporary Argentine painting, also sculptures and figureheads rescued from ships. Mon-Fri 0800-1800, Sat-Sun 1000-1700, T 301-1080, entrance free.

Museo de la Asociación Evaristo Carriego, Honduras 3784, tango museum of the writer, open Mon-Fri 1300-2000.

Museo de Motivos Populares Argentinos José Hernández, Av Libertador 2373, widest collection of Argentine folkloric art, with rooms dedicated to Indian, colonial and Gaucho artefacts; handicraft sale and library. Open Wed-Fri 1300-1900, Sat and Sun 1500-1900. T 802-7294 for guided visits in English or French. Entrance US$0.50 (closed in Feb).

Museo del Instituto Nacional Sanmartiniano, Gral Ramón Castilla and Av A M de Aguado; Mon-Fri 0900-1700. Replica of San Martín's house in exile in Grand Bourg near Paris, T 802-3311 in advance.

Museo del Cabildo y la Revolución de Mayo, Bolívar 65, is the old Cabildo building, converted into a museum in 1940. It contains paintings, documents, furniture, arms, medals, maps, recording the May 1810 revolution, and memorabilia of the 1806 British attack; also Jesuit art. In the patio is La Posta del Cabildo café and stalls selling handicrafts. Entry free. Open Tues-Fri 1230-1900, Sun 1500-

1900. T 334-1782 for English tours. Library, Mon-Fri, 1100-1900.

Museo de Arte Hispanoamericano Isaac Fernández Blanco, Suipacha 1422. Contains a most interesting and valuable collection of colonial art, especially silver, plus watercolours by Carlos Pellegrini, in a beautiful colonial mansion. Open Tues-Sun, 1400-1900, admission US$2. Thur free; closed January. For guided visits in English or French T 327-0228; guided tours in Spanish Sat, Sun 1600.

Museo y Biblioteca Ricardo Rojas, Charcas 2837 (Tues-Fri 1400-1800). The famous writer Rojas lived in this beautiful colonial house for several decades. It contains his library, souvenirs of his travels, and many intriguing literary and historical curios.

Museo Numismático del Banco Central, San Martín 216, 1st floor, T 394-8411, fascinating, well kept, Tues 1000-1400, Wed and Fri tour at 1400, free, overlooks central foyer, ask guard for directions. Not to be confused with **Museo Numismático e Histórico del Banco Nación**, B Mitre 326, 1st floor, coins and notes, furniture and historical documents, Mon-Fri 1000-1500, T 342-4041, ext 607.

Fragata Presidente Sarmiento, Av Dávila y Cangallo, Puerto Madero, a sailing ship used as a naval training ship until 1961; now a museum. Open daily 0800-2000, all year, US$2.

Bank of London and South America (now Lloyds Bank, BLSA), Bartolomé Mitre y Reconquista, has a miniature museum on its fifth floor. Open during banking hours; the building, designed by SEPRA (Santiago Sánchez Elia, Federico Peralta Ramos, and Alfredo Agostini) and completed in 1963 is worth seeing. Next door is the **Banco de Córdoba**, designed by the brilliant Córdoba architect Miguel Angel Roca, completed in the early 1970s.

Museo Nacional de Aeronáutica, Av Costanera Rafael Obligado 4550, next to Aeroparque/Jorge Newbery airport. Many civil and military aircraft, plus displays of navigational material, documents, equipment, US$3, Tues-Fri 0830-1630, Sun 1400-1900, T 773-0665.

Museo Nacional Ferroviario, Av del Libertador 405, behind Retiro station. For railway fans, locomotives, machinery, documents of the Argentine system's history. Building in very poor condition. Mon-Fri, 0900-1800, Sat 0900-1200, free, T 325-5353. Archives 1100-1800.

Museo del Teatro Colón, Tucumán 1161. Documents and objects related to the theatre since 1908. T 382-1430, Mon-Fri 0900-1600; Sat 0900-1200, closed in Jan.

Museo Histórico Saavedra (also known as the Museo Histórico de la Ciudad de Buenos Aires, not to be confused with Museo de la Ciudad), Crisólogo Larralde (Republiquetas) 6409. City history from the 18th century, furniture, arms, documents, jewellery, coins and religious art; daily guided tours. T 572-0746. Tues-Fri, 0900-1800, Sun 1400-1800. Free on Wed; closed February.

Museo de la Policía Federal San Martín 353, p 8-9. Interesting but extremely gruesome forensic section (for strong stomachs only, no one under 15 admitted),T 394-6857, Tues-Fri 1400-1800, US$1.

Museo Penitenciario Argentino Antonio Ballue, Humberto I 378, entrance US$1. Museum of the penal system; Tues-Fri 1000-1200, 1400-1700, Sun 1000-1200, 1300-1700.

Museo del Teatro Nacional Cervantes, Córdoba y Libertad, history of the theatre in Argentina, Mon-Fri 1430-1800, Sat, Sun 1000-1300, T 815-8881 in advance.

Museo Internacional de Caricatura y Humorismo, Lima 1037, originals of cartoons and caricatures of 20th century, but small international section, admission US$0.05, Mon, Tues, Thur, Fri, 1700-2000, Sat 1200-1700.

Museo de Armas, Av Santa Fe 750, T 311-1071. All kinds of weaponry related to Argentine history, including the 1982 Malvinas/Falkland Islands conflict, plus Oriental weapons, T 312-9774, Tues-Fri 1400-1930, Sat 1100-1700, Sun 1300-1800, closed 15 Dec-15 Mar, US$1.

Museo de Telecomunicaciones in a magnificent building on the Costanera

Sur, Av de los Italianos 851, T 312-5405 (used to belong to Cervecería Munich), Fri, Sat, Sun 1400-1800.

Jewish Museum, Libertad 773, religious objects relating to Jewish presence in Argentina, Tues-Thur 1600-1800.

Museo de Arte Español Enrique Larreta, Juramento 2291, Belgrano (entrance on Av Rafael Obligado). Sat-Sun 1500-1900; Mon, Tues, Fri 1400-1945. Closed Wed, Thur and January. The home of the writer Larreta, with paintings and religious art; T 783-2640 for guided tour in language other than Spanish. Also **Biblioteca Alfonso El Sabio**, Mon-Fri, 1300-1930.

Museo Histórico Sarmiento Cuba 2079, Belgrano, the National Congress and presidential offices in 1880; documents and personal effects of Sarmiento; library of his work, Thur-Sun 1500-1900 (2000 in summer), T 783-7555.

Museo Etnográfico JB Ambrosetti, Moreno 350, anthropological and ethnographic collections from around the world, including Bolivian and Mapuche silverwork, US$1, Mon-Fri 1400-1800 (1900 on Sat, Sun; closed Feb), T 331-7788.

Parks and squares

Parque Lezama, C Defensa y Brasil, originally one of the most beautiful in the city, has an imposing statue of Pedro de Mendoza, the founder of the original city in 1535. The tradition is that the first founding took place on this spot. The park is very lively on Sun.

The **Palermo Parks**, officially known as the Parque Tres de Febrero, with their magnificent avenues are the city's Bois de Boulogne. They are famous for their rose garden, Andalusian Patio, Japanese garden (admission US$2) with fish to feed and the Hipódromo Argentino, the Palermo race course, with seats for 45,000 (Sun, 1500, entry: US$3, senior citizens free). Opposite the parks are the Botanical and Zoological Gardens (the Zoo and Japanese Garden are closed on Mon). Nearby are the Municipal Golf Club, Buenos Aires Lawn Tennis Club, riding clubs and polo field, and the Club de Gimnasia y Esgrima (Athletic and Fencing Club).

The **Planetarium** (just off Belisario Roldán, in Palermo Park), is open Sat and Sun only (1500, 1630, 1800), entry US$5. At the entrance are several large meteorites from Campo del Cielo (see page 178). Reached by Subte line D.

The **Show Grounds** of the Argentine Rural Society, next to Palermo Park, entrance on Plaza Italia, stage the Annual Livestock Exhibition in July, known as Exposición Rural.

The **Municipal Botanical Gardens**, Santa Fe 2951, entrance from Plaza Italia (take Subte, line D), contain characteristic specimens of the world's vegetation. The trees proper to the several provinces of Argentina are brought together in one section. The Gardens, closed at 1800, contain the Museo del Jardín Botánico, whose collection of Argentine Flora is open Mon-Fri 0700-1600, T 831-2951. The Gardens are full of stray cats, fed regularly by local residents.

The **Zoo**, opp the Botanical Gardens, has been privatized and is open Tues-Sun 0930-1830, guided visits available, US$4 entry for adults, children under 13 free.

Plazas

On the Plaza de Mayo, the **Mothers of the Plaza de Mayo** march in remembrance of their children who disappeared during the crisis of the 1970s (their address is H Yrigoyen 1442). The Mothers still march anti-clockwise round the central monument every Thur at 1530, with photos of their 'disappeared' loved-ones pinned to their chests. Other squares include: the Plaza San Martín, with a monument to San Martín in the centre and, at the N end, a memorial with an eternal flame to those who fell in the South Atlantic conflict of 1982; the Plaza de la Fuerza Aérea (formerly Plaza Británica), with the clock tower presented by British and Anglo-Argentine residents, 'a florid Victorian sentinel, royal crest upon its bosom' (frequently vandalized); the Plaza Canadá (in front of the Retiro Station) in which there is a Pacific Northwest Indian totem pole, donated by the Canadian government; the Plaza Lavalle (see **Markets**, below); the Plaza del Congreso, the largest in the city, with a waterfall, floodlit at 2145; Plaza Francia, between Centro Cultural Recoleta and Museo de Bellas Artes, pleasant trees. There is also the great Plaza de la República, with a 67m obelisk commemorating the 400th anniversary of the city's founding at the junction between Av Roque Saenz Peña, Av 9 de Julio and Av Corrientes.

LOCAL INFORMATION

Security Buenos Aires is mostly a safe city, but street crime has risen since 1988, especially in the tourist season. Be particularly careful when boarding buses and near the Retiro train and bus stations. Beware of bagsnatching gangs in parks, markets and in the Subte, especially on Sun: they are not violent, but particularly skilful. See also **Safety**, page 236, on mustard-spraying. If your passport is stolen, remember to get a new 'entrada' stamp at the Dirección Nacional de Migraciones.

All hotels, guest houses, inns and camping sites are graded by the number of beds available, and the services supplied. The Dirección de Turismo fixes maximum and minimum rates for 1, 2 and 3-star hotels, guest houses and inns, but the ratings do not provide very useful guidance. 4 and 5-star hotels are free to apply any rate they wish. Hotels in the upper ranges can often be booked more cheaply through Buenos Aires Travel Agencies.

Hotel prices

L1	over US$200	L2	US$151-200
L3	US$101-150	A1	US$81-100
A2	US$61-80	A3	US$46-60
B	US$31-45	C	US$21-30
D	US$12-20	E	US$7-11
F	US$4-6	G	up to US$3

● **Accommodation**
The following list is only a selection; exclusion does not necessarily imply non-recommendation. Rates given below are generally the minimum rates. Room tax is 15% and is not always included in the price. Air conditioning is a must in high summer. Many of the cheaper hotels in the central area give large reductions on the daily rate for long stays. Hotels with red-green lights or marked *Albergue Transitorio* are hotels for homeless lovers (for stays of 1½-2 hrs).

5-star hotels in our L1-2 range: *Alvear Palace*, Av Alvear 1891, T 804-4031/4041, an older-style hotel, nr Recoleta, with roof garden, shopping gallery, elegant, extremely good; *Caesar Park*, Posadas 1232, T 814-5150, F 814-

5157, pool, solarium; *Claridge*, Tucumán 535, T 314-3700, F 314-8022, highly rec, but not its restaurant; *Etoile*, Presidente Roberto Ortiz 1835 in Recoleta, T 804-8603, outstanding location, rooftop pool, rooms with kitchenette, rec; *Libertador Kempinski*, Córdoba y Maipú, T 322-2095, F 322-9703; *Marriott Plaza*, Florida 1005, T 318-3000, F 318-3008, good restaurant; *Panamericano/Holiday Inn Crowne Plaza*, Carlos Pellegrini 525, T 393-6017, F 348-5250; *Park Hyatt*, Cerrito 1433, T 326-1234, F 326-3032; *Sheraton*, San Martín 1225, T 311-6330, F 311-6353, good buffet breakfast.

4-star: **L3** *Bisonte*, Paraguay 1207, T 394-8041, F 393-9086, a/c, TV, bar, modern, central, good value; **L3** *Bisonte Palace*, MT de Alvear y Suipacha, T 328-6621, F 328-6476, very good, welcoming; **A1** *Bristol*, Cerrito 286, T 382-3228, F 382-3384, good breakfast; **L3** *Carlton*, Libertad 1180, T/F 812-0080, with breakfast; **A1** *Carsson*, Viamonte 650, T 322-3601, F 392 3551, comfortable, friendly, quiet except rooms on street (ending in 17); **A1** *Gran Hotel Buenos Aires*, MT de Alvear 767, T/F 312-3003, rundown but clean; **L3** *Gran King*, Lavalle 560, T 393 4012/4052, helpful, English spoken; **L3** *Lancaster*, Córdoba 405, T 312-4061, F 311-3021, inc breakfast, expensive laundry service, charming; **L3** *Principado*, Paraguay 481, T 313-3022, F 313-3952, with breakfast, central, helpful, friendly; **A3** *Regidor*, Tucumán 451, T 314-9516, F 311-7441, a/c, clean, breakfast inc, rec; **L2** *Regente Palace*, Suipacha 964, T 328 6628, F 328-7460, very good, central, helpful, English spoken, buffet breakfast, sports facilities, stores luggage; *Salles*, Av 9 de Julio/Cerrito y J D Perón, 2 blocks from Obelisco, T 382-0091, F 382-0754, rec; **A1** *Savoy*, Av Callao 181, T 372-5972, F 325-9589, friendly and helpful.

3-star: **L2** *Camino Real*, Maipú 572, T 322-3162, F 325-9756, pleasant, clean, central; **A2** *City*, Bolívar 160, T 342 6481, F 342-6486, clean, rec; **A1** *Deauville*, Talcahuano 1253, T 811-5732, F 812-1560, a/c, restaurant and bar, garage, rec; **A2** *Ecuador*, Adolfo Alsina 2820, nr Plaza Once, T 956 0533, F 97 9987, rec; **A1** *Embajador*, Pellegrini 1181, T 393-9485, good; **A2** *Eibar*, Florida 328, T 325-0969, inc breakfast, quiet, friendly, helpful, dingy; **A2** *Gran Orly*, Paraguay 474, T/F 312-5344, good location, old fashioned, helpful, good lunches, English spoken, has some rooms for 4, holds mail for guests, arranges tours and taxis; **A1** *Impala*, Libertad 1215, T/F 816-0430, with breakfast; **A1** *Italia Romanelli*, Reconquista 647, T/F 312-6361, comfortable, rec; **A1** *Liberty*, Corrientes 632, T/F 325-0261, with breakfast, English spoken, luggage stored, clean, various sized rooms; **A3** *Promenade*, MT de Alvear 444, T/F 312-5681, no charge for credit cards, helpful, stores luggage, rec; **A2** *Regis*, Lavalle 813, T 327-2613, F 312-5681, good value, nice atmosphere, quiet at back; **A3** *San Carlos*, Suipacha 39, T 345-1022, F 345-1766; **A2** *Sarmiento Palace*, Sarmiento 1953, T 953 3404, clean, comfortable, English spoken, rec; **A2** *Victory*, Maipú 880, T 314-0655, F 322-8415, clean, a/c, modern, heating, TV, comfortable, front rooms noisy, luggage storage unreliable; **A3** *Waldorf*, Paraguay 450, T 312-2078, F 312-2079, clean, comfortable, rooms of varying standards, garage, a/c, rec.

2-star: **B** *Astoria*, Av de Mayo 916, T/F 334-9061, friendly, very clean; **A3** *Ayacucho Palace*, Ayacucho 1408, T 806-1815, F 806-4467, 10 mins from centre bus 10, rec; **A3** *Goya*, Suipacha 748, T 322-9269, with bath, a/c, quiet, clean, nr Buquebus; **A3** *Gran Hotel de la Paix*, Rivadavia 1187, T 383-7140, old but good, clean, large rooms; **A3** *Gran Hotel Hispano*, Av de Mayo 861, T 342-3472, spacious, clean, pleasant patio, stores luggage; **A3** *Mundial*, Av de Mayo 1298, T 383-0011, F 383-6318, with bath, clean, comfortable; **A3** *Plaza Roma*, Lavalle 110, T/F 311-0839, inc breakfast, rec; **A3** *San Antonio*, Paraguay 372, T 312-5381, with bath, nice atmosphere, garden, clean, rec; **A3** *Tres Sargentos*, Tres Sargentos 345, T 312-6081, clean, secure, new bathrooms, good value.

1-star or below: **A3** *Aguirre*, Aguirre 1041, T 773-5027, clean, safe; *Callao*, Callao y Sarmiento, T 476-3534, with bath, friendly, clean, noisy; **B** *Ceballos Palace*, Virrey Ceballos 261, 2 blocks from Congreso, T 372-7636, with bath, safe (next to police HQ); **A3** *Central Argentino*, Av del Libertador 174, T 312-6742, secure, clean, nr Retiro stations, noisy, overpriced; **A3** *Central Córdoba*, San Martín 1021, T/F 312-8524, very central, clean, helpful, quiet, good value; **A3** *Chile*, Av de Mayo 1297, T 383-

7877, clean, friendly, noisy; **A3** *El Cabildo*, Lavalle 748, T 392-6745, with bath, no breakfast; **B** *Hispano Argentino*, Catamarca 167, T 97-5543, some rooms with bath, clean, quiet, convenient; **B** *La Argentina*, Av de Mayo 860, with bath, clean, friendly, central, very noisy; **B** *Lisboa*, Mitre 1282, T 383-1141, with breakfast, clean, central; **B** *Maipú*, Maipú 735, T 322-5142, popular, hot water, clean, friendly, basic, stores luggage, laundry facilities, rec; **A3** *Majestic*, Libertad 121, T 351-949, Subte Lima, colonial-style, very clean, good value, inc breakfast; **B** *Marbella*, Av Corrientes 3193, T 382-8665, modernized, clean, friendly, quiet, breakfast pricey, fans, English spoken, highly rec, no credit cards; **B** *Mediterráneo*, Rodríguez Peña 149, T 476-2852, with bath, basic, central, helpful, safe, stores luggage, limited cooking facilities, fridge, rec; **B** *Micki*, Talcahuano 362, T 371-2376, clean, no a/c, basic, good value; **B** *O'Rei*, Lavalle 733, T 393-7186, without bath, basic, clean, central, gloomy, unfriendly, popular; **A3** *Orense*, Mitre 1359, T 476-3173, also **C** without bath, fan, good service, laundry and cooking facilities, rec; **B** *Uruguay*, Tacuarí 83, T 334 3456, central, clean, friendly, good value, rec; **A3** *Vedra*, Av de Mayo 1350, T 383-0584, clean, stores luggage, rec; **A3** *Versalles*, Arenales 1394, T 811-5214, W of Av 9 de Julio, friendly, basic, clean, shower, no breakfast, fine staircase and mirrors; **B** *Vila Seca*, Av de Mayo 776, T 340-952, basic, friendly, noisy.

C *Bahía*, H Yrigoyen 3062, hot showers, pleasant, clean, safe, central but noisy (10% discount to ISIC members); rec; **C** *Bolivia*, Corrientes 1212, T 382-1780, without bath; **C** *Frossard*, Tucumán 686, T 322-1811, inexpensive, hot showers (10% discount to ISIC members); **C** *Sportsman*, Rivadavia 1426, nr Plaza Congreso, T 381-8021/2, clean, old fashioned, without bath.

In San Telmo: **C** *Bolívar*, Bolívar 886, T 361-5105, with bath, clean; **D** *Hotel del Parque*, Defensa 1537, basic.

Youth hostels: *Youth Hostel*, Brasil 675 nr Constitución station, T 362-9133, **E** pp with YHA card (ISIC card accepted), inc breakfast, sheets provided, hot water 24 hrs, clean, basic, rec, no cooking facilities, cheap meals, doors closed 1200-1800 and from 0200, no single women. Women should be aware that they could attract unwelcome attention nr Constitución station as prostitutes operate there. **New Youth Hostel**: **E** pp *Del Aguila*, Espinosa 1628, hot water, cooking and laundry facilities, T 581-6663 (buses 24, 105, 106, 109, 146), rec. *Red Argentina de Alojamiento para Jóvenes*, Florida 835, p 3, T 315-1457, F 312-6840, has a network of hostels in the country.

Apartments: contracts are usually for at least 1 year and owners will demand a guarantor or a deposit covering at least 6 months rent (security or cash). One agent is Sr Aguilar, Florida 520, 3º-314, T 322-4074. An agency which arranges sharing apartments (often with senior citizens), is Martha Baleiron, Esmeralda 1066, 5ºF, T 311-9944. US$50 fee if an apartment is found, US$10 if not. All agencies should provide contracts which should be read carefully. To rent flats on a daily basis try *Edificios Esmeralda*, Marcelo T de Alvear 842, T 311-3929, inc cleaning; facilities for up to 6 persons. Also *Edificio Suipacha*, Suipacha 1235, T/F 322-6685, and *Aspen Apartment Hotel*, Esmeralda 933, T 313-9011; *Edificio Lemonde*, San Martín 839, T 313-2032, rec; *Res Trianon*, Callao 1869, T 812-3335.

Camping: about 15 km out at Lomas de Zamora, US$3 pp/night, inc swimming pool, take bus 141 from Plaza Italia to Puente La Noria then No 540 to Villa Albertini which passes the entrance.

Good camping equipment and fuel from *Fugate* (no sign), Gascón 238 (off Rivadavia 4100 block), T 982-0203, also repairs equipment. *Outside Mountain Equipment*, Donado 4660, T 541-2084, and Acampar, H Yrigoyen 2835, T 783-0209. *Munor*, H Yrigoyen 283, Martínez, and *Panamericana y Paraná*, Martínez (Shopping Unicenter, 3rd level). Good camping stores also at Guatemala 5908 and 5451. Camping gas available at Mitre 111, *Todo Gas*, Paraná 550, and El Pescador, Paraguay y Libertad. Every kind of battery (inc for Petzl climbing lamps) at Callao 373. *Cacique Camping* manufacture camping equipment and clothing, their two shops: Arenales 1435, Barrio Nte, and San Lorenzo 4220, Munro, Provincia Buenos Aires, T 762 0261, F 756 1392, also sell the *South American Handbook*.

● **Places to eat**

'The Buenos Aires Herald' publishes a handy *Guide to Good Eating in Buenos Aires* (with a guide to local wines) by Dereck Foster. There is also *El Libro de los Restaurantes de Buenos Aires*, published annually, describing the city's major restaurants. Eating out in Buenos Aires is very good but is getting more expensive. In 1996 good restaurants were charging US$30 pp and up; more modest places were charging US$20-25 pp. **NB** In many mid to upper range restaurants, lunch is far cheaper than dinner. Lunch or dinner in a normal restaurant cost US$9-12 (cutlet, salad, 1/4 of table wine, dessert); a portion at a *comidas para llevar* (take away) place cost US$2.50-3.50. Many cheaper restaurants are *tenedor libre*, eat as much as you like for a fixed price.

The following list, for reasons of space, not quality, gives only those restaurants easily accessible for people staying in the city centre. **In the banking district**, between Av Corrientes and Plaza de Mayo: *Clark's*, Sarmiento 645, in old English outfitter's shop (also at Junín 1777), well cooked food, very expensive, busy, fish and lamb specialities (set lunch very good value); *Bolsa de Comercio*, 25 de Mayo 359, downstairs at the Stock Exchange, good but expensive; *London Grill*, Reconquista 455, British, busy, famous for roast beef and turkey curries, closed in evenings; *Sabot*, 25 de Mayo 756, very good business lunches; *Brizzi*, Lavalle 445, business lunches, good and worth the price; *Blab*, Florida 325, sole, veal, pork specialities, lunchtime only; *La Pipeta*, San Martín 498, downstairs, serving for 30 years, good, noisy, closed Sun; *La Estancia*, Lavalle 941, popular with business people, excellent grills and service, expensive (US$30); *La Casona del Nonno*, Lavalle 827, popular, *parrilla* and pasta; *ABC*, Lavalle 545, traditional, good value (US$25 pp); *El Palacio de la Papa Frita*, Lavalle 735 and 954, Corrientes 1612, Laprida 1339, 10% discount for ISIC and youth card holders; *Emporio de las Papas Fritas*, Maipú 431, good *parrillas*, good value; *La Rural*, Suipacha 453, rec for *parrillada* and *bife de lomo*, expensive or cheaper *table d'hôte*, English-speaking head waiter is excellent; *Pizzería Roma*, Lavalle 800, cheap and good quality, delicious spicy *empanadas* and *noquis*, good breakfasts; *Los Inmortales*, Lavalle 746, specializes in pizza, also good. There are other locations: some serve *à la carte* dishes which are plentiful, and are open from 1500-2000 when most other restaurants are closed; *El Figón de Bonilla*, rustic style, L N Alem 673, good, another branch at Junín 1721; *Los Troncos*, Suipacha 732, good grills, US$18 *menú*; *Catalinas*, Reconquista 875, seafood, very expensive. **A few blocks from this district**: *El Aljibe*, at *Sheraton*, smoked salmon, tournedos Rossini, baby beef; *Dolli*, Av del Libertador 312, nr Retiro, very good food, fairly expensive; *La*

Chacra, Córdoba 941 between Suipacha and 9 de Julio, good but overpriced.

Walking up Av Quintana, you reach Plaza Recoleta. On the corner of Roberto M Ortiz is *La Biela* (see **Tea Rooms**, etc, below), and opp *Café de la Paix*. Turning left on Ortiz: *Lola*, No 1805, good pasta, lamb and fish but expensive; *Don Juan*, No 1827; *La Tasca de Germán*, No 1863, highly rec, European. Cross Guido to: *Gato Dumas*, Junín 1745, expensive but has good fixed price menus; *La Bianca*, Junín 1769, very good value for BsAs, lunch US$16 pp; *Harper's*, Junín 1773; *Hippopotamus*, Junín 1787, dinner expensive, good value executive lunch; *Munich Recoleta*, Junín 1871, good steaks, pleasant atmosphere, US$20 pp, no credit cards. Nearby, 2 blocks from Recoleta towards Av Callao, *Au Bec Fin*, Vicente López 1827, reservations needed, open 2000-0200 daily.

In the San Telmo area: *C de Angeles*, Chile 318, nice setting in an old, covered street, high standards; *La Convención de San Telmo*, Carlos Calvo 375, good, but very dear; *El Repecho de San Telmo*, Carlos Calvo 242, excellent, expensive, reserve in advance (T 362-5473); *La Casa de Esteban de Luca*, Defensa 1000, very good, good wines. For ice cream, *Sumo*, Independencia y Piedras.

The Costanera Rafael Obligado along the river front (far end of Aeroparque) is lined with little eating places (take taxi, or colectivo 45 from Plaza Constitución, Plaza San Martín or Retiro to Ciudad Universitaria): *El Rancho Inn* is best, try also *Happening*, *La Marea* and *Los Años Locos*, good beef, *parrilla*, cold buffet. *Clo Clo*, La Pampa y Costanera, reservation required. Typical *parrilla* at *Rodizio*, Costanera Nte, opp Balneario Coconor, self-service and waiter service, other branches, eg Av Callao y Juncal, good value, popular. In Puerto Madero, across the docks from Plaza de Mayo, are *Las Lilas*, excellent *parrilla*; *Cholila*, Dávila 102, Puerto Viamonte, chic; *Xcaret* Dávila 164; *Mirasol*, No 202, and opp, *Bice*, Dávila 192, mostly Italian, good; *Columbus*, popular (all about US$40 pp inc wine and tip); a bit cheaper (US$30-35) are *Bahía Madero*, Dávila 430, highly rec; branches of *Rodizio* and *Happening*.

Near the Teatro Colón: *Tomo Uno*, Carlos Pellegrini 521 (*Hotel Panamericano*), expensive, trout, mignon, shrimp, home-made pasta, closed Sun; *Posta del Gaucho*, Pellegrini 625, accepts Visa; *Edelweiss*, Libertad 432, tuna steaks, grill, expensive and famous. **By Congreso**: *Quorum*, Combate de los Pozos 61, behind Congress, popular with politicians.

Typical Boca restaurants on Necochea, but check the hygiene. They all serve antipasto, pasta and chicken; no point in looking for beef here. All bands are loud. The seafood restaurant *La Barca*, Av Pedro de Mendoza, on river bank nr Avellaneda bridge, rec; also rec for seafood and good value, *Viejo Puente*, Almte Brown 1499. *El Pescadito*, Mendoza 1483, rec for pasta and seafood.

Other recommendations: *Pepito*, Montevideo 381, very good; *Pippo*, Montevideo 341, large pasta house, simple food, very popular, also at Paraná 356; *Chiquilín*, Montevideo 321, pasta and meat, good value; *Nazarenas*, Reconquista 1132, good for beef, expensive, rec; *Ostramar*, Santa Fe 3495 y Julián Alvarez (Subte station Ortiz, then walk back towards town), good quality fish; *El Salmón II*, Reconquista 1014, large portions of good food, not cheap.

Other Italian: *Broccolino*, Esmeralda 776, excellent, very popular, try *pechuguitas*; *Mama Liberata*, Maipú 642, excellent. Three famous *pizzerías* in the centre are on Corrientes: *Banchero*, No 1298; *Las Cuartetas*, No 838, and *Los Inmortales*, No 1369, same chain as above; *Il Gatto*, Corrientes 959, popular and reasonably priced.

Spanish: *El Imparcial*, H Yrigoyen 1204, and opp, *El Globo*, No 1199, both rec. **Swedish**: food at *Swedish Club*, Tacuarí 147, open to non-members. **Hungarian**: *Budapest*, 25 de Mayo 690, cheap. **British**: *The Alexandra*, San Martín 774, curries, fish and seafood, nice bar, closed in evening.

Vegetarian: *Granix*, Florida 126 and 467 *tenedor libre* US$8, bland but filling, lunchtime Mon-Fri. *Ever Green* is a chain of *tenedor libre* vegetarian restaurants, branches: Paraná 746, Tucumán 666, Sarmiento 1728 and Cabildo 2979; *La Esquina de las Flores*, Córdoba 1599, excellent value, also good health-food shop; *Los Angeles*, Uruguay 707, US$7 for salad bar, main meal and dessert, rec; *La Huerta*, Paraguay 445, T 311-0470, macrobiotic, rec; *La Huerta II*, Lavalle 895, 2nd floor, *tenedor libre*, US$7, reasonable.

Oriental: *Nuevo Oriental*, Maipú nr Lavalle, Chinese *tenedor libre*, US$6, good choice; *Tsuru*, ground floor of *Sheraton*, authentic Japanese, small, rec.

Pumper-nic is a chain of rather pricey fast food restaurants. Many *McDonalds* in the centre. *The Embers*, Callao 1111, fast food, 10% discount for ISIC and youth card holders. Try also restaurants in Supercoop stores at Sarmiento 1431, Lavalle 2530, Piedras y Rivadavia and Rivadavia 5708.

Cheap meals at *Los Teatros*, Talcahuano 354, good (live music 2300-0100, open 24 hrs); *Pizzalandia*, on Brasil (nr Youth Hostel) serves cheap *empanadas*, *salteñas* and pizzas. Good snacks all day and night at Retiro and Constitución railway termini. For quick cheap snacks the markets are rec. The snack bars in underground stations are also cheap. *DeliCity* bakeries, several branches, very fresh pastries, sweets, breads, authentic American donuts; *Biscuit House*, bakery chain, 20 branches, media lunas, empanadas and breads.

For restaurants with shows, see **Nightclubs and folklore** below.

Tea rooms, cafés and bars: *Richmond*, Florida 458 between Lavalle and Corrientes, genteel (chess played between 1200-2400); well-known are the *Confitería Suiza*, Tucumán 753, and the *Florida Garden* at Florida and Paraguay. *Confitería Ideal*, Suipacha 384, old, faded, good service, cakes and snacks, rec. Many on Av del Libertador in the Palermo area. *Café Querandí*, Venezuela y Chacabuco, popular with intellectuals and students, good atmosphere, well known for its Gin Fizz. The more bohemian side of the city's intellectual life is centred on Av Corrientes, between Cerrito and Callao, where there are many bars and coffee shops, such as *La Paz* (open very late, No 1599, T 46-5542, 10% discount for ISIC and youth card members). *Pub Bar Bar O*, Tres Sargentos 415, good music and prices, gives similar discount. *El Molino*, Rivadavia y Callao, popular with politicians, nr Congress, Belle Epoque décor, frequent art sales, good value. *Café 1234*, Santa Fe 1234, good and reasonable; *Clásica y Moderna*, Callao y Paraguay, bookshop at back, expensive but very popular, jazz usually on Wed night, open 24 hrs. Excellent ice-cream at *Freddo*, de Melo y Callao, or Ayacucho y Quintana. Next door (Quintana y Recoleta) is café *La Biela*, restaurant and *whiskería*, elegant. Similarly popular, *Café Victoria*, Ortiz 1865, whiskería/sandwichería, typical of the Recoleta area. On Lavalle there are *whiskerías* and *cervecerías* where you can have either coffee or exotic drinks. *Barila*, Santa Fe 2375, has excellent confectionery. *Café Tortoni*, Av de Mayo 825-9, delicious cakes, coffee, a haunt of artists, very elegant, over 100 years old, interesting *peña* evenings of poetry and music. On Sat at 2315 it becomes a 'Catedral del Jazz', with Fenix Jazz Band, US$15 entrance. *Café El Verdi*, Paraguay 406, also has live music. *Parakultural New Border*, Chacabuco 1072, mostly avant-garde theatre, popular; *Die Schule*, Alsina 1760, hard rock bar with avant-garde theatre. A 'bohemian, bizarre' bar is *El Dorado*, H Yrigoyen 971. Good bars in San Telmo around Plaza Dorrego, eg *El Balcón de la Plaza*, and on Humberto I. Watch whisky prices in bars, much higher than in restaurants. Most cafés serve tea or coffee plus *facturas*, or pas-

tries, for breakfast, US$2.50-3 (bakery shops sell 10 *facturas* for US$2).

● **Airline offices**
Aerolíneas Argentinas (AR), Paseo Colón 185, T 343-2071, with 4 branches, plus airport offices, reservations T 362-5008, information T 393-5122, Mon-Fri 0945-1745; **Austral Líneas Aéreas**, LN Alem 1134, T 317-3605/340-7777; **Líneas Aéreas del Estado** (LADE), C Perú 714, T 361-7071/0853, erratic schedules, uninfomed office; **Líneas Aéreas Privadas Argentinas** (LAPA), Av Santa Fe 1970, ticket office MT de Alvear 790, T 812-3322 (reservations), or Aeroparque Puente Aéreo section, T 772-9920, cheapest fares to main tourist centres, good service; **DINAR**, Av R Sáenz Peña 933, T 326-0135, 322-8888 (reservations); **LAER**, Lavalle 347, p 2B, T 394-5641; **Kaiken**, Almafuerte Travel, Av de Mayo 580, p 6, T 331-0191; **AeroPerú**, Santa Fe 840, T 311-6431; **Varig**, Florida 630, T 329-9201; **Lan Chile**, Paraguay 609 p 1, T 311-5334, 312-8161 for reconfirmations; **Ladeco**, Santa Fe 920, T 480-0253; **United**, M T Alvear 590, T 326-9111; **Lufthansa**, M T Alvear 636, reservations T 319-0600; **Air France**, Santa Fe 963, T 311-0749; **British Airways**, Córdoba 690, T 322-7611; **American**, Santa Fe 881, T 318-1111; **KLM**, Reconquista 559, p 5, T 480-9470.

See **Introduction and Hints**, or Brazil chapter for Mercosur Airpass.

● **Banks & money changers**
Many shops and restaurants accept US dollar bills. Most banks charge very high commission especially on TCS (as much as US$10). Banks open Mon-Fri 1000-1500, be prepared for long delays. US dollar bills are often scanned electronically for forgeries, while TCs are sometimes very difficult to change and you may be asked for proof of purchase. American Express TCs are less of a problem than Thomas Cook. Practices are constantly changing. **Lloyds Bank** (BLSA) Ltd, Reconquista y Bartolomé Mitre, Visa cash advances provided in both US dollars and pesos. It has 10 other branches in the city, and others in Greater Buenos Aires. **Royal Bank of Canada**, Florida y Perón, branch at Av Callao 291. **Citibank**, B Mitre 502, changes only Citicorps TCs, no commission, also Mastercard; branch at Florida 746. **First National Bank of Boston**, Florida 99. **Bank of America**, JD Perón y San Martín changes Bank of America TCs are only, into US$ at very high commission. **Banco Tornquist**, Mitre 531, Crédit Lyonnais agents, advance cash on visa card. **Banco Holandés**, Florida 361; **Deutsche Bank**, B Mitre 401 (and other branches), changes Thomas Cook TCs, also Mastercard, both give cash advances. **Banco Roberts**, 25 de Mayo 258, changes Thomas Cook TCs without commission. Thomas Cook rep, **Full-**

ers, Esmeralda 1000 y M T Alvear. **American Express** offices are at Arenales 707 y Maipú, by Plaza San Martín, T 312-0900, where you can apply for a card, get financial services and change Amex TCs (1000-1500 only, no commission into US$ or pesos). **Client Mail** in same building, Mon-Fri 0900-1800, Sat 0900-1300. Mastercard ATMs (look for Link-Mastercard/Cirrus) at several locations, mostly **Banco Nacional del Lavoro** inc Florida 40 and Santa Fe y Esmeralda.

There are many *casas de cambio*, some of which deal in TCs. Most are concentrated around San Martín and Corrientes (*Cambio Topaz*, No 1394-1400, recently rec, also **Casa Piano**, San Martín 345-347, changes TCs into pesos or US$ cash for 2-3% commission, *Cambios Trade Travel*, San Martín 967, 3% commission on TCs, and *Exprinter*, Suipacha 1107), open from Mon-Fri 1000-1600, Sat closed. Many *cambios* will exchange US$, TCs for US$ cash at commissions varying from 1.25 to 3%. If all *cambios* closed, try Mercadería de Remate de Aduana, Florida 8, or *Eves*, Tucumán 702, open until 1800. On Sat, Sun and holidays, cash may be exchanged in the *cambio* in some of the large supermarkets (eg *Carrefour*, Paseo Alcorta Shopping Center, open daily 1000-2200). There is no service charge on notes, only on cheques. Major credit cards usually accepted but check for surcharges. General **Mastercard** office at H Yrigoyen 878, open 0930-1800, T 331-1022/2502/2549; another branch at Florida 274 (open 1000-1730). **Visa**, Corrientes 1437, 2nd floor, T 954-3333/2000, for stolen cards. Other South American currencies can only be exchanged in *casas de cambio*.

● **Cultural centres**
Argentine Association of English Culture, Suipacha 1333 (library for members only); **British Chamber of Commerce**, Av Corrientes 457; **British Council**, M T Alvear 590, p 4, T 311-9814/7519, F 311-7747 (open 1000-1200, 1430-1630); **Goethe Institut**, Av Corrientes 311, German library (open 1300-1900 excluding Wed, and 1000-1400 first Sat of month) and newspapers, free German films shown, cultural programmes, German language courses. In the same building, upstairs, is the German Club, Corrientes 327. **Alliance Française**, Córdoba 946; **USA Chamber of Commerce**, Diagonal Nte 567; **US Information Library** (Biblioteca Lincoln), Florida 935, reference and lending library, free, no identification needed, but take passport to become a member, on first 5 days of each month only, fixed address needed (closed Sat/Sun). **St Andrew's Society**, Perú 352.

Clubs: **American Club**, Viamonte 1133, facing Teatro Colón, temporary membership available; **American Women's Club**, Av Córdoba 632, p 11; **English Club**, 25 de Mayo 586, T 311-9121, open for lunch only, temporary membership available to British business visitors. The American and English Clubs have reciprocal arrangements with many clubs in USA and UK. **Swedish Club**, Tacuarí 147; **Organización Hebrea Argentina Macabi**, Tucumán 3135, T 962-0947, social and sporting club for conservative Jews.

● **Embassies & consulates**
All open Mon-Fri unless stated otherwise. **Bolivian Consulate**, Belgrano 1670, p 2, T 381-0539, open 0900-1400, visa while you wait; **Brazilian Consulate**, Carlos Pellegrini 1363, p 5, open Mon-Fri, 0930-1400, visa takes 1 day, T 394-5260/5264; **Paraguayan Consulate**, Las Heras 2545, 0900-1400, T 322-6536; **Peruvian Consulate**, San Martín 691, p 6, T 311-7582, 0900-1400, visa US$5, takes 1 day; **Uruguayan Consulate**, Ayacucho 1616, open 1000-1800, T 821-6031, visa takes up to 1 week; **Chilean Embassy**, Tagle 2762, T 394-6582, Mon-Thur 0930-1330, 1530-1830, Fri 0915-1430; **Ecuadorean Embassy**, Quintana 585, p 9 y 19, T 804-6408.

US Embassy and Consulate Gen, Cerviño 4320, T 777-4533/7007, 0900-1730, consulate, visas 0800-1100, calls between 1500 and 1700 (US Embassy Residence, Av Libertador 3502); **Australian Embassy**, Av Santa Fe 846 (Swissair Building), T 312-6841, Mon-Thur 0830-1230, 1330-1730, Fri 0830-1315; **Canadian Embassy**, Tagle 2828, T 312-9081; **South African Embassy**, Marcelo T de Alvear 590, p 7, T 311-8991/7, Mon-Thur 0900-1300, 1400-1630, Fri 0900-1330; **Israeli Embassy**, Av de Mayo 701, p 9, T 342-6653; **Japanese Embassy**, Paseo Colón 275, p 9 y 11, T 343-2561, 0900-1300, 1430-1800.

Austrian Embassy, French 3671, T 802-1400, 0900-1200; **Belgian Embassy**, Defensa 113-8, T 331-0066/69, 0800-1300; **British Embassy**, Luis Agote 2412/52 (nr corner Pueyrredón y Guido), T 803-7070, open 0915-1215, 1415-1615; **Danish Embassy**, L N Alem 1074, p 9, T 312-6901/6935, 0900-1230, 1500-1730; **Finnish Embassy**, Av Santa Fe 846, p 5, T 312-0600/70, Mon-Thur 0830-1700, Fri 0830-1200; **French Embassy**, Av Santa Fe 846, p 3, T 312-2425, 0900-1200; **German Embassy**, Villanueva 1055, Belgrano, T 771-5054/9, 0900-1200; **Greek Embassy**, R S Peña 547, p 4, T 342-4958, 1000-1300; **Irish Embassy**, Suipacha 1380, p 2, T 325-8588, 1000-1230; **Italian Embassy**, Billinghurst 2577, consulate at M T de Alvear 1149, T 325-6132, 0900-1300; **Netherlands Embassy**, Edif Buenos Aires, Av de Mayo 701, p 19, T 334-4000, 0900-1200, 1300-1530; **Norwegian Embassy**, Esmeralda

909, p 3 B, T 312-2204, 0900-1430; **Spanish Embassy**, Florida 943, T 811-0078, 0900-1330, 1500-1730. **Swedish Embassy**, Corrientes 330, p 3, T 311-3088/9, T 1000-1200; **Swiss Embassy**, Av Santa Fe 846, p 12, T 311-6491, open 0900-1200.

● **Entertainment**

Cinemas: the selection of films is as good as anywhere else in the world and details are listed daily in all main newspapers. Films are shown uncensored. Tickets best booked early afternoon to ensure good seats (average price US$8 in 1996, 50% discount Wed and for first show Mon-Fri). Tickets obtainable, sometimes cheaper, from ticket agencies (*carteleras*), such as *Vea Más*, Paseo La Plaza, Corrientes 1600, local 19 (the cheapest), *Cartelera*, Lavalle 742, T 322 9263, *Teatro Lorange*, Corrientes 1372, T 372-7386, and *Cartelera Baires*, Corrientes 1372, local 25. Almost all foreign films are shown with subtitles. Many cinemas on Lavalle, around Av Santa Fe and Callao and in Belgrano (Av Cabildo and environs). Film club at *Faro Gandhi*, Montevideo 453 on Fri and Sat evenings, showing old, foreign and 'art' films, US$1.50, open to non-members. Free films at Asociación Bancaria, Sarmiento 337/341, T 313-9306/312-5011/17, once a month (Wed); old films at Cine en la Cinemateca Argentina, Sarmiento 2255, T 952-2170 (half price of other cinemas, plus 20% discount for ISIC holders), and at Sarmiento 2150, T 48-2170. ISIC holders also entitled to discounts at Cine IFT Sala 1, Boulogne Sur Mer 549 (50%). On Sat nights many central cinemas have *trasnoches*, late shows starting at 0100.

Cultural events: the *Luna Park* stadium holds pop/jazz concerts, ballet and musicals, at Bouchard 465, nr Correo Central, T 311-5100, free parking at Corrientes 161. *Teatro Alvear*, Corrientes 1659, T 46-9470, has free concerts Fri at 1300, usually Orquesta de Tango de BsAs. *Tango Week*, leading up to National Tango Day (11 Dec), has free events all over the city, details posted around the city and at tourist offices. *Teatro Municipal Gen San Martín*, Av Corrientes 1530, organizes many cultural activities of which quite a few are free of charge, inc concerts Sat and Sun evenings; the theatre's Sala Leopoldo Lugones shows international classic films, Sat-Sun, US$2. Free concerts at ProMusica music shop, Florida 638; schedule in window. *Centro Cultural Gen San Martín*, Sarmiento 1551, and the *Centro Cultural de Recoleta*, Junín 1930, next to the Recoleta cemetery have many free activities. Look for details in main newspapers and weekly paper *La Maga*, US$5 from news stands. **NB** From mid-Dec to end-Feb most theatres and concert halls are closed.

Music: bars and restaurants in San Telmo district, with live music (usually beginning 2330-2400): *Players*, Humberto I 528 (piano bar); *Samovar de Rasputin*, Almte Brown, edge of Parque Lezama, good blues, dinner and/or show. Cover charges between US$5 and US$20, or more.

Jazz: *El Subsuelo*, JD Perón 1372, good bands featured; *Oliverio*, Paraná 328, excellent live jazz features the great Fats Fernández, Fri-Sat 2330 and 0100; *Café Tortoni*, Av de Mayo 829, T 342-4328, traditional jazz downstairs, Fri-Sun 2315, Fri tango concert 2130, rec.

Bailantas are music and dance halls where they play popular styles which for years have been despised as 'low class'. They are now fashionable among the upper classes. A popular place is *Terremoto Bailable*, Paraguay y Thames; *Metropolis*, Santa Fe at Plaza Italia. For salsa: *El Club*, Yerbal 1572, friendly, for all ages, not trendy, all welcome; *La Salsera*, Yatay 961, highly regarded salsa place.

Nightclubs and folklore: Tango: *Casablanca*, Balcarce 668, T 331-4621, excellent show, costing US$40 pp inc drinks; *Michelangelo*, Balcarce 433, T 334-4321, impressive setting, concert café in an old converted monastery, various types of music inc tango and folklore, Tues-Sun, and *La Ventana*, Balcarce 425, Mon-Sat shows at 2230, T 331-3648/334-1314, very touristy but very good show, US$50 for show, dinner and unlimited wine, through an agency, 20% discount for ISIC and youth card holders, from Asatej office (see **Useful addresses** below). Tango shows also at *La Cumparsita*, Chile 302, T 361-6880, authentic, US$50 for 2 inc wine; *Bar Sur*, Estados Unidos 299, and *Antigua Tasca de Cuchilleros*, Carlos Calvo 319, T 362-3811/28, pleasant surroundings, show US$20, show and dinner, US$32, both in San Telmo. Recommended are *Tarquino*, Brasil y Perú, and Cochabamba 444, pay US$5 when leaving, young crowd, rec, lessons also available. The best affordable tango bars are in the Boca, but it is difficult to find authentic tango for locals, most are tourist-oriented. Good show also at *La Veda*, Florida 1, reasonable meal with wine and other drinks. *Viejo Buzón*, Corrientes y Rodríguez Peña, good tango, no dinner but plenty of dancing, locals and tourists; *Café Mozart*, Esmeralda 754, tango, jazz, theatre, no dinner; *La Casa de Aníbal Troilo*, Carlos Calvo 2540, good singers and bands, for tourists; *Tango Danza*, José María Moreno 351, Fri, Sat, Sun, from 2200; *Salón La Argentina*, Rodríguez Peña 365, Thur-Sun, 2200, more modern-style tango. Also rec are *Café Homero*, JA Cabrera 4946, Palermo; *Italia Unita*, JD Perón 2535; *Mesón Español*, Rodríguez Peña 369, T 35-

0516, good folk music show and good food; *Galería Tango Argentino*, Boedo 722 y Independencia, T 93-1829/7527, Wed-Sat, less touristy than others, dinner (usually), show and dancing, has dancers and tango lessons (Mon-Fri, 1800-2100), well-known bands; *Paladium*, San Martín 954, tango/bolero dance hall; *Volver*, Corrientes 837, Mon-Fri, 1800-2100. Andean music at *Ollantaytambo*, Estados Unidos 541. Tango lessons at *Champagne Tango*, Rio de Janeiro 387, Tues, Fri, Sun.

Recommended nightclub/discos: inc *Hippopotamus*, Junín 1787, Recoleta, French restaurant (lunch and dinner), fashionable nightclub; *Le Club*, small and exclusive, Quintana 111; *Cemento*, Estados Unidos 700 block, disco with liveshows, usually hard rock and heavy metal, popular with younger crowds, as are *La City*, Alvarez Thomas y El Cano, and *Halley*, Corrientes 2020, heavy metal and hard rock.

Also rec: *Mama Baker*, Santa Fe 2800; *Cinema*, Av Córdoba 4633, inside a former cinema; *El Dorado*, H Yrigoyen y 9 de Julio, interesting, different; *El Nacional*, Reconquista 915, in tunnels formerly used for smuggling; *El Angel*, Corrientes 1768 y Callao; *Club Coco Bahiano*, Carlos Calvo y Balcarce, live Brazilian music, crowded and friendly, open Fri and Sat till 0700, entry inc one drink US$9, rec; *Cachaça Tropical*, on Brasil (1 block from Plaza Constitución), big disco with Latin American music, good meeting place; *Roxy*, Rivadavia 1900 block, rock and roll, reggae, rec; *New York City*, Alvarez Thomas 1391, T 552-4141, young and middle-aged clientele, popular, chic, well-established.

Gay discos: *Bunker*, Anchorena 1170, Thur-Sun; *Experiment*, C Pellegrini 1085, open nightly; *Enigma*, Esmeralda y Paraguay, also for heterosexuals. Some discos serve breakfast for additional charge at entry. Generally it is not worth going to discos before 0230 at weekends. Dress is usually smart.

Theatre: about 20 commercial theatres play the year round. Recommended is the *Teatro Liceo*. There are many amateur theatres. You are advised to book as early as possible for a seat at a concert, ballet, or opera. For ticket agencies, see **Cinemas**, above.

● **Hospitals & medical services**
Innoculations: *Centro Médico Rivadavia*, S de Bustamante 2531 y Av Las Heras, Mon-Fri, 0730-1900 (bus 38, 59, 60 or 102 from Plaza Constitución), or *Guardia de Sanidad del Puerto*, Mon and Thur, 0800-1200, at Av Ing Huergo 690, T 334-1875, free, bus 20 from Retiro, no appointment required (typhus, cholera, Mon-Fri 0800-1200; yellow fever, Tues-Thur 1400-1600, but no hepatitis, take syringe and needle, particularly for insulin and TB). Buy the vaccines in

Laboratorio Biol, Uriburu 159, or in larger chemists. Any hospital with an infectology department will do hepatitis A.

Urgent medical service: (day and night) (**Casualty ward**: *Sala de guardia*) T 34-4001/4. For free municipal ambulance service to an emergency hospital department, T 107 (SAME). In case of intoxication, T 962-6666 for information or first aid. *British Hospital*, Perdriel 74, T 23-1081, US$14 a visit; cheap dental treatment at Av Caseros y Perdriel 76; *German Hospital*, Pueyrredón 1657, between C Berutti and C Juncal, T 821-4083. Both maintain first-aid centres (*centros asistenciales*) as do the other main hospitals. *French Hospital*, Rioja 951, T 97-1031; *Children's Hospital* (Ricardo Gutiérrez), Bustamante 1399, T 86-5500; *Centro Gallego*, Belgrano 2199, T 47-3061; *Hospital Juan A Fernández*, Cerviño y Bulnes, good, medical attention. If affected by pollen, asthma sufferers can receive excellent treatment at the *Hospital de Clínicas José de San Martín*, Córdoba 2351, T 821-6041, US$6/treatment. *Dental Hospital*, Pueyrredón 1940, T 941-5555; *Eye Hospital*, San Juan 2121, T 821-2721.

● **Language schools**
Verbum Language School, Lavalle 357, p 3, C 2, T/F 393-8228, frequently rec, accommodation and social events offered; *Instituto de Lengua Española para Extranjeros*, Lavalle 1619, 7th C, T 375-0730, F 864-4942, US$15/hour, rec by individuals and organizations alike; *Bromley Institute*, Paraná 641, 1A, T 40-4113, courses in Spanish, Portuguese, French, English, high standards, well-regarded, rec. Free Spanish classes at *Escuela Presidente Roca*, Libertad 581, T 35-2488, Mon-Fri, 1945-2145 (basic level only). Spanish classes also at *Instituto del Sur*, Av Callao 433, 9 S, T/F 49-8421, individual lessons, cheap; *Estudio Buenos Aires, San Martín 881, p 4, T 312-8936, owner also lets out rooms*; *Link Educational Services*, Arenales 2565, p 5 B, T 825-3017; *Universidad de Buenos Aires*, 25 de Mayo, offers cheap, coherent courses; *AmerISpan Unlimited* has an affiliated school, contact PO Box 40513, Philadelphia, PA 19106, USA, T 800-879-6640 or, outside North America 215-985-4522, F 215-985-4524, Email info@amerispan.com (http://www.amerispan.com). CEDIC, Reconquista 719, p 11 E, T/F 315-1156, US$16/hour private tuition, US$11/hour in groups, rec. For other schools teaching Spanish, and for private tutors look in *Buenos Aires Herald* in the classified advertisements. Enquire also at Asatej (see **Useful addresses**).

Schools which teach English to Argentines inc: *International House*, Pacheco de Melo 2555, British-owned and run; Berlitz, Av de

Mayo 847; Santiago del Estero 324; *American Teachers*, Viamonte y Florida, T 393-3331. There are many others. Vacancies are advertised in the *Buenos Aires Herald*. Before being allowed to teach, you must offically have a work permit (difficult to obtain) but schools may offer casual employment without one (particularly to people searching for longer-teroom employment), if unsure of your papers, ask at Migraciones (address below). There are many 'coordinadoras', usually women, who do not have an institute but run English 'schools' out of their homes by hiring native English-speakers and sending them out on jobs. Pay varies between US$10 and 25, depending on where you teach and on negotiation, the pay is usually better than in a fixed institute. Adverts occasionally appear in the *Herald*, but most contacts are by word of mouth.

● **Laundry**

Many dry cleaners and many launderettes, eg Alvear 861, in centre; Junín 15 y Rivadavia, Mon-Sat 0800-2100; Junín 529 y Lavalle; Rivadavia 1340; *Laverap*, Paraguay 888 y Suipacha, Córdoba 466, Local 6, T 312-5460, US$6.50/load (10% discount to ISIC and youth card holders, also at Brasil y Bolívar and Rodríguez Peña 100-200), Arenales 894, Solís nr A Alsina (cheaper). The laundry at Brasil 554 costs US$4/load, more for valet service. *Marva*, J D Perón 2000 y Ayacucho.

● **Libraries**

Harrods (2nd floor) on Florida, 800 block (being remodelled). See also Biblioteca Nacional, under **Museums**, and **Cultural and Trade Associations**.

● **Places of Worship** (non-Catholic)

The *Holy Cross*, C Estados Unidos 3150, established by the Passionists; *St John's Cathedral* (Anglican), 25 de Mayo 282 (services, Sun 0900 in English, 1030 in Spanish), was built half at the expense of the British Government and dedicated in 1831; *St Paul's, St Peter's, St Michael and All Angels* and *St Saviour's* are Anglican places of worship in the suburbs; *St Andrew's*, C Belgrano 579, is one of the 8 Scottish Presbyterian churches. The *American Church*, Corrientes 718, is Methodist, built in 1863, service at 1100; *First Methodist* (American) Church, Av Santa Fe 839, Acassuso.

German Evangelical Church, Esmeralda 162; *Swedish Church*, Azopardo 1422; the *Armenian Cathedral* of St Gregory the Illuminator at the Armenian Centre, and the *Russian Orthodox Cathedral* of The Holy Trinity (Parque Lezama) are interesting.

Synagogue: the most important in Buenos Aires are the Congregación Israelita en la República Argentina, Libertad 705 (also has a small museum), and, the oldest, the Templo Israelita at Paso 423 (called the Paso Temple), traditional and conservative. An important orthodox temple is the Comunidad Israelita Ortodoxa, the seat of the rabbis of Argentina, Ecuador 530, T 862-2701. The Comunidad Betel, Av Elcano 3424, and the B'nai Tikvah, Vidal 2049, are for reformed worshippers. Congregación Emanu-El (reformed sect), Tronador 1455, take bus 140 from Av Córdoba to Alvarez Thomas block 1600, then turn right into Tronador.

● **Post & telecommunications**

General Post Office: (Correo Central – now privatized, Correos Argentinos), Sarmiento y L N Alem, Mon-Fri, 0800-2000. *Poste Restante* on 1st floor (US$2.25/letter), poor reports, very limited service on Sat (closes 1400). Fax service US$5/minute. Philatelic section open Mon-Fri 1000-1800. Centro Postal Internacional, for all parcels over 1 kg for mailing abroad, at Av Antártida Argentina, nr Retiro station, open 1100 to 1700. Check both Correo Central and Centro Postal Internacional for *poste restante*.

Telecommunications: the State company Entel has now been privatized and the city is split into two telephone zones, owned by Telecom and Telefónica Argentina. Av Corrientes 705 (open 24 hrs) for international phone calls, fax, public telex in basement; alternatively in Central Post Office (more expensive), also telex. Other offices at San Martín 322, on Santa Fe 1841, on Agüero/Las Heras, and at Lavalle 613. *Fichas* or *cospeles* (tokens) for calls in the city from public telephone boxes cost US$0.50, obtained at newspaper stalls, cigarette *kioskos* and Telecom or Telefónica Argentina offices. Many phones now use phone cards costing 5 and 10 pesos (break off the corner tab before using), the cards of the two companies are interchangeable. (Payphones in Telecom and Telefónica Argentina offices reportedly use 5 cent coins.) International telephone calls from hotels may incur a 40%-50% commission in addition to government tax of about the same amount. For more details see **Postage and Telephone Rates** in **Information for travellers**.

NB Since privatization, many phone prefixes in the city have been changed: 34 became 342, 30 – 343, 37 – 383, 38 – 381, 59 – 581, 45 – 476 or 372 depending on location, and 47 – 951. Further changes are likely and will be indicated on the first pages of the phone directory, or dial 110 to ask the operator.

● **Shopping**

Most shops close lunchtime on Sat. Visit the branches of *H Stern*, for fine jewellery at the *Sheraton* and *Plaza* hotels, and at the International Airport; *Kelly's*, Paraguay 431, has a very large selection of reasonably priced Argentine handicrafts in wool, leather, wood, etc; *Plata Nativa*, Galería del Sol, Florida 860, local 41, for Latin American folk handicrafts; *Campanera Dalla Fontana*, Reconquista 735, leather factory which is fast, efficient and reasonably priced for made-to-measure clothes. Good quality leather clothes factory at Boyacá 2030, T 582 6909 to arrange time with English speaking owner; *Aida*, Florida 670, can make a leather jacket to measure in 48 hrs; *El Guasquero*, Av Santa Fe 3117, traditionally made leather goods; *Galería del Caminante*, Florida 844, has a variety of good shops with leather goods, arts and crafts, souvenirs, etc; *Marcelo Loeb*, galería at Maipú 466, for antique postcards from all over the world, not cheap, same galería has several philatelic and numismatic shops. The main, fashionable shopping streets are Florida and Santa Fe (especially between 1,000 and 2,000 blocks). Av Cabildo in Belgrano district can be reached by bus 152 from Retiro for good shopping between 1,600 and 2,800 blocks. *Pasaje de Defensa* is a beautifully restored colonial house containing small shops, on Defensa 791 in the San Telmo area. Defensa is good for antique shops. There is a shopping mall, **Patio Bullrich**, between Av del Libertador y Posadas, at Montevideo, entrances on Posadas and Av del Libertador (No 750). Boutiques are very expensive, but leather goods are of high quality. A new mall, very smart and expensive, is **Alto Palermo**, at Col Díaz y Santa Fe; **La Plaza Shopping Centre**, at Corrientes 1600, has a few restaurants and an open-air theatre; **Paseo Alcorta**, Av Figueroa Alcorta y Salguero, 4 levels, cinemas, supermarket, stores, many cheap restaurants (take colectivo 130 from Correo Central); **Galerías Pacífico**, on Florida, between Córdoba and Viamonte, is a beautiful shopping mall with fine murals and architecture, many exclusive shops and fast food restaurants in basement. Also good set-price restaurant on 2nd floor and free lunchtime concerts on lower-ground floor (details in the press); *Casa Piscitelli*, San Martín 450, has a large selection of tapes and CDs. **Galerías Broadway**, Florida 575, for cheap electronic goods, CDs, tapes.

Bookshops: many along Av Corrientes, W of Av 9 de Julio, though most have no foreign language sections. Try *Yenny* (No 571) for new English classics (also 7 other branches) and *Distal*, No 913; also *Fausto* (No 1316 and 1243) for second-hand books. *ABC*, Av Córdoba 685 and Rawson 2105 in Martíntez suburb, good selection of English and German books, also sells *South American Handbook*; *Joyce Proust y Cía*, Tucumán 1545, 1st floor, T 40-3977, paperbacks in English, Portuguese, French, Italian; classics, language texts, etc,

good prices; *Librería Rodríguez*, Sarmiento 835, good selection of English books and magazines, has another branch on Florida, 300 block; French bookshop at Rivadavia 743; *Librería Goethe*, Lavalle 528, good selection of English and German books. Italian books at *Librería Leonardo*, Av Córdoba 335, also (with newspapers and magazines); *La Viscontea*, Libertad 1067. *Asatej Bookshop*, Florida 835, 1° Of 104, T 312-8476, sells this *Handbook* 'at the best price'; *El Ateneo*, Florida 340, basement has good selection of English books, other branches inc Callao 1380; *Kel Ediciones*, MT de Alvear 1369 and Conde 1990 (Belgrano), also maintain a good stock of English books and sells *South American Handbook*. *Acme Agency*, Suipacha 245, p 1, for imported English books. Prices at *Harrods* on Florida are lower than most (being remodelled 1995-96). *LOLA*, Viamonte 976, 20D, T 476 0518, specializes in Latin American Natural History books. **For used and rare books**: *Fernández Blanco*, Tucumán 712; *Casa Figueroa*, Esmeralda 970; and *L'Amateur*, Esmeralda 882. Second-hand English language books from *British and American Benevolent Society*, Catamarca 45 (take train to Acassuso). *Aquilanti*, Rincon 79, esp good on Patagonia; *Juan Carlos Pubill*, Talcahuano 353 (ring bell), and from *Entrelibros*, Av Cabildo 2280 and Santa Fe 2450, local 7.

Foreign newspapers at news stands on Florida, and at kiosk at Corrientes y Maipú.

Every April the Feria del Libro is held at the Centro De Exposiciones, Av Figueroa Alcorta y Pueyrredón, Recoleta; exhibitions, shows and books for sale in all languages.

Camera repairs and film developing: film developing to international standards. There are many Kodak labs around Talcahuano. *Fotospeed*, Av Santa Fe 4838 (20% discount to SAHB owners!) for quality 2-hr service. For developing slides Esmeralda 444, fast service, and *Kinefot*, Talcahuano 244. **Camera repairs**: several good shops on Talcahuano 100-400 blocks. Try also *Casa Schwarz*, Perú 989, international brands; *Golden Lab*, Lavalle 630, good prices for film; *Horacio Calvo*, Riobamba 183, all brands and variety of rare accessories, rec; fast service at Tacuarí 75; for Olympus cameras, *Rodolfo Jablanca*, Corrientes 2589. German spoken at *Gerardo Föhse*, Florida 890, fast, friendly.

Markets: Market for souvenirs, antiques, etc, **Plaza Dorrego** (San Telmo) with food, dancers, buskers, Sat and Sun 0900-1700, on Humberto I and Defensa (entertaining, not cheap, an interesting array of 'antiques'). **Feria Hippie**, in Recoleta, nr cemetery, big craft and jewellery market, Sat and Sun, good street atmosphere, expensive. Also **Feria de Las Artes** (Fri, 1000-1700) on Defensa y Alsina. Sat craft, jewellery, etc market, at **Plaza Belgrano**, nr Belgrano Barrancas station on Juramento, between Cuba y Obligado, 1000-2000. Handicraft markets at weekends at Parque Lezama (San Telmo). A secondhand book market is at **Plaza Lavalle** in front of Tribunales, a few English titles (ask around), weekdays only. **Plazoleta Santa Fe**, Santa Fe and Uriarte (Palermo) old books and magazines, Sat 1200-2000, Sun 1000-2000; plastic arts in the **Caminito**, Vuelta de Rocha (Boca), 1000-2000 summer, 0900-1900 winter. At **Parque Rivadavia**, Rivadavia 4900, around the *ombú* tree, records, books, magazines, stamps and coins, Sun 0900-1300, **Plazoleta Primera Junta**, Rivadavia and Centenera, books and magazines, Sat 1200-2000, Sun 1000-2000. **Parque Patricios**, Av Caseros entre Monteagudo y Pepiri, 1000-2000, antiques, books, art and stamps. Sat market in **Plaza Centenario**, Díaz Vélez y L Marechal, 1000-2100 local crafts, good, cheap hand-made clothes.

● **Sports**

Aerobics: try the *San Martín Club*, San Martín 645, T 311-9191, or the *Gimnasio Olímpico Cancillería*, Esmeralda 1042, no membership required.

Association and rugby football: are both played to a very high standard. Soccer fans should see Boca Juniors, matches Sun 1500-1800 (depending on time of year), Wed evenings, entry US$10 (stadium open weekdays for visits), or their arch-rivals, River Plate. Soccer season Sept-May/June, with a break at Christmas. Rugby season April-Oct/November.

Chess: *Club Argentino de Ajedrez*, Paraguay 1858, open daily, arrive after 2000, special tournament every Sat, 1800, high standards. Repairs for pocket chess computers, T 952-4913.

Cricket: is played at four clubs in Greater Buenos Aires between Nov and March.

Gambling: weekly lotteries. Football pools, known as *Prode. Bingo Lavalle*, Lavalle 842, open to 0300.

Golf: the leading golf clubs are the *Hurlingham, Ranelagh, Ituzaingó, Lomas, San Andrés, San Isidro, Sáenz Peña, Olivos, Jockey, Campos Argentinos* and *Hindú Country Club*. Visitors wishing to play should bring handicap certificate and make telephone booking. Weekend play possible only with a member. Good hotels may be able to make special arrangements. Municipal golf course in Palermo, open to anyone at any time.

Horse racing: at Palermo, a large, modern racecourse, popular throughout the year. Riding

school at Palermo. Also at San Isidro.

Ice-hockey: is becoming popular.

Motor racing: Formula 1 championship is no longer held in Argentina, but efforts are being made to restore it. There are lots of rallies, stock racing and Formula 3 competitions, mostly from Mar to mid-December.

Polo: the high handicap season is Oct to Dec, but it is played all year round (low season April-June). Argentina has the top polo teams. A visit to the national finals at Palermo in Nov or Dec is rec.

Tennis, squash and paddle tennis: are popular – there are five squash clubs. The Argentine Tennis Open is in Nov, ATP tour. There are many private clubs.

● **Tour companies & travel agents**

Tours: a good way of seeing Buenos Aires and its surroundings is by 3-hr tour. Longer tours inc dinner and a tango show, or a gaucho *fiesta* at a ranch (excellent food and dancing, although the gaucho part can be somewhat showy). Bookable through most travel agents, US$50-65. *BAT, Buenos Aires Tur*, Lavalle 1444, T 40-2304, almost hourly departures, *Eurotur* (T 312-6170), in English, or *Autobuses Sudamericanos* (TISA), information and booking office at Bernardo de Irigoyen 1370, p 1, Offices 25 and 26, T 307-1956, F 307-8899. Prices range from US$12 to US$60 (20 night time and *estancia* options). For reservations in advance for sightseeing tours, with a 20% courtesy discount to *South American Handbook* readers, write to Casilla de Correo No 40, Sucursal 1 (B), 1401 Buenos Aires. In USA T (New York) 212-524-0763, First Class Travel Service Ltd. TISA has other branches in Buenos Aires and publishes *Guía Latinoamericana de Omnibus*, organizes Amerbuspass (T 311-7373 for tickets, or USA 602-795-6556, F 795-8180) for bus travel throughout Latin America. At same address *Transporte Aereo Costa Atlántica* (TACA), passenger charter services to Pinamar, Villa Gesell, Bariloche, T 26-7933. Also *Indiana Cars*, T 307-1956/300-5591, for remise, car hire and taxi service with women drivers.

For river tours of Buenos Aires, Charles Ce saire, Dársena Nte, T 553-4380/314-1780, Sat, Sun, holidays 1500, 1700, 1900, with bar, US$10.

Travel agents: among those rec are *Exprinter*, Suipacha 1107, T 312-2519, and San Martín 170, T 331-3050, Galería Güemes (especially their 5-day, 3-night tour to Iguazú and San Ignacio Miní); *American Express*, Arenales y Maipú; *Furlong*, Esmeralda y M T de Alvear, T 318-3200, T 312-3043, Thomas Cook representatives; *ATI*, Esmeralda 561, mainly group travel, very efficient and helpful, many branches; *Turismo Feeling*, L Alem 762, T 311-9422, excellent and reliable horseback trips and adventure tourism; *Versailles*, Callao 257, p 13 N, helpful, friendly; *Giorgio*, Florida y Tucumán, T 327-4200, F 325-4210, also at Santa Fe 1653; *Germania*, Lavalle 414, T 393-1265/0035, excellent service (English not spoken), especially for tours to the N, branch in Salta; *Lihue Expeditions*, Maipú 926, T 311-9610, helpful with all arrangements, especially wildlife tours and *estancia* visits, rec; *Flyer*, Reconquista 621, p 8, T 312-9164, English, Dutch, German spoken, rec (details on fishing, polo, *estancias*, motorhome rental); *Eves Turismo*, Tucumán 702, T 393-6151, helpful and efficient, rec for flights; *City Service*, Florida 890 y Paraguay, p 4, T 312-8416/9; *Travel Up*, Maipú 474, p 4, T 326-4648; *Proterra Turismo*, Lavalle 750, p 20 D, T/F 326-2639; *Folgar*, Esmeralda 961, p 3 E, T 311-6937; *Ruta 40*, P O Box 5210, 1000 Buenos Aires, T 782-7427, F 783-5557, jointly run by Federico Kirbus, the traveller and author (see **Tourist offices** in **Information for travellers**). English is widely spoken.

● **Tourist offices**

National office at Santa Fe 883 with maps and literature covering the whole country. Open 1000-1700, Mon-Fri, T 312-2232, 312-5550. Has a guide to campsites throughout Argentina. Other offices at Aeroparque, T 773-9891/05 and at Ezeiza, T 480-0224/0011. There are tourist kiosks on Florida, junction with Diagonal Norte, in Galerías Pacífico and in Centro Cultural Recoleta. For free tourist information anywhere in the country T 0800-5-0016.

There are also helpful *Casas de Turismo* for most provinces (open Mon-Fri usually, 1000-1800, depending on office, check): **Buenos Aires**, Av Callao 237, T 371-7045/3587; others on Callao are **Córdoba** (332, T 373-4277, F 476-2615), **Chaco** (322, T 476-0961, F 375-1640), **Mendoza** (445, T/F 371-7301). **Others**: **Río Negro**, Tucumán 1916, T 371-7066, F 476-2128; **Chubut**, Sarmiento 1172, T/F 382-0822;

Entre Ríos, Suipacha 844, T/F 328-9327; **Formosa**, H Irigoyen 1429, T 381-7048, F 381-6290; **Mar del Plata**, Santa Fe 1175, T/F 811-4466; **Jujuy**, Santa Fe 967, p 6, T/F 393-6096; **Misiones**, Santa Fe 989, T 322-0677, F 325-6197; **Neuquén**, JD Perón 687, T/F 326-6812; **Salta**, Diagonal Nte (Roque Sáenz Peña) 933, T 326-1314, F 326-0110; **Santa Cruz**, 25 de Mayo 277, 1st floor, T 343-3653, F 342-1667; **Catamarca**, Córdoba 2080, T/F 374-6891; **Corrientes**, San Martín 333, p 4, T/F 394-7432; **La Pampa**, Suipacha 346, T/F 326-0511; **La Rioja** Viamonte 749, p 5, T/F 326-1140; **San Juan**, Sarmiento 1251, T 382-5291, F 382-4729; **San Luis**, Azcuénaga 1083, T/F 822-0426; **Santa Fe**, Montevideo 373, p 2, T/F 375-4570; **Santiago del Estero**, Florida 274, T 326-9418, F 326-5915; **Tucumán**, Suipacha 140, T 325-0564; **Tierra del Fuego**, Av Santa Fe 919, T/F 322-8855; **Patagonia**, Av de Mayo 801, T 342-0101; **Villa Gesell**, B Mitre 1702, T/F 374-5098; **Bariloche** hotel, Flat and bungalow service in Galería at Florida 520/Lavalle 617, room 116 (cheapest places not listed). Calafate bookings for *Refugio and Autocamping Lago Viedma*, excursions with Transporte Ruta 3 and lake excursions with Empresa Paraíso de Navegación booked from Turismo Argos, Maipú 812, p 13 C, T 392-5460. (For bookings for *Hotel La Loma*, Calafate and further information on the area contact Paula Escabo, Av Callao 433, p 8 P, T 371-9123.) For tourist information on Patagonia and bookings for cheap accommodation and youth hostels, contact Asatej, see **Useful addresses** below.

Municipalidad de Buenos Aires, Sarmiento 1551, p 5, open Mon-Fri 0930-1730, has an excellent free booklet about the city centre and maps. Further offices at Aeroparque (Aerolíneas Argentinas), Mon-Fri, 0830-2000 and Sat 0900-1900, and Ezeiza Airport, Mon-Fri 0830-2200.

On Fri, the youth section of *Clarín* (*Sí*) lists free entertainments; *Página 12* has a youth supplement on Thur called *NO*, the paper lists current events in *Pasen y Vean* section on Fri; also the weekly *La Maga* and Sun tourism section of *La Nación* (very informative). *Where in Buenos Aires*, a tourist guide in English, published monthly, is available free in hotels, travel agencies, tourist kiosks on Florida, and in some news stands. The *Buenos Aires Times* is a bilingual monthly newspaper covering tourist topics, available in some hotels. A good guide to bus and subway routes is *Guía Peuser*; there is one for the city and one covering Greater Buenos Aires. Similar guides are *Lumi* and *Guía T*; all are available at news stands, US$10. Also handy is Auto Mapa's pocket-size *Plano guía* of the Federal Capital, available at news stands, US$8, or from sales office at Santa Fe 3117; *Auto Mapa* also publishes an increasing number of regional maps, Michelin-style, high quality. Countrywide maps at Instituto Geográfico Militar, Cabildo 301 (see **Maps** in Information for Travellers).

● **Useful addresses**

Asatej: Argentine Youth and Student Travel Association, information for all South America, noticeboard useful for single travellers, booking for hotels and travel, the *Sleep Cheap Guide* lists economical accommodation in Argentina, Bolivia, Chile, Brazil, Uruguay and Peru; ISIC cards sold, English and French spoken, very helpful but limited travel information, Florida 835, p 3, oficina 315, T 311-6953, F 311-6840, also Student Flight Center at oficina 319 B, be prepared for a long wait and take US$ cash.

Central Police Station: Moreno 1550, T 38-8041 (emergency, T 101 from any phone, free).

Comisión Nacional de Museos y Monumentos y Lugares Históricos: Av de Mayo 556, professional archaeology institute.

Dirección Nacional de Parques Nacionales, Av Santa Fe 680, opp Plaza San Martín, T 311-0303.

Migraciones: (Immigration), Antártida Argentina 1365 (visas extended mornings only), T 312-3288/7985/8661, from 1230-1700.

Municipalidad: Av de Mayo 525, facing Plaza de Mayo.

Salvation Army: Rivadavia 3255.

Youth Hostel Association: information for all South America, Talcahuano 214, p 3, T 45-1001 (post code: 1013 Buenos Aires). **NB** A YHA card in Argentina costs US$20, ISIC cards also sold. Secretariat open Mon-Fri 1300-2000. (There are very few hostels nr Route 3, the main road S from Buenos Aires.)

YMCA: (Central), Reconquista 439. **YWCA**: Tucumán 844.

● **Transport**

Local Buses *Colectivos* (city buses) cover a very wide radius, and are clean, frequent, efficient and very fast (hang on tight). The basic fare is US$0.50, US$1 to the suburbs. Have correct coins ready for ticket machine as drivers no longer sell tickets. **NB** The bus number is not sufficient indication of destination, as each number has a variety of routes, but bus stops display routes of buses stopping there and little plaques are displayed in the driver's window. *Guía T* gives routes and livery of all buses and *Lumi* guide routes gives (see above).

Car hire: expensive, with an additional 20% tax. It is difficult to hire cars during holiday periods, best to book from abroad. Use of Avis Car Credit card with central billing in your home country is possible. See also **Information for travellers**. Driving in Buenos Aires is no problem, provided you have eyes in the back of your head and good nerves. Note that traffic fines are high and police increasingly on the lookout for drivers without the correct papers. **Avis**, Cerrito 1527, T 326-5542; **A1 International**, San Luis 3138, T 963-3489/961-6666; **Hertz**, Ricardo Rojas 451, T 312-1317. There are several national rental agencies, eg **ALV**, Av Alvear 1883, T 805-4403; **Ricciard Libertador**, Av del Libertador 2337/45, T 799-8514; **Localiza**, Paraguay 1122, T 375-1611. **Motoring Associations** See page 239 for details of service.

Underground railways ('**Subte**'): 5 lines link the outer parts of the City to the centre. 'A' line runs under C Rivadavia, from Plaza de Mayo to Primera Junta. 'B' line from central Post Office, Av LN Alem, under Av Corrientes to Federico Lacroze railway station. 'C' line links Plaza Constitución with the Retiro railway station, and provides connections with all the other lines. 'D' line runs from Catedral, under the Diagonal Nte, Córdoba, Santa Fe and Palermo to Ministro Carranza (5,300 block of Av Santa Fe). 'E' line runs from Bolívar (nr Plaza de Mayo) through San Juan to Avs Directorio and José María Moreno. Note that stations 9 de Julio (Line 'D'), Diagonal Nte (Line 'C') and Carlos Pellegrini (Line 'B') interconnect. The fare is US$0.45, the same for any direct trip or combination between lines; tokens (*fichas*) must be bought at the station before boarding; buy a few in advance to save time (dollars not accepted). System operates 0530-2215, but some lines close before 2200. Line A, the oldest was built in 1913, the earliest underground in South America. Many of the stations in the centre esp on Line E have fine tile-work designs and pictures which are worth seeing. Some trains date from the early part of the century too. The oldest and nicest station is Perú. Backpacks and luggage allowed. Map available free from stations and from tourist office.

Taxis: are painted yellow and black, and carry *Taxi* flags. Fares are shown in pesos. The meter starts at US$0.96 when the flag goes down; make sure it isn't running when you get in. A charge is sometimes made for each piece of hand baggage (ask first). Tips not usual. Four common taxi driver tricks are 1) to take you on a longer than necessary ride; 2) to switch low-denomination notes for higher ones preferred by the passenger (don't back down, demand to go to the police station); 3) to grab the passenger's baggage and prevent him/her from leaving the taxi (scream for help); 4) to quote 'old' prices for new, eg 'quince' (15) for 1.50 pesos, 'veinte y seis' (26) for 2.60 pesos, etc. If possible, keep your luggage with you. Worst places are the two airports and Retiro; make sure you know roughly what the fare should be before the journey. (As examples, from Aeroparque to: Ezeiza 32 pesos, Congreso 7 pesos, Plaza de Mayo 6 pesos, Retiro 5 pesos, La Boca 9 pesos.) Fares double for journeys outside city limits (Gen Paz circular highway). Alberto Pommerenck, T 654 5988, offers reasonable ½ day hire, knows suburban leather factories well, good driver.

Remise taxis operate all over the city; they are run from an office, have no meter (but charge about the same as yellow-and-black cabs), and the companies are identified by signs on the pavement. Fares can be verified by phoning the office and items left in the car can easily be reclaimed.

Tram: a green and white old-fashioned street car operates April-Nov on Sat and holidays 1600-1900 and Sun 1000-1300, 1600-1930 (not Easter Sun)and Dec-Mar on Sat and holidays 1700-2000, Sun 1000-1300, 1600-1900 free, on a circular route along the streets of Caballito district from Subte Primera Junta (Line A), no stops en route. Operated by Asociación de los Amigos del Tranvía, T 476-0476.

Air Ezeiza (officially Ministro Pistarini, T 620-0011), the international airport, is 35 km SW of the centre by a good dual carriageway, which links with the Gen Paz circular highway round the city. The airport has a duty free shop (expensive), exchange facilities (Banco de la Nación, 1.5% commission) and ATMs (Visa and Mastercard), post office (open 0800-2000) and (under the stairs) a left luggage office (US$10/piece). Its hotel, the *Internacional*, is closed for renovation (no other hotels nearby). There is a *Devolucion IVA* desk (return of VAT) for purchases such as leather goods. Airport information, T 480-0217. Reports of pilfering from luggage, to discourage this have your bags sealed after inspection by Your Packet International SA,

US$5-10/piece. Free hotel booking service at Tourist Information desk – helpful, with list of competitively-priced hotels. A display in immigration shows choices and prices of transport into the city. **Airport buses:** 2 companies run special buses to/from the centre: *Manuel Tienda León* (office at customs exit), service to the company office at Santa Fe 790, next to *Hotel Crillon* (T/F 315-0489, F 311-3722, or airport T/F 480-0597/0374 – 24 hrs), 0400, 0500, then every 30 mins till 2030, US$14, return US$25, credit cards accepted. Santa Fe office has check-in desk for AR flights. *San Martín* services from outside Alitalia office, to company office at Santa Fe 887 (next to Secretaría Nacional de Turismo), T 314-4747/3446, Ezeiza 480-9464, 15 mins past each hour, US$11 (will also collect passengers from hotels in centre for no extra charge, book previous day). **Local buses:** No 86 buses (white and blue, marked 'Fournier') run to the centre from outside the airport terminal to the right (*servicio diferencial* takes 1½ hrs, US$4, *servicio común* 2¼ hrs, US$1, coins only no change given) between 0500 and 2400. To travel to Ezeiza, catch the bus at Av de Mayo y Perú, 1 block from Plaza de Mayo – make sure it has 'Aeropuerto' sign in the window as many 86s stop short of Ezeiza. Only one bag is normally allowed and passengers with backpacks may be charged double fare. **Taxis:** both airport ('rojos') and city ('amarillos') taxis are allowed to operate from Ezeiza; they have separate departure points: 'rojos' in front of the central hall, 'amarillos' 50m to the left of the 'Espigón Internacional'. Taxis from centre to Ezeiza US$45-50 but bargain. Fixed-price **remise taxis** can be booked from the Manuel Tienda León counter at Ezeiza, US$49 (inc US$2 toll) payable in advance. Remise from the city to Ezeiza is about half this price, ie US$25-30. Avoid unmarked cars at Ezeiza no matter how attractive the fare may sound; drivers are adept at separating you from far more money than you can possibly owe them. Always ask to see the taxi driver's licence, if you think you have been cheated, T 343-5001 to complain. If you take an 'amarillo', the Policía Aeronáutica on duty notes down the car's licence and time of departure. **Trains** Local electric trains go to Ezeiza suburb from the Constitución station. The train, marked 'Ezeiza' costs US$0.80, and takes 40 mins. One block from the Ezeiza station, colectivo No 502 goes to the airport, US$0.60, and takes 20 mins.

Aeroparque (Jorge Newbury Airport) 4 km N of the centre nr the New Port, T 771-2071, handles all internal flights, services to Punta del Este and Montevideo and flights from Latin American countries with an intermediate stop in Argentina.The terminal is divided into two sections, one each for AR and Austral: both have cafés and car rental. AR section has duty free facilities, tourist information, Manuel Tienda León office (see below) and luggage deposit (US$3/piece). Exchange: Banco de la Ciudad (Austral section) and Aeromar (between sections). No post office or post box. **Buses** Manuel Tienda León buses to/from centre (see above for address), 0710-2110 every 30 mins, US$5. Local bus 45 runs from outside the airport to the Retiro railway station, then follows Av L N Alem and Paseo Colón to La Boca. Bus 37C goes from Plaza del Congreso to Aeroparque but make sure it has 'Aeroparque' sign, US$0.50. **Remise taxis**: are operated by Universalflet (office in Austral section) and Manuel Tienda León, US11-13 to centre, US$40 to Ezeiza. Ordinary taxi to centre US$8.

Manuel Tienda León operates buses between Ezeiza and Jorge Newbery airports, stopping in city centre, US$15. AR offer free transfers between Ezeiza and Aeroparque to passengers whose incoming and connecting flghts are both on AR: ask at AR desk for a voucher.

Aerolíneas Argentinas, Austral and Lapa offer daily flights to the main cities, for details see text under intended destination, see also page 238 for the Visit Argentina fare. If travelling in the S, book ahead if possible with LADE, whose Flights are cheaper than buses in most cases.

Trains There are 4 main terminals: Retiro: really three separate stations (Belgrano T 311-5287; Mitre T 312-6596, San Martín T 311-8704). Services in operation: to Tucumán, Mon and Fri, 1600, returning Thur and Sun, 14 hrs (23 hrs), US$50 pullman, US$36 1st, US$30 tourist (service run by Tucumán provincial government). Suburban services to Tigre, Capilla del Señor, Bartolomé Mitre and Zárate (tickets checked on train and collected at the end of the journey). The terminal has a left-luggage facility, US$1.50/bag/day.

Constitución: T 304-0021; frequent services to La Plata (US$1), Ezeiza (US$0.80), Ranelagh (US$0.50) and Quilmes (US$0.90). Also suburban servies.(Keep your ticket as you have to show this at your destination.) Service to Bariloche (via Bahía Blanca),run by Servicios Ferroviarios Patagónicos, Wed and Sun 0740, US$65 pullman, US$60 1st, US$44 tourist, food mediocre; San Antonio Oeste, US$30, 22 hrs; Mar del Plata 7 times daily from 0100-1830, US$30 pullman, US$19 1st, US$14 tourist; Necochea, Mon, Wed, Fri 2100 (daily in summer), returns Tues, Thur, Sun, US$20.50 pullman, US$16 1st class, US$14 2nd. The Automóvil Club Argentino provides car transporters for its members (see **ACA** in **Information for travellers**).

Federico Lacroze: Ferrocarril Nacional Urquiza (North-Eastern) – T 553-5213. No services except the Tren Histórico: every Sun a Scottish 1888 Neilson steam engine pulls old wooden carriages, either to Capilla del Señor with lunch or a folkloric show at an *estancia* (dep 1000, return 1900), or to Zárate across the Zárate-Brazo Largo bridges over the Paraná river (dep 0900). Prices from US$15-50, T 374-4186, operates in summer only.

Once: Ferrocarril Nacional Sarmiento (Western), T 87-0041/2/3, for services in the province of Buenos Aires.

Buses All long-distance buses leave from the Estación Terminal de Omnibus at Ramos Mejía y Antártida Argentina (Subte C), behind Retiro station, T for information 311-6073/6088. All offices are on the E side on the ground floor. The passage between the bus station and Retiro is packed with market stalls and is narrow (beware pickpockets), all designed to inconvenience those with luggage (although, as one correspondent points out, this also slows down anyone trying to make a speedy escape with someone else's belongings). There are two left-luggage offices (US$5/piece), open 0600-2300 (lockers, tokens from kiosks, US$2.50). Some bus companies charge extra for luggage (illegally). Fares may vary according to time of year and advance booking is advisable Dec-March. Some companies may give discounts, such as 20% to YHA or student-card holders and foreign, as well as Argentine teachers and university lecturers. Travellers have reported getting discounts without showing evidence of status, so it's always worth asking. For further details of bus services and fares, look under proposed destinations.

Hitchhiking: for Pinamar, Mar del Plata and nearby resorts, take bus for La Plata to Alpargatas *rotonda* roundabout. For points further S, take bus 96 to Ruta 3 – the Patagonia road. Best to hitch from a service station where trucks stop. The police control point at Km 43 (S) is reported to be friendly and will help to find a lift for you. For Mendoza try truck drivers at the wine warehouses nr Palermo station (take Subte to Puerto Pacífico, at Buenos Aires al Pacífico train station, at viaduct crossing Av Santa Fe/Av Cabildo; turn left into Av Juan B Justo for the warehouses).

Sea Passenger boats: the *Buenos Aires Herald* (English-language daily) notes all shipping movements. Flota Fluvial del Estado (Corrientes 489, T 311-0728) organizes cruises from Buenos Aires, Dársena Sur (dock T 361-4161/0346) up the Paraná river. South Coast, down to Punta Arenas and intermediate Patagonian ports, served by the Imp & Exp de la Patagonia and Elma (state shipping line). Very irregular sailings. For connections with Uruguay, see page 88.

TRAVEL INTO NEIGHBOURING
COUNTRIES

● By Road

Four branches of the Inter-American Highway run from Buenos Aires to the borders of Chile, Bolivia, Paraguay and Brazil. The roads are paved except when otherwise stated.

To Chile: via Río Cuarto, Mercedes, San Luis, and Mendoza, Total: 1,310 km paved throughout. (Direct buses to Santiago, 23 hrs, US$70-75, eg Ahumada, El Rápido Internacional and others, 1,459 km; US$70-75 to Valparaíso or Viña del Mar, TAC, Fénix Pullman Nte, cheaper to book to Mendoza and then rebook.) There are also road connections between Catamarca and Copiapó, Bariloche and Osorno and Puerto Montt, and between Salta and Antofagasta.

To Bolivia: via Rosario, Villa María, Córdoba, Santiago del Estero, Tucumán, and Jujuy. Total: 1,994 km. There is no direct bus service from Buenos Aires to La Paz but through connections can be booked (Sudamericanos, T 27-6591, goes via La Quiaca-Villazón, US$135, 48 hrs; Atahualpa, T 315-0601, goes via La Quiaca, US$95, or Pocitos, US$91, daily, then a new ticket to La Paz or Santa Cruz must be bought).

To Paraguay: via Rosario, Santa Fe, Resistencia, Clorinda and Asunción (via toll bridge). Total: 1,370 km. Buses take 20-22 hrs, with 11 companies (all close to each other at the Retiro bus terminal). You have choice between executive (luxury service, 15 hrs, US$80) *diferencial* (with food, drinks, 18 hrs, US$64) and *común* (without food, but has a/c, toilet, 21 hrs, US$48). Also five companies to Ciudad del Este, US$45; Caaguazú goes to Villarrica, and Expreso Río Paraná and La Encarnaceña go to Encarnación, US$46. Tickets can be bought up to 30 days in advance.

To drive to Paraguay, 3 main routes: 1) via Rosario, Santa Fe, Resistencia, Clorinda to Asunción; 2) cross the Zárate-Brazo Largo bridges to Route 12, then head W across Entre Ríos to Paraná and take the tunnel to Santa Fe, or head W across Corrientes to the bridge from Corrientes to Resistencia; 3) via Misiones, San Ignacio Miní and the Iguazú Falls: as for 2), but follow Routes 12 and 14 up the Río Uruguay via Colón and Concordia to Misiones province via Posadas.

To Brazil: to the Iguazú Falls, follow 3) above under **To Paraguay**. On this route you can cross from Paso de los Libres to Uruguaiana in Brazil. Direct buses to Brazil via Paso de los Libres by Pluma (T 313-3901): São Paulo, 40 hrs, US$145, Rio de Janeiro, 45 hrs, US$163; Porto Alegre, US$71; Curitiba, 38 hrs, US$128; Florianópolis, 32 hrs, US$115. To Rio, changing buses at Posadas and Foz do Iguaçu is almost half price, 50 hrs. A third route across the Río de la Plata

and through Uruguay is a bit cheaper, not as long and offers a variety of transport and journey breaks. Tickets from Buen Viaje, Av Córdoba 415 (31-2953) or Pluma, Av Córdoba 461 (311-4871 or 311-5986).

To Uruguay: direct road connections by means of two bridges over the Río Uruguay between Puerto Colón and Paysandú and between Puerto Unzué and Fray Bentos (much slower than the air or sea routes given below). '*Bus de la carrera*' (office 65-67 Retiro, T 313-3695) links Montevideo and Buenos Aires, 8½ hrs, US$20. Departure from each city at 1000, 2200, 2220 and 2300, with a *dormibus* at 2230 (US$22), via Zárate-Gualeguaychú-Puerto Unzué-Fray Bentos-Mercedes.

To Peru: Ormeño (T 313-2259) and El Rápido Internacional (T 393-5057) have a direct service to Lima, from Retiro bus station, 3½ days, inc all meals, one night spent in Coquimbo, Chile (if you need a visa for Chile, get one before travelling), the route is: Mendoza, Coquimbo, Arica, Tacna, Nazca, Ica, Lima. El Rápido Internacional at Bs As bus terminal, ticket office 89, US$160.

● Air, River and Railway Services

Brazil: daily air services to São Paulo, Rio de Janeiro and other Brazilian cities. No rail connections.

Chile: no passenger rail services, although freight trains run between Salta and Antofagasta. Foreign and national lines fly daily between Buenos Aires and Santiago, 1½-2 hrs.

Bolivia: no passenger rail services from Argentina to connect with the Bolivian lines from La Quiaca to La Paz and Pocitos to Santa Cruz de la Sierra. There are air services to La Paz and Santa Cruz de la Sierra by AR and LAB.

Paraguay: there are daily air services to Asunción by AR and Lapsa. See also Posadas, page 167. Occasional river boats to Asunción in May to Oct, 11 days, bed and private bath, food and nightly entertainment, US$400, reported good. Details from Tamul, Lavalle 388, T 393-2306/1533.

Uruguay: boat connections: 1) Direct to Montevideo, Buquebus, Córdoba 867, T 313-4444, 'Avión de Buquebus' 4 times a day, 0800 (0745 Sat), 1130, 1500, 1930 (Sun 0745, 1530 and 1930), 3 hrs or 2½ hrs by *K55* (summer schedule), US$38 tourist class, US$50 1st class one way inc transport from office to port, vehicles US$80-90, bus connection to Punta del Este, US$10.

2) From Dársena Sur to Colonia, services by 2 companies: Buquebus (US$16-21, or 24-31 depending on vessel) with bus connection to Montevideo (US$5 extra), 4 a day. Ferry turismo Sea Cat, Av Córdoba 699, T 394-6800 (port:

Dársena Sur, Ribera Este, T 361-4161) at 0815, 1330, 1830 (Mon-Fri), 0730, 1600 (Sat), 0930, 1900 (Sun), US$18, US$25 inc bus to Montevideo, 1 hr to Colonia, total of 4 to Montevideo. Free bus 1 hr before departure from Florida y Córdoba. Ferry turismo also run a ferry service BsAs-Colonia, with connecting bus to Montevideo, 3-hr crossing, US$8, US$15 inc bus to Montevideo. Mon-Thur 0730, 2330, Fri 0730, Sat-Sun 0800. Cars are carried on both services. Sailings may be cancelled in bad weather.

3) From Tigre to Carmelo, boats are operated by Cacciola at 0800, 1730 and 2245, 3 hrs, US$11 to Carmelo, and US$18.50 to Montevideo; Cacciola office: Lavalle y Florida 520, oficina 113, T 322-9374/0026 and Estación Fluvial, *local* 13, Tigre, credit cards accepted. It is advisable to book in advance; connecting bus from offices to port and from Carmelo to Montevideo.

4) From Tigre to Nueva Palmira, Lineas Delta Argentina, from Tigre 0730, 3 hrs, US$14.

Boats and buses heavily booked Dec-Mar, especially at weekends. **NB** No money changing facilities in Tigre, and poor elsewhere. Beware of overcharging by taxis from the harbour to the centre of Buenos Aires. US$3 port tax is charged on all services to Colonia/Carmelo, US$10 port tax in Buenos Aires. Do not buy Uruguayan bus tickets in BsAs; wait till you get to Colonia.

Several airlines fly from Jorge Newbery Airport (Aeroparque, Puente Aéreo section) to Colonia 12 mins, US$30. Buy tickets directly at the LAPA or AUSA counters preferably in advance especially at weekends when flights are fully booked. Continue by bus to Montevideo (or special car connecting with Lapa flight, US$3-4 to Montevideo. Also from Jorge Newbery, shuttle service to Montevideo, known as Puente Aéreo and run by AR and Pluna, daily 0730 and 0910, 40 mins. Book at Jorge Newbery Airport or T 393-5122/773-0440. Punta del Este, 5 Flights daily 15 Dec-1 Mar with AR, 40 mins, or Pluna (out of season, Fri only).

SUBURBS OF BUENOS AIRES

Quilmes (BsAs), with one of the world's largest breweries, an important industrial centre SE of the Capital Federal, was given that name because the Quilmes Indians were forcibly moved there in 1665 from the famous Inca site in Tucumán Province (see page 116).

The naturalist and writer WH Hudson (1841-1922) was born at Florencio Varela, near Quilmes, about 32 km from Buenos Aires. His birthplace is now a national

monument. Hudson's *The Naturalist in La Plata*, reedited by Dover, is very useful on Argentine fauna.

Olivos (*Pop* about 160,000), on the Río de la Plata coast, 20 mins by the Mitre Railway or 40 mins by Bus No 60, is a favourite residential district. The presidential residence is there.

From Olivos station, walk up C Corrientes with its neocolonial architecture and old, shady trees. Taking Corrientes to the river you reach the Puerto de Olivos, mainly used for construction materials, but there are a marina (private yacht club) and several *parrilladas* (popular). On Sat and Sun a catamaran sails to Tigre, 2 hrs, rec trip past riverside mansions, sailing boats and windsurfers.

Martínez, nearby, is an attractive residential area overloooking the Río de la Plata, with an interesting shopping area. Sailing and windsurfing are well represented and river launches and other craft may be hired.

San Isidro (*Pop* 80,000), just beyond Olivos, a resort for golf, yachting, swimming, and athletics, is one of the most attractive suburbs on the coast. Fashionable nightlife here, especially along the river bank. There is a magnificent turf racecourse, an attractive central plaza ('hippy' fair at weekends) and fine colonial buildings with a historical museum.

WEST OF THE CAPITAL

TIGRE

Tigre (*Pop* 40,000) on the Delta of the Paraná about 29 km NW, is a popular recreational centre. Regattas are held in Nov and March. The Tigre Boat Club was founded in 1888. There is an excellent fruit and handicrafts market at nearby Canal San Fernando on Sun. North of Tigre are innumerable canals and rivulets, with holiday homes and restaurants on the banks and a profitable fruit growing centre. The fishing is excellent and the peace is only disturbed by motor-boats at weekends. Regular launch services (lanchas) run to all parts of the Delta, including taxi launches – watch prices for these! – from the wharf. Tourist catamarans, run by Interislena (Lavalle 499, T 749-0397, weekends Lavalle 419, T 749-4529) leave from next to the Cacciola dock, Mon-Fri 1330, 1600, 1½ hrs, US$10, different schedule at weekends. Longer trips (4½ hrs) to the open Río de la Plata estuary are available.

Museums **The Museo Naval**, Paseo Victorica, is worth a visit (open Mon-Fri 0800-1230, Sat and Sun 1400-1800 US$2). Covers origins and development of Argentine navy. There are also relics of the 1982 South Atlantic war on display outside. **The Museo de la Reconquista**, Castaneda 470, T 749-0090, Wed-Fri 1000-1200, Sat/Sun 14-18, near the location of Liniers' landing in 1806, celebrates the reconquest of Buenos Aires from the British in 1806-07.

● **Accommodation** There are no good hotels in Tigre itself. On the islands of the Delta: **A3** pp *El Tropezón*, an old inn on Paraná de las Palmas island, formerly a haunt of Hemingway, now frequented by affluent *porteños*, highly rec despite the mosquitoes; **A1** *l'Marangatú*, on Río San Antonio, inc breakfast, pool, sports facilities. Delta **Youth Hostel** at Río Luján y Abra Vieja, **F** pp *Canal de San Fernando*, clean, hot showers, table tennis, volleyball, canoes, ask at Talcahuano 214, Buenos Aires. Take all food in advance, there are basic cooking facilities.

● **Places to eat** Restaurants on the waterfront in Tigre across the Río Tigre from railway line; cheaper places on Italia and Cazón on the nr side.

● **Transport Trains** By train from Buenos Aires to Estación Tigre (rebuilt 1995-96), US$0.65 one way, every 10 mins during peak hours, otherwise every 15 or 20 mins. Alternatively take train from platform 1 or 2 at Retiro station (FC Mitre) to Bartolomé Mitre and change to the Maipú station in Olivos for the new Tren de la Costa, US$1.50 return, US$2 at weekends (stamp ticket in machine before boarding, every 12 mins, 30 mins' journey). Several stations on this line have shopping centres (eg San Isidro) and the terminus, Estación Delta, will also have a *centro comercial*, T 732-6200. **Buses** Take *colectivo* 60 from Constitución: the 60 *bajo* takes a little longer than the 60 *alto* but is more interesting for sightseeing. **Ferries** To Carmelo, Uruguay leave from Cacciola dock (see page 89). Overnight trips to Carmelo (US$72-110 inc accommodation) and 3 day trips to Montevideo (US$118 inc accommodation) are also available from Cacciola.

Martín García island (Juan Díaz de Solís' landfall in 1516) in the Río de la Plata, 45 km N of Buenos Aires, used to be a military base. Now it is an ecological/historical centre and an ideal excursion from the capital, with many trails through the cane brakes, trees and rocky outcrops – interesting birds and flowers. Some of the old buildings have a colonial air. Boat trips daily except Tues and Thur from Tigre at 0800, returning 1700, 3 hrs' journey, US$45 including lunch and guide (US$22 transport only), 2-day trip US$120. Reservations can be made through Cacciola, Florida 520, p 1, Of 113, T 394-5520, who also handle bookings for the inn and restaurant on the island. For bungalow rental: T (0315) 24546.

LUJÁN

(*Pop* 30,000; *Phone code* 0323) 66 km W of the capital by bus from Once station (1 hr), Luján is a place of pilgrimage for all devout Catholics in Argentina. An image of the Virgin was being taken from church to church in the area in 1630 by ox cart. The cart got stuck, in spite of strenuous efforts by men and oxen to move it. This was taken as a sign that the Virgin willed she should stay there. A chapel was built for the image, and around it grew Luján. The chapel has long since been superseded by an impressive neo-Gothic basilica and the Virgin now stands on the High Altar. 8 May is her day. Each arch of the church is dedicated to an Argentine province, and two of the transepts to Uruguay and Paraguay. Very heavy traffic at weekends.

Museums **Museo Colonial e Histórico**, in the old Cabildo building, is one of the most interesting museums in the country. Exhibits illustrate its historical and political development. Open Wed-Sat 1200-1800. No cameras allowed, and nowhere to store them. General Beresford, the commander of the British troops which seized Buenos Aires in 1806, was a prisoner here, and so, in later days, were Generals Mitre, Paz, and Belgrano. There are also museums devoted to transport and to religious ex-votos.

● **Accommodation & places to eat** *La Paz*, 9 de Julio 1054, T 24034. Several others. There are numerous **restaurants**. An excellent one is

L'Eau Vive on the road to Buenos Aires at Constitución 2112, it is run by nuns, pleasant surroundings. The Río Luján is picturesque at this point, a favourite spot for picnic parties.

33 km W of Luján is **Mercedes**, a pleasant city (*Pop* 47,850) with many fine buildings. (Not to be confused with Villa Mercedes in San Luis Province – see below.) Tourist office on plaza, very friendly. **C** *Hotel Loren* (no sign), Salta 228, friendly, clean, parking.

SAN ANTONIO DE ARECO

113 km NW of Buenos Aires (bus, 2 hrs, US$4, every hour) is a popular location for visiting estancias. Many handicrafts are sold, mainly *gaucho* objects, ceramics, silver, leather, colonial furniture.

Museo Gauchesco Ricardo Güiraldes, on Camino Güiraldes y Aureliano, is a typical *estancia* of the late 19th century with manor house, mill, tavern, open daily except Tues, 1000-1500 (1645 Sat, Sun and holidays). Check if it is open in Jan-February. Güiraldes was a writer who described *gaucho* life, his best-known book is *Don Segundo Sombra*.

There is also a local natural history museum, Parque Metri, on Matheu and Moreno. Sub-Dirección de Turismo at Alsina and Lavalle, T 2101.

Día de la Tradición is a *gaucho* festival with traditional parades, games, events on horseback, music and dance, celebrated in the week up to 10 Nov each time. Accommodation is hard to find at this time.

● **Accommodation & places to eat B** *Hotel San Carlos*, Zapiola y Zerbione, T 22401, clean and friendly, ask in advance for meals; **C** *Res Areco*, Segundo Sombra y Rivadavia, T 22166, good, comfortable, clean. **Camping**: nr town centre, also *Auto-camping La Porteña*, 12 km from town on the Güiraldes *estancia*, good access roads. Many *parrilladas* on the bank of the Río Areco.

● **Estancias** Day visits can be made to working *estancias* such as *Cina-Cina*, tour inc typical lunch and riding display, rec. Other estancias which can be visited are: *La Bomba*, T 0326-4053; *Los Patricios*, T 0326-3823 and *El Ombú*.

South of Buenos Aires

THE ATLANTIC coast S of Buenos Aires with its many resorts, including Necochea, Bahía Blanca and, the most famous, Mar del Plata. This region also covers the inland towns of Tandil, Azul and Santa Rosa as well as the hills of the Sierra de la Ventana.

FROM BUENOS AIRES TO MAR DEL PLATA

From Buenos Aires Route 2 runs S, past the coastal city of La Plata, through Chascomús and Dolores to Mar del Plata, the most celebrated Argentine seaside resort.

LA PLATA

La Plata (*Pop* 545,000; *Phone code* 021), on the Río de la Plata 56 km SE of Buenos Aires was founded in 1882 as capital of Buenos Aires province after the city of Buenos Aires had become federal capital. It has a port and an oil refinery. A motorway is being built to link La Plata with Buenos Aires.

Places of interest

The **Muncipalidad** and **Cathedral** ('a magnificent building with a classical Gothic interior') are in the **Plaza Moreno**. From here Av 51 and Av 53 run NE to **Plaza San Martín** and beyond to the **Paseo del**

Bosque, a large park containing the Museo de Ciencias Naturales, zoological gardens, astronomical observatory and a racecourse. 8 km W of the city is the **República de los Niños**, an interesting children's village with scaled-down public buildings, built under the first Perón administration; take a green microbus 273 or a red and black 518 to República de los Niños from Plaza San Martín. To the NE are the **Islas del Río Santiago**, the Yacht Club, Arsenal and Naval Academy. At **Punta Lara**, an Argentine holiday resort nearby, there is a small, interesting nature reserve, slide show and tour, open to public Sat-Sun, 1000-1300 and 1400-1800.

Museo de Ciencias Naturales, in the Paseo del Bosque, famous for its collection of extinct animals. Its treasures are largely ethnological and include human skulls, mummies, and prehistoric implements. There are zoological, botanical, geological, mineralogical, palaeontological and archaeological sections, guided tours in Spanish. Highly recommended, open daily, 1000-1800, US$3, closed in Jan and on public holidays (T 39125).

Local festivals
Foundation of the City, 19 November.

Local information
● **Accommodation**
A3 *San Marco*, C 54 No 523, T 42249, good; *Corregidor*, C 26 No 1026, T 256800, 4-star, expensive.

C *Roga*, C 54 No 334, T 219553, 3 blocks from Paseo del Bosque; **C** *Plaza*, C 44 entre C3 y 4, with bath.

● **Places to eat**
Restaurants rarely open before 2100. *El Fogón*, Av 1, C 49; *Don Quijote*, Plaza Pasco, good value, best in town, can get very crowded; Chinese 'tenedor libre' at *Guinga*, Plaza Pasco; *La Linterna*, C 60 y Av 1, upmarket, good value; *El Chaparral*, good *parrillada*, C 60 y C 117 (Paseo del Bosque). Recommended bar, with steak sandwiches, *El Modelo*, C 54 y C5. Best *empanadas* at *La Madrileña*, a hole-in-the-wall on C 60 between Avs 5 and 6. Best bakery is *El Globo*, C 43 y C 5.

● **Entertainment**
Tango and tropical music at *El Viejo Almacén*, on Diagonal 74, C 2. There are free concerts during the summer in the *Teatro Martín Fierro*

in the Paseo del Bosque.

● **Tour companies & travel agents**
Turismo San Martín, C 51 between Avs 7 and 8, rec.

● **Tourist offices**
In the Municipality on Plaza Moreno.

● **Transport**
Trains To/from Buenos Aires (Constitución), frequent, US$1.20.

Buses To Buenos Aires, 1½ hrs, US$3.20, about every 30 mins. From Buenos Aires, from Retiro day and night and from Plaza Constitución, daytime.

CHASCOMUS

(*Pop* 22,200) 126 km from Buenos Aires, the town is on a wide plain on the shores of Lago Chascomús, which covers 3,000 ha and swells greatly in size during the rains. Its slightly brackish water is an important breeding place for *pejerrey* fish, amateur fishing competitions are held in the winter season. There is a *gaucho* museum, a Regatta Club and bathing beaches.

● **Accommodation**   Four campsites inc Monte Brown, on the far side of the lake (all nicely located, but poor facilities). **Tourist Farm**: 64 km S of Chascomús and 21 km N of Dolores, nr Castelli, **L3** *Estancia Haras La Viviana*, full board, watersports, bird-watching, fishing, horseriding. Contact Haras La Viviana, Castelli, Gaspar Campos 671, Vicente López CP138, Prov Bs As, T 541-791-2406.

DOLORES

204 km from Buenos Aires (district *pop* 30,000) **Dolores** was founded in 1818, destroyed by Indians 3 years later, and rebuilt. It is a grain and cattle farming centre, and has moved on little since the 1940s. The **Museo y Parque Libres del Sur**, commemorating the revolt of the district against Rosas in the early 19th century, is interesting and well displayed. **Museo de Bellas Artes**, Belgrano 134, Wed-Sun 1000-1700.

● **Accommodation B** *Hotel Plaza*, very pleasant; **C-B** *Avenida* Olavarría 362, T (0245) 7619, 4 blocks from Plaza, ugly but OK. *Parrilladas, heladerías* and nightlife on C Buenos Aires.

● **Transport Local Taxi**: taxi stand at Belgrano y Rico, 1 block from plaza, T 3507. **Trains** Station 15 mins from centre, 3½ hrs to Buenos Aires, US$8. **Buses** Río de la Plata, Buenos Aires

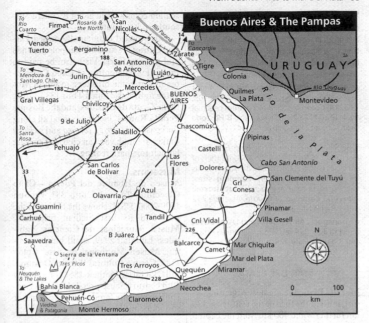

Buenos Aires & The Pampas

285, Cóndor/La Estrella, Buenos Aires 300 block, 3½ hrs to the capital.

SAN CLEMENTE DEL TUYÚ

107 km E of Dolores (*Phone code* 0252), is the nearest Atlantic coastal resort to Buenos Aires. A family resort with little nightlife, it is cheaper than the more fashionable resorts further S. 9 km away at **Punta Rasa**, there are an old lighthouse and a nature reserve owned by the Fundación Vida Silvestre, with interesting birdlife.

● **Accommodation** Many places along the promenade, inc **B** *Acuario*, Av San Martín 444, T 21357, clean, friendly, inc breakfast; **C** *Splendid*, C1 No 2430, T 21316; **C** *Res Bahía*, C 4, between C 1 y C 15, breakfast inc, good. Several campsites.

● **Places to eat** *Restaurante Yo y Vos*, C 4 y C 17, large and cheap portions, friendly, good.

● **Banks & money changers** US dollars can be changed at the **Banco de la Provincia de Buenos Aires**, C 1 y C 4, but TCs are not accepted anywhere in town.

● **Entertainment** 3 km from the centre, nr the harbour (micro bus 500) is **Mundo Marino**, the largest oceanarium in South America (T 0252-21071), with amusements and shows as well as whales, penguins, etc; open daily from 1000, closes 1530 May-Sept, 1630 Mar-April, Oct-Dec, 1800 Jan-February.

● **Buses** To Mar del Plata, frequent, Empresa Costamar, US$11, 5 hrs. To Buenos Aires, several companies, US$15-20.

PINAMAR

89 km S of San Clemente (*Phone code* 0254), a resort with a casino, which is eclipsing Mar del Plata. The water-skiing is good. Fish, including conger eel (*con grio*) may be bought on the beach from local fishermen. Tourist office, friendly and helpful, is on the main plaza.

● **Accommodation** Many, from *Arenas*, Av Bunge 700, T 82444, 4-star, to *Berlín*, Rivadavia 326, T 82320, 1-star. All hotels fully booked throughout January-March. Houses and apartments can be rented from Dec-Mar: 2-room flats about US$1,000/month, up to US$5,000 for a mansion. In Mar rates are halved. **Youth hostel**: Nuestras Malvinas y Sarmiento, T 82908, and *Moby Dick* campsite at Ostende, T 86045. Many other campsites close to town.

VILLA GESELL

(*Pop* 8,700; *Phone code* 0255) 22 km further S, a modern resort with a chocolate factory, fine beaches and over 100 hotels; it has become very popular although less crowded than Mar del Plata.

● **Accommodation** *Terrazas Club*, 4-star, suite accommodation, Av 2 entre C 104 y 105, T 63214; *Colón*, 2-star, 3 blocks from beach at Av 4, C 104, T 62310, restaurant; **B** *Hostería Gran Chalet*, Paseo 105 No 447 y Av 4-5, T 62913, clean, rec; **C** *Bero*, Av 4 y C 141, T 66077, opp bus terminal; **E** pp *Hosp San Hector*, Av 8, No 641, T 62052. Many others of all classes within 800m of sea. Many apartments for rent (rates as Pinamar). **Camping sites**: many, a few open all year round. **Youth hostel**: *Albergue Camping El Coyote*, Alameda 212 y 306, Barrio Nte, T 68448.

● **Transport Air** With AR and LAPA. **Buses** Direct to Buenos Aires, US$29, Empresas Antón and Río de la Plata, book in advance at weekends. Tourist office at terminal.

MAR DEL PLATA

Mar del Plata, the greatest Argentine resort, built at the turn of the century, is 130 km further S and 400 km from the capital (*Phone code* 023). The normal population is 407,000, but during the summer about 2 million visitors stay there; there are all classes of apartment blocks, boarding houses and lodgings. It is necessary to book in advance between late Dec and mid-Mar (when the night-life continues all night). For the rest of the year the town is fairly quiet and good value.

Places of interest

There are several fine squares, especially **Plaza San Martín**, and 8 km of beaches, including fashionable **Playa Grande**, with its private clubs and the summer estates of wealthy *porteños*; **Playa Bristol**, where the casino is (upper floor open to the public); and **Playa La Perla**, with moderately priced hotels. At **Punta Iglesia** there is a large rock carving of Florentino Ameghino, the palaeontologist who collected most of the fossils in the museum at La Plata. South of Playa Grande is the port, reached by bus, 15 mins from terminal. There are a large fishing fleet, excursion boats, seafood restaurants and a huge sealion colony (walk along Escollera Sur-southern breakwater).

The wooded municipally-owned **Parque Camet** is 8 km N. It has polo grounds and playing fields. Visits can be paid to the rocky promontory of **Cabo Corrientes** to watch the breakers; to **Punta Mogotes** lighthouse (open Thur 1330-1700); to the **Gruta de Lourdes**, and the **Bosque Peralta Ramos**. Fishing is good all along the coast and *pejerrey*, *corvina* and *merluza* (hake) abound; you can charter a private launch for shark fishing.

Museums

Museo de Hombre del Puerto – Cleto Ciocchini, Padre J Dutto 383, Fri-Sun 1600-2000, US$1, shows the history of the port and its first Sicilian fishermen. **Museo Municipal de Ciencias Naturales**, Libertad 2999, small but interesting. **Museo Municipal de Arte**, Colón 1189. **Centro Cultural Victoria Ocampo**, Villa Victoria, Matheu 1851, in an early 20th century house prefabricated in England, where the famous author spent her summers until her death in late 1970s.

Excursions

To the the – Mar Chiquita –, 34 km N, a lagoon joined to the sea by a narrow channel, offering good fishing, yachting, boating and bathing.

Local festivals

10 Feb (Foundation of City); 10 Nov (Day of Tradition); 22 Nov (Sta Cecilia).

Local information

● **Accommodation**

During summer months it is essential to book in advance. Many hotels open in season only. Out of season, bargain everywhere. 5-star *Provincial*, Blvd Marítimo 2500, T 916376; **A1** Many 4-star inc *Dos Reyes*, Colón 2129, T 912714; *Hermitage*, Blvd Maritimo 2657, T 519081, 150 rooms; *Gran Dora*, Buenos Aires 1841, T 911992; *Astor*, Entre Ríos 1649, T 23051/4, small, no credit cards, 3 mins from beach.

Among the 3-star hotels (**A2**) are: *Benedetti*, Colón 2198, rec, T 30031/2; *Gran Continental*, Córdoba 1929, T 23027; *Presidente*, Corrientes 1516, T 28819.

There are scores of other hotels at reasonable rates eg **A3** *O Sole Mío*, Av Independencia 1277, T 26685, half board, Italian run, highly rec.

Budget accommodation: B *Boedo*, Almte Brown 1771, T 24695, with bath, hot water, clean, good value, nr beaches (open Jan-Feb only); C *Monterrey*, Lamadrid 2627, T 23266, clean, good; C *Niza*, Santiago del Estero 1843 (E out of season), bath, clean, safe, friendly, rec.

Near the bus terminal: B *Europa*, Arenales 2735, T 40436, clean, quiet, hot water; C *Hosp Paraná*, Lamadrid 2749, T 42825, with bath; C *Peley*, on Alberti, clean, comfortable, open all year, rec, good value restaurant.

Camping: *Pinar de la Serena*, Ruta Provincial 11 y C 3, and other sites, reasonable prices. Several on the road S.

Youth hostel: Tucumán 2728, T 27927, E pp, friendly, clean, only a small discount for YHA card holders.

Apartment rental: there are many houses and apartments for rent. Monthly rates for summer 1995/6, excluding electricity, gas etc. Flats US$4,200-600, chalets US$550-1,000, houses US$800-1,800.

● **Places to eat**
El Caballito Blanco, Rivadavia 2534, excellent, German decor; *Gruta de Capri*, Belgrano 2161, not cheap but excellent value; *La Paella*, Entre Ríos 2025, good. Seafood restaurants in the Centro Comercial Puerto inc *La Caracola*, good but not cheap; *Teresa*, San Luis 2081, fresh pasta dishes, good value; *Lo de Terri*, Gascón y San Luis, good *parrilla*; *Raviolandia*, Colón y Las Heras, good, cheap, try the seafood with rice. Many *tenedor libre* restaurants of all kinds along San Martín. *Los Inmortales*, Corrientes 1662, good, moderately priced. Good value meals at *La Nueva Glorieta*, Alberti 1821, and *El Nuevo Hispano*, Alberti 1933. Many cheap restaurants along Rivadavia.

Vegetarian: *El Jardín*, San Martín 2463, *tenedor libre*, and *La Huerta*, San Martín 2300.

● **Banks & money changers**
Lloyds Bank (BLSA) Ltd, Av Luro 3101. Open 1000-1600. Casas de Cambio **Jonestur**, San Martín 2574 for TCs; **Amex**, Colón 2605, does not cash TCs; **La Moneta**, Rivadavia 2623; **Mar del Plata Cambio**, Buenos Aires 1910.

● **Cultural centres**
Cultural events: reduced price tickets are often available from *Cartelera Baires*, Santa Fe 1844, local 33 or from *Galería de los Teatros*, Santa Fe 1751. **La Cultura** (formerly Sociedad de Cultura Inglesa), San Luis 2498, friendly, extensive library.

● **Entertainment**
Casino: open Dec to end-April, 1600-0330; 1600-0400 on Sat. Winter opening, May-Dec, Mon-Fri 1500-0230; weekends 1500-0300. Entrance US$5.

● **Post & telecommunications**
Post Office: Av Luro 2460.

Telecommunications: Av Luro y Santiago del Estero.

● **Tourist offices**
Blvd Marítimo 2267, T 41325, open 0800-1900, good information, inc bus routes to all sites of interest.

● **Useful addresses**
Immigration Office: Chile y Alberti, open am.

● **Transport**
Air Camet airport, 10 km from town. Many flights daily to Buenos Aires, Austral, Lapa and AR. *Remise* taxi from airport to town, mini bus US$3.50.

Trains Station at Av Luro 4599, about 13 blocks from the centre. To Buenos Aires (Constitución) 5¼ hrs. See under Buenos Aires, **Trains**.

Buses Terminal at Alberti y Las Heras, convenient. To **Buenos Aires** 6 hrs, US$26, Micromar, Costera Criolla, also has *coche cama*, Empresa Argentina, Chevallier. Bus to **Miramar** hourly, 45 mins, US$4. El Cóndor and Rápido Argentino to **La Plata**, US$20. La Estrella to **San Martín de los Andes**, US$56; to **Bariloche**, US$60 (none direct, change at Bahía Blanca or Tres Arroyos). To **Bahía Blanca**, only Pampa, 6 daily, US$25, 5½ hrs. To **San Clemente del Tuyú**, Empresa Costamar, frequent, US$11, 5 hrs. To **Puerto Madryn** and **Trelew**, Wed and Sat night. For hitchhiking S, take a colectivo to the monument to El Gaucho.

INLAND FROM MAR DEL PLATA

Picturesque spots reached from Route 226 inland to Balcarce are (19 km) **Laguna de los Padres** (a **reserva provincial**), Sierra de los Padres and (32 km beyond) the **Laguna La Brava**, at the foot of the Balcarce hills.

68 km W of Mar del Plata, is the town of **Balcarce** (*Pop* 28,800), a centre for visits to the Cinco Cerros, five strangely shaped hills. Balcarce is the birthplace of the great racing driver **Juan Fangio**; it has a racing circuit and a motor museum with all Fangio's racing cars and trophies (C 17 y C 18, open 1100-1800, US$5, recommended). Frequent buses from Mar del Plata. Excellent *parrilladas* on the outskirts.

● **Accommodation** B *Balcarce*, C 17, T 22055, good.

TANDIL

(*Pop* 125,000; *Phone code* 0293) Beyond Balcarce Route 226 runs 103 km NW to **Tandil**, at the northern end of the Sierra de Tandil, a ridge of hills which run W from the sea into the pampa for 250 km. The air is splendidly clear and refreshing, and the Holy Week festivities are outstanding. There is a beautiful lake in the city. Excursions to the Sierra La Aurora.

● **Accommodation & places to eat** B *Plaza*, Gen Pinto 438, T 27160, 3-star, very friendly, clean, comfortable and quiet; **C** *Kaiku*, Mitre 902, T 23114, basic; **C** *Turista*, 14 de Julio 60, T22626, 1 star; *Libertador*, Mitre 545, T 22127, central, good value. Recommended restaurant is *El Estribo*, San Martín 759, friendly, good atmosphere.

● **Buses** To Buenos Aires, 6 hrs, US$15.

AZUL

(*Pop* about 45,000; *Phone code* 0281) 92 km from Tandil, 264 km SW of Buenos Aires, Azul is a cattle centre with an attractive plaza, a French Gothic-style Cathedral and an ethnographic museum. A good stopping place if driving S from Buenos Aires on Route 3 to Bahía Blanca. The river has been dammed to provide a water-sports centre.

● **Accommodation** B *Gran Hotel Azul*, Colón 626, T 22011, excellent cafetería; **C** *Res Blue*, Av Mitre 983, T 22742, clean, friendly, nr bus station; *Argentino*, Yrigoyen 378, T 25953; *Torino*, San Martín 1000, T 22749. Municipal campsite.

MAR DEL PLATA
TO BAHIA BLANCA

MIRAMAR

From Mar del Plata, there is a road (53 km) along the rocky sea-front SW to the resort of **Miramar** (*Pop* 17,500; *Phone code* 0563). Cheaper than Mar del Plata, the cliffs backing the beach are higher and the surrounding hills more picturesque. There is a fine golf course at *Hotel Golf Roca* and a casino. Immediately S of the city limits is an extensive forest park on the beach, the **Vivero Dunicola**, whose vegetation stays green and blooming throughout the year, despite winter night-time temperatures below freezing. 14 km S, among dunes and black rocks, is Mar del Sur (*Atlantic Hotel*) with good fishing in a lagoon and bathing on the beach.

● **Accommodation** Dozens of hotels and apartments. **B** *Santa Eulalia I*, C 26 No 851, T 20808, friendly but run down; **B** *Villa Cruz*, C 19, No 864, friendly, clean, nr the beach; *Gran*, C 29, No 586 esq 12, T 20358, 2-star; *Palace*, C 23, No 774, T 20258, 3-star. **Camping**: F pp *El Durazno*, 3 km from town, good facilities, shops, restaurant, take bus 501 marked 'Playas'. Many sites, reasonably priced.

● **Tourist offices** On central plaza, maps available.

● **Transport Trains** Ferrobus twice daily to/from Mar del Plata, connects with Buenos Aires trains. **Buses** To Buenos Aires, Chevallier, Micromar and Costera Criolla, 8 a day, US$31; to Mar del Plata, Rápido del Sud.

NECOCHEA

About 110 km further SW along the coast, **Necochea**, is another famous resort, second only to Mar del Plata (*Pop* 52,000 with a large Danish community; Danish club and consulate; *Phone code* 0262). Its 24 km long beach is one of the best in the country. There is a municipal recreation complex, with a large casino deteriorating in the salt air (open summer only 2200-0400), various sports facilities, including skating rink, swimming pool, bowling, a cinema and children's play area. The Parque Miguel Lillo (named after the Argentine botanist) faces the beach, comprising 400 ha of conifers, nature park, swan lake with paddle boats, an amphitheatre, museum and go-cart track. The surroundings are picturesque. Visits can be paid to the Paseo del Puente, Punta Negra, the Cascada (or waterfalls) 16 km up the Río Quequén Grande and Los Manantiales.

About 3½ km across the mouth of the river from Necochea is **Quequén**, with an excellent beach, good bathing, and pleasant scenery. The channel to the port, which exports grain, has to be dredged daily.

● **Accommodation** The Hotel Association is at Av 79 y C 4. Most hotels are in the downtown area from C 2 (parallel with beach) N between Av 71-91. There are at least 100 within 700m of the beach. **A3** *Hostería del Bosque*, C 89 No 350, entre 8 y 10, T/F 20002, 5 blocks from beach, quiet, upper rooms better, nice bar and garden, parking next door; on plaza, *San Miguel*, C 85 No 301 esq 6, T/F 25155, and *San Martín*, C 6 No 4198 esq 85, T/F 37000, restaurant; **B** *Doramar*, C 79, No 357, T 25815, family run, friendly, helpful; **C** *Hosp Solchaga*, C 62, No 2822, T 25584, clean, excellent; **E** *Hosp Bayo*, C 87, No 363, T 23334. Several in Quequén inc *Costa Azul*, *Continental*, *Quequén*. Campsites on beach reported expensive in season.

● **Places to eat** *Rex*, C 62, 'a trip to 1952 Paris'.

● **Language schools** *Instituto Argentino de Idiomas*, Galería Monviso, local 8, C 62 y 63, rec.

● **Tourist offices** At bus terminal and on beach front at Av 79.

● **Buses** Terminal at Av 47 y C 582, 4 km from the centre; bus from outside the terminal. To Buenos Aires, US$44, La Estrella, El Cóndor and Costera Criolla. To Mar del Plata US$6; to Bahía Blanca US$16.

TRES ARROYOS

(Pop 85,000; *Phone code* 0983) About 195 km E of Bahía Blanca, is a cattle and wheat growing centre. Many inhabitants are of Dutch origin (Dutch consulate and school). There is also an important Danish colony, with school, club and consulate. A 68 km paved road runs S to the sea at the pleasant little resort of **Claromecó**, with a beautiful beach of dark sand backed by high dunes.

● **Accommodation & places to eat** At Tres Arroyos: inc **A3** *Parque*, Pellegrini 23, T 27055, restaurant, rec; *Andrea*, Istilart 228, T 26214, good. *Restaurant Di Troppo*, Moreno 133, good; *Tres Amigos*, Chacabuco 102, popular parrilla **At Claromecó**: several hotels and restaurants. **Camping at Claromecó**: good campsite *Dunamar*, hot showers, fire pits and laundry facilities. Also ACA campsite.

● **Buses** Terminal a few blocks from the centre of Tres Arroyos. Buenos Aires-Claromecó, El Cóndor, US$40. Tres Arroyos-Claromecó twice daily off season, extra buses from mid-Dec in season. Pampa bus to Mar del Plata 0650, 4½ hrs.

BAHIA BLANCA

(Pop 300,000, *Phone code* 091) The most important centre S of Mar del Plata stands at the head of a large bay at the mouth of the Río Naposta. The region has over a million people. Bahía Blanca consists of the city itself, built back from the river front, and five ports at various distances from the city strung along the N bank of the Naposta: Arroyo Pareja and the naval base of Puerto Belgrano at the mouth of the estuary; Puerto Ingeniero White, 23 km inland (reached by buses 500, 501, 504 from the plaza), Puerto Galván, 3½ km beyond, and Cuatreros, 8 km upstream.

Places of interest

The city has some fine modern buildings and two parks. There is a modest **Jardín Zoológico** in Parque Independencia, Ruta 3 y Av Pringles, on the outskirts. The **Barrio Inglés** (direction Ingeniero White) is where the foremen and technicians of the port and railway construction teams lived; Brickman St is a row of late Victorian semi-detached houses. Managers lived at nearby Harding Green.

Museums

Museo Histórico, Alsina 425, including interesting photos of early Bahía Blanca. **Museo del Puerto**, Torres y Carrega, Ingeniero White. **Museo de Bellas Artes**, Alsina 65.

To the E of Bahía Blanca is an enormous stretch of sandy beaches, developed for visitors (in the afternoon, it is usually windy). **Pehuén-Có**, 70 km away (hotel, C, quiet and clean), is an example of the beaches with camping places, well shaded by pine trees (beware of jellyfish when wind is in the S). Signs to it on the main road 24 km from Bahía Blanca. Another fine beach, with hotels and camping places is **Monte Hermoso**, 106 km, 2 hrs by bus (4 a day in summer, 2 in winter) E of Bahía Blanca. Good cheap meals, several restaurants. (Its hotels are open only Jan-Mar, several campsites – including *Las Dunas*, 30 mins' walk W along the beach, US$3 pp, a friendly spot run by an elderly German couple.)

Local holidays

Sept 24 (Our Lady of Mercy); Nov 10 (Day of Tradition).

Local information
● Accommodation
A1 *Austral*, Colón 159, T 20241, F 553737, 4-star, restaurant; **A3** *Argos*, España 149, T/F 40001, 3-star.

A3 category: *ACA Motel Villa Borden*, Av Sesquicentenario, entre Rutas 3 y 35, T 40151, F 21098; *Belgrano*, Belgrano 44, T 20240/30498; *City*, Chiclana 226, T 30178; *Italia*, Brown 181, T 20121, simple, clean, restaurant; *Muñiz*, O'Higgins 23, T 20021, friendly, central; *Santa Rosa*, Sarmiento 373, T 20012/3.

B *Barne*, Hipólito Yrigoyen 270, T 30864/30294; **B** *Bayón*, Chiclana 487, T 22504, friendly, clean, safe; **A3** *Ameghino*, Valle Encantado 60, T 81098, clean, nr beach; **B** *Victoria*, Gral Paz 82, T 20522, basic, friendly, hot water, rec.

C *Chiclana*, Chiclana 370, **D** without bath, T 30436; **C** *Del Sur*, 19 de Mayo 75, T 22452, with restaurant, noisy with traffic; **C** *Res Roma*, Cerri 759, T 38500, with bath, cheaper without; **C/E** *Hosp Andrea*, Lavalle 88, a/c, very friendly. Many other *residenciales* nr railway station.

Camping: Balneario Maldonado, 4 km from centre, US$5/tent, US$1 pp, next to petrochemical plant, salt water swimming pool, bus 514 along Av Colón every hour but only when beach is open, ie when sunny and not in evening. Many others.

● Places to eat
La Cigala, Cerri 757, very good; *Il Vesuvio*, San Martín 337, good lunch, cheap; *La Casita de Miguel*, San Martín 510, cheap comedor, good food; *Da Sergio*, Gorriti 61, good food, large portions, good value; *Café La Bahía*, Chiclana 548, good value, rec; *Bar/Comedor*, Mitre y Casanova, similar. A few good fish restaurants at the harbour, eg *El Royal*. Very good seafood and fish at Ingeniero White.

● Banks & money changers
Lloyds Bank (BLSA), Chiclana 102; Citibank, Colón 58; Amex, Fortur, Soler 38, T 26290, *poste restante*, English spoken. *Casas de Cambio*: Pullman, Av San Martín 171, change US$, TCs to US$ notes, 3% commission on TCs, good rates (closes 1600); Viajes Bahía Blanca, Drago 63, good rates. All *casas de cambio* closed at weekends.

● Laundry
Laverap, Villarrino 87 and at Perú 122.

● Post & telecommunications
Post Office: Moreno 34.

Telephones: O'Higgins 203.

● Shopping
Good gaucho shop on Soler, nr Fortur (see above), genuine articles.

● Tourist offices
In town hall on main plaza, Alsina 25, very helpful.

● Transport
Air Comandante Espora, 15 km from centre. Austral, Lapa (T 46566) and AR flights to **Buenos Aires**. To **Comodoro Rivadavia, Río Gallegos** and **Río Grande** (Austral). Lapa and TAN to Neuquén.

Trains Station at Av Gral Cerri 780, T 21168. Buenos Aires-Bariloche train passes through (see Buenos Aires **Trains**).

Buses Terminal is 2½ km from centre at Estados Unidos y Brown, connected by *micro* bus service, no hotels nearby. To **Buenos Aires** frequent, 8-11 hrs, US$33-49 depending on service (eg Don Otto, La Estrella/Cóndor); to **Mar del Plata**, Río Paraná, US$25, 5½ hrs; to **Neuquén**, 6 a day, 9 hrs, US$16; to **Zapala** 3 daily, pullman service with food and drinks sold, 15 hrs, US$25 with Alto Valle; to **Río Colorado** US$8 Viedma 3 a day, 4 hrs; to **Trelew**, 3/week, US$32; to **Río Gallegos**, Don Otto US$80.

Hitchhiking: S or W from Bahía Blanca is possible but not too easy. Most southbound traffic takes Route 22 via Río Colorado. North to Buenos Aires on Route 3 is 'virtually impossible'.

SIERRA DE LA VENTANA

Some 100 km to the N is the **Sierra de la Ventana**, a favourite and recommended area for excursions from Bahía Blanca, and a **reserva provincial**.

The small town of **Tornquist**, 32 km N of Bahía Blanca by Route 33, with an attractive church on the central plaza, is a good starting point (**B** *Gran Central Hotel*, seedy but friendly; campsite). The town of Pigüe is also recommended as a good base. From Route 33 take Route 76 towards the town of Sierra de la Ventana. After 32 km is the entrance to the **Parque Provincial**, with massive ornate gates from the Tornquist family home. From here it's a 3-hr walk to the summit of Cerro La Ventana, which has fantastic views from the 'window' in the summit ridge (camping at the base, free, basic facilities, canteen). 5 km further is the forestry station, with audio-visual display, trips to see wild deer, wild horses, guanacos, and on Fri and Sun trips at

0900 to two caves, one an Indian cemetery, the other with petroglyphs (US$0.70). Villa Ventana, 10 km further, is a wooden settlement with excellent teashop, *Casa de Heidi*, and wholefood available from *Jardín de Aylem*. Municipal campsite by river with all facilities.

The town of **Sierra de la Ventana**, further E, is a good centre for exploring the hills. Tres Picos, rising bare and barren from the rich farmlands to 1,070m, is only 6¼ km away. There is a 9-hole golf course, and good trout fishing in the Río Sauce Grande. Excellent tourist information.

• **Accommodation A3** *Provincial*, Drago y Malvinas, T 915025; **D** *La Perlita*, San Martín y Roca, T 915020; **E** pp *Yapay*, Av San Martín nr bus terminal, clean, quiet, rec. **Youth hostel**: *Albergue Sierra de la Ventana* (sleeping bag necessary).

CARHUE

193 km N of Bahía Blanca by road through Saavedra is **Carhué** (*Pop* 18,000; *Phone code* 0936). Behind the town hall there is a museum of the wars against the Indians. Tourist information at bus station. Lago Epecuén, by the town, covers over 40,000 ha and is over 20 times saltier than the sea. No fish can live in the water, which is recommended for chronic rheumatism and skin diseases. There are many hotels and *residenciales* at the lake side, which is a tourist resort. The ghost town of Lago Epecuén, 15 km away, drowned by the lake in 1985, can be visited (unpaved road).

• **Accommodation & services** *Hotel Shalom*, Belgrano 880, T 2503, C, 'eccentric but clean', breakfast extra. Restaurant at bus terminal is reasonable. Free camping in the beach area, no facilities. Rotary Club campsite, 2 km from Carhué.

About 38 km by road NE of Carhué, on the Roca Railway, is **Guaminí** (*Pop* 3,500), a pleasant summer hill resort on the shore of Laguna del Monte, not as salty as Lago Epecuén; accommodation and camping at the lake; *pejerrey* fishing.

Córdoba and the Central Sierras

CORDOBA has some historic, colonial buildings and is an important route centre, especially for road travel to the NW. It is the Republic's second city. The Sierras de Córdoba contain many pleasant, small resorts in the hills.

FROM BUENOS AIRES TO CORDOBA

There are two main road routes: the shorter (713 km) is via Rosario (see page 160) and **Villa María**, an important crossroads where the Rosario-Córdoba highway meets the highway linking central Chile with Paraguay, Uruguay and Brazil. It is a prosperous agricultural town (*Pop* 68,000).

• **Accommodation B** *City*, Buenos Aires 1184, T 20948; **C** *Alcázar*, Alvear y Ocampo, T 25948, nr bus station, good value.

The longer (835 km) is via San Antonio de Areco, Pergamino, **Venado Tuerto** (154 km; *Pop* 58,000; Country Club; several hotels) and **Río Cuarto** (*pop* 138,000). There is a golf club and a fine old municipal building with a lookout tower worth seeing. In April/May one of the country's biggest motor races (*carrera de autos*) is held here.

• **Accommodation B** *Gran*, Sobremonte 725, T 33401, 3-star; **C** *Alihué*, Sarsfield 58, good value, very friendly, big rooms. Near bus station on Sobremonte 100-200 block are three cheap *Residenciales*, *El Ciervo*, *Hosp El Bambi*, *Res Monge*, all **C**. Municipal campsite, *El Verano*.

● **Banks & money changers** Lucero Viajes, Constitución 564, T 33656, only place changing TCs, 3% commission.

● **Buses** To Buenos Aires, US$34, frequent service; to Mendoza, US$24; to Córdoba US$10; to Santiago, Chile, frequent.

Córdoba is 225 km N of Río Cuarto across flatlands and rolling hills. About half-way between the two, the road runs on the retaining wall of the great Río Tercero dam; the artificial lake here is used for recreation. The town of Río Tercero (several hotels) has gained in importance with the development of groundnut plantations and a local military factory.

CORDOBA

Córdoba, capital of Córdoba Province and Argentina's second city (*Pop* 1.2 million; *Alt* 440m; *Phone code* 051). The city was founded as early as 1573. The site of the first university in the country, established in 1613 by the Jesuits, it now has two universities. It is an important industrial centre, the home of Argentina's motor industry, and a busy modern city with a flourishing shopping centre.

Places of interest

In the heart of the city is **Plaza San Martín** with a statue of the Liberator. On the W side is the old **Cabildo**, for many years used as the police headquarters, now a historical museum (see below). Next to it stands the **Cathedral**, the oldest in Argentina, started in 1697 and finished 1787, see the remarkable cupola. One of the features of this part of the city is its old churches. Near Plaza San Martín at Independencia 122 is the 16th century **Carmelo convent** and chapel of **Santa Teresa**. The church of **La Compañía**, Obispo Trejos y Caseros, with a simple façade, dates from about 1650 and is a far better building than the Cathedral; its façade was rebuilt in the 20th century. The barrel vault and cupola of the Capilla Doméstica of this church, built entirely of Paraguayan cedar, are unique. The basilica of **La Merced** at 25 de Mayo 83, was built in the early 19th century, though its fine gilt wooden pulpit dates from the colonial period. On its exterior, overlooking Rivadavia, are fine murals by local artist Armando Sica. There are some pleasant small 18th century churches with striking bell gables and undulating pediments. The neo-gothic church of the **Sagrado Corazón**, built in 1933, at Buenos Aires e Yrigoyen, is also worth a visit. Further E, at Blvd JD Perón, is the magnificent **Mitre railway station**, dating from the late 19th century, with its beautiful tiled *confitería*.

Museums

Museo Histórico, in the old Cabildo, Plaza San Martín, free guided tours 1100 and 1700, Tues, Wed and Fri; **Museo Histórico Provincial**, in the fine colonial Casa del Virrey Marqués de Sobremonte, Rosario de Santa Fe 318, 1 block E of Plaza San Martín; **Museo de Ciencias Naturales**, Yrigoyen 115, open Mon-Fri 0800-1900, Sat 0900-1200, good guided tours (in Spanish, entry free, 'interesting skeletons of prehistoric glyptodonts'); **Museo de Mineralogía y Geología** of the Universidad Nacional de Córdoba, V Sarsfield 299, open Mon-Fri, 1400-1600; **Museo de Zoología**, same address, open Mon-Fri 0900-1200, Wed-Fri 1600-1800, many birds but poorly displayed with no labels; **Museo del Teatro y de la Música**, in the Teatro San Martín, V Sarsfield 365, open Mon-Fri 0900-1200; **Museo Provincial de Bellas Artes**, Plaza España, open Tues-Fri 0900-1300, 1500-2000, Sat/Sun 1500-1900, good; **Museo Municipal de Bellas Artes**, Gral Paz 33, open Tues-Fri 0930-1330, 1630-2030, Sat/Sun 1000-2000; **Museo Histórico de la Ciudad**, Entre Ríos 40; **Centro de Arte Contemporáneo**, Parque San Martín; **Museo de Meteorología Nacional**, San Luis 801, open Tues-Fri 0900-1300, 1400-1800, Sat 0830-1230; nearby in Laprida is Argentina's main observatory, open Wed 2000-2200; **Museo de Arte Religioso**, in the convent of Santa Teresa, Independencia 122, Sat 1030-1230.

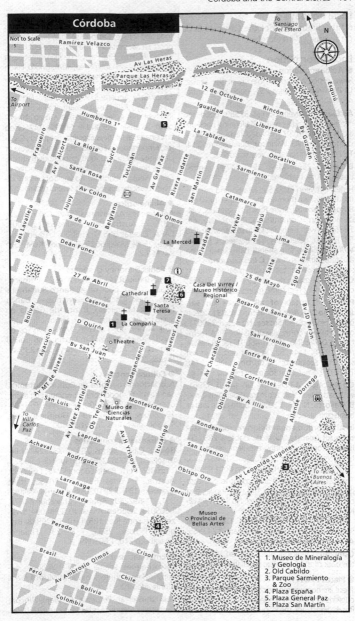

Córdoba

Not to Scale

To Santiago del Estero

N

To Airport

Ramírez Velazco

Av Las Heras

Parque Las Heras

Humberto 1°

12 de Octubre

Igualdad

Rincón

Libertad

La Tablada

Fragueiro

Av F Alcorta

La Rioja

Santa Rosa

Sucre

Tucumán

Av Gral Paz

Rivera Indarte

San Martín

Oncativo

Sarmiento

Catamarca

Jujuy

Av Colón

Belgrano

9 de Julio

Av Olmos

Alvear

Av Maipú

Lima

Bas Lavalleja

Deán Funes

La Merced

Rivadavia

Salta

25 de Mayo

90 Del Estero

27 de Abril

Cathedral

Caseros

Santa Teresa

Casa Del Virrey / Museo Histórico Regional

Rosario de Santa Fe

Bolívar

D Quirós

La Compañía

Buenos Aires

San Jerónimo

Ayacucho

Bv San Juan

Theatre

Independencia

Av Chacabuco

Entre Ríos

Corrientes

Balcarce

Av Mt de Alvear

San Luis

Av Vélez Sarsfield

Ob Trejo y Sanabria

Museo de Ciencias Naturales

Montevideo

Obispo Salguero

Bv A Illia

Allende

Dorrego

Laprida

Av H Yrigoyen

Ituzaingó

Rondeau

Achaval

Rodríguez

San Lorenzo

To Villa Carlos Paz

Larrañaga

JM Estrada

Obispo Oro

Av Leopoldo Lugones

To Buenos Aires

Peredo

Derqui

Museo Provincial de Bellas Artes

Brasil

Crisol

Perú

Av Ambrosio Olmos

Bolivia

Chile

Colombia

Esquiú

Bv Guzmán

Av 1D Perón

1. Museo de Mineralogía
   y Geología
2. Old Cabildo
3. Parque Sarmiento
   & Zoo
4. Plaza España
5. Plaza General Paz
6. Plaza San Martín

Local holidays

6 July (Foundation of the City); 30 Sept (St Jerome), 7-10 October.

Local information

● **Accommodation**

More expensive hotels, mainly in the centre: **L3** *Panorama*, Alvear 251, good pool central new.

A3 *Cañada*, Alvear 580, T 37589, good, inc conference facilities with full technical back-up, a/c, private bath, TV and video, restaurant, laundry, transport; **A3** *Windsor*, Buenos Aires 214, T 224012, comfortable, very good.

B *Garden*, 25 de Mayo 35, T 44739, central, clean, secure, highly rec.

Hotels between Plaza San Martín and bus terminal, most of them in the cheaper brackets: **B** *Roma Termini*, Entre Rios 687, spotless, welcoming; on Corrientes, **C** *Bristol*, No 64, T 236222, with bath, a/c; **C** *Hosp Camacho* (No 587), clean, quiet, very friendly, rec; **C** *Res Mi Valle* (No 586), fan, shared bath, small, clean and nice, family-run, rec; **C** *Res Corrientes* (s/n) shared bath, not too clean, pleasant rooms; **C** *Florida*, Rosario de Santa Fe 459, T 26373, clean, friendly, rec, some rooms with a/c.

Plenty of hotels of all classes on San Jerónimo: **A3** *Ritz* (No 495), T 45031, 'clean but dilapidated'; **A3** *Sussex*, No 125, T 229071, comfortable, roomy, discounts for ACA members; **B** *Dallas* (No 339), T 46091, rec; **B** *Felipe II* (No 279), T 44752, in new part, D in old section, adequate; **C** *Corona* (No 574), T 228789, clean, comfortable, friendly.

On Balcarce: **A3** *Del Sol*, No 144, T 33961, with bath, clean, fan, a/c extra, piped music, rec; **B** *Mallorca*, No 73, T 39234, quite clean and nr bus terminal, noisy.

In Alta Córdoba near Belgrano railway station: **A3** *Jolanda*, Av JL de Cabrera 285, delightful rooms, friendly, excellent restaurant, highly rec; **C** *La Amistad*, Sáenz Peña 1523, T 711943, basic, clean; others on both streets.

The following offer 10% discount to ISIC card holders: *del Sol*, Balcarce 144 (see above), and on Arturo Illia, *del Boulevard*, No 182, *Heydi*, No 615.

A2 *ACA Hotel Dr Cesar C Carman*, Av Sabattini (Ruta 9) y Bajada del Pucará, T 243565, **A1** for non-members, very good.

Camping: Municipal site, Gral San Martín, at the back of the Complejo Ferial (bus 31).

● **Places to eat**

There are numerous grills of all categories on the outskirts of the city, especially in the Cerro de las Rosas district, for meals out-of-doors when the weather is suitable. Many cheap restaurants along San Jerónimo inc *San Carlos*, No 431, good food and service; *Casino Español*, Rivadavia 63, good; *La Mamma*, Alcorta 270, excellent Italian, pricey; *Il Gatto*, Gral Paz y 9 de Julio, great pasta and pizzas, reasonably priced; *Romagnolo*, Perón y San Jerónimo, opp the Mitre railway station, rec; *Betos*, San Juan 454, good *parrilla*, rec, pricey; *Fancy Café*, Andarte 317, good, cheap; *Firenze*, 25 de Mayo 220, busy, pleasant, traditional cafe. Excellent fruit juices (*licuados*) at *Kiosco Americano*, Tucumán 185 and at Gral Paz 242. Good *empanadas* at *La Vieja Esquina*, Belgrano y Caseros; *Empanadería La Alameda*, Obispo Trejo nr University, reasonable food, good student atmosphere, best 2200-2400. Icecream at branches of *Dolce Neve* throughout town; *Soppelsa's* ice cream is also highly rec, with several outlets.

● **Airline offices**

Aerolíneas Argentinas, Av Colón 520, T 819676. **Austral**, Buenos Aires 59, T 228008. **LAPA**, Caseras 355, T 258000. **LAB** and **Alitalia**, 25 de Mayo 6625, 3rd floor. **KLM**, Gen Paz 159.

● **Banks & money changers**

Lloyds Bank (BLSA), Buenos Aires 23; **Citibank**, Rivadavia 104, poor rates; **Banco Sudameris** buys Amex TCs at 1% commission; **Banco Fegin** for Mastercard; **Banco de Galicia** on Sucre for Amex cards. Amex, **Simonelli Viajes**, Av F Alcorta 50, T 26186. Many *cambios* on Rivadavia just off Plaza San Martín; shop around for best rate. Also see **Currency**, page 235, on *bonos*.

● **Cultural centres**

Asociación Argentina de Cultura Británica, San Juan 137, good library, poor reading room, open Mon-Fri 0900-1200, Mon, Wed, Fri 1600-1945, Tues, Thur 1500-1945; **Goethe Institut**, Illia 356, open Tues-Fri 1700-2100.

● **Embassies & consulates**

Bolivia, Castro Barros 783, T 732827; **Chile**, Crisol 280, T 609622; **Paraguay**, 9 de Julio 573, T 226388; **Peru**, Poeta Lugones 212, T 603730. **Austria**, J Cortés 636, T 720450; **Italy**, Ayacucho 131, T 221020; **Germany**, A Olmos 501, T 692269; **Spain**, Chacabuco 875, T 605013; **Sweden**, Alvear 10, T 240094; **Switzerland**, Entre Ríos 185, L-10, T 226848; **Belgium**, F Posse 2533, T 813298; **Finland**, Chacabuco 716, T 605049.

● **Entertainment**

Discotheques: several on Av H Yrigoyen, expensive; late night rock music at *Música Pura*, Montevideo 100, Thur-Sat.

Folk music: at *Pulpería El Viejo Rincón*, Dumesnil y Mendoza, excellent music till 0500.

● **Hospitals & medical services**
English-speaking doctor, *Ernesto J MacLoughlin*, Centro Asistencial Privado de Enfermedades Renales, 9 de Julio 714, home Pérez del Viso 4316, T 814745. Dentist, *Dra Olga Olmedo de Herrera*, Fco J Muñiz 274, T 804378, daughter speaks English.

● **Language schools**
Comisión de Intercambio Educativo, San José de Calasanz 151, T 243606, offers classes mainly pre-arranged in Germany. (Contact Kommission für Bildungsaustausch, Wrangelstr 122, DW-2000 Hamburg 20.) Deutsch-Argentinische Gesellschaft Mariano Fragueiro 2676, Alta Córdoba, T/F 715442 (write to Eppendorfer Weg 287, 20251 Hamburg, Germany, T/F 40-484641) organizes stays abroad and language classes (about US$130/week, 25 hrs of classes) and accommodation at about US$10/day, also exchange programmes for any nationality.

● **Laundry**
Chacabuco 320; *Laverap*, Paraná y Rondeau; *La Lavandería*, Avellaneda 182, local 4.

● **Post & telecommunications**
Post Office: Colón 201, parcel service on the ground floor beside the customs office.
Telecommunications: Gen Paz 36 and 27 de Abril 27.

● **Shopping**
Handicraft market in Rodríguez y Canadá, Sat/Sun. *Librería Blackpool*, Dean Funes 395, for imported English books.

● **Tour companies & travel agents**
Carolina, San Jerónimo 270, local 13/14, good value excursions, minimum of 6 people; *El Delfín*, Gral Paz 250, local 140, p 1; *Argentina Turística*, Vélez Sarsfield 30, T/F 234520, rec; *Alexandria*, Belgrano 194, p 1.

● **Tourist offices**
Dirección Provincial de Turismo, Tucumán 25. Municipal tourist information,Rosario de Santa Fe 39. Information office also at bus station, has free maps, extensive information on accommodation and camping in the province, helpful. Tourist Office desk at airport often unmanned. A useful information booklet is the free monthly, *Plataforma 40*, put out by Nueva Estación Terminal de Omnibus de Córdoba (Netoc).
Club Andino: Deán Funes 2100, open Wed after 2100, closed January.

● **Transport**
Local Buses Municipal buses and electric buses (trolleys) do not accept cash; you have to buy tokens (*cospeles*) or cards from kiosks, normal US$0.65, diferencial US$1.30. **Car hire**: Avis at airport and Corrientes 452, T 227384.

A1, Entre Ríos 70, T 224867. **Localiza** at airport and Castro Barros 1155, T 747747.

Air Pajas Blancas airport, 13 km from the city, is modern and has a good restaurant and a bank (open Mon-Fri 1000-1500). Taxi to airport, US$15. Airport bus from bus terminal, irregular schedule, 30 mins, US$1.50. Alternatively take local bus No 55 from Santa Rosa y Avellaneda (Plaza Colón), allow 1 hr. Several flights to **Buenos Aires** daily, about 1 hr; to **Mendoza**, Austral and LAPA; to **Tucumán**, Austral. To **San Juan**, LAPA; to **Salta**, AR and Austral, who fly once a week to **Jujuy**.

Trains A new tourist service, the Tren de las Sierras, runs from Rodríguez del Busto station (15 km out of town) to Capilla del Monte. Dep 0830, returns 1530, Tues, Thur, Fri, Sat, Sun, US$10 one way, inc taxi transfer from bus terminal to Rodríguez del Busto.

Buses Excellent modern terminal at Blvd Perón 300, with Tourist Office, many public telephones, shops inc food supermarket on 3rd floor, bank (does not change TCs), post office, police, restaurants, and showers in bathrooms (about 6 blocks from centre), crowded at weekends. To **Buenos Aires**, Ablo, Costera Criolla, Chevalier or Cacorba, 10 hrs, US$30 *común* US$50 *diferencial*: to **Salta** (US$41) and **Jujuy** (US$45), Panamericano, 4 daily, La Veloz del Nte twice, about 12 and 15 hrs. To **Mendoza** (10 hrs), 6 a day with TAC, frequent delays and breakdowns, 1 daily with Uspallata US$29; to **Tucumán**, US$30, 8 hrs, about 8 a day, Panamericano has more than other companies. To **Posadas** Expreso Singer, Crucero del Nte (very good buses). To **Santa Fe**, frequent, 5½ hrs, US$18. To **La Rioja** 3-4 a day, Cotil and El Cóndor, 6½ hrs; some go on to Catamarca; to La Rioja-Aimogasta-**Tinogasta**- Fiambalá with El Cóndor, Tues, Thur, Fri; leaves Tinogasta 1140 arr Fiambalá 1240, returns from Fiambalá same day 1445, from Tinogasta at 1600 (see also page 151). To **Belén** (Catamarca) La Calera, Mon, Wed, Fri, 2100. Cacorba, efficient a/c buses, serve **Villa Carlos Paz** (1 hr, frequent service, every 15 mins), **Cosquín** and **La Falda** in the Sierras of Córdoba.

To **Asunción** (Paraguay) direct, Brújula, 4 times a week, and Cacorba 19 hrs, US$55. To **Montevideo** (Uruguay), US$55, dep 1700, Mon, Wed, Fri and Sun, Encon, 15 hrs. To **Lima**, Peru, Colta, dep Fri 2200, via Mendoza, 0700 Sat, arrives Lima Tues am, US$130. To **Pocitos** (Bolivian border) with Panamericano. In general, it is best to travel from Córdoba if you are going N, as it may be hard to get a seat if boarding en route; a seat is only guaranteed if you pay US$1 extra.

SIERRAS OF CORDOBA

Three ranges of undulating hills rise from the pampas, their lower slopes often wooded, particularly in the S. The Sierra Grande, the longest, is in between Sierra Chica to the E and Sierra de Guisapampa and its continuation, the Sierra de Pocho, to the W. The highest peak, Champaquí (2,975m) has a small lake about 2,550m up. The hills run, roughly, for 500 km from N to S; W of Córdoba they are 150 km wide. A network of good roads gives pleasant contrasts of scenery. The region's climate is dry, sunny and exhilarating, especially in winter.

At the foot of the Sierra Chica are large dams to contain the waters of the Río Primero at San Roque, the Río Segundo at Los Molinos and Río Tercero. There are two other large dams in the hills, at Cruz del Eje and La Viña. They provide power and irrigation, and the lakes themselves are attractive. Sailing and fishing are popular.

NB There are innumerable good hotels and *pensiones* in the Córdoba mountain region; names are therefore not always given. Many services in this area are closed out of season.

THE PUNILLA VALLEY

VILLA CARLOS PAZ

(*Pop* 46,000; *Alt* 642m; *Phone code* 0541; 36 km W of Córdoba) On an artificial lake, Lago San Roque, it is the nearest resort to Córdoba and is therefore often crowded. Tours available on amphibian buses as far as the two dams on the lake (US$10); launch trips also available. At the Casa de Gaspar, Miguel Cané and El Redentor, roller-skating and optical illusions, Fri-Sun 1400-1900 out of season. A chair-lift runs up the slopes to a tearoom and night-club overlooking the valley, between 0900 and 1900. Bus tours to areas such as Sierra Chica, for those who like snack bars, fun slides and gravity-defying houses.

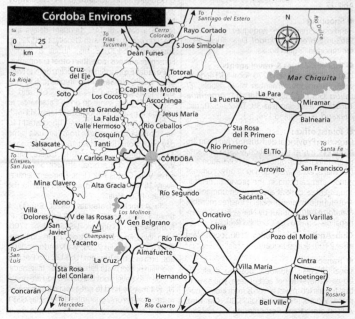

Córdoba Environs

Excursions North of Villa Carlos Paz, on Route 38, a road branches W to Tanti from where local buses go to Los Gigantes, a paradise for climbers, 2-day treks possible. Club Andino has several *refugios*; details in Villa Carlos Paz.

● **Accommodation** Plenty of hotels, big and small, in all price categories. **C** *El Monte*, Caseros 45, T 22001, F 22993, very good, rec; **C** *Mar del Plata*, Esquiú 47, T 22068, friendly, rec; **C** *Villa Carlos Paz Parque*, Santa Fe 50, T 25128, full board available, rec. **Camping**: at ACA site (Av San Martín y Nahuel Huapi, T 22132) and several others inc *Las Tolderías* (Comechingones y Barrio Costa Azul) and *Los Pinos*, rec, Curro Enriquez y Lincoln (open all year). There are many campsites nr the main road through the Punilla Valley, most open Dec-April only.

● **Banks & money changers** Banco de Córdoba, Av San Martín, accepts US$ cash only.

● **Laundry** San Martín y Libertad.

● **Post & telecommunications Post Office and telephone**: Av Gral San Martín 190.

● **Shopping Best buys**: leather mats, bags, pottery.

● **Tourist offices** At bus station, very friendly.

● **Buses** To Córdoba every 15 mins in summer, US$2; taxi to/from Córdoba airport, US$10.50. To/from Buenos Aires, Ablo, US$26; also Cacorba, Chevallier, Gen Urquiza.

COSQUÍN

From Villa Carlos Paz Route 38 runs N through the Punilla valley to a string of resorts. **Cosquín** (*Pop* 16,400; *Alt* 720m; 26 km from V Carlos Paz, 63 km from Córdoba), on the banks of the Río Cosquín, is known as the National Folklore Capital. It is the site of the most important folklore festival, beginning last week in January. A new arena seating 10,000 spectators has been built. There is also a national artesía festival in the same month; **Museo de Artesanías**, Tucumán 1031. **Museo Camin Cosquín** at Km 760, out of town, minerals and archaeology, recommended.

Take a bus (or walk 2 hrs) to the Pan de Azúcar hill from where there is a good view over the Punilla valley. Chairlift to top (all year round).

● **Accommodation C** *La Serrana*, P Ortiz 740, T 51306, nr bus station, friendly, good; **C** *Italia*, Ternengo y Vértiz, T 52255, opp bus station, rec; **E** pp *Res Cosquín*, Tucumán y Sabattini, T 51222, clean. Several campsites.

● **Tourist offices** San Martín 560, T 51105.

● **Buses** To Córdoba, US$2.60, Empresa La Capillense; 1½ hrs, via Carlos Paz or La Calera via the San Roque dam.

LA FALDA

19 km N of Cosquín is **Valle Hermoso** (*Alt* 850m). The old restored chapel of San Antonio is a little gem. Horseriding.

A few kilometres N of Valle Hermoso is **La Falda** (*Pop* 30,000; *Alt* 933m; *Phone code* 0548) 82 km from Córdoba). It is a good touring centre, friendly and peaceful.

There is a **Model Railway Museum** at **Las Murallas Zoo** at the end of Av 25 de Mayo. The privately run **Ambato Archaeological Museum**, Cuesta del Lago 1467, is well displayed, open Thur-Sun and public holidays 0900-2000, US$0.50 entrance.

Excursions Extensive hiking in surrounding hills. 3½ km N by Route 38 is **Huerta Grande**, at 971m, a bathing resort with good fishing and medicinal waters. Round trip excursion to **Cascadas de Olaén**. Take the road to Valle Hermoso S 10 km towards Cosquín, then follow dirt road about 12½ km to the crossing marked 'Cascadas de Olaén'; from here walk 4½ km to the falls: quite spectacular canyon – the water splashes into a small lake full of little fish. Return to the dirt road and 2½ km to a monolith and another dirt road, which leads to La Falda. On the Pampa de Olaén, there are many quartz mines. To La Candelaria, 53 km W along unpaved roads where there is a Jesuit *estancia* and chapel dating from 1693.

● **Accommodation** About 80 hotels in all categories, all full in Dec-Feb holiday season; La Falda is visited mostly by the elderly, most hotels belong to pension funds (eg **C** *Res Atenas*, Rosario 329, T 22424, clean, comfortable, rec), at other times a basic room with bath is in our **D** range. *Hostería Los Abrojos*, Goya s/n, Valle Hermoso, T/F 70430, with bath, hot water, full board, sports, excursions. Houses for rent 1 Mar to 30 Nov on a monthly basis. Various campsites.

● **Places to eat** *El Bochín*, España 117, good, cheap; *Pachamama*, 9 de Julio 160, vegetarian.

● **Banks & money changers** Bancos de la

Nación and de Suquía for exchange.

● **Entertainment** Jazz at 19th century *Hotel Edén*.

● **Tour companies & travel agents** *Aventura Club*, 9 de Julio 541, La Falda, T/F 23809, trekking, jeep tours, camping, birdwatching etc. *Wella Viajes*, Av Edén 412, loc 12, T 0548-21380, offers 15% discount to ISIC and youth card holders for trekking, climbing, etc to Cerro Champaquí.

● **Tourist offices** Av España 50 and at bus station.

● **Buses** To Córdoba, US$4, 2 hrs; to Buenos Aires, Cacorba, Cita, US$40.

NORTH OF LA FALDA

La Cumbre (12 km; *Alt* 1,141m): fine views from the statue of Christ on the hill. Trout streams with good fishing from Nov to April. Swimming, golf, tennis and hang gliding. Tourist office in old train station near the bus terminal.

● **Accommodation & places to eat A1** *Lima*, Moreno y Dean Funes, with breakfast, T 51727, excellent facilities, pool, quiet, clean; *Victoria*, Posadas s/n, T 51412, charming, small; *La Cumbre Inn*, 9 de Julio 753, T 51736, large and commercial, good views; **C** *Res Peti*, Paz y Rivadavia, good, friendly. *Pizza Luis*, Rivadavia 267, friendly, rec.

Cruz Chica, 2½ km N of La Cumbre, altitude, 1,067m, has English-style houses and gardens in pine woods. Museo Manuel Mujica Laínez, in former house of the Argentine writer, US$3.

Los Cocos, 8 km N of La Cumbre, is a popular mountain resort with three first rate hotels (eg *Blair House*, Av C Grierson, T 92147, English-style, recommended) and many holiday houses. Climb up El Mastil and beyond for the views and birds. Hang-gliding nearby at Cuchi Corral.

CAPILLA DEL MONTE

Capilla del Monte, in the heart of the Sierras (106 km from Córdoba; *Alt* 979m). Medicinal waters (good baths at La Toma, 4 km), rocks and waterfalls and wide views; El Zapato rock is 'graffiti-ridden', better are Los Mogotes, 3 km from town, reached through Paso del Indio. Excursions in the hills, particularly to Cerro Uritorco, 1,950m, 2½ hrs. Walk also to Los Alazanes dam. Many other walks after crossing

bridge at La Toma, recommended. You can walk on to the direct dirt road to San Marcos Sierra (22 km W); many parakeets and small farmhouses. Along the way you will also get views down to the Cruz del Eje dam. Horse riding costs US$20/half day and there are tours to meditation and 'energy' centres: the area is popular for 'mystical tourism'.

● **Accommodation B** *Hosp Italia*, Rivadavia 54, clean, showers, opp bus station. Municipal campsite Calabalumba on the way to Cerro Uritorco, E/tent, rec.

● **Buses** To Córdoba, 3 hrs, US$10; to BsAs, Gen Urquiza, US$38.

Cruz del Eje (58 km NW; *Pop* 25,500; *Phone code* 0549) is famous for its honey; try that made from carob blossom (*algarrobo* 1 kg about US$2). Boats for hire on the artificial lake where there is good fishing.

● **Accommodation A3** *Posta de las Carretas*, Ruta 38 y R Moyano, T 2517, good, service station and restaurants at the crossroads. Camping possible at foot of dam, or stay at friendly, family-run **C** *Hotel España* in village, Caseros y Alsina, T 2702.

NORTH FROM CORDOBA

A road runs N to **Ascochinga** through pleasant little townships such as Villa Allende, Río Ceballos, Salsipuedes and La Granja. At El Manzano, 40 km N of Córdoba, a road branches W to **Candonga**, altitude 810m. The historic church, now a National Monument, was built in 1730 as an oratory of the Jesuit Estancia de Santa Gertrudis.

14 km N of Ascochinga is **Santa Catalina**, originally a Jesuit mission founded in 1622 and the most elaborate Jesuit establishment in the Sierras de Córdoba. See the church, begun in 1754, workshops and stone conduits; the families who now use it as a summer homes will show you round. Buses from Jesús Maria, twice a day.

● **Accommodation In Río Ceballos: D** *La Gloria*, Av San Martín 5495, affiliated to IYHA, warmly rec. Three campsites. Several campsites also at **Salsipuedes**. **In Ascochinga: B** *Hostería El Cortijo*, full board only, good value, with bath, small swimming pool and river outside, horses for rent, US$1/hr; 5 km walk to Tres Cascadas falls and *balneario*. During winter, open weekends only. Campsite open all year.

JESUS MARIA

From Ascochinga a road runs E for 20 km to **Jesús María** (*Pop* 21,000; *Alt* 533m; 51 km N of Córdoba on Route 9; several hotels). There is a good 18th century Jesuit church and the remains of its once famous winery; in the cloister is an excellent Museo Jesuítico, said to be one of the best on the continent (Mon-Fri 0800-1200 and 1400-1900, Sat and Sun 1600-2000). Each Jan there is a gaucho and folklore festival, lasting 10 nights from 2nd week; very popular. Good fishing in winter. Direct bus from Córdoba, US$2, 1½ hrs.

Sinsacate, with an interesting church, is 4 km N of Jesús María. There is also a fine colonial posting inn, now a museum, with long, deep verandah and chapel attached.

At Rayo Cortado, 114 km N of Jesús María, a turning leads W to **Cerro Colorado**, 160 km N of Córdoba, the former home of the Argentine folklore singer and composer Atahualpa Yupanqui. His house, now a museum, can be visited, US$2, ask in the village for the curator. There are more than 30,000 rock paintings by the Comechingones Indians in the nearby Cerro Colorado archaeological park and a small archaeological museum (US$1 entry, includes guide in English or Spanish). There is cheap accommodation with families and camping. Daily bus from Jesús María at 1610.

Villa de María (136 km N of Jesús María) is the birthplace of Leopoldo Lugones, a poet of country life. His house is a museum.

MAR CHIQUITA

Some 200 km NE of Córdoba the Río Dulce, flowing in places through salt flats, runs into the shallow **Mar Chiquita** on the S margin of the Chaco and about 320 km SE of Santiago del Estero. Mar Chiquita is naturally salty and the water is warm. No river drains it, though two other rivers flow into it from the Sierras de Córdoba in the flood season. There are several islands in the lake. On its S shore is the small town of **Miramar**, which is being gradually overwhelmed by the expanding Mar Chiquita. The area is a very popular resort during the summer months; its salt waters are used in the treatment of rheumatic ailments and skin diseases.

NB This Mar Chiquita and Miramar should not be confused with the other Mar Chiquita and Miramar on the Atlantic coast.

● **Accommodation** *Savoy*, San Martín y Sarmiento, cheap, very friendly. **Camping**: *Autocamping Lilly*, Bahía de los Sanavirones.

A scenic road SW from Villa Carlos Paz passes **Ycho Cruz**, by the Río San Antonio (**D** *Hostería Avenida*, with bath; several campsites). Beyond, the road climbs into the Sierra Grande. 7 km N of the village of El Cóndor, a wide trail leads to Quebrada de los Condoritos (6-7 km), with superb landscape and the chance of seeing condors in their easternmost habitat. The road crosses the Pampa de Achala, a huge desert plateau of grey granite, before descending to another chain of resorts. (Bus Córdoba-Ycho Cruz, US$2, Cotap; to El Cóndor US$5.)

MINA CLAVERO

Three rivers, popular for swimming, pass through the town centre (*Pop* 5,100; *Alt* 915m; *Phone code* 0544; 140 km from Córdoba). It is a good centre for exploring the high *sierra*. There is a nice church and a most interesting museum, 'Rocsen', 13 km S and about 5 km from the village of Nono, entrance US$3, open 0900 till sunset, with furniture, minerals, instruments, animals, etc.

● **Accommodation & places to eat** Many hotels. Restaurant *Rincón Suizo*, C Champaquí 1200, serves good pastries.

● **Buses** To Córdoba, 6 a day, 4 hrs.

CHAMPAQUI

2,884m, the highest peak in the Sierras. It can be reached Villa de las Rosas, 35 km S of Mina Clavero (several hotels), or from San Javier, 12 km further S. The latter route goes by Capilla La Constancia, set in a river valley with pine and nut trees. To the summit takes 8-10 hrs, the descent to La Constancia 4 hrs. Neither route should be attempted in misty weather. A good base is *Vai Kunta*, 5885 Villa de las Rosas, run by Rolf Graf (Swiss), rooms for rent, good food, guiding service. Take any Córdoba-Villa Dolores bus to Villa de las Rosas; at bus station look for the *pizzería* where taxis to Los Molles can be arranged. From Los Molles it's a 2-hr walk to the house.

2 km S of San Javier, at the foot of Champaquí, in a region of woods and waterfalls is **Yacanto**, which has curative waters.

15 km E of Villa de las Rosas is **Villa Dolores** (*Pop* 21,000; *Alt* 529m; 187 km from Córdoba), with *balnearios* nearby.

● **Accommodation** **D** *Hosp Cáceres*, Brizuela 390; **D** *Res Champaquí*, F Germán 166, T 22358. **Camping**: nearest site is *Piedra Pintada*, 15 mins' bus ride away, pleasant village well situated for walks into mountains.

● **Buses** To San Luis 5¼ hrs; to Córdoba 5 hrs.

SOUTH FROM CORDOBA

ALTA GRACIA

39 km SW of Córdoba beside Lago Tajamar, **Alta Gracia** (*Pop* 39,000; *Alt* 580m; *Phone code* 0547) has an interesting colonial church, finished about 1762, open am and after 1700. The buildings housing **Museo del Virrey Liniers**, on the Estancia de Alta Gracia, were founded in 1588 and taken over by the Jesuits in 1643, open Tues-Fri 0900-1300, 1500-1830, Sat, Sun 0930-1230, 1530-1830, US$1 (all day in summer). There is also the **Museo Manuel de Falla** on Pellegrini Final, closed Mon, entry US$0.30, where the Spanish composer spent his last years. Beautiful views from the Gruta de la Virgen de Lourdes, 3 km W of town.

Excursions The Bosque Alegre and Observatory, 24 km NW, affords good views over Córdoba, Alta Gracia and the Sierra Grande. Open Thur 1600-1800, Sun 1000-1200 and 1600-1800.

● **Accommodation** *Hostería Reina*, Urquiza 229, T 21724, good. Two campsites, one scruffy, the other better (nr golf course) and free in winter.

● **Tourist offices** Tourist office inside clock tower by Lago Tajamar.

● **Buses** To Córdoba, US$1.50, every 15 mins, 1 hr.

VILLA GENERAL BELGRANO

The road from Alta Gracia to the Río Tercero dam (79 km S) passes La Serranita, the Embalse Los Molinos and Villa General Belgrano (58 km). A completely German town founded by the surviving interned seamen from the *Graf Spee*, some of whom still live in the town (*Phone code* 0546). It is a pleasant resort and a good centre for excursions in the surrounding mountains. Beer festival in October.

La Cumbrecita is a German village 30 km W of Villa Gen Belgrano. Good walking and riding.

● **Accommodation** **In Gen Belgrano**: **A3** *Bremen*, Route 5 y Cerro Negro, T 61133, restaurant, sports facilities; 2 **Youth Hostels**: **C** *El Rincón*, in beautiful surroundings nr terminal, cooking and laundry facilities, highly rec (reservations: Patricia Mampsey, Casilla 64, T 61323); and at *Estancia Alta Vista*, T 62238, 14 km from town on way to La Cumbrecita, both offer discounts to ISIC and YHA card holders (20% and 25% respectively). **At La Cumbrecita**: **A3** *Cascadas*, T 81015, with pool, tennis etc; **A3** *Panorama*, higher up hill (T 98406); 3 others.

● **Buses** From Gen Belgrano to Córdoba, 2 hrs, US$4, 8 a day; to Mendoza, US$28; to Buenos Aires, Colta, 1 a day, US$35. To La Cumbrecita from Gen Belgrano by taxi (US$33, 1-1½ hrs) or by bus, Sun only.

The Northwest: Santiago del Estero, Tucumán, Salta and Jujuy

THE ROUTE to the major tourist centre of Salta, from where trips can be made into Andean regions, the Quebrada de Humahuaca and the Calchaquí and Cachi valleys. There are prehispanic ruins near Tafí del Valle, Quilmes, Santa Rosa de Tastil and others. This is also a region in which there are a number of Amerindian groups.

The pattern of the land in Northern Argentina, from the crest of the Andes in the W to the Río Paraguay in the E, consists of a high, dry Altiplano rising to a windswept, stony and treeless Puna cut into on its E face by rivers which flow into the Lowlands. This configuration of the land, similar to Bolivia, is carried S into all the NW provinces of Argentina as far S as Tucumán, but the altitudes in Argentina are not so great as in Bolivia, and the whole area not so large. The E running rivers flow into the Chaco; their broad valleys, or *quebradas*, make access to the heights comparatively easy. Between the base of the Puna and the Chaco lie a series of front range hogback hills running roughly from N to S; the lowlands between them are known in Argentina as the *valles*. Tucumán is the southern boundary of this kind of land. North of Tucumán crops can be grown without irrigation (except where the soil is absorbent) but S of Tucumán is droughty land, with long N-S ranges of low hills such as the Sierras de Córdoba, set in plains which have salt flats and swamps in the depressions.

Settlement and economy

The first Spanish expedition from Bolivia entered Argentina in 1542. A little later a better and lower route was discovered – the main route used today – descending from La Quiaca to Jujuy through the Quebrada de Humahuaca, with rugged and colourful mountain ranges closing in on both sides. Along this new route the Spaniards founded a group of towns in the NW: Santiago del Estero (the first), Tucumán, Córdoba, Salta, La Rioja and Jujuy. Mendoza, San Juan and San Luis were all colonized by people who crossed the passes from Chile. All these colonies were hemmed in by the warlike tribes of the Pampas, and until the war of extermination in 1880 the route from Buenos Aires to Córdoba was often unsafe. The Indians raided frequently for cattle, which they drove S and over the Andes for sale in Chile.

During the whole of the colonial era the trade of the area, mostly in mules, was with Bolivia and Peru rather than with Buenos Aires. The mules were bred mainly in the plains between Rosario, Santa Fe, and Córdoba, and driven finally into Salta for the great fair in Feb and March.

Historically, Tucumán was always important, for the two river routes of the Salado and the Dulce across the dry belt forced the mule traffic to pass through Tucumán on the way to Salta. Tucumán still produces most of Argentina's sugar. Tobacco is a major crop, and an important factor in the NW is the growth of tourism.

● **Recommended reading** Federico Kirbus' *Guía de Aventuras y Turismo de la Argentina* (available at Librería La Rayuela, Buenos Aires 96, Salta and El Ateneo, Florida 340, basement, Buenos Aires).

SANTIAGO DEL ESTERO

Founded in 1553 by conquistadores pushing S from Peru, this is the oldest Argentine city. It is 395 km N of Córdoba and 159 km SE of Tucumán. (*Pop* 201,000; *Alt* 200m; *Phone code* 085.)

Places of interest

On the **Plaza Libertad** stand the **Municipalidad** and the **Cathedral** (the fifth on the site). The fine **Casa de Gobierno** is on Plaza San Martín, 3 blocks away. In the convent of **Santo Domingo**, Urquiza y 25 de Mayo, is one of two copies of the 'Turin Shroud', given by Philip II to his 'beloved colonies of America'. On Plaza Lugones is the church of **San Francisco**, the oldest surviving church in the city, founded in 1565. At the back of the church is the cell of San Francisco Solano, patron saint of Tucumán, who stayed in Santiago in 1593.

Beyond the church is the pleasant **Parque Aguirre**.

Museums

Museo Arqueológico, Avellaneda 353, containing a large collection of Indian pottery and artefacts from the Chaco, Mon-Fri, 0800-1300, 1400-1900, Sat, 0900-1200, free; **Museo Histórico**, Urquiza 354, Mon-Fri, 0830-1230, 1530-1830, Sat 0900-1200; **Museo de Bellas Artes**, Independencia between 9 de Julio and Urquiza, Mon-Fri, 0900-1300; **Museo Andrés Chazarreta**, Mitre 127, handicrafts.

Local festivals

Carnival in Feb: virtually everything throwable gets thrown by everyone at everyone else.

Local information

● **Accommodation**

A3 *Gran*, Avellaneda e Independencia,

North-West Argentina

T 214400, 4-star; *Libertador*, Catamarca 47, T 215766, 3-star; **A3 Rodas**, Gallo 432, T 218804, clean, safe.

C *Res Emausi*, Av Moreno 600 block, with bath, good value; *Santa Rita*, Santa Fe 273, nr bus terminal, clean, basic.

Camping: *Las Casuarinas* in the Parque Aguirre.

● **Places to eat**
Restaurant Sociedad Española, Independencia 236, popular, good value; *Centro de Viajes*, Buenos Aires 37, good value lunches; *Mía Mamma*, 24 de Septiembre 16, on Plaza, good restaurant/salad bar, pricey.

● **Banks & money changers**
Banco Francés, 9 de Julio y 24 de Septiembre; **Noroeste Cambio**, 24 de Septiembre 220, good rates. **Amex**, El Quijote Paladea Turismo, Independencia 342, T 213207.

● **Tourist offices**
On Plaza Libertad.

● **Transport**
Air Austral to Buenos Aires.

Buses To Buenos Aires, several daily, 12 hrs, US$37, Cacorba, La Unión and Atahualpa. To **Resistencia**, 3 a day, El Rayo, 9 hrs, US$25, El Rayo, via Quimili and Roque Sáenz Peña (8 hrs); to **Córdoba**, 12 a day, 7 hrs, US$16; to **Tucumán** (via Río Hondo) US$7. Four a day to **Salta**, US$23, Panamericano, 5½ hrs, and to **Jujuy**, 7 hrs.

TERMAS DE RIO HONDO

65 km N of Santiago del Estero along the road to Tucumán, a major spa town (*Pop* 25,000; *Phone code* 0858). The thermal waters are recommended for blood pressure and rheumatism; good to drink, too, and used for the local soda water. Swimming (free) in a public pool called La Olla near the bridge which crosses the Río Hondo (see **Camping** below). Tourist office at Pasaje Borges, s/n. The huge Río Hondo dam on the Río Dulce is close by; it forms a lake of 33,000 ha, used for sailing and fishing.

● **Accommodation** There are over 170 hotels, but at national holiday periods, and especially in Aug, accommodation is hard to find, so book well in advance. *Grand Hotel Río Hondo*, Hipólito Yrigoyen 552, T 21195; *Los Pinos*, Maipú 201, T 21043, pleasant; **B** *Ambassador*, Libertad 184, T 21196; *Aranjuez*, Av Alberdi 280, T 21108. **Camping**: Municipal site, Yrigoyen y Ruta 9, nr river bank; *La Olla*, left

bank of river; ACA 4 km from town; *El Mirador*, Ruta 9 y Urquiza.

● **Buses** To Santiago del Estero, 1 hr, US$2 and to **Tucumán**, 2 hrs, US$4; several to Buenos Aires US$38.

TUCUMAN

It proper name is San Miguel de Tucumán (*Pop* 400,000; *Alt* 450m; *Phone code* 081). Capital of its province, it is the busiest and the most populous city in the N. It stands on a plain, but to the W towers the Sierra de Aconquija. Summer weather can be very hot and sticky.

Places of interest
The city was founded by Spaniards coming S from Peru in 1565 and there are still some colonial buildings left. On the W side of the main Plaza Independencia is the ornate **Palacio de Gobierno**, next is the church of **San Francisco**, with a picturesque façade. On the S side is the **Cathedral**, with an old rustic cross, kept near the baptismal font, used when founding the city.

To the S, on C Congreso, is the **Casa Histórica** (see also below) where, in 1816, the Congress of the United Provinces of Río de la Plata met to draft the country's Declaration of Independence. A bas-relief on the museum walls shows the delegates proclaiming independence. Nightly (not Tues, except in July) at 2030, *son et lumière* programme at Casa Histórica, in garden, adults US$2, children US$1, tickets from tourist office on Plaza Independencia, no seats. Some distance to the W is **Plaza Belgrano**, with a statue to Gen Belgrano, who won a decisive battle against the royalists on this site in 1812. Two blocks E is the **University**, in the grounds of which is a good zoo, the **Reserva Biológica San Javier**.

In the large **Parque Nueve de Julio** (avoid at night) is the house of Bishop Colombres, who introduced sugar cane to Tucumán in the early 19th century. In the house is his first milling machine (open Tues-Fri 0900-1200, 1730-2030). There are several sugar mills nearby: the easiest to visit is **Ingenio Concepción**, on the outskirts of town, guided tours in Spanish during harvest period only (15 July-early Nov), Mon-Sat, 0930 and 1030, no booking required. Take Aconquija bus for Santo Cristo US$0.60, 15 mins.

Museums

Casa Histórica (see above), C Congreso, Tues-Fri 0830-1330,1500-1930, Sat 0830-1300, US$0.40. **Museo de Antropología y Etnografía**, 25 de Mayo 265 in University building, fine collection, Mon-Fri, 0800-1200, 1600-2000. **Museo Folklórico Provincial**, 24 de Septiembre 565, Mon 1730-2030, Tues-Fri, 0900-1230, 1730-2030, Sat, Sun, 1800-2100, free. **Instituto Miguel Lillo**, San Lorenzo y Lillo (30 mins' walk from bus terminal), associated with the natural sciences department of the University, has a small but well-presented museum containing sections on geology and biology with some stuffed animals and a dinosaur skeleton, Mon-Fri, 0900-1200, 1500-1800. **Casa Padilla**, Plaza Independencia, houses a collection of international art and antiques. **Museo Histórico de la Provincia** (Casa de Avellaneda) Congreso 56, Mon-Fri, 0900-1230, 1700-2000, Sat-Sun, 1700-2000; **Museo Iramaín**, Entre Rios 27, memorial to the sculptor, Mon-Fri, 0900-1900. **Museo de Bellas Artes**, 9 de Julio 48, entre 24 de Septiembre y Alvarez, Tues-Fri, 0900-1300, 1630-2100, Sat-Sun, 0900-1200, 1730-2030.

Excursions

North: **El Cadillal** dam, in the gorge of the Río Sali, 26 km, supplies electricity and water for the city and permanent irrigation for 80,000 ha. There are places to eat, a good ACA campsite, good swimming, and a small archaeological museum at the dam (Sierras y Lagos buses every 1½ hrs approximately, US$1.50, 45 mins, last buses back 1715 and 1945).

South: **Simoca**, 50 km on Route 157, has a Sat morning handicrafts and produce market (Posta bus, several, 1½ hrs, US$2.50; essential to get there early).

West in the Sierras de Aconquija: **Villa Nougués**, 36 km, the summer residence of the well-to-do Tucumanos (*Hostería Villa Nougués*, T 310048, small, excellent,

great views) and San Javier, 34 km (hotel), both reached by San Javier bus 1300. Aconquija park, with glorious trees, is at the foot of the mountains, 14 km. Bus at 1130 (the only one; returns immediately).

Local holidays

24 Sept (Battle of Tucumán). 29 Sept, San Miguel. 10 Nov, Día de la Tradición.

Local information
● Accommodation

L3 *Grand de Tucumán*, Av Soldati 380, T 245000, large, 5-star, opp the Parque 9 de Julio, efficient, outstanding food and service, pool (open to non-residents), tennis courts, discotheque.

A1 *Carlos V*, 25 de Mayo 330, T/F 221972, central, good service, a/c, bar, restaurant, rec; **A2** *Metropol*, 24 de Septiembre 524, T 311180, F 310379, good service, worth it.

A3 *Gran Hotel Corona*, 24 de Septiembre 498 on corner of Plaza Independencia, T 310985, good location and facilities; **A3** *ACA Motel Tucumán*, Av Salta 2080, T 266037; **A3** *Premier*, Alvarez 510, T 310381, a/c, good, friendly; **A3** *Colonial*, San Martín 35, T 311523, modern, very clean, private bath, fan, laundry service, breakfast inc, rec; **A3** *Mayoral*, 24 de Septiembre 364, T 228351, F 310080, 20% discount to *South American Handbook* readers; **B** *Congreso*, Congreso 74, T 216025, clean, old-fashioned but rec, with bath, plain, good location; **B** *Plaza*, San Martín 435, T 215502, built round a pretty patio, basic but clean; **B** *Viena*, Santiago del Estero 1050, T 310004.

C *La Vasca*, Mendoza 281, T 211288, with bath, clean, friendly, safe, rec; **C** *Casa de Huéspedes María Ruiz*, Rondeau 1824, clean, safe, rec; **C** *Florida*, 24 de Septiembre 610, T 221785, good value, clean, poorly-lit rooms, helpful; **C** *Independencia*, Balcarce, between San Martín and 24 de Septiembre, with fan, clean, quiet, poor water supply on first floor; **C** *Palace*, 24 de Septiembre 233, friendly, rec; **C** *Petit*, C Alvarez 765, T 214902, spacious, friendly, clean, quiet, without bath, highly rec.

Camping: Parque Nueve de Julio, two sites (US$0.25/tent, US$0.25 pp). Two roadside camp sites 3 km E and NE of city centre.

● Places to eat

There are several popular restaurants and cafés in Parque 9 de Julio and on Plaza Independencia. *Ali Baba*, Junín 380, Arab specialities (Syrian owners), intimate, inexpensive, good, rec, closed lunchtime; *Adela*, 24 de Septiembre 358, well prepared food, Arab specialities, good value; *La Leñita*, 25 de Mayo 377, expensive,

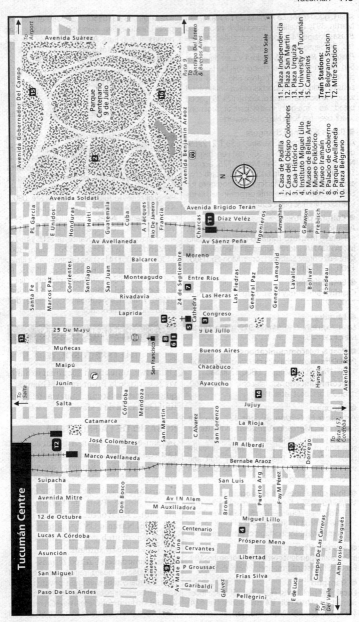

Tucumán Centre

Not to Scale

1. Casa de Padilla
2. Casa del Obispo Colombres
3. Casa Histórica
4. Instituto Miguel Lillo
5. Museo de Bellas Arte
6. Museo Folklórico
7. Museo Iramain
8. Palacio de Gobierno
9. Parque Avellaneda
10. Plaza Belgrano
11. Plaza Independencia
12. Plaza San Martín
13. Plaza Urquiza
14. University of Tucumán
15. Campsites

Train Stations:
T1. Belgrano Station
T2. Mitre Station

smart, good meat; *La Parrilla de La Plaza*, San Martín 391, excellent, reasonable prices; *Las Brasas*, Maipú 740, good but not cheap; *Augustus*, 24 Septiembre y Buenos Aires, good café; *Pastísima Rotisería*, Mendoza y Laprida and at San Martín 964, good cheap snacks, take out service; *La Vieja Casa*, Córdoba 686, good, inexpensive set lunch. Set lunches nr bus station good value. *Panadería Villecco*, Corrientes 751, good bread, also 'integral'. In this part of Argentina 'black beer' (eg Salta Negra) is available.

● **Banks & money changers**
American Express, Chacabuco 38, T 217269, does not change cash or TCs, but very helpful; **Noroeste Cambios**, San Martín 775, accepts TCs; **Dinar**, San Martín 645 and 742, cash only, and **Maguitur**, San Martín 763, good rates for cash, accepts TCs. (See note on provincial bonds used as currency, page 235.)

● **Cultural centres**
Alliance Française, Mendoza 255, free events in French; **Instituto Italiano di Cultura**, Salta 60; **ATICANA** (North American Centre) inc JF Kennedy Library, Salta 581, open Mon-Fri, 0800-1200, 1700-2100.

● **Entertainment**
Casino: Sarmiento y Maipú, open Fri, Sat, Sun, 2100-0230.

● **Laundry**
Lava Expreso, San Martín 929; *Lava Norte*, Mendoza 375.

● **Post & telecommunications**
Post Office: Córdoba y 25 de Mayo, open 0700-1300, 1600-2000 Mon-Fri, 0800-1300 Sat.
Telecommunications: Telecom, Maipú 360, open 24 hrs, best after 1900.

● **Shopping**
Artesanía El Cardón, Alvarez 427, excellent handicrafts; *Mercado Artesanal*, at the tourist office in Plaza Independencia, small, but nice selection of lace and leather work. All shops close 1200-1630. There is a lively fruit and vegetable market, *Mercado de Abasto*, at San Lorenzo y Lillo, worth a visit.

● **Tour companies & travel agents**
Viajes Ru-Mar, Alvarez 566, organizes day trips to Tafí del Valle, Quilmes etc, Sat, and Sun. Tours may be difficult to arrange out of peak season (eg Sept) owing to shortage of passengers.

● **Tourist offices**
In Plaza Independencia at 24 de Septiembre 484. For free tourist information, T 0800-5-8828.

● **Transport**
Local Car hire: Avis, *Hotel del Sol*, Plaza Independencia; **Liprandi**, 24 de Septiembre 524, T 311210/212665; **Movil Renta**, San Lorenzo

370, T 218635/310550, F 310080 and at airport; **Localiza**, San Juan 959, T 311352. **Car repairs**: Rubén Boss, Av Aconquija 947, rec esp for Volkswagen. **Motorists**: should not park on the street overnight; pay US$5 for garage parking.

Air Airport at Benjamín Matienzo, 15 km from town. Bus for each flight, US$1.50, starts from *Hotel Mayoral*, 24 de Septiembre 364. Taxi US$10. To Buenos Aires, AR, Lapa and Dinar. Austral to Córdoba, Salta (also Lapa and Dinar) and Jujuy.

Buses Modern bus terminal on Av Benjamín Araoz beside a huge shopping complex; to **Cafayate** (8 hrs, US$17) via Tafí and Santa María, Aconquija, daily at 0600 and 1400; direct to **Salta** (not via Cafayate), 4½ hrs, several daily, eg La Estrella, Veloz del Nte, US$18 (slow bus 5½ hrs). Plenty of buses to **Jujuy**, eg Veloz del Nte, 0900, 6 hrs. See note below on routes to Salta.

To **Buenos Aires**, Chevallier, La Estrella, Veloz del Nte, 16 hrs, all with toilet, a/c, bar, video, 3 stops; book in advance; fares US$48-70; to **Mendoza**, La Estrella, US$29 leaving 1300, 1400 and 2000 (14 hrs), via Catamarca, La Rioja, and San Juan; **La Rioja**, 7 hrs, US$15. To **Catamarca**, 5 a day with Bosio, plus other lines. To **Santiago del Estero**, US$7; to **Córdoba**, US$30, 7 hrs, many companies (inc Sol and El Tucumano Panamericano).

TUCUMAN TO SALTA

THE DIRECT ROUTE

Of the two routes from Tucumán to Salta, via Rosario de la Frontera and Güemes is quicker, but less scenic, than via the beautiful Quebrada de Cafayate.

ROSARIO DE LA FRONTERA

145 km N of Tucumán, a popular resort (with casino) from June to Sept (*Alt* 769m; *Phone code* 0876). 8 km away are sulphur springs.

Excursions About 20 km N is the historical post house, Posta de **Yatasto**, with museum, 2 km E of the main road; campsite. To **El Naranjo** (19 km) a Jesuit colonial town; church contains images and carvings made by Indians.

● **Accommodation A3** pp *Termas*, Route 34, T 81004, full board, rambling place, good food but many rooms without private bath (6 km from bus station), taxi US$1.50. About 1 km from *Hotel Termas* is *ACA hostería*, T 81143, opp is man-made lake owned by Caza y Pesca Club. **C** *Real*, Güemes, 185, T 81067, basic, clean, not all doors close.

● **Buses** To Tucumán, Güemes, Salta and Jujuy, frequent.

PARQUE NACIONAL FINCA EL REY

About 80 km N of Rosario de la Frontera, at Lumbreras, a road branches off Route 9 and runs 80 km NE to the Parque Nacional **Finca El Rey**, a 44,160 ha tropical forest and wildlife preserve set among 900-1,500m hills with clear streams (good fishing). It can also be reached from Salta (196 km) where there is a Park office, España 366, 3rd floor (helpful). Mosquitoes, ticks and chiggers thrive; take lotion.

● **Accommodation** None while *Hostería El Rey* is closed (it is due to be transferred to private hands). Camping is free, there are several tent sites, but few facilities. Horseback riding.

● **Transport** The access road is poor and fords the river 9 times; passable for ordinary cars except in the wet season. Best time to visit is winter (drier). There is no public transport to the park; ask the park office in Salta about alternatives, or take a tour from an agency, US$50pp for at least 6.

VIA CAFAYATE

TAFI DEL VALLE

46 km S of Tucumán Route 307 branches NW through a gorge with sub-tropical vegetation to **Tafí del Valle**. At Km 27 on this road is a statue to El Indio, with picnic area. Tafí del Valle (*Pop* 3,000, 97 km from Tucumán, not to be confused with Tafí Viejo which is 10 km N of the city) is known to archaeologists as a holy valley of the precolumbian Indian tribes. 10 mins from Tafí is Capilla Jesuítica y Museo La Banda in the 16th century chapel of San Lorenzo (open 0900-1200, 1400-1800 daily, US$1).

10 km S of Tafí del Valle are Dique El Mollar and, nearby, the menhir park of **El Mollar**, with 129 standing stones (collected in the early years of this centuy from various sites) and good views (best to visit am). Tafí del Valle and El Mollar are often shrouded in fog because of the dam.

Tours to El Mollar and Tafí are available from Travel Agencies in Tucumán, US$15 each for 4 people minimum. For tours throughout the NW from Tafí, contact Margarita and Bruno Widmer, T/F (0867) 21076, highly recommended.

● **Accommodation** **A3** *Hostería ACA*, T 21027, run down, restaurant, garden; **C** *Colonial*, T 21067, nr bus station, closed out of season, no singles, friendly, clean; **C** *Atep*, Los Menhires, nr bus station, D in winter, with bath, clean, friendly, rec; *Pensión*, opp *Colonial*, in billiard hall, ask in advance for hot water; **E** pp *hostal* run by Celia Correa, clean, nr church. Hotels and bungalows (**B**) at El Pinar del Ciervo. New hotel, *Luna Huaná* (no details). 1 km from the town at La Banda is **A1** *La Hacienda Le Pepe*, inc breakfast, English and French spoken, horses for rent. **Camping**: Autocamping *Los Sauzales*, T 21084, very clean, hot showers, rec.

● **Places to eat** *El Rancho de Félix*, rec; *El Portal de Tafí*, good, has video room (movies in summer only); *La Rueda*, at S entrance to village, inexpensive, rec; *Los Faroles*, pleasant cafe. Try local cheese.

● **Buses** To/from Tucumán, Aconquija, sit on left-hand side from Tucumán, 4 a day, 3½ hrs, US$9. To Cafayate 4 a day, 4 hrs, US$10. Tafí-El Mollar daily 1215, returns 1330, US$1.

NORTHWEST OF TAFI DEL VALLE

From Tafí the road runs 56 km NW over the 3,040m Infiernillo Pass and through attractive arid landscape to **Amaichá del Valle** which claims 360 sunny days a year. La Pachamama festival at end of pre-Lent Carnival. (**Accommodation** **B** *Hostería Provincial*, T 21019, full board, showers not always hot, clean and friendly, recommended; bus to Tucumán, US$7.)

From Amaicha the road is paved as far as the junction with Route 40 (15 km). A paved road also runs S from Amaicha 22 km to **Santa María** (*Pop* 18,000). Small archaeology museum on the plaza (Sarmiento 18). From Santa María Route 40 leads N to Cafayate (55 km) and S to Belén (176 km, see page 152).

● **Accommodation** **A3** *Plaza*, San Martín 350, T 20309, on plaza, clean, small rooms, slightly run down; **B** *Provincial de Turismo*, San Martín y 1 de Mayo, T 20240, friendly, rec, dining room, with bath; **C** *Res Alemán*, Quintana 13, T 20226, small rooms but clean, friendly, quiet. **Campsite**: Municipal campsite at end of Sarmiento.

● **Buses** leave from Belgrano 271 on main plaza. To Tucumán 6 hrs, 0220, 0800, US$8.50. To Cafayate, 4 hrs, daily at 0700 excluding Thur at 1030, US$10. Empresa Bosio goes to

Catamarca, Sat; via Tucumán Sun at 1230, 9 hrs; Cayetano to **Belén** 4 hrs, Mon, Wed, Fri at 0500.

From Santa María you can visit Cerro Pintado, 8 km, coloured sandstone mountains, and archaeological sites at **Fuerte Quemado**, 15 km N along Route 40, Loma Rica, 18 km, and Ampajango, 27 km S off Route 40.

None is as impressive as **Quilmes** (Tucumán) 37 km N, 5 km along a dirt road off the main Santa María-Cafayate road, 16 km from Amaicha del Valle. There are Inca ruins (dam, village and posting house – *tambo*), with splendid views and interesting cacti (guide 0700-1730, entry US$2). There is also a provincial archaeological museum.

● **Accommodation & services At Quilmes**: **A2** *Parador Ruinas de Quilmes*, T (0892) 21075, at the site, comfortable, underfloor heating in winter, a/c in summer, owners are tapestry and ceramics experts; shop selling good indigenous crafts, particularly textiles; good restaurant, bar, toilets and camping facilities.

● **Transport** For a day's visit take 0630 Aconquija bus from Cafayate to Santa María, alight at site, or take 0700 bus from Santa María; in each case take 1100 bus back to Cafayate. Taxi from Cafayate US$60 return.

CAFAYATE

Cafayate (*Pop* 8,432; *Alt* 1,660m; *Phone code* 0868) is a clean town, with low rainfall (none Mar-Oct), lying between two ranges of Andean foothills and surrounded by vineyards. A walk to Cerro San Isidro (3 hrs) takes you to a view of the Aconquija chain in the S to Nevado de Cachi in the N.

Vineyards

Cafayate is an important centre of wine production and home of several renowned *bodegas*. **La Rosa** owned by Michael Torino can be visited, Mon-Fri, 0800-1230, 1500-1830, weekends am only, no need to book, 30-min tours and tasting, reached by turning right 500m past the ACA *hostería*; **Etchart**, 2 km on Ruta 40 to Tucumán, also has tours (T 21310/2), Mon-Fri 0800-1200. **La Banda**, the oldest *bodega* in the valley (next to ACA *hostería*), is interesting because it is more primitive.

Museums

The **Museo de la Vidy El Vino** in an old *bodega* is on Av Güemes, 2 blocks S of the plaza, US$0.50, very well laid out. **Museo Arqueológico**, main plaza, local collection of the late Sr Rodolfi, pre-Inca funeral urns and 19th century domestic artefacts.

Local information

● **Accommodation**

Accommodation is hard to find at holiday periods (especially for a single person). **A3** *Briones*, Toscano 80, main plaza, T 21270, clean and comfortable, with bath and hot water, accepts Amex card; **A3** *Asembal*, Güemes y Almagro, T 21065, nice rooms with bath, good; **A3** *Asturias*, Güemes 158, T 21328, rec.

B *Hostería Cafayate* (ACA), T 21296, on N outskirts, modern, quiet (but cold), colonial-style, covered parking, good food, but restaurant may be closed; **B** *Gran Real*, Güemes 128, T 21016, without breakfast, pleasant, clean, rec.

C *Colonial*, Almagro 134, T 21233, charming patio; **C** *Confort*, Güemes 232, T 21091, with bath, clean, comfortable, member of Red Argentina de Alojamiento para Jóvenes; **C** *La Posta del Rey*, Güemes 415, T 21120, clean; **C** *Pensión Arroyo* (no sign), Niño 160, rec, friendly; **B** *Tinkunaku*, Diego de Almagro 12, 1 block from plaza, with bath, clean, friendly, rec; **C** *Vicano*, Toscana 273, clean, rec; **E** pp *Youth Hostel*, Av Güemes 441, T 21440, small, clean, hot water, friendly, stores luggage; another, **E** pp, at Buenos Aires 930, T 239910. Accommodation in private houses is available.

Campsite: Municipal campsite Lorohuasi at S access to town, hot water, swimming pool, well maintained, bungalows for rent, **D** for 4 people; private campsite to N of town, opp ACA *hostería*.

● **Places to eat**

Several good ones on the main plaza: *Cafayate*; *Confitería La Barra*; *El Gordo. La Carreta de Don Olegario*, Güemes y Quintana, rec; *El Criollo*, Güemes 254, clean, pricey, rec; *La López Pereyra*, Güemes 375, good food, friendly. Several *comedores* along Rivadavia (2 blocks N of Plaza), where the locals eat. Only the more expensive restaurants are open late.

● **Banks & money changers**

Banco de la Nación, main plaza, for cash, TCs and credit cards.

● **Shopping**

Handicrafts: locally woven tapestries are interesting and very expensive; visit the Calchaquí tapestry exhibition of Miguel Nanni on the main square. Also Platería of Jorge Barraco, Colón

147, for silver craft work. Oil paintings, wood-carving, metalwork and ceramics by Calixto Mamani can be seen in his art gallery at Rivadavia 452, or contact him at home at Rivadavia 254. Handicrafts in wood and silver by Oscar Hi-paucha on main plaza. Pancho Silva and his family have a workshop at 25 de Mayo selling and displaying their own and locals' handicrafts. Souvenir prices are generally high. Local pottery in the Mercado Municipal de Artesanía on the main plaza.

● **Tourist offices**
Kiosk on the main plaza.

● **Transport**
Rentals: bike hire from Rentavel, Güemes 175 US$2/hour, US$15/day. **Horses**: can be hired from La Florida, Bodega Etchart Privado (2 km from Cafayate on road to Tucumán) or from Tito Stinga (ask in village). **Buses** Aconquija bus to **Tucumán** daily at 0630, 8 hrs, US$15, also Sat 1500. Alternatively go to Santa María on 1100 El Indio bus, or 0630 Aconquija bus, 2 hrs, US$10, and then take bus to Tucumán. El Indio bus to and from **Salta** via the Quebrada de Cafayate, 3 a day, 4 hrs, US$12 (worth travelling in daylight); to **Angastaco** (El Indio) 1100 daily except Sun, US$4, sit on the right, leaves Angastaco for the return journey at 0630.

QUEBRADA DE CAFAYATE

Route 68 goes NE from Cafayate to Salta through the gorge of the Río de las Conchas (known as the **Quebrada de Cafayate**) with fascinating rock formations of differing colours, all signposted: Anfiteatro (a gorge), El Sapo, El Fraile, El Obelisco, Los Castillos. The road goes through wild and semi-arid landscapes with many wild birds, including *ñandúes*(rheas). North of the Quebrada is Col Moldes; Cabra Corral, one of the largest artificial lakes in Argentina, 81 km S of Salta; water skiing, fishing, no hotels, just a camping site, restaurant and sailing club; the **B** *Hostería Cabra Corral*, T 231965, is 4 km from the lake, Route 68, half board, swimming pool, 'delightful', recommended (paved road ends at the Presa Gen M Belgrano, impressive views of the bridge across the lake); El Carril. One way of seeing the Quebrada de Cafayate is by taking the El Indio bus for Salta as far as Los Loros, Km 32. From here you can walk back (and catch a returning bus from Salta); alternatively hire a bike

in Cafayate and take it on the early morning El INdio bus as far as Alemania (84 km) and then cycle back. **NB** The sun is very hot, take lots of water.

VALLES CALCHAQIES

North of Cafayate Route 40 runs 160 km through the Valles Calchaquíes to Cachi. The road is mainly gravel and can be very difficult after rain, but the views of the Andean-foothill desert country with its strange rock formations and unexpected colours, are fascinating. The population is largely Indian.

SAN CARLOS

About 24 km N of Cafayate, a small settlement (*Alt* 1,710m) destroyed four times by Indians. It has a pleasant white church completed 1854, a small archaeological museum There are artisans' shops and workshops, craft market near church.

● **Accommodation C** *Hostería*, T 218937. Municipal campsite.

● **Buses** To El Indio, on the Salta-Cafayate-Angastaco run, arrive in San Carlos by noon and on the return journey at 0745.

ANGASTACO

North of San Carlos Route 40 enters the Calchaquí valley and climbs to **Angastaco**, 50 km from San Carlos, 2 km off the main road. The road passes through the spectacular **Quebrada de las Flechas**, remarkable for its formations and colours, 5-10 km S of Angastaco. You can sample the local Vino Patero, red or sweet white, in a house close to the river bridge in Angastaco; *vino patero* is supposed to be made by treading the grapes in the traditional manner. The Fiesta Patronal Virgen del Valle is held on the second weekend of Dec, with processions, folk music, dancing, many gauchos and rodeos.

● **Accommodation C** *Hostería*, T 222826, negotiable in low season, good, cheap and delicious meals on request, has its own small but informative archaeological museum; **F** pp *Res El Cardón*, good, clean, comfortable.

● **Transport Buses** To Cachi and Salta, Fri, 1100 only; daily bus to San Carlos and Cafayate 0545 (Sat and holidays 0630). **Taxi**: to Molinos US$15.

MOLINOS

From the Angastaco turn-off it is 40 km on a winding road through beautiful and desolate rock formations to **Molinos**. The church, with its fine twin-domed bell-towers, built about 1720, contains the mummified body of the last Royalist governor of Salta, Don Nicolás Isasmendi Echalar. To protect it from visitors plucking its hair, this relic can no longer be viewed by the public. The priest is very knowledgeable about local history. A pleasant walk is down from the church, crossing a creek and then climbing a gentle hill, from which there are good views of Molinos and surrounding country.

● **Accommodation A3** *Hostería Molinos*, T 214871, rec, with breakfast, good meals, in Casa de Isasmendi, which also contains a small museum. *Sra de Guaymas* (known as 'Sra Silvia') runs a restaurant and rents rooms, **E**, double only, basic, clean. There are other rooms to rent around the main plaza.

● **Buses** To Salta via Cachi, Thur, Fri, Sat, Mon at 0645, also Mon, Wed, Thur, Sat at 1315, Marcos Rueda; 2 hrs to Cachi, US$4.50, 7 hrs to Salta. To Angastaco, Thur morning.

CACHI

From Molinos it is 46 km to **Cachi** (Quechua for 'salt'; *Alt* 2,280m), a beautiful little town renowned for its weaving, other crafts and invigorating climate. The church's roof and confessional are made from the wood of the *cardón* cactus. The Museo Arqueológico (open Mon-Sat, 0800-1800, Sun, holidays 0900-1200) presents a small but interesting survey of pre-colonial Calchaquí culture, US$1.

The Indian ruins at **Las Pailas**, 18 km W of Cachi, are barely excavated; in themselves, they are not especially impressive but the view is breathtaking, with huge cacti set against snow-topped Andean peaks. They can be reached on foot (4 hrs one way), or by bus from Cachi. Ask for directions or a guide in Las Pailas village.

● **Accommodation A3** *ACA Hostería Cachi*, T 210001, on hill above the town, good, clean, pleasant; **E** *Albergue Municipal*, also has good municipal campsite with swimming pool and barbecue pits, on hill at S end of town. **At Cachi Adentro**, 6 km W of Cachi, is the **B** *Hostal Samay Huasi*, a restored *hacienda*,

pleasant and helpful owners, heating and hot water at all times; **A1** *Finca El Molino de Cachi Adentro*, a restored working mill, beautiful views, horse riding, rec, minimum stay 3 days, book in advance, T 8039339, F 4762065 (Bs As), T 213968, F 233122 (Salta); 3 buses a day from Cachi. Hire horses in the village, US$5/hr. Fishing is also possible.

● **Buses** To Salta, 1400 daily (except Wed), also at 0900 Thur, Fri, Sat, Mon, 5 hrs, US$12; to Molinos 1200 daily; El Indio from Cafayate Thur am only, returning Thur pm.

CACHI TO SALTA

Follow Route 40 for 11 km N to Payogasta (new *Hostería*, clean), then turn right to Route 33. This road (gravel) climbs continuously up the Cuesta del Obispo passing a dead-straight stretch of 14 km known as La Recta del Tin-Tin with magnificent views of the **Los Cardones National Park** with the huge candelabra cacti, which grow up to 6m in height. (Elsewhere there are not many cacti left as they are used to make furniture.) It reaches the summit at Piedra de Molino (3,347m) after 43 km. Then it plunges down through the Quebrada de Escoipe. The road rejoins Route 68 at El Carril, from where it is 37 km. back to Salta.

North of Cachi Route 40 continues to San Antonio de los Colores via **La Poma**, 54 km, a beautiful hamlet (*Alt* 3,015m; *hostería*, **F**) and the Paso Abra de Acay (4,900m – the highest pass in South America negotiable by car, often closed in summer by landslides). This road is in very poor condition (no buses beyond La Poma).

SALTA

Situated on the Río Arias, in the Lerma valley, in a mountainous and strikingly beautiful district, Salta is capital of its province, founded in 1582, with fine colonial buildings. It is a great handicraft centre and the best starting place for tours of the NW. (*Pop* 370,000; *Alt* 1,190m; *Phone code* 087; from Bs As 1,600 km; from Güemes 148 km N of Rosario de la Frontera, Route 9 runs 43 km W through the mountains, to Salta).

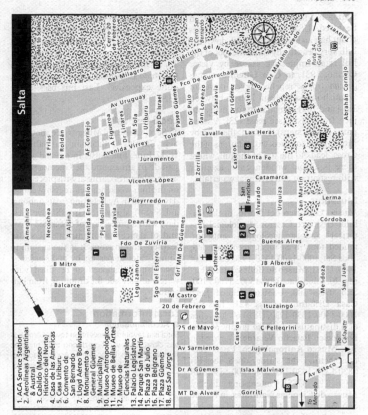

Salta

Places of interest

1. ACA Service Station
2. Aerolíneas Argentinas & Austral
3. Cabildo (Museo Histórico del Norte)
4. Casa de las Américas
5. Casa Uriburu
6. Convento de San Bernardo
7. LloydAéreo Boliviano
8. Monumento a General Güemes
9. Municipality
10. Museo Antropológico
11. Museo de Bellas Artes
12. Museo de Ciencias Naturales
13. Palacio Legislativo
14. Parque San Martín
15. Plaza 9 de Julio
16. Plaza Belgrano
17. Plaza Güemes
18. Res San Jorge

Places of interest

Follow the ceramic pavement plaques, or get map from Tourist Office, for an interesting pedestrian tour. The **Cathedral** (open mornings and evenings), on the N side of the central **Plaza 9 de Julio**, was built 1858-1878; it contains the much venerated images of the Cristo del Milagro and of the Virgin Mary, the first sent from Spain in 1592, and has a rich interior mainly in red and gold, as well as a huge late baroque altar. The miracle was the sudden cessation of a terrifying series of earthquakes when the images were paraded through the streets on 15 September 1692. They still are, each September. On the opposite side of the Plaza is the **Ca-**

bildo, built in 1783. The Convent of **San Bernardo**, at Caseros y Santa Fe, was built in colonial style in the mid-19th century; it has a famous wooden portal of 1762. Nuns are still living here so the inside of the convent is not open to visitors. **San Francisco** church, at Caseros y Córdoba, built in 1882, rises above the city centre skyline with its magnificent façade and red, yellow and grey coloured tower (open 0700-1200, 1730-2100, although the times are erratic).

East of the city centre is the **Cerro San Bernardo** (1,458m), accessible by cable car (*teleférico*), functions daily, 1600-2000, US$6 return, children US$3, from Parque San Martín, fine views. Near the *teleférico* station is a lake where rowing boats can be hired (US$3 for 20 mins). It takes about half an hour to walk back down the hill. Very beautifully set at the foot of the hill is an impressive **statue** by Víctor Cariño, 1931, **to Gen Güemes**, whose *gaucho* troops repelled seven powerful Spanish invasions from Bolivia between 1814 and 1821, which contains many objects from Tastil (see page 123). A steep path (1,136 steps) behind the nearby Museo Arqueológico, with Stations of the Cross, leads to the top of the hill, where there is an old wooden cross, together with restaurant and artificial waterfalls.

Museums

Museo Histórico del Norte, in the Cabildo Histórico, Caseros 549, colonial, historical and archaeological museum, guided tour in Spanish, recommended, Tues-Sat, 1000-1400, 1530-1930, Sun 1000-1400, US$1. **Museo de Bellas Artes**, Florida 20, Mon-Sat 0900-1300, 1700-2100, Sun 0900-1200, US$0.60 (closed Jan). **Casa Uriburu**, Caseros 421, Tues-Sat, 1000-1400, 1530-1930, US$0.60, has relics of a distinguished *salteño* family. **Museo Folclórico Pajarito Velarde**, Pueyrredón 106. **Museo Antropológico**, Paseo Güemes, behind the statue, open Tues-Fri 0830-1230, 1430-1830, Sat 1500-1830, Sun 1600-1830, US$1, interesting display. **Museo de Ciencias Naturales**, in Parque San Martín, has a full display of over 150 regional stuffed birds and an interesting display of armadillos, recommended, open Tues-Sun 1400-2000, US$0.25. **Museo de la Ciudad 'Casa de Hernández'**, La Florida 97, Tues-Sat, 0900-1230, 1600-2030. Check opening times in summer at tourist office; many close then.

Excursions

11 km NW of Salta is the wealthy neighbourhood of San Lorenzo (restaurant in high tower, *El Castillo*, good food and music, closed Mon, T 921052 for free taxi, 4-6 people); **A2** *Hostal Selva Montaña*, C Alfonsina Storni 2315, T 921184, luxurious, highly recommended; camping and picnicking beside rocky stream and natural woodland. Sibylle Oeschger and

Hansruedi Hintermann, T 921080, rent 1 room (**E** pp) and offer horseriding tours, US$24 pp/¹⁄₂-day. Hourly bus service from Salta terminal, Empresa Chavez, platform 15, 30 mins, US$1. Bus stops in front of *Quebrada* restaurant (good food, friendly, quite expensive). Last bus back about 2330.

Local festivals

15 Sept, Cristo del Milagro (see above); 24 Sept, Battles of Tucumán and Salta. On 16-17 June, folk music in pm and *gaucho* parade in am around the Güemes statue. Salta celebrates Carnival with processions on the four weekends before Ash Wednesday at 2200 in Av Belgrano (seats optional at US$2-4); also Mardi Gras (Shrove Tuesday) with a procession of decorated floats and of dancers with intricate masks of feathers and mirrors. It is the custom to squirt water at passers-by and *bombas de agua* (small balloons to be filled with water) are on sale for dropping from balconies.

Local information
● Accommodation

Salta is a favourite convention town. Some hotels close for a vacation during the Christmas season until Jan 10, so check. Accommodation is scarce in the last 2 weeks in July because of holidays and around 10-16 Sept because of the celebrations of Cristo del Milagro.

A2 *Salta*, Buenos Aires 1, in main plaza, T 21101/413, 1st class, pool, good restaurant; **A1** *Portezuelo*, Av Del Turista 1, T 310133, F 310133, breakfast extra, some rooms a/c, English, German, French, Italian spoken, pool, clean, helpful, good restaurant, rec; **A2** *California*, Alvarado 646, T 310266, 1 block from main plaza, rec; **A2** *Victoria Plaza*, Zuviría 16, T 310334, expensive but good restaurant, the foyer overlooking the plaza is one of the centres of *salteño* life.

A3 *Colonial*, Zuviría 6, T 310760, with bath, a/c, rec, but 1st floor rooms noisy; **A3** *Cristal*, Urquiza 616, T 222256, clean, helpful; **A3** *Las Lajitas*, Pasaje Calixto Guana 336, T 233796, modern, clean, good value, ACA reduction, rec; **A3** *Petit*, H Yrigoyen 225, T 213012, pleasant, small, friendly, expensive breakfasts, rooms around courtyard with small swimming pool, a/c extra, French spoken; **A3** *Regidor*, Buenos Aires 10, T 222070, English-speaking owner, good value lunch, clean, comfortable, friendly.

B *Astur*, Rivadavia 752, T 311305, with bath, rec; B *España*, España 319, T 217898, central but quiet, simple, rec; B *Florida*, Florida y Urquiza 718, T 212133, with bath, very friendly, clean, stores luggage, rec; B *Italia*, Alberdi 231, T 214050, next to jazz club/casino, very clean and friendly, rec; B *Res Elena*, Buenos Aires 256, T 211529, clean, friendly and quiet, 'charming', safe, try to get there early, even out of season; B *Res Balcarce*, Balcarce 460, T 218023, friendly, clean; *Res Provincial*, Santiago de Estero 555, T 219438, friendly, hot water; D pp *Res Crisol*, Ituzaingó 166, T 214462, hot water, clean; *Sanyor* San Martín 994, T 214440, clean, friendly, laundry facilities.

D pp *Res San Jorge*, Esteco 244 y Ruiz de los Llanos 1164 (no sign), T/F 210443, with or without bath (E single), parking, safe deposit, laundry and limited kitchen facilities, central heating, parking, homely, guide for climbing, horse-trekking advice by proprietor, also organizes local excursions by car, good value, highly rec (take buses 3 and 10 from bus station to San Martín y Malvinas); D *Casa de familia de María del Toffoli*, Mendoza 915 (about 10 blocks from bus station), T 21-7383, nice atmosphere, comfortable, clean, roof terrace, cooking facilities, rec, rooms also at Nos 917 and 919, D-C, belonging to Sra Toffoli's sisters (reservations at No 917), cosy, highly rec; also *Sra Dora de Batista*, Mendoza 947, T 310570. rec, laundry facilities, clean; E *Hosp Doll*, Pasaje Ruiz de los Llanos 1360 (7 blocks from centre), with bath, friendly, safe, rec. Many other cheap hotels nr railway station (eg E *Internacional*, Ameghino 651, hot water, basic, with good cheap restaurant), but few nr bus station.

Camping: Casino Provincial municipal grounds, by river, 300m artificial lake (popular Dec-Feb). Bus 13 to grounds. There is no signposting: leave the city heading S on C Jujuy, after 3 km you will see the Coca Cola plant on your left, turn left before the plant and then take the first road right. Charges US$3/tent plus US$2 pp. Free hot showers available if there is gas (not often), safe, bathrooms run-down, disappointing. At ACA's *Motel Huaico*, Bolivia y P Costas, T 310571. *Municipal Campsite* at Campo Quijano, 30 km W of Salta, at the entrance to Quebrada del Toro gorge, hot showers, bungalows, plenty of room for pitching tents, rec, bus from Salta bus terminal. Camping shops: *HR Maluf*, San Martín y Buenos Aires, and one at La Rioja 995.

Outside Salta: The *Finca San Antonio*, El Carril, T/F 908034, offers accommodation on a farm dating from 1621, pool, horseriding.

At **El Bordo**, 45 km E of Salta, Sr de Arias offers luxury accommodation on his finca, L3 pp full board; excursions also arranged. Contact: *Finca El Bordo De Las Lanzas*, 4432 El Bordo, Salta, T 310525.

Youth hostel: *Backpackers*, Buenos Aires 930, T 087-239910, bus 12 from bus terminal or 30 mins' walk, E pp in dormitories, laundry and kitchen facilities, stores luggage, information, bar, clean, hot showers, English, Greek and Hebrew spoken, friendly, frequently rec. E pp *No Me Olvides*, Av de los Pioneros, Km 0.800, shared rooms, cooking facilities, friendly, rec. NB Do not be tempted by touts at the bus station offering convenient accommodation.

● **Places to eat**

El Monumento, Gurruchaga 20 (opp Güemes monument), good food, slow service, good atmosphere, reasonably priced; *Maxims*, Mendoza y Florida, good; *La Posta*, España 476, food and atmosphere both excellent, reasonable prices, highly rec; *El Viejo Jack*, Virrey Toledo 145, good meat dishes, huge portions; *El Viejo Jack II*, Av Reyes Católicos 1465, gigantic servings of meat, reasonable prices; *Cantina*, Caseros y 20 de Febrero, pizzas, steaks; *9 de Julio*, Urquiza 1020, excellent lunch; *El Rescoldo*, Caseros 427, cheap lunches, rec; *Green Park*, Caseros 529, good snacks, and milk shakes; *El Mesón de Pepe*, Rivadavia 774, fish specialities, good but pricey. Several good places on Plaza 9 de Julio. Pleasant outdoor restaurants in Parque San Martín, at foot of Cerro San Bernardo; *Sociedad Española*, Balcarce 653, excellent cuisine; *de Pablo*, Mitre 399, excellent set lunch; *Alvarez*, Buenos Aires y San Martín, cafeteria style, cheap and good; *Casa de Té*, Paseo Alberdi 422, chocolate and cakes; *La Casona del Molino*, Caseros 2600, colonial house, good food and drink, good value, entertainment provided by guests; *Pub Yo Juan*, Balcarce 481, popular, live music at weekends; *Café del Paseo* at *Hotel Colonial*, Zuviría 6, open 24 hrs, superb breakfast, good value (ask for Té Paseo); *Heladería Gianni*, España 486, ask for *copa dell'Amore*, excellent coffee; *Cafe Río*, Mitre 40, good breakfasts. Cheap restaurants nr the railway and bus stations, which are also the cheapest places for breakfast. Many restaurants are lunch only, especially on San Martín nr the Municipal Market. Cheapest food is from the numerous *superpanchito* stalls. Good supermarket, *Disco*, on Alberdi y Leguizamon.

● **Airline offices**

Aerolíneas Argentinas, Caseros 475/485, T 310866; Austral, Caseros 475, T 310258; LAPA, Caseros 492, T 317080; Dinar, Buenos Aires 46, T/F 310606; Lloyd Aéreo Boliviano, Buenos Aires 120, T 217753 (will hold luggage and schedule a *colectivo* taxi).

● **Banks & money changers**
Banks open 0730-1300. **Banco de la Nación**, Balcarce y España; **Banco Provincial de Salta**, España 526 on main plaza, changes TCs, 2.5% commission; **Banco de Credito Argentino**, Urquiza, cash advance on Mastercard; **Banco de Galicia**, ATM for Visa cash advance; **Banco Roberts**, Mitre 143, good rates, changes cheques, 3% commission; **Amex**, Chicoana Turismo, Av Belgrano y Zuviria 255, does not cash TCs. Many *cambios* on España: **Cambio Dinar**, Mitre 101 (Plaza 9 de Julio and España 609), changes Amex cheques (3% commission) and cash (poor rates), long queues. **Maguitur**, España 666, only cash; **Golden Life**, Mitre 95 (Plaza 9 de Julio), local 1, first floor, best rates for cash. See also **Currency**, page 262, on *bonos*.

● **Cultural centres**
Alliance Française, Santa Fe 20, T 210827.

● **Embassies & consulates**
Bolivia, Los Almendros 161, T 223377, open Mon-Fri, 0900-1300 (unhelpful, better to go to Jujuy; **Chile**, Santíago del Estero, T 215757; **Peru**, 25 de Mayo 407, T 310201; **Spain**, Las Heras 1329, T 221420; **Italy**, Alvarado 1632, T 213881; **France**, Santa Fe 20, T 213336; **Germany**, Córdoba 202, T 216525, F 311772, consul Juan C Kühl, who also runs *Kuehl* travel agency and photo shop, helpful; **Belgium**, Pellegrini 835, T 233459.

● **Entertainment**
Music: folk music show and evening meal at *Boliche Balderrama*, San Martín 1126; *Gauchos de Güemes*, Uruguay 750; *Casa Güemes*, España 730. For something less touristy try *Manolo*, San Martín 1296. Some bars charge around US$7 pp for music, but don't display charges.

● **Laundry**
Sol de Mayo, 25 de Mayo 755, service wash. *Laverap*, Santiago del Estero 363 (open Sun am) good, fast service, US$6 for one load; *Marva*, Juramento 315; *La Baseta*, Alvarado 1170.

● **Post & telecommunications**
Post Office: Deán Funes 160, between España and Belgrano *poste restante* charges US$1.15/letter.
Telephone: Belgrano 824, 24 hrs; international calls at Vicente López 146, 0800-1930.

● **Shopping**
Mercado Municipal, corner of San Martín and Florida, for meat, fish, vegetables, *empanadas*, *humitas* and other produce and handicrafts, closed 1200-1700 and Sun. **Mercado Artesanal** on the outskirts of the city in the Casa El Alto Molino, a late 18th century mansion, at San Martín 2555, T 219195, Mon-Fri 0800-2000,

Sat 0900-2000 (sometimes closes in summer) take bus 2, 3, or 7 from Av San Martín in centre and get off as bus crosses the railway line. Excellent range of goods but expensive. Woodcarvings of birds etc from *Tres Cerritas*, Santiago del Estero 202. For objets d'art and costume jewellery made of onyx, visit *Onix Salta*, Chile 1663. *Feria del Libro*, Buenos Aires 83; *Librería Rayuela*, Buenos Aires 96, foreign-language books and magazines. Arts and handicrafts are often cheaper in surrounding villages.

Bicycles: *Manresa*, Pellegrini 824, imported equipment. Helpful mechanic, *S Fernández*, Urquiza 1051.

● **Tour companies & travel agents**
All agencies charge similar prices for tours: Salta city US$15; Quebrada del Toro US$18; Cachi US$45; Humahuaca US$50; San Antonio de las Cobres US$75; 2-day tour to Cafayate, Angastaco, Molinos, Cachi, US$80. Out of season, tours often run only if there is sufficient demand; check carefully that tour will run on the day you want. *Saltur*, Caseros 525, T 212012, very efficient and rec for local tours (no English-speaking guides). *Puna Expediciones*, Braquiquitos 399, T 212-797 (well experienced and qualified guide Luis H Aguilar can also be contacted through the *Res San Jorge*), organizes treks in remote areas, US$25 a day inc transport to trekking region, food, porters, highly rec. *Hernán Uriburu*, organizes trekking expeditions, Rivadavia 409, T 310605, expensive but highly professional. *Juan Kühl*, Córdoba 202, T 216525, F 311772 tours by light aeroplane, horseback, caravan, boat, German and English spoken, highly rec, also run photographic company.

● **Tourist offices**
Provincial Tourist Office (Emsatur), Buenos Aires 93 (one block from main plaza). Open every day, except Sun, till 2100. Very helpful, gives free maps. Municipal Tourist office, Buenos Aires 61, closed Sun, helpful, free maps. Both offices arrange accommodation in private houses in high season (July) and can arrange horse-riding, US$50 full day, US$30 ½-day inc horses, guide and meals, rec. Office at bus terminal, friendly, no maps.

● **Useful addresses**
Immigration Office: Maipú 35, 0730-1230.

● **Transport**
Local Car hire: Avis, Alvarado 537, T 216344, rec; **Rent A Car**, Caseros 489 and 221; local companies reported to be cheaper: **ALE**, Caseros 753, T 223469; **López Fleming**, Gral Güemes 92, T 211381, new cars, cheap, friendly; **Ruiz Moreno**, Caseros 225, in *Hotel Salta*, good cars, helpful; **Renta Autos**, Caseros 400, also

good. It may be cheaper and more convenient to hire a taxi for a fixed fee.

Air LAB to **Santa Cruz** (Bolivia) twice a week, once via Tarija. AR, Austral, Dinar and Lapa fly to **Bs As** (2 hrs, minimum) and **Tucumán; Austral** to **Córdoba**. Bus 22 to airport from San Martín. Also airport bus service to/from Aerolíneas Argentinas office on Caseros, 1 block from Plaza 9 de Julio, US$3; don't be fooled by taxi touts who tell you there is no bus. Taxi from airport to bus station US$7.

Trains For details of the Tren a Las Nubes and freight lines to Chile, see below. The surest direct route Salta-Antofagasta is by bus.

Buses Terminal is 8 blocks E of the main plaza (T 214716 for information). Behind terminal serving is a 24 Shell station serving cheap snacks, friendly. To **Buenos Aires**, several daily, US$80, 19 hrs (Atahuallpa, La Estrella, inc snacks, dinner and breakfast in restaurant, comfortable, rec, 4 daily) US$84 with La Veloz del Nte. To **Córdoba**, 4 a day, 12 hrs, US$41, Expreso Panamericano (T 212460), luxury service with hostess, twice daily, Veloz del Nte. To **Santiago del Estero**, 6 hrs, US$23. To **Tucumán**, 4 hrs, several firms (La Veloz del Nte rec, La Estrella), US$18. To **Puerto Iguazú**, via Tucumán, US$70. To **Mendoza** via Tucumán, several companies, daily, US$52, 20 hrs. To **Embarcación** daily with Atahualpa at 0700, US$14.50. To **Jujuy**, Balut Hnos, or Atahualpa hourly between 0700 and 2300, 'directo', US$7, 1¾ hrs; to **La Rioja**, US$33. To **Belén**, Wed, US$26.

Io **Cafayate**, US$10, 4 hrs, El Indio, 3 a day; to **Santa María**, El Indio, 6½ hrs, 0700. To **Cachi** (5 hrs, US$12), **Angastaco** (dep Thur 1300) and **Molinos** (7 hrs) Marcos Rueda daily (except Tues, Thur) at 1300, unreliable on Sun (sit on left). To **Rosario de la Frontera**, US$5, 2½ hrs, stewardess service, very pleasant trip. To **San Antonio de Los Cobres**, 5½ hrs, El Quebradeño,Mon-Sat 1600,Sun 1930, US$14. Extra service on Thur 1030 continues to the Tincalayu mining camp (arrives 2140), returning to Salta on Fri 1200, passing San Antonio at 1800. This bus is the only public transport going further into the puna than San Antonio.

To **Paraguay**: there is no direct bus from Salta to Asunción, but Salta provides the most reliable cheap land connection between Bolivia and Paraguay. Buses daily 1700, US$40 with La Veloz del Nte (20% reduction for students) Saenz Peña or Panamericano, 14 hrs to **Resistencia**, for crossing into Paraguay; for description of road, see page 178. Salta-**Formosa** with Atahualpa, which provides the quickest route to Asunción (change at Orán), operates only twice weekly because of the state of the road – Wed and Sun at 0630, 12 hrs, US$40.

To Chile: Services to Calama, San Pedro de Atacama (both US$39), and Antofagasta (US$50) are run by Géminis (behind bus terminal), Sat 1600 all year round, arduous 20 hrs to Antofagasta, 16 hrs to Calama. Bus can be caught in San Antonio de los Cobres, book ahead and pay full fare. Tramaca also has services to Calama (US$45), Tues and Fri in winter, plus Sun in summer, at 0700, 12 hrs, via Jujuy (0900) with three meals. Book well in advance, may be difficult to get a reservation, so try just before departure for a cancellation. Take warm clothes (at night ice sometimes forms on the insides of bus windows), a sheet to protect luggage against dust and food (**NB** Chilean customs will not allow fruit in). This route is usually closed for at least part of the winter and is liable to closure at other periods of the year.

Routes to Bolivia To La Quiaca, on Bolivian frontier, about 10 buses daily, Atahualpa (US$27), 11 hrs (via Jujuy, prolonged stop), can be very cold, dusty, not rec, best change to Panamericano in Jujuy. Buses also NE to **Orán** (see page 123), 6 hrs, and Aguas Blancas for Bermejo, Bolivia; thence road connection to Tarija. Also to Yacuiba, via **Pocitos** (Bolivian frontier, see page 142), for Santa Cruz, Bolivia, US$17 with Atahualpa to Pocitos, 7-10 hrs, very full, road paved.

FROM SALTA TO SAN ANTONIO DE LOS COBRES AND CHILE

SAN ANTONIO DE LOS COBRES

There is a 900 km long metre-gauge railway from Salta through the little town of **San Antonio de los Cobres** to Antofagasta, in N Chile. San Antonio (*Pop* 2,200; *Alt* 3,750m) is a squat, ugly mining town on a bleak, high desert. The inhabitants of this area are Coya Indians who bear a far closer resemblance to their cousins in Bolivia then to the Salteño lowlanders. A path leads to La Polvorilla railway viaduct (see below), 3 hrs, ask in town for details.

San Antonio can also be reached by Route 51 from Salta, which is being upgraded. From Campo Quijano it runs along the floor of the Quebrada del Toro (fords) before climbing the Abra Muñano in a long series of steep zig-zags (the section between Santa Rosa de Tastil and *Comedor Alfarcito* is very steep, not suitable for long vehicles).

At Santa Rosa de **Tastil** there are Indian ruins and a small museum (US$0.50), recommended. Basic accommodation next door to the museum, no electricity

Railway to the Clouds

🦶 The Argentine section of the railway to the Chilean frontier was engineered by Richard Maury, of Pennsylvania, who is commemorated by the station at Km 78 which bears his name. This remarkable project was built in stages between 1921 and 1948, by which time developments in road and air transport had already reduced its importance. No racks were used in its construction. The line includes 21 tunnels, 13 viaducts, 31 bridges, 2 loops and 2 zig-zags. From Salta the line climbs gently to Campo Quijano (Km 40, 1,520m), where it enters the Quebrada del Toro, an impressive rock-strewn gorge. At El Alisal (Km 50) and Chorrillos (Km 66) there are zig-zags as the line climbs the side of the gorge before turning N into the valley of the Río Rosario near Puerto Tastil (Km 101, 2,675m), missing the archaeological areas around Santa Rosa de Tastil. At Km 122 and Km 129 the line goes into 360° loops before reaching Diego de Almagro (3,304m). At Abra Muñano (3,952m) the road to San Antonio can be seen zig-zagging its way up the end-wall of the Quebrada del Toro below. From Muñano (3,936m) the line drops slightly to San Antonio, Km 196. The spectacular viaduct at La Polvorilla is 21 km further at 4,190m, just beyond the branch line to the mines at La Concordia. The highest point on the line is reached at Abra Chorrillos (4,475m, Km 231). From here the line runs on another 335 km across a rocky barren plateau 3,500-4,300m above sea level before reaching Socompa (3,865m).

or heating, take food, water and candles. Try the *quesillo de cabra* (goat's cheese) from Estancia Las Cuevas. Take El Quebradeño bus (see below), a tour from Salta, or share a taxi.

● **Accommodation A3** *Hostería de las Nubes*, edge of San Antonio on Salta road (T 087-909058, or Bs As 326-0126, Esmeralda 320), modern, inc breakfast, spacious, rec; **E** pp *Hosp Belgrano* (no sign) no heat; **C** pp *Hosp Los Andes*, breakfast extra, very friendly, both on main street and basic. Accommodation may also be available in the school.

● **Transport Buses** To Salta, El Quebradeño, daily except Thur and Sat, 5½ hrs, US$14; stops at Santa Rosa de Tastil (1130 basin). Two buses run in case of breakdown. **Trains** On all journeys on this line beware of *soroche* (altitude sickness): do not eat or drink to excess.

The Tren a las Nubes (Train to the Clouds) runs between Salta and La Polvorilla viaduct. The service operates every other Sat from April to Oct, weather permitting, and on additional days in the high season (July/Aug), depart 0700, return to Salta 2215, US$95, without meals, credit cards not accepted, US$250 from Buenos Aires (planned to run every Sat throughout the year). The train is well-equipped with oxygen facilities and medical staff as well as a restaurant car and snack bar. Explanations are available in English, Spanish, French and Italian. This service is operated privately and cannot be booked through Ferrocarriles Argentinos. Book in advance (especially in high season) through *Movitren*, Caseros 441, Salta, T 216394, F 311264, *Veloz del Nte*, Esmeralda 320, p 4, T 326-9623, Bs As, or through any good travel agency. It can be very difficult get on the train from Salta as it is often booked up from Buenos Aires. **Freight trains** still run on the line to Chile, but they no longer carry passengers, at least officially. A train leaves Salta Wed only about 1015 for San Antonio, 12 hrs, and Socompa, 26 hrs; passengers are not allowed to board this train, but boarding may be possible in Campo Quijano and Rosario de Lerma, which can be reached by bus from Salta 1800 (ask in the brake van and offer the guard yerba mate, sugar and cigarettes). Long delays are common on this route and you may do the entire journey in the dark. Take food, water and warm clothing.

Beyond Socompa there are irregular freight trains into Chile (Augusta Victoria, Baquedano or Antofagasta): officially the Chilean railway authorities do not permit passengers to travel on this line. To travel on by train or truck may involve a wait of several days. There is no food or accommodation, but try the Chilean customs building.

INTO CHILE BY ROAD

The road from San Antonio de los Cobres to San Pedro de Atacama now uses the Sico Pass, which runs parallel to the old Huaytiquina Pass (4,200m). Fork left just before Catúa, cross the border at **Sico** (4,079m) and continue via Mina Laco and

Socaire to Toconao (road very bad between these two points) where the road joins the Huaytiquina route. It is a very beautiful trip: you cross salt lakes with flamingoes and impressive desert. The road on the Argentine side is very good, but most traffic prefers the more northerly Jama Pass. Gasoline is available in San Pedro and Calama. Because of snowfalls, this route may be closed 2-3 times a year, for 2 or 3 days each time. A car must be in very good condition to cope with the heights. Ask the *gendarmes* in San Antonio de los Cobres about road conditions, and complete exit formalities there; entry formalities must also be carried out at San Antonio (no facilities at border). **NB** Hitchhiking across the Andes from here is not recommended.

JUJUY

The direct road **from Salta to Jujuy**, Route 9 via La Caldera and El Carmen, is picturesque with its winding 92 km subtropical stretch, now paved, known as *la cornisa* (huge trees and unexpected plants). The longer road, via Güemes, is the better road for hitchhiking.

San Salvador de Jujuy (pronounced Hoo-hooey) often referred to by locals as San Salvador, is the capital of Jujuy province and is completely surrounded by wooded mountains. The city (*Pop* 182,000; *Alt* 1,260m; *Phone code* 0882) was founded first in 1561 and then in 1575, when it was destroyed by the Indians, and finally established in 1593.

History The province of Jujuy bore the brunt of fighting during the Wars of Independence: between 1810 and 1822 the Spanish launched 11 invasions down the Quebrada de Humahuaca from Bolivia. In Aug 1812 Gen Belgrano, commanding the republican troops, ordered the city to be evacuated and destroyed before the advancing Spanish army. This event is marked on 23-24 Aug by festivities known as El Exodo Jujeño with gaucho processions and military parades. As a tribute to the city for obeying his orders, Belgrano donated a flag which is displayed in the Sala de la Bandera in the Casa de Gobierno.

Places of interest

In the eastern part of the city is the **Plaza Belgrano**, a fine square lined with orange trees. On the S side of the plaza stands the **Casa de Gobierno**, an elaborate French baroque-style palace (open Mon-Fri, 0800-1200, 1600-2000, but not always). On the W side is a colonial **Cathedral** with very fine 18th century images, pulpits, walls and paintings finished about 1746. It has been heavily restored, but in the nave is a superb wooden pulpit, carved by Indians and gilded, a colonial treasure without equal in Argentina. On C Lavalle you can see the doorway through which Gen Lavalle, the enemy of Rosas, was killed by a bullet in 1841, but the door is a copy; the original was taken to Buenos Aires. The **Teatro Mitre** is at Alvear y Lamadrid. In the western part of the city are the **Parque San Martín** and an open space, **La Tablada**, where horses, mules and donkeys used to be assembled in caravans to be driven to the mines in Bolivia and Peru. See the **Palacio de Tribunales** near the river, one of the best modern buildings in Argentina. Streets are lined with bitter-orange trees.

Museums

Museo Histórico Provincial, Lavalle 250, open daily 0830-1230, 1500-2000, including display of colonial art and history of Gen Lavalle; **Museo de Paleontología y Mineralogía**, part of the University of Jujuy, Av Bolivia 2335, Mon-Fri 0800-1300. **Museo de Bellas Artes**, Güemes 956, Mon-Fri, 0800-1200, 1700-1900. **Police Museum**, in the Cabildo, Mon-Fri 1000-1300, 1500-2100, Sat 1030-1230, 1830-2100, Sun 1830-2100; **Museo de la Iglesia San Francisco**, Belgrano y Lavalle, including 17th century paintings from Cuzco and Chuquisaca. The **Estación Biológica de Fauna Silvestre**, Av Bolivia 2335, is open to the public on Sun (for private tours on other days, contact Dr Arturo A Canedi, T 25617-25845), very interesting.

Excursions

19 km W of Jujuy is **Termas de Reyes**,

where there are hot springs. This resort, with the *Hotel Termas de Reyes* (**A3** with breakfast, or half-board, **A2** full board, restaurant, friendly, T 0882-35500), is set among magnificent mountains 1 hr by bus from Jujuy bus terminal, 6 times a day between 0630 and 1945, returning 0700-2040, US$1. US$3 to swim in the thermal pool at the hotel (weekends US$5); municipal baths US$1, open daily 0800-1200 and 1400-1700 (Thur 1400-1700 only). Free camping below the hotel. Cabins for rent beside river, **F** pp, shower and thermal bath.

Local festivals

Festival on 6 November. El Exodo Jujeno, 23/24 Aug (hotels fully booked).

Local information
● Accommodation

Panorama, Belgrano 1295, T 30183, 4-star, highly-regarded; **A2** *Augustus*, Belgrano 715, T 22668, 3-star, modern, comfortable but noisy; **A2** *Internacional*, Belgrano 501 (main plaza), T 22004; **A3** *Fenicia*, 19 de Abril 427, T 28102, quiet.

A3 *Avenida*, 19 de Abril 469, T 22678, on riverside, with good restaurant (**C** off season, cafeteria only); **A3** *Hostería Posta de Lozano*, Route 9, Km 18, friendly, clean, good restaurant, pools with fresh mountain water, covered parking; **A3** *Sumay*, Otero 232, T 22554, central, clean; **A3** *Alto La Viña*, Route 56, Km 5, T 26588, attractive, swimming pool, bus US$0.35 from town.

B *Res Los Andes*, Siria 456, T 24315, clean, hot water, a bit prison-like. Opp is **B** *Res San Carlos*, Siria 459, T 22286, modern, friendly, some rooms a/c, parking.

Budget Accommodation: **C** *Belgrano*, Belgrano 627, T 26459, old fashioned, hospitable, clean, noisy; **C** *Chung King*, Alvear 627, T 28142, friendly, dark, very noisy, many mosquitoes, good restaurant. Near the bus terminal only, **C** *San Antonio*, Lisandro de la Torre (opp), modern, clean, highly rec; **D** *Res Río de Janeiro*, Av José de la Iglesia 1536, very basic, clean, bit run down; **D** *El Aguila*, Alvear 400, basic.

Camping: *Autocamping Municipal*, US$4/tent, ask for a cheaper rate for one person, 14 km N of Jujuy on Humahuaca road. *Autocamping*, 3 km N outside city at Huaico Chico. Buses 4 or 9 frequent. Hot showers (if you remind the staff), clothes washing facilities, very friendly.

● Places to eat

El Cortijo, Lavalle y San Martín, interesting salads, good vegetarian food, reasonably priced; *Sociedad Española*, Belgrano y Pérez, elegant setting; *Bar La Royal*, Belgrano 770, good but expensive; *Restaurant Sirio Libanesa*, Lamadrid 568 (don't be put off by the uninviting entrance); *La Victoria*, Av El Exodo 642, away from centre, good; *Confitería Carena*, Belgrano 899, old-fashioned, good for breakfast; *La Ventana*, Belgrano 751, good cheap menu, good service, à-la-carte menu is expensive; *La Rueda*, Lavalle 320, good food and service, very popular, expensive; *Krysys*, Balcarce 272, excellent atmosphere; *La Pizzería*, Alvear 921, warm welcome, pleasant atmosphere; *Ruta 9*, Costa Rica 968, Barrio Mariano Moreno (take taxi), good local food, Bolivian owners. Cheaper places behind bus terminal on Santiago del Estero and Alem. Very good ice cream at *Helados Xanthi*, Belgrano 515, made by Greek owner. *Opus-Café*, Belgrano 856, good coffee, music and atmosphere. Good bread and cake shop at Belgrano 619. Good sandwiches at *Rada Tilly*, 2 locations on Belgrano.

● Banks & money changers

At banks: **Banco de la Provincia de Jujuy**, Lavalle, gives cash against Mastercard, no commission, also changes dollars; **Banco de Galicia**, Alvear, US$10 commission on Amex TCs; **Horus**, Belgrano 722, good rates for cash, no cheques; **Dinar**, Belgrano 731, 4% commission on TCs. Travel agencies on Belgrano also change cash and TCs. Thomas Cook TCs cannot be changed. If desperate, ask the dueña of the *confitería* at bus station, rates not too unreasonable. (See note on provincial bonds used as currency, page 235.)

● Embassies & consulates

Bolivia, Patricinio Argentino 641, T 23156, price of visa should be US$5, pay no more; **Spain**, R de Velasco 362, T 28193; **Italy**, Av Fascio 660, T 23199; **Paraguay**, Tacuarí 430, T 28178.

● Entertainment

Chung King, Alvear 627, live music and dancing at weekends.

● Laundry

Laverap, Belgrano y Ramírez de Velazco.

● Post & telecommunications

Post Office: at Independencia y Lamadrid, in Galería Impulso, Belgrano 775.

Telecom: Senador Pérez 141, open 0700-0100.

● Shopping

Handicrafts are available at reasonable prices from vendors on Plaza Belgrano nr the cathedral; *Regionales Lavalle*, Lavalle 268; *Centro de Arte y Artesanías*, Balcarce 427; *Librería*

Rayuela, Belgrano 636; *Librería Belgrano*, Belgrano 602, English magazines and some books; *Farmacia Avenida*, Lavalle y 19 de Abril, 0800-2400.

● **Tour companies & travel agents**
Many along Belgrano: *Alicia Viajes*, No 592, T 22541; *Giménez*, No 775, T 2924; *Turismo Lavalle*, No 340; *Pasajes Turismo* No 722; *Grafitti*, No 731 All offer tours along the Quebrada de Humahuaca, 12 hrs, US$25; *Be Dor Turismo*, No 860 local 8, 10% for ISIC and youth card holders on local excursions.

● **Tourist offices**
Belgrano 690, T 28153, very helpful, open till 2000.
    For information on bird watching, contact Mario Daniel Cheronaza, Peatonal 38, No 848-830, Viviendas 'El Arenal', Jujuy.

● **Useful addresses**
Migración: Antardida 1365

● **Transport**
Air El Cadillal, 32 km SE, T 91505; Tea Turismo vans leave *Hotel Avenida* to meet arrivals, 1 hr, US$4.50. Service to **Buenos Aires** by Austral, 1 flight a day direct with bus connection to Tartagal (in the NE of the province) via San Pedro and Embarcación. Austral also flies to **Salta, Santiago del Estero, Tucumán** and **Córdoba**.

Buses Terminal at Iguazú y Dorrego, 6 blocks S of centre. Young boys charge US$1 for loading luggage. To **Buenos Aires**, US$89, several daily with Balut, La Estrella, La Internacional. Via Tucumán to Córdoba, with Panamericano and La Veloz, daily; **Tucumán** 5 hrs, US$25, and **Córdoba**, 14 hrs US$45; to **Puerto Iguazú**, 2 a week, US$80, 30 hrs. To **Salta** hourly from 0700, 2¾ hrs, US$7. To **La Quiaca**, 6½ hrs, Panamericano (best) and Atahualpa, US$21.50, road paved only as far as Humahuaca, reasonably comfortable, but very cold at night. To **Humahuaca**, US$7, 3 hrs, sit on left side. To **Orán** daily at 1700; to **Embarcación**, US$7 with Balut, via San Pedro and Libertador San Martín. Jujuy-**Purmamarca-Susques**, leaves Purmamarca at 1330 on Wed and Sat, returning Thur and Sun, crossing the Abra Potrerillos (4,164m) and the Salinas Grandes of Jujuy. To **Tilcara** 1½ hrs, US$5.

To Chile via the **Jama** pass (*Alt* 4,200m), the route taken by most traffic crossing to northern Chile. In this region, the only accommodation is poor lodging at **Susques**, 105 km N of San Antonio de los Cobres on a road through utter desert. Buses from Jujuy to Antofagasta via San Pedro de Atacama and **Calama** (15 hrs), Tramaca, Tues and Fri, US$50 inc cold meal, breakfast; to **Iquique**, Wed and Sat, Panamericano, US$50. Check weather conditions in advance.

NORTH FROM JUJUY: THE ROUTE TO LA QUIACA

NB For drivers heading off main roads in this area, note that service stations are far apart: (there are ACA stations at Jujuy, Humahuaca and La Quiaca, and YPF stations at Tilcara and Abra Pampa. Spare fuel and water must be carried.

QUEBRADA DE HUMAHUACA

Route 9, the Pan-American Highway, runs through the beautiful Quebrada, which has a variety of rock colours and giant cacti in the higher, drier parts. In the rainy season (Jan-Mar) ask the highway police about flooding on the roads.

Beyond Tumbaya, where there is a church originally built in 1796 and rebuilt in 1873, a road runs 5 km W to **Purmamarca**, a very popular, picturesque village overlooked by a mountain: seven colours can be distinguished in the rock strata (arrive before noon when sun is in the E). At the entrance to Purmamarca a right turn leads to a new gravel road, which leads through another *quebrada* over a 4,170m pass to the Salinas Grandes salt flats at about 3,500m on the Altiplano (fantastic views especially at sunset). In the winter months, on both sides of the road, three different ancient types of salt mining by hand can be seen. There are also spectacular rock formations on this road which leads SW past the salt flats to San Antonio de los Cobres.

● **Accommodation Purmamarca: E** pp *Ranchito del Rincón*, Sarmiento, new, clean, owners Yolanda and Zulma are friendly and helpful, highly rec; also 2 rooms in shop, **F** pp, friendly, ask at the police station for the address, *comedor* on main square has good, cheap, local food.

About 7 km N of the turn is La Posta de Hornillos, a museum in a restored colonial posting house, of which there used to be a chain from Buenos Aires to the Bolivian border (open, in theory, Wed-Mon 0900-1800, free). 3 km further is **Maimará** (**C** *Pensión La Posta*, clean and friendly, the owners' son is a tourist guide and has helpful information, 5 km from Maimará).

TILCARA

22 km N of Purmamarca. The Museo Archaeológico here, attached to the University of Buenos Aires, contains a fine collection of precolumbian ceramics from the Andean regions of present day Argentina, Chile and Peru, open Tues-Sun 0900-1200, 1500-1800, highly recommended, US$2, free entry Tues. Admission includes a reconstruction of a *pucará*, or Inca fortified village (2 km from the museum), set in botanical gardens containing only high altitude and Puna plants. Beautiful mountain views, recommended. There are excellent craft stalls and shops around the main plaza, selling ponchos, sweaters and wooden items.

Local festivals *Fiestas* on weekends in January.

● **Accommodation** B *Hotel de Turismo*, Belgrano 590, swimming pool, usually dry; D *El Antigal*, Rivadavia, pleasant, good restaurant, colonial style, stores luggage, rec; E *Hostería La Esperanza*, spacious room, arranges walking tours; E *Res Frami*, nr hospital. **Youth hostel**: E *Malka*, San Martín s/n, 4 blocks from plaza. **Private houses**: E Juan Brambati, San Martín s/n, comfortable, hot water, meals, highly rec, also does tours. Also at Radio Pirca, E pp, 3 blocks from plaza, use solar energy. **Camping**: Municipal campsite, dirty; *Camping El Jardín*, US$5, clean, hot showers.

● **Places to eat** *Pucará*, good value; *Café del Museo*, good coffee.

The colonial churches of Huacalera, Uquía, and Humahuaca are on the main road. 2 km before Huacalera, a sundial 20m W of the road gives the exact latitude of the Tropic of Capricorn. At **Huacalera** is the B *Hotel Monterrey*, friendly but run down. At **Uquía** (church built 1691, with *cuzqueño* paintings), the walls of the naves are hung

with 17th century paintings of winged angels in military dress: the so-Called *ángeles arcabuceros*. Cactus-wood decoration is found in many local churches.

All along the Quebrada de Humahuaca the pre-Lent carnival celebrations are picturesque and colourful. In Tilcara and Humahuaca pictures of the Passion are made of flowers, leaves, grasses and seeds at Easter and a traditional procession on Holy Thursday at night is joined by thousands.

HUMAHUACA

The town dates from 1594 but was almost entirely rebuilt in the mid 19th century. (129 km N of Jujuy; *Pop* 4,000; *Alt* 2,940m.) It is an attraction for coach trips from Salta and Jujuy; few tourists stay for more than a couple of hours, but it is an attractive and peaceful centre from which to explore the Quebrada de Humahuaca.

Places of interest

The **church, La Candelaria**, originally built in 1631, was completely rebuilt in 1873-80; it has a bell from 1641. A mechanical figure of San Francisco Solano blesses the town from **El Cabildo**, the neo-colonial town hall, at 1200. Overlooking the town is the massive **Monumento a la Independencia Argentina**, built in 1924 and sited here because the valley was the scene of the heaviest fighting in the country during the Wars of Independence. There is a good **Feria Artesanal** on Av San Martín (on the far side of the railway line), but avoid the middle of the day when the coach parties arrive.

Colonial Churches of the North

Lovers of old churches will find Salta and Jujuy excellent centres. Franciscan and Dominican friars arrived in the area from Bolivia as early as 1550. The Jesuits followed about 1585. Some churches can be found along the old Camino de los Incas (now non-existent), eg Susques and Coranzulí. Many more are on or near the Panamericana through the Quebrada de Iturbe. The padres, in the course of two centuries, built simple but beautiful churches, of which about 20 survive. They are marked by crosses on the map on page 110. All of them can be visited by car from Salta or Jujuy, though some of the roads are very rough.

Museums

Museo La Casa, Buenos Aires 296, next to the post office, open daily 1000-2000, US$3, guided tours in Spanish only, offers a fascinating insight into social customs in the mid-19th century, recommended; **Museo Ramoneda**, Salta y Santa Fe, private collection of contemporary art; **Museo Arqueológico Municipal**, at one side of Independence monument, Mon-Fri 0800-1200, 1400-1700; **Museo Nicasio Fernández Mar**, Buenos Aires, opposite *Hotel de Turismo*, memorial to the sculptor, open daily, free. **Museo Folklórico Regional**, Buenos Aires 435, run by Sixto Vásquez, US$10 including guide.

Excursions

To **Coctaca**, 10 km NE, where there is an impressive and extensive (40 ha) series of pre-colonial agricultural terraces.

Local festivals

2 Feb, La Candelaria.

Local information

● **Accommodation**

C *Provincial de Turismo*, Buenos Aires 650, I 12, run down, poor service, modern building sadly out of keeping with surroundings; **C** *Res Humahuaca*, Córdoba y Corrientes, 1 block N of bus station, some a/c, traditional, clean, friendly, rec; **C** *Res Colonial*, Entre Ríos 110, nr bus terminal, T 21007, with bath, some windowless rooms, clean, laundry facilities.

Camping: across bridge by railway station, small charge inc use of facilities.

Youth hostel: **E** pp *Albergue Humahuaca*, Buenos Aires 447, T 21064 clean, laundry and very limited cooking facilities,cafeteria, cold, special price for ISIC and youth card holders. Offers tours, all with accredited local guides to popular and lesser-known sites, horse riding, trekking, local festivals, also to the Pacific via Lagunas Colorada and Verde (Bolivia) and the Ruta de Che Guevara (Bolivia).

● **Places to eat**

Most restaurants open only during the day, difficult to find breakfast and the mediocre restaurant at the bus terminal is often the only place open in the evenings. *La Cacharpaya*, Jujuy 295, excellent, pricey, Andean music; *Humahuaca Colonial*, Tucumán 22, good regional cooking, good value, but invaded by coach parties at midday; *El Rancho*, Belgrano s/n, just around the corner from market, lunches only, where the locals eat.

● **Banks & money changers**

Bank. Try the handicraft shops on the main plaza, or the *farmacia* at Córdoba 99. Better rates at Youth Hostel, but best to change elsewhere. Credit cards are not accepted anywhere.

● **Tourist offices**

Kiosk in main plaza in high season.

From Humahuaca Route 9 runs to La Quiaca on the Bolivian border. 20 km N of Humahuaca, at the turn off to Yrigoyen and Iruya, the paving ends and the road runs across the the bleak and barren *puna*.

IRUYA

An unpaved road runs NE from the Panamericana 8 km to **Yrigoyen** (railway station called Iturbe; **F** *Pensión El Panamericano*, basic) and then over the 4,000m Abra del Cóndor before dropping steeply into the Quebrada de Iruya. **Iruya** (*alt* 2,600m), 66 km from Humahuaca, is a beautiful walled village wedged on a hillside. It has a fine 17th century church and Rosario festival on first Sun in October.

● **Accommodation & places to eat F** pp *Albergue Belén*, very basic; **F** pp *Hosp Tacacho*, clean, friendly, *comedor*, on the plaza. Food at *Comedor Iruya*.

It is worthwhile staying in Iruya for a few days; it makes an extremely pleasant and friendly centre for horseback or walking trips (take sleeping bag). At Titiconte 4 km away, there are unrestored pre-Inca ruins (take guide). *Puna Expediciones* (see Salta page 122) runs a 7-day trek, Salta-Iruya-Nazareno-La Quiaca, walking between Iruya and Nazareno on small, remote paths where there are no tourists or motor vehicles, sleeping in local schoolhouses; rest of route is by truck. The trips to Iruya offered by *pensiones* in Humahuaca are overpriced.

● **Buses** Daily bus service from Jujuy and Humahuaca to Yrigoyen by Panamericano, 1400 and 1900, 45 mins; in Yrigoyen you may be able to get a seat on a truck. Empresa Mendoza bus from Humahuaca, 0730, Mon, Wed and Sat, 3½ hrs' journey, US$7 one way, waits 2-3 hrs in Iruya before returning; service varies according to time of year and is suspended in rainy season (esp Feb and Mar) details from *Almacén Mendoza*, Salta y Belgrano, Humahuaca.

ABRA PAMPA AND WEST OF THE HIGHWAY

Abra Pampa, an important mining centre (*Pop* 4,000), is at Km 91 on the Panamericana (**F** pp *Res El Norte*, Sarmiento 530, shared room, clean, hot water, good food).

Laguna Pozuelos (*Alt* 3,650m) 50 km NW of from Abra Pampa, is a flamingo reserve and natural monument. Bus daily at 1030 excluding Sun via the mines at Pan de Azúcar and Rinconada, 4 hrs, US$3, dropping you at the park ranger station. If driving, the Laguna is 5 km from the road; walk last 800m to reach the edge of the lagoon. Temperatures can drop to -30°C in winter; if camping warm clothing, drinking water and food are essential. By car it is possible to drive N along the E side of the Laguna via Cienaguillas to reach La Quiaca. 15 km from Abra Pampa is the vicuña farm at Miraflores, the largest in Argentina. Information offered, photography permitted; colectivos go am Mon-Sat from Abra Pampa to the vicuña farm.

From a point 4 km N of Abra Pampa roads branch W to Cochinoca (25 km) and SW to **Casabindo** (62 km). 'On 15 Aug at Casabindo, the local saint's day, the last and only *corrida de toros* in Argentina is held amidst a colourful popular celebration. The event is called *El Toreo de la Vincha*; in front of the church a bull defies onlookers to take a ribbon and medal which it carries.' The Casabindo church itself is a magnificent building, sometimes called 'the cathedral of the Puna'. (Federico Kirbus). La Quiaqueña bus daily on Route 40 from Jujuy to La Quiaca via Casabindo.

LA QUIACA

A concrete bridge joins the Argentine frontier town to its Bolivian neighbour, Villazón. The border is 292 km N of Jujuy (*Alt* 3,442m; *Phone code* 0885). Warm clothing is essential particularly in winter when temperatures can drop to -15°C, though care should be taken against sunburn during the day. Most commercial activity has moved to Villazón because everything is much cheaper in Bolivia.

Excursions

Yavi, with the fine church of San Francisco, which has magnificent gold decoration and windows of onyx (1690), is 16 km E of La Quiaca, reached by a good, paved road; taxi available – US$25 return, including 1 hr wait. (Find the caretaker at her house and she will show you round the church, open Tues-Sun 0900-1200 and Tues-Fri 1500-1800.) Opposite this church is the house of the Marqués Campero y Tojo. Only a precarious road for trucks and pick-ups leads on to the two churches of Santa Victoria (a forlorn Indian village in a rain forest valley) and Acoyte.

At **Santa Catalina**, 67 km W of La Quiaca, along a poor road, there is also a 17th century church. (Bus from Jujuy to Santa Catalina via La Quiaca, 19 hrs, Mon and Fri.)

Local festivals

On the third Sun in Oct the Manca Fiesta, or the festival of the pots, is held here, and the Colla Indians from Jujuy and the Bolivian *altiplano* come, carrying all sorts of pots.

Local information
● **Accommodation**

B *Turismo*, Siria y San Martín, T 2243, rec, clean, modern, comfortable, hot water 1800-2400, heating from 2030-2400 in winter, restaurant; **C** *Cristal*, Sarmiento 543, T 2255, clean and comfortable, friendly, with café and bus office adjacent; **C** *Victoria*, opp railway station, clean, good hot showers; *Alojamiento Pequeño*, Av Bolívar 236, friendly, cheap, clean; **C** *La Frontera* hotel and restaurant, Belgrano y Siria, downhill from Atahuallpa bus stop, good; **E** *Res Independencia*, rec, nr railway station and church, hot water but no room heating even in winter.

Camping: is possible nr the control post on the outskirts of town; also at the ACA service station about 300m from the frontier.

● **Places to eat**
Sirio-Libanesa, nr *Hotel Frontera*, good, cheap set meal.

● **Banks & money changers**
No facilities for changing TCs. Rates are better in Villazón.

● **Hospitals & medical services**
There is a good hospital in La Quiaca. *Farmacia Nueva*, ½ block from Church, has remedies for *soroche* (mountain sickness).

● **Transport**
Buses from new terminal, Av España y Belgrano. Difficult to obtain information in La Quiaca about buses leaving Villazón for points in Bolivia (see Bolivia, **South from La Paz** for Villazón); 6-8 buses a day to **Salta** (US$27) via Humahuaca and Jujuy with change in Jujuy (5 hrs to Humahuaca, 6 hrs to Jujuy, 10 hrs to Salta). Panamericano, 5 a day to **Jujuy**, US$21.50, 6½ hrs, some meal breaks, but take own food, as sometimes long delays. Buses may be stopped and searched for coca leaves; to **Buenos Aires**, via Jujuy, US$89 inc meals, 28 hrs.

FRONTIER WITH BOLIVIA

● **Argentine immigration and customs**
The frontier bridge is 10 blocks from La Quiaca bus terminal, 15 mins' walk (taxi US$1). Offices open 0800-2000 (signature needed from customs officer, who may be out for lunch); on Sat, Sun, and holidays there is a special fee of US$3 which may or may not be charged. Buses arriving outside these hours will have to wait, so check before travelling. You can cross the border at night, without luggage, and your passport will not be stamped.

If leaving Argentina for a short stroll into Villazón, show your passport, but do not let it be stamped by Migración, otherwise you will have to wait 48 hrs before being allowed back into Argentina.

NB Argentine time is 1 hr later than Bolivia.

● **Entering Argentina**
Formalities are usually very brief at the border but thorough customs searches are made 100 km S at Tres Cruces.

● **Bolivian consulate**
Travellers who need a visa to enter Bolivia are advised to get it before arriving in La Quiaca.

NORTHEAST FROM JUJUY

SAN PEDRO DE JUJUY

A sugar town (*Pop* 60,000) 63 km from Jujuy. The Ingenio La Esperanza, on the outskirts, is a sugar-mill with hospital, housing and a recreation centre, formerly owned by the English Leach brothers.

● **Accommodation B** *Hotel Alex 2*, R Leach 467, T 20269, private bath, fan, clean; *Alex I*, Tello 436, T 20299; **E** *Vélez Sarsfield*, V Sarsfield 154, T 20446.

● **Places to eat** Excellent restaurant at *Sociedad Sirio-Libanesa* on the plaza.

● **Transport** Buses to Jujuy, US$2.50, 1½ hrs; to Embarcación, Atahualpa, US$6.50, 2½ hrs.

PARQUE NACIONAL CALILEGUA

Libertador (formally Libertador Gen San Martín), another sugar town 50 km N of San Pedro, is a base for exploring the **Parque Nacional Calilegua**, an area of peaks and sub-tropical valleys, reached by dirt road from just N of the town. There are over 200 species of bird here including the very rare black and chestnut eagle and the red-faced guan and 60 species of mammal including tapir, puma, deer and otters. The two highest peaks in the park are Cerro Amarillo (the tallest at 3,720m with Inca ruins at the top) and Cerro Hermoso. Condors and taruca deer may be seen. The first park ranger's house is at Agua Negra. (Camping nearby; drinking water from river nearby, and some cooking facilities and tables). The ranger, Angel Caradonna, and his wife, Mony, are very friendly and knowledgeable. Mony sells hand-painted T-shirts featuring the park's wildlife. 13 km further along the trail is the 2nd ranger house, at Mesada de las Colmenas (ask permission at the 1st ranger house to camp here). 10 km from here is the N boundary of the park, marked by an obelisk, and where the most interesting birds can be seen.

● **Park services** Park headquarters are on San Lorenzo s/n, in Calilegua, 4 km from Libertador, T (0886) 22046. The park entrance is 10 km along the dirt road (hitching from Libertador possible), which climbs through the park and beyond to Valle Grande (no accommodation, basic food supplies from shops), 90 km from Libertador. From here it is possible to walk to Humahuaca and Tilcara (allow at least 3 days; these walks are described in *Backpacking in Chile and Argentina* by Bradt Publications).

● **Accommodation** At Libertador: **E** *Res Gloria*, Urquiza 270, clean, hot water; **E** *Ledesma*, Jujuy 473 just off plaza, friendly, large rooms but no keys, local radio station opp so can be noisy.

● **Places to eat** *Sociedad Boliviana*, Victoria 711, where the locals eat.

● **Banks & money changers** On Plaza San Martín, **Banco Roberts** changes dollars at a good rate.

● **Tourist offices** At bus terminal.

● **Transport** Trucks run by Empresa Valle Grande, Libertad 780, leave Libertador, Tues, and Sat, 0730, 6 hrs if road conditions are good, very crowded, returning Sun and Thur 1000. Check with Sr Arcona (the driver, everyone knows him) who lives opposite the railway station in Libertador whether the truck is going. Weather is unpredictable. Or contact Gustavo Lozano at Los Claveles 358, Barrio Jardín, T 21647, who will contact Angel Caradonna to pick you up.

ROUTES TO BOLIVIA

1 VIA POCITOS

From Libertador, Route 34 runs NE 244 km, to the Bolivian frontier at Pocitos and Yacuiba (see **Eastern Bolivia**, page 347).

The road goes via **Embarcación** (*Pop* 24,000; *Phone code* 0878), 101 km NE of Libertador. 2 km from Embarcación you can walk to the Loma Protestant mission for Mataes and Toba Indians, who sell unpainted pottery.

● **Accommodation & places to eat** C *Punta Norte*, España 277, clean, a/c friendly. Restaurant of *Sociedad Sirio-Libanesa*, H Irigoyen and 9 de Julio, cheap and good.

● **Transport** Buses to Orán, 1 hr, US$1.70 on a paved road; to Pocitos change at Tartagal, making sure your ticket is stamped with the next bus time or you won't be allowed on it; to **Buenos Aires** US$91; to **Salta** US$14.50, 3 a day. To **Formosa** daily at 1300, 17 hrs, US$40, Atahualpa, but frequently cancelled; alternative is to take bus to Pichanal, US$1.25, several, change for JV Gonzales, US$10, 1600, and change again for Resistencia, 2215, then take a bus to Formosa and Clorinda.

74 km N of Embarcación is **Tartagal** (*Pop* 70,000), an agricultural centre with a small museum featuring displays on animals of the Chaco and regional folk art. The director, Ramón Ramos, is very informative about the region. Animal masks and pottery are made by Indians nearby at Campo Durán.

● **Accommodation** *Argentino*, San Martín 54, T 21327, 3-star; *Espinillo*, San Martín 122, T 21007; *Res City*, Alberdi 79, T 21558.

The border town of **Pocitos** is 56 km N of Tartagal (E *Hotel Buen Gusto*, just tolerable). From Yacuiba, across the border, buses and trains go to Santa Cruz de la Sierra. Customs at Pocitos is not to be trusted (theft reported) and overcharging for 'excess baggage' on buses occurs.

2 VIA AGUAS BLANCAS

At Pichanal, 100 km NE of Libertador, 16 km before Embarcación, Route 50 heads N to **Orán**, an uninteresting place (*Pop* 34,000).

● **Accommodation** B *Gran Hotel Orán*, Pellegrini 617, T 21214; and several *residenciales*, inc C *Res Crisol*, López y Planes, hot water, friendly, rec.

There are frequent buses to **Aguas Blancas** on the frontier (53 km; no accommodation, nowhere to change money and Bolivianos are not accepted S of Aguas Blancas; restaurants include *El Rinconcito de los Amigos*; also shops). The passport office is open from 0700 to 1200 and 1500 to 1900. Insist on getting an exit stamp. There is no exit tax. Buses run twice daily from Bermejo, across the river (ferry US$0.50), to Tarija (10 hrs).

● **Transport** Buses between Aguas Blancas and Orán run every 45 mins, US$2, luggage checks on bus. From **Aguas Blancas** direct buses to Güemes, 8 a day, US$10; through buses to **Salta**, Veloz del Nte and Atahualpa, 3 daily each, US$17.50. From Orán to **Salta**, 7-10 hrs, 6 daily; direct bus to **Tucumán** at 2130, connecting for Mendoza bus which leaves at 1300; to **Jujuy** at 1200 daily; to **Formosa**, US$28, 14 hrs, leaving Tues, Thur, Sat at 0930; to **Embarcación**, US$3; to **Tartagal** daily at 0630 and 1800. There is no direct bus from Orán to Asunción, Paraguay; take bus to Embarcación, change for to Formosa, then change again for Asunción.

The West: San Luis, Mendoza, San Juan, La Rioja and Catamarca

FROM THE PAMPA to the heights of Aconcagua and the Uspallata Pass, en route to Santiago. Mendoza is a centre of wine making, fruit growing, winter sports (several ski resorts nearby) and climbing.

In the Cuyo region, in the W, there is little rain and nothing can be grown except under irrigation. The two most important oases in this area of slight rainfall are Mendoza itself and San Rafael, 160 km to the S. Of the 15 million ha in Mendoza Province, only 4% are cultivated. Of the cultivated area 40% is given over to vines, 25% is under alfalfa grown for cattle, and the rest under olive groves and fruit trees. Petroleum is produced in the Province, and there are important uranium deposits.

NB No fresh fruit, vegetables or cold meats may be brought into the provinces of Mendoza, San Juan, Río Negro or Neuquén.

ROUTE 7 TO SAN LUIS

256 km W of Buenos Aires across the pampa, **Junín** (*Pop* 63,700; *Phone code* 0362) is close to lagoons from which fish are taken to the capital. Eva Perón was born near the city.

● **Accommodation A2** *Copahue*, Saavedra 80, T 23390, F 29041, faded, ACA discount; *Embajador*, Sáenz Peña y Pellegrini, T 21433.

● **Places to eat** *Paraje del Sauce*, Km 258 on Route 7, picturesque, good food but 'don't stop there if you are in a rush'. *El Quincho de Martín*, B de Miguel y Ruta 7, good.

At Rufino (*Pop* 15,300), 452 km from Buenos Aires, is the recommended **L3** *Hotel Astur*, Córdoba 81, C with ACA discount; also at **Laboulaye**, 517 km from Buenos Aires, there are several good and cheap hotels, eg *Victoria*, and **B** *Motel Ranquel Mapu*, Km 489, very good, bottled water supplied.

SAN LUIS PROVINCE

VILLA MERCEDES

At **Villa Mercedes** (*Pop* 77,000; *Phone code* 0657), the old municipal market (Chacabuco y Mitre) is now an arts and community centre.

● **Accommodation & places to eat** ACA hotel **B** *San Martin*, Lavalle 435, T 22358, restaurant, garages, clean, friendly. The ACA restaurant at the service station on Route 7, outside town (just before junction with Route 8), is very good value. Cheaper places on Mitre, eg **C** *Res Cappola*, No 1134, clean, rec.

● **Transport Air** Airport at Villa Reynolds, 10 km from Villa Mercedes. **Buses** To Buenos Aires US$28.

VILLA MERCEDES TO CORDOBA

Route 8 runs NE to (122 km) Río Cuarto (*Pop* 110,000) in Córdoba province.

Route 148 runs N through San José del Morro, near a group of mountains which were originally volcanoes (there is a model in the Museo de Ciencias in Buenos Aires). You will find a lot of rosequartz. A short detour W, 70 km NE of San Luis, is **La Toma** (**C** *Hotel Italia*, Belgrano 644, T 21295, hot showers; the cheapest place to buy green onyx. From here you can make an excursion to Cerros Rosario, interesting hills and rock scenery, 10 km NW. Route 148 continues N to Villa Dolores (see page 108).

Provincial route 1 parallels Route 148 to the E; a scenic road through a string of pretty villages like Villa Larca, Cortaderas and Carpintería. Almost at the San Luis-Córdoba border is **Merlo**, (*Alt* 700m) some 150 km N of Villa Mercedes, a small town on the western slopes of the Sierra de Comechingones. It enjoys a fresher climate than the pampas in summer, and the area is being promoted for its rich wildlife, particularly birds. There are many walks (eg the climb to Cerro Linderos Alto via the hill with a cross; the Circuito de Damiana Vega, 3-4 hrs) and excursions to balnearios, waterfalls and other attractions. The tourist office is on the main plaza and the bus station 3 blocks away.

8 km N of Merlo is **Piedra Blanca**, a small settlement in attractive surroundings.

● **Accommodation** In Merlo and nearby are many hotels, *hosterías* and *residenciales*. **A2** *Rincón del Este*, T 75306, 3-star, 5 km from centre, rec. Others in Piedra Blanca.

● **Transport** Frequent buses to **San Luis**; TAC to **Buenos Aires** at 1800, US$35.

SAN LUIS

About 65 km W of Villa Mercedes, the rolling hills of San Luis begin; beyond there are stretches of woodland.

San Luis, 98 km from Villa Mercedes, is the provincial capital (*Pop* 150,000; *Alt* 765m; *Phone code* 0652). It stands at 765m at the S end of the Punta de los Venados hills. It was founded by Martín de Loyola, the governor of Chile, in 1596, and is still faintly colonial. The area is rich in minerals including onyx.

Places of interest

Visit the Centro Artesanal San Martín de Porras, run by the Dominican fathers, on 25 de Mayo, opp Palacio de Gobierno, where rugs are woven. Open 0700-1300 excluding Sat and Sun.

Excursions

A 'Via Crucis' sculptured in white marble skirts the mountainside at Villa de la Quebrada, 35 km N. Beyond Salto Grande, Salto Colorado and the Gruta de la Virgen

de las Flores is El Volcán (12 km; *balneario*, walks, picnics; *Hotel Andrea*) in whose neighbourhood is Cruz de Piedra dam (drives, fishing). Hotels and inns along the road.

Local information
● **Accommodation**

Several on Pres Illia: *Quintana*, No 546, T/F 29548, 4-star, best; **A2** *Aiello*, No 431, T 25639, F 25694, a/c, private bath, garages, rec; *Gran San Luis*, No 470, T 25049, pool, 50m from ACA; *Gran Hotel España*, No 300, T 25051. *Intihuasi*, La Pampa 815 (behind Casa de Cultura), spotless, very friendly, TV, lounge, highly rec (price unknown); **C** *Rivadavia*, Estado de Israel 1470, T 22437, with bath, hot water, friendly, opp bus station; next door is *17 de Octubre*, which should be avoided, basic, dirty.

16 km from San Luis is **L3** *Hotel Potrero de los Funes*, (0652) 30125/20889, F 23898 or BsAs 313-4886, F 312-3876 (25 de Mayo 516, p 11), a luxury resort and casino on lake of the same name, which has its own microclimate (sports and watersports, lovely views but upkeep a little lacking).

Camping: Rio Volcán, 4 km from town.

● **Places to eat**
The majority close at weekends; hotel restaurants are closed Sun, *San Luis'* closes Sat too. *El Cantón de Neuchatel*, San Martín 745, opp Cathedral on main plaza, is open Sun, modest. *Michel*, Lafinur 1361, good food and service.

● **Banks & money changers**
Very difficult to change TCs, try **Banco de Galicia**, Rivadavia y Belgrano, 1.5% commission.

● **Tourist offices**
Junín, opp Post Office, excellent.

● **Transport**
Bus terminal at Vía España between San Martín y Rivadavia.

SAN LUIS TO CORDOBA

Route 146 runs N from San Luis towards Córdoba through Villa de la Quebrada, San Francisco del Monte de Oro, Luján and Villa Dolores. An alternative is to take Route 9 via Trapiche (**A2** *Hostería Los Sauces*, bus from San Luis, US$4 return) to Carolina. A disused goldmine can be seen at Carolina, allegedly put out of action deliberately in the 1970s, in an attempt to force up the world price of gold. A statue of a gold miner overlooks the main street of what has become a ghost town. Near Carolina, at Gruta de Inti-huasi, a natural arch forms a cave in which the mummified body of a child was found, estimated to be 8,500 years old. 4WD vehicles can drive up Tomolasta mountain (2,000m) to see typical San Luis landscapes. From this road the Cuesta Larga descends to San Francisco. Route 146 then continues to Villa Dolores.

SIERRA DE LAS QUIJADAS

This national park, in the NW of the province can be reached from the San Luis Encón, San Juan road (Route 147). The area contains interesting geological formations, evidence of dinosaurs and pterosaurs, archaeological remains and flora and fauna of a traditional zone between wooded sierra and open, chaco-type terrain. The park is 97 km from San Luis.

MENDOZA

Beyond San Luis Route 7 climbs to 460m before descending to the valley of the Río Desaguadero, the provincial boundary with Mendoza. **Mendoza**, at the foot of the Andes, is an expanding and very pleasant city. Rainfall is slight, but irrigation has turned the area into an oasis of fruit trees and vineyards. The city was colonized from Chile in 1561 and named in honour of the then governor of Chile. It was from here that the Liberator José de San Martín set out to cross the Andes, to help in the liberation of Chile. Mendoza was completely destroyed by fire and earthquake in 1861, so today it is essentially a modern city of low dwellings (as a precaution against earthquakes), thickly planted with trees and gardens.

BASICS *Population*: of city 148,000, but with suburbs included, about 600,000. *Alt*: 756m. *Phone code*: 061. 1,060 km from BsAs; 264 km from San Luis. *Annual average temperature*: 19°C (summer 24°; winter 7°). *Annual average rainfall*: 236 mm.

Places of interest

See the **Cerro de la Gloria**, a hill above the great **Parque San Martín** on the W side of the city, crowned by an astonishing **monu-ment to San Martín**. There is a great rectangular stone block with bas-reliefs depicting various episodes in the equipping of the Army of the Andes and the actual crossing. In front of the block, San Martín bestrides his charger. In the park at the foot of Cerro de la Gloria steep and twisting paths run to the **Jardín Zoológico** (US$1). Nearby in the park there are watercourses and a 1 km-long artificial lake, where regattas are held, and views of the Andes (when the amount of floating dust will allow) rising in a blue-black perpendicular wall, topped off in winter with dazzling snow, into a china-blue sky. The entrance to the Parque San Martín is 10 blocks W of the Plaza Independencia, reached by bus 110 from the centre. An hourly bus ('Oro Negro') runs to the top of the Cerro de la Gloria from the E end of the park, on Av Libertad – it's a long walk (45 mins).

The best shopping centre is **Av Las Heras**, where there are good souvenir, leather and handicraft shops. **Plaza Pellegrini** (Av Alem y Av San Juan) is a beautiful small square where wedding photos are taken on Fri and Sat nights.

Tours

Official tours of the city are generally poor value. A large sign in Plaza Independencia shows a walking tour which takes about 2 hrs. There is also a bus service (Bus Turístico) which tours the city, with commentary from the driver. There are 14 stops and tourists can alight or join the bus at any point; the US$10 ticket is valid for 24 hrs (the service operates 1000-2000). Stops are clearly marked and the municipal tourist office issues a map. The bus waits for 15 mins at Cerro de la Gloria.

Museums

Museo Histórico San Martin, Av San Martín 1843, open Mon-Fri, 0900-1200, 1700-2000, US$1; **Museo del Pasado Cuyano**, Montevideo 444, beautifully furnished, has a collection on San Martín and history of Mendoza, open Mon-Fri 0930-1230, Tues and Thur, 1600-1730, but times vary; US$0.50; **Museo de Ciencias Naturales** and **Museo Arqueológico** (in the Ciudad Universitaria), Playas Serranes,

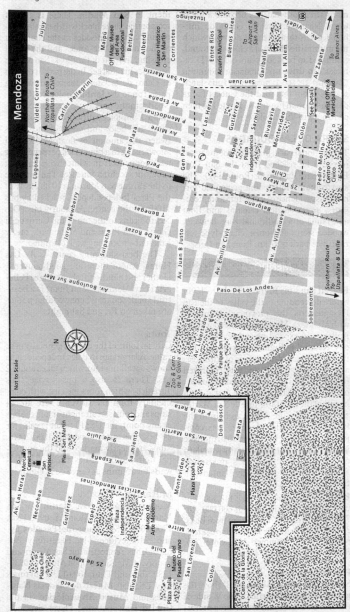

Mendoza

Not to Scale

Videla Correa

Jul22

Malipú
Off Map: Museo
del Área
Fundacional

Beltrán

Alberdi

Museo Histórico
San Martín

Corrientes

Iturzaingo

Carlos Pellegrini

Northern Route To
Uspallata & Chile

L. Lugones

Jorge Newberry

Suipacha

M De Rozas

T Benegas

Cnel Plaza

Av Mitre

P Mendocinas

Av España

Av San Martín

Entre Ríos

Acuario Municipal

Buenos Aires

To
Airport &
San Juan

Garibaldi

Av L N Alem

Av R Videla

Av Zapata

To
Buenos Aires

Gen Paz

Perú

Av Las Heras

Gutiérrez

Sarmiento

Rivadavia

Montevideo

Av Colón

San Juan

See Detail

Tourist Office &
Municipalidad

Espejo

Plaza
Independencia

25 de Mayo

Chile

Pedro Molina

Centro
Cívico

Av. Belgrano

Belgrano

Av. Juan B Justo

Av. Emilio Civit

Av. A. Villanueva

Paso De Los Andes

Sobremonte

Southern Route
To
Uspallata & Chile

Av. Boulogne Sur Mer

Av. Libertador

Parque San Martín

To
Zoo & Cerro
de la Gloria

Cerro de la Gloria

N

Detail

Av. Las Heras

Mercado

Cementerio

San
Francisco

Plaza San Martín

9 de Julio

Av. San Martín

Don Bosco

P de la Reta

Zapata

Necochea

Gutiérrez

Espejo

Av. España

Sarmiento

Patricias Mendocinas

Plaza
Independencia

Museo de
Arte Moderno

Montevideo

Plaza España

Perú

25 de Mayo

Chile

Av. Mitre

Rivadavia

Museo del
Pasado Cuyano

San Lorenzo

Colón

Plaza Chile

Plaza Italia

Parque San Martín, Tues-Fri 0900-1200, 1400-1800, Sat-Sun 1500-1900; **Museo Municipal de Arte Moderno**, underground (subsuelo) in Plaza Independencia, US$1.50, very small unless there is a special exhibition. The **Acuario Municipal** is underground at Buenos Aires e Ituzaingó, small but worth a visit, US$0.50, open Mon-Fri 1000-1200 and 1530-2000, Sat and Sun same times am. **Museo del Area Fundicional**, Alberdi y Videla Castillo, history of Mendoza, Tues-Sat 0800-1400, 1630-2230, Sun pm only, contains the mummified body of a child found on Aconcagua, US$2, recommended. Across Ituzaingó from the museum are the ruins of the Jesuit church of **San Francisco**, part destroyed in the 1861 earthquake (Ituzaingó y Beltrán).

On the road S of the city to Luján de Cuyo (buses go every 15 mins from near bus terminal) is the excellent Museo Provincial de Bellas Artes Emiliano Guiñazu, **Casa de Fader**, dedicated to Argentine artists, surrounded by sculpture in gardens, admission US$1.50, open Tues-Fri 0930-1330, 1500-1900, Sat, Sun 1630-2030, T 960224.

Wine

Wine *bodegas* (wine-making season Mar/April) and fruit preserving; visiting times available from Tourist Office. To *La Colina de Oro* (ex-*Giol*) winery, one of the world's biggest, take 150 or 151 bus marked 'Maipú' (every hour, 0900-1230, 1500-1800), but check if winery is open before going, T 972090. The tour is recommended in season. Also in Maipú district is *Peñaflor*, on Mitre, T 972388, bus 170, good visit and generous tasting. *Ruttini*, Coquimbito, Maipú, T 973590, a small bodega, is worth visiting, bus 170, tours 0900-1100, 1600-1800, tasting, Museo del Vino (fascinating), open Mon-Fri 0800-1100, 1500-1800. (In Maipú itself see the lovely square and eat at the *Club Social*, good simple food.) *Bodega Escorihuela* (bus 'T' G Cruz from centre Belgrano 1188, Godoy Cruz, T 220157); *Santa Ana*, Roca y Urquiza, Guaymallén, T 211000, visits 0800-1700; *Chandon*, Ruta Provincial 15, Km 29, T 980830, phone for appointment

0900-1700. The *Toso* bodega at JB Alberdi 808, T 380244, is small, old-fashioned, has excellent wines and an interesting, free guided tour, some tasting, highly recommended. The *Orfila* bodega in San Martín, T (0623) 20637, 40 km E, located in the house of the Liberator, also has a wine museum. Prices at the bodegas have roughly a 100% mark-up from supermarket prices. Many tourist agencies including the bodegas in their ½-day or day-long tours (US$4-8 but these visits are too short, with too few guides and little tasting – only of the cheaper wines, usually in plastic cups).

Excursions

TAC and Uspallata buses run to the hot springs at **Cacheuta**, US$3.15 round trip, US$8 entry (indoor thermal baths for a variety of ailments, for residents only), 45 km to the SW (**L** *Hotel Termas*, T 316085, full board; campsite, T 259000).

About 50 km N of Mendoza are the hot springs at **Villavicencio**, visited by many tourists. Pleasant walks in the area.

Local holidays

18 Jan (Crossing of the Andes); 25 July (Santiago Apóstol); 8 Sept (Virgin of Carmen de Cuyo). The wine vintage festival, Fiesta de la Vendimia, is held in the amphitheatre of the Parque San Martín at the end of March. Hotels fill up fast. Prices rise at this time, and in July (the ski season) and Sept (the spring festival).

Local information

● **Accommodation**

L3 *Aconcagua*, 4-star, comfortable, San Lorenzo 545, T 204455, F 311085, good but expensive restaurant, pool, disappointing, tourist advice and bookings available; *Huentala*, Primitivo de la Reta 1007, T 240766, 4-star, good.

In our A2-3 range: *Crillón*, Perú 1065, T 245525, F 248079, small, clean but overpriced; *Plaza*, Chile 1124 on main plaza, T/F 233000, not too clean, but obliging; **A2** *Nutibara*, Bartolomé Mitre 867, T 295428, F 296628 (discounts for cash), central, colour TV, a/c, parking, no breakfast, modern swimming pool, rec; *Palace*, Las Heras 70, T 234200, a/c, bath, inc breakfast, central; *San Martín*, Espejo 435, T 380677, rec; *Vecchia Roma*, España 1615, T 232529 (next door to restaurant of same name), comfortable, safe; **A3** *Balbi*, Las

Heras 340, T 233500, F 380626, small swimming pool, a/c, nice rooms; **A3** *Argentino*, Espejo 455, Plaza Independencia, T 254000, breakfast inc, quite comfortable; **A3** *1 de Mayo*, Garibaldi 80, T 204296; highly rec, breakfast inc; *Royal*, 9 de Julio 1550, T 380522/380675, breakfast inc, friendly, a/c, rec; *Center*, Alem 547, T 241184, with bath, very clean; *Imperial*, Las Heras 84, T 234671, washing facilities, friendly, rec, may offer cheaper price.

In our price range B: *City*, Gen Paz 95, T 251343, inc breakfast, clean, helpful; *Vendimia*, Godoy Cruz 101, T 250675, F 233099, good; *Petit*, Perú 1419, T 232099, without breakfast, 1½ blocks from railway station, clean, friendly, rec; *Pacífico*, San Juan 1407, T/F 235444, modern, comfortable, clean; *Milena*, Pasaje Babilonia 17 (off San Juan nr Don Bosco), T 200284, 2-star, clean, nice atmosphere; *Balcarce*, San Martín 1446, T 252579, clean, safe, very friendly, inc breakfast; *El Libertador*, España 247, T 290921, good; *Las Viñas*, Av Martinez de Rosas 1668, T 232501, clean.

The following are in our C range: *Galicia*, Av San Juan 881, nr Av LM Alem, T 202619, very clean, hot water, use of kitchen, rec; *San Remo*, Godoy Cruz 477, T 234068, clean, quiet, central, stores luggage, secure parking, highly rec; *El Piño Azul* apartments, San Martín 2848 (T 304240); *Mayo*, 25 de Mayo 1265, T 254424, inc breakfast, good value; *Zamora*, Perú No 1156, T 257537, reasonable and friendly.

On Juan B Justo: *Gutelcas* (No 67), T 252811, with bath, a/c and heating, good, snack bar; *Ideal* (No 270, T 256842), transport to bus station; *Hosp Ambajador*, No 365, T 259129, with bath, a/c, good value.

Necochea, Necochea 541, T 253501, pleasant, cheerful, English spoken; *Res Alberdi*, Alberdi 51, T 234110, family run, friendly, clean; *Quijote*, Av San Juan 1407, clean, friendly, restaurant; *Escorial*, San Luis 263, T 254777, very friendly and clean, rec.

Camping: in Parque Gen San Martín permitted, free. Three campsites at El Challao, 6 km W of the city centre, reached by colectivo No 11 leaving every hour, *Atsa*, friendly, swimming pool, good service, caters for families; noisy at weekends with disco; *Camping Suizo*, modern with pool, barbecues, hot showers, friendly, rec; *Saucelandia*, at Guaymallén, 9 km E of Mendoza. White gas (*bencina blanca*) can be bought at *Ferreteria Alsina*, Catamarca 37.

Youth hostel: Tirasso 2170, T 263300, **E**, take bus 26B, 'Paraguayo', takes 20 mins, ask driver.

● **Places to eat**
Trevi, Las Heras 70, good food and service, rec; *Posta Las Marías*, San Martín 914, English spoken, speciality is roast kid, pricey but good; *Sarmiento*, Av Sarmiento 658 (*parrilla*), good. *Parrillada Arturito*, Chile 1515, good steak, popular with locals; *Montecatini*, Gral Paz 370, wide variety, good food, good value, rec; *La Reja 14*, San Lorenzo 65, good meat, rec; *Club Alemán*, Necochea 2261, Godoy Cruz, rec; *Club Sociedad Libanesa*, Necochea 538-42, good value; *Govinda*, Salta 1538, vegetarian, good and cheap set meal, open 1200-1600, 1900-2200; *Comedor Línea Verde*, Montecaseros 1177, vegetarian, *tenedor libre*; *El Dragón de Oro*, Chinese, 25 de Mayo 1553 (nr Las Heras), very good. Ice cream at *Soppelsa*, Las Heras y España and at Paseo Sarmiento, rec. *Sr Cheff*, restaurant/confiteria at *Hotel 1 de Mayo*, Garibaldi 80. *Il Tucco*, Emilio Civit 556, also in centre at Paseo Sarmiento 68, excellent Italian restaurants; reasonable prices. Good value, and big 'super pancho' sandwiches in many places, inc *Pizzeria Seb*, Alem 431; *Pizzería Mi Querencia*, Las Heras 523, good pasta dishes and atmosphere. Huge sandwiches in *Belgrano*, on street of same name, crowded with locals, highly rec. Several places with cheap 3-course menus on San Juan, 1300 and 1400 blocks; *Aranjuez*, Lavalle y San Martín, nice cafe, good meeting place; *Mankie Snack Bar*, Las Heras y Mitre, excellent breakfasts; *Café de la Gente*, café/bookshop at Rivadavia 135, pleasant atmosphere. Several good snack bars (known as *carrito* bars): *Tío Paco*, Salta y Alem; *Torombola*, San Juan 1348; *Don Claudio*, T Benegas 744; *El Gran Lomo*, San Martín y Pedro Molina, open 24 hrs, rec. There is a good, cheap café (excellent ice creams) next to the bus station.

● **Airline offices**
Aerolíneas Argentinas and Austral, Paseo Sarmiento 82, T 204100; LAPA, España 1008, T 291081; TAN, España 1012, T 540240, Dinar, Sarmiento 69, T 256870; Ladeco, Paseo Sarmiento 144, T 242778.

● **Banks & money changers**
Lloyds Bank (BLSA), Gen Gutiérrez 72, cash advance on Mastercard, no commision; Banco de Crédito Argentino, España 1168, cash advance on Visa card, high commission; American Express, Galeria Piazza, local 72, San Martín 1207, T 295440; Citibank Av San Martín 1099, gives US$ cash for cheques. Many *cambios* along San Martín, inc Exprinter, No 1198, 5% commision on TCs; Santiago No 1199, rec; Maguitur, No 1203. *Casas de cambio* open till 2000 Mon-Fri, and some open Sat, am.

● **Cultural centres**
Alianza Francesa, Chile 1754; Instituto Dante Alighieri (Italy), Espejo 638; Instituto Cultural Argentino-Norteamericano, Chile 985; Instituto Cuyano de Cultura Hispánica (Spain), Villanueva 389; Goethe Institut, Morón 265, Mon-Fri, 0800-1200, 1600-2230.

● **Embassies & consulates**
Bolivia, Eusebio Blanco y 25 de Mayo, T 292458; Chile, Av Emilio Civit 599, T 255024; Spain, Agustín Alvarez 455, T 253947; Italy, Necochea y Perú, T 231640; France, Houssay 828, T 231542; Germany, Montevideo 127, p 1 D6, T 296539; Finland, Boulogne Sur Mer 631, T 972388; Israel, Olascoaga 838, T 380642.

● **Entertainment**
Casino: 25 de Mayo 1123, daily 2100-0300.

Cinema: Cine de Arte Eisenchlas, 9 de Julio 500, Thur-Sun 2200.

Discothèques: Saudades, Barraquero y San Martín; Kalatraba, Perú 1779.

● **Hospitals & medical services**
Gynaecology: there is a private gynaecological clinic at Gral Paz 445; helpful and relatively inexpensive.

● **Language schools**
Sra Inés Perea de Bujaldon, Rioja 620, T 290429, teaches Spanish to German speakers, rec.

● **Laundry**
Coin-operated laundromat, at corner of San Juan and Rondeau. Laverap, Av Colón 547.

● **Post & telecommunications**
Post Office: Av San Martín y Av Colón, unreliable poste restante.

Telephone: Chile 1584.

● **Shopping**
Mercado Central, Av Las Heras y Patricias Mendocinas, clean, well-stocked. Leather goods good and cheap, try Alain de France, Olegario V, Andrade 147. English language magazines and Buenos Aires Herald usually available from kiosks on San Martín.

● **Sports**
Mountain Climbing: information from Tourist Office.Club Andinista, F L Beltrán 357, Gillén, T 319870. There is a 3-day (Thur-Sat) climbing and trekking expedition via Godoy Cruz and Cacheuta to Cerro Penitentes (4,351m), sleeping in mountain refuge, food inc. See also page 141.

● **Tour companies & travel agents**
Travel agents: lots, especially on Paseo Sarmiento. Cuyo Travel, Paseo Sarmiento 162, 10% discount for ISIC and youth card holders for trekking and climbing on Aconcagua. Servicios Especiales Mendoza, c/o Annette Schenker, Amigorena 65, 5500 Mendoza,

F (061) 244721, 240131, or Radio, code 548, 242162/244505, only Spanish spoken, run by Bernard Klapproth, guided tours around all Argentina, many languages spoken, waterskiing on El Carrizal lake, climbing Aconcagua and Andes, trekking and other specialist programmes, access to Red Cross and Police, only company to cross Andes to Chile without papers. Turismo Cóndor, 25 de Mayo 1537, T 234019 (also at bus station), rec for tours in and around the city, and to El Cristo Redentor statue, good guides, Spanish only; Mylatours, Paseo Sarmiento 133, T 380717, rec; Turismo Sepeán, San Juan 1070, T 204162, friendly and helpful, have branch in Santiago; Turismo Cultural, Rivadavia 211, T 242579, helpful; Ibiza, Espejo 217, T 258141, helpful and efficient; Hunuc Huar Expediciones, Av España 1340, p 8, oficina 7, and Huera Pire, Emilio Civit 320, specialize in assistance to climbers, especially on Aconcagua; José Orviz, Juan B Justo 550/536, T/F 256950/380085, guides, mules, transportation and hire of mountain trekking equipment.

River rafting in the region is popular; ask agencies for details.

● **Tourist offices**
At airport, T 306484, helpful (frequently closed), at the bus terminal (helpful but limited English spoken), T 259709, at Municipalidad, 9 de Julio 500, T 495185, at San Martín 1143, T 202800, at Paseo Sarmiento/Garibaldi y San Martín, T 201333, central, very helpful, and at Mitre y Las Heras, T 257805. They have a list of reasonable private lodgings and a hotel booking service (B range and upwards), and other literature inc lists of bodegas and an excellent free town and province map; the latter is also available at most kiosks.

● **Transport**
Local Car hire: Avis, Rioja 1462, T 255601; Lis Car, San Lorenzo 110, T 291416; Localiza, at airport and Gutiérrez 453, T 491491. Motorcycle repairs: César Armitrano, Rubén Zarate 138, 1600-2100, highly rec for assistance or a chat; he will let you work in his workshop.

Air Plumerillo, 8 km from centre, T 487128, reached by remise taxis (US$9, inc US$1 to enter airport grounds) and bus No 68 from the corner of San Juan and Alem which takes you close to the terminal (10 mins' walk); make sure there is an 'Aeropuerto' sign on the driver's window. Flying time from Buenos Aires: 1 hr 50 mins, with AR, Lapa, Austral and Dinar. Ladeco and National to Santiago, daily. To Córdoba, Lapa and Austral, who also fly to San Rafael. TAN flies to Neuquén.

Buses Terminal on E side of Av Videla, 15 mins' walk from centre, T 313001. To Bariloche, Andesmar daily, TAC, 3 a week, US$70, 22 hrs, book well ahead; to Córdoba, TAC 5 daily, 9 hrs, US$29; to **San Rafael**, many daily, US$9; to **San Juan** frequent, US$11, 2 hrs (several companies, inc TAC, El Cumbre and Villa del Sur y Media Agua). To **La Rioja** US$25, 10 hrs, 5 a day, 3 companies; similarly to **Catamarca**, 12 hrs, daily, US$20. 6 daily to **Tucumán**, US$29; to **Salta**, Andesmar daily (via Tucumán) at 1300 and 2130, 20 hrs, US$52 (plus 4 other companies). To **Puerto Iguazú** at 1930, Mon, Wed, Sat with Cotal, US$70, 38 hrs; alternatively take daily Villa Marta bus to Santa Fe and change, about 40 hrs inc waiting time. To **Comodoro Rivadavia**, daily with Andesmar, at 2000, US$100, 32 hrs inc 4 meal stops; the Tues and Sat departures continue to Río Gallegos, arriving 1450 Thur. To **Rosario**, US$40, 12 hrs. To **Buenos Aires**, 2nd class US$45, 1st class daily, US$60 (lines inc Chevallier, TAC Coop, Jocoli); luxury service daily at 1800 (Chevallier), US$76 inc meals; via Route 7 (Junín-Mercedes) at 2020, arrive 1205. Dull scenery, and very cold across the Pampas at night. 20% student discount on some routes (eg Comodoro Rivadavia). A US$1 tip is expected for removing luggage from buses.

Transport to Chile Turismo cars (Chi-Ar – some adverse reports – and Nevada) carrying up to 11 passengers (US$27, 5 hrs) and minibuses (5½-6 hrs) do the trip to **Santiago** daily. When booking, ensure that the car will pick you up and drop you at your hotel; have this written on your receipt, if not you will be dropped at the bus station. Buses to Santiago daily at 0600-1430; several companies, Tur Bus and TAC have been recommended, mixed reports on other companies. Most buses are comfortable and fast (6½-8 hrs) and charge US$15-20, those with air-conditioning and hostess service (inc breakfast) charge more (US$25, TAC), worth it when crossing the border as waiting time can be a matter of several hours. Also three buses daily to Viña del Mar and 2 to Valparaíso, US$20-25. All companies in same part of Mendoza bus station: you can easily shop around. Children under 8 pay 66% of adult fare, but no seat, book at least 1 day ahead. If all seats booked try CATA, its service is reportedly less good than others thus it usually has some empty seats. Passport required, tourist cards given on bus. The ride is spectacular. Information at terminal. If you want to return, buy an undated return ticket Santiago-Mendoza; it is cheaper. A taxi Mendoza-Santiago costs about US$90 for 4-5 people. For Chilean side, see Chile, **Santiago and the Heartland** (Section 3), To Buenos Aires across the Andes.

International buses: to La Serena, Dec-Mar only. To **Lima**, El Rápido Mon, Wed, Sat 0900. To **Montevideo**, US$66, El Rápido, Tues. **Hitchhiking**: between Mendoza and Buenos Aires is quite easy. If hitching to San Juan, take bus No 6 to the airport nr the highway. Hitching from Mendoza to Los Andes (Chile) is easy; go to the service station in Godoy Cruz suburb (also bus No 6), from where all trucks to Chile, Peru and elsewhere leave.

SKI RESORTS

The charming resort of **Potrerillos** is 13 km from Cacheuta, with ski slopes not far away and excellent birdwatching in summer. **A1** *Gran Hotel*, T 233000, with meals; ACA campsite. *Restaurant Armando*, recommended.

In summer, you can hike 20 km from Potrerillos to **Vallecito**, a closed ski resort, taking 2 days. On the first you will see desert scenery, blooming cactus flowers, birds and an occasional goat or cow. The second you walk surrounded by peaks, a steep but not difficult climb to the San Antonio refuge, usually open with beds and meals.

The small ski resort of **Los Penitentes**, 165 km from Mendoza, is named after the majestic mass of pinnacled rocks, passed on the highway to Chile. From their base (easily reached with a guide from Puente del Inca, see below), the higher rocks look like a church and the smaller, sharper rocks below give the impression of a number of cowled monks climbing upwards. At the resort, daily ski hire is US$35, lift pass US$28. Skiing is good with few people on slopes. A visit on foot to the green lake of Laguna de los Horcones is worthwhile (walk along road towards Chile, then after 1 km follow signs to mountain, excellent views of Aconcagua, especially am). **A3-B** *Hotel Ayelén*, in middle of village, T 259990, clean, comfortable; **C** *La Taberna del Gringo*, Km 151, Villa Los Penitentes, recommended, and others. 5 km from Puente del Inca on the road to Mendoza is *Cruz de Caña* ski club, only open in season, friendly, with comfortable dormitories (**C** with 2 meals), and a good restaurant. The owner organizes trekking expeditions to Plaza de Mulas on Aconcagua; US$50 a day full board during expedition, and US$20/mule.

South of Mendoza, the resort of **Manantiales** is being developed W of

Tunuyán (63 km from the city). Expected open 1996. The best skiing is at Valle de las Leñas, S of San Rafael in the Valle Hermoso (see page 143).

MENDOZA TO CHILE

The route to Chile is sometimes blocked by snow in winter: if travelling by car in June-Oct enquire about road conditions from ACA in Mendoza (San Martín y Amigorena). Officially, driving without snow chains and a shovel is prohibited between Uspallata and the border, but this can be resolved in a friendly way with border police. Both ACA and Chilean Automobile Club sell, but do not rent, chains, but ask at YPF station in Uspallata about chain rental. If driving in mountains remember to advance the spark by adjusting the distributor, or weaken the mixture in the carburettor, to avoid the car seizing up in the rarified air.

USPALLATA

There are two alternates of Route 7, which meet at **Uspallata**, the only settlement of any size between Mendoza and the Chilean frontier. The fully-paved S branch, via Cacheuta and Potrerillos, is wider and better than the N branch, which goes via Villavicencio with a stretch of one-way traffic just beyond the resort, where the road leads up spectacularly to the 3,050m high Cruz del Paramillo. This N branch is still unpaved. 5 km from Uspallata are the ruins of Las Bóvedas, built by the Huarpe Indians under the Jesuits, and an Inca *tambería*; there is a small, interesting museum. They are just off the road which leads to Barreal and Calingasta (see page 147), unpaved for its first part and tricky when the snow melts and floods it in summer. The tourist office in Uspallata keeps unreliable hours.

● **Accommodation A2** *Valle Andino*, Ruta 7, T (0624) 20033, good rooms and restaurant, heating, pool, inc breakfast, ACA discount; **A3** *Hotel Uspallata*, T 20003, nice location, but run down, service friendly; **C** *Hostería Los Cóndores*, T 20002, clean, friendly, good restaurant. **Camping**: ACA site, US$3/head, full washing facilities, hot water.

The crossing of the Andes taken by San Martín is the old mountain trail the Spaniards named the Camino de los Andes. Beyond Uspallata is a vast, open, undulating plain, wild and bare. On all sides stand the grey, gaunt mountains. On the far side of this plain the valley narrows till Río Blanco is reached, and there the mountain torrents rush and froth into the river. At Punta de Vacas, look left up the Tupungato Valley at the majestic cone of **Tupungato**, one of the giants of the Andes, rising 6,550m. Walking tours in the Tupungato area can be arranged by Quinche Romulo, Alte Brown, Tupungato (a town 73 km SW of Mendoza), T 0622-88029.

PUENTE DEL INCA

A sports resort set among mountains of great grandeur (*Alt* 2,718m; 72 km W of Uspallata). The natural bridge after which the resort is named is one of the wonders of South America; it crosses the Río Mendoza at a height of 19m, has a span of 21m, and is 27m wide, and seems to have been formed by sulphur-bearing hot springs. Watch your footing on the steps; extremely slippery. There are hot thermal baths just under the bridge, a little dilapidated but a great place to soak. Puente del Inca is the best point for excursions into the higher Andean valleys. Los Penitentes for skiing is nearby. Horse treks go there.

● **Accommodation A3-B** *Hostería Puente del Inca*, T 380480, less off-season, very pleasant atmosphere, but overpriced and poor service, more expensive if booked in Mendoza. **Camping**: possible next to the church, if your equipment can withstand the winds.

● **Transport** Buses (Expreso Uspallata) from Mendoza for Uspallata and Puente del Inca, US$8, 4 hrs, 0600 and 1000, returning from Puente del Inca 1200 and 1615; local buses also go on from Puente del Inca to Las Cuevas, Expreso Uspallata, US$12 return (**NB** take passport). Also note that buses from Mendoza through to Santiago de Chile do not stop here.

ACONCAGUA

West of Puente del Inca (you can walk along the old railway), on the right, there is a good view of Aconcagua (6,959m), sharply silhouetted against the blue sky. It is the highest peak in the Americas and a provincial **park**. In 1985, a complete Inca mummy was discovered at 5,300m on the mountain. The mountain was first climbed by Zurbriggen of the Fitzgerald Expedition in 1897.

● **Access & accommodation** Best time for climbing Aconcagua is from end-Dec to February. For trekking or climbing it is first necessary to obtain a permit: 3-day trekking US$15, 5 days' trekking US$30. For climbing a 20-day permit is required. (Argentines US$40, foreigners US$80). Permits are sold only at **Dirección de Recursos Naturales Renovables**, Parque Gral San Martín, Mendoza, T 252090. From Mendoza take a bus or colectivo to Puente del Inca. From here mules are available (shop around; large differences in muleteers prices; more economical to travel with a group); you have to pay for 3 days there and back (1 day rest) and for the muleteer and his wages. This only takes you to the base camp at Plaza de Mulas (4,370m), where there is, nearby, the highest hotel in the world, (see below), and a rescue patrol, crowded in summer. Also at 4,200m is Plaza de Francia, facing the S face, less crowded in summer. Plaza de Francia is about 25 km from Puente del Inca and can be reached in two stages via Confluencia (camping also available here, recommended if pacing yourself).Refugios above this height unserviceable. Take a tent able to withstand 100 mph + winds, and clothing and sleeping gear for temperatures below -40°C. Allow at least 1 week for acclimatization at lower altitudes before attempting the summit (4 days from Plaza de Mulas). Hotel *Plaza de Mulas*, **L3** pp full, **B** pp without meals, good food, information, medical treatment, recommended, also camping area. In Mendoza you can book *refugio* reservations and programmes which inc trekking, climbing to the summit, with hotel accommodation or camping, prices from US$990 to US$1,890 for 10 days, T/F Mendoza 61-380383, Nueve de Julio 1126. In Buenos Aires, representation at Proterra Turismo, Lavalle 750, p 20 D, T/T 326-2639.

● **Climbing information** Treks and climbs organized by Sr Fernando Grajales, the famous climber, in *Hostería Puente del Inca*, or at Moreno 898, 5500 Mendoza, Telex 55-154. Information also from Eduardo Enrique Esteban, Emilio Civit 320, Maipú, Mendoza, CP 5515, T/F (61) 973393 and Carlos and Amalia Cuesta, *Los Gateados*, nr Cementerio de los Andinistas, 1 km before Puente del inca (Dec-Feb, or T Mendoza 391080/290410), rec for details on mules, trekking and climbing. Other guides can be found at the airport in Mendoza and further information from **Dirección de Recursos Naturales Renovables** (see also under Mendoza: **Travel agents**).

LAS CUEVAS AND CRISTO REDENTOR

Las Cuevas (16 km from Puente del Inca) is a neat, modern settlement being developed as a ski-ing resort (though there is no ski-lift as yet).

Beyond Las Cuevas, the road, completely paved, goes through the 4-km El Libertador-Las Cuevas toll road tunnel to Chile (US$2 for cars and VW buses). The old road over La Cumbre pass is now closed to through traffic so that it is no longer possible to go from Mendoza to Santiago via the statue of **El Cristo Redentor** (Christ the Redeemer) at 3,854m. All buses and cars go through the tunnel to Chile, leaving the statue unseen above. It was erected jointly by Chile and Argentina in 1904 to celebrate King Edward VII's decision in the boundary dispute of 1902. It is completely dwarfed by the landscape. (The road from the tunnel to the statue is closed for the season after the first snowfall in April.) To see the statue you must either go on a 12-hr excursion from Mendoza (weekends early am, all travel agencies, highly recommended; the excursion also includes Puente del Inca) or walk from Las Cuevas. This takes $4\frac{1}{2}$ hrs up, 2 hrs down. You should be in good condition and the weather should be fine.

● **Accommodation & places to eat** **A3** *Hostería Las Cuevas*, basic, warm rooms, friendly, food OK, price inc breakfast and supper. Food available at kiosk at Expreso Uspallata bus terminal point.

FRONTIER WITH CHILE

● **Argentine immigration**
The Chilean border is beyond Las Cuevas, but all Argentine entry and exit formalities are dealt with at Punta de Vacas, 30 km E of Las Cuevas.

● **Argentine customs**
A new customs post, Ingeniero Roque Carranza has been built near Laguna Los Horcones, nearer Las Cuevas. Customs at the frontier are closed 1200-1400.

● **Crossing by private vehicle**
Car drivers can undertake all formalities in advance at Uspallata while refuelling. Members of ACA need only the *Libreta de Pasos por Aduana*, otherwise you need the *Documento de Exportación* to enter Chile.

● **Chilean consulate**
See under Mendoza. **NB** No visas into Chile are available at the border. Tourist cards are given out on international buses.

● **Hitchhiking**
One can hitchhike, or possibly bargain with bus drivers for a seat, from Punta de Vacas to Santiago, but if one is dropped at the entrance to the tunnel in winter, one cannot walk through. Travellers report that customs men may help by asking motorists to take hitchhikers through to Chile.

SOUTH OF MENDOZA

SAN RAFAEL

At **San Rafael** (*Pop* 72,200; *Phone code* 0627; 273 km SW of San Luis, 242 km S of Mendoza), irrigation makes it possible to grow fruit in large quantities at the foot of the Andes.

Excursions

Two bodegas to visit, Suter and Bianchi (Monte Caseros y E Civit, recommended). There is a small but interesting natural history museum 6 km SE of town at Isla Río Diamante (Tues-Sun 0800-1200, 1500-1900, free; Isclin bus along Av JA Balloffet); zoo nearby. A road runs W over El Pehuenche pass to Talca (Chile).

Up the Río Atuel valley, there is beautiful scenery in the **Valle Hermoso** up to the three dams of El Nihuil which provide irrigation water and hydroelectric power to Mendoza. There is fishing in the reservoir above the highest dam. In the **Río Atuel** canyon there are polychrome rocks in the spectacular gorge. Three buses a day go to Valle Grande at the end of the canyon, US$3. Plenty of accommodation and campsites, river rafting and horse riding. Travel agencies in Mendoza run all-day excursions to the Atuel canyon.

Local information
● **Accommodation**
C *Kalton*, Yrigoyen 120, T 30047, excellent, clean, safe, good value; and others.

Campsites: 2 sites (one of them ACA) at Isla Río Diamante, 15 km SE.

● **Tourist offices**
Av H Yrigoyen y Balloffet, very helpful. Ask for Aldo or Hector Seguín at España 437 for trekking and climbing information.

● **Transport**
Buses to **Mendoza**, frequent, US$9; to **Neuquén**, US$20.

LAS LENAS

182 km SW of San Rafael, a road heads W into the Andes. It passes **Los Molles**, where there are thermal springs and the spa hotel of **Lahuenco**. Also off this road is the **Pozo de las Animas**, two natural pits, both filled with water (the larger is 80m deep); when the wind blows across the holes, a ghostly wail results, hence the name. At the end of Valle Los Molles is **Las Leñas**, 2,250m, a new resort with 33 pistes for good skiing, three T-bars, three ski-lifts (US$35-45/day; equipment hire US$20-24). It claims to be the foremost ski resort in the S hemisphere.

● **Accommodation** Three stonebuilt hotels: *Escorpio*, *Acuario* and *Gemini*, T for all 71100, and a disco, shop renting equipment and expensive restaurant. All the hotels are **L2**; for cheaper accommodation you have to stay in Los Molles where there is **A3** *Hotel La Huenca*, a/c, clean.

● **Transport** Buses from San Rafael US$5.30, colectivo US$20; buses from Buenos Aires, 15 hrs, in skiing season only.

MALARGUE

Further S on Route 40, **Malargüe** (*Pop* 8,600) is developing as a tourist centre, especially for adventure tourism. 8 km from the town is the Caverna de Brujas and 37 km SE the Laguna Llancanelo, a bird reserve. Details from the tourist office.

● **Accommodation** **A3-B** *Hotel del Turismo*, San Martín 224, T 71042, quiet, rec; **B** *Hotel-Restaurant El Cisne*, Villegas 278, T 71350, clean, rec; *Portal del Valle*, T 71536, provides multilingual tour guides. Several others.

● **Guides & tours** *AGAPE Mendoza*, Asociación Grupo Antropo-Paleonto-Espeleológico; contact Dora de and Héctor Rofsgaard, Beltrán 414, T (0627) 71536. *Expresos Payún*, Av Roca 430, T 71426.

● **Transport Air** Flights with TAN from Mendoza and Nuequén.

NORTH OF MENDOZA

The oases of San Juan, La Rioja and Catamarca between the plains and the Andes. Interesting natural rock formations can be seen, especially Valle de la Luna and Puerta de Talampaya.

Of the three oases in the more arid zone N of Mendoza, San Juan is the most prosperous, wine and olives support La Rioja, but Catamarca is economically depressed.

SAN JUAN

San Juan (*Pop* 122,000; *Alt* 650m; *Phone code* 064, 177 km from Mendoza), was founded 1562 by Don Juan Jufré de Loaysa y Montese and is capital of its namesake province. The city is proud of its sunny climate and clean, tree-lined streets. Nearly destroyed by a 1944 earthquake, the centre is well laid-out, with a modern cathedral.

Places of interest

The area is famous for its wine, 'to be between San Juan and Mendoza' is an Argentine expression for having drunk too much. One of the country's largest wine producers, **Bodegas Bragagnolo**, on the outskirts of town at Route 40 y Av Benavídez, Chimbas, can be visited (bus 20 from terminal; guided tours daily 0830-1330, 1530-1930, not Sun). **Escuela de**

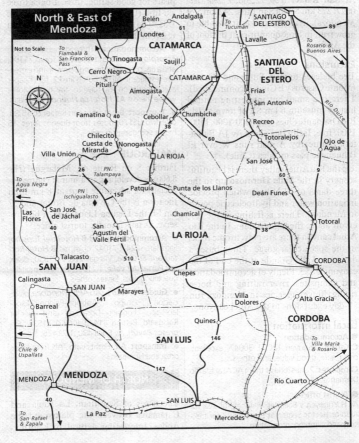

North & East of Mendoza

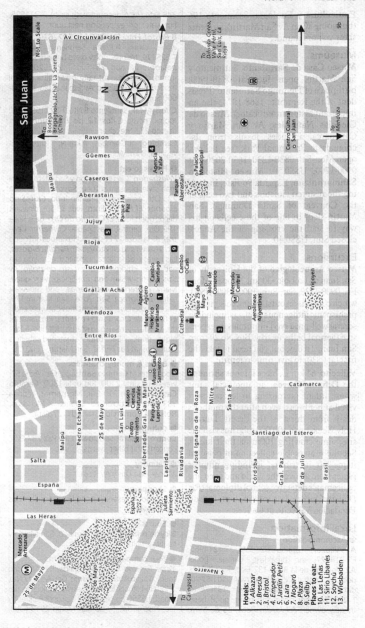

San Juan

Not to Scale

Av Circunvalación

To Difunta Correa,
Valle Fértil,
San Luis, La
Rioja

To Mendoza

Centro Cultural
o San Juan

9b

Rawson

Güemes

Caseros

Aberastain

Jujuy

Rioja

Tucumán

Gral. M Achá

Mendoza

Entre Ríos

Sarmiento

Catamarca

Maipú

To
Bodega
Braspagnolo,Jáchal, La Serena
(Chile)

Agencia
o Yalar

Parque M
Paz

Palacio
Municipal

Parque
Aberastain

Cambio
o Santiago

Agencia
o Agüero

Museo
Histórico
Marianiano

Cathedral

Cambio
o Cash

Bolsa de
Comercio

Parque 25 de
Mayo

Mercado
Central

Aerolíneas
Argentinas

Santiago del Estero

Catamarca

Yrigoyen

España

Salta

Pedro Echague

25 de Mayo

Maipú

San Luis

Teatro
Sarmiento

Museo
Ciencias
Naturales

Parque
Laprida

Av Libertador Gral. San Martín

Museo Casa
Sarmiento

Laprida

Rivadavia

Av José Ignacio de la Roza

Mitre

Santa Fe

Córdoba

Gral. Paz

9 de Julio

Brasil

Las Heras

Mercado
Artesanal

25 de Mayo

España

de Mayo

Santa
Julieta
Sarmiento

S Navarro

To
Calingasta

Hotels:
1. Alkazar
2. Brescia
3. Bristol
4. Emperador
5. Jardín Petit
6. Lara
7. Nogaró
8. Plaza
9. Selby
Places to eat:
10. Las Leñas
11. Sirio Libanés
12. Soychú
13. Wiesbaden

Fruticultura y Enología, Sarmiento 196 (bus going W on Av San Martín), students show visitors round.

Museums

Museo Casa de Sarmiento, Sarmiento y San Martín, open Tues-Sat 0830-1900; birthplace of Domingo Sarmiento (President of the Republic, 1868-1874, also an important historian/educator). **Museo de Ciencias Naturales**, Av San Martín y Catamarca, includes fossils from Ischigualasto Provincial Park (see below), open Mon-Sat, 0830-1230, 1630-2030, Sat 0900-1200, US$0.50. **Museo Histórico Sanmartiniano**, Laprida 96 Este, including the restored cloisters and two cells of the Convent of Santo Domingo. San Martín slept in one of these cells on his way to lead the crossing of the Andes, closed Sun, US$0.40.

Excursions

Museo Arqueológico of the University of San Juan at La Laja, 20 km N, open Mon-Fri, 0900-1830, Sat, Sun, 1000-1300, US$2, which contains an outstanding collection of prehispanic indigenous artefacts, including several well-preserved mummies. Inexpensive thermal baths nearby. Bus No 20 from San Juan, 2 a day, but you need to take the first (at 0830) to give time to return.

Vallecito, 64 km E, has a famous shrine to the **Difunta Correa**, an unofficial saint whose infant (according to legend) survived at her breast even after the mother's death from thirst in the desert. During Holy Week, up to 100,000 pilgrims visit the site, some crawling 100m on their knees. See the remarkable collection of personal items left in tribute, including number plates from all over the world and even one policeman's detective school diploma! (*Res Difunta Correa*). For information, consult Fundación Vallecito at Caucete.

Local information
● Accommodation

A1 *Alkázar*, Laprida 82 Este, T 214965, F 214977, inc breakfast, garage, good; **A2** *Nogaró*, de la Roza 132 Este, T 227501/5, pool, a/c, central, TV, parking (ACA and US AAA discounts); **A3** *Central*, Mitre 131 Este, T 223174, very clean and quiet, good beds, friendly owner; **A3** *Jardín Petit*, 25 de Mayo

345 Este (ACA discount with cash), T 211825, hot water, pricey, parking next door.

B *Bristol*, Entre Rios 368 Sur, T 222629, a/c, hot water, clean; **B** *Plaza* Sarmiento 344 Sur, T 225179, friendly, noisy disco behind; **A3** *Embajador*, Rawson 25 Sur, T 225520, large rooms, clean, pleasant, café, good value. Several residenciales (**B**) along Av España, blocks 100-600 Sur.

C *Jessy-Mar*, Sarmiento 8 Nte, T 227195, small rooms, noisy; **C** *Res 12 de Diciembre*, Sarmiento 272 Nte, clean.

Camping: at Chimbas, 7 km N; 3 sites at Rivadavia, 8 km W.

● Places to eat

Wiesbaden, Circunvalación y San Martín, German-style, pleasant setting; *Soychú*, de la Roza 223 Ote, excellent vegetarian food; *Club Sirio Libanés 'El Palito'*, Entre Rios 33 Sur, pleasant decor, good food; *El Castillo de Oro*, de la Roza 199 Ote, central, reasonable; *Comedor Central*, de la Roza 171 Este, not luxurious but good *locro* (stew) and *chivito* (goat); *Parrilla Bigotes*, Las Heras e de la Roza, inexpensive 'all you can eat' meat, chicken, salads; *Listo de pollo*, Av San Martín y Santiago del Estero, very good. Many *pizzerías*, *confiterías*, and sidewalk cafés. *Lomoteca San José*, San Martín 179, grills, inexpensive, late night music at weekends; *El Clavel de Oro*, Santa Fe y Entre Ríos, snacks, drinks; *Marilyn Bar*, San Martín y Mendoza, late night drinks. Eat under thatched shelters (*quinchos*) at *Las Leñas*, San Martín, 1600 Ote.

● Banks & money changers

Good rates at **Cambio Santiago**, Gen Acha 52, weekdays until 2100, Sat until 1300; **Cambio Cash**, Tucumán 210 Sur; **Montemar**, Laprida 133 Sur; **Multicrédito**, Laprida y Mendoza; **Bolsa de Comercio**, Gral Acha 278 Sur.

● Cultural centres

Centro Cultural San Juan: Gral Paz 737 Este, concerts and other events.

● Laundry

Marva, San Luis y Av Rioja.

● Shopping

Mercado Artesanal at Av España y San Luis worth a visit.

● Sports

Bicycle repairs: Ruedas Armado, San Martín y La Rioja, helpful.

● Tour companies & travel agents

Yafar Turismo, Caseros y Laprida, T 214476 (no tours); *Mario Agüero Turismo*, Gen Acha 17 Nte, T 220864, tours to Ischigualasto subject to demand, US$50 pp plus US$3 National Park entry fee; *Fascinatur*, Av Lib San Martín 2918 (Ote),

Rafael Joliat rec for 4WD treks to remote areas. For mountain climbing contact Pablo Schlögl, 543 Haité Este, T 225132, rec as probably the most experienced mountaineer in Argentina.

● **Tourist offices**
Sarmiento Sur 24 y San Martín, helpful, good brochures, open Mon-Sat, 0900-1330, 1430-2100, Sun 0900-1300; also at bus terminal. Arranges tours in summer only. Large-scale provincial maps available at bookshops. **ACA**, 9 de Julio 802 Este, useful information on routes, helpful. The **Diario de Cuyo** published a Guía de Turismo for San Juan province in Oct 1993 (similar to Chile's Turistel guides), very informative.

● **Transport**
Local Car hire: Parque Automotor, España y San Martín, T 226018. Cash discount on request. Localiza, España 274 (Sur), T 229243.

Air Chacritas Airport, 14 km SE. From Buenos Aires with AR (T 220205) and Lapa (T 216039). AR also from Mendoza; Lapa from Córdoba.

Buses Terminal at Estados Unidos y Santa Fe, 9 blocks E of centre (buses 33 and 35 go through the centre). Long distance services to **La Rioja**, 9 hrs, US$19, or go via Chepes, 0900 daily US$6, with connecting service from Chepes, Mon, Wed, Sun at 1600, 4 hrs, US$10, **Catamarca** (660 km over secondary roads, US$17, with connection to Salta, US$29), **Tucumán** (3 a day, 13 hrs, Libertador is cheapest), Córdoba, Santa Fe, Mar del Plata, Bahía Blanca and BsAs (Autotransporte San Juan, US$47). To **San Agustín** at 1800, US$11. Fifteen departures daily to and from **Mendoza** with TAC and El Cumbre, 2 hrs, US$11, try to sit in the shade (on W side in am, E in pm). Also service to provincial tourist destinations. **To Chile**: only connection with **Santiago (Chile)** is via Mendoza; catch the TAC bus at 0600, arrives in Mendoza 0830 in time for bus to Santiago.

Crossing to Chile Cars can now cross the Andes via the Agua Negra Pass (4,600) which is spectacular but it is only open Jan to early April; in winter it is closed by snow, in summer it may be closed by rain. No buses take this route. ACA, customs and immigration at Las Flores (see below) informs all the ACA stations in the country of road conditions. It takes approximately 6 hrs from Las Flores in Argentina to Rivadavia in Chile (where the first service station can be found).

Hitchhiking To La Rioja, take route 141 to Chepes (ACA Hostería), then N to Patquia; more traffic on provincial Route 29, a well paved, but less interesting road than that via San Agustín or Jachal (see below).

WEST OF SAN JUAN

Along scenic provincial route 12 (open westbound mornings, eastbound afternoons), 135 km W of San Juan, is **Calingasta**, in the valley of same name (annual cider festival in April).

● **Accommodation** B Calingasta, T 22014, remodelled, pool, full board available; **C** La Capilla, T 21033, inc breakfast, basic but very clean, family run and friendly, the family also sells the TAC bus tickets, and has the only public telephone in the village.

40 km S of Calingasta on the road to Uspallata is **Barreal**. At El Leoncito (2,348m), 26 km from Barreal there is an observatory (no public transport; tours can be arranged from San Juan or at Hotel Barreal).

● **Accommodation** Barreal, San Martín s/n, T (0648) 41000, reservations through Nogaró in San Juan, T 227501, improved and refurbished in 1996, restaurant, pool, riding; **Cabañas Doña Pipa**, see below; **E** Hotel Jorge, clean, very simple; **Posada San Eduardo**, small, few rooms with bath, open summer only; accommodation with Sr Patricio Sosa or Sr Cortez.

● **Places to eat** Restaurant Isidoro, owned by local baker and sandyacht champion, reasonable, ask waiter for the day's recommendation; food also available at Mama Rosa.

● **Adventure tours** Rafting trips can be arranged in Barreal, contact Sr Eduardo Conterno Sr Ramón Luis Ossa, physical education teacher at Barreal's high school, runs mule treks into the Andes, crossing the foothills in summer, from 10 to 21 days between Nov and April; he can be reached at **Cabañas Doña Pipa**, Mariano Moreno s/n, 5405 Barreal, Pcia San Juan, T (0648) 41004. The cabañas sleep 5, with bath, kitchen, sitting room, comfortable.

● **Transport** Buses from San Juan daily, El Trinfo, 0700, plus Mon, Wed, Fri, Sun at 2030 (return Mon, Wed, Fri, Sun 1330, 1600, Tues, Thur 1400, Sat 1600), 5 hrs, US$11. Remise service San Juan-Calingasta-Barreal, US$17 pp, T San Juan 262121 (or 1900-2300 252370), at Pablo D'Marco 5949 (0), Barrio Camus, Rivadavia, San Juan; in Barreal, Sr Pachá, Restaurante Isidoro. Omnibus Vitar from Mendoza (Las Heras 494, T 232876) Thur and Sat via Uspallata, continuing to Tamberías and Calingasta (return Fri and Sun); fare Barreal-Calingasta US$7.

Climbing
Mercedario (also El Ligua), 6,770m. No authorization is required, but it is advis-

able to inform the Gendarmería Nacional at Barreal. From Barreal go to Casas Amarillas on the Río Blanco, about 100 km on a gravel road. It may be possible to hire a Unimog 4 x 4 from the Gendarmería Nacional; guides (*baqueanos*) may also be hired, they can provide mules if necessary. The best time is mid-Dec to end-Feb; the types of terrain encountered are gravel, snow and rock. There is no rescue service. Nearby peaks include Pico Polaco (6,050m), La Mesa (6,200m), Alma Negra (6,120m) and Ramada (6,410m). More information is available from Club Andino Mercedario, 9 de Julio 547 Este, 5400 San Juan, or *Antonio Beorchia Nigris*, director, Ciadam (Research Centre for Andean Archaeology), República del Líbano 2621, 5423 San Juan. **NB** Do not enter this region from Chile, it is illegal.

NORTH OF SAN JUAN

Route 40, the principal tourist route on the E Andean slope, heads N toward Cafayate and Salta, via San José de Jachal. At Talacasto, 55 km from San Juan, route 436 branches toward Las Flores (Km 180) and the Chilean border at Agua Negra pass (4,600m – see above). Alternatively Route 141 runs directly N from Calingasta to Las Flores, a dirt road via Villa Nueva and Tocota, reported scenic but lonely.

At **Pismanta**, 5 km N of Las Flores, the **B** *Hotel Termas de Pismanta*, T 227501, has rooms for 120 guests, thermal baths between 38° and 44°C, a large swimming pool, medical attention, bowling, bingo occasionally, covered parking, well-maintained. Reservations in Buenos Aires (Maipú 331) and San Juan (San Martín y Sarmiento); **E** *La Olla*, family run, clean, restaurant. From San Juan, 2 buses daily with TAC, 4 weekly with Empresa Iglesia, also from Mendoza. 22 km further N, in Rodeo, Ing Meglioli raises guanaco and vicuña, and sells local produce and crafts.

From Pismanta, a scenic road, with several tunnels, follows the Río Jachal 61 km E to **San José de Jachal**, a wine and olive-growing centre (*Pop* 15,000), with many adobe buildings. Expreso Argentino bus from San Juan at 0730 arrives at 0940.

● **Accommodation & places to eat** C *Plaza*, San Juan 545, T 20256; *San Martín*, Juan de Echegaray 387, T 20431. Camping. *El Chato Flores* restaurant, good.

From Jachal, the undulating Route 40, paved to the La Rioja border, crosses dozens of dry watercourses. It continues unpaved to Villa Unión (see below).

EAST OF SAN JUAN

Route 141 runs across the S of the province towards La Rioja province and Córdoba. Just after Marayes (133 km), paved route 510 (poor) goes N 114 km to **San Agustín del Valle Fértil**. There is a municipal swimming pool, and a lake with fishing. Tourist information on the plaza. Local weavers offer ponchos and blankets.

● **Accommodation** *Hostería Valle de la Luna*, Rivadavia s/n, Dpto Valle Fértil, T (0646) 20015-7, new, good, overlooking Dique San Agustín. Res *Andacollo*; *Res Los Olivos*; **D** *Hosp Romero*; private houses also provide lodging.

● **Transport** Bus from San Juan US$9; San Juan-La Rioja bus stops in San Agustín about midnight, leaves at 0300, 4 hrs, US$9.50.

THE PARKS OF ISCHIGUALASTO AND TALAMPAYA

North of San Agustín, at a police checkpoint, 56 km by paved road, a side road goes NW for 17 km to the 62,000-ha **Ischigualasto** Provincial Park, also known as **Valle de la Luna** for its exotic desert landforms, entrance US$5. Here the skeletons of the oldest known dinosaurs have been found (230 million years).

● **Tours & access** All private vehicles must be accompanied by rangers whose knowledge and interest vary greatly, fee US$2 pp. The circular tour, on an unpaved road, lasts 2-3 hrs. Local bus from San Juan Mon and Fri to police checkpoint and on Sat afternoon, if demand is sufficient. Tours from San Juan, US$50 (not including lunch); from San Agustín US$18 for a guide (ask at tourist office). Rec guide is Barros Lito, US$40 for full day tour of Valle and Talampaya in private car. Taxi to park US$55 (rec if there are 4-5 people).

Just beyond the police checkpoint, near Los Baldecitos, paved Route 150 heads E to Patquía and then to La Rioja or Chilecito. From the junction provincial Route 26 heads N to Villa Unión. 58 km N of the junction a paved road goes E to

Puerta de Talampaya National Park (open 0800-1630, entrance US$3), another collection of spectacular desert landforms (*Refugio* near the entrance, sleeping bag essential). Herbert Levi writes: "There are 6,000-year-old petroglyphs with pictures depicting animals. The whole area is said to have been covered with water long ago; now there are two visible strata, the *tarjado* and the *talampaya*. After that one enters a canyon with 'balconies', sheer overhanging walls. Coming out of the canyon there are rocks shaped like a cathedral, a bird, a castle, a chessboard, a monk, and three kings on a camel". Better to visit park in the morning and avoid strong winds in the afternoon.

● **Tours & access** Tours follow the dry bed of the Río Talampaya in 4WD vehicles operated by park rangers (US$30 for 2-hr tour for 8 people, not inc entrance; also medium and long tour, latter US$130 shared between 8 people, almost full day, rec). Tours, arranged through Dirección Provincial de Turismo in La Rioja, or Sr Furlin, park director, in Pagancillo, who can also arrange accommodation in the village (eg with **D** pp *Familia Flores*, including breakfast and dinner). Chilecito-San Juan buses pass Talampaya, drop off at Km 144. Patquía-Villa Unión buses pass Pagancillo.

LA RIOJA PROVINCE

72 km N of Patquía, on Route 38, is the capital of La Rioja province.

LA RIOJA

In the city (*Pop* 106,000; *Phone code* 0822), founded 1592, some colonial buildings survive, despite a major earthquake in 1894. La Rioja is known as 'City of the Orange Trees', but there are also many specimens of the contorted, thorn-studded *palo borracho* tree, whose ripened avocado-like pods release large brown seeds in a kapok-like substance. It is also a common ornamental in Buenos Aires.

Places of interest

The **Convent of San Francisco**, 25 de Mayo/Bazán y Bustos, contains the Niño Alcalde, a remarkable image of the infant Jesus as well as the cell (*celda*) in which San Francisco Solano lived and the orange tree, now dead, which he planted in 1592.

To visit the tree when the church is closed, ring the bell at 25 de Mayo 218 next door. A visit may also be made to **Los Padrecitos**, 7 km from town, where a stone temple protects the remains of the 16th century adobe building where San Francisco converted the Indians of the Yacampis valley. The **Convent of Santo Domingo**, Luna y Lamadrid, is the oldest surviving temple in Argentina, dating from 1623. The **Casa González**, a brick 'folly' in the form of a castle, is at Rivadavia 950.

Museums

Museo Folklórico, P Luna 811, Tues-Fri, 0900-1200, 1600-2000, Sat, Sun, 0900-1200, US$1.50; **Museo Arqueológico Inca Huasi**, Alberdi 650, owned by the Franciscan Order, contains a huge collection of fine Diaguita Indian ceramics, open Tues-Fri, 0800-1200, 1500-1900, US$1. **Museo Histórico de la Provincia**, Dávila 87, opening hours variable. **Museo Municipal de Bellas Artes**, Copiapó 253, works by local, national, and foreign artists.

Excursions

Swimming and fishing at Los Sauces dam, 15 km W. Good views of La Rioja from Cerro de la Cruz (1,680m), 12 km W, now a centre for hang-gliding, where condors and falcons may be sighted. To Ischigualasto and Talampaya (via Nonogasta, Cuesta de Miranda and Villa Unión, by private car with guide), costs US$190 for up to 5 people plus entrance fees, departs 0900. To Samay Huasi (see Chilecito, page 150).

Local information

NB Avoid arriving on Sat night as most things are shut on Sun.

● **Accommodation**

Accommodation can be difficult to find, particularly in the lower price ranges.

A2 *Plaza*, San Nicolás y 9 de Julio, T 25215, rec but street noisy; **A3** *King's*, Quiroga 1070, T 25272; *Libertador*, Buenos Aires 253, T 27474, good value; *Talampaya*, Perón 951, T 24010; *Turismo*, Perón y Quiroga, T 25240, offstreet parking.

B *Imperial*, Moreno 345, T 22478, clean, helpful; **B** *Res Petit*, Lagos 427, basic, friendly; **C** *Savoy*, Roque A Luna 14, T 26894, excellent value, hot shower; **C** *Pensión 9 de Julio*, Copiapó y Vélez

150 Argentina

Sarsfield, rec; **C Res Florida**, 8 de Diciembre 524, clean, basic, cheap. Tourist Office keeps a list of private lodgings, such as Sra Vera, Dávila 343.

Camping: at Balneario Los Sauces, 13 km W.

● **Places to eat**
Café Corredor, San Martín y Pelagio Luna, good, cheap; *La Cantina de Juan*, Yrigoyen 190, excellent food, inexpensive; *Il Gatto*, Plaza 25 de Mayo, good pastas and salads; *Club Atlético Riojano*, Santa Fe between 9 de Julio and Buenos Aires, no atmosphere but cheap; good open air *churrasquería* next to *Hotel de Turismo*; *La Casona*, Rivadavia 449, very good and reasonably priced, rec; *Taberna Don Carlos*, Rivadavia 459, good fish and service; *Comedor Sociedad Española*, 9 de Julio 233, excellent pastas, inexpensive; *La Pomme*, Rivadavia y San Martín, open-air terrace, popular meeting place.

● **Banks & money changers**
US$ cash changed at **Banco de Galicia**, Plaza 25 de Mayo (no commission on Visa cash advance), and **Banco de Crédito**, San Nicolás 476. Cheques difficult to change – try **Banco de la Provincia**, Bazán y Bustos, commission 8%. Better to change plenty before arriving (see note on provincial bonds used as currency, page 235).

● **Laundry**
Laverap, Av Perón 944.

● **Post & telecommunications**
Post Office: Av Perón 258.
Telecommunications: Perón 764.

● **Tourist offices**
At Perón y Urquiza, T 28834.

● **Transport**
Air To/from Buenos Aires, AR (T 27257) and Lapa (T 35197); Lapa also **Catamarca**.

Buses Terminal 7 blocks S of the Cathedral at Artigas y España. To **Buenos Aires** with Gen Urquiza, US$47, combination Ablo, via Córdoba. To **Mendoza** (US$25) and **San Juan** (US$19), night service with La Estrella or Libertador, with Andesmar, 1000, 8 hrs. To travel to San Juan by day (good scenery), take 0715 Cotil bus to Chepes (new bus station and ACA motel), then Cotil again next day to San Juan at 0900 or 20 de Junio bus at 1000 for San Juan or 1230 to San Luis. To **Tinogasta**, 0620, 2200, daily, US$11. To **Tucumán** (US$15), with Bosio and La Estrella. To **Salta**, Andesmar, 10 hrs, US$33. Also provincial services.

CHILECITO

129 km NW of Patquía is La Rioja province's second town (*Pop* 20,000). Founded in 1715, it has good views of Sierra de Famatina, especially from the top of El Portezuelo, an easy climb from the end of C El Maestro. At Los Sarmientos, 2 km N of town, is the Santa Clara church, dating from 1764. The region is famous for its wines, olives and walnuts.

Museums
Samay Huasi, 3 km S of town, the house of Joaquín V González, founder of La Plata University, open 0800-1200 and 1500-1800, contains the **Museo de Ciencias Naturales, Mineralogía y Arqueología**, pleasant gardens, and good views of Chilecito, the Famatina ridge and connecting valley. **Molino San Francisco y Museo de Chilecito**, at J de Ocampo 63, has archaeological, historical and artistic exhibits, open Mon-Fri 0800-1300, 1400-1900.

Excursions
La Mejicana mine via Santa Florentina road: a cable car system (built 1903) which brought ore 39 km to the railhead at Chilecito is now out of use, although it runs on some weekends between stations 1 and 3. For treks, and trips to see gold washers at Famatina or to Talampaya, ask for Carlos de Caro, or enquire at tourist office. To **Famatina** (31 km N), a sleepy hamlet amid nut plantations, *hostería*, restaurants.

Local information
● **Accommodation**
A3 *Chilecito*, Dr L Martínez y 8 de Julio, T 2201/2, good, clean, friendly, no credit cards, safe parking, pool, good restaurant; **B** *Riviera*, Castro Barros 133, rec, clean, hot showers; **C** *Belsavac*, 9 de Julio y Dávila, T 2877, good but thin walls; **C** *Wamatinag*, Galería Victoria, W side of Plaza Sarmiento, T 2977, clean, pleasant, best value in town; **C** *Americano*, Libertad 68, T 8104. The Tourist Office has a list of families offering accommodation, but not for singles.

Camping: at Santa Florentina, 6 km NW of Chilecito and Las Talas, 2 km beyond.

● **Places to eat**
El Gallo, Perón e Illia, excellent. On Plaza Sarmiento are: *Chaplin*, best in town; *Robert Snak Bar*, light meals and drinks; *Vanesa*, good home-made ice-cream; *Toscanini*, Fátima y San Martín, good Italian food, inexpensive; *Ferrito*, Av Luna 661, very good.

● **Tourist offices**
Libertad e Independencia, T 2688, very helpful.

● **Transport**
Air Líneas Aéreas Riojanas fly La Rioja-Chilecito, 20 mins.

Buses To San Juan, Tues, Thur, Sat at 2200, arriving 0705; to Tinogasta (Catamarca), Mon-Fri, direct at 0700 via route 11, returning same day at 0600; to Tinogasta Mon and Thur 0600, returning 1330 the same days; to La Rioja, 3 times daily with Cotil, to Villa Unión daily at 1345 with Cotil. Connections with Catamarca and Córdoba via La Rioja only.

VILLA UNIÓN AND WESTERN LA RIOJA

16 km S of Chilecito, at Nonogasta, partly paved Route 40 heads W climbing through a deep narrow canyon in a series of hairpins to the Cuesta de Miranda. After rain, this canyon may be impassable owing to deep river crossings; check conditions in advance. After the Cuesta is **Villa Unión**, 92 km from Nonogasta.

● **Accommodation** E *Hosp Paola*, main street opp police station, basic; next door is E *Hosp Changuito*, restaurant.

From Villa Unión, jeep excursions can be made to Ischigualasto and Talampaya, and to Laguna Verde and Laguna Veladero. The remains of a huge volcano crater, La Caldera del Inca, can also be visited from here. It spans 40 km across, between the peaks Pissis (6,882m) and Bonete (6,872m). The bottom of the crater is desert-like but with glaciers beneath the sand in parts, and with a lake frequented by flamingos and other birds. A fascinating area, but hard to reach. Ask for Ursula Hofman in the town for directions, or for organizing an expedition. The tourist office in Chilecito may be able to help, or, in the same town, Jorge Llanos hires out vehicles.

ROUTES From Chilecito, old Route 40, now Route 11, goes via Famatina to Tinogasta. New route 40 goes to Pituil, where the paved section ends, and on to Salicas and Cerro Negro junction (59 km) with Route 60, the Tinogasta-Aimogasta road. From Cerro Negro it is 38 km SE to **Aimogasta** (national olive festival in May) and another 30 km to turnoff to **Termas Santa Teresita** (2 hrs by car from La Rioja).

TINOGASTA AND FIAMBALA

Tinogasta (*Pop* 9,000), a half-Indian former-copper mining town, is in an oasis of vineyards, olive groves, and poplars.

● **Accommodation** A3 *Provincial de Turismo*, Romero y Gordillo, T 23911, clean but run down, restaurant; *Hostería Novel*, nr airport.

● **Places to eat** *Persegani*, Tristán Villafañe 373; *Rancho Huairapuca*, on Moreno.

● **Transport** Buses to Tucumán, Empresa Gutiérrez, Tues, Fri, Sun 1700, Mon, Tues, Fri, Sun 0615, Fri 0845, US$22; return Tues, Fri, Sun. To Catamarca 1700 and 0030 daily; to La Rioja 0930, El Cóndor, US$11. Services twice a week to Chubut, Comodoro Rivadavia, and Caleta Olivia, with Empresa Ortiz, reflect that this is the source region for labour in the Patagonian oilfields.

Mountaineering

Tinogasta is the starting point for expeditions to the second highest mountain in South America. Most recent cartography has allowed for some corrections in altitude so that **Pissis** has been confirmed, at 6,882m, as higher than Ojos del Salado (6,879m). To get there take Route 60 which crosses Tinogasta in the direction of the San Francisco pass. Everyone has to register at the police station outside Fiambalá, take passport. Expeditions organized and horse riding with Omar Monuey, La Espiga de Oro, 25 de Mayo 436.

Fiambalá is 49 km N of Tinogasta. **B** *Hotel* with restaurant, and small, basic *pensión* (unsigned – ask), near which is a good restaurant. There is also a clean *hostería*. Drive or take a taxi from here to **Aguaditas**, hot springs, US$1 entry, temperatures from 30°C to 54°C (make sure taxi fare includes wait and return). The entire province is rich in thermal mineral waters. There are vineyards in the valley. 36 km beyond Fiambalá is Palo Blanco, in the *pre-puna* foothills.

● **Transport** Empresa Gutiérrez daily at 1345 to Catamarca via Tinogasta (1500) and Cerro Negro junction (1610), connect with Coop Catamarca bus to Belén (from Catamarca), about 2 hrs by bad road. Also 0530 departure from Fiambalá. 4WD vehicles may be hired for approaching the Pissis-Ojos region; ask at the Intendencia. For transport into the *puna* ask for Sr Jonson Hugo Reynoso (check state of vehicles).

BELEN

After flooding in 1981, the old Route 40, Tinogasta-Belén road via the Cuesta de Zapata, was closed. Turn W at Cerro Negro for 2 km, paved route 40 heads N to **Londres**, founded in 1558 and the second-oldest town in Argentina, named in honour of the marriage of Mary Tudor and Philip II. The town hall displays a glass coat-of-arms of the City of London and a copy of the marriage proposal.

15 km further (paved) is **Belén** (*Pop* 8,800). The weaving district is famous for weavings, ponchos, saddlebags and rugs. There are good views from the new statue of Virgin of Belén at the summit of the path beginning at C Gen Roca, and an interesting archaeological museum, Condor Huasi. Folklore festivals Oct and Christmas. Belén is encircled by mountains, except to the SE; lush vegetation along Río Belén. North of Belén Route 40 runs another 176 km, largely unpaved, to Santa María at Tucumán provincial border (see page 115), and on to Cafayate (page 116).

- **Accommodation A3** *Samai*, Urquiza 349, clean, friendly, rec; **C** *Turismo*, cheap and good, with bath; *Provincial*, dilapidated.

- **Places to eat** Good breakfast at bus terminal; *Restaurant Dalesio*, nr YPF gas station, excellent and cheap; *El Amigazo*, behind church, good.

- **Transport** Belén-Villavil (thermal springs – open Jan-April), inc side trip to Corral Quemado and end of line at Barranca Larga, 19 km N of Villavil, Tues, Thur, Sun at 0800, returns from Villavil at 1830. (Villavil may have to be abandoned, under threat of seismic collapse.) Sit on right-hand side for best views of impressive canyon and Rio Bolsón reservoir. Belén-**Santa María** Tues 1330, Fri and Sun 2020; return Tues and Thur 0930, Sun 1945. Belén-**Salta** via Hualfín, Santa María, Cafayate Thur 0600.

85 km E of Belén, but best reached by Route 40 which branches N from Route 60, 15 km E of Aimogasta, is **Andalgalá** (130 km; *Pop* 7,800), a beautiful town renowned for strong alcoholic drinks. (*Hostería Provincial*, often full; *Res Galileo*; 3 bus lines to Catamarca). The road, through Saryil, parallels the Salar de Pipanaco on the W and Sierra de Ambato on the E. At Minas Capillitas (N of Andalgalá), rhodochrosite, Argentina's unofficial national stone is quarried; it can be bought at shops around the plaza in Andalgalá.

BELEN TO SALTA

An alternative route to Salta is along Route 53 (43 on some maps), which branches W off Route 40 at a point 52 km N of Belén. It goes through Villavil (thermal springs, open Jan-April, 3 buses a week from Belén) to Antofagasta de la Sierra and San Antonio de los Cobres (petrol available – see page 123). This route is almost impassable in passenger cars after heavy rains, and requires enough fuel for 600 km at high altitudes on unmaintained roads (fill up at Hualfín – thermal springs – 10 km past turnoff to Route 53). Also, the stretch beyond the right turn at Puerto de Corral Quemado is very difficult (37 km of fords), to be avoided in summer rainy season. At Km 87 is Cerro Compo (3,125m), magnificent descent; at Km 99 the road turns right to Laguna Blanca, where there is a small vicuña farm (don't go straight at the junction).

ANTOFAGASTA DE LA SIERRA

(260 km) Together with El Peñón and Laguna Blanca in the *puna*, and Villavil and La Hoyada in the *pre-puna*, this is the main township of NW Catamarca. There are lunar landscapes, with salt lakes, around Antofagasta, and many peaks over 5,000m. Deposits of marble, onyx, sulphur, mica, salts, borates, and gold are present. Wildlife in the sparsely populated region including vicuña, guanaco, vizcacha, flamingoes, foxes and ostriches. No petrol station, but fuel obtainable from *intendencia*. **NB** Petrol/gasoline is rarely available in this region; remember that in the *puna* fuel consumption of carburettor engines is almost double that in the lowlands.

- **Accommodation B** *Pensión Darío*, blue door just off main square; *Almacén Rodríguez*, Belgrano y Catamarca, serves meals, inc breakfast).

- **Transport** Colectivo from Belén on Fri about 1000, arriving 2200, returning Mon 0700, or hire a pickup or hitch.

CATAMARCA

Paved Route 38 runs from La Rioja to the third oasis, **San Fernando del Valle de Catamarca**, (*Pop* 89,000; *Alt* 490m; *Phone code* 0833). It is capital of its province, on the Río del Valle, between two S slopes of the Sierra de Aconquija, about 89 km NE of La Rioja, 240 km S of Tucumán. Cattle, fruit, grapes and cotton are the main agricultural products, but it is also renowned for hand-woven ponchos and fruit preserves. Therapeutic mineral springs. There are traces of Indian civilizations, including extensive agricultural terraces (now mostly abandoned), throughout the province. The *Zonda*, a strong dry mountain wind equivalent to the European *Föhn* or North American chinook or Santa Ana, can cause dramatic temperature increases.

Museums

Instituto Cultural Esquiú, Sarmiento 450, with important archaeological section, open Mon-Fri 0700-1300, 1430-2000, Sat, Sun, am only; **Museo Folklórico**, underground (subsuelo), Paseo Gral Navarro.

Tours

Manzana de Turismo, Gen Roca, primera cuadra, with information, folders, typical handicrafts, visit to the centre where students learn how to make hand-woven rugs. Ask about the Torres y Campanas (towers and bells) tour, comprising many old chapels and churches mainly on the way to Las Pirquitas reservoir. Visitors can also see the place where murdered student, María Soledad Morales, was found in 1990. The affair led to lengthy criminal proceedings (as yet unresolved) and the site has become a shrine.

Excursions

To Dique Las Pirquitas, 3 hrs with local bus 1A from bus station. Bus stops at *Hostería de Turismo* (with restaurant) at Villa Pirquitas, about 45 mins' walk. Five morning buses from 0700, last returns at 2200. Opening hours Mon-Fri 1000-1900, Sat, Sun and holidays 0830-1900.

Local festivals

Pilgrimages to the church of the Virgen del Valle. In July, regional handicrafts are sold at Festival del Poncho, a *feria* with 4 nights of music, mostly folklore of the NW.

Local information

● **Accommodation & places to eat**

A3 *Ancasti*, Sarmiento 520, T 25001/4, restaurant; **B** *Inti Huasi*, República 297, T 24664; **B** *Arenales*, Sarmiento 544.

C *Colonial*, República 802, T 23502, no food, rec, clean, welcoming, good value; **C** *Delgado*, San Martín 788, basic, friendly; **C** *Suma Huasi*, Sarmiento 547, T 22301, avoid TV lounge and rooms above it.

D *Las Cumbres*, Plaza 25 de Agosto. Many *Residenciales* on Av Güemes. Discounts to ACA members at *Ancasti*, *Inti Huasi*, and *Suma Huasi*. Provincial tourist office has a list of families who rent rooms.

● **Places to eat**

Sociedad Española, Urquiza 703; *La Cabaña*, Tucumán 1115, has folk dancing. *La Tinaja*, Sarmiento 500 block, excellent, pricey, live music; warmly rec; *Pizzería Maryeli*, Esquiú 521, basic (but good *empanadas*); *Sociedad Italiana*, M Moreno (off Paseo Gen Navarro), pastas, inexpensive; *Comedor Unión Obrera*, Sarmiento 857, good value, speciality *cabrito*; *Parrilla de Adrián*, Av Güemes block 500, good *asado*; *Montmartre*, Paseo Gen Navarro, good food, reasonably priced; *Marco Polo Bar*, Rivadavia 916, drinks, snacks. Many cheap restaurants along Av Güemes, bars and cafés along Rivadavia (pedestrian street).

● **Banks & money changers**

Banco de Catamarca, Plaza 25 de Mayo, changes US$ cash but not TCs; **Banco de Galicia** changes TCs, US$10 commission.

● **Post & telecommunications**

Post Office: San Martín 753, slow, open 0800-1300, 1600-2000.

Telephones: Rivadavia 758, open 0700-2400, daily.

● **Shopping**

Catamarca specialities from. *Cuesta del Portezuelo*, Sarmiento 575; *Maica Regionales*, next to Aerolíneas Argentinas; *Casa Valdés*, Sarmiento 586; and *Suma Regionales*, Sarmiento y Esquiú. *Mercado Artesanal*, Urquiza y 945, wide range of handicrafts, open 0700-1300, 1400-2000, reached by infrequent colectivo 23 from centre.

● **Tourist offices**

Sarmiento 450, T/F 22695, open 0800-2000, helpful. In small surrounding towns, go to municipal offices for information and maps.

● **Transport**

Air AR (office on Sarmiento, next to *Hotel Suma Huasi*, T 24450/24460) and Lapa (Sarmiento 506, T 34772) to/from Buenos Aires and La Rioja.

Buses Good information at bus terminal. To **Tucumán**, 4-5 daily with Bosio, 4½ hrs, US$10, several other companies; road paved, in good condition except for rough stretch at provincial border (Cuesta del Totoral has steep gradients, hairpins, potholes). To **BsAs**, US$50, 2nd class at 2200, 1st class at 1900, daily. To **Belén** via Cerro Negro with Coop Catamarca, returns from Belén daily 1300 (see page 152). Also Belén-Catamarca via Andalgalá; Coop Catamarca via Saujil, Poman, Chumbicha, Tues, Thur 1000, Fri, Sun 1300, about 8 hrs. Catamarca-El Rodeo-Las Juntas daily at 1300, returns from Las Juntas 1700. Five buses daily to **Córdoba**. To **Santiago del Estero**, 1630, US$12. There are several buses daily to Mendoza.

Buses to Santiago del Estero province: a road runs NE to **Lavalle** (towards Santiago del Estero). This 116 km run over the **Cuesta El Portezuelo** (1,980m), is scenic, but steep and difficult (to be paved). No bus service over Portezuelo to Lavalle, but a service to Frías, E, and also in Santiago del Estero province – No 9 and not No 18 (which crosses the Totoral), run by Coop de Transportes de Catamarca. Leaves 0500 Tues, Thur, Fri and Sat, arrives at Frías 1000, returns 1400, arrives in Catamarca 1900. From Frías travel to Lavalle.

Catamarca-Frías via Totoral, No 18 Mon, Wed, Fri, Sat 0500, arrives 1030, return 1330, arrives Catamarca 1900. No 14 via El Alto, longer trip, arrives Frías 1045. Catamarca-Lavalle via Totoral, same No 18, leaves Tues, Thur, and Sun 1100, arrives Lavalle 1510.

The Northeast

THIS SECTION begins at the Río de la Plata and ends at the magnificent Iguazú Falls on the Brazilian border. Two routes are followed, the Ríos Uruguay and Paraná, describing the river towns and beaches, and the Jesuit missions near Posadas (in particular San Ignacio Miní). Crossings to Uruguay and Paraguay are also given.

Between the Ríos Uruguay and Paraná lies Argentine Mesopotamia: the provinces of Entre Ríos, Corrientes, and Misiones. The distance between the rivers is 390 km in N Corrientes, but narrows to about 210 km in the latitude of Santa Fe.

The province of Corrientes is marshy and deeply-wooded, with low grass-covered hills rising from the marshes. The normal rainfall is about 2,000 mm, but the rains are not spread uniformly and drain off quickly through the sandy soil. Entre Ríos has plains of rich pasture land not unlike those of Uruguay. Misiones is a hilly strip of land between the Uruguay and the Alto Paraná rivers, 80-100 km wide and about 400 km long; its capital is the river port of Posadas. Its boundary to the N is the river Iguazú, which here tumbles over the great Iguazú Falls. Misiones is on the Paraná Plateau; much of it is covered with

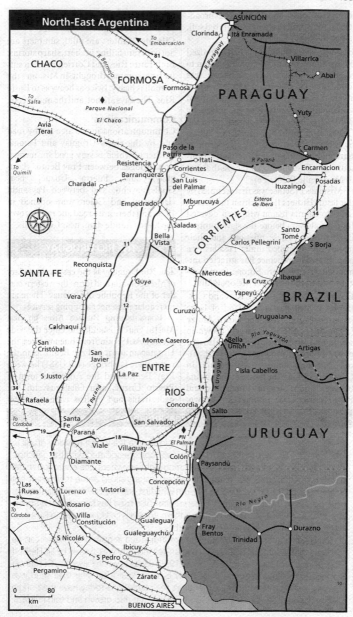

North-East Argentina

To Embarcación

ASUNCIÓN
Clorinda Itá Enramada

CHACO
FORMOSA

R Bermejo

81

R Paraguay

Villarrica

Abai

PARAGUAY

To Salta

Formosa

Parque Nacional
El Chaco

Avia
Terai

16

Yuty

Carmen

To Quimili

Paso de la Patria

Resistencia
Barranqueras

Itati

R Paraná

Encarnación

Corrientes
San Luis
del Palmar

Ituzaingó

Posadas

Charadai

Empedrado

Mburucuyá

Esteros
de Iberá

CORRIENTES

Saladas

14

N

Bella
Vista

Carlos Pellegrini

Santo
Tomé

SANTA FE

11

Reconquista

S Borja

Vera

Goya

12

123

Mercedes

La Cruz

Ibaqui

Yapeyú

BRAZIL

Calchaquí

Curuzú

Uruguaiana

San
Cristóbal

San
Javier

Monte Caseros

Bella
Unión

Artigas

S Justo

ENTRE

La Paz

Isla Cabellos

Río Yaguarón

34

Rafaela

RIOS

14

R Uruguay

To
Córdoba

Santa
Fe

19

Paraná

San Salvador

18

Concordia

Salto

URUGUAY

Viale

Villaguay

11

Diamante

PN
El Palmar

Colón

Paysandú

Las
Rusas

S
Lorenzo

Victoria

Concepción

Río Negro

9

To
Córdoba

Rosario

Villa
Constitución

Gualeguay

8

S Nicolás

Gualeguaychú

Fray
Bentos

Durazno

Ibicuy

Trinidad

Pergamino

S Pedro

Zárate

0   80
km

BUENOS AIRES

forests of pine and cedar and broad-leaved trees, and the land, with its red soil, is reminiscent of Brazil.

History Mesopotamia was first colonized by Spaniards pushing S from Asunción to reoccupy Buenos Aires; Santa Fe was founded in 1573, Corrientes in 1588. From about 1880 there were Jewish agricultural settlements in Entre Ríos, promoted by Baron Hirsch for victims of pogroms in the Czarist Empire (see 'Los gauchos judíos' by Alberto Gerchunoff). Vestiges of these settlements remain at Domínguez (museum) and Basavilbaso, and across the river in Moisesville (Santa Fe).

Misiones Province was first occupied by the Jesuit Fathers fleeing from the Brazilian Alto-Paraná region with their devoted Indian followers before the slave-hunting Bandeirantes. These missions and their history are described under Posadas (see page 167). The province has attracted immigrants from Eastern Europe, from Paraguay and from the rest of Mesopotamia.

Economy Much of Entre Ríos and Corrientes is still pastoral, a land of large *estancias* raising cattle and sheep. Maize (a gamble in the N) is largely grown in southern Entre Ríos, which is also the most important producer of linseed, citrus fruit and poultry in Argentina. In Corrientes, along the banks of the Paraná between the cities of Corrientes and Posadas, rice and oranges are grown.

Misiones is a large producer of *yerba mate*, citrus, tobacco, timber and tung oil.

Climate Winters are mild; summers are hot with rain falling in short, sharp storms. Both Entre Ríos and Corrientes often suffer from summer drought. In Misiones the rainfall is heavy: twice as heavy as in Entre Ríos. The days are hot, and the nights cool.

Communications

Communications in the area are by road and by the rivers Uruguay and Paraná, neither of which is very good for navigation. Bridges between Fray Bentos (Uruguay) and Puerto Unzué, near Gualeguaychú, and between Paysandú (Uruguay) and Colón were opened in 1976, and there are a road and railway over the Salto Grande dam, near Concordia.

THE RIO URUGUAY

The Río Uruguay is the eastern boundary of Mesopotamia and forms the western border of the Republic of Uruguay. There are no regular passenger shipping services.

Boats leaving Buenos Aires go past Martín García island, and enter the wide estuary. At 193 km from Buenos Aires, the Uruguayan town of Fray Bentos is to the right; there is a bridge (toll US$1) between Fray Bentos and the Argentine town of **Puerto Unzué**, near Gualeguaychú, but pedestrians and cyclists cannot cross it

Paraguayan Tea; Indian Tea

Yerba mate (ilex paraguayensis) is made into a tea which is widely drunk in Argentina, Paraguay, Brazil and Uruguay. Traditionally associated with the gauchos, the modern mate paraphernalia is a common sight anywhere: the gourd (*un mate*) in which the tea leaves are steeped, the straw (usually silver) and a thermos of hot water to top up the gourd. It was the Jesuits who first grew *yerba mate* in plantations, inspiring one of the drink's names: *té de jesuitas*. Also used has been *té de Paraguay*, but now just *mate* or *yerba* will do. In southern Brazil it is called *ximarão*; in Paraguay *tereré* when drunk cold with digestive herbs.

In NE Corrientes and in Misiones more Indian tea is now grown than can be absorbed by the internal market. The Indian-tea industry was started by Sir Herbert Gibson, who sent for seed from Assam in 1929; it was sown in Playadito, Corrientes province. Six seeds developed into sturdy bushes. Year after year their seed was given to anyone interested. All Argentina's tea plantations today have their origin in Sir Herbert Gibson's enterprise. Good Indian tea is also grown and sold in Brazil.

other than on motor vehicles; officials will give lifts on either side (customs formalities take about 10 mins). The river now becomes braided into channels and islands.

GUALEGUAYCHU

Opposite Fray Bentos, on the left, is the mouth of the Río Gualeguaychú; 19 km up is **Gualeguaychú**, a very pleasant town (*Pop*, 80,000, with quite a large German contingent; *Phone code* 0446). Since the opening of the bridges between Zárate and Brazo Largo, the journey time from Buenos Aires, 248 km S, has been reduced and Gualeguaychú has become a popular weekend resort for *porteños*. Airport.

Places of interest and museums

The cathedral was built in 1863. On the river is a promenade and on the opposite bank is the Parque Unzué. **Museo de la Ciudad**, San Luis y Jujuy, in former residence built in 1835, US$1; **Museo Arqueologico**, in the Casa de la Cultura, 25 de Mayo 734, with artefacts from indigenous cultures of the Uruguay basin. **Solar de los Haedo**, San José y Rivadavia, in the oldest house in the city, which served as Garibaldi's headquarters when he sacked the city in 1845. Filled with artefacts of the Haedo family, guided tour (Spanish) US$1, Wed-Sat 0900-1145, Fri/Sat also at 1600-1945. **Museo Ferroviario**, Piccini y Rocamora, open air railway museum in the former station.

Local festivals

Lively pre-Lenten Carnival.

Local information

● **Accommodation**

Accommodation is scarce at weekends (when few single rooms are to be found)and during carnival. The tourist office has a list of family accommodation.

A3 *Embajador*, San Martín y 3 de Febrero, T 24414, casino; **A3** *Alemán*, Bolívar 535, T 26153, German-spoken, clean, without breakfast rec; **A3** *París*, Bolívar y Pellegrini, T 23850, F 26260, with breakfast, fan, restaurant, clean, comfortable; **A2** *Berlin*, Bolívar 733, T/F 25111, German spoken, with breakfast, a\c, comfortable; **A3** *Viedma*, Bolívar 530, T 24262, clean, garage extra.

B *Victoria*, Bolivar 565, T 26469, opp terminal, small rooms, clean, modern, with breakfast.

C *Brutti*, Bolívar 591, T 26048, cleanish, shabby, good value, without breakfast, fan; **C** *Amalfi*, 25 de Mayo 571, T 25677, with breakfast, good beds, friendly.

D *Mayo*, 3 de Febrero y Bolívar, T 27661, uncomfortable beds, with bath.

Camping: *La Delfina* in the Parque Unzué, T 22293; *Costa Azul*, T 23984; *Puerta del Sol*, T 23700, and *Playa Chica*, T 25709, all nr the river; *Ñandubaysal*, 15 km E, T 26009, best.

● **Banks & money changers**

Banco Internacional Cooperativa, 25 de Mayo y Perón, changes cash; *Casa de Cambio*: Daniel, 3 de Febrero 128.

● **Tourist offices**

Av Costanera y 25 de Mayo, open 0800-2000.

● **Transport**

Bus terminal in centre of town at Bolívar y Chile. To **Fray Bentos**, 1 hr, US$3, 2 a day, ETA. To **Mercedes**, 1½ hrs, US$4, 2 a day, ETA; to **Concepción del Uruguay, Colón** and **Concordia**; to/from **Buenos Aires** US$15, 4 hrs, Flechabus and El Rápido, 6 a day each.

CONCEPCION DEL URUGUAY

Known locally as Concepción (*Pop* 65,000; *Phone code* 0442), the first Argentine port of any size on the river is 74 km N of Gualeguaychú. Founded in 1783, it was until 1883 capital of Entre Ríos province.

The old town is centred on Plaza Ramírez. Overlooking the main plaza is the church of the Immaculate Conception which contains the remains of Gen Urquiza.

Museums Museo Casa del Delio Panizza, Galarza y Supremo Entrerriano, in a mansion dating from 1793, containing 19th century furnishings and artefacts; **Museo Don Andrés García**, personal collection, open daily 0900-1200, 1500-1800. **Palacio San José**, Urquiza's former mansion, 35 km W of the town, is now a museum, with artefacts from Urquiza's life and a collection of period furniture, Mon-Fri 0900-1300, 1400-1800, Sat/Sun 0900-1245, 1400-1745, US$1.50, written explanations in Spanish, French and English (Itape buses to 3 km from the Palacio, US$3, 45 mins), highly rec.

● **Accommodation C** *Gran*, Rocamora y Colón, T 22851; **C** *Virrey*, González 2075,

T 25017, F 25007; **B** *Res Fiuri*, Sarmiento 779, T 27016, attractive; **C** *Ramírez*, Martínez 50, T 25106, above bus terminal; **E** *Hosp Los Tres Nenes*, Galarza 1233, nr terminal, clean, friendly.

● **Places to eat** *El Canguro*, opp terminal, good food, reasonably priced; *Rocamora*, Rocamora y Millán. Bus terminal bar for tenedor libre meals.

● **Tourist offices** 9 de Julio 844, T 25820.

● **Transport** Bus terminal at Rocamora y Martínez (bus 1 to centre or remise, US$1). To **Buenos Aires**, frequent, 4½ hrs, US$15; to **Paraná**, 5 hrs; to **Colón** 45 mins; to **Paysandú** (Uruguay) 1 hr.

COLON

350 km from Buenos Aires, 45 km N of Concepción del Uruguay, **Colón** (*Pop* 15,000) was founded in 1863. The river is more picturesque here with an attractive costanera and five sandy beaches, and cliffs visible from a considerable distance; a road bridge links Colón and Paysandú, Uruguay. The town is known for *artesanía* shops along 12 de Abril, and there is a large handicrafts fair at Carnival time (Feb).

● **Accommodation L3** *Quirinale*, Av Quirós s/n, T 21978, 5-star, (with casino); **A3** *Plaza*, 12 de Abril y Belgrano, T 21043; with breakfast, a/c, modern; **B** *Palmar*, Ferrari 285, T 21952, good; **A3** *Holimasú*, Belgrano 28, T 21305, F 21303, with breakfast, clean; **B** *Vieja Calera*, Bolívar 344, T 21139, with breakfast, a/c, clean; **C** *Ver-Wei*, 25 de Mayo 10, T 21972, without breakfast, new ownership, clean. Many **families** rent rooms – the Boujon family, Maipú 430, C, good breakfast and other meals extra, rec. Apartments for rent from Sr Ramón Gallo, Av Paysandú, T 472 3280, with kitchen, bathroom, hot showers, close to bus terminal. Several **campsites** along river bank (municipal site, excellent facilities, cheapest).

● **Places to eat** *Comedor El Rayo*, Paysandú 372; *Pizzería Luisa*, San Martín 346; *La Rueda*, San Martín y 3 de Febrero; *Marito*, Gral Urquiza y Andrade.

● **Tourist offices** Av Costanera y Gouchón.

● **Transport** Bus terminal Paysandú y Sourigues. To **Buenos Aires**, 4 a day, US$18, 5 hrs; to **Concepción del Uruguay**, Copay and Paccot, 4 a day, 2 on Sun, US$2; to **Concordia**, US$6 (2½ hrs) and **Paraná** daily. To **Córdoba** 4 a week.

To Uruguay: via the Artigas Bridge (US$4 toll) all formalities are dealt with on the Uruguayan side. Passports are collected on the bus. Easy crossing. Bus to Paysandú, US$3, 45 mins.

PARQUE NACIONAL EL PALMAR

8,500 ha, 51 km N of Colón, on the Rio Uruguay, off the Ruta Nacional 14: The Park (entrance US$2) contains varied scenery with a mature palm forest, sandy beaches on the Uruguay river, Indian tombs and the remains of an 18th century quarry and port, a good museum and many rheas and other birds. The Yatay palms grow up to 12m and some are hundreds of years old. It is best to stay overnight as wildlife is more easily seen in the early morning or at sunset. Very popular at weekends in summer.

● **Access & services** Buses from Colón, 40 mins, US$2.50, will drop you at the entrance and it is easy to hitch the last 6 km to the park administration. There are camping facilities (US$3 pp, electricity, hot water), a small hotel 8 km N of the Park, with restaurant opposite, and a small shop.

CONCORDIA

104 km N of Colón, a little downriver from Salto, Uruguay, this is a prosperous city (*Pop* 93,800). The river is impassable for large vessels beyond the rapids of Salto Chico near the city, and Salto Grande 32 km up-river, where there is a large international hydro-electric dam, providing a route for an international road and railway. Above Salto Grande the river is generally known as the Alto Uruguay. There is excellent fishing in the artificial lake.

Places of interest

In the streets around the main Plaza 25 de Mayo there are some fine public buildings. 5 km NE is Parque Rivadavia, in the centre of which is the Palacio San Carlos, briefly inhabited by Antoine de Saint-Exupéry. The park offers good views of the river and there is also a motor-racing track. To get to the park, take colectivo No 2, 1 block from Plaza 25 de Mayo, to corner of Av Justo and Av Salto Uruguay, from where entrance is 1 block N.

Museums

Museo Regional, Plaza Urquiza, in the Palacio Arruabarrena, local and natural history collections, open 0800-2100 daily, entry free.

Local information

● **Accommodation**

A1 *Salto Grande*, Urquiza 581, T/F 210034, with breakfast, comfortable; **A3** *San Carlos*, Parque Rivadavia, T 216725.

B *Colón*, Pellegrini 611, T 215510, fan, attractive but run down, poor beds, clean; **B** *Embajador*, San Lorenzo 75, T 213018, nr bus station, neat and clean; **A2** *Palmar*, Urquiza 521, T 216050, bright, clean, comfortable, also **B** in older part, with breakfast, clean, friendly; **C** *Argentino*, Pellegrini 560, T 215767, with bath, old fashioned, nice patio; **C** *Concordia*, La Rioja 518, T 216869, with bath, fan, clean; **C** *Colonial Pellegrini 443*, T 221448, with bath, without breakfast, fan, clean, pleasant; **C** *Central*, 1° de Mayo 148, T 212842, reasonable, but shared bathrooms not too clean; **A3** *Federico 1o*, 1° de Mayo 248, T 213323, with fan, clean; **A3** *Centro*, La Rioja y Buenos Aires, T 217776, F 217746, a/c, clean, comfortable, *comedor*; **C** *Victoria*, Urquiza next to Esso, 2 blocks from terminal, quite good.

Camping: *La Posada de Suárez – Club Viajantes* on Av Costanera nr the park, warmly rec, with good *parrillada* alongside.

● **Places to eat**

La Estancia, Plaza 25 de Mayo, good value; *Comedor Las Dos Naciones*, Plaza 25 de Mayo and Av 1° de Mayo, good, moderate prices, large portions; *Mafalda*, corner of Plaza Urquiza and Av Entre Ríos, very good home made ice cream and cakes.

● **Banks & money changers**

Banco Río de la Plata, on plaza, no commission on Visa advances; *Casa Julio*, 1 de Mayo, ½ block from plaza; *Casa Chaca*, on plaza; *Tourfé* on Mitre.

● **Post & telecommunications**

Post Office: La Rioja y Buenos Aires. **Telephone**: 700 block of San Luis (24 hrs).

● **Tourist offices**

Plaza 25 de Mayo, open 0700-2400 daily, lousy map.

● **Transport**

Buses Terminal 2 km from centre. No 2 bus goes to main plaza. To **Buenos Aires**, 6 daily, US$17, 6½ hrs; to **Córdoba**, US$25 with Expreso Singer, at 2200 and 0300, 9 hrs; to **Paraná** 5 a day, to **Posadas** at 1800 and 2300, with Expreso Singer (8½ hrs, US$32), to **Iguazú** at 1810, 13½ hrs, to **Corrientes** US$11. Bus to **La Paz** (Entre Ríos) – see page 163, 1100, US$10.50, 8 hrs. To **Paso de los Libres** direct, El Recreo 1500 Mon, Sat and

several at 0300, US$11, 3½ hrs.

To Uruguay: take No 4 bus from terminal marked 'Puerto', for ferry crossing to Salto US$3-4 (tickets obtainable at a small kiosk, which shuts 15 mins before departure, outside migration in building marked 'Resguardo', 5 departures Mon-Fri, 4 departures Sat, 2 departures, Sun, 20 mins, passengers only. Also buses via Salto Grande dam, Flecha Bus and Chadre 2 a day each, US$3, all formalities on Argentine side, passports checked on bus.

NORTH OF CONCORDIA

About 153 km upstream from Concordia lies the small port of **Monte Caseros** (*Pop* 18,400), with the Uruguayan town of Bella Unión, on the Brazilian border, almost opposite.

● **Accommodation** *Paterlini*, Colón y Salta, T 219; *Conte*, Salta 463; *Cortez*, 2 de Febrero 1663).

PASO DE LOS LIBRES

Above Bella Unión, the Alto Uruguay is the boundary between Argentina and Brazil. 96 km above Monte Caseros is **Paso de los Libres** (*Pop* 25,000), with the larger Brazilian town of Uruguaiana opposite: a bridge joins the two. Paso de los Libres was founded in 1843 by Gen Madariaga; it was here that he crossed the river from Brazil with his 100 men and annexed Corrientes province for Argentina. Road (paved) to Paraná.

● **Accommodation A2** *Alejandro I*, Col López 502, T 24102, pool, cable TV, best; **C** *Uruguay*, Uruguay 1252, T 25672, not clean but friendly, good *comedor*; opp is **C** *26 de Febrero*. Near terminal are **C** *Capri*, T 24126, with bath, and several others.

● **Transport Air** Líneas Aéreas Entre Ríos (LAER) flies from Aeroparque, Buenos Aires to Paraná, Gualeguaychú and Concordia with very low fares; enquire at Puente Aéreo desk at Aeroparque. **Buses** Terminal is 1 km from town centre, nr border. To Buenos Aires US$25. **To Brazil**: minibuses run between town and border, US$0.60. No bus service on Sun – taxi charges US$20. From Uruguaiana there are buses into Brazil.

YAPEYU

58 km N of Paso de los Libres, on the road to Alvear, is the site of a Jesuit mission, famous as the birthplace of the liberator, José de San Martín. Part of the house

where he was born is well preserved, and there is an interesting Jesuit Museum.

● **Accommodation** C *Hosteria ACA*, T 93020; the Carillo family on the main plaza rent rooms, **E**, good; *cabañas* on the outskirts of town; camping by the river.

BUENOS AIRES TO PARAGUAY: THE RIO PARANA

The only long-distance passenger services up the Río Paraná from Buenos Aires are those to Asunción, Paraguay. Depending on the tide, boats enter the Paraná river by either the Las Palmas reach of the delta, on which is Zárate, or the Paraná-Guazú reach, on which is Ibicuy.

BUENOS AIRES TO ROSARIO

Route 9 heads NW out of the capital to **Zárate** (90 km; *Pop* 77,000; *Phone code* 0328), on the W bank, an industrial centre with large *frigoríficos* and paper works. A link including two large and beautiful bridges has been built between Zárate and Brazo Largo, accelerating rail and road journeys alike (the bridge toll is US$6).

● **Accommodation B** *San Martín*, Ameghino 773, T 22713, clean. *Camping Club La Isla*, on the Paraná Guazú nr the Zárate bridge.

● **Places to eat** *Restaurant La Posta de Correa*, cheap, good service. Along the waterfront are many *parrillas* and restaurants.

● **Transport** Bus from Buenos Aires, Plaza Once, US$3, every 30 mins.

ROUTES The highway continues through **San Pedro** (*Pop* 35,500), 50 km further, with many fine campsites on the riverfront, and the grain exporting ports of San Nicolás and Villa Constitución.

North of Zárate, the Paraná de las Palmas and Paraná Guazú rivers, plus the lowlands between, are crossed by the Zárate and Brazo Largo suspension bridges. These beautiful bridges carry rail and road traffic (car toll US$6). Route 14 continues N up the W bank of the Río Uruguay.

GUALEGUAY

At Ceibas, Route 12 branches NW to **Gualeguay** (134 km from Zárate; *Pop* 30,000; *Phone code* 0444). It is the centre of

one of the richest cattle and sheep ranching regions in Entre Ríos. The house in which Garibaldi was tortured by the local chief of police in 1837, in the time of Rosas, still exists. 8 km S is its river port, Puerto Ruiz. Paved Route 11 runs W 224 km to Paraná; other routes go N through Mesopotamia.

● **Accommodation A3** *Gran Gualeguay*, Monte Caseros 217, T 23085; **E** *Italia*, Palacios 1, T 24575, with bath, friendly. There is a municipal **campsite**.

● **Places to eat** In the centre there are practically no restaurants, but the *Jockey Club* and the *Club Social*, both on the main square close to the *Gran Hotel Gualeguay*, cater also for non-members. The *Club Social* has a very nice atmosphere, good food, and you might be invited to see films on certain nights.

ROSARIO

Rosario, largest city in the province of Santa Fe, 320 km N of Buenos Aires, is the third largest city in Argentina (*Pop* about 1 million; *Phone code* 041). It is a great industrial and export centre. The city has a lively cultural scene. It is the home of many popular rock musicians and modern artists and there are good discothèques and theatres. It has a racecourse, two boat clubs and Saladillo Golf Club. The Aero Club is in the suburb of Gral Alvear. Swimming at sandy **Florida beach**, about 8 km N of Rosario. From Oct to early Mar it is warm, and from Dec to the end of Feb uncomfortably hot. Changes of temperature are sudden.

Places of interest

Monument of the Flag, a memorial on the river bank in honour of Gen Belgrano, designer of the Argentine flag, who raised it on this spot for the first time (lifts go to the top); **Parque Independencia**, in the centre of the city, 126 ha, containing lakes and monumental gardens. **Cathedral**, 25 de Mayo, in somewhat eclectic style, contains the Virgen of Rosario.

Museums

Museo Histórico Provincial, Parque Independencia, (open Thur and Sat 1500-1800, and Sun 1000-1200, 1500-1800; **Museo de Bellas Artes J B Castagnino**, Av Pellegrini

2202, 1,600 paintings, including works by El Greco, Goya and Titian; **Museo de Arte Decorativo Firma y Odilio Estévez**, Santa Fe 748, has some Caravaggios, Goyas and Murillos. A recommended pedestrian tour called 'Paseo Centenario' around C Córdoba touches on the interesting buildings and monuments of the 'Golden Days of Rosario' (1880-1950). There are explanation signs now installed.

Excursions

Boat trips to river islands can be made at weekends (eg *Ciudad de Rosario* from Estación Fluvial by the Monument of the Flag, Sat 1730, Sun 1600, 1830), or from Florida beach at any time (US$3-4 river trips; US$100 fishing trips). Canoes can be hired.

28 km N of Rosario is **San Lorenzo** (*Pop* 38,000), with one of the largest chemical works in Argentina. See the restored monastery of San Carlos de Borromeo on the river bank. Nearby is the Campo de la Gloria, where in 1813 San Martín won his first battle in the War of Independence. Visitors are shown a pine tree grown from a cutting of the tree under which the Liberator rested after the battle.

Local holidays

7 Oct (Foundation of the City).

Local information

● **Accommodation**

A1 *Riviera*, San Lorenzo 1460, T 253587, a/c; **A2** *Embajador*, Santa Fe 3554, T 386367; **A2** *Presidente*, Av Corrientes 919, T 242905, good; **A2** *Plaza*, Barón de Mauá 26, T 47097; on Santa Fe: **A3** *Micro*; No 3650, T 397192, opp bus station, and others; **B** *La Paz*, Barón de Mauá 36, T 210905, clean, quiet, friendly, rec, **C** *Río*, Rivadavia 2665, T 396421, opp railway station, clean, friendly; **C** *Normandie*, Mitre 1030, T 212694, friendly, helpful, central.

Camping: La Florida, nr the river.

● **Places to eat**

Don Rodrigo, Sante Fe 968, and *Fénix*, Santa Fe next to Citibank, are both very good. *Doña María*, Santa Fe 1371, does good Italian food; *Casa Uruguaya*, Alvear 1125 (T 69320), away from centre, good; *MariaIronn*, Santa Fe y Pres Roca, rec for dancing. Along the river are good cheap restaurants and fishing club barbeques, good atmosphere.

● **Airline offices**

Aerolíneas Argentinas, Santa Fe 1410.

● **Banks & money changers**

Lloyds Bank (BLSA), C La Rioja 1205; Citibank, Santa Fe 1101; First National Bank of Boston, Córdoba esq Mitre. Open 1000-1600. Most banks charge 2% commission on cheques and cash. Amex, Grupo 3 de Turismo, Córdoba 1147, T 244415. *Casas de Cambio*: *Transatlántica*, Córdoba 900; *Carey*, Corrientes 802; *Carbatur*, Corrientes 840.

● **Laundry**

Santa Fe 1578.

● **Post & telecommunications**

Post Office: Córdoba y Buenos Aires.

Telecommunications: San Luis, between San Martín and Maipú.

● **Shopping**

Bookshop: *Stratford*, Mitre 726, for imported English books.

● **Tourist offices**

Cafferata 729, T 301093.

● **Transport**

Air Airport at Fisherton, 8 km from centre. Minibus service connects with flights, US$4, to and from hotels and AR office (Transportes Ayolas, Dean Funes 1,525m T 839863. Taxi or *remise* US$18. Several flights daily to Buenos Aires with AR, 3 a week with Austral.

Buses Terminal expanded 1994. There are regular bus services to Arroyo Seco, Casilda, Cañada de Gómez, San Lorenzo and other important centres up to 80 km from the city. To **Buenos Aires**, via San Nicolás on Route 9 (4 hrs) or via Pergamino, less frequent, on Route 8 (Chevallier bus every hour, US$20-22; also Ablo, Gen Urquiza, La Unión), NW to **Córdoba** and **Tucumán**. To **Santa Fe**, US$10. To **Mendoza**, US$40. To **Puerto Iguazú**, US$50.

Rosario can be reached from Buenos Aires by Route 8 (marked Córdoba) to Pergamino, and then, following signs, by Route 188, and then 178 to Rosario. This is a better way than lorry-packed Route 9. Hitching to Salta along Route 34 is possible.

Ferry To Victoria, in Entre Ríos, which has a municipal campsite.

PARANA

Some 180 km above Rosario, on the E bank, is **Paraná**, capital of Entre Ríos (*Pop* 210,000; *Phone code* 043), founded in 1588. From 1853 to 1862 the city was the capital of the Republic.

Places of interest

The centre is situated on a hill offering fine views over the river and beyond to Santa Fe. There are many fine buildings; in the centre is the **Plaza Primero de Mayo**, where there are fountains and a statue of San Martín. Around the Plaza are the **Municipalidad**, the **Cathedral**, notable for its portico and its interior, and the tourist information office. The **Casa de Gobierno** at Santa Fe y Laprida has a grand façade. The city's glory is **Parque Urquiza**, to the NW. It has an enormous statue to Gen Urquiza, and a bas-relief showing the battle of Caseros, at which he finally defeated Rosas; also an open-air theatre. There are pleasant walks along the river bank and around the fishing *barrio* of **Puerto Sánchez**.

Museums

Museo de Bellas Artes, Buenos Aires 355; **Museo Histórico**, Buenos Aires y Laprida, open Mon-Fri, 0800-1200, 1500-1800, Sat, 0900-1200, 1600-1900, Sun, 0900-1200.

Local information

● **Accommodation**

There is a shortage of hotel space, especially at peak periods (Semana Santa and July), when the tourist office arranges accommodation with families. There is a greater selection of hotels – at lower prices – in Santa Fe.

A1 *Mayorazgo*, Etchevehere y Córdoba, on Costanera Alta, T 216111, 5-star, with fine view of park and river, has casino and swimming pool; **B** *Gran Hotel Paraná*, Urquiza 976, T 223900; **B** *Super Luxe*, Villaguay 162, T 212787; **C** *Almafuerte*, Av Almafuerte 1295, T 240644. Cheap hotels nr railway station, inc **D** *City*, Racedo 231, T 210086, basic, rec, and **C** *Bristol*, Alsina 221, T 213961, close to the bus terminal, good quality, refurbished, and **C** *Plaza*, San Martín 915, T 210720.

Camping: Balneario Thompson.

● **Laundry**

Laverap, Belgrano 650.

● **Tourist offices**

25 de Mayo 44, T 221632.

● **Transport**

Air Airport: Gen Urquiza, 12 km from town.

Buses New terminal on Av Ramirez under construction. East across Entre Ríos to Concordia on Río Uruguay, 5 a day, 5 hrs. To/from **Buenos Aires**, US$22.

Travelling between Santa Fe and Paraná

The two cities do not face one another, but are 25 km apart and are separated by several islands. From Paraná the Hernandarias tunnel, toll US$2/car, passes under the river to connect with the W bank; from here a road runs 23 km W to Santa Fe across two islands and bridges. Trucks with dangerous loads cross the river by a launch which also carries pedestrians and operates Mon-Sat, 0600-2100, 20 mins' journey, frequency depending on demand from trucks. Frequent bus service between the two cities by Etacer and Fluviales del Litoral, US$2, 1 hr.

SANTA FE

Santa Fe, a larger city of some 400,000 inhabitants, is the capital of its province and the centre of a very fertile region (165 km from Rosario; *Pop* 400,000; *Phone code* 042). It was founded by settlers from Asunción in 1573, though its present site was not occupied until 1660.

Places of interest

The S part of the city, around the **Plaza 25 de Mayo** is the historic centre. On the Plaza itself are the majestic **Casa de Gobierno**, built in 1908 in French-style on the site of the historic cabildo in which the 1853 constitution was drafted. Opposite is the **Cathedral**, with its twin towers capped by blue cupolas. On the E side is the **Colegio de la Inmaculada Concepción**, established by the Jesuits and including the Iglesia de **Nuestra Señora de los Milagros**, dating from 1694, more richly decorated with an ornate dome.

One block S of the plaza is the Iglesia y Convento de **San Francisco** built in 1680. The church has fine wooden ceilings, made from timber floated down the river from Paraguay, carved by indigeneous craftsmen and fitted without the use of nails. Inside are the remains of Estanislao López (see below). The Convent of **Santo Domingo**, a block W of the Plaza at 3 de Febrero y 9 de Julio, has a fine patio and museum; N of the centre at Javier de la Rosa 623, is the modern neogothic style Iglesia de **Nuestra Señora de Guadalupe**, with attractive stained glass windows (open daily 0730-2000, bus 4 from the centre, 20 mins).

Museums

Museo de San Francisco, in the Convent (see above) includes a reconstruction with wax figures of the Consitutent Congress of 1852-1853, daily 1000-1200, 1500-1800. **Museo Histórico Provincial**, 3 de Febrero y San Martín, in a building dating from 1680 (one of the oldest surviving civil buildings in the country), includes pieces from the Former Jesuit mision of San Javier and artefacts associated with the dictator Rosas and with Urquiza, who overthrew him. There are portraits of both men and of Estanislao López, Rosas's ally who ruled Santa Fe, Tues-Fri 0830-1230, 1430-1900, Sat/Sun 1500-1800. **Museo Etnografico**, 3 de Febrero y Av Costanera, includes large collection of artefacts from Santa Fe La Vieja (the original site of the city) and items from indigenous cultures in Santa Fe area, Mon-Fri 0900-1200, 1530-1900, Sat 1530-1830, Sun 1000-1200, 1530-1830. **Museo de Bellas Artes**, Gen López, Tues-Sun 1730-2030, exhibitions of local artists' work.

Local holidays

30 Sept (San Jerónimo); 15 Nov (Foundation of City).

Local information

● **Accommodation**

A1 *Conquistador*, 25 de Mayo 2676, T/F 551195, sauna, pool, gym; **A2** *Río Grande*, San Gerónimo 2586, T 551025, modern, rec; **A2** *Corrientes*, Corrientes 2520, T 592126, with breakfast, garage, restaurant, comfortable; **A2** *Hostal de Santa Fe de la Vera Cruz*, San Martín 2954, T 551740, best, genial, well-kept and run; **A3** *Castellar*, 25 de Mayo y Falucho, T 520141, a/c, parking, clean; **A3** *Hernandarias*, Rivadavia 2680, T 529752, fan, clean, gloomy; **A3** *Suipacha*, Suipacha 2375, T 521135, clean, safe, rec a/c, garage, clean, pleasant.

B *Niza*, Rivadavia 2755, T 522047, very clean, friendly, without breakfast, a/c; **B** *Brigadier*, San Luis 3148, T 537387, 2 blocks from bus station, good, clean, friendly, a/c, some English spoken, parking; **B** *Emperatriz*, Irigoyen Freire 2440, T 530061, clean, pleasant, good value.

Accommodation nr the terminal: **A3** *Bertaina*, H Irigoyen 2255, T/F 553068 parking, a/c, good beds, well maintained; **A3** *Zavaleta*, H Yrigoyen 2349, T/F 551840, cafeteria, with breakfast; **B** *Colón*, San Luis 2862, T 545167, with bath, D without, pleasant, large and clean rooms; **C-B** *Royal*, Irigoyen Freyre 2256,

T 527359, clean, with bath, fan, gloomy; **C** *Apolo*, Belgrano 2821, T 527984, clean, old fashioned, gloomy, poor beds, basic; **C-B** *Carlitos*, Irigoyen Freyre 2336, T 531541, clean, friendly; **C** *Humberto*, Crespo 2222, T 550409, without breakfast, poor beds, basic.

Camping: several sites on the lakes and rivers outside town inc: *Luz y Fuerza*, 7 km N nr Lago Guadalupe; *Cámara del Hogar*, 4 km E on Route 168; 2 sites on Río Colastine, 15 km E on Route 168.

● **Places to eat**

Many good ones, offering excellent meals with good wine. *El Quincho de Chiquito*, Obispo Príncipe y Almte Brown, excellent and good value, classic fish restaurant, huge helpings. Excellent grills inc *surubí* (local fish) at *Gran Parrillada Rivadavia*, Rivadavia 3299. Surubí also at *España*, San Martín 2644. *Baviera San Martín*, San Martín 2941, good salads; *Café de la Paix*, San Martín y Santiago del Estero.

● **Banks & money changers**

Lloyds Bank (BLSA), 25 de Mayo 2501, open 0715-1315; **Citibank**, San Martín 2609. **Amex** representative, Vacaciones Felices, San Martín 2347. *Casas de Cambio*: *Camsa*, 25 de Mayo 2466; *Carbatur*, San Martín 2520; *Tourfé*, San Martín 2901, Sat 0830-1230, changes TCs.

● **Laundry**

Servi Rap, Rivadavia 2834 (open Sat 0800-1300); *Laverap*, San Martín 1687.

● **Sports**

Swimming: on river at Guadalupe beach; local bus.

● **Tourist offices**

San Martín 2836 and at the bus terminal: maps, friendly.

● **Transport**

Air At Sauce Viejo, 17 km from the city. Daily AR flights to and from Buenos Aires, T 599461.

Buses Terminal nr the centre, Gen M Belgrano 2910. To **Córdoba**, US$18, 5 hrs. Many buses to **Buenos Aires** US$19-28; to **Paraná** frequent service US$2, 45 mins; to **Rosario** very frequent, 2½ hrs by autopista, US$10; daily to **Mendoza** (2100), **Posadas**, 12 hrs, US$30, several companies and **Santiago del Estero/Tucumán** (2010). To **Concordia** 4½ hrs, US$16.50. To **Asunción** (Paraguay), daily overnight, La Internacional US$31, común, US$57 diferencial.

UPRIVER FROM SANTA FE/PARANA

On the E bank a road more-or-less parallels the Río Paraná, passing through **La Paz (Entre Ríos)**, a small port (*Pop* 15,200) with regional museum, riverside park and golf club, and **Goya**, the second town of the Province of Corrientes (*Pop* 47,000; several hotels). On the opposite bank, joined by vehicle-ferry, is **Reconquista** (*Pop* 34,800; several hotels). Further N still, at Bella Vista, river crossing is possible at the port 5 km away.

THE IBERA MARSHES

The **Esteros de Iberá** (**Iberá marshes**) are a nature reserve containing more species, it is claimed, than the Pantanal in Mato Grosso, Brazil. Among the species are the endangered aguará-guazú (maned wolf), deer, otters, the Juan Grande stork, kingfishers, snakes, etc. Trips can be organized through Marcus Moncada, of Turismo Aventura 4WD, Junín 1062, Loc 4, Corrientes T/F 33269, from US$75 pp/day, advance booking essential.

Mercedes (140 km E of Goya; *Pop* 20,750) is a good base for visiting the marshes. 27 km S of Mercedes are the strange Ita Pucú rock formations, remnants of a mountain massif long disappeared.

● **Accommodation** *Turismo*, Caaguazú y Sarmiento, T 317; *Plaza*, San Martín 699, T 13, E, cheapest.

At **Carlos Pellegrini**, 110 km NE of Mercedes (3 buses a week), a new visitors centre to the marshes has been opened (take food, sleeping bag, light, binoculars). Workers at the visitors centre take boat trips in small punts, a recommended way of discovering the wildlife quietly, or tours can be arranged in Mercedes or Corrientes. The tap water here is not drinkable, but bottled water is sold at the main store in the village.

210 km SE of Corrientes, on the edge of the Iberá marshes, is the Estancia of **San Juan Poriahú** (16,500 ha), a wildlife reserve with a superb array of animals and birds. Visitors can explore the estancia on horseback, or in pick-ups or tractors.

CORRIENTES

40 km below the confluence of the Ríos Paraguay and Alto Paraná is **Corrientes**. The 2¾ km Gen Belgrano bridge crosses the Río Paraná (toll US$1/car) to Resistencia (25 km), from where Route 11 goes N to Formosa and Asunción. East of Corrientes, Route 12 follows the Alto Paraná to Posadas and Iguazú. The river can make the air heavy, moist and oppressive, but in winter the climate is pleasant. The city was founded in 1588 (*Pop* 258,000; *Phone code* 0783); it is capital of Corrientes province and the setting for Graham Greene's *The Honorary Consul*.

Places of interest

The main **Plaza 25 de Mayo** is one of the best preserved in Argentina. On the N side is the police station built in 19th century French style, On the E side is the Italianate **Casa de Gobierno** and on the N is the church of **La Merced**. Two blocks E at Quintanta y Martínez is the **Convent of San Francisco**, rebuilt in 1861 (the original dated from the early 17th century). The **Cathedral**, built in 1874 is on Plaza Cabral where there a statue to the sergeant who saved San Martín's life at the battle of San Lorenzo. The church of **La Cruz de los Milagros** (1897) houses a miraculous cross placed there by the founder of the city, Alonzo de Vera – Indians who tried to burn it were killed by lightning from a cloudless sky. A beautiful walk eastwards, along the Av Costanera, beside the Paraná river leads to **Parque Mitre**, from where there are good views of sunsets over the river. Up river from the bridge to Resistencia, is a **zoo** with animals of the region. Calle Junín is pedestrianized, with restaurants and shops, crowded at night.

Museums

Museo Histórico Regional, 9 de Julio 1044, Tues-Fri 0800-1200, 1600-1800, Sat 0900-1200, US$1; **Museo de Bellas Artes**, San Juan 643, open Tues-Fri, 0800-1200, 1600-2100, Sat, Sun, 0900-1200, 1800-2000; **Museo de Artesanía**, Buenos Aires y Quintana, Mon-Fri, 0730-1200, 1500-2000, Sat 0900-1200, 1600-1900.

Excursions

Northeast along Route 12 are: **Santa Ana de los Guacaras** (20 km), a 17th-century settlement with attractive colonial architecture. The small town of **Paso de la Patria** (38 km) is a paradise for *dorado* fishing, with plenty of bungalows to stay. (**A3** *Hostería*

Don Julián, T 94021, full board.)

A tiny port on the Alto Paraná, **Itatí**
(*Pop* 5,700), is reached by bus (73 km).
Here, on 16 July, is held a festival which
celebrates jointly the crowning of the Virgin of Itatí (housed in a sanctuary built
1638), and St Louis of France. Thousands
of pilgrims arrive on the 16th (when the
religious ceremonies begin) from San
Luis del Palmar (*Pop* 15,000). *Hospedajes*:
Antártida, El Promesero, El Colonial.

Local information
● **Accommodation**
More expensive than Resistencia, **A2** *Gran Hotel
Guaraní*, Mendoza 970, T 23663, F 24620, with
breakfast, very good a/c restaurant; **A3** *Corrientes*, Junín 1549, T 65019, F 65025, with breakfast,
a/c, parking, good value for Corrientes, good
restaurant; **A3** *Turismo*, Entre Ríos 650, T 23841,
pool US$3 a day to non-residents; **A3** *Hostal de
Pinar*, Martinez y Italia, T 69060, modern, parking, sauna; **A3** *Orly*, San Juan 867, T 27248, with
breakfast, a/c, parking; **A3** *San Martin*, Santa Fe
955, T 65004, F 32326, with breakfast, good
beds, clean, restaurant, parking.

Cheaper accommodation is difficult to find.
In the centre **C** *Robert* La Rioja 437, basic, clean,
without bath. Several nr the terminal inc
C *Caribe*, Av Maipú Km 3, T 69045, clean.

Camping: nr bus terminal and railway station is
Camping-club Teléfono, Av Maipú, hot showers or bath, friendly. There is another campsite
on the riverbank, go up through Parque Mitre
and continue along the road closest to the river;
the site is just past the water works.

● **Places to eat**
El Nuevo Balcón, Pelligrini 962, good food,
clean, reasonable prices; *Las Brasas*, Av
Costanera y San Martín (nr beach). Many others,
and various *pizzerías*. Several tea rooms on San
Juan, and on Junín. Try local baked delicacy
called *chipa*.

● **Banks & money changers**
Banco de la Provincia, 9 de Julio y San Juan,
cash advance on Mastercard; Banco de Ibera
for cash advance on Visa and Mastercard; *Casa
de Cambio El Dorado*, 9 de Julio 1343.

● **Entertainment**
Nightclubs: *Metal*, Junín y Buenos Aires; *Savage*, Junín y San Lorenzo.

● **Posts & telecommunications**
Post Office: San Juan y San Martín.
Telecommunications: Pelligrini y Mendoza.

● **Tour companies & travel agents**
Turismo Aventura 4WD, Galería Paseo del Sul,

Junín 1062, T 27698, Amex. *Quo Vadis*, Carlos
Pellegrini 1140, T 23096.

● **Tourist offices**
Plaza Cabral.

● **Transport**
Local Car hire: Avis at *Gran Hotel Guaraní* and
airport; only credit cards accepted from foreigners.

Air Camba Punta, 10 km from city. (Bus No 8
from urban bus terminal at river end of La Rioja).
Austral (T 27442) and Lapa (T 31625) to/from
Buenos Aires and Formosa.

Buses To Resistencia US$0.55, Cota, every 15
mins, 40 mins' journey, labelled 'Chaco', leave
from harbour; terminal 5 km S of centre (bus No
6 or 11), US$0.50. To **Posadas** US$18, 5½ hrs,
road paved; to **Buenos Aires**, US$30, but there
are more services from Resistencia to Buenos
Aires, Rosario and Santa Fe; to **Paso de los
Libres**, 5 hrs, US$10; to **Concordia** US$11,
Empresa Gualeguaychú, 2 a day; to **Asunción**
(Paraguay) US$18.

RESISTENCIA

Resistencia, the hot and energetic capital
of the Province of Chaco, 6½ km up the
Barranqueras stream on the W bank of the
Paraná. On the Paraná itself is the little
port of Barranqueras, about 600 km upstream from Santa Fe. The city (*Pop*
218,000; *Phone code* 0722) is known as the
'city of the statues', there being over 200
of these in the streets. The local products
are cotton, *quebracho* and cattle.

Places of interest
The **Fogón de los Arrieros**, Brown 350,
entre López y French, is a famous club
frequented by local artists and full of local
art and '*objets*' from abroad. It promotes
the city's statues. Open to non-members
Mon-Sat, 0800-1200, Tues, Wed, Thur
only, 2130-0100, US$2.

Museums
Museo Histórico Regional, Donovan
425, Mon-Fri, 0800-1200, 1600-1800, in
the Escuela Normal Sarmiento, traces the
development of the city (under restoration
Aug 1995); **Museo de Ciencias Naturales**,
Pelligrini 802 (former railway station),
Mon-Fri, 0830-1230, 1600-2000, Sat 0900-
1200; **Museo de Bellas Artes**, Mitre 150,
Tues-Sat, 0730-1200, 1500-1900, collection

of 19th and 20th century local works; **Museo Regional de Antropología**, Las Heras 727 in the Universidad Nacional del Nordeste, Mon-Fri 0800-1200, 1600-2100; **Museo Del Hombre Chaqueno**, Illia 655, sections on indigenous peoples, European immigration and the fauna of the Chaco; **Museo Policial**, Roca 233, Mon-Fri 0800-1200, 1500-2000, Sat 0800-1200, sections on marijuana and other drugs.

Excursions

To the Parque Nacional Chaco, see page 148.

Local information

● **Accommodation**
A3 *Colón*, Sta María de Oro 143, T 22862, old fashioned, clean, comfortable; **A3** *Covadonga*, Güemes 182, T 44444, F 43444, small rooms, clean, a/c, *Tabaré* snack bar.

B *Hotel A.M.C.S.A.P.CH.* (known as Esmirna), H Irigoyen 83 on corner of Plaza, T 22898, owned by local police, with bath, good, a/c; **C** *Alfil*, Santa Maria de Oro 495, T 20882, a/c extra, clean, English spoken.

C *Celta*, Alberdi 210, T 22986, with bath, basic; **C** *Res San José*, Rawson 304, basic; **D** *Aragón*, Santiago del Estero, 154; **C** *Res Alberdi*, Av Alberdi 317, basic but clean, restaurant, friendly owner, rec.

Camping: *Parque Dos de Febrero*, very pretty, nr artificial lake, tent US$3.

Places to eat
Círculo Residentes Santafecinos, Vadia 150, tasty meals, family style. Try *chupin de surubí*, a sort of bouillabaisse, delightful. *Restaurant Sociedad Italiana*, Yrigoyen 204, excellent cuisine, smart, pricey; *Charly*, Güemes 215, snacks, good breakfast.

● **Banks & money changers**
Banco del Chaco, Plaza 25 de Mayo, cash only; Banco de Crédito, Justo 200 block, cash advance on Mastercard. Banco de Iberá changes TCs (3% commission). It can take a long time to change TCs on Mon as locals queue for money; Cambio El Dorado, 9 de Julio 201, changes TCs at reasonable rate.

● **Laundry**
Tokio, Güemes y Brown.

● **Post & telecommunications**
Post Office: Plaza 25 de Mayo, Mon-Sat, 0700-1200, 1500-2000.

Telecommunications, Justo y Paz.

● **Shopping**
Regionales Pompeya, Güemes 154, sells local handicrafts and has an Indian handicraft display. Excellent leather goods at *CHAC*, Güemes 160.

● **Tourist offices**
Justo 135; kiosk in Plaza 25 de Mayo.

● **Transport**
Local Car hire: Avis, French 701 and at airport. Localiza, Roca 460, T 39255.

Air Airport 8 km from town (no bus). AR (T 22859/25360), Austral (T 45550) and Lapa (T 30201) to/from Buenos Aires; Austral and Lapa from Formosa.

Buses To **Corrientes** over the Río Paraná bridge, every 15 mins from Av Alberdi nr Plaza 25 de Mayo, 40 mins, US$0.55. Modern terminal on S outskirts (bus 3 or 10 to centre, US$0.60; remise US$4); to **Buenos Aires** 14 hrs, US$35 several companies, most services overnight; to **Santa Fe**, 8 hrs, US$26; to **Córdoba**, 12 hrs, US$43; to **Formosa** 2½ hrs, US$10; to **Iguazú** US$30; to **Posadas**, 5½ hrs, US$18; to **Tucumán** El Rayo, 1930 and 2200, 12 hrs, US$21; to **Salta** (for connections to Bolivia), Veloz del Nte and Central Saenz Peña, daily 1700, 14 hrs, US$40. To **Bolivian border at Aguas Blancas/Bermejo**, take bus for Salta, change at Güemes, for direct connection to Orán (Atahualpa buses every 2 hrs or so), from where it is a 45 mins ride to border. To **Clorinda** and Paraguayan border US$13, 5 hrs; to **Asunción** daily, via Formosa, La Internacional, 6½ hrs, US$21.

FORMOSA

The only Argentine port of any note on the Río Paraguay, 240 km above Corrientes and capital of Formosa Province (*Pop* 95,000; *Phone code* 0717). The surroundings are flat and swampy, the climate and vegetation tropical. On the opposite side of the river is Isla Alberdi, a Paraguayan duty-free spot, which can be visited only if you have a multiple entry visa.

Museums

Museo Histórico y Regional, 25 de Mayo y Belgrano, Mon-Fri 0730-1200, 1500-1930, entry free, large collection of artefacts with no particular logic.

Excursions

To Estancia Bouvier, 70 km N, an 80,000 ha estate which includes a wildlife reserve. Accommodation available on the Estancia which is accessible only by motorboat. Details: Santiago de la Vega, T 795-1727.

Local information

● Accommodation

A2 *Turismo*, best, San Martín 759, T 26004, best, parking, a/c; **A1** *Colón*, Belgrano 1068, T 26547, noisy, a/c, colour TV, spacious, **B** without a/c, good, inc breakfast; **B** *San Martín*, 25 de Mayo 380, T 26769, a/c, with breakfast, run down. **C** *Rivas*, Belgrano 1395, T 20499, with bath (E without), cold water, basic, run down, friendly; **C** *Colonial*, San Martín 879, T 26345, clean, basic, a/c, parking; **C** *Casa de Familia*, Belgrano 1056, friendly, good. Opposite bus terminal is **D** *Hosp El Extranjero*, Gutnisky 2660, T 28676, modern, a/c, with bath, clean, also short stay.

Camping: *Camping Banco Provincial*, Route 11 4 km S, good facilities inc pool, tennis courts, T 29877; *Las Arianas*, 10 km S (turn off Route 11 at El Pucu, Km 6), T 27640; *Club Caza y Pesca*, on banks of Río Paraguay.

● Places to eat

Ser San, 25 de Mayo and Moreno, good; *Pizzeria Italia*, 25 de Mayo y Rivadavia. Also on 25 de Mayo: *El Tono Maria*, No 55, good Italian food, nice atmosphere, expensive; *Parrillada La Cascada*, No 335.

● Banks & money changers

Banks close at about noon and there are no exchange shops; buy pesos in Asunción or Clorinda if en route when they're closed.

● Tour companies & travel agents

Turismo de Castro, Brandzen 75, T 34777; *Turinfort*, Moreno 58, T 27011.

● Tourist offices

Brandzen 117, T 26502, also at bus terminal very helpful.

● Transport

Air El Pucu airport, 7 km N; Austral and Lapa (T 35979) to Buenos Aires.

Bus Modern bus terminal on W outskirts (bus 4 or 11 to/from centre); to **Asunción**, 0400, 0800 and 1730, 3 hrs, US$10.50, delays at frontier common. Easier to go to Clorinda on the border (US$6.50) and then take a micro to Asunción. To **Puente Loyola**, US$5, Empresa Godoy, Mariano Moreno 1050 (surcharge for every 5 kg of luggage). 6 a day to **Resistencia**, US$10. To/from **Buenos Aires** US$41, La Internacional. Bus services to **Embarcación** are frequently cancelled (scheduled daily 1200; do not rely on this as a route to Bolivia, better to go from Resistencia to Salta and then N).

CLORINDA

137 km N of Formosa, almost opposite Asunción (Paraguay). The Puente Loyola crosses to Puerto Falcón, Paraguay. Border crossing is easy. Clorinda (*Pop* 40,000; *Phone code* 0718) has a banana festival in early October. From Puerto Pilcomayo, close to Clorinda (bus US$0.40) one can catch a ferry to Itá Enramada (Paraguay), a US$0.65, 5 mins' journey every 20 mins.

● Accommodation

B *Embajador*, San Martín 166, T 21148; **C** *Helen*, San Martín 320, T 21118; **D** *Res 9 de Julio*, San Martín y R Sáenz Peña, T 21221; *Res San Martín*, 12 de Octubre 1150, T 21211.

● Transport

Buses from Argentine end of Puente Loyola: to **Formosa** (10 a day), **Resistencia** (4) and **Santa Fe/Rosario/Buenos Aires** (3).

PARQUE NACIONAL RIO PILCOMAYO

50,000 ha, 65 km NW of Clorinda. Flora includes quebrachos, caranday palms and palo borachos. Viewing is in the company of guardaparques.

● Access

Buses run to Laguna Blanca, 4 km from the Park Entrance; 3 km further is the guardaparque office, near which camping is permitted.

MISIONES AND IGUAZÚ

At the confluence of the two rivers above Corrientes the Río Paraguay comes in from the N, the Alto Paraná from the E. The Alto Paraná is difficult to navigate, being shallow in parts, braided in others, its various channels embracing mid-stream islands. Much rice is grown on its banks.

POSADAS

The main Argentine port on the S bank of the Alto Paraná is the capital of the province of Misiones, 377 km above Corrientes (*Pop* 141,000; *Phone code* 0752; very hot in summer). The city's centre is Plaza 9 de Julio, on which stand the Cathedral and the Gobernación, in imitation French style. There is a good Mercado Artesanal at Alberdi 602 in the Parque Río del Paraguay, 11 blocks N of Plaza 9 de Julio, by the river (Mon-Fri, 0800-1200). A good way of seeing the city is to take the No 7 bus ('Circunvalación') from C Junín. Yerba mate, tea and tobacco are grown in the area.

Misiones Province

Ciudad del Este · Foz do Iguaçu
Puerto Iguazú · Iguazú Falls
101
Villarrica
Wanda
Esperanza
Caazapa
PARAGUAY
San Antonio
12
B de Irigoyen
Eldorado · 17
Tobuna
San Pedro
Pto Rico
Trinidad
Jardín América
Dos de Mayo
Cnl Bogado
Encarnación 12
San Ignacio
8
Posadas
Sta Ana
Río Uruguay · Moconá Falls
Ituzaingó 105
Candelaria LN Alem
Oberá · 105
To Corrientes
Alba Posse
ARGENTINA
5
BRAZIL
Apóstoles · San Javier
To Paso de los Libres
0   50
km

On the opposite bank of the river lies the Paraguayan town of Encarnación, joined to Posadas by the San Roque bridge.

Museums

Museo Regional, Alberdi 606 in the Parque Río del Paraguay, open 0800-1200, 1400-2000, rather neglected; **Museo del Hombre**, Gen Paz 1865, open Mon-Fri, 0700-1300, 1400-1900, housing archaeological pieces from the areas to be flooded by the Yacyretá hydroelectric project and a section on the Jesuit missionary era; **Museo de Ciencias Naturales**, San Luis 384, open Mon-Fri, 0800-1200, 1500-1900, Sat/Sun (summer) 0900-1200, US$1, including sections on the Guaraní, Jesuit missions especially San Ignacio Miní, European colonisation and endangered species; **Museo de Bellas Artes**, Sarmiento 1815, open 0700-1230, 1400-1830, entry US$2.

Excursions

To **San Miguel Apóstoles**, 65 km S, a prosperous town founded by Ukrainian and Polish immigrants, where a maté festival is held in Nov (**D** *Hotel Misiones*, clean).

87 km W of Posadas is **Ituzaingó** (*Pop* 10,000), a rapidly growing town serving the Yacyretá-Apipé hydroelectric project (all turbines due to be in place by 1998). Buses run to the Relaciones Públicas centre (free, no stops en route), where a video film is shown and other information given.

● **Accommodation** Several hotels, eg **A3** *Ituzaingó*, Entre Ríos y Iberá, T 20601; **E** *Hosp Dos Hermanos*, Pellegrini y Posadas, clean, friendly. About 15 km W of Ituzaingó on Ruta Nacional 12, Km 1237, is *Estancia San Gará*, full board **A2** pp, or in dormitory with hammock-style accommodation, **C** pp, inc pool and all excursions into the Iberá marshes, by boat, jeep or on horseback (highly rec); a lovely place with extraordinary hospitality. Book in advance: T 0786-20550, in Posadas 0752-27217, in Buenos Aires, 01-811-1132, F 476-2648 (office at Av Alvear 1668, p 5); always ask for owner Sr Pablo Prats.Take any bus going to/ from Posadas via Ituzaingó, get off at turning (drivers know it) and walk 1.5 km to the *estancia*.

Local information

NB After alterations to street numbering, all buildings have old and new numbers.

● Accommodation Posadas

Best is **A2** *Libertador*, San Lorenzo 2208, T 37601, F 39448, with breakfast, also cheaper rooms for travellers; **A2** *Continental*, Bolívar 314, T 38966, F 35302, comfortable but noisy, restaurant, parking, breakfast; **A2** *Posadas*, Bolívar 272, T 40888, F 30294, garage, a/c, TV, comfortable, good service, snack bar, laundry, highly rec.

B *Turismo*, Bolívar 171, T 37401, modern clean, a/c; **B** *City*, Colón 280, T 33901, with bath, a/c, clean and reasonable, central, good value, good restaurant.

Near bus terminal: **B** *Carioca*, Mitre 2437, T 24113, with bath, clean, next to expreso Singer; **B** *Colonial*, Barrufaldi 2419, T 36149; **B** *Horianski*, Libano 2655, T 22675, with bath, garage, fan, clean but poor value; **C** *Res Misiones*, Azara 382, basic; **C** *Gran Hotel Misiones*, Libano y Barrufaldi, T 22777, clean, run down, with bath and breakfast; **B** *Res Marlis*, Corrientes 234, T 25764, clean, German spoken, highly rec; **B** *Le Petit*, Santiago del Estero 1630, T 36031, with bath, parking.

C *Res Andresito*, Salta 1743, T 23850, youth hostel style, clean, noisy.

Camping: Municipal camping ground on the river, off the road to San Ignacio Miní, electric showers, dirty, shop, reached by buses 4 or 21 from centre.

● Places to eat

El Tropezón, San Martín 185, good, inexpensive; *El Encuentro*, San Martín 361, good value; *La Ventana*, Bolívar 1725, excellent; *Restaurant de la Sociedad Española*, La Rioja 1848, good food, popular lunches; *El Estribo*, Tucumán y Ayacucho, good cooking in attractive atmosphere, rec; *La Querencia*, Bolívar 322, on Plaza 9 de Julio, good value, rec; *Pizzería Los Pinos*, Sarmiento y Rivadavia, excellent and cheap; *Pizzería La Grata Alegría*, Bolívar y Junín, good; *Sukimo*, Azara nr San Martín, good for breakfast. The restaurant at San Martín 1788 serves excellent meals, good value. Several cheap places on Av Mitre nr the bus terminal, nr the market and on the road to the port.

● Banks & money changers

Banco de Iberá, Bolívar 1821 (main plaza), changes Amex cheques (4-5% commission); **Banco de La Nación**, Bolívar 1799, opens 0700-1215; **Banco Francés**, San Martín y San Lorenzo, Visa cash advance (am only) also **Banco Río**, Colón 1950. *Cambio Mazza*, Bolívar 1932 and Buenos Aires 1442, open Sat 0800-1200, TCs accepted. Street money changers on SW corner of Plaza 9 de Julio. If stuck when banks and *cambios* are closed, cross the river to Encarnación and use the street changers.

● Embassies & consulates

Paraguayan Consulate: San Lorenzo 179. **Brazilian Consulate**: Mitre 631, T 24830, 0800-1200, visas issued free, photo required, 90 days given.

● Entertainment

Discos: *Los Anos 60*, San Lorenzo y Entre Rios; *Power Bolívar*, between 3 de Febrero y 25 de Mayo and at San Martín y Jujuy, open 0100-0500 Thur-Sun.

● Post & telecommunications

Post Office: Bolívar y Ayacucho.

● Tour companies & travel agents

Viajes Turismo, Colón 1901, ask for Kenneth Nairn, speaks English, most helpful, good tours to Iguazú and local sights. Amex agent, *Express Travel*, Félix de Azara 2097, T 237687.

● Tourist offices

Colón 1985 y La Rioja, T 24360, helpful, maps and brochures in English of Posadas, Formosa and Iguazú Falls. Municipal kiosk on Plaza 9 de Julio, open 0800-1200, 1400-2000 daily. Hotel listings for Misiones province.

● Transport

Air Gen San Martín Airport(12 km), reached by Bus No 8 or 28 from nr bus terminal (ask at kiosk opp terminal) in 20 mins, US$0.45, taxi US$13. To/from **Buenos Aires** with Lapa (Junín 2054, T 40300) and Austral (Ayacucho 264, T 32889), who fly once a week via Corrientes.

Buses Terminal at Av Uruguay y Av Mitre. From **Buenos Aires**, US$40-80, 15 hrs; Expreso Singer and Tigre-Iguazú each have several buses a day: *común* US$47.50, *diferencial* US$58, *ejecutivo* (with hot meal) US$70. Some go via Resistencia, some via Concordia. Expreso Singer (Av Mitre 2447, T 24771/2) and Tigre bus terminal is 5 mins' walk from the main bus terminal. From the Argentine side of the international bridge bus tickets to Buenos Aires are sold which inc taxi to bus terminal and breakfast. Frequent services to San Ignacio Miní (1 hr), US$2 and Puerto Iguazú, *servicio común* US$19 (20% student discount), 7 hrs, *expreso*, US$23, 5 hrs. To **Córdoba** with Singer and Litoral on alternate days at 1200, arrive at 0735 next day. To **Corrientes** US$18; to **Formosa**, US$8. La Estrella bus to **Tucumán**, Tues, Thur, Sun at 1720, 16 hrs, US$28. To **Resistencia**, 6-7 hrs, US$18. To **Concordia** (Expreso Singer) US$32,

2100 daily, 10 hrs. To **Concepción del Uruguay**, Singer, US$29, 11 hrs.

International To **Asunción** (Expreso Singer, daily 1400, 7 hrs, and Empresa Godoy), US$14. To **Montevideo**, a roundabout journey because the main Asunción-Montevideo route passes through Corrientes. One can take Expreso Singer bus to the junction for Colón, at Villa San José (ACA hostel, C), local bus to Colón, bus over the bridge to Paysandú, then on to Montevideo. If going to Brazil (Uruguaiana) there are 3 daily buses (Singer) to **Paso de los Libres** for Puente Internacional. Expreso Singer bus to **Porto Alegre** (via Oberá, Panambí, Santo Angelo and Carazinho), Tues, Thur, Sun at 1400, arriving 0345 next day.

FRONTIER WITH PARAGUAY

● **Argentine immigration and customs**
On the Argentine side of the bridge to Encarnación. Buses across the bridge (from opp bus terminal every 15 mins, US$1) do not stop for formalities; alight, keep your ticket and luggage, and catch a later bus.

Pedestrians and cyclists are not allowed to cross; cyclists must ask officials for assistance. The ferry across the river is for locals only.

● **Exchange**
Pesos are accepted in Encarnación, so no need to change them back into dollars.

SAN IGNACIO MINI

63 km E of Posadas is the site of the most impressive Jesuit ruins in the Misiones region. San Ignacio (*Phone code* 0752) is a good base for visiting the other Jesuit ruins and for walking.

San Ignacio was founded on its present site in 1696. The 100m-square, grass-covered plaza, is flanked N, E and W by 30 parallel blocks of stone buildings with 10 small, one-room dwellings in each block. The roofs have gone, but the massive metre-thick walls are still standing except where they have been torn down by the *ibapoi* trees; each block was surrounded by a roofed gallery. The public buildings, some of them still 10m high, are on the S side of the plaza. In the centre are the ruins of a large church finished about 1724. To the right is the cemetery, to the left the cloisters, the priests' quarters and the workshops. The masonry, a red or yellow sandstone from the Río Paraná, was held together by a sandy

mud. There is much bas-relief sculpture, mostly of floral designs.

200m inside the entrance to the ruins is the **Centro de Interpretación Jesuítico-Guaraní**, generally known as the 'Museo Vivo', with representations of the lives of the Guaraníes before the arrival of the Spanish, the work of the Jesuits and the consequences of their expulsion, as well as a fine model of the mission in its heyday; well laid out. **Museo Provincial**, contains a small collection of artefacts from Jesuit reducciones, open 0700-1900 daily. Son et-lumière show at the ruins, 2000 (not Mon or Tues) US$2.50, weekends only out of season, cancelled in wet weather, Spanish only, tickets from museum.

The site is maintained by UNESCO as a National Monument (open 0700-1900, entry US$2.50, US$10 with guide, tip appreciated if the guards look after your luggage). Allow about 1½ hrs for a leisurely visit. Go early to avoid crowds; good birdwatching. There are heavy rains in February. Mosquitoes can be a problem.

Excursions

To the ruins of two other Jesuit missions: **Loreto**, reached by a 3 km dirt road (signposted) which turns off the main road 6 km W of San Ignacio. Little remains other than a few walls of this once substantial establishment. Note the number of old trees with stones encased between their buttresses and main trunk.

Santa Ana, 16 km W, much less well preserved but more extensive in area than San Ignacio. Santa Ana was the site of the Jesuit iron foundry. The ruins are 1½ km along a path from the main road (signposted), entry US$1.

To the house of Horacio Quiroga, the Argentine writer, beautifully secluded, 2 km outside town, entry US$2, recommended.

To the **Peñón Teyu-Cuare**, 11 km S, a 150m high hill overlooking the Río Paraná offering panoramic views. Tours and excursions on foot, on horseback and by canoe are offered by Dante and Eva Perroue, details from tourist information.

Local festivals

30-31 July.

Local information

● **Accommodation & places to eat**

A3 *Hostería San Ignacio*, T 70064, with bath and breakfast, nice rooms, pleasant grounds; **C** *San Ignacio*, San Martín 823, T 70047, with bath, friendly, good, clean, *cabañas*; **C** *Hosp El Descanso*, Pellegrini 270, T 70207, clean, modern, quiet, owner speaks German, rec, excellent camping; **F** pp *Hosp Alemán Los Salpeterer*, Sarmiento y Centenario, 100m from bus station, kitchen, nice garden, run down but pleasant, 'pool', camping, rec, English and German spoken, owner Peter Sutter is helpful and has good travel information; **E** *Hosp Italia*, San Martín 1291, artists' house, 1 room, laundry facilities; *Hosp de la Selva*, 5 km NE on Route 12, **D** pp with meals, also cabins, horse riding, canoeing and ecological tours, English and German spoken, a good way to experience life on a farm. Ask at *Rest Artemio* (see below) and you will be given a lift there, rec. *Restaurant Artemio I*, good and cheap lunches. There are two *comedores* opp the entrance to the ruins. A shop opp the entrance sells huge homemade ice creams for US$2.50.

Camping: outside the ruins in municipal site; cold showers and toilets. Two pleasant sites by small lake about 5 km S of San Ignacio, on Route 12, cold showers only.

● **Transport**

Buses to/from **Posadas** every 30 mins-1 hr, US$2, last return bus at 2100; to Puerto Iguazú, dep 0915, arr 1500, US$14; to **Buenos Aires**, US$35 inc dinner, 24 hrs, dep 1800 or 1900.

SAN IGNACIO TO PUERTO IGUAZU

Route 12 runs direct NE via Jardín América, 48 km from San Ignacio, where there is an excellent municipal campsite 2 km off Route 12. The main highway continues through **Capioví** (restaurant, *Salto*, and campsite, with a room with beds for budget travellers, pleasant, near Capioví Falls; owner speaks German and English), **Puerto Rico**, 21 km N of Jardín América (hotel, camping, restaurants), and **Montecarlo**, 38 km further N, where there is a zoo (ACA *hostería*, T 97023, highly recommended; *Hotels Ideal* and

---

The Real Mission

The Jesuits set up their first missions among the Guaraní Indians about 1609, in the region of Guaíra, now in Brazil. The missions flourished: cotton was introduced, the Indians wove their own clothes, dressed like Europeans, raised cattle, and built and sculpted and painted their own churches. But in 1627 they were violently attacked by the slave-hunting Bandeirantes from São Paulo, and by 1632 the position of the missions had become impossible: 12,000 converts, led by the priests, floated on 700 rafts down the Paranapanema into the Paraná, only to find their route made impassable by the Guaíra Falls. They pushed for 8 days through dense virgin forests on both sides of the river, then built new boats and continued their journey. 725 km from their old homes they founded new missions in what is now Paraguay, Argentine Misiones, and Brazilian Rio Grande do Sul. By the early 18th century there were, on both sides of the river, 30 mission villages with a combined population of over 100,000 souls. Only four of these show any signs of their former splendour: San Ignacio Miní, São Miguel (Brazil), and Jesús and Trinidad (Paraguay). (Note Trinidad can also be visited by bus from Posadas. See Paraguay section for details.) At the height of its prosperity in 1731 San Ignacio contained 4,356 people. In 1767, Charles III of Spain expelled the Jesuits from Spanish territory; the Franciscans and Dominicans then took over. After the Jesuits had gone, there was a rapid decline in prosperity. By 1784 there were only 176 Indians at San Ignacio Miní; by 1810, none remained. By order of the Paraguayan dictator Francia, all the settlements were evacuated in 1817, and San Ignacio was set on fire. The village was lost in the jungle until it was discovered again in 1897. In 1943 an agency of the Argentine Government took control. Some of the craft work produced at the settlement can be seen at two museums in Buenos Aires: the Museo Colonial Isaac Fernández Blanco and the municipal Museo de Arte Colonial.

Kayken, both **D**, clean, friendly).

ELDORADO

This prosperous small town (*Pop* 14,440; *Phone code* 0751), 16 km further N, is surrounded by flourishing *mate*, tung, citrus, eucalyptus and tobacco plantations. The ACA office is very helpful and has a large illuminated map of Eldorado and its surroundings. For information on the **Misiones Rainforest Reserve**, contact Daphne Colcombet, T (0751) 21351.

● **Accommodation** **A3** *Hostería ACA*, T 21370, pool, good facilities; **B** *Alfa*, Córdoba y Rioja, T 21097; **C** *Atlántida*, San Martín 3087, T 21441, a/c, pool, parking, good restaurants, friendly, rec; **C** *Esmeralda*, Av San Martín, Km 8, clean, basic; **C** *Ilex*, Av San Martín, Km 9, clean, safe; *Gran Riojano*, Av San Martín 314, T 22217, very friendly, 5 mins' walk from main road crossing, with restaurant. **Camping**: Municipal site in Parque Schweim, Av San Martín, Km 1, T 2154, free, good.

● **Banks & money changers** *Cambio Fonseca*.

Near **Wanda**, 42 km further N, there are two open-cast amethyst and quartz mines which sell gems. There are free guided tours to one of them, Salva-Irupé, daily. Regular buses from Posadas and Puerto Iguazu, then walk 1½ km. Nearby at **Puerto Esperanza** is the **C** pp *Hotel Las Brisas*, Swiss owned, English and German spoken, discount for Swiss nationals. (Buses between Posadas and Puerto Iguazú stop near the mines and the hotel.)

OBERA AND THE INTERIOR OF MISIONES

East of Santa Ana (95 km from Posadas) is **Oberá** (*Pop* 42,000), the second largest town in Misiones. There is a Parque de Naciones, with houses to commemorate the nationalities of all the immigrants who founded the town. In the first week of Oct is a Fiesta Nacional del Inmigrante; there are about 17 groups of immigrants.

Places of interest **Museo de Ciencias Naturales**; ceramics workshops; Criadero de Pájaros Wendlinger (with birds of the region); Serpentario, La Paz (with snakes of Misiones), best visited 1000-1200; and the many tea and maté-leaf drying factories can be visited.

● **Accommodation** *Premier*, 9 de Julio1164, T 21214, 3-star; *Cuatro Pinos*, Av Sarmiento 853, T 21306, good value; **C** *Real*, opp bus terminal, T 22761, basic, hot showers; *Res Anahí*, Santiago del Estero 36, T 21127, many others; cheap accommodation at Centro Deportivo; campsite 6 km outside town on road to Santa Ana, with swimming pool and waterfall nearby.

● **Places to eat** *Enqüete* restaurant, Cabeza de Vaca 340, good; excellent *empanadas* at *Bar Terminal* next to bus terminal.

● **Tourist offices** Plazoleta Güemes, Av Libertad 90, open 0700-1900, Sat 0700-1300, very helpful, lots of maps.

● **Transport** Buses to Posadas, 2 hrs, US$5.50, Expreso Singer; once a day to/from Iguazú, 5 hrs.

Route 14 runs NE from **Oberá** through the heart of Misiones. It passes through **Dos de Mayo** (**C** *Hotel Alex*, clean), **Paraíso** (Maconá falls 82 km away), **San Pedro** and **Tobuna** where there are the Alegría falls.

● **Accommodation** At **Palmera Boca**, 3 km from San Pedro: **C** *American Hotel*, Güemes 670, T 3364, meals served; *Camping Itarogo* on outskirts; **C** *Posada Itaroga*, T 0751-70165, a family farm with log houses beside a lake, swimming and rowing boats, inc breakfast, cooking facilities, peaceful, relaxed and friendly, rec.

From Tobuna Route 17 heads W to Eldorado through lovely vegetation, or NE to **Bernardo Yrigoyen**, on the Brazilian frontier, (**C** ACA *Motel*, T 0751-92026, Ruta Nacional 14, Km 1435, clean, friendly). The direct (dirt) road N from Bernardo Yrigoyen to Puerto Iguazu, 142 km, crosses the National Park of Iguazú, via the quiet attractive villages of Andrecito (**C** *Res Los Robles*, clean, quiet, nice), Cabuneí and San Antonio, offering fine views of rainforest.

● **Transport** There are buses to B Yrigoyen from Eldorado and Oberá; from B Yrigoyen local buses run to Iguazú through the national park in dry weather.

THE IGUAZU FALLS

For specific references to the Brazilian side of the Falls, with accommodation and transport links, see Southern Brazil section, the Paraná River. For a general description, local trans-

port arrangements, and specific Argentine references, see below.

The **Iguazú Falls**, on the Argentina-Brazil border 19 km upstream from the confluence of the Río Iguazú with the Río Alto Parana, are the most overwhelming falls in South America. The main falls are 20m higher than Niagara and about half as wide again. The Río Iguazú (*guazú* is Guaraní for big), which rises in the Brazilian hills near Curitiba, receives the waters of some 30 rivers as it crosses the plateau. Above the main falls the river, sown with wooded islets, opens out to a width of 4 km. There are rapids for 3½ km above the 60m precipice over which

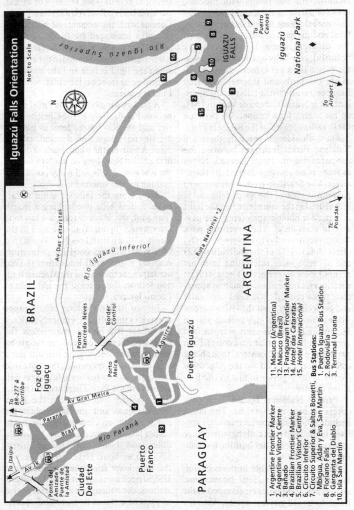

Iguazú Falls Orientation

Not to Scale

1. Argentine Frontier Marker
2. Argentine Vistor's Centre
3. Bañado
4. Brazilian Frontier Marker
5. Brazilian Visitor's Centre
6. Circuito Inferior
7. Circuito Superior & Saltos Bossetti, Mbigua, Adán y Eva, San Martín
8. Garganta del Diablo
9. Floriano Falls
10. Isla San Martín
11. Macuco (Argentina)
12. Macuco (Brazil)
13. Paraguayan Frontier Marker
14. Hotel das Cataratas
15. Hotel Internacional

Bus Stations:
1. Puerto Iguazú Bus Station
2. Rodoviaria
3. Terminal Urbana

the water plunges in 275 falls over a frontage of 2,470m, at a rate of 1,750 cubic metres a second.

Above the impact of the water upon basalt rock hovers a perpetual 30m high cloud of mist in which the sun creates blazing rainbows. Viewed from below, the tumbling water in its setting of begonias, orchids, fern and palms with toucans, flocks of parrots and cacique birds, swifts (*vencejos*) dodging in and out of the very falls, and myriads of butterflies (at least 500 different species), is majestically beautiful, especially outside the cool season (when the water is much diminished, as are the birds and insects). The first European visitor to the falls was the Spaniard Alvar Núñez Cabeza de Vaca in 1541, on his search for a connection between the Brazilian coast and the Río de la Plata.

On both sides of the falls there are National Parks. Transport between the two parks is via the Ponte Tancredo Neves as there is no crossing at the falls themselves. The Brazilian park offers a superb panoramic view of the whole falls and is best visited in the morning when the light is better for photography (entry fee payable in reais only). The Argentine park (which requires a day to explore properly) offers closer views of the individual falls and is much more interesting from the point of view of seeing the forest with its wildlife and butterflies, though to appreciate these properly you need to go early and get well away from the visitors areas. Busiest times are holiday periods and on Sun, when helicopter tours over the falls are particularly popular (and noisy). Both parks have visitors' centres, though the information provided by the Argentine Centre is far superior to that in the Brazilian Centre.

Parque Nacional Iguazú The park covers an area of 55,000 ha. The fauna includes the black howler monkey, capybara, jaguar and puma, along with a huge variety of birds; neither hunting nor fishing is allowed.

Entry US$5, payable in pesos or dollars only (guests at *Hotel Internacional* should pay and get tickets stamped at the hotel to avoid paying again). Visitors'

Centre includes a museum of local fauna and an auditorium for periodic slide shows (on request, minimum 8 people), no commentary, only music; it also sells a good guide book on Argentine birds.

The Garganta del Diablo or Devil's Throat, the most spectacular of the falls, can be visited from Puerto Canoas (reached by bus – see below – or by car, parking US$1). Boats (US$5) link Puerto Canoas with the remains of a series of catwalks (damaged by floods in 1980) which lead to a point above the Garganta, particularly recommended in the evening when the light is best and the swifts are returning to roost on the cliffs, some behind the water.

A trail starting behind the Hotel Internacional leads down to the Circuito Inferior and the Río Iguazu ferry to Isla San Martín, ferry leaves on demand, takes 3 mins. A path on the island leads to the top of the hill, where there are trails to some of the less visited falls and rocky pools (take bathing gear in summer to cool off).

Away from the falls are other attractions: a bird hide overlooking a marsh (Bañado); the Macuco trail, a 4 km-long interpreted (Spanish) nature trail in the forest, with a natural pool (El Pozón) fed by a waterfall and good for swimming. Another nature trail leads from the old airstrip, near the start of the Macuco trail, and follows the route of the old road to Puerto Iguazú.

Iguazu Jungle Explorer offer a range of services including Aventura Náutica, a powerboat trip on the river below the falls, US$25, and tours of the jungle by jeep (Spanish only) 'good fun but not a serious nature experience'; these are sold through agencies in Puerto Iguazú as well as direct in the Park. There are also nighttime walking tours between the Hotel Internacional and the falls when the moon is full; on clear nights the moon casts a blue halo over the falls. Mountain bikes and boats can also be hired, US$2.50 an hour. Helicopter rides over the falls leave from the Brazilian side, US$50 pp, 7 mins. Apart from disturbing visitors, the helicopters are also reported to present a threat to some bird species which are laying thinner-shelled eggs.

In the rainy season, when water levels are high, waterproof coats or swimming costumes are advisable for some of the lower catwalks and for boat trips. Cameras should be carried in a plastic bag. Wear shoes with good soles, as the rocks can be very slippery in places.

Park information
● Accommodation & food
See under Puerto Iguazú or Foz do Iguaçu. The latter, though less convenient, is much the larger town, tends to be cheaper with more choice. Food and drinks are available in the Park but are expensive so best to take your own.

● Transport
Transportes Cataratas buses run every 30-45 mins from Puerto Iguazú bus terminal, stopping at the National Park entrance for the purchase of entry tickets and continuing to Puerto Canoas. Fares US$2 to Visitors' Centre, US$2.50 to Puerto Canoas, payable in pesos, dollars or reais. First bus 0640, last 1700, last return 1900, journey time 30 mins. These buses are sometimes erratic, especially when it is wet, even though the times are clearly indicated. There are fixed rates for taxis, US$30, up to 5 people. A tour from the bus terminal, taking in both sides of the Falls, costs US$40. Hitchhiking to the Falls is difficult, but you can hitch up to the Posadas intersection at Km 11, then it is only 7 km walk. For transport between the Argentine and Brazilian sides see below under Puerto Iguazú.

Motorists visiting the Argentine side from Brazil can park overnight in the National Park, free. Taxis between the border and Puerto Iguazú cost US$15 and between the border and *Hotel Internacional Iguazú* cost US$35. Between Oct and Feb (daylight saving dates change each year) Brazil is 1 hr ahead of Argentina.

PUERTO IGUAZU

A small town (*Pop* 19,000; *Phone code* 0757) above the river on the Argentine side; at the far end of Av Tres Fronteras there is a *mirador* overlooking the confluence of rivers Iguazú and Alto Paraná, with several tourist souvenir and crafts stalls.

Museums
Museo Mbororé, San Martín 231, Mon-Sat 0900-1200, 1600-2000, Sun 1600-2000, exhibition on Guaraní culture.

Local information
● Accommodation
Crowded during summer (Jan-Feb), Easter and July holiday periods and busy at other times of the year. Accommodation is generally expensive. Outside the high season be prepared to shop around and to bargain.

L2-L3 *Internacional Iguazú*, T 20748, F 20311, 5-star, pool, casino, good restaurants, business facilities, overlooking the falls, rooms with garden views cost less, excellent, check-out can take ages. Reservations at Av Eduardo Madero 1020 (T 311-4259, or 313-6292), Buenos Aires (in UK through Utell Internacional); *Cataratas*, Route 12, Km 4, T 21390, 5-star, pool, gymnasium.

A1 *Esturión*, Av Tres Fronteras 650, T 20020, clean, comfortable, swimming pool, good restaurant, reservations at Belgrano 265, p10, Buenos Aires. **A3** *Saint George*, Av Córdoba 148, T 20633, F 20651, with breakfast, comfortable, pool and garden, good, expensive restaurant, B in older part, highly rec; **A3** *La Cabaña*, Av Tres Fronteras 434, T 20564, with shower and breakfast, a/c, good, clean and friendly, with an older part and a new annexe, swimming pool, rec; **A3** *Libertador*, Bompland 110, T 20416, modern, central, helpful, large bedrooms and public rooms, rooms at back have balconies overlooking garden and swimming pool; **A3** *Alexander*, Córdoba 685, T 20249, T 20566, opp bus station, a/c, inc meagre breakfast, pool; **A3** *Las Orquídeas*, Ruta 12, Km 5, T 20472, in the National Park, very comfortable, clean.

B *Hostería Casa Blanca*, Guaraní 121, T 21320, 2 blocks from bus station, with breakfast, fan, large rooms with phone, friendly, rec. Behind *Saint George* is **B** *Hostería Los Helechos*, Amarante 76 (off Córdoba), T 20338, with bath and breakfast, owner speaks German, clean, pleasant and friendly, fan, motel-style accommodation, 10% discount for ISIC and YHA card holders, pool; **B** *Res Gloria*, Av Uruguay 344, with bath and fridge, pool, clean, quiet, friendly; **C** *Res Lilian*, Beltrán 183, T 20968, 2 blocks from bus terminal, with bath, clean, helpful, safe, rec; **B** *Res Río Selva*, San Lorenzo 147, T 21555, clean, friendly, laundry facilities, large garden, use of swimming pool, communal barbecue, highly rec; **B** *Tierra Colorada*, Córdoba y El Urú 265, T 20649, very good, clean, with fan and bath, trips arranged; **C** *King*, Aguirre 209, T 20917, pool, hot showers, good value; **C** *Misiones*, Aquirre 304, T 20991, with bath and breakfast, fan, clean, friendly; **C** *Res Paquita*, Av Córdoba 158, T 20434, opp bus terminal, clean, nice setting, some rooms with terrace rec; **C** *Res San Fernando*, Córdoba y Guaraní, T 21429, close to bus station, with bath, clean, popular, D in low season.

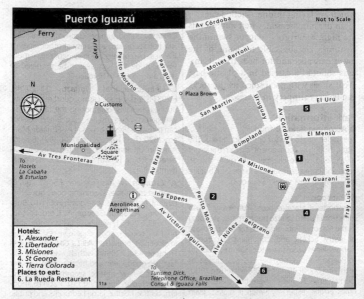

Puerto Iguazú

Not to Scale

Hotels:
1. Alexander
2. Libertador
3. Misiones
4. St George
5. Tierra Colorada
Places to eat:
6. La Rueda Restaurant

D *Hosp Uno*, Beltrán 116, T 20529, with bath, friendly, IYHA discount, clean, rec. The Tourist Office has a list of *Casas Familiares* (**E** pp), though it may be reluctant to find private accommodation unless the hotels are full.

Camping: free site 600m past parking area at Puerto Canoas. Tables, but no other facilities. Camping sometimes permitted at the school just inside the Park entrance. Municipal campsite in Puerto Iguazú reported 'grim'. Camping El Pindó at the edge of town, charges US$1.60 pp, plus charge for tent and for use of pool, friendly, but very run down. There are also facilities at Complejo Turístico Americano, Km 5, Route 12, T 2762 inc pool (open to non-guests, US$2.50) in pleasant, wooded gardens, but no food; US$3 pp, US$3/car, US$3/tent.

● **Places to eat**
La Rueda, Av Córdoba 28, good food at reasonable prices; *Pizzería Ser*, Victoria Aguirre 453, good pizzas; *Charo*, Córdoba 106, good food, popular with locals, no credit cards; *Don Nicola*, Bompland 555, good; *El Criollito*, Av Tres Fronteras 62, rec; *Casa de Comercio*, Aguirre 327; *Tomás*, Córdoba y Misiones, at bus terminal, open 24 hrs, *tenedor libre*; *Chapa*, behind bus station, cheap, highly rec; *Fechoria*, Ing Eppens 294, good *empanadas*; *Panificadora Real*, Cordoba y Guarani, good bread.

● **Airline offices**
Aerolíneas Argentinas, Brasil y Aguirre, T 20194; **Lapa**, Bompland 110, loc 7, T 20214.

● **Banks & money changers**
Banco de la Nación, Aguirre, cash only, am only. Three *casas de cambio* opp the tourist office and several on Av Aguirre towards the outskirts of town towards the falls inc **Dick**, changes TCs, at high commission (up to 10%). Kiosk at the bus terminal poor rates. Rates vary so shop around. Alternatively change dollars in Foz do Iguaçu and buy pesos in Puerto Iguazú.

● **Tour companies & travel agents**
Turismo Dick, Aguirre 226, T 20556, also in Foz do Iguaçu; *Reinhard Foerster*, Privat Servis, Av Tres Fronteras 335, T 2774, offers naturalists' and birdwatchers' programmes; *Macuco Tur*, Terminal, local 23, T 21696; *Turismo Caracol*, Aguirre 563, T 20064, does all-day tour of both sides of falls, inc good meal in Brazil, but mainly for 'non-English speaking clients with an interest in shopping'. *Turismo Cuenca del Plata*, Amarante 76, T 20338, offers 10% discount to ISIC and youth card holders on local excursions. Recommended taxi-guide, Juan Villalba, T 20973 (radiotaxi 044), good value, speaks basic English. Agencies arrange day tours to the Brazilian side (lunch in Foz), Itaipú and Ciudad del Este (US$30), and to a Wanda gem mine, San Ignacio Miní and a local zoo (10 hrs

driving time, US$30, not inc entry fees, may be cheaper for more than 2 in a taxi or hired car). *Africana Tours*, Esmeralda 358, Buenos Aires T/F 394-1720, are rec for their complete package, by plane or bus, inc all tours, hotels and half-board (US$167-598 depending on hotel). Many agencies eg Flyer Turismo run tours from Buenos Aires, starting at US$75 for 1-day.

● **Tourist offices**
Aguirre 396, T 20800, open Mon-Fri 0800-1200, 1500-2000, Sat/Sun 0800-1200, 1630-2000.

● **Transport**
Local Car hire: Avis at airport. Localiza, at airport and Aguirre 279, T 20975. Cars may be taken to the Brazilian side for an extra US$5.

Air There is an Argentine domestic airport nr the Falls, and a Brazilian international airport about half-way between Foz do Iguaçu and the Falls. Taxi between the two airports over the bridge costs US$25. Expreso A del Valle buses (T 20348) run between Argentine airport and hotels, about 2 hrs before plane departures, US$3; it stops at the bus terminal, check times at Aerolíneas Argentinas office in Puerto Iguazú. A bus meets each flight on arrival, tickets US$3. Taxis charge US$10 to *Hotel Internacional* and at least US$18 to Puerto Iguazú and US$14 to Foz do Iguaçu.

AR, Lapa and Dinar fly direct to/from Buenos Aires (1 hr 50 mins). For best view on landing, sit on left side of aircraft. Flights to **Buenos Aires** are very crowded.

Buses To/from **Buenos Aires**, 21 hrs, Expreso Singer, Expreso Tigre, Expreso Iguazú and other companies daily, US$40 *común*, US$65 *cama* (some offer student discounts). It is cheaper to take a local bus to Posadas and then rebook. To **Santiago del Estero**, Wed and Sat at 0130 (20 hrs) with Cotal, gives student discount. To **Córdoba**, daily at 1130, via Posadas 26 hrs, US$40, with Singer or El Litoral. To **Rosario** daily except Thur, 24 hrs, US$50. To **Posadas**, stopping at San Ignacio Miní, frequent, 5 hrs, US$23, expreso, 7 hrs, US$19 *servicio común*. To **San Ignacio Miní**, US$14 *servicio común*, US$17 *rápido*. To **Resistencia** daily 1430 and 2200, 11 hrs, US$30; change there for Bolivian border at Aguas Blancas/Bermejo, via Güemes and Orán. To **Eldorado**, 2 hrs, US$5 with Cotal. To **Salta**, via Tucumán, Tues, Thur, Sun at 1100, 12 hrs, US$80, with Itatí.

FRONTIER WITH BRAZIL

This crossing via the Puente Tancredo Neves is straightforward. If crossing on a day visit no immigration formalities are required.

Argentine immigration is at the Brazilian end of the bridge. If entering Argentina buses stop at immigration.

● **Brazilian Consulate**
In Puerto Iguazú, Guaraní y Beltrán, 0800-1200.

● **Transport**
Buses leave Puerto Iguazú terminal every 20 mins, US$1.50 but do not wait at the frontier so if you need exit and entry keep your ticket and catch the next bus.

FRONTIER WITH PARAGUAY

Ferry service from the port in Puerto Iguazú to Tres Fronteras is for locals only (no immigration facilities). Crossing to Paraguay is via Puente Tancredo Neves to Brazil and then via the Puente de la Amistad to Ciudad del Este. Brazilian entry and exit stamps are not required unless you are stopping in Brazil.

● **Paraguayan Consulate**
Bompland 355.

● **Transport**
Direct buses (non-stop in Brazil), leave Puerto Iguazú terminal every 30 mins, US$2, 45 mins, liable to delays especially in crossing the bridge to Ciudad del Este.

THE CHACO

Between the NW highlands and the Río Paraná to the E lies the Argentine Chaco, comprising the entire provinces of Formosa and Chaco, parts of Salta, Santiago del Estero and Santa Fe, and a tiny corner of the province of Córdoba. Its S limit is the Río Dulce valley, which forms a segment of the border between Santiago del Estero and Córdoba provinces. It is a sprawling alluvial lowland, rising gradually toward the W, covered by palm savanna and sometimes impenetrable thorn scrub; the birdlife is abundant and interesting.

Climate There are two climatic zones: the Dry Chaco and the Humid Chaco, each with distinct flora and fauna. South America's highest temperatures, exceeding 45°C, have been recorded here, but winters are mild, with an occasional touch of frost in the S. Rain falls mostly in summer, decreasing from E to W.

Numerous **Indian peoples**, who call themselves Wichi, inhabit the Chaco, including the Toba, Mataco, Mocoví, Pilagá, and some immigrant Mapuches from the S.

Economy The Chaco is mostly cattle country, consisting of large estancias with low stocking rates. Tannin and cotton are the traditional industries of the Chaco, although acreage planted to sunflowers has increased dramatically, along with maize and sorghum. The iron-hard *quebracho* (axe-breaker) tree, which grows only in the Argentine and Paraguayan Chaco, is the purest known source of tannin. The industry is struggling against competition from synthetic tannin and the huge mimosa plantations in South Africa. The more accessible eastern forests have nearly disappeared; deforestation of all species is proceeding rapidly in the N and W of the province, which produces charcoal for a military steel foundry in Jujuy. Small roadside factories also produce custom furniture.

Towns of the Chaco The most important ones – Resistencia and Formosa – are on the W bank of the Paraná and Paraguay and are described under Argentine Mesopotamia. Apart from Roque Sáenz Peña, the only other town of any importance is Santiago del Estero, on the W boundary of the Chaco.

ROQUE SAENZ PENA

Route 16, the main road across the Chaco runs NW from Resistencia to connect with Route 9, the main northern highway, N of Metán and provides the quickest route between Paraguay and NW Argentina. It is mostly paved. **Presidencia Roque Sáenz Peña** (*Pop* 75,000; *Phone code* 0714), 160 km NW of Resistencia on Route 16, offers almost no shade for relief from the overpowering summer heat. The Parque Zoológico, 3 km from the centre, is one of the best in the country, containing a wide variety of animals native to the Chaco, as well as a botanical reserve of local species.

● **Accommodation A2** *Gualok*, San Martín 1198, T 20521, inc use of thermal baths (also available to non-residents for a small charge); **A3** *Augustus*, Belgrano 483, T 22809, a/c; **B** *Orel*, San Martín 130, T 20101; *Res Asturias*, Belgrano 402, T 20210, fair; *Res Sáenz Peña*, Sub Palmira 464, T 20320, nr bus station, cheap, clean, friendly.

● **Transport** Buses to Buenos Aires, daily

2000, US$40 (from Buenos Aires also daily 2000), La Estrella and La Internacional alternate days; to **Santiago del Estero** and Tucumán, Empresa El Rayo daily; to **Resistencia** (connection for Salta 1700 daily), 2 hrs, US$4.

Central Sáenz Peña has buses at 1100, 1530 and 2000 to the village of **Castelli**, about 100 km N, which has a large Toba Indian community and an *artesanía* shop (**E** *Hotel Guc*, basic). On route 16, 23 km E of Sáenz Peña, is Quitilipi, a Toba community with a free municipal campsite.

PARQUE NACIONAL CHACO

Between Resistencia and Sáenz Peña, an ecological island of 15,000 ha, preserves some of the last remaining eastern Chaco forest and savanna. It is a good place to see the region's abundant bird life. Flora including three species of quebrachos as well as the palo borracho. The park keeper offers a 1-2-hr walk, explaining about plants, animals and the region, recommended.

● **Accommodation** Camping facilities, good, free, cold showers, but the nearest supplies are in Capitán Solari, 6 km from the park entrance.

● **Transport** Buses from Resistencia 4 buses daily, 2½ hrs, US$6, as far as Capitán Solari.

ROUTES ACROSS THE CHACO 31 km NW of Roque Sáenz Peña is **Avia Terai**, where the road forks. Provincial Route 94 goes SW to Gen Pinedo, then continues paved as national Route 89 to Quimilí and Santiago del Estero.

Federico Kirbus tells us that on the border of Chaco and Santiago del Estero provinces on this road is **Campo del Cielo**, a meteorite impact field about 15 km by 4 km where about 5,000 years ago a planetoid broke before landing into 30 main pieces. Some of the meteorites are on display in Buenos Aires (the Rivadavia Museum and the Planetarium), but the largest, 'El Chaco' (33.4 tonnes), is on display at the Campo. Access at Gancedo, where you travel 15 km S to Las Víboras.

From Avia Terai, Route 16, heading NW passes through **Pampa del Infierno** to the Santiago del Estero border. In Santiago province the road is good to Los Tigres, then less good to the Salta border. From this border to **Macapillo**, it is straight, well-paved. After Macapillo Route 16 continues to **Joaquín V González**, around which the road is appalling and difficult after rain, then to Ceibalito, El Tunal and on to Route 9. At Ceibalito, 18 km beyond González, an excellent lateral detour leaves Route 16 to connect with provincial Route 5 (passing Parque Nacional Finca El Rey, see page 115) and Route 9 at Lumbreras. The J V González stretch can be avoided by a dust-road detour between just past Macapillo to El Tunal, via Corral Quemado.

● **Services** There are service stations at Roque Sáenz Peña, Pampa del Infierno (ACA *Hostería*), Pampa de los Guanacos (good hot, clean and free showers at the YPF station, and good value set dinner at the *comedor* next door), **Taco Pozo** (basic *Hospedaje* ½ block from ACA station), **El Quebrachal** (gaucho festival in late Nov) and J V González (last fuel before Güemes en route to Salta). Fuel cannot be pumped during frequent power cuts. In general, Chaco roads are poor.

The Lake District

THE LAKE DISTRICT contains a series of great lakes strung along the foot of the Andes from above 40° to below 50° in the Los Glaciares National Park area. In the N the W ends of these lakes cut deeply into the mountains, their water lapping the forested skirts of some of the most spectacular snow-capped peaks in the world; their eastern ends are contained by the frontal moraines deposited there by the ancient glaciers which gouged out these huge lakes. The water is a deep blue, sometimes lashed into white froth by the region's high winds. The area is good for fishing, water-sports, walking, climbing and skiing.

See the Chilean chapter, **The Lake District**, page 767 for map and details of the system of lakes on the far side of the Andes. These can be visited through various passes.

NB Off season, from mid-Aug to mid-Nov, many excursions, boat trips, etc, run on a limited schedule, if at all. Public transport is also limited. For **Fishing**, see page 216.

ROUTES Neuquén is a major stop en route from the E coast to the northern lakes and Bariloche. From Buenos Aires, Route 5 goes via **Chivilcoy** (*Pop* 49,000) and **Pehuajó** (*Pop* 28,500) to **Santa Rosa** (*Pop* 75,000; *Phone code* 0954), capital of La Pampa province, 619 km from Buenos Aires.

● **Accommodation In Santa Rosa**: **A2** *Calfu-cura*, San Martín 695, T 23608, 4-star, no meals, but excellent steak restaurant round the corner; **B** *Hostería Río Atuel*, Luro 256, opp bus terminal, T 22597, very good, rec; **C** *San Martín*, Alsina 101, T 22549, clean, restaurant, garage; **C** *Motel Calden*, Route 35, Km 330, T 24311, good restaurant attached, large rooms.

79 km S of Santa Rosa on Route 35 a road heads 28 km W to **General Acha** after which desert has to be crossed either on Route 20 to Cruz del Desierto and Catriel (no fuel on this stretch), thence on Route 151 to Neuquén, or on Route 152 to Chelforó on Route 22.

Route 22 is the main alternative, direct from Bahía Blanca, cutting across the southern tip of La Pampa to Río Colorado (campsite with all facilities), on the river of the same name. (Bus to Buenos Aires 0100, 11 hrs, US$30.) It then runs through northern Río Negro to **Choele Choel** on the Río Negro itself, 308 km from Bahía Blanca. Large fruit growing areas at Choele Choel and Villa Regina are irrigated from the Río Negro dam. An un-broken series of groves of tall trees shelter the vineyards and orchards.

● **Accommodation Choele Choel**: **B** *ACA Motel* on edge of town, T/F 0946-2394, Ruta Nacional 22, Km 1,006, with bath, good restaurant at bus station, and fine modern *Hotel Choele Choel*; several other hotels; free municipal campsite beside Río Negro, shady, excellent, no showers.

NEUQUEN

Founded 1904 on the W side of the confluence of the Ríos Limay and Neuquén (223 km from Choele Choel by Route 22), Neuquén is a pleasant, clean provincial capital and industrial city (*Pop* 90,000; *Phone code* 099). It serves the oilfields to

the W with heavy equipment and con-struction materials, and the surrounding fruit orchards with farm machinery. There are also many wine *bodegas* nearby. At the Parque Centenario is a *mirador* with good views of the city and the confluence of the rivers, where they become the Negro (be sure *not* to take the bus to Centenario industrial suburb). Facing Neuquén and connected by bridge is Cipolletti, in Río Negro province (*Pop* 43,600) a prosperous centre of the fruit-growing region.

Museums
Museo Histórico Dr Gregorio Alvarez, San Martín 280; **Museo de Ciencias Naturales**, at entrance to airport (as is the Casino); **Museo Provincial Carlos Ameghino**, Yrigoyen 1047, modest but interesting.

Excursions
Paved roads lead 33 km N to the artificial and natural swimming pools at the Ballester dam (take bus marked 'Banda del Medio' from terminal); nearby is arti-ficial Lago Pellegrini, where watersports are held. A narrow-gauge railway with sporadic services runs via Cipolletti to Contralmirante Cordero, 7 km from the dam. Extensive irrigation has turned the Río Negro valley into a major fruit-pro-ducing region, with apples the princlipal crop. All the towns in the valley celebrate the Fiesta Nacional de la Manzana in the second half of March.

Local information
● **Accommodation**
A3 *del Comahue*, Av Argentina 387, T 480112, 4-star, very good; **A2** *Res Arrayán*, Ruta 22, T 466128, with breakfast, parking, clean, pool; **A2** *Apolo*, Av Olascoaga 361, T 422334, good, but overpriced; **B** *Cristal*, Av Olascoaga 268, T 422414, adequate; *ACA Cipolletti*, Ruta Nacional 22 y Av Luis Toschi, just outside Neuquén, T 71827; **B** *Hosp Neuquén*, Roca 109, T 422403, overpriced; others on San Martín and J B Justo, mostly **C**. 13 km S on Zapala road is *Hostal del Caminante*, T 466118, with pool and garden, popular. Mu-nicipal **camping** site nr river, free, local police warn that it's dangerous.

● **Places to eat**
Las Tres Marías, Alberdi 126, excellent. Cheap places on Av Mitre opp bus station.

● **Airline offices**
Austral, Santa Fe 54, T 422409; **Lapa**, Av Argentina 30, T 438555; **TAN**, 25 de Mayo 180, T 423076 (430096 at airport); **Kaiken**, Av Argentina 327, T 471333.

● **Banks & money changers**
Pullman, Alcorta 144, T 422438.

● **Post & telecommunications**
Post Office: Rivadavia y Santa Fe.

● **Tourist offices**
Félix San Martín y Río Negro, T 424089.

● **Transport**
Local Car mechanic: Normando Toselli, Mitre 801, Neuquén 8300 (Former South American superbike champion), for cars or motorbikes, highly rec.

Air Airport 7 km from centre. Taxi US$8. Austral and Lapa fly regularly to and from Buenos Aires. Lapa also flies to Bahía Blanca. The regional airline TAN flies to Bahía Blanca, Comodoro Rivadavia, Córdoba, Mar del Plata, Mendoza, Bariloche, San Martín de los Andes and, in Chile, Puerto Montt and Temuco. Kaiken flies to Comodoro Rivadavia, Esquel, Bariloche and Trelew.

Buses Bus terminal: Mitre 147. La Estrella/El Cóndor, El Valle and Chevallier to **Buenos Aires** daily US$44, 18½ hrs. Connections with **Copahue** and **Córdoba**; also with **San Rafael** (US$20) and **San Martín de los Andes** (US$22, 4 hrs) to **Zapala** daily, 7 hrs; to **Mar del Plata**, US$40, 12 hrs; to **Bariloche**, take La Estrella or Chevallier (not El Valle as it stops too often), and sit on left; to **Mendoza**, Andesmar, daily, US$46; La Unión del Sud to **Temuco** (Chile) via Zapala all year three times a week each way, and Ruta Sur twice a week, US$30, 16 hrs.

ROUTES Driving from Neuquén to **Bariloche**, go via El Chocón hydroelectric lake, Junín and San Martín (both 'de los Andes'), taking Routes 237, 40 and 234; route more attractive than that via Zapala. The most direct road to Bariloche (426 km) is by Route 237, then Route 40, missing Junín and San Martín. The road is fast, skirting the entire length of the reservoir formed by the Ezequiel Ramos Mejía dam. Then it drops over an escarpment to cross the Collón Curá river before following the Río Limay valley to Confluencia (see page 184) and the Valle Encantado.

ZAPALA

Route 22 and the railway go W from Neuquén to **Zapala** (179 km, *Pop* 20,000) through the oil zone at Challacó, Cutral-Có and Plaza Huincul (at the local Car-

men Funes municipal museum, there are the vertebrae of a dinosaur, Argentinosaurus Huinculensis, believed to be the largest that ever lived on Earth; its vertebra are estimated to have weighed 70 kg each; a recovered tibia is 1.60m in length). There is an excellent geology museum, visited by specialist groups from all over the world (open only to 1300, entry free, closed weekends). Among the collections of minerals, fossils, shells and rocks, is a complete crocodile jaw, believed to be 80 million-years-old. There is an airport and an ACA service station.

The **Parque Nacional Laguna Blanca** 35 km SW of Zapala is known for its animal and bird life (notably black-necked swans). The park has not yet become a tourist centre. It can be reached by an unmarked turning off Route 40 about 10 km S of Zapala. The park entrance is 10 km from this turning, and the lagoon lies amid flat and scrubby land 4-5 km beyond. No public transport and little traffic makes hitchhiking difficult. Advice may be available at the park warden's (*guardia fauna*) office on Vidal, next to *Hotel Pehuén*, in Zapala.

● **Accommodation A3** Hue Melén, Almte Brown 929, T 422407, good value, restaurant; **B** *Coliqueo*, Etcheluz 159, T 21308, opp bus terminal, good; **B** *Nuevo Pehuén*, Vidal y Etcheluz, 1 block from bus terminal, T 21360, rec; **C** *Huinclul*, Roca 313, restaurant; **C** *Odetto's Grill*, Ejército Argentino 455, 2 mins from bus terminal, OK. There is a municipal camping site.

● **Transport** Buses to **Bahía Blanca** 3 a day, 15 hrs, US$25, with Alto Valle. El Petróleo bus to **San Martín de los Andes** (5½ hrs) via Junín de los Andes. There is also an overnight (at 2200) Neuquén-Zapala-San Martín bus that comes through Zapala at 0230; same service at 0915 (US$23). To **Bariloche** direct buses about twice a week. To **Temuco** (Chile) all year, several companies inc La Unión del Sud and Ruta Sur, at 0500, US$22, 10-12 hrs, as under Neuquén (see above). Also Igi-Llaimi Wed and Fri at 0530, return 0330, twice weekly. Buy Chilean currency before leaving.

NORTH OF ZAPALA

North of Zapala on the Chilean border is the **Reserva Nacional Copahue**, best-known for its thermal baths and volcano of the same name. The **Termas de Copa-**

hue (*Alt* 1,980m) are enclosed in a gigantic amphitheatre formed by mountain walls, with an opening to the E (several hotels in the town of Copahue, 15 km from the Termas). Near Copahue, Caviahue is being developed; accommodation is available in prettier surroundings (there are trees), and a bus service connect the two. There are buses from Neuquén (5 hrs) and Zapala to Copahue, which may also be reached by road from Mendoza.

Route 40 N via Las Lajas is paved as far as **Chos Malal**, founded as a military fort in 1889 (restored as a historic monument, with Museo Histórico Olascoaga). ACA service station and hotels.

● **Accommodation** *Chos Malal*, San Martín 89, T 21469; on 25 de Mayo, *Hostería El Torreón*, T 21141, No 137, and *Hosp Baal Bak*, No 920, T 21495; *Hosp Lavalle*, T 21193.

Beyond Chos Malal, Route 40 to Mendoza via Malargüe is more scenic, but slower than the Neuquén-Mendoza route (Nos 151 and 143 via Santa Isabel and San Rafael).

SOUTHWEST NEUQUEN

JUNIN DE LOS ANDES

Junín de los Andes (*Pop* 7,350; *Phone code* 0944) is 38 km W of Route 40, between Zapala and Bariloche. It is known as the trout capital of Argentina. A short detour from Junín leads to the very beautiful lake of Huechulafquen (bus, Koko, US$6 one way, arrange return journey with driver).

● **Accommodation A3** *Hostería Chimehuín*, Suárez y 25 de Mayo, T 91132, fishing hostelry; **B** *Alejandro I*, Ruta 234, on edge of town, T 91184; **C** *Res Marisa*, Rosas 360, T 91175, cheapest; **C** *Res El Centro*, Lamadrid 409, T 91182, with bath, gloomy; *Posada Pehuén*, Col Suárez 560, T 91237, clean, good value, charming owners, Rosi and Oscar Marconi, rec; **L3** *Estancia Huechahue* (reached from the Junín-Bariloche bus), T 91303, English run, comfortable, farmhouse accommodation, horseriding, fishing, river trips. Municipal **campsite**, T 91296.

● **Places to eat** *Ruca Hueney*, Milanesio 641, main plaza, good trout and pasta dishes, friendly service, rec.

● **Transport Air** Between Junín and San Martín is Chapelco civil airport, served by Austral from Bs As and TAN (T 0972-27872) from Neuquén, Bariloche and Puerto Montt (Chile).

FRONTIER WITH CHILE: THE TROMEN PASS

● **Argentine immigration**
Formalities are carried out at the Argentine side of the Tromen Pass (Chileans call it Mamuil Malal). This route runs through glorious scenery to Pucón (135 km) on Lago Villarrica (Chile). It is less developed than the Huahum and Puyehue routes further S, and definitely not usable during heavy rain or snow (June to mid-Nov). Parts are narrow and steep. (Details of the Chilean side are given under **Puesco**, the Chilean customs post, **The Lake District**, page 777).

Camping: it is possible to camp in the area (though very windy), but take food as there are no shops at the pass.

● **Transport**
The international bus will officially only pick up people at Tromen but at the discretion of the driver can pick up passengers at Puesco (no hotel) at 0900 and Currarehue stops. Hitchhiking over to the Tromen Pass is difficult. Bus Igi-Llaima, daily Junín de los Andes-Pucón US$26.

LANIN NATIONAL PARK

This beautiful, large park has sparkling lakes, wooded mountain valleys and the snow capped **Lanín Volcano**. Geologically, Lanín (3,768m) is one of the youngest volcanoes of the Andes; it is extinct and one of the world's most beautiful mountains. A 4-hr hike from the Argentine customs post at Tromen pass (speak to the *guardaparque* at the border) leads to the *refugio* at 2,400m. The climb from *refugio* to summit is easy but crampons and ice-axe are essential. Dr González, President of the Club Andino in Junín, can arrange guides and equipment hire. Limited *refugio* space; entry of visitors without tents restricted. Park Administration is in San Martín, on main plaza, helpful but maps poor; entry US$3. The numerous deer in the park are the red deer of temperate Europe and Asia.

SAN MARTIN DE LOS ANDES

This lovely but expensive little town at the E end of Lago Lacar, is the best centre for exploring **Lanín National Park**. San Martín (*Pop* 14,000; *Phone code* 0972) is 40 km S of Junín. Mirador Bandurrias, 6 km from the centre offers good views. There is excellent skiing on Cerro Chapelco, and facilities for water skiing, windsurfing and sailing on Lago Lacar.

Excursions

The most popular trips by car are to Lagos Lolog, Aluminé, Huechulafquen and Paimún, to a campsite in the shadow of Lanín Volcano. Shorter excursions can be made on horseback or by launch. A small road runs W from San Martín along the S edge of Lago Lacar for 10 km to Quila Quina, where there are Indian engravings and a lovely waterfall. Boat trip on Lago Lacar from San Martín to Quila Quina, 45 mins one way, US$10 return.

Local information

● Accommodation

Single accommodation is scarce. Motel, **L2-L3** *El Sol de los Andes*, very expensive, set above the town (Cerro Cnl Díaz), T 27460, 5-star, shopping gallery, swimming pool, sauna, nightclub, casino, regular bus service to centre of town.

In our **L3-A1** range: *Alihuen Lodge*, Ruta 62, Km 5 (road to Lake Lolog), T 26588, F 26045, inc breakfast, other meals (very good) available, lovely location and grounds, very comfortable, highly rec; *El Viejo Esquiador*, San Martín 1242, T 27690, clean, friendly, rec. *La Cheminée*, Roca y Moreno, T 27617, very good, breakfast inc, but no restaurant; *La Masia*, Obeid 811, T 27688, very good.

A2 *Turismo*, Mascardi 517, T 27592, rec; *La Raclette*, Pérez 1170, T 27664, 3-star, charming, warm, excellent restaurant, rec; *Posta del Cazador*, San Martín 175, T 27501, very highly rec; **A3** *Villa Bibi*, Diaz 1186, T 72206, with breakfast, comfortable, clean, rec; **A3-B** *Curra-Huincla*, Rivadavia 686, T 27224, clean, modern, rec; **A3** *Hostería Los Pinos*, Almte Brown 420, T 27207 (cheaper low season), German-run, with a/c, breakfast and heating, clean, friendly, lovely garden; **A3** *Hostería Anay*, Cap Drury 841, T 27514, central, good value, rec; **A3** *Hostería Las Lucarnas*, Pérez 632, T 27085/27985, English and French spoken; **A3** *Res Peumayén*, San Martín 851, T 27232, very clean, with bath and breakfast.

B *Casa Alta*, Gabriel Obeid 659, T 27456, chalet in rose garden, 'beyond comparison and fantastic'; **B** *Hostería Cumelén*, Elordi 931, T 27304 (or BsAs T 502-3467), with bath, hot water, breakfast, rec; **B** *Casa del Amigo*, Obeid

y Col Pérez, very friendly.

Consult Tourist Office for other private addresses, but these are only supplied in high season. Cheapest is **E** pp *Posta del Caminante*, Caballería 1164, summer only, basic, friendly, good atmosphere, noisy; **E** pp *La Casa del Trabun*, Elordi 186, T 27755, sleeping bags essential, friendly, clean, kitchen facilities. The following offer discounts to ISIC and youth card holders: **C** pp *Hosp Turístico Caritas*, Capitán Drury 774, T 27313, shared rooms, run by church, friendly, clean, also floor space for sleeping bags in summer; *Albergue Universitario Técnico Forestal*, Pasaje de la Paz s/n, T 27618, youth hostel style, and *Hostería Los Pinos* (see above).

Camping: *ACA Camping*, Av Koessler 2176, with hot water and laundering facilities, **F** pp. *Camping Los Andes*, Juez del Valle 611, other side of bridge, accommodation, **C**, clean, bunk beds, shared bath. Pleasant site by the lake at Quila Quina, 27 km from San Martín, with beaches, and another on Lago Lacar at Catritre, 6 km from town.

● Places to eat

Try smoked venison, wild boar or trout, at *El Ciervo*, Villegas 724; *Piscis*, Villegas y Moreno, *Betty*, San Martín 1203, and *El Peñón*, Calderón, all good. *La Tasca*, Moreno 866, excellent trout and venison, home-baked bread, rec; *Parrilla La Tranquera*, Villegas 965, good value; and *Parrilla del Esquiador*, Belgrano 885, reasonable home-cooked food; *Mendieta*, San Martín 713, *parrillada*, popular; *Paprika*, Villegas 568, venison and trout, excellent, highly rec; *Jockey Club*, Villegas 657, also good; *Pizzería La Strada*, San Martín 721, good; *Fanfani*, Rodhe 786, has good pasta.

● Banks & money changers

Banco de la Nación, San Martín 687, cash only; American Express San Martín 1141, T 28453; Andino Internacional, San Martín 876, p 1, only place to change TCs, commission 3%.

● Laundry

Laverap, Drury 878, 0800-2200 daily and Villegas 986, cheaper, 0900-1300, 1600-2130 Mon-Fri, 0900-1300 Sat.

● Sports

Skiing: there are several chair-lifts of varying capacity on Cerro Chapelco and a ski-tow higher up. Bus from San Martín to slopes, US$7 return. Very good slopes and snow conditions. Lift pass US$20-35, ski hire US$13 a day from *Hostería Villa Lagos*. At the foot of the mountain are a restaurant and base lodge. There are three more restaurants on the mountain and a small café at the top. For information on trout **fishing** or duck and geese **shooting**, contact Logaine and David Denies at Trails, Pérez 662, San Martín.

● **Tour companies & travel agents**
Tiempo Patagónico, Av San Martín 950,
T 27113, excursions and adventure tourism,
10% discount to ISIC and youth card holders;
also *Pucará Viajes*, Av San Martín 943.

● **Tourist offices**
Tourist offices at Rosas 790, on main plaza,
corner of San Martín, open 0800-2200, very
helpful.

● **Useful addresses**
Police station: at Belgrano 611.

● **Transport**
Local Car hire: Avis office, San Martín 998.
Localiza, at airport and Villegas 977, T 28876.

Air See under Junín de los Andes above.

Buses Bus station at Gen Villegas 251, good
toilet facilities. **Buenos Aires**-San Martín,
US$60, daily at 1240 (Chevallier) and 2100 with
El Valle. To **Bariloche**, Ko Ko, 3 days a week,
0800, 4 hrs, US$22.50. To **Villa La Angostura**
via Seven Lakes, 3 days a week with La Petroule.

FRONTIER WITH CHILE: THE HUAHUM PASS

This route is open all year round and is an
alternative to the route via the Tromen
Pass (see above). A road along the N shore
of Lago Lacar through the Lanín National
Park crosses the border to Puerto Pire-
hueico. Buses daily at 0800, US$6, 2-hrs'
journey through Lanín National Park.
Huahum village at the W end of the lake
has camping and a shop; a boat leaves San
Martín at 0930, returns 1800, US$20
(T 27380). For connections from Puerto
Pirehueico to Panguipulli and beyond, see
Chile chapter, page 779.

● **Transport**
Daily bus San Martín-Puerto Pirehueico 0800,
US$6, 2 hrs.

There are also buses via Junín de los Andes
and the Tromen Pass to Pucón and Temuco:
mid-Nov to May Empresa San Martín Mon, Wed
and Fri, at 0700, returns from Temuco the following day at 0500, Igi-Llaimi Tues, Thur and Sat
at 0700, returns next day at 0630, US$25, 7 hrs,
rough journey. When the pass is closed buses
go via Huahum and do not pass through Pucón
en route to Temuco. For Pucón change to JAC
bus in Villarrica. From June to mid-Nov, schedules to Temuco are reduced and in winter when
Huahum is blocked by snow, there are no buses.

SAN MARTIN DE LOS ANDES TO BARILOCHE

There are two routes S to Bariloche: one, via
Lago Hermoso and Villa La Angostura,
known as the 'Seven Lakes Drive', is very
beautiful. (National Park permit holders
may camp freely along this route.) On this
route, from a bridge 7 km S of San Martín,
you can see the Arroyo Partido: at this very
point the rivulet splits, one stream flowing
to the Pacific, the other to the Atlantic. Some
bus services, however, take a rather less
scenic route to **Confluencia** on the paved
Bariloche highway (ACA station and a hotel, also motel *El Rancho* just before Confluencia). Neither El Valle buses, 4 a week, nor
Ko Ko buses, follow the Seven Lakes Drive.
Round trip excursions between San Martín
along the Seven Lakes Drive, 5 hrs, are
operated by several tour companies.

Villa Traful, beside Lago Traful about
half-way between San Martín and Bariloche on a side road, is described as a
'camper's paradise'. There are also hotels
on the lake. Marvellous views, fishing
(licence needed) excellent. All roads are
dirt; drive carefully, avoiding wild cattle!

PARQUE NACIONAL NAHUEL HUAPI

Lago Nahuel Huapi with its surroundings, an area of 7,850 sq km, was set aside
in 1903 as a National Park. It contains the
most diverse and spectacular natural phenomena: lakes, rivers, glaciers, waterfalls,
torrents, rapids, valleys, forest, bare
mountains and snow-clad peaks. Most of
the area is covered with abundant vegetation, though it is notably more abundant
on the Chilean side, which gets more rain.
Many kinds of wild animals live in the
region, but they are extremely shy and
seldom glimpsed by the explorer. Bird life,
on the other hand – particularly swans,
geese and ducks – is seen at any time and
everywhere in large flocks.

The outstanding feature of this National Park is the splendour of the lakes.
The largest is **Lago Nahuel Huapi** (*Alt
767m*), 531 sq km and 460m deep in
places. It is in full view of the snow-covered peaks of the Cordillera and of the

forests covering the lower slopes. Towering over the scene is Cerro Tronador. Some 96 km long, and not more than 12 km wide, the lake is very irregular in shape; long arms of water, or *brazos*, reminiscent of the Norwegian fjords, stretch far into the land. There are many islands: the largest is **Isla Victoria**, on which stands the forest research station where new species of vegetation are acclimatized. The Zoological Board is adding to the indigenous fauna; the trout and salmon of the lakes, for instance, have been introduced from abroad. Lago Nahuel Huapi is drained eastwards by the Río Limay; below its junction with the Río Neuquén it becomes the Río Negro, Argentina's second largest river.

A mere sand bar in one of the northern *brazos* separates Lago Nahuel Huapi from Lago Correntoso, which is quite close to Lago Espejo. Lago Traful, a short distance to the NE, can be reached by a road which follows the Río Limay through the Valle Encantado, with its fantastic rock formations. South of Nahuel Huapi there are other lakes: the three main ones are Mascardi, Guillermo, and Gutiérrez. The luxury *Hotel Tronador* is on Lake Mascardi, beautiful setting, highly recommended, also camping *La Querencia*. On the shore of Lago Gutiérrez, in a grotto, is the Virgen de las Nieves (Virgin of the Snows). There is a road to these lakes from Bariloche.

BARILOCHE

San Carlos de Bariloche, (*Pop* 77,750; *Phone code* 0944), on the S shore of Lago Nahuel Huapi, founded 1898, is the best centre for exploring the National Park. Renowned for its chocolate industry, it is a beautifully-situated, Swiss-looking town of steep streets, its wooden chalets perched upon a glacial moraine at the foot of Cerro Otto. The place is full of hotels and *hosterías*. To the S lie the heights of the Ventana and the Cerro Colorado (2,135m). The forests are particularly beautiful around May. Major fires in Jan 1996 burned some 2,000 ha of forest S of the city.

The town has experienced phenomenal growth and can be very busy. The best time to visit it is out of season either in the spring or autumn, although the weather is unpredictable Mainly in July, Bariloche is a major destination for secondary school students, who come to complete courses, ski and enjoy themselves in the evening. The main road into Bariloche from the E is paved and in good condition.

Places of interest
The **cathedral**, built in 1946, dominates the town; interior unfinished. There is a **belvedere** at the top of Cerro Otto with wide views over the town and the lake and mountain. The **Lido swimming pool** on the lake shore is beautifully sited but somewhat run down. The clock in the **Centro Cívico** has four figures which rotate at noon; photos with St Bernard dogs (including brandy keg) may be taken in the Centro Cívico plaza and on 12 de Octubre above the Lido.

Museums
The **Museo de La Patagonia** in the Centro Cívico has nice collections of stuffed animals and Indian artefacts, open 1000-1200, 1400-1900 Tues-Fri, 1000-1300, Sat US$2.50; the attached **Biblioteca Sarmiento** is open Mon-Fri, 1100-2200.

Llao-Llao
The 24 km road to the resort of Llao-Llao (bus No 20, 45 mins) is largely ribbon-developed. Hotels on this road and in the resort are given below. At Km 17.7 on the road to Llao-Llao there is a chairlift to Cerro Campanario (0900-1200, 1400-1800 daily, US$5), from the top of which there are fine views of Isla Victoria and Puerto Pañuelo. At Km 18.3 begins the Circuito Chico, a 60 km circular route around Lago Moreno Oeste, past Punto Panorámico and through Puerto Pañuelo and Llao-Llao itself. Tour companies do the circuit and it can be driven in half a day. It can be extended to a full day: Bariloche-Llao Llao-Bahía-Colonia Suiza (on Lago Moreno Este)-Cerro Catedral-Bariloche; the reverse direction misses the sunsets and afternoon views from the higher roads, which are negotiable in winter

(even snow-covered). The surrounding countryside offers beautiful walking, eg to Lago Escondido on a 3½ km trail off the Circuito Chico. A longer walk is to Cerro López (3 hrs, with a *refugio* after 2); take Colonia Suiza bus (from Moreno y Rolando) and alight at Picada. Longer still is the hike to *refugio Italia* (same bus, but alight at SAC); details of this and 3-5 day continuations from Club Andino.

Boat excursions

A ½-day excursion (1300-1830) may be taken from Bariloche to Puerto Pañuelo, then by boat to Isla Victoria. The full-day excursion (0900-1830, or 1300 till 2000 in season) at US$28 includes the Arrayanes forest on the Quetrihue peninsula further N, and 3 hrs on Isla Victoria, picnic lunch advised. It is best to book this trip through an agency, as the boat fare alone is US$21. Some boats going to Arrayanes call first at Isla Victoria, early enough to avoid boat-loads of tourists. These boats carry the names of Paraná river provinces – *Corrientes, Misiones, Santa Fe* – and they have no open deck. (Turisur have four catamarans with a bar and cafeteria.) All boats are very crowded in season, but operators have to provide seating for all passengers. The Arrayanes forest can also be visited by walking 12 km from Villa La Angostura (see page 191).

Other excursions

For climbing and skiing on Cerros Catedral and Otto, see **Sports** below. A ½-day excursion is possible taking a bus to Virgen de las Nieves on Cerro Catedral, walking 2 km to arrive at beautiful Lago Gutiérrez; walk along lake shore to the road from El Bolsón and walk back to Bariloche (about 4 hrs).

Tours

There are numerous tours: most travel agencies charge the same price. It is best to buy tours on the spot rather than in advance, although they get very booked up in season. Whole-day trip to Lagos Gutiérrez, Mascardi, Hess, the Cascada Los Alerces and Cerro Tronador (950m) leaves at 0800, US$29, and involves 1 hr walk to the Black Glacier, interesting but too much time spent on the bus. Catedral and Tur-

isur have a 9-hr excursion, leaving at 0900 (afternoon dep also Dec-Mar), to Puerto Pañuelo, sailing down to Puerto Blest and continuing by bus to Puerto Alegre and again by launch to Puerto Frías (US$19.50). A visit to the Cascada de los Cántaros is made (stay off the boat at the Cascada and walk around to Puerto Blest through beautiful forest, 1 hr, recommended). Several 12-hr excursions to San Martín de los Andes, US$34, recommended, through two national parks, passing seven lakes, returning via Paso de Córdoba and the Valle Encantado.

If one is staying only 1-2 days in the area the best excursions are to Cerro Tronador the 1st day, and on the 2nd to Cerro Catedral in the morning and Isla Victoria in the afternoon (possible only Dec-Mar when there are afternoon departures for the island).

Local information

● **Accommodation**

The most complete listing with map is published by the Oficina Municipal de Turismo, which you are advised to consult if you arrive in the high season without a reservation. It also has a booking service at Florida 520 (Galería), room 116, Buenos Aires. Out of season, prices are reasonable, in all ranges, but in season everything is very expensive. Most hotels outside the town inc half-board, and those in the town inc breakfast. Hotels with lake views normally charge US$3-4 extra/room/day, for the view in high season; the following selection gives lake-view high-season prices where applicable.

Hotels outside Bariloche: **L2** *Apart-hotel Casablanca* (road to Llao-Llao, 23.5 km), T 48117, good, on a peninsula between Lagos Nahuel Huapi and Moreno. Also at Llao-Llao is **L1** *Hotel Llao-Llao*, Bustillo, Km 25.5, reopened after complete redecoration, run by a US company, visitors welcome (reservations: Av Santa Fe 846, p 6, Bs As, T/F 311-3432); **B** *La Caleta*, Km 1.9 on Llao-Llao road, bungalows run by Neil Callwood, price for an apartment sleeping 4, shower, open fire, excellent value, self-catering, rec, T 25650; *Pájaro Azul*, Km 10.8 Ruta Llao-Llao, 4 rooms, friendly, bus No 20 passes the door; **A1** *La Cascada*, Av Bustillo, Km 6, T 41046, La Cascada district, 5-star, rec.

Hotels in Bariloche: **L2** *Bariloche Ski*, San Martín 352, 4-star, T 22913, Telex 18273, good; **L2** *Edelweiss*, Av San Martín 232, 5-star, T 26165, modern, spotless, excellent food, enclosed pool, highly rec; **L2** *Lagos de la Patagonia*, San Martín

536, T 25846, 5-star, heated swimming pool.

First class: **A2** *Bella Vista*, Rolando 351, T 22435, with breakfast, large well-appointed rooms with lake view, 2 good restaurants; **A2** *Italia*, Tiscornia 892, new, clean, friendly, good breakfast; **B** *Aguas del Sur*, Moreno 353, T 22995/24329, inc excellent 4-course meal and breakfast; **A3** *Colonial*, Quaglia 281 T 26101,

clean, helpful, lake views; **A3** *Internacional*, Mitre 171, T 25938, F 20072, clean, reduction for ACA members; **A3** *La Pastorella*, Belgrano 127, T 24656, with bath, English and French-spoken, central, rec; **A3** *Nevada*, Rolando 250, T 22778, with shower, and heating, nice room; **A2***Hostería Tirol*, Pasaje Libertad 175, T 26152, clean, friendly good, German spoken;

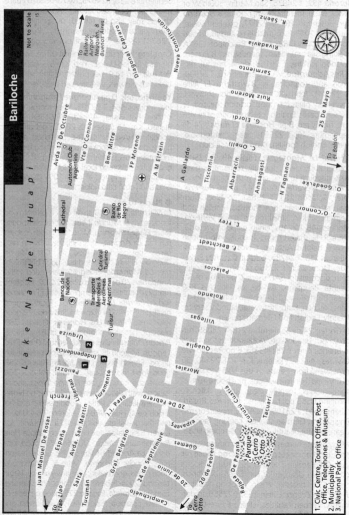

Bariloche

Lake Nahuel Huapi

1. Civic Centre, Tourist Office, Post Office, Telephones & Museum
2. Municipality
3. National Park Office

A3 *Ayelén*, same street, No 157, T 23611, 3-star, comfortable, TV, restaurant, rec.

B *Fontán*, Palacios 200 block, pleasant, friendly, family-run, new; **B** *Millaray*, Libertad 195, T 22229, good, shower, closed off season; **B** *Casita Suiza*, Quaglia 342, T 23775/26111, comfortable, rec; **B** *Res Elisabeth*, JJ Paso 117, T 24853, central, clean, quiet, safe; **B** *Res La Sureña* 432, T 24875, San Martín, 500m W of Civic Centre, friendly, clean, helpful; **B** *Hostería Sur*, Beschtedt 101, T 22677, excellent value, with bath, 10% discount to ISYC and youth card holders; opp is **C** *Res Piuké*, Beschtedt 136 (**A** in skiing season), clean, friendly, rec; **B** *Pucón*, Rolando y Mitre, T 26163, clean, helpful, rec; **B** *Res Adquintue*, VA O'Connor 776, T 22084, clean and comfortable; **B** *Hostería El Ñire* (T 23041), John O'Connor 94, hot showers, clean, very pleasant, good location, heated, Sr Golisch speaks English, prefers longer-stay visitors, highly rec; **B** pp *Hostería El Radal*, 24 de Septiembre 46, T 22551, clean, comfortable, warm, English spoken, D pp in low season.

C *Hotel Le Montagne*, Elflein 49, T 22500, comfortable, clean, friendly, restaurant, gives 10% discount to ISYC and youth card holders; **C** *Punta Nevada*, Onelli 347, rec; **C** *Res Premier*, Rolando 263, T 23681, ½ block from main street, clean, hot showers, English and German spoken, small rooms, rec; **C** *Venezia*, Morales 446, T 22407, clean, rec; **C** pp *Victoria*, Mitre 815, shared room, friendly, information service, helpful. Also rec, **C** *Hostería Güemes*, Güemes 715, T 24785, helpful; **C** pp *Res Puyehue*, Elordi 243, T 22196, clean, friendly, inc bath, discount for *SAH* users; **C** *pensión* of Sra Carlota Baumann, Av de los Pioneros 860 (T 29689), follow 20 de Febrero uphill for 10-15 mins, kitchen, bath, hot water, laundry service, friendly, English and German spoken.

D *Godec*, 24 de Septiembre 218, T 23085, run down but good value, restaurant (reservations in Buenos Aires T 751-4335); **E** pp *Res No Me Olvides*, Av Los Pioneros Km 1, T 29140, 30 mins walk' from centre or Bus 50/51 to corner of C Videla then follow signs, nice house in quiet surroundings, friendly, clean, use of kitchen, camping US$5 pp, highly rec; **E** pp *Res Rosán*, Güemes 691, T 23109 (Sra Arco), repeatedly rec, English and German spoken, cooking facilities, clean, helpful,beautiful garden, camping US$5.

Many private homes also offer accommodation, the tourist office keeps a list. **Among those rec are**: **C/E** *Familia Dalfaro*, Rolando y Tiscorra (SW corner), clean, quiet, rec; **E** *Pensión Venus*, Salta 571, heating, clean, cooking facilities; **F** pp *Casa Diego*, Elflein 163, T 22556, in dormitory, kitchen facilities, clean; **E** *Pire-Cuyen*, Anasagasti 840, clean, doubles only; **E** *Frey 635*,

clean, dormitory, cooking and laundry facilities, motorcycle parking; **E** Anasagasti 348, friendly; **E** pp *Sra Iris*, Quaglia 526, with bath; **E** *Eloisa Lamuniere*, 24 de Septiembre 71, T225614, homely, helpful, cooking facilities; **E** pp *Casa Nelly*, Beschtedt 658, T 22295, hot showers, kitchen, camping, friendly; **D** pp *Lo de Giani*, Elflein, with breakfast; **E** *Mariana Pirker*, 24 de Septiembre 230, T 24873, two 3-bedded apartments with bath and kitchen. Apartments and chalets may also be rented, prices vary enormously according to the season: try **C** Ruiz 1870, T 26781 (ask for Teo), small but very good.

Camping: list of sites from Tourist Office. Two sites on road to Llao-Llao: *El Yeti*, Km 5.6, good, rec; *Petunia*, Km 14.9, well protected from winds by trees, hot showers, well-stocked shop, rec.

Youth hostels: **D** pp *Albergue Patagonia Andina*, Morales 564, T 22783, small rooms, use of kitchen, hot water; *Alaska*, T/F 61564, on Av Bustillo, Km 7.5 (buses 10, 20, 21, get off at La Florida), IYHA-affiliated, **D-E** pp, good atmosphere, poor beds, cooking and washing facilities, mountain bikes, pleasant location, English spoken, good information on local treks,book in advance in summer, highly rec; all offer 10% discount to ISYC and youth card holders.

● **Places to eat**

La Marmita, Mitre 329, small, cosy, excellent mixed fondues rec; *El Mundo*, Mitre 700, excellent, good value; *El Viejo Munich*, Mitre 102, good meat and fish, rec; *La Andina*, Elflein 95, specializes in inexpensive but good 'fast food'; rec; *Caza Mayor*, Quaglia y Elflein, game and fish, good but expensive; *La Montaña*, Elflein 49, very good value; *Kandahar*, 20 de Febrero 698, T 24702, excellent, run by Argentine ski champion Marta Peirono de Barber; *Parrilla 1810*, Elflein 167, T 23922, good meat, rec; *Parrilla La Vizcacha*, Rolando 279, good value, rec; *Parrilla Los Pioneros*, Quaglia 259, pleasant, historical photographs of Bariloche; *El Rincón*, Villegas 216, good service, cheap, rec; *Lennon*, Moreno 48, small, good food, reasonably priced, English spoken; *La Jirafa*, Palacios 288, good food, good value; *Simoca*, Palacios 264, inexpensive Tucumán fare; *Familia Weiss*, also on Palacios (with delicatessen round corner on Mitre), excellent local specialities. Good pastries and hot chocolate at *Hola Nicolás*, Moreno 66 y Urquiza (see the graffiti-graven tables). *La Rondine*, San Martín 536, Italian, luxurious, good (above *Hotel Panamericano*). *Jauja*, Quaglia 370, good local dishes; *La Andinita*, Mitre 56, rec, pizzas, reasonable, friendly; *Cocodrilo*, Mitre 5, big choice of good pizzas, good value, take-away service; *Vegetariano*, 20 de Febrero y Belgrano, not expensive, friendly; *Pizzaiola*, Pagano 275, good pizzeria; *La Nueva Estancia*, Elflein 401, good meat and trout, occasional live entertainment; *La Alpina*

Confitería, Moreno 98, open fire, reasonably priced, cheese fondue rec, very popular; ***Ermitage***, tea rooms, on road to Llao-Llao at Km 18. Many good delicatessens in the area with take-away food, inc chicken, pizzas and cheeses, for picnics.

On Av Bustillo (the road to Llao-Llao), Km 10, is ***La Posta del Río***, reasonable, and ***La Glorieta***, Av Bustillo, Km 3.8, good.

● Airline offices

Aerolíneas Argentinas, Mitre 119 y Villegas, T 23161; **Austral**, Mitre 185, T 22548; **Lapa**, Villegas 121, T 23714; **TAN**, Villegas 142, T 27889.

● Banks & money changers

There are several banks and exchange shops, which buy and sell virtually all European and South American currencies, besides US dollars; Sat is a bad day. **Olano**, Quaglia 238, 2% commission on TCs. **American Express**, B Mitre 387, T 25414, no exchange facilities, sends you to **Banco Nación**, Mitre y Villegas, to buy TCs, but does have emergency cash service. **Banco Quilmes**, Mitre 300 block, cash advances on Visa. Beware forged Argentine banknotes. If everything closed try *Kiwanis* (boot rental), Mitre 210, 3% commission.

● Embassies & consulates

Consulates: **Chilean** JM de Rosas 180, friendly, helpful; **German**, Ruiz Moreno 45, T 25695; **Swiss**, Quaglia 342, T 26111.

● Entertainment

Cinemas: *Arrayanes*, Moreno 39; *Cine Club*, Tues 2115 only, Biblioteca Sarmiento in the Centro Cívico.

● Hospitals & medical centres

Clinic: Cruz Azul, Capraro 1216.

● Laundry

on Palacios, San Martín, Quaglia, and on Villegas nr Mitre.

● Post & telecommunications

Post Office: Centro Cívico (same building as tourist office). *Poste Restante* US$2.50/letter.

Telecommunications: San Martín e Independencia and Elflein y Frey (3 mins minimum charge); cheaper from *Hotel Bariloche*, San Martín 127. Outside the phone office is a telephone with links to several countries (eg UK, Chile, Japan).

● Shopping

The products of the local chocolate industry are excellent: ***Fábrica de Chocolate Cerro León*** on Av 12 de Octubre, nr railway station. You can watch chocolates being made at ***El Turista***, San Martín 252. 1 block away is ***Mamushka***, excellent. Very good chocolate at ***Estrella Alpina***, Villegas 216 or Albarracín 146, and ***Benroth***, Beschtedt 569, and at ***Abuela Goye***, Albarracín 157. Try 'Papas de Bariloche', the local chocolate speciality. Local wines are also good. Woollen goods are rec. Handicraft shops all along San Martín; some will change money. Artesanía co-operative on Moreno y Rolando, rec. ***Burton Cerámica***, 2/3 km on Llao Llao road, Av E Bustillo 4100, T/F 41102, makes and sells 'Patagonian pottery'. Winter clothing at ***Flying Patagonia***, Quaglia between B Mitre and VA O'Connor.

Bookshop: *Cultura*, Elflein 78, has a good range of technical books, some in English and German; *La Barca*, Mitre 131 and *Mileno*, Quaglia 262, local 19.

● Sports

Apart from sailing and boating, there are golf, mountaineering, walking, birdwatching, skiing, and fishing (for which you need a permit). Excellent trout fishing Nov-Mar; boat hire arranged with tackle shops. Racquet Club, Ruta Llao-Llao, Km 13.5, tennis and squash, snack bar.

Bicycles: may be hired beside the lake in high season (eg A Carlucci, Mitre 723, US$20 full day). Mopeds from Vertigo Rental, San Martin 594.

Hiking and trekking: before going hiking, buy moisturizing creams for exposed skin areas and lips. Horseflies (*tábanos*) frequent the lake shores and lower areas in summer; lemon juice is good for keeping them away, but can cause skin irritation. Club Andino (see below) has sketch maps of hikes. For horse trekking trips contact Carol Jones, Casilla 1436 (or through Hans Schulz – see below under **Tourist Agencies**), US$35 ½-day, US$60 day trips, spectacular, highly rec. Also *Cumbres Patagonia*, Villegas 222, US$40 for 3 hrs, suitable for all levels of experience, enjoyable. Or ask at Club Andino for Valerie, friendly, rec.

Mountain climbing: in the area there is something for every kind of mountaineer. National Park mountain guides are available but can be expensive. Book: *Excursiones, Andinismo y Refugios de Montaña en Bariloche*, by Tonek Arko, available in local shops, US$2, or from the author at Güemes 691. In treks to *refugios* remember to add costs of ski lifts, buses, food at *refugio* and lodging (in Club Andino *refugios*: US$5/night, plus US$3 for cooking, or US$5 for breakfast, US$8 for dinner). Take a sleeping bag. Best information from Club Andino Bariloche, 20 de Febrero 30, open 0900-1200 and 1500-2000 Mon-Fri and Sat 0900-1200. The Club arranges guides; ask for Sr Ricardo, the secretary, who organizes easy weekend climbs and walks. Its booklet 'Guía de Sendas y Picadas' gives details of climbs and it provides maps (1:150,000) and details of all campsites, hotels and mountain lodges. The climbing may mean a ride on horseback or a skilled ascent of the slopes of Cerro Tronador. The Government has built convenient rest lodges at from 1,000 to 2,000m on the mountains. Firing, light and food are provided at these points. Note that at higher levels, winter snow storms can begin as early as April, making climbing dangerous.

Skiing: there is good skiing during the winter season (July to early Oct), supervised by the Club Andino Bariloche. It is best organized with a tour company, through whom you can secure discounts as part of an inclusive deal. (Skiing is cheaper, however, at smaller resorts, such as Esquel, though more expensive at San Martín de los Andes.) The favourite skiing slopes are on Cerro Catedral (several hotels), and a new ski-lift is to be built higher up, to permit a longer skiing season. (Hourly bus service with seasonal timetable from Mercedes bus company at Mitre 161, US$5 return.) There is a cable car (US$10 single, 13 return) and a chair lift (US$120 full week, US$26-32 high season, US$18-22 low – full day from the foot of Cerro Catedral to points high on the ridge. Red and yellow markers painted on the rock mark a trail from the top, which leads to Refugio Frey (well equipped, blankets, meals, US$5-8, bed US$5 pp) on the edge of a small mountain lake (allow 6 hrs; you can return through the forest to the ski complex the next day and take a bus back to Bariloche). The seasonal cable car, with a chair lift from its upper terminal, takes you higher than the main (2-stage) chair lift. Check at tourist info if cable car is running, as everything closes in March. Bus tours from Bariloche to the foot of Cerro Catedral give time for less than 2 hrs on top of the mountain. Entrance to the Cerro Catedral ski slopes, below the snowline, is US$ 0.50. The only disadvantage at Bariloche is that the snow is unreliable except at the top. There are other skiing slopes 5 km out of Bariloche, on Cerro Otto (cable car, US$20 pp; open 0900-1900 Jan, Feb, July, Aug, and 1400-1800 rest of year; free bus service to cable car from National Parks office in San Martín, every 30 mins, entry to revolving restaurant at top, US$3.50, nice confitería belonging to Club Andino on Cerro Otto, 20 mins' walk from main confitería on summit). Cerro Otto can be reached in 2-3 hrs' walk from the town, rec; take the paved Av de los Pioneros, then switch to the signed dirt track 1 km out of Bariloche (splendid views), or in a minibus which goes every 30 mins from a car park near the National Park headquarters (closed public holidays), between 1400 and 1600, US$7 round trip (local bus US$2.10 return). Also at Piedras Blancas (bus US$7 return); on López (try a car trip, rough road, US$14 for a tour, 1400-1830), Dormilón and La Ventana. Ski hire US$9-16 a day, depending on quality, dearer at Cerro Catedral than in town. Ski clothes can also be rented by the day, at US$1-2/item, from Kiwanis sport stores, Mitre 210, or El

Iglú, Galería Arrayanes II, Rolando 244.

Swimming: in the larger lakes such as Nahuel Huapi and Huechulafquen is not rec, for the water is cold. But swimming in smaller lakes such as Lolog, Lacar, Curruhué Chico, Hermoso, Meliquina, Espejo, Hess and Fonck is very pleasant and the water – especially where the bottom shelves to a shingly beach – can be positively warm.

● **Tour companies & travel agents**
Tour buses pick you up from your hotel. *Catedral Turismo*, Mitre 399, T 25443/5, runs boats to Chile for Peulla-Puerto Montt trip, US$90 one way, rec (10% discount for ISIC and youth card holders on lake crossing to Chile and local excursions); *Turisur*, Quaglia 227, T 26109, organizes trips on lake and on land. *Limay Travel*, VA O'Connor 710, English and German spoken; *Hans Schulz*, Casilla 1017, T 23835/26508 (speaks Spanish, German and English) arranges tours and guides, highly rec. Arrange trekking with *Sr Daniel José Gorgone*, San Martín 127, DT 0706, T 26181. Also rec; *Cumbres y Lagos*, Villegas 222, T/F 23831, skiing, mountain biking, trekking and excursions. Rec guide *Daniel Feinstein*, T/F 42259, speaks fluent English, naturalist and mountaineer, very experienced in both Argentina and Chile. **NB** Check what the cost of your tour includes; funicular rides and chair lifts are usually charged as extras.

● **Tourist offices**
Oficina Municipal de Turismo in Centro Cívico, open in skiing season Mon-Fri 0800-2000, Sat 0900-1900. Daily at those times in summer but check times out of season (April, Oct-Nov) when closed at weekends. Has full list of city buses, and details of hikes and campsites in the area and is very helpful in finding accommodation. The book, *Guía Busch, Turismo y Comercio*, useful, is available free at the Río Negro or national tourist offices in Buenos Aires, but is not free in Bariloche. National Park information (scanty) at San Martín 24, open 0800-2000. Information also from Sociedad Profesional de Guías de Turismo, Casilla de Correo 51, 0400 5C de Bariloche (President: Ana Botroff).

NB Obtain maps and information about the district in Buenos Aires at the National Park Tourist Office at Santa Fe 690, or at the provincial offices (addresses given on page 84); it is hard to obtain these in the provinces themselves. Park wardens are also useful sources of information.

● **Useful addresses**
Immigration Office: next to *Hostería Tirol*, Libertad 175.

● **Transport**
Local Car hire: Hertz, Avis, and A1 International, at airport and in town (latter at Bartolomé Mitre 26, T 24869, 22038); no flat rates, unless reservation made outside Argentina.

Guiñazú del Campo, Libertad 118, good cars, English spoken, no office at airport but arranges transport to meet flights. Chapís Car, Libertad 120, and Carro's SACI, Mitre 26, T 24826 (out of season open Mon-Fri, am only) are both cheaper. Localiza, at airport and San Martín 570, reliable, helpful, competitive, better km allowance than others. To enter Chile a permit is necessary, US$50, allow 48 hrs. Car mechanic: Auguen SA, VA O'Connor 1068, fast, reasonable, highly rec. Taxis: Remise Bariloche, T 30222; Auto Jet, T 22408. Some drivers speak English or German.

Air Airport, 15 km from town. Taxi to or from airport, US$12; bus US$3 from Austral or Aerolíneas office. Many flights to **Buenos Aires**, with AR, Austral and Lapa. Austral also flies to **Viedma**. TAN and Kaiken fly to **Comodoro Rivadavia** and **Neuquén**; TAN also to **Puerto Descado**, **San Martín de los Andes** and, in summer only, to **Puerto Montt** (Chile). Kaiken also serves **Esquel** and **Trelew**.

Trains The railway station is 5 km E of centre (booking office closed 1200-1500 weekdays, Sat pm and all Sun), reached by local buses 70 and 71 (US$0.25), taxi US$5-6. Information from the Tourist Office; tickets also available from Hotel Pagano y Pamozzi, 3 blocks from Centro Cívico. See under Buenos Aires, **Trains**, for schedule and fares. The train goes via **Bahía Blanca** (about 24 hrs Bariloche-Bahía Blanca). Trip can be extremely dusty, take a wet towel in a plastic bag for face and hands. Scenery only interesting between Bariloche and Jacobacci (see page 195), 4½ hrs. Food on board reasonable (US$7.50 for 3 courses), but not always available and water sometimes runs out.

Buses Terminal 3 km E of centre (buses 20 and 21) buses also stop at railway station. To **Buenos Aires**, daily, Chevallier 22½ hrs, US$80, inc meals. Also La Estrella daily and El Valle via Neuquén, US$57 (not rec). For **Mar del Plata**, take Buenos Aires bus and change at Bahía Blanca or Tres Arroyos (eg La Estrella, 1500, arrive Tres Arroyos 0555, US$60). To **Mendoza**, TAC (Mitre 86), Tues, Thur and Sat, US$70, 22 hrs, via Zapala, Buta Ranquil and San Rafael. To **Córdoba**, TUS, 25 hrs, 4 a week, US$70. To **El Bolsón**, Don Otto (San Martín 283) or Mercedes, daily except Sun, 3½ hrs, US$10. To **Esquel**, Don Otto, daily, 6 hrs, US$30 (direct along Route 40) or Mercedes, US$28.50, 7 hrs (more scenic route through Los Alerces National Park, though the bus may get stuck after rainfall, sit on the right, rec). The Don Otto service continues 4 times a week to Comodoro Rivadavia, US$55. To **Puerto Madryn**, 24 hrs via Esquel (7-hr wait), and Trelew, US$56. To **San Martín de los Andes**, Ko Ko, Moreno 107, Mon-Sat 1430, US$22, 4 hrs; to **Junín de los**

Andes US$19. To **Neuquén**, US$18 by Transportes Mercedes on Bartolomé Mitre or daily with La Estrella, Palacios 246 at 1415, 6½ hrs (a dull journey). No direct bus to **Río Gallegos**; you have to spend a night in Comodoro Rivadavia en route. Don Otto fare to Río Gallegos US$88. For Punta Arenas it may be cheaper to go via Puerto Montt. To **Santiago** (Chile), Tues, Fri and Sun, 24 hrs with tea and breakfast served en route. To **Puerto Montt**, see the route to Chile from Bariloche, page 192.

Villa La Angostura is a picturesque town (*Pop* 3,000) 90 km NW of Bariloche on Lago Nahuel Huapi. The port, 3 km from town, is spectacular in summer.

12 km S of the port at the S end of the Quetrihue Peninsula is **Parque Nacional Los Arrayanes**, containing 300 year old specimens of the rare Arrayan tree.

● **Accommodation L2** Hostería Las Balsas, T 94308, small, exclusive, high standard, good location; **A3** Correntoso, T 94168, has a chalet next door, **B** for 2 bedrooms, shared use of kitchen and sitting room, luxurious; Hotel La Angostura, T 94151. Cheaper are La Cabañita and Don Pedro in El Cruce, dirty, both **C**. Ask in the tourist office, opp ACA, for lodgings in private houses, cheaper than hotels. **D-E** Hostal Nahuel, member of Red Argentina de Alojamiento para Jóvenes. **Camping**: El Cruce, 500m from centre, US$2 pp, dirty toilets; ACA Osa Mayor (2 km along Bariloche road, pleasant, open late Dec to mid-May), Municipal Lago Correntoso (Km 87 from Bariloche).

● **Tour companies & travel agents** Turismo Cerro Bayo, Av Arrayanes s/n, of 5, T (0944) 94401/94412, 10% discount for ISIC and youth card holders on ski packages, trekking, rafting, lake and adventure tours.

● **Transport** Villa La Angostura can be reached by excursion bus (day trip, 8 hrs) or local bus (at 1900 daily, returning 0800, Transportes Mercedes, US$7) which requires staying overnight. It is best to return to Bariloche if going on to Osorno (Chile): otherwise you have to pay twice the fare to Osorno from Bariloche and arrange for the bus company to pick you up at La Angostura. Daily bus at 1700 to San Martín de los Andes.

FRONTIER WITH CHILE

1 The Puyehue pass

A good broad highway, which is paved apart from a 55 km gravel section (difficult in winter) between the two customs posts, goes around the E end of Lago Nahuel Huapi, then follows the N side of the lake through

Villa La Angostura. It passes the junction with 'Ruta de Los Siete Lagos' for San Martín at Km 94, Argentine customs at Km 109 and the pass at Km 125 at an elevation of about 1,280m. Chilean customs is at Km 146 in middle of a forest. The frontier is closed at night. It is a 6-hr drive, but liable to be closed after snow-falls.

2 Via Lake Todos Los Santos

The alternative is to go via the lakes. The route is Bariloche to Llao-Llao by road, Llao-Llao to Puerto Blest by boat (2½ hrs), Puerto Blest Lago Frías by bus, cross the lake to Puerto Frías by boat (20 mins), then 1½ hrs by road to Peulla. Leave for Petrohué in the afternoon by boat (2½ hrs), cross Lago Todos Los Santos, passing the Osorno volcano, then by bus to Puerto Montt. This route is not recommended in wet or foggy weather. It is also long and tiring.

● **Immigration and customs**
The Argentine and Chilean border posts are open every day. The launches (and hence the connecting buses) on the lakes serving the direct route via Puerto Blest to Puerto Montt generally do not operate at weekends; check. There is an absolute ban in Chile on importing any fresh food – meat, cheese, fruit – from Argentina.

Further information on border crossings in the Lake District will be found in the **Chile chapter**.

● **Exchange**
You are strongly advised to get rid of all your Argentine pesos before leaving Argentina; it is useful to have some Chilean pesos before you cross into Chile from Bariloche. Chilean currency can be bought at Puyehue customs at a reasonable rate.

● **Transport**
Four bus companies run services from Bariloche to Osorno (6 hrs), Puerto Montt (7 hrs) and Valdivia, via the Puyehue pass: there is at least one bus every day from Argentine side and fares range from US$20-25 (US$35 for a 1-day excursion including city tour and Termas de Puyehue). Companies include Bus del Nte, San Martín 283, Mercedes, B Mitre 161, and Tas Choapa (at Turismo Algarrobal, San Martín 459, T 22774). Sit on left side for best views. You can buy a ticket to the Chilean border, then another to Puerto Montt, or pay in stages in Chile, but there is little advantage in doing this.

Turismo Catedral sells 1 and 2-day crossings to Puerto Montt via roads and lakes (route as stated above). The 1-day crossing costs US$104 + cost of lunch at Peulla (US$18), credit cards accepted; this excursion does not permit return to Bariloche next day. (1 Sept-31 Mar, take own food, buy ticket day in advance, departs 0700). For a 2-day crossing (operates all year round), there is an overnight stop in Peulla. Details about accommodation under Peulla, in **Chile,** page 791. Several tour companies sell this tour, inc transport, board and lodging. Book in advance during the high season. The other agencies sell excursions to Puerto Frías using a Mercedes bus to Puerto Pañuelo, a Turisur boat to Puerto Blest and share a bus and boat to Puerto Frías with excursion groups going on to Chile. Information from Turismo Catedral which owns the exclusive rights to the excursion via the lakes, using their own boats and bus from Puerto Pañuelo to Puerto Frías (Andina del Sud operates with them on the Chilean side).

By car: full-circle from Bariloche can be done by going first via Puyehue to Puerto Montt, returning via Tromen Pass (see the Villarrica volcano, good road), then Junín and San Martín de los Andes. No cars are taken on ferry on Lago Todos Los Santos.

SOUTH OF BARILOCHE

The road from Bariloche to El Bolsón is paved for about the first 40 km, after which it becomes narrow and steep with many S bends. It passes the beautiful lakes Gutiérrez, Mascardi and Guillelmo.

Villa Mascardi is the starting point for a 2-day walk from **Pampa Linda** over Paso de los Nubes to Laguna Frías and Puerto Frías on the Chilean frontier. To reach Pampa Linda take the Mercedes bus to Villa Mascardi then hitch the remaining 50 km. The road to Pampa Linda has a one-way system: up only before 1400, down only after 1600. Register at the Ranger station at Pampa Linda (entry US$5) and ask their advice about conditions (campsite at Ranger Station). The route is not always well marked, and should only be attempted if there is no snow on the pass (normally passable only between Dec and Feb). Allow at least 6 hrs to reach Puerto Frías from the pass. From Puerto Frías (campsite opposite the customs post) a 30 km road leads to Peulla (see **Chile, Section 5**). From Pampa Linda two other paths lead up Cerro Tronador: one leads to Refugio Otto Meiling, 2,000m, on the edge of the E glacier; the other leads to a refugio on the S side of the mountain.

Río Villegas, about 80 km S of Bariloche on the road to El Bolsón, is very beautiful (**D** *Hostería Río Villegas*, pleasant, friendly, restaurant, just outside the gates of the National Park, by the river).

EL BOLSON

130 km S of Bariloche on the old road to Esquel, this attractive small town (*Pop* 8,000; *Phone code* 0944) in beautiful country, with many mountain walks and waterfalls (dry in summer) nearby. As it lies in a hollow at about 300m, it can be very hot in summer. It has good fishing and is fully developed as a tourist resort. Within half an hour's drive are Lagos Puelo (see below) and Epuyén (shops and petrol available). The farms and the orchards sell their produce at Bariloche. Famous local fruit preserves can be bought at the factories in town. Handicraft market Thur and Sat. The Balneario Municipal is 300m from the town centre, pleasant river swimming.

Excursions

To **Lago Puelo**, about 20 km S in the Parque Nacional Lago Puelo. Regular buses from El Bolsón go to the lake via Villa Lago Puelo (*Hostería Enebros*, T 99054; *Hostería Lago Puelo*, T 99059; also *cabañas*) where there is a bank, shops and fuel. From here a path runs 12 km W to Chile. Inside the park is the *Albergue El Turbio*, T 92523, horse and kayak hire, 10% discount for ISIC and youth card holders (information from Turismo Translago in El Bolsón). Good information on the park is available from the wardens at the entrance. Turismo Translago excursions from the paying campsite, or from office in town: ½-day trip across the lake to Valle Río Turbio below Cerro Tres Picos, US$15; also to the Chilean border and Lago Interior. Canoes can be rented for US$3/hour to appreciate the beauty of the lake. Use 'Fletes' truck transport to get to more remote treks and campsites.

Local information

● **Accommodation**

Very difficult to find in the high season.

A3 *Hotel Cordillera*, San Martín 3210, T 92235, clean, warm; *Motel La Posta*, T 92297, smart (Route 258).

C *Hostería Steiner*, San Martín 300, T 92224, clean and pleasant, wood fire, lovely garden; **C** *Familia Sarakoumsky*, San Martín 3003, good; **C** *Hotel Salinas*, Rocas 641, T 92396, friendly, clean, rec; **D** *Hosp Los Amigos*, Las Malvinas y Balcarce, 2 cabins or camping, hot water, shared bath, cooking facilities, breakfast inc, rec (also have cabins and camping 6 km away on Río Azul, good hiking and swimming in river, owners will provide transport); **E** *Campamento Ecológico*, Pagano y Costa del Río, T 92-954, bunks, US$4 camping, hot water, cooking facilities, friendly.

Youth hostel: **E** *El Pueblito*, 3 km N in Luján, 1 km form Route 258. 6 km from town is *La Casona de Odile*, small farm, home cooking, reservations only (Apdo 83, 8430 El Bolsón, Pca Río Negro, T/F 92753). 20 km N of El Bolsón, at Rinconada del Mallín Ahogado (daily bus from El Bolsón) is **A3** *Hostería María y Pancho Kramer*, warmly rec, wholefood meals, hot shower, sauna, swimming pool, chess, volleyball, horseback and trekking excursions to lakes and mountains. At Lago Epuyén, 40 km S of El Bolsón, **E** pp *Refugio del Lago*, with breakfast, also full and half pension; meals with fresh food, tours, trekking, riding, French owned, Sophie and Jacques Dupont, Correo Epuyén, 9211 Chubut, or leave a message, T 0944-92753.

Camping: Del Sol, M Balneario Municipal, **F** pp, pleasant, friendly, cheap food. *La Chacra*, Route 288, 15 mins' walk from town, US$5 pp. *Aldea Suiza* camping site, 4 km N on Route 258, rec, tennis courts, hot showers, good restaurant; *Nokan Cani*, 4 km N on road towards Lago Puelo, pleasant site nr stream, picnic tables, toilets, hot showers, electricity, owner is an acupuncturist, rec. The paying campsite (US$5) at Lago Puelo has beautiful views across the lake to Tres Picos, but the walking is limited, expensive shop and café; free campsite also at Lago Puelo. Frequent public transport from El Bolsón.

● **Places to eat**

Don Diego, San Martín 3217, good; *Ricar-Dos*, Roca y Moreno, good coffee (food less good); *Parrilla Achachay*, San Martín y Belgrano, basic, but reasonable value; *El Viejo Maitén*, Roca 359, good; *Amacuy*, San Mateo 3217, good; *Lustra*, Sarmiento 3212, good value; *Parrilla Las Brasas*, Sarmiento y P Hube, clean, good.

● **Banks & money changers**

Hotel Cordillera, or *Inmobiliaria Turneo* shop, cash only.

● **Sports**

Horse riding: Horacio Fernández, Loma del

Medio, Apdo Postal 33, El Bolsón, CP 8430; trips of 1 or more days into the mountains, US$20/day, plus US$15 for Horacio and his horse, highly rec for all standards. Cross bridge over Río Azul, follow road to right, at power station turn left, follow path straight ahead and on hill is 'Cabalgatas' sign on left.

● **Tour companies & travel agents**
Turismo Translago, Perito Moreno 360, T 92523, 10% discount for ISIC and youth card holders on lake excursions to Chilean border and to Valle del Turbio, trekking to Lago Puelo and Cerro Plataforma.

● **Tourist offices**
Office on main plaza, open 0900-2000. Ask for sketch maps of the beautiful walks in the neighbourhood inc up Cerro Piltriquitrón, rec (6-7 hrs round trip, great views, food and shelter at *refugio*).

● **Buses**
Full-day tours from Bariloche are run by Don Otto and Mercedes, 11 hrs, very crowded and difficult to get on in high season. Also local bus by Mercedes from Bariloche, US$10, 3¼ hrs; Empresa Charter offers 10% to ISIC and youth card holders between Bariloche and El Bolsón.

CHOLILA

About 80 km S of El Bolsón is **Cholila**, with superb views of Lago Cholila, crowned by the Matterhorn-like mountains of Cerros Dos and Tres Picos. The ranch where Butch Cassidy, the Sundance Kid and Ethel Place lived between 1901 and 1905 is 13 km N along Ruta 258 and can be visited. A recommended journey for motorists is to spend the night at El Bolsón, enter the Los Alerces park via Cholila and drive right through it to Esquel, travelling the whole length of Lagos Rivadavia and Futalaufquén. Mercedes bus between Bariloche and Esquel passes daily.

Excursions Good walk around Lago Mosquito: continue down the road from *El Trébol* past the lake then take a path to the left, following the river. Cross the river on the farm bridge and continue to the base of the hills to a second bridge. Follow the path to the lake and walk between the lake and the hills, crossing the exit river via a suspension bridge just past *El Trébol* – 6 hrs (Nick Saunders and Sarah Jaggs, London W1).

● **Accommodation**   C pp *El Trébol*, T/F 98055, with bath and breakfast, comfortable rooms with stoves, meals and half board also available, popular with fishing expeditions, reservations advised, bus stops in village 4 km away; *Hostería El Pedregoso*, at Lago Cholila, 8 km W; *Casa de Te*, Ruta 258 13 km N, with breakfast. **Camping**: F pp *Autocamping Carlos Pelligrini*, next to El Trébol; free camping in El Morro park; *Camping El Abuelo*, 13 km S.

ESQUEL

Originally an offshoot of the Welsh colony at Chubut, nearly 650 km to the E, **Esquel** is now a modern town with reasonable amenities (*Pop* 18,800; *Phone code* 0945; 260 km S of Bariloche). Esquel is known for its tulips, chocolate, jellies and jams.

Local information
● **Accommodation**
A2 *Tehuelche*, 9 de Julio 825, T 2421, with shower, heating and breakfast, excellent restaurant, some staff speak English; **A3** *Angelina*, Alvear 758, T 2763, very friendly and clean good food, warm, run by Italian teacher, highly rec; **B** *Res Esquel*, San Martín 1040, T 2534, clean, friendly, heating, rec; **C** *Hostería Los Tulipanes*, Fontana 365, T 2748, good rooms and service; **C** *Hostal La Hoya*, Ameghino 2296, T 2473, on road to airport, 1 km (also **C** *Hostería La Hoya* at the Centro Deportivo de Ski at La Hoya itself); **C** *Vascongada*, Mitre y 9 de Julio, T 2361, with shower, friendly, good cheap food; **C** *Huentru Niyeu* (no sign), Chacabuco 606, T 2576, clean, quiet, friendly, modern, garage; **C** *Lago Verde*, Volta 1081, T 2251, doubles only, breakfast inc, modern, comfortable, highly rec; **C** *Zacarias*, Roca 634, T 2270; **C** *Res Huemul*, Alvear y 25 de Mayo, T 2149, clean, not very secure, good *confitería*; **C** *Res Argentino*, 25 de Mayo 862, T 2237, no singles, basic, clean, heating, camping in season; **C** *Res Gingins*, Rivadavia 1243, T 2452, friendly, grubby; **C/E** Sra Helga Hammond, Antártida Argentina 522, friendly, clean, German spoken; **E** Mrs Megan Rowlands' guesthouse at Rivadavia 330, T 2578, Welsh spoken, rec; **E** Sra Olga Daher, Sarmiento 269, friendly, quiet. Ask at tourist office for lodgings in private houses. Hotels are often full in February. **Youth hostel**: **E** *Lihuen*, San Martín 820, T/F 2589, open all year.

Camping: Municipal site 5 km from centre on Trevelin road, nr gravel-crushing plant, hot showers, rec. Free campsite at Laguna Z, 5 km along C Fontana. La Colina, on hill overlooking town, Darwin 1400, US$3 pp, hot showers, kitchen facilities, lounge with log fire, highly rec. Those with sleeping bags can go to the Salesian school and sleep in the school classrooms, Dec to Mar; get recommendation from tourist office.

● **Places to eat**
Jockey Club, Alvear 949, reasonably priced; *Ahla Wasahla*, Sarmiento y San Martín, good cheap, friendly, closed Sun; *Red Fox*, Sarmiento 795 y Alvear, a British-style pub with light, but expensive meals, open from 2200, closed Tues; *Confitería Suiza*, Antártida Argentina 569, good homemade food; *Parrilla La Estancia*, 25 de Mayo 541, quite good; *El Mesón*, Rivadavia 1034, reasonable, but slow service; *Parrilla de María*, Rivadavia 1024, popular; *Pizzería Don Pipo*, Fontana 649, good pizzas and *empanadas*; *Atelier*, 25 de Mayo y San Martín, good coffee, cheap, open 24 hrs. Rugby fans will enjoy the *Confitería Las Tejas*, 25 de Mayo 745, which shows videos of the game. Home made chocolate and the famous local mazard berry liquor is sold at the *Braese Store*, 9 de Julio 1540.

● **Banks & money changers**
Banco de la Nación Güemes y San Martín, accepts TCs, no commission on Mastercard, open 0730-1300; **Viajes Sol del Sur**, 9 de Julio 1086, accept TCs, open Mon-Fri, 1000-1300; **Viasur**, 9 de Julio 1027, Amex TCs only accepted.

● **Post & telecommunications**
Post and telecommunications office opp the bus terminal on Fontana and Alvear (open 0800-2000).

● **Laundry**
Laverap, B Mitre 543, open Mon-Sat, 0900-2100; *Marva*, San Martín 941, cheaper.

● **Sports**
Skiing: La Hoya, 15 km N, has 7 ski-lifts and is cheaper than Bariloche. For skiing information ask at Club Andino Esquel; bus to La Hoya from Esquel, 3 a day, US$7 return, ski pass US$10-18 depending on season, gear hire US$7 a day.

● **Tour companies & travel agents**
Esquel Tours, Fontana 754, T 2704, and at airport, good for local tours, to Lagos Menéndez and Cisnes. *Fairway Sports and Adventures*, San Martín 1-43, T 3380, varied programme of tours, highly rec.

● **Tourist offices**
Alvear y Sarmiento, very friendly, can arrange lodgings in private homes. Closed Sat and Sun off-season.

● **Transport**
Local Car hire: Fiocaci, 9 de Julio 740, T 2299/2704. **Mechanic**: Claudio Peinados, Brown 660, T 0945-3462, highly rec.

Air Airport, 20 km E of Esquel, by paved road, US$14 by taxi. US$2.50 by bus; US$4 by Esquel Tours bus 1 hr before each LADE flight. To **Buenos Aires** with Austral (T 3413/3614), via San Martín de los Andes. Kaiken to Bariloche, Comodoro Rivadavia, Trelew and Neuquén.

Accommodation Hotel in Jacobacci: **B Gran Hotel Argentino**, nearly opp station, with shower and heating, only place in town, very

The Old Patagonian Express Train

👣 Esquel is the terminus of a 330-km (approx) narrow-gauge railway from Ingeniero Jacobacci (*Pop* 6,000), a junction on the Buenos Aires-Bariloche line, 194 km E of Bariloche. On the Jacobacci-Esquel branch line runs a steam-operated train (described by Paul Theroux in *The Old Patagonian Express*) dating from 1922. The schedule of the train, called *La Trochita*, changes often, T (0945) 95190 for details. In mid-1996 the train was running only between Esquel and El Maitén, leaving Esquel on Wed, returning on Thur. Bookings can be made at *Turismo Catedral* in Bariloche. If you want to see railway engines, there are only two at Esquel, so go to **El Maitén** where there is a steam engine cemetery, rec. From El Maitén it is possible to hitch to Bariloche (166 km) or take the Esquel-Bariloche bus (4 times a week at 1100, US$17, 6 hrs).

From Buenos Aires, Constitución, train leaves Sun and Wed as for Bariloche (above), arriving in Ingeniero Jacobacci, after 31 hrs, returning Wed and Sat 0125. (Infrequent buses from Bariloche to Ing Jacobacci.) Enquire in advance to check if the *Trochita* is running to Jacobacci. Sleepers from Jacobacci to BsAs are usually fully booked from Bariloche; only a small quota of first class tickets are available in Esquel for connections to BsAs.

Two hotels in El Maitén, same owner, both overpriced, one is *Accomazzo* with good restaurant, the other is **A3** *La Vasconia*, nr station, basic, hot showers.

good, may be closed when late trains arrive, restaurant nearby.

Buses None direct from Buenos Aires to Esquel so travel via Bariloche. To **Comodoro Rivadavia** (paved), Don Otto, 4 times a week, US$25 (but usually arrives from Bariloche full in season) or Angel Giobbi, Tues, and Fri 0600, US$25, via Río Mayo. Don Otto to **Bariloche**, US$30, direct. Empresa Mercedes goes daily (9 hrs) to **Bariloche** at 0800, best bus for views (and at 2200), US$28.50. To **El Bolsón**, 5 hrs, US$10, rough road, goes alternate days via El Maitén (for train buffs) and via Cholila (for views). To **Trelew**, US$32, 9 hrs, leaves 0900 Tues, Thur, Sat, and 2200 Mon, Wed, Fri; other bus companies on Av Fontana and Alvear (bus terminal) are Empresa Don Otto, Chubut, Denis. Bus terminal T 2233, also for taxis.

TREVELIN

Trevelin (*Pop* 5,000), 23 km SW of Esquel (local bus, US$0.85, every 30 mins, 0700-1900), is an offshoot of the Welsh Chubut colony (see page 200). There is a modern Anglican church beside the Catholic church. It has a Welsh historical museum (entrance US$2) in the old mill.The Hogar de Mi Abuelo, is a private park and museum, with a meticulous reproduction of the owner's home, entry US$2.

Excursions 17 km on road to frontier are Nant-y-fall Falls, entrance US$0.50 pp including guide to all seven falls (1½-hr walk).

● **Accommodation & places to eat** *Hostería Estefanía*, Perito Moreno s/n, T 8148; *Hosp Trevelin*, San Martín 327, T 8102. Grills at *Che Ferrada*, good mixed *parrillada* at *El Quincho*, and several tea rooms offering *té gales* and *torta negra* (eg *El Adobe* on AV Patagonia; *Nain Maggie*, rec). *La Cabaña*, 7 km out on the road from Trevelin to Lago Futalaufquen, serves Welsh teas. There is a custom of giving a newly-married couple a 'black cake' on their wedding day, to be eaten on their first anniversary. Municipal campsite nr centre. On the road to Esquel 3 km from Trevelin, signposted on the righthand side, is *La Granja Trevelin*, owned by Domingo Giacci, macrobiotic meals and good Italian cooking, sells milk, cheese and onions; camping US$1, hot water and wc, bungalows US$15 a day; excellent horses for hire.

● **Tourist offices** Good office in central plaza.

PARQUE NACIONAL LOS ALERCES

60 km W of Esquel, the National Park includes centuries-old larch trees and **Lago Futalaufquen**, entry US$5 (even if just passing through on Route 258). The E side of Los Alerces has much the same natural attractions as the Nahuel Huapi and Lanín parks, but is much less developed for tourism. Lago Futalaufquen has some of the best fishing in this huge area, season begins 15 November.

At the S tip of the lake is the park administration building (or Intendencia); it has a small museum about the park and a slide show of Argentina's National Parks. Service station, two expensive supermarkets in Villa Futalaufquen and a lady sells bread and vegetables from her house (buy bread early, or order the day before).

An interesting part of the park can be reached from a separate entrance through Trevelin following the Río Futaleufú, but one can go only 22 km W because of the Futaleufú hydroelectric dam. Behind it is Lago Amutui Quimei, which has swallowed Lago Situación and three others stretching almost to the frontier. (Futaleufú supplies power to the alumina plant at Puerto Madryn, 500 km to the E.) Entrance by car to see Futaleufú dam is only allowed at 1500, under police supervision; photography not permitted, except on top of the dam itself. There is no public transport to the dam.

Trekking and tours The W side of Lago Futalaufquen is untouched by tourism, by law. There is good walking eg to Cinco Saltos, and El Dedal. The latter is a 6-hr hike from *Hotel Futalaufquen* and up and back, with great views of the lakes and the cordillera from the top. A good information leaflet describing the flora and fauna encountered along the trail up to Cerro Dedal is available at the park headquarters. Regular full day launch trip from Puerto Limonao (reached by early morning minibus) on Lago Futalaufquen (a sheer delight) through Río Arrayanes to windless Lago Verde (2 campsites, one US$1 pp, one free, very crowded in summer, the free campsite is nicely situated and has a small shop; *Camping Agreste Lago Verde* offers 10% discount to ISIC and youth card holders). From there one can walk out to Lagos Rivadavia and Cholila (see above) – 2 days minimum, and to the end of Lago Menéndez, famous for its giant larch trees (US$52 including launch trip on Lago Menéndez, with *Tehuelche Viajes y Turismo*, Av Fontana 574, from Esquel); the boat leaves at 1400 but book the day before in Esquel, preferably, as it will not leave if there are not enough passengers; arrive early to claim your space, crossing 90 mins. The dock can be reached by a 30-min walk across the bridge between lakes Futalaufquen and Verde. There are local guides with outboard motor boats for fishing. Lovely view of Lago Cisne (Swan Lake) to the NW end of Lago Menéndez. One then walks a 3 km nature trail looking across the Andes to Chile before returning. Tours arranged at Esquel (eg *Elentur's* Lacustre excursion visiting lakes Futalaufquen, Verde, Menéndez and a guided tour around the 2 km walk to Lago Cisne, on which you will see a 2,600-year-old alerce, leaves from Puerto Limonao, take food and drink). Other excursion tours offered are less interesting because they only involve short stops in front of points of interest. A road connects all the lakes. The tourist office in Esquel has a pamphlet on all the walks in the Park. **NB** *Refugio Lago Krüg-ger* in the Park offers 10% discount to ISIC and youth card holders; camping and fishing also available.

● **Accommodation** On the E side of Lago Futalaufquen: *Quime Quipán*, T 22272, rec for fishing, closed in winter; **A2** *Hostería Los Tepúes*, simple, rustic, open all year, family bungalow for rent; **A2** *Pucón Pai*, T 3799, good restaurant, rec for fishermen (holds a fishing festival to open the season); open out of season for large groups only; has campsite; next door **C** *Cabañas Tejas Negras*, good facilities for camping. *Cume Hué*, T 2858, also rec for fishing. *Trevelin Lodge*, also specializes in fishing, run by O'Farrell Safaris, organizes tours, white-water rafting and horse-riding. (Contact Telluride Flyfishers, PO Box 1634, Telluride, Colorado, T 800-828-7547.) Camping at Villa Futalaufquen and at Los Maitenes (closed May-Sept), hot water, store. **On the W side:** **L2** *Hotel Futalaufquen* just N of Puerto Li-

monao, T 2648, rec, especially rooms 2/3 and 4/5 which have balconies overlooking the lake, open all year (no heating in rooms); good walking around the hotel.

● **Transport** Bus (Mercedes) to Lago Verde passing along the E side of Lago Futalaufquen at 0700, 1300 and 1700 daily in season (it passes 3 hotels and drives into 2 camp sites). Buses also from El Bolsón. Off season transport is difficult but the Esquel – Bariloche bus, twice weekly, passes the lake.

FRONTIER WITH CHILE: LA BALSA

● **Immigration and customs**
The frontier is 70 km SW of Esquel via Trevelin. Campsite (Camping Río Grande) on Argentine side of river. Cross the frontier river by bridge after passing Argentine customs; Chilean customs is 1 km on the other side of river (1 hr for all formalities). At the Futaleufú and Palena border crossings, Argentine border officials only give transit visas: legalize your stay within 10 days either by leaving the country or by renewing your entry stamp at an immigration office.

● **Transport**
Colectivo Esquel-La Balsa, 2 hrs, US$3. Colectivo from Argentine customs to Futaleufú (10 km) is US$3. Very little traffic for hitching. (For transport from Futaleufú to Chaitén (Chile) see Chile chapter.)

ROUTES South of Esquel, Route 40 is paved S through the towns of Tecka and **Gobernador Costa** (**D** *Hotel Jair*, clean, friendly; **D** *Hotel Vega*; municipal campsite with all services, US$2) in Chubut province; to the W, on the Chilean border, is Lago Gen Vintter, plus smaller lakes with good trout fishing. 34 km S of Gobernador Costa, gravelled Route 40 forks SW through the town of Alto Río Senguer, while provincial Route 20 heads almost directly S for 81 km (ACA petrol station at isolated La Laurita), before turning E toward Sarmiento and Comodoro Rivadavia. At La Puerta del Diablo, in the valley of the lower Río Senguer, Route 20 intersects provincial Route 22, which joins with Route 40 at the town of Río Mayo (see page 211). This latter route is completely paved and preferable to Route 40 for long-distance motorists; good informal campsites on the W side of the bridge across the Río Senguer.

Patagonia

THE VAST, WINDY, treeless plateau S of the Río Colorado: the Atlantic coast is rich in marine life, most easily seen around Puerto Madryn. In the S of the region is the Parque Nacional de los Glaciares, with journeys on lakes full of ice floes and to the Moreno glacier. In the Chubut Valley is Argentina's Welsh community.

Patagonia is sub-divided into the provinces of Neuquén, Río Negro, Chubut, Santa Cruz and Tierra del Fuego. The area covers 780,000 sq km: 28% of the national territory, but has a population of only 600,000, little over 2.7% of the total population; and 57% of it is urban. Wide areas have less than one person to the sq km, and there are virtually no trees except in the N and the Andean foothills.

Climate and economy

Over the whole land there blows a boisterous, cloud-laden strong wind which raises a haze of dust in summer, but in winter the dust can turn into thick mud. Temperatures are moderated by the proximity of the sea and are singularly mild, neither rising high during the summer nor falling low during the winter. Even in Tierra del Fuego, where the warmest summer months average 10½°C, the winter days' average can reach a high of about 2°C. Make sure you have plenty of warm clothing, and anti-freeze in your car, available locally. Rain falls mostly in the winter, but not more than 200-250 mm a year. The whole E part of the area suffers from a lack of rainfall and the land is more or less desert. Deep crevices or canyons intersect the land from E to W. Few of them contain permanent water, but ground water is easily pumped to the surface. The great sheep *estancias* are along these canyons, sheltered by the wind, and in the depression running N from the Strait of Magellan to Lagos Argentino and Buenos Aires and beyond. During a brief period in spring, after the melting of the snows, there is grass on the plateau. Most of the land is devoted to sheep raising. The wool, which is shipped N to Buenos Aires, is mostly the fine and finecrossbred wool used by the Argentine mills, and is often heavy with sand. Over-grazing leads to much erosion. Wild dogs and the red fox are the sole enemies of the sheep. Because of the high winds and insufficient rainfall there is little agriculture except in the N, in the valleys of the Colorado and Negro rivers. Some cattle are raised in both valleys where irrigation permits the growing of alfalfa.

Patagonia is rich in extractive resources: the oil of Comodoro Rivadavia and Tierra del Fuego, the little exploited iron ore of Sierra Grande, the coal of Río Turbio, the hydro-electric capacity of El Chocón, plentiful deposits of minerals (particularly bauxite) and marine resources, but their exploitation has been slow. Tourism is opening up too.

In all Patagonia there is only one town – Comodoro Rivadavia – with a population over 100,000. Most of the towns are small ports, which used only to work during the wool-shipping season but have livened up since the local economy began to diversify. The high tidal range makes it impossible in most of them for ships to tie up at docks (except at Madryn and Punta Arenas, Chile).

Wildlife

Guanacos and rheas are a common sight: there are also *maras*, Patagonian hares. On and off parts of the coast, particularly the

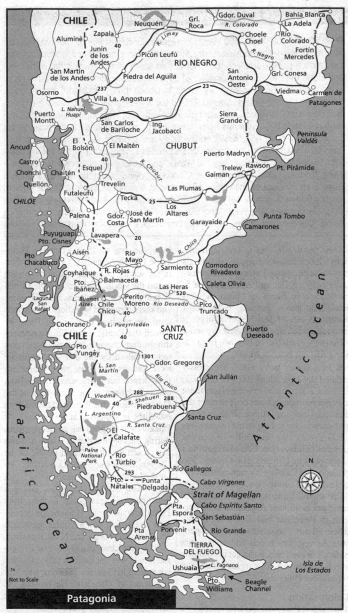

The Welsh Settlement

On 28 July 1865, 150 Welsh immigrants landed at Puerto Madryn, then a deserted beach deep in Indian country. After three weeks they pushed, on foot, across the parched pampa and into the Chubut river valley, where there is flat cultivable land along the riverside for a distance of 80 km upstream. Here, maintained in part by the Argentine Government, they settled, but it was three years before they realized the land was barren unless watered. They drew water from the river, which is higher than the surrounding flats, and later built a fine system of irrigation canals. The colony, reinforced later by immigrants from Wales and from the United States, prospered, but in 1899 a great flood drowned the valley and some of the immigrants left for Canada. The last Welsh contingent arrived in 1911. The object of the colony had been to create a 'Little Wales beyond Wales', and for four generations they kept the Welsh language alive. The language is, however, dying out in the fifth generation. There is an offshoot of the colony of Chubut at Trevelin, at the foot of the Andes nearly 650 km to the W, settled in 1888 (see page 196). It is interesting that this distant land gave to the Welsh language one of its most endearing classics: *Dringo'r Andes* (Climbing the Andes), written by one of the early women settlers.

Valdés peninsula, seals, sea-elephants, right whales and other aquatic mammals may be seen, as well as penguins, especially between Oct and April. Further S, particularly in Tierra del Fuego, the antarctic wild goose (*quequén*) is the most commonly seen of the 152 species of birds (recommended reading, *Aves de Argentina y Uruguay*, available, in English, from *Librería ABC* in Buenos Aires).

NB In summer hotel prices are grossly inflated (by as much as 100% in Ushuaia, 75% in Calafate); also in some places there may not be enough hotel beds to meet the demand. Camping is increasingly popular, and *estancias* seem hospitable to travellers who are stuck for a bed. During Argentine summer holidays (Jan, Feb, Mar) getting a hotel room in Ushuaia, Río Grande, Río Gallegos and Calafate is practically impossible. In this connection, remember that ACA establishments, which charge the same prices all over Argentina, are a bargain in Patagonia and Tierra del Fuego, where all other accommodation is expensive. As very few hotels and restaurants have a/c or even fans, it can get uncomfortably hot in January. TCs are hard to change throughout Patagonia.

Colonization

The coast of Patagonia was first visited by a European late in 1519, when the Portuguese Fernão Magalhães (Magellan), then in the service of Spain, was on his voyage round the world. Early in 1520 he turned W into the strait which now bears his name and there struggled with fierce headwinds until he reached that Sea of Peace he named the Pacific. Later European expeditions that attempted to land on the coast were repulsed by the dour and obdurate local Indians, but these were almost entirely wiped out in the wars of 1879-1883, generally known as the 'Campaign of the Desert'. Before this there had been a long established colony at Carmen de Patagones; it shipped salt to Buenos Aires during the colonial period. There had also been a settlement of Welsh people in the Chubut Valley since 1865 (see below). After the Indian wars colonization was rapid, the Welsh, Scots and English taking a great part. Chilean sheep farmers from Punta Arenas moved N along the depression at the foot of the Andes, eastwards into Tierra del Fuego, and N to Santa Cruz.

The first European to traverse Patagonia S to N was the English sailor, Carder, who saved his life in a 1578 shipwreck in the Strait of Magellan. He crossed the Strait, walked to the Río de la Plata and arrived in London 9 years later.

Recommended reading

In Patagonia by Bruce Chatwin, a good introduction to the area and its people. *Patagonia*, by Metzeltin and Buscaini (Dall' Oglio, Milan). *At Home with the Patagonians*, by George Musters (history of 19th century life of Patagonian Indians), ed John Murray, London 1871/1973. *Argentine Trout Fishing. A Fly Fisherman's Guide to Patagonia* by William C Leitch (ISBN 1-87817-5-06-8)

Communications

Air Main air services are given in the text below. Check for discounts on flights. Prepare for delays in bad weather.

Many air force LADE flights in the region S of Bariloche must be booked in advance from departure point of flight. The planes are small and fly low; passengers miss little of what there is to be seen, highly recommended for those who enjoy flying. The baggage allowance is 15 kg. Flights are often heavily booked ahead, but always check again on the day of the flight if you are told beforehand that it is sold out. Sometimes, through LADE, individual passengers are allowed to fly on air force carriers if planes are full or inopportune. LADE tickets are much cheaper for a long flight with stops than buying separate segments. LADE's computer reservation system is linked to Aerolíneas Argentinas, so flight connections are possible between these airlines.

Road The main road, Route 3, which runs near the coast, is now paved from Buenos Aires via Fitz Roy and down to Río Gallegos. South of this town to Ushuaia is all-weather in a bad state of repair as it is awaiting asphalt. Sometimes passengers going S have to pay for baggage by weight. Many buses do not operate between early April and late October.

The principal roads in Patagonia roughly form an inverted triangle. Route 3 has regular traffic and adequate services. At the southern end, this route enters Chile and crosses the Magellan Straits to Tierra del Fuego by the car ferry at Primera Angostura. The western route (Route 40) zigzags across the moors, is lonely and is good in parts, poor in others

(more details given below); there is hardly any traffic except in Dec, Jan and Feb, the tourist season. However, it is by far the more interesting road, with fine views of the Andes and plenty of wildlife as well as the Alerces and Glaciares National Parks. Camping is no problem, and there are good hotels at Esquel, Perito Moreno, Calafate and (in Chile) Coyhaique and Puerto Natales. Third class accommodation also at Gobernador Gregores and Río Mayo. The northern part of the triangle is formed by the paved highway running from Bariloche through Neuquén to San Antonio Oeste.

Many of the roads in Southern Argentina are gravelled. The price of a good windscreen protector varies according to make of car, but can be US$50 in Buenos Aires. For a VW Kombi they are hard to find at a reasonable price. More primitive versions can be bought for much less – eg US$5 in San Julián, and probably elsewhere – or made from wire mesh, wood and string. The best types are the grid-type, or inflatable plastic ones which are made for some standard-type vehicles, the only disadvantage being some loss of visibility. Drivers should also look out for cattle grids (*guardaganados*), even on main highways. They are signed; cross them very slowly. Always carry plenty of fuel, as service stations may be as much as 300 km apart. Fuel prices are very low in Chubut and Santa Cruz provinces (except Bariloche), US$0.35/litre, which is about half the price of the rest of the country.

Hitchhiking is generally difficult except on Route 3 in spring and summer; camping equipment is useful as long delays can be expected even in the tourist season.

NORTHERN PATAGONIA

The upper course of the Río Colorado is the northern limit of Patagonia.

VIEDMA

160 km S of where it reaches the sea (250 km S of Bahía Blanca), about 27 km from the mouth of the Río Negro, is **Carmen de Patagones** (*Pop* 16,000), standing on high ground on the N bank, with **Viedma** (*Pop*

26,000; *Phone code* 0920) the capital of Río Negro Province, across the river, which is spanned by a connecting rail and road bridge, pleasant setting. There is also a frequent ferry service for pedestrians. On a hill behind Patagones a monument commemorates an attack on the twin towns by a Brazilian squadron in 1827. There are three museums, open 1000-1200 only. The swimming is recommended on the Viedma side of the river, where there is a nice shady shore.

Excursions Beautiful beach, El Cóndor, 30 km S of Viedma, 3 buses a day from Viedma in summer, hotel open Jan-Feb, restaurants and shops, free camping on beach 2 km S. 30 km from El Cóndor is a sealion colony (*lobería*); daily bus in summer from Viedma; hitching easy in summer.

● **Accommodation & places to eat At Viedma: B** *Austral*, Villarino 292, T 22019, rec, modern; **C** *Peumayen*, Buenos Aires 334, T 25243; *Restaurant Munich*, Buenos Aires 150, open late. **Camping**: good municipal site 500m after crossing the river on the new road bridge on the right, US$14/tent plus US$4 pp, all facilities inc hot showers, but can be noisy at weekends.

Further camping sites on the Río Negro where the main route into Patagonia meets the river (some 170 km from Viedma due NW) with all facilities including a small shop. Additional shops at Gen Conesa, 2 km away. Mosquito repellent needed.

● **Banks & money changers** Travel agency at Namuncurá 78, Viedma, exchanges Amex cheques.

● **Tourist offices** Belgrano 544, p 9, Viedma.

● **Transport Air** From Buenos Aires and Bariloche with Austral (the city is also served by LADE). **Buses** Terminal at C A Zatti y Lavalle about 6 blocks from main plaza. To/from Buenos Aires US$45, La Estrella/Cóndor. To San Antonio Oeste, US$7.50.

SAN ANTONIO OESTE

Almost due W and 180 km along the coast, on the Gulf of San Matías, is **San Antonio Oeste** (*Pop* 10,000; *Phone code* 0934). 17 km S is a popular seaside resort, **Las Grutas**, developed in the 1960s with good safe beach (the caves themselves are not really worth visiting); bus from San Antonio hourly US$1.30. The whole of Las Grutas closes down in mid-Mar and retires to Buenos Aires.

● **Accommodation At San Antonio: B** *Kandava*, Sarmiento 240, T 21430, with bath, hot water, clean, good; **C** *Golfo Azul*, simple, clean; **C** *Iberia*, Sarmiento 241, with bath, but without breakfast, small rooms, but rec. **In Las Grutas**: ACA has a *Unidad Turística*, T 97095, with 6-bed rooms, no restaurant. **C** *Tour du Golfe*, Av Bariloche y Sierra Grande, friendly, 3 bedrooms, cooking facilities. There are also many good camping sites (eg *La Entrada*, US$5/tent, on edge of town above beach). Seafood restaurants.

● **Transport Trains** Railway via Viedma to **Bahía Blanca** and **Buenos Aires** and W to **Bariloche**. Timetable from Buenos Aires as for Bariloche; train passes through San Antonio Oeste at 1953 en route to Bariloche, 1002 to Bahía Blanca. **Buses** N to **Bahía Blanca** and S to **Río Gallegos** and **Punta Arenas** by Transportes Patagónicos. To **Viedma** 0700 daily, US$7.50. To **Puerto Madryn** and Trelew, Don Otto, 0200 and 1530, 4 hrs, US$20. To **Buenos Aires**, US$46 via Bahía Blanca, frequent.

ROUTES From San Antonio Oeste a road runs N 91 km through bush country providing fodder for a few cattle, with a view to the W of the salt flats called Salina del Gualicho, before joining Route 250 which meets the Zapala-Bahía Blanca highway (Route 22) at Choele Choel, 178 km N of San Antonio Oeste (see page 180, and **Road** page 181). Between San Antonio and Puerto Madryn is Sierra Grande (ACA garage and café, camping at rear, no facilities but free hot showers at YPF garage in town), where iron-ore deposits are extracted and piped in solution to an ocean terminal 32 km E.

PUERTO MADRYN AND PENINSULA VALDES

Puerto Madryn (*Pop* about 50,000; *Phone code* 0965), about 250 km S, along Route 3 (paved) in Chubut province, is a port on a wide bay, Golfo Nuevo. Founded by the Welsh colonist, Parry Madryn, in 1865, the town has a giant alumina plant (for visits enquire at the tourist office) and fish processing plants. The town is becoming a popular tourist centre, with a casino, skindiving and nature reserves, both close to town and on the nearby Valdés peninsula.

Museums
Museo de Ciencias Naturales y Oceanográfico, Domecq García y J Menéndez, informative and worth a visit,

open Tues-Sat 1500-1830, entry US$2, ask to see video.

Local information

● **Accommodation**

Often full in summer, when prices rise; make bookings early. Many smaller places close out of season.

A1 *Península Valdés*, Roca 155, T 71292 4-star, sea view, suites available, sauna, comfortable, rec; **A2** *Playa*, Roca 187, T 50732, overpriced but safe, clean, cafeteria; **A2** *Bahía Nueva*, Roca 67, T/F 51677, with breakfast, bar, very comfortable; **A3** *Tolosa*, sáenz Peña 250, T 71850, 3-star, friendly; **A3** *Gran Madryn I*, Lugones 40, T 72205, 2-star, friendly, clean, good; **A3** *Hostal del Rey*, Brown 681, T 71156, on beach, rec, 2-star, clean, breakfast extra, restaurant with fixed price menu; **A3** *Marina*, Roca 7, T 74044, heated, showers, clean, warm, kitchen facilities; **B** *Yanco*, Av Roca 626, T 71581, on beach, without breakfast, nightly entertainment programme, free, has rooms for up to 6; **B** *Muelle Viejo*, Yrigoyen 38, T 71284, opp pier, good restaurant, expensive breakfast, good, clean, quiet; **B** *Gran Palace*, 28 de Julio 390, T 71009, clean; **B** *Res Petit*, Alvear 845, T 51460, with bath, clean, quiet, good; **B** *Res La Posta*, Av Roca 33, T 72422, good, heating,

fan, light rooms; **C** *Hostería Hipocampo*, Vesta 33, clean, helpful; **C** *Res Manolo's*, Roca 763, T 72390, inc breakfast, small, quiet, homely; **C** *Español*, 28 de Julio y San Martín, clean, basic, hot water, restaurant, parking, difficult to find; **C** *Anclamar*, 25 de Mayo 875, T 51509 clean, quiet, rec; **C** *Antiguo/Central*, 28 de Julio 170, T 71742, good, clean, basic, friendly, hot water; **C** *Res J'os*, Bolívar 75, T 71433, pleasant; **C** *Vaskonia*, 25 de Mayo 43, T 72581, without bath, central, clean, good value; **E-D** pp *Backpackers*, 25 de Mayo 1136, T 74426, clean, friendly, laundry and kitchen facilities.

Camping: all closed out of season. At Punta Cuevas, 3.5 km S of town, is ACA site with evening hot showers, good facilities and shady trees (ACA members only, US$8/tent for 2) but many people camp on beach. There is a swimming pool in the rocks nr the ACA camp site, which gets its water at high tide, very pleasant, and free. Two municipal sites: one at Ribera Sur, 1 km before ACA site on same road along beach (gives student discount). All facilities, very crowded, US$3 pp and US$2/tent for first day. Also room with bunkbeds, F pp. Bus from town stops 100m before entrance. The other is N of town at Barrio Brown. Camping out can be interesting as one can watch foxes, armadillos, skunks and rheas roaming around in the evening.

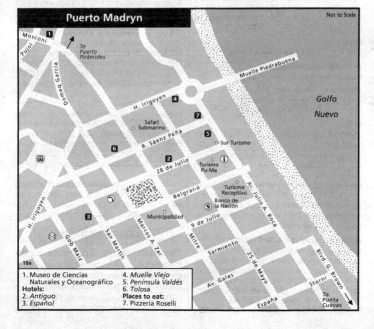

Puerto Madryn

Not to Scale

- 1. Museo de Ciencias Naturales y Oceanográfico
  Hotels:
- 2. *Antiguo*
- 3. *Español*
- 4. *Muelle Viejo*
- 5. *Península Valdés*
- 6. *Tolosa*
  Places to eat:
- 7. Pizzería Roselli

● **Places to eat**

Las Aguilas, MA Zar y Sáenz Peña, rec, good for seafood; *Cantina El Náutico*, Roca y Lugones, good food, especially fish; *París*, Sáenz Peña by Muelle Piedrabuena, good and reasonably priced; *Pizzería Roselli*, Sáenz Peña y Roca, good, with vegetarian selections; *Quijote*, Belgrano 138, reasonable prices, very good; *Barbarians*, 25 de Mayo y 28 de Julio, good coffee. For excellent Welsh afternoon teas, *La Goleta*, Roca 87, 1700-1900. Several local chocolate makers; try *Península* on Roca nr *Turismo Receptivo*.

● **Airline offices**

Aerolíneas Argentinas, 25 de Mayo 150, T 50110; **LAPA** at *Turismo Receptivo*. **LADE** office at Roca 119, T 51256.

● **Banks & money changers**

Banks open Mon-Fri 0830-1330 (0800-1300 in summer). **Banco de la Nación**, 25 de Mayo y 9 de Julio, US$10 commission for changing TCs; **Banco del Sud**,Sáenz Peña, ATM for Visa; **Banco Provincia Chubut**, 25 de Mayo, changes US$ cash, no commision, Mastercard and Amex ATM. There are no *casas de cambio*, apart from *Turismo Pu-Ma*, 28 de Julio 46 (2% commission for TCs), but fair rates from travel agents (eg *Safari Submarino*, address below; go in the morning); **La Moneda**, Roca y 28 de Julio, will exchange large sums, not very good rates. High commission on changing TCs.

● **Laundry**

Laverap, 25 de Mayo 529, highly rec.

● **Post & telecommunications**

Post Office: Belgrano y A Maiz.

Telephone: 28 de Julio 326, also fax, 0700-2400; Telefónica Milano, Roca y 9 de Julio; phone and fax at kiosk at Roca 733.

● **Sports**

Puerto Madryn is a diving centre. Tours, inc for those who have never dived before, are organized by several agencies. *Safari Submarino*, Mitre 80, T/F 74110, only one open all year; *Ocean Divers*, Brown entre 1 y 2 Rotundas; *Abismo*, Roca 516, prices inc equipment, US$50 beginners, US$40 experts (less with own equipment) courses on video, photography and underwater communication; PADI instruction US$200. No courses in January-February.

● **Tour companies & travel agents**

Several agencies do tours to the Valdés Peninsula, all are for 12 hrs, see below. Prices are fixed by law, but some agencies run larger buses than others. Note that return distances of some tour destinations are high: Peninsula Valdés 380 km, Punta Tombo 400 km, Ameghino Dam 400 km. The largest agency is *Sur Turismo*, Roca 175, T 73585;

Safari Submarino, Mitre 80, Tito Botazzi, small groups, plenty of time at sites (10% reduction to SAH owners) see also under Puerto Pirámides. Other agencies inc: *Pu-Ma*, 28 de Julio 48, T 71482, rec; *Mar y Valle*, Roca 37, T 72872, rec; *Receptivo*, Roca 303 y Belgrano, T 51048, Amex agent, weekend and off-season tours, rec; *Prima Tur*, 28 de Julio; *Coyun Co*, Roca 171, T 51845. *Franca del Sur*, Reconquista 378, T 50710, small groups, Spanish only, rec; *Aquatours*, Muelle Piedrabuena, T 51954, rec.

● **Tourist offices**

Roca 223, T 73029, Mon-Fri 0700-1300, 1500-2100, Sat/Sun 0800-1300,1700-2100 but only Mon-Fri in winter; helpful, has notice board for messages, list of current hotel rates and interesting video on the region.

● **Transport**

Local Car hire: very expensive (US$150/day). *Fiorasi*, on Sarmiento; *Localiza*, Belgrano 196, T 71660; *Cuyun-Co*, Roca 171. Cycle Hire: *XT*, Roca 700 block.

Air Daily from Buenos Aires via Trelew with Austral; from Ushuaia with Kaiken; from Comodoro Rivadavia with LADE. Airport is 7 km from town, no buses, taxi or *remise* only, US$7-8.

Buses Terminal in old railway station.To **Buenos Aires**, daily, Don Otto (US$57), La Puntual (US$50), QueBus (daily except Wed); to **Río Gallegos**, about 20 hrs, Don Otto, 1745 daily US$49, also Andesmar US$58; to **Comodoro Rivadavia**, Don Otto US$26; to **Bahía Blanca** and Viedma, 12 hrs, US$36; to **Mar del Plata**, change at Bahía Blanca; to **Bariloche**, Andesmar daily US$56; to **Córdoba**, US$72, 1900, Tus Tur; to Caleta Oliva, US$20, 0700; to **Mendoza**, US$68, Andesmar to **Neuquén**, US$31, Andesmar; to **Santiago** (Chile) via Neuquén, Andesmar, US$ 89; to **Trelew**, joint service by 28 de Julio and Mar y Valle, approx every 30 mins, US$4.50, 1 hr, driver stops nr entrance to Trelew airport if asked; direct to Trelew airport, Puma, US$5, leaves 1½ hrs before flight and takes arriving passengers back to Puerto Madryn (taxi to airport US$45). **Taxis**: outside bus terminal and on main plaza.

For hitching N, try on the industrial estate road, or take a Trelew bus to the main highway then walk 3 km to the service station/truck stop. With luck it is possible to get to Bahía Blanca in 1 day.

NATURE RESERVES

The natural history of the region is most interesting, with elephant seal and penguin colonies, breeding grounds for right whales in the Golfo Nuevo, fossils in the cliffs, and guanacos, rheas and armadillos in the countryside. Oct-Nov is the time to see the greatest variety of wildlife. Whales can be seen from perhaps as early as June to, at the very latest, end-December. There is less wildlife after Dec, a point not always made by tour agencies.

The **Punta Loma** sealion reserve is 15 km SE of Puerto Madryn. It is open 0900-1200, 1430-1730; Sept and Oct are the best months. Information and video. Entry US$2. Taxis US$25. Sea-lions can even be seen in Puerto Madryn harbour.

PENINSULA VALDES

The Golfos Nuevo and San José are separated by the Istmo Carlos Ameghino, which leads to Península Valdés. The peninsula is private property, but around its coast much marine life can be seen. In depressions in the heart of the peninsula are large salt pans; Salina Grande is 42m below sea level. The entrance to the peninsula is on the isthmus (US$5 entry fee); a conservation officer is stationed here. About 79 km E of Puerto Madryn, near the entrance, Isla de los Pájaros can be seen in Golfo San José. Its seabirds can only be viewed through fixed telescopes (at 400m distance), except for recognized ornithologists who can get permission to visit. The centre for visits to the Peninsula is **Puerto Pirámides** (*Pop* 100), 90 km E of Puerto Madryn. It is from here that whale-watching boat trips depart; sailings are controlled by the Prefectura, according to weather and sea conditions.

At Punta Norte (176 km) at the N end of the Valdés Peninsula, there are elephant seals (breeding time in first fortnight in Aug, best seen at low tide), reasonably priced restaurant for meals and snacks. At Caleta Valdés, 45 km S of Punta Norte you can see penguins and elephant seals at close quarters, but not at any specific point. At Punta Delgada (at the S of the peninsula) elephant seals and other wildlife can be seen, but not penguins. The beach on the entire coast is out of bounds; this is strictly enforced.

Tours Excursions are organized by tourist agencies in Puerto Madryn (addresses above). Full-day tours take in Puerto Pirámides (with whale-watching in season), plus some, but not necessarily all, of the other wildlife viewing points. Prices are fixed by law but shop around for quality: about US$25-30 pp plus the entry to the National Park; boat trip to see whales US$20 extra. On all excursions take drink with you, food too if you don't want to eat in the expensive restaurants (binoculars are also a good idea). Most tour companies stay 50-60 mins on location. Tito Bottazzi, T 95050, recommended, can also be contacted via *Safari Submarino* in Puerto Madryn. *Hydro Sports* rents scuba equipment and boats, has a small restaurant, and organizes land and sea wildlife tours (ask for Mariano). Off season tours run when demand is sufficient, usually on Thur and Sun, departing at 0955 and returning at 1730. To avoid disappointment check all excursion dates and opening times in advance if possible.

The peninsula is easily reached if you have your own transport, in fact the best way to see the wildlife is by car. See above for car hire; taking a taxi is worth considering if you can get a group together (taxi US$30 pp for the day). Hitching is very difficult, even at weekends in season. Peninsular roads all gravel except the road from Puerto Madryn to Puerto Pirámides (tours will not run after heavy rain in the low season).

There are also tours from Puerto Madryn to Punta Tombo (see page 1117) and to the Florentino Ameghino Dam, but these usually include 'sight-seeing' in the Chubut valley and a lot of time is spent travelling. It is cheaper to visit from Trelew.

● **Accommodation & places to eat At Puerto Pirámides**: **A2** *ACA Motel*, T 72057, poor restaurant, camping; there is also an ACA service station (open daily) with good café and shop; **A3** *Res El Libanés*, T 95007; **C** *Español*, basic but clean, friendly; *Posada del Mar*, T 95016, friendly, restaurant; **D** pp *Paradise Pub*, T 95030, helpful, rec, good value food and beer, good atmosphere; municipal campsite by the black sand beach, US$5 pp (free out of season), hot showers in evening only, dirty, busy, get there early to secure a place. **At Punta Delgada**: **A2** pp *Faro*, T 71910, full board, comfortable, excellent food, rec (reservations at *Hotel Península Valdés* in Puerto Madryn); there is also a separate restaurant.

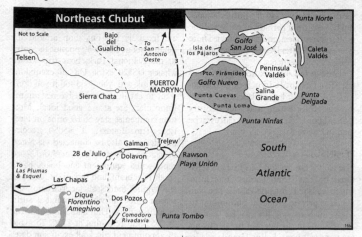

Northeast Chubut

Not to Scale

Punta Norte

Bajo del Gualicho

To San Antonio Oeste

Telsen

Isla de los Pájaros

Golfo San José

Caleta Valdés

PUERTO MADRYN

Pto. Pirámides
Golfo Nuevo

Península Valdés

Sierra Chata

Punta Cuevas

Salina Grande

Punta Delgada

Punta Loma

Gaiman Trelew

Punta Ninfas

28 de Julio Dolavon

Rawson
Playa Unión

South

To Las Plumas & Esquel

Las Chapas

Atlantic

Dique Florentino Ameghino

Dos Pozos

Ocean

To Comodoro Rivadavia

Punta Tombo

- **Shopping** In summer there are several well-stocked shops, but if staying take sun and wind protection and drinking water. There is a shop that sells original Patagonian Indian work.

- **Tourist offices** There is a small tourist office on the edge of Puerto Pirámides, useful information for hikes and driving tours.

- **Transport** Buses (Empresa 28 de Julio) from Puerto Madryn, Thur, Sun at 1000 returns 1800, US$6.50 each way.

THE CHUBUT VALLEY

RAWSON

The capital of Chubut Province, 7 km from the sea, is a town of official buildings (*Pop* 15,000; *Phone code* 0965). Above the Ciné Teatro Rawson is the Museo de la Ciudad, containing a collection of historical objects and old photos. 5 km down river is Puerto Rawson, and, nearby, Playa Unión, a beach with casino and many restaurants. Tourist Office, 9 de Julio 280.

- **Accommodation** A3 *Provincial*, Mitre 551, T/F 81400, clean, good restaurant; **C** *Res Sampedrano*, Belgrano 744.

- **Places to eat** *La Plaza*, M Moreno y B Vacchina; *Petit Café*, Belgrano y Costa.

- **Transport** Bus terminal, Av Antártida nr 25 de Mayo, but buses to Trelew and La Unión are best caught from the plaza. To Trelew US$2; to Playa Unión US$1, 20 mins.

ROUTES A paved road (Route 25) runs from Rawson through Trelew, Gaiman (see page 209) and Dolavon, all on the Río Chubut, to Las Plumas (mind the bridge if driving) and the upper Chubut Valley, all the way to Esquel (see page 194) and Trevelin. Spectacular scenery and lots of wildlife can be seen from the road.

TRELEW

Some 20 km up the Río Chubut is **Trelew**, pronounced 'TrelAYoo' (*Pop* 61,000; *Phone code* 0965), a prosperous town which has lost its Welsh look.

Places of interest

The **Capilla Tabernacle** on Belgrano between San Martín and 25 de Mayo is a red brick chapel dating from 1889. Nearby is another brick building from the same period, the Asociación San David. On the road to Rawson, 3 km S is **Chapel Moriah**, the oldest standing Welsh chapel. Built in 1880, it has a simple interior and a cemetery with the graves of many original settlers.

Museums

The **Museo Paleontológico** Egidio Feruglio, 9 de Julio 655, Mon-Fri 0830-1230 1330-2000, Sat 0900-1200, 1400-2100, Sun/holidays 1400-2100, US$4, located in the Parque Paleontológico Bryn-Gwyn, traces the history of dinosaurs with models made from moulds of dinosaur bones (not all from Patagonia). Note the dinosaur eggs filled with quartz. **Museo Regional**, Fontana y 9 de Julio, 0700-1300, 1400-2000, US$2, displays on indigenous societies, on failed Spanish attempts at settlement and on Welsh colonization; interesting.

Tours

Agencies run excursions to the Valdés Peninsula, more expensive and longer than from Puerto Madryn; ½-day tour to Punta Tombo US$30; ½-day tour of the Chubut valley includes Gaiman, Dolavon, Rawson US$15; to the Florentino Ameghino dam, US$30, 110 km inland on the Río Chubut. The dam covers 7,000 ha with water and irrigates 28,000 ha in the lower Chubut valley, as well as producing electric power, recommended for change of landscape.

Local holidays

28 July (Founding of Chubut); 13 Dec (Petroleum Day).

Local information

● **Accommodation**

L3 *Rayentray*, San Martín y Belgrano, T 34702, pool, restaurants, helpful, comfortable.

A2 *Centenario*, San Martín 150, T 30042, F 21524, expensive restaurant, Punta Tombo travel agency; **A3** *Libertador*, Rivadavia 31, T 35132, T 20220, without breakfast, good rooms, poor restaurant, quiet, friendly, good value; **A3** *Touring Club*, Av Fontana 240, T 33998, excellent, with bath and breakfast, TV.

B *Galicia*, 9 de Julio y Rivadavia, T 33803, F 24273, very warm, without bath, clean; **B** *City*, Rivadavia 254, F 33951/2; **B** *Res San Carlos*, Sarmiento 758, T 31538, rec; **B** *Rivadavia*, Rivadavia 55, T 34472, F 23591, with bath, clean, helpful, rec.

C *Argentino*, Abraham Matthews 186, T 36134, with bath, clean, quiet, good, nr bus terminal; **C** *Res Patterson*, Moreno 280, T 31636; **C** *Hostal Avenida*, Lewis Jones 49, T 34172, close to bus station, lots of character, basic but clean, friendly, quiet. Raul G Lerma, Rucahue 964, T 30208, offers free camping space in garden and local information, speaks English (taxi US$5 or ask at Estrella del Sur Turismo).

Camping: by the river, S of the town on the road to Rawson, on right about 200m beyond the bridge over Río Chubut, US$12, dirty, run-down, beware of mosquitoes; take Rawson bus, No 7 or 25. The site belongs to the Sports Club and has a public swimming pool.

● **Places to eat**

Don Facundo, Fontana 213, good, cheap, rec; *Eulogia Fuentes*, Don Bosco 23, good pasta; *El Quijote*, 25 de Mayo 90, good seafood; *Sugar*, 25 de Mayo 247, good *minutas*; *El Mesón*, Rivadavia 588, seafood; *El Marfil*, Italia 42, good, cheap; *La Primera*, Rivadavia y Pasaje Mendoza, *rotisería* and meat; *El Galeón*, San Martín 118, seafood specialities, good; *Cabildo Star*, Roca 76, excellent and cheap pizzas; *Napoli*, Rivadavia y 9 de Julio, old fashioned *confitería*; *Capítulo II*, Roca 393, *tenedor libre*, good and cheap; *La Casa de Juan*, Moreno 360, cosy, good pizzas; *La Empanadas de Isidro*, Bell 220; *Café Vittorio*, Belgrano 341, good service; café at *Hotel Touring Club*, popular, good coffee.

● **Airline offices**

Austral and Aerolíneas Argentinas, 25 de Mayo 33, T 20170; LADE, Fontana 227, T 35925; LAPA, Fontana 285, T 23438; TAN, T 34550.

● **Banks & money changers**

Banco de la Nación, 25 de Mayo y Fontana, accepts Amex and Thomas Cook TCs; Lloyds Bank (BLSA), Av 9 de Julio y Belgrano, does not change TCs, cash advance on Visa but high charge for call to verify card; Banco Provincia del Chubut, Rivadavia y 25 de Mayo; Banco del Sud, 9 de Julio 370, cash advance on Visa, high commission; Banco Almafuerte, 9 de Julio 270; Cambio at Caja de Ahorro y Seguro, San Martín y Fontana. Banks change currencies before midday only.

● **Post & telecommunications**

Post Office: 25 de Mayo and Mitre.

Telephone: *Teléonica Fontana*, Fontana 418; *Telefónica Argentina*, Roca nr Fontana; *Los alerces*, Pellegrini 321, for Fax.

● **Shopping**

Chocolates Patagónicos, Belgrano y Pasaje Mendoza, for local chocolate. *Camping Sur*, Pellegrini 389 for camping equipment.

● **Tour companies & travel agents**

Sur Turismo, Belgrano 326-330, organize good excursions, T 34550; *Estrella del Sur Turismo*, San Martín 129, T 31282, English spoken, rec; *Nievemar*, Italia 20, T 34114; *Punta Tombo Turismo*, San Martín 150, T 20358; and others.

● **Tourist offices**

On ground floor of bus terminal, at airport and in Municipalidad, entrance on San Martín. Free maps, hotel prices and self-guided city tour.

● **Transport**

Local *Car hire*: expensive (cheaper to take a tour to Punta Tombo and Península Valdés). Avis, Localiza and Renta Car Patagonia, desks are manned only at flight arrival times and cars are snapped up quickly. **Localiza**, Urquiza 310, T 35344; **Avis**, Paraguay 105, T/F 34634; **Rent A Car**, San Martín 125, T 20898.

Air Airport 5 km from centre; taxis cost about US$8. Local buses to/from Puerto Madryn stop at the airport entrance if asked, turning is 10 mins' walk, US$3.50; AR runs special bus service to connect with its flights. Lapa and AR have flights to/from **Buenos Aires**, **Río Gallegos** and **Ushuaia**. Lapa also to **Comodoro Rivadavia**. Kaiken flies to Comodoro Rivadavia, **Esquel**, **Neuquén** (also TAN), and Bariloche; also to **El Calafate** daily, 2 hrs 50 mins, 0830, US$127 one

way with overflight of Perito Moreno Glacier.

Buses To Buenos Aires, 4 daily, 21½ hrs US$60; to Bahía Blanca, US$32 daily with Don Otto, 0600, several a week with La Puntual, 0600; to **Mar del Plata**, changing at Bahía Blanca, US$35 with La Puntual; to **Esquel**, US$35, 2130, 11 hrs, Empresa Chubut; to **Bariloche** daily; to **Rawson** every 15 mins; frequent buses to **Gaiman**, US$1.15; hourly to **Puerto Madryn**, US$3.50 with 28 de Julio and Mar y Valle; to **Comodoro Rivadavia** daily at 2000, and Sun, Wed, Thur and Fri at 1035, US$26, 4 hrs; to **Río Gallegos**, daily, TAC, 6 hrs, US$55. If **hitching** S from Trelew, take the Rawson bus

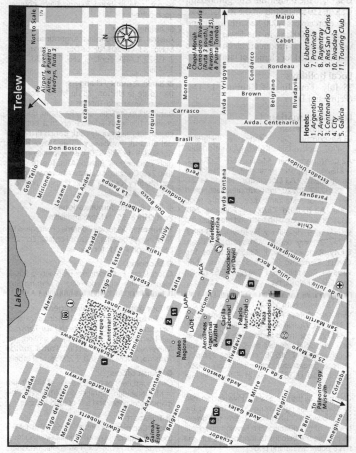

to the flyover 5 km out of town; there is a junction N of town for Puerto Madryn traffic.

GAIMAN

18 km W of Trelew, it is a pretty town (*Pop* 4,400) of well-built brick houses. It hosts the annual Eisteddfod (Welsh festival of arts) in October. In the old railway station is the museum of the Welsh colony, US$1 (open in summer, Mon-Sat 1600-2000, in winter, Tues-Sat 1500-1900, curator Mrs Roberts is 'full of stories'). El Desafío, two blocks W of the plaza, is a private theme-park, 16 years work by Sr Joaquín Alonso. It is constructed entirely of rubbish (drinks cans, bottles, piping and wire), a labyrinth of coloured plastic, glass and aluminium with mottos at every turn, US$5, tickets valid 2 months.

● **Places to eat** Welsh teas are served from about 1500 (US$10-12) by several **Tea Rooms**, inc *Casa de Té Gaiman*, Yrigoyen 738, excellent; *Plas y Coed*, Miguel D Jones 123 (oldest, excellent tea 'and enough food for a week', Marta Rees speaks English and is very knowledgeable about the area, highly rec); *Ty Gwyn*, 9 de Julio 111, rec; *Ty Nain*, Yrigoyen 283 (frequented by tour buses, display of historical items), and *Fima*, Tello 571. Small municipal **campsite** beyond Casa de Té Gaiman (poor, no facilities). Most facilities are closed out of season.

Dolavon, is a small town 20 km further W. The main street runs parallel the irrigation canal built by the settlers; there is a chapel over the canal. The old flour mill at Maipú 61, dates from 1930 and can be visited: key kept in the Municipalidad, Roca 188 (next to Banco Provincial del Chubut). Campsite near the service station on the way into town, good facilities, free. Some Trelew-Gaiman buses continue to Dolavan; check at Trelew bus station.

PUNTA TOMBO

117 km S of Trelew, on a dirt road which branches off the road to Rawson, 5 km SE of Trelew: driving time 1¾ hrs. Park entrance US$5. The wildlife is very varied: penguins, guanacos, etc. Season for penguins, Sept-Mar (Dec-Jan is the time when the young are taking to the water); the Reserve closes after March. Check with the Tourist Office that it is all right to visit the penguins as from late Mar they

are 'off limits' as they prepare to migrate. When visits are permitted it is a fantastic experience. You can share a taxi from Trelew (US$30 pp). Trelew and Puerto Madryn travel agencies run tours, spending 30 mins at the site; the fixed fee does not include park entry. About mid-way between Rawson and Punta Tombo, a road leads off Ruta 1 to Isla Escondida (9 km, signed), no facilities, but lovely rock and sand beach with bird and wildlife (badly littered unfortunately); secluded camping. Good place to camp if you are visiting the wildlife at Punta Tombo early am (the best time).

CAMARONES

275 km S of Trelew and 300 km N of Comodoro Rivadavia. There is a large **penguin colony** 35 km away at Cabo Dos Bahías along a dirt road (US$5, open all year); free camping is possible there and in the town itself

● **Accommodation B** *Kau-i-Keuken*, clean, friendly, good food, rec, owner runs trips to penguin colony; 2 others, **C**, the one by the power station is not rec).

● **Transport** Local buses very scarce; two a week, US$10, on Mon and Fri from Trelew (Don Otto), book at Uruguay 590, Trelew; bus leaves 0800 from San Martín and Belgrano, arrives 1130, returns to Trelew same day 1600. In Camarones ask the Guardia Fauna on Mon or Fri for a lift, hitchhiking is difficult, but possible at weekends and taxis are unavailable (a private car will charge US$50-60, ask at Busca Vida).

COMODORO RIVADAVIA

The largest city in the province of Chubut (*Pop* 158,000; *Phone code* 0967), is 387 km S of Trelew. Petroleum was discovered here in 1907 and about 30% of all Argentina's oil production comes from wells to the S and W. A 1,770-km pipeline carries the natural gas to Buenos Aires, and there is a petrochemical plant. Renewed interest in the local oil industry is making the town boom. There is an Oil Museum, with exhibits on exploration and production, 3 km N in Gral Mosconi (bus No 6 from San Martín y Abasolo). From here southward, prices begin to rise very rapidly, so stock up before reaching Río Gallegos (although bear in mind you are not allowed to take food into Chile). Good beach at Rada Tilly, 12 km S (buses every 30 mins); walk along beach at low tide to see sealions.

Local holidays
28 July (Founding of Chubut); 13 Dec (Petroleum Day).

Local information
● **Accommodation**
A3 *Austral*, Rivadavia 190, T 32200, noise from traffic but otherwise comfortable, reasonable restaurant; **A3** *Comodoro*, 9 de Julio 770, T 32300, overpriced, restaurant, nightclubs, car rental; **A3** *Res Azul*, Sarmiento 724, T 24874, comfortable, spotless, rec.

C *Colón*, San Martín 341, T 22283, run down, but quiet and safe; **C** *Comercio*, Rivadavia 341, T 22341, friendly, old fashioned, dirty, nr bus station, hot showers, good meals; **C** *Hosp Belgrano*, Belgrano 546, T 24313, with bath, clean, hot water; **C** *Hosp Praga*, España y Sarmiento, shower, clean; **C** *Rada Tilly*, Piedrabuena, in Rada Tilly 5 km S, T 51032, modern, clean; *Motel Astra*, S access of Route 3, T 25394.

Camping: Municipal, 12 km S at Rada Tilly, may be reached by Expreso Rada Tilly bus from town, hot and cold water. There is another, free, campsite at N end of beach, cold water only (watch out for clayslides when it rains).

● **Places to eat**
La Rastra, Rivadavia 384, very good for *churrasco*, but not much else; *Pizzería El Nazareño*, San Martín y España, good. *Bom-Bife*, España 832, good food, inexpensive. Several *rotiserías*, much cheaper, on 400 block of Rivadavia, in municipal market.

● **Airline offices**
Austral, 9 de Julio 870, T 40050; **LAPA**, Rivadavia 396, T 471685; **LADE**, Rivadavia 360, T 36181; **TAN**, T 23855.

● **Banks & money changers**
Lloyds Bank (BLSA), Av Rivadavia 276, Oct-Mar 0700-1300; April-Sept 1200-1800; no exchange transactions after 1000 in summer, 6% commission on TCs, pays US$ cash on TCs but minimum US$300; the **Banco de la Nación**, San Martín 108, has the best rates on US$ but does not change TCs. Amex agent is **Orbe Turismo Show**, San Martín 488, T 29699, 5% commission for US$, does not change TCs. Several travel agencies also change money inc **Roqueta Travel**, Rivadavia y Pellegrini, **Ceferino**, 9 de Julio 852, and **CRD Travel**, Moreno 844 (TCs accepted).

● **Embassies & consulates**
Belgian Vice-Consul, Rivadavia 283; **Chilean Consul**, Sarmiento 936; **Italian Vice-Consul**, Belgrano 1053.

● **Post & telecommunications**
Post Office: San Martín y Moreno.

● **Tour companies & travel agents**
Puelche EVT, Rivadavia 527; *Richard Pentreath*, Mitre 952; *San Gabriel* and *Atlas* at San Martín 488 and 263, respectively; *Monitur*, 9 de Julio 948.

● **Tourist offices**
On Rivadavia.

● **Transport**
Local VW dealer: Comercial Automotor, Rivadavia 380, rec. VW concession in Barrio Industrial, Av Irigoyen, also rec.

Air Airport, 9 km. Bus to airport from bus terminal, hourly (45 mins), US$0.40; take bus No 6. Taxi to airport, US$7. To/from **Buenos Aires** with LAPA or Austral (latter via **Bahía Blanca**, except Sun, continuing to **Río Gallegos** and **Río Grande**); LAPA also to Río Gallegos, Río Grande and Trelew. TAN and Kaiken to Neuquén, Río Gallegos, Río Grande, Bariloche, Trelew; TAN also to Puerto Deseado; Kaiken to Esquel and Ushuaia. LADE flies once a week (Wed) Comodoro Rivadavia-Perito Moreno-Gobernador Gregores Calafate/Lago Argentino-Río Gallegos-Río Grande-Ushuaia, and on Mon to Puerto Deseado-San Julián-Gob Gregores-Calafate-Río Turbio-Río Gallegos-Santa Cruz; once a week to Bariloche via Trelew and Viedma, or Trelew and Esquel, or via Esquel, El Maitén and El Bolsón; other services to Neuquén via the Lake District and to Trelew.

Buses Bus station conveniently located in city centre; has luggage store, good *confitería* upstairs, lousy toilets, *remise* taxi booth, some kiosks. Bus service to **Buenos Aires** daily at 1200 and 2115, 32 hrs, US$108 (same fare on Costera Criolla; also daily with La Estrella/Cóndor at 1335). Angel Giobbi buses to **Coyhaique** (Chile), US$30, 12 hrs, twice a week (Mon and Thur) 0100, June-Sept and 3 a week (Mon, Wed, Fri), 0100, Oct-May (weather permitting), also Turibus, Tues and Sat 0800. Three buses a week to **Bariloche**, US$55 (Don Otto at 2150, Sun, Tues, Thur, stops at Sarmiento midnight, Esquel at 0600 and for 30 mins at El Bolsón at 0900, arrives 0600 at Bariloche). To **Esquel** (paved road) direct, Fri 1230, 10 hrs, via Río Mayo, Mon, Thur, 0100, 15½ hrs, to Río Mayo Tues, Thur, Sun, 1700 and 1900, 5½ hrs. In summer buses heading S usually arrive full. To **Río Gallegos**, Don Otto 2345 daily, and Transportes Patagónica 2200 daily, 11 hrs US$40, reserve or standby. To **Puerto Madryn** and **Trelew**,

US$26, at 1200. La Unión colectivo to **Caleta Olivia**, hourly, US$3.50. To **Sarmiento**, US$7, 2½ hrs at 0700, 1300, 1900. To **Mendoza**, daily at 0130, 20 hrs; to **Córdoba**, Tues, Fri, Sun, 1200, 33 hrs.

Hitchhiking: there is a truck stop outside Comodoro Rivadavia on Route 3, the road to Bahía Blanca, where you can contact drivers whether heading N or S. Hitch out of the centre on Ruta 3 to 'Astra Km 20', or take any bus going N. Expensive truckdrivers' restaurants along the road; buy food in supermarkets.

FROM COMODORO RIVADAVIA TO CHILE

SARMIENTO

The road to Chile runs inland from Comodoro Rivadavia, amid oil wells, to (156 km) Colonia colectivo to (commonly known just as **Sarmiento**; *Pop* 7,000). Archaeological museum on Lago Musters, near the large Lago Colhué Huapi, with tourist office next to cathedral, check opening times, may be closed at weekends.

This is the area of the **petrified forests**, 70,000,000 years old, of fallen araucaria trees, nearly 3m round and 15-20m long: a remarkable sight. There are two sites you can visit: the **Bosque Petrificado José Ormachea**, 32 km S of Sarmiento on good gravel road, entry US$5, and the Víctor Szlapelis park, some 40 km further SW along the same road (follow signposts, road from Sarmiento in good condition). Taxi, Sarmiento to forests, US$39 (3 passengers), including 1 hr wait, for each extra hour US$9. Hitching is difficult, even in summer. Contact Sr Valero, the park ranger, for guided tours, ask at *Hotel Colón* (see also the *Monumento Natural Bosques Petrificados*) below, page 213).

● **Accommodation** B *Hostería Los Lagos*, Roca y Alberdi, T 93046, good, friendly, heating, restaurant; **E** *Colón*, P Moreno 645, restaurant, cheap, friendly; *Lago Musters*, P Moreno y Col, T 93097; *San Martín*, San Martín y P Moreno, cheap, good restaurant; **D** *Ismar*, Patagonia 248, with bath, clean, restaurant. In Dec-Mar you may be permitted to sleep in the Agricultural School (take sleeping bag) on the road to petrified forest, opp the ACA petrol station. **Camping**: Municipal site 2 km N of centre on Route 24, basic, no shower, US$3 for tent, US$1 pp, beside river.

● **Transport** Overnight buses to **Esquel** on Sun, Tues and Thur, stop at Río Mayo, 0630, take food for journey as cafés on route tend to overcharge. Three buses a day to **Comodoro Rivadavia**, 0700, 1300, 1900 and Giobbi buses to Chile leave at 0200.

From Sarmiento you can reach Esquel (448 km N along Routes 20 and 40), at the S edge of the Lake District (see page 194). Hitching along this road is very difficult, even in summer.

84 km W of Sarmiento, Route 22 branches SW to **Río Mayo** (*Pop* 2,260; 4 hotels: **C** *Covadonga*, very good; **C** *Hotel Pingüino*; **C** *A'Ayones*, T 20044, clean, modern, heating; **F** pp *San Martín*). 114 km W is the Chilean frontier at Coyhaique Alto for Coyhaique and Puerto Aisén in Chile.

South of Río Mayo Route 40 becomes quite rough, with no public transportation and very few vehicles of any kind even in mid-summer; persistent enquiries around town may locate a lorry heading to Perito Moreno, 124 km to the S. At Km 31 on this road a turning leads W to Lago Blanco, where there is a small *estancia* community, 30 km from the border with Chile (about 150 km from Río Mayo). No hotel, but police are friendly and may permit camping at the police post; wild but beautiful place. No public transport to Chile. From here the road continues to Chile via Paso Huemules and Balmaceda.

● **Transport Buses** The Giobbi buses from Comodoro Rivadavia to Coyhaique, Chile, pass through Río Mayo at 0600 on Mon, Wed and Fri (Mon and Thur, June-Sept), US$14, 6 hrs, but seats are scarce. Mon and Thur at the same hour Giobbi takes Route 40 N from Río Mayo direct to Esquel.

PERITO MORENO

The town (*Pop* 1,700; *Alt* 400m) is close to Lago Buenos Aires, which extends into Chile as Lago Gen Carrera. Do not confuse it with the famous glacier of the same name on Lago Argentino near El Calafate, nor with nearby **Parque Nacional Perito Moreno**, see below.

● **Accommodation** B *Argentino*, Buenos Aires 1236, dirty, no showers; B *Belgrano*, San Martín 1001, T 2019, with shower, clean, friendly, no heating, restaurant, rec; **C *Santa Cruz***, on Belgrano, heating, shared bath and hot water. 25 km S on Route 40, **B** pp ***Telken***, sheep station of the Nauta family offers accommodation Oct-April, discounts for families with two children, breakfast inc, other meals extra, English and Dutch spoken. **Camping**: Parque Laguna in town, opp Laguna Cisnes, well shielded, but dirty, US$1.50 pp, US$1 extra for showers, also cabins (slide shows at the tourist office there, information given).

● **Places to eat** *Pipach III*, good pizzas and *empanadas*.

● **Banks & money changers** US$ cash can be exchanged at **Banco de la Provincia de Santa Cruz**. Better rates from Plácido Treffinger, San Martín opp town hall. Difficult to exchange TCs, though the *Hotel Belgrano* may do so.

● **Transport Air** Airport is a long way from town, try to hitch as there is only one taxi; LADE flies from Perito Moreno to **Río Gallegos** on Wed, check in well in advance. **Hitchhikers** to the S are warned that, outside the tourist season (Jan-mid-Feb), it is usually quicker to head for the coast at Caleta Olivia and go S from there than to take Route 40 via Gobernador Gregores and Piedrabuena.

FRONTIER WITH CHILE: LOS ANTIGUOS

From Perito Moreno Route 43 runs S of Lago Buenos Aires to **Los Antiguos**, 67 km W, 2 km from the Chilean frontier (**B** *Hotel Argentino*), comfortable, restaurant; outstanding municipal campsite; service station; salmon fishing; annual cherry festival in early Jan).

At Km 29 **A3** *Hostería La Serena* offers accommodation in *cabinas*, 10% reduction to *South American Handbook* readers, good restaurant and organizes trips in both the Chilean and Argentine Lake Districts, open Oct-June; further details from Geraldine des Cressonières, Estancia La Serena, Casilla 87, 9040 Perito Moreno, Santa Cruz. Nearby is Los Chilcas where Indian remains can be found (trout fishing).

● **Transport** There is a bus connection (Empresa Co-Mi) from Caleta Olivia (see below) through to Los Antiguos every Mon, Thur, and Sat, at 1030 (from Perito Moreno, leaves from *Hotel Argentino*) and back to Caleta Olivia every Tues, Fri and Sun at 0830 (1030 from Perito Moreno), daily in Feb (at least), US$10. From Los Antiguos Transportes VH buses cross the border

by new bridge to Chile Chico, 8 km W, US$3, 45 mins (for routes from Chile Chico to Coyhaique and Puerto Aisén see **Chile**, page 821).

Another route to Chile is to follow the roads which go around the N side of Lago Buenos Aires to Puerto Ibáñez. At the roundabout, N edge of town, go straight, on the biggest road (do not follow signs to Puerto Ibáñez); at the police checkpoint, turn right onto a small road. Follow this to the road between Lago Blanco and Balmaceda; turn left Paso Huemules border crossing. The road is passable for jeeps or motorbikes.

SOUTH OF PERITO MORENO

118 km S of Perito Moreno on Route 40, a marked road goes directly to the famous **Cuevas de las Manos** (44 km). The series of galleries with 10,000-years-old paintings of human hands and of animals in red, orange, black, white and green, are interesting even for those not interested in rock art. The canyon in which the caves are situated is very beautiful, especially in the evening light (entrance US$1). A ranger lives at the site; he looks after the caves and is helpful with information. Camping is permitted but very windy. If it is not busy the ranger may let you sleep inside the park building. No buses, but the tourist office at Perito Moreno can supply names of drivers who can take you there, prices between US$80-100, to be split among a party of visitors. On leaving Perito Moreno on the way to the caves you will pass Cerro de El Volcán, its crater is accessible; after passing the Gendarmería on your right, take the first left (dirt road) at the 3-road junction with Route 40. It is 12 km to the path to the crater – ask permission at the Estancia to continue.

Corrugated Route 40 is dismal until tiny, forlorn **Bajo Caracoles** (**C** *Hotel Bajo Caracoles*, decent but relatively expensive meals). There is a good grocery store here. 92 km further S of Bajo Caracoles is the turning off W to Lago Belgrano and Parque Nacional Perito Moreno. 7 km E, along Route 521 is *Hotel Las Horquetas* with a café/bar, and 15 km beyond this is the Tamel Aike village (police station, water). 'Super' grade fuel is available in most places; carry extra, since the only other available source of fuel before Tres Lagos involves a 72-km detour to Gobernador

Gregores (see page 214). From the Parque Moreno junction to Tres Lagos (accommodation at *Restaurant Ahoniken*, Av San Martín, E pp), Route 40 improves considerably, but after Tres Lagos (one restaurant and supermarket) it deteriorates rapidly and remains very rugged until after the turnoff to the Fitz Roy sector of Parque Nacional Los Glaciares. 21 km beyond is the bridge over Río La Loma, with a hotel which has a bar/café. The remainder of the highway to Calafate, while slow, holds no major problems.

NB It is nearly impossible to hitchhike between Perito Moreno and Calafate. There is no public transport, at any time of year along this road.

PARQUE NACIONAL PERITO MORENO

Midway between Perito Moreno and Gobernador Gregores, at the end of a 90-km spur in bad condition is **Parque Nacional Perito Moreno**, one of the Argentine park system's wildest and most remote units, where guanaco and other wildlife roam among a large, interconnected system of lakes below glaciated peaks. The largest of the lakes is Lago Belgrano. Here the mountains are streaked with a mass of differing colours. This is excellent hiking country (ammonite fossils can be found), and a downhill expedition into Chile is possible for intrepid walkers (take all food). On the way to Cerro León is *Estancia La Oriental*, T 0966 2445/2196, guest house and camping site, D pp, A full board, clean, horses for hire. Good chance of spotting condors here. There are few visitors and no formal facilities, but camping (US$2-4/night) is among the best in South America. The park is situated S of Cerro San Lorenzo, highest peak of the Patagonian Andes. Entrance fee US$5, park ranger has maps and information. There is no public transport into the park but it may be possible to arrange a lift with *Estancia* workers from *Hotel Las Horquetas*. For more detail, see William C Leitch's *South America's National Parks* (Seattle: The Mountaineers, 1990).

COMODORO RIVADAVIA TO RIO GALLEGOS

CALETA OLIVIA

South of Comodoro Rivadavia, Route 3 continues to **Caleta Olivia** (Km 66; *Pop* 13,000). A good start-point for hitching S, Caleta Olivia is the urban centre for important oilfields, and is near Pico Truncado, the gas field which feeds the pipeline to Buenos Aires. On the central roundabout in front of the bus station is a huge granite monument of an oil driller with the tools of his trade.

● **Accommodation B** pp *Robert*, San Martín 2151, T 61452; **A3** *Grand*, Mosconi y Chubut, T 61393; **B** *Capri*, Hernández 1145, T 61132. Camping at Yacht Club.

● **Transport** Buses to Rio Gallegos, Pingüino, US$34, dep 2100, arr 0900. Many buses to Comodoro Rivadavia, 1 hr, US$3.50. To Calafate, dep 1400, 5 hrs.

73 km further S is **Fitz Roy**, named after the captain of Darwin's ship, *Beagle*. Fuel is available. (**B** *Hotel Fitzroy*, good, clean, cheap food, camping sometimes possible.)

The **Monumento Natural Bosques Petrificados**, surrounding the Laguna Grande on a road SW from Fitz Roy, 113 km away, can also be reached from Jaramillo (14 km S of Fitz Roy). This site has the largest examples of petrified trees (open 1000-2000). A 50 km new unpaved road has been built from Route 3 at Km 30 S of Fitz Roy to the Bosques Petrificados, which reduces the journey by several kilometres.

PUERTO DESEADO

10 km S of Fitzroy Route 281 branches off Route 3 and runs 123 km SE to **Puerto Deseado** (*Pop* 4,100; *Phone code* 0967; airport), at the mouth of the river Deseado which drains Lago Buenos Aires, far to the W. The town was founded on 15 July 1884; its harbour takes large ships. A local tourist attraction is the Cañadón de las Bandurrias, sometimes known as the Grotto of Lourdes, 40m high. Nearby are islands with penguins and other birds, including the unique grey cormorant; local launches available.

Local holidays 31 Jan (San Juan Bosco); 9 Oct (Coat of Arms day).

- **Accommodation A3** *Los Acantilados*, Pueyrredón y España, T 70167; **A3** *Colón*, Almte Brown 450, T 70304, dormitory-style; accommodation may also be available in the sports centre – ask at the Municipalidad.
- **Places to eat** *El Quincho*, Av Costanera Marcelo Lotufu, T 70977, rec.

ROUTES Inland Lago Buenos Aires is reached by road in 7 hrs; 280 km to Las Heras, then 177 km to Perito Moreno (see above).

SAN JULIAN

From Fitz Roy Route 3 runs S 268 km to **San Julián**, founded 1901 (*Pop* 4,480; *Phone code* 0962), the best place for breaking the 834 km run from Comodoro Rivadavia to Río Gallegos. There is much wildlife in the area: red and grey foxes, guanacos, wildcats in the mountains, rheas, etc. The main activities are sheep raising for export, fish canning, and production of kaolin and clay. Clay grinding can be seen at Molienda Santa Cruz and ceramics made at the Escuela de Cerámica; good handicraft centre at Moreno y San Martín. There is a regional museum at the end of San Martín on the waterfront. The ruins of Florida Blanca, a colony 10 km W of town, founded in 1870 by Antonio Viedma, can be visited. The cascade of San Julián is formed by two different tides. Punta Caldera is a popular summer beach. The first mass in Argentina was held here after Magellan had executed a member of his crew. Francis Drake also put in here to behead Thomas Doughty, after amiably dining with him. Near San Julián (15 km) is Cabo Curioso beach, with an attractive cave.

- **Accommodation A3** *Municipal*, 25 de Mayo 917, T 2300/1, very nice, well-run, good value, but no restaurant; **A3** *Res Sada*, San

Naming the Penguin

It was at Puerto Deseado that a Welshman in Cavendish's expedition of 1586 gave the name of *pengwyn* (white head) to a certain strange-looking bird. It is only fair to mention the opposing theory that the name is derived from a Spanish word, *pingüe*, meaning fat.

Martín 1112, T 2013, nice, clean, hot water, own bathroom, but sited on busy main road. Also older **B** *Colón*, Av San Martín 301 and **C** *Aguila*, San Martín 500 block, sleazy, cheapest in town. Good municipal campsite on the waterfront, US$2 pp, repeatedly rec, all facilities, Av Costanera betweeen Rivadavia and Roca.

- **Places to eat** *Sportsman*, Mitre y 25 de Mayo, excellent value; *Rural*, Ameghino y Vieytes, good, but not before 2100; a number of others. Also bars and tearooms.
- **Banks & money changers** Banco de la Nación, Mitre y Belgrano, and Banco de la Provincia de Santa Cruz, San Martín y Moreno.
- **Post & telecommunications** Post Office: Belgrano y San Martín.
- **Hospitals & medical services** Pharmacy: *Del Pueblo* on San Martín 570. Hospital, Av Costanera entre Roca y Magallanes.
- **Tourist offices** In centre of San Martín.
- **Transport Air** Weekly services (Mon) with LADE to Santa Cruz, Río Gallegos, Puerto Deseado, Gob Gregores, Comodoro Rivadavia, Calafate/Lago Argentino and Río Turbio. **Buses** Transportadora Patagónica comes from Río Gallegos en route to **Buenos Aires** (also Pingüino, 6 hrs, US$14 to/from Río Gallegos); Transportes Staller goes weekly (Sat) to **Lago Posadas** stopping in Gobernador Gregores, Hotel Las Horquetas, Bajo Caracoles and Río Blanco. For hitching, walk 5 km to petrol station on Ruta 3.

ROUTES An unpaved road (Route 521) runs NW from San Julián to Route 40 along the foothills of the Andes. After 215 km is **Gobernador Gregores** (*Hotel San Francisco*; municipal campsite; good mechanic in town and all grades of fuel available).

PIEDRABUENCA AND SANTA CRUZ

Piedrabuenca (*pop* 2,600) on Route 3, 146 km S of San Julián, a paved road heads E 75 km to **Santa Cruz**, one of the best of the coastal harbours (*pop* 3,000; airport). The port is near the mouth of the Santa Cruz river which drains Lago Argentino. It was founded on 1 December 1878 and was capital of Santa Cruz province until 1904. A deep-water port is being built 22 km outside Santa Cruz at **Punta Quilla**. Isla Monte León, 66 km away (Route 1601, then Route 3 and dirt track) has penguins, beaches and fishing.

- **Accommodation & places to eat Piedrabuena**: **A3** *ACA Motel*, T 7145, simple, functional but good, warm and nice food; **A3** *Hostería El Alamo*, Lavalle 08, T 7249, shower, clean, quiet, breakfast extra, rec; *Andalucia*, Belgrano Ote 170, hotel and restaurant (good pasta); **C** *Res Internacional*, Ibáñez 99, T 7197, rec; **C** pp *Hotel Vani*; also campsites N of town on Route 3. Several other restaurants. **Santa Cruz**: **A3** *Hostal de la Ría*, 25 de Mayo 645, T 8038; *Hostería Turística*; *Anel Aike*, both **C**.

ROUTES Inland Provincial Route 9 (1603 on some maps, unpaved, no petrol) from 43 km S of Piedrabuena to Calafate runs along the edge of a plateau with occasional panoramic views across the valley of the Río Santa Cruz below. Then at about 170 km it drops down into the valley itself to follow the river into the hills and to Lago Argentino. A pleasant run, without being spectacular. Route 288 runs direct from Piedrabuena via Laguna Grande (fuel) and Tres Lagos on Route 40, thence W and S to Lagos Viedma and Argentino. Most traffic to El Calafate goes via Río Gallegos.

RIO GALLEGOS

The capital of Santa Cruz Province, at the mouth of the Río Gallegos, is 265 km S of Santa Cruz. It has a deep-water port with a dry-dock and a large military base. The city was founded on 9 December 1885 (*Pop* 75,000; *Phone code* 0966). There is a large trade in wool and sheepskins. It is somewhat drab, but has a good shopping centre on Roca. Beyond Roca and Zapiola, the streets turn to dust and stones. The small Plaza San Martín, 1 block from the post office is well tended, with flower beds and statues; outside the post office is the remarkable sight of a balcony (preserved from a demolished house) commemorating the meeting of Presidents Errázuriz and Roca to end Chile and Argentina's 1883 Magellan Strait dispute.

Museums
Museo Provincial Mario Echevarría Baleta, Moreno 45 entre Zapiola y Roca, has collections of local history, flora, fauna, rock samples (open 0800-1900, weekends 1500-2000); **Museo de los Pioneros**, Alberdi y Elcano in the house of a German pioneer family, free, open 1500-2000, recommended.

Local holidays
31 January.

Local information
● **Accommodation**
L3 *Aparthotel Niza*, Alcorta 190, T 20958, quiet, inc good breakfast, clean, rec.

A1 *Costa Río*, San Martín 673, new, comfortable, discounts for ACA members; **A3** *Alonso*, Corrientes 33, T 22414, simple, very clean, room very hot; **A3** *Santa Cruz*, Roca 701, T 20601, with shower and heating, receptionist speaks English, good coffee bar, breakfast; **A3** *Covadonga*, Roca 1214, T 20190, clean, with shower, comfortable, warm, rec; **A3** *Nevada*, Zapiola 480, T 25990 (opp bus station for Punta Arenas), with bath, English spoken, good; **A3** *Piscis*, Avellaneda y Magallanes, T 25064, pleasant rooms, friendly.

B *Cabo Vírgenes*, Comodoro Rivadavia 252, T 22141, with bath, rec; **B** *Oviedo*, Libertad 746, T 20118, with bath, clean, comfortable, kitchen facilities, rec; **B** *Colonial*, Urquiza y Rivadavia, T 22329, shower, cheaper without, hot water, heating, friendly, clean.

C *Central*, Av Roca 1127, central, quiet, cold shower, no heating; close by is **C** *Entre Ríos*, Entre Ríos 170, T 20125, good; **C** *Pensión Belgrano*, Belgrano 123, dirty, basic but friendly, good restaurant; **C** *Res Internacional*, Sphur 78, with heating, friendly, but insecure; **C** *Río Turbio*, Zapiola 486, T 22155, good value; **C** *Viejo La Fuente*, Vélez Sarsfield 64-70, T 20304, basic, run down, rooms nr bar are noisy, hot water, one key fits several locks, restaurant.

D pp *Residencia* at Alberdi 458, meals, friendly, rec; **D** *Puerto Santa Cruz*, Zapiola 238, T 20099, with bath, passable. **Private house**: Barrio Codepro II, Casa 71, T 23789, E pp, rec.

NB Accommodation is hard to find in Río Gallegos because of the number of transient workers in town. Apparently no **camping** is allowed around Río Gallegos because it is a military zone apart from the authorized site 1 block S of bus terminal (Ruta 3 Nte), US$3 pp + US$1 for tent. Also try the YPF service station. Ask at tourist office for new site, being developed alongside a children's playground, cheap, free, hot showers. Taking photographs was not allowed either, for the same reason. **NB** Do not confuse C Comodoro Rivadavia with (nearby) C Rivadavia.

● **Places to eat**
Plenty and good, some specializing in seafood. *Restaurant Díaz*, Roca 1143, good but dirty, cheap; *La Casa de Miguel*, Roca 1284, good; *Biferia La Vasca*, Roca 1084, good value, young crowd, rock music, open till 0300; *Jardín*, Roca 1315, good, cheap, popular; *Club Británico*, Roca 935, excellent, reasonably priced; *El Palenque*, Corrientes 73, rec; *Café Carrera*,

Fagnano y Roca, good but expensive breakfast; *Le Croissant*, Zapiola y Estrada, good bakery.

● **Airline offices**
Aerolíneas Argentinas, San Martín 545, T 20181; **Austral**, Roca 917, T 22038; **LAPA**, Estrada 71, T 28382; **LADE**, Fagnano 53, T 22316; **TAN**, T 25259.

● **Banks & money changers**
Lloyds Bank (BLSA), Sarmiento 47, open 1000-1600, cash advance on Visa and Mastercard. Many banks on Av Roca inc **Banco de Santa Cruz**, 900 block, fair rates, Mastercard, best rates for TCs, no commission, change TCs here if going to Calafate, where it is even more difficult. Fair rates at **Cambio El Pingüino**, Zapiola 469, may also change European and South American currencies; **Cambio Sur**, San Martín y Roca, often has good rates; **Banco del Sud**, Alcorta 100 block, changes TCs without commission; **Banco de Crédito Argentino**, quick cash advance on Visa upstairs.

● **Embassies & consulates**
Chilean Consulate, Mariano Moreno 136, Mon-Fri, 0900-1300; tourist cards issued at border.

● **Laundry**
Alberdi y Rawson. *Laverap*, Corrientes 277.

● **Post & telecommunications**
Post Office: Roca 893 and at the airport.
Telephones: Roca 613.

● **Shopping**
Artesanías Koekén, San Martín 336, leatherwork, woollen goods, local produce; *Artesanías Santacruceñas*, Roca 658; *Tía* department store, Roca 700 block, good supermarket section; Supermarket *La Anónima*, Roca y España. Most places take a 2-3-hr lunch break.

● **Sports**
Fishing: the S fishing zone inc the Ríos Gallegos, Grande, Fuego, Ewan, San Pablo and Lago Fagnano, nr Ushuaia. It is famous for runs of sea trout. See **Fishing** in **Information for travellers**, page 241.

● **Tourist offices**
Roca y Córdoba, Mon-Fri, 0800-1400, friendly, helpful, English spoken. They will phone round hotels for you.

● **Transport**
Local Car rental: *Localiza*, Sarmiento 237, T 24417; Eduardo Riestra, San Martín 1508, T21321. **Car parts and repairs**: at Repuestos Sarmiento, on Sarmiento, owner very friendly and helpful. **Motorcycle mechanic**: Juan Carlos Topcic, Costa Rica 25, friendly and helpful. **Taxis**: hiring a taxi for group excursions may be

no more expensive than taking a tour bus *A1*, Entre Ríos 350, T 22453, for taxis and car rental, not cheap.

Air Airport 15 km from town. Taxi (*remise*) to/from town, eg opp *Hotel Colonial* US$8 (beware overcharging); hitching from car park is easy. It is permitted to spend the night at the airport prior to early am flights. In summer, it is best to make your bookings in advance. AR's Buenos Aires-Auckland-Sydney flight (twice a week) stops at Río Gallegos, but the return journey does not. To/from **Buenos Aires**: AR (direct or via Trelew), Austral (via Bahía Blanca and Comodoro Rivadavia), LAPA (via Trelew or Comodoro Rivadavia). TAN from **Neuquén** via Trelew and Comodoro Rivadavia. Several flights to **Ushuaia** (Tierra del Fuego), direct (AR, always booked, but standby seats available), Kaiken or LAPA. To **Río Grande**, AR, Austral, LAPA, TAN, Kaiken. Kaiken also to Comodoro Rivadavia and Calafate. LADE (Fagnano 53, T 20316) to **Río Turbio** and Calafate, twice a week, to Ushuaia and **Comodoro Rivadavia** once a week.
NB Flights may leave early, sometimes up to 40 mins. LADE flights should be booked as far in advance as possible.

Buses New terminal at corner of Route 3 and Av Parque, 3 km from centre (no left luggage, small bank, *confitería*, few toilets, kiosks); taxi to centre US$3, bus US$1 (Nos 1 and 12 from posted stops on Roca). To **Calafate**, 4-5 hrs, US$30, very crowded; turn up with ticket 30 mins before departure: 2 companies – Interlagos and Pingüino – run daily services at 1345 and 1600 between Sept and May, which wait at the airport for incoming flights. In winter both companies operate 3 times a week; El Pingüino has reclining seats, video, toilet, etc, US$50 return, mixed reports; Pingüino offers 2-night excursion to Calafate, sold at airport only, US$93 in single room, credit cards accepted. Quebele Tours and LAPA offer direct connections from airport to Calafate.
Pingüino daily at 2100 to **Caleta Olivia**, US$34, 11 hrs. To **Trelew** and **Puerto Madryn** daily (18 hrs), US$71. To **Comodoro Rivadavia**, 834 km, Patagónico at 2100, stops at Fitz Roy daily at dawn, arr 1000 next day, US$40. For **Bariloche**, take this bus to Comodoro Rivadavia, then the 2150 Don Otto bus to Bariloche (fare to Bariloche US$88). A bus (Andesmar) goes all the way to **Mendoza**, leaves Fri 1300, arrives 0900 Sun, via Comodoro Rivadavia, Puerto Madryn and Neuquén.
To **Buenos Aires**, 2,575 km, 36 hrs, Pingüino, Mon, Wed, Fri, 2200, daily, 2115, with Costera Criolla, US$107.
To **Río Turbio**: Expreso Pingüino goes at 1300 daily excluding Sat (Sat 1230), 5½-6½

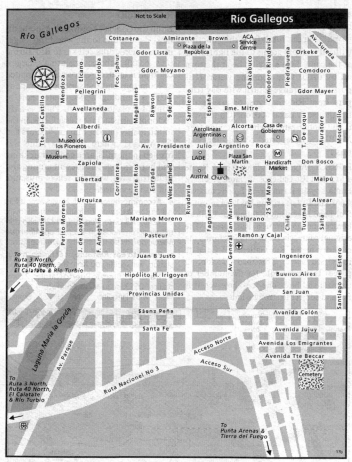

Río Gallegos

Not to Scale

hrs, US$20 (hitching practically impossible); also Mansilla, Sat 1330, and Vera, Mon-Fri 1200. No buses to/from Río Grande.

To Chile buses: to **Puerto Natales**, Bus Sur and Pingüino twice a week each, 7½ hrs, US$22. To **Punta Arenas**, 260 km, US$23.50 daily at 1300, by Pingüino, also Ghisoni at 1730, except 1415 Tues and Thur, none on Sat, 6½ hrs inc border-crossing process.

By car: make sure your car papers are in order (go first to Tourist Office for necessary documents, then to the customs office at the port, at the end of San Martín, very uncomplicated).

For road details, see Tierra del Fuego sections in Argentina and Chile.

Hitchhiking: to Buenos Aires is possible in about 5-7 days; appearance important; hitching to Tierra del Fuego possible from service station on Ruta 3 at edge of town, trucks stop here for customs check, be there before 0700. To Calafate, from police control outside town.

134 km S, there is a penguin colony at **Cabo Vírgenes** (US$3, run by local authority which puts money directly into conservation). The Navy allows visitors to climb up Cabo Vírgenes lighthouse for

a superb view. Follow Route 3 then branch off on Route 1 for 3½ hrs (unpaved). You can hitch from this junction with oil workers going to the lighthouse at the cape. Take a taxi to be at the turn off by 0700. Take drinking water. It is possible to arrange return with day trippers from Río Gallegos, or ask at the lighthouse or naval station. (On the way is El Cóndor ranch, where the manager, Mr Blake, is reported to welcome visitors.)

ROUTES Argentina's longest road, Route 40, ends at Río Gallegos, or, more precisely, Punta Loyola; it runs from Bolivia for over 4,667 km. Its last section has been rerouted S of Lago Argentino to follow the Chilean border and go through Río Turbio. The original route, via La Esperanza, forms the majority of the Río Gallegos-El Calafate route (see below). This road (323 km, all paved) is worth while for the number of animals and birds one sees; however, it is flat and subject to strong winds.

RIO TURBIO

From Río Gallegos a railway, the southern-most regular line in the world (no longer in operation), runs 260 km to **Río Turbio** (*Pop* 6,000), where Argentina's largest coalfield is located; reserves are estimated at 450m tons and the state coal company YCF is building a deep-water port at Punta Loyola to service it. There is a director of tourism, Prof César Cetta, in the municipality on San Martín. Visitors can see Mina 1, where the first mine was opened in the hills; area good for trekking and horse riding. The present mining and industrial area, with the school museum, can also be visited.

● **Accommodation** Hotels always almost full: **A3** *Hostería Capipe*, Dufour (9 km from town, T 91240); **A3** *Gato Negro*, T 91226, also dormitory accommodation **E** pp; **E** pp *Albergue Municipal*, by ski-run in hills, 6 km from town.

● **Places to eat** *Restaurant El Ringo*, nr bus station, will shelter you from the wind.

● **Transport** Buses to **Puerto Natales**, 2 companies, US$3, regular. To **Calafate** 4 times a week with Pingüino, 7 hrs, US$27. Expreso

El Calafate & Environs

Refugio Onelli

Reserva Nacional Zona Centro

Lago Onelli

Brazo Upsala

Canal Spegazzini

Brazo Norte

Cerro Negro 1650 m

Boca del Diablo

Lago Argentino

Peninsula Avellaneda

Seno Mayo

Glaciar Mayo

Gl. Ameghino

Cerro Negro 2011 m

Canal de los Témpanos

Puerto Bandera

Peninsula Magallanes

R. Mitre

Isla Solitaria

Calafate   To Río Gallegos

Glaciar Moreno

Cerro Cervantes 2380 m

Brazo Rico

Lago Roca

Brazo Sur

R Rico

ARGENTINA

Parque Nacional los Glaciares

Reserva Nacional Zona Roca

CHILE

CHILE

N

17e

0   10
km

Pingüino runs daily at 0600 (plus 1300 Tues, Thur, Sat, 6 hrs) in summer or 1300 Wed, Thur, Sat in winter to **Río Gallegos**, but LADE flights are cheaper and avoid the numerous passport checks. (airport 15 km from town, taxi US$5pp. **To Chile**: Río Turbio is 39 km by road from Puerto Natales (Chile). This road is open open all year, daytime only. Alternatively, 55 km N of Río Turbio is Cancha Carrera, from where there is a border crossing, only open during the summer, into Torres del Paine National Park (Argentine customs are fast and friendly). 8 km beyond is the Chilean border post, where you have to register at the *carabineros'* office.

CALAFATE AND THE PARQUE NACIONAL DE LOS GLACIARES

CALAFATE

El Calafate (to give its proper name; *Pop* 3,000; *Phone code* 0902) is on Lago Argentino, 312 km (paved) NW of Río Gallegos. It is the southern gateway to the **Parque Nacional de los Glaciares**, which is 50 km away (the northern end is at Lago Viedma). The Lago Argentino area is very popular, booking all transport in advance is a *must*; in Jan-Feb accommodation can be difficult to find. Credit cards are not popular, apart from hotels, and high commissions are charged; most places quote in US dollars.

Places of interest

From the Centro Cívico, visit Capilla Santa Teresita in Plaza San Martín. Behind it is C Perito Moreno; walk to the top of the hill for the views of the silhouette of the southern end of the Andes, the Laguna Redonda and Isla Solitaria on Lago Argentino. On the alluvial plain by the lake there are many interesting birds, and in the other direction there is scope for good hill-walking.

Excursions

For the main excursion to the Moreno glacier, see below. Travel by road to the most interesting spots is limited and may require expensive taxis. Tours can be arranged at travel agencies, or with taxi drivers who await arrivals. Walk down to **Lago Argentino**; 15 km along the lakeside are the painted caves at **Punta Gualichó**

(badly deteriorated) but there are fascinating geological formations caused by erosion, on the edge of Lago Argentino, 12 km from Calafate on the road to Río Gallegos. A recommended walk is from the Intendencia del Parque, follow the new road among cultivated fields and orchards to **Laguna de Los Cisnes**, a bird reserve, with flamingoes, ducks, and abundant birdlife. 21 km W of Calafate is **El Galpón**, an estancia which offers evening visits (from 1730) to see sheep shearing, birdwatching and a barbecue, also horseriding (or visits at other times on request); in Calafate T/F 91793; BsAs, Av Paseo Colón 221, p 7, T 343-8185, F 334-2669.

An excursion can also be made to **Lago Roca**, 40 km S from Calafate. Trout and salmon fishing, climbing, walking, camping and branding of cattle in summer. Good camping here in wooded area, restaurant.

Local festivals

People flock to the rural show on 15 Feb (Lago Argentino Day) and camp out with much revelry; dances and *asados* (barbecued sides of sheep). There are also barbecues and rodeo etc on Día de la Tradición, 10 November.

Local information

● **Accommodation**

Many hotels are open only from Oct to April/May.

L2 *Los Alamos*, Moyano y Bustillo, T 91144, F 91186, comfortable, good food and service, rec; **L3** *Hostería Kau-Yatún*, with bath, many facilities, 25 de Mayo (10 blocks from town centre), T 91059, F 91260, old *estancia* house, comfortable, restaurant and barbecues, horse-riding tours with guides; **L3** *El Mirador del Lago*, Libertador 2047, T/F 91176, good accommodation, acceptable restaurant (wines not rec), better not to take half-board; **A2** *Michelangelo*, Espora 1020, T 91045, F 91058, modern, clean, reasonable, good restaurant, accepts TCs (poor rates); **A3** *ACA Hostería El Calafate*, San Martín, T 91004, F 91027, modern, good view, open all year; **A3** *Amado*, Av del Libertador 1072, T 91023, good; **A3** *Upsala*, Espora 139, T 91075, inc breakfast, warm, friendly, rec; **B** *Cabañas Del Sol*, Av del Libertador 1956, T 91439 (D in low season), friendly, clean, good meals, highly rec; **B** *Hosp del Norte*, Los Gauchos 813, T 91117, open all year, kitchen facilities, clean, comfortable, owner organizes tours, highly rec, a similar place

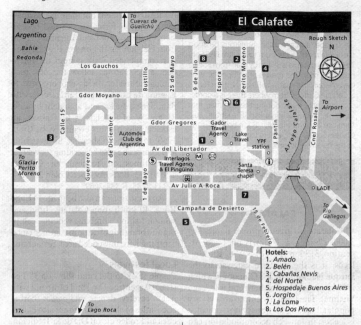

El Calafate

Rough Sketch

Hotels:
1. Amado
2. Belén
3. Cabañas Nevis
4. del Norte
5. Hospedaje Buenos Aires
6. Jorgito
7. La Loma
8. Los Dos Pinos

across the street; **A3** *Hostería Schilling*, Roca 895, T 91453, with bath, lovely rooms, manager speaks good English, safe parking for motorcycles. On the road to Parque Nacional de los Glaciares, 40 km W of Calafate is **L3** *Los Notros*, T/F 91438, half-board, spacious, rooms with glacier views, rec.

B *Hostería Kapenke*, 9 de Julio 112, T 91093, with bath, inc breakfast, good, rec; **B** *La Loma*, B Roca y 15 de Febrero (100m from bus station), T 91016 (can be booked in Buenos Aires at Av Callao 433, 8a 'P', T 371-9123), with bath, inc breakfast, modern, highly rec, multilingual, restaurant, tea room, cheaper in low season, free audio-visual of the last breaking of Moreno Glacier in 1988; **B** *Las Cabañitas*, V Feilberg 218, T 91118, cabins, hot water, kitchen and laundry facilities, helpful, rec; **B** *Res Dos Lagos*, 25 de Mayo 220, T 91170, with bath, very comfortable and clean, good value, rec; **C** pp *Cabañas Nevis*, about 1 km from town towards glacier, Libertador 1696, T 91180, for 4 or 8, lake view, full board good value.

Several slightly cheaper hotels but none less than E pp, eg **C** *Lago Azul*, Perito Moreno 83, T 91419, only 2 double rooms, highly rec; **C** *Hosp Belén*, Los Gauchos 300 y Perito Moreno, T 91028, clean, warm, hot water, cooking facilities, friendly, family

welcome, highly rec; **C** *Hosp Jorgito*, Gob Moyano 943, T 91323, clean, basic, hot water, cooking facilities, heating, breakfast extra, often full, rec; **C** *Hosp Los Dos Pinos*, 9 de Julio 358, T 91271, hot water, cooking and laundry facilities, clean, also cabins **C**, dormitory accommodation **F** pp, and camping **F** pp, arranges tours to glacier, popular; **E** pp *Hosp Familiar Buenos Aires*, Buenos Aires 296, 200m from terminal, T 91147, kitchen facilities, helpful, hot showers, luggage store; **E** pp *Hosp Alejandra*, Espora 60, T 91328, good value, rec; **D** pp *Youth Hostel Albergue del Glaciar*, Los Pioneros, 200m off Av Libertador, T/F 91243 (reservations in Buenos Aires T 541-447 2338 or 54-321 69416), discount for ISIC or IYHA members, open 1 Oct-31 Mar, rec, hot water, kitchen facilities, English spoken, travel agency, Perito Moreno Tours, runs tours to Moreno glacier (US$28 pp, constantly rec as good value) and elsewhere, free shuttle service from bus station and airport book in advance in summer. *Youth Hostel La Loma*, Roca 849, multilingual, restaurant, room for 2-3 people with bath, or **E** pp sharing, IYHA affiliated, 2 blocks from bus station. Some private houses offer accommodation such as Enrique Barragán, Barrio Bahía Redonda, Casa 10, T 91325, **E**, rec. **F** pp *Apartamentos Lago Viedma*, Paralelo 158, T 91159, F 91158, hostel, 4 bunks to a room, cooking facilities. **F** pp *La Cueva de Jorge Lemos*, Gob Moyano 839, behind YPF station, bunk beds, bathroom, showers, kitchen facilities, popular and cheap. If in difficulty, ask at tourist office from which caravans, tents (sleep 4) and 4-berth *cabañas* may be hired, showers extra.

Camping: campsite behind YPF service station, US$4 pp. Three campsites in the Park en route to the glacier: *Camping Río Mitre*, nr the park entrance, 52 km from Calafate, 26 km E of the glacier, US$3 pp; *Camping Bahía Escondida*, 7 km E of the glacier, toilets and hot showers, US$3 pp; unmarked site at Arroyo Correntoso, 10 km E of the glacier, no facilities but nice location and lots of firewood. Take food to all three. Another campsite is *Camping Río Bote*, 35 km, on road to Río Gallegos.

● **Places to eat**
Prices rise during Nov and high season lasts until May. *Pizzería Onelli*, Libertador 1197, reasonable, stays open out of season; *Michelangelo*, Espora 1020, very expensive but absolutely magnificent steaks, rec; *Paso Verlika*, Av Libertador 1108, small, 2 courses with wine US$16, credit cards 10% extra, good value; *Mi Viejo*, Av Libertador 1111, *parrilla*; *El Rancho*, 9 de Julio y Gob Moyano, large, cheap and good pizzas, popular, free video shows of the glacier, highly rec; *La Loma* (address above), friendly, home food, picnic lunches supplied, good cakes and chocolates, beautiful view, reasonable prices, discounts for IYHA. Tea rooms: *Maktub*, Libertador 905, excellent pastries, pricey; *Bar Don Diego de la Noche*, Av del Libertador 1603, lamb and seafood, live music, good atmosphere.

● **Banks & money changers**
Banco de la Provincia de Santa Cruz (Av del Libertador) changes cash (commission 1%) and TCs. Advances on Visa and Mastercard (high commission). Travel agencies such as Interlagos also change notes; YPF garage and Chocolate El Calafate and some other shops give good

rates for cash; also El Pingüino bus company for good rates (but watch the commission); the Scorpio snack bar in the main street is reported to give best rates; try also the supermarket in the main street and the *Albergue del Glaciar*. High commission on cheques.

● **Post & telecommunications**
Telephones: public office on Espora, 0700-0100, also has telex and fax facilities.

● **Shopping**
Supermarket, Libertad y Perito Moreno, accepts US$ cash.

● **Tour companies & travel agents**
Interlagos, Libertador 1175, tours to Moreno glacier, plenty of time allowed, provide cheapest transport to Fitz Roy (but double check return!), English and Spanish speaking guide, highly rec; *Navimag*, Av El Bosque Nte 0440, p 1, T 203-5030, F 203-5025, Tx 240208-240224 NISA CK, Metro Tobalaba for services Puerto Montt-Puerto Natales and Puerto Montt-Puerto Chacabuco; *El Pingüino*, Libertador 1025, T 91273, changes TCs, rec; *Los Glaciares*, Libertador 1303, T 91159, rec, good value; *Tur Aike*, Libertador 1080, T 91436, and *Gador Viajes*, Libertador 900 block; *Upland Goose*, Libertador (1st floor), T 0902-91424, rec; *Hielo y Aventura*, 25 de Mayo, T 91053, organizes 2-hr trek on glacier with champagne, rec. Most agencies charge the same rates for excursions. to the Moreno Glacier US$25 for a trip leaving 0830, returning 1800, without lunch, 3 hrs at glacier; to Lago Roca, at 0930 return 1700, US$25; Cerro Fitz Roy, at 0600 return 1900, US$50, Gualichó caves, 2 hrs, US$16 (see **Excursions**, above). Several hotels also organize tours by minibus inc *Hosp del Norte* and *Albergue del Glaciar*. Jorge Lemos, *Aventrek*, Gob Moyano 839, Aptdo Postal Esp No 7 (9405) El Calafate, Telex Cab pública 86905, runs rec treks with small groups in Glaciers National Park and Fitzroy. Mountain bikes can be hired from Sr Daniel Alvarez, also rec as source of information, at the Mercado Artesanal on Libertador.

● **Tourist offices**

Tourist office in new building by bridge over Río Calafate and in bus terminal. Hotel prices detailed on large chart at tourist office; has a list of taxis but undertakes no arrangements. Helpful staff. Sr Jorge Antolín Solache owner of *Hotel La Loma*, Casilla de Correo 36, 9405 Calafate (T 0902-91016, Dec-May), rest of the year Callao 433-8a 'P', 1022 Buenos Aires (T 371-9123), has kindly offered to provide any information to travellers in the region. He speaks English, French, Italian and Portuguese. Many shops on main street have maps.

● **Transport**

Air There is a new airport, called Lago Argentino, with an all-weather runway (though flights may be suspended in severe weather). By air with Kaiken from Río Gallegos, Río Grande, Ushuaia, Bariloche, Esquel and Trelew (returns at 1830 daily); LADE twice a week to Río Turbio, 3 a week in summer to connect with buses to Puerto Natales and Torres del Paine. Once a week to Perito Moreno, LADE. Air fares can be cheaper than buses.

Buses Terminal on Roca, 1 block from Libertador. Journey to **Ushuaia** requires four changes, and ferry, total cost US$43. Interlagos Turismo bus runs daily at 0800 (summer) or 0915 Tues, Thur, Sat (winter) to **Río Gallegos** and its airport; in addition El Pingüino runs daily at 0600 and 1630 (Wed, Fri, Sat, in winter) 4½ hrs, US$30, passengers on this bus wishing to go to Chile get off at Güer Aike to catch Pingüino's Gallegos-Río Turbio bus 50 mins later, arriving at 1700. To Río Turbio with Pingüino 4 times a week, 7 hrs, US$27. Taxi to Río Gallegos, 4 hrs, US$200 irrespective of number of passengers, up to 5 people.

Direct services to Chile: COOTRA to **Puerto Natales** via Río Turbio, several times a week, US$25, 7 hrs (rec to book in advance). Travel agencies inc Albergue del Glacier run regular services in summer, on demand in winter, up to US$50, 5 hrs.

PARQUE NACIONAL DE LOS GLACIARES

At the far end of Lago Argentino (80 km from Calafate) the **Ventisquero Moreno**, one of the few glaciers in the world that has been growing larger, descends to the surface of the water over a 5-km frontage and a height of about 60m. In a cycle of roughly 3 years it used to advance across the lake, cutting the Brazo Rico off from the Canal de los Témpanos; then the pressure of water in the Brazo Rico would break up the ice and reopen the channel. Owing to rising temperatures from the thinning of the ozone layer, the glacier is reportedly not growing any more (since 1992) and the 3-year cycle has been disrupted (it is estimated at 7 years now). Pieces break off and float away as icebergs. The vivid blue hues of the ice floes and the dull roar as they break away from the snout are spectacular, especially at sunset. Wooden catwalks prevent you from going to the water's edge; there is a fine of up to US$500 for leaving the catwalks.

● **Access** From Calafate to the glacier's edge there are buses by Pingüino, Interlagos and Albergue del Glaciar (daily Nov-Mar, less frequent at other times), US$25-28 return (plus US$3.50 park entry) leaving 0830 returning 1800, giving 3 hrs at glacier, book through any agency in Calafate, return ticket valid if you come back next day (student discount available). Albergue del Glaciar trips go out via an *estancia* and return past the lake and have been repeatedly rec. They also do walking tours on the glacier, book ahead. Taxis, US$80 for 4 passengers round trip. Out of season, trips to the glacier are difficult to arrange, but one can gather a party and hire a taxi (remise taxis T 91745, 91044); take warm clothes, and food and drink. It may be possible to camp in the *guardaparque's* backyard, but you must ask first. Ask rangers where you can camp out of season, no facilities except a decrepit toilet block. Boat trips are organized by *Hielo y Aventura* travel agency, T 91053, large boats for up to 60 passengers, US$20 pp on 'Safari Náutico' (1 hr), or a day trip ('Minitrekking') including boat trip and 2½ hrs' walk on the glacier, US$67, rec, but not for the fainthearted, take your own lunch.

A worthwhile trip is by motor-boat from Punta Bandera, 50 km from Calafate, to the **Upsala Glacier** at the NW end of Lago Argentino (check before going that access to the glacier face is possible). The trip also goes to Lago Onelli and glacier (restaurant) and Spegazzini glacier. From the dock on Bahía Onelli to Lago Onelli is an easy 2-km trail done with a guide (in English, German or Spanish) through a lovely southern forest wreathed in bearded moss. Small **Lago Onelli** is quiet and very beautiful, beech trees on one side, and ice-covered mountains on the other. The lake is full of icebergs of every size and sculpted shape.

Southern Santa Cruz & P.N. Los Glaciares

PN Los Glaciares:
1. Ventisquero Moreno
2. ACA Restaurant
3. Canal de los Témpanos
4. Brazo Rico
5. Lago Onelli
6. Upsala Glacier
7. Spegazzini Glacier
8. Punta Gualichó
9. Punta Bandera

● **Access** Tour boats usually operate a daily trip to the glacier, the catamaran *Serac*, US$90, or the *Nunatak* (slightly cheaper). The price includes bus fares and park entry fees – pay in dollars and take food. Bus departs 0730 from Calafate for Punta Bandera. 1 hr is allowed for a meal at the restaurant near the Lago Onelli track. Return bus to Calafate at 1930; a tiring day, it is often cold and wet, but memorable. Out of season it is extremely difficult to get to the glacier. Many travel agencies make reservations.

Another worthwhile excursion is to the N end of the Glaciares National Park around Lago Viedma to **Cerro Fitz Roy** (Tehuelche name El Chaltén) and Cerro Torre, 230 km NW of Calafate. The Fitz Roy massif can be seen from the village of **El Chaltén**, which is becoming very popular (stupendous views: "anyone within 500 miles would be a fool to miss them" – Julian and Cordelia Thomas).

On the way to Cerro Fitz Roy on Route 40, is the Southern Astronomical Observatory, managed by the Observatory of La Plata.

Día de la Tradición (10 Nov) is celebrated with gaucho events, riding and barbecue (US$5).

Local information

● **Accommodation & places to eat**

North Glaciares: **A3** *Fitz Roy Inn*, I 9111 /, with breakfast, restaurant; cabins sleep 2, 3 or 4. Opposite is **E** pp *Albergue Patagonia*, Av San Martín, T 61564/93019, also dormitory accommodation Fpp, kitchen and laundry facilities, TV and video, book exchange, accepts TCs; **B** pp *Estancia La Quinta*, 3 km from Chaltén, half-board, no heating, prepares lunch for trekkers, rec; **E** pp *Hotel Lago del Desierto*, good, small, showers, new 6-berth cabins D pp with bath. *Confitería La Senyera*, excellent bread, rec; *Josh Aike*, excellent *confitería*, homemade food, beautiful building, rec; *The Wall Pub*. *Camping Madsen* (free) at end of village nr the paths to Cerros Fitz Roy and Torre (the bus from Calafate goes to and from this site), no facilities; *Ruca Mahuida*, 400m N on route to treks, very helpful, camping US$5, showers, stores gear, rec.

Southern shore of Lago Viedma: A1 *Hostería Helsingfors* (T/F 0966-20719, San Martín 516, Río Gallegos, or BsAs T/F 824-6623/3634), with bath and breakfast, all other meals available, many treks and boat trips available, also riding, sheep-shearing.

Camping: a stove is essential for camping as firewood is scarce. Take plenty of warm clothes and a good sleeping bag. Buy supplies in Calafate (cheaper and more choice). It is possible to rent equipment in El Chaltén, ask at park entrance. Two small shops sell food, gas and batteries.

● **Sports**

Hiking: there are three main trails in the park from the entrance (all well signposted): 'Río Blanco' to Fitz Roy glacier, 5 hrs each way; 'Cerro Torre' 3 hrs each way; and to the Salto, 1 hr each way. Cerro Fitz Roy base camp is 3 hrs easy walk from *Camping Madsen* (which is a better place to stay). It is possible to hike from Chaltén to Cerro Torre base camp and back in 1 day, crossing the Río Fitz Roy by the new bridge.

Beware of straying from the paths. A map is essential, even on short walks (the information centre at park entrance provides photocopied maps of treks). The best is one published by Zagier and Urruty, 1992, US$10 (Casilla 94, Sucursal 19, 1419 Buenos Aires, F 572-5766) and is now available in several shops in Calafate.

Climbing: Fitz Roy (3,375m) is approached from Chaltén to Río Blanco, 2-3 hrs, walk, then to Laguna Torre (base camp for Cerro Torre), 3-4 hrs' walk. Ask the guide Sr Guerra in Chaltén about hiring animals to carry equipment(another guide is Alberto del Castillo, T 93017). The best time is mid-Feb to end-Mar; Nov-Dec is very windy; Jan is fair; winter is extremely cold. There are no rescue services; necessary gear is double boots, crampons, pickaxe, ropes, winter clothing; the type of terrain is ice and rock. Possible targets nearby inc Cerro Torre, Torre Egger, Cerro Solo, Poinclennot, Guilleaulmet, Saint-Exupery, La Bífida, La Indómita, Cardón Adela and Hielo Continental (Continental Ice Shelf). Ask for a permit to climb at the Parques Nacionales office in Chaltén. There is no access at all from Chile.

● **Transport**

A new road has been built from Route 40 to Chaltén. Daily buses in summer from Calafate are run by Caltur, daily at 0600, returning at 1600 (back in Calafate 2000), and Los Glaciares, leaving at 0600 to El Chaltén, at the base of Cerro Fitz Roy, 5 hrs, returns 1600, allowing 2-3 hrs at site, US$50

return. Best to book return before departure during high season (private drivers go off season and charge more). Ask at the *gendarmería* (border-police) in Calafate if you can join their truck which goes once or twice a week.

Organized trips to the northern part of Glaciares National Park are too short to appreciate it fully; either go on a tour bus, then camp (good gear essential) or hire a taxi/minibus. The travel agencies charge US$200 for up to 8 people, US$300 to take you and return later to collect you; private drivers in Calafate charge US$300 for up to 8 to take you and collect later.

EL CALAFATE TO CHILE

The road trip from Calafate to Punta Arenas is very interesting for wildlife enthusiasts, who will see guanacos and condors at frequent intervals. About 40 km before reaching the border there are small lagoons and salt flats with flamingos. From Calafate take the almost completely paved combination of provincial Route 11, national Route 40 and provincial Route 5 to La Esperanza (165 km), where there is a petrol pump and a large but expensive *confitería*. (90 km SE of Calafate Route 40 takes a rough, unpaved and sometimes difficult to follow shortcut which avoids the circuitous La Esperanza route, but even high-clearance vehicles may be unable to cross the unbridged Río Pelque and Chorrillo de Barrancas Blancas after any significant rain. Work has started to improve this section.) From La Esperanza, gravelled Route 7 heads W to join Route 40 at the Río Coyle. At nearby Fuentes del Coyle, there is a small but acceptable bar/*confitería* with 2-3 rooms for travellers and a Hotel, D pp, cold, dirty. Road continues to Cancha Carrera (border post Dec-April, no town), then 14 km to Chilean border post, Cerro Castillo, then unpaved but good road (63 km) to Puerto Natales and 254 km to Punta Arenas, all paved. There is no direct route from Calafate to Torres del Paine National Park, unless you are prepared to hitch, with some patience, from Cerro Castillo. To take the bus coming from Puerto Natales to the Park, you have to board it in Puerto Natales itself. It is not possible to change Argentine pesos once inside the Park.

Tierra del Fuego

THE ISLAND at the extreme S of South America is divided between Argentina (E side) and Chile (W). The S has beautiful lakes, woods and mountain scenery, and there is much birdlife to see. Boat trips can be made on the Beagle Channel; there is skiing in winter.

Tierra del Fuego is bounded by the Magellan Strait to the N, the Atlantic Ocean to the E, the Beagle Channel to the S – which separates it from the southern islands – and by the Whiteside, Gabriel, Magdalena and Cockburn Channels etc, which divide it from the islands to the W. The local Ona Indians are now extinct. Throughout Tierra del Fuego the main roads are narrow and gravelled. The exceptions are San Sebastián (Argentina)-Río Grande, which is paved, the road for about 50 km out of Porvenir (Chile), which is being widened, and Río Grande-Ushuaia. Part of the S is a National Parks Reserve: trout and salmon in nearly all the lakes and rivers, and in summer wild geese, ducks, 152 other species of birds, and imported musk rats and beaver. Mar-April is a good time to visit because of the beautiful autumn colours. **NB** Accommodation is sparse and the island is becoming popular among Argentines in summer. Hotel beds and seats on aircraft may begin to run short as early as November. Fruit and meat may not be taken onto the island.

● **Recommended reading** *Tierra del Fuego* (3rd edition), in English, by Rae Natalie Prosser de Goodall, US$7.50 (obtainable in Ushuaia and Buenos Aires), colourful maps by the same author. Also *Tierra del Fuego: The Fatal Lodestone*, by Eric Shipton, and *Uttermost Part of the Earth*, by E Lucas Bridges. Available in USA: *Birds of Isla Grande* (Tierra del Fuego) by Philip S Humphrey, and *A Guide to the Birds of South America*, by Rodolphe Meyer de Schauensee.

ROUTES TO TIERRA DEL FUEGO

Via Punta Delgada

There are no road/ferry crossings between the Argentine mainland and Argentine Tierra del Fuego. You have to go through Chilean territory. From Río Gallegos, Route 3 reaches the Chilean frontier at Monte Aymond (55 km approx), passing Laguna Azul (3 km off main road in an old crater; an ibis breeding ground, beautiful colours). For bus passengers the border crossing is very easy; similarly for car drivers if papers are in order (see page 217). 41 km into Chile is **Punta Delgada**, from where a 16 km road goes to the dock for the 30-min ferry-crossing over the Primera Angostura (First Narrows) to **Punta Espora**. Some 40 km S, on Chilean Tierra del Fuego, is Cerro Sombrero, from where the road continues 85 km to Chilean San Sebastián. 14 km E, across the frontier, is Argentine San Sebastián, from where the road is paved to Río Grande (see below). **NB** For details of all transport and accommodation on Chilean territory, see the **Chile** chapter, **Chilean Patagonia**. It is not always possible to cross the Chilean part in 1 day because of the irregularity of the ferry.

VIA PUNTA ARENAS

The alternative ferry crossing is Punta Arenas-Porvenir. The road from Punta Delgada goes on 103 km to the intersection with the Punta Arenas-Puerto Natales road, 54 km before Punta Arenas. 5 km E of Punta Arenas, at Tres Puentes, there is a daily ferry crossing to Porvenir, from where a 225-km road runs E to Río Grande (6 hrs) via San Sebastián. Border police at San Sebastián will sometimes arrange lifts to Ushuaia or Río Grande. Hitching after San Sebastián is easy. The best way to hitch from Río Gallegos to Punta Arenas is to take any lorry as far as the turn-off for Punta Delgada ferry. Then there is plenty of Chilean traffic from Punta Delgada to Punta Arenas. *Hotel San Gregorio* will put you up if you get stuck near the turn-off.

Entering Argentina from Chile, be firm about getting an entry stamp for as long as you require. Going in the other direction, don't stock up with food in Argentina, as Chilean border guards will confiscate all fruit, vegetable, dairy and meat products coming into Chile.

RIO GRANDE

Río Grande (*Pop* 35,000; *Phone code* 0964), is a port in windy, dust-laden sheep-grazing and oil-bearing plains. The oil is refined at San Sebastián in the smallest and most southerly refinery in the world (**A3** *ACA* motel; service station open 0700-2300). The *frigorífico* (frozen meat) plant in Río Grande is one of the largest in South America; so is the sheep-shearing shed. Government tax incentives to companies in the 1970s led to a rapid growth in population; the subsequent withdrawal of incentives has produced increasing unemployment and emigration. Accommodation is difficult if arriving at night. Food is cheaper here than in Ushuaia (*Tía* supermarket rec, good choice). ACA garage on sea-front has free hot showers for men, as has the gymnasium. Fill up with gasoline here.

Excursions

To Estancia Punta María, 38 km S where horses can be hired.

11 km N lies the Salesian mission and the regional museum housed in the original chapel and first parish church of Río Grande. Although the exhibits are not classified, there is a great deal to see. There are Ona Indian materials, Salesian mission works, fossils, handicrafts and Flora, fauna and mineral exhibits of the area. Just past the mission, on the right side of the road, is the old cemetery.

Local festivals

Trout Festival, 3rd Sun in Feb; **Snow Festival**, 3rd Sun in July; **Woodsman Festival**, 1st week of December.

Local information

● **Accommodation**

A3 *Atlántida*, Av Belgrano 582, T 22592, said to be best, always full; **A3** *Los Yaganes ACA*, Av Belgrano 319, T/F 23897, clean, comfortable, good expensive restaurant; **A3** *Federico Ibarra*, Rosales 357, T 21071, excellent restaurant; **B** *Res Rawson*, Estrada 750, T 30352/30623, with bath, clean, rec; **B** *Villa*, San Martín 277, T 22312, very warm.

C *Hosp Irmary*, Estrada 743, clean and pleasant, rec; **C** *Miramar*, Mackinlay 595, T 22462, without bath, no breakfast, heated, hot water, kitchen facilities, rec; **E** pp *Hosp Noal*, Rafael Obligado 557, lots of bread and coffee for breakfast, clean, cosy, friendly, rec.

● **Places to eat**

Don Rico, Belgrano y Perito Moreno, in ultra-modern building in centre, interesting, closed Mon; *Pizzería La Colonial*, Rosales 666, home made food, friendly. *Confitería Roca*, Roca 629, open all hours, reasonably priced food and bar.

● **Airline offices**

Aerolíneas Argentinas, T 22711; **LAPA**, 9 de Julio 747, T 32620; **LADE**, Lasarre 425, T 22968; **Kaiken**, Perito Moreno 937, T 30665; **Aerovías**, 9 de Julio 597, T 30249; **TAN**, T 22885.

● **Banks & money changers**

Banco de la Nación Argentina, San Martín 200; Banco del Sud, Rosales 241, cash advance on Visa; Superkiosko, Piedrabuena y Rosales, cash only. Exchange is difficult: if coming from Chile, buy Argentine pesos there.

● **Laundry**

El Lavadero, P Moreno y 9 de Julio.

● **Post & telecommunications**

Post Office: Piedrabuena y Ameghino.

● **Tour companies & travel agents**

Yaganes, friendly and helpful.

● **Tourist offices**

Tourist information at the Municipalidad, Mon-Fri, on Sebastián Elcano.

● **Transport**

Local Car hire: Rent-a-Car, Belgrano y Ameghino, T 22657. Localiza, at airport, T 30482. **Car mechanic**: and VW dealer Viaval SRL, P Moreno 927.

Air Airport 4 km W of town. Bus US$0.50. Taxi US$5. Río Grande-**Buenos Aires** flights with Aerolíneas Argentinas, daily, 3 hrs 20 mins direct. Austral daily (except Sun) via Bahía Blanca, Comodoro Rivadavia and Río Gallegos. TAN flies to Neuquén, Trelew, Comodoro Rivadavia and Río Gallegos. To **Ushuaia**, AR and Kaiken, daily. LADE also to **Río Gallegos**, 50 mins (book early in summer, 1 a week, Thur), continuing to **Comodoro Rivadavia** via Calafate, Gob Gregores and Perito Moreno. Kaiken flies to **Calafate** weekly. To Punta Arenas in Chile, through Kaiken Agency, or Aerovías DAP.

Buses Leave at 0630 Tues and Sat US$25 (Senkovic, San Martín 959, T 22345), for **Porvenir**, Chile, no food or drink provided, no toilets, nor stops, for 7 hrs, always heavily booked but especially over Christmas/New Year period, meticulous passport and luggage control at San Sebastián. To Punta Arenas, Pacheco (Bilbao 873), runs buses via Porvenir on Tues, Thur, Sat 0700, US$36, 10 hrs, tickets available on day of departure, also with Los Carlos on Mon, Thur, 0730, same price. Best to book bus connection in Ushuaia. Very difficult to hitch to Porvenir or N into Argentina (try the police post 7 km out of town). Daily bus service with Transportes Los Carlos, to **Ushuaia**, 234 km on an unpaved road (sit on right for better views), US$21, 4 hrs, times vary, stopping at Hostería El Kaikén, Lago Fagnano, for a drink (rec for the views). Bus departs from Los Carlos office (Estrada 568); arrive 15 mins early. Summer service also by Tecni Austral, daily (excluding Sat) at 0730, 3 hrs, US$22.

USHUAIA

The most southerly town in Argentina, and among the most expensive, **Ushuaia** (*Pop* 50,000; *Phone code* 0901) is 236 km SW of Río Grande by a new road via Paso Garibaldi. Its steep streets overlook the green waters of the Beagle Channel, named after the ship in which Darwin sailed the Channel in 1832, on Captain Fitzroy's second expedition. The people are engaged in timber cutting, fishing and, nowadays, in the electronics industry. The tourist industry is also expanding rapidly.

Places of interest
The old prison, **Presidio**, at the back of the Naval Base can be visited, interesting: tours start from the Museum daily 1600-2300, US$3 (not including tip for guide). There are impressive views of the snow-clad peaks, rivers, waterfalls and dense woods. There is a naval station at **Isla Redonda**. Ushuaia and its environs are worth a 2-3 day visit.

Museums
Museo Territorial, Maipú y Rivadavia, T 21863, open Mon-Sat 1600-2000, US$2, small but interesting display of early photos and artefacts of the local Indian tribes; relics from the missionaries and first settlers, etc. Known as the 'museum at the end of the world' (you can get a stamp in your passport). Highly rec. The building also contains an excellent library with helpful staff, a good bookshop with books in English, and post office, open afternoons when the main one is closed.

Excursions
To the **Cerro Martial** and the glacier (itself unspectacular but fine views down the Beagle Channel and to the N) about 7 km behind the town; to reach the chairlift (US$5) follow Magallanes out of town, allow 1½ hrs, or take Turismo Pasarela minibus, several departures daily in summer, US$5 return. The glacier is a 3-hr walk from town. (In winter the Cerro is inaccessible, even on foot.)

Other excursions include: to the **Río Olivia** falls; to **Lagos Fagnano** and **Escondido** (tours depart 0930, 5-6 hrs, US$5; Los Carlos bus to Lago Fagnano, 2½ hrs, US$10, then from Lake to Río Grande 2 hrs, US$11). A bus runs to **Puerto Almanza** on the Beagle Channel, 75 km, 4-5 hrs, US$18.

The Estancia **Harberton**, the oldest on the island, now run by descendents of a British missionary, Mr Bridges, offers guided walks through protected forest (not Mon) and tea, in Manacatush confitería (T 22742). You can camp. It can be reached by rented car from Ushuaia and by boat. By car, leave Ushuaia on Route 3, after 40 km fork right on Route J, passing Lago Victoria, then 25 km through forest before the open country around Harberton (85 km in all). Some parts of the road are bad; tiring driving, 5 hrs there and back. Agency tours by land cost US$30 plus US$6 entrance; take your own food if not wishing to buy meals at the Estancia. Tours to the Estancia and to the penguin colony by boat and bus, Mon, Tues, Fri, Sun, US$72 plus US$6 entrance, 12 hrs, from all agents, take own food (the sea can be very rough). Some tour agencies in Ushuaia imply that their excursions go to the Estancia though in fact they only go to the bay; others go by inflatable launch from main boat to shore. Check thoroughly in advance.

Sea Trips

Rumbo Sur does a whole-day trip by catamaran down the Beagle Channel to see wildlife, with return by bus, highly rec (see below under **Travel Agents**). Similar tours operated by Aventura Travel, US$70. *Tres Marías* is a fishing boat, tours are 4 hrs, twice a day, maximum 8 passengers, snack included, through agencies Antartur, All Patagonia, Caminante. In summer, chartered trips may be taken to see the sealions on Isla de Los Lobos, 4-5 hrs, or by catamaran, dep 0930, 1430, 2½ hrs. Ask at Rumbo Sur; the *Ana B* leaves 0930 and 1430 daily, English and Spanish-speaking guide. Catamaran trips cost US$40-60 depending on duration. Take food and drinks on all these trips as those sold on board are expensive.

Local festivals

12 Oct: *Founding of Ushuaia.*

Local information

NB Prices double on Dec 12 and accommodation may occasionally be hard to find Dec-Mar – the tourist office will help with rooms in private homes and with campsites. Hotel prices are higher than on the mainland. It is best not to drink tap water in Ushuaia.

● **Accommodation**

L3 *Canal Beagle*, Maipú 590, T 21117, restaurant (catering usually for tour groups), overpriced; **L3** *Tolkeyen*, at Estancia Río Pipo 5 km from town, T 22637, with rec restaurant Tolkeyen, 100m (see below); **L3** *Albatros*, Maipú 505, T 33466, F 30636, clean, modern, inc breakfast, but rooms a bit cold; **L3** *Las Lengas*, Florencia 1722, T 23366, superb setting, heating, good dining room. 2 new hotels overlooking the city (addresses not known): **L2** *Las Hayas*, colourful large rooms, pool, friendly, and **L2** *del Glacier*, nr Martial Glacier, casino, pool rooms, shuttle to town.

A2 *Malvinas*, Deloqui 615, T 22626, with bath, inc breakfast, pleasant, helpful, central heating, rec; **A2** *Antártida*, San Martín 1600, T 21896, friendly, restaurant with fine views, rec; **A2** *Cabo de Hornos*, San Martín y Rosas,

T 22187, F 22313, comfortable, often full, TV, spotless, good value, restaurant not open to non-residents; **A2** *César*, San Martín 753, T 21460, F 32721, with bath, comfortable, often full (book in advance), friendly, clean, inc breakfast, rec; **A3** *Fernández*, Onachaga y Fitzroy, T 21192, very friendly, hot water, good but expensive meals, cheaper in bunk-bed accommodation (dank and dirty); **A3** *Maitén*, 12 de Octubre 140, T 22745, good value, clean, but 2 km from centre, 10% discount for ISIC and youth card holders; **A3** *Monte Cervantes*, San Martín y Sarmiento, T 30600, rec; **A3** *Mustapic*, Piedrabuena 230, T 21718, multi-lingual owner (Sr Miro, from Croatia, his daughter runs travel agency next door, T 23557, rec), 10% discount for ISIC card holders, no singles, highly rec, exceptionally clean, can leave luggage, rooftop restaurant for breakfast; **A3** *Posada Fin del Mundo*, Valdez 281, T 22530, family atmosphere, rec; **A3** *Hosp Turístico*, Deloqui 271, T 21316, with private bath, very clean, friendly, parking, TV, kitchen, English spoken, rec.

B *Garbin-Casalaga*, Gob Paz 1380, clean, comfortable, friendly, heating, good breakfast, no sign, rec; **B** *Hostal Julio Linares*, Deloqui 1522, nr airport, new, clean good value; **B** *Hosp María Cristina Navarrete*, 25 de Mayo 440, T 23068, clean, friendly, cooking facilities; **B** *Familia Cárdenas*, 25 de Mayo 345, T 21954, nr top of hill, rec; **B** *Sra Marta Loncharich*, Magallanes 229, T 24150, shared bathroom, good food and comfort, clean, but overpriced.

D pp *Alojamiento Internacional*, Deloqui 395, 1st floor, T 23483/23622, spartan, scruffy, friendly, dormitory, take sleeping bag, no security, good meeting place, changes money; **C** pp *María Guercio*, Kuanip 67, T 22234, also large chalet outside town to let; **D** pp *Hosp Torres al Sur*, Gob Paz 1437, T 30745, heating, clean, hot water, kitchen facilities; **C** rooms, at home of Ismael Vargas, Kayen 394 (T 21125) 15 mins from centre, clean, doubles only, Sra Vargas speaks English.

Accommodation in private homes (all **B-C**): *Familia Beltrame*, Gob Valdez 311, T 22819, rec; *Familia Galeazzi*, Gob Valdez 323, T 23213, speak English and French, rec; *Familia Velásquez*, Fadul 361, T 21719, dormitory accommodation, clean, warm, helpful, not enough showers, skimpy breakfast, can leave luggage when hiking. *Zulema R Saltzmann*, Roca 392 (esq Campos), **C** pp, clean and friendly; *Sr Ueno*, 12 de Octubre 432, T 24661, full board US$10 pp, rec. *La Fiaka*, Deloqui 641, T 22669, **C** pp, clean, warm, cooking facilities, rec.

There is no YHA in Ushuaia. Hostel for sporting groups only at Sports Complex. Many people go to the airport to offer rooms in private houses, in our **E** pp range (minimum).

At Lago Escondido: **B** *El Petrel Inn*, 54 km

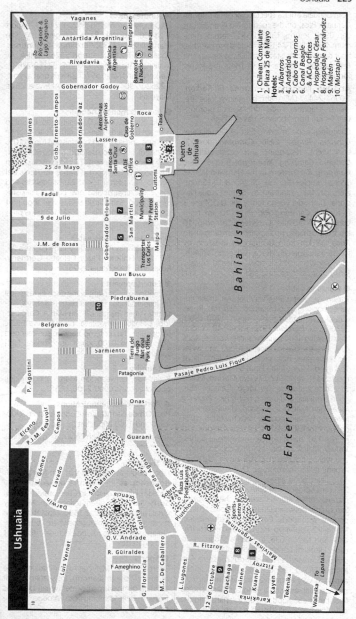

Ushuaia

Key

1. Chilean Consulate
2. Plaza 25 de Mayo

Hotels:
3. Albatros
4. Antártida
5. Cabo de Hornos
6. Canal Beagle
   & ACA Offices
7. Hospedaje César
8. Hospedaje Fernández
9. Maitén
10. Mustapic

Bahía Ushuaia

Bahía Encerrada

To Grande &
Lago Fagnano

Yaganes

Antártida Argentina

Rivadavia

Gobernador Godoy

Magallanes

Gob. Ernesto Campos

Gobernador Paz

25 de Mayo

Fadul

9 de Julio

J.M. de Rosas

Don Bosco

Piedrabuena

Belgrano

Sarmiento

Patagonia

Onas

P. Agostini

Guarani

Elcano

P.J.M. Beauvoit

Campos

L. Gómez

Lavado

Darwin

San Martín

Luis Vernet

Q.V. Andrade

R. Güiraldes

F Ameghino

G. Florencia

M.S. De Caballero

L. Lugones

12 de Octubre

Onachaga

Jainen

Karukinka

Kuanip

Kayen

Tekenika

Walanika

To Lapataia

R. Fitzroy

Florencia

Sobral

Plaza Luis
Piedrabuena

Pluschow

Sports
Centre

Malvinas Argentinas

Fitzroy

28 de Agosto

Immigration

Museum

Telefónica
Argentina

Banco de
la Nación

Aerolíneas
Argentinas

Casa de
Gobierno

Roca

Taxis

Lassere

Banco de
Santa Cruz

LADE
Office

Customs

Municipality

YPF Petrol
Station

San Martín

Gobernador Deloqui

Maipú

Transportes
Los Carlos

Tierra del
Fuego
National
Park Office

Pasaje Pedro Luis Fique

Puerto
de
Ushuaia

N

18

from Ushuaia after a spectacular climb through Garibaldi Pass, on the road to Río Grande (bus dep 0900, returns 1500, US$17 return, minimum 4 people), T 24390, trout fishing possible, boat rides, friendly staff. Facilities at *Kaiken* and *Petrel* are open all year round. These inns are rec for peace and quiet.

At Lago Fagnano: C *Hostería El Kaiken*, T 0964-24427 (ACA) also bungalows, nice site, well-run facilities, cheap drinks, on a promontory 93 km from Ushuaia, has real bath.

Camping: none in town. East of Ushuaia are: *Ushuaia Rugby Club Camping* (Km 3) US$415/tent, restaurant and good facilities; *Ushuaia Camping Municipal* (Km 8) free; *Camping Río Tristen*, in the Haruwen Winter Sports complex (Km 19), T/F 24058, US$5/tent, electricity, bar, restaurant. Inside the Parque Nacional Tierra del Fuego (entry fee US$5) are 3 free sites: *Camping Río Pipo*, 10 km from Ushuaia, no facilities; *Ensenada Camping*, 15 km from Ushuaia, no facilities; *Camping Lago Roca*, 18 km from Ushuaia, at Lapataia, by forested shore of Lago Roca, with good facilities, dirty, showers (US$3), noisy, reached by bus Jan-Feb, small shop, cafeteria.

● **Places to eat**

Tía Elvira, Maipú 349, very popular, make advance booking, good seafood; *Asturias*, Rosas 45, pleasant, reasonable, open 1200-1500, 2030-2300; *Barcleit 1912*, Fadul 148, cordon bleu cooking at reasonable prices; *Kaupé*, Roca 470, English spoken, excellent food and wine, rec, expensive. Best place to eat lamb is at *Tolkeyen*, Estancia Río Pipo, 5 km from town, meal US$15, taxi US$7; *El Viejo Marino*, Maipú 229, nice ambience; *Mi Viejo*, Campos 758, good *parrillada* and buffet, highly rec; *Pizzería Ideal*, San Martín 393, good, cheap, *tenedor libre* US$13, very popular with travellers, 10% discount for ISIC card holders; *Los Amigos*, San Martín 130, quick service, some cheap dishes; *Volver*, Maipú 37, interesting decor, good food and service, not cheap; *El Aborigen*, Antártida Argentina 75, inexpensive; *Quick*, San Martín 130, clean, good service, rec, 10% discount for ISIC card holders; also *Split*, Piedrabuena 238, pizzería, offers same discount, cheap; *Turco*, San Martín between Onas y Patagonia, cheap, popular with locals. *Café de la Esquina*, San Martín y 25 de Mayo, rec; *Der Garten*, *confitería*, San Martín 638, in Galería shopping arcade. Excellent homemade chocolate sold at a shop at San Martín 785. *Helados Massera*, San Martín 270-72, good. The coffee bar at the airport is very expensive. Ask around for currently available *centolla* (king crab) and *cholga* (giant mussels). Food and drink (apart from the duty-free items) in Ushuaia are very expensive.

● **Airline offices**

LADE, Av San Martín 542, T 21123, airport T 21700; **Austral**, Barberis agency, Av San Martín 638, T 23235; **Aerolíneas Argentinas**, Roca 160, T 21218, airport 21265; **LAPA**, Av Malvinas Argentinas 120, T/F 22150/22637; **Kaiken**, San Martín 857, T 23663, or at airport, T 22620/23049; **DAP**, Agencia Akawala, 25 de Mayo 64.

● **Banks & money changers**

Banks open 1000-1500 (in summer). Useful to have credit cards here as difficult to change cheques and very high commission (up to 10% reported), but **Banco del Sud**, Maipú 600 block, only place for changing TCs (downstairs). Cash advance on Mastercard at **Banco de Tierra del Fuego**, San Martín 1044. Tourist agencies and the *Hotel Albatros* also give poor rates. *Listus* record shop, San Martín 973, sweet shop next door, or *Caminante*, Deloqui 368 for better rates for cash.

● **Embassies & consulates**

Chile, Malvinas Argentinas y Jainen, Casilla 21, T 21279; **Finland**, Paz y Deloqui; **Germany**, Rosas 516; **Italy**, Yaganes 75.

● **Entertainment**

A popular spot at night is the disco *Extasis* at 9 de Julio y Maipú; another disco is *Barny's*, Antártida Argentina just off San Martín. *Café Latino*, Deloqui y Rivadavia, bar with live music (Argentine and contemporary), in summer gets going around 0200, great atmosphere, high standard.

● **Laundry**

Rosas 139, between San Martín and Deloqui, open weekdays 0900-2100, US$8.

● **Post & telecommunications**

Post Office: San Martín y Godoy, Mon-Fri 0900-1300 and 1700-2000, Sat 0830-1200.

Telephones: and fax on Roca next to Aerolíneas Argentinas.

● **Shopping**

Good boots at *Stella Maris*, San Martín 443. **Bookshop** at San Martín y 9 de Julio (Lapataia Arcade). Film is cheaper in Chile. Supermarkets: *Surty Sur* (with clean toilets, San Martín y Onas) and *Sucoop*, Paz 1600. Most things are more expensive than elsewhere but some cheap imported goods, eg electrical equipment and cigarettes.

● **Sports**

Sports Centre on Malvinas Argentinas on W side of town (close to seafront). Ice skating rink at Ushuaia gymnasium in winter (when lagoon is frozen). Beachcombing can produce whale bones.

Fishing: trout, contact Asociación de Caza y Pesca at Maipú y 9 de Julio, with small museum. Fishermen may be interested in visiting the fish hatchery 7 km E of Ushuaia, visiting hours daily 1400-1700. There are brook, rainbow and brown trout and land-locked salmon. Take No 1 bus east-bound on Maipú to the end of the line and continue 2½ km on foot to the hatchery. Birdwatchers will also find this ride rewarding.

Skiing, hiking, climbing: contact Club Andino, Solís 50, or *Caminante*. **Skiing**: A downhill ski run (beginner standard) on Cerro Martial. There is another ski run, Wallner, 3 km from Ushuaia, open June-Aug, has lights for night-skiing and is run by Club Andino. The area is excellent for cross country skiing; *Caminante* organizes excursions 'off road'. 20 km E of Ushuaia is Valle Tierra Mayoria, a large flat valley with high standard facilities for cross country skiing, snow shoeing and snowmobiling; rentals and a cafeteria; bus am and 1400 from *Antartur*, San Martín 638. The Haruwen Winter Sports complex is 21 km E on Route 3.

● **Tour companies & travel agents**

All agencies charge the same fees for excursions; with 3 or 4 people it is often little more expensive to hire a *remise* taxi. *Rumbo Sur*, San Martín 342, T 21139, runs a range of tours on water and on land and offers a 2-day package to Cafayate, US$150 inc transport and hotel, good value. Also organizes bus to ski slope, very helpful; *Antartur*, San Martín 638, T 23240; *All Patagonia*, 25 de Mayo 31, of A, T 24432, F 30707, Amex agent; *Onas Tours*, 25 de Mayo 50, T 23429, just off main street, very friendly; *Aventura Austral*, Maipú 237, catamaran trip to Estancia Harberton, highly rec. *Tolkeyen*, 12 de Octubre 150, T 22237, rec; *Caminante*, Don Bosco 319, T 32723, F 31040, organizes walking, climbing tours and horse riding to suit all levels of experience, provides food, tents, equipment, outdoor clothing, detailed map, very friendly and helpful, English and German spoken, highly rec; *Kilak*, Kuanip 67, T 22234, for horse-riding tours. Recommended guide: Domingo Galussio, Intervú 15, Casa 211, 9410 Ushuaia, bilingual, not cheap (US$120), rec.

● **Tourist offices**

San Martín 660, T/F (0901) 24550, 'best in Argentina', literature in English, German and Dutch, helpful, English spoken. Large chart of hotels and prices and information on travel and staying at Estancia Harberton. Has noticeboard for messages. Open Mon-Fri 0830-2030, Sat and Sun 0900-2000. **National Park Office**, on San Martín between Patagonia y Sarmiento, has small map but not much information. The **ACA** office on Maipú also has maps and information.

● **Transport**

Local Car hire: Tagle, San Martín y Belgrano, T 22744, good, also **Río Grande**, Elcano 799, T 22571, and **Localiza**, in *Hotel Albatros* and at airport, rec, T 30663.

Air The airport was upgraded in late 1995. Taxi to airport, US$3, or 30 mins' walk (no bus). Services are more frequent in high season; in winter weather often impedes flights. In the summer tourist season it is sometimes difficult to get a flight out. Aerolíneas Argentinas and LAPA to BsAs via Río Gallegos and/or Trelew, all year round, over 4½ hrs. To **Río Grande**, AR and Kaiken. To **Río Gallegos**, LADE once a week, Kaiken, LAPA and AR. Kaiken daily to **Calafate**. LADE to **Comodoro Rivadavia** via Río Grande, Río Gallegos, Calafate/Lago Argentino, Gob Gregores and Perito Moreno on Thur (to Calafate only in summer). To **Punta Arenas**, Aerovías DAP twice a week.

At the airport ask around for a pilot willing to take you on a 30 mins flight around Ushuaia, US$38 pp (best to go in pm when wind has dropped). Alternatively ask about flights at the tourist office in town. Aerial excursions over the Beagle Channel with local flying club, hangar at airport, 3-5 seater planes, 30 mins: Lago Fagnano, Lapataia and Ushuaia Bay.

Trains A Decauville gauge train for tourists runs along the shore of the Beagle Channel between the Fin del Mundo station in Ushuaia to the boundary of the Tierra del Fuego National Park, 4.5 km, 3 departures daily, US$15 (tourist), US$27 (first class), plus US$5 park entrance and US$3 for bus to the station; it is planned to continue to Lapataia. Run by Ferrocarril Austral Fueguino with new locomotives and carriages, it uses track first laid by prisoners to carry wood to Ushuaia; tickets from Tranex kiosk in the port, T 30709. Sit on left outbound.

Buses Run daily between Ushuaia and Río Grande 4 hrs, times vary, US$21, Transportes Los Carlos, Rosas 85, T 22337, and Tecni Austral (summer only), San Martín 657, T 21945. There is a twice-weekly service to Punta Arenas on Mon and Fri, dep 0300 with Transportes Los Carlos, 14 hrs, US$58, a comfortable and interesting ride via Punta Delgada. Trucks leave Ushuaia for the refinery at San Sebastián Mon-Fri, but hitching is very difficult (easier via Bahía Azul and Punta Delgada where there is more traffic). A good place to hitch is from police control on Route 3.

To Puerto Williams: Chile, *Tres Marías*, once a week, US$65; alternatively put together a group and hire a private yacht, or book through a travel agency (*El Caminante*, US$120 pp, rec) or ask at the Club Náutico for trips in private launches or catamarans, US$60 pp. Luxury cruises around

Cape Horn via Puerto Williams are operated by the Chilean company, *Tierra Austral*, 7/8 days, US$1,260.

PARQUE NACIONAL TIERRA DEL FUEGO

12 km W is the entrance to the park, which stretches to the Chilean frontier. At Km 30 from Ushuaia is **Lapataia Bay**. US$5 National Park fee (free before 31 Oct).

In winter the temperature drops to as low as -12°C, in summer it goes up to 25°C. Even in the summer the climate can often be cold, damp and unpredictable.

Beaver inhabit the Parque Nacional near the Chilean border; one may see beaver dams and with much luck and patience the beavers themselves. Stand still and down-wind of them: their sense of smell and hearing are good, but not their eyesight. There are many beautiful walks. No maps of the Park are available and hiking can be interrupted by the Chilean border. Good climbing on Cerro Cóndor, rec. It is reported that most of the park has been closed off to preserve nature.

● **Access** Minibus to National Park from Turismo Pasarela, Fadul 40, T 21735, US$5 one way, 4 times a day from YPF service station (Maipú y Fadul, first at 1000, last back 2000 from Lago Roca in the Park). In summer Caminante run minibuses to the National Park, departing from Don Bosco 319, 2 or 3 a day, US$15 return. A similar service is operated by two other agencies. Caminante also runs a 1 day excursion to the Parque Nacional, including trek, canoeing, *asado* lunch, US$70 inclusive (small groups, book early). Ask at the tourist office about cycling tours in the park, US$65 full day, also 'Eco Treks' available and cultural events. It is

possible to hitchhike, as far as Lapataia. A ranger truck leaves Ushuaia every weekday at 1300 and picks up hitchhikers.

● **Accommodation** See above for **Camping** possibilities. Rangers in the park are friendly and will sometimes put people up for a couple of days (as will police) and help with places to visit.

ISLA DE LOS ESTADOS

Robert T Cook writes: "This long (75 km) and guarded island lies E of Tierra del Fuego. Except for the caretakers of the lighthouse and an occasional scientist few people ever set foot on this cloud-shrouded reserve of Fuegian Flora and fauna that no longer exist on the main island. During the 18th and 19th centuries large numbers of ships were wrecked or lost in the treacherous waters surrounding this island. Much gold, silver and relics await salvage." Information and tours from Rumbo Sur, San Martín 342, Ushuaia.

Argentina apparently has plans for tourist developments in **Antarctica** (accommodation at Marambio and Esperanza stations). Flights can be arranged in Buenos Aires in Jan-Feb through Surexpress, Esmeralda 629, 4th floor, T 325-0252. The plane goes to Ushuaia and you take a boat from there. Also try Andy Macfarlane at Macren Travel, T 322-7988. Complete trips for US$6,000-8,000 for 11 days can be booked at Corrientes 536, 10th floor, T 394-5399. The National Institute of the Antarctic is at Cerrito 1248, T 816-6313/1689, 0900-1500.

Information for Travellers

BEFORE YOU GO

ENTRY REQUIREMENTS

● **Documents**

Check visa requirements in advance. Passports are not required by citizens of neighbouring countries who hold identity cards issued by their own Governments. No visa is necessary for US citizens, British citizens and nationals of other Western European countries, Canada, Mexico, El Salvador, Nicaragua, Honduras, Costa Rica, Colombia, Ecuador, Peru, Haiti, Dominican Republic, Barbados, Jamaica, Hong Kong, Malaysia, Israel, Hungary, Poland, Turkey, Croatia, Slovenia and Japan, who may stay for 3 months, a period which can be renewed for another 3 months at the National Directorate of Migration. For all others there are three forms of visa: a business 'temporary' visa (US$28, valid 1 year), a tourist visa (US$28), and a transit visa. Australians, New Zealanders and South Africans need visas. (Australians applying for a visa in London must have a return ticket.) Tourist visas are usually valid for 3 months and multiple entry. If leaving Argentina on a short trip, check on re-entry that border officials look at the correct expiry date on your visa, otherwise they will give only 30 days. Renewing a visa is difficult and can only be done for 30-day periods. Visitors should carry passports at all times; backpackers are particular targets for thorough searches – just stay calm; it is illegal not to have identification handy. When crossing land frontiers, remember that though the migration and customs officials are generally friendly, helpful and efficient, the police at the control posts a little further into Argentina tend to be extremely bureaucratic.

At land borders, 90 days permission to stay is usually given without proof of transportation out of Argentina. If you need a 90-day extension for your stay in Argentina, get a new stamp at the first opportunity. Do not be put off by immigration officials in provincial cities who say that the stamp is not necessary, or too complicated to obtain. You can also leave the country, at Iguazú or to Uruguay, and 90 further days will be given on return. Without a valid stamp you will be fined US$40 on leaving.

NB At Argentine/Uruguayan borders one immigration official will stamp passports for both countries. Under Mercosur regulations (1992), borders between Argentina, Uruguay, Paraguay and Brazil are open 24 hrs a day. Argentine immigration and customs officials wear civilian dress. The border patrol, *gendarmería*, in green combat fatigues, operate some borders.

● **Representation overseas**

Australia, 100 Miller Street, Suite 6, Level 30, North Sydney, New South Wales 2060, T 2922-7272, F 2 923-1798; **Belgium**, 225 Avenue Louise B.3, 1050 Brussels, T 2 647-7812, F 2 467-9319; **Canada**, 90 Sparks Street, Suite 620, Ottawa KIP 5B4, T 613 236-2351, F 613 235-2659; **France**, 6 Rue Cimarosa 75116 Paris, T 1 4553-3300, F 1 4553-44633; **Germany**, Wiesenhuettenplatz 26, 8th Floor, 6000 Frankfurt, T 496 923-1050, F 496 923-6842; **Netherlands**, Herengracht 94 1015 BS, Amsterdam, T 2 023-2723/6242, F 2 062-67344; **New Zealand**, 11 Floor, Harbour View Bldg, 52 Quay Street, PO Box 2320, Auckland, T 9 39-1757, F 9 373-5386; **Spain**, Paseo de la Castellana 53, Madrid 1, Madrid, T 1 442-4500, F 1 442-3559;

UK, 100 Brompton Rd, London SW3 1ER, T 0171 589-3104, F 0171 584-7863; **USA**, 12 West 56th Street, New York 10019, T 212 603-0400, F 212 397-3523.

● **Tourist information**
Addresses of tourist offices are given in the text.

● **Tourist offices overseas**
Delegations abroad: Bonn, Eduardo Piva, Penthouse 1, Suite F, Bldg AmeriFirst, Adenauerallee 52, 5300 Bonn, T 228-222011; New York, López Lecube, 12 West 56 St, NY10019, T 603-0400; Rome, Luis Ruzzi, Via B Ammamati 6, T 963-60-1485; São Paulo, Ruben Eduardo Ali, Av Paulista 2319, Argentine Embassy, F (5511) 881-4063.

● **Specialist tours**
An increasing number of foreign visitors are birdwatchers. Since at least 980 of the 2,926 species of birds registered in South America exist in Argentina, in places with easy access, enthusiasts head for Península Valdés, Patagonia, the subtropical forests in the NW, or the Chaco savannah in the NE. Tours to observe and photograph the animals are led by expert guides.

● **Maps**
The best road maps are those of the ACA (see below). Topographical maps are issued by the Instituto Geográfico Militar, Cabildo 301, Casilla 1426, Buenos Aires (reached by *Subte* D to Ministro Carranza – or Palermo while Min Carranza is closed for repair – where IGM is one block from station – turn right from station, or take bus 152 from Retiro). 1:500,000 sheets cost US$3 each and are 'years old'; better coverage of 1:100,000 and 1:250,000, but no general physical maps of the whole country or city plans. Helpful staff, sales office accessible from street, no passport required, map series indices on counter, open Mon-Fri, 0800-1300.

HEALTH

Argentina is generally a healthy country to visit, with good sanitary services. In some provinces, like Neuquén and Salta, medical assistance, inc operations, X-ray and medication, is free in provincial hospitals, even for foreigners. Sometimes, though, one must pay for materials. All private clinics, on the other hand, charge. Medicines are more expensive than in Europe (eg US$8.20 for Paracetamol drops for children). Smallpox vaccination no longer required to enter Argentina. If intending to visit the low-lying tropical areas, it is advisable to take precautions against malaria. Chagas' disease (see **Health Information**) is found in NW Argentina. To counter the effects of altitude in the NW, chew coca leaves or take *te de coca* (use of coca is legal, its trade is not). In the S take plenty of sunscreen to prevent burning owing to the thinning of the ozone layer. Certain shellfish from the Atlantic coast are affected once or twice a year by red algae '(*Marea roja*), at which time the public is warned not to eat them. Buy seafood, if self-catering, from fishmongers with fridge or freezer. To be certain, soak fish for 30 mins in water with a little vinegar. Cholera presents no problem except in some remote villages on the Bermejo and Pilcomayo rivers in the tropical lowlands of the Salta and Jujuy provinces, where the Mataco and Toba tribes have been affected by the disease. If travelling through this region, use bottled water and take your own food.

MONEY

● **Currency**
– The peso –, which is at par with the dollar, is divided into 100 centavos. Peso notes in circulation: 1, 2, 5, 10, 20, 50 and 100. Coins in circulation: 5, 10, 25 and 50 centavos and 1 peso. It is often difficult to change TCs, particularly at weekends and in the smaller towns. There is a 3% tax on cheques and commissions can be as high as 10% and in banks is generally 4%. Commission can be avoided if you go to a branch of the issuing bank, especially if changing small amounts. Cheque transactions can take a long time and many forms. Cheques are often scrutinized very closely: any variation between signatures can lead to their being refused. It is best to take US$ cash (which is widely accepted, but take only utterly unblemished notes, as dirty or torn notes are usually refused) and American Express TCs, which can be changed at the American Express bank in Buenos Aires. (In N Argentina, while Amex card is widely accepted, Amex TCs are hard to change.) Emergency cash from Amex is available only in Buenos Aires and Bariloche. Citibank TCs have been rec; no commission is charged at their own branches around the country. Because of TCs fraud there are periodic crackdowns on particular types; take more than one type to avoid being stuck without funds. Thomas Cook Mastercard TC refund assistance point, 25 de Mayo 195, 6° p, Buenos Aires, T 343-8371. Most major towns have exchange shops (*casas de cambio*). Exchange rates are quoted in major newspapers daily. Money remitted to Argentina from abroad is normally paid out in local currency. It is possible to obtain money from Europe through an express transfer, which takes 2-3 days, and the currency will be subject to tax. For Western Union, T (1) 322-7774. If staying for a long time in Argentina and especially Buenos Aires, you can transfer money from your bank in your home country to a local bank, opening an account in pesos or dollars. Paperwork is not complicated and your money is safe and gaining interest. Check with your bank before leaving.

ATMs are available in Buenos Aires and a few other cities (known as Cajeros Automaticos). Dollar bills are widely accepted. Visa can be used at Banelco ATMs. Cirrus card can be used at ATMs with Link sign, eg Banco Nacional de Lavore.

The provinces of Córdoba, Salta, Jujuy, Catamarca and possibly San Juan (1996) issue *bonos* (bonds) which circulate at face value alongside the national currency. Tucumán issues *cheques predatos*. Two warnings: they are not accepted outside the province of issue and even inside province of issue they are not accepted for some transactions, eg trains, long distance buses. Also, they bear redemption dates, after which they are valueless. Try always to use cash in these provinces and pay the exact amount; change may be given in *bonos*.

When crossing a land frontier into Argentina, make sure you have some Argentine currency as there are normally no facilities at the border.

● **Cost of living**

In 1995-96, Argentina was very expensive for the foreign visitor. Budget travellers should allow US$35-40 a day minimum. High costs can be expected for items such as slide film, and clothing as well as basics, although you can save money by camping and preparing your own food. Imported electronic goods are cheap.

● **Credit cards**

American Express, Diners Club, Visa and Mastercard cards are all accepted. There is a 10% surcharge on credit card transactions in many establishments; many hotels offer reductions for cash. Credit cards are readily accepted in all main towns, even in the S, but outside main towns their use is limited. In the S very few service stations accept credit cards (ACA stations only take cards from members; YPF accepts Visas). All shops, hotels and places showing Argencard (head office, H Yrigoyen 878, Buenos Aires, T 331-2088) signs will accept Eurocard and Access, but you must state that these cards are affiliated to Mastercard. Argencard will not permit cash advances on these cards in outlying regions, and is itself very slow in advancing cash. Lloyds Bank, in many cities, handles Mastercard.

● **Value-added tax**

VAT is not levied on most medicines and some foodstuffs but on all other products and services 21%.

GETTING THERE

BY AIR

● **From Europe**

British Airways (non-stop, 3 times a week) and Aerolíneas Argentinas (AR, via Madrid) each fly from London. Aerolíneas also fly to the following European destinations (with other carriers in parentheses): Frankfurt (once a week, Lufthansa); Madrid (6 a week, Iberia, daily); Paris (4 a week, Air France); Rome (4 a week, also Alitalia); Zurich (2, Swiss Air). KLM flies 3 times a week from Amsterdam. Aeroflot flies from Moscow once a week.

● **From North America**

Aerolíneas Argentinas fly from the following US destinations (with other carriers in brackets): Los Angeles (6 times weekly); Miami (daily, LanChile, American, United); New York (daily, Lan Chile, American, United). American from Dallas daily via Miami. Canadian Air International fly 5 times a week from Toronto; Aerolíneas fly once a week from Toronto and Montreal. **NB** AR is part of Continental's frequent flier programme.

● **From Australasia and South Africa**

Aerolíneas Argentinas fly from Sydney, Australia, via Auckland, New Zealand, twice a week. On the outward flight from Argentina, Aerolíneas stop at Río Gallegos, but it is difficult to board there in high season. Malaysia Airlines fly twice a week from Johannesburg and Cape Town. South African Airways fly from Johannesburg.

● **From Latin America**

Aerolíneas Argentinas and Lapsa daily from Asunción; AR and Avianca from Bogotá; Viasa from Caracas; AR and LAB from La Paz via Santa Cruz, and direct from Santa Cruz; from Lima, AR (3), AeroPerú; from Montevideo (apart from those given in the Buenos Aires section), AR, Pluna, United and Iberia; frequent flights also to Punta del Este, with many more in holiday season; from Santiago, Chile, daily with AR, Ladeco and LanChile and other Latin American, European and North American carriers on various days.

From Brazil, AR, Varig and Vasp fly daily from Rio de Janeiro and São Paulo (plus European airlines stopping over at both cities), Varig stops over in Porto Alegre, Transbrasil flies daily from Brasília, São Paulo and Porto Alegre. See under Brazil, or **Introduction and Hints**, for the Mercosur Air Pass.

BY ROAD

For entering Argentina by automobile see **Motoring, Additional Notes** in **Introduction and Hints**. Tourists can bring into Argentina their own cars, vehicles bought or hired in neighbouring countries for up to 8 months under international documentation. No specific papers are usually required to bring a Brazilian registered car into Argentina.

CUSTOMS

No duties are charged on clothing, personal

effects, toilet necessities, etc. Cameras, typewriters, binoculars, radios and other things which a tourist normally carries are duty-free if they have been used and only one of each article is carried. This is also true of scientific and professional instruments for the personal use of the traveller. Travellers may only bring in new personal goods up to a value of US$200 (US$100 from neighbouring countries); the amount of duty and tax payable amounts to 50% of the item's cost. There are red and green divisions at airport customs. Baggage claim tags are inspected at the exit from the customs inspection area.

2 litres of alcoholic drinks, 400 cigarettes and 50 cigars are also allowed in duty-free; for tourists originating from neighbouring countries the respective quantities allowed are 1 litre, 200, 20 and 2 kg. You can buy duty-free goods *on arrival* at Ezeiza airport.

If having packages sent to Argentina, do not use the green customs label unless the contents are of real value and you expect to pay duty. For such things as books or samples use the white label if available.

WHEN YOU ARRIVE

● Airport information
Do not send unaccompanied luggage to Argentina; it can take up to 3 days of form-filling to retrieve it from the airport. Paying overweight, though expensive, saves time.

● Clothing
Shorts are worn in Buenos Aires and residential suburbs in spring, summer and autumn, but their use is not common outside the capital. Bermuda-type shorts are very fashionable, as are jogging suits. In general, dress tends to be formal (unless casual wear is specified on an invitation) in Buenos Aires and for evening outings to shows, etc. The general standard of dress among Argentines is very high: collar and tie, with jacket, are very much the standard for men, and women 'should always err on the side of elegance' – David Mackintosh. Men wearing earrings can expect comments, even hostility, in the provinces.

● Hours of business
Banks, government offices, insurance offices and business houses are not open on Sun. *Government Offices*: 1230-1930 in the winter and 0730-1300 in summer. *Banks*: Generally 1000-1600 but time varies according to the city, and sometimes according to the season. (See under names of cities in text.) *Post Offices*: stamps on sale during working days 0800-2000 but 0800-1400 on Sat. *Shops* are open from about 0900 to 1900, though many close at midday on Sat. Outside the main cities many close for the daily afternoon siesta, reopening at about 1700. 24-hr opening is allowed except on Mon; this applies mainly to restaurants, foodshops, barbers, newspaper shops, art, book and record stores.

Dance halls open at 2300 but don't fill up till after midnight; nightclubs open after midnight. In city centre, cafés and restaurants are busy till after midnight and many evening events, such as lectures, may not start before 2200.

● Official Time
3 hrs behind GMT.

● Safety
Argentina is one of the safest countries in South America but in Buenos Aires and other major cities beware of the increasingly common trick of spraying mustard (or ketchup) on you and then getting an accomplice to clean you off (and remove your wallet). If you are sprayed, walk straight on.

NB Never carry weapons, or drugs without prescriptions.

● Shopping
Local leather goods in Buenos Aires, eg coats (leather or suede), handbags and shoes. **NB** Leather from the *carpincho* is from the capybara and should not be purchased. A gourd for drinking *yerba mate* and the silver *bombilla* which goes with it, perhaps a pair of *gaucho* trousers, the *bombachas*. Ponchos (red and black for men, all colours for women). Articles of onyx, specially in Salta. Silver handicrafts. Knitted woollens, especially in Bariloche and Mar del Plata.

● Voltage
220 volts (and 110 too in some hotels), 50 cycles, AC, European Continental-type plugs in old buildings, Australian 3-pin flat-type in the new. Adaptors can be purchased locally for either type (ie from new 3-pin to old 2-pin and vice-versa).

● Weights and measures
The metric system is used.

ON DEPARTURE

● Airport tax
US$15 for all international flights, except to Montevideo from Aeroparque, which is subject to US$5 tax; US$3-6, payable only in pesos also for internal flights (US$1.75 in Ushuaia). When in transit from one international flight to another, you may be obliged to pass through immigration and customs, have your passport stamped and be made to pay an airport tax on departure. There is a 5% tax on the purchase of air tickets. Airport tax can be prepaid.

WHERE TO STAY

● Camping and youth hostels
Camping is very popular in Argentina (except in

Buenos Aires) and there are sites with services, both municipal, free, and paying private campsites in most tourist centres. Most are very noisy and many are closed off-season. Camping is allowed at the side of major highways and in all national parks (except at Iguazú Falls). Wild camping in deserted areas is possible, but note that in Patagonia strong winds make camping very difficult. Many ACA and YPF service stations have a site where one can camp (usually free) and in general service station owners are very friendly to campers, but ask first. Service stations usually have hot showers. A list of camping sites is available from ACA (labelled for members, but should be easily available) and from the national tourist information office in Buenos Aires, which has a free booklet, *1ra Guía Argentina de Campamentos*; see Autoclub magazine. References to sites will be found in the text. ACA campsites offer discounts to members, and to holders of the International Driving Licence; European automobile clubs' members are allowed to use ACA sites. The Danmark Organization, Junín 1616, p 3, Buenos Aires, T (54-1) 803-3700, has a network of clean, cheap youth hostels throughout Argentina (no age limit, but card needed): in Bariloche, El Bolsón, Pinamar, Calafate and the Tigre Delta. See also under Buenos Aires. There are few other youth hostels (many open only Feb to Mar), but some towns offer free accommodation to young travellers in the holiday season, on floors of schools or church halls; some fire stations will let you sleep on the floor for free (sometimes men only). Regular (blue bottle) Camping Gaz International is available in Buenos Aires, at an electrical goods store on Av 9 de Julio, near Teatro Colón, and *Suntime*, Lima 225, Guatemala 5908 (Palermo), Juramento 2452 (Belgrano) and *América Pesca*, Alfredo Pollini Alvear 1461. White gas (*bencina blanca*) is readily available in hardware shops (*ferreterías*). *Camping Center*, Acoyte 1622, Buenos Aires, T 855-0619, rents camping, fishing and backpacking equipment, 5% discount for ISIC holders.

FOOD AND DRINK

FOOD

National dishes are based in the main upon plentiful supplies of beef. Many dishes are distinctive and excellent; the *asado*, a roast cooked on an open fire or grill; *puchero*, a stew, very good indeed; *bife a caballo*, steak topped with a fried egg; the *carbonada* (onions, tomatoes, minced beef), particularly good in Buenos Aires; *churrasco*, a thick grilled steak; *parrillada*, a mixed grill, mainly roast meat, offal, and sausages, *chorizos* (inc *morcilla*, black pudding to the British, or blood sausage), though do not confuse this with *bife de chorizo*, which is a rump steak (*bife de lomo* is fillet

steak). A *choripán* is a roll with *Arroz con pollo* is a delicious combination inside chicken, eggs, vegetables and strong sauce. *Puchero de gallina* is chicken, sausage, maize, potatoes and squash cooked together. *Empanada* is a tasty meat pie; *empanadas de humita* are filled with a thick paste of cooked corn/maize, onions, cheese and flour. *Milanesa de pollo* (breaded, boneless chicken) is usually good value. *Ñoquis* (gnocchi), potato dumplings normally served with meat and tomato sauce, are tasty and often the cheapest item on the menu; they are also a good vegetarian option when served with either *al tuco* or Argentine roquefort (note that most places only serve them on the 29th of the month, when you should put a coin under your plate for luck). *Locro* is a thick stew made of maize, white beans, beef, sausages, pumpkin and herbs. Pizzas come in all sorts of exotic flavours, both savoury and sweet. **NB** Extras such as chips, *puré* (mashed potato), etc are ordered and served separately, and are not cheap. Almost uniquely in Latin America, salads are quite safe. A popular sweet is *dulce de leche* (especially from Chascomús), milk and sugar evaporated to a pale, soft fudge. Other popular desserts are *almendrado* (ice-cream rolled in crushed almonds), *dulce de patata* (sweet potato preserve), *dulce de membrillo* (quince preserve), *dulce de zapallo* (pumpkin in syrup); these *dulces* are often eaten with cheese. *Postre Balcarce*, a cream and meringue cake and *alfajores*, maize-flour biscuits filled with *dulce de leche* or apricot jam, are also very popular. Note that *al natural* in reference to fruit means canned without sugar (fresh fruit is *al fresca*). Croissants (known as *media lunas*) come in two varieties: *de grasa* (dry) and *de mantequilla* (rich and fluffy). Sweets: the Havana brands have been particularly is rec. Excellent Italian-style ice-cream with exotic flavours. For local recipes (in Spanish) *Las Comidas de Mi Pueblo*, by Margarita Palacios, is rec.

Offices close for 2 to 2½ hrs for lunch between 1200 and 1500. Around 1700, many people go to a *confitería* for tea, sandwiches and cakes. Dinner often begins at 2200 or 2230; it is, in the main, a repetition of lunch. Eating out is expensive: the cheapest option is to have the set lunch as a main meal of the day and then find cheap, wholesome snacks for breakfast and supper. Budget travellers should note that especially in Buenos Aires a number of cheaper restaurants are advertised as *tenedor libre* – eat all you want for a fixed price. Those wishing to prepare their own food will find supermarkets fairly cheap for basics.

DRINK

Argentine wines (inc champagnes, both charmat and champenoise) are sound throughout the price range. The ordinary *vinos de la casa*,

or *comp...-*.... ...e and relatively
chea-.....tter than the whites. The local
beers, mainly lager-type, are quite acceptable.
In restaurants wines have become more expensive (up to US$20/bottle for a good quality wine).
Hard liquor is relatively cheap, except for imported whisky. *Clericó* is a white-wine *sangría*
drunk in summer. It is best not to drink the tap
water; in the main cities it is often heavily chlo-
rinated. It is usual to drink soda or mineral water
at restaurants, and many Argentines mix it with
their cheaper wine, with ice, as a refreshing drink
in summer.

GETTING AROUND

AIR TRANSPORT

Internal air services are run by Aerolíneas Argentinas (AR), Austral, LAPA (reliable turbo-prop and
Boeing 737 services, cheaper than main airlines),
TAN (Transporte Aéreo Neuquén) in the S (book
tickets through Austral), Dinar (based in Salta,
serving the capital, Mar del Plata and the N, cheap
fares), LAER (Entre Ríos, Mesopotamia), and the
army airline LADE (in Patagonia), which provides
a good extended schedule with new Fokker F-28
jets. **NB** LADE will not accept IATA MCOs. Deregu-
lation and privatization has permitted the introduction of discounts by the major carriers. Ask at
a travel agency. (Even though sometimes offices
in various towns may tell you the flights are full, it
is usually worth a try out at the airport.) The naval
air passenger service, Aeronaval, carries paying
civilian passengers, one third cheaper than LADE.
No firm schedule though; 2 flights a week between Ushuaia, Río Grande and Río Gallegos; once
a week between Ushuaia and Buenos Aires. Some
airlines, like Air Kaiken operate during the high
season, or are air taxis on a semi-regular schedule.
AR and Austral offer discounted, *banda negativa*
fares on a limited number of seats on many flights,
but reserve well in advance. LAPA and Dinar maintain low fares as long as a flight is not fully booked.
All airlines operate standby systems, at half regular
price, buy ticket 2-3 hrs before flight. It is only
worth doing this off season. *Plan familiar* tickets
allow couples to travel with a 25% discount for
the spouse. Children under 3 travel free. LADE also
operates discount spouse (65%) and children
(35%) tickets. If travelling by AR or Austral a long
linear distance, eg Río Gallegos-Buenos Aires, but
wishing to stop en route, it is cheaper to buy the
long flight and pay extra (about US$2) for stop-
overs. **NB** All local flights are fully booked way in
advance for travel in December. Don't lose your
baggage ticket; you won't be able to collect your
bags without it. Some travellers have rec checking
in 2 hrs before flight to avoid being 'bumped off'
from overbooking.

Visit Argentina fare Aerolíneas Argentinas sells
a Visit Argentina ticket: 4 flight coupons costing
US$450, with US$120 for each extra coupon up
to a maximum of 8. It is valid for 30 days and must
be purchased outside Argentina and in conjunction with an international flight ticket. Austral sell
similar tickets (known as Jetpaq) and they are
interchangeable (but cannot be used on Inter
Austral, its subsidiary). Routing must be booked
when the coupons are issued: one change of date
and of destination is free (but subsequent changes
cost US$50). One stop only is permitted per town;
this includes making a connection (as many flights
radiate from Buenos Aires, journeys to and from
the capital count as legs on the airpass, so a
4-coupon pass might not get you very far). If you
start your journey outside Buenos Aires on a Sun,
when Aerolíneas Argentinas offices are closed, you
may have difficulty getting vouchers issued at the
airport. If you wish to visit Tierra del Fuego and
Lago Argentino it is better fly on the Visit Argentina
pass to Río Grande or Ushuaia and travel around
by bus or LADE from there than to stop off in Río
Gallegos, fly to Ushuaia and thence back to Buenos
Aires, which will use 3 coupons. Infants under 2
years not occupying a seat pay 10%. Domestic
timetables are given in *Guía Argentina de Tráfico
Aéreo* and *Guía Internacional de Tráfico*. It is
unwise to set up too tight a schedule because of
delays which may be caused by bad weather.
Flights between Buenos Aires and Río Gallegos are
often fully booked 2 to 3 weeks ahead, and there
may be similar difficulties on the routes to Bariloche
and Iguazú. If you are 'wait-listed' they cannot
ensure a seat. Reconfirmation at least 24 hrs ahead
of a flight is important and it is essential to make
it at the point of departure. Extra charges are made
for reconfirming LADE flights but they are not high.

LAND TRANSPORT

● **Train**
The future of rail services in Argentina is most
uncertain. On 10 March 1994, the government
withdrew its funding for Ferrocarriles Argentinos, handing responsibility for all services to the
provinces through which the lines run. Few
provinces accepted the responsibility, because
of lack of resources. Most trains have therefore
been suspended. Those that were operating in
May 1995 are given in the text, but note that
this can change at any moment.

● **Bus**
Fares are charged at about US$4.50/100 km.
Sleeper services from the capital to Mendoza,
Córdoba and Bariloche cost US$7/100 km.
There are also 'ómnibus truchos' (fake buses),
which do not start or end services at bus stations
and which have less reliable equipment or time-
keeping; they charge less than US$4/100 km

(ask at travel agents or hotels). Most bus companies give a 20% student discount if you show an international student card; a YHA card is also useful. The same discount may also be given to foreign, as well as Argentine, teachers and university professors but you must carry documentary proof of your employment. It can be difficult to get reductions between Dec and March. Express buses between cities are dearer than the *comunes*, but well worth the extra money for the fewer stops. When buying tickets at a bus office, don't assume you've been automatically allotted a seat: make sure you have one. Buses have strong a/c, even more so in summer; take a sweater for night journeys.

● **Motoring**

All motorists are required to carry two warning triangles, a fire-extinguisher, a rigid tow bar, a first aid kit, full car documentation together with international driving licence (for non-residents, but see **Car hire** below), and the handbrake must be fully operative. Safety belts must be worn if fitted. Although few checks are made in most of the country, with the notable exceptions of roads into Rosario and Buenos Aires, checks have been reported on cars entering the country. **NB** Police checks around Buenos Aires can be very officious, even to the point of charges being invented and huge 'fines' demanded. You may not export fuel from Argentina, so use up fuel in spare jerry cans while you are in the country. Always fill up when you can in less developed areas like Chaco and Formosa and in parts of Patagonia as filling stations are infrequent. Diesel fuel 'gas-oil' prices are US$0.27/litre. Octane rating for gasoline ('nafta') is as follows: regular gasoline 83 (US$0.65/litre); super 93(US$0.78/litre). Unleaded fuel is not widely available but its use is increasing (it is called Ultra SP and costs a little more than super). ACA sells petrol vouchers (*vales de nafta*) for use in ACA stations. Shell and Esso stations are slightly more expensive.

To obtain documents for a resident (holder of resident visa, staying at least 6 months in the country) to take a car out of Argentina, you can go to ACA in Buenos Aires, which may take up to 4 working days, or you can ask for a list of other ACA offices that can undertake the work; take forms with you from Buenos Aires, and papers may be ready in 24 hrs. You will need at least one passport-size photo, which you can have taken at ACA at a fair cost. If the car is not your own (or is hired), you require a special form signed by the owner and witnessed by a notary public. **NB** Non-residents may buy a car in Argentina but are in no circumstances allowed to take it out of the country; it must be resold in Argentina, preferably in the province where it was purchased. Third party

insurance is obligatory; best travellers ACA, for members only.

Most main roads are paved, if rather narrow (road maps are a good indication of quality), and roadside services are good. Road surface conditions vary once one leaves main towns: on the dirt and gravel roads a guard for the windscreen is essential. Most main roads now have private tolls, ranging from US$2 to US$10; tolls are spaced about every 100 km. Secondary roads (which have not been privatized) are generally in poor condition. Sometimes one may not be allowed to reach a border if one does not intend to cross it, stopping eg 20 km from the border.

Automóvil Club Argentino (ACA), Av Libertador Gen San Martín 1850, 1st floor, touring department on 3rd floor, 1425 Buenos Aires, T 802-6061/9, open 1000-1800 (take colectivo 130 from LN Alem and Corrientes down Alem, Libertador and F Alcorta, alight opp ACA and walk 1 block through park; to return take the 130 from corner of Libertador on left as you leave building), office on Florida above Harrod's, 2nd floor, has a travel document service, complete car service facilities, insurance facilities, road information, road charts (*hojas de ruta*- about US$2.35 each to members, if available) and maps (dated with the code letters in the bottom corner – road map of whole country, with service stations and *hosterías* shown, US$4 to members, US$9.50 to non-members, and of each province), a hotel list, camping information, and a tourist guide book sold at a discount to its members and members of other recognized, foreign automobile clubs upon presentation of a membership card. (YPF, the state oil agency, also produces good maps for sale.) **NB** Members of other recognized automobile clubs are advised to check if their club has reciprocity with ACA, thus allowing use of ACA facilities and benefit from lower prices for their rooms and meals at ACA *hosterías*. The Club has service stations, some with parking garages, all over the country. If you are not a member of ACA you will not get any help when in trouble. ACA membership, US$20/month, permits you to pay with Eurocard (Argencard) for fuel at their Service stations, gives 20% discount on hotel rooms and maps, and discounts at associated hotels, and 10% discount on meals.

ACA accommodation comes in 4 basic types: *Motel*, *Hostería*, *Hotel*, and *Unidades Turísticas*, and they also organize campsites. A *motel* may have as few as 3 rooms, and only 1 night's stay is permitted. *Hosterías* have very attractive buildings and are very friendly. *Hotels* are smarter and more impersonal. All have meal facilities of some kind. Anyone can get in touch with the organization to find out about accommodation aos, as well as motorists, are rec to contact the ACA for its wealth of information.

Touring Club Argentino, Esmeralda 605 and Tucumán 781, p 3, T 392-6742, has similar travel services but no service stations.

● **Motorcycle**

Repairs at Eduardo Olivera, Mecánica Ruben SA, Lavoiser 1187-1674, Sáenz Peña, Buenos Aires, T 757-4285, excellent BMW mechanic with good selection of spares. Juan Carlos Topcic, Costa Rica 25, casa 48, 9400 Río Gallegos, T 0966-23572, all makes.

● **Motorhomes**

Casa Import Trailer, Av Juan de Garay 331, T 361-5674, sells articles for motorhomes. *Casa Car*, Humberto Primo 236, T 30-0051, rents motorhomes. *Rancho Móvil*, Luis Viale 2821, T 59-9470, is club for motorhome owners; all in Buenos Aires. Porta-Potti toilets are widely sold in Argentina, sometimes under a different name.

● **Car hire**

To rent a small car (for 4 plus luggage) costs from US$40 to US$110 a day, not inc mileage, fuel, insurance and tax (20%); highest prices are in Patagonia. Discounts are available for several days', or weekly rental. Minimum age for renting is 25 (private arrangements may be possible). A credit card is useful. You must ensure that the renting agency gives you ownership papers of the vehicle, which have to be shown at police and military checks. At tourist centres such as Salta, Posadas, Bariloche or Mendoza it may be more economical to hire a taxi with driver, which includes the guide, the fuel, the insurance and the mechanic. Avis offers a good and efficient service with the possibility of complete insurance and unlimited mileage for rentals of 7 days or more, but you should prebook from abroad. No one-way fee if returned to another Avis office, but the car may not be taken out of the country. Localiza, a Brazilian company, accepts drivers aged at least 21 (according to Brazilian rules, but higher insurance). They also offer 4WD vehicles, though only from Buenos Aires. Taking a rented car out of Argentina is difficult with any company. Other companies are given in the text.

If you do not have an international driver's licence, you can get a 3-month licence from Dirección de Transportes de la Municipalidad, Av Roca 5225, Buenos Aires, T 602-6925, Mon-Fri 0800-1300; bring documentation from home.

● **Hitchhiking**

Argentina seems to be getting increasingly difficult for this. Ask at petrol stations. Traffic can be sparse, especially at distances from the main towns, and in Patagonia, which is popular with Argentine hitchhikers. It may be useful to carry a letter from your Consulate. Though they tend to be more reserved in manner than most Latin Americans, Argentines are generally friendly and helpful, especially to foreigners (display your flag, but not the Union Jack).

COMMUNICATIONS

● **Language**

Spanish, with variant words and pronunciation. English comes second; French and Italian (especially in Patagonia) may be useful.

The chief variant pronunciations are the replacement of the 'll' and 'y' sounds by a soft 'j' sound, as in 'azure' (though note that this is not done in Mendoza), the omission of the 'd' sound in words ending in '-ado' (generally considered uncultured), the omission of final 's' sounds, the pronunciation of 's' before a consonant as a Scottish or German 'ch', and the substitution in the N and W of the normal rolled 'r' sound by a hybrid 'rj'. In grammar the Spanish 'tú' is replaced by 'vos' and the second person singular conjugation of verbs has the accent on the last syllable eg *vos tenés, podés*, etc. In the N and NW, though, the Spanish is more akin to that spoken in the rest of Latin America.

● **Newspapers**

Buenos Aires dailies: *La Nación, La Prensa, Clarín, La Razón*. Evening papers: *Crónica*. English language daily: *Buenos Aires Herald*. Magazines: *Noticias, Gente, Redacción, Mercado, El Gráfico* (sports). The daily, *Página Doce*, is very popular among students and intellectuals. *La Maga* is a weekly cultural review, Wed, US$5. English language magazines: *The Review of the River Plate* (commercial, agricultural, political and economic comment), and *The Southern Cross* (Irish community). German-language weekly, *Argentinisches Tageblatt*, available everywhere, very inforoomative. There is a weekly international edition of *La Nación*, priced in Europe at US$1.50. Write for further information to. La Nación, Edición Internacional, Bouchard 557, 1106 Buenos Aires.

● **Postal services**

Letters from Argentina take about 10 days to get to the UK and the USA. Rates for letters up to 20 grams: US$0.75 Mercosur, US$1 rest of Latin America, US$1.25 rest of world (add US$2 for *certificado*); up to 150 grams, US$1.50, US$2.25, US$3 respectively.

Small parcels only of 1 kg at post offices; larger parcels from Encomiendas Internacionales, Centro Postal Internacional, Av Antártida Argentina, near Retiro station, Buenos Aires, and in main provincial cities, about US$40 for 5 kg. Larger parcels must first be examined, before final packing, by Customs, then wrapped (up to 2 kg, brown paper; over 2 kg must be sewn in linen cloth), then sealed by Customs, then taken to Encomiendas Internacionales for posting. Cheap packing service available. Open 1100-1700 on weekdays. Used clothes have to be fumigated before they will be accepted. Having parcels sent to Argentina inclurs a customs tax of about US$3/package. *Poste restante* is available in every town's main post office, fee US$1.

● **Telephone services**

Two private companies operate telephone services, Telecom in the N and Telefónica Argentina in the S. Buenos Aires Federal District and the country as a whole are split roughly into two halves. For the user there is no difference and the two companies' phone cards are interchangeable. For domestic calls public phones operate on *cospeles* (tokens) which can be purchased at news stands (different tokens for local and inland calls). On weekdays, 2200-0800, and from Sat 1300 to 0800 Mon inland and local calls cost one third (Telefónica Argentina) and international calls are reduced by 20%; other offices have different reduced rate hours Rates/minute for international calls, full rate: USA US$3.52; Paraguay, Chile US$3.55; Spain, Italy US$4.22; Canada, UK, Germany, France US$5.10; Japan, Hong Kong US$6.37. All charges are payable only in pesos. In main cities there are also privately-run 'Centros de Llamadas', offering a good telephone and fax service. International public phones display the DDI sign (Discado Directo Internacional); DDN (Discado Directo Nacional) is for phone calls within Argentina. Provide yourself with enough tokens or phone cards in Buenos Aires because, in the regions, phone booths exist, but the tokens and cards are not on sale. Most telephone company offices in principal cities have a phone for USA Direct; if they do not, they can direct you to one. BT Chargecard can be used to the UK via the operator. There is frequently a high mark-up on calls made from hotels. No reverse-charge calls to South Africa. It is now easy to call reverse charge to Australia. Operator speaks English. Fax: American Express in Buenos Aires allows card holders to receive faxes at US$1/sheet and to send them at US$8/sheet (to Europe). Telefónica and Telecom send faxes abroad for US$1.23/page, plus cost of the call, and US$1.82/page to receive. (You get charged for sending the fax even if it does not get through.) Communications on the internet are difficult. Some Centros de Llamadas have compatible equipment but static on the lines makes data transmission difficult and you are charged regardless.

NB Owing to modernization, many 2- and 3-digit prefixes are being changed (see page 81).

● **Radio**

English language radio broadcasts can be heard daily on short wave: 0100-0130 on 6060 KHz 49m, 0230-0300 on 11710 KHz 25m, 0430-0500 and 2230-2300 on 15345 KHz 19m; Radiodifusión Argentina al Exterior, Casilla de Correo 555, 1000, Buenos Aires. This is a government station and broadcasts also in Japanese, Arabic, German, French, Italian and Portuguese. Broadcasts by foreign radio stations (inc the BBC) are receivable on short wave.

SPORT

Fishing The three main areas for fishing are the Northern Zone, around Junín de los Andes, extending S to Bariloche; the Central Zone around Esquel; the Southern Zone around Río Gallegos and Río Grande.

The waters of the Lake District are full of fish, and the best time for fishing is at the beginning of the season, that is, in Nov and Dec (the season runs from early Nov to the end of Mar). Among the best are: Lagos Traful, Gutiérrez, Mascardi, Futalaufquen (in Los Alerces National Park), Meliquina, Falkner, Villarino, Nuevo, Lacar, Lolog, Curruhué, Chico, Huechulafquen, Paimún, Epulafquen, Tromen (all in Lanín National Park), and, in the far N, Quillén. In the far S, the fishing in Lago Argentino is also good. The Río Limay has good trout fishing, as do the rivers further N, the Quilquihue, Malle, Chimehuin, Collon-Cura, Hermoso, Meliquina and Caleufú. All rivers are 'catch and release'. They are all in the neighbourhood of San Martín de los Andes. To fish anywhere in Argentina you need a permit, which costs US$10/day, US$30/week, US$100/year. In the Northern Zone forestry commission inspectors are very diligent. For tours arranged from the UK, contact Sport Elite (JA Valdes-Scott), Woodwalls House, Corscombe, Dorchester, Dorset, DT2 0NT.

Walking and skiing Details on outdoor activities in Argentina can be found in *Weekend* (Spanish), good photos and excellent maps. Information on trails in NW Argentina, the Lake District, Patagonia and Tierra del Fuego is given in *Backpacking in Chile and Argentina*, 3rd edition 1994 (Bradt Publications, 41 Nortoft Road, Chalfont St Peter, Bucks, SL9 0LA, UK). Note that Bradt Publications' *South America Ski Guide* (1992) gives details of Argentine ski resorts.

The skiing season is May to end-Oct; best sites are Las Leñas (Mendoza, which has many other small sites), Chapelco, San Martín de los Andes, Bariloche and La Hoya (nr Esquel, cheapest, but shorter runs).

On the basis of treks made with Sr Ramón

Ossa de Barres .....owing additions to the or- ......om's list of recommendations for equipment on any Andean trip: metal drinking mugs, metal containers to prevent tubes of toothpaste etc emptying themselves in mule packs, long underpants to protect against chafing, woollen cap, insect repellent, sunburn cream, laxatives, soap, nylon groundsheet for sleeping bag (depending on weather), portable tent for privacy, and fishing gear for those who prefer catching their own meals (No 3 spoons best for Andean streams – permit required).

HOLIDAYS AND FESTIVALS

The main holiday period, generally to be avoided by business visitors, is Jan-Mar, though some areas, such as Tierra del Fuego, begin to fill up in November/December. Winter school holidays, in which travelling and hotels may be difficult, are the middle 2 weeks of July. No work may be done on the national holidays (1 Jan, Good Friday, 1 May, 25 May, 10 June, 20 June, 9 July, 17 Aug, 12 Oct and 25 Dec) except where specifically established by law. There are no bus services on 25 and 31 December. On Holy Thursday and 8 Dec employers are left free to decide whether their employees should work, but banks and public offices are closed. Banks are also closed on 31 December. There are gaucho parades throughout Argentina, with traditional music, on the days leading up to the Día de la Tradición, 10 November. On 30 Dec (not 31 because so many offices in centre are closed) there is a ticker-tape tradition in downtown Buenos Aires: it snows paper and the crowds stuff passing cars and buses with long streamers.

FURTHER READING

Federico B Kirbus has written the highly informative Guía de Aventuras y Turismo de la Argentina (with comprehensive English index – 1989), obtainable at El Ateneo, or from the author at Casilla de Correo 5210, 1000, Buenos Aires. Kirbus has also written the Guía Ilustrada de las Regiones Turísticas Argentinas, 4 volumes, NW, NE, Centre, S, with about 300 black and white photos, colour pictures and colour plates on Flora and fauna (published by El Ateneo, US$18-21 each); also La Argentina, país de

Maravillas, Manrique Zago ediciones (1993), a beautiful book of photographs with text in Spanish and English. YPF have published a 6 volume guide in Spanish with extensive maps, good background information, US$10/volume. Also rec is the Pirelli Guide, edited by Diego Bigongiari, US$18, inc map for cultural, historical and nature information. Nuestros Paisanos Los Indios by Carlos Martínez Sarasola is an excellent compendium on the history and present of Argentine Indian communities, rec. The Fundación Vida Silvestre (conservation organization and bookshop), Defensa 245/251, has information and books on Argentine Flora and fauna. Field guide to Argentine birds: Guía para la identificación de las aves de Argentina y Uruguay by T Narosky and D Yzurieta, with drawings and colour illustrations.

British business travellers are strongly advised to read 'Hints to Exporters: Argentina', obtainable from DTI Export Publications, PO Box 55, Stratford-upon-Avon, Warwickshire, CV37 9GE. Similar information is provided for US citizens by the US Department of Commerce.

ACKNOWLEDGEMENTS

We wish to offer our thanks to Charlie Nurse for doing the updating. For their generous assistance we wish to thank Federico Kirbus, Herbert S Levi, Brad Krupsaw, Gloria Pacheco and Nidia Baldomá (Secretaría Nacional de Turismo) and Giselle Levy (all from Buenos Aires). The editor would like to thank the following for their hospitality and help when he was in Argentina in Nov/Dec, 1995: Herbert and Inés Levi, Federico and Marlú Kirbus, Brad and Gilda Krupsaw, Leo Fainboim and Marta Beckermann, Dereck Foster, Harry Ingham, Isabel and Sarah Wagener (Flyer Turismo), Julio Emiliani (LAPA), Diego Bigongiari and Judith Ravin (Pirelli Guide), Encarnación Ezcurra (La Nación), Armando S Schlecker (TISA), Guillermo Paats and Tono Giuggia (Receptivo Puerto Madryn), Herman Müller and Alicia Sachs (Secretaría de Turismo, Puerto Madryn), Teresa María Kaminski de Bottazzi (Tito Bottazzi Viajes y Turismo), Ruben Coll (Interventor, Organismo Provincial de Turismo, Rawson), Emilio Antonio Balado (Director de Turismo, Trelew).

Bolivia

HORIZONS

THE LAND

Bolivia, straddling the Andes, is a land of gaunt mountains, cold desolate plateaux and semi tropical lowlands. In area it is about twice the size of Spain. It is landlocked, with Chile and Peru to the W, Brazil to N and E, and Argentina and Paraguay to the S.

The Andean range is at its widest, some 650 km, in Bolivia. The Western Cordillera, which separates Bolivia from Chile, has high peaks of between 5,800 and 6,500m and a number of active volcanoes along its crest. The passes across it are above 4,000m. To the E of this range lies the bleak, treeless, windswept Altiplano, much of it 4,000m above sea-level. It has an average width of 140 km, is 840 km long, and covers an area (in Bolivia) of 102,300 sq km, or nearly 10% of the country. Its surface is by no means flat, for the Western Cordillera sends spurs into it which tend to divide it into basins. The more fertile northern part is the more inhabited; the southern part is parched desert and almost unoccupied, save for a mining town here and there. Nearly 70% of the population lives on it, for it contains most of the major cities; almost half of the people are urban dwellers.

The Altiplano is a harsh, strange land, a dreary grey solitude except for the bursts of green after rain. The air is unbelievably clear – the whole plateau is a bowl of luminous light. A cold wind blows frequently in the afternoons, causing dust storms.

From the Altiplano rises, to the E, the sharp façade of the Eastern Cordillera. As luck would have it there is a gently graded passageway along the plateau at the foot of the Eastern Cordillera from Lake Titicaca, in the N, to the Argentine frontier, in the S. From Viacha, near La Paz, a railway line runs S along this passageway to Villazón on the Argentine border with connections to Chile (from Uyuni). The giant masses of the northern parts of the Eastern Cordillera rise to very great heights in the Cordillera Real to the E of Lake Titicaca: six peaks soar to above 6,000m. This magnificent sight can be seen on a clear day from the top of a ridge on the more southern Titicaca-La Paz road, which goes past Tiahuanaco. The far sides of the Cordillera Real fall away to the NE, very sharply, towards the Amazon basin.

Lake Titicaca

Lake Titicaca, at the northern end of the Altiplano, is an inland sea of 8,965 sq km at 3,810m: the highest navigable water in the world. Its maximum length and

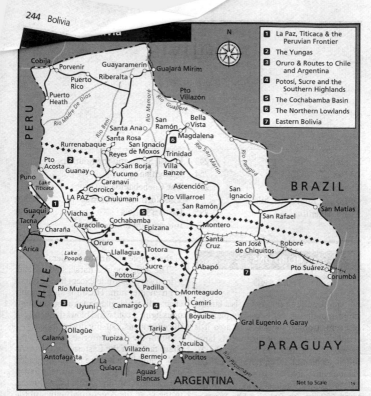

1	La Paz, Titicaca & the Peruvian Frontier
2	The Yungas
3	Oruro & Routes to Chile and Argentina
4	Potosí, Sucre and the Southern Highlands
5	The Cochabamba Basin
6	The Northern Lowlands
7	Eastern Bolivia

breadth are 171 and 64 km, and the greatest known depth is 280m. There are large annual variations between high and low water levels; 95% of the water flowing into it is lost by evaporation, making it more salty than most freshwater lakes. The immense depth of the water keeps the lake at an even all-the-year-around temperature of 10°C. This modifies the extremes of winter and night temperatures on the surrounding land, which supports a large Aymara indian population, tilling the fields and the hill terraces and tending their sheep and llamas.

Wildlife of the Altiplano

Llamas serve as pack animals. They carry up to 22 kg loads up to 20 km a day and yield about 2½ kg of wool when sheared at intervals of from 2-5 years. The alpaca, bred not for work but for wool, belongs to the same group; alpacas have smaller noses, thicker coats and are smaller than llamas. The vicuña, chinchilla and red fox are the main wild animals. The vicuña, an untamed smaller member of the family to which the llama and the alpaca belong, is found, though in diminishing numbers, on the bleak pampas. It may not be hunted, but its fine silky, tawny coloured wool may be sold.

Agriculture in the Altiplano

The potato and the *oca* (another tuber), eaten in the dehydrated form of *chuño* and *tunta*, are the main crops. *Quinoa*, a kind of millet, and *cañava*, a smaller and darker grain, are the main cereals; both are extremely nutritious. *Chicha*, the national intoxicant, is brewed from maize (corn).

Edible fish (small *boga*, large white-fleshed *pejerrey* and the rainbow and salmon trout with which Lake Titicaca has been stocked) are widely sold in the towns of the Altiplano.

Mining

Since the colonial period mining has been far more important to the economy of the Altiplano than agriculture. In 1545 the Spanish discovered Indian mine workings and vast reserves of silver, tin, bismuth and tungsten in a mountain which they called Cerro Rico (the 'rich hill'). Interested only in silver, they built Potosí at its base, 4,070m above sea level. Today a much more important mining centre is Oruro, 210 km S of La Paz at the base of the Eastern Cordillera, where a low belt of hills supplies tin, copper, silver and tungsten. Nearby are the mines of Huanani, formerly owned by the tin magnate Simón Patiño, and Colquiri. Since the collapse of the world tin market in 1986, most of the other mines in the area have been closed or are now worked as small-scale cooperatives. Lack of investment and the high cost of producing Bolivian tin was a major contributor to the industry's decline. Silver is still mined or extracted from the tailings left by past generations, and variable amounts of lead, bismuth, antimony, tungsten and zinc from pockets in the Cordillera are exported. Large deposits of silver have been found S of the Altiplano, near Lípez, and mines are being reopened, and their tailings reprocessed, two centuries after the Spaniards abandoned them.

● **Recommended reading** *We Eat the Mines and the Mines Eat Us* by June Nash, New York, 1979; *The Potosí Mita 1573-1700* by Jeffery Cole, Stanford University Press, 1985; *The Great Tin Crash – Bolivia and the world tin market* by John Crabtree (Latin America Bureau, London, 1987).

THE YUNGAS AND THE PUNA

The heavily forested northeastern slopes of the Cordillera Real are deeply indented by the fertile valleys of the Nor Yungas and Sud Yungas, drained by the Río Beni and its tributaries, where cacao, coffee, sugar, coca and tropical fruits are grown. The problem of transport from here to the

consuming centre of ... the connecting all-weather road, ...dable: ing in places, climbs 3,430m in 80 km to surmount La Cumbre pass, at 4,725m within 24 km of La Paz.

Further S, from a point just N of Cochabamba the Eastern Cordillera is tilted, not to the NE, but to the E. This part of the Eastern Cordillera rises abruptly in sharp escarpments from the Altiplano, and then flattens out to an easy slope E to the plains: an area known as the Puna. The streams which flow across the Puna are tributaries of the Río Grande flowing NE to the basin of the Amazon, and of the Pilcomayo flowing SE through the Chaco to the Río de la Plata system. They cut increasingly deep incisions as they gather volume until, to the E, the Puna is eroded to little more than a high remnant between the river valleys. These valleys are densely inhabited; a variety of grain crops and fruits is grown. All these semi-tropical mountain valleys are known as Yungas: the generic name is not confined to the valleys of the Provinces of Nor and Sud Yungas to the E of La Paz.

THE LOWLANDS

The lowland tropics, stretching from the foothills of the Eastern Cordillera to the frontiers with Brazil to the NE and E and with Paraguay and Argentina to the SE and S, take up 70% of the total area of Bolivia, but contain only about 20% of its population. In the N and E the Oriente has dense tropical forest. Open plains covered with rough pasture, swamp and scrub occupy the centre. Towards the end of the 18th century this was a populous land of plenty; for 150 years Jesuit missionaries had controlled the area and guided it into a prosperous security. A symbol of their great effort is the cathedral at San José de Chiquitos: a gem of elegance and dignity. But the Jesuits were expelled in 1767; years of maladministration, spoliation and corruption reduced the area to lethargy.

This once rich land, drained by the Madre de Dios, Beni and Mamoré rivers into the Madeira, a tributary of the Amazon, has been isolated from the rest of the country. It is as difficult to get at from the

E as from the ~~delta~~ which limit naviga-
~~falls~~ in its heart lie the seasonally inun-
dated tropical Llanos de Mojos, ringed in
by rain forest or semi-deciduous tropical
forest: 230,000 sq km with only 120,000
people. Roads and river connections are
being improved; roads link Trinidad with
La Paz and Santa Cruz, Guayaramerín
and Riberalta with La Paz and Todos
Santos and Puerto Villarroel with
Cochabamba. Meat is now shipped from
Trinidad, capital of Beni Department,
and from airstrips in the area, to the
urban centres of La Paz, Oruro, and
Cochabamba.

The forests and plains beyond the
Eastern Cordillera sweep S towards the
Río Pilcomayo, getting progressively less
rain and merging into a comparatively
dry land of scrub forest and arid savanna.
The main city of this area is Santa Cruz
de la Sierra, founded in the 16th century,
now the second city of Bolivia and a large
agricultural centre. Here conditions favour the growing of sugar-cane, rice, oil
plants and citrus fruit. The plains to the
E are mainly used as grazing lands with
small areas under cultivation, but in this
area are extensive oil, gas, and iron-ore
deposits, possibly Bolivia's greatest asset
when developed.

CLIMATE

There are four distinct climatic zones: (1)
The tropical lowlands; altitude between
150 and 750m; rainfall is high but seasonal
(heaviest Nov-Mar, but can fall at any
season); large areas suffer from alternate
flooding and drought. The climate is hot,
ranging from 23° to 25°C in the S and to
27°C in the N. Occasional cold dust-laden
winds from the S, the *surazos*, lower the
temperature considerably. (2) The Yungas
N of La Paz and Cochabamba, among the
spurs of the Cordillera; altitude, 750-
1,500m; average temperature, 24°C. (3)
The Valles, or high valleys and basins
gouged out by the rivers of the Puna; average temperature, 19°C. Rainfall in the
Yungas valleys is from 700 to 800 mm a
year (heaviest Dec-Feb), with high hu-

midity. (4) The Puna and Altiplano; average temperature, 10°C, but above 4,000m
may get down to -25°C at night in June-
August. By day the tropical sun raises
temperatures over 20°C. Rainfall on the
northern Altiplano is 400 to 700 mm,
much less further S. Little rain falls upon
the western plateaux between May and
Nov, but the rest of the year can be wet.
The period from Dec to Mar is considered
the rainy season throughout Bolivia.

HISTORY

PRE-CONQUEST

At Tiwanaku (Tiahuanaco), near Lake Titicaca, stand the impressive remains of a
pre-Inca civilization. The Aymara speaking
Indians in this area emerged around 1000
BC into a civilization characterized by massive stone buildings and monuments, ex-
quisite textiles, pottery and metalwork. This
phase seems to have been ended abruptly
by some unexplained calamity around AD
900 (possibly the failure of the agricultural
system). When the Quechua-speaking Incas of Cusco conquered the area around AD
1200, they found the Aymaras at Tiahuanaco living among ruins they could no
longer explain. The Aymaras resisted obsti-
nately and were not finally conquered until
the latter part of the 15th century in the reign
of Inca Túpac Yupangi (1471-93). Even so,
they kept their traditional social structures
and language, and fought for the Incas under their own leaders. Only religion was
formally imposed by the Incas. Kollasuyo,
Inca Bolivia, was only a small part of the
Inca Empire and lasted only about 80 years.

CONQUEST AND AFTER

Francisco Pizarro landed in Peru in 1532.
6 years later Spain conquered Bolivia, and
the next year La Plata, now Sucre (still the
official capital), was founded. The excellent Inca communications system and economic organization fell into ruin. In 1559
La Plata became capital of the *audiencia* of
Charcas, in the Viceroyalty of Peru. As a
result of the discovery of silver at Potosí in
1545, Charcas became one of the most
important centres of the Spanish colonial

economy, sending a constant supply of silver to Spain. By 1610 Potosí, with a population of over 160,000 was the largest city in the Americas, but, as the richest deposits were exhausted and new mines opened in Mexico, Alto Peru, as present day Bolivia was known, went into decline.

Revolutionary movements against Spanish colonial rule began early; there were revolts at La Paz in 1661, at Cochabamba in 1730 and at Sucre, Cochabamba, Oruro and La Paz from 1776 to 1780. In 1809 the University of San Francisco Xavier, at Sucre, called for the independence of all Spain's American colonies. Finally, on 9 December 1824, Simón Bolívar's general, Gen Antonio José de Sucre, won the decisive battle of Ayacucho in Peru and invaded Alto Peru, defeating the Spaniards finally at the battle of Tumusla on 2 April 1825. On 9 February 1825, when he first entered La Paz, Sucre had already promulgated the decree of independence, but his second in command, Santa Cruz, was for retaining links with Peru; Bolívar was in two minds. Sucre had his way and Bolivia was declared independent.

POST INDEPENDENCE

For most of the period since independence, three main features have dominated Bolivian history: the importance of mining; the loss of territory through disputes and wars with neighbouring countries; and chronic political instability. Although silver had been so important in the colonial period, the Bolivian economy has depended for much of this century on exports of tin. The construction of railways and the demand for tin in Europe and the USA (particularly in wartime) led to a mining boom after 1900. By the 1920s the industry was dominated by three entrepreneurs, Simón Patiño, Mauricio Hochschild and the Aramayo family, who exercised great influence over national politics. The importance of mining and the harsh conditions in the isolated mining camps of the Altiplano led to the rise of a militant miners movement.

Bolivian politics have been even more turbulent than elsewhere in Latin America. Although in the 19th century the army was very small, officers were key figures in power-struggles, often backing different factions of the landowning elite. Between 1840 and 1849 there were 65 attempted coups d'etat. The longest lasting government of the 19th century was that of Andrés Santa Cruz (1829-1839), but when he tried to unite Bolivia with Peru in 1836, Chile and Argentina intervened to overthrow him. After the War of the Pacific (1879-1883) there was greater stability, but opposition to the political dominance of the city of Sucre culminated in a revolt in 1899 led by business groups from La Paz and the tin-mining areas, as a result of which La Paz became the centre of government.

Since independence Bolivia has suffered continual losses of territory, partly because of communications difficulties and the central government's inability to control distant provinces. The dispute between Chile and Peru over the nitrate-rich Atacama desert in 1879 soon dragged in Bolivia, which had signed a secret alliance with Peru in 1873. Following its rapid defeat in the War of the Pacific Bolivia lost her coastal provinces. As compensation Chile later agreed to build the railway between Arica and La Paz. Railways traded for valuable territory has been Bolivia's fate. A railway to Yacuiba was Argentina's return for annexing some of the Chaco. When Brazil annexed the rich Acre Territory in 1903, Bolivia was compensated by yet another railway, but this Madeira-Mamoré line never reached its destination, Riberalta, and proved of little use; it was closed in 1972.

There was not even an unbuilt railway to compensate Bolivia for its next loss. A long-running dispute with Paraguay over the Chaco erupted into war in 1932. Defeat in the so-called Chaco War (1932-1935) resulted in the loss of three quarters of the Chaco (see Paraguay chapter, page 1165).

MODERN BOLIVIA

Instability after the loss of the Chaco

The Chaco War was a turning point in

Bolivian history, increasing the political influence of the army which in 1936 seized power for the first time since the War of the Pacific. Defeat bred nationalist resentment among junior army officers who had served in the Chaco and also led to the creation of a nationalist party, the Movimiento Nacionalista Revolucionario (MNR) led by Víctor Paz Estenssoro. Their anger was directed against the mine owners and the leaders who had controlled Bolivian politics. Between 1936 and 1946 a series of unstable military governments followed. This decade witnessed the apparent suicide in 1939 of one president (Germán Busch) and the public hanging in 1946 of another (Gualberto Villarroel). After a period of civilian government, the 1951 elections were won by the MNR but a coup prevented the party from taking office.

The 1952 revolution

In April 1952 the military government was overthrown by a popular revolution in which armed miners and peasants played a major role. Paz Estenssoro became president and his MNR government nationalized the mines, introduced universal suffrage and began the break-up and redistribution of large estates. The economy, however, deteriorated, partly because of the hostility of the US government. Paz's successor, Hernán Siles Zuazo (president 1956-1964), a hero of the 1952 revolution, was forced to take unpopular measures to stabilize the economy. Paz was re-elected president in 1960 and 1964, but shortly afterwards in Nov 1964 he was overthrown by his vice president, Gen René Barrientos, who relied on the support of the army and the peasants to defeat the miners.

Military rule in the '70s

The death of Barrientos in an air crash in 1969 was followed by three brief military governments. The third, led by Gen Torres, pursued left-wing policies which alarmed many army officers and business leaders. In Aug 1971 Torres was overthrown by Hugo Banzer, a right-wing general who outlawed political parties and trade unions. Banzer's government, though repressive, was mild by compari-

son with contemporary regimes in Argentina and Chile. After Banzer was forced to call elections in 1978, there was another period of short-lived military governments, which overruled elections in 1978 and 1979 giving victories to Siles Zuazo. One of these, led by Gen García Meza (1980-1981) was notable for its brutal treatment of opponents and its links to the cocaine trade which led to its isolation by the international community.

Return to democracy and economic stabilization

In Aug 1982 the military returned to barracks and Dr Siles Zuazo assumed the Presidency in a leftist coalition government with support from the communists and trade unions. Under this regime inflation spiralled out of control. The elections of 14 July 1985 were won again by Víctor Paz Estenssoro, who imposed a rigorous programme to stabilize the economy. In the elections of 7 May 1989, Gonzalo Sánchez de Lozada of the MNR (chief architect of the stabilization programme) won most votes but the result was so close that Congress had to choose a president from the three leading contenders. Jaime Paz Zamora of the Movimiento de la Izquierda Revolucionaria (MIR) who came third in the elections, was inaugurated as President on 6 August 1989 after having made an unlikely alliance with the former military dictator, Gen (retired) Hugo Banzer (Acción Democrática Nacionalista), in return for certain cabinet posts.

At the end of Paz Zamora's term, the former military dictator Gen Luis García Meza was sentenced to 30 years in prison at a much-publicized trial. Although several of his accomplices were imprisoned at the same time on human rights charges, García Meza himself managed to escape during the trial. He was captured in Brazil in early 1994 and held there by the military until Feb 1995, when he was extradited to Bolivia. He is now held in solitary confinement in a prison outside La Paz.

In the presidential election of 6 June 1993 Gonzalo Sánchez de Lozada won

COMMUNICATIONS

After centuries of isolation new roads are now integrating the food-producing eastern zones with the bulk of the population living in the towns of the Altiplano or the W-facing slopes of the Eastern Cordillera. Under Spanish rule there were four great trails in use within the country: three of them led through passes in the western Cordillera to the Pacific; the fourth led from La Paz S into Argentina. At the turn of the century, railways replaced the llamas and mules. By far the shortest line is the one from La Paz to Arica (Chile), completed in 1913. Arica ships a large part of the exports together with Antofagasta (Chile) and Matarani (Peru).

Bolivia has 3,774 km of railway. There are two private railways: Machacamarca-Uncia, owned by the Corporación Minera de Bolivia (108 km) and Uyuni-Pulacayo (52 km) owned by the Empresa Minera Pulacayo. A railway to link Cochabamba and Santa Cruz, as part of a Pacific-Atlantic rail network, has been under study with Inter-American Development Bank assistance since 1989. Bolivia has over 14,000 km of navigable rivers, which connect most of the country with the Amazon basin. The national highway system at the end of 1988 totalled 41,642 km, of which only 4% were paved and under 25% gravel-surfaced.

La Paz

L A PAZ, Lake Titicaca and Mt Illimani are probably the three most familiar sights of Bolivia, set amid high Andean Altiplano and the Cordillera Real. The region around La Paz is known as Little Bolivia, containing snow-peaks, desert and sub-tropical jungle in Coroico, just one day's breathtaking bus-ride away.

The highest capital in the world, lies in a steep canyon; Plaza Murillo in the centre, at 3,636m, is about 370m below the level of the Altiplano and the new city of El Alto. Mt Illimani, with its snow-covered peaks (6,402m), towers over the city. One of the best ways to appreciate the setting is from the air. East-west flights pass by Illimani with beautiful views of the summit; the rim of the Altiplano, with El Alto built up to the edge, the old city descending the canyon, is very dramatic. The Spaniards chose this odd place for a city on 20 October 1548, to avoid the chill winds of the plateau, and because they had found gold in the Río Choqueyapu, which runs through the canyon.

BASICS In 1993, the *population* of La Paz was estimated at 1.2 million, over half of it Indian. The mean average *temperature* is 10°C, but it varies greatly during each day, and the nights are cold. It rains almost every day from Dec to Feb, but the sun usually shines for several hours. The rest of the year is mostly clear and sunny. Snow is rare. Beware of *soroche* (altitude sickness), especially if arriving from much lower altitudes by air. *Phone code* 02.

Orientation is relatively simple; a major avenue, changing its name from Av Mcal Santa Cruz to Av 16 de Julio (this section is generally known as Prado) runs SE from Plaza San Francisco down to the Plaza del Estudiante. The business quarter, government offices, central university (UMSA) and many of the main hotels and restaurants are situated in this area. On the hills above Plaza Mendoza are the poorer parts of the city. From the Plaza del Estudiante, Av Villazón and its extensions lead further SE towards the wealthier residential districts, which run from Sopocachi to the bed of the valley at Obrajes, 5 km from the centre and 500m lower than Plaza Murillo. Sopocachi, through which runs Av 6 de Agosto, has many restaurants, discos, bars, etc; the Mercado Sopocachi, on F Guachalla, is good but not cheap (a bimonthly *Sopocachi* magazine of cultural events, with map, is sold at newsstands). Beyond Obrajes are the upper-class districts of Calacoto and La Florida. The main sports and social clubs are in these districts.

El Alto is now a city in its own right. Apart from the district known as Ciudad Satelite, it is almost 100% indigenous; almost everyone is an emigrant from the countryside. It is growing at 10%/year, compared with 4% growth in the wealthier districts of La Paz. Costs are much lower than in La Paz, but construction, etc is much more basic. There is a market on Thur and Sun in Av Alfonso Ugarte, more interesting for its size than the items for sale. El Alto is connected to La Paz by motorway (toll US$0.50, cycles free). Buses from Plaza Aguino and Pérez Velasco leave regularly for Plaza 16 de Julio, El Alto.

PLACES OF INTEREST

There are few colonial buildings left in La Paz; probably the best examples are in **Calle Jaén**. Late 19th/early 20th century architecture, often displaying heavy European influence, can be found in the streets around Plaza Murillo, but much of La Paz is modern. Emilio Villanueva added local features to European styles, eg the Tiwanaku-style decorations on the University building, but much 20th-century architecture was influenced by Frank Lloyd Wright, eg the new Correo. The **Plaza del Estudiante** (Plaza Franz Tamayo), or a bit above it, marks a contrast between old and new styles, between the traditional commercial and the more elegant. The **Prado** itself is lined with high-rise blocks dating from the 1960s and 1970s. **Plaza Murillo**, three blocks N of the Prado, is the traditional centre. Facing its formal gardens are the huge **Cathedral** (very graceful); the **Palacio Presidencial** in Italian renaissance style, usually known as the Palacio Quemado (burnt palace) twice gutted by fire in its stormy 130-year history; and on the E side the **Congreso Nacional**. In front of the Palacio Quemado is a statue of former President Gualberto Villarroel who was dragged into the plaza by an angry mob and hanged in 1946. Across from the Cathedral on C Socabaya is the **Palacio de los Condes de Arana**, dating from 1775, now the Museo Nacional del Arte. Calle Comercio, running E-W across the Plaza, has most of the stores and shops. On Av Libertador Simón Bolívar (to which Mt Illimani provides a backdrop), is the **Central Market** (called 'Mercado Camacho'), a picturesque medley of Indian victuals and vendors. Further E is the residential district of Miraflores. Another good view of Illimani can be had from the top of the rise on C Illimani.

At the upper end of Av Mcal Santa Cruz is the **Plaza San Francisco** with the church and monastery of San Francisco, dating from 1549, well worth seeing. The church (opens at 1600) is richly decorated on native religious themes (the mestizo baroque façade clearly displays how the traditional baroque vine motif is transformed into an array of animals, birds, fruits and plants), the interior contains huge, square columns and gilt altars on which stand many saints; Indian weddings can be seen on Sat 1000-1200. Behind the San Francisco church a network of narrow cobbled streets rise steeply. Much of this area is a permanent street market. Handicraft shops line the lower part of **Calle Sagárnaga**; further up, from Illampu to Rodríguez and in neighbouring streets, is the local **Rodríguez market**. Turning right on Max Paredes, heading W, is Av Buenos Aires, one of the liveliest streets in the Indian quarter, where small workshops turn out the costumes and masks for the Gran Poder festival. Continuing W along Max Paredes towards the **cemetery district**, the streets are crammed with stalls selling every imaginable item. Transport converges on the cemetery district (for more information see **Buses** below). Do not expect to go anywhere in a hurry in this part of the city; there are good views of Illimani from these heights.

Other churches include **Santo Domingo** (originally the cathedral), Calles Ingavi y Yanacocha, with its decorative 18th-century façade; **La Merced**, on a plazuela at Calles Colón and Comercio; **San Juan de Dios**, on Loayza between Merced and Camacho, with a carved portico, circular paintings of the life of Christ and, above the altar, figures holding lighted electric candles around a statue of the Virgin; and **San Sebastián**, the first church to be built in La Paz, in Plaza Alonso de Mendoza (named after the church's builder). On **Plaza Sucre** (with trees, benches and photographers) is **San Pedro** church, Av 20 de Octubre y Colombia, built 1720; large paintings of the life of Christ along the nave, a huge chandelier below the dome and a gilt altar.

A worthwhile walk is to **Mirador Lai-**

cacota on Av del Ejército: one of the delights of La Paz is the change from day to night, when all the lights begin to twinkle on the surrounding hillsides.

MUSEUMS

Museo Nacional de Arte, C Socabaya 432, housed in the 18th century baroque palace of the Condes de Arana, with beautiful exterior and patio. It has a fine collection of colonial paintings including many works by Melchor Pérez Holguín, considered one of the masters of Andean colonial art, and also exhibits the works of contemporary local artists. Tues-Fri 0900-1230, 1500-1900, US$0.25, Sat 1000-1300, US$0.50, students US$0.25.

Museo Tiahuanaco (Tiwanaku), or Museo Nacional de Arqueología, easily reached by going down the flight of stairs by María Auxili church on the Prado. This modern building, simulating the Tiwanaku style, contains good collections of the arts and crafts of ancient Tiwanaku and items from the E jungles. It also has a 2-room exhibition of gold statuettes and objects found in Lake Titicaca. Tues-Fri 0900-1230, 1500-1900, Sat 1000-1230, 1500-1830, Sun 1000-1300; US$1.20.

Museo Semisubterráneo, or Templete del Estadio, in front of National Stadium, with restored statues and other artefacts from Tiahuanaco. It's in a sunken garden and much can be seen from street level. No explanations are given and the statues are being badly eroded by pollution.

Museo Nacional de Etnografía y Folklore, C Ingavi 916, in the palace of the Marqueses de Villaverde, exhibits on the Chipaya and Ayoreo Indians, quite good library adjoining. Mon-Fri 0830-1200, 1430-1830.

The following four museums are included on a single ticket, which costs US$0.75, from Museo Costumbrista. All are open Tues-Fri 1030-1300, 1600-2030, Sat and Sun 1030-1300, with well-displayed items in colonial buildings. All are on C Jaén, a picturesque colonial street with many craft shops, worth seeing for itself.

Museo Costumbrista, Plaza Riosinio, at top of Jaén. Miniature displays depict incidents in the history of La Paz and well-known Paceños. Also has miniature replicas of reed rafts used by Norwegian, Thor Heyerdahl and Spaniard, Kitin Muñoz, to prove their theories of ancient migrations, T 378478.

Museo Casa Murillo, T 375273, was originally the home of Pedro Domingo Murillo, one of the martyrs of the abortive La Paz independence movement of 16 July 1809. This colonial house has been carefully restored and has a good collection of paintings, furniture and national costumes of the period; there is also a special room dedicated to herbal medicine and magic (Kallawaya) along with two rooms of paintings.

Museo de Metales Preciosos, Jaén 777, well set out with Inca gold artefacts in basement vaults, also ceramics and archaeological exhibits, T 371470.

Museo del Litoral Boliviano, Jaén 789, with artefacts of the War of the Pacific, and interesting selection of old maps.

Casa Museo Marina Núñez del Prado, Ecuador 2034, Mon-Fri, 1000-1300, 1500-1900, Sat, 1000-1300, excellent collection of her sculptures housed in the family mansion.

Museo Tambo Quirquincho, C Evaristo Valle, nr Plaza Mendoza (Tues-

La Paz: Key to map

1. Cathedral; 2. Museo Costumbrista, Museo Casa Murillo, Museo de Metales Preciosos and Museo del Litoral Boliviano; 3. Museo Nacional de Arte; 4. Museo Nacional de Etnografía y Folklore; 5. Palacio Quemado; 6. Parque Prehistórico Tiahuanaco (Museo Semisubterráneo). **Parks and squares:** 7. Plaza Murillo; 8. Plaza del Estudiante/Franz Tamayo; 9. Plaza Mendoza; 10. Plaza Sucre/San Pedro; 11. Plaza Venezuela; 12. Plaza Vicente Eguino; 13. Plaza Velasco; 14. Plaza Riosinio; 15. Plaza Antofagasta; 16. Garita de Lima. **Hotels:** 17. *Continental*; 18. *Copacabana*; 19. *El Dorado*; 20. *España*; 21. *Gloria*; 22. *Libertador*; 23. *Max Inn*; 24. *Milton*; 25. *Panamericano*; 26. *Plaza*; 27. *Presidente*; 29. *Res Rosario*; 30. *Sagárnaga* and *Alem*; 31. *Sucre Palace*; 32. *Viena*; 33. *Hostal Claudia*; 34. *Hostal República*. **Restaurants/Peña:** 35. Casa del Corregidor; 36. Los Escudos.

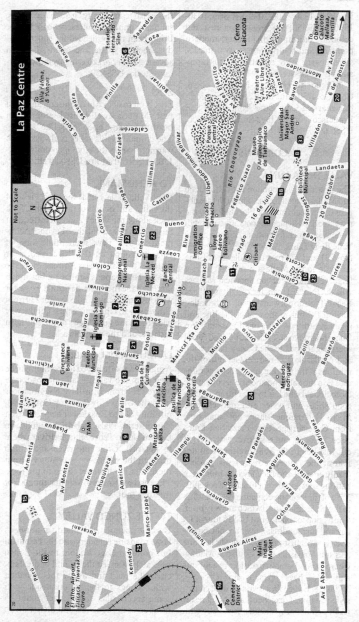

Fri, 1030-1300, 1600-2030, Sat-Sun, 1030-1300, US$0.50, Sat free), in a restored colonial building, displaying modern painting and sculpture, carnival masks, silver, early 20th century photography and city plans.

Museo de Historia Natural, C 26, Cota Cota, 30 mins from centre by microbus marked Cota Cota from Plaza San Francisco, open Tues-Sun 1000-1700, US$0.60.

EXCURSIONS

VALLE DE LA LUNA

The best nearby excursion is to Río Abajo and Mallasilla golf course. Through the suburbs of Calacoto and La Florida follow the river road past picnic spots and through some weird rock formations, known as the **Valle de la Luna**, 'Moon Valley'. Kombi A, Nos 231 and 273 pass the Valle de la Luna en route to the Mallasa recreation area, a large weekend excursion area near Mallasa village. (No 231 can be caught at Plaza Belzu; if you do not want to walk in the valley, stay on the bus to the end of the line and take a return bus, 2 hrs in all.) About 3 km from the bridge at Calacoto the road forks; sharp right leads to the Caza y Pesca Club and Mallasilla golf course. Get out of the minibus at the turning and walk a few minutes E to the Valle entrance, or get out at the football field which is by the entrance. Take good shoes and water. Alternatively take Micro 11 ('Aranjuez'-large, not small bus) from C Sagárnaga, near Plaza San Francisco, US$0.65, and ask driver where to get off. Just before the Valle are the Aranjuez Forest, the Aniceto Arce cactus gardens (badly eroded) and the *Playa de Aranjuez*, a bathing spot popular for lunch at weekends. Most of the local travel agents organize tours to the Valle de la Luna (which are very brief, 5 mins stop for photos in a US$15 tour of La Paz and surroundings); taxis are not expensive (US$6). Just past the Valle de la Luna and the Mallasilla Golf Course is Mallasa where several small roadside restaurants and cafés have opened; also *Oberland*, T 796818, F 796389, a Swiss-owned, chalet-style restaurant (excellent) and hotel resort (**A2**), popular at weekends, especially with

the expat community: gardens, cabañas, sauna, swimming pool, racket ball, tennis. It has been recommended for superb fondue, raclette, pasta and salads. Book in advance. Also *Los Lobos*, highly rec for *churrasco* steaks, US$4.50.

ZOO

Zoo, is on road to Río Abajo, entrance just past Mallasa, well-housed animals in beautiful, wide open park-like setting. The climate in this valley is always much warmer than in the city. Open daily 0900-1700, US$0.40 adults, US$0.20 children.

TO ACHUMANI

(Past Valle de la Luna) for good views of the valley and houses of the wealthy. Walk back along the valley and catch frequent buses into town. Further beyond Achumani is the new residential zone of Chasquipampa on the Palca road, near which is the Valle de las Animas. Here the eroded landscape is similar to, but much larger than, the Valle de Luna; good for walking and picnics. Take Kombi 239 from University to Chasquipampa. On the way back there are good views of the southern districts and the city above.

LA MUELA DEL DIABLO

A gigantic, toothshaped rock which can be seen from the Valle de la Luna road, take Micro 'N' from Murillo y Sagárnaga or from the University (last stop Cota Cota), minibus 213 to Rosales, or *trufi* 288 from Cementerio, Plaza Isabel La Católica to Urbanización Pedregal (ask driver where to get off). Cross the river and climb through the village to the cemetery; from there it is 1½ hrs easy climb to the rock. The road continues to Ventilla, the start of the Inca trail.

TO THE ZONGO VALLEY

Pass the abandoned Milluni tin mine, its large roadside cemetery and the colourful but polluted Lago Milluni to the Zongo pass at 4,700m. At the far end of the dam, cross the road and follow the aqueduct which clings to the mountainside with some spectacular drops. After about 45 mins cross the aqueduct and then walk up

The Alacitas Fair

🐌 "It is dedicated to Ekeko, an Indian household god. You can buy plaster images of him at many of the booths. He is a red-nosed cheerfully-grinning little personage laden with an assortment of miniature cooking utensils, coins, balls of wool, tiny sacks of sugar, coffee, salt, rice and flour; a kind of Bolivian Santa Claus. Ekeko is said to bring prosperity and to grant wishes. If you buy a toy house, or a cow, or a sheep at the Alacitas, you will get a real one before the year is out. There are also model motor-cars and planes, for the extreme optimists." (Christopher Isherwood, 'The Condor and the Cows'.) The most popular purchase is miniature dollar bills.

to reach the base of the Charquini glacier – do not go on the glacier unless you have crampons and are roped. Alternatively continue round for great views of Huayna Potosí. From the dam the road drops almost 3,000m in less than 40 km past various hydroelectric plants – popular with mountain bikers.

● **Transport** Either arrange a jeep through a tourist agency for US$70; or go to Plaza Ballivián in El Alto to catch a *camión* at midday Mon, Wed and Fri, US$1, or haggle with drivers of empty minibuses for US$10; or hire a taxi for US$30 for the return trip (make sure the driver knows where he's going); or contact *Refugio Huayna Potosí* which organizes regular transport. If driving, make sure you have your passport and driving documents as there is a police check point immediately before the mine. To get back from the dam if you haven't arranged transport, the truck returns passing the Zongo dam at about midday Tues, Thur and Sat. There are La Paz-bound jeeps and minibuses at irregular intervals during the season.

OTHER EXCURSIONS

To see Puya Raimondii plants, go to the village of Comanche, 2½ hrs from La Paz (micros from railway station to Viacha – 1 hr – then truck to Comanche – rough, dusty and cold, or by train, Tues 2200, back on Wed only at 1500, US$2 each way); some travel agencies arrange tours.

URMIRI

Take road S towards Oruro, turn left at Urmiri sign at Km 75. To get this far take Flota Bolívar or Flota Copacabana bus; lifts from the crossroads are few and far between. A steep scenic descent leads to pool filled by mineral springs and a pleasant primitive inn. Worth visiting, it's a

2½ hrs trip one way. The La Paz Prefectura runs buses to Urmiri, where they have a hotel (D), price includes food.

LOCAL FESTIVALS

The **Alacitas Fair**, from last week of Jan to first week of Feb, on the upper part of Plaza Villarroel, mostly on C Tejada Zorzano (take *micro* B, K, H, 131 or X). Beginning of June, **Corpus Christi**.

End May/early June, **Festividad del Señor de Gran Poder**, the most important festival of the year, with a huge procession of costumed and masked dancers. **Fiestas de Julio**, a month of concerts and performances at the Teatro Municipal, offers a wide variety of music, including the University Folkloric Festival. **8 December**, festival around Plaza España, not very large, but colourful and noisy. On **New Year's Eve** fireworks are let off and make a spectacular sight, and a din, view from higher up. See also page 354 for festivals outside La Paz.

LOCAL INFORMATION

Try to arrive in La Paz early in the day as accommodation, especially at the cheaper end of the market, can be hard to find. Prices inc tax and service charge (20% in all).

Hotel prices

L1	over US$200	**L2**	US$151-200
L3	US$101-150	**A1**	US$81-100
A2	US$61-80	**A3**	US$46-60
B	US$31-45	**C**	US$21-30
D	US$12-20	**E**	US$7-11
F	US$4-6	**G**	up to US$3

● **Accommodation**
L3 *Radisson Plaza*, formerly *Hotel La Paz* (still referred to as *Sheraton*), Av Arce 2177,

T 316163, F 343391, good 5-star hotel with all facilities, sauna; **L3 *Plaza***, Av 16 de Julio 1789, T 378317, F 343391, excellent, good value restaurant (see under Places to eat), peña show on Fri; **L3 *Presidente***, Potosí 920 y Sanjines, T 368601, F 354013, inc breakfast, 'the highest 5-star in the world', pool, gymnasium and sauna all open to non-residents, bar, disco, excellent service, comfortable, good food, rec; **L3 *Ritz Aparthotel***, Plaza Isabel La Católica 2478, T 433131, F 433080, 5-star self-catering apartments, inc breakfast.

A1 *El Rey Palace*, Av 20 de Octubre 1947, T 393016, F 367759, inc breakfast, large suites, excellent restaurant, stylish, modern; **A1 *Gran Hotel París***, Plaza Murillo esq Bolívar, T 319170, F 372547, inc breakfast, cable TV, English spoken, elegant restaurant; **A2 *Camino Real***, Ravelo 2123, T 314542, F 365575, self-catering apartments, inc breakfast, TV, parking; **A3 *Gloria***, Potosí 909, T 370010/18, F 391489, central, 2 restaurants, one on top floor with good view, one vegetarian, excellent food and service (see under Places to eat); rec; **A3 *Libertador***, Obispo Cárdenas 1421, T 351792, F 391225, very good value, colour TV, good cheap restaurant, helpful (baggage stored), highly rec.

B *Eldorado*, Av Villazón, T 363355, F 391438, with breakfast, safe luggage deposit, secure parking nearby; **B *Max Inn***, Plaza Sucre 1494, T 374391, F 341720, small but clean rooms with bath, heating, TV, smart, poor service.

C *Hostería Blanquita*, Santa Cruz 242, T 352933, 'baroque', inc breakfast, hot showers, comfortable; **C *Copacabana***, Av 16 de Julio 1802, T 352244, with bath, central, restaurant and grill room (lunch only at latter), good service, safe deposit, rooms a bit small, rec; **C *Hostal Embajador***, Juan de la Riva 1438, T 392079, with bath, TV, heating, inc breakfast, German spoken, helpful; **C *Hostal República***, Comercio 1455 (T 357966), with bath, D without, café, beautiful old house of former president, very clean, warm water, inadequate shared bathrooms, luggage stored, helpful, laundry service, very popular with cyclists, usually full, rec, also a separate house is available, sleeps 6, all facilities; **C *Residencial Copacabana***, Illampu 734, T 367896/375378, hot water, renovated 1995, D without bath, inc breakfast, changes TCs; **C *Residencial Rosario***, Illampu 704, T 326531, F 375532, Turisbus travel agency downstairs (see under Travel Agents), with bath (electric shower – safe design), D without, very popular with foreigners, avoid noisier rooms nr foyer, sauna, laundry, excellent restaurant (see under Places to eat), stores luggage, friendly, highly rec; **C *Sagárnaga***, Sagárnaga 326, T 350252, F 360831, with bath, D without, inc basic breakfast, good location, laundry, English spoken,

poor service; **C** *Viena*, Loayza 420, T 323572, with bath, E without, beautiful old building with elegant entrance and patio, gloomy rooms, good lunch in restaurant, friendly, clean, rec, arrive early, often full, tours with Vicuña Tours, good.

D *Continental*, Illampu 626, T 378226, with bath, hot water, clean; **D** *España*, Av 6 de Agosto 2074, T 354643, hot water, TV, quiet, friendly, rec; **D-C** *Hostería Claudia*, Av Villazón 1965, T 372917, with bath, E without, clean, secure, friendly, rec; **D** *El Alem*, Sagárnaga 334, T 367400, hot water, E without bath, clean, helpful, secure, rec, has helpful travel agency; **D** *La Joya*, Max Paredes 547, T 324346, F 350959, with bath and TV, phone, E without bath or TV, clean, modern and comfy, laundry, in the heart of market district, rec; **D** *Milton*, Illampu y Calderón No 1124, T 368003/353511, F 365849 (PO Box 5118), with bath, hot water, inc breakfast, laundry, safe parking around corner, popular with travellers, will store luggage, excellent views from roof, good restaurant, rec, local market outside; **D** *Res La Estancia*, Mexico 1559, T 324308, with bath and breakfast, helpful, good restaurant; **D** *Res Sucre*, Colombia 340, on Plaza San Pedro, T 328414, F355506, cheaper without bath, quiet area, warm water, big rooms, clean, luggage stored, friendly and helpful; **D** *Tambo de Oro*, Armentia 367, T 322763, nr bus station, hot showers, clean, friendly, helpful and safe for luggage.

E *Andes*, Av Manco Kapac 364, T 323461, clean, hot water 24 hrs a day, motorcycle parking, good value (one of the few that offers single rooms at F), discount for IYHA card holders, rec; **E** *Austria*, Yanacocha 531, T 351140, without bath (F pp in shared room), clean, hot water, but insufficient showers, safe deposit, very cosy, good for longer stays, use of kitchen, laundry, TV, friendly and helpful staff, very popular, arrive early, highly rec; opp is **E** *Hostal Yanacocha*, large clean rooms, hot water, secure; **E** *Bolivia*, Manco Kapac 287, T 375030, opp railway station, clean, shared tepid showers, good views from back, upper rooms, very noisy; **E** *Alojamiento Illimani*, Av Illimani 1817, T 325948, hot water, friendly, clean, quiet and safe, uncomfortable beds, laundry facilities, often full; **E** *Ingavi*, Ingavi 727, T323645/355178,nice rooms, good value; **E** *La Paz*, Acosta 487, very clean, friendly, quiet, stores luggage, safe, hot showers; **E** *Hostal Latino*, Junín nr Sucre, clean, hot water, motorcycle parking, luggage stored, helpful; **E** *Panamericano*, Manco Kapac 454, T 340810/378370, with hot showers, nr railway station and main bus terminal, helpful, good restaurant, rec; **E** *Res Plaza*, Plaza Pérez Velasco 785, T 322157, nice old building, clean, hot water, F without bath, washing and luggage

storage facilities, helpful; **E** *Torino*, Socabaya 457, T 341487, central, hot water on request (electric showers) with bath (F without), formerly the gringo hotel but run down, poor beds, dirty, noisy, from disco especially at weekends till 0300, 2400 curfew, has noticeboard, stores luggage, book exchange, bar.

F *Hostal Chiquiago*, Plaza San Francisco, simple, friendly, secure, luggage stored; **F** *Res Imperial*, Pando, esq Incachaca, clean, friendly, hot water 24 hrs, stores luggage, cheap laundry, rec; **F** *Max Paredes*, Max Paredes 660, T 362726, with bath (cheaper without), modern, clean; **F** *Alojamiento Universo*, Inca 575, G pp in dormitories, clean, friendly, stores luggage, laundry, very popular, usually hot water, motorcycle parking, rec; **F** *Posada El Carretero*, Catacora 1056, y Pichincha y Sanjinés, T 322233, 5 beds to a room, helpful, pleasant, hot shower extra, can use kitchen for breakfast.

Youth Hostel association, Asociacón Boliviana de Albergues Juveniles, ABAJ, Edif Alborada p 1, of 105, C Juan de la Riva 1406 y Loayza, T 361076/321597, has hostels at *Hostal Duendes*, Av Uruguay 470, T 351125, Casilla 8765, and *Hotel Andes*, Manco Kapac 364, US$3.50 and 3.00 respectively, pp, without breakfast; other hostels around the country are given in the text. To use hostels you must have a Bolivian YHA card, US$2, two photos needed, available from ABAJ, which also sells international cards, US$20.

Camping No organized site, but Mallasa (Municipal Park, unmarked, turn left at Aldeas Infantiles SOS), Valencia and Palca below the suburb of La Florida have been rec. *Caza y Pesca*, Edif Handal Center, Av Mcal Santa Cruz y Socabaya, *Condoriri*, Sagárnaga 339, T/F 316369, or *Epcot*, Av 6 de Agosto 2190, local 9, T 342424, for camping equipment and camping gas. Kerosene for pressure stoves is available from a pump in Plaza Alexander. Public showers at Duchas La Paz, 20 de Octubre 1677.

● **Places to eat**
Restaurants with international cuisine are to be found mainly on three streets, Av 16 de Julio (the Prado), Av 6 de Agosto and Av 20 de Octubre. Service charges and tax of up to 23% are usually inc on the bill but it is customary to leave a tip of 10% anyway.

Av 16 de Julio (street numbers given in brackets): there are many snack bars, inc *Confitería Elis* (1497 and 1800), with good plate lunches, excellent soups, breakfasts (waffles, pancakes, French toast, pay extra for coffee refills) and pastries, not cheap, also *Eli's Pizza Express* in same block, English spoken, rec; opp is *Unicornio*, great ice cream, pizza, lunch buffet upstairs, good; *Patito Pekín* (1687), good Chinese, reasonably priced; *California Donuts II*

(1695), American-style food, expensive, US$2-10, opens 1230 (*No I* is at Av Camacho 1248, *No III* is on Av Arce); *Utama*, in *Plaza* hotel (1789) excellent salad bar, great value lunch, excellent view, highly rec; *Tokio* (1832), good, also has tea room and patisserie and rec for *salteñas*, but look out for high prices not written on menus; *Super 10* (1991 y Villazón), very good, open Sun evenings. On Plaza Estudiante, *Pizza I'Passo II*, good; *Café Ciudad*, 24-hr coffee shop, full menu, change US$ for customers. *Mary's Tee*, nr Plaza Estudiante, for excellent pies and cakes.

South of Plaza del Estudiante and Av Arce: *Andromeda*, Arce 2116, T 354723, European-style and vegetarian, excellent, quite expensive, live music at weekends, book ahead; *El Batau*, Landaeta 402, T 342518, German owner, Bolivian and international cuisine, rec; *Pizzeria Morello*, Av Arce 2132, very good but very expensive; excellent buffet Mon and Wed, 2000-2300, at *Radisson Plaza Hotel*, US$5.25, delicious and friendly to backpackers; *Kranky*, Av Villazón 1987, good, cheap sandwiches, burgers, ice cream, rec; *Chifa Emy*, Cordero 257, Chinese, very good service, takes credit cards; *Rigo's*, Plaza Organo, nr Museo Semisubterráneo, pleasant and good set lunch; *Vienna*, Federico Zuazo 1905, T 391660, German, Austrian and local food, excellent food and service, very fashionable with Bolivians and popular with foreigners, too.

In the Sopocachi district: up-market Italian cuisine at *Pronto*, Jauregui 2248, T 355869, Mon-Sat 1830-2230 (below Imprenta Quipus behind 6 de Agosto between Guachalla and Rosendo Gutiérrez), beautiful decor, serves three different types of pasta: regular, integral and 'pasta de quinoa', popular, good service; *Montesano*, Sánchez Lima 2329, nr Plaza Abaroa, excellent Italian, also fish and steaks. Several restaurants on Belisario Salinas. Among those **on Av 6 de Agosto**: *El Arriero* (No 2535, Casa Argentina), best barbecue with large portions; *Sergiu's Pizza*, No 2036, good; *Mocambo*, 6 de Agosto y Rosendo Gutiérrez 319, good food and service, Spanish; *Kuchen Stube*, Rosendo Gutiérrez, Edif Guadalquivir, closed Mon, excellent cakes, coffee and German specialities, also at Mercado 1328, Mon-Fri 0930-1230, 1500-1900; *Oriental*, very good, cheap, Chinese; while **on Av 20 de Octubre** there is *Mamma Mia*, art gallery by day, good Italian restaurant at night, good pizzas; *La Quebecoise*, nr Plaza Abaroa, French Canadian, pleasant atmosphere; *El Gaucho*, No 2041, steakhouse, good. Close to 20 de Octubre: Brazilian *feijoada* on Sat and Sun, at *Ipanema*, Av Ecuador 2139, between Aspiazu and F Guachalla, T 372306, rec, closed Mon; *Gringo Limón*, Plaza Abaroa, delicious; *Filippo*, just off Plaza Abaroa, good *salteñas*; *La Caldera Mágica*, JJ Pérez 322 y 20 de Octubre, nice atmosphere, good lunches, bar.

On the continuation of the **Prado going West**, in Av Mcal Santa Cruz, is *Los Escudos* (Edif Club de La Paz, T 322028/350586), Munich-type bierkeller with fixed 4-course lunch, good *peña* on Fri and Sat nights (2100-0100), US$5 cover charge. On the corner of Colón with Santa Cruz is *Restaurant Verona* for good economical *plato del día*, very popular in the evenings; *La Fiesta*, Santa Cruz 1066, excellent, good lunches, rec; *Tambo Colonial*, in *Res Rosario*, excellent local and international cuisine, rec, peña at weekend. On Plaza Velasco is *Kory Punku*, which serves excellent *parrilladas*, cheap and popular, live music some evenings.

On Calle México, running parallel S of the Prado: *La Estancia*, No 1553, good *almuerzo*, rec; *Capullito*, No 1490, pleasant café and *confitería*. México continues W as Murillo: at No 1040 is *Casa del Corregidor*, T 353633, centrally heated, behind Correo, Spanish colonial restaurant with Bolivian and European dishes, excellent food, bar; *El Horno*, open Mon-Sat, lunches inc vegetarian, free *peña* at nights (see **Entertainment** below); *Crístal*, No 726, outdoor, quite cheap, good.

On Sagárnaga: *Naira*, next to *Peña Naira* (No 161 downstairs), which serves good food (see

Entertainment below), and above the Peña, is *Resolana*, often confused with the *Naira* restaurant, very good pizzas and puddings, live jazz most evenings, rec; *El Montañés* (No 323), opp *Hotel Sagárnaga*, good, clean, family-run, homemade dishes; *Imperial*, Sagárnaga 213, 2nd floor, no sign, international vegetarian menu, set lunch US$2, clean, balcony tables, rec. In same area, *El Lobo*, Santa Cruz 441, huge portions, clean (Israeli dishes, good meeting place, noticeboard, limited menu, very popular); *Snack América*, Av América 192, good hamburgers; *Los Laureles*, on Evaristo Valle, good 4-course lunch, rec; *Clávida*, opp train station, excellent set lunch.

In the shopping and business district N of the Prado: there are numerous snack bars and cheap restaurants. *Club de la Prensa*, C Campero, set in a pleasant garden, the limited menu is typical Bolivian – meat only, in copious quantities – and the company is lively; *Café Club de la Paz*, Camacho 1202, on the corner where Ayacucho joins Av Mcal Santa Cruz, good tea room, traditional, meeting place for businessmen and politicians, great coffee and cakes; *Café Paris*, in *Gran Hotel Paris*, Plaza Murillo esq Bolívar, good food; *Torino*, at the hotel in Socabaya, is rec for excellent set lunch; next to *Torino*, *Chifa Jardin*, Socabaya 48, good, cheap Chinese; *Confitería California*,

Potosí 1008, Centro Comercial Cristal, does good set lunches. Also on Potosí, *Repostería Alemana* (*Nollo*) for breakfasts, *La Kantuta*, in *Hotel Presidente*, No 920, excellent food, good service, *Subterráneo* (No 1120), cheap and OK, *Chez Pierre* (1320), good lunches, *Rincón Tarijeño La Choza*, good food at reasonable prices; *Hogar Austriaco*, good lunches, pleasant; *Solo Café* (1108), excellent coffee and cappucino (closed lunchtime). On Yanacocha, *La Fregata* (No 525), good value, and *La Tertulia*, nr Ingavi, small, simple, charming, hot drinks and pastries. *Dumbo*, Camacho y Loayza, large portions, clean, very good; *Confitería Arabesque*, Mercado y Loayza, excellent *café con crema*; *Casa Chang*, Juan de la Riva y Bueno, good set course Chinese meals; *Los Pinochos*, Sanjines 553, excellent cheese empanadas and steaks, good food in large portions, popular café; *La Casa de los Paceños*, Sucre 856, very good, especially its *fritanga*. There are many other snack bars and Chinese restaurants on C Comercio (eg *La Fuente de Soda*, No 801, good burgers, and *Salteñería Comercio*, No 1439, excellent *salteñas* and Bolivian food, outdoor seating); *La Diligencia Churrascaría*, Comercio 803, good grill and set meals, rec; also on Colón, *Taiwan*, opp Mercado Camacho, large portions, good; *Confitería Rivoli*, Colón 415, small and pleasant snack bar, good and cheap

food; also *Las Carabelas*, Colón, just above Comercio, good lunches.

Vegetarian restaurants to recommend are the *Hotel Gloria*, Potosí 909, buffet lunch, very popular, be there by 1200 for a table, also breakfast, closed Sun, good coffee at *Café Pierrot*, and at *Café Oro*, Av Villazón 1962; *La Huerta*, Plaza Isabel La Católica, Av Arce, 1st floor, excellent salads, lunchtime and early evening, rec; *Natur Center*, Cañada Strongest 1852, lunches only, closed Sun. *Lila Vatty*, Santa Cruz 266, p 1, good value. Vegetarian dishes served at *Palacio del Buen Gusto*, 18 de Julio 1698, closed weekends, not cheap.

Burgers: a good chain is *Clap's*, Centro Comercial El Patio, Av Arce, C Ayacucho, C Belisario Salinas, another chain is *Denny's*, at Av 16 de Julio 1605. Stalls in the Indian quarter sell hamburgers for US$0.75 each inc chips, egg and tomato, but don't have ají, mayonnaise or mustard if worried about hygiene and watch your burger being cooked.

Comedor Popular, often referred to as *Comedor Familiar*, for strictly limited budgets, cheap but filling local meals around US$0.80-1.50, available at Camacho and Lanza markets. Bread from street vendors and Cochabamba wholemeal bread (*pan integral*) sold at the main markets, is rec. *Kremrik* is a chain of ice-cream parlours, with outlets at Plaza Murillo 542, and on Av Villazón, just off Plaza del Estudiante, good.

The **Calacoto** district situated in The Valley 15 mins S of the city, 'La Zona Sur' (US$0.40 by *trufi* or minibus), is home of the resident foreign community. Calacoto has recently developed into an important area in its own right: international shopping centres, supermarkets stocked with imported items and some of the best restaurants and bars in La Paz. The area begins after the bridge at La Florida where there is an attractive park, Plaza Humbolt – exhibitions of local art work on Sun and a collection of kiosks selling cheap snacks. The main road, Av Ballivián begins here at C 8 and continues up the hill to the shopping district of San Miguel on C 21 (about a 20 mins walk). On the main avenue, corner of C 8 is *El Viejo Tonel*, Brazilian rodizio restaurant, bar and disco (young crowd). Next, on the right side of the avenue, between C 9 y 10 is *Rumors*, an American/Mexican bar, restaurant, excellent music, popular late night place. *Puerto del Sol*, good Chinese on the left on the corner of C 11. Opposite, still on the main road, is an excellent arts and handicrafts shop, weavings, ceramics, silver etc. Continuing up the hill on Av Ballivián between C 15 y 16 on the left is *The Britannia*, Bolivia's only authentic English pub, owned by Englishman Tom Clough, open Tues-Sun from 1700, cosy, popular with regular ex-pat crowd.

Batemans XXXB best English bitter, bar snacks, darts etc, highly rec. Next door to The Britannia on the avenue is *Abracadabra*, open 7 days for lunch and dinner, ribs, hamburgers and pizza, American owner, rec. 5 mins walk further up the hill on the right is C 21 – the church of San Miguel on the corner of the avenue is an easy landmark – which has a huge variety of shops, fast-food cafés, banks and a post office. Back on the main avenue and continuing up the hill between C 24 y 25 is *The Suisse Chalet*, excellent fondue, steaks, expensive but rec, and almost next door *The Galeon* for some of the city's best seafood. *Zur Mönchsklause*, C 13 y Ovanda Candia, Irpavi, German, open Fri-Sun and holidays, garden, meat dishes and some fish.

● **Airline offices**
Lloyd Aéreo Boliviano (LAB), Camacho 1460, T 367701/7/367718/371020; **Aero Sur**, 16 de Julio 1607, T 371834, F 390457; **British Airways** at Edif Ballivián on C Mercado; **KLM**, Av Arce 2355; **American Airlines**, Av 16 de Julio 1440, Edif Herman, T 372009. **AeroPerú**, Edif Av, 16 de Julio 1490, 2nd floor, T 370002-4; **Aerolíneas Argentinas**, Edif Banco de la Nación Argentina, Av 16 de Julio 1486, T 351711/351624; **Qantas**, Av 16 de Julio, Ed Cosmos, planta baja, T 322903; **Varig**, Av Mcal Santa Cruz 1392, Edif Cámara de Comercio, T 314040, F 391131; **LanChile**, Av 16 de Julio 1566, 1st floor, T 358377; **Viasa**, Cap Ravelo 2334, T 432325.

● **Banks & money changers**
Citibank, Av 16 de Julio 1434 (cashes its own TCs, very high commission and will receive money sent from any US bank), but will not advance cash to holders of Citibank Mastercard. **Banco Industrial**, Av Gral Camacho 1333, open 0830-1700, Sat 1000-1300, good service, changes cash and TCs. Cash advance (in bolivianos) on Visa and Mastercard at **Banco de La Paz** on Prado (limit US$300/day, no commission), **Banco Santa Cruz de la Sierra**, **Banco Mercantil**, Mercado 1124 (good, quick service), **Banco Popular**, **Banco Nacional** and **Banco Boliviano Americano**, among others; **Bidesa**, Potosí 1285, good service; Banco Santa Cruz branch in Shopping Norte is open Sat pm. **Visa** has an office on Av Camacho 1448, 11th and 12th floors, T 369975/357014, F 354066, for cancelling lost or stolen credit cards. Automatic cash dispensers for Visa and Mastercard can be found at many sites in the city inc Av Camacho 1223, the airport and Shopping Norte shopping centre (look for the sign Enlace – Visa at branches of ATC). **Amex**, Av 16 de Julio 1490, p 5, T 323954/341201.

Exchange houses: Sudamer, Colón 256, good rates also for currencies other than US$ (1.5%

commission on TCs into dollars, frequently rec); **Unitours**, Mercado 1300, 1% commission on TCs. **Casa de Cambio Silver**, Mercado 979, charges 1% commission to change TCs into dollars, good rates; **Kantuta**, Av Mcal Santa Cruz 1326. Some *cambios* verify passports. Very few deal in Argentine and Chilean pesos. Street changers can be found at corners around Plaza del Estudiante, Camacho, Colón and Prado (poor rates out of banking hours, but convenient, always count money in their presence). **NB** If arriving on Fri night, bring bolivianos or US dollars cash as it is difficult to change TCs at the weekend (try *El Lobo* restaurant, which usually changes TCs at any time, good rates, or *Hotel Gloria* which gives good rates for most western currencies). If you leave Bolivia with bolivianos you may not be able to change them in neighbouring countries. Watch out for forged currency, especially dollars and Chilean pesos.

● **Embassies & consulates**
Argentine Consulate, Sánchez Lima 2103, T 353089/343516, 24 hrs for visa; **Brazilian Consulate**, Av 20 de Octubre, 20-38 Edif Fonconain, Embassy p 11, visa office, p 9, T 352108, 0900-1300, Mon-Fri (visas take 2 days). **Chilean Consulate**, H Siles 5843, esq C 13, Obrajes district, T 785269, open Mon-Fri 0830-1130 (visa same day if requested in the morning, take microbus N, A or L from Av 16 de Julio). **Ecuador**, 16 de Julio 1440, p 14, T 321208. **Paraguayan Consulate**, Edif Illimani, Av 6 de Agosto (very good visa service), T 322018; **Peruvian Consulate and Embassy**, 6 de Agosto 2190 y C F Guachalla, Edif Alianza, T 353550, 0930-1300 (a visa costs US$10 in US$ bills, issued same day if you go early); **Venezuelan Embassy and Consulate**, Av Arce 2678, Edif Illimani, p 4, T 375023 (consulate open Mon, Wed, Fri 0900-1200 – visas are only given to Bolivian residents, if you need one, get it in your home country).

United States Embassy and Consulate, Av Arce 2780, T 350120/430251, F 359875, Casilla 425. **Canadian Consulate**, Av 20 de Octubre 2475, Plaza Avaroa, T 375224, Mon-Fri. 0900-1200. **Japanese Embassy**, Rosendo Gutiérrez 497, esq Sánchez Lima, PO Box 2725, T 373151.

Austrian Consulate, Edif Petrolero, p 7, Oficina 1, Av 16 de Julio 1616, T 326601, 1600-1800; **British Embassy and Consulate**, Av Arce 2732-2754, T 433424, F 431073, Casilla 694, Mon-Thur 0900-1200, 1400-1600, Fri 0900-1300, has a list of travel hints for Bolivia, doctors, etc; **Danish Consulate**, Federico Zuazo 1598, Edif Park Inn, p 11, Casilla 662, T 360655/1, F 376380; **Finnish Consulate**, Mercado 1004, c/o Sibo SA, T 350900/367227; **French Consulate**, Av Hernando Siles 5390, esq C 08, Obrajes,

T 786114 (take bus No 11 or microbus N, A or L down Av 16 de Julio); **Belgian Embassy** is 1 block from French at No 5290, T 784925; **German Embassy**, Av Arce 2395, T 390850, Mon-Fri 0900-1200; **Italian Embassy**, 6 de Agosto 2575, PO Box 626, T 323597, F 391075; **Netherlands Embassy**, C Rosendo Gutiérrez 481, T 392064, F 391027, PO Box 10509, cellular phone (emergency 012-91173); **Norwegian Consulate**, Av 6 de Agosto 2410, T 322528; **Spanish Consulate**, Av Arce y C Cordero, T 343518; **Swedish Consulate**, Av Arce 2856, Casilla de Correo 852, T 327535, open 0900-1200; **Swiss Embassy**, Av 16 de Julio 1616, p 6, T 353091, F 391462, Casilla 9356, open 0900-1200, 1400-1500; **Israeli Embassy**, Av Mcal Santa Cruz, Edif Esperanza, p 10, T 358676/371287, Casilla 1309/1320.

● **Entertainment**
Best entertainment for visitors are the folk shows (*peñas*). At these, visitors will be able to listen to the wide variety of local musical instruments, the different types of flutes and the *charango*, a small guitar with five strings, the body of which was originally made from the shell of an armadillo. Outstanding show at *Peña Naira* (US$5, inc first drink), Sagárnaga 161, T 325736, every night about 2230. Enquire at the *Rumillajta* shop (in the *galería* close to San Francisco church) about future performances by the famous folk group of that name. Good *peña* at *Casa del Corregidor*, C Murillo 1040 (T 363633), dinner show Mon-Thur, no cover charge, Fri and Sat *peña* US$4, colonial atmosphere, traditional music and dance (see also under **Places to eat**); nearby is *La Luna*, Oruro y Murillo, great live bands, contemporary music. See under **Places to eat** for *Los Escudos*. Another *peña* is *Marko Tambo* on C Jaén, US$7 (all inc) repeatedly rec (also sells woven goods). Indian dance halls, eg on Max Paredes, should only be visited in the company of Bolivians. If you wish to learn a local instrument, contact *Academia 'Walisuma'*, Av Apumalla 512 (old Cemetery District between José M Asin and José M Aliaga): Pedro Mar teaches bi-lingual courses, English/Spanish, for *quena*, *zampoña* and *charango*.

Good salsa disco at *El Loro en su Salsa*, on Rosendo Gutiérrez on corner of Av 6 de Agosto, open Thur, Fri and Sat pm (salsa lessons at *Gym Cec*, Illampu 868, p 1, T 310158, US$4/hr). *Bar Socavón*, Aspiazu y 20 de Octubre 2172, Sopocachi, T 353998, has live rock music Thur-Sat, music videos Wed, very popular. On C Belisario Salinas in Sopocachi Bajo, is *Piano Bar*, cosy, with a fireplace, live piano music, good drinks and snacks. On the same street in *Michelob*, live music, rec; and *Caras y Caretas*, live music, food, good atmosphere. *Café Montmarte*, Fernando Guachalla, 399 y 20 de Octubre, next to

Alliance Française, good French menu, set lunch US$4, bar with live music Thur, Fri, Sat. Excellent jazz at *Marius Club*, Presbitero Medina y Salazar (nr Plaza Avaroa). *Planet – the Funky Nachos Bar*, Prol Ecuador 2638 (Montículo), Wed-Sat from 2100, rock and grunge, Mexican food; *Bavaria*, Av 20 de Octubre, Plaza Avaroa, German-run, Tues-Sat from 1830, Sun lunchtime, good but expensive food; *Pig and Whistle*, Goitia 155, serves Guinness and a selection of beers and whiskies; *Green Bar*, Av Belisario Salinas 596, very small, interesting bar. Local radio station, *Radio Fides*, C Sanjines y Sucre, Andean music on Thur, when it is open to public (2000, US$0.75), not all year round, check in advance, T 359191.

Teatro Municipal has a regular schedule of plays, opera, ballet and classical concerts, at Sanjines y Indaburo. Next door is the new **Teatro Municipal de Camera**, a small studio-theatre which shows small-scale productions of dance, drama, music and poetry. There are some good **cinemas**, films being mainly in English with Spanish subtitles. The excellent Cinemateca Boliviana, Pichincha y Indaburo, is La Paz's art film centre with festivals, courses, etc, US$1.20, students US$0.60. **Casa Municipal de la Cultura 'Franz Tamayo'**, almost opp Plaza San Francisco, hosts a variety of exhibitions, paintings, sculpture, photography, videos, etc, most of which are free. The **Palacio Chico** (Ayacucho y Potosí, in old Correo), operated by the Secretaría Nacional de Cultura, also has exhibitions (good for modern art), concerts and ballet. It is also in charge of many regional museums. Listings available in Palacio Chico.

There are clown and mime shows in Parque del Ejército on Sun, colourful and popular; the Parque Central has a children's amusement park, US$0.20.

● **Hospitals & medical services**

Clínica del Accidentado, Plaza Uyuni 1351, T 328632/321888 offers first aid. Efficient and well run nursing homes such as *Clínica Americana* (Av 14 de Septiembre 78, T 783509), *Clínica Alemana* (6 de Agosto 2821, T 323023/327521/373676, good), *Clínica Rengel* (T 390792/8), *Clínica Santa María*, Av 6 de Agosto 2487, efficient and not too expensive, *Clínica del Sur*, Av Hernando Siles y C Siete, Obrajes. *Red Cross* opp Mercado Camacho will give inoculations if required, T 323642. *The Methodist Hospital* (12th block of Obrajes, T 783809, take 'A' *micro* from the Prado) runs clinic at US$5, telephone for appointment.

Dentists: Dr and Dra Osorio at *Hostal Austria*, Yanacocha 531. Dr Horacio M Rosso, Av 20 de Octubre, Edif Guadalquivir, T 35475, his wife speaks German, rec. Also rec: Dr Benjamín Calvo

Paz, Edif Illimani, Av Arce esq Campos, T 343706, and Dra Esperanza Eid, Edif Libertad, Potosí, p 9, No 909, both speak English. Tourist Office has a list of doctors and dentists who speak foreign languages.

Doctors: contact your embassy for rec doctor who speaks your language. Check that any medical equipment used is sterilized. *Dr Ricardo Udler*, Edif Mcal de Ayacucho, C Loayza, T 360393/327046, speaks very good German, rec. *Dr César H Moreno*, Pinilla 274, Edif Pinilla, T 433805/792665 (home), rec. *Dr Eduardo Fernández*, Edif Av, Av 16 de Julio, p 9, T 370385 (surgery)/795164 (home), speaks English, US$30 for consultation, rec.

Health and hygiene: malaria pills and yellow fever vaccination, US$15.50 inc certificate are available at *Centro Piloto de Salva*, Av Montes y Basces, T 369141, about 10 mins walk from Plaza San Francisco, N of the main bus station, rec as helpful and friendly. *Laboratorio Inti*, Socabaya 266, rec for vaccines (human immunoglobulin, cholera, typhoid, rabies vaccine – but make sure you know precisely how it should be administered). Tampons may be bought at most *farmacias* and supermarkets; others say they are impossible to find, especially outside La Paz. The daily paper, *Presencia*, lists chemists/pharmacies on duty (*de turno*). For contact lenses, *Optaluis*, Comercio 1089, a stock of 5,000 lenses, inc 'semiduros'.

● **Language schools**

Centro Boliviano Americano (address under **Libraries** below) US$140 for 2 months, 1½ hrs tuition each afternoon. *Alliance Française* (see also below). *Fastalk*, T 812341, offers Spanish and Portuguese courses, 1 week or 1 month, 3 hrs a day; *Instituto de La Lengua Española*, C 14 esq Aviador No 180, Achumani, T 796074, expensive, rec. Private Spanish lessons from: Alice, T 783064; William, T 340676/812341 and Cecilia T 365428; *María Isabel Daza*, Murillo 1046, p 3, T 360769, US$3/hr, individual or group lessons, speaks English and Danish, rec. For English language teaching try *Pan American English Centre*, Edif Avenida, p 7, Av 16 de Julio 1490, T 340 796, Casilla 5244, native speakers only, minimum stay 3 months; similarly Goethe-Institut, Alliance Française, CBA and foreign schools.

● **Laundromats**

Wash and dry, 6-hr service, at *Gelmi-Lava-Sec*, 20 de Octubre 2019, suite 9, T 352930, helpful service, US$1.40 for 1 kg; *Lavandería Cinco Estrellas*, 20 de Octubre 1114, US$3 for 3 kg. *Limpieza Rosario*, Av Manco Kapac, nr Hotel Andes, highly rec; *Lavandería Bandel*, Av Mcal Santa Cruz 1032, local 10, T 353563; *Limpieza Finesse*, Illampu 865, good but closed Sat pm. Normally leave laundry early morning and collect same evening. Sra Elena Aranda offers laundry and repairs service, meets people on ground floor of Post Office.

● **Libraries**

Centro Boliviano Americano (CBA), Parque Zenón Iturralde 121, T 351627/342582 (10 mins walk from Plaza Estudiante down Av Arce), has public library and recent US papers (Mon-Wed 0900-1230, 1500-1930, till 2000 Thur and Fri). *USIS* has lending library and 2nd-hand paperbacks. *Alliance Française*, F Guachalla 399 y Av 20 de Octubre, T 324075 (open Mon-Fri 1000-1200, 1500-1930), good for French newspapers and magazines. *Goethe-Institut*, Av 6 de Agosto 2118, T 374453 (Mon and Wed, 0900-1200, 1500-2000, Tues and Thur 1500-2000, Fri 0900-1200, 1500-1900), excellent library, recent papers in German, CDs, cassettes and videos free on loan.

● **Places of worship**

Protestant Community Church (inter-denominational), in English, American Co-operative School, C 10, No 7825, Calacoto (T 795639 or 792052). Sunday service at 1100, but there are lots of activities during the week. Anglican-Episcopalian services are held at the Community Church on the 3rd Sun of each month.

Synagogues: C Landaeta 330 (Sat am services only); Colegio Boliviano Israëlito, Cañada Strongest 1846 for Fri service.

● **Post & telecommunications**

Post Office: Correo Central, Av Mcal Santa Cruz y Oruro (Mon-Sat 0800-2200, Sun 0900-1200 only). Stamps are sold only at the post office. Good philately section on 1st floor. There are a number of shops selling good postcards, etc. Poste Restante keeps letters for 3 months, good service, no charge. Procedure for sending parcels: all is arranged downstairs (open office hours only, Mon-Fri 0800-1200, 1430-1830); have contents inspected by customs, then seal parcel with glue, US$1 for each parcel. Find out the price of postage before mailing parcels as the service is very expensive. Don't forget moth balls (difficult to buy – try C Sagárnaga) for textile items. To collect parcels costs at least US$0.50. Express postal service is on the top floor, expensive. **DHL**: Av Mcal Santa Cruz 1297; **UPS**, Mercado 1448, T 360687, F 391072.

Telecommunications: Entel (T 367474) office for telephone calls is at Ayacucho 267 (the only one open on Sun), and in Edif Libertad, C Potosí. Long wait for incoming calls. Fax also from Ayacucho 267. Many small offices throughout the city, with quicker service.

● **Shopping**

Look around and bargain first. There are good jewellery stores throughout the city (eg *Joyería*

Cosmos, Handal Center, Loc 13, Socabaya y Av 16 de Julio, Inca and Bolivian designs in gold and silver, colonial objects; *Joyería Kings*, 16 de Julio 1636, in *Hotel Sucre Palace*, specializing in fine silver) but visit the gold factories for lower prices and special orders. There is inexpensive silver and jewellery in the little cabinets outside Lanza market on Av Santa Cruz. Up Sagárnaga, by the side of San Francisco church (behind which are many handicraft stalls in the Mercado Artesanal), are booths and small stores with interesting local items of all sorts, best value on Sun am when prices are reduced. The lower end of Sagárnaga is best for antiques. At Sagárnaga 177 is an entire gallery of handicraft shops: *Artesanía Nacional Tiwanaku*, for paintings, silver jewellery and woven goods. Upstairs is *Artesanía Sajama*, rec for woollens. *Millma*, Sagárnaga 225, and in *Hotel Radisson*, for alpaca sweaters (made in their own factory) and antique and rare textiles. *Wari* on Sagárnaga will make to measure very quickly, English spoken, prices reasonable; also *Toshy* on Sagárnaga for top quality knitwear. *Artesanía Sorata*, Linares 862, and Sagárnaga 311, 0900-1930, Mon-Sat, specializes in dolls, sweaters and weavings made by a women's cooperative and handmade textiles. For musical instruments: *Rumillajta*, one of the Galería shops adjacent to the San Francisco church entrance; many shops in Linares, eg *Sumaj Supay*, No 851, also sell woollen goods, also *Coral* at No 852 (very good waistcoats, rugs, etc.). Alpaca goods are about 50% dearer than in Puno; sweaters are much more expensive than Peru (beware of moths in woollen goods). The maximum you can bargain prices down is 20%. Handmade clothing for children is good value. Most shops close Sat pm and Sun. Very cheap rubber stamps are made on Sagárnaga, to your own, or local designs. See also the 'witchcraft market' on Calles Melchor Jiménez, and Linares, which cross C Santa Cruz above San Francisco, fascinating items for sale.

Artículos Regionales in Plaza de los Estudiantes is rec. *Suma Ampara*, Av Villazón 1958, wide variety of woven goods, but prices not as low as in street markets. The rec *Casa Fisher* (see Cochabamba **Shopping**) has an outlet in Handal Center, Store No 2, Calles Mcal Santa Cruz y Socabaya, T/F 392948. Antique stores at El Prado 1615, Javier Núñez de Arco downstairs, his father upstairs, nice items, very expensive, also old photographs.

The Indian market is a good place for ponchos and local handicrafts. Many Indian objects are sold nr Av Buenos Aires, and Indian musical instruments on C Granier, nr the General Cemetery. On C Los Andes, above Buenos Aires, there are several embroidery shops. At Gallardo 1080, 1 block above Buenos Aires, there is the small workshop of the late master mask-maker, Antonio Viscarra, now run by his daughter and son-in-law. Costume, mask and trinket shops for Gran Poder abound above Buenos Aires. Food market is the Mercado Camacho (Camacho y Bolívar). The Tourist Office has a full list of all markets.

Shopping Norte, Potosí y Socabaya, is a new, modern mall with restaurants and expensive merchandise.

Bookshops: large stock of English, French and German books, and US magazines, at *Los Amigos del Libro*, Mercado 1315, also Edif Alameda, Av 16 de Julio (1 block from *Plaza Hotel*) and El Alto airport, rec; they also sell a few tourist maps of the region from Puno to the Yungas, and walking-tour guides. Amigos del Libro will ship books. *Gisbert*, Comercio 1270, books, maps, stationery, will ship overseas, rec. *Multi-Libro*, Loayza 233, T 391996, small, good for maps, politics, religion, psychology etc, open till 2100 Mon-Fri, and am Sat and Sun. *El Umbral*, Potosí 1375, T 361282, and *Hisbol*, Zapata 178, for academic subjects. *Librería La Paz*, Colón y Ballivián (wide selection of maps). Historian Antonio Paredes-Candia has a kiosk selling rare historical works on Villazón, opp San Andrés University. *Librería Martínez Acchini*, Arce 2132, good for technical books. There are 2nd-hand stalls on Av Ismael Montes; there are occasional book fairs on the Prado. German books available at Goethe Institut (see above).

Cycle spares: try the shop at the Velódromo in Alto Irpavi, about 10 km out of town; the cheap cycle chains made in India and sold in shops in the centre of La Paz are not rec.

Films: any film can be developed at a decent developer. It is normal to get a free film, album or 15 x 21cm print. *Foto Visión*, 6 de Agosto 2044 and other branches, cheap, good prints. *Foto Linares*, Mercado y Loayza, expensive but best for anything out of the ordinary. *Linares* and *Kavlin*, Potosí 1130, develop black and white. *Agfa Centre*, Loayza 250, for slide film,

US$4. Fuji and Kodak slide film is more expensive. All slide film should be developed 'solo revelado', ie without mounts because they tend to get scratched, about US$2/film. **Repairs** at Av Sánchez Lima 2178 by Rolando Calla C, rec, just ring bell (1400-1700), there is no sign.

Maps: Instituto Geográfico Militar head office is at Estado Mayor Gen, Av Saavedra Final, Miraflores, open 0900-1100, 1500-1700, take passport to purchase maps immediately; or go to Oficina 5, Juan XXIII 100, cul-de-sac off Rodríguez between Murillo y Linares, 0830-1200, 1430-1800, maps delivered within 24 hrs. Topographic maps cost US$5.25/sheet, US$4 for a photocopy (scale 1:50,000) and US$8, US$7 photocopy (scale 1:250,000). A 3-sheet map of La Paz costs US$5.25/sheet; a 3-sheet map of La Paz Department, inc Lake Titicaca, costs US$9.20; 1-sheet national communications map, US$6; 4-sheet country map, political 1988, 1:1,500,000 US$10.50; 9-sheet hydrographical map, 1990 1:1,000,000, US$17. Liam P O'Brien has produced a 1:135,000, full colour, shaded relief topographic map of the Cordillera Real, US$10/copy, from 28 Turner Terrace, Newtonville, MA02160, USA (add US$2 for shipping), or from map distributors (Bradt, Stanfords, etc). Walter Guzmán Córdova colour maps of Choro-Takesi-Yunga Cruz, Mururata-Illimani, Huayna Potosí and Sajama, available from bookshops. The German Alpine Club (Deutscher Alpenverien) produces 2 good maps of Cordillera Real North and South, best bought before arrival. Senac (the national road service) publishes a Red Vial 1989 map, which is probably the best, but is still inaccurate, about US$4.50 from the office on 8th floor of Ministerio de Transporte y Comunicaciones, Av Mcal Santa Cruz, tall building behind Correo, open till 1800, have to show passport. Also reported as inaccurate are the maps of the Automóvil Club Boliviano. Maps are generally hard to find. Maps are sold at Ichthus bookshop on the Prado, No 1800; also at Librería La Paz and Amigos del Libro (see page 270).

Sports

Golf: there are two golf clubs (Mallasilla, the world's highest, and Pinos). Non-members can play at Mallasilla on weekdays: club hire is possible, green free, clubs, balls, and caddie US$37, the course is empty on weekdays, no need to book; it is in good condition and beautiful. After your round have a drink in the small outside bar.

Snooker/pool: *San Luis*, Edif México, 2do Sótano, C México 1411, *Picco's*, Edif 16 de Julio, Av 16 de Julio 1566, both places rec for good tables and friendly atmosphere.

There are two tennis clubs (La Paz Tennis and Sucre Tennis). Football is popular and played on Wed and Sun at the Siles Stadium in Miraflores, two clubs (Micro A); there are reserved seats. YMCA sportsground and gymnasium, opp the University of San Andrés, Av Villazón, and clubhouse open to the public, Av 20 de Octubre 1839 (table tennis, billiards, etc); regular meetings Tues and Thurs 1930 of a mountaineering group which runs weekend excursions. See also under **Skiing** and **Mountaineering** under **Excursions** below.

● Tour companies & travel agents

Crillon Tours, Av Camacho 1223, Casilla 4785 (T 374566, F 391039), with 24-hr ATM for cash on credit cards; in USA, 1450 South Bayshore Dr, suite 815, Miami, FL 33131, T (305) 358-5353, F (305) 372-0054, joint scheduled tours with Lima arranged; see also under **Lake Titicaca**, page 282; *Transturin*, Camacho 1321 esq Colón (T 328560/363654, F 391162, Telex 2301 TRTURIN BV), and Mcal Santa Cruz 1295, p 3, T 342164: these two agencies offer full travel services, with tours ranging from La Paz to the whole country; full details of their Lake Titicaca services will be found on page 284. *Turismo Balsa*, Capitán Ravelo 2077 (T 357817, F 391310) and Av 16 de Julio 1650 (T 354049), PO Box 5889, city and local tours (rec), see also under **Puerto Pérez**, page 282; *Turisbus* (Illampu 702, Casilla 442, T 325348/369542, F 375532), helpful, trekking

equipment rented, agent for Peruvian railways, ENAFER, tickets (to Puno and Cusco – US$12 and US$31, also local and Bolivian tours), rec; *Exprinter*, Edif Herrman, Plaza Venezuela (also operates exchange facilities, helpful) to Cusco, US$28, 21 hrs, 3 times a week, via Desaguadero with a stop in Puno; *Magri Turismo*, Av 16 de Julio 1490, 5th floor, T 323954/341201, F 366309, Amex representative: gives TCs against American Express card, but cannot give cash or exchange TCs, offers all other Amex emergency services and clients' mail, rec for tours in Bolivia, travel services; *Pachamama Tours*, Av Mcal Santa Cruz y Colón, Galería Ed Litoral, subsuelo, of 17, T 322311, rec for tours of La Paz, Tiwanaku, Titicaca, etc, also arranges tours throughout Bolivia; *Diana Tours*, Sagárnaga 328, T 340356/375374/350252, F 360831, some English spoken, good tour to Coroico, cheapest for Tiwanaku and buses to Perú; *Titikaka Tours*, Loayza between Riva and Camacho, good for flights; *Tawa Tours*, Sagárnaga 161 and Rosenda Gutiérrez 701, T 325796, French-run, run jungle tours to their own camp as well as the Salt Lake areas, friendly, good guides (also charter flights to Europe and USA); *Shima Tours*, Potosí 1310, very helpful, good for flight tickets; *Combi*, Illampu next to *Res Copacabana*, classical tours and transport to Copacabana; *Transamazonas*, Edif V Centenario, p 3, Av 6 de Agosto above lower end of new underpass, T 350411, F 360923, Casilla 14551, German-run, top-end adventure tourism, English, German, French, Spanish spoken; *Fremen*, Plaza Abaroa, T 327073/ 376336, F 367329, own Flotel in Trinidad for jungle cruises in the Beni; *Paititi SRL*, Av 6 de Agosto y Aspiazu, and *Aparthotel Camino Real*, Capitán Ravelo 2123, 0900-1900, T 340108/ 341018/ 353558, F 329625, organizes adventure tours, rec, Javier Palza is helpful and speaks English, German, French, Italian; *Peru Bolivian Tours*, Loayza, Ed Mcal de Ayacucho PB – Of 8, T 363720, F 365845; *America Tours*, Av 16 de Julio 1490, T 328584, F 374204, Casilla 2568, Swiss-Bolivian owned,

cultural and ecotourism trips to many parts of the country, English, German, French spoken; *Andes Expediciones*, Plaza Alonso de Mendoza, Edif Santa Ana, p 3, of 314, T 320901/375240, F 392344, treks and mountaineering to many lesser-known and remote destinations, highly rec, manager Bernardo Guarachi is a very experienced mountain guide; also *Carmoar Tours*, C Bueno 159, which is headed by Günther Ruttger (T/F 340633), has information and maps for the Inca Trail to Coroico, rents trekking gear. For information on and arrangement of climbing and adventure tours, *Colibrí*, Sagárnaga 309, see under **Mountaineering** below. *Reinaldo Pou Munt*, Capitán Ravelo 2401, T 327226, Casilla 13632, expensive, offers excellent tours of the city and environs, speaks English and German; *Nuevo Continente*, Manco Kapac 366, T 373423/812479, rec for trip to Zongo, Clemente is a good driver, cheap service to airport, very friendly and helpful. Many agencies arrange excursions or travel to Perú (Puno, Cusco, Arequipa), as well as local tours. See also names and addresses under 'Exchange Houses', page 266. *Bracha*, T 327472, has details of and sells tickets for trains from Santa Cruz.

NB Flight tickets can be bought more reliably from airlines than through agencies.

● **Tourist offices**
Information office at the bottom end of Av 16 de Julio (Prado) on Plaza del Estudiante on corner with C México, helpful, English and French spoken, ask here for information on train services, free leaflets, map of La Paz US$2.50. Telephone directories in La Paz have economic and tourist information in English on all the provinces.

● **Useful addresses**
Asociación Boliviana de Agencias de Viajes y Turismo, Edif Litoral, Mcal Santa Cruz 1351, Casilla 3967. **Instituto Nacional de Ar-**queología de Bolivia, C Tiwanaku 93.

Immigration: to renew a visa go to Migración Bolivia, Av Camacho 1433 (opp Banco de Santa Cruz), T 379385/370475, Mon-Fri 0900-1200, 1600-1800, fast and efficient.

Tourist Police: Plaza del Estadium, Miraflores, next to *Love City* disco, T 225016, for insurance claims after theft, English spoken, helpful.

YMCA: 20 de Octubre 1839, Casilla 963.

● **Transport**
Local Bus: there are three types of city bus: large Fiat buses run by the city corporation, on fairly limited routes; *micros* (Bluebird-type buses), which charge US$0.18 in the centre, US$0.24 from outside centre; and *Kombis* (minivans), US$0.20/0.34, but quicker than *micros*.
Car hire: cars may be hired direct from **Imbex**, Av Montes 522, T 316895, F 379884, well maintained Suzuki jeeps (from US$50/day, inc 100 km free for 4-person 4WD, highly rec); **National**, F Zuazo 1935, T/F 376581, rec; **Avis** at Martin Travel, Plaza del Estudiante 1920; **Rent-a-Car International**, F Suazo 1942, T 357061; **Kolla Motors**, Rosendo Gutiérrez 502, T 341660/351701 who have well-maintained 4WD Toyota jeeps (which seat 6), insurance and gasoline extra. **Petita Rent-a-car**, Cañada Strongest 1857-A, T 379182, F 322596, Swiss owners Ernesto Hug and Aldo Rezzonico, rec for well-maintained VW 'beetles' and 4WD jeeps, etc, also offer adventure tours, **Jeeping Bolivia**, German, French, English spoken, rec. **Garage**: for VW and other makes: Ernesto Hug, Av Jaime Freyre 2326, T 342279 (see also **Car hire** above) highly rec. **Car Park** on corner of Ingavi and Sanjines, US$1.75 for 24 hrs, safe and central. **Motorcycle rental**: Moto Rent, Av Busch 1255, Miraflores Norte, T 357289, 650 Kawasaki endurance type, US$50/day unlimited mileage, US$250/week. **Taxis**: normal taxis charge US$0.40, radio taxis

US$1.20-2.20, for short trips within city limits. *Trufis* are fixed route collective taxis which charge US$0.28-0.40 pp within city limits. Taxi drivers are not tipped. Don't let the driver turn the lights out at night. Radio taxis, many companies, eg Alfa T 322427, La Rápida 392323 (standard fare in centre US$1.45, to suburbs US$2.80; good value for tours for 3 people, negotiate price). Eduardo Figueroa, T 786281, taxi driver and travel agent, rec. Adolfo Monje Palacios, in front of *Hotel El Dorado* or T 354384 highly rec for short or long trips. Oscar Vera, Simón Aguirre 2158, Villa Copacabana, La Paz, T 230453, specializes in trips to the Salar de Uyuni and the Western Cordillera, speaks English, rec.

Air El Alto, above La Paz, the highest commercial airport in the world (4,018m) connected to the city by motorway, T 810122/3. A taxi between the centre and airport takes about 30 mins, US$7 but may be negotiated down; current prices, inc luggage, should be on display at the airport exit (enquire at the tourist office in town, or at the airport). Cotranstur minibuses, white with 'Cotranstur' and 'Aeropuerto' written on the side and back, go from Plaza del Estudiante, anywhere on the Prado and Av Mcal Santa Cruz to the airport between 0800-0830 to 1900-2000, US$0.55 (allow about 1 hr), best to have little luggage, departures from the airport every 5 mins or so; colectivos from Plaza Isabel La Católica charge US$3.45 pp, carrying 4 passengers. There is a duty-free shop. Bank in international departures hall will change cash, rates OK. Enlace ATM for Visa and Mastercard. The international departures hall is the main concourse, with all check-in desks and is the hall for all domestic arrivals and departures. Small tourist office at the Airport, some maps available, English spoken, helpful (when staffed). The coffee shop is inexpensive and serves good breakfasts. **Services** LAB, Aero Sur (T 371833), TAM and Kantuta (T 390290) fly to the main cities and towns. Fares are comparatively low for internal flights. (For details, see under destinations.)

Trains It is imperative to check times because ENFE has been privatized and changes can be expected. For this reason, schedules given in the text (under destinations) should be treated with caution. For information T 353510/352510/373069. Towns served are Oruro, Potosí, Sucre, Cochabamba, Villazón, Arica in Chile and intermediate stops. Micros which go to the station are A, M, N, P, 130, 131, C. The ticket office, at the rear of the building at the N end of main station, opens 0700, but get there at least 2 hrs beforehand.

To **Villazón** (minimum 20 hrs) for Argentina, dep Fri at 1300, *Expreso del Sur*, via Oruro (US$6.30 pullman, US$7.40 salón), Uyuni (US$11.20/12.70), Atocha (US$12.70/14.40), Tupiza (US$14.40/16.50), Villazón (US$16.40/18.60). Book ahead at central station; queue at 0600 on previous day (queuing numbers are given out), take passport. If all train tickets are sold out, go to station 2 hrs before departure for returned tickets, try Exprinter travel agency, try and board train anyway and pay the guard, or fly to Tarija and then go by road to Villazón.

Railways to/from the Coast (1) By the Southern Railway of Peru from Arequipa to Puno, on Lake Titicaca then by road to La Paz, incorporating if desired one of the lake crossings described below under **Lake Titicaca** and **Crossing the Peruvian Frontier**.

(2) **La Paz-Arica International Railway**, 447 km: In the Bolivian section the line climbs to El Alto and then runs SW to Viacha (Km 32) the junction of lines to Antofagasta, Guaqui (freight only) and Villazón. It coninues to Corocoro, the copper mining town, crosses the Río Desaguadero at Calacoto (Km 98) and then runs SW to the border at Charaña (Km 208 – see below) a very cold place to change trains or wait for a bus. The mountain peaks visible inc Illimani, Huayna-Potosí, Mururata, and many others. For description of the Chilean part, see Chile, **The Desert North. NB** Chilean pesos can be bought in La Paz at good rates.

There is a Bolivian *ferrobus* service straight through to Arica, on Mon and Fri at 0715, arrives 1935, US$52 pullman, US$96 *especial*, inc breakfast and lunch, meals and refreshments after this charged extra ('bill in bolivianos, paid for in US dollars, change given in Chilean pesos'), max 20 kg baggage is free, extra charge for excess, worth it for the views, change at Arica station (poor rates), book ticket 1-2 weeks in advance at Estación Central, especially in high season (when extra trains are added). Alternatively take a train to **Charaña** on Wed from Viacha at 0300 (no chance of seeing the spectacular scenery), then change to a colectivo to Arica (US$10), or, on 2nd and 4th Wed of each month a train leaves Charaña at 0930, arriving Arica at 1800 (every Wed Jan-Mar). The return from Charaña to Viacha dep at 1600. Fares: Viacha-Charaña: US$3 pullman. Bus Charaña-La Paz US$9.75.

(3) **La Paz-Antofagasta**, by Antofagasta and Bolivia Railway, 1,173 km, definitely a trip for the adventurous who are impervious to cold at night, or blazing sunshine at tedious daytime border changes. The train is full of contrabandistas, impromptu folk music, and the ride is very rough and subject to long delays. The train starts at Oruro, which you must reach by bus, then train as far as Calama in Chile, then by bus (240 km) to Antofagasta. This, the most S of the three railway routes connecting La Paz with the Pacific coast, passes through magnificent scenery. The

train leaves Oruro at 1930 on Sun only (schedules often change), reaching Uyuni sometime after 0230 on Mon (US$4.10 Oruro-Uyuni), then there is a wait of up to 11 hrs, then another 4 hrs to Avaroa, the border (US$5 Uyuni-border, US$6.65 Oruro-border); 1 hr to change trains, then 40 mins to Ollagüe, where Chilean customs take 4-12 hrs. After that it is 6 uncomfortable hrs to Calama (US$18 Oruro-Calama, US$5 border-Calama). In Bolivia, seats can be reserved as far as the border; tickets are sold in Oruro 0730-1100 on day of departure, in Uyuni 30 mins before train arrives, or at 1800 the day before. Restaurant car and waiter service. If taking your own food, eat fresh things first as the Chileans do not allow dairy produce, teabags (of any description), fruit or vegetables to be brought in. There are no exchange facilities at the border. It is advisable to buy Chilean currency and sell bolivianos before journey, or on the train. All passports are collected and stamped in the rear carriage, they should be ready for collection after 1-2 hrs; queue for your passport, no names are called out (beware, as the train goes down to Chile, carriages are added; the reverse happens in the other direction).

Buses For information, T 367275/367274; buses to: **Oruro, Potosí, Sucre, Cochabamba, Santa Cruz, Tarija** and **Villazón**, leave from the main terminal at Plaza Antofagasta (micros 2, M, CH or 130), see under each destination for details. Beware of taxi rip-offs, false police and theft from buses as they pull in at the bus station. The terminal (open 0700-2300) has a post office, ENTEL, restaurant, luggage store and agencies, such as Turisbus, Diana, Vicuña (cheaper than their offices in town). Touts find passengers the most convenient bus and are paid commission by the bus company.

Buses to **Sorata, Copacabana** and **Tiahuanaco** do not leave from the bus station but from the Cemetery district. Companies located here inc Flota Copacabana, Manco Kapac, 2 de Febrero, Ingavi, Trans Perla Andina. To get to the Cemetery district, take any bus or kombi marked 'Cementerio' going up C Santa Cruz (US$1); the route is Santa Cruz, Max Paredes, Garita de Lima, Mariano Bautista, Plaza Félix Reyes Ortiz/Tomás Katari (look out for the cemetery arch on your left). On Plaza Reyes Ortiz are Manco Kapac, rec (T 350033) and 2 de Febrero (T 377181) for Copacabana and Tiquina. From the Plaza go up Av Kollasuyo and at the 2nd street on the right (Manuel Bustillos) is the terminal for kombis to Huatajata and Huarina, and buses for Sorata (eg Trans Unificada). Several micros (20, J, 10) and kombis (223, 252, 270, 7) go up Kollasuyo; look for 'Kollasuyo' in the windscreen in most, but not all, cases.

Buses to **Coroico and the Yungas** leave from Villa Fátima (25 mins by micros B,V,X,K, 131, 135, or 136, or *trufis* 2 or 9, which pass Pérez Velasco coming down from Plaza Mendoza, and get off at the service station, C Yanacachi 1434).

International buses: to Buenos Aires, daily at 1630, San Roque, T 329769, via Yacuiba US$125; or 1700, San Lorenzo, T 328911, US$130, either takes 2½ days. Alternatively, go to Villazón and change buses in Argentina. To **Arica** via the frontier at Tambo Quemado and Chungará the only reliable service is at 2030 Tues and Fri, US$22, with Litoral, T 358603 (office No 19 bus terminal), 18 hrs. To Arica via the frontier at Charaña and Visviri in stages (no direct service), Senobus (C Hujutri, 400m from train station in direction of Cementerio), Tues, Fri, Sat evenings (US$11) or (cheaper) El Cariñoso. In Charaña take taxi to Visviri (US$0.65), then colectivo taxi to Arica US$13. It is a beautiful, exhausting trip, but doing it in stages, rather than straight through, involves extra waiting at the border, all companies involve several changes of bus, 18 dusty hrs. Military checks can be expected both sides of the frontier. To **Iquique**, Tues, Sat and Sun 1700, US$32, 22 hrs, Litoral. To **Tacna**, also with Litoral, Thur and Sat, 0700, US$20, 10 hrs, road repaired 1996 (there are no Bolivian customs or immigration at the border for exit stamp, Peruvian entry is given in Tacna). To **Cusco**, Cruz del Sur, 3 a week, US$18, 'not luxurious'. Colectivos and agencies to **Puno** daily with different companies (eg Colectur) most easily booked through travel agencies, US$13-15.50, 10 hrs. **NB** Of the various La Paz-Puno services, only Transturin does not make you change to a Peruvian bus once over the border. Exprinter/Cruz del Sur, T 362708, go via Desaguadero Tues, Thur, Sat 0800, US$7.20. For luxury and other services to Peru see under **Lake Titicaca** below.

By **Road from La Paz to the Pacific Coast** There are 2 routes: the shortest and most widely used is the road from La Paz to Arica via border towns of Tambo Quemado (Bolivia) and Chungará (Chile). The majority of Bolivia's imports, inc foreign cars, jeeps and large vehicles from Chile's Pacific sea-ports, Arica and Iquique, are brought to La Paz by truck via this route. From La Paz take the main highway S towards Oruro to **Patacamaya** (104 km – about 1½ hrs from central La Paz on good paved road – 130 km N of Oruro); Sun market, no tourist items; **G** *Los Angeles*, basic, other cheap accommodation and restaurants. At Patacamaya turn right (W towards the cordillera) at green road sign to Puerto Japones on the Río Desaguadero (sign only visible coming from La Paz), thence to Tambo Quemado. The sections either side of the Río Desaguadero are being upgraded and paved, due for completion (except for a bridge over the river) July 1996. When complete, the La Paz-Arica journey should be less than 6 hrs (not counting border formalities). Take extra petrol (none available after Chilean border until Arica) food and water. Seek advice before travelling during or just after rainy season (Dec-April).

The journey is, in itself, worthwhile; the views, particularly to the W, of the volcanoes in distant Lauca National Park, Chile (see Chile – **The Desert North** (1) are breathtaking (Tom Clough, La Paz).

Midway between Patacamaya and Tambo Quemado is the town of Curahuara de Carangas (Alojamiento on plaza, G, dirty, no electricity). Watch for speed restrictions upon entering town past military school. Possible overnight stop in Sajama Village (4,200m) 22 km E of Tambo Quemado at the foot of Mt Sajama (see **South from La Paz – Excursions from Oruro**). Bolivian customs is at Lagunas, 12 km further on, a popular 'truck-stop'. Petrol available. Restaurant/bar Lagunas offers cheap set menu, helpful, friendly. Owner can usually find accommodation somewhere in the village, US$1, take your own sleeping bag, extra blankets, warm clothing. Facilities are at best very basic; you may well be sleeping on a straw mattress on a dirt floor. No water or electricity, gas lamps or candles are usual. It may be possible for men to sleep at Puesto Militar, beside the new road, 100m from village. Nights can be bitterly cold and very windy. In the daytime there are spectacular views of nearby snowcapped Mt Sajama.

The Bolivian border control at Tambo Quemado, 10km from Lagunas, consists of 'tránsito' (highway police), immigration, and international police. Approximately US$4.50/'particular' (private non-commercial) vehicle. Check with Automóvil Club Boliviano, La Paz for any special documents which may be required, depending on the registration of your vehicle. Bolivian vehicles require a temporary Export Certificate in order to leave Bolivia (to be obtained in La Paz prior to travel), and Temporary Import Certificate approx US$2.50 from customs at Chungará on entering Chile. Best to change a small amount of currency into Chilean pesos in La Paz. Temporary Import/Export Certificates are normally valid 90 days. It is worth double checking all documents inc visa requirements with the Consulate of Chile in La Paz before travelling. From Tambo Quemado there is a stretch of about 7 km of 'no-man's land' before you reach the Chilean frontier at Chungará. Here the border crossing, which is set against the most spectacular scenic backdrop of Lake Chungará and Volcán Parinacota is strictly controlled. Open: 0800-1200; 1430-1800. Ex-

pect a long wait behind lines of lorries; avoid Sun; best to travel midweek. Drivers must fill in 'Relaciones de Pasajeros', US$0.25 from kiosk at border, giving details of driver, vehicle and passengers. Border control consists of Ministry of Agriculture and Livestock (SAG – control of animals entering Chile is rigidly enforced; do not take any fruit, vegetables, or dairy products into Chile). Immigration, Customs and Police.

From Chungará, the road is paved; the first 50 km section to Putre goes through spectacular Lauca National Park. Look out for some treacherous bends as the road descends dramatically to sea-level where it meets the Pan Amerian Highway (Route 5) 12 km N of Arica.

An alternative, on which there are no trucks, is to go by good road from La Paz via Viacha to Santiago de Machaco (130 km, petrol); then 120 km to the border at **Charaña** (**G** Alojamiento Aranda; immigration is behind the railway station, only 30-day permit given on entry), very bad road. In Visviri (Chile) there is no fuel, accommodation, bath or electricity, ask for restaurant and bargain price. From Visviri a regular road runs to Putre, then as above.

A variation from Viacha is take the roads which more-or-less follow the railway to Charaña (4WD essential). On this scenic route, with interesting rock formations, you pass Comanche (see **Excursions**, above) and Gen Campero in the Ciudad de Piedra (nr the football field in Gen Campero is a house which lets a room and has water). From Gen Campero roads go to Gen Pérez, Abarao and Charaña. From this route treks can be made S to the mountains towards Sajama and, from Charaña, to Sajama itself.

TREKKING NEAR LA PAZ

● **Maps** All treks in the Cordillera Real are covered by the map of the Cordillera Real, 1:135,000, Liam O'Brien. Takesi, Choro and Yunga Cruz are covered by the Walter Guzmán Córdova 1:50,000 map; see **Maps** above. There are also the IGM 1:50,000 sheets: Takesi Chojlla 6044 IV; Choro Milluni 5945 II, 6045 III and Coroico; Yunga Cruz Lambate 6044 II and 6044
● **Guidebooks**: Backpacking and Trekking in Peru and Bolivia (6th edition) by Hilary Bradt (published by Bradt, 1995) and Trekking in Bolivia by Yossi Brain (published May 1997 by The Mountaineers).

TAKESI (MINA SAN FRANCISCO TO YANAKACHI)

Start at Ventilla (see **Transport** below), walk up the valley for about 3 hrs passing the rough Choquekhota until the track crosses the river and to the right of the road, there is a falling down brick wall with a map painted on it. The Takesi and Alto Takesi trails start here following the path to the right of the wall. The road continues to Mina San Francisco where the La Reconquistada trek starts. From the wall head up to the right to join excellent stone paving which is Inca or pre-Inca – depending on who you believe – to reach the pass at 4,630m in about an hour. Descend following more paving to *Estancia Takesi* in another hour; possible camping. A couple of km later the path rises right and above the river, passes by a hut marked 'CGI' selling drinks and goes through *Estancia Ekapi*, passing café *Don Pepe* (camping possible) after another 3 hrs. Drop down to a river crossing and then climb out and over a hill before dropping back down to the river and following an aqueduct to the unpleasant mining settlement of Chojlla in 2 hrs. Continue along the road passing through a gate where it is necessary to register and often pay a small 'fee', to Yanakachi which has a number of places to stay and takes another 2 hrs. Buy a minibus ticket on arrival in Yanakachi or be prepared to walk down to the La Paz-Chulumani road for transport in 45 mins. The trek can be done in one long day, especially if you organize a jeep to the start of the trail, but is more relaxing in two – or three if you take it really slowly – though you'll have to carry camping kit. Mules can be hired in Choquekhota for US$8 per day plus up to US$8 for the mulateer.

● **Transport** Take a Palca bus from C Venacio Burgoa esq C Boquerón, San Pedro, 0600 during the week, more often at weekends, and get off at Ventilla, or get a Bolsa Negra, Tres Ríos or Pariguaya bus Mon-Sat 0900 from C Gen Luis Lara esq Venacio Burgoa near Plaza Líbano, San Pedro. Not possible to buy tickets in advance – no ticket office, send someone up between 0700 and 0800 on the day to ensure ticket; drivers may not want to take you just to Ventilla so you may have to pay more, eg up to US$2 which is the fare to Chunavi. Alternatively, take any micro or minibus from central La Paz to Chasquipampa or Ovejuyo and then get on any transport going further, most transport goes to Palca, and get off at Ventilla. If there isn't any transport, haggle with drivers of empty minibuses in Ovejuyo; you should be able to get one to go to Ventilla for about US$10. Alternatively, haggle with a radio taxi in La Paz, it should be possible to get one to go to Ventilla for under US$20. The most comfortable way to get to the start of the trek is to hire a jeep from La Paz to Mina San Francisco for US$50 which takes 1½ to 2 hrs.

CHORO (LA CUMBRE TO COROICO)

Immediately before the road drops down from La Cumbre to start the descent to Los Yungas there is a falling down plastered brick wall on the left which marks the start of the trail. However there is nothing to help you get across the featureless moonscape to the *apacheta* where the trail starts properly. Cloud and bad weather are normal at the 4,700m La Cumbre: follow the left hand of the statue of Christ, take a map and compass or guide to get you to the start of the trail which is then well-signposted. It takes about 4 hrs to get to Achura and then another hour to get to Achapalla Pampa where it is possible to camp; the locals will ask for money or food. After 2 hrs you will reach the Choro bridge. Fill your water bottles, the next 2 hrs until you cross the Río Jacun-Manini are dry. Another dry 3 hrs to Sandallani where it is possible to camp in the carefully-tended garden of a Japanese man who keeps a book with the names of every passing traveller. He likes to see postcards and pictures from other countries. There is good paving down to Villa Esmeralda and another 2 hrs to Chairo. If you've got the money, stay at the 5-star *Hotel Río Selva*, otherwise continue. It is 17 km to Yolosa. Allegedly there is a truck at 0600 but you are unlikely to get there on time. A truck will run if there are enough people willing to pay US$2.25 each. From Yolosa it is 8 km uphill to Coroico with regular transport for US$0.60 pp. It takes 3 days to trek from La Cumbre to Chairo. If you use transport you can get to Coroico (or La Paz) the same day. If you walk from Chario it will take a long day to get to Coroico.

● **Transport** To get to the start take a bus or *camión* from Villa Fátima, but make sure the driver knows you want to get off at La Cumbre. Alternatively, get a radio taxi from central La Paz for about US$12.

YUNGA CRUZ (LAMBATE OR CHUNAVI TO CHULUMANI)

The best but the hardest of the three 'Inca' trails and therefore less popular so there is less litter and begging. From Chunavi follow path left (east) and contour gently up. Camping possible after 2 hrs. Continue along the path staying on left hand side of the ridge to reach Cerro Khala Ciudad (literally, Stone City Mountain,

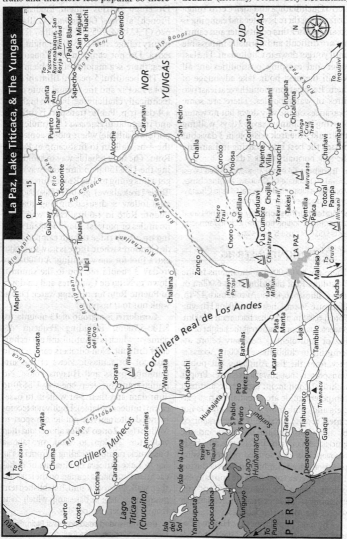

La Paz, Lake Titicaca, & The Yungas

you'll see why). Good paving brings you round the hill to join the path from Lambate. From Lambate head uphill for 2 days through Quircoma and then to Cerro Khala Ciudad after which you descend to join the path from Chunavi. Head N to Cerro Cuchillatuca and then Cerro Yunga Cruz where there is water and camping is possible. After this point water and camping are difficult and normally impossible until you get down to Chulumani. The last water and camping possibilities are all within the next hour, take advantage of them. Each person should have at least two litres of water bottles. There are some clearances on the way down but no water. Starting in Chunavi saves 2 days' walking and makes the trek possible in 3 days but misses the best bits. Starting in Lambate the trek normally takes 5 days.

● **Transport** Take the Pariguaya bus (see Takesi above) to Lambate or Chunavi, all other buses stop in Tres Ríos or Bolsa Negra; 6 hrs to Chunavi by bus, another hour to Lambate.

● **Water purification** Only use iodine-based preparations. Iodine tincture, *iodo* in *farmacias* costs US$0.50: use 5 drops/litre.

MOUNTAINEERING

There are 600 5,000m+ mountains in the Cordillera Real including six at 6,000m or above: Illimani 6,439m, Ancohuma 6,427m, Illampu 6,368m, Chearoco 6,104m, Huayna Potosí 6,088m and Chachacomani 6,000m. A week's acclimatization at the height of La Paz or equivalent is necessary before attempting to climb above 5,000m. Access is easy from the flat Altiplano, but public transport is not always possible. Proper technical equipment, experience and/or a competent guide are essential to cross glaciers and climb snow and ice safely. Do not expect rescue; a system is being organized by the Club Andino Boliviano and the guides' association, but is basically body recovery. Six people died or are missing presumed dead climbing in Bolivia during 1995. However, conditions are normally excellent during the season May-Sept and climbing is far safer than in Scotland in winter, the Alps or the Rockies.

The most popular peak is **Huayna Potosí**, normally climbed in 2 days, including one night camped on a glacier at 5,600m. To get to the start of the normal route take transport to the Zongo Pass as described in **Excursions** above. The *Refugio Huayna Potosí* organizes regular transport plus guides and porters: contact Dr Hugo Berrios (fluent English and French) at *Hotel Continental*, C Illampu 626 (T 323584, 795936), Casilla 731. The luxury refuge costs US$10 per night, food extra. Do not camp in the Zongo Pass area; there is a major theft problem.

The beautiful 5-peaked **Illimani** overlooks La Paz and the normal route is not technically challenging, but it is high and a 4-day trip. Public transport is difficult and irregular to *Estancia Una* (mules and porters available) where most people start the 4-hr walk-in to first camp at Puente Roto. The only reliable way to avoid paying the US$150 jeep fare (one way) is to get a bus going to Tres Ríos or further (see **Takesi trek** above), get off at Paso Pacuani and follow a disused mining road to Puente Roto in 4-6 hrs (carry your kit – no mules or porters). Day 2 is spent moving up a rock ridge to high camp at Nido de Cóndores where there is no water; take extra fuel for snow melting. A 0300 start to day 3 should see you to the summit, down to Nido de Cóndores and on down to Puente Roto for running water. Day 4, walk out to Estancia Una.

Condoriri is a group of 13 mountains, 5,100-5,700m, including Pequeño Alpamayo, which is beautiful and not technically difficult. Non-climbers can go up to Mirador for fantastic views of the surrounding peaks and Huayna Potosí. No public transport, jeep one way US$70 to Tuni dam and then 3-hr walk-in to basecamp (mules available). Highly not recommended alternatives: public transport to Milluni (see **Zongo Valley** above) and then walk for 24 km to Tuni, or take a bus/truck/minibus heading N from La Paz (eg to Lake Titicaca or Huarina or Achacachi) to Patamanta (garage on the left) and then walk 20 km+ to Tuni. Established tent guarding system at basecamp which costs from US$1 per tent per day.

● **Recommended reading** Yossi Brain, Secretario de Andinismo of the Club Andino Boliviano and author of *Climber's Guide to Bolivia* (published in April 1997 by The Mountaineers, Seattle).

Quimza Cruz: still 'the future of Bolivian mountaineering' because few people make the effort to get there despite the easy access. Roads go within 30 mins of glaciers and the area is covered in mining tracks. Rock climbing on granite near Mocaya (6 km after Viloco), beautiful lakeside campsites, snow peaks up to 5,800m, including Gigante Grande, and trekking possibilities, eg Viloco to Mina Caracoles in 2-3 days. It takes a day to get in and another to get out. Buses to Quimsa Cruz take 12 hrs, Santa Cruz, 0700 Mon-Sat, not possible to book seat, get there at least an hour before. A jeep can do the river in under 7 hrs for about US$300 but make sure the driver knows where to go. One driver who does is Vitaliano Ramos (T La Paz 416013). There are a number of accesses if you have a jeep: La Paz-Oruro road to Konani at Km 149 (garage – check everything and fill up tank plus extra containers with petrol) and turn left. After Caxata the Quime road is red due to the rock and there is a left turn-off which goes down and continues to Viloco. Alternatively, take the road to Ventilla then turn off up and left, through Tres Ríos and down to Lambate and then follow the Río Bajo to Araca (dry season only – wet season go via Quime).

For the Western Cordillera with the peaks of Sajama, Parinacota and Pomerape, see under Sajama, page 300, below.

The Cordillera Apolobamba, the N extension of the Cordillera Real, with many 5,000m-plus peaks, can be reached by public transport from La Paz, the main starting out points being **Charazani**, see page 289 (bus from C Reyes Cardona, Cemetery district, Wed 1100, US$6, 18-24 hrs, to Pelechuco, also truck at Wed 0630, takes even longer, buy returns Fri 2000).

● **Equipment** The best selections are *Condoriri*, Local 8, Galería Sagárnaga, C Sagárnaga 339 (T/F 319369) opp *Hotel Alem*, open Mon to Fri 0930-1300, 1430-2000, Sat 0930-1200. They also do an excellent repair service and rent equipment. *Andean Summits*, C Sagárnaga 189, T/F 317497, Casilla 6976, good selection of new camping and climbing gear. Best hire selection is at *Colibrí*, C Sagárnaga 309,

T 371936, F 355043, Casilla 7456. The cheapest way to buy kit is from outgoing climbers. CAB has a noticeboard where you can advertise your wares for sale; many adventure travel agencies, inc those mentioned above, will buy secondhand kit.

● **Guidebooks** Due in April 1997 is *Climber's Guide to Bolivia*, Yossi Brain, The Mountaineers, Seattle. Photocopies of *La Cordillera Real de los Andes, Bolivia*, by Alain Mesili (Los Amigos del Libro, 1984) are sometimes available in Spanish.

● **Guides**
Club Andino Boliviano, C México 1638, T 324682, Casilla 5879 (closed Sat). *Dr Hugo Berrios* (see above for contact) is an excellent guide, rec for Huayna Potosí. *Ozono*, Edif Labtec, PB, Av Bollivian y C14, Calacoto, La Paz, T/F 722240, e-mail: brain@schatz.bo, British-Bolivian owned agency specializing in mountaineering, trekking, rock climbing and other types of adventure tourism, inc skiing, can also organize radio cover. *Colibri SRL*, address above, specialize in climbing, with up-to-date information, trips arranged for all levels of experience and adventure tourism in all parts of Bolivia, very helpful, rec, full range of equipment hire. José Miranda, José Camarlinghi and Javier Thellacche of *Condoriri*, address above. *Andean Summits*, address above, is the contact point for *Asociación de Guías de Montaña y Trekking*, which has almost 30 members and is formalizing its procedures. *Colonial Travel*, México 1733, provide information and advice on routes, organizes transport. Also recommended, *Ricardo Albert* at Inca Travel, Av Arce 2116, Edif Santa Teresa. *Dr Juan Pablo Ando*, Casillo 6210, T 783495, trained in Chamonix, for mountaineering, rock climbing, trekking and ecological tours.

The *Club de Excursionismo, Andinismo y Camping*, CEAC, helps people find the cheapest way to go climbing, trekking, etc; foreigners may join local groups, T 783795, Casilla 8365, La Paz, or ask at the University or for Catherina Ibáñez at Plaza Tours, Av 16 de Julio 1789, T 378322, F 343301 (she has an information service for CEAC). Each week there is a meeting and slide show.

SKIING

90 mins by car from La Paz (36 km) is **Chacaltaya**, the highest ski run in the world. Season: Dec-April, depending on conditions. Skiing equipment may be hired, and a rope-tow reaches a maximum altitude of 5,221m. The facilities are sub-standard, emergency services non-existent and the rope-tow should be used with extreme caution. Midweek skiing is not possible unless

a group makes prior arrangement with the Club Andino Boliviano (address above). The Club runs its own Sat and Sun excursions (mixed reports). The day trip, beginning at 0730 and returning at 1600, is US$9 for bus ticket, plus US$13 for equipment rental and hook. Your ticket gives free access to the ski station restaurant (otherwise US$2 entrance, hot drinks only). Out of season the lift only goes if there are 5 or more people. Equipment is very limited, poor quality, queue at once; better take your own. A good tip is to share equipment since, at that altitude, you will need a long break between activities. No one should attempt to ski unless acclimatized at La Paz for at least a week. Sunglasses should block 100% of UV to avoid snowblindness. One can walk to the summit of Chacaltaya for views of Titicaca on one side, La Paz on the other, and Huayna Potosí. Tiring, as it is over 5,000m, but one has most of the day to do the climb. Laguna de Milluni, near Chacaltaya, is a beautiful lake to visit, but do not drink its heavily contaminated water. Take plenty of mineral water when going to the mountains as it's thirsty work in the rarefied air. (Chacaltaya skiing is described in Bradt's *South America Ski Guide*.)

● **Accommodation** For the really hardy, accommodation at the Chacaltaya ski station is free, but take very warm clothes, sleeping bag and bed roll, food and water, as there is no heating, or bedding. Meals are available at the hut at weekends.

● **Transport** Taxi or minibus US$30 (whole car) for a 1/2-day trip, or similar to the top by rented car costs about US$60, and really only at weekends. However, the trip can be hair-raising, buses carry no chains. Often the buses and tours only go half way. Many agencies do day trips, US$12.50, often combined with Valle de la Luna.

TIAHUANACO (TIWANAKU)

The ruins of Tiwanaku, not far from the village of Tiahuanaco, are 72 km W of La Paz, near the S end of Lake Titicaca.

LA PAZ TO TIWANAKU

The road from El Alto is graded and dusty. It passes through the village of **Laja**

(Laxa), the first site of La Paz, at the junction of the roads between Potosí and Lima and Potosí and Arica. Because there was no water, La Paz was moved to its present site on the Río Choquepayu. Laja's church was the first cathedral of the region. Its façade is mestizo baroque; the faces of King Ferdinand and Queen Isabella as Indians can be seen on the left bell tower (the right bell tower was built in 1903). The church has a solid silver altar, but is closed to visitors. Simple meals at US$1 available in village. At the highest point on the road between Laja and Tiwanaku are wide views of the Cordillera and a site where offerings to Pachamama are made.

HISTORY

Many archaeologists believe that Tiwanaku existed as early as 1600 BC, while the complex visible today is estimated to have been built between the 8th and 10th centuries AD. Recent research suggests that the site was a ceremonial complex at the centre of an empire which covered almost half Bolivia, S Peru, N Chile and NW Argentina. It was also a hub of trans-Andean trade. The reason for the demise of the Tiwanaku civilization is not entirely clear, although studies by Alan Kolata of the University of Illinois indicate that the area had an extensive system of raised fields (*Sukakollu*), capable of sustaining a population of 20,000, which may have been flooded by rising water levels in Lake Titicaca. This could have precipitated the empire's fall. The Pumapunka section, 1 km S of the main complex may have been a port, as the waters of the lake used to be much higher than they are today. The raised field system is being reutilized in the Titicaca area.

THE SITE

The main structures are: Kalasasaya, meaning 'standing stones', referring to the statues found in that part. Two of them, the Ponce monolith (centre of inner patio) and the Fraile monolith (SW corner), have been re-erected. In the NW corner is the Puerta del Sol, originally at Pumapunku:

the split in the top probably occurred in the move. Its carvings, interrupted by being out of context, are thought to be either a depiction of the creator God, or a calendar. The motifs are exactly the same as those around the Ponce monolith. This figure displays many of the typical Tiwanaku features: puma faces looking downwards, condor faces, two left hands, the snake with a human face on his left arm, the crying god. The Templo Semisubterráneo is a sunken temple whose walls are lined with faces, all different, according to some theories depicting states of health, the temple being a house of healing. The Akapana, originally a pyramid, was the largest structure, but is now no more than a hill. At Pumapunku, some of whose blocks weigh up to 100 tonnes, the widespread confusion of fallen stones suggests a natural disaster putting a sudden end to the construction before it was finished.

The entrance ticket to Tiwanaku costs US$2.50 for foreigners, including entry to museum; the site opens at 0900. There is a small museum at the ticket office. A new museum, Museo Regional Arqueológico de Tiwanaku, opened 1994, on the other side of the railway from the main site, it contains a well-illustrated explanation of the raised field system of agriculture. It has clean toilets. Most of the best statues are in the Museo Tiahuanaco or the Museo Semisubterráneo in La Paz. Locals trade arrowheads and bronze figures (almost all fakes). Allow 4 hrs to see the ruins and village.

TIAHUANACO VILLAGE

Tiahuanaco, the present-day village, has arches at the four corners of its square, dating from the time of independence. The church, built 1580-1612, used precolumbian masonry. In fact, Tiwanaku for a long while was the 'quarry' for the altiplano.

Local festivals

At Tiwanaku, 21 June, before sunrise, colourful dances, llama sacrifices, etc. In Tiahuanaco village, on the 8th day of carnival (Sun), local carnival, colourful, souvenirs for sale, bargain hard, do not take photographs. Market day in Tiahuanaco is Sun;

do not take photos then either.

Local information
● **Accommodation & places to eat**
G pp *Hostal-Restaurant El Puerto del Sol* is on the road out of Tiahuanaco village to La Paz, new, clean, friendly, meals US$0.50-1.00, owner is very knowledgeable about ruins. There are 3 restaurants on Tiahuanaco's main street serving *almuerzo* and *comida familiar*.

● **Guidebooks in English**
Tiwanaku, by Mariano Baptista, Plata Publishing Ltd, Chur, Switzerland, or *Discovering Tiwanaku* by Hugo Boero Rojo. They are obtainable from Los Amigos del Libro (or 2nd-hand from stalls in Av Ismael Montes). *Guía Especial de Arqueología Tiwanaku*, by Edgar Hernández Leonardini, a guide on the site, rec. Written guide material is difficult to come by; hiring a good guide costs US$10.

● **Transport**
Transportes Ingavi, José María Azin y Eyzaguirre (take any Micro marked 'Cementerio') US$1, 2 hrs, almost hourly, first dep 0700 (frequency may change according to demand – the earlier you go the better). They are usually full. Tickets can be bought in advance. Taxi for 2 costs about US$25 (can be shared), return, with unlimited time at site. (US$40 inc El Valle de la Luna). Some buses go on from Tiahuanaco to Desaguadero; virtually all Desaguadero buses stop at Tiahuanaco, US$0.65. Return buses (last one back 1730-1800) leave from Plaza in village. Road is being upgraded, when complete buses will take 1½ hrs.

Most tours from La Paz cost US$15 return; they stop at Laja and the highest point on the road before Tiwanaku. Some tours include El Valle de la Luna.

LAKE TITICACA

Lake Titicaca is two lakes joined by the Straits of Tiquina: the larger, northern lake (Lago Mayor, or Chucuito) contains the Islas del Sol and de la Luna at its southern end; the smaller lake (Lago Menor, or Huiñamarca) has several small islands. The waters are a beautiful blue, reflecting the hills and the distant cordillera in the shallows of Huiñamarca, mirroring the sky in the rarified air and changing colour when it is cloudy or raining. Periodically the water level rises, inundating low-lying land, but its size is much reduced from prehispanic times. There are various legends concerning the origin of the name, some surrounding the *titi*, a wild cat of the lake shore, whose pelt is much prized by witch doctors. The trout fished in the lake and served in many restaurants is not native. There is some trout farming but stocks are low enough for trout to have become too expensive for many locals, who catch *pejerrey* and *karachi*. Also beginning to be farmed are the Lake's giant frogs, whose legs are served, fried, with chips, in several places. The totora-reed boats are still made, more as museum pieces than for practical purposes. Wood and fibreglass vessels last much longer. A trip on the lake is a must if in the area; boat services are given below.

● **Recommended reading**

Tristan Jones, who crossed South America in his sailing cutter *Sea Dart*, spent over 8 months cruising Lake Titicaca, see his book *The Incredible Voyage*, Futura Publications. *An Insider's Guide to Bolivia*, by Peter McFarren, gives a good historical background, inc an interesting article about archaeological discoveries in Lake Titicaca, by Johann Reinhard (available in many bookshops and large hotels in La Paz). Reinhard also contributed a chapter on 'Underwater Archaeological Research in Lake Titicaca' to *Ancient America, Contributions to New World Archaeology*, edited by Nicholas J Saunders (Oxford: Oxbow Monograph 24, 1992).

LA PAZ TO COPACABANA

A paved road runs from La Paz to the Straits of Tiquina (114 km El Alto-San Pablo).

PUERTO PEREZ

Puerto Pérez is the closest point to La Paz on Lake Titicaca (72 km, less than 1 hr by car). The road to the port turns off the main road at **Batallas**, a typical Altiplano market town so named because of the final battles between Almagro and Pizarro. The views of the lake and mountains from Puerto Pérez are superb; the sunsets are spectacular, too. The port was the original harbour for La Paz, founded in the 19th century by British navigators as a harbour for the first steam boat on the Lake (the vessel was assembled piece-by-piece in Puno). Colourful fiestas are held on New Year's Day, Carnival (Mon and Tues before

Ash Wed), 3 May and 16 July.

● **Accommodation & places to eat A3** *Hotel Las Balsas*, owned and operated by Turismo Balsa (see La Paz **Travel Agents**), T La Paz 357817, F 391310, in a beautiful lakeside setting, with views of the cordillera; all rooms have balcony over the lake. Large new salon caters for groups, seminars. Hotel is advertised as 5-star; willing to negotiate to reduce price out of season; fitness facilities inc massage. jacuzzi, sauna, racket ball; T/F (2) 813226; restaurant expensive, but fixed price lunch or dinner good value at US$12. Turismo Balsa operate boat trips to Suriqui and Kalahuta, and services to Puno and Cusco.

Small restaurants in town serve trout.

● **Transport** There is a regular minibus service from La Paz Cementerio district: across from the cemetery, above the flower market, ask for buses to Batallas, price US$0.75.

HUARINA AND HUATAJATA

At **Huarina**, 42 km before Tiquina, a road turns off Achacachi, Sorata and the road along the E shore of Titicaca to Puerto Acosta. The next town is **Huatajata**, with *Yacht Club Boliviano* (restaurant open to non-members, open Sat, Sun lunch only, sailing for members only) and Crillon Tours International Hydroharbour and *Inca Utama Hotel* (see below). Beyond here is **Chúa**, where there is fishing, sailing and Transturin's catamaran dock (see below). The public telephone office, Cotel, is on the plaza just off the main road.

● **Accommodation & places to eat** In Huatajata, next to Crillón's *Inca Utama*, is *Restaurant Huatajata Utama*, highly rec, then *Inti Raymi*, with boat trips, *El Lago*, *Panamericano*, *La Playa* and **E** *Hostal Restaurante Lago Azul* (cramped rooms, basic, overpriced). The restaurants are of varying standard, most seem to come to life at weekends and in the high season. Beside *Lago Azul* is Máximo Catari's *Inti Karka* restaurant on the road (full menu, open 7 days, average prices, good fish), and hotel, a 3-storey building on the waterfront (F pp, breakfast extra, basic, shower, water unreliable, some rooms with lake view, ask for extra blankets, T 813212).

Between Huatajata and Huarina (at Km 65 from La Paz) is the **B** *Hotel Titicaca*, T La Paz 374877, F 391225, beautiful views, friendly, sauna, pool, good restaurant, very quiet during the week (address in La Paz, Potosí y Ayacucho 1220, p 2).

About 2 km before Chúa is a turning to the right (signed) to *La Posada del Inca* restaurant,

open Sat, Sun and holidays for lunch only, in a beautiful colonial *hacienda* setting (good trout, average prices).

● **Buses** La Paz-Huatajata/Tiquina, US$0.85, Transportes Titikaka, Av Kollasuyo 16, daily from 0400, returning between 0700 and 1800.

TOURS

1) Crillon Tours (address under La Paz **Travel Agents**), run a hydrofoil service on Lake Titicaca with a bilingual guide – 'excellent and willing to resolve any problem'. Crillon's tours stop at the Anden Roots cultural complex at *Inca Utama*: in the daytime visitors see the four different museums (recorded commentary, quite brief, but interesting), in the evening at the Kallaway (Native Medicine) museum, a meeting with a Kallaway fortune teller is offered. In all seven cultures are represented. The *Inca Utama* hotel has a health spa based on natural remedies; the 60 rooms are comfortable, with heating, electric blankets, good service, bar, good food in restaurant (5-star accommodation, **A1**, reservations through Crillon Tours, T La Paz 374566/350363). Also at *Inca Utama* are an observatory (*Alajpacha*) with retractable thatched roof for viewing the night sky, a new restaurant (*La Choza Nautica*), a bar on the lake, a new colonial-style tower with 15 de-luxe suites, panoramic elevator and 2 conference rooms. Health, astronomical, mystic and ecological programmes are offered. The hydrofoil trips include visits to Andean Roots complex, Copacabana, Isla del Sol and de la Luna, Straits of Tiquina and past reed fishing boats. See Isla del Sol below for *La Posada del Inca*. Trips can be arranged to/from Cusco and Machu Picchu, hydrofoil and train one way, flight the other; other combinations of hydrofoil and land-based excursions can be arranged (also jungle and adventure tours). Charge: US$173 from La Paz to Puno, US$145 for day excursion from La Paz. Expensive but fascinating, not least for the magnificent views of the Cordillera on a clear day. All facilities and modes of transport connected by radio.

2) Transturin (see also La Paz **Travel Agents**) run catamarans on Lake Titicaca, either for sightseeing or on the La Paz-Puno route (US$129 La Paz-Copacabana; overnight at *Hotel Titicaca* and tour US$168). From their dock at Chúa, 3-hr trips go to Copacabana, with bar, video, sun deck and music on board. One-night tours to Copacabana are also available. The catamarans are slower than the hydrofoils of Crillon so there is more room and time for on-board entertainment. Transturin runs through services to Puno without a change of bus, and without many of the usual formalities at the border. Transturin has offices in Puno, Jr Libertad, T352771/351316, and Cusco, Av Portal de Panes 109, of 1, T 222332.

ISLANDS OF LAKE HUINAMARCA

On **Suriqui** (1½ hrs from Huatajata) you can visit the museum/craft shops of the Limachi brothers (now living at the *Inca Utama* cultural complex) and Paulino Esteban, who helped in the construction, out of totora reeds, of Thor Heyerdahl's *Ra II*, which sailed from Morocco to Barbados in 1970. Heyerdahl's *Tigris* reed boat, and the balloon gondola for the Nazca (Peru) flight experiment (see Peru chapter, Section 4), were also constructed by the craftsmen of Suriqui. Reed boats are still made on Suriqui, probably the last place where the art survives. On **Kalahuta** there are *chullpas* (burial towers), old buildings and the town of Kewaya (no one lives there). On **Pariti** there is Inca terracing; the weaving on the island is very good.

● **Boat trips** Máximo Catari (see above) arranges boats to the islands in Lago Huiñamarca, Pariti, Kalahuta and Suriqui: prices, to Suriqui US$22 for 4-5 people, to all 3 islands US$40, 1 hr boat trip US$7.50, sailing boat for 3 US$16 for a day (boat trips rec). Paulino Esteban (see above) is also rec, contact through Servitur, PO Box 8045, La Paz, T 340060, F 391373. Boats can also be hired in Tiquina for trips to Suriqui, US$3 pp in a group.

From Chúa the main road reaches the E side of the Straits at San Pablo (clean blue restaurant with good toilets). On the W side is San Pedro, the main Bolivian naval base, from where a road (being paved) goes to Copacabana. Vehicles are transported across on barges, US$4. Passengers cross separately, US$0.80 (not included in bus fares) and passports are checked. Expect delays during rough weather, when it can get very cold.

COPACABANA

158 km from La Paz, is an attractive little town on Lake Titicaca. It has a heavily restored, Moorish-style cathedral containing a famous 16th century miracle-working Dark Virgin of the Lake, also known as the Virgin of Candelaria, the patron saint of Bolivia.

Places of interest

The cathedral itself is notable for its spacious atrium with four small chapels; the main chapel has one of the finest gilt altars in Bolivia. The basilica is clean, white, with coloured tiles decorating the exterior arches, cupolas and chapels. Vehicles are blessed in front of the church daily, especially on Sun. An *hospicio* (serving now as an almshouse) with its two arcaded patios is worth a visit; ask permission before entering. There are 17th and 18th century paintings and statues in the sanctuary, entrance at side of Basilica opp ENTEL, open Mon-Fri, 1100-1200, 1400-1800, Sat and Sun, 0800-1200, 1400-1800, only groups of 8 or more.

There are good walks beside the lake, or on the hills around the town. On the headland which overlooks the town and port, **Cerro Calvario**, are the Stations of the Cross. On the hill behind the town (Cerro Sancollani) overlooking the lake, roughly SE of the Basilica, is the **Horca del Inca**, two pillars of rock with another laid across them (probably a sun clock rather than a gallows, now covered in graffiti). With the church entrance behind you turn right up PD Murillo towards the green house at the street end. At the green house turn right and immediately left up a rocky hill. There is a path marked by white stones. Boys will offer to guide you: fix price in advance if you want their help. Above the Horca, on the other side of the ridge, is the Flecha del Inca, an arrow-shaped hole in a rock. Back down at the green house, turn left instead of right to the cemetery at the Asientos (Seats) del Inca, close to town. Further from town is **El Baño del Inca**, about 2 km, entrance US$0.60, small museum.

Follow C Junín out of town for 1½ km, then head for a large group of eucalyptus trees on hillside 500m away.

Excursions

There is a lovely walk along the lakeside N to Yampupata, 15 km (allow 3½ hrs), through unspoilt countryside, but it is too rough for cycling. At the village of Sequañe ask for Señor Hilario Paye Quispe who will row you across to the Isla del Sol and bring you back another day if you plan to stay on the island, or José Quispe Mamani who provides a motor launch, plus meals and accommodation.

Copacabana's water supply can be intermittent. Beware of sunburn especially on the lake, even when it does not feel hot. **NB** The local police have been known to accuse travellers of 'photographing secret buildings' and 'fine' them US$10-20, or confiscate 'false' US$ bills or TCs. New arrivals may also be pressurized into paying for 'entry' to the town; the fee is in fact for the sanctuary.

Local festivals

Easter, with candlelight procession on Good Friday. 2-5 May, very colourful; 5-8 Aug, when the town gets very full, hotel prices quadruple and theft is common in broad daylight; 15 Nov, Dark Virgin of the Lake.

Local information

● **Accommodation**

C *Playa Azul*, 6 de Agosto, full board (rooms fair, but chilly, half-board a possibility), tepid electric showers, water supply and toilets poor, good food, T 320068; **C** *Residencial Rosario del Lago*, Rigoberto Paredes between Av Costanera and Av 16 de Julio, same ownership as Res Rosario, La Paz, inc breakfast, colonial style, hot water (solar power), Turisbus office, due open mid 1996.

D *Ambassador*, Bolívar y Jauregui, T 216, balcony, heater US$2/day, clean, with bath, cheaper without, rooftop restaurant, great beds, reduction for more than night or with YHA card, rec; **D** *Prefectural*, with good meals, some rooms have lake view, very mixed reports.

E *Boston*, Conde de Lemos, nr basilica, T 0862-2231, with bath (F without), good, clean, quiet; **E** *El Solar*, Av Jauregui 140, T 0862-2009, with bath, F without, same owners, **G** *Res El Solar*, Oruro 110, T 0862 2014, without bath; **E** *Residencial Sucre*, Murillo 228, T 2080, hot water,

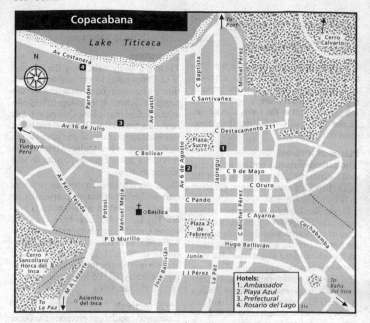

Copacabana

Hotels:
1. Ambassador
2. Playa Azul
3. Prefectural
4. Rosario del Lago

with bath, parking, quiet, clean, friendly, good cheap breakfast, poor beds.

F *Alojamiento Aransaya*, Av 6 de Agosto 121, T 229, basic but clean and friendly, hot shower but water problems, good restaurant (specializes in trout); **F** *Alojamiento Aroma*, Av Jauregui, towards beach, clean, hot showers, helpful and informative owner; **F** *Alojamiento Imperio*, C Visconde de Lemos, some hot water (shower US$0.50 extra), will change money; **F** *Kota Kahuaña*, Av Busch 15, blue house, hot showers on request, cheap, clean, quiet, some rooms with lake view; rec; **F** *Res Copacabana*, Oruro 555, T 220, warm water, reasonable; **F** *El Turista*, Pando 378, rec, friendly, cheap and clean, inadequate shower facilities; **F** *Res Porteña*, by market on Jauregui, clean, safe, rec; **F-G** *Emperador*, C Murillo, behind the Cathedral, clean, popular, laundry service and facilities, shared bath, excellent hot showers, breakfast may take a while, helpful for trips to Isla del Sol, highly rec; **G** *San José*, next to *Ambassador*, T 215, clean, basic, hot water, some rooms with lake view; *Alojamiento Bolívar*, Jauregui 158, bright blue, good views, hot shower, pleasant, simple, clean, rec. Many other residenciales in F and G categories. Prices increase at Easter and during fiestas.

● **Places to eat**

On Plaza 2 de Febrero are *Napolés*, clean, reasonable prices, does vegetarian tortilla, changes money; *Colonial*, decent lunch, good trout, has coin-operated phone. Several on 6 de Agosto inc *Snack 6 de Agosto*, good trout, big portions, some vegetarian dishes, serves breakfast; *Tourist Palace*, cheap, reasonable; *Puerta del Sol*, good, and *Pensión Flores*, lunch only. Many other restaurants offer acceptable US$2 meals; trout rec; good breakfasts and other meals, especially fish, in the market. Watch out for Gringo pricing.

● **Banks & money changers**

Bank changes Amex and Citicorps TCs. Several *artesanías* on Av 6 de Agosto buy and sell US$ and soles. Many shops (and bank) are closed on Mon and Tues, as they are open on Sun.

● **Post & telecommunications**

ENTEL: behind the church on road from La Paz.
Post Office: on Plaza 2 de Febrero, open Wed to Sun 0900-1200, 1400-1800.

● **Tourist offices**

Tourist Information kiosk on Plaza 2 de Febrero helpful when open. Motorcycles and bicycles can be hired; ask boys at the beach, but bargain. (If planning to cycle far hire mountain bikes.)

● **Transport**

Road By car from La Paz to Copacabana (direct), 4 hrs, take exit to 'Río Seco' in El Alto; the road is paved as far as Tiquina. **Bus** from **La Paz**: either take an agency bus for US$15 (pick up at your hotel; eg Turisbus, Diana Tours); or public bus: 2 de Febrero, T 377181, 6 a day; Manko Kapac, T 350033, 3 a day, 4½ hrs, US$4, last bus 1700, book day before; both companies' offices in La Paz are in Plaza Reyes Ortíz, opp entrance to cemetery. Note that buses for La Paz are very full on Sun afternoons. 1-day trips from La Paz are not rec as they allow only 1½-2 hrs in Copacabana. To reach Copacabana you cross the lovely straits of Tiquina (for details of the ferry crossing see below). Bus Copacabana-**Yunguyo** (Peru), hourly when full, US$1.30, 20 mins, from Plaza Sucre below *Hotel Playa Azul*. Agency buses between La Paz and Puno can be picked up, tickets from *Restaurant Aransaya*, US$4, 3 hrs, dep from *Hotel Ambassador*. No public bus services to Puno, you have to go to Yunguyo and catch a bus from there. It is also possible to catch a tour bus to Cusco, usually dep around 1400, tickets about US$15, change bus in Puno, tour company arranges connection. Bus to **Huatajata**, US$2.10 and to **Huarina**, US$2.50. **NB** It is impossible to travel from Copacabana to Guaqui direct, because of border crossings.

ISLA DEL SOL

The site of the Inca creation legend is a short distance by boat from Copacabana. A sacred rock at its NW end is worshipped as the birthplace of Manco Kapac and Mama Huaca, the first Incas. On the E shore near the jetty for Crillon Tours' hydrofoils and other craft is the Fuente del Inca, a pure spring, and Inca steps leading up from the water. A 2-km walk from the landing stage takes one to the main ruins of Pilko Caima (the Sun Gate from the ruins is now kept in the main plaza in Copacabana), a 2-storey building with false domes and superb views, entry US$1.20. Southeast of the Isla del Sol is the **Isla de la Luna** (or Coati), which also may be visited – the best ruins are an Inca temple and nunnery, but they have been sadly neglected.

Local information
● **Accommodation**

It is worthwhile staying overnight on the Isla del Sol for the many beautiful walks through villages and Inca terraces, some still in use. It is not possible to see all the sites on the Isla del Sol (a 4-hr round trip on foot) and return to Copa-

cabana in 1 day. Take camping equipment, all food and water (or water sterilizers), or ask Don Juan, next to the school on the beach at Challas (NW coast) for lodging in one of his rooms (US$0.80). He serves thirsty walkers with beer or refrescos. Also enquire nr the Inca steps for lodging. *La Posada del Inca* is a restored colonial hacienda above Yumani village, owned by Crillon Tours, solar-powered electricity and hot water, with bath, dining room, 2-4 day trekking opportunities, stays linked with hydrofoil itineraries. **G** *Hotel Inti Wayna*, known locally as *Casa Blanca* in the main village above the landing area, no electricity or running water but friendly and cosy with good beds, meals cooked to order, highly rec. Also **G** pp *Albergue Inca Sama*, next to Pilko Caima, restaurant serving fish dishes, excellent views, basic accommodation at Yumani, 30 mins walk from Pilko Caima, campsite (contact via *Hotel Playa Azul*, Copacabana, or La Paz T 356566/357817). The owner, Sr Pusari, offers boat service from Copacabana, US$33 one way, US$50 return.

● **Transport**

Boats can be hired in Copacabana, at the beach or through many *residenciales* (inc *Emperador*), to go to Islas del Sol and de la Luna. Few boats are available in the low season. You can go either to the S end of Isla del Sol, or to the N, or both, and on to La Luna. Whatever you choose to do it is imperative to agree with the boatman what is inc in the price, how long you will stay ashore and, if staying overnight, when you will be collected (preferably in writing). It is possible to be dropped off at N end of island and picked up later at Temple of the Sun at the S end. Fares vary according to type of boat, length of trip and number of passengers; motor boat to N end, US$5 pp, to S end, US$3 pp approximately, prices are negotiable. 1 day tour, US$8.50-12 depending on numbers. Note that sailing boats may suffer from lack of wind and that motor boats generally hold more passengers. **NB** Several reports have been received of boat excursions giving less than value for money, and often giving free rides to the owner's friends and relatives encountered en route. Many boat owners are also reluctant to do more than a morning trip (0730-1300). Don't always take the cheapest possible offer, ask around and check what is inc for your money.

Tour boats to Isla del Sol often stop only briefly at the jetty by the Fuente del Inca. Crillon's hydrofoils stop for 45 mins. All the time visitors are ashore they are pestered by people with llamas and children for photographs to be taken, after which payment is demanded.

To hire a rowing boat in Copacabana costs US$4.50/hr.

CROSSING THE PERUVIAN FRONTIER

There are three routes from La Paz to Puno.

ALONG THE WEST SIDE OF LAKE TITICACA

The road and railway (no passengers) go from La Paz 91 km W to **Guaqui**, formerly the port for the Titicaca passenger boats. On the last weekend of July, Guaqui celebrates the festival for the Apóstol Santiago. Arrive early morning to join in the end of all-night carousing (what little accommodation there is, is all fully occupied). The road crosses the border at **Desaguadero** 22 km further W and runs along the shore of the lake to Puno. The crossing can be hectic. If Peruvian police ask for a fee for registration, do not pay. If you need a visa get it elsewhere. The route La Paz-Guaqui-Puno is being paved so that, eventually La Paz to the Peruvian ports of Matarani/Mollendo will be paved throughout.

● **Accommodation** Guaqui: G *Residencial Guaqui*, nr port, good value, basic, friendly; tiny restaurant on the Plaza de Armas has been rec. Desaguadero: *Hotel Bolivia*, nr Bolivian customs, reasonable 4-course meals.

● **Transport** Buses from La Paz to Guaqui and Desaguadero depart from Ingavi office (José María Asu y Eyzaguirre) 0745 and 1000, US$2, 3½ hrs, avoid putting luggage on roof. From Desaguadero to La Paz 1430. To Puno US$8.50, 3 hrs. To Puno from La Paz US$18, 8 hrs.

VIA COPACABANA

From Copacabana an unpaved road leads S to the frontier near Yunguyo. For La Paz tourist agency services on this route see under International Buses (page 274) and under Lake Titicaca above.

This is now a very straightforward border crossing, with customs and immigration posts at either side of the border; the buses/colectivos stop at each one (or you can walk, 400m, and a small hill, between the two posts; transport does not start till Yunguyo, a further 600m). Taxis and tricycles run between the border and Yunguyo (shared taxi border to Yunguyo plaza, US$0.25 pp). Make sure, if arranging a through ticket La Paz-Puno, that

you get all the necessary stamps en route, and ascertain whether your journey involves a change of bus. Note the common complaint that through services La Paz-Puno (or vice versa) deteriorate once the border has been crossed, eg smaller buses are used, extra passengers taken on, passengers left stranded if the onward bus is already full, drivers won't drop you where the company says they will.

At Yunguyo, do not photograph the border area. There should be a statutory 72 hrs period outside Bolivia before renewing a visa but 24 hrs is usually acceptable. Ask for 90 days on return. Money can be changed in Yunguyo and soles can be changed in Copacabana (see above).

If crossing into Bolivia with a motorcycle, do not be fooled into paying any unnecessary charges to police or immigration.

ALONG THE EAST SIDE OF LAKE TITICACA

The Peruvian authorities do not officially recognize the road as being a border crossing. (Officially, you must get your entry stamp in the Department of Puno, but as this is next to impossible on this route, you will run into difficulties later on.) The road passes through Achacachi (see page 295), Ancoraimes (small Sun market), Carabuco (with colonial church), **Escoma**, which has a large Aymara market every Sunday (it finishes before 1300, watch out for drunks in the afternoon) and **Kasiri Puerto Acosta**. The area around Puerto Acosta is good walking country and the locals are friendly. From La Paz to Puerto Acosta the road is fine during the dry season (approximately May to Oct). North of Puerto Acosta towards Peru the road deteriorates rapidly and should not be attempted except in the dry season.

There is an immigration office, but it is advisable to get an exit stamp in La Paz first.

● **Accommodation** G *Alojamiento Espinosa*, basic, friendly, but no restaurants.

● **Transport** Buses La Paz (Cementerio district)-Puerto Acosta, US$3.25, Fri 1130, Sat/Sun 0630. Many trucks travel La Paz-Puerto Acosta on Tues and Fri afternoons. The only transport beyond Acosta is early on Wed and Sat mornings when a couple of trucks go to the markets, some 25 km from Puerto Acosta on the border (no formalities).

ESCOMA TO CHARANAZI

At Escoma a road branches N, roughly parallel with the border, going to Chuma, and to **Charazani** (official name Juan José Pérez; Ulla-Ulla *fiesta*, 16 July; witch doctor; thermal baths, small entry fee; **G** pp *Hotel Charazani*, good, clean, friendly; 2 restaurants; buses from 4 blocks above Cementerio in La Paz, Fri, Sat, Sun 0600, US$4.40, 10 hrs, Sat bus continues to Curva, return Sun, Mon, Tues. The road ends at Apolo.

The road from Escoma to Charazani is very scenic, climbing to 4,500m. At the highest point is a sign to the **Reserva Ulla Ulla**, where llamas, alpacas, vicuñas, vizcachas and many birds can be seen, with the backdrop of the Cordillera de Apolobamba. Camping is possible (but cold), ask for the thermal springs, or for permission at farms (payment welcome). Ulla Ulla-Charazani by car 3-4 hrs. Charazani is in the Yungas, with thermal springs. 2-3 hrs away is Curva, one of the bases of the Kallawaya (native medicine doctors), now reported to be unwilling to practice for visitors (too many of the latter).

Also in the area is **Iskanwaya**, a major archaeological site on the eastern Andean slopes. A road from the Escoma-Charazani road crosses a 5,000m pass before descending to Aucapata; continue down a very poor jeep track then hike 1 hr down a cactus-filled canyon to the ruin (at about 1,500m). The city stands on two built-up platforms, with delicate walls, plazas, narrow streets, storerooms, niches, pot shards, etc. Admission to the museum in Aucapata is by donation. Great care is needed not to damage this site. Guidebook: *Iskanwaya: la ciudadela que sólo vivía de noche*, Hugo Boero Rojo (Los Amigos del Libro, 1992).

● **Transport** Truck from Cementerio, La Paz, Fri 0200 to Aukapata, 27 hrs, then walk to ruins. Hire a jeep for US$400 round trip: one driver who knows the way is Oscar Vera, La Paz T 230453. Alternatively take irregular transport from Sorata to Consata, get off above bridge called Boca de Lobo over Río San Cristóbal (which becomes the Llica).

The Yungas

THE lush forested slopes behind the mountains to the N of La Paz is the main production area of citrus, bananas, coffee and coca leaves for the capital. It is also a favourite retreat for those escaping the Andean chill.

NB The Yungas is a coca-growing region, so it is advisable not to wander too far off the beaten track.

LA PAZ TO THE YUNGAS

The Yungas can be approached either via La Cumbre, NE of La Paz, or by turning off the road which skirts the E shore of Lake Titicaca and crossing the Cordillera to Sorata. Both routes join at Caranavi, so a circular route can be made (see map, page 277).

The route NE out of La Paz circles cloudwards over La Cumbre pass at 4,725m; the highest point is reached in an hour; all around are towering snow-capped peaks. Then at Unduavi the paving ends, the road becomes 'all-weather' and drops over 3,400m to the green semi-tropical forest in 80 km. The roads to Chulumani and Coroico divide just after Unduavi, where there is a *garita* (check point), the only petrol station, but no good place to eat. Note, if travelling by truck from La Paz to the Yungas via La Cumbre, the best views can be seen in May and June, when there is least chance of fog and rain on the heights. If you want to alight at La Cumbre, tell the driver beforehand for it is easy to miss in fog or cloud. It is very cold at La Cumbre and, further down, there are waterfalls at San Juan that baptise open vehicles – be prepared. For details of the La Cumbre-Coroico hike (Choro), see page 276.

CHULUMANI

Chulumani (*alt* 1,700m), the capital of Sud Yungas, is a pretty, relaxed little town with beautiful views. Coca, citrus fruits and coffee are the main products.

Excursions
Apa Apa Ecological Park, 8 km away, is the last area of original Yungas forest, T 0811-6106, or La Paz 790381, Ramiro Portugal (speaks English), to arrange lift, or write to Casilla 10109, Miraflores, La Paz. US$10 entry; campsite nearby. From Chulumani you can continue to **Irupana** (Fiesta 5 Aug; **F** *Hotel Casablanca*, with pool, rec); the road passes through fruit, coffee and coca plantations. Bus from Chulumani 1 hr, US$1, or take any passing truck at the *tránsito*. In Irupana you can hire transport for **Chicaloma**, one of several centres of black population in Sud Yungas (30 mins, US$10 with waiting, or 2 hrs walk). The village is in a tremendous location.

Local information
● **Accommodation**
A3 *Villas San Bartolomé* (T 358386), pleasant, superb setting with fabulous views of mountains, swimming pool, can be booked through the *Hotel Plaza*, La Paz, T 378311, Ext 1221 (or Plaza Tours in La Paz).

C *Hotel San Antonio*, pleasant cabins and swimming pools. Both hotels are 3 km from *tránsito* down Irupana road, arrange hotel transport beforehand if arriving by bus, no taxis.

D *Monarca*, on outskirts, full board, swimming pool (open to non-residents for US$0.50); **D** *Res El Milagro*, good views, at entrance to town by *tránsito*, very clean, very attentive landlady, garden; **D** *La Hostería*, Junín, T (0811) 6108, with bathroom (E without), inc breakfast, clean and friendly, good restaurant, excellent value, rec.

F pp *García*, on Plaza Libertad, with toilet, cheaper without, basic, clean and cheap, rec, restaurant, noisy at weekends from disco;

F *Bolívar*, very basic but clean and friendly.

25 km away, just outside Puente Villa, is **C** *Hotel Tamapaya*, beautiful setting, with shower, good rooms, swimming pool, rec.

● **Places to eat**
Don Miguel in lane at bottom of Junín, doesn't look much, but very good; *El Mesón*, on main Plaza, good cheap meals; *Yerko*, on Lanza, good food, great value.

● **Transport**
Buses From La Paz, Flota Yungueña, Av Las Américas 354, Villa Fátima, 120 km, Sat 0830, 4 hrs, US$4.30. Buses and minibuses every hour in am from C Yanacochi, Villa Fátima, book return from agencies on plaza, throughout am, US$2.60, 4 hrs.

The other branch from Unduavi leading to Yolosa, the junction 7 km from Coroico, has been described as 'life-endangering'. True, it is steep, twisting, clinging to the side of sheer cliffs, and it is very slippery in the wet, but the danger lies in not knowing the rules of the road, especially at weekends. Uphill vehicles always have right of way; downhill must wait or reverse to a passing place. Uphill drives on the cliff side, be it left or right, downhill on the outside. Speed and ignorance on the narrow road leads to drivers plunging over the edge.

COROICO

The little town of **Coroico** is perched on a hill at 1,760m; the scenery is beautiful. The hillside is covered with orange and banana groves; coffee is also grown. There are delightful walks through paths down to the river where warm pools are ideal for bathing (and if you're not up to 2-3 hrs walk each way, lifts are usually available in Coroico). The trail to the river starts at the left corner of the football pitch, looking downhill; it forks often, keep right. Another pleasant short walk starts at El Calvario (follow the Stations of the Cross by the cemetery, off C Julio Zuazo Cuenca which leads uphill from the plaza). Facing the chapel at El Calvario, with your back to the view of the town and its setting, look for a path on the left, which soon becomes well-defined. It leads in 1 hr to the Cascada y Toma de Agua de Coroico (the source of the town's water supply); the path runs quite level along the hill's edge.

Local festivals

There is a colourful 4-day festival on 19-22 Oct, when accommodation is hard to find. It is great fun, but wait a day or two before returning to La Paz (hung-over drivers). On 2 Nov, All Souls' Day, the local cemetery is festooned with black ribbons.

Local information

● Accommodation

San Carlo, 1 km outside town, 3-star, T 813266 (La Paz T 372380), with restaurant, pool and sports facilities, modern, rec. Also out of town is El Viejo Molino, 4-star, with pool, T 0811-6004 (or represented in La Paz by Valmar Tours, T 361076, F 352279).

D Don Quijote, 800m down Coripata road (up from square, then left, then right), pool, restaurant;D Esmeralda, T 0811-6017, 5 mins uphill from plaza (Casilla 9225, La Paz), free pick-up service, German owned, English spoken, pool, restaurant, hikes arranged, Visa, Mastercard taken,great views, hot showers, videos, excellent restaurant, garden, pool, laundry service, highly rec; D-E Hostal Kory, at top of steps leading down from square, swimming pool (open to all, US$1), with bath, cheaper without (weekly rates available), very popular, very helpful, lovely terrace, restaurant; D Prefectural, down the steps from plaza, past the convent and beyond the football pitch, building a bit dated, but clean and pleasant, nice garden, good views, swimming pool (may not have water), full board (E without food), food quite good.

E Lluvia de Oro, on street off square by Daedalus pub, good value, food rec, cheap, swimming pool, top floor rooms are best; E-F La Casa, just down the hill from Hostal Kory, small, swimming pool, clean, with restaurant (below), rec; E-F Sol y Luna, uphill past cemetery, and Umopar (narcotics police) station, 30 mins walk from town, dormitory accommodation G pp, meals available (Indonesian food), also 2 cabañas for rent with kitchen, D, camping US$1 pp, small pool, garden, laundry service, highly rec, reserve through Chuquiago Turismo, Planta Baja, Edif La Primera, Av Santa Cruz 1364, Casilla 4443, La Paz, T 362099/359227.

G pp Don Pesante, S Cuenca 30, clean, very friendly, restaurant with local and international food, breakfast rec; G pp Res de la Torre, on S Cuenca, showers, nice garden; Res 20 de Octubre is ABAJ youth hostel affiliate, US$2.50 pp. Camp site by the small church on the hill overlooking the town – a stiff climb though. Hotels can be difficult at holiday weekends and, as the area is a popular retreat for the rich from La Paz, prices are higher.

● **Places to eat**
La Casa is German-run, good food and setting, excellent salads, vegetarian dishes, fondue and raclette for dinner (reserve in advance), wonderful views, rec; the convent opp sells biscuits, peanut butter, wine and coffee liqueurs. *Balneario-restaurant Claudia Paola*, next to Turbus Totai on Sagárnaga, large pool, very good food, good value; *Daedalus Bar*, on plaza, for cocktails; *Back-Stube*, next to Hostal Kory, good cakes, muesli, delicious vegetarian lunch and dinner (not Tues), friendly atmosphere. Honey is sold in various places.

● **Banks & money changers**
No banks. Nowhere to change TCs.

● **Post & telecommunications**
Post Office and Tourist Info on plaza.

Entel, on Sagárnaga next to Totai, for international and local calls; **Cotel** next to church, phones, public TV.

● **Transport**
Buses, minibuses, trucks and pick-ups from La Paz all leave from Villa Fátima, where transport companies have their offices (eg Turbus Totai, Yanacochi 1434), US$2.60, 3 hrs, each company 4 times daily to/from La Paz 0800-1430 in 14 seater minibuses, worth booking in advance; Nuestra Señora de Candelaria, on plaza, trucks (best for views) US$2.50. Also pick-ups, usually from company offices. Sit on right in the mountains, on left hand side on the descent to Yungas. Extra services run on Sun. It can be difficult to book journeys to La Paz on holidays and on Sun evenings/Mon mornings (though these are good times for hitching). Trucks and pick-ups from La Paz may drop you at Yolosa, 7 km from Coroico; there is usually transport Yolosa-Coroico, US$0.65, or you can walk, uphill all the way, 2 hrs. In Coroico trucks leave from the market. Buses, trucks and pick-ups run from Yolosa to **Caranavi**, 3-4 hrs, US$3.25, **Guanay**, 7 hrs, US$5.20 and **Rurrenabaque**.

COROICO TO CHULUMANI

The countryside changes as you approach **Coripata** (**F** *Hotel Florida*), beyond which you enter the main coca growing area of N Bolivia. At Puente Villa the road joins the Unduavi-Chulumani road.

CARANAVI

From the road junction at Yolosa the lower fork follows the river NE to **Caranavi**, a very ugly town 164 km from La Paz, 75 km from Yolosa, at times the road follows a picturesque gorge, towards the settled area of the Alto Beni. Market day is Sat; lots of transport in late afternoon.

● **Accommodation** Mainly along Av Mcal Santa Cruz, the main street: **E** *Landivar*, most expensive, pool; **F** *Caranavi*, clean and friendly, rec; **F** *Res Avenida*, friendly, basic and cheap; **F** *Alojamiento Capitol*, basic; **G** *Hostal La Paz*, clean, basic.

● **Places to eat** *Paradiso*, cheap; *Tropical*, good set menu and cheap.

● **Buses** From Villa Fátima in **La Paz**; Yungueña, US$9, daily, 6-7 hrs; Turibus Totai, 4 a day, and trucks, 12½ hrs; to **Rurrenabaque**, 2000, 12 hrs, US$11.75. Direct bus **Coroico-Caranavi** on Sun, or you can take a truck, US$2.15. If you want to continue into the Beni Lowlands without going into Caranavi, wait at the checkpoint before the town where all transport has to stop and ask for a ride there. Rurrenabaque and Trinidad can be reached by road.

GUANAY

Some 70 km NW of Caranavi is the gold mining town of **Guanay**, an interesting, friendly place at the junction of the Tipuani and Mapiri rivers. Other gold mining sites are Tipuani and Mapiri (see below).

● **Accommodation E** *Panamericana*, helpful, popular with tour groups; **F pp** *Perla Andina*, clean, friendly, cold water, rooms on street less hot than those on courtyard, fans in rooms but electricity 1800-2400 only; **F** *Hotel Ritzy*, on main plaza, very clean, with mosquito nets; **G pp** *Alojamiento Los Pinos*, opp football pitch, cold water, basic, clean, may arrange exchange of TCs (with commission – cash can be changed with shopkeepers or gold dealers); **G pp** *Estrella Azul*, basic, friendly; **G pp** *Pahuichi*, clean, nice restaurant. Camping is possible next to the football field.

● **Places to eat** *Restaurant La Bamba*, opp *Panamericana*, good value, English spoken. Many other eating places on main street have fixed-price meals; one, with courtyard, monkey and parrot, serves excellent value breakfast. Electricity is rationed – every 10 mins or so – and water is available before 1200 only.

● **Transport** Buses direct from La Paz, Yungueña and Estrella Azul, about US$8, also trucks, which make frequent stops and diversions. Frequent transport to Caranavi. **River** To **Mapiri**: from Guanay dock, 3 blocks from plaza, boats leave at 0700 daily, or when full, US$5. Do not rely on cargo boats at other times. En route mines can be seen among the tropical vegetation. Boats go down the Río Beni to

Rurrenabaque (see page 330), 8-12 hrs, US$11-18 depending on how successfully you negotiate and availability of vessels. Cargo is now carried by road so you have to wait till the boat is full, which can take several days. Boats may not go with fewer than 10 passengers. 'Expreso' boats can be hired from Flota Fluvial, opp *Perla Andina*, at a price (US$150-300 depending on size and your ability to bargain). The journey goes through gold mining settlements, then narrow, fertile river banks sown with peanuts.

MAPIRI

This ugly mining town on the river of the same name (**G** pp *Alojamiento Porvenir*, best in town) is the starting point for an adventurous route up into the mountains. It goes via Sorata Limitada (a mining town, not to be confused with Sorata) and Santa Rosa to Sorata, thence, completing the Yungas circuit, back to La Paz. *Camionetas* run (2 hrs in dry season), to Santa Rosa (*Res Judith*, nice, with pool, wait here for lift to La Paz or Sorata). At Sorata Limitada there are 2 basic *alojamientos*, both G, the one beside the football pitch is quieter than the one beside the bar. *Camionetas* leave for Sorata from Sorata Limitada, US$13, 14 hrs and from Santa Rosa, US$9, 10 hrs. The scenery is superb, but the road is narrow, slippery, dangerous and dirty, especially in the rainy season. Try to sit in front with driver; there is usually a carpet to protect passengers against rain, but there is also a lot of dust. Have warm clothing handy for the road crosses the pass at 4,700m before dropping to Sorata.

SORATA

Rather than going straight through to La Paz, it is worth breaking the journey at **Sorata**, a beautiful place at 2,695m. There is also good transport from La Paz (see below). All around Sorata are lovely views and ideal country for hiking and climbing since it is in a valley at the foot of Illampu. The plaza, with its trees and, on a clear day, the snow-capped summit of Illampu as a backdrop, is delightful. The market area is beside the plaza; market day is Sun. Fiesta 14 Sept.

Local information
● **Accommodation**

D *Prefectural*, at entrance to town, C full board, bath, hot water, good but expensive food, bar, pool (US$0.80 for non-residents), nice building and garden, rec.

E *Paraíso*, Villavicencio 117, with bath, breakfast extra, hot water, smart, restaurant.

F pp *Copacabana*, 20 mins downhill from the centre (look for the signs), shared hot showers, expensive restaurant, clean, simple rooms; **F** *San Cristóbal*, Muñecas 350, nr market, basic, shared bath, no single rooms, meals available, friendly;

F pp *Res Sorata*, just off plaza, T (0811) 5044, shared bathrooms, huge rooms, very friendly, beautifully-furnished public rooms, excellent restaurant, big garden, laundry facilities, Louis from Quebec has good info and maps on local walks, 'best value in the Americas', highly rec.

G pp *Hostal Panchita*, on plaza, T5038, shared bath, good restaurant *El Ceibo*, good value, also houses Entel office.

● **Places to eat**
Ristorante Italiana, follow signs from plaza, good Italian cuisine inc vegetarian dishes, homemade ice cream, friendly, not cheap but worth it; *La Terraza*, good, friendly, cheap, good breakfast; *Santa Rosa*, on plaza, cheap meals; *El Tigre*, C Ingavi just off plaza, cheap lunches, open late, good value; *Girasol*, plaza at 143, excellent food, rec.

● **Banks & money changers**
Change dollars in shops on plaza displaying signs.

● **Post & telecommunications**
Two Entel offices on plaza (one in *Hostal Panchita*).
Post Office: on N side of plaza.

● **Shopping**
For handicrafts, *Artesanía Sorata* on plaza, also cashes TCs and accepts them as payment.

● **Transport**
Buses From La Paz with Trans Perla Andina, Larecaja, Trans Unificada and Bustillos (all from Kollasuyo in Cemetery district); at least hourly 0630-1330, 5 hrs, US$2; Perla Andina and Larecaja have offices on N side of plaza in Sorata; from Sorata 10 per day daily 0500-1430 (more at weekends). Plenty of trucks in am from Cemetery district, La Paz, to Sorata. Sit on left from La Paz.

HIKING AND CLIMBING
The climbing season is end of April to beginning of September. Sorata is the starting point for climbing **Illampu** (experience and full equipment necessary).

Louis at *Res Sorata* can arrange guides (US$7/day plus food), mules (US$8) and will provide up-to-date information (Francisco has been rec as reliable and friendly). Club Sorata (at *Hotel Copacabana*) rents equipment and can arrange treks, guides and mules, very expensive; much cheaper to make arrangements yourself (which is permissible, despite claims to the contrary). Bring all equipment if not doing tour with Club Sorata, there is none for hire otherwise.

When trekking in this area do not trust any water, it may be infected by vizcacha urine or with micah from the snow melt; it is best to filter it.

There are lots of walking possibilities. The most popular is to **San Pedro cave**, beyond the village of San Pedro (where the road splits, take the lower road and look for the white building above). You can swim in the underground 'lake'. Entry US$0.60, toilets at entrance; a good flashlight is essential; best not to go alone. It is reached either by road, a 12 km walk (2 hrs) each way, or by a path along the Río San Cristóbal (about 3½ hrs one way); on leaving Sorata on the San Pedro road, look for the round sign to the Seminario. Go down that road and join the river. Get clear directions before setting out. It is imperative to take water, at least 1 litre pp (or else take sterilizing tablets and fill up at the tap in San Pedro). Ask for the house selling refrescos by the litre in San Pedro.

A highly recommended hike is to Laguna Chillata and Inca Marka, a strenuous full-day walk, climbing from Sorata to 4,207m (either take plenty of water, or a water filter). Go with a guide because this is a sensitive area; the lake is sacred and Inca Marka is a burial place, dating back to the precolumbian Mollu culture. Camping is forbidden; do not touch anything, not even bits of paper, bottles, etc, which may be offerings.

The **'Circuito Illampu'**, a 5-7-day high-altitude trek (5 passes over 4,500m) around Mt Illampu, is excellent. It can get very cold and it is a hard walk, though very beautiful with nice campsites on the way. Some food can be bought in Cocoyo

on the 3rd day. You must be acclimatized before setting out.

It is also possible to hike from Sorata to Lake Titicaca. It is much cheaper to go to Sorata and ask about trekking there than to book up a trek with an agency in La Paz.

See warning in **Hiking**, page 354.

Gold digger's trail

Sorata is the starting point for two treks into the Yungas. The **'Camino del Oro'**, a 7-8 days hike to Guanay, rises to 4,741m (Abra Illampu) before going to Ancoma (1½ days from Sorata), then Wainapata, Chusi, 18 hrs from Ancoma (shop), Llipi, 8 hrs from Chusi and Unutulumi (2-3 hrs from Llipi, from here a *camioneta* runs daily to Guanay, US$5, 0930, winding through the many gold-digging towns in the Tipuani valley). After Ancoma it is very hot. The Ancoma-Llipi section is the most interesting, following the Tipuani River, climbing Inca staircases, crossing rivers on precarious plank bridges and going through an Inca tunnel. Very strenuous, not much flat ground for camping.

The Mapiri trail

Claimed by some to be prehispanic and paved since Mollu times and used by Colonel Faucett, this road was certainly used by quinine and rubber traders, gold miners as well as the Bolivian army on the way to defeat by Brazil in 1903. It is 150 km, 7-8 days, and tough; a guide is essential. Travel light, take water purification and capacity for at least 3 litres pp. From Mapiri, you continue to Guanay by boat.

Anne Girardet (Nyon, Switzerland) writes: "It starts in the freezing cold town of Ancoma at 4,200m, follows for much of its length a ridge allowing beautiful views and ends in tropical Mapiri at 800m" adding "It is not a luxury to hire mules to carry the heavy load for the first 3 days." Matthew Parris, author of *Inca Kola: a traveller's tale of Peru*, adds: "Your camps must be waterproof and insect-excluding. If you don't like flies, wasps, bees and ants, don't go. Much of your time will be spent crawling along rock-bottomed trenches and under logs. You will be rewarded with parrots, butterflies, flowers, tree-ferns, millions of tons of moss and with unbelievable views over thousands of square miles of near-vertical cloud forest, utterly unpenetrated by man."

SORATA TO LA PAZ

The road to the capital leaves Sorata, descends to the river, crosses a bridge and climbs up the side of the valley. It continues climbing, in a landscape of huge valleys and ridges, to a pass in fields with stone walls and boulders before reaching the openness of the altiplano. Between Warisata and Achacachi is a tremendous marsh, with sheets of water, dykes, farms, cattle, people working the fields and many birds; in the distance snow-capped peaks can be seen.

ACHACACHI

There are good views of Lake Titicaca from the church up the hill from the left side of the plaza (which looks as if it was once prosperous). Interesting Sun market. Fiesta 14 September. The market is behind the main plaza. It is possible to walk to the lake in 1½ hrs.

● **Accommodation & places to eat** Three *alojamientos*: *Huancayuno*, opp school, bathroom, water, *San Pedro*, no bathroom, *Tu Residencial*, all **G**, none too clean and all reported hostile, better stay somewhere else; 2 restaurants to the left of *Huancayuno*.

● **Transport** Plenty of buses to La Paz in the morning, US$1.30; from La Paz to Achacachi every 15 mins from Cemetery district (opp side of Av Kollasuyo from Sorata buses). Achacachi is a good place for connections if coming from Peru to Sorata: from Copacabana take a bus to Huarina, change there for a bus direct to Sorata. Sorata to Peru: take a La Paz bus and get out at Huarina; from there take a bus to Copacabana (best done in the morning).

Oruro and Routes to Chile and Argentina

FLAMINGOES shimmering in the glare of salt-flats, geysers and volcanoes on the Chilean border and, around Oruro, the poverty of the mines belies former wealth.

ORURO

Oruro, built on the slopes of a hill, is famous as a mining town, but there are no longer any working mines. It is, however, an important railway junction and the commercial centre for the mining communities of the altiplano. (*Pop* 195,000, mostly Indian; *alt* 3,740m; 230 km SE of La Paz; *phone code* 052).

Places of interest

Several fine buildings in the centre hint at the city's former importance, notably the **baroque concert hall** (now a cinema) on Plaza 10 de Febrero and the **Casa de la Cultura** (see below under **Museums**) built as a mansion by the tin 'baron' Simón Patiño. There is a good view of the city from the **Cerro Corazón de Jesús**, near the church of the **Virgen del Socavón**, 5 blocks W of Plaza 10 de Febrero at the end of C Mier. Excellent daily **market**, near railway station. The **zoo** is not really worth a special visit. The disused **San José mine**, worked for over 450 years for silver, tin and other minerals, lies 3 km W of the city. It can be visited with a permit from Comibol, the state mining company; contact Tourist Office which will help obtain permit; the *Intendencia* of the mine will provide a guide at mine. A 20,000 tons-a-year tin smelter has been built nearby at **Vinto**; open to visitors, but a permit has to be applied for, 24 hrs in advance, in Oruro.

Museums

Museo Etnográfico Minero, under the Church of the Virgen del Socavón, W end of C Mier, containing mining equipment and other artefacts from the beginning of the century as well as a 'tío', entry via the church 0900-1200, 1430-1800, US$0.50; **Casa de la Cultura**, Soria Galvarro 5755, formerly one of the Patiño residences, now run by the Universidad Técnica de Oruro, contains European furniture and a coach imported from France, also houses temporary exhibitions, open Mon-Fri 0900-1200, 1430-1800, US$1.45; **Museo Antropológico**, S of centre on Av España (take micro A heading S or any trufi going S) has a unique collection of stone llama heads as well as impressive carnival masks, open Mon-Fri 0900-1200, 1400-1800; Sat/Sun 1000-1200, 1500-1800, US$0.75; **Museo Mineralógico**, part of the University (take micro A South to the Ciudad Universitaria), with over 3,000 mineral specimens, claimed as one of the best in South America, open Mon-Fri 0800-1200, 1430-1700.

Local festivals: La Diablada

On the Sat before Ash Wednesday, Oruro Carnival stages the Diablada ceremony in homage to the miraculous Virgen del Socavón, patroness of miners, and in gratitude to Pachamama, the Earth Mother. The procession is led by a condor and a pack of frolicking bears and apes. Behind them, two gigantic and magnificently costumed masqueraders representing Lucifer (Luzbel/Satanás) stride ahead of their army of devils. St Michael the Archangel urges on the horde of leaping, gesticulating dancers wearing demoniacal masks. Prancing seductively at the head of the columns of demons, a band of female dancers, wearing red wigs and masks, represent China Supay, Lucifer's consort, who plays the role of carnal temptress. A mighty brass band in the rear drives on the first great team of devils. Behind it follow at least 50 other groups, each with its own band. These include more Diabladas, Morenos and Caporales (each satirizing the Spaniards' treatment of African slaves), Tobas, Negritos, Suri Sicuris, Tinkus and others representing different indigenous cultural traditions. The entire procession starts its 5 km route through the town at 0700, reaching the Sanctuary of the Virgen del Socavón at 0400 on Sun. There the dancers invoke her blessing and ask for pardon. The company then proceeds to the Av Cívica amphitheatre, where the Angel and the Devils perform two masques: the first is a contest between good and evil, in which St Michael routs the Devils. In the second, the **relato de los diablos**, seven devils are forced to confess to the Seven Deadly Sins. After the performance the dancers all enter the sanctuary, chant a hymn in Quechua and pray for pardon. The Diablada was traditionally performed by Indian miners, but several other guilds have taken up the custom.

The costume always features the heavy, gruesome mask modelled in plaster, with a toad or snake on top, huge glass eyes, triangular glass teeth, a horsehair wig and pointed, vibrating ears. Tied around the neck is a large silk shawl embroidered with dragons or other figures, and the dancer also has a jewelled, fringed breastplate. Over his white shirt and tights he wears a sash trimmed with coins, and from it hang the four flaps of the native skirt, embroidered in gold and silver thread and loaded with precious stones. Special boots equipped with spurs complete the elaborate outfit. The Lucifer dancers wear scarlet cloaks and carry a serpent twisted around one arm and a trident. The working-class Oruro district known as La Ranchería is particularly famous for the excellence of the costumes and masks made there.

The **Gran Curso del Carnaval** takes place on the Sun, a very spectacular display. Monday is **El Día del Diablo y del**

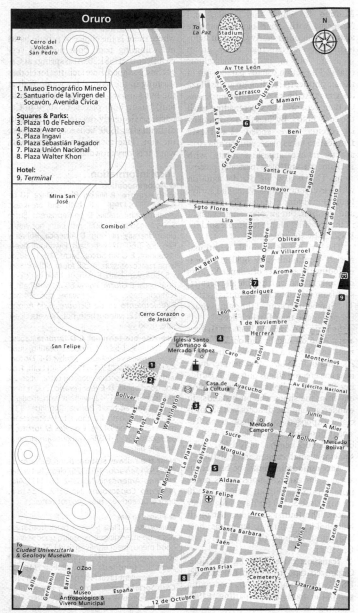

Oruro

22 Cerro del
Volcán
San Pedro

1. Museo Etnográfico Minero
2. Santuario de la Virgen del
Socavón, Avenida Cívica

Squares & Parks:
3. Plaza 10 de Febrero
4. Plaza Avaroa
5. Plaza Ingavi
6. Plaza Sebastián Pagador
7. Plaza Unión Nacional
8. Plaza Walter Khon

Hotel:
9. *Terminal*

To
La Paz

Stadium

N

Mina San
José

Comibol

Cerro Corazón
de Jesus

San Felipe

To
Ciudad Universitaria
& Geology Museum

Av Tte León

Barrientos
Carrasco

Cap Ustáriz
C Mamani

Gran Chaco

Av La Paz

Beni

Santa Cruz

Sotomayor

Pagador

Av 6 de Agosto

Sgto Flores

Lira

Vásquez

6 de Octubre

Oblitas

Av Villarroel

Aroma

Velasco Galvarro

Av Beizi

Rodríguez

León

1 de Noviembre

Herrera

Caro

Potosí

Monterinos

Iglesia Santo
Domingo &
Mercado F López

Casa de
la Cultura

Ayacucho

Av Ejército Nacional

Bolívar

Linares

Av Petot

Camacho

Washington

La Plata

Soria Galvarro

Sucre

Murguia

Mercado
Campero

Junín

A Mier

Av Bolívar

Mercado
Bolívar

Buenos Aires

Sim Montes

Aldana

San Felipe

Arce

Buenos Aires

Brasil

Tarapacá

Santa Barbara

Jaén

Tejerina

Tacna

Zoo

Museo
Antropológico &
Vivero Municipal

España

Tomas Frías

12 de Octubre

Cemetery

Lizárraga

Arica

Salle

Germania

Barriga

Moreno in which the Diablos and Morenos, with their bands, compete against each other on Av Cívica in demonstrations of dancing. Every group seems to join in, in 'total marvellous chaos'. The action usually parades out of the amphitheatre, ending up at the Plaza de Armas. At dusk dancers and musicians go their separate ways, serenading until the early hours. By Tues the main touristic events have ended; **La Fiesta Doméstica** takes place, with ch'alla rituals to invoke ancestors, unite with Pachamama and bless personal possessions. This is also the **día del agua** on which everyone throws water and sprays foam at everyone else (usually teenagers and children, but anyone can get caught in the crossfire; plastic tunics are sold for US$0.20 by street vendors).

The Fri before carnival, traditional miners' ceremonies are held at mines, including the sacrifice of a llama. Visitors may only attend with a guide and permission from Comibol, via the tourist office. The Sun before carnival the groups practise and make their final pledges.

Seating Around the Plaza de Armas, along Av 6 de Agosto and on Av Cívica, seats cost US$3 a day, bought from the Alcaldía in the plaza, or whichever business has erected stands outside its building. Seats on Av Bolívar, etc, cost US$2 a day from the shops who built stands. To wander among the dancers you are officially supposed to purchase a professional photographer's ticket for US$15, but amateurs can pay only US$1.50 by showing a small camera and insisting.

Accommodation must be booked in advance for carnival; hotel prices range from US$15 pp without bath, to US$20 pp with, to US$100 pp/day in the better places. The tourist office has list of all householders willing to let rooms: host and guest arrange the price, at least US$10 pp.

Transport prices from La Paz triple. Organized day trips from La Paz cost US$50, including transport, food and a seat in the main plaza, departing at 1900 (missing the last 8-9 hrs).

Excursions

To the hot springs at **Obrajes**, 23 km N, where there is the choice of private baths or swimming pool, both hot (not very clean), entry US$1.20. Also springs at Capachos, less good. Free facilities for clothes washing in the natural hot water. Wait at the bus stop at C Caro for the (intermittent) bus to both places, US$0.50 to Capachos. Go early as return transport difficult after 1600. Taxis sometimes make the run. Take picnic lunch. Avoid Sun, when it is very crowded.

Local information
● Accommodation

In the centre: **B** *Nikkei Plaza*, Plaza 10 de Febrero, T 54799, with bath and breakfast, modern, comfortable; **D** pp *Repostero*, Sucre 370 y Pagador, T 50505, with bath, hot water, clean, friendly, parking; **D** *América*, Bolívar y Pagador, T 60707, with bath, **E** without, clean, restaurant; **E** *Gran Sucre*, Sucre 510, T 53838, large new exnersion, rec; **E** *Ideal*, Bolívar 386, T 52863, with bath, **F** without, basic but clean, poor beds; **E** *Gloria*, Potosí 6059, with bath, **F** without, basic, clean, hot water, open 24 hrs; **F** *Alojamiento 15 de Octubre*, 6 de Agosto 890, T 40012, without bath, hot showers, clean, safe, good value.

Near the bus terminal: **C-D** *Terminal*, above bus terminal, T 53797, modern, heating, good views, expensive restaurant, noisy; **D-E** *Lipton*, Av 6 de Agosto 225, T 41538, with bath, **F** pp without, clean, secure, parking extra, open 24 hrs, good value; **D-E** *Res Verano*, 200m from bus terminal, T 41742, without bath, modern, clean, open 24 hrs; **F** *Bolivia*, Rodríguez 131, T 41047, with bath, **F** without, hot water, clean, restaurant, open 24 hrs; **F** pp *Res El Turista*, 6 de Agosto 466, T 41888, without bath, unhelpful, safe parking.

Near the railway station: all on Galvarro, **E-F** *Res San Salvador* (No 6325), clean, hot water. *Hispano-Americano* (No 6392, T 61117); *Alojamiento Copacabana* (No 6352, T 54184), both **G** pp and very basic, no hot water.

● Places to eat

Unicornio, La Plata 5955, 1 block from main plaza, open evenings only, smart, good service, good menu, main dishes around US$4; *La Casona*, Pres Montes 5970, opp Post Office, good pizzeria; *Confitería Capri*, Bolívar 749, on plaza, excellent breakfast, bar café, open late; *Club Social Croata*, Junín y Pres Montes, good value lunches; *La Cabaña*, Junín 609, comfortable, smart, good international food, bar, reasonable prices, closed Mon; *Brujas*, Junín y 6 de Octubre, café-concert, open 2100 till late for snacks, bar, live music weekends, good atmosphere, rec; *Mateos*, Bolívar y 6 de Octubre, good, reasonable prices, also ice cream; *SUM Confitería*, Bolívar esq Galvarro, good coffee, popualr at lunch, open late; *Confitería M y M*, Bolívar 490, good salteñas, pizzas, ice cream; *Libertador*, Bolívar 347, excellent set lunch for US$1.50; *Pasteleria La Polar*, Montes 5921, rec; *El Huerto*, Bolívar 359, good cheap vegetarian food. Excellent food stalls on Galvarro and Ayacucho, chicken and chips for US$0.50.

● **Banks & money changers**
Cash advances on credit cards at **Banco de La Paz**, US$3.75 authorization charge. TCs can be changed at **Banco Boliviano Americano**, 5% commission and at **Banco de Santa Cruz**, Bolívar 670 (also office at Pagador y Caro, open Sat 0900-1200). It is quite easy to change dollars (cash) on the street: good rates on Av V Galvarro, opp train station, or at Ferretería Findel, C Pagador 1491, nr the market (large hardware store), or try Don Ernest at Av V Galvarro 5998, T 60520.

● **Embassies & consulates**
German Consulate: at Adolfo Mier y Galvarro.

● **Entertainment**
Nikkei Disco in basement of hotel, separate entrance, state-of-the-art sounds, lights, reasonable prices.

Public baths: *Duchas Oruro*, 500 block of 6 de Agosto.

● **Laundry**
Alemania, Aldana 280.

● **Post & telecommunications**
Post Office: Presidente Montes 1456.

Telecommunications: Entel, Bolívar, 1 block E of plaza.

● **Shopping**
Reguerín 6 de Octubre 6001 esq Mier, good Diablada dolls and masks. On Av La Paz the 4 blocks between Leon and Beizu, 48-51, are largely given over to workshops producing masks and costumes for Carnival. There are 3 daily markets, all equally authentic and interesting: *Mercado Bolívar*, nr rail station; *Mercado Campero*, on Mier and Galvarro; *Mercado Fermín López*, on Cochabamba, has an interesting *brujería* section where you can find *curanderos'* magical concoctions.

● **Tour companies & travel agents**
Jumbo Travel, 6 de Octubre 6080, T 55005/55203, friendly and efficient. A rec driver and guide is *Freddy Barron*, Casilla 23, Oruro, T (052) 41776, who offers a programme of excursions and aventure tours. *Juan Carlos Vargas*, T 40333, also rec as tour guide, contact via tourist office.

● **Tourist offices**
in Prefectura, ground floor next to Migración, on W side of plaza, T 50144, open Mon-Fri 0830-1200, 1430-1830, Sat/Sun 0900-1000, very helpful, has list of hotels with approved prices. Map/guide US$1.

● **Transport**
Trains Check in advance which services are running, T 60605. To Cochabamba, *pasajero local*, 1 a week, 12 hrs, US$3. To Potosí and Sucre, Mon at 2040. To Villazón, Mon/Thur, 1900 (US$7.50), Wed/Sun, 1930 (US$5.60), 15-17 hrs; goes via Uyuni (6½ hrs). Ticket office opens at 0700, best to be there early. **Calama**, for Antofagasta (Chile), 22 hrs, very prone to delay, Sun 1930, US$16. For details see above under La Paz, **Railways to/from the Coast** (3).

Buses Bus terminal 10 blocks N of centre at Buenos Aires y Aroma, T 53689. To/from **La Paz**, 3 hrs, at least 10 *flotas* work the route, hourly, US$3.20, also at night US$4; to **Potosí**, 7 hrs, US$5.40-6.70; to **Cochabamba**, 4 hrs on paved road, US$5.15, Cometa 14 a day 0600-1900, several other companies. Roads to **Río Mulatos** and **Uyuni** are very bad; 11 de Julio and Flecha Norte daily, Panasur Mon and Thur, US$5.20; some trucks work the route. Trans Sabaya dep Tues and Sat at 2130 to Tambo Quemado and Chungará, connection to Arica; Geminis to Iquique Mon, Thur and Sat, also to Arica, Calama, Antofagasta and Santiago. Trucks to Potosí and Sucre leave from Av Cochabamba nr the Mercado Bolívar.

LAGO POOPO

About 80 km S is the **Santuario de Aves Lago Poopó**, an excellent bird reserve on the lake of the same name. Can be visited from Challapata, 120 km S of Oruro; bus dep 0800 and 1430, 2½ hrs, US$1.25, always full; 2 or 3 very basic places to stay; food poor; *fiesta* 15-17 July; rent a bike or motorbike to ride to lake shore, 10 km. The lake dries up completely in summer and it's possible to drive on it.

LLALLAGUA

Near this mining town, 95 km SE (*alt* 3,881m) is the famous Siglo Veinte, once the largest tin mine (ex-Patiño) in the country (now closed), but being worked by small cooperatives (welcoming). There is an acute water shortage. The Incatem adult school can be visited by Spanish speakers. Also nearby at **Uncia** (Km 102; small *alojamiento* near the prison, G, clean, safe, basic; poor restaurants, eat at the market) there are more former Patiño mines and good hot springs (reached by *trufi*). *Fiesta*: Asunción.

● **Accommodation** F *Hotel Bustillo*; *Santa María*; G *Hotel Llallagua*, small beds, no bath, seldom has water, perhaps the best, but not really rec; few restaurants.

● **Transport** Llallagua can be reached by bus from Oruro (Bustillo, 7 a day, Enta 0900, 1700 daily, 3 hrs, US$2.50). Also buses 1900 from La Paz.

SOUTHWEST FROM ORURO

Travellers with a 4WD vehicle might explore the country SW of Oruro towards the Chilean frontier. It's a day's drive to the western mountains following tracks rather than roads. There are no hotels in any of the towns, but lodging can often be found by asking a local school-teacher or mayor. At Toledo, 38 km SW, there is a colonial church. **Escara**, further SE, is a lovely village with a beautiful plaza; it is a friendly place, has bike rental. From Escara it is only 25 km S to **Chipaya**, 190 km from Oruro, which is less welcoming, the main settlement of the most interesting Indians of the Altiplano. They speak a language closely related to the almost extinct Uru; their distinctive dress and unique conical houses are beginning to disappear as the community changes. This is a very difficult trip without your own transport; there is transport once a week in either direction from Huachacalla on the Oruro-Sabaya road. In Chipaya, the town council charges visitors US$50 for free access and hospitality. For a smaller, or no, contribution you will be much less welcome. There is very little for the visitor to do and it is very cold.

SAJAMA NATIONAL PARK

A 1-day drive to the W is the **Parque Nacional Sajama**, established in 1945 and covering 60,000 ha. The park contains the world's highest forest, consisting mainly of the rare Kenua tree (Polylepis Tara-

pana) which grows up to 5,200m. The scenery is wonderful and includes views of three volcanoes (**Sajama** – Bolivia's highest peak at 6,530m – Parinacota and Pomerape). The road is very bad. There are restaurants in the park but no fresh food, so take plenty from La Paz (water no problem, but take purifying tablets). Crampons, ice axe and rope are needed for climbing the three volcanoes which are not technically difficult; the routes to base camp and beyond are fairly obvious. In Sajama village (*pop* 500; *alt* 4,200m), Peter Brunnhart (Señor Pedro) and Telmo Nina have a book with descriptions of the various routes to the summit (Telmo Nina keeps the visitors book, Park entry fee US$1); basic accommodation available. It can be very windy and cold at night (good sleeping bag essential). Mules can be hired, US$6/day. Good bathing in hot springs 5 km N of village, interesting geothermic area 6 km W of village. The Sajama area is a major centre of alpaca wool production and llama meat is still the main food.

● **Transport** Take the Litoral La Paz-Arica bus (La Paz 0530 Tues and Fri; from Arica Mon and Thur 2400), ask for Sajama, pay the full fare. If continuing into Chile (same buses) remember that no meat, dairy products, fruit or vegetables may be taken across the border. This area will become more accessible when the new La Paz-Arica highway is completed.

ROUTES A road and railway line run S from Oruro, through Río Mulato, the junction for trains to Potosí, to Uyuni (323 km). The road is sandy, and after rain very bad, especially S of Río Mulato.

UYUNI

Uyuni (*pop* 10,000; *alt* 3,665m), lies bitterly cold and unprotected near the eastern edge of the Salar de Uyuni. Still a commercial and communication centre, Uyuni was, for much of this century, important as a major railway junction. A giant statue of an armed railway worker, erected after the 1952 Revolution, dominates Av Ferroviaria. Most services are near the station. Water is frequently cut off and may only be available between 0600 and midday. Market Sun. Uyuni's main point of interest is as a centre for excursions to the Salar de Uyuni, Laguna Colorada and Laguna Verde (see below).

20 km E is **Pulcayo**, on the road to Potosí: a largely abandoned mining town with a railway cemetery and alpaca wool factory (**G** *Hotel Rancho No 1*, without bath, large old rooms, hot water, good meals).

Local information
● Accommodation
D *Avenida*, Av Ferroviaria, opp station, T 2078, in renovated wing, rooms with bath, hot water, **E** without bath in old wing, clean, washing facilities, timed hot showers US$1 extra, motorcycle parking, best place to make up group for tour; **F** *Res Sucre*, C Sucre, clean, padlocks on doors, basic; **F** *Hostal Tuyupa*, Av Ferroviaria, unlimited hot water, 4 rooms, quiet, cosy, friendly; **G** pp *Residencial Urkupiña*, basic and quite clean, hot water.

● Places to eat
Pizzería Paso Dorado, very good food, not cheap; other places on main plaza: *16 de Julio*, Av Arce, opens 0700, not cheap, good meeting place; *Pizzas Internacional*, opens 0800, excellent breakfasts; *Cafetería El Repostero*; *Urquipiña*. *Restaurant-Bar Los Andes*, C Bolívar, good. *Salteñas* go on sale about 0900 daily; good breakfast in market for US$0.50.

● Banks & money changers
Bidesa, Av Potosí, changes TCs in bolivianos or dollars cash (2% commission). Outside banking hours, try photographer's shop on Av Potosí, changes dollars or Chilean pesos. Tour agencies and some shops accept payment in TCs.

● Useful addresses
The Immigration Office is at Av Potosí 10; only issues 30-day stamps, for 90 days go to Potosí. The tourist office, Av Potosí 13, is helpful.

● Transport
Trains The train service to Calama, Chile, is described under **Railways To/From the Coast** (3), page 273. Uyuni is also a stop on the La Paz-Oruro-Villazón line: Oruro-Villazón arrives at 0130 Mon/Thur, 0230 Wed/Sun and at 2330 Fri. Uyuni-La Paz (Expreso del Sur, Sat 2030, US$11.55; to Oruro, pullman Mon and Fri 0130, US$3.50; local train Thur 0240, 7 hrs. Daily freight train to Ollagüe, US$4.50, 6 hrs.

Buses To La Paz and Oruro, direct night bus with Panasur, Wed/Sun 1800, US$10.50, 13 hrs, terrible road as far as Huari; buses also dep hourly day and night for La Paz but have to change in Oruro (7 hrs, US$6.75, 11 de Julio 1900, Flecha del Norte 2000); to Tupiza, 11 de

Julio, Wed and Fri 1500, US$5.20, 7½ hrs; to **Potosí**, 5 lines all daily at 1030, 6 hrs, US$4.15-5.20, spectacular journey on unpaved roads.

By Road to Chile Motorists must be warned against the direct route from Uyuni into Chile by way of Ollagüe. There is the danger of getting lost on the many tracks leading over the deserted salt lakes, no gasoline between Uyuni and Calama (Chile), and little hope of help with a breakdown on the Bolivian side unless you don't mind waiting for perhaps a week. After rain the route is impassable and even experienced guides get lost. Maps give widely differing versions of the route. "Where the road has been built up, *never* forsake it for the appealing soft salt beside it. The salt takes a man's weight but a vehicle breaks through the crust into unfathomable depths of plasticine mud below." – Andrew Parkin.

To hitch to Chile via Ollagüe, trucks first go N, then across the Salar de Ollagüe. The scenery on this route is amazing and, once in Chile, you will see lakes similar to Lagunas Colorada and Verde. There is nowhere to stay in Ollagüe, but police and border officials will help find lodging and transport for hitchers.

SALAR DE UYUNI

The salt lake is claimed to be the largest in the world. "When it still has water in it (up to 4 or possibly 6 ins), being in the middle of the Salar de Uyuni is like being an ant on a gigantic mirror. The blue sky merges into the blue water, the islands are perfectly reflected and since there is no horizon they appear suspended in space. Some areas may be dry, in which case the salt crust is as blinding-white and featureless as the most perfect snowfield (sunglasses essential)." – Stephen Saker.

On its W side, 5 hrs from Uyuni, is **Llica**, capital of Daniel Campos province. Good for llama and other wool handicrafts, but there are no shops or electricity. **F** *Alojamiento Municipal*, basic; Angel Quispe in the plaza has 3 beds; meals available in private houses. Bus from Uyuni 1200 daily, truck 1100.

TOURS TO LAGUNA COLORADA AND LAGUNA VERDE

Laguna Colorada (4,775m), 346 km SW of Uyuni, 12 hrs straight driving over unmarked, rugged truck tracks, is one of Bolivia's most spectacular and most isolated marvels. The shores and shallows of the lake are crusted with gypsum and salt, an arctic-white counterpoint to the flaming red, algae-coloured waters in which the rare James flamingoes, along with the more common Chilean and Andean flamingoes, breed and live. The leg and bill colorations are the easiest way to distinguish the three breeds. Chilean: brownish-blue legs with red knee-joints; almost white bill with brown-black tip. Andean: bright yellow legs; black front half on yellow bill. James: dark, brick-red legs; small black tip on bright yellow bill. See: *The Birds of Chile*, AW Johnson, or *Land Above the Clouds*, Tony Morrison.

The standard outing (see below for operators) lasts 4 days and takes visitors from Uyuni N to the Salar de Uyuni, S on to Lagunas Colorado and Verde, and then back to Uyuni. Day one: Uyuni to Colchani, thence to the Salar, including a salt-mine visit, lunch on the cactus-studded Isla Pescado, and overnight at a village, eg San Juan, S of the Salar (simple lodging, US$4.15-5.50, electricity 1900-2100, running water). Between Colchani (17 km) and Isla Pescado is **D** *Hotel Playa Blanca* run by Teodoro Colque, built entirely of salt, furniture and all. Day two: to Laguna Colorada, passing active Volcán Ollagüe and a chain of small, flamingo-specked lagoons. Overnight at Laguna Colorada. (Eustaquio Berna runs the *campamento*, US$1.90 to stay, dirty, no washing facilities, windy. Day three: drive past belching geysers at Sol de Mañana (do not walk over the geysers) and through the Pampa de Challviri (4,800m, via a pass at 5,000m) where telluric outcroppings sprout from sand dunes surrounded by wind-scoured mountains, to the wind-lashed, frothy jade waters of the **Laguna Verde** (4,600m) at the foot of Volcán Licancábur, and back to Laguna Colorada. At Aguas Termales Pulque, between the two lakes, hot springs feed the salty water at about 30°C (hottest early am), makes up for the lack of facilities at Laguna Colorado. *Refugio* at Laguna Verde, US$2, small, mattresses, running water, view of lake. Day four: Return to Uyuni. A 3-day version eliminates the Salar de Uyuni.

● **Tour operators**
The normal vehicle used by agencies is the Toyota Land Cruiser, taking, usually, 6 passengers. The cost for a trip is US$300 (or US$50 pp), but it may vary according to the number of days and the demand. (Whether you return to Uyuni or proceed into Chile, you pay for a round-trip.) Price incl gas and meals but excludes lodging. Tents are not required, but a warm sleeping bag is essential (can be hired from an agency).

Temperatures at Laguna Colorada can easily drop below -20°C even out of the persistent strong winds. It is imperative that trips carry sufficient food, water and fuel and that the vehicle is equipped with spares and is up to the task. Take warm bedding, candles, hat, swimming costume and high factor sun tan lotion. **NB** Reports vary on the quality of tours. Obtain a written contract and be firm. Try to check the vehicle before agreeing terms. Insist on taking spares and try to ensure the vehicle is filled with fuel the evening before (in case of power cuts). It is worth taking two drivers and choosing an agency with experienced drivers and radio contact. We have received reports of drivers getting so drunk they are incapable of setting off on time the following day; also reported to try to cut a day off a 4-day tour.

Tours can be organized in Uyuni, in Potosí or La Paz (some of the Uyuni companies are connected with Potosí and La Paz travel agencies). In Uyuni there are 17 agencies; rec are: *Transandino Tours* (Wilma Ignacio Apala, Casilla 18, T 0693-2132, or La Paz 820353); *Pucara Tours* (Jhovana Valiz Rojas), Av Arce 04, T (0693) 2055, Nelson Blas Quisbeth is a good driver and guide, good food; *Brisa Tours*; *Tunupa Tours* (Elias Cruz Romero, good value); *Esmeralda Tours*; *Olivos Tours*; *Juliet Tours* (Juliet is very helpful, her husband, Omar, is a knowledgeable guide, good vehicles). Prices are higher in La Paz and Potosí. It is quite easy to get a group together in Uyuni, except at Carnival; everyone is at Oruro. Tours do not run at Christmas/New Year.

CROSSING INTO CHILE

If you plan to enter Chile via one of the unattended border crossings in the SW region, you must get an exit stamp at the Bolivian immigration office in Uyuni (Mon-Fri only). There are no immigration offices SW of Uyuni. The stamp is valid for 3 days, ie you have 72 hrs to get out of Bolivia, but more than 72 hrs may be permitted if you state the exact date you intend to leave Bolivia. Before issuing the exit stamp, Bolivian immigration requires that you present proof of travel, ie your excursion contract. Your tour company can arrange passport formalities on the morning you are leaving. Buy Chilean pesos in Uyuni.

To **San Pedro de Atacama (Chile)** From Laguna Verde it is 7 km to Hito Cajones, the frontier post with Chile. Tour agencies will, if requested beforehand, leave travellers here. A further 8 km is La Cruz, the junction with the E-W road used by trucks carrying borax and sulphur from the mines to San Pedro. There are reports of a daily bus Hito Cajones-San Pedro, but it is much safer to ask tour agencies to arrange for transport from Hito Cajones to San Pedro de Atacama (eg *Nativa*: see San Pedro de Atacama **Tourist Agencies**, page 732, and **Frontier with Bolivia**). The meteorological station at Laguna Verde will radio for a pick-up from San Pedro. This service costs US$10 pp Hito Cajones-San Pedro. The chance of finding other transport is remote. Adequate, food, water and clothing essential. **Do not underestimate the dangers of getting stuck without transport or lodging at this altitude. Do not travel alone.**

TUPIZA

South of Uyuni, 200 km, is **Tupiza** (*pop* 20,000; *alt* 2,990m), a centre of the silver, tin, lead, and bismuth mining industries. The statue in the main square of Tupiza is to Victor Carlos Aramayo, the founding member of the Aramayo mining dynasty, pre-eminent in the late 19th, early 20th centuries, together with the Patiños and the Hoschilds. Chajra Huasi, a palazzo-style, abandoned home of the Aramayo family across the Río Tupiza, may be visited. It was expropriated by the government after the 1952 revolution. Local history museum, on 2nd floor of *Casa Municipal de Cultura*, just off plaza, free entry, open late pm. IGM office, for maps, is in the Municipal building. Beautiful sunsets over the fertile Tupiza valley can be seen from the foot of a Christ statue on a hill behind the plaza.

Local information
● **Accommodation & services**

F *Mitru*, Av Chichas, run down, private shower and bath, water unreliable, poor plumbing, downstairs rooms preferable, laundry can take 3 days, but still the best, restaurant has good *almuerzo*, but no dinner, annex has snack shop and restaurant, both open for dinner; **F** *Res Valle Hermoso*, Av Pedro Arraya, T 589, hot showers, good, will let you park motorbikes in restaurant; **F** *Centro*, 2 blocks from station, clean, friendly and quiet; **F** *Res My Home*, Abaroa 288, shared bath, hot water, clean, friendly, rec; **G** pp *El Rancho*, Av Arraya 200 block, without bath; also **G** pp *Res Monterrey*, opp railway station, clean, hot water. *Picantería Las Brisas*, on opp side of river, open Sat and Sun only, large helpings; on C Chorolque nr plaza are, *Los Helechos* and *Il Bambino*, both rec; good ice cream at *Cremelin*, on plaza; *El Flamingo*, good cheap meals; good breakfast at Mercado Negro.

TCs can be changed at *Empresa Bernall Hmnos*, but only in the presence of the owner, good rates, many shops will also change dollars at better rates than in Villazón. Hospital Ferroviário (nr *Hotel Mitru*), Dr Rolando Llano Navarro and staff, very helpful.

● **Transport**
Trains To Villazon, Mon/Thur arr 0700 from Oruro, Wed/Sun arr 0845, Fri at 0415, 3 hrs. To Uyuni, Mon, Tues, Thur, Fri and Sat. To La Paz, dep Sat 1530.
Buses To Villazón 3 hrs, US$2.50, 1000 and 1500; to Potosí, US$5.40, O'Globo at 1000, 8 hrs, Expreso Tupiza daily 2030, US$7.75; to Uyuni, US$5.20, 7½ hrs. No direct bus to La Paz, only via Potosí. A new road is being built from Uyuni to Atocha. Bad road from Potosí which goes on S to Villazón; often closed in rainy season because road fords the Río Suipacha.

TO SAN VICENTE

Tupiza is the centre of Butch Cassidy and the Sundance Kid country. On 4 November 1908, they held up an Aramayo company payroll N of Salo. (Aramayo *hacienda* in Salo, 1 hr N of Tupiza, still stands. Roadside kiosks serve excellent roast goat, *choclo, papas*, soup.) 2 days later they encountered and were killed by a four-man military-police patrol in **San Vicente** (*pop* 400; *alt* 4,500m), 103 km, 4 to 6 hrs on a good dirt road, NW of Tupiza. Shootout site off main street – ask locals. Cassidy and Sundance are buried in an unmarked grave in the cemetery, but the grave has yet to be found. An investigation of the supposed grave, by the Nova project in 1991, proved negative, but see *Digging Up Butch and Sundance*, by Anne Meadows (New York: St Martin's Press, 1994). Whether Butch and Sundance did die here or not, San Vicente has been described by one correspondent as "a very sad place to die".

● **Accommodation** Basic *alojamiento* on main street marked 'Hotel'; restaurant 'El Rancho' next-door; several *tiendas* sell beer, soda, canned goods, etc.

● **Tour companies & travel agents** Dr Félix Chalar Miranda, President of the local historical society offers jeep tours to the hold-up site nr Salo, the escape route and San Vicente; T 467 (office), 509 (home) or contact via *Inquietud* newspaper editor at Av Cul Arraya 205. *Tupiza Tours*, Av Chichas 187, T/F (694) 3001, Casilla 67, offer 2-day tours which follow Butch and Sundance's movements in 1908, US$80-100 pp, inc transport, guide, meals and lodging, run by Fabiola Mitru whose parents run *Hotel Mitru*; also through *Potosí Tours*, Galeria Chuquiago, C Sagárnaga 213, T/F 350870, La Paz, Casilla 11034.

● **Transport** Trucks from Tupiza on Thur early am from Av Chichas nr *Hotel Mitru*. Alternatively hire a vehicle: Fermín Ortega at Taller Nardini, Barrio Lourdes, rec; Don Manuel at *Hotel Mitru* can suggest others, US$30 to US$80 one-way. (Also accessible and a bit closer from Atocha, but fewer vehicles for hire.)

SOUTH TO ARGENTINA

VILLAZON

The Argentine border is at **Villazón** (*pop* 13,000; *alt* 3,443m) 81 km S of Tupiza. Little to see in Villazón (has two cinemas) and not at all welcoming; border area must not be photographed.

Local information
● **Accommodation & places to eat**
E *Res El Cortijo*, clean, good value, intermittent hot water, restaurant; **F** pp *Grand Palace*, behind bus station, safe; **F** *Hotel Bolivia*, 1 block from border, clean small rooms, good value breakfast, hot showers extra; **F** *Panamericano*, clean, laundry facilities, rec. **F** *Res Martínez*, ½ block from bus station, well signed, hot water when town's supply is on, basic but clean and well-maintained; **F** *Res 10 de Febrero*, next door, very basic. Restaurants opp bus station and

on 1st floor of covered market, eg *Repostería*, about US$1 a head. The Mercado Municipal de Vivanderos is nr the frontier, parallel with main street, across the railway.

● **Banks & money changers**
Money changing at *Cambio Porvenir* or other *cambios* on main street, good rates (some take TCs), also at *Cambio Trébol*, shop by border that sells train tickets (see below) but with 6% commission on TCs; Banco del Estado does not change TCs. Out of hours try the Ciné Rex. No exchange facilities in La Quiaca.

● **Transport**
Road An improved road goes to Tarija. The road linking Potosí with Villazón via Camargo is in poor condition and about 100 km longer than the better road via Tupiza.

Buses To Potosí several between 0830 and 1830, 10-15 hrs, US$7-8 (unsurfaced road – terrible in the wet, can take 24 hrs); to Tupiza, 0700 and 1500, US$2.50; to Tarija, beautiful journey but most buses overnight only, daily at 1900/2000, US$6.50, 6 hrs, very cold on arrival but passengers can sleep on bus until daybreak. From La Paz, several companies: journey takes 25 hrs, costs US$17.25, eg Panamericana and Chicheña, even though buses called 'direct', you may have to change in Potosí, perhaps to another company, eg Villa Imperial. 1830 depart La Paz, 0700 arrive Potosí, 0830 leave Potosí, 1930 arrive Villazón. The same procedure applies from Villazón to La Paz. Bus station is nr plaza, behind Ciné Teatro Libertador Bolívar; it is 5 blocks from the border. Taxi to border, US$0.35 or hire porter, US$1, and walk across.

Trains Station about 1 km N of frontier on main road, taxi US$2.35. To Oruro for La Paz (very dusty and cold journey), Mon/Thur 1630, US$5.60, Tues/Fri 1600, US$7.50, *Expreso del Sur*, Sat at 1300, US$15. Train stops at Tupiza, Atocha, Uyuni and Oruro. The express from La Paz/Oruro connects with a bus to Tarija, tickets from railway station. Ticket office opens 0800, long queues.

FRONTIER WITH ARGENTINA
● **Bolivian immigration**
The Bolivian offices open at 0700. Bolivian officials tend to stamp papers in the morning only, so a night in Villazón is usually required; border guards will allow this. There is an entry/exit tax of US$4. This is an easy crossing.

NB Bolivian time is 1 hr earlier than Argentina.

● **Argentine consulate**
In main plaza, Villazón, open Mon-Fri 1400-1700.

Potosí, Sucre and the Southern Highlands

THE WORLD Cultural Heritage sites of Potosí, with its rich mining past and current mining misery, and Sucre, the white city. In the S of this region, Tarija is known for its fruit and wines and its traditions which set it apart from the rest of the country.

POTOSI

Potosí (*pop* 110,000; *alt* 4,070m; *phone code* 062), 551 km SE of La Paz, is the highest city of its size in the world. The climate is often bitterly cold and fireplaces are few; warm clothes essential. It was founded by the Spaniards on 10 April 1545, after they had discovered Indian mine workings at Cerro Rico, the hill at whose foot it stands.

Immense amounts of silver were once extracted. In Spain 'éste es un Potosí' (it's a Potosí) is still used for anything superlatively rich. By the early 17th century Potosí was the largest city in the Americas, but over the next two centuries, as its lodes began to deteriorate and silver was found elsewhere, Potosí became little more than a ghost town. It was the demand for tin – a metal the Spaniards ignored – that lifted the city to comparative prosperity again. Silver, copper and lead are also mined.

Places of interest

Large parts of Potosí are colonial, with twisting, narrow streets and an occasional great mansion with its coat of arms over the doorway. UNESCO has declared the city to be 'Patrimonio de la Humanidad'. Some of the best buildings are grouped round the Plaza 10 de Noviembre. The old Cabildo and the Royal Treasury – Las Cajas Reales – are both here, converted to other uses. **The Cathedral** (open Mon-Fri 0930-1000, 1300-1500, Sat 0930-1000, guided tour only, US$1) faces Plaza 10 de Noviembre, and nearby is the Mint, the **Casa Real de Moneda** (founded 1572, rebuilt 1759-1773), one of the chief monuments of civil building in Hispanic America (C Ayacucho, T 22777).

The **Moneda** (entrance US$1.65, US$2 to take photos), has a museum in many sections occupying 30 of its 160 rooms. The main art gallery is in a splendid salon on the 1st floor. One section is dedicated to the works of the 17th-18th century religious painter Melchor Pérez de Holguín, one of Bolivia's most acclaimed artists. Elsewhere are coin dies and huge wooden presses which made the silver strip from which coins were cut. The smelting houses have carved altar pieces from Potosí's ruined churches. There are also sections on armaments and on mineralogy. You cannot fail to notice the huge, grinning mask over an archway between two principal courtyards; its significance is uncertain, perhaps to hide a coat of arms at the time of Independence. You are advised to wear warm clothes, as it is cold inside; a guided tour (obligatory) starts at 0900 and 1400 sharp, and lasts for 2½ hrs, Spanish only. The rooms are only opened for the tours. Open Mon-Sat 0900-1200 and 1400-1700.

The **Convento y Museo de Santa Teresa** at Chicas y Ayacucho, T 23847 (entry US$2, US$2 to take photos, Mon-Fri 0900-1200, 1300-1800, Sat 0900-1200, but check at Tourist Office, tour is Spanish) has an interesting collection of colonial and religious art, obligatory guide. Among Potosí's baroque churches, typical of the Andean or 'mestizo' architecture of the 18th century, are the **Compañía** (Jesuit) church, on

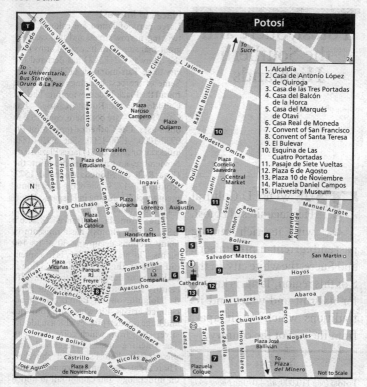

Potosí

1. Alcaldía
2. Casa de Antonio López de Quiroga
3. Casa de las Tres Portadas
4. Casa del Balcón de la Horca
5. Casa del Marqués de Otavi
6. Casa Real de Moneda
7. Convent of San Francisco
8. Convent of Santa Teresa
9. El Bulevar
10. Esquina de Las Cuatro Portadas
11. Pasaje de Siete Vueltas
12. Plaza 6 de Agosto
13. Plaza 10 de Noviembre
14. Plazuela Daniel Campos
15. University Museum

Ayacucho, with an impressive bell-gable (1700, closed for restoration since 1992), **San Francisco** (Tarija y Nogales) with a fine organ (can be visited in morning and evening, worthwhile for the views from the tower and roof, museum of ecclesiastical art, underground tunnel system, open 1400-1600, Mon-Fri, entry US$1.45, US$2 to take photos), and **San Lorenzo**, with a rich portal (1728-1744, C Héroes del Chaco); fine views from the tower. **San Martín** on C Hoyos, with an uninviting exterior, is beautiful inside, but is normally closed for fear of theft. Ask the German Redemptorist Fathers to show you around; their office is just to the left of their church. Other churches to visit include **Jerusalén**, close to the *Hotel Centenario*, and **San Agustín** (only by prior

arrangement with tourist office) on Bolívar y Quijarro, with crypts and catacombs (the whole city was interconnected by tunnels in colonial times). Tour starts at 1700, US$0.10 admission. From **San Cristóbal**, at Pacheco y Cañete, one gets a fine view over the whole city. **Teatro Omiste** on Plaza 6 de Agosto is under restoration; it has a fine façade. The University has a museum with some good modern Bolivian painting (Mon-Fri, 1000-1200, 1500-1700, entrance US$1, C Bolívar, T 22248).

In Potosí, 2,000 colonial buildings have been catalogued. For example, C Quijarro, one of Potosí's best-preserved streets, was, in colonial times, C Ollería – potmakers – and C de los Sombreros. The whole block behind San Agustín belonged to the monastery; there are many wooden balconies, many houses retain colonial interiors with balconies, patio, rings for tying horses, etc, but much restoration is needed. At Quijarro and Omiste is the Esquina de las Cuatro Portadas (four houses with double doors), or Balcón de Llamacancha. There is a fine stone doorway (house of the Marqués de Otavi) in Junín between Matos and Bolívar. Off Junín, see the Pasaje de Siete Vueltas (the passage of the seven turns). At Lanza 8 was the house of José de Quiroz and of Antonio López de Quiroga (now a school). Turn up Chuquisaca from Lanza and after 3 blocks right into Millares; here on the left is a sculpted stone doorway and on the right a doorway with two rampant lions in low relief on the lintel. Turning left up Nogales you come to an old mansion in a little plaza. Turn left along La Paz and 1 block along there is another stone doorway with suns in relief. At La Paz y Bolívar is the Casa del Balcón de la Horca. Turn left for the Casa de las Tres Portadas.

Local festivals

San Bartolomé, or the Fiesta de Chutillos, is held from the middle of Aug, with the main event being processions of dancers on the last weekend, Sat featuring Potosino, and San national, groups. Costumes can be hired in artesanía market on C Sucre. In May there is a market on C Gumiel every Sun, with lotteries and lots of fun things for sale. On three consecutive Sat at the end of May, beginning of June llama sacrifices are made at the cooperative mines in honour of Pachamama; the same occurs on 1 Aug, the Ritual del Espíritu. Other mining festivals are the Carnaval Minero and the Fiesta de los Compadres in Feb, for decorating El Tío (the Dios Minero) and one's workplace. Potosí is sometimes called the 'Ciudad de las Costumbres', especially at Corpus Cristi, Todos Santos and Carnaval, when special cakes are baked, families go visiting friends, etc. In Oct, Festival Internacional de la Cultura, in Potosí and Sucre.

Local information

● **Accommodation**

Unless otherwise stated hotels have no heating in rooms. **C** *Claudia*, Av Maestro 322, 3-star, T 22242, helpful, modern, highly rec; **C** *Hostal Colonial*, Hoyos 8, a pretty colonial house (T 24809) nr the main plaza, rec, with heating, has names and T numbers of guides, even if you're not staying there very helpful, very expensive for long-distance phone calls; **C** *Hostal Libertador*, Millares 58, T 27877/24629, Casilla 324, heaters in rooms, with bath, clean, quiet, comfortable, parking (owner is Sr Wilson Mendieta Pacheco, director of Casa Real de la Moneda); **C** *Hostal Felimar*, Junín 14, T 24357, 2-star, hot water, breakfast, 2 roof-top suites, solar-powered (so no hot water early morning), 1st floor rooms have no exterior windows but warm, quiet;

D *Hostal Santa María*, Av Serrudo 244, T 23255, clean, hot water, comfortable, friendly, good cafetería, rec; **D** *Jerusalem*, Oruro 143, T/F 22600, pleasant, helpful, comedor, with bath, E without, parking, laundry, highly rec; **D** *El Turista*, Lanza 19 (T 22492), also LAB office, helpful, hot showers all day, breakfast (US$1) highly rec, with bath and TV, good value; **D** *Hotel IV Centenario*, Plaza del Estudiante, T 22751, hot water all day, large cold rooms, central, very run down, poor service.

E *Central*, Bustillos 1230 y Linares, T 22207, hot shower, breakfast, basic, friendly; **E** *Hotel Carlos V*, Linares 42 on Plaza 6 de Agosto, T 25151, friendly, breakfast, without bath, occasional hot water, clean, luggage store, rec; **E-F** *Res Sumaj*, Gumiel 10, T 23336, small rooms, double room on top floor good views, not always hot water, shared bathrooms only, mixed reports; **E** *Res Felcar*, Serrudo 345 y Bustillos, T 24966, F without bath, clean, hot water, 0800-1200, friendly, popular.

F *Alojamiento La Paz*, Oruro 262, T 22632, central, basic, clean; **F** *Residencial Copacabana*, Av Serrudo 319, T 22712, individual or shared rooms, restaurant, clean, separate hot showers, will change $ cash, safe car park (owner, Dr Hugo Linares Fuentes will give medical assistance).

G *Alojamiento Ferrocarril*, Av E Villazón 159, T 24294, basic, clean (hot showers US$0.55), friendly, close to the railway station; **G** *Alojamiento San Lorenzo*, Bustillos 967, T 24842, close to market, very basic, no shower or hot water; **G** pp *Casa de María Victoria*, Chuquisaca 148, T 22132, clean, stores luggage, popular, friendly, laundry facilities, often no water pm, breakfast available, rec.

Youth Hostels: **D-E** *San Antonio*, Oruro 136, T 23566, US$2 pp without breakfast, dirty;

F *Alojamiento El Barquito*, Oruro 7, T 22600 (not obviously spotted, good, rustic, rec).

5 km from Potosí in the village of San Antonio is *Hotel El Tambo*, Km 5 Carretera a Oruro, T 25597, F 22985, 3-star, colonial/rustic architecture, 3 restaurants, Bodega Bar, all details from Hidalgo Tours (see below).

● **Places to eat**
Sumaj Orcko, Quijarro 46, excellent, large portions, cheap set lunch, reasonably priced, very popular with travellers, heating, slow service; *Plaza*, Quijarro 38, serves a cheap set lunch, good and friendly; *Pastelería Royal*, Linares 32 esq Padilla, small selection of good snacks and cakes; *El Mesón*, corner of Plaza 10 de Noviembre nr Tarija, irregular opening, European-style, reasonably priced, mixed reports; *Las Vegas*, Padilla 1, 1st floor, cheap *almuerzos*, dinner more expensive, good; *Anexo El Criollo*, Bolívar 581, good, excellent steaks; *Don Lucho*, Bolívar 789, large and tasty servings, but not cheap, meat good, *peñas* on Fri, check entrance fee for show before eating. *The Sky Room* at Bolívar 701 has interesting views of the town and the Cerro, pricey, slow service; *La Carreta*, Gumiel s/n, excellent, pleasant service, mid-price range; *Quillahuasi*, Junín 56, good; *Kivo's*, Quijarro 12, very good Italian food; *Coffee Snack El Farol*, Tarija 28, opp San Francisco, high kitsch decor, bohemian atmosphere, popular with artists, open late; *Confitería Cherys*, Padilla 12 y Linares, friendly, good cakes, coffee, burgers, very popular, good breakfast, cheap, rec, open 0800. Other *confiterías*: *Santa Clara*, Plaza 10 de Noviembre, open 0800 for breakfast and pizzas, and *Chaplin*, Bustillos 979, open 0730 for breakfast. Good value food in Mercado Central, between Oruro, Bustillos, Héroes del Chaco and Bolívar; breakfast from 0700, fresh bread from 0600.

● **Banks & money changers**
Banco Nacional, Junín 4-6, exchange for US$ TCs and cash. Many shops on Plaza Alonso de Ibañez and on Bolívar, Sucre and Padilla display 'compro dólares' signs. TCs can also be changed at Distribuidora Cultural Sud, Matos 19. **Banco Popular**, Bolívar y Sucre, cash withdrawals on Visa.

● **Entertainment**
Public baths: Sauna Florida, Plaza Chuquimina, nr bus station, open Fri, Sat, Sun, US$1.50 (also has racquetball).

● **Hospitals & medical services**
Clinics: Clínica Británica, on Oruro nr *Alojamiento La Paz*, clinics am and pm, English spoken.

● **Laundry**
Limpieza la Veloz, C Quijarro, corner of Mattos, Edif Cademin, and at Camacho 258,

US$1.30/kilo.

● **Post & telecommunications**
Post Office: Lanza 3, open Sat till 1900, Sun 0900-1200; unreliable for overseas mail.

Telecommunications: Entel, on Plaza Arce at end of Av Camacho, T 43496; also at Av Universitaria nr bus terminal.

● **Shopping**
Mercado Central (see address above) sells mainly food and produce but silver is sold nr the C Oruro entrance. *Mercado Gremial*, between Av Camacho and Oruro, only sells household goods. There is an informal swap market every Fri night at the Plazuela, at Bolívar and Quijarro. Handwoven cloth is sold only in *Mercado Artesanal*, at Sucre y Omista, which has a wide variety of regional handicrafts at reasonable prices. Some Fri the merchants organize music, food and drink (*ponche*), not to be missed. Almost opp is *Andina*, Sucre 94, for handicrafts and antiques. For musical instruments, Arnaud Gerard (Belgian), workshop *Killay* at the back of Mercado Artesanal, makes beautifully made and tuned pieces, designed to be played, will make to order, open Mon-Fri, 1700-1930. The best bookshop is at the University, open Mon-Fri, 1000-1200, 1500-1700. Postcards, gifts etc from gift shop at entrance to Post Office.

● **Tour companies & travel agents**
Hidalgo Tours, Junín y Bolívar, T 28293, F 22985, Casilla 310, specialized services within the city and to Salar de Uyuni, highly rec for mine visits (see below); *Potosí Tours*, corner of Padilla, on the Plaza, good tours of the city and mine (see below); *Transamazonas*, Quijarro 12, Edif Cámara de Minería, T 27175, F 24796; *Koala Tours*, Ayacucho 5, opp Casa de la Moneda, PO Box 33, T 24708, F 22092 mine tours (see below); *Turismo Balsa*, Plaza Alonzo de Ibáñez, T 26272, English spoken, daily city and mine tours (see also La Paz **Travel Agents**). Also rec for mine tours are: *Altiplano Tours*, Ayacucho 19, T25353/27299. *Transandino Tours*, on Quijarro, changes TCs at reasonable rates.

Some agencies offer trips to the Salar de Uyuni, Laguna Colorada and Laguna Verde (see above page 301) but this is more expensive and time-consuming than excursions to these places from Uyuni. Tours from Potosí cost US$160-180 pp and last 5-6 days. It is essential to get a written contract (a tourist police requirement) and make sure that the guide is approved by the police. Other important hints are given under Uyuni.

● **Tourist offices**
On 2nd Floor, Cámara de Minería, C Quijarro (T 25288), ½ block from main plaza, and kiosk on Plaza Alonso de Ibañez (both closed Sat and Sun and unreliable opening times during the

week); sells town maps (US$0.25), information booklet (US$2.50), helpful. Instituto Geográfico Militar, C La Paz, possible to buy maps, 0900-1200, 1400-1800.

● **Useful addresses**
Migración: La Paz 1001.

Police station: on Plaza 10 de Noviembre.

● **Transport**
Local Taxi: within city limits US$0.55; approx US$1.30/km for longer journeys. Buses US$0.15.

Air Aerosur (Bolívar and Junín, T 22087) to La Paz daily except Sun at 1005, with connections to Cobija, Cochabamba, Guayaramerín, Santa Cruz, Tarija and Trinidad. LAB fly to La Paz, also Santa Cruz, Sucre and Cochabamba. Book flights well in advance. Airport is 5 km out of town on the Sucre road.

Trains Potosí is on the La Paz, Oruro, Potosí, Sucre line. Trains leave La Paz for Potosí Tues and Sat 1700, US$10.40. Service is good, with blankets, heating, meals and drinks for sale. Full information from Enfe at the station, T 23101.

Buses Terminal out of town, on Av Universitaria, below railway station, 30 mins walk, steeply uphill to main plaza (or *micros* C, I or L); through buses from La Paz call here at the toll gate, as they are not allowed to enter city limits. There is an information office at the terminal, T 26075, an express mail service, an Entel office and a terminal bar, 50 centavos. To **Tarija**, Andesbus daily 0930, 1400, US$13.65, rec; San Jorge daily at 1600, US$10.75; Emperador (T 25580), daily, US$13.65 at 1600; 10 de Noviembre daily at 0830. To **Villazón**, several companies daily, usually departing 1800-1900, 12 hrs (O'Globo and Trans Villa Imperial at 0800), US$7-8 (Trans Tupiza, T 24264, rec). To **Cochabamba**, US$6.75-9.50, San Miguel, direct, 1800 (via Oruro at 0700), Trans and Flota Copacabana and El Dorado at 1900. Many buses to **La Paz** (mostly overnight in either direction, 10-14 hrs, US$6.75-11, you get what you pay for), Flota Copacabana, good, Trans Copacabana luxury service with heat and video, US$16.35, 10 hrs, spacious, rec. To **Oruro**, US$5.40-6.70, Bustillos (T 25672) and San Miguel, 8 hrs, dep 0700 and 1900, Universo dep 0630 (but poor time-keeping, chaotic, not rec). To **Uyuni**, TransAmerican (office on Av Universitario opp terminal, T 27162), comfortable, dep 1200, 5-6 hrs; 11 de Julio (T 28126, rec), dep 1800, US$4.15; Emperador and Flecha Norte dep 1200, US$5.20; all have offices on Av Villa Imperial Toledo y Av Antofagasta and leave from here; rough unpaved road, book in advance, especially on the day when the bus connects with the Oruro-Calama train. To **Sucre**, 2½ hrs:

two types of service, the more luxurious being Andesbus, Bustillos 1094, T 25050, US$6.50, rec; similar service with Transtin, Plaza Arce, T 22056, dep 0700 and 1700; Emperador, Bustillos and San Jorge all have offices in terminal, dep 0630, 0700 and 0800; all buses dep from terminal. To **Santa Cruz**, Trans Copacabana and El Dorado, 1900, and Flota Copacabana, 1930, both US$16.30.

VISITS TO THE MINES

The state mines in Cerro Rico were closed in the 1980s and are now worked as cooperatives by small groups of miners. A 4½ hrs morning tour to the cooperative mines and ore-processing plant involves meeting miners and seeing them at work in medieval conditions. Visitors need to be reasonably fit as parts are very hard going, not recommended for claustrophobics or asthmatics. Guided tours are offered by former miners, who provide essential equipment – helmet, lamp and usually protective clothing (but check when booking). Wear old clothes and take torch and a handkerchief to filter the dusty air. The price of tours is US$6 pp and includes transport. A contribution to the miners' cooperative is appreciated as are medicines for the new health centre (*Posta Sanitaria*) on Cerro Rico. New projects (a radio, drinking water) have been, or will shortly be realized. You will also be asked to contribute towards buying presents for the miners – dynamite, coca leaves, cigarettes. The Pailaviri State mine is closed temporarily as of April 1995.

● **Guides** By law all guides have to work with a travel agency. Guides rec inc: Eduardo Garnica Fajardo, Hernández 1035, Casilla 33, T 24708/22092 (Koala Tours), he speaks English, French and some Hebrew (frequently rec, and sometimes impersonated by unprofessionals). Koala Tours offer breakfast at 0600, 'plato típico' with llama meat; they also donate 15% of their fee to support on-site health-care facilities (donations can be sent to Eduardo Garnica). Also highly rec as an English-speaking guide for small groups is Julio César Morales (Sumaj Tours, *Hotel Jerusalém*, address above). Raul Braulio, Millares 147 (Transamazonas Tours), T 25304, experienced guide, speaks some English, will take only 1 or 2 people; Santos and Marco Mamami, Pacheco 60, T 27299; Roberto Méndez E, Campamento Pailaviri 4, T 26900, runs tours organized by *Casa de María Victoria* (see above) speaks English, very knowledgeable, small groups, rec;

Salustio Gallardo, C Betanzos 231, nr Plaza Minero; Juan Carlos González, Av Japón 10, T 26349 (Turismo Balsa), rec, Spanish spoken only. Efraín Huanca (Hidalgo Tours) warmly rec as friendly and very informative. The size of tour groups varies – some agencies, eg Koala, limit groups to 10, some groups are as large as 20 people, which is excessive.

THERMAL BATHS AT TARAPAYA

On the road to Oruro, a good place to spend a lazy day resting, or to freshen up after visiting the mines (mine guides often offer transport after a mine tour). There are public baths, US$0.30, and private, US$0.60; the private baths, higher up, may be cleaner. If you get out of the truck or bus at the bridge at Km 25, cross the bridge and take any trail up, you reach the 50m-diameter crater lake on the other side of the river from Tarapaya. The temperature of the lake is 30°C, a beautiful spot; take sun protection. Below the crater lake are boiling ponds. Trucks go straight to Tarapaya. Buses, micros and colectivos from market nr train station, Av Antofagasta, US$0.75. Taxi US$7.50 for a group. Last colectivo back to Potosí at 1800. On the way to Tarapaya is the village of El Molino (15 km), in a green valley; no accommodation or shop, but nice landscape. Take a colectivo from Plaza Chuquimia.

CAIZA

About 2 hrs from Potosí, on a road which forks off the Tarija road at Ingenio Cucho, Caiza is at a much lower altitude than Potosí, so is hotter and can provide relief from *soroche*. Cooperatives produce handicrafts in tin and some silver, which is being encouraged. On 4 Aug, the entry of the Virgen de Copacabana is celebrated with dancing and traditional costumes. For information go to the tourist office in Potosí, or *Programa de Autodesarrollo Campesino*, Av Argentina y Gareca, Ciudad Satélite, Potosí, T 32013/32028. *Hotel San Martín de Porres*, nr plaza, clean, restaurant. Two daily buses from Plaza del Minero, Potosí, 1330.

ROUTES **Potosí 164 km NE to Sucre** The road is fully paved. It passes San Diego (thermal baths, restaurant), Chaqui (pleasant thermal baths, clean, closed Wed; truck or bus from Plaza Uyuni, 1 hr) and goes through **Betanzos** (1 hr, frequent buses from terminal; a few *alojamientos*, G, also hotel, E). The Feria de Papas is held within the first 2 weeks of May: folk dances, music and costumes; large and interesting market; a few kms away are the famous Umajalanta caves with well-preserved rock paintings.

Sucre 366 km to Cochabamba, via Epizana on the old Santa Cruz-Cochabamba road (see page 328): the first hour out of Sucre is OK, then it is terrible to Epizana. Thereafter the road is paved to Cochabamba.

SUCRE

Founded in 1538 as the city of La Plata, it became capital of the audiencia of Charcas in 1559. Its name was later changed to Chuquisaca. The present name, Sucre, was adopted in 1825 in honour of the first president of the new republic. It is the official capital of Bolivia. In 1992 UNESCO declared the city a 'Patrimonio Histórico y Cultural de la Humanidad'. There are two universities, the oldest dating from 1624. Long isolation has helped it to preserve its courtly charm; by tradition all buildings in the centre are painted in their original colonial white. It is sometimes referred to as La Ciudad Blanca.

BASICS *Pop* 112,000; *alt* 2,790m; *climate* is mild (mean temperature 12°C, but sometimes 24°C in Nov-Dec and 7°C in June); *phone code* 064.

Places of interest

Plaza 25 de Mayo is large, spacious, full of trees and surrounded by elegant buildings. Among these are the **Casa de la Libertad**, formerly the Assembly Hall of the Jesuit University (open Mon-Fri 0900-1130 and 1430-1830, Sat, 0930-1130, US$1, US$0.40 to take photographs, US$2.65 to use video), where the country's Declaration of Independence was signed (it contains a famous portrait of Simón Bolívar by the Peruvian artist Gil de Castro "... hecho en Lima, con la más grande exactitud y semejanza" – the greatest likeness); also on the Plaza is the beautiful 17th century **Cathedral**, entrance through the museum in C Ortiz (open Mon-Fri 1000-1200, 1500-1700, Sat 1000-1200, US$1, if door is locked wait for the guide). Worth seeing are the famous jewel-encrusted Virgin of Guadalupe, 1601, works by Viti, the first great painter of the New World, who studied under Raphael, and the monstrance and other church treasures including giant lanterns of pure silver weighing 46 kilos. Four blocks NW of Plaza 25 de Mayo is the modern **Corte Suprema de Justicia**, the seat of Bolivia's judiciary (entry free but must be smartly dressed, leave passport with guard, guide can be found in library). The nearby **Parque Bolívar** contains a monument and a miniature of the Eiffel tower in honour of Bolivia's richest 20th century tin baron, Francisco Arcandona, who created much of Sucre's latter-day splendour. The obelisk opposite the **Teatro Gran Mcal**, in **Plaza Libertad**, was erected with money raised by fining bakers who cheated on the size and weight of their bread. Also on this plaza is the **Hospital Santa Bárbara**. Sucre University was founded in 1624.

Southeast of the city, at the top of C Dalence, lies the Franciscan monastery of **La Recoleta** (see **Museums**) with good views over the city. Behind the monastery a road flanked by Stations of the Cross ascends an attractive hill, **Cerro Churuquella**, with large eucalyptus trees on its flank, to a statue of Christ at the top. The cemetery is worth a visit, to see mausoleums of presidents and other famous people, boys give guided tours; take C Junín S to its end, 7-8 blocks from main plaza.

Church opening times seem to change frequently, or are simply not observed. **San Miguel**, completed in 1628, has been restored and is very beautiful with Moorish-style carved and painted ceilings, *alfarjes* (early 17th century), pure-white walls and gold and silver altar. In the Sacristy some early sculpture can be seen. It was from San Miguel that Jesuit missionaries went S to convert Argentina, Uruguay and Paraguay (open 1130-1200, no shorts, short skirts or short sleeves). **San Felipe Neri**, church and monastery, neoclassical, attractive courtyard with cloisters (note above the crucifix an inscription in Hebrew letters saying, from right to left, TALE – lamb, one of the signs

for Christ in the zodiac, on each side of the cross are two replicas of the Israeli *menora*, the lamp from the Temple). The monastery is used as a school. The church, sadly, is closed. Access to the roof (note the penitents' benches), which offers fine views over the city, is only open for an hour between 1600 and 1800 (times change) US$1 entrance with a free guide from Universidad de Turismo office, opposite the convent, at N Ortiz 182. **Santa Mónica** (Arenales y Junín) is perhaps one of the finest gems of Spanish architecture in the Americas, note the main altar and pulpit in filigree (it is no longer a church and was closed to visitors mid 1995). **San Francisco** in C Ravelo has altars coated in gold leaf and 17th century ceilings; the bell is the one that summoned the people of Sucre to struggle for independence (0700-0930, 1600-1930). **Capilla de la Rotonda** (Av L Cabrera, near the railway station), **Santa Rita**, **San Sebastián** (reconstructed in 1990). **Santo Domingo**, corner of Calvo and Bolívar (1545), open only Fri and Sun night. **San Lázaro**, Calvo y Padilla, built in 1538, is regarded as the first cathedral of La Plata (Sucre). On the nave walls are six paintings attributed to Zurbarán; it has fine silverwork and alabaster in the Baptistery, open daily for mass 0700-0745. **La Merced** (Azurduy and Pérez) has gilded altar pieces.

Museums

These include the University's anthropological, archaeological, folkloric, and colonial collections at the **Museo Universitario Charcas** (Bolívar 698), and its presidential and modern-art galleries (Mon-Fri 0830-1200, 1500-1800, Sat 0830-1200, US$1, photos US$1.50). The **Museo de Santa Clara** (C Calvo 212), displays paintings, books, vestments, some silver and musical instruments (including a 1664 organ); there is a window to view the church; small items made by the nuns on sale, entry US$0.65, Mon-Sat 1000-1130, 1430-1700. The **Museo de la Recoleta** (C Pedro de Anzúrez, Mon-Fri 0900-1130, 1500-1630, US$0.85 for entrance to all collections, guided tours only) is at the Recoleta monastery, notable for the beauty

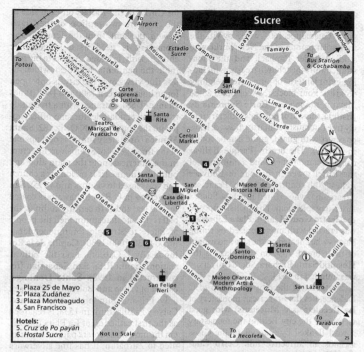

Sucre

1. Plaza 25 de Mayo
2. Plaza Zudáñez
3. Plaza Monteagudo
4. San Francisco

Hotels:
5. Cruz de Po payán
6. Hostal Sucre

Not to Scale

of its cloisters and gardens; the carved wooden choirstalls above the nave of the church are especially fine (see the martyrs transfixed by lances); in the grounds is the Cedro Milenario, a 1,000-year-old cedar. **Museo de Historia Natural**, C San Alberto 156 (Mon-Fri 0830-1200/1400-1800), US$0.50. **Caserón de la Capellanía**, San Alberto 413, houses the textile museum run by Antropológicas del Surandino. Rec for explanations of Indian groups and their distinctive textiles, Mon-Fri 0830-1200, 1500-1800, Sat 0900-1200, US$50, English-speaking guide.

Excursions

To the **Castillo de la Glorieta**, 5 km S on the Potosí road (*trufi* 4 or E from Arce y Siles), the former mansion of the Argandaña family, built in a mixture of contrasting European styles with beautiful painted ceilings and standing in gardens which must once have been delightful (now run down). Damaged by years of military use and neglect, there are plans for its restoration. It is in the military compound, entry free, passports surrendered at the gate, open daily 0900-1200, 1500-1700.

Local festivals

Independence celebrations, 24-26 May, most services, museums and restaurants closed. 8 Sept: Virgen de Guadalupe, 2-day fiesta. Oct: Festival Internacional de la Cultura, 10 days, shared with Potosí. Día del Estudiante, 21 Sept, music and dancing around main plaza.

Local information
● **Accommodation**

A3 *Real Audiencia*, Potosí 142, T 32809, F 30823, excellent restaurant, modern, rec.

B *Hostal Cruz de Popayán*, Loa 881, T 25156/31706, rec, a beautiful colonial house with interior courtyard, no heating, colour TV, excellent breakfast served in room or in patio;

B-C *Colonial*, Plaza 25 de Mayo 3, T 24709/25487, F 21912, expensive, some rooms noisy, but generally rec, good breakfast.

C *Hostal Libertad*, Arce y San Alberto, 1st floor, T 23101/2, clean, spacious and comfortable rooms, friendly and efficient with excellent restaurant, highly rec; **C** *Hostal Sucre*, Bustillos 113, T 21411/31928, good, clean, patio, friendly staff, great American breakfast for US$2, rec; **C** *Municipal Simón Bolívar*, Av Venezuela 1052 (T 21216), rec, restaurant.

D-E *Grand*, Arce 61, T 22104, large rooms, with hot showers, inc breakfast, restaurant, laundry service, safe, rec. Many cheap and basic places opp central market; **D** *Hostal España*, España 138, T 25765, inc breakfast, TV, clean, pleasant; **D** *Hostal los Pinos*, Colón 502, T 24403, clean, comfortable, hot showers, TV in room, garden, quiet, peaceful, inc breakfast, long way from centre; **D** *Hostal San Francisco*, Av Arce 191 y Camargo, T 22117, with shower, E without, pleasant, meals available, clean, quiet, comfortable, safe motorcycle parking, rec; **D** *Londres*, Av H Siles 949, T 24792, 3 blocks uphill from station, with shower, restaurant, good; **D-E** *Res Bolivia*, nr plaza, San Alberto 42, T 24346, with electric showers, cheaper without bath, clean, spacious rooms, hot water, breakfast inc, clothes washing not allowed, arranges transport to Tarabuco.

On Av Ostria Gutiérrez: E *Alojamiento Austria*, No 518, T 24202, hot showers, good value, restaurant, nr bus station; **E** *Alojamiento Central*, No 456, T 23935, hot showers charged extra; **F** *Alojamiento Chuquisaca*, No 33, T 24459, shared bathrooms, clean, friendly, safe car parking (US$0.50/day); **E** *Res Avenida*, Av H Siles 942, T 21245, clean, hot showers, breakfast extra, laundry, friendly and helpful, rec, good Argentine restaurant next door; **E** *Res Bustillo*, Ravelo 158, T 21560, without bath (D with bath), tiny rooms, clean, hot water, stores luggage; **E** *Charcas*, Ravelo 62, T 23972, with bath, F without, good value breakfast, hot showers, clean, helpful, opp market, laundry facilities, will arrange bus to Tarabuco, highly rec.

F *Alojamiento Abaroa*, Loa 419, hot showers, uncomfortable beds, friendly, basic; **F** *Alojamiento La Plata*, Ravelo 26, T 22102, without bath, limited shower facilities, basic, opp market, noisy; **F** *Alojamiento El Turista*, Ravelo 118, T 23172, hot showers 0700-1200 only, safe, basic, cheap meals, terrace, doors closed at 2300; **F** *Res Oriental*, San Alberto 43, T 21644, with bath, clean, bit run down but good value, unlockable interior windows, hot water, motorcycle parking.

● **Places to eat**

Piso Cero, Venezuela 1241, good but expensive; *Las Vegas* on SE side of Plaza, Nos 36-37, main restaurant and annex (less grand), good, main dishes about US$4; *Pizzería Napoletana*, on Plaza 25 de Mayo 30, excellent pizzas (evenings and some lunchtimes) and good home-made ice cream, not cheap; *Plaza*, on Plaza 25 de Mayo 33, with balconies, good food and pisco sours, good live music on Fri nights, very popular with locals; *Kactus*, C España 5, just off main plaza, nice bar and restaurant, pizzas, pricey but good value, highly rec; *El Huerto*, Ladislao Cabrera 86, in beautiful garden, highly rec; *La Taverne* of the *Alliance Française*, Aniceto Arce 35, ½ block from plaza, closed Sun, decent French food, not cheap, also regular films and cultural events, good meeting place; *Picolíssimo*, San Alberto 237, very good Italian food, not expensive, popular; *Bibliocafé Sureña* N Ortiz 30, nr plaza, good pasta and light meals, music, opens 1800, closed Mon; *Suizo* N Ortiz 42, good service, pricey but good value, *peña* on Sat, excellent *roesti*, live music some nights; *Kultur-Café Berlin*, Avaroa 326, open 1500-2400, good food but limited selection and small portions, German newspapers, *peña* every other Fri, closed Sun (in same building as Instituto Cultural Boliviano Alemán – ICBA), popular meeting place; *El Germen*, Camargo 574, very good vegetarian food and set lunches (US1.35), clean and attractive, pleasant ambience, excellent breakfast, US$0.75-1.50, open Mon-Sat 0800-2100, book exchange, German magazines, warmly rec; *Nirvana*, Loa 777, nr Olañeta, vegetarian, open daily for lunch and dinner, good food and atmosphere; *Confitería Palet*, Plaza 25 de Mayo 8, good coffee; *Le Repizza*, Calvo 70, very good value lunches, small but good pizzas in evening, rec; *Chorizería Los Bajos*, Loa 759, serves special sausages (*chorizo chuquisaqueño*), good, daytime only; *El Solar*, Bolívar 800, good (Sun closed); *Snack Miriam*, España 136, good *salteñas*; also on España, No 140 is *Snack Lucy*, rec; *Amanecer*, Pasaje Junín 810-B, German *pastelería*, run by social project supporting disabled children, excellent; *New Hong Kong II*, 25 de Mayo 30, expensive but good, authentic Chinese; *Charcas*, San Alberto 242, excellent 4-course lunch for US$2.50, good value local dishes; *El Tropezón*, Junín 725, good set meal; *Bunkers*, Ravelo 28, good breakfasts, bar, open 0800 till late; *Chop Clock Café*, Audiencia Grau, 1 block from plaza, good breakfasts; *Café Hacheh*, Pastor Sainz 233, coffee bar, open 1100-2400, art gallery, tasty sandwiches and fresh fruit juices, highly rec; *Salon de Té Las Delicias*, Estudiantes 50, favourite student hangout; *La Casona*, Ostria Guitierez 401, nr bus terminal, stylish, *platos típicos*, good value. Good chicken and chips cafés on Camargo between Arce and Loa and on Loa and H Siles. Many fruit juice and snack stalls in the central market, stall No 11, Rosa, is rec for her *vitaminico*; stalls also sell cheap meals (US$0.75-1.40). The local sausages and chocolate are rec.

● **Banks & money changers**

Banco Nacional, C España, cash given on Visa card, good rates, TCs changed, 1% commission. **Banco de la Paz**, Plaza 25 de Mayo, for cash on Visa and Mastercard. Travel agencies' rates are good and at *El Arca*, España 134, T30189, good rates for TCs. **Ambar**, *casa de cambio*, San Alberto 7, T 31339, poor rates for TCs. Stalls at corner of Camargo and Arce buy and sell cash $ as well as Argentine, Chilean and Brazilian currency at good rates. Many shops and street changers on Hernando Siles/Camargo buy and sell $ cash.

● **Cultural centres**

The **Instituto Cultural Boliviano – Alemán** (Delegación de Enseñanza del Goethe Institute), Avaroa 326, Casilla 304, T 22091, shows films, has German newspapers and books to lend (0930-1230 and 1500-2100), runs Spanish, German, Portuguese and Quechua courses and it has the *Kulturcafé Berlín* (see above). Spanish lessons cost from US$3.50 for 45 mins for one person, with reductions the more students there are in the class. The ICBA also runs a folk music *peña* on Fri. **Alianza Francesa**, Aniceto Arce 35, T 23599, noticeboard on Plaza 25 de Mayo (Casa de Libertad side) announces events. **Centro Boliviano Americano**, Calvo y Potosí, library open Mon-Fri 1500-2000, rec for reference works. The *Centro Cultural Hacheh* (see address for *Café Hacheh* above), run by Felix Arciénega, Bolivian artist who organizes folk and jazz concerts, conferences and discussions, and is the editor of an art and poetry journal 'Hacheh'. The café also puts on exhibitions by other local artists, has an extensive library and a large collection of native, jazz and classical records. *Casa de la Cultura*, Argentina 65, in beautiful colonial building, presents art exhibitions, concerts, folk dancing etc, open Mon-Sat 0900-1200, 1430-2000.

● **Embassies & consulates**

Germany, Arenales 215 (T 21862). **Spain**, Pasaje Argandoña (T 21455), **Italy**, Vice Consul, Dalence 33.

● **Entertainment**

Folklore: Centro Cultural Masis promotes the traditional Yampara culture: textiles, ceramics, figurines and music. It offers instruction in Quechua, traditional Bolivian music (3 hrs a week for US$12 a month, rec) and handicrafts; once or twice a week there are musical events and the snack bar holds exhibitions of textiles and photographs. Items are for sale, inc musical instruments to the highest professional standard. Open 1530-2130. Contact the director, Roberto Sahonero, at Bolívar 561 DS (T 23403, Casilla 463), or at the centre Mon, Wed and Fri, 1900.

● **Hospitals & medical services**

Dentist: Dr Carlos Sánchez C, San Alberto 75.

Doctor: *Dr Gaston Delgadillo Lora*, Colón 33, T 21692, speaks English, French, German, highly rec.

Hospital: rec, staffed by Japanese and locals.

● **Laundry**

Laverap, Bolívar 617, between Audiencia and Dalence, quick, US$2.50 wash and dry. *Lavandería Paola*, Bolívar 543, T 32477, rec.

● **Post & telecommunications**

Post Office: Ayacucho 100 y Junín, open till 2000. *Poste Restante* is organized separately for men and women.

Telephone and Fax: Entel, España 271, open till 2245.

● **Shopping**

Permanent market is bounded by Ravelo, Loa, Camargo and Junín, situated in nice colonial building, clean and colourful, wide variety of goods. A bus from the central market will take you to the *campesino* market. *Artesanías Calcha*, Arce 103, opp San Francisco church, rec, very knowledgeable proprietor. *ASUR*, Antropológicos del Surandino, have a museum and project shop at San Alberto 413, Caserón de la Capellanía, T 23841, weavings from around Tarabuco and from the Jalq'a (Chuquisaca and Potosí departments); weavings are more expensive, but of higher quality than elsewhere (see above for the museum). *Charcas*, Camargo 481 y España, high quality hats. *Charangos* and weavings from Tarabuco and Candelaria are obtainable in the main plaza. Camping gas can be bought at Alberto 25.

● **Sports**

Swimming: pool on Av Venezuela, US$1 pp.

Tennis: Sucre Tennis Club, Av Venezuela, good clay courts, US$5 pp inc equipment hire. Racquetball Club also on Venezuela.

● **Tour companies & travel agents**

Fremen, Plaza 25 de Mayo 15, T 30351/32211, rec; *Turbo Tours*, España 66, German and English spoken; *Sur Andes*, N Ortiz 6, T 21983, F 21677, organizes trekking from half a day to 5 days, inc the Camino Prehispánico (must take sleeping bag and good shoes, all else provided, but no porters); also tours to Salar de Uyuni, Laguna Colorada and Laguna Verde. *Highland Pioneer*, T 2-5659, English, Dutch, French, German, Spanish spoken, safe 4WD jeep tours, rec, good value.

● **Tourist offices**

Calle Potosí 102 esq San Alberto, T 25983, good map and guide for sale, US$2; in the same building as the ASUR textile museum, the Caserón de la Capellanía, but has a different entrance. Check church and museum opening hours. Sub-office at airport, helpful. Tourist information office opp San Felipe Neri, at Nicolás Ortiz 182 (open 0800-1200, 1400-1800 Mon-Fri), is run by students studying tourism, who will show you around tourist sites for free (see above under **Churches**). All offices closed Sat and Sun. For country maps Instituto Geográfico Militar, Dalence, 2, p 1, T 25514, open 0830-1200, 1430-1800, Mon-Fri.

● **Useful addresses**

Car Mechanic: at Camargo 450, rec for Toyotas.

Immigration: Plaza 25 de Mayo, in *Palacio de Gobierno.*

Motorcycle mechanic: Sr Jaime Medina, Motorservi Honda, C René Calvo Arana, T 25484. Will service all makes of machine.

Police radio patrol: T 110 if in doubt about police or security matters.

● **Transport**

Local Taxi: US$0.55 pp within city limits.

Air By LAB there is a Mon, Wed, Fri La Paz-Sucre direct air service, to Cochabamba on Tues, Thur, Sat and Sun and to Santa Cruz Mon, Wed and Fri. To Puerto Suárez, for Brazil, you have to go via Santa Cruz, then take Aero Sur's daily flight. There are also LAB flights to Tarija (Wed, Sat). The private Aero Sur (Arenales 204A, T 064-24895) flies from Sucre to La Paz and Santa Cruz. All flights heavily booked but some 'stand by' available. Tucsupaya Airport 5 km NW of town (T 24445). LAB office is at Bustillos 131 (T 21140/21943 for reservations, poor information). Airport minibus leaves from corner of Siles and Junín, 1½ hrs before flight (not always). Taxi US$4 (US$2 shared); buses from main road (difficult to get on with luggage). *Trufis* No 1 and F go from entrance to H Siles y Loa, 1 block from main plaza, US$0.55, 25 mins. Beware of pickpockets at airport.

Trains Enfe information, T 31115; station is on Plaza Aniceto Arce. Train from La Paz and Potosí, US$13.90.

Buses Terminal is on N outskirts of town, 3 km from centre on Ostria Gutiérrez, T 22029; closed 1900-0700; taxi US$0.65; Micro C or *trufi* No 3. Information T 22029. Daily to/from **La Paz** via Cochabamba (19 hrs, US$13.50), many companies with frequent deps between 0700 and 1700, 3 hrs wait at Cochabamba, very cold at night, Illimani rec and Flota Copacabana, good facilities in Cochabamba; or via Potosí, US$13 (20-24 hrs) at least 4 companies, departures in am (Trans La Paz not rec). To **Cochabamba** daily, several companies 1800-1830 departures (San Francisco not rec), 10-12 hrs, US$9.75; **Potosí**, a number of companies have offices in centre of town: Andesbus, Bolívar 621, T 24251/30751, daily 0700

(complimentary breakfast, snack meal en route), and 1700, US$6.50; Transtur (on Loa, but tickets etc from Sur Andes Travel Agency), all deps from bus terminal; Bustillos dep 1100, US$4 (10 de Noviembre not reliable). Trans O'Globo goes daily at 0800 to Potosí, continuing to Tupiza (US$12.35) and Villazón (US$13); To **Villazón** via Potosí daily with Emperador at 0715 and Andesbus at 0700. To **Uyuni**, Americana and Emperador, 0700, 10 hrs, US$9, change buses in Potosí. To **Santa Cruz**, with Bolívar direct Tues, Fri, Sun, dep 1230, 17 hrs; or via Cochabamba, Flota Unificada, highly rec with video, Tues and Fri, 1700, also Mopar, Tues, Fri, Sun (rec) and others, US$13-17, most departures 1130-1300. To **Tarija** 10 de Noviembre, Tues, US$20, Andesbus' service to Potosí on Mon, Thur and Sat at 0700 continues to Tarija, US$20, 19-20 hrs, daily with Emperador via Potosí at 0715. To **Camiri** and **Monteagudo**, daily with Emperador at 1730, also Andesbus.

TARABUCO

Tarabuco, 3,295m, 64 km by good road SE of Sucre, has a most colourful Indian market on Sun, starting about 0930. The market is popular with tourists and yet is very enjoyable. The main appeal is the Indians in their authentic dress. Best bargains are to be had before the bulk of tourists arrive (from 1030), or late in the day. It helps if you have an idea about the quality on offer. Note: the market is not held at Carnival (when all Tarabuco is dancing in Sucre), Easter Sunday or on a holiday weekend in November.

Festival with fair: Virgen de Rosario, 1st Sun in Oct and 12 Mar, the Phujllay independence celebration, very colourful and lively with even more costume and dance than the Rosario; no one sleeps during this fiesta so no accommodation problems!

● **Accommodation & places to eat** There are at least 2 budget hotels, inc **G** *Residencial Florida*, basic, cold, dirty but friendly, good almuerzo in garden, with music and dancing, good fun; 3 other decent restaurants on plaza and lots of food stalls in market offering tasty local dishes.

● **Transport** Buses (US$2) and trucks (US$1.30) leave from 0630 or when full from Plaza Huallparimachi (take bus C from Mercado), 2½ hrs journey (or taxi, US$45). Shared *trufi* taxis can be arranged by hotels, with pick-up service, starting at 0700, US$3.25 return. First bus back 1300. Transport more difficult on weekdays; take an early bus and return by truck. Guide to Tarabuco, Alberto from Sucre tourist office, US$45 for a full day in a car for 4 people.

The weavers' villages nearby include **Candelaria** (2 hrs by truck from Tarabuco) or **Macha** (8 hrs from Sucre); **Pocata** (1 hr from Macha), or **Ravelo** (59 km NW of Sucre; travel to Ravelo: by truck between 0900-1000 from departure point near airport, 3 hrs; *micro*, US$1.65, check at shop at Hernando Siles 843 if it's running, it's supposed to leave at 0900, return 1600 – lorries back to Sucre invariably full). At Punilla, on the road to Ravelo, there is a 2½ hrs walk to **Incamachay** where there are precolumbian drawings. Punilla is also where you leave the truck for Challanaca and thence to Potolo, where they weave red animals on a black or brown background. You can buy direct from the weavers, no stores, but it can be difficult to find them. Trucks (Thurs and Fri in the dry season) go direct from near Sucre airport; in the wet, you can only get to Challanaca and you walk for 3 hrs to get there – the prices will probably be lower in the wet season.

Besides Incamachay, there is a precolumbian site at Pumamachay, where cave drawings can be seen; 'very hard to find', recommended to ask at student tourist office (address above). Also in the vicinity is the prehispanic road at Chataquila, possibly Inca. Tours to these sites are run by Sur Andes Travel Agency in Sucre.

EAST AND SOUTH OF SUCRE

A main road runs SE from Sucre through Tarabuco, Monteagudo, Camiri and Boyuibe to the frontier with Paraguay at Hito Villazón (not to be confused with the other Villazón on the frontier with Argentina, see above page 304). At Padilla (Km 190, altitude 2,080m, hotels on plaza) a turn-off heads N 20 km to **Villa Serrano**, where the musician Mauro Núñez lived. A music festival is held on 28-29 Dec. (The journey is beautiful through wild mountains.) At **Monteagudo** (Km 323, altitude 1,138m) there are direct buses to Santa Cruz, twice a week, US$8, 14 hrs. Several basic hotels: **F** *Alojamiento los Naranjos* be-

hind plaza, hot showers, *Alojamiento las Tablitas*, and *Alojamiento Oriental*, both on the main road.

CAMIRI

Further SE at Km 456 is **Camiri** (*pop* 20,000; *alt* 827m), growing rapidly because of nearby oilfields – the oil refinery may be visited.

● **Accommodation & services** As a garrison town it has some hotels: **E** *Hotel Ortuño*, C Comercio; **E** *Residencial Marieta*, Av Petrolera 15; **E** *Residencial Premier*, Av Busch 60; **E** *Gran Hotel Londres*, Av Busch 36, motorcycle parking; **F** pp *Residencial Chaqueña*, C Comercio, clean, good; **F** *Residencial Familiar*, C Comercio; restaurants, bars (nothing is cheap). There is a post office.

● **Transport** Emperador and Andesbus runs from Sucre daily in each direction, at least 20 hrs, US$20. From Camiri there is a bus to Santa Cruz, office on Av Busch next to *Gran Hotel Londres*, goes 4 times a week if enough passengers, 8 hrs, US$14.50; *camioneta* leaves from in front of the market when there are enough passengers, US$13-15.50, 7 hrs (dusty). **Road** A paved road heads S from Camiri, through Boyuibe (see below), Villa Montes (see page 321) and Yacuiba to Argentina (see page 347).

CROSSING INTO PARAGUAY

It is possible to drive from Camiri into Paraguay direct in a truck or 4WD, high clearance vehicle, carrying insect repellent, food and water for a week. No help can be relied on in case of a breakdown; a winch is advisable, especially after rain. There are some rivers to ford and although they are dry in the dry season they can be impassable if there is rain in the area. 3 buses a week from Santa Cruz to Asunción via Abapó, Camiri, Boyuibe and Hito Villazón. **Boyuibe**, Km 519, alt 817m, the last town in Bolivia (*Hotel Guadalquivir*, or *Hotel Chaqueño* next door, both **F**, both serve meals), is also on regular bus route Tarija-Entre Rios-Villamontes-Santa Cruz. Fuel and water are available, and it is on the Yacuiba railway (rail fare Santa Cruz-Boyuibe: *ferrobus* US$13 and US$10; *rápido* US$5.50 and US$4). Passports are stamped at military checkpoint. If travelling by bus, passports are collected by driver and returned on arrival at Mcal Estigarribia,

Paraguay, with Bolivian exit stamp and Paraguayan entry stamp.

¾ km after the military checkpoint turn left past a large water tower. From then on just follow the most used road; accurate directions may be obtained from the army before leaving Boyuibe. If hitching be at customs post before 0600. It is about 115 km from Boyuibe to the Bolivian border post at Hito Villazón (manned by a Bolivian army unit), 3 hrs by bus. You can camp at Hito Villazón, but no food is available, nor is there much water.

The frontier is 12 km E of Villazón at Guaraní and the Paraguayan post is 10 km further E at Fortín Gen Eugenio A Garay. Camping is possible here and for a small contribution the troops may give you use of showers and kitchen. There is a military post (water available) at Fortín Mister Long, about 15 km, further on. "There are long stretches where the road disappears beneath ridges of soft dust; be prepared to spend many hours digging/pushing/pulling your bus out of the countless dust pits in 40° heat" (Simon Watson Taylor, London NW6).

Beyond Fortín Mister Long the road improves through Colonia La Patria and beyond. Entry stamps are given at Mcal Estigarribia where there is a large military base; if you arrive after Fri 1700, you must wait until Asunción and report to immigration there. (For Mcal Estigarribia and the continuation of this route see **Paraguay: The Paraguayan Chaco**.)

TARIJA

ROUTES A road runs S from Potosí to Tarija. At **Camargo**, 186 km from Potosí, is an excellent restaurant, *Media Luz*. Guest rooms have been built for overnight stop. Around Camargo, vines are cultivated, using the traditional method of training them up pruned *molle* trees. The road continues for 182 km to Tarija.

Tarija (*pop* 100,000; *alt* 1,840m; *phone code* 066) was founded 4 July 1574, in the rich valley of the Guadalquivir River. The city had a tumultuous struggle against Spain, declaring itself independent in 1807, and has a strong cultural heritage. Its people are markedly religious and strongly individualistic, and the Indian strain is less evident here than elsewhere in Bolivia. Tarija is a delightful small city, a nice, peaceful place to enjoy the sun. The streets and plazas are planted with flowering trees, quite a contrast if coming from the treeless altiplano. **Plaza Luis de Fuentes** has palm trees, jacarandas, orange trees (both in flower/fruit in Oct), and roses. There is a statue, erected in 1991, to the city's founder, Capitán Luis de Fuentes Vargas. The modern Av Las Américas, or **Costanera** gracefully flanks the curves of the river.

Places of interest

The **Cathedral**, on C La Madrid, is open in the morning and from 1700. **San Francisco** church (La Madrid y Daniel Campos), is beautifully painted inside, with praying angels depicted on the ceiling; note the four evangelists at the four corners below the dome. The library is divided into old and new sections, the old containing some 15,000 volumes, the new a further 5,000. The oldest book is a 1501 *Iliad* incorporating other works. There are also old manuscripts and 19th century photograph albums. To see the library, go to the door at Ingavi 0137 (open 0830-1130, 1530-1730, Sat 0830-1130). Tarija's **university** was founded in 1946; the university's museum, Trigo y Lema, contains a palaeontological collection (dinosaur bones, fossils, remains of an Andean elephant), as well as smaller mineralogical, ethnographic and anthropological collections; open Mon-Fri 0830-1200, 1430-1800, brochure US$0.65. The **Casa Dorada**, Trigo y Ingavi (entrance on Ingavi), also called the Maison d'Or, has been reconstructed and is now the Casa de Cultura (open 0830-1200, 1430-1800, Sat 0900-1200, guided tours only; voluntary donation). The house and emporium of importer/exporter Moisés Narvajas and his wife Esperanza Morales was begun in 1886, inaugurated 1903, but had fallen into disrepair by 1980. It has been repainted in original colours, silver and ochre on the outside, cerise, green and dark blue, with white trim, inside; it has

Italian murals, art nouveau copies on ceiling panels and much gold in the rooms. Tours view the private oratory, sacristy with beautiful vestments, etc; the reception room – damask curtains, Persian carpets, Victorian chairs, Venetian mirrors, red cedar piano, bronze peacock with original tungsten illumination in the tail; the photography room (pictures of Tarijan history and the restoration of the house); and the dining room (note the opal table lamps in the form of bunches of grapes and lilies). It has been described as a superb example of Kitsch decorative art. Near Parque Bolívar (shady, pleasant) is another of Narvajas' houses, the **Castillo de Beatriz**, painted bright blue and white (Bolívar entre Junín y O'Connor; ask the owner if it is possible to visit).

A good view can be had from **La Loma de San Juan**; follow C D Paz to the top of the rise where the buses gather, turn right on the cobbled street, then right through the gate and follow the Stations of the Cross to the top (124 steps up, equestrian statue of Moto Méndez, see **Excursions** below, at the top).

Maize, vegetables, wheat, potatoes and splendid grapes thrive in the basin. The best time to visit Tarija is from Jan onwards, when the fruit are in season. Bolivia's best wines are produced here; see **Excursions** below.

Excursions

Recommended tours of Tarija, the city, surrounding areas and vineyards, are offered by *Hostal Carmen* (see **Hotels**, below).

The outskirts of the city can be a good place to look for fossils: take a micro or taxi in the direction of the airport. 5 km out of town, before the police control (*garita*), you see lovely structures of sand looking like a small canyon (*barrancos*). Here have been found bones, teeth, parts of saurian spines, etc; things come to the surface each year after the rains. You may have to go a long way from the city. If in luck, compare your finds with the objects in the University museum.

At **San Jacinto** (8 km, *trufi* from Ingavi y Daniel Campos, by Palacio de Justicia, every 30 mins, 35 mins journey, US$0.45), is a tourist complex beside the lake formed by a dam completed in 1991. At the dam there is a café, several shacks selling food and drink, boats for hire. There is a level lakeside walk which is very pleasant. Cross the dam, go past the food stalls and follow the clear track to the head of the lake. The track passes farms and animals in the fields. It takes about an hour until climbing a shoulder and then descending to more houses. Either return the same way (in which case you miss the best part), or climb the hill to the left (a bit of a scramble to the top) for a good, all-round view. Walk back along the ridge path which descends directly back to the steep ravine which is blocked by the dam (take care on the final descent, in particular do not walk over the cliff where the dam is; keep left, the lake side).

To **San Lorenzo** (15 km, *trufis* from La Loma, top of D Paz, return from San Lorenzo plaza, 45 mins, US$0.40). The road passes Tomatitas river bathing (5 km), and the **Parque Nacional Los Barrancos**, an area of erosion. San Lorenzo's plaza is very pleasant, with palms, oranges and flowers; the church is huge and unadorned. Around the town the land is agricultural; you can walk down to the river (head N and turn right) and ask directions in the fields for the way up the eroded cliffs (45 mins, fine views). Just off the plaza is the Museo Méndez, the house of the independence hero Eustaquio Méndez, El Moto (he lost his right hand, many stories as to how it happened). The small museum exhibits his weapons, his bed, his 'testimonio', entry US$0.30, open Mon-Fri 0900-1230, Sat 0900-1200, 1500-1700, Sun 1000-1200. **Los Chorros de Jurina** with natural rock pools, 22 km from Tarija, are 5 km beyond San Lorenzo, you need a guide to walk there (check first if there is water in the falls).

Bodegas

To visit the Aranjuez bodega, ask Sr Milton Castellanos at the Agrochemical shop at Trigo 789. To the Rugero Singani bodega at **El Valle de Concepción**, an appointment must be made with Ing Sergio Prudencio Navarro, Bodegas y Viñedos de la

Concepción, Casilla 99, Tarija, La Madrid y Suipacha s/n, T 25040. Ing Prudencio will show visitors round the vineyards and the bodega. To Concepción, 36 km S of Tarija, *trufis* go from Plazuela Sucre every 20-30 mins, US$0.55, return from plaza. The route to Concepción takes the road past the airport, at the *garita* the road forks left to Yacuiba/Pocitos, right to Bermejo. Take the latter and after a while take an unmade road to the right. This area is called Santa Ana. Look on your left for the ex-Russian observatory (signpost; a good place to go at night to see the stars). Then you pass the Colonial winery, the Santa Ana bridge and Santa Ana Grande vineyards and the Centro Vitivinicola, Cooperación Española, before reaching Concepción. The town is a mixture of the old and new; the plaza is filled with bitter orange and ceibo trees. The houses on the road that leads out to Rugero are of adobe or stone-clad.

Zoo

On Av Costanera, a tatty park for children, but worth the US$0.15 to see the condors.

Local festivals

The city is famous for its *niño* (child) processions: colourful and charming. During processions of **San Roque** in a 3-day festival from the first Sun in Sept the richly dressed saint's statue is paraded through the streets; wearing lively colours, cloth turbans and cloth veils, the people dance before it as it goes, and women thow flowers from the balconies. Dogs are decorated with ribbons for the day. On the second Sun in Oct the flower festival commemorates the **Virgen del Rosario**, and another takes place in **Easter** week. Also in Oct, on two weekends mid-month, there is a **beer festival** on Av de las Américas. Colourful processions take place on 15 April, **Day of Tarija**.

Santuario Chaguaya, S of El Valle, beyond Padcaya by road, is 60 km S of Tarija. At the fiesta for **La Virgen de Chaguaya**, 15 Aug, people walk all the way from the city (the pilgrimage route is 45 km). Línea P *trufi* from Plaza Sucre, Tarija, to Padcaya, US$1; bus to Chaguaya and Padcaya from terminal daily, 1600, US$1.35.

Local information

Street numbering works as follows: all blocks W of C Colón have a small O before number (oeste), and all blocks E have an E before number (este); blocks are numbered from Colón outwards. All streets N of Av Las Américas are preceded by N.

● Accommodation

A3 *Los Ceibos*, Av Víctor Paz Estenssoro y La Madrid, T 34430, F 42461 (formerly *Prefectural*), inc excellent buffet breakfast, large rooms with bath, TV, phone, mini-bar, good restaurant, outdoor pool and cocktail bar, free transport to airport, rec.

B *Victoria Plaza*, on Plaza Luis de Fuentes, T 42700, F 22600, with bath, hot water, TV, phone, inc buffet breakfast, laundry service, highly rec; **B** *Grand Hotel Tarija*, Sucre 0770, T 42684, F 44777, modernized, comfortable, central; **B** *Hostal Costanera*, Av Las Américas, T 42851, modern, with breakfast; **B** *Hostal Cristal*, Plaza Luis de Fuentes, T 45533/4, with breakfast, hot water, phone, TV, transport from airport.

D *Hostal Libertador*, Bolívar O-0649, T 44231, with bath, phone, sporadic hot water, breakfast extra, family-run, nr cathedral, rec; **D** *Hostal Carmen*, Ingavi O-0784 y R Rojas, T 43372/44342, shower, clean, good value, some ground floor rooms without exterior windows, good breakfast, sometimes has transport to/from airport, organizes tours of the area, rec; opp is **F** pp *Res Rosario*, Ingavi O-0777, with bath, cheaper without, breakfast, clean and friendly, highly rec; **D** *Gran Hotel Max*, Junín 930, T 24549, with bath, E without, cheaper still in 3, 4-bedded rooms, inc breakfast, 20 mins walk from main plaza; **D** *Hostal Bolívar*, Bolívar O-0256, T 42741, with bath, rec, clean, comfortable, hot water, poor breakfast, laundry; **E** *América*, Bolívar O-0257, T 42627, hot showers, good, run down but quiet, inc small breakfast, restaurant attached (good); **F** *Hostería España*, Alejandro Corrado 0-0546, T 43304, clean, hot showers, pleasant; **F** *Hostal 15 de Abril*, Campos 1079, without bath, bright; **F** pp *Res Familiar*, Sucre 656, with bath, cheaper without, most downstairs rooms without windows; **F** *Alojamiento Ocho Hermanos*, Sucre 782, nr main plaza, clean, collective rooms only. *Terminal*, behind bus station, family-run, good lunches, suitable for a night's stop-over; **F** *Alojamiento El Hogar*, across Av Las Américas from bus terminal, clean; **F** *Res Zeballos*, Sucre 0966, T 42068, clean.

● Places to eat

Best is *Milano*, in elegant white house at W end of Bolívar where it meets Av Víctor Paz, T 34093, home-made pastas and pizzas around US$2.50, fondue and raclette more expensive, excellent meat, good wine list, rec, annex which houses *Churrasquería*, good value. In the evening lots of eating places can be found around the plaza. *La Cabaña de Don Pepe*, N-Campos 0136, nr Av Las Américas, some way from centre, has excellent steaks at reasonable prices; *Cabaña Don Pedro*, in lane off Av Victor Paz, 1 block W of terminal, good typical food, outdoor patio, moderate prices; *Don Ñato*, 15 de Abril O-0844, good food and service; *Club Social Tarija*, on E side of plaza, pleasant, old-fashioned, excellent *almuerzo* for US$2, rec; *Snack Te Ve*, Sucre N-0624, just off plaza, open pm only; *Tonmy*, La Madrid E-0178, local food; *Viejo Bar*, Madrid 0358, on the plaza, good *confitería*, pizzas, ice cream, popular meeting place, bar atmosphere in evening, good food, rec. Also on the plaza: *La Taberna Gatopardo*, pizza, *parrillada* with Argentine beef, hot dogs, snacks, local wines, good value, lively atmosphere; next door is *La Esquina*, burgers etc, bar; *Chingos*, popular with young crowd, hamburgers, on E side of plaza; *Pizzería Issabella* and *Fechorias*, good *saulteñas* in am, both on W side next to Prefectura; *El Solar*, Campero y V Lema, vegetarian, set lunch, closes 1400; *Heladería Gloria*, Trigo 0676 tea, refrescos, sandwiches; *La Fonatana*, Campos N-0597 esq La Madrid, for coffee, ice cream. For breakfast try the market (cheap). Typical dishes inc *keperi*, meat that is first boiled, then fried, *saice*, beef and chickpeas spiced with cumin and picante, *ranga-ranga*, tripe, *chancao*, a chicken soup. Try the local wines, eg Aranjuez, La Concepción, Santa Ana de Casa Real or Kohlberg, the *singani* (a clear brandy, San Pedro de Oro and Rugero are rec labels), also local beer, Astra. **NB** Many restaurants (and much else in town) close between 1400 and 1600.

● **Banks & money changers**
Banco del Estado will change money. **Banco Mercantil de Bolivia**, Sucre y 15 de Abril, exchanges cash and gives cash against Visa and Mastercard (US$5 authorization charge). Cash also advanced on Visa cards at **Banco Popular del Perú**, Sucre. For TCs, try *Café Irupana*, Av Domingo Paz 351, 3% commission. Dollars and Argentine pesos can be changed at a number of *casas de cambio* on Bolívar between Campos and Sucre.

● **Embassies & consulates**
German Sucre 685, helpful. **Argentine** Ballivián 0699 y Bolívar, Mon-Fri, 0800-1300. Spanish Ingavi y Méndez.

● **Hospitals & medical services**
Dentist: Dra Marta Bass-Werner, opp Casa Dorada, highly rec, inexpensive and good.

● **Laundry**
At D Campos 420, US$1/kg.

● **Post & telecommunications**
Post Office: V Lema y Sucre; also at bus terminal.

Telecommunications: V Lema y D Campos, T 42676; also at terminal.

● **Shopping**
The market is in the block encompassed by Domingo Paz, Sucre, Bolívar and Trigo. *La Nueva Italia*, Ingavi y Sucre; hat shop selling and making men's hats of various regional styles.

● **Sports**
Swimming: Tomatitas, trip of 5 km, popular picnic area (same transport as for San Lorenzo, see above). At lunchtime on Sun in Tomatitas, many courtyards serve very cheap meals. For those with their own transport El Rincón de la Victoria, 18 km, or Tolomosita, 7 km, sandy beach on river bank, or the Ancón gorge.

● **Tour companies & travel agents**
Internacional Tarija, Sucre 721, T 44446/7, helpful. *Mara Tours*, Gral Trigo 739, T 43045/43490, most helpful.

● **Tourist offices**
On main plaza in Prefectura, very helpful, city map and guide for US$0.20 each.

● **Transport**
Air LAB to Santa Cruz, La Paz 3 a week, to Cochabamba 4 a week; Sucre (Wed, Sun), and Salta (Sun). Aero Sur flies to La Paz, 4 a week. Flights are frequently cancelled and/or delayed. LAB office on plaza S side; TAM office La Madrid O-0470, T 45899, Aero Sur office, Ingaví O-0339, T 45820. Taxi to airport, US$1.30 pp, or *micro* drops you 2 blocks away. Some hotels have free transport to town, you may have to phone for it. On arrival at Tarija, reconfirm your return flight immediately. Airport information T 43135.

Buses Daily on the 935-km route Potosí-Oruro-La Paz, dep 0700 and 1700 (26 hrs, US$23.25; check which company operates the best buses, San Lorenzo, eg has heating). To Potosí (386 km), daily, US$13.65 with San Lorenzo, San Jorge and Emperador; for Sucre, you must change buses in Potosí. To Villazón: several companies daily, deps am and pm. On Tues and Fri there is a combined bus/train service to Villazón and La Paz, US$24.50, leaves Tarija 0630; seat guaranteed on both services. To Santa Cruz, US$19.50, 32 hrs over incredibly bad roads, last 140 km from Abapó is paved; via Villamontes, Boyuibe and Camiri, San Lorenzo and Expreso Tarija Mon and Thur at 0730, Gran Chaco Thur at 1800; between Entre Rios and Villamontes is life-threatening or spectacular, depending on your point of view. The new bus station is in the outskirts on Av de Las Américas (30 mins walk from centre, 7-8 mins from airport). Cía El Chapaco and Expreso del Sur use poor quality vehicles. Trucks to all destinations leave from Loma, nr the market.

TO ARGENTINA

The road to Villazón, 189 km, is the shortest route to Argentina. There is no railway (see above for transport). The alternative route to Argentina via Bermejo is the most easily reached from Tarija, 210 km, the views are spectacular (sit on right); not recommended in the rainy season or a month or so after. The road is in an appalling condition apart from 50 km which are paved. Do not try to cycle. Daily buses, usually at night, some early am, take 5-9 hrs (4 hrs in a car), US$7.75, truck US$4.50. At **Bermejo** (*pop* 13,000; *alt* 415m; at least 3 hotels, 2 *casas de cambio* on main street, thorough customs searches) cross river by ferry to Agua Blanca, Argentina. From Tarija to Yacuiba/Pocitos border is 290 km. Buses to Yacuiba, 4 times a week at 2000 by Flota Tarija. **NB** Crossing to Argentina, expect up to 4 hrs to pass through customs and immigration. Electronic goods must be entered in your passport for later checks. Also note Bolivia is 1 hr behind Argentina.

VILLAMONTES

Villamontes, 260 km E of Tarija is famous for the highest temperatures in Bolivia; take mosquito repellent. It is renowned for fishing and holds a Fiesta del Pescado in August. Villamontes is a friendly town on the edge of the Gran Chaco and is on the road and rail route from Santa Cruz to the Argentine border at Yucuiba. Another dry-season road runs E to Paraguay which is OK for high clearance vehicles.

● **Accommodation D** pp *Gran Hotel Avenida*, T 2106/2297, very clean, TV, fridge bar, helpful owner, parking. On street to railway station is **G** *Res Miraflores*, friendly, clean, helpful.

● **Buses** From Tarija Mon, Thur at 0700 and Thur at 1800, US$9.75; to Tarija, 1700, 12 hrs.

The Cochabamba Basin

THE fertile foothills surrounding the colonial city of Cochabamba provide much of the country's grain, fruit and coca. Colonial villages and precolumbian sites are also within reach.

It is 394 km from La Paz to Cochabamba by road, now completely paved.

COCHABAMBA

Bolivia's third largest city (*pop* 300,000; *alt* 2,570m; *phone code* 042) was founded in 1571. It has an excellent climate with an average temperature of 18°C. Located in one of the richest agricultural regions in Bolivia, the Cochabamba valley attracted settlers from Spain who prospered as landowners producing foodstuffs for the mining areas. Land reform since 1952 has created a class of relatively prosperous and conservative small farmers. Today Cochabamba is an important commercial and communications centre with a greater vitality than the cities of the altiplano.

Places of interest

At the heart of the old city is the arcaded **Plaza 14 de Septiembre**, with the **Cathedral** dating from 1571, but much added to (open mornings only). Nearby are several colonial churches: **Santo Domingo** (Santiváñez y Ayacucho) begun in 1778 and still unfinished; **San Francisco** (25 de

Mayo y Bolívar) 1581, but heavily modernized in 1926; the **Convent of Santa Teresa** (Baptista y Ecuador) original construction 1753; and **La Compañía** (Baptista y Achá), whose whitewashed interior is completely innocent of the usual riot of late Baroque decoration. From **Plaza Colón**, at the N end of the old town, the wide Av Ballivián (known as **El Prado**) runs NW to the wealthy modern residential areas. To the S of the old town lie the bus and train stations and some of the best produce markets in Bolivia. Overlooking the bus station is the **San Sebastián hill**, offering grand views of the city. From here you can walk to the adjoining **La Coronilla hill**, topped by an imposing monument commemorating the defence of Cochabamba by its womenfolk from Spanish troops in 1812. (Beware of robbery and of bogus policemen.) At the E end of Av Heroínas is another hill the **Cerro de San Pedro**, with a statue to Cristo de la Concordia.

Cochabamba was the birth-place of Simón Patiño, the tin baron, who built two houses in the city. One of these, in the centre, is now part of the **Universidad San Simón**; next door on the corner of Calama and Aguirre is his bank, the Banco Mercantil (see the domed interior of the main banking hall). To the N of Plaza Colón at Av Potosí 1450 (T 43137) lies **Palacio de Portales**, the Patiño mansion, now the *Centro Cultural Pedagógico Simón J Patiño*, is reached by micro G from Av San Martín. Built in French renaissance style, furnished from Europe and set in 10 ha of gardens inspired by Versailles, the house was finished in 1927 but never occupied; open Mon-Fri 1700 and 1730, and Sat at 1100 for guided tours in Spanish, entrance US$1, don't be late; useful library. There is an excellent art gallery in the basement (open Mon-Fri 1430-1830, Sat 0900-1200, Sun 1000-1200). The educational centre for teachers and students works to promote literacy in the surrounding countryside. For Patiño's country mansion at Pairumani, see under **Excursions**.

Museums

Museo Arqueológico, 25 de Mayo y Heroínas, part of the Universidad de San Simón, Mon-Fri 0900-1200, 1500-1900, Sat 0900-1300, US$1.50, free student guide (Spanish or English) small but interesting display of artefacts including amerindian heiroglyphic scripts and pre-Inca textiles, good 1½ hrs tour; **Museo de la Casa de la Cultura**, 25 de Mayo y Heroínas, Mon-Fri 0900-1200, 1400-1800, free, exhibitions of paintings, occasionally shows films.

Excursions

To the N, in a high fault-block range of mountains, is **Cerro Tunari**, 5,180m. A road runs to within 300m of the top, usually sprinkled with a little snow. There are beautiful views of the Cochabamba valley from the mountain road which goes into the Parque Tunari from Cala Cala, ending at the lake which supplies drinking water; best in the afternoon, but no public transport.

Quillacollo (*pop* 20,000), 13 km W, has a good Sun market but no tourist items; the *campesinos* do not like being photographed. **Fiesta de la Virgen de Urkupiña** lasts 4 days with much dancing and religious ceremony, its date varies each year between June and Aug. Plenty of transport from Cochabamba, hotels all full throughout the festivities. Be there before 0900 to be sure of a seat, as you are not allowed to stand in the street. The first day is the most colourful with all the groups in costumes and masks, parading and dancing in the streets till late at night. Many groups have left by the second day and dancing stops earlier. The third day is dedicated to the pilgrimage. (Many buses, micros and *trufis* from Heroínas y Ayacucho, 20 mins, US$0.30.)

2-3 km beyond Quillacollo is a road to the beautiful Pairumani *hacienda*, centre of the Patiño agricultural foundation. Known also as **Villa Albina**, it was built in 1925-32, furnished from Europe and inhabited by Patiño's wife, Albina. The house and Patiño mausoleum may be visited by prior arrangement (T 60082, open Mon-Fri 1500-1600, Sat 0900-1130, Bus 7 or 38, or *trufi* 211 from Cochabamba).

At Marquina (US$0.65 by bus from Quillacollo, US$10.50 taxi from Cochabamba) is **D-E** *Hostal Los Nuevos Inkas*, PO Box 318, Cochabamba, T 41505, F 61234, cheaper rate involves community work; all meals included; it is an ecological Quechua hostal, part of the Movimiento Pachamama Universal; also solar heating, sauna, gardens, pool.

The Inka-Rakay ruins Near the village of Sipe-Sipe, 27 km W of Cochabamba; the main attraction is the view from the site of the Cochabamba valley and the mountains ringing the ruins. From Sipe-Sipe to the ruins there is either a 6 km footpath, or a 12 km road with almost no traffic, taking 3 to 4 hrs to walk. It is a beautiful trip, slightly less terrifying on foot than in a vehicle. Start early for it is a full day. Get full directions for the footpath before setting out, or walk there along the road and return by the path (it is easier to find that way). It may be possible to hitch; alternatively hire a guide (Norberto Rojas Mcal, who runs a shop in the plaza, is rec, he speaks English). **NB** Take food and plenty of water as there is none available and beware of theft on the footpath. Also worth taking a hat and sunblock as there is no shade on the path or road. In Sipe Sipe are *La Cabaña* thermal baths, open all year, with restaurant, good food, book in advance. Bus 245 goes direct from Cochabamba to Sipe-Sipe, also *trufi* 145 (more frequent than bus). From Quillacollo, buses for Sipe-Sipe wait until there are enough passengers.

Tarata 33 km SE, a colonial town with a traditional arcaded plaza on which stand the church, containing an 18th-century organ and other colonial artefacts (open 0800-1300 daily), the Casa Consistorial, and the Municipalidad. Inside the Franciscan Convent overlooking the town are the remains of the martyr, San Severino, patron saint of the town, more commonly known as the 'Saint of Rain'; a lively and colourful celebration of the feast takes place on the last Sun of Nov and attracts thousands of local people. Large procession on 3 May, day of Santa Vera Cruz, with fireworks and brass band. Market day Thur (bus US$0.65, 1 hr, frequent,

last return 1800, see **Transport** below). Ask for Doña Prima Fernández who sells sweaters at 'amazing prices'; she lives opposite the monastery.

At **Cliza**, 6 km further SE, there is a large Sun market (**G** *Alojamiento*, near bus terminal; see **Transport** below). **Punata**, 48 km E of Cochabamba, has a very lively and colourful market on Tues. Behind the main church, new vehicles are lined up to be blessed by the priest. The local speciality is *garapiña*, a mixture of *chicha* and ice-cream. Beyond Punata, at Villa Rivera, woven wall hangings are produced. At **Arani**, 7 km E of Punata, there is an *artesanía* market on Thur.

Local festivals

Carnival is celebrated 15 days before Lent. Rival groups (*comparsas*) compete in music, dancing, and fancy dress, culminating in El Corso on the last Sat of the Carnival. Drenching from water-throwing is likely the day after Carnival. *Mascaritas* balls also take place in the carnival season, when the young women wear long hooded satin masks.

14 Sept, Day of Cochabamba.

Local information

Street numbering Street numbering works as follows: the city is divided into 4 quadrants based on intersection of Av Las Heroínas running W to E, and Av Ayacucho/Av Libertador Simón Bolívar running N to S. In all longitudinal streets N of Heroínas the letter N precedes the 4 numbers. South of Heroínas the numbers are preceded by S. In all transversal streets W of Ayacucho the letter O (Oeste) precedes the numbers and all streets running E are preceded by E (Este). The first 2 numbers refer to the block, 01 being closest to Ayacucho or Heroínas; the last two refer to the building's number.

● **Accommodation**

L3 *Portales*, Av Pando 1271, T 48700, F 42071, 5-star, swimming pool, a long way from centre.

A1 *Aranjuez*, Av Buenos Aires E-0563, T 41935, F 40158, Casilla 3056, 4-star, rec, 2 blocks from Los Portales, small, colonial style, good restaurant, jazz in the bar, Fri and Sat night; **A1** *Caesar's Plaza*, 25 de Mayo S-210 y Bolívar, T 50088/54092, F 59324, modern, 4-star, good buffet breakfasts; **A2** *Gran Hotel Cochabamba*, Plaza Ubaldo Anze, T 82551, F 42823, beautifully set in the N part of the city (2 blocks from Los Portales at La Recoleta), with

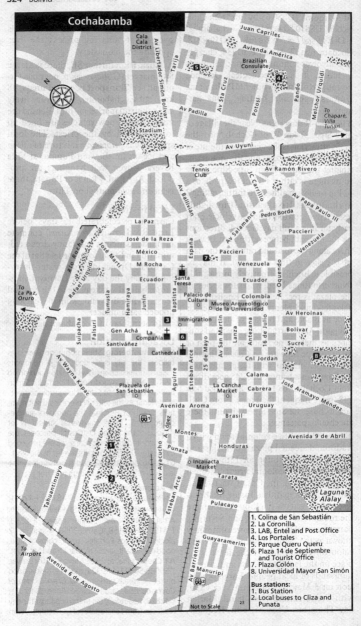

Cochabamba

1. Colina de San Sebastián
2. La Coronilla
3. LAB, Entel and Post Office
4. Los Portales
5. Parque Queru Queru
6. Plaza 14 de Septiembre and Tourist Office
7. Plaza Colón
8. Universidad Mayor San Simón

Bus stations:
1. Bus Station
2. Local buses to Cliza and Punata

Not to Scale

garden, swimming pool (guests only) and tennis courts, popular with tour groups, rec. In the city: **A3** *Ambassador*, C España N-0349 (T 48777, F 28778), private bath, hot water, telephone, modern, central and reasonable, good restaurant.

B *Americana*, Av Aroma y Esteban Arce, T 50554, F 50484, clean, TV, fridge, fan, helpful, good service.

C *Boston*, C 25 de Mayo 0167, T 28530, clean and friendly, restaurant, luggage deposit, quiet rooms at back, safe parking; rec; **C** *Capitol*, Colombia 0415 y 25 de Mayo, T 24510, private bath, TV, clean and modern, no parking; **C** *Uni-hotel*, Baptista S-0111 Esq Av Heroínas, T 51228, with bath and breakfast, pleasant, helpful, modern, clean, central.

D *City Hotel*, Jordán E-341, T 22993, nr centre, with shower, cheaper rooms on upper floors, clean, noisy but modern; **D** *Colonial*, Junín N-0134 entre Colombia y Heroínas, T 21791, with garden and terrace, rooms with big balcony, peaceful, secure, laundry facilities, breakfast served on terrace, highly rec; **D** *El Dorado*, 25 de Mayo 1034, T 21940, rec, clean, hot water; **D** *Hostal Central*, Gral Acha 0235, T 23622, with bath, modern, relaxed, friendly; **D** *Res Buenos Aires*, 25 de Mayo 329, T 29518, with bath, E without, pleasant, clean communal baths; **D** *Hostería Jardín*, Hamiraya N-0248 (entre Colombia y Ecuador), T 47844, with bath, E without, garden, very friendly, safe car-park, renovated, rec; **D** *Hostal Elisa*, Agustín López, S-0834, T 27846, with bath, E without, good breakfast US$1.25, modern, clean, garden, 2 blocks from bus station, laundry service, friendly, main gringo place, highly rec.

E *Alojamiento Escobar*, Aguirre S-749, clean, a good budget place (not to be confused with *Residencial* at Uruguay E-0213); **E-F** *Florida*, 25 de Mayo S-0583, T 27787, clean and friendly, but noisy, popular, laundry service, safe deposit box, quite clean, breakfast, rec (hot showers); **E** *Res Copacabana*, Av Arce S 0875 y Brasil, T 27929, nr bus station, hot showers, spotless, friendly, rec, motorcycle parking; **E** *Res El Salvador* Montes E-0420, T 27307, with electric shower, clean, will store luggage, rec, close to market but inconvenient for restaurants; **E** *Res Familiar*, Sucre E-0554, T 27988, with annex at 25 de Mayo S-0234, T 27986, old fashioned, pleasant, clean, secure, good showers; **E** *Jerusalem*, Aroma y 25 de Mayo, nr bus station, with bath, warm water, clean, friendly, big rooms.

F *Res Agustín López*, Agustín López 0859, T 27250, nr bus station, basic, without bath, clean, hot water; **F** *Res Kennedy*, Av Aroma 750, T 24732, hot water, quiet, clean, water only at certain times, small rooms, with washing facilities; **F** *Res Urkupiña*, Av Arce 750,

T 23502, very clean, basic, hot water, shared bath. Many cheap and basic places to stay nr the bus station.

Youth Hostel: ABAJ affiliate, **D** *Res Jordán*, C Antesana S-0671, modern, clean, basic. For long-term accommodation, Sra Nora de Durán, Ecuador E-0479, entre 25 de Mayo y San Martín, full board available, good value.

● Places to eat

José, Plaza 14 de Setiembre 0209, popular Chinese, not expensive; *Suiza*, Av Ballivián 820, T 45485, popular, rec for international cuisine, good value; *BJ*, Av Libertador Bolívar 1580, T 48629, excellent, international cuisine, well prepared, rec; *América's*, Bolívar E-0971, a bit simpler and cheaper; *Miraflores*, Av Tarija N-0314, Bolivian food, large, popular, weekend speciality roast pig; *El Caminante*, Arce S-0628, pleasant patio, excellent food inc duck with salad and vegetables; *La Estancia* Anecito Padilla block 7, serves best steak in town, also grilled fish and chicken (in side street off Plaza Recoleta), also has a salad bar, rec; *Los Troncos*, Junín 0-0942, barbecued meats, stylish, good; *Las Palmeras*, Lanza N-0248, very good food; *Paso del Toro*, Junín y Aroma, cheap and good; *Papichín*, Aroma y 25 de Mayo, cheap and friendly, very good chicken and *churrasco*; *Gopal*, C España 250, Galeria Olimpia, harekrishna, hence no smoking or alcohol, good vegetarian lunch, US$1.45, good spiced bread, and Italian in the evenings, pleasant garden, English spoken, closed Sun; *La Cantonata*, España y Mayor Rocha, Itallan, highly rec, though expensive; *Lai-Lai*, Aniceto Padilla 729, best Chinese, also takeaway service; *Los Escudos*, Heroínas 0460, good food but not cheap; *Snack Uno*, Av Heroínas E-0562, good lunches and dinners inc vegetarian; *Cevichería Arriba Alianza*, Av Oquinda S-06 s/n, highly rec for lovers of Peruvian ceviche, inexpensive; *Chifa Hong Kong*, Hamiraya N-0260, excellent Chinese, huge portions, main dishes about US$3; *Pizzería Don Corleone*, España N-0350, expensive but great pizzas; *España*, España N-0272, limited menu, good value; *Carajillo*, España N-0386, Spanish-style, snacks and drinks, highly rec. Excellent pastries and ice cream at the *Zurich Tea Room*, Av San Martín Norte 143, open 1500-2000; *Pastelería Oriental*, Mayor Rocha E-0358, Santa Cruz-style, popular for tea; *California Burgers*, 25 de Mayo S-0123, good burgers. Good ice-cream parlours on Av Heroínas: *Dumbo* 0440, popular eating and meeting spot, also does cheap meals; *Kivon* 0440, 3 doors away, similar but smaller and quieter; *Unicornio*, Heroínas y Baptista, large, attractive, popular gringo hangout, pricey. Good salteñas at *Salteñería Illimani*, 25 de Mayo S-0608, cheap. *La Chatarra del Cronopio*, Ballivián 0674, pleasant bar. Excellent food in Incallacta market for under US$1.

● **Banks & money changers**
Cash on Visa or MasterCard from many banks; no commission on bolivianos. Visa and Mastercard at 'Enlace' cash dispensers in *Hotel Portales*, Centro Comercial Cavero (Av Heroínas), bus terminal and Av Heroínas y Tumusla. **Bidesa**, Jordán E-0224, changes TCs, 1% commission for cash dollars or bolivianos, good rates. **Exprint-Bol**, Plaza 14 de Septiembre 252 (will change TCs into dollars at 2% commission); **América**, Acha 0162, good rates. Money changers congregate at most major intersections, especially outside the Post Office, safe, good rates. Also *Unicornio Cafetería*.

● **Cultural centres**
Centro de Cultura El Umbral, España N-0261, video-cinema with good films, theatre with resident company, concerts, dance, art gallery, café with traditional music, library and reading room. At 25 de Mayo N-0365, T 21288, is the **Centro Boliviano Americano** with a library of English-language books, open 0900-1200 and 1500-1900. **Alianza Francesa**, Santiváñez O-0187. **Goethe Institute**, Sucre y Antezana.

● **Embassies & consulates**
USA, Av Libertador Bolívar 1724, T 43216, 0900-1200 (will also attend to needs of British and Canadian travellers); Netherlands, Heroínas 473, *Gitano Tours*, T 28836/29409; Brazil, 9th floor Edif Los Tiempos Dos, Av Oquendo, T55860, open 1400-1800; Argentina, F Blanco E-0929, T 55859, visa applications 0900-1300.

● **Entertainment**
Frequent concerts and plays at the elegant *Teatro Achá*; more popular stage productions (stand-up comedy, music and dance) at *Tra La La*, Plazuela 4 de Noviembre, opp Chilean consulate, or *Champagne*, C Ballivián 0658. Cinemas on 25 de Mayo opp *Dumbo*; 25 de Mayo y Colombia; 25 de Mayo y Bolívar; and 25 de Mayo y Sucre. Discos: *Arlequín*, Uyuni between Plaza Recoleta and stadium, big, popular, young crowd; *Reflejos*, Libertador y América, both popular. Nightlife is moving to the N area on América between Libertador and Pando. *Wunderbar* in the centre (Antesana 2 blocks from Plaza Colón), good music, darts upstairs.

● **Hospitals & medical services**
Health: Doctor rec by the Tourist Office, James Koller, C Baptista N-0386, T 24191, call between 1700-1800.

● **Language classes**
Sra Blanca de La Rosa Villareal, Av Libertador Simón Bolívar 1108, esq Oblitas, Casilla 2707 (T 44298) charges US$5 for a 45 mins lesson. *Runawasi*, J Hinojosa, Barrio Juan XXIII s/n, Casilla 4034, T/F 48923, Spanish and Quechua,

also arranges accommodation, rec. *Sra Alicia Ferrufino*, JQ Mendoza N-0349, T 81006, US$10/hr, is a rec Spanish teacher. Courses available at the Centro Boliviano Americano (address below).

● **Laundry**
Superclean, 16 de Julio y Jordán, US$1/kg; *Limpieza Económico*, 16 de Julio entre Venezuela y Paccieri, safe, fast service; also at Women's Prison, Plazuela San Sebastián, good and cheap (possible to visit if you ask guards).

● **Post & telecommunications**
Post Office: Av Heroínas y Ayacucho, next to LAB office; Mon-Sat 0800-1900, Sun 0800-1200, helpful, reliable. Telecommunications Entel, same location, phone, cable, Fax (not possible to make AT&T credit card calls), open till 2245, T 25210.

● **Shopping**
Artesanías Casa Fisher, C Ramón Rivero E-0204, opp the Tennis Club, PO Box 3782, T and F 49846, beautiful woollen goods, prices about US$85 locally, US$225-265 in USA, Casa Fisher will be happy to provide information for travellers. *Fotrama* Cooperative for alpaca sweaters, stoles, rugs, alpaca wool, etc (expensive – run by Maryknoll Mission, factory at Av Circunvalación 0413, T 25468. *Asarti*, Mayor Rocha E-0375, beautiful hand-made and machine-knitted sweaters, can make to order, expensive. For made-to-measure leather goods and alpaca, *Chenza*, 25 de Mayo N-0344, mostly modern designs, highly rec; similarly rec is *Arizona*, Juan Capriles E-0133; export-quality leather garments and goods at *Roger's*, Av San Martín S-0427; or *D'Luca*, España N-0320.

Markets are very good for tourist items and souvenirs. The main market is called San Antonio. La Cancha market (nr railway station) is packed on Wed and Sat with campesinos, 'huge and well worth a visit'; woollen items are expensive but high quality, US$35-50 for an alpaca sweater. There is a Sat market at Av América y Libertador, best before 0900. Mercado Incallacta for fruit and vegetables excellent and very cheap, except for 2 touristy avenues which sell souvenirs. Try local hot drink, *api*, made from maize. Kiosks behind the post office sell interesting crafts.

A very good **bookshop** is *Los Amigos del Libro*, Av de Heroínas 311 y España, Gral Achá 110, in *Hotel Portales* and *Gran Hotel Cochabamba*, and in the new Torres Sofer shopping centre, stocks US and English magazines as well as *South American Handbook*. Good city map and guide in colour for US$2.50.

Camera repairs: rec at *Maxell* on Plaza 14 de Setiembre, reasonable prices rec. For developing film *Foto Broadway*, España y Colombia, reasonable prices, inc slide transparencies. *Germán Grunbaum*, 25 de Mayo N-0345, good quality, rec.

Camping equipment: available at shop on 25 de Mayo, just before plaza Colón; wide variety of goods, very helpful owner, speaks English and perhaps German. Also try Heroínas 225, T 29711. Camping gas available at several shops on Av San Martín.

● **Sports**
Swimming: Tourist complex *El Carmen*, road to Quillacolla, US$2, popular, catch micro on Junín. Pool at Club Social, C Méjico y Plaza Colón (US$1.50), is open to the public. Pool, restaurant at Estancia El Rosedal at Tiquipaya, take bus number 12 from Antesana y Cabrera to end of line. See also Sipe Sipe, under **Inka-Rakay**, below. Most are open only at weekend in summer only ('too cold' in winter, check before going).

Tennis: Club de Ténis de Cochabamba admits non-members for US$5/day.

● **Tour companies & travel agents**
Fremen, Tumusla N-0245, T 43827, F 47126, city and local tours, but specializes in travel in Bolivian Amazonia, using the *Reina de Enin* floating hotel out of Puerto Varador nr Trinidad; *Tai Tours*, Av Heroínas E-0620, T 51723/21267, adventure tourism. *Turismo Balsa*, Av Heroínas O-0184, T 27065, daily city tours, excursions to Quillacollo, Inca-Rakay, Samaipata, Torotoro, etc, airline reservations (see also under La Paz **Travel agents**).

● **Tourist offices**
Plaza 14 de Septiembre E-0249, open Mon-Fri 0900-1200, 1430-1700, helpful, sell city map and guide for US1.25, good service. Also at Jorge Wilstermann airport.

● **Useful addresses**
Immigration Office: Plaza 14 de Septiembre E-0231.

● **Transport**
Local Micros and colectivos, US$0.15; *trufis*, US$0.17; anything marked 'San Antonio' goes to the market. Trufis C and 10 go from bus terminal to the city centre. Taxis: agree fare before getting in and beware overcharging; about US$0.65 from anywhere to the Plaza; double after dark.

Drivers: in Cochabamba should note that, when approaching a junction, the driver who blows his/her horn first has right of way.

Air Jorge Wilstermann airport. Airport bus is Micro B from Plaza 14 de Septiembre, US$0.40; taxis from airport to centre US$5.20 (no set rates, so bargain). Reconfirm all flights (and obtain reconfirmation number), and arrive early for international flights. Daily by LAB to and from **La Paz** (30 mins, 20 kg baggage allowance), book early for morning flights, and to **Santa Cruz** (40 mins). 4 a week to Sucre; 5 flights a week to **Tarija** and to **Trinidad**. LAB has flights to Lima (daily except Fri), Quito, Panama, Mexico City, Santiago and Salta (once a week each). LAB in town at Ayacucho and Heroínas, open 0800; at airport LAB office, T 50750/50650, opens 0500. Aero Sur (Av Ayacucho S-0170, T 28385), has daily flights to La Paz and Santa Cruz, with connections to other cities.

Trains To Oruro, *pasajero local* Sun 0800, 12 hrs, US$3.

Buses The main bus terminal is at Av Aroma y Ayacucho. Buses (early am and evening) to **Santa Cruz**, taking 8-15 hrs, US$9-15; buses take the Chapare route, as opposed to the old mountain road via Epizana (except Cinta de Plata, once a week). See page 328, below. To/from La Paz many companies, shop around for best times, services and prices (about US$7.75), by night or day, 7 hrs on paved road. Bus to **Oruro**, US$5.15, 4½ hrs, eg Flota Cometa, 1 a day. To **Potosí**, US$6.75-9.50 via Oruro, several companies. Daily to **Sucre**, US$9.75, several companies between 1900 and 2015, eg Flota Bolívar (meal and coffee stops), Flota Copacabana 2000, arr 0600, Trans Copacabana 2015, arr 0615, both rec (latter *bus-cama* US$10.40), Azul or Mopar, rec, 10 hrs, overnight only. To Sucre by day; take a bus to Aiquile, Trans Campero, Av Barrientos S-2291 (100m past Av 6 de Agosto junction, *trufis* 1, 10, 14, 16, 20 pass in front), Mon, Tues, Thur, Fri 1300, Wed, Sat 1400, 5 hrs, then a bus at midnight-0100 passing en route to Sucre (if you want to take a truck in daylight, wait till next day). To **Iquique**, TEPP (Punata) Mon, Wed 1430 via Oruro. Local buses leave from Av Barrientos y Av 6 de Agosto, nr **La Coronilla** for Tarata, Punata and Cliza; Av Oquendo 985 (at the edge of Lake Alalay; be careful around this area) to Villa Tunari, US$4.50, 5 hrs (1030, or when full); Chimoré, US$5.75; Eterazama, US$5.75; Puerto Villarroel, US$7.75, 6 hrs (from 0800 when full, daily); Puerto San Francisco, US$6.50.

TOROTORO NATIONAL PARK

In the province of Potosí is **Torotoro**, a small village best reached from Cochabamba (120 km), set amid beautiful rocky landscape. The village is in the centre of the **Torotoro National Park**, writes Linda Slater, a peace corps worker from Cochabamba. Attractions include caves, a canyon, waterfalls, pictographs, ruins, dinosaur tracks and fossils. Tourist information is available at the national park office in Torotoro. Dinosaur tracks (fossilised?) can be seen by the stream just outside the village. Ask at Santiago, the only shop, for the key to the Umajalanta cave, about 8 km NW of Torotoro; a guide is necessary for both the cave and the dinosaur tracks, US$2.50 pp for whole day.

● **Services** Trucks and *micros* go to Torotoro from Av República y Punata, nr the market in Cochabamba, at 1800 Sun and Thur, US$4, 12 hrs, or a truck also goes from the market at Cliza at about 0800, 10 hrs. Trucks return to Cochabamba every Mon and Fri. Alternatively, hire a jeep, US$220 for 3 days inc mileage and fuel; quite an adventure. Take your own food as only a limited range is sold at the shop. New *alojamiento* nr bus terminal, **G**, friendly; ask the priest for other places to sleep, rooms are available in locals' homes, cheap and friendly. The village has no electricity. A small travel agency on C 25 de Mayo in Cochabamba offers 5-day trips for US$80 pp inc transport, highly rec 'for the adventurous traveller with time and energy'.

From 24-27 July, the Fiesta de Santiago, the people from surrounding communities congregate here to sing, dance, and drink. **NB** Travel to Torotoro is all but impossible in the wet season (end Nov-May), as flooded rivers wash out roads. Check bus schedules in advance at all times of year.

THE MOUNTAIN ROAD TO SANTA CRUZ

The 500-km road via the mountains and Epizana to Santa Cruz (page 336) is paved, but the new lowland route is preferred by most transport.

INKALLAJTA

Before the Siberia pass, 5 km beyond Montepunco (Km 119), the 23-km road to Pocona and **Inkallajta** turns off. The Inca ruins, on a flat spur of land at the mouth of a steep valley, are extensive and the main building of the fortress is said to have been the largest roofed Inca building.

● **Accommodation & services** To get there without your own transport, take a micro to the checkpoint 10 km from Cochabamba, then a truck to Km 119, walk towards Pocona or take a truck for 15 km, to where a large yellow sign indicates the trail. After approx 10 km the trail divides, take the downhill path and the ruins are a further 2 km. Take food and camping gear.

There are several good camping sites. The Cochabamba Archaeological Museum has some huts where visitors can stay, free, but take sleeping bag and food. Water available at nearby waterfall.

EPIZANA

Epizana, 13 km beyond Montepunco, Km 128, is the junction for the road to Sucre, 233 km, 7-8 hrs scenic drive, all but the last hour rough, and narrow in parts. (**F** *Hotel España*, other so-called hotels are restaurants; also service stations.) At Km 386 on the road to Santa Cruz is Samaipata (see page 341).

TOTORA AND AIQUILE

Totora, on the Sucre road, is described as one of the loveliest, friendly colonial villages, better to stay in than Epizana, with two hotels (**F** *Gran Hotel Totora*, colonial style, huge rooms) and restaurants (truck to Sucre daily 1100, 11 hrs).

Aiquile, 215 km from Cochabamba, is famous for its wooden *charangos*: *charango* festival in Oct or Nov, ask tourist office; weekend market. Museo Arqueológico Regional, with extensive exhibits on Omereque and Yampara cultures. **F** *Hostal Campero*, Bolívar 960, clean, water all day, good food; **F** *Hotel Escudo*, basic, no water in toilets, cooking water unsafe but clean beds. See Cochabamba **Transport** for buses.)

COCHABAMBA TO SANTA CRUZ VIA CHAPARE

The lowland road from Cochabamba to Santa Cruz, which most buses take, runs through Villa Tunari, Sinahota and Chimoré. The road is good all the way and the Cochabamba-Villa Tunari stretch is picturesque.

● **Accommodation & places to eat** About an hour's drive from Cochabamba is an artificial lake, beside which is *Hotel Poseidon*, cabins for rent; large restaurant popular at weekends.

VILLA TUNARI

In **Villa Tunari** (see Cochabamba, **Transport**, **Buses**, above) ask for the Piscinas Naturales for beautiful swimming. Annual Fish Fair 5 and 6 Aug, music and dancing, delicious meals.

• **Accommodation D** *Las Palmas*, T 47554, 1 km out of town, clean, friendly, with pool and good restaurant, rec; **D** *El Puente*, Av de la Integración, with bath in cabins from 2 people to family-size (book in advance at Fremen Travel Agency in Cochabamba or La Paz), to get there continue on the highway through town, cross the second bridge, turn right on the first road to the right, then go 1 km, the turn is clearly marked, the hotel has a beautiful stream and 14 natural pools; *Sumuqué*, cheaper, away from main road, decent; **F** *Pilunchi*, quiet and rundown, in centre; **F** *La Querencia*, pleasant terrace on river front, avoid noisy rooms at front, friendly, good cheap food, clothes washing facilities, insect repellent provided, and toads. On eastern outskirts, **A3** *Country Club Los Tucanes*, inc breakfast, a/c, 2 swimming pools.

• **Banks & money changers** One bank in Villa Tunari, then none until Yapacaní, the first town in Santa Cruz department, across the Río Ichilo from Bulo Bulo.

In **Chimoré**: *Hotel Copacabana*, used by military and prostitutes; water cuts common June-Sept; *Restaurants El Tamarindo*, on right entering village from Cochabamba, and *El Curichi*, on left, mostly for bus passengers, token system, limited menu, but OK. In **Ivirgarzama**, *Hotel El Torero*, very basic; *Restaurant Punata*, 100m from bus station, popular.

The Northern Lowlands

FROM SCRUBBY east lowlands to dense tropical jungle in the north, this is pioneer country: missionaries, rubber tappers and cocaine refiners. Improved roads to Rurrenabaque and Trinidad are opening up the area and wildlife expeditions are becoming increasingly popular.

Bolivia's Northern lowlands, the Cuenca Amazónica, account for about 70% of national territory. Beni department has 53% of the country's birds and 50% of its mammals, but destruction of forest and habitat is proceeding at an alarming rate. A **Beni Biosphere Reserve**, under the auspices of Unesco, has been set up. As much archaeological work is taking place in Beni as in the altiplano; the same efforts to reinstate precolumbian agricultural methods are being made in each zone.

ROUTES There are two main land routes into the northern lowlands: one from La Paz and one from Villa Tunari on the Cochabamba-Santa Cruz road.

CARANAVI TO SAN BORJA

From Caranavi, a road runs N to **Sapecho**, where there is an interesting cocoa cooperative (**E-F** *Alojamiento Rodríguez*, very friendly and pleasant, recently upgraded) and a bridge over the Río Beni. This bridge has cut off Puerto Linares, the old port for river access to the lowlands. Across the river is Santa Ana, originally an Indian village, more interesting than Puerto Linares, but no services exist in either town. Beyond Sapecho, the road passes through Palos Blancos 7 km from the bridge (market day, Sat; several cheap lodgings). The road between Sapecho and Yucumo is now a very good all-weather gravel surface, 3 hrs from Sapecho *tránsito*. There are *hospedajes* (F) and restaurants in **Yucumo**. 550,000 ha of jungle are under cultivation, rice, sugar, corn and fruit being planted. The Chimanes indians are trying to survive the influx of settlers from the altiplano. At Yucumo a road branches NW, fording rivers 21 times on its way to Rurrenabaque.

● **Buses** Yucumo is on the La Paz-Caranavi-Rurrenabaque or San Borja routes. Rurrenabaque-La Paz bus passes through about 1800. If travelling to Rurrenabaque by bus or truck take extra food in case there is a delay for river levels to fall.

SAN BORJA

From Yucumo it is 50 km (1-2 hrs) to **San Borja**, a small, dusty cattle-raising centre with hotels and restaurants clustered near the plaza. This is a coca-growing region and it is unwise for travellers to wander alone inside the Parque Nacional Isiburo in case they are mistaken by coca farmers for DEA agents.

● **Accommodation** **D-E** *Hostal Jatata*, T 3103, 2 blocks from plaza, modern, comfortable, friendly,fans in rooms, good snack bar, highly rec; **F** *Trópico*, 1 block from main plaza, clean, rec; **E-F** *Res Manara*, just off plaza, clean, comfortable, some rooms with a/c; **G** *Jaropa*, clean, basic, friendly.

● **Places to eat** *Taurus*, good food, cheap; *Club Social*, 2 blocks from plaza, covered open-air restaurant, good *almuerzos*.

● **Banks & money changers** Good rate for dollars at *Joyería San Borja* next to entrance to supermarket round corner from central market.

● **Transport** Flota Yungueña daily except Thur at 1300 to La Paz (19 hrs); also to Rurrenabaque, Santa Rosa, Riberalta, Guayaramerín Thur, Sat, Sun. **To Trinidad** From San Borja the road goes E to Trinidad via San Ignacio de Moxos. There are 5-6 river crossings and, in the wetlands, flamingoes, blue heron and a multitude of waterfowl. The road surface Caranavi-San Borja is very good;

San Borja-San Ignacio poor, long stretches are rutted and pot-holed; San Ignacio-Trinidad is good. Gasoline available at Yolosa, Caranavi, Yucumo, San Borja and San Ignacio. Minibuses and Camionetas run daily between San Borja and Trinidad throughout the year, about 7 hrs inc 20 mins crossing of Río Mamore on ferry barge. 1 de Mayo daily to San Ignacio (US$8), Trinidad and Santa Cruz at 0850; daily micros and camionetas to Trinidad, US$15, or hitch on a timber truck. Aero Sur flies San Borja-Trinidad and from there, to most main cities.

RURRENABAQUE

Rurrenabaque is a small, picturesque jungle town, on the Río Beni, with San Buenaventura on the opposite bank. Mosquito nets can be bought here much more cheaply than in La Paz. Public swimming pool in town, US$1.

Jungle tours

Agencia Fluvial, at *Hotel Tuichi* runs jungle tours on the Río Tuichi, normally 4 days, but shorter by arrangement, for a group of 5 or more, US$20 pp/day (payable in dollars) including food, transport and mosquito nets. (Write to Tico Tudela, Agencia Fluvial, Rurrenabaque.) 3 nights are spent in the jungle, learning about plants, survival and the foods of the region. You must take swimming costume, insect repellent to ward off sandflies and mosquitoes and a camera. Fluvial also run 3-day 'Pampas Tours' on a boat to Río Yacuma, US$20 pp/day, lots of wildlife, rec as better value than jungle tours. Fluvial tours can be arranged through Hotel Tuichi; rec guide is Negro. *Ecotour* also run tours to Pampas, office opp *Hotel Berlín*, experienced, family-run, US$20 pp/day. The jungle is very hot in the rainy season with many more biting insects and far fewer animals to be seen. 1 day trips are reportedly a waste of time as it takes 3 hrs to reach the jungle. Note that an increase in tourism is putting pressure on animal populations.

Local information
● **Accommodation**
Most hotels in Rurrenabaque are noisy owing to all night discos.

E *Santa Ana*, with bath, **F** without, nr plaza, clean, basic, cold water, laundry, pretty courtyard; rec; **E** *Porteño*, with bath, less without, quite good.

F *Rurrenabaque*, clean, safe, cooking and laundry facilities; **F** *Tuichi*, kitchen and laundry facilities, fan, very clean, friendly; **G/F** *Berlín*, nr wharf, all rooms dirty, insanitary, cold water, to be avoided.

● **Places to eat**
Best meals at *Club Social Rurrenabaque*, vegetarian dishes on request. Good ice-cream at *Bambi*, opp Flota Yungueña office, good meeting place. Three restaurants with terrace seating facing canoe dock, offer good cheap fish, beef or chicken kebabs with rice, empanadas and chicha, all under US$1.

● **Banks & money changers**
Exchange at Agencia Fluvial, 5% commission on TCs.

● **Transport**
Air LAB flies from La Paz, Fri. Itemox Express flies from Trinidad to Reyes, 30 km N (lodging, restaurants), a useful alternative to the bus ride.

Buses To/from La Paz via Caranavi Mon-Sat with Flota Yungueña and Totai, dep 1200 and 1500, 19 hrs, US$13. Bus to Riberalta, Tues, Thur, Sat, Sun 2330, 12 hrs, continues to Guayaramerín; trucks also go to Riberalta but few boats. To Trinidad, Tues, Thur, Sat, Sun at 2230 with Trans Guaya via Yucumo and San Borja.

From Rurrenabaque an all-weather road leads via **Santa Rosa** (**F** *Hotel Oriental*, changes dollars. *Restaurant and Confitería El Triángulo*, very friendly, rec) to **Riberalta**.

RIBERALTA

The town (*pop* 40,000; *alt* 175m), at the confluence of the Madre de Dios and Beni rivers, which together flow into the Mamoré N of Guayaramerín. The whole region attained temporary importance during the natural-rubber boom of the late 19th century; the cattle industry is providing a new boost for expansion.

Local information
● **Accommodation**
Ask for a fan and check the water supply.

C-D *Hostal Tahuamanu*, M Hanicke 75, T8006, modern, smart, very comfortable, with bath and a/c, inc excellent breakfast, highly rec; **E** *Res Los Reyes*, nr airport, with fan, clean, safe, pleasant and friendly but noisy disco nearby on Sat and Sun; **E-F** *Colonial*, Plácido Méndez 1, charming colonial casona, large, well-furnished rooms, nice gardens and courtyard, comfortable, good beds,

spotlessly clean, helpful owners, highly rec.

F pp *Comercial Lazo*, C NG Salvatierra, D with a/c, clean, comfortable, laundry facilities, good value; **F-G** *Nor-Oeste*, Av Moreno y Av Molina, T597, clean, simple rooms, good for budget travellers; **F-G** *Res El Pauro*, Salvatierra 157, clean, simple, shared baths, nice café at front.

● **Places to eat**
Club Social Progreso, on plaza, good value *almuerzo*, excellent fish; *Club Social Riberalta*, on Maldonado, good *almuerzo* US$3.50, smart dress only; *Quatro Ases*, C Arce, good. Nameless café on N side of plaza with pavement seating, good coffee and *salteñas*; *Tucunare*, M Chávez/Martínez, rec. Good lunch at *comedor popular* in market, US$1.50.

● **Banks & money changers**
Banco Internacional de Desarollo (Bidesa) on Maldonado, changes cash and TCs for $ or bolivianos. Lots of street changers outside or in shops.

● **Transport**
Air Aero Sur, on plaza (T 2798), flies daily except Sun to Trinidad with connections to Cobija, Guayaramerín, La Paz, San Borja, Santa Cruz and Cochabamba. Expect delays in the wet season. LAB office M Chávez 77, T 2239, to Guayaramerín daily except Wed, Trinidad 4 a week, Santa Cruz (3), Cobija, Cochabamba and La Paz (2). TAM office Av Suárez/Chuquisaca, T 2646, to Cochabamba Tues, Santa Cruz Wed and Sun, La Paz Thur; 25% discount for students and over-60s.

Road Several companies (inc Yungueña) to La Paz, via Rurrenabaque and Caranavi Tues-Sat at 1100, also Tues, Thur, Sat at 1000; to Trinidad with 8 de Diciembre Mon, Wed, Thur, Sat, Sun at 0830, also Trans Guaya daily at 0930, via Rurrenabaque; to Guayaramerín 12 weekly services on Tues, Thur, Sat, Sun at 0630, 1400 and 1700, daily with TransAmazonas at 0730 and 1630; to Cobija on Wed, Fri, Sat at 0900 with 8 de Diciembre, Mon, Thur at 1000 with TransAmazonas. Buses stop in Santa Rosa for meals.

River Cargo boats carry passengers along the Río Madre de Dios, but they are infrequent. There are few boats to Rurrenabaque.

GUAYARAMERIN

From Riberalta the road continues E, crossing the Río Yata before reaching **Guayaramerín**, a cheerful, prosperous little town (*pop* 12,500) and centre for gold prospectors on the bank of the Mamoré River, opposite the Brazilian town of Guajará-Mirim. Passage between the two towns is unrestricted; boat trip US$1.65 (more at night).

Local information

● Accommodation

B *Esperanza*, Cachuela Esperanza, Casilla 171, reserve through Aero Sur, T 0855 2201, or in La Paz *American Tours*, T 374204, F 328584, eco-friendly.

C *San Carlos*, 6 de Agosto, 4 blocks from port, T 2152/3, with a/c (D without), hot showers, clean, money exchange (dollars cash and TCs and reais), swimming pool, reasonable retaurant.

E *Santa Ana*, 25 de Mayo, clean, with bath, F without, close to airport, rec.

F *Litoral*, on 25 de Mayo, nr LAB office, cold water only, friendly; **F** *Plaza Anexo*, on Plaza, clean, good value, cold water only, ceiling fan.

● Places to eat

All on Plaza: *Made in Brazil*, good coffee; *Gipssy*, good *almuerzo*; *Los Bibosis*, popular with visiting Brazilians. *Only*, 25 de Mayo/Beni, good *almuerzo* for US$2.50, plus Chinese; on road to airport *Heladería Tutti-Frutti*, excellent ice-cream.

● Transport

Air Aero Sur, on plaza (T 2493) to Riberalta daily except Sun, connections to Santa Cruz and La Paz; TAM at 16 de Julio (road to airport), to Cochabamba Tues, Thur; Santa Cruz Wed, Sun; La Paz on Fri; LAB, on 25 de Mayo, T 2040, daily except Thur to Trinidad, except Fri to Riberalta, 3 a week to Santa Cruz, 2 a week to Cobija, Cochabamba and La Paz.

Buses To/from La Paz, Flota Yungueña, 5 a week, 36 hrs, US$33; to Riberalta 2 hrs, US$5.75, 7 deps daily 0700-1730; to Trinidad Fri, 30 hrs, US$28; to Rurrenabaque, US$20; to Cobija 4 a week, US$15.50; to Santa Cruz via Trinidad, 1-2 a week, US$33, 2½ days. All buses dep from Gral Federico Román.

River Check the notice of boats leaving port on the Port Captain's board, prominently displayed nr the immigration post on the river's bank. Boats up the Mamoré to Trinidad are fairly frequent – a 3-day wait at the most.

FRONTIER WITH BRAZIL

● Bolivian immigration

Av Costanera nr port; open 0800-1100, 1400-1800. Passports must be stamped here when leaving, or entering Bolivia.

Entering Bolivia: passports must be stamped at the Bolivian consulate in Guajará-Mirim.

● Brazilian consulate

On 24 de Septiembre, Guayaramerín, open 1100-1300; visas for entering Brazil are given here.

● Banks & money changers

Exchange money here (TCs at 2% commission in Bidesa bank on plaza) as this is very difficult in the State of Rondônia in Brazil.

COBIJA

The capital of the lowland Department of Pando lies on the Río Acre which forms the frontier with Brazil. It is an unattractive town (*pop* 7,000; *alt* 252m), whose only redeeming feature is the fact that it is a duty-free zone. Shops in centre have a huge selection of imported consumer goods at bargain prices. Brazilians and Peruvians flock here to stock up. The rainy season is Nov to Mar; the rest of the year is dry and hot. Temperatures average 29°C but can reach 40°C, or fall to 15°C when the *surazo* blows. This area has many Brazilian residents. Foodstuffs are much more expensive than in La Paz.

Local information

● Accommodation & places to eat

D-E *Prefectural Pando*, Av 9 de Febrero, T 2230, inc breakfast, *comedor* does good lunch, poor value, manager Sr Angel Gil, helpful; **F** *Res Frontera*, basic, cheap, fan; **E** *Res Crocodilo*, Av Molina, comfortable, good atmosphere, rooms with fan. *La Esquina de la Abuela*, opp Res Crocodilo, good food, not cheap. Good cheap meals in *comedor popular* in central market.

● Banks & money changers

Bidesa Bank on Av 2 de Febrero changes TCs.

● Hospitals & medical services

There is an old hospital, a recently built one (Japanese-funded), and the Red Cross.

● Post & telecommunications

Entel: on C Sucre, for telephone calls internal and abroad and fax, much cheaper than from Brazil. Post to/from La Paz 3 times a week. New building on plaza should be ready in 1996.

● Transport

Local Taxis are very expensive, charging according to time and distance, eg US$10 to the outskirts, US$12 over the international bridge to Brasileia. Besides taxis there are motobike taxis (much cheaper). Brasileia can also be reached by canoe, US$0.35.

Air Aero Sur, in *Hotel Pando*, T 2230, flies daily except Sun to Trinidad, with connections for La Paz, Santa Cruz. LAB office on Av Molinos, to Riberalta, Guayaramerín, Trinidad, Santa Cruz and La Paz. TAM office on 2 de Febrero, check schedule with them.

Buses Flota Yungueña to La Paz via Riberalta and Rurrenabaque Sat at 0700 (check times first,

T2318); to Riberalta with several bus companies and trucks, dep from 2 de Febrero, most on Wed, Fri, Sun at 0600; good all-weather surface; 5 river crossings on pontoon rafts, takes 10-11 hrs.

VILLA TUNARI TO THE LOWLANDS

PUERTO VILLARROEL

Another route into Beni Department is via the lowland road between Cochabamba and Santa Cruz. At Ivirgazama, E of Villa Tunari, the road passes the turn-off to **Puerto Villarroel**, 27 km further N, from where cargo boats ply irregularly to Trinidad in about 4-10 days (see below). You can get information from the Capitanía del Puerto notice board, or ask at docks.

● **Accommodation & services** *Hotel Hannover*, no fans, dirty toilets, facilities shared with late night disco; *Alojamiento El Jazmín*, 4 rooms, 11 beds, helpful, pleasant, meals served, restaurant planned; also *Alojamiento Petrolero*. There are very few stores in Villarroel. Sr Arturo Linares at the Cede office organizes boat trips to the jungle – not cheap.

● **NB** As this is coca-growing territory the police advise: don't stray from the main road, don't talk to strangers and don't guard or carry other people's luggage.

● **Transport** *Camionetas* go from the junction on the main road to Puerto Villarroel a few times a day, 1 hr, US$1.20. From Cochabamba you can get a bus to Puerto Villarroel (see Cochabamba **Transport, Buses**), Puerto San Francisco, or Todos Santos on the Río Chapare.

● **By boat to Trinidad**: Puerto Villarroel is the main port for the river transport to the N of Bolivia. The road network is being extended, but many roads can only be used in the dry season, so river transport is still an important means of communication. Boats sail between Puerto Villarroel, Trinidad and Guayaramerín on the Brazilian border, taking passengers. This trip is only for the hardy traveller. In the rainy season when the river is high it takes about 3 to 5 days to Trinidad (45 hrs sailing, but boats stop from sunrise to sunset; US$15 for 3 days and nights inc meals – prices and quality vary); in the dry season, ie between May or June and Aug-Dec, it may last 8 to 10 days (the river is lower, cleaner and there may be more animals to see on the shore – there may be no boats Oct-Dec). It is another 5 days to Guayaramerín. The food consists of all kinds of fish, dishes like *massaca* (stewed yuca with cooking bananas, *charque* or dried meat, oil and salt) and turtle eggs. If you are concerned about wildlife preservation, do not eat the turtle eggs; if you are fussy about food in general, don't make the trip because the kitchen is beyond description and the toilet facilities, too. Take your own drinking water, or water sterilizing tablets as the water served is taken from the river. Supplement the diet with fruit and any other interesting food you can find beforehand. The countryside between Puerto Villarroel and Trinidad is more or less cultivated, with plantations of bananas and cattle ranches. One can see *petas* – small turtles basking in the sun, capibara, river dolphin, jumping fish, now and then monkeys on the beach, and many types of birds. At night, there are never-ending frog concerts. A mosquito net is a 'must', a hammock a good idea, and binoculars for watching the wildlife a useful extra. Bathing in the river can be done without any harm.

TRINIDAD

The capital of the lowland Beni Department, founded 1686, is a dusty city in the dry season, with many streets unpaved (*pop* 50,000; *alt* 237m). A family of sloths lives in the trees in the plaza. There are two ports, Almacén and Varador, check which one your boat is docking at. Puerto Varador is 13 km from town on the Río Mamoré on the road between Trinidad and San Borja; cross the river by the main bridge by the market, walk down to the service station by the police checkpoint and take a truck, US$1.70. Almacén is 8 km from the city. The main mode of transport in Trinidad (even for taxis, US$0.40 in city) is the motorbike. Motorcycle rental on plaza, costs US$5/hr, US$12.50/half day.

Excursions

Interesting for wildlife, as is the river trip (hire a motorbike or jeep to go to the river; good swimming on the opposite bank; boat hire US$5). 5 km from town is the Laguna Suárez, with plenty of wildlife; the water is very warm, the bathing safe where the locals swim, near the café with the jetty (elsewhere there are stingrays and alligators). Motorbike taxi from Trinidad, US$1.30.

17 km N is **Chuchini** with the Madriguera del Tigre, an ecological and archaeological centre, accessible by road in dry season and by canoe in wet season. Contact Efrém Hinojoso at C Santa Cruz 658, T 22534, or through Tourist Office; advisable to book in advance. Plenty wildlife to be seen; accommodation and meals;

also **Museo Arqueológico del Beni**, containing human remains, ceramics and stone objects from precolumbian Beni culture, said to be over 5,000 years old.

Local information
● **Accommodation**

A3 *Gran Moxos*, Av 6 de Agosto y Santa Cruz, T 22240, all rooms with a/c, fridge bar, cable TV, phone, good restaurant, accepts Visa and Mastercard; **B** *Ganadero*, Av 6 de Agosto, Edif Big Beni, T 21099/21644, small, rec, friendly, good restaurant, rooftop pool.

C *El Bajío*, Av Nicolás Suárez 632, T 2240/22252, with bath and fan, breakfast extra, modern, swimming pool; **D** *Hostal Triny*, C Sucre 353, T22613, good value, fan, clean; **D-E** *Paulista*, Av 6 de Agosto 36, T 20013, ½ block from plaza, cheaper without bath, clean, comfortable, good restaurant.

E *Monteverde*, 6 de Agosto 76, T 22342/22738, with or without a/c, all rooms have TV and mini-fridge, great breakfast, daily excursions organized to Balneario Topacare, rec; **E** *Mi Residencia*, Manuel Limpias 76, nr plaza, T 21529/21376, friendly, clean, comfortable.

F *Yacuma*, La Paz y Santa Cruz, T 20690, run down, poor bathrooms, cold water, helpful, laundry facilities, fan; **F** *Brasilia*, 6 de Agosto, ½ block from plaza.

G *Res Palermo*, Av 6 de Agosto 123, T 20472, clean with hot water, basic, noisy, friendly, restaurant.

● **Places to eat**

Brasilia, Av 6 de Agosto, good dinner; *Carlitos*, on Plaza Ballivián, rec; *Pescadería El Moro*, Bolívar and 25 Diciembre, excellent fish and another fish restaurant, out of town on the road to the airport, is *El Tiburón*; *La Casona*, on the main plaza, for good pizzas and set lunch, closed Tues; *La Estancia*, on Ibare entre Muibe y Velarde, excellent steaks. Burgers, ice cream and snacks at *Kivón* cafeteria on main plaza; also on plaza, *Heladería Oriental*, good coffee, ice-cream, cakes, popular with locals (see above); *Balneario Topacare* is a restaurant and bathing resort 10 mins out of town on Laguna Suárez; delicious local specialities, lunch or dinner, beautiful location, excellent bird spotting, favourite spot for locals at weekends. It is hard to find a good cheap restaurant, but cheap meals, inc breakfast, are served at the fruit and vegetable market. Try sugar cane juice with lemon – delicious.

● **Banks & money changers**

TCs changed at Bidesa, 6 de Agosto, 2% commission. Street changers are nearby on 6 de Agosto.

● **Post & telecommunications**

Entel and **Correos** in same building at Av Barace, just off plaza.

● **Tour companies & travel agents**

All on 6 de Agosto: *Tarope Tours*, No 731, T 21468. *Paraíso Travel*, No 138, T 20692, Casilla 261, does 'Conozca Trinidad' packages. *Moxos*, No 745, T 21141, rec; *Fremen*, No 140, T 22276, F 21400. Most agents offer excursions to local *estancias* and jungle tours down river to Amazonia. Most *estancias* can also be reached independently in 1 hr by hiring a motorbike. It is worth shopping around for jungle tours – prices around US$25 pp/day. Do not be surprised if, whoever you book with, Moxos runs the tour. Fremen operate speed boat trips along the Mamoré and Iboré rivers and to Isiboro National Park. *Flotel Reina de Enin* (of Fremen Tours) offers tours of more than 1 day, US$70 pp/day, good food, ensure that the itinerary is fixed in advance and adhered to. Note: tours to Isiboro are at present too dangerous owing to violent disputes between *cocaleros* and the authorities.

● **Tourist offices**

In Prefectural building on plaza, ground floor, T21722, very helpful, sells guide and city map, US$2.

● **Transport**

Air LAB, at Santa Cruz 324, 200595, twice a week to La Paz, 5 a week to Cochabamba; Tues, Thur, Sun to Magdalena daily except Thur to Guayaramerín, twice weekly to Riberalta, once to Cobija. To Guayaramerín, Santa Cruz, Riberalta, La Paz, San Borja and Cobija, most daily with Aero Sur (Cipriano Baraci 51, T 20765/21117); also to Sucre and Tarija. TAM, at airport, T 20355, Fri to Baures, Bella Vista, Magdalena and Huacaraje, all in the lowlands, Wed to Riberalta, Guayaramerín, Fri to Santa Cruz, Sat to La Paz. Itemox Express (Av 6 de Agosto 281, T 22306) has flights to Baures, Huacaraje, Bella Vista, Magdalena, Reyes (nr Rurrenabaque) and Santa Rosa, fares about US$30 to all but Reyes and Santa Rosa. Airport authority, AASANA, T 20678. Taxi to airport US$2 pp.

Buses Several flotas daily to/from La Paz via San Borja and Caranavi, 20-21 hrs. See under San Borja, **Transport**. To Santa Cruz and Cochabamba; many flotas with daily deps (Copacabana and Mopar have 3 deps daily); Trinidad to Casabare is paved and Santa Cruz to El Puente; good gravel surface on all sections of unpaved road (12 hrs to Santa Cruz, slower in the wet). To Riberalta and Guayaramerín; Urkupiña dep Wed and Thur at 1100, about 26 hrs, connecting with bus to Cobija; also Guaya Tours and Trans Trópico Thur at 1000. Motorbike taxis will take people with backpacks from bus station to centre for US$0.45; bus station is on Mendoza, between Beni and

Pinto, 9 blocks E of main plaza.

River Cargo boats down the Río Mamoré to Guayaramerín take passengers, 3-4 days, assuming no breakdowns, best organized from Puerto Varador (speak to the Port Captain). *Argos* is rec as friendly, US$22 pp, take water, fresh fruit and toilet paper. Ear-plugs are also rec as hammocks are strung over the engine on small boats. Monique Wong (Artamon, NSW) writes, "Cargo gets first preference for space but hammock space isn't too difficult to come by ... you just have to hope it doesn't rain. Meals will not be the highlight of your journey. The food was cooked in river water – don't look when they collect water because the kitchen is next to the toilet and everything from the toilet goes straight into the river."

SAN IGNACIO DE MOXOS

90 km W of Trinidad, known as the folklore capital of the Beni Department. The traditions of the Jesuit missions are still maintained with big *fiestas*, especially during Holy Week; 31 July is the town's patron saint's day, one of the country's most famous and colourful celebrations. 60% of the population are *Macheteros*, who speak their own language.

● **Accommodation** There are a few cheapish *residencias*: **E-F** *Don Joaquín*, on the main plaza, with bath, very clean, fan, family atmosphere; **E** *Plaza*, on main plaza, with or without bath, clean and friendly, fan, good value, restaurant, rec. Several other basic *alojamientos* on and around plaza. Electricity is supplied in town from 1200 to 2400.

● **Places to eat** Restaurants do not stay open late. *Isireri*, on plaza, good and cheap set lunches and delicious fruit juices; *Casa Suiza*, good European food; *Donchanta*, rec for tasty meat dishes.

● **Buses** Bus Trinidad to San Borja stops at *Restaurant Donchanta* for lunch, otherwise difficult to find transport to San Borja. Minibus to Trinidad daily at 0730 from plaza, also *Camionetas*, check times beforehand.

MAGDALENA

This charming town (*pop* 5,000) NE of Trinidad stands on the banks of the Río Itonama. It was founded by Jesuit missionaries in 1720, made a city in 1911 and is now the capital of the province of Iténez. Beef is the main product of the region and the river is the means of transporting cattle and other agricultural produce. 7 km upriver is the Laguna La Baíqui, popular for

fishing. Around the city is an abundance of wildlife and birds. The city's main festival is on 22 July, Santa María Magdalena, attracting many groups and visitors from all over Beni and beyond.

● **Accommodation & places to eat** Three *pensiones*: **F** *San Carlos*, private toilet, fan, shower and water bed! *Res Iténez* and **F** *Ganerero*; all are modest but clean. Restaurants: *El Gato*, on road off plaza beside church, drinks and nightly dancing; *Heladería Laidi*, 1 block from plaza, simple meals and good juices. Drinking water is available and electricity runs from 1800-2400.

● **Useful information** There is a bank (changes TCs) and an Entel office and Correos on plaza.

● **Transport Air** Itemox Express has daily flights to Trinidad (US$31, in 5-seater); also flights to Bella Vista, Baures and Huacaraje. LAB flies from Trinidad Tues, Thur and Sun. **Roads** An unpaved road goes to Trinidad via San Ramón, passable only in the dry season. A road is being constructed to Bella Vista (see below), should be open by mid 1996.

EAST OF MAGDALENA

Bella Vista on the Río Blanco is considered by many to be one of the prettiest spots in NE Bolivia. Lovely white sandbanks line the Río San Martín, 10 mins paddling by canoe from the boat moorings below town (boatmen will take you, returning later by arrangement; also accessible by motorcycle). Check that the sand is not covered by water after heavy rain. Other activities are swimming in the Río San Martín, canoeing, hunting, good country for cycling.

● **Accommodation & services F-G** *Hotel Cazador*, owner Guillermo Esero Gómez very helpful and knowledgeable about the area, shared bath, provides meals for guests (restaurant to be built). Three well-stocked shops on plaza, but none sells mosquito repellent or spray/coils: many mosquitoes at the beginning of the wet season (apply repellent before leaving the plane). No bank or Entel office. Flights by Itemox Express, no fixed schedule, from Magdalena or Trinidad.

Baures, SE of Magdalena, is the centre of an archaeological study by the University of Pennsylvania of a civilization dating back some 2,000 years. Flights by Itemox Express.

Eastern Bolivia

THE VAST and rapidly developing plains to the east of the Eastern Cordillera are Bolivia's richest area in natural resources. It probably has least to offer most visitors, but the Inca ruins of Samaipata, and the beautiful churches of former Jesuit missions east of Santa Cruz are worth a visit.

SANTA CRUZ DE LA SIERRA

Santa Cruz de la Sierra, capital of the Department of Santa Cruz, is 851 km by road, 552 km by air from La Paz. The city was founded in 1561 by the Spaniard Ñuflo de Chávez, who had come from Paraguay. Until the 1950s Santa Cruz was fairly isolated, but rail and road links ended this isolation. Now there is an ever-increasing flow of immigrants from the highlands as well as Mennonites mostly from USA and Canada and Japanese settlers, such as the Okinawan colony 50 km from Montero, to grow soya, maize, sugar, rice, coffee and other crops, which yield profusely. Cattle breeding and timber projects are also important. The exploitation of oil and gas in the Department of Santa Cruz has greatly contributed to the city's rapid development.

BASICS *Pop* 615,125 (Bolivia's second city); *alt* 437m; *phone code* 03. It is usually hot and windswept from May to Aug. When the cold *surazo* blows from the Argentine pampas during these months the temperature drops sharply. The rainy season is Dec-Feb.

Places of interest

The **Plaza 24 de Septiembre** is the city's main square with the **Cathedral** (interesting hand-wrought colonial silver), the Casa de Cultura (see **Museums** below) and the Prefectura set around it. Look for the sloths who live in the trees of the plaza. The Cathedral museum is open on Tues and Thur (1000-1200, 1600-1800), and Sun (1000-1200, 1800-2000). It has collections of silver, vestments, painting and some furniture (entry US$0.75). The heart of the city, with its arcaded streets, retains a colonial air, despite the variety of modern shops and the new building that surrounds it. Five blocks N of the Plaza is **Parque El Arenal** with a lake and a mural by Lorgio Vaca depicting Santa Cruz' history. Pleasant residential areas are being developed on the outskirts of town. About 7 km E of town new **Botanical Gardens** are being developed. At the N edge of town (Barrio Equipetrol, Tercer Anillo, W of road to airport) is a depressing **zoo** with a variety of tropical animals in small concrete cages, US$0.70. Take micro 12 or 76 (taxi from centre US$1.30).

Museums

Casa de la Cultura, on the plaza, with occasional exhibitions and also an archaeological display; has plays, recitals, concerts and folk dancing. **Museo de Historia Natural** at Av Irala s/n, entre Velasco y Independencia. **Museo Etno-Folklórico**, in the Parque Arenal, entry free, very small collection of artefacts from lowland cultures. *RC Antigüedades*, Bolívar 262, p 2, Small Inca, Tiwanaco and antiques collection.

Excursions

Las Lomas de Arena del Palmar The country surrounding the city is flat and scenically uninteresting – except to the agriculturist. The sand-dunes, 20 km to the S, are worth a visit. You may be able to get there by taxi, but private transport is best. It may be possible to hitch at weekends, but a 4WD vehicle is normally required.

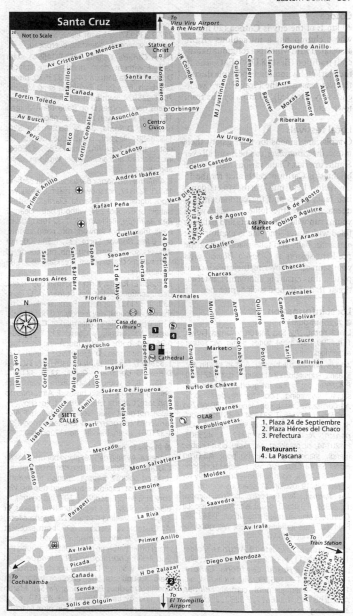

Santa Cruz

26°   Not to Scale

To
Viru Viru Airport
& the North

Statue of
Christ

Av Cristóbal De Mendoza

Santa Fe

Mons Rivero

JR Coimbra

MJ Justiniano

Quijarro

Campero

C Llanos

Segundo Anillo

Acre

Itenes

Fortín Toledo

Platanillos

Cañada

Asunción

D'Orbingny

Baurés

Moxás

Mamoré

Abuna

Av Busch

Perú

P Rico

Fortín Corrales

Centro
Cívico

Riberalta

Primer Anillo

Av Cañoto

Andrés Ibáñez

Av Uruguay

Celso Castedo

Rafael Peña

Vaca Diez

Parque El Arenal

6 de Agosto

6 de Agosto

Los Pozos
Market

Obispo Aguirre

Cuellar

Seoane

24 De Septiembre

Caballero

Suárez Arana

Sara

Santa Bárbara

España

21 de Mayo

Libertad

Charcas

Charcas

Buenos Aires

Florida

Arenales

Arenales

N

Junín

Casa de
Cultura

S

Murillo

Aroma

Quijarro

Campero

Bolívar

José Callali

Valle Grande

Ayacucho

Independencia

Ben

S

Chuquisaca

Cochabamba

Sucre

Cordillera

Ingavi

Colón

Market

La Paz

Potosí

Tarija

Ballivián

Pol

Cathedral

Camiri

Suárez De Figueroa

Ñuflo de Chávez

SIETE
CALLES

Isabel la Católica

Pari

Velasco

René Moreno

Warnes

LAB

Republiquetas

Av Cañoto

Mercado

Mons Salvatierra

Moldes

Lemoine

Saavedra

Parapeti

La Riva

Av Irala

José Callali

Av Irala

Picada

Primer Anillo

Diego De Mendoza

Potosí

To
Train Station

To
Cochabamba

Cañada

Senda

H De Zalazar

To
El Trompillo
Airport

Av Argentina

Tte A Peña

Solís de Olguin

1. Plaza 24 de Septiembre
2. Plaza Héroes del Chaco
3. Prefectura

Restaurant:
4. La Pascana

Cotoca

20 km E of the city is **Cotoca** (20 mins), whose church has a miraculous virgin, associated with which is a religious handicraft tradition (*fiesta* 8 Dec). Eat *sonzos* in the market. Swimming is possible during the wet season in the Piray River (weekends very crowded), 10 mins by bus from town centre.

Local festivals

Cruceños are famous for their gaiety, their music, the *carnavalitos*, can be heard all over South America. Of the various festivals, the brightest is Carnival, celebrated for the 15 days before Lent: music in the streets, dancing, fancy dress and the coronation of a queen. Beware the following day when youths run wild with buckets and balloons filled with water – no one is exempt. The *mascaritas* balls also take place during the pre-Lent season at *Caballito Blanco*: girls wear satin masks covering their heads completely, thus ensuring anonymity. International Trade Fair held each September.

Local information
● Accommodation

L1-L3 *Yotaú*, Av San Martín y James Freyre, T 367799, new 1994, suites, 5-star, a/c, sauna, all services.

A1 *Los Tajibos*, the biggest, Av San Martín 455 in Barrio Equipetrol out of town, 5-star, T 421000, F 426994, a/c, restaurant good (*ceviche* is rec), sauna, swimming pool for residents only; **A1** *Cortez*, Av Cristóbal de Mendoza 280, on 2nd Anillo nr the Cristo, T 331234, F 351186, pool, good, a/c, rec for medium or long stays; **A2** *Caparuch*, Av San Martín 1717, T 423303, F 420144, inc breakfast, a/c, clean, comfortable, friendly, inadequate swimming pool; **A2** *Gran Hotel Santa Cruz*, Pari 59, T 348811/348997, F 324194, pool, open to non-residents, fully restored to its 1930s glory, a/c, spacious, friendly, rec. *Las Palmas*, Av Trompillo, nr city airport, T 520366, F 330533, 4-star, a/c, friendly, rec; *La Quinta*, 4-star, Arumá, Barrio Urbari, T 342244, F 342667, has individual chalets, a/c, good for families but out of town.

In the centre of town is the **B** *Asturias*, Moldes 154, T 339611, F 350897, 2 pools, a/c, also has cabins; **B** *Hostal Confitería Cañoto*, Florida 45-7, T 331052/3, with breakfast, a/c, TV, small, open air pool, central; *Felimar*, Ayacucho 445, T 346677, F 323232, central, 3-star, English spoken.

C *Colonial*, Buenos Aires 57, T 323568, central, comfortable, warmly rec; **C** *Copacabana*, Junín 217, T 339937, with bath, clean, friendly, cheap laundry service, inc breakfast, overpriced.

D *Res Cañada*, Cañada 145, T 345541, with bath, E without, clean, good, nr bus station; **D** *Brasil*, Santa Bárbara 244, T 323530, breakfast, bath, friendly; **D** *Excelsior*, René Moreno 70, T 325924, with bath and breakfast, good rooms, good lunches; **D** pp *Italia*, René Moreno 167, T 323119, with bath, a/c, phone, TV, inc breakfast; **D** *Roma*, 24 de Septiembre 530, T 338388, pleasant, good value, helpful, no restaurant; **D** *Viru-Viru*, Junín 338, T 322687, inc breakfast and a/c, cheaper with fan, clean and pleasant, rec.

E *Alojamiento Santa Bárbara*, Santa Bárbara 151, T 321817, hot showers, helpful, clean, will store luggage, rec; **E** *Santa Clara*, Cañoto y Isabela La Católica 294, without bath, clean; **E** *Res Ballivián*, Ballivián 71, T 321960, clean, basic, friendly, hot showers, nice patio, central, rec; **E** *Res Bolívar*, Sucre 131, T 342500, hot showers, some rooms with bath, nice courtyard with hammocks, excellent breakfast US$1, repeatedly rec.

F *Posada El Turista*, Junín 455, small basic room, clean, central, quiet; **F** *Res Comercio*, Quijarro 439, T 321127, opp Los Pozos market, dirty, shared bathrooms, very friendly and helpful.

In vicinity of Siete Calles market: **C** *Mediterráneo*, Vallegrande y Camiri 71, T 338804, F 361344, bath, a/c, TV, fridge, inc breakfast, cheaper with fan; **D** *Ejecutivo*, Camiri 118, T 338654, F 332843, with bath, a/c, TV; and **D** *Res 26 de Enero*, Camiri 32, T 321818, F 337518, E without bath, extra clean, with patio. For those taking buses, **E** *Alojamiento San José*, Cañada 136, T 328024, hot showers, clean, not great value. Near train station, **F** *Alojamiento Ferrocarril*, Av Capitán Arrien 131, T 321061, clean, friendly, stores luggage.

● Places to eat

Floresca, Av Velarde 136, piano bar upstairs; *La Castañuela*, Velasco 308 esq Pari, in beautifully-restored colonial Casona, Spanish restaurant, fine wine list, expensive but good quality; *Victory* in Galería Casco Viejo 102 (old centre), nr Plaza, expensive, but rec for lunch and cakes; *El Fogón*, Av Viedma 434 and *La Buena Mesa*, Av Cristobal de Mendoza 538, both excellent for *parrillada* and *churrasquería*, and there are many other barbecue restaurants all around the 2nd Anillo; *Churrasquería El Palenque*, Av El Trompillo y Santos Dumon, good; *Michelangelo*, Chuquisaca 502, excellent Italian, not cheap; *Amadeus Pizzería*, at Av San Martín 201 and Av Irala/G Villaroel, T 45319, good (closed Sun lunchtime, open Sun pm); *Machi's*,

Av Velarde block 1, for pizzas; *Pizzería Mesón de René*, 24 de Septiembre 285, bright and clean, good; *Pizzería La Bella Napoli*, Independencia 635, good selection, pricey. *El Boliche*, Arenales 135, open 1930 onwards, serves good crêpes, expensive. Chinese restaurants inc: *El Patito Pekín*, 24 de Septiembre 307, basic cheap Chinese food (open Sun pm); *Shanghai*, Av 26 de Febrero 27; *Mandarin 2*, Av Potosí 793, both excellent. *Naturcenter*, Arenales 638, vegetarian self service, good value, also at Warnes 138; *Vegetarismo*, Ayacucho 491, 1st floor, good set lunch. *Café España*, Junin y Colón, good coffee, *salteñas* (am only), cheap snacks all day; *Hawaii*, Sucre y Beni, open 0700, good breakfasts and coffee. Many cheap restaurants nr the bus terminal on Av Cañoto serving fried chicken. Also on the extension of C 6 de Agosto behind Los Pozos market (daytime). Excellent *empanadas* are sold in the food section of Los Pozos market. The bakeries on Junín, Los Manzanos and España look scruffy but sell the local specialities: *empanadas de queso* (cheese pies), *cuñapés* (yuca buns), rice bread and *humitas* (maize pies). Try local speciality *arroz con leche* in markets, only available before 1100. *Ciné Palace* on the main Plaza sells good cakes; *La Pascana* on the Plaza is a favourite of tourists and locals alike for meals, ice-cream and snacks, nice atmosphere, not cheap; *California*, Independencia 481, burgers, donuts, hot dogs. *Dumbos*, Ayacucho 247, burgers, great ice-cream and full meals, rec; *Heladería Pastelería Manolo*, 24 de Septiembre 170, good sandwiches, cakes and ice cream, reasonable prices; *Kivón*, Ayacucho 267, highly rec for ice cream, also at Quijarro 409 in Mercado Los Pozos. *Salteñería San Andres*, C Charcas 64, cheap set lunch for US$1.

● **Airline offices**
LAB, Warnes y Chuquisaca, T 344411; *Aero Sur*, Irala/Colón, T 367400; *Varig*, Junín 284, T 391105, open till 1200 on Sat; *Aeroperú*, Beni/Bolívar, T 365385; **American Airlines**, Arenales/Beni, T341314; **Aerolíneas Argentinas**, Edif Banco de la Nación Argentina, T339776; **Lan Chile**, Libertad 144, T335951; **Iberia**, main Plaza, T327448.

● **Banks & money changers**
Bank of America, Velasco 19; Banco Popular del Perú, 24 de Septiembre 156; *Banco de la Nación Argentina*, Sucre 31; *Banco de Santa Cruz*, Junín 154 will pay bolivianos on Visa and Mastercard, no commission. Open 0830-1130, 1430-1730. Banks won't change TCs Sat am. **Enlace** cash dispensers accept Mastercard and Visa at Comercial Cañoto, Comercial Oriental, Slam supermarket and Floresca restaurant. *Casas de cambio*: **Mendicambio** on Plaza 24 de Sep-

tiembre will change TCs into dollars at 3% commission; also on main plaza **Alemana** (changes TCs at 2% commission for $ or bolivianos) and **Sudamer**. **Cambios** can also be found on Libertad, eg **Latina** and **Oriente** in first block. **Magri Turismo**, Ingavi 14, T 345663, 2 blocks from main plaza, the American Express agent doesn't change American Express TCs, but you may have to go there to have cheques certified before a *casa de cambio* will accept them. Street money changers on Plaza 24 de Septiembre and around bus terminal.

● **Cultural centres**
Centro Boliviano Americano, Cochabamba 66, T 342299, library with US papers and magazines, English classes, some cultural events; **Instituto Cultural Boliviano Alemán**, Junín 363, T 329906 (library, films, language courses, etc); **Centro Iberoamericano de Formación**, Arenales 583, T 351311, F 322217, Casilla 875 (concerts, films, art exhibitions, lectures, etc), very good.

● **Embassies & consulates**
Brazil, Av Busch 330, nr Plaza Estudiantes, T 336888, opens at 0830, 24 hrs to process visa applications, reported as very unhelpful, Puerto Suárez may be better; **Argentina**, Junín 22, p 3, T 324153; **Uruguay**, Moldes 436, T 329317, Mon-Fri 0900-1100; **Paraguay**, Cristóbal de Mendoza 441, T 425233, colour photo required for visa; **Peru**, Libertad 349, T 330482; **USA**, Chuquisaca y Ballivián, Edif Oriente, p 3, of 313, T 330725; **Chile**, C de Mendoza 441, T327907; **British**, Parapetí 28, p 2, T 345682; **French**, Avaroa 69, T 334818; **Dutch**, Ayacucho 284, p 2, T 367613; **Italian**, La Paz 532, T 322949; **Swiss**, Florida 48, T 346404; **Danish**, Km 5½ Carretera al Norte, T 421816, Mon-Fri, 0830-1200, 1430-1800; **German**, Av Las Américas 241, T 324825; **Belgium**, Junín 124, T343597.

● **Entertainment**
Discotheques: The bar at *Hotel Los Tajibos* usually has live music. *Doña Icha*, René Moreno 239, 2 blocks from plaza, Whiskería with 'pub' atmosphere, rec; also good are *Wall Street*, at Chuquisaca 113, and *Dalí Bar de Tapas*, at Beni 222, open 2000.

Check listings in local press for discos and bars.

● **Hospitals & medical services**
Clínica Lourdes, René Moreno 362, T 25518.

● **Laundry**
Bolívar 490, no sign, knock on door, US$1/kg, same day service. *Rápido*, Pasaje Callejas 70, side street on Republiquetas, Plaza Callejás, rec, cheap and quick.

● **Post & telecommunications**
Post Office: C Junín 146.

Telecommunications: Entel, Warnes 83 (entre Moreno y Chuquisaca), T 325526, local and international calls and fax; open Mon-Fri 0730-2300, Sat, Sun and holidays 0800-2100. There is also a small Entel office at Quijarro 267.

● **Shopping**

Many smart shops in Galería Casco Viejo, 21 de Mayo y Junín. Cameras and lenses are a good buy, same prices as in USA. Artesanía shops on Libertad and on Plaza 24 de Septiembre y Bolívar. *Artecampo*, Salvatierra esq Vallegrande, T 341843, run by a local NGO, sells handicrafts made in the Bolivian lowlands, high quality, rec. Leather goods (*Dorian*, Florida 39, esq Libertad, honest), baskets, fine quality hammocks. Carvings and other objects made from beautiful woods. *RC Limitada*, Bolívar 262, for jewellery and Bolivian gems, the manager also produces and sells good maps of Santa Cruz City and department. *Los Pozos market*, taking up the whole block between 6 de Agosto, Suárez Arana, Quijarro and Campero, is clean, good for midday meals, food aisles serve local and Chinese food, and worth going to in summer for its exotic fruits: *ambaiba* (looks like a glove and the fruit is sucked out of the 'fingers'), *guaypurú* (like a cherry), *ocoro* (like a prickly mandarin), *achachayrú* (mandarin-like with hard skin), *pitón* (like sour grapes) as well as better-known tropical fruits. The market is open daily. Beware of bag-snatching. There are plenty of smuggled Brazilian goods on sale, exchanged for Bolivian coca. Another market (nothing for tourists, mainly for clothing, but food and fruit is sold outside) is *Bazar Siete Calles*: main entrance is in 100 block of Isabel La Católica, also on Camiri and Vallegrande, past Ingavi. There is a fruit and vegetable market at Sucre y Cochabamba. *El Aventurero Caza y Pesca*, Florida 126-130, has absolutely everything you need for fishing, climbing, trekking, or arctic and tropical regions.

Books: *Los Amigos del Libro*, Velasco 37, sells foreign language books and magazines, inc *Time* and *Newsweek*. International magazines and newspapers often on sale in kiosks on main Plaza, eg *Miami Herald*, after arrival of Miami flight.

Film: processing *ABC*, Junín 467, top quality, 36 prints, plus new film, US$9.50. *Foto Relieve*, Ingaví 256, excellent processing, English spoken.

Hairdresser: *Pippo*, Colón 58, T 326868, 'an experience', very good.

● **Sports**

Clubs: *Club Las Palmas*, 2½ km on road to Cochabamba, has 18-hole championship golf course and olympic-length pool. *Club Hípico*, riding club, nearby. *Racquet Club*, Barrio Ubari, racquet ball courts and saunas; *Club de Caza y Pesca*, Av Argentina 317, T 35707, advice on fishing, hunting and safaris.

● **Tour companies & travel agents**

Exprinter, Av Busch 127, T335133; *Magri Turismo*, address under **Banks & money changers**, helpful, rec; *Fremen*, Libertad 320, T/F 360265; *Bracha*, C Florida 23, T 366640/322209 and at train station, T467795, local 11, open daily 0830-1230, 1430-1900, for rail tickets to Quijarro and Yacuiba and Empresa Yacyretá buses to Asunción; *Anavin*, 21 de Mayo 208, T 352009, rec; *Amazonas Adventure Tours*, Centro Comercial Cañoto, local 122, T 338350, F 337587, PO Box 2527, operates tours to Perseverancia, a centre for ecotourism and scientific research, in the **Ríos Blanco y Negro Wildlife Reserve**, NE Bolivia; contact AAT for all details. Mario Berndt, *Kayara Tours*, Casilla 3132, home address Tapiosí 113 (nr zoo), T 420340, is highly rec for tours in the high Andes and the lowlands; he is a professional photographer, is knowledgeable about culture, flora and fauna, speaks English, German and Spanish, is safe and attentive. *Selva Tours*, Bolívar 262, T332725, F360471, city and area tours, trips to Amboró, Samaipata, Jesuit Missions, gold pospecting; 10-day regional tour inc all the above, airport pick-up, US$165 pp/day, English and German spoken.

● **Tourist offices**

Edif Cordecruz 3rd floor, Av Chávez Ortiz, T 363900, F 368901, open Mon-Fri, business hours only, good free city map. Also kiosk at airport. *Guía de Santa Cruz*, published by Rede, available in bookshops, gives all details on the city.

● **Useful addresses**

Migración: is at España 383 esq Seoane.

● **Transport**

Local Taxis: about US$1.30 inside first Anillo, US$1.65 inside 2nd Anillo, fix fare in advance.

Air LAB flies at least twice daily to La Paz and Cochabamba. International flights are given in **Information for travellers**, but note that flying is the only straightforward way from Santa Cruz to Paraguay. LAB flies to Trinidad (once a week), Sucre (3 times), Puerto Suárez (4 times a week), book well in advance, Tarija and other Bolivian destinations. Aero Sur flies to La Paz, Potosí (via La Paz), Cochabamba, Trinidad (for connections to the N Lowlands), Puerto Suárez and Sucre.

The international airport is at Viru-Viru, about 16 km from the town. Information on 181; has Emigration/Immigration office, Entel office, luggage lockers, duty free shop, restaurant, bank – when closed, small amounts of cash may be exchanged at LAB *caja*, or at the very helpful Tourist Information kiosk in Check-In hall, English spoken, free map. Airport bus every 30 mins from the bus terminal, 35 mins (US$1). Taxi, US$5 (beware of overcharging). From Trompillo airport in the S part of the city, companies offer flights in small planes to local destinations.

Trains To Puerto Suárez, for Brazil, and Yacuita, for Argentina, see below.

Buses Bus terminal on corner of Av Cañoto and Av Irala, T 338391 or 340772 (taxi to centre US$1). Daily buses to **Cochabamba** (US$9-15, 10 hrs, sit on left for best views), many *flotas* leave between 0830 and 2030. All buses to Cochabamba now take the new, lowland route, via Montero, Buena Vista and Villa Tunari, which is no quicker than the old mountain route via Epizana and much less scenic (only Cinta de Plata goes via Epizana, Sun 1700). Direct to **Sucre** daily with Mopar, Unificado, Copacabana and Bolívar at 1700, 12 hrs, US$13-17 (20% discount for students with Copacabana). **Oruro** and **La Paz** 16 hrs direct with Flota Copacabana, US$18.75, 8 a day (plus Bus Cama at 1900, Mon, Thur, Sat, US$36, 19 hrs). To **San Ignacio**, see under **The Chiquitano Jesuit Missions**. To **Yacuiba** and **Tarija**, daily, several companies; 26-32 hrs to Tarija. To **Camiri**, **Cotoca**, **Montero**, many colectivos and micros from outside *Hotel España* (US$10-12 to Camiri). To **Trinidad**, several daily, 12-13 hrs, US$7.50-10, all dep 1800 or 1830.

ON THE OLD ROAD TO COCHABAMBA

Los Espejillos, where a mountain stream plunges over a waterfall and carves its way through limestone rocks down a beautiful green and forested valley, is worth the effort to get to – 4WD, only in the dry season. Turn right at Km 26, cross the Piray River and drive some 12 km up a forested valley. At a green field on the left (football goal posts) stop and walk a few hundred metres up to the stream.

The drive along the Piray gorge and up into the highlands makes a splendid trip.

SAMAIPATA

The town of Samaipata (*alt* 1,960m; median temperature 24°C) is a popular tourist resort, famous for its plant nurseries (*viveros*), experimental orchards, jams and sweet wines. Local *artesanías* include ceramics. The **Museo Arqueológico Regional** (open daily 0900-1200, 1430-1830, US$1) has a collection of pots and vases with anthropomorphic designs, dating from 200 BC to 200 AD and, most importantly, provides information on the nearby,

pre-Inca ceremonial site commonly called El Fuerte. This sacred structure consists of a complex system of channels, basins, high-relief sculptures, etc, carved out of one vast slab of rock. Latest research suggests that Amazonian people created it around 1500 BC; there is evidence of subsequent occupations and that it was the eastern outpost of the Incas' Kollasuyo (their Bolivian Empire). El Fuerte is 9 km from the town (3 km along the highway, then 6 km up a signposted road: 2 hrs 10 mins' walk one way, taxi US$4 pp, or drive to the entrance). Entry US$2.

● **Accommodation & places to eat** Several hotels: *Casa Blanca*, T 6076, *Hostería Mi Casa*, T 6061, both just off the plaza; **F** *Miny*, T 6151, on highway at entrance to town, with bath, good value; **F** *Don Jorge*, T 6086, clean, friendly, warm showers; fully equipped chalets for 5-7, 10 mins from town, poor, swimming in the river, waterfalls, information and reservations at *Selva Tours* (see Santa Cruz **Tour companies**); *La Víspera*, organic farm/guesthouse, Dutch owners, very peaceful. Many restaurants on and around the plaza, most cheap, but some like *Chancho Rengo*, expensive. *Achira Sierra Resort*, 7 km from town, in Santa Cruz, T 52256 (Igmiri 506, Barrio Urbari, Casilla 1020), cabins, camping, horse riding, sports facilities, restaurant, 6 km from an access point for Amboró National Park (see below).

● **Transport** 24-hr taxi service from Santa Cruz, C Lemoine y Av Cañoto, 2 hrs, US$4 pp, return by taxi or on any micro or bus passing Samaipata en route to Santa Cruz between 1600-1800. Many buses and micros leave Santa Cruz for Vallegrande, Sucre and other towns in pm, 1600-1800, passing Samaipata; colectivos from C Tundy 70, nr bus terminal, 2 hrs, US$3 pp.

VALLEGRANDE AND HIGUERA

Some 45 km S of the Santa Cruz-Cochabamba road is **Vallegrande** (Sun handicraft market; *Hotel Copacabana*, Bolívar 100; *Res Valle Grande*, Sucre 102; *Alojamiento Pinto*, on Plaza de Armas; *Restaurant El Castillo*, Plaza de Armas y 26 de Enero). Flota Bolívar and Trans Vallegrande run daily from Santa Cruz; Bolívar on Thur from Sucre and Cochabamba. South of here is Pukara, from where a 4-5 km walk will take you to the village of **Higuera**, where Che Guevara was killed. On 8 Oct each year, many people gather there to celebrate his memory; ask at the Universidad Gabriel René Moreno or Radio Santa Cruz about collective transport.

ON THE NEW ROAD TO COCHABAMBA

The new road route to Cochabamba passes through fertile lowland to the NW of Santa Cruz. It goes N through Warnes (note the statue of a man leading an ox-cart-load of bananas at the town entrance), then N to **Montero** (37 km, *pop* 30,000), where sugar and cotton are grown and processed, and on to Puerto Grether, high on the Río Ichilo, a tributary of the Mamoré. It then connects at Todos Santos with the 200-km road to Cochabamba. A non-stop shuttle minibus service leaves from Santa Cruz bus station for Montero when full; US$1, 50 mins. The town is named after the Independence hero, Marceliano Montero; the statue to him in the main square is in the same style as the statue of Bolívar in Santa Cruz, the horse supported by broken cannon.

AMBORO NATIONAL PARK

From Santa Cruz buses and from Montero minibuses run to Buena Vista (2 *alojamientos*). Near Buena Vista is the **Amboró National Park** (180,000 ha) – walk to Cerro Amboró (guide required) recommended. The park is home to butterflies, humming birds, macaws, hoatzin and other native fauna (many of them endangered species). Beware of the insects – do not wear shorts or short-sleeved shirts; much wading is required to get around the park (see also below).

● **Transport** Transport to the park from Buena Vista: either truck to El Terminal and then walk to the Río Surutú, the park's E boundary, or daily bus to Santa Fe, 0800, then motorcycle taxi to the river, US$5, 1 hr, very rough. At the park guardhouse there are 3 beds (free), take own food. To return ask park guard to radio for a motorcycle taxi.

● **Access** There is a national park office in Buena Vista (permit free; guide US$7).

Beyond Buena Vista is the **Yapacaní** bridge where *surubí* from the river or *jochi* and *tatú* (armadillo) from the forest may be eaten in one of the riverside eating houses.

THE CHIQUITANO JESUIT MISSIONS

Six Jesuit churches survive E of Santa Cruz, San Javier, Concepción, Santa Ana, San Rafael, San Miguel and San José de Chiquitos. All are Unesco World Heritage sites. The first four were built by the Swiss Jesuit, Padre Martin Schmidt, the other two (plus that at San Ignacio de Velasco, which was demolished in 1948, see below) were built by other priests. Besides organizing *reducciones* and constructing churches, for each of which he built an organ, Padre Schmidt wrote music (some is still played today on traditional instruments) and he published a Spanish-Idioma Chiquitano dictionary based on his knowledge of all the dialects of the region. He worked in this part of the then Viceroyalty of Peru until the expulsion of the Jesuits in 1767 by order of Charles III of Spain.

Access to the mission area is by bus or train from Santa Cruz: the simplest is the former, by paved highway N to San Ramón (139 km), then N on a good, all-weather gravel road through San Javier (45 km), turning E here to Concepción (68 km) and San Ignacio. One road continues E to San Matías and the Brazilian border; others head S either through San Miguel, or Santa Ana to meet at San Rafael for the continuation S to San José de Chiquitos. By rail, one would leave the Santa Cruz-Quijarro train at San José and from there travel N. We describe the missions according to the bus route, but an option is to use San Ignacio as a base for exploring the area.

SAN JAVIER

The first Jesuit mission in Chiquitos (1691), its church completed by Padre Schmidt in 1752. The original wooden structure has survived more or less intact and restoration was undertaken between 1987 and 1993 by the German Hans Roth. Subtle designs and floral patterns cover the ceiling, walls and carved columns. One of the bas-relief paintings on the high altar depicts Martin Schmidt playing the piano for his Indian choir. The modern town prospers from extensive cattle ranching. Many fine walks in the surrounding countryside; also good for cycling with an all-terrain bike. Local *fiesta*, 3 December.

- **Accommodation & places to eat C** *Gran Hotel El Reposo del Guerrero*, with bath, more expensive Sat-Sun, **E** pp with shared bath, inc breakfast, comfortable, T 0963-5022, or Santa Cruz 327830, restaurant, bar; **E** *Alojamiento San Javier*, inc breakfast, hot water, garden, *artesanía* shop, good value, rec; **F** *Alojamiento Ame-Taunus*, on plaza; **F** *Posada Pinto*, clean, nice, and **F-G** *Alojamiento Hnos Añez*, both 1 block from plaza. Best restaurant is **Ganadero**, in Asociación de Ganaderos on plaza, excellent steaks; others on plaza. *Helad-ería Alpina* on main road.

- **Buses** Many late at night to Santa Cruz and San Ignacio. Micros to Santa Cruz, 4 hrs, several between 0700 and 1830.

CONCEPCION

The magnificent cathedral was completed by Padre Schmidt in 1756; it was totally restored by Hans Roth 1975-1982, whose team of European experts had to recreate the building from the crumbling original. The interior of this beautiful church is very fine, with an altar of laminated silver. In front of the church is a bell-cum-clock tower housing the original bells and behind it are well-restored cloisters. The town's pretty plaza has lawns, trees and flower beds. Entel office on the corner of the plaza; private Centro Médico 1 block from plaza. Here again, cattle farming is the main activity.

- **Accommodation & places to eat B** *Gran Hotel Concepción*, on plaza, very comfortable, excellent service, inc buffet breakfast, pool, bar, highly rec; **E** *Res Westfalia*, 2 blocks from plaza on same street as Centro Médico, German-owned. Several restaurants around the plaza: *El Buen Gusto* opens early, delicious *empanadas*, snacks, meals; *Club Social Ñuflo de Chávez*, good *almuerzos*. *Don Beto*, 2 blocks from plaza, good *almuerzos*, popular.

- **Buses** Many buses between Santa Cruz and San Ignacio pass through, about midnight. Flota La Veloz del Norte micros to San Javier and San Ramón at 0700, 0800 and 1800; Flota 31 del Este 0700 to Santa Cruz.

SAN IGNACIO DE VELASCO

A lack of funds for restoration led to the demolition of San Ignacio's Jesuit church in 1948. A modern replacement contains the elaborate high altar, pulpit and paintings and statues of saints. A museum in the Casa de la Cultura on the plaza has a few musical instruments from the old church. A lake on the outskirts of town is good for swimming, boating and fishing. Horses can be hired.

- **Accommodation & places to eat D** *Plaza*, with bath, hot water, TV, inc breakfast, comfortable, rec; **E** *Casa Suiza*, at the end of C Sucre, small guesthouse run by Horst and Cristina, German and French spoken, good Swiss cooking, family atmosphere, full board or half board; **E** *Palace*, on plaza, restaurant; **E-F** *Guapamó*, Sucre, nr several bus offices, clean, pleasant, restaurant; **F** *31 de Julio*, on plaza, basic, clean; several other cheap lodgings. Best restaurant is *Mimi*, 1 block from plaza, good food and service, smart, all main courses about US$3; several on the plaza, inc *Pizzería Pauline*, *Snack Marcelito*, good *salteñas*, *Cayoni's Bar*, pleasant in the evening.

- **Transport Air** TAM on Wed from Santa Cruz, returns Thur, also serves San Matías on the Brazilian border. **Buses** From Santa Cruz, Flota Chiquitana, from terminal 1900 daily, 10 hrs, US$9; at least 7 other companies, most from C Suárez Arana, Av Uruguay end, en route to San Matías for Brazil, eg Trans Bolivia, at No 332, 2000, and Flota Veloz del Este, No 318, 1800. From San Ignacio these companies leave for Santa Cruz or **San Matías** for Brazil (see below) between 1800-2100. Trans Brasil micros to Santa Cruz, Tues, Thur, Sat 0830 (check in advance). To **San José de Chiquitos**, Flota Universal on Tues, Wed, Sat, Sun 1000 from market area (look for big yellow bus), US$5, goes via San Miguel and San Rafael, 6 hrs. Micros to **Santa Ana, San Rafael, San Miguel** from market area, about 0700 and 1000 but check, return same day.

SANTA ANA, SAN RAFAEL, SAN MIGUEL

A day trip by taxi from San Ignacio to these villages costs US$30-35 (negotiate).

The church in **Santa Ana** is in fine condition (finished 1755), a lovely wooden building, entirely unrestored. In a sky-blue house on a corner of the plaza, the lady will prepare a meal for a visiting couple and has a spare room for an overnight stay.

San Rafael's church was completed by

Padre Schmidt the year after Santa Ana: beautifully restored with frescoes in beige paint over the exterior (*Alojamiento*, pink house at entrance to village; 2 restaurants on plaza; public phone).

The frescoes on the façade of the church (1754) at **San Miguel** depict St Peter and St Paul; designs in brown and yellow cover all the interior and the exterior side walls. The high altar and pulpit are ornate, carved and gilded; fine square bell-tower. On the outskirts is a fish-filled lake. (**F** *Alojamiento y Restaurant La Pascana*, pleasant, cheap; *Restaurant Avenida* has rooms, public phone.)

SAN JOSE DE CHIQUITOS

The whole of one side of the plaza of this dusty little town is occupied by the superb frontage of the Jesuit mission. The buildings, in Baroque style, are of stone, connected by a wall. They are the restored chapel (1750); the church, unfinished at the expulsion of the Jesuits, with a triangular façade and side walls standing (restoration work in progress); the 4-storey bell-tower (1748); the mortuary (*la bóveda* – 1754), with one central window but no entrance in its severe frontage, behind is a long colonnaded hall.

On Mon, Mennonites bring their produce to sell to shops and to buy provisions. The colonies are 50 km W and the Mennonites, who speak English, German, plattdeutsch and Spanish, are happy to talk about their way of life.

4 km from San José is the **Parque Nacional Histórico Santa Cruz la Vieja**, which includes the ruins of the original site of Santa Cruz (about 1540), a *mirador* giving views over the jungle and, 5 km into the park, a sanctuary. The park's heavily-forested hills contain much animal and bird life; various trails; guides available from the small village in the park (take insect repellent). 2 km past the entrance, at the end of the road at the foot of high hills, is a large swimming pool fed by a mountain stream (open daily, free, no facilities other than changing rooms; take refreshments). The park and pool are best visited by car or taxi because it is a very hot, dusty walk there (allow over 1 hr on foot).

● **Accommodation & places to eat E** *Hotel Raquelita*, on the plaza, good, clean, laundry service, restaurant serves good breakfast; **F** *Victoria*, also on plaza, friendly, basic; **F** *San Silvestre*, opp train station, basic, clean, good food. Restaurants on plaza inc: *Sombrero e' Sao*, with sidewalk seating under trees, and *Casa e' Paila*, with *artesanías* for sale, both serve good *almuerzo*, not cheap.

● **Services** Electricity is cut from 0200-0630; the town is lighted when trains arrive. Bidesa changes TCs into dollars cash or bolivianos. Entel. Hospital.

● **Transport Trains** Schedule from Santa Cruz as for Quijarro (see **Travel to Brazil**), 8 hrs to San José, US$3.20 by Expreso del Oriente, US$7 by Tren Rápido 1st class, US$5 2nd. San José-Santa Cruz trains leave about 8 hrs after departure from Quijarro, check expected arrival time in advance. It is impossible to reserve seats on either service. **Buses** To San Ignacio, Flota Universal, T 2198, Mon, Tues, Fri, Sat, 0800 from station area, reserve seat and check time in advance at company's terminal (some distance from town, take taxi), goes via San Rafael and San Miguel, 6 hrs (5 hrs by car avoiding San Miguel detour).

TRAVEL TO BRAZIL

There are three routes: two via Puerto Suárez and/or Quijarro, one via San Matías. Puerto Suárez, reached by air, is near Quijarro which is the terminus of the railway from Santa Cruz. On the Brazilian side of the border is Corumbá and the southern Pantanal. San Matías is reached by road from Santa Cruz, with road links to Cáceres, Cuiabá and the northern Pantanal in Brazil.

THE BRAZILIAN BORDER AREA

The populated area by the Brazilian border is made up of several towns which are gradually growing into each other: Puerto Suárez, Puerto Quijarro and Arroyo Concepción. Trade here grew due to increasing prices in Brazil during 1995-1996. With gradually improving infrastructure on the Bolivian side of the border, and much lower prices, it now represents a viable alternative to Corumbá for visitors and local businessmen alike. A *Zona Franca* (customs free zone) has been established in the area to encourage development and woo Brazilian shoppers.

PUERTO SUAREZ

Puerto Suárez (*pop* 15,000) on the shore of Laguna Cáceres, a large backwater of the Paraguay River, was an important commercial port at the beginning of the 20th century, until a dam built by Brazil upriver reduced the water level of the lake and put an end to shipping and the town's prosperity. It is today a friendly, quiet, small town; a good place to stay on the way from/to Santa Cruz and an access point for the Bolivian Pantanal. The main square is shady and pleasant; there is a nice view of the lake from the park at the N end of Av Bolívar. The area around the train station is known as *Paradero*.

Excursions Fishing and photo tours to the Pantanal can be arranged in Puerto Suárez, a cheaper alternative to the Brazilian side in 1996. Stewart and Sandra Williams of *Tours Aguas Tranquilas* (inquire at Hotel Frontera Verde) offer air-boat trips along small tributaries of the Paraguay river, which are not accessible with other types of water craft, lots of wildlife, good fishing, US$10 pp/hr (min US$40), US$150 to hire boat for 4 hrs, includes lunch and fishing gear, US$250/7 hrs, max capacity 9, English spoken.

● **Accommodation** **C** *Frontera Verde*, Vanguardia 24 y Simón Bolívar, T 62468, F 62470, best in town, with bath, a/c, TV, D with fan, clean, breakfast included, parking, friendly, helpful, English spoken, can arrange for Pantanal tours; **C** *Bamby*, Santa Cruz 31 y 6 de Agosto, T 62015, with bath, a/c, D with fan, cheaper with shared bath, comfortable, friendly; **D** *Roboré*, 6 de Agosto 78, T 62170, with bath, fan, TV, E with shared bath, basic, friendly, restaurant next door; **D** *Palace*, at the S end of Bolívar, T 62098, with bath, a/c, TV; **D** *Ejecutivo*, at S end of Bolívar, T 62267, with bath, a/c, TV, parking, cheaper with fan, comfortable, friendly; **D** *Sucre*, Bolívar 63 on main plaza, T 62069, with bath, a/c, TV, E with shared bath and fan, very clean, pleasant, good restaurant; **D** *Beby*, Av Bolívar 111, T 62270, with bath, a/c, E with shared bath and fan, clean, welcoming; **E** *Res Puerto Suárez*, Bolívar 105, shared bath, clean, fans, showers, basic, friendly; **E** *Progreso*, Bolívar 21, shared bath, basic.

● **Places to eat**
Parillada Jenecherú, Bolívar near plaza, grilled meats; opp is *Al Paso*, Bolívar 43, very good value set meals and à la carte, popular; *El Taxista*, Bolívar 100 block, several other small inexpensive restaurants near it.

● **Banks & money changers**
Supermercado Tocale changes Bolivianos, Reales and US$, cash only. Banco de la Unión in Paradero is reported to change TCs.

● **Tour companies & travel agents**
Tours Aguas Tranquilas, see **Excursions** above; *R B Travel*, Bolívar 65 by Plaza, T62014, for airline tickets. Airline offices: *LAB*, La Paz 33, T 62241; *AeroSur*, Bolívar near the Plaza, T/F 62155; *Transportes Aéreos Militares TAM*, C del Chaco s/n, T 62205.

● **Embassies & consulates**
Brazilian Consulate, Santa Cruz entre Bolívar y 6 de Agosto.

● **Post & telecommunications**
Post Office: La Paz opp main plaza. **Entel:** La Paz. 3 blocks from Plaza and in Paradero.

● **Shopping**
Supermercado Tocale, Bolívar next door to Residencial Puerto Suárez, wide selection of Brazilian, Bolivian and imported goods. Several fishing and hunting supply shops.

● **Transport**
Local Taxis: to Paradero US$1.65; to airport US$2; to Quijarro or the border (Arroyo Concepción) US$5 (day), US$6 (night) or US$0.80 pp in a colectivo.

Air Airport is 6 km N of town, T 62347; airport tax US$2. To Santa Cruz, US$71, with Aerosur, daily at 1645, continuing (daily except Sat) to Cochabamba US$95 and La Paz US$147; Lloyd to Santa Cruz, Mon, Wed, Fri and Sat about 1600; to São Paulo, US$203, Sat at 1110. TAM to Santa Cruz, US$59, Tue at 1300 continues to La Paz, US$105, Sat at 1000 continues to Trinidad and La Paz. 25% discount for family groups (can be as few as 2 family members). **NB** Do not buy tickets for flights originating in Puerto Suárez in Corumbá, you will have to pay more. There is an airport immigration office where they will issue Bolivian exit/entry stamps.

Trains The station for Puerto Suárez is about 3 km from town. It is the 1st station W of Quijarro. Bracha agent, Bolívar 86, T/F 62577.

PUERTO QUIJARRO

The eastern terminus of the Bolivian railway is at Puerto Quijarro (*pop* 15,000), the gateway to Brazil, a town created because of, and around the railway station. Once a muddy, unsafe, disorganized village; it is, in the mid-1990s, struggling to improve its infrastructure and image; efforts are being made to develop tourism in the Bolivian Pantanal. There have been reports of drug trafficking and related problems in this border area and caution is recommended.

● **Accommodation NB** Water supply is frequently unreliable, try the tap before checking in.

C *Santa Cruz*, Av Brazil 2 blocks E of station, T 82113, F 82044, with bath, a/c, TV, cheaper with fan, D with shared bath, clean, good rooms, nice courtyard, restaurant, parking, friendly, highly rec.

D *Cochabamba*, Av Brazil 100m from the station, T 82158, with bath, a/c, E with shared bath and fan, basic, friendly, not too clean, quiet; **D** *La Frontera*, Rómulo Gómez s/n, 5 blocks from the station on the S side of the tracks, T 82010, with bath, fan, TV, clean, parking; **D** *Gran Hotel Colonial*, Av Brazil y Panamá, T/F 82037, with bath, a/c, TV, cheaper with fan, E with shared bath, restaurant; **D** *Oasis*, Av Argentina 20, T 82159, with bath, a/c, TV, fridge, cheaper with shared bath and a/c, E with fan, OK, friendly; **D** *Yoni*, Av Brazil opp the station, T 82109, with bath, a/c, fridge, TV, E with shared bath and fan, clean, comfortable, mosquito netting on windows.

F *Res Paratí*, Guatemala s/n, shared bath, fan, clean, laundry facilities, friendly. On Av Brazil across from the station are; **F** *Alojamiento Urkupiña*, shared bath, basic, unfriendly; **F** *Res Ariane*, T 82122, shared bath, basic, friendly, new rooms with bath and a/c under construction in 1996; **F** *Vasco de Gamma*, very basic, cheap.

● **Places to eat**
The best restaurant in the area is in Arroyo Concepción (see below), restaurants at *Hotel Santa Cruz* and *Hotel Colonial* have been rec, due to poor hygienic conditions, the food stalls by the station and market are best avoided.

● **Banks & money changers**
Bolivianos, Reales and US$ cash traded along Av Brazil opp the station by changers with large purses sitting in lawn chairs; good rates, but beware of tricks.

● **Tour companies & travel agents**
Santa Cruz, in hotel of same name, sells Bracha and airline tickets, organizes tours to Pantanal.

● **Post & telecommunications**
Post Office: in Puerto Suarez. **Entel**: at the S end of Av Naval, national and international calls, Mon-Sat 0700-2300, Sun 0700-2000; also small office at Guatemala y Brazil nr the station.

● **Shopping**
A duty free zone was created in 1994 at Puerto Aguirre, 700m N of Quijarro, to boost the regional economy. Mostly electronics and luxury goods for Brazilian shoppers. Construction of a new, larger, duty free centre started in 1996.

● **Transport**
Local Taxis: to the border (Arroyo Concepción) US$0.40 pp; to Puerto Suarez US$0.80 pp or US$5 (day), US$6 (night).

Train See **Travel to Brazil** above.

BORDER WITH BRAZIL

The Municipality by the border is known as **Arroyo Concepción**. The fanciest hotel on either side of the border is here, 1½ km from the frontier: **L3** *El Pantanal Hotel Resort & Casino*, T 82089, F 82020, 5 star luxury resort, a/c, buffet breakfast and airport transport included, restaurants, disco ,pool, modern buildings on nice grounds, horseback riding, tours to Pantanal and nearby caves; one of the better restaurants in the area is also here: *Pescadería Ceará*, 250m from the border, with excellent fish (moved from Corumbá).

Going to Brazil: you need not have your passport stamped if you visit Corumbá for the day. Otherwise get your exit stamp at Bolivian immigration, in a blue building to your right, just before the bridge, formalities are straightforward. There are no formalities on the Brazilian side, you must get your entry stamp in Corumbá at the Polícia Federal, Praça da República, next door to the NS da Candelária church, T 231-5848, open 0800-1900 (knock after hours); there is also an office at the bus station which is usually closed. Yellow Fever vaccination is compulsory to enter Brazil, have your certificate at hand when you go for your entry stamp, otherwise you will be sent to get revaccinated. Just past the bridge, on a small side street to the right is the bus stop for Corumbá, it goes to Praça da República, US$0.50, every 45 mins between 0630 and 1915, don't believe taxi drivers who say there is no bus. Taxi to centre US$10.

● **Bolivian immigration**
At the border at Arroyo Concepción, blue building on right just before bridge, opens 0700; at Puerto Suárez airport; in San Matías. Passports

From Ollagüe (Chile) to Uyuni, see page 301.

From Arica (Chile) via Tambo Quemado or via Visviri (see By Road from La Paz to the Pacific Coast, page 274).

Travel to Paraguay Apart from the journey described on page 316 (also taken by Santa Cruz-Asunción buses), an alternative way of getting to Paraguay is to travel by bus to Salta or Orán (Argentina), then on to Asunción via Resistencia (Argentina).

CUSTOMS

● **Duty-free imports**
200 cigarettes, 50 cigars and 1 lb tobacco; one opened bottle of alcoholic drink.

WHEN YOU ARRIVE

● **Clothing**
Visitors to the Altiplano and the Puna should be prepared for the cold at night. The climate in the Eastern Lowlands is tropical. Oruro and Potosí are colder than La Paz, Cochabamba can be very warm.

● **Hours of business**
Hours of business are normally 0900-1200 (sometimes 1130 in La Paz), and 1400-1800. Sat is a half day. Opening and closing in the afternoon are several hours later in the provinces. Government offices are closed on Sat. Banks 0900-1200, 1400-1630, but closed on Sat.

● **Official time**
4 hrs behind GMT.

● **Security**
Bolivian law states that the police may only search bags at a police station, not on the street. Identity must be checked only by immigration officials; see their identity card and verify the date. Insist on going to the police station, or call the uniformed police if in doubt. In La Paz and Sucre particularly tourists are often approached by bogus policemen. If at all possible, insist on your right not to show your passport to anyone on the street. If you can get a witness, so much the better.

The procedure for reporting a robbery is to go to the Dpto de Criminalística, or the office for stolen property, in the town where the theft took place. Purchase official paper from the police for them to write the report, then, with patience and politeness, you may get a report costing between US$1.30 and US$5.25.

NB In some cities there is hostility to foreigners, mainly out of resentment from involvement in anti-narcotics policies.

● **Shopping**
Best Buys Llama-and alpaca-wool knitted and woven items are at least as good as those from Peru and much cheaper. Ponchos, *mantas*, bags, *chullos* (bonnets). Gold and silverware. Musical instruments such as the *charango* (mandolin traditionally with armadillo-shell sound-box, now usually of wood) and the *quena* (Inca flute), and other assorted wooden items.

● **Tipping**
Up to 10% in restaurants; in all other cases a tip is given in recognition of a service provided, eg to a taxi driver who has been helpful (an extra Bs 0.50-1), to someone who has looked after a car, carried bags, etc. Usual tip Bs 0.50-1.

● **Voltage**
Varies considerably. Generally 110 volts, 50 cycles AC in La Paz, 220 volts 50 cycles AC elsewhere, but check before using any appliance. (You may even find 110 and 220 in the same room). US-type plugs can be used in most hotels.

● **Work opportunities**
See under La Paz **Language schools** for teaching possibilities. Voluntary work at the Hogar Mixto La Paz, Av Arce, nr British Embassy, beside Centro Boliviano Americano.

ON DEPARTURE

● **Airport and border taxes**
Tax of US$20, payable in dollars or bolivianos, cash only, is levied on leaving (US$30 extra if you have stayed over 3 months). On internal flights B$15 is paid at La Paz and Santa Cruz, B$10 at smaller airports. Tax on airline tickets 18%. Entry/exit tax at land borders is US$4 (beware of spurious charges). If you stay in Bolivia less than 24 hrs, no tax is charged.

WHERE TO STAY

● **Camping**
One can camp almost anywhere in safety, except near settlements (unless unavoidable). Warm sleeping gear essential, even in the lowlands in the winter. Sleeping bags are also useful for getting some sleep on the buses or long distance trains, especially those crossing the Andes. Mosquito nets can be purchased in La Paz, but they are not cheap. Beware sandstorms S of Oruro. Camping gas-style and Epigas cannisters are available in La Paz and all large cities; white gas for Coleman stoves is difficult to find. Kerosene is much easier to find outside La Paz, even in small towns. *Alcohol potable* (meths) is widely available.

● **Hotels**
Hotels must display prices by law. Throughout Bolivia the cheaper hotels impose their own curfews. In La Paz it tends to be midnight (check) but it can be as early as 2130 in Copacabana.

These locking up times are strictly adhered to by hotel keepers. Ask for the hot water schedule, it changes with the season, water pressure, etc. Clothes washing is generally not allowed. Many mid-range hotels will keep money and valuables in the safe if there are no safety-deposit boxes. Cheaper hotels rarely have heating in the rooms. Youth Hostels are not necessarily cheaper: many middle range *residenciales* are affiliated to the IYHA.

FOOD AND DRINK

FOOD

The normal international cuisine is found at most good hotels and restaurants.

Salteñas are meat stew pies (originating from Salta, Argentina, but popular throughout the Andean countries), eaten regularly by Bolivians, mostly in the morning. Some are *muy picante* (very hot) with red chili peppers, but *medio picante* and *poco picante* ones can normally be obtained. *Marraqueta* is bread from La Paz, crusty, with a soft centre; *pan de Batallas* is a sandwich loaf.

In the N lowlands, many types of wild meat are served in tourist restaurants and on jungle tours. Bear in mind the turtles whose eggs are eaten are endangered and that other species not endangered soon will be if they stay on the tourist menu.

NB Bolivian highland cooking is usually very tasty and often *picante*. Local specialities, which visitors should try, inc *empanadas* (cheese pies) and *humitas* (maize pies); *pukacapas* are *picante* cheese pies. Recommended main dishes inc *sajta de pollo*, hot spicy chicken with onion, fresh potatoes and *chuño* (dehydrated potatoes), *parrillada* (a Bolivian kind of mixed grill), *fricase* (juicy pork dish served with *chuño*), *silpancho* (fried breaded meat with eggs, rice and bananas), *saice*, a dish of minced meat with picante sauce, served with rice, potatoes, onions and tomatoes, *pique macho*, roast meat with chips, onion and pepper, and *ají de lengua*, ox-tongue with chilis, potatoes and *chuño* or *tunta* (another kind of dehydrated potato). The soups are also good, especially a *chairo* soup made of meat, vegetables, *chuño* and *ají* (hot pepper) to which the locals like to add *llajua* or *halpahuayca* (hot sauces always set on restaurant tables) to make it even more *picante*. Fried vizcacha is eaten in some places, mostly outside the main towns and cities.

In the lowland Oriente region, the food usually comes with cooked banana and yuca; eg *Pollo Broaster* is chicken with rice, chips, yuca and fried banana. The bread in this region is often sweet with cheese on top, and the rice bread is also unusual.

In the *pensiones* and cheaper restaurants a basic lunch (*almuerzo* – usually finished by 1300) and dinner (*cena*) are normally available. The *comida del día* is the best value, in any class of restaurant. Good cheap and clean breakfasts are served in the markets in most towns (most restaurants do not open very early in the morning). Lunch can also be obtained in many of the modern market buildings in the main towns; eat only what is cooked in front of you. Dishes cooked in the street are not safe. Llama meat contains parasites (similar to those in pork), so make sure it has been cooked for a long time and is hot when you eat it. Be very careful of salads; they may carry a multitude of amoebic life as well as vile green bacteria.

DRINK

The several makes of local beer, lager-type, are recommendable; El Inca is a dark beer, sweet, like a stout; the local hot maize drink, *api* (with cloves, cinnamon, lemon and sugar), should be tried (usually US$0.12), as well as *singani*, distilled from grapes, good, cheap and bracing. *Chuflay* is *singani* and 7 Up or Canada Dry (or whatever carbonated drink is available). *Chicha* is a fermented maize drink, popular around Cochabamba. It is not always alcoholic. In the countryside, look for the white flag outside the houses selling *chicha*. Bottled water, Viscachani, is easily available but make sure the seal is unbroken (rain water is sometimes offered as an alternative); there are also several brands of flavoured mineral water, Cayacayani, La Cabaña, Mineragua. Naturagua is purified water. The local tap water should not be drunk without first being sterilized. Local water purifier is 'Lugol Fuerte Solución', an iodine-based product, US$1.75/small bottle; also *iodo* from *farmacias*, US$0.50. For milk, try sachets of Leche Pil (plain, chocolate or strawberry-flavoured), at US$0.25 each.

GETTING AROUND

AIR TRANSPORT

Internal air services are run by Lloyd Aéreo Boliviano (LAB), Aero Sur, and TAM (not too reliable) between the main towns. LAB uses American Airlines Sabre computer system with immediate access to worldwide flight information. Boarding passes are issued only at airports; after obtaining one, pay airport tax (see above). LAB offers a 28-day unlimited domestic flight ticket for US$135 for international travellers using LAB, which must be bought outside Bolivia (only one stopover per city is allowed, except for connecting flights; note that many flights radiate from La Paz, Santa Cruz or Cochabamba).

To avoid paying the 18% tax on the air-pass, purchase it as an MCO outside the country, then exchange this for flight tickets later. You must enter Bolivia using LAB or on a foreign carrier with whom LAB may have a pooling arrangement. LAB have 20% discounts for family members if they travel together (take passport). LAB and Aero Sur offer discounts of 25% to students and passengers over 60. Delays are common on LAB; a 'through' flight may require a change of plane, or be delayed waiting for a connecting flight coming from elsewhere. Only on international flights is overnight lodging provided during delays. Insure your bags heavily as they tend to get left around.

NB If your internal flight is delayed keep your baggage with you and do not check it in until the flight is definitely announced. There have been robberies of prematurely checked-in baggage.

LAND TRANSPORT

● **Trains**

Empresa Nacional de Ferrocarriles (ENFE), was privatized in 1996. Schedules change frequently. Always check departure times in advance. Tickets can be bought in advance.

● **Road**

Descriptions of all major roads are given in the text, above. Nearly all Bolivian road surfaces, even the paved sections, are bad, and after flooding or rough weather they are even worse. Even main roads may be closed in the rainy season.

NB On election day no public transport runs whatsoever; only cars with a special permit may be on the road.

● **Buses**

Buses ply most of the roads (interurban buses are called *flotas*, urban ones *micros*, also minibuses and *trufis*). Reporting time is half an hour before the bus leaves, but you should always try to reserve, and pay for, a seat as far as possible in advance and arrive in good time. In the wet season, bus travel is subject to long delays and detours at extra cost. In the dry season journeys can be very dusty. On all journeys, take food and toilet wipes. Bus companies are responsible for any luggage packed on the roof. A small charge is made for use of major bus terminals; payment is before departure.

● **Motorists** (including motor-cyclists)

For necessary documents, see **Introduction and Hints – Motoring**: motorcyclists may be asked for a *carnet de passages* (*tríptico*), but it is not officially necessary. If hiring a car, the company can arrange a 'blanket' driving permit for tourist purposes which is valid for several

days and destinations. Tolls vary from US$0.50 to US$2.50 for journeys up to 100 km. In theory, you need an International Driving Permit (and, since a driving licence number is requested, also your national driving licence, or some ingenuity). Just a national licence will do when hiring a car and the rental document usually suffices at police controls. Two authorization certificates are required in La Paz: the first from the Automóvil Club Boliviano, corner of 6 de Agosto and Arce, T/F 372139, and the second from the traffic police at the Comando Departamental, Organismo Operativo de Tránsito, corner of Mcal Santa Cruz and Plaza San Francisco. For hints on high-altitude motoring, see **Introduction and Hints** at front of book.

Take great care when driving at night (it is best not to): cyclists do not usually have lights; truck drivers almost never dip their headlights (keep your own on full beam to make the truck dip his); some truck drivers are drunk, or fall asleep at the wheel; at the slightest sign of danger, pull out of the way. Day or night, watch out for people asleep at the roadside in lowland areas; they tend to lie with head and torso in the road where there are fewer mosquitoes.

Petrol (gasoline) 2 grades: 85 and 92 octane. 85 octane costs US$0.44, super US$0.56; diesel costs US$0.38/litre. Costs are higher in Guayaramerín, Riberalta and Puerto Suárez. Around Lake Titicaca, there are no petrol stations as such, the only two that exist frequently run out; ask in villages for where petrol is sold from the drum.

● **Trucks**

Trucks congregate at all town markets, with destinations chalked on the sides. They are normally about half the cost when there is competition. Otherwise they charge what they judge the market will bear and can therefore seem expensive.

COMMUNICATIONS

● **Media**

In La Paz: morning papers – *Presencia*, daily, the largest circulation, largely Catholic; *La Razón*, *Primera Plana*, *Hoy* and *El Diario* (sensationalist). *Meridiano* (midday): *Ultima Hora*, and *Jornada* (evenings). In Cochabamba – *Los Tiempos*, *Extra*. In Oruro – *La Patria*, mornings (except Mon). *El Día*, *La Estrella del Oriente*, *El Mundo* and *El Deber* are the Santa Cruz daily papers; *Deber* also appears in Trinidad. In Sucre, *El Correo*. *Presencia*, *El Diario*, *El Mundo*, *La Razón* all have good foreign coverage. Weekly: *Nueva Economía*. La Paz papers are on sale in other cities. English language weekly *The Bolivian Times*, published Fri, US$1.50, available in major cities, many local reports (details T 340062,

F 390700, address Jauregui 2248, Sopocachi, La Paz, casilla 1696). International papers are available in La Paz. Also, there are about 85 radio stations, a commercial government TV station as well as a university TV service.

● **Postal services**

Post offices use the post box (*casilla*) system. Items sent by post should therefore bear, not the street address, but the *casilla* number and town. Hours are Mon-Sat 0800-2000, Sun 0800-1200. For security, send mail 'certificado'. There is a national and international express post system; special counters and envelopes provided. Air-mail letters to and from Europe take between 5 and 10 days. To send a letter up to 20 grammes to USA/Canada costs US$0.60, to Europe US$0.70, more than 20g to USA US$1.70, to Europe US$2.30. Parcels to Europe can only be sent by air. There are 2 classes – fast (taking 7-10 days) and slow (taking a month): slow rates – US$16 for 1 kg, US$90 for 5 kg, US$120 for 20 kg. Parcels are checked by customs officers before being sealed. Several reports of customs officers attempting to charge for inspecting parcels: refuse to pay (politely).

● **Telecommunications**

The national telecommunications company is Entel, which handles all phone, telex and fax services. In the Department of La Paz, Cotel operates local services, alongside Entel. There is now direct satellite communication with Bolivia. Direct calls possible from major cities to Europe, USA, Australia and elsewhere, clear lines, delays minimal; US$2.06/min to Europe and Mexico, US$1.76 to USA and South America, US$3.44 to Australia. Collect calls can only be made to the USA. BT Chargecard calls available direct to UK. At the La Paz exchange you can pay by credit card and the phone shows the cost as you speak. Outside La Paz you may have to wait a while for an overseas connection, but otherwise there are no problems. Fax to Europe costs US$5/page, to the USA US$3.80, to Australia, New Zealand US$6. Phone calls within city limits are free for private calls; for public phones, coins/fichas or phone cards are necessary. Fichas and phone cards only work in the city in which they are bought.

Direct collect-call numbers: US AT&T 0800 1111, MCI 0800 2222, Sprint 0800 3333, IDB (TRT) 0800 4444; UK BT 0800 0044; Spain Telefónica 0800 0034; Brazil 0800 0055; Chile Entel 0800 0056; Canada Teleglobe 0800 0101; Japan KDD 0800 0081.

SPORT

● **Hiking**

Various treks are described in the text, especially nr La Paz and from Sorata. Note that all these trails are remote in parts and that robbery and violent attacks have been made on tourists and Bolivians alike. It is advisable to hike these trails in large, organized groups. *Backpacking and Trekking in Peru and Bolivia*, published by Bradt Publications, describes 3-9 day hikes in the Cordillera Real within easy reach of La Paz (Bradt Publications also publish *South America Ski Guide*). Due May 1997 *Trekking in Bolivia*, Yossi Brain (The Mountaineers, Seattle). The local tourist office also produces leaflets with sketch maps on walks in the vicinity of La Paz. There are also some excellent guides available through local clubs.

HOLIDAYS AND FESTIVALS

● **Public holidays**

1 Jan, New Year's Day; Carnival Week, Mon, Shrove Tuesday, Ash Wednesday; Holy Week, Thur, Fri and Sat; 1 May, Labour Day; Corpus Christi (movable); 16 July, La Paz Municipal Holiday; 5-7 Aug, Independence; 12 Oct, Columbus Day; 2 Nov, Day of the Dead; Christmas Day.

There are local holidays at Tarija, on 15 April; at Sucre on 25 May; at Cochabamba, 14 Sept; at Santa Cruz and Cobija 24 Sept; at Potosí, 10 Nov; in the Beni, 18 Nov, and at Oruro, 22 Feb.

● **Festivals**

In addition to those given in the text: 2 Feb: Virgen de la Candelaria, in rural communities, Copacabana, Santa Cruz. 3 May: Fiesta de la Invención de la Santa Cruz, various parts. 2 June: Santísima Trinidad in Beni Department. 24 June: San Juan, all Bolivia. 29 June: San Pedro y San Pablo, at Tiquina and Tihuanaco. 28 July: Fiesta de Santiago (St James), Altiplano and lake region; Achocalla a convenient place to go to. 16 Aug: San Roque, patron saint of dogs, the animals are adorned with ribbons and other decorations. 1 and 2 Nov: All Saints and All Souls, any local cemetery. 18 Nov: Beni's Departmental anniversary, especially in Trinidad. For other festivals on the Altiplano enquire at hotels or tourist office in La Paz. Remember that the cities are very quiet on national holidays, but colourful celebrations will be going on in the villages. Beware of water-filled balloons thrown during carnival in most cities – even the coldest. Hotels are often full at the most popular places, for instance Copacabana on Good Friday, worth booking in advance.

FURTHER READING

An Insider's Guide to Bolivia, by Peter McFarren (Fundación Cultural Quipus, Casilla 1696, La Paz, 3rd edition, 1992, US$25) has been recommended, especially for its section on culture. *Descubriendo Bolivia*, Hugo Boero Rojo, 1989 on archaeology and precolumbian history, with road routes (also available in English). *La Pintura En los Museos de Bolivia*, by José de Mesa and Teresa Gisbert, published 1991 by Los Amigos del Libro. *Guía Boliviana de Transporte y Turismo* (GBT) published monthly at Plaza del Estudiante 1920, T 321027, F 391641, US$6 a month, US$65 a year, gives information on transport, accommodation, restaurants, useful data etc, with town plans, for the whole country.

British Business Visitors are strongly advised to consult 'Hints to Exporters: Bolivia', which can be obtained from DTI Export Publications, PO Box 55, Stratford-upon-Avon, Warwickshire, CV37 9GE. Similar publications for US business visitors may be obtained from the Department of Commerce.

ACKNOWLEDGEMENTS

For updating this chapter, we are most grateful to Alan Murphy. Our warmest thanks are also due to Yossi Brain, Secretario de Andinismo of the Club Andino Boliviano, resident correspondent in La Paz, and to Robert and Daisy Kunstaetter for a thorough review of Eastern Bolivia (they wish to thank Juan Currubí, Puerto Suárez, Steward and Sandra Williams, Puerto Suárez, Blanca de España, Quijarro and Eduardo Vega, Arroyo Concepción). We are also very grateful to Simon Watson Taylor for a very detailed series of letters. Travellers who have written are acknowledged at the end of the book.

Brazil

HORIZONS

THE LAND

Brazil, the fifth largest country in the world, has the sixth largest population. It is almost as large as the United States of America and its area is nearly half that of South America. For neighbours it has all the South American countries save Chile and Ecuador. Distances are enormous: 4,320 km from N to S, 4,328 km from E to W, a land frontier of 15,719 km and an Atlantic coast line of 7,408 km. Its population is over half that of all South America, and over 65% is under 30 years of age. It was named for the tropical redwood, *pau do brasil*, exported by the first settlers.

Brazil's topography may be divided roughly into five main zones: the Amazon Basin; the River Plate Basin; the Guiana Highlands N of the Amazon; the Brazilian Highlands S of the Amazon; and the coastal strip. The two great river basins account for about three-fifths of Brazil's area.

The river basins

The **Amazon Basin**, in northern and western Brazil, takes up more than a third of the whole country. This basin is plain, broadly based on the Andes and funnelling narrowly to the sea; most of the drained area has an elevation of less than 250m. The rainfall is heavy, for the winds from the NE and SE lose their moisture as they approach the Andes. Some few places receive from 3,750 to 5,000 mm a year, though over most of the area it is no more than from 1,500 to 2,500 mm. Much of the basin suffers from annual floods. The region was covered by tropical forest, with little undergrowth except along the watercourses; it is now being rapidly cut down. The climate is hot and the humidity high throughout the year.

The **River Plate Basin**, in the southern part of Brazil, has a more varied surface and is less heavily forested than the Amazon Basin. The land is higher and the climate cooler.

Brazil's highlands

Most of the remainder of Brazil's territory is highland. The **Guiana Highlands**, N of the Amazon, are partly forested, partly hot stony desert. Those that face the NW winds get heavy rainfall, but the southern slopes are arid. The rainfall, which comes during the hot season, is about 1,250 mm a year. The summers are hot and the winters cool.

The **Brazilian Highlands** lying SE of the Amazon and NE of the River Plate Basin form a tableland of from 300 to 900m high, but here and there, mostly in SE Brazil, mountain ranges rise from it. The highest peak in southern Brazil, the Pico da Bandeira, NE of Rio de Janeiro, is 2,898m; the highest peak in all Brazil, the Pico da Neblina on the Venezuelan border, is 3,014m.

For the most part the Highlands cascade sharply to the sea. South of Salvador as far as Porto Alegre the coast rises steeply to a protective barrier, the **Great Escarpment**. In only two places is this Escarpment breached by deeply cut river beds – those of the Rio Doce and the Rio Paraíba; and only in a few places does the land rise in a single slope making for comparatively easy communication with the interior. Along most of its course, the Great Escarpment falls to the sea in parallel steps, each step separated by the trough of a valley.

The few rivers rising on the Escarpment which flow direct into the Atlantic do so precipitously and are not navigable. Most of the rivers flow deep into the interior. Those in southern Brazil rise almost within sight of the sea, but run westward through the vast interior to join the Paraná. In the central area the Escarpment rivers run away from the sea to join the São Francisco river, which flows northwards parallel to the coast for 2,900 km, to tumble over the Paulo Afonso Falls on its eastward course to the Atlantic.

The Great Escarpment denies to most of Brazil the natural valley outflows and lines of travel from the interior to the sea. Of its rivers the Amazon alone is directly navigable for a great distance inland.

CLIMATE

The average annual temperature increases steadily from S to N, but even on the Equator, in the Amazon Basin, the average temperature is not more than 27°C. The highest recorded was 42°C, in the dry northeastern states. From the latitude of Recife S to Rio de Janeiro, the mean temperature is from 23° to 27°C along the coast, and from 18° to 21°C in the Highlands. From a few degrees S of Rio de Janeiro to the boundary with Uruguay the mean temperature is from 17° to 19°C. Humidity is relatively high in Brazil, particularly along the coast.

It is only in rare cases that the rainfall can be described as either excessive or deficient: few places get more than 2,000 mm – the coast N of Belém, some of the Amazon Basin, and a small area of the Serra do Mar between Santos and São Paulo, where the downpour has been harnessed to generate electricity. The rainy season in Amazônia is Mar-May, but is getting steadily shorter and less severe, possibly as a result of deforestation. The northeastern droughts are caused by irregular rainfall.

The rainy season in the S is from Dec to Mar; this is also the holiday season when Brazilians flock to the coastal resorts, and when prices are higher.

NATIONAL PARKS

This chapter gives details on many of Brazil's national parks, which are run by Ibama (the Brazilian Institute of Environmental Protection). The Institute is underfunded, often understaffed and visitors may find it difficult to obtain information. National parks are open to visitors, usually with a permit from Ibama. Ecological Stations and Biological Reserves are open to researchers and educational groups, but not tourists.

POLITICAL AND SOCIAL HISTORY

THE PORTUGUESE COLONY

The Portuguese, Pedro Alvares Cabral, landed in Brazil in 1500. He left after a week, shortly followed by Amerigo Ves-

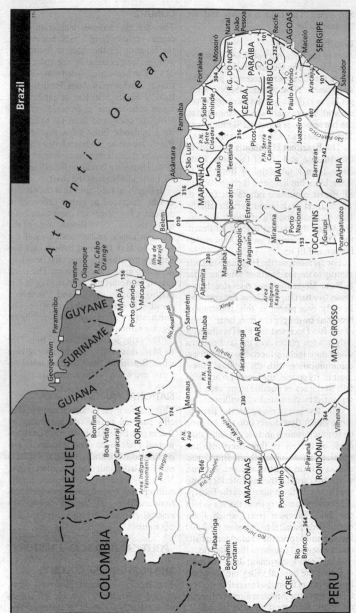

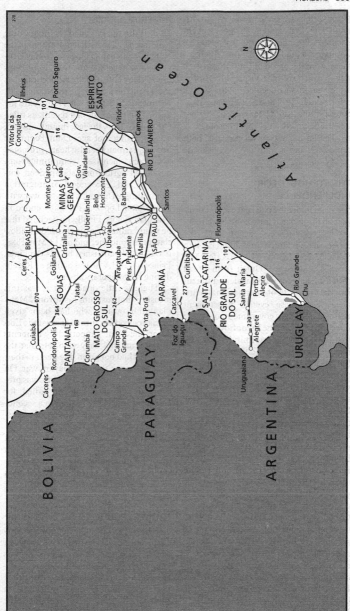

pucci who had been sent to explore further. The first system of government adopted by the Portuguese was a Capitânia, a kind of feudal principality – there were 13 of them, but these were replaced in 1572 by a Viceroyalty. In the same year it was decided to divide the colony into two, N and S, with capitals at Salvador and Rio de Janeiro; it was not until 1763 that Rio became the sole capital. The Portuguese crown expected both a personal and a state revenue from its colony.

THE STRUGGLE FOR INDEPENDENCE

300 years under the paternal eye of Portugal had ill-prepared the colonists for independent existence, except for the experience of Dutch invasion (1624 in Salvador, and 1630-1654 in Recife). The colonists ejected the Dutch from Brazil with little help from Portugal, and Brazilians date the birth of their national sentiment from these events. Resentment against Portuguese government and trade intervention led to the **Inconfidência**, the first revolution, masterminded by **Tiradentes** with 11 other citizens of Minas Gerais. They were unsuccessful (Tiradentes was executed), but when France invaded Portugal in 1807, King João VI was shipped to safety in Brazil, escorted by the British navy. Rio was temporarily declared the capital of the Portuguese Empire. The British, as a price for their assistance in the Portuguese war, forced the opening of Brazil's ports to non-Portuguese trade. King João VI returned to the mother country in 1821, leaving his son, the handsome young Pedro, as Regent. Pedro refused to return control of Brazil to the Portuguese Côrtes (parliament), and on 13 May 1882, by popular request, he agreed to stay and assumed the title of 'Perpetual Defender and Protector of Brazil'. On 7 Sept he declared Brazil's independence with the cry 'Independence or Death' by the Rio Ipiranga; on 12 Oct he was proclaimed constitutional emperor of Brazil, and on 1 Dec he was crowned in Rio de Janeiro.

IMPERIAL BRAZIL

Dom Pedro the First had the misfortune to be faced by a secession movement in the N, to lose the Banda Oriental (today Uruguay) and to get too involved in his complicated love life. Finally, he abdicated as the result of a military revolt in 1831, leaving his 5-year-old son, Dom Pedro the Second, in the hands of a regent, as ruler. On 23 July 1840, the lad, though only 15, was proclaimed of age. Dom Pedro the Second, a strong liberal at heart, promoted education, increased communications, developed agriculture, stamped on corruption and encouraged immigration from Europe. Under his rule the war with the dictator López of Paraguay ended in Brazilian victory. Finally, he declared that he would rather lose his crown than allow slavery to continue, and on 13 May 1888, it was finally abolished by his daughter, Princess Isabel, who was acting as Regent during his temporary absence.

There is little doubt that it was this measure that cost him his throne. Many plantation owners, who had been given no compensation, turned against the Emperor; they were supported by elements in the army and navy, who felt that the Emperor had not given due heed to their interests since the Paraguayan War. On 15 November 1889, the Republic was proclaimed and the Emperor sailed for Europe. 2 years later he died in a second-rate hotel in Paris, after steadfastly refusing a pension from the conscience-stricken revolutionaries. At the time of the first centenary of independence in 1922 the imperial family was allowed to return to Brazil, and the body of Dom Pedro was brought back and buried in the cathedral at Petrópolis.

FROM REPUBLIC TO DICTATORSHIP

The history of the 'Old Republic' (1889-1930), apart from the first 10 years which saw several monarchist rebellions, was comparatively uneventful, a time of expansion and increasing prosperity. Brazil declared war on Germany during both wars and Brazilian troops fought in the Italian campaign in 1944-45. In 1930 a revolution headed by Getúlio Vargas, Governor of Rio Grande do Sul, who was to become known as 'the Father of the Poor' for the social measures he introduced, deposed President Wáshington Luís. Vargas assumed executive power first as provisional president and then as dictator. He was forced to resign in Oct 1945. In 1946 a liberal republic was restored and the following 18 years saw considerable economic development and social advance.

An increase in government instability and corruption prompted the military to intervene in civil affairs. From Mar 1964 until Mar 1985, the military governed Brazil with the use of political repression and torture, yet achieving great economic success (up to 1980). Between 1964-74 average growth was 10% a year but the divide between rich and poor widened. Labour leaders were oppressed, dissenters were jailed and *favelas* mushroomed. Political reform did not occur until 1980 and free elections were not held until 1989.

THE RETURN TO DEMOCRACY

In Jan 1985 a civilian, Tancredo Neves, representing a broad opposition to the military regime, was elected President by the electoral college introduced under the military's 1967 constitution. He was unable, because of illness, to take office: the vice-president elect, Sr José Sarney, was sworn in as acting President in Mar 1985, and in April became President on Sr Neves' death. After complete revision by a Constituent Assembly in 1987-88, Brazil's new constitution of 1988 permitted direct presidential elections in Nov 1989. The elections, held in two rounds, gave Fernando Collor de Melo, of the small Partido da Reconstrução Nacional, 53% of the vote, narrowly defeating his left-wing rival, Luis Inácio da Silva (Lula). Just over half way through his 5-year term, Collor was suspended from office after a landslide congressional vote to impeach over his involvement in corruption. He avoided impeachment by resigning on 29 December 1992. Vice-president Itamar Franco took over, but had scant success in tackling poverty and inflation until the introduction of an anti-inflation package which introduced the real as the new currency.

RECENT DEVELOPMENTS

The success of the **real** plan was the principal reason for its architect, finance minister Fernando Henrique Cardoso, winning the presidential elections of Oct 1994. After trailing Luis Lula da Silva of the Workers Party (PT), Cardoso's popularity grew so rapidly between July and Oct that a second round of voting was not required. Cardoso represented an alliance of the Brazilian Social Democrat Party (PSDB), the Liberal Front (PFL) and the Labour Party (PTB), which failed to gain a majority in either house of congress. This severely hampered the president's plans to reform the tax and social security systems and the civil service. As business pressed for faster economic reform and unemployment began to rise, Cardoso's popularity started to wane. The government was also criticized for its slowness in addressing social problems such as land reform and the violence associated with landlessness; the slave-like working conditions in some agricultural areas; human rights; the demarcation of Indian land. A national plan for human rights was announced in May 1996, but swift congressional approval was not expected.

SETTLEMENT AND ECONOMIC HISTORY

The first European settlement was at Salvador da Bahia, and the settlers came mainly from southern Portugal, with its feudal tradition of great estates. For the first few years Portugal, then much concerned with the Orient, paid little attention to Brazil. In about 1507 a second colony was settled at São Vicente, near Santos, and in 1537 a third at Olinda, near Recife. The settlers at São Vicente, who founded the first settlement in the highlands at São Paulo in 1534, were unlike those at Salvador and Recife: they came from the poorer and more energetic N of Portugal. All of them were attracted less by the prospect of earning their living by self-supporting labour than by opportunities of speculative profit. To do the work they used the primitive Tupi-Guarani Indians, many of whom died from European diseases (see *Red Gold*, by John Hemming). They cohabited freely with the Indians and, later, with slaves imported from Africa to run the huge estates.

Sugar cane had been introduced at São Vicente in 1532, but it was the wealthy settlers of the NE who had the necessary capital to establish the crop and to buy African slaves to work it; the Indian, with a hunting-and-gathering culture, was a disappointment as a labourer. In the matter of sugar, Salvador and Recife had the advantages over São Vicente of being very much nearer home, and of having better ports and easier access to the interior. During the latter half of the 16th and the whole of the 17th centuries, the provinces of Bahia, Pernambuco, and Paraíba were the world's prime source of sugar.

The settlers at São Paulo, envious of the more fortunate NE, sent out expeditions to explore the interior for gold, which had already been found in small quantities in their own streams. These hardy Bandeirantes pushed as far S as Colonia, opposite Buenos Aires, as far W as the Río Paraguay, and N into the area W of the sugar plantations of the NE. In 1698 they struck gold in central Minas Gerais. More was found soon after in central Mato Grosso, and in 1725 in Goiás. Diamonds were discovered in 1729 N of the goldfields of Minas Gerais.

There followed a great gold and diamond rush. The gold boom started early in the 18th century, lasted a 100 years, and then petered out. Minas Gerais was transformed from a wilderness into a well populated agricultural, pastoral, and mining region. It was as an outlet for this area that Rio de Janeiro was developed. Some of the wealth went to create the extraordinarily beautiful city of Ouro Preto, to-day a national monument of superb building, painting and sculpture, and the similarly attractive cities of São João del Rei, Mariana, Congonhas do Campo, Diamantina and others.

Brazil was ready for the next specula-

tion, coffee, introduced about 1720 from French Guyana. Coffee planting began near Rio de Janeiro and at many places round the coast as far as the Amazon, but by 1825 it had mainly been concentrated in the Paraíba valley, W of the capital. From there it spread into São Paulo, where its cultivation attracted a large number of immigrants after 1850.

There have been many other typical Brazilian booms and recessions. The best known is the rubber boom in the Amazon valley; competition from SE Asia wiped it out after 1912. Sugar, coffee, and cocoa were alike the subject of booms. In each case Brazil was challenged by other sources of supply, where more intensive methods of production were applied.

This boom tradition still holds, but it is shifting from agriculture to industry: Brazilians today prefer to think of themselves as a rising industrial nation. Nevertheless, a great increase in production and export of manufactured goods has not prevented oases of prosperity being edged by deserts of poverty and wilderness.

CULTURE

PEOPLE

At first the Portuguese colony grew slowly. From 1580 to 1640 the population was only about 50,000 apart from the million or so indigenous Indians. In 1700 there were some 750,000 non-indigenous people in Brazil. Early in the 19th century Humboldt computed there were about 920,000 whites, 1,960,000 Africans, and 1,120,000 Indians and *mestiços*: after 3 centuries of occupation a total of only 4 million, and over twice as many Africans as there were whites.

Modern immigration did not begin effectively until after 1850. Of the 4.6 million immigrants from Europe between 1884 and 1954, 32% were Italians, 30% Portuguese, 14% Spanish, 4% German, and the rest of various nationalities. Since 1954 immigrants have averaged 50,000 a year. There are some 1 million Japanese-descended Brazilians; they grow a fifth of the coffee, 30% of the cotton, all the tea, and are very active in market gardening.

Today the whites and near-whites are about 53% of the population; people of mixed race about 34%, and Afro Brazilians 11%; the rest are either Indians or Asians. There are large regional variations in the distribution of the races: the whites predominate greatly in the S, which received the largest flood of European immigrants, and decrease more or less progressively towards the N.

Most of the German immigrants settled in the three southern states: Santa Catarina, Rio Grande do Sul, and Paraná. The Germans (and the Italians and Poles and other Slavs who followed them) did not in the main go as wage earners on the big estates, but as cultivators of their own small farms. Here there is a settled agricultural population cultivating the soil intensively.

The arid wastes of the Sertão remain largely uncultivated. Its inhabitants are people of mixed Portuguese and Indian origin (*mestiço*); most live off a primitive but effective method of cultivation known as 'slash and burn', which involves cutting down and burning the brushwood for a small patch of ground which is cultivated for a few years and then allowed to grow back.

The decision to found a new federal capital, Brasília, deep in the interior, was a symbolic act of faith in the future of the Sertão: a bold attempt to deflect population from the coastal regions to the under-developed central and western plateaux of the country.

Though there is no legal discrimination against black people, the economic and educational disparity – by default rather than intent of the Government – is such that successful Afro Brazilians are active almost exclusively in the worlds of sport, entertainment and the arts.

Indigenous peoples

It is estimated that, when the Portuguese arrived in Brazil, there were more than 5 million Indians living in the area. Today there are only about 200,000. Tribal groups number 221; each has a unique dialect, but most languages belong to four main linguistic families, Tupi-Guarani, Ge, Carib and Arawak. A few tribes remain uncontacted, others are exclusively nomadic, others are semi-nomadic hunter-gatherers and farmers, while some are settled groups in close contact with non-Indian society. The struggle of groups such as the Yanomami to have their land demarcated in order to secure title is well-documented. The goal of the Statute of the Indian (Law 6.001/73), for demarcation of all Indian land by 1978, is largely unmet. It was feared that a new law introduced in Jan 1996 would slow the process even more. Funai, the National Foundation for the Support of the Indian, a part of the Interior Ministry, is charged with representing the Indians' interests, but lacks resources and support. There is no nationwide, representative body for indigenous people. Most of Brazil's indigenous people live in the Amazon region; they are affected by deforestation, encroachment from colonizers, small-and large-scale mining, and the construction of hydroelectric dams. Besides the Yanomami, other groups include the Xavante, Tukano, Kreen-Akrore, Kaiapó, Arawete and Arara.

Rural and urban population

The population has historically been heavily concentrated in a comparatively small area – chiefly along the coastal strip where the original Portuguese settlers exploited the agricultural wealth, and further inland in the states of Minas Gerais and São Paulo where more recent development has followed the original search for gold, precious stones and slaves. Much of the interior of Pará, Amazonas, Goiás and the Mato Grosso has densities of one person per sq km or less. Brazil's attention is officially focused on these relatively underpopulated regions as a means of syphoning off some of the population excess in the urban centres.

The urban population of Brazil increased at rates more than double the overall average rate, until the 1980s, and much of this growth has been concentrated in the larger cities. Internal migration is the major cause of these phenomenal growth rates, bringing to the cities problems of unemployment, housing shortage, and pressure on services which are already stretched to breaking point; shanty towns – or *favelas, mocambos, alagados*, according to the region – are an integral part of the urban landscape and a constant reminder of the poverty of some of the rural areas from which these people come. But while the NE, because of its poverty, has lost many workers to the industries of the SE, many rural workers from southern Brazil have moved N, drawn by the rapid development of Amazônia, creating unprecedented pressures on the environment.

Education

Of the 13 million children between 7 and 14, 2 million have no school to go to. Of those who go to school, not all stay long enough to learn how to read and write. Adult literacy campaigns have, however, recently improved the picture.

MUSIC AND DANCE

Perhaps because of its sheer size, Brazil has a greater musical inventory than any other Latin American country, not only reflected in the immense regional spread of folk music but also in its successive waves of urban popular music. The Brazilian expresses him/herself through music and dance to an extraordinary degree and the music covers the whole spectrum from the utmost rural simplicity to the ultimate state-of-the-art commercial sophistication. The far N of the country is virtually in the Caribbean, while the extreme S shares its culture with the Rio de la Plata countries.

The South

In Paraná, Santa Catarina and Rio Grande do Sul, the music is strictly European in origin, rhythm and instrumentation. Rio Grande do Sul shares Gaucho dances such as the Pericom and song styles such as the Milonga, Trova and Pajada with neighbouring Uruguay and Argentina. The Chula is a competitive dance for men to show off with (comparable to the Argentine Malambo), while the Pexinho is for men and women. The guitar and the accordion are the favourite instruments, also true for Santa Catarina and Paraná, where

the names of the dances denote their European origins: Mazurkas, Valsas, Chotes, Polquinhas and Rancheiras. The Chimarrita is a song style that came straight from the Azores. If you are feeling sentimental, you sing a Toada, if energetic, you stamp your feet to a Fandango. Except for the Batuque de Rio Grande do Sul in Porto Alegre, closely related to the Candombe of nearby Montevideo, there is no African influence in the music of this region and none of that classic Brazilian syncopation.

São Paulo, Rio de Janeiro, Minas Gerais

Moving N into São Paulo, we enter an area rich in traditional folk dances and music, with the African admixture beginning to show up. At many religious festivals will be found the Cōngadas (European 'Moors & Christians', but danced by blacks) and Moçambique (a stick dance for men), while the Samba de Lenço, Fandango and Batuque are recreational dances for one or more couples. The instrumental accompaniment branches out into shakers (the *ganzá*), drums (*caixas* and *tambores*) and above all the guitar (*viola*). Try the great pilgrimage church at Aparecida do Nte on a Sun. You might well see a group of religious dances. In the hinterland of Rio de Janeiro the Folias de Reis are out on the street from Christmas to Epiphany, singing from house to house, accompanying themselves on the *caixa* and *adufe* drums and the guitar, while in the old coastal towns of Parati and Angra dos Reis are to be found the Dança de Velhos (the old men), performed to the accordion. The Jongo is a dance of African origin for men and women, naturally with a drum accompaniment. And there is hardly need to mention Rio de Janeiro at carnival and its Samba Schools. Further N again, we come to the states of Espíritu Santo, Minas Gerais and Goiás. In colonial Ouro Preto, in Minas, you can hear the old Modinha sung to the Portuguese guitar as a serenade and be transported into the past. Espíritu Santo is home to the Ticumbi, a kind of Congada, danced to the guitar and shakers (*chocalhos*). Goiás shares with Minas Gerais a very rich heritage of Portuguese derived religious folk song and dance, centred on Folias, Modas and Calangos.

Bahia

Bahia is the heart of African Brazil and a very musical heart it is, born of the Yoruba religion that came with the slaves from what is now Nigeria. The resulting syncretic religion is known as Candomblé in Bahia and the gods or 'Orixás' are worshipped through song, dance and possession in the 'Terreiros', directed by the priests (Pães-de-Santo) and priestesses (Mães-de-Santo). The mainly female adepts, dressed entirely in white, circle gracefully to the background chant of 'Pontos' and the thunderous pounding of the *atabaques*, the tall drums. The two most revered priestesses are Mãe Olga de Alakêto and Mãe Menininha de Gantois. Similar syncretic African religions are found elsewhere in Brazil. Macumba in Rio, Xangô in the NE and Umbanda all over. Another vital African element in Bahian folk music is the spectacular dance-cum-martial arts form of Capoiera. Bodies whirl and cartwheel around each other to the sound of the *berimbau* (a one-stringed bow with resonator) and the accompanying chant. Related to the Capoiera is the stick dance Maculelê. Two of the best *berimbau* groups on record are Camafeu de Oxossí and the Cordão de Ouro. Bahia has a carnival almost as celebrated as that of Rio and here you can see the Afoxé, a serious religious dance, performed to drums alone.

The North East

North of Bahia is the Nordeste, with music that runs the whole gamut from black African to mediaeval Portuguese. In colonial times the church directed the peoples' musical energies into religious plays, songs and dances and a large number of these are still performed. The Bumba-Meu-Boi is a folk drama in the course of which a bull is killed and then brought back to life. Particularly popular in Piauí and Maranhão, its variants are found as far afield as Amazônia, where it is called the Boi-Bumbá, and Paraná in the far S, where it is known as Boi-Mamão. Also popular along the coast from Ceará to Paraíba is a nautical drama of Portuguese origin called Marujada or Nau Catarineta, a version of Moors and Christians, accompanied by Portuguese guitar (*violão*), drums and the *ganzá* scraper. In Alagoas, Sergipe and Pernambuco we find the sword dance called Reisado, danced after Christmas, the Caboclinhos, who are dressed like Indians and dance with bows and arrows, and the Guerreiros Alagoanos, a mixture of both. The last named are accompanied by the classical northeastern musical group called Terno de Pífanos, with the *pífano* vertical flute, accompanied by *maracas* and *ganzá*. The Banda de Pífanos de Caruaru in Pernambuco can be found on record. Recreational dance music in the Nordeste goes under the generic name of 'Forró', said to be derived from the expression 'For All', because the English companies operating at the turn of the century organized weekend dances for their workmen to which all comers were invited. Four very popular recreational folk dances of this region are the Ciranda (a round dance), the Coco, the Bate-Coxa (where the dancers bump bellies) and the Bambelô. Carnival in Recife, the largest city, is when and where to see the energetic and gymnastic Frevo, danced by young men with an umbrella in their hands, and the very stately and superbly costumed Maracatu dancers, with their queen and king. The Nordeste is equally rich in song styles, notably the Desafios, Emboladas, Cocos and Aboios. The Desafios are performed by so-called Repentistas or Violeiros, who accompany themselves on the Portuguese guitar and whose repertoire includes a large inventory of verse styles. They will sing about individual spectators, who then pay willingly for the compliment. The Emboladas and Cocos are similar, but faster and accompanied solely by tambourines, while the Aboios are haunting songs related to cattle and cattlemen. Repentistas and Emboladores can normally be found at work in markets throughout the region. The premier Repentista is Otacílio Batista do Pajeú, who sang to the Pope during the latter's visit to Brazil.

The music of the Nordeste has also been well propagated by more sophisticated groups that have based themselves on folk roots, such as the Quinteto Violado, Ariano Suassuna's Orchestra Armorial and Cussy de Almeida's Quinteto Armorial, not forgetting the veteran accordionist Luiz Gonzaga and the popular Alçeu Valença. As a result of the huge migration of *nordestinos* to the urban S, moreover, it is just as easy to hear this regional music in São Paulo as it is in Recife.

Pará and the Amazon

Finally to Pará and the Amazon in the far N, where the music has been heavily influenced from the Caribbean. The most popular musical genre here is the Carimbó, danced to a Merengue-type rhythm and played on drums, wind or brass (usually the clarinet) and strings, particularly the banjo. Notable performers are Pinduca ('O Rei do Carimbó'), Veriquete and Vieira. It is the last-named who thought up the term 'Lambada' for his particular version of the Carimbó and the spectacular, thigh-entwining dance form introduced to the world in Paris by Karakos and Lorsac in 1988 had already been popular among young people at 'Forrós' throughout the region for some years. The very traditional island of Marajó in the mouth of the Amazon has preserved versions of 18th century dances, such as the Lundú and Chula.

Urban popular music

The vast range of Brazilian regional folk music is only equalled by the chronological depth of its urban popular music, which surges like endless waves on a beach. For the origins we have to go back to Jesuit missions and Portuguese folk music, influenced and blended by African slaves, from which emerged the 19th century Lundús, Polcas and Maxixes that in turn gave way to the romantic and sentimental Choro song genre (from *chorar*, to weep), accompanied by guitar, flute and *cavaquinho* (small guitar), which became all the rage and indeed still has its adepts in Brazil today. Around the turn of the

century the instrumentation turned to brass and Rio's urban Samba was born, a birth that was announced by the recording in 1917 of Donga's 'Pelo Telefone'. Names from this early period are Pixinguinha, Sinhô, Heitor dos Prazeres, Ary Barroso, Noel Rosa and of course Carmen Miranda, who took the Samba to Hollywood and the rest of the world. It also became intimately connected with the carnival in the form of Marcha Ranchos and Sambas de Enredo as the first samba schools were formed, of which Salgueiro, Mangueira, Partido Alto, Portela, Mocidade Independente and Beija-Flor are some of the most famous. With the Escolas de Samba came the Batucada or percussion groups playing the *pandeiro* (tambourine), *atabaque* and *tamborim* (drum), *agogô* (cowbell), *reco-reco*, *chocalho*, *afoxê* and *cuíca*. This is the real engine room of Samba. Listen to Lúcio Perrone or Mocidade Independente de Padre Miguel. A new phase was ushered in with an invasion from Bahia and the Nordeste in the early 50's. From Bahia came Dorival Caymmi, who dropped his fishermen's songs in favour of the Samba, and Luiz Gonzaga, who brought his accordion, *zabumba* drum and *triangulo*, with which to play his Baiãos (his 'Asa Branca' is a classic) and almost put the Samba itself into eclipse for several years. Almost, but not quite, for out of the ashes there soon arose Bossa Nova – white, middle class and silky smooth. Vinícius de Moraes and Tom Jobim were its heroes; 1958 to 1964 the years; Copacabana, Ipanema and Leblon the scene; 'Samba de uma Nota Só', 'A Garota de Ipanema' and 'Desafinado' the songs and Nara Leão, Baden Powell, To quinho, João Gilberto, Luis Bonfá and Astrud Gilberto the main performers. Stan Getz, the American jazz saxophonist, helped export it to the world. What was now being called MPB (Música Popular Brasileira) then took off in several directions. Chico Buarque, Edu Lobo and Milton Nascimento were protest singers. Out of Bahia emerged 'Tropicalismo' in the persons of Gilberto Gil, Caetano Veloso and his sister Maria Bethânia, Gal Costa, João Gilberto and 'Som Livre'. The words were important, but the rhythm was still there. Brazilian rock also now appeared, with such stars as Roberto Carlos, Elis Regina, Rita Lee, and Ney Mattogrosso. Recently, in turning towards international black consciousness, the Bahianos have mixed Reggae and Samba to produce 'axê'. Still, Samba has survived, although now called 'Pagóde' and amazingly, 40% of all Brazilian records sold are of Música Sertaneja, a highly commercialized pseudofolk genre which is closer to American Country and Western than to most other Brazilian music. Listen to the 'Duplas' of Tonico & Tinoco, Jaco e Jacozinho or Vieira & Vieirinha and you'll see. In the meantime a series of brilliant Brazilian instrumentalists have become international names and often live abroad – Sérgio Mendes, the guitarist Sebastião Tapajós, flautist Hermêto Paschoal, saxophonist Paulo Moura, accordionist Sivuca, percussionists Airto Moreira and Nana Vasconcelos, singer Flora Purim and all-rounder Egberto Gismonti are but a few. On the top of a huge recording industry, we're now a long way from the grassroots and the haunting flute music of the forest Indians.

THE ECONOMY

Structure of production Brazil's economy is the largest in Latin America and the tenth in the world, but its gdp per capita has grown little since 1980 and is less than the average for the whole of Latin America and the Caribbean. It has abundant and varied natural resources, not all of which are fully explored or exploited. The 40 years after 1945 were a period of massive state intervention and industrialization with public sector investment in energy, heavy industry, transport equipment and capital goods, but in the 1990s the country has moved towards a market economy with a smaller role for the state.

Brazil remains a large farming country; processed and unprocessed agricultural products account for about a third of exports and agriculture, forestry and fishing account for 11% of gdp. Brazil is the world's largest producer and exporter of coffee and maintains a dominant position in international markets for soya and orange juice, mostly grown in the state of São Paulo. São Paulo state also produces over half Brazil's harvest of about 220 million tonnes of sugar cane, most of which is distilled into fuel alcohol for cars or electricity generating power plants. Although Brazil used to be the world's largest cocoa grower, with Ilhéus the main area of production, the industry has declined because of underinvestment, fungus and low prices and it is now ranked fourth. Most of Brazil's agricultural land is held by large landowners, with 10% of the farmers owning 80% of the land. Land reform is contentious and has proceeded very slowly with much conflict and violence. Up to 5 million families are believed to want land although only 130,000 were resettled in 1986-94. Holdings must be confirmed unproductive before they can be appropriated for settlement.

The country is richly endowed with metals and other minerals. Brazil has up to a third of the world's iron ore reserves, found mainly in Minas Gerais and certain parts of the Amazon basin, especially the Serra dos Carajás region (Pará). Brazil also exports manganese and produces increasing amounts of tin and copper. In 1996, the state mining company, Companhia Vale do Rio Doce (CVRD), announced a 150-tonne gold find near Carajás, which would make it the largest gold mine in Latin America. It is expected to produce 10 tonnes a year, about 20% of Brazil's present output. The mine is also near Serra Pelada, an open mine which in the 1980s attracted a gold rush of 80,000 garimpeiros, wildcat goldminers, but the new one is much deeper and not suitable for being dug by hand. CVRD is one of the world's largest natural resources groups and owns mining and exploration rights worth an estimated US$40bn, including Carajás, where reserves of iron ore are sufficient for 500 years. As well as gold and iron ore, it is involved in steel, aluminium, forestry, railways and port and shipping facilities. The Government has gradually reduced its stake in CVRD to 51% and this holding is due for privatization in 1996/97.

Industrial production accounts for 36% of gdp and sales of mechanical equipment, cars, chemicals, textiles and other manufactures account for the majority of exports. The steel and vehicle industries are among the top 10 in the world. Brasmotor, a consumer goods conglomerate, is the world's second largest producer of compressors. Ceval and Sadia, two large food processing companies, have annual exports of over US$1bn, while Brahma, the largest brewer in Latin America, also exports. The Mercosur free trade area has encouraged exporters to look for markets in neighbouring countries instead of concentrating on the USA and Europe. Privatization, the abolition of price controls and falling tariffs have forced increased efficiency and productivity on to Brazilian companies, which have had to invest in modernization and gear their strategy to coping with competition rather than hyperinflation.

Energy sector development was aimed at substituting local for imported energy. The oil industry was nationalized in 1953 and the state monopoly, Petrobrás, controlled exploration, production, refining and distribution of oil and gas. In 1995, however, Congress voted to end that monopoly and allow private sector companies to compete with Petrobrás. Oil production averages 800,000 b/d; reserves are 10.3 billion barrels, of which 5.1 billion are proven, while gas reserves are 147 billion cu m. Large investments have been made in hydroelectricity, alcohol and nuclear power. A 620-MW nuclear power plant at Angra dos Reis (Rio de Janeiro) came on stream in 1985, but financial restrictions have slowed nuclear and other electricity development. The system's total capacity in 1995 was 52,700MW, but investment was not keeping pace with demand of about 5% a year, so shortages and power cuts were affecting parts of the country. It is estimated that 10% of homes are not connected to the electricity grid, having improved from 47% in 1970, and some 16% of energy distributed is not paid for because of illegal connections. Constitutional restrictions prevent sweeping privatization, although some states are pursuing sales of their

Brazil : fact file

Geographic

Land area	8,547.404 sq km
forested	57.7%
pastures	21.9%
cultivated	5.8%

Demographic

Population (1995)	155,822,000
annual growth rate (1990-95)	1.5%
urban	70.8%
rural	29.2%
density	18.2 per sq km
Religious affiliation	
Roman Catholic	70%
Birth rate per 1,000 (1994)	21.0
	(world av 25.0)

Education and Health

Life expectancy at birth,	
male	57.0 years
female	67.0 years
Infant mortality rate	
per 1,000 live births (1994)	60
Physicians (1992)	1 per 715 persons
Hospital beds (1990)	1 per 271 persons
Calorie intake as %	
of FAO requirement	118%
Population age 10 and over	
with no formal schooling	18.1%
Literate males (over 15)	83.3%
Literate females (over 15)	83.2%

Economic

GNP (1993 market price)	
	US$471,978mn
GNP per capita	US$3,020
Public external debt (1993)	
	US$86,650mn
Tourism receipts (1993)	
	US$1,449mn
Inflation (annual av 1989-94)	1,525%
Radio	1 per 2.9 persons
Television	1 per 5.3 persons
Telephone	1 per 13 persons

Employment

Population economically active (1990)	
	64,467,981
Unemployment rate (1994-registered)	
	6.0%
% of labour force in	
agriculture	22.0
manufacturing	14.6
mining and public utilities	1.3
construction	5.9
Military forces (1995)	295,000

Source *Encyclopaedia Britannica InterAmerican Development Bank*

Debt – the Rise and ....

During the 1970s large, costly development projects were financed by foreign borrowing. Brazil accumulated the region's largest external debt which became unsustainable in the 1980s. From 1982 annual rescheduling agreements were concluded with creditors, with new money and, in 1983-85, IMF standby facilities. These arrangements did not, however, help to reduce the burden of interest payments and in 1987 Brazil declared a moratorium on interest in order to preserve foreign exchange reserves and halt the net transfer of resources to creditors. The plan failed and a year later reserves were even lower as lenders declined to extend credit. In 1988 Brazil negotiated a financing package from all creditors aimed at restoring its creditworthiness, but by 1989 it had moved back into arrears. In 1992 another IMF standby agreement was made, allowing further debt rescheduling with the Paris Club of creditor governments, but the facility collapsed later in the year. Despite the lack of IMF approval for its economic management, Brazil managed to clinch a deal with its commercial bank creditors to restructure US$49bn of debt in 1994, using so-called Brady bonds as collateral. By 1995 all the collateral for the bonds had been deposited and with reserves of US$40bn, Brazil was expected to start a buy-back programme, taking advantage of the market discount.

regional utilities. Parts of the state company, Eletrobrás', operations are planned for eventual sale, leaving nuclear power and the Itaipú hydroelectric dam (jointly owned with Paraguay) in state hands. Independent energy producers have been permitted to operate since 1995 but the lack of enabling legislation delayed progress.

Recent trends High inflation in the 1980s and the early 1990s proved intractable as successive governments introduced stabilization programmes with new currencies but limited success. The principal cause of failure was the lack of political will to tackle the structural causes of inflation, namely the public accounts disequilibrium, supply bottlenecks, inefficiencies and corruption in state governments and enterprises, and widespread indexation of wages, prices and financial instruments. It was not until May 1993, with the appointment of Fernando Henrique Cardoso as Finance Minister that a plan was implemented which contained stringent measures to strengthen the public accounts and thus reduce inflation. However, cooperation from powerful political interests was not forthcoming and inflation soared. On 1 July 1994, a new currency, the real, was introduced at par with the US dollar.

Inflation immediately plummeted from over 50% a month to less than 2% and while interest rates remained high, the real appreciated. As confidence in the programme grew and price stability led to a rise in real wages, consumer spending also increased. The feelgood factor helped the election of Cardoso to the Presidency. Imports soared while exports were diverted to the domestic market. Investment picked up and gdp rose by 5.7%, the highest growth rate since 1986. By the end of the year Brazil was recording monthly trade deficits for the first time since the mid-1980s. Despite reserves of some US$40bn to support the real, the Mexican financial crisis at the same time brought a bad case of nerves in the financial markets. The Government adjusted the exchange rate regime, introducing a range of floating bands within which the real would trade, raised some tariffs to curb imports and imposed emergency measures to balance the budget. By mid-1995 the trade account was in surplus again.

The Government's reform programme encompasses three main areas, all requiring changes to the 1988 Constitution: the responsibilities and spending obligations of the central government to be devolved to local government and the private sector; government revenue to be raised by an overhaul of the tax system; the social security system to be reformed (beneficiaries exceed contributors, costing US$28bn in 1995 compared with US$14bn in 1992). Bills for the reform of the tax and social security systems were sent to Congress, where progress was painfully slow. Privatization was to be extended to cover energy, transport, telecommunications and mining, while removing some constitutional restrictions on competition, allowing the private sector to compete with or enter into joint ventures with state enterprises such as the oil company, Petrobrás. Priority spending plans have been announced for social spending (particularly health, education and sanitation) and infrastructure (roads, railways, waterways and telecommunications) amounting to US$161bn by the end of the century, some of which will be in joint ventures with the private sector.

GOVERNMENT

Constitution
The 1988 constitution provides for an executive president elected by direct popular vote, balanced by a bicameral legislature (81 seats in the Federal Senate, 513 seats in the Chamber of Deputies) and an independent judiciary. The vote has been extended to 16-year-olds and illiterates. Presidential elections are held every 5 years, with a second round 1 month after the first if no candidate wins an outright majority. Congressional elections are held every 4 years, the deputies being chosen by proportional representation.

Local administration
Each state has a popularly-elected Governor who exercises the executive power, and

a Legislative Assembly which legislates on all matters affecting provincial administration and provides for state expenses and needs by levying taxes. Each municipality has a similar structure, with a mayor (*prefeito*), also popularly elected, and a local council (*câmara de vereadores*).

COMMUNICATIONS

Railways
There are 30,379 km of railways originally built to supply export markets, but not combined into a unified system. Brazil has two gauges and there is little transfer between them (some sections have been made mixed gauge). Two more gauges exist for the isolated Amapá Railway and the tourist-only São João del Rei line. Many lines have been closed in recent years.

Roads
Though the best paved highways are heavily concentrated in the SE, those serving the interior are being improved to all-weather status and many are paved. Brazil has over 1.65 million km of highways, of which 150,000 km are paved, and several thousand more all-weather. Recent road-building programmes have emphasized inter-regional connections and the opening up of the Centre, N and W of the country. Nationwide bus services are frequent and good.

Air services
The first commercial flight in Brazil was in 1927. Because of the great distances, aircraft have eased the traveller's lot spectacularly in Brazil. The larger cities are linked with each other several times a day, and even the more remote points can be reached by light aircraft.

Brasília

THE PURPOSE-BUILT federal capital of Brazil, with its late 20th century design and its overflow communities, succeeded Rio de Janeiro (as required by the Constitution) on 21 April 1960.

(*Pop* 411,000 (census); 1,600,000 (1992 est); *Alt* 1,150m; *CEP* 7000, *DDD* 061)

Brasília is 960 km away from Rio de Janeiro on undulating ground in the unpopulated uplands of Goiás, in the heart of the undeveloped Sertão. The official name for central Brasília is the Plano Piloto.

The Federal District has an area of 5,814 sq km. The climate is mild and the humidity refreshingly low, but trying in dry weather. The noonday sun beats hard, but summer brings heavy rains and the air is usually cool by night. Only light industry is allowed in the city and its population was limited to 500,000; this has been exceeded and more people live in a number of shanty towns, with minimal services, located well away from the main city.

History and design

The creation of an inland capital had been urged since the beginning of the last century, but it was finally brought into being after President Kubitschek came to power in 1956, when a competition for the best general plan was won by Professor Lúcio Costa, who laid out the city in the shape of a bent bow and arrow. (It is also described as a bird, or aeroplane, in flight.)

Along the curve of the bow are the residential areas made up of large 6-storey apartment blocks, the 'Super-Quad-

ras'. They lie on either side (E and W) of the 'bow' (the Eixo Rodoviário) and are numbered according to their relation to the Eixo and their distance from the centre. Thus the 100s and 300s lie W of the Eixo and the 200s and 400s to the E; Quadras 302, 102, 202 and 402 are nearest the centre and 316, 116, 216 and 416 mark the end of the Plano Piloto. The numbering applies equally on either side of the centre, the two halves of the city being referred to as Asa Sul and Asa Nte (the N and S wings). Thus, for example, 116 Sul and 116 Nte are at the extreme opposite ends of the city. Each Super-Quadra houses 3,000 people and has a primary school and playgroup. Each group of four Super-Quadras should have a library, police station, club, supermarket and secondary school. All Quadras are separated by feeder roads, along which are the local shops. There are also a number of schools, parks and cinemas in the spaces between the Quadras (especially in Asa Sul), though not as systematically as was originally envisaged. On the outer side of the 300s and extending the length of the city is the Av W3 and on the outer side of the 400s is the Av L2, both of these being similarly divided into N and S according to the part of the city they are in.

Asa Sul is almost complete and Asa Nte is growing very fast, with standards of architecture and urbanization that promise to make it more attractive than Asa Sul in the near future. The main shopping areas, with more cinemas, restaurants and so on, are situated on either side of the old bus station (rodoviária). There are now several parks, or at least green areas. The private residential areas are W of the Super-Quadras, and on the other side of the lake.

At right angles to these residential areas is the 'arrow', the 8-km long, 250m wide **Eixo Monumental**. The main N-S road (Eixo Rodoviário), in which fast-moving traffic is segregated, follows the curve of the bow; the radial road is along the line of the arrow – intersections are avoided by means of underpasses and cloverleaves. Motor and pedestrian traffic is segregated in the residential areas.

PLACES OF INTEREST

At the tip of the arrow, as it were, is the **Praça dos Três Poderes**, with the Congress buildings, the Palácio do Planalto (the President's office), the Palácio da Justiça and the Panteão Tancredo Neves. 19 tall Ministry buildings line the Esplanada dos Ministérios, W of the Praça, culminating in two towers linked by a walkway to form the letter H, representing Humanity. They are 28 storeys high: no taller buildings are allowed in Brasília. Where the bow and arrow intersect is the city bus terminal (rodoviária), with the cultural and recreational centres and commercial and financial areas on either side. There is a sequence of zones westward along the shaft of the arrow; a hotel centre, a radio city, an area for fairs and circuses, a centre for sports, the **Praça Municipal** (with the municipal offices in the Palácio do Buriti) and, lastly (where the nock of the arrow would be) the combined new bus and railway station (rodoferroviária) with the industrial area nearby. The most impressive buildings are all by Oscar Niemeyer, Brazil's leading architect.

The **Palácio da Alvorada**, the President's official residence (not open to visitors), with a family of emus on the lawn, is on the the lakeshore. The 80-km

drive along the road round the lake to the dam is attractive. There are spectacular falls below the dam in the rainy season. Between the Praça dos Três Poderes and the lake are sites for various recreations, including golf, fishing and yacht clubs, and an acoustic shell for shows in the open air. The airport is at the eastern end of the lake. Some 395 ha between the lake and the northern residential area (Asa Nte) are reserved for the Universidade de Brasília, founded in 1961. South of the university area, the Av das Nações runs from the Palácio da Alvorada along the lake to join the road from the airport to the centre. Along it are found all the principal embassies. Also in this area is the attractive vice-presidential residence, the **Palácio do Jaburu**, not open to visitors. This area is almost completed and very scenic.

Overview

A fine initial view of the city may be had from the **television tower**, which has a free observation platform at 75m up; also bar and souvenir shop; closes for maintenance on Mon mornings. If the TV tower is closed, the nearby *Alvorada* hotel has a panoramic terrace on the 12th floor (lift to 11th only): ask at reception. A general impression can be gained in a day by bus or taxi tour – don't try walking much unless fit and fairly impervious to heat. This impression is best gained at weekends when the city is quieter, though then there are fewer buses to move you around (some say the city is "totally dead" at weekends). The city can also be seen at night by taking the Alvorada circular bus from the old rodoviária. Bus maps are not available although buses are plentiful; each bus stop has a list of the services that stop there, but you still need to know which one you require. It is worth telephoning addresses away from the centre to ask how to get there. An urban railway, Metrô, is under construction.

Tours A good and cheap way of seeing Brasília is by taking bus rides from the municipal rodoviária at the centre: the destinations are clearly marked. The circular bus routes 106, 108 and 131 go round the city's perimeter. If you go around the lake by bus, you must change at the Paranoá dam; to or from Paranoá Nte take bus 101, 'Rodoviária', and to and from Sul, bus 100, bypassing the airport. Tours, from 1300-1700, start from the downtown hotel area and municipal ro-

doviária (US$12-20). Many hotels arrange city tours.

● **Tour companies** All tour operators have their offices in the shopping arcade of the *Hotel Nacional*; *Toscana* has been rec as cheap and

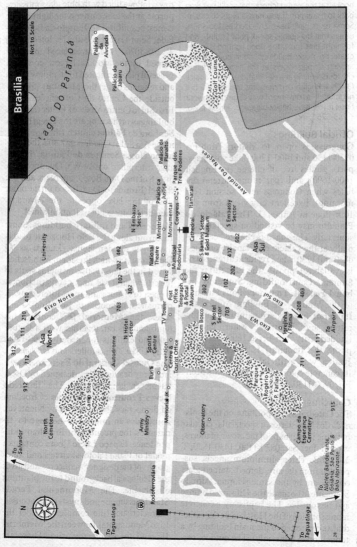

Brasília

Not to Scale

Lago Do Paranoá

Palácio da Alvorada

Palácio da Jaburu

Golf Course

Palácio da Planalto

Parque dos Três Poderes

Avenida das Nações

N Embassy Sector

Palácio Ea Justiça

Ministries

Palácio Itamaratí

Monumental

Congress

Cathedral

S Embassy Sector

602

University

National Theatre

Municipal Rodoviária

S Banking Setor & Gold Museum

412

202

Asa Sul

Eixo Norte

102 202 402

Eixo

302

Post Office

Telegraph & Postal Museum

102

302

Eixo Sul

703 210 410

703

TV Tower

S Hotel Sector

703

208 409

312 111

912 712

Asa Norte

N Hotel Sector

Autodrome

Sports Centre

Dom Bosco

Eixo W3

Igrejinha Fátima

311 111

To Airport

711

Convention Centre & Tourist Office

Burití

915

To Salvador

Camp Site

Memorial JK

Army Ministry

Observatory

Parque Rogério P Farias

Campo da Esperança Cemetery

North Cemetery

N

Rodoferroviária

Rodoviária

To Taguatinga

To Taguatinga

To Núcleo Bandeirante, Goiânia, São Paulo & Belo Horizonte

28

good. *Presmic Turismo*, Galeria do Hotel Nacional, lojas 33/34, T 225-5515, offers full-, half-day and night-time tours (0845, 1400 and 1930 respectively). *Kubitschek Turismo* (Lucas Milhomens – speaks English), T 347-1494, rec for city tour and information. Tours can also be booked at the airport (check that you'll be taken back to the airport if you have a flight to catch). Some tours have been criticized as too short, others that the guides speak poor English, and for night-time tours, the flood lighting is inadequate on many buildings. Tour guides meet arriving air passengers at the airport, offering city tours, ending at a destination of your choice (3-4 hrs, English commentary, inexpensive but negotiate) – a convenient way of getting to your hotel if you have heavy baggage. Teresa Tasso, T 243-5251, rec.

Official Buildings

Congress is open to visitors Mon-Fri 0930-1130 and 1400-1700 (take your passport), guides free of charge (in English 1400-1600), and visitors may attend debates when Congress is in session (Fri morning). Excellent city views from the 10th floor in Annex 3. The **Palácio do Planalto** may be visited on special occasions only. The guard is changed ceremonially at the Palácio do Planalto on Tues, 0830 and 1730. The President attends if he is available. Opposite the Planalto is the Supreme Court building, **Supremo Tribunal Federal**. The marvellous building of the Ministry of Foreign Affairs, the **Itamarati**, has modern paintings and furniture and beautiful water gardens (guided visits Mon-Fri at 1600, free). Opposite the Itamarati is the **Palácio de Justiça**, with artificial cascades between its concrete columns, visiting hours Mon-Fri, 0900-1130, 1500-1700.

Churches

The **Catedral Metropolitana**, on the Esplanada dos Ministérios, a spectacular circular building in the shape of the crown of thorns, is open Tues-Sat, 0830-1130, 1430-1830, T 224 4073. Three aluminium angels, suspended from the airy, domed, stained-glass ceiling, are by the same sculptor, Alfredo Scesciatte, who made the 4 life-sized bronze apostles outside. The baptistery, a concrete representation of the Host beside the cathedral, is connected to the main building by a tunnel (open Suns only). The outdoor carillon was a gift from the Spanish government: the bells are named after Columbus's ships. West of the TV tower on Av W3 Sul, at Quadra 702, is the Sanctuary of **Dom Bosco**, a square building with narrow windows filled with blue glass mosaics, purple at the four corners; the light inside is most beautiful. The **Templo da Boa Vontade**, Setor Garagem Sul 915, lotes 75/76, T 245-1070, is a seven-faced pyramid topped by the world's largest crystal, a peaceful place dedicated to all philosophies and religions (to get there take bus 151 from outside the Centro do Convenções or on Eixo Sul to Centro Médico). Other religious buildings worth seeing are the **Igreja Nossa Senhora de Fátima** church (the Igrejinha) in the Asa Sul at Quadras 307-308, the **Santuário Nossa Senhora de Fátima**, the 'orange caterpillar' on Av W5, Quadra 906, a little S of the Dom Bosco sanctuary, and the chapel (**Ermida**) of Dom Bosco, on the other side of the lake opposite the Alvorada, though the site is not well maintained.

Memorials and military buildings Some 15 km out along the Belo Horizonte road is the small wooden house, known as '**O Catetinho**', in which President Kubitschek stayed in the late 1950s during his visits to the city when it was under construction; it is open to visitors and most interesting. A permanent memorial to Juscelino Kubitschek, the '**Memorial JK**', contains his tomb and his car, together with a lecture hall and exhibits (open daily 0900-1800, entry US$0.50, has toilets and *lanchonete*). The **Quartel-General do Exército**, Brazilian Army headquarters, designed by Oscar Niemeyer, is interesting. The **Tancredo Neves Pantheon** is a 'temple of freedom an democracy', built 1985-6 by Niemeyer. It includes an impressive homage to Tiradentes, the precursor of Brazilian independence. **Espaço Lúcio Costa** contains a model of Plano Piloto, sketches and autographs of the designer's concepts and gives the ideological background to the planning of Brasília. The **Monumental Parade Stand** has unique and mysterious acoustic characteristics (the complex is N of the Eixo Monumental, between the 'Memorial JK' and the rodoferroviária). There are

also at airport. **Banco Econômico**, Setor Comercial Sul, Subterraneo (currency and Amex cheques), 1045-1630; **American Express**, *Buriti Turismo*, CLS 402 Bloco A, Lojas 27/33, T 225-2686. **Diners Club** office, Av W3 Nte 502. **Mastercard**, for cash against a card, SCRN 502, bl B, lojas 30 e 31, Asa Nte. Good exchange rates at *Hotel Nacional*. Good exchange rates from hotels with 'exchange-turismo' sign.

● **Cultural centres**
British Council: SCRN 708/709 B1 F No 1/3, T 272-3060, F 272-3455. **Cultura Inglesa**, SEPS 709/908 Conj B, T 243-3065. **American Library**: Casa Thomas Jefferson, Av W4 Sul, quadra 706, T 243-6588. **Aliança Francesa**, Sul Entrequadra 707-907, Bloco A, T 242-7500; **Instituto Cultural Goethe**, Edifício Dom Bosco, Setor Garagem Sul 902, Lote 73, Bloco C, T 224-6773, Mon-Fri, 0800-1200, also 1600-2000, Mon, Wed, Thur.

● **Electric current**
220 volts, 60 cycles.

● **Embassies & consulates**
British: SES, Quadra 801, Conjunto K (with British Commonwealth Chamber of Commerce), or Av das Nações, Caixa Postal 070586, T 225-2710. **USA**: SES, Av das Nações 3, T 321-7272. **Australian**: Caixa Postal 11-1256, SHIS QI-09, Conj 16, Casa 1, T 248-5569 (in residential district, S of the lake). **Canadian**: SES, Av das Nações 16, T 223-7665. **Danish**, Av das Nações 26, CP 07-0484, T 242-8188, open 0900-1200, 1400-1700. **German**: SES, Av das Nações 25, T 243-7466. **Netherlands**: SES, Av das Nações 5, T 321-4769. **Swiss**: SES, Av das Nações 41, T 244-5500; **Austrian**: SES, Av das Nações 40, T 243-3111; **Finnish**: SES, Av das Nações, lote 27, T 242-8555; **Swedish**: Av das Nações 29, Caixa Postal 07-0419, T 243-1444. **Venezuela**: SES, Av das Nações 13, T 223-9325; **Guyana**: SDS, Edifício Venâncio III, 4th floor, sala 410/404, T 224-9229; **Greek**: T 248-1127 248-0920, Shis Q1, 4 Conjunto 1, Casa 18, 704610.

● **Entertainment**
There are three auditoria of the *Teatro Nacional*, the Sala Villa-Lobos (1,300 seats), the Sala Martins Pena (450), and the Sala Padre José Maurício (120); the building is in the shape of an Aztec pyramid.

The Federal District authorities have two theatres, the *Galpão* and *Galpãozinho*, between Quadra 308 Sul and Av W3 Sul. Concerts are given at the *Escola Parque* (Quadras 507-508 Sul), the *Ginásio Presidente Medici* (Eixo Monumental, nr TV tower), the *Escola de Música* (Av L2 Sul, Quadra 602) and the outdoor *Concha Acústica* (edge of lake in the Setor Hoteleiro Nte). *Planetarium*, on the Eixo next to the TV tower, gives shows Sat and Sun at 1600 and 1700.

Information about entertainment etc is available in two daily papers, *Jornal de Brasília* and *Correio Brasiliense*. Any student card (provided it has a photograph) will get you into the cinema/theatre/concert hall for half price. Ask for 'uma meia' at the box office.

Cinema: there are 15 cinemas in the Plano Piloto; programmes are available daily by phoning 139, entrance is half price on Wed.

Nightclubs: in Conjunto Venâncio, in Centro Gilberto Salomão and in the main hotels.

● **Post & telecommunications**
Post Office: Poste restante, Central Correio, 70001; SBN-Cj 03, BL-A, Ed Sede da ECT, the central office is in the Setor Hoteleiro Sul, between *Hotels Nacional* and *St Paul*. Another post office is in Ed Brasília Rádio, Av 3 Nte.

● **Shopping**
There are eight big shopping complexes, inc the vast *Conjunto Nacional* on the N side of the rodoviária, the *Conjunto Venâncio* on the S side, the *Centro Venâncio 2000* at the beginning of Av W3 Sul, the *Centro Venâncio 3000* in the Setor Comercial Nte, *Parkshopping* and the *Carrefour* hypermarket just off the exit to Guará, 12 km from centre. For fine jewellery, *H Stern* has branches in the *Nacional* and *Carlton* Hotels and at the Conjunto Nacional and Parkshopping. The embassy sector is good for low-priced, high quality men's wear. For handicrafts try *Galeria dos Estados* (which runs underneath the *eixo* from Setor Comercial Sul to Setor Bancário Sul, 10 mins' walk from municipal rodoviária, S along Eixo Rodoviário Sul) with shops selling handicrafts from all the Brazilian states; for Amerindian handicrafts, *Artíndia* in the rodoviária and at the airport. Dried flowers (typical of the region) outside the Cathedral (but not always). There is a *feira hippy* at the base of the TV tower every Sat, Sun and holiday: leather goods, wood carvings, jewellery, bronzes. English books (good selection) at *Livraria Sodiler* in Conjunto Nacional and at the airport.

● **Tour companies & travel agents**
Buriti Turismo Ltda, Cls 402, Bloco A, Lojas 27/33, T 225 2686. *Jahjah Turismo*, CRS 504, bloco A, Loja 11, friendly.

● **Tourist offices**
At the Centro de Convenções (Detur, helpful, good map of Brasília, open to public 1300-1800 – ask for Eliane, who speaks English, T 321-3318); small stand at rodoferroviária, friendly but not very knowledgeable (open 24 hrs, every day). Tourist office at the Air Terminal is on the international arrival side only, will book hotels, generally helpful; French and English spoken. Detur publishes a book called *Brasília, Coração*

Brasileiro, which is full of practical information. **Touring Club do Brasil**, on Eixo, has maps (members only). The information office in the centre of Praça dos Tres Poderes has a colourful map and lots of useful text information. The staff are friendly and have interesting information about Brasília and other places in Goias – only Portuguese spoken. **Maps** 'Comapa', Venâncio 200 business complex, 2nd floor, have expensive maps. 'Didactica', a schoolbook shop in the city rodoviária sell maps of Brazil for US$8.4.

● **Transport**
Car hire: about 9 agencies, inc Budget, Hertz, Locarauto.

Air Varig to Rio and São Paulo regular service (1½ hrs in both cases); daily flights to other main cities; regional services to the interior of Goiás, São Paulo, Pará, Manaus (2½ hrs), etc. Very few services for individual travellers. Airline offices are in the *Hotel Nacional* building. Bus 102 or 118 to airport, regular, US$0.65, 30 mins. Taxi is US$10 after bargaining, worth it. Left luggage facilities at airport (tokens for lockers, US$0.50). Airport tax US$1.25.

Buses The bus terminal (rodoferroviária) beside the railway station, from which long-distance buses leave, has post office (0800-1700, Sat 0800-1200), telephone and telegram facilities. Bus 131 between rodoviária, the municipal terminal, and rodoferroviária, US$1; taxi rodoferroviária to Setor Hoteleiro Nte, US$7. There are showers (US$0.50). Both bus stations have large luggage lockers. To **Rio**: 17 hrs, 6 *comuns* (US$38) and 3 *leitos* (about US$74) daily. To **São Paulo**: 16 hrs, 7 *comuns* (about US$33) and 2 *leitos* (about US$66) daily (Rápido Federal rec). To **Belo Horizonte**: 12 hrs, 9 *comuns* (US$23) and 2 *leitos* (US$46) daily. To **Belém**: 36 hrs, 4 daily (US$66, Trans Brasília T 233-7589, buses poorly maintained, but no alternative), *leito* (US$132) Tues, Wed and Sat. To **Recife**: 40 hrs. To **Salvador**: 24 hrs, 3 daily (US$45). **Mato Grosso**: generally Goiânia seems to be the better place for Mato Grosso destinations. There is a bus which goes as far as Vila Rica on the BR150 Xavantes. **Barra do Graças**: 0830 and 2000, takes 9 hrs with Araguarina, T 233-7598, US$15.25 return: **Marabá**: no direct connection, from Brasília: Manaus via Porto Velho and Cuiabá involves several changes, taking up to 6 days (road is good as far as Porto Velho). All major destinations served. Bus tickets for major companies are sold in a subsidiary office in Taguatinga, Centro Ote, C8, Lotes 1 and 2, Loja 1; and at the city rodoviária.

ROUTES From Saída Sul (the southern end of the Eixo) the BR-040/050 goes to Cristalina where it divides; the BR-040 continues to Belo Horizonte and Rio de Janeiro, the BR-050 to Uberlândia and São Paulo (both paved).

Also from Saída Sul, the BR-060 to Anápolis, Goiânia and Cuiabá; from Anápolis the BR-153 (Belém-Brasília) heads N to Belém (paved – for a description of this road, see page 627) and from Goiânia the BR-153 goes S through the interior of the states of São Paulo and Paraná (also paved).

From Saída Nte (the northern end of the Eixo) the BR-020 goes N to **Formosa** (1½ hrs by frequent buses from Brasília, **E** *Hotel Mineiro* and one other, G, clean and friendly; cheap restaurants), Barreiras, and after Barreiras on the BR-242 (all paved) to Salvador and Fortaleza. The BR020 is in good condition for 120 km. At Alvorado do Nte (130 km) there are cheap but very basic hotels. **Posse** (295 km) is picturesque. **Accommodation** on Av Padre Trajeiro (inc *Hoki Mundial*, friendly). The road is slow with many potholes until Barreiras.

● **Road distances** in km: Belém, 2,120; Campo Grande, 1,134; Corumbá, 1,531; Cuiabá, 1,133; Foz do Iguaçu, 1,573; Goiânia, 209; Manaus, 3,490; Porto Alegre, 2,027; Recife, 2,220; Rio, 1,148; Salvador, 1,531; São Paulo, 1,015.

DISTRITO FEDERAL

Of the seven *cidades satélites* that contain between them over half the Federal District's population, five are new and two (Brazlândia and Planaltina) are based on pre-existing settlements.

Planaltina

Planaltina, 40 km N of the Plano Piloto via Saída Nte, the town (*pop* 50,000) was originally a settlement on the colonial pack route from the mines of Goiás and Cuiabá to the coast. The old part still contains many colonial buildings. There are two good *churrascarias* on the main street and it is a good place for a rural Sun lunch. 5 km outside Planaltina is the Pedra Fundamental, the foundation stone laid by President Epitácio Pessoa in 1922 to mark the site originally chosen for the new capital.

Just before Planaltina, at Km 30 on the road from Brasília, lies the point known as **Águas Emendadas**: from the same point spring two streams that flow in opposite directions to form part of the two great river systems – the Amazon and the Plate. Permission from the biological institute in Brasília is now required to visit the site. Continuing along the same road (BR-020), at Km 70 is the town of Formosa (see above). Some 20 km N of the town is the Itiquira waterfall (158m high).

From the top are spectacular views and the pools at the bottom offer good bathing. It is crowded at weekends. There are four smaller falls in the area. Camping is possible. To get there take the road into the centre of Formosa and follow the signs or ask. It is not possible to get by bus to the Itiquira falls from Brasília in one day; the only bus from Formosa to Itiquira leaves at 0730 and returns at 1700.

Cristalina
In the other direction (S), take the BR-040 (Belo Horizonte road) and at Km 104 take a left turn along a dirt road, just after the highway police post, to the Cristalina waterfall (11 km along this road). The town of **Cristalina** (*pop* 24,900) is famous for its semi-precious stones, which can be bought cheaply in local shops. The panning and mining sites amid magnificent rock formations are about 6 km away, an interesting excursion. Small municipal museum R 21 de Abril 156, 0800-1100, 1300-1700, except Tues. **D** *Hotel Goyás*, R da Saudade 41, fan, fridge, OK.

PARQUE NACIONAL DE BRASILIA
Northwest of Brasília, but only 15 mins by car from the centre is the **Parque Nacional de Brasília** (about 28,000 ha), founded in 1961 to conserve the flora and fauna of the Federal Capital. Only a portion of the park is open to the public without a permit. There is a swimming pool fed by clear river water, a snack bar and a series of trails through gallery forest (popular with joggers in early am and at weekends). The rest of the park is rolling grassland, gallery forest and *cerrado* vegetation. Large mammals include tapir, maned wolf and pampas deer; birdwatching is good (especially Brasília Tapaculo, Horned Sungem, Yellow-faced parrot, Least Nighthawk). Contact Focus Tours, Belo Horizonte (page 429) for birding and nature tours. For information, contact Delegacia Estadual do Ibama, Av W3 Nte, Quadra 513, Edif Imperador, rooms 301-320, or T 233-4055/234-9057.

For information on the State of Goiás, which surrounds the Federal District, see page 624.

State of Rio de Janeiro

THE world-renowned Rio, with its beautiful location, carnival and much more besides (not all of it delightful), plus the hill and beach resorts nearby.

The State of Rio de Janeiro covers 43,305 sq km (the size of Denmark) and in 1991 had a population of 12.6 million, 88% of whom lived in metropolitan areas. The State is Brazil's second-largest industrial producer.

Rio de Janeiro (*Pop* 5,336,180 – 1991 estimate; *CEP* 20000; *DDD* 021) is on the south-western shore of Guanabara Bay, 24 km long and from 3 to 16 km wide. The setting is magnificent. The city sweeps 20 km along a narrow alluvial strip between the mountains and the sea. The combination of a dark blue sea, studded with rocky islands, with the tumbling wooded mountains and expanses of bare grey rock which surround the city is very impressive. Brazilians say: God made the world in six days; the seventh he devoted to Rio (pronounced Heeoo by locals). God's work is now under threat from too many high-rise buildings and failure to maintain or clean the city adequately.

The best known of these rocky masses are the Pão de Açúcar (Sugar Loaf), the highest peak of a low chain of mountains on the fringe of the harbour, and the Corcovado (Hunchback), a jagged peak rising behind the city. There are other peaks, including Tijuca, the tallest point in the foreground, and 50 km away rise the strangely shaped Serra dos Órgãos.

Climate

Rio has one of the healthiest climates in the tropics. Trade winds cool the air. June, July and Aug are the coolest months with temperatures ranging from 22°C (18° in a cold spell) to 32°C on a sunny day at noon. Dec to Mar is hotter, from 32°C to 42°C. Humidity is high. It is important, especially for children, to guard against dehydration in summer by drinking as much liquid as possible. Oct to Mar is the rainy season, and the annual rainfall is about 1,120 mm.

History

The Portuguese navigator, Gonçalo Coelho, arrived at what is now Rio de Janeiro on 1 January 1502, but it was first settled by the French, who, under the Huguenot Admiral Villegaignon, occupied Lage Island on 10 November 1555, but later transferred to Sergipe Island (now Villegaignon), where they built the fort of Coligny. The fort has been demolished to make way for the Naval College (Escola Naval), and the island itself, since the narrow channel was filled up, has become a part of the mainland. In Jan 1567, Mem de Sá, third governor of Brazil, defeated the French in a sea battle and transferred the Portuguese settlement to the São Januário hill – the Esplanada do Castelo covers the site today. Though constantly attacked by Indians, the new city grew rapidly, and when King Sebastião divided Brazil into two provinces, Rio was chosen capital of the southern captaincies. Salvador became sole capital again in 1576, but Rio again became the southern capital in 1608 and the seat of a bishopric. There was a further French incursion in 1710-11.

Rio de Janeiro was by now becoming the leading city in Brazil. On 27 January 1763, it became the seat of the Viceroy. After independence, in 1834, it was declared capital of the Empire, and remained the capital for 125 years.

PLACES OF INTEREST

Two of the main streets are particularly impressive. The Av Rio Branco, nearly 2 km long and 33m wide, is intersected by the city's main artery, the Av Presidente Vargas, 4½ km long and over 90m wide, which starts at the waterfront, divides to embrace the famous Candelária church, then crosses the Av Rio Branco in a magnificent straight stretch past the Central do Brasil railway station, with its imposing clock tower, until finally it incorporates the palm-lined, canal-divided avenue formerly known as the Av Mangue. The Av Rio Branco is lined with ornate buildings, including the Museo Nacional de Belas Artes (in the old Academia de Belas Artes), Biblioteca Nacional and the Teatro Municipal. The R do Ouvidor, crossing the Av Rio Branco half way along its length, contains the centre's principal shops. Other shopping streets are the RR Gonçalves Dias, Sete de Setembro, Uruguaiana, Assembléia, and also the arcade running from Av Rio Branco to the R Gonçalves Dias. The most stylish shops, however, are to be found in Ipanema, Leblon and in the various large shopping centres in the city (see under **Shopping** below). The Av Beira Mar, with its royal palms, bougainvillaeas and handsome buildings, coasting the Botafogo and Flamengo beaches (too polluted for bathing), makes a splendid drive; its scenery is shared by the urban motorway along the beach over reclaimed land (the Aterro), which leads to Botafogo and through two tunnels to Copacabana, described on page 388. Some of the finest modern architecture is to be found along the Av República do Chile, such as the Petrobrás and National Housing Bank buildings, and the new Cathedral, dedicated in Nov 1976. There are many fine trees in the city.

Churches and religious foundations

Check opening hours before attempting to visit.

The oldest foundation is the convent of the **Ordem Terceiro do Monte do Carmo**, built early in the 17th century, now used as a school on R Primeiro de Março close to Praça 15 de Novembro. Its present church, the Carmo Church in R Primeiro de Março, next to the old cathedral, was built in the 1770s and rebuilt between 1797 and 1826. It has strikingly beautiful portals by Mestre Valentim, the son of a Portuguese nobleman and a slave

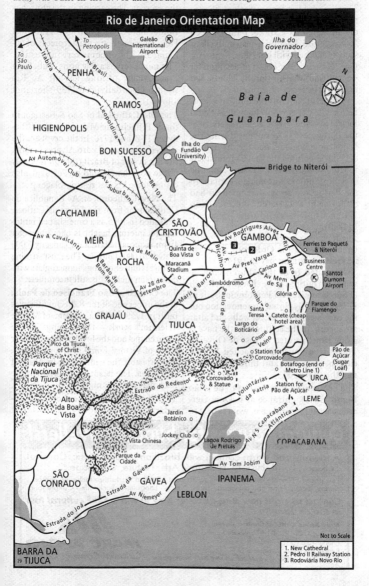

Rio de Janeiro Orientation Map

To Itabira
To Petrópolis
To São Paulo

Galeão International Airport

Ilha do Governador

PENHA

Av Brasil

RAMOS

Baía de Guanabara

HIGIENÓPOLIS

Av Automóvel Club

BON SUCESSO

Ilha do Fundão (University)

Bridge to Niterói

BR 101

Av Suburbana

CACHAMBI

Av A Cavalcánti

MÉIR

24 de Maio

Barão do Bom Retiro

ROCHA

Av 28 de Setembro

Maris e Barros

SÃO CRISTOVÃO

Quinta de Boa Vista

Maracanã Stadium

Sambódromo

Av Rodrigues Alves

GAMBOA

Av Pres Vargas

Ferries to Paquetá & Niterói

Business Centre

Santos Dumont Airport

Carioca

Av Mem de Sá

Glória

Parque do Flamengo

Paulo de Frontin

Santa Teresa

Catumbi

Cosme Velho

Largo do Boticário

Catete (cheap hotel area)

GRAJAÚ

TIJUCA

Pico da Tijuca of Christ

Parque Nacional da Tijuca

Estrada do Redentor

Station for Corcovado

Corcovado & Statue

Pão de Açúcar (Sugar Loaf)

Botafogo (end of Metro Line 1)

Station for Pão de Açúcar

URCA

LEME

Alto da Boa Vista

Voluntárias da Patria

Jardin Botánico

Vista Chinesa

Jockey Club

Lagoa Rodrigo de Freitas

Av S Copacabana

Atlântica

COPACABANA

Parque da Cidade

SÃO CONRADO

GÁVEA

Estrada da Gávea

Av Niemeyer

LEBLON

Av Tom Jobim

IPANEMA

Estrada do Joá

BARRA DA TIJUCA

Not to Scale

1. New Cathedral
2. Pedro II Railway Station
3. Rodoviária Novo Rio

girl. He also created the main altar of fine moulded silver, the throne and its chair, and much else.

The second oldest convent is the 17th century **Convento de Santo Antônio**, on a hill off the Largo da Carioca, built between 1608 and 1615. Its church has a marvellous sacristy adorned with blue tiles. Santo Antônio is a particular object of devotion for women who want to find husbands, and many will be seen in the precincts.

The crypt contains the tomb of a Scottish soldier of fortune known as 'Wild Jock of Skelater'. He was in the service of the Portuguese Government during the Napoleonic War, and had the distinction of being appointed the first Commander-in-Chief of the Army in Brazil. The statue of Santo Antônio was made a captain in the Portuguese army after his help had been sought to drive out the French in 1710, and his salary paid to the monastery. In 1810 the statue became a major, in 1814 a lieutenant-colonel, and was granted the Grand Cross of the Order of Christ. He was retired without pay in 1914.

Separated from this church only by some iron railings is the charming church of **São Francisco da Penitência**, built in 1773. Currently closed for renovation but the carving and gilding of walls and altar are superb. In the ceiling over the nave is a fine panel painted by José de Oliveira. There is a museum attached to the church, open first and third Sun of the month, 0700-1000.

The **Mosteiro** (monastery) **de São Bento** (1641); entrance at R Dom Gerardo 68, contains much of what is best in the 17th and 18th century art of Brazil. 'O Salvador', the masterpiece of Brazil's first painter, Frei Ricardo do Pilar, hangs in the sacristy. The carving in the church is particularly good. The Chapels of the Immaculate Conception and of the Most Holy Sacrament are masterpieces of colonial art. The organ is very interesting. The monastery is a few mins' walk from Praça Mauá, turning left off Av Rio Branco. Open daily 0800-1730 (shorts not allowed).

The **Old Cathedral** of São Sebastião, in the R Primeiro de Março, was built between 1749 and 1770. In the crypt are the alleged remains of Pedro Alvares Cabral, the discoverer of Brazil (though it is only fair to note that Santarém, Portugal, also claims to be his last resting-place).

The **New Cathedral**, on Av República do Chile not far from the Largo da Carioca, dedicated in 1976, is a cone-shaped building. Its internal height is 68m, diameter 104m, external height 83m; capacity 5,000 seated, 20,000 standing. The most striking feature is four enormous stained-glass windows (60m high). It is still incomplete.

The Church of **São Francisco de Paula**, at the upper end of the R do Ouvidor, was built in 1759. It contains some of Mestre Valentim's work – the carvings in the main chapel and the lovely Chapel of Our Lady of Victory. Some of the paintings, and probably the ceiling, are by Manuel da Cunha. The beautiful fountain at the back plays only at night.

The Church of **Nossa Senhora da Candelária** (1775-1810), on Praça Pio Dez, at

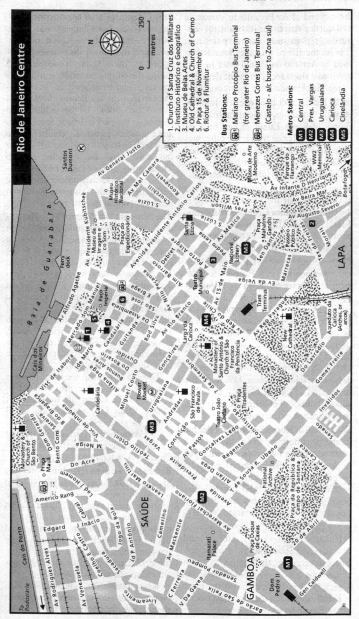

Rio de Janeiro Centre

N

0   250
metres

Bus Stations:

B1 Mariano Procópio Bus Terminal
    (for greater Rio de Janeiro)

B2 Menezes Cortes Bus Terminal
    (Castelo - a/c buses to Zona sul)

Metro Stations:

M1 Central
M2 Pres. Vargas
M3 Uruguaiana
M4 Carioca
M5 Cinelândia

1. Church of Santa Cruz dos Militares
2. Instituto Histórico e Geográfico
3. Museu de Belas Artes
4. Old Cathedral & Church of Carmo
5. Praça 15 de Novembro
6. Riotur & Flumitur

Santos Dumont

Av General Justo

Baía de Guanabara

Ferry dock

Cais dos Mineiros

Av Alfredo Agache

Mercado Dom Manuel

Av Mal Câmara

Churchill

S Luzia

Roosevelt

Avenida Presidente Antônio Carlos

Museu Histórico Nacional

Av Presidente Kubitschek

Museu da Imagem e do Som

Praça do Expedicionário

Debret

Graça Aranha

Porto Alegre

Santa Luzia

Padre Lessa

S Luzia

Av México

Beira Mar

Pres Wilson

Museu de Arte Moderno

WW2 Memorial

Parque do Flamengo

Av Infante D Henrique

Av Beira Mar

Av Augusto Severo

To Botafogo

National Library

Praça Mahatma Gandhi

Passeio Público

Marrecas

Sen Dan. Gandhi

Ev da Veiga

Paço Imperial

São José

Av Assembleia

Nilo Peçanha

Av Nilo Peçanha

Alm Barroso

Teatro Municipal

Av 13 de Maio

Av Rio Branco

Av Graça Aranha

Chile

R Sete de Setembro

Rosário

Do Rosário

Uruguaiana

Gonçalves Dias

Larga da Carioca

Carioca

Monastery & Church of Santo Antônio & Church of São Francisco da Penitência

Tram Terminus

Aqueduto da Carioca (Arches, or arcos)

Cathedral

Do Lavradio

Av Rep Paraguai

Gomes Freire

LAPA

Candelária

Ouvidor

Vist de Itaboraí

Miguel Couto

Visc de Inhaúma

Flower Market

Andradas

São Francisco de Paula

Teatro João Caetano

Praça Tiradentes

Constituição

Do Lavradio

Invalidos

Senado

Conceição

Av Passos

Gonçalves Ledo

Regente

Alfandega Dega

Rua da Alfandega

Buenos Aires

B do Bragança

Saravia

Bento Cons

Dom Gerado

Do Acre

Monastery & Church of São Bento

São Bento

Praça Mauá

Americo Rang

Teófilo Otôni

Senador Pompeu

Leandro Martins

Av Marechal Floriano

SAÚDE

Camerino

Av Mackenzie

Presidente

T de Sousa R. Ubano

National Archive

Praça da República & Campo de Santana

Gonçalves Dias

Praça Duque de Caxias

Nanãrati Palace

20 de Abril

Cais do Porto

To Rodoviária

Av Rodrigues Alves

Av Venezuela

Coelho E Castro

Sacadura

Jogo da Bola

J P Antônio

J Inácio

Edgard

C Ferreira

V Da Gávea

Barão de São Felix

Livramento

Senador Pompeu

GAMBOA

Dom II Pedro II

Gen Caldwell

the city end of Av Presidente Vargas, is well worth a visit to see its beautiful ceiling decorations and romantic paintings. It is on the site of a chapel founded in 1610 by Antônio da Palma after he had survived a shipwreck, an event depicted by paintings inside the present dome.

In the R de Santa Luzia, overwhelmed by tall office buildings, is the attractive little church of **Santa Luzia**. When built in 1752 it had only one tower; the other was added late in the 19th century. Feast day: 13 Dec, when devotees bathe their eyes with holy water, considered miraculous.

In the R Primeiro de Março, at the corner of Ouvidor (near the Old Cathedral), is the church of **Santa Cruz dos Militares**, built 1780-1811. It is large, stately and beautiful and has inside has been well renovated in a 'light' baroque style.

The beautiful little church on the Glória hill, overlooking the Parque do Flamengo, is **Nossa Senhora da Glória**. It was the favourite church of the imperial family; Dom Pedro II was baptized here. Built in 1791, it contains some excellent examples of blue-faced Brazilian tiling. Its main altar, of wood, was carved by Mestre Valentim. The church, open 0900-1200 (only Sat-Sun) and 1300-1700 weekdays, is reached by bus 119 from the centre and 571 from Copacabana. The adjacent museum of religious art is open on application to the priest.

The church of **Nossa Senhora da Penha**, in the N suburb of Penha (early 20th century), is on a bare rock in which 365 steps are cut. This staircase is ascended by pilgrims on their knees during the festival month of Oct; there is a funicular for those unable to do this. Bus 497 from Copacabana, 340 and 346 from centre.

When the Morro do Castelo was levelled to build the Esplanada do Castelo, the old church of **São Sebastião** had to be demolished. Its successor, the Capuchin church of São Sebastião in the R Haddock Lobo, Tijuca, built in 1936, contains the tomb of Estácio de Sá, founder and first Governor of Rio de Janeiro.

Parks, Squares and Monuments

On the Glória and Flamengo waterfront, with a view of the Pão de Açúcar and Corcovado, is the **Parque do Flamengo**, designed by Burle Marx, opened in 1965 during the 400th anniversary of the city's founding, and landscaped on 100 ha reclaimed from the Bay. Behind the War Memorial (see below) is the public yacht marina. In the park are many sports fields and a botanical garden; for children, there are a sailboat basin, a marionette theatre, a miniature village and a staffed nursery. There are night amusements, such as bandstands and areas for dancing. Security in the park is in the hands of vigilante policemen and it is a popular recreation area.

The National War Memorial to Brazil's dead in WW2 (Monumento aos Mortos na Segunda Guerra) and the Museu de Arte Moderna (see page 386) are at the city end of the park, opposite Praça Paris. The Memorial takes the form of two slender columns supporting a slightly curved slab, representing two palms uplifted to heaven. In the crypt are the remains of the Brazilian soldiers killed in Italy in 1944-45. It is well worth a visit, but beach clothes and rubber-thonged sandals are not permitted. The crypt and museum are open Tues-Sun 1000-1700.

Those who want to see what Rio was like early in the 19th century should go by bus to the **Largo do Boticário**, R Cosme Velho 822, a charming small square in pure colonial style. Buses to Cosme Velho from all parts of the city. The square is close to the terminus for the Corcovado rack railway (see page 390).

Botanical Gardens (Jardim Botânico) founded 1808, open 0800-1730 (US$1); well worth a visit. The most striking features are the transverse avenues of 30m royal palms. There are over 7,000 varieties of plants, herbarium, aquarium, and library (some labels are unclear). Many improvements were carried out before the 1992 Earth Summit, including a new Orquidário, an enlarged bookshop, a *lanchonete*, replanting and cleaning up. Visitors needing information in English should ask for Beatriz Heloisa Guimarães, of the Society of Friends of the Garden. The Gardens are 8 km from the centre, 140 ha in area; take any bus from the centre, eg 104, to Leblon, Gávea or São Conrado marked 'via Jóquei'. From Copacabana take bus 592.

Bird-watchers should visit the Botanical Gardens, preferably early in the morning. 140 species of birds have been recorded there. Flycatchers are very prominent (the social flycatcher, great and boat-billed kiskadees, cattle tyrant); also tanagers (the sayaca and palm tanagers, and the colourful green-headed tanager), and over 20 different kinds of hummingbird. Birds of prey include the roadside hawk, the laughing falcon and the American kestrel, and there are doves, cuckoos, parakeets, thrushes and woodpeckers, and occasional flocks of toucans. (John and George Newmark, Eastbourne).

Parque Laje, near the Jardim Botânico at R Jardim Botânico 414, almost junglelike, has small grottoes, an old tower and lakes, pleasant. (The Instituto Nacional de Belas Artes is housed in the mansion.) Open daily, 0730-1730, admittance free.

Quinta da Boa Vista, formerly the Emperor's private park, contains the zoo (see below) and many specimen trees. The Palace now houses the Museu Nacional (see page 386).

Jardim Zoológico, which contains Brazilian and imported wild animals, and a fine collection of birds (as well as many 'visitors' – also good for bird-watchers), is in the Quinta de Boa Vista (admission US$2). Open 0800-1800 daily, except Mon (best in the morning). The gateway is a replica of Robert Adam's famous gateway to Syon House, near London. Near the Zoological Gardens is the Museu de Fauna (see below). Take bus 474 or 472 from Copacabana or Flamengo; bus 262 from Praça Mauá.

Parque da Cidade A pleasant park a short walk beyond the Gávea bus terminus. It was previously the grounds of the home of the Guinle family, by whom it was presented to the City. Admission to the park is free; open Tues-Fri 0730-1730, Sat, Sun and holidays 1100-1700. The proximity of the Rocinha favela means that the park is not very safe. It is advisable to carry a copy of your passport here because of frequent police checks.

Jockey Club Racecourse, at Praça Santos Dumont, Gávea, meetings on Mon and Thur evenings and Sat and Sun 1400, entrance US$1-2, long trousers required, a table may be booked. Take any bus marked 'via Jóquei'. Betting is by totalizator only.

Praça da República and **Campo de Santana** is an extensive and picturesque public garden close to the Central Railway station. At Praça da República 197 lived Marshal Deodoro da Fonseca, who proclaimed Brazil a republic in 1889 (plaque). The Parque Júlio Furtado in the middle of the square is populated by agoutis (or gophers), best seen at dusk; there is also a little artificial grotto, with swans.

Passeio Público (turn right at S end of Av Rio Branco) is a garden planted by the artist Mestre Valentim, whose bust is near the old former gateway. Coin and stamp market on Sun, am.

Praça Quinze de Novembro contains the original royal palace (see page 386). Every Sat 0900-1900, flea market; nearby on the waterfront is a Sun antiques market, 1000-1800.

Praça Tiradentes, old and shady, has a statue to D Pedro I. Shops in nearby streets specialize in selling goods for *umbanda* and *macumba* – African-based religion and magic respectively.

Praça Mahatma Gandhi, at the end of Av Rio Branco, is flanked on one side by the cinema and amusement centre of the city, known as Cinelândia. The fountain (1789) by Mestre Valentim in the ornamental garden was moved here from Praça Quinze de Novembro in 1979.

Parque do Catete is a charming small park between the Palácio do Catete (Museu da República) and Praia do Flamengo; it has many birds and monkeys.

Praça Paris, built on reclaimed ground near the Largo da Glória, is much admired for the beauty of its formal gardens and illuminated fountains.

Largo da Carioca, remarkable ensemble of old and new plus the muddle of the street vendors who have occupied the square beween R da Carioca and the Metro.

Fountains The oldest, the Fonte da Glória (1789), has eight bronze spouts. Possibly the finest, although now sadly neglected, is at the back of the church of São Francisco de Paula, at the inland end of the R do Ouvidor. These, and nine other old fountains, are illuminated by night.

Museums and other Public Buildings

All museums and the Jardim Botânico are closed over Carnival.

The **Museu Nacional** in the Quinta da Boa Vista has important collections which are poorly displayed. The park surrounding it is dangerous. The building was the principal palace of the Emperors of Brazil, but only the unfurnished Throne Room and ambassadorial reception room on the 2nd floor reflect past glories. In the entrance hall is the famous Bêndego meteorite, found in the State of Bahia in 1888; its original weight, before some of it was chipped, was 5,360 kg. Besides several foreign collections of note, the Museum contains collections of Brazilian Indian weapons, dresses, utensils, etc, of minerals and of historical documents. There are also collections of birds, beasts, fishes, and butterflies. Open 1000-1630, closed Mon; entrance US$1. Buses: 472, 474, 475 from centre, Flamengo and Copacabana, 583 from Largo do Machado. Nearest Metrô São Cristóvão, but thieves operate by park entrance and in the park, taxi to the main door is safer. Some of the collections are open to qualified research students only.

Museu de Fauna also at Quinta da Boa Vista, contains a most interesting collection of Brazilian fauna. Open Tues-Sun 1200-1700.

The **Biblioteca Nacional** at Av Rio Branco 219, was founded in 1810. Its first collection came from the Ajuda Palace in Lisbon, and today it houses over 2 million volumes and many rare manuscripts. Open Mon-Fri 0900-2000, and Sat 0900-1500.

Museu Nacional de Belas Artes, Av Rio Branco 199, has about 800 original paintings and sculptures and some thousand direct reproductions. Exhibitions of works by contemporary Brazilian artists from 17th to 20th century. The collection is not very large but interesting. There are several paintings by Cândido Portinári (1903-61), Alberto de Vergo Guignard and Frans Janszoon Post (NL 1612-80) who painted Brazilian landscapes in classical Dutch style. Open Tues-Fri 1000-1800; Sat, Sun and holidays 1400-1800; US$1.

Those interested in contemporary art will also visit the former Ministry of Education (Le Corbusier designs modified by Oscar Niemeyer), to see the great murals of Cândido Portinári.

Opposite the Art Museum is the **Teatro Municipal**. Opera and orchestral performances are given here; the small museum that used to be below the theatre is now at R São João Batista 103/105, Botafogo, open 1300-1700 Mon-Fri.

The **Paço Imperial** (former Royal Palace on Praça 15 de Novembro), a beautiful colonial building begun in 1743, has been restored. It has several galleries, one theatre, one cinema, library, the *Bistro* and the *Atrium* restaurants, rec.

The **Museu de Arte Moderna** is a spectacular building at Av Infante D Henrique 85, near the National War Memorial (see page 384). It suffered a disastrous fire in 1978; the collection is now being rebuilt, and several countries have donated works of art. There is also a non-commercial cinema. The collection of contemporary Brazilian art, which includes very expressive drawings by Cândido Portinári from the 1940s and 50s and drawings and etchings of everyday work scenes by Gregório Gruber, made in the 1970s, is worth going to see. Entrance US$1, Tues-Sun 1200-1800.

The **Museu Histórico Nacional** on Praça Rui Barbosa (formerly Praça Marechal Âncora) contains a most interesting collection of historical treasures, colonial sculpture and furniture, maps, paintings, arms and armour, silver, and porcelain. The building was once the old War Arsenal of the

Empire, part of which was built in 1762. Open Tues to Sun, 1000-1600; Sat, Sun and holidays 1430-1730; admission US$1.20.

Museu da Imagem e do Som, also on Praça Rui Barbosa, has many photographs of Brazil and modern Brazilian paintings; also collections and recordings of Brazilian classical and popular music and a non-commercial cinema Fri-Sun. Open Mon-Fri, 1300-1800.

Museu Naval e Oceanográfico, R D Manoel 15, daily 1200-1630, has large collection of paintings and prints, besides the more usual display of weapons and figureheads.

Museu do Índio, R das Palmeiras 55, Botafogo, T 286 8799, being partly renovated so there is only a small exhibition. Among the 12,000 objects from many Brazilian Indian groups there is series of pencil drawings by an Indian artist, explaining an Indian creation myth. There is also a small, well-displayed handicraft shop (shop closes for lunch 1200-1400). Open Mon-Fri 1000-1730. You can get there by Metrô to Botafogo plus a 10-min walk, or (from Catete) bus 571 (Glória-Leblon) which passes R Bento Lisboa and R São Clemente, rec.

The **Chácara do Céu**, or Fundação Raymundo Ottoni de Castro Maia, R Murtinho Nobre 93, has a wide range of art objects and particularly modern painters, including Brazilian. Take Santa Teresa tram to R Dias de Barros, then follow signposts. Open Wed-Sun, Sun 1200-1700, US$1. Castro Maia's former residence, **Museu Açude**, Estrada do Açude 764, Alto da Boa Vista, Tijuca, is also a museum, currently under restoration, T 238 0368.

Museu do Instituto Histórico e Geográfico, Av Augusto Severo 8 (10th floor), just off Av Beira Mar, has an interesting collection of Brazilian products and the artefacts of its peoples. Open Mon-Fri 1200-1700.

The **São Cristóvão Pavilion**, designed by Sérgio Bernardes, has the world's largest open floor space without columns or transverse walls, but is now closed to the public. It is in very poor condition. Sunday market is worth visiting for northeastern food and hammocks. Bus 472 or 474 from Copacabana or centre.

The **Museu de Astronomia/National Observatory** (founded 1827) is on São Januário hill, R Gen Bruce 586, São Cristóvão. Hours: Tues-Fri 0900-1700, guided tours 1000-1200; 1400-1600. Visitors advised to call 580-7010 after 1700 to arrange a night viewing.

The **Casa de Rui Barbosa**, R São Clemente 134, Botafogo, former home of the Brazilian jurist and statesman, containing his library and other possessions, is open Tues-Fri 1000-1630, Sat, Sun and holidays 1400-1700. The large garden is also open to the public. Buses 106, 176, 178 from centre; 571 from Flamengo; 591 from Copacabana.

Palácio do Itamarati (Historical and diplomatic Museum), Av Marechal Floriano 196, Centro, Mon, Wed, Fri 1400-1700, with guided tours on the hour, rec.

Museu da República, R do Catete 153, Tues-Fri, 1200-1700, Sat-Sun and holidays 1400-1800 US$1, highly rec. The former palace of a coffee baron, later converted into the presidential seat, until the move to Brasilia, this museum now exhibits historical paintings; the first floor is devoted to the history of the Brazilian republic. You can also see the room where Getúlio Vargas shot himself. Behind the museum is the Parque do Catete.

Museu do Folclore Edison Carneiro, R do Catete 179, not to be missed. Very interesting objects, well selected and arranged. There is a collection of small ceramic figures representing everyday life in Brazil, some very funny, some scenes animated by electric motors. There are fine Candomblé and Umbanda costumes, religious objects, ex-votos. A brochure containing a general description of the objects in English is available at reception. Photography is allowed, but without flash. Tues-Fri 1100-1800 free. Bus 571 from Copacabana, and close to Catete Metrô station.

Museu Carmen Miranda, Tues-Fri 1300-1600, Flamengo park area in front of Rui

Barbosa 560 (small display of the famous singer's gowns etc); US$0.30, Sun free, but not always open Sun. **Museu de Imagens do Inconsciente**, Ramiro Magalhães 521, Engenho de Dentro, Mon-Fri 0900-1600. **Museu Villa-Lobos**, R Sorocaba 200, Botafogo, Mon-Fri 0930-1730, with instruments, scores, books, recordings. **Capão do Bispo Estate**, Av Suburbana 4616, Del Castilho, Mon-Fri 1400-1700, with archaeological exhibition.

Planetarium, Padre Leonel Franco 240, Gávea, Wed 1830, Sat and Sun at 1530 and 1830: inaugurated in 1970, sculpture of Earth and Moon by Mario Agostinelli. Free *choro* concert Fri at 2100. Buses 176 and 178 from centre and Flamengo; 591 and 592 from Copacabana.

Museu Aeroespacial, Av Marechal Fontenelle 2000, Campo dos Afonsos, Tues-Fri 0900-1600, Sat, Sun and holidays 0930-1600, early Brazilian civil and military aircraft.

Museu do Carnaval, Passarela do Samba, entrance by R Frei Caneca, Tues-Sun 1000-1700, good.

Museu Antônio Lago, R Andradas 96, centre, Mon-Fri 1400-1900. Reproduction of historical apothecary's shop.

Amsterdam Sauer Museum, Garcia d'Avila e Visconde de Pirajá 105, reproduction of a Brazilian mine and exhibition of gemstones. Mon-Fri 1000-1700, Sat 0930-1300.

Museu Internacional de Arte Naïf do Brasil, R Cosme Velho, 561, Mon-Fri 1000-1900, Sat-Sun 1200-1800, US$5, opened Oct 1995, rec.

Museu do Telefone, R 2 de Decembro, 63, Tues-Sun 1000-1700. The museum exhibits old telephones; on the top floor there is a semi-mechanical telephone exchange from the 1940s plus Getúlio Vargas' golden telephone and a replica of the telephone of Dom Pedro II, rec.

THE SUBURBS OF RIO DE JANEIRO

COPACABANA

Built on a narrow strip of land (only a little over 4 sq km) between mountain and sea, **Copacabana** has one of the highest population densities in the world: 62,000 per sq km, or 250,000 in all. Its celebrated curved beach backed by skyscraper apartments is a must for visitors. Tourist police patrol Copacabana beach until 1700.

Copacabana began to develop when the Old Tunnel was built in 1891 and an electric tram service reached it. Weekend villas and bungalows sprang up; all have now gone. In the 1930s the Copacabana Palace Hotel was the only tall building; it is now one of the lowest on the beach. The opening of the New Tunnel in the 1940s led to an explosion of population which shows no sign of having spent its force. Unspoilt Art Deco blocks towards the Leme (city) end of Copacabana are now under preservation order.

There is almost everything in this 'city within a city'. The shops, mostly in Av Copacabana and the R Barata Ribeiro, are excellent; this is the area in which to watch, or participate in, the city's glamorous night life. A fort at the far end of the beach commands the entrance to Rio Bay and prevents a seashore connection with the Ipanema and Leblon beaches. Parts of the military area are now being handed over to civilian use, the first being the Parque Garota de Ipanema at Arpoador, the fashionable Copacabana end of the Ipanema beach.

• **Transport** Buses to and from the city centre are plentiful and cheap, about US$0.40. If you are going to the centre from Copacabana, look for 'Castelo', 'Praça 15', 'E Ferro' or 'Praça Mauá' on the sign by the front door. 'Aterro' means the expressway between Botafogo and downtown Rio (not open Sun). From the centre to Copacabana is easier as all buses in that direction are clearly marked. Aterro bus does the journey in 15 mins.

IPANEMA AND LEBLON

Beyond Copacabana are the beautiful seaside suburbs of **Ipanema** (a good place from which to watch the sunset) and **Leblon**. They are a little less built-up than Copacabana, and their beaches tend to be cleaner. There is now night-time illumination on these beaches and the section in front of the *Caesar Park* hotel is patrolled

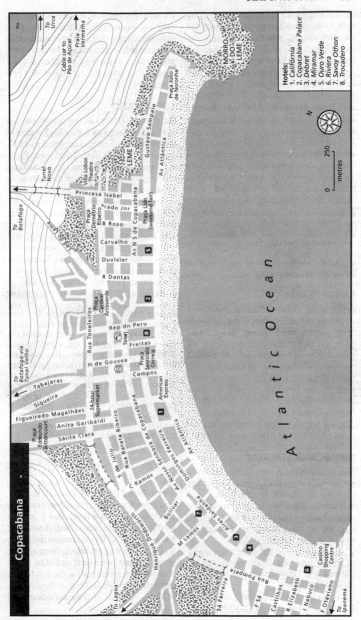

Copacabana

Hotels:
1. Califórnia
2. Copacabana Palace
3. Debret
4. Miramar
5. Ouro Verde
6. Riviera
7. Savoy Othon
8. Trocadero

N

0   250
metres

Atlantic Ocean

To Urca

Cable car to
Pão de Açúcar

Praia
Vermelha

MORRO
DO
LEME

Praça Júlio
de Noronha

Gustavo Sampaio

Av Atlântica

LEME

Villa Lobos
Theatre

Tunel
Novo

Princesa Isabel

Praça
Demétrio
Ribeiro

rado Jnr

B B Roxo

Praça Lido
(weekend fair)

Carvalho

Av N S de Copacabana

Duvivier

R Dantas

Praça
Cardeal
Arcoverde

Rua Toneleiros

Rep do Peru

Tele

Freitas

H de Gouvea

Praça
Serzedelo
Correia

Campos

American
Express

Tabajaras

Siqueira

24-hour
Supermarket

Figueiredo Magalhães

Anita Garibáldi

Praça
Edmundo
Bittencourt

Salita Clara

5 de Julho

Rua Barata Ribeiro

Av Nossa Senhora de Copacabana

Henrique Dodsworth

C Ramos

Bolivar

Av Atlântica

Domingos Ferreira

Aires Saldanha

M Lemos

Rua Pompéia

Sá Ferreira

F Sá

Castilhos

R Elizabeth

J Nabuco

F Otaviano

Casino Shopping
Centre

To Lagoa

To Ipanema

To Botafogo

To Botafogo via
Tunel Velho

To Lagoa

by the hotel's security staff: this, along with 24-hr video surveillance during the summer season, makes it probably the safest patch of sand in Rio. Backing Ipanema and Leblon is the middle-class residential area of Lagoa Rodrigo de Freitas, by a salt-water lagoon on which Rio's rowing and small-boat sailing clubs are active; too polluted for bathing. Beyond Leblon the coast is rocky; the Av Niemeyer skirts the cliffs on the journey past Vidigal, a small beach where the *Sheraton* is situated, to the outer seaside suburbs of São Conrado (beach polluted) and Barra da Tijuca (see below). The flat topped Gávea rock can be climbed or scrambled up for magnificent views, but beware snakes.

● **Transport** Buses from Botafogo Metrô terminal to Ipanema: some take integrated Metrô-Bus tickets; look for the blue signs on the windscreen. Many buses from Copacabana to Ipanema (buses 154 and 158 from Flamengo) and Leblon (buses 158, 434 and 488 from Flamengo, continuing to Barra da Tijuca).

SANTA TERESA

A hilly inner suburb SW of the centre, well known as the coolest part of Rio. It boasts many colonial and 19th-century buildings, set in narrow, curving, tree-lined streets. See particularly the Convent (only the outside; the Carmelite nuns do not admit visitors), the Chácara do Céu Museum (see page 387), the Hotel Santa Teresa (the oldest house in the area), Vista Alegre, the R Aprazível, and Largo de Guimarães. Santa Teresa is best visited on the traditional open-sided tram, described on page 405.

MARACANÃ STADIUM

This is one of the largest sports centres in the world. The football ground has seating capacity for 200,000 spectators (matches are worth going to for the spectators' samba bands, even if you're not a football fan; **NB** agencies charge much more for tickets than at the gate).

● **Transport** Buses 455 from Copacabana; 434 from Flamengo; from Leblon, 464 via Ipanema and Copacabana; also Metrô from Botafogo and centre.

Guided tour of stadium (in Portuguese), US$2.50, and museum, US$0.50, highly rec to football fans. Maracanã is now used only for major games; Rio teams play most matches at their home grounds (still a memorable experience). Hotels can arrange visits to football matches: a good idea on Sun when the metro is closed and buses very full.

CORCOVADO

Corcovado (710m) is the hunch-backed peak surmounted by a 40m high statue of Christ the Redeemer completed in 1931, weighing, with its base, 1,200 tons. There is a superb view from the top (sometimes obscured by mist), to which there are a cog railway and a road; both car and train put down their passengers behind the statue – there is a climb of 220 steps to the top, near which there is a café. To see the city by day and night ascend at 1500 or 1600 and descend on the last train, approx 1815. Mass is held on Sun in a small chapel in the statue pedestal. The floodlighting was designed in 1931 by Marconi himself.

● **Transport** Take a Cosme Velho bus (180184 or 422 from Centro or Flamengo) to the **cog railway station at R Cosme Velho 513**; from Copacabana take No 583, 584 back. Service every 20-30 mins according to demand between 0800 and 1830, journey time 10 mins (cost: US$15 return; single tickets available). Also, a 206 bus does the very attractive run from Praça Tiradentes (or a 407 from Largo do Machado) to Silvestre (the railway has no stop here now). An active walk of 1 hr will bring one to the top, and the road is shady. (Best done in company.) Coach trips tend to be rather brief, but taxis do wait in front of the station offering tours for US$30 which include Corcovado and Mirante Dona Marta for groups of 3 or more.

PÃO DE AÇÚCAR

The Sugar Loaf (396m) is a massive granite cone at the entrance to Guanabara Bay. The bird's eye view of the city and beaches is very beautiful. There is a restaurant (excellent location, mixed reports on food, closes 1900) and a playground for children on the Morro da Urca, half way up, where there are also shows at night (weekends and Mon, 2200). You can get refreshments at the top. On the small path that leads down in the direction of Morro Cara de Cão there are toucans and macaws in cages.

There are 35 rock routes up the mountain, with various degrees of difficulty (best months for climbing: April to Aug; see **Sports**, below, for climbing clubs).

It is possible to walk or jog on the S side in the military area at the foot.

● **Transport Buses** Bus 107 (from the centre or Flamengo) and 511 or 500 'jardinière', or those marked 'Urca' (from Copacabana) take you to the cable-car station, Av Pasteur 520, at the foot. The **cable car** timetable: Praia Vermelha to Urca: first car goes up at 0800, then every 30 mins (or when full), until the last comes down at 2200. From Urca to Sugar Loaf the first connecting cable car goes up at 0815 then every 30 mins (or when full), until the last leaves the summit at 2200; the return trip costs US$10 (US$5 to Morro da Urca, half-way up). The old cableway has been completely rebuilt. Termini are ample and efficient and the present Italian cable cars carry 75 passengers. Even on the most crowded days there is little queuing.

TIJUCA NATIONAL PARK

The Pico da Tijuca (1,012m) gives a good idea of the tropical vegetation of the interior and a fine view of the bay and its shipping. A 2-3 hr walk leads to the summit: on entering the park at Alto de Boa Vista (open 0600-2100), follow the signposts (maps are displayed) to Bom Retiro, a good picnic place (1½ hrs' walk), passing by the Cascatinha Taunay, Mayrink Chapel (built 1860) and the restaurant *A Floresta*. At Bom Retiro the road ends and there is another hour's walk up a fair footpath to the summit (take the path from the right of the Bom Retiro drinking fountain; not the more obvious steps from the left). The last part consists of steps carved out of the solid rock; look after children at the summit as there are several sheer drops, invisible because of bushes. The route is shady for almost its entire length. The panels painted in the Mayrink Chapel by Cândido Portinári have been replaced by copies and the originals will probably be installed in the Museu de Arte Moderna. Maps of the Park are available.

Other places of interest not passed on the walk to the peak are the Paul and Virginia Grotto, the Vista do Almte and the Mesa do Imperador (viewpoints). Allow at least 5 to 6 hrs for the excursion. Also, one of the Raymundo Castro Maia museums, Museu Açude, is nearby (see page 387).

● **Buses** Take a 221 from Praça 15 de Novembro, 233 or 234 bus from the rodoviária or 454 from Copacabana or from Praça Sáenz Pena, Tijuca (reached by Metrô) to Alto da Boa Vista, for the park entrance.

Viewpoints not already mentioned under Tijuca, Corcovado and Pão de Açúcar include the Vista Chinesa (420m), where from a Chinese-style pavilion one can see the inland lake (the Lagoa), Ipanema and Leblon; and the Mirante de Dona Marta (340m) off the Corcovado road, with the same direction of view as the Corcovado, but as it is lower the details can be seen more clearly. There is no public transport to these places.

BARRA DA TIJUCA

This rapidly developing residential area is also one of the principal recreation areas of Rio, with its 20-km sandy beach and good waves for surfing. There are innumerable bars and restaurants, clustered at both ends, campsites (see page 398), motels and hotels: budget accommodation tends to be self-catering. On Av Sernambetiba (the beach boulevard), **A1** *Aparthotel Barraleme*, No 600, T 389-3100, has been rec. Travel agency and car hire in same building. The facilities include Riocenter, a 600,000 sq m convention complex and the huge Barra Shopping and Carrefour shopping centres. The stylish Fashion Mall is opposite the golf club. Hang-gliders jump from the hilltops at weekends. View the beaches and hills from the air, Ultra Força Ltda, Av Sernambetiba 8100, T 399-3114, 15 mins.

South of Barra are beaches at Recreio dos Bandeirantes (small, ocean very rough), Prainha (a little cove, good for surfing), and Grumari (very attractive, rustic beach bar), the last two inaccessible by public transport, therefore less crowded and safer. They attract heavy traffic at weekends and this stunning coastal road (the start of the Costa Verde highway) is becoming obliterated by executive housing developments – visit soon, if you can.

The **Autódromo** (motor racing track) is beyond Barra in the Jacarepaguá district. The Brazilian Grand Prix is held here or at Interlagos, São Paulo, alternately in January.

● **Transport** Buses from the Tijuca Forest continue on the 233 or 234 bus (from Praça Sáenz Pena, very good views of São Conrado and Barra), or from the city bus station at R São José, from Santos Dumont airport, bus 591 or 592 from Leme, and from Copacabana via Leblon beach bus 523. Taxi to Zona Sul, US$15 (US$22.50 after midnight). From Botafogo, Glória or Flamengo take bus 179. A comfortable bus, Pegasus, goes along the coast from the Castelo bus terminal to Barra da Tijuca and continues to Campo Grande or Santa Cruz, or take free 'Barra Shopping' bus. Bus 700 from Praça São Conrado (terminal of bus 553 from Copacabana) goes the full length of the beach to Recreio dos Bandeirantes.

PAQUETÁ ISLAND

The island, in Guanabara Bay, is noted for its gigantic pebble shaped rocks, butterflies and orchids. The house of José Bonifácio, the opponent of slavery, may be seen. Horse-drawn carriages may be hired (many have harnesses which cut into the horse's flesh), but they do not stop at the interesting Parque Darke de Mattos. Tour by 'trenzinho', a tractor pulling trailers, US$1.25, or on foot, quieter and free. Bicycles also can be hired. Very crowded at weekends and public holidays, but usually very quiet during the week. Reasonable food and drink prices.

● **Transport** Paquetá Island can be visited by more or less 2-hourly ferry services from Praça 15 de Novembro, between 1015 and 1300, last back at 1900 (fare US$1.25 by boat, 1 hr, US$6.25 by hydrofoil, 20 mins' journey, which more than doubles its price Sats, Suns and holidays). Bus to Praça 15 de Novembro: 119 from Botafogo; 154, 134, 455, 474 from Copacabana or 415 passing from Leblon via Ipanema.

Other boat trips: Aquatur (T 230-9273), Brazilian Marina Turismo, Camargo (T 275-0643), Passamar, Siqueira Campos 7 (T 236-4136), Greyline (T 274-7146), Soletur (Bay trips Sat and Sun only) and American Sightseeing, Av NS de Copacabana 605, Sala 1204 (T 236-3551). The last three offer a day cruise, inc lunch, to Jaguanum Island (see page 413, under Itacuruçá) and a sundown cruise around Guanabara Bay, also deep-sea fishing expeditions and private charters.

CARNIVAL

Carnival in Rio is spectacular. On the Fri before Shrove Tues, the mayor of Rio symbolically hands the keys of the city to King Momo, a sequinned Lord of Misrule, signifying the start of a five-day party. Imagination runs riot, social barriers are broken, the main avenues are colourfully lit, full of people, and children wear fancy dress. Special bandstands throughout the city are manned for public street-dancing (see local press for where and when) and organized carnival groups, the *blocos carnavalescos*, are everywhere, dancing, drumming and singing (among others, look out for the entertaining Banda da Ipanema, a parade of transvestites, most evenings in that suburb). There are numerous samba schools in Rio, divided into 2 leagues. The first league is split into 5 groups: the top 3 of these parade in the Sambódromo. 12 Group B schools parade on Fri; 9 Group A schools on Sat. The 18 Special Group schools parade on Sun and Mon, 9 schools per night; the order of appearance is determined by lottery, so both days are good. The 10 selected winners (5 each from the Special Group and Group 1) perform a celebratory parade the following Sat night at the Sambódromo. The third and fourth divisions parade on Av Rio Branco (less spectacular, but free).

Every school presents 3,000-5,000 participants, divided into 40 *alas* (wings) and as many as 30 floats. Each school chooses a theme, then composes a samba, and designs costumes and floats to fit it. The theme must be national (often an element of Brazilian history or a current political topic). The samba song (*enredo*) is a poetic, rhythmic and catchy expression of the theme, which is then developed – with breathtaking flights of imagination – through the *alas'* floats and costumes. A percussion wing, the *bateria*, maintains a reverberating beat that must keep the entire school, and the audience, dancing frenetically throughout their pageant.

Schools are given between 65 and 80 mins to parade, losing points for failure to keep within the limits. Judges award points to each school for components of their procession, such as costume, music and design, and make deductions for lack of energy, enthusiasm or discipline. The best schools are promoted to a higher division, those with fewest points being relegated, as in a football league. Competition is intense. For the winners there is a monetary prize, funded by the entrance fees. It may be possible to join a Samba school if you are in Rio prior to Carnival (see below).

The Carnival parade is by no means created as a tourist attraction; it is the culmination of months of intense activity by community groups, mostly in the city's poorest districts. To understand the traditions of the schools, the meanings of the different parts of the parade, and carnival as a whole, visit the carnival museum in the Sambódromo; although small, it has lots of photographs and the English-speaking staff are very informative (entrance in R Frei Caneca; T 293-9996; Tues-Sun 1000-1700; free). Suggested reading: *The Insider's Guide to Rio* (in English; Christopher Pickard, from Rio bookshops); *Samba* (paperback; a personal account by Alma Guillermoprieto, Bloomsbury Press). The **Sambódromo**, a permanent site at R Marquês de Sapucaí, Cidade Nova, not far from the centre, is 600m long, with seats for 60,000 people. Designed by Oscar Niemeyer, it handles sporting events, conferences and concerts during the rest of the year; it also houses a public education centre which presently teaches 5,000 children.

The Sambódromo parades start at 1900 and last about 12 hrs. Gates (which are not clearly marked) open at 1800. Spectator accommodation comprises seats ('cadeiras') at ground level, terraces ('arquibancadas') and boxes ('camarotes'). The best boxes, which are reserved for tourists and VIPs, sell for around US$1,000 pp. Seats are closest to the parade, but you may have to fight your way to the front. Seats and boxes reserved for tourists have the best view; sectors 4, 7 and 11 are preferred (they house the judging points); 6 and 13 are least favoured, being at the end when dancers might be tired, but have more space. The terraces, while uncomfortable, house the most fervent fans, tightly packed; this is where to soak up the atmosphere (but not take pictures – too crowded). Tickets (maximum 4) are sold through Banco do Brasil or the Banco Meridional in most big cities, and start at about US$40; they are also sold at the Maracanã Stadium box office, but not during Carnival weekend: touts outside will try to sell you places at double the price. Check availability, even if they say all tickets are sold. Samba schools have an allocation of tickets which members sometimes sell off; if you are offered one of these, check its date. Tourist tickets start at US$100; available through Riotur or travel agencies. Taxis to the Sambódromo are negotiable (around US$15) and will find your gate; nearest Metrô is Praça 11: an enjoyable ride in the company of costumed samba school members. Main Metrô and bus routes run all night during Carnival (erratically).

Most Samba schools will accept a number of foreigners: you will be charged upwards of US$150 for your costume; your money helps to fund poorer members of the school. You should be in Rio for at least 2 weeks before Carnival (Portuguese speakers can telephone the schools direct), but in 1996 several schools were still recruiting from booths at the start of the holiday. It is essential to attend fittings and rehearsals on time, to show respect for your section leaders, and to enter into the competitive spirit of the event. For those with the energy and the dedication, it will be an unforgettable experience. The 'concentration area' at the entrance to the Sambódromo, where schools line up before their parade, is an excellent point from which to see the chaotic preparations on the night; people who cannot afford tickets gather here to see the costumes: Av Presidente Vargas (drinks and food on sale; canal can be unpleasant in hot weather). All schools hold a preview of their entire parade in their own neighbourhood, usually the week before Carnival; well worth seeing, admission often free for women, otherwise around US$4, photography OK but don't take valuables;

listed in local press under 'ensaios'. It's wise to go by taxi, as most schools are based in poorer districts.

Carnival week comprises an enormous range of official contests and events, as well as many unofficial ones. Exhibitions and competitions reach a peak on the Tues; Riotur's guide booklet (also available from better hotels) gives concise information in English; *Veja, Manchete* (weekly magazines) and the Jornal do Brasil's *Programa* (Fri) are also invaluable sources: an equally wide programme exists for those looking for entertainment but not wishing to 'play' at Carnival.

Rio's fancy-dress balls range from the sophisticated to the wild. The majority of clubs and hotels host at least one. The *Copacabana Palace* hotel's is elegant and expensive (US$250), with costumed mime artists parading on a backlit terrace for the benefit of spectators on the Av Atlântica below; the *Scala* club's licentious parties are televised nightly. It is not necessary to wear fancy dress; just join in, although you will feel more comfortable if you wear a minimum of clothing to the clubs (crowded, hot and rowdy). Two of the most famous (both at *Scala*) are the Red & Black Ball (Fri) and the Gay Ball (Tues). Prices vary: from about US$15 pp; US$100 per table for 4; US$750 for a box. Drinks are expensive (beer/soft drink US$3). *Scala* gives free tickets to attractive young women, which their boyfriends then sell outside the entrance: expect to pay about US$15, and check the date. The tourist office has a full list of balls.

The expensive hotels offer special Carnival breakfasts from 0530 at US$10-15, all good; *Caesar Park* (Ipanema) highly rec, wonderful meal, top-floor view of sunrise over beach.

Essential information
● Addresses
Copacabana Palace Hotel, T 255-7070, ext 187 (reservations); *Scala*, Av Afrânio de Mello Franco, Leblon, T 239-4448.

● Lodging and security
Visitors wishing to attend the Carnival are earnestly advised to make sure of their accommodation well in advance. Virtually all hotels raise their prices during Carnival, although it should be possible to find a room.

Your property should be safe inside the Sambódromo, but the crowds outside can attract pickpockets: as ever, don't brandish your camera, and take with you as much money as you need for fares and refreshments (food and drink are sold in the Sambódromo, glass and cans are not allowed if you take your own). It gets hot! Wear as little as possible (shorts or Bermudas and a T-shirt).

● Samba Schools
Salgueiro (Andaraí) T 238-5564; Beija-Flor (Nilópolis) T 791-2866; Mangueira (Mangueira) T 234-4129; Estácio de Sá (Cidade Nova) T 293-8944; Imperatriz (Ramos) T 270-8037; Mocidade Independente (Padre Miguel) T 332-5823; Portela (Madureira) T 390-0471; Tradição (Campinho) T 350-5868; União da Ilha (Ilha do Governador) T 396-4951; Vila Isabel (Santa Isabel) T 268-7052; also see local press and Riotur booklet.

● If you can't be there at Carnival time
Rehearsals are held at various places from Nov onwards; eg the Portela *escola* at R Arruda Câmara 81, Madureira, late Sat nights. See addresses above. Tour agents sell tickets for glitzy samba shows, which are nothing like the real thing. When buying a Carnival video, make sure the format is compatible (Brazilian format matches the USA; VHS PAL for most of Europe).

● Carnival dates
9 Feb 1997; 22 Feb 1998; 14 Feb 1999; 5 Mar 2000.

OTHER FESTIVALS

Less hectic than Carnival, but very atmospheric, is the festival of **Iemanjá** on the night of 31 Dec, when devotees of the sea spirit gather on Copacabana, Ipanema and Leblon beaches, singing and dancing around open fires and making offerings, and the elected Queen of the Sea is rowed along the seashore. At midnight small boats are launched as sacrifices to Iemanjá. The religious event is dwarfed, however, by a massive **New Year's Eve party** at Copacabana. The beach is packed as thousands of revellers enjoy free outdoor concerts by big-name pop stars, topped with a lavish midnight firework display. Most crowded in front of *Copacabana Palace Hotel*.

The festival of **São Sebastião**, patron saint of Rio, is celebrated by an evening procession on 20 Jan, leaving Capuchin-hos Church, Tijuca, and arriving at the cathedral of São Sebastião. The same evening an *umbanda* festival is celebrated at the Caboclo Monument in Santa Teresa.

Local information

● Security

The majority of visitors enjoy Rio's glamour, and the rich variety of experience it has to offer, without any problems. It is worth remembering that, despite its beach culture, carefree atmosphere and friendly people, Rio is one of the world's most densely populated cities. If you live in London, Paris, New York or Los Angeles and behave with the same caution in Rio that you do at home, you will be unlucky to encounter any crime. There is extreme poverty in Rio: most robberies that occur are committed out of desperation. Overseas visitors are an obvious target: simply by having been able to afford the ticket, you are comparatively wealthy. Brazilians can usually tell you are foreign just by the way you carry yourself, but there is no sense in looking as if you have something worth stealing (by wearing expensive clothes, valuable jewellery, a large daypack, or your camera – put it in your shoulder bag, worn in front of you, or buy disposable cameras as often as you need them). If you are unfortunate enough to be threatened, try to remember that the assailant is probably as scared as you are, and will not hurt you if you give him what he's asking for (keep some money easily accessible, just in case). If you see someone having trouble, don't interfere, but try making a lot of noise to frighten the attacker away; if you think you are being followed, go up to a policeman. The streets are not excessively dangerous at night, but if you're going out in your best clothes, don't know the way, or are drunk, it's wisest to get a taxi. All the above advice comes from the **tourist police** (see **Useful addresses** below), who publish a sensible advice leaflet (available from hotels and consulates: consulates also issue safety guidelines). Officers are helpful, efficient, and multilingual. All the main tourist areas are patrolled. If you have any problems, **contact the tourist police first**.

The following are risky places: the tunnels are not safe to walk through; the city centre on Sun when it is deserted; quiet alleyways; jostling crowds; dark corners. Locals don't walk on the beaches at night: if you must, do not go out of sight of the pavement. The Tijuca forest is best explored with a group of 6 or more, except the stretch between Afonso Vizeu square and Cascatinha which is well policed during the day; the tram (see page 405) attracts pickpockets; robberies sometimes happen in city buses: don't use them if guarding your property is essential (private 'frescão' buses are more secure). The main bus station is patrolled inside, but uncomfortable outside. If you go to the North Zone at night, use a taxi; wandering around *favelas* at any time of day is both ill-advised and in questionable taste. Street vendors and children working the tables at your bar or restaurant will have been permitted by the management and there is little risk, though children can be light-fingered, so watch your wallet.

It seems that far too many crimes against tourists are the result of thoughtlessness: remember that you are in a busy city, and that the beaches are a pivot of daily life; leaving things unattended on the sand is equivalent to leaving them on Times Square while you go for a walk. We have been asked to advise male readers that all the usual risks apply if hiring prostitutes of either sex (police may well take your companion's side in a dispute over prices – don't argue). The 'red light' districts of the South Zone are unlikely to offend anyone walking about at night, even children or unaccompanied women. Do, however, be suspicious of any club that you are invited into by a stranger (have your drink opened in front of you), and of anyone offering drugs. You have the most to lose when carrying all your belongings and as you go in and out of banks, exchange houses, and expensive shops, so take extra care then. At other times, put your passport, TCs, etc in the hotel safe. Don't take too much out with you, have some sense, and relax.

On all Rio's beaches you should take a towel or mat to protect you against sandflies; in the water stay near groups of other swimmers; there is a strong undertow.

● Accommodation

Hotel prices

L1	over US$200	**L2**	US$151-200
L3	US$101-150	**A1**	US$81-100
A2	US$61-80	**A3**	US$46-60
B	US$31-45	**C**	US$21-30
D	US$12-20	**E**	US$7-11
F	US$4-6	**G**	up to US$3

All hotels 2-stars and above in the following list are a/c. A 10% service charge is usually added to the bill and tax of 5% or 10% may be added (if not already inc). Note that not all higher-class hotels inc breakfast in their room rates. The following list begins with expensive hotels and then gives economy establishments, by area.

Centre: well placed for transport, 30 mins from the beaches. Most offices and commerce are located here, but no night life, so not a secure area and not rec for tourists: **L2** *Luxor Hotel do Aeroporto* at Galeão Airport, T 398-5960,

F 398-3983 (3-star); **A1** *Ambassador*, Senador Dantas, 25, T 297-7181, F 220-4783; **A1** *Grande Hotel OK*, Senador Dantas, 24, T 292-4114, F 533-0163.

Flamengo: residential area midway between centre and Copacabana: **L2** *Novo Mundo*, Praia Flamengo 20, T 205-3355, F 265-2369, well rec but noisy; **L3** *Glória*, R do Russel, 632, T 205-7272, F 245-1660, stylish and elegant old building, two swimming pools, highly rec; **A1** *Flamengo Palace*, Praia Flamengo 6, T 205-1552, F 265-2846, appears a bit old-fashioned.

Copacabana: the famous seaside residential and commercial area: many hotels on Av Atlântica charge about 30% more for a room with a sea view, but some town-side upper rooms have equally fine views of the mountains. 5-star hotels (**L1-2**): *Copacabana Palace*, Av Atlântica 1702, T 255-7070, F 235-7330, swimming pool, good; *Meridien*, Av Atlântica 1020, T 275-9922, F 541-6447, Air France hotel, world-renowned, but very expensive, pool, rooms quite small; *Rio Othon Palace*, Av Atlântica 3264, T 521-5522, F 521-6697, pool, very good, as is *Rio Palace*, Av Atlântica 4240, T 521-3232, F 247-1752, all rooms locked by central system at 0130. There are two excellent suites hotels: **L3** *Rio Atlântica*, Av Atlântica 2964, T 255-6332, F 255-6410 with pool, 2 restaurants and other facilities (Swiss management, very high standards) rec; and *Rio Internacional*, Av Atlântica 1500, T 295-2323, F 542-5443, pool.

4-star hotels in Copacabana: there are 4 Othon hotels in this category, all in the **L3-A1** range (some rooms more): *Califórnia Othon*, Av Atlântica 2616, T/F 257-1900, good; *Savoy Othon*, Av Copacabana 995, T/F 521-8282, very central, popular, commercial, quite noisy; *Olinda*, Av Atlântica 2230, T/F 257-1890, also good, and the *Lancaster*, Av Atlântica 1470, T/F 541-1887, rec, easy to change TCs, non-smoking rooms, helpful management. Next door to the *Lancaster* is *Ouro Verde*, Av Atlântica 1456, T 542-1887, F 542-4597, good value, excellent all round; 3 Luxor hotels: *Luxor Continental*, Gustavo Sampaio 320, T 275-5252, F 541-1946, *Luxor Copacabana*, Av Atlântica 2554, T 235-2245, F 255-1858, *Luxor Regente*, Av Atlântica 3716, T 287-4212, F 267-7693, all good hotels in this range, well-placed. *Leme Palace*, Av Atlântica 656, T/F 275-8080, also good, but poorer location, popular with tour groups. *Royalty Copacabana*, Toneleros 154, T/F 255-5699, 4 blocks from beach, a/c, swimming pool on 13th floor with view.

Copacabana 3-stars (except where indicated A1-A2): *Castro Alves Othon*, Av Copacabana 552, T/F 255-8815, central, very comfortable and elegant, rec; *Debret*, Av Atlântica 3564,

T 521-3332, F 521-0899, good, helpful staff, some inner rooms dark, but well-furnished; *Plaza Copacabana*, Av Princesa Isabel 263, T 275-7722, F 275-8693, highly rec (being refurbished in Jan 1996).

Copacabana 2-stars: **B** *Atlantis Copacabana*, Av Bulhões de Carvalho 61, T 521-1142, F 287-8896, a/c, TV, very good, close to Ipanema and Copacabana beaches; *Biarritz*, R Aires Saldanha 54, T 521-6542, F 287-7640, good, accepts American Express; **B** *Santa Clara*, R Décio Vilares 316, T 256-2650, best rooms at front, quiet, friendly, rec; **B** *Toledo*, R Domingos Ferreira 71, T 257-1990, 1 block from beach, good breakfast, single rooms are gloomy, but excellent value; **B** *Acapulco Copacabana*, R Gustavo Sampião 854, T 275-0022, F 275-3396, a/c, TV, simple, rec.

Ipanema/Leblon: outer seaside residential and commercial area: all the following are good, starting with the most luxurious, **L1** *Caesar Park*, Av Vieira Souto 460, T 287-3122, F 521-6000, pool, beach patrol; **L3** *Everest*, Prudente de Morais 1117, T 287-8282, F 521-3198, pool; **L3** *Marina Palace*, Av Delfim Moreira 630, T 259-5212, F 259-0941, and **L3** *Marina Rio*, Av Delfim Moreira 696, T 239-8844, F 259-0941; **L3** *Praia Ipanema*, Av Vieira Souto 706, T 239-9932, F 239-6889, pool, helpful; **A1** *Sol Ipanema*, Av Vieira Souto, 320, T 267-0095, F 521-6464, rec; **A3** *Ipanema Inn*, Maria Quitéria 27, behind *Caesar Park*, T 287-6092, F 511-5094, good location, friendly; **A3** *Arpoador Inn*, Francisco Otaviano 177, T 247-6090, F 511-5094, only hotel on beach, rec.

São Conrado and further out: spectacular settings, but isolated and far from centre: the first two are luxury hotels with pools: **L1** *Intercontinental*, Av Pref Mendes de Moraes 222 (São Conrado), T 322-2200, F 322-5500; **L1** *Sheraton*, Av Niemeyer 121 (Vidigal), T 274-1122, F 239-5643; **A2** *Atlântico Sul*, Av Sernambetiba 18000 (Recreio), T 437-8411, F 437-8777.

Economy hotels: are found mainly in three districts of Rio: Flamengo/Botafogo (best), Lapa/Fátima and Saúde/Mauá. Rates are for doubles, and inc continental breakfast.

Flamengo/Catete: (Residential area between centre and Copacabana, with good bus and Metrô connections.) From the centre, you will come across the hotels in this order: **E** *Opera*, Santa Amaro 75, T 242-3585, recently reopened. On the hillside is Ladeira da Glória: **C** *Turístico*, Ladeira da Glória 30, T 265-1698, with bath, inc breakfast, a/c, tourist information provided, mixed reports, some highly favourable. **D** *Victória*, R do Catete 172, with breakfast, bath and hot water, a/c, clean and friendly, rec; also on R do Catete: No 233,

D *Rio Claro*, small rooms, breakfast, shower, a/c, safe, rec; No 160, **D** *Monte Blanco*, breakfast, bath, a/c, radio, refurbished, clean, friendly (try for a room about 1200). To the left is R Silveira Martins: **C** *Inglês*, No 20, T 265-9052, reasonable breakfast. Walking down Praia de Flamengo you will come across the next streets: Ferreira Viana: **A3** *Florida*, No 71/81, T 245-8160, F 285-5777, sauna, pool, safe, quiet, good views, great breakfast, highly rec; **B** *Regina*, No 29, T 225-7280, 2-star, a/c, bath, rooms vary; **D** *Unico*, Buarque de Machado 54, T 205-9932, bath, TV, a/c, fridge, clean, friendly, rec; also nr Largo do Machado Metrô: **D-C** *Monterrey*, R Artur Bernardes 39, T 265-9899, with bath, fan, TV, clean; at No 29, **E** *Rio Lisboa*, with bath, a/c, cheaper rooms without bath, clean, safe, rec – both hotels in this quiet street are family hotels. R Paissandu: No 34, **D** *Venezuela*, with bathroom, very clean, but rooms small and breakfast poor; **B** *Paysandu*, opp *Venezuela* at No 23, T 225-7270, very clean, comfortable and good value. Beyond Largo de Machado: R Gago Coutinho: No 22, **D** *Serrano*, pleasant, helpful; and **B** *Argentina*, Cruz Lima 30, T 225-7233, F 285-4573, best rooms on 5th floor, cheapest on 1st, rec.

Lapa/Fátima: between Lapa and Praça Tiradentes is an inner residential area, less desirable than Flamengo. Parts of this area are deserted from 2200 on. Near Cinelândia Metrô station are a lot of cheap hotels, but many are short stay. In Lapa itself, nr the Arches just beyond Passeio Público, is R Joaquim Silva: No 99, **D** *Marajó*, with breakfast, varied rooms, clean; also **E** *Love's House*, R Joaquim Silva, ask for room with window, safe, respectable, good value. Passing under the Arches you come to Av Mem de Sá (bus 127 from bus terminal): No 85, **E** *Mundo Novo*, clean, a/c. Turning towards Praça Tiradentes is R Resende, No 31, **D** *Estadual*, good; No 35 **D** *Pouso Real*, T 224-2757, good, gay area, rec; **D** *Marialva*, Gomes Freire 430 (nr New Cathedral, convenient for Av Rio Branco, buses etc), 2-star, with bath, a/c, breakfast in room, rec. Praça Tiradentes: **D** *Rio* *Hotel*, clean, noisy rooms on Praça, quieter overlooking São Sebastião cathedral, with breakfast (only served in rooms).

Saúde/Mauá: (area between the railway station and the docks): the very cheapest hotels in town are in this area, but it is not too safe at night.

In the traditional **Santa Teresa** district, R Almte Alexandrino 660, is the **B** *Santa Teresa Hotel*, with swimming pool. Also Dona Ana's hostel on the same street at No 501, B, T 232-9603. Take the 'Dois Irmãos' tram from Largo da Carioca or bus 206/214.

Youth hostels: R Almte Alexandrino 2840, Santa Teresa (*Pousada do Garuda*, T 225-0393/236-1419), Santa Amaro 162, Glória, T 222-8576, noisy; *Chave do Rio de Janeiro*, Gen Dionísio 63, Botafogo, T 286-0303, US$12, clean, washing facilities, superb breakfast, noisy but frequently rec; *Copacabana Praia* (also called *Indy*), R Ten Marones de Gusmão 85, Bairro Peixoto, CEP 22041, T 235-3817/237-5422, US$6; *Saint Roman*, R Saint Roman 48, Copacabana, T 227-7685; *Copacabana Chalet*, R Pompeu Loureiro 99, T 236-0047, US$23, noisy, nr beach, shops, YHA card not necessary, but you pay a bit more without it. Associations: both at R da Assembleia 10: ALBERJ (for Rio), room 1616, T 531-1302/2234; Federação Brasileira (Brazil), room 1211, T 531-1129. Youth hostels are fully booked between Christmas and Carnival; if intending to stay at this time reserve well in advance.

Remember that 'motels' are mainly for the use of very-short-stay couples.

The city is noisy. An inside room is cheaper and much quieter. (If you are desperate and it is late, some smaller hotels and hostelries may let you sleep on the floor.)

Self-catering apartments: a popular form of accommodation in Rio, available at all price levels: for example, furnished apartments, accommodating up to 6, cost US$240/month in Maracanã, about US$360/month in Saúde, Cinelândia, Flamengo. Copacabana, Ipanema and Leblon prices range from about US$15/day for a simple studio, up to US$2,000 a month for a luxurious residence sleeping 4 to 6. Heading S past Barra da Tijuca, virtually all the accommodation available is self-catering. Renting a small flat, or sharing a larger one, can be much better value than a hotel room. Blocks consisting entirely of short-let apartments can attract thieves, so check the (usually excellent) security arrangements; residential buildings are called *prédio familial*. Higher floors (*alto andar*) are considered safest.

The following **rent apartments in residential blocks**: *Hamburg Imobiliária*, Av Copacabana 195, Loja 104, T 542-1446, F 236-4541, German run, specialize in flats, very reasonable, helpful, highly rec, also offer tours at good rates, flights and exchange; *Yvonne Reimann*, Av Atlântica 4.066, Apto 605, T 227-0281/267-0054, rents apartments, all with phone, nr beach, a/c, maid service, English, French, German spoken, all apartments owned by the agency, prices from US$48 up (check if per flat or pp); *Yolanda Thiémard*, Av Prado Junior 165 CO2, T 295-2088, multilingual, good value, rec; *Dona Lígia*, R Ministro Viveiros de Castro 141 apto 101, T 541-6367, speaks English, lower-price apartments. European agent: Mr Peter Corr, Friedrichsplatz 6, D-6816, Mannheim, Germany, T 0049-621-402721, F 0049-6234-801177, rec. 'Apart-Hotels' are listed in the *Guia 4 Rodas* and Riotur's booklet; the *Praia Leme Hotel*, Av Atlântica 866, has apartments (expensive), with maid and laundry service at Av Princesa Isabel 7, close to the beach; in high season reservation is necessary; *Rio Beach*, R Prado Júnior 48, Loja 2, Copacabana, T 547-2395, well-equipped flats for US$18/day and US$400/month; *Rio Flat Service*, Almte Guilhém 322, Leblon, reservations through SASS Ltda, Ataulfo de Paiva 566/305, T 274-9546, Tx 30245. Also try *Copacabana Holidays* at R Barata Ribeiro 90, room 204, Copacabana, T 542-1597/542-1525, and at R Barata Ribeiro 87/ 202, T 255-2016 or 237-1133; *New Rio Home Service*, Visconde de Pirajá 414, sala 102, Ipanema, T 521-2332, F 267-6090, Swedish-run, rec; *Mellow Holidays*, R Paula Freitas 45/1101, T 256-5061, have apartments at a range of prices in the Copacabana and Ipanema districts. Agents and private owners advertise in *Balcão* (like *Exchange and Mart*), twice weekly, *O Globo* or *Jornal do Brasil* (daily); under 'Apartamentos – Temporada'; advertisements are classified by district and size of apartment: 'vagas e quartos' means shared accommodation; 'conjugado' (or 'conj') is a studio with limited cooking facilities; '3 Quartos' is a 3-bedroom flat. There should always be a written agreement when renting.

Camping: Camping Clube do Brasil has 2 beach sites at Barra da Tijuca: Av Sernambetiba 3200, T 493-0628 (bus 233 from centre, 702 or 703 from the airport via Zona Sul, US$5 – a long way from the centre), sauna, pool, bar, café, US$12 (half price for members), during Jan and Feb this site is often full and sometimes restricted to members of the Camping Clube do Brasil; a smaller site at Estrada do Pontal 5900, T 437-8400, lighting, café, good surfing, US$6. Both have trailer plots. *Ostal*, Av Sernambetiba 18790, T 437-8350; and *Novo Rio*, at 17.5 km on Rio-Santos road, T 437-6518. If travelling by trailer, you can park at the Marina Glória car park, where there are showers and toilets, a small shop and snack bar. Pay the guards to look after your vehicle. Camping gear for sale at *Montcamp*, Teixeira de Melo 21, Ipanema, T 287-1143.

● **Places to eat**

In Rio, avoid mussels! In 1996, prices were similar to São Paulo, see page 451. The best restaurants in Rio are those at the quality hotels (good value for world-class food and service); most close at midnight, many lack atmosphere. There are much livelier, and cheaper, places to eat as well if going out for an evening meal, Cariocas eat late (2200; later at weekends).

Centre: *Republique*, Pça da República 63 (2nd floor), T 532 4000, new and chic in 1996, designed by architect Chicô Gouveia, good food, expensive (US$50 without wine); *Café do Teatro*, Rio Branco, Teatro Municipal, good food in grand manner, shorts and scruffy gear not admitted; *Fiorino*, Av Heitor Beltrão 126, Tijuca, T 567 4476/567 9189, very good and cheap, rec; *Bistro do Paço*, Praça XV de Novembro 48, Centro, T 252 6353, excellent food, cheap prices, cosy surroundings, fancy place, Swiss run, rec; *Alba Mar*, fish, very good and reasonable, Praça Mal Ancora 184-6; *A Cabaça Grande*, Casa das Peixadas, R do Ouvidor 12, best for fish, closed Sun/holidays; *Rio Minho*, R do Ouvidor 10, for seafood, expensive, old-fashioned, very good. *Spaghetti*, Av Rio Branco 26, Italian, self-service, good salads, cheap. There are several Arab restaurants on Av Senhor dos Passos, also open Sat and Sun. *Luciano*, R das Marrecas 44, all you can eat at buffet, and others on this street. *Salad Market*, Av 13 de Maio 33/c, s/loja, weekday lunches only, US$16/kg; many *lanchonetes* for good, cheap meals in the business sector.

Santa Teresa: *Bar do Arnaudo*, Alm Alexandrino 316, B, rec; **Lapa**: *Semente*, R Joaquim Silva 138, vegetarian. **Glória**: *Casa da Suíça* in same building as Swiss Consulate, R Cândido Mendes 157, T 252-5182, bar/restaurant, good atmosphere; several others on this street; *Hobby Lanches*, R da Glória, nr Metrô, good, cheap.

Flamengo and Catete: there are a lot of eating places on R do Catete: *Bar KTT*, excellent; No 239, *Pastelaria Wong*, very cheap, good; No 234B, *Amazônia*, downstairs, one-price counter service, upstairs for good, reasonably-priced evening meals, rec; *Catelandia*, No 204, excellent and cheap; *Restaurante e Pizzaria Guanabara*, No 150, excellent value and selection; *Rio Galícia*, No 265, very good pizza, good service; *Machado*, No 286, good Italian food at reasonable prices; *Parmé*, No 311, one of a chain, friendly and reasonable; *No 128*, no name, lunch only, communal tables, rec; *Alcaparra*, Praia do Flamengo 144, elegant Italian, reasonable; close by *Lamas*, Marquês de Abrantes 18-A, excellent value, good food, great atmosphere, opens late, popular with Brazilian arts/media people, rec; *Alho E Oleo*, R Buarque de Macedo 13, T 205 2541/225 3418, fashionable, pleasant, rec; *Gaúcha*, R das Laranjeiras 114, good.

Botafogo: *Maxim's*, 44th floor of Rio Sul shopping centre, French, closed Sun; *Manolo*, Bambina e M de Olinda, very good value; *Raajmahal*, R Gen Polidoro 29, Indian, reasonable; *Zen Japanese Restaurant*, Praia de Botafogo 228, highly rec.

Copacabana and Leme: the main hotels (see above); most expensive is *Le Saint Honoré* at the *Meridien*, Leme, good food and wonderful view; *Churrascaria Marius*, at Leme end of Av Atlântica, 290-B, all you can eat US$20 with drinks, excellent; *Churrascaria Palace*, R Rodolfo Dantas 16-B, 22 different kinds of meat, very good; *Nino*, R Domingos Ferreira 242-A, good but not cheap; *Arataca*, Figueiredo de Magalhães 28, try *carne-de-sol* and *lagosta ao molho*; *A Marisquera*, Barata Ribeiro 232, good seafood; *Ponto d'Encontro* at No 750, Portuguese, try baked *bacalhau*; *Rian*, Santa Clara 8 (international), excellent and reasonable, very popular; *Maximix*, R Siquera Campos 12, loja A, buffet by weight, opens late, very popular, cheap, rec; *Arosa*, No 110, *lanchonete*, very good and cheap. *Frango na Brasa*, R Constante Ramos 35; *La Tratoria*, Av Atlântica (opp *Hotel Excelsior*), Italian, good food and service very reasonable, rec.

Ipanema: *Bardo Beto*, R Farme de Amoedo 51, excellent food, big servings, good value; *Il Capo*, Visconde de Pirajá 276, rec; *Banana Café*, Barão da Torre 368, trendy, lively nightclub upstairs after 2400; *Alho e Oleo*, next door, fashionable, friendly, rec; *Porção*, Barão de Torre 218, a very good *churrascaria*, US$8; *Pax Délicia*, Praça Nossa Senhora de Paz, good food, lively crowd; *Amarcord*, R Maria Quitéria 136, T 287 0335, rec; *Mostarda*, Av Epitácio Pessoa 980, not cheap but food excellent, nightclub

upstairs, rec. Ipanema is quieter than Copacabana, many nice places round Praça Gen Osório, such as *Romanos*; *Del Mare*, rec, at corner of Prudente de Morais and Vinícius de Morais. *Amarelinho*, R Farme de Amoedo 62, great corner lanchonete with tables outside, fresh food, lunch US$5, friendly, open until 0300, rec. *Casa da Feijoada*, Prudente de Morais 10, serves an excellent *feijoada* all week. Health food at *Restaurante Natural*, R Barão de Torre 171. *Delicats*, Av Henrique Dumont 68, good Jewish deli.

Leblon: *Un, Deux, Trois*, R Bartolomeu Mitre 123, very fashionable, restaurant, nightclub; *Antiquarius*, R Aristides Espínola 19, restaurant-cum-antique shop, seafood and international cuisine; *Mediterráneo*, R Prudente de Morais 1810, excellent fish, reasonable prices. In **Jardim Botânico**: *Claude Troisgros*, R Custódio Serrão 62, T 537 8582, elegant French restaurant, rec; *Enotria*, R Frei Leandro 20, T 246 9003, excellent Italian food, service, atmosphere and prices, rec. **Lagoa**: *Mistura Fina*, Av Borges de Medeiros 3207, T 266-5844/537-2844, classy, popular, friendly nightclub upstairs (US$25). **São Conrado**: *El Pescador*, Praça São Conrado 20, Spanish-style fish restaurant, excellent value and variety of paellas. **Barra**: *Amarelinho*, Av Ayrton Senna 3000, warmly rec lanchonete, see Ipanema above; *Caffe Milano*, R Rodolfo Amoedo 360, T 494-4671, new, good Italian, US$35 (no credit cards).

Grill or barbecue houses (churrascarias) are relatively cheap, especially by European standards. There are many at São Conrado and Joá, on the road out to Barra da Tijuca (see page 391). Look for the 'Churrascaria Rodízio', where you are served as much as you can eat. There are plentiful hamburger stands (literally 'stands' as you stand and eat the hamburger) and lunch counters all over the city. *McDonalds* and *Big Bob's* (similar) can be found at about 20 locations each (Big Mac US$3). *Galetos* are lunch counters specializing in chicken and grilled meat, very reasonable. In the 'shopping centres' there is usually a variety of restaurants and snack bars grouped around a central plaza where you can shop around for a good meal. Most less-expensive restaurants in Rio have basically the same type of food (based on steak, fried potatoes and rice) and serve large portions; those with small appetites, and especially families with children, can ask for a spare plate, and split helpings. *La Mole*, at 11 locations, serves good, cheap Italian food: very popular. *Comida por quilo* is about US$15/kg in Rio. There are many juice bars in Rio with a wide selection. Most restaurants are closed on 24 and 25 December.

Tea rooms: for those who like their teas served

English style, the sedate (100 years old in 1994) *Confeitaria Colombo*, R Gonçalves Dias 32 nr Carioca metro station, is highly rec for atmosphere, being the only one of its kind in Rio, with the original Belle Epoque décor, open 0900-1800, lunch available, no service charge so tip the excellent waiters. More modern but similar establishments in some of the main hotels, and at *Casarão*, Souza Lima 37A, Copacabana; *Traiteurs de France*, Av Copacabana 386, delicious tarts and pastries, not expensive; *La Bonne Table*, Visc de Pirajá 580 sala 407, Ipanema; and *Ponto de Encontro*, Barata Ribeiro 750B, Copacabana. *Café de la Paix*, Av Atlântica 1020; *Chá e Simpatia*, Av Atlântica 4240; *Um Chorinho Chamado Odeon*, Gávea Shopping Centre; *Bolo Inglês*, Cassino Atlântico Shopping Centre; *Concorde*, Av Prudente de Morais 129. These establishments have become very fashionable. Chicest *chá* in 1996: *Pergula*, Copacabana Palace Hotel, Av Atlântica 1702, run by Englishwoman Anne Phillips, Mon to Fri 1400 – 1700, rec.

Bars: wherever you are, there's one near you. A beer costs around US$1.50, rarely more than US$3 even in expensive bars. A cover charge of US$3-7 may be made for live music. Snack food always available. Single drinkers/diners are usually welcome, though you may not remain alone for long unless you stick your nose in a book. Copacabana, Ipanema and Leblon have many beach *barracas*, several open all night. On the town (more protected) side, the seafront bars on Av Atlântica are great for people-watching. The big hotels have good cocktail bars (*Copacabana Palace*, poolside, rec); *Alla Zingara*, corner of Min Viveiros de Castro and Belfort Roxo, is friendly. There are only 4 seafront bars in Ipanema: *Barril 1800*, Av Tom Jobim 110, highly rec, nice place to watch the sunset. *A Garota de Ipanema*, R Vinícius de Morais 49, is where the song 'Girl from Ipanema' was written, very lively. Lots more bars opening in districts to the S. *Bar Lagoa*, Av Epitácio Pessoa 1674, Lagoa, rec ('arty crowd', evenings only). British ex-pats meet at *Porão*, under the Anglican church hall, R Real Grandeza 99, Botafogo, Fri only.

● **Banks & money changers**
Banks: Lloyds Bank, R da Alfândega 33; Banco Internacional (Bank of America and Royal Bank of Canada), R do Ouvidor 90; Banco Holandês Unido, R do Ouvidor 101; Citibank, R Assembléia 100, changes large US$ TCs into smaller ones, no commission; The First National Bank of Boston, Av Rio Branco 110; many others. Banco do Brasil, there are only 2 branches in Rio which will change US$ TCs, Praia de Botafogo, 384A, 3rd floor (minimium US$200) and central branch R Senador Dantes 105, 4th floor (minimum US$500 – good rates. Banco do Brasil

at the International Airport is open 24 hrs a day. Visa cash withdrawals at Banco do Brasil (also TCs) and Bradesco (machines). Banco Noroeste, R Buenos Aires 56, advances cash on Eurocard/Mastercard; Mastercard and Cirrus cash machines at Itaú, on Av Atlântica (next to *Copacabana Palace*), R Visconde de Parajá, close to Pça Osório (Ipanema), and other locations. Banks use the legal tourist exchange rate. See **Currency**, page 658.

Money changers: American Express, Av Atlântica 1702, Loja B, *Hotel Copacabana Palace*, T 255-2148/2677. Most large hotels and reputable travel agencies will change currency and TCs. Copacabana (where rates are generally worse than in centre) abounds with *câmbios*; Eurocheques, TCs and currency at *Hamburg Imobiliária*, Av Copacabana 195, Loja 104, T 542-1446. NB Many *câmbios* will give you the parallel rate for cash, but a worse rate for cheques; some will also change US$ cheques for US$ cash with a 4% commission. These transactions are not strictly legal, so you will have to look around for the *câmbios* that do them. For credit/cash card withdrawals, see *Banks* above.

● **Cultural centres**
The British Council, R Elmano Cardim 10, Urca, T 295-7782, F 541-3693. The British School of Rio de Janeiro, R Real Grandeza 99. Sociedade Brasileira de Cultura Inglesa, Av Graça Aranha 327, and in Copacabana, T 227-0147. American Chamber of Commerce for Brazil, Praça Pio Dez 15, 5th floor. American Society and American Club, Av Rio Branco 123, 21st floor. USICA Reference Library, US Consulate General, Av Presidente Wilson 147. The American School of Rio de Janeiro, Estrada da Gávea 132. Marc Apoio Cultural Contact Center, PO Box 1736, 20001-970, T/F (21) 275-8605; German Cultur-Institut (Goethe), Av Graça Aranha 416, 9th floor; open Mon-Thur 1200-1900, Wed-Thur 1000-1100. Centro Cultural Banco do Brasil, R Primeiro de Março 66, free concerts. Australian Trade Commission, R Voluntários da Pátria 45, 2°, Botafogo, T 286-7922 (for visas etc you must go to Brasília).

● **Electric current**
110-220 volts, 60 cycles, AC.

● **Embassies & consulates**
Argentine, Praia de Botafogo 228, T 551-5498, very helpful over visas, 1130-1600; Uruguay, R Artur Bernardes 30, T 285-0195; Paraguay, Av NS de Copacabana 583, room 404, T 255-7572, visas US$5; Venezuela, Praia de Botafogo 242, 5th floor, T 551-5698 (will not issue visas, see under Manaus and Boa Vista).

US Consulate General, Av Presidente Wilson, 147, T 292-7117. Canada, R Dona Gerardo 46, 11th floor, T 233-9286.

UK, Praia do Flamengo 284, T 552-1422; **Ireland**, Av Princesa Isabel 323, 1208, T 275 0196; **Switzerland**, R Cândido Mendes 157, 11° andar, T 221 1867; **German Consulate-General**, R Presidente Carlos de Campos 417, T 553-6777; **France**, Av Pres Antônio Carlos, 58, T 210-1272; **Austria**, Av Atlântica 3804, T 227-0040/048/049; **Netherlands**, Praia de Botafogo 242, 7th floor, T 552-9028 (Dutch newspapers here; also at KLM office on Av Rio Branco); **Swedish Consulate-General**, Praia do Flamengo 344, 9th floor, T 552-2422; **Denmark**, Av das Américas 3333, Apt 805, T 431-2080.

Israel, Av NS Copacabana 680-C, T 255-5432; **South Africa**, Av Pres Antônio Carlos 607, T 533-0216; **Greece**, T 552-6849, 552-6749, Praia do Flamengo 344/201 22210.

● **Entertainment**

Cinemas: new American releases (with original soundtrack), plus Brazilian and worldwide films, and classics. A very few give cheaper tickets to students, but not at weekends. See local press. Normal seat price US$4, discount on Wed and Thur.

Nightclubs: Rio nightlife is rich and infinitely varied, one of the main attractions for most visitors. If you are not in Rio for Carnival, it's worth seeing a samba show, cheaper if you pay at the door. *Hotel Nacional* at São Conrado has the most lavish show in town; also *Plataforma I*, R Adalberto Ferreira 32, Leblon, T 274-4022, arrive by 2000, show finishes 2300. For about 2 months before Carnival, samba schools give public rehearsals, cheap and great fun (see page 394).

Many young Cariocas congregate in Botafogo for live music. There are free concerts throughout the summer, along the beaches, in Botafogo and at the parks: mostly samba, reggae, rock and MPB (Brazilian pop): information from local press (see below). January sees Hollywood Rock, a vast 3-day open air concert featuring international bands, Praça da Apoteose; there are live concerts every weekend at the Arpoador park, between Copacabana and Ipanema.

Trendiest club in 1996 (contemporary dance music) was *Le Boy*, Raul Pompéia 94, Copacabana, T 521 0367; also try *Dr Smith*, R da Passagem 169, Botafogo, T 295-3135, Wed-Sun; *Banana Café*, Barão da Torre 368, Ipanema, T 5211460; *Papillon*, Av Prefeito Mendes de Moraes 222, São Conrado, T 322 2200; *Mostarda*, Av Epitácio Pessoa 980, Ipanema; *Resumo da Ópera*, Av Borges de Medeiros 1426, Lagoa, T 274-5875 ('rich Brazilians at play'); *The Basement*, Av NS de Copacabana 1241, new, alternative; also rec is *Torre de Babel*, Visconde de Parajá (close to hippy market), Sats only; and at the *Jardim Botânico* (weekends). There are dozens of other good clubs, most open Wed-Sun,

action starts around midnight, lone women and male-only groups may have trouble getting in.

Canecão is a big, inexpensive venue for live concerts, most nights, see press for listings: R Venceslau Braz 215, Botafogo, T 295-3044.

Rio's famous jazz, in all its forms, is performed in lots of enjoyable venues, see press. The following are sophisticated sit-down places (you have to eat something, budget around US$20 each, comfortable for lone women): *Jazzmania*, Av Rainha Elisabeth, Ipanema, T 227-2447; *Mistura Fina*, Av Borges de Medeiros 3207, Lagoa, T 266-5844; *Rio Jazz Club*, annexe of *Meridien Hotel*, Av Atlântica, Leme, T 541-9046. Check time of show, usually around 2200.

Gafieiras, for Samba dancing, inc *Elite Club*, R Frei Caneca 4, 1st floor, Centro, T 232-3217; *Estudantinha*, Praça Tiradentes 79, T 232-1149, Thur-Sun: there are many cheaper *gafieiras*: one, enthusiastically rec, under the beach highway at Botafogo. All types of music and entertainment are represented: *Forró da Copacabana*, Av NS de Copacabana 435, has been rec for forró fans (safe, disco upstairs); *Reggae Rock Cafe*, Largo de São Conrado 20, T 322-4197; *Raizes*, Av Sernambetiba 1120, T 389-6240, for Afro-Brazilian beats.

Copacabana is full of discos where the girls are for hire: biggest and most entertaining is *Help*. Entry charge (US$9) does not inc drink. Music is usually good, trade is low-pressure, women with female friends and a sense of humour can have a lot of fun (but not rec for couples). Sleazier shows are concentrated around Leme, as are gay clubs; many gay clubs also around Lapa (Cinelândia), but good ones exist all over the city. *Stop-Night*, a disco bar at Av Atlântica (nr *Copacabana Palace* hotel) is a popular gay pick-up joint: please be extremely careful.

Many people look for Macumba religious ceremonies. Those offered on the night tours sold at hotels are not genuine, and a disappointment. You need a local contact to see the real ones, which are usually held in *favelas* and are none too safe for unaccompanied tourists.

Theatres: there are about 40 theatres in Rio, presenting a variety of classical and modern performances in Portuguese. Seats about US$15; some children's theatre is free. Rio's stages attract top-name Brazilian artists – check local papers.

● **Hospitals & medical services**

Vaccinations at *Saude de Portos*, Praça 15 de Novembro (international vaccination book and ID required). *Policlínica*, Av Nilo Peçanha 38, rec for diagnosis and investigation. *Hospital Miguel Couto*, Mário Ribeiro 117, Gávea, has a casualty ward (free), but no eye doctors T 274-2121; these can be found at *Hospital Souza Aguiar*, Praça da República III (casuality ward also free),

T 296-4114. The *Rio Health Collective* will help you contact an English-speaking doctor: dial 294-0282/325-3327/239-7401; ask for the 'dona da casa'.

Take note of local advice on water pollution; air pollution also occurs.

Dentist: English-speaking, Amílcar Werneck de Carvalho Vianna, Av Pres Wilson 165, suite 811. Dr Djorup, Av Beira Mar Mauro Suartz, R Visconde de Pirajá 414, room 509, T 287-6745, speaks English and Hebrew, helpful.

Public conveniences: there are very few in Rio de Janeiro, but many bars and restaurants (eg Macdonalds) offer facilities; just ask for the 'banheiro' (banyairoo). Good conveniences are to be found in the Shopping Centres.

● **Language courses**
Instituto Brasil-Estados Unidos, Av Copacabana 690, 5th floor, T 255-8332, offers 8-week courses in Portuguese, 3 classes a week, US$200, 5-week intensive course US$260. Good English library at same address. *Curso Feedback*, branches in Botafogo, Centre, Barra and Ipanema, T 221-1863.

● **Laundry**
Fénix, R do Catete 214, Loja 20; R Marques de Abrantes, about No 80 (Flamengo); Praça G Osório, Ipanema; *Lavlev Flamengo*, RC de Baepinédi 78, or R das Laranjeiras 43, L28. Laundromat at 1216 Av NS de Copacabana; R Barata Ribeiro 662, Copacabana, self-service, US$1.50/machine. In Rio Sul are self-service laundrettes such as *Lavlev*, about US$3-4 for a machine, inc detergent and drying, 1 hr, also at R Voluntário da Patria 248, Botafogo, Av Prado Jnr 6313, Copacabana.

● **Places of worship**
Places where worship is conducted other than in Portuguese: **Christ Church**, R Real Grandeza 99, Botafogo (Church of England/American Episcopalian). The British School, for children of 5-16, is nearby. **Chapel of Our Lady of Mercy**, R Visconde de Caravelas 48, Botafogo (Roman Catholic, with primary school). **Union Church**: (Protestant nondenominational) services held at R Parque da Lagoa de Marapendi, CP 37154-CEP 22609 Barra da Tijuca. **International Baptist Church**, R Desembargador Alfredo Russel 146, Leblon. **First Church of Christ Scientist**, Av Marechal Câmara 271, room 301. **Masonic Temple**, in the British School at R da Matriz 76, Botafogo. **Synagogues**, R Pompeu Loureiro 48, Botafogo, T 257-4299; R Barata Ribeiro 489, Copacabana. Includes kosher bakery. **Swedish Church**, Igreja Escandinava, Av Rui Barbosa 170, Bloco B 1, 5 And, T 551-6696, open 1300-2200, Sun 1700-2100, will store luggage. **British Cemetery**, R da Gamboa 181, granted to the British community by Dom João, Regent of Portugal, in 1810. It is the oldest cemetery in Rio.

● **Post & telecommunications**
Cables: Embratel, Av President Vargas 1012. Telegrams may be sent through any post office. Larger offices have telex and fax.

Post Office: central Post Office, R Primeiro de Março 64, at corner of R do Rosário; Av NS de Copacabana 540, and many other locations; all handle international post. There is a post office at the airport. **Poste Restante**: American Express, Av Atlântica 1702 loja B, Copacabana (for customers), and all large post offices (letters held for a month, rec, US$0.10/letter); Kontik Franstur will forward mail to their branches in Brazil without charge. Federal Express, Av Calógeras 23 (nr Sta Luzia church) T 262-8565, is reliable.

Telephones: international calls at Av Copacabana 540, 2nd floor, international airport, international telephone booths (blue), rodoviária, R Dias da Cruz 192, Méier-4, 24 hrs, 7 days a week, or at Santos Dumont airport, 1st floor (0530-2300). Also at Praça Tiradentes 41, a few minutes' walk from Metrô Carioca. R Visconde Pirajá, 111. Av NS de Copacabana, 540. R do Ouvidor, 60 centro.

● **Shopping**
Buy precious and semi-precious stones from reputable dealers. *H Stern* have shops at the airport, and all over Copacabana and Ipanema; they also offer a tour, with head-phone commentary, of their lapidary and designing workshops, on request; *Roditi* and *Amsterdam Sauer* offer free taxi rides to their workshops. There are several good jewellery shops at the Leme end of Av NS de Copacabana: *Lido*, R Rodolfo Dantas 26B, T 541-8098, rec. For mineral specimens as against cut stones, try *Mineraux*, Av Copacabana 195, Belgian owner. *Saara* is a multitude of little shops along R Alfândega and R Sen dos Passos (between city centre and Campo Sant'ana) where clothes bargains can be found (especially jeans and bikinis). Little shops on Aires Saldanha, Copacabana (1 block back from beach), good for bikinis and cheaper than in shopping centres. *Malamada*, R da Carioca 13, rec for rucksacks.

Bookshops: for international stock, *Livraria Kosmos*, R do Rosário 155, good shop (in the centre and Av Atlântica 1702, loja 5) and there are many others, eg *Livros Técnicos*, R Miguel Couto 35, wide selection; *Nova Livraria Da Vinci*, Av Rio Branco 185 lojas 2, 3 and 9, all types of foreign books, *SAH* available; *Livraria Argumento*, R Dias Ferreira 417, Leblon, sells imported English books; also branches of *Solider* at airports and shopping centres. *Livrarias Siciliano*, Av Rio Branco 156, loja 26, European books, also at NS de Copacabana 830 and branches; French books at No 298. *Unilivros*, Largo do Machado 29C, French and English bestsellers (7 branches); *Livraria Nova Galeria de Arte*, Av Copacabana 291D, international stock. *El Dorado*, Av das Américas 4666, loja 207. Second-hand books also at *Livraria São José*, R Carmo 61 (only a few in English); *Livraria Brasileira*, Av Rio Branco 156, S/Loja 229; Aimée Gilbert, R da Carioca 38 (some in English); *Livraria Antiquário*, Sete de Setembro 207 and in R Pedro I, all in centre. Also on Av Marechal Floriano, nr Av Rio Branco, especially at No 63. On S side of Praça Tiradentes, *Casa dos Artistas* trades in second-hand paperbacks. Second-hand English books at the Anglican church, R Real Grandeza 99, Botafogo.

Cameras and film processing: *Dino's*, R Buenos Aires 241; others in same street. Camera repair, Av Rio Branco 151, 2nd floor, room 204. Kodachrome slide film difficult to get in Rio. For processing, *Flash Studio*, R Visconde de Pirajá 156, expensive; *One Hour Foto*, in the Rio Sul and Barra shopping centres, is rec; also a laboratory at R do Russel 344, Glória (1 hr for transparencies). *Honório*, R Vinícius de Moraes 146-E, stocks lithium batteries. Nikon camera repairs, *T Tanaka cia Ltda*, Av Franklin Roosevelt 39, of 516, T 220-1127.

Electronics repair: (radio, walkman, etc), *Eletrônika Tekron*, R Figueiredo Magalhães 870, Copacabana, T 235-4096, efficient, friendly.

Local press: *Balcão*, an advertising newspaper, US$1.50, twice weekly, offers apartments in and around Rio, language lessons, discounted tickets, items for sale, and advertises shops; similar advertisements in the classified sections of *O Globo* and *Jornal do Brasil*, daily. Both dailies have entertainments pages. *O Globo* inc a travel section on Thur; the *Jornal do Brasil*'s Friday *Programa* is an essential 'what's-on' magazine, as is the *Rio* supplement to *Veja*, a weekly news magazine (*Veja* publishes similar supplements in other major cities). *Riotur's* monthly booklet listing main attractions; *Rio This Month* (less reliable), free from hotels. *IurisRio's* free magazine about the State of Rio de Janeiro is interesting; if your hotel does not have the above 3 publications, just ask at the reception of one of the larger establishments.

Markets: Northeastern market at Campo de São Cristóvão, with music and magic, on Sun mornings. Saturday antiques market on waterfront, nr Praça 15 de Novembro (1000-1800), rec, and flea market Sat (0900-1900) in Praça 15; another in Largo da Carioca. Sunday stamp and coin market in Passeio Público. Sunday open-air handicrafts market (hippie fair) at Praça Gen Osório, Ipanema, 0800-1300 or 1400, touristy but fun. Markets on

Wed 0700-1300 on R Domingos Ferreira and on Thur, same hours, on Praça do Lido, both Copacabana; also on Thur, good leather and jewellery market on 1 de Março in centre. Sunday market on R da Glória, colourful, cheap fruit, vegetables and flowers; early-morning food market, 0600-1100, R Min Viveiros de Castro, Ipanema. Excellent food and household-goods markets at various places in the city and suburbs (see newspapers for times and places).

Shopping centres: Rio Sul, at Botafogo end of Túnel Novo, Cassino (Copacabana), Nte Shopping (Todos os Santos), Plaza Shopping (Niterói), Barra on Barra de Tijuca (see page 391). At São Conrado The Fashion Mall is smaller and more stylish.

● **Sports**

There are hundreds of excellent gyms and sports clubs; most will not grant temporary (less than 1 month) membership: big hotels may allow use of their facilities for a small deposit. *Paissandu Athletic Club*, Av Afrânio de Melo Franco 330, Leblon – tennis, bowls, swimming, Scottish dancing, Tues, April-Oct, 2000-2230, may admit non-members. *Sociedade Hípico Brasileiro*, Av Borges de Medeiros 2448, T 246-8090, Jardim Botânico – riding; horse racing Sat, Sun, entrance US$1-2, long trousers required. *late Clube do Rio de Janeiro*, Av Pasteur, Urca, T 295-4482 – yachting.

Cycling: tours (hire available) with *Rio Bikers*, R Domingos Ferreira 81, room 201, T 274-5872.

Golf clubs: there are both 18-hole and 9-hole courses at the Itanhangá Golf Club, Jacarepaguá, visiting cards from Av Rio Branco 26, 16th floor. The Gávea club, São Conrado, T 399-4141 and the Teresópolis Golf Club, Estrada Imbuí (Várzea) both have 18 holes. 9 holes at Petrópolis Country Club, Nogueira.

Hang gliding: with Rejane Reis (US$100), T 322-6972.

Paragliding: from Leblon beach with Sr Marra, T 226-5207 or find him at the beach: "Just fantastic!"

Rock climbing and hill walking: *ECA*, Av Enasmo Braga 217, room 305, T 242-6857/571-0484, personal guide US$100/day, owner Ralph speaks English; *Clube Excursionista Carioca*, also rec for enthusiasts, R Hilário Gouveia 71, room 206, T 255-1348, meets Wed, Fri.

● **Tour companies & travel agents**

American Express, see **Banks & money changers** above; *Roxy*, est 1948, Av Franklin Roosevelt, 71/601, Centro, CEP 20.021-120, T 532-0141, F 532-3165, ask for Michael or Ricardo Werwie who speak English, rec; *Exprinter*, Av Rio Branco, 128; *Manhattan Turismo Ltda*, R da Assembléia 10, GR 3503, Centro,

T 242-3779/3064, very helpful, English spoken; *Tour Brazil*, R Farme de Amoeda 75/605, nr Ipanema, T 521-4461, F 021-521-1056, very good English spoken; *Victor Hummel*, Av Presidente Vargas 290/4, T 223-1262, Swiss-run, rec, T 231-1800. *Marlin Tours*, Av Copacabana 605/1201, T 255-4433, rec, Robin and Audrey speak English. *Quality Travel*, Av NS Copacabana 387, T 235-6888, F 236-6985, helpful with hotel bookings; *Hamburg Imobiliária*, Av Copacabana 195, Loja 104, T 542-1446, F 236-4541, German run, flights, accommodation, tours, exchange, very helpful (English, Spanish, Port), rec; *Hanseatic*, R Sete de Setembro 111/20, T 224 6672, centro, German run (English, French, Port), rec.

The tourist office in Praça da República offers hourly tourist buses for US$0.50: leave the bus at sites you wish to visit, and rejoin the next one. Organized trips to Samba shows cost US$50 inc dinner, good but it's cheaper to go independently. Regular sightseeing tours operated by *Gray Line* (294-0393), *American Sightseeing* (236-3551), *Sul América* (257-4235), *Canbitur* (of Copacabana), *Passamar Turismo*, Av Rio Branco 25 (233-8883, 233-4833, 253-1125; also at *Hotel Nacional*). *Adrianotour*, T 208-5103, for guided tours, reservations and commercial services (English, French, German and Spanish spoken). *Sangetur*, Largo de Machado, 29 (Galeria Condor), Loja 39, T 205 0993 or 0245, credit cards only accepted for airplane tickets. *Dantur*, Largo de Machado, 29 (Galeria Condor) Loja 47, T 205 1144, Helena speaks English and is friendly and helpful.

● **Tourist offices**

There are several information centres. **Embratur**, R Mariz e Barros 13, nr Praça da Bandeira, T 273-2212, gives information on the whole country. **Riotur** (for the city of Rio): small, helpful information desk at R da Assembleia 10, 9th floor, has good city maps and a very useful free brochure 'Rioguia' written in both Portuguese and English. More information stands can be found at Pão de Açúcar cablecar station (0800-2000); Marina da Glória, Flamengo; Rodoviária Novo Rio (the bus station – 0600-2400; very friendly and helpful in finding accommodation but has no printed information) and at Copacabana, Av Princesa Isabel 183, T 542 8080 or 8084. Riotur also has a multilingual telephone service operating 24 hrs, T 580-8000. English information service, T 242-8000. **Flumitur** (for the state of Rio de Janeiro) at Rio International Airport, helpful with hotel information and booking, can sometimes arrange discounts, and R da Assembléia 10, 8th floor, very helpful. **Touring Clube do Brasil**, Pres Antônio Carlos 130 and Av Brasil 4294 (out of town) no English

spoken. **Centro Cultural Banco do Brasil**, Primeiro Março 66, has a free, computerized information service.

Best guide to Rio, with excellent map, *Guia Quatro Rodas do Rio* in Portuguese and English (the *Guia Quatro Rodas do Brasil*, published annually in Nov also has a good Rio section). Also, *The Insider's Guide to Rio de Janeiro*, an annual guide book by Christopher Pickard, available from Rio bookshops, or enquire at Marlin Tours (T 255-4433). Many hotels provide guests with the weekly *Itinerário (Rio This Month)*; also see **Local Press**, above.

NB Tourist packs are sold for US$25 at the International Airport – they are completely unnecessary.

Maps: *Guia Rex* street guide. *Guia Schaeffer Rio de Janeiro* is a good map. Maps are also available from Touring Clube do Brasil, newsstands, touring agencies and hotels; Geomapas tourist map is clear. Paulini, R Lélio Gama 75 (outside the entrance of the downtown tram station): topographical and other maps of Brazil and of South America. **NB** Tourist agencies do not normally provide lists of cheap accommodation for travellers; some initiative is required.

● **Useful addresses**

Tourist Police: Av Afrânio de Melo Franco, Leblon (opp Scala nightclub), T 511-5112. Renewal of 90-day visa, US$4.

● **Transport**

Local Buses Good services to all parts, very crowded and not for the aged and infirm during rush hours. Hang on tight, drivers living out Grand Prix fantasies. Fare normally about US$0.55. Bus stops are often not marked. The route is written on the side of the bus. Private companies operate a/c buses which can be flagged down practically anywhere: Real, Pegaso, Anatur. They run from all points in Rio Sul to the city centre, Rodoviária and the airports. Fares about US$2 (US$5 to international airport). **Car hire:** Avis, Rio International airport, less helpful than office at Praia do Flamengo 224 (205-5796); **Nobre**, Gustavo Sampaio 826 (275-5297) and Av Princesa Isabel 350 (T 541-4646), Copacabana. **Telecar**, R Figueiredo Magalhães 701 (257-2620). Many agencies on Av Princesa Isabel, Copacabana. Credit card virtually essential. Recent reports suggest it is cheaper to hire outside Brazil, you may also obtain fuller insurance this way. Remember service stations are closed in many places on Sat and Sun. **Car repairs:** Kyoso Team Mecânico Siquero Campos, at the entrance to the old tunnel, T 255-0506, a good mechanic who enjoys the challenge of an unusual car, rec. **Taxis:** the fare between Copacabana and the centre is US$9. Between 2300 and 0600 and on Suns and holidays 'tariff 2' is used. Taxis have red number plates with white digits (yellow for private cars, with black digits) and have meters. Smaller ones (mostly Volkswagen) are marked TAXI on windscreen or roof. Make sure meters are cleared and on tariff 1, except at those times mentioned above. Only use taxis with an official identification sticker on the windscreen. Don't hesitate to argue if the route is too long or the fare too much. Radio Taxis are safer but more expensive, eg Cootramo, 270-1442, Coopertramo, 260-2022, Cooper-Transpa, 593-2598, Transcoopass, 278-4888. Luxury cabs are allowed to charge higher rates. Inacro de Oliveira, T 225-4110, is a reliable taxi driver for excursions, only speaks Portuguese, rec. Grimalde, T 267 9812, has been rec for talkative daytime and evening tours, English, Italian, negotiate price. **Trams:** the last remaining tram runs from Largo da Carioca (where there is a museum, open only Fri 0830-1700) across the old aqueduct (Arcos) to Dois Irmãos or Paula Matos in Santa Teresa – historical and interesting, US$0.10. Service is cut in low season. The trams are open sided, do not carry valuables. **Underground railway**: Metrô, good service, clean, a/c and fast. Line 1 operates between Tijuca and Botafogo, via the railway station and Glória, with 19 km in operation; it is being extended 1 km at the Tijuca end and 7 km at the other. It will go from Botafogo via Copacabana and on to Ipanema and Leblon (Jardim de Allah); still not open in March 1996. Line 2, running past the Maracanã stadium northward to Irajá, will eventually run from Praça 15 de Novembro (Estação das barcas Rio-Niteroi), through the city centre, to Estácio. Operates 0600-2300, Sun 1400-2000 closed holidays. Fare US$0.50 single (12 tickets US$5); integrated bus/Metrô tickets available. Substantial changes in bus operations are taking place because of the extended Metrô system; buses connecting with the Metrô have a blue-and-white symbol in the windscreen.

Air Rio has two airports. The Santos Dumont airport on Guanabara Bay, right in the city, is used exclusively for Rio-São Paulo shuttle flights (US$300 return), air taxis and private planes. The shuttle services operate every 30 mins throughout the day from 0630 to 2230. Sit on right-hand side for views to São Paulo, other side coming back, book in advance for particular flights. The main airport (Galeão), on Governador Island, some 16 km from the centre of Rio, is in two sections, international and domestic (inc Vasp and Transbrasil's jet shuttle from Rio to São Paulo). Duty-free shops are well-stocked, but not especially cheap. Duty-free at Galeão is open

to arrivals as well as departures.

The a/c 'Alvorada' bus runs very frequently from the first floor of Galeão to Recreio dos Bandeirantes via the municipal rodoviária and city centre, Santos Dumont Airport, Flamengo, Copacabana, Ipanema and Leblon. Luggage is secured in the hold (receipted), passengers are given a ticket and fares collected during the journey; Zona Sul about US$5. The driver will stop at requested points (the bus runs along the seafront from Leme to Leblon), so it's worth checking a map beforehand so that you can specify your required junction. Returns by same route. A/c taxis (Cootramo and Transcopass) have fixed rates (US$40 Copacabana), buy a ticket at the counter nr the arrivals gate before getting into the car. The hire is for taxi, irrespective of number of passengers, and therefore it is possible to share with other passengers. Make sure you keep the ticket, which carries the number to phone in case of difficulty. Check at the Riotur counter before leaving, for folders, maps and advice. Ordinary taxis also operate with the normal meter reading. Do not negotiate with a driver on arrival, unless you are a frequent visitor. Town buses M94 and M95, Bancários/Castelo, take a circular route passing through the centre and the interstate bus station.

There are câmbios in the departure hall of airport; there is also a câmbio on the first floor of the international arrivals area, but it gives worse rates than the Banco do Brasil, 24 hr bank, 3rd floor, which will give cash advances against Visa card (beware 'officials' who say there are no câmbios or banks). There is a wider choice of restaurants outside passport control.

Trains There are suburban trains to Nova Iguaçu, Nilópolis, Campo Grande and elsewhere. Buses marked 'E Ferro' go to the railway station. The Silver Train, deluxe, overnight, runs to **São Paulo** Sun, Tues, Thur 2030, from Av Francisco Bicalho s/n, T 293-6328; a cabin on the 9-hr journey costs US$100 single.

Buses Rodoviária Novo Rio, T 291-5151 (Av Rodrigues Alves, corner with Av Francisco Bicalho, just past the docks). Some travel agents sell interstate tickets, or will direct you to bus ticket office in centre. Buses run from Rio to all parts of the country; it is advisable to book tickets in advance. Details of journey times and fares are given under destinations throughout the chapter.

International: Asunción, 1,511 km via Foz do Iguaçu, 30 hrs (Pluma), US$42; **Buenos Aires** (Pluma), via Porto Alegre and Santa Fe, 44 hrs, US$163 (book 2 days in advance); **Montevideo**, only from São Paulo; **Santiago** de Chile, with Pluma or Gral Urquiza, about 70 hrs. The Buenos Aires and Montevideo services are fully booked a week in advance.

The main bus station is reached by buses M94 and M95, *Bancários/Castelo*, from the centre and the airport; 126, 127, 136, *Rodoviária/Copacabana*; 170, *Rodoviária/Gávea*; 128, 172, *Rodoviária/Leblon*; these buses pass Botafogo and Flamengo. It has a Riotur information centre, very helpful. Left luggage, US$2.50. The local bus teminal is just outside the rodoviária: turn right as you leave and run the gauntlet of taxi drivers – best ignored. The rodoviária attracts thieves; exercise caution. The a/c Real bus (opp the exit) goes along the beach to São Conrado and will secure luggage. **If you need a taxi collect a ticket**, which ensures against overcharging, from the office inside the entrance. The fare to Copacabana in 1996 was US$16. On no account give the ticket to the taxi driver.

Hitchhiking To hitch to Belo Horizonte or Brasília, take a C-3 bus from Av Presidente Antônio Carlos to the railway station, cross through the station to a bus station, and catch the Nova Iguaçu bus. Ask to be let off at the Belo Horizonte turn off. For the motorway entrance N and S take bus 392 or 393 from Praça São Francisco.

Roads Distances in km to some major cities with approximate journey time in brackets: Juiz de Fora, 177 (2¾ hrs); Belo Horizonte, 429 (7 hrs); São Paulo, 434 (6 hrs); Vitória, 519 (8 hrs); Curitiba, 839 (12 hrs); Brasília, 1,148 (20 hrs); Florianópolis, 1,154 (20 hrs); Foz do Iguaçu, 1,500 (21 hrs); Porto Alegre, 1,603 (26 hrs); Salvador, 1,690 (28 hrs); Recife, 2,309 (38 hrs); Fortaleza, 2,861 (48 hrs); São Luís, 3,093 (50 hrs); Belém, 3,187 (52 hrs).

Entering Rio from the W, an alternative to the BR-101 and Av Brasil, is to leave BR-101 on the road to Santa Cruz, continuing 6 km to the fishing village of Sepetiba, quiet other than at weekends. Along the coast is Pedra de Guaratiba, from where you join Av das Américas, turning off right soon afterwards to Ponta do Picão and Guaratiba, a pretty seaside resort on a rocky, narrow, steep ledge between mountain and sea (good beaches and a playground for the rich). Another 2 km along the main road is another (unmarked) right turn leading to a restaurant at the summit, with fantastic views, then down to Praia de Grumari (see above). It is then 30 km to Copacabana, via Recreio dos Bandeirantes.

THE STATE OF RIO DE JANEIRO: EAST FROM RIO

NITERÓI

(*Pop* 416,125; *CEP* 24000; *DDD* 021) Founded in 1573, the ex-capital of the State of Rio de Janeiro, is reached across Guanabara bay by bridge or ferries.

Places of interest

On this side of the bay are beaches which, though calm, are often overcrowded and polluted, but no more so than those opposite in Rio. The forts on this side of the bay include Santa Cruz (16th century, still a military establishment), Barão do Rio Branco (1633), Gragoatá and Nossa Senhora da Boa Viagem. You should also visit the church of Boa Viagem (1633), built on an island connected to the mainland by a short causeway, a few minutes' walk from Icaraí beach. Nearby, on R Tiradentes, is the **Museu Antônio Parreira**, opens 1300, dedicated to the eponymous artist. The **Museu de Arqueologia de Itaipu** is in the ruins of the 18th century Santa Teresa Convent, and also covers the archaeological site of Duna Grande on Itaipu beach.

Local information
● **Accommodation**

A2 *Bucsky*, R Cel Tamarindo 150, Praia do Gragoatá, T 717-3322, F 717-3841.

C *Niterói Palace*, R Andrade Neves 134, T 719-2155, F 719-2800; *Icaraí Praia*, R Belisário Agusto 21, T 714-1414, F 710-6142, similar price. Youth Hostel, *AJ Solar dos Díos*, R Santo Eduardo 63, T 709-0686.

● **Electric current**
110 volts, AC, 60 cycles.

● **Entertainment**
Clubs: *Rio Cricket*, bus 57 from ferry. *Rio Sailing*, bus 33 marked 'via Froes'.

● **Laundry**
Lavlev, R Presidente Backer 138.

● **Tourist offices**
Flumitur information booth to the right of the ferry station.

● **Transport**
Crossing from Rio Ferry: from the 'barcas' at Praça 15 de Novembro, ferry boats and launches cross every 10 mins to Niterói (20-30 mins, US$0.40). There are also hydrofoils ('aerobarcas') every 10 mins (about 10 mins, US$4.50).

The Niterói ferry service is still being maintained, despite the competition from the 14 km bridge linking the two sides of Guanabara Bay. Of the frequent ferry boat and hydrofoil services from Praça 15 de Novembro, Rio, the slow, cheaper ferry gives the best views.

Bus/car: the Rio-Niterói bridge (Ponte Costa e Silva) is 14 km long. Toll for cars, US$0.50. (The approach to the bridge is on the elevated motorway from the centre, or via Av Rio de Janeiro, in the Caju district; take Av Rodrigues Alves past the docks.) Bus 999 from the corner of Senador Dantas and Av Beira Mar, Rio, crosses the bridge to Niterói and Icaraí (US$0.75); also 996 and 998 from the Jardim Botânico (all three go to the Rodoviária in Rio).

LOCAL BEACHES

Near the Flumitur office you can take the 33 bus (marked 'via Froes') to the beaches of Icaraí, São Francisco and Jurujuba on the bay, a beautiful ride. Sit on the right-hand side. A few minutes' walk from where the bus route ends at Jurujuba are the attractive twin beaches of Adão and Eva, with lovely views of Rio across the bay. From Praça Gen Gomes Carneiro, take a 38 or 52 bus to Piratininga, Itaipu and Itacoatiara, fabulous ocean beaches and the best in the area, about 40 mins' ride through picturesque countryside (buses leave from the street directly ahead of the ferry entrance, at right angles to coast street). The undertow at Itacoatiara is dangerous, but the beach itself is safe.

LAGOS FLUMINENSES

To the E of Niterói lie a series of salt-water lagoons, the Lagos Fluminenses. Two small lakes lie behind the beaches of Piratininga, Itacoatiara and Itaipu near Niterói, but they are polluted and ringed by mud. The next lakes, Maricá and Saquarema, are much larger, though they are still muddy, the waters are relatively unpolluted, and wildlife abounds in the scrub and bush around the lagoons. At the outlet to the lake of Saquarema (turn right off the main road at Bacaxá) is the holiday village of **Saquarema**. The little white church of Nossa Senhora de Nazaré (1675) is on a green promontory jutting into the ocean. Saquarema is the centre for surfing in Brazil, and the national championships

are held here each year in May. Beware of strong currents, though. Mil e Um bus Rio-Saquarema, every 2 hrs 0730-1800, 2 hrs, US$3.60.

The largest lake is **Araruama**, famous for its medicinal mud. The salinity is extremely high, the waters calm, and almost the entire lake is surrounded by sandy beaches, making it very popular with families looking for safe, unpolluted bathing. The major industry of the area is salt, and all around one can see the saltpans and the wind pumps used to carry the water into the pans. At the eastern end of the lake is **São Pedro de Aldeia**, which, in spite of intensive development, still retains much of its colonial charm and has a lovely Jesuit church built in 1723.

The ocean beaches beside these lagoons, except for the sheltered coves of Ponta Negra and Saquarema, are rough and lonely.

● **Accommodation In the lake district**: Saquarema: **C** *Pousada do Holandés*, Av Vilamar 377, at Itaúna beach, highly rec, many languages spoken by Dutch owner and his Brazilian wife (who runs the local day-care centre), good meals – follow the signs, or take a taxi (US$0.80), from Saquarema. Restaurant in Saquarema, *Tem Uma Né Chama Teré*, very good, in main square. Araruama: **A1** *Chalés do Coqueiral*, chalets on lake beach, T 65-1159; **A1** *Parque Hotel* R Argentina 502, T 65-2129; **A1** *Senzala*, on Iguabinha beach, 10 km from Araruama, T 24-2230, F 24-1212, with meals; **B** *La Gondola*, on the lake beach, T 65-1364, overpriced; **São Pedro de Aldeia: B** *Solar de Iguaba*, T 24-2162. **At Ponta Negra** are **A3** *Pousada Colonial*, suites and bungalows in this range, inc breakfast, T Rio, 451-6254 for reservations, and **A3** *Solar Tabauna*, T 748-1626, pool, both highly rec. The whole area is perfect for camping; there are campsites (inc Camping Clube do Brasil) at Araruama (close to the *Parque Hotel*) and São Pedro de Aldeia.

● **Transport Road** A very steep road connects the beaches of Itaipu and Itacoatiara with BR-106 (and on to Araruama) via the village of Itaipu-Açu, with beach and good camping. Most maps do not show a road beyond Itaipu-Açu; it is certainly too steep for buses. An alternative to the route from Niterói to Araruama through the lagoons is via Manilla, Itaboraí and Rio Bonito, on the BR-101 and RJ-124; this is a fruit-growing region.

CABO FRIO

(*Pop* 86,615) 156 km from Rio, is a popular holiday and weekend haunt of Cariocas because of its cool weather, beaches, scenery, sailing and good under-water swimming (but mosquitoes are a problem). The ocean beach is much less frequented than the bay beach. The São Mateus fort nearby was built by the French; it is in a state of disrepair. If in the area, take a look at the huge church under construction at Arraial do Cabo nearby; it totally dominates the town (bus every 20 mins from Cabo Frio). There are random car searches for drugs on the road to Búzios.

● **Accommodation** A wide selection, from expensive down to **C** *Jangada*, Granaola 220, nr canal, very friendly, good breakfast, rec. Youth Hostel, both sexes, open all year to IYHF members (E pp, more for non-members), on R Kubitschek, 1 block from bus station, very friendly. 3 youth hostels in the area around Cabo Frio rodoviária and one in Arraial do Cabo, at R Joaquim Nabuco 23, nr Praça de Bandeiras. **Camping**: Clube do Brasil sites at Estrada dos Passageiros, nr town; at Km 135 on the Rio road, 4 km outside town, in Palmeiras; and at Arraial do Cabo on Praia dos Anjos, crowded beach. Also site at Cabo Yacht club.

● **Transport Buses** Rodoviária is 2 km from centre. Bus from Rio every 30 mins, 2½ hrs, US$7.20. To Búzios, from local bus terminus in town centre, every hour, US$1.

BÚZIOS

(*Pop* 26,000; *CEP* 28905; *DDD* 0246) NE of Cabo Frio, an expensive, fashionable resort sprawling with low-rise (but attractive) development. It has 27 sandy coves, best seen by boat (*Queen Lori*, rec), US$22 – schooner trips of 2-3 hrs around the bay are very popular, calm unpolluted waters (superb for windsurfing), beautiful scenery, thriving nightlife. Tourist information office near bus stop. Very crowded during Brazilian holiday season and extremely difficult to get hotel bookings. Notable beaches are: Ossos, close to town; Azeda, very relaxed, topless OK; Geriba, about 2½ km out of town (turn left down the path between two Shell stations – it is marked); Tartaruga, not marked and not developed (take dirt road up small hill opp *Pousada Baer Búzios*); there is a restaurant and snack bar in season.

● **Accommodation** Plenty of good hotels and pousadas: eg **A1** *Pousada Happy*, on road to Raza on opp side of crossing to Rio, on beach, inc breakfast, rec, good windsurfing, German owner; **A2** *Pousada Hibiscus Beach*, R 1 No 22, Quadra C, Praia João Fernandes, T/F 23-6221, run by its British owners, 15 nice bungalows, garden, pool, inc breakfast, light meals available, help with car/buggy rentals and local excursions; **A3** *Pousada dos Búzios*, T 231155, a/c, terrace bar with lovely view; all central, rec; **C** *Pousada Casa de Pedra*, Trav Lúcio A Quintanilha 57, T 231499, TV, fridge, safe; **C** *Pousadinha em Búzios*, T 231448, very pretty, friendly; **C** *Bougainville Flats*, T 236501, Estrada Jose Bento Ribeiro Dantas 100 (on the main road that leads to the R de Pedra), friendly, comfortable, bath, ceiling fan, fridge, central, rec; **C** *Brigitta's Guest House*, T 236157, R das Pedras 131, 28925-00. Private rooms can be rented in family homes. Camping is allowed but dangerous.

● **Places to eat** Several good restaurants (try the *camarão tropical*) and popular bars (*Chez Michou*, R das Pedras, is reportedly the mecca for trendy travellers).

● **Entertainment Watersports**: there are several agencies selling tours around the Bay of Buzios and its islands. *Buziana* offers a 5-hr trip for US$10 pp, rec; *Casamar*, T 232441 (located in Rio de Janeiro), a highly professional dive operation offers one day diving trips costing US$25 pp if you bring your own equipment, US$50 pp if you rent equipment, both prices inc 2 bottles of air, Casamar is closed in May and Tues during low season, rec.

● **Tour companies & travel agents** *Ekoda Agencia de Viagens e Turismo Ltda*, R Jose B Ribeiro Dantas, 13, T 23 1490.

● **Transport** Best route from Rio (2 hrs by car) is the paved road towards Macaé, with a paved turnoff to Búzios (1001 bus from Rio, 4-5 a day, 2½ hrs, US$7). Direct road from Cabo Frio (bus 45 mins) is unpaved.

OTHER SEASIDE RESORTS

Continuing to the N, one comes to Barra de São João, **Rio das Ostras** (**C** *Hotel Mirante do Poeta*, T 64-1910, and others) and **Macaé** (**Accommodation B** *Colonial*, Av Elias Agostinho 140, T 62-5155, friendly, helpful, comfortable; **B** *Panorama*, same avenue No 290, T/F 62-4455; **D** *Central*, R Rui Barbosa, clean, nice, friendly, good breakfast, secure parking), all containing sheltered coves with good swimming and scuba diving. Macaé is also the supply centre for the offshore oil industry (bus Rio-Macaé 2½-3 hrs, every 30 mins, Mil e Um or Rápido Macaense; bus Macaé-Campos, 1¾ hrs, US$3).

POÇO DAS ANTAS BIOLOGICAL RESERVE

From Rio and Niterói a first class highway, the BR-101, runs NE past Macaé to Campos. At Km 222 is the **Biological Reserve of Poço das Antas** (2 hrs' drive from Rio; it is not open to the general public, for details, Delegacia Estadual do Ibama, Av Pres Antônio Carlos 607-12°, CEP 20.000, Rio de Janeiro). Many animals (including the *mico-leão*, Golden Lion Tamarin – this is its only natural habitat) roam in the forest. Tours are very restrictive: visitors must be accompanied by Reserve staff to track radio-collared tamarins. Once an animal is seen, the tour ends, with no further opportunity for birdwatching, or looking for the maned sloth (also endangered).

CAMPOS

(*Pop* 368,800) A busy industrial city, some 276 km (4½ hrs by Mil e Um bus, hourly) from Rio de Janeiro (70 km from Macaé). It stands 56 km from the mouth of the Rio Paraíba, up which coffee planting originally spread to São Paulo state. Coffee is still grown near Campos, though the region is now one of the largest sugar-producing zones in Brazil. Important offshore oil discoveries have been made nearby. Town is quite interesting.

● **Accommodation C** *Palace*, Av 15 de Novembro 143, T 22-7755, F 22-3661; **C** *Planície*, R 13 de Maio 56, T 23-4455; **C** *Terrazo Tourist*, Joaquím Tavora 22, T 22-1405, 2-star; **D** *Silva*, some way behind church on municipal square, breakfast, clean, safe parking.

INTO ESPÍRITO SANTO

Travelling N, as an alternative to BR-101 to Vitória, one can take a detour inland, going through São Fidélis, Cambiasca, Itoacara and on to **Santo Antônio de Pádua** (*Pop* 36,330), 130 km from Campos, a pleasant town on the Rio Pomba. (**C** *Hotel das Águas*, a short walk from the centre, in a park with pool, health centre and bottling plant for the local mineral water

which is used for treating cardiovascular illness; **D** *Braga*, in town, clean, friendly, good food.) Take road No 393 to Itaperuna, Bom Jesus do Itabapoana and into Espírito Santo, then road No 484 to **Guaçuí** (**E** *Grande Hotel Minas*, friendly, clean; *Restaurant Kontiki*, very good), one of the starting points for the Parque Nacional do Caparaó (see page 438). Then take the road 482 to Cachoeira do Itapemirim and the BR-101 (see page 416).

INLAND RESORTS

PETRÓPOLIS

(*Pop* 255,210; *CEP* 25600; *DDD* 0242) A summer hill resort and industrial city, 68 km N of Rio, it is reached by bus along a steep, scenic mountain road. Until 1962 Petrópolis was the 'summer capital' of Brazil; it was founded in 1843 as a summer refuge by Dom Pedro II. Now it combines manufacturing industry (particularly textiles) with floral beauty and hill scenery.

Places of interest

The **Museu Imperial** (Imperial Palace), which seems to express very faithfully what we know of Dom Pedro II's character, is a modest but elegant building, fully furnished and equipped, containing the Crown Jewels and other imperial possessions. It is assiduously well-kept: one might think the imperial family had left the day before one's visit, rather than in 1889. Open Tues-Sun, 1200-1730. Entry US$1.

Well worth a visit is the Gothic-style **Cathedral**, completed in 1925, which contains the tombs of the Emperor and Empress (guide in English, US$0.50).

Museu Ferreira da Cunha, Fernandes Vieira 390 (old road to Rio) shows large collection of arms, open Sat and Sun (groups only; arrange in advance) 0900-1700.

See also the Summer home of air pioneer **Santos Dumont**, showing early inventions. **Palácio de Cristal** in Praça da Confluência, former imperial ballroom and now exhibition centre.

Excursions

Orquidário Binot, R Fernandes Vieira 390 (take bus to Vila Isabel; open Mon-Sat, 0800-1100, 1300-1700), a huge collection of orchids from all over Brazil (plants may be purchased).

Local information
● **Accommodation**

A3 *Casa do Sol*, T 43-5062, 4-star hotel 8 km out on road to Rio; **A3** *Casablanca Center*, Gen Osório 28, T 42-2612, F 42-6298; **A3** *Riverside Parque*, R Hermogéneo Silva 522, T 43-2312, F 43-2430.

B *Casablanca*, R da Imperatriz 286, T 42-6662, F 42-5946, good atmosphere in older part, pool, very clean; **B** *Casablanca Palace*, 16 de Março 123, T 42-0162; **B** *Margaridas*, R Bispo Pereira Alves 235, T 42-4686, chalet-type hotel set in lovely gardens with swimming pool, charming proprietors.

Camping: Associação Brasileira de Camping and YMCA, Araras district. Can reserve space through Rio YMCA, T 231-9860.

● **Places to eat**

Churrascaria Majórica, Av do Imperador 754; *Dom Giovanni*, same street, rec; *Bauernstube*, João Pessoa 297.

● **Sports**

Whitewater rafting: at Três Rios, on the junction of rivers Paraibuna, Piabanha and Paraíba do Sul, is arranged by *Klemperer Turismo*, T 43-4052 (also from Rio, T 252-8170), highly rec. (It is cheaper – but complicated – to book direct with the owners of the restaurant at Pontal, no phone.)

● **Transport**

Buses leave from Rio every 15 mins throughout the day (US$3.50), Sun every hour, 1½ hrs, sit on the left hand side for best views. Return tickets are not available, so buy tickets for the return on arrival in Petrópolis. 75 mins each way. The ordinary buses leave from the rodoviária in Rio; a/c buses, hourly from 1100, from Av Nilo Peçanha, US$4.25. There is a direct overnight bus from São Paulo.

TERESÓPOLIS

(*Pop* 120,700; *alt* 910m) Near the Serra dos Órgãos, 124 km NE of Rio, it was the favourite summer residence of the Empress Teresa Cristina. Building in recent years has destroyed some of the city's character. See the Colina dos Mirantes hill (30-min steep climb, sweeping view of the city and surroundings, a taxi up is not dear), the Sloper

and Iaci lakes, the Imbui and Amores waterfalls, and the Fonte Judith.

Local festivals São Pedro, 29 June, is celebrated with fireworks.

● **Accommodation** **L3** *São Moritz*, Swiss-style, outside on the Nova Friburgo road, Km 36, T 741-1115, F 741-1135, with meals; **A1** *Montebello*, at Km 17, same road, T/F 742-2116, modern hotel with pool, friendly, with 3 meals, rec; **A2** *Alpina*, Parque Imbui, on Petrópolis road, T/F 742-5252; **D** *Várzea Palace*, R Sebastião Teixeira 41, T 742-0878, highly rec. Many cheap hotels in R Delfim Moreira, nr the Praça. **Youth hostel**: Retiro da Inglesa, 20 km on road to Friburgo, Fazenda Boa Esperança (reservations, R Papa Pio XII 50, Jardim Cascata, 25963 Teresópolis). **Camping**: National Park, entrance to Teresópolis from Rio, full facilities; Quinta da Barra, Km 3 on Petrópolis road, T 742-1825; Vale das Choupanas, Km 30 on Rio road.

● **Places to eat** *Taberna Alpina*, Duque de Caxias 131; *Bar Gota d'Água*, Praça Baltasar da Silveira 16 for trout or *feijoada* (small but rec and for *batidas*). Cafeteria in the ABC supermarket, clean and cheap, rec.

● **Banks & money changers** Cash or TCs at Teretur, Trav Portugal 46 (English spoken).

● **Tourist offices** In the bus station, T 742-0999.

● **Transport** Buses **Rio-Teresópolis**: Buses leave every 30 mins from rodoviária. Book the return journey as soon as you arrive at Teresópolis. Fare US$3. From Teresópolis to Petrópolis, every 2 hrs from 0900-2100, US$3.50. **Suggested day trip**: leave Rio 0800 or before (Viação Teresópolis) for the 1¾-hr ride into the mountains to Teresópolis (sit on right side). Upon arrival, buy a ticket right away for Petrópolis (Viação Teresópolis) for the 1200 bus. This gives you 2¾ hrs to wander around. The 90-min drive from Teresópolis to Petrópolis is beautiful. (Sit on left side.) The views on either side are spectacular. Again, upon arrival in Petrópolis, buy your ticket to Rio (Facil or Unica). Take the 1715 bus 'via Quitandinha', and you might catch the sunset over the mountains (in May, June, July, take the 1615 bus). This gives you time to visit most of the attractions listed above.

SERRA DOS ÓRGÃOS

About 30,000 ha of the **Serra dos Órgãos**, so called because their strange shapes are said to recall organ-pipes, are now a **National Park**. The main attraction is the precipitous Dedo de Deus (God's Finger) Peak. There is also the rock formation Mulher de Pedra 12 km out on the Nova

Friburgo road, and the Von Martius natural-history museum. The highest point is the Pedra Açu, 2,400m. A path leads up the 2,260m Pedra do Sino, 3-4 hrs' climb. The park is the home of the very rare and endemic grey-winged cotinga, as well as a number of other cotingas, berryeaters and other rare endemic birds. Anyone can enter the park and hike the trails from the Teresópolis gate, S of the town. Entrance to park, US$1, US$1.65 for the path to the top. Ibama (T 742-0266/0260) has some hostels, US$5.75 full board, or US$3.75 first night, US$2 thereafter, a bit rough. Camping, US$1. A good way to see the Park is to do the Rio-Teresópolis-Petrópolis-Rio circuit; a scenic day trip. Tours of the park with Francisco of Lazer Tours are recommended, T 742-7616, or find him at the grocery shop on R Sloper 1. Focus Tours of Belo Horizonte (see page 429) offers birdwatching tours.

NOVA FRIBURGO

(*Pop* 166,940; *Alt* 850m) A popular resort during summer months, in a beautiful valley with excellent walking and riding. It was founded by Swiss settlers from Fribourg. Cable car from Praça dos Suspiros 650m up the Morro da Cruz, for view of rugged country.

● **Accommodation A2** *Bucsky*, T 22-5052, F 22-9769, 5 km out on Niterói road, with meals; **A2** *Garlipp*, German-run, in chalets, with meals, at Muri, km 70.5 from Rio, 10 km from Nova Friburgo, T 42-1330, F 42-1444; **A2** *Sans-Souci*, T/F 22-7752, 1 km out, with meals, C without, **B** *Fabris*, Av Alberto Browne 148, T 22-2852, central, TV, hot showers, plentiful breakfast buffet. Under same ownership as *Garlipp* is **B** *Fazenda São João*, T 42-1304, 11 km from *Garlipp* up a side road, riding, swimming, sauna, tennis, hummingbirds and orchids, owner will meet guests in Nova Friburgo or even in Rio. **C** *Everest*, R Manoel António Ventura 75, T 22-7350, comfortable, good breakfasts; **C** *Maringá*, R Monsenhor Miranda 110, T 22-2309, with bath, D without, good breakfast, rec. **Camping**: camping Clube do Brasil has sites on Niterói road, at Caledônia (7 km out) and Muri (10 km out). Cambrás site also at Cônego, and private site at Fazenda Sanandu, 20 km out on same road.

● **Transport** Buses from Rio (every hour), 2 hrs, US$5.

THE STATE OF RIO DE JANEIRO: WEST FROM RIO

VOLTA REDONDA

(*Pop* 220,085; *alt* 565m; *CEP* 27180; *DDD* 0243) On a broad bend of the Rio Paraíba, 113 km W of Rio along the railway to São Paulo, **Volta Redonda** has one of the largest steel works in Latin America. The mills are on the river bank and the town spreads up the surrounding wooded and gardened slopes. To visit, apply for a permit from the Companhia Siderúrgica Nacional, Av Treze de Maio 13, Rio de Janeiro (10 days in advance), or locally from the *Bela Vista* hotel. Visits start at 0900, and last 2½-3 hrs.

● **Accommodation A2** *Bela Vista*, Alto de Boa Vista, on a hill overlooking town, T 43-2022, F 42-4190; **B** *Sider Palace*, R 33 No 10, T 42-0885/1032, F 42-6116; **D** *Embaixador*, Tr LA Félix 36, T 42-3665, 1-star.

● **Transport** Buses from Rio by buses or minibuses, 2½ hrs, US$3.

MOUNTAIN TOWNS NORTH OF VOLTA REDONDA

North of Volta Redonda is **Miguel Pereira**, with an excellent mountain climate; nearby is the Javari lake, a popular recreational spot (**B** *Hotel-Fazendas Javari*, Praça Nações Unidas 35, near town, T 84-3611, restaurant, swimming pool, sports grounds, etc). A tourist train runs 56 km to Conrado on Sat, Sun and holidays, 0945, 3½ hrs, US$18 round trip, beautiful views of mountains, rivers and waterfalls. Further N, and still in the mountains are the university centres of **Vassouras** and **Valença**; both are historical monuments. 35 km from Valença is **Conservatória**, another colonial town. This region can also be reached via the Japeri turn-off on the BR-116 (a beautiful mountain drive).

WEST OF VOLTA REDONDA

Some 30 km W of Volta Redonda, in the town of **Resende** (*Pop* 91,575), is the Military Academy of Agulhas Negras. Grounds, with captured German guns of WW2, are open to the public. (Accommodation and restaurants in town.)

• **Transport** Buses from Aparecida do Nte (see page 465), several daily, US$2.50; from Rio, frequent, 1¾ hrs, US$3.60, also from São Paulo and Volta Redonda. From Resende buses go to Barra Mansa (Resendense, 40 mins, US$1.25) where you can change for Belo Horizonte (Util 1230, 8-9 hrs, US$14.50).

In the same region, 175 km from Rio, is the small town of **Penedo** (5 buses a day from Resende) which in the 1930s attracted Finnish settlers who brought the first saunas to Brazil. This popular weekend resort also provides horseback riding, and swimming in the Portinho river. (Accommodation: **A3** *Bertell*, T 51-1288, with meals; **C** *Pousada Penedo*, T 51-1309, safe, clean, pool, rec, and others, 2 campsites.)

HILL RESORTS

Some 33 km beyond Penedo (part of road unpaved) is the small village of **Visconde de Mauá**, where the tourist officer speaks no English but plays guitar (closed out of season). There are lots of places offering acupuncture, shiatsu massage, macrobiotic food, etc. Fine scenery and walks, lots of holidaymakers, pleasant atmosphere. There are roads to three other small hill towns: delightful 2 hrs' walk to **Maringá**, to Marumbá and to Mirantão, at about 1,700m, with semitropical vegetation. The Rio Preto, the border between Rio de Janeiro and Minas Gerais states, runs through the region. 6 km up river from Maringá are the Santa Clara falls; between Visconde de Mauá and Maringá is a natural pool in the river (turn left before crossing the bridge). After Marumbá follow signs to Cachoeira Escorrega, a small fall with cold natural swimming pool, 2 km. Horse rental in Visconde de Mauá from Berto (almost opp *Vendinha da Serra*), or Pedro (Lote 10); many places in Maringá.

• **Accommodation** Limited cheap lodgings: enquire at *Vendinha da Serra*, excellent natural food restaurant and store; next door is **F** pp *Dona Mariana*, rec, shared bath. *Pousada Beira Rio*, T 54-1801; *Pousada Vale das Hortênsias*, T 54-3030, both provide all meals, rec; ½ km on road to Maringá is *Hotel Turístico*, with handicrafts and homemade food, Italian owner, Nino, and his Brazilian wife, run excursions. Everywhere in town shuts at about 1900, except *Adega Bar*, open till mid-

night, live music and dancing (Sat only), reasonable pizza, and a restaurant in Lote 10, open till 2200. Youth Hostel, 5 km along the road to Maringá. Several **D** hotels, *Bar do Jorge* café; *Forró da Marieta* for forró dancing.

• **Transport** Buses to Visconde de Mauá from Resende, 1500 and 1630, 2 hrs, return 0900-0830, US$1.25. Direct bus Rio-Visconde de Mauá, Cidade de Aço, 0900 daily, plus one in evening, 3½ hrs, US$8.50.

ITATIAIA NATIONAL PARK

Founded 1937 on the Serra de Itatiaia in the Mantiqueira chain of mountains, the park is a few kilometres N of the Via Dutra (Rio-São Paulo highway). The road to it is paved. The town of Itatiaia is surrounded by picturesque mountain peaks and lovely waterfalls. This is a good area for climbing (Pico das Agulhas Negras 2,787m, Pico da Prateleira 2,540m), trekking and bird-watching (specialities include swallow-tailed, shrike-like and black-and-gold cotingas, white-bearded antshrike, black-capped manakin, various tanagers and humming birds). The southern masked titi monkey is common, recognizable by its loud hee-haw-like call. Information and maps can be obtained at the park office. Worth seeing are the curious rock formations of Pedra de Taruga and Pedra de Maçã, and the waterfall Véu de Noiva (many birds). The Administração do Parque Nacional de Itatiaia operates a refuge in the park which acts as a starting point for climbs and treks: information on these from Clube Excursionista Brasileira, Av Almte Barroso 2, 8th floor, T 220-3695, Rio. Tres Picos wildlife trail near *Hotel Simon*; very difficult to visit park without a car (70 km from *Hotel Simon* to other side), but hotel is helpful. There is a Museum of Flora and Fauna, closed Mon. Entrance to Park, US$1.

• **Accommodation** Basic accommodation in cabins and dormitories is available in the park; you will need to book in season, say 30 days in advance, by writing to Administração do Parque Nacional de Itatiaia, Caixa Postal 83657, Itatiaia 27580-000, RJ, T (0243) 52-1652. **L3** *Simon*, Km 13 park road, T 52-1122, with meals, lovely views, beautifully set, rec; **A2** *Repouso Itatiaia*, Km 11 park road, T 52-1110, F 52-1509, with meals; **A3** *Fazenda da Serra*, Via Dutra Km 151, T 52-1611, with meals; **A3** *Hotel do Ypé*,

Km 13 park road, T 52-1453, with meals; **B** *Pousada do Elefante*, 15 mins' walk back down hill from *Hotel Simon*, good food, swimming pool, lovely views, may allow camping; lodging in **F** range at R Marica 255, T 52-1699, possibility of pitching a tent on the premises, located close to the National Park. **Camping Clube do Brasil**: site is entered at Km 148 on the Via Dutra.

● **Transport** A bus from Itatiaia, marked *Hotel Simon*, goes to the Park, 1200, returns 1700; coming from Resende this may be caught at the crossroads before Itatiaia. Through tickets to São Paulo sold at a booth in the large bar in the middle of Itatiaia main street.

ENGENHEIRO PASSOS

Further along the Dutra Highway (186 km from Rio) is the small town of **Engenheiro Passos**, from which a road (BR-354) leads to São Lourenço and Caxambu in Minas Gerais (see page 439), passing **Agulhas Negras**. One can climb Agulhas Negras from this side by taking the road from Registro pass (1,670m) to the Abrigo Rebouças refuge, which is manned all year round (take your own food, US$1.25 to stay), at 2,350m.

● **Accommodation A2** *Villa Forte*, 1 km from town, T 52-1219, with meals. Nine campsites in the area.

THE NEW RIO-SANTOS HIGHWAY

This section of the BR101, is one of the world's most beautiful highways, hugging the forested and hilly 'Green Coast' SW of Rio. It is now complete through to Bertioga (see page 459), which has good links with Santos and São Paulo. Buses run from Rio to Angra dos Reis, Parati, Ubatuba, Caraguatatuba, and São Sebastião, where it may be necessary to change for Santos. Hotels and *pousadas* have sprung up all along the road, as have expensive housing developments, though these have not spoiled the views. The coast is littered with islands, beaches, colonial settlements and mountain fazendas: the drive should take 7 hrs, but it would be better to break the journey and enjoy some of the attractions.

ITACURUÇÁ

91 km from Rio, a delightful place to visit:

there is fine scenery, peace and quiet, with islands off the coast.

The sea is too polluted for bathing, but you can walk along the railway to Castelo where the beach is cleaner. Ilha de Itacuruçá can also be reached from **Muriqui**, a popular beach resort 9 km from Itacuruçá; bathing also in the Véu de Noiva waterfall. The next beach along the coast is Praia Grande.

● **Accommodation** On Ilha de Itacuruçá, is **L2** *Hotel Pierre*, reached by boat from Coroa Grande, N of Itacuruçá on the mainland, 5 mins (boats also go from Itacuruçá); restaurant, bars, sporting facilities. For bookings T/F 788-1560, T Rio 247-8938, or Saveiros Tours, 267-2792. **L3** *Hotel Jaguanum*, Ilha de Jaguanum, Itacuruçá, has apartments and chalets with private bathrooms, full board. There are beautiful walks around the island. Reservations for the hotel inc the boat trip to and from the island (at 1000 and 1700). The only extra is the bus, US$6 return, which picks you up at your hotel. T 235-2893 or 237-5119, in Rio, or enquire at *Sepetiba Turismo*, Av NS de Copacabana 605, s 202.

MANGARATIBA

(*Pop* 17,920) This fishing village half-way from Rio to Angra dos Reis has muddy beaches, but pleasant surroundings and better beaches outside town, for example Ibicuí, São Brás, Praia Brava, Saco, Guiti and Cação.

● **Accommodation D** *Mendonça*, without breakfast or bath, good, clean; 2 others, more expensive; **F** *Sítio Santo Antônio 12*, T 789-2192, family run, owner Carlito is proud of his shell collection, rec. At Rio das Pedras is *Club Med*, Km 55, Mangaratiba, CEP 23880, RJ, T 021-789-1635, F 021-789-1312.

● **Transport Buses** From Rio Rodoviária 7 a day, US$3. **Ferry**: daily ferry (Conerj) to Ilha Grande island (see below), at 0800 daily, 1½ hrs, highly rec; return ferry Mon, Wed, Fri at 1700, Tues, Thur at 1100, Sat, Sun at 1600. Fare US$3.60. Tues and Thur departures continue to Angra dos Reis. Ferry departures and destinations can be checked at ferry station at Praça Quinze de Novembro, Rio.

ANGRA DOS REIS

Angra dos Reis (*Pop* 85,220; *CEP* 23,900; *DDD* 0243), said to have been founded in 1502, is 197 km SW of Rio by road. A small port with an important fishing and shipbuilding industry, it has several small bays with good bathing within easy reach and is situated on an enormous bay full of islands. Boat trips around the bay are available, some with a stop for lunch on the island of Jipóia (5 hrs, US$9 pp; boats for hire US$12/hr). Of particular interest are the convent of Nossa Senhora do Carmo, built in 1593, the parish church (1626), the ruins of the Jacuecanga seminary (1797), and the Senhor do Bonfim church (1780).

● **Accommodation L3** *Frade*, road to Ubatuba (Km 123 on BR-101, 36 km), T/F 65-1212; **L3** *Porto Aquarius*, Saco de Itapirapuã, T 65-1642, F 65-1766, out of town (access from Km 101 on BR-101, 13 km) lots of facilities, pleasant, helpful staff. At Km 115 on BR-101 is **A2** *Hotel Porto Brachuy* (T 65-3939) with lots of facilities for watersports, nightly shows and dancing, restaurant, etc (23 km from Angra dos Reis). **B** *Londres*, R Pompéia 75, T 65-0044, F 65-0511; **B** *Palace*, Carvalho 275, T 65-0032, F 65-2656; **C** *Caribe*, R de Conceição 255, T 65-0033, F 65-3450, central, rec. Youth Hostel at Km 115 on Estrada Rio-Santos.

● **Places to eat** *Taberna 33*, Raul Pompéia 110, good, popular, moderate prices; *Tropicalitá*, Largo do Convento do Carmo.

● **Sports Diving** *Aquamaster*, Praia da Enseada, US$60 for two dives with drinks and food, take bus marked 'Retiro' from the port in Angra.

● **Transport Trains** The historic *trem da mata atlântica* has been reopened, making the coastal trip to Lidice on weekends only, 1030 (has restaurant car). **Buses** Hourly from Rio's rodoviária, Viação Eval, take the 'via litoral' bus and sit on the left, US$7, 2½ hrs. Tourist information opp the bus station, very good.

ROUTES A road runs inland (about 18 km beyond Angra), through Getulândia, to join the BR-116 either just S of Pirai or near Volta Redonda, through nice mountain scenery.

ILHA GRANDE

2 hrs by ferry boat, US$3.75 (Mon, Wed, Fri at 1500, return 1000 – so you have to stay 2 nights; for day trips, go from Mangaratiba). A 2-hr ferry makes a most attractive trip through the bay to Abraão, on **Ilha Grande**, once an infamous pirate lair, and now occupied principally by fishermen and one of Brazil's larger prisons. Ask in the port at Angra dos Reis for a fishing boat going to Proveta, where you can stay in boat sheds or, if lucky, with a fisherman. It is a beautiful village, from which you can walk through tropical forest on a mountain to Praia do Aventureiro (a day's leisurely walk each way). Take mosquito precautions and register with police post in Abraão. Exchange is difficult on the island.

● **Accommodation A1** *Paraiso do Sol* (full board, 2 hrs' walk from Abraão, or hire a boat, reservations, Rio, T 262-1226) and **A2** *Mar da Tranqüilidade* (reservations T 780-1861 or Rio, T 288-4162). Hotel reservations are necessary. Many new *pousadas*: eg **B** *Pousada da Vanda*, T 285-2429, friendly and clean in green surroundings; **C** *Beto's*, T 780-1202, friendly, central, rec; **D** *Hotel Ori*, R Prof Lima, rec; **D** *Sonia/Tuti*, R Antonio Moreira 80, T 654512, clean, 5 mins from beach, small house with 2 rooms, rec; **D** *Albatroz*, R das Flores 108, T 627-1730, rec); alternatively you can camp on beaches, or rent a room (E) in Abraão.

PARATI

Beyond Angra dos Reis, the road continues 100 km along the coast, past the nuclear-power plant at Itaorna, to **Parati** (*Pop* 23,870; *CEP* 23,970; *DDD* 0243), a charming colonial town only recently accessible. The centre has been declared a national historic monument in its entirety. It used to be the chief port for the export of gold in the 17th century. The churches were built separately for each race, Indian, black and white. There is a great deal of distinguished Portuguese colonial architecture in delightful settings. On the northern headland is a small fort, 15 mins' walk, pleasant views. There is reputedly health-giving mud at one end of Jabaquara beach behind the fort (lively, safe for children). The town centre is out of bounds for motor vehicles, in spring the roads are flooded, while the houses are above the water level. It is now very popular with tourists, and an expensive place to visit. Local patchwork is for sale in the community centre on the waterfront, quilts for sale in gift shop in Santa Rita de Cassia church.

Excursions

Enjoyable walk through a wood (lots of

mosquitoes) to Trinidad beach. Also visit Muricana Fazenda: 6 km walk, or buses: zoo, restaurant and rum refinery with 10 different varieties of rum. 7 km from town is the natural water slide of Tubarão.

Tours

Boat trips round the bay daily from 1100, returning 1700, US$14.50 pp, beautiful trip; alternatively you can hire small boats by the hour. Take mosquito repellent. Scuba-diving trips from a schooner owned by Frederico are available from the shops around the quay, US$50 for ½ day, highly rec, especially at weekends.

Local festivals

In Sept, festival of sacred music.

Local information
● Accommodation

A1 *do Ouro*, Dr Pereira 145, T 71-2033, F 71-1311; **A1** *Pousada Pardieiro*, Ten Francisco Antônio 74, T 71-1370, F 71-1139, attractive colonial building with lovely gardens, but always full at weekends, does not take children; **A1** *Pousada Parati*, R do Comércio, T 71-1205, F 71-2111, good value, clean, highly rec; **A2** *Coxixo*, Ten Francisco Antônio 362, T 71-1460, F 71-1568, central, pool, attractive patio, rec; **A2** *Pousada do Príncipe*, Roberto Silveira 289, T 71-2266, F 71-2120, all facilities, pool, highly rec.

B *Pousada del Arte*, R Dona Geralda 79, artist owner Urquijo speaks English, Spanish, rec; **B** *Aconchego*, Domingos Gonçalves de Abreul, T/F 71-1598; **B** *das Canoas*, R Silveira 279, T 71-1133, F 71-2005, rec, clean, swimming pool, a/c; **B** *Pescador*, Av Beira-Rio, T 71-1154, F 71-2145, central.

C *Estalagem Colonial*, R de Matriz 9, T 71-1626, clean, rec; **C** *Marendaz*, R Patitiba 9, T 71-1369, with breakfast, simple, charming; **C** *Morro do Forte*, R Orlando Carpinelli, T/F 71-1211, lovely garden, good breakfast, pool, German owner Peter Kallert offers trips on his yacht, rec; **C** *Pouso Familiar*, R J V Ramos 262, run by Belgian (Joseph Yserbyt) and his Brazilian wife (Lucia), nr bus station, laundry facilities, English, French, German and Flemish spoken, T 71-1475, rec; **C** *Pousada do Corsário*, Beco do Lapeiro 26, T/F 71 1866, a/c, TV, fridge, swimming pool, rec.

D *Pousada Miramar*, Abel de Oliveira 19, T 71-2132, friendly, good value, 1 room has own kitchen, rec; **D** *Tia Palminas*, opp Entel caravan, basic.

Camping: there is a small Camping Club site on

the fine Pontal beach, good, very crowded in Jan and Feb, US$8 pp, and also a private camping site and a site next to the police station after the bridge, hot showers, US$2.50 pp. Apart from camping, very little cheap accommodation.

● Places to eat

Good restaurants, oldest and most famous is *Verde Mar*, on the sea front at Praça Lopes Trovão 35, T 65-2065, expensive but worth it. *Cavallino*, R da Lapa, enjoyable atmosphere, rec. Snack bars; *Chez Regine*, R da Praia 310, Centro Histórico, T 71 1608, cheap, fast and good, rec.

● Tourist offices

Praça Chafariz.

● Transport

7 buses a day to **Rio** (4 hrs, US$12) and to **Angra dos Reis** (1½ hrs, every 2 hrs, US$4.20); 3 a day to **Ubatuba** (70 km), **Taubaté** (170 km) and **Guaratinguetá** (210 km); 4 a day to **São Paulo** (5½ hrs, US$12, booked up quickly) and São Sebastião.

The coast road continues from Parati into the State of São Paulo. Another road, rough but scenic, climbs the Serra do Mar to Cunha and Guaratinguetá, also in São Paulo.

Espírito Santo

THE COASTAL state, north of Rio de Janeiro, which has a mountainous interior and a hot, damp seaboard. It is an important grower of coffee. In the north there are large forests containing hardwoods.

CAMPOS TO VITÓRIA

North of Campos (see page 409) is the State of Espírito Santo (*Pop* 2,598,230) with its capital at Vitória. The people are known as Capixabas, after a former Indian tribe. The main road N passes **Cachoeiro do Itapemirim** (*Pop* 140,400), a busy city on both banks of the fast-flowing Rio Itapemirim; many hotels of all classes.

Beach resorts

Just across the frontier between the states is the resort town of **Marataízes**, with good beaches.

● **Accommodation A2** *Praia*, Av Atlântica 99, T 532-2144, F 532-3515, on beach; **A2** *Saveiros Palace*, Av Miramar 119, T 532-1413, F 532-1285, on beach; **B** *Dona Judith*, Av Lacerda de Aguiar 353, T 532-1436, F 532-1305. **Camping:** Municipal site on Praia do Siri, 10 km from centre; Xodó private site, Av Atlântica, 2 km from centre.

Continuing up the coast At **Anchieta** is **A3** *Hotel Thanharu Praia*, T 536-1246, F 536-1466, good. Fishing/diving boat hire from Sr Romildo, Peixaria do Onça (2 km N of Anchieta) eg to Ilha dos Franceses. Near Anchieta are Praia dos

Castelhanos and Praia Iriri, 30 km from Guarapari, served by a regular bus; 2 beaches, beautiful setting, lodging in private houses is possible. A little further N is the fishing village of **Ubu** with **A3** *Pousada Alba Ubu*, R Aleixo Neto 1762, T 361-1320, fully equipped, half board.

GUARAPARI

Further N, 58 km S of Vitória, is **Guarapari** (*Pop* 61,600), whose beaches attract many people seeking cures for rheumatism, neuritis and other complaints, from the radioactive monazitic sands.

The Casa de Cultura is the former seat of the prefeitura, which was built in 1749 (open from 1300). Downstairs there are paintings by local artists, newspaper articles about local events. Upstairs there is a museum exhibiting old photographs and information about radioactive sand, monazite mining and small samples, also various handicrafts.

The Antiga Matriz church on the hill in the town centre was built in 1585. At the entrance the brochure 'Guarapari é o seu nome' by Padre Antonio Nunez is sold, US$3. The brochure contains historical information, descriptions of the Indian mission, information about the radioactive sands and its alleged benefits, and samples of Anchieta's poetry.

Like Marataízes, Guarapari is very crowded mid-Dec to end-February.

● **Accommodation A1** *Porto do Sol*, Av Beira Mar 1, Mediterranean style village on rocky point overlooking a calm beach, pool, sauna, etc, rec, T 361-1100, F 261-2929; **A2** *Atlântico*, Av Edísio Cirne 332, T 261-1237 on beach, rec; **C** *Mariland*, R Silva Mello 98, T 261-0553, nr beach, rec; **C** *Vieira 323*, R Joaquim da Silva, T 261-0185, rec; **C** *do Angelo*, R Pedro Caetano 254, T 261-0230, rec; **C** *Costa Sul*, R Getulio Vargas 101, bath, breakfast, loads of mosquitoes, otherwise rec; **C** *Bom Jesus*, R Pedro Caetano 156, T 261 1184, bath, breakfast, fan, simple, central, good, rec; **C** *Pousada Lisboa*, opp rodoviária, bath, simple, clean, rec; **C** *Guarapari Tourist*, R Joaquim da Silva Lima 167, T 361 0388, bath, TV, rec. **Camping:** Camping Clube do Brasil, Setiba beach, 9 km from centre, T 262-1325. Cambrás site off Vitória highway close to beach, 4 km from centre. Private site nr Cambrás site.

● **Places to eat** *Sonho do Mel*, R Joaquim da

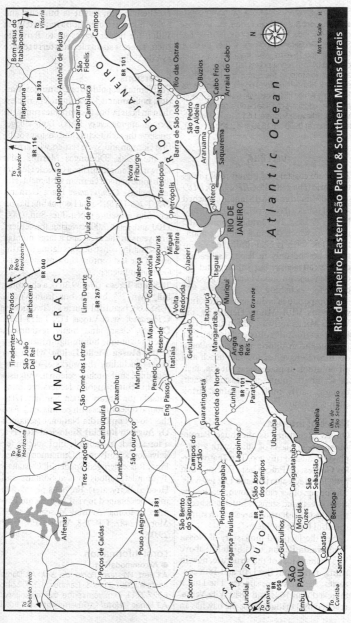

Rio de Janeiro, Eastern São Paulo & Southern Minas Gerais

Not to Scale

Silva Lima, sorvetes, sopas, tea-room, very good.

● **Transport Buses** Guarapari has 2 rodoviárias, one for Alvorada, the other for Itapemirim/Penha, Sudeste, São Gerardo and others. They are close together and 15 mins' walk from the city centre or US$8 by taxi. Penha tickets (eg to Rio) are sold at *R-Tur Turismo*, in the centre opp Banco Baneste, at R Manoel Severo Simões e R Joaquim da Silva Lima where air tickets, free brochures, maps, and hotel addresses can also be obtained. Bus from **Vitória**, 1 hr with Sudeste, US$2.10. To **Rio** with Itapemirim at 0900 arr 1630 and 2300 arr 0500, US$11.

VITÓRIA

There are coastal and inland road routes to **Vitória** (*Pop* 258,245; *CEP* 29,000; *DDD* 027) 509 km from Rio de Janeiro, reached several times a day by plane (80 min), and by bus (9 hrs). Two bridges connect the island on which it stands with the mainland. The town is beautifully set, its entrance second only to Rio's, its beaches quite as attractive, but smaller, and the climate is less humid. Vitória is a growing centre for sea fishing.

Its importance is due to its connection westwards with Minas Gerais by the Vitória-Minas railway, which transports for export iron ore, coffee and timber. Port installations at Vitória and nearby Ponta do Tubarão have led to some beach and air pollution at places near Vitória, such as Camburi (quite a pleasant beach, though, partly built up, palms, drink stands, fair surf).

Places of interest

On Av República is the huge **Parque Moscoso**, an oasis of quiet, with a lake, playground and tiny zoo. The **Teatro Carlos Gomes**, on Praça Costa Pereira, often presents plays, also jazz and folk festivals. The upper, older part of town, reached by steep streets and steps, is much less hectic than the lower harbour area which suffers dreadful traffic problems.

See the fortified monastery of **Nossa Senhora da Penha**, on a high hill above Vila Velha. Most of the structure, now in ruins, dates from the 17th and 18th centuries; the views are superb. The Dutch attacked it in 1625 and 1640. **Vila Velha**, reached by a bridge across the bay, has an excellent beach, but it is built up and noisy: take bus from Vitória marked Vilha Velha; for bigger waves go to Barra do Jucu. There is also a pleasant ferry service to Vila Velha.

Excursions

Visit **Santa Leopoldina** or **Domingos Martins**, both around 45 km from Vitória, less than an hour by bus (2 companies run to the former, approx every 3 hrs). Both villages preserve the architecture and customs of the first German and Swiss settlers who arrived in the 1840s. Domingos Martins (also known as Campinho) has a Casa de Cultura with some items of German settlement (Hotels include **C** *Imperador*, Praça Gerhardt 275, T 268-1115). Santa Leopoldina has interesting museum (open Tues-Sun, 0900-1100 and 1300-1800) covering the settlers' first years in the area, and a large number of fascinating constructions dating from the end of the last century showing Swiss and German influence.

To **Santa Teresa** (*Pop* 39,365), a charming hill town 2½ hrs by bus from Vitória (US$3.60, beautiful journey). Two hotels, **C** *Pierazzo*, Av G Vargas 115, T 259-1233, **D** *Glebo*, clean, and many restaurants. There is a unique hummingbird sanctuary at the **Museu Mello Leitâo**, which is a library including the works of the hummingbird and orchid scientist, Augusto Ruschi. Hummingbird feeders are hung outside the library (open Sat-Sun 1200-1700, at other times with permission). Also the Nova Lombardia National (renamed **Dr Augusto Ruschi**) **Biological Reserve**, a forest rich in endemic bird species (eg Salvadori's Antwren, Cinnamon-vented Pina, Russet-winged Spadebill, Oustalet's Tyrannulet, Rufous -brown Solitaire and Hooded Berryeater). Previous permission must be obtained to visit from Bento Ferreira at Ibama, Av Mal Mascarenhas de Moraes 2487, CP 762, Vitória ES, CEP 29.000.

Local information
● **Accommodation**
A1 *Best Western Porto do Sol*, Av Dante Michelini 3957, Praia de Camburi, T 327-2244, F 327-2711, 7 km from centre, overlooking sea; **A3** *Senac Hotel* (Government-run hotel

school), luxurious, swimming pool, restaurant, guests attended by student staff, on the ocean at R Bráulio Macedo 417, Ilha do Boi, T 325-0111, F 325-0115.

B *São José*, Av Princesa Isabel 300, T 223-7222, F 223-5746.

D *Avenida*, Av Florentino Avidos 350(ish), T 223-4317/0770, with breakfast, friendly, clean, rec; **D** *Vitória*, Cais de São Francisco 85, nr Parque Moscoso, with bath, excellent restaurant, changes money, good, clean, rec.

E *Europa*, Sete de Setembro, corner of Praça Costa Pereira, clean, noisy but cheap, good value restaurant (nearby is a good value vegetarian restaurant and a money changer, ask at the hotel). Adequate hotels opp Rodoviária. Hotels located in beach areas, Camburi to the N, Vila Velha to the S, both about 15 mins from city centre.

Youth hostel R Hugo Viola 135, T 325-6010, take 'Universitário' bus, get off at first University stop.

● **Places to eat**
Mar e Terra opp Rodoviária, good music, live music at night; *Lavacar* and many others at Praia Camburi offer food and live music; *Lambahias* is a lively dancing place for the young, ½ km W of Bambini, buses each hour on the hour.

● **Banks & money changers**
Local banks Plumatur, Av Governador Bley 465, Edif Glória, Conj 101 (also tourist information, coffee). Mastercard, cash against card, Av Jerônimo Monteiro 1000, Grupo 414/424, Ed Trade Center, Centro.

● **Embassies & consulates**
Danish, R do Sol 141, Sala 210, T 222-4075, open 0900-1300, 1500-1900.

● **Post & telecommunications**
Telecommunications: Embratel, Palácio do Café, Praça Costa Pereira 52.

● **Tourist offices**
Emcatur, Av Getúlio Vargas (corner of Av Jerônimo Monteiro), and at rodoviária (friendly, good tree map).

● **Transport**
Trains Daily passenger service to Belo Horizonte, 14 hrs, US$10 1st class, US$7 2nd.

Buses Rodoviária is 15 mins' walk W of centre. Rio, 8 hrs, US$14.25 (*leito* 18.50). To hitch to Rio, take Itapemirim bus to Aracatiba (26 km). **Salvador**, 18 hrs, US$30; **Porto Seguro** direct 11 hrs with lots of stops, US$15.50 (also *leito* service); alternatively, take bus to Eunápolis, then change buses which run every hour, US$2. To hitch to Salvador, take a bus to Sara, which is beyond Carapina; alight where the bus turns off to Sara. Enquire at rodoviára for other destinations.

NORTH OF VITÓRIA

At Ibiraçu, 57 km N of Vitória on BR-101, an 11 km road goes E to **Aracruz** (*Pop* 52,425), with an impressive Scandinavian/Brazilian cellulose plant, surrounded by vast new eucalyptus forests.

136 km N of Vitória is **Linhares** (*Pop* 119,500) on Rio Doce, with good hotels and restaurants.

Linhares is close to three **nature reserves**: the **Linhares Reserve** owned by CVRD (the state-owned mining company) is possibly the largest remaining lowland tract of Atlantic forest; permission from the reserve's director must be obtained to visit (very good birdwatching). The **Sooretama Biological Reserve**, NW of the CVRD Reserve, on left of highway, protects tropical Atlantic rain forest and its fauna and birds (it contains several bird species not found in CVRD Reserve). For permission to visit contact Ibama at address above.

The **Comboios Biological Reserve**, just S of Linhares, is designed to protect the species of marine turtles which frequent this coast (for information, contact Ibama).

● *Focus Tours*, Belo Horizonte (page 429) offers 1-week birding and general nature tours combining Museu Mello Leitão, Nova Lombardia, CVRD Reserve and Sooretama; many bird and orchid species are found in these reserves and apparently nowhere else.

CONCEIÇÃO DA BARRA

84 km N of Linhares is **Sao Mateus**, a pleasant town, 13 km from good beaches (buses). The most attractive beaches in the State, however, are around **Conceição da Barra** (*Pop* 22,290) 242 km N of Vitória. Corpus Christi (early June) is celebrated with an evening procession for which the road is decorated with coloured wood chips.

Itaúnas, 21 km up the coast, is an interesting excursion; the small town has been swamped by sand dunes, so it has been moved to the opposite river bank. There is now a fantastic landscape of huge dunes and deserted beaches. There are a few *pousadas* and a small campsite. Bus from the *padaria* in Conceição da Barra at 0700, returns 1700.

● **Accommodation** Conceição da Barra, pleasant beach hotels, also **D** *Rio Mar*, Av Dr Mário Vello Silvares, T 762 1228, rec; **D** *Sombra e Água Fresca*, Rodovia Bento Daher 1800, T 762-1206, *pousada*, and campsite, US$3 pp, both with excellent facilities, many languages spoken, enthusiastically rec; **D** *Caravelas*, Av Dr Mário Vello Silvares 83, T 762-1188, 1 block from beach, basic, clean, shared bathroom, light breakfast, rec. *Camping Clube do Brasil* site with full facilities, Rodovia Adolfo Serra, Km 16, T 762-1346.

Minas Gerais

A STATE with a number of fine colonial cities built during the gold rush in the 18th century, some splendid caves, the Rio São Francisco in the N, and several spas and hill resorts. The capital is Belo Horizonte, the country's first modern planned city, now a major industrial centre.

The inland State of Minas Gerais (*Pop* 15,746,200) somewhat larger than France, is mountainous in the S, rising to the 2,787-m peak of Agulhas Negras in the Mantiqueira range, and in the E, where there is the Caparaó National Park containing the Pico da Bandeira (2,890m). From Belo Horizonte N are undulating grazing lands, the richest of which are in the extreme W: a broad wedge of country between Goiás in the N and São Paulo in the S, known as the Triângulo Mineiro. Most of the upland is also good grazing country. Being frost-free, Minas Gerais is again becoming one of the main producers of coffee.

History and economy

Minas Gerais was once described as having a heart of gold and a breast of iron. Half the mineral production of Brazil comes from the State, including most of the iron ore. Diamonds and gold are still found. Its exports move through Rio de Janeiro, Santos, Vitória and Angra dos Reis. The easy

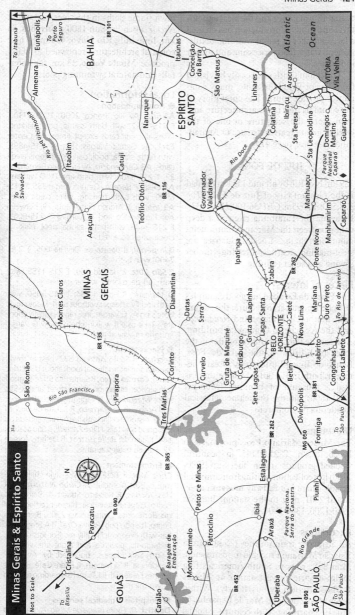

Minas Gerais & Espírito Santo

Not to Scale

availability of power and the local agricultural and mineral production has created a large number of metal-working, textile, mineral water, food processing and timber industries.

The colonial cities can easily be visited from Rio or Belo Horizonte; many companies provide tours. The chief glory of the colonial cities is the architecture and, even more, the sculpture of one of the world's great creative artists, 'O Aleijadinho' (see box, page 424).

JUIZ DE FORA

129 km N of Rio by air and 155 km by road is the pleasant city of **Juiz de Fora** (*Pop* 378,500; *Alt* 695m; *CEP* 36,100; *DDD* 032). It lies on the Paraibuna river, in a deep valley between the Mar and Mantiqueira mountain chains. Local industries are steel-making, textiles, brewing, timber sawing and sugar refining.

Places of interest

The **Praça da Estação** has good examples of Belle Epoque architecture, the station hall, the hotels *Príncipe* and *Renascença* and the Associação Comercial building. Also see the Portinári mural of tiles in the foyer of Edifício Clube Juiz de Fora; Banco do Brasil building by Oscar Niemeyer, both in R Halfeld where there is also a museum of banking (Mon-Fri 1300-1600) and the French neo-classical Academia de Comércio.

Museums

The **Museu Mariano Procópio**, Mariano Procópio s/n, T 211-1145, in beautiful wooded grounds (open Tues-Sun 1200-1800) has collections dating from Imperial Brazil. There is a **railway museum** at Av Brasil 2001, next to the station; Tues-Sat 0900-1200, 1330-1800.

Excursions

An attractive train journey (25 km) from Estação Mariano Procópio (opp museum, Mon-Sat), runs to South America's first hydro-electric power station at **Matias Barbosa** (return by bus, hourly). Within reach of Juiz de Fora: **Mar de Espanha**, 62 km E, charming 19th-century colonial town (tame sloths in the trees, restaurant *Nectar*, open Fri-Sun 1800); **Torreões**, 33 km, lime hills; **Rio Novo**, 48 km N, nice colonial architecture, renowned for dairy produce; **Monte Verde**, 33 km, for waterfalls and natural swimming pools.

Local information

● Accommodation

A1 *Ritz*, Av Rio Branco 2000, T 215-7300, F 215-1892, with bath, sauna, pool, parking, takes all credit cards except Amex; **A1** *Center Park*, Av Getúlio Vargas 181, T/F 215-4898, with bath, sauna, pool, parking, accepts credit cards; **A3** *Centenário*, Av Francisco Bernardino 33, T 215-3700, with bath and TV, D without; **A3** *César Palace*, Av Getúlio Vargas 335, T 215-6599, with bath, parking, takes credit cards; **A3** *Joalpa*, R Afonso Pinto Mota 29, between Avs Rio Branco and G Vargas, T 215-6055, F 215-3446, with bath, sauna, pool, parking, credit cards accepted.

B *Imperial*, R Batista de Oliveira 605, T 215-7400, with bath.

C *São Luiz*, R Halfeld 360, T 215-1155, with bath, art deco lobby, winter garden.

D *Majestic*, R Halfeld 284, T 215-5050, with bath and TV, cheaper without bath. Many cheap hotels on Av G Vargas, in E range, mostly short-stay. Take care if walking betwen Av G Vargas and the railway at night.

● Places to eat

Berttu's, R Santo Antônio 572, best in town; *mineira* and international food (about US$20 inc wine); *Cantão Suíço*, R Santa Rita 557/59, good self-service; others on same street and R São João; *Marrakech*, R Espíritu Santo 1081, bar and Arab cuisine; *Barroco*, R Batista de Oliveira 1126, restored cellar with live music, *feijoada* on Sat, good cocktails; *I Due Fratelli*, R São Mateus 144, Italian; *La Belle Bistrot*, R Delfim Moreira 22, French bar/restaurant.

● Entertainment

Chez Moi, R Tietê 40, Swiss-style chalet, live music. Best nightclub is *Clube Noturno Vila das Tochas*, R Roberto Stigert 4, Bairro São Pedro, crêperie, American bar, dance floor; *Bar do Bené*, Pres Costa e Silva 2305, Bairro São Pedro, friendly pub; *Prova Oral*, R A Braga 210, bar with live music, highly rec. For lots of bars, restaurants, pizzerias and night life, visit the Bairro São Mateus, bounded by Av Independência, R Sã Mateus, R Padre Café, R Mons Gomes Freire with R Manoel Bernardino running down the middle.

● Hospitals & medical services

Dentist: Dr Elsom Braga de Mello, Av Barão do

Rio Branco 25555 sala 1203 (some English).

Doctor: *Alberto Moutinho*, R António Dias 475-A, Granbery, T 213-5083 (no English).

Hospital: *Reunidos*, R Delfim Moreira 62, T 215-6400, serious injuries only.

● **Language courses**
At the federal university, UFJF, T 229-3732, F 231-1342. Students may be able to stay at the *república*, R Dimas Bergo Xisto 155 (bairro São Pedro, 36037-510 Juiz de Fora, 7 km from centre), T 231-1263. From Juiz de Fora rodoviária, take bus 630 to Av Getúlio Vargas esq R Marechal Deodoro, walk to corner of Bargas e R São João, take bus 530 to the *república*, or 532 to corner of Av Senhor dos Passos e Dimas Bergo Xisto.

● **Shopping**
Locally produced clothing, try bargain shops in R Fonseca Hermes; *Priscila Joiais*, gold and silver workshop, Galeria Solar, loja 228; many interesting antique shops; plentiful regional foods.

● **Tour companies & travel agents**
Serra Branca, R Aristóteles Braga 186, Cidade Universitária, T 231-1245, local tours and to further afield in Minas Gerais. *Beijaflor*, Shopping Santa Cruz, loja 1148, T 215-0249, French, Italian, some English spoken.

● **Transport**
Air Av Guadalajara, T 233-1089; bus 520 on the hour to centre. Nordeste Linhas Aéreas, T 233-1040, once a day Mon-Fri to São Paulo and Ipatinga.

Buses Bus station outside town, Av Brasil 4501, T 215-7696, take bus 630 to town. To/from **Rio**, 19 a day, Útil, US$6, 2¾ hrs (a spectacular trip through mountains and tropical forest); Útil to **Belo Horizonte**, 10 a day, US$8 (Viaçao Útil, T 215-3976, Rodoviária, or in town R Henrique Surerus 22, T 215-6759, Mon-Fri 0800-1800, Sat 0800-1200). To **São João del Rei** via Conselheiro Lafaiete, 6 hrs, US$6.

PARQUE FLORESTAL DE IBITIPOCA

85 km from Juiz de Fora, in the municipality of Lima Duarte is the **Parque Florestal de Ibitipoca** at 1,760m, which preserves birds, animals and vegetation of the region, plus several quartzite caves and rock formations. Local guide US$10. For guided tours contact Dale Jaume, T (032) 211-7008, US$70 for full day including transport and lunch, US$80 with simple overnight accommodation and breakfast. In the nearby village of Conceição de Ibitipoca, hand-dyed and woven bedspreads are made; **B** *Pousada do Rodrigo*, T Juiz da Fora, 032-215-8659.

ACCESS By unpaved road (4WD rec) from Lima Duarte to Conceição de Ibitipoca. Bus Rio Preto from Juiz da Fora to Lima Duarte, T 221-4461, then seek out Sr Pedro Moreira's taxi, T 281-1200 (Banco do Brasil) or 281-1296 (home); US$18 to Conceiçao and US$23 to the park, one way.

SÃO JOÃO DEL REI

From **Barbacena** (*Pop* 100,050), 103 km on (with an important horse and cattle fair, and a rose festival in Oct), a paved road runs W to the colonial city of **São João del Rei** (*Pop* 72,740; *CEP* 36300; *DDD* 032), at the foot of the Serra do Lenheiro. The streets are paved with fossilized plants: 'almost sacrilegious to walk on them'. A good view of the town and surroundings is from Alto da Boa Vista, where there is a Statue of Christ (Senhor dos Montes). São João del Rei is very lively at weekends.

Places of interest

A fine bridge and three splendid 18th century churches, open most mornings: **Pilar** (the Cathdral, R Getúlio Vargas), the earliest, with rich altars and bright ceiling, and good *azulejos* in choir, and a sacristy with portraits of the Evangelists; **São Francisco de Assis** (1764), Praça Frei Orlando, with two sculptures by Aleijadinho, and others of his school (restoration has removed the plaster from the altars, revealing fine carving in sucupira wood); **Carmo**, Largo do Carmo, designed by Aleijadinho and with interior sculptures by him, very well restored, all in white.

Museums

Near São Francisco is the house of **Bárbara Heliodora** (1759-1819), one of the Inconfidentes (see page 431), which also contains the municipal museum. The **railway museum** (Av Hermílio Alves 366, T 371-2888 see below) is well worth seeing. **Museu da Arte Sacra**, Praça Gastão da Cunha 8, by Cathedral small but well recommended (Tues-Sun 0900-1700, US$0.50). There are also the **Tancredo Neves Museum**, R Padre José Maria Xavier 7 (weekends and holidays 0900-1700); the **Museu de Arte Regional do Patrimônio Histórico**, in Praça Severiano de Resende (open Tues-Sun, 1200-

O Aleijadinho

Antônio Francisco Lisboa (1738-1814), the son of a Portuguese architect and a black slave woman, was known as O Aleijadinho (the little cripple) because in later life he developed a maiming disease (possibly leprosy) which compelled him to work in a kneeling (and ultimately a recumbent) position with his hammer and chisel strapped to his wrists . His finest work, which shows a strength not usually associated with the plastic arts in the 18th century, is probably the set of statues in the gardens and sanctuary of the great Bom Jesus church in Congonhas do Campo, but the main body of his work is in Ouro Preto, with some important pieces in Sabará, São João del Rei and Mariana.

1730, US$0.50), and a **pewter factory** (with exhibition and shop), Av Leite de Castro 1150, T 371-4422, run by an Englishman, John Somers.

Local festivals

The morning masses on Sun and religious festivals at São Francisco (0915) and Mercês (1030), Praça Br de Hambé, behind and above Pilar, are accompanied by a choir and orchestra who maintain a tradition of over 200 years of local composition.

Local information

● **Accommodation & places to eat**

In Barbacena: **B** *Grogotó*, excellent, operated by Senac, T 331-7755, F 32-2234.

In São João del Rei: **A3** *Porto Real*, Av Eduardo Magalhães 254, T/F 371-1201, comfortable, good restaurant; **B** *Lenheiro Palace*, Av Pres Tancredo Neves 257, T/F 371-3914, good; **B** *Pousada Casarão*, opp São Francisco church, converted mansion, Ribeiro Bastos 94, T 371-1224, swimming pool, delightful; **C** *Colonial*, Manoel Anselmo 22, T 371-1792, clean and comfortable; **E** *Brasil*, Av Pres Tancredo Neves 395, T 371-2804, lovely colonial house, opp railway station so back rooms much quieter, clean, friendly, cheap, rec, no breakfast (*Cafeteria Globo* in the same street, 2 blocks away, is good, though). Cheap *pousadas* in R Marechal Deodoro: **F** *S Benedito*, No 254, clean; **F** *Santa Rita*, No 242, clean, friendly, shared rooms; **F** *Pousada Ramón*, opp bus station. *Restaurant Quinta do Ouro*, Praça Severiano de Rezende 4, all rec. Good *Churrascaria* next to railway station.

● **Tourist offices**

In old bus station in São João del Rei.

● **Transport**

Rodoviária is 2 km W of centre of São João. Buses to **Rio**, 3 daily, 5 hrs, Sun 0800 only, **São Paulo**, 8 hrs, US$12, and **Belo Horizonte**, 3½ hrs. To **Ouro Preto** via Congonhas, US$13, **Juiz de Fora**, US$6, frequent service to Tiradentes.

TIRADENTES

(Originally São José del Rei; *Pop* 10,220; *CEP* 35325; *DDD* 032) John Parsons writes: The centre of this charming little town, 15 km from São João, with its nine streets and eight churches, at the foot of the green Serra São José, hardly belongs to this century. The town is very busy during Holy Week, when there are numerous religious processions.

Places of interest

The **Santo Antônio** church, first built in 1710, contains some of the finest gilded wood carvings in the country and a small but fine organ brought from Oporto in the 1790s. The reconstructed façade is said to follow a design by Aleijadinho. There is also a sun-dial by him. The charming **Rosário** church has fine statuary and ornate gilded altars; this and **Nossa Senhora das Mercês** have interesting painted ceilings and the latter a notable statue of the Virgin.

At the bottom of the stone paved road which descends from Santo Antônio is the fountain (*chafariz*), installed in 1749, whose water is brought by a stone aqueduct from springs in the forest at the foot of Serra São José. Fine walks in the Serra include the lane beside the aqueduct. The **museum**, housed where Padre Toledo (another Inconfidente) once lived, exhibits some good pieces of furniture. The simple pilgrimage church of **Santíssima Trindade** is also well worth seeing. See the artists' lithographic printing shop of Largo do Ó. There are attractive walks in the neighbourhood, and a 1½-hr walk to the fountains and pools of Águas Santas.

Excursions

Recommended is the train trip between São João del Rei and Tiradentes (13 km). The train has been in continuous operation since 1881, using the same locomotives and rolling stock, running on 76 cm gauge track, all now lovingly restored and cared for. Maximum speed is 20 km per hr. Price: US$2.50 return, one class only. Fri, Sat, Sun and holidays, 1000 and 1415, returning 1300 and 1700. Railway museum at the railway station in São João del Rei; open daily 0900-1130, 1300-1700, entrance included in rail fare; there are also a round house which has 16 vintage locomotives in superb condition, an engine shed and a steam-operated machine shop, still working.

Local information
● **Accommodation**
A1 *Solar da Ponte*, Praça das Mercês (prop John and Anna Maria Parsons) T 355-1255, F 355-1201, atmosphere of country house, inc breakfast and tea, only 12 rooms, fresh flowers in rooms, bar, sauna, garden, swimming pool, light meals for residents only, for larger meals, the hotel rec five local restaurants. Also *Pousada Maria Barbosa*, R Antônio Teixeira Carvalho 134, T 355-1227, pool, very pleasant; *Hotel Wellerson*, R Fogo Simbólico 218, T 355-1226; *Hotel Ponto do Morro das Forras 2*, T/F 355-1342; *Pousada de Laurito*, Direita 187, T 355-1268.

● **Places to eat**
Local food: *Quinta de Ouro*, Direita 152, rec; *Estalagem*, R Min G Passos 280; *Padre Toledo*, Direita 202.
Italian: *Donatello*, Direita 205; *Aluarte*, Largo do Ó 1, cheap, garden, sells handicrafts, rec.
Vegetarian: *Opção Saúdavel*, Av Tiradentes 792, tiny, cheap, rec.

● **Tourist offices**
In the Prefeitura, R Resende Costa 71.

ROUTES From Belo Horizonte, the shortest road to São João del Rei is via Lagoa Dourada. Just past Lagoa Dourada is the turning (12 km) for **Prados**, a small town 15 km from Tiradentes (local bus, 30 mins) known for its musical and handicrafts traditions, excellent leather clothing, good prices from *Mara e Café*, R Magachães Gomes 90.

The capital of Minas Gerais is the third largest city in Brazil (*Pop* 2,048,861; *Alt* 800m; *CEP* 3000; *DDD* 031). It is surrounded by mountains, and enjoys an excellent climate (16°-30°C) except for the rainy season (Dec-Mar). It was founded 12 December 1897. Belo Horizonte is one of the fastest growing of Brazil's main cities, now suffering from atmospheric pollution.

The industrial area, about 10 km from the centre, has now become the third largest industrial centre of Brazil, and apart from being the traditional centre of mining and agricultural industries (as well as diamond cutting and precious stones), it has steelworks and an automobile industry. The city has a good public transport system (red buses serve central and express routes, yellow circular routes, and blue diagonal routes), and taxis are plentiful, although hard to find at peak hours.

Places of interest

On the **Praça da Assembléia** are three fine modern buildings: Legislative Assembly, church and Banco do Brasil; the **Palácio da Liberdade**, in Praça da Liberdade amid other fine *fin-de-siècle*-style public buildings (every Sun morning and Thur evening an open-air craft market operates here, very good; also a flower market each Fri from 1800 and an antique and occultism market each Sun: at night the fountain is illuminated in a variety of colours); the **Palácio das Artes**, Afonso Pena 1567, which is in the Parque Municipal and contains the Centro de Artesanato Mineiro (craft shop open 0900-1700, Tues-Sun). The **Parque Municipal** (an oasis of green, right in the centre of the city, small amusement park and playground, closed at night and on Mon, except for a small section in the SW corner). In 1984, the **Minascentro**, a convention centre for exhibitions and congresses, was opened in the city centre.

Museums

Museu Mineiro, Av João Pinheiro, 342, religious art in old Senate building near centre (open Tues, Wed, Fri 1230-1830,

Thur 1500-2100, Sat, Sun 1000-1600); **Museu da Mineralogia Prof Djalma Guimarães**, R da Bahia 1149, a Gothic building near the Parque Municipal, with interesting exhibits; **Museu Histórico Abílio Barreto**, R Bernado Mascarenhas, Cidade Jardim, T 296-3896, in an old *fazenda* which is the last reminder of Belo Horizonte's predecessor, the village of **Arraial do Curral d'el Rey**, built by João Leite da Silva Ortiz in the 18th century, houses most interesting historical exhibits (open 1000-1700 Wed-Mon, take bus 2902 from Av Pena); **Museu da Telecomunicaçao**, Av Afonso Pena 4001, Mangabeiras (open Mon-Fri, 0800-1700); the **railway station**, with museum on 2nd floor showing a model railway and the railway headquarters in a mansion on the hill above the station, with locomotive and railway coach used by Dom Pedro II; **Museo Histórico Natural**, in the Instituto Agronómico, R Gustavo da Silveira 1035, T 461-7666, has a local geological and palaeontological display and good archaeological exhibits (take bus 3803A from Praça Rio Branco). An obelisk in Praça Sete de Setembro, commemorating Independence, is the centre for political protests.

Suburbs

8 km from the centre is the picturesque suburb of **Pampulha**, famous for its modern buildings and the artificial lake (many infestations, do not swim in it). Many buildings were designed by Oscar Niemeyer. In Pampulha the glass and marble **Museu de Arte de Belo Horizonte** is at Av Octacílio Negrão de Lima, Km 11 (open 0800-1800 daily); the **Chapel of São Francisco de Assis**, same avenue, Km 12, has interior decorations by the painter Cândido Portinári). There is a bus (not the 4403) from the city centre to the **Jardim Zoológico** (at the far end of the lake from the dam – small selection of birds with some rarities, animals well kept for the most part) that passes the chapel and also the **Mineirão** stadium about ¾ km away (the second largest in Brazil after the Maracanã stadium in Rio); bus 2004 goes from Av Afonso Pena to the chapel.

In the southern zone of the city, on the Serra do Curral, the **Parque de Mangabeiras** has a good view of the city, forest trails, sports facilities and snack bars. The natural amphitheatre where the Pope spoke in 1982 is nearby; there is an iron monument marking the occasion (take bus 2001 from Afonso Pena between Av Amazonas and R Tamóios, closed Mon).

Excursions

Within easy motoring distance from Belo Horizonte are several of the 400 caves and grottoes for which Minas Gerais is famous. The best and most famous is the **Gruta de Maquiné** with 6 chambers open to visitors, well lit, but hot, 26°C (entry US$2), 126 km NW of Belo (well signposted and with restaurants nearby, which greet potential customers with combined history and menu leaflet; bus at 0915, return at 1500, 3½ hrs, US$4.50). In the nearby town of **Cordisburgo** is a museum to the writer João Guimarães Rosa. The **Gruta de Lapinha**, almost as good, is only 51 km N of the city (entrance to caves and small museum, US$1, closed Mon); bus at 1015, 1¼ hrs, US$2 one way.

10 km before Lapinha is the town of **Lagoa Santa** (*Pop* 24,890), a weekend resort for Belo Horizonte. The sandy beach on the lake (close to the town centre and bus station) is used for fishing, sun-bathing and boating (do not swim, the water is infected with schistosomiasis). Along the beach are bars and restaurants, with more in the nearby main square which also has two small hotels and an interesting modernistic church. The road to Belo Horizonte (½-hourly bus service, US$1) passes Belo Horizonte's international airport. Bus Lagoa Santa-Lapinha every 30 mins. Local bus stop for Lagoa Santa is 2 km downhill from Lapinha caves.

To the NE of the city, a few kilometres off the BR-262, is the **Serra de Piedade**, a high peak giving spectacular views over the surrounding countryside, only accessible by car or special bus service. There are a small chapel and a *churrascaria*. From the peak can be seen the small town of **Caeté** (*Pop* 33,440), which has one or two interesting churches and the remains of an old ironworks near the railway sta-

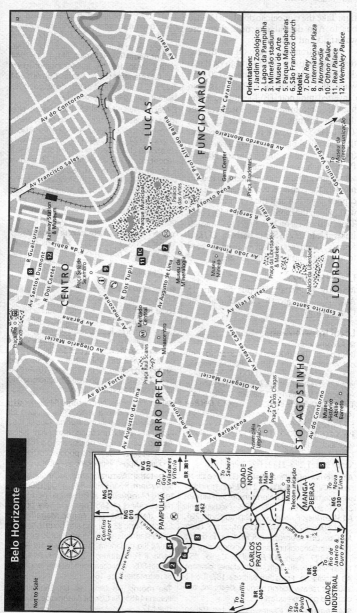

Belo Horizonte

Not to Scale

N

Orientation:
1. Jardim Zoológico
2. Lagoa da Pampulha
3. Minerão stadium
4. Museu de Arte
5. Parque Mangabeiras
6. São Francisco church

Hotels:
7. Del Rey
8. International Plaza
9. Normandie
10. Othon Palace
11. Real Palace
12. Wembley Palace

S. LUCAS

FUNCIONÁRIOS

CENTRO

BARRO PRETO

STO. AGOSTINHO

LOURDES

Av do Contorno

Av Brasil

Av Carandaí

Av Bernardo Monteiro

Av Prof Alfredo Balena

Av Francisco Sales

Av Afonso Pena

Av Getúlio Vargas

Av João Pinheiro

Av Bias Fortes

Av Olegário Maciel

Av Amazonas

Av Augusto de Lima

Av Álvares Cabral

Av Augusto de Lima

Av do Contorno

Av Barbacena

R Sergipe

R Espírito Santo

R Guaicurus

R Dos Caetés

R Dos Tupis

R Santos Dumont

R Paraná

Railway Station
& Museum

Praça da Estação

Palácio das Artes

Parque Municipal

Praça Sete de Setembro

Mercado Central

Minascentro

Praça Raul Soares

Museu da Mineralogia

Museu de Mineiro

Praça da Liberdade
& Market

Palácio da Liberdade

Gem Center

Praça Tiradentes

Assembléia Legislativa

Praça Carlos Chagas

Museu Histórico Abílio Barreto

Praça da Liberdade

Banco

— *inset map* —

To Confins Airport

To Guy Valadares & Vitória

To Sabará

MG 433

MG 010

MG 020

BR 381

BR 262

BR 040

MG 030

Av Pedro I

Av José Pinto

Av Gabriela

PAMPULHA

CIDADE NOVA

see Main Map

MANGA BEIRAS

CARLOS PRATOS

CIDADE INDUSTRIAL

Museu da Telecomunicação

To Brasília

To São Paulo

To Rio de Janeiro & Ouro Preto

To Nova Lima

tion. Take the Conceição do Mato Dentro bus to Alto do Palácio; near there are waterfalls and campsites.

Further from Belo, turn off the BR-262 (towards Vitória) at Km 73 and go via Barão de Cocais and Brumal to Caracá (120 km), where the seminary, at 1,220m, has been converted into a hotel (B), the site and region highly recommended. Reservations through Instituto São Vicente in Belo, T 031-441-5399 (space is very limited and there is no public transport). *Focus Tours* (below) runs tours to the **Caracá Natural Park**, which contains many bird species, some rare, and the endangered masked titi monkey, the common marmoset, the black-capped capuchin and the very rare maned wolf (which the monks feed at dusk). Focus Tours will advise on how to get to Caracá. It is possible to stay in Santa Bárbara (**D** *Hotel Karaibe*; **D** *Sta Inés*, 25 km away on the road to Mariana) and hitchhike to Caracá.

Local holidays

Maundy Thursday; Corpus Christi; 15 Aug (Assumption); 8 Dec (Immaculate Conception).

Local information
● **Accommodation**
(Number of stars in brackets) **L2** *Brasilton* (4), out of town at Km 3.65 on Rodovia Fernão Dias, Contagem, T 396-1100, F 396-1144, very good restaurant; **L3** *Boulevard Plaza* (3), Av Getúlio Vargas 1640, Savassi district (obis), T 223-9000, F 225-8438, very nice; **L3** *Del Rey* (4), Praça Afonso Arinos 60, T 273-2211, F 273-1804; **L3** *Othon Palace* (5), Av Afonso Pena 1050, T 273-3844, F 212-2318, deluxe, excellent, safe deposit boxes, pool on roof, helpful staff; **L3** *Real Palace* (4), R Espírito Santo 904, T 273-3111, F 273-2643.

A1 *Internacional Plaza Palace* (3), R Rio de Janeiro 109, T 201-2300, F 212-2347, good but seedy part of town; **A1** *Normandie* (3), R Tamóios 212, T 201-6166, F 222-6133, excellent grill; **A1** *Wembley Palace* (3), R Espírito Santo 201, T 201-6966, F 224-9946, excellent, central, clean; **A2** *Casa dos Municípios*, R Rio Grande do Nte 1017, Funcionários (in Savassi, chic shopping area), T 226-5177, clean; **A3** *Estoril*, R Carijós 454, T 201-9322, with bath, comfortable, pleasant; **A3** *Itatiaia* (2), Praça Rui Barbosa 187, T 212-3300, nr railway station, central, clean, a/c, with bath and good breakfast.

B *Ambassy* (3), R Caetés 633, nr bus station,

T 201-0222, helpful, English spoken, clean, a/c, noisy, good restaurant; **B** *Sul América Palace* (2), Av Amazonas 50, T 201-1722, clean, friendly, TV and fridge in rooms, run down; **C** *Continental* (2), Av Paraná 241, T 201-7944, central, clean, friendly, quieter interior rooms rec; **C** *Esplanada* (2), Av Santos Dumont 304, T 273-5311 (E without bath), clean, good restaurant, own garage, good value.

E *Maciel*, Av Ol Maciel 95, basic, clean. Near rodoviária and in R Curitiba many hotels are for very-short-stay couples, rec: **D** *Magnata*, R Guarani 124, with breakfast, nr rodoviária, cheap and clean, bath, good hot shower, safe deposit, rec; **E** *Minas Bahia*, No 173, friendly; **E** *Madrid*, opp rodoviária, rec. Within 10 mins' walk of rodoviária, turn left along main road to R Espírito Santo, No 284, **D** *Majestic*; No 227, **E** *São Salvador*; No 237, rec. You may spend the night in the rodoviária only if you have an onward ticket (police check at midnight).

Youth hostels: *Pousadinha Mineira*, R Januária 206, T 446-2911, 15 mins from rodoviária, rec; *Chalé Mineiro*, R Sta Luzia 288, Sta Efigênia, T 467-1576, attractive, splash pool, highly rec.

● **Places to eat**
Chinese: *Yun Ton*, R Santa Catarina 946, rec.

Local food: *Tavares*, R Santa Catarina 64, excellent value; *Dona Lucinha*, R Sergipe 811; *Chico Mineiro*, R Alagoas 626, corner of Av Brasil, local chicken specialities, good, closed Sun; *Santa Felicidade*, R Prof Morais 659 (Funcionários) and da Bahia 1204 (Centro); good; *Arroz com Feijão*, Av Contorno 6510, Av Contorno 7438 and R Antônio de Albuquerque 440, all friendly, reasonably-priced.

Italian: *Pizzaiolo*, Av Contorno 8495, good for pizzas; *Dona Derna*, R Tomé de Souza 1380 (Funcionários), highly rec; *Buona Távola*, R Sta Rita Durão 309, Funcionários, excellent Italian; *Alpino* (German), Av do Contorno 5761 (Funcionários), good value and popular, corned beef and fresh boiled vegetables available.

Vegetarian: *Naturalmente*, Av Andradas 367; *Superbom*, R São Paulo, 971, 1100-1500, Mon to Fri. *Mangueiras*, at Pampulha, next to Niemeyer chapel of São Francisco, very popular; *Flor de Líbano*, opp *Hotel Magalhães* at Espírito Santo 234, cheap and good. Many bars and restaurants around Praça Raúl Soares; more on Av Rio de Janeiro. Two rec bars are *Americana*, R Pernambuco 1025; *Janis*, Av Getúlio Vargas 809. Very cheap and friendly *lanchonete* nr rodoviária, Acre 164.

Tea rooms: *Era Uma Vez Un Chalezinho*, R Paraíba 1455; *Tia Clara*, R Antônio de Albuquerque 617.

● **Banks & money changers**
Lloyds Bank, Av João Pinheiro 580; Citibank, R Espírito Santo 871; Banco do Brasil, R Rio de Janeiro 750, Av Amazonas 276; Banco Econômico, R Bahia 360, 9th floor, and other local banks, 1000-1630. American Express, *Master Turismo*, Av Afonso Pena 1967, T 273-3122. Mastercard, cash against card, Banco Meridional, R dos Inconfidentes 1051, 4th floor, Funcionários (for information only), R da Bahia 1255, Centro (for cash); Sr Cláudio, R Espírito Santo 466, 16th floor, office 1608, very good rates. São Paulo Joias, Amazonas 105, good rates. Changing TCs is difficult, but hotels will change them for guests at a poor rate.

● **Electric current**
120-220 AC 60 cycles.

● **Embassies & consulates**
British Vice-Consulate: Av Afonso Pena 952, s 500, Caixa Postal 576, T 222-6318; German, R Carijós 244, T 222-3411; Austrian; R José Américo Cancado Bahia 199, T 333-3622. French, R Prof Antônio Aleixo 843, 5th Floor, T335-5563; Italian, Praça Carlos Chagas 49, 2nd floor, T 335-5394; Netherlands, R Alagoas 1460, 11th floor, T 221-0615; Finland, Av Contorno 6283, sala 604/8, T 227-2725; Denmark, R Prof Jerson Martins 166, T 448 6013, F 261 7561. US: Serviço de Divulgação e Relações Culturais, Av Alvares Cabral 1600, 3rd floor, T 335-3555.

● **Entertainment**
Music school: Av Afonso Pena, opp Palácio das Artes: 'brilliant' classical concerts, entrance free or nominal (US$2).

Nightlife: *L'Apogée*, R Antônio de Alberquerque 729; *Pantheon*, Rio Janeiro do Nte 1470; *Máscaras*, R Sta Rita Durão 667; *Ao Bar*, R Cláudio Manoel 572, Funcionários; *Sausalito*, R Tomé de Souza 912, street café.

Theatre: *Teatro da Cidade*, R da Bahia 1341, for Portuguese speakers.

● **Hospitals & medical services**
Mater Dei, R Gonçalves Dias 2700, T 335-2200, has been rec; *Alfredo Balena MedCentre*, R dos Otoni 927, a private hospital. *Dr Ricardo Queiroz Guimarães*, Av Brasil 1474, Funcionários, T 224-2020 for contact lenses and eye problems.

● **Places of worship**
Synagoga Beth Yacou, R Pernambuco 326, T 224-6013; Catholic Church, Av Antônio Carlos 2747, T 442-7743, R Bahia 1596, T 222-6059; Presbyterian Church, R Ceará 1434, T 226-1844; Baptist Church, R Joaquim de Figueiredo 332, T 384-1322; Mormon Church, R Levindo Lopes 214, T 233-7883; Adventist Church, R Timbras 683, T 226-6144.

● **Post & telecommunications**
Post Office: with poste restante, Av Afonso Pena 1270.

UPS: Salima, T 222-9002.

● **Shopping**
Mercado Central, Av Aug de Lima 744, large and clean, open every day, Sat social centre. Market for fruit, vegetables, meat and other items at corner of R Santa Catarina and Av Amazonas (nr Praça Raúl Soares). There are huge hypermarkets just outside the city on the highways to Rio and to São Paulo. Splendid delicatessen with foreign food and wines – and liquors – *Au Bon Gourmet*, R Tupinambás 187. Gemstones are a good buy here, try *Manoel Bernardes*, R Espírito Santo 835, very reasonable, ask for US saleswoman Manuela, who can arrange tours of workshops. For records, *Cogumelo*, Av Augusto de Lima 399. 'Hippie fair' Thur evenings in Praça da Liberdade. Food and Antique fair, Av Afonso Pena, opp park, Sun; good home-made food; other fairs on Fri and Sat. Belo is said to be very good for slide film, cheese and chocolate.

Bookshop: *Daniel Vaitsman*, R Espírito Santo 466, 17th floor, for English language books. Foreign language books at *Livraria Van Damme*, R das Guajajaras 505, also good local and Portuguese selection (and said to change TCs); *Acaiaca*, R Tamóios 72, good for dictionaries. Used foreign-language books at *Livraria Alfarrábio*, R Iamóios 320.

● **Tour companies & travel agents**
Focus Tours, R Alagoas 1460/s 503, Savassi, 30130 Belo Horizonte, T 223-0358, F (031) 223-0599, Tx 039 1976, run by Douglas and Nancy Trent, offer specialized tours all over Brazil and have a special interest in ecology and tours to the Pantanal. Tours in Minas to see a great variety of wildlife. Reliable information and a portion of their profits is used for conservation project in Brazil (office in USA 14821 Hillside Lane, Burnsville, MN 55306, T/F 612-892-7830). *Master Turismo*, Aeroporto Internacional, Suite 45, T 689-2044, and Av Afonso Pena 1967, T 273-3122.

● **Tourist offices**
Belotur (municipal information office), R Tupis 149, 17th floor, T 222-5500; Turminas, Av Augusto de Lima 785, T 201-0122/201-3875; Praça Sete de Setembro; at rodoviária (particularly polyglot, reasonable free map of centre) ask for the *Guia Turístico* for events, opening times etc, airport (very helpful). Touring Clube do Brasil, Av Afonso Pena 1913.

● **Transport**
Local Car hire: Nobre, Confins Airport and Av Francisco Sales 1424, T 227-5700; and others.

Air A new international airport nr Lagoa Santa, at Confins, 39 km from Belo Horizonte, has been opened. Taxi to centre, US$24; airport bus, either *executivo* from the exit, US$6, or comfortable normal bus from far end of car park every hr on the ½-hr, US$2.40, both go to/from rodoviária.

Closer to the city is the national airport at Pampulha, which has shuttle services from several cities, inc Rio and São Paulo. Flights, as well as transportation to/from this airport, are cheaper. From airport to town blue bus 1202 leaves across the street from the aiport, 25 mins, US$0.15, bus passes the rodoviária and cheaper hotel district.

Trains To Vitória, daily 0700, tickets sold at 0530, US$10 1st class, US$7 2nd, 14 hrs.

Buses Rodoviária is by Praça Rio Branco at end of Av Afonso Pena (left-luggage lockers, attended service 0700-2200). To **Rio**, 7 hrs, US$14.25 (ordinary), *leito*, US$28.50; to **Brasília**, 10 hrs, 9 a day inc 2 *leitos*, only one leaves in daylight (0800), US$23, *leito* US$46. To **São Paulo**, 10 hrs, US$7.25; route passes the great Furnas reservoir. To **Salvador** US$39, 24 hrs, at 1800 and 1900 daily. **Porto Seguro** 18 hrs, direct, via Nanuque and Eunápolis; **Recife**, US$60; **Belém**, US$91. To **Campo Grande** 2000, with Gontijo, a good route to Bolivia, avoiding São Paulo. All major destinations served. For buses within Minas Gerais, see under destination.

Hitchhiking To Rio or Ouro Preto, take a bus marked 'Shopping', to the shopping centre above Belo Horizonte on the Rio road.

About 120 km NE of Belo Horizonte, 33,400 square km of the Serra do Espinaço has been named as the **National Park of Serra do Cipó**, in view of its scenic beauty and rich variety of plant and animal life. The park is between 1,140 and 1,560m, with rocky outcroppings, although there are more outcroppings, better scenery and rich birdlife outside the park. There are several endemic plants, insects and birds (the Cipo Canestero – only found outside the park in one small area). There are also several carnivorous plants (Ibama office: Av do Contorno 8121, Cidade Jardim, CEP 30.110-120, Belo Horizonte, T 335-6611).

THE COLONIAL CITIES

The road from Belo Horizonte to the picturesque colonial cities described below follows the Rio das Velhas.

NOVA LIMA

(*Pop* 52,200) About 27 km SE of Belo by a good road, set in eucalyptus forests. Its houses are grouped round the gold mine of Morro Velho, opened by a British firm in 1834 but sold to Brazilians in 1959, the deepest mine in the Americas. The shaft has followed a rich vein of gold down to 2,591m (not open to tourists). There are interesting carvings by Aleijadinho, recovered from elsewhere, in the (modern) parish church.

SABARÁ

A paved road branching off the Belo Horizonte-Brasília highway leads (30 km, 30 mins) to the colonial gold-mining (and steel-making) town of **Sabará** (*Pop* 89,680). Return by the old road over the mountain range of Serra do Curral for fine views. Sabará is strung along the narrow steep valleys of the Rio das Velhas and Rio Sabará.

Places of interest

Its old churches and fountains, its rambling cobbled streets, its simple houses with their carved doors, and its museum of 18th century gold mining in the **Intendência de Ouro** (built 1732, closed for repairs, 1995) are of great interest. The mineral museum in the **Escola da Minas** is worth a visit for those interested in minerals and rock formations.

The other main sights are the **Prefeitura**, in R Pedro II, an old mansion with oratory and main reception room (*salão nobre*); the **Teatro Municipal** (former Opera House) (1770, restored 1960) in the same street, has a fine interior; the portal of the **Casa Azul**, in the same street; the Churches of **Nossa Senhora do Carmo** (1774), with doorway, pulpits and choir-loft by Aleijadinho and paintings by Athayde; **Nossa Senhora do Rosário dos Pretos** (left unfinished at the time of the slaves' emancipation); **São Francisco**; **Nossa Senhora da Conceição** (1720) with much gilding, and paintings by 23 Chinese artists brought from Macau; and **Nossa Senhora da Ó**, built in 1698 and showing unmistakable Chinese influence (paintings much in need of restora-

D *Pousada Ciclo do Ouro*, Felipe dos Santos 241, T 581-3201/2210, clean, laundry facilities, rec; **D** *Pousada São Francisco de Paula*, 100m from Rodoviária (next to the São Francisco de Paula), panoramic view, clean, rec; **D** *Pousada Casarão*, R Direita, quiet, clean, shared bathroom, breakfast, rec.

East at R Conselheiro Quintiliano 26, Rosana lets rooms, basic, clean, friendly, clothes washing; **E** *Hospedaria* of Consuêlo Perdigão, R Pandiá Calógeras 59, Barra, T 551-2318, price pp in shared room, use of kitchen, living room, shared bathroom, very good, English spoken, rec; **E** *Pousa Ouro Preto*, Praça Tiradentes 71, cheap, nice, clean, hot water, shared bathroom rec; **E** *Villa dos Pilares*, Praça Monsenhor C Barbosa 19, T 551-1324, very relaxed, 'slightly weird'; **E** *Vermelha Dormitório*, Praça São Francisco de Assis 30, T 551-1138, quiet, clean, shared shower, laundry facilities. Youth hostel in R das Mercês, accepts student cards as membership. Also try *casas de família*, reasonably-priced, can be booked through tourist office, or with people offering accommodation on Praça Tiradentes.

Difficult to get hotel rooms at weekends and holiday periods; a good idea to telephone ahead. In the low season prices can be negotiated.

Students: may be able to stay, during holidays and weekends, at the self-governing student hostels, known as *repúblicas* (very welcoming, 'best if you like heavy metal music'). Many are closed between Christmas and Carnival.

Camping: Camping Clube do Brasil, 2 km N of city, is quite expensive but very nice. Also a site reached by car up a very steep hill at the top end of town: about 5 km. Also at picnic site 4 km W of Ouro Preto, and at Rio Acima nearby.

● **Places to eat**
Pasteleria Lampião, Praça Tiradentes, good views at the back (better at lunchtime than in evening); *Casa Grande* and *Forno de Barro*, both on Praça Tiradentes, good local dishes; *Café & Cia*, R São José 187, closes 2300, very popular, *comida por kilo* at lunchtime, good salads, juices, rec; *Chafariz*, R São José 167, good local food; *Calabouço*, good, Conde de Bobadela 132, with an antique shop; *Sobrenatural* on the same street, rec; *Tacho de Ouro Preto*, Conde de Bobadela 76, good lunch buffet, popular; *Casa do Ouvidor*, Conde de Bobadela 42, above De Bernardis jewellery shop, nr main square, good; *Adega*, R Teixeira Amaral, 1130-1530, vegetarian smorgasbord, US$6, all you can eat, highly rec. Try the local *licor de jaboticaba*. A candlelit bar, *Acaso 85*, Praça Largo Rosário, is not cheap but marvellous for romantics; *Vide Gula*, R Senador Rocha Lagoa, food/kilo, good, friendly atmosphere, rec.

● **Banks & money changers**
Banco do Brasil, R São José, good rates, also for TCs.

● **Electric current**
110 volts AC.

● **Post & telecommunications**
Post Office: on R Direita.

● **Shopping**
For precious stones, *Videmaju*, owned by Vincente Júlio de Paula, a professor at the School of Mines, sells stones at very good prices from his house at R Conselheiro Santana 175. Buy soapstone carvings at roadside stalls and bus stops rather than in the cities; they are much cheaper. Many artesans sell soapstone carvings, jewellery and semi-precious stones in the square in front of São Francisco de Assis church. Gems are not much cheaper from freelance sellers in Praça Tiradentes than from the shops around the square, and in the shops themselves, the same quality of stone is offered at the same price – *Brasil Gemas* and *De Bernard* are rec.

● **Tourist offices**
Praça Tiradentes 41. Enquire here for details of accommodation in *casas de família*, *repúblicas* and other places. Note, though, that foreigners are expected to want expensive hotels. The tourist office at the bus station is sometimes open, map US$1.10 from either office.

Guides: Bandeira's *Guia de Ouro Preto* in Portuguese and English (US$3.50 with coloured map, US$1 with black and white one), normally available at Tourist Office. Also available is Lucia Machado de Almeida's *Passeio a Ouro Preto*, US$6 (in Portuguese, English and French). A local guide for a day, Associação de Guias de Turismo, T 551-2655, is more expensive if obtained through Tourist Office (rec guide: Cassio Antunes). *Ourotur* runs a tour of Ouro Preto in a vintage-style bus, 0900 and 1430, from the rodoviária (T 551-2764).

● **Transport**
Buses The rodoviária is above the town nr the São Francisco de Paula church. It's an easy downhill walk to the centre (10 mins), or a town bus passes every 30 mins; taxis charge exorbitant rates. An early plane from Rio to Belo Horizonte and a bus (11 a day) gets to Ouro Preto by lunch (2 hrs); bus fare, each way, US$4, taxi US$50. Day trips are run; alternatively take bus from **Rio**, Útil at 2300 (US$18, 6½ hrs), return bus to Rio leaves at same time. Book your return journey to **Belo Horizonte** early if returning in the evening; buses get crowded. There are also buses to **Conselheiro Lafaiete** for connections to Belo Horizonte and Congonhas, and direct to **Congonhas** at 1400 and 1530, or to Rio via

Barbacena and Juiz da Fora (direct bus to Rio is often fully booked 2-3 days, or weekends, in advance). Direct bus Ouro Preto to **Vitória** at 2100, US$13, 5½ hrs (connection to Porto Seguro), daily. To **Salvador** with Gontijo (change at Belo Horizonte), 1945, 24 hrs, US$40, buy ticket at Útil desk. Direct bus to **São Paulo**, 1900, 11 hrs, US$24. Check that your bus ticket from Ouro Preto is in fact from Ouro Preto and not from Belo Horizonte. Two buses an hour to Mariana, if return buses are full walk to the next village. Hitchhiking to Mariana is said to be easy, start in Praça Tiradentes.

MARIANA

(*Pop* 38,115; *Alt* 697m; *CEP* 35420; *DDD* 031) Another old mining city, founded 1696, much less hilly than Ouro Preto, is 12 km E of Ouro Preto on a road which goes on to join the Rio-Salvador highway.

Places of interest
The beautiful old prison on Praça João Pinheiro (**Cadeia**, 1768, now the Prefeitura Municipal); on the same square the **Carmo** church (1784, steatite carvings, Athayde paintings, chinoiserie panelling – closed for repairs since 1992), next to it is the fine **São Francisco** church (1762, pulpits designed by Aleijadinho, Athayde paintings and tomb, fine sacristy, one side-altar by Aleijadinho, entry, US$0.50) and the old **Palácio dos Governadores** connected with it; the **Museu Arquidiocesano** has fine church furniture, a gold and silver collection, Aleijadinho statues and an ivory cross (R Frei Durão 49, open 0900-1300 except Mon and 1400-1645; entrance US$1, good guide book); **Capela de Santo Antônio**, wonderfully simple and the oldest in town. The **Cathedral**, Basílica de NS da Assunção, built 1711-1760, Praça da Sé, has a wooden German organ (1701), façade by Aleijadinho, beautiful interior and side altars (entry US$0.50). Organ concerts are given on Fri, 1100 and Sun, 1200 (US$5). Between the old prison and São Francisco is a stone monument to Justice, at which slaves used to be beaten. The house of the poet Afonso de Guimarães (buried behind the Igreja Santuaria), R Direita 35, is open to visitors: photographs and letters (free). There are viewpoints at the churches of **NS do Rosário**, R do Rosário (1752, with work

by Athayde and showing Moorish influence) and **São Pedro dos Clérigos** (built in 1753), Largo de São Pedro. Some people still pan for gold in the river running through the town.

Minas de Passagem
Between Ouro Preto and Mariana is the Minas de Passagem gold mine, dating from 1719. A guided tour visits the old mine workings and underground lake (take bathing suit), entrance US$10, visiting hours 0900-1800, T Ouro Preto 551-1068, Mariana 557-1340/1255. Buses leave Ouro Preto from beside the Escola de Minas, nr *Restaurante Casa das Contas*, for Mariana, US$0.75, all passing Minas de Passagem, US$0.25; bus from Belo Horizonte (via Ouro Preto), US$2, 2¼ hrs. Taxi from Ouro Preto, US$7.80. There is a waterfall, Cachoeira Serrinha, where swimming is possible, 30 mins' walk from the bus stop to the mine. Ask for directions. Initially you have to walk 100m towards Mariana then ask.

Excursions
24 km N of Mariana (infrequent bus US$0.50), is the small village of Antônio Pereira where the imperial topaz is mined. Tours of an interesting cave with stalactites: pay local children a few centavos to show you round.

Local information
● **Accommodation**
C *Faísca*, R Antônio Olinto 48, T 557-1206, inc breakfast; **C** *Müller*, Av G Vargas 34, T 557-1188; **C** *Pousada do Chafariz*, R Côn Rego 149, T 557-1492, TV, fridge, parking, breakfast inc, friendly family atmosphere, rec.

D *Providência*, R Dom Silverio 233, T 557-1444, run by nuns, small rooms, pool, clean, quiet.

E *Central*, R Frei Durão 8, on attractive square, pleasant, quiet, rec but avoid downstairs rooms. The modern service station (*posto*) on the highway above the town offers good clean rooms at E, with hot showers.

● **Places to eat**
Alvorada, Praça Cláudio Manoel 42; *Tambaú*, Praça da Sé; *Papinha della Nonna*, D Viçoso 27, Italian, rec. *Portão da Praça*, Praça Gomes Freire 108, excellent, 20% discount given to guests of *Pousada do Chafariz*, rec.

● **Tourist offices**
Terminal Turístico, 500m beyond rodoviária towards colonial centre, Praça Tancredo Neves, guides' association, small tourist office, map US$1.50. Tourist agency, **Transcolta**, Praça JK, T 557-2056; enquire also at **Embratur**, Praça Tancredo Neves, T 557-1533.

CONGONHAS DO CAMPO

(*Pop* 41,070; *Alt* 866m; *CEP* 36404; *DDD* 031) A hill town, it is connected with Ouro Preto by a good road through pleasant farming country (a worthwhile day trip, taking 0900 bus to Cons Lafaiete and changing at Murtinho). A paved 3½-km road links with the Rio-Belo Horizonte highway.

The town is dominated by the great pilgrimage church of **Bom Jesus do Matozinho** (1773), which opens at 0815; indeed there is little else of architectural interest. There is a wide view of the country from the church terrace, below which are six small chapels set in attractive sloping gardens, showing scenes with life-size Passion figures carved in cedar wood. The church is mainly famous for its group of prophets sculpted by Aleijadinho, standing on the parapets of the terrace. These 12 great dramatic statues (thought of as Aleijadinho's masterpieces), carved in soapstone with dramatic sense of movement, constitute one of the finest works of art of their period in the world – not just in Latin America. Inside the church, as well as the Room of Miracles, there are paintings by Athayde and the heads of four sainted popes (Gregory, Jerome, Ambrose and Augustine) sculpted by Aleijadinho for the reliquaries on the high altar. (Bus 'Basílica', on the hour from opposite the Rodoviária to Bom Jesus, US$0.20.)

Excursions Pleasant excursion to waterfall with park and swimming, at Cachoeira Santo Antônio.

Local festivals Congonhas is also celebrated for its Holy Week processions, which have as their focus the Bom Jesus church. The most celebrated ceremonies are the meeting of Christ and the Virgin Mary on the Tues, and the dramatized Deposition from the Cross late on Good Fri. Pilgrimage season, first half of Sept, draws many thousands.

● **Accommodation D** *Colonial*, Praça da Basílica 76, opp Bom Jesus, T 731-1834, good and comfortable, breakfast extra, no showers or toilets in room, blankets only, fascinating restaurant downstairs full of colonial handicrafts and good local food; **E** *Freitas*, R Marechal Floriano 69, T 731-1543, basic. There are handicraft shops selling soapstone artefacts.

● **Transport Buses** Rodoviária is 1½ km outside town. To/from **Belo Horizonte**, 1½ hrs, US$3.25, 6 times a day, best to buy a return ticket. To **São João del Rei**, either direct (US$13), or go via Murtinho. Bus to **Ouro Preto**: direct (US$13), or go via Belo Horizonte, Murtinho or Conselheiro Lafaiete.

ROUTES None direct from Rio; you have to change buses at **Conselheiro Lafaiete** (**C** *Rhud's Hotel and Restaurant*, R José Nicolau de Queiroz 11, T/F 721-4199; **B** *Hotel Cupim*, on main Rio road, 18 km, T 721-5022, F 721-5375).

DIAMANTINA

(*Pop* 42,980; *Alt* 1,120m; *CEP* 39100; *DDD* 037) The most revered of these cities is reached from Belo Horizonte by taking the paved road to Brasília. 30 km N of Belo Horizonte on this road, is the *Hotel Fazenda* at Ipê Amarelo – horses to ride, etc. Further on, between Caetanópolis and Paraopeba, is the *Flora Eunice* (*Leite ao Pé de Vaca*) snack-bar (good toilets) with small private botanic garden and zoo with contented animals, recommended. 19 km beyond Paraopeba is **Curvelo** (a lively town, *Hotel Sagarana*, 5-star, very good; *Restaurant Denise* with sleeping accommodation, on main highway, very clean), beyond which the road passes through the impressive rocky country of the Serra do Espinhaço.

Diamantina, centre of a once active diamond industry founded in 1729, has excellent colonial buildings. Its churches (difficult to get into, except for the modern Cathedral) are not as grand as those of Ouro Preto, but it is possibly the least spoiled of all the colonial mining cities, with carved overhanging roofs and brackets; try walking through the lower part of the town. This very friendly town is in the deep interior, amid barren mountains; it is the birthplace of President Juscelino Kubitschek, the founder of Brasília. His house has been converted into a museum.

After repeated thefts, the diamonds of the Diamond Museum, in the house of Padre Rolim, one of the Inconfidentes (see under Ouro Preto) have been removed to the Banco do Brasil. Diamonds are still sought; see traditional methods at Guinda, 7 km away. *Passeio a Diamantina*, an excellent guide, is written by the author of *Passeio a Sabará*. The town's latest industry is the making of Portuguese Arraiolos-style tapestry carpets by hand, at a cooperative in the centre; it was started by a diplomat, Sr Flecha da Silva, who was perturbed by the amount of local unemployment, and it has become very successful. Also etchings on leather are made locally.

The house of Chica da Silva, an 18th-century slave who married a rich diamond contractor, is at Praça Lobo Mesquita 266, entry free; Chica has become a folk-heroine among Brazilian blacks.

Excursions

Walk along the **Caminho dos Escravos**, the old paved road built by slaves between the mining area on Rio Jequitinhonha and Diamantina. A guide is essential (ask at the Casa de Cultura – cheap), and beware of snakes. Along the river bank to (12 km) **Biribiri**, a pretty village with an abandoned textile factory. About half-way, swimming pools in the river; opposite them, on a cliff face, animal paintings in red, age and origin unknown. Interesting plant life along the river, and beautiful mountain views.

Local information
● **Accommodation**

B *Tijuco*, Macau do Melo 211, T 931-1022, best, good food.

D *Dália*, Praça JK (Jota-Ka) 25, T 931-1477, fairly good.

E *JK*, opp rodoviária, with breakfast, clean, friendly; **E** *Pensão Comercial*, Praça M Neves 30, basic. Wild camping nr waterfall just outside town.

● **Places to eat**
Bar-Restaurant Confiança, R da Quitanda 39, good. *Capistrana*, R Campos Carvalho 36, nr Cathedral square, rec. *Serestas* (serenades) Fri and Sat nights; many young people in bars in Beco da Mota.

● **Electric current**
110 AC.

Tourist offices
Depto de Turismo in Casa de Cultura in Praça Antônio Eulálio 53, 3rd floor, pamphlets and a reliable map, also information about churches opening times, friendly and helpful, will arrange free tour of churches with guide who has access to keys (tip guide).

● **Transport**
Air An airport was due for completion in 1995.

Buses 6 a day to **Belo Horizonte**, via Curvelo, for connections to Brasília, with Pássaro Verde: $2\frac{1}{2}$ hrs to **Curvelo**, US$3.25, to **Belo Horizonte**, US$10.75, $5\frac{1}{2}$ hrs. A slow but interesting trip to the N is possible by taking the bus to **Aracuaí**, 6 hrs, then to Itaobim, $1\frac{1}{2}$ hrs, from where there are connections along the BR116 to **Bahia**.

SERRO

(Pop 19,445; *CEP* 39150; *DDD* 037) 92 km by paved road from Diamantina and reached by bus from there or from Belo Horizonte is this unspoiled colonial town on the Rio Jequitinhonha. It has six fine baroque churches, a museum and many beautiful squares. It makes *queijo serrano*, one of Brazil's best cheeses, being in the centre of a prosperous cattle region. The most conspicuous church is **Santa Rita**, on a hill in the centre of town, reached by steps. On the main square, by the bottom of the steps, is the **Carmo**, arcaded, with original paintings on ceiling and in choir. The town has two large mansions: those of the **Barão de Diamantina**, now in ruins, and of the **Barão do Serro** across the river, beautifully restored and used as the town hall and Casa de Cultura; there are old mine entrances in the hillside behind the courtyard.

Just by the Serro turnoff is the town of **Datas**, whose spacious church (1832) decorated in red and blue, contains a striking wooden image of Christ with the crown of thorns.

● **Accommodation** **C** *Pousada Vila do Príncipe*, T 941-1485, very clean, in an old mansion at R Antônio Honório Pires 38, contains its own museum, the artist Mestre Valentim is said to have been born in slave quarters; other cheap hotels (eg **F** *Dormitório*, R Rio Branco, opp Banco do Brasil).

● **Places to eat** *Itacolomi*, Praça João Pinheiro 20, fair; good one on main square, also *Churrascaria Vila do Príncipe* nearby on RA H Pires.

NORTH OF BELO HORIZONTE

THE RIO SAO FRANCISCO

Some 240 km NW of Belo Horizonte is a lake five times as large in area as Rio de Janeiro bay, formed by the **Tres Marias** dam on the upper reaches of the São Francisco river. The town (*Pop* 21,410) is at the lake's northern end. At Barreiro Grande is the **C** *Clube Náutico Tres Marias*, BR-040, 5 km from centre, T 754-2015, also campsite.

PIRAPORA

North of Tres Marias is the terminus for boat journeys on the Rio São Francisco (see also page 534). The cutting down of trees, in part as fuel for the boats, and the low rainfall in recent years, has greatly reduced the flow. The town itself (*Pop* 46,230; *CEP* 39270; *DDD* 037) is a tourist attraction because of the falls in the river which make for excellent fishing. The fishermen use punt-like canoes. The sandy river beaches are used for swimming. The riverboats' grotesque figureheads, *carrancas*, are made in the workshops of Lourdes Barroso, R Abaeté 390.

- **Accommodation B** *Pirapora Palace*, on Praça Melo Viana (7 blocks W and 1 block S of Rodoviária), T 741-1330, ask for room on garden, clean, friendly, safe; **C** *Canoeiras*, Av Salmeron 3, T 741-1946, used by river-tour parties; **C** *Daila*, Praça JK 13, with breakfast but without bath; **D** *Grande*, R da Quintande 70, with bath but without breakfast. Camping nr the Praça on riverside.

- **Places to eat** *Lá em Casa*, 'meals by the kilo, huge *caipirinhas* US$0.50, excellent value'; *Borretos* on the riverfront.

Passenger services on the river have been discontinued, but it is still sometimes possible to arrange journeys on cargo boats if you talk to the masters, in the port. If you succeed, the regular stops are at Januária (famous for Brazil's reputed best *cachaça*) and Bom Jesus da Lapa (a pilgrimage centre with a church built in a grotto inside a mountain, but a very poor town); hotels inc **B** *Hansão das Pedras*, **C** *Real*, **F** *Brasília*; a choice of bars on the river beach). Between Pirapora and Januária is the colonial town of **São Francisco**, with many attractive houses and a good handicraft market in the town

hall; the boats do not always stop there. If you want to see the real Sertão, get off at Xique-Xique and take a bus to Utinga, Rui Barbosa and Itaberaba, then on to Salvador. Of the two remaining wood-burning stern-wheel boats, allegedly built for Mississippi services in the 1860s and imported from the USA in 1922 to work on the Amazon, one, the *Gaiola*, has been restored for tourist-agency use. An expensive weekly trip (starting Sun) is made downriver visiting various ports as far as São Francisco, organized in Belo Horizonte by *Unitour* (Av Tupis 141) or *Mangebeira Turismo* (R Goitacases 71, 8th floor).

ROAD TO BAHIA

If you can't get a boat, an adventurous journey to the Bahia coast is by bus from Pirpora to Montes Claros, next morning bus Montes Claros – Almenara (12 hrs) then bus Almenara-Salto da Divisa (2½ hrs). Stay the night in Salto at hotel facing bus station, then take a bus to Porto Seguro. **Montes Claros** is a pleasant town with many hotels (eg **E** *Giovanni*, close to rodoviária, clean, modern), restaurants and cinemas.

- **Transport** Buses to Montes Claros from Diamantina, weekdays 0600, US$10, 6 hrs. An alternative route to Bahia is the daily 1000 bus to Vitória da Conquista (see page 518, Gontijo line US$13); interesting journey through hilly country, pine and eucalyptus plantations, and many remote towns.

EASTERN MINAS

Eastern Minas Gerais is a centre of semi-precious stone processing and crystal carving, and also contains the Serra do Caparaó, where are found several of Brazil's highest mountains. The two principal towns, Governador Valadares and Teófilo Otôni, are both on the BR-116 inland Rio-Salvador road, and both have good connections with Belo Horizonte. Only through *Focus Tours* (see Belo Horizonte, page 429) can the private Caratinga Biological Station be visited, 880 ha of mountainous, inland Atlantic forest which is home to four rare primates: the muriqui (formerly called the woolly spider monkey, the largest primate in the Americas and the largest mammal endemic to Brazil), the black-capped capuchin, the brown howler monkey and the buffy-headed marmoset. Also at the station are brown-throated, three-toed sloths and an incredible array of birds. The primates and many of the birds are not bothered by human presence. Entrance fee is US$20 pp per day.

GOVERNADOR VALADARES

A modern planned city (*Pop* 230,490; *Alt* 170m; *CEP* 35100; *DDD* 0332), 324 km from Belo Horizonte, 5½ hrs by bus (US$9.50, US$19 leito) and also by regional air service, is a good place to break the Belo Horizonte-Salvador journey. It is a centre of semi-precious stone mines and lapidation, as well as for the cut-crystal animals one finds in tourist shops all around Brazil.

Excursions To the top of the Pico de Ibituruna, 960m.

- **Accommodation A3** *Governador Palace*, Av Minas Gerais 550, T 271-7474, F 271-4750; **B** *Panorama*, Mal Floriano 914, T 221-7833; **B** *Real Minas*, Praça Serra Lima 607, T 271-6751. Many **F** hotels nr bus station.

- **Places to eat** Main hotels; *JB*, R Bárbara Heliodora 384, rec, huge servings; *Joazeiro*, R Pessanha 639.

- **Transport Air** Airport is on the BR-381, 6 km from the city centre with flights to Belo Horizonte and Ipatinga.

TEŚFILO OTŚNI

(*Pop* 140,640; *Alt* 335m; *CEP* 39800; *DDD* 033) 138 km from Governador Valadares, this is a popular buying spot for dealers of crystals and semi-precious stones, with the best prices in the state.

- **Accommodation** *Nobre Palace*, Av Francisco Sá 43, T 521-5824, F 522-3272; *Teófilo Otôni*, BR-116 Nte km 275, 5 km from centre, T 521-4822; **C** *Lancaster*, R Frei Gonzaga 142, T 522-3131; **C** *Presidente*, Av Getúlio Vargas 183, clean, good breakfast, laundry facilities; **D** *Pousada Tio Miro*, R Dr Manoel Esteves 389, T 521-4343, clean, relaxed atmosphere, rec.

- **Transport** Buses to **Porto Seguro** via Nanuque (can break Belo Horizonte-Salvador journey here; **F** *Hotel Minas*, at rodoviária, adequate, and others nearby).

CAPARAÓ NATIONAL PARK

In the park are the Pico da Bandeira (2,890m), Pico do Cruzeiro (2,861m) and the Pico do Cristal (2,798m). The park features rare Atlantic rainforest in its lower altitudes and Brazilian alpine on top. From the park entrance (small fee) it is 6 km on a poorly-maintained road to the car park at the base of the waterfall. From the hotel (see below) jeeps (US$20 per jeep) run to the car park at 1,970m (2½ hrs' walk), then it's a 3-4-hr walk to the summit of the Pico da Bandeira, marked by yellow arrows; plenty of camping possibilities all the way up, the highest being at Terreirão (2,370m). This is good walking country. It may also be possible to visit local fazendas, for example Fazenda Modelo, 8 km from the town of **Manhumirim** (*pop* 27,625). It is best to visit during the dry season (April-Oct). It can be quite crowded in July and during Carnaval. Contact via Caixa Postal 17, alto Jequitibá, MG, CEP 36976-000, T 255, via operator on 101, Alto do Caparaó.

- **Accommodation C** *Caparaó Parque*, 2 km from park entrance, 15 mins' walk from the town of Caparaó, nice, T (032) 741-2559. Ask where **camping** is permitted in the park. In **Manhumirim: E** *São Luiz*, good value, but *Cids Bar*, next door, Travessa 16 do Março, has better food.

ACCESS Caparaó National Park is 49 km by paved road from Manhuaçu (about 190 km S of Governador Valadores) on the Belo Horizonte-Vitória road (BR-262). There are buses from Belo Horizonte, Ouro Preto or Vitória to **Manhumirim**, 15 km S of Manhuaçu. From Manhumirim, take a bus direct to Caparaó, 0930, 1630 US$0.80, or to Presidente Soares (several, 7 km), then hitch 11 km to Caparaó. By car from the BR-262, go through Manhumirim, Pres Soares and Caparaó village, then 1 km further to the *Hotel Caparaó Parque*. Coming from Rio, leave BR-116 at Fervedouro and take BR-482 to Carangola. Just before this town branch N to Espera Feliz. About half way about turn left again to Pres Soares.

THE SPAS OF SOUTHERN MINAS GERAIS

Some 240 km SW of Belo is the huge lake

formed by the Furnas dam. It can be seen from the BR-381 road to São Paulo.

The spas are easily reached by road and in some cases by air from Rio de Janeiro and São Paulo. They are also popular holiday places with a great many hotels; Dec-Mar is the high season.

POÇOS DE CALDAS

(*Pop* 110,150; *Alt* 1,180m; *CEP* 37700; *DDD* 035) The city is sited on the crater of an extinct volcano in a mountainous area on the SW border of the state. It is reached by road or plane from São Paulo (272 km), Rio (507 km) or Belo Horizonte (510 km). Venetians from Murano settled here and established a crystal-glass industry. A well-known resort, it is a traditional honeymoon centre and has complete and up-to-date thermal establishments for the treatment of rheumatic, skin and intestinal diseases; you need a local doctor's certificate to use these facilities. Excursions include several lakes within a few kilometres of the city with boating and restaurants; the Véu das Noivas with its three waterfalls illuminated at night; the tall statue of Cristo Redentor at an altitude of 1,678m, which can be reached by cable car; nearby is an 80m granite rock, Pedra Batão. There are also the lovers' well, Fonte dos Amores, and the Japanese tea-house at the Recanto Japonês. A tourist train runs from Poços de Caldas to Águas da Prata and back each Sat (dep 0915 and 1500, return 1130 and 1700, 1 hr 15 mins' journey). Hippie fair every Sun in Praça Pedro Sanches. Festivals include Carnival, São Benedito ending on 13 May, and the Festival de Música Popular Brasileira (Festa UAI, 2nd half of Aug). Excellent climate. There is now a small industrial estate.

● **Accommodation** Some 80 hotels and pensions. **A1** *Palace*, Praça Pedro Sanches, T 722-1392, old fashioned but well run, with sulphur baths; **A1** *Pousada Vale das Rosas*, Av N Brás 4500, T 713-1759, F 713-1315; **A3** *Continental*, Av Francisco Salles 235, T 722-1166. The following are **E** pp and good: *Real*, R Minas Gerais 390, T 721-4152; *Virginia*, R Minas Gerais 506, T 722-2694.

● **Places to eat** *Sem-Sem*, R Assis Figueiredo 1080; *Cantina do Araújo*, R Assis Figueiredo 1705. Local specialities: smoked cheese, sausages, sweets and jams (try squash-and-coconut).

● **Transport Buses** Rodoviária 3 km from centre. **Rio**, 8 hrs, US$11.50; **São Paulo**, 4½ hrs, US$6.60.

● **Banks & money changers** Meridional, R Prefeito Chagas, 138, for Mastercard cash.

HILL RESORTS NEAR TRES CORAÇÕES

8 km E of BR381 is **Tres Corações** (*Pop* 57,040; *DDD* 035), also in southern Minas but not a spa. It is the birthplace of Pelé, the legendary football star (statue). Reached by daily buses from Rio, São Paulo and Belo Horizonte.

● **Accommodation** **D** *Italian Palace*, Av Dep R Azeredo 1009, T/F 232-2112; **E** *Capri*, Av Getúlio Vargas 111, T 231-1427. Good food at *Hotel Cantina Calabresa*, R J Bento de Carvalho 65, T 231-2108.

There are two daily buses to (35 km, US$1.80, 2 hrs) **São Tomé das Letras**, a beautiful hilltop village, one of the five highest places in Brazil (*Pop* 5,710; *Alt* 1,291m). A traditional quarry town, it has some charming old-style buildings with frescoed 17th-century church and many caves in surrounding hills. Cave inscriptions have lent the town a mystical reputation, attracting 'new age' visitors, very popular at weekends. Waterfalls: Cachoeira de Eusebiose, 4 km; Véu de Noiva 8 km.

● **Accommodation & places to eat** *Hospedaria do Gê*, R Gabriel Luis Alves 28; restaurant opp, *Das Letras*, both rec. **Other resorts Pocinhos de Rio Verde**, a friendly hill resort, bus 1 hr; *Hotel Bosque das Fontes*, rec, at entrance to town, chalets, camp sites, restaurant, low cost steam and mineral baths; *O Portal*, R Armando Vilela 7, camping, good lasagne on offer; lake, horses and many trails. Rainy season Oct-March. Downhill, on road to Sobrachinha is the quiet community of **Harmonia**, 'new age', cheap vegetarian food, clean accommodation (**E** pp); *Hospedaria dos Sonhos I and II*, T 237 1235, restaurant, swimming pool, sauna, television in rooms, rec.

OTHER HYDRO RESORTS

São Lourenço (*Pop* 29,510; *Alt* 850m; *CEP* 37470; *DDD* 035) is easily accessible from Rio de Janeiro (5-6 hrs by bus) or São Paulo (6-7 hrs by bus). There is a splendid park, tennis, boating, swimming, a flying field, and fishing from the Ilha dos Amores in a lake ringed by gardens and forests. Its rich mineral waters are used in the treatment of stomach, liver, kidney and intestinal complaints. There is an up-to-date hydro establishment for douches and for the famous carbo-gaseous baths, unique in South America. There is a grand ride through fine scenery to the Pico de Buqueré (1,500m). On Sat and Sun a tourist train goes to São Lourenço from Cruzeiro (São Paulo state), 0900, US$15 including guide and snack.

Caxambu (*Pop* 19,470; *Alt* 900m; *CEP* 37440; *DDD* 035), N of São Lourenço, is one of the more sophisticated of these resorts. Its waters are used for treating stomach, kidney and bladder diseases, and are said to restore fertility. They seemed to work for Princess Isabel, daughter of Dom Pedro II, who produced three sons after a visit. The little church of Santa Isabel da Hungária stands on a hill as a thank-offering. The mountains and forests around are very beautiful. View over the city from Morro Caxambu, 1,010m. Excellent hotels.

Lambari (*Pop* 16,080; *Alt* 900m; *CEP* 37480; *DDD* 035) is 56 km W of Caxambu by road. Hotels are not luxurious but fairly comfortable. The Parque das Águas has seven springs and a swimming pool. There are boat trips on the Lago Guanabara. Casino. **Cambuquirá** (*Pop* 11,600; *Alt* 946m; *CEP* 37420; *DDD* 035) is a little N of Lambari by road, very popular, with friendly atmosphere and picnic sites close by.

WESTERN MINAS

ARAXÁ

(*Pop* 69,860; *Alt* 970m) A quiet little place in the Minas Triangle with thorium and radio-active waters and sulphur and mud baths. It can be reached from Rio (848 km), São Paulo (549 km) or Belo Horizonte (374 km), by bus. Airport.

- **Accommodation** A1 *Grande de Araxá*, luxury, 8 km away, T 661-2011; **A3** *Colombo*, same location, T 661-3016, F 661-5367; *Pinto*, Pres O Maciel 284, T 661-2551.

SERRA DA CANASTRA NATIONAL PARK

South of Araxá is the **Serra da Canastra National Park**, in which the Rio São Francisco rises. It is a cool region (temperatures in May and June average 18°C), best reached from Piumhi, on state road 050, 267 km W of Belo Horizonte. (Ibama, address as for Serra do Cipó, above.)

UBERABA AND UBERLÂNDIA

Uberaba (*Pop* 210,800; *Alt* 700m; *CEP* 38100; *DDD* 034), also in the Minas Triangle, is on the Rio da Prata, 120 km W of Araxá, 718 km from São Paulo. It is an important rail and road junction, being on the direct highway between São Paulo and Brasília, and serves a large cattle raising district. At the beginning of May each year the Rural Society of the Minas Triangle holds a famous cattle and agricultural exhibition at Uberaba. Several hotels and restaurants. Bus from Belo Horizonte, US$11.50 (leito US$23), 7 hrs.

About 100 km N of Uberaba is **Uberlândia** (*Pop* 366,710; *CEP* 38400; *DDD* 034), founded in 1888 as São Pedro do Uberabinha (the current name was adopted in 1929); good communications by air and road (buses to Brasília, 6 hrs, US$9; to Belo Horizonte, 9 hrs, US$14.50, to São Paulo, US$15.25). **D** *Hotel Nacional*, Higino Guerra 273, T 235-4983, opp rodoviária, with view (cheaper without), shower and breakfast, clean; many others, also restaurants. In the rodoviária is a helpful tourist information kiosk.

The State of São Paulo

THE state is the industrial heart of Brazil, with much agriculture too; the city is the financial centre. The metropolis does have much of cultural interest in the way of museums, and the famous Butantã Snake Farm. On the coast there are many fine beaches, although pollution is a problem; inland there are hill resorts.

The State of São Paulo (*Pop* over 31,000,00), with an area of 247,898 square km, is larger than the states of New York and Pennsylvania together and about the same size as Great Britain and Northern Ireland. A narrow zone of wet tropical lowland along the coast rises in an unbroken slope to the ridge of the Great Escarpment – the Serra do Mar – at from 800 to 900m above sea level. The upland beyond the Great Escarpment is drained westwards by the tributaries of the Rio Paraná. The broad valleys of the uplands are surmounted by ranges of low mountains; one such range lies between the São Paulo basin and the hinterland of the state. West of the low mountains between the basin and the rest of the state lie the uplands of the Paraná Plateau, at about 600m above the sea. One of the soils in this area is the terra roxa, the red earth in which coffee flourishes. When dry it gives off a red dust which colours everything; when wet it is sticky and slippery. There is ample rainfall in São Paulo State; indeed, the highest rainfall in Brazil (3,810 mm) is over a small area between Santos and São Paulo; at São Paulo itself it is no more than 1,194 mm. Temperatures on the plateau are about 5°C lower than on the coast, but it is only S of the latitude of Sorocaba that frosts occur and then not frequently. Temperatures are too low for coffee in the São Paulo basin itself, but the State produces, on average, about 7 million bags a year.

Between 1885 and the end of the century a boom in coffee and the arrival of large numbers of Europeans transformed the State out of all recognition. By the end of the 1930s there had arrived in São Paulo State a million Italians, half a million each of Portuguese and immigrants from the rest of Brazil, nearly 400,000 Spaniards and nearly 200,000 Japanese. It is the world's largest Japanese community outside Japan. Today the State produces some 20% of Brazil's agricultural output and 65% (40% in São Paulo city alone) of its industrial production, being also responsible for 60% of the country's industrial consumption of electric energy. São Paulo provides 33% of the total exports of Brazil and takes 40% of the total imports: nearly all pass through the port of Santos.

SÃO PAULO

São Paulo (*Pop* 10,998,000 – metropolitan population est 19,000,000; *Alt* 730m; *CEP* 01000; *DDD* 011) is 429 km from Rio de Janeiro, and is connected with it by air, the Via Dutra highway, and the Central do Brasil railway. It is one of the fastest growing cities in the world and is already the most populous city in South America, and the continent's leading industrial centre. Visitors find the characteristic sharp changes of temperature troublesome and even Paulistanos seem to catch cold often. (Incidentally, one differentiates between Paulistas – inhabitants of the State – and Paulistanos – inhabitants of the city.) The traffic pattern is extremely exasperating:

you may have to drive around 10 blocks to reach a point half a block away. Buy a *Guia de São Paulo* from a newstand if you plan to stay any length of time. Also exasperating is the amount of air pollution: in dry weather eyes and nose are continually troubled.

History

São Paulo was founded in 1554 by two Jesuit priests from São Vicente, Blessed José Anchieta and Padre Manuel Nóbrega, as a mission station. The original settlement, not yet effectively preserved, was at the Pátio do Colégio in the centre of the city, where a copy of Anchieta's original church has been built, using one of the surviving mud-packed walls of the original 16th century structure (it is open Tues to Sun, 1300-1700).

Until the 1870s it was a sleepy, shabby little town known as 'a cidade de barro' (the mud city), as most of its buildings were made of clay and packed mud. The city was transformed architecturally at the end of the 19th century when wealthy landowners began to invest in São Paulo as a financial and residential centre. The main reasons for the city's development lie in its position at the focus of so much agricultural wealth, and the availability of plentiful hydro-electric power. Nowadays, it covers more than 1,500 square km – three times the size of Paris – but little remains of its 19th century architecture. Although most of its citizens are proud of its skyscrapers, of its well-lit streets, and especially of its Metro system, they also mourn the loss of innumerable historical buildings and green areas through short-sighted planning policies in the 1980s.

Districts

The shopping, hotel and restaurant centre embraces the districts of Av São Luís, the Praça da República, and R Barão de Itapetininga. The commercial quarter, containing banks, offices and shops, is contained within a central district known as the Triângulo, bounded by R Direita, Quinze de Novembro, São Bento and Praça Antônio Prado, but it is already rapidly spreading towards the apartment and shopping district of Praça da República. R Augusta begins close to Av São Luis, extends as far as **Avenida Paulista**, and continues beyond into one of the most affluent areas, Jardins. Both sides of R Augusta have a variety of shops, snackbars and restaurants, but the Jardins side contains the more exclusive boutiques and fashion houses, while the part which leads to the centre is a rather curious but colourful mix of seedy bars, saunas (mixed, or men only) and 5-star hotels. Cinemas are found on both sides as well as a number of shopping malls (close to Paulista). Avenida Paulista, once the home of coffee barons and São Paulo's wealthy citizens, is now Brazil's largest financial centre housing most banking head offices (most consulates as well), and the **Museu de Arte de São Paulo** (MASP – opened by Queen Elizabeth II in 1968). It is becoming a new downtown area, more dynamic, but considerably less colourful than the old centre with its maze of bustling pedestrianized streets. Another new centre is Av Faria Lima, 8 km from Praça da República. Other popular areas are Vila Madalena and Pinheiros; in the latter is Espaço Paulista on Depto La Cerda Franco 87, with entertainers on Fri and Sat pm.

PLACES OF INTEREST

The park in **Praça da República** is worth going into between 0800 and 1400 on Sun: birds, trees and Brazilians in all their variety, and a famous handicrafts fair; on Sat pm there is live music, and stalls sell sweets and salgados. Near the Praça is the city's tallest building, the **Edifício Itália** on the corner of Av Ipiranga and Av São Luís. There is a restaurant on top and a sightseeing balcony (see **Places to eat**). Also worth a visit is the **Martinelli building**, the city's first skyscraper, R Líbero Badaró and Av São João, Mon-Sat, 0900-1600, entry to 26th floor, free. Two central parks are **Parque da Luz**, Av Tiradentes (110,000 sq metres) and **Siqueira Campos** (Parque Trianon), Peixoto Gomilde 949 and Av Paulista, open daily 0700-1830, a welcome green area in the busiest part of the city.

The **Viaduto do Chá**, which bridges the central avenue, Anhangabaú, leads to

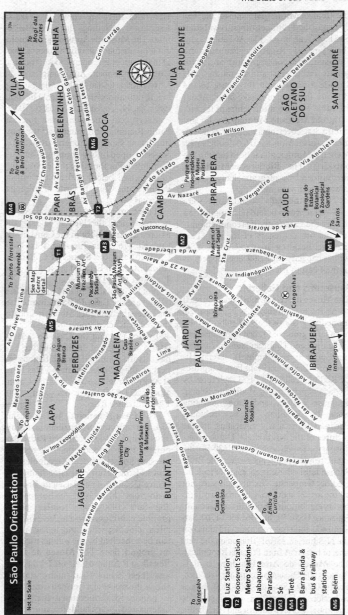

São Paulo Orientation

Not to Scale

T1 Luz Station
T2 Roosevelt Station

Metro Stations:
M1 Jabaquara
M2 Paraiso
M3 Sé
M4 Tietê
M5 Barra Funda & bus & railway stations
M6 Belém

the **Teatro Municipal**, one of the few distinguished 19th-century survivals that São Paulo can boast. The Av Paulista and the 'jardins' América, Paulista and Paulistano still contain some mansions of beauty and interest and are on the 702U Cidade Universitária bus route to the Butantã Institute or 'snake farm'. About 10 mins' walk from the centre of the city is the old **Mercado Municipal** at R Cantareira 306, covering an area of 27,000 sq metres (open Mon-Sat 0400-1600); a new Mercado Municipal has been built in the outskirts. The **Biblioteca Municipal**, surrounded by a pleasant shady garden, is well worth visiting.

The **Cathedral's** foundations were laid over 40 years before its inauguration during the 1954 festivities commemorating the 4th centenary of the city. This massive building in neo-Gothic style, with a capacity for 8,000 worshippers, is in the heart of the city.

Museums and Galleries

The **Museu de Arte de São Paulo** (founded by Assis Chateaubriand, Av Paulista 1578, immediately above the 9 de Julho tunnel) has a large group of French Impressionists, Florentine and Umbrian painters (including Botticelli and Raphael), several Hieronymus Bosch and Frans Post, sculptures by Rodin, a collection of 73 sculptures by Degas and paintings by Modigliani, Renoir, Toulouse- Lautrec, and some interesting work by Brazilian artists, including Portinári. Particularly interesting are the pictures of the NE made by Dutch artists during the Dutch occupation (1630-54): the exotic tropical landscapes – even the Paulo Afonso falls! – have been made to look incredibly temperate. (Exhibitions vary, not all the artists above may be on view.) Temporary exhibitions are held in the basement. Entrance US$0.50, Tues-Fri 1300-1700, Sat-Sun 1400-1800 (nearest metro is Paraíso on the N-S line, or MASP-Trianon on the new line, or bus 805A from Praça da República). The **Museu de Arte Brasileira** is at R Alagoas 903, Pacaembu, entrance free, Tues-Fri 1400-2200, Sat-Sun 1300-1800, houses collections of Brazilian artists such as Portinári, Anita Malfatti and Brecheret.

Here also there are copies of Brazilian sculptures, including those of Aleijadinho. The **Museu de Arqueologia e Etnologia** is on the fourth and fifth floors of Bloco D in the students resident blocks (known as Crusp) in the main Arts Complex of the Universidade de São Paulo (USP), bus stop before the entrance to the Butantã Institute (see page 447); open Tues-Fri 0900-1700.

Every odd-numbered year the São Paulo Bienal at Ibirapuera has the most important show of modern art in Latin America, open from beginning of Sept till November. For the other museums at Ibirapuera, see below, and for the Museu Paulista and Casa do Grito at Ipiranga, see page 447.

There are two museums on Av Tiradentes, near the Jardim da Luz; the **Museu de Arte Sacra** in the Convento da Luz, No 676 (open Tues-Sun 1300-1700, US$0.20) and the **State Art Collection** (**Pinacoteca do Estado**) at No 141 (open Tues-Sun 1300-1800, free).

Not far from the Butantã Institute (see below) are the **Casa do Bandeirante** (being renovated) at Praça Monteiro Lobato, the reconstructed home of a pioneer of 400 years ago; and the **Casa do Sertanista**, a museum of Indian folklore and handicrafts mounted by the famous expert on the Indians, Orlando Villas Boas, at Av Prof Francisco Morato 2200, Caxingui, T 211-5341, open Tues-Sun, 0900-1700, entrance free.

The **Casa Brasileira**, Av Faria Lima 774, is a museum of Brazilian furniture, Tues-Sun, 1300-1700. **Museo Padre Anchieta**, Pátio do Colégio, is a restored mission house; inside are examples and relics of the Jesuit era, same hours, entrance US$0.50. The **Museu da Imagem e do Som** (MIS) is at Av Europa 158, Tues-Sun 1400-2200, regular photographic exhibitions and archives of Brazilian cinema, video and music, which can be consulted by the public, nice café on ground floor. The **Museu de Lasar Segall**, at R Alfonso Celso 362, Vila Mariana (near Santa Cruz metro station), shows the works of a German expressionist painter who emigrated to Brazil, with cinema and library, holds free courses and

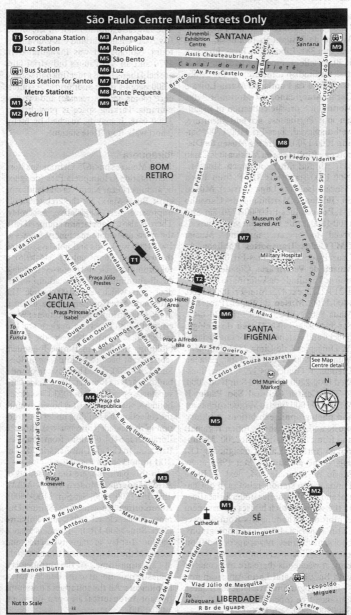

São Paulo Centre Main Streets Only

- **T1** Sorocabana Station
- **T2** Luz Station
- **Bus Station**
- **Bus Station for Santos**
- **Metro Stations:**
- **M1** Sé
- **M2** Pedro II
- **M3** Anhangabau
- **M4** República
- **M5** São Bento
- **M6** Luz
- **M7** Tiradentes
- **M8** Ponte Pequena
- **M9** Tietê

Not to Scale

seminars (arrive early), Tues-Fri 1430-1800, Sat 1430-2000, Sun 1430-1830. **Museu da Imigração Japonesa**, R São Joaquim 381, Liberdade, Tues-Sun 1330-1730, excellent, nice roof garden, ask at desk for English translation of the exhibits. **Museu da Fundação Maria Luisa e Oscar Americano**, Av Morumbi 3700, Morumbi, a private collection of Brazilian and Portuguese art and furniture, well-displayed, Tues-Fri 1100-1700, Sat-Sun 1000-1700. There is a **Museu da Discoteca e Biblioteca da Música** at R Catão 611, 5th and 6th floors, open Mon-Fri, 0900-1300 (take bus 819 P from Praça Princesa Isabel to Lapa district). **Museu do Telefone**, Martiniano de Carvalho 851, Paraíso, Tues-Fri 0900-1730, Sat-Sun 1400-1800, quite good, but you're not allowed to operate anything. **Museu CMTC dos Transportes Públicos**, Av Cruzeiro do Sul 780, Tues-Fri, 0900-1700. **Museu de Veterinária**, Cidade Universitária, Facultade de Veterinária, bloco 7, T 210-2122, ext 475, Mon-Fri 0900-1200, 1400-1700. **Museu do Papel** (Paper), R Mauá 836, casa 25, Tues-Fri 1330-1700, Sat-Sun 1000-1400; **Museu do Relógio** (clocks and watches), rec for enthusiasts, Av Diógenes R de Lima 2333, Pompéia, Mon-Fri 0800-1130, 1300-1700; **Estação Ciência**, R Guaicurus 1274, Lapa, Tues-Wed 1200-2200, Thur and Sun 1000-2000.

The **Centro Cultural São Paulo**, R Vergueiro 1000 (metro Vergueiro) has art and photographic exhibitions, a library, music and dance shows (often regional) and films; open daily until 2200. **Memorial da América Latina**, designed by Oscar Niemeyer, built in Mar 1989, at Av Mário de Andrade 664, next to Barra Funda metro station, relief map of Central and South America under a glass floor in the section which houses a permanent exhibition of handicrafts from all over Latin America, library of photographs, books, magazines, newspapers and films shown on video, very impressive, restaurant; at weekends there are free concerts with Brazilian and Latin American musicians, programme available on request, entrance free (open Tues-Fri 0900-2100, Sat 0900-1800, Sun 1000-1800).

Anhembi

The largest exhibition hall in the world (Av Assis Chateaubriand e R Olava Fontoura, Santana), it was inaugurated in 1970 and all São Paulo's industrial fairs are held there. It has a meeting hall seating 3,500 people, three auditórios, 24 conference rooms (*salas de reunião*) and two restaurants. Parking space is provided for 3,500 cars. It may be reached by metro (short walk from Tietê station).

Ibirapuera

Take a Monções bus (675-C) from Ana Rosa metro station to Ibirapuera Park (designed by architect Oscar Niemeyer and landscape artist Burle Marx) for the architecturally impressive new **Legislative Assembly**. There is also a **planetarium** equipped with the most up-to-date machinery (shows at 1600-1800 weekends and holidays, during the week for groups only, T 544-4606); a velodrome for cycle and motor-cycle racing; an all-aluminium covered stadium for indoor sports which seats 20,000 people. The **Museu de Arte Contemporâneo**, founded in 1963, has an important collection of Western and South American modern art. The collection is divided between the Bienal building, 3rd floor, in Parque Ibirapuera (entrance at back of building, open Tues-Sun, 1200-1700, closed holidays, free) and a building at R da Reitoria, 109, Cidade Universitária, open Wed-Sun 1000-1700, closed holidays, students free (it is hoped to unite the collection in a building under construction in the Cidade Universitária). Buses to Ibirapuera, 6414 (Gatusa) from Praça da Bandeira; to Cidade Universitária 702U or 7181 from Praça da República.

In this park, too, are the museums of **Arte Moderna** (Modern Art – MAM, Tues-Fri 1300-1900, Sat-Sun 1100-1900), **Aeronáutica** (showing the Santos Dumont plane; closed 1995), and **Folklore** (Tues-Sun 1400-1700). There is also a unique display of nativity scenes and scenes of the life of Christ. (Concerts held at Christmas-time.) At the entrance is a majestic monument to the Bandeirantes, or pioneers. All the Ibirapuera museums (except Aeronáutica) are open Tues-Sun, 1400-1700.

Shopping centres

Typical of modern development are the huge Iguatemi, Ibirapuera and Morumbi **shopping centres**. They include luxurious cinemas, snack bars and most of the best shops in São Paulo. Parking in each for over 1,000 vehicles. On a rather humbler level are the big supermarkets of El Dorado (Av Pamplona 1704) and Pão de Açúcar (Praça Roosevelt, near the *Hilton*); the latter is open 24 hrs a day (except Sun).

CITY EXCURSIONS

The large municipal stadium in the **Pacaembu** valley, a flourishing residential district, is well worth seeing. Built on Olympic lines in an area of 75,500 sq metres, it holds nearly 70,000 spectators. Besides the flood-lit football ground inluding athletics field and basketball court, there are also a covered gymnasium, open-air and covered tennis courts, an illuminated 50m long swimming pool, and a great hall for receptions and rallies. There is a larger stadium holding 100,000 people in **Morumbi**, one of the more elegant residential districts. Motor racing fans might like to visit the Morumbi cemetery, last resting place of Ayrton Senna.

The palatial **Jockey Club** racecourse is in the Cidade Jardim area with easy access by bus (Butantã from República, among others). Race meetings are held on Mon, Wed and Thur at 1730 and Sat and Sun at 1500. The new town premises of the Jockey Club (R Boa Vista) are well worth a visit.

The Butantã Snake Farm and Museum, Av Dr Vital Brasil 1500, Pinheiros, is the most popular tourist attraction. The snakes are milked for their poison six times a day but you may not witness this; the antidotes made from the venom have greatly reduced deaths from snakebite in Brazil. It also deals with spider and scorpion venom, has a small hospital and is a biomedical research institute. Open daily from 0900-1700 (except Mon), entrance US$1.50. Informative museum; details in English and Portuguese. From Praça da República take bus marked 'Butantã' or 'Cidade Universitária' (Nos 701U or 792U) along Av Paulista, and ask to be let out at Instituto Butantã.

Parque da Independência, in the suburb of Ipiranga, contains the famous Ipiranga Monument to commemorate the declaration of Brazilian independence; beneath the monument is the Imperial Chapel, with the tomb of the first emperor, Dom Pedro I, and Empress Leopoldina (open Tues-Sun, 1300-1700). Take bus 4612 from Praça da República. The **Casa do Grito**, the little house in which Dom Pedro I spent the night before his famous cry of Ipiranga – 'Independence or Death' – is preserved in the park (open Tues-Sun 0930-1700). The **Museu Paulista**, housed in a huge palace at the top of the park, has old maps, traditional furniture, collections of old coins and of religious art and rare documents, and a department of Indian ethnology. Behind the Museum is the **Ipiranga Botanical Garden**. Open Tues-Sun and holidays, 0900-1700. Take bus 478-P (Ipiranga-Pompéia for return) from Ana Rosa. There is a *son et lumière* show on Brazilian history in the park on Wed, Fri and Sat evenings at 2030.

Parque do Estado (Jardim Botânico), out at Água Funda (Av Miguel Estefano 3687), has a vast garden esplanade surrounded by magnificent stone porches, with lakes and trees and places for picnics, and a very fine orchid farm worth seeing during the flowering season, Nov-December. Over 32,000 different kinds of orchids are cultivated. Open Tues-Fri, 0900-1130, 1230-1700, Sat-Sun 0900-1600. The astronomical observatory nearby is open to the public Thur afternoons. Take metro to São Judas on Jabaquara line, then bus.

Zoological Gardens, Av Miguel Estefano 4241, near the Jardim Botânico, are not more than half an hour's drive from the city centre. A very large variety of specimens can be seen in an almost natural setting of about 35 ha of forest. Open 0900-1700, admission US$0.45 (bus 4742, 'Jardim Celeste', from São Judas). There is a wild-life park, **Simba Safari**, nearby, admission US$0.80 per pedestrian, US$3 pp with a car (children under 11 free), open Tues-Fri 1000-1630, Sat-Sun 0900-1630 (1730 in summer).

Parque Água Branca (Av Água Branca 455) has beautiful gardens with specimens of tropical plants, Brazilian birds and wildlife. Pavilions house a well stocked aquarium, a zoo, and exhibitions of food produce.

In Tremembé, a little beyond Cantareira, 30 mins from the down-town area, is the **Horto Florestal** (R do Horto, in Parque Estadual da Cantareira, 7,900 ha), containing examples of nearly every species of Brazilian woodland flora, 15 km of natural trails, museum with exhibits of regional flora and fauna, view of São Paulo from Pedra Grande on the right of entrance to the park (admission US$0.80, daily, 0700-1730).

Miraporanga Botanical and Wildlife Sanctuary in the foothills of the Serra do Mar, is 1 hrs' drive from São Paulo city centre. It is a 100 ha botanist's paradise, with a vast collection of orchids, carnivorous and aquatic plants, waterlily pools, a lake and 20 glasshouses. It also contains armadilloes, deer and other mammals, monitor lizards and a variety of hummingbirds, T Sr Samuel Jorge de Mello, 816-0817, weekends 476-6716 for information on times and prices of admission.

Santo Amaro Dam (Old Lake), is 3 km from the centre of Santo Amaro suburb. This is a popular boating resort with several sailing clubs and many attractive cottages along the shore. There is a bus (30 min) from São Paulo to Santo Amaro.

Interlagos (Av Interlagos, T 577-0522), which has a motor-racing circuit with 18 km of track, is São Paulo's lake resort on the Santo Amaro dam. It can be reached from Santo Amaro by bus. Close to the track, where the Brazilian Grand Prix takes place every second year, usually in Feb, is the 32-km long **Guarapiranga** artificial lake with good restaurants and several luxurious sailing and sports clubs (Av Guarapiranga 575, open 0600-1700 daily). Camping Clube do Brasil site. Guarapiranga is less polluted than the other artificial lake, Billings, which also has restaurants.

Pico de Jaraguá (1,135m) the highest peak in the neighbourhood, gives good views of Greater São Paulo on a fine day. Lots of hang gliding here at weekends, many people go to watch. This peak is reached from Km 18 on the Campinas highway (Via Anhanguera) by a good road through Taipas and Pirituba.

Embu (*Pop* 138,520), 28 km from São Paulo, is a colonial town which has become a centre for artists and craftsmen. On Sun afternoons there is a large and popular arts and crafts fair (0900-1800). Buses from close to the Largo de Pinheiros, São Paulo, or Santo Amaro bus.

LOCAL HOLIDAYS

25 Jan (Foundation of City). Note that during carnival most museums and attractions are closed.

LOCAL INFORMATION

Warning Beware of assaults and pickpocketing in São Paulo. Thieves often use the mustard-on-the-back trick (see **Introduction and Hints**, **Security**). The areas around Luz station and Centro are not safe at night, and visitors should not enter *favelas*.

● **Accommodation**

Hotel prices

L1	over US$200	**L2**	US$151-200
L3	US$101-150	**A1**	US$81-100
A2	US$61-80	**A3**	US$46-60
B	US$31-45	**C**	US$21-30
D	US$12-20	**E**	US$7-11
F	US$4-6	**G**	up to US$3

Among the most luxurious (corporate rates available), all with swimming pools, nightclubs and convention halls, are the **L1** *Caesar Park*, R Augusta 1508, T 253-6622, F 288-6146; **L1** *Maksoud Plaza*, Alameda Campinas 150, T 253-4411, F 253-4544; **L1** *Mofarrej Sheraton*, Alameda Santos 1437, T 253-5544, F 280-8670 (rec); **L1** *Grand Hotel Cà d'Oro*, R Augusta 129, T 256-8011, F 231-0359; **L1** *Hotel Deville*, Av Monteiro Lobato s/n, Guarulhos, T 968-0400, F 964-0594, comfortable, excellent food, nr airport; **L1** *Brasilton*, R Martins Fontes 330, T 258-5811, F 258-5812; **L1** *Hilton*, Av Ipiranga 165, T 256-0033, F 257-3137; **L1** *Holiday Inn Crowne Plaza*, R Frei Caneca 1360, T 253-2244, F 251-3121, 5-star, central, small swimming pool, very comfortable; the

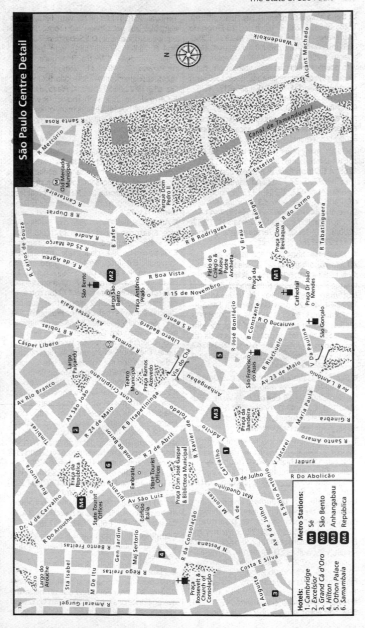

São Paulo Centre Detail

Metro Stations:
M1 Sé
M2 São Bento
M3 Anhangabau
M4 Republica

Hotels:
1. Cambridge
2. Excelsior
3. Grand Cá d'Oro
4. Hilton
5. Othon Palace
6. Samambaia

L1 *Della Volpe Garden*, R Frei Caneca 1199, T 285-5388, F 288-8710, is rec; **L3** *Eldorado Boulevard*, Av São Luís 234, T 214-1833, F 256-8061 (excellent); **A1** *Linson*, R Augusta 440, Consolação, T 256-6700, F 258-5371, all apartments with double bed, kitchenette, sitting room, bath, TV security system, restaurant, pool; **L3** *Grand Corona*, Basílio da Gama 101, T 259-8177, F 257-5025, good; **A1** *Planalto*, Cásper Líbero 117 (Varig-Tropical chain), T 230-7311, F 227-7916, secure, helpful, good service, good dining room; **A1** *San Juan*, Aurora 909, nr Praça da República airport bus terminal, T 250-9100, rec.

There are many other good hotels, inc **L2** *Bristol*, R Martins Fontes 277, T 258-0011, F 231-1265; **A1** *Othon Palace*, R Líbero Badaró 190, T 239-3277, F 37-7203; **A1** *Samambaia*, R Sete de Abril 422, T 231-1333 (discounts for cash and at weekends); **L3** *Jaraguá*, R Major Quedinho 44, T 256-6633, F 256-1377; **A1** *Solar Paulista*, R Francisca Miquelina 343, T 257-2800, F 257-2800; **A3** *Terminus*, Av Ipiranga 741, T 222-2266.

A residential hotel, rec for longer stays, is **A1** *Metropolitan Plaza*, Alameda Campinas 474, T 287-4855, F 285-3158. A rec 'Apart-hotel' for longer stays is *Residencial Alameda Nothman* (A1 Nothman 682, T 222-6144); **A2** *Hores Belgrano*, R Marquês de Paranaguá, 88, T 258-0255, F 257-7803, central, English spoken, special rates for long stays; *Service-Flat Monterey*, Alameda Itu 265, Jardim Paulista, T 285-6111, F 283-3247, has been rec for longer stays; safe parking, comfortable accommodation.

B *Banri*, R Galvão Bueno 209, T 270-8877, F 278-9225, good, nr metro station Liberdade (Japanese quarter); **B** *Center Bela Vista*, 13 de Maio 198, T 255-4042, nr plenty of restaurants in an old Italian suburb (R Santo Antônio/R 13 de Maio, nr Praça da Bandeira).

There are scores of cheaper hotels, of which we append a selection: **D** *Continental*, R Vitória 223, clean, safe, highly rec; **D** *Itauna*, Av Rio Branco 280, well furnished, rec; **D** *Las Vegas*, R Vitória 390 (corner Av Rio Branco)rec; **D** *Lincoln*, Av Rio Branco 47, excellent breakfast, friendly, safe, rec; **D** *Joamar*, José de Barros, Centro, in the pedestrian area, hot showers, clean, safe, TV, room service, rec; **D** *Serrano*, R Gago Coutinho 22, T 285-3233, warmly rec; **D** *Natal*, R Guaianazes 41, T 220-6722, recently rebuilt, very well rec; **D** *Itamarati*, Av Viera de Carvalho 150, T 222-4133, ½ block from Praça da República, good location, friendly, safe, highly rec; **D** *Plaza Marabá*, Av Ipiranga 757, T 220-7811, very clean, rec. Also suggested: **C** *Riviera*, Av Barão de Limeira 117, T 221-8077, excellent value, highly rec; **D** *Ofir*, R dos

Timbiras 258, T 223-8822, with bath, stores valuables but not money, big rooms, TV, well equipped, good value; **D** *S Sebastião*, 7 de Abril 364 (T 257-4988/255-1594), with bath, rec, cheap and clean; **E** *Metro*, R Vergueiro 1563, nr Paraíso, T 549-8531, without breakfast, quiet, convenient. In Av São João **B** *Cineasta*, No 613, T 222-5533, a/c; **C** *Plaza*, No 407; **E** *Central*, No 288, with shower, F without, clean, good, helpful, central; many others in the district. Many of the cheap hotels accommodate short-stay couples.

Take the metro to Luz station and in the block behind the old Rodoviária, off Av Rio Branco, there are scores of cheap hotels with prices ranging from E to C; try: R Santa Ifigênia: **C** *Uai*, No 66, clean and pleasant, rooms on street are good, rec; **D** *Luanda*, No 348, with breakfast, English-speaking owner, helpful, rec; **E** *Trinidade*, No 737, clean, friendly, good value; **E** *Aliança*, R Gral Osório 235, crnr Sta Ifigênia, nice; **E** *Saturno*, Largo Osório 39, T 223-9561, hot water, soap and towel. R dos Gusmões: **E** *Galeão*, No 394, clean, safe, helpful, hot showers; **E** *Itaipu*, No 467, good, clean; **E** *Lepanto*, R Cásper Líbero 359, shower, TV, clean; **E** *Lima*, Ipiranga 710, friendly, rec; **E** *Tatuí*, Praça Princeza Isabel 171 (on corner of Av Duque de Caxias, 2 blocks from old bus station), clean with bath. **NB** The red light district is in the blocks bounded by RR Santa Ifigênia, dos Andradas, dos Gusmões and Av Ipiranga, and is definitely not rec for women travelling alone. The whole area around Av Rio Branco is rather seedy and not entirely safe late at night.

E *Casa do Politécnico*, R Afonso Pena 272, cheap accommodation; **E** *São José*, Alameda Barão de Piracicaba 221, without breakfast, basic. **Youth hostel** at R Mariz e Barros 350, Vila Santa Eulália (bus 4491 from Parque Dom Pedro in the centre), F, cooking and washing facilities, good fruit and vegetable market directly across R Ricardo Jafet on Tues. YHA for membership, 15 de Novembro e Av São João – office in centre, about US$5 a year. Also Magdalena Tagkiaferro, Estrada Turística do Jaguará 651, Km 18, via Anhanguera, 05173 São Paulo (T 229-3787/3011); *Sampa City*, R dos Franceses 100, T/F 288-1592, 500m from Brigadeiro metro station, US$6.50, and *Bela Vista*, R João Passalacqua 181, T 607 3662, US$7 rec.

Camping: list of sites can be obtained from Camping Clube do Brasil, R Minerva, 156 – Perdizes (T 864-7133).

● **Places to eat**

Apart from the international cuisine in the first-class hotels, here are a few out of many (the average price of a meal in 1996 was US$20-30 in trattorias, US$40-60 in 1st class places rising to US$100 in the very best restaurants; remember that costs can be cut by sharing the large portions served.

The best (by all accounts): *Bassi*, R 13 de Maio 334, T 34-2375, Bela Vista, for meat; *Don Curro*, R Alves Guimarães 230, T 852-4712, Piaheiros, closed Mon, for seafood, especially paella; *Le Bistingo*, Al Franca 580, T 289-3010; *Massimo*, Al Santos 1826, T 284-0311, international cuisine; *Antiquarius*, Al Lorena 1884, T 282-3015, Portuguese; *La Tambouille*, Av 9 de Julho 5925, Itaim Bibi, T 883-6276, French and Italian, closed Mon, reserve in advance.

Portuguese: *Abril em Portugal*, R Caio Prado 47, reasonable and good; *Bocage*, Al Joaquim Eugênio de Lima 1377, excellent.

Italian: *San Genovese*, R Bela Cintra 1849, very reasonable, US$29 pp, *salada Lellis* is a must, and fresh squid in batter; *Famiglia Mancini*, R Avanhandava 81, Bela Vista, excellent, especially salads and cold dishes, always queues between 2000-2400; *Gigetto*, Avanhandava 63, good pasta, reasonable prices; *Trattoria del Sargento*, Al Pamplona 1354, Jardim Paulista, good, popular; *Leonardo*, Al Santos 1508, Bela Vista (opp *Sheraton*), good; *Da Fiorella*, R Bernardino de Campos 294, Brooklin (closed Mon and Sun pm), top quality vegetarian pasta; *Don Cicillio*, Praça Tomás Morus 185, Perdizes, good homecooking in traditional surroundings; *Via Veneto*, Al Barros 909, Sta Cecília, good pasta and meat, very popular; *La Trattoria*, R Antônio Bicudo 50, Pinheiros, closed Mon, midweek until 1900, Fri, Sat till 0100, very good, reasonably priced food, *strozzapreti* a must; *La Farina*, Av Ipiranga 924, for good cheap pasta, popular. Many Italian restaurants in Bela Vista/Bixiga area, especially R 13 de Maio; good pizzerias are *Torre do Bixiga*, 13 de Maio 848, *Capuano*, R Consarrão 416, *Margherita*, Al Tietê 255.

French: *L'Affiche*, R Campos Bicudo 141, small, intimate, décor inc owner's collection of antique French posters; *La Casserole*, Largo do Arouche 346, (centro), best known bistro in São Paulo, closed Mon (US$40-60 pp). *Freddy*, Praça Dom Gastão Liberal Pinto 11; *Marcel*, R da Consolação 3534, sensational soufflés.

German: *Jucalemão*, R Álvaro Rodrigues 320; *Bierhalle*, Av Lavandisca 249, Indianópolis; *Arnold's Naschbar*, R Pereira Leite 98, Sumarezinho; *Eisbein peruruca*, rec; *Bismarck* (excellent draught beer) and *Paprika* (very reasonable), on Av Ibirapuera 3178 and 573 respectively.

Swiss: *Chamonix*, Al Lorena 1052, and *Le Jardin Suisse*, Al Franca 1467, both in Jardim Paulista, expensive, very good.

Russian: *Samovar*, R Baronesa de Bela Vista 602, Aeroporto, good food, typical shows at

weekends, closed Sun. **Hungarian**: *Hungaria*, Al Joaquim Eugênio de Lima 776, Jardins, old world décor, good food, expensive; *Hungaria Express*, Av Jaú 310, cheap and good.

Greek: *Zorba*, R Henrique Monteiro 218.

Arabic: *Almanara*, good and reasonable, Av São João 1155 (Centro), Oscar Freire 523 (Cerqueiro César), R Basilio da Gama 70 and Av Vieira de Carvalho 109 (Consolação); *Mandalun*, Al Itú 1564, Jardim Paulista, mainly Lebanese, high standard, not cheap; *Bambi*, Al Santos 59, cheapish, good; *Rubayat*, Av Vieira de Carvalho 116, Al Santos 86 and Av Faria Lima 583, excellent meat, fixed price meals.

Oriental: (Japanese tends to be expensive) *Sino-Brasileiro*, R Alberto Torres 39 (Perdizes); *Iti Fuji*, Al Jaú 487; typical Japanese, excellent; *Sushigen*, Av Brig Luis Antônio 2367, Lojas 13 and 14, very good *sushi* and *sashimi* but a bit overpriced; *Komazushi*, same street No 2050, Loja 7, reasonably priced and good; *Korea House*, Galvão Bueno 43 (Liberdade). *Kar Wua* Chinese restaurant, at R Mourato Coelho 30, highly praised. Many other Chinese and Japanese restaurants in Liberdade, the Japanese quarter, where there is a Japanese food market in the square by the metro station.

Indian: *Govinda*, R Princesa Isabel 379, good, expensive.

Vegetarian: almost always the cheapest option in São Paulo. *Sattva*, R da Consolação 3140; *O Arroz de Ouro*, Largo do Arouche 42-44 (shop as well, central); *Cheiro Verde*, Peixoto Gomilde 1413, Jardins, very good, more expensive than most; *Nutri Som*, R 9 Júlio 160, new, rec; *Intergrão*, R Joaquim Antunes 377, macrobiotic; *Delícia Natural*, Av Rio Branco 211 (4th floor), corner Av Ipiranga, lunch only, good; *Sabor Natural*, same building, 1st floor, lunch only, good; *Folhas e Raízes*, Líbero Bádaro 370, buffet lunch US$3.20; *Saúde Sabor*, São Bento 500, lunch only; *Vegetaliano*, D Sampaio 155, Sto Amaro, Italian vegetarian. 'Vida Integral' newspaper gives details of all health food restaurants and stores in São Paulo.

General: *Terraço Itália*, on top of Edifício Itália (Ipiranga e São Luis), 41 floors up, good fixed price lunch and excellent other meals, dancing with excellent band and superb view (must consume to be allowed to see the view), US$85 pp inc wine in dancing part, US$65-70 otherwise, dress smartly; *Mexilhão*, R 13 de Maio 626, Bela Vista, very good seafood; *Paulista*, João Moura 527, Pinheiros, top quality meat, popular; *Dinho's Place*, Al Santos 45 and Largo do Arouche 246, Fri excellent seafood buffet, good meat, US$45, has daily bargains; *Mate Amargo*, Av Pompéia 1603, churrascaria, live music, rec; *Paddock*, Av São Luís 258 and Av

Faria Lima 1541, traditional fare, excellent *feijoada*; *Um, Dois, Feijão e Arroz*, Praça de Sé 42 and R Ipiranga 940, modest but very good traditional food; *Cantina Amigo Piolin*, R Augusta 902, good, US$20; *Novo Olido*, Largo do Arouche 193, closed Sat, regional dishes from interior of São Paulo; *Bolinha*, Av Cidade Jardim 53 for *feijoadas* (on Wed and Sat); *Oxalá*, Tr Maria Antônia 72, just off Consolação, Bahian specialities at modest prices; *Bronx*, R Haddock Lobo 1576, very reasonable traditional home cooking.

McDonalds and other fast food chains can be found all over the city as well as many other not quite so fast, but infinitely more interesting alternatives. *Frevinho Lanches*, R Augusta 1563, famous for its *beirute* (speciality of São Paulo), as well as many other toasted sandwiches with pitta bread; *Baguette*, Consolação 2426, nr Paulista, opp Belas Artes cinema, good sandwiches, especially lively around midnight; *Absolute*, Al Santos 843, best hamburgers in town; *Rock Dreams*, Al Tietê 580, good hamburgers and sandwiches; *Restaurante do MASP*, Av Paulista 1578, in basement of museum, reasonably priced, often has live music; *Casa da Fogazza*, R Xavier de Toledo 328 and R 7 de Abril 60 (both close to Praça da República), Calzone, with different fillings, juices, rec.

Bars and cafés: *Ritz*, Al Franca 1088, Jardins, always lively, friendly, predominately gay clientèle; *Riviera*, R da Consolação 2450, traditional haunt of students and 'counter' revolutionaries since early 60s, noisy, a bit rough but kept under control by surly waiters. *Café com Arte*, R Oscar Freire 1051 (Jardins), small coffee shop, 1000-2000 (later weekends); *Fran's Café*, open 24 hrs, Av Paulista 358; R Heitor Penteado 1326 (Sumaré); R Haddock Lobo 586; Estac Alameda Lorena 1271 (Jardim Paulista); *Café Columbia*, R Augusta 3008 (Jardim América); *Café das Flores*, R dos Pinheiros 953; *Café Paris*, Av Waldemar Ferreira 55, Butantã; *Café do Bixiga*, 13 de Maio 76 and lots of others in Bixiga/Bela Vista area with live music, eg *Café Piu Piu* (closed Mon) and *Café Pedaço*, at 13 de Maio 134 and 140. Bixiga is traditionally known as the 'Bohemian' area and bars here are usually cheaper than Jardins and Pinheiros areas. *Euro Bar*, R Min José Geraldo R Alkimin 2338, quiet; *Baguette*, good breakfasts, R Consolação 2426 (Consolação) and R 13 de Maio (Bela Vista); in Itaim Bibi: *Hard Rock Café*, R Brigadeiro Haroldo Veloso 707, fake but still sells the T-shirts; *Blue Note Jazz Bar*, Av São Gabriel 558, as the name describes.

● **Banks & money changers**

Banks: opening hours vary from bank to bank, but most are open between 1000-1630. Many national and international banks, most on R 15

de Novembro, Av Paulista, Av Brig Faria Lima and R Líbero Badaró. **Banco do Brasil**, R 7 de Abril, nr República will accept payment orders from overseas but with a US$30 charge and payment in reais. **Citibank**, Av Ipiranga 855, or Av Paulista 1111 (T 576-2211) will receive money from abroad (US$20 charge, takes 5 days). **Banco Mercantil de São Paulo**, Av Paulista 1450, for cash advances on Access/Mastercard; **Mastercard**, cash against card, R Campo Verde 61, 4° andar, Jardim Paulistano. Thomas Cook/Mastercard TC refund assistance point: R Haddock Lobo 337, 2 andar, 01414 São Paulo, T 259-3022. **Western Union** at Banco Itamarati, T 0800-11-9837.

Money changers: many *câmbios* nr Praça da República; none nr rodoviária or Tietê hotels. **American Express**, Al Santos 1437 (*Hotel Mofarrej Sheraton*) T 284-2515 and Kontik Franstur (address below) very helpful; **Exprinter**, Barão de Itapetininga 243, also deals in foreign currencies (cash only). **Interpax**, Praça da República 177, loja 13, changes cash but not cheques; **Amoretur**, Praça da República 203, will change cheques. Most travel agents on Av São Luis change TCs and cash at good rates.

● **Cultural centres**

British Chamber of Commerce of São Paulo, R Barão de Itapetininga 275, 7th floor; Caixa Postal 1621, T 255-0519. **British Council**, R Maranhão 416, Higienópolis, Caixa Postal 1604, T 826-4455, F 66-3765, library at R Dep Lacerda Franco 333, Pinheiros, T 814-4155. **Sociedade Brasileira de Cultura Inglesa**, Av Higienópolis 449, has cinema (films US$1.50). **American Chamber of Commerce for Brazil**, R Formosa 367, 29th floor, T 222-6377. **American Library**, União Cultural Brasil-Estados Unidos, R Col Oscar Porto 208, T 287-1022. **Goethe-Instituto**, R Lisboa 974, T 280-4288 (open Mon-Thur 1400-2030). **Instituto Hans Staden**, R Cons Crispiniano 53, 12th floor. See under **Entertainment** for Alliance Française Theatre.

● **Education**

There are three universities: the official university of São Paulo, the Pontifical Catholic University, and the Mackenzie University. The official University of São Paulo is now situated in the Cidade Universitária (buses from main bus station), outside the city beyond Pinheiros. There are a number of architecturally interesting buildings housing different faculties and the four museums of archaeology, ethnology, anthropology and mineralogy. They have courses available to foreigners, inc a popular Portuguese course, registry is through the International Bureau, Comissão de Cooperação Internacional, R do Anfiteatro 181, Bloco das Colmdias 05508, Cidade Universitária, São Paulo.

● **Electric current**
110-220 volts AC, 60 cycles.

● **Embassies & consulates**
Argentine, Av Paulista 1106, T 284-1355 (open 0900-1300, very easy to get visa here); **Bolivian**, R da Conso lação 37, 3rd floor (open 0900-1300), T 255-3555; **Chilean**, Av Paulista 1009, T 284-2044; **Paraguayan**, Av São Luiz 50, 10th floor, T 255-7818; **Peru**, R Laplace 739, T 531-0943; **Uruguayan**, Al Campinas 433, 7th floor, T 284-5777; **Venezuelan**, R Veneza 878, T 887-4583.

American Consulate General, R Padre João Manuel 933, T 881-6511; **Canadian Consulate General**, Av Paulista 854, 5th floor, T 287-2122; **British Consulate General**, Av Paulista 1938, 17th floor, Caixa Postal 846, T 287-7722; **Irish**, Av Paulista 2006, 5th floor, T 287-6362; **Danish Consulate General**, R João Tibiriçá 900, T 831-9799, open 0900-1200, 1300-1700, Fri until 1400 only; **German**, Av Brig Faria Lima 1383, 12th floor, T 814-6644; **Swiss Consulate-General**, Av Paulista 1754, 4th floor, Caixa Postal 30588, T 289-1033; **Austrian Consulate-General**, R Augusta 2516, 10th floor, T 282 6223; **French**, Av Paulista 1842, T 287-9522; **Swedish Consulate-General**, R Oscar Freire 379, 3rd floor, T 883-3322 (Caixa Postal 51626); **Dutch**, Av Brigadeiro Faria Lima 1698, T 813-0522; **Greek**, T 285-5571, 285-5582, 289-0178, Av Paulista No.1499, 11 Andar -s/1104.

● **Entertainment**
The **Teatro Municipal** (magnificent interior) is used by visiting theatrical and operatic groups, as well as the City Ballet Company and the Municipal Symphony Orchestra who give regular performances. There are several first-class theatres: **Aliança Francesa**, R Gen Jardim 182, T 259-0086; **Itália** (Av Ipiranga 344, T 257-3138); **Cacilda Becker** (R Tito 295, T 864-4513); **Paiol** (R Amaral Gurgel 164, T 221-2462); **Ruth Escobar** (R dos Ingleses 209, T 251-4881), among others. Free concerts at **Teatro Popular do Sesi**, Av Paulista 313, at midday, under MASP (Mon-Sat) and at weekends at the **Memorial América Latina**. Free films are shown at the **Centro Cultural São Paulo**, R Vergueiro 1000, and the **Museu Lasar Segall**, R Afonso Celso 362. The biggest cinema is reckoned to be the **Marabá**, Av Ipiranga 757, which has 1665 seats. In cinemas entrance is usually half price on Wed; normal seat price is US$2.50.

See *Ilustrada* selection of *Folha de São Paulo* for listings of concerts, theatre, museums, galleries and cinema. *Veja São Paulo* of weekly news magazine *Veja* lists bars, restaurants, clubs and shows as well as the above.

Nightclubs: São Paulo is teeming with clubs catering to most preferences.

We list a small section: **Disco bars**: Entrance/cover charges US$5-10: *Banana-Banana Café*, Av 9 de Júlio 5872 (Itaim Bibi), closed Mon; *HB Club*, R Cardeal Arcoverde 2958 (Pinheiros), closed Sun, bar, snooker, and informal dance lessons; test your new skills at *Blen-Blen*, same address weekends, live Latin bands; *Cervejaria Continental*, packed, mixed music, R dos Pinheiros 1275 and R Haddock Lobo 1573.

Clubs: Entrance US$5-20 which may inc a drink: *Columbia* upstairs, R Estados Unidos 1570, lively; *Hell's Club* downstairs, opens 0430, techno, wild; *Cha-Cha-Cha*, R Tabapuã 1236, closed Mon, no Brazilian music, art on walls, candles, gay and straight; *Balafon*, R Sergipe 160, Wed-Sun, small, Afro-Brazilian; *Reggae Night*, Av Robert Kennedy 3914, Thur-Sun, outdoors on lakeside; *Limelight Industry*, R Franz Schubert 93, pop hits, Japanese restaurant upstairs; *Plataforma 1*, Av Paulista 424, dinner and folkloric show, very touristy but extremely popular.

● **Hospitals & medical services**
Doctors: (English-speaking) *Edwin Castello*, José Maria Lisboa 861, s/104, T 884-9132; *Ruy Silva*, Conselheiro Brotero 1505, No 64, T 67-2470; *Wilson Frey*, Barão de Jacegua 1103, T 241-4474. *Christel Schlúnder*, R Alvares de Azevedo 127, Santo Amaro, T 247-5963, German speaking, and for children. Also *Samaritans' Hospital*, R Conselheiro Brotero 1486, T 825-1122.

Emergency and ambulance: T 192, no charge. **Fire**: T 193.

● **Places of worship**
St Paul's Anglican (Episcopal) Church, R Comendador Elias Zarzua 1231, Santo Amaro, T 246-0383. **Igreja Metodista**, Av Liberdade 659, T 278-5895. **Adventist**, R Jaguá 88, T 279-8206. **Presbyterian**, R Néstor Pestanha 106, T 255-6111. **Mormon Church**, Av Prof Francisco Morato 2430, T 570-2483. **Synagogue** Congregação Shalom, R Comendador Elias Zarzur 568; Israelita Paulista, R Antonio Carlos 553. **Templo Budista**, Av do Cursino 753, T 63-4015. **Lutheran church**, Av Rio Branco 34. **Swedish Church**, Igreja Evangelica Luterana Escandinava, R Job Lane 1030, T 247 88 29.

● **Post & telecommunications**
Post Office: Correio Central, Praça do Correio, corner Av São João and Prestes Máia, T 831-5222. Booth adjoining tourist office on Praça da República, weekdays only 1000-1200, 1300-1600, for letters and small packages only. *UPS*, Brasinco, Alameda Jaú 1, 1725, 01420 São Paulo, T 852-8233, F 853-8563; *Federal Express*, Av São Luiz 187, is reliable.

International Telephone: R 7 de Abril 295, nr

Praça da República. **Telecommunications**: Embratel, Av São Luís 50, and Av Ipiranga 344.

● **Shopping**

All types of stores at **Shopping Centers Iguatemi, Ibirapuera** and **Morumbi** (see page 446), also **El Dorado Shopping Centre** (corner of Av Rebouças and Marginal Pinheiros). Souvenirs from *Mimosa*, Joaquim Nabuco 275, Brooklin Paulista; *Artindia*, R Augusta 1371, loja 119 (Galeria Ouro Velho), T 283-2102; *Coisarada*, R Tabapuã 390, Itaim Bibi (T 881-4810); *Casa dos Amazonas*, Av São Luis 187, Galeria Metrópole, loja 14; *Ceará Meu Amor*, R Pamplona 1551, Loja 7, good quality lace from the NE. *H Stern*, jewellers, at Praça da República 242, R Augusta 2340 and at Iguatemi, Ibirapuera and Morumbi shopping centres and main hotels; designer jewellery, *Our Collection*, R São Benedito 1747, Alto da Boa Vista. *Tatuagem Polaco*, R 24 de Maio, is a professional and hygienic tattoo parlour, who will work to your own designs. Haggling with the price is suggested, but maybe not too much.

Open air markets: **'Hippy' fair**, Praça da República, daily 0800-1400, very varied, many tourists, good selection of inexpensive fossils, Bahian food, lots of artists, items from Peru and Bolivia; **'Oriental' fair**, Praça de Liberdade Sun pm, good for Japanese snacks, plants and some handicrafts, very picturesque, with remedies on sale, tightrope walking, gypsy fortune tellers, etc. Below the Museu de Arte de São Paulo, an **antiques** market takes place on Sun, 0800-1700. There are **flea markets** Suns in the main square of the Bixiga district (Praça Don Orione) and in Praça Benedito Calixto in Jardim América. São Paulo is relatively cheap for film and clothes (especially shoes). The **Ceasa flower market** should not be missed, Av Doutor Gastão Vidigal 1946, Jaguaré, Tues and Fri 0700-1200. **Handicraft market** at Praça Campos de Bagatelle, Sun 0800-1300.

Bookshops: *Livraria Cultura*, Av Paulista 2073, loja 153, Conjunto Nacional, new books in English; *Livraria Freebook*, R da Consolação 1924, T 259-1120, ring bell for entry, wide collection of art books and imported books in English; *Livraria Triângulo*, R Barão de Itapetininga 255, loja 23, Centro and *Ilco*, Barão do Triúnfo 371, Brooklin Paulista, books in English; *Livraria Kosmos*, Praça Dom José Caspar 134, loja 30, international stock. In various shopping malls *Livrarias Saraiva* and *Laselva* (also at airports) sell books in English; *Livraria Alemã*, R Laplace 159, Brooklin; *Librairie Française*, R Barão de Itapetininga 275, 6th floor, wide selection; *Letraviva*, Av Rebouças 2080, Mon-Fri 0900-1830, Sat 0900-1400, specializes in books and music in Spanish; *Book Centre*, R Gabus Mendes 29 loja 5, Consolação area books in

English and German; *Duas Cidades*, R Bento Freitas 158, nr República, good selection of Brazilian and Spanish American literature; *Cinema Elétrico*, R Augusta 973, Centro, and *Sola Cinemateca*, R Fradique Coutinho 361, sell postcards and books on cinema and art.

Camera repairs: Canon and other makes: *Cine Camera Service*, R Cons Crispiano 97, 2nd floor.

● **Sports**

The most popular is association football. The most important matches are played at Morumbi and Pacaembu grounds. At Interlagos there is a first-class racing track (see page 448). There is yachting, sailing and rowing on the Santo Amaro reservoir. For nature trails, etc, Free Way, R Leôncio de Carvalho 267, Paraíso, T 285-4767/283-5983.

Golf courses: about half an hour's drive from the centre there are 18-hole golf courses at the São Paulo Golf Club, Praça Dom Francisco Souza 635, in Santo Amaro, in beautiful surroundings; Clube de Golf de Campinas, Via Anhanguera, Km 108, Campinas; Clube de Campo São Paulo and Guarapiranga Golf e Country, both at Reprêsa Guarapiranga, Estrada Paralheiros, Km 34; São Fernando Golf Club, Estrada de Cotia, Km 29; a lakeside club at Km 50 on the Santos road. Outside the city are Terras de São José, Itú, 110 km; PL Golf in Arujá; Bastos golf club, 400 km.

9-hole courses at São Francisco club, Estrada de Osasco, Km 15; Anglo Sports Center, Barretos; International golf club, Via Dutra Km 232, Guaratinguetá; PL Golf and Arujá Golf Club, in Arujá; Lago Azul Golf Club, Araçoiaba da Serra, 120 km from city. There are also two 9-hole courses in Santos (see page 458).

● **Tour companies & travel agents**

Woehrle Turismo, R do Tesouro 47, CEP 01013, T 37-7594, USA T (011) 532-1105, helpful, German spoken; *Lema Turismo*, Av Marquês de Itú 837, personalized excursions, Marta Schneider speaks 8 languages, inc Hungarian; *AmEx* office in *Hotel Sheraton Mofarrej*, Al Santos 1437, T 284-3515; *Kontik-Franstur* (American Express representative), R Marconi 71, T 259-4211; *Student Travel*, Estados Unidos 153, T 887 4242; *Audiotur* (ask for Janice Kawasake), Estados Unidos 627, T 887-3400, gives information about trains; *Ambiental Viagens e Expedições*, Av Brig Faria Lima 1684-S/L 40, Jardim Paulista, T 814-8809, English and Spanish spoken, helpful, rec for trips to less well known places; *Terra Expedições*, Osmar e Valdir, R Silva Jardim 429, Sta Terezinha, Santo André, CEP 09250, T 446-3381/447-3535, rec for motocycle tours and information, Spanish and Italian spoken (English improving). Visits to coffee fazendas (May-June) and round trips into the surrounding country are organized by the travel agencies.

● **Tourist offices**
Praça da República (very helpful, most regularly open), Praça da Sé and Liberdade metro entrances, Praça Dom José Gaspar (corner Av São Luis), R Augusta esq Av Paulista, R Barão de Itapetininga, nr Teatro Municipal; excellent free map at all these offices. Office at Guarulhos airport is helpful. For information on São Paulo State, Praça Antônio Prado 9, 6th floor, Av São Luís 115. Very cheap tours leave tourist office at Praça da República every 30 mins Tues-Sat from 0900 to 1700 and Sun 0900-1600; there are 8 different itineraries visiting places of cultural interest. Each tour lasts approximately 3 hrs, tickets and full programme from tourist office in Praça da República, T 267-2122, ext 627/640, Mon-Fri, CMTC tours by metro on Sat-Sun from 0900-1000, 1400-1500 from Praça da Sé; information at Praça da Sé, T 229-3011. Tourist offices have free magazines in Portuguese and English: *Where* and *São Paulo This Month* (also available from most travel agencies and better hotels). Also rec is Quatro Rodas guide to the City.

Maps: of São Paulo in train timetables at newsstands (US$3.50), and in the monthly tourist guide published by the Prefeitura (US$0.70 – poor map but good for what's on). Also obtainable from the tourist offices, the rodoviária (upstairs), the better hotels, American Express and H Stern, the jeweller. Map shops: **Mapolândia**, 7 de Abril 125, shop 40; **Metrópole Mapas**, Av São Luís 153, Loja 1 (Galeria Metrópole). 2 private map producers: Geo Mapas, R Líbero Badaró 336, CEP 01008, T 259-2166 (40% discount for volume purchases, excellent 1988 1:5,000,000 map of Brazil, town maps), and Editorial Abril, R do Cartume 769, bl G, 11° andar, Lapa, CEP 05066-900, T 831-0599, F 831-0599 ext 2270.

● **Useful telephone numbers**
Police: T 228-2276; Radio Patrol, T 190. Federal Police, Av Prestes Maio 700, open 1000-1600 for visa extensions.

● **Transport**
Local City buses and taxis: buses are normally crowded and rather slow, but clean. Maps of the bus and metro system are available at depots, eg Anhangabaú. Taxis display cards of actual tariffs in the window. For 'especial taxis', dearer but fewer hassles, T 223-1975 (Tele Taxi), call out charge US$1, calls not accepted from public phones.

Metro: the metro, the first in Brazil, began operating in 1975. It has two main lines intersecting at Praça de Sé: N-S from Santana to Jabaquara; E-W from Corinthians Itaquera to Barra Funda (the interchange with Fepasa and RFFSA railways and site of the São Paulo and Paraná Rodoviária). A third line runs from Clínicas in the W, along Av Paulista, to Ana Rosa in the S, joining the Jabaquera line at Paraíso and Ana Rosa. The system is clean, safe, cheap and efficient; it operates from 0500-2400. Fare US$0.60, book of 10 tickets US$5; backpacks are allowed. Combined bus and metro ticket are available, eg to Congonhas airport.

Motorcycle repairs: BMW São Paulo, R Funchal 551, CEP 04551, São Paulo, T 820-8633, few parts but helpful and they have all BMW motorcycle special tools; can order parts from Miami.

Air There are air services to all parts of Brazil, Europe, North and South America from the international airport at Guarulhos, also known as Cumbica, Av Monteiro Lobato 1985, T 945-2111 (30 km from the city). Varig has its own, new terminal for international flights, adjoining the old terminal which all other airlines use. Money exchanges open 0800-2200 daily, post office, etc, 2 information booths.

The local airport of Congonhas, 14 km from the city centre, is used for the Rio-São Paulo shuttle, some flights to Belo Horizonte and Vitória and private flights only.

From Guarulhos there are airport taxis which charge US$43 on a ticket system (go to the second booth on leaving the terminal and book a Co-op taxi at the Taxi Comum counter, the best value). Fares from the city to the airport are higher and vary from cab to cab. Emtu bus service every 30 mins to Guarulhos from Praça da República (NW side, corner of R Arouche), US$8.50, very comfortable (in airport buy ticket at booth in Domestic Arrivals); the same company runs services from Guarulhos to Tietê (hourly), Congonhas airport (hourly 0600-2200) and Av Paulista (hourly 0600-0700 from airport to 2100, passing in front of, or nr many major hotels on its route to the city: *Bristol, Brasilton, Cá d'Oro, Caesar Park, Della Volpe, Crowne Plaza, Sheraton, Maksoud Plaza*). Cheap buses from Bresser and Jabaquara bus terminals to Guarulhos, without luggage space, usually crowded. Inter-airport bus US$12. There are about 400 flights/week to Rio de Janeiro (US$300 return). All airline offices in triangle formed by Av São Luís, Av Ipiranga and R da Consolação.

Air freight: Varig will send anything, anywhere, but involves some red tape.

Trains São Paulo has four stations: **1) Estação da Luz**, T 681-3039/3062, for long-distance trains to **Ribeirão Preto** and **Campinas** (8 a day); trains from Campinas go to **Araguari** via **Uberlândia**, dep 2345 (the Campinas-Brasília line had no passenger service in 1995-96). Express trains to **São**

José do Rio Preto. Passenger services to Bauru ceased in 1994 and those on the Campo Grande-Corumbá section were discontinued in 1995. Beyond Corumbá, trains run from Quijarro (Bolivia) to Santa Cruz de la Sierra by the Estrada de Ferro Brasil-Bolívia (see page 634).

2) **Barra Funda**, T 284-7759, has a metro station and handles Sorocabana and Santos a Jundiaí commuter services; all long distance trains into and out of Luz stop at Barra Funda; a new, weekend service 'down the hill' to **Santos** dep Barra Funda 0820, arr Santos 1205, return – in the dark – 1700 (superb scenery). Also from this station, the Silver Train to **Rio de Janeiro**, Mon, Wed, Fri, 2030, T 825-7022 (office R Cap Mor Goncalo Monteiro 6), US$100 with meals. Express from Barra Funda to **Presidente Prudente**, about 15 hrs, daily at 2135, all facilities, reservations essential.

3) **Júlio Prestes station**, T 220-8862, for commuter services to SW of the state (former Sorocabana railway, metre gauge); 4) **Roosevelt**, T 942-1132, for commuters to Mogi das Cruzes (ex Central do Brasil) and eastern suburbs. Slower metre guage trains to Pres Prudente.

Buses To get to the main rodoviária (T 235-0322), take the metro to Tietê, very convenient. Left luggage US$0.80/day/item. You can sleep in the bus station after 2200 when the guards have gone; tepid showers US$2.50. Bus to centre, US$0.60. Buses to the interior of São Paulo state, state capitals and international buses (see next paragraph): to **Rio**, 6 hrs, every 30 mins, US$20 (leito, 40), special section for this route in the rodoviária, request the coastal route ('via litoral') unless you wish to go the direct route; to **Porto Alegre**, 18 hrs, US$37 (leito, 82); **Belo Horizonte**, 10 hrs, US$7.25; buy ticket and get on bus at Terminal Bresser (Metro Bresser, T 692-5191); **Salvador**, 30 hrs, US$58 (leito, 116); **Recife**, 40 hrs, US$80 (leito, 160); **Cuiabá**, 24 hrs, US$50; **Porto Velho**, 60 hrs (or more), US$108; **Brasília**, 16 hrs, US$33 (leito, 66); **Foz do Iguaçu**, 16 hrs, US$29 (leito, 58); **São Sebastião**, 4 hrs US$7.80 (say 'via Bertioga' if you want to go by the coast road, beautiful journey but few buses take this route). To **Santos**, US$3 (there is a bus station for Santos and São Vicente at the southern end of the Metro line, at Jabaquara, buses from here leave every 5 mins, taking about 50 mins). There are two other bus terminals, Barra Funda, T 235-0322 or 66-4682 (same as metrô and rail station), to cities in southern São Paulo state and many destinations in Paraná; Bresser, T 299-0177 (Cometa) or 267-7411 (Transul), for destinations in Minas Gerais.

To **Montevideo**, via Porto Alegre, with TTL, departs 2200, 31 hrs, US$77 (semi-cama), cold a/c at night, plenty of meal stops, bus stops for border formalities, passengers disembark only to collect passport and tourist card on Uruguayan side. To **Buenos Aires**, Pluma, 36 hrs, US$145; to **Santiago**, Pluma or Gral Urquiza (both start from Rio), 56 hrs, US$110 (leito US$220), Chile Bus, Av Paulista 1009, SL 1909, T 251-5388, or Terminal Tietê, T 267-6239, US$107 (poor meals, but otherwise good, beware overbooking); to **Asunción** (1,044 km), 18 hrs with Pluma or RYSA, US$33 (leito US$48); to **Puerto Suárez** (Quijarro, Bolivia), 22 hrs.

ROUTES To take the beautiful coast road to Rio, take the Via Anchieta to the Guarujá turn, before Guarujá take Bertioga turn and you're on the Santos-Rio highway. Motorists leaving the ring road for Curitiba and Iguaçu should follow Regis de Bittencourt signs. To hitch to Rio, take the metro to Ponte Pequeno, then a bus to Guarulhos, alighting where the bus turns off the Rio road for Guarulhos.

ATIBAIA

A weekend resort, 70 km N of São Paulo on the Dom Pedro I highway (*Pop* 86,190); nearby is the strangely-shaped Pedra Grande mountain summit. There are two campsites, *Pedra Grande*, and *Taba*, which is near the *Hotel Village Eldorado* (with sports facilities, American-plan accommodation).

CAVERNS OF THE VALE DO RIBEIRO

The caves are SW of the state capital, W of the BR-116; among the best known is the 8-km **Gruta da Tapagem**, known as Caverna do Diabo (Devil's Cave – as huge 'as a cathedral' with well-lit formations), 45 km from Eldorado Paulista. The caves are open 0800-1100 and 1200-1700; bar and toilets.

43 km from Caverna do Diabo is **Caverna de Santana**, 10 km from the town of Iporanga; it has 5.6 km of subterranean passages and three levels of galleries. (Iporanga is the most convenient town for visiting both sets of caves; it is 42 km E of Apiaí, which is 257 km SW of São Paulo.)

● **Transport** Bus to Eldorado Paulista from Santos or São Paulo, US$4.75, 4-5 hrs, then hitchhike on banana trucks; alternatively, tourist buses run from both cities; most traffic on Sat and Sun. From Curitiba, change buses at Jacupiranga for Eldorado Paulista.

A suitable stopping place for visiting the caves area is **Registro** (*Pop* 48,860) on BR-116, in the heart of the tea-growing region, populated mainly by Japanese Brazilians. (**C** *Lito Palace Hotel*, Av J Banks Leite 615, T 21-1055, F 21-4470; **F** *Hotel Brasília*, R Brasília, round corner from rodoviária, no breakfast, shower, clean, airy; good *Churrascaria* next to bus station; international telephone exchange in town centre).

THE COAST OF THE STATE OF SÃO PAULO

SANTOS

(*Pop* 428,525; *CEP* 11000; *DDD* 0132) 63 km SE of São Paulo and 5 km from the open sea, **Santos** is the most important Brazilian port. (Over 40% by value of all Brazilian imports and about half the total exports pass through it.) It is reached from Rio by a direct highway (see pages 413 and 459). Although best known for its commerce, Santos is also a holiday resort, with magnificent, but polluted, beaches, and views. The port is approached by the winding Santos Channel; at its mouth is an old fort (1709). It is sometimes possible to visit naval shipyards, for details see the local press. A railway and the Anchieta and Imigrantes highways run to São Paulo. A free-port zone for Paraguay, 1,930 km by rail or road, has been established. A few kilometres outside the city there is an important industrial area round the steelworks, oil refinery and hydroelectric plant at Cubatão.

The island upon which the city stands can be circumnavigated by small boats. The city has impressive modern buildings, wide, tree-lined avenues, and wealthy suburbs.

Places of interest

The streets around **Praça Mauá** are very busy in the daytime, with plenty of cheap shops. In the centre, an interesting building is the **Bolsa Oficial de Café**, in R 15 de Novembro. The night-life is best in the **Gonzaga** area which has the large hotels.

There are many monuments: one in Av Ana Costa to commemorate the brothers Andradas, who took a leading part in the movement for independence; one in the Praça Rui Barbosa to Bartolomeu de Gusmão, who has a claim to the world's first historically recorded airborne ascent in 1709; one in the Praça da República to Bras Cubas, who founded the city in 1534; and one in the Praça José Bonifácio to the soldiers of Santos who died in the Revolution of 1932. There are a disappointing municipal **aquarium** on Av Bartolomeu de Gusmão (Ponta da Praia) and a **Museu do Mar**, R República do Equador 81. In the eastern district of José Menino are the orchid gardens in the **Praça Washington** (flowering Oct-Feb). There is an open-air cage containing humming-birds of 20 different species and the park is a sanctuary for other birds.

Excursions

The **Ilha Porchat**, a small island reached by a bridge at the far end of Santos/São Vicente bay, has beautiful views over rocky precipices, of the high seas on one side and of the city and bay on the other. At the summit is a splendid nightclub, the *Top House Restaurante e Discoteca*. No entrance fee but there is a minimum charge of US$10.

To **Alto da Serra**, the summit of the forest-clad mountain range; magnificent views. The return journey can be done in under 2 hrs by road.

Monte Serrat At the summit there is a semaphore station and look-out post which reports the arrival of all ships in Santos harbour. There is also a quaint old church, dedicated to Nossa Senhora da Monte Serrat, said to have performed many miracles. The top can be reached on foot. Seven shrines have been built on the way up; annual pilgrimages are made by the local people. Fine views.

Local holidays

26 Jan (Foundation of Santos); Good Fri; Corpus Christi.

Local information

● **Accommodation**

A2 *Mendes Plaza*, Av Floriano Peixoto 42, T 37-4243, F 4-8253; **A2** *Parque Balneario*, complex at the centre of Gonzaga, Ana Costa 555, T 34-7211, F 4-0475, with shopping centre.

B *Mendes Panorama*, R Euclides da Cunha 15, T 37-2627, F 4-8253; **B** *Atlântico*, Av Pres Wilson 1, T 37-8823, F 37-8837, good value.

Beach front hotels on Av Pres Wilson: **A3** *Gonzaga*, No 36, T 4-1411, with bath, poor value; **B** *Avenida Palace*, No 10, T 4-1166; **B** *Maracanã Santos*, No 172, T 37-4030; **B** *Indaiá*, Av Ana Costa 431, T 4-1134. Many cheap hotels nr the Orquidário Municipal (Praça Washington), 1-2 blocks from the beach.

● **Places to eat**
Cibus, Av Vicente de Carvalho 1, beach end, considered the best; *Hong Kong Palace*, Av Conselheiro Nébias 288 (Chinese); first class *Pizzaria Zi Tereza*, Av Ana Costa 449; *Churrascaria Tertúlia*, Av Bartolomeu de Gusmão 187, T36-1461.

● **Banks & money changers**
Banks: **Banco Internacional**, R Gen Câmara 24; **Banco Holandês Unido**, **Citibank**, **Banco do Brasil**, all on R 15 de Novembro. The **First National Bank of Boston**, Praça Visc de Mauá 14. Banks open: 1000-1630.

Money changers: **Casa Faro**, R 15 de Novembro, 80 & 260; **Casa Bancaria Branco**, Praça de República 29 and **Gonzaga**, R Galeão Carvalhal 52/4.

● **Electric current**
220 AC 60 cycles.

● **Embassies & consulates**
British, R Tuiuti 58, 2nd floor, Caixa Postal 204, T 33-6111/34-6656. **Danish**, R Frei Gaspar 22, 10th floor, 106, CP 726, T 235 5165, F 232 8752, open 1000-1100, 1500-1700.

● **Places of worship**
All Saints Church: Praça Washington 92, José Menino. Services in English held every Sun.

● **Post & telecommunications**
Telecommunications: Embratel, Largo Senador Vergueiro 1 and 2.

● **Sports**
Golf courses: two 9-hole courses: Santos Golf Club, Av Pérsio de Queiroz Filho, São Vincente; Guarujá Golf Club (see below).

● **Tourist offices**
Praça dos Expedicionários 10, 10th floor; booths at Aquarium (Av Bartolomeu de Gusmão, Ponta da Praia), rodoviária, Casa do Café, Orquidário Municipal.

● **Transport**
Local Taxis: all taxis have meters. The fare is a fixed charge of US$0.50 plus US$0.20/km. Taxi, Gonzaga to bus station, US$4.

Trains The British-built Santos a Jundiaí up the hill to São Paulo is one of the railway wonders of the world; it passes through Cubatão and

then, running on toothed tracks up the escarpment, interesting hill scenery. The schedule for weekend passenger services is given under São Paulo. From Ana Costa station, a Fepasa (mixed) train may be taken to Embu Guaçu from where there is a bus to São Paulo.

Buses For most suburbs buses start from Praça Mauá, in the centre of the city. There are buses to **São Paulo** (50 mins, US$2.40) at intervals of approximately 15 mins, from the rodoviária nr city centre. Enquire about being picked up or put down outside usual terminal points. Express cars also run to São Paulo at regular intervals. Fare, US$4.50 each way, per passenger. (The two highways between São Paulo and Santos are sometimes seriously crowded, especially at rush hours and weekends.) Buses for Santos are caught in São Paulo in the Jabaquara bus station, not the Tietê rodoviária. To **Rio** (Normandy company, 6 a day, 7½ hrs, US$20, leito at 2230, US$40); to Rio along the coast road is via São Sebastião (US$12, change buses if necessary), Caraguatatuba and Ubatuba.

GUARUJÁ

(*Pop* 206,750) The route from Santos to the resort of Guarujá is along Av Conselheiro Nébias to the seafront, continuing along the beach to the Guarujá ferry (every 10 min, free for pedestrians) at Ponta da Praia. On the other side proceed as far as Enseada das Tartarugas (Turtle Bay). During the season and weekends there is a long delay at the Ponta da Praia vehicle ferry; to avoid this take the ferry on foot and get the bus on the Guarujá side; motor boats also cross for US$0.10. There is a strong undertow on nearly all the Guarujá beaches; the Jequiti-Mar beach (officially called Praia de Pernambuco) is the safest. The beaches are built-up and polluted. Golf club at Guarujá. (Trolleybus from Praça Mauá in Santos to the ferry, then buses.)

● **Accommodation & services** Turn left in centre of Guarujá and drive less than 1 km to reach **L2** *Delphin Hotel* and its restaurant *La Popote* at the beginning of the long beach of Praia da Enseada, Av M Stéfano 1295, T 86-2111, F 86-6844. Close by, at Av M Stéfano 999, is **L2** *Casa Grande Hotel*, luxury, in colonial style, with clean beach, T/F 86-2223. Facing sea is the luxurious **A1** *Ferraretto Hotel*, R Ribeiro 564, T 86-1112 (nightclub, swimming pool). Camping Clube do Brasil site at Praia do Perequê (where the best fish restaurants are), nr municipal nursery. Good *churrascaria* opp rodoviária.

The *Jequiti-Mar* holiday complex, 8 km beyond Guarujá on the road to Bertioga, is extremely attractive, T 53-3111, F 53-2325. There are private beaches (excellent swimming and boating) and very fine fishing grounds, and chalet accommodation, **A1-3**, according to size and situation. There is an excellent restaurant and two nightclubs; they are open each weekend and every night from Dec to Mar, in the holiday season. 2 km further N is a beach where fishing boats land their catch – a number of good seafood restaurants line the seafront.

BEACHES EAST OF SANTOS: BERTIOGA AND SÃO SEBASTIÃO

There are good sea-food restaurants on the road to **Bertioga**, an overcrowded place, where the fort of São João houses the João Ramalho museum (bus Guarujá-Bertioga, 1 hr, US$0.30). (Hotels: *Marazul*, Av Tomé de Souza 825; *Indaiá Praia*, same street, No 1079, both **A2**; restaurants include *Zezé e Duarte*, same street No 10.) The coastal road beyond Bertioga is paved, and the Rio-Santos highway, 1-2 km inland, provides a good link to São Sebastião. Going NE, the beaches are Praia de Bertioga, Praia São Lourenço, Praia Guaratuba and Praia Boracéia (campsite, meals served).

Beyond Boracéia is **Camburi**, surrounded by the Mata Atlântica. The sea is clean and good for bathing and watersports, including surfing. You can walk on the Estrada do Piavú into the Mata Atlântica to see streams, vegetation and wildlife (bathing in the streams is permitted, but use of shampoo and other chemicals is forbidden). 5 km from Camburi is Praia Brava, reached by 45 mins' walk through the forest, camping and nude bathing possible.

● **Accommodation** There are a number of good hotels and restaurants: **A2** *Pousada da Rosa*, R das Rosas 139, T 0124-651412, **B** in low season, with bath and breakfast, clean, friendly, pool.

● **Transport** Three daily buses from São Paulo, 160 km, en route to São Sebastião/Ilhabela, US$6.

30 km beyond Boracéia is the beach resort of **Maresias**, a fashionable place for surfers. Several hotels in town: **A2** *Maresias Praia*, on beach. *Mr Harris Jazz Bar*, rec.

From Maresias it is 21 km to **São Sebastião** (*Pop* 32,845; *CEP* 11600; *DDD* 0124). There is a **Museu de Arte Sacra** in the chapel of São Gonçalo in the town centre. Tourist Office: Av Dr Altino Arantes 174, friendly and helpful except regarding Ilhabela. The beaches within 2-3 km of São Sebastião harbour are polluted; others, Barra do Una, Boiçucanga, Praia da Balcia, are clean and very inviting. Ilhabela tends to be expensive in season, when it is cheaper to stay in São Sebastião.

● **Accommodation**   **A2** *Arrastão*, T 62-0099, most facilities; **B** *Recanto dos Pássaros*, Porto Grande, T 52-2046; **C-B** *Hotel Roma*, on the main square, T 52-1016, has more expensive rooms, excellent, very well rec; **D** *Bariloche*, R Tres Bandeirantes 133, 1 block from main square towards harbour, basic but clean; next door is **D-C** *Santa Rosa*. Non-members can stay in the *Camping Clube do Brasil* grounds for US$4 a night. 6 km S of São Sebastião is *Camping do Barraquecaba Bar de Mar de Lucas*, hot showers, English spoken, cabins available, rec. Halfway between Bertioga and Sao Sebastiao, on the Praia de Juqueí beach, are **L3** *Encanto da Praia*, with dinner, on the hill leading to Barra da Una, rec; **B** *Hotel Timão*, German-owned, with excellent fish meals.

● **Transport Buses** Two buses a day from **Rio**, 0830 and 2300, to Rio 0600 and 2330, heavily booked in advance; 4 a day from **Santos**, $3^{1}/_{2}$ hrs, US$12; buses from **São Paulo** (US$8) run inland via São José dos Campos, unless you ask for the service via Bertioga, only 2 a day. Free **ferry** to Ilhabela (4 hrs by bus from Santos, 3 a day, US$6).

ILHA DE SÃO SEBASTIÃO (Ilhabela)

The island of São Sebastião, known popularly as Ilhabela, is now easily accessible by car or bus from Santos. A bus runs along the coastal strip facing the mainland. Cavendish, the English pirate, had his secret anchorage in one of the sheltered caves there. Last century it was used as a landing place for illegal slave-traffic.

The island is of volcanic origin, roughly about 390 sq km in area. Its highest peak, Morro do Papagaio, rises 1,300m above sea-level, with its bare peak often obscured by mist; the slopes are densely wooded. There are many beautiful waterfalls, which can be reached on foot. Most of the flatter ground is given over to sugar-cane.

The only settled district lies on the coastal strip facing the mainland, the Atlantic side being practically uninhabited except by a few fisherfolk. The place abounds in tropical plants and flowers, and many fruits grow wild, whose juice mixed with cachaça and sugar makes as delicious a cocktail as can be imagined.

The energetic can climb over the hump of the island down towards the Atlantic, sometimes through dense tropical forest following the old slave trail, but for this 50-km return journey a local guide is required. There is a rough road to the Atlantic side, but it is very difficult to drive. The terraced Toca waterfalls amid dense jungle close to the foot of the 970m Baepi peak give cool freshwater bathing (entry, US$0.50). In all shady places, especially away from the sea, there abounds a species of midge known locally as *borrachudos*. A locally sold repellant (Autan) keeps them off for some time, however. Those allergic to insect bites should remain on the inhabited coastal strip. There is a small hospital (helpful) by the church in town.

Ilhabela

No alterations are allowed to the frontage of the main township, **Ilhabela** (*Pop* 9,500). It is very popular during summer weekends; at such times it is very difficult to find space for a car on the ferry. It is, however, a nice place to relax on the beach, with good food and some good value accommodation.

Places of interest Visit the old **Feiticeira** plantation, with underground dungeons. The road is along the coast, sometimes high above the sea, towards the S of the island. You can go by bus, taxi, or horse and buggy. *Gipsy Tur*, T 72-1518, helpful.

Pedras do Sino (Bell Rocks) These curious seashore boulders, when struck with a piece of iron or stone, emit a loud bell-like note. Campsite nearby.

Bathing On the mainland side it is not recommended because of oil, sandflies and jelly fish on the beaches and in the water. **Praia dos Castelhanos**, reached by a rough road over the island (no buses), is recommended.

● **Accommodation** **L2** *Ilhabela*, Av Pedro Paulo de Morais 151, T 72-1083, F 72-1031, good breakfast, rec; next door is **L3** *Itapemar*,

T 72-1329, F 72-1329, windsurfing equipment rented. **A3** *Colonial*, Av Brasil 1541, T 72-1033; **A3** *Petit Village*, Morro da Cruz 241, T 72-1393; **A3** *Pousada dos Hibiscos*, Av PP de Morais 714, T 72-1375, good atmosphere, swimming pool, rec. There are several other less expensive hotels in B-C range, mostly on the road to the left of the ferry. *Camping Porto Seguro*, T 72-9147, accessible by 2-hourly bus from Ilhabela.

● **Places to eat** *Perequê*, Av Princesa Isabel 337, reasonable. *Farol*, Av Princesa Isabel 1634, Perequê, good, especially seafood, rec.

● **Transport Ferry** Passenger ferry every 2 hrs; stops at Perequê and Ilhabela; car ferry runs through the night and serves Perequê only (fare for cars is US$7 weekdays, double at weekends).

NORTH OF SÃO SEBASTIÃO

On the Santos-Rio road, is São Francisco, good beaches. Further on is **Caraguatatuba** (*Pop* 52,915) with 17 good beaches to the NE and SW (several hotels, popular at weekends, good restaurants). Good camping site on beach and other sites. Direct buses to Caraguatatuba from Rio de Janeiro, São Paulo and Santos; direct buses from São Paulo do not use the coast road. Further E is **Lagoinha**, 34 km W of Ubatuba, with chalets and sailing boats for hire. Exotic birdlife and forest.

UBATUBA

(*Pop* 47,295; *CEP* 11680; *DDD* 0124) In all, there are 72 beautiful beaches (Iperoig, Itaguá and Saco da Ribeira are officially designated polluted), quite spread out, most with campsites (Grande, just S, and one 6 km N of Ubatuba are rec). There is also a yacht haven. The area gets very crowded at Carnival time as people from Rio come to escape the crowds in their city. Jewellery market on beach, Sats.

● **Accommodation** At all holiday times it is expensive, with no hotel less than US$15 and camping costing US$8. **A1** *Saveiros*, Praia do Lázaro T 42-0172, pool, restaurant, English spoken; **A2** *Solar das Águas Cantantes*, Praia do Lázaro, T 42-0178, reached by local bus, swimming pool, restaurant; **C** *Xaréu*, JH da Costa 413, T 32-1525, central nr beach, clean, quiet, friendly, rec; **C-D** *Jangadeiro*, Av Abreu Sodre (15 mins' walk from centre, cross bridge, next to beach), with bath, good value; *Mauricio*, Av Abreu Sodre 607, nr Praia do Perequê-Açu, has cheap rooms, friendly, clothes washing possible; *Pousada do Page*, T 32-4515, breakfast, on beach, rec. **Camping**: two Camping Clube do Brasil sites at Maranduba and Perequê-Açu beaches.

ROUTES The road from São Sebastião is paved, so a journey from São Paulo along the coast is possible, 5 buses daily. 25 km S of Ubatuba at Baia Fortaleza is *Refúgio de Corsário*, T 43-1126, C and up, a clean quiet hotel on the water front, sailing and swimming, a good place to relax. Ubatuba is 70 km from Parati (see page 414), several buses daily, on the hour, from *Lanchonete Nice*, near rodoviária. If driving from Ubatuba along the coast to Rio, one can stop for lunch at Porto Aquarius, where there is a cave and hotel in a beautiful setting (not cheap). Direct buses from Rio (US$12), São Paulo and Santos.

PARQUE NACIONAL SERRA DA BOCAINA

Straddling the border of São Paulo and Rio de Janeiro states is the **Parque Nacional Serra da Bocaina**, which rises from the coast to heights of over 1,900m, encompassing three strata of vegetation (Ibama, T 021-294-6497, or 0125-77-1225).

SOUTHWEST FROM SANTOS

It is 50 km beside the Praia Grande to **Itanhaém** (*Pop* 33,210) with its pretty colonial church and semi-ruined Convento da Conceição on a small hill. There are several good sea-food restaurants along the beach, hotels and camping (many more sites 29 km away at Peruíbe beach). There are many attractive beaches here, and hot springs with medicinal mud. The whole stretch of coast is completely built up with holiday developments. The beaches of Praia Grande and Itanhaém were officially declared polluted in 1990. Frequent buses from Santos US$1.50, 1 hr.

IGUAPE AND ILHA COMPRIDA

Further S is the town of **Iguape** (*Pop* 27,890; *DDD* 0138) founded in 1538. Typical of Portuguese architecture, the small municipal museum is housed in a 16th century building. It has a market, hotels and restaurants. Opposite Iguape is the northern end of the **Ilha Comprida** with 86 km of beaches (some dirty and disappointing). The island is being developed as a resort; good restaurants, hotels, supermarket – fresh fish is excellent. At the southern end **Cananéia** (*Pop* 9,905) is more commercialized than Iguape; it has several hotels (from **C**).

● **Accommodation** At **Iguape**: **C** *Silvi*, R Ana Cândida Sandoval Trigo 515, T 41-1421, with bath and breakfast, good; **C** *Rio Verde*, R Antônio José de Morais 86, T 41-1493, good rooms but humid; **D** *Pousada Aguape*, R Padre Homer. *Camping Clube do Brasil* site 15 km from Iguape; other sites on Ilha Comprida, inc *Britânia*, US$10 for 2, good, clean, friendly.

● **Transport Buses** To Iguape: from São Paulo, Santos, or Curitiba, changing at Registro (see above). **Sea** A continuous ferry service runs from Iguape to Ilha Comprida (passengers free; cars at a small charge); buses run until 1900 from the ferry stop to the beaches. From Iguape it is possible to take a boat trip down the coast to Cananéia and Ariri. Tickets and information from Dept Hidroviário do Estado, R Major Moutinho 198, Iguape, T 41-1122. Boats leave Iguape on Mon, Thur (but check in advance), returning next day, or bus back from Cananéia. It is a beautiful trip, passing between the island and the mainland. The boat has a toilet, fresh water, and meals. In wet weather, the cabin gets crowded and uncomfortable. Ariri has no road connections; there is a hostel, E, run by the shipping line.

Towns in the State of São Paulo

BOUT 13% of Brazil's population lives within 200 km of São Paulo city, a circle which includes 88 municipalities. Four of them – the big ABCD towns – sharing a population of over a million, are Santo André, São Bernardo, São Caetano and Diadema; they have many of the largest industrial plants. There are some 70 cities in the State with populations of over 50,000 and São Paulo is linked with all of them by road, and several of them by railway.

NORTHWEST OF SÃO PAULO

JUNDIAÍ

An important railway, the broad-gauge Santos a Jundiaí, runs from Santos to São Paulo and across the low mountains which separate São Paulo city from the interior to its terminus at **Jundiaí** (*Pop* 312,520; *CEP* 13200; *DDD* 011), 58 km from São Paulo, which has textile factories and other industries. The district grows coffee and grain and there is an annual Grape Festival.

● **Accommodation C** *Grande Hotel*, R do Rosário 605, T 434-5355, with good restaurant.

CAMPINAS

Campinas (*Pop* almost 1 million; *CEP* 13100; *DDD* 0192), 88 km from São Paulo by the fine Via Anhanguera highway, is important as a clearing point for coffee, for its Agricultural Institute, and its rapidly growing industries. The Viracopos international airport is 11 km from Campinas, which also has its own airport.

Places of interest

See fine cathedral, old market, colonial buildings, several museums (including Arte Contemporânea, Arquidiocesano, Carlos Gomes and, in the Bosque de Jequitibás, Histórico and Folclore), arts centre (noted symphony orchestra; the city is the birthplace of the noted 19th century Brazilian composer Carlos Gomes), and the modern university outside the city. Visits can be made to the Agricultural Institute to see all the aspects of coffee. A tourist train operates in Parque Taquaral.

Local information
● **Accommodation**

L2 *Royal Palm Plaza* Praça Rotatória 88, T 2-9085, F 2-7085; **L2** *Solar das Andorinhas*, a health farm with pool, sauna, horses, sports, etc 18 km outside city on the Mogi-Mirim road, with meals, T 39-4411, F 39-5899. **L2** *Vila Rica*, R Donato Paschoal 100, T 31-5242.

A1 *Savoy*, R Regente Feijó 1064, T 32-9444, F 2-9207.

B *Opala Avenida*, Av Campos Sales 161, T 8-4115, F 31-6983, central; **B** *Parati Palácio*, R Bernardino de Campos 426, T 32-0395/8368, German spoken, bath, TV, clean, rec; **B** *Hotel IPE*, R Bernardino de Campos 1050, T 31 7746, friendly, clean, rec.

● **Places to eat**

Bar Restaurante Barão, Barão de Jaguará 1381 and *Churrascaria Gaúcha*, Av Dr Campos Sales 515, excellent for Brazilian food. *Cenat*, R Barão de Jaguara 1260, 2nd floor, closed Sat (and Fri for dinner). *Nutrir*, R Dr Quirino 1620, vegetarian, very good value. *Sucão*, R Benjamin Constant 1108, good variety of juices; *Pastelaria do Sr Júlio*, R de 13 Maio 143, friendly, helpful, cheap, rec.

● **Banks & money changers**

The First National Bank of Boston, Av Francisco Glicério 1275, and local banks.

● **Entertainment**

Nightlife on weekends is busy around the Centro

de Convivência, Praça Imprensa Fluminense, in city centre. There are cinemas in the city centre and the Iguatemi and Galleria shopping centres.

● **Places of worship**
Community Church: services in English at School of Language and Orientation, R Eduardo Lane 270.

● **Shopping**
H Stern jewellers at Shopping Centre Iguatemi.
Bookshops: *Pontes Editores*, R Dr Quirino 1223, has English books; second-hand at *Sebo Comércio*, R Bareto Leme 1265, and *O Livrão*, R B Jaguara 936, Loja 11.

● **Transport**
Local Trains and buses to São Paulo (bus US$3), Ribeirão Preto and Araguari; buses to Rio de Janeiro, 7 hrs, US$11.50.

Trains The metre-gauge Mogiana line, connecting with the broad-gauge Paulista at Campinas, serves the northeastern part of the state. It goes through Ribeirão Preto to Uberlândia and Araguari in the Triângulo of Minas Gerais, a great area for fattening cattle which are trucked to the *frigoríficos* of São Paulo. No São Paulo-Ribeirão Preto tickets are sold, so you may have to wait a day at Campinas for a connection (or go by bus). From Araguari there is a line into the state of Goiás and to Brasília (no passenger services). 25 km from Campinas, at Jaguariúna, is a railway preservation group with steam engines and wagons; hourly bus from Campinas US$1, or take the steam train itself from Campinas (station behind Carrefour, Anhumas, reached by town bus), Sat and Sun, T 53-6067 for schedule. Tourist train one Sat a month to Peruibe, 0700, 6 hrs, run by Pettená-Tur.

SERRA NEGRA

(*Pop* 21,660; 78 km NE of Campinas) A very pleasant spa town and summer holiday resort in the mountains at 1,080m, 145 km from São Paulo. Visitors tour the countryside in horse-drawn buggies. There are a *balneário* and a small zoo.

20 km from Serra Negra is the even better-known spa town of **Lindóia** (*Pop* 4,665), whose still waters are bottled and sent all over Brazil.

● **Accommodation L2** *Rádio Hotel*, Serra Negra, T 92-3311, very nice indeed, and several others of a good standard.

Americana (*Pop* 142,580), an interesting town, is 42 km from Campinas. This area was settled by Confederate refugees from the S of the USA after the Civil War. Most of the original settlers soon returned to

the States, but some stayed, and there still exist reminders of their occupation here. A visit to the cemetery reveals an unusual number of English surnames.

RIBEIRÃO PRETO

(*Pop* 430,805; *Alt* 420m; *CEP* 14100; *DDD* 016) The centre of a rich coffee-growing district, the town also has a steel industry. It is a distribution centre for the interior of São Paulo State and certain districts in Minas Gerais and Goiás. Products: coffee, cotton, sugar, grain and rice. It is 300 km from São Paulo by rail via Campinas and paved road (4 hrs by bus); airport has TAM flights to São Paulo, Rio, Poços de Caldas.

● **Accommodation L3** *Holiday Inn*, R Alvares Cabral 1120, T 625-0186, F 635-1279; **A3** *Stream Palace*, R Gen Osório 850, T 636-0660, F 636-7834, with TV; **B** *Umuarama Recreio*, Praça dos Cafeeiros 140, T 637-3790, 6 km from centre, very pleasant, pool, gardens.

Barretos Some 115 km NW of Ribeirão Preto is where, in the third week in Aug, the **Festa do Peão** is held. This is the biggest annual rodeo in the world. Trips from the UK are run by *Last Frontiers*, Swan House, High St, Long Crendon, Bucks, HP18 9AF, T/F 01844-208405.

WEST OF SÃO PAULO

SOROCABA

(*Pop* 377,270; *Alt* 540m; *CEP* 18100), 110 km W of São Paulo, **Sorocaba** is an important industrial centre. The climate temperate. It has textile mills; produces cement, fertilizers, footwear, hats, alcohol, wines; there are railway workshops, extensive orange groves and packing house installations. It is an important cotton centre. Other products are timber, sugar, cereals, coffee, and minerals. Communications with São Paulo are better by road than by rail; the Castello Branco highway passes nearby.

● **Accommodation B** *Terminus*, Av Gen Carneiro 474, T 21-6970; **D** *Manchester*, R 15 de Novembro 21, basic, friendly.

PIRAPORA DE BOM JESUS & ITU

There is a picturesque paved road along the Tietê valley from São Paulo to Bauru, via the colonial towns of **Pirapora de Bom Jesus** (*Pop* 7,935), a popular place of pilgrimage, in a most attractive setting on both sides of the river, and **Itu** (*Pop* 106,870), founded by the Bandeirantes in the 17th century. The beautiful falls of Salto de Itu, 8 km N, are flanked by a park and a textile mill.

• **Accommodation At Itu**: **C** *International*, R Barão do Itaím 93, T 482-4577; **D** *Sabará*, Praça Padre Miguel 90. **Camping**: *Casarão do Carmo*, Km 95 on the Jundiaí road; *Alemão*, at Km 90 on the Cabreúva road.

BAURU

(*Pop* 260,380; *CEP* 17100; *DDD* 0142) Founded at the end of the last century, the town is used by Paulistanos as a weekend resort.

• **Accommodation A3** *Bekassin*, Av Duque de Caxias 1717, T 24-3700, swimming pool; **B** *Alvorada Palace*, R Primeiro de Agosto 619, T 22-5900. **C** *Colonial*, Praça Rui Barbosa 248, T 22-3191. Cheaper hotels in the vicinity of the rodoviária and the railway station.

• **Places to eat** *H 2 Churrascaria*, Piauí 8-55; *Cantina Bello Nápoli*, 1° de Agosto 6-52.

• **Transport** Passenger train services to Bauru were discontinued in 1995. Connections with São Paulo and Campo Grande must be made by bus.

Marília (*Pop* 151,760), W of Bauru, is a pleasant clean town with a good hotel, **A3** *Sun Valley Park*, R Aimorés 501, T/F 33-5944, friendly.

Ourinhos (*Pop* 76,900), founded in 1924, is 95 km S of Marília near the border with Paraná state. It is surrounded by sugar cane plantations. A possible stop-over on the road from São Paulo to Foz do Iguaçu or Campo Grande, it is on the railway which runs to Presidente Epitácio (see page 499) on the Paraná river. **Accommodation C** *Pousada Ourinhos*, R Mons Córdova 333, T 22-5898, good value; **D** *Comercial*, R Amornio Prado 38, friendly.

Further W is **Presidente Prudente** (*Pop* 165,450), another useful place to make bus connections for Campo Grande, Porto Alegre, São Paulo, Ribeirão Preto, 9 hrs. **A1** *Hotel Aruá*, Av Marcondes 1111, T 22-4666, F 22-0765, doubles better than single rooms; **D** *Hotel Alves* opp rodoviária, clean, nice but noisy.

NORTHEAST OF SÃO PAULO

CAMPOS DO JORDÃO

(*Pop* 36,850; *Alt* 1,710m; *CEP* 12460; *DDD* 0122) A mountain resort between Rio de Janeiro and São Paulo in the Serra da Mantiqueira, it is prettily set in a long valley. The climate is cold and dry in winter and cool in summer, a great relief from the coastal heat and humidity.

Places of interest

Palácio Boa Vista, 4 km from Abernéssia Centre, Governor's residence and museum, open Wed, Sat, Sun, 1000-1200, 1400-1700; **Pedra do Baú** (1,950m), to get there take a bus to São Bento do Sapucaí at 0800 or 1500, then walk to Paiol Grande and then on an unmarked path to the Pedra. Return buses from São Bento at 0915 and 1615. Near Paiol Grande is the small waterfall of **Cachoeira dos Amores**. **Pico do Itapeva** (2,030m) and **Imbiri** (1,950m) command a beautiful view of the Paraíba valley; see also **Morro do Elefante** (chairlift available); **Gruta dos Crioulos**; nature reserve at **Horto Florestal** (20 km), signposted from chairlift station, very pretty – go in the morning to avoid crowds; lots of streams with bridges, waterfalls nearby. Campos do Jordão is a popular place for hikers; most of the roads leading off the main avenue lead to quiet areas with nice views, eg up Av Dr Antônio Nicola Padula, turn left 500m past Refúgio na Serra for waterfalls and Pico do Itapeva. The villages of **Emílio Ribas** and **São Cristóvão** are connected by a railcar which runs frequently, US$0.15.

Local information
• **Accommodation**

Book accommodation in advance if going June/July. Many hotels inc *Toriba*, Av E Diederichsen, T 62-1566, F 63-2793; *Vila Inglesa*, Sen R Simonsen, T 63-1955, F 63-2699; *Refúgio Alpino*, Av Roberto Simonsen 885, T 63-1660, and others at Capivari.

B *Refugio na Serra*, Av Dr Antônio Nicola Padula 275, T 63-1330, comfortable, good breakfast, very helpful owners (some English spoken), rec.

Camping: *Clube do Brasil* site in the Descansópolis district, T 63-1130.

Youth hostel: R Diogo de Carvalho 86, T 229-3787/3011, ramal 286; membership card and permission from Dr Fernando at Tourist Office in the rodoviária required.

● **Places to eat**

Sole Mio, Av Dr Emilio Lang 485 (on road to Horto Florestal), Italian, big portions; *Baden Baden*, R Djalma Forjaz 93, German, good.

● **Shopping**

There are plenty of chocolate shops, also jams and cheese for sale. Stalls on main square Thur-Sun sell local produce. 'Milbaho' mineral water is produced here.

● **Transport**

Road The resort is reached by an 87 km paved road from São José dos Campos, 100 km from São Paulo, on the Presidente Dutra (BR-116) highway. By car it takes about 3 hrs from São Paulo, 6 to 7 from Rio.

Trains No through rail service: railcars make round trips between Campos do Jordão and Santo Antônio do Pinhal, in season between 0800 and 0900 and at 1310, out of season (Oct-Nov, Mar-April) at 1310 only, a bit bumpy, but beautiful views (sit on the right on the way there, left coming back): hills, valleys, tight corners. The train is very crowded even though you are assigned a seat; fare US$1.50 (buy ticket in advance, and get return immediately on arrival in San Antônio; watch your belongings on board). Whole trip takes about 3 hrs: 1 hr each way on train, 40 mins-1 hr in Santo Antônio (not much on offer there: a few snack bars, nice views, statue of Madonna and Child). There is a local railcar service within São José (very crowded but cheap).

Buses From **São Paulo**, US$6, 3 hrs; from **Rio**, changing at São José dos Campos, US$9.50.

ROUTES The short road down to **Pindamonhangaba**, starting from the paved road 24 km SW of Campos do Jordão, is paved (5 buses daily, 50 mins). Railcar to 'Pinda' leaves 1705 Mon-Thur and weekends, from Pinda 0600 Tues-Fri, 0930 weekends. A new road branching off the BR-116 near Caçapava provides a quicker drive from Rio, or São Paulo, to Campos do Jordão than the route via São José dos Campos. From 'Pinda' buses run to **São Paulo** and to **Aparecida do Norte**, 1030, US$2.

APARECIDA DO NORTE

(*Pop* 35,060) Nearer to Rio than the Pindamonhangaba turn, just off the BR-116, is Brazil's chief place of pilgrimage and the seat of its patron saint, Nossa Senhora

Aparecida. This small black image of the Virgin is said to have been taken by a fisherman from the nearby Río Paraíba, and quickly acquired a miraculous reputation. It is now housed in a huge modern basilica in Romanesque style on top of a hill, with the clean white-walled, red-roofed town below.

Southern Brazil: Rio Grande do Sul

THIS consists, from south to north, of the three states of Rio Grande do Sul, Santa Catarina and Paraná. Rio Grande do Sul is gaúcho (cowboy) country; it is also Brazil's chief wine producer. Throughout the south European settlement, especially from Germany, heavily influences cultural and agricultural activity. The coast offers a variety of beaches and scenery while in the far west is one of Latin America's major natural attractions, the Iguaçu falls, and one of its largest manmade constructions, the Itaipu dam.

The conformation of the land is not unlike that further N; the Great Escarpment runs down the coastal area as far as Porto Alegre, receding from the coast in a wide curve between Paranaguá and Florianópolis. South of Tubarão to the borders of Uruguay the hills of southern Rio Grande do Sul, which never rise higher than 900 to 1,000m, are fringed along the coast by sand bars and lagoons.

North of the Rio Uruguai the land is deeply forested, but the area of prairie, small in São Paulo, Paraná and Santa Catarina, grows more extensive than the forest in Rio Grande do Sul, S of the Uruguai valley. In southern Rio Grande do Sul, S and W of the Rio Jacuí (draining into the Lagoa dos Patos) there are great grasslands stretching as far as Uruguay to the S and Argentina to the W. This is the distinctive land of the gaúcho, or cowboy (pronounced ga-oo-shoo in Brazil), of the flat black hat, of bombachas (the baggy trousers worn by the gaúcho), of the poncho and ximarão (or mate without sugar), the indispensable drink of southern cattlemen. There are many millions of cattle, sheep and pigs, and some 75% of all Brazilian wine comes from the state. Its population (who all call themselves gaúchos) now number over 9 million. Rio Grande do Sul has the highest proportion of literate people in Brazil. The gaúcho culture is quite vigorous, increasingly developing a sense of distance from the African-influenced culture of further N. This separationist strain was most marked in the 1820s and 1830s when the Farroupilha movement, led by Bento Gonçalves, proclaimed the República Riograndense in 1835. The subsequent war with the federal government ended with the Treaty of Ponche Verde in Feb 1845.

There are three sharply contrasted types of colonization and land owning in Rio Grande do Sul. During the colonial period, wars with the Spaniards of Uruguay were frequent, and the Portuguese government brought into the grasslands of the S a number of military settlers from the Azores; these soldiers inter-married with the Brazilian herdfolk in the area. In the colonial period, also, the Jesuits built several settlements to acculturate the local Indians; relics of this process include the impressive ruins of the **Sete Povos das Missões Orientais** (São Borja, São Nicolau, São Luiz, São Lourenço, São Miguel, São João, Santo Ángelo). West from Porto Alegre, in the floodlands of the Rio Jacuí and its tributary, the Rio Taquari, rice is cultivated in typical Brazilian fashion: large estates with tenant workers.

At São Leopoldo, N of Porto Alegre, a group of Germans were settled in 1824 on their own small farms, and during the next 25 years over 20,000 more were brought into the area by the Brazilian Government. The Germans concentrated on rye, maize, and pigs. Between 1870 and 1890, settlers from northern Italy arrived, bringing viticulture with them, and settled N of the Germans at Alfredo Chaves and Caxias do Sul.

PORTO ALEGRE

(*Pop* 1,262,630; *CEP* 90000; *DDD* 051) The capital of Rio Grande do Sul, lies at the confluence of five rivers (called Rio Guaíba, although it is not a river in its own right) and thence into the great freshwater lagoon, the Lagoa dos Patos, which runs into the sea. Porto Alegre is the most important commercial centre S of São Paulo. Standing on a series of hills and valleys on the banks of the Guaíba, with its business centre jutting out into the water on a promontory, it is one of the most heavily industrialized cities in Brazil. The climate is temperate through most of the year, though the temperature at the height of summer can often exceed 40°C and drop below 10°C in winter. The surrounding suburbs are pleasant. The city's many bars and clubs cluster around the Zona Norte.

Porto Alegre is a fresh-water port for ocean-going vessels of up to 7,000 tons and 4.87m draught. Vessels must come up through Rio Grande and the Lagoa dos Patos, some 275 km from the open sea. Large areas of reclaimed land have been

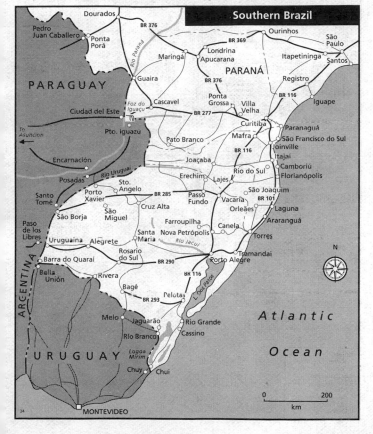

Southern Brazil

used for residential building and to extend the port facilities and quays, now among the most up-to-date in Brazil. Mosquitoes are plentiful.

The city's most important industries are food and farm products, textiles, metal-processing, chemicals and leather products. Chief exports are pinewood, rice, wheat, soya, meat, hides, wool, animal hair, semi-precious stones, wine and tobacco. A visit to Varig's installations and workshops is worth while. Varig's museum, R Augusto Severo 851 e 18 de Novembro 800, São João, is open Tues-Fri

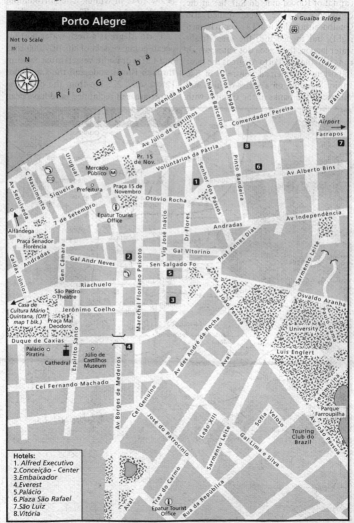

Porto Alegre

Not to Scale

To Guaiba Bridge

To Airport

Rio Guaiba

Hotels:
1. Alfred Executivo
2. Conceição - Center
3. Embaixador
4. Everest
5. Palácio
6. Plaza São Rafael
7. São Luiz
8. Vitória

and 0900-1300 Sun. *Cervejaria Brahma*, Av Cristovão Colombo 545, offers tours of its brewery (but not Dec-Mar).

Citizens of Porto Alegre (which means 'happy port') call themselves *gaúchos*. A frequent source of amusement to them is visitors' confusion over place names: many streets and squares are known by a traditional name whose origin is lost in history, and which bears no relation to its postal address. Where possible, we give both names – but it's worth identifying your destination on a map before setting out.

Places of interest
The older residential part of the town is on a promontory dominated previously by the **Palácio Piratini** (Governor's Palace), the imposing modern **cathedral**, and the two high white towers of the old church of **Nossa Senhora das Dores**, but Governor and God have now been utterly dwarfed by the skyscraper of the **Assembléia Legislativa**. The streets in the centre are famous for their steep gradients.

Do not miss that section of the **R dos Andradas** (R da Praia) that is now permanently closed to traffic. It is the city's principal outdoor meeting place, the main shopping area, and by around 1600 it is jammed full of people.

The **Parque Farroupilha** (called Parque Rendação) is a fine park near the city centre. The interesting cathedral of the **Anglican-Episcopal church** of Brazil, the **Jardim Zoológico do Estado** near São Leopoldo (bus US$0.80), the **Botanic Gardens** (Bairro Jardim Botânico, bus 40 from Praça 15 de Novembro) and the **Cidade Universitária** are worth a visit. The **Mercado Público** is next to the Prefeitura, in the centre of town. In the **Cidade Baixa** quarter are the colonial **Travessa dos Venezianos** (between RR Lopo Gonçalves and Joaquim Nabuco) and the **house of Lopo Gonçalves**, R João Alfredo 582, which houses the Museu do Porto Alegre, free, 0900-1700 Tues-Sun. The 5-km wide Rio Guaíba lends itself to every form of boating and there are several sailing clubs. Boat trips leave from Av Mauá opp the Ministério da Fazenda, US$3.50, 1 hr. **Ipanema beach**, on

the southern banks of the river, offers spectacular sunsets. A good view of the city, with glorious sunsets, may be had from the **Morro de Santa Teresa** (take bus 95 from the top end of R Salgado Filho, marked 'Morro de Santa Teresa TV' or just 'TV').

Museums
The **Museu Júlio de Castilhos**, Duque de Caxias 1231, has an interesting historical collection (Tues-Sun 0900-1700), and there is the **Museu do Trem** in the old railway station of São Leopoldo, decrepit but interesting exhibits: entrance free, Mon-Fri 1400-1800, sometimes closed Mar-November. **Museu de Arte do Rio Grande do Sul**, Praça Senador Florêncio (Praça da Alfândega), Tues 1000-2100, Wed-Sun 1000-1700, entry free, is interesting.

Local festivals
The main event is on 2 Feb (local holiday), the festival of **Nossa Senhora dos Navegantes** (Iemanjá), whose image is taken by boat from the central quay in the port to the industrial district of Navegantes. **Semana Farroupilha**, celebrating *gaúcho* traditions with parades in traditional style, main day 20 Sept. The **Carnival** parade takes place in Av A do Carvalho, renamed Av Carlos Alberto Barcelos (or Roxo) for these 3 days only, after a famous carnival designer.

Local information
● Warning
The market area in Praça 15 de Novembro and the bus terminal are dangerous at night; thefts have been reported in Voluntários da Pátria and Praça Parcão.

● Accommodation
L2 *Plaza São Rafael*, Av Alberto Bins514, T 221-6100, F 221-6883, *Conceição-Center*, Av Senador Salgado Filho 201, T 225-7774, good; **L3** *Alfred Executivo*, Av Otávio Rocha 270, T 221-8966; **L3** *Embaixador*, Jerônimo Coelho 354, T 228-2211, 4-star, comfortable, unexciting restaurant; **L3-A1** *Ritter*, Largo Vespasiano J Veppo 55, T 228-4044, 221-8155, F 228-1610, conveniently located opp rodoviária, good service, English, French, German, fine restaurant, bar, small pool,rec; **L3** *Continental*, next door (No 77, T 225-3233, F 228-5024), all facilities, high standards, rec.

A1 *Porto Alegre Residence*, R Des André da

Rocha 131, T 225-8644, large rooms, TV, a/c, friendly, rec; **A1** *Ritter*, see above, has 3-star rooms (good); **A2** *Everest*, R Duque de Caxias 1357, T 228-3133.

B *São Luiz*, Av Farrapos 45, T 228-1722, spotless, good service, but nr rodoviária so a bit noisy; **B** *Terminaltur*, opp rodoviária, next to *Continental* No 125, T 227-1656, with bath, a/c, TV, breakfast, heating, small rooms and tiny bathrooms, not too comfortable.

C *Palácio*, Av Vigário José Inácio 644, central, clean, friendly, hot water, rec; **C** *Açores*, R dos Andrades 885, T 221-7588, central, cramped but friendly; **C** *Savoy*, Av Borges Medeiros 688, T 224-0511, good value; **C** *Santa Catarina*, R Gen Vitorino 240, T 224-9044.

Marechal, R Andrade Neves 123, basic, clean (not far from Mercado Municipal); **D** *Ritz*, André da Rocha 225, friendly, central, helpful, Spanish spoken; next door is *Finks*, same price range; **D** *Uruguay*, Dr Flores 371, clean, simple, rec; **D** *Curitibano*, R Dr Barros Cassal 82, T 228 2343, rec.

E *Porto Alegre*, Pinto Bandeirantes 339, good, clean, quiet, rec. Hotels in the area around R Garibáldi and Voluntários da Patria between Av Farrapos and rodoviária are overpriced and used by low-rent girls.

Camping: Praia do Guarujá, 16 km out on Av Guaíba.

Youth hostel: The hotel *Ritz* is temporarily acting as a youth hostel (1996), André da Rocha 225.

● **Places to eat**

Many good ones. *Gaúcho* cooking features large quantities of meat – churrascaria (barbecue) is a fundamental part of daily life here, the ritual family meal on Sunday afternoons and Wednesday nights. At restaurants, it's often served by staff in traditional dress. German cuisine is also a very strong influence. Regional farm (*campeiro*) food, now a dying art, uses plenty of rice, vegetables, and interesting sauces. Vegetarians might try some of the *campeiro* soups and casseroles, otherwise stick to Italian restaurants or churrascaria salad bars: this high-protein city only had one strictly vegetarian restaurant in 1996, closed evenings and weekends.

General: *Mosqueteiro*, Estádio Olímpico (belongs to football club); *Komka*, Av Bahia 1275 (San Geraldo), T 222-1881, reasonable, rec; *Chalé da Pça 15*, Praça 15 de Novembro, average food but rec for early evening drinks and snacks.

Regional: *Recanto do Tio Flor*, Av Getúlio Vargas 1700 (Menino Deus), T 233-6512, *comida campeira*, reasonable, rec; *Pulperia*, Tr do Carmo 76 (Cidade Baixa), T 227-1172, inexpensive, music, opens to 0400, closed Sun lunch; *Porky's*, Av

Cristóvão Colombo 1971 (Floresta), T 222-7552, serves wild boar and buffalo, closed Sun, rec; *Grumete*, 24 de Outubro 905; *Barranco*, Av Protásio Alves 1578; *Farroupilha*, Fernando Machado 973 (corner of Borges de Medeiros), delicious *prato feito* US$3.

Churrascarias: all rec: *Gauchão* at Rodoviária, inexpensive, live entertainment nightly; *Santo Antônio*, R Dr Timotéu 465 (Moinhos de Vento), T 222-3541/ 222-3138, more expensive; *Zequinha*, Av Assis Brasil 1294 (Passo D'Areia), T 341-8157, with regional dances; *Galpão Crioulo*, Parque Mauricio Sirotsky Sobrinho (in park, Cidade Baixa), T 226-8194, show and dancing; *Moinhos de Vento*, R Dona Laura 424, T 331-1847, closed Sun pm; *Capitão Rodrigo*, Av Albert Bins 514 (in *Plaza São Rafael* hotel), T 221-6100, closed Mon.

German: *Sociedade Germânia*, Av Independência 1269, 6th floor, T 222-9094, Sat night dinner-dance, reasonable, closed Mon, Sat lunch, Sun eves, rec; *Hannover*, Av C Colombo 2140 (Floresta), T 222-7902, inexpensive, closed Mon, rec; *Chopp Stübel*, R Quintino Bocaiúva 940, T 332-8895, closed Sun, rec; *Wunderbar*, R Marquês do Herval 5981, T 222-4967, opens 2000-0400, very busy, rec (both in Moinhos de Vento); *Steinhaus*, Paulino Teixeira 415.

Portuguese: *Casa de Portugal*, João Pessoa 579; *Galo*, João Alfredo 904.

Italian: *Copacabana*, Praça Garibáldi; *Pizzeria 4 Climas*, Av Vigario José Inacio 695.

Vegetarian: (Mon-Fri, lunch only) *Ilha Natural*, R Gen Câmara 60, self service, cheap; also try *Associação Macrobiotica*, R Mal Floriano 72, T 225-4784, weekdays only.

Bars: (beer and sandwiches, music) *Cía Sandwiches*, Getúlio Vargas 1430; *João de Barro*, R da República 546, Cidade Baixa, good jazz; *Julius*, José de Alencar 1348; *Sgt Peppers*, Dona Laura 329. There is a pleasant bar at the **Casa de Cultura Mário Quintana**, R dos Andradas 736.

Late bars, see **Nightclubs** below.

● **Banks & money changers**

Exchange on Av Borges de Medeiros, good rate, cash only. **Platino Turismo**, Dos Andrades e Av Borges de Medeiros (only one to change TCs, Amex, but 6% less than cash), **Exprinter**, Sen Salgado Filho 247 (best for cash); **Mastercard**, cash against card, R 7 de Setembro 722, 8th floor, Centro; for other addresses consult tourist bureau brochure. **Lloyds Bank**, R Gen Câmara 249 (open 1000-1630). **Banco do Brasil**, Uruguai 185, 9th floor (open 1000-1500), good rates for TCs. **Bradesco**, Praça Senador Florência, Visa machine.

● **Cultural centres**

Sociedade Brasileira da Cultura Inglesa, Praça Mauricio Cardoso 49, Moinhos de Vento. **Instituto Goethe**, 24 de Outubro 122 (open Mon-Fri, 0930-1230, 1430-2100), occasional concerts, bar rec for German *Apfelkuchen*. **Instituto Cultural Americano Brasileiro**, Mon-Fri, 0800-2000 (Sat 0800-1700).

● **Electric current**

110-120 AC 50 cycles.

● **Embassies & consulates**

Argentine, R Prof Annes Dias 112, 1st floor, T 24-6799/6810/6786. **Uruguayan**, R Siquera Campos 1171, 6th floor, T 224-3499. **US**, Genuíno 421, corner of Medeiros, T 226-4288. **British**, R Itapeva 110, Sala 505, Edif Montreal Bairro D'Areia, T 41-0720; **Austrian**, R 7 de Setembro 1069, conj 1714, Caixa Postal 1771, T 2460 77/85. **Danish**, Av Ipiranga 321, 5th floor, Bairro Menino Deus, Caixa Postal 500, T 231 7344, F 233 6158, open 0800-1200, 1400-1800. **Finnish**, R Comendador Azevedo 224, T 222-7188.

● **Entertainment**

The old Hotel Majestic has become the **Casa de Cultura Mário Quintana**, at R dos Andrades 736: this is a lively centre for the arts, with exhibitions, theatre etc. Plays by local and visiting companies at the theatres of **São Pedro** (opp Government Palace) free noon and late afternoon concerts Sat, Sun, art gallery, café, and **Leopoldina** (Av Independência). Modern cinemas. **Centro de Tradição Gaúcha** has *gaúcho* shows every Sat, starting at 2200.

Nightclubs: *Crocodillo's*, 24 de Outubro (Auxiliadora), disco, rec. *Descretu's*, Venâncio Aires 59, gay disco, shows at 0230. *Gaúchos* congregate at late-night bars. Most popular in 1996 were: *Amsterdam*, Av Nilo Peçulha 1690 (3 Figueras), 1900-0200, closed Sun, sophisticated; *Best Bier*, Av C Colombo 3000, esq R Germano Petersen Júnior (Higienópolis), Mon-Fri 1800-0100, weekends 2000-0200, mixed crowd, live music, choice of ambiences; *Barong*, R Mostadeiro 517, T 222-1663, Balinese style, Indian snack food, varied music, closed Sun.

● **Language courses**

Portuguese and Spanish, Matilde Dias, R Pedro Chaves Barcelos 37, apto 104, T 31-8235. US$10 for 90 mins, rec.

● **Post & telecommunications**

Post: R Siqueria Campos 1100, Centro, Mon-Fri 0800-1700, Sat 0800-1200. *UPS*: T 43-4972/42-4602 (Alvaro).

Telecommunications: Embratel, R Siqueira de Campos 1245. T 41233.

● **Shopping**

H Stern jewellers at Shopping Center Iguatemi and international airport. The Praia de Bello shopping centre, claimed to be the largest in Latin America, is a US$1.50 taxi ride from town. There is a street market (leather goods, basketware, etc) in the streets around the central Post Office. Good leather goods sold on the streets. Sun am handicraft and bric-a-brac market (plus sideshows) Av José Bonefácio (next to Parque Farroupilha). Very good food market.

Bookshops: *Livraria Kosmos*, R dos Andradas 1644 (international stock); *Livraria Lima*, Borges de Medeiros 539; *Papyrus*, R dos Andrades e Caldos Jnr, cheap English books; *Livraria Globo*, Andradas 1416; airport bookshop. *Livres e Artes* bookstall in book market, Praça Senador Florêncio, English books. Brasil-America Cultural Centre has free English library, next door used books are sold and exchanged.

● **Sports**

Jockey Club holds races on Sat and Sun. British Club, Av Carlos Gomes 534 (Montserrat). Weights and aerobics at *Academia do Parção*, 24 de Outubro 684.

Golf: Porto Alegre Country Club, Av Líbero Badaró, 18 holes, closed to non-members. Several 9-hole courses in nearby towns.

Swimming: from the beaches nr or in the city is forbidden because of pollution. See **Beaches**, below.

● **Tour companies & travel agents**

Mercatur, Av Salgado Filho, 97, T 225 8055. Several tour companies offer trips to Foz do Iguaçu and Ciudad del Este, overnight journey each way (12 hrs in Paraguay). 3-day trips with 1 night's hotel accommodation, US$56 including sightseeing (time at the falls may be limited). See Turismo section in 'Zero Hora' classifieds (Thur, Sat, Sun) for tour companies' ads.

● **Tourist offices**

Epatur, Travessa do Carmo 84 (head office), 0830-1800, maps and literature, helpful. **Setur**: Salgado Filho airport, friendly; interstate bus station, very helpful (free city maps). **CRTur** (Companhia Riograndense de Turismo), R dos Andradas 1137, 6th floor. A monthly booklet is available. City bus tour US$6, regional tour US$18, Spanish or Portuguese only. Enjoyable boat tours (daytime or evening) on the *Cisne Branco* and *Noiva do Caí*, information from hotels. **Touring Clube do Brasil**, Av João Pessoa 623.

● **Transport**

Local First-class minibuses (*Lotação*), painted in a distinctive orange, blue and white pattern, stop on request. Safer and pleasanter than normal buses, fare about US$1. There is also a

metrô service, the Trensurb, from the southern terminal at the Mercado Modelo (station beside the market) going as far N as Canoas. The second station serves the rodoviária and the fifth the airport (10 mins), 0500-2300, single journey US$0.30.

Air There is a large modern international airport, Salgado Filho, 8 km from the city, connected to the centre by train (see above). There are daily flights to Rio, São Paulo, Curitiba, Buenos Aires and Montevideo, and many other Brazilian cities. The airport is served by all Brazilian airlines, Pluna and Aerolíneas Argentinas.

Buses The busy terminal on Av Mauá with Garibáldi has good facilities, inc a post office and long-distance telephone service until 2100. A regular bus runs from the rodoviária to the airport, also the Trensurb metrô service (see above), just outside. There are 2 sections to the terminal; the ticket offices for interstate/ international destinations are adjacent to the regional ticket office. Regional ticket widows are very busy – ask for travel information at the very helpful booth on the station concourse. To **Rio**, US$50 (*leito* 113), 24 hrs; **São Paulo**, US$37 (*executivo* 45, *leito* 82), 18 hrs; **Brasília**, US$69, 33hrs; **Uruguaiana**, US$17, 8 hrs; **Florianópolis**, US$10.50, 7 hrs with Viação São Cristóvão (beware of overbooking and of stopping buses – eg Santo Anjo – on this route); **Curitiba**, US$31, 11 hrs; **Rio Grande**, US$11.50, 8/day, 0600 to 2000, 4½ hrs. **Foz do Iguaçu**, US$24, 15 hrs. Very many other destinations. To **Cascavel** (Paraná) for connections to Campo Grande, Cuiabá and Porto Velho: daily except Sat with Aguia Branca, 21 hrs, or Unesul, 19 hrs. To **Jaguarão** on Uruguayan border at 2400, 6 hrs, US$10.50.

International buses: to **Montevideo**, with TTL (daily 1700 and 2000, US$38, US$60 *leito*; see page 478), alternatively take bus to border town of Chuí at 1200 daily, 7½ hrs, US$13.25, then bus to Montevideo (US$11-12, cheaper bought in Porto Alegre or Chuí than in Uruguay). *Leito* to **Punta del Este** (Uruguay), departs Fri 2100, arriving Sat 0700, US$70. Ouro e Prata operates a 2-3 times weekly service to Salto and Paysandú (Uruguay), via Santana do Livramento/Rivera. To **Asunción** with Unesul at 1900, Tues, Fri, US$44 *executivo*, 18hrs via Foz do Iguaçu. **Santiago** US$90, 0800 Mon. There are bus services to **Buenos Aires**, US$53, 19 hrs (depending on border) with Pluma, 1700 daily (*leito* US$90, 1715 Mon), route is Uruguaiana, Paso de los Libres, Entre Ríos and Zárate. For Misiones (Argentina), take 2100 bus (not Sat) for Porto Xavier on Río Uruguay, 11 hrs, US$20, get exit stamp at police station, take a boat across to San Javier, US$2, go to Argentine immigration at the port, then take a bus to Posadas (may

have to change in LN Além). **NB** Take your passport when purchasing international bus tickets.

ROUTES Good roads radiate from Porto Alegre, and Highway BR-116 is paved to Curitiba (746 km). To the S it is paved (though some stretches are in poor condition), to Chuí on the Uruguayan frontier, 512 km. In summer visibility can be very poor at night due to mist, unfenced cows are a further hazard. The paved coastal road to Curitiba via Itajaí (BR-101), of which the first 100 km is a 4-lane highway, is much better than the BR-116 via Caxias and Lajes. The road to Uruguaiana is entirely paved but bumpy.

BEACHES

The main beach resorts of the area are to the E and N of the city. On the road N, 112 km from Porto Alegre, is **Osório** (*Pop* 36,775) a pleasant town near sea and lakes, with, **E** *Big Hotel*, good.

TRAMANDAÍ AND TORRES

The towns of **Tramandaí** (126 km, *Pop* 20,070) and **Torres** (209 km, *Pop* 37,505) have the most popular beaches, with lots of luxury and other hotels, motels, bars, restaurants, and other standard seaside amenities. To celebrate independence in 1836, a cavalcade of horses reaches Torres on 16 Sept from Uruguay. Hotels tend to be very full during the summer season.

Between the two towns are the resorts (heading S to N) of **Atlântida** (*Hotel Azul*), **Capão da Canoa** (*Hotel Kolman*, R Sepé 1827, T 665-2021, and others), **Arroio Teixeira** (Camping Clube do Brasil) and **Arroio do Sal** (**D** *Hotel D'Itália*, Av Assis Brasil 11, T 09, on beach, highly rec; *Casa da Sogra*, good food).

● **Accommodation At Tramandaí**: **C** *São Jorge*, F Amaral 19, T 661-1154, quiet, clean, bath, rec. Many more. **At Torres**: many, inc **A1** *Dunas da Praia*, on beach, T 664-1011, F 664-2080; **A3** *A Furninha*, R Joaquim Porto 281, good service, T 664-1655, F 664-1437; **B** *Grande Hotel Torres*, R Júlio de Castilhos 124, T 664-1887, with bath, balcony and breakfast; **C** *Central*, Borges de Medeiros 296, T 664-2580, clean and friendly; **C** *Salth*, Borges de Medeiros 209, T 664-1881, with bath, friendly, clean, Dec-Feb; **C** *Pousada Brisa do Mar*, R

Julio de Castilhos, T 664 2019, good breakfast, rec; **C Oceano Hotel**, Av Barão do Rio Branco 400, T 664 1154, rec; **E São Domingo Youth Hostel** in a school building, Júlio de Castilhos 875, T 664-1865, clean. **Camping**: there are fully equipped campsites at both towns, and camping is also allowed on some beaches.

● **Places to eat** Bom Gosto, Rio Branco 242, churrascaria; **Sol Macrobiótico**, J Castilhos 746, good cheap vegetarian with a cosy, personal atmosphere.

● **Banks & money changers**
In Torres, **Banco do Brasil** and at Rodoviária.

ROUTES There is a paved road from Torres and Tramandaí (mostly prohibited to trucks) along the coast to Quintão, giving access to many beaches. A track continues to Mostardas, thence along the peninsula on the seaward side of the Lagoa dos Patos to São José do Nte, opposite Rio Grande. There is accommodation in **Palmares do Sul** (across the peninsula from Quintão) and Mostardas. South of Mostardas is **Tavares** on the **Lagoa do Peixe**, a national park, which is a resting place for migrating birds (details from Praça Luís Martins 30, Mostardas, CEP 96270-000, T 051-673-1464). The road to the park is called the Estrada do Inferno. In Tavares, the red house on the Praça is a hotel, no sign, rec; several buses a week Tavares – São José do Nte (130 km) and several daily to Porto Alegre. To reach Florianópolis, take a bus from Torres to Araranguá and change.

SÃO LOURENÇO DO SUL

Another popular beach area is S of Porto Alegre, around Cassino, near Rio Grande (see page 476). 40 km to the S (towards Rio Grande) begins the Costa Doce of the Lagoa dos Patos; noted bathing points are Tapes, Barra do Ribeiro, Arambaré, **São Lourenço do Sul** and Laranjal. São Lourenço is a good place to enjoy the lake, the beaches, fish restaurants and watersports. The town hosts a popular festival in March, a 4-day extravaganza of local and latin music, with lots of night-time activity.

● **Accommodation** At São Lourenço do Sul is **Hotel Vilela**, R Almte Abreu 428, family hotel, clean, friendly. Good **camping** facilities nearby, at Reponte by the beach.

THE SERRA GAÚCHA

Inland is the pleasant Serra Gaúcha, the

most beautiful scenery being around the towns of **Canela**, about 130 km from Porto Alegre. There is a distinctly Bavarian flavour to many of the buildings in both towns. In spring and summer the flowers are a delight, and in winter there are frequently snow showers. This is excellent walking and climbing country among hills, woods, lakes and waterfalls. There are many excellent hotels at all prices in both towns, but it is difficult to get rooms in the summer. Local crafts include knitted woollens, leather, wickerwork, and chocolate.

GRAMADO

(Pop 22,045) The town has two fine parks, Parque Knorr and Lago Negro, and Minimundo, a collection of miniature models. The town is decorated and, on Sat, about 1 week before 24 Dec there is outdoor Christmas music; book hotels in good time as the town is crowded.

● **Accommodation** **L3** Serra Azul, R Garibáldi 152, T 286-1082, F 286-3374; **L3** Serrano, Costa e Silva 1112, T 286-1332; **A1** Hortensias, R Bela Vista 83, T 286-1057; **A1** Ritta Höppner, R Pedro Candiago 305, T 054-286-1334, in cabins, very good value, friendly, good breakfasts, German owners, cabins have TV, fridge, pool and miniature trains in grounds; **A2** Pequeno Bosque, R Piratini 486, T 286-1527, with bath, fridge, TV, good breakfast, located in wood close to Véu da Noiva waterfall; **A3** Pousada Zermatt, A Acorsi e R da Fé, T 286-2426, rec; **B** Luiz, Senador Salgado Filho 432, T 286-1026, good breakfast, clean; **B** Parque, Leopoldo Rosenfeldt 818, T 286-1326, bungalows, good breakfast, friendly, maid will do laundry reasonably; **C** Dinda, R Augusto Zatti 160, T 286-1588, one of the cheapest; Planalto, Borges de Medeiros 2001, T 286-1210, opp rodoviária, clean and friendly; a private house in this street, No 1635, rents rooms, rec.

● **Places to eat** Saint Hubertus, R da Carriere 974; Nápoli, Av Borges de Medeiros 2515, good Italian; Lancheira, R Garibáldi 321, cheap and good. Coffee shop, Tia Nilda, das Hortênsias 765. Pyp yoghurt factory, Av S Diniz 1030, has snack bar serving health food sandwiches and yoghurt. The local speciality is café colonial, a 5 o'clock meal of various dishes, inc meats, rec at Café da Torre, das Hortênsias 2174. Visitors should also sample hot pinhões (nuts from the Paraná pine) and quentão (hot red wine, cachaça, ginger, cloves, sugar and cinnamon, often topped with *gemada* – beaten egg yolks and sugar).

● **Banks & money changers** Banco do Brasil, R Garibáldi esq Madre Verónica, Gramado.

● **Tourist offices** Corner of Borges de Medeiros and Col Diniz, Gramado (2 blocks from Rodoviária, no English spoken) and on main square in Canela, good maps and hotel lists.

● **Transport** Frequent bus service to Canela, 10 mins.

CANELA

(*Pop* 24,375; *DDD* 054) 6 km from Canela is the **Parque Estadual do Caracol**; a well-marked nature trail leads to the foot of the falls, which are 130m high (allow $1\frac{1}{2}$ hrs of daylight), and to smaller falls above Caracol. From the high point at Ferradura, 7 km from the park, there is a good view into the canyon of the Rio Cai. Good views also from Moro Pelado, follow signs from behind the town (nice walk through forest).

● **Accommodation** L2 *Laje de Pedra*, Av Pres Kennedy Km 3, T 282-1530, F 282-1532, all amenities; **A1** *Vila Suzana Parque*, Theoboldo Fleck 15, T 282-2020, chalets, heated pool attractive; **C** *Bela Vista*, R Oswaldo Aranha 160, T 282-1327, nr rodoviária, clean, good breakfasts; **C** *Canela*, Av Osvaldo Aranha 223, T 282 2774, breakfast, English speaking staff, rec; *CNEC*, youth hostel, R Melvin Jones 151, T 282-1134; **D** *Central*, Av Júlio de Castilhos 146, clean, safe, rec; **D** pp *Pousada do Viajante*, R Ernesto Urbani 132, clean, kitchen facilities, friendly, rec, T 282-2017. **Camping**: *Camping Clube do Brasil*, 1 km from waterfall in Parque do Caracol, 1 km off main road, signposted (6 km from Canela); excellent honey and chocolate for sale here, highly rec. *Sesi*, camping or cabins, $2\frac{1}{2}$ km outside Canela, T (054) 282-1311/1697, clean, restaurant, rec.

● **Electric current** 220 volts AC.

● **Transport** Several buses daily Canela-Caxias do Sul, 2 hrs, US$3. From Florianópolis, you have to go via Porto Alegre.

PARQUE NACIONAL DE APARADOS DA SERRA

80 km from São Francisco de Paula (38 km E of Canela, 117 km N of Porto Alegre) is the **Parque Nacional de Aparados da Serra**, where the major attraction is the 7.8-km canyon, known locally as the Itaimbezinho (check in advance if open –

Ibama, R Miguel Teixeira 126, Cidade Baixa, Caixa Postal 280, Porto Alegre, CEP 90050-250, T 225-2144). Here, two waterfalls cascade 350m into a stone circle at the bottom. There is a free campsite and a restaurant, which has a few rooms, in the park. From the restaurant one can walk to the canyon of Malacara. For experienced hikers (and with a guide) there is a difficult path to the bottom of Itaimbezinho. One can then hike 20 km to Praia Grande in Santa Catarina (see page 479). As well as the canyon, the park and surrounding region have several bird specialities (eg speckle-breasted Antpitta, Black-and-White Monjita, Hellmayr's Pipit, Giant Snipe, Straight-billed Reed haunter, and others). Red-legged Seriema, a large conspicuous bird, can be seen on the way to the park, and there are two fox species.

● **Access & accommodation** Tourist excursions, mostly at weekends, from **São Francisco de Paula** (hotel: **A1** *Veraneio Hampal*, RS-235 road to Canela, Km 73, T 644-1363). At other times, take a bus to Cambara, get off at the crossroads, from where it is 15 km to the park – walk or hitchhike if you're lucky. *Pousadas* in Cambará: **C** *Mirão*, R Benjamin Constant, breakfast, rooms and apartments, rec; **D** *Fortaleza*, with bath; **F** *São Jorge*.

NOVA PETRÓPOLIS

24 km W of Gramado (bus US$0.65) is another city (*Pop* 16,715) with strong German roots. Nova Petrópolis has a Parque do Imigrante, an open-air museum of German settlement. North of Nova Petrópolis is **Jammerthal**, a valley in the Serra Gaúcha with German farms, many of whose inhabitants still speak German (go to Joanette and walk from there).

● **Accommodation** Nova Petrópolis hotels inc *Recanto Suiço*, Av 15 de Novembro 2195, T 281-1229, on Parque dos Imigrantes, 3-star; *Petrópolis*, R Steglich 81, T/F 281-1091; *Veraneio Schoeller*, RS-235, Km 8.5, T 281-1778, 1-star; youth hostel *Bom Pastor*, at Km 14, Linha Brasil RS 235, T 281 1195 ext 14.

CAXIAS DO SUL

(*Pop* 290,970; *CEP* 95100; *DDD* 054) 122 km from Porto Alegre is the centre of the Brazilian wine industry. Caxias' population is principally of Italian descent, and it is an expanding and modern city. Vines were first brought to the region in 1840 but not until the end of the century and Italian immigration did the industry develop.

Places of interest

The church of **São Pelegrino** has paintings by Aldo Locatelli and 5m-high bronze doors sculptured by Augusto Murer. Good **municipal museum** at R Visconde de Pelotas 586 (open Tues-Sat, 0800-1200, 1400-1800), with displays of artefacts of the Italian immigration. Jan-Feb is the best time to visit.

Excursions

Caxias do Sul's festival of grapes is held in Feb-March. Many *adegas* accept visitors (but do not always give free tasting). Good tour and tasting (6 wines) at *Adega Granja União*, R Os 18 de Forte 2346. Visit also the neighbouring towns of **Farroupilha**, **Bento Gonçalves** and **Garibáldi** (*Pop* 25,900); dry ski slope and toboggan slope – equipment hire, US$2.50/hr. A good *adega*, with free tasting, is *Cooperativa Viti Vinícola Emboaba Ltda*, in Nova Milano (bus to Farroupilha, then change – day trip).

A restored steam train leaves Bento Gonçalves Sat at 1400 for Carlos Barbosa; called 'a rota do vinho' (the wine run), it goes through vineyards in the hills. US$10 round trip; reserve in advance through *Giodani Turismo*, R Emy H Dreher 197, T 451-2788.

Local information

● **Accommodation**
Caxias do Sul: **L3** *Alfred Palace*, R Sinimbu 2302, T/F 221-8655; **L3** *Samuara*, 10 km out on RS-122, road to Farroupilha, T 227-2222, F 227-1010.

A1 *Alfred*, R Sinimbu 2266, T 221-8655; **A1** *Cosmos*, 20 de Setembro 1563, T/F 221-4688; **A1** *Volpiano*, Ernesto Alves 1462, T 221-4744, F 221-4445; **A3** *Itália*, Av Júlio de Castilhos 3076, T/F 225-1177.

B *Real*, R Marquês de Herval 606, T 221-4400, F 221-2911.

D *Bandeira*, R Sinambu 2435, with TV and bath; **D** *Peccini*, R Pinheiro Machado 1939, shared bath, good breakfast; **D** *Pérola*, corner Ernesto Alves and Marquês de Herval (No 237), clean, good value. Hotels fill up early pm.

At Farroupilha: *Don Francesco*, R Dr J Rossler 88, T 261-1132, 2-star.

At Bento Gonçalves: **B** *Dall'Onder*, R Emy Hugo Dreher 197, T/F (054) 451-3555; **C** *Vinocap*, R Barão do Rio Branco 245, T 452-1566.

At Garibáldi: **A3** *Pietá*, João Pessoa 1728, T 262-1283.

Camping: *Palermo*, 5 km out on BR-116 at Km 118, T 222-7255. At Garibáldi, Camping Clube do Brasil, estrada Gen Buarque de Macedo Km 4.

● **Places to eat**
Good restaurants inc *Cantina Pão e Vino*, R Ludovico Cavinato 1757, Bairro Santa Catarina, Caxias, good value; *Dom Rafael*, Praça Rui Barbosa, good value.

● **Tourist offices**
Kiosk in Praça Rui Barbosa.

SOUTH OF PORTO ALEGRE

PELOTAS

(*Pop* 289,495; *CEP* 96100; *DDD* 0532) On the BR-116, 266 km S of Porto Alegre, 56 km N of Rio Grande, **Pelotas** is the second largest city in the State of Rio Grande do Sul, on the left bank of the Rio São Gonçalo which connects the Lagoa dos Patos with the Lagoa Mirim. Its proximity to Rio Grande has hindered the development of its own port. Pelotas is prosperous, with an array of shops and pleasant parks. Like Rio Grande, it is rather damp.

Within a radius of 60 km, say an hour's drive, there are numerous excursions into the hilly countryside. Simple and clean accommodation and cheap, good and plentiful food can be found on the farms of settlers of German descent. 5 km from Taím there is an ecological station with a small museum of regional animals; some accommodation for interested visitors.

● **Accommodation** **B** *Estoril*, R Gen Osório 718, T 25-2411, a/c, reasonable. **B** *Rex*, Praça Pedro Osório 205, T 22-1163, friendly, dowdy.

D *Grande*, Praça Pedro Osório 51, T 25-8139/6659, 'wonderful colonial hotel', some rooms with electric shower.

Camping: Municipal camp site on coast N of town, take bus Z3 from centre, superb site, fresh fish in village 2 km away.

● **Banks & money changers** Banco do Brasil will change TCs. It is difficult to change money at weekends.

● **Transport Air** One plane a day Mon-Fri to Porto Alegre and Rio Grande. **Buses** Rodoviária is far out of town, with bus every 15 mins to centre. Frequent daily buses to **Porto Alegre**, 244 km (US$8.50, 3-4 hrs, paved road); **Rio Grande**, 90 mins (paved but in poor condition) buses stop at Praça 20 de Setembro; **Jaguarão**, on frontier with Río Branco, Uruguay (police post for passport checks 3 km before the Maná bridge, customs at the bridge), paved; and inland to **Bagé** and other towns. The road to the Uruguayan frontier at **Chuí** (paved), has international bus service, but only a couple of daily buses Pelotas-Chuí. TTL bus services (Montevideo-Porto Alegre) stop at the bus station for Montevideo, US$30-46 (RR Chile and Venezuela); tickets must be purchased from agency during day. Bus service to Buenos Aires via Uruguaiana. From Bagé, where there is a police post, the Uruguayan company Núñez runs buses 3 times a week to Melo, via Aceguá. Good direct road NW to Iguaçu via **São Sepe** (C *Trevo Parque Hotel*, a/c, very friendly), Santa Maria (see page 477) and São Miguel mission ruins (see below).

RIO GRANDE

(*Pop* 172,435; *CEP* 962000; *DDD* 0532) At the entrance to the Lagoa dos Patos, 274 km S of Porto Alegre, **Rio Grande** was founded in 1737. The city lies on a low, sandy peninsula 16 km from the Atlantic Ocean. Today it is the distribution centre for the southern part of Rio Grande do Sul, with significant cattle and meat industries.

During the latter half of the 19th century Rio Grande was an important centre, but today it is a rather poor town, notable for the charm of its old buildings. (**Museu Oceanográfico**, US$0.50, 0900-1100, 1400-1700 daily, interesting, 2 km from centre; bus 59 or walk along waterfront.) At Praça Tamandaré is a small zoo.

Excursions

To **Cassino**, a popular seaside town on the Atlantic Ocean, 24 km, over a good road.

The breakwater (the Barra), 5 km S of Cassino, no bus connection, through which all vessels entering and leaving Rio Grande must pass, is a tourist attraction. Barra-Rio Grande buses, from E side of Praça Ferreira pass the Superporto. Very good fishing. The coastline is low and straight, lacking the bays to the N of Porto Alegre; unfortunately the beach is used as a roadway. One attraction is railway flat-cars powered by sail, settle the price in advance; the railway was built for the construction of the breakwater.

Local information
● **Accommodation**
A1 *Charrua*, R Duque de Caxias 55, T 32-8033, rec, good value.

B *Europa*, R Gen Neto 165, main square, T 32-8133.

D *Paris*, R Marechal Floriano 112, T 32-8944, old, charming; **D** *Ritter*, Silva Paes 373.

At Cassino: **B** *Atlântico*, Av Rio Grande, 387, T 36-1350, clean, special rates for students; **B** *Marysol*, Av Atlântica 900, T 36-1240, near beach, friendly. Private campsite on Av 33, on the way out to Rio Grande. Camping Clube do Brasil site nr town.

● **Places to eat**
Recanto Doce, Silva Paes 370, cheap, friendly; *China Brasil*, R Luís Loréa 389, good but not cheap; *Pescal*, Mal Andréa 389, for fish, fairly expensive; *Caumo's*, Dr Nascimento 389, good churrascaria; *Jensen*, Al Abreu 650, nr rodoviária, good and cheap; *Bar Brejeiro*, Andrades 193, jazz upstairs; *Tia Laura*, 29 km from town on BR-392 N to Pelotas, excellent, specializes in home cooking and café *colonial*.

● **Embassies & consulates**
British, R Francisco Marques 163, Caixa Postal 455, Centro, 96-200 Rio Grande, T 32-7788. **Danish**, R Mal Floriano 122, CP 92-96000, T 532-32-4422, open 0800-1200, 1330-1800.

● **Post & telecommunications**
Telecommunications: Embratel, R Andrade Neves 94.

● **Tourist offices**
R Riachuelo, on the waterfront, behind the Câmera de Comércio and beneath the Hidroviária; good map and information.

● **Transport**
Buses Frequent daily buses to and from **Pelotas** (56 km), **Bagé** (280 km), **Santa Vitória** (220 km), and **Porto Alegre** (US$11.50, 4½ hrs). To **Itajaí**, 14 hrs, US$24. All buses to these destinations go through Pelotas. Road to Uruguayan border at **Chuí** is paved, but the surface is poor (5 hrs by bus, at 0700 and 1430, US$7.75). Bus tickets to Punta del Este or Montevideo at *Bentica Turismo*, Av Silva Paes 373, T 32-1321/32-1807.

Sea Boat trip across mouth of Lagoa dos Patos, to pleasant village of São José do Nte, US$0.30, every hour from Porto Velho.

TUBARÃO AND THE SOUTH OF THE STATE

Just across the border from Rio Grande do Sul (but not on the main highway – BR101) is **Praia Grande** (hotel, E, and churrascaria, just off praça, good and cheap). Buses from Praia Grande go to **Araranguá** (*Pop* 48,220), on the BR101, 13 km from which is the beautiful beach of **Arroio do Silva**.

● **Accommodation** D *Hotel Scaini Palace*, T/F 22-1466, good food, clean, rec; *Hotel Paulista*, R Dionizio Mondardo No 58, T/F 26-1244. *Bar Nabar*, Av Getulio Vargas 970, T 526 1290, cheap drinks, English speaking owners, live music, close to beach, rec.

Some 75 km N of Araranguá is the coal-field town of **Tubarão** (*Pop* 95,060). In-land from the main road are the coalfields of Criciúma and Içara, all interesting, and the nearby beaches are good.

Termas do Gravatal can be visited from Tubarão (There is one first class hotel, and two others: **E** *Petit Village*, a/c, mineral pool, good value, quiet, good food.)

About 60 km inland from Tubarão is **Orleães**. It has one of the most interesting and least known museums in the area, which has an original water-powered workshop and sawmill, complete with waterwheel. It dates from the original settlers (late 19th century), and is still in working order. To get there one must get off the bus at the junction about 3 km from the town.

SÃO JOAQUIM

Buses from Tubarão go inland to Lauro Müller, then over the Serra do Rio do Rastro (beautiful views of the coast in clear weather) to **Bom Jardim da Serra** which has an apple festival every April. The road continues to **São Joaquim** (*Pop* 22,285; *Alt* 1,360m). The highest town in Southern Brazil, it regularly has snowfalls in winter; a very pleasant town with an excellent climate. From São Joaquim NE over Pericō to Urubici is unpaved. These roads go around the **Parque Nacional de São Joaquim** (33,500 ha) in the Serra Geral. It has canyons containing sub-tropical vegetation, and araucaria forest at higher lev-

els. There is no bus (local Ibama office, T 0482-22-6202, Secretaria de Turismo de São Joaquim, T 0492-33-0258).

● **Accommodation in São Joaquim** *Nevada* (expensive meals) and **D** *Maristela* (good breakfast), both on R Manoel Joaquim Pinto, 213 and 220 respectively (5 mins' walk from Rodoviária). Camping Clube do Brasil site.

● **Transport** Bus to **Florianópolis** 0830 and 2230, 7½ hrs, US$9.50. To **Caxias do Sul**, 4½ hrs, US$7.25.

LAGUNA

386 km NE of Porto Alegre, 15 km from Tubarão, is the small fishing port of **Laguna** (*Pop* 44,825; *DDD* 0486), in southern Santa Catarina. At Laguna is the **Anita Garibáldi Museum**, containing documents, furniture, and the personal effects of the Brazilian wife of the hero who fought in the 1840s for the independence of Rio Grande do Sul and later helped to unify Italy (US$0.10). Laguna's beach, 2 km from the centre, is not very good, but 16 km away (by ferry and road) are beaches and dunes at **Cavo de Santa Marta**. Also from Laguna, take a Lagunatur or Auto Viação São José bus to **Farol** (infrequent, US$0.85). You have to cross the mouth of the Lagoa Santo Antônio by ferry to get to Farol; look out for fishermen aided by dolphins (*botos*). Here is a fishing village with the alleged third oldest lighthouse in the world (Farol Santa Marta) – guided tours available (taxi, US$10, not including ferry toll). It may be possible to bargain with fishermen for a bed.

● **Accommodation** *Hotel Laguna Tourist*, Praia do Gi, 4 km, T 44-0022, F 44-0123, first class; *Hotel Itapirubá*, 4-star with beach and pool, 24 km away, T 44-0294, F 55-1822; **B** *Turismar*, Av Rio Grande do Sul 207, T 44-0024, F 44-0279, view over Mar Grosso beach, TV; several others, medium-priced, **C** *Hotel Farol de Santa Marta*, T 44-0370; **D** *Grande*, opp post office, clean, without breakfast; **E** *Recanto*, close to bus terminal, clean, basic.

● **Transport** Buses to/from Porto Alegre, 5½ hrs, with Santo Anjo Da Guarda; same company goes to Florianópolis, 2 hrs, but you can't buy a ticket before the bus arrives in Laguna – as soon as it comes in, follow the driver to ticket office.

Another 32 km to the N of Laguna is the

port of **Imbituba** (*Pop* 30,975) where there is a carbo-chemical plant, from which air pollution is very bad. Imbituba sends the coal mined in the area between Araranguá and Tubarão in coastal vessels to Rio de Janeiro, where it is railed to the steel mills at Volta Redonda for coking. The rail link between Imbituba and Tubarão is one of the busiest steam services in South America (freight only apart from an occasional tourist steam train on Sun, probably summer only). There are good beaches (particularly those near Garopaba and Araçatuba), and bus services to Porto Alegre.

FLORIANÓPOLIS

124 km N of Laguna is **Florianópolis** (founded in 1726, *Pop* 254,945; *CEP* 88000; *DDD* 0482), capital of the State, on the Ilha de Santa Catarina joined to the mainland by two bridges, one of which is Ponte Hercílio Luz, the longest steel suspension bridge in Brazil (closed in 1994). The newer Colombo Machado Salles bridge has a pedestrian and cycle way beneath the roadway. It is a port of call for coastal shipping, 725 km from Rio de Janeiro and 420 from Santos. The natural beauty of the island, beaches and bays make Florianópolis a popular tourist centre (only Jan and Feb are very crowded and expensive). The southern beaches are usually good for swimming, the E for surfing, be careful of the undertow. It seems a pity that the city's waterfront, scene of a traditional market, has been filled in and reclaimed and that the city is not in general better maintained.

Places of interest

The **Cathedral** on Praça 15 de Novembro has a life-size sculpture in wood of the flight into Egypt, originally from the Austrian Tyrol. **Forts** include the **Santana** (which houses a **Museu de Armas de Polícia Militar**), **São José da Ponta Grossa** (at the N end of the island) and **Nossa Senhora da Conceição** (at the S end). There are three other museums, the **Museu Histórico** in the old Palácio Cruz e Souza, on Praça 15 de Novembro (1000-2000, Tues-Fri, 1000-1800 Sat-Sun), the **Museu de Antropologia** at the Federal University (0900-1700 Mon-Fri 1300-1800 Sat-Sun) and the **Museu do Homem Sambaqui** at the Colégio Catarinense, R Esteves Júnior 159 (open 0800-1100, 1400-1700, Mon-Sat). There is a look-out point at **Morro da Cruz** (take Empresa Trindadense bus, waits 15 mins). Carnival is recommended as beautiful.

Excursions

Excursions can be made on the mainland to the hot springs at **Caldas da Imperatriz** (41°C) and **Águas Mornas** (39°C); at the former are two spa hotels (**B** *Caldas da Imperatriz*, including meals and baths, built in 1850 under the auspices of Empress Teresa Cristina, houses public baths; from **A3** *Plaza Caldas da Imperatriz*, with baths, swimming pools, very well appointed), at Águas Mornas, the **A1** *Palace Hotel* is on the site of the springs, baths open to public Mon-Fri am only. Boat trips can be made from Florianópolis in the bay, T 22-1806, from US$4.50.

See below for a description of the island.

Local information

NB All Florianópolis phone numbers are being changed from 6 to 7 digits. We give new ones where available.

● **Accommodation**

L3 *Florianópolis Palace*, R Artista Bittencourt e R dos Ilhéus 26, T 22-9633, F 23-0300, best, a/c, clean, TV, rec.

A1 *Ivoram*, Av Hercílio Luz 652, T 24-5388, F 24-5890, discount in off season; **A3** *Royal*, Trav João Pinto 34, T 22-2944, F 22-2537, good.

C *Veleiro*, R Silva Jardim 234, T 23-6622, with breakfast, a/c and TV, rec, clean, friendly, pier for yachts, 10 mins from bus station, take Cidade Universitária bus.

Within 10 mins' walk of the rodoviária: **A3** *Querência Palace*, R Jerônimo Coelho 95, T 24-2677, F 22-3874, highly rec; **A3** *Diplomata Hotel*, T 23 4455, F 22 7082, Av Paulo Fontes 1210, very good views, rec; R Felipe Schmidt, **A1** *Faial*, No 603, T 23-2766, F 22-9435, good restaurant; **D** *Cacique*, No 53, good, clean, good value but rooms vary; **B** *Baia Sul*, R Tiradentes 167, T 223-2269, F 224-0810, nr Praça 15 de Novembro, TV, bath, a/c, safe, inc breakfast, rec; **B** *Felippe*, 1 block from 15 de Novembro at R João Pinto 25, good, clean, friendly, small rooms, 10% off to Youth Hostel members.

On the mainland: **B** *Bruggeman*, R Santos

D *Pousada-Lanchonete Sem Nome*, Praia do Moçambique, in 4-bunk rooms, bathrooms separate, kitchen, laundry, rec; **E** *Albergue do Mar*, basic, friendly, good for lone travellers; *Pousada Sol Mar* operates as a youth hostel but only 2 bathrooms for all; **E** *Hotel Camping Duvalerim*, on beach, overpriced; *Camping da Barra*, T 32-3199, beautiful site, clean, helpful

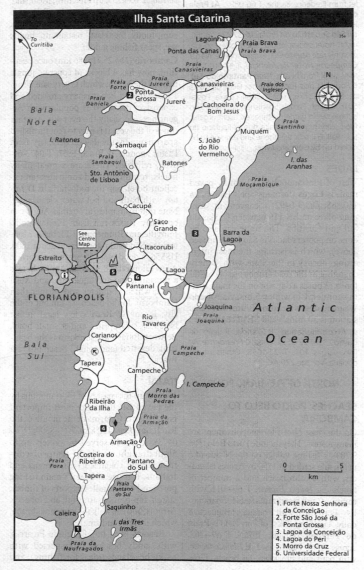

Ilha Santa Catarina

1. Forte Nossa Senhora da Conceição
2. Forte São José da Ponta Grossa
3. Lagoa da Conceição
4. Lagoa do Peri
5. Morro da Cruz
6. Universidade Federal

owner. **At Joaquina**: **A1** *Hotel Cris*, T 32-0380, F 32-0075, luxurious, rec). **At Ponta das Canas**: B *Hotel Moçambique*, T/F 66-1857, in centre of village, noisy at weekends; houses to let from Frederico Barthe, T 66-0897. **At Praia dos Ingleses**: B *Sol e Mar*, T 62-1271, excellent, friendly, rec. **At Praia de Campeche**: *Hotel São Sebastião da Praia*, T/F 37 4247/4066, resort hotel on s splendid beach, offers special monthly rate April to Oct, excellent value; *Natur Campeche Hotel Residencial*, T 37-4011, 10 mins walk from beach. **Near Pantano do Sul**: B *Pousada dos Tucanos*, Estra Geral da Costa de Dentro 2776, T 237-5084, Caixa Postal 5016, English, French, Spanish spoken, spacious bungalows in garden setting, excellent organic food, very highly rec; take bus to Pantano do Sul, walk 6 km or telephone and arrange to be picked up by German owner.

LAGES

West of Florianópolis, 212 km by paved road, is **Lages** (formerly spelt Lajes; *Pop* 150,865; *DDD* 0492) a convenient stopping place on BR-116 between Caxias do Sul and Curitiba. The route can also be done on poorer roads via São Joaquim (see above), which is perhaps the most interesting journey in the State, with scenery changing as the road climbs out of coastal forest (3 buses a day run on the main road in summer, 1 in winter, 5 hrs, via Alfredo Wagner, otherwise go via Blumenau). Bus station is 30 mins' walk SE of centre.

• **Accommodation** B *Grande*, R João de Castro 23, T/F 22-3522, good; C *Presidente*, Av Pres Vargas 101, T 22-1058. Others nr rodoviária. Voltage 220 AC.

NORTH OF FLORIANÓPOLIS

BEACHES: PORTO BELO TO CAMBORIÁ

On the coast N of Florianópolis there are many resorts. They include **Porto Belo** (*Pop* 9,700), a fishing village on the N side of a peninsula settled in 1750 by Azores islanders, with a calm beach and a number of hotels (eg *Baleia Branca*, T 69-4011, with camping) and restaurants (bus Florianópolis – Porto Belo with Praiana or Biguaçu, 8 daily, 3 on Sun). West of Port Belo is **Praia de Perequê** (Hotels: E *Tati*, T 69-4363, across from beach, and E *Blumenauense*, with bath and breakfast, on beach, T 69-

4208). Around the peninsula are wilder beaches reached by rough roads: Bombas (2 hotels), Bombinhas (*Pousada do Arvoredo*, T 69-4355, up on a hill), Mcal, and, on the southern side, Cantinho (**B** *Pousada Zimbros*, T 69-4225, less off season, on beach, sumptuous breakfast, restaurant, highly rec, spear fishing guide).

Camboriú (*Pop* 25,715; 86 km) once beautiful, now has 4 blocks of concrete jungle behind the beach, which is very safe. From 15 Dec to end-Feb it is very crowded and expensive; the resort is popular with Argentines, especially the over 40s. At other times of the year it is easy to rent furnished apartments by the day or week (try Bom Pastor agency, Av Brasil 1861, T 0473-66-0769, reliable). There are a great many hotels, restaurants and campsites (an excellent hotel, opp the rodoviária, is **D** *Jaitur*, with bath and hot water, clean, safe). Note that from mid-July to mid-Aug it can be chilly. Buses run from Florianópolis, Joinville and Blumenau. TTL buses Montevideo-São Paulo stop here at about 1800, US$56, a good place to break the journey. A few kilometres S, at Lojas Apple, there is a museum, zoo and aquarium; and Meia Praia, which is quieter and cleaner than Camboriú. Pinho beach, 15 km out of the city, is one of Brazil's few legal nudist beaches; 2 campsites and a small hotel. Between Itajaí and Camboriú is the beautiful, deserted (and rough) beach of Praia Brava.

ITAJAÍ

100 km up the coast N of Florianópolis by the paved BR-101 is the most important port in Santa Catarina at the mouth of the Rio Itajaí (*Pop* 119,585; *CEP* 88300; *DDD* 0473). It is well served by vessels up to 5½m draught, and is the centre of a district largely colonized by Germans and Italians. It is one of Brazil's main fishing ports and also handles exports of timber, starch, tapioca, sassafras oil, and tobacco. Airport. You can walk to Cabeçudas beach, which is quiet and small.

Resorts N of Itajaí include Piçarras, with sandy beaches interspersed with rocky headlands (ideal for fishing), and

Barra Velha (D *Hotel Mirante*, good, cheap restaurant, and 2 dearer hotels).

● **Accommodation** A1 *Marambaia Cabeçudas*, at Cabeçudas beach, best, 6 km out of town, T 44-0999; C *Grande*, R Felipe Schmidt 44, T 44-0968, good value. Recommended bar, *Trudys*, on riverfront at end of main street, a good place for changing cash.

● **Embassies & consulates** Finnish Consulate, R Almte Tamandaré 100, T 44-6511.

BLUMENAU

There is a 61 km paved road to **Blumenau** (*Pop* 211,175; *CEP* 89100; *DDD* 0473), 47 km up the Rio Itajaí. It is in a prosperous district settled mostly by Germans; the city is a notable textile centre. A clean, orderly city with almost caricatured Germanic architecture, Blumenau offers a charming alternative to the less-organized Brazilian way of life. It is very popular with people from São Paulo.

Places of interest

See the **Museo da Família Colonial**, German immigrant museum, Av Duque de Caxias 78, open Mon-Fri, 0800-1130, 1330-1730, Sat am only, US$0.15. **German Evangelical Church**. Also the houses, now **museums** (open 0800-1800) of **Dr Bruno Otto Blumenau** and of **Fritz Müller** (a collaborator of Darwin), who bought the Blumenau estate in 1897 and founded the town.

Excursions

By bus to Timbo and Pomerode (from riverside road opp Prefeitura) past rice fields and wooden houses set in beautiful gardens. At **Pomerode** (*Pop* 18,790) 32 km, US$1 (D *Hotel Central*, big lunches) there is an interesting zoo. Tourist office. The N German dialect of Plattdeutsch is still spoken here. The *Tortenparadies* serves excellent German cakes. Rex Bus goes to Iraguá from Pomerode; change for connection to Joinville, US$3. ½-day excursion to Gaspar to visit the cathedral set high above the river (Verdi Veli bus company from stop outside the huge supermarket on R 7 de Setembro in the centre).

Local festivals

A 'traditional' Oktoberfest beer-festival was started in 1984 here, and was expected to become the second largest in the world after Munich's (bands come from Germany for the event). Visitors report it is worth attending on weekday evenings but weekends are too crowded. It is repeated, but called a 'summer festival', in the 3 weeks preceding Carnival ('5 visitors').

Local information
● **Accommodation**
Reservations essential during Oktoberfest.

L2 *Plaza Hering*, 5-star, 7 de Setembro 818, T 26-1277, F 22-9409, heating and a/c.

A1 *Garden Terrace*, R Padre Jacobs 45, T 26-3544, F 26-0366; **A1** *Garden Convention Center*, Alameda Rio Branco 21, T 26-0145; **A1** *Himmelblau Palace*, R 7 de Setembro 1415, T/F 22-5800; **A3** *Glória*, R 7 de Setembro 954, T 22-1988, F 22-5370, German-run, excellent coffee shop.

C *Blumenau Tourist Hotel*, R Francisco Margarida 67, T 23-4640, 200m from bus station, helpful (all aforementioned hotels have heating in rooms).

D *Central*, R 7 de Setembro 1036, T 22-0570, basic, with bath, E without, both without breakfast, clean; **D** *City*, R Ângelo Dias 263, T 22-2205.

E *Herrmann*, central, Floriano Peixoto 213, T 22-4370, rec, shower, clean. Many cheap hotels do not inc breakfast. Most hotels and restaurants very clean. Youth Hostel at R Paraíba 66 (T 22-8420).

Camping: Municipal campsite, 3 km out on R Pastor Osvaldo Hesse; Paraíso dos Poneis, 9 km out on the Itajaí road, also Motel; Refúgio Gaspar Alto, 12 km out on R da Glória.

● **Places to eat**
Good German food at *Frohsinn*, Morro Aipim (panoramic view) and *Cavalinho Branco*, Av Rio Branco 165, huge meals; international eating at *Moinho do Vale*, Paraguai 66. *Amigo*, Peixoto 213, huge cheap meals; *Caféhaus Glória*, in Hotel Glória, excellent coffee shop. *Deutsches Eck*, R 7 de Setembro 432, rec, esp carne pizzaiola; *Gruta Azul*, Rodolfo Freygang 8, good, popular, not cheap. *Internacional*, Nereu Ramos 61, Chinese, very good, not particularly expensive; *Chinês*, R 15 de Novembro 346, nr Tourist office, good.

● **Banks & money changers**
At *Câmbios*/travel agencies: *Vale do Itajaí Turismo e Cambio*, Av Beira Rio 167, very helpful, German spoken; *Ilhatur Turismo*, Rodolfo Freygang 5, 1st floor. *Tilotur Turismo*, Alameda Rio Branco e 15 de Novembro, 2nd floor; *Casa Rowder*, R Curt Herring 20.

● **Shopping & amenities**
Teatro Carlos Gomes, 15 de Novembro between Kennedy and N Deeke, is also exhibition centre; public library open 0800-1800; German bookshops, *Librerias Alemãs*, at bus station and RR 7 de Setembro (also stocks English books), and 15 de Novembro. Craft shop, *Casa Meyer*, 15 de Novembro 401.

● **Post & telecommunications**
International Telephones: corner of Av Brasil and República Argentina.

● **Voltage**
220 AC.

● **Transport**
Bus to rodoviária from Av Pte Castelo-Branco (Beira Rio). Good bus connections in all directions from Blumenau. Blumenau to **Caxias do Sul** at 1930 only, arrives 0400, US$14.50.

To Iguaçu: as an alternative to a direct bus, daily from Florianópolis and Itajaí to Iguaçu via Blumenau, you can travel through rich and interesting farming country in Santa Catarina and Rio Grande do Sul, stopping at **Joaçaba**, a town of German immigrants (*Pop* 28,145; Hotels *Erexim* (strong *gaúcho* influence; hotels), or **Iraí**, Italian immigrant area, town with thermal springs (*Pop* 11,595; **D** *Hotel São Luís*, R Antônio Siqueira 332, T 345-1324, with full board, town good for semi-precious stones), thence from any of these places to Pato Branco and Cascavel (see page 494 for connections to Foz do Iguaçu).

2 hrs from Joaçaba is **Treze Tílias**, a little village where 19th-century Tyrolean dialect is still spoken and the emigrant culture is perfectly preserved.

SÃO FRANCISCO DO SUL

(*Pop* 29,550) 80 km up the coast, this is the port for the town of Joinville, 45 km inland at the head of the Cachoeira Rio. Most of the colonial architecture has been replaced by modern buildings. There are some excellent beaches nearby, such as Ubatuba, Enseada (hotels, pensions and 3 camp sites, *Pascerella* rec) and Cápri. (At weekend trips to Ilha do Farol in port's supply boat.) Petrobrás oil refinery, but oil pollution has been reported. Take mosquito repellent.

● **Accommodation B** *Kontiki*, Camacho 33, T 44-0232; **B** *Zibamba*, R Fernandes Dias 27, T 44-0077, F 44-0823, central, good restaurant.

● **Places to eat** The *Restaurante Franciscano*, on the Praia dos Coqueiros, is rec, so are the *Metralhas* and *Flutuante* (good seafood.)

● **Transport** Bus terminal is 1½ km from centre. Direct bus (Penha) daily to Curitiba at 0730, US$6, 3½ hrs.

JOINVILLE

(*Pop* 346,095; *CEP* 89200; *DDD* 0474) The state's largest city lies 2 km from the main coastal highway, BR-101, by which Curitiba and Florianópolis are less than 2 hrs away. At Expoville, 4 km from centre on BR-101 (continuation of 15 de Novembro) is an exhibition of Joinville's industry. The industry does not, however, spoil the considerable charm of the city. There is an annual flower festival in the first fortnight of September.

Places of interest

See the **Museu Nacional da Imigração e Colonização** in the Palácio dos Príncipes, R Rio Branco 229 (Tues-Fri 0900-1800, Sat-Sun 0900-1200, 1400-1800), which has a collection of objects from the original German settlement. The interesting **Museu de Arte** is in the old residence of Ottokar Doerfell, R 15 de Novembro 1400 (open Tues-Sun, 0900-1200, 1400-2200). The **Museu Arqueológico do Sambaqui**, R da Francisca 600, has a collection dating back to 5000 BC (open Tues-Fri, 0900-1200, Sat, Sun, and holidays, 0900-1200, 1400-1800; US$0.25). **Museum** of the sculptor **Fritz Alt**, R Aubé (0800-1800, closed Mon).

Excursions

Four daily buses go to **Ubatuba** beach, a weekend resort (see above under São Francisco do Sul). The Sambaqui site of **Rio Comprido** can be reached by Gideon Bus, but there is not much to see. It is a pleasant trip to **Jaraguá do Sul**, European, hilly landscape.

To Guaratuba (see page 492) by bus, 1¼ hrs, US$2 (connections to Paranaguá). The **festival of São João** in June can be seen best in Santa Catarina at **Campo Alegre**, the first town on the road inland to Mafra. There are bonfires, a lot of (German) folk dancing, and large quantities of *quentão* and *pinhões* (see under Gramado, **Places to eat**, above). It is a beautiful climb on the road from the BR-101 to Campo Alegre. The road continues through São Bento and Rio Negrinho to Mafra, from where a good road (the BR-116) goes to Curitiba.

João Negrão e Mal Deodoro.

● **Sports**
Golf: Graciosa Country Club, Av Munhoz da Rocha 1146: 9 holes.

● **Tourist offices**
Guía Turística de Curitiba e Paraná, annual, US$4, on sale at all kiosks, has been rec. **Paranatur** has booths at Rodoferroviária, and at airport, helpful, English spoken, but no maps. Free maps from R Ebano Pereira 187, 5th floor. Free weekly leaflet, *Bom Programa*, available shops, cinemas, paper stands etc.

● **Useful addresses**
Visa extensions: Federal police, Dr Muricy 814, 1000-1600.

● **Tour companies & travel agents**
BMP Turismo Passagens e Servicos Ltd, R Brigadeiro Franco, 1845, T 224 7560.

● **Transport**
Local The city has a very efficient bus system; all bus stops have maps. Express buses on city routes are orange: eg from centre (Praça Rui Barbosa) take Leste bus marked 'Villa Oficinas' or 'Centenário' for Rodoferroviária (combined bus and railway station). A tourist bus, US$3, stops at the Botanic Garden, the Opera, the University and other sites; 4 stops permitted.
Rodoferroviária at end of Av 7 de Setembro (bus to centre US$0.15).

Air An international air terminal is under construction (1995).

Trains Passenger trains to Paranaguá, see below. Also tourist train on first Sun of month to Lapa, 85 km, 3 hrs, tickets from travel agencies or from the railway station at Praça Eufrásio Correa (Railway Museum here is officially closed, but permission may be given to see the steam locomotives).

Buses Short-distance bus services (up to 40 km) begin at old bus station at R João Negrão 340. Frequent buses to São Paulo (6 hrs, US$7.25; *leito* 14.50) and Rio de Janeiro (12 hrs, US$24, *leito* 50). To Foz do Iguaçu, 10 a day, 10 hrs, US$27.50; Porto Alegre, 10 hrs; Florianópolis, 4½ hrs; good service to most destinations in Brazil. Pluma bus to Buenos Aires US$128 and to Asunción US$32. TTL runs to Montevideo, 26 hrs, US$64, 0340 departure (*semi-cama*). If travelling by car to Porto Alegre or Montevideo, the inland road (BR-116) is preferable to the coastal highway (BR-101).

LONGER EXCURSIONS

CARITIBA TO PARANAGUÁ

Popular expeditions during the summer are by paved road or rail (4½ hrs) to Paranaguá. The railway journey is the most **spectacular** in Brazil. There are numerous tunnels with sudden views of deep gorges and high peaks and waterfalls as the train rumbles over dizzy bridges and viaducts. Near Banhado station (Km 66) is the waterfall of Véu da Noiva; from the station at Km 59, the mountain range of **Marumbi** can be reached: see below.

● **Transport** Trains leave Curitiba twice daily during the summer and in July. For the rest of the year, there are return services on Sun only, plus one-way trains to Morretes on Tues and Thur. On Sun the year round ordinary service is at 0730, arriving in Paranaguá at 1030 (US$4 one class, tickets on sale at 0630, except for Sun when the ticket office is closed: buy ticket for weekend as early as possible (Mon); sandwiches, chocolate and drinks for sale on board; the schedule may vary, ask at the station). Avoid the front coach. A modern a/c rail-car (the Litorina, called the automotriz) leaves at 0900, daily in summer, winter Sun, arriving in Paranaguá at 1130 (US$8 each way, reserved seats bookable 2 days in advance; the service varies); recorded commentary (in Portuguese, French, Spanish and English) and stops at the viewpoint at the Santuário da NS do Cadeado and at Morretes (only a few minutes). Sit on the left-hand side on journey from Curitiba. If Litorina is full, take bus to Paranaguá, US$3.50, then take Litorina back: return journeys start at 1500 (Litorina) and 1600 (ordinary train) so remember that in winter part of the ordinary train's journey is covered in the dark (also, on cloudy days there's little to see on the higher parts). The train is usually crowded on Sat and Sun. Many travellers recommend returning by bus (1½ hrs, buy ticket immediately on arrival), if you do not want to stay 4½ hrs. A tour bus meets the train and offers a tour of town and return to Curitiba for US$6.

ANTONINA AND MORRETES

You can also visit **Antonina** (a port, not on main route, *Pop* 17,055) and **Morretes** (on main route, *Pop* 13,130), two sleepy colonial towns which can be reached by bus on the old Graciosa road, which is almost as scenic as the railway. 14 km N of Morretes is the beautiful village of **São João de Graciosa**, 2 km beyond which is a flower reserve. The Graciosa road traverses the **Marumbi** range for 12 km, with 6 rest stops with fire grills, shelters and camping. Marumbi is very beautiful; you can also hike the original trail which follows the road and passes the rest-stops. Take food, water and plenty of insect repellent.

● **Accommodation   At   Morretes:** C *Nhundiaquara*, in town centre, well located but hot and cramped, good restaurant; good restaurants in town (try 'barreado', beef cooked for 24 hrs, especially good in the two restaurants on the river bank, highly rec) and a river beach.

● **Transport** Buses from Paranaguá to Morretes at 1830, US$1.25, to Antonina, stopping en route at Morretes, 6 a day (US$2). 12 buses daily Morretes-Curitiba US$2; 20 buses a day Curitiba-Antonina.

PARANAGUÁ

(*Pop* 107,585; *CEP* 83200; *DDD* 041) Chief port of the state of Paraná and one of the main coffee-exporting ports, **Paranaguá** was founded in 1585, 268 km S of Santos. It is on a lagoon 29 km from the open sea and is approached via the Baia de Paranaguá, dotted with picturesque islands. Paranaguá is a free port for Paraguay.

Places of interest

The **fort of Nossa Senhora dos Prazeres** was built in 1767 on a nearby island; 1-hr's boat trip. The former Colêgio dos Jesuitas, a fine baroque building, has been converted into a **Museu de Arqueológia e Artes Populares** (Tues-Sun 1200-1700; entrance US$1). Other attractions are a 17th century fountain, the church of **São Benedito**, and the shrine of **Nossa Senhora do Rocio**, 2 km from town. There are restaurants and craft shops near the waterfront. The part of town between the waterfront, railway station and new bus station has been declared a historic area.

Excursions

Cruises on Paranaguá Bay by launch, daily from Cais do Mercado.

Matinhos (*Pop* 11,315) is a Mediterranean-type resort, invaded by surfers in Oct for the Paraná surf competition; several cheap hotels, inc *Bolamar* (**E**, basic, cheapest) and *Beira Mar*. Four camp sites in the vicinity. Bus from Paranaguá at 1000, 1400 and 1615, US$1. 8 km S is Caiobá, at the mouth of a bay the other side of which is **Guaratuba** (*Pop* 17,990 less built up than Caiobá). The ferry between the two towns

is frequent, beautiful crossing, free for pedestrians, US$1.50 for cars. Both towns have hotels; also camping at Guaratuba, where restaurant *Sol Nascente*, R Vicente Machado 967, is superb.

Local information

● **Accommodation**

C *Auana*, R Correia de Freitas 110, T 422-6531, good value, rec.

D *Karibe*, F Simas 86, T 422-1177, good value; D *Litoral*, R Correia de Freitas 66, without breakfast, clean and comfortable; **D** *Monte Líbano*, R Júlio da Costa 152, T 422-2933, overpriced.

Camping: *Arco Iris* at Praia de Leste, on the beach, 29 km S of Paranaguá, 30 mins (beach said to be better than Matinhos, see above).

● **Places to eat**

Bobby's, Faria Sobrinho 750, highly rec, esp for seafood. *Danúbio Azul*, 15 de Novembro 91, good, not cheap, view of river, classical piano music; *Aquarius*, Av Gabriel de Lara 40, good but not cheap seafood; there are cheap restaurants in the old market building, and plenty of cheap ones nr the markets on the waterfront; the *Yacht Club*, beyond *Danúbio Azul* is impressive and has a good bar.

● **Banks & money changers**

Banco do Brasil, Largo C Alcindino 27; Câmbio, R Faria Sobrinho, for cash.

● **Tourist offices**

Tourist information kiosk outside railway station.

● **Transport**

All buses operated by Graciosa. To Curitiba, US$3.50, many, 1½ hrs (only the 0745 in either direction and the 1545 to Curitiba take the old Graciosa road); direct to Rio at 1915, 15 hrs, US$38.50.

ILHA DO MEL

On the island, which is an ecological reserve (no cars permitted), well-developed for tourism, there are two beach villages, 5 km apart. From Praia dos Encantados to Nova Brasília there are boats (US$10, or US$2 pp if more than 5), or you can walk on a track (1½-2 hrs) or follow the coast, walking in the sea. From Nova Brasília, a 20-min walk leads to El Farol for good views. Praia dos Encantados is more suitable for swimming than Brasília. The beaches, caves, bays and hill walks are beautiful. 4 hrs' walk from the villages is an old Portuguese fort. In summer and at holiday times the island is very crowded with an active nightlife and are some steps that lead down the steep slope to the river bank. Beautiful walk. It can be misty early in the morning at the Falls. Entry to the Brazilian side of the Falls is US$2, payable only at the National Park entrance. If possible, visit on a weekday when the walks are less crowded.

● **Access**   From Foz do Iguaçu, Dois Irmãos buses (from local bus station – *Terminal Urbana* – on Av Juscelino Kubitschek, opp Infantry Barracks) marked 'Cataratas' run the 32 km to the falls every 2 hrs Sat, Sun, hourly Mon-Fri, past airport and *Hotel das Cataratas*; schedule is usually 0800 to 1800, but sometimes buses start and finish earlier, journey takes 40 mins; those marked 'Parque Nacional' stop at the park entrance, take a 'Cataratas' bus the rest of the way (this works out more expensive). Buses of either route can also be picked up at any of the stops on Av Juscelino Kubitschek, sometimes more convenient than going to the Terminal Urbana. At weekends, holidays and other high seasons, frequency increases to every hour. Buses return 0700-1800. US$1 one way, payable in *reais* only. The driver waits at the Park entrance while passengers purchase entry tickets. (The taxi fare is US$6, plus US$2.50 for each hour of waiting.) The tours of the Falls organized by the various hotels have been recommended in preference to taxi rides.

To the Argentine side: buses between Foz do Iguaçu and Puerto Iguazú (Argentina) run half-hourly from the Terminal Urbana, crossing the frontier bridge; 20 mins' journey, no stops for border formalities (Pluma and Tres Fronteiras companies, tickets interchangeable between the two, US$1.50). There are many advantages in staying in Foz and commuting to the Argentine side (better and cheaper hotels and restaurants, for example). If you decide to stay in Brazil, do not rely on spending *reais* in Argentina; they are accepted, but at very poor rates. It is better to change dollars into pesos for the day, which is easily done at Puerto Iguazú bus station or nearby before taking the bus to the Falls. A poorer rate for pesos is given in Brazil. **NB** Be sure you know when the last bus departs from Puerto Iguazú for Foz (usually 1900) and remember that in summer Argentina is an hour earlier than Brazil. Combined tickets to Puerto Iguazú and the Falls cost more than paying separately; when returning from Puerto Iguazú, ask to be let off in Foz. Taxi Foz-Argentina US$33. Crossing the frontiers in a private vehicle, if only intending to visit the National Park, presents no problems.

● **Frontier crossings**   Be sure to get a stamp on your passport if intending to stay in Brazil, but if going nowhere other than Iguaçu there is no need for citizens of countries requiring visas to have one. There is an entry tax on the Brazilian side for car passengers only, not for bus passengers. If driving into Brazil insist on visiting customs. You must get entry papers for your car here or you'll have serious problems later.

There are Brazilian immigration offices on the Brazilian sides of the bridges into Paraguay and Argentina; if you are just visiting Ciudad del Este or Puerto Iguazú and the Argentine side of the Falls and returning to Brazil the same day, you must take your passport; no need to have it stamped. There are Brazilian customs patrols looking for undeclared goods on the roads past the frontier. Note that if entering or leaving a country and you have to visit customs and immigration, buses won't wait; take a taxi instead.

See under **Transport** below for crossing to Paraguay.

FOZ DO IGUAÇU

(*Pop* 188,190; *CEP* 85890; *DDD* 045) A rapidly developing and improving town, with a wide range of accommodation and good communications by air and road with the main cities of southern Brazil, and with Asunción, Paraguay.

Excursions

From Foz, you can make an excursion to the 12,600-megawatt **Itaipu** dam, the largest single power station in the world, which Brazil and Paraguay have built nearby. The dam is 8 km long. The power house 1½ km. Paraguay does not use all its quota of power so this is sold to Brazil, which powers all of Southern Brazil and much of Rio, São Paulo and Minas Gerais from Itaipu. The Paraguayan side may also be visited from Ciudad del Este. Santa Helena on Lake Itaipu, has an artificial beach and relaxing leisure park, US$2.50.

● **Tours of Itaipu**   Bus marked Canteira da Obra from Terminal Urbana (stand 50 Batalhão) goes every 40 mins to the Public Relations office at the main entrance (US$0.35), Conjunto C-via Nte or via Sul bus goes more frequently to within 250m. Visits are free, but in groups only, a film in Portuguese is shown (half of which is about protecting animals and the environment) and then the dam is visited (one stop for taking photos); ask in reception if you may see turbines. Four tours daily. 300m before Public Relations is the Eco Museum, about the Itaipú dam, free visit with guide, rec (closed Sun). There are also an 'executive' bus and agency tours but these are an unnecessary expense. You get a better view sitting on the right-hand side. If it's sunny, go in the morning as the sun is behind the dam in the afternoon and you will get poor photographs.

Good reports on the **Parque das Aves** bird park, entrance US$8, at Rodovia das Cataratas Km 10.5, just before the falls. To book a guided tour, T 523-1007. Several other excursions, by bus or boat, into the surrounding countryside, enjoyable, book with a reputable company. **Fishing** for dourado and surubi with Simon Williams at Cataratas Iate Club, Av Gen Meira, Km 5, T 523-2073.

Local information
● Security

At bus terminals watch out for pickpockets who pose, with a coat over their arm, as taxi drivers. Taxis are only good value for short distances when you are carrying all your luggage.

● Accommodation

On a height directly overlooking the Falls, 32 km from Foz, is the **L3** *Hotel das Cataratas*, T 523-2266, F 574-1688 (but 15% discount for holders of the Brazil Air Pass) highly rec, an attractive colonial-style building with nice gardens and a swimming pool. Much wildlife can be seen in the grounds at night and early am. It is reported money is exchanged only at the official rate, check before paying. Non-residents can have US$15 meal here (midday and evening buffets, or else wait 45 mins for *à-la-carte* dishes), dinner (churrasco) with show, US$30.

Many out-of-town hotels on the Falls road state their address as km from Foz. On road to Falls (Rodovia das Cataratas) are **L2** *Bourbon*, all facilities, excellent buffet dinner, open to non-residents (US$12), Km 2.5, T 523-1313, F 574-1110; **L3** *Colonial* (Km 16.5), T 574-1777, F 76-1960, nr airport, swimming pool, fine location; **A1** *Carimã* (Km 16), T 523-1818, F 574-3531, 3-star, very good value, a/c, pool, restaurant, bars, rec; **A3** *Panorama* (Km 12), good value, pool, T 23-1200, F 574-1490; many others.

Hotels:
1. *Bogari*
2. *Continental Inn*
3. *Foz do Iguaçu*
4. *Internacional*
5. *Lanville*
6. *Pousada Verde Vale*
7. *Salvatti*

🚉¹ Terminal Urbana
🚉² Rodoviária (off map)

Foz do Iguaçu

To Itaipu, Paraguay

To Curitiba &

Infantry Barracks
Av República Argentina

Rebouças

Xavier da Silva

Av Brasil

Barroso

Floriano Peixoto

Marechal Deodoro

Santos Dumont

Castelo Branco

Patrulheiro Verísati Otemba

Av Paraná

Rui Barbosa

Paraguayan Consulate

Bartolomeu do Gusmão

Paranatur

Jorge Sanways

Av Juscelino Kubitschek

Naipi

Tarob

das Missões

N

Quintino Bocaiúva

Almirante Barroso

Tiradentes

Banco do Brasil

Barão do Rio Branco

Prefeitura

José Bonifácio

Argentine Consulate

Duque de Caxias

Dom Pedro II

Benjamin Constant

Av Brasil

Edmundo Barros

Av Jorge Schimmelpfeng

Belarmino de Mendonça

Antônio Raposo

Padre Montoya

18 de Junho

São Paulo

To Falls

Rio Paraná

0   100
metres

In 1994, many street numbers were changed. Both old numbers (lower) and the new higher ones were still in use. We have altered numbers where known: bear changes in mind when looking for your hotel. If you know which hotel you wish to stay in (there are over 180), note that touts may say it no longer exists, or quote room rates below what is actually charged. There is a scam in which children will escort you to a cheap hotel, receiving commission for doing so. Your luggage is then stolen from the hotel. In high season (eg Christmas-New Year), you will not find a room under US$15.

L2 *Internacional*, Almte Baroso 345, T 523-1414, F 574-5201, good.

A1 *Continental Inn*, Av Paraná 485, T/F 574-4122, good restaurant; **A1** *Salvatti*, R Rio Branco 651, T 523-1121, F 574-3674, all a/c (with restaurant and cinema); **A3** *Foz Presidente*, R Marechal Floriano 1851, T 523-2318, F 574-5155, shower, a/c, overpriced, restaurant, swimming pool, trips arranged to Falls, inc breakfast, convenient for buses, rec; **A2** *Rafahin*, Mal Deodoro 984, T 523-1213, F 523-2007, good restaurant, pool, well spoken of; **A2** *Suiça*, Av Felipe Wandscheer 3580, new, Swiss manager, helpful, pool.

On Av Brasil: **A1** *Bogari Palace*, No 106, T 523-2243, F 523-1125, excellent restaurant, swimming pool; **A3** *Foz do Iguaçu*, No 97, T 574-4455, F 574-1775, good, expensive laundry, will look after luggage; **B** *City*, No 938, T 574-2074, with bath, fan, hot water, clean; **B** *Diplomata*, No 678, T 523-1615, some a/c, with shower, run down, swimming pool, arranges taxi tours to Argentine side; **C** *O Astro*, No 660, T 72-3584, clean, OK, a/c; **C** *Dani Palace*, No 509, comfortable, good buffet breakfast, bath, clean; **C** *Imperial*, No 168, T 574-2422, with bath, clean; **D** *Ortega*, No 1140, T 574 1288, good breakfast.

In R Rebouças: **B** *Pietá*, No 84, T 574-5581, pool, clean, friendly, good breakfast, car and guide, rec; **C** *Minas*, No 641, T 574-5208, clean and basic, hot water, safe, no breakfast; **D** *German Pension*, No 907, friendly, rec; **E** *Trento*, No 665, T 574-5111, a/c and bath, clean, rec; **E** *Pousada Verde* Vale, No 335, T 574-2925, youth hostel style, cramped but popular, buses to Falls stop outside. **D** *Piratini*, No 101, hot showers, shabby but friendly rec. Rec accommodation: house of Gertrudis Roth, No 1091, T 574-5603, E inc breakfast, 3 rooms, highly rec.

B *Estoril*, Av República Argentina 694, T 523-1233, F 523-2311, breakfast, pool, TV, rec.

C *Bastos*, Castelo Branco 931, T 574-5839, a/c with bath, clean, secure, helpful, rec; **C** *Luz*,

Almte Barroso, T 573-1891, nr Rodoviária, clean, rec; **C** *Patt's Hotel*, R Marechal Floriano Peixoto, 1368, T 574-2507, bath, good breakfast, a/c, TV, rec; **C** *Hotel Tarobá*, R Tarobá 1048, T 574-3670 or 574-3890, friendly, helpful, clean, good breakfast, rec; **C** *San Remo*, Kubitschek e Xavier da Silva 467, T 572-2956, good, bath, good breakfast, a/c.

D *Pousada Pôr do Sol*, R Santos Durmont 41, T 574-3122, family-run, helpful, rec; **D** *Hospedaria Britos*, Santos Dumont e Xavier da Silva, shared shower, large breakfast, clean, good value; **D** *Hospedaria Janice*, Santos Dumont 1222, very friendly and helpful; **D** *Riviera*, Mal Deodoro 559 e Bartolomeu de Gusmão, clean, friendly; **D** *Piratini*, R Rui Barbosa 237, T 523-3370, hot showers, good breakfast, very friendly, safe, rec; **D** *Pousada Evelina Navarrete*, R Irlan Kalicheski 171, Vila Yolanda, T/F 574 3817, very clean, lots of tourist information, helpful, good breakfast and location, nr Av Cataratas on way to the Falls, rec.

E *Senhor do Bonfin*, Almte Barroso 6, breakfast, fans, hot water, family atmosphere, clean, not very secure, convenient for the Cataratas bus which departs from the TTU square 4 blocks away; **E** *Holiday*, Xavier da Silva 1407, T 574-5948, good, breakfast. Lots of cheap (**F**) accommodation on Almte Baroso, Nos 2000-2200; **E** pp *Pousada da Laura*, R Naipi 629, T 574-1799, secure, friendly, Spanish, English and French spoken, excellent; **E** *Maria Schneider*, Av Jorge Schimmelpfeng 483, T 574-2305, German spoken; **E** *Hotel Evalina*, T 574-3817, R Irlan Kalichewski 171, good breakfast, private bath, good kitchen, friendly, Spanish, French, English and a bit of Italian spoken, not central but good shops and buses to centre available, rec. Many hotels have a minibus service to the airport for guests for a small fee and also offer excursions to Falls.

Camping: (pretty cold and humid in winter). By National Park entrance *Camping Clube do Brasil*, 17 km from Foz, US$10 pp a night (half with International Camping Card), swimming pool, clean; park vehicle or put tent away from trees in winter in case of heavy rain storms, no restaurants, food there not very good, closes at 2300. *Camping Ecológico*, Fazenda São João Batista (W Keller), T 574-1794, 8 km from Foz, turn left just before park entrance, basic, nice scenery, dormitory and space for tents. Not permitted by hotel and Falls. Sleeping in car inside the park also prohibited.

● **Places to eat**

Many open till midnight, most accept a variety of currencies. *Rafain*, Av das Cataratas, Km 6.5, with Paraguayan harp trio, good *alcatra* (meat), excellent buffet, but expensive. *Rafain Center*,

Rebouças 600 block, next to *Minas Hotel*, a collection of food stalls for different tastes and budgets, with live music and dancing 2000 to 0200, lively, rec; *Calamares*, No 686, all you can eat buffet US$5, closes 2300, rec. *Santos De-lavy*, Av J Kubitschek 393, Argentine owner, cheap and friendly; *Ali Baba*, No 998, very good Arabic food. *Churrascaria Cabeça de Boi*, Av Brasil 1325, large, live music, buffet US$9, also for coffee and pastries. *Cantina*, Av Rodrigues 720, buffet, all you can eat, rec; *Clarks*, No 896, excellent food, reasonable; *El Club Caxos*, No 249, cheap; *Scala*, Santos Dumont e Xavier da Silva, good atmosphere and value.

● **Banks & money changers**
Very difficult to exchange on Sun, but quite possible in Paraguay where US dollars can be obtained on credit cards. There are plenty of banks and travel agents on Av Brasil: **Banco do Brasil**, good rates for TCs (note that you cannot obtain US dollars in Brazil); **Bradesco**, No 1192, cash advances on Visa.

● **Electric current**
110 volts a/c.

● **Embassies & consulates**
Argentina, ER Bianchi 26, T 74-2877/2969, open 0800-1300; **Paraguay**, Bartolomeu de Gusmão 480.

● **Entertainment**
Discotheque Whiskadão with three different dance halls, Alm Barroso 763, reasonable, lively at weekends. Fun fair, *Centro de Diversões Imperial*, on Av Brasil. There is a cinema on Barão do Rio Branco, also a late-opening super-market.

● **Hospitals & medical services**
There is a free 24-hr clinic on Av Paraná, opp Lions Club. Few buses: take taxi or walk (about 25 mins). Ask for Sra Calça: friendly and helpful. Her son speaks English.

● **Post & telecommunications**
Post Office: Praça Getúlio Vargas 72, next to Tourist Office.
International phone: calls from the office on Rui Barbosa.

● **Tour companies & travel agents**
Beware of overcharging for tours by touts at the rodoviária. There are many travel agents on Av Brasil. *Dicks Tours* is said to change up to US$100/day, 10% charge, and has been rec for its all-day tour to the Brazilian side of the Falls, to Paraguay (Ciudad del Este) and to the Itaipú dam. Recommended guides, *Wilson Engel*, T 574-1367, friendly, flexible. Ruth Campo Silva, *STTC Turismo Ltda*, Hotel Bourbon, Rodovia das Ca-taratas, T 574-3557; *Chiderly Batismo Pequeno*, R Almte Barroso 505, Foz, T 574-3367.

● **Tourist offices**
Praça Getúlio Vargas 56; **Paranatur**, very help-ful, Almte Barroso 1300, T 574-2196. Kiosk on Av Brasil, by Ponte de Amizade (helpful), will book hotels. Airport tourist information is also good, open for all arriving flights, gives map and bus information. Helpful office, free map, at rodoviária, English spoken. A newspaper, *Triplice Fronteira*, carries street plans and other tourist information. *Kunda Livraria Universitária*, R Almte Barroso, T 523-4606, for guides and maps of the area, books on the local wildlife, novels etc in several languages inc French and English. There is a help line number, 1516.

● **Transport**
Air The Iguaçu international airport has daily flights from Río, São Paulo, Curitiba and other Brazilian cities. Taxis to town from the Brazilian airport 18 km from Foz, are expensive (up to US$54); Dois Irmãos town bus for US$0.50, first at 0530, does not permit large amounts of luggage (but backpacks OK). Varig office in Foz: Av Brasil 821, T 523-2111; staff speak foreign languages; Vasp, T 574-2999. Money exchange is on the 1st floor and a small commission is charged.

Buses Rodoviária, Av Costa e Silva, 4 km from centre on road to Curitiba; bus to centre, Anel Viario, US$0.35. Book departures as soon as pos-sible. Foz is reached by buses from **Curitiba** (Su-lamericana, 9-11 hrs, paved road, US$27.50), from Guaíra via Cascavel only (5 hrs, US$9.50), and from **São Paulo** (15 hrs, about US$29 with Pluma, *leito* US$58). To **Campo Grande**, 15 hrs by Maringá company (3 hrs to Cascavel, and 12 from there to Campo Grande) 15hrs by Medianeira company direct, US$29, rec; to **Brasília**, 26 hrs, 1800, US$50; to **Rio** 22 hrs, several daily, US$37 (*leito* 74). **Buenos Aires**, Pluma daily 1630, 18 hrs, US$45. It is cheaper to go to **Posadas** through Paraguay than through Argentina. Very many other destinations.

Travel To/From Paraguay Three Varig flights a week between Asunción and Foz do Iguaçu. Paved road from Asunción: Nuestra Señora, Rysa, Pluma and Unesul ply the route, US$14. From Ciudad del Este, take a bus to the Ponte de Amizade (Friendship Bridge, Brazilian post open until 0200, pay US$2 in dollars, guaraníes or *reais* at the Paraguayan end), pass Brazilian Customs and take Ponte-Cidade bus (US$0.12) to Terminal Urbana where buses go to the Falls or to Argentina. Do use the buses to cross no-man's-land.

GUAÍRA

In the far NW of the state, also on the Rio Paraná, were the tremendous waterfalls

Climate

It rains somewhat all the year but the main rainy season is between May and September. The climate is pleasant and the sun is never far away. Temperatures range from 25°C to 32°C, never falling below 19° in winter.

Salvador stands on the magnificent Bahia de Todos os Santos, a sparkling bay dotted with 38 islands. The bay is the largest on the Brazilian coast covering an area of 1,100 sq km. Rising above the bay on its eastern side is a cliff which dominates the landscape and, perched on top, 71m above sea level, are the older districts of Salvador with buildings dating back to 17th and 18th centuries.

History

The bay was discovered by Amérigo Vespucci on 1 November 1501, All Saints Day. The first Governor General, Tomé de Sousa arrived on 23 March 1549 to build a fortified city to protect Portugal's interest from constant threats of Dutch and French invasion. Salvador was the capital of Brazil until 1763 at which stage it was the most important city in the Portuguese Empire after Lisbon, ideally situated in a safe, sheltered harbour along the trade routes of the New World.

African presence The city's first wealth came from the cultivation of sugar cane and tobacco, the plantations' workforce coming from the W coast of Africa. For three centuries Salvador was the site of a thriving slave trade and this major influx is responsible for Salvador being described as the most African city in the Western Hemisphere. The influence permeates the city: food sold on the street is the same as in Senegal and Nigeria, Bahian music is fused with pulsating African polyrhythms, men and women nonchalantly carry enormous loads on their heads, fishermen paddle dug out canoes in the bay, the pace of life is a little slower than elsewhere. The pulse of the city is *candomblé*, an Afro-Brazilian religion in which the African deities of Nature,

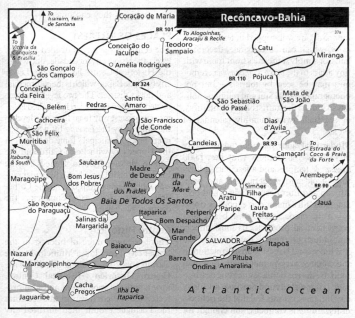

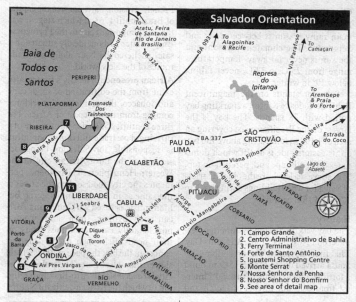

Salvador Orientation

1. Campo Grande
2. Centro Administrativo de Bahia
3. Ferry Terminal
4. Forte de Santo Antônio
5. Iguatemi Shopping Centre
6. Monte Serrat
7. Nossa Senhora da Penha
8. Nosso Senhor do Bomfirm
9. See area of detail map

the Goddess of the sea and the God of creation are worshipped. These deities (or *orixás*) are worshipped in temples (*terreiros*) which can be elaborate, decorated halls, or simply someone's front room with tiny altars to the *orixá*. *Candomblé* ceremonies may be seen by tourists – but not photographed – on Sun and religious holidays. Contact the tourist office, Bahiatursa, or see their twice monthly calendar of events.

Modern Salvador Salvador today is a city of 15 forts, 166 Catholic churches, 1,000 *candomblé* temples and a fascinating mixture of old and modern, rich and poor, African and European, religious and profane. It is still a major port exporting tropical fruit, cocoa, sisal, soya beans and petrochemical products. Its most important industry, though, is tourism; after Rio it is the second largest tourist attraction in the country, very popular with Brazilian tourists who see Bahia as an exotic destination. It is mostly a rundown, poor and dirty city, but most visitors feel that the richness of its culture is compensation enough for

any problems they encounter.

PLACES OF INTEREST

The centre of the city is divided into two levels, the Upper city (or Cidade Alta) where the Historical Centre lies, and the Lower city (Cidade Baixa) which is the commercial and docks district. The two levels are connected by a series of steep hills called *ladeiras*. The easiest way to go from one level to the other is by the *Lacerda* lift which connects Praça Municipal (Tomé de Sousa) in the Upper city with Praça Cairu and the famous Mercado Modelo. There is also the Plano Inclinado Gonçalves, a funicular railway which leaves from behind the Cathedral going down to Comercio, the commercial district.

Centro Histórico

There is much more of interest in the Upper city. From Praça Municipal to the Carmo area 2 km N along the cliff is the **Centro Histórico** (Historical Centre), now a national monument and also protected by Unesco. It was in this area that the Portuguese built their fortified city side altars in honour of black saints. The painted ceiling is also very impressive, the overall effect being one of tranquillity in contrast to the complexity of the other two churches. A small entrance fee is charged.

At the corner of Alfredo Brito and Largo do Pelourinho is a museum to the work of Jorge Amado (**Casa da Cultura Jorge Amado**, mainly photos, book covers and a lecture room, Mon-Fri 0900-1800), who lived in, and set many of his books, in this section of the city. His works have been published in 47 languages. A good way to get a feel of the city and its people is to read *Dona Flor and her two husbands*. The Carmo Hill is at the top of the street leading out of Largo do Pelourinho. The **Carmo** (Carmelite Third Order) church (1709) houses one of the sacred art treasures of the city, a sculpture of Christ made in 1730 by a slave who had no formal training, Francisco Xavier das Chagas, known as O Cabra. One of the features is the blood made from whale oil, ox blood, banana resin and 2000 rubies to represent the drops of blood. Opening hours are 0800 to 1200 and 1400 to 1730, entry US$0.30.

South of the Praça Municipal

In the direction of the mouth of the bay, is the more modern section of the city with many skyscrapers. R Chile leads to **Praça Castro Alves**, with its monument to Castro Alves, who started the campaign which finally led to the Abolition of Slavery in 1888. Two streets lead out of this square, Av 7 de Setembro, a bustling street of shops and street vendors selling everything imaginable, and, parallel to it, R Carlos Gomes. **São Bento** church (rebuilt after 1624, but with fine 17th century furniture) is on Av 7 de Setembro.

Campo Grande to Barra

Both eventually come to **Campo Grande** (also known as Praça Dois de Julho). In the centre of the square is the monument to Bahian Independence, 2 July 1823. The British Club is just off the square on R Banco dos Ingleses. Av 7 de Setembro continues out of the square towards the Vitória area, indeed this stretch is known as Corredor da Vitória (Vitória Corridor). There are some fine homes along this street built during the last century as the city expanded in this direction. The Corredor da Vitória comes to Praça Vitória and continues down Ladeira da Barra (Barra Hill) to **Porto da Barra**. The best city beaches are in this area. Also in this district are the best bars, restaurants and nightlife. A little further along is the **Forte de Santo Antônio**, 1580, built on the spot where Américo Vespucci landed in 1501. It is right at the mouth of the bay where Bahia de Todos Os Santos and the South Atlantic Ocean meet.

Atlantic beach suburbs

The promenade leading away from the fort and its famous lighthouse is called Av Oceânica, which goes along the coast to the new beach suburbs of Ondina, Amaralina and Pituba. The road is also called Av Presidente Vargas, but the numbering is different. Beyond Pituba are the best ocean **beaches** at Jaguaripe, Piatã and Itapoan (take any bus from Praça da Sé marked Aeroporto or Itapoan, about 1 hr, sit on right hand side for best views). En route the bus passes small fishing colonies at Amaralina and Pituba where *jangadas* can be seen. A *jangada* is a small raft peculiar to the northeastern region of Brazil used extensively as well as dug out canoes. Near Itapoan is the **Lagoa do Abaeté**, surrounded by brilliant, white sands. This is a deep, fresh water lake where local women traditionally come to wash their clothes and then lay them out to dry in the sun. The road leading up from the lake offers a panoramic view of the city in the distance, the coast, and the contrast of the white sands and fresh water less than a kilometre from the sea and its golden beaches. Near the lighthouse at **Itapoan** there are two campsites on the beach. A little beyond the campsites are the magnificent ocean beaches of Stella Maris and Flamengo, both quiet during the week but very busy at the weekends. Beware of strong undertow at these beaches.

Bomfim and Itapagipe

See also the famous church of **Nosso Sen-**

hor do Bomfim on the Itapagipe peninsula in the suburbs, whose construction began in 1745; it draws endless supplicants (particularly on Fri and Sun) offering favours to the image of the Crucified Lord set over the high altar; the number and variety of ex-voto offerings – often of parts of the body deemed to have been cured by divine intervention – is extraordinary. The processions over the water to the church on the third Sun in Jan are particularly interesting.

Also on the Itapagipe peninsula is a colonial fort on **Mont Serrat** point, and at Ribeira the church of **Nossa Senhora da Penha** (1743). The beach here has many restaurants, but bathing from it is not recommended because of pollution (bus from Praça da Sé or Av França).

MUSEUMS

The city has 27 museums. The **Museu de Arte Contemporânea**, converted from an old estate house and outbuildings off Av Contorno, is only open for special exhibitions. The good restaurant(*Solar do Unhão*) is still there, and the buildings are worth seeing for themselves (take a taxi there as access is dangerous).

There is a remarkable **Museu de Arte Sacra** in the 17th century monastery and church of Santa Teresa, at the bottom of the steep Ladeira de Santa Teresa, at R do Sodré 276 (off R Carlos Gomes). Many of the 400 carvings are from the Old World, but a number are local. Among the reliquaries of silver and gold is one of gilded wood by Aleijadinho. Open Mon-Fri 0700-1800, US$0.40. Many of the treasures which used to be in an old mansion, the Casa de Calmon, Av Joana Angélica 198, are here now. This important collection is well worth a visit. Opposite is **Tempostal**, a private museum of postcards, open Tues-Sat, 1000-1130, 1400-1600, at R do Sodré 276 (proprietor, Antônio Marcelino do Nascimento).

The **Museu do Carmo**, in the Convento do Carmo, has a museum with a collection of icons and colonial furniture, open Mon-Sat 0800-1200, 1400-1800, Sun 0800-1200; don't miss the carving of

Christ by Francisco Xavier das Chagas (see above), entry US$0.10.

Museu Abelardo Rodrigues, in the Solar Ferrão, Pelourinho (R Gregório de Mattos 45, open Mon-Fri 1000-1200, 1400-1700, closed Tues, Sat-Sun 1100-1700), is another religious art museum, with objects from the 17th, 18th, and 19th centuries, mainly from Bahia, Pernambuco and Maranhão. **The Pelourinho Renovation Exhibition**, R Gregório de Matos (next door), pictures showing houses before and after the renovation, very interesting.

Museu Afro-Brasileiro, in former Faculty of Medicine building, Terreiro de Jesus, open Mon-Sat, 0900-1700, US$0.30, comparing African and Bahian Orixás (deities) celebrations, beautiful murals and carvings, highly rec. **Museu Arqueológico a Etnográfico**, in the basement of the same building, archaeological discoveries from Bahia (stone tools, clay urns etc), exhibition on Indians from the Alto Rio Xingu area (artefacts, tools, photos) rec a museum in same complex.

Casa do Benin, below NS do Rosario dos Pretos, shows African crafts, photos, video show on Benin and Angola, open Tues-Sat 1000-1800.

Museu da Cidade, Largo do Pelourinho, arts and crafts, old photographs, entrance free, Tues-Fri 1000-1800, Sat, Sun, 1300-1700. From the higher floors of the museum you can get a good view of the Pelourinho.

Museu Costa Pinto, Av 7 de Setembro 2490, US$2, daily 1430-1800, is a modern house with collections of crystal, porcelain, silver, furniture etc. It also has the only collection of *balangandãs* (slave charms and jewellery), highly rec.

Museu de Arte da Bahia, Av 7 de Setembro 2340, Vitória, Tues-Fri 1400-1900, Sat-Sun 1430-1830, US1, interesting paintings of Brazilian artists between 18th and early 20th century. The **Museu Geológico do Estado** is at Av 7 de Setembro 2195, Vitória, open Mon-Fri 1330-1830.

Museu Hidrográfico, Forte de Santo Antônio (Mon-Fri 0700-2100, Tues and Wed free, Thur-Sat US$0.50); recently restored and housed in the upper section from the great variety of local fish, vegetables and fruits.

See Capoeira, a sport developed from the traditional foot-fighting technique introduced from Angola by African slaves. The music is by drum, tambourine and *berimbau*; there are several different kinds of the sport. If you want to attempt Capoeira, the best school is Mestre Bimba in Terreiro de Jesus, at R Francisco Muniz Barreto 1. Classes are held in evenings (if you want to get the most out of it, knowledge of Portuguese is essential). There are two more schools in Forte de Santo Antônio behind Pelourinho, but check addresses at tourist office. Exhibitions take place in the Largo do Pelourinho, very picturesque, in the upper city (cost: US$2). You can also see the experts outside the Mercado Modelo on most days, around 1100-1300, and at Campo Grande and Forte de Santo Antônio on Sun afternoons; they often expect a contribution. Negotiate a price before taking pictures or demands may be exorbitant. At the Casa da Cultura at Forte de Santo Antônio there is also free live music on Sat night.

MUSIC IN BAHIA

The best time to hear and see artists and groups is during carnival but they are also to be seen outside the carnival period. Olodum, Ilê Aiye, Muzenza and Araketu are the most famous of the numerous drumming troupes where up to 100 drummers form the powerful rhythms for the sweet melodies. For Olodum and Ilê Aiyê, see **Nightlife** below.

Artists and bands using electronic instruments and who tend to play in the *trios elèctricos* draw heavily on the rich rhythms of the drumming groups creating a new musical genre known as *Axé*. The most popular of such acts is Daniela Mercury, following the steps to internationals stardom of Caetano Veloso, Maria Bethânia, João Gilberto, Gilberto Gil. Other newer, interesting acts are Margareth Menezes who has travelled extensively with David Byrne. Gerónimo was one of the first singer/songwriters to use the wealth of rhythms of the Candomblé in his music

and his song 'E d'Oxum' is something of an anthem for the city. Other artists worth investigating are Roberto Mendes, Carlinhos Brown and his vibrant drumming group Timbalada. The most famous of the trio bands are Chiclete com Banana, Banda Mel, Banda Beijo and Banda Reflexus.

All of the above have albums released and you can find their records easily in most record stores. *Mini Som*, in Praça da Sé has a wide collection in a very small store, but has a good collection of older recordings upstairs (watch the steep steps) and is more than willing to let you hear the records before buying. Another good record store is *Billbox* in the Shopping Barra on the third floor. See also **Shopping in the Pelourinho**, below.

EXCURSIONS

From the lower city the train (Trem do Leste) leaves Calçada for a 40 min journey through the bayside suburbs of Salvador – Lobato, Plataforma (canoes and motor boats for Ribeira on the Itapagipe peninsula), Escada (17th century church), Praia Grande, Periperi and Paripe (take bus for 17th century church at São Tomé de Paripe). The train runs Mon-Fri only; the same trip can be made by bus, less picturesquely.

LOCAL INFORMATION

Warning Be very careful of your money and valuables at all times and in all districts. Avoid the more distant beaches out of season, when they are empty (eg Itapoan, Piatã, Placafor); on Sun they are more crowded and safer. At night, the area around and in the lifts and buses are unsafe. On no account change money on the streets; this is a guaranteed way to be robbed. Leave valuables securely in your hotel (inc wristwatch and cameras if possible: disposable cameras are widely available), particularly at night. Carry a small amount of money that you can hand over if you are threatened. One is warned not to walk down any of the links between the old and new city, especially the Ladeira de Misericôrdia, which links the Belvedere, near the Lacerda lifts, with the lower city. Should a local join you at your table for a chat, leave at once if drugs are mentioned. The civil police are reported to be very sympathetic and helpful and more resources have been put into policing the old part of the city, which is now well-lit at night.Police are little in evidence after 2300, however.

● **Accommodation**

Hotel prices

L1	over US$200	**L2**	US$151-200
L3	US$101-150	**A1**	US$81-100
A2	US$61-80	**A3**	US$46-60
B	US$31-45	**C**	US$21-30
D	US$12-20	**E**	US$7-11
F	US$4-6	**G**	up to US$3

A 10% service charge is often added to the bill. Check which credit cards are accepted. All have swimming pools.

Luxury hotels: **L2** *Enseada das Lajes*, Av Oceânica 511, Rio Vermelho, T 336 1027, family run, 9 rooms in what used to be a private house, antique furniture, excellent pieces of art, wonderful setting, 2 mins beach. **L3** *Bahia Othon Palace*, Av Oceânica 2456, Ondina, T 247 1044, F 245 4877, 5-star, nice rooms and views, excellent swimming pool, next to beach; **L3** *Grande Hotel da Barra*, Av 7 de Setembro 3564, Barra, 4-star, T 336 6011, F 247 6223, excellent location on beach, small, friendly, ask for room with sea view; **L3** *Hotel da Bahia* (Tropical), Praça 2 de Julho 2, Campo Grande, T 321 3699, F 321 9725, 5-star, refurbished, well-run, owned by Varig, location noisy but convenient for city centre, daily courtesy bus to beach; **L3** *Marazul*, Av 7 de Setembro 3937, Barra, T 336 2110, F 235 2121, 4-star, on seafront, heartily rec, good discounts for longer stays; **L3** *Meridien*, R Fonte do Boi 216, Rio Vermelho, 5-star, T 248 8011, F 248 8902, well-run, ocean views, no beach, nothing within walking distance so taxis must be used. **L3** *Ondina Apart Hotel*, Av Oceânica 2400, Ondina, T 203 8000, 5-star, self-contained apts, on beach, highly rec; **L3** *Sofitel* (Quatro Rodas), R da Passargada, Farol de Itapoan, T 249 9611, F 249 6946, 5-star, a complete resort hotel 22 km from city centre, extensive grounds, peaceful but plenty of activities available eg golf, tennis, etc, shuttle bus to city centre; **L3** *Victória Marina Apart Hotel*, Av 7 de Setembro 2068, Vitória, T 336 7736, F 336 0507.

A1 *Itapoan Praia*, Jardim Itapoan, Placafor, T 249 9988, F 248 7111, 3-star, 20 km from centre nr excellent beaches; **A1** *Ondina Praia*, Av Oceânica 2275, Ondina, T 336 1033, F 247 9434, 3-star, nr beach; **A1** *San Marino*, Av Oceânica 889 Barra, T 336 4363, 3-star, on ocean.

Centre: (includes old city and main shopping area): **B** *Bahia de Todos os Santos*, Av Sete de Setembro 106 (Ladeira de São Bento), T 321 6344; **B** *Palace*, R Chile 20, T 243 1155, F 243 1109, rec; **D** *Chile*, opp, clean, big rooms, some have harbour view; **C** *Pousada do Boqueirão*, R Direita do Santa Antônio 48, T/F 241 2262, family run,

beautiful house overlooking the bay, relaxed atmosphere, most European languages spoken, great food, especially breakfast, highly rec; **B-C** *Imperial*, Av 7 de Setembro 751, Rosario, T 321 3389, a/c, helpful, breakfast, highly rec; **D** *Internacional*, R da Faisca 88, T 243 6151, clean, convenient, good value; **D** *Paris*, R Ruy Barbosa 13, T 321 3922, a/c rooms more expensive, shared showers, breakfast, restaurant in same building, rec; also **E** *Pousada da Praça*, at No 5, T 321 0642, breakfast, rooms with and without bath, clean, friendly, rec; **D** *São Bento*, Largo de São Bento 3, T 243 7511, friendly, good cheap restaurant; **D** *São Bento*, Albergue das Laranjeiras, R Inácio Acciolli 13, T 321-1366, hostal accommodation, new, clean, friendly, cooking facilities, English spoken, rec. Cheaper hotels on Av 7 de Setembro: **E-D** *São José*, No 847, T 321 4928, safe, rec; **F** *Madrid*, No 186, Mercês, T 321 9505, very cheap and basic, damp, not too secure; **E** *Pousada Pampulha*, No 76, 1st floor, São Pedro, T 243 1240, breakfast, restaurant, laundry service; **F** *Pousada*, No 2349, price pp, warmly rec. **F** *Joana Angêlica* in street of same name, friendly, no breakfast.

There are many hotels nr the Praça da Sé. The following have been rec: **C** *Pelourinho*, R Alfredo Brito 20, T 321 9022, run down but central and charismatic; **D** *Solara*, R José Alencar 25, Largo do Pelourinho, T 321 0202, with shower, toilet, breakfast, clean, laundry facilities; **D** *Themis*, Praça da Sé 398, Ed Themis, 7th floor, T 243 1668, bath, fan, wonderful views over bay and old city, rec restaurant with French chef; Spanish is spoken in all of the following: **D-E** *Ilheus*, Ladeira da Praça 4, 1st floor, T 243 2329, breakfast; **E** *Vigo*, R 3 de Maio 18, 2 blocks from Praça da Sé, with bath and breakfast (F without), fairly clean; **F** *Jequié*, off Praça da Sé at Ciné Liceu, clean, no breakfast, mixed reports, some rooms better than others.

Campo Grande/Vitória: this is a much quieter area, still central and convenient for museums: **B** *Bahia do Sol*, Av 7 de Setembro 2009, T 336 7211, F 336 7776, comfortable, safe and frigobar in room, clean, family run, good breakfast, rec; **D** *Mater Café Teatro*, R Marechal Floriano 5, Canela T 235 1958, with breakfast, clean (but poor locks on doors); **D** *Caramuru*, Av Sete de Setembro 2125, Vitória, T 336 9951, breakfast, very friendly, clean, safe parking, rec; **D** *Do Forte*, R Visc de São Lourenço 30, Campo Grande, T 321 6915, breakfast, bath; **D** *Santiago* at No 52, breakfast, bath, T 245 9293.

Barra: the best location to stay in: it is safe, has good beaches (but the sea may be polluted), is a short bus ride from the centre, has good restaurants in all price ranges and good nightlife (but note that the bars around Porto da Barra have become meeting places for prostitutes and

European tourists). On Av 7 de Setembro: **B** *Barra Turismo*, No 3691, Porto da Barra, T 245 7433, breakfast, bath, a/c, TV, fridge, on beach, rec; **C** *Porto da Barra*, No 3783, Porto da Barra, T 247 7711, friendly, clean, some rooms very small, on beach; **C** *Solar da Barra*, No 2998, Ladeira da Barra, T 336 4917, some rooms with bay view; **C** *Pousada Malu*, No 3801, T 237 4461, small and friendly with breakfast, on beach; **C** *Villa da Barra*, No 3959, Porto da Barra, T 247 7908, F 247 9667, chalets in front of the beach, English spoken, rec; **B** *Barra Praia*, Av Alm Marqués do Leão 172, Farol da Barra, T 235-0193, a/c, clean, one street from beach, rec; **C** *Enseada Praia da Barra*, R Barão de Itapoã 60, Porto da Barra, T 235 9213, breakfast, clean, safe, friendly, money exchanged, accepts credit cards, laundry bills high otherwise good value, nr beach; **C** *Pousada Village Paulista*, R Lord Cochrane 148, Barra, T 245 9099, fan, clean, English spoken, mixed reports, annexe opp is cheaper but not as good; **C** *Seara Praia*, R Belo Horizonte 148, Barra Av, T 235 0105, good breakfast; **D** *Bella Barra*, R Afonso Celso 439, T 237 8401, a/c, good, rec; **E** *Pousada da Carmen Simões*, R 8 de Dezembro 326, safe, friendly, helpful; **E** *Pousada Marcos*, Av Oceânica 281, T 235 5117, youth hostel style, great location nr lighthouse, very busy, many notices in Hebrew for potential travelling companions, good value, rec; **F** pp *Pousada do Porto*, R Barão de Serqy 197, Porto da Barra, T 247 0228, hostel-type but more luxurious than normal in beautiful turn-of-the-century house, inc breakfast, nr beach, convenient, English spoken, highly rec. Also rooms to let in private apartment, rec, from Gorette, R 8 de Dezembro 522, Apt 002, T 237-3584.

Atlantic Suburbs: this is the modern suburban area built along the coast from Ondina to Itapoan stretching for 20 km towards the airport. The best beaches are in this area. **A3** *Catharina Paraguaçu*, R João Gomes 128, Rio Vermelho, T 247 1488, charming, small, colonial-style, tastefully decorated, rec; **A3** *Maravista*, R H C Ribeiro 4, Ondina, T 247 3866, rec, nr beach; **A3** *Ondina Plaza*, Av Pres Vargas 3033, Ondina, T 245 8188, a/c, pool, good value, on beach, rec; **B** *Amaralina*, Av Amaralina 790, Amaralina, T 248 6347, a/c, nr beach. Two in Pituba: **B** *Paulus*, Av Otavio Mangabeira, T 248 5722, a/c, pool; **D** *Pituba*, Av Manoel Dias da Silva 1614, T 248 5469, no breakfast. Two nr excellent beach, in Placaford: **B** *Praia Dourada*, R Dias Gomes 10, T 249 9639, a/c, rec; **B** *Praia dos Coqueiros*, Av Otavio Mangabeira 25, Placaford, T 249 9828, a/c, rec. **A3** *Pituaçu Praia*, Jardim Iracema, Lote 27, Corsario, T 371 9622, a/c, 2 blocks from good beach. In Itapoan: **A3** *Praia da Sereia*, Av Dorival Caymmi 14, T 249-4523, F 249-4550, very good, pool, clean, friendly,

safe; **B** *Grão de Areia*, Loteamento Jardim Piatâ, Quadra 25, Lote 23/24, T 249 4818, a/c, pool, nr good beach; **B** *Pousada de Itapoan*, Av D Caymmi, V dos Ex Combatentes, Quadra 1, Lote 3, T 249 9634, with bath, D without, excellent breakfast, clean, good value, laundry, parking; **C** *Europa*, R Genibaldo Figueiredo 53, T 249 9344, breakfast; **D** *Pousada Glória*, R do Retiro 46, T 249 1503, with bath, no breakfast, nr beach.

A1 *Solar Diana*, Av Yemanjá, R U, Lote 16, Jardim Armação, nr Convention Center, T 231 1017, F 231 7927, sophisticated, small, most European languages spoken, highly rec; **A3** *Portal Da Cidade*, Av Antonio Carlos Magalhães 4230, next to rodoviária, T 371 0099, a/c, pool.

Youth hostels: Albergues de Juventude, E-F pp inc breakfast but cheaper if you have a YHA membership card. In Pelourinho: *Albergue Solar*, R Ribeiro dos Santos 45-47, T 241 0055; *Albergue do Pelô*, same street No 5, T 242 8061; *Pousada do Passo*, No 3, T 321-3656, highly rec. *Casa Grande*, R Minas Gerais, 122, Pituba, T 248 0527; *Albergue da Barra*, R Florianopolis 134, Jardim Brasil, Barra, T 247 5478, good location.

Pensionatos are places to stay in shared rooms (up to 4 persons/room); part or full board available. Houses or rooms can be rented for US$5-35 a day from Pierre Marbacher, R Carlos Coqueijo 68A, Itapoan, T 249 5754 (Caixa Postal 7458, 41600 Salvador), he is Swiss, owns a beach bar at R K and speaks English, French and German. At Carnival its a good idea to rent a flat; the tourist office has a list of estate agents (eg José Mendez T 237 1394/6). They can also arrange rooms in private houses, however caution is advised as not all householders are honest.

Apart Hotels: these are self-contained apartments with fully equipped kitchen and a/c, with all the facilities of a hotel, which can be rented by the day; standards are generally high. *Jardim Paraiso*, Av Dunas 259, Itapoan, T 249 3397, pool, nr beach; *Bahia Flat*, Av Pres Vargas 235, Barra, T 336 4233, on beach, pool, sauna; *Barra Apart Service*, R Marques de Caravelas 237, Barra, T 247 5844; *Flat Jardim de Alá*, Av Otavio Mangabeira 3471, Armação, T 371 5288, beautiful location nr beach, pool, sauna, rec; *Manhattan Residence Service*, R Maranhão 445 Pituba, T 248 9911, pool, gym, popular with business visitors; *Parthenon Farol da Barra Flat*, Av Oceânica 409, Barra, T 336 6722, pool, sauna, on beach, rec; *Pituba Apart Hotel*, R Paraíba 250, Pituba, T 240 7077, pool, sauna; *Barra Summer Flat*, Av Princesa Isabel 526, Barra, T 336 3699; all in A1-A3 range rec; *Lucia Arleo*, R Miguel Bournier, 59-Ap 203, 237-2424, specially furnished apartments nr the beach, rec.

Camping: *Ecológica*, nr the lighthouse at Itapoan, take bus from Praça da Sé direct to Itapoan, or to Campo Grande or Barra, change there for Itapoan, about 1 hr, then 30 mins' walk: bar, restaurant, hot showers, highly rec. *Camping de Pituaçu*, Av Prof Pinto de Aguiar, Jardim Pituaçu. Sea bathing is dangerous off shore nr campsites.

● **Places to eat**

Bahian cuisine: is spiced and peppery. The main dish is *moqueca*, seafood cooked in a sauce made from coconut milk, tomatoes, red and green peppers, fresh coriander and *dendê* (palm oil). It is traditionally cooked in a wok-like earthenware dish and served piping hot at the table. Served with *moqueca* is *farofa* (manioc flour) and a hot pepper sauce which you add at your discretion, it's usually extremely hot so try a few drops before venturing further. The *dendê* is somewhat heavy and those with delicate stomachs are advised to try the *ensopado*, a sauce with the same ingredients as the *moqueca*, but without the palm oil.

Nearly every street corner has a Bahiana (see above under **Folklore**) selling a wide variety of local snacks, the most famous of which is the *acarajé*, a bean dumpling fried in palm oil. To this the Bahiana adds *vatapá*, a dried shrimp and coconut milk paté (also delicious on its own), fresh salad and hot sauce (*pimenta*). For those who prefer not to eat the palm oil, the *abará* is a good substitute. *Abará* is steamed, wrapped in banana leaves. The Bahianas are being given lessons on hygiene, but seek local advice on which are safest.

Three good Bahianas are *Chica*, at Ondina beach (on street at left side of *Mar A Vista Hotel*), *Dinha* at Largo da Santana (in a newly opened public square, very lively late afternoon), serves *acarajé* until midnight, extremely popular, and the one in front of *Tiffany's* restaurant on R Barão de Sergy at Porto da Barra. Bahians usually eat *acarajé* or *abará* with a chilled beer on the way home from work or the beach at sunset.

Another popular dish is *Xin-Xin de Galinha*, chicken on the bone cooked in *dendê*, with dried shrimp and squash.

Pelourinho (Historical Centre): *Cantina da Lua*, Terreiro De Jesus, open daily, popular but hangers-on can sometimes be a nuisance; *El Mesón*, Alfredo Brito 11 (upstairs), open Mon-Sat, 1100-2330, Sun 1800-2330, good seafood, meat, English spoken; *Pizzaria Micheluccio*, Alfredo Brito 31, best pizzas in Pelourinho, open daily 1200 till late, rec (T 321 5884). *Senac*, Praça José Alencar 8 (commonly known as Pelourinho Square), state run catering school, a selection of 40 local dishes, buffet, lunch 1130-1530, dinner 1830-2130, all you can eat for US$12, inconsistent quality but very popular, folkloric show Thur-Sat 2030, US$5. *Casa do Benin*, Praça José Alencar 29, Afro-Bahian restaurant, great surroundings, try the shrimp in the cashew nut sauce, closed Mon, open 1200-1600, 1900-2300, expensive but highly rec. *Bar Banzo*, Praça José Alencar 6 (upstairs) Mon-Sat 1100 to 2300, Sun 1800 to 2300, reasonably priced, good view of streetlife in Largo do Pelourinho below, friendly, good music. *Celina*, R dos Passos nr Casa do Benin, good, cheap, popular with locals.

First right on Alfredo Brito is R J Castro Rabelo: *Atelier Maria Adair*, No 2, specializing in various kinds of coffee, interesting cocktails, Maria is a well known artist, the café gives a glimpse of her highly original work, rec. Good wholemeal snacks and juices at *Saúde Brasil*, No 16, open daily 0900-2330, rec; *Dona Chika-Ka*, No 10, 1100-1500 and 1900-0200, good local dishes. Open gates beside *Dona Chika-Ka* lead to an open square (known locally as Quadra 2M) with many bars and restaurants. On the next block down is *Tempero da Dadá*, R Frei Vicente 5, open daily 1130 till late, closed Tues, the best Bahian cuisine in the Pelourinho, owners Dadá and Paulo are genial hosts, extremely popular, try the *bobó de camarão* (shrimp in yam sauce) and the shrimp *moqueca* which is served with the best *pirão* (thick manioc gravy) in Bahia, highly rec. Next door is *Mustafá*, R Frei Vicente 07, open 1200-2400 except Sun 1200-1500, closed Tues, Middle Eastern dishes, try the *mezze*, a selection of starters and main dishes, enough for two people. Across the street is *Abará da Ró*, specializing in *acarajé* and *abará*, popular late afternoon and early evening.

Uauá, R Gregório de Matos 36 (upstairs), 1130-1500 and 1900-2330, closed Tues, has the best in northeastern Brazilian cuisine, try the *carne de sol*, very reasonably priced, highly rec. Next door is the new branch of the famous *Casa da Gamboa*, R João de Deus 32, 1st floor, 1200-1500 and 1900-2400, closed Mon; *Uauá*, same street above *Bar do Reggae*, good Bahian and NE food, good value.

Good *feijoado* at *Alaide do Feijão*, R Fransisco Muniz Barreto 26, open daily 1100-2400. Also at *da Dinha* on Praça José Alencar 5, Mon-Sat 0800-2000; *Encontro dos Artistas*, R Ribeiro do Santos 10, Passo – Pelourinho, vegetarian food, cheap, rec.

Between Historical Centre and Barra: at Praça Da Sé, *Café Brasil*, good breakfast; also *Hotel Themis* (see above). *Bar Padrão*, R José Gonçalves, nr Praça Da Sé; rec. There are some good snack bars on Av 7 de Setembro; *Nosso Cantinho*, nr *Hotel Madrid*, good value; *Kentefrio*, No 379, the best, clean, counter service only, closed Sun, rec; on same street, 600 block, *La Portuguesa*, good, cheap; *Casa D'Italia*, corner of Av 7 and Visconde de São Lourenço, reasonable prices, good service; *Grao de Bico*, No 737, very good vegetarian. *Suave Sabor*, R Cons Lafaiete, vegetarian, US$2.50 for all you can eat. Another good vegetarian restaurant nearby is *Nutrebem*, Av Joana Ângêlica 148. *Casa Da Gamboa*, R da Gamboa, beautifully located in old colonial house overlooking the bay, good reputation, open Mon to Sat 1200-1500 and 1900-2300, not cheap. *Manjur*, R Banco dos Ingleses 20, Campo Grande, good, friendly, vegetarian dishes, 0900-1900, great view of bay. An excellent Japanese restaurant is *Gan*, Praça A Fernades 29, Garcia, intimate atmosphere, Tues-Sun 1900 till midnight, rec. The best churrascaria in Salvador is *Baby Beef*, Av AC Magalhães, Iguatemi, top class restaurant, excellent service, extremely popular, not expensive, highly rec, open daily 1200-1500 and 1900-2300.

At the bottom of the Lacerda Lift is Praça Cairu and the famous *Mercado Modelo*: on the upper floor of the market are two very good restaurants, *Camafeu De Oxossi* and *Maria De São Pedro*, both specializing in Bahian dishes, great atmosphere, good view of the port, daily 1130 till 2000, Sat lunchtime particularly busy. Opposite Mercado Modelo, the Pães Mendonça supermarket self-service counter is good value, 1100-1500, 1st floor. At the base of the Lift is *Cinquenta Saladas*, not only salads, very reasonable. On Av Contorno, *Solar Do Unhão*, beautiful manor house on the edge of the bay, lunch and dinner with best folklore show in town, expensive. *Juárez*, Mercado de Ouro, Comércio, good steaks, cheap, rec.

Barra section: *Xangai*, Av 7 de Setembro 1755 (Vitória), Chinese, reasonable; *Nan Hai*, No 3671, good Chinese, lunch and dinner (Porto da Barra); good cheap snacks at Goethe Institute and American Institute, also restaurant at *Hotel Bahia Do Sol*, No 2009, on first floor, good, reasonably priced; *Tiffany's*, Barão do Sergy 156, 1900-2400, French, rec; on same street are *Alface e Cia*, wide range of salads and juices; *Via Brera* No 162, T 247-6973, upmarket Italian; *Unimar* supermarket, good cheap meals on 2nd floor. Good cheap meal at *Sorbon*, Av Doutora Praquer Fries, Porto da Barra.

Near the lighthouse at the mouth of the bay (Farol Da Barra area) there are a number of good fast food places: *Micheluccio*, Av Oceânica 10, best pizza in town, always busy, friendly, rec; next door is *Baitakão*, good hamburger and sandwiches. *Mon Filet*, R Afonso Celso 152, good steaks, pastas, open 1830 till midnight; on same street, *Pastaxuta*, pizza, pasta, reasonable prices; a number of other good cheap restaurants on R Afonso Celso, eg *Maná*, opens 1100 till food runs out, different menu each day, closed sun, popular, owner Frank speaks a little English; also *Luar da Barra*, No 447; Shopping Barra has good cheapish places to eat, *Pizza e Cia* on ground floor, good selection of fresh

salads, also good pizzas, good value, rec; opp is *Perini*, great ice cream, chocolate, savouries and cakes; *MacDonald's* also on this floor; *Saúde Brasil*, on the top floor (L3, above C&A's), for very good wholefood snacks, cakes and a wide variety of juices, rec. The best Bahian restaurant in the area is *Frutos Do Mar*, R Marques De Leão 415. A very good vegetarian restaurant is *Rama*, R Lord Cochrane, great value, rec. *Don Vitalone*, D M Teixeira 27, nr lighthouse, off seafront, excellent Italian, open daily for lunch and evening meal, highly rec.

In Ondina: *Double Gula*, in *Mar A Vista Hotel*, and *Baby Beef Martínez*, in *Ondina Apart Hotel*, for excellent meat. Further along Av Oceânica towards the Rio Vermelho district is *Sukiyaki*, No 3562, an excellent Japanese restaurant, open 1200-1500, and 1900 till midnight, not cheap, rec. Also highly rec is *Extudo*, Largo Mesquita 4, T 237-4669, good varied menu, lively bar at night, attracts interesting clientele, open 1200-0200, closed Mon, not expensive. *Manjericão*, R Fonte do Boi (the street leading to *Meridien Hotel*), excellent wholefood menu, Mon-Sat 1100-1600, highly rec. *Philippe Camarao*, same street, bar and restaurant, specializes in shrimp dishes, expensive. *Marisco*, at Paciencia Beach nearby, good seafood, 1100-1500 and 1800-2100, good value. Zona Franca, Largo da Santana, top floor of Free Shopping Center, open air, varied menu, popular, Mon-Sat lunch and dinner.

There is an interesting fish market at Largo Da Mariquita with a number of stalls serving food from noon until the small hours, clean, good atmosphere, popular with locals. A good kiosk is *Riso e Nega* (kiosk with green tables), friendly, good basic food; nearby is *Brisa*, R Augusto Severo 4, Mon-Sat 1100-1500, excellent wholefood restaurant, small, simple, cheap, owner Nadia is very friendly.

Further along Avenida Oceânica at Jardim Armação are three very good restaurants: *Yemanjá*, excellent Bahian seafood, open daily from 1130 till late, very typical, always busy, reasonably priced, good atmosphere, highly rec. Nearby is *Tamboril*, busy seafood restaurant, 1200-1600 and 1900-2400. *Deutsches Haus*, Av Otávio Mangabeira 1221, good German cooking. The very best Bahian restaurant in the city is *Bargaço*, open daily 1200-1600 and 1900-2400, great selection of starters, oyster, lobster, fresh water shrimp, crab meat, etc, highly rec, expensive but worth it.

A Porteira at Boca do Rio specialises in northeastern dishes inc *carne do sol* (beef dried in the sun), 1200-1600 and 1800-2300, seafood dishes also served. A popular bar/restaurant is *Casquinha De Siri* at Piatã beach, daily from

0900 until last customer leaves, live music every night, cover charge US$2. The beaches from Patamares to Itapoan are lined by Barracas, thatched huts serving chilled drinks and freshly cooked seafood dishes, ideal for lunch and usually very cheap. Try *Ki-Muqueça*, Av Otávio Mangabeira 36 (Av Oceânica), for large helpings of excellent Bahian food in attractive surroundings. At Itapoan the road goes left towards the airport along Av Dorival Caymmi. *Restaurant Uauá*, Av Dorival Caymmi 46, specialses in northeastern dishes, meat based, seafood also served, open Thur to Sun. Fri and Sat are very busy with forró dancing till 0400.

● **Banks & money changers**
Do not be tempted to change money on the street (see above) especially in the Upper City where higher rates are usually offered. Changing at banks can be bureaucratic and time-consuming. Banks are open 1000-1600. All major banks have exchange facilities but these are only available at selected branches. **Citibank**, R Miguel Calmon 555, Comércio, centre, good rates, will change large denomination TCs into smaller ones with a commission. **Lloyds Bank**, R Miguel Calmon 22, Comércio. **Banco Econômico**, R Miguel Calmon 285, Comércio is the American Express representative. Visa at **Banco do Brasil**, Av Estados Unidos 561, Comércio, in shopping centre opp Rodoviária (also a *câmbio* here), and at R Miguel Bournier 4, Barra. Mastercard at **Credicard**, 1st floor, Citibank building, R Miguel Calmon 555, Comércio. **Banco do Brasil** is to open an exchange office in Shopping do Pelô on R Francisco Muniz Barreto 2; also at the airport is open 0830-1530 and 1600-2100 Mon-Fri and 0900-1600 Sat, Sun and holidays. **Carlos**, Bazaar Colon, Praça Anchieta 17, in front of São Francisco church in the old city gives good rates, but doesn't always accept TCs (will require passport when he does). In the Barra section, exchange at **Banco do Brasil**, R Miguel Bournier and in Shopping Barra; also in Ondina. **Banco do Nordeste**, R Marqués de Leão 41. Banking hours only. **Figueiredo**, opp *Grande Hotel da Barra* on Ladeira da Barra will exchange cash at good rates. Also in Ondina is **Banco Econômico** in the parade of shops under *Ondina Apart Hotel*. If stuck, all the big hotels will exchange, but at poor rates. **Banespa**, Av dos Estados Unidos, changes TCs without commission.

● **Cultural centres**
British Club, Inglesa 20B, just off Campo Grande. **Cultura Inglesa**, R Plínio Moscoso 357, Jardim Apipema. **Associação Cultural Brasil-Estados Unidos**, Av 7 de Setembro 1883, has a library and reading room with recent US magazines, open to anyone, and at No 1809 on the same avenue is the German **Goethe Institut**, also with library and reading room with recent papers.

● **Embassies & consulates**
British Vice-Consulate, Av Estados Unidos 4, Salas 1109/1113, Ed Visc de Cairu, Caixa Postal 38, Comércio, T 243-9222, Mon-Fri, 0800-1200, 1400-1730. **USA**, Av Antonio Carlos Magalhães, Ed Cidadella Center 1, Sala 410, Itaigara, T 358 9166, Mon-Fri, 1430-1630. **Germany**, R Lucaia 281, Rio Vermelho, T 247 7106, Mon-Fri 0900-1200. **Austria**, R Alm Marqués do Leão 46, Apto 33, Barra, T 247 6013, Mon, Wed, Fri 1400-1700. **Belgium**, Centro Empresarial Iguatemi, Bloco B, Sala 809, Iguatemi, T 358 9542, Tues and Thur 1430-1800, Fri 0900-1200. **Denmark**, Av Sete de Setembro 3959, Barra, T 247 9667, Mon-Fri 0900-1200, 1400-1700. **Spain**, R Marechal Floriano 21, Canela, T 336 9055, Mon-Fri 0900-1300. **Finland**, C Portinári 19, Barra, T 247 3312, Mon-Fri 1000-1600, closes for lunch. **France**, Trav Francisco Gonçalves 1, Sala 805, Comércio, T 371-0410, Mon-Fri 0800-1130. **Holland**, R Lauro Miller 8, Sala 503, T 241 7645 Mon-Fri 0800-1130, 1400-1730. **Italy**, Av Sete de Setembro 1238, Mercês, T 321-8335, Mon, Wed, Fri, 0900-1100, 1500-1700. **Norway and Sweden**, R Quintino de Carvalho 153, Apto 601, Jardim Apipema, T 247 0528, Mon-Fri 0900-1200. **Portugal**, Praça Piedade, Gabinete Português de Leitura, T 241-1633, Mon-Fri 0800-1400. **Chile**, R Chile 22, Sala 401, T 321 9457, Mon-Fri 1330-1630.

● **Electric current**
110-220 AC, 60 cycles.

● **Entertainment**
Nightlife: in the historical centre, there is live music on the streets on Tues and Sun evening (especially the first and last Tues of the month) and Fri and Sat nights (particularly lively, especially in the summer months). *Pagôde*, a samba style from Rio, is becoming very popular, and bands play in the Pelourinho Square in front of the Casa de Jorge Amado. The main attraction is the rehearsal of the Olodum drummers on Tues; these are the most innovative of the carnival drumming groups and have attracted much attention after being featured on Paul Simon's 1990 album, *Rhythm of the Saints*. They rehearse in an open space known as the Quadra behind Teatro Antônio Miguel on R João de Jesus from 1900-2300, tickets on sale from 1700, US$4, buy tickets in advance from Casa do Olodum on R Gregório de Matos and go early. They usually also rehearse on Sun in Largo de Pelourinho from 1800-2300, but these rehearsals can be very crowded (at both, beware pickpockets and fights, police use tear gas to quell trouble). Other drumming groups, Levado do

Pelo and Primeiro Odum de Dida (a drumming group of girls), play for free on Tues at the same time as Olodum in the Largo do Pelourinho. Ilê Ayê, plays every Sat from 2200 in Forte Santo Antônio de Carmo. It is recommended to get as close as the crowds permit by taxi at night.

Araketu, a fusion of samba and African rhythms, rehearses in R Chile on Fri night; very popular, US$12. Two more squares in Pelourinho were renovated in 1995: Praça Teresa Batista, behind the Sebrae building, usually hosts a good jazz band called *Garagem* on Wed night in the summer months (entry free). A good bar on the square is *Oratório*. The *Cailleur Bar* across the street leads onto the Praça Pedro Arcanjo. The best night here is Sat, when a local big band under the baton of the great local musician Fred Dantas plays to a packed square. Check with Bahiatursa for details on both squares.

Good bars are *Atelier Maria Adair* (see above), *Casa do Olodum*, *Estação Pelô* and *Bar Do Reggae* and *Alamabique Cachaçaria*, all on R João de Deus, the latter has a great selection of cachaças from all over Brazil, watch out for the steep stairs, especially after a few cachaças! Also good is *Café Impresso*, R João de Deus 3, interesting clientele, rec. Many bars on the Quadra 2M (see above), *Dom Crepe*, *Habeas Copos* are very busy. There is often live music in this square. Good bars in the Pelourinho Square are *Bar Banzo* and *Kalundo*. Good café and great chocolate at *Cailleur*, R Gregório de Matos 17, open daily 0930-2100, bar service continues till 0100. Popular disco is *Gueto*, R Alfredo Brito, plays techno mainly, but does vary.

Barra section: *Mordomia Drinks*, Ladeira Da Barra, enter through narrow entrance to open air bar with spectacular view of the bay, very popular. Most Barra nightlife happens at the Farol da Barra (lighthouse). R Marques de Leão is very busy, with lots of bars with tables on the pavement: *Habeas Copos*, R Marques de Leão 172, famous street side bar, very popular; also *Aladim*, *Bali*, *Ponte de Safena* and *Psicoanalista*, all busy. In the next street, R Afonso Celso, is *Casco Grosso*. *Barril 2000*, on Av Oceânica, is very busy, with live music (MPB – popular Brazilian music) at weekends; *Barra Vento 600*, popular open air bar on the beach front.

Further along the coast at Ondina is the *Bahia Othon Palace Hotel* with a good disco called *Hippotamus*, busy at weekends. In **Rio Vermelho** district are *Rio de Janeiro Bar*, Largo Mesquita, small bar attracting bohemian clientele, few tables, most people drink in the street, Thur-Sat, 1900-0300. *Via Brasil*, rooftop bar in *Bahia Park Hotel*, Largo da Mariquita, open Wed-Sun 2130-0300, live music, cover charge. In same square, *Bar Canoa* at the *Meridien Hotel* has live

music every night, jazz, popular Brazilian music, cover charge US$6, 2100 till 0100. Dancing at *Carinhoso*, Av Otavio Mangabeira, T 248-9575; *Champagne* at *Salvador Praia Hotel*, T 245-5033; *New Fred's*, Av Visc de Itaboraí 125, T 248-4399 (middle-aged market, singles bar). *Bell's Beach* disco at Boca Do Rio, open Tues to Sat 2200-0400, up-market, expensive; *Concha Acústica*, Ladeira da Fonte (behind Teatro Castro Alves, Campo Grande), concerts every weekend with best Brazilian musicians, Rock, MPB, mainly during summer months, usually very cheap, open air, good venue.

Theatres: *Castro Alves*, at Campo Grande (Largo Dois de Julho), frequent concerts; *Teatro da Gamboa*; *Teatro Vila Velha*; *Senac*; *Instituto Cultural Brasil-Alemanha* (ICBA): *Teatro Santo Antônio*, part of the Escola de Teatro da Universidade Federal da Bahia; *Teatro de Arena*.

● **Hospitals & medical services**

Clinic: Barão de Loreto 21, Graça. *Dr Argemiro Júnior* speaks English and Spanish. First consultation US$40, second free. *Dr Manoel Nogueira* (from 1000-1200), Av Joana Angélica 6, T 241-2377, English-speaking.

Doctors: German-speaking doctor, *Dr Josef Stangl*, R Conselheiro Pedro Luiz 179, Rio Vermelho, T 237-1073.

Medical: yellow fever vaccinations free at *Delegação Federal de Saúde*, R Padre Feijó, Canela. Ensure that a new needle is used. Israeli travellers needing medical (or other) advice should contact *Sr Marcus* (T 247-5769), who speaks Hebrew and is glad to help.

● **Language classes**

Casa do Brasil, R Milton de Oliveira 231, Barra, T 245-5866.

● **Laundry**

Lavanderia Lavalimpo, R do Pilar 31, Comércio, Mon-Sat 0800-1800. *Lavanderia Comficha*, Av Doutora Praquer Fries, Porto da Barra, automatic, not too dear.

● **Post & telecommunications**

Post Office: main post office and poste restante is in Praça Inglaterra, in the Lower City, open Mon-Fri 0800-1700, Sat 0800-1200. Other offices at Praça da Sé in Ed Associação Bahiana de Imprensa on R Guedes de Brito 1, T 240-6222; R Alfredo Brito 43, Mon-Sat 0800-1700, Sun 0800-1200, has philatelic section (only pink post office in Brazil!); Rodoviária, Mon-Sat 0800-1800 (till 1200 on Sun); airport; Barra and Iguatemi Shopping Malls (Mon-Fri); Av Princesa Isabel, Barra, and R Marqués de Caravelas; in Ondina by the hotels there is a booth by the beach next to *Ondina Apart Hotel*.

Telecommunications: Embratel, R do Carro

120. Telebahia has branches at Campo da Pólvora, on R Hugo Baltazar Silva (open 0700-2200 daily), Barra and Iguatemi Shopping Centres (Mon-Fri 1000-2200 and Sat 0900-2000), airport (daily 0700-2200) and rodoviária (Mon-Sat 24 hrs and Sun 0700-2200).

● **Shopping**

H Stern jewellers at *Hotels Meridien*, *Othon* and *Bahia*, also at Barra and Iguatemi Shopping centres. Visit the stone-cutting workshops at *Breis* in the Largo do Carmo; best prices for cut stones and jewellery made to order in 24 hrs with a genuine guarantee. The Barra and Iguatemi shopping centres are big, modern and a/c with big department stores. Quality *artesanato* at the 3 official FIEB-SESI shops: Av Tiradentes 299 (Bonfim); Av Borges dos Reis 9 (Rio Vermelho); Av 7 de Setembro 261 (Mercês).

Shopping in Pelourinho: there are many new shops in the area. The major carnaval *afro blocos* have boutiques selling tee-shirts etc. *Boutique Olodum*, on Praça José Alencar, *Ilê Aiyê*, on R Fransisco Muniz Barreto 16 and *Muzenza* next door. On the same street is *Modaxé*, a retail outlet for clothes manufactured by street children under the auspices of the pioneering and highly successful Projeto Axé, expensive but these are the trendiest T-shirts in town. Also on this street at No 18 is *Brazilian Sound*, latest in Brazilian and Bahia music, CDs mainly. Another good record store is *Mini Som* in nearby Praça de Sé (see **Music in Bahia**, above).

Instituto Mauá, R Gregorio de Matos 27 (T 321 5638), open Tues-Sat 0900-1800, Sun 1000-1600, good quality Bahian handicrafts at fair prices, better value and better quality for traditional crafts than the Mercado Modelo. A similar store is *Loja de Artesanato do SESC*, Largo Pelourinho (T 321 5502), Mon-Fri 0900-1800 (closed for lunch), Sat 0900-1300. Both stores rec.

Trustworthy, reliable jewellery stores are *Lasbonfim* (T 242 9854) and *Simon* (T 242 5218), both in the Terreiro de Jesus. They both have branches in the nearby Carmo district. Excellent hand-made lace products at *Artesanato Santa Barbara*, R Alfredo Brito 7. For local art the best stores are *Atelier Portal da Cor*, Ladeira do Carmo 31 (T 242 9466), run by a cooperative of local artists, Totonho, Calixto, Raimundo Santos, Jô, good prices, rec. Also across the street at *Casa do Indio*, Indian artefacts and art, restaurant and bar open here till late, good surroundings. Also good *naif* art at *Koisa Nossa* on R Alfredo Brito 45. Good wood carvings next door by a cooperative of sculptors, Palito and Negão Barão being the most famous. Hand-made traditional percussion instruments (and percussion lessons) at *Chez Lua*, Alfredo Brito 27, made by percussionist Dilson Lua.

Also percussion lessons at *Oficina de Investigação Musical*, Alfredo Brito 24 (T 321 0339), Mon to Fri, 0800-1200 and 1300-1600. *Shopping do Pelô*, R Fransisco Muniz 02 (T 321 4200), is run by SEBRAE, the Brazilian small business authority, open daily until 1800, stalls with varied goods, clothes, jewellery etc.

Bookshops: *Livraria Brandão*, R Ruy Barbosa 104, Centre, T 243 5383, secondhand English, French, Spanish and German books. *Livraria Civilizaçao Brasileira*, Av 7 de Setembro 912, Mercês, and in the Barra, Iguatemi and *Ondina Apart Hotel* shopping centres have some English books; also *Graúna*, Av 7 de Setembro 1448, and R Barão de Itapoan 175, Porto da Barra, many English titles; *Livraria Planeta*, Carlos Gómez 42, loja 1, sells used English books. The bookshop at the airport has English books and magazines.

Markets: the Mercado Modelo, at Praça Cairu, lower city, offers many tourist items such as wood carvings, silver-plated fruit, leather goods, local musical instruments. Lace items for sale are often not handmade (despite labels), are heavily marked up, and are much better bought at their place of origin (eg Ilha de Maré, Pontal da Barra and Marechal Deodoro, see page 541). Cosme e Damião, musical instrument sellers on 1st floor, has been rec, especially if you want to play the instruments. Bands and dancing, especially Sat (but very much for money from tourists taking photographs), closed at 1200 Sun. Photograph exhibition of the old market in basement. (Many items are often cheaper on the Praça da Sé.) Largest and most authentic market is the **Feira de São Joaquim**, 5 km from Mercado Modelo along sea front: barkers, trucks, *burros*, horses, boats, people, mud, all very smelly, every day (Sun till 1200 only), busiest on Sat morning; interesting African-style pottery and basketwork; very cheap. (Car ferry terminal for Itaparica is nearby.) **Iguatemi Shopping Centre** sells good handicraft items, it is run by the government so prices are fixed and reasonable; similarly at Instituto Mauáy Porto da Barra. Every Wed from 1700-2100 there is a **handicrafts fair** in the 17th century fort of Santa Maria at the opp end of Porto da Barra beach. On Fri from 1700-2100, there is an open air market of handicrafts and Bahian food in **Porto da Barra**, a popular event among the local young people. Daily market of handicrafts in **Terreiro de Jesus** in the old city from 1000-1800. Mosquito nets from *Casa dos Mosquiteros*, R Pedro Sá 6F, Calçada, T 226 0715.

Photography and repairs: *Pepe*, R da Ajuda, ed Triúnfo, 1st floor, Centre. *Maxicolor*, R Estados Unidos (Mercado Modelo), for cut-price developing. *Fotocolor*, R da Misericordia, 3, rec place for slide film. *Gil Filmes*, R da Misericordia 5, rec for

Fujichrome and Ektachrome (well priced).

Videotapes: HAL Video Produções, R da Paz, 1 (nr Largo da Graça), T 235-7946, copies produced for US$15/tape or US$20 inc new tape, transcodificação (Brazilian NTSC – European PAL system) US$25; Videovic, Vitória-Centre, Av Centenário 2883, opp Shopping Barra, copying and transcodificação US$28-35.

● **Tour companies & travel agents**
Bus tours are available from several companies: LR Turismo, Itaparica Turismo and Alameda Turismo: city tour (US$25 pp), Bahia by Night includes transport to Moenda restaurant, show and dinner (US$45 pp). All day boat trip on Bahia de Todos Os Santos from 0800-1700 inc visit to Ilha das Frades, lunch on Itaparica (US$10 extra) US$35 pp. Tatu Tours, Ed Victória Center, Sala 1108, Av Centenário 2883, 40147-900 Salvador, BA, in front of Shopping Barra, T 245 9322, F 237 7562, run by an Irishman, specialise in Bahia, give private guided tours and can make any necessary travel, hotel and accommodation arrangements, rec. They are represented in the USA by Brazil Nuts, 1150 Post Rd, Fairfield, CT 06430, T (203) 259-7900, F 259-3177. Submariner, R de Paciência 223, Rio Vermelho, T 237-4097, hire diving equipment, friendly. Kontik-Franstur Viagens e Turismo Ltda, R da Argentia 1, Terreo Comércio, POB 973, T 242-0433. Turitravel, Av Centenário 2883, Ed Vitória Center, Sala 1106, T 245 9345 or 237 4596, helpful, English spoken.

● **Tourist offices**
(With lists of hotels and accommodation in private homes) Bahiatursa, Palácio Rio Branco (see above), R Chile on Praça Municipal, open 0800-1830, Mon-Fri, English and German spoken, helpful. Visitors can obtain weekly list of events and itineraries (on foot or by car) planned by the city, well worth doing. Map, US$2, good; offices have noticeboard for messages. Also at R Francisco Muniz Barreto 12, Historical Centre, T 321 2463, open daily 0830-1930; at rodoviária (good, English spoken); airport (T 204-1244, open daily 0800-2000), friendly (but inefficient); in the Mercado Modelo (T 241-0242, Mon-Fri 0800-1800, Sat 0800-1200); Porto da Barra (T 247-3195, Mon-Fri, 0800-1800, Sat Sun 0800-1200). Also details of travel throughout Sate of Bahia. Phone 131 0600-0030 for tourist information in English. Emtursa, at airport, T 377 2262, Mon-Sat 0800-2200, has good maps. Maps from Departmento de Geografia e Estatística, Av Estados Unidos (opp Banco do Brasil, lower city): also from newsstands inc airport bookshop, US$1.50.

● **Useful addresses**
Immigration: (for extensions of entry permits), Polícia Federal, Av O Pontes 339, Aterro de Água de Meninos, Lower City, T 321-6363, open 1000-1600. Show an outward ticket or sufficient funds for stay, visa extension US$11.
Tourist Police: R Gregório de Matos 16.

● **Transport**
Local Bus: Local buses US$0.35, frescões (or executivos) US$1. On buses and at the ticketsellers' booths, watch your change and beware pickpockets. To get from the old city to the ocean beaches, take a 'Barra' bus from Praça da Sé to the Barra point and walk to the nearer ones; the Aeroporto frescão (last 2130) leaves Praça da Sé, passing Barra, Ondina, Rio Vermelho, Amaralina, Pituba, Costa Azul, Armação, Boca do Rio, Jaguaripe, Patamares, Piatá and Itapoan, before turning inland to the airport. The glass-sided Jardineira bus goes to Flamengo beach (30 km from the city) following the coastal route; it passes all the best beaches; sit on right hand side for best views. It leaves from the Praça da Sé daily 0730-1930, every 40 mins, US$1.50. For beaches beyond Itapoan, take the frescão to Stella Maris and Flamengo beaches. These follow the same route as the Jardineira. During Carnival, when most streets are closed, buses leave from Vale do Canela (O Vale), nr Campo Grande. **Taxi**: Taxi meters start at US$0.60 for the 'flagdown' and US$0.15/100m. They charge US$15/hr within city limits, and 'agreed' rates outside. Taxi Barra Centro US$3 daytime; US$4 at night. Watch the meter, especially at night; the night-time charge should be 30% higher than daytime charges. Teletaxi (24-hr service), 321-9988. **Car rental**: Avis, Av Sete de Setembro 1796, T 237-0155, also at airport, T 377-2276 (toll free 0800-118066); Budget, Av Presidente Vargas 409, T 237-3396; Hertz, R Baependi, T 245-8364, Unidas, Av Oceânica 2456, Ondina, T 336 0717. If renting a car check whether credit card or cash is cheapest. National Car Rentals allow decision at the end of the rental. **Hitchhiking** Out of Salvador, take a 'Cidade Industrial' bus from the rodoviária at the port; it goes on to the highway.

Air Daily flights to Rio, São Paulo, Recife, Aracaju, Belém, Belo Horizonte, Brasília, Fortaleza, Goiania, Ilheus, João Pessoa, Maceió, Manaus, Natal, Porto Alegre, São Luis, and Vitória. Nordeste Regional Airlines, Av Dom João VI 259, Brotas T 244 3355 has daily flights to Porto Seguro and several flights a week to Barreiras, Bom Jesus da Lapa, Guanambi, Paulo Afonso and Vitória da Conquista in the interior of Bahia. Also to Petrolina. Dois de Julho Airport is 32 km from city centre. Buses from airport to Centre Aeroporto-Campo Grande US$0.35, at least 1 hr. Special Executivo bus Aeroporto-Praça da Sé along the coast road for hotels, US$1.30. Special taxi (buy ticket at airport desk)

US$30; taxis airport to city are controlled by certain drivers. From the city to airport is less restricted, fare US$17.50.

Trains From Salvador there are only local train services.

Buses Rodoviária is 5 km from city with regular services to centre (US$0.30); bus RI or RII, 'Centro-Rodoviária-Circular'; in centre, get on in lower city at foot of Lacerda lift; buses also to Campo Grande; journey can take up to 1 hr especially in peak periods. Executive bus, quicker, from Praça da Inglaterra (in front of MacDonalds), Comércio, runs to Iguatemi Shopping Centre, weekdays only, from where there is a walkway to the rodoviária (take care in the dark, or a taxi, US$10). To **Recife**, US$24 (*leito*, 47), 13 hrs, 4 a day and 1 *leito*, Itapemerim, T 388-0037, all at night; plenty to **Rio** (28 hrs, US$47, *leito* 115, Itapemirim, good stops, clean toilets, rec), **São Paulo** (30 hrs), US$58, *leito* US$116 (0815 with Viação Nacional, 2 in pm with São Geraldo, T 533-0188), to **Fortaleza**, 19 hrs, US$40 at 0900 with Itapemerim; **Ilhéus**, 7 hrs, Aguia Branca, T 533-1515, *comercial* US$14, *expresso* US$17, *executivo* US$19, *leito* US$28, several; **Belo Horizonte**, Gontijo T 358-7448, at 1700, US$40, São Geraldo at 1800, US$39. **Foz do Iguaçu**, 52 hrs, US$65. There are daily bus services to **Brasília** along the fully paved BR-242, via Barreiras, 3 daily, 23 hrs, Paraíso, T 358-1591, US$45. Frequent services to the majority of destinations; a large panel in the main hall of the terminal lists destinations and the relevant ticket office.

ROUTES To Rio can do the trip on the BR-116 highway in 3 days, stopping at **Vitória da Conquista** (524 km from Salvador), a busy town with large market Mon-Sat, and a man-made lake with fountains and waterfalls: **C** *Hotel Aliança*, Tr Z Nunes 20, T 424-1006, **C** *Hotel Livramento*, Praça Barão do Rio Branco, T 424-1906, with restaurant, and **F** *Tel-Aviv Palace*, good breakfast, one block from final stop of urban bus from rodoviária; also Camping Clube do Brasil site at Km 831 (bus to Salvador, 8 hrs, US$10; to Feira Santana; to Itaobim, 6 hrs, US$4.50; to Lençóis – change at Bominal – 8 hrs); Teôfilo Otôni, 946 km, or Governador Valadares, 1,055 km (see page 438), and Leopoldina (1,402 km). There are also various motels; two in the State of Bahia are at Vitória da Conquista; and at Feira de Santana; also between Feira and Salvador. Fairly good hotels are also available in **Jequié** (*Itajubá*, *Rex*, and motels), and basic ones in Milagres. Stopovers

on the BR-101 coastal road can be made at Vitória and Itabuna (or Ilhéus), and there are many other towns on or near the coast.

ISLANDS IN THE BAY

From Ribeira (see **Excursions**) a small boat goes 25 km to **Ilha da Maré** between 0900 and 1100, connecting the island's villages of Itamoaba, Praia Grande and Santana (US$1); boat returns next day from Santana at 0400-0500. Santana is a centre for lace making, Praia Grande for basket-weaving. None of the villages has a hotel, but there are restaurants and bars and camping is possible. From São Tomé de Paripe, near the naval base at Aratu, irregular boats go to **Ilha dos Frades**, sparsely populated, no electricity, one *pousada* (**C** *Ponta de Nossa Senhora de Guadalupe*, beachfront, T Salvador 245-8536). The beach is busy lunchtimes with excursions from Salvador, but otherwise is quiet, good snorkelling.

ITAPARICA

Across the bay from Salvador lies the island of **Itaparica**, 29 km long and 12 km wide. The town of Itaparica is very picturesque, with a fair beach in the town, and well worth a visit. Take a bus or kombi by the coast road (Beira Mar) which passes through the villages of Manguinhos, Amoureiras and Ponta de Areia. The beach at Ponta de Areia is one of the best on the island and is very popular. There are many *barracas* on the beach, the best and busiest is *Barraca Pai Xango*, always very lively.

In Itaparica there are many fine residential buildings from the 19th century, plus the church of São Lourenço, one of the oldest in Brazil, a delightful walk through the old town. During the summer months the streets are ablaze with the blossoms of the beautiful flamboyant trees. The beaches at Mar Grande are fair but can be dirty at times. There are many *pousadas* in Mar Grande and the nearby beaches of Ilhota and Gamboa (both to the left as you disembark from the ferry).

From Bom Despacho there are many buses to other towns such as Nazaré das

Farinhas, Valença (see below) and also **Jaguaribe**, a small, picturesque colonial port. Both of these towns are on the mainland connected by a bridge on the SW side of the island, turn off between Mar Grande and Cacha Pregos (bus company is Viazul). There are good beaches across the bay on the mainland, but a boat is needed to reach these (US$8.25). Visits to the marine reseach Station on Ilha do Medo, a project run by the Federal University of Bahia, have to be arranged through their visitors' centre beside the handicraft centre in the historical centre of Itaparica.

Local information

● Accommodation

A good simple *pousada* at Amoureiras is **C** *Pousada Pé na Praia*, good breakfast, good sized rooms, English and French spoken (T 831 1389).

There is a popular **Club Med** on the island (Fazenda Boca do Rio, 44470 Vera Cruz, Bahia, T 071-833-1141, F 071-241-0100). There are few *pousadas* in the town. The best is **L3** *Quinta Pitanga* (T 831 1554), beautifully decorated by the owner Jim Valkus, 3 suites and 2 singles, beachfront property, a retreat, excellent restaurant, expensive but highly rec, accepts day visitors. **A1** *Grande Hotel da Itaparica* (Av Beira Mar, T 831 1120); **C** *Pousada Santa Rita*, and **E** *Restaurant/Pousada Cantinha da Ilha*, clean; **C** *Pousada Icarai*, charming, good location.

In Mar Grande: **A3** *Pousada Arco Iris*, Estrada da Gamboa 102, T 833 1130, magnificent building and setting in mango orchard, expensive, good if slow restaurant, *Manga Rosa*, rec. They have camping facilities next door, shady, not always clean. **C** *Pousada Estrela do Mar*, Av NS das Candeias 170 (T 833 1108), good rooms, clean, fan or a/c, rec. Next door is **C** *Pousada Mar de Ilhota* (T 833 1486). **E** *Pousada Samambaia*, same street, No 61, good breakfast, French spoken, rec; **C** *Lagoa e Mar*, R Parque das Dunas, 01-40, T/F 823-1573, very good breakfast, spacious bungalows, swimming pool, 200m to beach, restaurant, friendly and helpful, highly rec; **C** *Pousada Scórpio*, R Aquárius, T 823-1036, breakfast, beach, swimming pool, simple rooms, weekend restaurant, friendly, rec; **C** *Água no Toco*, Av Atlántica, T 823-1190, 20m to beach, restaurant, friendly, weekend busy, rec; **C** *Pousada Sonho do Verão* (R São Bento 2, opp *Pousada Arco Iris*), chalets and apartments, cooking facilities, French and English spoken, T 833 1616. Like other *pousadas* they rent bicycles

(US$3/hr); they also rent horses (US$5/hr). Near the church in the main square is the **C** *Pousada Casarão da Ilha* (T 833 1106), spacious rooms with a great view of Salvador across the bay, swimming pool, a/c, rec.

At Gamboa **B** *Hotel Pousada Ponta Caieira* (T 833 1080), beachfront, take bus to Gamboa and it's a 5-min walk to the *pousada*, quiet.

At Aratuba there is an excellent hostel, *Albergue da Juventude*, **F** (for students) – **E**, on the beach, clean, friendly, shady, rec.

At Cacha Pregos: *Club Sonho Nosso*, T 837 1040 or 226 1933, very clean huts on clean beach, good service, collect you from anywhere on the island – also Bom Despacho Kombis stop in front of entrance, 5-min walk, rec; **D** *Pousada Cacha Pregos*, next to the supermarket, with fan, bath, no breakfast, good, T 839 1594. Also **C** *Pousada Casa da Praia*, T 837 1058; **C** *Pousada Babalú*, T 837-1193, spacious bungalows, frigobar, fan, good breakfast, friendly, rec.

● Places to eat

Good restaurants in Mar Grande are *Philippe's Bar and restaurant*, Largo de São Bento, good French and local cuisine, information in English and French. *O Pacifico* is good, friendly, peaceful. *Restaurant Rafael* in main square for pizzas and snacks. Also pizzas at *Bem Me Quer*, opp *Pousada Samambaia* down alley. There are many Baiana's selling *acarajé* in the late afternoon and early evening in the main square by the pier.

● Transport

Ferry The island is reached from the main land by two ferries. The main passenger ferry leaves for Bom Despacho from São Joaquim (buses for Calçada, Ribeira stop across the road from the ferry terminal; the 'Sabino Silva – Ribeira' bus passes in front of the Shopping Barra). The first ferry from Salvador leaves at 0600 and, depending on demand, the ferries leave at intervals of 45 mins. Last ferry from Salvador is at 2230. Returning to Salvador the first ferry is at 0515 and the last one is at 2230. During the summer months the ferries are much more frequent. Enquiries at the Companhia de Navegação Baiano (CNB), T 321 7100 from 0800 to 1700. One way ticket for foot passengers Mon-Fri US$0.80, Sat-Sun US$1.20.

Mar Grande can be reached via minibus from Bom Despacho, or by a smaller ferry (Lancha) from the Terminal Marítimo in front of the Mercado Modelo in Salvador. The ferries leave every 45 mins and the crossing takes 50 mins, US$0.45. They ask that no swimming costumes be worn on board.

Road From Bom Despacho there are many buses, kombis and taxis to all parts of the island. The best beaches are at Ponta de Areia, Mar

Grande (US$0.50 by kombi), Berlinque, Aratuba and Cacha Pregos. Kombi and taxis can be rented for trips around the island but be prepared to bargain, US$20-30 for a half-day tour.

Tours of the Bay

Small boats for trips around the bay can be hired privately at the small port by the Mercado Modelo called Rampa do Mercado. A pleasant trip out to the mouth of the bay should take 1½ hrs as you sail along the bottom of the cliff. When arranging to hire any boat ensure that the boat is licensed by the Port Authority (Captânia dos Portos) and that life-jackets are on board. Boats are regularly checked to ensure that they are sea worthy and boats not complying with these regulations are not permitted to carry paying passengers. The Companhia de Navegação Bahiana (T 321 7100) sails 5 times a week to **Maragojipe** on the Rio Paraguaçu to the W (see under **The Recôncavo** below). The trip takes 3 hrs. It sails across the bay and then up the valley of the river. There are some very beautiful views along the way. The ship makes two stops along the way, at Barra do Paraguaçu and also at Mutuca where locals row out to the ship in dug out canoes to disembark passengers leaving the ship at that point. A good trip would be to continue to Cachoeira by bus from Maragogipe and return to Salvador the following day. Departure from Salvador from Terminal Turístico in front of the Mercado Modelo Mon-Thur 1430 (1530 in summer). Fri departure is at 1130. Departure Maragogipe Mon-Thur 0500 and Fri 0830, US$3.

Itaparica Turismo (T 248 3187/248 3433) and *LR Turismo* (T 248 3333) run daily schooner trips to islands in the bay visiting Frades and Itaparica islands; boats leave from Terminal Turístico at 0830. American yachtsman Steve Lafferty is highly rec for enjoyable sailing trips, US$120 a day for up to 4 people: R do Sodre 45, apt 301, T 241-0994.

NAZARE DAS FARINHAS

(*Pop* 25,940) 60 km inland from Itaparica, and reached over a bridge by bus from **Bom Despacho**. This 18th-century town is celebrated for its market, which specializes in the local ceramic figures, or *caxixis*. There is a large market in Holy Week, particularly on Holy Thursday and Good Friday. 12 km from Nazaré (taxi US$5.50, also buses) is the village of **Maragojipinha**, which specializes in making the ceramic figures. Bus from Salvador, 1530, takes 5 hrs.

FEIRA DE SANTANA

(*Pop* 405,690) 112 km NW of Salvador on both the coastal BR-101 and the inland BR-116 roads to Rio, the centre of a great cattle breeding and trading area; its Mon market, known as Feira do Couro (leather fair), said to be the largest in Brazil, attracts great crowds to its colourful display of local products. The permanent Artesanato market in the centre has a bigger selection, including leather, than the Mon market. Bus every 30 mins from Salvador, 2 hrs, US$3. (Rodoviária has a wall of painted tiles made by Udo-Ceramista, whose workshop is Brotas, Av Dom João VI 411, Salvador.)

● **Accommodation A1** *Luxor*, BR-116 Sul, Km 437, T 221-5922; **C** *Flecha*, about 20 km away at Km 171 BR-101, T 221-5999; several cheap ones in Praça da Matriz and nr the rodoviária, which is quite nr the centre; **C** *Senador*, R Senador Quintino 10, rec, Bahian restaurant in same street, No 259, *Panela de Barro*, good.

THE RECÔNCAVO

The area around Salvador, known as the Recôncavo Baiano, was one of the chief centres of sugar and tobacco cultivation in the 16th century.

Leaving Salvador on the Feira road, at Km 33 one forks left on the BR-324 to the **Museu de Recôncavo Vanderlei de Pinho** (see page 507). Further W, round the bay, is **São Francisco do Conde**, 54 km from Salvador, with a church and convent of 1636 and the ruins of Don Pedro II's agricultural school, said to be the first in Latin America.

At 60 km from Salvador the BA-026 road branches off the BR-324 to Santo Amaro, Cachoeira and São Félix.

SANTO AMARO DA PURIFICAÇÃO

73 km from Salvador is **Santo Amaro da Purificação** (*pop* 54,145) an old sugar centre sadly decaying, noted for its churches (often closed because of robberies), municipal palace (1769), fine main square, house of the poet and singer Caetano Veloso (his sister, the singer Maria Bethânia, is also from here), and ruined mansions including the Araújo Pinto, former residence of the Barão de Cotegipe. Other attractions include the splendid beaches of the bay, the falls of Vitória and the grotto of Bom Jesus dos Pobres. Festivals in Jan and Feb (Santo Amaro and NS da Purificação) are interesting. Craftwork is sold on the town's main bridge. No good hotels or restaurants.

3 km beyond Santo Amaro on BR-420, turn right onto BA-878 for **Bom Jesus dos Pobres**, a small, traditional fishing village with a 300-year history. One good hotel: **B** *Água Viva*, T (075) 696 1178, reservations (Salvador 071) 359 1132, beach front, chalets or apartments, a/c or fan, good breakfast and restaurant, on one of the oldest farms in the region, good beach, rec. Bus from Salvador rodoviária 4 a day (Camurjipe), US$3.75.

CACHOEIRA AND SÃO FÉLIX

At 54 km from Santo Amaro, and only 4 km from the BR-101 coastal road, are the twin towns of **Cachoeira** (Bahia's 'Ouro Preto', *pop* 28,255), and **São Félix** (*pop* 12,095) on either side of the Rio Paraguaçu below the Cachoeira dam. Cachoeira, recently declared a national monument, was twice capital of Bahia: once in 1624-5 during the Dutch invasion, and once in 1822-3 while Salvador was still held by the Portuguese. It was the birthplace of Ana Néri, known as 'Mother of the Brazilians', who organized nursing services during the Paraguayan War (1865-70). There are beautiful views from above São Félix.

Places of interest Cachoeira's main buildings are the **Casa da Câmara e Cadeia** (1698-1712), the **Santa Casa de Misericórdia** (1734 – the hospital, someone may let you see the church), the 16th-

century **Ajuda** chapel (now containing a fine collection of vestments), and the Convent of the **Ordem Terceira do Carmo**, whose church has a heavily gilded interior. Other churches: Carmo (1548) and its Third Order (fine *azulejos* and gilding), the **Matriz** with 5m-high *azulejos*, and **Nossa Senhora da Conceição da Monte**. Beautiful lace cloths on church altars. All churches are either restored or in the process of restoration. Ruined Jesuit seminary. Tourist office in the Casa de Ana Néri. Craftwork in ceramics and wood readily available.

Excursions 6 km from Cachoeira, on the higher ground of the Planalto Baiano, is the small town of Belém (turning 2½ km on road to Santo Amaro). Church and seminary of Carmo. It is a healthy spot where people from Salvador have summer homes.

Maragojipe (*pop* 38,800) a tobacco exporting port 22 km SE of Cachoeira along a dirt road (BA-123), can also be reached by boat from Salvador. See the old houses and the church of São Bartolomeu, with its museum. The main festival is São Bartolomeu, in August. Good ceramic craftwork.

The tobacco centre of Cruz das Almas can also be visited, although transport is poor.

Local festivals São João (24 June) 'Carnival of the Interior' celebrations inc dangerous games with fireworks, well-attended by tourists; Boa Morte (early Aug); a famous *candomblé* ceremony at the Fonte de Santa Bárbara on 4 December.

● **Accommodation In Cachoeira:** **B** *Pousada do Convento de Cachoeira* (run by Bahiatursa), T 725 1716, in newly restored 16th-century convent, good restaurant; *Pousada do Guerreiro*, 13 de Maio 14, T 724-1203, no restaurant; **E** *Santo Antônio* nr the rodoviária, basic, clean, safe, friendly, laundry facilities, rec; **E** *Colombo*, nr the river, basic, friendly, meals available, rec. *Youth Hostel*, Av Parnamirim 417, T 268-4844/3390.

● **Places to eat** *Cabana do Pai Thomaz*, 25 de Junho 12, excellent Bahian food, good value, also an hotel, **D** with private bath and breakfast; *Recanto de Oxum*, nearby, *Gruta Azul*, Praça Manoel Vitorino, lunch only; *Do Nair*, R 13 de

Maio, delicious food and sometimes Seresta music. **São Félix**: *Xang-hai*, F, good, cheap food, warmly rec. Try the local dish, *maniçoba* (meat, manioc and peppers).

● **Transport** Buses from Salvador (Camurjipe) every hour or so; Feira Santana 2 hrs US$1.70.

INLAND FROM SALVADOR

ROUTES Motorists to Brasília can save a little time by taking the ferry to Itaparica, book in advance to avoid long queues, and then going across country to Itaberaba for the BR-242 highway. The journey can be broken at Itaberaba, Lençóis (see below), or Ibotirama on the Rio São Francisco; at Barreiras on the Rio Grande, where buses stop for 2-3 hrs; or at Posse or Alvorada do Norte (Goiás). All have hotels of varying quality. The road is paved from Salvador to Brasília, but it is reported poor between Salvador and Lençóis and full of potholes between Barreiras and Alvorado do Norte.

LENÇÓIS

400 km W of Salvador on the BR-242 is **Lençóis** (*pop* 7,590; *DDD* code 075), a historical monument and a colonial gem, founded in 1844 because of diamonds in the region. There are still some *garimpeiros*. In the town, *Artesanato Areias Coloridas*, R das Pedras, owned by Tourino, is the best place for local sand paintings made in bottles. These are inexpensive and fascinating to see being done. They will make one as you wait. For ceramic work, the best is *Jota*, who has a workshop which can be visited. Take the steps to the left of the school near the *Pousada Lençóis*. His work is very original, rec. Market day is Mon, in the morning, rec. It is difficult to change money in Lençóis.

Local information
● **Accommodation**
A3 *Pousada de Lençóis*, T 334-1102, with breakfast, swimming pool, rec.

B *Estalagem Alcino e Silvinha*, R Gen Vieira de Morais 139, T 334-1171, with bath, **D** pp shared bath, beautiful, restored 19th-century house, superb breakfast, highly rec; **B** *Canto de Águas*, Av Senhor dos Passos s/n, T 334-1154, F 334-1188, comfortable, good location, swimming pool, a/c or fan, good service, rec; **B** Ze Carlos and Lia Vieira de Moraes have 2 excellent

chalets in their huge garden at the entrance to the town, R Gen Viveiros 187, T 334 1151, English spoken, good breakfast (he is a keen birdwatcher and an authority on the region, she makes excellent jams).

C *Colonial*, Praça Otaviano Alves, T 334-1114; **C** *Pousada do Parque*, BR-242, T 334-1173, quiet, by first bridge before town; **C** *Pousada Village Lapão*, nearby, chalets of various size, quiet, T 334-1117.

D *Pousalegre*, R Boa Vista 95, T 334-1124, with good regional breakfast, friendly, safe, hot showers, good vegetarian restaurant; **D** *Repousada*, R Boa Vista, next door, good breakfast, safe, rec; **D** *Tradição*, R José Florêncio, T 334-1120, with bath, breakfast, fridge, mosquito net, pleasant.

E *Bicho de Mata*, contact in Salvador 240-4337, Alto da Estrele s/n (nr Zion Reggae Bar), new, very friendly, quiet, relaxed, good breakfast, highly rec; **E** *Casa de Hélia*, R das Pedras 102, t 334 1143, English and some Hebrew spoken, good facilities, renowned breakfast, rec.

Two campsites, one 2 km before Lençóis, one in the town centre (friendly, rec). There are also houses to rent in the town. Most of these are basic, with cooking and washing facilities. Juanita on R do Rosário rents rooms with access to washing and cooking facilities, US$3.50 pp. Isabel rents a house on the main square in front of the Correios, US$4 pp without breakfast.

● **Places to eat**
Lajedo, good food with good view of town, popular meeting place at night; *Goody*, R da Rodoviária s/n, good simple cooking, reasonably priced. A busy local bar is *Ynave*, with live music on weekends. The busiest spot at weekends is *Amigo da Onça*, R José Florêncio, nr municipal market, lambada, forró and samba-reggae until the small hours, good fun.

● **Post & telecommunications**
Communications: Telebahia, open daily 0800-2200.

● **Tour companies & guides**
Reliable tour company: *Pé de Trilha Turismo Aventura*, Praça Horácio de Matos s/n, T/F 334-1124, nr Banco do Brasil, guiding, trekking, rents camping equipment, etc, can make reservations for most of the *pousadas* in the Chapada Diamantina (see below), represented in Salvador by Tatu Tours (071-245-9322, F 071-237-7562). A reliable guide is Edmilson (known locally as Mil), who can be found at Sectur; he knows the region extremely well and is very knowledgeable. Roy Funch, the ex-director of the Chapada Diamantina National Park, is an excellent guide and can be found at his craft shop, *Funkart*, in the main square. Another rec guide to Chapada

Diamantina is João (contact at *Pousalegre*, above), experienced and knowledgeable on biology and geology, group tours, US$30 (eg to Gruta do Lapão, 6 people; Cachoeira da Fumação and Capão, 8 people, US$13 extra for food, 3-day tour.

● **Tourist offices**
Sectur, nr *Pousada Lençóis*, open daily 0800-1200, 1400-1800. Also on Praça Oscar Maciel, next to the church across the river from town, T 334-1121. There are many guides offering their services at most *pousadas*, about US$18; most of them are very young.

● **Transport**
Paraíso bus from **Salvador** 0730, 1200 and 2200, US$14 (bus goes to Seabra, 80 km beyond Lençóis, make sure driver knows you want to go to Lençóis); **Feira de Santana**, returns at 0900, 2100; buses also from Recife, Ibotirama, Barreiras or **Brasília**, 16 hrs, US$22.

PARQUE NACIONAL DA CHAPADA DIAMANTINA

Lençóis is the headquarters of the **Parque Nacional da Chapada Diamantina** (founded 1985), which contains 1,500 sq km of mountainous country, with waterfalls, large caves (take care, and a strong torch, there are no signs and caves can be difficult to find without a guide), rivers with natural swimming pools and good walking tours. Information, T (075) 332-2175, or Ibama, Av Juracy Magalhães Jr 608, CEP 40295-140, Salvador, T (071) 240-7322.

Excursions near Lençóis and in the Chapada Diamantina Near the town, visit the **Serrano** with its wonderful natural pools in the river bed, which give a great hydro massage. A little further away is the **Salão de Areia**, where the coloured sands for the bottle paintings come from. **Ribcirão do Meio** is a 45-min walk from town; here locals slide down a long natural water shute into a big pool (it is best to be shown the way it is done and to take something to slide in). **Gruta do Lapão**, 3 hrs from Lençíos, guide essential is in quartz rock and therefore has no stalagmites. Some light rock climbing is required. **Cachoeira da Primavera**, two very pretty waterfalls close to town, rec. **Cachoiera Sossego**, 2 hrs from town, a 'picture postcard' waterfall, swimming in pool, rec.

Morro de Pai Inácio, 30 km from Lençóis, has the best view of the Chapada, rec at sunset (bus from Lençóis at 0815, 30 mins, US$0.75). In the park is the **Cachoeira de Glass** (or Smoke Waterfall), 400m, the highest in Brazil. To see it, go to Palmeiras, from where it is 18 km on a dirt road to the point where you then walk 2 hrs to the falls. The view is astonishing; the updraft of the air currents often makes the flow of water stand up. Well worth the effort of getting there.

Other excursions are: **Lapa Doce**, a cave with fine stalagmites and stalactites, 70 km, **Andaraí**, 101 km, and the diamond ghost town of **Igatu**, a further 14 km on the other side of the Rio Paraguaçu. There is a bridge across the river. The town has a good *pousada*. A good day trip from Lençóis is to **Poço Encantado** (23 km SE of the Chapada itself, 55 km from Andaraí), a mountain cave with a lake of crystal clear water, 60m deep, very spectacular, known locally as the 8th wonder of the world. From April to Aug, the sunlight enters the cave from the mountain side, hits the water and is dispersed into the colours of the spectrum. A visit is highly recommended and can be followed by a trip to Igatu on the return to Lençóis. Southeast of the park is **Mucujé** (*Hotel Mucujé*, opp rodoviária, good food, basic, take mosquito coils), lovely walks among hills or along Rio Paraguaçu. It is possible to walk from Mucujé to Lençóis, about 50 km, but seek expert advice on the route through the park before doing so. Buses from Mucujé to Seabra run Tues, Thur, Sat at 0500; frequent service from there to Lençóis and Palmeiras.

Cachoiera da Fumaça and Capão is a 3 day excursion, including the Rio Capivara and the top of Cachoeira da Fumaça, reached on the third day. The village of **Capão** is near the base of the climb.

● **Accommodation** C *Candombá*, good breakfast, excellent food, home-grown vegetables, run by Claude and Suzana (Claude speaks French and English and guides in the region); F (075) 332 2176, or through Tatu Tours in Salvador (address above); D *Pousada Verde*, at entrance to town, very good breakfast, rec;

E *Pouso Riacho do Our*, friendly, rec; **E** *Tatu Feliz*, no breakfast.

● **Transport** From Salvador you can get a bus to Chapada Diamantina, US$11, 3 times daily, last bus from Salvador departs 2200 arrives 0430 via Alto Paraiso. **NB** Book in advance. Local guides can often arrange transport to the more remote excursions, certainly this is possible when groups are involved.

SOUTH FROM SALVADOR

VALENCA

271 km from Salvador, on an asphalted road, is this small, attractive and bustling town (*pop* 66,785), at the mouth of the Rio Una. Two old churches stand on rising ground above the town; the views from Nossa Senhora do Amparo are recommended. The town is in the middle of an area producing black pepper, cloves and *piaçava* (used in making brushes and mats). Other industries include the building and repair of fishing boats (*saveiros*). Valença and the beaches towards Ilhéus are being developed. The Rio Una enters an enormous region of mangrove swamps. The main attraction of Valença is the beaches on the mainland (Guabim, 14 km N) and on the island of Tinharé. Avoid touts at the rodoviária, they give misleading information and then offer an overpriced alternative; better to visit the friendly tourist office opposite the rodoviária.

● **Accommodation B** *Rio Una*, R Maestro Barrinha, T 741-1614, swimming pool; **C** *Guabim*, Praça da Independência, T 741-1110, modest, rec, good *Akuarius* restaurant; next door, **D** *Rafa*, new, large rooms, well rec; **E** *Tourist Hotel*, Mal Floriano 167, good, friendly; **E** *Valença*, R Dr H Guedes Melo 15, T 741-1807, clean, comfortable, good breakfast, rec.

● **Transport** Long-distance buses run from the new rodoviária, Av Maçônica, T 741-1280, while the old one is for local buses. Eight buses a day to/from Valença, 5 hrs, US$9, Camarujipe (T 071 358-0109) and São Jorge companies; São Jorge to **Itabuna**, 5 hrs, US$7, very slow. A new road has been opened, greatly shortening the journey to Valença; take the ferry from São Joaquim to Bom Despacho on Itaparica island. From there it is 130 km to Valença via Nazaré das Farinhas (see page 429). To/from Bom Despacho on Itaparica, Camarujipe and Águia Branca companies, 16 a day, 1 hr 45 mins, US$7.

TINHARÉ AND MORRO DE SÃO PAULO

Tinharé is a large island (with good walking, beaches and camping, but no banks or exchange) separated from the mainland by the estuary of the Rio Una and mangrove swamps, so that it is hard to tell which is land and which is water. The best beaches and *pousadas* are at Morro de São Paulo.

Morro de São Paulo is very popular in summer, situated on the headland at the northernmost tip of the island, lush with ferns, palms and birds of paradise, dominated by the lighthouse and the ruins of a Dutch colonial fort (1630). The village has a landing place on the sheltered landward side, dominated by the old gateway of the fortress. From the lighthouse a path leads to a ruined lookout with cannon, which has panoramic views. The place is expensive Dec-Mar, crowded at holiday times, but cheaper during the rest of the year. All roads are unmade, but beaches are good. Fish can be bought from the fishermen in summer, or borrow a pole and catch your own at sunset. Secondhand books (English, German, and others) sold at the back of the craft shop: the bearded owner will trade 2 for 1 if he's in the mood.

Galeão is another village in the island, but has no beach, only mangrove swamps. The church of São Francisco Xavier looks imposing on its hill.

Local information

● **Accommodation** in **Morro de São Paulo** *Pousada da Tia Glória*, friendly, quiet; next door is **D** *Pousada da Praça*, clean, friendly, fan, rec. There are many cheap *pousadas* and rooms to rent nr the fountain (Fonte Grande) but this part of town is very hot at night. **E** pp *Pousada Mare Sol*, simple, friendly, nr Fonte Grande, rec. Senhora Preta rents rooms **E**, ask at quay; **D** *Pousada Village da Ponte*, R da Fonte Grande, T in Salvador 071-248 2699, a/c fridge, fan, rec; **E** pp *Pousada Trilha do Riacho*, without breakfast, fan, friendly; **D** pp *Pousada Escorregue no Reggae*, with breakfast, reggae played all day, rec. Highly rec are **C** *Pousada Porto da Cima* (200m past **D** *Pousada Casarão*) chalets with fans, very friendly; **C-D** *Pousada Gaúcho*, huge breakfast, shared bath. A little further along and up some steep steps to the left is **B** *Pousada Colibri*, cool, always a breeze blowing, excellent views, only six apartments, Helmut, the owner, speaks English and German, highly rec.

Beach hotels: the beaches on Morro de São Paulo are at the bottom of the main street where one turns right on to the first beach (Primeira Praia). **B** *Pousada Vistabella*, is very clean, owner Petruska is extremely friendly, good rooms with bathrm, rooms to the front have good views and are cooler, all have fans, hammocks, rec, T (073) 254 1272; **C** *Pousada Farol do Morro*, all rooms with sea view, cool, T (071) 243 4144, F 243 4207; **D** *Pousada Ilha da Saudade*, good breakfast, simple, friendly; **C** *Pousada Ilha do Sol*, good views, rec. On second beach (Segunda Praia) is **C** *Pousada Oxum*. On third beach (Terceira Praia) is **B** *Pousada Gaimu*, 14 rooms, in lush tropical setting, secluded (T 071-321 1936). Nearby is **B** *Pousada Fazenda Caeira*, large grounds, private, well stocked library with snooker and other games, friendly T (075) 741 1272, both of these are rec. A new 5-star hotel, *Hotel Ville Gaignon*, has opened, swimming pools, games rooms, convention rooms, etc. On fourth beach (Quarta Praia) is **C** *Pousada Catavento*.

● **Places to eat**

Restaurant Gaúcho for good, reasonably priced, typical regional cooking. *Ebano* offers a good varied menu. *Belladonna* on the main street is a very good Italian restaurant with great music, a good meeting point; owner Guido speaks Italian, English and French and is a willing source of information on the Morro; open daily from 1800 till the small hours, rec. Across the street in a very good pizzeria called *Pizzas!*, rec. *Casablanca* is a good simple restaurant, open daily till late. Good breakfasts at *Doceria da Paula* on main street and at *Pousada Natureza*, nr church, US$5. The second beach is the liveliest with many beach huts offering cool drinks, meals etc. *Barraca Caita* opens till late with good music, dance music at weekends. They have snorkelling equipment for hire, popular meeting point, potent cocktails! Another *barraca* is *Ponto da Ilha* alongside. There are many other *barracas* on the third beach but a short walk to the fourth beach is *Barraca da Piscina*, good swimming in front, good ambience, dominos, draughts etc, reasonable seafood menu, open till late during summer months; *Comida Natural*, on main street, *comida a kilo*, good juices, rec. *Bahiana*, main square, good food, rec.

● **Transport**

From Salvador, a direct ferry service sails from the Terminal Marítimo in front of the Mercado Modelo to Morro de São Paulo (*Lancha Executiva*): daily in high season, Fri, Sat, Sun in low season, 0830, returns 1730, US$30 one way, 2½ hr trip. Also, the *Bonanza III* from Rampa do Mercado Modelo, US$15, daily at 1300, 4 hrs, T 226-7523 (Salvador), 783-1062 (Morro de São Paulo). Part of the trip is on the open sea, which can be rough (not rec for those who suffer from seasickness).

It is sometimes possible to get a direct boat from Salvador to Galeão, 2-3 times a week in summer, 6-7 hrs, ask for Sr Cacu and the *Natureza* at the fishing port next to the Mercado Modelo.

Boats (US$1.50) leave every day from Valença for Galeão (1½ hrs), Gamboa (1½ hrs) and Morro de São Paulo (1½ hrs).

Boats to the Morro leave from the main bridge in Valença 5 times a day (signalled by a loud whistle). The fare is US$2.50. Only buses between 0530-1100 from Salvador to Valença connect with ferries. Private boat hire can be arranged outside these times. A responsible local boatman is Jario, T (075) 741 1681; he can be contacted to meet travellers arriving at the rodoviária for transfer to the Morro. He also offers excursions to other islands, especially **Boipeba**, a small simple fishing village. Overnight excursions to this village are possible; **D** *Pousada Luar das Águas* (T 741 2238), simple, good.

ITACARÉ

On the coast, S toward Ilhéus, is the picturesque fishing village of **Itacaré**. It is a beautiful area with a protected beach with crystal-clear water to the right of town; across the river there are beaches with good surfing. It is becoming a popular weekend spot, especially for surfers.

● **Accommodation** **C** *Pousada Litoral*, R de Souza 81, 1 block from where buses stop, with bath, owner João Cravo, speaks English and can organize tours to out of the way beaches, hiring fishing boats, etc, rec; **C** *Sage Paint*, owned by a Cuban Ana Cubana, ocean-front *pousada*, showers, outings organized to nearby beaches etc, rec.

● **Transport** Buses to Ilhéus, 3-4 hrs, US$4.75; to Salvador, change at Ubaituba (3 hrs, US$2), Ubaituba-Salvador, 6 hrs, US$9.50, several daily.

ILHÉUS

(*Pop* 223,350; *CEP* 45660; *DDD* 073) Near the mouth of the Rio Cachoeira, 462 km S of Salvador, the port serves a district which produces 65% of all Brazilian cocoa. Shipping lines call regularly. A bridge links the Pontal district (airport) to the mainland. The town is the scene of the famous novel by Jorge Amado, *Gabriela, Clove and Cinnamon*. The local beaches are splendid (but the central beach is polluted) and the place is highly recommended for a short stay.

Places of interest

Among the churches to visit are **Nossa Senhora da Vitória**, in Alto da Vitória, built in 17th century to celebrate a victory over the Dutch; **São Jorge**, in city centre; and the cathedral of **São Sebastião** on sea shore; **Santana**, in Rio de Engeho is one of the oldest in Brazil.

Excursions

Buses run every 30 mins to **Itabuna** (32 km; *pop* 185,180), the trading centre of the rich cocoa zone (also many lumber mills). Ceplac installations at Km 8 on the Itabuna-Ilhéus road show the whole processing of cocoa. Tours of cocoa plantations can be arranged through the *Ilhéus Praia* hotel; Jorge Amado's novel *The Violent Lands* deals with life on the cocoa plantations. Bus from Salvador, 6½ hrs, US$8.50. The paved BA-415 links Itabuna to Vitória da Conquista (275 km) on the BR-116.

The **beaches** between Ilhéus and Olivença are good, eg Cururupe, and frequent buses run to Olivença. For the good beaches at Pontal, take 'Barreira' bus and get off just past *Hotel Jardim Atlântico*. Hot baths (*balneário*) 18 km away, are reached by Viaçao São Jorge or Canavieiras buses.

Local festivals

Include Festa de São Sebastião (17-20 Jan), Carnival, Festa de São Jorge (23 April), Foundation day, 28 June, and Festa do Cacau (Oct).

Local information
● **Accommodation in Ilhéus**
A3 *Hotel Barravento* on Malhado beach, R NS das Graças, T 231-3223, ask for the penthouse – usually no extra charge, inc bath, breakfast and refrigerator; **A3** *Ilhéus Praia*, Praça D Eduardo (on beach), T 231-2533, pool, helpful, rec; **A3** *Pontal Praia*, T 231-3033, Praia do Pontal, swimming pool.

C *Britânia*, T 231-1722, R 28 de Junho 16, and at No 29 **D** *San Marino*, T 231-3668, friendly, clean. **D** *Pousada Kazarão*, Praça Coronel Pessoa 9, clean, friendly, no breakfast, noisy; **D** *Pousada Sol Atlantico*, Av Lomanto Júnior,

1450, Pontal T 231-8059, ouside city but frequent buses passing, good view over bay, fan, TV, balcony, clean, friendly. *Tio San*, R Antonio Levigne de Lemos, T 231-3668.

Plenty of cheap hotels nr municipal rodoviária in centre; **E** *Hotel Atlântico Sul*, R Bento Berilo 224, Centro, T 231 4668 or 8051, clean, good bar/restaurant, rec.

Campsite: *Estancia das Fontes*, 19 km on road S to Olivença, cheap, shady, rec.

In Itabuna: of the hotels, the **A3** *Itabuna Palace* (Av Cinquentenário 1061, T/F 211-1233, restaurant) is probably the best; also **B** *Príncipe*, R Miguel Calmon 234, T 211-3272, and **C** *Lord*, Quintino Bocaiúva 1017, T/F 211-1233.

● **Places to eat**
Os Velhos Marinheiros, Av 2 de Julho, on the waterfront, rec; *Come Ben*, nr Praça Cairu, cheap and good; *Vesúvio*, Praça D Eduardo, next to Cathedral, made famous by Amado's novel (see above), now Swiss-owned, very good but pricey; *Nogar*, Av Bahia 377, close to the sea, good pizzas and pasta. Local drink, *coquinho*, coconut filled with cachaça, only for the strongest heads! Also try *suco de cacau* at juice stands.

● **Tourist offices**
Situated on beach opp Praça Castro Alves (a few minutes from cathedral), friendly, maps US2, rec.

● **Transport**
Buses Rodoviária is 4 km from centre on Itabuna road, but Itabuna-Olivença bus goes through centre of Ilhéus. Several daily to **Salvador**, 7 hrs, US$14-19 (*leito* US$28, Expresso São Jorge); 0620 bus goes via Itaparica, leaving passengers at Bom Despacho ferry station on the island – thence 50-mins ferry to Salvador. To **Itacaré**, 4 hrs, US$4.75; to **Eunápolis**, 7 hrs, US$6, this bus also leaves from the central bus terminal. Other destinations also served; local buses leave from Praça Cairu. Insist that taxi drivers have meters and price charts.

115 km S is **Canavieiras** (*pop* 32,960), a developing beach resort (**B** *Pousada Maria*; **C** *Mini-Hotel*; Camping at Praia de Atalaia).

PORTO SEGURO

About 400 km S of Ilhéus on the coast is the old town of **Porto Seguro** (*pop* 34,520; *CEP* 45820; *DDD* 073), now developed for tourism; the airport has been enlarged to take jets, frequent buses from the new rodoviária. Building is, however, subject to controls on height and materials, in keeping with traditional Bahian styles (colonial or Indian). In the area are remains of original Atlantic coastal forest, with parrots, monkeys, marmosets and snakes.

It was N of the site of Porto Seguro that Cabral first landed on 22 April 1500; a cross marks the supposed site of the first mass in Brazil on the road between Porto Seguro and Santa Cruz Cabrália. A tourist village, Coroa Vermelha, has sprouted at the site, 20 mins by bus to the N, souvenir shops selling Pataxó-Tupi Indian items, beach bars, hotels and rental houses, all rather uncoordinated. From the roundabout at the entrance to Porto Seguro take a wide, steep, unmarked path uphill to the historical city (**Cidade Histórica**), three churches (NS da Misericórdia-1530, NS do Rosário-1534, and NS da Pena-1718), the former jail and the cross; a small, peaceful place with lovely gardens and panoramic views.

There are *borrachudos*, little flies that bite feet and ankles in the heat of the day; coconut oil keeps them off; at night mosquitoes can be a problem (but there is no malaria, dengue or yellow fever).

Excursions

Guided tours of the area with BPS, at the Shopping Centre, T 288-2373. *Companhia do Mar* (Praça dos Pataxós, T 288-2981) does daily trips by schooner to coral reefs off the coast. The most popular is to Recife de Fora, with good snorkelling; leaves daily 1000, returns 1630, about US$18, US$3 extra for snorkelling gear. Other good trips to Coroa Vermelho and Coroa Alta, and S to Trancoso. 10 mins N of Coroa Vermelha, **Santa Cruz Cabrália** is a delightful small town with a splendid beach, river port, a 450-year old church with a fine view, and several hotels (eg *Pousada Xica da Silva* near bus stop, cheap, nice, good restaurant *Coqueiro Verde* – try *pitu*, a kind of crayfish). Across the river (dugout US$1) is Santo André, a small village on the ocean, also with a beach and inns. Hourly buses from Santa Cruz to Porto Seguro (23 km). Schooner trips to the reef also from Santa Cruz. For equipment hire, see below.

Local information
● **Accommodation**

The town is a popular holiday resort – prices rise steeply Dec-March.

A3 *Porto Seguro Praia*, 3 km N of city on coast road, T 288-2321, F 288-2069; *Cabanas do Tio João*, BR-367, Km 64, 2 km N of Porto Seguro, T 288-2315, a/c, pool, English and French spoken, rec; **A3** *Phonécia*, Av 22 de Abril 400, T 288-2411.

B *Estalagem Porto Seguro*, R Mal Deodoro 66, T 288-2095, old colonial house, a/c, fan, rec; **B** *Pousada Albatroz*, Av dos Navegantes 600, a/c, pool, rec, T 288-2394, F 288-2047; **B** *Pousada Casa Azul*, 15 de Novembro 11, T 288-2180, with bath, English spoken, good, swimming pool; **B** *Pousada Chauá*, same Av No 800, T 288-2894, a/c; **B** *Pousada Coqéiro Verde*, R 'A' No 01, T 288-2621, F 288-2623, a/c, pool, sauna; **B** *Pousada do Caís*, Portugal 382, T 228-2111, with bath, colonial house on sea-front, good; several others on same street; **B** *Pousada Gaivota*, Av dos Navegantes 333, T/F 288-2826, a/c, pool, sauna; **B** *Pousada Solar da Praça*, Praça da Bandeira, bath, a/c, good seafront location; **B** *Vela Branca*, Cidade Histórica, T 288-2316, top of cliff, good.

C *Chica da Silva*, Av dos Navegantes 94, T 288-2280, friendly, family run; **C** *Pousada Aquarius*, R Pedro Alvares Cabral 176, T 288-2738, bath, fan, English, French, Italian spoken, rec; *Pousada Coral*, R Assis Chateaubriand 74, T 288-2630, good breakfast, fan; **C** *Pousada Las Palmas*, Praça Antonio Carlos, Magalhães 102, Centro, T 288 2643, 281 1179, highly rec; **C** *Pousada Saveiros*, Av Navegentes 151, T 288-2122, good breakfast, will change TCs; **D** *Mar Azul* at No 109, with bath, breakfast, clean, friendly, rec. A number of good *pousadas* on Av Getúlio Vargas, most without breakfast: **C** *Pousada da Praia*, No 153, T 228 2908, a/c, fridge, showers, nice and clean, no breakfast; **C** *Pousada Raizes*, Praça dos Pataxós 196, T 288-2198, with bath, fan, rec; same square No 278 is **C** *Pousada Travessia*, T 288-2616, with good breakfast; **C** *Pousada Mar e Sol*, No 223, T 228-2137, clean, safe, filtered drinking water, very helpful manager (who teaches *lambada*), highly rec; **D** *Pousada Peixinho*, No 228, attractive, friendly; **D** *Pousada Coroa Vermelha*, No 12, T 288-2132, with bath, no breakfast, clean, good, friendly owners.

D *Porto Brasília*, Praça Antonio Carlos Magalhães 234, with breakfast, E without; *Pousada Navegantes*, Av 22 de Abril 212, T 288-2390, rec; **D** *Pousada Vera Cruz*, Av 22 de Abril 100, T 288-2162, with bath, good breakfast, clean. Some good, cheap *pousadas* on R Mal Deodoro at the port: **D** *Cavalo Marino*, No 100; **D** *Estalagem da Yvonne*, No 298, with breakfast, more with a/c, T 288-2045; **D** *Hospedaria do Pirata*, No 249, with good breakfast, bath, rec. **D** *Pousada de Sagres*, R 15 de Novembro, T 288-2031, with good breakfast, family run; **D** *Pousada Sonho Meu*, same street No 86, with bath, breakfast, fan, good; **E** house of Luisiana Silva Mercedes, No 214, T 288-1137.

Outside Dec-Feb rooms with bath and hot water can be rented for about US$150/month.

Camping: *Camping dos Marajas*, Av Getúlio Vargas, central; *Camping Gringa*, Praia do Cruzeiro, T 288-2076, US$2.50 pp/night, laundry, café, pool, excellent; *Camping do Sitio*, R da Vala, mosquitoes can be a problem here.

● **Places to eat**
Cruz de Malta, R Getúlio Vargas 358, good seafood; *Preto Velho*, on Praça da Bandeira, à la carte or self-service, good value; also good value is *Hall of Hunger*, R Rui Barbosa 194, home cooking daily from 1200 to 2200, cheap; good breakfast at *Pau Brasil*, Praça dos Pataxós, and *Club dos Sem Casa*, R Pedro Alvares Cabral 185, open 0800-2100, good, cheap lunches here also. On Praça Pataxós: *do Japonês*, No 38, excellent value with varied menu, open 0800-2300, rec; *Ponto do Encontro*, No 106, good simple food, friendly, owners rent rooms, open 0800-2400; *Sambuca*, good for pizzas; *Prima Dona*, No 247, Italian, good. *Anti-Caro*, R Assis Chateaubriand 26, good, rec, also antique shop, good atmosphere. The best meat restaurant is *Churrascaria do Maça*, R Mal Deodoro 342, open 1500-2400, very good *picanha*, enough for 3 people, not expensive, rec; *Les Agapornis*, Av dos Navegantes 180, wide selection of crêpes and pizzas; *Tres Vintens*, Av Portugal 1246, good imaginative seafood dishes, rec; *Ninô*, 22 de Abril 100, good pizzas; *Vida Verde*, R Dois de Julho 92, good vegetarian, open 1100-2100 except Sun, T 288 2766, rec.

● **Banks & money changers**
Banco do Brasil, Av 22 de Abril e Av Carlos Alberto Paracho, Dec-Mar for exchange 1800-2200, but not Sun. Other banks will not change money, but managers may privately. Good rates in the new shopping centre, nr Banco do Brasil; good rates at *Agência do Descobrimento*, Av Getúlio Vargas, lower rate for TCs, also arranges flight tickets and house rental. Rates are not as good as in the big cities.

● **Entertainment**
Porto Seguro is famous for the *lambada* (see **Music and Dance**). The best place to see it is at *Boca da Barra* at Praia do Cruzeiro. Instructors are on hand from 1800-2000, then the locals take the floor until the small hours. No entry charge, not to be missed, nightly throughout the year. The strong

local liqueur, *guarachaça*, a mixture of guaraná and cachaça, keeps the dancers going during the long hours; don't underestimate its strength. Another place to see *lambada* is **Lambaporto**, busy only at weekends.

A good bar for live music is *Porto Prego* on R Pedro Alvares Cabral, small cover charge. *Sotton Bar*, Praça de Bandeira, is lively. There are lots of bars and street cafés on Av Portugal.

● **Post & telecommunications**
Telephones: Telebahia service post, Praça dos Pataxós beside ferry terminal, open daily 0800-2000, cheap rates after 2000 so can be very busy at this time.

● **Sports**
Diving equipment, Portomar Ltda, R Dois de Julho 178, also arranges diving and snorkelling trips to the coral reefs offshore, professional instructors.

● **Tourist offices**
Casa de Lenha, Praça Visconde de Porto Seguro, nr port, has basic information.

● **Transport**
Local Rentals: Car hire, Itapoan, Av Portugal 1350, T 288-2710; **motorcycles**, Lupa Motos, Praça dos Pataxós, T 288-2868, expensive, heavy deposit required; **bicycles**, Oficina de Bicicleta, Av Getúlio Vargas e R São Pedro, about US$10 for 24 hrs; also at Praça de Bandeira and at Dois de Julho 242.

Air Nordeste Sat and Sun from Rio, direct 2 hrs 15 mins with 2 stops; Nordeste on same days from Belo Horizonte and Salvador; Rio Sul daily to Salvador and São Paulo; Vasp once a week to São Paulo and Belo Horizonte, twice to Salvador.

Buses From Porto Seguro to: **Salvador** (Águia Branca), daily, 12 hrs, US$28 (*leito* 44), once a day each service; **Vitória**, daily, 11 hrs, US$15.50; **Ilhéus** daily 0730, 5½ hrs, US$12; **Eunápolis**, 1½ hrs, US$2. For **Rio** direct buses (São Geraldo), leaving at 1745, US$36, 18 hrs, from Rio direct at 1600, or take 1800 for Ilhéus and change at Eunápolis. To Belo Horizonte daily direct. To **São Paulo** direct, 1045, 25 hrs, US$45, not advisable, very slow, much better to go to Rio then take Rio-São Paulo express. Other services via Eunápolis (those going N avoid Salvador) or Itabuna (5 hrs, US$7.80). (For the routes from Vitória see page 418 and from Belo Horizonte page 430.) At Brazilian holiday times, all transport N or S should be booked well in advance. There is new rodoviária, with reliable luggage store and lounge on 3rd floor, on the road to Eunápolis, 2 km from the centre, regular bus service (30 mins) through city to the old rodoviária near port. For local trips a taxi is an economic proposition for two or more passengers wishing to visit various places in 1 day.

ARRAIAL DA AJUDA

Across the Rio Buranhém S from Porto Seguro (10 mins, US$0.25, ferries take cars day time only, every 30 mins day and night), and a further 5 km (US$0.45 in bus), is the village of **Arraial da Ajuda**; about 15 mins' walk from the beach (better for camping than Porto Seguro). Pilgrimage in Aug to the shrine of Nossa Senhora da Ajuda (interesting room in church, full of ex-voto offerings – fine view from behind church). Ajuda has become very popular with tourists and there are many *pousadas*, bars and small shops. Known as a 'hippie' resort: drugs are said to be widely available, but easily avoided. Parties almost every night, on the beach or in the *Broadway*. At the *Jatobar* bar the *lambada* is danced, on the main square, by the church (opens 2300 – *pensão* at the back is cheap, clean and friendly). There is also a *capoeira* institute; ask for directions. Beach protected by coral reef. At Brazilian holiday times it is very crowded and, with the coastline up for sale, it may become overdeveloped in a few years. The beaches in this neighbourhood are splendid, for instance Pitinga, also protected by coral reef, Lagoa Azul and Mucugê. Porto Belo or Sta Cruz Cabrália buses go to the beaches frequently from the port.

● **Accommodation B** *Pousada das Brisas*, T 875-1033, clean, panoramic views, English, German, French and Spanish spoken; **B** *Ivy Marey*, nr centre on road to beach, T 875-1106, 4 rooms and 2 bungalows, showers, nice décor, good bar, French/Brazilian owned, rec; nearby *Le Grand Bleu*, T 875-7272, same French owner, similar prices, good *pizzaria*; **B** *Sole Mio*, T 875-1115, just off beach road leading from ferry to Arraial, different French owners, English spoken, laid back, 4 chalets, excellent *pizzaria*; **B** *Pousada Canto d'Alvorada*, on road to Ajuda, T 875-1218, in season, D out of season, Swiss run, 7 cabins, restaurant, washing facilities; **C** *Vila do Beco*, beautiful garden, good value; **C** *Pousada Caminho do Mar*, T 875-1099, English spoken, rate depending on season, owners very informative and helpful, also highly rec; **C** *Pousada Natur*, run by German environmentalist, clean, friendly, rec, English spoken T 288-2738; **D** *Pousada Le Cottage* (across ferry from Porto Seguro, but before Ajuda, T 875-1029), French owner, Sr Georges, with bath, C in chalet; **C** *Thaina Plage*, highly

rec, reserved in São Paulo, T 011-533-5898, or in Paris T 43-26-31-41, and **C** *Pousada Torrorão*, between village and beach, T 875-1260, restaurant, rec; **C** *Pousada Erva Doce*, T 875-1114, owners very friendly, good restaurant, well appointed chalets, highly rec; **C** *Pousada Tubarão*, R Bela Vista, beyond the church on the right, T 875-1086, good view of the coastline, cool, good restaurant, rec; **C** *Pousada Maravilha*, Av São João, with good breakfast; **D** *Pousada Aberta Mar*, on road to beach, with bath, good breakfast; **D** *Pousada Flamboyant*, pleasant, good breakfast, rec; **D** *Pousada Flor*, on square, T 875-1143, owner Florisbela Valiense takes good care of female guests, warmly rec; **D** *Pousada do Paulista*, with breakfast, fan, laundry facilities, clean, rec; **E** *Pousada Mangaba*, on way to the beach, bath, washing facilities, without breakfast, friendly, rec; **E** *Pousada Nova Esperança*, nearby, without breakfast, bath, rec; **E** *Pousada Tamarind*, on Praça Brigadeiro Eduardo Gomés, nr church, without breakfast; bath; **E** *Pousada Tio Otto*, without breakfast, alongside church; **F** *Pousada Miramar*, without breakfast, cheapest accommodation in town, rec; also, next door, **F** *La Nuit des Temps*; **D** *Pousada Gabriela*, R Projetada s/n – cep 45820, T 875-1237, with breakfast, rec. **NB** Above prices are high season prices unless otherwise stated, if staying for a long period they are negotiable; this is certainly true in the low season. **Camping**: *Praia*, on Mucugê Beach, good position and facilities, US$1 pp/night; *Chão do Arraial*, 5 mins from Mucugê beach, shady, good snack bar, also hire tents, rec. Also *Camping do Gordo*, on left shortly after leaving ferry, on beach but beach is not as good as Mucugê.

● **Places to eat** *São João*, nr the church, is the best typical restaurant; *Robin Wood*, opp police station, garden/restaurant, fresh food, excellent value, US$5, rec; *Asa Branca*, R Santa Rita, very good *carne do sol de picanha*; *Manda Brasa*, on Broadway, good *prato feito*, cheap; also on Broadway, *Spaghetti Point*, good, US$3; *Le Gourmet*, R São João, good international cuisine, specialise in French dishes, not cheap, rec; *Mão na Massa*, an excellent Italian restaurant, behind the church, rec; also rec is *Varanda Grill*, good grilled fish, meat and chicken; *Paulinho Pescador*, open 1200-2200, excellent seafood, also chicken and meat, English spoken, good service, *bobó de camarão* highly rec. *Café das Cores*, on way to the beach, good cakes and snacks, expresso coffee. Two good 'barracas' on Pitinga beach are *Bar da Pitinga* and *Bar do Genésio*, fresh fried fish, shrimp etc.

● **Post & telecommunications Telepho**

Telebahia has a service post on the main square, open 0800 until 2200.

TRANCOSO

25 km to the S of Porto Seguro and 15 km from Ajuda is **Trancoso**, reached by bus, 5 a day (US$0.60, 50 mins, last returns at 1630, more buses and colectivos in summer), by colectivo, hitchhiking or by walking along the beach; the road bridges are not safe, bus passengers alight and walk across. The village is simple but also popular with Brazilian tourists, beautiful beaches (some nude) and many Europeans have built or bought houses there. There are good restaurants around the main square. From the end of Praça São João there is a fine coastal panorama. Trancoso has a historic church. Colectivos run from Trancoso to Ajuda (US$1.90). Between Ajuda and Trancoso is the village of Rio da Barra. Caraiva with beautiful beaches, no electricity, can be reached by boat, 4 hrs from Porto Seguro, 2 hrs from Trancoso, or by bus, two daily. The sandy road from Trancoso is a difficult drive, ending at the river which must be crossed by boat. There are *pousadas* and restaurants with electricity generators, but no exchange facilities.

● **Accommodation A3** *Hotel de Praça*, bath, games room, good breakfast (T São Paulo 211-2239); **B** *Pousada Calypso*, good apartments, comfortable, rooms at lower price also available, good library, German and English spoken, rec (T Rio 267-3741); **C** *Caipim Santo*, to the left of main square, with breakfast, the best restaurant in Trancoso (natural cuisine), very friendly, bath, rec; **C** *Posada Canto Verde*, with breakfast, bath, restaurant only in high season, rec (T 0242-43-7823). Also on main square, **C** *Gulab Mahal*, oriental style, lovely garden, vast breakfast, highly rec; **C** *Pousada do Bosque*, on the way to the beach, English, German and Spanish spoken, with breakfast, camping facilities also available, good value; **D** *Pousada Sol da Manhã*, with breakfast; **E** *Pousada Terra do Sol*, without breakfast, good, rec. About 500m inland away from main square (known as the 'quadrado') lies the newer part of Trancoso (known as the 'invasão') with two good value *pousadas*: **D** *Pousada Quarto Crescente*, English, German, Dutch and Spanish spoken, cooking facilities, washing also, very friendly and helpful owners, library, highly rec, about 15 mins from beach. Another good *pousada* is **D** *Luna Pousa*, further along on the left, with

breakfast, well ventilated, only 4 rooms. There are many houses to rent, very good ones are rented by Clea who can be contacted at *Restaurant Abacaxi* on main square on right. You can leave a message for any one of the above mentioned *pousadas* by calling the Telebahia service post 867-1116, most people in town check there for messages on a daily basis. As in Porto Seguro and Ajuda if you stay for a longer period you can nearly always negotiate a better price, this is certainly true in the low season.

● **Places to eat** *Urano*, just before the main square is rec, good portions, usually enough for two; *Rama* has also been rec; *Abacaxi* on main square does good breakfasts, light snacks and very good crêpes; *Galub Mahal* for Eastern dishes; good breakfast also at *Pé das Frutas*, *Maré Cheia* next door good simple dishes. Good ice cream at *Tão Vez*. Apart from restaurants which serve breakfast most others open at 1500 until 2200 or so.

PARQUE NACIONAL DE MONTE PASCOAL

South of Porto Seguro, reached by a paved access road from the BR-101 16 km N of Itamaraju, is the **Parque Nacional de Monte Pascoal**, set up in 1961 to preserve the flora, fauna and birdlife of the coastal area in which Europeans made landfall in Brazil (Caixa Postal 076, CEP 45830-000 Itamaraju, T 073-281-2419). The Pataxó Indian reservation is located at Corombau village, on the ocean shore of the park. Corombau can be reached by schooner from Porto Seguro. A small luxury resort has been built at Corombau.

CURUMUXATIBA

From Itamaraju (93 km S of Eunápolis) the coastal towns of **Curumuxatiba** (**D** *Pousada Guainamby*, R Bela Vista, CEP 45983, German and Brazilian owned, small, clean, comfortable chalets, good views to long beach, good breakfast and fish and Italian meals, rec) and Prado. Also reached from Itamaraju is the *Jacotoka* holiday village, which offers diving, surfing and riding in a tropical paradise. US$50/day, reservations at 7 de Setembro 149, Porto Seguro, T 288-2291, F 288-2540; it can also be reached by boat from Porto Seguro.

CARAVELAS

Further S still, 130 km S of Porto Seguro, a charming little town (*pop* 21,650), rapidly developing for tourism, but a major trading town in 17th/18th centuries. It had a rail connection to Minas Gerais. Caravelas is in the mangroves; the beaches are about 10 km away at Barra de Caravelas (hourly buses), a fishing village.

• **Accommodation A1** *Marina Porto Abrulhos*, on beach front, very luxurious; **C** *Pousada Caravelense*, 50m from rodoviária, T 297-1182, bath, TV, fridge, good breakfast, clean, excellent restaurant, friendly, rec; **E** *Grande Hotel São Benedito*, close by, breakfast, dirty, noisy; **D** *Shangri-la*, Barão do Rio Branco 216, bath, breakfast, clean. **At Barra de Caravelas**: **C** *Pousada das Sereias*, French-owned; **E** *Pousada Jaquita*, use of kitchen, clean, big breakfast, bath, airy rooms, owner is Secka who speaks English; some food shops, restaurants and bars.

• **Tourist offices** Helpful tourist information at Ibama **Centro de Visitantes**, Barão do Rio Branco 281.

• **Useful services** Teresa and Ernesto (from Austria) organize boat trips (US$40/day), jeep and horse hire (turn left between bridge and small supermarket). 'Alternative' beach holidays (organic vegetarian food, yoga, meditation, other activities) with Beky and Eno on the unspoilt island of Coçumba, rec; contact *Abrolhos Turismo*. Banco do Brasil does not change money (Praça Dr Imbassahi); on same square, No 8, *Abrolhos Turismo* rents diving gear and arranges boat trips.

• **Transport** Buses to Texeira de Freitas (4 a day), Salvador, Nanuque and Prado.

Prado (*pop* 20,000) has some 16th-century buildings and beautiful beaches N and S. It is 200 km S of Porto Seguro. The proprietors of the *Casa de Maria*, R Seis, Novo Prado, T (073) 298-1377, claim to serve the best breakfast in the region. **D** *Pousada Talipe* (1125 Central Ave, 23rd St, Los Alamitos, T 555 6539, USA), friendly, good breakfast, rec.

PARQUE NACIONAL MARINHO DOS ABROLHOS

John Raspey writes: The **Parque Nacional Marinho dos Abrolhos** is 70 km E of Caravelas: 5 small islands (Redonda, Siriba, Guarita, Sueste, Santa Bárbara), and several coral reefs. The archipelago is administered by Ibama, and a navy detachment mans a lighthouse on Sta Bárbara, which is the only island that may be visited. Permission from Parque Nacional Marinho dos Abrolhos, Praia do Kitombo s/n, Caravelas, Bahia 45900, T (073) 297-1111, or Ibama, Av Juracy Magalhães Jr 608, CEP 40295-140, Salvador, T (071) 240-7322. The islands and surrounding reefs are home to birds, whales, fish turtles, and giant fire corals (also goats). Darwin visited them in 1830. A master authorized by the Navy to take tourists is Mestre Onofrio Frio in Alrobaça, Bahia, T (073) 293-2195. Tours also available from Abrolhos Turismo, see above, Caravelas, T 297-1149 (about US$170 for a slow 2½ day tour by *saveiro*). 1-day tours in a faster boat (US$100) from Abrolhos or the Marina Porto Abrolhos.

NORTH FROM SALVADOR

The paved BA-099 coast road from near the airport is known as the Estrada do Coco (Coconut Highway, because of the many coconut plantations) and for 50 km passes some beautiful beaches. The best known from S to N are Ipitanga (with its reefs), Buraquinho, Jauá, Arembepe, Guarajuba, Itacimirim, Castelo Garcia D'Avila (with its 16th century fort) and Forte. Buses serve most of these destinations. The Estrada do Coco was extended in 1994 to the state of Sergipe. The road is called the Linha Verde (Green Line), because of the concern to disturb the environment as little as possible.

AREMBEPE

Some 50 km to the N of Salvador this former fishing village is now a quiet resort. There is an 'alternative' village of palm huts, 30 mins' walk along the beach, behind the sand dunes, café and swimming. Best beaches 2 km N of town. *Pousada da Fazenda* on the beach, thatched huts, good seafood, not cheap; **E** *Pousada*; and restaurant *Mar Aberto*, T 824-1257, rec, food very good, English and French spoken; Verá's restaurant, try *pastel de banana*. Bus from Terminal Francés, Salvador, every 2 hrs,

1½ hrs, US$1.20, last one back at 1700; or from Itapoan.

PRAIA DO FORTE

The fishing village, 80 km N of Salvador, takes its name from the castle built by a Portuguese settler, Garcia D'Ávila, in 1556. He built the fortification as a lookout post to warn the city to the S of any attempt of invasion by enemy forces. Garcia D'Ávila was given a huge area of land which extended from Praia do Forte to Maranhão on the northern coast of Brazil. His was the first farm in Brazil and it was he who brought the first head of cattle to the country. To create pasture lands for these cattle he cleared the virgin Atlantic forest; he also brought the first coconut and mango trees to Brazil. Praia do Forte is now a tranquil resort with a strong emphasis on preservation of the local flora and fauna. Inland from the coast is a *restinga* forest, which grows on sandy soil with a very delicate ecosystem. *Restinga* forests are found in very few areas in Brazil. Near the village is a small *pantanal* (marshy area) and this is host to a large number of birds, caymans etc. Early morning and late afternoon the *pantanal* resounds to the calls of snail kites, kingfishers, cormorants and chattering parakeets. Birdwatching trips on the *pantanal* are rewarding. The Tamar Project was set up 12 years ago to preserve the sea turtles which lay their eggs in the area. Praia do Forte is now the headquarters of the national turtle preservation programme and is funded by the Worldwide Fund for Nature. There is a visitors centre at the project which explains the aims and success of the programme.

● **Accommodation** (Prices rise steeply in summer season.) Most hotels are in the **A1** price range. It may prove difficult to find cheaper accommodation. *Praia do Forte Resort Hotel*, apartment with seaview, very good sports facilities, 4 swimming pools, watersports equipment for hire, T 832 2333 or 835 1111, F 832-2100; *Pousada Praia do Forte*, 18 chalets in peaceful setting, more private than larger *Resort Hotel*, rec, T 835 1410, F 876-1050; *Pousada Solar da Lua*, R do Forte, T 876-1029, good location, spacious rooms; *Pousada Sobrado da Vila*, on main street, T 876-1088, F 235-7886, pleasant, good value restaurant; *Pousada Tatuapara*, T 876 1015, friendly; **B** *Pousada João Sol*, R da Corvina, T 876 1054, owner speaks English, Spanish and German, good, friendly, rec, only 6 apts, great breakfast; **B** *Pousada Canto da Sereia*, R da Corvina, with fan, good breakfast; **C** *Pousada Oxumaré*, verandah; **B** *Pousada Sol Nascente*, on street parallel to main street, clean, friendly, good, bath, frigobar, fan, breakfast; **C** *Tia Helena*, Helena being the motherly proprietor who provides an excellent meal and enormous breakfast, nice rooms, price reduced to US$20/night for 3 day stay, highly rec. Two-bedrm apartments at *Solar dos Arcos*, on beach, US$90, with pool, gardens, lawns, warmly rec.

● **Places to eat** *Bar Da Souza*, on the right as you enter the village, best seafood in town, open daily from 1000 until last customer leaves, live music at weekends by excellent local musicians, highly rec, reasonably priced; *Brasa Na Praia*, specializes in grilled seafood and meat, open daily from 1100 till midnight, peaceful setting, rec; *La Crêperie*, excellent crêpes, Tues to Sun, 1100 until the early hours, good music, a very popular meeting place, owner Klever very friendly, highly rec; *Pizzaria Le Gaston*, good pizza and pasta, also good home made ice-creams, open daily from 1000 until midnight. There are many other restaurants in the village: good ones are at *Pousada Solar Da Lua*, open daily until late, *Nora*, on main street, and *Restaurant Tropical* can also be rec.

● **Tour companies & travel agents** **Tours**: *Odara Turismo*, in the *Resort Hotel*, T 876 1080, F 876 1018, imaginative tours to surrounding areas and outlying villages and beaches using 4WD vehicles. They are very friendly and informative, rec. The owners, Norbert and Papy, speak English and German. Praia do Forte is ideal for windsurfing and sailing owing to constant fresh Atlantic breezes.

● **Transport** Buses to Praia do Forte from Salvador (US$2.50): Santa Maria/Catuense leaves 5 times daily from rodoviária, 1½ hrs.

TO THE SERGIPE BORDER

The Linha Verde runs for 142 km to the Sergipe border, the road is very scenic, especially near Conde. There are very few hotels or *pousadas* in the more remote villages. The most picturesque are **Imbassaí**, Subaúma, **Baixios** (very beautiful, where the Rio Inhambupe meets the sea) and **Conde**. Sítio do Conde on the coast, 6 km from Conde, has many *pousadas*, but the beaches are not very good. Sítio do Conde is a good base to explore other beaches at Barra do Itariri, 12 km S, at the mouth of a river (fine sunsets). The road passes unspoilt beaches (the best are Corre Nu and Jacaré). You can also go to Seribinha, 13 km N of Sítio do Conde (the road goes along the beach through coconut groves and mangroves; at Seribinha are beach huts serving cool drinks or food, one *pousada* reported on beach). The last stop on the Linha Verde is **Mangue Seco**. Access from Sergipe is by boat or canoe on the Rio Real from Pontal (10 min crossing). A steep hill rising behind the village to tall white sand dunes offers a superb view of the coastline. The encroaching dunes have caused the mangrove to dry up. Bus Salvador-Conde (São Luis, T 071 358-4582), 3 a day, 4 on Fri, US$7.50.

- **Accommodation & places to eat Imbassaí: C** *Pousada Imbassaí*, T 235-3599, chalets and apartments of varying sizes; **B** *Pousada Anzol de Ouro*, T 971-9025, reservations, T/F 243-2614, 12 chalets, ventilation, swimming pool; **B** *Pousada Lagoa da Pedra*, T 971-7095, reservations 359-3512/245-2506, large grounds, a little English spoken, friendly. **Subaúma: B** *Pousada da Praça*, simple, clean. **Sítio do Conde: A3** *Hotel Praia do Conde*, T (075) 429-1229, reservations (071) 321-2542, a/c, pool; **C** *Pousada Oasis*, T (075) 421-2397, simple; **C** *Pousada Beira Mar*. Cheaper are **D** *Pousada do Boliviano* and **E** *Pousada de Dona Dulce*. **Restaurants:** *Bar e Restaurante Zeca*, typical dishes; *Pizzaria Marcos*; *Restaurante Harmonioso*. **Mangue Seco: B** *Pousada Mangue Seco*, T (071) 359-8506, in main square, ceiling fan; further away, left from boat landing, 15 mins' walk, **B** *Pousada Village Mangue Seco*, T (071) 241-7355, swimming pool, fan. Seafood restaurants at boat landing.

INLAND, NORTH FROM SALVADOR

MONTE SANTO AND CANUDOS

About 270 km N of Feira da Santana, and 38 km W of Euclides da Cunha on the direct BR-116 road to Fortaleza, is the famous hill shrine of **Monte Santo** in the Sertão, reached by 3½ km of steps cut into the rocks of the Serra do Picaraça (about 45 mins' walk each way – set out early). This is the scene of pilgrimages and great religious devotion during Holy Week. The shrine was built by an Italian who had a vision of the cross on the mountain in

1765. One block N of the bottom of the stairs is the Museu do Sertão, with pictures from the 1897 Canudos rebellion. **Canudos** itself is 100 km away at the junction of the BR-116 and BR-235 (direct buses from Salvador); religious rebels led by the visionary Antônio Conselheiro defeated three expeditions sent against them in 1897 before being overwhelmed. These events are the theme of two great books: *Os Sertões* (Revolt in the Backlands) by Euclides da Cunha, and *La Guerra del Fin del Mundo* (The War of the End of the World) by the Peruvian Mario Vargas Llosa. The Rio Vaza Barris, which runs through Canudos has been dammed, and the town has been moved to Nova Canudos by the dam. Part of the old town is still located 10 km W.

- **Accommodation D** *Grapiuna*, Praça Monsenhor Berenguer 401 (T 275-1157), with bath (cheaper without, downstairs), rec; **E** *Santa Cruz*, opp Banco do Brasil, shared bath, basic but clean; pleasant bars. At Euclides da Cunha, on the BR-116 and 39 km from Monte Santo, are *Hotel Lua*, simple and *Hotel Conselheiro*.

PARQUE NACIONAL DE PAULO AFONSO

Part of the northern border of Bahia is the Rio São Francisco; on the opposite bank are Pernambuco and Alagoas. From Salvador, the BR-110 runs N to the river at Paulo Afonso; the road is paved for all but 30 km between Cícero Dantas and Antas. At Jeremoaba, 41 km further N, BR-235 heads W to Canudos, 111 km. 76 km N of Jeremoaba is the **Parque Nacional de Paulo Afonso**. The Falls of **Paulo Afonso**, once one of the great falls of the world but now exploited for hydroelectric power, are 270 km from the mouth of the São Francisco river, which drains a valley 3 times the size of Great Britain. There are 2,575 km of river above the Falls to its source in Minas Gerais. Below the Falls is a deep, rock gorge through which the water rushes. The national park is an oasis of trees and the lake amid a desert of brown scrub and cactus. The best time to visit the Falls is in the rainy season (Jan-Feb); only then does much water pass over them, as almost all the flow now goes through the power plant. The best view is from the northern (Alagoas) bank. The Falls are in a security area; no admission for pedestrians, so you need to visit by car or taxi (US$4.50 an hour). Admission is from 0800 onwards, but it depends on the availability of guides, without whom one cannot enter; go to the tourist information office in the centre of the town and sign up for a tour of the hydroelectric plant, 2 hrs, US$6/car.

● **Accommodation A3** *Grande Hotel de Paulo Afonso* (a/c, TV, pool, T 281-1914) and a guest house (apply for room in advance) at the Falls. The town of Paulo Afonso (*pop* 86,560) is some distance from the Falls, reached by bus from Salvador, by paved road from Recife, bus, 7 hrs, US$8, or from Maceió (306 km) via Palmeira dos Índios, partially paved. **C** *Belvedere*, Apolônio Sales 457, T 281-1814, a/c, swimming pool and **C** *Palace*, T 281-1521, with bath, a/c, swimming pool, 'best value in town', next door. Plenty of restaurants, eg *Kilanche*, next to Tourist Office.

● **Shopping** Handicrafts (embroidery, fabrics) from Núcleo de Produção Artesanal, Av Apolônio Sales 1059.

TRAVEL ON THE RIO SÃO FRANCISCO

Travel between Paulo Afonso and Penedo (see page 538) is complicated because there are no direct buses.

Piranhas (Alagoas), 80 km E of Paulo Afonso (road almost completely paved, buses difficult), is a charming town with good beaches on the Rio São Francisco; it has picturesque houses and an old railway station which is now a *Pousada* (3-4 room, **E**, restaurant) with a small museum (photographs of the severed head of Lampião, the Brazilian 'Robin Hood').

PETROLINA AND JUAZEIRO

The river is navigable above the Falls from above the twin towns (linked by a bridge) of Juazeiro, in Bahia, and Petrolina, in Pernambuco, thriving towns compared to many on the upper São Francisco. Navigation is possible as far as Pirapora in Minas Gerais, linked by road to the Belo Horizonte-Brasília highway (see page 437).

Like Pirapora, **Petrolina** (*pop* 174,970)

is famous for the production of *carrancas* (boat figureheads, mostly grotesque) of wood or ceramic. Petrolina has its own airport and close to this is the small Museu do Sertão – relics of rural life in the NE and the age of the 'coronéis' and the bandit Lampião.

Juazeiro (*pop* 128,380) is the poorer of the two cities. Market on Fri and Sat.

● **Accommodation & places to eat** Petrolina: **B** *Grande Rio*, R Padre Praga; **D** *Pousada da Carranca*, BR-122, Km 4, T 961-3421; **E** *Hotel Newman*, Av Souza Filho 444, T 961-0595; **E** *Espacial*, EF Leste Brasileiro Km 2; and *Restaurante Rancho Grande. Restaurante Panorâmico*, the only one on the river front, is good. **Juazeiro**: *Grande Hotel*, R Pititinga, T 811-2710, *Vitória*, T 811-2712, and *União* (rec) and *Oliveira*, the last two in R Conselheiro Saraiva. **B** *Hotel Pousada de Juazeiro*, 6 km S on BR-407, T 811-2820, with bath, a/c, pool, restaurant, bar, pleasant. Unique restaurant known as the *Vaporzinho* is high and dry on the river front, a side-wheel paddle steamer (poor food), the *Saldanha Marinho*, built at Sabará in 1852.

● **Transport** River transport has changed rapidly in the past few years; for information T Juazeiro (075) 811-2465.

ROUTES The BR-253 runs W from Canudos to Juazeiro, alternatively, from Salvador go to Feira de Santana, take the paved BR-324, then the BR-407, which continues through Petrolina to Picos in Piauí (see page 573) junction for Fortaleza or Teresina. On the BR-324, 124 km S of Juazeiro is **Senhor do Bonfim** (*pop* 83,260), a busy market town with lots of life (also banks and post office).

WINERIES

Margy Levine and Jordan Young (Lexington, MA) write:

There are three wineries in the area: one in Casa Nova (Bahia); Ouro Verde in Lagoa Grande (Pernambuco); and Fazenda Milano in Santa Maria da Boa Vista (Pernambuco), on the N shore of the Rio São Francisco. Fazenda Milano (24 km from Lagoa Grande, towards Santa Maria da Boa Vista) was the first winery in the NE, and makes wine from European grapes, with 150 ha of vines. Owned by Forestier, a winemaker from the S, they make red, white and rosé, blended and varietals. You can visit the winery on Thur, if you call in advance on (081) 961-4669 or, in Recife (081) 251-2200. Wine can be bought at US$3 for 3 bottles. When you get to the Fazenda Milano sign on the Lagoa Grande-Santa Maria road, turn S towards the river, and drive 8 km on a dirt road to the gate.

The Northeast: Sergipe and Alagoas

THE EIGHT northeastern states are generally poor economically, but are neither poor historically (see Recife, Olinda, São Luis), nor culturally (eg 'Forró' and other musical styles, many good museums, lacework, ceramics). There is a multitude of beaches: those in established resorts tend to be polluted, but you don't have to travel far for good ones, while off the beaten track are some which have hardly been discovered.

Climate South of Cabo São Roque (Rio Grande do Norte) there is abundant rain fall, but in Pernambuco the zone of ample rain stretches only 80 km inland, though it deepens southwards. São Luís in Maranhão also gets plenty of rain, but between eastern Maranhão and Pernambuco lies a triangle, with its apex deep inland, where the rainfall is sporadic, and occasionally non-existent for a year. Here the tropical forest gives way to the *caatinga*, or scrub forest bushes which shed their leaves during drought. In this area grow the palms that

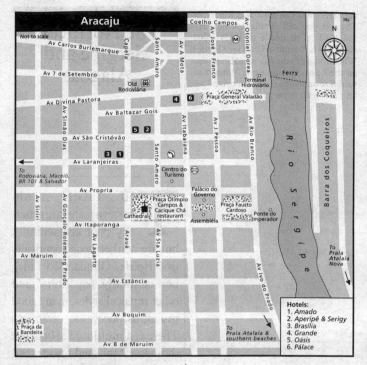

Aracaju

Not to scale

Av Carlos Burlemarque
Av 7 de Setembro
Old Rodoviária
Av Divina Pastora
Av Baltazar Gois
Av São Cristóvão
Av Laranjeiras
To Rodoviária, Maceió, BR 101 & Salvador
Av Propria
Av Itaporanga
Av Maruim
Av Estância
Av Buquim
Av B de Maruim
Praça da Bandeira

Coelho Campos
Capela
Santo Amaro
Av A Mota
Av José P Franco
Av Otoniel Dorea
Ferry
Terminal Hidroviário
Praça General Valadão
Av Itabaiana
Av J Pessoa
Av Rio Branco
Santo Amaro
Centro do Turismo
Praça Olímpio Campos & Cacique Chá restaurant
Cathedral
Av Simão Dias
Palácio do Governo
Praça Fausto Cardoso
Assembléia
Ponte do Imperador
Av Siriri
Av Gonçalo Rolemberg Prado
Av Lagarto
Araua
Av Sta Luzia
Av Ivo do Prado

Rio Sergipe
Barra dos Coqueiros

To Praia Atalaia Nova

To Praia Atalaia & southern beaches

Hotels:
1. Amado
2. Aperipê & Serigy
3. Brasília
4. Grande
5. Oásis
6. Pálace

produce carnauba wax and babaçu nuts, and the tree that produces oiticica oil.

History There was a brief period of colonization from northern Europe in the NE, when the Dutch West India Company, based at Recife, controlled some seven captaincies along the coast. They gained control in 1630, when Portugal was subject to Spain. After 1640, when Portugal freed itself, the colonists fought the Dutch and finally expelled them in 1654.

247 km N of Salvador, on BR-101, almost midway between the Sergipe-Bahia border and Aracaju is **Estância**, with pleasant hotels: **E** *Turista*, and **E** *Dom Bosco*, opposite, slightly cheaper, bath and breakfast. The town boasts a small Jorge Amado museum and the June festival of São João. Many buses stop at the Rodoviária, which is on the main road. Bonfim buses on the Aracaju-Salvador run make a mandatory stop at Entre Rios on the Bahia-Sergipe border.

ARACAJU

(*Pop* 401,245; *CEP* 49000; *DDD* 079) Capital of Sergipe (*state pop* 1,492,400), 327 km N of Salvador, founded 1855, it is a clean and friendly town. It stands on the S bank of the Rio Sergipe, about 10 km from its mouth, and can be reached from Salvador or Maceió by road.

Places of interest

In the centre is a group of linked, beautiful parks: **Praça Olímpio Campos**, in which stands the cathedral, **Praça Almirante Barroso**, with the Palácio do Governo, and **Praças Fausto Cardoso** and **Camerino**. Across Av Rio Branco from these two is the river. The streets are clean (parts of Laranjeiras and João Pessoa in centre reserved for pedestrians). There is a handicraft centre, the **Centro do Turismo**, open 0900-1300, 1400-1900, in the restored Escola Normal, on Praça Olímpio Campos; the stalls are arranged by type (wood, leather, etc). The commercial area is on Ruas Itabaianinha and João Pessoa, leading up to R Divina Pastora and Praça General Valadão. At R Itabaianinnha 41 is the **Instituto Geográfico e Histórico de Sergipe** (Mon-Fri 0800-1200, 1400-1700).

Beaches

A 16-km road leads to the fine **Atalaia** beach: oil-drilling rigs offshore. Beaches continue S down the coast. There is an even better beach, **Nova Atalaia**, on Ilha de Santa Luzia across the river, reached by boat from the Hidroviária (ferry station), which is across Av Rio Branco from Praça General Valadão. Boats cross the river to **Barra dos Coqueiros** every 15 mins (US$0.25); the boats at a quarter past the hour combine with a bus to Nova Atalaia (US$0.35). Buses return to Barra on the hour. Services are more frequent at weekends, when it is very lively. The river at Barra dos Coqueiros is busy with fishing and pleasure craft.

Excursions

15 km NW from Aracaju is **Laranjeiras** (*pop* 15,600), reached by São Pedro bus, from old rodoviária in centre, 30 mins-1 hr. A small pleasant town, with a ruined church on a hill, it has three museums (Museu Afro-Brasileiro, Centro de Cultura João Ribeiro, and Sacro in the Conceição church), and the 19th century Capela de Sant'Aninha with a wooden altar inlaid with gold. **C** *Pousada Vale dos Outeiros*, rec.

70 km W of Aracaju is **Itabaiana**, which has a famous gold market on Sat.

Local festivals

On 8 Dec there are both Catholic (Nossa Senhora da Conceição) and Umbanda religious festivals.

Local information
● **Accommodation**
In **Atalaia** (Velha) there are many hotels and aparthotels, mostly mid-to-high priced.

L2 *Parque dos Coqueiros*, Atalaia beach, R F R Leite Neto 1075, T 243-1511, F 243-2186, large pool, luxurious, attractive, only hotel on beach; **A1** *Beira Mar*, Av Rotary, T 243-1921, F 243-1153; **D** *Pousada da Praia*, R Niceu Dantas 667, T 223-1700. At Atalaia Nova is the **A2** *Da Ilha*, T262-1221, F 262-1359.

In the centre: **A2** *Palace de Aracaju*, Praça Gen Valadão, T 224-5000, 3-star, a/c, TV, fridge, central, restaurant, pool, parking; **A2** *Grande*, R Itabaianinha 371, T 211-1383, F 222-2656, a/c, TV, fridge, central, *Quartier Latin* resturant; **B** *Aperipê*, R São Cristóvão 418, T 211-1880, central, a/c, phone, fridge, restaurant; **A3** *Serigy*, R Santo Amaro 269, T 211-1088, same management and facilities, comfortable; **C** *Brasília*, R Laranjeiras 580, T 224-8022, good value, good breakfasts, rec; **C** *Oásis*, R São Cristóvão 466, T 224-2125, with good breakfast, hot water, fair, a bit tatty; **D** *Amado*, R Laranjeiras 532, a/c (less with fan), laundry facilities; **E** *Turista*, R Divina Pastora 411, noisy, mosquitoes, no hot water or breakfast, friendly. **F Youth Hostel**, T 223-2802, on road to Ataláia (take bus Os Campos, from Centre), no card needed, clean, friendly; new youth hostel, R Braulio Costa 675, with pool, rec.

Camping: *Camping Clube do Brasil* site at Ataláia Velha beach.

● **Places to eat**
Very many in Ataláia, on Av Oceânica try *Chapéu de Couro*, No 128, rec; *Cantinha da Bahia*, No 180, rec for fresh crab. In town, there is a good bar and restaurant, *Cacique Chá*, in the cathedral square, lively at weekends; also on Praça Olímpio Campos is *Rancho Gaúcho*, No 692, quite good, very friendly; *Bar e Lanchonete Dom Qui Chopp*, Laranjeiras opp Telergipe, popular.

● **Post & telecommunications**
Post Office: Laranjeiras e Itabaianinha.

Telephones: Telergipe, Laranjeiras 296, national and international calls until 2200.

● **Shopping**
Artesanato interesting: pottery figures and lace particularly. Fair in Praça Tobias Barreto every Sun. Municipal market is a block N of the Hidroviária.

● **Tourist offices**
Bureau de Informaçes Turísticas de Sergipe, R 24 Horas, T 224-5168, very friendly, helpful, abundant leaflets. In the centre, go to **Aracatur**, R Maruim 100, Sala 10, T 224-1226, which has leaflets and maps such as *Aracaju no bolso* and *Onde?*, helpful, English spoken.

● **Transport**
The rodoviára for interstate buses is 4 km from the centre, linked by local buses from the ad-

jacent terminal (buy ticket before going on to the platform). Bus 004 'T Rod/L Batista' goes to the centre, US$0.25; look for route plates on the side of buses and at termini in town. The old bus terminal in town is at Santo Amaro e Divina Pastora, Praça João XXIII: buses from here to new rodoviária, Laranjeiras and São Cristóvão (45 mins, US$0.70). Buses to the rodoviária also can be caught at the terminal nr the Hidroviária and from Capela at the top of Praça Olímpio Campos.

To **Salvador**, 6-7 hrs, 11 a day with Bonfim, US$10.50, executive service at 1245 US$14.50, saves 1 hr. To **Maceió**, US$8.50 with Bonfim. Many coastal destinations served; also Vitória (US$44), Rio (US$60), São Paulo, Belo Horizonte (US$50).

SÃO CRISTÓVÃO

(*Pop* 41,300) The old state capital of Sergipe, SW of Aracaju on the road to Salvador, was founded in 1590 by Cristóvão de Barros. It is the fourth oldest town in Brazil. Built on top of a hill, its colonial centre is unspoiled, the majority of buildings painted white with green shutters and woodwork. (No hotels, but families rent rooms near the rodoviária at the bottom of the hill, straight down from Praça G Vargas.)

Places of interest Worth visiting are the **Museu de Arte Sacra e Histórico de Sergipe** in the **Convento de São Francisco** (open Tues-Sun 0800-1800), and the **Museu de Sergipe** in the former **Palácio do Governo**, both on Praça de São Francisco. Also on this square are the churches of **Misericórdia** (1627) and the **Orfanato Imaculada Conceição** (1646, permission to visit required from the Sisters). On Praça Senhor dos Passos are the churches of **Senhor dos Passos** and **Terceira Ordem do Carmo** (both 1739), while on the Praça Getúlio Vargas (formerly Praça Matriz) is the **Igreja Matriz Nossa Senhora da Vitória** (all are closed Mon). Also worth seeing is the old **Assembléia Legislativa** on R Coronel Erundino Prado. Outdoor arts festival in second half of October.

• **Transport** Buses (São Pedro) from Aracaju, from old rodoviária in centre, see above. A tourist train runs between Aracaju and São Cristóvão each Sat and Sun, 0900, 3½ hrs.

The Rio São Francisco marks the boundary between Sergipe and Alagoas. The BR-101 between Aracaju and Maceió – the next port to the N – is paved, crossing the São Francisco by bridge between Propriá and Porto Real do Colêgio.

PENEDO

Another crossing can be made by boat from **Neópolis** in Sergipe, to **Penedo** (*pop* 40,665) in Alagoas, near the mouth of the Rio São Francisco. Neópolis has a small market place by its central landing stage and, up the hill, a square with two churches.

Penedo is a charming town, with a nice waterfront park, Praça 12 de Abril, with stone walkways and walls. Originally the site of the Dutch Fort Maurits (built 1637, razed to the ground by the Portuguese), the colonial town stands on a promontory above the river. Among the colonial architecture, modern buildings such as the Associação Commercial and *Hotel São Francisco*, both on Av Floraino Peixoto, do not sit easily.

Places of interest

On the Praça Barão de Penedo is the neo-classical **Igreja Matriz** (closed to visitors) and the 18th century **Casa da Aposentadoria**. East and a little below this square is the Praça Rui Barbosa, on which are the **Convento de São Francisco** (1783 and later) and the church of **Santa Maria dos Anjos** (1660). As you enter, the altar on the right depicts God's eyes on the world, surrounded by the three races, one Indian, two negroes and the whites at the bottom. The church has fine *trompe-l'oeil* ceilings (1784). The convent is still in use. Guided tours are free. The church of **Rosário dos Pretos**, on Praça Marechal Deodoro, is open to visitors, while **Nosso Senhor da Corrente** (1764), on Praça 12 de Abril, and **São Gonçalo Garcia** (1758-70) on Floriano Peixoto are closed, the latter for restoration to its façade. Also on Floriano Peixoto is the pink **Teatro 7 de Setembro** of 1884; between it and the old covered market are fruit and vegetable stalls. The **Casa de Penedo**, at R João Pessoa 126 (signs point the way up the hill from F Peixoto), displays photographs and books on, or by, local figures such as the Barão de Penedo (Francisco Ignácio de Carvalho Moreira), Elysio de

Carvalho (writer and poet), and others. It also has a few historical exhibits and a small lecture room.

River traffic

Very few of the long two-masted sailing vessels that used to cruise on the river can be seen now, although there are plenty of smaller craft. Boats can be rented at the waterfront for excursions to the river islands, the mouth of the river and to beaches (eg Praia do Peba).

Local information
● **Accommodation**
C *Pousada Colonial*, Praça 12 de Abril 21, T 551-2677, all rooms with bath, *luxo* and suite have phone, TV and fridge, suites have a/c, spacious, clean, good cheap restaurant, front rooms with view of Rio São Francisco; **C** *São Francisco*, Av Floriano Peixoto, T 551-2273, standard rooms have no a/c, others have a/c, TV, fridge, rec except for poor restaurant.

E *Turista*, R Siqueira Campos 143, T 551-2237, with bath, fan, hot water, rec.

F *Impérial*, Av Floriano Peixoto, basic.

● **Places to eat**
Forte da Rocheira, R da Rocheira (take either of the alleys running W off the hill between Praças Barão de Penedo and 12 de Abril, turn right), good food, especially *ensopada de jacaré* (alligator stew); continue along the cliff walkway to the riverside for *Churrascaria O Scala*, at the end of R 15 de Novembro.

● **Banks & money changers**
Banks open 0830-1300. **Banco do Nordeste do Brasil** on Av F Peixoto; **Banco do Brasil** and **Bradesco** on Av Duque de Caxias, opp Bompreço. *Restaurant e Bar Lulu*, Praça 12 de Abril, will change cash if conditions suit the owner, fair rates.

● **Post & telecommunications**
Post Office: Av Floriano Peixoto, opp *Hotel Imperial*.
Telephones: Telasa on Barão de Penedo.

● **Shopping**
Daily market on streets off Av Floriano Peixoto. Good hammocks. Ceramics for sale outside Bompreço supermarket on Av Duque de Caxias.

● **Tourist offices**
Tourist office in Casa da Aposentadoria, Praça Barão de Penedo (if open).

● **Transport**
Buses 451 km from **Salvador** (US$16, 6 hrs, by daily bus at 0600, book in advance), at same time for **Aracaju** (US$8.50); buses S are more

frequent from Neópolis, 6 a day (0630-1800) to Aracaju, 2 hrs, US$5. 115 km from **Maceió**, 5 buses a day in either direction, US$5-6, 3-4 hrs. One bus to **São Paulo** daily, 1500, 2 a day to **Recife**, 0700, 2100. The Penedo rodoviária is on Av Duque de Caxias, behind Bompreço, little information; timetables posted in *Pousada Colonial*.

Ferries Frequent launches for foot pasengers and bicycles across the river to Neópolis, 25 mins, US$0.35. The dock in Penedo is on Av Duque de Caxias, below Bompreço. The ferry makes three stops in Neópolis, the second is closest to the rodoviária (which is near the Clube Vila Nova, opp Texaco station). Heading S, if you take the 0730 ferry from Penedo, you will have plenty of time to get out at the third stop, walk through Neópolis and catch the 0900 bus to Aracaju. Also half-hourly car ferry (US$1; take care when driving on and off).

MACEIÓ

(*Pop* 527,440; *CEP* 57000; *DDD* 082) The capital of Alagoas state (*pop* 2,513,000) is about 287 km NE of Aracaju by road, and 244 km S of Recife. It is mainly a sugar port, although there are also tobacco exports and a major petrochemical plant. A lighthouse stands in a residential area of town (Farol), about one km from the sea. The commercial centre stretches along the seafront to the main dock and climbs the hills behind. Alagoas is one of the poorest and least developed states. Be prepared for delays, cancellations and changed opening times. Maceió, however, is a friendly city with a low crime rate.

Places of interest

Two of the city's old buildings, the **Palácio do Governo**, which also houses the Pierre Chalita museum (see below), and the church of **Bom Jesus dos Mártires** (covered in tiles), are particularly interesting. Both are on the Praça dos Martírios (or Floriano Peixoto). The recently restored **cathedral**, Praça Dom Pedro II, is also interesting. The Associação Comercial has a museum on R Sá e Albuquerque, Jaraguá, near the sea, in a beautiful, though deteriorating building.

Museums

Instituto Histórico e Geográfico, R João Pessoa 382, T 223-7797, good small collection of Indian and Afro-Brazilian arte-facts. **Fundação Pierre Chalita**, Praça Floriano Peixoto 49, centre, T 223-4298, Alagoan painting and religious art. **Museu do Folclore Theo Brandão**, Praça Sinimbu 206, centre. All closed Sat and Sun.

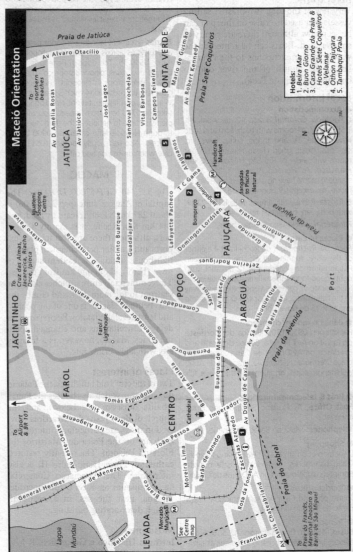

Maceió Orientation

Hotels:
1. Beira Mar
2. Buon Giorno
3. Casa Grande da Praia &
   Hotels Siete Coqueiros
   & Velamar
4. Othon Pajuçara
5. Tambaqui Praia

Lagoa do Mundaú

An enjoyable lagoon, Lagoa do Mundaú, whose entrance is 2 km S at **Pontal da Barra**, limits the city to the S and W: excellent shrimp and fish at its small restaurants and handicraft stalls; a nice place for a drink at sundown. Boats make excursions in the lagoon's channels.

Beaches

Beyond the city's main dock the beach-front districts begin; within the city, the beaches are posher the further from the centre you go. The first, going N, is Pajuçara beach, where there is a nightly craft market. At weekends there are wandering musicians and entertainers and patrols by the cavalry on magnificent Manga Larga Marchador horses. There are periodic *candomblé* and *axé* nights and rituals to the goddess Iemanjá. Next is Ponta Verde, then Jatiúca, Cruz das Almas, Jacarecica (9 km from the centre), Guaxuma (12 km), Garça Torta (14 km), Riacho Doce (16 km), Pratagi (17 km) and Ipioca (23 km). Jatiúca, Cruz das Almas and Jacarecica are all good for surfing. Taxis from town go to all the northern beaches (eg 30 mins to Riacho Doce), but buses run as far as Ipioca. The Jangadeiras bus marked 'Jacarecica-Center, via Praias' runs past all the beaches as far as Jacarecica. From there you can change to 'Riacho Doce-Trapiche', 'Ipioca' or 'Mirante' buses for Riacho Doce and Ipioca. These last three can also be caught in the centre on the seafront avenue below the Praça Sinimbu (US$0.25 to Riacho Doce). To return take any of these options, or take a bus marked 'Shopping Center' and change there for 'Jardim Vaticana' bus, which goes through Pajuçara. Beaches fronting the old city, between Salgema terminal and the modern port area (Trapiche, Sobral) are too polluted for swimming. The beaches, some of the finest and most popular in Brazil, have a protecting coral reef a kilometre or so out. Bathing is much better 3 days before and after full or new moon, because tides are higher and the water is more spectacular. For beaches beyond the city, see **Excursions** below.

Jangadas take passengers to a natural swimming pool 2 km off Pajuçara beach (Piscina Natural de Pajuçara), at low tide you can stand on the sand and rock reef (beware of sunburn). You must check the tides, there is no point going at high tide. *Jangadas* cost US$2.50 pp/day (or about US$12 to have a *jangada* to yourself). On Sun or local holidays in the high season it is overcrowded, take mask or goggles (at weekends lots of *jangadas* anchor at the reef selling food and drink).

Excursions

By bus (22 km S) past Praia do Francês to the attractive colonial town and former capital of Alagoas, **Marechal Deodoro** (*pop* 31,000), which overlooks the Lagoa Manguaba. The 17th century **Convento de São Francisco**, Praça João XXIII, has a fine church (Santa Maria Magdalena) with a superb baroque wooden altarpiece, badly damaged by termites. You can climb the church's tower for views, but if you want to take photos you will have to collect your camera from the baggage store at the entrance. Adjoining it is the **Museu de Arte Sacra**, open Tues-Sun, 0900-1700, US$0.30 (guided tours available, payment at your discretion). Also open to visitors is the Igreja **Matriz de NS da Conceição** (1783). Remains of other 18th century churches include NS do Rosário, do Amparo and the Convento do Carmo. The town is the birthplace of Marechal Deodoro da Fonseca, founder of the Republic; the modest house where he was born is on the R Marechal Deodoro, close to the waterfront, open Mon-Sat, 0800-1700 (entry free). Good local lacework. *Restaurant São Roque*, simple but good. **NB** Schistosomiasis is present in the lagoon.

On a day's excursion, it is easy to visit the town, then spend some time at beautiful **Praia do Francês**. The northern half of the beach is protected by a reef, the southern half is open to the surf. Along the beach there are many *barracas* and bars selling drinks and seafood; try *agulhas fritas*.

● **Accommodation** A2 *Cumaru*, T 231-2223, 3-star, good; C *Água Praia*, good, clean; C *Pousada Bougainville e Restaurant Chez Patrick*, T 231-1079, a/c, TV, pool, seafood and

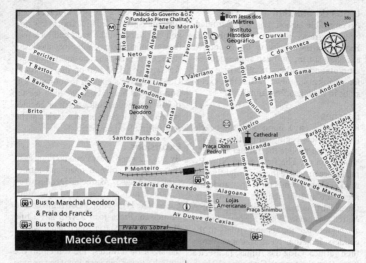

Bus to Marechal Deodoro & Praia do Francês

Bus to Riacho Doce

Maceió Centre

international cooking, very nice; **C** *Pousada Manguaba*, good; **D** *Pousada Le Baron*, T 235-3061, on road from beach to highway, good; **D** *O Pescador*, T 231-6959, with restaurant. Recommended **restaurant** *Panela Mâgica*; several others.

Further out from Maceió is the beach of **Barra de São Miguel** , entirely protected by reef, now very popular, crowded at weekends, with *Pousada da Barra*, good, new, and **A3** *Village Barra Hotel*, T 272-1207, pool, restaurant, excursions to other beaches. Several good, cheap *barracas* for food and drink (*do Amizade*, rec). Carnival here has a good reputation.

Local holidays

27 Aug (Nossa Senhora dos Prazeres); 16 Sept (Freedom of Alagoas); 8 Dec (Nossa Senhora da Conceição); Christmas Eve; New Year's Eve, half-day.

Local information
● Accommodation

Many hotels on Praia Pajuçara, mostly along Av Dr Antônio Gouveia and R Jangadeiros Alagoanos. **A1** *Enseada*, Av A Gouveia 171, T 231-4726, F 231-5134, rec; **A1** *Pajuçara Othon*, R Jangadeiros Alagoanos 1292, T 231-2200; **A2** *Sete Coqueiros*, Av A Gouveia 1335, T 231-8583, F 231-7467, 3-star, a/c, TV, phone, popular restaurant, pool; next door is the smaller **B** *Velamar*, T 231-5888, a/c, TV, fridge, safes in rooms.

Many good *pousadas* R Jangadeiros Alagoanos, one block back from the beach (it can be hard to find a room during the Dec-Mar holiday season, when prices go up): **B** *Verde Mar*, No 1, with bath, a/c, hot water, TV, T 231-2669, very good; **B** *Maceió Praia*, No 3, T 231-6391, highly rec; **B** *Pousada Sete Coqueteiros*, No 123, T 231-5877, rec; **B** *Laguna Praia*, No 1231, T 231-6180, clean, highly rec; **C** *Buongiorno*, No 1437, T 231-7577, F 231-2168, a/c, fridge, clean, English-speaking owner, helpful; **D** *Costa Verde*, No 429, bath, fan, good family atmosphere, English, German spoken, rooms on 1st floor are best, T 231-4745; **D** *Casa Grande da Praia*, No 1528, T 231-3332, with bath, a/c and TV, cheaper without, rec; *Amazona*, No 1095, clean, friendly, great breakfast; **D** *Pousada Quinta Pruma*, No 597, T 231-6065, clean, friendly. On Antônio de Mendonça: **E** *Pousada Rex*, No 311, with bath, clean, friendly, honest, helpful, highly rec (esp the breakfast); **E** *Pousada Maramar*, No 343, clean and bright, some rooms with sea view, exchange library; **E** *Pousada Shangri-La*, No 1089, T 231 3773, clean, friendly and safe. *Mandacaru*, Almte Maranenhas 85, 2 corners from beach, clean, safe, good value.

At Ponta Verde beach: **A1** *Tambaqui Praia*, R Eng Mário de Gusmão 176, T 231-0202, a/c, TV, phone, restaurant; **C** *Dos Corais*, R H Guimarães 80, helpful; **C** *Hotel do Mar*, Av R Kennedy 1447, T 231-3171, good; **D** *Pousada Bela Vista*, Av Eng Mario de Gusmão, 1260, T 231 8337, well situated, clean, excellent breakfast, a/c, TV, rec; **D** *Baleia Azul*, Av Sandoval

Arroxeias 822, a/c, fridge, TV; **D** *Sol de Verão*, R Eng Mário do Gusmão 153, with bath, E in small rooms without, clean, friendly.

Further from centre, **L2** *Matsubara*, on Cruz das Almas beach, T 231-6178, F 235-1660, pool, tennis, all facilities, rec; **D** *Hospedaria de Turismo Costa Azul*, Av João Davino and Manoel Gonçalves Filho 280, T 231-6281, clean, shower, fan, English spoken, discounts over a week.

C-D *Pousada Cavalo Marinho*, R da Praia 55, Riacho Doce (15 km from centre), facing the sea, T 235-1247, T 235-3260, use of bicycle, canoes and body boards inc, hot showers, clean, German and English spoken, tropical breakfasts, Swiss owner, very highly rec (nearby is *Lua Cheia*, good food and live music at night).

In the centre: **A1** *Beiriz*, R João Pessoa 290, T 221-1080, comfortable, pool; **A3** *Sobral Praia*, Av Assis Chateaubriand 8022 (Praia do Sobral), T 221-6665, shower, a/c, restaurant, pool, run down; **C** *Parque*, Praça Dom Pedro II 73, T 221-9099, a/c; **D** *Pousada Sol e Mar*, Av Rosa da Fonseca s/n, T 221-2615, with bath, helpful owners, safe, rec; **E** *Golf*, R Prof Domingos Moeda 38A (nr the Cathedral), clean. Cheap hotels (mostly without windows) in R Barão de Ataláia. Owing to pollution, few visitors now stay on Av or Sobral beaches: hotels in the area are being allowed to run down.

Youth hostel: **F** *Nossa Casa*, R Prefeito Abdon Arroxelas 177, T 231-2246.

Camping: there is a Camping Clube do Brasil site on Jacarecica beach, T 235-3600, a 15-min taxi drive from the town centre. Camping Pajuçara at Largo da Vitória 211, T 231-7561, clean, safe, food for sale, rec.

● **Places to eat**
Ao Lagostão, Av Duque de Caxias 1348, seafood, fixed price (expensive) menu; *Pizzeria Sorrisa*, Av Alagoana e J Pessoa Imperador, very cheap, good food, popular with Brazilians; *Bar das Ostras*, R Cruzeiro do Sul 487, Vergel do Lago, expensive but good. Vegetarian: *O Natural*, R Libertadora Alagoana (R da Praia) 112; *Nativa*, Osvaldo Sarmento 56, good views. *Spettus*, Av R Kennedy 1911, Ponta Verde, *churrascaria rodízio*. Many good bars and restaurants in Pajuçara: rec places on Av Antônio Gouveia are: *Paraíso*, No 631, vegetarian, open late; *O Dragão*, No 21, Chinese; *Comes e Bebes*, No 981, Italian and Arabic, good, take-away service; *Tempeiro Paulista*, No 1103, typical food, good service, cheap. *Massarella*, Jangadeiras Alagoanas 1255, Italian, small, good. *Mello's Bar*, R Epaminondas Gracindo 194, excellent food and value. The beaches for 5 km from the beginning of Pajuçara to Cruz das Almas in the N, are lined with *barracas* (thatched bars) providing music, snacks and meals until midnight (later at weekends). Vendors on the beach sell beer

and food during the day: clean and safe. At Ponto da Barra, on the lagoon side of the city, *Alípio*, and many others. Local specialities include oysters, *pitu*, a crayfish (now becoming scarce), and *sururu*, a kind of cockle. Local ice cream, *Shups*, rec.

● **Banks & money changers**
Banco do Brasil, etc. Open 1000 to 1500. Good rates at **Banespa**. **Banorte**, cash against Mastercard, R de Comercio, 306, Centro. **Banco Meridional**, cash against Mastercard, Praça Dom Pedro II, 95, Centro.

● **Electric current**
220 volts AC, 60 cycles.

● **Entertainment**
Teatro Deodoro, Praça Marechal Deodoro, in centre; *Cinema São Luiz*, R do Comércio, in centre; *Arte 1* and *2* Pajuçara and Iguatemi shopping centre; the other cinemas tend to be fleapits; *Bar Chapéu de Couro*, José Carneiro 338, Ponto da Barra, is a popular music bar for young people.

● **Entertainment**
Nightlife is relaxed and varied. The beach *barracas* offer live music, especially good at week ends: popular ones are *Bar Lampião* (or *Tropical*) and *Ipaneminha* on Pajuçara (Brazilian pop), and *Fellini* on Ponta Verde (varies: good blues and jazz). There are nightclubs to suit most tastes; *Calabar*, in Pajuçara, for *forró* and *lambada*, *Lambadaõ* at Cruz das Almas (excellent *lambada*, weekends only).

● **Post & telecommunications**
Post Office: R Joã Pessoa 57, centre, 0700-2200.

Telecommunications R do Comércio 508, almost opp Bandepe. Small Telasa office on Pajuçara beach, opp *Othon* hotel. Also at rodoviária.

● **Tourist offices**
Ematur, Duque de Caxias 2014, Centro, T 221-8987. Also at airport and rodoviária (latter not always open). Helpful, has good maps and leaflets. The municipal tourist authority is **Emturma**, R Saldanha da Gama 71, Farol, T 223-4016; information post on Pajuçara beach, opp *Hotel Solara*.

● **Transport**
Local Bus: Frequent buses, confusingly marked, serve all parts of the city. Bus stops are not marked, best to ask where people look as if they are waiting. The 'Ponte Verde/Jacintinho' bus runs via Pajuçara from centre to rodoviária, also take 'Circular' bus (25 mins Pajuçara to rodoviária, the stop in Pajuçara is opp the petrol station by Bompreço supermarket); 'Feitosa' also goes to the rodoviária, by a different route.

See also **Beaches**, above. Buses and kombis to Marechal de Deodoro, Praia do Francês and Barra de São Miguel leave from R Barão de Anádia, outside the ferroviária, opp *Lojas Americanas*: bus US$0.50, kombi US$0.55 to Marechal Deodoro, 30 mins, calling at Praia do Francês in each direction. Last bus back from Praia do Francês to Maceió at 1800.

Air 20 km from centre, taxi about US$15. Buses to airport from nr *Hotel Beiriz*, R João Pessoa 290 or in front of the Ferroviária, signed 'Rio Largo'; alight at Tabuleiro dos Martins, then 7-8 mins' walk to airport, bus fare US$0.50. Tourist flights over the city.

Trains The ferroviária is in the centre, R Barão de Anádia 121. 5 trains a day, Mon-Sat, from 0630-1855 to Rio Largo (35 km, US$0.12), via Fernão Velho, Satuba and Utinga. Worth taking in one direction at least since it passes the Lagoa Mundaú, through places where buses do not go.

Buses Rodoviária is 5 km from centre, on a hill with good views and cool breezes. Luggage store. Take bus marked 'Ouro Preto p/centro' or see above (taxi quicker, US$3.50) to Pajuçara. Bus to Recife, 10 a day, 3½ hrs express (more scenic coastal route, 5 hrs) US$7; to **Aracaju**, US$8.50, 5 hrs (potholed road); to **Salvador**, 10 hrs, 4 a day, US$19 (*rápido* costs more). Buses to most large cities including Belém, Fortaleza, Brasília, Belo Horizonte, Rio, São Paulo.

NORTH TO PERNAMBUCO

There are many interesting stopping points along the coast between Maceió and Recife. At **Paripueira**, 40 mins bus ride from Maceió (Rodoviária), the beach is busy only during high season. **Barra de Santo Antônio**, 45 km N, is a busy fishing village, with a palm fringed beach on a narrow peninsula, a canoe-ride away; boats also go to the Ilha da Croa; many beautiful beaches nearby. **Accommodation E** *São Geraldo*, simple, very clean, restaurant; *Pousada Buongiorno* in Maceió has 6 modest rooms to rent in a farmhouse, bathrms but no electricity, many fruit trees (T Maceió 231-7577, F 231-2168); accommodation can be found through local people. **Places to eat** *Peixada da Rita*, try prawns with coconut sauce, rec for local seafood; *Estrela Azul*, more expensive, good, popular with tourists. Also **Japaratinga** (**E** *Pousada Rei dos Peixes*, rooms for 12 or 24 hrs, bit dirty, fan, toilet, simple, opposite sewer; 3 km S is **B** *Praia Hotel Bitingui*, nicely situated – bus from Maceió at 0515) and **São José da Coroa Grande** (**D** *The Pousada*, Av Pedro Cavalcante 535, T 291-1112, rec; a few families rent rooms); at low tide watch colourful fish in the rock pools on the reef.

Pernambuco

About 244 km N of Maceió and 835 km N of Salvador is **Recife** (*pop* 1,290,150; *CEP* 50000; *DDD* 081), founded on reclaimed land by the Dutch prince Maurice of Nassau in 1637 after his troops had burnt Olinda, the original capital. It is the capital of Pernambuco State (*pop* 7,110,000). The city centre consists of three portions, Recife proper, Santo Antônio and São José, and Boa Vista and Santo Amaro. The first two are on islands formed by the rivers Capibaribe, Beberibe and Pina, while the third is made into an island by the Canal Tacaruna, which separates it from the mainland. The centre is always very busy by day; the crowds and the narrow streets, especially in the Santo Antônio district, can make it a confusing city to walk around. Recife has the main dock area, with commercial buildings associated with it. South of the centre is the residential and beach district of Boa Viagem, reached by bridge across the Bacia do Pina. Olinda, the old capital, is only 6 km to the N (see page 554).

PLACES OF INTEREST
Churches
The best of them are the churches of **Santo Antônio do Convento de São Francisco** (1606; beautiful Portuguese tiles), in the R do Imperador, and adjoining it the **Capela Dourada** (Golden Chapel, 1697, the finest sight of all, Mon-Fri 0800-1130 and 1400-1700, Sat 0800-1130: US$0.15, no flash photography; it is through the Museu Franciscano de Arte Sacra, entry US$1); **São Pedro dos Clérigos** in São José

district (1782), for its façade, its fine wood sculpture and a splendid *trompe-l'oeil* ceiling, open Tues-Fri 0800-1200, 1400-1630, Sat 0800-1000; **Santo Antônio** (1753), in Praça da Independência, rebuilt in 1864, open daily 0800-1200 and Mon-Fri 1400-1800, Sun 1700-1900; **Conceição dos Militares**, R Nova 309 (1708), grand ceiling and a large 18th century primitive mural of the battle of Guararapes (museum next door), open Mon-Fri, 0700-1130, 1330-1600, Sat 0730-1100; **Nossa Senhora do Carmo**, Praça do Carmo (1675), open Mon-Sat 0800-1200, 1400-1800, Sun 1000-1100, 1900-2000; **Madre de Deus** (1706), in the street of that name in the district of Recife, with a splendid high altar, and sacristy, Mon-Fri 0800-1100, Sun 1000-1100; the **Pilar Church** (1680), R do Pilar, Recife district; the **Divino Espírito Santo** (1642), the original church of the Jesuits, Praça 17 in Santo Antônio district, Mon-Fri 0730-1630, Sat 0730-1200; **S José do Ribamar** (19th century), in São José, open Thur only. There are many others. Most of them are closed to visitors on Sun because of services.

14 km S of the city, a little beyond Boa Viagem and the airport, on Guararapes hill, is the historic church of **Nossa Senhora das Prazeres**, open daily 0800-1700. It was here, in 1648-9, that two Brazilian victories led to the end of the 30-year Dutch occupation of the NE in 1654. The church was built by the Brazilian commander in 1656 to fulfil a vow. Boa Viagem's own fine church dates from 1707.

Other Attractions
Forte do Brum (built by the Portuguese in 1629, before the founding of Recife), is an army museum – open Tues-Fri 1000-1700, Sat-Sun 1400-1700. **Forte das Cinco Pontas** (with **Museu da Cidade do Recife** – cartographic history of the settlement of Recife – open Mon-Fri 1300-1800, Sat-Sun 1400-1800, free), built by the Dutch in 1630 and altered by the Portuguese in 1677. The two forts jointly controlled access to the port at the northern and southern entrances respectively. The first Brazilian printing press was installed in 1706 and Recife claims to publish the

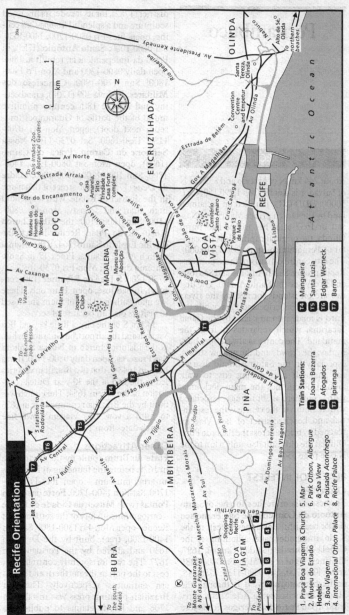

Recife Orientation

Train Stations:
T1 Joana Bezerra
T2 Afogados
T3 Ipiranga
T4 Mangueira
T5 Santa Luzia
T6 Edgar Werneck
T7 Barro

Hotels:
1. Praça Boa Viagem & Church
2. Museu do Estado
3. Boa Viagem
4. Internacional Othon Palace
5. Mar
6. Park Othon, Albergue & Sea View
7. Pousada Aconchego
8. Recife Palace

OLINDA
Av. Presidente Kennedy
Alto da Sé, Olinda
J. Nabuco
To northern beaches
Santa Teresa, Olinda
Convention Centre and Empetur
Av de Olinda
Rio Beberibe
Atlantic Ocean
RECIFE
A Lisboa
Av Cruz Cabugá
Cemitério Santo Amaro
Parque 13 de Maio
Gov A Magalhães
Estrada de Belém
ENCRUZILHADA
Av Norte
Estrada Arraia
Estr do Encanamento
Casa Amarela, sítio Trindade & Casa Forte complex
J Bonifácio
A Rosa e Silva
POÇO
Museu do Homem do Nordeste
Rio Capibaribe
MADALENA
Av Caxanga
Museu da Abolição
Av Rui Barbosa
Av João de Barros
BOA VISTA
Dom Bosco
Dantas Barreto
To Várzea
Av San Martim
Iaque Clube
Av Gonçalves da Luz
Estr dos Remédios
R São Miguel
R Imperial
H Bandeira
A de Gois
PINA
To the north, Rio João Pessoa
Av Abdias de Carvalho
5 stations to Rodoviária
Av Central
Dr J Rufino
BR 101
Rio Tijipió
IBURA
IMBIRIBEIRA
Rio Jordão
Rio Pina
Av Recife
Av Sul
Av Marechal Mascarenhas Morais
Gen MacArthur
Shopping Center Recife
BOA VIAGEM
Canal Jordão
Av Domingos Ferreira
Av Boa Viagem
To Monte Guararapes & NS das Prazeres
Canal Jordão
To Piedade
To the south, Maceió

N
km

oldest daily newspaper in South America, *Diário de Pernambuco*, founded 1825. The building is on the Praça da Independência.

The artists' and intellectuals' quarter is based on the **Pátio de São Pedro**, the square round São Pedro dos Clérigos (see under **Churches**). Folk music and poetry shows in the square on Fri, Sat and Sun evenings and there are pleasant little restaurants, with good atmosphere, at Nos 44, 46 and 47, and No 20 *Caldeira de Cana e Petisqueira Banguê*. The square is an excellent shopping centre for typical NE craftware (clay figurines are cheapest in Recife). Not far away is the **Praça do Sebo**, where the city's second-hand booksellers concentrate; this Mercado de Livros Usados is off the R da Roda, behind the Edifício Santo Albino, near the corner of Av Guararapcs and R Dantas Barreto. Visit the city markets in the São José and Santa Rita sections.

The former municipal prison has now been made into a cultural centre, the **Casa da Cultura** (open Mon-Sat 0900-1900, Sun 1400-1800), with many cells converted into art or souvenir shops and with areas for exhibitions and shows (also public conveniences). Local dances such as the ciranda, forró and bumba-meu-boi are held as tourist attractions on Mon, Wed and Fri at 1700 (T 241-2111 to check in advance). Among other cultural centres are Recife's three traditional **theatres**, **Santa Isabel** (Praça da República, open to visitors Mon-Fri 1300-1800), **Parque** (R do Hospício 81, Boa Vista, restored and beautiful, open 0800-1200, 1400-1800) and **Apolo** (R do Apolo 121, open 0800-1200, 1400-1700).

Boa Viagem is the finest residential and hotel quarter. The 8 km promenade commands a striking view of the Atlantic, but the beach is crowded at weekends and not very clean. During the Jan breeding season, sharks come close to the shore. Go fishing on *jangadas* at Boa Viagem with a fisherman. The main square has a good market Sat, with forró dancing. Bus from centre, take any marked 'Boa Viagem'; from Nossa Senhora do Carmo, take buses marked 'Piedade', 'Candeias' or 'Aeroporto' – they go on Av Domingos Ferreira, two blocks parallel to the beach, all the way to Praça Boa Viagem (at Av Boa Viagem 500). Back to centre take buses marked 'CDU' or 'Setubal' from Av Domingos Ferreira.

MUSEUMS

The **Museu do Homem do Nordeste**, Av 17 de Agosto 2223, Casa Forte (open Tues-Sun, 1100-1700, entry US$1), comprises the **Museu de Arte Popular**, containing ceramic figurines (including some by Mestre Alino and Zé Caboclo); the **Museu do Açúcar**, on the history and technology of sugar production, with models of colonial mills, collections of antique sugar bowls and much else; the **Museu de Antropologia**, the **Nabuco Museum** (at No 1865) and the modern museum of popular remedies, **Farmacopéia Popular**. Take the 'Dois Irmãos' bus (check that it's the correct one, with 'Rui Barbosa' posted in window, as there are two) from in front of the Banorte building near the post office on Guararapes, 30 mins' ride 10 km outside the city to the **zoo** (US$0.20, not very good) and **botanical gardens**; it passes the museum complex, and together with the zoo they make a pleasant day's outing. It is easier to get to the museum complex by taxi.

The **Museu do Estado**, Av Rui Barbosa 960, Graças (closed am on Sat and Sun, and all day Mon), has excellent paintings by the 19th-century landscape painter, Teles Júnior. **Museu do Trem**, Praça Visconde de Mauá, small but interesting, especially the Henschel locomotive, built to the Beyer-Garrett pattern (open Tues-Fri, 0900-1200, 1400-1700, Sat 0900-1200, Sun, 1400-1700). **Museu da Abolição (of Slavery)**, R Benfica 150, Madalena, is worth a visit, in an early 19th-century tiled house, once owned by the abolitionist João Alfredo (closed since 1990). **Museu de Imagem e Som**, R da Aurora 379, Boa Vista, open Mon-Fri, 0900-1200, 1400-1800. You may like to visit **Cerámica Brennand**, a factory in the western suburbs at Várzea, 16 km from the centre, on the Camaragibe road, T 271-2784 (take a taxi, or walk the 3 km

Recife

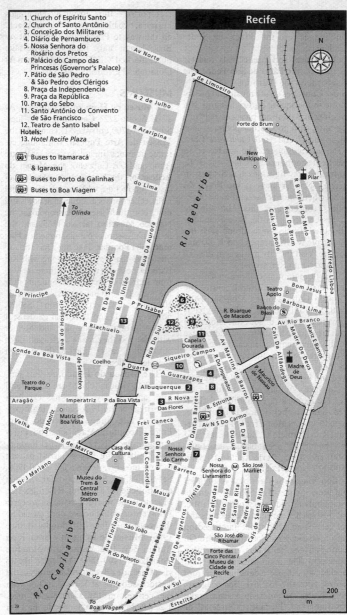

1. Church of Espírtu Santo
2. Church of Santo Antônio
3. Conceição dos Militares
4. Diário de Pernambuco
5. Nossa Senhora do Rosário dos Pretos
6. Palácio do Campo das Princesas (Governor's Palace)
7. Pátio de São Pedro & São Pedro dos Clérigos
8. Praça da Independencia
9. Praça da República
10. Praça do Sebo
11. Santo Antônio do Convento de São Francisco
12. Teatro de Santo Isabel
Hotels:
13. *Hotel Recife Plaza*

🚌1 Buses to Itamaracá & Igarassu

🚌2 Buses to Porto da Galinhas

🚌3 Buses to Boa Viagem

along R Gastão Vidigal – past hotels *Costa Azul* and *Tropical* – from the end of the bus line along Av Caxangá). They make ceramic tiles, and one of the brothers is a sculptor of idiosyncratic works. Entry is free, and it is very friendly. They also have a shop at Av Conselheiro Aguiar 2966, loja 4, convenient for Boa Viagem.

EXCURSIONS

Any bus going S of Boa Viagem passes the **Ilha do Amor**; ask a fisherman to row you out to it and collect you at a set time, US$2.50. Walk across the island (10 mins) to the Atlantic side for a fine, open, uncrowded beach. Take care here as it is a little isolated. About 30 km S of Recife, beyond Cabo, is the beautiful and quiet **Gaibu** beach (take bus 'Centro do Cabo' from airport, frequent buses – 20 mins – from Cabo), *Pousada Beto Qualhado*; rooms, E, at *Oliver y Daniel*, Av Laura Cavalcante 20, German, very relaxed, cheap restaurants; 1 km on foot from Gaibu is **Praia Calhetas**, which is very nice. **Itapuama** beach is even more empty, both reached by bus from Cabo. **Cabo** (*pop* 121,000), Pernambuco's main industrial city, has interesting churches and forts and a Museu da Abolição, and at nearby Suape are many 17th-century buildings and a biological reserve. **Porto de Galinhas**, further S still, is a beautiful beach, reached by bus from Cais de Santa Rita, Recife US$2, via the town of Nossa Senhora do Ó, 2 hrs, 0900, 1230, 1530 (not Sun), 0740 Sun only, take 0900 since others don't allow enough time; last back at 1600, packed out. It has cool, clean water, and waves. **A1** *Solar Porto de Galinhas*, T 325-0772, F 325-1331, on beach, many facilities, beautiful place; *pousada* of Dona Benedita in the street where the bus stops, very basic, clean; several other hotels and *pousadas*; food at *Rang Bem* in same street as *Benedita*. Further S (80 km from Recife) are the beaches of **Barra do Sirinhaém**, with little tourist development as yet, 3 hotels including **E** *dos Cataventos*; fishermen make trips to offshore island (good views).

Carpina (*pop* 71,950), 54 km from Recife, is well known for its carnival and for the traditional Epiphany festival early in Jan,

and also for the carpets made in nearby village of Lagoa do Carro. There is a historical museum. Hotels (**A3** *Pousada das Acácias*, BR-408, Km 77, T 621-0594; **C** *São João da Escócia*, Av João Alfredo 136, T 621-0365) and restaurants. **Tracunhaém** (*pop* 13,700), is a peaceful town where fine ceramics are made; there are two interesting early 19th-century churches. It is just N of Carpina, on to the road to Nazaré da Mata.

LOCAL HOLIDAYS

1 Jan (Universal Brotherhood). 12-15 Mar, parades to mark the city's foundation. 24 June (São João), celebrated with bonfires and fireworks, see also below. 16 July (Nossa Senhora do Carmo, patron saint of the city). 8 Dec (Nossa Senhora da Conceição).

Carnival

The carnival groups dance at the doors of all the churches they pass; they usually go to the Church of Nossa Senhora do Rosário dos Pretos, patron saint of the slaves (R Estreita do Rosário, Santo Antônio), before proceeding into the downtown areas. A small car at the head bears the figure of some animal; it is followed by the king and queen under a large, showy umbrella. The *bahianas*, who wear snowy-white embroidered skirts, dance in single file on either side of the king and queen. Next comes the *dama do passo* carrying a small doll, or *calunga*. After the *dama* comes the *tirador de loas*: he chants to the group which replies in chorus, and last comes a band of local percussion instruments.

Still flourishing is the dance performance of the *caboclinhos*. The groups wear traditional Indian garb: bright feathers round their waists and ankles, colourful cockades, bead and animal teeth necklaces, a dazzle of medals on their red tunics. The dancers beat out the rhythm with bows and arrows; others of the group play primitive musical instruments, but the dance is the thing: spinning, leaping, and stooping with almost mathematical precision.

There is a *pre-carnavalesca* week, followed by the main days Sun to Tues; on the Sat the *bloco* 'Galo da Madrugada' officially opens carnival (wild and lively), see local press for routes and times. The groups taking part are *maracatu*, *caboclinhos*, *trocas*, *blocos*, *ursos*, *caboclos de lança*, *escolas de samba* and *frevo*. Usually they start from Av Conde da Boa Vista and progress along R do Hospício, R da Imperatriz, Ponte da Boa Vista, Praça da Independência, R 1° de Março and R do Imperador. During Carnival (and on a smaller scale throughout the year) the Casa de Cultura has frevo demonstrations where visitors can learn some steps of this unique dance of Pernambuco (check press for details of 'Frevioca' truck and frevo orchestras during Carnival in the Pátio de São Pedro). The best place to see the groups is from the balconies of *Hotel do Parque*. Information from Casa da Carnaval, office of Fundação da Cultura de Recife, Pátio de São Pedro, lojas 10-11.

Festivais Juninos

In the June *festas* of São João and São Pedro, the forró is danced. This dance, now popular throughout the NE, is believed to have originated when the British builders of the local railways held parties that were 'for all'.

LOCAL INFORMATION

Warning Opportunistic theft is unfortunately common in the streets of Recife and Olinda (especially on the streets up to Alto da Sé). Keep hold of bags and cameras, and do not wear a watch. The police in Olinda are reported to be far less helpful than those in the city.

● **Accommodation**

Hotel prices

L1	over US$200	**L2**	US$151-200
L3	US$101-150	**A1**	US$81-100
A2	US$61-80	**A3**	US$46-60
B	US$31-45	**C**	US$21-30
D	US$12-20	**E**	US$7-11
F	US$4-6	**G**	up to US$3

(For Olinda hotels see page 555). In general, there is a shortage of good, mid-range hotels, plenty of multi-star hotels and plenty of flea-pits.

Hotels in the **centre** and away from the beach: in Casa Forte, NW of centre, is **A1** *Pousada Casa Forte*, Av 17 de Agosto 735, T 268-0524, 3-star; **A3** *Recife Plaza*, R da Aurora 225, T 231-1200, Boa Vista, 3-star, overlooking the Rio Capibaribe, every comfort, highly rec, fine restaurant (very popular lunchtime); **B** *4 de Outubro*, R Floriano Peixoto 141, Santo Antônio, T 424-4477, 4 standards of room, with bath, hot water, TV, phone, a/c.

In the cheaper categories: **D** *América*, Praça Maciel Pinheiro 48, Boa Vista, T 221-1300, 2-star, with a/c (cheaper without), front rooms pleasanter, clean, quiet; **D** *Lido*, R do Riachuelo 547, T 222-4660, good breakfast, hot water, friendly, rec; **D** *Nassau*, Largo do Rosário 253, T 224-3977/3520, clean, hot showers, but a bit noisy (breakfast only, served on 7th floor, with a balcony overlooking the city); **E** *Recife*, R do Imperador 310, T 224-0799, with bath (cheaper without), central, OK but grubby; **E** *Interlaine*, R do Hospício 186, T 222-3762, good value in town centre, highly rec; **E** *Parque*, R do Hospicio 51, inc breakfast, good view, good value, rec.

Hotels on or near the beach in Boa Viagem: **L2** *Recife Palace*, Av Boa Viagem 4070, T 325-4044, F 326-8895, 5-star; **L2** *Mar*, nr beach at R Barão de Souza Leão 451, T 341-5433, F 341-7002, 5-star; **L2** *Vila Rica*, No 4308, T 326-5111, F 326-5511, 4-star; **A1** *Do Sol*, No 978, T 326-7644, F 326-7166, 4-star; **A1** *Internacional Othon Palace*, No 3722, T 465-5022, F 326-7661, 4-star; **A1** *Savaroni*, No 3773, T 325-5077, F 326-4900, 4-star; **A3** *Aguamar Praia*, R dos Navegantes 492, T 326-4604, a/c, TV, safe, good breakfast; **A3** *Arcada*, Av Cons Aguiar 3500, T 326-9922, F 326-9622, hotel, fondue restaurant and travel agency with exchange; **A3** *Boa Viagem*, No 5000, T 341-4144, F 341-1627, 4-star, nr beach; **A3** *Casa Grande e Senzala*, Av Conselheiro Aguiar 5000, T/F 341-0366, 3-star; *Castelinho Praia*, No 4520, T 326-1186, F 465-1150, 3 stars, pool, bar, restaurant; **A3** *Recife Monte*, R Petrolina e dos Navegantes 363, T 326-7422, F 326-2903, good value, rec; **B** *Pousada da Praia*, Alcides Carneiro Leal 66, T 326-7085, with bath, a/c, fridge, TV, safe, rooms vary (some tiny), helpful; **B** *Setúbal*, R Setúbal 932, T 341-4116, clean, helpful, good breakfast; **B** *Uzi Praia*, Av Cons Aguiar 942, T 325-2741, a/c, bath, rec; **C** *Pousada Aconchego*, Félix de Brito 382, T 326-2989, F 326-8059, 3 levels of tariff, all with bath, a/c, pleasant, swimming pool, good meals, safe is closed on Sun and in evening, English-speaking owner, will collect you from the airport; **C** *Praia Mar*, Av Boa Viagem 1660, T 326-6905, small, clean, rec; **C** *200 Milhas*, No 865, T 326-5292, safe, highly rec; **C** *Saveiro*, R Conselheiro Aguiar 4670, T 326-6073, no pool, mosquitoes, but clean, a/c; **C** *Sea View*, R Navegantes 101, T 326-5891, Dutch-owned (Dutch, English, French spoken), a/c, small, very friendly, rec; **D** *Guest House Pousada*, Luis

Marques Teixeira 155, T 341-0559, a/c, secure, proprietor Ricardo Teixeira is a Sevagtur guide, helpful, highly rec, English and German spoken, rec; **D** *Solar da Tia Cléo*, R Joaquim Carneiro da Silva 48, T 326-3460/1090, no sign outside, fans, family atmosphere, fine garden, English spoken, clean, rec.

Youth hostels E *Albergue do Mar 81*, R dos Navegantes 81, T 326-2196, cheaper for IYHA members, good breakfast and atmosphere; **E** *Albergue Mandacaru*, R Maria Carolina 75, T 326-1964, stores luggage, English and German spoken, good breakfast, rec; *Maracatus do Recife*, R Maria Carolina 185, T 326-1221, good breakfast, pool, clean, safe, friendly, membership not needed, rec. Membership information from Associação Pernambucano de Albergues da Juventude (APEAJ), from Empetur (see below – take 2 photos).

Paulo Bezerra de Mello, DHL, R do Riachuelo 201, T 221-2000, rents an apartment for 3 at Boa Viagem, rec. Hotels in the Santa Rita area are not rec as this area is dangerous at night.

During Carnival and for longer stays at other times, private individuals rent rooms and houses in Recife and Olinda; Lins Turismo has listings as does the *Diário de Pernambuco*, or ask around the streets of Olinda. This accommodation is generally cheaper, safer and quieter than hotels. Many hotels sell 5-day Carnival packages (at high prices), which you must take regardless of the length of time you wish to stay. Shop around.

● **Places to eat**
There are many good restaurants, at all prices, in the city, and along beach at Boa Viagem.

City: *Leite* (lunches only), Praça Joaquim Nabuco 147/53 nr Casa de Cultura, old and famous, good service, smart (another branch in Boa Viagem, at Prof José Brandão 409). *Le Buffet*, R do Hospício 147-49, good, helpful, friendly, English-speaking owner; *Fuji* (Japanese), No 354, economical, good tofu dishes; *Lisboa á Noite*, Hospício nr Conde da Boa Vista, good, reasonable, open Sun evenings (unlike many); *Tivoli*, R Matias de Albuquerque, Santo Antônio, lunches downstairs, a/c restaurant upstairs, good value; *Galo D'Ouro*, Gamboa do Carmo 83, rec, good value; at No 136, *Casa de Tia*, lunch only, must arrive by 1215, try *cosido*, a meat and vegetable stew, enough for 2, highly rec. *O Vegetal*, R Cleto Campelo e Av Guararapes (2nd floor) behind Central Post Office, lunch only, highly rec, closed Sat-Sun. *Casa dos Frios*, da Palma 57, loja 5, delicatessen/sandwich bar, salads, pastries etc, very good. *Boa Opçion* on the corner of Barão de Souza Leão and Av Domingos Ferreira, cheap, delicious local specialities, open for lunch and dinner, food/kilo, rec.

Boa Viagem: Main hotels. *Maxime*, Av Boa Viagem 21, is where the locals eat seafood; *O Porção*, Av Domingos Ferriera 4215, very good rodizio and salad bar, expensive; *Oficina da Massas*, No 2232, Italian; pizzas at *Mr Pizza*, Av Cons Aguiar 3553 and *Fiorentino*, R Laete Lemos 60 (another branch at Av Bernardo Vieira de Melo 4738, Candeias); *Mediterráneo*, R Setúbal, 100m from *Hotel Setúbal*, Italian, pasta, fish, reasonable, rec; *Shangai Palace* (Chinese), Av Domingos Ferreira 4719, excellent, plenty of food, another branch at Av Boa Viagem 5262; *China Especial*, Av Domingos Ferreira 3470, good value, large helpings; *Futuba*, R Mauoel de Brito 44, a tiny side street towards beach from Av Conselheiro Aguiar 1313, Japanese, good; *Chinés*, Herculano Bandeiro 875, Pina (just after bridge, on Boa Viagem side), good value, another branch at Av Bernardo Vieira de Melo, Piedade; *Prá Vocês*, Av Herculano Bandeira 115, Pina (town end of Boa Viagem beach), good but pricey seafood. *Snack Bar Flamingo*, Av Cons Aguiar 542, good hamburgers and ice cream; *Churrascarla o Laçador*, R Visconde Jequitinhonha 138, good meat, superb salads of all kinds, rec.

For Olinda restaurants see under Olinda, page 556. Be careful of eating the local small crabs, known as *guaiamum*; they live in the mangrove swamps which take the drainage from Recite's *mocambos* (shanty towns).

Bars: the Graças district, W of Boa Vista, on the Rio Capibaribe, is popular for bars and evening entertainment. Recommended is *Depois do Escuro*, R da Amizade 178, Graças, but there are many others. *Shoparia*, 2 doors from *Maxime* restaurant, rec for beer and atmosphere, live rock music after 2200; *Highlander*, English pub at Av Domingos Ferreira 2222, Boa Viagem.

● **Banks & money changers**
Banks open 1000-1600, hours for exchange vary between 1000 and 1400, sometimes later. **Banco do Brasil**, next to shopping centre, Boa Vlagem (Visa), very helpful. In Boa Viagem, **Banorte** branches on Avs Domingos Ferreira and Cons Aguiar. **Mastercard**, cash against card, Av Cons Aguiar 3924, Boa Viagem. **Banco Meridional**, cash against Mastercard, Av Rio Branco, 155, Centro, **Lloyds Bank**, R do Fogo 22. Moneychanger hangs out at *Casa dos Frios* deli, R da Palma corner with Guararapes. **Edifício Bancomércio**, 3rd floor, R Matias de Alberquerque 223, takes cash and TCs. *Restaurante Leite*, Praça Joaquim Nabuco 147/53, good rates for TCs and cash.

● **Embassies & consulates**
British, Domingos Ferreira 222, sala 203, Boa Viagem, T 326 3733, open 0800-1130. **Danish**,

Av M de Olinda 85, Ed Alberto Fonseca 2°, CP 3450030, T 224-0997, open 0800-1200, 1400-1800. **Swedish**, Av Marquês de Olinda 126, sala 101, T 326-3144. **Finnish**, Av Conde da Boa Vista 708. **German**, Dantas Barreto 191, Edif Santo Antônio, 4th floor, T 424-3488. **French**, Av Dantas Barreto 1200, 9° floor, Edif San Diego, São José, T 224-6722. **US**, Gonçalves Maia 163, Boa Vista, T 221-1412.

● **Cultural centres**
British Council, Domingos Ferreira 4150, Boa Viagem, CP 6104, T 272-3060, F 272-3455, 0800-1500, reading room with current English newspapers, very helpful. **Instituto Brasileiro Alemã**, R do Sossego 364. **Alliance Française**, R Amaro Bezerra 466, Derby, T/F 222-0918.

● **Electric current**
220 volts AC, 60 cycles.

● **Entertainment**
Discotheques: tend to be expensive and sophisticated – best of these are in Casa Forte. Best times are around midnight on Fri or Sat. Take a taxi.

Recife Ballet: shows in the Recife/Olinda Convention Center, US$10, traditional dances in full costume, rec.

The following have live regional music: *O Catedral da Seresta*, R Real da Torre 1435, Bairro Torre, T 228-0567; *O Pirata*, Av 17 de Agôsto 1738, Bairro Casa Forte; *Maria Bonita*, R Jack Ayres s/n, Boa Viagem, T 325-5402. Also visit a typical northeastern 'Forró' where local couples dance to typical music, very lively especially on Fri and Sat: several good ones at Candeias.

● **Laundry**
Av Conselheiro Aguiar 1385, Boa Viagem.

● **Places of worship**
Church: Episcopalian, R Carneiro Vilela 569.

● **Post & telecommunications**
Post Office: including poste restante, Central Correios, 50001, Av Guararapes 250 (or American Express, R Félix de Brito 666, T 465-5000 for poste restante). In Boa Viagem, Av Cons Aguiar e R Cel Sérgio Cardim.

Telecommunications: Embratel, Av Agamenon Magalhães, 1114, Parque Amorim district, T 221-4149; also Praça da Independência. Telpe, Av Cons Aguiar e R Padre Carapuceiro, closes 1200 on Sun. **International telephones**: R Diário de Pernambuco, 38 (closes 2230); also at airport (first floor), noisy.

● **Shopping**
Markets: permanent craft market in **Casa da Cultura** (see above); prices for ceramic figurines are lower than Caruaru (see below). Also in the Casa da Cultura is *Sucos da Terra*, Ralo Norte, wide selection of juices made with mineral water. Mercado São José (1875) for local products and handicrafts. **Casa Amarela** for a truly typical market on Sat and Sun evening; **'hippy fair'** at Praça Boa Viagem, on the sea front, life-sized wooden statues of saints (a good meeting place is the *Bar Lapinha* in the middle of the square). Sat craft fair at **Sítio Trindade**, Casa Amarela: during the feast days of 12-29 June, fireworks, music, dancing, local food. On 23 April, here and in the Pátio de São Pedro, one can see the *xangô* dance. Herbal remedies, barks and spices at Afogados market.

Bookshops: *Livraria Brandão*, R da Matriz 22 (used English books and some French and German) and bookstalls on the R do Infante Dom Henrique. *Livro 7*, a huge emporium with a very impressive stock, R Sete de Setembro 329. *Solider* at Guararapes airport has books in English, newspapers, magazines. *Livraria do Nordeste*, between cells 118 and 119, Ralo Leste, Casa da Cultura, for books in Portuguese on the NE. *Livraria Nordeste*, R Imperatriz 43, Boa Vista. A great local character, *Melquísidec Pastor de Nascimento*, second-hand bookseller, at R Bispo Cardoso Aires, 215; also has a second-hand stall at Praça de Sebo (see page 548).

● **Sports**
Golf: Caxangá Golf & Country Club, Av Caxangá 5362: 9 holes.

● **Tour companies & travel agents**
Trilhas, T 222-6864, rec for ecologically oriented excursions; *Souto Costa Viagens e Turismo Ltda*, R Felix de Brito Melo 666, T 465-5000, and Aeroporto de Guararapes.

● **Tourist offices**
Empetur (for the State of Pernambuco), main office, Centro de Convençes, Complexo Rodoviário de Salgadinho, T 241-2111, F 241-9011, between Recife and Olinda, branch at airport – 24 hrs (will book hotels, helpful but few leaflets, English spoken). Maps available, or can be bought at newspaper stands in city; also sketch maps in monthly guides *Itinerário Pernambuco* and *Guia do Turista*.

Hours of opening of museums, art galleries, churches etc are published in the *Diário de Pernambuco*.

● **Transport**
Local Bus: city buses cost US$0.35; they are clearly marked and run frequently until about 2230. Many central bus stops have boards showing routes. On buses, especially at night, look out for landmarks as street names are written small and are hard to see. Integrated bus-**metrô** (see **Train** below) routes and tickets (US$0.75) are explained in a leaflet issued by

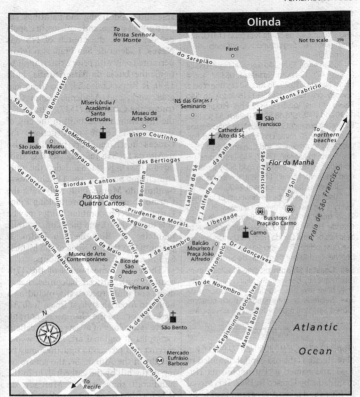

Olinda

To Nossa Senhora do Monte

Not to scale

Farol

do Sarapião

Av Mons Fabricio

São João

do Bonsucesso

Misericórdia / Academia Santa Gertrudes

NS das Graças / Seminario

Museu de Arte Sacra

São Francisco

São Miséricórdia

Bispo Coutinho

Cathedral, Alto da Sé

To northern beaches

São João Batista

Museu Regional

Amparo

das Bertiogas

Flor da Manhã

da Floresta

Cel Joaquim Cavalcante

Biordas 4 Cantos

do Bonfim

Pousada dos Quatro Cantos

Ladeira da Sé

T.I Alfredo T.S

da Palha

São Francisco

do Sol

Praia de São Francisco

Av Joaquim Nabuco

Bernardo Vieira

Prudente de Morais

Seguro

Liberdade

Bus stops / Praça do Carmo

13 de Maio

Museu de Arte Contemporáneo

Henrique Dias

7 de Setembro

Bico de São Pedro

São Bento

Balcão Mourisco Praça João Alfredo

Vasconcelos

Dr J Gonçalves

Carmo

Prefeitura

10 de Novembro

Av Segismuneo Gonçalves

Manoel Borba

Atlantic Ocean

15 de Novembro

São Bento

N

Santos Dumont

Mercado Eufrásio Barbosa

To Recife

CBTU Metrorec, T 251-5256. See below for buses to Olinda and other destinations outside the city. Trams run in the city centre. Taxis are plentiful; fares double on Sun.

Air The principal international and national airlines fly to Guararapes airport, 12 km from the city. Direct flights from Europe with Air Portugal, Varig and Vasp (see **Information for travellers**, see page 659. From Miami, Vasp and Varig. Internal flights to all major cities. Bus to airport, No 52, US$0.60, 30 mins from NS do Carmo, or 'Aeroporto' from city centre and Av Domingos Ferreira, Boa Viagem (US$0.25, 10 mins). Tourist taxis at the airport cost US$5 to Boa Viagem, while ordinary taxis picked up on the main road cost about US$1 less. There is a bank desk before customs which gives much the same rate for dollars as the moneychangers in the lobby.

Trains Recife is the centre of the Rede Fer-

roviária do Nordeste, with lines N to Paraíba and Natal (no passenger services). Commuter services, known as the **Metrô** but not underground, leave from the central station; they have been extended to serve the rodoviária (frequent trains, 0500-2300, US$0.25). If going to Boa Viagem from the rodoviária, get off the Metrô at Joanna Bezerra (20 mins from rodoviária) and take a bus or taxi (US$5.25) from there.

Buses The rodoviária, mainly for long-distance buses, is 12 km outside the city at São Lourenço da Mata (it is called Terminal Integrado dos Passageiros, or TIP, pronounced 'chippy'). T 455-1999/1503. There is a 30-mins metrô connection to the central railway station, entrance through Museu do Trem, opp Casa da Cultura (US$0.25), 2 lines leave the city, take train marked 'Rodoviária'. From Boa Viagem a taxi all the way costs US$18, or go to Joana Bezerra Metrô station and change there. Bus US$0.60, 1 hr, from centre or from Boa Viagem. The train to the centre is much quicker than the bus. Real Alagoas bus tickets (for Maceió and Aracaju) also sold at Cais de Santa Rita (opp EMTU) and *Fruir Tur*, Av Segismundo Gonçalves 487, Carmo, Olinda.

To **Salvador**, 13 hrs, 4 a day (all at night) US$24 (1 *leito*, 47); 12 hrs to **Fortaleza**, US$22, and 4 hrs to **Natal** US$9.25. To **Rio**, 50 hrs (the road is severely pot-holed), US$59 (118 *leito*); to **São Paulo**, 40 hrs; to **São Luís**, 28 hrs, Progresso at 1430 and 1945, US$48.50; to **Belém**, 34 hrs (Boa Esperança bus rec). Good roads N to **João Pessoa** (buses every 30 mins, US$3.60), Natal and Fortaleza, W to Arcoverde and Caruaru (US$4.75, 2 hrs). South to **Maceió**, US$7, 3½ hrs (express), 6 hrs (slow), either by the main road or by the coast road daily 'via Litoral'. Efficient service to most Brazilian cities, last bus leaves at 2400.

Buses to the nearby destinations of Igarassu (every 15 mins) and Itamaracá (every 30 mins) leave from Av Martins de Barros, in front of *Grande Hotel*; to Olinda, see below; those to beaches beyond Olinda from Av Dantas behind the post office. To Cabo (every 20 mins) and beaches S of Recife from Cais de Santa Rita.

Sea Coastal Shipping: Lóide Brasileiro ships run frequently between Brazilian coastal ports. They have several up-to-date vessels, some de luxe. Recife is an international port; customs (closed Sat, Sun) reportedly can be obstructive.

OLINDA

(*Pop* 340,675; *CEP* 53000; *DDD* 081) 6 km N of Recife is the old capital, founded in 1537 and named a 'Patrimônio da Humanidade' by Unesco in 1982. It is served by buses and taxis. A programme of restoration, partly financed by the Netherlands government, was initiated in order to comply with the recently conferred title of National Monument. Despite adoption by Unesco and the Dutch, the need for restoration and cleaning has grown.

Places of interest

Of particular interest are: on R São Bento, the **Prefeitura**, once the palace of the viceroys, and the monastery of **São Bento**, founded 1582 by the Benedictine monks, restored 1761, the site of Brazil's first law school and the first abolition of slavery (paintings, sculpture, furniture; the monastery is closed to anyone without written permission to visit); the convent of **Santa Teresa** (1687), Av Olinda 570; the **Convento de São Francisco** (1585), with

splendid woodcarving and paintings, superb gilded stucco, and azulejos, in Capela de São Roque; the church of **NS das Neves**, Ladeira de São Francisco (visits permitted only with prior written application); the **Igreja da Misericórdia**, built 1540, R Bispo Coutinho, fine tiling and gold work, and Acádemia Santa Gertrudes; the **Cathedral** (1537), Alto da Sé, the first church to be built in the city, of simple and severe construction; the **Graças** church (seminary) built 1582, also in Alto da Sé; **São João Batista dos Militares** (1581), R da Saudade, the only church not burnt by the Dutch; **Nossa Senhora do Monte**, built early 16C; the **Carmo** church (1588) overlooking Praça Carmo (under restoration, guides may be able to get you in), and the colonial public fountain, the **Bica de São Pedro**, R Joaquim Cavalcanti. None of the historic buildings has fixed opening hours.

There are some houses of the 17th century with latticed balconies, heavy doors and pink stucco walls, including a house in Moorish style at Praça João Alfredo 7, housing the *Mourisco* restaurant. There is a colony of artists and excellent examples of regional art, mainly woodcarving and terracotta figurines, may be bought in the Alto da Sé, the square on top of the hill by the cathedral, or in the handicraft shops at the **Mercado da Ribeira** (the former slave market), R Bernardo Vieira de Melo (Vieira de Melo gave the first recorded call for independence from Portugal, in Olinda in 1710). Handicrafts are also sold at good prices in the Mercado Eufrásio Barbosa, by the junction of Av Segismundo Gonçalves and Santos Dumont, Varadouro; the bars serve good value meals. There is a **Museu de Arte Sacra** in the former Palácio Episcopal (1696) at Alto da Sé 7, open Mon-Fri, 0700-1300. At R 13 de Maio 157, in the 18th-century jail of the Inquisition, is the **Museu de Arte Contemporânea** (Tues-Fri 0900-1700, Sat-Sun 1400-1700). The **Museu Regional**, R do Amparo 128, is excellent (same hours).

Guides

Guides with identification cards wait in

Praça do Carmo. They are former street children and half the fee for a full tour of the city (about US$20) goes to a home for street children. If you take a guide you will be safe from mugging which, unfortunately, occurs (see below). If in doubt about this system, ask at the *Pousada Flor da Manhã*.

Beaches

The beaches close to Olinda are reported to be seriously polluted. Those further N from Olinda, beyond Casa Caiada, are beautiful, usually deserted, palm-fringed; at **Janga**, and **Pau Amarelo**, the latter can be dirty at low tide (take either a 'Janga' or 'Pau Amarelo' bus). At many simple cafés you can eat *sururu* (clam stew in coconut sauce), *agulha frita* (fried needle-fish), *miúdo de galinha* (chicken giblets in gravy) and *casquinha de caranguejo* (seasoned crabmeat and *farinha de dendê* served in crabshells). Visit the Dutch fort on Pau Amarelo beach; small craft fair here on Sat nights. Near the fort is *Bar Lua Cheia*, which has music and dancing.

Local festivals

At Olinda's **carnival** thousands of people dance through the narrow streets of the old city to the sound of the Frevo, the brash energetic music which normally accompanies a lively dance performed with umbrellas. The local people decorate them with streamers and straw dolls, and form themselves into costumed groups to parade down the R do Amparo; Pitombeira and Elefantes are the best known of these groups. Foundation Day is celebrated with 3 days of music and dancing, 12-15 Mar, night time only.

Local information

NB Olinda has been severely afflicted by rapidly-worsening poverty, the effects of which are perhaps more noticeable in this attractive and comparatively prosperous area. Please exercise caution, and sympathy.

● **Accommodation**

At Casa Caiada, Av José Augusto Moreira 2200 (T 431-2955, F 431-0670), is **L2** *Quatro Rodas* with swimming pool, excellent restaurant, tennis courts, gardens, very good.

A3 *Pousada dos Quatro Cantos*, R Prudente de Morais 441, in a converted mansion, very

good, highly rec, prices rise to L2 for 5-night package during Carnival, T 429-0220, F 429-1845, sometimes has live entertainment, expensive restaurant.

B *Marolinda*, Av Min Marcos Freire (Beira Mar) 1615, Bairro Novo, T 429-1699, F 326-6934, 2-star, rec, rooms at front very noisy at weekends; **B** *Pousada São Francisco*, R do Sol 127, T 429-2109, F 429-4057, clean, comfortable, pool, rec, modest restaurant; **B** *Quatorze Bis*, Av Beira Mar 1414, T 429-0409, friendly, helpful, clean, run by Dutchman; **B-E** *Pousada d'Olinda*, P João Alfredo 178, T/F 439-1163, happy, warmly rec, 10% discount with *South American Handbook*, 5 luxury a/c apartments, 2 colonial suites, 16 rooms with shared bath, two communal rooms with good view, pool, breakfast, other meals if requested in advance, English, French, German and Spanish spoken.

C *Oh! Linda Pousada*, Av Marcos Freire 349, Bairro Novo, T 439-2116, clean and friendly, rec; **C** *Circular do Bonde*, Av Min Marcos Freire 223, T 429-3485, shared bath, sea views, communal breakfast, garage, pool, friendly, rec.

D *Hospedaria do Turista*, Av Beira Mar 989, excellent, T 429-1847; **D** *São Pedro*, Praça Cons João Alfredo 168, T 429-2935, cosy, helpful, laundry, Danish run, English spoken, rec; **D-E** *Flor da Manhã*, R São Francisco 162, T 429-2266, clean, good food, beautiful views, friendly, safe, multilingual, consistently rec.

E *Albergue da Olinda*, R do Sol 233, T 429-1592, reasonable, clean, friendly, popular with gringos, suites with bath and communal bunk rooms, clothes washing facilities, discounts for IYHA members, highly rec.

Several **youth hostels**: *Portalinda*, Av Min Marcos Freire (Beira Mar) 295, Bairro Novo, T 429-3198; **E** *Cheiro do Mar*, No 95, T 429-0101, more expensive for non-members, very good small hostel with some double rooms (room No 1 is noisy from disco), cooking facilities, ask driver of 'Rio Doce/Piedade' or 'Bairra de Jangada/Casa Caiada' bus (see below) to drop you at Albergue de Juventude on sea front; *Palanquim*, Prof Cândido Pessoa 1833, Bairro Novo, T 429-0101; **E** *Do Bomfim*, R do Bomfim 115, Carmo, T 429-1674, more for non-members, clean, safe, breakfast, cooking and laundry facilities. **NB** Hotels on R do Sol and in Bairro Novo are below the old city and on the roads heading N.

At Carnival, the price of accommodation rises steeply. Houses or rooms may be rented at this time for 5-10 days.

Camping: *Olinda Camping*, R Bom Sucesso 262, Amparo, T 429-1365, US$5 pp, space for 30 tents, 5 trailers, small huts for rent, quiet, well-shaded, town buses pass outside, rec.

● **Places to eat**
L'Atelier, R Bernardo Vieira de Melo 91, Ribeira, small converted workshop with beautiful view, run by Swiss tapestry artists, excellent international food, local dishes with reservation (necessary) T 429-3099, open Wed-Sun evenings. *Mourisco*, R João Alfredo 7, calm and pleasant, discotheque attached; *Samburá*, Av Ministro Marcos Freire 1551 (with terrace) rec to try *caldeirada* and *pitu* (crayfish), also lobster in coconut sauce or daily fish dishes, very good; on Av Beira Mar, *Ouriço*, local food good; *Gouiaba*, charcoal grill, facing sea, good value, rec; *Cantinho da Sé 305*, lively, good view of Recife, views just as good and prices lower upstairs; *O Rei do Vatapá*, on seafront nr Praça do Carmo, friendly, good, quite cheap; *Tony*, 2 blocks from Praça do Carmo towards Recife, good, reasonable; *Chin Lee*, excellent Chinese food; many others, mostly for fish. The traditional Olinda drinks, *Pau do Índio* (which contains 32 herbs) and *Retetel*, are both manufactured on the R do Amparo.

● **Entertainment**
At Janga beach on Fri and Sat, you can join in a *ciranda* at the bar-restaurant *Ciranda de Dona Duda*. For the less active, there is the *Casa da Seresta*, also in Janga on the beach side of the main road. On Praça do Carmo is *Clube Atlântico*, a *forró* dance hall. *Capoeira* is practised on Sun at about 1800 in the Mercado da Ribeira.

Beginning at dusk, but best after 2100, the Alto da Sé becomes the scene of a lively street fair, with arts, crafts, makeshift bars and barbecue stands, and impromptu traditional music. The fair becomes even more animated at Carnival.

● **Post & telecommunications**
Post Office: in Santa Tereza, nr Santa Tereza church, on way out of Olinda to Recife.

● **Tour companies & travel agents**
Viagens Sob O Sol, Prudente de Moraes 424, T 429-3303/432-5109, 24 hrs, transport offered to all parts, any type of trip arranged, contact Mauro and Felipe. *FruirTour*, Av Segismundo Gonçalves, close to Praça do Carmo, bus tickets sold, rec.

● **Tourist offices**
Secretaría de Turismo, R do Sol 127, Carmo, T 429-1039.

● **Transport**
From Recife: take any bus marked 'Rio Doce', No 981 which has a circular route around the city and beaches, or No 33 from Av NS do Carmo, US$0.60 or 'Jardim Atlântico' from the central post office at Siqueiro Campos; from Boa Viagem, take bus marked 'Piedade/Rio Doce' or 'Bairra de Jangada/Casa Caiada' (US$0.65, 30 mins). From airport to Olinda by bus, take 'Aeroporto' bus to Av Domingos Ferreira, Boa Viagem, ask to be let off, and catch a 'Piedade/Rio Doce' or 'Bairra de Jangada/Casa Caiada' bus; from the Recife Rodoviária, take the metrô to Joana Bezerra station and then catch a 'Piedade/Rio Doce' or 'Bairra de Jangada/Casa Caiada' bus. In all cases, alight in Praça do Carmo. Taxis between Olinda and Recife put their meters onto higher rates at the Convention Centre (between the two cities), best to start a journey either way there (taxi to Recife US$6, US$10.75 to Boa Viagem at night).

BIOLOGICAL RESERVES

For information on Pernambuco's two reserves, contact Ibama, Av 17 de Agosto 1057, Casa Forte, CEP 50.000, Recife. They are **Saltinho**, which preserves some of the last vestiges of Atlantic Forest in the NE, and **Serra Negra**, which has some of the last remaining forest at higher altitude in the interior.

NORTH OF RECIFE

IGARASSU

(*Pop* 79,400) 32 km N of Recife on the road to João Pessoa, Igarassu has the first church built in Brazil (SS Cosme e Damião), the Livramento church nearby, and the convent of Santo Antônio with a small museum next door. The church of Sagrado Coração is said to have housed Brazil's first orphanage. Much of the town (founded in 1535) has been declared a National Monument; it is an attractive place, with a number of colonial houses and Brazil's first Masonic hall. Hotel: **A2** *Fazenda Praia da Gavoa*, Estrada do Ramalho (Nova Cruz), T 543-0110, F 541-1088; Camping Clube do Brasil has site nearby at Engenho Monjopè, an old sugar estate, now a historical monument and interesting (it is 3 km before Igarassu coming from Recife – bus US$0.65 – alight at the 'Camping' sign and walk 5-10 mins, T 543-0528). Igarassu buses leave from Av Martins de Barro, Recife, 45 mins, US$0.70.

ITAMARACA

North of Igarassu you pass through coconut plantations to Itapissuma, where there is a bridge to **Itamaracá** island, where, the locals say, Adam and Eve spent their holidays (so does everyone else on Sun, now). It has the old Dutch Forte Orange; an interesting penal settlement with gift shops, built round the 1747 sugar estate buildings of Engenho São João, which still have much of the old machinery; charming villages and colonial churches, and fine, wide beaches. Buses from Recife (Av Martins de Barros opp *Grand Hotel*, US$0.75, very crowded) and Igarassu.

Excursions Pleasant trips by *jangada* to Coroa do Avião, a recently-formed sandy island (developing wildlife, migratory birds) with rustic beach bars, crossing (US$2 return) from Forte Orange, S of Igarassu bridge; Praias do Sossego and da Enseada, quiet, some bars but relatively undiscovered, crossing 3 km N of Itamaracá town, rec for sun worshippers.

Further N again, 2 hrs from Recife by bus, is **Pontas de Pedra**, an old fishing village, nice beach, fishing and diving expeditions, lots of bars; try **C** *Pousada Calanda*, R do Meio 269, T 626-0500.

● **Accommodation A2** *Itamaracá Parque*, Estrada do Forte, T 544-1030; **B** *Caravela*, Praça João Felipe de Barros Dias, T 544-1130, with shower, good restaurant, on beach, rec; **B** *Pousada Itamaracá*, R Fernando Lopes 205, T 544-1152, pool etc, some minutes from beach; *Hospedaria do Turismo*, Pilar 9, fan, clean; **C** *Santa Ina*, on main square, with good restaurant, *Barretinha*; **D** *Pousada Jaguaribe*, R Rios 355 (close to bus terminal), close to beach, fans and mosquito nets in all rooms, kitchen, laundry facilities, swimming pool, close to beach.

● **Places to eat** Those with a car and above budget means should have lunch and a swim at *Porto Brasílis*, a restaurant at tiny, hidden, charming Vilha Velha (T 081-543-0366 for reservation); allow all afternoon. There is good, relaxing music, fine artefacts and furnishings and a majestic panorama.

GOIANA

(*Pop* 64,060; *CEP* 55900; *DDD* 081) On the Recife-João Pessoa road; founded 1570, this is one of the most important towns for ceramics. Visit the workshop of Zé do Carmo, opposite the *Buraco da Giá* restaurant (excellent seafood; owner has tame crab which will offer you a drink), R Padre Batalha 100.

Places of interest Carmelite church and monastery, founded 1719, impressive but poorly restored; Matriz do Rosário, only open for 1800 mass, Soledade convent (1755); Amparo church with sacred art museum; Misericôrdia church (1723). The uniformity of many of the dwellings is due to their construction, for his workforce, by the owner of a now-defunct textile factory. Just N of Goiana is a sugar-mill, Usina Nossa Senhora das Maravilhas, which can be visited during the week; ask for Dr Jairo.

At the Pernambuco-Paraíba border, a 27 km dirt road goes to the fishing village of **Pitimbu**, with *jangadas*, lobster fishing, surf fishing, lobster-pot making. No tourist facilities but camping is possible; food from *Bar do Jangadeiro*. Bus from Goiana, US$0.60.

WEST OF RECIFE

85 km W of Recife is **Gravatá** (*pop* 60,000), known as the Switzerland of Pernambuco for its scenery and good hill climate. (**A1** *Hotel Fazenda Portal*, BR-232, Km 88, T 533-0288; **C** *Grande da Serra*, BR-232, Km 83, T 533-0014; **C** *Centro*, Av C B de Oliveira/BR-232, Km 82, T 533-0016, 2-star.)

CARUARU

(*Pop* 250,000) 130 km W of Recife. The paved road there passes through rolling hills, with sugar cane and large cattle fazendas, before climbing an escarpment. As the road gets higher, the countryside becomes drier, browner and rockier. Caruaru is a busy, modern town with a big Fri to Sun market: a combination of the *feira da Sulanca* (clothes), *feira do Gado* (livestock), *feira do Troca-Troca* (barter market), and *feira de Antigüidades* (antiques). A separate site, *Feira do Artesanato*, across the river for leather goods, ceramics, hammocks and basketware, although now disappointingly tourist-oriented, is open daily. See the hand-painted textiles of Sr Valério Cristóvão, R 13 de Maio 94, 1st floor; he is very helpful and his work depicts local history. The little clay figures (*figurinhas de barro*) originated by Mestre

Vitalino, and very typical of the NE, are a local speciality; many local potters live at Alto da Moura 6 km away, where a house once owned by Vitalino is open, but has no examples of his work. Bus, 30 mins, bumpy, US$0.35.

Local festivals 22 Dec-2 Jan, Festa de Comércio; 18-22 May, city's anniversary; São João, June, huge *forró* festival; 15-22 Aug, folklore week; carnival; Semana Santa; Sept, Micaru; Oct, Vaquejada (Brazilian cross between rodeo and bull fighting), biggest in the NE.

● **Accommodation A1** *Do Sol*, Cidade Alta, T 721-3044, F 721-1336 (3-star) on hill outside town, good restaurant, pool; **B** *Grande Hotel São Vicente de Paulo*, Av Rio Branco 365, T 721-5011, bar, restaurant, laundry, a/c, pool, TV; *Trevo*, opp rodoviária, and *Village*, on road to Recife from rodoviária, 3 km out, T 721-5974, food rec. Cheap *hospedarias* around central square, Praça Getúlio Vargas; **C** *Central*, R Vigario Freire 71, T 721-4669, good breakfast, in centre, rec; **C** *Centenário*, 7 de Setembro 84, T 722-9011, good breakfast, in town centre, rec (at both of these, bookings must be made in advance because of nearby *Teatro Nova Jerusalém*).

● **Transport** Rodoviária is 4 km from town; buses from Recife stop in the town centre. Alight here and look for the *Livraria Estudiantil* on the corner of Vigario Freire and R Anna de Albuquerque Galvão. Go down Galvão, turn right on R 15 de Novembro to the first junction, 13 de Maio; turn left, cross the river to the Feira do Artesanato. Bus from centre, same place as Recife bus stop, to Rodoviária, US$0.20. Many buses from TIP in **Recife**, 2 hrs express, US$4.75, also *comum*. Bus to **Maceió**, 0700, 5 hrs, US$5.50. Bus to **Fazenda Nova** 1030, 1 hr, US$2, returns for Caruaru 1330.

FAZENDA NOVA AND NOVA JERUSALEM

During Easter Week each year various agencies run package tours to the little country town of **Fazenda Nova**, 23 km from Caruaru. Just outside the town is **Nova Jerusalém**, where for the week up to Easter Sun, an annual passion play, suggested by Oberammergau's, is enacted. The site is one third the size of the historic quarter of Jerusalem, with 12 permanent stages on which scenes of the Passion are presented; the audience moves from one to another as the story unfolds. Performances begin at 1800, lasting around 3 hrs – well worth a visit if you are in the region at this time of year.

● **Accommodation In Fazenda Nova**: *Grande*, Av Poeta Carlos Penha Filho, T 732-1137, best; and others.

GARANHUNS

Good roads via Caruaru or Palmares run to the city of **Garanhuns** (*pop* 113,470), 243 km SW of Recife. It claims to be the best holiday resort in the NE, partly because of its cool climate – it stands at 890m, and has an average temperature of 21°C – and partly because of its mineral waters and beautiful landscapes and parks.

● **Accommodation A2** *Tavares Correia*, Av Rui Barbosa 296, T 761-0900, 4-star; **B** *Petrópolis*, Praça da Bandeira 129, T 761-0125. **Camping**: *Camping Treze*, BR-432, Km 105.

Arcoverde (*pop* 54,150), about 126 km W of Caruaru (bus 2½ hrs, US$3), is a market town in the Sertão, market every Sat, cool at night. Hotels: **C** *Grande Majestic*, Av Cel Japiassu 326, T 821-1175 (fair), with breakfast; **E** *Dormitório O Barão*, clean.

TRIUNFO

(*Pop* 28,900) About 200 km W of Arcoverde via Serra Talhada is a delightful small town in Serra de Borborema, good climate, with great variety of crops, flowers and fruits. There are also a sugar mill that can be visited (Engenho Boa Esperança), waterfalls, sounding rocks, the convent of São Boaventura, and the Museu do Cangaça, showing the lives and relics of the traditional bandits of the Nordeste.

● **Accommodation** Stay at **B** *Pousada Baixa Verde*, R Manoel Paiva dos Santos 114, T 846-1103, nice rooms, good breakfast; **B** *Hospedaria Santa Terezinha* (Centro), abundant and good meals; **D** *Pousada Baixa Serote*, superb breakfast, friendly, highly rec.

● **Transport** Two buses daily to and from Recife (6½ hrs).

FERNANDO DE NORONHA

A small archipelago 345 km off the NE coast declared a Marine National Park in 1989 (T Parnamar 081-619-1210). Only one island is inhabited. It used to be an independent dependency under military control but is now part of the state of Pernambuco administered from Recife. The islands were discovered 1503 and were for a time a pirate lair. In 1738 the Portuguese built the Forte dos Remédios, later used as a prison in this century; remains still exist as well as a semi-deserted village nearby. Many locals are now dependent on tourism and it can be difficult to find fish as the fishermen are busy taking tourists on boat trips. Most food is brought from the mainland and prices are about double. Repellent is not available for the many mosquitoes. The island, which is dominated by a 321m peak, has many unspoilt beaches, interesting wildlife and fishing; scuba-diving and snorkelling are excellent. It is now prohibited to swim with the dolphins but they can be seen from the beach. Take sufficient *reais* as dollars are heavily discounted. The time is 1 hr later than Brazilian Standard Time. Entry to the island has been limited to 120 tourists per day because of the serious problems of energy and water supply.

Tours

Boat trips and jeep tours around the island are available; also possible to hire a jeep or beach buggy. You can hitch everywhere as everyone stops. Scuba-diving is organized by *Águas Claras* (T 619-1225, US$50) in the hotel grounds, staff are regarded as entertaining but unqualified; 2 dives (with superannuated equipment).

Local information
● **Accommodation**

The only hotel, *Pousada Esmeralda*, T 619-1355, is expensive and none too comfortable. Large a/c apartments at *Solar dos Ventos* (full board) have been rec, ask for 'o capitanão'. Overpriced packages from mainland travel agents usually place visitors in the *Esmeralda*. Beware of similar packages at lower prices in other 'pousadas' because they turn out to be rooms in family homes. Independent travellers can go much cheaper as many local families rent out rooms with full board, US$20 pp/day. The best known is that of Suzanna and Rocha, rooms with fan and bathrm, but they never refuse a reservation and farm people out to other families with much inferior levels of accommodation. Vanilda across the street has been highly rec.

● **Places to eat**

There is only one restaurant, called *Ilha Encantado*, nr the hotel.

Bars: *Bar da Vila* in the village of Remédios, only open in the daytime; *Bar Idade* on the Çonceição beach, daytime only with loud rock music; *Mirante Bar*, nr the hotel, with spectacular view over Boldró beach, has loud music and at night is an open-air disco and the only nightlife on the island.

● **Transport**

Air Sea landing is difficult but an airport has been built. Three flights daily from Recife, 4 on Sat and Sun, some flights via Natal, on 13 and 17 seater planes by Nordeste, T 341-3187, 1 hr 40 mins. An entry fee of US$13 a day is payable at the airport.

Paraíba

JOÃO PESSOA

It is a bus ride of 2 hrs through sugar plantations over a good road from Recife (126 km) to **João Pessoa** (*pop* 497,215; *CEP* 58000; *DDD* 083), capital of the State of Paraíba (*pop* 3,200,620), on the Rio Paraíba. Ocean-going ships load and unload at Cabedelo (see **Excursions**).

PLACES OF INTEREST

The old monasteries are worth seeing, and the 18th century church of **São Francisco** is a beauty (open 0800-1700). At São Francisco is an excellent cultural centre with a magnificent collection of colonial and popular artefacts. This is also the best point to see the sun set over the forest. Other tourist points include the **Casa da Pólvora**, an old gunpowder store which has become the city museum; the city parks; and trips on the Rio Paraíba. See the booklet *Relíquias da Paraíba*, by Padre Antônio Barbosa.

Excursions

The principal beach resort is **Tambaú**, 7 km from João Pessoa, take a taxi or bus (No 510 'Tambaú' from outside the rodoviária, or 'Lagoa' from city centre, alight at *Hotel Tropical*); excellent bathing. North of Tambaú is Manaira beach (the section near *Hotel Tropical/Tambaú* is too polluted for bathing. Cabo Branco club on Tambaú beach, open to visitors: good food, beautiful views.

14 km S down the coast is the **Cabo Branco** lighthouse at Ponta do Seixas, the most easterly point of continental Brazil and South America; there is a panoramic view from the cliff top. The beaches below are palm-lined but oil-polluted. (Hotel: *Pousa das Águas*, Praia do Cabo Branco,

T 226-5103/7268, seafront; youth hostel *Cabo Branco*, Av Pe-José Trigueiro 104, Praia de Cabo Branco, T 221-2903/226-6171). Take bus 507 'Cabo Branco' from outside the rodoviária, or 'Lagoa' bus from centre and get out at last stop; hike up to the lighthouse. The **Fundação José Américo de Almeida**, halfway between Tambaú and Cabo Branco, on the esplanade, should be visited by those interested in modern literature and politics; it is in the former house of the novelist and sociologist.

At **Cabedelo** (*pop* 28,925), 18 km by road or rail, are the impressive walls of the 17th-century fortress of Santa Catarina. If you take a Cabedelo bus and alight at Jacaré, about 12 km from João Pessoa, there is an excellent beach with food stalls at weekends. In Jacaré, where the yachts tie up, is a bar run by an Englishman.

Local information
● Accommodation
Central hotels: **D** *Aurora*, Praça João Pessoa 51, T 241-3238, with a/c and bath, clean, friendly, rec; **D** *Guarany*, R Almeida Barreto 181 e 13 de Maio, T 241-2161 (more with a/c and TV), clean, safe, friendly, good value, good breakfast; **D** *Pedro Américo*, Praça Pedro Américo, 109, clean (no breakfast on Sun); cheap hotels nr the old rodoviária, eg **E** *São Pedro*, R Irineu Pinto 231, clean, basic, friendly. *Villa Mare Apartment Hotel*, Av Nego 707, T 226-2142, new apartments for 2 or 3 people, US$600/month, clean, friendly, helpful, rec.

Also in Tambaú: **L3** *Tropical Tambaú*, Av Alm Tamandaré 229, Tambaú, T 226-3660, F 226-2390, comfortable, good service, rec; **B** *Costa Bela Praia*, Av Négo 131, T 226 1570, rec, small; **B** *Sol-Mar*, Rui Carneiro 500, T 226-1350, F 226-3242, pool, superb restaurant, highly rec; **D** *Gameleira*, Av João Maurício 157, T 226-1576, good breakfast, dirty, noisy at night.

Youth hostels: on Av das Trincheiras, at Palácio dos Esportes, T 221-7220/1, and R Bezerra Reis 82, T 226-5460/1988.

● Places to eat
Two good restaurants on Tambaú beach are *Adega do Alfredo* (Portuguese) and *Wan Li* (Chinese); *Pescador*, nr Cabo Branco lighthouse.

● Banks & money changers
Banco do Brasil, nr Praça João Pessoa, 3rd floor, helpful. Banco Meridional, cash against Mastercard, R Duque de Caixas, 454, Centro.

● Electric current
220 volts AC, 60 cycles.

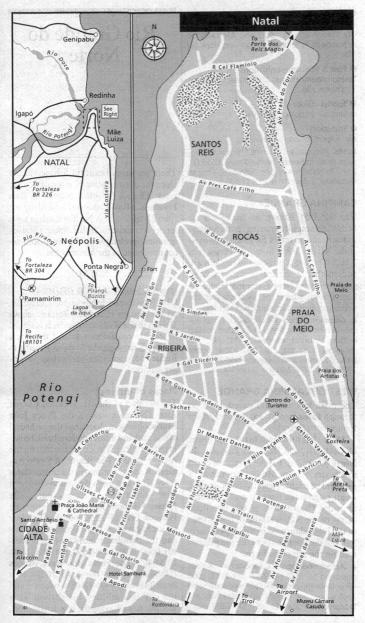

Natal

To Forte dos Reis Magos

R Cel Flaminio

Av Praia do Forte

SANTOS REIS

Av Pres Café Filho

R Décio Fonseca

ROCAS

R Vietnam

Av Pres Café Filho

R S João

Praia do Meio

Fort

Av Eng H Go

R Simões

PRAIA DO MEIO

Av Duque de Caxias

R S Jardim

R do Areial

RIBEIRA

F Gal Elicério

Praia dos Artistas

R Gen Gustavo Cordeiro de Farias

R do Motor

R Sachet

Centro do Turismo

Rio Potengi

Getúlio Vargas

Dr Manoel Dantas

To Via Costeira

de Contorho

R V Barreto

Nilo Peçanha

São Temé

R Serídó

Joaquim Fabrício

To Areia Preta

Av Rio Branco

Ulisses Caldas

Av Princesa Isabel

Av Deodoro

Av Floriano Peixoto

Prudente de Morias

R Potengi

R Traíri

Cordoro

R Mipibu

To Mãe Luiza

✠ Praça João Maria & Cathedral

Santo Antônio

João Pessoa

Mossoró

Av Afonso Pena

Av Hermes da Fonseca

CIDADE ALTA

R S Antônio

Padre Pinto

R Gal Osório

To Alecrim

Hotel Samburá

R Apodi

To Rodoviária

To Tirol

To Airport

Museu Câmara Cascudo

Inset map (top left):

N

Genipabu

Rio Doce

Redinha

See Right

Igapó

Rio Potengi

Mãe Luiza

NATAL

via Costeira

To Fortaleza BR 226

Rio Pirangi

Neópolis

To Fortaleza BR 304

Ponta Negra

Fort

To Pirangi, Búzios

Parnamirim

Lagoa da Tiqui

To Recife BR101

40

● **Shopping**
Crafts at *Casa do Artesão*, R Maciel Pinheiro nr
city rodoviária; very good new *Mercado de
Artesanato* in Tambaú, almost opp *Hotel Sol
Mar*.

● **Post & telecommunications**
Telecommunications: Embratel, R das
Trincheiras 398.

● **Tourist offices**
In Tambaú shopping centre (helpful).

● **Transport**
Air Airport for internal services.

Buses Rodoviária is 10 mins from centre; luggage store. To **Recife**, every 60 mins, US$3.60,
2 hrs. To **Natal**, every 2 hrs, US$4.75, 3 hrs; to
Fortaleza, 4 daily, 16 hrs, US$15.25.

CAMPINA GRANDE

(*Pop* 326,155) Known as the 'Porta do
Sertão', this rapidly growing centre for light
industry and an outlet for goods from most
of the NE is 120 km from João Pessoa (bus
2 hrs). There is a museum of modern art,
and another of the cotton industry. Most
genial climate. Near Campina Grande is
Lagoa Seca, where the local craft is the
making of figures in wood and sacking.

● **Accommodation** *Rique Palace Hotel* (excellent) is on the top floors of the tallest building
in town, Venâncio Neiva 287, T 341-1433: the
restaurant is on the 11th floor. Other hotels:
B *Ouro Branco*, João Lourenço Porto 20, T 341-
2929, F 322-5788. Many nr old rodoviária.

WEST OF CAMPINA GRANDE

The main highway, still paved, leads on
through **Patos** (*pop* 81,300, **E** *Hotel JK*) to
Ipaumirim (Ceará).

Here a left turn leads to the twin towns
of **Crato** (*pop* 90,360) and **Juazeiro do
Norte** (Ceará, *pop* 173,300), oases of green
in the dry Sertão. Mosquitoes can be a
problem at night. Juazeiro do Norte is a
small pilgrimage town; it was the home
of Padre Cícero, one of the unofficial
saints of the NE. A statue to him stands
in the Logradouro do Horto, a park overlooking the town; either take the pilgrim
trail up the hill or go by bus.

● **Accommodation** **C** *Panorama*, R Sto
Agostinho 58, T 511-2399, F 511-2173, good
value; **D** *Vieira*, corner of R São Pedro and R Santo
Antônio, private bathrm and breakfast; and
D *Municipal*, Praça P Cícero, T 511-2299, rec.

Rio Grande do Norte

There are many beautiful fishing villages
along the coast heading N, often difficult to
reach. One of the most popular is **Baía
Formosa** in Rio Grande do Norte (daily bus
from Natal, 2½ hrs). No hotel; ask in town
for accommodation in fishermen's houses,
infinitely preferable to the overpriced accommodation at the *Miramar* bar.

NATAL

(*Pop* 606,540; *CEP* 59000; *DDD* 084) Capital of Rio Grande do Norte (*pop* 2,413,620),
on the estuary of the Rio Potengi, about
180 km to the N of João Pessoa. It is served
by weekly coastal vessels and there is a
railway S through the State of Paraíba to
Recife and Maceió (only suburban passenger services).

Places of interest

The old part of the city is called **Cidade
Alta**. The main square, the **Praça João
Maria**, oblong in shape, has the cathedral
at one end and a fine modern bank building at the other. The city is centred on the
Av Rio Branco. The church of **Santo Antônio**, R Santo Antônio in the centre, dates
from 1766, and has a fine, carved wooden
altar and a sacred art museum. The
Museu Câmara Cascudo, Av Hermes da
Fonseca 1440 (T 222-2860), has exhibits
on archaeological digs, Umbanda rituals
and the petroleum industry (open Tues-
Fri, 0800-1100, 1400-1600, Sat 0800-1100,
US$1.40). The **Forte dos Reis Magos**
(16th-century) on the coast at Rocas is
open Tues-Sun 0900-1700; between it and
the city is a military installation. It is
possible to walk along the beach to the fort,

or to go in a tour, or by taxi; it is worth it for the views (entry US$1.40). The **Marine Research Institute** at the Praia da Areia Preta can be visited; bus marked 'Areia Preta' from Av Rio Branco. Good local craftware Sat at **Mercado do Alecrim**, along R Quaresma near R Gonçalves. At Mãe Luiza is a lighthouse with beautiful views of Natal and surrounding beaches (take city bus marked Mãe Luiza; get key from the house next door).

Beaches

Natal has excellent beaches: **Ponta Negra**: many hotels (see below). It is 20 mins by bus from centre; pleasant and 'quaint' atmosphere (not safe to wander alone on the dunes as there are robberies). Some beaches are on the far side of the Potengi river, for example Redinha and **Genipabu** – where you can toboggan down the sand-dunes – reached by direct bus from old Rodoviária, last bus back from Genipabu at 1830. Few people are there from June-October. You can hire buggies to drive on the dunes for US$30 a day, or by the hour, these are making the most popular beaches very noisy. More beautiful beaches to the S: Pirangi, Tabatinga, **Búzios**. Litoral Sul bus from rodoviária follows coastline, US$1. The friendly village of **Pipa** lies 80 km S of Natal, There is a bus from Natal to Pipa that departs from Rodoviária Nova everyday at 0830 and 1515 and from Pipa to Natal at 0500 and 1600 US$3.50. Pipa has lovely beaches and several pousadas. Hotels arrange transport to the stunning bay N of the village, visited most mornings by dolphins. Reached by the Natal-Goianinha bus.

Excursions

At **Pirangi**, 25 km S, or 30 mins by bus from new rodoviária, is the world's largest cashew-nut tree (*cajueiro*); branches springing from a single trunk cover an area of some 7,300 sq metres. From Natal (Viação Campos), US$0.60, 5 times a day from 0630 to 1815, 3 on Sun, 0730, 0930, 1645; the snack bar by the tree has schedules of buses back to Natal. A number of good beaches and attractive villages may be found along this coast. North of Natal are extensive cashew plantations.

Local festivals

In mid-Oct there is a country show, **Festa do Boi**, bus marked Parnamirim to the exhibition centre, it gives a good insight into rural life. Mid-Dec sees **Carnatal**, a lively 4-day music festival with dancing in the streets.

Local information

● **Accommodation**

Marsol Natal, Via Costeira 1567, Km 7, Parque das Dunas, T/F 221-2619, 3-star; Via Costeira is a good place to stay, but hotels mostly in **A1-A3** range: eg *Barreira Roxa Praia*, T/F 222-1093, 5 km from the centre, clean, helpful, good; *Imirá Plaza*, Costeira 4077, T 211-4105, F 211-5722, on beach, pool, tennis, rec.

B *Oásis*, R Joaquim Fabrício 291, Casa 08, Petrópolis, T 221-3570, F 221-5699, Swiss-owned, pool, massive breakfasts, exceptional value; **B** *Praia do Sol*, Av Pres Café Filho 750, Praia do Meio, T/F 211-4562, opp beach, renovated, clean, quiet, a/c, TV, friendly, rec; **B** *Samburá*, R Prof Zuza 263, T 221-0611, rec.

D *Beira Mar*, Av Pres Café Filho, Praia dos Artistas, T 222-4256, on the beach front, with breakfast, but no a/c, small, good value, popular; **D** *Farol*, Av Gouv Silvio Pedrosa 174 (on beach), T 222 4661, with a/c; **D** *Le Bateau*, Praia de Areia Preta, on beach front, clean, helpful, good breakfast, English and French spoken; **D** *Pousada Marina*, at No 860, T 222-0678, a/c, TV, fridge, 'lovely'; **D** *Pousada Terra do Sol*, Av Pres Café Filho, 11, Praia dos Artistas, T 211 4878, noisy but arranges good Passeio de Buggy, rec.

E *Casa Grande*, R Princesa Isabel 529, T 211-4895, with a/c, F without bath, good breakfast, pleasant, excellent value, rec; **E** *Fenícia*, Av Rio Branco 586, T 222-1366 (more with a/c), with breakfast and shower, friendly, English spoken; **E** *Flat*, R 31 de Março, Morro de Careca, T 219 2541, breakfast, fridges in rooms, fans, hot showers and a nice garden, warmly rec; **E** *Natal*, Av Mar Floriano Peixoto 104, clean, English spoken; *Born Jesús*, Av Rio Branco 384, good value, popular; **E** *Pousada Bejo Tropical*, R Valentim de Almeida 10, T 221-5361, clean, helpful, warmly rec; **E** *Pousada Esquina de Mar*, Av Roberto Freire, T 236-2843, rec, baths, pool, breakfast, meals available; **E** *Pousada Zur Kurve*, Av Silvio Pedrosa 97, good breakfast, clean, safe, rec; **E** *Parque das Dunas*, T 222 2252, R João XXIII 601, excellent breakfast, safe, clean; *Papa Jerimum*, R Rodrigues Dias 445, Praia do Meio, English spoken, rec.

Beach hotels At Ponta Negra: C *Maria Bonita 2*, T 236-2941, rec; *Caminho do Mar*,

R Des HH Gomes 365, nr Ponta Negra beach, T 219-3363, very friendly, clean; **C** *Ponta Negra*, R Des João V da Costa 8896, T 219-3264, pool, friendly, rec; **C** *Pousada do Mar*, T 236-2509, pool; *Bella Napoli*, Av da Praia 3188, T 219-2666; *Miramar*, Av da Praia 3398, T 236-2079; **D** *Pousada Porta do Sol*, R Francisco Gurgel 9057, T 236 2555, room with bar, TV, excellent breakfast, pool, steps down onto beach, friendly, good value, rec. Also restaurants.

At Genipabu: A3 *Aldeia*, Caixa Postal 274, T 225-2011, has 5 luxury bungalows and a restaurant; **D** *Genipabu*, 2 km from beach, marvellous views, isolated; **D** *Mar-Azul*, T 225-2065; **E** *Pousada Porta Alberta*, on beach, good breakfast.

At Buzios: C *Balneário Rio Doce*, pool, games, highly rec; **C** *Pousada da Lagosta*, rec. Other *pousadas* and bars.

At Pipa: F *Pousada do Pipa*, French-owned, highly rec, good food, good music, clean, bath in room; **D** *Tropical*, good food, rec.

Youth hostels: head office of Associação Potiguar de Albergues da Juventude, Av Deodoro 249, Petrópolis, T 221-3751, open 1300-1730. *Lua Cheia*, Av Estrela do Mar 2215, Conj Algamar, Ponta Negra, T 236-3696; *Verdes Mares*, R das Algas 2166, Conj Algamar, T 236-2872; *Ladeiro do Sol*, R Valentin de Almeida 10, Praia dos Artistas, T 221-5361. *Meu Canto*, R Mandel Dantas 424 Petroplis, Cep 59012-270, T 211 3954, highly rec.

Camping: *Camping Clube do Brasil* site at Sítio do Jiqui, expensive. Vale das Cascatas, Ponta Negra beach, swimming pool, leisure facilities.

● **Places to eat**
Casa de Mãe, R Pedro Afonso 153 (Petrópolis), regional food, rec; *Bom Demais*, R Princesa Isabel No 717-C, cheap, good; *Pietro's*, Av Marechal Deodoro, opp cathedral, cheap, good; *Raizes*, Av Campos Sales, e C Mossoró, good regional dishes; *Thin-San*, Av Hermes da Fonseca 890, Tirol, Chinese, quite good, not expensive. Vegetarian (with shops): *Amai*, General Varela 624, and *A Macrobiótica*, Princesa Isabel 524. For snacks try the stalls on Praia do Meio, there are also various restaurants along the beach road nearby, where itinerant musicians play. Try the restaurants on the point that separates Praias dos Artistas and da Areia Preta (eg *Calamar*). *Chaplin*, Av Pres Café Filho 27 (Praia dos Artistas), very good seafood, sociable.

● **Banks & money changers**
Cash advances against Visa card at **Banco do Brasil**, Av Rio Branco 510.

● **Electric current**
220 volts AC, 60 cycles.

● **Entertainment**
Dance is an important pastime in Natal. The *Casa da Música Popular Brasileira* has dancing on Fri and Sat night and Sun from 1700, very popular. Daily shows also at *Mandacaru*, Av do Jiquí 21, Neopolis, T 217-3008 (US$8) and *Zás-Trás*, R Apodi 500, Tirol, T 222-6589; many other enjoyable venues where visitors are encouraged to join in.

● **Post & telecommunications**
Telecommunications: Embratel, Av Duque de Caxias 99, T 221-2209. International phone calls, Telern, R João Pessoa e Princesa Isabel.

● **Tourist offices**
Centro de Turismo (a converted prison with wide variety of handicraft shops), R Aderbal de Figueiredo s/n, off R General Cordeiro, Petrópolis (only Portuguese spoken, poor information); Rodoviária and airport.

● **Transport**
Air Augusto Severo, 15 km from centre; flights to Belém, Brasília, Cuiabá, Fernando de Noronha, Fortaleza, Manaus, Recife, Rio, Salvador, São Paulo and other cities. Bus every 30 mins from old rodoviária nr centre US$0.65, taxi US$15.

Buses Rovoviária, with luggage store, is about 6 km out of town, bus 'Cidade de Esperança Av 9', 'Areia Preta via Petrópolis' or 'Via Tirol' to centre. To **Recife**, 4 hrs, US$9.25; to **Fortaleza**, 5 hrs, US$9; to **Maceió**, buses go either direct, or via Recife, 4-6 hrs; to **João Pessoa**, US$4.75, 3 hrs.

ROUTES The state of Rio Grande do Norte (whose people are called 'Potiguares' after an Indian tribe that now resides at Jacaré de São Domingos, municipality of Rio Tinto in neighbouring Paraíba state) has three main paved roads radiating from Natal: S to João Pessoa and Recife, SW to Caicó and W to Mossoró and Fortaleza. Between **Caicó** (*pop* 50,660) and **Mossoró** (*pop* 191,960; **A3** *Hotel Termas*, comfortable, with a hot, mineral water pool system, each pool on a terrace, with temperatures ranging from 54°C at the top to 30°C at the bottom; there are cheaper alternatives) there is a turning to **Patu** with its huge basilica on a hillside, with passable 'hotels', rather primitive. From Mossoró you can visit the salt pans at Grossos on the coast, but get written permission from the administrative offices in Mossoró. Bus Mossoró-Aracati (Ceará) at 0800 with Emp Nordeste, 2 hrs, US$2.

Ceará

ARACATI AND CANOA QUEBRADA

From Mossoró the main road, BR304, enters Ceará and continues about 50 km to **Aracati** (*pop* 60,710).

10 km from Aracati is the fishing village **Canoa Quebrada** on a sand dune, famous for its *labirinto* lacework and coloured sand sculpture, for sand-skiing on the dunes, for the sunsets, and for the beaches. To avoid jiggers (*bicho de pé*), it is best to wear shoes. Nowhere to change money except Banco do Brasil in Aracati.

Beyond Canoa Quebrada is **Majorlândia**, reached by paved road from the main highway. A very nice village, with many-coloured sand dunes (used in bottle pictures) and a beach; the arrival of the fishing fleet in the evening is an important daily event. 4-5 km S along the beach is the village of Camo.

● **Accommodation Aracati**: **D** *Hotel Litorânea*, R Cel Alexandrino 1251, T 421-1001, clean, nr rodoviária. **Canoa Quebrada**: **D** *Pousada Alternativa*, with or without bath, central, clean, rec; **D** *Pousada Cultural*, basic, clean, friendly; **D** *Pousada Ma Alice*, clean, safe, friendly; **D** *Pousada do Rei*, highly rec; 2 rooms **D** behind *Sol de Manhã* café on mainstreet, clean, with shower, good breakfast in the café; **D** *Tenda do Cumbe*, at end of road on cliff, thatched huts, restaurant, warmly rec; also on cliff above beach, **D** *Pousada Ao Nascer do Sol*, clean, shower, friendly, hammocks for rent; villagers will let you sling your hammock or put you up cheaply (Veronica is rec, European books exchanged; Sr Miguel rents good clean houses for US$10 a day). **Youth hostel**: *Lua Estrela*, T 421-1401, restaurant and café. **Majorlândia**: **D** *Apartamento Beira Mar*, on beach; **C** *Pousada Dunas Praia*; **D** *Pousada do Gaúcho*; **D** *Pousada e Restaurante Reouinte*, 100m before beach on main road,

clean, airy rooms, friendly, use of kitchen, rooms with or without bath, rec.

● **Places to eat Canoa Quebrada**: bars and restaurants, vegetarian food in *Espácio Cultural*, cheap seafood (don't drink the water); *Casaveide*, good food – Chinese, Mexican and typical Brazilian, good atmosphere, cards and darts available, good music.

● **Transport** Bus Natal-Aracati via Mossoró, 6 hrs, US$9; Fortaleza-Aracati, 174 km, São Benedito bus 11 a day, US$3.50; 4 a day Fortaleza-Majorlândia, US$5. Aracati-Canoa Quebrada from Gen Pompeu e T João Paulo, US$1; taxi US$6.

MORRO BRANCO

87 km from Fortaleza (too far for a day trip) is **Morro Branco** (4 km from Beberibe – bus from Aracati, 2 hrs) with spectacular beach, craggy cliffs and beautiful views. *Jangadas* leave the beach at 0500, returning at 1400-1500. Beach buggies and taxi for hire, Marrambaia can be visited, some accommodation. Very crowded at holiday times.

● **Accommodation A1** *Praia das Fontes*, T 338-1179, F 338-1269, luxurious, rec; **C** *Recanto Praia*, clean, good breakfast, rec; **D** *Cabana do Morro*, *Pousada do Morro*, clean, but mosquitoes, fan and shower, both with pool; **D** *Novo*, clean, noisy at weekends; **D** *Pousada Sereia*, on the beach, clean, good breakfast, friendly, highly rec; **E** *Rosalias'*, with use of kitchen, 50m from bus stop, strongly rec; or you can rent fishermen's houses; meals can also be arranged at beach-front bars (try *O Jangadeiro*). Double room at **E** *Bar São Francisco*, or 7-room house for rent.

● **Transport** São Benedito bus from Fortaleza, US$2, 2½ hrs, 4 a day. To get to Natal, take 0600 bus to Beberibe, then 0800 bus (only one) to Aracati, US$1, then on to Natal.

BEACHES SE OF FORTALEZA

Further up the coast is **Caponga** beach. A 30-min walk S along the deserted white-sand beach leads to a river mouth, offering a combination of fresh-and salt-water bathing. *Jangadas* set sail in the early morning (arrangements can be made to accompany fishermen on overnight trips); there is a fish market on the beach. Weekend houses now being built here.

● **Accommodation** Accommodation at *Caponga Praia*, on the beach front, simple rooms and good meals, **D** *Mon Kapitan*, on the

cast into the surf. Well worth attending (members of the public may 'pegar um passo' – enter into an inspired religious trance – at the hands of a *pai-de-santo*). Beware of pick-pockets and purse-snatchers.

Local information

NB At night the centre of town is dead, but by day it is very busy with vendors and crowds. Still, it is not over-agitated. Generally the level of policing is high, except in the centre at night.

NB The road which runs along the sea front (Av Pres Kennedy) is often known as Av Beira Mar. Many new hotels and apartment blocks have been built along this stretch.

● Accommodation

L2 *Esplanada Praia*, Av Presidente Kennedy 2000, T/F 224-8555; **L2** *Marina Park*, Av Pres C Branco 400, T 252-5253, F 253-1803, huge new luxury leisure complex with all facilities, modern mooring for yachts at reasonable prices, day rates available for non-residents, strongly rec; **L3** *Beira Mar*, on Meireles beach, Av Pres Kennedy, T 244-9444, F 261-5659, swimming pool; **L3** *Colonial Praia*, 4-star (Best Western), R Barão de Aracati 145, T 211-9644, F 252-3501, pleasant grounds and big pool, laundry service (10 mins' walk from Av Kennedy); **L3** *Novotel*, Av Pres Kennedy 2380, T 244-9122, F 261-2793.

A1 *Othon Palace*, 5-star, Av Pres Kennedy 2500, T 244-9177, F 224-7777, beach front location; *Nordeste Palace*, R Assunção 99 in centre, T 221-1999, large rooms, friendly, good value; **A2** *Pousada Jardim*, run by Sr Abelardo Bezerra at Ildefonso Albano 950, no sign outside (T 231-7991) in Aldeota district, by Iracema beach, very clean, friendly, nice garden, excursions arranged, many languages spoken, warmly rec, 20% discount to *South American Handbook* users; **A2** *Samburá Praia*, Av Pres Kennedy 4530, T 263-1999, F 263-2177, cheaper than most beach hotels, friendly.

B *Apart-hotel Aquidabá*, Av Raimundo Girão (was Aquidabá) 630, T 226-1405, at beginning of Praia Iracema, 20 mins' walk from centre, with bath, pool and bar, clean, quiet; **B** *Cabana Praia II*, at R João Lourenço 441 (T261-1399) and No I at Av Rui Barbosa 555, T 261-4954, both small, friendly; **B** *Caxambu*, General Bezerril 22 (T 231-0339), a/c, with breakfast, and bath, clean, central (opp Cathedral, in market area); **B** *Paraíso da Praia*, R dos Pacajus 109, T 231-3387, Iracema, small, on beach, helpful and friendly, good *trattoria* next door; **B** *Pousada d'Antonietta*, Carlos Vasconcelos 660, T 224-3454, clean, quiet, 5 mins from beach, buses to centre and other beaches

nearby, with bath; **B** *Pousada da Praia*, Av Mons Tabosa 1315, Iracema, 2 blocks from beach, best rooms on 2nd and 3rd floors, a/c, clean, friendly, also cheaper rooms, fan, rec, buses to centre stop at door.

C *Ondas Verdes*, Av Pres Kennedy 934, T 226-0871, fan, TV, shower, clean, rec; **C** *Passeio*, R Dr João Moreira 221, with bath, fan, good breakfast, safe, storage, good value; **C** *Pousada Central*, Av Dom Manuel, nr Costa Barrios, T 252-5040, good value; **C** *Pousada Village Mar e Sol*, R Idelfonso Albano 614, Praia Iracema, T 252-3206, with or without bath, friendly, rec.

D *Chevalier*, Av Duque de Caxias 465, T 231-4611, with bath and fan, pleasant; **D** *Pousada Vida da Praia*, José Vilar 252, T 244-6444, in Aldeota district, clean, safe, helpful, English spoken; **D** *Pousada Tropicália*, Almte Barroso 617, T 244-4019, laundry, kitchen, English-run, rec.

On Av Abolção, Meireles, **C** *Zen Praia*, No 1894, clean, friendly, rec; **D** *Nossa Pousada*, No 2600, T 261-4699, without bath, nr beach, friendly, helpful.

Several hotels along R Senador Pompeu, eg **D** *Universo*, at No 1152, without breakfast, clean, friendly, may rent by the bed (ie single sex clients 3 to a room), smokers unwelcome, some rooms have mosquito nets. Try student houses on Av Universitários, cheap or even free.

E *Pousada Abril em Portugal*, Av Almte Barroso 1006, with bath, breakfast, fan, good value, rec;

Youth Hostel: *Albergue Praia de Iracema*, Av Al Barroso 998, T 252-3267, US$12 for members, US$20 for non-members, use of kitchen and laundry, clean, helpful, good location; another at R Rocha Lima 1186, Aldeota, T 244-1850.

Camping: official site about 10 km S of city, 2 km along a bumpy road off the highway, T 273-2544, signposted, US$4.50 pp.

● Places to eat

Several good fish restaurants at far end of Av Presidente Kennedy, where the boats come ashore between 1300 and 1500, for example, *Trapiche*, No 3956 (seafood, expensive, but excellent). At Praia de Iracema, a collection of cafés on the beach serve good fast food and great coffee; on Av Kennedy *Alfredo* (good fish), No 4616, and, next door, No 4632, *Peixada do Meio* (better). Italian are *La Trattoria*, R dos Pacajus 125, Praia de Iracema between Tabajaras and Av Kennedy, *Sandras*, Av Eng Luis Vieirra 555, Praia do Futuro, lobster has been specially rec, as has *Francés-Italiano*, Av Desem Moreira 155. *Churrascaria Tourão*, Av Mons Tabosa 825, all you can eat at fair prices.

Good Chinese: *HongKong*, Av Pres Kennedy 4544, Mucuripe. Vegetarian: *Alivita*, Barão do Rio Branco 1486, good, has fish, lunch only, Mon-Fri; *Céu da Boca*, R Franklin Távora 136, lunch and 1800-2000 Mon-Fri, good and inexpensive; *Fonte de Saúde*, R Pedroi 339, excellent vegetarian food, sold by weight, and a wide range of fruit juices; *Kury*, R Senador Pompeu 959, good food at reasonable prices; opp is a good Chinese restaurant. Another good place in centre is *Belas Artes*, Major Facundo 82, just up from Passeio Público. Cheap meals at railway station. Emcetur restaurant, *Xadrez*, in old prison, good atmosphere, open to 2400, reported safe to 2100. Good view of Fortaleza from *Restaurant Panorámico*, R Mirante, in Mucuripe district, nr the lighthouse. At *Pirata* club, Praia de Iracema, forró is danced. Many good bars and clubs along the beach. *El Mirante*, on a hill with spectacular views, has many lively bars and restaurants, accessible by car or taxi.

● **Banks & money changers**
Banco do Nordeste, Major Facundo 372, a/c, helpful, rec; and other national banks; **Banorte** gives good rates. Open 0900-1630. **Master card**, cash against card, Av Dom Luiz 880, Aldesta. **Banco Económico**, R Major Facundo 322, T 211-1834, sells TCs on Amex card; TCs exchanged and cash with Visa at **Banco do Brasil**, R Barão do Rio Branco 1500, also on Av Abolição. Exchange at **Tropical Viagens**, R Barão do Rio Branco 1233, English spoken; **Libratur**, Av Abolição 2794, rec; **Ari**, Sapataria Brasileira, R Gen Bezerril 259, or at the **Zely** shop in the old prison.

● **Electric current**
220 volts AC, 60 cycles.

● **Embassies & consulate**
Danish, Av Marquês de Olinda 85, Ed Alberto Fonseca 2, Caixa Postal 34, T 224 0311, 0376, 0421, F 224 0997, open 0900-1200, 1400-1700; **Honorary British Consulate**, Annette de Castro, Edson Queiroz Building, esq Av Desembargador Moreira e Av Antônio Sales.

● **Entertainment**
Forró is danced at the *Clube dos Vaqueiros* out on the BR-116 S, Wed 2230; or at *Viva Maria*, Vieira e Estados Unidos, Sat at 2200 (check by phone first); *Chico do Caranguejo*, Praia do Futuro, lively bar, Thur nights, rec.

Theatre: Teatro José de Alencar, nr railway station in centre, built 1810, building contains also newer theatre built 1910.

● **Hospitals & medical services**
R Vincente Leite 631, English-speaking doctor.

● **Post & telecommunications**
Post Office: Praça Ferreira in centre. Parcels must be taken to Receita Federal office at Barão de Aracati 909, Aldeota (take 'Dom Luiz' bus).

Telecommunications: Embratel, Av Pontes Vieira 1554. **Telephone**: International calls from Emcetur hut on Iracema beach and from Teleceará offices (R João Moreira esq R Floriano Peixoto).

● **Shopping**
Fortaleza has an excellent selection of textiles at reasonable prices (among the cheapest in Brazil) and some handicrafts. The local specialities are lace (some hand-made) and embroidered textile goods; also hammocks (US$3-20), fine alto-relievo wood carvings of NE scenes, basket ware and clay figures (*bonecas de barro*). Bargaining is OK at the **Mercado Central** in the Praça da Sé, and the **Emcetur tourist market** in the old prison (more expensive). The *SINE* shop, at R Dr João Moreira 429, is part of a state government initiative to promote small independent producers, high quality traditional handicrafts at reasonable prices. Every night (1800-2300), there are stalls along Av Pres Kennedy (the beach), lively, fair prices. The **Centro de Artesanato Luiza Távora**, Av Santos Dumont 1589, has been rebuilt and is worth a visit. Boutiques along Monsenhor Tabosa between Senador Almino and João Cordeiro. Cashew nuts at the Mercado Central are excellent.

● **Sports**
Golf: The Ceará Golf Club has 9 holes.

● **Tour companies & travel agents**
Hippopotamus Turismo, Prai de Iracema, tour to Jericoacoara rec, as is the tour by *Pousada Ondas Verdes* (US$90); *Lafuente Turismo*, Av Senador Virgilio Tavora 496, T 244 8558.

● **Tourist offices**
Emcetur, in ex-municipal prison, helpful, has maps (sometimes), enquire about beach tours. Open 0700-1800, Sun 0700-1200. Also at Praça Ferreira and on Iracema beach.

● **Transport**
Local Car hire: beach buggies rentable from *Junna's Buggy*, Av Abolição 2480, T 244-7872.

Air Direct flights to Belém, Recife, Rio and other cities in Brazil. Flights from Europe with Varig and Transbrasil, see page 659. Bus 404 from airport to Praça José de Alencar, taxis US$5. The airport is nr the rodoviária.

Trains South to Baturité (tourist train round trip Sun).

Buses Rodoviária 6 km from centre, bus from Av Grl Sampaio marked 'Aguanambi' 1 or 2, or 'Bairra de Fátima-Rodoviária' bus from Praça Coração de Jesus, US$0.35 (and others); no luggage store, only lockers. The 'Expresso de Luxo' runs daily to **Recife** (12 hrs, US$22, leave at night), book early for weekend travel; also **Rio**

de Janeiro, 48 hrs, US$86 (*leito* 110), São Paulo, 48 hrs, US$88 (*leito* 176); Jericoacoara daily 0900, 2100, US$9, 7 hrs; Salvador, daily 0900, US$40, and many other cities. Belém US$42, 5 buses a day, 23 hrs (2 companies, Exp Timbira good: also sells Belém-Manaus boat tickets). Piripiri, for Parque Nacional de Sete Cidades, US$12, 9 hrs, a good stop en route to Belém.

To hitch to Teresina, take a bus W to the BR-222, the Teresina road.

INLAND EXCURSIONS

The Serra de Maranguape with tropical growth and distant views back to the city is 30 km inland from Fortaleza. The pilgrimage centre of **Canindé** may be visited, 108 km SW of Fortaleza, 3-hr bus ride from the rodoviária (office 21, Viação Nova Esperança). Large modern church on hill with carved baptistery doors, many ex-votos, interesting dry-land vegetation along route. (Hotels: *Plaza*, by basilica, food OK; *Santo Antônio*). Another inland town, **Baturité**, can be seen, 3 hrs from rodoviária (office 45) by Redenção bus, mornings only, also a tourist train round trip Sun.

NORTHWEST OF FORTALEZA

2 hrs NW of Fortaleza by bus is **Paracuru** (*pop* 20,940), a fishing port which is being developed as Ceará's carnival city (restaurant *Ronco do Mar*, good fish dishes, also *Balança do Mar* and a pizzaria; breakfast at Dona Luci's *sitio*, No 25 in the market; *Boca do Poço* bar has *forró* at weekends). It has some lovely deserted white sand beaches with good bathing, and the people are very friendly. Some 7 hrs from Fortaleza, passing lovely Lagoinha and Fleixeras beaches, is the sleepy fishing village of **Almofala**, served by many buses. There is electricity, but no hotels or restaurants, although locals rent hammock space and cook meals. Bathing is better elsewhere, but the area is surrounded by dunes and is excellent for hiking along the coast to explore beaches and lobster-fishing communities. In Almofala, the church with much of the town was covered by shifting sands and remained covered for 50 years, reappearing in the 1940s.

JERICOACOARA

Nestled in the dunes 165 km before the border with the state of Piauí is the fishing community of **Jericoacoara** (known as Serrote by locals). It is popular with travellers and Brazilians, crowded Jan to March. The visitor is rewarded with towering sand dunes, deserted beaches with little shade, cactus-covered cliffs rising from the sea, and a chance to savour village life, although it is becoming ever more geared to tourism. Electricity depends on generators. There is forró nightly.

● **Accommodation** A2 *Papagaio*, is said to be the best (has organized tours); **A2** *Hippopotamus*, with pool; **A3** *Matusa*, pool and bar; **B** *Isalana*, R São Francisco, light and shower. **On R do Forró**: **C** *Acuara*, by beach, gas lamps; **C** *Isabel*, light and shower, rec; on R São Francisco, **E** *Dona Belinha*, the oldest *pousada*, very basic; **E** *Estrela do Mar*, light and shower, no breakfast; **E** *Pousada Parahiso*, friendly, clean; **F** *Natur*, basic, hammocks, friendly. Other rec *pousadas; Recanto das Araras* clean, good breakfast, friendly, washing facilities, rec based; **E** *São Francisco*; **E** *do Coqueiro*; *O Alemão*. Many locals rent hammock space, hammocks, and cook food.

● **Places to eat** There are several restaurants serving vegetarian and fish dishes: *Laricau; Acuara do Jèrico*, reasonable; for *pratos feitos* try *As Paulistas; Pousada São Francisco; Verandhao*; pasta and pizza at *Casinha da Barra*; juices, snacks and beer until late at *Jacaré*; *Tenda Popular* for the cheapest breakfast; *Espaço Aberto* also rec for breakfast. Several shops sell basic provisions, so camping is possible. *Restaurante Central*, in Jijoca, is rec; *Sorrisa de Natureza* cheap, tasty food, rec.

● **Entertainment Nightlife** is interesting: *Forró e Lambateira* has dancing every night (unless raining); *Cabaret do Lopez*, video shows, dancing when Lambateira rained off; *Tochas (bar do Loco)*, on beach by church, reggae, salsa and rock by candlelight; *GP Rangos Biritas* for blues and jazz.

● **Transport** Horses can be hired to visit beautiful lagoons, but the animals may be badly treated. A jeep meets buses at Jijoca de Cruz for the 1½ hrs onward journey to Jericoacoara. If coming from Belém (20 hrs, US$30, difficult journey) you may be able to change at Sobral for Jijoca, but it is much more reliable to go to Fortaleza, from where there are regular buses to Jijoca. Jeep transfer is free with some bus lines, eg Redenção, otherwise about US$3, less if the jeep is full. Returning, the bus leaves Jijoca for

Fortaleza at midnight and 0600. A direct journey from Fortaleza on a 2 or 3-day tour is possible in a VW Kombi, book through an hotel or T 244-5974, Maria do Carmo. You can also get there by boat 'seasickness guaranteed', or bus from **Camocim** (a little further W; **F** *Hotel Lusitania*). Take a truck from Camocim to Guriú where hammock space can be found. The village musician sings his own songs in the bar. Walk 4 hrs, or take boat across the bay to Jericoacoara. Many other marvellous beaches in this region; some like Nova Tatajuba, recently discovered, with simple *pousadas*; others like Maceió, also reached from Camocim, an unspoilt paradise.

WEST TO PIAUÍ

The road to Sobral and Teresina, BR-222, is paved, but in poor condition. **Sobral** (*pop* 127,450), the principal town in western Ceará and well-known for straw hats, has **C** *Hotel Visconde*, 10 mins from rodoviária, friendly, good breakfast, and **D** *Francinet's Hotel, Hotel Vitória*, cheap good lunch buffet, rec. At **Tianguá**, 311 km from Fortaleza on the Teresina road, is **B** *Serra Grande* hotel, all amenities, good (bus from Fortaleza US$9, from Belém, US$32.50).

UBAJARA NATIONAL PARK

The Ubajara caves in the **Ubajara National Park** are worth seeing; they are 18 km off the road to Teresina, on a good paved road, 3 km from Ubajara town. A cablecar descends the cliff to the cave entrance, 0830-1600, US$3.50. Lighting has been installed in the nine caverns of the complex, but a torch and spare batteries may be useful. Ibama office at the park entrance, 5 km from the caves; not always helpful, T 634-1388. There is a 3-km cobbled path from the cablecar (take drinking water). The views of the *sertão* from the upper cablecar platform are superb, beautiful walks among forest and waterfalls and old sugar-mills scattered around the plateau. To walk all the way up to the top of the plateau takes 14 hrs; if you want to do this take plenty of water, from the trail entrance the walk is 3 hrs.

● **Accommodation** Nearby is the **C** *Pousada Neblina*, T 634-1270, in beautiful cloud forest, with swimming pool, rustic campground (US$1.25), with breakfast and private shower (D

without breakfast) restaurant open 1100-2000, meals rec; opp is **F** *Pousada Gruta da Ubajara*, with bath, clean, friendly, rustic, restaurant, rec. Near the park, at Sítio Santana (ask taxi driver for 'Sítio do Alemão'), is the coffee plantation of *Herbert Klein*, on which there are 3 small chalets, D, warmly rec, with full facilities, excursions, bicycle hire offered (postal address Caixa Postal 33, CEP 62.350, Ubajara, Ceará), if chalets are full the Kleins accommodate visitors at their house.

In **Ubajara** town (*pop* 23,350, 2 hotels; **C** *Le Village*, on Ibiapina road, T 634-1364, restaurant, pool, sauna, good value; **D** *Ubajara*, R Juvêncio Luís Pereira 370, T 634-1261, small restaurant). Most restaurants US$10, big meals in the old market cost US$3. An interesting Sun morning market sells produce of the *sertão*. Buses to Fortaleza.

Crateús South of Sobral is a remote town (*pop* 66,635), paved road all the way to Fortaleza, with the **D** *Crateús Palace Hotel*, very reasonable and clean, with breakfast. Good restaurant, *Churrascaria Pequena Cabana*, at back of hotel. Bus service from Crateús over very bad road to Teresina, every 2 days.

Piauí

PARNAÍBA

Between the states of Maranhão and Piauí runs the Rio Parnaíba. Near the river mouth is the anchorage of Luís Correia, where ships unload for final delivery by tugs and lighters at **Parnaíba** (*pop* 127,990; *CEP* 64200; *DDD* 086) 15 km up river, the collecting and distributing centre for the trade of Piauí: tropical products and cattle. There is a regular connection here to Tutóia, for boats across the Parnaíba delta (see page 574).

Beaches

Beaches at Luís Correia, which with Parnaíba has radioactive sands. Some 15 km from Parnaíba is Pedra do Sal: dark blue lagoons and palm trees. At Lagoa de Portinho there are bungalows, a bar and restaurant and it is possible to camp; canoes for hire.

● **Accommodation B** *Cívico*, Av Gov Chagas Rodrigues, T 322-2470, with bath and a/c, good breakfast, friendly, rec; **E** *Rodoviária*, and other basic hotels in the centre.

TERESINA

(*Pop* 598,450; *CEP* 64000; *DDD* 086) About 435 km up the Rio Parnaíba, is the capital of the State of Piauí (*pop* 2,581,055), possibly the poorest in Brazil. There are paved road and rail connections (freight only) with the neighbouring state capitals. The city itself is reputed to be the hottest after Manaus (temperatures rise to 42°C).

Places of interest

The **Palácio de Karnak** (the old governor's palace), just S of Praça Frei Serafim, can be visited, Mon-Fri, 1530-1730; it contains lithographs of the Middle East in 1839 by David Roberts RA. Also see the **Museu do Piauí**, Praça Mal Deodoro, Mon-Fri 0800-1730, Sat, Sun, 0800-1230, US$0.60. There is an interesting **open market** by the Praça Mar Deodoro and the river is picturesque, with washing laid out to dry along its banks. The market is a good place to buy hammocks, but bargain hard. Every morning along the river bank there is the **troca-troca** where people buy, sell and swap; an under-cover complex (**Mercado Central do Artesanato**) has been built at R Paissandu 1276 (Praça Dom Pedro II), open daily 0800-2200 (not weekends). Most of the year the river is low, leaving sandbanks known as *coroas* (crowns).

Local information
● **Accommodation**

A1 *Luxor Hotel do Piauí*, T 222-4911, F 222-4171, and *Teresina Palace*, Paissandu 1219, T 222-2770.

B *Sambaíba*, R Gabriel Ferreira 230-N, 2-star, T 222-6711, central, good; **B** *São José*, João Cabral 340, T 223-2176, F 223-2223, reasonable restaurant.

E *Fortaleza*, Felix Pacheco 1101, Praça Saraiva, T 222-2984, fan, basic, rec; many cheap hotels and *dormitórios* around Praça Saraiva; **E** *Grande*, Firmino Pires 73, very friendly and clean. Many cheap ones in R São Pedro and in R Alvaro Mendes; **E** *Glória*, at 823 (clean, best), blocks 800 and 900 on each street.

● **Places to eat**
For fish dishes, *Pesqueirinho*, R Domingos Jorge Velho 6889, nr the confluence of the rivers in Poti Velho district. Many eating places for all pockets in Praça Dom Pedro II.

● **Banks & money changers**
Try **Alda Tur**, R A de Abreu 1226. Larger hotels may be helpful.

● **Shopping**
Supermarket on Praça Marechal Deodoro 937, clean, good, fresh food. Local handicrafts include leather and clothes.

● **Tourist offices**
Piemtur, R Alvaro Mendes 2003, Caixa Postal 36, information office at R Magalhães Filho s/n (next to 55 N, English spoken); kiosks at rodoviária and airport.

● **Transport**
Air Flights to Fortaleza, Brasília, Rio de Janeiro, São Paulo, Goiânia, São Luis.

Trains Local services only, on a diesel service called the 'metrô'.

Buses The bus trip from **Fortaleza** is scenic and takes 9 hrs (US$12.25, *leito* US$24.50). There are direct buses to Belém (16 hrs, US$20), Recife (16 hrs, US$30) and to **São Luís** (7 hrs, US$9.50).

ROUTES A road, very bad, leads inland to Porto Franco and **Imperatriz** on the Belém-Brasília highway (see page 577); daily bus takes 26-40 hrs for the trip to Imperatriz (US$17), depending on the state of the road; these buses are very crowded. Another main road, runs SE to **Picos** (*pop* 78,425; **E** *Hotel Picos*, basic, but a/c); from there a good road runs via Salgueiro (many *pousadas*) to Recife (800 km) and another to **Petrolina**, on the River São Francisco opposite the Bahian town of Juazeiro. Buses from Petrolina/Juazeiro (see page 534) SE to Salvador.

PARQUE NACIONAL DE SETE CIDADES

Some 190 km NE of Teresina and 12 km from Piracuruca is the interesting 20-sq km Parque Nacional de **Sete Cidades** with its strange eroded rock formations, just off the Fortaleza-Teresina road. From the ground it looks like a medley of weird monuments. The inscriptions on some of the rocks have never been deciphered; one Austrian researcher in the 1920s suggested links with the Phoenicians, and the Argentine Professor Jacques de Mahieu, considers them to be Nordic runes left by the Vikings. There is plenty of birdlife, and iguanas, descending from their trees in the afternoon. If hiking in the park, beware of rattlesnakes. Ibama provides a free bus, returns 1700, or else walk (takes all day, very hot, start early). Ibama, Av Homero Castelo Branco 2240, Teresina, CEP 64048-400, T 232-1142. Small booklet with sketch map (not really good enough for walking), entrance US$1.25. There are camping facilities (US$2) and two natural swimming pools, although several years of drought have lowered their water level drastically. Local food is limited and monotonous: bring a few delicacies, and especially fruit. Guided tours with Tropicália Turismo, Piracuruca, T (086) 343-1347. 50 km away Pedro Segundo is a good place to buy opals.

● **Accommodation** 6 km from the park entrance is the hotel **B** *Fazenda Sete Cidades*, with private bathrm, swimming pool, good restaurant and bicycle or horse transport (it is at Km 63 on BR-222, T (086) 261-3642); also has a free pick-up to the park (and a most unpleasant zoo). In the park is an Ibama hostel, F pp, rooms with bath, pleasant, good restaurant, natural pool nearby, rec. **Hotels in Piripiri**: 26 km away (*Pop* 63,015), **F** *Dos Viajantes*, basic and clean; *Piripiri*, both nr bus offices and behind the church. Exchange at the bank only. Piripiri is a cheap place to break the Belém-Fortaleza journey.

● **Transport** A free bus service leaves the Praça in Piripiri (in front of Telpisa office), at 0700, passing *Hotel Fazenda Sete Cidades* at 0800, reaching the park 10 mins later; return at 1630, or hitchhike. Taxi from Piripiri, US$14, or from Piracuruca, US$18. Bus Teresina-Piripiri and return, throughout the day 2½ hrs, US$3.50. Bus São Luis-Piripiri, 1200, 1630, 2130, 10 hrs, US$12. Several daily buses Piripiri-Fortaleza, 9 hrs, US$12. Bus Piripiri-Ubajara (see above), marked 'São Benedito', or 'Cratéus', 2½ hrs; US$3.60, first at 0700 (a beautiful trip).

OEIRAS

In the S of the state, some 300 km S of Teresina, is **Oeiras** (*pop* 51,890) old capital of Piauí, where the state government is restoring some of the old buildings, such as the bishop's palace and the church of Nossa Senhora da Vitória.

Maranhão

MARANHÃO state
(*pop* 4,922,340) is
about the size of Italy;
its land is flat and low-lying, with
highlands to the S. The Atlantic
coastline – a mass of sandbanks
and creeks and sandy islands on
one of which stands São Luís – is
480 km long. A quarter of Maranhão is covered with *babaçu* palms,
and by far the most important
products are *babaçu* nuts and oil.
Rice often takes second place, but
well behind *babaçu*. There are salt
pans along the coast. The huge
Boa Esperança hydroelectric
plant on the Parnaíba river now
floods the State with energy, and
some petroleum has been discovered.

The main road from Teresina passes
through the Maranhense town of Caxias,
which has a good churrascaria, *Selva do
Braz* (Av Central 601), live music in the
evening.

Crossing the Parnaíba delta, which separates Piauí from Maranhão, is possible by
boat arriving in **Tutóia**: an interesting
trip through swamps sheltering many
birds. Trucks from Tutóia go to Barreirin-
has, gateway to the Parque Nacional dos
Lençois Maranhenses, a vast protected
area of sand dunes with rare birds and
other wildlife (see below).

SÃO LUÍS

São Luís (*pop* 695,780; *CEP* 65000; *DDD*
098), the capital and port of Maranhão
state, founded in 1612 by the French and
named for St Louis of France, is about 560
km W of Fortaleza (1,080 km by road) and
400 km SE of Belém (830 km by road) in
a region of heavy tropical rain, but the
surrounding deep forest has been cut
down to be replaced by *babaçu* palms. The
city stands upon São Luís island between
the bays of São Marcos and São José. The
urban area extends to São Francisco island, connected to São Luís by three
bridges. An old slaving port, the city has a
large black population and has retained
much African culture.

Places of interest

The old part, on very hilly ground with
many steep streets, is still almost pure
colonial. Part of it, known as the Reviver,
has been restored with generally splendid
results: the damp climate stimulated the
use of ceramic tiles for exterior walls, and
São Luís shows a greater variety of such
tiles than anywhere else in Brazil, in Portuguese, French and Dutch styles. The
commercial quarter (R Portugal, also
called R Trapiche) is still much as it was
in the 17th century; best shopping area is
R de Santana near Praça João Lisboa.

See the **Palácio dos Leões** (Governor's
Palace – closed since Jan 1995), beautiful
floors of dark wood (*jacarandá*) and light
(*cerejeira*), marvellous views from terrace,
and the old slave market. The restored
Fortaleza de Santo Antônio, built originally by the French in 1614, is on the bank
of the Rio Anil at Ponta d'Areia. The **Fonte
do Ribeirão**, Largo do Ribeirão, was begun
in 1796.

Churches

The best colonial churches to see – some
of them rebuilt and not improved by it –
are the **Cathedral** and the churches of

ROUTES To Belém: direct paved road via **Santa Inês** (convenient stopping place, **E** *Hotel Novo Horizonte*, nr rodoviária, with bath, others nearby with restaurants) and Alto Bonito, in reasonable condition (sometimes washed out but still passable – fascinating swamplands), with petrol stations not far apart (about 9 hrs driving with stop for lunch). There is a bus service 13 hrs, US$22, Transbrasiliana at 1900 and 2000 (no *leito*).

ALCANTARA

Some 22 km away by boat is **Alcântara** (city *pop* 4,000, municipality 19,620) the former state capital, on the mainland bay of São Marcos. Construction of the city began at the beginning of the seventeenth century and it is now a historical monument. There are many old churches (eg the ruined **Matriz de São Matias**) and colonial mansions (see the **Casa**, and **Segunda Casa, do Imperador**, also the old cotton barons' mansions with their blue, Portuguese tiled façades), the traditional pillory, the **Pelourinho**, in the Praça Gomes de Castro, also a small museum in the square (US$0.20) and the **Forte de São Sebastião** (1653) now in ruins. See also the **Fonte de Miritiva**. Good beaches, good walking around the coast (can be muddy after rain), mosquitoes after dark. A rocket-launching site has been built nearby. Principal festival: **Festa do Divino**, at Pentecost (Whitsun).

● **Accommodation B** *Pousado do Mordomo Régio*, R Grande 134 (T 337-1221 or São Luís 227-0110), rooms with bath, TV, refrigerator, good restaurant; **C** *Pousado do Imperador*, R Grande 13, some rooms with bath; **C** *Pousada do Pelourinho*, Praça Gomes de Castro (E without breakfast), clean, friendly, good restaurant, communal bathrm. Try bargaining for hammock space in private houses. Children who offer themselves as guides can help arrange accommodation in private houses, friendly but no great comfort; provide your own mineral water.

● **Places to eat** *Bar do Lobato*, on the praça, is pleasant, with good, simple food, fried shrimps highly rec. The restaurants are not cheap, so take a picnic if on a tight budget.

● **Transport** Ferries cross the bay daily, leaving São Luís at about 0800, returning from Alcântara about 1400: check time and buy the ticket at the *hidroviária* (W end of R Portugal, São Luís) the day before as departure depends on the tides. The journey takes 90 mins, return US$15, worth paying extra for 'panorámica' seat. Sea can be very rough. There are also catamaran tours bookable through tour operators in São Luís, meals not included.

PARQUE NACIONAL LENCOIS MARANHENSES

To the E of São Luis, on the Atlantic Coast is the **Parque Nacional Lençóis Maranhenses**, 155,000 ha of beaches, lakes and dunes, with very little vegetation and largely unstudied wildlife. For information, phone the Ibama office, T 221-2125/2776, or Baluz Turismo, T 222-6658, or Jaguarema Turismo, T 222-4764.

IMPERATRIZ

On the Eastern bank of the Rio Tocantins, at Maranhão's western border with Tocantins, is **Imperatriz** (*pop* 276,450), a city serving a large cattle region. Go down Av Getúlio Vargas and see the range of goods on offer. To get to the ferry across the river, go along R Luis Domingues, which runs parallel to Av Getúlio Vargas.

● **Accommodation B** *Poseidon*, R Paraíba 740, T 721-4466, central, best, a/c, TV, swimming pool, rec; **D** *Anápolis*, BR-010, Km 1345, T 721-2255, opp rodoviária, a/c, fridge, swimming pool, friendly; a lot of cheap hotels nr rodoviária.

● **Entertainment** There is a good, expensive discotheque at Beira Rio, N of the ferry crossing, *Fly Back Disco Club*; it has two dance floors, one fast, one slow (for couples only).

● **Post & telecommunications Telephone Office**: on R Rio Grande do Norte, a side street off Av Getúlio Vargas, nr *Hotel Poseidon*.

ROUTES Lying on the Belém-Brasília highway, Imperatriz has bus connections with both cities; there is a slow, crowded bus service to Teresina. To get to Marabá on the Transamazônica, you can either take a Transbrasiliana bus direct, 7-10 hrs (starting on the Belém highway, the bus then turns W along a poorer road, passing finally through destroyed forest, new fazendas and unplanned cities), or, a faster route, involving taking a ferry across the river in the early morning (0600-0700) to catch a pick-up on the other side, takes about 5 hrs, but is more expensive.

Northern Brazil

BRAZILIAN amazônia, from the mouth of the great river to the Colombian and Peruvian borders. The cities of Belém, Santarém and Manaus are described, together with river travel between and excursions into the jungle. Also dealt with are the land and water routes to Venezuela and the Guianas.

Northern Brazil consists of the states of Pará, Amazonas, Amapá and Roraima. The states of Rondônia and Acre are dealt with under Section 10, Southern Amazônia.

Brazilian Amazônia

The area is drained by the Amazon, which in size, volume of water – 12 times that of the Mississippi – and number of tributaries has no equal in the world. At the base of the Andes, far to the W, the Amazonian plain is 1,300 km in width, but E of the confluences of the Madeira and Negro rivers with the Amazon, the highlands close in upon it until there is no more than 80 km of floodplain between them. Towards the river's mouth – about 320 km wide – the plain widens once more and extends along the coast southeastwards into the state of Maranhão and northwards into the Guianas.

Brazilian Amazônia, much of it still covered with tropical forest, is 56% of the national area. Its jungle is the world's largest and densest rain forest, with more diverse plants and animals than any other jungle in the world. It has only 8% of Brazil's population, and most of this is concentrated around Belém (in Pará), and in Manaus, 1,600 km up the river. The population is sparse because other areas are easier to develop; the rainfall is heavy, the humidity high and the climate hot; and the soil, as in all tropical forest, is poor.

Successive Governments have made strenuous efforts to develop Amazônia. Roads have been built parallel to the Amazon to the S (the Transamazônica), from Cuiabá (Mato Grosso) northwards to Santarém (Pará), and NE from Porto Velho through Humaitá to the river bank opposite Manaus. Some maps show a road N of the Amazon, marked Perimetro (or Perimetral) Norte; this road does not exist, never has and probably never will. Agricultural settlements are being established along these roads; major energy and mining projects for bauxite and iron ore are bringing rapid change. Much environmental damage has been caused to the region by gold prospectors (*garimpeiros*), especially by their indiscriminate use of mercury. The most important cause of destruction, however, has been large scale deforestation to make way for cattle ranching. Choosing the best path towards development in Amazônia remains the subject of much controversy throughout Brazil, and foreign interference in the matter (there has been no shortage of it) is generally not welcome. Nonetheless, there is a gradually growing awareness among many Brazilians that their northern hinterland is a unique treasure and requires some form of protection. Most recently, much attention has been focused on ecotourism as a potentially nondestructive source of income for the region. Just how benign this activity actually is, remains to be confirmed. There are increasing numbers of Brazilians from the S taking holidays in Amazônia.

Anyone interested in the Amazonian development programme and its ecological, social, economic and political effects should read Richard Bourne's masterly *Assault on the Amazon* (London, Gollancz, 1978), *Dreams of Amazonia*, by Roger D Stone (Penguin, 1986), or *Amazon* by Brian Kelly and Mark London (Harcourt Brace Jovanovich, New York, 1983). *The Fate of the Forest* by Suzanne Hecht and Alexander Cockburn (Penguin, 1991) has also been rec.

ALONG THE TRANSAMAZÔNICA

The Transamazônica, about 5,000 km in length, represents the greater part of a direct road connection between Brazil's furthest E and furthest W points. It skirts the southern edge of the Amazonian plain, linking the following places: Estreito (junction with the Belém-Brasília highway, N of Araguaína, see page 628), Marabá (on the Tocantins river), Altamira (on the Xingu), São Luís do Tapajós, near Itaituba (on the Tapajós), Jacarèacanga, Humaitá (on the Madeira), Rio Branco, and Japim, in the far W of the State of Acre. The road was officially opened in Dec 1973. Parts of it have been paved, but the harsh climate and inadequate maintenance have caused much deterioration. Some sections are often totally intransitable throughout the rainy season (eg Santarém to the Belém-Brasilia Highway). Others may require 4WD and winch. There are stretches with regular truck traffic and scheduled bus services, but as conditions are constantly changing, detailed local inquiry is essential before heading out. Also ensure that you have sufficient *reais* for your journey. Despite all the resources invested in road construction, the rivers remain the principal avenues of transport throughout Amazônia. In April 1995 the government announced plans to extend and pave the Transamazonian highway system, to improve the road links with Peru and Venezuela, and to Cuiabá in Mato Grosso.

MARABÁ

Near **Marabá** (*pop* 121,815; *alt* 84m); are beaches on the Rios Tocantins and Itacaiúnas, best June-October. With the filling of the Tucuruí dam the town has been moved; even so it suffers from flooding.

There is a bridge across the Toncantins at Marabá. There are essentially three parts of Marabá: Marabá Velha (also called Marabá Pionera), Marabá Nova (where the rodoviária is situated), and Cidade Nova. The distance between Marabá Nova and Velha is about 2.5km. A good, friendly and rec travel agent is *IBR Travel* on the main street of Marabá Velha. Banco do Brasil will not cash TCs; parallel market in larger stores, eg *Supermercado Bato Logo*.

Excursions The **Serra Pelada** gold mines are now worked by heavy machinery. This massive excavation was the scene of much human misery (and some fabulous fortunes). Bus to Km 6, change there to Serra Pelada bus (US$3, 3 hrs, last bus back 1400). 11 km before the town is a police post: search for weapons and alcohol (forbidden); second search at the airport 2 km from the mine. No prior permission is needed to visit the mines. The miners are usually friendly and like being photographed, but enquire about conditions before going there.

● **Accommodation B** *Vale do Tocantins*, Folha 29, Cidade Nova, 7 km, T 322-2321, modern, restaurant, travel agency; of similar standard are **B** *Itacaiúnas*, nearby, T 322-1715, and *Del Príncipe*, Av Mal Rondon 95, Cidade Nova, I 324-1175; **C** *Dallas*, Nova Marabá, next to rodoviária, rec; **C** *Bahia*, Nova Marabá, also next to the rodoviária; **C** *Plaza*, Folha 32, Quadra 10, lote 06, T 322 1610/1611/1612, fan, quiet, friendly helpful, very good breakfast, some English spoken rec; **C** *Keyla*, Rod Transamazônica 2427, 3 km, a/c, some cheaper rooms; *Victória*, Av Espírito Santo 130, 2 km, both similar to *Plaza* but not as friendly; **E** *Serra de Ouro*, all of wood, shower; others nr rodoviária.

● **Places to eat** *Kome Aki no Chikāo*, Av Antônio Maia 997, central, a/c, modest, 1200-1500, 1800-2300 (in theory); *Bambu*, Pedro Cameiro 111, Cidade Nova, 3 km, mainly fish, clean, good value, 1100-1500, 1800-2300. Good *Churrascaria* in main square nr public TV set; juice bars and *DiscoTony* discotheque; *Lanchonete Domino*, opp rodoviária, rec.

● **Transport Air** Airport in Cidade Nova, 3 km. There are no direct flights to Altamira or Santarém, only via Belém with Brasil Central or Varig. Brasil Central flies to several local destinations, eg São Luis, Imperatriz. **Buses** Rodoviária in Nova Marabá, 4 km on PA-150, T 321-1892. Buses leave daily for Belém (654 km, paved), for **Santarém** (34 hrs) and many daily for **Imperatriz** (7-10 hrs,

US$9.50, there is also a pick-up to the bank of the Tocantins opp Imperatriz, 5 hrs, but more expensive, US$12); buses can be caught going S at **Toncantinópolis**, opp Porto Franco on the Belém-Brasília road. Also a bus can be taken to **Araguaína**, 12½ hrs, US$19; bus Marabá-Goiânia (change at Araguaína), US$48. Bus to **Santa Inês** (Maranhão, on Belém-Teresina road), 19 hrs, US$23. Transbrasiliana bus to **Altamira** daily, 1300 (if road is passable); direct to **Rio** US$60, **São Paulo** US$52. On these bus trips take plenty of food and drink – local supplies are expensive. From rodoviária to **Railway Station** take colletivo bus US$0.31 from opposite the rodoviária to 'Km 6' (a kind of suburb of Marabá), then another colletivo bus US$0.31 to the Estação Ferrovia. The colletivos are not frequent but are crowded. Alternatively taxis, which can be shared cost US$11 from railway station to town. **River Boat**: trips to Belém (24 hrs), Altamira (6 hrs) and Santarém (18 hrs).

Between Marabá and Belém, on the Rio Tocantins, is the **Tucuruí** hydroelectric scheme (which is causing much ecological damage). To go to the dam, take bus 'V Temp I II' or 'Vila Temporária'; it is difficult to obtain a permit to visit the inside of the hydroelectric plant.

● **Accommodation & places to eat** *Transamérica* best in Tucuruí (*pop* 81,655); **E** *Marajoara*, R Lauro Sodré 685, T 787-1776, simple but OK. Floating bar (light meals), *Fluente*, 1½ km N, take a taxi or motorboat, or walk, popular.

● **Transport** From Marabá to Tucuruí, take Transbrasiliana bus, 0730, 1100, 1800, 8 hrs, US$9.50, road good to Itupiranga, deteriorates thereafter. Day and night river boat from Belém, 32 hrs.

CARAJÁS MINE

Companhia Vale Rio Doce (CVRD) operates the very impressive iron mine at **Carajás** (the largest mineral development in Brazil) which looks like a giant red hole in a green jungle. The ore is almost pure iron oxide and is therefore extremely profitable. It is ground, washed and shipped to São Luis by trains up to 2km long, without further treatment or chemical processing. Apart from iron other metals like manganese are also mined by the CRVD in the area. To get into Carajás (checkpoint 35 km from the project), you must have a permit, available from CVRD in Marabá, São Luis, São Paulo or Rio: Av Groça

Aranha 26, 16° andar, Centro, Rio 20030000 – attention Dr Hugo Mourão (hotel bookings handled here too); apply in advance and have a good reason. **Parque Zoo-Botaniquo** is a very pleasant zoo with local animals, and like everything else in the region is run by CVRD. The animals have very spacious, quasi-natural cages. There is a lot to see including a small shop with Funai articles from the local indians.

37 km before the mine is **Parauapebas**. Originally intended as a temporary settlement for the Carajás construction workers, it is now a big city and still growing. Many people have moved from Carajás, CVRD have even built new houses for its employees here. Both cities however are expensive, especially Carajás. In the dry season, summer, there are frequent bush fires in the region, ignited mainly as *fazendeiros*. The old part of Parauapebas is where the colorful fruitmarket, shops and banks are situated and is very busy.

● **Accommodation Parauapebas**: **B** *Almaribe*, T 346 1048, very pleasant and friendly, manager Alipio speaks excellent English, some French and German, clean, safe, a/c, refrigerator, TV, good breakfast, restaurant, gym machines, good atmosphere, highly rec; **D** *Ouro Verde*, Rio Verde district nr market, basic, cheap, rec. *Florida Bar*, T 346 1038, has good cocktails and food, the friendly owner Neuma speaks good Austrian/German. Opens from 2000 closed Mon, Tues, rec; *Pit Dog*, on main street has fast food and live music, rec.

● **Transport Air** There are flights to Carajás from Belém, Marabá and Tucuruí. Parauapebas is the final station of the Carajás railway line. To Marabá, dep 1930, 2 hrs, US$1.55. To São Luis, see page 576. **Buses** There are 8 daily buses to Marabá between 0545 and 1900. There is 1 daily bus to Conceição de Araguaia. Direct buses from Rio, São Paulo and Vitória to Parauapebas with Aguia Branca. Plenty of Transbrasiliana buses daily Marabá-**Carajás**, 4-5 hrs, US$5.75. Military Police check for weapons and drugs at Curianópolis.

OTHER TOWNS IN THE TRANSAMAZONICA

The Transamazônica crosses the Rio Xingu at Favânia, 41 km E of **Altamira**, a busy, booming Amazônian town with many gold dealers (*pop* 120,565). A road is being paved 46 km N to the fishing village of Vitória on the lower Xingu, from which boats go to Belém; a good place to watch the *garimpeiros* working below the last rapids. No organized trips but a boat can be hired, US$25/day, for a trip up the Xingu which is highly rec. Many animals. The area is an Assurine Indian reservation and it is not allowed to enter villages; buy food in Altamira.

● **Accommodation & places to eat C** *Alta Palace*, Av Tancredo Neves 3093, bar/restaurant, a/c, good, T 515-2057; **D** *Pae e Filho*, simple, rec; **D** *Requinte*, rec; **D** *Lisboa*, Lindolfo Aranha 405, a/c, TV, good value, slightly better than **D** *Imperatriz*, R Beto Somez nr market, bath, a/c, rec; good *churrascos* and shopping in the market; *Restaurante Casa Grande*, R Anchieta, centre, good *churrascos*, cheap, 1130-1430, 1930-2330; *Restaurante Esquina*, next to hotel *Lisboa*, good *sucos*, closed sun, rec.

● **Transport Air** The airport is 8 km from centre, no bus, exchange is difficult; flights to Belém, Santarém, Cuiabá and other Amazon destinations. **Buses** Rodoviária on Av Perimentral, T 515-1879, no left luggage. Buses run from Tucuruí via Repartimento.

Rurópolis (Presidente Medici) lies at the junction of the Transamazônica and the Santarém highway. Hotel run by Incra, "by all accounts, like the rest of the place: cracked, empty, dreaming of a future that never came" (Kevin Healey).

Itaituba is the jumping-off place for the **Amazônia National Park**; see Father Paul Zoderer, who may help to arrange a visit, at church on waterfront – nearest Ibama information, T (091) 224-5899/2621. The Transbrasiliana company has a rodoviária on the Rio Tapajós, near the ferry docks (**E** *Hotel 3 Poderes*, clean, friendly, rec). Bus to Marabá, about 34 hrs, US$30.

In **Humaitá** (*pop* 38,755) there are several basic hotels on the eastern edge of town; try *Hotel Meire*, on main street. The Soltur rodoviária is in the centre.

● **Transport** There is very little traffic on the Transamazônica between Itaituba and Humaitá (1,028 km); local drivers may give lifts. A ferry crosses the Rio Aripuanã at Vila do Carmo. The road is good for about 350 km from Humaitá, then it deteriorates badly. It is hilly, narrow, and the jungle usually grows over the side of the road. Expresos Humaitá daily bus takes 24 hrs from Humaitá to Jacarèacanga, 597 km (the town is 8

km off the highway). One must stay overnight and catch the Transbrasiliana bus to Itaituba (24 hrs, schedule erratic; the bus is replaced occasionally by a truck). There are two insanitary and expensive hotels in Jacarèacanga (try the filling station on the Transamazônica near the Jacarèacanga turn-off, they may have hammock space). Bus fare Humaitá-Jacarèacanga, US$30; Jacarèacanga-Itaituba, US$14.50; travel time depends on the weather conditions, the condition of the bus, and whether the driver decides to stop somewhere for the night.

UP THE AMAZON RIVER

The Amazon system is 6,577 km, long, of which 3,165 km are in Brazilian territory. Ships of up to 4-5,000 tons regularly negotiate the Amazon for a distance of about 3,646 km up to Iquitos, Peru. Distances upstream from the river mouth to Manaus in nautical miles are:

Belém	80
Narrows (entrance)	225
Narrows (exit)	330
Garupa	334
Prainha	452
Santarém	538
Óbidos	605
Parintins	694
Itacoatiara	824
Manaus	930

RIVER TRANSPORT IN AMAZONIA

Although air service is widespread throughout the region, and road transport is gradually increasing, rivers remain the arteries of Amazônia for the transport of both passengers and merchandise. The two great ports of the region are Belém, at the mouth of the Amazon, and Manaus at the confluence of the Rio Negro and Rio Solimões. The strategic location of the latter makes it the hub of river transport. From Manaus there is regular shipping service E to Santarém and Belém along the lower Amazon, S to Porto Velho along the Rio Madeira, W to Tabatinga (the border with Colombia and Peru) along the Rio Solimões, NW to São Gabriel da Cachoeira along the Rio Negro, and N to Caracaraí (for Boa Vista) along the Rio

Branco. There is also a regular service connecting Belém and Macapá, on the N shore of the Amazon Delta, Santarém and Macapá, as well as Santarém and Itaituba S along the Rio Tapajós. All of the above services call at many intermediate ports and virtually every village has some form of riverboat service. There is no regular direct service between Belém and Tabatinga, or Manaus and Iquitos (Peru).

The size and quality of vessels varies greatly, with the largest and most comfortable ships generally operating on the Manaus – Belém route; acceptable conditions can be found, however, on some boats to almost all destinations. Since 1991 there has been more stringent government control (see **Health** below) as well as increased competition among ship owners. Thus conditions have generally improved, with less overcrowding, better hygiene, better food, and friendlier service. Many of the larger ships now offer a/c berths (not really necessary), and even suites with double beds and private bath, in addition to first class (upper deck) and second class (lower deck) hammock space. Most boats have some sort of rooftop bar serving drinks and snacks (generally overpriced).

Riverboat travel is not a substitute for visiting the jungle. Except for a few birds and the occasional dolphin, little wildlife is seen. However it does offer an insight into the vastness of Amazônia and a chance to meet some of its people. It can be a very pleasant and satisfying experience.

The vessels operating on a particular route and their schedules are frequently changing and it is generally not possible to book far in advance. Extensive local inquiry and some flexibility in one's schedule are indispensable for river travel. The following are some suggestions on how to choose a riverboat. Refer to the appropriate city sections for details of port facilities in each.

Whenever possible, avoid purchasing tickets from agents or touts (hawkers) for a boat you have not seen. See the vessel yourself and have a chat with the captain or business manager to confirm departure date and time, length of voyage, ports of call, price, etc. Have a careful look around, inspecting cleanliness in the kitchen, toilets and showers. All boats are cleaned up when in port, but if a vessel is reasonably clean upon arrival then chances are that it has been kept that way throughout the voyage. You can generally arrange to sleep onboard a day or 2 before departure and a day or two after arrival, but be sure to secure carefully your belongings when in port. If you take a berth, choose exactly the one you want, lock it and keep the key even if you will not be moving in right away. If you are travelling hammock class, it is best to board ship at least 8 to 12 hrs before sailing in order to secure a good spot (away from the toilets and the engine). Be firm but considerate of your neighbours as they will be your intimate companions for the duration of the voyage. Always keep your gear locked. Take some light warm clothing, it can get chilly at night in the hammock area.

Compare fares for different ships. As a general rule of thumb they will be about half of the prevailing one-way airfare, including all meals. (Drinks not included. Many ships sail in the evening and the first night's supper is not included.) Shop around and bargain for the best fares. Payment is usually in advance. Insist on a signed ticket indicating date, vessel, class of passage, and berth number if applicable.

All ships carry cargo as well as passengers and the amount of cargo will affect the length of the voyage because of weight (especially when travelling upstream) and loading/unloading at intermediate ports. All but the smallest boats will transport vehicles, but these are all too often damaged by rough handling. Insist on the use of proper ramps and check for adequate clearance. Vehicles can also be transported aboard cargo barges. These are usually cheaper and passengers may be allowed to accompany their car, but check about food, where you will sleep, and adequate shade.

The following are the major shipping routes in Amazônia indicating intermediate ports, average trip durations, and fares. Not all ships stop at all intermedi-

● **Shopping**
Shopping in Av Presidente Vargas; also try the Indian handicrafts shop at Praça Kennedy, set in a garden with Amazonian plants and animals. *Parfumaria Orion*, Trav Frutuoso Guimarães 268, has a wide variety of perfumes and essences from Amazonian plants, much cheaper than tourist shops. Belém is a good place to buy hammocks, look in the street parallel to the river, 1 block inland from Ver-O-Peso. Also good for secondhand English books, in the Trav Campos Sales.
Camera repairs: *Neemias Texeira Lima*, R Manoel Barata 274, Sala 211, T 224-9941.

● **Sports**
Golf: Maracangalha Golf Club has 9 holes.

● **Tour companies & travel agents**
Ciatur, Av Presidente Vargas 645, T 224-1993, good half-day tour on water and in forest and 32-hr trip to Marajó. *Gran-Para Turismo Ltda*, *Hilton Hotel*, Av Presidente Vargas 882 LJ8, T 224-2111.

● **Tourist offices**
Municipal office, **Detur**, in airport and Rodoviária. Hotel reservations made, including low-priced hotels. Map, US$1, from rodoviária bookshop. **Paratur**, Praça Kennedy on the waterfront, by the handicraft shop, helpful, many languages spoken; has a good map of Belém in many languages (but some references are incorrect). Town guidebook, US$2.75.

● **Useful information**
Police: for reporting crimes, R Santo Antônio e Trav Frei Gil de Vila Nova. To avoid crime, take sensible precautions and stay out of dark corners.

● **Transport**
Air Bus 'Perpétuo Socorro-Telégrafo' or 'Icoaraci', every 15 mins from Prefeitura, Praça Felipe Patroni, to airport, 40 mins, US$0.30. Taxi to airport, US$10 (ordinary taxis cheaper than Coop taxis, buy ticket in advance in Departures side of airport). Airport has a hotel booking service but operated by, and exclusive to, 5 of the more expensive hotels, discounts offered. Weekly flights N to **Miami** by Varig, S to **Brasília** and other Brazilian cities, and W to **Santarém** and **Manaus**. To **Paramaribo**, and **Cayenne** 4 times weekly. Air France, R Boaventura Da Silva 1457, T 223-7547/7928. Surinam Airways, R Santo Antônio 432, Edif Antonio Velho, 4th floor, English spoken, helpful with information and documentation. Travellers entering Brazil from Guyane may find it necessary to obtain a 60-day visa (takes 2 days) before airlines will confirm their tickets.

Buses The rodoviária is at the end of Av Gov José Malcher 5 km from centre, take Aeroclube,

Cidade Novo, No 20 bus, or Arsenal or Canudos buses, US$0.35, or taxi, US$5 (day) US$7 (night) (at rodoviária you are given a ticket with the taxi's number on it, threaten to go to the authorities if driver tries to overcharge). It has a good snack bar and showers (US$0.10). Regular services to all major cities. There are direct buses from Belém to Marabá (16 hrs) on the Transamazônica, Transbrasiliana US$16, then change to Santarém. Direct bus Belém-Santarém once a week (US$75, more expensive than by boat and can take longer). To **São Luís**, 2 a day, 13 hrs, US$22, interesting journey through marshlands. If going to Campo Grande or Cuiabá, it may be better change in Goiânia than in Brasília.

Sea Shipping: regular coastal services to Southern Brazil. Agency for international services, Agências Mundiais Ltda, Av Pres Vargas 121, T 224 4078.

To **Santarém**, **Manaus**, and intermediate ports (see **River Transport in Amazônia**, page 581). The larger ships berth at Portobrás/Docas do Pará (the main commercial port) either at Armazem (warehouse) No 3 at the foot of Av Pres Vargas, or at Armazem No 10, a few blocks further N (entrance on Av Marechal Hermes esq Av Visconde de Souza Franco). The guards will sometimes ask to see your ticket before letting you into the port area, but tell them you are going to speak with a ship's captain. Many touts will spot you as you approach the area, they are best ignored. Many smaller vessels (sometimes cheaper, but usually not as clean, comfortable or safe) sail from several small docks along the Estrada Nova (not a safe part of town). Take a Cremaçao bus from Ver-o-Peso.

To **Macapá (Porto Santana)**. *Silja e Souza* of Souzamar, Trav Dom Romualdo Seixas corner R Jeronimo Pimentel, T 222-0719, and *Almirante Solon* of Sanave (Servico Amapaense de Navegação, Castilho Franca 234, opp Ver-o Peso, T 222-7810). ENAL, T 224-5210; *Macamazônia*, R Castilho Franca (see **River Transport in Amazônia**, page 581). There is a desk selling tickets for private boats in the rodoviária; some hotels (eg *Furtaleza*) also sell tickets. They are good for information on the boats for which they sell tickets, but will not tell you anything about alternatives. Purchase tickets from offices 2 days in advance. Smaller boats to Macapá also sail from Estrada Nova.

There is weekend service to **Souré** on Ilha Marajó, for beaches, departing from the old ENASA dock next to Ver-o-Peso market.

Hitchhiking Going S, take bus to Capanema, 3½ hrs, US$3.80, walk ½ km from rodoviária to BR-316 where trucks stop at the gas station.

ROUTES A good asphalted road, BR-316, leads E out of the city. A branch goes N to the coast town of Salinópolis, some 223 km, at the extreme end of the eastern part of the Amazon Delta. Various paved roads branch off: 118 km out of Belém the BR-010 turns right, paved highway S to Brasília (2,120 km). Straight on, the road leads to Bragança, the centre of an early, unsuccessful, attempt in the 1900s to transfer population to Amazônia. At **Capanema** (**E** *Hotel São Luís*, good), 54 km before Bragança, the BR-316 for São Luís, Teresina, Fortaleza and Recife branches right.

Tomé-Açu South of Belém on the Rio Acará-Mirim, affords a view of life on a smaller river than the Amazon; 3 buses a day from Belém, US$8.75. **E** *Hotel Las Vegas*, owner Fernando is very friendly. Boat back to Belém on Sun at 1100, arriving 1800, US$7.50.

MARAJÓ

The world's largest river island (a claim disputed by the Bananal): flooded in rainy Dec-June, it provides a suitable habitat for the water buffalo, said to have swum ashore after a shipwreck. They are now farmed in large numbers (try the cheese and milk). It is also home to many birds, crocodiles and other wildlife, and has several good beaches. It is becoming crowded at weekends and in the July holiday season. The island was the site of the precolumbian Marajoaras culture.

Ponta de Pedras

Boats leave Belém (near Porto do Sal, seat US$3.60, cabin US$38 for 2, 5 hrs) most days for **Ponta de Pedras** (**E** *Hotel Ponta de Pedras*, good meals, buses for Souré or Salvaterra meet the boat). Bicycles for hire (US$1/hr) to explore beaches and the interior of the island. Fishing boats make the 8 hr trip to Cachoeira do Arari (one hotel, **E**) where there is a Marajó museum. A 10 hr boat trip from Ponta de Pedras goes to the Arari lake where there are two villages, Jenipapo (one *pousada*, **E**) built on stilts, forró dancing at weekends, and Santa Cruz which is less primitive, but less interesting (a hammock and a mosquito net are essential). There are water buffalo on

the lake. There is a direct boat service to Belém twice a week.

Trips to the island are arranged by the *Grão Pará Hotel* (rec) and travel agents in Belém.

Souré

The Enasa service to **Souré** (*pop* 17,200), 'capital' of the island, sails weekends only (4 hrs, US$5). Flights to Souré (infinitely preferable), Mon and Wed, 0700 and 1600, US$30 (return Mon, Wed, Fri). Colectivos into town, US$2. There are fine beaches, Araruna (2 km – take supplies and supplement with coconuts and crabs, beautiful walks along the shore), do Pesqueiro (bus from Praça da Matriz,1030, returns 1600, eat at *Maloca*, good, cheap, big, deserted beach, 13 km away) and Caju-Una (15 km). Small craft await passengers from the Enasa boats, for Salvaterra village (good beaches and bars: seafood), US$12, 10 mins, or trips bookable in Belém from Mururé, T 241-0891, **B** *Pousada das Guarás* (on beach, well-equipped), or *Hotel Marajó*, T 741-1396 (Belém 225-2880), cheaper.

● **Accommodation & Services Souré**: **D** *Cosampa*, Travessa 14, T 229-3928, hot showers, clean, friendly, free transfer from docks; **D** *Waldeck*, Trav 12, T 741-1414, clean, friendly, only 4 rooms; **E** *Soure* (3a R, Centro: walk straight on from Enasa dock, then take 3rd street on left), with bath, a/c, basic; *Pousada Marajoara*, and **E** *Pousada Parque Floresta*, nearby, friendly and clean, good meals; **F** *Pensão* at 2nda R 575 (*Bar Guarani*), simple, rec. *Canecão*, Praça da Matriz, sandwiches, meals, rec. Changing money is only possible at very poor rates. Take plenty of insect repellent.

SALINÓPOLIS

(*Pop* 22,688) This seaside resort with many small places where you can eat and drink at night by the waterfront, and fine sandy beach nearby (buses and cars drive on to the beach), is a peaceful place mid-week. Best during holiday month of July. Atalaia, opposite Salinópolis, is pleasant, reached by taxi (US$10) or with a fisherman.

● **Accommodation C** *Atalaia*, on island of Atalaia, 15 km from Salinópolis, T 724-1122, simple, clean, beautiful setting, reserve in advance and take a taxi; **C** *Solar*, Av Beira Mar s/n, with bath, best in town, good restaurant; **D** *Jeanne d'Arc*, with breakfast; **E** *Salinas*, on beach.

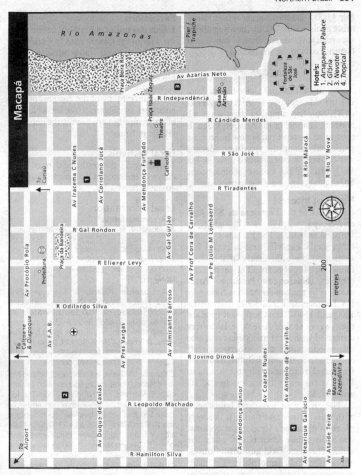

Macapá

Río Amazonas

Pier / Trapiche

Av Azarias Neto

Praça Beira Rio

R Independência

Praça Isaac Zagury

Casa do Artesão

Fortaleza de São José

Hotels:
1. Amapaense Palace
2. Glória
3. Novotel
4. Tropical

R Cândido Mendes

Theatre

Cathedral

Av Mendonça Furtado

R São José

R Rio Maracá

R Rio V Nova

Av Coriolano Jucá

Av Iracema C Nunes

To Curiaú

R Tiradentes

N

R Gal Rondon

Praça da Bandeira

Av Procópio Rola

Prefeitura

R Eliezer Levy

Av Prof Cora de Carvalho

Av Pe Júlio M Lombaerd

200

0   metres

R Odilardo Silva

Av Almirante Barroso

To Curicorne & Oiapoque

Av F.A.B.

Av Pres Vargas

R Jovino Dinoá

Av Caraci Nunes

Av Antonio de Carvalho

To Marco Zero Fazendinha

To Airport

R Leopoldo Machado

Av Duque de Caxias

Av Mendonça Junior

Av Henrique Galúcio

Av Ataíde Teive

R Hamilton Silva

• **Places to eat** *Bife de Ouro* opp filling station, simple, but excellent fish and shrimp, always crowded for lunch; *Gringo Louco*, further out than Atalaia (take taxi or hitch), at Cuiarana beach, follow signs, gringo owner serves good, unusual dishes, and some 'wild' drinks known as 'bombs', popular.

• **Transport** Buses 4 hrs from Belém on good road, US$5.50.

AMAPÁ

Rubber was almost the only product of Amapá until the 1950s, when manganese was discovered 150 km NW of Macapá. A standard-gauge railway, 196 km long, the only one in Brazil, has been built from the mining camp to Porto Santana, from which there is an excellent road. Other products are gold, coal, timber and agricultural. The state is one-quarter the size of France but with only 289,050 inhabitants. Malaria is rampant in the state; the illiteracy rate is 85%; smuggling goes on in a big way. The mining area – Icomiland (*pop* 4,000) – is a startling exception: swimming pools, football fields, bowling alleys, supermarkets, dance halls, movies, a healthy oasis in the wilderness.

MACAPÁ

There are ferries and daily flights from Belém to **Macapá** (*pop* 179,610; *CEP* 68900; *DDD* 096), the capital of Amapá on the northern channel of the Amazon Delta. It used to be decrepit but is now improving, particularly along the riverfront. Macapá was declared a customs free zone in Jan 1993, raising hopes for an economic boom. So far, though, nothing has happened.

Places of interest

Each brick of the **Fortaleza de São José do Macapá**, built 1764, was brought from Portugal as ballast. The Fortaleza is used for concerts, exhibits, and colourful festivities on the anniversary of the city's founding, 4 February. The handicraft complex (**Núcleo de Produção Artesanal**) is located on Av Azárias Neto e Av JM Lombaerd, T 222-3681, daily 0800-1200 and 1500-2000. Craftsmen produce their wares onsite. A feature is pottery decorated with local manganese ore, also nice woodcarvings and leatherwork; staff are very friendly and helpful. **São José Cathedral**, inaugurated by the Jesuits in 1761, is the city's oldest landmark. Its aisles are lined with gravestones.

The riverfront has been landscaped with trees, lawns and paths. It is a very pleasant place for a stroll in the evening, when the whole town is out doing the same. There are food and drink kiosks, and a nice lively atmosphere. The main avenue along the river is closed to vehicles on weekends. The pier (*trapiche*) is decaying, but is still a lovely spot for savouring the cool of the evening breeze, or watching sunrise over the Amazon. There is a monument to the equator, **Marco Zero** (take Fazendinha bus from Av Mendonça Furtado). The equator also divides the nearby football stadium in half, aptly named O Zerão. South of these, along the road to Fazendinha, are the **zoo** and **botanical gardens**. **Fazendinha** itself is a popular local beach, very busy on Sun.

Excursions

Lagoa dos Indios, 4 km W of the city along the Duque de Caxias road is a lake with snowy egrets and water buffaloes. Also fishing and swimming. **Curiau**, a town 8 km from Macapá, is inhabited by the descendants of African slaves who have maintained many of the customs of their ancestors. Analogous to the Bush Negroes of Suriname, but apparently the only such village in Brazil.

Local festivals

Marabaixo is the traditional music and dance of the state of Amapá, festival held 40 days after Easter.

Local information

● **Accommodation**

A1 *Novotel*, French-owned, Av Azarias Neto 17, on waterfront, T 223-1144, F 231-1115, small, 4-star, all rooms a/c, swimming pool rec; **A3** *Ekinox*, R Jovino Dinoá 1693, T/F 222-4379, central, a/c, clean, helpful, excellent restaurant, highly rec.

D *Amapaense Palace*, R Tiradentes 109, T 222-3366, F 222-0703, 2-star, a/c, cold showers, comfortable, clean; **D** *Santo Antônio*, Av Coriolano Jucá 485, T 222-0226, nr main square, very clean, fan, shower, good breakfast extra; **D** *Tropical*, Av Antônio Coelho de Carvalho 1399, 20 mins from centre, 1-star, T 223-4899, with a/c (cheaper without), rec.

E *Kamilla*, Av Padre JM Lombaerd, behind *Novotel* tennis courts, clean, friendly, with fan and bath; **E** *Meruno*, central, good value. The following are 10-mins' walk from port and from Praça São José (where bus from Porto Santana stops): **E** pp *Mara*, R São José 2390, with bath, a/c, TV, fridge, good, clean, breakfast; **E** *Mercúrio*, R Cândido Mendes, 1300 block (no sign), T 223-4123. Cheap, basic hotel above churrascaria at Av Cora de Carvalho e R Independencia.

● **Places to eat**

Kamilla, below hotel of same name, good buffet, pay by weight. Another buffet is *Kilo's*, Hamilton Silva 1398, T 223-1579, elegant, overpriced; *O Boscão*, Hamilton Silva 997, no sign, quite good; *O Paulistano*, Av Henrique Galúcio 412, a/c, good; *Churrascaria Tropeiro*, Av Pres Vargas 450; *Clip*, Av Duque de Caxias 848; *Pizza San Carlos*, Cândido Mendes 1199, good for lunch; *Lennon*, good pavement café, no meals, at R Gen Rondon esq IC Nunes. Excellent ice cream sold in Macapá, eg *Sorveteria Santa Helena*, Av Feliciano Coelho 1023, Bairro do Trem, excellent; *Sorveteria Macapá*, R São José

1664, closer to centre.

● **Banks & money changers**
Banco do Brasil, Av Independência 250, cash and TCs. Câmbios (cash only): *Lantur*, Cândido Mendes 1085, *Casa Francesa*, on same street, *Monopólio*, Av Isaac Alcoubre 80. The rates in Macapá are similar to other cities in northern Brazil. Both US$ and French francs can be exchanged here. Best to buy francs in Belém if heading for Guyane as câmbios in Macapá are reluctant to sell them and they are more expensive and hard to obtain at the border.

● **Embassies & consulates**
There is a French consular agent in Macapá, some distance from town (ask taxi drivers or at *Novotel*), but visas are not issued for non-Brazilians. Only French and Portuguese spoken.

● **Post & telecommunications**
Post Office: Praça da Bandeira.

● **Transport**
Local Car rentals: National, Av Independência 30, nr Praça Beira Rio, T 223-2799, at airport 231-4799. Localiza, Alameda Serrano, T 223-2799. **Locauto**, Av Pres Vargas 519, T 222-1011/1511.

Air Varig, office on R Cândido Mendes 1039, T 223-1755, flies to Belém, Iguaçu, Rio and São Paulo

Sea Shipping service: most ships now dock at Porto Santana, 30 km from Macapá (frequent buses US$0.55, shared taxis US$3.60 pp), however some smaller vessels still arrive at the pier in Macapá itself. This pier is also used when all of Porto Santana's dock space has been occupied by ore freighters.

To Belém, *Silja e Souza* of Souzamar, R São José S of cathedral, and *Almirante Solon* of Sanave (Serviço Amapaense de Navegação, Av Azárias Neto, Praça Beira Rio). Both ships operate twice a week (see **River Transport in Amazônia**, page 581). Purchase tickets from offices 2 days in advance. Also smaller boats.

There is also regular direct service to **Santarém**, not going via Belém.

Buses To Oiapoque: Estrela de Ouro has its office on the main square, in front of the cathedral; it leaves daily at 2000. Cattani, office on Nunes between São José and Cándido Mendes, leaves daily at 0630. Journey time about 12 hrs (dry season) with several rest stops, 14-24 hrs in rainy season. Both leave from opposite Polícia Técnica, 30 mins from centre, take bus 'Jardim' and get out at Polícia Técnica. Fare US$40. The Oiapoque bus does not go into Amapá or Calçoene and it is therefore difficult to break the trip at these places. One would have to walk several kilometres from town to the main highway to catch the northbound bus when it passes in the small hours of the morning. Bus fare to Amapá and Calçoene US$25, 7 hrs, daily at 0700.

Pickup **trucks** (office Av Pres Vargas between São José and Tiradentes, can reserve in advance) also run daily to various locations throughout the state of Amapá, crowded and dusty on narrow benches in the back, or pay more to ride in the cab. Despite posted schedules, they leave when full. To **Oiapoque** at 0800, 10-12 hrs, US$40 cab, US$25 in back. To **Lourenço** at 0900, to **Laranjal do Jari** at 1000.

Ibama office, R Hamilton Silva 1570, Santa Rita, CEP 68.900, Macapá, has details on the **Cabo Orange National Park** in the extreme N of the Territory, and the **Lago Piratuba Biological Reserve**, neither accessible by road.

NORTH OF MACAPÁ

The road N to the Guyane border (BR-156) has been improved and although still precarious in places, it is now open throughout the year with both bus and pickup truck service operating even in the wet season. At all times however, it is prudent to take food and water for the journey as services are scarce in this sparsely populated region. Gasoline and diesel (not alcohol) are available along the road but there are occasional shortages. Those driving should take extra fuel from Macapá.

North of Macapá the road passes through **Porto Grande** (*Recanto Ecológico Sonho Meu*, resort at Km 108, Macapá T 234-1298) and on to **Ferreira Gomes** on the shores of the Rio Araguari, where the pavement ends. Further on are the towns of **Amapá** (formerly the territorial capital; *D Tourist Hotel* and one other, clean, comfortable, one block from square towards docks, turn right, 2nd house on left) and **Calçoene** (**D** government-owned hotel by bus stop, expensive food in adjoining canteen; sleeping space advertized in a café on Oiapoque road, very cheap). North of Calçoene a road branches W to **Lourenço**, whose gold fields continue to produce even after various decades of prospecting.

FRONTIER WITH GUYANE

The main road continues N across the Rio Caciporé and on to the border with French

Guyane at **Oiapoque**, on the river of the same name. It is 90 km inland from Cabo Orange, Brazil's northernmost point on the Atlantic coast. 7 Km to the W is Clevelândia do Norte, a military outpost and the end of the road in Brazil.

Oiapoque is a remote town, with its share of contraband, illegal migration, and drug trafficking. It is also the gateway to gold fields in the interior of both Brazil and Guyane. Quite a rough place, and the visitor should be cautious, especially late at night. Prices here are at least double those of anywhere else in Brazil, but still substantially lower than in neighbouring Guyane. The **Saut Maripa** rapids can be visited, 20 mins upstream along the Oiapoque River.

● **Accommodation & places to eat** D *Government Hotel*, at E end of riverfront, now privately operated, refurbished, best in town, restaurant; **E** *Kayama*, on riverfront street above Taba office, with fan, 1 room has private bath, good. Another **F** next door, basic. **F** *Sonho Meu*, one street back from river, basic. *Restaurant Paladar Drinks*, one block up from river, very expensive. There are several cheap hotels (F) along the waterfront. They are often full of Brazilians waiting to cross to Guyane.

● **Exchange** It is possible to exchange US$ and *reais* to francs, but dollar rates are low. Visa users can withdraw *reais* at Bradesco, exchanging these to francs. Gold merchants, some shops, and one *câmbio* in the market will sell *reais* for US$ or French francs, but are reluctant to sell francs. Rates are even worse in St-Georges. Best to buy francs in Belém, or abroad.

● **Transport Buses** *Estrela de Ouro* leaves for Macapá from the waterfront, daily at 1000, 12 hrs (dry season), 14-24 hrs (wet season), US$40, also Cattani. Pickup **trucks** depart from the same area when full, US$40 in cab, US$25 in the back. **Sea** Occasional cargo vessels to Belém or Macapá (Porto Santana). **Crossing to Guyane**: motorized canoes cross to St-Georges de L'Oyapock, 10 mins downstream, F20 pp, slightly cheaper in *reais*, bargain. There is no vehicle ferry and no bridge. *Catraias* (decrepit canoes) carry illegal migrants for nighttime landing expensive, dangerous, definitely not rec. There is no road from St-Georges to Cayenne, you must fly or take a boat (details given on page 1635). While awaiting flights to Cayenne it is much cheaper to wait on the Brazilian side. Polícia Federal for Brazilian exit stamp is on the road to Calçoene, about 500 meters back from the river.

BELÉM TO MANAUS

A few hours up the broad river the region of the thousand islands is entered. The passage through this maze of islets is known as 'The Narrows'. The ship winds through 150 km of lanes of yellow flood with equatorial forest within 20 or 30m on both sides. In the Furo Grande the vessel rounds a hairpin bend almost touching the trees, bow and stern.

After the Narrows, the first point of special interest is formed by the curious flat-topped hills, on one of which stands the little stucco town of **Monte Alegre** (airport), an oasis in mid-forest. Monte Alegre has some simple hotels (E), offering lagoon cruises to see lilies, birds, pink dolphins; boat trips to ancient cave paintings; village visits (US$25-40 per day), rec guide lives next door to a small brown and white hotel near the end of terrace at E side of docks.

SANTARÉM

(*Pop* 265,105; *CEP* 68100; *DDD* 091) 2-3 days upstream on the southern bank, the city stands at the confluence of the Rio Tapajós with the Amazon, just half-way between Belém and Manaus. It was founded in 1661, and is the third largest town in the Brazilian Amazon. Nevertheless, it is a sleepy town with attractive colonial squares overlooking the waterfront. There is a movement for statehood for the Tapajós region, with Santarém as its capital. There is now a road southwards to Cuiabá (Mato Grosso), meeting the Transamazônica at Rurópolis (see page 581). Timber, bauxite and gold discoveries promoted very rapid growth. Although the gold is running out, the city is the jumping off point for gold prospectors in the Mato Grosso territories to the S.

Places of interest

The yellow Amazon water swirls alongside the green-blue Tapajós; the **meeting of the waters**, in front of the market square, is nearly as impressive as that of the Negro and Solimões near Manaus. A small **museum** was opened in Jan 1993 in the old city hall on the waterfront, downriver from where the boats dock. It has a collection of ancient Tapajós ceramics, as well as various 19th century artefacts and publications. The unloading of the fish catch between 0500 and 0700 on the waterfront is an interesting scene. There are good beaches nearby on the Rio Tapajós.

Excursions

To **Alter do Chão**, a friendly village amid Amazonian vegetation on the Rio Tapajós, at the outlet of Lago Verde; hotel (D), comfortable; *Pousada* near the church, quiet, clean; luxury hotel to be built shortly; *Restaurant Mongote*, Praça 7 de Setembro, good fresh fish, huge portions; *Lago Verde*, try *caldeirada de tucunaré*; good swimming in the Tapajós from the beautiful, clean beach. From Santarém: bus stop on the square opposite Mercado Modelo, very close to *Hotel Plaza*, US$0.70, about 1 hr, timetable at hotel reception desk.

To **Porto Novo**: by 0800 (0930 on Sun) bus, 3 hrs into the jungle by a lake, bus returns 0500 next morning and at 1230 Sun, Tues, Wed (you can sleep in it). Interesting wildlife on the lake; canoes can be hired.

Local information
● Accommodation
A *Tropical*, Av Mendonça Furtado 4120, T 522-1533, F 522-2631, swimming pool (being renovated in early 1996), friendly, cheaper rooms with no view or fridge, reserved for business travellers.

B *Brasil Grande Hotel*, Trav 15 de Agosto 213, T 522-5660, clean, family-run, with restaurant; **B** *Santarém Palace*, close to city centre, Rui Barbosa 726, T 522-5285, good, with bath and TV.

C *Central Plaza*, Praça Rodrigues dos Santos 877, with bath and fan, run-down, friendly; **C** *City*, Trav Francisco Correia 200, T 522-4719, with bath, a/c, TV, radio, frigobar, good, will collect from airport.

D *Brasil*, Travessa dos Mártires, 30, inc breakfast, good meals served, clean, good service, English spoken, owner plays chess; **D** *Greenville*, Av Adriano Pimenal 44, T 522-5820, good bathrm facilities and balcony view across the river.

E *Horizonte*, Travessa Lemos 737, clean.

● Places to eat
Mascotinho bar/pizzeria, on riverfront, popular, good view; *Storil*, Travessa Turiano Meira, 2 blocks from Rui Barbosa, good fish, live music,

takes credit cards; *Ritz*, Praça do Pescador, good; *Lanchonete Luci*, Praça do Pescador, good juices and pastries; *Sombra do Jambeiro*, Trav 15 de Novembro, Norwegian-owned bar and lanchonete, excellent meals.

● Banks & money changers
It is very difficult to change dollars (impossible to change TCs anywhere), try **Farmácia Java**, opp *Coruá-Una Turismo*, 15 de Novembro, or **Ouro Minas**, a gold dealer, Travessa dos Martires, close to Banco do Brasil on Av Rui Barbosa (next to *Santarém Palace Hotel*); also try travel agencies. Cash withdrawals on Visa at **Banco do Brasil**.

● Hospitals & medical services
Dr Ihsan Youssef Simaan, T 522-3886/3982, speaks English and Spanish.

● Tour companies & travel agents
Gil Serique, Praça do Pescador 131, T 522-5174, English-speaking guide, rec. **Coruá-Una Turismo**, 15 de Novembro 185-C, T 522-6303/7421 offers various tours, Pierre d'Arcy speaks French, rec. **Tapam Turismo**, Travessa 15 de Agosto, 127 A, T 522 3037/1946/2334, rec. **Amazon Tour**, Travessa Turiano Meira, 1084, T 522 1098, the owner Steve Alexander is a very friendly, helpful man who can give you lots of hints what to do. He also organizes excursions for groups to remote areas which are quite expensive, rec. **Santarém Turismo**, in *Hotel Tropical* (above), owned by Perpétua and Jean-Pierre Schwarz (speaks French), friendly, helpful, also quite expensive group tours (for a group of 5 US$50/day pp), rec.

● Transport
Air 15 km from town. Internal flights only. To Manaus with Varig US$129. To São Paulo via Manaus (stop over possible) with Varig US$357 (11-day advance purchase), daily. Varig office, R Siqueira Campos, block between Travessas 15 de Agosto and 15 de Novembre. Buses to centre or waterfront. From centre bus leaves in front of cinema in Rui Barbosa every 80 mins from 0550 to 1910, or taxis (US$12 to waterfront). The hotels *Tropical* and *New City* have free buses for guests; you may be able to take these.

Buses Rodoviária is on the outskirts, take 'Rodagem' bus from the waterfront near the market, US$0.25. Santarém to **Itaituba**, 8 hrs, US$10.25; there connecting service E to **Marabá** on the River Tocantins, 28 hrs (if lucky; can be 60 hrs, or even 6 days), US$48, with Transbrasiliana. Also to **Imperatriz**, 46 hrs, US$54, office on Av Getúlio Vargas and at rodoviária. Enquire at rodoviária for other destinations. (Beware of vehicles that offer a lift, which frequently turn out to be taxis.) Road travel during the rainy season is always difficult, often impossible.

Shipping services: to Manaus, Belém, Macapá, Itaituba, and intermediate ports (see **River Transport in Amazônia**, page 581). Most boats, in particular the smaller ones, dock at the waterfront by the centre of town, but at times they may dock at the Cais do Porto, 4 km W, take 'Circular' or 'Circular Externo' bus. Check both places for departures to your destination. Also local service to Obidós, Oriximiná, Alenquer, and Monte Alegre (US$10, 5-8 hrs).

BELTERRA AND HENRY FORD

37 km S from Santarém on a dirt road is **Belterra** (*pop* about 8,000), where Henry Ford established one of his rubber plantations, in the highlands overlooking the Rio Tapajós. Ford built a well laid-out new town; the houses resemble the cottages of Michigan summer resorts. Many of the newer houses follow the white paint with green trim style. The town centre has a large central plaza that includes a band stand, the church of Santo Antônio (circa 1951), a Baptist church and a large educational and sports complex. A major hospital, which at one time was staffed by physicians from North America, is now closed. Ford's project was unsuccessful: now the rubber forest is in bad condition. (**E** *Hotel Seringueira*, with about 8 rooms and pleasant restaurant).

Fordlândia was the Ford Motor Company's first rubber plantation, founded in 1926; it is a friendly town since there are few visitors. *Hotel Zebu*, in old Vila Americana (turn right from dock, then left up the hill); one restaurant, two bars and three shops on town square. There is a little pebble beach N of the town. Km 83, South of Santarém on BR 163, there is a section of the **Floresta Nacional do Tapajós** which has a vehicle track running due W through it; beautiful rainforest which can be entered with permission from IBAMA if accompanied by one of their guides. It is well worth a visit if only to see the butterflies.

• **Transport** Bus from Santarém to Belterra (from unmarked *Café Amazonas*, Travessa Moraes Sarmento between Rui Barbosa and São Sebastião), 1000 and 1230, Mon-Sat, return 1300 and 1530, US$2, about 2 hrs. **NB**: 1 hr time difference between Santarém and Belterra so if you take the 1230 bus you'll miss the 1530

return bus. If driving, take Av Santarém-Cuiabá out of town, which is paved for 8 km. At Km 37 is a small Shell station; fork right and stop at the guardhouse; it's 15 km into town, following the electricity cables. Boats from Santarém to Itaituba may stop at Fordlândia if you ask (leave Santarém 1800, arrive 0500-0600, US$12 for 1st class hammock space); ask the captain to stop for you on return journey, about 2300. Boats may stop for Belterra, but it's a walk of several kilometres from the river to town.

Óbidos (*Pop* 42,195), 110 km up-river from Santarém, is a picturesque and clean city with many beautiful, tiled colonial buildings. It is located at the narrowest and deepest point on the river. For many kilometres little is seen except the wall of the great Amazonian forest. Small airport.

MANAUS

The next city upstream, Manaus was at one time an isolated urban island in the jungle. It is the collecting-point for the produce of a vast area which includes parts of Peru, Bolivia and Colombia. There is superb swimming in the natural pools and under falls of clear water in the little streams which rush through the woods, but take locals' advice on swimming in the river; electric eels and various other kinds of unpleasant fish, apart from the notorious *piranhas*, abound and industrial pollution of the river is growing.

Until recently Manaus' only communications were by river and air. A road SW to Porto Velho, which is already connected with the main Brazilian road system, has been completed, but officially closed since 1990. Another, not yet fully paved, has been built due N to Boa Vista, from where other roads already reach the Venezuelan and Guyanese frontiers.

Manaus (*pop* 1,010,560; *CEP* 69000; *DDD* 092) is the capital of the State of Amazonas, the largest in Brazil (1.6 million sq km), which has a population of 2.1 million. Though 1,600 km from the sea, it is only 32m above sea-level. The average temperature is 27°C. The city sprawls over a series of eroded and gently sloping hills divided by numerous creeks (*igarapés*).

Manaus is building fast; 20-storey

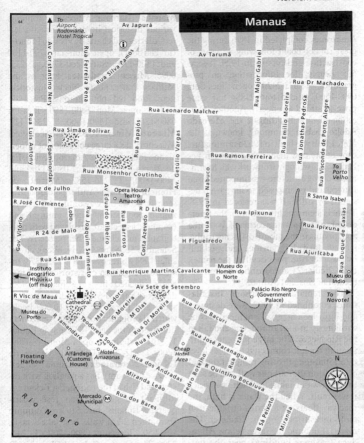

Manaus

modern buildings are rising above the traditional flat, red-tiled roofs. It was the first city in South America to instal trams, but they have now been replaced by buses. A rather heavy-handed clean-up campaign between 1989 and 1993 brought major changes to the Zona Franca, the old city and the port area: better public sanitation; the eviction of street vendors (*camelos*) and beggars; the enforcement of building and hygienic standards in cheaper hotels; the completion of a concrete retaining wall from behind the market to Montecristi, improving the waterfront; opening one of the floating docks to regional shipping.

Places of interest

Dominating the centre is a **Cathedral** built in simple Jesuit style on a hillock; nothing distinguished inside or out. Nearby is the main shopping and business area, the tree-lined Av Eduardo Ribeiro; crossing it is Av Sete de Setembro, bordered by ficus trees. The area between Av Sete de Setembro and the rear of *Hotel Amazonas* is now reserved to pedestrians. There is a modern air-conditioned theatre.

The main attractions are the **Botanic**

Gardens, the well stocked public library, and the legendary Opera House, the **Teatro Amazonas**, completed in 1896 during the great rubber boom following 17 years of construction and rebuilt in 1929. It seats 685 people; for information on programmes, T 622-2420 (open Tues-Sun, 0900-1500, guided tour US$4 but same price to attend a concert). Another interesting historic building is the **Mercado Adolfo Lisboa**, commonly known as the Mercado. It was built in 1902 as a miniature copy of the now demolished Parisian Les Halles. The wrought ironwork which forms much of the structure was imported from Europe and is supposed to have been designed by Eiffel. It was restored in 1978. There is a curious little church, the **Igreja do Pobre Diabo**, at the corner of Avs Borba and Ipixuna in the suburb of Cachoeirinha; it is only 4m wide by 5m long, and was built by a worker (the 'poor devil' of the name); take Circular 7 Cachoeirinha bus from cathedral to Hospital Militar.

The remarkable **harbour installations**, completed in 1902, were designed and built by a Scottish engineer to cope with the up to 14m annual rise and fall of the Rio Negro. The large passenger ship floating dock is connected to street level by a 150m-long floating ramp, at the end of which, on the harbour wall, can be seen the high water mark for each year since it was built. When the water is high, the roadway floats on a series of large iron tanks measuring 2½m in diameter. The material to build the large yellow **Alfândega** (customs building) near the harbour was brought block by block from Scotland as ballast. Tourists can visit the docks 0730-2000 daily.

Museums

Museu do Índio (Indian Museum), kept by the Salesian missionaries: this interesting museum's collection includes handicrafts, ceramics, clothing, utensils and ritual objects from the various Indian tribes of the upper Rio Negro, R Duque de Caxias (nr Av 7 Setembro); excellent craft shop, rec; open Mon-Fri 0800-1200 and 1400-1700, Sat 0800-1130, closed Sun, T 234-1422, US$3; **Museu do Porto de Manaus** (Harbour Museum), contains various historical items, documents, letters, diaries and charts, R Vivaldo Lima 61 (nr Harbour); open Mon-Sat 0700-1100 and 1300-1700, Sun 1200-1700, T 232-0096; **Museu Tiradentes**, kept by the Military Police, holds selected historical items and old photographs, Praça da Polícia; open Mon 1400-1800, Tues-Fri 0800-1200 and 1400-1800, T 234-7422; **Museu de Minerais e Rochas** (Geological Museum) has a large collection of minerals and rocks from the Amazon region, Est do Aleixo 2150; Mon-Fri 0800-1200 and 1400-1800, T 236-1582; **Museu do Homem do Norte** (Anthropological Museum) reviews the way of life of the Amazonian population; social, cultural and economic aspects are displayed with photographs, models and other pieces, Av 7 de Setembro 1385 (nr Av J Nabuco); closed since 1994 for renovation, T 232-5373; **Instituto Geográfico e Histórico do Amazonas**, located in a fascinating older district of central Manaus, houses a museum and library of over 10,000 books which thoroughly document Amazonian life through the ages, R Bernardo Ramos 117 (nr Prefeitura); open Mon-Fri 0800-1200, T 232-7077, US$0.20; **Museu de Ciências Naturais da Amazônia** (Natural Science Museum), has a pavilion with insects and fish of the region, Est Belém s/n (difficult to get to, 'São José-Acoariquarape/Tropolis' bus 519 to Conjunto Petro, then 2 km walk, best take a taxi), US$3.50, Tues-Sun 0900-1700, T 244-2799. The **Centro Cultural Chaminé**, R Isabel, near R Q Bocaiuva bridge, has occasional art exhibitions mounted in a restored water treatment works, built by the British in 1896.

Jardim Botânico 'Chico Mendes' (Horto Municipal). The botanical gardens contain a collection of plants from the Amazon region. Unfortunately the plants are not well named. Av André Araujo s/n (Buses 'Aleixo', 'Coroado'). Daily 0800-1200 and 1400-1700.

Zoo Run by CIGS, the Brazilian Army Unit specializing in jungle survival. About 300 Amazonian animals are kept in the Gardens (reported run-down with small cages). Est Ponta Negra 750 (no sign). Bus 120 or 207 (marked 'Ponta Negra'), US$0.45, every 30 mins from R Tamandaré, opp cathedral in centre, alight 400m past the 1st Jungle Infantry Barracks (a big white building), look for the sentries. Open 0800-1700. Entrance for foreigners, US$0.75, free on Sun. Small zoo also at *Hotel Tropical*, see below. **Instituto Nacional de Pesquisas Amazonas** (INPA), Estrada de Aleixo, at Km 3, not far from the Natural Science Museum (any bus to Aleixo), has named trees and manatees (best seen Wed and Fri at 0830 when water is changed), caimans and giant otters; worth a visit and good for birdwatchers.

Excursions

Meeting of the waters About 15 km from Manaus is the confluence of the Solimões (Amazon) and the Rio Negro, which is itself some 8 km wide. Here you can see the meeting of the blue-black water of the Rio Negro with the yellow-brown Solimões flood; the two rivers run side by side for about 6 km without their waters mingling. Tourist agencies run boat trips to this spot (US$50). The simplest way to see the waters meeting is to take a taxi or No 617 'Vila Buriti' bus to the Careiro ferry dock, and take the car ferry across. The ferry goes at 0700, returning 0900 and 1500, returning 1830 (approx). You can also take small private launches across, 40 mins journey, about US$12/seat, ask for the engine to be shut off at the confluence, you should see dolphins especially in the early morning. Alternatively, ask in the dock area for boats which may be going to the confluence, or hire a motorized canoe from near the market (US$15 approx; allow 3-4 hrs to experience the meeting properly). A 2-km walk along the Porto Velho road from the Careiro ferry terminal will lead to a point from which Victoria Regia water lilies can be seen in April-Sept in ponds, some way from the road. If you continue over the Capitari bridge, you reach unspoilt jungle. There are several small restaurants on the S bank in Careiro, where the road SW to Porto Velho and the S begins.

Manacapura A typical Amazon town, 84 km on AM-070 by bus, 4 daily, US$5, 2 hrs including ferry crossing. A small market town on the Solimões W of Manaus, with three basic hotels, *Rio Branco*, clean, friendly, and *Il Maccarone* pizzeria, Av Eduardo Ribeiro 1000, with its friendly Italian owner Mário.

Araçá Another village one can visit, a 3-hr bus ride from Rodoviária in the direction of Castanho; the journey includes a ferry crossing at the confluence of the Negro and Solimões (fare to Araçá US$0.85, bus leaves 0600 and 1100). The village is on the banks of the Rio Mamori; canoes can be hired for US$5 for a day (night trips also possible) and you may be able to sling your hammock in a private house. Plenty of wildlife close at hand. 3 buses a day return to Manaus.

Local holidays

6 Jan (Epiphany); Ash Wednesday, half-day; Maundy Thursday; 24 June (St John); 14 July; 5 Sept; 30 Oct; 1 Nov, All Saints Day, half-day; Christmas Eve; New Year's Eve, half-day.

14 Jan: **Anniversary of Praça 14 de Janeiro**, commemorates the founding of the bairro; Samba Schools, street market, and fun fair. Feb: **Carnival** dates vary – 5 days of Carnival, culminating in the parade of the Samba Schools (see below). 3rd week in April: **Week of the Indians**, Indian handicraft, talks, photographic exhibition, various localities. First fortnight of June: **Festival Marquesiano**, 3 days of festival, regional and Afro-Brazilian dancing, Arabian, Russian and European folklore, held at the Campo da Amizade, São Raimundo; **Festival Folclórico do Amazonas**, second fortnight, Praça Francisco Pereira da Silva, Bola da Suframa. Second fortnight of Aug: this is reported to be second only to Carnival. 10 Sept: **Travessia Almirante Tamandaré**, swimming race across the Rio Negro (8,500m) leaving from Praia da Ponta Negra; also in Sept: **Festival de Verão do Parque Dez**, second fortnight, summer festival with music, fashion shows, beauty contests, local foods, etc, Centro Social Urbano do Parque Dez; **Festival da Bondade**, last week, stalls from neighbouring states

and countries offering food, handicrafts, music and dancing, SESI, Est do Aleixo Km 5. Nov: **Festival Universitário de Cultura** (entire month) with music, art and book exhibition, organized by the students on the University Campus. 8 Dec: **Processão de Nossa Senhora da Conceição**, from the Igreja Matriz through the city centre and returning to Igreja Matriz for a solemn mass.

Carnival in Manaus

Carnival in Manaus is rapidly becoming one of Brazil's most famous. It is a carnival of samba, with spectacular parades in a sambadrome modelled on Rio's, but with 3 times the capacity. Brazil's most famous performers appear at the Manaus carnival. Tourists may purchase grandstand seats, but admission at ground level is free, with every samba school member guaranteed entrance. This may make it rather unsafe for those carrying valuables, but ensures a memorable occasion with plenty of dancing.

NB Manaus time is 1 hr behind Brazilian standard time (2 hrs behind during Oct-Mar when the rest of Brazil is on summer time).

Local information

Crime Since 1991, Manaus has suffered a more serious economic downturn than the rest of Brazil. As lower national customs duties have undermined the Zona Franca, leading to increased unemployment, many people are seeking greener pastures, and there has been a substantial rise in crime and prostitution. The tourist industry continues to flourish, making the visitor a common target. One should take appropriate precautions, but also bear in mind that Manaus is still a good deal safer than the big cities of southern Brazil (see **Information for visitors**).

● **Accommodation**

Hotel prices

L1	over US$200	L2	US$151-200
L3	US$101-150	A1	US$81-100
A2	US$61-80	A3	US$46-60
B	US$31-45	C	US$21-30
D	US$12-20	E	US$7-11
F	US$4-6	G	up to US$3

10% tax and service must be added to bills. There is a hotel booking service at the airport.

The Zona Franca is reported to be safer than the area around Av Joaquim Nabuco.

L1-L2 *Tropical*, Praia de Ponta Negra, T 658-5000, F 658-5026, a lavish, 5-star Varig hotel 20 km outside the city (taxi to centre, US$20), very expensive, 30% discount with a Varig air pass, *Restaurant Tarumã* open for dinner only, *churrascaria* by pool, 24-hr coffee shop, open to well-dressed non-residents, take minibus from R José Paranaguá in front of Petrobras building esq Dr Moreira, US$6 return, 0830, 0930, 1130 to Hotel, 1200, 1400, 1500, 1800 to town, or take Ponta Negra bus, US$0.35, then walk. Hotel collects guests from the airport. It is rarely full, except in Jan-February. Parkland setting, wave pools, small zoo with animals in small cages, beach with new dock, departure point for many river cruises, glossy nightclub Thur-Sat, tennis. Exchange at official rate only. Also away from centre, **L2** *Novotel*, Av Mandii 4 in the Industrial Area, T 237-1211, F 237-1094, 4-star, luxurious, T 663-1213/3323, F 611-3721, pool, US$1.75 taxi ride from centre, less good than *Tropical*; **A2** *Da Vinci*, R Belo Horizonte 240, 3 km from centre, T 663-1213/3323, F 611-3721, pool, friendly service.

Central hotels: L3 *Best Western*, Marcílio Dias 217/225, T 622-2844, F 233-5984, some rooms a/c, expensive for what is offered, with good breakfast, good service; has a cheaper annex; **L3** *Amazonas*, Praça Adalberto Vale, T 622-2233, F 622-2064, 4-star, the ground floor is not rec, but rooms are reasonable, hot water, a/c; opp is **A1** *Ana Cassia Palace*, expensive, R dos Andradas 14, T 622-3637, F 622-4812; **L3** *Imperial*, Av Pres Vargas 227, T 622-3112, F 622-1762. A highly rec Aparthotel is **L3** *St Paul*, R Ramos Ferreira 1115, T 622-2131/36, F 622-2137, best in town, suites with bath, kitchen, living room, has pool, gym and sauna. **A2** *Mônaco*, R Silva Ramos 20, T 622-3446, F 622-3637, 3-star, rooms have good view, pleasant (some rooms noisy), rooftop restaurant/bar, delicious breakfast; **C** *Premier*, Av Eduardo Ribeiro 124, T 234-0061, some rooms with TV and fridge, friendly, good value; **C** *Sulista*, R Pedro Botelho, with bath, a/c, breakfast, safe, with friendly restaurant, good value, rec; **D** *Janelas Verdes*, Leovegildo Coelho 216, T 233-1222, a/c, shower, TV, small, quiet (except Sun), safe, rec; **D** *Dona Joana*, R dos Andradas 553, T 233-7553, a/c, clean, good value, insecure; **D** *Especial*, Av Pres Vargas 198, T 234-0389, a/c, fridge, TV, bath, inc breakfast; **D** *Fortaleza*, R dos Bares 238, with bath, a/c, fridge, reasonable, rec, cheaper without a/c, also dormitory (F), next door are *Allison* and *Asa Branca*, both a little cheaper; **D** *Neide*, opp rodoviária, with fan, clean, rec; **D** *Hospedária*

Turístico 10 de Julho, Dez de Julio 679, T 232 6280, a/c, clean, rec; **D** *Sun*, R Lima Bacuri 67B, centre, T 233-5668; **E** *Cheap*, R dos Andrades, friendly, clean, safe; **E** *Jangada*, R dos Andrades 473, basic, friendly, breakfast, cooking facilities, cheap, rec.

In R G Moreira (Zona Franca): **B** *Internacional*, No 168, T 234-1315, F 234-5396, 2-star, a/c, friendly, central, coffee most of the day, good exchange rates; **B** *Rey Salomão*, No 119, T 234-7374, clean, breakfast; **B** *Central*, No 202, T 232-7887, some a/c, quiet; **B** *Nacional*, No 59, T 233-0537, with bath, fridge, a/c; **B** *Rio Mar*, No 325, T 234-7409, inc breakfast and bath, poor service, central.

In Av Joaquim Nabuco (by no means a safe area): **E** *Arteiro*, No 471, T 622-1343, nr corner with R Lima Bacuri, with a/c or fan, clean, large rooms with bath; **E** *Aurora*, No 120, F 234-5121, with bath, a/c, friendly, clean, noisy TV in front rooms, good, simple breakfast; **E** *Luz* and **E** *Iguaçu*, T 232-9339 (Nos 779 and 711 respectively) are better than most on this street: the former is singles only above a gym, clean, breakfast inc at *Iguaçu*; **E** *Manauara*, No 129, with bath, a/c, fridge, coffee all day, friendly, has TV; **E** *Ideal*, No 491, a/c, F with fan, bath, no windows; **E** *Pensão Sulista*, No 347, breakfast, clean, rec; **E** *Rio Branco*, No 484, T 233-4019, rec, avoid damp rooms on ground floor, clean, safe, laundry facilities, a/c, popular, friendly, highly rec; **E** *Jangada*, No 473, cooking allowed, laundry facilities, very basic, fan, without bath. Other cheaper places in same area; **E** *Turista*, R Miranda Leão 356, basic; **E** *Hospedaria Olinda*, R L Coelho y J Paranaguá, rec, has soccer evenings.

NB When taking a taxi from the airport, insist on being taken to the hotel of your choice, and not to the one which pays the driver commission.

10 km E of the city is the small but growing town of **Iranduba**, cheaper than Manaus and with a good beach. **D** *Hotel Verdes Matas*, T 367-1133, rec. Easy bus ride from Manaus, includes ferry crossing.

Camping: there are no campsites in or nr Manaus; it is difficult to find a good, safe place to camp wild.

● **Places to eat**

Novotel serves a rec *feijoada completa* on Sat; *Tropical Hotel*, see above; *Canto da Peixada*, R Emilio Moreira 1677 (Pça 14), T 234-3021, superb fish dishes, lively atmosphere, unpretentious, close to centre; *La Barca*, R Recife 684, wide variety of fish dishes, classy, popular, often has live music; *São Francisco*, Blvd Rio Negro 195, 30 mins' walk from centre (or bus 705), in Educandos suburb, good fish, huge portions, highly rec; *Panorama* next door, No 199, T 624-4626, also good for fish, balcony overlooking river, cheap, highly rec.

Caçarola, R Maués 188, Cachoerinha, T 233-3021, very good local fish dishes (take a taxi); Japanese at *Miako*, R São Luís 230, also *Suzuran*, Blvd Álvaro Maia 1683, Adrianópolis, good, closed Tues, take taxi; *Búfalo*, churrascaria, Joaquim Nabuco 628, all you can eat (high quality); *Fiorentina* R José Paranaguá 44 (Praça da Polícia), Italian, very good, half price on Sun; *Esquina do Lanche*, Paranaguá e Dr Moreiro, good, cheap; *Fiorella*, R Pará 640, good Italian; *Olinda*, Pedro Botelho 93, nr Miranda Leão, good regional dishes, *caldeirada* rec; *Frangolandia*, Joaquim Nabuco nr 7 de Setembro, good grill. *Chapaty*, Saldanho Marinho 429B; also R Costa Azevedo 105, vegetarian, closed pm. *Mandarim*, Av Eduardo Ribeiro 650, Chinese, all you can eat lunches US$5, closed Sun; *Schnaps bar and restaurant*, R Recife 1005, Casa 17-A, typical German, friendly, evenings only, closed Sun; *Skina dos Sucos*, E Ribeiro e 24 de Maio, rec for juices; pizzeria next door also good; *Casa do Guaraná*, R Marcilio Dias, marvellous juices mixed with *guaraná*; *Casa dos Sucos*, 7 de Setembro between Joaquim Nabuco and G Vargas, regional fruit juices and snacks; *Maté Amargo*, R Saldanha Marinho 603, good buffet, all you can eat; *Veneza*, Av Getúlio Vargas 570, good Sat *feijoada*; *Floresta*, R dos Andradas 335, friendly, English-speaking, good vegetables; *Jangada Bar*, opp *Hotel Amazonas*, good for snacks; good, but expensive snacks in *Hotel Amazonas* itself; *Alemã*, cafeteria, R José Paranaguá/Praça da Polícia, good for juices, sandwiches; *Sorveteria Glacial*, Getúlio Vargas 161 and other locations, highly rec for ice cream. *Restaurante Natalia*, Av Epaminondas s/n, downtown, with garden, has Pagode music and dancing on Fri nights. Many restaurants close on Sun nights and Mon. City authorities grade restaurants for cleanliness: look for A and B. Good juice bars along Av Joaquim Nabuco, try *cupuaçu*.

The fishing catch is brought to the waterfront between 2300 0100, including the giant *pirarucu*. Good fruit and vegetable market by the port.

● **Banks & money changers**

Banco do Brasil, R Marechal Deodoro (5th floor) and Airport changes dollars cash, 8% commission, Visa withdrawals at Pça Dom Pedro II (in front of docks), efficient; many local banks, open 0900-1600. Most offices shut afternoons; foreign exchange operations 0900-1200 only, or close even as early as 1100. **Banco Meridional**, 7 de Setembro 691 (Mastercard). Thomas Cook cheques changed by **Banespa** (good rates, cheques and cash). **Bamerindus**, R Marcilio Dias 196, TCs only, good rates, fast and friendly service; **Banco Amazonas**, R Henrique Martins Cavalcante, good rates; **Credicard**, Av Getúlio Vargas 222 for Mastercard and Diner's cash advances. **American Express** for money transactions and mail, Selvatur, Praça Adalberto Valve, T 622-2577, adjacent to *Hotel Amazonas*. Cash at main hotels; Sr Lima, R Quintino Bocaiúva 189, Sala 34; *Câmbio Cortez*, 7 de Setembro e Getúlio Vargas, converts TCs into US$ cash at 3-5% commission. It is not safe to change money on the streets.

● **Electric current**

110 volts AC; some hotels 220 volts AC, 60 cycles.

● **Embassies & consulates**

Most open am only. **Peruvian**, Conjunto Aristocratais, Chapada, R A, Casa 19 (T 656-3267, open 0800-1400). **Colombian**, R Dona Libânia 62, nr opera house, T 234-6777, please note that apparently a Colombian tourist card can be obtained at the border. We advise double-checking. **Venezuelan**, R Ferreira Pena 179, Cep 60,010,140, T 233 6004, F 233 0481, 0800-1400; everyone entering Venezuela overland needs a visa, the requirements are: 1 passport photo, an onward ticket and a yellow fever certificate (check with a Venezuelan consulate in advance for changes to these regulations). **Bolivian**, the consulate is now apparently run from a restaurant, *Los Palmas*, R Rio Jauari.

British, Eduardo Ribeiro 520, Sala 1202, T 622-3879. **United States**, Geral Recife 1901, T 234 4546 (office hours) and 232 1611 (outside office hours); will supply letters of introduction for US citizens. **Spain**, R Monsenhor Coutinho, T 234-0842; **Dutch**, R M Leão 41, T 234-8719/223-6874; **Austria**, Av Eduardo Ribeiro 500, 1st floor; **Italy**, R Belo Horizonte 240, T 611-4877; **Japanese**, R Ferreira Pena 92, T 234-2521; **Danish**, R M Leão 45, T 622-1356, also handles **Norway**; **Finnish**, T 234-5084; **Belgium**, 13 qd D conj Murici, T 236-1452; **Portugal**, R Terezina 193, T 234-5777.

● **Entertainment**

For *Teatro Amazonas*, see above. *Spectrum*, R Lobo D'Almada 322, very young. Cachoeirinha has a number of bars offering music and dancing, liveliest at weekends. The *Tropical Hotel*'s nightclub attracts Manaus's wealthy citizens on Thur-Sat, as does its bingo club; nearby Ponta Negra beach becomes extremely lively late on weekend nights and during holidays; *Kalamazon Night Club*, Km 12 on Torquato Tapajós road, T 651-2797, Wed-Sat, all kinds of music, disco; *Studio 5* disco, R Contorno, Distrito Industrial, T 237-8333; *Superstar*, next to the rodoviária; *Orvalho da Noite*, R Santa Isabel 1000; *Nostalgia Clube*, R Ajuricaba 800; *Clube de Samba*, R Manicoré.

Cinema: 6 screens at the new Amazonas shopping centre, bus Cidade Nova 5, or 204, 207, 208, 307. Most foreign films are shown with original soundtrack and Portuguese sub-titles. Afternoon performances are rec as long queues often form in the evenings.

● **Hospitals & medical services**

Hospital of tropical medicine, Av Pedro Teixeira (D Pedro I), T 238-1711, treatment free, some doctors speak a little English. Take 'Dom Pedro' bus from rodoviária, about a 20-min ride.

● **Post & telecommunications**

Post Office: main office including poste restante in Marechal Deodoro. On the first floor is the philatelic counter where stamps are sold, avoiding the long queues downstairs. Staff don't speak English but are used to dealing with tourists. For airfreight and shipping, Alfândega, Av Marones Santa Cruz (corner of Mal Deodoro), Sala 106. For airfreight and seamail, Correio Internacional, R Monsenhor Coutinho e Av Eduardo Ribeiro (bring your own packaging). **UPS** office, T 232-9849 (Custódio).

Telephone: TeleAmazon, R Guilherme Moreira, 326 e 7 de Setembro; Av Getúlio Vargas, 950 e R Leo Malcher.

● **Shopping**

Bookshop: *Livraria Nacional*, R 24 de Maio, stocks some French books, the *Livraria Brasília* has some English books.

Markets and souvenirs: go to the *Mercado Adolfo Lisboa* (see above) early in the morning when it is full of good quality regional produce, food and handicrafts; look out for *guaraná* powder or sticks, scales of *pirarucu* fish (used for manicure), and its tongue used for rasping *guaraná* (open daily 0500-1800). In Praça da Saudade, R Ramos Ferreira, there is a Sun *Festa de Arte* from 1700; try prawns and calaloo dipped in *tacaca* sauce. In the Praça do Congresso, Av E Ribeiro, there is a very good Sun craftmarket. See the two markets nr the docks, best in the early morning. The *Central Artesanato*, R Recife s/n, nr Detran, has local craft work. *Casa de Beija-Flor*, in the *Hotel Tropical*, good. *Selva Amazônica*, Mercado Municipal, for wood carvings and bark fabric. Ponta Negra beach boasts a small 'hippy' market, very lively at weekends; for hammocks go to R dos Andrades where there are many shops. In R Duque de Caxias is a rubber factory open to the public. Since Manaus is a free port, the whole area a few blocks off the river front is full of electronics shops. Note that all shops close at 1400 on Sat and all day Sun.

Photographic: highly rec for camera repairs: *Oficina Kawasky*, R Floriano Peixoto; film processing at *Studio Universal*, R 24 de Mai 146, cheap, good quality.

● **Sports**

For **swimming**, go to Ponta Negra beach by Soltur bus for US$0.35, though beach virtually disappears beneath the water in April-August. The whole area has been remodelled with a new sidewalk and snack bars; popular by day and at night with outdoor concerts and samba in the summer season. Good swimming at Bolívar Falls in the Rio Tarumã, where lunch is available, shade, it is crowded at weekends; take Tarumã bus from R Tamandaré or R Frei J dos Inocentes, 30 mins, US$0.35 (very few on weekdays), getting off at the police checkpoint on the road to Itacoatiara.

Cycling Bicycle repairs: 3 shops on R Com Clementino, nr Av Alvaro Maia.

● **Tour companies & travel agents**

Agencia Selvatur Ltda, Praça Adalberto Vale s/n, T 622-2577. *Tucumaré Turismo*, R Henrique Martins, T 234-5071, will give information and make reservations.

● **Tourist offices**

Emamtur, Praça 24 de Outubro, R Tarumã 379 helpful, 0730-1330, weekdays only, at Teatro Amazonas, corner of Eduardo Ribeiro, and airport. Town map from *Hotel Amazonas* or from Amazon Explorers. *Guide Book of Manaus*, US$3, available from *Hotel Amazonas* and other places, in English, useful. *A Notícia*, newspaper, lists local entertainments and events. *Mananara Guia*, a very detailed Manaus street index and guide, is available from news kiosks, US$18.

● **Useful addresses**

Police: take bus from *Hotel Amazonas* to Kissia Dom Pedro for Polícia Federal post, people in shorts not admitted.

● **Transport**

Air International flights: Varig to Miami and Mexico City once a week each; LAB to La Paz, Santa Cruz, Miami and Caracas. Viasa to Caracas twice a week. Vasp twice a week to Aruba. To the Guyanas, connection must be made in Belém. Transbrasil to Buenos Aires daily (2-3 stops); also once a week to Amsterdam and Vienna. Make reservations as early as possible, flights may be full. Do not rely on travel agency waiting lists; go to the airport 15 hrs early and get on the airport waiting list. Varig, M Dias 284, T 622-3161, English spoken, helpful; LAB, T 232-7701; Vasp, T 622-1141/3470; Transbrasil, T 622-3738.

Internal flights: There are frequent internal flights with Varig, Vasp and Transbrasil. The most frequent routes are Rio-São Paulo, Rio-Brasília, São Paulo-Brasília and the NE Coast milk run Santerém-Belém-São Luís-Fortaleza-Recife. Varig flies to Boa Vista, 2230, US$99.

The taxi fare to or from the airport is US$12, fixed rate, buy ticket at airport and in most hotels; or take bus 608 or hourly bus 201 marked Aeroporto Internacional from R Tamandaré nr cathedral, US$0.45, or 1107 from Ed Garagem on Av Getúlio Vargas. No buses 2200-0700. (Taxi drivers often tell arrivals that no bus to town is available, be warned!) It is sometimes possible to use the more regular, faster service run by the *Tropical Hotel*; many tour agenices offer free transfers without obligation. Check all connections on arrival. **NB** Check in time is 2 hrs in advance. Allow plenty of time at Manaus airport, formalities are very slow. The restaurant serves good à la carte and buffet food through the day. It is possible to sleep on the airport observation deck if catching an early morning flight. Local flights leave from airport terminal 2: make sure in advance of your terminal.

Buses Manaus rodoviária is 5 km out of town at the intersection of Av Constantino Nery and R Recife; take local bus from centre, US$0.45, marked 'Aeroporto Internacional' or 'Cidade Nova' (or taxi, US$7.50). Local buses to Praça 14 or airport leave from opposite *Hotel Amazonas* (take airport bus and alight just after Antártica factory) or take local bus to Ajuricaba.

ROUTES To **Itacoatiara**, 285 km E on the Amazon, with Brazil-nut and jute processing plants (bus service 8 a day, 4 hrs); now paved route AM-010, 266 km, through Rio Preto da Eva.

The road N from Manaus to Boa Vista (770 km) is described on page 610. Hitchhiking with truckers is common, but not recommended for women travelling alone. To hitch, take a Tarumã bus to the customs building and hitch from there, or try at 'posta 5', 2 km beyond rodoviária.

The Catire Highway (BR 319) from Manaus to Porto Velho (868 km), has been officially closed since 1990, several bridges are out, and there is no repair in sight. It may, however, be passable in the dry season with a 4WD and winch (ask Embratel, whose vehicles use the road to maintain the telephone lines). Those who would undertake such an expedition must be entirely self-sufficient and obtain a permit from the military in Manaus. Without this you will be turned back at the second ferry crossing. The 250 km middle stretch is uninhabited: if taking this route, sling your hammock high and check your shoes for spiders in the morning. The alternative for drivers is to ship a car down river on a barge, others have to travel by boat (see below). There is, at present, no bus service on this road.

Shipping To Santarém, Belém, Porto Velho, Tefé, **Tabatinga** (for Colombia and Peru), **Caracaraí** (for Boa Vista), **São Gabriel da Cachoeira**, and intermediate ports (see **River Transport in Amazônia**, page 581). Almost all vessels now berth at the first (downstream) of the floating docks which is open to the public 24 hrs a day. A ticket sales area has been built by the pedestrian entrance to the port (bear left as you enter) where bookings can be made up to 2 weeks in advance. The names and itineraries of departing vessels are displayed here as well as on the docked boats themselves; travellers still recommend buying tickets from the captain on the boat itself. The port is relatively clean, well organized, and has a pleasant atmosphere.

ENASA (the state shipping company) sells tickets for private boats at its office in town (prices tend to be high here). A few local boats and some cargo barges still berth by the concrete retaining wall between the market and Montecristi.

NB See introduction to **Up the Amazon River** section on **Health**. You may need a visa to travel to Peru; consulate address above. Those arriving from Leticia should go to the police for their immigration entrance stamp, but you should get this in Tabatinga. Departures to the less important destinations are not always known at the Capitânia do Porto, Av Santa Cruz 265, Manaus. Be careful of people who wander around boats after they've arrived at a port: they are almost certainly looking for something to steal.

Immigration For those arriving by boat who have not already had their passports stamped, the immigration office is on the first of the floating docks next to the tourist office. Take the dock entrance opposite the cathedral, bear right, after 50m left, pass through a warehouse to a group of buildings on a T section.

TOURS

There are many different kinds of tours: 'luxurious', which are comfortable but 'set up' for tourists; some aiming at seeing lots of animals, and others at seeing how the people in the jungle live. Be sure to ascertain in advance the exact itinerary of the tour, that the price includes everything (even drink and tips), that the guide is knowledgeable and he himself will accompany you, and that you do not want to kill anything rare. Be very clear about what you want from your trip, and ensure that others in your party share the same expectations, and are going for the same length of time. Choose a guide who speaks a language you can understand. A shorter tour may be better than a long, poor one. It is worth shopping around for the best service and bargaining may reduce prices. Packaged tours, booked overseas, are usually of the same price and quality as those negotiated locally. **NB** Guides must be officially registered with Embratur and must carry an identity card. It is potentially very dangerous to go with an unofficial guide. Do not employ freelance guides touting at the airport or the river port. Wait until you get to your hotel and seek advice on reputable companies there. Then book direct with the company itself. Ask for a detailed, written contract.

Flights over the jungle give a spectacular impression of the extent of the forest.

Bill Potter, resident in Manaus, writes: "opposite Manaus, near the junction of the Rio Negro and the Rio Solimões, lies the **Lago de Janauri**, a small nature reserve. This is where all the day or half-day trippers are taken usually combined with a visit to the 'meeting of the waters'. Although many people express disappointment with this area because so little is seen and/or there are so many 'tourist-trash' shops, for those with only a short time it is worth a visit. You will see some birds and with luck dolphins. In the shops and bars there are often captive parrots and snakes. The area is set up to receive large numbers of tourists, which ecologists agree relieves pressure on other parts of the river. Boats for day trippers leave the harbour constantly throughout the day, but are best booked at one of the larger operators such as Amazon Explorers or Selvatour. Remember that in the dry season, 1-day tours may not offer much to see if the river is low."

Those with more time can take the longer cruises and will see various ecological environments, but bear in mind that most tour operators will make a trip up the Rio Negro because it is easier to navigate, generally calmer and there are many fewer biting insects. There is also much less animal life in general, so to see any patience and luck are needed. To see virgin rainforest a 5 day trip by boat is needed. On the Rio Solimões there is more wildlife, but you are less likely to see anything because you'll be constantly fighting the mosquitoes and sandflies.

Another alternative is to go up river to

rates found at *Câmbio Cortez*, Av da Amizade 2205 (near Banco do Brasil). Airport to Tabatinga by minibus, US$0.75. The Port Captain in Tabatinga is reported as very helpful and speaking good English. **NB** The port area of Tabatinga is called Marco. Mosquito net for hammock essential if sailing upstream from Tabatinga; much less so downstream.

THE BRAZILIAN/COLOMBIAN/ PERUVIAN FRONTIER

It is advisable to check all requirements and procedures before arriving at this multiple border. As no foreign boat is allowed to dock at the Brazilian, Colombian and Peruvian ports, travellers should enquire carefully about embarkation/disembarkation points and where to go through immigration formalities. If waiting for transport, the best place for accommodation, exchange and other facilities is Leticia, Colombia.

● **Brazilian immigration**

Entry and exit stamps are given at the Polícia Federal, 10 mins' walk from the Tabatinga docks, opp *Café dos Navegantes* (walk through docks and follow road to its end, turn right at this T-junction for 1 block to white building), Mon-Fri 0800-1200, 1400-1800; also at airport, open Wed and Sat only. Proof of US$500 or onward ticket may be asked for. There are no facilities in Benjamin Constant. One-week transit in Tabatinga is permitted.

In this frontier area, carry your passport at all times.

If coming from Peru, you must have a Peruvian exit stamp and a yellow fever certificate.

NB When crossing these frontiers, check if there is a time difference (eg Brazilian summer time, usually mid-Oct to mid-Feb).

● **Colombian consulate**

Near the border on the road from Tabatinga to Leticia, opp *Restaurant El Canto de las Peixadas* (0800-1400). Tourist cards are issued on presentation of 2 passport photos.

● **Transport**

Travel between Tabatinga and Leticia is very informal; taxis between the two towns charge US$3 (more if you want to stop at immigration offices, exchange houses, etc), or US$0.80 as a colectivo (more after 1800).

Boats From Manaus to Benjamin Constant normally go on to Tabatinga, and start from there when going to Manaus. Boats usually wait 1-2 days in both Tabatinga and Benjamin Constant before returning to Manaus; you can stay on board. Tabatinga and Leticia are $1\frac{1}{2}$-2 hrs from Benjamin Constant (ferry/*recreio* US$2.50; much quicker by speedboat, US$13).

For information on boats to/from Manaus, see Manaus **Shipping** and **River Transport in Amazônia**.

● **Colombian immigration**

DAS, C 9, No 8-32, T 27189, Leticia, and at the airport. Exit stamps to leave Colombia by air or overland are given only at the airport. If flying into Leticia prior to leaving for Brazil or Peru, get an exit stamp while at the airport. Check both offices for entry stamps before flying into Colombia.

Entering Colombia To enter Colombia you must have a tourist card to obtain an entry stamp, even if you are passing through Leticia en route between Brazil and Peru (the Colombian consul in Manaus may tell you otherwise; try to get a tourist card elsewhere). The Colombian Consular Office in Tabatinga issues tourist cards. 24-hr transit stamps can be obtained at the DAS office. If visiting Leticia without intending to go anywhere else in Colombia, you may be allowed to enter without immigration or customs formalities (but TCs cannot be changed without an entry stamp).

● **Colombian customs**

No customs formalities for everyday travel between Leticia and Tabatinga.

● **Consulates**

Brazilian, C 11, No 10-70, T 27531, 1000-1600, Mon-Fri, efficient, helpful; onward ticket and 2 black-and-white photos needed for visa (photographer nearby); allow 36 hrs. Peruvian, Cra 11, No 6-80, T 27204, F 27825, open 0830-1430; no entry or exit permits are given here.

● **Transport**

Travel between Colombia and Brazil and Peru is given above and below respectively. Travel from/into Colombia is given under Leticia.

● **Peruvian immigration**

At the border, immigration for entry/exit formalities is at Aguas Verdes, opposite Leticia/Tabatinga. Every boat leaving Peru stops here. There is also an immigration office in Iquitos, where procedures for leaving can be checked.

● **Consulates**

Brazilian and Colombian consulates are in Iquitos.

● **Exchange**

At Islandia, on the Peruvian side of a narrow creek.

● **Transport**

Boats sail from Iquitos to a mud bank called Islandia, on the Peruvian side of a narrow creek a few metres from the Brazilian port of Benjamin Constant (11-36 hrs downstream, depending on the speed of the boat). Passengers leaving Peru must visit immigration at Aguas Verdes when the boat stops there. For entry into Brazil, formalities are done in Tabatinga; for Colombia, in Leticia. Boats to Peru leave from Islandia, calling at Aguas Verdes (2-3 days upstream to Iquitos).

Boats between Iquitos and Brazil are listed under Iquitos.

UP THE RIO NEGRO

It is possible to get a launch from Manaus up the Rio Negro; see **River Transport in Amazônia**, see page 581. There are hardly any villages of more than a few houses; these places are important in terms of communications and food resources. It is vital to be self-sufficient in food and cash and to be able to speak Portuguese or have a Brazilian guide. **Nova Airão**, on the W bank of the Negro, is about 2 days upstream. It has a large boat-building centre at the S end, and a fish and vegetable market at the N end. Ice and bread can also be purchased here. The town has many similar houses of wood and corrugated-iron construction. It has a telephone (from which international calls can be made – after a fashion).

Nova Airão is the starting point for the **Parque Nacional Jaú** (Ibama office in Manaus, BR-319, Km 01, Distrito Industrial, Caixa Postal 185, CEP 69.000, T 237-3721).

Moura is about 5 days upstream from Manaus; it has about 120 people based around the military-run granite quarry. There are basic medical facilities and the military base has an airstrip (only usable Sept to Dec) and telecommunications. About a day further upstream is **Carvoeira**, almost opposite the mouth of the Rio Branco; although small, it has a vibrant festival in the first week of August. More than a day beyond is **Barcelos**, with an airstrip (Hotel *Oasis*, German spoken; *Macedo*).

A great distance further upstream is **São Gabriel da Cachoeira**, from where you can continue to Venezuela (see Venezuela section). In São Gabriel, Tom Hanly, an Irish Salesian brother, is helpful, friendly and informative. Hotels: **E** *Valpes*; another (better class) on the island, restaurant, rec, shops, 2 banks, no exchange, beautiful white beaches and, in the river, rapids for 112 km. São Gabriel is near the **Pico de Neblina National Park** (Pico de Neblina is the highest mountain in Brazil, 3,014m, Ibama office in Manaus, see above).

Cargo boats ply to **Cucuí** at the Brazil/Colombia/Venezuela border, also twice-weekly bus, US$2.50 (1 hotel, ask for Elias, no restaurants); with your embassy's assistance it may be possible to fly with the military (airport 8 km from São Gabriel). From Cucuí daily boats to Guadalupe (Colombia), infrequent boats to Santa Lucía (Venezuela).

Many of the **gold prospectors** (*garimpeiros*) expelled from the Yanomami reserves in Roraima have begun to move W to the middle and upper reaches of the Rio Negro, bringing conflict and destruction in their wake. The environment and indigenous populations in the area have been affected and relations with Venezuela strained. Get detailed local information and exercise considerable caution if travelling to this region.

THE RIO BRANCO

About 2 days up the Rio Branco is **Santa Maria de Boiaçu**, a village of about 30 families. There is a military airstrip which is in use in July and Aug, very basic medical facilities and an indirect radio link with Manaus. There are three small shops selling basic necessities (but they aren't often open), and several tiny, but lively churches. The Rio Branco is yellowish in colour, and less acidic than the Negro. Therefore, biting insects and their associated diseases are more prevalent outside the wet season. The river is better for fishing, though, and there is more wildlife to see.

CARACARAÍ

River traffic on the Rio Branco connects Manaus with **Caracaraí**, a busy, but un-

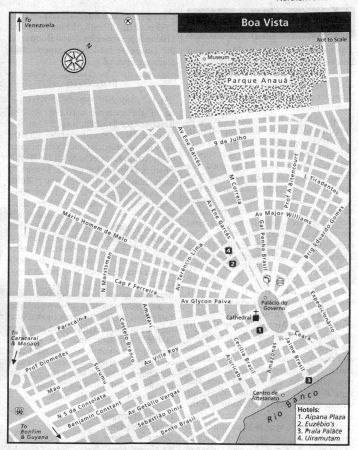

Boa Vista

Not to Scale

To Venezuela

Museum

Parque Anauá

9 de Julho

M Correia

L Tiradentes

Av Ene Garcés

Prof A Bitencourt

Av Major Williams

Gal Penha Brasil

Brig Eduardo Gomes

Mário Homem de Melo

Av Terêncio Lima

Av Ene Garcés

N Moristsman

Cap F Ferreira

Av Glycon Paiva

Palácio do Governo

Cathedral

Expedicionário

Ceará

Paracaíma

Castelo Branco

Amatari

Surumu

Cecília Brasil

Aluricaba

Amazonas

Jaime Brasil

To Caracaraí & Manaus

Prof Diomedes

Mau

Av Ville Roy

N S da Consolata

Benjamin Constant

Av Getúlio Vargas

Sebastião Diniz

Bento Brasil

Centro de Artesanato

Rio Branco

To Bonfim & Guyana

Hotels:
1. *Aipana Plaza*
2. *Euzébio's*
3. *Praia Palace*
4. *Uiramutam*

attractive river port with modern installations. It is also on the the Manaus-Boa Vista road (see below). If this road is washed out, the Rio Branco is the only route through to Venezuela. In the rainy season, April-Sept, river transport is quite easy to arrange (bargain for your fare, and sling your hammock under a truck); empty trucks offer cheaper fares for cars, talk to the drivers; it's an interesting journey, 96 hrs upstream, 48 down, take water or purifying treatment. The river banks are closer, so there is more to see than on the Amazon and stops in the tiny riverside settlements are fascinating.

● **Accommodation & places to eat** D *3 Irmãos*, behind rodoviária, clean, rec; **E** *Caracaraí*, down street from rodoviária, friendly but dirty; *Sorveteria Pizzaria Lidiany*, rec.

● **Exchange** Silas in the Drogaria on S side of town will change dollars.

● **Transport** Bus on from Caracaraí to Boa Vista costs US$6, 3 hrs. **NB** The Perimetral Norte road marked on some maps from Caracaraí E to Macapá and W to the Colombian frontier does not yet exist; it runs only about 240 km W and 125 km E from Caracaraí, acting at present as a penetration road.

MANAUS TO VENEZUELA AND GUYANA

The road which connects Manaus and Boa Vista (BR-174 to Novo Paraíso, then the Perimetral, BR-210, rejoining the BR174 after crossing the Rio Branco at Caracaraí, ferry during daylight hours) is of dirt between Manaus and Caracaraí, but is regularly maintained. Paving of the entire route is due for completion in 1997. It is generally passable, even during the rainy season (when it is slower, bus takes between 1 and 3 days: good idea to pack food, drink and a raincoat). The road is fully paved from Caracaraí to Boa Vista. For drivers on this route, some advise being defensive with regard to lorry drivers (who drive for too long, haul too much and drink), but they can be very helpful to anyone in difficulties. There are service stations with toilets, camping, etc, every 150-180 km, but all petrol is low octane; take a tow cable and spares. At Km 100 is Presidente Figueiredo, with shops and a restaurant. About 100 km further on is a service station at the entrance to the Uaimiri Atroari Indian Reserve, which straddles the road for about 120 km. Private cars and trucks are not allowed to enter the Indian Reserve between sunset and sunrise, but buses are exempt from this regulation. Nobody is allowed to stop within the reserve at any time. At the northern entrance to the reserve there are toilets and a spot to hang your hammock (usually crowded with truckers overnight). At Km 327 is the village of Vila Colina with *Restaurante Paulista*, good food, clean, can use shower and hang hammock. At Km 359 there is a monument to mark the equator. At Km 434 is the clean and pleasant *Restaurant Goaio*. Just S of Km 500 is *Bar Restaurante D'Jonas*, a clean, pleasant place to eat, you can also camp or sling a hammock. Beyond here, large tracts of forest have been destroyed for settlement, but already many homes have been abandoned.

Boa Vista has road connections with the Venezuelan frontier at Santa Elena de Uairen (237 km, a dirt road, improved in 1993 but still difficult, the only gasoline 110 km S of Santa Elena) and Bonfim for the Guyanese border at Lethem. Both roads are open all year.

BOA VISTA

(*Pop* 142,815; *CEP* 69300; *DDD* 095) Capital of the extreme northern State of Roraima (*pop* 215,790), it is 759 km N of Manaus. Mount Roraima, after which the Territory is named, is possibly the original of Sir Arthur Conan Doyle's 'Lost World'. There is swimming in the Rio Branco, 15 mins from the town centre (too polluted in Boa Vista), reachable by bus only when river is low. This town has a modern functional plan, which often necessitates long hot treks from one function to another. South of town is an industrial estate S of town; NW is a new government district. Interesting modern cathedral; also a museum of local Indian culture (poorly kept). Under heavy international pressure, the Brazilian government expelled some 40,000 gold prospectors (*garimpeiros*) from Yanomami Indian Reserves in the W of the state of Roraima in 1991/92 and again in 1993. Although some have since returned, the economic consequences have been very severe for Boa Vista, which went from boom to bust. There has been some increase in cattle ranching in the area, but this has not taken up the slack.

Local information
● **Accommodation**

Generally expensive.

A1 *Aipana Plaza*, Praça Centro Cívico 53, T 224-4800, F 224-4116, modern, friendly service; **A1** *Praia Palace*, on river, with beach, hard beds but service friendly, T 224-8111, F 224-8496 (good food in restaurant next door); **A1** *Uiramutam*, Av Cap Ene Garcez 427, T 224-9912.

C *Eusébio's*, R Cecília Brasil 1107, T 224-0300, always full, book ahead, demand single if on your own, very good restaurant, swimming pool, free transport to rodoviária or airport, rec.

D *Colonial*, Ajuricaba 532, T 224-5190, nr Consolação church, a/c with bath and breakfast, clean; **D** *Roraima*, Av Cecília Brasil e Benjamin Constant, with bath, rec, restaurant opp is also rec.

E *Beija-Flor*, Av Nossa Sra da Consolata 939 W,

Southern Amazônia

R ONDÔNIA and Acre, frontier areas, not just between Brazil and Peru and Bolivia, but also between the forest and colonization. Much of Rondônia, now colonized, has been deforested. Acre is still frontier country with great expanses of forest in danger of destruction.

Rondônia, with a population of 862,000 in 1985, which had reached 1,130,400 in 1991, is the focus of experimental development in agriculture, with concomitant colonization of the area. At the same time, much of the state is being reserved for Indians and national forests.

The Rio Madeira on which Porto Velho, the state capital stands, is one of the major tributaries of the Amazon. The four main rivers which form it are the Madre de Dios, rising a short distance from Cuzco (Peru); the Beni, coming from the southern Cordillera bordering Lake Titicaca; the Mamoré, rising near Sucre, Bolivia; and the Guaporé, coming out of Mato Grosso, in Brazil.

PORTO VELHO

(*Pop* 296,400; *CEP* 78900; *DDD* 069) **Porto Velho** stands on a high bluff overlooking a curve of the Rio Madeira. The city prospered during the local gold and timber rush but as this has slowed; unemployment has grown and some of the population, that had grown too rapidly in previous decades, has emigrated.

Places of interest

At the top of the hill, on Praça João Nicoletti, is the **Cathedral**, built in 1930, with beautiful stained glass windows and a carved wooden ceiling; the **Prefeitura** (town hall) is across the street. The principal commercial street is Av Sete de Setembro, which runs from the railway station and market hall to the upper level of the city, near the rodoviária. The centre is hot and noisy, but not without its charm, and the port and old railway installations are interesting. There is a **Geological Museum** and a crafts centre *Casa do Artesão* (Thur-Sun 0800-1800) at the old railway yards, known as Praça Madeira Mamoré. (See page 616 for the Madeiro-Mamoré railway.) A neoclassical **Casa do Governo** faces Praça Getúlio Vargas, while Praça Marechal Rondon is spacious and modern. There are several viewpoints overlooking the river and railway yards: the **Mirante I** (with restaurant) is at the end of R Carlos Gômes, **Mirante II** (with a bar and ice cream parlour), at the end of R Dom Pedro II. There are some bars by the riverfront, behind the rail sheds, with a good sunset view, but the surrounding area is not safe. There is a clean fruit and vegetable market at the corner of R Henrique Dias and Av Farqhuar and a dry goods market 3 blocks to the S, near the port.

Excursions

The Cachoeira de Santo Antônio, rapids on the Rio Madeira, 7 km upriver from Porto Velho, is a popular destination for a swim during the dry season; in the rainy season the rapids may be underwater and the strong current makes swimming dangerous. Access is by boat, taking a tour from Porto Cai N'Água, 1 hr; or by train on Sundays (see Madeira-Mamoré Railway, below); or by bus, take city bus No 102, *Triângulo*, which runs every 50 mins from the city bus terminus or from bus stop on R Rogerio Weber, across from Praça Marechal Rondon. Gold dredges may be seen working near Porto Velho, ask around if interested.

Local information

NB Malaria is common; the drinking water is contaminated with mercury (from gold panning). With rising unemployment, crime has increased in the city and outside. Caution is recommended in the evenings and even during the day nr the railway station and port.

● **Accommodation**

L3 *Vila Rica*, Av Carlos Gomes 1616, T/F 224-3433, tower block, 'flashy, flamboyant and mechanically efficient', restaurant, pool, sauna; **A1** *Aquarius Selva*, R Roberto Souza 1760, 3km from centre, T 222-4334, F 2223198, a/c, minibar, TV, restaurants, pool, sauna; **A1** *Rondon Palace*, Av Gov Jorge Teixeira corner Jacy Paraná, away from the centre, T/F 223-3422, a/c, fridge, restaurant, pool, travel agency; **A3** *Selton*, Av Brasília 2323, T 221-7535, F 221-2900, a/c, fridge, TV, restaurant, central, rec; **B** *Central*, Tenreiro Aranha 2472, T 224-2099, F 223-2302, a/c, TV, fridge, rec; **B** *Aline Park*, Av Campos Sales 2645, T 221-1764, F 221-1054, a/c, fridge, TV.

On Av Carlos Gomes: **A3** *Novo*, No 2776, nr rodoviária, T 221-4284, with bath, a/c, fridge, TV, parking, clean, comfortable; **E** *Erica*, opp rodoviária, convenient but short-stay; much better is **E** *Líder*, nr rodoviária, honest, reasonably clean, fan, coffee, rec for new arrivals; *Ouro Fino*, No 2844, *Amazonas*, No 2835, both E; **D-E** *Karme (Tía Carmen)*, No 2995, T 221-7910, very good, honest, good cakes in *lanche* in front of hotel, highly rec. From rodoviária, take bus No 301 'Presidente Roosevelt' (outside *Hotel Pontes*), which goes to railway station at riverside, then along Av 7 de Setembro as far as Av Marechal Deodoro, passing: **C** *Pousada da Sete*, No 894, T 221-8344, with bath, a/c, cheaper with fan, D with shared bath; **D** *Guaporé Palace*, No 927, T 221-2495, a/c, restaurant; **D** *Sonora*, No 1103, clean, fan, clothes washing facilities; **D** *Cuiabano*, No 1180, T 221-4080, friendly, good, clean, with bath, a/c, cheaper with fan, E with shared bath, fan, no breakfast, rec; **D** *Nunes*, No 1195, T 221-1389, with bath, fan, basic; **E** *Sonora*, No 1209, bath, fan, basic, not too clean; **E** *Laira*, Joaquim Nabuco, just off 7 de Setembro, good, clean, cheap.

● **Places to eat**

Churascaria Natal, Av Carlos Gomes 2783, good meat and chicken; *Assados na Brasa*, Carlos Gomes 2208, similar; *Mister Pizza II*, Carlos Gomes e José de Alencar, good. *Almanara*, R José de Alencar 2624, good authentic Lebanese food, popular, not cheap, rec; *Chá*, Av Pres Dutra 3024, by kilo buffet, pricey. A

number of good restaurants around the intersection of Dom Pedro II and Av Joaquim Nabuco: *Champagne*, rec for pizzas, and a good Chinese, J Nabuco 2264, oriental food; *Bella Italia*, J Nabuco 2205, Italian, pizza and comida caseira. Many *lanches* in town: rec are *Petiskão*, Av 7 de Setembro e Joaquim Nabuco, excellent juices; *Panificadora Popular*, Av Mal Deodoro between 7 de Setembro e Dom Pedro II, good juices and soups; *Xalezinho*, opp, for an even bigger bowl of soup. *Banana Split*, Av 7 de Setembro, popular, good by the kilo meals; also *Sorvette Pinguim* for ice creams. Avoid eating much fish because of mercury contamination.

● **Banks & money changers**

Banks in mornings only; **Banco do Brasil**, Dom Pedro IIOK 607 e Av José de Alencar, cash and TCs with 2% commission, min commission US$10, min amount exchanged US$200. *Marco Aurélio Câmbio*, R José de Alencar 3353, T 223-2551, quick, efficient, poor rates, Mon-Fri 0900-1500. *Parmetal* (gold merchants), R J Nabuco 2265, T 221-1566, cash only, good rates, open Mon-Fri 0730-1800, Sat 0730-1300. Local radio news and papers publish exchange rates. Difficult elsewhere in Rondônia.

● **Electric current**

110 volts AC, Guajará-Mirim also, elsewhere in Rondônia 220 volts.

● **Hospitals & medical services**

Dentist: at Carlos Gomes 2577; 24-hr clinic opp.

● **Laundry**

Lavanderia Marmoré, Pinheiro Machado 1455b.

● **Post & telecommunications**

Post Office: Av Pres Dutra 2701, corner Av 7 de Setembro.

Telephones: Teleron, Av Pres Dutra 3023 e Dom Pedro II, 0600-2300 daily.

● **Shopping**

Bookshop *Livraría da Rose*, Av Rogério Weber 1967, opp Praça Mal Rondon, a few English paperbacks; Rose, the proprietor, speaks English, friendly; other bookshops nearby. Indian handicrafts at *Casa do Índio*, R Rui Barbosa 1407 and *Casa do Artesão*, Praça Madeira-Mamoré, behind the railway station, open Thur-Sun 0800-1800. Hammocks more expensive than in Manaus. *Supermercado Maru*, 7 de Setembro e Joaquim Nabuco. Camping supplies and gas at *Casa do Pescador*, J Nabuco e Pinheiro Machado. Film developing at 7 de Setembro e José de Alencar.

● **Transport**

Local Car hire: Silva Car, R Almte Barroso 1528, Porto Velho, T 221-1423/6040,

US$50/day.

Air Airport 8 km W of town, take bus marked 'Aeroporto' (last one between 2400-0100). Twice daily Varig flights to Manaus, daily to Brasília (Vasp), Cuiabá (several airlines), Rio Branco (Varig); twice a week to Cruzeiro do Sul, via Rio Branco; also flights to other Brazilian destinations.

Buses Rodoviária is on Jorge Teixeira between Carlos Gomes and Dom Pedro II. From town take 'President Roosevelt' bus No 301 (if on Av 7 de Setembro, the bus turns at Av Mal Deodoro); 'Aeroporto' and 'Hospital Base' (No 400) also go to rodoviária. Health and other controls at the Rondônia-Matto Grosso border are strict. União Cascavel has bought out most of the smaller regional carriers such as Colibri and Serra Azul, service is good but prices are high. To break up a long trip is much more expensive than doing it all in one stretch. Bus to **Humaitá**, US$8, 3 hrs; to **São Paulo**, 60-plus hrs, US$108; to **Cuiabá**, 23 hrs, US$63, expensive food and drink is available en route. To **Rio** US$142, 72 hrs; **Belo Horizonte** US$99, 44 hrs; **Curitiba** US$137, 52 hrs; **Fortaleza** US$175, 72 hrs. To **Guajará-Mirim**, see below. To **Rio Branco**, Viaçao Rondônia, 5 daily, 8 hrs, US$19. Daily bus with Eucatur from **Cascavel** (Paraná, connections for Foz do Iguaçu) via Maringá, Presidente Prudente, Campo Grande and Cuiabá to Porto Velho (Porto Velho-Campo Grande 36 hrs, US$94). To **Cáceres** for the Pantanal, 18 hrs, US$52. To **Vitória**, daily, 61 hrs. Hitching difficult, try the gasoline stations on the edge of town. There is no bus service to **Manaus** as the road remains closed (1996).

Road To Cuiabá (BR-364 – Marechal Rondon Highway), 1,450 km, fully paved; see below and page 649; to Rio Branco, 544 km, BR-364, poorly paved; N to Humaitá (205 km) on the Madeira river, BR-319, paved, connecting with the Transamazônica, BR 230 (frequently closed, ascertain conditions before travelling). The BR-319 N from Humaitá to Manaus is closed indefinitely. Road journeys are best done in the dry season, the second half of the year.

River services: see **River Transport in Amazônia**, page 581. Passenger service from *Porto Cai N'Água* (which means 'fall in the water', watch out or you might!), for best prices buy directly at the boat, avoid touts on shore. The Rio Madeira is fairly narrow so the banks can be seen and there are several 'meetings of waters'. Shipping a car: São Matheus Ltda, Av Terminal dos Milagros 400, Balsa, takes vehicles on pontoons, meals, showers, toilets, cooking and sleeping in car permitted. Wait at the Capitânia do Porto in the centre of town for a possible passage on a cargo boat; these boats

leave from the Porto Bras docks, down river from Porto Velho. **NB** From Manaus to São Paulo is cheaper by boat Manaus-Porto Velho, then bus to São Paulo, than by flying direct or by boat to Belém then bus.

Boats usually call at Humaitá (paved road and regular bus service from Porto Velho, see above, 1st class hammock Humaitá-Manaus US$61), Manicoré (see below), Novo Aripuanã, Borba and Nova Olinda. Passengers can disembark or embark at these ports, if that is your intention confirm the itinerary beforehand; if embarking at an intermediate port you will not have your choice of hammock space.

6 days a week a boat leaves at 1800 for Manaus from Manicoré, at the confluence of the Rios Madeira and Manicoré, two nights and 1 day's journey, food included; boats from Porto Velho to Manicoré on Mon, Wed and Sat (1800, arr 0200, but you can sleep on the boat), connecting with Manicoré-Manaus boats (a rec boat is *Orlandina*). **Manicoré** (*pop* 37,810) is a pleasant town; the Praça de Bandeira is at the corner of Av Getúlio Vargas and Av Pedro Tinoco (one block to left of road that goes up from the dock). **E** *Hotel Silviani*, 4 blocks left from Praça on Av Vargas, just before the big church; *Restaurant Tapuia*, 1 block from Praça in opp direction to river on Av Tinoco; slow but good restaurant at floating dock. Fruit market on Av Vargas.

If you want to see a typical river community, get off at Calama, about 10 hrs from Porto Velho. Stay with Dona Morena in her 'hotel' and eat *en famille* (F). The people are friendly and Tyer, the school teacher, enjoys a chat. From Calama you may be able to get a boat up the Ji-Paraná river; very attractive with waterfalls and a few isolated settlement schemes.

THE BR-364

A result of the paving of BR-364 is the development of farms and towns along it; cattle ranches can be seen all along the road, with least population density in the S between Pimenta Bueno and Vilhena. From Porto Velho S, the towns are: **Ariquemes** (202 km from Porto Velho; *pop* 65,899; *CEP* 78930; *DDD* 069; buses hourly from 0600, 3-4 hrs, Banco do Brasil); Nova Vida (200 km), Jaru (257 km), Ouro Preto d'Oeste (297 km).

• **Accommodation Ariquemes: E** *Valérius Palace*, Av T Neves 3113, T 535-3311, *Ariquemes*, Av Cap Sílvio 1141, T 535-2200, a/c, fridge, parking). About 250 km S of Porto Velho it is possible to stay on a working *fazenda*, the

Rain Forest Lodge Rancho Grande at Caixa Postal 361, Ariquemes, Rondônia 78. 914, F (069) 535-4301 (reservations and tours can be arranged through Focus Tours, Belo Horizonte). Not cheap but rec, esp for butterfly lovers. About 450 bird species and numerous mammals can be seen on the 20 km of trails. Harald Schmitz speaks English, German and Spanish, highly rec.

Ji Paraná (376 km; *pop* 106,457; *DDD* 069; *CEP* 78960; bus to Porto Velho, US$23, 16 hrs; to Cuiabá, 15 hrs, US$47), on the shores of the Rio Machado. It is a pleasant town with a small riverside promenade, which has several bars, lively at night; there is swimming at the river, beware of the current; a telegraph museum is on Av Marechal Rondon.

• **Accommodation A2** *Transcontinental*, R J Guerra 258, centre, T 422-1212, F 422-2064, a/c, TV, fridge, restaurant, pool, overlooking the river, rec; **A3** *Vitória Regia*, R Júlio Guerra 172, centre, T 422-1432, a/c, fridge, TV, parking, view of the river; **B** *Plaza*, R Martins Costa 336, across the bridge from the centre, T 422-2524, a/c, fridge, TV, parking; **D** *Nova Era*, Av Marechal Rondon 1845, 2 blocks from the rodoviária, with bath, a/c, TV, cheaper with fan, parking, good value, rec; **E** *Sol Nascente*, R Dr Osvaldo 101, accross the bridge from the centre, T 421-1997, with *churrascaria*; *Casablanca*, R Padre Rohl 465, centre, T 421-5894, with bath, a/c, fridge, TV, cheaper with fan; cheap hotels in front of rodoviária are filthy – not rec.

Trips to frontier towns possible, eg Nova Colina, Presidente Médici (373 km; *pop* 50,000), **Cacoal** (481 km; *pop* 74,691; *DDD* 069; *CEP* 78975), a spread-out town, **Pimenta Bueno** (440 km; *pop* 50,000), with a gasoline station, rodoviária, and **Vilhena** on the Rondônia-Mato Grosso border (*pop* 41,452; *DDD* 069; *CEP* 78995), 704 km from Porto Velho (bus US$42, 11 hrs), 752 km from Cuiabá (bus US$34, 11 hrs), a good place to break the Cuiabá-Porto Velho trip.

• **Accommodation Cacoal: A3** *Estoril Palace*, R São Luis 1065, T 441-4810, a/c, fridge, TV, pool; **B** *Cacoal Palace*, R Gen Osório 718, T 441-5011, a/c, TV, fridge; **D** *Ramadas*, R R Branco, T 441-5379, safe parking, rec, and *Amazônas*, T 441-5463. **Pimenta Bueno:** *Píritiba Pálace*, Pres Dutra 1036, T 451-2131, a/c, TV, parking; *Casarão*, R Moura 42, T 451-3056; *Nacional*, F Peixoto 211, T 451-2077 and several restaurants. **Vilhena:** hotels in the centre, **A2** *Mirage*, Av Mcal Amarantes 3536, T/F 321-

2166, a/c, TV, fridge, parking, pool, on the main commercial street; **C** *Comodoro*, Av Cap Castro 3663, T/F 321-1244, with bath, TV, fridge. In Nova Vilhena ('Circular' bus to the centre), nr the rodoviária, are: **A3** *Diplomata*, R Francisco Tildre 63, T 321-3173, F 321-3233, a/c, fridge, TV, pool; **B** *Santa Rosa Palace*, R Dal Toé 191, T 321-3900, a/c, fridge, TV, parking, C with fan; also on this street **D** *Paraná*, cheaper with shared bath, run down, unfriendly; **D** *Vitória*, at No 117, T 321-3918, with bath, fan, cheaper with shared bath, parking, friendly; on Av Sabino Bezerra de Queiroz are: **B** *Olinda Pálace*, No 5173, T 321-2531, a/c, fridge, TV, C with fan; **B** *Campinense*, No 5227, T/F 321-3156, with bath, fan, parking, E with shared bath, good value, rec; **B** *Nacional*, No 5363, T 321-3952, a/c, TV, fridge, C with fan, parking, clean; **C** *Rover Pálace*, No 5423, T/F 321-2253, with bath, fan, TV, parking, simpler rooms D; **D** *Luz*, No 5341, T/F 321-1825, with bath, fan, parking, good value; **D** *Rodoviário*, No 5537, T 321-3785, with bath, fan, E with shared bath, basic, run down. Restaurants, on Av Sabino Bezerra de Queiroz by the rodoviária are *Tókio*, at No 5489 for oriental food and *Bom Papão II*, No 5261, good *caseira*.

At the Mato Grosso state border proof of yellow-fever inoculation is required: if no proof, new shot.

PACAÁS NOVOS NATIONAL PARK

The **Pacaás Novos National Park**, 765,800 ha, lies W of the BR-364; it is a transitional zone between open plain and Amazonian forest. Details from Ibama, T (069) 223-2599/3597, Porto Velho; also enquire here about the Jaru Biological Reserve in the E of the State.

On the Rio Guaporé is the Guaporé Biological Reserve, in which is the Forte Príncipe da Beira, begun in 1777 as a defence of the border with Bolivia. The fort, which is being restored, can be reached from Costa Marques (20 km by road), which is some 345 km by unpaved road W of **Rolim de Moura**. This unplanned town (*pop* 110,000) has several hotels, including **B** *Transcontinental*; it is 40 km W of Pimenta Bueno.

THE MADEIRA-MAMORÉ RAILWAY

Porto Velho was the terminus of the Madeira-Mamoré railway of 367 km (closed 1971), Brazil's price to Bolivia for annexing the Acre territory in the rubber boom. During construction, it cost a life for every 100 sleepers, 6,208 in all, earning it the nickname 'the devil's railroad'. The line, built 1907-12, by-passed the 19 rapids of the Madeira and Mamoré rivers, and gave Bolivia an outlet of sorts to the Atlantic. It was supposed to go as far as Riberalta, on the Rio Beni, above that river's rapids, but stopped short at Guajará Mirim. It still runs the 7 km from Porto Velho to the Madeira river rapids at Santo Antônio. Woodburning steam trains, built in 1925 in Philadelphia, use a narrow-gauge track. The line works all week but tourist excursions are on Sun only, 7 departures from 0830 to 1700, US$1.50, crowded with people going to bathe at the falls during the dry season – good fun. The roundhouse, recently restored, has two other antique locomotives on display.

GUAJARA MIRIM

From Porto Velho, the paved BR-364 continues 220 km SW to **Abunã** (**E** *Hotel Thalita;* **E** *Dormitório Oliviera*), where the BR-425 branches S to Guajará Mirim. 9 km E of Abunã is a ferry crossing over the Rio Madeira, where it receives the waters of the Rio Abunã. The BR-425 is a fair road, partly paved, which uses the former rail bridges (in poor condition). It is sometimes closed Mar-May. Across the Mamoré from Guajará Mirim is the Bolivian town of Guayaramerín, which is connected by road to Riberalta, from where there are air services to other Bolivian cities. **Guajará Mirim** (*Pop* 32,530; *DDD* 069) is a charming town. The **Museu Municipal** is at the old Guajará Mirim railway station beside the ferry landing; interesting and diverse, well organized and presented, highly rec. An ancient stern wheeler plies on the Guaporé; 26-day, 1,250 km trips (return) can be made on the Guaporé from Guajará Mirim to Vila Bela (see page 655) in Mato Grosso, fare includes food.

● **Accommodation B** *Jamaica*, A Leopoldo de Matos 755, T 541-3721, F 541-2007, with bath, a/c, TV, fridge, parking; **B** *Lima Palace*, Av 15 de Novembro 1613, T 541-3521, F 541-2122, with bath, a/c, TV, fridge, parking; *Cen-*

tral Palace, Av Marechal Deodoro 1150, T 541-2610, rec. *Alfa*, Av Leopoldo de Matos 239, T 541-3121, F 541-3149, with bath, a/c, TV, fridge; **C** *Mini-Estrela*, Av 15 de Novembro 460, T 541-2399, with bath, a/c, parking; **D** *Chile*, Av Q Bocaiuva, good value, inc breakfast, rec; **E** *Fénix Palace*, Av 15 de Novembro 459, T 541-2326, higly rec; **E** *Mamoré*, R M Mor_es, T 541-3753, clean, friendly. **Youth Hostel**: Av 15 de Novembro, Centro Deportivo Afonso Rodrigues, T 541-3732. There is a basic *dormitório*, **E**, opp rodoviária.

● **Places to eat** Best is *Oasis*, Av 15 de Novembro 464, rec (on main dishes 10% service charge is added); *Lanchonates*, self-service, good value, rec.

● **Banks & money changers** Banco do Brasil (foreign exchange am only). **Loja Nogueira**, Av Pres Dutra, esq Leopoldo de Matos (cash only). There is no market in Brazil for bolivianos.

● **Post & telecommunications Post Office**: on Av Pres Dutra. **Telephone**: office on Av B Ménzies 751.

● **Shopping** Brazilians shop here for imported goods brought through Bolivia.

● **Transport** Buses from Porto Velho to Guajará Mirim, 5½ hrs or more depending on season, 8 a day with Viaçã0 Rondônia, US$18. Taxi from Porto Velho rodoviária, US$25 pp for 4-5, 3 hrs, leaves when full.

FRONTIER WITH BOLIVIA

● **Brazilian immigration**
Brazilian exit/entry stamps from Polícia Federal, Av Pres Dutra 70, corner of Av Q Bocaiuva, T 541-2437.

● **Bolivian consulate**
Av C Marqués 495, T 541-2862, Guajará Mirim; visas are given here.

● **Transport**
Speedboat across the Mamoré River (border), US$1.50, 5-min crossing, operates all day, tickets at waterside; ferry crossing for vehicles, T 541-3811, Mon-Sat 0800-1200, Mon-Fri 1400-1600, 20-min crossing.

ACRE

NB Rio Branco time is 1 hr behind Porto Velho and Manaus time; this means 2 hrs behind Brazilian Standard Time.

This intriguing state, rich in natural beauty, history and the *seringeiro* culture, is still very much off the beaten track. The area is beginning to develop its considerable tourist potential for adventure tourism and historians as links are opened up with neighbouring Peru and Bolivia.

RIO BRANCO

From Abunã, the BR-364 continues W in excellent condition, 315 km to **Rio Branco** (*pop* 195,943; *CEP* 69900; *DDD* 068) the capital of the State of Acre (*pop* 417,440). During the rubber boom of the late 19th Century, many *Nordestinos*, particularly from the State of Ceará, migrated to the western frontier in search of fortune. As a result, the unpopulated Bolivian territory of Acre was gradually taken over by Brazil and formally annexed in the first decade of the 20th century. This transfer of power is known locally as the *Revolução Acreana*. In compensation, Bolivia received the Madeira-Mamoré railroad, as described above. In 1913, Rio Branco became capital of the new Território Federal do Acre, which attained statehood in 1962. The main industries remain rubber and *castanha* (Brazil nut) extraction, but timber and ranching are becoming increasingly important and improved road access is putting the state's tropical forests at considerable risk. The cultural influence of the original Cearense colonists is still noticeable. Despite improved air and road links, Rio Branco remains at the 'end of the line', a frontier outpost from where there is nowhere left to go. The chronically depressed economy, high unemployment and prevalent drug-running make the city unsafe at night, and some caution is advised at all hours.

Places of interest

The Rio Acre is navigable upstream as far as the Peru and Bolivia borders. It divides the city into 2 districts called Primeiro (W) and Segundo (E), on either side of the river. In the central, Primeiro district are **Praça Plácido de Castro**, the shady main square; the **Cathedral**, NS de Nazaré, along Av Brasil; the neoclassical **Palácio Rio Branco** on R Benjamin Constant, across from Praça Eurico Gaspar Dutra. Two bridges link the districts. In the Segundo district is the **Calçadão da Gameleira**, a pleasant promenade along

the shore, with plaques and an old tree marking the location of the original settlement. There are some interesting old wooden houses nearby and *palafitos*, houses on stilts at the edge of the river, can be seen from here. The airport and rodoviária are in the Segundo district. There are several large parks in the city; the **Horto Forestal**, popular with joggers, in Vila Ivonete (1° distrito), 3 km N of the centre ('Conjunto Procon' or 'Vila Ivonete' city-buses), has native amazonian trees, a small lake, walking paths and picnic areas; the **Parque Zoo-Botânico**, on the UFAC campus (1° distrito), 5 km from the centre, along BR-364, has samples of tropical plants, rubber plantations and some virgin forest; **Parque Capitão Ciriaco**, rodovia AC-40 (2° distrito, not far from the bridge), is an urban park.

Museums

Museu da Borracha (Rubber Museum), Av Ceará 1177, Mon-Fri 0900-1800, Sat-Sun 1600-2000, in a lovely old house with a tiled façade, has information about the rubber boom, archaeological artefacts, a section about Acreano Indians (13 groups in the state today, from the Pano, Aruak and Arawá linguistic groups, the Kashinawá living in the centre of the state are the most numerous group), documents and memorabilia from the Revolução Acreana and a display about the Santo Daime doctrine (see excursions below), rec. **Casa do Seringueiro**, Av Brasil 216, corner of Av Getúlio Vargas, has a good exhibit on rubber tappers and on Chico Mendes in particular; the Sala Hélio Melo has a display of Melo's paintings, mainly on the theme of the forest.

Excursions

8 km SE of town, upriver along the Rio Acre is **Lago do Amapá**, a U-shaped lake good for boating and watersports; access is by river or by land via route AC-40. 2 km beyond along the AC-40 is **Praia do Amapá**, a bathing beach on the Rio Acre; there is an annual arts festival here in September. Excursions can be made to **rubber plantations** and rubber extraction areas in native forest (*seringães nativos*).

One *seringal nativo* is on road AC-40, Km 21, another is on the shores of the Rio Acre (access by river); there is a rubber plantation on the road to Brasilea, 1 km from where it meets road AC-40. 13 km from Rio Branco is **Colônia Cinco Mil** (access along AC-10), a religious centre of the followers of the Santo Daime doctrine: its members (many originally from outside Acre and Brazil) live a communal life, working in agriculture and producing crafts made of latex; the religion centres around the use of *Ayahuasca*, a hallucinogenic potion adopted from local indians and made of herbs and barks including Japurana leaves (*Pychotica viridis*) and Jagube bark (*Baristeriopsis caapi*). Visitors are usually welcome, but enquire beforehand.

Local information
● Accommodation
There are few economical hotels in the centre, but a reasonable selection of these by the rodoviária.

In 1° distrito (W bank): **L3** *Pinheiro Palace*, Rui Barbosa 91, T 224-7191, F 224-5726, a/c, pool, friendly, rec; **A2** *Inácio Palace*, R Rui Barbosa 72, T 224-6397, F 224-5726, fridge, TV, overpriced, fair restaurant; **A3** *Rio Branco*, R Rui Barbosa 193, T 224-1785, F 224-2681, by Praça Plácido de Castro, a/c, fridge, TV, nice but simple, friendly.

B *Triângulo*, R Floriano Peixoto 727, T 224-9265, a/c, TV, fridge, restaurant; **B-C** *Albemar*, R Franco Ribeiro 99, T 224-1938, with bath, a/c, fridge, TV, good breakfast, friendly, good value, rec.

D *Xapuri*, Naçoes Unidas 187, T 225-7268, shared bath, fan, basic, 15 mins' walk from centre.

In 2° distrito (E bank), in Cidade Nova by the rodoviária: **A3** *Rodoviária*, R Palmeiral 268, T 224-4434, with bath, a/c, fridge TV, D with shared bath, fan, clean, good value; **C** *Skina*, Uirapuru 533, T 224-0087, with bath, a/c, fridge, TV, fan; **D** *Nacional*, R Palmeiral 496, T 224-4822, with bath, fan, both cheaper with shared bath.

By the airport: **C** *Cuzco*, Rodovia AC-40, Km 01, T 224-4348. **Youth hostel**: Fronteira Verde, Trav Natanael de Albuquerque, 2° distrito, T225-7128.

● Places to eat
Kaxinawa, Av Brasil at corner of Praça Plácido de Castro, best in town for Acreano regional food; *Dona Bela*, on the outskirts of town,

along the road S to Senador Guiomard, regional food, popular on weekends; *Pizzaria Tutti Frutti*, Av Ceará 1132, across from Museu da Borracha, pizzas, ice cream, not cheap; *Casarão*, Av Brasil 310, next to telephone office, good food and drink; *Churrascaria Triângulo*, R Floriano Peixoto 727, as much charcoal-grilled meat as you can eat, rec; *Churrascaria Modelo*, R Marechal Deodoro 360, less good; *Remanso do Tucunaré*, R José de Melo 481, Bairro Bosque, fish specialties; *Anexos*, R Franco Ribeiro 99, next door to *Albemar Hotel*, popular for meals and drinks. A local delicacy is tacacá, similar to that eaten in the states of Pará and Amazonas; a soup served pipping hot in a gourd (*cuia*), it combines glue-like mandioc starch (*goma*), cooked *jambú* leaves which numb the mouth and tongue, shrimp, spices and hot pepper sauce; rec from Sra Diamor, Boulevar Augusto Monteiro 1046, Bairro 15 in the 2° distrito (Bus Norte-Sul from the centre), other kiosks in town, ask around. For ice cream *Sorveteria Arte Sabor*, Travessa Santa Inés 28, corner Aviario, 1° distrito, 15 mins' walk from the centre, excellent home made ice cream, many jungle fruit flavours, highly rec; *Sorvete & Cia*, Av Brasil 394, ice cream by kilo and fix it yourself hot dogs.

● Post & telecommunications
Post Office: on corner of R Epaminondas Jacome and Av Getúlio Vargas.

Telephone: Teleacre, Av Brasil between Mal Deodoro and Av Getúlio Vargas, long delays for international calls.

● Shopping
Market: 1° distrito, off R Epaminondas Jacome. *Inacio's Tur*, runs shopping trips to Guajará Mirim, 3/week US$40 leaving 2330, returning the next day at 2130.

● Tour companies & travel agents
Nilce's Tour, R Quintino Bocaiúva 20, T/F 223-2611, for airline tickets, helpful, 15 mins' walk from the centre; *Serra's Tur*, R S Coelho 372, T 224-4629; *Inácio's Tur*, R Rui Barbosa 91, at *Hotel Pinheiro*; *AcreTur*, R Rui Barbosa 193, by *Rio Branco Hotel*.

● Tourist offices
DETUR/AC, Departamento de Turismo, Av Getúlio Vargas 659, Centro, T 224-3997, ramal 20, part of the Acre Secretaria de Indústria e Comércio.

● Transport
Local Car hire: prices for car rentals with the nationwide agencies are higher in Acre than in other states; **Interlocadora**, Rodovia AC-40, Km 0, 2° distrito, T 224-7041; **Localiza**, T 224-7746; **Unidas**, T 224-5044.

Air The airport is on AC-40, Km 1.2, in the 2°

distrito. Taxi from the airport to the centre US$20 flat rate, but going to the airport the meter is used, which usually comes to less. By bus, take 'Norte-Sul' or 'Vila Acre'. Flights with Varig daily to **Porto Velho** and Manaus; daily to Cuiabá and Campo Grande; Tues and Thur to **Cruzeiro do Sul**. Cheaper daily flights with Tavaj, to Cruzeiro do Sul and Manaus. There are several air taxi companies for charter flights to the interior, inc Rio Branco, T 224-1384, Tacezul, T 224-3242 and Regional, T 224-2465. Ote Redes Aéreas, T 223-2390 (airport), 224-2830 (manager, Pasco at home), operates a twin engine Bandeirante with capacity for 18, to **Puerto Maldonado**, Peru, irregular departures (1-3/week), US$100 (payable in US$ cash or *reais*), a 1 hr interesting flight over the jungle; Puerto Maldonado office, González Prada 360, T 571-656; the Polícia Federal are at the airport for exit/entry stamps when these international flights operate. Airport tax is US$6.

Buses Rodoviária on Av Uirapuru, Cidade Nova, 2° distrito (E bank); city bus 'Norte-Sul' to the centre. To **Porto Velho**, Viação Rondônia, 5 daily, 8 hrs, US$19. To **Guajará Mirim**, daily with Rondônia at 1130 and 2200, 5-6 hrs, US$17; see **Shopping** above for a more luxurious service. To **Brasiléia** with Acreana, daily at 0600, 1115 and 1300, 5 hrs in the wet season, faster in the dry, US$17, continuing to **Assis Brasil** in the dry season only. There is no bus service to Cruzeiro do Sul at any time of the year.

ROUTES From Rio Branco the BR-364 continues W (in principle) to Cruzeiro do Sul and Japim, with a view to reaching the Peruvian frontier further W when completed; it is hoped that it will be continued by the Peruvians to Pucallpa. It is very difficult to get from Rio Branco to Cruzeiro do Sul by road because there is no bus service, and the occasional truck goes mainly in the dry season; the road is frequently impassable (it is open, on average, 20 days a year). In early 1996, Brazil and Peru declared their intention to foster development along their common border, starting with improved road links in the Assis Brasil/Iñapari area (see below).

WEST OF RIO BRANCO: CRUZEIRO DO SUL

(*Pop* 66,600) An isolated Amazonian town on the Rio Juruá in western Acre; cheap excursions can be made on the river, for example to the village of Rodrigues Alves (2-3 hrs, return by boat or by road, 15 km). In the jungle one can see rubber-tapping, and collecting the latex into 'borrachas' which weigh up to 45 kg.

● **Accommodation & places to eat** E *Novo do Acre*, rec, a/c, clean; E *Flor de Maio*, facing river, clean, showers, full board available. Several other hotels and restaurants.

● **Banks & money changers** Money changing is very difficult.

● **Transport Air** Besides the scheduled Varig flights to Rio Branco, air taxis go to Rio Branco (Tavaj) and Pucallpa (Tasa). **Road** is described under **Routes** above. In rainy season, **river** transport to Manaus is possible.

FRONTIER WITH PERU AND BOLIVIA

The BR-317 from Rio Branco heads S and later SW, parallel to the Rio Acre; it is paved as far as **Xapuri** (the location of the Fundação Chico Mendes in memory of the environmentalist and union organizer murdered in 1989); one very basic lodging and two restaurants. The road continues to **Brasiléia** (three buses daily to Rio Branco, 5 hrs in the wet, US$17, three hotels, two basic lodgings, several restaurants, Polícia Federal give entry/exit stamps), opposite the Bolivian town of Cobija on the Rio Acre, and finally to Assis Brasil where the Peruvian, Bolivian and Brazilian frontiers meet. Across the Rio Acre are Iñapari (Peru) and Bolpebra, Bolivia. Bus service operates only in the dry season beyond Brasiléia to Assis Brasil, access in the wet season is by river. **Quixadá**, 30 km W of Brasiléia has no facilities, poor roads, crossing to Bolivia unreliable, but a friendly community. In **Assis Brasil**, there are two hotels (one basic but clean, friendly, E), two restaurants, some shops, a bank which does not change US dollars (the hotel owner may be persuaded to oblige), river transport in the wet season, and bus service in the dry. You get between Iñapari and Assis Brasil by wading across the river. The Brazilian side is reported to be somewhat more expensive, but much pleasanter and offering more variety. **NB** There is no Polícia Federal in the village, get entry/exit stamps in Brasiléia.

The Centre-west

THE so-called Centre-West (*Centro-Oeste*) of Brazil, occupied by the states of Goiás, Mato Grosso and Mato Grosso do Sul (divided from Mato Grosso in 1977), was the most isolated part of the nation until President Vargas' 'Drive to the West' in the 1940s (when many of the Xingu Indian tribes were first contacted).

Today Goiás, with an area of 364,714 sq km and 4,024,550 inhabitants, is one of Brazil's most rapidly-developing frontier agricultural areas, producing coffee, soya and rice, most of Brazil's tin and tungsten, and raising beef on the country's largest cattle ranches. The Federal District of Brasília was subtracted from its territory in 1960, which was further split in half in 1990 to form the new state of Tocantins in the N (see page 627). Old colonial mining towns in the state sprang from gold rushes which began in 1722, as Paulistas and Bandeirantes pushed out from Minas Gerais in search of precious stones and new mineral wealth. The eroded Brazilian Plateau, clothed in woodland savannah and varying from 600m to 900m in height, ripples across the S of the state; most of its clearwater rivers flow N to feed the Araguaia and Tocantins rivers. Elsewhere, the climate is sub-tropical, with distinct wet and dry seasons.

The Centre-West provides 6% of the country's internal income, mainly from farming and cattle raising. With over 100 million fertile ha, the region produces 10% of national bean production, while Goiás alone has about 12% of the nation's cattle (about 18 million head) and produces 7% of Brazil's milk (about 1 billion litres). Corn (maize) is abundant the year round, so much so that many regional corn dishes have been created: cakes, ice cream, soufflés and *pomonhas* (see under Goiânia, **Restaurants**).

GOIÂNIA

(*Pop* 920,840; *CEP* 74000; *DDD* 062) Just off the BR-060, 209 km SW of Brasília: the second (after Belo Horizonte) of Brazil's planned state capitals, Goiânia was founded in 1933 and replaced Goiás Velho as capital 4 years later. In general, commercial and industrial sectors are to the N, with administration in the centre and residential zones to the south.

Places of interest

The unremarkable **Metropolitan Cathedral**, corner Ruas 14 e 19, stands two blocks E of the Praça. Walk due N on broad Av Goiás to see the painted walls of the **Projeto Galería Aberto**; many city buses are also painted with colourful and eye-catching designs.

It is a spacious and modern city, with many green spaces and well-lit main avenues, ornamented with plants, radiating out from the central **Praça Cívica**, on which stand the Government Palace and main Post Office. 1½ km out along the Av Araguaia (which runs diagonally NE from the Praça) is the shady **Parque Mutirama**, with recreational and entertainment facilities and a planetarium (Sun sessions at 1530 and 1630); there is also a pleasant **Parque Zoológico**, Av Anhangüera, some distance W of the main square, with good zoo, zoological museum, playground, lake and sports fields (park open Tues-Sun 0900-1830). Other pleasant places to visit are Bosque dos Buritis, just W of the Centro Cívico, and the Lagoa das Rosas, also W of the centre.

Museums

Museu Antropológico do UFG on the Praça Universitária (1 km E of Praça Cívica) with wide-ranging ethnographic displays on the Indians of the Centre-W (Mon-Fri 0900-1700), **Museu de Ornitologia**, Av Pará 395 (Sétor Campinas), with more than 8000 stuffed birds and animals from many countries (open 0900-1900, except Mon). Just off the Praça Cívica is the **Museu Estadual 'Zoroastro Artiaga'**, Praça Dr P L Teixeira 13, with a collection of local handicrafts, religious objects, animals and Indian artefacts.

Excursions

To Goiás Velho, Caldas Novas and Pirenópolis (see below), the thermal springs at Cachoeira Dourada (240 km S on the Paranaíba River), the fantastic rock formations of the Serra das Galés at **Paraúna** (160 km SSW off BR-060) and a host of delightful, colonial mining villages within 2 hrs' drive on good (often paved) roads. Travel agents in town can arrange day tours, eg *Turisplan Turismo*, R 8 No 388, T 224-1941 (which also sells regular bus tickets).

Local information

● **Accommodation**

Many hotels located along Av Anhangüera, which runs E-W 4 blocks N of the Central Plaza; as one of the main arteries through the city it is busy and noisy.

L3 *Castro's Park*, Av Rep do Líbano 1520, Setor Ote, T 223-7766, F 225-7070, warmly rec.

A1 *Papillon*, Rep do Líbano 1824, T 223-8511, F 223-8381, good; **A3** *Samambaia*, Av Anhanguera 1157, T/F 261-1444; *Bandeirantes*, same street No 3278, T/F 224-0066; *Umuarama*, R 4 No 492, T 224-1555, F 224-1673, all three good; **A3** *Karajás*, Av Goiás e R 3, T 224-9666, F 229-1153, 3 blocks N of Praça, convenient and comfortable; **A3** *Cabiúna Palace*, Av Parnaíba 698 (close to Parque Mutirama), T/F 224-4355, good value.

B *Augustus*, Praça Antônio Lizita 702, T 224-1022, F 224-1410, good; **B** *Vila Rica*, Anhangüera 3456, T 224-0500, F 225-0551, 2-star Embratur hotel, a/c, convenient.

C *Mundial*, R 10A No 69 (nr airport), T 224-6629; **C** *Presidente*, Anhangüera 5646, T 224-0500.

Cheaper (**C-D**) are: *Príncipe*, Anhangüera 2936 e Av Araguaia, T 224-0085, fans, clean, good value; *Paissandú*, Av Goiás 1290 e R 55, T 224-

4925, fans, clean, 8 long blocks N of Praça; *Hotel del Rey*, R 8 No 321, T 225-6306, good location on pedestrian mall, fans, good value.

Several cheap hotels (**D-E**) nr the rodoviária: eg *Star*, R 68 No 537, basic, interesting clientele; *Itaipú*, R 29A No 178 at the old rodoviária (Setor Aeroporto), T 212-4055; *J Alves*; opp rodoviária. Northwest of the rodoviária are many cheap *dormitórios*.

Camping: at *Itanhangá* municipal site, Av Princesa Carolina, 13 km, attractive wooded location, reasonable facilities, US$5.50 pp.

● **Places to eat**

Goiânia is much cheaper for eating than Brasília, and the variety of eating places is too wide to list here. Many *churrascarias*, eg *Boi na Brasa*, on Praça Germano Roriz (the first large square due S of Praça Cívica on R 84), open 1100-0100, and the more expensive *Lancaster Grill*, R 89 No 117, a/c, live music; *Le Steak*, Av 85 No 352, excellent, a/c, good atmosphere, expensive by Brazilian standards; *Fim de Tarde*, Av 85 No 301, good meat dishes (inc *picanha* and *kibe*, Arabic appetizer) and beer, open from 1700; *Costelería do Marcão*, Av 31 de Março, past Praça do Cruzeiro, best ribs in Goiás, rec, open from 1700; *Bom Gourmet*, Av 85 No 1676, for meat and chicken dishes, very good, seats on street or in a/c room. Varied menu at *Cliff Piano Bar e Restaurante*, R 23 No 72, esq Av Rep do Líbano, expensive, elegant, good food and service, nice atmosphere, highly rec. *Palatinum*, in *Hotel Augustus*, Italian, very good, elegant, a/c, piano music. Good array of restaurants and watering holes around the Praça Tamandaré (Ruas 8 e 5, just beyond the Bosque dos Buritis, 1 km W of Praça Cívica), including *Modiglianni* for good pizzas.

Vegetarians are well-catered for: eg *Arroz Integral*, R 93 No 326 (1100-1400, 1800-2100, self-service), or *Naturalmente Natural*, R 15 No 238, 1 block from the cathedral. Many small eating places nr the rodoviária, which also has good food at low prices.

For **regional specialities** try the *Centro de Tradições Goiánas*, R 4 No 515 (above the Parthenon Centre), traditional rice and fish cuisine. *Piquiras*, Av Rep do Líbano 1758 (nr *Castro's Hotel*) and R 139 s/n, Setor Marista, try the *pastelzinho de piquí* as an appetizer: *piquí* is a regional fruit used in many traditional Goiás dishes, the most famous of which is *galinhada* (fried chicken, *piquí*, rice cooked with saffron). If eating *piquí*, be very careful of the little thorns on the inside. Street stands (*pamonharías*) throughout the city sell *pamonha* snacks, tasty pastries made with green corn, some are sweet, some savoury, some *picante*/spicy; all are served hot and have cheese in the middle, some include sausage. Rec *pomonharias* are: *Pomonharia*

18th-century sugar *fazenda* now listed as an historical site, small museum, original mill, no public transport.

Local festivals

Festa do Divino Espírito Santo, 45 days after Easter (Pentecost), is one of Brazil's most famous and extraordinary folkloric/religious celebrations, lasting 3 days, with medieval costumes, tournaments, dances and mock battles between Moors and Christians, a tradition held annually since 1819.

Local information

● **Accommodation**

A3 *Hotel Fazenda Quinta da Santa Bárbara*, in garden setting at R do Bonfim 1, T 331-1304, all facilities inc *Restaurante Brasília*; **A3** *Pousada dos Pirineus*, Chácara Mata do Sobrado, Bairro do Carmo, T 331-1345, a/c, TV, restaurant, bar, 2 pools, gym, tennis and other sports, boat hire.

C *Pousada das Cavalhadas*, Praça da Matriz, T 331-1261, central, fans, fridges in rooms, best of the budget choices.

More basic are: D *Rex*, also on the Praça da Matriz, T 331-1121, 9 sparse rooms, small restaurant; *Pousada Tavares*, *Pensão Central* and *Dormitório da Geny* are all **E** and mostly for the desperate. All accommodation is filled during the Festa (see above) and even the downtown municipal camping site beside the Rio das Alvas overflows; better to visit from Brasília at this time.

CALDAS NOVAS

(*Pop* 24,060; *CEP* 76940; *DDD* 062) 187 km SE of Goiânia, a newly developed thermal resort with good hotels and camp sites with hot swimming pools. There are three groups of springs within this area: Caldas Novas, Fontes de Pirapetinga (7 km from the town) and Rio Quente (29 km from the town, bus from Caldas Novas); water temperatures are 37-51°C.

● **Accommodation** 48 in all. Very fashionable is **L2** *Hotel Turismo* (5-star) – *Pousada do Rio Quente* (4-star) complex at Rio Quente, T 452-1122, F 452-1177, or F São Paulo 282-5281, T 852-5733, or Brasília 224-7166, breakfast and lunch, transportation to main pools and recreation facilities inc in price, other extras paid for with hotel's own currency, good hotel, accommodation in main buildings or chalets. (The *Turismo* has a private airstrip; flights from Rio and São Paulo with agencies.) **L3** *Parque das Primaveras*, R do Balneário, T 453-1355, F 453-1294, rec by locals, cheaper than the Rio Quente places; **A1** *Tamburi*, R Eça de Queirós, 10, T 453-1455, OK; **C** *Serra Dourada*, Av Correia Neto 574, T 453-1300, rec; **E** *Imperial*, nr Rodoviária, clean, friendly. **Camping**: at Esplanada, and *Camping Clube do Brasil* site on the Ipameri road, 1 km from the centre. Many other 'Clubes e Campings', all with snack bars, eg *Tropical*, 2 sites in town, and *Berro d'Água*, Bairro do Turista, rec.

● **Places to eat** *Caminho do Natural*, R José Borges 550 vegetarian, good, but expensive.

● **Transport** Many buses from Goiânia; best reached from Morrinhos on BR-153 (Goiânia-São Paulo). Daily bus from Morrinhos US$1, 30 mins.

CHAPADA DOS VEADEIROS

Goiás has two major National Parks. In the elevated region 200 km N of Brasília is popular **Chapada dos Veadeiros** (US$0.60 fee). The main attractions are a number of high waterfalls (including a series along the Rio Negro, 7 km from São Jorge by rough track) complete with palm-shaded oases and natural swimming pools, and the varied wildlife: capibara, rhea, tapir, wolf, toucan, etc (Ibama R 219 No 95, Setor Universitário, 74605-800 Goiânia, T 062-224-2488, or T 061-646-1109).

● **Access** The park is reached by paved state highway 118 to Alto Paraíso de Goiás, then gravel road W towards Colinas for 30 km where a sign marks the turnoff (just before the village of São Jorge). Buses Brasília-Alto Paraíso 1000 and 2200, US$6; occasional local buses Alto Paraíso-São Jorge, inc 1600 departure, 5-km walk to park entrance. By jeep it is possible to cross from Alto Paraíso to the Brasília-Salvador highway (BR-242) via Nova Roma (ferry crossing) and Posse, a very slow but beautiful journey of 220 km.

● **Accommodation** There is a small hotel (E) by the rodoviária in Alto Paraíso and a very basic *dormitório* in São Jorge (take sleeping bag or hammock), but camping in the park is the most pleasant option, about US$2/night and busy on weekends in the best visiting season (May-Oct).

EMAS NATIONAL PARK

In the far SW of the state, covering the watershed of the Araguaia, Taquari and Formoso Rivers, is the small **Emas National Park**, 110 km S of Mineiros (*pop* 33,600) just off the main BR-364 route between Brasília and Cuiabá (112 km beyond Jataí).

Douglas Trent of Focus Tours writes: "The near 132,868 ha of undulating grasslands and 'campo sujo' cerrado forests host the world's largest concentration of termite mounds. They provide a surreal setting for large numbers of pampas deer, giant anteater and greater rhea, or 'ema' in Portuguese. Maned wolf are frequently seen roaming the grasses in search of tinamou and other prey. Other animals which may be seen include yellow and giant armadillos, Amazonian anaconda, Brazilian tapir, grisons and white-lipped peccary. The park holds the greatest concentration of blue-and-yellow macaws outside Amazônia, and blue-winged, red-shouldered and red-bellied macaws can also be seen. Other bird specialities include the endemic white-winged nightjar, cock-tailed tyrant, white-vented violetear, lesser tinamou and the rare lesser northura, dwarf tinamou, and crested eagle. A pair of bare-faced currasow, white-woodpeckers, streamer-tailed tyrants and other showy birds visit the park HQ building daily.

Along with the grasslands, the park supports a vast marsh on one side and rich gallery forests on the other. The crystal clear waters of the Rio Formosa pass right by the headquarters and wander through the park. Many have compared this park with the African savannas. As many of the interesting mammals are nocturnal, a spotlight is a must."

● **Access** The park is most easily reached from Campo Grande (approx 6 hrs by car, compared with about 20 hrs from Goiânia, paved road poor). The road to the National Park is now paved; there is no regular transport but tour operators can organize 4WD trips. The São José monastery, Mineiros, can arrange the necessary permission to visit, turn left out of rodoviária and walk ½ km along dirt road (or from Ibama, as above, also from Secretaria de Turismo, Praça Cel Carrijo 1, T 661-1551). A 4-day, 3-night visit to the Park can be arranged through agencies (eg Focus Tours, Belo Horizonte, see page 429).

● **Accommodation In Mineiros**: are **C** *Pilões Palace*, Praça Alves de Assis, T 661-1547, restaurant, comfortable; and **D** *Boi na Brasa*, R Onze 11, T 661-1532, no a/c, good *churrasco* restaurant attached; next door **E** *Mineiros Hotel*, with bath and huge breakfast, good lunch, rec. Camping within the park costs about US$2

pp and there is simple, dormitory accommodation at the park headquarters; kitchen and cook available but bring own food.

THE RIO ARAGUAIA: WEST AND NORTH OF GOIÂNIA

Of Goiás' many natural attractions it is the Rio Araguaia which is most being promoted as a vacation destination. Brazilians are firmly convinced that the 2630-km-long river is richer in fish than any other in the world; a visit to the 220-km stretch between Aruanã and the Ilha do Bananal during the fishing season is quite an experience. As the receding waters in May reveal sparkling white beaches along the Araguaia, thousands of Brazilian and international enthusiasts pour into the area, intent on getting the best camping spots. As many as 400 tent 'cities' spring up, and vast quantities of fish (*pirurucu, pintado, pacu, suribim, tucanaré* and various types of catfish) are hauled in before the phenomenon winds down in Sept, when the rivers begin to rise again and flood the surrounding plains. Without Brazilian contacts, the traveller's best way of experiencing this annual event is with one of the specialist tour operators; rec are *Transworld*, R 3 No 560, Goiânia, T 224-4340 (one week group trips in a 'botel' out of Aruanã to Bananal), and *KR International Travel*, R Mexico 11-Gr 1701, Rio de Janeiro, T 210-1238, ex-Peace Corps manager, good for info on the Centre-West region. Boats (US$10-25 an hour) and guides can also be hired in Aruanã, Britânia, Barra do Garças or **Porto Luis Alves** (**A1** *Pousada do Jaburu*, including meals; **A3** *Pousada do Pescador*, a/c, access to boats and guides), guide Vandeir will arrange boat trips to see wildlife, take food and water. Interesting walks in surrounding jungle with Joel, ask at the hotel. There is good fishing for *tucanaré* in the Rio Cristalino. Beware of currents and do not swim where the bed is muddy or where sting rays are said to lurk. Piranhas are reported not to be a problem where there is a current and provided swimmers have no open wounds. Yellow-fever vaccination is also rec for the region. *Borrachudas*, tiny biting insects, are an unavoidable fact of life in Central Brazil in June and July; repellent helps a little.

ARUANÃ

The Araguaia is most readily accessible from **Aruanã** (*pop* 5,400) a port 165 km NW of Goiás Velho by paved highway, which sees little excitement outside the winter fishing season (when its comfortable hotels are booked out for months). Boats can be rented to visit some of the beautiful lakes and beaches nearby. Buses from the rodoviária serve Araguapaz, Britânia and Goiânia. The Brazilian Canoeing Championships are also held along the river in July.

- **Accommodation & places to eat A2** *Recanto Sonhado*, on river at end of Av Altamiro Caio Pacheco (2 km), T 376-1230, self-service restaurant, boutique, inc lunch, no hardships whatever (reservations can be made through T 062 241-7913 in Goiânia); **C** *Araguaia*, Praça Couto Magalhães 53 (opp the docks), T 376-1251; both have pools, a/c, and meals available; restaurants in town rather poor, but try *Columbia*, R João Artiaga 221 (opp Municipal Stadium), clean, good menu. The official campground is a 20-min boat ride away on Ilha Redonda, but open (and full) only in July.

BARRA DO GARÇAS

A direct dirt road (250 km, via Jussara) and a more circuitous paved route through Iporá (340 km) connect Goiás Velho with Aragarças (on the Goiás side) and **Barra do Garças** (on the Mato Grosso side of the Araguaia). Barra (*pop* 45,600) is the pleasanter of the two and has the better facilities, including several banks and hotels. 6 km E of Barra on the road to Araguaiana is **Parque Balneário das Águas Quentes**, with thermal pools (42°C), river bathing and recreational opportunities. The abrupt 600m-high Morro do Cristo (10 km) gives a wide view over the Araguaia and surrounding country.

Local festivals A *Festival de Praia* is held locally in July: fishing tournaments, displays, boat races, etc.

- **Accommodation In Barra do Garças**: **C** *Esplanada Palace*, R Waldir Rabelo 81, T 861-2515, a/c, safe parking; various **D-E** hotels along Av Min João Alberto, eg *Novo Mundo*, *Presidente* and *Avenida*, all clean and

a/c. *Churrascarías* also on this avenue and nr the bridge (eg *Del Fronteyra*, live music, 1100-1400, 1900-2200); pleasant river beach with bars and snacks; campsite on island in river; nighttime entertainment by the port. In Aragarças: (4 km) is the new **A1** *Hotel Toriuá Park*, T 861-2232, pool, minizoo, own launch, lakeside location rec.

- **Transport** Buses to Barra to/from São Paulo direct, 20 hrs, US$30; to São Felix do Araguaia at 2000, US$24, arrives early afternoon, wildlife may be seen in early am.

ROUTES If heading for the Pantanal, note that BR-070 from Barra to Cuiabá is in poor condition after the turn to Poxoréo; better to go to Rondonópolis, either for Cuiabá or Campo Grande.

The road N to Marabá (BR-158), paralleling the Araguaia on the Mato Grosso and Pará side, leaves Barra do Garças and runs 140 km to **Xavantina** (*pop* 13,000) on the Rio das Mortes, the famous 'River of Deaths' which once marked the territorial boundary of the intractable Xavante Indians. The road is paved for a further 310 km to Alô Brasil, then marginal dirt (465 km) to beyond the Pará state border; it is again paved for the remaining 650 km to Marabá via Redenção and Xinguara (see below).

- **Accommodation** (on BR-158, in Mato Grosso): At **Xavantina**: is **E** *Hotel Xavantina*, basic but nothing better; *Churrascaria Arca de Noé*, highly rec. At **Água Boa** (*pop* 16,570), 76 km N of Xavantina, are **C** *Palace* and *Manga Rosa*, good churrascaria.

On the other (E) side of the Araguaia, the Brasília-Belém highway (BR-153) runs N through the heart of Goiás and Tocantins states.

TOCANTINS

The new state of Tocantins (277,321.9 sq km; *pop* 920,135) is technically an Amazonian state, the boundary of the Norte region running along the border between it and Goiás. Its main attractions are the Ilha do Bananal and the Araguaia National Park, and fishing, although additional sites of interest might be the various diamond workings in the state and the Kraolândia and Xerente Indian Reserves between Miracema and Carolina.

TOWNS IN TOCANTINS

Miracema do Tocantins is the provisional
capital until the purpose-built **Palmas** is
complete (*pop* in 1993, 6,000, mostly government personnel and construction workers).
The small town of **Gurupi** on the BR-153,
90 km N of the Tocantins border, has been
rec as a pleasant place to break the journey.
Hotel (E) near the rodoviária. Entry to the
Bananal is not permitted from here.

At Fátima, on the BR-153, a paved road
heads E 52 km to a new bridge over the
Rio Tocantins to **Porto Nacional** (*pop*
43,225). From here a road is being built
N to Palmas, 55 km, a few kilometres
inland from the village of Canela (which
is opposite Molha – ferry across the Tocantins). Porto Nacional has 3 habitable
hotels, 3 restaurants, an airport with regional flights, 7 banks, the regional hospital and a small rodoviária on Praça do
Peso Boiadeiro. The church of Nossa Senhora das Mercês (1903) on the main
square is probably the only major point
of interest; a regional festival of N Sra das
Mercês is on 24 September. 2-hr boat trips
up the Tocantins from the old ferry port
go the Carreira Comprida rapids and island beaches (best May-Sept).

77 km upriver from Palmas, on the W
bank, **Miracema do Tocantins** (*pop*
20,850) has 5 hotels, an airport, sightseeing at nearby Cachoeiras do Lajeado
Grande and a 24-hr ferry to Tocantínia on
the E bank. From the BR-153 to Miracema is 23 km. Much of the area is
under threat of flooding if a hydroelectric
dam is built at Lajeada (Miracema):
Canela would vanish, and Palmas and the
bridge at Porto Nacional have been designed with the hypothetical lake in
mind.

At Guaraí the road forks, one branch
continuing W into Pará, then turning N
to Marabá on the Transamazônica and on
to Belém. The other branch goes to Araguaína, whereafter the BR-226 goes to
Estreito in Maranhão, from where the
BR-010 runs N through Imperatriz to
Belém. A pleasant overnight stop on the
road to Araguaiana is the hilly town of
Uruaçu, cheap hotels near rodoviária.

ARAGUAÍNA

(*Pop* 103,395) In Tocantins, on the
Brasília-Belém road (Brasília, 1,102 km;
Belém 842 km; Imperatriz, 174 km); several hotels near rodoviária including
D *Esplanada*, may have to share a room,
friendly, clean, fan, no breakfast, good;
Líder, *São Jorge*, *do Norte* and *Goiás* (all **E**).
● **Transport Air** Varig **flights** twice a week
from Brasília, Imperatriz and São Luiz. **Buses** Bus
leaves Araguaína for Marabá 0700 and 1400.
Ordinary bus to Goiânia takes 24 hrs: try to get
an express. If travelling to Belém or Brasília by
bus, reservations are not normally accepted: be
at the terminal 2 hrs before scheduled departure
as buses tend to leave early; as soon as bus pulls
in, follow the driver to the ticket counter and
ask if there are seats. Brasília 1200, 2400, US$36
(22 hrs). Buses also to Santarém.

TO CONCEIÇÃO DO ARAGUAIA

Off the Brasília-Belém road are fast-devel-
oping frontier regions between the lower
Araguaia and Xingu rivers. Kevin Healey
writes: There is now a soaring concrete
bridge spanning the Araguaia just S of
Conceição do Araguaia, and the road connection to the Belém highway at Guaraí is
being paved. (This is the only bridge
across the Araguaia between Barra dos
Garças and Marabá.)

North and W of Conceição are many
new townships and ranches. Places like
Redenção (*pop* 54,365) and Xinguara are
raw, dusty and not very salubrious for
tourists, especially at night. At **Xinguara**
(*pop* 40,315 already) is the **E** *Hotel Rio
Vermelho*, not too bad. To the W, Cumaru
is a *garimpeiro* settlement, from where the
local military governor keeps 'law and
order' over the gold mining centres near
the Rio Fresco. Here, the miners and
prospectors are already on the edge of the
Gorotiré Indian Reserve and a road is
poised to enter the Indian land. To the S
is **Campo Alegre** (*pop* 8,400), the centre
of cow country, with a huge new slaugh-
terhouse serving the corporate ranches
around the region (eg the experimental
ranch of Cristalino, owned by VW Brasil).
This is a perfect place to see the destruction of the rainforest and the changing
climate pattern.

CONCEIÇÃO DO ARAGUAIA

The town (*pop* 54,490) has a frontier atmosphere, although mudhuts are being replaced by brick: cowboy hats, battered Chevrolet pick-ups, skinny mules and a red light district. Airport 14 km SW. Conceição would be a useful base for visiting the Ilha do Bananal.

● **Accommodation & places to eat** The best hotel is the **B** *Taruma Tropical* (T 421-1205), pool, conference centre, garage, sauna, frigobars, expanded restaurant, clean and functioning bathrms, a/c – when it works; the hotel is well patronized by ranchers and absentee landowners from Brasília; also *Marajoara*, Av JK 1587, T 421-1220, some a/c, safe parking, breakfast; *Araguaia*, R Conto de Magalhães 2605, breakfast, both small, overpriced. Best place to eat is *Café Taboquinha*, Av Francisco Vitor, well-prepared fish, open 1200-1500, 1800-2300.

ILHA DO BANANAL

Douglas Trent, of Focus Tours, Belo Horizonte (who arrange tours, see page 429), writes:"**Bananal** is the world's largest river island, located in the state of Tocantins on the northeastern border of Mato Grosso. The island is formed by a division in the S of the Rio Araguaia and is approximately 320 km long. The entire island was originally a national park (called **Parque Nacional Araguaia**), which was then cut in half and later further reduced to its current size of 562,312 ha (of an original 2 million). The island and park are subject to seasonal flooding and contain several permanent lakes. The island, and especially the park, form one of the more spectacular wildlife areas on the continent, in many ways similar to the Pantanal. The vegetation is a transition zone between the *cerrado* (woody savanna) and Amazon forests, with gallery forests along the many waterways. There are several marshlands throughout the island.

The fauna is also transitional. More than 300 bird species are found here, including the hoatzin, hyacinthine macaw, harpy eagle and black-fronted piping guan. The giant anteater, maned wolf, bush dog, giant otter, jaguar, puma, marsh deer, pampas deer, American tapir,

yellow anaconda and South American river turtle also occur here. The island is flooded most of the year, with the prime visiting (dry) season being from June to early Oct, when the beaches are exposed. Unfortunately, the infrastructure for tourism aside from fishing expeditions (the island is a premier spot for big fish) is very limited.

Permission to visit the park should be obtained in advance from Sr Levi Vargas, Director of the Park, Ibama, R 219, No 95, Setor Universitário, 74605-800 Goiânia."

Local information
● **Accommodation & Access**

Access to the park is through the small but pleasant town of **Santa Teresinha** (*pop* 8,900) which is N of São Felix (see below), and is the gateway to the park. A charming hotel is the **A3** *Bananal*, Pça Tarcila Braga 106, CEP 78395 (Mato Grosso), with full board. There is room only for 10; reserve well in advance, either by mail, allowing several months for the mail to get through, or by phoning the town's telephone operator, asking the hotel to call you back and hoping that you hear from them.

There is some simple accommodation for scientists at the park, which can sometimes be reserved at the address above or from IBDF, the National Parks department in Brasília. Bring your own food and bedding, and the severely underpaid but dedicated staff would appreciate any extra food or financial help, although it will not be solicited. A boat to the park can be lined up at the *Hotel Bananal*.

Bananal can be visited from São Félix do Araguaia – see below (with permission from Funai in the town) by crossing the river to the Carajá village of **Santa Isabela de Morra** and asking to see the chief, who can tell you the history of the tribe. The island can be crossed from São Félix to **São Miguel de Araguaia** by taking an 8-hr trip (contact the *Bar Beira*). From São Miguel a 5-hr bus trip brings you to **Porangatu** (E *Hotel Mauriti*, shower, restaurant) on the Belém-Brasília highway.

SÃO FÉLIX DO ARAGUAIA

São Félix do Araguaia (*pop* 14,365) is a larger town with more infrastructure for fishing than Santa Teresinha. Many Carajás indians are found in town; a depot of their handicrafts is between the *Pizzaria* and *Mini Hotel* on Av Araguaia. Mosquito nets are highly recommended: high incidence of malaria.

Tours Many river trips available for fishing or to see wildlife. Juracy Lopes, a very experienced guide, can be contacted through *Hotel Xavante*; he has many friends, inc the chief and council, in Santa Isabela (see above). Morning or afternoon trips to the village or to see wildlife, cost US$15 for 2; longer trips can be made to the meeting of the waters with the Rio das Mortes, or spending a night in the jungle sleeping in hammocks. *Icuryala* is recommended, T (062) 223-9518 (Goiâna), excellent food, drink, and service, US$100/day, independent visitors also welcomed. Fazenda owners may invite you as their guest – do not abuse this privilege, and remember to take a gift.

● **Accommodation & places to eat** A very simple hotel with the best view in town is the **D** *Mini Hotel Araguaia*, Av Araguaia 344, T (065) 522-1154, inc breakfast. They have a/c rooms, not rec, electricity is turned off at night and the closed-in room gets very hot. Rec is **D** *Xavante*, Av Severiano Neves 391, T 522-1305, a/c, shower, frigobar, excellent breakfast, delicious *cajá* juice, Sr e Sra Carvalho very hospitable rec. A good restaurant is the *Pizzaria Cantinho da Peixada* on Av Araguaia, next to the Texaco station, overlooking the river: the owner, Klaus, rents rooms, **E**, better than hotels, T 522-1320, he also arranges fishing trips rec. *Bar Paralelos* has live music.

● **Transport Air** Access to both Santa Teresinha and São Félix is by Brasil Central/TAM flights, and to São Félix by bus from Barra do Garças, see above. The air service is unreliable and, as the planes hold just 15 passengers, it is common to get held over for a day or two. There is a daily Votec flight from São Felix to Belém, stopping at Redenção, Tucumã, and many other places. **Buses** Rodoviária is 3 km from centre and waterfront, taxi US$3; buses to Barra do Garças at 0500, arr 2300, or 1730, arr 1100 next day; also to Tucumã, 6-8 hrs, and to São José do Xingu, 10 hrs. No buses to Marabá. In Sta Teresinha look out for a man in a yellowish taxi who kindly offers a free ride and then tries to collect outrageous sums from foreigners. There are legitimate taxis available – use them.

Mato Grosso do Sul and Mato Grosso

TO THE west of Goiás are the states of Mato Grosso and Mato Grosso do Sul, with a combined area of 1,231,549 sq km and a population of only about 3.8 million, or about three persons to the sq km. The two states are half covered with forest, with a large wetland area (230,000 sq km) called the Pantanal (roughly west of a line between Campo Grande and Cuiabá, between which there is a direct road), partly flooded in the rainy season (see page 641).

East of this line the pasture plains appear. Cattle ranching is very important, with over 21 million head of beef cattle on 16 million ha of free range pasture in Mato Grosso do Sul alone. The Noroeste Railway (passenger service indefinitely suspended) and a road run across Mato Grosso do Sul via Campo Grande to Porto Esperança and Corumbá, both on the Rio Paraguai; much of the road is across the wetland, offering many sights of birds and other wildlife.

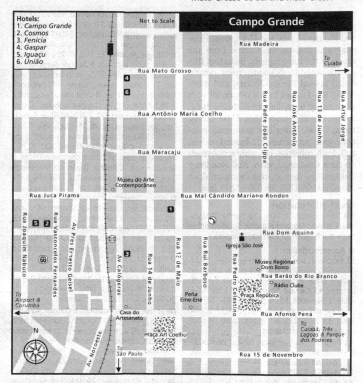

Campo Grande

Hotels:
1. Campo Grande
2. Cosmos
3. Fenícia
4. Gaspar
5. Iguaçu
6. União

CAMPO GRANDE

(*Pop* 565,620; *CEP* 79100; *DDD* 067) Capital of the State of Mato Grosso do Sul (*pop* 1,778,500). It was founded in 1899 and became state capital in 1979 when Mato Grosso do Sul separated from Mato Grosso. It is a pleasant, modern city. Because of the *terra roxa* (red earth), it is called the 'Cidade Morena'.

Places of interest

In the centre is a shady park, the **Praça República**, commonly called the Praça do Rádio after the Rádio Clube on one of its corners. Three blocks W is **Praça Ari Coelho**. Linking the two squares, and running through the city E to W, is Av Afonso Pena; much of its central reservation is planted with yellow ypé trees. Their blos-

som covers the avenue, and much of the city besides, in spring. The city also has a great many mango trees, consequently it is very leafy. The **Parque dos Poderes**, a long way from the centre, extends for several hectares; as well as having the Palácio do Governo and state secretariats, it has a small zoo for the rehabilitation of animals from the Pantanal (phone the Secretaria do Meio Ambiente to visit), lovely trees and cycling and jogging tracks.

Museums

Museu Dom Bosco (Indian Museum), R Barão do Rio Branco 1843 (open daily 0700-1100, 1300-1700, US$0.50, T 383-3994), is a superb museum with the following collections: exhibits from the 5 Indian groups with which the Salesian missionaries have had contact in the 20th century: the Bororó, from the region between Bolivia to the border with Goias and between the Rio Garças and Rio das Mortes; the Moro, from Paraguay and Bolivia; the Carajá, from the shores of the Rio Araguaia, including Ilha do Bananal; the Xavante, from central Brazil beyond Rio das Mortes, and tribes of the Rio Uaupés in Amazônia, all with explanatory texts; fossilised shells, malacology (shells), entomology, 2,800 stuffed birds, 7-8,000 butterflies, mammals, minerals and 'monstruos' (2-headed calves, etc). Each collection is highly rec. **Museu do Arte Contemporâneo**, Mal Rondón e Calógeras, modern art from the region, open Mon-Fri 0900-1700, Sat 0900-1200, free.

Local information

NB The important street in the centre, R Marechal Cândido Mariano Rondon, is called either Marechal Cândido Rondon, or Cândido Mariano.

● Accommodation

L2 *Exceler Plaza*, Av Afonso Pena 444, T 721-0102, F 721-5666, 4-star, very good, luxury, art gallery, pool, tennis, all-you-can-eat business lunches; **L2** *Campo Grande*, R 13 de Maio 2825, T 384-6061, F 724-8349, central, a/c, luxury, cash discounts; **L3** *Buriti*, Av A M Coelho 2301, T/F 384-2211, a/c, fridge, cable TV, pool, sauna, parking, restaurant.

A1 *Concord*, Av Calógeras 1624, T 384-3081, F 382-4987, very good, swimming pool, a/c, mini bar; **A1** *Indaiá Park*, Av Afonso Pena 354, T 384-3858, F 721-0359, a/c, pool, restaurant; **A1** *Vale Verde*, Av Afonso Pena 106, T 721-3355, a/c, mini bar, restaurant, pool; **A3** *Advanced*, Av Calógeras 1909, T 721-5000, F 725-7744, a/c, fridge, TV, B with fan, modern, clean; **A3** *Fenícia*, Av Calógeras 2262, T 383-2001, F 383-2862, a/c, mini bar, TV; **A3** *Paris*, Av Costa e Silva 4175, T 787-1795, F 725-7744, a/c, mini bar, C with fan.

B *Anache*, Marechalo Rondón 1396, T 383-2841, with bath, fan, TV.

C *Americano*, R 14 de Julho 2311 e Marechal Rondón, T 721-1454, a/c, fridge, TV, cheaper with fan, a bit run down, friendly; by Praça Ari Coelho are **C** *Pousada LM*, R 15 de Novembro 201, T 383-3300, with bath, fan, fridge, also rents by the month; and **D** *Central*, R 15 de Novembro 472, T 384-6442, fan, basic, cheaper with shared bath.

Near the rodoviária: A3 *Internacional*, Allan Kardec 245, T 384-4677, F 721-2729, a/c, fridge, B with fan, modern, clean, pool; on Dom Aquino are **A3** *Iguaçu*, No761, T 384-4621, F 721-3215, a/c, fridge, TV, B with fan, modern,

clean, pleasant, rec; **A3** *Palace*, No1501, T 384-4741, a/c, fridge, TV, B with fan, clean, some rooms small; **B** *Nacional*, No 610, T 383-2461, a/c, TV, cheaper with fan, C with shared bath; **B** *Village Palace*, No 802, T 724-1954, a/c, fridge, TV, C with fan; **B** *Saigali*, Barão do Rio Branco 356, T 384-5775, with bath, a/c, mini bar, TV, parking, clean, cheaper with fan, comfortable, friendly, rec; **B** *Carandá*, J Nabuco 62, T 382-8384, a/c, TV, cheaper with fan; **C** *Cosmos*, Dom Aquino 771, T 383-4270, with bath, fan, good value; **C** *Novo*, J Nabuco 185, T 721-0505, with bath, clean, without breakfast, good value, rec; **C** *Turis*, Allan Kardec 200, T 382-7688, with bath, a/c, clean, cheaper with fan, D in basement; **C** *Rocha*, Barão do Rio Branco 343, 1 block from rodoviária, T 7256874, without breakfast, with bath, fan, TV, parking, clean; **D** *Vânia*, Marechal Rondón 1004, T 384-2338, with bath, fan, cheaper with shared bath, laundry, clean, rec; **D** *Santa Inês*, Afonso Pena 1413, T 724-2621, with bath, fan, clean, comfortable, cheaper with shared bath; **D** *Paulista*, J Nabuco 233, T 382-9120, shared bath, fan, basic; **D** *Pamella*, J Nabuco 245, T 724-3209, shared bath, fan, buffet restaurant. There is a wide variety of hotels in the streets around the rodoviária; if you have time, leave bags in the *guarda volumes* and shop around.

Near the railway station: B *Gaspar*, Av Mato Grosso 2, T/F 383-5121, opp station, with bath, a/c, fridge, C with fan, ask for quiet room, good breakfast, clean, comfortable; next door is **C** *União*, Calógeras 2828, T 382-4213, with bath, TV, cheaper with shared bath, good breakfast, clean, ask for quiet room, friendly; **D** *Continental*, R Maracaju 229, 2 blocks from railway, 5 from rodoviária, clean, comfortable; **D** *Plaza*, R Maracaju 140, with bath, fan, cheaper with shared bath. **D** *Rio Negro*, R Maracaju 171, with fan, clean; **D** *Esperança*, R Dr Temistocles 93, 1 block from station, hot and cold showers, basic, no a/c or fan, clean, restaurant, very helpful; **D** *Caçula*, Calógeras 2704, T 721-4658, with bath, fan, TV, cheaper with shared bath, basic, hot showers, laundry, friendly; others in R Maracaju.

● Places to eat

Churrascarias: *Vitório*, Av Afonso Pena 1907, live music evenings; *Terracus Gaúcho*, at rodoviária, huge meal; *Campo Grande*, Av Calógeras 2199, good value; *Nossa Querência*, Av Afonso Pena 1267, rodizio, good value and quality, nr rodoviária, 2-for-1 special in evenings, rec. **Comida caseira:** *Carinca*, SE corner of main square, modern, clean, good plain food; *Bandeirantes*, Dom Aquino 803, good and economical; *Papa Gula*, Dom Aquino 1761, central, good value meals and snacks; *Re-*

staurante da Gaúcha, Allan Kardek 238, nr rodoviária.

Oriental: *Hong Kong*, R Maracaju 131, centre, good Chinese food, also a legal outlet for *jacaré* meat, closed Mon.

Other: *Optimus*, Shopping Center Campo Grande, 2nd floor, T 726-1020; *Cafeteria Lojas Americanas*, Marechal Rondón 1336, in a supermarket, and *Meio Kilo* opp, good value buffet; *El Café*, R Dom Aquino 1248, both rec. *Nutre Bem*, vegetarian, Pedro Celestino 1696, good. Plenty of good, cheap places in R Barão de Rio Branco, eg *Maracaju*. *Confidência Mineira*, 14 de Julho 945, Mineiro food and 49 types of *cachaça* on sale, open daily, shows Sun and Tues.

Regional specialities include *caldo de piranha* (soup), *chipa* (Paraguayan cheese bread), sold on the streets, delicious when hot, and the local liqueur, *pequi com caju*, which contains *cachaça*.

● **Banks & money changers**
Banco do Brasil, 13 de Maio e Av Afonso Pena, open 1000-1500, commission US$10 for cash, US$20 for TCs, commission of amount exchanged; **Banco Frances Brasileiro**, Marechal Rondon 1672, open 1000-1200 and 1330-1430, US$ cash and TCs, no commission; **Overcash Câmbio**, R 13 de Maio 2892, open Mon-Fri 1000-1600, poor rate for TCs, 7% commission to change TCs to US$ cash; **Campo Grande Câmbio**, R 13 de Maio 2484, open Mon-Fri 0930-1630, cash only; **Origem & Destino Câmbio**, R Dom Aquino 1682, cash only, fair rates. On weekends, try: *Hotel Fenícia*, 10% commission on TCs, check notes carefully; *Hotel Carandá*; Sr Abdala in the clothes shop at 14 de Julho 2581; Las Vegas billiard hall, Barão do Rio Branco 1130.

● **Consulates**
Bolivia, R Dom Aquino 1353, T 382-2190; **Paraguay**, R João Crippa 1065, T 721 4430.

● **Entertainment**
See below for *Peña Eme-Ene*. *Cameleão*, 15 de Novembro 1131, Wed-Sat, bar with shows, live music, entrance US$1-5 depending on what's on; owned by local artist, Humberto Espíndola, who specializes in depicting and criticizing cattle culture (*boicultura*). Ask at *Cameleão* if you want to find out more.

● **Hospitals & medical services**
Yellow and Dengue fevers are both present in Mato Grosso do Sul. There is a clinic at the railway station, but it's not very hygienic, best to get your immunizations at home.

● **Post & telecommunications**
Post Office: on corner of R Dom Aquino e

Calógeras 2309 and Barão do Rio Branco corner Ernesto Geisel, both locations offer fax service, US$2.10/page within Brazil.
Telephone: TELEMS, R Dom Aquino 1805, between P Celestino and Rui Barbosa, open 0600-2200 daily.

● **Shopping**
The *Casa do Artesão*, Av Calógeras 2050 e Av Afonso Pena, open Mon-Fri 0800-1800, Sat 0800-1200, has a good collection of native crafts, Indian jewellery and arrows on sale. *Eme-Ene*, Av Afonso Pena 2303, T 382-2373, regional handicrafts, open 0700-1900, Sat 0700-1700, Sun 0800-1200, good, has a *peña* (folk music show) each Wed at 2100, rec; *Arte do Pantanal*, Av Afonso Pena 1743, regional crafts. A local speciality is Os Bugres da Conceição, squat wooden statues covered in moulded wax. There is a market (Feira Livre) on Wed and Sat. Mato Grosso do Sul is a good region for buying cheap, good leather shoes.

Bookshop: R 15 de Junho e R Dom Aquino, highly rec, English spoken, will exchange English books.

● **Tour companies & travel agents**
Vox Tour, R Cândido Mariano 1777, T 3843335, F 725-8663, English and Spanish spoken, helpful; *Tainá Turismo*, R Sete de Setembro 1966, T 384-6544, F 384-2510; *Impacto*, R Padre João Crippa 1065, sala 101, T 382-5197, T/F 724-3167, Pantanal and Bonito tour operators and wholesalers, helpful; *Origem e Destino*, R Dom Aquino 1682, T 721-1430, F 721-1470, English, French and Spanish spoken.

● **Tourist offices**
Tourist information from the state run *Casa do Turismo*, R Arthur Jorge 622, by Parque Belmar Fidalgo, T/F 724-5104, friendly, helpful. Maps and books for sale at the municipal *Centro de Informação Turística e Cultural*, Av Noroeste 5140 corner Afonso Pena, housed in Pensão Pimentel, a beautiful mansion built in 1913, also has a data base about services in the city and cultural information, but not the friendliest. Kiosk at airport. Town information in Secretária de Turismo, Indústrias e Comércio, Parque dos Poderes, T 726-4012.

● **Transport**
Local Car hire: Laredo, R Dom Aquino 1878, T/F 382-2984; on Av Afonso Pena are: **Localiza**, No 318, T 382-8786, T (airport) 763-1401; **Hertz**, No 2620, T 383-5331; **Locagrande**, No 466, T 721-3282, F 721-3282; **Unidas**, No 829, T 384-5626, F 384-6115, T (airport) 763-2145. Daily rates from US$37.

Air Daily flights to São Paulo, Rio, Corumbá, Cuiabá, Presidente Prudente, Goiânia, Ponta Porã, Brasília, Manaus, Porto Velho. Airport tax

US$6.50. City bus No 158, 'Popular' stops outside airport. Taxi to airport, US$6. Banco do Brasil at airport exchanges dollars. Post office, fax and phones in same office.

Trains The railway station is on Av Calógeras, 8 blocks from the bus terminal. **Ponta Porã** (9 hrs), via Sidrolândia and Maracaju, Mon, Wed, Fri at 0920, US$6.80 1st class, US$4.80 2nd, ticket office opens at 0800 on same day. A sad vestige of a once important railroad. Passenger **trains to Bauru** were withdrawn in 1994 and service to Corumbá ceased in Jan 1995. There was talk in 1996 of service being reinstated following privatization of the state railway system.

Buses Rodoviária is in the block bounded by Ruas Barão do Rio Branco, Vasconcelos Fernandes, Dom Aquino and Joaquim Nabuco, T 383-1678, all offices on 2nd floor; at the V Fernandes end are town buses, at the J Nabuco end state and interstate buses. In between are shops and *lanchonetes*. 8 blocks' walk from Praça República; cinema in rodoviária, US$1.20. (Taxi to rodoviária, US$3.60.) Campo Grande has good connections throughout the country: **São Paulo**, US$36, 14 hrs, 9 buses daily, 1st at 0800, last at 2400, 3 *leito* buses US$71. **Cuiabá**, US$25, 10 hrs, 12 buses daily, *leito* at 2100 and 2200 US$48. To **Brasília**, US$46, 23 hrs at 0900 and 1900. To **Goiânia**, São Luis company 1100, 1630, 1900, 2300, 15 hrs on 1900 service, US$39, others 24 hrs, US$1 cheaper. **Rio de Janeiro**, US$50, 21 hrs, 4 buses daily, *leito* at 1745 US$100. **Corumbá**, with Andorinha, 8 daily from 0600, 6 hrs, US$22. Campo Grande-Corumbá buses connect with those from Rio and São Paulo, similarly those from Corumbá through to Rio and São Paulo. Good connections to all major cities. **Ponta Porã**, 4 hrs, 9 buses daily, US$9. **Dourados**, 4 hrs, 14 daily (Queiroz), US$9. Beyond Dourados is Mundo Novo, from where buses go to Ponta Porã (0530) and to Porto Frajelli (very frequent); from Mundo Novo ferries for cars and passengers go to Guaíra for US$0.50. Twice daily direct service to **Foz do Iguaçu** (17 hrs) with Integração, 1200, 1600, US$29; same company goes to Cascavel, US$23. To **Pedro Juan Caballero** (Paraguay), del Amambay company, US$10.

CAMPO GRANDE TO SÃO PAULO

The Campo Grande-São Paulo journey can be broken at **Três Lagoas** (*pop* 68,070), 9½ hrs from São Paulo (motorway) and 6 hrs from Campo Grande by paved highway BR-262 (buses dep Campo Grande.

16 km E of Três Lagoas is the massive **Jupiá** Dam on the Rio Paraná, which can be visited with prior permission (T 521-

2753) on weekends and holidays only, 0800-1800.

Further N are other hydroelectric dams, most impressive of which is at **Ilha Solteira** (50 km, several hotels and good fish restaurants on São Paulo state side); guided tours at 1000 and 1500 weekends and holidays. Excellent swimming is to be had at **Praia Catarina**, with bars, playground and kiosks (6 km). Overlooking the river 35 km S of Ilha Solteira is restored **Fort Itapura**, built during the War of the Triple Alliance, with beach and restaurants nearby.

• **Accommodation & places to eat** B *Três Lagoas*, Av Rosário Congro 629, T 521-2500, a/c, best; **C** *Regente Palace*, R Paranaíba 580, a/c, good value; **E** *Novo*, Av Antônio de Souza Queiroz, nr rodoviária, friendly. *Restaurant Casarão*, R Munir Tomé 30, has good selection of dishes; *Boi na Brasa*, Av Antônio Trajano 487, for *churrascos*, rec.

• **Transport** Buses Campo Grande-Três Lagoas 0800, 1200, 2230, US$15.75, an interesting journey, 'especially for cattle farmers'.

CAMPO GRANDE TO PARAGUAY

DOURADOS

The paved road from Campo Grande to the Paraguayan frontier at Ponta Porã passes through **Dourados** (224 km; *pop* 135,780; *alt* 430m), the supply centre of a developing agricultural region carved from the red *sertão*, in large part by Japanese immigrants. Apart from a couple of pleasant parks and lakes for swimming there is little of note for the traveller.

• **Accommodation & places to eat** B *Alphonsus*, Av Pres Vargas 603, T 421-5211, F 421-9178, best; **C** *Figueira Palace*, R Toshinobu Katayama 553, T 421-5611, a/c, pleasant; **C** *Bahamas*, R Cândido da Câmara 750, T 421-4714, a/c, simpler but excellent value. *Restaurante Boxexa*, R Araújo 780, good pizzas; *Churrascaria Guarujá* (No 595 same street) for *churrascos* in enjoyable surroundings.

• **Transport Air** Scheduled flights to Campo Grande, Ponta Porã, Ourinhos, Pres Prudente and São Paulo from the small airport (10 km). **Buses** Good bus connections for Campo Grande, Ponta Porã, Mundo Novo, and Presidente Prudente and Maringá to the E of the Rio Paraná;

PONTA PORÃ

The highway continues 115 km to **Ponta Porã** (*pop* 55,830), separated from Pedro Juan Caballero in Paraguay only by a broad avenue. With paved streets, good public transport and smart shops, Ponta Porã is decidedly more prosperous than its neighbour, although Brazilian visitors flock across the border to play the casino and buy cheaper 'foreign' goods. At the **Parque das Exposições**, by the rodoviária (see below), an animal show is held each October.

● **Accommodation** B *Porta do Sol Palace*, R Paraguai 2688, T 431-3341, F 431-1193, a/c, pool, very nice; **B** *Pousada do Bosque*, Av Pres Vargas 1151, 3 km out of town, T 431-1181, F 431-1741, good motel type, a/c, pool, restaurant; **B** *Guarujá*, R Guia Lopes 63, T 431-1619, rec; opp is **C** *Barcelona*, maze-like building, a/c, restaurant, pool; **C** *Alvorada*, Av Brasil 2977, T 431-5866, good café, close to post office, good value but often full; **C** *Internacional*, R Internacional 1267, T 431-1243, with a/c and bath, D without a/c, hot water, clean, good breakfast, rec; **E** *Dos Viajantes*, across park opp railway station, very basic, clean. Brazilian hotels inc breakfast in tariff, Paraguayan ones do not.

● **Places to eat** *Top Lanches*, beside *Hotel Barcelona*, cheap and friendly. *Chopão*, R Mal Floriano 1877, good food at reasonable prices.

● **Banks & money changers** Banco do Brasil changes TCs. Several *cambios* on the Paraguayan side. Many in the centre of town (but on Sun change money in hotels).

● **Electric current** 220 volts AC.

● **Transport** *Air* Services to São Paulo, Marília and Pres Prudente; daily except Sun to Campo Grande with TAM. *Trains* A railway also connects the city with Campo Grande, a 9-hr trip through rolling hills, departures Tues, Thur and Sat at 0750, US$6.80 1st class, US$4.80; the station is some 8 blocks from the centre, take 'Ferroviária' bus (US$1). *Buses* To Campo Grande: 9 a day from 0100-2130, 4 hrs, US$9; the rodoviária is 3 km out on the Dourados road ('São Domingos' bus, taxi US$5).

FRONTIER WITH PARAGUAY

There are no actual border posts between the two towns and people pass freely for local visits.

● **Brazilian immigration**
The Brazilian Federal Police office (for entry/exit visas) is on the 2nd floor of the white engineering supply company building at R Marechal Floriano 1483, T 431-1428, officially open 24 hrs but weekdays 0730-1130, 1400-1700 is more realistic.

● **Paraguayan consulate**
The two nations' consulates face each other on R Internacional (border street) a block W of Ponta Porã's local bus terminal; some nationalities require a visa from the Paraguayan consul (next to *Hotel Internacional*), open only 0800-1200 Mon-Fri. **Check requirements carefully**, and ensure your documents are in order: without the proper stamps you will inevitably be sent back somewhere later on in your travels.

● **Transport**
Taking a taxi between offices can speed things up if pressed for time; drivers know border crossing requirements.

BONITO

The municipality of **Bonito** in the Serra do Bodoquena yields granite and marble and is clad in forest. (*Town pop* 16,388; *CEP* 79290; *DDD* 067; distance from Campo Grande 248 km.) The area's main attractions are in its rivers and caves (the formations are comparable to those found in the Lagoa Santa region of Minas Gerais). There are spectacular walks through mountains and forest; wildlife includes birds, rheas, monkeys, alligators and anaconda. Most excursions require authorization; this is not an obstacle to those with their own transport but as there is no public transport, those without a car will need to use an agency (see below). Bonito has become very popular with Brazilian vacationers, especially during Dec-Jan, Carnival, Easter, and July (at these times advance booking is essential). Prices are high. The wet season is Jan-Feb; Dec-Feb is hottest, July-Aug coolest.

Local attractions: Caves

The first cave to be opened is **Lagoa Azul**, 26 km from Bonito. Lagoa Azul has a lake 50m long and 110m wide, 75m below ground level. The water, 20°C, is a jewel-like blue as light from the opening is refracted through limestone and magnesium. The startling blue, in combination with the browns and yellows of the stalactites, is beautiful. Prehistoric animal bones have been found in the lake. The light is at its best Jan-Feb, 0700-0900, but is fine at other times. A 25-ha park surrounds the cave. You must pay a municipal tax, US$5; if not using your own transport, a car for 4 costs US$20. Also open is **NS Aparecida cave**, which has superb stalactites and stalagmites; no tourism infrastructure.

River excursions

The **Balneário Municipal** on the Rio Formoso (7 km on road to Jardim), with changing rooms, toilets, camping, swimming in clear water, plenty of fish to see (strenuous efforts are made to keep the water and shore clean). **Hormínio** waterfalls, 13 km, eight falls on the Rio Formoso, suitable for swimming; bar and camping, entry US$0.15. **Rafting** on the Rio Formoso: 12 km, 2½ hrs, min 4 people, US$15 pp, a mixture of floating peacefully downriver, swimming and shooting 4 waterfalls, lifejackets available; arranged by *Hapakany Tour* and many other agencies, see below. The **Aquário Natural** is one of the **springs of the Rio Formoso**; to visit you must have authorization from *Hapakany Tour*; you can swim and snorkel with 5 types of fish. Do not swim with suntan oil on. Other tours are: from the springs of the Rio Sucuri to its meeting with the Formoso (permission from *Hapakany* or *TapeTur*), about 2 km of crystal-clear water, with swimming or snorkelling, birdwatching, very peaceful; **Aquidaban**, a series of limestone/marble waterfalls in dense forest; **Rio da Prata** a spring with underground snorkelling for 2 km, very beautiful. The **fishing** season is from 1 Mar to 31 October. In late Oct, early Nov is the *piracema* (fish run), when the fish return to their spawning grounds. Hundreds can be seen jumping the falls.

NB Bonito's attractions are nearly all on private land and must by visited with a guide. Owners also enforce limits on the number of daily visitors so, at busy times, pre-booking is essential.

Local information
● **Accommodation**
A1 *Zagaia Resort*, Rodovia Bonito-Três Morros, T/F 255-1280, new in 1996, luxurious, pool, L1 full board including tours; **A2-B** *Pousada Olho d'Água*, just outside Bonito, Km 1 on road to Três Morros, T 255-1430, F 255-1470, accommodation in cabins, inc breakfast, fan, showers

with solar-heated water, fruit trees, fresh vegetables, small lake, own water supply, horse riding, bicycles.

B *Tapera*, on hill above Shell station on road to Jardim, T 255-1700, fine views, cool breezes, a/c, comfortable, good.

C *Bonanza*, R Cel Pilad Rebuá (main street) 628, T 255-1315, F 255-1235, suites and family rooms available, a/c, TV, frequently rec, opp is parking lot, with bar from 1800, darts and *churrascaria* on Fri; *Canãa*, Pilad Rebuá 1293, T 255-1255, parking, TV, a/c, fridge, phone, restaurant and *churrascaria*; *Muito Bonito*, R Cel Pilad Rebuá 1444, T/F 255 1645, rec.

D *Gemila*, R Luís da Costa Leite 2085, clean, bath, fan, hot water, laundry; **D** *Pousadinha da Praça*, Pilad Rebuá 2097, T 255-1135, 2-4 bedded rooms (latter cramped), fan, hot water.

E pp *Pousada Muito Bonito*, Pilad Rebuá 1448, T/F 255-1645, with bath, or rooms with bunkbeds, nice patio, clean, excellent, helpful owners, inc breakfast, also with tour company (Mario Doblack speaks English, French and Spanish), rec.

Camping: at *Ilha do Padre*, 12 km N of Bonito, very pleasant, no regular transport (Hapakany's raft trip ends here), T/F 255-1430; 4 rustic cabins with either 4 bunk beds, or 2 bunks and a double, US$10 pp, youth hostel with two sets of 12 beds, US$6 pp, same price for camping, toilets, showers, clothes washing, meals available, bar, electricity, lots of trees, can swim anywhere, to enter the island for a day US$3. Managers are Henrique Ruas and Jane Tatoni. Camping also at *Poliana* on Rio Formosa, 100m past Ilha do Padre, very pleasant.

● **Places to eat**
Tapera, Pilad Rebuá 480, T 255-1110, good, home-grown vegetables, breakfast, lunch, pizzas, meat and fish dishes, opens 1900 for evening meal; *Comida Caseira*, Luis da Costa Leite e Santana do Paraiso, good local food, lunch and dinner, not open Sun pm; *Verdo-Frutos e Sucos Naturais*, Pilad Rebuá 1853, next to *Bonanza* car park, good juices and fruits.

● **Banks & money changers**
Banco do Brasil, for Visa; some hoteliers may change money.

● **Post & telecommunications**
Post Office: on R Cel Pilad Rebuá.
Telephones: on Santana do Paraiso.

● **Tour companies & travel agents**
There are 13 agencies and 54 guides in Bonito who accompany visitors to the private sites. Sérgio Ferreira Gonzales, R Cel Pilad Rebuá 628, T 255-1315 (opp *Bonanza*), is an authority on the caves, rec. *Hapakany Tour*, Pilad Rebuá

628, T 255-1315, F 255-1235, Jason and Murilo, for all local tours, rec. *TapeTur*, next to *Tapera* restaurant, guides, information, tours, clothes shop, also rec. For information in English and French, contact Henrique Ruas, T/F 255-1430, see *Ilha do Padre* or *Pousada Olho d'Água* above.

● **Transport**
Rodoviária is on edge of town. From Campo Grande, US$15, 5½-6 hrs, 1500, returns at 0530. Bus uses MS-345, with stop at Autoposto Santa Cruz, Km 60, all types of fuel, food and drinks available. For Aquidauana, take Campo Grande bus. Bus Corumbá-Miranda-Bonito-Jardim-Ponta Porã, Mon-Sat, leaves either end at 0600, arriving Bonito 1230 for Ponta Porã, 1300 for Miranda; can change in Jardim (1400 for 1700 bus) or Miranda (better connections) for Campo Grande; fare Corumbá-Bonito US$18. Also connections on 1230 route in Bela Vista at 2000 for Asunción and Coronel Oviedo. Ticket office opens at 1200.

ROUTES The road to **Jardim** is paved. In Jardim, which has a wide, tree-lined main street, there is a rodoviária for Cruzeiro do Sul buses. A few blocks uphill is *Panificadora Massa Pura*, clean and bright, and other eating places. Buses: to Campo Grande 0730, 1300, 1700 and 2 in middle of night, US$10.15; Aquidauana 0730 and 1700; Bonito (US$5); Miranda and Corumbá at 1130; Dourados

0600; Bela Vista (Paraguayan border) 0200, 1030, 1500, 1930; Porto Murtinho 0010 and 1530 (bus from Bonito connects); Ponta Porã 0600, 1500; Sun only at 1400 to São Paulo. From Bonito there is a road to **Porto Murtinho** where a boat crosses to Isla Margarita in Paraguay (entry stamp available on the island). Hotels **E** *Eldorado*, friendly, clean, good food; **E** *Beira Rio*, basic; **E** *Caicaras*; **E** *Americano*, 2 *lanchonetes*, *Churrascaria Gaspão*. Elia, taxi driver, will change money.

CAMPO GRANDE TO CORUMBÁ AND BOLIVIA

BR-262 is paved most of the way from Campo Grande to Corumbá and the Bolivian border, rail service along this route was suspended indefinitely in 1995. It is best to make this journey during the day, to take advantage of marvellous scenery.

AQUIDAUANA
131 km W of Campo Grande, just N of the road but on the railway, is **Aquidauana** (*pop* 39,300, several daily buses from Campo Grande). BR-412 heads S from here to Jardim, with connections to Paraguay (see

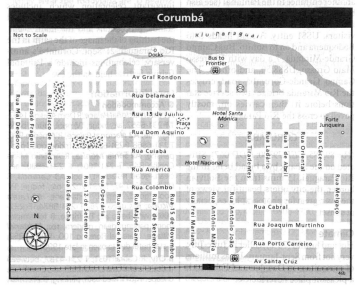

● **Post & telecommunications**

Post Office: main at R Delamaré 708 (has fax service) branch at R 15 de Novembro 229.

Telephone: TELEMS, R Dom Aquino 951, nr Praça da Independência, open 0700-2200 daily. There is a direct telephone link between Corumbá and Quijarro/Puerto Suarez, Bolivia, it costs slightly more than a local call, dial 214 + the Bolivian number.

● **Shopping**

Shops tend to open early and close by 1700. *Pro-Sol, Casa do Artesão*, R Dom Aquino Correa 405, in a converted prison, open Mon-Fri 0800-1200 and 1400-1800, Sat 0800-1200, good selection of handicrafts and a small bookshop with works by local authors, friendly staff but high prices. *CorumbArte*, Av Gen Rondon 1011, for good silk-screen T shirts with Pantanal motifs. *Livraria Corumbaense*, R Delamaré 1080 for state maps.

Supermarkets: *Ohara*, Dom Aquino corner Antônio João; *Frutal*, R 13 de Junho 538, open 0800-2000.

● **Tour companies & travel agents**

Corumbá has many travel agencies selling tours to the Pantanal; we list some. For more information see page 645: *Mutum Turismo*, R Frei Mariano 17, T 231-1818, F 231-3027; for airline tickets, tours, helpful; *Pantanal Tours/Sairú Turismo*, R M Cavassa 61, T 231-4683, F 231-2523, fishing trips, agents for Cabexy I and II, luxurious floating hotels with 4 double a/c berths, US$2,000/day for 8 persons, min 5 days, day trips on land, US$55 pp, river trips US$15 pp/3 hrs, stays at *Fazenda Santa Clara*, happily rec; *Pantanal Service*, R Dom Aquino 700, T/F 231-5998, fishing and photo trips by boat, agents for Hotel Porto Vitória Régia; *Corumbatur*, Antônio M Coelho, T/F 231-1532, combined Pantanal/Bonito tours; *JMS Turismo*, R M Cavassa 215, T 231-5235, small fishing boats for rent US$60/day for 3 persons, minivans for trips to Bolivia US$10 pp; *Itajiloma*, R M Cavassa 267, T 231-1046, small craft for fishing trips, US$65/day for 2 persons, US$120/day for 5 persons; *Pérola do Pantanal*, R M Cavassa 255, T 231-1470, F 231-6585, river and land tours, good 1-day river tour with *Lancha Pérola*; *Taimã*, R Antônio M Coelho 786, T/F 231-6696, river trips, flights over Pantanal, airline tickets; *Pantur*, R América 969, T 231-4343, F 231-6006, tours, agents for Hotel Fazenda Xaraes in Nhecolândia; *Receptivo Pantanal*, R Frei Mariano 502, T 231-5795, helpful (1-day tour US$50, 3-day US$100, 4-day US$130).

● **Tourist offices**

Emcotur, R America 969, T 231-6996, municipal tourist office, for general information and city maps.

● **Transport**

Local Car hire: Localiza, airport and R Frei Mariano 51, T 231-6379, F 231-3741, daily rates from US$90 (unlimited km), weekly from US$540; Unidas, R Frei Mariano 633, T/F 231-3124.

Air Daily flights to Campo Grande, 2 airlines, TAM and Pantanal (much cheaper); TAM also to Cuiabá, daily, Londrina and São Paulo (via Campo Grande). See **Bolivia**, **Section 5**, for flights between Puerto Suárez and Santa Cruz. Daily private flights to Santa Cruz, Bolivia, cheaper to travel overland to Asunción and fly from there.

Trains Passenger trains from Corumbá to Campo Grande stopped running in Jan 1995.

Buses The rodoviária is located on R Porto Carreiro at the S end of R Tiradentes, next to the railway station. Andorinha services all pointws east. To **Campo Grande**, 7 hrs, US$22, 13 buses daily, between 0630 hrs and midnight, interesting journey ('an excursion in itself') – take an early bus to see plentiful wildlife, connections from Campo Grande to all parts of Brazil. To **São Paulo** direct, 22 hrs, US$58, 1100 and 1500, confirm bus times in advance as these change(T 231-2033). To **Rio** direct, 28 hrs, US$72, daily 1100. Cruzeiro do Sul operates the route S to the Paraguayan border. To **Ponta Porã**, 12 hrs, US$36, via Bonito (6 hrs, US$18) and Jardim (9 hrs, US$22), Mon-Sat at 0600; ticket office open 0500-0600 only, at other times call T 231-2383. City bus to rodoviária from Praça da República. **Taxis**: are extortionate.

River Shipping In 1996, the *Acurí*, a luxury vessel, began sailing between **Cáceres** and Corumbá, once a week, US$600 including return by air. (See page 653, under Cáceres.) Ships from **Asunción**, Paraguay, have not called at Corumbá since 1995.

FRONTIER WITH BOLIVIA

Over the border from Corumbá are Arroyo Concepción, Puerto Quijarro and Puerto Suárez. From Puerto Quijaro a 650-km railway runs to Santa Cruz de la Sierra. There is a road of sorts.

● **Brazilian immigration**

Immigration and emigration formalities are constantly changing so check procedure in advance. You need not have your passport stamped to visit Quijarro or Puerto Suarez only for the day. Otherwise, get passport stamped by Brazilian Polícia Federal at their main office, Praça da República, next door to the NS da Candelária church, T 231-5848, open 0800-1900 (knock after hours); there is also an office at the rodoviária, which is frequently closed. Brazilian exit stamp is valid for 5 days. If exiting Brazil merely to obtain a new visa, remember that exit and entry must not be on the same day.

Entering Brazil If you arrive in Brazil without a yellow fever vaccination certificate, you may have to go to R 7 de Setembro, Corumbá, for an inoculation.

● **Bolivian consulate**
R Antônio Maria Coelho 852, Corumbá, Mon-Fri, 0700-1100, 1500-1730, Sat and Sun closed. Check **Documents** in **Bolivian Information for travellers** for requirements. A fee is charged to citizens of those countries which require a visa. A yellow fever vaccination certificate is required.

● **Exchange**
Money changers at the border and in Quijarro offer same rates as in Corumbá.

● **Transport**
Leaving Brazil, take Canarinho city bus marked Fronteira from port end of R Antônio Maria Coelho to Bolivian border (15 mins), walk over the bridge to the Bolivian border post (blue building), go through formalities, then take colectivo to Quijarro or Puerto Suarez.

When travelling from Quijarro, take a taxi or walk to the Bolivian border to go through formalities. Just past the bridge, on a small side street to the right is the bus stop for Corumbá, it goes to Praça da República, US$0.50, every 45 min between 0630 and 1915, don't believe taxi drivers who say there is no bus. Taxi to centre US$10. Find a hotel then take care of Brazilian formalities at Polícia Federal, address above.

Trains Services to **Santa Cruz** in Bolivia, from Quijarro, the Bolivian frontier station, are given on page 347. The schedule of each appears to change frequently so check on arrival in Corumbá. Tickets may be booked through travel agencies, which charge higher prices than if booked direct. If purchasing your own ticket, you must do so in Quijarro on day of departure, except for the luxury *Bracha* coach (from travel agents only). Go as early as possible (it may be best to stay in Quijarro to get a good place in the queue).

PANTANAL

This vast wetland, measuring 230,000 sq Km between Cuiabá, Campo Grande and the Bolivian frontier, is one of the world's great wildlife preserves. Parts spill over into neighbouring Bolivia and Paraguay, and the entire area has been opened up to tourism. The water in the Pantanal is not stagnant, a gentle gradient ranging for 1 to 3 cm/km, from N to S, keeps it flowing in that direction, hence during the wet season flooding gradually advances southwards. The region is drained by the São Lourenço, Cuiabá, Piquiri, Taquari, Aquidauana, Miranda and Apa rivers, all of which are tributaries of the Rio Paraguai.

Flora and fauna
Similar in many ways to the Amazon basin, though because of the more veldt-like open land, the wildlife can be viewed more easily than in the dense jungle growth. Principal life seen in this area is about 300 species of birds, including the hyacinth macaw, jabiru stork (the *tuiuíu*, almost 1.2m tall), plumbeous ibis, yellow-billed cardinal, great rufous woodcreeper, buff-bellied hermit, Mato Grosso antbird, Chaco suiriri, white-naped xenopsaris, white-eyed atilla, Chaco chachalaca, bare-faced currasow, both blue-throated and red-throated piping guans, chestnut-bellied guan, red-billed scythebill, roseate spoonbill, black-hooded and yellow-chevroned parakeets, and turquoise-fronted parrot. There are some 230 varieties of fish, from the giant *pintado*, weighing up to 80 kilos, to the tiny, voracious *piranha*. Fishing here is exceptionally good (best May-Oct). Animal life is represented among others by giant and collared anteaters, 4 species of opossum, 5 armadillo species, black-tailed marmoset, brown capuchin, black howler monkey, maned wolf, crab-eating racoon, South American coati, grison, tayra, southern and giant river otters, ocelot, margay, jaguarundi, puma, 3 peccary species, marsh deer and two other species, Brazilian porcupine, yellow anaconda and the ubiquitous *capivara*, a species of giant aquatic guinea-pig. Probably the most impressive sight is the *jacaré* (Yacare Caiman). The extraordinary thing is that man and his domesticated cattle thrive together with the wildlife with seemingly little friction. Local farmers protect the area jealously.

Ecology and conservation
Only one area is officially a national park,

the **Parque Nacional do Pantanal Matogrossense** in the municipality of Poconé, 135,000 ha of land and water, only accessible by air or river. Permission to visit at Ibama, R Rubens de Mendonça, Cuiabá, CEP 78008-000, T 644-1511/1581.) Hunting in any form is strictly forbidden throughout the Pantanal and is punishable by 4 years imprisonment. Fishing is allowed with a licence (controlled by Ibama, issued by Banco do Brasil, enquire at travel agents); it is not permitted in the spawning season or *piracema* (Oct 1 to Feb 1 in Mato Grosso do Sul, Nov 1 to Mar 1 in Mato Grosso). Like other wilderness areas, the Pantanal faces important threats to its integrity. Agrochemicals and *garimpo* mercury washed down from the neighbouring *planalto* are a hazard to wildlife. The potential impact of planned completion and paving of the Transpantaneira Highway (see below) from Cuiabá, past Porto Jofre to Corumbá, is also of concern, as is the proposed dredging of the Rio Paraguai to create an international waterway, although neither project is anywhere near implementation. Visitors must share the responsibility of protecting the Pantanal and you can make an important contribution by acting responsibly and choosing your guides accordingly: take out your rubbish, don't fish out of season, don't let guides kill or disturb fauna, don't buy products made from endangered species, don't buy live birds or monkeys, and report any violation of these norms to the authorities.

The International Union for the Conservation of Nature is concerned at the amount of poaching, particularly of jacaré skins, birds and capivaras. The Forestry Police have built control points on all major access roads to the Pantanal. Biologists interested in research projects in the area should contact the Coordenador de Estudos do Pantanal, Departamento de Biologia, Universidade Federal do Mato Grosso do Sul, Caixa Postal 649, Campo Grande, CEP 79070-900, T (067) 787-3311 ext 2113, F (067) 787-5317.

Climate

There are two distinct seasons. In the rainy season (Dec-Mar, wettest in Feb), most of the area floods, mosquitoes abound, and cattle crowd on to the few islands remaining above water. In the southern part, many wild animals leave the area, but in the N, which is slightly higher, the animals do not leave. An ordinary vehicle should be able to manage the Transpantaneira out of Cuiabá throughout most of the year, but in the wet season you should be prepared to get stuck, and muddy, pushing your car from time to time. The dry season (July to Oct) is the nesting and breeding season. The birds form vast nesting areas, with hundreds and thousands crowding the trees creating an almost insupportable cacophony of sounds; the white sand river beaches are exposed, *jacarés* bask in the sun, and *capivaras* frolic amid the grass.

In winter (June-Aug), temperatures fall to 10°, warm clothing and covers or sleeping bag are needed at night, but it's very hot and humid during summer.

Wear long sleeves and long trousers and spray clothes as well as skin with insect repellent (less of a problem July-Aug). Take insect repellent from home as mosquitoes, especially in the N Pantanal, are becoming immune to local brands.

Access

The Pantanal is not easy or cheap to visit. The best starting points are Corumbá, Cuiabá, and to a lesser extent Campo Grande, from where one finds public transport all around the perimeter, but none at all within. Wild camping is possible if you have some experience and your own transport. Remember that the longer you stay and the further you go from the edges (where most of the hotels are located), the more likely you are to see rare wildlife.

From Corumbá there is access to the Pantanal by both road and river, offering a variety of day trips, luxury house boat excursions, and connections to many surrounding *fazendas*. Along the road from Corumbá to Campo Grande (BR-262), are Miranda and Aquidauana, both important gateways to various fishing and tourist lodges. The BR-163 which connects Campo Grande and Cuiabá skirts the E edge of the Pantanal; Coxim, 242 Km N of Campo Grande offers access via the Rio Taquari but few facilities. From Cuiabá there is year-round road access to Barão de Melgaço and Poconé, both of which can be starting points for excursions. The Transpantaneira Highway runs S from Poconé to Porto Jofre, through the heart of the Pantanal, providing access to many different lodges, but does not have any bus service. Finally Cáceres, 215 Km W of Cuiabá at the NW corner of the Pantanal, offers access along the Rio Paraguai to one of the least developed parts of the region.

Tourist facilities in the Pantanal currently cater to four main categories of visitors. **Sports fishermen** usually stay at one of the numerous speciality lodges scattered throughout the region, which provide guides, boats, bait, ice and other related amenities. Bookings can be made locally or in any of Brazil's major cities. **All-inclusive tours** combining air and ground transportation, accommodations at the most elaborate *fazendas*, meals, guided river and land tours, can be arranged from abroad or through travel agencies in Brazil's gateway cities. This is the most expensive option. **Moderately priced tours** using private guides, camping or staying at more modest *fazendas* can be arranged locally in Cuiabá (where guides await arrivals at the airport) or through the more reputable agencies in Corumbá. **The lowest priced tours** are offered by independent guides in Corumbá, some of whom are unreliable and travellers have reported at times serious problems here (see below). For those with the barest minimum of funds, a glimpse of the Pantanal and its wildlife can be had on the bus ride from Campo Grande to Corumbá, by lodging or camping near the ferry crossing over the Rio Paraguai (Porto Esperança), and by staying in Poconé and day-walking or hitching S along the Transpantaneira. Whatever your budget, take binoculars.

How to choose a guide

A tour of the Pantanal could be the highlight of your travels, so it is best to do some research before contracting a guide. Many budget travellers en route to or from Bolivia make Corumbá their base for visiting the Pantanal. Such tourists are often approached, in the streets and at the cheaper hotels, by salesmen who speak foreign languages and promise complete tours for low prices. They then hand their clients over to agencies and/or guides, who often speak only Portuguese, and may deliver something quite different. Some travellers have reported very unpleasant experiences and it is important to select a guide with great care anywhere. By far the best way to do so, is to speak with other travellers who have just returned from a Pantanal tour. Most guides also have a book containing comments from their former clients. Do not rush to sign up when first approached, always compare several available alternatives. Discuss the planned itinerary carefully and try to get it in writing (although this is seldom possible). Do not pay everything in advance of departure, and try to deal directly with agencies or guides, not salesmen (it can be difficult to tell who is who). Always get an itemized receipt. Bear in mind that a well-organized 3-day tour can be more rewarding than 4 days with an ill-prepared guide. There is fierce competition between guides who provide similar services, but with very different styles. Although we list a few of the most reputable guides below, there are other good ones and most economy travellers enjoy a pleasant if spartan experience. Remember that travellers must shoulder part of the responsibility for the current chaotic guiding situation in Corumbá. Act responsibly and don't expect to get something for nothing. (See also Corumbá guides section.)

Camping allows you to see the wildlife at its greatest period of activity – dawn and dusk but protection against mosquitoes is essential. Care should also be taken to avoid dangerous animals: snakes (especially in the rainy season), piranhas (especially in the dry season), killer bees and the larger *jacarés*. The inexperienced are cautioned not to strike out on their own.

● **Further reading** The Pantanal: Brazil's Forgotten Wilderness, Vic Banks (Sierra Club Books, 1991, 730 Polk St, San Francisco, CA 94100).

Local information
● Accommodation

There are many lodges with fair to good accommodation, some only approachable by air or river; most are relatively expensive. One option is to hire a car and check accommodation for yourself: in June-Sept, especially July, it is necessary to book accommodation in advance. Following is a list of some of those presently operating:

From Campo Grande: **L1** full board Pousada São Francisco, 135 km from Aquidauana in the Rio Negro area of Nhecolândia, accessible only by air during the wet, with bath, fan, screening, horseback riding, price inc transport, meals, tours, bookings through Impacto Turismo, Campo Grande, T/F (067) 724-3167 as above; **L1** full board Refúgio Ecológico/Caimã, 36 km from Miranda, 236 km from Campo Grande, first class, full board, excursions, US$690 pp/4 days T (067) 242-1102, or 725-5267, or São Paulo 246-9934; **L3** full board Pousada Aguapé, Fazenda São José, 59 Km N of Aquidauana, 202 km from Campo Grande, farmhouse hotel, screened rooms, some with a/c, pool, horse riding, boat trips, trekking, meals and tours inc, friendly and clean, bookings through Impacto Turismo, as above; **L3** full board Hotel Fazenda Carandá, 60 km from Aquidauana, cabins, a/c, full board, horses, boat trips on Rio Aquidauana, bookings through Panbratur, Aquidauana, T/F (067) 241-3494; **A1** Cabana do Pescador, 65 km from Aquidauana on the Rio Miranda, T (067) 241-3697, access by Bonito bus from Campo Grande (see page 635), fishing lodge, inc breakfast; **A1** Fazenda Beira Rio, 8 km from Miranda, T (067) 242-1262, fishing lodge; **A1** Fazenda Salobra, T (067) 242-1162, 6 km from Miranda, 209 km from Corumbá, 198 from Campo Grande, is rec, with bath, inc all meals, tours, boat rentals and horses are extra; it is by the Rio Salobra (clear water) and Rio Miranda, with birds and animals easily seen. Take bus from Campo Grande to Miranda, and alight 50m from the bridge over Rio Miranda, turn left for 1,200m to the Fazenda; **A1** Pousada Caiman, US$620 for 3 nights, everything inc, airport pickup/drop-off, boats, trucks, horses, day and night hikes, great guides, excellent food, pool, highly rec. Fazenda Rio Negro, 13,000 ha farm on the shores of the Rio Negro, farm house dating to 1920, tours, horses, fishing, bookings through Panbratur, Aquidauana, T/F as above; Pousada

Mangabal, in Nhecolândia, farm setting, horses, tours, walks, bookings through Panbratur, Aquidauana, T/F as above; Pousada Toca da Onça, 10 km from Aquidauana on the shores of the Rio Aquidauana, cabins, a/c, restaurant, boats, bookings through Panbratur, Aquidauana, T/F as above. **B** Pousada Águas do Pantanal, Av Afonso Pena 367, Miranda, T/F (067) 242-1314, F 242-1242, contact Fátima or Luis Cordelli, very good, clean, friendly, good food, restaurant serves jacaré legally (closed in Feb/96). There is a good campsite 30 km past Miranda. Alternatively, hire a car in Corumbá and drive to Miranda, but note that the dirt road is bad after rain (consequently not much traffic and more wildlife can be seen). Car with driver can be hired at Salobra for US$25. There are several camping possibilities along the shores of the Rio Aquidauana including **Camping Baía**, 50 km from Aquidauana, on a bay on the river, trees for shade, boats; Pequi Camping, 48 km from Aquidauana, with toilets, electricity; **Camping Itajú**, sandy beach, cabins, lanchonete, shower, electricity, boat rental.

A1 Hotel dos Camalotes, Porto Murtinho, T (067) 287-1160, 440 km from Campo Grande; access by bus long, tedious, bumpy and dusty; best access by air taxi; 4-star luxury hotel on the shores of the Paraguai river, favoured by wealthy Paulista fishermen, full board.

Another access to the Pantanal from the E is **Coxim** (pop 28,276; DDD 067; CEP 79400; 242 Km N of Campo Grande) on the BR-163, half way between Campo Grande and Rondonópolis; it sits in a green bowl, on the shores of the Rio Taquari; the area has great potential for tourism, but there are no official tours to the Pantanal at this time (1996), a great place if you have your own boat. **Accommodation** **A3** Coxim, 4 km S of town, T 291-1480, F 291-1479, a/c, fridge, TV, restaurant; **A3** Santa Ana, R Miranda Reis on the river bank, T 291-1602 cabins for 4, pool; **C** Santa Teresa, 5 km S of town, T 291-2215, F 291-1289, with bath, fan; Piracêma, by the bridge over the Rio Taquari, with restaurant; Sinhazino, N of the Taquari bridge; there are several simpler hotels in town.

From Corumbá: 1 day river trips available on river boats with a capacity of 80 passengers, US$15 half-day; US$30 full day, inc transfers and hot fish meal. Smaller boats US$15 pp for 3 hrs. Tickets at travel agents and by port. Boats may be hired, with fishing tackle and guide, at the port (US$100/day, up to 3 people, in season only). Cattle boats will on occasion take passengers on their round trips to farms in the Pantanal, but take your own boat – it is not always possible to disembark. Ask at Bacia da Prata, 10 mins out of Corumbá on the Ladário bus (the gatekeeper is unhelpful).

Lodges: **L1** full board *Pousada do Pantanal*, T (067) 231-5797, 125 km from Corumbá nr the Campo Grande road at Fazenda Santa Clara (still a working cattle ranch), very comfortable, easy access by bus, reservations from all agencies in Corumbá; US$190 pp for 3 days/2 nights, minimum 2 persons, good food (but drinks not inc), with horseback, car and boat excursions, guides inc, canoes, simple fishing gear, motor boats for rent (try bargaining in the off-season for reduced rates). **L1** full board *Hotel Fazenda Xaraés*, T (067) 231-6777, Rio Abobral, 130 km from Corumbá, luxurious, a/c, pool, restaurant, horses, boats. **A2** *Fazenda Santa Blanca*, on the Rio Paraguai, 15 mins by boat S of Porto Esperança (where the BR-262 crosses the Rio Paraguai), full board, very clean and friendly, good kayak excursions, horse riding, information from R 15 de Novembro 659, 79300 Corumbá, T 231-1460, or *Flins Travel* (Walter Zoss), R do Acre 92, 6th floor, 602, CEP 20081, Rio de Janeiro, T (021) 253-8588/0195 or *Safari Fotográfico*, R Frei Mariano 502, Corumbá, T 231-5797. *Fazenda Leque*, Roberto Kassan (contact through R América 262, Corumbá, T 231-1598), take mosquito coils, unlimited use of horses and boats, on small lake behind the farm, good food, plenty of wildlife to be seen. *Pousada Do Castelo*, 3 hrs by boat from Corumbá, T (067) 231-5151. The going rate for a 3-day camping photo safari by jeep is US$70-80 pp for 4-6 people; US$80-90 pp for 4 days. Fishing trips in luxurious floating hotels for 8 (eg Tuiuiú T/F 231-2052 and Cabexy II from *Pantanal Tours*, Corumbá – must be booked in advance), US$1,200-2,000/day, minimum 5 days. Hotels specializing in fishing, all reached from Corumbá by road: **L2** full board *Pesqueiro da Odila*, on the Rio Paraguai, reservations from Belo Horizonte T (031) 221-4003, a/c, fridge, restaurant. **L3** full board *Porto Morrinho*, on the Rio Paraguai, T 231-1360, a/c, fridge, TV, pool. **L3** full

board *Pesqueiro Tarumã*, Rio Paraguai, 65 km from Corumbá, Corumbá office at R M Cavassa 109, T/F 231-4771. **L3** full board *Pesqueiro Paraíso dos Dourados*, 72 km from Corumbá, Rios Paraguai e Miranda, Corumbá office at R Antônio João, T/F 231-3021, a/c, fridge, tours. **L3** *Pantanal Park*, 20 min by boat from Porto Esperança (where the BR 262 crosses the Rio Paraguai), with a/c, restaurant. **A1** *Pesqueiro Cabana do Lontra*, including meals T (067) 383-4532, 180 km from Aquidauana on the Corumbá road.

● **Tour companies & travel agents**
Travel agents in Corumbá: some of Corumbá's many agencies are listed on page 640. Tours out of Corumbá are of 3-4 days, costing between US$50-90 (includes all food, accommodation and transport). Travel is in the back of a pick-up (good for seeing animals), up to a maximum of 6. Accommodation is in a hammock under a palm thatch on a *fazenda*. Food can be good. If you want flushing toilets, showers or luxury cabins, approach an agency. Guides provide bottled mineral water (make sure enough is carried), but you must take a hat, sun screen and mosquito repellent. Some guides go to *fazendas* without permission, have unreliable vehicles, or are inadequately equipped, so try to check their credentials (see **Ecology and Conservation** and **How to Choose a Guide**, above).

Guides will generally not make the trip with fewer than 5 people, so if you have not already formed a group, stay in touch with several guides (most important during Mar-Oct, when fewer tourists are around). Decide on your priorities: try to ensure that your guide and other group members share your ideas.

We list below those guides who have received positive reports from travellers: *Natureza Tours*, Durvanil Pereira Rodrigues, R Dom Aquino 255, T 231-1218, 2-4 day trips to his own family *fazenda*, including boat trip, fishing, horse riding, cheap but very good; *Coli-

bri Pantanal Safari, run by Claudine (Swiss) out of one of the *Pousadas Pantaneiras*, popular; *Green Track*, R Ladorio 271, rec; *Tucantur*, at *Hotel Londres*, Corumbá, 3-5 day trips; *Katu*, R Dom Aquino 220, T 231-1987, rec; *Gil Tours*, R Porto Carrero 612, T 231-1772, tours with Gil himself or guide Elísio Rodríguez da Silva; the company has a commitment to preservation. There are many other guides not listed here; lots have received criticisms (some repeatedly) from correspondents. There may be others on whom we have received no feedback.

TO THE PANTANAL FROM CUIABÁ

The Transpantaneira Highway, built in 1976, was originally projected to connect Cuiabá with Corumbá but currently goes only as far as Porto Jofre on the Rio Cuiabá. Work has been suspended indefinitely because of difficulties, costs and ecological considerations, but completion and paving of this road was once again proposed in 1996.

POCONÉ

A paved road turns S off the main Cuiabá-Cáceres road to **Poconé** (*pop* 31,190; *DDD* 065; *CEP* 78175; 102 km from Cuiabá), was founded in 1781. It is known as the Cidade Rosa. Until 1995 there was much *garimpo* activity north of town and many slag heaps can be seen from the road.

● **Accommodation & places to eat** D *Hotel Skala*, in the Praça Matriz; E *Pousada Pantaneira*, good restaurant, clean and simple, on Transpantaneira, T 721-1220, to hitchhike to Pixaim or Porto Jofre (see below), start at 0600 outside the hotel; E *Hotel Joá*, with bath, basic, acceptable, car parking; also on the Transpantaneira just S of town are *Aurora do Pantanal* T 721-1339 and *Hotel Santa Cruz*. 3 *Poderes Restaurant*, R Beri, cheap good food; *Doce e Mel*, Praça Matriz, pleasant café serving good sweets and coffee.

● **Transport Buses** From Cuiabá US$7.65 by TUT, T 322-4985, 6 a day between 0600 and 1900. Poconé has a 24-hr **gas station** with all types of fuel, but closed on Sun.

From Poconé the Transpantaneira runs 146 km S to Porto Jofre (just a gas station, gasoline and diesel, but no alcohol available). At the entrance to the Pantanal, there is a gate across the road where drivers are given a list of rules of conduct. The road is of earth, in poor condition, with ruts, holes and many bridges that need care in crossing. Easiest access is in the dry season (July-Sept), which is also the best time for seeing birds and, in Sept, the trees are in bloom. In the wet, especially Jan-Feb, there is no guarantee that the Transpantaneira will be passable. The wet season, however, is a good time to see many of the shier animals because more fruit, new growth and other high calorie foods are available, and there are fewer people. It is easier to see the animals listed above from the Transpantaneira than from other areas of the Pantanal, but you need to go to the last 40 km of the road to gain the full benefit. Campos de Jofre, about 20 km N of Porto Jofre is said to be magnificent between Aug and Oct, with very large concentrations of birds and animals. In Poconé one can hitch (not much traffic, bumpy, especially in a truck) to Porto Jofre, or hire a vehicle in Cuiabá. You will get more out of this part of the Pantanal by going with a guide; a lot can be seen from the Transpantaneira in a hired car, but guides can take you into *fazendas* and will point out wildlife. Recommended guides in Cuiabá are listed below. Driving on the Transpantaneira during the wet season can be difficult. Although there are gas stations in Pixaim and Porto Jofre, they are not always well stocked, best to carry extra fuel.

PIXAIM

63 km from Poconé is **Pixaim** (2 hrs in the dry, up to 5 in the wet season), a bridge across the Rio Pixaim, where there are two hotels, with a fuel station (all types available, check that the pump is set to zero) and a tyre-repair shop (*borracheria*).

● **Accommodation** In Pixaim and The Transpantaneira: **A2** *Pousada Pixaim*, built on stilts, T 721-1899, full board (meals also available separately), 10 rooms with a/c or fan, mosquito-netted windows, hot water, electricity 24 hrs, pleasant setting, boat trips – US$30/hr with driver, camping possible US$10/tent or free if you eat in the restaurant, rec, bookings through Faunatur in Cuiabá. On the opp bank of the Rio Pixaim is **A1** *Hotel Beira Rio*, T/F (065) 321-9445, modern cabins, 35 rooms for 3-6 people, with full board, fan, clean, hot water (also family-size apartments with a/c), good home-grown food, in radio contact with office on R Barão de Melgaço in Cuiabá, camping possible, boat rental with driver US$30/hr; **A2** *O Pantaneiro*, full board, 6 rooms with 2-3 bunk beds each, bath, simple, owned and operated by *pantaneiros* (reservations through *Focus Tours*, Belo Horizonte, see page 429, or through *Faunatur* in Cuiabá), about 45 km from Pixaim, not as far S as **L3** *Hotel Fazenda Santa Rosa*, 150 km from Poconé, in Porto Jofre, with full board, no electricity, an old *fazenda*, refurbished and under new management in 1996, occasional water problems, river trips not inc and expensive, breakfast-eating parrot (reservations through *Focus Tours*, Belo Horizonte).

L2 *Pousada Araras*, Km 30 on Transpantaneira, 10 rooms with bath, good food, homemade *cachaça*, book through *Expeditours* in Cuiabá; **A1** *Hotel-Fazenda Cabanas do Pantanal*, 142 km from Cuiabá, 50 km from Poconé by the Rio Pixaim, on the northern edge of the Pantanal, 10 chalet bedrms with bath, restaurant, boat trips (few in dry season), horse-riding, fishing, helpful proprietor and staff, everything except boat trips and bar drinks inc in price (booking: *Confiança*, Cuiabá). **L2** *Sapé Pantanal Lodge*, Caixa Postal 2241 – CEP 78020.970, Cuiabá, T/F (065) 322-3426/361-4069, 8 rooms, 4-day, 3-night all-inclusive programme US$490, fishing, wildlife observation and photography excursions, holder of the Embratur 'Ecológico Especial' classification. A complete programme includes road transport from Cuiabá airport to Barão de Melgaço (wet season), or Porto Cercado (dry season) with onward river transportation (2 hrs and 1½ hrs respectively), and return; full board; outboard powered boats with experienced guides at guests' disposal during entire stay; optional trekking in dry season, paddling in wet; English, French, Spanish spoken. Sapé is closed 20 Dec-31 Jan, highly rec.

BARAO DE MELGAÇO

130 km from Cuiabá (TUT bus at 0730 and 1500, US$6.50) on Rio Cuiabá, **Barão de Melgaço** is reached by two roads: the shorter, via Santo Antônio de Leverger, unpaved from Sto Antônio to Barão (closed in the wet season), or via São Vicente, longer, but more pavement. As you approach Barão, the hills which limit the eastern edge of the Pantanal come into view and the last part of either route skirts the *mata* (forest), with babaçu and açori palms. The way to see the Pantanal from here is by boat down the Rio Cuiabá. Boat hire, for example from *Restaurant Peixe*

Vivo on waterfront, up to US$85 for a full day; or enquire with travel agencies in Cuiabá. The best time of day would be sunset, but it would need some organizing to be in the best part at the best time, without too much boating in the dark. Protect against the sun when on the water. Initially the river banks are farms and small habitations, but they become more forested, with lovely combinations of flowering trees (best seen Sept-Oct). After a while, a small river to the left leads to the Baia and Lakes Chacororé and Sia Mariana, which join each other. Boats can continue beyond the lakes to the Rio Mutum, but a guide is essential because there are many dead ends. The area is rich in birdlife and the waterscapes are beautiful.

● **Accommodation** In the town are *Barão Tour Hotel*, apartments with a/c, restaurant, boat trips and excursions (T Cuiabá 322-1568, or Melgatur), and, much humbler, *NS do Carmo Hotel* on the waterfront, and *Pousada e Lanchonete Francisco de Asis* on main road down to waterfront. *Mercadinho do Povo* minimarket sells provisions, including cheap hats. **Hotels reached from Barão de Melgaço**: on Sia Mariana are *Pousada do Barão*, 6 chalets with bath, swimming pool, 1st class, boat and trekking expeditions (book through Melgatur); *Restaurant Flamingo*, simple food, rooms, camping with permission, popular with fishermen; one other restaurant. Barão de Melgaço is also the starting point for the *Pousada Passargada*, programmes from 3 days up, full board, boat, car and trekking expeditions, transport from Barão de Melgaço, owner speaks English, French and German, food excellent, highly rec, closed Dec to Feb; reservations in Barão de Melgaço on riverside, through *Nature Safaris*, Av Mal Rondon, Barão de Melgaço, or Av NS de Copacabana 330, Rio de Janeiro, CEP 22020, T 235-2840, F 236-5285. Much cheaper if booked direct with the owner, Maré Sigaud, Mato Grosso, CEP 786807, *Pousada Passargada*, Barão de Melgaço.

● **Tour companies & travel agents in Cuiabá**: *Confiança*, Mariano 434, T 321-4147, very helpful travel agency, tours to Pantanal are expensive. Also rec *Expeditours*, Av Gov Ponce de Arruda 670, T 381-4959/5674, sightseeing, fishing trips for 4-5 days by boat; *Anaconda*, R Comandante Costa 649, T 624-4142, F 624-6242, tour operators for Pantanal, Chapada dos Guimarães and Southern Amazonia, Pantanal day tour as far as Pixaim US$60 pp, 2 day US$155 pp, 3 day US$210, day tour to Chapada

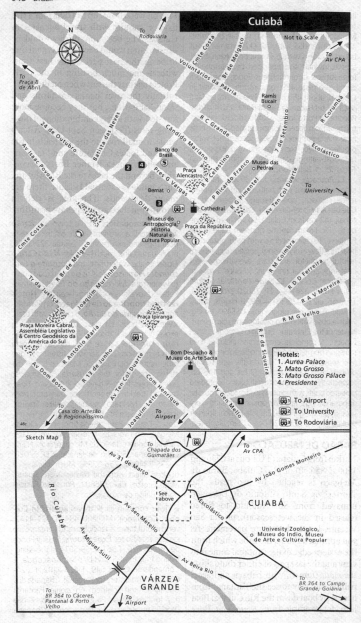

Cuiabá

Not to Scale

To Rodoviária
To CPA
Av CPA

To Praça 8 de Abril

Cmte Costa
Voluntários da Pátria
Br de Melgaço

Ramis Bucair

R Corumbá

R C Grande

24 de Outubro
Batista das Neves
Cándido Mariano
Celestino
7 de Setembro
Ecolástico

Av Isac Povoas

Banco do Brasil
Pres G Vargas
Praça Alencastro
P Ricardo Franco
Museu das Pedras

Bemat

J. Dias
Cathedral

Museus do Antropologia, Historia Natural e Cultura Popular
Praça da República

R G Pimental

Av Ten Col Duarte

To University

Cmte Costa
R Br de Melgaço
Tr da Justiça
Joaquim Murtinho

R M Coimbra
R D D Ferreira
R A V Moreira
R M G Velho

Praça Ipiranga

Praça Moreira Cabral, Assembléia Legislativo & Centro Geodésico da América do Sul

R Antônio Maria

Bom Despacho & Museu de Arte Sacra

R F de Siqueira

Av Dom Bosco
R 13 de Junho
Av Ten Col Duarte
Com Henrique

To Casa do Artesão & Regionalíssimo

Joaquim Leite
To Airport
Av Gen Mello

Hotels:
1. Aurea Palace
2. Mato Grosso
3. Mato Grosso Pálace
4. Presidente

To Airport
To University
To Rodoviária

Sketch Map

To Chapada dos Guimarães
To Av CPA

Av 31 de Março
Av João Gomes Monteiro

Rio Cuiabá

Av Sen Metello
See above
Ecolástico

CUIABÁ

Univesity Zoológico, o Museu do Indio, Museu de Arte e Cultura Popular

Av Miguel Sutil

Av Beira Rio

VÁRZEA GRANDE

To BR 364 to Campo Grande, Goiânia

To BR 364 to Cáceres, Pantanal & Porto Velho

To Airport

46c

or Aguas Quentes US$50 pp, Amazon trips to Alta Foresta/Rio Cristalino region US$100 pp/day + airfare; *Ametur,* R Joaquim Murtinho 242, T 624-1000, very helpful, good for air tickets; Adriana Coningham of *Ararauna Turismo Ecológica,* R Barão de Melgaço, highly rec. All these agencies arrange trips to the Pantanal; for longer or special programmes, book in advance. *Focus Tours* of Belo Horizonte (see page 429) specializes in tours in this part of the Pantanal and, starting from Cuiabá, to the southern Amazon, with bases at Alta Floresta and on the Rio Cristalino (see page 654).

Recommended guides (in alphabetical order): Laércio Sá, *Fauna Tour,* Real Palace Hotel, Praça Ipiranga 102, CEP 78020-600, T/F 321-5375 (Attn Faunatours) or Av Beira Rio, Quadra 28, Casa 21, CEP 78.065-780, has own car, well-informed, helpful, speaks English, Spanish and Italian, 2 day Pantanal tours US$140 pp, 3 day US$190 pp (inc transport, accommodation, meals, trekking, horse riding, boat trips, fishing) can arrange longer tours and camping (Aug-Oct) on request, also excursions to Chapada das Guimarães, rec. Joel Souza, can be contacted at the airport, speaks English well, checklists for flora and fauna provided, will arrange all transport, farm accommodation, fishing, horse riding, trekking, night excursions (US$140 for 2-night tours). Most guides await incoming flights at airport; compare prices and services in town if you don't wish to commit yourself at airport.

CUIABÁ

(*Pop* 435,647, unofficially much larger; *alt* 165m; *CEP* 78000; *DDD* 065) **Cuiabá**, the capital of Mato Grosso state (*pop* 2,020,580) on the Rio Cuiabá, an upper tributary of the River Paraguai, is in fact two cities: Cuiabá on the E bank of the river and Várzea Grande, where the airport is, on the W. It is very hot; coolest months for a visit are June, July, and Aug, in the dry season. It has a number of squares and is known as the *Cidade Verde* (green city).

Places of interest

Cuiabá has an imposing government palace and other fine buildings round the green **Praça da República**. On the square is the **Cathedral**, with a plain, imposing exterior, two clock-towers and, inside, coloured-glass mosaic windows and doors. Behind the altar is a huge mosaic of Christ in majesty, with smaller mosaics in side chapels. Beside the Cathedral is another

leafy square, **Praça Alencastro**. On **Praça Ipiranga**, at the junction of Avs Isaac Póvoas and Ten Cel Duarte, a few blocks W of the central squares, there are market stalls and an iron bandstand from Huddersfield. On a hill beyond the square is the church of **Bom Despacho** (closed for restoration, 1996). In front of the Assembléia Legislativa, Praça Moreira Cabral, is a point marking the **Geogedesic Centre of South America** (see also under Chapada dos Guimarães, below).

Museums

Museus de Antropologia, História Natural e Cultura Popular in the Fundação Cultural de Mato Grosso, Praça da República 151, US$0.50, historical photos, documents, furniture, one room of religious art, contemporary art gallery, stuffed fauna, stones and woods from the region, Indian items and weapons, archaeological finds and pottery, open Mon-Fri 0800-1730. **Museu de Arte Sacra**, beside Bom Despacho church. **Museu de Pedras**, US$2 entry, Galdino Pimentel 195, Mon-Fri 0800-1100 and 1300-1700, exhibits stones from the Chapada dos Guimarães. At the entrance to Universidade de Mato Grosso, 10 mins by bus from the centre, is the **Museu do Índio/Museu Rondon** (by swimming pool), small, well-displayed exhibits. Carrying on along the road through the campus, signed on the left before a right turn in the road, is the **Zoológico**, open 0800-1100, 1330-1700 (closed Mon); free; the jacaré, capivara, tortoise and tapir pen can be seen at any time, but best early am or late pm, also has coatis, otters, emu, monkeys, peccaries, birds, etc. Opposite the zoo is the theatre. Its museum, **de Arte e Cultura Populares**, is closed indefinitely.

Excursions

Good fishing in the Cuiabá and smaller Coxipó rivers. The **Águas Quentes** hot springs, 86 km (9 km S of the BR 163, 77 km E of Cuiabá) can be visited; **L3** *Hotel Águas Quentes* at the springs, all meals inc, reservations through *Hotel Mato Grosso Palace*, address below, T 624-6637. The waters fill pools of 42° and 36° C; no buses go there, arrange transport through *Hotel*

Mato Grosso Palace.

Local information

NB The prot area is best avoided, even in daylight.

● Accommodation

L2 *Eldorado Cuiabá*, Av Isaac Póvoas 1000, T 624-4000, F 624-1480, very smart; **L2** *Global Garden*, Av Miguel Sutil 5555, T 6241660, F 6249966, a/c, fridge, TV, pool, bar, restaurant; **L3** *Mato Grosso Palace*, Joaquim Murtinho 170, T 624-7747, F 321-2386, 4-star (Best Western), with bath, a/c, fridge, TV, central, good; **L3** *Novotel Paiaguas*, Av Rubens de Mendonça 1718, T 624-5353, F 322-2910, a/c, fridge, TV, pool, sauna, restaurant; **L3** *Taiamã Plaza*, Av Rubens de Mendonça 1184, Bosque de Saúde, T/F 624-1490, 3-star, very good, pool, excellent breakfast; **L3** *Veneza Palace*, Av Cel Escolástico 738, T 321-4847, F 322-5212, 3-star, rec.

A2 *Jaguar*, Av Getúlio Vargas 600, T 322-9044, F 322-6698, use of swimming pool; **A2** *Las Velas*, Av Filinto Müller 62, opp airport, T 6823840, F 6823734, clean, pool, good value; **A3** *Aurea Palace*, Gen Melo 63, T 322-3377, pleasant rooms, restaurant, swimming pool, good; **A3** *Almanara*, Av Cel Escolástico 510, T 323-1244, F 323-2049, with a/c, fridge, TV; opp but less good is **A3** *Bandeirantes*, at No 425, T 321-0920, F 624-5363, a/c, fridge, TV, SE of centre; **B** *Abudi Palace*, No 259, T 322-7399, a/c, TV, good.

B *Lord*, Av G Vargas 1406, by Praça 9 de Abril, T 321-4113, with bath, a/c; **B** *Mato Grosso*, R Comandante Costa 2522, T 321-9121, 2-star, a/c, cheaper with fan, clean, good restaurant, good value; **B** *Presidente*, Barão de Melgaço e Av G Vargas, T 321-6162, on a busy central corner, convenient but lots of traffic outside, a/c, C with fan, TV, fridge, cheaper with shared bath; **B** *Real Palace*, 13 de Junho 102, Praça Ipiranga, T 321-5375, F 611-1141, with bath, large rooms, some with a/c, good breakfast.

C *Panorama*, R Barão de Melgaço, N of Telemat, T 322-0072, with bath, fan; **C** *Samara*, R Joaquim Murtinho 270, T 322-6001, central, with bath, hot shower, fan, basic but good, clean, friendly, cheaper with shared bath.

E *Lagunas*, Av Gen Melo 166, small rooms, basic.

By the rodoviária, on Jules Rimet are: **A3** *Skala Palace*, at No 26, T 322-4347, with a/c, fridge, TV, restaurant, smart lobby, front rooms noisy; **B** *Brazil*, No 20, T 621-2703, with bath, a/c, fridge, TV, parking, D with fan, cheaper with shared bath; **C** *Ipanema*, s/n, T 621-3069, with bath, a/c, TV, D with fan, cheaper with shared bath, clean, good value, good breakfast, rec; **C** *Grande*, No 30, T 621-3852, with bath, a/c, TV, D with fan, cheaper with shared bath, basic; **D** *Cuiabano*, No 28, with bath, fan, E with shared bath, basic, dirty; **E** *Modelo*, No 221, with bath, fan, basic; **D** *União*, R Poxoréu 13, T 621-1589, with bath, fan, TV, E with shared bath, basic, friendly; **D** *Rondônia*, R Poxoréu 124, with bath, a/c, D with fan, E with shared bath, basic, dirty; others in same area.

● Places to eat

Bierhaus, Isaac Póvoas 1200; *Tio Ari*, R Comandante Costa 770, buffet with a wide variety of vegeterian and a few meat dishes, good quality and value, rec; *Sachimi*, Av Isaac Póvoas across from *Eldorado Hotel*, Japanese. *O Choppão*, Praça 9 de Abril, very good, popular; *Cacalo Peixaria*, Av Lavapés 203, Santa Rosa, traditional fish dishes, popular, good; *Salambô*, Av 31 de Março 720, accross from *Shopping Goiabeiras*, good buffet, not cheap, open evenings; *Getúlio Grill*, Av Getúlio Vargas 1147, meat specialties; *Cedros*, Praça 8 de Abril 750, goiabeiras, Arab food; *Casa Suiça*, Av Miguel Sutil 4200, Swiss food, trout. Restaurants in the city centre are closed at night, try Av Getúlio Vargas, between Praças Santos Dumont and 9 de Abril, about 10 mins' walk from centre, has several popular pizza and other restaurants, also along Isaac Póvoas in the same direction (NW). On Av CPA are many good restaurants and small snack bars. There are several restaurants and lanchonetes on R Jules Rimet across from the rodoviária, *Paladar*, at No 60, good value, rec.

● Banks & money changers

Banco do Brasil, Av Getúlio Vargas e R Barão de Melgaço, commission charged: US$10 for cash, US$20/transaction for TCs, very slow for TCs, but best rates; fewer people at **Banco do Estado de Mato Grosso** (Bemat), Pedro Celestino s/n, Praça Alencastro, cash and TCs, 1000-1500; **Banespa**, Av Getúlio Vargas 240, cash and TCs, min transaction US$500, 1000-1330. The following travel agents or gold dealers change cash only at poor rates (generally open Mon-Fri): *Mattos-Tur*, R Cândido Mariano 465; *Goldmine*, R Cândido Mariano 400, 0800-1600; *Ourominas*, R Cândido Mariano 401, 0800-1700, may change on Sat 0800-1200 if cash is available, enquire first, T 624-9400; *Portobello*, R Comandante Costa 555, 0900-1600. It is difficult to get cash advances on credit cards especially Mastercard, for Visa try Banco do Brasil or Bradesco.

● Electric current

110 volts AC, 60 cycles.

● Entertainment

Cuiabá is quite lively at night, bars with live music

and dance on Av CPA; *Tucano* bar/restaurant, Av CPA, beautiful view, rec. Four cinemas in town.

● **Post & telecommunications**
Post Office: main branch at Praça da República, fax service.

Telecommunications: Telemat, R Barão de Melgaço 3209, 0700-2200, also at rodoviária, 0600-2130, international service.

● **Shopping**
Handicrafts in wood, straw, netting, leather, skins, Pequi liquor, crystallized *caju* fruit, compressed *guaraná* fruit (for making the drink), Indian objects on sale at airport, rodoviária, craft shops in centre, and daily market, Praça da República, interesting. The **Casa de Artesão**, Praça do Expedicionário 315, T 321-0603, sells all types of local crafts in a restored building, rec. Fish and vegetable market, picturesque, at the riverside.

● **Tourist offices**
Secretaria de Desenvolvimento do Turismo, **Sedtur**, Praça da República 131, next to post office building, T/F 624-9060, Mon-Fri, 0700-1800. Good maps, friendly, helpful regarding general information, hotels and car hire, some English and Spanish spoken. **Ramis Bucair**, R Pedro Celestino 280, is good for detailed maps of the region.

● **Transport**
Local Buses Many bus routes have stops in the vicinity of Praça Ipiranga. To/from airport, see below; bus 501 or 505 (Universidade) to University museums and zoo (ask for 'Teatro') from Av Ten Cel Duarte by Praça Bispo Dom José, a triangular park just E of Praça Ipiranga. To rodoviária, No 202 from R Joaquim Murtinho behind the cathedral, about 20 mins. **Car hire**: **Unidas**, Av Isaac Póvoas 720, T 682-4062; **Nobre**, at airport, T 381-1651; **Localiza**, Av Dom Bosco 963, T 624/979; **Atlântida**, Av Isaac Póvoas, T 623-0700.

Air Airport in Várzea Grande, T 682-2213. By air to Corumbá, São Paulo, Manaus, Campo Grande, Goiânia, Brasília, Rio de Janeiro, Belém and Porto Velho. Also many smaller Brazilian cities. Night flights for those routes available cost approx 30% less. No bank at airport; there is a post office and a Turimat office (not always open). Taxi to centre US$10-15, bus US$0.40 (take any white Tuiuiú bus, name written on side, in front of airport to Av Ten Cel Duarte; to return take 'Aeroporto' bus from Praça Ipiranga).

Buses Rodoviária is on R Jules Rimet, Bairro Alvorada, N of the centre; town buses (see above) stop at the entrance. Comfortable buses (toilets) to **Campo Grande**, 10 hrs, US$25, 12 buses daily, *leito* at 2000 and 2100, US$48. **Goiânia**, 14 hrs,

US$30; direct to **Brasília**, 24 hrs, US$37, leito US$59. To **Porto Velho**, 6 União Cascavel buses a day, US$63, road paved, 1,450 km, bus journey takes 21 hrs. Andorinha 1700 bus São Paulo-Cuiabá connects with Porto Velho service. Eventually a paved road from Brasília to Caracas is envisaged. Several to **São Paulo**, eg Motta, US$50. Integração buses go to Ponta Porã, Foz do Iguaçu and Cascavel; União Cascavel also go to the NE and Fortaleza via Imperatriz; Açailândia to the NE via Tocantins; to Curitiba via Londrina and Ponta Grossa, with a service continuing to Florianópolis. To **Barra do Garças**, Xavante 0800, 1300 and 2030, US$17, also Barattur. Connections to all major cities.

ROUTES There is a paved road to Campo Grande (712 km); the 2,400 km BR-364 road from Brasília to Porto Velho and Rio Branco passes through Cuiabá; it is paved all the way between Brasília, Cuiabá (1,127 km) and is in good condition, but between Cuiabá and Porto Velho there are many pot-holes. Service stations often provide free hot showers and the *prato comercial* is a cheap meal. The more direct road to Brasília through Barra do Garças and Goiás Velho (the BR-070) is paved also. Several paved feeder roads connect the BR-070 and BR-364.

CHAPADA DOS GUIMARÃES

68 km NE of Cuiabá lies one of the oldest plateaux on earth. The pleasant town of **Chapada dos Guimarães** (*pop* 13,416; *DDD* 065; *CEP* 78195), the main population centre, is a base for many beautiful excursions in this area; it has the oldest church in the Mato Grosso, **NS de Santana** (1779), a bizarre blending of Portuguese and French baroque styles, and a huge spring-water public swimming pool (on R Dr Pem Gómes, behind the town). Formerly the centre of an important diamond prospecting region, today Chapada is a very popular destination for Cuiabanos to escape the heat of the city on weekends and holidays.

The Chapada is an immense geological formation rising to 700m, with rich forests, curiously-eroded rocks and many lovely grottoes, peaks and waterfalls. A **National Park** has been established in the area just W of the town, where the **Salgadeira** tourist centre offers bathing, camping and a restaurant close to the Salgadeira waterfall. The beautiful 85m

Véu da Noiva waterfall (Bridal Veil), 12 km before the town near Buriti (well-signposted, ask bus from Cuiabá to let you off), is reached by a short route, or a long route through forest. Other sights include the **Mutuca** beauty spot, **Rio Claro**, the viewpoint over the breathtaking 80m-deep **Portão do Inferno** (Hell's Gate), and the falls of **Cachoeirinha** (small restaurant) and **Andorinhas**. 8 km E of town is the monument **Mirante do Ponto Geodésico**, a monument officially marking the Geodesic Centre of South America, which overlooks a great canyon with views of the surrounding plains, the Pantanal and Cuiabá's skyline on the horizon; to reach it take R Fernando Corrêa E, drive 8 km then turn right at the 'Centro Geodésico' sign. Continuing E, the road goes through agricultural land and later by interesting rock formations including a stone bridge and stone cross; 45 km from Chapada you reach the access for **Caverna do Francês** or Caverna Aroe Jari ('the dwelling of the souls' in the Bororo language), a sandstone cave over 1 km long, the second largest in Brazil; it is a 2-km walk to the cave, in it is Lagoa Azul, a lake with crystaline blue water, a good place for a dip. Other excursions are to the **Cidade de Pedra** rock formations, 25 km from town along the road to the diamond prospecting town of Agua Fria, nearby is a 300m wall formed by the Rio Claro and 60 km from town, are the **Pingador** and **Bom Jardim** archaeological sites, caverns with petroglyphs dating back some 4,000 years. The Chapada dos Guimarães is one of the most scenic areas of Brazil and retains much of the mystery attributed to it for centuries. In the 1920s Colonel Fawcett was told of many strange things hidden in its depths, and an unusual local magnetic force which reduces the speed of cars has been documented. The birdwatching is very good and mammals, such as puma, giant river otter and black-tailed marmoset, live here. Unfortunately, the national park is not regulated so that soil erosion, mercury used by the *garimpeiros* and uncontrolled tourism are threatening both the Chapada's own features and the waters that run from it into the Pantanal.

Tours Hiring a car in Cuiabá is the most convenient way to see many of the scattered attractions, although access to several of them is via rough dirt roads which may deteriorate in the rainy season; drive carefully as the area is prone to dense fog. Hitchiking from Chapada town to the National Park is feasible on weekends and holidays, when many Cuiabanos flock to the area, but expect crowds at the swimming holes. Travel agencies in Chapada and Cuiaba offer expensive tours to all the sights. The small Tourist Office run by the Secretaria de Turismo e Meio Ambiente, R Quinco Caldas 100, near the praça, provides a useful map of the region and organizes tours; José Paulino dos Santos is a guide working with this office (weekdays 0800-1100, 1300-1800, T 791-1245). Rec tours with Jorge Belfort Mattos from *Ecoturismo Cultural*, Praça Dom Wunibaldo 464, T/F 791-1393; he speaks English and knows the area well; several 4- to 6-hr itineraries from US$20-56 pp (min 4 people or prices increase). Also with Cássio Martins of *AC Tour*, R Tiradentes 28, T 791-1122, who often waits at the rodoviária. 4 hr tours are about US$20 pp, min 5 persons; 7-8 hr tours, US$25 pp, min 5; horseback day tour, US$25 pp, min 2; an 8-10 km hike with a guide, US$20 pp, min 2; bicycle tour with guide, US$20 pp, min 2. Tours from Cuiabá cost US$35-40 pp.

Local festivals The **Festival de Inverno** is held in last week of July, and **Carnaval** is very busy. Accommodation is scarce and expensive at these times, as up to 60,000 Cuiabanos flock to Chapada.

● **Accommodation A1** *Pousada da Chapada*, 2 km out on Cuiabá road (MT 251, Km 63), T 791-1171, F 791-1299, a/c, fridge, TV, A2 with fan, very comfortable, restaurant, bar, pool, sports facilities, parking; **A3** *Turismo*, R Fernando Corrêa 1065, a block from rodoviária, T 791-1176, F 791-1383, a/c, fridge, TV, B with fan, restaurant, very friendly and popular, German-run; **B** *Estância San Francisco*, at the entrance to town from Cuiabá (MT 251, Km 61), T 791-1102, F 791-1537, on 42 ha farm with 2 lakes, a/c, fridge, TV, said to have the best breakfast in town fresh from the farm, new in 1996; **B** *Rio's Hotel*, R Tiradentes 333, T 791-

1126, a/c, TV, fridge, C with fan, cheaper with shared bath, clean, good breakfast, rec; **B** *Chapadense*, R Ver José de Souza 535, T/F 791-1410, a/c, fridge, TV, C with fan and TV, restaurant serves *comida caseira*; **C** *Pousada Bom Jardim*, Praça Bispo Dom Wunibaldo s/n, T 791-1244, with bath, fan, clean, comfortable, parking, friendly, good breakfast, new end-1995, rec; **C** *Quincó*, Praça Bispo Dom Wunibaldo 464, T 791-1404, with bath, fan, clean; **D** *São José*, R Ver José de Souza 50, T 791-1152, with bath, fan, cheaper with shared bath and no fan, hot showers, basic, good, owner Mário sometimes runs excursions; **D** *Dormitorio*, R Tiradentes s/n, basic, with bath, no fan, cheaper with shared bath. **Camping: E** pp *Aldeia Velha*, in the Aldeia Velha neighbourhood at the entrance to town from Cuiabá, T 322-7178 (Cuiabá), fenced area with bath, hot shower, some shade, guard; Salgadeira, unorganized camping 16 km from town at the tourist centre, watch your belongings.

● **Places to eat** *Nívios*, Praça Dom Wunibaldo 631 for good regional food; *Fogão da Roça*, Praça Dom Wunibaldo 488, *comida Mineira*, generous portions, good quality, rec; **O** *Mestrinho*, R Quinco Caldas 119, meat, speciality is ribs, regional dishes, rodízio on weekends; *Choppada* (*O Chopp da Chapada*), R Cipriano Curvo s/n nr praça, drinks and meals, regional dishes, live music at weekends; *Trapiche*, R Cipriano Curvo 580, pizza, drinks, regional dishes; **O** *Mestrinho*, *Peixaria Serrano*, R Dr Pem Gómes 505 (nr pool), fish specialities and *comida caseira*, cheaper than those nr the praça; *Veu da Noiva*, R Dr Pem Gómes 524, regional dishes, fish in season (*piracema* fishing ban 1 Oct-1 Mar). *Pequí* is a regional palm fruit used to season many foods; *arroz com pequí* is a popular rice and chicken dish.

● **Post & telecommunications Post Office**: R Fernando Corrêa 848.

● **Shopping** Crafts, indigenous artefacts, sweets and locally-made honey from *Casa de Artes e Artesanato Mato Grossense* (Praça Dom Wunibaldo). Regional sweets from *Doceria Olho de Sogra*, Praça Dom Wunibaldo 21. João Eloy de Souza Neves is a local artist, his paintings, music and history about Chapada (*Chapada dos Guimarães da descoberta aos dias atuais*) are on sale at *Pousada Bom Jardim*.

● **Transport** There are bus services from the rodoviária to Brasilândia and Paranatinga (350 km away to the N by seasonal road in the headwaters of the Rio Xingu, 1330 daily), and 7 departures daily to and from Cuiabá (Rubi, 0700-1900, last back to Cuiabá 1800), 1½ hrs, US$4.

CACERES AND TO BOLIVIA

River trips from Cuiabá to Corumbá are very difficult since boats on the Cuiabá river are few and irregular. You can sometimes get to Corumbá by river from **Cáceres** (*pop* 77,821; *DDD* 065; *CEP* 78200), on the banks of the Rio Paraguai, 200 km W of Cuiabá, very hot but clean and hospitable. The city has many well maintained 19th century buildings, painted in pastel colours. The Municipality runs the **Museu Histórico de Cáceres** (R Antônio Maria by Praça Major João Carlos). The main square, Praça Barão de Rio Branco, has one of the original border markers from the Treaty of Tordesillas, which divided South America between Spain and Portugal; it is pleasant and shady during the day. In the evenings, between Nov and Mar, the trees are packed with thousands of chirping swallows (*andorinhas*), beware of droppings; the square is surrounded by bars, restaurants and ice cream parlours and comes to life at night. The city is known for its many bicycles as most people seem to get around on two wheels. Until 1960, Cáceres had regular boat traffic, today it is limited to a few tour boats and pleasure craft; the riverfront is an attractive place for a stroll, there is a yacht club, with swimming pool, volley ball and children's playground. Brazilians go to Cáceres to shop for bargains brought in from neighbouring Bolivia. Tourism is still limited however, despite its location by the scenic Serra da Mangabeira and at the edge of the Pantanal. Vitória Regia lilies can be seen N of town, just across the bridge over the Rio Paraguai along the BR-174. There are archaeological sites on the river's edge N of the city.

Local festivals The **Piranha Festival** is held in mid Mar, an International Fishing Festival in mid Sept as well as an annual cattle fair.

● **Accommodation A2** *Turbo*, Av São Luiz 1399 by BR 070, T 223-1984, luxury, a/c, TV, fridge, restaurant, pool; **A2** *Ipanema*, R Gen Osório 540, T 223-1177, F 223-1743, with a/c, fridge, TV, garage, good restaurant; **A3** *Comodoro*, Praça Duque de Caxias 561, T 223-2078, a/c, fridge, TV; **A3** *Caiçaras*, R dos Operários 745, corner R Gen Osório, T 223-3187, F 223-

2692, with bath, a/c, fridge, TV, B with bath and a/c, clean, pleasant, modern, parking; **B Fénix**, R dos Operários 600, T 223-1027, F 221-2243, fridge, a/c, TV, comfortable; **B Rio**, Praça Major João Carlos 61, T 223-3387, F 2233084, with bath, a/c, fridge, TV, C with bath, a/c, D with shared bath, fan; **C Charm**, Col José Dulce 405, T/F 223-4949, with bath, a/c, D with shared bath, friendly; nr the rodoviária are: **C Capri**, R Getúlio Vargas 99, T 223-1711, with bath, a/c, clean, comfortable; **C 13 de Junho**, R 13 de Junho s/n, T 223-3871, with bath, a/c, clean, pleasant; **C Gasparin**, Av Sangradouro 162, T 223-4579, with bath, a/c, fridge, cheaper with fan; **D União**, R 7 de Setembro 340, with bath, fan, E with shared bath, basic, friendly, good value; **D Rio Doce**, R 7 de Setembro, with bath, a/c, cheaper with shared bath, good value; **E Santa Terezinha**, R Tiradentes 485, with fan, breakfast, not clean, friendly. Many other cheap hotels.

● **Places to eat** *Corimbá* on riverfront, fish specialities, good, not cheap; *Bistecão*, R General Osório 977, meat, opens erratically; *Kaskata*, floating restaurant at the end of R Coronel José Dulce, by the port, nice setting, fish and *jacaré* specialties, fanciest in town, expensive; *Gulla's*, R Col José Dulce 215, buffet by kilo, good quality and variety, rec; *Hispano*, Praça Barão de Rio Branco 64, buffet by kilo; *Kaskata Pizzaria*, R Col José Dulce 250, pricey; *Panela de Barro*, R Frei Ambrósio 34, nr rodoviária, *comida caseira*.

● **Banks & money changers** *Casa de Câmbio Mattos*, Comandante Bauduino 180, next to main square, changes cash and TCs at good rates.

● **Post & telecommunications** Telecommunications: Praça Barão de Rio Branco s/n.

● **Tour companies & travel agents** *Cáceres*, Av Getúlio Vargas 408, T 223-1428, F 223-2440, fishing and photo tours to Pantanal, boat rentals, Claudio Duarte helpful guide; *Pantanal Tour*, R Com Farías 180, T 223-1200, boat rentals, fishing trips, tickets; *Vereda Turismo*, R Padre Cassemiro 1121, T 223-4360, Tours, boat rentals, fishing.

● **Shopping** *Náutica Turismo*, R Bom Jardim 119A, by the waterfront, for fishing/camping supplies and boat repairs.

● **Transport Local Car hire**: Localiza, Padre Cassemiro 640, T 223-4562. **River** The *Acuri*, brand new in 1996, a luxury tourist vessel sails to Corumbá, 1 week cruise including return by air from Corumbá to Cuiabá US$600 pp.For information on other boat sailings, ask at the Capitânia dos Portos, on the corner of the main square at the waterfront. If possible phone in advance to Cáceres, Posto Arrunda, 221-1707

to find out if any boats are going. Also Portobrás on the outskirts at the waterfront (T 221-1728). You may (with a lot of luck) be able to get passage on a boat; 3 days to Corumbá (up to 8 the other way). These boats are officially not allowed to take passengers. In the dry season there are practically no boats to Corumbá. At the waterfront you can hire a boat for a day trip, US$5/hr/pp, min 3 people; on holidays and some weekends there are organized day trips on the river. **Buses** Colibri/União Cascavel buses Cuiabá-Cáceres, US$13.50, many daily between 0630-2400 (book in advance, very crowded), 3½ hrs. Nice ride through rolling hills and cattle ranches, about 15 km before Cáceres, the road crosses the beautiful Serra da Mangabeira. To San Matías, Bolivia, Transical-Velásquez, Mon-Sat at 0630 and 1500, Sun 1500 only (return at same times), US$4, 3 hrs; connecting service to Santa Cruz, US$23.50, 24 hrs in the dry season, 30 hrs or more in the wet; Trans Bolivia to San Matías, Sun, Mon, Fri at 1500, Tues, Wed, Thur and Sat at 0700.

FRONTIER WITH BOLIVIA

An unpaved road runs from Cáceres to the Bolivian border at San Matías.

● **Brazilian immigration**
Polícia Federal, R Coronel Farías, Cáceres, for exit and entry formalities.

● **Transport**
Buses between Cáceres and the border take 15 hrs, US$22.

OUTLYING DISTRICTS OF MATO GROSSO: NORTH

The road due N from Cuiabá to Santarém (1,777 km) has been completed and is all-weather, through **Sinop** (*pop* 41,057), with a branch W to **Colíder** (*pop* 31,155), and **Alta Floresta** (*pop* 68,217; *DDD* 065; *CEP* 78580): daily bus from Cuiabá with São Luis at 2000, 12 hrs, US$46. Yellow fever inoculations insisted on when travelling this route. Outside Alta Floresta, the *Cristalino Jungle Lodge*, on the Cristalino river, is a basic lodge, with shared baths, in a very rich and well-preserved section of southern Amazônia. Many rare mammals are found here (including the short-eared dog), as well as five species of macaw, harpy eagle and a few hundred other bird species. *Anaconda Operators* in Cuiabá run tours to *Cristalino Jungle Lodge*, US$100 pp/day plus airfare (US$200 return);*Focus*

Tours of Belo Horizonte can also make reservations or arrange guided tours.

● **Accommodation Sinop: C** *Italian Palace*, Av das Figueras 493, T 531-2109, restaurant, bar, sauna. **Alta Floresta: B** *Floresta Amazônica*, Av Perimetral Ote 2001, T 521-3601, F 521-3801, in park, lovely views, pool, sports, all facilities; **C** *Pirâmide Palace*, Av do Aeroporto 445, T 521-2400, with bath, a/c, fridge, restaurant; **D** *Grande Hotel Coroados*, R F 1 118, T 521-3022, not too well kept but has a/c, pool and bar.

SOUTHEAST: RONDONÓPOLIS

From **Rondonópolis** (*pop* 125,110), about 215 km SE of Cuiabá on the road to Goiânia, a paved road branches southwards to Campo Grande and thence to the western parts of the State of São Paulo.

● **Accommodation** Many hotels, **A1** *Novotel*, R Floriano Peixoto 711, T 421-9355, F 421-9322, a/c, fridge, TV, pool; **A2** *Guarujá*, R Fernando Corrêa 624, T/F 421-8611, a/c, TV, fridge; **A2** *Thaani*, Av Amazonas 472, T 4219288, a/c, TV, fridge, pool; **A3** *Nacional*, R Fernando Corrêa 978, T 421-3245, F 421-4848, a/c, fridge, TV; **D** *Dormitório Beija Flor*, nr rodoviária.

● **Transport Air** For internal flights. **Buses** From Rondonópolis, **Brasília**, US$23, 14½ hrs; **Goiânia**, US$19, 11 hrs; **Campo Grande**, US$9.50, 6½ hrs; **Presidente Epitácio**, US$7.75; **Presidente Prudente**, US$11.50. Beware of overbooking on Viação Motta buses.

WEST OF CUIABÁ

A journey along the Porto Velho road from Cuiabá (BR-364) demonstrates the amount of development and deforestation along Brazil's 'Far West' frontier, see page 615. At Km 168 of the BR-174 there is a sign marking the divide between the Amazon and River Plate watersheds. Further N, a side road off the BR-174, at **Pontes e Lacerda** (**A3** *Verona Palace Hotel*, T 266-1507, with bath, a/c, restaurant, pool; also 2 dormitories by rodoviária) goes to **Vila Bela** on the Rio Guaporé, which used to be the capital of Mato Grosso. It has a ruined church, cannon balls lying around, and is very interesting.

NB When travelling N of Cuiabá, yellow fever vaccination is obligatory; if you do not have a certificate, you will be (re)vaccinated.

Information for travellers

BEFORE YOU GO

ENTRY REQUIREMENTS

● **Documents**

Consular visas are not required for stays of up to 90 days by tourists from Western European (except for French nationals) or South American (except Bolivia and Guyana) countries, Finland, Morocco, Bahamas, Barbados, Trinidad and Tobago, and the Philippines. For them, only the following documents are required at the port of disembarkation: valid passport (or *cédula de identidade* for nationals of Argentina, Chile, Paraguay and Uruguay); and a return or onward ticket, or adequate proof that you can purchase your return fare, subject to no remuneration being received in Brazil and no legally binding or contractual documents being signed. Some consulates (eg Frankfurt) insist that your passport be valid for at least 6 months from date of entry. If coming from Bolivia, Colombia or Peru (or certain African countries), you must have valid yellow fever vaccination certificate. Venezuelan passport holders can stay in Brazil for 60 days on filling in a form at the border. (Some consulates, eg Santiago, ask to see an onward ticket: persistence, adequate money and showing a credit card may overcome this.) 90-day renewals are easily obtainable, but only at least 15 days before the expiry of your 90-day permit, from the Polícia Federal: the procedure is, give your name, passport data and Brazilian address to the clerk, who will type this on the form for extension (US$0.50); take this to a bank; pay US$3 tax; then return to Polícia Federal who will

stamp the extension in your passport after they have seen onward flight tickets and receipt from the bank for the tax; sometimes proof of sufficient funds for your continued stay is requested. Some points of entry refuse entry for longer than 30 days, renewals are then for the same period, insist if you want 90 days. For longer stays you must leave the country and return (not the same day) to get a new 90-day permit. If you overstay your visa, or extension, you will be fined US$1/day, up to US$75. After paying the fine to Polícia Federal, you will be issued with an exit visa and must leave within 8 days. If you cannot pay the fine you must pay when you next return to Brazil. US, Canadian and French citizens and people of other nationalities, and those who cannot meet the requirements above, *must* get a visa before arrival, which may, if you ask, be granted for multiple entry. (Visa fees vary, eg free for USA, US$32 for Canadians, US$40 for French and Russians; for most others a tourist visa costs US$16.) Do not lose the emigration permit they give you when you enter Brazil. Leaving the country without it, you may have to pay up to US$100 pp.

Officially, if you leave Brazil within the 90-day permission to stay and then re-enter the country, you should only be allowed to stay until the 90-day permit expires. Usual practice, though, is to give another 90-day permit, which may lead to charges of overstaying if you apply for an extension.

You must always carry identification when in Brazil; it is a good idea to take a photocopy of the first 5 pages of your passport, plus that with your Brazilian immigration stamp, and leave your passport in the hotel safe deposit. Always keep an independent record of your passport details. In Rio it is a good idea to register with your consulate to expedite document replacement if yours gets lost/stolen.

● **Vaccinations**

Vaccination against smallpox is no longer required for visitors, but vaccination is necessary against yellow fever if you are visiting Amazônia and the Centre-West, or are coming from countries with Amazonian territories, eg Bolivia, Colombia, Ecuador, Peru. It is strongly rec to have a yellow fever inoculation before visiting northern Brazil since those without a certificate will be inoculated on entering any of the northern and centre-western states, probably in unsanitary conditions. Poliomyelitis vaccination is required for children from 3 months to 6 years. If you are going to Amazônia, or to other low-lying forested areas, malaria prophylaxis is advised (this can be difficult to obtain in some areas – the local name for paludrine is doroprim) and water purification tablets are essential. Dengue fever is now endemic in Brazil, and Rio is one of the worst places: protect yourself against mosquitoes. Sporadic outbreaks of cholera have occurred in the Amazon region and on the NE coast (eg Recife), but numbers have been in the tens, rather than the hundreds. Take care to drink only sterilized water. Also, in the Amazon basin, sandflies abound; take a good repellent and get inoculations against hepatitis and typhoid.

Yellow fever (see page 655) and some other vaccinations can be obtained from the Ministério da Saúde, R Cais de Pharoux, Rio de Janeiro. Less common vaccinations can be obtained at Saúde de Portos, Praça 15 de Novembro, Rio de Janeiro. It is reported that shots of immunoglobulin against hepatitis are not screened against Aids, which is widespread.

● **Representation overseas**

Canada, 2000 Mansfield, Suite 1700, Montreal H3A 3AS, T 514-0499; **Denmark**, Ryvangs Alle 24, 21 Copenhagen, T 20-6478; **France**, 34 Cours Allert IER, 75008 Paris, T 4225-9250; **Germany**, Stephanstrasse 3, 4 Stock, 6000 Frankfurt, T 290709; **UK**, 32 Green St, London WIY 4AT, T 0171-499-0877, consulate at 6 St Albans St, London SW1Y 4SQ, T 0171-930-9055; **USA**, 630 Fifth Ave, 27 Floor, New York NY 10111, T 212 916-3251/3200; **USA**, 8484 Wilshire Blvd, Suites 730-711, Los Angeles, California, T 213 651-2664.

● **Tourist information**

All Brazil's States, and most cities and towns have their own tourist information bureaux. They are not usually too helpful regarding information on very cheap hotels, tending to imagine that no foreign tourist should consider staying in anything of that kind. It is also difficult to get information on neighbouring states. *Quatro Rodas*, a motoring magazine, publishes an excellent series of maps and guides in Portuguese and English from about US$10. Its *Guia Brasil* is a type of Michelin Guide to hotels, restaurants (not the cheapest), sights, facilities and general information on hundreds of cities and towns in the country, including good street maps. These guides can be purchased at street newspaper vendors throughout the country. Quatro Rodas Guides may be bought in Europe from 33 rue de Miromesnil, 75008 Paris, T 42.66.31.18, F 42.66.13.99, or Distribuidora Jardim, Quinta Pau Varais, Azinhaga de Fetais, Camarate 2685, Lisbon, Portugal, T Lisbon 947-2542. In USA: Lincoln Building, 60 East 42nd St, Suite 3403, New York, NY 10165, T 557-5990/3, F 983-0972. Note that telephone yellow pages in most cities (but not Rio) contain good street maps which, together with the Quatro Rodas maps, are a great help for getting around.

Many of the more expensive hotels provide locally-produced tourist information magazines for their guests. Travel information can be very unreliable and it is wise to recheck details thoroughly.

WHEN TO GO

● **Best time to visit**

The best time for a visit is from April to June, and Aug to Oct, inclusive. Business visitors should avoid from mid-Dec to the end of Feb, when it is hot and people are on holiday. In these months hotels, beaches and means of transport tend to be crowded. July is a school holiday month.

Conditions during the winter (May to Sept) are like those of a N European summer in Rio de Janeiro (including periods of rain and overcast skies), but more like a N European autumn in São Paulo and the southern states. Summer-weight woollens can be worn without discomfort in winter in Rio de Janeiro (temperatures vary at this season from 14°C to the high 20s), but further S something heavier is often required. It can get very cold in the far S. In São Paulo, which is in the Highlands, light-weight clothing is only required in the summer; the climate can be treacherous, however, with large temperature changes in a brief space of time. It can get surprisingly cold S and W of Rio, and on high ground anywhere in Brazil; at night, warm clothes are needed. The season of heavy rains is from Nov to Mar in Rio and São Paulo, Jan to April in the N, and from April to Aug around Recife.

Summer conditions all over the country are tropical, but temperatures of 40°C are comparatively rare. On the coast there is a high degree of humidity. The luminosity is also very high; sunglasses are advisable.

HEALTH

Be very careful about bathing in lakes or slow rivers anywhere in Brazil: harmful parasites abound (including the snails that carry schistosomiasis – this disease is rampant in Minas Gerais and most of central Brazil). South of the Amazon beware of *borrachudos*, small flies with a sharp bite that attack ankles and calves; coconut oil deters them. Water should not be drunk from taps unless there is a porcelain filter attached or unless you have water sterilizing tablets ('Hydrosteril' is a popular local brand); there is mineral water in plenty and excellent light beer, known as 'chopp' (pronounced 'shoppi'), and soft drinks. For those who have been in Brazil for a while, *água gelada* (chilled water) is usually safe to drink, being filtered water kept in a refrigerator in most hotels, restaurants and stores. Avoid ice in cheap hotels and restaurants; it is likely to be made from unfiltered water. Colestase is the rec local treatment for upset stomachs.

Brazilians are famous for their open sexuality: appearances can be deceptive, however, and attitudes vary widely. To generalize, the coastal cities are very easy-going, while in smaller towns and the interior, traditional morals are strictly enforced. Aids is widespread, commonly transmitted by heterosexual sex, and tolerance of male homosexuality is diminishing. You should take reliable condoms with you, even if you are sure you won't be needing them. The primary means of HIV infection in Brazil is now heterosexual sex. Local condoms are reported not to be reliable.

Tampons are available, as are Hydrocare contact lens products (expensive).

● **Medical facilities**

An excellent hospital, supported by the American and British colonies in São Paulo, is Hospital Samaritano, R Conselheiro Brotero 1486, São Paulo (T 51-2154). If staying in Brazil for any length of time, it is rec to take out Brazilian health insurance; Banco Econômico and Citibank are reported to provide good advice on this matter.

MONEY

● **Currency**

Until 1 July 1994, the currency unit was the cruzeiro real (called 'cruzeiro'), introduced in Sept 1993, and having 1,000 times the value of the cruzeiro introduced in Mar 1990. A new currency unit, the *real*, R$ (plural *reais*), was introduced on 1 July 1994. The value of the *real* was the same as one Real Unit of Value (URV), a transitionary accounting unit introduced on 1 March 1994 at a par with the US dollar. By Dec 1994 the *real* had risen to US$0.84, but revaluations in early 1995 permitted it to float and by mid-June 1996 the official rate for the *real* was R$1 = US$1. Any amount of foreign currency and 'a reasonable sum' in *reais* can be taken in; residents may only take out the equivalent of US$4,000. Notes in circulation are: 100, 50, 20, 10, 5 and 1 *real*; coins 1 *real*, 50, 25, 10, 5, 2 and 1 centavo.

Money sent to Brazil is normally paid out in Brazilian currency, so do not have more money sent to Brazil than you need for your stay in the country itself. In most large cities Citibank will hold US personal cheques for collection, paying the day's tourist dollar rate in *reais* with no charge. Banco do Brasil offers the same service with small charge. From the UK the quickest method of having money sent is Swift Air. Tourists cannot change US$ TCs into US$ notes (though some exchange houses will do this illegally), but US$ TCs obtained on an American Express card (against official policy).

● **Cost of living**

Since the introduction of the *real* in July 1994, prices for residents and visitors have increased. Eating in smart restaurants is very costly. While hotel accommodation has risen steeply in price since 1995, budget hotels have responded by cutting extras, cramming more beds into rooms, etc. A cheap room cost about US$10. Shopping prices are equivalent to Europe. Hotel price categories and transport fares in this chapter reflect the appreciation of the *real*, but travellers may find variations as the *real* fluctuates within the floating exchange rate system introduced in 1995. Prices are higher in Amazônia than elsewhere.

● **Banks & money changers**

Banks in major cities will change cash and TCs. For the latest exchange rate, see tables nr end of book. If you keep the exchange slips, you may convert back into foreign currency up to 50% of the amount you exchanged. This applies to the official markets only; there is no right of reconversion unless you have an official exchange slip. The parallel market, found in travel agencies, exchange houses and among hotel staff, was of no benefit compared with bank rates in 1996. TCs are a safer way to carry your money, but rates for cheques are usually lower than for cash and they are less easy to change, commission may be charged. Many banks may only change US$300 minimum in cash, US$500 in TCs. Dollars cash are becoming more frequently used for tourist transactions and are also useful for those places where TCs cannot be changed and for when the banks go on strike: damaged dollar notes may be rejected. Parallel market and official rates are quoted in the papers and on TV news programmes.

● **Banks**

Banks open between 1000-1600 or 1630 Mon-Fri.

● **Credit cards**

Credit cards are widely used; Diners Club, Master Card, Visa and American Express are useful. Master Charge/Access is accepted by Banco Econômico, Banco Meridional and Banco Real. Overseas credit cards need authorization from São Paulo, this can take up to 2 hrs, allow plenty of time if buying air tickets. Mastercard and Diners are equivalent to Credicard, and Eurocheques can be cashed at Banco Alemão (major cities only). Banco Bradesco handles the international Visa automatic teller machine (ATM) network, Visa cash advances also at Banco do Brasil (in case of lost or stolen cards T 000-811-933-5589). A rapidly increasing number of Banco Itaú's ATMs give cash withdrawals on Mastercard/Cirrus. Both Bradesco and Itaú have machines at airports, shopping centres and major thoroughfares; Banco 24 Horas machines, at similar locations, operate with Amex, Diners, Boston and Citibank among others. Credit card transactions are charged at the tourist official rate. Cash advances on credit cards will only be paid in *reais* at the tourist rate, incurring a $1\frac{1}{2}$% commission. Banks in small remote places may still refuse to give a cash advance: if you have run out of cash and TCs, try asking for the manager ('gerente'). Automatic cash dispensers are now common in Brazil: it's worth remembering your PIN number since queues can be extremely long.

GETTING THERE

BY AIR

● **From Europe**

Brazil is connected with the principal cities of Europe by Air France, KLM, Lufthansa, Alitalia, Iberia, Aerolíneas Argentinas, Varig and TAP. Varig flies from London to Rio and São Paulo 5 times a week. British Airways flies 3 times a week London-São Paulo-Rio. Varig flies to Salvador and Fortaleza from Milan, Rome and Paris. Vasp flies to Brussels from Rio, São Paulo, Salvador and Recife. There are flights with Varig to Recife from Lisbon (also TAP), Madrid, Milan and Rome. Transbrasil flies from Vienna and Amsterdam to Rio and São Paulo.

● **From USA**

Brazil is connected to the USA direct by Varig, Transbrasil, American Airlines, United Airlines and Vasp (LA-Rio and São Paulo, Miami-São Paulo and Rio). The cheapest route is probably from Miami. There are also daily flights from the USA to Belo Horizonte with United and American.

● **From Latin America**

All South American capitals are connected by air services to Rio. Caracas, 3 weekly (Varig, Viasa; there are 3 flights a week from Caracas to Manaus); Bogotá, 4 weekly (Varig, Avianca); Lima, 3 weekly (Varig); La Paz, 5 weekly (Varig, via Santa Cruz and São Paulo); Quito/Guayaquil, twice a week with Varig and Lacsa joint operation; Asunción, daily with Varig (American flies Asunción-São Paulo daily; Lapsa flies Asunción-São Paulo 5 times a week); Santiago, several (Ladeco, LAN-Chile, Varig, Iberia; São Paulo is also served, LAN-Chile and European carriers in addition); Montevideo, about 15 weekly (Pluna, also Varig to São Paulo); Buenos Aires, several daily. Paramaribo, 4 a week by Surinam Airways to Belém via Cayenne. If buying a ticket to another country but with a stop over in Brazil, check whether two tickets are cheaper than one.

There are 3 flights a week from Mexico City to Rio with Varig and 2 flights a week from San José, Costa Rica to Rio (Varig, Lacsa).

Varig and Aerolíneas Argentinas operate the Mercosur Airpass, in conjunction with other carriers in Brazil, Argentina, Uruguay and Paraguay. Valid for a minimum of 10 days, the pass is for a maximum of 8 flight coupons, no more than 4/country. At least two countries must be included; rerouting is not permitted. The airpass must be bought outside the region by holders of an international return ticket. Price is worked out on a kilometre basis: the further you go and the more countries you visit, the cheaper it is: prices range from US$225 to US$870. Varig also has an extensive 'Stopover' programme which gives reduced rates on transfers and hotel rooms in many cities in Brazil and throughout South America (plus San José, Costa Rica).

● **From elsewhere**

Varig (twice a week) and SAA (once) fly between Rio and Johannesburg. Varig and Japan Airlines fly several times a week between Tokyo and Rio and São Paulo, some flights stopping in Los Angeles. Airline tickets are expensive in Brazil, buy internal tickets with *reais* (you can pay by credit card). External tickets must be paid for in dollars.

NB Regulations state that you cannot buy an air ticket in Brazil for use abroad unless you first have a ticket out of Brazil.

BY ROAD

To drive in Brazil you need either a translation of your home driving licence, or an international licence. There are agreements between Brazil and all South American countries (but check in the case of Bolivia) whereby a car can be taken into Brazil (or a Brazilian car out of Brazil) for a period of 90 days without any special documents; an extension of up to 90 days is granted by the customs authorities on presentation of the paper received at the border, this must be retained; this may be done at most customs posts and at the Serviço de Controle Aduaneiro, Ministerio da Fazenda, Av Pres A Carlos, Sala 1129, Rio de Janeiro.

This now applies to cars registered in other countries; the requirements are proof of ownership and/or registration in the home country and valid driving licence (international or from home country). It is better to cross the border into Brazil when it is officially open (from 1300 to 1800 Mon to Fri) because an official who knows all about the entry of cars is then present. The motorist should in any case insist on getting the correct paper 'in accordance with Decree No 53.313/63', or he/she might find it impossible to get the 90-day extension. You must specify which border station you intend to leave by, but application can be made to the Customs to change this. If you want to leave by ship the Touring Club in Rio (possibly also elsewhere, but this is less definite) will arrange it at a cost; you can also arrange the paper yourself by taking your car away by ship, but it takes about 2 days and costs about US$15 in port and police charges; the Touring Club provides information on how to go about it. (Klaus Elgner, of Hannover, reports this can be done with a letter in Portuguese saying you wish to leave by ship plus passport number, vehicle number, entry forms data plus an *ordem de embarque* supplied and stamped by the shipping agent. These should be presented to the Customs.) Crossing by a land border is, in any case, easier and probably cheaper.

BY SEA

For shipping lines that carry passengers to Brazil, see **Introduction and Hints**. **NB** There is an 8% tax on international shipping-line tickets bought in Brazil.

CUSTOMS

Clothing and personal articles are free of import duty. Such articles as cameras, movie cameras, portable radios, tape-recorders, typewriters and binoculars are also admitted free if there is not more than one of each. Tourists may also bring in, duty-free, 12 bottles of alcohol, 400 cigarettes, 25 cigars, 280 grams of perfume, up to 10 units of cosmetics, up to 3 each of any electronic item or watch, up to a total value of US$500. Duty free goods may only be purchased in foreign currency.

WHEN YOU ARRIVE

● Clothing

Fashions are provocative, and while women are advised to dress in the local style, this can have unnerving effects. It is normal to stare and comment on women's appearances, and if you happen to look different or to be travelling alone, you will undoubtedly attract attention. You are very unlikely to be groped or otherwise molested: this is disrespectful, and merits a suitable reaction. Be aware that Brazilian men can be extraordinarily persistent, and very easily encouraged; it is safest to err on the side of caution until you are accustomed.

In general, clothing requirements in Brazil are less formal than in the Hispanic countries. It is, however, advisable for men visiting restaurants to wear long trousers (women in shorts may also be refused entry), trousers and jackets or pullovers in São Paulo (also for cinemas). As a general rule, it is better not to wear shorts in official buildings, cinemas, inter-state buses and on flights.

● Conduct

Men should avoid arguments or insults (care is needed even when overtaking on the road); pride may be defended with a gun. Gay men, while still enjoying greater freedom than in many countries, should exercise reasonable discretion.

Colour   The people of Brazil represent a unique racial mix: it is not uncommon for the children of one family to be of several different colours. Individuals are often described by the colour of their skin (ranging through several shades of brown), and 'white' can refer to people who would not necessarily be thought white in Europe or North America. Generally speaking, the emphasis is on colour rather than racial origins.

Racial discrimination is illegal in Brazil. There is, however, a complex class system which is informed both by heritage and by economic status. This effectively discriminates against the poor, who are chiefly (but by no means exclusively) black due to the lack of inherited wealth among those whose ancestors were servants and slaves. Some Brazilians might assume that a black person is poor, therefore of low status. Black visitors to the country may encounter racial prejudice. We have also received a report from a black North American woman who was the subject of sexual advances by non-Brazilian, white tourists. Black women travelling with a white man may experience some problems, which should disappear with the realisation that your partnership is not a commercial arrangement. A surprising number of Brazilians are unaware that black Europeans exist, so you could become the focus of some curiosity.

Brazilian culture is rich in African influences. Those interested in the development of Afro-Brazilian music, dance, religion, arts and cuisine will find the whole country N of São Paulo fascinating, and especially the cities of Bahia and São Luis which retain the greatest African influences. Black Pride movements are particularly strong in Bahia. Further reading: *Samba* by Alma Guillermoprieto, paperback, Bloomsbury Press; *Towards the Abolition of Whiteness* by David Roediger, Verso, £11.95 (a sociological study of how 'colour' is determined by economic status, mostly in the USA and UK).

● **Hours of business**
Hours of business are 0900-1800 Mon to Fri for most businesses, which close for lunch some time between 1130 and 1400. Shops are open on Sat till 1230 or 1300. Government departments are open from 1100-1800 Mon to Fri. Banks 1000-1500, but closed on Sat.

● **Official time**
Brazilian standard time is 3 hrs behind GMT; of the major cities, only the Amazon time zone, Manaus, Cuiabá, Campo Grande and Corumbá are different, with time 5 hrs behind GMT. The State of Acre is 4 hrs behind GMT. Clocks move forward 1 hr in summer for approximately 5 months (usually between Oct and Feb or Mar) but times of change vary. This does not apply to Acre.

The days of the week are: segunda feira (Mon), terça feira (Tues), quarta feira (Wed), quinta feira (Thur), sexta feira (Fri), sábado (Sat), domingo (Sun).

● **Police**
There are 3 types of police: Polícia Federal, civilian dressed, who handle all federal law duties, including immigration. A subdivision is the Polícia Federal Rodoviária, uniformed, who are the traffic police. Polícia Militar is the uniformed, street police force, under the control of the state governor, handling all state laws. They are not the same as the Armed Forces' internal police. Polícia Civil, also state-controlled, handle local laws; usually in civilian dress, unless in the traffic division.

● **Safety**
Personal safety in Brazil has deteriorated of recent years, largely because of the economic recession, and crime is increasing. Some recommend avoiding all large cities; the situation is far less insecure in smaller towns and in the country. The police are reported to be charging for documents reporting crimes if these are required quickly.

Apart from the obvious precautions of not wearing jewellery (wear a cheap, plastic *digital* watch), do not camp or sleep out in isolated places and if you are hitchhiking, never accept a lift in a car with two people in it. Money belts are safer than bags for your valuables. Consider buying clothing locally to avoid looking like a gringo. If you are held up and robbed, it is worth asking for the fare back to where you are staying. It is not uncommon for thieves to oblige. Do carry some cash, to hand over if you are held up. Do not leave valuables in hotel rooms, except where a safe is provided. Hotel safe deposits are generally (but not always) secure. If you cannot get a receipt for valuables in a hotel safe, seal the contents in a plastic bag and sign across the seal. Always photocopy your passport, air ticket and other documents, make a record of TC and credit card numbers and keep them separately from the originals. Leave another set of records at home. Never trust anyone telling 'sobstories' or offering 'safe rooms', when looking for a hotel, always choose the room yourself. Take only your towel and lotion to the beach, tuck enough money for your cold drinks into your trunks/bikini bottom. A few belongings can safely be left at a bar. Ted Stroll of San Francisco advises, "remember that economic privation has many Brazilians close to the edge, and that they are probably as ashamed of exploiting you as you are angry at being exploited". The corollary is be generous to those who give you a good deal. Travellers are most vulnerable when carrying baggage, if possible take a taxi, but don't leave the driver in the car with your bags.

● **Shopping**
Gold, diamonds and gemstones throughout Brazil. Innovative designs in jewellery: buy 'real' at reputable dealers (best value in Minas Gerais); cheap, fun pieces from street traders. Interesting furnishings made with gemstones, marble; clay figurines from the NE; lace from Ceará; leatherwork; strange pottery from Amazônia; carvings in soapstone and in bone; tiles and other ceramic work, African-type pottery and basketwork from Bahia. Many large hotel gift shops stock a good selection of handicrafts at reasonable prices. Brazilian cigars are excellent for those who like the mild flavours popular in Germany, the Netherlands and Switzerland. Recommended purchases are musical instruments, eg guitars, other stringed, and percussion instruments.

Excellent textiles: good hammocks from the NE; other fabrics; design in clothing is impressive, though unfortunately not equalled by manufacturing quality. Buy your beachwear in Brazil: it is matchless. For those who know how to use them, medicinal herbs, barks and spices from street markets; coconut oil and local skin and haircare products (fantastic conditioners) are better and cheaper than in Europe, but known brands of toiletries are exorbitant. Other bad buys are film (including processing), cameras and any electrical goods (including batteries). Sunscreen, sold in all department stores and large supermarkets, is expensive.

As a rule, shopping is easier, quality more reliable and prices higher in the shopping centres (mostly excellent) and in the wealthier suburbs. Better prices at the small shops and street traders; most entertaining at markets and on the beach. Bargaining (with good humour) is expected in the latter.

● **Tipping**
Tipping is usual, but less costly than in most other countries, except for porters. Restaurants, 10% of bill if no service charge but small tip if there is; taxi drivers, none; cloakrm attendants, small tip; cinema usherettes, none; hairdressers, 10-15%; porters, fixed charges but tips as well; airport porters, about US$0.50/item.

● **Weights and measures**
The metric system is used by all.

● **Working in Brazil**
Work-permit restrictions are making it harder to find work as an English language teacher than it used to be, though many people do it unofficially and leave Brazil every 90 days in order to re-enter as tourists. One's best bet would be in a small language school. Or advertise in the Press.

ON DEPARTURE

● **Airport tax**
The equivalent of about US$20 is charged for international flights and, for internal flights, US$10 depending on the class of airport. It must be paid on checking in, in *reais* or US$. Tax is waived if you stay in Brazil less than 24 hrs.

WHERE TO STAY

● **Accommodation**
The best guide to hotels in Brazil is the *Guia Brasil Quatro Rodas*, with good maps of towns. Motels are specifically intended for very short-stay couples: there is no stigma attached and they usually offer good value (the rate for a full night is called the *pernoite*), though the decor can be a little unsettling. The type known as *hotel familiar*, to be found in the interior – large meals, communal washing, hammocks for children – is much cheaper, but only for the enterprising. *Pousadas* are the equivalent of bed-and-breakfast, often small and family run, although some are very sophisticated and correspondingly priced. Usually hotel prices include breakfast; there is no

reduction if you don't eat it. In the better hotels (our category B and upwards) the breakfast is well worth eating: rolls, ham, eggs, cheese, cakes, fruit. Normally the *apartamento* is a room with a bath; a *quarto* is a room without bath. The service stations (*postos*) and hostels (*dormitórios*) along the main roads provide excellent value in room and food, akin to truck-driver type accommodation in Europe, for those on a tight budget. The star rating system for hotels (5-star hotels are not price-controlled) is not the standard used in North America or Europe. For information about Youth Hostels contact Federação Brasil Albergues Juventude, R da Assambleia 10, room 1211, T 531-1129, Rio de Janeiro; its brochure provides a full list of good value accommodation. Low-budget travellers with student cards (photograph needed) can use the Casa dos Estudantes network. Leave rooms in good time so frigobar bills can be checked; we have received reports of overcharging in otherwise good hotels.

Business visitors are strongly rec to book accommodation in advance, and this can be easily done for Rio or São Paulo hotels with representation abroad. Varig has a good hotel reservation service, with discounts of up to 50% for its passengers.

NB Taxi drivers will try to take you to the expensive hotels, who pay them commission for bringing in custom. Beware!

● **Camping**
Members of the Camping Clube do Brasil or those with an international campers' card pay only half the rate of a non-member, which is US$10-15 pp. The Club has 43 sites in 13 states and 80,000 members. For enquiries, Camping Clube do Brasil, Divisão de Campings, R Senador Dantas 75° andar (T 262-7172), Rio de Janeiro. It may be difficult to get into some Camping Clube campsites during the high season (Jan-Feb). Private campsites charge about US$5 pp. For those on a very low budget and in isolated areas where there is no camp site, service stations can be used as camping sites (Shell stations rec); they have shower facilities, watchmen and food; some have dormitories; truck drivers are a mine of information. There are also various municipal sites; both types are mentioned in the text. Campsites often tend to be some distance from public transport routes and are better suited to those with their own transport. Never camp at the side of a road; wild camping is generally not possible.

Good camping equipment may be purchased in Brazil and there are several rental companies. Camping gas cartridges are easy to buy in sizeable towns in the S eg in HM shops. *Guia de Camping* is produced by Artpress, R

Araçatuba 487, São Paulo 05058; it lists most sites and is available in bookshops in most cities. Quatro Rodas' *Guia Brasil* lists main campsites. Most sizeable towns have laundromats with self service machines. *Lavanderias* do the washing for you but are very expensive.

FOOD AND DRINK

FOOD

The most common dish is *bife (ou frango) com arroz e feijão*, steak (or chicken) with rice and the excellent Brazilian black beans. The most famous dish with beans is the *feijoada completa*: several meat ingredients (jerked beef, smoked sausage, smoked tongue, salt pork, along with spices, herbs and vegetables) are cooked with the beans. Manioc flour is sprinkled over it, and it is eaten with kale (*couve*) and slices of orange, and accompanied by glasses of *aguardente* (unmatured rum), usually known as *cachaça* (booze), though *pinga* (drop) is a politer term. Almost all restaurants serve the *feijoada completa* for Sat lunch (that means up to about 1630). Bahia has some excellent fish dishes (see note on page 512); some restaurants in most of the big cities specialize in them. *Vatapá* is a good dish in the N; it contains shrimp or fish sauced with palm oil, or coconut milk. *Empadinhas de camarão* are worth trying; they are shrimp patties, with olives and heart of palm. A mixed grill, including excellent steak, served with roasted manioc flour (*farofa*; raw manioc flour is known as *farinha*) goes under the name of *churrasco* (it came originally from the cattlemen of Rio Grande do Sul), normally served in specialized restaurants known as *churrascarias* or *rodizios*; good places for large appetites. Minas Gerais has two splendid special dishes involving pork, black beans, *farofa* and kale; they are *tutu á mineira* and *feijão tropeiro*. A white hard cheese (*queijo prata*) or a slightly softer one (*queijo Minas*) is often served for dessert with bananas, or guava or quince paste. Meals are extremely large by European standards; if your appetites are small, you can order, say, one portion and one empty plate, and divide the portion. However, if you are in a position to do so tactfully, you may choose to offer the rest to a person with no food (many Brazilians do – observe the correct etiquette) alternatively you could as for an *embalagem* (doggy bag) or get a take away called a *marmita* or *quentinha*, most restaurants have this service but it is not always on the menu. Many restaurants now serve *comida por kilo* where you serve yourself and pay for the weight of food on your plate. Unless you specify to the contrary many restaurants will lay a *coberto opcional*, olives, carrots, etc, costing US$0.50-

0.75. **NB** The main meal is usually taken in the middle of the day; cheap restaurants tend not to be open in the evening. **Warning** Avoid mussels, marsh crabs and other shellfish caught nr large cities: they are likely to have lived in a highly polluted environment. In a restaurant, always ask the price of a dish before ordering.

For vegetarians, there is a growing network of restaurants in the main cities. In smaller places where food may be monotonous try vegetarian for greater variety. We list several. Most also serve fish. Alternatives in smaller towns are the Arab and Chinese restaurants.

There is fruit all the year round, ranging from banana and orange to mango, pawpaw, custard-apple (*fruta do conde*) and guava. One should try the *manga de Uba*, a non-fibrous small mango. Also good are *mora* (a raspberry that looks like a strawberry), *jaboticaba*, a small black damson-like fruit, and *jaca* (jackfruit), a large yellow/green fruit.

The exotic flavours of Brazilian ice-creams should be experienced. Try *açaí*, *bacuri*, *biribá*, *buruti*, *cupuaçu* (not eveyone's favourite), *marimari*, *mucajá*, *murici*, *pajurá*, *pariri*, *patuá*, *piquiá*, *pupunha*, *sorva*, *tucumá*, *uxi* and others mentioned below under 'drinks'.

If travelling on a tight budget, remember to ask in restaurants for the *prato feito* or *sortido*, a money-saving, excellent value table-d'hôte meal. The *prato comercial* is similar but rather better and a bit more expensive. *Lanchonetes* are cheap eating places where you generally pay before eating. *Salgados* (savoury pastries), *coxinha* (a pyramid of manioc filled with meat or fish and deep fried), *esfilha* (spicey hamburger inside an onion-bread envelope), *empadão* (a filling – eg chicken – in sauce in a pastry case), *empadas* and *empadinhas* (smaller fritters of the same type), are the usual fare. In Minas Gerais, *pão de queijo* is a hot roll made with cheese. A *bauru* is a toasted sandwich which, in Porto Alegre, is filled with steak, while further N has tomato, ham and cheese filling. *Cocada* is a coconut and sugar biscuit.

DRINK

Imported drinks are expensive, but there are some fair local wines. Chilean and Portuguese wines are sometimes available at little more than the cost of local wines. The beers are good and there are plenty of local soft drinks. *Guaraná* is a very popular carbonated fruit drink. There is an excellent range of non-alcoholic fruit juices, known as *sucos*: *caju* (cashew), *pitanga*, *goiaba* (guava), *genipapo*, *graviola* (= *chirimoya*), *maracujá* (passion-fruit), *sapoti* and *tamarindo* are rec. *Vitaminas* are thick fruit or vegetable drinks with milk. *Caldo de cana* is sugar-cane juice, sometimes mixed with ice. Remember that *água mineral*, available in many varieties at bars and restaurants is a cheap, safe thirst-quencher (cheaper still in supermarkets). Apart from the ubiquitous coffee, good tea is grown and sold. **NB** If you don't want sugar in your coffee or *suco*, you must ask when you order it. *Água de côco* or *côco verde* (coconut water from fresh green coconut) cannot be missed in the Northest.

Among the better wines are Château d'Argent, Château Duvalier, Almadén, Dreher, Preciosa and Bernard Taillan. The red Marjolet from Cabernet grapes, and the Moselle-type white Zahringer have been well spoken of. It has often been noticed that a new *adega* starts off well, but the quality gradually deteriorates with time; many vintners have switched to American Concorde grapes, producing a rougher wine. Greville Brut champagne-type is inexpensive and very drinkable. A white-wine *Sangria*, containing tropical fruits such as pineapple and papaya, is worth looking out for. The Brahma, Cerpa and Antártica beers are really excellent, of the lager type, and are cheaper by the bottle than on draught. Buying bottled drinks in supermarkets, you may be asked for empties in return.

Some genuine Scotch whisky brands are bottled in Brazil; they are very popular because of the high price of Scotch imported in bottle; Teacher's is the most highly regarded brand. Locally made gin, vermouth and campari are very good. The local firewater, *aguardente* (known as *cachaça* or *pinga*), made from sugarcane, is cheap and wholesome, but visitors should seek local advice on the best brands; São Francisco, Praianinha, Maria Fulô, '51' and Pitu are rec makes. Mixed with fruit juices of various sorts, sugar and crushed ice, *cachaça* becomes the principal element in a *batida*, a delicious and powerful drink; the commonest is a lime batida or *batida de limão*; a variant of this is the *caipirinha*, a *cachaça* with several slices of lime in it, a caipiroska is made with vodka. *Cachaça* with Coca-Cola is a *cuba*, while rum with Coca-Cola is a *cuba libre*.

GETTING AROUND

AIR TRANSPORT

Internal air services are highly developed and very expensive. A monthly magazine, *Guia Aeronáutico*, gives all the timetables and fares. All national airlines – Varig, Vasp and Transbrasil – offer excellent service on their internal flights. Between 2200 and 0600, internal flights cost 30% less than daytime flights. (Ask for the *vôo coruja*.) On some flights couples can fly for the price of one-and-a-half. A 30% discount is of-

fered on flights booked 7 days or more in advance; there are also seasonal and other discounts. It is well worth enquiring in detail. Double check all bookings (reconfirm frequently) and information given by ground staff as economic cutbacks have led to pressure on ground service (but not to flight service).

Varig, Vasp and Transbrasil offer good value 21-day airpasses. The Varig airpass covers 3 zones: US$490 for all cities; US$400 Central South; and US$290 North East. Routes must be specified before arrival. Up to 5 journeys are permitted on the all-cities pass, up to 4 on the other two. Additional journeys cost US$100 and on the North East pass there is a US$50 supplement for a return from Rio or São Paulo. The pass is available to travellers arriving in Brazil with Varig or the national airline of the country of origin which shares the route with Varig (eg it is available to TAP passengers who start their journey in Lisbon, but not London). The Vasp/Transbrasil airpass costs US$440. The airpass must be purchased outside Brazil by holders of an international flight ticket to Brazil, no journey may be repeated, it may not be used on the Rio-São Paulo shuttle. The airpass is limited to 5 coupons, to which a maximum of 4 may be added (purchased outside Brazil) at US$100 each. No sector may be repeated in the same direction; the itinerary may be changed in Brazil. Make sure you have two copies of the airpass invoice when you arrive in Brazil; otherwise you will have to select all your flights when you book the first one. Remember that domestic airport tax has to be paid at each departure. Hotels in the Tropical and Othon chains, and others, offer discounts of 10% to airpass travellers; check with Varig, who have a hotel reservation service. Promotions on certain destinations offer a free flight, hotel room, etc; enquire when buying the airpass. We have been told that it is advisable for users of the airpasses to book all their intended flights in advance or on arrival in Brazil, especially around summer holiday and Carnival time. Converting the voucher can take some hours, do not plan an onward flight immediately, check at terminals that the air pass is still registered, faulty cancellations have been reported. Cost and restrictions on the airpass are subject to change. An alternative is to buy an internal flight ticket which includes several stops.

The small feeder airlines have been formed into scheduled domestic airlines, and now operate Brazilian-built *Bandeirante* 16-seater prop-jets into virtually every city and town with any semblance of an airstrip. **NB** Internal flights often have many stops and are therefore quite slow. Foreigners are not allowed to travel on Brazilian air force flights. Most airports have left-luggage lockers (US$1 for 24 hrs). Seats are often unallocated on internal flights: board in good time.

LAND TRANSPORT

● Train

Trains are appreciably slower than buses. There are passenger services in the state of São Paulo and between São Paulo and Rio. More and more services are being withdrawn; travellers are normally advised to go by air or road. Timekeeping is good on the whole.

● Motoring

Most main roads between principal cities are now paved. Some are narrow and therefore dangerous. Many are in poor condition.

Any foreigner with a passport can purchase a Brazilian car and travel outside Brazil if it is fully paid for or if permission is obtained from the financing body in Brazil. Foreigners do not need the CPF tax document (needed by Brazilians – you only have to say you are a tourist) to purchase a car, and the official purchase receipt is accepted as proof of ownership. Sunday papers carry car advertisements and there are second-hand car markets on Sun mornings in most cities – but don't buy an alcohol-driven car if you propose to drive outside Brazil. It is essential to have an external intake filter fitted, or dust can rapidly destroy an engine. VW Combi vans are cheapest in Brazil where they are made, they are equivalent to the pre-1979 model in Europe. Be sure to travel with a car manual and good quality tools, a VW dealer will advise. There are VW garages throughout the continent, but parts (German or Latin American) are not always interchangeable. In the main, though, there should be no problems with large components (eg gears). If a lot of time is to be spent on dirt roads, the Ford Chevrolet pickup is more robust. A letter in Spanish from your consul explaining your aims and that you will return the vehicle to Brazil can make life much easier at borders and checkpoints. Brazilian cars may not meet safety regulations in N America and Europe, but they can be easily resold in Brazil.

● Bus

There is no lack of transport between the principal cities of Brazil, mostly by road. Ask for window seats (*janela*), or odd numbers if you want the view. Brazilian bus services have a top speed limit of 80 kph (buses are supposed to have governors fitted). They are extremely comfortable (many have reclining seats), stopping fairly frequently (every 2-4 hrs) for snacks; the cleanliness of these *postos* is generally good, though may be less so in the poorer regions. Standards of comfort on buses and in *postos* vary from line to line, which can be important

on long journeys. Buses only stop at official stops. Take something to drink on buses in the N. The bus terminals are usually outside the city centres and offer fair facilities in the way of snack bars, lavatories, left-luggage stores ('guarda volume'), local bus services and information centres. *Leito* buses ply at night between the main centres, offering reclining seats with foot and leg rests, toilets, and sometimes in-board refreshments, at double the normal fare. For journeys over 100 km, most buses have chemical toilets. Air conditioning can make *leito* buses cold at night, so take a blanket or sweater (and plenty of toilet paper); on some services blankets are supplied. Some companies have hostess service. Rodoviárias for interstate services and other long-distance routes are usually called *rodoviárias*. Buy bus tickets at rodoviárias (most now take credit cards), not from travel agents who add on surcharges. Reliable bus information is hard to come by, other than from companies themselves. It is not easy to sell back unused bus tickets. Some bus companies have introduced a system enabling passengers to purchase return tickets at point of departure, rather than individual tickets for each leg. Buses usually arrive and depart in very good time; you cannot assume departure will be delayed. In the SE and S a *Horário de Ônibus* is available at *rodoviárias* (not available for N or NE). Many town buses have turnstiles which can be inconvenient if you are carrying a large pack. Urban buses normally serve local airports.

● Car hire

It is essential to have a credit card in order to hire in Brazil; tour agencies accept TCs, dollars cash may not be accepted, but *reais* cash may qualify for a discount. Check insurance carefully, as few policies give full cover, unless purchased outside Brazil. Avis is found only in the major cities and has only a time-and-mileage tariff. National, ie Localiza, is represented in many places, often through licencees; connected with Inter-Rent/Europcar in Europe, will accept credit cards from InterRent/Europcar and offers unlimited mileage if booked in advance from Europe on a fixed US$ rate. Compare prices of renting from abroad and in Brazil. If you intend to hire a car for a long time, buying and reselling a vehicle within Brazil may be a reasonable alternative (see above).

NB It is virtually impossible to buy premium grades of petrol/gasoline anywhere. With alcohol fuel you need about 50% more alcohol than regular gasoline. Larger cars have a small extra tank for 'gasolina' to get the engine started; remember to keep this topped up. Fuel is only 85 octane (owing to high methanol content), so be prepared for bad consumption and poor performance and starting difficulties in non-Brazilian cars in winter. Diesel fuel is cheap and a diesel engine may provide fewer maintenance problems for the motoring tourist. Service stations are free to open when they like. Very few open during Carnival week.

● **Hitchhiking**

Information on hitchhiking (*carona* in Portuguese) suggests that it is difficult everywhere; drivers are reluctant to give lifts because passengers are their responsibility. Try at the highway-police check points on the main roads (but make sure your documents are in order) or at the service stations (*postos*).

● **Taxis**

Taxi meters measure distance/cost in 'taxi units' (UT), not *reais*. Taxi units are converted into *reais* with a price list. In many cities this list is taped to the side window of the taxi; in others the driver has the list. Be sure that the list is not a photocopy. The original either has colours inset on the black and white, or, if black and white only, is laminated. Whether or not you see the conversion sheet, you can work out the price by knowing the *real* value of each UT. This rate will either be posted near the meter in the front window, or written on the bottom of the conversion sheet. The rate varies from city to city, but is consistent within each city. At the outset, make sure the meter is cleared and shows tariff 1, except 2300-0600, Sun, and in Dec when 2 is permitted. Check that the meter is working, if not, fix price in advance. The radio taxi service costs about 50% more but cheating is less likely. Taxis have a 40% surcharge on Sun. If you are seriously cheated note the number of the taxi and insist on a signed bill, threatening to go to the police; it can work.

COMMUNICATIONS

● **Language**

The language is Portuguese. Efforts to speak it are greatly appreciated and for the low-budget traveller, Portuguese is essential. If you cannot lay your tongue to 'the language of the angels', apologize for not being able to speak Portuguese and try Spanish, but note that the differences in the spoken languages are very much greater than appears likely from the printed page and you may well not be understood: you will certainly have difficulty in understanding the answers.

One important point of spelling is that words ending in 'i' and 'u' are accented on the last syllable, though (unlike Spanish) no accent is used there. This is especially important in place names: Parati, Iguaçu. Note also that 'meia' (half) is frequently used for number 6. Audio-

forum, Microworld House, 2-6 Foscote Mews, London W9 2HH, T 0171-266 2202 does cassette courses on Brazilian Portuguese (US$195/£155 and US$245/£165), orders by mail or phone with credit card no. There are Brazilian tutors in most cities (in London, see *Time Out* for advertisements).

● **Postal services**

Postal charges are high: the overseas rate for letters, aerogrammes and postcards is the same. Air mail takes 4 to 6 days to or from Britain or the US; surface mail takes some 4 weeks. 'Caixa Postal' addresses should be used when possible. Postes restantes usually only hold letters for 30 days. You can buy charge collected stamps, Compraventa de Francamento (CF) for letters only, to be paid on delivery. The Post Office sells cardboard boxes for sending packages internally and abroad (they must be submitted open); pay by the kilo; you must fill in a list of contents; string, official sellotape is provided in all post offices. Franked and registered (insured) letters are normally secure, but check that the amount franked is what you have paid, or the item will not arrive. Aerogrammes are most reliable. It may be easier to avoid queues and obtain higher denomination stamps by buying at the philatelic desk at the main post office. Poste Restante for Amex customers efficiently dealt with by the Amex agents in most large towns. Courier services such as DHL, Federal Express and UPS (rec) are useful, but note that they may not necessarily operate under those names.

● **Telephone services**

There is a trunk-dialling system linking all parts: for the codes see DDD in the text, or look in the telephone directory. There are telephone boxes at airports, post offices, railway stations, hotels, most bars, restaurants and cafés, and in the main cities there are telephone kiosks *for local calls only* in the shape of large orange shells, for which *fichas* can be bought from bars, cafés and newsvendors; in Rio they are known as *orelhões* (big ears). Phone cards are available from telephone offices, newstands, post offices and some chemists. Public boxes for intercity calls are blue; there are boxes within main telephone offices for international calls, make sure you buy a card worth at least 100 international units. Collect calls within Brazil can be made from any telephone – dial 9, followed by the number, and announce your name and city. Local calls from a private phone are normally free. International phone calls are priced on normal and cheaper rates, depending on time of day. Check with the local phone company. Peak rate to Europe is US$4/minute, to USA US$3. There is a 40% tax added to the cost of all telephonic and telegraphic communications, which makes international service extremely dear. Local phone calls and telegrams, though, are quite cheap. **NB** Brazil is now linked to North America, Japan and most of Europe by trunk dialling (DDI). Codes are listed in the telephone directories. Embratel operates Home Country Direct, available from hotels, private phones or blue public phones to the following countries (prefix all numbers with 00080); Argentina 54, Australia 61, Bolivia 13, Canada 14, Chile 56, Denmark 45, France 33, Germany 49, Israel 97, Italy 39, Japan 81, Holland 31, Norway 47, Portugal 35, Spain 34, Sweden 46, UK 44 (BT Direct), USA 10 (AT&T), 12 (MCI), 16 (Sprint), Uruguay 59. For collect calls from phone boxes (in Portuguese: 'a cobrar'), dial 107 and ask for the *telefonista internacional*. No collect calls available to New Zealand, though to Australia is OK. To use the telephone office, tell the operator which city or country you wish to call, go to the booth whose number you are given; make your call and you will be billed on exit. Not all offices accept credit cards.

Cable facilities are available at all post offices, and the main ones have public telex booths. Post offices are recognizable by the ECT (Empresa de Correios e Telégrafos) signs outside. Make sure that hotels equipped by telex facilities can send outgoing telexes; some are unable to do so, or only at certain times of day.

Fax services operate in main post offices in major cities, or from private lines. In the latter case the international fax rates are as for phone calls; from the post office the rates are US$3-4/page within Brazil, US$10.50 to Europe and US$9 to the USA. To receive a fax costs US$1.40.

ENTERTAINMENT

● **Newspapers**
The main **Rio** papers are *Jornal do Brasil, O Globo,* and *Jornal do Commércio*. **São Paulo** Morning: *O Estado de São Paulo, Folha de São Paulo, Gazeta Mercantil* and *Diário de São Paulo*. Evening: *A Gazeta, Diário do Noite, Ultima Hora*.

● **Radio**
English-language radio broadcasts daily at 15290 kHz, 19m Short Wave (Rádio Bras, Caixa Postal 04/0340, DF-70 323 Brasília).

HOLIDAYS AND FESTIVALS

National holidays are 1 Jan (New Year); 3 days up to and including Ash Wed (Carnival); 21 April (Tiradentes); 1 May (Labour Day); Corpus Christi (June); 7 Sept (Independence Day); 12 Oct, Nossa Senhora Aparecida; 2 Nov (All Souls' Day); 15 Nov (Day of the Republic); and 25 Dec (Christmas). The local holidays in the main cities are given in the text. Four religious or traditional holidays (Good Friday must be one; other usual days: 1 Nov, All Saints Day; 24 Dec, Christmas Eve) must be fixed by the municipalities. Other holidays are usually celebrated on the Mon prior to the date.

FURTHER READING

British visitors are referred to 'Hints to Exporters: Brazil', obtainable from DTI Export Publications, PO Box 55, Stratford-upon-Avon, Warwickshire, CV37 9GE.

ACKNOWLEDGEMENTS

This chapter has been updated by Cherry Austin and Wendy dos Santos, to whom we are most grateful. We are also grateful to Steve Talbert and Piet Snell (Recife) for their surfing guide; Robert and Daisy Kunstaetter (Quito) researched and rewrote the Southern Amazonia and Pantanal sections; they would like to thank Marlene of Corumbarte; Sr Durvanil of Fazenda Natureza; Dona Joana of Pousada Pantaneira (all of Corumbá); Marilene Mazini, Casa do Turismo; Dra Maria Eugênia C Amaral, Biology Dept, Universidade Federal do Mato Grosso do Sul; Dr Masao Vetanabaro, Co-ordinator of Pantanal Studies, Universidade Federal do Mato Grosso do Sul (all of Campo Grande); Laercio Sá, of Faunatour, Cuiabá; Michelle Bancardi of the Cuiabá Tourist Office; Sâmia Cosson; Geraldo and Eva-Christina Marques (all of Rio Branco) Thanks are also due to Peter Bossew (Vienna, Austria) for very thorough research. Travellers who wrote to the *Handbook* are acknowledged at the end of the book.

Chile

HORIZONS

Chile is smaller than all other South American republics save Ecuador, Paraguay, Uruguay and the Guianas. Its territory is a ribbon of land lying between the Andes and the Pacific, 4,329 km long and, on average, no more than 180 km wide. Of this width the Andes and a coastal range of highland take up from a third to a half. There are wide variations of soil and vast differences of climate; these are reflected in the density of population and the occupations of its people.

THE LAND

In the extreme N Chile has a frontier with Peru running 10 km N of the railway from the port of Arica to the Bolivian capital of La Paz. Its eastern frontier – with Bolivia in the far N and with Argentina for the rest of its length – is along the crest of the Andes, gradually diminishing in height from Santiago southwards to the southern seas, where the Strait of Magellan lies, giving access to the Atlantic. Chile's western and southern coastline is 4,500 km long.

Down the whole length, between the Andes and the coastal range, there runs a valley depression, though it is less well defined in the N. North of Santiago transverse ranges join the two massifs and impede transport, but for 1,044 km S of the capital the great longitudinal valley stretches as far as Puerto Montt. South of Puerto Montt the sea has broken through the coastal range and drowned the valley, and there is a bewildering assortment of archipelagos and channels.

From N to S the country falls into five sharply contrasted zones:

A The first 1,250 km from the Peruvian frontier to Copiapó is a rainless hot desert of brown hills and plains devoid of vegetation, with a few oases. Here lie nitrate deposits and several copper mines.

B From Copiapó to Illapel (600 km) is semi-desert; there is a slight winter rainfall, but great tracts of land are without vegetation most of the year. Valley bottoms are here cultivated under irrigation.

C From Illapel to Concepción is Chile's heartland, where the vast majority of its people live. Here there is abundant rainfall in the winter, but the summers are perfectly dry. Great farms and vineyards

Chile

1. Santiago &
   The Heartland
2. Valparaíso &
   Viña del Mar
3. From Santiago
   to La Serena
4. North of La Serena
5. Antofagasta, Calama
   & San Pedro
6. Iquique, Arica &
   The Far North
7. South through
   The Central Valley
8. The Lake District
9. Chiloé
10. Archipelagic Chile
11. Chilean Patagonia

cover the country, which is exceptionally beautiful.

D The fourth zone, between Concepción and Puerto Montt, is a country of lakes and rivers, with heavy rainfall through much of the year. Cleared and cultivated land alternates with mountains and primeval forests.

E The fifth zone, from Puerto Montt to Cape Horn, stretches for 1,600 km. This is archipelagic Chile, a sparsely populated region of wild forests and mountains, glaciers, fjords, islands and channels. Rainfall is torrential, and the climate cold and stormy. There are no rail links S of Puerto Montt, but the Carretera Austral now provides almost unbroken road access for more than 1,000 km S of that city. Chilean Patagonia is in the extreme S of this zone.

A subdivision of the fifth zone is Atlantic Chile – that part which lies along the Magellan Strait to the E of the Andes, including the Chilean part of Tierra del Fuego island. There is a cluster of population here raising sheep and mining coal. Large offshore oilfields have now been discovered in the far S, and the area is developing rapidly.

National parks

Chile has an extensive system of protected natural areas, 7 million ha in all. The areas, managed by Conaf (the Corporación Nacional Forestal), are divided into 30 national parks, 36 forest reserves and 10 natural monuments. Of the 76 areas, 46 have public access, and details of the majority are given in the text.

HISTORY

A century before the Spanish conquest the Incas moved S into Chile from Peru, crossing the desert from oasis to oasis at the foot of the Andes. They reached the heartland and conquered it, but were unable to take the forest S of the Río Maule; there the fierce Mapuches (Araucanians) held them. In 1537 Diego de Almagro, at the head of a 100 Spaniards and some thousands of Indians, took the Inca road from Peru S to Salta and across the Andes. Many of the Indians perished, but the heartland was reached; bitterly disappointed at not finding gold they returned to Peru. The next *conquistador*, who took the desert road, was Pedro de Valdivia; he reached the heartland in 1541 and on 12 Feb founded Santiago. Reinforced by fresh colonists from Peru and Spain, Valdivia pushed S into Mapuche land and founded a number of forts. Valdivia was killed in 1553 and the Mapuches soon overran all the Spanish settlements apart from the town to which he had given his name. The Mapuches were fearsome opponents; they soon mastered the use of horses and were effective guerrilla fighters. In 1598 they began a general offensive which destroyed most of the Spanish settlements S of the Río Biobío. The Spanish were forced to create a special frontier army and to build a string of forts along the Biobío. For the rest of the colonial period the Spanish presence S of the river was limited to the coastal fortress of Valdivia and the Island of Chiloé.

In addition to constant wars against the Mapuches, the colonial period was marked by internal dissensions, particularly between the landowners and the priests who strongly objected to a system of Indian serfdom. There were also natural disasters in the form of earthquakes and tidal waves which wiped out cities again and again. From the end of the 16th century British and French pirates frequented the coasts. For most of the colonial period, Chile formed part of the Viceroyalty of Peru; it was controlled from Lima, and trade was allowed only with Peru. This led to uncontrolled smuggling and by 1715 there were 40 French vessels trading illegally along the coast. It was not till 1778 that trading was allowed between Chile and Spain.

In 1810 a group of Chilean patriots, including Bernardo O'Higgins – the illegitimate son of a Sligo-born Viceroy of Peru, Ambrosio O'Higgins, and a Chilean mother – revolted against Spain. This revolt led to 7 years of war against the occupying troops of Spain – Lord Cochrane was in charge of the insurrectionist navy – and in 1817 Gen José de San Martín crossed the Andes with an army

from Argentina and helped to gain a decisive victory. O'Higgins became the first head of state: under him the first constitution of 1818 was drafted. But there was one thing which was dangerous to touch in Chile: the interests of the dominant landed aristocracy, and O'Higgins's liberal policies offended them, leading to his downfall in 1823. A period of anarchy followed, but in 1830 conservative forces led by Diego Portales restored order and introduced the authoritarian constitution of 1833. Under this charter, for almost a century, the country was ruled by a small oligarchy of landowners.

After 1879 Chilean territory was enlarged in both N and S. During the 1870s disputes arose with Boliva and Peru over the northern deserts which were rich in nitrates. Although most of the nitrates lay in Bolivia and Peru, much of the mining was carried out by Anglo-Chilean companies. In the ensuing war (War of the Pacific, 1879-1883) Chile defeated Peru and Bolivia, mainly because her stronger navy gave her control over the sea and even allowed her to land troops in Peru and occupy Lima. Chile gained the Bolivian coastal region as well as the Peruvian provinces of Tarapacá and Arica and for the next 40 years drew great wealth from the nitrate fields.

In the S settlers began pushing across the Río Biobío in the 1860s, encouraged by government settlement schemes and helped by technological developments including repeating rifles, telegraph, railways and barbed wire. At the end of the War of the Pacific the large Chilean army was sent to subdue the Mapuches who were confined to ever-diminishing tribal lands. The territory was then settled by immigrants – particularly Germans – and by former peasants who had fought in the North.

The rule of the Right was challenged by the liberal regime of President Arturo Alessandri in 1920. Acute economic distress in 1924, linked to the replacement of Chilean nitrates with artificial fertilizers produced more cheaply in Europe, led to army intervention and some reforms were achieved. The inequalities in Chilean society grew ever sharper, despite the maintenance of political democracy, and gave rise to powerful socialist and communist parties. President Eduardo Frei's policy of 'revolution in freedom' (1964-70) was the first concerted attempt at overall radical reform, but it raised hopes it could not satisfy. In 1970 a marxist coalition assumed office under Dr Salvador Allende; the frantic pace of change under his regime polarized the country into Left- and Right-wing camps. Gradually increasing social and economic chaos formed the background for Allende's deposition by the army and his death on 11 September 1973. After the overthrow of President Allende, Chile was ruled by a military president, Gen Augusto Pinochet Ugarte, and a 4-man junta with absolute powers. In its early years particularly, the regime suppressed internal opposition by methods which were widely condemned. Despite economic prosperity and efforts to make the regime more popular, Pinochet's bid for a further 8 years as president after 1989 was rejected by the electorate in a plebiscite in 1988.

As a result, presidential and congressional elections were held in 1989. A Christian Democrat, Patricio Aylwin Azócar, the candidate of the Coalition of Parties for Democracy (CPD, or Concertación), was elected President and took office in March 1990 in a peaceful transfer of power. The CPD won 71 of the 120 seats in the Chamber of Deputies, but only 22 seats in the 47-seat Senate, its majority wiped out by nine seats held by Pinochet appointees, who could block constitutional reform. Gen Pinochet remained as Army Commander although other armed forces chiefs were replaced. The new Congress set about revising many of the military's laws on civil liberties and the economy. In 1991 the National Commission for Truth and Reconciliation published a report with details of those who were killed under the military regime, but opposition by the armed forces prevented mass human rights trials. In Dec 1993 presidential elections resulted in the election of the Christian Democrat Eduardo Frei, son of the earlier president,

but in congressional elections held at the same time the Concertación failed to achieve the required two-thirds majority in Congress to reform the constitution, replace heads of the armed forces and end the system of designated senators. In Aug 1995, Frei presented bills to make the necessary constitutional reforms to these non-elected powers. He also proposed that investigations continue into the disappearance of some 500 political prisoners in the 1970s. On both issues the military and their political allies appeared to have sufficient support to prevent government success, contrary to public opinion and despite some opposition members favouring reform.

CULTURE

PEOPLE

There is less racial diversity in Chile than in most Latin American countries. Over 95% of the population is *mestizo*. There has been much less immigration than in Argentina and Brazil. The German, French, Italian and Swiss immigrants came mostly after 1846 as small farmers in the forest zone S of the Biobío. Between 1880 and 1900 gold-seeking Serbs and Croats settled in the far S, and the British took up sheep farming and commerce in the same region. The influence throughout Chile of the immigrants is out of proportion to their numbers: their signature on the land is seen, for instance, in the German appearance of Valdivia, Puerto Montt, Puerto Varas, Frutillar and Osorno.

There is disagreement over the number of indigenous people in Chile. The Mapuche nation, 95% of whom live in the forest land around Temuco, between the Biobío and Toltén rivers, is put at 1 million by Survival International, but much less by other, including official, statistics. There are also 15,000 Aymara in the northern Chilean Andes and 2,000 Rapa Nui on Easter Island. A political party, the Party for Land and Identity, unites many Indian groupings, and legislation is proposed to restore indigenous people's rights.

The population is far from evenly distributed: Middle Chile (from Copiapó to Concepción), 18% of the country's area, contains 77% of the total population. The Metropolitan Region of Santiago contains, on its own, about 39% of the whole population.

The rate of population growth per annum is slightly under the average for Latin America. The birth rate is highest in the cities, particularly of the forest zone. The death rate is highest in the cities. Infant mortality is highest in the rural areas.

Since the 1960s heavy migration from the land has led to rapid urbanization. Housing in the cities has not kept pace with this increased population; many Chileans live in slum areas called *callampas* (mushrooms) on the outskirts of Santiago and around the factories.

MUSIC AND DANCE

At the very heart of Chilean music is the Cueca, a courting dance for couples, both of whom make great play with a handkerchief waved aloft in the right hand. The man's knees are slightly bent and his body arches back. It is lively and vigorous, seen to best advantage when performed by a Huaso wearing spurs. Guitar and harp are the accompanying instruments, while handclapping and shouts of encouragement add to the atmosphere. The dance has a common origin with the Argentine Zamba and Peruvian Marinera via the early 19th century Zamacueca, in turn descended from the Spanish Fandango. For singing only is the Tonada, with its variants the Glosa, Parabienes, Romance, Villancico (Christmas carol) and Esquinazo (serenade) and the Canto a lo Poeta, which can be in the form of a Contrapunto or Controversia, a musical duel. Among the most celebrated groups are Los Huasos Quincheros, Silvia Infante with Los Condores and the Conjunto Millaray. Famous folk singers in this genre are the Parra Family from Chillán, Hector Pávez and Margot Loyola. In the N of the country the music is Amerindian and closely related to that of Bolivia. Groups called 'Bailes' dance the Huayño, Taquirari,

Cachimbo or Rueda at carnival and other festivities and precolumbian rites like the Cauzulor and Talatur. Instruments are largely wind and percussion, including *zampoñas* (pan pipes), *lichiguayos*, *pututos* (conch shells) and *clarines*. There are some notable religious festivals that attract large crowds of pilgrims and include numerous groups of costumed dancers. The most outstanding of these festivals are those of the Virgen de La Tirana near Iquique, San Pedro de Atacama, the Virgen de la Candelaria of Copiapó and the Virgen de Andacollo.

In the S the Mapuche nation, the once greatly feared and admired 'Araucanos', who kept the Spaniards and Republicans at bay for 400 years, have their own songs, dance-songs and magic and collective dances, accompanied by wind instruments like the great long *trutruca* horn, the shorter *pifilka* and the *kultrun* drum. Further S still, the island of Chiloé, which remained in the hands of pro-Spanish loyalists after the rest of the country had become independent, has its own unique musical expression. Wakes and other religious social occasions include collective singing, while the recreational dances, all of Spanish origin, such as the Vals, Pavo, Pericona and Nave have a heavier and less syncopated beat than in central Chile. Accompanying instruments here are the *rabel* (fiddle), guitar and accordion.

THE ECONOMY

Structure of production Chile is endowed with a diversified environment, allowing the production of all temperate and Mediterranean products. Traditional crops, such as cereals, pulse, potatoes and industrial crops (sugarbeet, sunflowerseed and rapeseed) account for about a third of the value added of agriculture, and vegetables for a quarter. Fruit growing has grown rapidly and fresh fruit now accounts for over US$1bn in exports a year, making fruit the second most important earner after copper. Another area of expansion is forestry; timber and wood products make up the third place in exports. More than 80% of the 1.6 million ha of cultivated forest is planted with insignis radiata pine, a species which in Chile grows faster than in other countries. However, native forest has been declining rapidly, partly because of demand by wood chippers. Chile is the most important fishing nation in Latin America and the largest producer of fishmeal in the world. Industrial consumption absorbs about 93% of the fish catch; fresh fish and fish products contribute about 10% of merchandise exports. Salmon farming is being expanded.

The dominant sector of the economy is mining. Chile has been the world's largest producer of copper since 1982 and also produces molybdenum, iron ore, manganese, lead, gold, silver, zinc, sulphur and nitrates. Chile has a quarter of the world's known molybdenum ore reserves and is believed to have around 40% of the world's lithium reserves. Mineral ores, most of which is copper, account for half of total export revenue. Fluctuations in world prices for minerals can have a great impact on the balance of payments. Foreign investment is the driving force in mining, which has averaged almost US$900mn a year in the 1990s in exploration and mine development. By 2000 output of copper will be 4 million tonnes a year, over 40% of world production, of which 1.4 million tonnes will be produced by the state company, Codelco, from its five mines, Chuquicamata, El Tte, Salvador, Andina and Radomiro Tomic (to come on stream in 1998). Privately owned, high-tech mines or joint ventures are responsible for most of the expected growth, the largest being Escondida, which will produce 800,000 tonnes in 1997.

Chile is fortunate in possessing reserves of oil, natural gas and coal, and abundant hydroelectricity potential. Almost all the country's hydrocarbon reserves are in the extreme S, on Tierra del Fuego, in the Strait of Magellan and the province of Magallanes. Natural gas is likely to be piped across the Andes from Argentina from 1997. Two pipelines are planned and up to six new gas-fired power plants may be built in 1998-2002, reducing electricity costs and pollution around

Chile : Fact File

Geographic

Land area	756,626 sq km
forested	22.0%
pastures	18.2%
cultivated	5.7%

Demographic

Population (1995)	14,210,000
annual growth rate (1989-94)	1.6%
urban	85.5%
rural	14.5%
density	18.8 per sq km
Religious affiliation	
Roman Catholic	76.7%
Birth rate per 1,000 (1992)	21.6
	(world av 25.0)

Education and Health

Life expectancy at birth,	
male	70.4 years
female	76.0 years
Infant mortality rate	
per 1,000 live births (1992)	14.3
Physicians (1992)	1 per 889 persons
Hospital beds	1 per 312 persons
Calorie intake as %	
of FAO requirement	106%
Population age 25 and over	
with no formal schooling	5.7%
Literate males (over 15)	81.3%
Literate females (over 15)	80.9%

Economic

GNP (1993 market prices)	
	US$42,454mn
GNP per capita	US$3,070
Public external debt (1993)	
	US$16,031mn
Tourism receipts (1993)	US$824mn
Inflation	
(annual av 1989-94)	17.5%
Radio	1 per 3.2 persons
Television	1 per 7.0 persons
Telephone	1 per 9.1 persons

Employment

Population economically active (1993)	
	5,219,300
Unemployment rate	4.6%
% of labour force in	
agriculture	15.8
mining	1.8
manufacturing	16.0
construction	7.7
Military forces	93,000

Source *Encyclopaedia Britannica*

Santiago if coal-fired plants are closed.

Manufacturing activity is mostly food processing, metalworking, textiles, footwear and fish processing. The sector has been vulnerable to changes in economic policy: nationalization during the Allende administration in the early 1970s; recession brought about by anti-inflation policies in the mid-1970s; increased competition resulting from trade liberalization in the early 1980s and greater exports together with import substitution in the mid-1980s. The contribution of manufacturing to total gdp fell from 25% in 1970 to 20% in 1994, but its share of exports rose and the sector grew by over 6% a year in the 1990s.

Recent trends The policies used to bring inflation down from over 500% at the end of 1973 to less than 10% by end-1981 resulted in fiscal balance but an overvalued currency. Freeing the exchange rate in 1982 caused renewed inflation; this was restricted by tight monetary control and a lower public sector borrowing requirement which caused a severe recession and contraction in gdp. IMF help was sought following a sharp fall in international commercial lending in 1982 and a decline in Chile's terms of trade. In the 1980s Chile negotiated several debt refinancing packages and reduced its foreign debt through schemes which converted debt into equity in Chilean companies. Renewed growth in debt in the 1990s was offset by rising gdp and exports which meant that the debt:gdp ratio fell from 94% in 1985 to an estimated 40% in 1995, while the debt service ratio declined from 48% to about 15% in the same period.

The Government follows anti-infla-tionary policies, accompanied by structural adjustment and reform. Privatization has been widespread, although certain key companies such as Codelco remain in state hands. Privatizing the pension system and corporate savings have doubled domestic savings to 27% of gdp. Pension funds now manage assets of US$25bn, about 40% of gdp. Rising investor confidence has brought economic growth every year since the mid-1980s and the Chile model has been held up as an example for other debtor countries to adapt to their own needs. Unemployment has fallen and progress is being made in reducing poverty with increased public spending on health and education. Infant mortality dropped from 33 per thousand in 1980 to 14.3 per thousand in 1992; the literacy rate rose from 90.8% to 95.3% in the same period and the percentage of malnourished children fell from 8.8% in 1982 to 5.3% in 1993.

GOVERNMENT

The pre-1973 constitution was replaced, after a plebiscite, on 11 March 1981. This new constitution provided for an 8-year non-renewable term for the President of the Republic (although the first elected president was to serve only 4 years), a bicameral Congress and an independent judiciary and central bank. In Feb 1994, the Congress cut the presidential term of office from 8 years to 6. Congress is composed of a 120-seat Chamber of Deputies and a 47-seat Senate, eight of whose members are nominated, rather than elected. In 1974 the country was divided into 13 regions, replacing the old system of 25 provinces.

Santiago and the Heartland

The capital and its surroundings, from north of the Río Aconcagua to the Río Maipo; within easy reach are several vineyards and Andean ski resorts.

From a third to half of the width of the area is taken up by the Andes, which are formidably high in the northern sector; at the head of the Río Aconcagua the peak of Aconcagua (in Argentina), the highest in the Americas, rises to 6,964m. The region suffers from earthquakes. There is a mantle of snow on the mountains: at Aconcagua it begins at 4,300m. The lower slopes are covered with dense forests. Between the forest and the snowline there are alpine pastures; during the summer cattle are driven up to these pastures to graze.

The coastal range, over 2,130m high, takes up another third of the width. It is lower here than in the northern desert, but the shoreline is unbroken; it is only at Valparaíso and San Antonio that good harbourage is to be found.

Between the coastal range and the Andes lies the Central Valley; rivers cross it at right angles and cut their way to the sea through narrow canyons in the coastal highland.

Nearly 70% of the people of Chile live in the comparatively small heartland. The rural population density in the area is exceptional for Latin America: it is as high as 48 to the square km to the S of Santiago.

Climate

There is rain during the winter in the heartland, but the summers are dry. The rain increases to the S. On the coast at Viña del Mar it is 483 mm a year, but is somewhat less inland. Temperatures, on the other hand, are higher inland than on the coast. There is frost now and then, but very little snow falls.

Temperatures can reach 33°C in Jan, but fall to 13°C (3°C at night) in July. Days are usually hot, the nights cool.

SANTIAGO

Santiago, founded by Pedro de Valdivia in 1541, is the fifth largest city in South America and one of the most beautifully set of any, standing in a wide plain. The city is crossed from E to W by the Río Mapocho, which passes through an artificial stone channel, 40m wide, spanned by several bridges. Public gardens are filled with flowers and kept in good order. The magnificent chain of the Andes, with its snow-capped heights, is in full view for much of the year, rain and pollution permitting; there are peaks of 6,000m about 100 km away. More than half the country's manufacturing is done here; it is essentially a modern capital, full of skyscrapers, bustle, noise, traffic and smog (tables for which are published in the daily papers, as are the registration numbers of those cars which are not allowed into the city each day).

BASICS *Pop* almost 5 million; *Alt* 600m; *Phone code* 02.

PLACES OF INTEREST

The centre of the old city lies between the Mapocho and the Av O'Higgins usually known as the **Alameda**. From the **Plaza Baquedano** (**Plaza Italia**), in the E of the city's central area, the Mapocho flows to the NW and the Av O'Higgins runs to the SW. From Plaza Baquedano the C Merced runs due W to the **Plaza de Armas**, the heart of the city; it lies 5 blocks S of the Mapocho. On the eastern and southern sides of Plaza de Armas there are arcades with shops; on the northern side is the Post Office and the Municipalidad; and on the western side the Cathedral and the archbishop's palace. The **Cathedral**, much rebuilt, contains a recumbent statue in wood of San Francisco Javier, and the chandelier which lit the first meetings of Congress after independence; it also houses an interesting museum of religious art and historical pieces. In the **Palacio de la Real Audiencia** on the Plaza de Armas is the Museo Histórico Nacional (see **Museums**, below). A block W of the Cathedral is the **former Congress** building now occupied by the Ministry of Foreign Affairs (the Congress, which held no sittings after 1973, has been moved to Valparaíso to a purpose-built building). Nearby are the law courts. At C Merced 864, close to the Plaza de Armas, is the **Casa Colorada**, built in 1769, the home of the Governor in colonial days and then of Mateo de Toro, first President of Chile. It is now the Museum of the History of Santiago. From the Plaza de Armas Paseo Ahumada, a pedestrianized street lined with cafés runs S to the Alameda 4 blocks away, crossing Huérfanos, which is also pedestrianized.

The Av O'Higgins runs through the heart of the city for over 3 km. It is 100m wide, and ornamented with gardens and statuary: the most notable are the equestrian statues of Generals O'Higgins and San Martín; the statue of the Chilean historian Benjamín Vicuña Mackenna who, as mayor of Santiago, beautified Cerro Santa Lucía (see **Parks and Gardens** below); and the great monument in honour of the battle of Concepción in 1879.

From the Plaza Baquedano, where there is a statue of Gen Baquedano and the Tomb of the Unknown Soldier, the Alameda skirts, on the right, Cerro Santa Lucía, and on the left, the Catholic University. Beyond the hill the Alameda goes past the neo-classical **Biblioteca Nacional** on the right, which also contains the national archives. Beyond, on the left, between C San Francisco and C Londres, is the oldest church in Santiago: the red-walled church and monastery of **San Francisco**. Inside is the small statue of the Virgin which Valdivia carried on his saddlebow when he rode from Peru to Chile. Near the church cloisters is the Museo de Arte Colonial. South of San Francisco is the Barrio París-Londres, built in 1923-1929, now restored and pedestrianized. Two blocks N of the Alameda on C Agustinas is the **Teatro Municipal**. A little further W along the Alameda, is the **Universidad de Chile**; the **Club de la Unión** is almost opposite. Nearby, on C Nueva York is the **Bolsa de Comercio**.

One block further W is the Plaza de la Libertad. To the N of the Plaza, hemmed in by the skyscrapers of the Centro Cívico, is the **Palacio de la Moneda** (1805), the Presidential Palace containing historic relics, paintings and sculpture, and the elaborate 'Salón Rojo' used for official receptions (guided visits only with written permission from the Dirección Administrativa – 3 weeks notice required). Although the Moneda was damaged by air attacks during the military coup of 11 September 1973 it has been fully restored. In front of the Palace is the statue of former President Arturo Alessandri Palma. (Ceremonial changing of the guard every other day, 1000, never on Sun; Sun ceremony is performed Mon.)

The Alameda continues westwards to the **Planetarium** (Av O'Higgins 3349, T 776-2624, US$2.50) and, opposite it on the southern side, the railway station (Estación Central or Alameda). On Av Matucana, running N from here, is the very popular **Parque Quinta Normal**. About 7 blocks W of the Estación Central is the southern bus terminal.

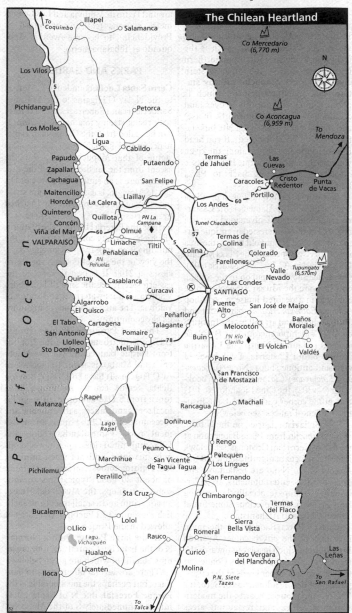

The Chilean Heartland

Four blocks N of the Plaza de Armas is the interesting **Mercado Central**, at Puente 21 de Mayo. The building faces the Parque Valenzuela, on which is the Cal y Canto metro station, the northern terminus of Line 2, and, at its western end, the former **Mapocho railway station**, now a cultural centre, which is planned to extend eventually over land occupied by the prison (currently in use) and the former Terminal del Nte bus station 4 blocks W (now closed). If you head E from Mapocho station, along the river, you pass through the Parque Forestal (see below), before coming back to Plaza Baquedano.

Between the Parque Forestal, Plaza Baquedano and the Alameda is the **Lastarria** neighbourhood (Universidad Católica metro). For those interested in antique furniture, objets d'art and old books, the area is worth a visit, especially the **Plaza Mulato Gil de Castro** (C José V Lastarria 305). Occasional shows are put on in the square, on which are the Museo Arqueológico de Santiago in a restored house, a bookshop (*Librería Latinoamericana*), handicraft and antique shops, and art gallery, the Instituto de Arte Contemporáneo and the *Pergola de la Plaza* restaurant. Nearby, on Lastarria, are the **Jardín Lastarria**, a cul-de-sac of craft and antique shops (No 293), *Gutenberg, Lafourcade y Cía*, an antiquarian bookseller (No 307), the Ciné Biógrafo (No 131) and, at the corner with Merced, the Instituto Chileno-Francés (see below).

The **Bellavista** district, on the N bank of the Mapocho from Plaza Baquedano at the foot of Cerro San Cristóbal (see below), is the main focus of nightlife in the old city. Around C Pío Nono are restaurants and cafés, theatres, entertainments, art galleries and craft shops (especially those selling lapis lazuli, a semi-precious stone found only in Chile and Afghanistan).

East of Plaza Baquedano, the main E-W axis of the city becomes **Avenida Providencia** which heads out towards the residential areas, such as Las Condes, at the eastern and upper levels of the city. It passes the new headquarters of Sernatur (the national tourist board), the modern shopping, office and restaurant areas around Pedro de Valdivia and Los Leones metro stations (collectively known as Providencia), to become Avenida Apoquindo at Tobalaba metro.

PARKS AND GARDENS

Cerro Santa Lucía, bounded by C Merced to the N, Av O'Higgins to the S, Calles Santa Lucía and Subercaseaux is a cone of rock rising steeply to a height of 70m. It can be scaled from the Caupolicán esplanade, on which, high on a rock, stands a statue of that Mapuche leader, but the ascent from the northern side of the hill, where there is an equestrian statue of Diego de Almagro, is easier. There are striking views of the city from the top (reached by a series of stairs), where there is a fortress, the Batería Hidalgo (the platform of which is its only colonial survival – the building is closed). Even on smoggy days, the view of the sunset is good; the Cerro closes at 2100. It is best to descend the eastern side, to see the small Plaza Pedro Valdivia with its waterfalls and statue of Valdivia. The area is famous, at night, for its gay community.

The great **Parque O'Higgins** (Parque O'Higgins metro station on Line 2, or bus from Parque Baquedano via Avs Mackenna and Matta), is about 10 blocks S of Av O'Higgins. It has a small lake, playing fields, tennis courts, swimming pool (open from 5 Dec), an open-air stage for local songs and dances, a discothèque, the racecourse of the Club Hípico, an amusement park, Fantasilandia (admission US$7, unlimited rides, open at weekends only in winter, and not when raining), kite-fighting contests on Sun, and a group of about 20 good 'typical' restaurants, some craft shops, the Museo del Huaso, an aquarium and a small insect and shellfish museum at El Pueblito. Cars are not allowed in the Parque.

In the large **Parque Quinta Normal**, N of the Estación Central, are four museums, details of which are given below.

There are several other parks in Santiago, but perhaps the most notable is the **Parque Forestal**, due N of Santa Lucía hill and immediately S of the Mapocho.

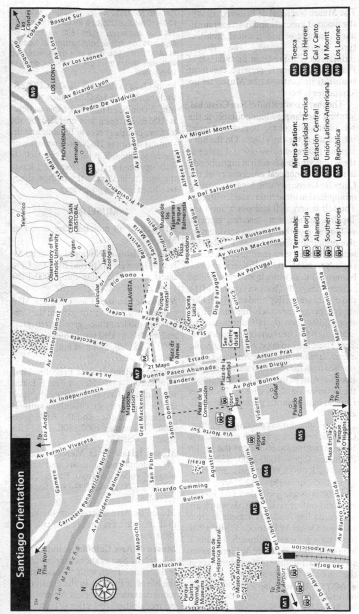

Santiago Orientation

To The North

To Los Andes

To Las Condes

Bosque Sur

Apoquindo

Av Tobalaba

Av Lota

LOS LEONES

Av Los Leones

M9

Av Ricardo Lyon

Av Pedro De Valdivia

PROVIDENCIA

Sta María

Sernatur

Av Eliodoro Yáñez

Av Miguel Montt

M8

Av Providencia

Alférez Real

Av Francisco

Av Del Salvador

Rancagua

Av Andrés Bello

Museo de
Tajamares /
Parque
Balmaceda

Plaza
Baquedano

Av Bustamante

Av Vicuña Mackenna

Av Portugal

Av Santa María

BELLAVISTA

Bellavista

Pío Nono

Loreto

Funicular

Virgen

Jardín
Zoológico

CERRO SAN
CRISTÓBAL

Observatory of the
Catholic University

Teleférico

Av Perú

Av Recoleta

Av Santos Dumont

Av La Paz

Av Independencia

Former
Mapocho
station

Gral Mackenna

Santo Domingo

Puente Paseo Ahumada

Bandera

21 Mayo

Plaza de
Armas

Estado

M

M7

Parque
Forestal

Sta Lucía De La Barra

Cerro Santa
Lucía

Diag Faraguay

Curicó

Tarpacá

Arturo Prat

San Diego

Av Pdte Bulnes

Plaza de la
Constitución

M6

Airport
Bus

Plaza de la
Libertad

See
Centre
detail

Vidurre

Conaf

Palacio
Cousiño

To
The South

M5

Via Norte Sur

Airport
Bus

M4

Agustinas

Brasil

Ricardo Cumming

Bulnes

M3

Av Diez de Julio

Av Manuel Antonio Marta

San Pablo

Santo Domingo

Av Fermín Vivaceta

Gamero

Carretera Panamericana Norte

Av Presidente Balmaceda

Matucana

Museo de
Historia Natural

Parque
Quinta
Normal &
Museums

M2

Av Del Libertador General O'Higgins

Av Exposición

Parque
O'Higgins

Av Blanco Encalada

Plaza Ercilla

M1

To
Valparaíso
& Airport

San Borja

Av 5 De Abril

Río Mapocho

N

Bus Terminals:

BT1 San Borja
BT2 Alameda
BT3 Southern
BT4 Los Héroes

Metro Station:

M1 Universidad Técnica
M2 Estación Central
M3 Unión Latino-Americana
M4 República

M5 Toesca
M6 Los Héroes
M7 Cal y Canto
M8 M Montt
M9 Los Leones

The Museo Nacional de Bellas Artes is in the wooded grounds and is an extraordinary example of neo-classical architecture (details below). The Parque Balmaceda (Parque Gran Bretaña), E of Plaza Baquedano, is perhaps the most beautiful in Santiago (the Museo de los Tajamares is here).

The sharp, conical hill of **San Cristóbal**, forming the Parque Metropolitano, to the NE of the city, is the largest and most interesting of the city's parks. On the hill's summit (300m) stands a colossal statue of the Virgin, which is floodlit at night; beside it is the astronomical observatory of the Catholic University which can be visited on application to the observatory's director. The hill is very well laid out around the Tupahue station, with terraces, gardens, and paths; in one building is a good, expensive restaurant (*Camino Real*, T 232-1758) with a splendid view from the terrace, especially at night, and an Enoteca, or exhibition of Chilean wines from a very limited range of vineyards. (You can taste one of the three 'wines of the day', and buy if you like, though prices are much higher than in shops.) The Casa de la Cultura has art exhibitions and free concerts at midday on Sun. There are two good swimming pools: one at Tupahue; the other, Antilen, can be reached from the road that starts below the Enoteca. Also in the Tupahue vicinity are the Botanical Gardens, with a collection of Chilean native plants, guided tours available.

A funicular railway goes up from Plaza Caupolicán at the northern end of C Pío Nono, stopping on its way at the Jardín Zoológico (open 1000-1300, 1500-1800 Tues-Fri, 1000-1800 Sat, Sun and holidays), US$2 in week, US$2.25 weekends. The zoo is being extended and has an excellent collection of animals which are well-cared for. A *teleférico* ascends from Estación Oasis, Av Pedro de Valdivia Nte (only taxis go there, although it is not a long walk from Pedro de Valdivia metro station), via Tupahue to the summit, near the funicular's upper station.

• **ACCESS By funicular**: every few minutes from 1000-1900 Mon-Fri, 1000-2000 Sat and Sun (closed for lunch 1330-1430). Fares: from Plaza to zoo US$2.40 (easily walked); from zoo to San Cristobal US$3.20. **By teleférico**: 1030-1900 at weekends, 1500-1830 weekdays except Tues (in summer only), so to get to Tupahue at other times you must take the funicular up and walk down from the summit (or drive, or take a taxi).

From Oasis to the top is US$2.80, US$2.85 to Tupahue and US$2.80 return to Tupahue. A combined funicular/*teleférico* ticket is US$6. An open bus operated by the *teleférico* company runs to Tupahue and the summit from the Pío Nono terminal with the same schedule as the *teleférico* itself. To walk up, head up C Pío Nono for 1 km to the sign 'A la Virgen'; the path is shady, tree-lined and has good views.

MUSEUMS

NB Almost all museums are closed on Mon.

Museo Histórico Nacional, Plaza de Armas 951, covers the period from the Conquest until 1925; Tues-Sun, 1000-1230, 1400-1700 (US$0.75).

Museo de Santiago, Casa Colorada, Merced 860, history of Santiago from the Conquest to modern times, excellent displays and models, guided tours; Tues-Sat, 1000-1800 (US$1.50), Sun and holidays, 1000-1300.

Museo Chileno de Arte Precolombino, Bandera 361, in the former Real Aduana, recommended, representative exhibition of objects from the precolombian cultures of Central America and the Andean region; Tues-Sun 1000-1800, US$1.25, Booklet, US$0.35.

Museo Iglesia de la Merced, MacIver 341, colonial religious art and archaeological collection from Easter Island; Tues-Fri 1000-1300, 1500-1800, Sat 1000-1300, US$1.

Museo de Arte Sagrado, in the Cathedral, Mon and Fri only, 0930-1230, 1530-1830, free.

Museo de Arte Colonial, Londres 4, beside Iglesia San Francisco, religious art, includes one room with 54 paintings of the life of St Francis; in the cloisters is a room containing Gabriela Mistral's Nobel medal; also a collection of locks; Tues-

Sat 1000-1800, Sun 1000-1400, US$1.

The Palacio de la Alhambra, Compañía 1340 corner of Amunátegui, is a national monument sponsored by the Society of Arts; it stages exhibitions of paintings as well as having a permanent display; Mon-Fri 1100-1300, 1700-1900, T 80875.

Biblioteca Nacional, Moneda 650, temporary exhibitions of books, book illustrations, documents, posters, etc.

Palacio Cousiño, C Dieciocho 438, 5 blocks S of the Alameda, a large elaborate mansion amongst crumbling buildings and shanties; it contains some good oriental rugs and 19th-century European furniture. It is run by the Corporación Cultural as a museum; Tues-Sun 0930-1330, US$3, but donations welcome. Visitors must be accompanied by a guide and wear cloth bootees to protect the floors.

In the Parque Quinta Normal are: **Museo Nacional de Historia Natural**, which has exhibitions on zoology, botany, mineralogy, anthropology, ethnography and archaeology; Tues-Fri 1000-1230, 1400-1730, Sat-Sun 1100-1300, 1500-1700, US$0.80. The **Museo Ferroviario** containing 13 steam engines built between 1884 and 1953 (Tues-Fri, 1000-1230, 1400-1700, Sat, Sun and holidays, 1100-1315, 1500-1715, US$1, photography permit, US$2.50). **Museo Ciencia y Tecnología**, US$1, same hours as **Ferroviario**. Nearby on Av Portales is the **Museo Artequín**, in the Chilean pavilion built for the 1889 Paris International Exhibition, containing prints of famous paintings and activities and explanations of the techniques of the great masters, rec, daily 1000-1800, US$1.25.

Museo Aeronáutico, Camino a Melipilla 5100, Cerrillos Airport, Tues-Sun 1000-1700, free, in a new building, well displayed, worth a visit.

Museo Arqueológico de Santiago, in Plaza Mulato Gil de Castro, Lastarria 307, temporary exhibitions of Chilean archaeology, anthropology and precolombian art; Mon-Fri 1030-1400, 1530-1900, Sat, 1030-1400, free.

In the Parque Forestal is the **Museo Na-**cional de Bellas Artes**, which has a large display of Chilean and foreign painting and sculpture, and contemporary art exhibitions are held several times a year (Tues-Sat 1000-1800, Sun and holidays 1100-1800, US$0.70). In the W wing of the building is the **Museo de Arte Popular Americano**, a collection of N and S American folk art (this wing is awaiting renovation, so only a small part of the exhibition is on display). Similarly, the **Museo de Arte Contemporáneo** is on limited view as it is normally housed in the W wing.

Museo Tajamares del Mapocho, Parque Balmaceda, Av Providencia 222, an exhibition of the 17th and 18th century walls built to protect the city from flooding by the river, and of the subsequent canalization; Tues-Sat 1000-1800, Sun 1000-1330.

Museo Benjamín Vicuña Mackenna, Av V Mackenna 94, recording the life and works of the 19th century Chilean historian and biographer; occasional exhibitions.

In Parque O'Higgins, at Pueblito: **Museo del Huaso**, a small, interesting collection of criollo clothing and tools; Tues-Fri 1000-1300, 1430-1715, Sat, Sun and holidays 1000-1800, free; **Municipal Aquarium** at Local 9, Tues-Fri 1000-2000 (till 2100 Sat, Sun, holidays – small charge); **Museo de Insectos y Caracoles**, Local 12, a collection of indigenous items, same hours as the aquarium but open till 2200 at weekends and holidays.

Museo de la Escuela Militar, Los Militares 4500, Las Condes, with displays on O'Higgins, the Conquest, the Pacific War and a room devoted to the medals of Gen Pinochet (not on general display so ask), Mon-Fri 0930-1230, 1500-1800, Sat 0930-1430, Sun 1430-1800, free (passport essential).

Museo Ralli, Sotomayor 4110, Vitacura, collection of works by modern European and Latin American artists, including Dali, Chagall, Bacon and Miró; Tues-Sun 1100-1700, free.

Museo de Artes Decorativos, Casas Lo Matta, Av Pdte Kennedy 9350, Vitacura, a beautiful museum containing Don Hernán Garcés Silva's bequest to the nation: antique silverplate from South America and Europe, 16th-18th century Spanish colonial and European furniture, 15th century Books of Hours, housed in an 18th century country mansion. Guided tours available; by bus, take Intercomunal No 4 from Mapocho station, or take a taxi; in either case ask to be let out at 'Casas lo Matta'.

The house of Pablo Neruda, the poet, **La Chascona**, is at F Márquez de la Plata 0192, Bellavista, T 777-8741, now headquarters of the Fundación Pablo Neruda. Closed Sun and Mon. Hourly guided visits only, US$2 entry; can book an English guide (see page 709).

LOCAL FESTIVALS

During Nov there is a free art fair in the Parque Forestal on the banks of the Río Mapocho, lasting a fortnight. In Oct or Nov there are a sumptuous flower show and an annual agricultural and industrial show (known as Fisa) in Parque Cerrillos. Religious festivals and ceremonies continue throughout Holy Week, when a priest ritually washes the feet of 12 men. The image of the Virgen del Carmen (patron of the Armed Forces) is carried through the streets by cadets on 16 July.

LOCAL INFORMATION

● Warning
Like all large cities, Santiago has problems of theft. Pickpockets and bagsnatchers, who are often well-dressed, operate especially on the Metro and around the Plaza de Armas. The Cerro Santa Lucía area is reported to be dangerous even in daytime.

● Accommodation
Check if breakfast and 18% tax is inc in the price quoted (if foreigners pay in US$ cash or with US$ TCs, the 18% IVA/VAT should not be charged; if you pay by credit card, there is usually a 10% surcharge).

Hotel prices

L1	over US$200	L2	US$151-200
L3	US$101-150	A1	US$81-100
A2	US$61-80	A3	US$46-60
B	US$31-45	C	US$21-30
D	US$12-20	E	US$7-11
F	US$4-6	G	up to US$3

Expensive hotels in the Providencia area: L1 *San Cristóbal Sheraton*, Santa María 1742, T 233-5000, F 223-6656, best in town, good restaurant, good buffet lunch, and all facilities, also **Sheraton Towers**, slightly cheaper; L1 *Park Plaza*, Ricardo Lyon 207, T 233-6363, F 233-6668, good.

In Las Condes: L1 *Hyatt Regency Santiago*, Av Kennedy N 4601, T 218-1234, F 218-2279, superb, beautifully decorated, highly rec.

A1 *Aloha*, Francisco Noguera 146, T 233-2230/7, F 233-2494, helpful, good restaurant; **A1** *Santa María*, Santa María 2050, T 232-6614, F 231-6287, excellent, friendly, small, good breakfast, other meals good value, highly rec; **A1** *Orly*, Pedro de Valdivia 27, metro Pedro de Valdivia, T 232-8225, but has smaller, cheaper rooms with less comfort, small, comfortable, has apartments for rent on Juana de Arco, good, US$70 a day (reductions may be possible); **A1** *Montebianco*, Isidora Goyenechea 2911, T 233-0427, F 233-0420, small, smart motel; **A1** *Parinacota*, Av Apoquindo 5142, Las Condes, T 246-6109, F 220-5386, 4-star, small, all services, no pool; **A1** *Torremayor*, Ricardo Lyon 322, T 234-2000, F 234-3779, clean, modern, good service, good location; **A2** *Presidente*, T 235-8015, F 235-9148, Eliodoro Yáñez 867, almost at Providencia, good value and good location; **A2** *Posada del Salvador*, Eliodoro Yáñez 893, T 235-9450, F 251-8697, metro Salvador, with bath.

Expensive hotels in the central area: L1 *Carrera*, Teatinos 180, T 698-2011, F 672-1083, enormous rooms, pool, rooftop restaurant (good buffet lunch); L1 *El Conquistador*, Miguel Cruchaga 920, T/F 696-5599, and L1 *Galerías*, San Antonio 65, T 638-4011, F 639-5240, excellent, welcoming; L1 *San Francisco Kempinski*, O'Higgins 816, T 639-3832, F 639-7826, Lufthansa affiliated, 5-star, good; L2 *Fundador*, Paseo Serrano 34, T/F 632-2566, helpful, good value; L2 *Holiday Inn Crowne Plaza*, O'Higgins 136, T 638-1042, F 633-6015, all facilities, also good, spacious, a/c (book through travel agent for better rates); L3 *Hostal del Parque*, Merced 294, opp Parque Forestal, T 639-2694, F 639-2754, comfortable, quiet, friendly, rec.

A1 *Tupahue*, San Antonio 477, T 638-3810, F 639-5240, comfortable; **A2** *Ducado*, Agustinas 1990, T 696-9384/672-6739, F 695-1271, with breakfast, clean, quiet at back, rec, secure parking; **A2** *Gran Palace*, Huérfanos 1178, T 671-2551, F 695-1095, overpriced, clean, good restaurant; **A2** *Panamericano*, Teatinos 320 y Huérfanos, T 672-3060, F 696-4992, comfortable, serves popular business lunch between 1230 and 1530; **A3** *City*, Compañía 1063, T 695-4526, F 695-6775, old-fashioned, clean, rec; **A3** *Conde Ansúrez*, Av República 25, T 699-6368, F 671-8376, metro República, convenient for central station and bus terminals, clean, helpful, safe, luggage stored; **A3** *Don Tito*, Huérfanos 578, T 639-1987, good service, excellent breakfast, English spoken; **A3** *Libertador*, O'Higgins 853, T 639-4212, F 633-7128, helpful, rec, stores luggage, good restaurant, bar, roof-top pool; **A3** *Majestic*, Santo Domingo 1526, T 695-8366, F 697-4051, with breakfast, pool, English spoken, rec; **A3** *Monte Carlo*, Subercaseaux 209, T 633-9905, F 633-5577, at foot of Santa Lucía, modern, restaurant, with heating, stores luggage; **A3** *Santa Lucía*, San Antonio 327 y Huérfanos, 4th floor, T 639-8201, garage 2 blocks away, clean, comfortable, good, small, quiet restaurant.

Mid-price hotels in the centre: **B** *Imperio*, O'Higgins 2879, T 689-7774, F 689-2916, nr central station, with bath, good restaurant, parking, clean; **B** *Principado*, Arturo Burhle 015, just off Vicuña Mackenna 1 block S of Plaza Baquedano, T 635-3879, F 222-6065, convenient location, very nice; **B** *Lira*, Lira 314, T 222-2492, F 634-3637, excellent; **B** *Hotel Turismo Japón*, Almte Barroso 160, T 698-4500, convenient location, intermittent hot water, helpful, friendly, clean, good breakfast, manager speaks English, best rooms at top, rec; **B** *Res Alicia Adasme*, Moneda 2055, T 696-0787, hot water, friendly, with breakfast; **B** *Santa Victoria*, Vicuña MacKenna 435, T 634-5753, quiet, small, safe, family run, rec; **B** *Vegas*, Londres 49, T 632-2514, F 632-5084, clean, large comfortable rooms, friendly, good breakfast; **B** *Hostal Vía Real*, Marín 066, T 635-4676, F 635-4678, charming, friendly, helpful, small, with bath, TV, laundry, rec; **C** *Res Alemana*, República 220 (no sign), T 671-2388, Metro República, hot water, clean, pleasant patio, central, heating on request, good cheap meals available, rec; **C-D** *Res Londres*, Londres 54, T/F 638-2215, nr San Francisco Church, former mansion, large old-fashioned rooms and furniture, few singles, no heating, English spoken, very popular, rec repeatedly (often full by 0900); **C-D** *París*, C París 813, T 639-4037, with bath, no singles, quiet, clean, good meeting place, good value, luggage store, also short-stay.

In Providencia: **C** *Hostal Parada*, Grau Flores 168, T 460-6640, spacious, clean.

Cheaper central hotels: **D** *Res Mery*, Pasaje República 36, off 0-100 block of República, T 696-8883, big green building down an alley, hot showers, quiet, rec; **D** *Hostal Aula Magna*, Vergara 541, T 698-0729, laundry facilities, nr Metro Toesca; **C** *España*, Morandé 510, T696-6066, with bath, hot water, clean, run down; **D** *Res del Norte*, Catedral 2207, T 696-9251, inc breakfast, friendly, safe, clean, large rooms,

convenient, credit cards accepted; **D** pp *San Patricio*, Catedral 2235, T 695-4800, with bath, **E** pp without, with breakfast, clean, safe, friendly, good value; **D** *Maury*, Tarapacá 1112, T 672-5889, F 697-0786, clean, friendly, safe, meals, English and French spoken; **D** *Santo Domingo*, Santo Domingo 735, with bath, **E** without, cleanish, basic, gloomy; **E** *Indiana*, Rosas 1339, T 714-251, convenient for buses to centre, very basic; **E** pp *Nuevo*, Morandé y San Pablo, T 671-5698, simple but OK, central, erratic hot water, safe, basic, poor beds, use of kitchen (no utensils), cable TV, popular, good meeting place; **E** pp *Olicar*, San Pablo 1265, quiet, clean, rec.

Convenient accommodation for bus terminals and Estación Central: **C** *Elisa*, Manuel Rodríguez 140, T 695-6464, with bath, clean, quiet; **C** *Res Midi*, Unión Americana 134, huge rooms with ancient furniture, basic, clean, hot water, laundry facilities, rec; **E** *Res Sur*, Ruiz Tagle 55, meals available; **E** *Alojamiento Diario*, Sanfuentes 2258 (no sign), T 699-2938, shared rooms, clean, safe, kitchen facilities, Metro República. On N side of Alameda opp bus terminals: **F** pp Federico Scotto 130, T 779-9364, use of phone and fax, good meals, cooking facilities, hot water, clean, often full; **E** pp Federico Scotto 079, T 7766484, with breakfast, helpful, luggage stored; **E** pp Sazie 2107, Metro Republica, T 672-2269, basic; **E** pp Huérfanos 2842, T 681-4537, kitchen, laundry, dormitory accommodation.

North of the Plaza de Armas near the Mapocho Station: **D** *Res Buen Hogar*, San Martín 70, T 671-0737, central, old, good clean rooms; **D** *Res Miraflores*, Riquelme 555, T 696-3961, clean, friendly, safe, meals available, rec; **D** *Res Amunátegui*, Amunátegui 652, T 652, clean, friendly; **E** *Souvenir*, Amunátegui 862, old, rambling place with 'adventurous plumbing' and chatty parrots around entrance. Many on Gen MacKenna inc **E** *San Felipe*, No 1248, T 713816, secure, cheap laundry service, kitchen, some single rooms are poor, second floor quieter, luggage stored, good beds; **E** *Ovallino*, No 1477 y San Martín, clean, hot water, secure; **E** pp *Casa Andina*, Recoleta 895, T 737-2831, clean, cheap, across the river from Cal y Canto Metro. **NB** Morandé, Gen Mackenna, San Martín and San Pablo are in the red light district.

As the above list shows there is little good accommodation under US$20 a night. Travellers can find good accommodation in comfortable family guesthouses through *Amigos de Todo el Mundo*, Av Pdte Bulnes, Paseo, 285, dept 201, Casilla 52861 Correo Central, T 672-6525, F 698-1474, Sr Arturo Navarrete, prices from

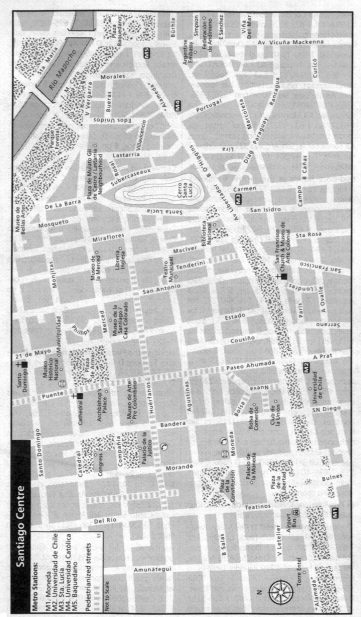

Santiago Centre

Metro Stations:
M1: Moneda
M2: Universidad de Chile
M3: Sta. Lucia
M4: Universidad Católica
M5: Baquedano

Pedestrianized streets

Not to Scale

US$16 with breakfast, other meals extra, monthly rates available, also transport to/from airport, rec; **E** pp *Alberto and Paola Peirario*, Chapultepec 5657, T 218-2101, F 204-4652, offer family accommodation, minimum 5 days, Spanish classes; also **E** pp Sra Marta, same address depto 401, T 779-7592, similar; **E** pp *Sra Lucía*, Catedral 1029, p 10, dept 1001, T 696-3832, central, friendly, safe, cooking facilities, basic; **E** pp *Sra Fidela*, San Isidro 261, Apt H, T 222-1246, shared bathroom, breakfast, rec; **D** *Casa Paxi*, Llico 968, T 522-9947, F 521-6328, 1 block from Metro Departamental, washing machine, gardens, quiet; **D** *Sra Marta*, Amengual 035, Alameda Alt 4.400, T 779-7592, lado Nte (metro Ecuador), good, hospitable, kitchen facilities, motorcycle parking; **E** *Sra Eliana Zuvic*, Almte Latorre 617, T 696-8700, Metro Toesca, hot water, nice atmosphere, highly rec; **D** pp *Alicia Bravo*, Artemio Gutiérrez 1328, T 556-6620, with breakfast,helpful, friendly, clean, not very central, rec.

For longer stay accommodation, read the classified ads in *El Mercurio*, flats, homes and family *pensiones* are listed by district, or in *El Rastro* (weekly), or try the notice board at the tourist office. In furnished apartments; if you want a phone you may have to provide an *aval*, or guarantor, to prove you will pay the bill, or else a huge deposit will be asked for. Estate agents handle apartments, but often charge ⅓ of the first month's rent as commission, while a month's rent in advance and 1 month's deposit are required. Rec apartments are *Edificio San Rafael*, Miraflores 264, T 633-0289, F 222-5629 US$29 a day single, US$46 a day double, minimum 3 days, US$600 a month, very central. Staying with a family is an economical and interesting option for a few months. Providencia and Las Condes are residential districts, but the latter is some way from the centre; the area W of Plaza Baquedano, E of Cerro Santa Lucía and S of Parque Forestal is good and central; or you could try Bellavista, but not C Pío Nono where the nightlife goes on until 0300.

Youth hostels: information available from Av Providencia 2594, oficina 420, metro Tobalaba, T 233 3226 (worth getting list of YH addresses around country as these change year by year). Supplies student cards (2 photos required and proof of student status, though tourist card accepted), US$11. Hostels in the capital inc **E** pp Cienfuegos 151, T 671-8532 (5 mins from metro Los Héroes), clean, satellite TV, no cooking facilities, breakfast and snacks, laundry facilities, parking, highly rec; **E** pp *Res Gloria*, Almte Latorre 447, T 698-8315, Metro Toesca, clean, popular, meals, difficult to use kitchen).

Camping: on the Farellones road nr the river; or S of Santiago nr Puente Alto (take Av J Pedro Alessandri S to Las Vizcachas and La Obra where there is a small park on left side of road). At Km 25 S of city on Panamericana, Esso garage offers only a vacant lot nr highway. Excellent facilities about 70 km from Santiago at Laguna de Aculeo, called *Club Camping Maki*: inc electricity, cold water, swimming pool, boat mooring, restaurant, but only available to members of certain organizations. An alternative site is *El Castaño* camping (with casino), 1 km away, on edge of lake; very friendly, café sells fruit, eggs, milk, bread and kerosene; good fishing; no showers, water from handpump.

● **Places to eat**
In addition to those at the main hotels and those in Parque O'Higgins there are, in the centre of the city: *Nuria*, MacIver 208, wide selection, US$20 plus; *Da Carla*, MacIver 577, Italian food, good, expensive; and *San Marco*, 2 doors away, better still; *Casa Suiza*, Huérfanos 648, good Swiss food; *Jacaranda*, Huérfanos 614, elegant, good service, good pasta and seafood. *Les Assassins*, Merced 297, very good, highly rec; *La Omelette*, Agustinas nr Amex, clean and good, closes 2100. *Gran Parrillada la Brasileña*, San Diego, huge portions, rec.

Seafood: *El 27 de Nueva York*, Nueva York 27, central, pricey, good; *Savory Tres*, Ahumada 327, good but limited choice and closed evenings. Some of the best seafood restaurants are to be found in the Mercado Central (by Cal y Canto metro; lunches only), or at the Vega Central market on the opp bank of the Mapocho.

For mainly local food in the centre. *Chez Henry*, on Plaza de Armas, expensive restaurant and delicatessen at Alameda 847, which is highly rec; also in Plaza de Armas, *Faison d'Or*, good *pastel de choclo*, pleasant place to have a drink and watch the world go by; *Torres*, O'Higgins 1570, traditional bar/restaurant, good atmosphere, live music at weekends; *Fuente de Soda Orion*, O'Higgins y Manuel Rodríguez, cheap, good pizzas; *Silvestre*, Huérfanos 956, open 0800-2400, good buffet-style; *Mermoz*, Huérfanos 1048, good for lunches; *Bar Nacional No 1*, Huérfanos 1151 and *Bar Nacional No 2*, Bandera 317, good restaurants, popular, local specialities; *Guima*, Huérfanos y Teatinos, good, reasonable prices, good value *almuerzo*; *Café Dante*, Merced 801 y San Antonio, for *pastel de choclo*, lunchtime only; *Bar Central*, San Pablo 1063, typical food, rec; *Fra Diavolo*, París 836 (nr *Res Londres*), lunches only,local and Italian, excellent food and service, popular; *Verdijo*, Morandé 526, noisy, cheap and popular; *Bar-restaurant Inés de Suárez*, Morandé 558, cheap; *El Lugar de Don Quijote*, café, and *Parrilladas de Don Quijote*, restaurant, good, Morandé y Catedral; two doors away is *Con-

greso, popular at lunchtime. *Círculo de Periodistas*, Amunátegui 31, p 2 unwelcoming entrance, good value lunches, rec; *Los Adobes de Argomedo*, Argomedo 411 y Lira, hacienda-style, good Chilean food and floor show inc cueca dancing, salsa and folk, Mon-Sat, only place in winter which has this type of entertainment on a Mon. Several cheap *fuentes de soda* for cheap lunches along Av Santa Rosa between the Alameda and C París.

Oriental in the centre: *Guo Fung*, Moneda 1549, rec; *Lung Fung*, Agustinas 715, delicious food, pricey, excellent fixed price lunch, large cage in the centre with noisy parrots; *Pai Fu*, Santa Rosa 101, good; *Kam Thu*, Santo Domingo 771, nr San Antonio, good, large helpings; all Chinese. *Izakaya Yoko*, Merced 456, good, Japanese, rec.

Many in the Lastarria and Bellavista neighbourhoods, inc: *La Pergola de la Plaza* in Plaza Mulato Gil de Castro, but better and close by are *Quiche Lorraine* in the Instituto Chileno-Francés, Lastarria 345, highly rec for food, drink and ambience; *Gatopardo*, Lastarria 192, good value and *R*, highly rec. *Café Universitario*, Alameda 395 y Victoria Suberceaseaux (nr Sta Lucía), good, cheap *almuerzos*. Many restaurants/bars on Pío Nono inc: *Venezia*, huge servings, good value; *Eladio*, good steaks; *Zingarrella*, Italian, good: *La Puña*, *Los Ladrillos*, popular, lively, and *La Maviola*, speciality pizzas. *Café del Cerro*, Ernesto Pinto Lazarrigue 192, T 778-308, with live music (check *El Mercurio* for programme), door charge, highly rec; *Cipriani*, Pinto Lazarrigue 195, pasta, elegant atmosphere, US$25-30, top class; *Picoroco*, Pinto Lagarrigue 123, good seafood; *Al Mazzat*, de Bello 82, Arab dishes, good; *El Otro Sitio*, Antonio de Bello 53, excellent food, elegant not cheap; *Caramaño*, Purísima 257, good seafood, reasonably priced, ring doorbell, rec; *Les Copains*, Purísima 65, French, good food; *La Tasca Mediterránea*, Purísima 100 block, good food, rec; *La Divina Comida*, Purísima 215, Italian with 3 rooms – Heaven, Hell and Purgatory, highly rec; *La Esquina al Jérez*, Mallinkrodt 102, excellent Spanish; *San Fruttuoso*, Mallinkrodt 180, Italian, rec.

Outside the centre, in Providencia: *La Pizza Nostra*, Av Las Condes 6757, Providencia, sells good Italian food as well as pizzas, real coffee, pricey, also at Av Providencia 1975 and Luis Thayer Ojeda 019; *da Renato*, Mardoqueo Fernández 138 (metro Los Leones), Italian, good; *El Parrón*, Av Providencia 1188, *parrilladas*, rec, the local dice game of 'dudo' is played in the bar; *Lomit's*, Av Providencia 1980, good; *Gatsby*, Av Providencia 1984, American food, as-much-as-you-can-eat buffet and lunch/dinner,

snack bar open till 2400, tables outside in warm weather, good; *La Mía Pappa*, Las Bellotas 267, Italian, very popular lunches; *Olé Olé*, Guardia Vieja 136, Spanish, good food, wide selection; *Coco*, La Concepción 236, good seafood, expensive, rec, reservation advised; *Centre Catalá*, Av Suecia 428 nr Lota, good, reasonably-priced; *München*, German, Av El Bosque Nte 204, rec; *Carrousel*, Los Conquistadores 1972, very good, nice garden, over US$20.

Many first-class restaurants out of the centre can be found in the Las Condes district, inc grills, Chilean cuisine (often with music), French cuisine and Chinese. They tend to be more expensive than central restaurants. Good examples are *Seriatutix*, Av Colón 5137, restaurant and disco, live music, café, great atmosphere; *Delmónico*, Vitacura 3379, excellent, reasonably priced; *El Madroñal*, Vitacura 2911, T 233-6312, excellent, booking essential; *Praga*, Vitacura 3917, Czech; *La Tasca de Altamar*, Noruega y Linneo, good seafood, reasonably priced; *Pinpilinpausha*, Isadora Goyenechea 2900, good; *Martín Carrera*, Isidora Goyenechea 3471, good nouvelle cuisine; *Taj Mahal*, Isidora Goyenechea 3215 (Metro El Golf), T 232-3606, only Indian in Santiago, expensive but excellent; *El Club*, Bosque Nte 280 (approx), popular, good value (US$15-20); *Coco Loco*, opp at No 215, good, US$20-30. On Av Las Condes: *La Estancia*, No 13810 (US$20-25), *La Querencia*, No 14980, a bit cheaper, both good; *Santa Fe*, No 10690, excellent Mexican.

It is difficult to eat cheaply in the evening apart from fast food. If on a budget make the *almuerzo* your main meal. Cheap lunches *Casino La Blanquita*, San Martín 75, popular with locals. *Food Garden*, in galeria at Estado/Ahumada and Huérfanos/Agustinas, p 2, is collection of fast food kiosks, good resting place.

Vegetarian restaurants: *El Huerto*, Orrego Luco 054, T 233-2690, rec, open daily, live music Fri and Sat evenings, varied menu, very good but not cheap, popular; *Rincón Vegetariano*, Monjitas 558, good fixed price lunches, good, juices, rec, closes 1800.

● **Cafés & bars**

In the city centre: *Bucaneros*, Morandé 564, good value lunches and snacks; *Café Paula*, several branches, eg Estado at entrance to Galería España, excellent coffee and cake, good breakfast, also on San Antonio opp the Teatro Municipal. *Café Colonia*, MacIver 133, rec; *Café Santos*, Huérfanos 830, popular for 'onces' (afternoon tea); *La E*, San Pablo 1310, good coffee. Try *Café Haití*, *Café Brasil* and *Café Caribe*, all on Paseo Ahumada and elsewhere in centre and Providencia, for delicious coffee. *Bon Bon Oriental*, Merced 345, superb Turkish cakes. *Cafetería Berri*, Rosal 321, live music at weekends; *Tip-Top Galetas* rec for freshly baked biscuits, branches throughout the city, eg Merced 867. Many in Bellavista inc: *Café de la Dulcería Las Palmas*, de Bello 190, good pastries and lunches and several on Purísima 100-200, inc *La Candela*. In Lastarria: *El Biógrafo*, Villavicencio 398, bohemian style, rec.

In Providencia: *Geo Pub*, Encomenderos 83, owner Francisco Valle speaks English, pub and expensive restaurant with travel films once a week in winter, music occasionally, popular with travellers, rec; *Villa Real*, Pedro de Valdivia 079, rec. Many on Av Providencia inc: *Phone Box Pub*, No 1670, T 496627; *El Café del Patio*, next door, student hang-out; *Violin Pub*, No 1684, good lunch; *Salón de Té Tavelli*, Drugstore precinct, No 2124, rec. *Golden Bell Inn*, Hernando Aguirre 27, popular with expatriates; *Cross Keys Pub*, Las Bellotas 270 local 5 (opp *La Mía Pappa*), nr Los Leones metro, with darts, pints, etc, good value. Many other good bars nearby on Av Suecia inc *Mr Ed (No 1552)*; *Brannigan Pub (No 35)*, good beer, live jazz; *Red Pub (No 29)*. In Las Condes: *El Vikingo*, Rotunda Atena, good atmosphere, cheap; *El Metro* and *Country Village*, Av Las Condes y Estoril; further E on Av Las Condes at Paseo San Damían are several popular bar-restaurants inc *Tequila* and *Mississippi*; *Café Iguana*, Av Vitacura y La Tranquera. Note that almost all hotel bars are closed Sun.

For snacks and ice cream: try *Coppellia*, Av Providencia 2211, *Bravissimo*, same avenida No 1406, and *El Toldo Azul*, at No 1936.

● **Airline offices**
LanChile, sales office: Agustinas 640, Torre Interamericana, T 699-0505; reservations T 632-3211; Ladeco, Huérfanos 1157, T 698-2233 and Pedro de Valdivia 0210, T 251-7204; National Airlines, Huérfanos 725, p 3, B, T 633-9288/632-2698; Aerovías DAP, Luis Thayer Ojeda 0180, of 1304, Providencia, T 334-9672, F 334-5843; Alta, Las Urbinas 30, T/T 244-1777; British Airways, Isidora Goyenechea 2934, Oficina 302, T 601-8614, 232-9560 (for conformation); Aerolíneas Argentinas and Viasa, Moneda 756; Varig, Miraflores, between Agustinas and Moneda, T 639-5976; Aero Perú, Fidel Oteiza 1953, p 5, T 274-3434; Lacsa, Av Providencia 2083, Oficina 22, T 233-6400; KLM, San Sebastián 2839, Oficina 202, T 233-0011; Aeroflot, Agustinas 640, Local 5, T 632-3914; South African Airlines, Moneda 970, p 18, next to Lufthansa (T 698-6490); LAP, Agustinas 1141, p 2, T 671-4404; Swiss Air, Estado 10, p 10.

● **Banks & money changers**
Banks, open from 0900 to 1400, but closed on Sat. Official daily exchange rates are published in *El Mercurio* and *La Epoca*. Banco Central de Chile, Ahumada entre Huérfanos y Agustinas, demands the minimum of formalities, but may charge commission. Banco O'Higgins, Bandera 201, will change TCs into dollars with commission on transactions between US$100-1,000. American Express, Agustinas 1360 (Turismo Cocha, Av El Bosque Nte 0430, Providencia, for travel information and mail collection), no commission, poor rates (better to change TCs into dollars – no limit – and then into pesos elsewhere). Citibank, Ahumada 40. Thomas Cook/Mastercard agent, *Turismo Tajamar*, Orrego Luco 23, T 231-5112.

Casas de Cambio (exchange houses) close on Sat except in summer when they open till 1300 (check first). Normally there is no commission on TCs though rates may be lower. Shop around as terms vary. Most exchange houses are on Agustinas and Huérfanos. Casa de Cambio Blancas, opp *Hotel Orly* on Pedro de Valdivia, and Exprinter, Agustinas 1074, are rec for good rates, low commission, also Inter, Moneda 940, upstairs office at Ahumada 131 (oficina 103), Cambios Andino, Ahumada 1062 and Teletour, Guardia Vieja 55. Afex, Moneda 1160, good rates for TCs; Sr Fernando Sáez (travel agent), M Cousiño 150, Oficina 327, T 638-2885, for good exchange rates (and australes). Casa de Cambio, C Bombero A Ossa 1010, Of 214 (nr Ahumada/Agustinas), open 0900-2200 (Mon-Fri only, but operates from travel agency next door on Sat am). In Providencia several around Av Pedro de Valdivia, eg at Gral Holley 66, good rates; Mojakar, Pedro de Valdivia 072. Mastercard at Fincard, Alameda 1427, T 698-4260, 2465/7, 3855, 7229, offers its full range of services (even lost or stolen cards are replaced in a couple of days); open 24 hrs. Visa at Banco Concepción, Huérfanos y Bandera, but beware hidden costs in 'conversion rate', and Banco Osorno, Av Providencia and Pedro de Valdivia, no commission. For stolen or lost Visa cards go to Transbank, Huérfanos 777, p 3. Unless you are feeling adventurous avoid street money changers (particularly common on Ahumada and Agustinas): they will usually ask you to accompany them to a Casa de Cambio or somewhere more obscure. Rates for such transactions are no better and the passing of forged notes and mugging are reported. For Cirrus ATMs go to Banco Santander and Banco de Santiago and other banks with Redbank sign.

● **Cultural centres**
Instituto Chileno Británico de Cultura, Santa Lucía 124, T 638-2156, 0930-1900, except

1330-1900 Mon, and 0930-1600 Fri, has English papers in library (also in Providencia, Dario Urzúa 1933, and Las Condes, Renato Sánchez 4369), runs language courses; **British Chamber of Commerce**, Av Suecia 155-c, Providencia, Casilla 536, T 231-4366; **British Council**, Av Eliodoro Yáñez 832, nr Providencia, T 223-4622. The British community maintains the **British Commonwealth Society** (old people's home etc), Av Alessandri 557, T 223-8807, the interdenominational Santiago Community Church, at Av Holanda 151 (Metro Tobalaba), Providencia, which holds services every Sun at 1045.

Instituto Chileno Francés de Cultura, Merced 298, T 639-8433, in a beautiful house; **Instituto Chileno Alemán de Cultura**, Goethe-Institut, Esmeralda 650, T 638-3185; **German Chamber of Commerce**, Ahumada 131. **Instituto Chileno de Cultura Hispánica**, Providencia 927; **Instituto Chileno Italiano de Cultura**, Triana 843; **Instituto Chileno Israelí de Cultura**, Moneda 812, oficina 613; **Instituto Chileno Japonés de Cultura**, Providencia 2653, oficina 1902.

Instituto Chileno Norteamericano de Cultura, Moneda 1467, T 696-3215, good for US periodicals, cheap films on Fri; also runs language courses and free Spanish/English language exchange hours (known as Happy Hours) which are a good way of meeting people. (Ask also about Mundo Club which organizes excursions and social events).

Instituto Cultural del Banco del Estado de Chile, Alameda 123, regular exhibitions of paintings, concerts, theatrical performances; **Instituto Cultural de Providencia**, Av 11 de Septiembre 1995 (Metro Pedro de Valdivia), art exhibitions, concerts, theatre; **Instituto Cultural Las Condes**, Av Apoquindo 6570, nr beginning of Av Las Condes, also with art exhibitions, concerts, lectures, etc.

● **Embassies and consulates**

Argentine Embassy, Miraflores 285, T 633-1076; Consulate Vicuña Mackenna 41, T 222-6853, Australians need letter from their embassy to get visa here, open 0900-1400 (visa US$25, free for US citizens), if you need a visa for Argentina, get it here or in the consulates in Concepción, Puerto Montt or Punta Arenas, there are no facilities at the borders; **Brazilian Embassy**, Alonso Ovalle 1665, MacIver 225, 15 p, visas issued by Consulate, MacIver 225, 15 p, Mon-Fri 1000-1300, US$10 (visa takes 2 days); take: passport, 2 photos, ticket into and out of Brazil, photocopy of first 2 pages of passport, of tickets, of credit card and of Chilean tourist card; **Bolivian Embassy**, Av Santa María 2796, T 232-8180 (Metro Los Leones), open 0930-1400; **Panamanian Embassy**, Del Inca 5901, T 220-8286 (open 1000-

1330); **Paraguayan Consulate**, Huérfanos 886, Oficina 514, T 639-4640, open 0900-1300 (2 photos and copy of first page of passport required for visa); **Peruvian Embassy**, Av Andrés Bello 1751, T 232-6275 (Metro Pedro de Valdivia).

US Embassy, Edif Codina, Agustinas 1343, unit 4127, T 232-2600, F 330-3710; **US Consulate**, T 710133, Merced 230 (visa obtainable here); **Canadian Embassy**, Ahumada 11, p 10, T 696-2256 (prints a good information book). **Australian Embassy**, Gertrudis Echeñique 420, T 228-5065, 0900-1200. **New Zealand Embassy**, Ave Isadora Goyenechea 3516, Las Condes, T 231-4204. **South African Embassy**, Av 11 de Septiembre 2353, Edif San Román, p 16, T 231-2862; **Japanese Embassy**, Av Providencia 2653, p 19; **Israeli Embassy**, San Sebastian 2812, T 246-1570.

British Embassy and Consulate, El Bosque Nte 0125 (Metro Tobalaba), Casilla 72-D, T 231-3737, F 231-9771, will hold letters, open 0900-1200; **German Embassy**, Agustinas 785, p 7 y 8, T 633-5031; **Netherlands Embassy**, C Las Violetas 2368, T 223-6825, open 0900-1200; **French Embassy**, Condell 65, T 225-1030; **Norwegian Embassy**, Av Vespucio Nte 548, T 228-1024; **Belgian Embassy**, Av Providencia 2653, depto 1104, T 232-1071; **Danish Embassy**, Av Santa María 0182, T 737-6056; **Austrian Embassy**, Barros Errázuriz 1968, p 3; **Italian Embassy**, Clemente Fabres 1050, T 223-2467; **Spanish Consulate**, Av Providencia 329, p 4, T 40239; **Finnish Embassy**, Sótero Sanz de Villalba 55, Oficina 71, T 232-0456; **Swedish Embassy**, 11 de Septiembre 2353, Torre San Ramón, p 4, Providencia, T 231-2733, F 232-4188; **Swiss Embassy**, Av Providencia 2653, Oficina 1602, T 232-2693, open 1000-1200 (metro Tobalaba).

● **Entertainment**

Cinemas: 'Ciné Arte' (quality foreign films) is very popular and a number of cinemas specialize in this type of film: *El Biógrafo* (Lastarria 181), *Alameda Cultural Centre*, Av Providencia 927, *Casa de Extensión Universidad Católica*, Av B O'Higgins 390, T 222-1157, *Espaciocal* (Goyenechea y Vitacura), *Tobalaba* (Av Providencia 2563), and others, full details are given in the press. Try also Goethe Institut, and Instituto Chileno-Francés (addresses above). Other cinemas tend to show 'sex, violence and war'. Seats cost US$3-5 with reductions on Wed (elsewhere in the country the day varies).

Discotheques: *Gente*, Av Apoquindo 4900, also *Baltas*, Av Las Condes 10690, both expensive, but good. *El Baile*, de Bello, Bellavista. *Maestra Vida*, Pío Nono 380. Many more, mainly in the Providencia and Las Condes areas.

Nightclubs: some of the restaurants and cafés which have shows are given above. Listings are given in *El Mercurio*, or *La Epoca*. Clubs in Bellavista are cheaper and more down market generally than those in Providencia. *La Cucaracha*, Bombero Núñez 159 (Bellavista) is very popular, floorshow at 2330, US$3.50 cover charge, orchestras, dancing. *Varadero*, on Pío Nono, good. Several tango clubs inc *Club Troilo*, Cumming 795, cheap, unpretentious (tango classes 1800-2000, Fri and Sun). *El Tucano Salsateca*, P de Valdivia 1783, p 4, Wed-Sun 2200-0600, fashionable. *Peña Nano Parra*, San Isidro 57, good folk club, cheap.

Theatres: *Teatro Municipal*, Agustinas y San Antonio, stages international opera, concerts by the Orquesta Filarmónica de Santiago, and the Ballet de Santiago, throughout the year; on Tues at 2100 there are free operatic concerts in the Salón Claudio Arrau; tickets range from US$5.60 for a very large choral group with a symphony orchestra, and US$7 for the cheapest seats at the ballet, to US$80 for the most expensive opera seats. Some cheap seats are often sold on the day of concerts. *Teatro Universidad de Chile*, Plaza Baquedano, is the home of the Orquesta y Coro Sinfónica de Chile and the Ballet Nacional de Chile; prices from US$1.25-3.50 for concerts to US$1.25-13.50 for ballet.

Free classical concerts are sometimes given in San Francisco church in summer; arrive early for a seat.

There are a great number of theatres which stage plays in Spanish, either in the original language or translations, eg *La Comedia*, Merced 349, *Abril*, Huérfanos 786, *Camilo Henríquez*, Amunátegui 31, *Centro Arrayán*, Las Condes 14891, *El Galpón de los Leones*, Av Los Leones 238, *El Conventillo*, Bellavista 173. Four others, the *Opera*, Huérfanos, *California*, Irarrázaval 1546, *Humoresque*, San Ignacio 1249 and *Picaresque*, Recoleta 345, show mostly Folies Bergères-type revues. *Santiago Stage* is an English-speaking amateur drama group. Outdoor rock concerts are held at the *Estadio Nacional*, Av Unión Latino Americana (metro of same name), at the Teatro Teletón, Rosas 325 (excellent sound system), and elsewhere. Events are listed in *El Mercurio* and *La Epoca*. The most comprehensive listings appear in *El Mercurio's Wikén* magazine on Friday.

● **Hospitals & medical services**
Emergency Pharmacy: Portugal 155 (T 382439).

Hospitals: emergency hospital at Marcoleta 377 costs US$60. If you need to get to a hospital, it is better to take a taxi than wait for an ambulance. For yellow fever vaccination and others (but not cholera), *Hospital San Salvador*, J M Infante 551, T 225-6441, Mon-Thur 0800-1300, 1330-1645; Fri 0800-1300, 1330-1545. Also *Vaccinatoria*

Internacional , Hospital Luis Calvo, Mackenna, Antonio Varas 360. *Clínica Central*, San Isidro 231, T 222-1953, open 24 hrs, German spoken. *Clínica Alemana*, Vitacura 5951, Las Condes, German and English spoken (bus 344 from centre). Physician: Dr Sergio Maylis, T 232-0853 (1430-1900). Dentist: Antonio Yazigi, Vitacura 3082, Apto 33, T 487962, English spoken, rec. Dr Torres, Av Providencia 2330, Depto 23, excellent, speaks English.

● **Language schools**
Centro de Idiomas Bellavista, Dominica 25, T 777-5933/227-7137, offers Spanish in groups or individually and organizes accommodation. *Escuela de Idiomas Violeta Parra*, Lagarrigue 362A, Recoleta, T 284-4708, F 229-8246, arranges accommodation and visits to local organisations; *AmeriSpan Unlimited* has an affiliated school in Santiago, details from PO Box 40513, Philadelphia, PA 19106, USA, T 215-985-4522/800-879-6640, F 215-985-4524, E-mail info@amerispan.com. Many private teachers (much cheaper), inc Carolina Carvajal, T 623-8405, highly rec, and Patricia Vargas Vives, Monitor Araucano 0680, Depto 25AC, Providencia, T 777-0595, qualified and experienced. Lucla Araya Arevalo, Puerto Chico 8062, Villa Los Puertos, Pudahuel, T 236-0531, speaks German and English. Patricio Ríos, Tobalaba 7505, La Reina, T 226-6926, speaks English, rec

An increasing number of private language institutes, most of them small, offer English courses. Most English teachers are badly paid and schools are increasingly reluctant to employ foreigners without work permits. (These are difficult to obtain and can only be acquired by the teacher themselves). More unscrupulous schools are reported to employ teachers with 90-day tourist visas and 'discover' as this expires that the teacher is not entitled to work, at which point it is difficult to obtain unpaid wages. English language teachers seeking work should apply in mid-Feb/early March with a full curriculum vitae and photo (smart appearance essential); before accepting employment check how much tax is deducted (10% is normal).

● **Laundry**
Wet-wash places in the centre: at Agustinas 1532, also *Nataly*, Bandera 72, another at Bandera 572, at Catedral y Amunátegui and *Lava Facil*, Huérfanos 1750, Mon-Sat 0900-2000, US$4/load. There are plenty of dry-cleaners, eg Merced 494. Nearby, just S of Metro Universidad Católica there are several, inc *American Washer*, Portugal 71, Torre 7, local 4, US$3, open 0900-2100 inc Sun, can leave washing and collect it later, also at Monjitas 650. Wet wash laundries in Providencia inc *Marva*, Carlos Antúñez 1823 (Metro Pedro de Valdivia), wash and

dry US$8; Providencia 1039, full load, wet wash, US$5, 3 hrs; **Laverap**, Av Providencia 1600 block; Manuel Montt 67. At the corner of Providencia and Dr Luis Middleton there are several self-service dry cleaners (Metro Pedro de Valdivia, 11 de Septiembre exit).

● **Places of worship**

Anglican Church, Holanda 151 (service 1030); Synagogues Tarapacá 870, T 393872, and Las Hortensias 9322, T 233-8868.

● **Post & telecommunications**

Telephones: Compañía de Teléfonos de Chile, Moneda 1151, closed Sun. International phone calls also from: Entel, Huérfanos 1133, Mon-Fri 0830-2200, Sat 0900-2030, Sun 0900-1400, calls cheaper 1400-2200; Fax upstairs. Fax also available at CTC offices, eg Mall Panorámico, 11 de Septiembre, 3rd level (phone booths are on level 1). There are also CTC phone offices at some metro stations, La Moneda, Escuela Militar, Tobalaba, Universidad de Chile and Pedro de Valdivia for local, long-distance and international calls. International telex service, Bandera 168. Local calls 50 pesos, only 50 peso coins accepted.

Post Office: Plaza de Armas (0800-1900), poste restante well organized (though only kept for 30 days), US$0.20, passport essential, list of letters and parcels received in the hall of central Post Office (one list for men, another for women, indicate Sr or Sra/Srita on envelope); also has philatelic section, 0900-1630, and small stamp museum (ask to see it). Another office at Moneda 1155. If sending a parcel, the contents must first be checked at Post Office; paper, tape etc on sale; open Mon-Fri 0800-1900, Sat 0800-1400.

● **Shopping**

El Almacén Campesino, Purísima 303, Bellavista, handicrafts from all over Chile. Best bargains are handicraft articles, pottery (best bought in Pomaire, 50 km away, see page 696) and beautiful wrought copper and bronze. The gemstone lapis lazuli can be found in a few expensive shops in Bellavista but is cheaper in the arcades on S side of the Plaza de Armas and in the *Centro Artesanal Santa Lucía* (Santa Lucía metro, S exit) which also has a wide variety of woollen goods, jewellery, etc. *Amitié*, Av Ricardo León y Av Providencia (Metro Los Leones); *Dauvin Artesanía Fina*, Providencia 2169, Local 69 (Metro Los Leones) have also been rec. *H Stern* jewellery shops are located at the *San Cristóbal Sheraton*, *Hyatt Regency* and *Carrera* hotels, and at the International Airport. *Cema-Chile* (Centro de Madres), Portugal 351 and at Universidad de Chile metro stop, *Manos Chilensis*, Portugal 373, *Artesanías de Chile*,

Varas 475, *Artesanía Popular Chilena*, Av Providencia 2322 (nr Los Leones metro), and *Artesanía Chilena*, Estado 337, have a good selection of handicrafts. *Talleres Solidarios*, de la Barra 456, small selection. Antique stores in Plaza Mulato Gil de Castro and elsewhere on Lastarria (Merced end).

Beside and behind the Iglesia de los Dominicos, on Av Nueva Apoquindo 9085, is *Los Graneros del Alba*, or *El Pueblo de Artesanos*, open daily except Mon, 1130-1900; all types of ware on sale, classes given in some shops, interesting. *Restaurant El Granero* is here. To get there, take a small, green Los Dominicos bus from Av Providencia, marked 'Camino del Alba', or an Apoquindo bus, similarly marked, from Metro Escuela Militar; get out at the children's playground at the junction of Apoquindo y Camino del Alba, at the foot of the hill leading up to the church, and walk up.

Mercado Central, between Puente y 21 de Mayo by the Río Mapocho (Cal y Canto metro) is excellent but quite expensive; there is a cheaper market, the *Vega Central*, on the opp bank of the river. There are other craft markets in an alleyway, 1 block S of Av B O'Higgins between A Prat and San Diego, on the 600 to 800 blocks of Santo Domingo (inc pieces from neighbouring countries) and at Pío Nono y Av Santa María, Bellavista. The shopping arcade at the Central Station is good value, likewise the street market outside. Cheap clothes shops in the city, eg on Bandera esp 600 block, are good for winter clothes for travellers who need them (look for sign Ropa Europea). There is a flea market at Franklin y Santa Rosa on Sun am and a good outside fruit market at Puente 815, by *Frutería Martínez*. There is an antique fair on Sun (1000-1400) in the summer and a Fiesta de Quasimodo on the first Sun after Easter at Lo Barnechea, 30 min by bus from Santiago. Parque Arauco is a large modern shopping mall on Av Kennedy, N of Metro Escuela Militar.

Bookshops: book prices tend to be high compared with Europe. *Librería Albers*, Vitacura 5648, Las Condes, T 218-5371, F 218-1458, and 11 de Septiembre 2671, Providencia, T 232-7499 (Spanish, English and German – good selection, cheaper than most, helpful, also German and Swiss newspapers); *Librería Catalonia*, Huérfanos 669; *Feria Chilena del Libro*, Huérfanos nr McIver, and in Drugstore precinct, Providencia 2124; *Librería Inglesa*, Huérfanos 669, local 11, and Pedro de Valdivia 47, Providencia, T 231-9970, good selection of English books, sells *South American Handbook*. *South American Way*, Av Apoquindo 6856, Las Condes, T 211-8078, sells books in English. There are many bookshops in the Pedro de Valdivia area on Providencia. Second-hand English books from *Librería El Patio*, Providencia 1652, nearest Metro stop Pedro de Valdivia; exchange for best deal. Also, from Henry at Metro station, Los Leones, and *Books*, next to *Phone Box Pub*, in the courtyard at Providencia 1670 (the artist's shop in same precinct sells attractive cards). *Librairie Française*, books and newspapers, C del Estado 337. As well as the antiquarian bookshop mentioned above in the Lastarria district, there are other good antiquarian bookshops on Merced around the corner from Lastarria, eg *América del Sur Librería Editorial*, No 306, *Libros Antiguos El Cid*, No 344. Many stalls on Paseo Ahumada/Huérfanos sell foreign newspapers and journals.

Camera repairs & film: *Harry Müller*, Ahumada 312, Oficina 402, not cheap but good and fairly quick, rec; speaks German and English. For Minolta and Canon repairs, *TecFo*, Nueva York 52, p 2, T 695-2969, rec. Many developers on Ahumada offer 24-hr service of varying quality (some develop, but not mount, slides, slow service). *Tecnofoto*, Ahumada 131, p 7, Oficina 719, T 672-5004 rec as quick and efficient. *Moretto*, Merced 753, rec as cheap and good. *Fototeknika*, Lira 45, develops and mounts slides on same day, US$5.30 for 36, also handles prints, Mon-Fri 0800-1800. *Black Box*, Gral Flores 229 (Metro Mannel Montt), highly rec. For camera batteries and other spares try *Fotocenter*, Ahumada y Huérfanos.

Camping equipment: standard camping gas cartridges can be bought at *Fabri Gas*, Bandera y Santo Domingo, or *Unisport*, Av Providencia 2503. Other equipment for camper-vans from *Bertonati Hnos*, Manuel Montt 2385. Tent repairs: *Juan Soto*, Silva Vildosola 890, Paradero 1, Gran Avenida, San Miguel, Santiago, T 555-8329. *Reinaldo Lippi*, Grenado 566 (nr Santa Lucía hill), T 639-1180, F 639-9169, makes tents, sleeping bags, back packs, etc, sells secondhand kit, and does repairs, most helpful. Camping goods from *Club Andino* and *Federación de Andinismo* (see page 691 below): expensive because these articles are imported. *Lomas*, Santa Rosa y 10 de Julio, good selection of sleeping bags, helpful. Good sleeping bags from *Fuc*, Rengo 1670 (off M Montt), T 225-8862. For packs also try Sr Espinosa, San Martín 835. Repair of camping stoves at *Casa Italiana*, Tarapacá 1120. For second hand equipment try Luz Emperatrie Sanhuela Quiroz, Portal de León, Loc 14, Providencia 2198 (Metro Los Leones).

● **Sports**

Bicycles: for parts and repairs *Importadora Caupolicán*, San Diego 863, T 697-2765, F 696-1937, wide range, helpful. Ask for Nelson Díaz 'a walking encyclopaedia' on bikes.

Clubs: Ñuñoa (T 223 7846), with swimming pool, tennis courts and school; Chess Club, Alameda O'Higgins 898, Mon-Sat 1800, lively.

Football: main teams inc Colo Colo who play at the Estadio Monumental, reached by any bus to Puente Alto; tickets from Cienfuegos 41. Universidad de Chile (Estadio Nacional, Av Grecia 2001, T 239-2212) and Universidad Católica who play at San Carlos de Apoquindo, reached by bus from Metro Escuela Militar.

Other sports: **Running**: the Hash House Harriers hold runs every other week; information through the British Embassy and Consulate. **Tennis**: Santiago Tennis Club; also, Club de Tenis Jaime Fillol, Rancho Melnichi, Par 4. **Bowling**: Bowling Center, Av Apoquindo 5012. **Gymnasium**: Gimnasio Alicia Franché, Moneda 1481, T 696-1681, aerobics and fitness classes (women only); another at Huérfanos 1313, T 671-1562. **Tai Chi** and other martial arts: Raul Tou-Tin, Irarrázaval 1971, T 204-8082. **Cricket**: Sat in summer at Club Príncipe de Gales, Las Arañas 1901 (bus from Tobalaba metro).

Racecourses: Club Hípico, racing every Sun and every other Wed afternoon (at Viña del Mar, Jan-Mar); Hipódromo Chile every Sat afternoon; pari-mutuel betting.

Skiing & climbing: Club Andino de Chile, Enrique Foster 29, ski club (open 1900-2100 on Mon and Fri). **Federación de Andinismo de Chile**, Almte Simpson 77 (T 222-9140), open daily; has a small museum (1100-1330, 1700-2000, free) and library (open weekday evenings, not Wed), sells limited range of equipment and guides to the mountains around Santiago (US$2.50) and the extreme S (eg Paine, US$4.35). Little other information available, apart from the addresses of all the mountaineering clubs in the country. It has a mountaineering school. **Club Alemán Andino**, El Arrayán 2735, T 242-5453, open Tues and Fri, 1800-2000, May-June. Also try **Skitotal**, Apoquindo 4900, Oficina 32,33,43, T 246-0156, for 1-day excursions, and **Anke Kessler**, Arzobispo Casanova 25, T 737-1958, F 274-5146, for individually-tailored packages inc hotels and transport for budget skiers. Equipment hire is much cheaper in Santiago than in ski resorts. Sunglasses are essential. For ski resorts in the Santiago area see below page 696. **Skiing and climbing equipment**: *Mountain Service*, Ebro 2805, Las Condes (Metro Tobalaba) T 242-9723, English spoken, tents, stoves, clothing, equipment rental, rec; *Panda Deportes*, Paseo Las Palmas 2217 (Metro Los Leones), T 232-1840.

Swimming Pools: Tupahue (large pool with cafés, entry US$9 but worth it) and Antilen), both on Cerro San Cristóbal, open daily in summer except Mon 1000-1500 (check if they are open in winter, one usually is). In Parque O'Higgins, 1330-1830 summer only, US$3. Olympic pool in Parque Araucano (nr Arauco Shopping Centre, closest Metro E Militar), open Tues-Sat 0900-1900 November-March.

● **Tour companies & travel agents**
Wagons-Lits Cook, Carmencita, Providencia, T 233-0820, rec; *Turismo Cocha* (American Express representatives with mail service), Av El Bosque Nte 0430, PO Box 191035, Providencia, Metro Tobalaba, T 230-1000. *Passtours*, Huérfanos 886, Oficina 1110, T 639-3232, F 562-633-1498, many languages spoken, helpful, rec. *VMP Ltda*, Huérfanos 1160, Local 19, T/F 696-7829, for all services, German, English, French, Italian and Portuguese spoken, helpful, repeatedly rec. *All Travels*, Huérfanos 1160, local 10, T 696-4348, good for flight tickets; *Eurotur*, Huérfanos 1160, local 13, for cheap air tickets to Europe. *Blanco*, Pedro de Valdivia nr Av Providencia, good for flight information and exchange. *Rapa-Nui*, Huérfanos 1160, specializes in trips to Easter Island. *Turismo Grace*, Victoria Subercaseaux 381, T 693-3740, good service. For local tours: *Ace Turismo*, O'Higgins 949, T 696-0391, city tour, US$12 for ½ day. *Maysa*, Paseo Ahumada 6, Of 43, T/F 696-4468, good tours of bodegas and Valparaíso, US$35.

For adventure tours and trekking: *Sportstours*, Teatinos 330, p 10, T 696-8832/698-3058, German-run, helpful, 5 day trips to Antarctica (offices also at Hotels *Carrera*, and *San Cristóbal*); *Altue Expediciones*, Encomenderos 83, T 232-1103, for wilderness trips inc 15 day tour of Patagonia, rec (above *Geo Pub*). Climbing and adventure tours in the Lake District and elsewhere, *Antu Aventuras*, Casilla 24, Santiago, T 271-2767, Tx 440019, RECAL CZ. *Azimut 360*, Monte Carmelo 360, Dept 36, T 777-2375, highly rec, low prices; *Mountain Service*, Ebro 2805, Las Condes, T 242-9723, F 234-3438, and *Evasión*, Sotero Sanz 95, Providencia, T 231-1876 both rec for climbing trips; *Racies*, Plaza Corregidor Zañartu 761, cultural tours, inc Robinson Crusoe Island and Antarctica, T/F 638-2904. *Turismo Grant*, Huérfanos 863, Oficina 516, T 639-5524, helpful, English spoken; *Patagonia Chile*, Constitución 172, Bellavista, T 351871, offer mountain trips, river rafting, trekking. *Turismo Cabo de Hornos*, Agustinas 814, Of 706, T 6338481, F 6338486, for DAP flights and Tierra del Fuego/Antártica tours. *Andina del Sud*, Bombero Ossa 1010, p 3, Of 301, T 697-1010, F 696-5121, for tours in the Lake District. Ask at *Hotel Maury*, address above, for tours with Fernández (Tony), who speaks English, inc riding, rafting and barbecue, US$50 pp, rec. For skiing in the Santiago area see below page 696.
Turismo Joven, Av Suecia Nte 0125, T 232-

9946, F 334-3008, E-mail turjoven@mail-ent.rdc.cl, youth travel services for young people and students for travel, studies, leisure with links in Latin America and worldwide.

● **Tourist offices**
Servicio Nacional de Turismo (Sernatur – the national tourist board), Av Providencia 1550 (Casilla 14082), T 236-1416, Tx SERNA CL 240137, between metros Manuel Montt and Pedro de Valdivia, next to Providencia Municipal Library, open Mon-Fri 0900-1900, Sat 0900-1300. English and German spoken and maps (road map US$1.50), brochures and posters are available. Good notice board. Ask for the free booklet, *Paseos en Santiago* (City Walks in Santiago), which is very useful for those with time to explore on foot. Kiosk on Ahumada nr Agustinas (erratic opening times). Information office also at the airport, open 0900-2100 daily. Municipal Tourist Board, Casa Colorada, Merced 860, T 336700/330723, offers walking tours of the city, Wed 1500, or from kiosk on Paseo Ahumada. **NB** Many tourist offices outside Santiago are closed in winter, so stock up on information here.

Excellent road maps (US$1.75) and information may be obtained from the **Automóvil Club de Chile**, Vitacura 8620, T 212-5702/3/4 (Metro P de Valdivia then bus to Vitacura, or a US$6 taxi ride from the centre), which also gives discounts to members of affiliated motoring organizations; open Mon-Fri 0845-1815, Sat 0900-1300, very helpful. Geophysical and topographical maps (US$11) are available from **Instituto Geográfico Militar**, at the main office Dieciocho 369, T 698-7278, open 0900-1800 Mon-Fri, closed in Jan/February. In 1991 the Insituto Geográfico published a *Guía Caminera*, with roads and city plans, for US$8.75 (available only at IGM offices, not 100% accurate). *Turistel* (see **Tourist Information** in **Information for travellers**) publishes a *Mapa Rutera*. The Biblioteca Nacional, Moneda 650, has an excellent collection of maps which can be photocopied, particularly useful for climbing. **Conaf** (Corporación Nacional Forestal), Presidente Bulnes 259, oficina 206 (main office at No 285), T 696-0783/699-2833, publishes a number of booklets (see **Information for travellers**) and has documents and maps about the national park system that can be consulted or photocopied (not very useful for walking). CODEFF (Comité Nacional Pro-Defensa de la Fauna y Flora), Sazie 1885, T 696-1268, can also provide information on environmental questions. Walkers' maps are not available outside Santiago. Write to the Dpto de Estudios Vialidad Nacional, Morandé 59, oficina 344, Santiago, to see if their set of 14 maps of the country (scale 1:500,000 – border areas 1:1,000,000) is available. Maps on sale from news kiosks: Esso road and town plans, Copec, Inupal and others (see also **Information for travellers** for details of other publications).

● Useful addresses

Immigration: Ministerio del Interior, Palacio de la Moneda, *Extranjería* section; extension of tourist card US$8.

Policía Internacional: for lost tourist cards, etc, Santo Domingo y MacIver.

● Transport

Local **Buses & taxis**: there are three kinds of buses: the small fast kind called *liebres* (hares) which cost US$0.50 a ride; the regular buses at US$0.30, and the large buses marked Expreso, US$0.40. Taxis (black with yellow roofs) are abundant, and not expensive, with a minimum charge of US$0.40, plus US$0.12/200m. Taxi drivers are permitted to charge more at night, but in the day time check that the meter is set to day rates. At bus terminals, drivers will charge more – best to walk a block and flag down a cruising taxi. Large blue taxis do not have meters. Avoid taxis with more than one person in them especially at night. There are also colectivo taxis to the suburbs, US$0.70. For journeys outside the city arrange the charge beforehand. The private taxi service which operates from the bottom level of *Hotel Carrera* has been rec (same rates as city taxis), as has Radio Taxis Andes Pacífico, T 225-3064/2888; similarly Rigoberto Contreras, T 638-1042, ext 4215, available at *Holiday Inn Crowne Plaza*, but rates above those of city taxis

Car hire: prices vary a lot so shop around first. Hertz, Avis and Budget available from airport. **Hertz**, Av Andrés Bello 1469, T 225-9328, and airport, T 601-9262, has a good network in Chile and cars are in good condition. **Avis** at La Concepción 334, T 495-757, poor service reported. **Automóvil Club de Chile** car rental, Marchant Pereira 122, Providencia, T 274-4167/6261, discount for members and members of associated motoring organizations. A credit card is usually asked for when renting a vehicle. Tax of 18% is charged but usually not inc in price quoted. If possible book a car in advance. Note that in the capital driving is restricted according to licence plate numbers; look for notices in the street and newspapers.

Metro: the first line of the underground railway system runs W-E between San Pablo and Escuela Militar, under the Alameda, and the second line runs N-S from Cal y Canto to Callejón Ovalle. The connecting station is Los Héroes. Line 5, from Baquedano S to La Florida is under construction. The trains are fast, quiet, and very full. The first train is at 0630 (Mon-Sat), 0800 (Sun and holidays), the last about 2245. Fares vary according to time of journey; there are 3 charging periods: high 0715-0900, 1800-1900, US$0.45; medium 0900-1800, 1930-2100 and weekends, US$0.40; low 0630-0715, 2100-2230, US$0.25. The simplest solution is to buy a *boleto valor*, US$3.50; a charge card from which the appropriate fare is deducted. Metrobus services connect with the metro at Lo Ovalle for southern Santiago and at Escuela Militar for Vitacura, Las Condes and Apoquindo.

Motorcycles: small BMW workshop, Av San Camilo 185, Sr Marco Canales. BMW car dealer *Frederic*, Av Portugal, has some spares. Also tyre shops in this area. BMW riders can also seek help from the *carabineros* who ride BMW machines and have a workshop with good mechanics at Av Rivera 2003.

Air International and domestic flights leave from Arturo Merino Benítez Airport at Pudahuel, 26 km NW of Santiago. A new international terminal was opened in 1994. Airport information T 601-9709. Airport taxi, about US$15 but bargain hard and agree fare beforehand: more expensive with meter. Taxi to airport is much cheaper if flagged down in the street rather than booked by phone. Bus service to/from city centre by 2 companies: *Tour Express* (Moneda 1529, T 671-7380) and *Metropuerto* (T 601-9883/695-8058), US$2, approx every 15 mins, plenty of luggage space. First bus from city centre 0530, first from airport 0645, last from airport 0030. Buses leave from outside airport terminal and, in Santiago, from Moneda y San Martín calling at Plazoleta Los Héroes (nr the yellow 'Línea 2' sign) and Estación Central. Empresa Turismo Bar-C from your house or hotel to airport (or vice-versa), any time day or night, T 246-3600/1 for reservation (cheaper than taxi). *Empresa Navett*, Av Ejército Libertador 21 (nearest metro Los Héroes), T 695-6868 has a round-the-clock service, US$7. Also *Blue Line*, US$7, very efficient, order before passing through customs. On arrival, get entry card from desk at entrance to arrivals hall before proceeding to immigration, otherwise you will be sent back. Bank and Afex *cambio* (better rates, but not as good as in town) outside customs hall; Sernatur office in same area will book accommodation. There are some shops, but they are very expensive, as are the bar and restaurant. Buy your wine etc in town. Left luggage US$2.50/bag/day. For schedules of domestic flights from Santiago, see under destinations.

Accommodation nearby at **B** pp *Hacienda del Sol y La Luna*, 4 Hijuela 9978, Pudahuel, T/F 601-9254, clean, English, German, French spoken, rec.

Trains No passenger trains to northern Chile. All trains leave from Estación Central at Alameda

O'Higgins 3322. The line runs S to Rancagua, San Fernando, Curicó, Talca, Linares, Parral and Chillán, thereafter services go to 1) **Concepción**, 2) **Puerto Varas** (for Puerto Montt) via **Temuco**, with a bus connection to **Valdivia**. Schedules change with the seasons, so you must check timetables before planning a journey. See under destinations for fares and notes on schedules. *Expreso* services do not have sleepers; some *rápidos* do (in summer *rápidos* are booked up a week in advance). *Dormitorio* carriages were built in Germany in 1930's, bunks (comfortable) lie parallel to rails, US-Pullman-style (washrooms at each end, one with shower-bath – often cold water only); an attendant for each car; bar car shows 3 films – no cost but you must purchase a drink ticket in advance. There is also a newer, *Gran Dormitorio* sleeping car (1984), with private toilet and shower, US$10 extra for 2, rec. For the *expresos* there are no reservations (get your ticket the morning of the day the train leaves and sit on the train as soon as you can get on; otherwise you'll stand for the whole journey). Free hot water supplied, so take own mug and coffee. Also a car-transporter service to Chillán, Temuco and Puerto Montt. Trains are still fairly cheap and generally very punctual, although 1st class is generally dearer than bus; meals are good though expensive. Check for family, senior citizen and student discounts. Trains can be cold and draughty in winter and spring. Booking offices: for State Railways, Alameda O'Higgins 853 in Galería Hotel Libertador, Local 21, T 632-2801, Mon-Fri 0830-1900, Sat 0900-1300; or Metro Esc Militar, Galería Sur, Local 25, T 228-2983, Mon-Fri 0830-1900, Sat 0900-1300; central station, open till 2230, T 689-5718/689-1682. For Calama-Oruro, contact Tramaca, Ahumada 11, Of 602, T 698-5536. Left luggage office at Estación Central.

A steam train runs tourist services between Santiago and Los Andes, 5-hrs' journey, T 698-5536 for details.

Buses There are frequent, and good, interurban buses to all parts of Chile. (**NB** Many leave early because of tight competition: arrive at bus station early.) Check if student rates available (even for non-students), or reductions for travelling same day as purchase of ticket; it is worth bargaining over prices, especially shortly before departure and out of the summer season. Also take a look at the buses before buying the tickets (there are big differences in quality among bus companies); ask about the on-board services, many companies offer drinks for sale, or free, and luxury buses have meals and wine, colour videos, headphones. Reclining seats are common and there are also *salón cama* sleeper buses. Fares from/to the capital are given in the text. On Fri evening, when night departures are getting ready to go, the terminals are murder.

There are 4 bus terminals: 1) Terminal de Buses Sur, O'Higgins 3878, T 791-385, nearest metro Universidad Técnica/Universidad de Santiago (both names are used); buses from here go to Valparaíso, Viña del Mar and southern destinations. 2) Terminal de Buses Alameda, O'Higgins 3712, metro Universidad de Santiago, and next to the Terminal Sur: Pullman-Bus and Tur-Bus services go from here to Valparaíso, Viña del Mar and southern destinations. 3) Terminal San Borja, O'Higgins y San Borja, 1 block W of Estación Central, 3 blocks E of Terminal Alameda, metro Estación Central, for northern destinations. 4) Terminal Los Héroes on Jiménez, just N of the Alameda, has booking offices of about 10 companies for N and S routes as well as some international services. Varmontt buses, who run an expensive service to Puerto Montt, have their own terminal at Av 21 de Septiembre 2212 (office on 2nd floor), metro Los Leones; many companies have offices away from the terminals, at which their buses call.

See the note under **Taxis** about not taking expensive taxis parked outside bus terminals. Also, do not change money at the bus terminals; if coming from Argentina, try to get some Chilean pesos before you arrive.

International buses Long distance: to **Buenos Aires**, from Los Héroes terminal US$70-75, 22 hrs (TAC and Ahumada rec); to **Montevideo**, also from Los Héroes, several companies, most involving a change in Mendoza, eg Tas Choapa, 27 hrs, meals inc; to **Córdoba** direct, Tas Choapa and TAC, 18 hrs (El Rapido not rec); **Caracas** (Tues and Fri 0900); **Lima**, 51 hrs, it is cheaper to take a bus to Arica (US$40 and up), a colectivo to Tacna (US$5), thence bus to Lima. Services also to **Bogotá** (7 days); **São Paulo** and **Rio de Janeiro** (eg Chile-bus, Tues, Thur, Sat, US$107-110, 52 hrs); **Asunción** (4 a week, 28 hrs, US$75); **Guayaquil** and **Quito**. Tramaca, runs a *combinación* service which links with the train from Calama to **Uyuni** and **Oruro** in Bolivia. Géminis goes on Tues to **Salta**, Argentina, changing in Calama, US$60. Short distance: there are frequent bus and *colectivo* taxi services from Terminal San Borja over the Andes to **Mendoza** 6-7 hrs, US$15-20; taxis also go from the southern terminal, touts will approach you. All buses go through the Cristo Redentor tunnel. Many *colectivos* for Mendoza go from the 800/900 blocks of Morandé, more expensive than the buses, but with shorter waiting time at customs (US$27): Chi-Ar taxi company, Morandé 890, rec, leaves at 0800; Chile-Bus, Morandé 838, at 0830; Cordillera Nevada, Morandé 870, T 698-4716, or Local 61 at southern terminal, drive very fast.

Hitchhiking To Valparaíso, take Metro to Pajaritos and walk 5 mins to W – no difficulty. Or, take bus 'Renca Panamericana' from MacIver y Monjitas. To hitch S, take Metro to Estación Central, then Buses del Paine at C Borja as far as possible on the highway to the toll area, about US$1, 75 mins. To Buenos Aires (and Brazil) take a bus to Los Andes, then go to Copec station on the outskirts (lots of trucks early morning).

Shipping 'Navimag, Av El Bosque Nte 0440, p 1, T 203-5030, F 203-5025, Tx 240208-240224 NISA CK, Metro Tobalaba for services Puerto Montt-Puerto Natales and Puerto Montt-Puerto Chacabuco. **Transmarchilay**, Agustinas 715, Oficina 403, T/F 633-5959, for services between Chiloé and the mainland, ferry routes on the Carretera Austral and on Lake General Carrera. M/n *Skorpios*: luxury cruise out of Puerto Montt to Laguna San Rafael, Augusto Leguía Nte 118, Las Condes, T 231-1030, F 232-2269. Navimag and Transmarchilay also sail to the Laguna San Rafael in summer. Check shipping schedules with shipping lines rather than Sernatur.

DAY-TRIPS AND ACTIVITIES OUTSIDE SANTIAGO

On the NE outskirts in Las Condes is the **Santuario de la Naturaleza Yerba Loca**, administered by Conaf (maps available), open Sept to April (small entrance fee).

Peñalolén, 16 km E, provides opportunities for hiking and a beautiful view of the city if there's no smog (bus in front of Mapocho station at Av Independencia and Balmaceda).

Termas de Colina (915m), an attractive, popular spa in the mountains 43 km to the N: take a bus from Cal y Canto metro station to the town of Colina (hourly in summer only, 40 mins), then another to the military base 1½ km from town. From here a rough road leads 6 km to **L3** *Hotel Termas de Colina*, T 844-1408, modern, thermal baths, beautiful swimming pool (closed Fri), formal restaurant; facilities open to public: swimming pool US$6 (crowded at weekends), thermal baths US$10; last return bus at 1900. On the walk to the hotel, beautiful countryside, do not take photos or even show your camera when passing the military base. Taxi from Colina to the hotel, US$6.

The small towns in the Aconcagua Valley to the N – San Felipe, Jahuel and Los Andes – are described in the section 'To Argentina', page 698.

45 km S of Santiago is the **Reserva Nacional Río Clarillo**, reached by Micro No 32 to El Principal, 2 km from the entrance, US$2.50. It is in the precordillera and can be visited at any time of year for its landscapes.

CAJON DEL MAIPO

Southeast of Santiago, in the Upper Maipo valley (Cajón del Maipo) are a number of resorts including: **San José de Maipo**, some 50 km from the capital, buses every 30 mins from Metro Parque O'Higgins, Av Nte-Sur, or W side of Plaza Ercilla (return fare US$2, 2 hrs each way), particularly beautiful in spring. The mountain town of **Melocotón** is 6 km further S, and **San Alfonso**, 4 km on. The walk to the *Cascada de las Ánimas* is pleasant; ask permission to cross the bridge at the campsite (see below) as private land is crossed. Buses at hourly or 2-hr intervals from Metro Parque O'Higgins, Av Nte-Sur, Santiago.

● **Accommodation San José**: **E** *Alojamiento Inesita*, Comercio 301, good. **Melocotón**: **D** pp *Millahue*. **San Alfonso**: **B** *Posada Los Ciervos*, with breakfast and bath, **A** full board, good; **C** *Res España*, clean, comfortable, restaurant, also others, campsite at the *Comunidad Cascada de las Ánimas*, T 251-7506, also rents cabins – **C** for 4, hot water, cooking equipment etc – sauna, horseriding.

● **Places to eat** *Restaurant El Campito*, Camino al Volcán 1841, very good.

31 km further SE is **El Volcán** (1,400m) reached by three buses a day (US$2) from Parque O'Higgins; there are astounding views, but little else (the village was wiped away in a landslide). **NB** If visiting this area or continuing further up the mountain, be prepared for military checks: passport and car registration numbers may be taken. From El Volcán the road (very poor condition) runs 14 km E to the **B** pp *Refugio Alemán Lo Valdés*, stone-built chalet accommodation, full board, good food, rec, a good place to stay for mountain excursions, open all year. A splendid region which deserves the journey required to get there. Nearby are warm natural baths at **Baños Morales**, open from Oct, entry to baths, US$1. North of Baños Morales is **El Morado**

National Park with a glacier. 12 km further E up the mountain is **Baños Colina**, not to be confused with Termas de Colina, see above; hot thermal springs, entry free, horses for hire (**D** pp *Res El Tambo*, full board; restaurant, also camping). This area is popular at weekends and holiday times, but is otherwise deserted.

● **Accommodation & places to eat** At Baños Morales: **D** *Pensión Díaz*, friendly, good food, excellent café in the village, serving homemade jam, it closes at Easter for the winter; **C** pp *Refugio Baños Morales*, full board, hot water; **D** pp *Res Los Chicos Malos*, comfortable, fresh bread, good meals; free campsite. No shops so take food (try local goats cheese).

● **Transport** Bus leaves daily in Dec/Jan, weekends only off season, from Metro Parque O'Higgins, Av Nte-Sur, at 0730, US$3, 3 hrs, returns at 1800; buy return on arrival to ensure seat back; alternatively, hitch back to Santiago on quarry lorries.

MAIPU AND POMAIRE

In this suburb 10 km SW of Santiago a monument marks the site of the Battle of the Maipú, 5 April 1818, which resulted in the final defeat of the Spanish royalist forces in mainland Chile. Nearby is the **National Votive Temple of Maipú**, of fine modern architecture and stained glass; interesting (open daily 0800-2100, also daily mass at 1830, 1730 Sat, 1000-1400, 1600-2000 Sun and religious holidays), and so is the attached **Museo del Carmen** of carriages, furniture, clothing and other colonial and later items, Sat 1600-2000, Sun and holidays, 1100-1400, 1600-2000. Bus from Teatinos y O'Higgins, 45 mins.

Pomaire is a little town 65 km W of Santiago, where pottery can be brought and the artists can be observed at work. The area is rich in clay and the town is famous for its cider (*chicha de uva*, 3 strengths: *dulce*, *medio* and *fuerte*) and Chilean dishes; highly rec: *Restaurant San Antonio*, welcoming, semi-outdoor, good food and service.

● **Transport** Pomaire may be reached by Melipilla bus from C San Borja, Santiago, bus station behind Estación Central metro station, every few minutes, US$1 each way, Rutabus 78 goes on the motorway, 1 hr, other buses via Talagante take 1 hr 25 mins (alight at side road

to Pomaire, 2-3 km from town, colectivos every 10-15 mins); en route, delicious *pastel de choclo* can be obtained at *Restaurant Mi Ranchito*.

Vineyards Several vineyards in the Santiago area can be visited. *Cousiño-Macul*, Av Quilin on E outskirts of the city offer tours Mon-Fri, phone first T 238-2855. At Pirque, near Puente Alto, 40 km S of Santiago is the vineyard of *Concha y Toro*, T 850-3168, free entry, Mon-Sat and Sun pm, short tour (Spanish, English, French, German, Portuguese). Take 'La Puntilla' bus from Metro O'Higgins, 1 hr, US$1, asking to be dropped at Concha, or colectivo from Plaza Italia, US$2.50. The *Undurraga* vineyard at Santa Ana, SW of Santiago, T 817-2346, also permits visits with prior reservation only, 0930-1200, 1400-1600 on weekdays (tours given by the owner-manager, Pedro Undurraga). Take a Melipilla bus (but not Rutabus 78) to the entrance.*Viña Santa Carolina*, Rodrigo de Araya 1341, in Nuñoa, offers tours at weekends.

Horse-Breeding A specially rec excursion is to **Los Lingues**, a private *hacienda* 120 km S of Santiago, where it is said the best horses in Chile are bred. Rosie Swale was lent two of them for her epic ride from Antofagasta to Cape Horn, described in *Back to Cape Horn* (Collins, London, 1986). Visits can be arranged to the 17th century house, a gift of the King of Spain, at Hacienda Los Lingues, Torre C de Tajamar, Of 205, Santiago, T 235-2458/5446/7604, F 235-7604, Tx 346060 LINGUES CK. To 6060 LINGUE. 1-day tours including transport, rodeo and lunch are available, also accommodation with extra charge for breakfast or full board, very expensive (the Hacienda is a member of the French Hotels et Relais et Chateaux).

SKIING

There are 6 main ski resorts nr Santiago, 4 of them E of the capital.

Farellones, 51 km E of Santiago at 2,470m, and reached by road in under 90 mins is an excellent centre. High season: June to Sept/Oct, weather permitting. An excellent network of five ski-lifts. Beautiful views for 30 km across 10 Andean peaks. Incredible sunsets. Busy at weekends. Large restaurants. There are excursions for a day from Santiago at US$5 plus US$30 ski-lifts ticket ; enquire Ski Club Chile, Goyenechea Candelaria 4750, Vitacura (N of Los Leones Golf Club), T 211-7341.

● **Accommodation** *Motel Tupungato* (Candelaria Goyenechea 4750, Santiago, T 218-2216), **A3** pp *Refugio Club Alemán Andino* (address under **Skiing and Climbing**, above), hospitable, good food; *Colorado Apart Hotel* (Av Apoquindo 4900, Oficina 43, Santiago, T 246-0660, F 246-1447); *Posada Farellones*, highly rec.

Farellones is easily reached by buses from front of Omnium building, Av Apoquindo, 4 blocks from Escuela Militar Metro, daily at 0830, essential to book in advance, US$7. It is easy to hitch from the junction of Av Las Condes/El Camino Farellones (petrol station in the middle): take a Las Condes bus from C Merced almost to the end of the line.

La Parva 6 km further E. The upper class Santiago weekend resort which has 12 lifts, 0900-1730, where the runs are a little easier, though the snow may not be as good. In summer, this is a good walking area: a good trail leads to the base of Cerro El Plomo (6,050m, the southernmost Inca sacrificial peak – the ruins nr the summit are in good repair). Allow 3-4 days for the climb; ice axe and crampons necessary. Lift ticket, US$40, and equipment rental, US$10-15 depending on quality. (*Condominio Nueva Parva*, good hotel and restaurant, reservations in Santiago: Roger de Flor 2911, T 220 8510/206-5068.)

8 km SE of Farallones is **El Colorado** (accommodation in *Edificios Los Ciervos* and *Monteblanco*, in Santiago, San Antonio 486, Oficina 151), with 3 triple chairlifts and a ski lodge.

Valle Nevado (owned by Spie Batignolles of France), the site of the 1993 Pan American winter games is also nearby. Valle Nevado aims to be the largest ski resort in South America. Although incredibly expensive and not to everyone's taste, the resort is very highly regarded and much less crowded than the nearby resorts at weekends. There are 25 runs, two chairlifts, six skilifts and many more are planned; daily ski lift pass US$30 weekdays, US$42 weekends, joint El Colorado/Valle Nevado pass US$50 peak season, US$40 off-peak; similar prices for joint La Parva/Valle Nevado pass.

● **Accommodation L1** *Hotel Valle Nevado*, and more; *Hotel Puerta del Sol; Condominium Mirador del Inca*; 6 restaurants. *Casa Valle Nevado*, Gertrudis Echeñique 441, T 206-0027, F 228-8888.

Portillo (*Alt* 2,855m), 145 km N of Santiago and 62 E of Los Andes, on the route to Argentina, is another great centre for skiing and winter sports. The weather is ideal, the snow conditions excellent, the runs many and varied; 12 lifts carry skiers up the slopes. The season is from June to Sept/Oct, weather permitting. Lift pass US$40. Cheap packages can be arranged at the beginning and out of the season. There are some gentle ski slopes for beginners near the hotel. The major skiing events are in Aug and September. On three sides the mountains soften into snow-clad fields and finally slope gently into the Laguna de Inca, 5½ km long and 1½ km wide; this lake, at an altitude of 2,835m, has no outlet, is frozen over in winter, and its depth is not known. There are boats for fishing in the lake; but beware the afternoon winds, which often make the homeward pull 3 or 4 times as long as the outward pull. Out of season this is another good area for walking, but get detailed maps before setting out. Mules can be hired for stupendous expeditions to the glacier at the head of the valley or of the Cerro Juncal, to the pass in the W side of the valley.

● **Accommodation & places to eat L2** *Hotel Portillo*, cinema, night club, swimming pool, sauna and medical service, on the shore of Laguna de Inca; accommodation ranges from lakefront suites, full board, fabulous view, to family apartments to bunk rooms without or with bath (much cheaper, from C up), parking charges even if you go for a meal, jacket and tie must be worn in the dining room, self-service lunch, open all year. Reservations, Roger de Flor 2911, T 231-3411, F 699-2575, Tx 440372 PORTICZ, Santiago. Cheaper food available at *Restaurant Yuly* across the road, and *Restaurant Los Libertadores* at the customs station

1 km away. **L3** *Hostería Alborada*, inc all meals, tax and service. During Ski Week (last in Sept), about double normal rate, all inc. Reservations, Agencia Tour Avión, Agustinas 1062, Santiago, T 72-6184, or C Navarro 264, San Felipe, T 101-R.

● **Transport** In winter Portillo is easily reached from Santiago by daily bus services (except in bad weather). In summer, take any bus from Santiago or Los Andes to Mendoza and ask the bus driver to stop, you may have to hitch back.

Lagunillas is a favourite ski-resort 67 km SE of Santiago in the Maipo Valley (see above for details of transport to San José de Maipo). Accommodation in the lodges of the Club Andino de Chile (bookings may be made at Ahumada 47, Santiago). Tow fee US$20; long T-bar and poma lifts; easy field.

TO ARGENTINA

See under Santiago, **International Buses**. Check in advance on weather and road conditions before travelling beyond Los Andes. Route 57 runs N from Santiago to the rich Aconcagua Valley, the so-called Vale of Chile. North of Llaillay, at Km 69, the road forks – the E branch going to Los Andes, the W branch to **San Felipe** (*Pop* 42,000; *Alt* 635m; *Phone code* 034), the capital of Aconcagua Province, 96 km from Santiago and 128 km from Valparaíso. It is an agricultural and mining centre with an agreeable climate. Part of the Inca highway has recently been discovered in the city; previously, no traces had been found further S than La Serena. A paved highway (13 km) runs N from San Felipe to the old town of Putaendo.

● **Accommodation C** *Hostería San Felipe*, Merced 204, T 510508.

Termas de Jahuel is high in the Cordillera (1,190m) 18 km by road from San Felipe. The hill scenery includes a distant view of Aconcagua.

● **Accommodation L2** *Termas de Jahuel*, T 511240 or Santiago 393-810.

Curimón, between San Felipe and Los Andes, has a historic church, with a small museum attached.

Los Andes (*Pop* 30,500; *Alt* 730m; *Phone code* 034), 16 km SE of San Felipe and 77 km N of Santiago, is situated in a wealthy agricultural, fruit-farming and wine-producing area, but also the site of a large car assembly plant. It is a good place for escaping from Santiago and a convenient base for skiing at nearby Portillo. There are monuments to José de San Martín and Bernardo O'Higgins in the Plaza de Armas, and a monument to the Clark brothers, who built the Transandine Railway to Mendoza (now disused). Good views from El Cerro de la Virgen, reached by a trail from the municipal picnic ground on Independencia (1 hr).

Museums Museo Arqueologico de los Andes, O'Higgins y Santa Teresa, 10.30-1300,1500-1830, entry US$0.60.

● **Accommodation A1** *Baños El Corazón*, at San Esteban, T 421371, with full board, use of swimming pool but thermal baths extra, take bus San Esteban/El Cariño (US$0.50); **B** *Plaza*, Esmeralda 367, T 421929, good but restaurant expensive; **D** *Central*, Esmeralda 278, T 421275, reasonable and very friendly (excellent bakery opp, try the *empanadas*); **E** *Alameda*, Argentina 576, T 422403, without bath, clean; **F** pp *Res Maruja*, Rancagua 182, cheap, clean; **F** pp *Estación*, Rodríguez 389, T 421026, cheap restaurant; **F** *Valparaíso*, Sarmiento 160, clean.

● **Banks & money changers** Cambio Inter at Plaza Hotel, good rates, changes TCs.

● **Post & telecommunications Telephones**: CTC, O'Higgins 405.

● **Automovil Club de Chile** Chacabuco 33, T 422790.

● **Transport Trains** Rail service to Viña del Mar and Valparaíso (see under **Valparaíso**). **Buses** To Mendoza (Argentina) Tas Choapa, Fenix Pullman Nte, Cata and Ahumada. (Any of these will drop passengers off for Portillo, US$6). **Hitchhiking** Over Andes possible on trucks from Aduana building in Los Andes.

East of Los Andes the road to Argentina passes into the Cordillera and winds along the Río Aconcagua for 34 km until it reaches the village of **Río Blanco** (1,370m), set at the confluence of two rivers which form the Río Aconcagua: the Blanco and the Juncal. There is a fish hatchery with small botanical garden at the entrance of the Andina copper mine.

● **Accommodation** *Hostería Luna*, 4 km W, good value, clean, helpful, good food; *Hostería Guardia Vieja*, 8 km E, expensive but untidy, campsite.

● **Transport** Buses run daily from Los Andes; from Santiago, Ahumada, at 1930 daily, direct, 2 hrs, US$2.

FRONTIER WITH ARGENTINTA: LOS LIBERTADORES

The Redentor tunnel is open from 0800-1800 Chilean time, toll US$3. The old pass, with the statue of Christ the Redeemer (Cristo Redentor), is 8 km beyond the tunnel on the Argentine side. On the far side of the Andes the road descends 203 km to Mendoza.

● **Immigration & customs**
The Chilean border post at Caracoles is at Km 33 E of Río Blanco. There may be long delays during searches for fruit, meat and vegetables, which may not be imported into Chile. All luggage is X-rayed; remove all camera film before boarding bus as hand-luggage is not X-rayed.

Valparaiso and Viña del Mar

PACIFIC beaches close to the capital include the international resort of Viña del Mar and a variety of others. On the same stretch of coast is the port of Valparaíso.

VALPARAISO

Valparaíso (*Pop* 277,000; *Phone code* 032) capital of V Región (Valparaíso), is the principal port and second-largest city of Chile, and an important naval base. With the construction of a new congress building on Plaza O'Higgins, it is now the seat of the Chilean parliament. The city is situated on the shores of a sweeping bay and on a crescent of hills behind. Seen from the ocean, it presents a majestic panorama: a great circle of hills is backed by the snow-capped peaks of the distant Cordillera. The climate is good, for the summer heat is tempered by fresh breezes and sunshine mitigates the unkindness of a short winter. (The mean annual temperature is 15°C, with -1°C and 31°C as the extremes.)

Founded in 1536, the city became in the 19th century the major centre of British naval and commercial activity on the Pacific coast of South America, before declining in importance with the opening of the Panama Canal in 1914. Little of its colonial past has survived the sequence of pirates, tempests, fires and earthquakes, although a remnant of the old colonial city can be found in the hollow known as El Puerto, grouped round the low-built stucco church of La Matriz. Until recently, all buildings were low, as a precaution against earthquakes, but during the last few years modern multi-storey blocks have appeared. Most of the principal buildings date from after the devastating earthquake of 1906. There was another serious earthquake in July 1971 and, most recently, in Mar 1985.

Places of interest

There are two completely different cities. The lower part, known as **El Plan**, is the business centre, with fine office buildings on narrow streets strung along the edge of the bay. Above, covering the hills ('cerros'), is a fantastic agglomeration of fine mansions, tattered houses and shacks, scrambled in oriental confusion along the narrow back streets. Superb views over the bay are offered from most of the 'cerros'. The lower and upper cities are connected by steep winding roads, flights of steps and 16 *ascensores* or funicular railways dating from the period 1880-1914. The most unusual of these is **Ascensor Polanco** (entrance from C Simpson, off Av Argentina a few blocks SE of the bus station), which is in two parts, the first of which is a 160m horizontal tunnel through the rock, the second a vertical lift to the summit on which there is a *mirador*. Note that the lower entrance is in a slum area which is unsafe: do not go alone and do not take valuables.

The heart of the city is the **Plaza Sotomayor**, dominated by the former **Intendencia** (Government House), now used as the Regional Naval Headquarters. Opposite is a fine statue to the 'Heroes of Iquique' (see page 760). The passenger quay is 1 block away (handicraft shops on quay) and nearby is the railway station, from which passenger services run on the metropolitan line to Los Andes. The streets of El Puerto run on either side from Plaza Sotomayor. C Serrano runs NW for 2 blocks to the Plaza Echaurren, near which stands the church of **La Matriz**, built in 1842 on the site of the first church in the city. Further NW, along Bustamante lies the Plaza Aduana from where there is an *ascensor* to the bold

hill of **Cerro Artillería**, crowned by the huge Naval Academy and a park. To the W of the Cerro the Av **Playa Ancha** runs to a stadium, seating 20,000 people, on Cerro Playa Ancha. Avenida Altamirano runs along the coast at the foot of Cerro Playa Ancha to **Las Torpederas**, a picturesque bathing beach. The **Faro de Punta Angeles**, on a promontory just beyond Las Torpederas, was the first lighthouse on the W Coast; you can get a permit to go up. On another high point on the other side of the city is the **Mirador de O'Higgins**, the spot where the Supreme Dictator exclaimed, on seeing Cochrane's liberating squadron: 'On those four craft depends the destiny of America'.

Southeast of Plaza Sotomayor Calles Prat, Cochrane and Esmeralda run through the old banking and commercial centre to Plaza Aníbal Pinto, the most attractive square in Valparaíso. Further E is Plaza O'Higgins (flea market on Sat mornings), which is dominated by the imposing new Congress building. Several of the Cerros are worth visiting, notably Cerro Concepción, where the Anglican church dating from 1854 can be visited, and Cerro Bellavista, where you can visit the 'Museo Al Cielo Abierto', a collection of 20 murals painted on the exteriors of buildings (reached from Plaza de la Victoria).

The New Year is celebrated by a firework display on the bay, which is best seen from the Cerros.

Museums

Museo Municipal de Bellas Artes, with Chilean landscapes and seascapes and some modern paintings, housed in Palacio Baburizza, Paseo Yugoslavo, art nouveau palace overlooking harbour (free), open Tues-Sun 1000-1800; take *Ascensor El Peral* from Plaza Justicia, off Plaza Sotomayor. **Museo del Mar Almirante Cochrane**, housing collection of naval models built by local Naval Modelling Club, good views over port, Tues-Sun 1000-1800, free, take Ascensor Cordillera from C Serrano, off Plaza Sotomayor, to Cerro Cordillera; at the top, Plazuela Eleuterio Ramírez, take C Merlet to the left. **Museo Naval**, in the old Naval Academy on Cerro Artillería,

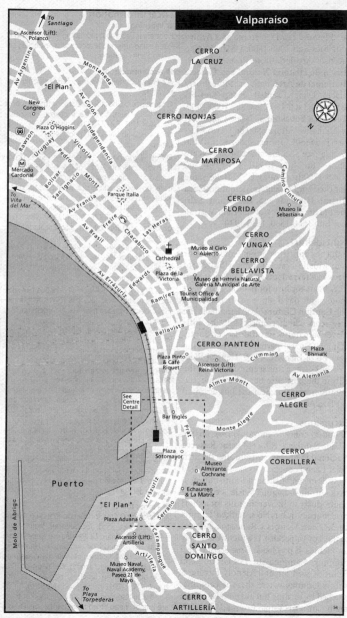

Valparaíso

To Santiago

Ascensor (Lift): Polanco

CERRO LA CRUZ

Av Argentina

Montaneda

"El Plan"

Av Colón

New Congress

Plaza O'Higgins

CERRO MONJAS

Rawson

Uruguay

Victoria

Pedro

Independencia

Mercado Cardonal

Bolívar

San Ignacio Montt

CERRO MARIPOSA

To Viña del Mar

Av Francia

Parque Italia

Camino Cintura

CERRO FLORIDA

Av Brasil

Freire

Chacabuco

Las Heras

Museo la Sebastiana

CERRO YUNGAY

Cathedral

Museo al Cielo Abierto

CERRO BELLAVISTA

Edwards

Plaza de la Victoria

Museo de Histrria Natural, Galeria Municipal de Arte

Av Errázuriz

Ramírez

Tourist Office & Municipalidad

Bellavista

CERRO PANTEÓN

Plaza Bismark

Plaza Pinto & Café Riquet

Ascensor (Lift): Reina Victoria

Cumming

Almte Montt

Av Alemania

CERRO ALEGRE

See Centre Detail

Bar Inglés

Pratt

Monte Alegre

CERRO CORDILLERA

Plaza Sotomayor

Museo Almirante Cochrane

Puerto

Plaza Echaurren & La Matriz

Molo de Abrigc

"El Plan"

Errázuriz

Plaza Aduana

Serrano

CERRO SANTO DOMINGO

Ascensor (Lift): Artillería

Artillería

Carrampangue

Museo Naval, Naval Academy, Paseo 21 de Mayo

To Playa Torpederas

CERRO ARTILLERÍA

54

Paseo 21 de Mayo, naval history 1810-1880, includes exhibitions on Chile's two naval heroes, Lord Cochrane and Arturo Prat, Tues-Sun 1000-1800, US$0.35 (take Ascensor Artillería from Plaza Aduana). **Museo de Historia Natural** and **Galería Municipal de Arte**, both in 19th-century Palacio Lyon, Condell 1546, Tues-Fri 1000-1300, 1400-1800, Sat/Sun 1000-1400. **Museo La Sebastiana**, Pasaje Collado 1, Av Alemania, Altura 6900 on Cerro Florida, T 256606, former house of Pablo Neruda (see also his house at Isla Negra below), Tues-Sun 1030-1430, 1530-1800 (closes 1700 June-Aug), US$2 (take Verde Mar Bus O or D along Av Alemania); **Casa Mistral**, Higueras 118, exhibition dedicated to life and work of Gabriela Mistral, Tues-Sun 1000-1330, 1530-1930.

Sightseeing

Launches run trips around the harbour from Muelle Prat, 30 mins, US$1.20, to Playa Las Torpederas and to Viña del Mar; other boats for hire for fishing. **NB** Don't photograph naval ships or installations. The **Camino Cintura**/Av Alemania is the only road which connects all the hills above Valparaíso; it affords constantly changing views, perhaps the best being from Plaza Bismark. No 9 'Central Placeres' bus gives a fine scenic drive over the hills to the port; also bus 'Mar Verde' (O) from Av Argentina near the bus terminal to Plaza Aduana.

Excursions

About 25 mins from Valparaíso, on the road to Santiago (Ruta 68) is the **Reserva Nacional Peñuelas**, surrounding the artificial Lago Peñuelas. Access is permitted for walking and fishing; administration at park entrance. Laguna Verde, a couple of hours' dusty walk over the hills (or a short road journey by bus No 3, marked 'Laguna Verde' from Victoria y Rancagua, hourly) to the S of Valparaíso, is a picturesque bay for picnics. **E** pp *Posada Cruz del Sur*, also camping. Camping site *Los Olivos*, good facilities, well run and friendly. Further S still is Quintay where there is camping; reached by turning left at Peñuelas on the main Santiago- Valparaíso road.

Local information

● **Warning**

Robbery is becoming increasingly common in El Puerto and around the *ascensores*, especially on Cerro Santo Domingo.

● **Accommodation**

A2 *Prat*, Condell 1443, T 253082, gloomy, restaurant.

C *Lancaster*, Chacabuco 2362, with bath and breakfast, clean; **C** *Reina Victoria*, Plaza Sotomayor 190, T 212203, D on top floors, without bath, with breakfast, poor beds, run down, clean.

D *Res Dinamarca*, Dinamarca 539 (from Plazuela Ecuador – just S of Condell y Bellavista – take any micro marked 'Carcel'; or climb 10 mins up Av Ecuador), hot water, clean, good value, also short stay, parking, not nr restaurants but serves full breakfast and snacks; **D** *Garden*, Serrano 501, T 252776, friendly, hot water, use of kitchen; **D** *Res Lily*, Blanco Encalada 866, T 255995, 2 blocks from Plaza Sotomayor, clean, safe (despite no locks on doors); **D** *Enzo and Martina Tesser*, Av Quebrada Verde, T 288873, with breakfast, German spoken, friendly (reached by bus 1).

E pp *Res Mi Casa*, Rawson 310, nr bus terminal, friendly, basic, fleas, also has rooms at Yungay 2842, quiet; **E** pp *Sra Mónica*, Av Argentina 322, Casa B, T 215673, 2 blocks from bus terminus, friendly; **E** pp *Sra Silvia*, Pje La Quinta 70, Av Argentina, 3 blocks from Congress, T 216592, clean, quiet, kitchen facilities, rec; **E** pp *Sra Anita*, Higuera 107, Cerro Alegre, with good breakfast, clean, hot water, wonderful views; **E** pp *María Pizarro*, Chacabuco 2340, Casa No 2, T 230791, clean, lovely rooms, central, quiet, kitchen, highly rec; her neighbours, Francisca Escobar and Guillermo Jones, Chacabuco 2326, T 214193, also rent rooms, same price, equally rec, English spoken. Many cheap hotels on Cochrane and Blanco Encalada, S of Plaza Sotomayor, but very few are recommendable. Many of the 'cheap' hotels in the Chacabuco area are for short-term occupation only. Youth hostel office at Edwards 695, p 3, will extend membership; nearest hostel in Viña del Mar.

● **Places to eat**

Al Galeone D'Oro, Independencia 1766, Italian, not cheap but good; *Tentazione*, Pedro Montt 2484, good, cheap; *La Parrilla de Pepe*, Pedro Montt 1872, good food and service; *Hamburg*, O'Higgins 1274, German management, German beer, beware of overcharging. *Del Mónico*, Prat 669, good, cheap lunches, popular; *La Rotunda*, Prat 701, good food; *Nantón*, Brasil 1368, Chinese, good. Around the market there are lots of cheap lunch restaurants, specialising

Valparaíso Centre

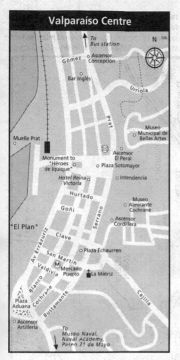

To Bus station
N
Gómez
Ascensor Concepción
Bar Inglés
Urriola
Prat
Muelle Prat
Museo Municipal de Bellas Artes
Monument to "Héroes de Iquique"
Ascensor El Peral
Plaza Sotomayor
Hotel Reina Victoria
Intendencia
Hurtado
Museo Almirante Cochrane
Goñi
Serrano
Ascensor Cordillera
"El Plan"
Clave
Plaza Echaurren
Av Errázuriz
San Martín
Valdivia
Mercado Puerto
La Matriz
Blanco
Cochrane
Cajilla
Bustamante
Plaza Aduana
Ascensor Artillería
To Museo Naval, Naval Academy, Paseo 21 de Mayo

in seafood inc *Los Porteños*, Valdivia 169, very good. At Caleta Membrillo, 1 km NW of Plaza Sotomayor there are several good fish restaurants inc *Club Social de Pescadores*, Altamirano 1480, good; opp are *San Pedro*, shabby but friendly, and *El Membrillo*, more expensive; other good places for lunch: *Nahuel*, Donoso 1498, popular, cheap; *Mesón del Lord*, Cochrane 859; *Bambú*, Pudeto 450, vegetarian.

Cafés and bars: *Riquet*, Plaza Anibal Pinto 1199, traditional, comfortable, expensive, good coffee and breakfast, rec; *Bar Inglés*, Cochrane 851 (entrance also on Blanco Encalada), good food and drink, traditional, rec, not cheap; *Cinzano*, Plaza Anibal Pinto 1182, old style bar/restaurant, popular; *Westfalia*, Cochrane 847, coffee, breakfasts, vegetarian lunches; *Café do Brasil*, Condell 1342, excellent coffee, juices, sandwiches; *Turri*, Templemann 147, on Cerro Concepción, T 259196, overlooking port, good food and service.

● **Airline offices**
LanChile, Esmeralda 1048, T 251441; Ladeco, Blanco Encalada 951, T 216355.

● **Banks & money changers**
National banks. Open 0900 to 1400, but closed on Sat. Good rates at **Banco de Santiago**, Prat 816, and **Banco de Crédito e Inversiones**, Cochrane 820; **Fincard** (Mastercard), Esmeralda 1087; **Exprinter**, Prat 887 (the building with the clocktower at junction with Cochrane), good rates, no commission on TCs, open 0930-1400, 1600-1900; **Inter Cambios**, Errázuriz esq Plaza Sotomayor, good rates; **Gema Tour**, Esmeralda 940; **New York**, Prat 659, good rates for cash; **Afex**, Cochrane 828. When *cambios* are closed, street changers operate outside *Inter Cambios*.

● **Cultural centres**
Instituto Chileno-Norteamericano, Esmeralda 1069, shows foreign films.

● **Embassies & consulates**
British Consul, Blanco Encalada 725, oficina 26, T 256117, Casilla 82-V; Argentine Consul, Cochrane 867.

● **Entertainment**
Proa Al Canaveral, Errázuriz 304, good seafood restaurant downstairs, pleasant bar upstairs with dancing from 0100, poetry reading on Thur; several popular bars on Ecuador, some with live music and small entry charge.

● **Hospitals & medical services**
Dentist: *Dr Walther Meeden Bella*, Condell 1530, Depto 44, T 212233.

● **Laundry**
Las Heras 554, good and cheap

● **Post & telecommunications**
Telecommunications: VTR Telecommunications, Cochrane 825; CTC, Esmeralda 1054 or Pedro Montt 2023; Entel, Condell 1491.

● **Shopping**
Bookshop: *Librería Universitaria*, Esmeralda 1132, good selection of regional history. *Librería Ivens*, Plaza Anibal Pinto, specializing in up-to-date French and German newspapers; many others.

● **Tourist offices**
In the Municipalidad building, Condell 1490, Oficina 102, open Mon-Fri 0830-1400, 1530-1730. Kiosks at bus terminal (good map available), helpful, open 0900-1300, 1530-1930 (closed Thur, Mar-Nov), Muelle Prat, open Nov-March 1030-1430, 1600-2000, and in Plaza Victoria, open 1030-1300, 1430-2000 Nov-March.

● **Useful addresses**
YMCA: (Asociación Cristiana de Jóvenes), Blanco Encalada 1117; **YWCA**: (Asociación Cristiana Feminina), Blanco 967. **Valparaíso Seamen's Institute**: Blanco Encalada 394.

● **Transport**
Local Taxis: are more expensive than Santiago:

a short run under 1 km costs US$1. **Buses** Buses and modern electric buses, US$0.20 within city limits. **Funiculares** US$0.30.

Trains Regular service on Merval, the Valparaíso metropolitan line between Valparaíso, Viña del Mar, Quilpue, Limache, Quillota, La Calera, Llaillay, San Felipe and Los Andes (and intermediate stations); to Viña del Mar every 15-30 mins,

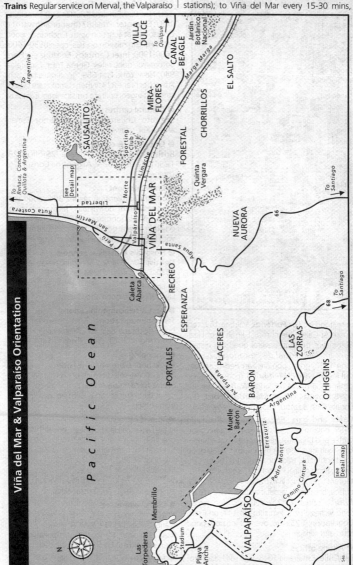

Viña del Mar & Valparaíso Orientation

trains that run the entire route are 1800 daily, 1430 Mon-Fri (not holidays), 0805, Sat, Sun and holidays, fare to Los Andes US$1.50, 3 hrs. *El Porteño* tourist train runs on Sun, 1 Jan-28 Feb and on most public holidays.

Shipping For shipping services from Valparaíso to the Juan Fernández Islands and Easter Island see below under **The Chilean Pacific Islands**.

Buses Excellent and frequent bus service to **Viña del Mar** (25 min) US$0.25 from Plaza Aduana, passing along Av Errázuriz; colectivos to Viña US$0.40. Terminal is on Pedro Montt 2800 block, corner of Rawson, 1 block from Av Argentina; plenty of buses between terminal and Plaza Sotomayor. To **Santiago**, 2 hrs, US$3-4, shop around, frequent (book on Sat to return to the capital on Sun); to **Concepción**, 11 hrs, US$12; to **Puerto Montt**, 17 hrs, US$18. **La Serena**, 8 hrs, US$10. To **Calama**, US$35. To **Arica**, US$40, Fénix *salón cama* service, US$50. To Argentina: to **Mendoza**, 4 companies, 6-7 hrs, US$25; to **Córdoba**, US$40.

If driving from Santiago the main road passes through two tunnels, toll of US$3.25 paid at the first, but this can be avoided by turning off onto the old road over the mountains about 1 km before the tunnels; there is another toll just before the start of the motorway, 56 km from Santiago.

Hitchhiking To Santiago is easy from service station on Av Argentina.

FROM VALPARAISO TO ARGENTINA

If driving from Valparaíso to the Argentine border, Route 62 runs through Viña del Mar, climbs out of the bay and goes through (16 km) **Quilpue**, 1½ km E of El Retiro, a popular inland resort with medicinal springs and a municipal zoo. It crosses a range of hills and reaches the Aconcagua Valley at **Limache**, a sleepy market town, 40 km from Valparaíso (*Pop* 22,511). 8 km E of Limache is Olmué, beyond which is **Parque Nacional La Campana**, an area of native woodland, including the Chilean palm (*kankán*), much varied birdlife, and the Cerro La Campana which Darwin climbed in 1836. Extensive views from the top, but a guide may be necessary because there are a number of ascents, some of which are very difficult. Route 62 joins Route 60 just before **Quillota**, an orchard centre (**B** *Balneario El Edén*, 5 km out of town, cabins for rent, up to 6 people, very good restaurant in an old estate building, T 311963, F 312342, good swimming), continuing to La Calera (88 km from Valparaíso), where it joins the Pan-American Highway; turn SE and E for Llaillay, San Felipe, Los Andes and the Redentor tunnel to Mendoza.

VINA DEL MAR

Viña del Mar (*phone code* 032), one of the foremost South American seaside resorts, is 9 km NE of Valparaíso by one of the innumerable express buses, which run along a narrow belt between the shore and precipitous cliffs. Halfway, on the hill of Los Placeres, is the Universidad Técnica. The popular bathing resort of El Recreo is passed, then Caleta Abarca with its crowded beaches, floral clock and big *Hotel Miramar*. Beaches are often closed because of pollution.

Places of interest

Follow the street signs for a self-guided tour of Viña del Mar's sights. At the entrance to Viña del Mar there is a steep bluff, worth climbing for the views over Viña from its *paseos*. Here also is **Cerro Castillo**, the summer palace of the Presidents of the Republic. Below, to the left, is the lagoon of the **Marga Marga**, crossed by a bridge which leads direct to the **Casino**, built in the 1930s and set in beautiful gardens, US$6 to enter, jacket and tie for men required (open all year).

The **Teatro Municipal** is on Plaza Vergara. The **Palacio Rioja**, the former mansion of a Spanish banker, dating from 1906, can be visited (Quillota y 3 Nte – see **Museums** below). Near the **Valparaíso Sporting Club** with its racecourse and playing fields are the Granadilla Golf Club and a large stadium. In the hills behind is a large artificial lake, the **Laguna Sausalito**, adjacent to Estadio Sausalito (home to Everton soccer team, among many other sporting events). It possesses an excellent tourist complex with swimming pools, boating, tennis courts, sandy beaches, water skiing, restaurants, etc. Entry US$2.50, children under 11, US$1.75; take colectivo No 19 from C Viana.

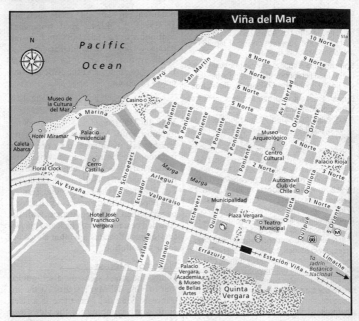

One of the sights is the municipally owned **Quinta Vergara**, superb gardens with a double avenue of palms (highly recommended). The **Palacio Vergara**, in the gardens, houses the Museo de Bellas Artes and the Academia de Bellas Artes. Part of the grounds is a children's playground, and there is an outdoor auditorium where concerts and ballet are performed in the summer months, and in Feb an international song festival is held.

The Song Festival is lively, with the emphasis more on the 'shows' of the special guests, famous latino singers, and European and local rock bands than on the unknown contestants. Schedules may be delayed to fit in with TV programming. Take warm clothes if staying till the end. Tickets from the Municipalidad US$3-US$15, seats are numbered so no need to arrive till 2100. For the final evening touts sell tickets outside the Quinta Vergara.

Southeast of the city is the **Jardín Botánico Nacional**, formerly the estate of the nitrate entrepreneur Pascual Baburizza, administered by CONAF. There are over 3,000 species but they are not labelled. Take bus 20 from Plaza Vergara, entry US$1.

Museums

Museo de la Cultura del Mar, in the Castillo Wulff, contains a collection on the life and work of the novelist and maritime historian, Salvador Reyes, Tues-Sat 1000-1300, 1430-1800, Sun 1000-1400; **Museo de Bellas Artes**, Quinta Vergara, Tues-Sun 100-1400, 1500-1800, US$0.25; **Palacio Rioja**, Quillota 214, built at turn of century by a prominent local family and now used for official municipal receptions, ground floor preserved in its original state, open to visitors 1000-1400, 1500-1800, Tues-Sun, rec. **Museo Sociedad Fonk**, C 4 Nte 784, archaeological museum, with objects from Easter Island and the Chilean mainland, including Mapuche silver, open Tues-Fri 1000-1800, Sat-Sun 1000-1400, entry US$0.20. An Easter Island statue stands on the lawn between the railway and the beach just beyond Caleta Portales, between Viña del Mar and Valparaíso. **Centro Cultural**, Libertad 250, holds regular exhibitions.

Local festivals

El Roto, 20 Jan, in homage to the workers and peasants of Chile.

Local information

● **Accommodation**

Many in L3-A3 range, some with beach.

L3 *San Martín*, San Martín 667, T 689191, with breakfast.

A2 *Alborada del Mar*, San Martín 419, T 975274, tastefully decorated; **A2** *Español*, Plaza Vergara 191, T/F 685145, with bath, TV, phone and *Restaurante Colonial*; **A2** *José Francisco Vergara*, Dr von Schroeders 392, T 626022, has garden houses for up to 5; **A3** *Res Offenbacher Hof*, Balmaceda 102, T 621483, clean, friendly, rec; **A3** *Monte Carlo*, V MacKenna 136, 6 km N in Reñaca, T 830397, very modern, comfortable.

B *Alejandra*, 2 Pte 440, T 974404, with shower and breakfast (C in low season); **B** *Balia*, von Schroeders 36, T 978310, F 680724, bath, TV, phone, parking; **B** *Petit Palace*, Paseo Valle 387, T 663134, small rooms, good, central, quiet, **B** *Quinta Vergara*, Errázuriz 690, T 685073, clean, friendly, large rooms, beautiful gardens, rec.

C *Capric*, von Schroeders 39, T 978295, with bath, TV, good value; **C** *El Escorial*, two places: one at 5 Pte 114, the other at 5 Pte 441 (T 975266), with breakfast, shared bath, clean, central. **C** *Res Magallanes*, Arlegui 555, T 685101, with breakfast, clean, mixed reports; *Res Victoria*, Valparaíso 40, T 977370, without bath, with breakfast, clean, central; **C** *Res Villarica*, Arlegui 172, good, friendly.

D *Res Agua Santa*, Agua Santa 34, basic, hot shower; **D** *Res Blanchait*, Valparaíso 82, T 974949, clean, with breakfast, hot water, good service; **D** *Res Familiar*, Batuco 147, clean, friendly; **D** *Res France*, Montaña 743, clean, safe, helpful; **D** *Sra Nalda*, 2 Nte 849 (Pasaje Klamer), T 970488, good garden, cooking facilities, rec; **D** *Res Tajamar*, Alvarez 884, opp railway station, old-fashioned, central, huge rooms, atmospheric. There are a great many more places to stay inc private accommodation (E pp). Out of season furnished apartments can be rented through agencies (with commission). In season it is cheaper to stay in Valparaíso and commute to the Viña beaches.

Camping: *Camping Reñaca*, Santa Luisa 401,

expensive, dirty, also cabins.

Motels: several at Reñaca (6 km N of Viña del Mar).

Youth hostels: **E** pp *Res La Montaña*, Agua Santa 153, T 622230, for YHA card holders, with breakfast, other meals available, dingy, dirty bathroom, no cooking facilities, also family rooms; **E** pp *Lady Kinnaird Hostal*, 1 Ote 1096, T 975413, YWCA, central, friendly, English spoken, women only, highly rec.

● **Places to eat**

At hotels. *Cap Ducal*, Marina 51, expensive; *Raul*, Valparaíso 533, live music; *Casino Chico*, Valparaíso 99, Chilean and international dishes; *Panzoni*, Pasaje Cousiño 12-B, good lunches, Italian; *Machitún Ruca*, San Martín 529, excellent. *Pizzería Mama Mía*, San Martín 435, good, reasonably priced; *Armandita*, San Martín 501, *parrilla*, large portions, good service; *El Encuentro*, San Martín 477, fish, very good; *Las Gaviotas*, 14 Nte 1248, Chilean meat dishes, not expensive, live music. Many restaurants on Av Valparaíso, try in the Galerías (arcades), eg *Café Big Ben*, No 469, good coffee, good food; *Alster*, No 225, expensive; *Samoiedo*, No 637, *confitería*, grill and restaurant. Several pleasant restaurants and cafés along the renovated Muelle Vergara inc *La Mía Pappa*, Italian, good lunches and evening buffets. *Centro Vital*, Av Valparaíso 376, vegetarian, excellent lunches.

In Reñaca: *El Pancho*, Av Borgoño 16180, excellent seafood and service; *Anastassia*, Av Borgoño 15000, excellent international menu, expensive; *Rincón Marino*, Av Borgoño 17120, good seafood, pricey; *Hotel Oceanic*, Av Borgoño, T 830006, very good, expensive.

● **Banks & money changers**

Many *casas de cambio* on Arlegui inc *Afex*, No 641 (open 0900-1400 Sat); *Cambio Norte*, No 610; *Cambio Andino*, No 644; also in the tourist office. *Fincard* (Mastercard), Ecuador 259.

● **Cultural centres**

Instituto Chileno-Británico, 3 Nte 824, T 971061; Instituto Chileno – Norteamericano de Cultura, 3 Nte 532, T 662145; Casa Italia (cultural centre, consulate, restaurant), Alvarez 398; Goethe Institut, El Salto, 20 mins from town; Instituto Chileno-Francés, Alvarez 314, T 685908.

● **Entertainment**

Discotheques: *Topsy Topsy*, Santa Luisa 501 and *La Cantina del Cocodrilo*, Av San Martín, both in Reñaca, expensive, rec; *El Gato de la Luna*, Arlegui 396, good bar, live music and dancing.

● **Post & telecommunications**

Telephone: CTC, Valparaíso 628; Global Telecommunications/Entel, 15 Nte 961.

● **Shopping**
Market: at intersection of Av Sporting and river, Wed and Sat.

● **Tourist offices**
Valparaíso 507, Of 303, T 882285. Arrangements may be made at the Tourist Office for renting private homes in the summer season. **Automóvil Club de Chile**: 1 Nte 901, T 689509.

● **Transport**
Local Car hire: Euro Rent-A-Car, in *Hotel O'Higgins*, clean cars, efficient.

Air Ladeco Santiago-Viña del Mar (to naval airfield nr Concón), several daily, 10 mins, US$15, T 978210; National T 883505; Alta, Av Libertad 22, local 1, T 692920, F 692917.

Trains Services on the Valparaíso Metropolitan line (Merval) stop at Viña (details under Valparaíso).

Buses Terminal at Av Valparaíso y Quilpué. To **Santiago**, US$3-4, 2 hrs, frequent, many companies (heavily booked in advance for travel on Sun afternoons); to **La Serena**, 6 daily, 8 hrs, US$10, to **Antofagasta**, 20 hrs, US$35.

RESORTS NORTH OF VIÑA DEL MAR

There is a very fine drive N of Viña del Mar along the coast (many motels) through Las Salinas and Reñaca to Concón, then inland to Quintero. Las Salinas, a beach between two towering crags, is very popular. Beyond Reñaca beach, 6 km N, very popular, is Cochoa with its large sealion colony, 100m offshore.

Concón, on the S shore of a bay at the mouth of the Río Aconcagua, is 12 km N of Reñaca. Main attractions: tennis, bathing, fishing, and riding. Main eyesore: an oil refinery (not visible from beach; some pollution). Near the Concón beach there is a pelican colony. There is also an inland road, much faster than the coast road, between Viña del Mar and Concón.

● **Accommodation L2** *Hostería Edelweis*, Av Borgoño 19200, T 903600, modern cabins, clean, comfortable, sea views, inc breakfast, excellent food in attached restaurant, German spoken, highly rec; several motels; **D** *Cabañas Koala Place*, Los Pescadores 41, T 813026.

● **Places to eat** Good seafood *empanadas* at bars; *Vista al Mar*, Av Borgoño 21270, T 812-221, good fish restaurant, good value; *Don Chico*, Av

Borgoño 21410, good seafood; *Mirador Cochoa*, Av Borgoño 17205, good, pricey.

Quintero, another 16 km N of Concón, is a fishing village and the naval aviation centre. On the N shore of the bay at Las Ventanas are a power station and copper processing plant.

● **Accommodation A2** *Yachting Club*, Luis Acevedo 1736, T 930061; **D** *Isla de Capri*, 21 de Mayo 1299, T 930117, pleasant, sea views; **D** *Monaco*, 21 de Mayo 1530, T 930939, run down but interesting, good views. A number of Residenciales.

Horcón (also known locally as Horcones), set back in a cove surrounded by cliffs, is a pleasant small village, mainly of wooden houses. On the beach hippies sell cheap and unusual jewellery and trinkets. Vegetation is tropical with many cacti on the cliff tops. Seafood lunches with the catch of the day, sold at any number of stalls on the seafront, are recommended. It is best avoided in Jan-Feb when it is packed out. Drinking alcohol on the beach is forbidden – and enforced by the *carabineros*.

● **Accommodation B** *El Ancla*, cabañas, pleasant; **C** *Cabañas* on Playa Cau Cau, good; **C-B** *Aranciba*, with bath, **D** without, pleasant gardens, good food, friendly, rec; also rooms in private houses; no campsite but camping possible at private houses.

● **Places to eat** *El Ancla* rec; *Reina Victoria*, cheap, good.

From Las Ventanas the road continues N past Maitencillo (wonderful beach; hotels, *cabañas*) to the fashionable resort of **Zapallar** (33 km N of Las Ventanas). There are several fine mansions along Av Zapallar. 3 km S at Cachagua a colony of penguins may be viewed from the northern end of the beach. No cars are allowed on the Zapallar seafront. Excellent bathing, but water is cold.

● **Accommodation A1** *César*, T 711313, very nice but dear; **A3** *Isla Seca*, T 711508, small, pool, good restaurant; good, reasonably-priced food in *Restaurant César* (different management from hotel), on seafront; no *Residenciales*, no campsite.

Papudo, 10 km further N, rivalled Viña del Mar as a fashionable resort in the 1920s but has long since declined.

● **Accommodation D** *Moderno*, F Concha

150, T 711496; *D' Peppino*, No 609, T 711482; many more.

● **Transport** Buses from Valparaíso and Viña del Mar: To **Concón** bus 9 or 10 (from Av Libertad between 2 and 3 Nte in Viña), US$0.50; to **Quintero** and **Horcón**, Sol del Pacífico, every 30 mins, US$1, 2 hrs; to **Zapallar** and **Papudo**, Sol del Pacífico, 4 a day (2 before 0800, 2 after 1600), US$3.

RESORTS NEAR THE MOUTH OF THE RIO MAIPO

SAN ANTONIO

112 km S of Valparaíso and 113 km from Santiago, the Río Maipo flows into the sea near the port of **San Antonio** (*Pop* 60,000; *Phone code* 035). Its shipping has grown considerably, mostly at the expense of Valparaíso, and it has a fishing port and fishmeal plants. The port exports copper brought by rail from the large mine at El Tte, near Rancagua. A motorway connects it to the capital. South of San Antonio are **Llolleo** (4 km) at the mouth of the Maipo, a famous resort for those who suffer from heart diseases, and 7 km further than **Rocas de Santo Domingo**, the most attractive and exclusive resort in this area with 20 km of beaches and a golf course; even in high season it is not very crowded.

● **Accommodation** At **San Antonio**: **C** *Jockey Club*, 21 de Mayo 202, T 31302, best good views, restaurant; **D** *Colonial*, Pedro Montt 196. At **Llolleo**: **D** pp *Oriente*, Inmaculada Concepción 50, T 32188; *Res El Castillo*, Providencia 253, T 373821. At **Santo Domingo**: **B** *Rocas de Santo Domingo*, La Ronda 130, T 231348; no cheap accommodation – try Llolleo.

● **Transport** Buses to Valparaíso, Pullman Bus, every 45 mins until 2000, US$2; to **Santiago**, Pullman Bus, every 20 mins, US$2.

CARTAGENA

8 km N of San Antonio is the biggest resort on this part of the coast. The administrative centre lies around the Plaza de Armas, situated on top of the hill. To the S is the picturesque Playa Chica, overlooked by many of the older hotels and restaurants; to the N is the Playa Larga. Between the two a promenade runs below the cliffs; high above hang old houses, some in dis-

repair but offering spectacular views. Cartagena is a very popular resort in summer, but out of season especially it is a good centre for visiting nearby resorts; there are many hotels and bus connections are good.

● **Accommodation** **D** *Biarritz*, Playa Chica, T 32246; **D** *La Bahía*, Playa Chica, T 31246; **D** *Violeta*, Condell 140, T 234093, swimming pool, good views; **E** pp *El Estribo*, just off Plaza de Armas, with breakfast, **E** pp full board, basic, cheap *comedor*; **E** pp *Res Carmona*, Playa Chica, T 212199, small rooms, basic, clean, good value.

NORTH OF CARTAGENA

There are several small resorts including **Las Cruces**, **El Tabo** and **El Quisco**, a small fishing port with 2 beautiful white beaches (very expensive and crowded during Chilean holidays).

Algarrobo, 29 km N of Cartagena, is the largest of these and the most chic, with its large houses, yacht club, marina and penguin island (no entry). In summer there are boat tours round the island from the jetty.

In the village of **Isla Negra**, on the road between El Tabo and El Quisco is the beautifully-restored **Museo-Casa Pablo Neruda**, containing artefacts gathered by Neruda from all over the world. It is open for guided tours in Spanish, English or French (last two only after 1500), Tues-Sun 1015-1230, 1500-1800, in summer 1000-1745, US$2, T 035-212284 for opening hours or to book English guide (see also his house, La Chascona, under Santiago **Museums**, and La Sebastiana, under Valparaíso **Museums**). Tours from Santiago, departing at 0900 from Plaza de Armas (Compañía y Ahumada), cost US$23.75 and include seaside resorts, T 232-2574.

● **Accommodation** At **Las Cruces**: **D** *La Posada*, T 233520, good birdwatching.

At **El Tabo**: **C** *Hotel El Tabo*, T 33719, quite nice, and *Motel El Tabo*, T 212719, next door (overfull in Jan-Feb); 2 cheap and basic campsites. At **Isla Negra**: **B** *Hostería Santa Elena*, beautiful building and location, restaurant, some rooms damp and gloomy. At **El Quisco**: (accommodation generally expensive); **C** *Motel Barlovento*, T 481030; *Residenciales* 100-200m from beach in **C** range, eg *Res Oriental*,

T 481662, with breakfast, good, clean, hot water; **D** pp *Cabañas del Irlandés Volador*, Aguirre 277, T 473464; **D** *Res Julia*, Aguirre 0210, T 481546, very clean, quiet, good value, rec; **D** *Cabañas Pozo Azul*, Capricornio 234, SE of town, quiet; **D** *El Quisco*, Dubournais 166, with breakfast, clean, open weekends only; others on this avenue. Excellent seafood restaurant *La Caleta*, Isidoro Dubournais 166 (main street).

At Algarrobo: C *Costa Sur*, Alessandri 2156, T481151; **D** *Uribe*, behind *Costa Sur*, T 481035, pleasant, quiet; **D** *Vera*, Alessandri 1521, with breakfast, good; **E** pp *Res San José*, Av Principal 1598, basic, no hot water.

• **Transport** Buses between Algarrobo and Santiago, Pullman Bus, every 20 mins, 2 hrs, US$3, stopping in Cartagena and the resorts along the coast (but not San Antonio). Services between Algarrobo and San Antonio also by Empresa de Buses San Antonio (frequent, last bus around 2000) and Empresa Robles.

From Santiago to La Serena

THE chief interest remains on the coast as the land becomes less fertile. The largest resort is La Serena, from where access can be made to the pisco-producing Elqui Valley and to one of the world's astronomical centres.

From the Río Aconcagua to the Río Elqui is a transitional zone between the fruitful heartland and the northern deserts. The Andes and coastal *cordillera* merge; several rivers, the largest being the Limarí, cut through the highlands. The first stretch of the Pan-American Highway from Santiago is through green valleys with rich blue clover and wild artichokes. Then it mainly follows the coastline, which is relatively flat, passing many beautiful coves, alternatively rocky and sandy, with good surf, but the water is very cold, as is the air. It only rains in winter so the vegetation is characteristic of semidesert (dry scrub and cactus), except in those areas where condensation off the sea provides sufficient moisture for woods to grow. On the coast the average temperature is 14°C, rising to 16-17° inland. Irrigated land produces abundant fruit.

LOS VILOS

Los Vilos (*phone code* 051), 216 km N of

Santiago, is a former mineral port, now a small seaside resort with frequent launches to the off-shore Isla de Los Huevos and Isla de Los Lobos. 26 km S is a beautiful beach at **Pichidangui** (*phone code* 053). **Los Molles**, 10 km S of Pichidangui is a small town where many wealthy residents of Santiago have their summer homes. There are two small hotels, one down at the beach and the other on the cliff overlooking the beach.

- **Accommodation Los Vilos**: *C Hostería Arrayán*, Caupolicán 1, T 541005, clean; *C Lord Willow*, Hostería 1444, T 541037, overlooking beach and harbour, with breakfast and bath, pleasant, parking, weekend disco next door; *D Bellavista*, Rengo 20, T 541073, with breakfast, without bath, hot water, clean; *F pp Res Angelica*, Caupolicán 627, central, warm water, restaurant attached, expensive camping

(US$13/site). The *American Motel* is right on the highway, Km 224, T 541020, and is a convenient stopping place between Viña del Mar or Santiago and La Serena, quite good. In **Pichidangui**: *Motel El Bosque*, El Bosque s/n, T 541182, rec; *B Motel Pichidangui*, Francis Drake s/n, T 594010, swimming pool; *C Puquen*, 2 Pte s/n, attractive, good value; various other hotels and *pensiones* in every price range. **Camping**: No campsite in Los Vilos; two good sites in Pichidangui, US$10 in season, bargain for lower price off season.

- **Places to eat** In Los Vilos *Restaurant Costanera*, good views over ocean, good meals, expensive. Restaurants in Pichindangui tend to be pricey although there is a food shop.

- **Transport** Only 1 bus daily Pichidangui-Santiago, but N-S buses (eg Inca Bus) on the Highway pass 3 km from the towns. **Driving** See page 746 for list of service stations between Santiago and the Peruvian border.

Illapel, 59 km NE of Los Vilos, 287 km N of Santiago, lies in the basin of the Río Choapa (hotels; *Pop* 25,600). Fruit, grains and cattle are raised in the valley.

OVALLE

The centre of a fruit, sheep-rearing, and mining district 412 km N of Santiago, **Ovalle** (*Pop* 53,000; *Phone code* 053) lies inland in the valley of the Río Limarí. Market days are Mon, Wed, Fri and Sat, till 1600; the market (*feria agrícola*) is on Benavente. The town is famous for its *talabarterías* (leather workshops) and for its products made of locally-mined lapis lazuli. The Paloma dam, at the confluence of the Ríos Grande and Huatulame, SE of Ovalle, is one of the largest in Chile.

Museums
Museo del Limarí, Independencia 329, open Tues-Sun 1000-1600, displays on petroglyphs and a good collection of Diaguita ceramics and other artefacts.

Excursions
The **Monumento Nacional Valle del Encanto**, about 22 km SW of Ovalle, has Indian petroglyphs as well as dramatic boulders, its own microclimate, cacti and lizards (open Mon-Fri 0900-1300, 1500-1900, Sat 0900-1300, 1500-1800, Sun 1000-1300, US$2). No local bus service; you must take a long distance bus and ask to

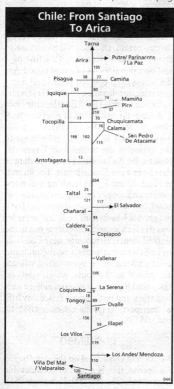

Chile: From Santiago To Arica

Tacna

Arica — Putre/ Parinacota / La Paz
195
Pisagua — 38 — 77 — Camiña
Iquique — 52 — 80
— 74 — Mamiña
243 — 43 — 210 — Pica
Tocopilla — 73 — 70 — Chuquicamata
— 16 — Calama
189 — 102 — 115 — San Pedro De Atacama
Antofagasta — 13
264
Taltal — 25
121 — 117 — El Salvador
Chañaral — 93
Caldera — 74
— Copiapoó
150
— Vallenar
198
Coquimbo — La Serena
18
Tongoy — 89 — Ovalle
37
156 — 59 — Illapel
Los Vilos
119
Viña Del Mar / Valparaiso — 110 — Los Andes/ Mendoza
120
Santiago
64A

be dropped off – 5 km walk to the valley; flag down a bus to return. Camping facilities.

Termas de Socos, 35 km SW of Ovalle, has fine thermal springs (entrance US$5), a good hotel (**A2**, T Ovalle 621373, Casilla 323) and a campsite (US$10 per tent, but bargain) nearby. Bus US$2.

Parque Nacional Fray Jorge, 50 km W at the mouth of the Río Limarí, is approached by a poor road leading off the Pan-American Highway (very poorly signposted). Its forests, usually covered in fog, contrast with the otherwise barren surroundings. Open Sat, Sun and public holidays only, 0830-1830; visits closely controlled due to risk of fire. (Scientific groups may obtain permission to visit from The Director, Conaf, Cordóvez 281, La Serena, T 211124.) Round trip in taxi, US$30.

Some 47 km NE along an unpaved and largely winding road is the **Monumento Nacional Pichasca** (open 0830-1700, US$3). It has petrified tree trunks, archaeological remains, including a vast cave (comparable to the Cueva Milodón outside Puerto Natales) with remains of ancient roof paintings, and views of gigantic rock formations on the surrounding mountains. Daily bus from Ovalle to Río Hurtado passes the turn off (to San Pedro) about 42 km from the city. From here it is 3 km to the park and about 2 km more to sites of interest.

Local information
● **Accommodation**
D *Res Bristol*, Araucano 224, pleasant spacious building, restaurant. On Libertad: **D** *Francia*, No 231, T 620828, pleasant, friendly, restaurant; **D** *Roxy*, No 155, T 620080, constant hot water, clean, friendly, patio, *comedor*, highly rec; **E** *Venecia*, No 261, T 620968, clean, safe, friendly, rec; **E** *Res Socos*, Socos 22, T 624157, clean, quiet, family run, rec. For cheaper accommodation try **G** *Res Lolita*, Independencia 274, without bath, F with, clean, basic, rec. Several other cheap *Residenciales* in C Socos (short stay).

● **Places to eat**
Club Social, V MacKenna 400 block, excellent fish dishes though pricey; *Club Social Arabe*, Arauco 255, spacious glass-domed premises, limited selection of Arab dishes, good but not cheap; *El Quijote*, Arauco 294, intimate atmosphere, good seafood, inexpensive; *Alamar*, Santiago 259, excellent seafood, good value. Good value *almuerzos* at *Casino La Bomba*, Aguirre 364, run by fire brigade. For drinks and snacks try *Café Caribe Express*, V MacKenna 241; *Yum Yum*, V MacKenna 21, good, cheap, lively; *D'Oscar Bar*, Plaza de Armas; *Pastelería Josti*, Libertad 427. *Club Comercial*, Aguirre 244 (on plaza), open Sun.

● **Shopping**
For articles made of Lapis Lazuli try Sr Wellington Vega Alfaro at his workshop at Vicente Ovando 660, Población Yungay, T 621951.

● **Tourist offices**
Two kiosks on the Plaza de Armas. **Automóvil Club de Chile**, Libertad 144, T 620011, very helpful, overnight parking.

● **Transport**
Buses to **Santiago**, several, 6½ hrs, US$7; to **La Serena**, 12 a day, 1¼ hrs, US$2; to **Antofagasta**, US$20.

ANDACOLLO

The good inland road from Ovalle N to La Serena makes an interesting contrast to Ruta 5 (Panamericana), with a fine pass and occasional views of snowcapped Andes across cacti-covered plains and semi-desert mountain ranges. 61 km N of Ovalle a side road runs 44 km SE to the little town of **Andacollo**, last 20 km of road very bad. Here, on 24 to 28 Dec a picturesque religious ceremony is held, the pilgrimage to the shrine of the miraculous Virgen del Rosario de Andacollo. The ritual dances date from a pre-Spanish past. The church is huge. Alluvial gold washing and manganese and copper mining in the area. No hotel, but some *pensiones*; during the festival private houses rent beds and some let you pay for a shower. Colectivos run to the festival from C Benavente, near Colocolo, in La Serena, but 'purists' walk (torch and good walking shoes essential). 2 villages are passed on the route, which starts on the paved highway, then goes along a railway track and lastly up a steep, dusty hill.
● **Transport** To **Ovalle** colectivo, US$2.40; bus, US$1.70.

COQUIMBO

84 km N of Ovalle and on the same bay as La Serena, this is a port of considerable importance (*Pop* 106,000; *Phone code* 051).

It has one of the best harbours on the coast and major fish-processing plants. The city is strung along the N shore of a peninsula. Most of the commercial life is centred on 3 streets which run between the port and the steep hillside on which are perched many of the poorer houses. On the S shore of the peninsula lies the suburb of Guayacán, with an iron-ore loading port and a steel church designed by Eiffel. Nearby is **La Herradura**, 2½ km from Coquimbo which has the best beaches. Also nearby is a resort complex called *Las Tacas*, with beach, swimming pool, tennis, flats, *apart-hotel*, etc.

Museums

In 1981 heavy rain uncovered 39 ancient burials of humans and llamas which had been sacrificed. A small museum has been built in the Plaza Gabriela Mistral to exhibit these.

Excursions

To **Totoralillo**, 12 km S where there are good beaches (good swimming).

25 km further S is **Guanaqueros** a fishing village with beaches (**D** *Hotel La Bahía*, clean, simple). A further 13 km S is **Tongoy**, an old fishing port occupying the whole of a small peninsula. It is now a rapidly growing resort and well worth a visit: to the Sthe Playa Grande is 14 km long; to the N the Playa Socos is 4 km in length.

Local information
● **Accommodation**
Coquimbo: generally much cheaper than in La Serena. **B** *Lig*, Aldunate 1577, T 311171, comfortable, friendly, good value, nr bus terminus; **C** *Prat*, Bilbao y Aldunate, T 311845, comfortable, pleasant; **C** *Iberia*, Bandera 206, p 8, T 671-4510, friendly, rec; **D** *Punta del Este*, Videla 170, T 312768, nice rooms; **E** *Claris*, Aldunate 669, run-down, old-fashioned, rambling hotel with bar and *comedor*, live music on Fri and Sat, popular with sailors; **E** *Mi Casa*, Varela 1653, clean, friendly, good value. Several hotels in La Herradura, inc **C** *Hotel La Herradura*, Costanera 200, T 321320.

Camping: *Camping La Herradura*, T 312084.

Tongoy: **A2** *Panorámico*, Mirador 455, T 391944, inc breakfast, all rooms with view of bay and fishing boats, excellent, clean, friendly; **A1-B** *Hotel Yachting Club*, Costanera 20,

T 391154, good; *Samay*, overlooking fishing port, T 391355; **E** *Plaza*, on main square, T 391184; several basic *Residenciales*.

● **Places to eat**
Lots of good fish restaurants in **Coquimbo** inc *Sal y Pimiento del Capitán Denny*, Aldunate 769, one of the best, pleasant, old-fashioned, mainly fish, US$12-20 pp; *La Picada*, Costanera nr statue of O'Higgins, excellent, pricey; *Crucero*, Aldunate 1326, excellent; *La Barca*, Ríos y Varela, modest but good; and *La Bahía*, Pinto 1465, excellent, good value. Several good seafood restaurants (known as *pensiones*) at the municipal market, Melgarejo entre Bilbao y Borgoño (*El Callejón* rec); *Mai Lai Fan*, Av Ossandón 1, excellent Chinese, rec; *Tavola Calda*, Bilbao 451, good Italian, good value.

In **Tongoy**: try the *marisquerías* nr the fishing port, excellent value. *Restaurant El Buque*, Puesto 17 on seafront, nr fishing harbour, fish and meat with superb sauces, good service, highly rec.

● **Post & telecommunications**
Telephones: CTC, Aldunate 1633.

● **Tourist offices**
Kiosk in Plaza de Armas (open summer only).

● **Transport**
Buses leave from new bus terminal at Varela y Garriga. To La Serena, every few mins, US$0.30. To Guanaqueros, US$0.80, 45 mins, and to Tongoy, US$1, 1 hr, with Ruta Costera, frequency varies according to day (more on Sun) and season. Colectivos US$1.40 and US$1.70 respectively.

LA SERENA

La Serena (*Pop* 120,000; *Phone code* 051), 12 km N of Coquimbo, 473 km N of Santiago, is the capital of IV Región (Coquimbo). Built on a hillside 2 km inland from Bahía de Coquimbo, it has many neo-colonial buildings and pretty gardens.

Places of interest

Around the attractive Plaza de Armas are most of the official buildings, including the Post Office, the **Cathedral** (built in 1844 and featuring a carillon which plays every hour) and the Historical Museum (see below). There are 29 other churches, several of which have unusual towers. **San Francisco**, Balmaceda y de La Barra, has a nice façade and is on a small plaza with handicraft stalls and arcades covered with purple flowers. **Santo Domingo**, half a block from the Plaza de Armas is fronted by a small garden with statues of sealions. **La Recova**, the new market, at Cienfuegos y Cantournet, includes a large display of handicrafts and, upstairs, several good restaurants. On the W edge of the old city is the Parque Pedro de Valdivia, which includes a children's zoo and the Parque Japonés, open daily 1000-2000, US$1.25. A *moai* from Easter Island can be seen on Av Colo Colo, direction Vicuña, about 15 mins' walk from the centre; there is a view of the city from here. A pleasant boulevard, Av Francisco de Aguirre (known as the **Alameda**), runs from the centre to the coast, terminating at the **Faro Monumental**, a neo-colonial style mock-castle (US$0.45 entry). A series of beaches stretch from here to Peñuelas, 6 km S, linked by the Av del Mar. Many apartment blocks, hotels, *cabañas* and restaurants have been built along this part of the bay.

History

La Serena was founded by Juan de Bohón, aide to Pedro de Valdivia, in 1544, destroyed by Diaguita Indians in 1546, rebuilt by Francisco de Aguirre in 1552, and sacked by the English pirate Sharpe in 1680. Legends of buried treasure at Bahía la Herradura de Guayacán, frequented by pirates, persist. The present-day layout and architectural style has its origins in the 'Plan Serena' drawn up in 1948 on the orders of Chilean president, Gabriel González Videla, a native of the city.

Museums

Historical museum in the Casa Gabriel González Videla on the Plaza de Armas, including several rooms on the man's life. Open Tues-Sat 0900-1300, 1600-1900, Sun 1000-1300, entry US$0.60, ticket also valid for **Museo Arqueológico**, Cordóvez y Cienfuegos, interesting collection of Diaguita and Molle Indian exhibits, especially of most attractively decorated pottery; open Tues-Sat 0900-1300, 1600-1900, Sun 1000-1300, entrance, US$0.30. There is a **mineralogical museum** in the University of La Serena, C A Muñoz between Benavente and Infante (for geologists, open Mon-Fri 0930-1200, free).

Local information

● Accommodation

Accommodation in the centre of town is expensive. Route 5 from La Serena to Coquimbo is lined with cheaper accommodation, from hotels to *cabañas*, and restaurants. There are no buses along Av del Mar, but it is only ½ km off Route 5. The tourist office in the bus terminal has accommodation information, helpful.

L3 *El Escorial I*, Colón 617, T 224793, F 221433, good; **L3** *Los Balcones de Alcalá*, Av de Aguirre 452, T 225999, F 211800, comfortable, clean, TV; **L3** *Mediterráneo*, Cienfuegos 509, Casilla 212, T 225837, inc good breakfast, rec.

A2 *Francisco de Aguirre*, Córdovez 210, T 222991, with breakfast, shower, good rooms, reasonable restaurant; **A2** *Pucará*, Balmaceda 319, T 211966, F 211933, with bath and breakfast, modern, clean, quiet; **A3** *Berlín*, Córdovez 535, T 222927, F 223575, clean, safe, efficient, rec.

C *Londres*, Córdovez 550, T 214673, with bath, **D** without, restaurant, old fashioned; **C** *Brasilia*, Brasil 555, T 225248, friendly, small rooms, overpriced; **C** *Hostal Croata* Cienfuegos 248, T/F 224997, with bath, **D** without, with breakfast, laundry facilities, cable TV, patio, hospitable, rec; **C** *Hostal Del Mar*, Cuatro Esquinas 0680 (nr beach), T 225816, also *cabañas*, clean, friendly.

D *Alameda*, Av de Aguirre 450, T 213052, run down, clean and comfortable; *Hostal Santo Domingo*, Bello 1067, 10 mins' walk from bus station, with breakfast, highly rec; **D** *Lido*, Matta 547, T 213073, hot water, clean, friendly; **D** *Res Chile*, Matta 561, T 211694, basic, small rooms, clean, hot water am only; **D** *El Cobre*, Colón y Matta, large rooms, spotless, friendly owners, highly rec; **D** *Res El Loa*, O'Higgins 362, with shower, good inexpensive home cooking, friendly; **D** *Res Petit*, de la Barra 586, T 212536, hot water; **D** *Turismo 2000*, Lautaro 960, T 215793, hot water, bargain; **D** *Lautaro 880*, hot water, clean, rec; **D** *Gabriela Matos*, Cienfuegos 230, T 214588, in beautiful old building, use of kitchen, helpful, rec; **D** *Casa del Turista*, Colón 318, clean, back rooms better, laundry facilities, helpful; **D** *San Juan*, Balmaceda 827, clean, central.

E *Gregoria Fernández G*, Andrés Bello 979A, T 224400, highly rec, clean, friendly, good beds; **E** *Rosa Canto*, Cantournet 976, T 213954, hot water, kitchen, comfortable, family run, rec; **E** pp Las Rojas 21, T 215838, nr terminal, use of kitchen, clean, friendly; **E** pp *Alejandro Muñoz*, Brasil 720, T 211619, with breakfast, good showers, English and French spoken, helpful, rec; **E** Adolfo Ballas 1418, T 223735; **E** pp *Ana Jofre*, Rgto Coquimbó 964 (entre Perú y Amunátegui), T 222335, kitchen facilities, nr bus terminal, rec.

F pp unnamed *Res* at Av de Aguirre 411, in dormitories, clean.

Youth Hostel: **E** pp *Res Zimmat*, Lautaro 974, T/F 211373 central, breakfast extra, patio, tours offered, English and German spoken, IYHA reduction, rec.

Motels: **A1** *Canto del Agua*, Av del Mar 5700, T 242203, F 241767, very good, pleasant cabins; **A3** *Les Mouettes*, Av del Mar 2500, T 225665, F 226278, good restaurant, inc breakfast, rec; **B** *Cabañas Los Papayos*, Huerto 66, 2 km S of city (Vista Hermosa bus), much cheaper out of season, 2 bedroom cabins, rec, pool, gardens; **B** *La Fuente*, Av del Mar 5665, T 245755, F 541259, appartments, cable TV, parking, very good; several more motels along the beach.

Camping: *Camping Peñuelas*, Los Pescadores 795, T 313818. *Maki Payi*, 153 Vegas Nte, T 213628, about 5 km N of La Serena, nr sea, friendly, rec, self-contained cabins available. *Hipocampo*, 4 km S on Av del Mar (take bus for Coquimbo and get off at Colegio Adventista, US$2.50 pp by Playa El Pescador), T 214276.

● **Places to eat**
El Granero, Colón 360, excellent steaks, reasonably priced; *Club Social*, Córdovez 516, p 1, unpretentious but excellent value; *El Rincón Colonial*, Córdovez 578, good fish; *Hotel La Serena*, Córdovez 610, good meat. *Ciro's*, Aguirre 431, T 213482, old-fashioned, good lunch, rec; *El Cedro*, Prat 572, Arab cuisine, expensive; *Mesón Matias*, Balmaceda 1940, excellent Spanish, elegant, expensive but highly rec; *La Mía Pizza*, O'Higgins 460, Italian, good value, inexpensive (branch on Av del Mar in summer); *Mai Lai Fan*, Córdovez 740, good Chinese, reasonably priced; *Salón Las Tejas*, Francisco de Aguirre 395, cheap, local dishes; *Chopería Don Antonio*, Vicente Zorrilla 837-9, 20m from *La Recova* market, friendly, good value. For good, fish lunches try the restaurants on the upper floor of the Recova market.

Several good cafés: *Tito's*, O'Higgins y Córdovez, popular meeting place; *Café do Brasil*, Balmaceda 461, good coffee; *Casa Miró*, Balmaceda 265, good for coffee and late evening drinks; *Café La Créperie*, O'Higgins y de la Barra, crêpes, light meals, occasional live music; *Bocaccio*, Prat y Balmaceda, good cakes, modern, smart, popular; *Café del Patio*, Prat 470, sandwiches, cakes and coffee, English spoken, rec; *Vadinho*, Balmaceda 545, open late. Note that the quality of restaurants, especially

on Av del Mar, varies considerably; often the majority of what is on the menu is not available.

● **Airline offices**
LanChile, T 225981; Ladeco, Córdovez 484, T 225753; National, Eduardo de la Barra 435, T 214460, F 232808; Alta, Los Carrera 515, T 212832, F 215671.

● **Banks & money changers**
Fincard (Mastercard), Balmaceda 383, Local 217, Mon-Fri 0900-1400, 1600-2030. Banco Concepción, O'Higgins 529, Visa. *Casas de Cambio*: La Reconquista, in a galería on Córdovez between Balmaceda and O'Higgins, excellent rates; US$100 Money Exchange, Prat 645, Mon-Fri 0900-1400, 1600-2100, Sat 0900-1400; Viajes Val, Prat 540 (open Sat 1100-1400); La Portada, Balmaceda 515; Serena Cambios at bus terminal and airport, open 1100-2300 daily; Cambio Fides, Caracol Colonial, Balmaceda 460, good rates, changes TCs (another *cambio* in the basement, building closed 1400-1600). If heading N note that La Serena is the last place to change TCs before Antofagasta.

● **Laundry**
Ro-Ma, Los Carrera 654, open 0900-1300, 1600-2000; another at Balmaceda y Brasil.

● **Post & telecommunications**
Telecommunications: long distance calls from Córdovez 446 and La Recova market. Entel, Prat 571. CTC administration on Plaza de Armas sells *Turistel*.

● **Shopping**
La Recova handicraft market, though many items imported from Peru and Bolivia; *Cema-Chile*, Los Carrera 562; *Las Brisas* supermarket, Cienfuegos y Córdovez, food not as cheap as in *La Recova*. 24-hr supermarket on corner of Cienfuegos, 30m from *alojamiento* at No 324.

● **Sports**
Gimnasio GFU, Amuñategui 426, T 222420, and *Vitalia*, Córdovez 756, T 221939.

● **Tour companies & travel agents**
Ingservitur, Los Lirios 300, Coquimbo, T 313821, F 312943, varied programme of tours, inc Parque Nacional Fray Jorge (see page 712), depending on demand; *San Bartolmé*, Brasil 415, T/F 221992; *Gira Tour*, Prat 689, T 223535; *Turismo Elquitur*, Los Carrera 594, T 227875.

● **Tourist offices**
Main **Sernatur** office in Edificio de Servicios Públicos (next to the Post Office on the Plaza de Armas), T 225138, open Mon-Fri 0900-1300, 1500-1730. Kiosks at bus terminal (summer only) and at Balmaceda y Prat (open in theory

Mon-Sat 1100-1400, 1600-1900), helpful. **Automóvil Club de Chile**: Eduardo de la Barra 435, T 225279.

● **Transport**
Local Buses City buses US$0.25; taxis US$0.75 + US$0.10/every 200m. **Car hire**: Hertz, Francisco de Aguirre 0225, T 225471/226171, Budget, Av de Aguirre 0240; Daire, Prat between O'Higgins and Cienfuegos, rec as cheapest, good service. **Bicycle repairs**: Green Go Club, Panamericana Nte y Aguirre, T 224454, North American run, good parts, information on local cycle routes.

Air Ladeco flies to **San Juan**, Argentina, in summer only. To **Santiago** and **Copiapó**, Lan Chile, Ladeco and National.

Buses Bus terminal, El Santo y Amunategui (about 8 blocks S of the centre). Buses daily to **Santiago**, several companies, 7-8 hrs, US$14; to **Arica**, US$30; to **Calama**, US$18, 16 hrs. To **Valparaíso**, 7 hrs, US$10; to **Caldera**, 7 hrs, US$10; to **Antofagasta**, 11 hrs, several companies, US$20 (Flota Barrios cama US$38), and to **Iquique**, 17 hrs, US$25. Bus to **Vicuña**, Frontera Elqui, Av Perú y Esmeralda, frequent service, 1 hr, US$1.50; *colectivo* to Vicuña, Empresa Nevada del Sol de Elqui, Domeyko 550, T 21450, others from Av Aguirre y Balmaceda, US$2; to **Coquimbo**, bus No 8 from Av Aguirre y Cienfuegos, US$0.30, every few mins.

OBSERVATORIES

The La Serena district is one of the astronomical centres of the world, with three observatories:

El Tololo, 89 km SE of La Serena in the Elqui Valley, 51 km S of Vicuña, which belongs to Aura, an association of US and Chilean universities. This possesses the largest telescope in the southern hemisphere, eight others and a radio telescope. It is open to visitors every Sat 0900-1200, 1300-1600, only by permit obtained from Casilla 603, La Serena, T 051-225-415, and then pick up your free permit the day before (the office is at Colina Los Pinos, on a hill behind the new University – personal applications can be made here for all three observatories). During holiday periods apply well in advance. At other times you may be able to book the day before. They will insist that you have private transport; you can hire a taxi, US$33, but you will require the registration number when you book.

La Silla, 150 km NE of La Serena, which belongs to ESO (European Southern Observatory), financed by 8 EC countries, comprising 14 telescopes. Open first Sat of the month, 1430-1730, no permission required; for prior information and registration (essential), Alonso de Córdoba 3107, Santiago, T 228-5006/698-8757, or write to Casilla 567, La Serena, T 224-527. Office also at bus terminal. From La Serena it is 114 km to the turn-off (**D** *Posada La Frontera*, cabañas), then another 36 km.

Las Campanas, 156 km NE of La Serena, 30 km N of La Silla, belonging to the Carnegie Institute, has 4 telescopes and is altogether a smaller facility than the other two. It is open without permission every Sat 1430-1730, T 224680/211254, or write to Casilla 601, La Serena. Go to the same junction as for La Silla, then 40 km in a different direction. For La Silla and Las Campanas those without private transport can take the 1100 Pullman Fichtur bus towards Vallenar (2 hrs, US$3.25) and get out at the junction (*desvío*); hitch from there.

Tours Travel agents in La Serena inc Ingservitur, Gira Tour and Turismo Cristóbal, receive tickets from the observatories and arrange tours (to Tololo US$22 pp), though you may need to reserve several days in advance in holiday periods.

THE ELQUI VALLEY

La Serena is at the mouth of the Elqui river valley, where the Nobel Prize-winning poet Gabriela Mistral was born. She described the valley as "confined yet lofty, many-sided yet simple, rustic yet a mining area". The branches of the road up the valley all lead to "fertile nooks, to shady vegetation, to dense groves, to gardens fed by the very sap of the hills". Of the *elquinos*, the people of the valley, she says that "even the most taciturn of them come out with witty and charming remarks". There are still a few descendants of the Diaguitas, the tribe that inhabited the valley at one time. The road up the valley is paved as far as Varillar, 24 km beyond Vicuña, the capital of the valley. Except for Vicuña, most of the tiny towns have but a single street. There are mines, orchards, orange groves and vineyards in the valley, which is the main pisco-producing area of Chile, the climate and soil being ideally suited to the cultivation of grapes with a high sugar-content. Of the 9 Pisco distilleries in the valley, the largest is Capel in Vicuña. Huancara, a delicious liqueur introduced by the Jesuits, is also produced in the valley.

VICUNA

66 km E of La Serena, a small, clean, friendly, picturesque town (*Pop* 6,000; *Phone code* 051). On the W side of the plaza are the municipal chambers, built in 1826 and topped in 1905 by a prefabricated medieval-German-style tower – the Torre Bauer – imported by the German-born mayor of the time. Inside the chambers is a gallery of past local dignitaries. Also on the plaza is the Iglesia Parroquial. Tourist office on Plaza de Armas. There are good views from Cerro La Virgen, N of town. The Capel Pisco distillery is 1½ km E of Vicuña, to the right of the main road; guided tours (in Spanish) are offered Dec-Feb, Mon-Sat 0930-1200, 1430-1800, Sun 1000-1230; Mar-Nov, Mon-Fri 0930-1200, 1430-1800, Sat 1000-1230; free; no booking required.

Museums The **Museo Gabriela Mistral** is at C Gabriela Mistral y Riquelme (open Tues-Sat 0900-1300, 1500-1900, Sun 1000-1300, entry US$0.40).

● **Accommodation L3** *Hostería Vicuña*, Sgto Aldea 101, T 411301, F 411144, swimming pool, tennis court, excellent restaurant; **A2** *Yunkai*, O'Higgins 72, T 411195, F 411593, cabañas for 4/6 persons, pool, restaurant. On Gabriela Mistral: **C** *Valle Hermoso*, No 706, T 411206, clean, comfortable, rec; **D** *Sol del Valle*, at No 743, hot water, TV, vineyard, restaurant; **E** *Hostal Michel*, No 573, large gardens; **E** *Res Moderna*, at No 718, full board available, no hot water, nothing modern about it, but quiet, clean, very nice; **E** pp *Res Mistral*, at No 180, restaurant, basic, hot water, clean. **Camping**: *Camping y Piscina Las Tinajas*, E end of Chacabuco, swimming pool, restaurant.

● **Places to eat** Mainly on G Mistral: *Club Social de Elqui*, at No 435, very good, attractive patio, good value *almuerzo*; *Mistral*, at No 180, very good, popular with locals, good value

almuerzo; *Halley*, at No 404, good meat dishes, also *chopería*, swimming pool (US$5 pp); *Yo Y Soledad*, No 364, inexpensive, good value; *Pizzeria Virgos*, on plaza.

● **Transport** Buses to **La Serena**, about 10 a day, most by Frontera Elqui, first 0800, last 1930, 1 hr, US$1.50, *colectivo* from Plaza de Armas US$2; to **Santiago** via La Serena, Expreso Nte at 1145 and 2200; to **Pisco Elqui**, 4 a day, Vía Elqui and Frontera Elqui, 1 hr, US$2.

From Vicuña the road continues up the valley another 18 km to Rivadavia where it divides: the main route (Route 41) winding through the mountains to the Argentine frontier at Agua Negra (see below). The other branch of the road runs through Paihuano (camping) and **Monte Grande** (where the tomb of Gabriela Mistral is situated) to **Pisco Elqui** (one bus a day to La Serena).

● **Accommodation C** *Carillón*, pool, also cabanas (B); **E** pp *Hostería de Don Juan*, with breakfast, fine views, noisy; **E** *El Elqui*, hot shower, good restaurant, rec, not always open; *Las Vegas* campsite, **F** pp, *Sol de Barbosa*, also camping; *Camping El Olivo*, G pp, no hot water.

Beyond Monte Grande, on the road to El Colorado, are several Ashram places, some of which welcome visitors; one can camp. Bus from Vicuña plaza to Monte Grande US$1.20.

FRONTIER WITH ARGENTINA: PASO AGUA NEGRA

Paso Agua Negra (4,775m) is reached by unpaved road from Rivadavia, 18 km E of Vicuña.

● **Immigration**
Chilean emigration and customs at Juntas, 84 km W of the frontier, 88 km E of Vicuña. Open 0800-1700; US$2/vehicle, 1700-2200, Jan-April only.

● **Accommodation**
Basic accommodation at Huanta (Guanta on many maps) Km 46 from Vicuña, G, clean, ask for Guillermo Aliaga. Huanta is the last chance to buy food.

● **Transport**
No public transport. El Indio mine transport may give lifts to Juntas.

North of La Serena

T HE northern desert begins beyond the mining and agro-industrial centre of Copiapó.

North of the Río Elqui, the transitional zone continues to Copiapó. Thereafter begins the desert, which is of little interest, except after rain. Then it is covered with a succession of flowers, insects and frogs, in one of the world's most spectacular wildlife events. Rain, however, is rare: there is no rain in summer; in winter it is light and lasts only a short time. Annual precipitation at Copiapó is about 115 mm. Drivers must beware of high winds and blowing sand N of Copiapó.

VALLENAR

(*Pop* 47,000; *Phone code* 051; airport) This is the chief town of the Huasco valley, 194 km N of La Serena. The valley is an oasis of olive groves and vineyards. It is rugged and spectacular, dividing at Alto del Carmen into the Carmen and Tránsito valleys. There are Pisco distilleries at Alto del Carmen (30 km) and San Félix (**F** *Res San Félix*, basic). A sweet wine known as Pajarete is also produced.

Museums

Near the municipal stadium is the **Museo del Huasco**, containing artefacts from the valley (Tues-Fri 1030-1230, 1530-1900; Sat-Sun 1000-1230).

To **Freirina**, 36 km W of Vallenar, easily reached by colectivo. Founded 1752, Freirina was the most important town in

the valley, its prosperity based upon the nearby Capote goldmine and on later discoveries of copper. On the main plaza are the Municipalidad (1870) and the Santa Rosa church. No accommodation.

At Domeyko, 51 km S of Vallenar, a turning W goes to Caleta Chañaral on the coast, where is the **Humbolt Penguin Natural Reserve**. On Isla Chañaral, besides penguins, there are seals, sea lions, a great variety of seabirds and, offshore, a colony of grey dolphin. Permission to visit must be sought from Conaf in Caleta Choros.

Local information
● Accommodation
L3 *Hostería Vallenar*, Ercilla 848, T 614538, excellent, pool, Hertz car hire office, restaurant reputed to be among the best in Chile; **C** *Real*, Prat 881, T 613963, parking; **C** *Vall*, Aconcagua 455, T 611226, rec.

D *Cecil*, Prat 1059, T 614071, with bath and hot water, clean, rec; **D** *Viña del Mar*, Serrano 611, T 611478, clean, *comedor*, smoking disapproved of. Several *Residenciales*.

● Places to eat
Bavaria, Santiago 678, good, not cheap; *El Fogón*, Ramírez 944, for meat dishes, *almuerzo* good value; *Shanghai*, Ramírez 1267, Chinese; cheap places along S end of Av Brasil.

HUASCO

(*Pop* 7,000) A pleasant town and interesting port 56 km W at the mouth of the river. 1½ km S of Huasco is a terminal for loading iron ore from the deposits at Algarrobal, 52 km N of Vallenar.

● **Accommodation & places to eat** **B** *Hostería Huasco*, Craig y Carrera Pinto, T 531026; *Restaurant Escorial*, best; cheap seafood restaurants nr port.

COPIAPO

Copiapó (*Pop* 100,000; *Phone code* 052), capital of III Región (Atacama), 144 km N of Vallenar, is situated 60 km inland in a ribbon of farms, vineyards and orchards about 150 km long on the Río Copiapó, the river generally regarded as the southern limit of the Atacama desert. It is an important mining centre with a big mining school.

Places of interest

There is a monument to Juan Godoy, a mule-driver, who, in 1832, discovered silver at Chañarcillo (see below). The plaza is interesting, with a wooden Cathedral dating from 1851.

Museums

The best **mineralogical museum** in Chile is at Colipí y Rodríguez, 1 block E from Plaza de Armas; Mon-Fri 1130-1300, 1500-1900, Sat 1000-1300, US$0.50. Many ores shown are found only in the Atacama desert. Also **Museo Regional del Atacama**, Atacama y Rancagua, entrance US$0.75 (free on Sun), interesting. Open Mon-Sat 0900-1245, 1500-1830, Sun 1000-1245. The museum at the **railway station** is dull, but the steam locomotive used in the inaugural journey between Copiapó and Caldera in 1851 (the earliest railway line in South America) can be seen at the Universidad de Atacama on the northern highway.

Excursions

90 km SE up the river valley from Copiapó is the **Centro Metalúrgico Incaico**, a largely reconstructed Inca bronze foundry, connected by a paved road. By public transport: take Casther bus, 0845, to Valle del Cerro, US$1.50, 2 hrs and get off at Valle Hermoso (foundry is 1 km walk from main road). Return buses pass about 1400 and 1600. No accommodation in nearby villages of Los Loros, Villa Hermoso, Las Juntas.

59 km S of Copiapó on the Pan-American Highway is a signposted turning to **Chañarcillo**. This was one of the 19th century's richest silver mines, becoming the second largest in the Americas. The tips are being reworked and this has destroyed much of the ruins.

Local information
● **Accommodation**

A2 *Hostería Las Pircas*, Av Kennedy s/n, T 213220, bungalows, pool, dining room, out of town; **A2** *San Francisco de la Selva* Los Carrera 525, T 217013, modern.

C *Derby*, Yerbas Buenas, 396, T 212447, clean; **C** *Inglés*, Atacama 337, T 212797, old-fashioned, spacious; **C** *Palace*, Atacama 741, T 212852, patio, pleasant, parking; **C** *La Ca-*

sona, O'Higgins 150, T 217277/8, clean, friendly, tours organized; **C** *Marcoan*, Yumbel 351, T 211397, modern.

E pp *Res Chacabuco*, C Chacabuco 271, T 213428, nr bus terminal, quiet, clean; **E** *Res Nuevo Chañarcillo*, Rodríguez 540, T 212368, without bath, comfortable, rec; **E** *Res Rodríguez*, Rodríguez 528, T 212861, basic, friendly, good *comedor*, rec; **E** *Res Rocío*, Yerbas Buenas 581, T 215360, good value, clean, attractive patio, rec.

● **Places to eat**

La Carreta, on Carretera de Copayapu, 5 km S, ranch-style, very good meat and fish; *Bavaria*, on main square, good but not cheap. *Chifa Hao Hua*, Colipí 340, good Chinese; *Pampas*, Maipú y Atacama, smart, pleasant.

● **Banks & money changers**

Fincard (Mastercard), Chacabuco 389, open Mon-Fri 0900-1400, 1630-1930, Sat 1030-1300. **Banco Concepción**, cash advance on Visa.

● **Post & telecommunications**

Telephones: CTC, Atacama 566.

● **Tour companies & travel agents**

Exploration and Adventure Tour, Rodríguez 771, T 212459, organize a wide range of excursions.

● **Tourist offices**

Los Carrera 691, N side of Plaza de Armas, T 212838, helpful.

● **Transport**

Local Car hire: expensive: Av Kennedy 310, T 2964; **Hertz** at Copayapu 173, T 211333. **Cycle repairs**: *Biman*, Atacama 360B, T/F 217391, excellent.

Air LanChile, O'Higgins 640, T 213512, daily to/from Santiago, also to El Salvador; National (Colipí 350, T 218951) direct to La Serena and on to Santiago.

Buses To Santiago US$15, 12 hrs; to La Serena US$7, 5 hrs; to Caldera, US$2, 1 hr.

FRONTIER WITH ARGENTINA: PASO SAN FRANCISCO

Paso San Francisco is reached either by unpaved road NE from Copiapó, via the Salar de Maricunga and Laguna Verde or by an unpaved road SE from El Salvador: the two roads join near the Salar de Maricunga. Officially open all year, this crossing is liable to closure in winter. On the Argentine side a poor road continues to Tinogasta (suitable only for 4WD vehicles).

● **Chilean immigration and customs**
Near the Salar de Maricunga, 100 km W of the frontier, open 0830-1830; US$2/vehicle charge for crossing Sat, Sun and holidays.

South of the pass rises the **Ojos del Salado** mountain, believed to be the third highest peak in the Americas; its height is now thought to be 6,864m (although the latest Chilean IGM map says 6,879m – 1994; it seems to depend which side of the border you are on).

To climb Ojos del Salado, allow 12-14 days for a climbing expedition. Base camp for the climb is at the Argentine frontier post (4,500m). There are 2 refugios, at 5,200m (4 beds) and 5,700m (6 beds). From the latter it is 10-12 hrs climb to the summit, approx grade 4. Take water from Capiapó. Guides and equipment can be hired in Capiapó (Rubén E Rubilan Cortes, O'Higgins 330, T 216536, and others) US$450-600.

NORTH FROM COPIAPO

There are 2 alternative routes N: W to Caldera and then N along the coast to Chañaral, 167 km; the inland route via Diego de Almagro and then W to meet the Pan American Highway near Chañaral, 212 km.

CALDERA

73 km W of Copiapó is the port of **Caldera** (*Pop* 12,000; *Phone code* 052), which has a pier of 230m; 1½ km to the S there is a terminal for the loading of iron ore. There is a fruit inspection for all passing through Caldera going S; this applies to bus passengers, whose luggage is searched.

Bahía Inglesa, 6 km S of Caldera, 6 km W of the Highway, is popular with Chileans for its beautiful white sandy beaches and unpolluted sea (can get crowded Jan-Feb and at weekends). The climate is warm and dry the year round. It was originally known as Puerto del Inglés after the arrival in 1687 of the English 'corsario', Edward Davis.

● **Accommodation Caldera**: **B** *Hostería Puerta del Sol*, Wheelwright 750, T 315205, inc tax, cabins with bath and kitchen, view over bay; **C** *Costanera*, Wheelwright 543, T 316007, takes credit cards, simple rooms,

friendly; **A3** *Portal del Inca*, Carvallo 945, T 315252, shower, cabins with kitchen, English spoken, restaurant not bad, order breakfast on previous night; **C** *Pucará*, Ossa Cerda 460, T 315258; **D** *Res Fenicia*, Gallo 370, T 315594, eccentric owner, rec; **E** *Res Millaray*, main plaza, clean, friendly. **Bahía Inglesa**: **B** *Los Jardines de Bahía Inglesa*, Av Copiapó, *cabañas*, T 315359, open all year, good beds, comfortable; **Camping Bahía Inglesa**, Playa Las Machas, T 315424, **B**/tent site, fully equipped *cabañas* for up to 5 persons, **A3**. *El Coral* restaurant has some cabins **C**, T 315331, Av El Morro, overlooking sea, good seafood, groups welcome, open all year.

● **Places to eat In Caldera**: *Miramar*, Gana 090, at pier, good seafood. *El Pirón de Oro*, Cousiño 218, good but not cheap; *Charles*, Ossa Cerda, good seafood, clean.

● **Transport** Buses to Copiapó and Santiago, several daily; to Antofagasta, US$18, 7 hrs; to travel N, it may be better to take a bus to Chañaral (Inca-bus US$2), then change. Hourly buses between Bahía Inglesa and Caldera; taxis and colectivos US$1, all year; frequent micro service Jan-Feb US$0.25.

CHAÑARAL

A neglected looking town (*Pop* 10,000) with wooden houses perched on the hillside is 93 km N of Caldera and 968 km N of Santiago. In its heyday it was the centre for the nearby copper mines of El Salado and Las Animas.

● **Accommodation B** *Hostería Chañaral*, Miller 268, T 480055, excellent restaurant; **C** *Mini*, San Martín 528, T 480079, good value restaurant; **D** *Nuria*, Costanera 302, good; **D** *Jiménez*, Merino Jarpa 551, without bath, friendly, patio with lots of birds rec, restaurant good value; **E** *La Marina*, Merino Jarpa 562, basic.

● **Places to eat** In hotels; *Rincón Porteño*, Merino Jarpa 567, good and inexpensive. *San Remo*, Torreblanca, good seafood; *Restaurante de los Pescadores*, in La Caleta, good fish, clean, cheap, rec.

● **Banks & money changers** Poor rates for cash; nowhere to change TCs.

● **Tourist offices** Kiosk on the Pan-American Highway at S end of town (closed winter).

● **Transport** Bus terminal Merino Jarpa 854. Frequent services to Antofagasta US$11, 5 hrs, and Santiago.

PARQUE NACIONAL PAN DE AZUCAR

The park, N of Chañaral, consists of the Isla Pan de Azúcar on which Humboldt penguins and other sea-birds live, and some 43,700 ha of coast whose vegetation, mainly cacti, is nourished by frequent sea mists (*camanchaca*). After rain in some of the gullies there are tall purple lilies. The park is home to 103 species of birds, guanaco and 26 varieties of cacti. There are fine beaches (popular at weekends in summer). Fishermen near the Conaf office offer boat trips round Isla Pan de Azúcar to see the penguins which are normally not visible from the mainland. **NB** There are heavy fines for driving in 'restricted areas' of the park.

● **Park information** Two entrances: N by good secondary road from Chañaral, 28 km to Caleta Pan de Azúcar; from the Pan-American Highway 45 km N of Cañaral, along a side road 20 km (road in parts deep sand and very rough). Taxi from Chañaral US$15, or hitch a lift from fishermen at sunrise.

● **Conaf** office in Caleta Pan de Azúcar, maps available; park entry US$2.50, camping, US$5, no showers, take all food.

EL SALVADOR

An important mining town, 129 km E of Chañaral in the valley of the Río Salado, reached by a road which branches off the Pan-American Highway 12 km E of Chañaral. All along the valley there are people extracting metal ore from the water by building primitive settling tanks.

● **Accommodation** *Hostería El Salvador*, Potrerillos 003, T 472492; *Camino del Inca*, El Tofo 333, T 472311; *Res Linari*, Potrerillos 705.

● **Transport Air** Lan Chile from Santiago and Copiapó (T 056-121-2590). **Buses** Pullman Bus daily to Santiago.

TALTAL

The next important port to the N is 146 km N of Chañaral, along the Pan-American Highway. Taltal (*Pop* 9,000; *Phone code* 055) is a town of wooden buildings, many dating from the late 19th century when it prospered as an important mineral port of 20,000 people. It is now a nitrate and copper ore centre. There is an airport, but few flights. The **Museo Arqueológico** is on Av Prat. 72 km N of Taltal is the Quebrada El Médano, a gorge with ancient rock-paintings along the upper valley walls.

● **Accommodation** C *Hostería Taltal*, Esmeralda 671, T 101, excellent restaurant, good value *almuerzo*; **D** *Verdy*, Ramírez 345, T 105, with bath, E without, clean, spacious, restaurant; opp is **E** *Taltal City*, clean, no hot water; **E** *San Martín*, Martínez 279, T 88, without bath, good *almuerzo*; **E** *Viña del Mar*, Serrano 762.

● **Places to eat** *Caverna*, Martínez 247, good seafood.

● **Transport** Buses to Santiago 2 a day; to Antofagasta Tramaca, 3 a day, US$5.

Antofagasta, Calama and San Pedro

NTOFAGASTA and Calama are export and service centres respectively for the copper industry in the area. Calama is also the starting point for one of the rail journeys to Bolivia. Around San Pedro de Atacama (which has remains of Atacameño culture) are superb Andean landscapes; San Pedro itself is growing increasingly as a tourist centre.

The next two sections deal with the 1,255 km between Copiapó and Arica, a desert without vegetation, with little or no rain. The inhospitable shore is a pink cliff face rising to a height of from 600 to 900m. At the bottom of the cliff are built the towns, some of considerable size. The far from pacific Pacific often makes it difficult to load and unload ships. The nitrate fields exploited in this area lie in the depression between Taltal and Pisagua. Major copper deposits are mined in the Cordillera.

Life in the area is artificial. Water has to be piped for hundreds of kilometres to the cities and the nitrate fields from the Cordillera; all food and even all building materials have to be brought in from elsewhere.

There is some difference of climate between the coast and the interior. The coast is humid and cloudy; in the interior the skies are clear. The temperatures on the coast are fairly uniform; in the interior there is often a great difference in the temperature between day and night; the winter nights are often as cold as -10°C, with a cruel wind.

ANTOFAGASTA

Antofagasta (*Pop* 185,000; *Phone code* 055), 1,367 km N of Santiago and 699 km S of Arica, is the largest city in Northern Chile. It is the capital of the Second Region and is a major port for the export of copper from Chuquicamata. It is also a major commercial centre and home of two universities. The climate is delightful (apart from the lack of rain); the temperature varies from 16°C in June/July to 24°C Jan/Feb, never falling below 10°C at night.

Places of interest

In the main square, **Plaza Colón**, is a clock tower donated by the British community. **Paseo Prat**, which runs SE from Plaza Colón, is the main shopping street. Two blocks N of Plaza Colón, near the old port, is the **Ex-Aduana**, built as the Bolivian customs house in Mejillones and moved to its current site after the War of the Pacific. Opposite are two other buildings, the former **Capitanía del Puerto** (now occupied by the Fundación Andrés Sabella, which offers occasional workshops on weaving, painting, etc) and the **ex-Resguardo Marítimo** (now housing Digader, the regional coordinating centre for sport and recreation). East of the port are the buildings of the **Antofagasta and Bolivia Railway Company** (FCAB) dating from the 1890s and beautifully restored, but still in use and difficult to visit. These include the former railway station, company offices and workers' housing. The former main square of the **Oficina Vergara**, a nitrate town built in 1919 and dismantled in 1978, can be seen in the campus of the University of Antofagasta, 4 km S of the centre (bus 3 or 4). Also to the S on a hill (and reached by Bus B) are the ruins of

Huanchaca, a Bolivian silver refinery built after 1868 and closed in 1903. From below, the ruins resemble a fortress rather than a factory.

Museums

Museo Histórico Regional, in the former Aduana, Balmaceda y Bolívar, Tues-Sat 1000-1300, 1530-1830, Sun 1100-1400, US$0.80, children half-price, fascinating new displays (many in Spanish only) on life on land and in the oceans, development of civilization in South America, minerals, human artefacts, rec. **Museo Geológico** of the Universidad Católica del Nte, Av Angamos 0610, inside the university campus, open Mon-Fri, 0830-1230, 1500-1800, free (colectivo 3 or 33 from town centre).

Excursions

The fantastic cliff formations and symbol of the Second Region at **La Portada** are 16 km N, reached by taking airport bus No 20 (see below), minibuses from Latorre y Sucre (US$3 return) or any bus for Mejillones from the Terminal Centro. Taxis charge US$11. Hitching is easy. From the main road it is 2 km to the beach which, though beautiful, is too dangerous for swimming; there is an excellent seafood restaurant (*La Portada*) and café (open lunch-time only). A number of bathing beaches are also within easy reach.

Juan López, 38 km N of Antofagasta, is a windsurfers' paradise (Hotel *La Rinconada*, T 268502; *Hostería Sandokan*, T 692031). Buses at weekends in summer only, also minibuses daily in summer from Latorre y Sucre. For those with their own transport, follow the road out of Juan López to the beautiful cove at Conchilla. Keep on the track to the end at Bolsico. The sea is alive with birds, including Humboldt penguins, especially opposite Isla Santa María.

72 km NE of Antofagasta (on the Pan-American Highway) is **Baquedano**, formerly an important railway junction. The old railway station (still used by goods trains) and the Parque Histórico Ferrocarril, a large and neglected collection of old (and rusting) locomotives, can be seen.

30 km further N and just off the Pan-American Highway is **Chacabuco**, a large nitrate town, opened in 1924, closed in 1938 and used as a concentration camp by the Pinochet government between 1973 and 1975. Workers' housing, the church, theatre, stores and the mineral plants can be visited. Free guided tour (in Spanish). Take any bus from Antofagasta towards Calama, get off at the Carmen Alto junction and walk the last 4 km.

Local holiday

29 June, **San Pedro**, patron saint of the fishermen: the saint's image is taken out by launch to the breakwater to bless the first catch of the day. **Festivals** On the last weekend of Oct, the foreign communities put on a joint festival on the seafront, with national foods, dancing and music.

Local information

● **Accommodation**

A1 *Nadine*, Baquedano 519, T 227008, F 265222, bath, TV, bar, café, parking, etc; opp is **A2** *Ancla*, Baquedano 508, T 224814, F 261551, bath, TV, bar, restaurant, exchange (see below); **A2** *Antofagasta*, Balmaceda 2575, T/F 268259, garage, swimming pool, lovely view of port and city, run down, with breakfast (discount for Automóvil Club members), beach; **A2** *Diego de Almagro*, Condell 2624, T 268331, good for the money but a bit tatty; **A3** *Colón*, San Martín 2434, T 261851, F 260872, with breakfast, quiet, clean.

B *Pieper*, Sucre 509, T 263603, clean, modern, warmly rec; **B** *San Marcos*, Latorre 2946, T 251763, modern, comfortable, avoid rooms at the back (loud music), overpriced; **B** *San Martín*, San Martín y Bolívar, T 263503, with bath, TV, parking, clean, safe and friendly; **B** *Tatio*, Av Grecia 1000, T 247561, modern building, out of old town on the beach, has buses converted into caravans, D, friendly, beautiful views, acts as youth hostel, no cooking facilities.

C *Latorre*, Latorre 2450, T 221886, pleasant; **C** *San Antonio*, Condell 2235, T 268857, clean, helpful, modern but noisy from bus station.

D *Res La Riojanita*, Baquedano 464, T 268652, basic, old-fashioned, hot water on demand, noisy; **D** *Res El Cobre*, Prat 749, T 225162, central, noisy, basic; **D** *Res O'Higgins*, Sucre 665, T 267596, big, old, dirty, no hot water; **D** *Rawaye*, Sucre 762, T 225399, without breakfast, basic, hot water am only, no towels; **D** *Res Toconao*, Bolívar 580, clean.

E pp *Brasil*, Bolívar 568, clean; **E** *Res Paola*, Prat

766, T 222208, without bath, noisy, poor bathroom facilities.

Camping: to the S on the road to Coloso are: *Las Garumas*, Km 6, T 247758, US$10 for tent (bargain for lower price out of season), US$15 for cabins; cold showers and beach (reservations Av Angamos 601, casilla 606). *Rucamóvil*, Km 13, T 231913 and 7 *cabañas*, T 221988. Both open year-round, expensive. Also *La Rinconada*, 30 km N of city, off road to Mejillones, between La Portada and Juan López, T 261139.

● **Places to eat**
Marina Club, Av Ejército 0909, good fish and seafood dishes and a view, expensive but worth it; *Tío Jacinto*, Uribe 922, friendly, good seafood; *El Arriero*, Condell 2644, good service, good set lunch otherwise pricey, live music; *Bavaria*, J S Ossa 2428, excellent meat and German specialities, not cheap; *Flamingo*, Condell y Baquedano, rec; *D'Alfredo*, Condell 2539, pizzas, good; *Chicken's House Center*, Latorre 2660, chicken, beef and daily specials, open till 2400; *Casa Vecchia*, O'Higgins 1456, good value. Difficult to find any coffee, etc, before 0900. *Café Bahía*, Prat 452, and *Café Caribe*, Prat 482, good coffee, open 0900; *Piccolo Mondo*, Condell 2685, expresso coffee, snacks, drinks, opens 0930, good; ice cream at *Fiori di Gelatto*, Baquedano 519, in new *Hotel Nadine*, highly rec; *Chico Jaime* above the market, surrealistic decor, seafood, *almuerzo* US$3, mixed reports; good reports of *El Mariscal* in same area. Many eating places in the market. Good cheap lunches at *El Rincón de Don Quijote*, Maipú 642. Good fish restaurant at Coloso, 8 km S nr the Playa Amarrilla (take your own wine). *Chez Niko's*, Ossa 1951, restaurant, bar, bakery, *pastelería*, good pizzas, *empanadas* and bread. *Chifa Pekín*, Ossa 2135, Chinese, smart, reasonable prices. Good seafood restaurants in *terminal de pescadores*.

● **Airline offices**
LanChile, Washington 2552, T 265151; Ladeco, Washington 2589, T 269170, F 260440; National, Latorre 2572, T 224418, F 268996; Alta, Balmaceda 2584, T 226089, F 282202.

● **Banks & money changers**
Banco de Concepción, Plaza Colón for Visa. Banco Edwards, Prat 461, TCs changed at high commission. Fincard, Prat 431, for Mastercard. Foreign money exchange (all currencies and TCs) is best at *Hotel Ancla*, Latorre 2478 y Baquedano 508, T 224814, open all day every day. **NB** Impossible to change TCs S of Antofagasta until you reach La Serena.

● **Embassies & consulates**
Bolivia, Av Grecia 563, Oficina 23, T 221403; France and Belgium, Baquedano 299, T 268669.

● **Entertainment**
Discotheques: *Con Tutti*, Av Grecia 421; *Popo's*, Universidad de Chile (far end from town); *Parador 63*, Baquedano 619, disco, bar-restaurant, live shows, good value.

Theatre: *Teatro Municipal*, Sucre y San Martín, T 264919, modern, state-of-the art; *Teatro Pedro de la Barca*, Condell 2495, run by University of Antofagasta, occasional plays, reviews.

● **Laundry**
París, Condell 2455, laundry and dry cleaning, expensive, charges/item; *Laverap*, 14 Febrero 1802.

● **Post & telecommunications**
Post Office: on Plaza Colón, 0830-1900, Sat 0900-1300.

Telephones: Entel Chile, Baquedano, 753; CTC, Condell 2529.

● **Shopping**
Galería del Arte Imagen, Uribe 485, sells antiques inc artefacts from nitrate plants.

Bookshop: *Librería Universitaria*, Latorre 2515, owner Germana Fernández knowledgeable on local history; opp is *Multilibro*.

Market: Municipal market, corner of Matta and Uribe.

● **Sports**
Swimming: olympic pool at Condell y 21 de Mayo, US$1.20, open till 1800, best in am. Sauna: Riquelme y Condell.

Tennis: Club de Tenis Antofagasta, Av Angamos 906.

● **Tour companies & travel agents**
Many inc *Tatio Travel*, Latorre 2579, T 263532, Tx 225242 TATIO CL, English spoken, tours arranged for groups or individuals, highly rec. *Turismo Cristóbal* in *Hotel Antofagasta*, helpful. *Turismo Corssa*, San Martín 2769, T/F 251190, rec. Alex Joseph Valenzuela Thompson, Edif Bulnes, Sucre 220, p 4, Oficina 403, T 243322/F 222718, Aptdo Postal 55, offers to guide German speakers around the area.

● **Tourist offices**
Maipú 240, T 264044, Mon-Fri 0830-1300, Mon-Thur 1500-1930, Fri 1500-1930; kiosk on Balmaceda nr *Hotel Antofagasta* Mon-Fri 0930-1300, 1530-1930, Sat/Sun 0930-1300 kiosk at airport (open summer only). **Automóvil Club de Chile**: Condell 2330, T 225332.

Customs agent: Luis Piquimil Bravo, Prat 272, oficina 202, excellent, fast service, efficient.

● **Transport**
Local Car rental: Rent-a-Car, Prat 810, T 225200; Avis, Prat 272, T 221668; Budget, Prat 206, T 251745; Hertz, Balmaceda 2566

(T 269043), offer city cars and jeeps (group D, Toyota Landcruiser) and do a special flat rate, with unlimited mileage; **Felcar**, 14 de Febrero 2324, T 224468, English spoken, reported to be the cheapest.

Air Cerro Moreno Airport, 22 km N. Taxi to airport US$7, but cheaper if ordered from hotel. Bus No 20 from San Martín y Prat, US$0.50, every 2 hrs from 0730. LanChile, Ladeco and National fly daily to Santiago, Iquique and Arica.

Trains There are no passenger services from Antofagasta. The journey to Bolivia starts from Calama (see below) – tickets from Tramaca, Uribe 936 or in Calama.

Buses Main terminal is at S end of town, Av Argentina y Díaz Gana, but each company has its own office in town (some quite a distance from the centre). Some, like Tramaca, go only from their own terminal. Buses for **Mejillones** and **Tocopilla** operated by Barrios, Tramaca, Camus and others depart from the Terminal Centro at Riquelme 513. Minibuses to Mejillones leave from Latorre 2730. Bus company offices are as follows: Tramaca, Uribe 936, T 223624; Flota Barrios, Condell 2764; Géminis, Latorre 3099; Fénix Pullman Nte, San Martín 2717; Incatur, Maipú 554; Turis Nte, Argentina 1155; Libac, Argentina 1155; Pullman Bus, Latorre 2805; Chile-Bus (to Argentina and Brazil) and Tur-Bus, Latorre 2751. To **Santiago**, 18 hrs (Flota Barrios, US$60, *cama* inc drinks and meals); 30% reduction on Inca, Tramaca, and Géminis buses for students, but ask after you have secured a seat; many companies: fares US$35-40, book 2 days in advance. If all seats to the capital are booked, catch a bus to **La Serena** (13 hrs, US$20, or US$38 *cama* service), or **Ovalle**, US$20, and re-book. To **Valparaíso**, US$35. To **Arica**, US$16 (Tur-Bus), 13½ hrs, Tramaca, US$18. To **Chuquicamata**, US$6, frequent, 3 hrs. To **Calama**, several companies, US$5, Tramaca, 3 hrs; to **San Pedro de Atacama**, no direct services – go via Calama. Direct to **Copiapó** on Thur and Sat at 2230, US$10.50. Frequent buses to **Iquique**; US$13, 8 hrs.

Buses to Salta, Argentina Géminis, Wed, US$50, 22 hrs; via Calama, San Pedro and Paso Sico, immigration check at San Pedro de Atacama, then on to high Cordillera and to San Antonio de los Cobres (Argentine customs) all year round, although April-Sept dependent on weather conditions. Also Atahualpa/Tramaca joint service in summer only, Tues, Fri 0700 via Calama, San Pedro, Paso Sico and Jujuy US$50, student discount if you are persistent. Book in advance for these services, take food and as much warm clothing as possible. There is nowhere to change Chilean pesos en route. These services can be picked up in San Pedro, but book

first in Calama or Antofagasta and notify bus company.

Hitchhiking If hitching to Arica or Iquique try at the beer factory a few blocks N of the fish market on Av Pinto, or the lorry park a few blocks further N. If hitching S go to the police checkpoint/restaurant/gas station La Negra, about 15 km S of the city.

MEJILLONES

This good natural harbour protected from westerly gales by high hills is 60 km N of Antofagasta (*Pop* 4,000; *Phone code* 055). Until 1948 it was a major terminal for the export of tin and other metals from Bolivia: remnants of that past include a number of fine wooden buildings: the Intendencia Municipal, the Casa Cultural (built in 1866) and the church (1906), as well as the Capitanía del Puerto. Today the town lives mainly by fishing, coming alive in the evening when the fishermen prepare to set sail. The sea is very cold because of the Humboldt current. A Mediterranean-style tourist complex is planned for Mejillones Bay, once paving of the coastal road is finished.

- **Accommodation** **A2** *Costa Del Sol*, M Montt 086, T 621590, 4-star, new; **D** *Res Marcela*, Borgoño 150, with bath, pleasant; **F** *Res Elisabeth*, Alte Latorre 440, T 621568, friendly, basic, restaurant. No campsite but wild camping possible on the beach.

- **Places to eat** *Juanito*, Las Heras 241, excellent *almuerzo*; *Sion-Ji*, Alte Latorre 718, Chinese, good value.

CALAMA

202 km NE of Antofagasta on the Río Loa at an altitude of 2,265m is the oasis town of **Calama** (*Pop* 100,365; *Phone code* 055). The town is modern, expensive and a commercial and residential centre for workers at nearby Chuquicamata.

Places of interest

2 km from the centre on Av B O'Higgins is the **Parque El Loa** (open 1000-1800 daily), which contains a reconstruction of a typical colonial village built around a reduced-scale reproduction of Chiu Chiu church. Nearby in the park is the **Museo Arqueológico y Etnológico**, with an exhibition of pre-hispanic cultural history

(open Tues-Fri 1000-1330, 1430-1800, Sat-Sun 1100-1830; colectivos 4, 5, 6 or 18 from the centre). Although there is little to do, Calama may be a useful point to stay for a day or 2 to get used to the altitude before going higher.

Travellers by car coming from the N can drive via Chuquicamata, although the road is quite poor on either side of that town, or, from the S, by a paved road leaving the Pan-American Highway 98 km N of Antofagasta at Carmen Alto (petrol and food). This road passes many abandoned nitrate mines (*oficinas*).

Local information
● Accommodation
L3 *Lican Antai*, Ramírez 1937, T 341621, with breakfast, good service and good restaurant, TV, phone, safe, rec.

A1 *Park*, Camino Aeropuerto 1392, T 319900, F 319901, 233-8509 in Santiago, first class, swimming pool, popular, bar and restaurant, rec; **A2** *Alfa*, Sotomayor 2016, T 342565, comfortable; **A2** *Hostería Calama*, Latorre 1521, T 341511, comfortable, good food and service; **A2** *Quitor*, Ramírez 2116, T 314159, good. **A3** *Mirador*, Sotomayor 2064, T/F 340329, with bath, D without, clean, helpful, rec.

B *Casablanca* on Plaza, Sotomayor 2160, T 312966, clean.

C *Res John Keny*, Ecuador 1991, T 211430, modern, clean, friendly, parking; **C** *Hostal Coco*, Sotomayor 2215, clean, hospitable.

D *El Loa*, Abaroa 1617, T 311963, English spoken; **D** *Res Splendid*, Ramírez 1960, T 211841, with bath, E without, clean, hot water, good; **D** *Res Internacional*, Velázquez 1976, T 211553, hot water, friendly but noisy; **D** *Genesis*, Granaderos 2148, T 212841, nr Tramaca and Geminis bus terminals, clean, kitchen, rec; **D** *Res Casa de Huéspedes*, Sotomayor 2079, poor beds, basic, clean, hot shower; **D** *Res Toño*, Vivar 1973, T 211185, next to Kenny bus, hot shower, basic, clean.

E *Universo*, Sotomayor 1822, T 313299, clean, friendly; **E** *Prat*, Vivar 1970, cheap, cold water; **E** *Res El Tatio*, P L Galo 1987, T 212284, basic, friendly, noisy, clean, reasonable; **E** pp *Capri 2*, Ramírez 1880, basic, safe; **E** *Los Andes*, Vivar 1920, T 341073, renovated, good beds, noisy; **E** *Luxor*, Vargas 1881, T 310292 basic, safe.

● Places to eat
Bavaria, Sotomayor 2095, modern, clean, good coffee and delicatessen, open early morning; *Club Croata*, Abaroa 1869 (Plaza de Armas), serves good set lunches and evening meals;

good, cheap lunches also at *Hotel Quitor*, *Comedor Camarino*, Latorre 2033, *Lascar*, Ramírez 1917, and in the market. *Mariscal JP*, Felix Hoyos 2127, good seafood. Good ice cream at *Fior di Gelalo*, Plaza de Armas.

● Banks & money changers
Rates are generally poor especially for TCs. **Banco de Crédito E Inversiones**, Latorre, good rates, no commission (US$100 minimum); **Banco Osorno** (Visa), Sotomayor; **Fincard** (Mastercard), Latorre 1763, p 1, Mon-Fri 0900-1400, 1600-2000, Sat 1100-1300. *Casa de Cambio*, Sotomayor 1818, Mon-Fri, 0830-1400, 1500-1900 (closes 2300 for passengers on train to Bolivia). Try also shop at Ramírez 1434 and *La Media Luna* clothes store, Ramírez 1992 (poor rates). Money changers selling Bolivian money outside the railway station. At weekends try Tramaca or Morales Moralitos bus offices or *farmacias* (poor rates).

● Embassies & consulates
The **Bolivian Consulate**, Sr Reynaldo Urquizo Sosa, Bañados Espinoza 2232, Apdo Postal 85, T 341976, is open (in theory only) 0900-1230 and 1530-1830, Mon-Fri, friendly, helpful.

● Laundry
Laverap, Felix Hoyos y Abaroa, Paris, Vargas 2178 and Latorre 1955; *Universal*, Antofagasta 1313 (cheapest).

● Post & telecommunications
Post Office: Granaderos y V Mackenna, 0830-1300, 1530-1830, Sat 0900-1230, will not send parcels over 1 kg.
Telecommunications: CTC, Abaroa 1756; Entel, Sotomayor 2027.

● Shopping
Supermarkets, *El Cid*, Vargas 1942, *El Cobre*, Vargas 2148; market at Antofagasta between Latorre and Vivar.

● Tour companies & travel agents
Several agencies run 1-day and longer tours to the Atacama region, inc San Pedro; these are usually more expensive than tours from San Pedro and require a minimum number for the tour to go ahead. Reports of tour quality are increasingly mixed – poorly maintained vehicles and poor guides. Those with positive recommendations inc: *Talikuna*, Gral Velázquez 1948, T 212595; *Turismo El Sol*, Abaroa 1796, T 210152; *Desierto Diferente*, Sotomayor 2261, T 315111; *Nativa*, Avaroa 1780, T 319834, F 340107; *Livia Tours*, Vivar 1960, T 211664, rec for their 3-day desert tour.

● Tourist offices
Latorre 1689, T 211314. Map of town, helpful. Open Mon-Fri 0900-1300, 1430-1900 Sat-Sun (summer only) 0900-1300. **Automóvil Club de Chile**, Av Ecuador 1901, T 342770.

● **Transport**
Local Car hire: Comercial Maipo SA, Balmaceda 3950, T 212204; **Hertz**, Latorre 1510,
T 211380; **Avis**, Granaderos 2895; **Avis**, Latorre
1512, T 319797; **Maxso**, Abaroa 1930,
T 212194; **Budget**, Granaderos 2925, T 341076.
A 4WD jeep (necessary for the desert) costs between US$87-118 a day. Rates are sometimes
much lower at weekends. A hired car or taxi,
shared between several people, is an economic
alternative for visiting the Atacama region. **NB** Car
hire is not available in San Pedro de Atacama.

Air LanChile (Latorre 1499, T 341477/341494),
daily, and Ladeco (Ramirez 1858,
T 312626/315183), to Santiago, via Antofagasta. Taxi to town US$6 (courtesy vans from
Hotels *Calama*, *Alfa* and *Lican Antai*).

Trains To Oruro (Bolivia). This, the only section
of the old Antofagasta and Bolivia Railway line
still open to passenger trains, is a long slow
journey but well worthwhile for the scenery.
Weekly train to Uyuni and Oruro, Wed 2300,
US$12 to Uyuni, US$18 to Oruro, passport essential, journey time to Oruro up to 48 hrs. Book
seats in advance from Tramaca in Calama (Sotomayor 1961) or Antofagasta. (The 2 offices
sell tickets for different carriages and do not
know of reservations made at the other office.)
Catch the train as early as possible: although
seats are assigned, the designated carriages may
not arrive; passengers try to occupy several seats
(to sleep on) but will move if you show your
ticket. The journey is very cold, both during the
day and at night (-15°C). Sleeping bag and/or
blanket essential. Restaurant car; food is also
available at Ollagüe and Río Mulato (only for the
conditioned). The highest point of the line is
reached at Ascotán (3,960m) and the line then
descends to 3,735m at Cebollar, where it skirts
a great borax basin 39 km long. Chilean customs
are at Ollagüe, where there is a delay of 5-6 hrs
while an engine is sent from Uyuni. The train is
searched at Bolivian customs at Avaroa and
passengers are required to disembark at both
border posts for passport-control. There are
money changers at Ollagüe and Avaroa. From
the border the line runs NE to Uyuni, 174 km,
crossing the Salar de Chiguana and running at
an almost uniform height of 3,660m. Uyuni is
the junction with the line S to the Argentine
frontier at Villazón.

Río Mulato is the junction for Potosí, but it is
much quicker to travel by bus from Uyuni. The
train terminates at Oruro (see Bolivia chapter: **La
Paz Railways to/from the Coast**).

A freight train with one or two passenger
cars attached leaves Calama for Ollagüe Sat
2300, return departure unknown, check details
beforehand, buy ticket a few hours before de-

parture, US$5 one way, not crowded. Note that
there is no connecting passenger train and riding
on goods trains from Ollagüe into Bolivia is not
allowed. No accommodation in Ollagüe.

Buses No main terminal, buses leave from
company offices: Tramaca, terminal at Granaderos 3048 (colectivo 1A from centre), office at
Sotomayor 1961; Morales Moralitos, Sotomayor 1802; Yusmar, Antofagasta 2041,
T 318543; Geminis, O'Higgins 078; Kenny Bus,
Vivar 1954; Flota Barrios, Ramírez 2298. To
Santiago 23 hrs, US$35-40; to **Arica**, often
involves a change in Antofagasta (Geminis,
2130 and Tramaca, 4 until 1730 daily, may be
more in summer) US$16, 8 hrs; to **Val-
paraíso/Viña del Mar**, US$35; to **Iquique**, 8
hrs, US$13, overnight only (Geminis rec, Kenny
Bus not rec). To **La Serena**, 15 hrs, US$18. To
Chuquicamata (see below). For services to **San
Pedro de Atacama** and Toconao, see below;
to **Antofagasta**, 3 hrs, several companies, eg
Tramaca, hourly on the half-hour till 2130, US$5.

To **Salta**, Argentina Géminis services from
Iquique and Antofagasta call at Calama, details
above, book well in advance, US$39, 22 hrs.
(Géminis service can also be picked up in San
Pedro but book in Calama and tell the booking
office). Also Tramaca, service from Antofagasta,
dep Mon and Fri 1000, US$45, via Jujuy.

NB Remember that between Oct and March,
Chilean time is 1 hr later than Bolivian.

CHUQUICAMATA

Here, a clean, modern town (*Pop* 20,000; *Alt*
2,800m), 16 km N of Calama, is the world's
largest open-cast copper mine, employing
11,000 workers and operated by Codelco
(the state copper corporation). It is an as-
toundingly large hole, 4 km long, 2 km wide
and 600m deep. The giant trucks, carrying
225 ton loads, work 24 hrs a day, extracting
rock which is processed in other parts of the
plant. Guided tours in Spanish (by bus, also
in English if enough people) leave from the
office of Chuqui Ayuda (a local children's
charity) near the entrance at the top end of
the plaza, Mon-Fri 1000 (though less frequently in low season – tourist office in
Calama has details), 1 hr, US$2.50 donation,
be there by 0915. Register in the café near
entrance at least 30 mins in advance. Be in
good time because space is sometimes limited; passport essential. No filming permitted, but photographs may be taken at
specified points in tour.

● **Places to eat** Cheap lunches available at the

Club de Empleados and at *Arco Iris*, both facing the bus terminal.

● **Transport** From Calama: yellow colectivo taxis (marked 'Chuqui') from the corner of the main plaza, US$0.75. Buses to **Arica** at 2200 (weekends at 2300), US$16, 9 hrs; to **Antofagasta**, 10 a day, US$6; to **Iquique**, US$14; to **Santiago**, US$28, 24 hrs.

NORTH ALONG THE RIO LOA

Near Calama there are several small towns and villages in the valley of the Río Loa. 33 km E is the village of **Chiu Chiu**, with a very interesting church, dating from 1611, and nearby a unique, perfectly circular, very deep lake, called Chiu Chiu or Icacoia. Ancient rock carvings are to be found a few kilometres N in the Río Loa valley. 8 km N of Chiu Chiu at **Lasana** are the ruins of a pre-Incaic *pukará*, a national monument, with explanatory tablets (soft drinks and beer on sale). At **Conchi**, 25 km N of Lasana, there is a spectacular view from the bridge over the Río Loa, but it is a military zone, so no photographs allowed. Access to the river is by side tracks, best at Santa Bárbara; interesting wildlife and flower meadows, trout fishing in season (permit from Gobernación in Calama). **Estación San Pedro** (16 km NE of Conchi) has quite an interesting old village and small gorge, away from the railway station. Possible to camp at the station (ask the station master).

From Chiu Chiu a road runs to Ollagüe, 240 km N on the Bolivian frontier. There is a *carabinero* checkpoint at Ascotán, the highest point of the road at 3,900m. North of Ascotán the road becomes worse, especially where it crosses the Salares de Ascotán and Ollagüe (ask at Ascotán or Ollagüe before setting out about the conditions, especially in Dec/Jan or Aug). There are many llama flocks along this road and flamingoes on the salares. **NB** The desert to the eastern side of the road is extensively covered with minefields.

5 km S of Ollagüe is the sulphur mining camp of Buenaventura. It is possible to camp here. The mine at 5,800m (only 150m short of the summit of Ollagüe Volcano) can be reached by hiring a 4WD vehicle or by walking. Amazing views of volcanoes and salt flats.

High Altitude Husbandry

The main stock animals are llamas and alpacas, whose principal forage is the *ichu* bunch-grass covering the lower slopes. There is no timber. *Taqui* – dried llama dung – and *tola* scrub are used for cooking fires, but the main fuel is *yaretal*, a resinous moss growing in pillow-like masses in rocky outcrops from 3,500 to 5,000m high. Its calorific value is half that of bituminous coal. It apparently is an Ice Age relic, growing very slowly but now worked out in this area. Across the border in Bolivia there is plenty, which is used as fuel for the Laguna Verde sulphur mine. It is broken up with dynamite into chunks for transport.

NB There is no petrol between Calama and Uyuni in Bolivia. If really short try buying from the *carabineros* at Ollagüe or Ascotán, the military at Conchi or the mining camp at Buenaventura. The only real answer is to take enough.

OLLAGUE

419 km from Antofagasta on the dry floor of the Salar de Ollagüe, surrounded by a dozen volcanic peaks of over 5,000m. The village (*Pop* 200; *Alt* 3,690m) has one basic *alojamiento*, one bus a week to Calama. Ollagüe can be reached by taking the Calama-Oruro train (see above) but, if you stop off, you will have to hitch back as the daily freight trains are not allowed to carry passengers. (Hitching is difficult but the police may help you to find a truck.)

A 77-km spur railroad of metre gauge runs to the copper mines of Collahuasi, and from there one can reach the highest mine in the world: the Aucanquilcha, at 5,700-5,900m. Its sulphur is taken to Amincha, a town at the foot of the volcano, to be refined. The mine closes for Bolivian winter; it is served by road, which is sometimes impassable. On site are the ruins of an aerial tram system. From the mine you can scramble to the summit of Aucanquilcha at 6,176m; superb views. High clearance vehicle needed to drive to the mine. The highest passenger station on this spur is Yuma, at 4,400m.

At this altitude nights are cold, the days warm and sunny. Minimum temperature at Ollagüe is -20°C, and at the mine, -37°C. There are only 50 mm of rain a year, and water is very scarce.

An interesting excursion can be made N from Ollagüe to the village of **Coska** with its traditional agriculture and herds of llamas and alpacas.

FRONTIER WITH BOLIVIA: OLLAGUE

Open 0800-2100; US$2 per vehicle charge for crossings 1300-15, 1850-2100. Bad unmade road from Ollagüe into Bolivia (see Bolivia, **Oruro and Routes to Chile & Argentina**).

SAN PEDRO DE ATACAMA

103 km SE of Calama by a paved road is **San Pedro de Atacama**. There is no fuel, food or water along this road. At Paso Barros Arana (Km 58) there is an unpaved turning to the left which leads through interesting desert scenery to the small, mud-brick village of Río Grande. Look out for vicuñas and guanacos on the pass. The main road skirts the Cordillera de la Sal about 15 km from San Pedro. Spectacular views of sunset over to the Western Cordilleras. The old unmade road to San Pedro turns off the new road at Km 72 and crosses this range through the Valle de La Luna (see **Excursions** below), but should only be attempted by 4WD vehicles. This road is partly paved with salt blocks.

San Pedro de Atacama is a small town (*Pop* 1,600; *Alt* 2,436m; *Phone code* 055) more Spanish-Indian looking than is usual in Chile, now attracting large numbers of visitors. Both Diego de Almagro and Pedro de Valdivia stopped in this oasis.

Places of interest

The church, dating from the 17th century but heavily restored, has a roof of cactus wood; inside, the statues of Mary and Joseph have fluorescent light halos, quite arresting

Museums

Museo Arqueológico, the collection of Father Le Paige, a Belgian missionary who lived in San Pedro between 1955 and 1980, is now under the care of the Universidad Católica del Nte (Mon-Fri, 0800-1200, 1500-1900; Sat, and Sun, 1000-1200, 1500-1800; summer, Mon-Fri 0900-1200, 1400-1800, Sat-Sun 1000-1200, 1400-1800, entry US$2.50). It is a fascinating repository of artefacts, well organized to trace the development of prehispanic Atacameño society. Labels on displays are good and there is a comprehensive booklet in Spanish. Graham Greene tells us that "the striking feature of the museum is ... the mummies of Indian women with their hair and dresses intact dating from before the Conquest, and a collection of paleolithic tools which puts the British Museum in the shade". There is no heating nor electricity: wear warm clothing even in warm weather and go when sunlight is strongest.

Excursions

The **Valle de la Luna** , 12 km W of San Pedro, with fantastic landscapes caused by the erosion of salt mountains, is crossed by the old San Pedro-Calama road. Although buses on the new Calama-San Pedro road will stop to let you off where the old road branches off 13 km NW of San Pedro (signposted to Peine), it is far better to travel from San Pedro on the old road, either on foot (allow 3 hrs there, 3 hrs back; no lifts), by bicycle or by car. Take water, hat, camera and torch. Also consider spending the night to see the sunset (take warm clothes and plenty of water).

3 km N of San Pedro along the river is the **Pukará de Quitor**, a pre-Inca fortress restored in 1981. The fortress, which stands on the W bank of the river, was stormed by the Spanish under Pedro de Valdivia, 1,000 defenders being overcome by 15 horsemen who vaulted the walls (the path involves fording the river several times). A further 4 km up the river there are Inca ruins at Catarpe. The archaeological site at **Tulor**, 12 km SW of San Pedro, is a stone-age village; worth a visit on foot (you can sleep in two reconstructed huts), or take a tour, US$5 pp.

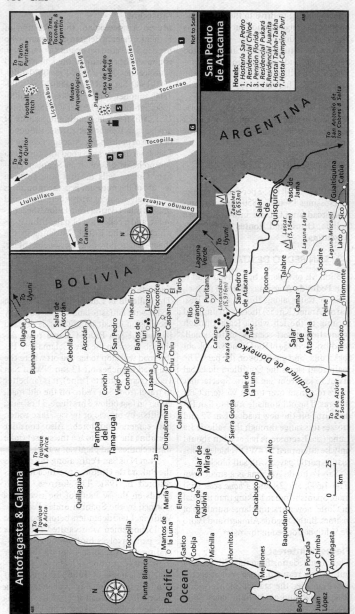

San Pedro de Atacama

Hotels:
1. Hostería San Pedro
2. Residencial Chiloé
3. Pensión Florida
4. Residencial Pukará
5. Residencial Juanita
6. Hostal Takha-Takha
7. Hostal-Camping Puri

Not to Scale

To Pozo Tres, Toconao, & Argentina

To El Tatio, Puritama

To Pukará de Quitor

To Calama

Caracoles

Tocornao

Tocopilla

Licancabur

Padre Le Paige

Museo Arqueológico

Casa de Pedro de Valdivia

Plaza

Football Pitch

Municipalidad

Domingo Atienza

Llullaillaco

N

Antofagasta & Calama

To Iquique & Arica

Pacific Ocean

BOLIVIA

ARGENTINA

To Uyuni

To Uyuni

Salar de Ascotán

Ollagüe

Buenaventura

Cebollar

Ascotán

San Pedro

Conchi Viejo

Conchi

Lasana

Chiu Chiu

Baños de Turi

Ayquina

Caspana

Inacaliri

Linzor

Toconce

El Tatio

Río Grande

Puritama

Licancabur (5,916m)

Laguna Verde

Zapaleri (5,653m)

Salar de Quisquiro

Paso de Jama

Lascar (5,154m)

Laguna Miscanti

Laguna Lejía

Guatiquina

Catúa

Sico

Laco

Tilomonte

Socaire

Camar

Peine

Tilopozo

Salar de Atacama

Valle de La Luna

Catarpe

Pukará Quitor

Tulor

San Pedro de Atacama

Toconao

Talabre

Cordillera de Domeyko

To Paz de Azúcar & Socompa

To San Antonio de los Cobres & Salta

Pampa del Tamarugal

Quillagua

Chuquicamata

Calama

Sierra Gorda

Salar de Miraje

Carmen Alto

Chacabuco

Pedro de Valdivia

María Elena

Baquedano

Tocopilla

Mantos de la Luna

Gatico

Cobija

Michilla

Hornitos

Mejillones

La Portada

La Chimba

Punta Blanca

Antofagasta

Bolsico

Juan López

N

0   25
km

Nearby are the ruins of a 17th century Spanish-style village, abandoned in the 18th century due to lack of water. For Toconao, 37 km S of San Pedro, see below.

Local information

San Pedro has electricity 1800-2230, but take a torch (flashlight) for walking at night. *Residenciales* supply candles, but better to buy them in Calama beforehand. Accommodation is scarce in Jan/Feb and expensive.

● Accommodation

A2 *Hostería San Pedro*, on Solcor, T 11, reserve in advance, swimming pool (residents only), petrol station (leaded fuel only), tents for hire, cabins, hot water, electricity am-1200 and 1800-2300, restaurant (good lunch) and bar, rec, no credit cards or TCs; **C** *Kimal*, Atienza y Caracoles, T/F 55-851030, traditional style, parking, good.

D *La Quinta Adela*, Toconao, friendly; **D** *Res Corvatch* , Antofagasta s/n, T 87, good rooms, good beds clean, friendly, German spoken highly rec; **D** *Res Juanita*, on the plaza, T 39, hot water on request, friendly, restaurant, rec; **D** *Hostal Takha-Takha*, on Caracoles, T 38 (F camping), hot water, very small rooms, some tents for rent, friendly and clean; **D** *Res Andacollo*, Tocopilla 11, T6, clean, basic, laundry facilities, cheap restaurant; **D** *Res Licancábur*, Toconao, T 7, clean, cooking facilities,safe, good.

E pp *Pensión Florida*, Tocopilla, temperamental hot water, basic, clean, laundry facilities, poor beds; **E** pp *Pukará*, Tocopilla 28, cold water, basic; **E** pp *Res Chiloé*, Atienza, T 17, hot water, good meals, laundry facilities, good beds, safe, popular; **F** pp *Res Solcor*, Atienza, dormitory accommodation, friendly; **E** pp *Camping Tulor*, off Atienza, T 27, good food, camping F pp, rents camping equipment, rec; **E** pp *Hostal-Camping Puri*, Caracoles s/n, T 49, restaurant, clean, quiet, friendly, camping F, rental of camping and

climbing gear.

● Places to eat

Best food in town at *Hostería San Pedro*. On Caracoles are *Estaka*, good set lunches and evening meals, popular; *Tambo Cañaveral*, live music at weekends, own generator, open late. Apart from these try Residenciales: *Juanita*, good set lunch and evening meal; *Andacollo*; *Chiloé* for cheap lunches. *Chañar Luminoso*, Caracoles, good coffee and juice. *Sonchek*, coffee, fruit juice, vegetarian dishes, also motorbikes for hire US$5/hr; *Chapaka*, opp Morales Moralitos bus stop sells health foods, bread, muesli.

● Banks & money changers

Cambio Atacama, Caracoles, open daily, poor rates, changes TCs, but often closed, best to change elsewhere. If stuck try *Hostería San Pedro* (worse rates still), or Hostal Takha-Takha.

● Post & telecommunications

Post Office: Granaderos y MacKenna sells excellent postcards.

Telephone: office on Tocopilla, 0830-2000.

● Sports

Climbing: San Pedro is a good centre for climbing Mt Lincancábur (5,916m) and other peaks on the Chile/Bolivia border. Allow at least 8 hrs to climb Lincancábur and 4 hrs to descend. Take plenty of water and your passport and hire a 4WD vehicle in Calama.

Horse riding: *Galopea*, run by Eleanor Merrill and Roberto Plaza Castillo ('Guatita') run guided horseback tours, US$5/hr, speak 6 languages, ask in post office.

Swimming Pool: *Piscina Oasis*, at Pozo Tres, 3 km SE, was drilled in the late 1950s as part of a mineral exploration project, open all year 0500-1730 daily (except Mon). US$1.50 to swim, sometimes empty. Worth asking around before walking there. Camping US$3 and picnic facilities, very popular at weekends.

● Tour companies & travel agents
About 10 agencies, most charging the same rates and organizing joint tour groups. Agencies inc: *Nativa*, Toconao, T 44, rec; *Cosmo Andino Expediciones*, Caracoles s/n, T/F 340107, English, German, French and Dutch spoken, book exchange in the above languages, wide selection, owner Martin Beeris (Martín El Holandés) rec; *Atacama Inca Tour*, Toconao s/n, T 34, F 52, rec; *Desert Adventure*, Caracoles s/n; opp is *Merakopp*, rec; *Pachamama*, Toconao, rec; *Ochoa*, Toconao, Spanish only, rec; *Antai*, Caracoles s/n, English and French spoken, also sell handicrafts, rec; *Cactus* offers horseriding with good guides to Valle de la Luna and other sites. Tours are also run by several *Residenciales*. Usual tour rates: to Valle de la Luna (best at sunset) US$6; to Toconao and the Salar de Atacama (best at sunset) US$11; to El Tatio (begin at 0400) US$16 (take swimming costume and warm clothing). These run most days in season, subject to demand at other times. Several agencies' tours to Laguna Verde, Mt Lincancábur and other sites in Bolivia no longer run because the Bolivian authorities refuse permits for Chilean tour vehicles.

There has been a boom in travel agencies since 1993, but many lack experience, dependable vehicles, suitable equipment (eg oxygen for El Tatio) or professionalism. Check that a guide speaks English if so advertised; ask to see the vehicle to be used (4WD land-cruisers are best); check if the company is recognized by the municipality. At the time of writing the first in the above list had formed the Asociación de Operadores Turísticos de San Pedro de Atacama; others are expected to join. Report any complaints to the municipality.

● Transport
Local Bicycle hire: from several places inc *Takha-Takha*; *Dada Atacama*, US$2.50/hr, US$10-12 a day; *Pangea*, Caracoles, English spoken, also cycle repairs. **Car hire**: is impossible. Try Calama. Pick up truck with 4WD best. Agency authorization essential to go to Bolivia.

Buses From Calama: two companies, both from Balmaceda y Sotomayor, opp railway station. Yusmar services leave **Calama** daily, 1100, 1600 and 1800, returning from San Pedro 0800, 1400 and 1800. Morales Moralitos buses 1000, 1530 and 1800, returning 0800, 1400 and 1800, 1½ hrs. Fare US$3 one way. Frequencies vary with more departures in Jan/Feb and some weekends, fewer out of season. Book in advance to return from San Pedro Sun pm. Both Morales Moralitos and Yusmar also run to Toconao. Geminis buses from Iquique and Antofagasta to Salta (Argentina) stop in San Pedro on Wed and Sat – book in Calama, Iquique or Antofagasta.

FRONTIER WITH BOLIVIA: HITO CAJONES

Hito Cajones is reached by a poor road E from San Pedro, 45 km. From the frontier it is 7 km N to Laguna Verde (see Bolivia chapter).

● Immigration
Chilean immigration and customs in San Pedro. Incoming vehicles are searched for fruit.

● Bolivian consulate
See under Calama.

● Transport
There are reports of a daily bus service from San Pedro to Hito Cajones to meet tour vehicles from Uyuni, US$10 pp. At Hito Cajones you may be able to find space in a tour vehicle (about US$20 to Uyuni). *Nativa* will take people to the frontier, US$120/vehicle.

FRONTIER WITH ARGENTINA: PASO DE JAMA AND PASO SICO

The Paso de Jama (4,200m) is reached by an improved road, suitable for all vehicles, which continues on the Argentine side to Susques and Jujuy. This is more popular than the Laguna Sico route but note but there is no accommodation in Susques.

Laguna Sico (4,079m) is reached by poor road which runs S and E of San Pedro, 207 km via Toconao. On the Argentine side this road continues to San Antonio de los Cobres and Salta.

● Immigration
Chilean immigration and customs in San Pedro. Incoming vehicles are searched for fruit.

● Crossing by private vehicle
Check road conditions before setting out as Paso de Jama can be closed due to heavy rain in summer and blocked by snow in winter.

● Transport
For bus services from Antofagasta, Calama and San Pedro to Jujuy and Salta see above.

NORTH OF SAN PEDRO

A maintained road runs NE, past the Baños de Puritama (28 km), then on a further 94 km to the geysers at El Tatio (*alt* 4,500m). The geysers are at their best 0630-0830, but there is no public transport and hitching is impossible, if going in a hired car, make sure the engine is suitable for very high altitudes and is protected with antifreeze; 4WD is advisable. If driving in the dark it is almost impossible to find your way: the sign for El Tatio is N of the turn off. A swimming pool has been built at El Tatio. Nearby is a workers' camp which is empty apart from one guard, who will let you sleep in a bed in one of the huts, G pp, take food and sleeping bag. From here you can hike to surrounding volcanoes if adapted to altitude. Tours arranged by agencies in San Pedro and Calama. **NB** People have been killed or seriously injured by falling into the geysers, or through the thin crust of the mud.

There are 3 alternative routes from El Tatio W to Calama: direct, on an atrocious track, to Caspana (basic accommodation at village store, G pp), beautifully set among hills, with a museum with interesting displays on Atacameño culture, and then W along the valley of the Río Salado.

North of El Tatio to Linzor (Represa Toconce); here you can turn W to **Toconce**, which has extensive prehispanic terraces set among interesting rock formations. Between Toconce and Caspana to the S are valleys of pampas grass with llama herds. If visiting Toconce, check in with the *carabineros* in the square. From Toconce follow the road W to Calama via Lasana and Chiu Chiu. 20 km W of Toconce is **Ayquina**, in whose ancient church is enshrined the statue of the Virgin of Guadalupe. Her feast-day is 8 Sept, when pilgrims come from far and wide. There is day-long group dancing to Indian rhythms on flute and drum. Towards sunset the Virgin is carried up a steep trail to a small thatched shrine, where the image and the people are blessed before the dancing is renewed at the shrine and all the way back to the village. The poor people of the hills gather stones and make toy houses all along the route: miniatures of the homes they hope to have some day.

6 km N of Ayquina are the luke-warm thermal waters of the **Baños de Turi** and the ruins of a 12th-century *pukará* which was the largest fortified town in the Atacama mountains. A further 35 km N of Turi is **Cupo**, which has a *fiesta* on 19 Mar (San José). Between this village and Turi

is a large, ruined prehispanic settlement at **Paniri** with extensive field systems, irrigation canals (including aqueducts) and a necropolis. Some of the fields are still in use. The area around Cupo is one of the best for seeing the Atacama giant cactus (*Notocereus atacamensis*). Flamingos can be seen on the mudflats. The Vega de Turi is an important site for the llama and sheep herders, who believe it has curative properties. At several times in the year, especially Sept, herders from a wide area congregate with their flocks.

The third alternative route to Calama is to continue N from Linzor to Inacaliri and the Ojo de San Pedro saltflat. Follow the road along the Río San Pedro Valley and cross the Río Loa at Conchi. The Río San Pedro has been a route for herders and silver caravans for centuries and there are many sites of interest, although access is on foot. For details on Conchi, Lasana and Chiu Chiu, see page 728 above.

SOUTH OF SAN PEDRO

From San Pedro to Toconao, 37 km S, the road (well-surfaced) runs through groves of acacia and pepper trees. There are many tracks leading to the wells (*pozos*) which supply the intricate irrigation system. Most have thermal water but bathing is not appreciated by the local farmers. The groves of trees are havens for wildlife especially rheas (ñandu) and Atacama owls.

About 4 km before you reach Toconao, there are some vehicle tracks heading E across the sand. They lead to a hidden valley 2 km from the road where there is a small settlement called **Zapar**. Here are some well-preserved pre-hispanic ruins on the rocky cliffs above the cultivated valley. The sand is very soft and 4WD is essential. **Toconao**, with some 500 inhabitants is on the eastern shore of the Salar de Atacama. All houses are built of bricks of white volcanic stone, which gives the village a very characteristic appearance totally different from San Pedro. The 18th century church stands next to the colonial bell tower, also built of volcanic stone. East of the village is an attractive oasis called the Quebrada de Jérez. The quarry where the stone (*sillar*) is worked can be visited. Worth visiting also are the vineyards which produce a unique sweet wine, and the tree-filled gorges with their hidden fields and orchards.

● **Accommodation** Three basic *residenciales* – ask around in the village. **Camping** possible along the Quebrada de Jérez.

● **Transport** Yusmar buses daily from San Pedro, 1300 and 2000, return 0700, 1645, US$1.30.

SALAR DE ATACAMA

South of Toconao is one of the main entrances to the Salar de Atacama, the third largest expanse of salt flats in the world. Rich in minerals including borax, potassium and an estimated 40% of world lithium reserves, the Salar is home to the pink flamingo and other birds (though these are usually only visible at a distance). Entry is controlled by Conaf in Toconao, US$1.50.

From Toconao the road heads S through the scenic villages of **Camar** (where handicrafts from cactus may be bought) and **Socaire** (which has domesticated llamas, knitwear for sale). 20 km S of Socaire is the beautiful **Laguna Miscanti** where wildlife abounds; 3 types of flamingo may be seen: Andean, Chilean (white and pink, no black) and James (small, with yellow legs). After Socaire the road goes on to the mine at Laco (one poor stretch below the mine), before proceeding to Sico, which has replaced the higher, more northerly Guaytiquina pass (4,295m, also spelt Huaytiquina) to Argentina.

10 km S of Toconao the old road branches E towards Guaytiquina. In a deep *quebrada* below Volcán Láscar is the small agricultural settlement of **Talabre**, with terracing and an ancient threshing floor. Above the *quebrada* is an isolated, stone-built cemetery. Large flocks of llamas graze where the stream crosses the road below Láscar. After a steep climb, you reach the **Laguna Lejía** (4,190m), where flamingos abound. You then pass through the high plains of **Guaytiquina** (4,275m), where only a few herdsmen are

found. This crossing is not open for road traffic to Argentina.

67 km S from Toconao, on a road that branches initially W between Camar and Socaire, is the attractive village of **Peine**, which is the site of the offices of the lithium extraction company. There is also a pool filled by thermal springs where you can swim. Woollen goods and knitwear are made here. To the E of the village lies a group of beautifully coloured hills (colours best at sunset) with good views over the Salar de Atacama. A path leads across these hills to Socaire (allow 2 days). It is worth asking if the offices' access road can be used to visit the Salar de Atacama's spectacular salt formations. Other villages worth visiting include Tilomonte and Tilopozo, S and W of Peine.

From Peine a road crosses the Salar de Atacama and then runs S until it joins the road to Argentina via the Portezuelo de Socompa, 13 km E of Pan de Azúcar. From the junction of Pan de Azúcar a good road leads back to San Pedro de Atacama along the western side of the Salar.

Pan de Azúcar is on the road which leads from the Pan-American Highway, 50 km S of Antofagasta to Socompa on the Argentine border. The road passes the mining centre at La Escondida (owned by RTZ) and continues, after Pan de Azúcar, in bad condition to Monturaqui. This is the source of the green onyx which is much used for carving in northern Chile.

FRONTIER WITH ARGENTINA: SOCOMPA

● **Immigration**
Chilean immigration is at Socompa. The Chilean side is open 0800-2200. On the Argentine side the road carries on to San Antonio de los Cobres and Salta. Argentine immigration is at San Antonio de los Cobres.

● **Crossing with a private vehicle**
US$2 is charged for crossing between 1300-1500 and 1860-2100.

Iquique, Arica and the Far North

THE continuation of the desert zone to the Peruvian border. The main cities are Iquique and Arica; between them are old mineral workings and even older geoglyphs. Large areas of the Andean highland have been set aside as national parks.

NORTH FROM ANTOFAGASTA

There are 2 routes from Antofagasta N to Iquique. 1) The Pan-American Highway continues N via Baquedano and Carmen Alto (Km 98), the turning to Calama.

At Km 167 a road turns off W to Pedro de Valdivia and **María Elena**, the two nitrate mines still functioning in Chile.

Museums Museo **Arqueológico y Histórico**, María Elena, on main plaza, with exhibits on prehispanic cultures.

● **Accommodation** E *Chacance*, T 632749, nice, secure; cheap meals at the *Casino Social*.

● **Transport** Buses to Iquique 6 hrs, US$10.

2) The coast road N of Antofagasta and Mejillones to Tocopilla, 187 km, is paved all the way, but there is no fuel N of Mejillones. The route runs at the foot of 500m cliffs, behind which are mountains which are extensively mined for copper, often by *piquineros* (small groups of self-employed miners). There are larger mines, with the biggest concentration in-

land of Michilla (107 km N).

Reminders of the area's mining past can be seen at several points, principally the ruins of **Cobija** (127 km N), formerly the coastal end of the silver trail from Potosí. This town was destroyed by an earthquake in 1877, and captured by the Chileans in the War of the Pacific 2 years later. Adobe walls, the rubbish tip (right above the sea) and the wreckage of the port are all that remains. The atmospheric ruins of the port of Gatico are at Km 144. About 5 km further N there is an amazing ransacked cemetery.

A zig-zag road (very steep) winds up the cliffs to the mine at Mantos de la Luna about 152 km N of Antofagasta. At the top there are rather dead-looking groves of giant cactus living off the sea mist which collects on the cliffs. Wildlife includes foxes (*zorros*).

There are good, weekend beach resorts at Hornitos (88 km N of Antofagasta) and Poza Verde (117 km N).

TOCOPILLA

Tocopilla (*Pop* 24,600; *Phone code* 055) is 187 km S of Antofagasta via the coastal road and 365 km via the Pan-American Highway. The town is dominated by a thermal power station, which supplies electricity to the whole of northern Chile, and by the port facilities used to unload coal and to export nitrates and iodine from María Elena (68 km E), and Pedro de Valdivia (85 km). In the centre is the copper concentrate plant of Cía Minera de Tocopilla. There is a sports stadium and two good beaches: Punta Blanca (12 km S) and Caleta Covadonga. Tocopilla Yacht Club, 45 km S, has a good beach, restaurant and bar. There is also fine deep sea fishing if you can find a boat and a guide.

● **Accommodation** C *Chungará*, 21 de Mayo 1440, T 811036, comfortable, clean, rec; **C** *Vucina*, 21 de Mayo 2069, T 811571, modern, good restaurant; **C** *Casablanca*, 21 de Mayo 2054, T 813222, F 813104, friendly, helpful; **D** *Hostería Bolívar*, Bolívar 1332, T 812783, modern, helpful, meals, clean, friendly, highly rec; **E** *Hostal Central*, Aníbal Pinto 1241, friendly, clean; **F** *Res La Giralda*, 21 de Mayo 1134.

The Far North

● **Places to eat** *Club de la Unión*, Prat 1354, good *almuerzo*, cheap; *Kong Jong*, 21 de Mayo 1833, reasonable value, Chinese; *El Pirata*, 21 de Mayo 1999, *parrilladas*. Good seafood at the Muelle Pesquero opp the old wooden clock tower.

● **Transport** Buses to **Antofagasta** 8 a day, several companies inc Barrrios, Tramaca and Camus, US$3, 2½ hrs; to **Iquique**, by bus and minibus along coastal road, Barrios, Tramaca and Turisnorte, 4 hrs, US$7, frequent. To **Chuquicamata** and **Calama**, Camus, 2 a day, 3 hrs, US$5. No direct services to **Santiago**, go via Antofagasta or take Tramaca or Flota Barrios to Vallenar or La Serena and change. Bus company offices are on 21 de Mayo.

Routes North and East of Tocopilla

East of Tocopilla a good paved road runs up the narrow valley 72 km to the Pan-American Highway. From here the road continues E in a very bad state (requires careful driving) to Chuquicamata.

81 km N of the crossroads is Quillagua (customs post, all vehicles and buses are searched) and 111 km further is the first of three sections of the **Reserva Nacional del Tamarugal**. In this part are the **Geoglyphs of Pintados**, some 400 figures on the hillsides (3 km W of the highway). Beyond the Reserve are Pozo Almonte and the turn-off for Iquique. The second part of Tamarugal is by La Tirana (see **Local festivals**, below), the third 60 km N of Pozo Almonte.

The coastal road from Tocopilla N to Iquique, 244 km, offers fantastic views of the rugged coastline and tiny fishing communities. Basic accommodation is available at San Marcos, a fishing village, 131 km N. At Chanaballita, 184 km N there is a hotel, cabanas, camping, restaurant, shops. There are also campsites at Guanillos, Km 126, Playa Peruana, Km 129 and Playa El Aguila, Km 160.

IQUIQUE

Iquique (*Pop* 140,000; *Phone code* 057), the capital of I Región (Tarapacá) and one of the main northern ports, is 304 km by road S of Arica. The name of the town is derived from the Aymara word *ique-ique*, meaning place of 'rest and tranquillity'. It was founded in the 16th century on a rocky peninsula at the foot of the high Atacama pampa, sheltered by the headlands of Punta Gruesa and Cavancha. The city, which was partly destroyed by earthquake in 1877, became the centre of the nitrate trade after its transfer from Peru to Chile at the end of the War of the Pacific.

A short distance N of town along Amunátegui is the Free Zone (Zofri), a giant shopping centre selling mainly imported electronic goods: it is worth a visit (much better value than Punta Arenas), good for cheap camera film (Fuji slide film available)(open Mon-Sat 0900-1330, 1630-2000). Colectivo taxi from the centre US$0.35. Limit on tax free purchases US$650 for foreigners, US$500 for Chileans. All vehicles travelling S from Iquique are searched for duty-free goods at Quillagua and at Chipana on the coastal road.

Places of interest

In the centre of the old town is **Plaza Prat** with a clock tower and bell dating from 1877. On the NE corner of the Plaza is the **Centro Español**, built in Moorish style in 1904; the ground floor is a restaurant, on the upper floors are paintings of scenes from Don Quijote and from Spanish history. On the S side of the Plaza is the **Teatro Municipal**, built in 1890; the façade features 4 women representing the seasons. Three blocks N of the Plaza is the old **Aduana** (customs house) built in 1871; in 1891 it was the scene of an important battle in the Civil War between supporters of President Balmaceda and congressional forces. Part of it is now a **Naval Museum**. Five blocks E along Sotomayor is the Railway Station, now disused, built in 1883. Along C Baquedano, which runs S from Plaza Prat, are the attractive former mansions of the 'nitrate barons'. Adorned with columns and balconies, these date from between 1880 and 1903 and were constructed from imported oregon pine. The finest of these is the **Palacio Astoreca**, Baquedano y O'Higgins, built in 1903, subsequently the Intendencia and now a museum.

The main exports are fishmeal, fish oil, canned fish and salt. Sealions and pelicans can be seen from the harbour. There are cruises around the harbour from the passenger pier, US$2.65, 45 mins, minimum 10-15 people.

Museums

Museo Naval, Sotomayor y Baquedano, focussing on the Battle of Iquique, 1879 (see page 760) open Tues-Sat 0930-1230, 1430-1800, Sun and holidays 1000-1300, entry US$0.50; **Museo Regional**, Baquedano 951, containing an archaeological section tracing the development of prehispanic civilizations in the region and a section devoted to the Nitrate Era which includes a model of a nitrate *oficina* and the collection of the nitrate entrepreneur, Santiago Humberstone, open Mon-Fri 0830-1300, 1500-1900, Sat 1030-1300, Sun (in summer) 1030-1300, US$0.50; **Palacio Astoreca**, Baquedano y O'Higgins, fine late 19th century furniture and exhibitions of shells, open Tues-Sun 1000-1300, 1600-2000, entry free.

Excursions

To **Humberstone**, a large nitrate town, now abandoned, at the junction of the Pan-American Highway and the road to Iquique. Though closed since 1961, you can see the church, theatre, *pulpería* (company stores) and the swimming pool (built of metal plating from ships' hulls). Entry US$2.50, guided tours Sat-Sun, leaflets available. Opposite, on the other side of the Iquique road, is the Oficina Santa Laura, the earliest nitrate plant in Chile, through which you can walk. Transport to/from Iquique: take any bus to/from Arica or Antofagasta, or a colectivo taxi for Pozo Almonte from Sgto Aldea y Barros Arana, US$2. To Pintados (see page 741) take any bus S, US$2.50, and walk from the Pan-American Highway then hitch back or flag down a bus. Many other sites around Iquique, including the Giant of the Atacama (see page 741), are difficult to visit without a vehicle. Hire a car and drive S along the Pacific coast to see sealions, *guano*, fishing settlements and old salt works, including the ghost town of Guanillos, complete with castle.

Local festivals

During the 10 days before 16 July there is a religious festival at the village of **La Tirana** (*Pop* 250), 70 km E of Iquique (near Pica, see page 740). Over 100 groups dance night and day, starting on 12 July, before making their pilgrimage to the church of the Virgen del Carmen. All the dances take place in the main plaza in front of the church; no alcohol is served. Accommoda-

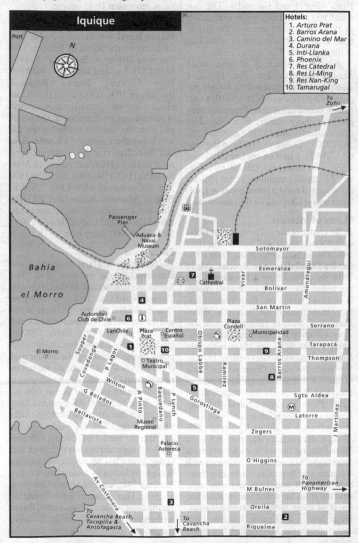

Iquique

Hotels:
1. *Arturo Prat*
2. *Barros Arana*
3. *Camino del Mar*
4. *Durana*
5. *Inti-Llanka*
6. *Phoenix*
7. *Res Catedral*
8. *Res Li-Ming*
9. *Res Nan-King*
10. *Tamarugal*

tion is impossible to find, other than in organized camp sites (take tent) which have basic toilets and showers.

Local information

● Accommodation

Accommodation is scarce in the weeks before Christmas as many Chileans visit Iquique to shop in the Zofri.

L3 *Hostería Cavancha*, Los Rieles 250, T 431007, 4-star, S of city, on water's edge.

A2 *Atenas*, Los Rieles 738, T 431100, F 424349, good service and food, rec; **A2** *Playa Brava*, Los Rieles 2503, T 431167, with breakfast, good; **A2** *Primeras Piedras*, street of same name, T 421358, 3 km from city, good food, friendly; **A3** *Tamarugal*, Tarapacá 369, T 424365, central, clean and modern, good restaurant.

B *Durana*, San Martín 294, T 412511, helpful; **B-C** *Inti-Llanka*, Obispo Labbe 825, T 412511, helpful.

C *Barros Arana*, Barros Arana 1330, T 412840, clean, modern, good value; **C** *Camino del Mar*, Orella 340, T 420465, restored building, clean, simple; **C** *Hostal Cuneo*, Baquedano 1175, T 428654, modern, clean, pleasant; **C** *Phoenix*, Aníbal Pinto 451, T 421315, with bath and breakfast, old but pleasant, noisy juke box.

D *Res Condell*, Thompson 684, T 423079, with bath, clean, friendly; **D** *Plaza*, Plaza Prat, T 414268, clean, friendly; **D** *Res Nan-King*, Thompson 752, T 423311, clean, good value; **D** *España*, Tarapacá 465, nr Plaza Condell, without bath, friendly, warm water, dirty; **D** *Hostal América*, Rodríguez 550, T/F 427524, nr beach, clean, good value; **D** *Hostal San Francisco*, Latorre 990, clean, hot water, noisy; **D** *Res José Luis*, San Martín 601, spacious, clean; **D** *Res Marclaud*, Juan Martínez 753, rec, clean, motor-cycle parking.

E *Playa*, Gral Hernán Fuenzalida 938, T 22911, small, friendly; **E** *Res Araucano*, San Martín 777, T 420211, friendly, cooking facilities, grubby, noisy; **D** *Res Li Ming*, Barros Arana 705, T 421912, clean, good value; **E** *Res Centro*, Lynch 621, cheap, run down, basic; **E** *Res Sol del Norte*, Juan Martínez 852, T 421546, cold water, basic, small rooms.

F pp *Hosp Tarapacá*, Tarapacá 1348, T 426040, clean, friendly, no hot water; **F** pp *Centenario*, Amunátegui 845, clean.

Camping: no site but wild camping possible on La Brava beach. Equipment: *Tunset*, in Zofri; *Lombardi*, Serrano 447.

● Places to eat

Club de la Unión, Plaza Prat, roof terrace, good views, good, not cheap; *Sociedad Protectora de los Empleados de Tarapacá*, Plaza Prat, reasonable prices; *Centro Español*, Plaza Prat, good meals well served in beautiful building, attractive, expensive; *José Luis*, Serrano 476, good, pleasant atmosphere, good value *almuerzo*; *Bavaria*, Wilson y Pinto, good but not cheap; *Rapa Nui*, Amunátegui 715, for good, cheap, local food; *Grecia*, Thompson 865, cheap but good; *Balcón*, Lynch 656, snacks, live music; *Pizzería D'Alfredo*, Vivar 631, expensive, good coffee; *Italianissimo*, Edificio España, Vivar y Latorre, very good coffee. Several good, inexpensive seafood restaurants (eg *Bucanero*) can be found on the second floor of the central market, Barros Arana y Latorre; also cafés opp the bus station, on the wharf, sell good, cheap fish lunches. *Bahía*, on seafront, cheap, good fish. *Club de Yates* at the harbour serves very expensive meals. *El Rey del Pescado*, Bulnes y Juan Martínez, very nice local place with good and cheap seafood dishes, *menú de la casa* a bargain; also *El Pescado Frito*, Bulnes y Juan Martínez, large portions. *Chifa Fu-Wa*, Barros Arana 740, Chinese.

Cafés: *Salón de Té Chantilly*, Tarapacá 520; *Café Diana*, Vivar 836; *Pinina*, Ramírez y Tarapacá, juices, ice-cream; *Samoa Grill*, Bolívar 396, good coffee and snacks.

● Airline offices

LanChile, Aníbal Pinto 641, T 414378; **Ladeco**, San Martín 428, T 413038; **National**, Galería Lynch, Local 1-2, T 427816, F 425158.

● Banks & money changers

National banks. **Fincard** (Mastercard), Serrano 372, open Mon-Fri 0900-1400, 1600-1800. Difficult to change TCs in town. Best rates for cheques and cash at *casas de cambio* in the Free Zone.

● Embassies & consulates

Bolivia, Serrano Pasaje Alessandri 429, p 2, Of 300, Mon-Fri 0930-1400; **Peru**, Los Rieles 131, T 431116.

● Entertainment

Cinema: *Cine Tarapacá*, Serrano 202, shows foreign films.

● Language schools

Academia de Idiomas del Norte, Ramírez 1345, T 411827, F 429343, Swiss run, Spanish classes and accommodation for students.

● Laundry

Bulnes 170, expensive; Obispo Labbé 1446.

● Post & telecommunications

Post Office: Correo Central, Bolívar 458.

Telecommunications: CTC, Serrano 620, Ramírez 587; Entel, Gorostiaga 287; Diego Portales 840; Telegrams at TelexChile, Lynch y San

Martín. **NB** Correos, Telex/Telefax and Entel all have offices in the Plaza de Servicios in the Zona Franca.

● **Sports**

Bathing: beaches at Cavancha just S of town centre, good, and Huaiquique, reasonable, Nov-March. Restaurants at Cavancha. Piscina Godoy, fresh water swimming pool on Av Costanera at Aníbal Pinto and Riquelme, open pm, US$1.

Fishing: equipment: *Ferretería Lonza*, Vivar 738; *Ferretería La Ocasión*, Sgto Aldea 890; fishing for broadbill swordfish, striped marlin, yellowfin tuna, oceanic bonito, Mar till end of August.

● **Tour companies & travel agents**

Iquitour, Tarapacá 465B, Casilla 669, T 422009, no English spoken, tour to Pintados, La Tirana, Humberstone, Pica, etc, 0900-1900, lunch inc, a lot of time spent eating and bathing; *Lirima*, Baquedano 823, rec; *Taxitur*, Sgto Aldea 791, 5-6 hr tour to local sites, maximum 5 passengers.

● **Tourist offices**

Aníbal Pinto 436, T 411523; open Mon-Fri, 0830-1300, 1500-1800, little information, poor maps. **Automóvil Club de Chile**: Serrano 154, T 426772.

● **Transport**

Local Car hire: expensive: Hertz, Souper 650, T 426316. **Continental**, Thompson 159, T/F 411426; **J Reategui**, Serrano 1058-A, T 429490/446079; **GP Car Rental**, O'Higgins 179. **Mechanic**: Sergio Cortez, *Givet*, Bolívar 684, highly rec for motorcycles. In the Zona Franca there is a wide range of motorcycle tyres.

Air Diego Aracena international airport, 35 km S at Chucumata, T 424577. Taxi from outside *Hotel Prat*, Plaza Prat, US$3, T 426184. Airport bus to city centre, US$2. LanChile, Ladeco and National all fly daily to Arica, Antofagasta and Santiago.

Buses Terminal at N end of Patricio Lynch (not all buses leave from here); bus company offices are nr the market on Sgto Aldea and B Arana. All luggage is searched for duty-free goods before being loaded onto buses; all southbound buses are then searched again, at Quillagua on the Pan American Highway and at Río Loa on the coastal Route 1. To **Arica**, buses and colectivos, frequent, US$8, 4½ hrs; to **Antofagasta**, US$13, 8 hrs. To **Calama**, 8 hrs, US$13, Kennybus not rec. To **Tocopilla** along the coastal road, buses and minibuses, several companies, 4 hrs, US$7; to **La Serena**, 17 hrs, US$25; to **Santiago**, 28 hrs, several companies, US$30 (US$50 for Barrios *salón cama*).

International buses: Geminis (Obispo Labbé y Sotomayor) to **La Paz** (Bolivia) via Oruro, Thur and Sat 2300, 22 hrs, US$32; also Litoral, Esmeralda 974, T 423670, Tues, Sat, Sun 2300, US$32. To **Salta** (Argentina) via Calama and San Pedro, Geminis, once a week, US$50; Tramaca twice a week to Jujuy via Paso de Jama, US$50.

INLAND FROM IQUIQUE

MAMINA

From Pozo Almonte, an unpaved road runs 73 km NE to the hot mineral springs in the mountains at Termas de **Mamiña** (2,700m), where there is also an interesting church (1632), a prehispanic *pukará* (fortress), a mud spring (Baño El Chino; open 0930-1300) and good accommodation. Electricity till 2230. The rainy season in Mamiña is mainly in Jan and is called *Invierno Boliviano* ('Bolivian winter').

● **Accommodation C** pp *Termas de Salitre*, full board, thermal pool in each room, electricity till midnight, swimming pool open 0930-1300; **B** *Termal La Coruña*, T 796298, good, nice views; **C** *Tamarugal*, T 424365, thermal pool in each room; **D** *Res Sol de Ipla*, cheapest, 2 others; *cabañas* to let and campsite; basic accommodation may also be available at the military refuge.

● **Transport** Minibuses from Iquique leave B Arana y Latorre, Mon-Sat 1600; from Mamiña, 0800; Sun from Iquique 0930, from Mamiña 1600, US$4.50.

PICA

9 km S of Pozo Almonte a road runs SE to La Tirana 10 km – see page 738, and the fertile oasis of **Pica** (*Pop* 1,500; *Alt* 1,300m) a centre of Spanish settlement during the colonial period. The town is famous for its pleasant climate, its citrus groves and its two natural springs, the best of which is Cocha Resbaladero (open 0700-2000 all year, changing rooms, snack bar, beautiful pool, entry US$0.70).

● **Accommodation & places to eat D** *Resbaladero*, Ibáñez 57, T 741316, full pension, good pool; **E** *San Andrés*, Balmaceda 197, T 741319, with large breakfast; **E** *O'Higgins*, Balmaceda 6, T 741322; **E** *El Tambo*, Ibáñez 60, T 741320, old fashioned, good restaurant; also *cabañas* for rent. Campsite at **Camping Miraflores**, T 741333. *Restaurant Palomar*, Balmaceda 74, excellent *almuerzo*.

● **Transport** Buses from Iquique operated by Santa Rosa, Latorre 973, daily 0930, 2 hrs; from

Pica 1800, US$3. Several companies (Flonatur, Sgto Aldea 790; Julia, B Arana 965) operate minibuses from Iquique but services vary. If travelling by car, a quicker route to Pica is by turning E off the Pan-American Highway at Pintados, 43 km S of Pozo Almonte.

IQUIQUE TO THE BOLIVIAN FRONTIER

33 km N of Pozo Almonte is **Huara** (last fuel before Arica; basic accommodation at *Restaurante Frontera*). A road turns off the Panamericana to **Colchane**, 173 km NE on the Bolivian frontier (open 0800-1300, 1500-1800 daily).

At Km 13 the road passes, on the right, the **Giant of the Atacama**, 86m high, reported to be the largest geoglyph in the world (best viewed from a distance). From Km 25 the road is unpaved. At **Chuzmisa**, 3 km off this road at Km 77 there are thermal springs: the water is bottled and sold throughout northern Chile. Basic accommodation is available.

● **Transport** Colchane can be reached by Kennybus from Iquique, one a week, returns after 2 hrs. Geminis bus from Iquique to La Paz also passes through Colchane.

PARQUE NACIONAL VOLCAN ISLUGA

The national park contains some of the best volcanic scenery in northern Chile. There is a Conaf refugio at Enquelga, but guardaparques are seldom there: ask the carabineros at Colchane where the key is. 6 km W of Colchane, the village of **Isluga** has an 18th century Andean walled church and bell tower. Mountain roads in poor condition lead NW from Isluga across the Parque Nacional to Camiña (see below), 171 km from Colchane. It is, in theory, possible to drive N from Isluga through the Salar de Surire via Guallatiri to the Parque Nacional del Lauca, and from there to Bolivia, or via Putre and Poconchile to Arica or Peru.

HUARA TO ARICA

The Pan-American Highway runs across the Atacama desert at an altitude of around 1,000m, with several steep hills which are best tackled in daylight (at night, sea mist, *camanchaca*, can reduce visibility).

At Zapiga, 47 km N of Huara there is a cross roads: one branch leads W for 41 km to the run down nitrate port of **Pisagua**. There is little left of this place, though there are a few quite good fish restaurants in the town and it makes a pleasant stop for a meal. Mass graves dating from just after the 1973 military coup were discovered near here in 1990.

The branch which leads E is not in very good condition, with deep sand and dust causing problems. After 67 km there is the picturesque village of Camiña where there is a basic hostal. 45 km further on is the Tranque de Caritaya, a dam which supplies water for the coastal towns set in splendid scenery with lots of wildlife and interesting botany (especially *llareta*). From here mountain roads lead across the Parque Nacional Volcán Isluga to Colchane.

At Km 57 N of Huara there is an interesting British cemetery dating from 1876. 64 km further N are the **Geoglifas de Chiza** (sign-posted, to left, and easily accessible). 70 km before Arica a road runs E to **Codpa**, an an agricultural community in a deep gorge with interesting scenery. From Codpa poor roads lead N and E through **Tignamar** and **Belén** to Putre. Belén, a tiny village founded by the Spanish in 1625, was on the silver route between Potosí and the coast: it has two colonial churches.

ARICA

Arica is Chile's most northerly city, 19 km S of the Peruvian border (*Pop* 174,064). It is built at the foot of the Morro headland, fringed by sand dunes. The Andes can be clearly seen from the anchorage.

Arica is an important port and routecentre. A 448 km railway runs E to the Bolivian capital La Paz: about half the legal trade of Bolivia passes along this line. An oil pipeline also runs to La Paz. The completion of the international highway to the Bolivian frontier at Tambo Quemado has added to the city's importance. It is frequented for sea-bathing by

Bolivians as well as the locals. A 63 km railway runs N to Tacna in Peru. Regrettably there are indications that Arica is also becoming a key link in the international drugs trade. There are large fishmeal plants and a car assembly factory.

BASICS *Pop* 174,064; *Phone code* 058. Air pollution at night can be bad. There is no

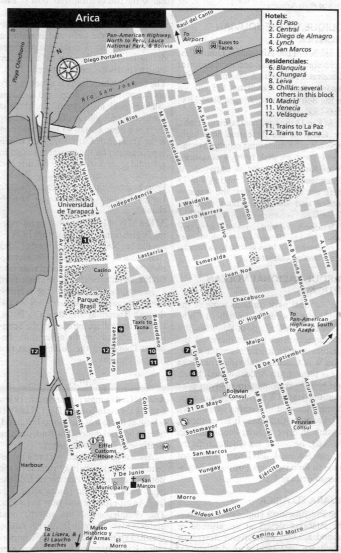

Arica

Hotels:
1. El Paso
2. Central
3. Diego de Almagro
4. Lynch
5. San Marcos

Residenciales:
6. Blanquita
7. Chungará
8. Leiva
9. Chillán: several others in this block
10. Madrid
11. Venecia
12. Velásquez

T1. Trains to La Paz
T2. Trains to Tacna

rain, winter or summer. The average, daytime winter temperature is 19°C, and the average summer temperature 24°C.

Places of interest

The **Morro**, with a good view from the park on top (10 mins' walk by footpath from the southern end of Colón), was the scene of a great victory by Chile over Peru in the War of the Pacific on 7 June 1880.

At the foot of the Morro is the Plaza Colón with the cathedral of **San Marcos**, built in iron by Eiffel. Though small it is beautifully proportioned and attractively painted. It was brought to Arica from Ilo (Peru) in the 19th century, before Peru lost Arica to Chile, as an emergency measure after a tidal wave swept over Arica and destroyed all its churches. Eiffel also designed the nearby **customs house** which is now the Casa de la Cultura (open Mon-Sat 1000-1300, 1700-2000.) Just N of the Aduana is the La Paz railway station; outside is an old steam locomotive (made in Germany in 1924) once used on this line. In the station is a memorial to John Roberts Jones, builder of the Arica portion of the railway, and a small museum (key at booking office).

Museums

Museo Arqueológico of the University of Tarapacá, see under **Excursions** below. **Museo Histórico y de Armas**, on the summit of the Morro, containing weapons and uniforms from the War of the Pacific.

Excursions

To the Azapa valley, E of Arica, by yellow colectivo from P Lynch y Chacabuco, US$1. At Km 13 is the **Museo Arqueológico de San Miguel**, part of the University of Tarapacá, containing an important collection of mummies from the Chinchorro culture, reputed to be the oldest collection in the world, as well as sections on Andean weaving, basketwork and ceramics (open Mon-Fri 0830-1300, 1500-1800, Sat, Sun, and holidays 1200-1800, Latin Americans US$1, others US$4, worth a visit). In the forecourt of the museum are several boulders with precolumbian petroglyphs. On the road between Arica and San Miguel images of humans

and llamas ('stone mosaics') can be seen to the S of the road. On the opposite side of the valley at San Lorenzo are the ruins of a *pukará* (pre-Inca fortress) dating from the 12th century.

To the **Lluta valley**, N of Arica along Route 11, bus from MacKenna y Chacabuco, 4 a day: At Km 14 and Km 16 there are ancient images of llamas and humans on the hillside. The road continues through the Lauca National Park and on to Bolivia.

Local festivals

Fiestas for the **Virgen de las Peñas** at the Santuario de Livircar in the Azapa Valley are held on the first Sun in Oct and a lesser festival on 7-9 Dec (on 8 Dec the festival moves to Arica). Take a bus from Av Chacabuco y Vicuña Mackenna, then walk 12 km from where it stops to the sanctuary. The Dec festival is not particularly outstanding but it takes place in a part of the valley not normally accessible. **NB** The arrival of Africans during the colonial period has created an Afro-Chilean folklore here.

Local information

● **Accommodation**

NB In this area, *pensión* means restaurant, not hostel.

L3 *Arica*, San Martín 599, T 254540, F 231133, best, price depends on season, good value, good and reasonable restaurant, other services expensive, about 2 km along shore (buses No 7, 8, frequent), tennis court, pool, lava beach (not safe for swimming), good breakfast, poor water supply; **L3** *El Paso*, bungalow style, pleasant gardens, swimming pool, Gen Velásquez, 1109, T 231965, with breakfast, good food; **L3** *San Marcos*, Sotomayor 382, T 232970, F 254815, clean, helpful, restaurant, parking.

A1 *Saint Georgette*, Camino a Azapa 3221, T 221914, F 223830, 5-star, pool, tennis court, restaurant, bar; **A2** *Azapa*, Sánchez 660, Azapa, T 222612, attractive grounds but several kilometres from beaches and centre, also cheaper cabins, restaurant; **A2** *Central*, 21 de Mayo 425, T 252575, central, nicely decorated; **A3** *Amadís de Gaula*, Prat 588, T/F 232994, central, modern; **A3** *Savona*, Yungay 380, T 232319, comfortable, friendly, quiet, highly rec.

B *Diego de Almagro*, Sotomayor 490, T 224444, F 221248, helpful, clean, comfortable, rec, stores luggage; **C** *Lynch*, Lynch 589,

T 231581, D without bath, pleasant but poor beds, clean, rec, parking; **C** *Res América*, Sotomayor 430, T 254148, clean, friendly, central; **C** *El Refugio*, Km 1½ Valle de Azapa, T 227545.

D *Hostal 18 de Septiembre*, 18 de Septiembre 524, T 251727, clean, hot water, breakfast; **D** *Res Caracas*, Sotomayor 867, T 253688, cheap, clean, hot water, TV, breakfast; **D** *Res Blanquita*, Maipú 472, T 232064, clean, hot water; **D** *Res Chungará*, Lynch 675, T 231677, with bath, clean, hot water am only, small rooms; **D** *Res Las Condes*, Vicuña Mackenna 628, T 251583, helpful, hot water, rec; **D** *Res Puerta del Sol*, 21 de Mayo 480, T 252597, shared bath, meals available, clean, quiet, excellent service; **D** *Pensión Donoso*, Baquedano y Maipú, downstairs with bath, gloomy, E upstairs without bath, bright; **D** *Res Ecuador*, Juan Noé 989, T 251573, clean, noisy, helpful, meals available.

E *Res Las Vegas 120*, Baquedano 120, T 231355, basic, friendly, dark rooms, hot water, safe, central; **E** *Res Leiva*, Colón 347, T 232008, without bath, French spoken, cooking facilities, motorcycle parking with difficulty; **E** *Casa Blanca*, Gen Lagos 557, modern, clean, rec; **E** *Res Española*, Bolognesi 340, T 231703, central, clean, basic, quiet; **E** *Res Madrid*, Baquedano 685, T 231479, without bath, clean, good value but poor beds, reductions for IYHA cards; **E** *Res Maipú*, Maipú 479, T 252157, basic, clean, hot water, safe; **E** *Hostal Raissa*, San Martín 281, T 251070, without bath, with breakfast. On Velásquez are: **E** *Res Valencia*, No 719, T 253479, friendly, cooking and laundry facilties, motorcycle parking; **E** *Res Velásquez*, No 685, T 231989, central, basic, friendly; **E** *Res Chillán*, No 749, T 251677, safe, friendly, clean, good value; **E** *Res Ine'sa*, No 725, T 231609, comfortable, breakfast available, kitchen, laundry, good; **E** pp Sra Eliana, Arteaga 50, T 232304, with breakfast, luggage stored, laundry facilities, rec; **E** *Res Venecia*, Baquedano 739, T 252877, spotless, hot water, small rooms, rec; **E** *La Posada*, 21 de Mayo 186, small rooms, good beds, central, without bath; **E** *Res Tropical*, Gen Lagos 649, friendly, basic; **E** *Res El Sur*, Maipú 516, very clean, small rooms, hot water, basic; **E** pp Raul del Canto 947, nice, friendly, clean, nr bus terminal; **E** Gloria Martínez, pasaje 7, Población Juan Noé, T 241971, friendly, helpful; **E** pp Sra Leony Vidiella, Gonzálo Cerda 1030, close to bus station, with breakfast, cooking facilities, clean, safe, tepid water, English spoken. In Jan-Feb the municipality supplies cheap basic accommodation, ask at the tourist office.

Camping: *Gallinazos*, at Villa Frontera, 15 km N, T 232373, and at the *Res El Refugio* (see above).

● **Places to eat**

Acuario, Máximo Lira, Terminal Pesquero, for food and atmosphere, expensive; *El Rey del Marisco*, Maipú y Colón, seafood, pricey, rec; *Maracuyá*, San Martín 0321, seafood, splendid location on the coast, pricey; plenty of seafood lunch places in the market; *Los Aleros del 21*, 21 de Mayo 736, rec for seafood and service; *Don Floro*, V MacKenna y Chacabuco, steaks; *Snack Suceso Inn*, 18 de Septiembre 250, good set meal and coffee; *La Jaula*, 18 de Septiembre 293, cheap lunches; *Casanova*, Baquedano 397, excellent but not cheap; *Yuri*, Maipú 500, good service, cheap, rec; *Bavaria*, Colón 613, expensive, with delicatessen and expresso coffee, repeatedly rec; *Govinda*, Bolognesi 430, vegetarian, good value lunches, repeatedly rec; *Scala*, 21 de Mayo 201, excellent fruit juices; *Carpaccio*, Velásquez 510, restaurant and bar, live music from 2330 Wed-Sat; *El Tambo*, in Poblado Artesanal, Hualles 2025, for lunches, folk music and dancing on Sun. Several good Chinese restaurants inc *Si Lom*, Sotomayor 593; *Chin Huang Tao*, Lynch 317. Several places for cheap breakfasts and set meals on Baquedano 700 block. *Casino de Bomberos*, Colón 357, at fire station, good value *almuerzo*; *Schop*, 18 de Septiembre 240, cheap sandwiches.

● **Airline offices**

LanChile, 7 de Junio 148, T 224738; Ladeco, 21 de Mayo 443, T 252021; Lloyd Aéreo Boliviano, P Lynch 298, T 251472; AeroPerú, 7 de Junio 148, T 232852; National, 21 de Mayo 627, T 253447, F 251283.

● **Banks & money changers**

Many money changers on 21 de Mayo and its junction with Colón, some accept TCs but with high commision. **Banco Osorno**, 21 de Mayo, cash on Visa, no commission; **Fincard** (Mastercard), 21 de Mayo 252, Mon-Fri 0900-1400, 1600-1730, only pesos given, at varying rates. *Casas de Cambio*: **Inter-Santiago** and **Cambio Fides**, Shopping Centre del Pacífico, Diego Portales 840; **Daniel Concha**, Chacabuco 300; **Sol y Mar**, Colón 610; **Tacora**, 21 de Mayo 171, good rates for cash; **Yanulaque**, 21 de Mayo 175, which stay open until 2000 but close all day Sun. Most large hotels also change cash. Rates for TCs are generally poor, you may even get better rates in the street.

● **Embassies & consulates**

United Kingdom, the only one in Chile N of Valparaíso, and Instituto Chileno – Británico de Cultura (library open Mon-Fri 0900-1200, 1600-2100), Baquedano 351, T 231960, Casilla 653; **Brazil**, Las Margaritas 717, Pob Prat, T 231142; **Bolivia**, 21 de Mayo 575, T 231030; **Denmark**, 21 de Mayo 399, T 231399; **Peru**, San Martín

220, T 231020; **Germany**, 21 de Mayo 639, T 231551, open 0900-1300; **Spain**, Santa María 2660, T 224655; **Italy**, San Martín y Chacabuco, T 229195; **Norway**, 21 de Mayo 399, T 231298; **Instituto Cultural Chileno Norteamericano**, San Marcos 581; **Instituto Chileno-Alemán de Cultura**, 21 de Mayo 816.

● **Entertainment**

Cinemas: *Colón*, 7 de Junio 190, T 231165; *Cine Arte Universidad,* University Campus, T 251813.

Discotheques: 3 S of town along front, also *Sunset* and *Swing*, both 3½ km out of town in the Valle de Azapa, 2300-0430 weekends (taxi US$3).

Theatre: *Teatro Municipal de Arica*, Baquedano 234, new, wide variety of theatrical and musical events, exhibitions, rec.

● **Hospitals & medical services**

Dentist: *Juan Horta Becerra*, 18 de Septiembre 1154, T 252497, speaks English; *Rodrigo Belmar Castillo*, 18 de Septiembre 1051, T 252047.

Health: *Dr Juan Noé*, 18 de Septiembre 1000, T 231331 (T 232242 for urgent cases).

● **Laundry**

Lavandería La Moderna, 18 de Septiembre 457, next day service, closed weekends, good; *Americana*, Lynch 260, T 231808.

● **Post & telecommunications**

Post Office: Prat 375. To send parcels abroad, contents must be shown to Aduana (under main post office) on weekdays, except Iues, between 1500 and 1700. Your parcel will be wrapped, cheaply, but take your own carton.

Telephones: Entel-Chile, 21 de May 345, open 0900-2200; CTC, Colón 430 and at 21 de Mayo 211; VTR Telecommunications, 21 de Mayo 477, telex, fax, telegrams.

● **Shopping**

Poblado Artesanal, Plaza Las Gredas, Hualles 2025 (take bus 2, 3 or 7): local 2, expensive but especially good for musical instruments; *Mercado Central*, Sotomayor, between Colón and Baquedano, mornings only. **Feria Turística Dominical**, Sun market, W end of Chacabuco extending N on Av Costanera Nte, good prices for llama sweaters. Fruit, vegetable and old clothes market at Terminal Agropecuario at edge of town; take bus marked 'Terminal Agro'. Arica, as a duty free zone, is an important centre for cheapish electronic goods for Bolivian and Peruvian shoppers. Supermarket at San Martín y 18 de Septiembre.

● **Sports**

Bathing: Olympic pool in Parque Centenario, Tues-Sun, US$0.50; take No 5A bus from 18 de Septiembre. The best beach for swimming is Playa Chinchorro, N of town. Buses 7 and 8 run to beaches S of town – the first two beaches, La Lisera and El Laucho, are both small and mainly for sunbathing. Playa Brava is popular for sunbathing but not swimming (dangerous currents). Strong currents also at Playa Las Machas which is popular with surfers. Good surfing also beyond seawall at Club de Yates. Playa Corazones, 15 km to S (no buses, take taxi or hitch), rec, not for swimming but picnics and fishing.

Golf: 18-hole course in Valle de Azapa, open daily except Mon.

Tennis: Club de Tenis Centenario, Av España 2640, open daily.

● **Tour companies & travel agents**

Jurasi, Bolognesi 360 A, T 251696, will hold mail, helpful, good city tour; *Eco Tours*, Bolognesi 460, T 250000, rec; *Huasquitur*, Sotomayor 470, T 223875, helpful, English spoken, will cater for individual itineraries, rec for flights; *Vicuña Tour*, 18 de Septiembre 399, oficina 215, T 253773, F 252404, rec; *Globo Tour*, 21 de Mayo 260, T 232807, F 231085, very helpful; *Aricamundi*, Prat 358, T 252263, F 251797, for airline tickets; *Latinorizons*, O'Higgins 440, T/F 250007, specialize in tours to Lauca National Park, small groups in 4WD Landcruiser and many others. Agencies charge similar prices for tours: Lauca National Park US$20, Valle de Azapa US$12; city tour US$10. Alex Figares, Casilla 2007, T/F 213643, rec as guide, speaks English

● **Tourist offices**

Sernatur, Prat 375, p 2; open Mon-Fri 0830-1300, 1500-1830, T 232101. Very helpful, English spoken, good map; Kiosk on 21 de Mayo between Colón and Baquedano, open Mon-Fri, 0830-1300, 1500-1900; **Automobile Club** Chacabuco 460, T 252678; **Conaf**, Valle de Azapa 3444 (Km 1.5), T 231559, closed weekends (bus 8 to Azapa intersection).

● **Transport**

Local Bus: buses run from C Maipú, US$0.25. Collective taxis on fixed routes within city limit, US$0.30 pp (US$0.50 pp after 2000). **Car hire**: Hertz, *Hotel El Paso*, Gen Velázquez 1109, T 231487; **Budget**, 21 de Mayo 650, T 252978; **Klasse**, Velásquez 762, Loc 25, T 254498; **American**, Gen Lagos 559, T 252234; *GP*, Copacabana 628, T 252594; **Viva**, 21 de Mayo 821, T 251121; 4WD and antifreeze are essential for Lauca National Park.

Motoring Automóvil Club de Chile: Chacabuco 469, T 237780. **Car insurance**: at Dirección de Tránsito; may insist on car inspection. **Car service**: Shell, Panamericana Nte 3456; Esso, Portales 2462; Autocentro, Azola 2999, T 241241. **Bicycle parts**: *Bicicletas Wilson*, 18 de Sept 583, also Portales 1479.

Air Airport 18 km N of city at Chacalluta, T 222831. Taxi to town US$9, collective taxi US$4-5 pp from Lynch y 21 de Mayo. Flights: to **La Paz**, LanChile and LAB; to **Santiago**, Ladeco (via Iquique and Antofagasta), LanChile (via Iquique or Antofagasta), and National (via Iquique or Antofagasta). Book well in advance. To **Lima**, AeroPerú and others from Tacna (Peru), enquire at travel agencies in Arica.

Trains To **La Paz** (Bolivia): direct ferrobus services operated by Enfe (Bolivian Railways) leave Arica Tues and Sat at 0830, 12 hrs, US$52 (in clean US$ bills only) inc breakfast, lunch and drinks up to lunchtime (extra food and drinks sold). Book well in advance in Jan-Mar, tickets from the station at 21 de Mayo 51, T 232844. Baggage allowance, 25 kg plus hand luggage (luggage is weighed and searched at the station). Additional trains may run in Jan-Mar, reduced service off season. Local trains run to the frontier towns of Visviri (Chile) and Charaña (Bolivia) every other Tues (every Tues in Jan-Mar) at 2300, 9 hrs, US$12 1st class, US$7 2nd class; from Charaña a service runs to Viacha, 32 km from La Paz, US$3.05 pullman. Check details in advance. (For train and bus connections from Charaña to La Paz see under La Paz, page 273) On all journeys, take plenty of warm clothing; long delays, particularly at the frontier are common. Search for fruit, vegetables and dairy products at Arica station for passengers arriving from Bolivia.

The line from Arica skirts the coast for 10 km and passes into the Lluta Valley, whose vegetation is in striking contrast with the barrenness of the surrounding hills. From Km 70 there is a sharp rise of 2,241m in 42 km through a series of tunnels. At Puquíos station, Km 112, the plateau is reached at 4,168m. The line continues through Col Alcérreca (Km 140) and Villa Industrial (Km 165), before reaching its highest point at General Lagos (4,247m). In the distance can be seen the snowcapped heights of Tacora, Putre, Sajama, and their fellows. The frontier station of Visviri is at Km 205, with a customs house. Beyond, the train enters Bolivia and the station of Charaña. In summer a tourist train runs from Arica to Col Alcérreca and back on Sun, 0800, returning to Arica 2100.

Buses Bus terminal at Av Portales y Santa María, T 241390, bus or colectivo No 8 or 18 (US$0.15, or US$0.30), taxi to centre US$2 (terminal tax US$0.25). All luggage is carefully searched for fruit prior to boarding and is then searched again at Cuya on the Pan American Highway. All long-distance buses are modern, clean and air-conditioned, but ask carefully what meals are inc. Bus company offices at bus terminal. Local services: Flota Paco (La Paloma), Germán Riesco 2071 (bus U from centre); Humire, P Montt 662, T 231891;

Martínez, P Montt 620, T 232265; Bus Lluta, Chacabuco y V Mackenna. To **Antofagasta**, US$18, 10 hrs. To **Calama** and **Chuquicamata**, 10 hrs, US$16, several companies, all between 2000 and 2200; to **Iquique**, frequent, US$8, 4½ hrs, also collective taxis, several companies, all with offices in the terminal; to **Santiago**, 28 hrs, a number of companies, eg Carmelita, Ramos Cholele, Fénix and Flota Barrios US$40-45, also *salón cama* services, run by Fichtur, Flota Barrios, Fénix and others, US$60, Tramaca rec (most serve meals and the more expensive, the more luxurious; student discounts available); to **La Serena**, 18 hrs, US$30; to **Viña del Mar** and **Valparaíso**, US$40, also *salón cama* service, US$50.

International buses: to **La Paz**, Bolivia, Internacional Litoral, Chacabuco 454, T 254702, Mon and Thur, 2400, 20 hrs, US$22, no food; service via border towns of Chungará (Chile) and Tambo Quemado (Bolivia, very cold at border – take blanket/sleeping bag, food, water and sense of humour), subject to cancellation in wet season. Also Geminis, Wed 2400, US$32, some food, 20 hrs, more comfortable via Huara and Challapata (Bolivia). To **Salta** (Argentina), Geminis, Tues 2130, US$50, connects at Calama next day with Antofagasta-Salta service. Computerized booking ensures seat reservation; passport details required, book in advance.

Motorists It is illegal to take fruit and dairy products S of Arica: all vehicles are searched at Cuya, 105 km S, and at Huara, 234 km S. **Service stations** between the Peruvian border and Santiago can be found at: Arica, Huara, Iquique, Pozo Almonte, Oficina Vitoria, Tocopilla, Oficina María Elena, Chuquicamata, Calama, Carmen Alto, Antofagasta, La Negra, Agua Verde, Taltal, Chañaral, Caldera, Copiapó, Vallenar, La Serena, Termas de Soco, Los Vilos, and then every 30 km to capital.

Hitchhiking Not easy to hitch South: try the Terminal Agropecuario (trucks leave Mon, Thur and Sat before 0700) and the Copec station opp (bus from Arica marked 'Agro').

By road to Bolivia There are 2 routes: 1) Via Chungará (Chile) and Tambo Quemado (Bolivia). This, the most widely used route, begins by heading N from Arica on the Pan-American Highway (Route 5) for 12 km before turning right (E towards the cordillera) on Route 11 towards Chungará via Putre and Lauca National Park (see below). This road is now paved as far as the border and the Bolivian section to La Paz is being paved, which will cut the journey time to 5 hrs. For the Bolivian portion of this route and the journey in reverse, see Bolivia, page 274. 2) Via Visviri (Chile) and (Charaña) Bolivia, following the La Paz-Arica railway line. This route should not be attempted in wet weather.

FRONTIER WITH PERU: CHACALLUTA

● **Immigration**

Open 0800-2400; a fairly uncomplicated crossing.

NB Between Oct and March Chilean time is 1 hr later than Peruvian, 2 hrs later Oct to Feb or March, varies annually.

● **Crossing by private vehicle**

US$2/vehicle is charged for crossing 1300-1500, 1850-2400 and on Sat, Sun, holidays. Drivers entering Chile are required to file a form, *Relaciones de Pasajeros*, giving details of passengers, obtained from a stationery store in Tacna, or at the border in a booth near Customs. You must also present the original registration document for your car from its country of registration. The first checkpoints outside Arica on the road to Santiago also require the *Relaciones de Pasajeros*. If you can't buy the form, details on a piece of paper will suffice or you can get them at service stations. The form is *not* required when travelling S of Antofagasta.

● **Exchange**

Facilities at the frontier but reproted better rates in Tacna.

● **Transport**

Collective taxis: run from the bus terminal and bus company offices in Arica to **Tacna**, US$4 pp, 1 hr, drivers take care of all the paperwork. Four companies: Chile Lintur, Baquedano 796, T 232048; Chasquitur, Chacabuco 320, T 231376; San Marcos, Noé 321, T 252528; Colectivo San Remo, Chacabuco 350, T 251925. Bus from the terminal, US$2, also Taxibus, 2 hourly, US$4. For Arequipa it is best to go to Tacna and catch an onward bus there.

Trains Services for passengers to Tacna leave Arica 3 times a week, US$1.60, 2½ hrs, from the station at Máximo Lira 889, T 231115. In Tacna there is a customs check at the station but no immigration facilities.

FRONTIER WITH BOLIVIA: VISVIRI

● **Immigration**

Open 0800-2400. Chilean formalities at Visviri, Bolivian formalities at Charaña, 10 km E.

● **Crossing with a private vehicle**

US$2/vehicle charge for crossing 1300-1500, 1850-2100 and Sat, Sun and holidays.

● **Transport**

No regular buses to/from Arica. Collective taxi from Arica US$10. In Visviri take a jeep across the border to Charaña. Bus from Charaña to La Paz, US$8.50, 7 hrs.

LAUCA NATIONAL PARK

A visit to the Parque Nacional Lauca, 176 km E of Arica stretching to the frontier with Bolivia, is highly recommended. Situated at over 3,200m (beware of soroche unless you are coming from Bolivia), the park covers 137,883 ha and includes numerous snowy volcanoes including 10 peaks of over 6,000m, two large lakes (Cotacotani and Chungará) and lava fields at Cotacotani. The park contains over 130 species of birds including a wide variety of waterfowl as well as vicuña, puma and vizcacha. It is administered by Conaf. During the rainy season (Jan and Feb) roads in the park may be impassable although the main Arica-La Paz road is now paved as far as the frontier; check in advance with Conaf in Arica from whom further information and map may be obtained. On the way, at Km 90 there is a pre-Inca *pukará* (fortress) and a few kilometres further there is an Inca *tambo* (inn). At the entrance to the park is **Putre** (3,500m), a scenic village with a church dating from 1670 and surrounded by terracing dating from Inca times. Putre is a good base for acclimatization. At **Parinacota** (4,392m), at the foot of the Payachatas volcano, there is an interesting 17th century church – rebuilt 1789 – with frescoes and the skulls of past priests. Local residents knit alpaca sweaters, US$26 approx; weavings of wildlife scenes also available. Weavings are sold from a tin shed with an orange roof opposite the church. From here an unpaved road runs N to the Bolivian frontier at Visviri (see above). From the Conaf hut you can climb Guane Guane, 5,300 m, in 2-3 hrs, ask the wardens. 20 km SE of Parinacota is **Lago Chungará**, one of the highest lakes in the world at 4,600m, a must for its views of the Parinacota, Sajama and Guallatire volcanoes and for its varied wildlife. From here it is about 10 km to the Bolivian frontier at Tambo Quemado. About 30 km S of Parinacota by road is Choquelimpie, the highest gold mine in the world, with an attractive colonial church in the precinct.

Park information

● Accommodation

At Putre: **B** *Hostería Las Vicuñas*, T 224466, 3 classes of room, bungalow-type; does not accept TCs, US$ cash or credit cards; **F** pp *Oasis*, basic, no showers, cheap, good restaurant; **F** pp *Rosamel*, clean, pleasant, hot water, restaurant; **E** *Supermercado Cali*, clean, hot shower, rec.

At **Chucuyo**, a village 30 km E of Putre, there are two shops/restaurants, one of which has 2 rooms to let, a good place to stock up on food. In **Parinacota**, cheap accommodation at the local school, **G** pp, rec.

There are three Conaf refuges in the park, but check in advance with Conaf in Arica that they are open: at **Parincota** (there is supposed to be oxygen for those suffering from soroche, but it is often not available), at **Lago Chungará** and at **Chucuyo**; all have cooking facilities, but no heating, US$12 pp, sleeping bag essential, take your own food, candles and matches. Camping US$6 tent. Advance booking rec. On arrival in Putre you are supposed to register with Conaf. Maps of the park (unreliable) are available from Conaf in Arica and from the tourist office.

● Transport

Buses go daily from Arica to the gold mines in the park at 0600 and 1400. Flota Paco buses (known as La Paloma) leave Arica for Putre daily at 0700, 4 hrs, US$4, returning Sun/Wed 1200, otherwise 1300; Bolivia Litoral bus from Arica to La Paz also runs along this route (charges full Arica-La Paz fare).

Hitching back to Arica is not difficult; you may be able to bargain on one of the tour buses. Trucks on the Arica-La Paz road seldom give lifts. For trucks from Arica you can try at the Poconchile control point, 37 km from Arica. Most trucks for Bolivia pass Parinacota between 0700-1100; it may be easier to get a lift from Parinacota to Visviri, further N on the Bolivian border on Tues with lorries going to meet the train; catch the train to La Paz at Charaña.

● Tours

Birding Altoandino, Baquedano 299 (Correo Putre) T/F (messages) 58-222735, run specialist tours to remote areas of the park and to the Parque Nacional Isluga for birdwatchers, photographers and naturalists, English spoken.

1-day tours are offered by most travel agencies in Arica (addresses above), daily in season, according to demand at other times, US$23 pp with breakfast and light lunch; but some find the minibuses cramped and dusty. You spend all day in the bus and, if not acclimatized, you will suffer from soroche. You can leave the tour and continue on another day as long as you ensure that the company will collect you when you want (tour companies try to charge double for this). For 5 or more, the most economical proposition is to hire a vehicle; fuel is available in Putre, ask at the shop, take at least one spare fuel can.

FRONTIER WITH BOLIVIA: CHUNGARA

● Immigration

Open 0800-2100; US$2 charge/vehicle crossing 1300-1500, 1850-2100 and Sat, Sun and holidays. Long delays are reported at this crossing.

● Transport

For details of through buses between Arica and La Paz see above under Arica.

RESERVE NACIONAL LAS VICUNAS

South of Lauca is the beautiful **Reserva Nacional Las Vicuñas** at 4,300 to 5,600m, which is suitable for 'adventure tourism', to use Conaf's phrase. Be prepared for cold, skin burns from sun and wind, etc; there is no public transport. A high clearance vehicle is essential and, in the summer wet season, 4WD: take extra fuel. Administration is at **Guallatiri**, reached by turning off the Arica-La Paz road onto the A147 2 km after Las Cuevas, where there is also a Conaf office. Open Mar-November.

MONUMENTO NATURAL SALAR DE SURIRE

The same road leads into the **Monumento Natural Salar de Surire** (4,200m), which is open for the same months and for which the same conditions apply. Administration is in **Surire**, 7 hrs from Arica. This can be reached by getting a ride in a borax truck; these run every day between July and Nov from Zapahuira (a road junction between Bolivia and Arica). At Surire there is a Conaf *refugio* (8 beds, very clean, solar heating).

The following advice on travelling off the beaten track in this region has been supplied by vulcanologist Dr Lynsdsey O'Callaghan. In all of the mountain areas of the N of Chile, it is important to note that weather and road conditions are very variable. The *carabineros* and military are very active trying to control the borders with Bolivia and Argentina, so they know about the conditions and are quite willing to tell, but only if asked. Some frontier areas are closed to visitors.

If you plan to stay in the mountains for any length of time, take small gifts for the locals, such as tea, sugar, coffee, salad oil, flour, or a few litres of fuel. Drivers should carry a tow-rope to assist other drivers. It is often possible to get people to bake bread etc for you, but you need to supply flour, yeast and salt. If you are planning to do much cooking, then a good pressure cooker is indispensible (remember water boils at only 90°C at these altitudes). You may also have problems with kerosene stoves; petrol ones, though rather dangerous, are much more reliable.

South through the Central Valley

ONE of the world's most fruitful and beautiful countrysides, with the snowclad peaks of the Andes delimiting it to the east, the Central Valley contains most of Chile's population. It is a region of small towns, farms and vineyards, with several protected areas of natural beauty. To the south are the major city of Concepción, the port of Talcahuano and the main coal-mining area.

ROUTES Road and railway run S through the Central Valley; the railway has been electrified from Santiago to just S of Temuco. Along the road from Santiago to Temuco there are several modern motels. From Santiago to San Javier (S of Talca), the highway is dual carriageway, with two tolls of US$2.50. The highway between Santiago and Rancagua is dangerous for cyclists (inattentive truck drivers).

RANCAGUA

The capital of VI Región (Libertador Gen Bernardo O'Higgins), 82 km S of Santiago, is an agricultural centre (*Pop* 167,000; *Phone code* 072).

The Battle of Rancagua

Rancagua was the scene of an important battle during the Wars of Independence. On 1/2 Oct 1814 O'Higgins and his 1,700 Chilean patriots were surrounded in the centre of Rancagua by 4,500 Royalist (pro-Spanish) troops; O'Higgins, who commanded his forces from the tower of the Merced church, managed to break out and escape. Defeated, he was forced into exile in Argentina and the Royalists re-established control over Chile. Plaques mark the sites of the battle and a diagram in the main Plaza de los Héroes shows the disposition of the troops.

Places of interest

At its heart is an attractive tree-lined plaza, the **Plaza de los Héroes**, and several streets of 1-storey colonial-style houses. In the centre of the plaza is an equestrian statue of O'Higgins. The **Merced** church, 1 block N, several times restored, dates from 1758. The **Museo Histórico**, 3 blocks S of the plaza, housed in a colonial mansion, contains collections of religious art and late 19th century furniture. The main commercial area lies along Av Independencia which runs W from the plaza towards the bus and rail terminals.

Excursions

To the thermal springs of **Cauquenes**, 28 km E, reached by colectivo from Rancagua market (*A3 Hotel Termas de Cauquenes*, T 297226, excellent, clean, excellent food, chapel, gardens, rec). 5 km N of Cauquenes is the village of **Coya**, where the Chilean President has a summer residence.

Local festivals

The **national rodeo championship** is held there at the end of Mar (plenty of opportunities for purchasing cowboy items). **Festival del Poroto** (Bean Festival), 1-5 February.

Local information

● **Accommodation**

B *Aguila Real*, Brasil 1055, T 222047, inc breakfast; **B** *Santiago*, Brasil 1036, T 230855, poorly maintained, friendly; **B** *Rancagua*, San Martín 85, T 232663, F 241155, with bath, quiet, clean, secure parking, rec.

C *España*, San Martín 367, T 230141, with bath, less without, central, hot water, pleasant, clean. Many hotels do not accept guests before 2000, or may charge you double if you arrive in the afternoon. Some 50 km S (22 km N of San Fernando) is *Hacienda Los Lingues*, see page 696.

● **Places to eat**

Café Haiti, Paseo Independencia 690, p 2, lively at night; *Bravissimo*, Astorga 307, for ice cream; *Lasagna*, W end of Plaza, for bread and empanadas.

● **Banks & money changers**

Afex, Campos 363, for US$ cash; *Fincard*, Av Campos 376, Mon-Fri 0900-1400, 1530-1930, Sat 1000-1300, for Mastercard.

● **Tourist offices**

Germán Riesco 277, T 230413, helpful, English spoken. **Automóvil Club de Chile**: Ibieta 09, T 239930.

● **Transport**

Motorists For car parts try Aucamar, Brasil 1177, T 223594, and several others around Brasil 1100-1200, better selection and prices in Santiago.

Trains Main line services between Santiago and Concepción and Chillán stop here. Also regular services to/from Santiago on Metrotren, 1¼ hrs, 11 a day, US$2.

Buses Main terminal at Ocarrol y Calvo; local buses leave from the Terminal de Buses Regionales, just N of the market. Frequent services to Santiago, US$3, 1 hr 10 mins.

Southwest of Rancagua, in the valleys of rivers Cachapoal, Claro and Zamorano, the land is given over to fruit growing (including the estates of Viña Concha y Toro). Towns such as Doñihue, San Vicente de Tagua Tagua and Peumo have their roots in an Indian past which has been replaced by the *huaso* (cowboy) and agroindustry. West of Peumo is **Lago Rapel**, the largest artificial lake in the country (Camping Punta Arenas, 3 km N of El Manzano, basic, cheap; watersports, etc at Bahía Skorpios). The lake feeds the Rapel hydroelectric plant (59 km SW of Melipilla).

The small **Chapa Verde** ski resort, 50 km E of Rancagua, on a private road above the El Tte copper mine, is operated by

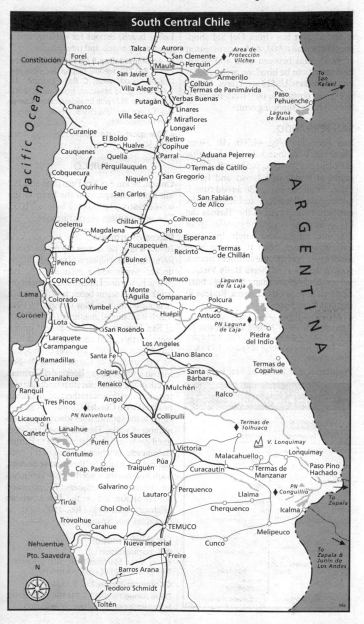

South Central Chile

Codelco (the national copper corporation). In season it can only be reached by mine-transport bus (from Del Sol shopping centre, daily 0900, weekends in season every 15 mins between 0800 and 0930). Equipment can be hired, no accommodation, lift tickets US$18 weekdays, US$25 weekends, obtainable only from resort office in Del Sol shopping centre.

SAN FERNANDO

San Fernando (*Pop* 44,500; *Alt* 340m; *Phone code* 072), founded in 1742, capital of Colchagua Province, is 51 km S of Rancagua. It stands in a broad and fertile valley. From San Fernando a road runs E towards the Cordillera and divides: the northern branch runs to the **Termas del Flaco**, near the Argentine frontier (poor campsite, *cabañas* and hotels, but open only in summer when it attracts large numbers of visitors); the southern branch goes to the resort of **Sierra Bella Vista**, a private *fundo* where many Santiago businessmen have holiday houses. Rodeos in Oct and November.

● **Accommodation** On Av Rodríguez: **C** *Español*, No 959, T 711098; **D** *Marcano*, No 968, T 714759; **E** *Imperio*, No 770, T 714595, with bath, clean; **D** *Pérez*, No 1028, T 713328, without bath.

Pichilemu, 120 km W of San Fernando (road 86 km paved) is a coastal resort with several beaches, including the Punta Los Lobos beach, famous for surfing, and a great many hotels and *residenciales*.

● **Accommodation B** *Chile-España*, Ortúzar 255, T 841270, friendly, helpful, excellent restaurant, good value; **C** *Rex*, Ortúzar 34, T 681003, good breakfast, good value; **E** *Bahía*, Ortúzar 262, with breakfast, clean. **Camping** Campsites, US$15/site, more expensive than residenciales.

● **Transport** Andimar bus to Santiago, 4 hrs, US$5.50.

CURICO

Curicó, 54 km S of San Fernando and 192 km from Santiago, is in the heart of the wine country (*Pop* 85,000; *Phone code* 075). The surroundings are picturesque.

Places of interest

In the **Plaza de Armas** there are lovely fountains with sculptures of nymphs, black-necked swans and a monument to the Mapuche warrior, Lautaro, carved from the trunk of an ancient beech tree. There is a steel kiosk, built in New Orleans in 1904, which is a national monument. The church of **San Francisco**, also a national monument, partly ruined, contains the 17th century Virgen de Velilla, brought from Spain. At the junction of Carmen and Av San Martín is the imposing **Iglesia del Carmen**. Overlooking the city, the surrounding countryside and with views to the distant Andean peaks is **Cerro Condell** (100m); it is an easy climb to the summit from where there are a number of walks. The fine, broad and tree-lined Av Manso de Velasco leads to **Parque Balmaceda**, in which is a bust of the poet, Gabriela Mistral. The **Torres wine bodega**, 5 km S of the city, is worth a visit: take a bus for Molina from Henríquez y O'Higgins and get off at Km 195 on the Pan-American Highway, open 0900-1300, 1500-1800, no organized tour, Spanish only.

Local information
● **Accommodation**
B *Luis Cruz Martines*, Prat 301 y Carmen, T 310552, breakfast extra, overpriced.
C *Comercio*, Yungay 730, T 312442, rec.
D *Res Rahue*, Peña 410, T 312194, basic, meals, hot water, annex rooms have no ventilation.

Chile: From Santiago To Puerto Montt

Valparaíso & Viña Del Mar	120 Santiago
San Antonio	109 87 Rancagua
	87 San Fernando
Curicó	55
	62 Talca
	49 Linares
	101
Concepción	86 Chillán
	105
	82 Los Angeles
Victoria	114
	71 56 Curacautín
	17 Temuco
Loncoche	54 55 Villarrica/ Pucón
	42 33
Valdivia	34 15 Panguipulli
	140 49
Osorno	35 Entre Lagos
	67 Frutillar
	43 Puerto Montt
Pargua/ Chiloé	Carretera Austral
	648

D *Res Central*, Av Prat, 2 blocks from station, good value.

E *Prat*, Peña 427, T 311069, pleasant patio, friendly, clean, hot water, laundry facilities; **E** *Res Colonial*, Rodríguez 461, clean, patio, friendly.

● **Places to eat**

El Fogón Chileno, Yungay 802, good for meat and wines; *American Bar*, Yungay 647, coffee, small pizzas, good sandwiches, pleasant atmosphere, open early am to late pm inc weekends, rec; *Café-Bar Maxim*, Prat 617, light meals, beer and wine. *Club de la Unión*, Plaza de Armas, good; *Centro Italiano Club Social*, Estado 531, good, cheap meals.

● **Banks & money changers**

Fincard, Carmen 498, for Mastercard. Casa de Cambio, Merced 255, Local 106, no TCs.

● **Laundry & dry cleaners**

Limpiabien, Prat 454 (and other branches), quick, efficient.

● **Post & telecommunications**

Telephones: CTC, Peña 650-A.

● **Tourist offices**

Tourist information supplied by the Mayor's secretary, Gobernación building, p 2, Plaza de Armas, helpful, has street map. **Automóvil Club de Chile:** Chacabuco 759, T 311156. **Conaf:** p 1, Gobernación, Plaza de Armas.

● **Transport**

Trains Station is at the end of Prat, 4 blocks W of Plaza de Armas, T 310028. To/from Santiago, 5 a day, US$4 *económico*, US$5 *superior*. To/from Concepción 1 a day.

Buses Companies have their own terminals for interprovincial destinations. Local buses, inc to coastal towns, from Terminal Rural, O'Higgins y Prat, 1 block E of railway station. Many southbound buses by-pass Curicó, but can be caught by waiting outside town. Io **Santiago** US$3, 3 hrs; to **Temuco**, LIT and Tur Bus, US$7.

ROUTES There is a toll (US$3) on the Longitudinal Highway S of Curicó. The city has a good road connection with Argentina, via Paso Vergara (Paso del Planchón, 92 km from Curicó) to San Rafael (transport schedules from Turismo Bucalemu, Yungay 621).

PARQUE NACIONAL SIETE TAZAS

A river flows through seven rock bowls, each with a pool emptying into the next by a small waterfall. The river then passes through a canyon, 15m deep but only 1½m wide, which ends abruptly in a cliff and a beautiful waterfall. Go to Molina, 26 km S of Curicó, from where buses run to the

Park, on Tues and Thur returning Wed and Fri. Daily bus from Curicó in summer, 1545, 4½ hrs, returns 0745 (Sun 0700, returns 1900). The park is open Oct to March.

● **Accommodation D** *Hostería La Flor de la Canela*, at Parque Inglés, 5 km away, inc breakfast, T 491613, good food, highly rec, camping, open summer only. **Camping:** nr park entrance, dirty.

COASTAL RESORTS WEST OF CURICO

A road runs W to the mouth of the Río Mataquito and the popular sea beaches of **Iloca**. North of Iloca is a popular resort, **Llico**, reached either by a coastal route or by an inland road which branches off at Hualañe (Km 74).

● **Accommodation D** *Res Atlántida 2000*, nr beach, good restaurant, bar, friendly, discount for *South American Handbook* readers; **D** *Hostería Llico*; *Res Miramar*, good seafood restaurant; **D** *Pensión Chile*, clean, friendly, rooms with bath have hot water, cheap meals.

● **Transport** Buses run from Terminal Rural in Curicó.

Just before Llico are **Lago Vichuquén**, very popular with the wealthy, road unpaved for 30 km (**A1-A2** *Hostería El Club de Yates*, well-equipped, restful, good food; other hotels, camping at Bahía Mansa, and watersports) and **Laguna de Torca**, a natural sanctuary for wildlife especially black-necked swans and other water birds. There are *miradores* for birdwatching 5 km before Llico, the administration is 2 km from Llico, take the trail from administration to Puente Llico; open Sept-April.

TALCA

56 km S of Curicó (258 km from Santiago, all dual carriageway), this is the most important city between Santiago and Concepción and a major maufacturing centre (*Pop* 300,000; *Phone code* 071); it is the capital of VII Región (Maule). It was founded in 1692, and destroyed by earthquake in 1742 and 1928; it has been completely rebuilt.

Places of interest

Just off the Plaza de Armas at 1 Nte y 2

Ote is the **Museo O'Higginiano** (open Tues-Sat, 0915-1245, 1500-1845, US$1) located in a colonial mansion which belonged to Juan Albano Pereira, tutor to the young Bernardo O'Higgins who lived here between the ages of 4 and 10. The house was later the headquarters of O'Higgins Patriot Government in 1813-14 (before his defeat at Rancagua). In 1818 O'Higgins signed the declaration of Chilean independence here: the room (Sala Independencia) is decorated and furnished in period style. 8 km SE is **Villa Huilquilemu**, a 19th century hacienda, now part of the Universidad Católica del Maule, housing 4 museums, of religious art, handicrafts, agricultural machinery and wine.

Local information
● Accommodation
On the Panamericana Sur, Km 250, are **A3** *Cabañas Entre Ríos*, T 223336, F 220477 (Santiago San Antonio 486, of 132, T 633-3750, F 632-4791), very good value, excellent breakfast, pool, very helpful owner, highly rec.

A3 *Plaza*, 1 Pte 1141, T 226150, good commercial standard; **C** *Amalfi*, 2 Sur 1265, T 225703, old-fashioned, central, very clean; **D** *Alcázar*, 2 Sur 1359, breakfast and meals available, rec as reasonable and clean; **E** pp *Cordillera*, 2 Sur 1360, T 221812, F 233028, nr bus terminal.

● Banks & money changers
Edificio Caracol, Oficina 15, 1 Sur 898, for US$ cash; Fincard (Mastercard), 1 Sur 826.

● Post & telecommunications
Post Office: 1 Ote s/n.
Telephones: CTC, 1 Sur 1156 and 1 Sur 835.

● Tourist offices
1 Pte 1234, T 233669. **Automóvil Club de Chile**: 1 Pte 1267, T 223-2774.

● Transport
Trains Station at 2 Sur y 11 Ote, T 226254. To Santiago, 5 a day, US$5; to Concepción, 1 a day, to Temuco 1 a day.
Buses Bus terminal, 12 Ote y 2 Sur. To Chillán, frequent service, US$2; also frequent to Constitución, 2 hrs, US$1.20.

VILCHES

Vilches, 63 km E of Talca, is the starting point for the climb to the volcanoes Quizapu and Descabezado (3,850m). 2 km beyond the town is the **Area de Protección Vilches**, with 20 km of beautiful walks; visit the lakes Los Patos, La Encantada and El Toro, and the Piedras Tacitas, a stone construction supposedly made by the aboriginal inhabitants of the region. For walks on Descabezado Grande and Cerro Azul (ice axe and crampons needed) contact recommended guide Carlos Verdugo Bravo, Probación Brilla El Sol, Pasaje El Nickel 257, Talca (Spanish only). The administration is near the *Hotel Altos de Vilches* (closed); there is a visitors' centre in the park (2 daily buses from Alto Vilches).

● **Accommodation C** pp *Hostería Rancho Los Canales*, with breakfast, use of kitchen, good food, log cabins C for 4 people, hospitable, knowledgeable family (postal address: Casilla 876, Talca).

● **Transport** Two buses a day, US$1.50, 2-2½ hrs, leave Talca 1300 and late pm, leave Vilches 0700 and 1730.

South of Vilches a road from Talca runs 175 km SE along **Lago Colbún** (*Hotel Casa El Colorado*, T/F 221750) and the valley of the Río Maule, passing through some of the finest mountain scenery in Chile to reach Paso Pehuenche.

FRONTIER WITH ARGENTINA: PASO PEHUENCHE

Paso Pehuenche (2,553m) is reached by unpaved road SE from Lago Colbún (see above). On the Argentine side the road continues to Malargüe and San Rafael. The border is open Dec-March 0800-2100, April-Nov 0800-1900.

CONSTITUCION

West of Talca and reached by road (89 km) from San Javier, **Constitución** is the centre of a prosperous district producing grain and timber, but its main attraction is as a seaside resort. The beach, an easy walk from the town, is surrounded by very picturesque rocks. There are good views from Cerro Mutrún, at the mouth of the river (access from C O'Higgins). The scenery is attractive, despite a nearby factory. There are plenty of hotels and *pensiones*, but accommodation is difficult from Jan to Mar, and bookings must be made well in advance.

● **Accommodation A2** *Hostería Consti-*

tución, Echeverria 460, T 671450, best; **C** *Avendaño*, O'Higgins 681, pleasant patio, restaurant, friendly, safe; **D** *Res Urrutia*, Freire 238, inc breakfast, some rooms gloomy, laundry facilities; **D** *Res Fadiz*, Bulnes nr bus terminal, clean, laundry facilities.

There are two **Reservas Nacionales** S of Constitución, in the vicinity of Chanco, 63 km S: **Los Ruiles**, protecting woods and flowers (open Oct-Mar, daily buses from Constitución or Cauquenes, on the road to the coast from Parral), and **Federico Albert**, ½ km N of Chanco (bus), which covers a marginal zone of woods and encroaching sand (visitors' centre, 4 paths of 5 km, open Oct-Mar). Near these is **Curanipe**, which has a beautiful beach (**C** *Hotel Pacífico*, Comercio 509, T 495903, pleasant, clean).

Parral, about half-way between Talca and Chillán, 342 km S of Santiago, is celebrated as the birthplace of the Nobel Prize-winning poet Pablo Neruda.

● **Accommodation D** *Brescia*, Igualdad 195, T 422675, without bath, clean, good restaurant; **D** *Santiago*, opp station, large old-fashioned rooms, clean; **E** *Res do Brasil*, C 18, clean, quiet; campsite.

CHILLAN

When the city was destroyed by earthquake in 1833, a new city was built slightly to the N; that, too, was destroyed by earthquake in 1939 and there was a further earthquake in 1960. It is a pleasant city and agricultural centre, 105 km S of the road junction for Linares and capital of Ñuble province (*Pop* 134,000; *Phone code* 042). It has a modern cathedral. Chillán was the birthplace of Bernardo O'Higgins (Arturo Prat, Chile's naval hero, was born 50 km away at Ninhue).

Places of interest
In **Chillán Viejo** (SW of the centre) there is a monument and park in honour of O'Higgins; it has a 60m long mural depicting his life (an impressive, but sadly faded, mosaic of various native stones), and a **Centro Histórico y Cultural**, with a gallery of contemporary paintings by regional artists (park is open 0900-1300, 1500-1900). In the **Escuela México** (at Av

O'Higgins between Vega de Saldías and Gamero), donated to the city after the 1939 earthquake, are murals by the great Mexican artists David Alvaro Siqueiros and Xavier Guerrero which present allegories of Chilean and Mexican history. The **Mercado y Feria Municipal** (covered and open markets) sells regional arts and crafts, and has many cheap, good restaurants, serving regional dishes; open daily, Sun until 1300. The Chillán area is well-known for its *pipeño* wine (very young) and its *longanizas* (sausages).

Museums
Museo Naval Arturo Prat, Collin y I Riquelme, contains naval artefacts and models Chilean vessels, Tues-Fri 0930-1200, 1500-1730.

Excursions
27 km SW of Chillán is **Quinchamalí**, a little village famous for the originality of its craftsmen in textiles, basketwork, black ceramics, guitars and primitive paintings (all on sale in Chillán market).

Local information
● **Accommodation**
A2 *Isabel Riquelme*, Arauco 600, T 213663.

B *Cordillera*, Arauco 619, on Plaza de Armas, T 215221, 3-star, small, all rooms with heating and bath, good; **B** *Rucamanqui*, Herminda Martín 590 (off Plaza de Armas), T 222927, clean, spartan; **B** *Floresta*, 18 de Septiembre, 268, quiet, old fashioned, friendly.

C *Quinchamalí*, El Roble 634, T 223381, central, quiet, clean, hot water, heated lounge; **C** *Nevado de Chillán*, O'Higgins 497, T 221013, with bath, D without, good value.

D *Libertador*, Libertad 85, T 223155, large rooms, clean, hot water; **D** *Real*, Libertad 219, T 221827, good; these two are a few minutes' walk from the railway station and are much better than the closer hotels such as *Chillán*, Libertad 85, and **E** *Bahía*, opp station, no hot water, clean but basic, good restaurant below; **D** *Res Su Casa*, Cocharcas 555, T 223931, inc breakfast, clean, parking; **D** *Claris*, 18 de Septiembre 357, T 221983, 2 blocks from plaza, friendly, good value, hot water, highly rec; **D** *Barcelona*, at bus terminal, without bath, clean, friendly, above noisy restaurant; **E** *Hosp Sonia Seguí*, Itata 288, T214879, good breakfast, small rooms, run down, but friendly.

● **Places to eat**
Centro Español, Plaza de Armas, separate bar with snacks, excellent; *Fuente Alemana*, Arauco 661, for *churrasco*; *Café París*, Arauco 686, expresso coffee, fine restaurant upstairs; *Club Comercial*, Arauco 745, popular at lunchtime, good value *almuerzo*, popular bar at night; *Quick Lunch*, El Roble 610, open 0800-2400 for good value meals with good service; *O'Higgins*, O'Higgins y Libertad, good value; *Jai Yang*, Libertad 250, good Chinese; *La Copucha*, 18 de Septiembre y Constitución, inexpensive meals and sandwiches; *Café Madrid*, 5 de Abril 608, good for coffee; *La Masc'a*, 5 de Abril 544, excellent cheap meals, *empanadas de queso*, drinks, rec. In Chillán Viejo, *Los Adobes*, on Parque O'Higgins, good food and service, reasonable prices.

● **Banks & money changers**
Both Banco de Concepción and Banco Sudamericano give poor rates. Better rates at *Casa de Cambio*, Constitución 550, or *Café París* on Arauco (ask for Enrique Schuler). **Fincard** (Mastercard), El Roble 553.

● **Language schools**
Interswop JB Turismo, Constitución 633, Of o3, T223526, F210744, offers exchange programmes with opportunities for work and language courses, US$180 for 25 hrs study. (Address in Germany: Bornstrasse 16, 20146 Hamburg, T/F 40-410-8029).

● **Tourist offices**
In Gobernación building on main plaza, central courtyard, left-hand gallery; street map of city, leaflets on skiing, Termas de Chillán, etc. **Automóvil Club de Chile**: O'Higgins 677, T 212550.

● **Transport**
Trains Station, Brasil opp Libertad, 5 blocks from plaza, T 222424. To Santiago, 2 daily, 5½ hrs, *Salón* US$7-7.35 depending on the service, *económico* US$5-5.35.

Buses Long distance buses leave from Constitución y Brasil (opp railway station).Local buses leave from Maipon y Sgto Aldea. To Santiago, 7 hrs, US$7.50; to Concepción, every 30 mins.

Termas de Chillán

The thermal baths 82 km E of Chillan, 1,850m up in the Cordillera, are reached by a good road (paved for the first 50 km). There is excellent skiing on the slopes and views of the Chillán volcano, E of the Termas; 4 chair lifts, 2 T-bars, lift pass US$30/day, US$20/half-day. Cheaper than centres nearer Santiago; packages available. This ski resort is to be expanded.

Season: middle Dec to the end of March. Information from Chillán Ski Centre, Barros Arana 261, or from Libertador 1042. Equipment hire from Chillán Ski Centre (about US$25 pp) or on slopes.

● **Accommodation** Ski Club de Chile has a tourist centre with hotel (full board, T 223887 Chillán, Casilla 247, office at Arauco 600, or Santiago T 251-5776, Av Providencia 2237, locales 42-4). On the road to the Termas, 70 km from Chillán are **A2** *Hotel Los Pirineos*, T 293839, and **A2** *Parador Jamón, Pan y Vino*, 18 de Septiembre 661, oficina 23, T 492241, Casilla 22, Chillán (Don Emilio Chamorro), arranges rec horse riding expeditions. Camping 2 km from the slopes.

● **Transport** Ski buses run from Libertador 1042 at 0800 and from Chillán Ski Centre, subject to demand, US$30 (inc lift pass). Taxi US$30 one way, 1½ hrs. At busy periods hitching may be possible from Chillán Ski Centre.

ROUTES From Chillán there are various road routes to Concepción: (1) W to Tomé then S along the coast through Penco; (2) along the Longitudinal Highway to Bulnes, where a branch road goes SW to Concepción; or to Cabrero from where there is a paved road W to Concepción.

CONCEPCION

Concepción, the capital of VIII Región (Bío-Bío), 15 km up the Biobío river and 516 km from Santiago, is the third biggest city in Chile. The most important city in the south, it is one of Chile's major industrial centres; to the S are coalfields and an important forestry area. Talcahuano, Chile's most important naval base is 15 km N. Founded in 1550, it has been badly damaged by earthquakes on several occasions and its site has been moved more than once in its history.

BASICS *Pop* 240,000 (with Talcahuano: 468,000); *Phone code* 041. The climate is very agreeable in summer, but from April to Sept the rains are heavy; the annual average rainfall, nearly all of which falls in those 6 months, is from 1,250 to 1,500 mm.

Places of interest

In the attractive Plaza de Armas at the centre are the **Intendencia** and the **Cathedral**. It was here that Bernardo O'Higgins proclaimed the independence of Chile on 1 January 1818. Every Feb in the **Parque**

Ecuador (on Victor Lamas, at the foot of Cerro Caracol), there is a craft fair. At the edge of the park is the Galeria de la Historia (see below).

Cerro Caracol can easily be reached on foot starting from the statue of Don Juan Martínez de Rozas in the Parque Ecuador, arriving at the Mirador Chileno

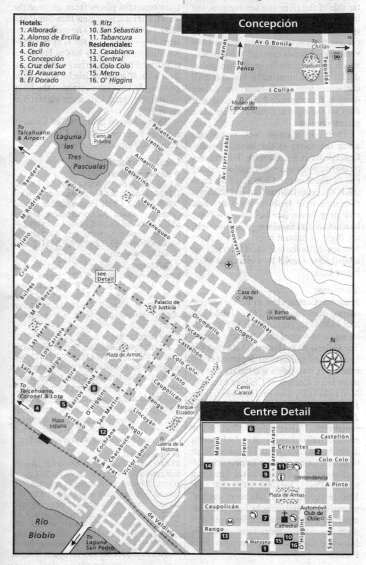

Hotels:
1. Alborada
2. Alonso de Ercilla
3. Bio Bio
4. Cecil
5. Concepción
6. Cruz del Sur
7. El Araucano
8. El Dorado
9. Ritz
10. San Sebastián
11. Tabancura

Residenciales:
12. Casablanca
13. Central
14. Colo Colo
15. Metro
16. O' Higgins

Concepción

To Talcahuano & Airport

Laguna las Tres Pascualas

Cerro la Polvora

Av G Bonila

To Chillán

Stadium

Teguaida

To Penco

I Collao

Museo de Concepción

Arenas

Pelantaro

Lientur

Ainavillo

Galvarino

Lautaro

Janequeo

Av Irarrazabal

Av Roosevelt

Casa del Arte

Barrio Universitario

E Larenas

see Detail

Palacio de Justicia

Orompello

Tucapel

Castellón

Colo Colo

A Pinto

Caupolicán

Rengo

Lincoyán

Angol

Ongolvo

Plaza de Armas

Cerro Caracol

Parque Ecuador

Galeria de la Historia

N

Bandera

M Rodriguez

Paicavi

Prieto

Cruz

Bulnes

Las Heras

M de Rozas

Los Carrera

Salas

Maipú

Freire

Barros Arana

O'Higgins

San Martin

Serrano

Cochrane

Chacabuco

Av A Prat

Victor Lamas

de Valdivia

To Talcahuano, Coronel & Lota

Plaza España

Río Biobío

To Laguna San Pedro

Centre Detail

Maipú

Freire

Barros Arana

Cervantes

Castellón

Colo Colo

Intendencia

A Pinto

Caupolicán

Plaza de Armas

Automóvil Club de Chile

Cathedral

Rengo

A Manzano

O'Higgins

San Martin

after 15 mins. From here it is another, 20 mins climb to **Cerro Alemán**. Chile's largest river, the Biobío, and its valley running down to the sea lie below. On the far side of the river you see lagoons, the largest of which, **San Pedro**, is a watersport centre. On the city side, among cypress trees, is the modern **Barrio Universitario**. A stroll through the grounds, which are beautifully kept with geese, ducks, swans, hummingbirds and a small enclosure with *pudu-pudu* (miniature deer) is recommended. La Posada golf club, on the road to Coronel, is beside a picturesque lake.

There are massive rock formations along the banks of the Biobío estuary. Concepción is linked with Talcahuano, on the bay, by 2 good roads, half-way along one of which is the Club Hípico's racetrack. Races are held on Sun and holidays. A branch road leads to good beaches, including Penco (see below). Two other beaches are Las Escaleras (a private club) – a flight of natural stairs down a sheer 53m sea cliff leads to it – and Ramuntcho, named after a novel by a visitor in 1875: Pierre Loti.

Museums

Museo de Concepción, nr Barrio Universitario, Tues-Sat 1000-1300, 1400-1700, Sun 1430-1730; entrance US$0.50; interesting on history of the Mapuche nation. The **Galería de la Historia**, Lincoyan y V Lamas, is an audiovisual depiction of the history of Concepción and the region; upstairs is a collection of Chilean painting, Mon 1500-1830, Tues-Fri 1000-1330, 1500-1830, Sat/Sun 1000-1400, 1500-1930, free. The **Casa del Arte**, Roosevelt y Larena, contains the University art collection; the entrance hall is dominated by *La Presencia de América Latina*, by the Mexican Jorge González Camerena, an impressive allegorical mural depicting Latin American history. Open Tues-Fri 1000-1800, Sat 1000-1600, Sun 1000-1300, entry free, explanations are given free by University Art students. There is another fine mural in the entrance hall of the railway station, *The History of Concepción* by Gregorio de la Fuente.

To the **Museo y Parque Hualpen**, a house built around 1885 (now a national monument) and its gardens, donated to the city by Pedro del Río Zañartu; it contains beautiful pieces from all over the world, 2 hr visit, rec (open Tues-Sun 0900-1230, 1400-1800, free). The park also contains Playa Rocoto, which is at mouth of Río Biobío. Take a city bus to Hualpencillo from Freire, ask driver to let you out then walk 40 mins, or hitch. You have to go along Av Las Golondrinas to the Enap oil refinery, turn left, then right (it is signed).

To the **Museo Stom**, SE of Concepción, at Progreso 156, in Chiguayante, T 362014, Mapuche artefacts.

Local information

● Accommodation

A1 *Alborada*, Barros Arana 457, Casilla 176, T 242144, good; **A1** *Eldorado*, Barros Arana 348, T 229400, F 231018, comfortable, central, cafeteria, parking; **A2** *Concepción*, Serrano 512, T 228851, F 230948, central, comfortable, heating, English spoken, rec; **A3** *San Sebastián*, Rengo 463, T 244529, F 243412, with breakfast, parking.

B *Casablanca*, Cochrane 133, T 226576, with bath, **C** without, clean; **B** *Ritz*, Barros Arana 721, T 226696, reasonable; **B** *Tabancura*, Barros Arana 790, p 8, T 238348, clean, highly rec. *Cecil*, Barros Arana 9, T 226603, nr railway station, formerly great hotel, with breakfast, clean, quiet, highly rec.

C *Res Antuco*, Barros Arana 741, flats 31-33, T 235485, rec; **C** *Res San Sebastian*, Barros Arana 741, flat 35, T 242710, F 243412, rec, reductions for IYHA (both of these are entered via the Galeria Martinez); **C** *Res Metro*, Barros Arana 464, T 225305, without bath, clean.

E pp *Pablo Araya*, Salas 643-C; **E** *Silvia Uslar*, Edmundo Larenas 202, T 227449, good breakfast, quiet, clean, comfortable. *El Naturista* restaurant lets out 2 rooms, **E** pp clean, central. Good budget accommodation is hard to find.

● Places to eat

El Rancho de Julia, Barros Arana 337, Argentine *parrillada*; *Piazza*, Barros Arana 323, good pizzas; *Rincón de Pancho*, Cervantes 469 (closed Sun), excellent meat, also pasta and congrio, good service and ambience; *Novillo Loco*, Portales 539, good, efficient service. *Le Château* Colo Colo 340, French, seafood and meat, expensive, closed Sun. Oriental: *Yiet-Xiu*, Angol 515, good, cheap; *Chungwa*, Barros Arana 270. *Big Joe Saloon*, O'Higgins 808, just off plaza, popular at lunchtime, closed Sun am but open in pm, good breakfasts, vegetarian meals, snacks and pizzas. *Saaya 1*, Barros Arana 899, excellent *panadería/pastelería/rotisería*, highly rec. Vegetarian: *El Naturista*, Barros Arana 244, good fresh juices, soups and other dishes, closes 1800, highly rec. Several *fuentes de soda* and cafés on Caupolicán nr the Plaza de Armas inc: *Fuente Alemana*, No 654, rec; *Café El Dom*, No 415, and *Café Haiti*, No 515, both open Sun am, good coffee; *Royal Pub*, O'Higgins 790, a posh snack bar; *Nuria*, Barros Arana 736, very good breakfasts and lunches, good value; *QuickBiss*, O'Higgins between Tuscapel and Castellón, salads, real coffee, good service, good lunches; *Café Colombia*, Aguirre Cerda, good coffee, good atmosphere; *Treinta y Tantos*, Prat 356, nice bar, good music, wide selection of *empanadas*, rec; good breakfasts and lunches at the market.

● **Airline offices**
LanChile, Barros Arana 541, T 25014/240025; Ladeco, Barros Arana y Lincoyán, T 248824; National, Barros Arana 348, T 246710; Alta, Campolicán 246, T 223371, F 223173; Aerolíneas Argentinas, O'Higgins 650, Of 602.

● **Banks & money changers**
Several *cambios* in Galería Internacional, entrances at Barros Arana 565 and Caupolicán 521: Cambios Fides, local 58, good rates for TCs; Inter-Santiago, local 31, T 228914; Afex, local 57, no commision on TCs. Fincard (Mastercard), O'Higgins 412, open 24 hrs. Banks such as Banco Concepción (which handles Visa) charge high commission on TCs.

● **Cultural centres**
Aliance Française, Colo Colo y Lamas, library, concerts, films, cultural events; Chilean-British Cultural Institute, San Martín 531 (British newspapers, library); Chilean-North American Institute, Caupolicán 301 y San Martín, has library; Chileno-Italiano, Barros Arana.

● **Embassies & consulates**
Argentine: San Martín 472; British Consul: Dr John F Pomeroy, Castellón 317, T 225655, Casilla 452.

● **Laundry**
Lincoyán 441; *Lavandería Radiante*, Salas 281, open 0900-2030, very good; *American Cleaning*, Freire 817.

● **Post & telecommunications**
Post Office: O'Higgins y Colo Colo.
Telephone CTC, Colo Colo 487, Angol 483. Entel, Barros Arana 541, Caupolicán 567, p 2; Colo Colo 487.

● **Shopping**
Main shopping area is N of Plaza de Armas.

Galería Internacional, Caupolicán y Barros Arana is worth a visit (*El Naturista* vegetarian restaurant has a shop here at local 22). The market has excellent seafood, fruit and vegetables. *Las Brisas* supermarket, Freire y Lincoyán.

● **Sports**
Country Club: Pedro de Valdivia, outdoor swimming pool, tennis.

● **Tour companies & travel agents**
South Expeditions, O'Higgins 680, p 2, oficina 218D, T/F 232290, rafting and trekking expeditions, 1 and 2-day programmes.

● **Tourist offices**
Aníbal Pinto 460 on plaza, T 227976. Information on the more expensive hotels and *Residenciales*. Automóvil Club de Chile: O'Higgins 630, Of 303, T 245884, for information and car hire (T 222070).

● **Transport**
Local Bicycle repairs: *Martínez*, Maipú y Lincoyán, very helpful. Car hire: Hertz, Prat 248, T 230152; Budget, Arana 541, T 225377. Automóvil Club de Chile, Caupolicán 294, T 2250939.

Air Airport N of the city, off the main road to Talcahuano. In summer, flights daily to and from Santiago (fewer in winter) and connections to Temuco, Puerto Montt and Punta Arenas. Airlines run bus services to airport from their offices, leaving 1 hr before flight, US$2.50, also meet flights. Taxi US$8.

Trains Station at Prat y Barros Arana, T 226925. Regular daily train to/from Santiago, plus Rapido del Bío Bío overnight service, 9 hrs; *salón* US$20, upper bunk US$30, lower bunk US$39; *departamento* US$80. Also local services to Laja and Yumbel. Booking offices at the station and at Galería Alessandri, Aníbal Pinto 478, local 3, T 225286.

Buses Main long distance terminal, known as Terminal Collao, is 2 km E, on Av Gen Bonilla, next to athletics stadium. (To the city centre take a Bus marked 'Hualpencillo' from outside the terminal and get off in Freire, US$0.40, taxi US$4.) Tur Bus, Línea Azul and Buses Bío Bío services leave from Terminal Camilo Henríquez 2 km NE of main terminal on J M García, reached by buses from Av Maipú in centre. To Santiago, 8½ hrs, US$10; to Valparaíso, 9 hrs, US$12; to Loncoche, 7 hrs, US$6.50; to Puerto Montt several companies, US$15, about 12 hrs; to Pucón, 8 hrs, US$8; to Valdivia, US$10; to Los Angeles, US$2.50. Best direct bus to Chillán is Línea Azul, 2 hrs, US$2. For a longer and more scenic route, take Costa Azul bus which follows old railway line, through Tomé, Coelemu and Ñipas on to Chillán (part dirt-track, takes 5½ hrs). Services to Coronel (US$0.45) Lota, Lebu,

Cañete and Contulmo are run by J Ewert (terminal next to railway station on Prat) and Los Alces (terminal at Prat y Maipú). To Talcahuano frequent service from Plaza de Armas (bus marked 'Base Naval'), US$0.20, 1 hr, express US$0.30, 30 mins.

NORTH OF CONCEPCION

A road runs N from Concepción along the coast through the suburbs of **Penco**, Km 12, and **Lirquén**, Km 15, a small, old, pretty town of wooden houses with a beach (walk along railway to reach it). Recommended. Plentiful cheap seafood for sale.

13 km further N is **Tomé**, 1½ hrs, US$0.70, a small town set in a broad bay with long beaches. An interesting cemetery, Miguel Gulán Muñoz, is set on a cliff overlooking the ocean.

Dichato, 9 km further N along a hilly road offering fine views, is a beautiful fishing village and has the oceanographic centre of the University of Concepción. In summer it is a busy holiday resort. Private Museo del Mar, by Benjamín Ortega, interesting, free. Take a local bus to the tiny village of Cocholgüe.

● **Accommodation & places to eat** In Penco: **D** *Hotel La Terraza*, T 451422, **E** *Hosp Miramar*, good, and *Casinoriente*, good seafood restaurant. **In Tomé**: **D** *Hotel Roxy*, Sotomayor 1077, T 650729, and **E** *Linares*, Serrano 875, T 651284. 7 km before Tomé, on a hill, is *El Edén*, restaurant, bar and *cabañas*, D. **In Dichato**: **A3** *Chamaruk*, Daniel Vera 912, T 683022, with bath, **C** without, clean, pleasant; **A2** *Manantial*, on seafront, T 683003; **B** *Kalifa*, Casimiro Vera 766, T 681027, with bath, restaurant; **D** *Chicki*, Ugalde 410, T 683004, with bath, **C** without; **E** pp *Res Santa Inés*, República 540, without bath; *albergue* in the school in summer.

● **Transport** Línea Azul and Costa Azul buses from Concepción pass through all these villages, which can also be reached cheaply by collective taxi.

TALCAHUANO

Talcahuano (*Pop* 228,000), on a peninsula jutting out to sea, has the best harbour in Chile. It is Chile's main naval station; its dry docks accommodate vessels of 30,000 tons. 1½ km away the steel plant at Huachipato has its own wharf to unload the iron ore shipped from the N.

On N edge of town is Parque Tumbes, on Península Tumbes. Owned by CODEFF (Comité Nacional pro Defensa de la Fauna y Flora), paths lead along the coast, no services, no admission charge (details from local CODEFF office, Caupolicán 346, Oficina E, p 4, T 226649).

The *Huáscar*, a relic of the War of the Pacific, is in the naval base. At the outbreak of the war the Chilean navy blockaded Iquique, then an important Peruvian nitrate port. On 21 May 1879, the Peruvian Navy's huge ironclad, the *Huáscar*, and the smaller *Independencia* reached Iquique to lift the siege. Chile sent out two small wooden ships, the *Covadonga* and the *Esmeralda*, under Captain Arturo Prat to challenge them. Prat fought with ferocity. When his damaged vessel, the *Esmeralda*, was rammed by the *Huáscar* Prat called upon his men to follow him, boarded the enemy and continued fighting until he was killed. Chile later captured the *Huáscar* at the battle of Angamos nr Mejillones, on 8 October 1879. The ship is open Tues-Sun 0900-1130, 1400-1700, US$1.25. Photography is permitted, but passports must be handed in at main gate.

● **Accommodation C** *De La Costa*, Colón 630; **D** *Res San Pedro*, Rodríguez 22, T 542145.

● **Places to eat** *Benotecas*, on seafront, a row of four restaurants sharing one window facing the harbour, superb fish and seafood in each one, rec, reasonable prices. *El Alero de los Salvo*, Colón 3396; *La Aguada*, Colón 912, shellfish dishes; *Domingo Lara*, Aníbal Pinto 450, seafood specialities, excellent.

SOUTH OF CONCEPCION

A road links Concepción with the coal-producing districts to the S of the Río Biobío. Between Concepción and Lota are the Lagunas San Pedro Chica (swimming) and Grande (watersports), just across the Río Biobío. Nearer Lota are Playa Negra (small, few people, black sand) and Playa Blanca (bigger, bars, cafés, crowded, white sand, free campsite), both on the Bahía de Coronel.

The town of **Coronel**, in the heart of the coal area, 29 km from Concepción, was the scene of a British naval defeat in 1914 (the *Good Hope* and *Monmouth* were sunk by the *Scharnhorst* – a monument was dedicated in Nov 1989), which was later avenged at the Battle of the Falklands/Malvinas with the destruction of the German squadron.

LOTA

The Lota coalmine, now state-owned, formerly the property of the Cousiño family, is the largest in Chile (*Pop* of town 52,000). In the church on the main plaza you can see a virgin made of coal.

The **Parque de Lota**, on a promontory to the W of the town, was the life's work of Isadora Cousiño. Laid out by an English landscape architect in the last century, it contains plants from all over the world, romantic paths and shady nooks offering views over the sea, and peafowl and pheasants roaming freely. (Admission US$1.25, no picnicking; open 1000-1800 daily, till 2000 in summer.)

The Coalmine, the tunnels of which run almost entirely under the sea, can be visited. Guided tours (Spanish only) Tues-Sat 1000, 3 hrs (minimum party of 5) US$13 pp, meet at the Park entrance, tiring but highly rec. Advance booking advisable, T 876362 Anexo 204, or at Tourist Office in Concepción from whom further details can be obtained. Ask to see the mining museum before you leave.

● **Accommodation** *Res Rome*, Galvarino 233, clean, friendly.

● **Transport** Buses to **Concepción**, 1½ hrs, US$0.50. Many buses by-pass the centre: catch them from the main road.

South of Lota the road runs past the seaside resort of **Laraquete** where there are miles of golden sands, and on to **Arauco**, past the Celulosa Arauco woodpulp plant.

● **Accommodation In Laraquete**: **D** *Laraquete*, on Gabriela Mistral, main street, friendly, small rooms, baths in poor repair; **D** *Hostería El Quinto*, helpful, basic, good breakfast. Several *residenciales* close to beach; campsite nr beach. **In Arauco**: **B** *Hostería Arauco*, P de Valdivia 80, T 551131. **D** *Plaza*, Chacabuco 347, T 551265.

LEBU

From Lota a road runs S, 76 km to Tres Pinos, where a bus can be taken W to **Lebu**, 31 km, a fishing port and coal washing centre (*Pop* 17,000; *Phone code* 041). It lies at the mouth of the Río Lebu, and is the capital of Arauco province. There are enormous beaches to both N and S, popular on summer weekends: 3 km N at Playa Millaneco are caves with steep hills offering good walks and majestic views.

● **Accommodation** **A1** *Hostería Millaneco*, T 511540, T 511904 at Playa Millaneco, offers *cabañas*, sleep 7, good restaurant, rec; **C** *Central*, Pérez 183, T 511904, with bath, **E** pp without, clean, parking, rec; **D** pp *Gran* Pérez 309, T 511939, with bath, **E** pp without, old fashioned, clean, *comedor*; **E** *Res Alcázar*, Alcázar 144, with breakfast, cold water, friendly.

CANETE

24 km S of Tres Pinos is **Cañete** (*phone code* 041), a small town on the site of Fort Tucapel where Pedro de Valdivia and 52 of his men were killed by Mapuche warriors in 1554.

Museums **Museo Mapuche de Cañete**, 3 km S on the road to Contulmo, in a modern building inspired by the traditional Mapuche *ruca*; includes Mapuche ceramics and textiles. Behind the museum is a reconstruction of a *ruca*. Open 0930-1230, 1400-1830, daily in summer, closed Mon in winter. Entry US$0.75.

● **Accommodation** **C** *Alonso de Ercilla*, Villagran 641, T 611974, with bath, clean; **D** *Derby*, Mariñan y Condell, T 611960, without bath, clean, basic, restaurant; **D** *Nahuelbuta*, Villagran 644, T 611073, clean, pleasant, parking; **E** *Comercio*, 7º de la Línea, T 611218, very pleasant, rec; **E** *Gajardo*, 7º de la Línea 817 (1 block from plaza), without bath, old fashioned, friendly, pleasant.

● **Places to eat** *Don Juanito*, Riquelme 151, very good, friendly, rec by the locals; real coffee at *Café Nahuel*, off the plaza.

● **Transport** Buses leave from 2 different terminals: J Ewert, Inter Sur and Thiele from Riquelme y 7 de la Línea, Jeldres, Erbuc and other companies from the Terminal Municipal, Serrano y Villagran. To **Santiago**, Inter Sur, daily, 12 hrs; to **Purén**, US$1.50; sit on right for views of Lago Lanalhue; to **Concepción**, 3 hrs, US$2.50; to **Lebu** US$1.50; to **Angol** US$3.50; to **Tirúa**, Jeldres, frequent and J Ewert, 3 a day, 2 hrs, US$2.

Tirúa, at the mouth of the Río Tirúa, is 78 km S of Cañete (turn off at Peleco, 11 km S of Cañete). The island of **Mocha**, visited by Juan Bautista Pastenes in 1544 and later by Sir Francis Drake, lies 32 km offshore. Most of the island's 800 inhabitants live around the coast, the interior being of forests. The main settlement is La Hacienda where accommodation is available with families. Transport from Tirúa: ferry daily 0600, US$14; plane US$56 (ask the police to radio the plane which is based on Mocha).

● **Accommodation in Tirúa** 3 *hospedajes* all E.

● **Transport** Buses from Cañete.

Lago Lanalhue

The lake, S of Cañete, is surrounded by forested hills from which there has been extensive logging. Much less popular than the Lake District this area offers good opportunities for walking. A road runs S from Cañete along the N side of the lake to Contulmo at its southern end. Playa Blanca, 10 km N of Contulmo, is a popular beach in summer. (take any bus between Contulmo and Cañete). For further information on the area ask at the *Hostal Licahue*.

Contulmo (*Pop* 2,000) is a sleepy village at the foot of the Cordillera which hosts a Semana Musical (music week) in January. The wooden Grollmus House and Mill, 3 km NW along the S side of the lake, are well worth a visit. The house, dating from 1918, has a fine collection of every colour of *copihue* (the national flower) in a splendid garden. The mill, built in 1928, contains the original wooden machinery. From here the track runs a further 9 km N to the *Posada Campesina Alemana*, an old German-style hotel in a fantastic spot at the water's edge.

● **Accommodation** C *Contulmo*, Millaray 116, with bath, **E** pp without, an attractive retreat, friendly and hospitable, highly rec; **E** pp *Central*, Millaray 131, without bath, no sign, very hospitable. **On the lake: A3** *Posada Campesina Alemana*, open Dec-March, poor beds, own generator, fish come to hotel steps to be fed by guests, details from Millaray 135 in Contulmo; **B** *Hostal Licahue*, 4 km N towards Cañete (Casilla 644, Correo Contulmo) T Santiago 273-8417, with breakfast, also full board, attractively set overlooking lake, pool, highly rec, also *cabañas*, **A1**, sleep 8, on far side of lake (connected by boat); *Hostería Lanalhue*, reached from Tirúa road, on S lakeside. **Camping**: at Playa Blanca: *Camping Elicura*, clean, rec, US$6; *Camping Playa Blanca*, clean; *Camping Huilquehue*, 15 km S of Cañete on lakeside.

● **Transport** Buses to **Concepción**, Thiele, US$4.50, 4 hrs; to **Temuco**, Thiele and Erbuc, US$4; to **Cañete**, frequent, US$1.

From Contulmo the road climbs the Cordillera through dense forest (do this journey in daylight) and then descends to **Purén**, where there is a full-scale reconstruction on the original site of the wooden Chilean fort used in the last campaign against the Mapuche (1869-1881). Purén is in the middle of a big logging area.

● **Accommodation** D *Hotel Tur*, Dr Garriga 912, T 22, clean, good; *Central Hotel*, on the plaza, meals excellent, rooms in tourist season only.

LOS ANGELES

Travelling S from Chillán on the Longitudinal Highway, the next major centre is **Los Angeles** (*Pop* 106,000; *Phone code* 043), capital of Bío-Bío province, in a wine, fruit and timber district. Founded in 1739 as a fort, it is now a pleasant, expanding city, with a large Plaza de Armas; Colón is the main shopping street. There is a good daily market.

Excursions

There is swimming in the Río Duqueco, 10 mins S by bus, US$0.80. The **Salto El Laja**, 25 km N, is a spectacular waterfall in which the Laja plunges 47m over the rocks. It costs a few pesos to enter and walk up to the falls, or to walk on the hotel side.

● **Accommodation** *A3-B Hotel y Hosteria Salto de Laja Resort*, address: Casilla 562, Los Angeles, T 321706/313956, F 313996 with fine restaurant, 2 swimming pools and chalet-type rooms on an island overlooking the falls; nearby are *Camping Los Manantiales*, T 323606, and Motels *El Pinar* and *Los Coyuches*.

● **Transport** Buses (Bus Bio Bio) from Los Angeles, US$1, 30 mins – frequent; to Chillán, frequent, US$2.

Local information
● **Accommodation**

A3 *Mariscal Alcázar*, Lautaro 385 (Plaza de Armas), T 311725.

B *Gran Hotel Müso*, Valdivia 230 (Plaza de Armas), T 313183, good restaurant open to non-residents.

C *Winser*, Rengo 138, overpriced but clean and friendly; **C** *Res Santa María*, Plaza de Armas, hot shower, TV, good beds.

Private house at Caupolicán 651, E, large breakfast, good value; opp is another, also No 651, basic, cheaper. 10 km N is **E** pp *Casa de familia/Cabañas El Rincón*, Panamericana Sur Km 494, Cruce La Mona 1 km E, T (09) 441-5019, F 043-317168, Elke and Winfried Lohmar, beautiful property beside a small river, restful, South American and European cuisine, inc vegetarian (**B** pp full board), tours arranged, English, French, German and Spanish spoken, highly rec.

● **Places to eat**

El Arriero, Colo Colo 235, T 322899, good *parrillas* and international dishes; *Di Leone*,

Colón 265, good lasagna; *Julio's Pizzas*, Colón 542 and *Rancho de Julio*, Colón 720, excellent *parrilla*. *Bavaria*, Colón 357, good.

● **Banks & money changers**
Banco Santander, Colón 500, Mastercard; Banco Concepción, Colón 300; Banco Sudamérica, Valdivia 276.

● **Cultural centres**
British Cultural Institute, Vicuña 648.

● **Post & telecommunications**
Post Office: on Plaza de Armas.
Telephone: CTC, Paseo Quilpué, or Valdivia 326; Entel, Colo Colo 393.

● **Travel agents**
Cultura Tours, arranges rafting, excursions, tracking, 164 Lautaro St, T 318467, F 314135.

● **Tourist offices**
Proto-Turismo, Edif Cámara Comercio No 24, beside Lautaro 267. **Conaf**, Ercilla 936, 0900-1300. **Automóvil Club de Chile**: Villagrán y Caupolicán, T 322149.

● **Transport**
Long distance bus terminal on NW outskirts of town, local terminal at Villagrán y Rengo in centre. To **Santiago**, 9 hrs, US$12; to **Viña del Mar** and **Valparaíso**, 10 hrs, US$14; 4 daily to **Concepción**, US$2.50, 2¼ hrs; to **Temuco**, US$4, hourly; to **Curacautín**, daily at 0600, 3 hrs, US$4.

PARQUE NACIONAL LAGUNA DE LAJA

A road runs from Los Angeles to the **Parque Nacional Laguna de Laja**, 88 km E, past the impressive rapids of the Río Laja. The lake is surrounded by stark volcanic scenery of scrub and lava, and dominated by the Antuco volcano and the glacier-covered Sierra Velluda.

● **Access** Take a bus to Abanico (**E** pp *Hostería del Bosque*, restaurant, also good campsite), 20 km past Antuco (US$1.35, 2 hrs, 5 a day but only 0830 in am, last return 1730), then 4 km to park entrance (details from Conaf in Los Angeles, Ercilla 936, 0800-1300, 1430-1800 Mon-Fri).

● **Accommodation** *Cabañas y Camping Lagunillas*, T 314275, 50m from the river, 4 km from the ski slopes, poor campsite US$2.50 pp.(During off-season, ie summer, only place to stay is Casino, **E** pp in ski huts). Camping not permitted on lake shore. 21 km from the lake is the *Refugio Chacay* offering food, drink and bed (**B**, T Los Angeles 222651, closed in summer); two other *refugios*: *Digeder*, **E**, and Uni-

versidad de Concepción, both on slopes of Volcán Antuco, for both T Concepción 221561, office O'Higgins 734. Nearby is the Club de Esquí de los Angeles with two ski-lifts, giving a combined run of 4 km on the Antuco volcano (season, May-Aug).

SOUTH OF LOS ANGELES

The Pan-American (or Longitudinal) Highway (Ruta 5) bypasses **Mulchén**, a small, old-fashioned town (32 km; bus 45 mins). It continues via Collipulli (campsite), Victoria, Púa and Lautaro to Temuco.

ANGOL

From Collipulli and Los Angeles paved roads run W to **Angol** (*Pop* 35,000; *Phone code* 045), capital of the Province of Malleco (IX Région), founded by Valdivia in 1552, seven times destroyed by the Indians and rebuilt. Worth visiting are El Vergel experimental fruit-growing station, the Dillman S Bullock regional museum with precolumbian Indian artefacts (open daily 0830-1300, 1500-1800, US$0.50, a 5 km bus-ride from town, colectivo No 2) and the San Francisco church. The Plaza de Armas is pleasant, as is the whole town.

● **Accommodation** **A1** *Millaray*, Prat 420, T 711570; **C** *Olimpia*, Lautaro 194, T 711517; **D** pp *La Posada*, at El Vergel, T 712103, full board, clean, friendly; **D** *Res Olimpia*, Caupolicán 625, T 711162, good; **D** pp *Casa Matriz*, Caupolicán 579, T 711771, with breakfast, clean, good food; **E** *El Parrón*, O'Higgins 345, T 711370; **E** Vergara 651, chaotic but cheap.

● **Tourist offices** On O'Higgins, across bridge from bus terminal, excellent.

● **Transport** Bus from **Santiago** US$6.50, **Los Angeles**, US$1.20, or **Collipulli**. To **Temuco** US$2.50.

Parque Nacional Nahuelbuta

35 km W of Angol is the **Parque Nacional Nahuelbuta**, in the coastal mountain range. The park has many araucaria trees (monkey-puzzles) and viewpoints over both the sea and the Andean volcanoes.

● **Access** Bus to Vegas Blancas, 0645 and 1600 daily except Sun, return 0900 and 1800, 1½ hrs, US$1.20, 27 km from Angol, then walk (or possibly hitch) 7 km to park gate, and a further 7 km to the campsite (US$2.45 to enter park, US$8 to camp – there are many free campsites on the way to the entrance). Rough maps are available at the park entrance for US$0.25. **Conaf**, Prat 191, p 2, Angol, T 711870.

CURACAUTIN

A small town which has hot springs nearby, is 56 km SE of Victoria by paved road; bus from Los Angeles or Temuco; bus station on the plaza (timetables posted on window are fiction).

● **Accommodation C** *Hostería La Rotonda del Contiu*, restaurant; **D** pp *Plaza*, Yungay 157, T 56, main plaza, restaurant good but pricey; **E** pp *Hostería Abarzúa*, full board C pp, camping; **E** pp *Res Rojas*, Tarapacá 249, without bath, good meals, rec; **E** pp *Turismo*, Tarapacá 140, T 116, clean, good food, comfortable, best value; **E** pp Rodríguez 705 (corner of plaza) with breakfast, clean, kitchen facilities. *Camping Trahuilco*, 3 km S, expensive.

● **Places to eat** *El Refugio*, popular.

HOT SPRINGS EAST OF CURACAUTIN

18 km E are the indoor **Termas de Manzanar** (US$5, open all year), reached by bus from Temuco and Victoria. The road passes the Salto del Indio (Km 14), before which is a turn-off to Laguna Blanca (25 Km away, take fishing gear, ask Sernatur about trucks), and Salto de la Princesa, just beyond Manzanar.

● **Accommodation B** *Termas*, also simple rooms with bath; **E** *Hostería Abarzúa*, simple, friendly.

32 km SE are the hot springs and mud baths of **Termas de Río Blanco** (hotel), at 1,046m on the slopes of the Sierra Nevada and nr Lago Conguillio (bus to Conguillio National Park – see page 771 below – only at 1800).

The beautiful pine-surrounded **Termas de Tolhuaca** (open 1 Nov-30 April) are 35 km to the NE of Curacautín by unpaved road, or 57 km by unpaved road from just N of Victoria (high clearance 4WD essential).

● **Accommodation A2** *Termas de Tolhuaca*, with full board, inc use of baths and horse riding, very good, T 164, Casilla 48 Curacautín, or T Temuco 220975; **E** pp *Res Roja*, hot water, food, camping nr the river, good.

It is about 9 km from the hotel to the **Parque Nacional Tolhuaca**, in which are the waterfalls of Malleco and Culiebra, and Lago Malleco; superb scenery and good views of volcanoes from Cerro Amarillo (the park is open Dec-April).

Lonquimay volcano

Northeast of Curacautín is the **Lonquimay volcano** with the Puelche ski-run, season May-November. The volcano begun erupting on Christmas Day 1988; the new crater is called Navidad. To see it, access is made from Malalcahuello, 15 km S and half-way between Curacautín and Lonquimay town. In Malalcahuello is a steam-powered carpenter's shop. The **Reserva Nacional Malalcahuello-Nalcas** on the slopes of the volcano is a popular centre for fly-fishing.

● **Access & accommodation** The teacher at Malalcahuello school charges US$10 for transport to and from the volcano (crampons, ice-axe and ropes essential); Sra Naomi Saavedra at *Res Los Sauces* also arranges lifts (**D** pp full board, or **F** pp with use of kitchen, hot water, good value); there is also a Conaf lodge. Accommodation is also available at the Centro de Ski Lonquimay, 5 km from the summit (10 km from the bus stop) **B** pp with breakfast, full board also available, free camping, ski pass US$17.

Bus Erbuc from Temuco, US$2 to Malalcahuello, 4 a day, 4 hrs, 5½ to Lonquimay town, US$3. There is accommodation in Lonquimay, but no public transport to the volcano.

FRONTIER WITH ARGENTINA: PASO PINO HACHADO

Paso Pino Hachado (1884 m) can be reached either by unpaved road, 77 km SE from Lonquimay or by unpaved road 103 E from Melipeuco. On the Argentine side this road continues to Zapala.

● **Chilean immigration & customs**
In Liucura, 22 km W of the frontier, open Dec-March 0800-2100, April-Nov 0800-1900. Very thorough searches and 2-3 hr delays reported.

● **Transport**
Buses from Temuco to Zapala and Neuquén use this crossing: see under Temuco.

The Lake District

YET more beautiful scenery: a variety of lakes, often with snow-capped volcanoes as a backdrop, stretch southwards to the salt water fjords which begin at Puerto Montt. There are a number of good bases for exploring (Valdivia has the added attraction of colonial forts a river trip away) and many national parks.

The Land and people

South from the Río Biobío to the Gulf of Reloncaví the same land formation holds as for the rest of Chile to the N: the Andes to the E, the coastal range to the W, and in between the central valley. The Andes and the passes over them are less high here, and the snowline lower; the coastal range also loses altitude, and the central valley is not as continuous as from Santiago to Concepción. The climate is cooler; the summer is no longer dry, for rain falls all the year round, and more heavily than further N. The rain decreases as you go inland: some 2,500 mm on the coast and 1,350 mm inland. This is enough to maintain heavy forests, mostly beech, but agriculture is also important; irrigation is not necessary. The farms are mostly medium sized, and no longer the huge *haciendas* of the N. The characteristic thatched or red tiled houses of the rural N disappear; they are replaced by the shingle-roofed frame houses typical of a frontier land rich in timber. The farms raise livestock, fruit and food crops, and timber is a major industry.

Between parallels 39° and 42° S is found one of the most picturesque lake regions in the world. There are some 12 great lakes of varying sizes, some set high on the Cordillera slopes, others in the central valley southwards from Temuco to Puerto Montt. Here, too, are imposing waterfalls and snowcapped volcanoes. Anglers revel in the abundance of fish, the equable climate, and the absence of troublesome insects (except for enormous horseflies, *tavanos*, between mid-Dec and mid-Jan – do not wear dark clothes). Out of season many facilities are closed, in season (from mid-Dec to mid-Mar), prices are higher and it is best to book well in advance, particularly for transport. It is a peaceful area, with fewer tourists than across the border in the Argentine lake district.

About 20,000 **Mapuches** live in the area, more particularly around Temuco. There are possibly 150,000 more of mixed blood who speak the Indian tongue, though most of them are bilingual.

Crossing to Argentina There are four main routes from the Chilean Lake District to Argentina: 1) The Tromen Pass, from Pucón and Curarrehue to Junín de los Andes (see page 777); 2) the Huahum Pass, from Panguipulli via Choshuenco and Lake Pirehueico to San Martín de los Andes (see page 779); 3) The Puyehue Pass, from Osorno and Entrelagos via the Parque Nacional Puyehue to Bariloche (see page 786); 4) The Lakes Route, from Puerto Montt or Osorno via Ensenada, Petrohue and Lago Todos Los Santos to Bariloche (see page 791).

TEMUCO

The Lake District proper does not begin until we reach Chile's newest city, **Temuco**, founded 1881 after the final treaty with the Mapuches. 679 km S of Santiago, the city (*Pop* 225,000; *Phone code* 045) is the capital of IX Región (Araucanía), and one of the most active centres in the S. Wheat, barley, oats, timber and apples are the principal products of the area.

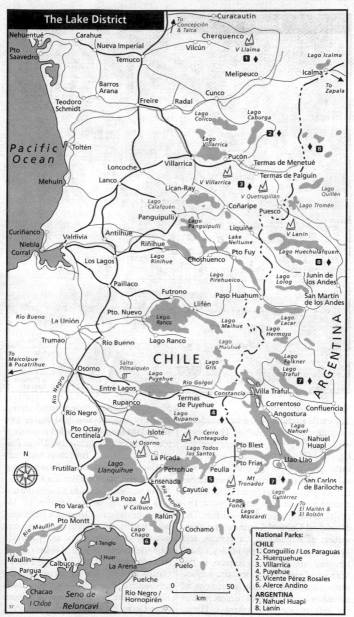

The Lake District

Pacific Ocean

CHILE

ARGENTINA

Nehuentué
Pto Saavedro
Carahue
Nueva Imperial
Temuco
Barros Arana
Teodoro Schmidt
Toltén
Mehuin
Loncoche
Lanco
Curiñanco
Niebla
Corral
Valdivia
Antilhue
Los Lagos
Paillaco
La Unión
Trumao
Río Bueno
Osorno
Entre Lagos
Rupanco
Río Negro
Pto Octay
Centinela
Frutillar
Maullín
Pargua
Calbuco
Pto Varas
Pto Montt
Chacao
I Chiloé

To Concepción & Talca
Curacautín
Cherquenco
Vilcún
V Llaima
Melipeuco
Lago Icalma
Icalma
To Zapala
Cunco
Freire
Radal
Lago Colico
Lago Caburga
Lago Villarrica
Pucón
Termas de Menetué
Termas de Palguín
Villarrica
Lican-Ray
V Villarrica
V Quetrupillán
Lago Quillén
Lago Tromén
Coñaripe
Puesco
Lago Calafquén
Panguipulli
Lago Panguipulli
Liquiñe
V Lanín
Riñihue
Choshuenco
Pto Fuy
Lake Neltume
Lago Huechulafquen
Lago Riñihue
Lago Pirehueico
Lago Lolog
Junín de los Andes
San Martín de los Andes
Futrono
Llifén
Paso Huahum
Lago Maihue
Lago Lacar
Lago Hermoso
Pto. Nuevo
Lago Ranco
Lago Ranco
Lago Huishué
Lago Gris
Lago Falkner
Lago Traful
Salto Pilmaiquén
Lago Puyehue
Río Golgoi
L. Constancia
Villa Traful
Termas de Puyehue
Correntoso
Confluencia
Angostura
Lago Rupanco
Cerro Punteagudo
Islote
Lago Nahuel
Nahuel Huapi
V Osorno
La Picada
Lago Todos los Santos
Pto Blest
Pto Frias
Llao Llao
Lago Llanquihue
Petrohue
Peulla
Mt Tronador
San Carlos de Bariloche
Ensenada
Cayutué
Lago Fonck
Lago Gutiérrez
To El Maitén & El Bolsón
La Poza
V Calbuco
Ralún
Río Petrohué
Cochamó
Lago Mascardi
Lago Chapo
I Tenglo
I Huar
Puelo
Puelche
La Arena
Río Negro / Hornopirén
Maicolpue & Pucatrihue
Río Negro
Río Bueno
Mehuin
Río Maullín
Seno de Reloncaví
Puelche

To Maicolpue & Pucatrihue

0   50
km

N

National Parks:

CHILE
1. Conguillio / Los Paraguas
2. Huerquehue
3. Villarrica
4. Puyehue
5. Vicente Pérez Rosales
6. Alerce Andino

ARGENTINA
7. Nahuel Huapi
8. Lanín

57

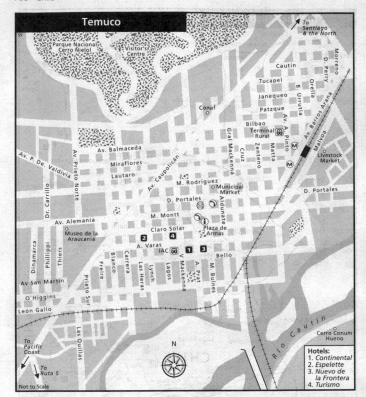

Temuco

Parque Nacional
Cerro Ñielol

Visitor's Centre

To Santiago & the North

Conaf

Cautin
Tucapel
Janequeo
Patzque
Bilbao
Terminal Rural

Morreno
D. Perry
Orella
B. Urrutia
Av. Pinto
Av. Barros Arana
Malvoa

Av. Balmaceda
Miraflores
Lautaro

Av. P. De. Valdivia
Av. Prieto Norte
Av. Caupolicán
Gral Mackenna
Cruz
Zenteno
Matta

Livestock Market

M. Rodríguez
Municipal Market

D. Portales

Dr. Carrillo
Av. Alemania
M. Montt
Claro Solar
Aldunate
Plaza de Armas

D. Portales

Museo de la Araucanía

Dinamarca
Phillippi
Thiers
A. Varas
JAC
Bello

Carrera
Blanco
Freire
Las Heras
Lynch
Lagos
V. Mackenna
A. Prat
M. Bulnes

Prieto Sur

Av San Martin
O'Higgins
León Gallo

Las Quillas

To Pacific Coast

To Ruta 5

Not to Scale

N

Río Cautín

Cerro Conum Hueno

Hotels:
1. Continental
2. Espelette
3. Nuevo de la Frontera
4. Turismo

Places of interest

The **cattle auctions** in the stockyards behind the railway on A Malvoa, Thur mornings, are interesting; you can see the
huasos, or Chilean cowboys, at work. Also,
cattle sales at Feria Agroaustral, just outside Temuco on the road to Nuevo Imperial, on Fri (take bus 4 from C Rodríguez),
auction starts at 1400, and at Nuevo Imperial, 35 km away, on Mon and Tues. The
Municipal Cultural Centre at the intersection of Balmaceda, Caupolicán and
Prat houses the municipal library, a theatre, and art galleries. Temuco is the
Mapuches' market town and you may see
some, particularly women, in their typical
costumes in the produce market next to
the railway station (Lautaro y Pinto).

Mapuche textiles, pottery, woodcarving,
jewellery etc are also sold inside and
around the **municipal market** in centre of
town (corner of Aldunate and Diego Portales – it also sells fish, meat and dairy
produce), but these are increasingly touristy and poor quality. The *Casa de la Mujer
Mapuche*, Gen Mackenna 83, sells the textiles made by a co-operative of 135
Mapuche weavers; all items are 100% wool
with traditional designs (spinning and
weaving demonstrations are planned).
Also highly recommended is the *Casa de
Arte Mapuche*, Matta 25-A, T 213085,
Casilla 1682, for information on Mapuche
arts and crafts speak to the director Rayen
Kvyeh. There is a good view of Temuco
from **Cerro Ñielol**, a park (entry US$1),

where there is a fine collection of native plants in the natural state, including the national flower, the *copihue rojo*. There is also a bathing pool (US$0.40) and a restaurant (open 1200-2400). On Cerro Ñielol is also La Patagua, the tree under which the final peace was signed with the Mapuches in 1881.

Museums

Museo de la Araucanía, Alemania 84, a well-arranged collection devoted to the history and traditions of the Mapuche nation. Open Tues-Sat 0800-1300, 1500-1800; Sun 1000-1400 (at some times of year Tues-Fri 0800-1300, 1500-1900), US$1.

Excursions

A pleasant trip through Mapuche country is to take a minibus from the Central Market to the country town of **Chol Chol**, 30 km unpaved to the NW. There are daily buses (Huincabus from Terminal Rural, 1 hr, 4 times between 1100 and 1800, US$0.60, or García/Gangas from same terminal at 1000), laden with corn, vegetables, charcoal, animals, as well as the locals. The trip traverses rolling countryside with panoramic views. On a clear day it is possible to see five volcanoes. Nearer Chol Chol, a few traditional round *rucas* can be seen. For an overnight stay and information, contact Sra Lauriza Norváez, C Luzcano (s/n), who prepares meals, and is very helpful. Daily bus at 1330 to Nueva Imperial and on to Puerto Saavedra, but bus connections few and slow (stay overnight in Puerto Saavedra – see below).

Local information

NB Do not confuse the streets Vicuña MacKenna and Gen MacKenna.

● **Accommodation**

A1 *Nuevo Hotel de la Frontera*, Bulnes 726, T 210718, inc breakfast, excellent; **A2** *Bayern*, Prat 146, small rooms, clean, helpful; **A2** *Apart Hotel Don Eduardo*, Bello 755, T 215554, parking, suites with kitchen, rec; **A3** *C'Est Bayonne*, Vicuña Mackenna 361, T 235510, F 714915, with breakfast, modern, German and Italian spoken.

B *Continental*, Varas 708, T 238973, F 233830, popular with business travellers, clean, friendly, colonial-style wooden building, excellent restaurant, the bar is popular with locals in the evening, cheaper rooms without bath, rec; **B** *Turismo*, Claro Solar 636, T 210583, nr main square, slightly run-down restaurant, good value, with bath, **C** without, good service, IYHA reductions.

C *Oriente*, M Rodríguez 1146, T 233232, clean, rec.

D *Hosp Adriane Becker*, Estebáñez 881, without bath, good breakfast, basic, friendly; **D** *Alba Jaramillo*, Calbuco 583, T 240042, by Av Alemania, with breakfast, clean; **D** *Hosp Aldunate*, Aldunate 187, T 213548, friendly, cooking facilities, also E dormitory accommodation; **D** *Casa Blanca*, Montt 1306 y Zenteno, T 212740, good breakfast, friendly, rec; **D** *Casa de huéspedes Centenario*, Aldunate 864, with breakfast, hot water, clean; **D** *Flor Acoca*, Lautaro 591, hot water, breakfast, clean; **D** *Hosp Millarey*, Claro Solar 471, simple, basic; **D** *Hostal Montt*, Manuel Montt 965, T 211856, parking, clean, friendly; **D** *Rupangue*, Barros Arana 182, hot shower, clean, helpful, good value. The following are in our **D** or **E** pp range: on Av Alemania, Sra Veronica Kiekebusch, No 0649, T 247287, with breakfast, clean, quiet, rec, buses No 1 or 9 from rural bus terminal; No 035, large rooms, hot water, use of kitchen, pleasant; A Bello y Las Heras, basic, clean; Blanco Encalada 1078, T234447, use of kitchen, friendly, rec; Bulnes 1006 y O'Higgins, good double rooms, hot water, above drugstore, ask for house key otherwise access limited to shop hours; on Claro Solar, No 151, with breakfast; No 483, clean, poor shower, Gen MacKenna 46, clean, Jan-Mar only; other private houses in same street; on Rodríguez, No 1311, friendly, clean, meals served; No 1341, *Res Temuco*, T 233721; Zenteno 486 (Sra Ruth Palominas), T 211269, friendly, clean, hot water, rec; **E** *Res Ensueño*, Rodríguez 442, hot water, clean; **E** *Hosp González*, Lautaro 1160, p 2, friendly, safe, clean, rec; **E** San Martín 01760 (Sra Eyla de González), T 246182, with breakfast, clean. Accommodation in private houses, category D, can be arranged by Tourist Office. Other *residenciales* and *pensiones* can be found in the market station area.

Camping: *Camping Metrenco*, 10 km S on Route 5.

● **Places to eat**

Café Marriet, Prat 451, Local 21, excellent coffee; on Bulnes: *Dino's*, No 360, good coffee; *Il Gelato*, No 420, delicious ice cream; *Julio's Pizza*, No 778, wide variety, not cheap; *Centro Español*, No 483; *Della Maggio*, No 536, good coffee and light meals. *D'Angelo*, San Martín 1199, good food, pleasant, pricey. Plenty of good eating places inside the municipal market. *Pront Rapa*, Aldunate 421, for take-away lunches and snacks, rec; *Ñam-Ñam*, Portales 802, pizzas, sandwiches etc, good; *Café Arte-*

sanía Raíces Indoamericanas, Manuel Montt 645, T 232434, specializes in Mapuche dishes, good coffee, adjoining shop sells handicrafts and textiles. *La Cumbre del Cerro Ñielol* (dancing), on top of Cerro Ñielol.

● **Airline offices**
LanChile, Bulnes 667, T 211339; **Ladeco**, Prat 565, Local 102, T 214325; **National**, Claro Solar 780, Local 7, T 215764; **Varig**, Mackenna 763, T 213120; **TAN**, T 210500.

● **Banks & money changers**
Good rates for TCs at **Banco Osorno** and **Global** both on Plaza de Armas; also **Turcamb**, Claro Solar 733; **Christopher Money Exchange**, Prat 696, Oficina 419; also at Bulnes 667, Local 202; **Inter-Santiago**, Bulnes 443, local 2. All deal in dollars and Argentine pesos. **Fincard** (Mastercard), Claro Solar 922. **Banco Concepción** (for Visa), M Montt 901; **Banco de Chile**, Varas 818, rec for money transfers by Switch.

● **Embassies & consulates**
Netherlands, España 494, Honorary Consul, Germán Nicklas, is friendly and helpful.

● **Laundry**
Caupolicán 110, Nos 4 and 5, open 0900-2100 daily, good, cheap, quick; Portales 1185, expensive; automatic at M Montt between Las Heras and Lynch.

● **Post & telecommunications**
Post Office: Portales 839.

Telephones: Centro de Llamadas CTC, A Prat just off Claro Solar and Bulnes, Mon-Sat 0800-2400, Sun and holidays 1030-2400. Entel, Bulnes 303, daily 0830-2200.

● **Shopping**
Cameras: *Ruka*, Bulnes 394, helpful, owner speaks German.

Supermarket: *Las Brisas*, Carrera 899; *Frutería Las Vegas*, Matta 274, dried fruit (useful for climbing/trekking).

● **Tourist offices**
Bulnes 586, T 211969. Open 0830-2030, all week in summer, 0900-1200, 1500-1800 Mon-Fri in winter. Also at Balmaceda y Prat. **Automóvil Club de Chile**: Varas 6878, T 213949. **Conaf**: Bilbao 931, T 234420.

● **Transport**
Local Car hire: Hertz, Las Heras 999, T 235385, US$45 a day. Budget, Lynch 471, T 214911; Automóvil Club de Chile, Varas 687, T 213949 and at airport; Puig, Portales 779; Fatum, Varas 983, T 234199; Euro, Mackenna 426, T 210311, helpful, good value.

Air Manquehue Airport 6 km from the city. LanChile, Ladeco and National to Santiago. Lan-Chile and Ladeco to Osorno and Valdivia; National to Puerto Montt and once a week to Punta Arenas; TAN flies to Neuquén, Argentina.

Trains Station at Barros Arana y Lautaro Navarro, T 233416. To **Santiago**: 2 a day, 12 hrs,: fares *económico* US$16, *superior/salón* US$22 (depending on service), sleeper US$24, double compartment, restaurant car expensive. To **Osorno** and **Puerto Montt** daily 0850, 9 hrs. Ticket office at Bulnes 582, T 233522, open Mon-Fri 0900-1300, 1430-1800, Sun 0900-1300 as well as at station.

Buses No long-distance bus terminal – buses leave from company offices. Buses to neighbouring towns leave from Terminal Rural, Pinto y Balmaceda. Bus company offices: Igi Llaima and Narbus, Barros Arana y Miraflores; Erbuc, Miraflores y Bulnes; LIT, San Martín y Bulnes; Cruz del Sur V Mackenna 671; JAC, Mackenna y Andres Bello; ETTA, Longitudinal Sur and Thiele, V Mackenna 600 block, nr Varas; Power, Bulnes 174; Pangui Sur, Miraflores 871.

Buses to **Santiago** US$16; to **Curacautín**, Erbuc, US$2, 7 daily, 2¾ hrs; to **Lonquimay**, Erbuc, 4 daily, 5½ hrs, US$3; to **Laguna Captren**, Erbuc, Mon and Fri 1645, 4 hrs, US$3; to **Contulmo**,US$3, 2 hrs,**Cañete**, US$4 and **Lebu**, Erbuc and Thiele; Cruz del Sur, 3 a day to **Castro**, 10 a day to **Puerto Montt** (US$9, 5½ hrs), to **Valdivia** US$4; to **Osorno** US$6; to **Villarrica** and **Pucón** many between 0705 and 2045, 1½ hrs, US$3, and 2 hrs, US$3.50; to **Coñaripe**, 3 hrs, and **Lican Ray**, 2 hrs; to **Panguipulli**, Power and Pangui Sur at 0730, 3 hrs, US$2; Pangui Sur to **Loncoche**, **Los Lagos**, **Mehuin** in summer only; to **Concepción**, Bío Bío, US$5, 4½ hrs; to **Arica**, US$55 or US$70 *cama*; to **Antofagasta**, US$45.

Buses to Argentina: JAC from Terminal Rural to **Junín de los Andes** (US$25), San Martín de los Andes (US$25) and Neuquén (US$30), Wed and Fri 0400; also Igi Llaima and San Martín 3 a week each to **San Martín**, US$25. Nar Bus from Terminal Rural to San Martín and Neuquén, Mon-Fri (San Martín buses go via Villarrica and Pucón when the Tromen Pass is open); Ruta Sur, Miraflores 1151, to **Zapala** (US$22) and Neuquén (US$28),via Paso Pino Hachado, Wed and Sat 0400; La Unión del Sud, Miraflores 1285, same destinations Wed, Fri and Sat Fénix (address above) to **Buenos Aires** and **Mendoza**.

Coastal resorts near Temuco

A paved road runs W to (55 km) **Carahue** (accommodation available). About 30 km further, S of the mouth of the navigable Río Imperial, is **Puerto Saavedra**, where there is a stretch of beach with black volcanic sand. It comprises 3 distinct towns:

the first administrative; the second, 2 km away, the fishing port with one poor *residencial*; the third, a further 2 km, the tourist area. From Puerto Saavedra there are interesting excursions to Nehuentue, on the N bank of the river, and to Trovolhue, reached by a specially chartered launch which takes 4 hrs to go up the Río Moncul.

● **Accommodation E** Sra Rita Sandoval Muñoz, Las Dunas 01511, lovely, knowledgeable; many *hosterías* in D-E category.

● **Transport** Buses to Temuco (Terminal Rural), Nar Bus, 3 a day, 3¼ hrs, US$2.50.

Puerto Domínguez, 40 km S of Carahue on an unpaved road is a picturesque little town on **Lago Budi**, the only inland, saltwater lake in Chile. Over 130 species of bird, aquatic and marine, including black-necked swans, visit it. Puerto Domínguez is famous for its fishing. The *Carlos Schalchli* ferry (free) leaves Puerto Domínguez for Isla Huapi (also spelt Guapi), Mon-Fri 0800 and 1630, returning 1030 and 1700. It takes about 30 mins. The Isla has a Mapuche settlement with traditional thatched houses (*rucas*) and fine views of both the lake and the Pacific. Ideal for camping.

● **Accommodation E** pp *Hostería Rucaleufú*, Alessandri 22, with good meals, clean, lake views, highly rec.

● **Transport** Bus from Temuco, 2 hrs.

LOS PARAGUAS AND CONGUILLIO NATIONAL PARKS

The 3,050m Llaima volcano at 1,500m, 80 km E of Temuco, is still active and last erupted in 1994. It stands in the middle of two large **national parks**, **Los Paraguas** (named after the umbrella-like araucaria, or monkey puzzle, pine trees – best visited Aug-Oct according to Conaf) and **Conguillio** (open 20 Nov-13 Mar). The latter, which contains the Laguna Conguillio and the snow-covered Sierra Nevada, is the best place to see araucaria forest, which used to cover an extensive area in this part of Chile. It is one of Chile's most popular parks, but is deserted outside the Jan/Feb season. The best way to get to the park is to drive, preferably in a high-clearance vehicle (roads are very bad, especially after rain) and with clear instructions on which roads shown in

maps are suitable and exist. There are three routes, on all of which there is public transport in season only: via Curacautín (42 km N of the Park), via Melipeuco (to the S) or via Cherquenco (to the W).

From Curacautín (see page 765) take a bus at 1830, Mon and Fri towards the park, 1 hr, US$1, or hitch (not difficult in summer). From the bus stop it is 10 km to Laguna Captren situated in araucaria forest, where you pay a park entrance fee of US$4; good hiking. 6 km further on is Laguna Conguillio, with a visitor's centre (closed off-season), from where you can hike into the Sierra Nevada, or take a shorter, interesting walk on the Sendero de los Carpinteros (impassable under snow).

15 km S of Laguna Conguillio, mostly across deserted lava fields, at Truful, is the southern entrance to the park, which is 13 km N by road from the village of **Melipeuco**.

The third entrance to the park is via paved road to Cherquenco, then by very poor road another 30 km (high clearance vehicle essential) to Llaima ski resort, one of the prettiest in Chile (daily buses Temuco-Cherquenco). It is then a 2-3 day hike around Volcán Llaima to Laguna Conguillio, dusty, but beautiful views of Laguna Quepe, then on to the Laguna Captren *guardería*.

To climb **Llaima**, crampons and iceaxe are essential. Climb NE from *Guardería Captren*, allow 5 hrs to ascend, 2 hrs to descend. Information on the climb is available from Sr Torres at *Guardería Captren*.

A brief résumé of the route on foot through the park from the S end: from entrance, 600m trail to Río Truful-Truful canyon and waterfall; 8 km to Laguna Verde (camping possible); 3 km to Laguna Arco Iris (beautiful, camping, possible); 3 km to Laguna Conguillio; 6 km from Centro de Información Ambiental on Conguillio to Laguna Captrén; 10 km to Park limits and *guardería*.

For details of these excursions visit the Conaf, IX Región, Caupolicán y Bulnes, Temuco. For best touring, hire a 4WD vehicle in Temuco. Buy supplies in Temuco or Melipeuco: much cheaper than shop in the park.

● **Accommodation** In the park, **Laguna Captren**: campsite US$20/site inc firewood but no other facilities. **Laguna Conguillio**: campsite (US$15/tent, hot water, showers, firewood), cheaper campsite (*camping de mochileros*, US$5 pp); *cabañas* (**A3** summer only, sleep 6, no sheets or blankets, gas stove, and café/shop). In **Melipeuco**: **E** *Germania*, Aguirre 399, basic, good food; **E** *Pensión Hospedaje*, Aguirre 729, more spacious, rec; **C** *Hostería Hue-Telén*, Aguirre 15, Casilla 40, T 693032 and leave message, good restaurant; free municipal campsite; also *Camping Los Pioneros*, 1 km out of town on road to the park, hot water. *Restaurant Los Troncos*, Aguirre 352, rec.

● **Transport** Bus from Temuco Terminal Rural, Flota Erbuc, 5 daily, 0900-1830, 4 hrs, US$1.30, ask driver to drop you at the road fork, 10 km from park entrance, last back to Temuco at 1630. Transport can be arranged from Melipeuco into the park (ask in grocery stores, US$20 one way).

FRONTIER WITH ARGENTINA: PASO DE ICALMA

Paso de Icalma (1,298 m) is reached by unpaved road, 53 km from Melipeuco. On the Argentine side this road continues to Zapala.

● **Chilean immigration**
Open Dec-March 0800-2100, April-Nov 0800-1900.

VILLARRICA

The town of Villarrica can be reached by a 63-km paved road SE from Freire (24 km S of Temuco on the Longitudinal Highway), or from Loncoche, 54 km S of Freire, also paved. Wooded Lago Villarrica, 21 km long and about 7 km wide, is the most beautiful in the region, with snow-capped Villarrica volcano (2,840m) to the SE.

Villarrica (*Pop* 36,000; *Phone code* 045), pleasantly set at the extreme SW corner of the lake, was founded in 1552 but destroyed by the Mapuches in 1602; the present town dates from 1882.

Local festivals

Festival Cultural Mapuche, with market, usually in second week of Feb; enquire at the Santiago or Temuco tourist office.

Local information
● **Accommodation**

A3 *Hotel El Ciervo*, Gen Koerner 241, T 411215, German-run, beautiful location, pool, rec; **A3** *Yachting Club*, San Martín 802, T 411191, pleasant atmosphere, terraced gardens, swimming pool, restaurant, boating and fishing, cheaper rooms in motel annex; **A3** *Hostería la Colina*, Ríos 1177, overlooking town, T 411503, Casilla 382, run by North Americans, with breakfast, large gardens, good service, good restaurant, highly rec; **A3** *Hotel y Cabañas El Parque*, 3 km out of Villarrica on Pucón road, T 411120, Casilla 65, lakeside with beach, tennis courts, with breakfast, good restaurant set meals, highly rec.

B *Hostería Kiel*, Gen Koerner 153, T 411631, **D** off season, lakeside, clean, friendly, good; **B** *Cabañas Traitraico*, San Martín 380, T 411064, 100m from lake, cabins sleep 6, TV, heating, kitchenette, parking; **B** *Hostería Bilbao*, Henríquez 43, T 411452, clean, small rooms, pretty patio, good restaurant.

C *Rayhuen*, Pedro Montt 668, T 411571 (**B** in summer), clean, good restaurant, good breakfast, lovely garden, rec.

D *Yandaly*, Henríquez 401, T 411452, small rooms, good; **D** *Fuentes*, Vicente Reyes 665, T 411595, basic, clean, friendly, restaurant; **D** *Hosp Dalila Balboa*, San Martín 734, clean, cheap; **D** *Res Villa Linda*, Valdivia 678, T 411392, hot water, clean, basic, cheap, good restaurant.

E pp *Res Victoria*, Muñoz 530, friendly, cooking facilities; **E** pp Vicente Reyes 854, nr JAC terminal, good breakfast, poor bathroom facilities.

Youth hostel: **E** pp *Res San Francisco*, Julio Zegers 646, shared rooms. Also, rooms in private homes, all **E** pp, inc several in Francisco Bilbao; Eliana Castillo, No 537, clean, friendly; Urrutia 407, large breakfast, kitchen, clean; Matta 469, cooking facilities, clean.

Camping: 2 sites just outside town on Pucón road, *Los Castaños*, T 65-250183, and *du Lac*, quiet, but buy supplies at *Los Castaños* which is cheaper. Many more on S side of Lake Villarrica, see under Pucón (below). Summer houses available in Dec-February.

● **Places to eat**

Club Social, P de Valdivia 640, good; *El Rey de Mariscos*, Letelier 1030, good seafood; several good and cheap places for seafood in the market; *Rapa Nui*, V Reyes 678, good and cheap, closed Sun; *Hotel Yandaly*, Henríquez 401, good food, rec; *Café 2001*, Henríquez 379, coffee and ice-cream, good.

● **Banks & money changers**
Banco de Osorno changes TCs; *Casa de Cambio*, O'Higgins 210, poor rates for TCs; **Cristophe Exchange**, Valdivia 1061, good rates for TCs. Rates are generally poor.

● **Laundry**
Lavandería y Lavaseco Villarrica, Andrés Bello 348, T 411449.

● **Post & telecommunications**
Post Office: Muñoz y Urrutia, open 0830-1230, 1400-1800 (Mon-Fri), 0830-1230 (Sat).
Telephones: Entel, Reyes 721. CTC, C Henríquez 430.

● **Tourist offices**
Valdivia 1070; information and maps (open all day all week in summer).

● **Transport**
Buses to **Santiago**, 10 hrs, US$15-20. To **Pucón**, in summer every 30 mins, 40 mins' journey, US$1; to **Valdivia**, JAC, US$3.50, 3 a day, 2½ hrs; daily service to **Panguipulli** at 0700, US$2, scenic ride; to **Coñaripe** (US$1.50) and **Liquiñe** at 1600 Mon-Sat, 1000 Sun; to **Temuco**, JAC, US$3; to **Loncoche** (road and railway junction), US$1.50. **NB** JAC has 2 terminals: long distance at Reyes y Montt, local on Reyes between Henríquez y Muñoz.

Io **Argentina** at 0615 on Tues, Thur and Sat with Empresa San Martín (Av A Muñoz 417) and at 0730 on Mon, Wed and Fri with Igi-Llaima, but if the Tromen pass is blocked by snow buses go via Panguipulli instead of Pucón.

Some 65 km NE of Villarrica is **Lago Colico** in a wild, remote setting. A road follows the lake's northern shore leading to the northern tip of Lago Caburgua (see **Excursions** from Pucón).

PUCON

A most attractive town on the south-eastern shore of Lago Villarrica, 26 km E of Villarrica. Pucón (*phone code* 045) has a good climate and first-class accommodation. The black sand beach is very popular for swimming and watersports. The season is from 15 Dec to 15 Mar, when the town is crowded and expensive. Off season it is very pleasant but many places are closed. The town is scheduled for major development, with plans to build on La Península and around La Poza, the yacht harbour. It now supersedes Villarrica as the tourist centre for the lake.

Places of interest

There is a pleasant walk to **La Península** for fine views of the lake and volcano, pony rides, golf, etc (private land owned by an Apart-Hotel, you must get permission first). There is another pleasant *paseo*, the **Otto Gudenschwager**, which starts at the lake end of Ansorena (beside *Gran Hotel Pucón*) and goes along the shore. Launch excursion from the landing stage at La Poza at end of O'Higgins at 1500 and 1900, US$4 for 2 hrs. There is a large handicraft centre where you can see spinning and weaving in progress. Besides the lake, other attractions nearby include whitewater rafting. A Villarrica-Pucón Centro de Ski has been built (see **Skiing** below) so that Pucón is also a winter sports centre.

Excursions

Two excursions from Pucón close to Lago Villarrica: 2-km walk N along the beach to the mouth of the Río Pucón, with views of the volcanoes Villarrica, Quetrupillán and Lanín. To cross the Río Pucón: head E out of Pucón along the main road, then turn N on an unmade road leading to a new bridge, upstream from the old ferry crossing to La Reducción de Quelhue, near the N bank. This is supposed to be a Mapuche village, but no traditional dress, language or customs are used, and the children ask for money. From here there are pleasant walks along the N shore of the lake to Quelhue and Travilelfu, or NE towards Caburgua, or up into the hills through farms and agricultural land, with views of three volcanoes and, higher up, of the lake.

Local information
● **Accommodation**
In summer, Dec to Feb, add 20% to hotel prices; at this time rooms may be hard to find – plenty of alternatives (usually cheaper) in Villarrica. Off-season it is often possible to negotiate for accommodation.

L1 *Antumalal*, luxury class, 30m above the shore, 2 km from Pucón, T 441011, F 441013, very small, picturesque chalet-type, magnificent views of the lake (breakfast and lunch on terrace), lovely gardens, excellent, with meals, open year round, good beach, swimming pool and good fishing up the river; state owned **L3** *Gran Pucón*, Holzapfel 190, T 441001, half board, L2 full board, restaurant, disco, sports centre (swimming, gym, squash, etc) shared with **L3** *Condominio Gran Hotel* apartments; **L3** *Interlaken*, Caupolicán, on lakeside 10 mins from town, T 441276, F 441242, Swiss run, chalets, rec, water skiing, golf, pool, TCs changed, credit cards not accepted (open Nov-April), no restaurant.

A1 *Araucarias*, Caupolicán 243, T 441963, F 441286, clean, comfortable but not luxurious; **A2** *Gudenschwager*, Pedro de Valdivia 12, T 441904, classic Bavarian type, views over lake, volcano and mountains, attentive staff, comfortable, excellent restaurant (open in summer only); **A2** *Hostería El Príncipito*, Urrutia 291, T 441200, with bath, good breakfast, clean, very friendly, rec; **A3** *La Posada*, Valdivia 191, T 441088, with bath, cheaper without, full board available, also spacious cabins (C low season).

C *Hosp La Casita*, Palguín 555, T 441712, clean, laundry and kitchen facilities, English and German spoken, large breakfast, garden, motorcycle parking, ski trips, Spanish classes, **D** off season, rec; **C** *La Tetera*, Urrutia 580, T 441462, with bath and breakfast, German spoken, warmly rec; **C** *Salzburg*, O'Higgins 311, T 441907, with bath and breakfast, rec, German spoken, some rooms with view over volcano (possible to borrow crampons); **C** *Turista*, O'Higgins 136, T 441153 (D low season), with bath, friendly, clean.

D *Goldapfel*, O'Higgins 136A, clean, cooking facilities; **D** *Hosp De La Montaña*, O'Higgins 472, T 441267, good value, clean, TV, central, restaurant, next to JAC buses; **D** *Hostería Milla Rahue*, O'Higgins 460, T 441904, clean, good inexpensive restaurant, convenient for JAC; **D** *Res Lincoyán*, Av Lincoyán, T 441144, with bath, cheaper without, clean and comfortable; **D** pp *Saint John*, hostería and campsite, 2 km on Villarrica road, open Dec-March, full board available, Casilla 154, T 441165/92; **D** *Hosp Gerlach*, Palguín 460, clean, kitchen facilities, helpful.

D *Hostería ¡école!*, Urrutia 592, T 441675, F 441660, inc breakfast, run by Ancient Forest International, good vegetarian and fish restaurant, ecological shop, forest treks, information. Accommodation in private houses, all **D** or **E** pp unless stated: Familia Acuña, Palguín 233 (ask at *peluquería* next door), without breakfast, hot water, kitchen and laundry facilities, dirty, good meeting place. On Lincoyán: Juan Torres, No 445, T 441248, clean, cooking facilities, talkative; *El Refugio*, No 348, with breakfast, good; *Hosp Sonia*, No 485, T 441269, hot showers, use of kitchen, very noisy and crowded, meals, friendly; No 815, cooking facilities (information on climbing Villarrica); **F** pp Irma Torres, No 545, with breakfast, cooking facilities, clean; **F** pp No 565, friendly, clean, safe, quiet, rec, cooking facilities; next door is *Casa Eliana* (Pasaje Chile 225, T 441851), kitchen facilities, highly rec; **E** Adriana Molina, No 312, with breakfast, clean, helpful; **F** pp No. 630, T 441043, kitchen facilities, good value; *Hosp Cherpas*, Fresia 161, T 441089, kitchen facilities, warm and friendly; *Hosp Graciela*, Pasaje Rolando Matus 521 (off Av Brasil), good food and atmosphere; Irma Villena, Arauco 460, clean, friendly, rec; Perú 720, use of kitchen, helps organize excursions to Volcán Villarrica and Huerquehue National Park; **F** pp Roberto y Alicia Abreque, Perú 170, basic, noisy, popular, kitchen and laundry facilities, information on excursions; *Casa Richard*, Uruguay 539, basic but friendly, cooking facilities, rec; Brasil 464, clean, kitchen facilities; many other families have rooms, especially on Calles Perú, Uruguay and Paraguay – look for the signs or ask in bars/restaurants.

Camping: buy supplies in Villarrica (cheaper). There are several campsites between Villarrica and Pucón: *Acapulco*, *Playa Linda* (Villarrica), *Suyay*, *Lorena*, 10 km from Villarrica (also rents *cabañas*); *Huimpalay*, 12 km from Villarrica; *Millaray*, 7 km S of Pucón; *Trancura* and *Saltos del*

Molco; La Poza, 300m out of town on road to Villarrica, E pp, all facilities. In fact, there are so many establishments along the lake's southern shore that you cannot get to the water's edge unless staying in one. Camping is also possible in gardens, US$2.50 pp with use of bathroom. On the road to Tromen Pass, *Cabañas El Dorado*, US$18 for 2, good site, poorly maintained. Cheaper sites en route to Caburga. **Camping equipment**: *Eltit*, O'Higgins y Fresia; *Mawinda*, Ansorena 485.

● **Places to eat**
Pizzería Che Thomas, Palguín 465, good value, small place run by Jorge; *El Fogón*, O'Higgins 480, very good; *El Refugio*, Lincoyán 348, some vegetarian dishes, expensive wine; *Le Demago*, Lincoyán 361 (plus *Pub Naf-Naf*); *Carnes Orlando*, bar/restaurant/butcher's shop, Ansorena nr Urrutia; *Club 77*, O'Higgins, excellent trout; *Puerto Pucón*, on Fresia, Spanish, stylish; *Pastelería Suiza*, next to *Hostería Suiza*, O'Higgins 116, good; *Café de Brasil*, Fresia 477, for real coffee; *Holzapfel Backerei*, Clemente Holzapfel 524, German cafe, rec; *La Tetera*, Urrutia 580, wide selection of teas, good coffee, snacks, German spoken, book exchange, rec; *Bar de Julio Parra*, Ansorena 370, English-style pub.

● **Banks & money changers**
Banco del Estado de Chile, O'Higgins casi Lincoyán, does not change cash or TCs. Many *casas de cambio* on O'Higgins, poor rates. Big supermarket on O'Higgins changes TCs.

● **Laundry**
Fresia 224; Colo-Colo 475 and 478.

● **Post & telecommunications**
Post Office: Fresia 813.
Telephone: CTC, Gen Urrutia 472; Entel, Ansorena 299.

● **Sports**
Fishing: Pucón and Villarrica are celebrated fishing centres, for the lake and the very beautiful Lincura, Trancura and Toltén rivers. Local tourist office will supply details on licences and open seasons etc. Some tourist agencies also offer fishing trips, US$12-20.
Hiking: to the Cañi Forest Sanctuary, overnight hikes are rec; enquire at *Hostería ¡école!*
Horse riding: horse hire US$5/hr.
Skiing: on the slopes of the Villarrica volcano, where there are 7 lifts (US$12 full day, US$18 weekends). Season is from July to November. Equipment rental US$15/day, US$82/week; lessons available.
Watersports: water-skiing, sailing, windsurfing at the beach by *Gran Hotel* and La Poza beach end of O'Higgins (more expensive than hotel, not rec); hotel rates: waterskiing US$10 for 15 mins, Laser sailing US$11/hr, sailboards US$6/hr, rowing boats US$3/hr.
Whitewater rafting: is very popular; many agencies offer trips (see below), basic course: US$9; advanced US$30.

● **Tour companies & travel agents**
Travel agents: on O'Higgins: *Sol y Nieve* (esq Lincoyán, also at *Gran Hotel Pucón*), good reports; *Altue*, No 371, *Nacional Travel Club*, No 323, *Trancura*, No 211, T 441959/441189 (good guides and equipment, some English spoken, rec); *Apumanque*, No 412, T 441085; *Turismo Florencia*, T/F 441267. All arrange trips to thermal baths, trekking to volcanoes, whitewater rafting, etc (prices: whitewater rafting and riding, see above; climbing Villarrica, US$40-45, 12 hrs, equipment provided; mountain bike hire from US$5/hr to US$20/day; tours to Termas de Huife, US$20 inc entry. Shop around: prices vary at times, quality of guides and equipment variable. *Sergio Catalán*, T 441269 (office) or 441142, Geronimo Alderete 192, tours, excursions and taxi service all year round. For falls, lakes and termas it is cheaper, if in a group, to flag down a taxi and bargain.

● **Tourist offices**
Sernatur, Caupolicán y Brasil, very helpful, ask here about all types of accommodation. Municipal Tourist Office at O'Higgins y Palguín provides information and sell fishing licences (US$1/month).

● **Transport**
Local Bicycle hire: *Taller el Pollo*, Palguín 500 block and Trancura, O'Higgins 261, US$10-12/day. Try also travel agencies, eg *Sol y Nieve*. **Car hire**: Hertz, Fresia 220, US$65 for cheapest car (inc tax, insurance, and 200 km free); same prices/day at *Gran Hotel*. **Taxis**: Cooperative, T 441009; individual member Oscar Jara Carrasco, T 411992 (home in Villarrica).

Buses No main terminal: each company has its own terminal: JAC, O'Higgins 480, T 441923; LIT, O'Higgins y Palguín; Cordillera, Av Miguel Ansorena nr O'Higgins.
JAC to **Villarrica**, **Temuco** (frequent, US$3, 2 hrs, *rapido* US$3.50, 1 hr) and **Valdivia** (US$4.50); for **Puerto Montt** go to Valdivia and change; to **Santiago**, 10 hrs, US$18-25, many companies, Power cheapest (and least comfortable), overnight only; daytime go via Temuco; *cama* service by Tur-Bus; Cordillera, for **Paillaco** and **Lago Caburgua** – see below. Colectivos to **Villarrica** from O'Higgins y Palguín. **Buses to Argentina**: Buses from Temuco to Junín pass through Pucón, fares are the same as from Temuco.

PARQUE NACIONAL VILLARRICA

Excursions from Pucón may be made to the active **Villarrica** volcano in the **Villarrica National Park** 8 km S of the town (entry US$6). The volcano can be climbed up and down in 8-9 hrs (go in summer when days are longer), good boots, iceaxe and crampons, sunglasses, plenty of water and sun block essential. Beware of sulphur fumes at the top – take a cloth mask moistened with lemon juice.

● **Access** Following a number of deaths in recent years, restrictions on access to the park have been imposed: entry is permitted only to groups with a guide and to individuals who can show proof of membership of a mountaineering club in their own country. Several agencies offer excursions, US$45-52.50 (plus park entry, US$6) including guide, transport to park entrance and hire of equipment (no reducction for those with their own equipment); at the park entrance equipment is checked; entry is refused if the weather is poor. Note that travel agencies will not start out if the weather is bad and some travellers have experienced difficulties in obtaining a refund: establish in advance what terms apply in the event of cancellation and be prepared to wait a few days. Guides, see above under Travel Agents. Also Alvaro Martínez, Cristóbal Colón 430; Juan Carlos, at Oliva's *pensión*, or his pool room on main street, rec. Many others, all with equipment; beware charlatans, ask at the tourist office. Crampons, ice axe, sunglasses can be rented for US$4/day from the *Taller El Pollo* bicycle shop (address above).

● **Accommodation** There is a refuge without beds 4 km inside the Park, insecure and in desperate need of renovation. Campsite with drinking water, toilets, below refuge.

CABURGUA AND PN HUERQUEHUE

Just off the road to volcanic **Lago Caburgua** are the **Ojos de Caburgua**, some 30 km NE of Pucón, beautiful pools fed from underground, particularly attractive after rainfall (entry US$0.50). The lake itself is very pretty, in a wild setting (row-boats may be hired, US$1.50 per hour). Lago Caburgua is unusual for its beautiful white sand beach whereas other beaches in the area are black sand of volcanic origin.

● **Accommodation B** *Hostería Los Robles*, 3 km from village, lovely views, good restaurant; campsite, T 236989, expensive in season, but cheap out of season. No shops, so take own food.

Three more beautiful lakes are Verde, Chico and Toro in the **Huerquehue National Park**, E of Lago Caburgua. The park entrance is 7 km (3 uphill, 3 down, 1 along Lago Tinquilco) from Paillaco, beyond Caburgua; entry US$2. The park is open officially only Jan-Mar, but you can get in at other times. Warden very helpful; people in park rent horses and boats. Take your own food.

From the car park at Lago Tinquilco there is a well-signed track to Lagos Verde, Chico and Toro (for those with cars there is a private car park, US$0.50, 1½ km along the track). The track zig-zags up (sign says 5 km, but worth it) to Lago Chico, then splits left to Toro, right to Verde. From Toro you can continue to Lago Huerquehue and Lago de los Palos (camping); there is no connecting path from Toro to Lago Verde, which is beautifully surrounded by trees. In Huerquehue there are 20 lakes in all and their outlines keep changing.

● **Accommodation** At the park entrance there is a campsite, US$8. 1½ km before the park entrance, two German speaking families – the Braatz and Soldans offer accommodation (**E** pp, no electricity, food and camping (US$6); they also rent rowing boats on the lake. Camping in park not allowed but 2 sites on route to Park, inc Conaf site US$6 and cheaper one just past it.

● **Transport** For all these lakes, the turn off from the main road is 8 km E of Pucón. 3 km before Caburgua a dirt road (dusty and slippery in dry weather, very slippery after rain) turns right to Paillaco. Taxi day trips from Pucón, US$25 return. Cordillera bus departs 1230 for Caburgua, returns 1400, 2nd bus (in summer only) leaves 1700 and returns next morning (US$1 single), but there are colectivos or you can try hitching. For Huerquehue, take JAC bus to Paillaco, 1½ hrs, US$1, 3 a day. If walking or cycling to Lago Caburgua, turn left 3 km E of Pucón (sign to Puente Quelhue) and follow track for 18 km through beautiful scenery, rec.

Hot springs East of Pucón

Outside the Huerquehue Park are the **Huife** thermal baths (*Hostería Termas de Huife*, T 441222, PO Box 18, Pucón), US$8, including use of one pool, modern, pleasant, picnicking not allowed (taxi from Pucón, US$23 return with taxi waiting, US$16 one way). Termas de **Quimaico** can be reached from the road to Huife: new, less ostentatious than Huife, camping allowed, 2 cabins and *hostería (centro turístico* under construction). There are also thermal baths at **San Luis**, 25 km E of Pucón and N of the road to Curarrehue (bus Pucón-Curarrehue passes 2 km from the baths; entry US$12.50), small hotel, 30 mins' walk to Lago del León.

South of the same road, and 36 km SE of Pucón, there are further baths at **Palguín** (**A1** *Hotel* – address, Casilla 1D, Pucón, T 441968 – full board, B in small huts with bath, run down, poor food, German-speaking owner, cool swimming pool, baths US$6). Taxi rates are same as for Huife. Nearby is the **D** *Rancho de Caballos*, offering accommodation, also *cabañas* and camping, good food, horse riding excursions (write to Cristina Bonninghoff, *Rancho de Caballos*, Casilla 142, Pucón). There are many hikeable waterfalls in the area; eg, 6-7 km from the turn-off for Termas de Palguín, Salto Palguín can be seen, but not reached, a further 2 km Salto China (spectacular, entry US$0.60, restaurant, camping); one more km to Salto del Puma (US$0.60) and Salto del León (US$1.25), both spectacular and 800m from the Termas. From Pucón take Bus Regional Villarrica from Palguín y O'Higgins at 1100 to the junction (10 km from Termas); last bus from junction to the Termas at 1500, so you may have to hitch back. Nearby is the entrance to the **Quetrupillán** section of the Villarrica National Park (high clearance vehicle necessary, horses best), free camping, wonderful views over Villarrica Volcano and 6 other peaks. Ask rangers for the route to the other entrance.

FRONTIER WITH ARGENTINA: PASO MAMUIL MALAL TROMEN

A road runs SE from Pucón to the the Argentine frontier. The route runs E to Curarrehue, with the volcanoes of Villarrica and Quetrupillán to the S and then turns S to Puesco. From here the road

deteriorates, though work was in progress in March 1996 to improve parts of it, running E via Lago Quellelhue, a gem set between mountains at 1,196m above sea level to the frontier at the Mamuil Malal or Tromen Pass. The road from the border runs S to Junín de los Andes, San Martín de los Andes and Bariloche. To the S of the Pass is the graceful cone of Lanín volcano (see under Junín de los Andes, **Argentina**, page 182).

● **Chilean immigration & customs**
At Puesco, open Dec-March 0800-2100, April-Nov 0800-1900, US$2/vehicle at other times.

● **Accommodation**
CONAF campsites at Puesco and 5 km from the frontier nr Lago Tromen, free, no facilities.

● **Transport**
Daily bus from Pucón, 1800, 2 hrs, US$2.

LAGO CALAFQUEN: LICAN-RAY

30 km S of Villarrica (fully paved) and 125 km SE of Temuco is **Lican-Ray**, with 2 good beaches, on the N shore of Lago Calafquén, full of islands. Boats can be hired from the beach (US$1.50 an hour). The resort is very crowded in season. 6 km to the E is the river of lava formed when the Villarrica volcano erupted in 1971.

Note that by the end of Mar almost everything has closed for the season.

● **Accommodation A3** *Refugio*, Canadian-owned, on Playa Grande, open all year, has a Travellers' Exchange Library for English-language books, all donations of paperbacks (in reasonable condition) welcome; **E** pp *Res Temuco*, G Mistral 515, clean, hot water, good; **E** Hugo Linolilli 235; several motels (eg at **C** *Cabañas El Eden*, Huenuman 105, for a chalet for 6 with hot water; *El Conquistador*, Cacique Millaqueo s/n), *hosterías*, and camping sites (eg *Camping Las Gaviotas*, 3 km E).

● **Places to eat** *Café Ñaños*, Urrutia 105, very good, reasonable prices, helpful owner. Also on Urrutia, *Restaurant-Bar Guido's*, good value.

● **Transport** Buses from Villarrica, 1 hr, US$1, several daily in summer from Villarrica (JAC – 7 a day, 3 on Sun – and García, Reyes y Henríquez, also frequent colectivos, US$0.60); in Jan-Feb, there are frequent direct buses from Santiago and Temuco; to Panguipulli, Mon-Sat 0730.

COÑARIPE

A road runs 14 km SE along the N shore

to **Coñaripe**, at the eastern end of Lago Calafquén. At first sight, the village is dusty and nondescript, but its setting, with a black sand beach surrounded by mountains, is very beautiful. There is a good walk from the left-hand side of the beach back through the fields to Coñaripe. This is a popular Chilean tourist spot: the lake is reputedly one of the warmest and is good for swimming. A road around the lake's southern shore leads to Lago Panguipulli (see below).

● **Accommodation**　**D** *Antulafquen*, homely; **E** pp *Hosp House*, with breakfast; **E** pp good *hospedaje* in bus terminal building, good meals; cheap campsites nr private houses (closed off season)

● **Transport** Buses to **Panguipulli**, 3 a day, US$1 and **Villarrica** US$1.50.

Hot springs

From Coñaripe a road runs SE climbing the steep Cuesta Los Añiques, with views of Lago Pellaifa. The **Termas de Pellaifa** (accommodation, restaurant etc at *Centro Termal Coñaripe ex-Pellaifa*), and the **Termas de Liquiñe** (hotel, **B** pp, cabins, restaurant, hot swimming pool, small native forest; accommodation in private houses, **E** pp; tours from Lican-Ray in summer, US$17, 0830-1830 with lunch). 6 km before Liquiñe is a road going S (50 km) to meet the Choshuenco-Puerto Fuy road (see below).

FRONTIER WITH ARGENTINA: PASO CARIRRINE

Paso Caririñe is reached by unpaved road from Termas de Liquiñe. It is open 15 Oct-31 August. On the Argentine side the road continues to San Martín de los Andes.

ROUTES South of Temuco The Longitudinal Highway (Ruta 5) runs from Loncoche (81 km S of Temuco, good place for hitching) through Lanco to Paillaco and Osorno. At San José de la Mariquina, a road branches off Ruta 5 to Valdivia, 42 km from the Highway (bus Lanco-Valdivia, Chile Nuevo, US$0.85, 4 a day, fewer at weekends). The road from Valdivia to Ruta 5 going S is not in very good condition; the Highway is rejoined near Paillaco.

LAGO PANGUIPULLI

A paved road SE from Lanco goes to **Panguipulli**, on the W bank of the lake of the same name, in a beautiful setting, with roses planted in all the streets (the name is Mapuche for 'hill of lions'). For fishermen, daily excursions on Lago Panguipulli are recommended. Excursions can also be made to Lagos, Calafquén, Neltume, Pirehueico and to the northern tip of Lago Riñihue at **El Desagüe** (this road was reported to be impassable due to damaged bridges in March 1996). There is a road from Panguipulli to Coñaripe, on Lago Calafquén, which offers superb views of the lake and of Villarrica volcano, whether you are travelling on foot or by bus.

Local festivals Last week of Jan, **Semana de Rosas**, with dancing and sports competitions.

● **Accommodation B** *Riñimapu*, in El Desagüe, T 388, good value, excellent; **C** *Hostería Quetropillán*, Etchegaray 381, T 348, comfortable, food; **D** *Central*, clean, hot water, friendly, good breakfast, rec; **E** pp *Res La Bomba*, quiet, friendly; **E** pp private house opp *Quetropillán*, clean, beautiful garden; **E** pp Etchegaray 464, for longer stays, clean, good breakfast; **E** pp Sra Pozas, Pedro de Valdivia 251, clean, clothes washing extra; **E** pp Olga Berrocal, JM Carrera 834, small rooms; **E** pp Eva Halabi, Los Ulmos 62, T 483, clean, good breakfast. **Camping**: Municipal campsite 1½ km outside town, US$5 with all facilities, rec (closes at end-Feb); free camping on lakeside at Panguipulli possible.

● **Places to eat** *Didactico El Gourmet*, restaurant of professional hotel school, excellent food and wine, pricey but high quality; *Café de la Plaza*, O'Higgins 816, good food and coffee; *Café Central*, M de Rosas 880, good cheap lunches, expensive evening meals; several cheap restaurants in O'Higgins 700 block.

● **Banks & money changers** in Panguipulli **Banco de Crédito e Inversiones**; Casa de Cambio, M de Rozas. Some shops accept US$ cash. Rates poor, TCs not accepted anywhere.

● **Tourist offices** In plaza next to police station.

● **Transport** Bus terminal at Gabriela Mistral y Portales. To Santiago daily at 1845, US$20; to **Valdivia**, frequent (Sun only 4), several lines, 2 hrs, US$3; to **Temuco** frequent, Power and Pangui Sur, US$2, 3 hrs; to **Puerto Montt**, US$5; to **Calafquén**, 3 daily at 1200, 1545 and 1600; to **Choshuenco** 1530, 1630, US$3, 2½ hrs; to **Puerto Fuy**, 1800, 2½ hrs; to **Coñaripe** (with connections for Lican Ray and

Villarrica), 4 a day, 1½ hrs, US$2; to **Neltume**, **Choshuenco**, **Puerto Fuy** 1200, dep Pto Fuy 1700 (means you can visit Huilo Huilo falls – see below – and return same day).

Choshuenco, at the eastern tip of Lago Panguipulli, can be reached by a 23-km road around the N shore along a beautiful coastline, wooded, with cliffs and sandy beaches. South of Choshuenco is the Choshuenco volcano, on which Club Andino de Valdivia has ski-slopes and a *refugio*. This can be reached by a turning from the road which goes S from Choshuenco to Enco at the E end of Lago Riñihue (see page 783).

● **Accommodation** D *Choshuenco*, run down, clean, good meals; various *hosterías*, inc D *Hostería Rayen Trai* (former yacht club), María Alvarado y O'Higgins, good food, open all year, rec; *Restaurant Rucapillán*, lets out rooms. **Camping**: on the beach.

● **Transport** Buses to Panguipulli 0645 and 0700.

LAGO PIREHUEICO

Puerto Fuy lies 21 km SE of Choshuenco at the N end of Lago Pirehueico, via the waterfalls of **Huilo Huilo**, which are most impressive, the river channelling its way through volcanic rock before thundering down into a natural basin. The falls are 3 hrs' walk from Choshuenco, or take the Puerto Fuy bus and get off at *Alojamiento Huilo Huilo*, Km 9 (1 km before Neltume) from where it is a 1½-hr walk to the falls. At the southern end of the lake is **Puerto Pirehueico**. From Puerto Fuy a scenic road runs S through rainforest around the Choshuenco volcano to the Río Pillanleufú, Puerto Llolles on Lago Maihue and Puerto Llifén on Lago Ranco (see below); we have no up-to-date information on the condition of this road, or whether it is open.

● **Accommodation In Neltume**: E *Pensión Neltume*, meals. **At Huilo Huilo**: E pp *Alojamiento Huilo Huilo*, basic but comfortable and well situated for walks, good food, highly rec. **In Puerto Pirehueico and Puerto Fuy**: beds available in private houses inc the white house near bus terminal, very basic F pp. **Campsite**: Puerto Fuy on the beach (take your own food).

● **Buses** Daily Puerto Fuy to Panguipulli at 0600, 3 hrs, US$2, except Sun when it runs at 1700. **Ferries** From Puerto Fuy across the lake to Puerto Pirehueico US$3, 2-3 hrs. A beautiful crossing (to take vehicles reserve in advance at the *Hotel Quetropillán* in Panguipalli). Schedule varies according to season (Tues and Thur 0700 out of season).

FRONTIER WITH ARGENTINA: PASO HUAHUM

Paso Huahum (659m) is a 4-hr walk from Puerto Pirehuico. On the Argentine side the road leads to San Martín de los Andes and Junín de los Andes.

● **Chilean immigration**
Open summer 0800-2100, winter 0800-2000.

VALDIVIA

Valdivia (*Pop* 110,000; *Phone code* 063), 839 km S of Santiago by road, is situated at the confluence of two rivers, the Calle Calle and Cruces which form the Río Valdivia. It is set in rich agricultural land receiving some 2,300mm of rain a year and is the capital of Valdivia province. The city was destroyed in the 1960 earthquake.

Valdivia was one of the most important centres of Spanish colonial control over Chile. Founded in 1552 by Pedro de Valdivia, it was abandoned as a result of the Mapuche insurrection of 1599 and the area was briefly occupied by Dutch pirates In 1645 it was refounded as a walled city, the only Spanish mainland settlement S of the Río Biobío. The coastal fortifications at the mouth of the Río Valdivia also date from the 17th century, but were greatly strengthened after 1770 owing to Spanish fears of war with Britain. The capture of Valdivia by the Chilean Navy under Lord Cochrane in 1820, when he seized the forts of Corral, Amargos and San Carlos, was one of the most important stages in the Chilean struggle for independence. From 1850 to 1875 a comparatively small number of German colonists settled in the area; their imprint in terms of architecture and agricultural methods, order, education, social life and custom is still strong. In particular they created numerous industries, some of them on Isla Teja, the island on the N side of the river, where the Universidad Austral de Chile is also situated.

Places of interest

On the tree-lined, shady **Plaza de la República**, a new cathedral is under construction. A pleasant walk is along **Avenida Prat** (or **Costanera**), which follows the bend in the river, from the bus station to the bridge to Isla Teja, the boat dock and the riverside market. On **Isla Teja**, near the library in the University, are a **botanic garden** and **arboretum** with trees from all over the world. **Lago de los Lotos** in Parque Saval on the island has beautiful blooms in Nov, entry US$0.30.

Museums

Museo Austral, on Isla Teja, run by the University, contains cartography, archaeology, history of German settlement (in-

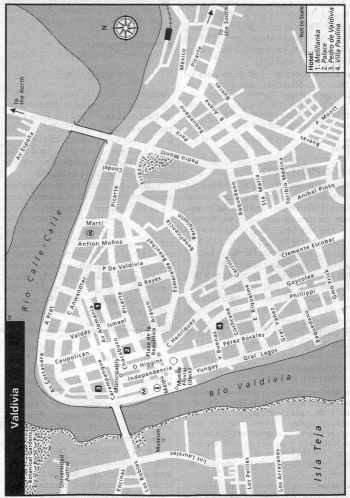

Valdivia

Hotel:
1. Melillanka
2. Palace
3. Pedro de Valdivia
4. Villa Paulina

Not to Scale

cluding cemetery), local Indian crafts, etc. Open Tues-Sun, 1000-1300, 1500-1800, US$1.

Excursions
The district has lovely countryside of woods, beaches, lakes and rivers. the various rivers are navigable and there are pleasant journeys by rented motor boat on the Ríos Futa and Tornagaleanes around the Isla del Rey. Among the waterways are countless islands, cool and green.

The **Santuario de la Naturalez Río Cruces**, flooded as result of 1960 earthquake, where lots of bird species are visible, can also be visited; tours by boat. *Isla del Río*, daily 1415, 6 hrs, US$15 pp.

Local festivals
Semana Valdiviana, in mid Feb, culminates in Noche Valdiviana on the Sat with a procession of elaborately decorated boats which sail past the Muelle Fluvial. Accommodation is scarce at this time.

Local information
● **Accommodation**
L3 *Pedro de Valdivia*, Carampangue 190, T/F 212931, with bath, good; **A3** *Melillanca*, Alemania 675, T 212509, F 222740, rec; **A2** *Naguilán*, Gen Lagos 1927, T 212851/52/53, F 219130, clean, quiet, swimming pool, good restaurant; **A2** *Villa del Río*, with bath, España 1025, T 216292, F 217851, restaurant expensive (try salmon in almond sauce), rents apartments with kitchen; **A3** *Palace*, Chacabuco y Henríquez, T 213319, F 219133, good, comfortable; **A3** *Villa Paulina*, Yerbas Buenas 389, T/F 216372, hot showers, clean, good.

B *Raitúe*, Gen Lagos 1382, T 212503, with bath; **B** *Hostal Centro Torreón*, P Rosales 783, T 212622, with breakfast, shared bath, old German villa, nice atmosphere, car parking.

C *Hosp Turístico*, Henríquez 745, with bath, **E** pp without, lovely villa in large gardens, friendly, large rooms, kitchen and laundry facilities, English spoken, clean, highly rec.

Around the bus terminal: on Picarte **C** *Hostal Montserrat* No 849, T 215410, with breakfast, clean, comfortable, highly rec; **D** *Res Germania*, No 873, T 212405, with breakfast, poor beds, clean, German spoken, IYHA reductions, lovely garden; **E** pp *Hostal del 900*, No 953, with breakfast, good value, clean, heated lounge; **D** *Hosp Elsa Martínez*, No 737, T 212587, clean, friendly, highly rec; several

others. On A Muñoz, outside terminal: **E** pp No 345, with breakfast, clean, friendly; **E** pp No 353, breakfast, hot water, rec. On C Anwandter: **E** pp *Hostal Casa Grande*, No 880, T 202035, attractive old house, laundry facilities, highly rec; **E** *Hosp Aredi*, No 624, Casa 2, T 214162, with breakfast, friendly, good value, comedor; **B** *Hostal La Terraza* No 624, Casa 4, T 212664, with breakfast, very comfortable, lovely views, parking; **E** pp *Hosp Andwandter*, No 482, clean, hot water; **F** pp No 490, without breakfast, use of kitchen.

Other, cheaper accommodation: **D** Arauco 935, clean, friendly; **D** *Prat*, Prat 595, T 222020, with good breakfast, clean; **D** *Unión*, Prat 514, T 213819, central, good value; **E** pp, Gen Lagos 874, T 215946, with breakfast, old German house, pleasant family atmosphere, rec; **E** *Hosp Universitaria*, Serrano 985, T 218775, breakfast, kitchen facilities, family atmosphere, clean, cheap meals, rec; **B** *Hosp Pérez Rosales*, Pérez Rosales 1037, T 215607, with bath, **E** pp without, modern, small rooms, good beds, over priced; **E** pp *Hostal Cochrane*, Cochrane 595, with breakfast; **E** pp Baquedano 664, inc breakfast (but avoid laundry service); Aníbal Pinto 1335, friendly and cheap; **E** pp Riquelme 15, T 218909, with breakfast, friendly, clean, good value; **E** pp *Ana María Vera*, Beauchef 669, T 218542, clean, friendly, hot water, good breakfast; **E** pp García Reyes 658, T 212015, Mario and Marcela, clean, helpful, English and German spoken, bikes to rent, use of kitchen, rec; Sra Paredes, García Reyes 244, **D** with breakfast, hot water, rec; **G** pp *Albergue Juvenil*, García Reyes s/n, off Picarte, Jan/Feb only.

Campsite: Camping Centenario, in Rowing Club on España, **E**/tent, overlooking river. Also in Parque Saval. White gas impossible to find, other than in pharmacies/chemists.

● **Places to eat**
Centro Español, Henríquez 436, good, lunch US$3.50; *Sociedad Protectora de EECC*, Independencia y Libertad, good seafood; *Dino*, Maipú y Rosales, good coffee; *Palace*, Arauco y P Rosales, popular, good atmosphere, expensive; *Pizzerón*, Henríquez 314, cheap, good, popular; *Delicias*, Henríquez 372, rec for meals and cakes (open Sun am) real coffee; *Selecta*, Picarte 1093, pleasant, excellent fish and meat, not cheap; *Shanghai*, Andwandter y Muñoz, pleasant Chinese, reasonably priced. *Fértil Provincia*, San Carlos 169, café, bookshop, cultural events, good meeting place, rec; *Café Haussmann*, O'Higgins 394, good tea and cakes; *Café Express*, Picarte 764, real coffee; *Phoenix Haus*, Av Viel s/n, on Isla Teja; restaurant in boat house, good seafood; several restaurants on the Costanera facing the boat dock,

have good food and good atmosphere: *Bar Olimpia*, Libertad 28, always full, 24 hrs, cheap, good meeting point; *Entrelagos*, Pérez Rosales 622, ice cream and chocolates. Bakery: *La Baguette*, Libertad y Yungay, French-style cakes, brown bread, repeatedly rec.

● **Banks & money changers**
Banco del Estado at Arauca y Camilo Henríquez (huge commission on TCs). Good rates for cash at **Banco Osorno**, P Rosales 585, **Banco Concepción** (Visa), Picarte 370, will change cash and TCs. **Banco Santiago**, Arauco y Independencia, Mastercard. **Turismo Cochrane**, Arauco y Caupolicán. **Fincard** (Mastercard), Picarte 334, Mon-Fri 0900-1400, 1500-1930, Sat 0900-1330. *Casa de Cambio* at Carampangue 325, T 213305, open 0800-2100 Mon-Fri, 0930-1800 Sat, 0930-1400 Sun; *Turismo Austral*, Arauco y Henríquez, Galería Arauco, accepts TCs.

● **Entertainment**
Cinema in Chacabuco 300 block, also in University.

● **Laundry**
Au Chic, Arauco 436; *Lavazul*, Chacabuco 300, slow. Coin laundry *Lavamatic*, Schmidt y Picarte (Mon-Sat 0930-2030); *Manantial*, Henríquez 809, T 217609.

● **Shopping**
Supermarket: *Hiper-Unico*, Arauco 697.
Film: *Fotoquideon*, Picarte 417, for developing.

● **Sports**
Clubs: Santa Elvira Golf Club (9 holes); tennis, sailing, motor, and rowing clubs like Phoenix on Teja Island.

● **Tour companies & travel agencies**
Paraty Club, Independencia 640, T 215585; for excursions to Corral and Niebla, try the kiosks along the Muelle Fluvial.

● **Tourist offices**
Prat 555, by dock, T 213596. Good map of region and local rivers, list of hotel prices and examples of local crafts with artisans' addresses. Helpful kiosk in bus terminal, mainly bus information. **Conaf**: Ismael Váldez 431. **Automóvil Club de Chile**: Caupolicán 475, T 212378, also for car hire.

● **Transport**
Car hire: Hertz, Aguirre Cerda 1154, T 218316; Turismo Méndez, Gral Lagos 1249, T 233205.
Air LanChile (Arauco 159, of 201, T 213042) and Ladeco (Caupolicán 579, local 18, T 213392) to/from Santiago every day via Temuco.
Trains Station at Ecuador 2000, off Av Picarte,

T 214978. To **Santiago**, one a day, 14 hrs, bus Valdivia-Temuco 2¾ hrs, then change to train.
Buses Terminal at Muñoz y Prat, by the river. To **Santiago**: several companies, 13 hrs, most services overnight, US$12-17 (TurBus good) *salón cama* US$45; Pullman daily to and from central and southern towns. Half-hourly buses to **Osorno**, 2 hrs, several companies, US$5; to **Lifén**, 4 a day, US$2.50; to **Panguipulli**, US$3, Empresa Pirehueico, about every 30 mins, US$3; many daily to **Puerto Montt**, US$7, 3 hrs; to **Puerto Varas**, 2 hrs, US$6; to **Frutillar**, US$4, 3 hrs; to **Villarrica**, by JAC, 6 a day, 2½ hrs US$3.50 continuing to Pucón, US$4.50, 3 hrs. Frequent daily service to Riñihue via Paillaco and Los Lagos.

To Argentina: to Bariloche via Osorno, 10 hrs, Bus. Nte, US$20, and Tramaca; to **Zapala**, Igi-Llama, Mon, Thur, Sat, 2300, change in Temuco at 0200, arrive Zapala 1200-1500, depending on border, US$34. To **Mendoza**, Fénix and Andesmar.

COASTAL RESORTS NEAR VALDIVIA

At the mouth of the Río Valdivia are remains of the fortifications built by the Spanish to defend the entry to Valdivia.

There are two centres for visiting the area, **Niebla** on the N bank and **Corral** on the S. In all there are the ruins of 17 forts but the principal ones to see are the following: the Fuerte de la Pura y Limpia Concepción de Monfort de Lemus, a substantial earthwork fort on a promontory W of Niebla (entry US$0.75, Sun free, open daily in summer 1000-1900, closed Mon in winter). It was partially restored in 1992 and has an interesting museum on this area of Chilean maritime history.

Opposite it, in Corral, the Castillo de San Sebastián, with 3m wide walls was defended by a battery of 24 guns. It has a museum and offers a view upriver to Volcán Llaima in the distance, entry US$2.50; Castillo San Luis de Alba, in poor condition, in Amargos, 40 mins' walk along the coast from Corral; and, in midstream, the Castillo de San Pedro de Alcántara on **Isla Mancera**. This last has the most standing buildings; all are national monuments. Niebla is also a resort with seafood restaurants and accommodation (**D** *Hostería Riechers*; *Cabañas Fischers*, **C** per cabin; 2 campsites, worth bargaining out of season; **E** *Santa Clara; Las Delicias* with restaurant under 'a view that would be worth the money even if the food weren't good', also *cabañas* and camping; *Hosp Plaza*); information and telephone office by the fort. 6 km further round the coast is **Los Molinos**, a seaside resort set among steep wooded hills (campsite, lots of seaside restaurants). The fishing port of Corral has several restaurants (eg *Español*, Av 6 de Mayo, good seafood), and **E** *Res Mariel*, Tarapacá, modern, clean, friendly, good value, and *Hostería La Nave*. Also in Corral is a small tourist office (closed 1300-1400) with a museum attached, entry US$0.25. 4 km along the coast from Corral is **San Carlos**, with its **E** *Hostería los Alamos*, a delightful hideout for those seeking a quiet life. West and S of San Carlos the coastal walks are splendid. Isla Mancera is a pleasant place to stopover on the boat trips, but it can get crowded when an excursion boat arrives. (**C** *Hostería Mancera*, T/F 216296, open Dec-March, depending on weather, no singles, phone first: water not drinkable, electricity due to be connected in 1996/97)

● **Transport** The tourist boats (*Neptuno* or *Calle-Calle*) to Isla Mancera and Corral, inc a guided half-day tour (US$20 with meals – cheaper without) leave the Muelle Fluvial, Valdivia (behind the tourist office on Av Prat 555), 1330 daily. The river trip is beautiful, but you can also take a bus to Niebla from Chacabuco y Yungay, Valdivia, roughly every 20 mins between 0730 and 2100, 30 mins, US$0.75 (bus continues to Los Molinos), then cross to Corral by boat, frequent, US$1. There are occasional buses from Valdivia to Corral.

Mehuin

Mehuin, on the coast, 2 hrs bus ride N from Valdivia, US$2, through San José de La Mariquina; post office, good sea bathing and several hotels: **C** *Hostería Millalafquen*, T 279; **D** *Mehuin*, not very inviting; *Playa*; **E** *Hosp Marbella*, clean, cheapest. Queule, 6 km from Mehuin, has two simple *residenciales*. Good beach but bathing dangerous at high tide because of undercurrents; safer to bathe in the river near ferry.

A beautiful, unpaved road runs 61 km E from Valdivia along the Río Calle Calle to **Los Lagos** (**D** *Hotel Roger*, Lynch 42, T 261, disco on Sat, rec; *Turismo Tell*, 10 km E, cabañas and campsite, T 09-653-2440, English, French and German spoken; 2 buses a day in summer), and on to the beautiful **Lago Riñihue** (39 km). The road around the southern edge of the lake from Riñihue to Enco is now closed (except in jeeps in summer only), so Choshuenco at the SE end of Lago Panguipulli can only be reached by road from Panguipulli or Puerto Fuy. Riñihue, a beautiful but very small and isolated village at the western end of the lake, is worth a visit. Campsite by the lake; *Restaurant del Lago* has rooms, **E** (no meals).

LAGO RANCO

Access from the Longitudinal Highway to lovely, island-starred **Lago Ranco** and to **Lago Maihue** further E is made from Los Lagos, or from a point 18 km S of Los Lagos, 11 km N of Paillaco. These two roads join to meet the road around the lake some 5 km W of **Futrono** on the northern shore. From Futrono (accommodation in the Casa Parroquial, **F** pp) the road curves round the N of Lago Ranco to **Llifén**, a picturesque place on the eastern shore. From Llifén, a visit can be paid to Lago Maihue (Cordillera Sur bus Valdivia-Llifén twice daily, once Sun).

● **Accommodation A1** *Huequecura*, Casilla 4, T 09-653-5450, inc meals and fishing services, good restaurant. **B** *Hostería Chollinco*, 3 km out of town on the road towards Lago Maihue, T 0638-202, limited electricity, swimming pool; **C** *Hostería Lican*, T 09-653-5315, F Valdivia 218921. 4 campsites in the vicinity, eg at Chollinco.

From Llifén the road continues round the lake to **Riñinahue** (*hostería*, **A3**, 2 campsites inc La Playa, US$6 per site) and Lago Ranco, an ugly little town on the S shore (several small hotels, *Residenciales*, houses to let in summer – see below for bus from Osorno). The road is terrible (lots of mud and animals, including ox-carts), but is worth taking to see an older lifestyle, the beautiful lake, waterfalls and sunsets on the distant volcanoes (if walking, beware the numerous guard dogs in the area). There is excellent fishing on the S shore of the lake. On the western shore is **Puerto Nuevo** (hotel of same name, **A1**, very good, watersports, fishing on the Río Bueno). Roads from Puerto Nuevo and Lago Ranco run W to La Unión (*Hotel Club Alemán*, Letelier 497, T 322695), which is bypassed by the Longitudal Highway.

Río Bueno is at the crossroads of the Lago Ranco-La Unión road and the Highway (Ruta 5). Some 42 km S of this point is Osorno, another centre for exploring the Lakes.

OSORNO

Osorno (*Pop* 103,000; *Phone code* 064), 921 km from Santiago and 105 km N of Puerto Montt, was founded in 1558 but was destroyed shortly afterwards. It was refounded by Ambrosio O'Higgins and Juan Mackenna O'Reilly in 1796. It was later settled by German immigrants, whose descendants are still of great importance in the area.

Places of interest

On the large **Plaza de Armas** stands the modern, concrete and glass cathedral, with many arches, repeated in the tower, itself an open, latticed arch with a cross superimposed. West of the centre on a bend overlooking the river is the **Fuerte María Luisa**, named after the Spanish queen much painted by Goya, built in 1793, restored 1977, with only the river front walls and end turrets standing. East of the main plaza along Mackenna are a number of late 19th century mansions built by German immigrants, now preserved as National Monuments.

Museums

Museo Histórico Municipal, Matta 809. Entrance in Casa de Cultura, US$1; Mon-Fri 1000-1200, 1430-1830, also Sat 1000-1300, 1500-1800 and Sun 1500-1800 in summer. Includes displays on natural history, Mapuche culture, refounding of the city and German colonisation.

Excursions

Drive or take bus (US$0.60, frequent) N of Osorno to Río Bueno, celebrated for its scenery, to La Unión, and to **Trumao**, a river port on the Río Bueno, whence a launch may be taken to La Barra on the coast; leaves Wed and Sat only at 0900, 5 hrs, US$6; returns Sun at 0900, no service in winter.

The sea beaches at **Maicolpue** (60 km from Osorno – **D** *Hostería Müller*, on the beach, clean, good service, rec, campsite) and **Pucatrihue** (*Hostería Incalcar*, summer only) are worth a visit in the summer (daily bus service).

Local information
● Accommodation

L3 *Del Prado*, Cochrane 1162, T 235020, swimming pool, garden, good meals, well-located, charming.

A1 *Waeger*, Cochrane 816, T 233721, PO Box 802, F 237080, 4-star, restaurant, comfortable, rec; **A2** *Gran*, O'Higgins 615, T 233990, F 239311, cable TV, comfortable; **A3** *Inter-Lagos*, Cochrane 515, T 234695, F 232581, with breakfast, garage, restaurant; **A3** *Pumalal*, Bulnes 630, T 243520, F 242477, with breakfast, modern, airy, clean; **A3** *Res Riga*, Amthauer 1058, T 232945, clean, pleasant, highly rec but heavily booked in season; **A3** *Eduviges*, Eduviges 856, T/F 235023, spacious, clean, quiet, attractive, gardens, also *cabañas*, rec; **A3** *Res Rucaitué*, Freire 546, T 239922, with breakfast, cable TV, overpriced; **A3** *Res Schulz*, Freire 530, T 237211, with bath, **B** without, cable TV.

B *Millantúe*, Errázuriz 1339, T 242072, opp bus terminal, with breakfast, parking; **B** *Res Hein*, Cochrane 843, T 234116, with bath, **C** without, old-fashioned, spacious, family atmosphere; **B** *Res Bilbao*, Bilbao 1019, T 236755, F 321111 and *Res Bilbao II*, Mackenna 1205, T 242244, with breakfast, parking, restaurant.

D *Amunátegui* 520, nr bus terminal, good; **D** *Germania*, Rodríguez 741, no hot water, cooking facilities; **D** *Res Ortega*, Colón y Errázuriz, 1 block from bus terminal, parking, basic, clean, terrible beds, toilet facilities limited; others nr bus terminal: at A Pinto 1758, E inc breakfast and hot water, T 238024.

E pp *Res Sánchez*, Los Carrera 1595, use of kitchen, hot showers, clean, noisy on ground floor, with breakfast; **E** pp *Hosp de la Fuente*, Los Carrera 1587, basic, friendly; **E** pp Colón 844, with breakfast.

F pp *Res Carillo*, Angulo 454, basic, clean; *La*

Paloma, Errázuriz 1599, basic; *Richmond*, Lastarria 530, basic; *Silvane*, Errázuriz y Lastarria, T 234429, fairly basic. Private houses at Germán Hube, pasaje 1, casa 22, población Villa Dama, E pp, hot water, clean, use of kitchen, rec.

Camping: Municipal site at S entrance to city, open from Jan only, free.

● **Places to eat**
Peter's Kneipe, M Rodríguez 1039, excellent German restaurant, not cheap; *Dino*, Ramírez 898, on the plaza, restaurant upstairs, bar/cafeteria downstairs, good. *Los Troncos*, Cochrane 527, good pizzas, French spoken; *Chung Hwa*, Freire 543, Chinese, good value set menus; *Casa del Atillo*, MacKenna 1011, good food and service, pleasant atmosphere, rec; *La Paisana*, Freire 530, Arab specialities, not cheap; *Waldis*, O'Higgins next to *Gran Hotel*, good coffee; *Travels* in bus terminal for cheap snacks. Bakery at Ramírez 977 has good wholemeal bread.

● **Banks & money changers**
Fincard for Mastercard, Mackenna 877, Mon-Fri 0900-1400, 1530-1900, Sat 0930-1330. For good rates try *Cambio Tur*, Mackenna 1010, T 4846; *La Frontera*, Ramírez 949, local 5 (Galería Catedral); if stuck try *Travels* bar in bus terminal.

● **Laundry**
Prat 678 (allow at least a day).

● **Post & telecommunications**
Post Office: O'Higgins 645, also Ielex.
Telephone: Ramírez at central plaza and Juan Mackenna y Cochrane.

● **Shopping**
Reinares and Thone, Ramírez 1100, for good fishing gear.

● **Sports**
Club Andino: Mackenna y Bulnes, p 3, better for skiing than mountaineering.

● **Tourist offices**
Provincial government office, on Plaza de Armas, O'Higgins s/n, p 1, left, T 234104. **Automóvil Club de Chile**: Bulnes 463, T 232269, information and car hire.

● **Transport**
Local Garage: *Automotriz Salfa Sur SA*, Fco Bilbao 857; *Automotriz Amthauer*, Amthauer 1250.
Air LanChile, Matta 862, T 236688, Ladeco, Mackenna 975, T 234355; both operate daily flights Osorno-Santiago, via Temuco.

Trains Station at Mackenna 600, T 232992. Daily train to/from Santiago (18 hrs) and to Puerto Montt (3 hrs).

Buses Main terminal 4 blocks from Plaza de Armas at Errázuriz 1400. Left luggage open 0730-2030. Bus from centre, US$0.30. To **Santiago**, frequent, US$16, *salón cama* US$25, 16 hrs; to **Valparaíso** and **Viña del Mar**, Tas Choapa, US$25; to **Arica**, Tas Choapa, US$55; to **Concepción**, US$12; to **Temuco**, US$6; to **Pucón** and **Villarrica**, Tur Bus, frequent, US$6; to **Valdivia**, frequent, 2 hrs, several companies, US$5; to **Frutillar**, US$2.50, **Llanquihue**, **Puerto Varas** and **Puerto Montt** (US$5) services by Varmontt every 30 mins; to **Puerto Octay**, US$1.50, Vía Octay company 6 daily between 0815-1930 (return 0800-1930) Mon-Sat, Sun 5 between 0800 and 2000 (4 return buses); to **Punta Arenas**, US$60-75, Cruz del Sur, Turisbus, Eurobus and Bus Nte, all twice a week.

Local buses to **Lago Ranco**, **Entre Lagos**, **Puyehue** and **Aguas Calientes** leave from the Mercado Municipal terminal, 1 block W of the main terminal. To **Lago Ranco**, 6 a day from 0810, Empresa Ruta 5, 2 hrs, US$1.50; to **Entre Lagos** frequent services in summer, Expreso Lago Puyehue and Buses Puyehue, 45 mins, US$1, reduced service off-season; some buses by both companies also continue to Aguas Calientes (off-season according to demand) 2 hrs, US$2; in summer there are also services Maicolpué on the coast if demand is sufficient.

PUYEHUE

Route 215 runs E to **Entre Lagos** at the western end of Lago Puyehue. The road follows the lake's southern shore to the thermal waters at **Termas de Puyehue** (US$3.50 pp for bathing, 0900-2000); 2 hrs by car, 2½ by bus (schedule under Osorno **Buses**). The bus does not stop at the lake (unless you want to get off at *Gran Hotel Termas de Puyehue* and clamber down), but turns off Route 215 and goes 4 km further to Aguas Calientes. The main road continues to Anticura and the Puyehue pass (see below).

● **Accommodation In Entre Lagos**: *Pub del Campo*, highly rec restaurant, reasonable prices, owner is of Swiss descent; **C** *Hosp Vista Hermosa*, with breakfast; **D** *Hostería Entre Lagos*, Ramírez 65, lake view, T 647225; **D** *Villa Veneto*, Gral Lagos 602, T 647203; **E** pp *Hosp Millarey*, with breakfast, excellent, clean, friendly; *Restaurant Jardín del Turista*, very good.

On the S lakeshore are: *Chalet Suisse*, Ruta 215, Km 55 (Casilla 910, Osorno, T Puyehue 647208, Osorno 064-234073), *hostería*, restaurant with excellent food; a few kilometres beyond, *Hosp y cabañas* at Almacén Valenciana; **B** *Posada Puntillo*, at Shell station, Km 62, before **A1** *Motel Ñilque*, T Santiago 231-3417, or (0647) 218, cabins, half-price May-Oct, fishing trips, watersports, car hire. **B** *Hostería Isla Fresia*, located on own island, T 236951, Casilla 49, Entre Lagos, transport provided.

At Lago Puyehue: L2-A1 pp *Gran Hotel Termas de Puyehue*, hot-springs swimming pool (T Osorno 235157), large and well kept (cheaper May to mid-Dec), meals expensive, in beautiful scenery, heavily booked Jan-Feb (postal address Casilla 27-0, Puyehue, or T Santiago 231-3417); accommodation also in private house nearby, **E** pp full board).

Camping: *Camping No Me Olvides*, Km 56, US$10; *Playa Los Copihues*, Km 56.5 (hot showers, good), all on S shore of Lake Puyehue; *Camping Playa Puyehue*, Km 75.

PARQUE NACIONAL PUYEHUE

The headquarters of the National Park are about 80 km E of Osorno at **Aguas Calientes**, where there is an open air pool with very hot thermal water beside the Río Chanleufú, open 0830-1900, US$1.50, children US$1, and a very hot indoor pool, open Mon-Fri (in season only) 0830-1230, 1400-1800, Sat, Sun and holidays (all year) 0830-2030, US$5, children US$3. In the Puyehue National Park is surviving temperate rainforest. Three marked paths can be followed: Los Rápidos, 1 km to falls on the Río Chanleufú (the trail starts at the entrance to the outdoor pool, if you don't want to swim, just say you're going to Los Rápidos); El Recodo, a continuation of Los Rápidos up the river bank; El Pionero, 1,800m up to a viewpoint (good for the exercise before you bathe). The trees are lovely: listen to the birds and watch for kingfishers by the river.

The road beyond Aguas Calientes continues 18 km to **Antillanca**, past three of small lakes and through forests. It is beautiful here, especially at sunrise, with the snow-clad cones of Osorno, Puntiagudo, and Puyehue forming a semicircle. The tree-line on Antillanca is one of the few in the world made up of deciduous trees (southern beech). It is possible to hike from Antillanca to **Volcán Casablanca** for even better views of the surrounding volcanoes and lakes; no path, information from Club Andino in Osorno.

● **Accommodation & transport** There is a Conaf campsite at **Aguas Calientes** (no hot water) with private sites (US$18/site), cabin type accommodation (**A3** in season, **C** off season, T 236988, a small shop – better to take your own food), and an expensive café; **A** *Hotel Antillanca*, T 235114, without food, at foot of Volcán Casablanca, 4 km from crater, excellent hotel/restaurant/café, with pool, sauna and small ski resort, 3 ski lifts. In winter chains can be hired; a one way traffic system operates, up in am, down pm. No public transport from Aguas Calientes to Antillanca; try hitching – always difficult, but it is not a hard walk.

FRONTIER WITH ARGENTINA: PASO PUYEHUE

Paso Puyehue is reached by Route 215, paved most of the way, from Osorno via Entre Lagos and Lago Puyehue. On the Argentine side the road continues to Bariloche.

● **Chilean immigration**
Open second Sat in Oct-second Sat in March 0800-2100, otherwise 0800-1900. The Chilean frontier post is at **Anticura**, 22 km W of the border (*Hostería y Canañas Anticura*; *Camping Catrue*).

NB This route is liable to closure after snow.

● **Crossing by private vehicle**
For vehicles entering Chile, formalities are quick (about 15 mins), but includes the spraying of tyres and shoes have to be wiped on a mat (pay US$2 to 'Sanidad') and US$1.25 at the documents counter. Passage will be much quicker if you already have Chilean pesos and don't wait to change at the border.

● **Transport**
To Anticura, bus at 1620 from Osorno, 3 hrs. Several bus companies run daily services from Puerto Montt via Osorno to Bariloche along this route (see under Puerto Montt for details). Although less scenic than the ferry journey across Lake Todos Los Santos and Laguna Verde (see page 791) this crossing is cheaper, more reliable and still a beautiful trip.

Lago Rupanco

A 13 km road from Entre Lagos goes S to El Paraíso at the western end of **Lago Rupanco** (*Hostería y Cabañas El Paraíso*, T 236239). To reach the S shore take the road from Osorno to Puerto Octay and turn E after 33 km. This lake is very beautiful and much less developed than most of its neighbours. A 40 km dirt road runs along the S shore, passing through the village of Piedras Negras.

• **Transport Buses** Osorno to Piedras Negras from either *Minimarket El Capricho*, Mackenna y Colón, or Estación Viejo (old railway station), leaves 1645, 1545 on Sat, returns from Piedras Negras 0700.

LAGO LLANQUIHUE

From Osorno it is 106 km S to Puerto Montt, including 25 km along the shore of **Lago Llanquihue**. Across the great blue sheet of water can be seen two snowcapped volcanoes: the perfect cone of Osorno (2,680m) and the shattered cone of Calbuco, and, when the air is clear, the distant Tronador (3,554m). Lago Llanquihue covers over 540 square km and is the third largest natural lake in South America. There is a road, 187 km long, around it. The N side of the lake is hilly; road from Frutillar to Puerto Octay runs through rolling hills with German-style farmhouses.

PUERTO OCTAY

At the northern tip of the lake in a lovely setting 56 km SE of Osorno is **Puerto Octay**, a small town (*Pop* 2,000; *Phone code* 064) founded by German settlers in 1851. The town has several fine buildings dating from its boom period in the late 19 century, notably the church and the enormous German-style former convent. 3 km S along an unpaved road is the Peninsula of **Centinela** with lodging, camping, a launch dock, bathing beaches, watersports. From the headland are fine views of the volcanoes Osorno, Calbuco, Puntiagudo and the Cordillera of the Andes; a very popular spot in good weather (taxi US$2.50 one way).

Museums Museo el Colono, Independencia 591, with displays on German colonisation, open Tues-Sun 0900-1300, 1500-1900, Dec-Feb only; another part of the museum, housing agricultural implements and machinery for making chicha, is just outside town on the road to Centinela.

• **Accommodation & places to eat B** *Haase*, Pedro Montt 344, T 193, with breakfast, attractive old building; **C** *Posada Gubernatis*, Santiago s/n, lakeside, clean, comfortable; **E** pp *Hosp La Naranja*, Independencia 361, without bath, with breakfast, restaurant; **E** pp *Hosp Fogón de Anita*, 1 km out of town, T 34523, good breakfast; **F** pp *Hosp Raquel Mardorf*, Germán Wulf 712, with enormous breakfast, clean, comfortable, owners have *Restaurante La Cabaña* at No 713, good; *Restaurante Baviera*, Germán Wulf 582, cheap and good. **Camping**: *El Molino*, beside lake, US$5 pp, clean, friendly, rec. **Centinela**: *Hotel Centinela*, T Santiago 234-4010, in beautiful former mansion, sadly neglected, meals available, friendly staff, also has *cabañas*; **E** pp *Hostería La Baja*, Casilla 116, T 391269, beautifully situated at the neck of the peninsula, with breakfast and bath. **Camping**: Municipal site on lakeside, US$15/site.

• **Tourist offices** Pedro Montt s/n, T 276, open Dec-Feb daily 0900-2100.

• **Transport** Buses to Osorno 7 a day; to Frutillar (1 hr), Puerto Varas (2 hrs) and Puerto Montt (3 hrs) Thaebus, 8 a day; to **Las Cascadas** (see below) Mon-Fri 1700, return next day 0600. Bus to Ensenada 0600, daily in season, less frequent out of season; no public transport to Puerto Octay; hitching to Puerto Octay and Entre Lagos is very difficult.

For a circuit of Lago Llanquihue by car, follow the road from Puerto Octay along the eastern lakeside, with the Osorno volcano on your left, to Ensenada (see below), with a turning to Petrohué and Lago Todos los Santos; continue along the S shore of the lake to Puerto Varas, then N along the W side via Frutillar (see below) to Octay. Note that the road round the N and E sides of the lake is narrow with lots of blind corners, necessitating speeds of 20-30 kph at best in places.

10 km E of Puerto Octay is Playa Maitén, 'highly recommended, nice beach, marvellous view to the Volcán Osorno, no tourists'. 24 km further on is **Las Cascadas**, surrounded by picturesque agricultural land, old houses and German cemeteries. The small settlement at Las Cascadas also has vacation houses.

• **Accommodation** *Centro de Recreación Las Cascadas*, T 235377; **E** *Hostería Irma*, on lake, 2 km past Las Cascadas, run by Tres Marías, attractive former residence, good food, very pleasant. Several farms on the road around N and E side of the lake offer accommodation, look for signs. **Camping**: *Centro de Recreación Las Cascadas* and Villa Las Cascadas picnic area (free); at Playa Maitén, rec.

FRUTILLAR

About half-way along the W side of the lake is **Frutillar** (*phone code* 065), in fact two towns: Alto Frutillar, with a railway station, just off the main highway, and Bajo Frutillar beautifully situated on the lakeside, 4 km away. (Colectivos run between the two towns, 5 mins, US$0.50). Bajo Frutillar is possibly the most attractive – and expensive – town on the lake. There is a large open-air chess board in the square outside the Club Alemán. In late Jan to early Feb there is a highly-regarded classical music festival (accommodation must be booked well in advance).

Museums Museo Colonial Alemán, including watermill (which does not turn), replicas of two German colonial houses with furnishings and utensils of the period, a blacksmith's shop (personal engravings for US$5), and a *campanario* (circular barn with agricultural machinery and carriages inside), gardens and handicraft shop. Well worth a visit. Open daily 0930-1900 summer, Tues-Sun 0930-1400, 1530-1800 winter, US$2. The nearby University collection of native trees and commercially-grown farm produce is also worth visiting.

● **Accommodation** N of Frutillar Bajo: **L3** *Salzburg*, T 589 or Santiago 2061419, new, excellent, country style, restaurant, sauna, mountain bikes, arranges tours and fishing; *Hostal Cinco Robles*, Casilla 100, T 351, with bath, breakfast, other meals on request, parking. In Frutillar Bajo: **B** *Casona del 32*, Caupolicán 28, T 369, Casilla 101, with bath and breakfast, comfortable old house, central heating, English and German spoken; **C** *Hosp El Arroyo*, Philippi 989, T 560, with breakfast, highly rec; **C-D** *Hosp Costa Azul*, Philippi 1175, T 388, mainly for families, good breakfasts; also on Philippi: **C** *Winkler*, No 1155, T 388, discount to YHA members, cabins, friendly, rec; **D** pp *Hosp Vivaldi*, No 851, T 382, Sra Edith Klesse, quiet, comfortable, excellent breakfast and lodging, also family accommodation, rec; **D** *Las Rocas*, No 1235, T 397, with breakfast; **D** *Residenz/Café am See*, No 539, good breakfast; **C** No 451, T 204, clean, good breakfast; **D** *Hotel Philippi*, on lake shore, good rooms, rec; **D** *Hosp Trayén*, No 963, T 346, basic, clean; **E** pp *Hosp Kaisersseehaus* (Viola Herbach), No 1333 (Casilla 13, T 387), hot water, good, cheap food, very comfortable and welcoming, English, German, Spanish spoken, highly rec;

D Pérez Rosales 590, excellent breakfast. In Frutillar Alto: **D** *Faralito*, Winkler 245, hot water, cooking facilities (owner can be contacted at shop at Winkler 167, T 440).Several along Carlos Richter (main street). Cheap accommodation in the school in Frutillar Alto, sleeping bag required. **Camping**: *Playa Maqui*, 7 km N of Frutillar, T 9139, fancy, expensive; *Los Ciruelillos*, 2 km S, T 9123, most services. Try also Sr Guido González, Casa 3, Población Vermont, T 385, G pp, rec.

● **Places to eat** *Club Alemán*, Av Philippi 747, good but not cheap, hostile to backpackers; Bar Restaurant upstairs at the Fire Station, *Bomberos*, opp *Hotel Frutillar* (which burnt down in 1993), best value, open all year, memorable painting caricaturing the firemen in action. *Bierstube*, Varas, open 1600-2400. Many German-style cafés and tea-rooms on C Philippi (the lakefront) eg *Salón de Te Frutillar*, No 775. *Der Volkladen*, O'Higgins y Philippi, natural products, chocolates and cakes, natural cosmetics. *Café Hermosa*, good breakfast. Budget travellers should eat at *Kaisersseehaus* (see **Accommodation**) 'and explode'.

● **Services** Toilet, showers and changing cabins for beach on O'Higgins. *Cema-Chile* shop, Philippi y O'Higgins.

● **Tourist offices** On lakeside opp *Club Alemán*, helpful; *Viajes Frutillar*, Richter y Alissandre in Alto Frutillar, run tours.

● **Transport** Buses to Puerto Varas (US$0.75) and Puerto Montt(US$1.25), frequent, Varmontt and Full Express; to Osorno, Varmontt 1¼ hrs, US$3; to Puerto Octay, Thaebus, 6 a day. Most buses leave from opposite the Copec station in Alto Frutillar.

PUERTO VARAS

This beauty spot on the shore of Lago Llanquihue, has roses growing along the streets (*Pop* 26,000; *Phone code* 065). It is 996 km from Santiago and only 20 by paved road from Puerto Montt. The church, in monumental Baroque style, built by German Jesuits in 1918, is a copy of the church in Marieenkirche in the Black Forest; worth a visit. **Parque Philippi**, on top of hill, is a pleasant place to visit; walk up to *Hotel Cabañas del Lago* on Klenner, cross the railway and the gate is on the right. The views are a bit restricted by trees and the metal cross at the top is unattractive (so is the electric clock which chimes the quarter-hours in town). Casino charges US$2.65 entry, including first drink.

Excursions

Puerto Varas is within easy reach of many famous beauty spots: Desagüe, Totoral, Frutillar, Los Bajos, Puerto Octay, Puerto Chico, Puerto Fonck, La Poza, Isla Loreley, Volcán Calbuco, La Fábrica, Puerto Rosales, Playa Venado, Ralún and Río Pescado. The whole countryside with its primeval forest, deep blue rivers and snowcapped volcanoes is very beautiful; interest is added by the timber-frame buildings with shingle roofs, even the churches.

La Poza is a little lake to the S of the main lake and reached through narrow channels overhung with vegetation; a concealed channel leads to yet another lake, the Laguna Encantada. The motor-boats that tour La Poza stop at Isla Loreley, very beautiful and well worth a visit.

Buses from Puerto Montt run every day on the southern side of the lake between Puerto Varas and (50 km) Ensenada, in the S-eastern corner of the lake, continuing to Ralún, Cochamó and Río Puelo (see below). In summer, buses go daily from Puerto Montt and Puerto Varas in the morning to Ensenada, Laguna Verde, Petrohué Falls and Lago Todos Los Santos, US$7, good value. The drive around the lake is very picturesque.

Local information

● **Accommodation**

Accommodation is expensive, it is cheaper to stay in Puerto Montt.

L3 *Los Alerces*, Pérez Rosales 1281, T 233039, 4-star hotel, with breakfast, new cabin complex, attractive.

A1 *Colonos del Sur*, Del Salvador 24, T 233369, with bath, good views, good restaurant, tea room; **A1** *Cabañas del Lago*, Klenner 195, T 232291, F 232707, rooms or remodelled cabins, central heating, TV, phone, parking, superb location; **A1** *Antonio Varas*, Del Salvador 322, T 232375, F 232352, very comfortable; **A2** *Bellavista*, Pérez Rosales 60, T 232012, cheerful, rec, restaurant, overlooking lake; **A3** *Motel Ayentemo*, Pérez Rosales 950, clean, comfortable cabins, friendly, T/F 232270; **A3** *Licarayén*, San José 114, T 232305, F 232955, with bath, overlooking lake, comfortable, 'enthusiastically rec', book in season, C out of season, clean, friendly, 'the perfect place for bad weather or being ill'.

B *Merlín*, Walker Martínez 584, T/F 233105,

quiet, excellent restaurant, highly rec; **B** *Motel Altué*, Pérez Rosales 1679, T 232294, inc breakfast. **C** *El Greco*, Mirador 134, T 233388, modern, good; **B** *Hosp Loreley*, Maipo 911, T 232226, rec, homely, quiet.

D María Schilling Rosas, La Quebrada 752, rec; **D** pp *Hosp Las Carmelas*, Imperial y Rosario, new, excellent, helpful, good meals, highly rec; **D** pp *Cabañas Amancay*, Martínez 564, with breakfast, German spoken, rec; **D** pp Andrés Bello 321, nice atmosphere, good breakfast; **D** *Res Alemana*, San Bernardo 416, T 232419, with breakfast, without bath, clean; **D** *Hosp Don Raúl*, Salvador 928, laundry and cooking facilities, very friendly, clean, rec, camping F pp; **C** Imperial 8 (opp *Motel Trauco*), good breakfast, good views, highly rec; other family *hospedajes* on same street inc **D** *Hosp Imperial*, No 653, T 232451, clean, inc breakfast, central, rec; **F** pp Pío Nono 489, T 233172, with breakfast; **E** pp Elsa Pinto, Verbo Divino 427, clean; **E** *Hosp Ellenhaus*, Martínez 239, T 233577, use of kitchen, lounge, hospitable, highly rec.

Camping: on S shore of Lago Llanquihue starting at Puerto Varas: Km 10, Playa Hermosa, T Puerto Varas 8283, Puerto Montt 252223, fancy, rec, take own supplies. Km 11, Playa Niklitschek, full facilities; Km 20, Playa Venado; Km 49, Conaf site at Puerto Oscuro, beneath road to volcano, very good.

● **Places to eat**

Donde El Gordito, downstairs in market, immense portions, very popular, good value; *Domino*, Del Salvador 450, good, cheap; *Café Danés*, Del Salvador 441, good coffee and cakes; *El Amigo*, San Bernardo 240, large portions, good value. At the Puerto Chilo end of Pérez Rosales are *Costa Azul*, No 01071, rec and *Ibis*, No 1117, warmly rec, expensive motel restaurants just beyond it aren't worth visiting, although service is friendly. *Café del Turismo*, next to Cruz del Sur office, cheap, good; *El Molino*, café next to an old water mill, on road to Ensenada 22 km from Pto Varas.

● **Banks & money changers**

Turismo Los Lagos, Del Salvador 257 (Galería Real, local 11), open daily 0830-1330, 1500-2100, Sun 0930-1330, accepts TCs, good rates. Banco Osorno, Del Salvador 399, good rates.

● **Laundry**

Del Salvador 553.

● **Post & telecommunications**

Post Office: San José y San Pedro.

Phone Office: Del Salvador y Santa Rosa.

● **Shopping**

VYH Meistur Supermarket, Walker Martínez, good selection, reasonably priced.

● **Sports**
Fishing: the area around Puerto Varas is popular for fishing. A licence costs US$2.50 a year, obtainable from the Municipal offices.

Cycle hire: *Travel Art*, Imperial 0661, T 232198, but check equipment carefully.

● **Tour companies & travel agents**
Andina del Sud, Del Salvador 243, T 232511, operate 'lakes' trip to Bariloche, Argentina via Lago Todos los Santos, Peulla, Cerro Tronador (see under Puerto Montt, **To Argentina**), plus other excursions, good. Also *Eco Travel*, Av Costanera s/n, T 233222, *Turismo Nieve* (on San Bernardo, rec), *Aqua Motion*, Imperial 0699, T/F 232747, for trekking, rafting and climbing, German and English spoken, good equipment; several others. Most tours operate in season only (1 Sept-15 April).

● **Tourist offices**
Del Salvador 328, 0900-2100 in summer, helpful, find cheap accommodation; also art gallery.

● **Transport**
Trains To Santiago daily, 1600, details under Puerto Montt.

Buses Varmontt terminal, San Francisco 500 block. To **Santiago**, Varmontt, Igi Llaima and others, US$20; to **Puerto Montt**, 30 mins, Varmontt and Full Express every 15 mins, US$0.50; same companies, same frequency to Frutillar (US$0.75, 30 mins) and **Osorno** (US$3.50, 1¼ hrs); to Valdivia US$6. To **Bariloche**, Andina del Sud, see above. Bohle bus from Puerto Montt departs 1130, daily except Sun, from *Res Hellwig* (San Pedro 210) to Petrohué, connecting with the ferry service to Peulla.

ENSENADA

50 km E of Puerto Varas, beautifully situated at the SE corner of Lago Llanquihue and a good centre for excursions. A half-day trip from Ensenada is to Laguna Verde, about 30 mins from *Hotel Ensenada*, along a beautiful circular trail behind the lake (take first fork to the right behind the information board), and then down the road to a campsite at Puerto Oscuro on Lago Llanquihue. The site is quiet and secluded, a good spot for a picnic

● **Accommodation A2** *Hotel Ensenada*, Casilla 659, Puerto Montt, T 232888, with bath, olde-worlde, good food (closed in winter) good view of lake and Osorno Volcano, runs tours, hires mountain bikes (guests only); also *hostal* in the grounds, cooking facilities, much cheaper but not that cheap. **B** *Hosp Ensenada*, T 8278, very clean, excellent breakfast, **D** off-season, rec;

C *Cabañas Villa Ensenada*, sleep 4, bargain off season; **C** *Hostería Los Pumas*, 3 hrs up the hill also highly rec, in season only; about 2 km from town is **C** *Pucará*, also with good restaurant (the steaks are rec); **C** *Ruedas Viejas*, T 312, for room, or **D** in cabin, about 1 km W from Ensenada, IYHA reductions, basic, damp, hot water, restaurant; **C** *Hosp Arena*, on same road, with breakfast, rec; **D** *Cabañas Brisas del Lago*, T 252363, chalets for 6 on beach, good restaurant nearby, highly rec for self-catering, supermarket next door; **D** *Moteles Hostería*, with breakfast, clean, poor service, comfortable; **D** *Hosp Opazo*, with breakfast, friendly; **E** pp *Hosp* above Toqui grocery, cheapest in town, basic, quiet, hot water, use of kitchen, beach in the back yard, rec. **Camping**: *Camping Montaña*, opp *Hotel Ensenada*, US$10, fully equipped, highly rec; also at Playa Larga, 1 km beyond *Hotel Ensenada*, US$10 and at Puerto Oscuro, 2 km N, US$8.

● **Places to eat** *Canta Rana* rec for bread and *kuchen*; *Ruedas Viejas*, the cheapest; most places closed off season, a few pricey shops; take your own provisions.

● **Transport** Minibuses run from Puerto Montt via Puerto Varas in summer. Hitching from Puerto Varas is difficult.

Volcán Osorno

Volcán Osorno lies N of Ensenada. It can be reached either from Ensenada, or from a road branching off the Puerto Octay-Ensenada road at Puerto Klocker, 20 km SE of Puerto Octay. The Club Andino Osorno (address under Osorno) has three shelters (US$3 pp): to the N at La Picada (20 km SE of Puerto Klocker) at 950m; to the S at *Las Pumas*, 12 km from Ensenada at 900m, with plenty of beds and cooking facilities, very friendly guards (apply at the Oficina de Turismo de Osorno); also to the S, 1.5 km from Ensenada at 1,200m **Refugio Teski Club**, E, bunk accommodation, restaurant and bar, sleeping bag useful, bleak site above the tree line; a good base for walking. Weather permitting, *Aqua Motion* (address under Puerto Varas), organize climbing expeditions with local guide, transport from Puerto Montt or Puerto Varas, food and equipment, US$150 pp (maximum group of 2) all year. Only experienced climbers should attempt to climb right to the top, ice climbing equipment and guide essential: there are many deep crevasses, the weather can change suddenly, never go alone, and set off early in the morning; there is a shelter for hikers. Before setting out ask first at Las Pumas or Refugio Teski for advice.

LAGO TODOS LOS SANTOS

16 km E of Ensenada, along a scenic, partially paved road, is **Lago Todos los Santos**, a long irregularly shaped sheet of water, the most beautiful of all the lakes in southern Chile. The lake, which lies within the **Parque Nacional Vicente Pérez Rosales**, has no roads round it. The waters are emerald green; the shores are deeply wooded and several small islands rise from its surface. Private launches can be hired for trips, for instance to Cayutué on a southern arm of the lake. In the waters of the lake are reflected the slopes of Volcán Osorno. Beyond the hilly shores to the E are several graceful snow-capped mountains, with the mighty Tronador in the distance. To the N is the sharp point of Cerro Puntiagudo (2,278m), and at the North-eastern end Cerro Techado (1,720m) rises cliff-like out of the water. The ports of **Petrohué** at its western and **Peulla** at its eastern ends are connected by boat. For walking, ask for the park guard, who organizes expeditions from Petrohué in the summer months. Trout and salmon fishing at Petrohué are excellent. The Salto de Petrohué (entrance, US$1.50) is 6 km (unpaved) from Petrohué, 10 km (paved) from Ensenada (a much nicer walk from Petrohué). Near the falls is a snackbar; there are also two short trails, the Senderos de los Enamorados and Carileufú.

Puella is a good starting point for hikes in the mountains. The Cascadas Los Novios signposted above the *Hotel Peulla*, are a steep walk, but are stunning once you reach them. Good walk also to Laguna Margarita, 4 hrs, take water.

Isla Margarita, the largest island on the lake, with a lagoon in the middle, can be visited (in summer only) from Petrohué, boats by Andino del Sud leave 1500, US$30.

On the S shore of Lago Todos Los Santos is the little village of **Cayutué**, reached by hiring a boat from Petrohué, US$30. From Cayutué it is a 3-hr walk to Laguna Cayutué, a jewel set between mountains and surrounded by forest. Good camping and swimming. From here it is a 5 hr hike S to Ralún on the Reloncaví Estuary (see below). This is part of the old route used by missionaries in the colonial period to travel between Nahuel Huapi in Argentina and the island of Chiloé. It is now part of a logging road and is good for mountain bikes.

Petrohué and Peulla are infested by *tavanos* in Dec and January. Cover up as much as possible with light-coloured clothes which may help a bit.

- **Accommodation At Petrohué: A2** *Hostería Petrohué*, with bath, excellent views, modernized and expanded, commercialized for tour groups (lunch with Chilean folksinging), comfortable, also self-service restaurant next door, better value; **A3** *Fundo El Salto*, nr Salto de Petrohué, very friendly, run by New Zealanders, mainly a fishing lodge, good home cooking, fishing trips arranged, Casilla 471, Puerto Varas; **E** pp *Familia Kuschel* on other side of river (boat across), with breakfast, meals available, electricity only 3 hrs in pm, dirty, noisy, poor value, camping possible. Albergue in the school in summer. There is a shop with basic supplies in the village. **At Peulla: A1** *Hotel Peulla*, PO Box 487, Puerto Montt, T 253253 (inc dinner and breakfast, direct personal reservations A3, PO Box 487, Puerto Montt, cheaper out of season), beautiful setting by the lake and mountains, restaurant and bar, good but expensive meals, cold in winter, often full of tour groups (tiny shop at back of hotel); **D** pp *Res Palomita*, 50m W of Hotel, half board, family-run, simple, comfortable but not spacious, separate shower, book ahead in season, lunches; accommodation is also available with local residents: Elmo and Ana Hernández Maldonado (only house with a balcony), **D** with breakfast, use of kitchen, helpful, clean. Small shop in Andino del Sud building but best to take your own food. **Camping**: at Petrohué on far side beside the lake, US$4/site, no services. At Peulla, opp Conaf office, US$1.50. Ask the commander of the military garrison at the beach nearest the hotel if you can camp on the beach; no facilities. Good campsite 1¾ hrs' walk E of Puella, take food.

- **Transport Minibuses** from Puerto Montt to Ensenada continue to Petrohué in summer. At other times of year there is a bus from Puerto Varas to Petrohué US$2, 1 hr, but it only waits 5 mins in Petrohué before returning to Puerto Varas.

The **boat** between Petrohué and Peulla costs US$20 one way (book in advance); it leaves

Petrohué at 1030, Peulla at 1500 (not Sun, 2½ hrs – most seating indoors, no cars carried, cycles free), commentaries in Spanish, English and German plus loud music. This is the only public service across the lake and it connects with the Andina del Sud tour bus between Puerto Montt and Bariloche (see under Puerto Montt). Local fishermen make the trip across the lake, but charge much more than the public service. If planning to go to Bariloche in stages, book through to Bariloche in Petrohué, not Peulla because onward connections from Peulla may be full and the accommodation is not so good there.

FRONTIER WITH ARGENTINA: PASO PEREZ ROSALES

● **Chilean immigration**

In Puella, 30 km W of the frontier, open summer 0800-2100, winter 0800-2000.

NB It is impossible to do this journey independently out of season as then there are buses only as far as Ensenada, there is little traffic for hitching and none of the ferries take vehicles.

RELONCAVI ESTUARY

The Reloncaví estuary, the northernmost of Chile's glacial inlets, is recommended for its local colour, its sealions, dolphins and its peace.

Ralún, a small village situated at the northern end of the estuary, is 31 km SE from Ensenada by a paved road along the wooded lower Petrohué valley. The road continues, unpaved, along the E side of the estuary to Cochamó and Puelo. In Ralún there is a village shop and post office, with telex.

● **Accommodation** E pp *Restaurant El Refugio* rents rooms; E pp *Navarrito*, restaurant and lodging; F pp *Posada Campesino*, simple, clean, without breakfast, very friendly; E pp *El Encuentro*; the *Hotel Ralún*, at S end of the village, which burnt down in 1992, has cabins.

● **Transport** Bus from Puerto Montt, 5 a day, Bohle, between 1000 and 1930, 4 on Sat, return 0700-1830, US$2. Also bus from Ensenada daily, US$1.

The road which goes to *Hotel Ralún* continues round the base of the mountains to Lago Chapo, giving access at the eastern end to Parque Nacional Alerce Andino (see page 811). There is, as yet, no

connection between the eastern and western shores of Lago Chapo.

Cochamó, 17 km S of Ralún on the E shore of the estuary is a pretty village, with a fine Chiloé-style church in a striking setting, with the estuary and volcano behind.

● **Accommodation D** *Cochamó*, T 212, basic but clean, friendly, often full with salmon farm workers, good meals, rec, and a large number of *pensiones* (just ask), eg **E** pp *Mercado Particular Sabin*, Catedral 20, next to *Hotel;* **E** pp Sra Flora Barrientos offers floorspace in her bar/restaurant/drugstore, same street No 16; **E** pp *Restaurant Copihue;* **E** pp *Res Gato Blanco;* cheapest accommodation at Catedral 2, by the pier (floor space only). *Camping Los Castaños*, T 214 (Reservations Casilla 576, Puerto Montt).

● **Sports Horseriding**: *Campo Aventura* (Casilla 5, Correo Cochamó) T/F 232747, offer accommodation at their base camp 2 km S of Cochamó (**E** pp, kitchen, sauna, camping) and at their other base, a renovated mountain house in the valley of La Junta. Specialize in horseback and trekking expeditions between the Reloncaví Estuary and the Argentine frontier, 2-10 days.

The **Gaucho Trail** E to Paso León on the Argentine frontier was used in the colonial period by indians and Jesuit priests and later by gauchos. The route runs along Río Cochamó to La Junta, then along the N side of Lago Vidal, passing waterfalls and the oldest surviving Alerce trees in Chile at El Arco, 3-4 days by horse, 5-6 days on foot, depending on conditions (best done Dec-March). From the border crossing at Paso León it is a 3-hr walk to the main Bariloche road.

Puelo, further S, on the S bank of the Río Puelo, is a most peaceful place (ferry crossing); lodging is available at the restaurant (F pp) or with families – try Roberto and Olivia Telles, simple, clean, no bath/shower, meals on request, or Ema Hernández Maldona; 2 restaurants.

● **Transport** Buses Fierro services from Puerto Montt, Mon-Sat 1230 and 1600, Sun 0900 1500 (from Puerto Varas 30 mins later). Daily buses from Cochamó 1515 and 2000. From here the road continues to Llaguepe. In summer boats sail up the Estuary from Angelmó. Tours from Puerto Montt US$30. Off season the *Carmencita* sails once a week, leaving Puelo Sun 1000 and Angelmó Wed 0900 (advisable to take warm clothes, food and seasickness pills if windy).

PUERTO MONTT

The capital of X Región (Los Lagos), 1,016 km S of Santiago, was founded in 1853 as part of the German colonization of the area (*phone code* 065). Good views over the city and bay are offered from outside the Intendencia Regional on Av X Region. The port is used by fishing boats and coastal vessels, and is the departure point for vessels to Puerto Chacabuco, Aisén, and for the long haul S to Punta Arenas. A paved road runs 55 km SW to Pargua, where there is a ferry service to Chiloé.

Places of interest

The **Iglesia de los Jesuitas** on Gallardo, dating from 1872, has a fine blue-domed ceiling; behind it on a hill is the **campanario** (clock tower). The little fishing port of **Angelmó**, 2 km W, has become a tourist centre with many seafood restaurants and handicraft shops (reached by Costanera bus along Portales and by collective taxi Nos 2,3,20 from the centre, US$0.30pp).

Museums

Museo Regional Juan Pablo II, Portales 997 near bus terminal, local history and a fine collection of historic photos of the city; also memorabilia of the Pope's visit. Open daily 1030-1800, US$0.50.

Excursions

Puerto Montt is a popular centre for excursions to the Lake District. The wooded **Isla Tenglo**, close to Puerto Montt and reached by launch from Angelmó (US$0.30), is a favourite place for picnics. Magnificent view from the summit. The island is famous for its *curantos*, a local dish. **Chinquihue**, W of Angelmó, has many seafood restaurants, with oysters as a speciality. East of Puerto Montt, **Chamiza**, up the Río Coihuin, has fine fishing. There is a bathing beach with black sand (polluted) at **Pelluco**, 4 km E of Puerto Montt (accommodation including *cabañas*; several good seafood restaurants, including *Pazos*, best *curanto* in Puerto Montt, rec). **Isla Guar** may be visited by boat from Angelmó harbour (1600, 2 hrs); boat returns from the other end of the island at 0730. The N shore is rocky. Accommodation, if lucky, at the church; best to camp.

West of Puerto Montt the Río Maullin, which drains Lago Llanquihue, has some attractive waterfalls and good fishing (salmon). The little fishing village of **Maullin**, founded in 1602 (**B** *Motel El Pangal*, 5 km away, T 244), at the mouth of the Río Maullin, is worth a visit. Southeast of here, on the coast, is Carelmapu; 3 km away is an excellent beach, Playa Brava. **Calbuco**, centre of the fishing industry (*Restaurant San Rafael*, rec) with good scenery, is on an island linked to the mainland by a causeway. It can be visited direct by boat or by road (the old coast road from Puerto Montt is very beautiful).

Local information
● **Accommodation**
Accommodation is expensive in season, much cheaper off season. Check Tourist Office.
A1 *Vicente Pérez Rosales*, Varas 447, T 252571, with bath and breakfast, some rooms

noisy, excellent restaurant, seafood, tourist and climbing information, rec; **A2** *Burg*, Pedro Montt y Portales, T 253813, modern, central heating, centrally located, good, interesting traditional food in restaurant; **A1** *Club Presidente*, Portales 664, T 251666, 4-star, with breakfast, very comfortable, also suites; **A1** *Don Luis*, Urmeneta y Quillota, T 259001, very good, no restaurant; **A3** *Montt*, Varas y Quillota, T 253651, with bath, C without, clean, friendly, good value, good restaurant; **A3** *Raysan*, Benavente 480, T 256151, helpful; **A2** *Viento Sur*, Ejército 200, T 258701, F 258700, excellent, good restaurant, sauna, gym, excellent views; **A3** *Millahue*, Copiapó 64, T 253829, F 253817, and apartments at Benavente 959, T/F 254592, with breakfast, modern, good restaurant.

B *Colina*, Talca 81, T 253813, with bath, clean, restaurant, bar, car hire, rec; **B** *Le Mirage*, Rancagua 350, T 255125, F 256302, with breakfast, small rooms, clean; **B** *El Candil*, Varas 177, T 253080, clean, attractive; also has **C** *Res Candil*, Illapel 87 nearby.

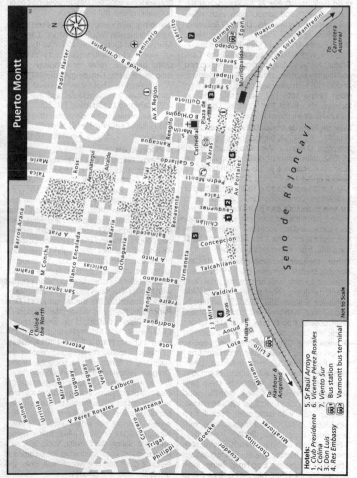

Puerto Montt

Seno de Reloncaví

Not to Scale

Hotels:
1. Club Presidente
2. Colina
3. Don Luis
4. Res Embassy
5. Sr Raúl Arroyo
6. Vicente Pérez Rosales
7. Viento Sur
B1 Bus station
R2 Varmontt bus terminal

C pp *Hostal Pacífico*, JJ Mira 1088, T 256229, with bath, **D** pp without, with breakfast, cable TV, parking, comfortable, rec; **C** *Res Embassy*, Valdivia 130, T 253533, with bath, **E** pp without, clean, stores luggage, rec; **C** pp *Res Urmeneta*, Urmeneta 290, T 253262, with bath, **D** pp without, clean, comfortable, rec, IYHA accepted; **C** pp *Res La Nave*, Ancud y Varas, T 253740, with bath, **E** pp without, clean, pleasant, inexpensive restaurant.

Near the bus terminal: **C** *Hosp Polz*, J J Mira 1002, T 252851, with breakfast, clean, warm, good beds, rec; **D** *Res El Turista*, Ancud 91, T 254767, with and without bath, with breakfast, clean, comfortable, rec; **D** *Res El Talquino*, Pérez Rosales 114, T 253331, hot water, clean; **D** *Res Punta Arenas*, J J Mira 964, with breakfast, hot water, basic but clean; **E** pp *Casa Gladis*, Ancud y Mira, dormitory style, kitchen and laundry facilities, crowded; **E** pp *Walglad*, Ancud 112, with breakfast, clean, friendly; **E** pp *Hosp Leticia* Lota 132, basic, safe, cooking facilities, rec; **E** pp *Res Central*, Lota 111, T 257516, clean, use of kitchen, rec.

Near the Plaza de Armas: **D** *Res Calipso*, Urmeneta 127, T 254554, without bath, clean IYHA accepted; **D** *Res La Alemana*, Egaña 82, T 255092, with breakfast, German spoken, run down; in **C** Huasco: **E** pp No 16, with breakfast, basic; **E** pp No 126, friendly, better, rec; **E** pp No 130, hot showers, cooking facilities, rec; **E** pp Sr Raúl Arroyo, Concepción 136, T 262188 (go to the 'inland' end of Concepción, turn right to end of alley), with breakfast, basic, crowded, run down, poor kitchen and bathroom facilities, English spoken, also has a cabaña 3 km away, sleeps 10; **D** Varas 840, basic, inc breakfast; cheaper.

Other cheaper accommodation: **D** *Casa Haraldo Steffen*, Serrano 286, T 253823, with breakfast, 15 mins' walk from centre, small clean rooms, run down, only 1 bathroom; **D** pp *Alda González*, Gallardo 552, T 253334, with bath, **E** pp without, with breakfast, cooking facilities, clean, popular; **F** pp *El Tata*, Gallardo 621, floor space, very basic, popular, packed in summer; **D** *Aníbal Pinto* 328, with breakfast, popular, laundry facilities, 10 mins' walk from centre, rec; **E** pp, Balmaceda 300, with breakfast, clean, friendly; **E** pp Balmaceda 283, clean, hospitable; **E** pp Balmaceda y Vial, reached by steep path behind Balmaceda 283, very friendly, good breakfast, safe, clean, rec; **E** pp *Vista Hermosa*, Miramar 1486, with bath, quiet, helpful; **E** pp Trigal 309, T 259923, use of kitchen, clean, with breakfast; **E** pp *Casa Perla*, Trigal 312, T 262104, with breakfast, French, English spoken, helpful, friendly, meals, Spanish classes offered off season, rec; **E** pp *Hosp Reina*, Trigal 361, family run, clean, welcoming; **E** pp Bilbao

380, T 256514, hot water, very clean, comfortable; **E** pp Sra María Oyarzo, Subida Miramar 1184, T 259957, inc breakfast, friendly, basic (no heating, hot water next door), clean, good beds; **E** pp *Res Emita*, Miraflores 1281, inc breakfast with homemade bread, clean, friendly, safe; **E** pp Vivar 1141, T 255039, inc breakfast, hot water; **E** pp Baquedano 247, T 252862, friendly, clean; on Petorca: **E** pp No 119, T 258638, clean, friendly, rec; **E** pp *Hosp Montesinos*, No 121, T 255353, with breakfast, clean, rec; **E** pp No 132, clean. *Albergue* in disused school opp bus station, sleeping bag on floor, very cheap, but no security.

Camping: 'wild' camping possible along the sea front. Several sites W of Puerto Montt: *Camping Municipal* at Chinquihue, 10 km W (bus service), open Oct-April, fully equipped with tables, seats, barbecue, toilets and showers. Small shop, no kerosene. *Camping Anderson*, 11 km W, American run, hot showers, private beach, home-grown fruit, vegetables and milk products. *Camping Los Alamos*, T 256067, 13 km W, nice views, poor services, stray dogs, US$17/site; *Camping Metri*, 30 km SE on Carretera Austral, T 251235, Fierro bus, US$2/tent.

● **Places to eat**

Embassy, Ancud 106, very good, pricey; *Club de Yates*, Juan Soler s/n, excellent, expensive seafood; *Centro Español*, O'Higgins 233, moderate prices; *Super Yoco*, Quillota 259, good value; *Kiel*, Capilla 298, excellent food and atmosphere, not cheap; *Club Alemán*, Varas 264, old fashioned, good food and wine; *Café Real*, Rancagua 137, for *empanadas*, *pichangas*, *congrio frito*, and cheap lunches; *Costa de Reloncaví*, Portales 736, good, moderate prices; *Café Central*, Rancagua 117, good atmosphere, meals and pastries; *Suerte Rincón*, Talca, excellent lunches, large portions, popular with locals. *Dino*, Varas 550, restaurant upstairs, snacks downstairs (try the lemon juice). *Don Pancho*, by the sea, in railway station, good. *Di Napoli Pizzas*, Gallardo 119, limited choice; *Café Amsel*, Pedro Montt y Portales, superb fish but not cheap; *Plato's*, Portales 1014, Galería Comercial España, cheap, good; also in the Galería is *El Rinconcito*, a good bar. *Super Dragon*, Benavente 839, Chinese, not cheap. Excellent and cheap food at bus terminal (all credit cards accepted). In **Angelmó**: many small seafood restaurants in the old fishing port, very popular – lunches only, ask for *té blanco* (white wine – they are not legally allowed to serve wine); *Asturias*, Angelmó 2448, limited menu, often rec. Bakery: *La Estrella*, Varas 984, self-service, good. Local specialities inc *picoroco al vapor*, a giant barnacle whose flesh looks and tastes like crab, and *curanto*.

● **Airline offices**

LanChile, San Martín 200, T 253141/253315; Ladeco, Benevente 350, T 253002; National, Benevente 305, T 258277, F 250664; Aerosur, Urmeneta 149, 252523; TAN, T 250071; Don Carlos, Quillota 127, T 253219.

● **Banks & money changers**

Impossible on Sun (but try Hotel Pérez Rosales). Exorbitantly high commission and low rates at Banco del Estado. For Visa try Banco Concepción, Pedro Montt y Urmaneta, good rates. Banco Osorno, Varas y Garrardo, good for Visa cash, but does not change TCs. Commission charges vary widely. Good rates at Galería Cristal, Varas 595, El Libertador, Urmeneta 529-A, local 3, and Turismo Latinoamericano, Urmeneta 531; Travellers travel agent in Angelmó (address below) has exchange facilities. Fincard (Access), Varas 437. La Moneda de Oro at the bus terminal exchanges Latin American currencies (Mon-Sat 0930-1230, 1530-1800). Obtain Argentine pesos before leaving Chile.

● **Embassies & consulates**

Argentine, Cauquenes 94, p 2, T 253996, quick visa service; German, Varas y Gallardo, p 3, of 306, Tues/Wed 0930-1200; Spanish, Rancagua 113, T252557; Dutch, Seminario 350, T 253428.

● **Laundry**

Center Varas 700; Lavatodo, O'Higgins 231; San Martín 232; Unic, Chillán 149; Yessil't, Edif Caracol, Urmaneta 300; Nautilus, Av Angelmó 1564, cheaper, good service; also in Las Brisas supermarket. Laundry prices generally high (US$7 for 3 kg).

● **Post & telecommunications**

Post Office: Rancagua 120, open 0830-1830 (Mon-Fri), 0830-1200 (Sat).

Telephone Office: Pedro Montt 114 and Chillán 98.

● **Shopping**

Woollen goods and Mapuche-designed rugs can be bought at roadside stalls in Angelmó and on Portales opp the bus terminal. Prices are much the same as on Chiloé, but quality is often lower. Supermarkets: Las Brisas opp bus terminal, very good, open 0900-2200 daily; Mondial, 2 blocks W is cheaper with better selection. Libros, Portales 580, small selection of English novels, also maps.

● **Sports**

Gymnasium: Urmeneta 537.

Sailing: Yacht Club, Marina del Sur, 3 km W (take bus marked Chinquihué); MDS Charters office at Yacht Club, T/F 251958 (also Santiago T/F 231-8238) specialize in cruising the Patagonian channels. Charters US$2,200-8,500/week

depending on size of boat. Yacht club has a notice board for crew (tripulante) notices.

● **Tour companies & travel agents**

Andina del Sud, very close to central tourist kiosk, Varas 437, T 257797, sells a daily tour at 0830 (not Sun) to Puerto Varas, Parque Nacional V Pérez Rosales, Petrohué, Lago Todos los Santos, Peulla and back (without meals US$27, with meals US$37), and to other local sights, as well as skiing trips to the Osorno volcano (see below for trip to Bariloche). Travellers, Av Angelmó 2270, T/F 258555, Casilla 854, close to 2nd port entrance and Navimag office, open Mon-Fri 0900-1330,1500-1830, Sat 0900-1400 for booking for Navimag ferry Puerto Edén to Puerto Natales, Osorno volcano trips and other excursions, money exchange, flights. Also sells imported camping equipment and runs computerized tourist information service, book swap,('best book swap south of Santiago'), English-run, rec. Petrel Tours, San Martín 167, of 403, T/F 255558, rec. Many other agencies. Most offer 1-day excursions to Chiloé and to Puerto Varas, Isla Loreley, Laguna Verde, and the Petrohué falls: both these tours are much cheaper from bus company kiosks inside the bus terminal, eg Bohle, US$15 to Chiloé, US$11 to the lakes.

● **Tourist offices**

Sernatur is in the Intendencia Regional, Av Décima Región 480 (p 3), Casilla 297, T 254580/256999, F 254580, Tx 270008. Open 0830-1300, 1330-1730 Mon-Fri. Ask for information on Chiloé as this is often difficult to obtain on the island. Also kiosk on Plaza de Armas run by the municipality, open till 1800 on Sat. Town maps available, but little information on other places. Telefónica del Sur and Sernatur operate a phone information service (INTTUR), dial 142 (cost is the same as a local call). Dial 149 for chemist/pharmacy information, 148 for the weather, 143 for the news, etc. The service operates throughout the Tenth Region. Sernatur in Puerto Montt has a reciprocal arrangement on information with Bariloche, Argentina. Conaf: Ochogavia 458, but cannot supply details of conditions in National Parks. Automóvil Club de Chile: Esmeralda 70, T 252968.

● **Transport**

Local Car hire: Hertz, Varas 126, T 259585, helpful, English spoken; Automóvil Club de Chile, Ensenada 70, T 254776, and at airport. Others are Avis, Egaña 64, T 256575 and at airport; Budget, San Martín 200 and at airport; Dollar (Hotel Vicente Pérez Rosales), Varas 447; First, Varas 437; Formula Uno, Santa María 620, T 254125, highly rec; Autovald, Portales 1330, T 256355, cheap rates; Travicargo, Urmeneta 856, T 257137/256438;

Automotric Angelmó, Talca 79, cheap and helpful. *Famas*, Portales y Gallardo, friendly, helpful, has vehicles that can be taken to Argentina.

Air El Tepual Airport, 13 km NW of town. ETM bus from terminal 1½ hrs before departure, US$1.25. To Santiago at least 2 daily flights by LanChile, Ladeco and National (cheaper). To Punta Arenas, LanChile, Ladeco and National daily; in Jan, Feb and Mar you may well be told that flights are booked up; however, cancellations may be available from the airport. National also flies to Concepción and Temuco. Flights to Bariloche, San Martín de los Andes and Neuquén (Argentina), TAN, twice a week, 40 mins. To Balmaceda, LanChile and Ladeco, daily. To Coyhaique, LanChile daily. Don Carlos flies to Chaitén, 1115 and 1515 Mon-Fri, Sat 1115 (fares under Chaitén), and runs regular charters for 5 passengers to Bariloche, Chaitén, and Coyhaique. Alta to Chaitén and to Balmaceda, Puerto Natales (3 hrs, US$70, highly rec for views) and Punta Arenas. Aerosur, also flies to Chaitén, daily except Sun and Tues and Futaleufú and Palena on Tues and Fri.

Trains New station under construction at Alerce, 10 km N of town. Old station at San Felipe 50, T 254908 functions only as ticket office (0830-1130, 1300-1700). Daily service to **Santiago** departs from Puerto Varas, 1600, Rápido with 1930s German built sleepers, 19 hrs. Seats: *turista* US$21, *salón* US$35; sleepers: US$44 lower bunk, US$59 upper bunk, US$130 double compartment, bicycles US$10, restaurant car, car transporter, book 3 days in advance, but 2 weeks in advance in high season.

Buses Terminal on sea front at Portales y Lota, has telephones, restaurants, *casa de cambio* (left luggage, US$1/item for 24 hrs). Varmontt has its own terminal at Copiapó y Varas, but Varmontt buses also call at main terminal. To **Puerto Varas** (US$0.50), **Llanquihue**, **Frutillar** (US$1.25) and **Osorno** (US$5) every 30 mins, Varmontt and Full Express. To **Ensenada** and **Petrohué** Buses JM at least 3 a day. To **Pucón**, US$7. To **Santiago**, express 15 hrs, US$18-25, *cama* US$45, Tur-Bus, very good, 14 hrs, Tas Choapa *Royal Class* US$33; to **Punta Arenas**, Austral, Turbus and Ghisoni, between 1 and 3 times a week, US$60-75 depending on company, departing either 0800 or 1100 (bus goes through Argentina via Bariloche – take US$ cash to pay for meals etc in Argentina), 32-38 hrs; book well in advance in Jan-Feb and check if you need a multiple-entry Chilean visa; also book any return journey before setting out; to **Temuco** US$9, to **Valdivia**, US$7; **Concepción**, US$15. For services to **Chiloé**, see page 803.

Motoring: when driving N out of Puerto Montt (or out of Puerto Varas, Frutillar, etc), look for signs to 'Ruta 5'.

Boat hire: Lucinda Cárdenas, Manuel Montt Pasaje 7, Casa 134, Angelmó, for trips around the harbour or to Tenglo island.

TO ARGENTINA
Via Lago Todos Los Santos

This popular route to Bariloche, involving ferries across Lago Todos Los Santos, Lago Frías and Lago Nahuel Huapi is outstandingly beautiful whatever the season, though the mountains are often obscured by rain and heavy cloud. The route is via Puerto Varas, Ensenada and Petrohué falls (20 mins stop) to Petrohué, where it connects with cataraman service across Lago Todos Los Santos to Peulla. Lunch stop in Peulla 2 hrs (lunch not inc in fare: *Hotel Peulla* is expensive, see page 791 for alternatives). Chilean customs in Peulla, followed by a 2 hr bus ride through the Paso Pérez Rosales to Argentine customs in Puerto Frías, 20 min boat trip across Lago Frías to Puerto Alegre and bus from Puerto Alegre to Puerto Blest. From Puerto Blest it is a beautiful 1½ hr catamaran trip along Lago Nahuel Huapi to Puerto Panuelo, from where there is a 1 hr bus journey to Bariloche (bus drops passengers at hotels, camping sites or in town centre). Out of season this trip is done over 2 days with overnight stay in Peulla, add about US$89 to single fare for accommodation in *Hotel Peulla*. (Baggage is taken to *Hotel Peulla* automatically but for alternative accommodation see under Peulla above.)

● **Transport** The route is operated only by Andino del Sud (address above). Bus from company offices daily at 0800; the fare is US$104 one way. Note that the trip may be cancelled if the weather is poor; there are reports of difficulty in obtaining a refund. Try both Puerto Montt and Puerto Varas offices if you want to take the Andina del Sud trip in sections.

Osorno and the Puyehue pass Daily services to Bariloche on this route via Osorno, US$20-25, 6-10 hrs, are run by Cruz del Sur, Andesmar, Turismo Lanín (not rec), Tas Choapa and Bus Nte. Tas Choapa services also run to Mendoza, Buenos Aires, Montevideo and Rio de Janeiro. Out of season, services are reduced. Buy tickets for international buses from the bus terminal, not through an agency. If intending to return by this route, buy an open return ticket as higher fares are charged in Argentina. Book well in advance in Jan and February. Hitchhiking on this route is difficult and may take as long as 4 days.

SEA ROUTES SOUTH OF PUERTO MONTT

To Puerto Natales

The dramatic 1,460 km journey first goes through Seno Reloncaví and Canal Moraleda. From Bahía Anna Pink along the coast and then across the Golfo de Peñas to Bahía Tarn it is a 12-17 hrs sea crossing, usually rough. The journey continues through Canal Messier, Angostura Inglesa, Paso del Indio and Canal Kirke (one of the narrowest routes for large shipping). The only regular stop is made off Puerto Edén (1 hr S of the Angostura Inglesa), where there are 3 shops, with scant provisions, one off-licence, one café, but no hotel or camping facility, nor running water. Population is 180, plus 5 *carabineros* and the few remaining Alacaluf Indians. It is, though, the drop-off point for exploring Isla Wellington, which is largely untouched, with stunning mountains. If stopping here, take all food; maps (not very accurate) are available in Santiago.

● **Shipping offices in Puerto Montt: Navimag** (Naviera Magallanes SA), Terminal Transbordadores, Angelmó 2187, T 253318, F 258540. **Constantino Kochifas C**, Angelmó 1660 y Miraflores (Castilla 588), T 252619, Tx 370161 NATUK CL. **Transmarchilay Ltda**, Angelmó 2187, T 254654, F 253683.

● **Shipping services**
Taxi from centre to ferry terminal, US$2. All shipping services should be checked in advance; schedules change frequently.

Navimag's *Puerto Edén* sails **to Puerto Natales** every 8 days, taking 4 days and 3 nights; the fare ranges from US$160 pp economy (inc meals) to US$660 pp in various classes of cabin (also inc meals); 10% discount on international student cards in cabin class only. The summer 1996 schedule was expected to be: leave Puerto Montt Mon, return from Puerto Natales Fri. Payment by credit card or foreign currency generally not accepted. Economy class accommodation is basic, in 24-berth dormitories and there is limited additional space for economy class passengers when weather is bad. Apart from videos, entertainment on board is limited. Economy class and cabin passengers eat in separate areas. Some report good food, others terrible. Standards of service and comfort vary, depending on the number of passengers and weather conditions. Take seasickness tablets.

Another Navimag vessel, the *Amadeus*, carries cargo between Puerto Montt, Puerto Cha-

cabuco and Puerto Natales, with a few passenger, same price as cheaper cabins on the *Puerto Edén*, no fixed timetable.

● **Booking** Economy class can only be booked, with payment, through Navimag offices in Puerto Montt and Puerto Natales. Economy tickets are frequently sold just before departure. Cabin class can be booked in advance through *Travellers* in Puerto Montt or Puerto Natales (see **Travel agents**, above), through Navimag offices in Puerto Montt, Puerto Natales and Punta Arenas, or through Cruceros Austalis (Navimag parent company) in Santiago. All of these have their own ticket allocation: once this is used up, they have to contact other offices to request spare tickets. Book well in advance for departures between mid-Dec and mid-Mar especially for the voyage S (Puerto Natales to Puerto Montt is less heavily booked). It is well worth going to the port on the day of departure if you have no ticket. Note that departures are frequently delayed – or even advanced.

To Puerto Chacabuco

● **Shipping services**
The roll on/roll off vehicle ferry m/v *Evangelistas* of Navimag, runs twice weekly to Puerto Chacabuco (80 km to the W of Coyhaique), usually Wed and Sat, returning from Puerto Chacabuco on the following day. From end-Dec to mid, or end-March the schedule changes to include a Sun-Tues trip from Puerto Chacabuco to Laguna San Rafael, so Pto Montt to Pto Chacabuco is Wed and Sat, but return to Pto Montt is Tues and Thur. The cruise to Puerto Chacabuco lasts about 24 hrs. First class accommodation includes 2 cabins with bath (US$125-250 depending on which cabin and number of occupants); tourist class, 14 bunks (about US$145 double); and third class, 400 reclining seats (US$68, type 'B', US$40, type 'A'). Fare to Laguna San Rafael US$155-220, reclining seat, or US$285-510 in cabin. First class reservations must be made in advance at the Santiago offices (see page 695). There is a small canteen; long queues if the boat is full. Food is expensive so take your own.

The *Colono* of Transmarchilay sails to Puerto Chacabuco on Tues and Fri between 1 Jan and early Mar, 26 hrs; passengers US$24-164 pp, vehicles US$165. Transmarchilay also runs a ferry service on the route Quellón (Chiloé)-Chaitén-Puerto Montt-Chaitén-Quellón (see under Quellón and Chaitén for details). Overbooking and long delays reported.

To Laguna San Rafael

● **Shipping services**
The m/n *Skorpios 1* and 2 of Constantino Kochifas C leave Pto Montt on Sat at 1100 for a

luxury cruise with stops at Puerto Aguirre, Melinka, Laguna San Rafael, Quitralco, Castro (each ship has a slightly different itinerary) and returns to Puerto Montt on Fri at 0800. The fare varies according to season, type of cabin and number of occupants: a double ranges from US$465 (low) to US$660 (high) on *Skorpios 1* and from US$770 (low) to US$1,100 (high) on *Skorpios 2*, which is the more comfortable of the two. It has been reported that there is little room to sit indoors if it is raining on *Skorpios 1*, but generally service is excellent, the food superb and at the glacier, you chip your ice off the face for your whisky.

Patagonia Connection, Fidel Oteíza 1921, Oficina 1006, T 225-6489, F (562) 204-9118, Santiago (D Portales 872, T 259790, Puerto Montt), operates *Patagonia Express*, a catamaran which runs from Puerto Montt to Laguna San Rafael via Termas de Puyuguapi see page 814 and Puerto Chacabuco. Stops can be made at any of these points on the weekly service, high season 16 Dec-Mar 15, low season 16 Mar-April 27 and 16 Sept-Dec 15. High season fares for a 4 day cruise from US$980, all inclusive, highly rec; also runs a 7-day package with 4-day stopover at Termas de Puyuguapi.

● **Other services** The m/n *Bohemia* makes 6 day/5 night trips from Puerto Montt to Río Negro, Isla Llancahué, Baños Cahuelmó and Fiordo Leptepu/Coman, US$545-720 pp depending on season (Antonio Varas 947, T 254675, Puerto Montt).

See also under Chaitén for passenger services on Terminales Marítimos Chilenos.

● **Boat hire** Lucinda Cárdenas, Manuel Montt Pasaje 7, Casa 134, Angelmó, for trips around the harbour or to Tenglo island.

Chiloé

THE culture of the island of Chiloé has been heavily influenced by isolation from Spanish colonial currents, the mixture of early Spanish settlers and Mapuche indians and a dependence on the sea. Religious and secular architecture, customs and crafts, combined with delightful landscapes, all contribute to Chiloé's uniqueness.

Land and climate
The **Isla de Chiloé** is 250 km long, 50 km wide, 9,613 sq km, and has a population of 116,000. There are two main towns, Ancud and Castro (airport), and many fishing villages. Seaweed is harvested for export to Japan. The hillsides in summer are a patchwork quilt of wheat fields and dark green plots of potatoes. Inland are impenetrable forests. Though the weather is often cold and foggy, the island is extremely beautiful when the sun is out.

History
Chiloé was claimed for Spain by Martín Ruiz de Gamboa in 1567 and the few Spaniards who settled divided the indigenous population and their lands between them. The rising of the Mapuche after 1598 which drove the Spanish out of the mainland S of the Río Biobío left the small Spanish community on Chiloé (some 200

settlers in 1600) isolated. During the 17th century Chiloé was served by a single annual ship from Lima. In 1600 and 1642 the island was attacked by Dutch pirates. Following a violent earthquake in 1646 the Spanish population asked the Viceroy in

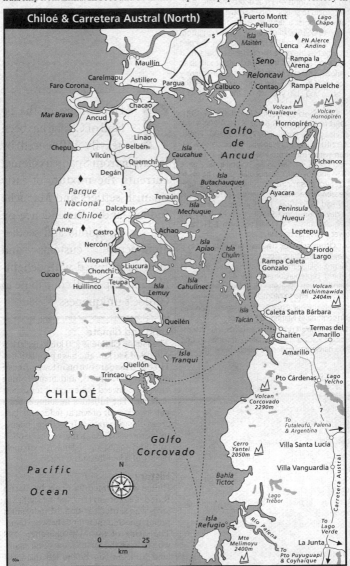

Chiloé & Carretera Austral (North)

Lima for permission to leave but this was refused.

Much of the island's distinctive character derives from its 200 years of isolation from the mainstream of Spanish colonial development. A major role in the island's cultural development was played by the Jesuits, who established missions (*reducciones*) for the indigenous population and ordered the building of schools and churches. By 1767, when the Jesuits were expelled, there were 79 churches on the island. Today it is dotted with nearly 150 churches, several of them dating from the 18th century. Chiloé was also used by the Jesuits as a base for missionary activity on the mainland; from here expeditions were sent out to the Río de la Plata and to the far S. The islanders were the last supporters of the Spanish Crown in South America. When Chile rebelled the last of the Spanish Governors fled to the island and, in despair, offered it to Britain. Canning, the British Foreign Secretary, turned the offer down. The island finally surrendered to the patriots in 1826.

Since independence the relatively high birth rate and the shortage of employment on Chiloé have led to regular emigration. Chilotes have settled throughout Chile, were prominent as shepherds in late 19th century Patagonia and are an important source of labour for the Argentine oil industry.

The availability of wood and the lack of metals have left their mark on the island. Some of the oldest churches are built entirely of wood, using wooden pegs instead of nails. Although the earliest houses were thatched, this was replaced by thin tiles (*tejuelas*) made in a wide variety of styles from alerce wood. However another typical feature of the island, *palafitos* or wooden houses built on stilts over the water, is a late 19th century innovation. The island is also famous for its traditional handicrafts, notably woollens and basket ware. Music is popular, with many players in the waterfront cafés in Castro.

Transport to Chiloé

Regular ferries cross the straits of Pargua between **Pargua**, 55 km SW of Puerto Montt on the mainland and **Chacao** on Chiloé.

- **Accommodation At Pargua**: *Hotel La Ruta*; *Res El Porvenir*. **At Chacao**: **E** pp *Pensión Chiloé*; **E** pp *Hosp Angelino*.

- **Transport Buses** From Puerto Montt, frequent, US$2, 1 hr, though most buses go right through to Ancud (3½-4 hrs) and Castro. Transport to the island is dominated by Cruz del Sur, who also own Trans Chiloé and Regional Sur and run their own ferries. Cruz del Sur run most services: 10 a day to Ancud and Castro, 5 to Chonchi and Quellón; in busy periods they are faster (their buses have priority over cars on Cruz del Sur ferries) and their fares are highest (Trans Chiloé lowest but sell out quickly). Fares from Puerto Montt: to **Ancud**, Cruz del Sur US$$5.75, Trans Chiloé US$4.50; to **Castro**, Cruz del Sur US$7.50, Trans Chiloé US$6; to **Chonchi**, US$7, **Quellón**, US$9. Note that there are direct bus services from Santiago, Osorno, Valdivia, Temuco and Los Angeles to Chiloé. Buses drive on to the ferry (passengers can get out of the bus). **Ferries** About 24 crossings a day, 30 min crossing, operated by several companies inc Transmarchilay and Cruz del Sur; all ferries carry buses, private vehicles (cars US$10 one way) and foot passsengers (who travel free).

ANCUD

Ancud (*Pop* 20,000; *Phone code* 065) is 30 km W of the Straits of Chacao.

Places of interest

The port is dominated by the **Fuerte San Antonio**, built by the Spanish in 1770, the site of the Spanish surrender to the Chileans in 1826. Close to it are the ruins of the **Polvorín del Fuerte** (a couple of cannon and a few walls). 1 km N of the fort is a secluded beach, **Arena Gruesa**. 2 km E is a **Mirador** offering good views of the island and across to the mainland.

Museums

Near the Plaza de Armas is the **Museo Regional** (open summer daily 1100-1900 winter Tues-Fri 0900-1300, 1430-1830, Sat 1000-1330, 1430-1800, US$1), with an interesting collection on the early history of Chiloé as well as replicas of a traditional Chilote thatched wooden house and of the small sailing ship *Ancud* which, in 1843, sailed to the Straits of Magellan to claim

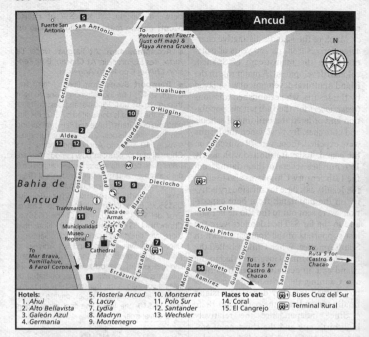

Ancud

Hotels:
1. Ahui
2. Alto Bellavista
3. Galeón Azul
4. Germania
5. Hostería Ancud
6. Lacuy
7. Lydia
8. Madryn
9. Montenegro
10. Montserrat
11. Polo Sur
12. Santander
13. Wechsler
Places to eat:
14. Coral
15. El Cangrejo

🚌1 Buses Cruz del Sur
🚌2 Terminal Rural

the Peninsula for Chile.

Excursions

Walk from Ancud W along the beach towards **Faro Corona** (34 km to Punta Corona), good views, interesting birdlife, dolphins can be seen, but the beach is not suitable for swimming. To **Pumillahue**, 27 km SW, and **Mar Bravo** on W coast, bus 1230 Mon-Fri. Near Pumillahue (bus daily 0700, details from tourist office) there is a penguin colony: hire a fishing boat to see it, US$2.50 pp.

Local information

● Accommodation

A1 *Hostería Ancud*, San Antonio 30, T/F 622340/622350, overlooking bay, attractive, very comfortable, friendly and helpful, restaurant; **A3** *Galeón Azul*, Libertad 751, T 622567, F 622543; **A3** *Lydia*, Pudeto y Chacabuco, T 622990, F 2879, with bath, **B** without bath, poor beds, small rooms, overpriced; **A3** *Lacuy*, Pudeto 219 nr Plaza de Armas, T/F 623019, with breakfast, rec; **A3** *Montserrat*, Baquedano 417, T/F 622957, with break-

fast, clean, good views, attractive.
B *Cabañas Las Golondrinas*, end of Baquedano at Arena Gruesa, T 622823, superb views, with bath, hot water and kitchenette; **B** *Hostería Ahui*, Costanera 906, T 622415, with bath and breakfast, modern, clean, good views; **B** *Polo Sur*, Costanera 630, T 622200, with bath, hot water, good value; avoid rooms overlooking disco next door; **B** *Res Weschler*, Cochrane 480, T 2318, clean, view of bay; **B** *Res Germania*, Pudeto 357, T/F 622214, with bath, **C** without, parking, comfortable, clean.

D *Caleta Ancud*, Bellavista 449, good breakfst, good restaurant; **D** *Hosp Alto Bellavista*, Bellavista 449, T 622384, with sleeping bag on floor much cheaper; **E** *Hosp Capri*, Ramírez 325, good breakfast; **D** *Hosp Alinar*, Ramírez 348, clean, hot water, hospitable; **D** *Hosp Santander*, Sgto Aldea 69, with bath, **E** without, clean, rec; **E** pp *Res Montenegro*, Blanco Encalada 531, T 2239, fair, no hot water; **E** pp Edmundo Haase Pérez, Ramírez 295, with breakfast, clean, basic, good value; **E** pp Errázuriz 442, with breakfast, cold water; **E** pp Elena Bergmann, Aníbal Pinto 382, clean, friendly, use of kitchen, parking; **E** pp Puedeto 331, T 622535, without bath, old fashioned; **E** pp Lautaro 947, T 2980, clean, friendly; **E** pp Familia Reuter-Miranda, Errázuriz 350, T 622261, good breakfast, clean, spacious, opp Cruz del Sur terminal, rec; Errázuriz 395, T 622657, without bath, clean; **F** pp Puedeto 619, clean, friendly, with breakfast. In summer, the school on C Chacabuco is open for lodging.

Camping: *Arena Gruesa* at N end of Baquedano; *Playa Gaviotas*, 5 km N; *Playa Larga Huicha*, 9 km N, **E**/site, bath, hot water, electricity.

● **Places to eat**

Seafood restaurants in market area. Good lunches at *Hotel Polo Sur*. *Carmen*, Puedeto 159, Chilean cooking, pasteles; *Coral*, Puedeto 346, good, not cheap; *Jardín*, same street No 263, good local food, not cheap; *Macaval*, Chacabuco 691; *El Trauco*, Blanco y Prat, seafood excellent, highly rec; *La Pincoya*, next to harbour, friendly, good seafood; *Lydia*, Puedeto 254, Chilean and international; *El Cangrejo*, Dieciocho 155, seafood highly rec; *Hamburguería*, Av Prat, much better than name suggests, good seafood; *Mar y Velas*, Serrano 2, p 2, beautiful views, good food.

● **Post & telecommunications**

Post Office: Puedeto y Blanco.

Telephone: Plaza de Armas, open Mon-Sat 0700-2200.

● **Tour companies & travel agents**

Turismo Ancud, Puedeto 219, Galería Yurie, T 2235, Tx 297700 ANCD CL.

● **Tourist offices**

Sernatur, Libertad 665, T 622665, open Mon-Fri 0900-1300, 1430-1800.

● **Transport**

Buses Cruz del Sur, Trans Chiloé and Regional Sur use the terminal at Errázuriz y Los Carrera; local buses leave from municipal terminal at Pedro Montt 538 though a new terminal is under construction at the E outskirts at Aníbal Pinto y Marcos Vera. To **Castro**, US$3, frequent (see below), 1½ hrs. To **Puerto Montt**, 2 hrs, Cruz del Sur 10 a day, Varmontt 3 a day from *Hotel Polo Sur*, Trans Chiloé also 3.

Sea Shipping: Transmarchilay Libertad 669, T 622317/2279, Tx 375007 MARCHI CK.

Longer excursions

To **Chepu**, on the coast SW of Ancud, famed for its river and sea fishing.(It is also the entrance to the N part of the Parque Nacional Chiloé, see under Cucao). There is a 2 day coastal walk between Ancud and Chepu: you can take the daily bus to Pumillahue, 27 km SW (0700, return 1330) or hitch. The route is difficult to follow so take food for 3 days and wear light-coloured clothes in summer to protect against *tavanos*.

East of Ancud on the N coast is **Caulín**, with good beaches; fresh oysters in *Hotel Lyon*. The road goes along the beach, only passable at low tide.

CASTRO

From Ancud, Route 5 leads S to Castro, 88 km in good condition and from there on through Chonchi to Quellón. An alternative route S runs from near Chacao along the E coast of the island through Quemchi and Dalcahue before joining Route 5 N of **Castro** (*Pop* 20,000; *Phone code* 065) capital of the island and a very friendly town.

Places of interest

There is a tremendous variety of styles in housing, including houses on stilts (*palafitos*) above the water, on the northern side of town and by the bridge over the Río Gamboa. Local woollen articles (hats, sweaters, gloves) can be found at **Feria**, or Mercado Municipal de Artesanía on the waterfront. *Palafito* restaurants have been put up behind the market. The large **cathedral** (1906), on the Plaza de Armas, strikingly decorated in lilac and orange, with a splendid wood panelled interior, was built by Italian architect, Eduardo Provosoli. Views of the city from **Mirador La Virgen** on Millantuy hill above the cemetery. On the road out of town to Quellón, walk to the Peninsula and Puntilla Ten Ten (2 hrs round trip), through woods and fields, nice views.

Museums

Museo Regional on Esmeralda, opp *Hotel La Bomba*, contains history, folklore, handicrafts and mythology of Chiloé and photos of 1960 earthquake, open summer Mon-Sat 0930-2000, Sun 1030-1300; winter Mon-Sat 0930-1300, 1500-1830, Sun 1030-1300; **Museo de Arte Moderno**, near the Río Gamboa, in the Parque Municipal, about 3 km NW of the centre (open 1000-2000).

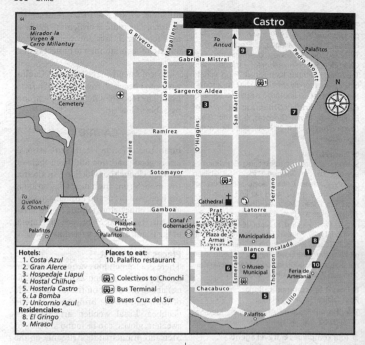

Castro

Hotels:
1. Costa Azul
2. Gran Alerce
3. Hospedaje Llapui
4. Hostal Chilhue
5. Hostería Castro
6. La Bomba
7. Unicornio Azul

Residenciales:
8. El Gringo
9. Mirasol

Places to eat:
10. Palafito restaurant

Colectivos to Chonchi
Bus Terminal
Buses Cruz del Sur

Local information
● Accommodation

A1 *Unicornio Azul*, Pedro Montt 228, T 632359, F 632808, good views over bay, comfortable, restaurant; **A2** *Cabañas Centro Turístico Nercón*, 5 km S, T 632985, rooms with bath, hot water, heating, restaurant, tennis court; **A3** *Hostería Castro*, Chacabuco 202, T 632301, F 635668 with bath and breakfast, hot water, good restaurant, attractive building, wonderful views; **A3** *Cabañas Truyen*, 5 km S of Castro, B off season, lovely views; **A2** *Gran Alerce*, O'Higgins 808, T 632267, with bath, heating, helpful, breakfast, also has *cabañas* and restaurant 4 km S of Castro.

B *Casita Española*, Los Carrera 359, T 635186, heating, TV, parking, rec; **B** *Chilhue*, Blanco Encalada 278, T 632956, with bath, good; **B** *Moteles Auquilda*, Km 2, Panamericana Nte, T 632458.

C *Quinta Niklitschek*, Panamericana Nte 331 (3 km N), T 632137, better inside than out; **C** *Costa Azul*, Lillo 67, T 632440, with bath, **D** without, friendly.

Cheaper accommodation on San Martín (all convenient for bus terminals): **D** *Res Mirasol*, No 815, basic, friendly, noisy; **E** pp *Hosp Chiloé*, No 739, breakfast, clean, rec; **E** pp *Hosp Angie*, San Martín 747, small rooms, clean, pretty; **E** pp *Hosp Guillermo*, No 700, clean, cheap; **E** pp *Res Capullito*, No 709, clean, friendly, quiet; **F** pp No 879, with big breakfast, central, clean, highly rec; **F** pp Lidia Low, No 890, with good breakfast, warm showers, use of kitchen; **E** pp No 638, clean; **E** pp No 581, helpful.

Other budget accommodation: **D** *Hilton*, Ramírez 385, good value, friendly, restaurant; **E** pp *Hosp* of Jessie Toro, Las Delicias 287, with good breakfast, hot water, helpful, clean, spacious, good bathrooms, also cabinas, warmly rec; **D** *La Bomba*, Esmeralda 270, T 632300, without bath, cheaper on 3rd floor, clean, good value, hot water, good 3 course menu; **E** pp *Casa Blanca*, Los Carrera 300, inc breakfast, clean, modern, warm; **D** Los Carrera 658, no sign, with breakfast, clean, friendly, rec; **E** pp *Res La Casona*, Serrano 488, above TV shop, with breakfast, rec; **E** Serrano 407, breakfast, friendly, warm water; **D** *Res El Gringo*, Lillo 51, without bath, good views, overpriced; **E** *Hosp Llapui*, O'Higgins 657, run down, with breakfast; **E** pp Euzaguirre 469, comfortable, rec; **E** pp María

Zuñiga, Barros Arana 140, T 635026, inc breakfast, clean, comfortable, cooking facilities, friendly, secure, rec; **E** pp Freire 758, breakfast, clean, good value; **E** pp O'Higgins 415, Dpto 41, quiet, very clean, hot water; **E** pp O'Higgins 865, clean, friendly, hot water; **E** pp Chacabuco 449, good beds, clean, quiet, friendly, water only warm; **E** pp Los Carrera 560, T 632472, clean, hot water; **D** *Hosp Sotomayor*, Sotomayor 452, T 632464, with breakfast, quiet, small beds; **E** pp *Hosp Tonque*, Pasaje Díaz 170, T 632773, without breakfast, clean, hot water; **F** pp *Hosp Polo Sur*, Barros Arana 169, T 635212, clean, safe, cooking facilities, wonderful views. Basic accommodation Dec-Feb in the Gimnasio Fiscal, Ramírez, T 632766, F with breakfast, clean; **E** pp *Hospedaje El Mirador*, Barros Arana 127, T 633795, friendly, good breakfast.

Camping: Camping Pudú, Ruta 5, 10 km N of Castro, cabins, showers with hot water, sites with light, water, children's games. Several sites on road to Chonchi.

● **Places to eat**

Palafito restaurants nr the Feria Artesanía on the waterfont offer good food and good value, inc *Brisas del Mar, Mariela, La Amistad; Sacho*, Thompson 213, good sea views, clean; *Don Camilo*, Ramírez 566, good food, not expensive, rec; *Pizzería La Niña*, Serrano 300 block, good pizzas, welcoming staff; *Stop Inn Café*, Prat y Chacabuco, good coffee; *Chilo's*, San Martín 459, good lunches; *El Curanto*, Lillo 67, seafood inc curanto, rec. *Maucari*, Lillo 93, good seafood, not expensive. In the market, try milcaos, fried potato cakes with meat stuffing; also licor de oro, like Galliano; *La Brújula del Cuerpo*, Plaza de Armas, good coffee, snacks; breakfast before 0900 is difficult: try *Café Paula*, Serrano 331.

● **Banks & money changers**

Banco del Estado de Chile, Plaza de Armas, accepts TCs (at a poor rate). **BCI** on plaza, Mastercard and Visa ATM. Better rates from Luis Barrientos Bilisco, Chacabuco 286, cash and TCs.

● **Hospitals & medical services**

Doctor: Muñoz de Las Carreras, nr police station, surgery 1700-2000 on weekdays, rec.

● **Laundry**

Lavandería Adolfo, Blanco Encalada, quick, reasonably priced.

● **Post & telecommunications**

Post Office: on W side of Plaza de Armas. Telephone: Latorre y San Martín.

● **Shopping**

See above for market. Cema-Chile outlet on Esmeralda, opp Hotel La Bomba. *Libros Chiloé*, Serrano y Blanco Encalada, books in Spanish on Chiloé. Cassettes of typical Chilote music are widely available.

● **Sports**

Bicycle hire: San Martín 581.

● **Tourist offices**

O'Higgins 549, T 635699; kiosk on main square opp Cathedral. *Conaf* at Gobernación, Plaza de Armas, p 3.

● **Tour companies & travel agents**

Varmontt, Plaza de Armas, day trips around the island, Jan and Feb only. *Pehuén Expediciones*, opp craft market; *Chiloé Tours*, Blanco Encalada 318; *Turismo Queilén*, Gamboa 502, good tours to Chonchi and Chiloé National Park, rec. **Lan**Chile agency, Thompson 245. **Ladeco** agency on Serrano, opp *Hostería Castro*. **Transmarchilay** agency at Suzuki Car Hire, San Martín y Blanco Encalada. Local guide Sergio Márquez, Felipe Moniel 565, T 632617, very knowldegeble, has transport. Tour prices: to Parque Nacional Chiloé US$25, to Mechuque US$37.

● **Transport**

Buses leave from 2 terminals: Cruz del Sur, T632389, Trans Chiloé and Arriagada from Cruz del Sur terminal on San Martín behind the cathedral. Other services leave from the Municipal Terminal, San Martín, 600 block (2 blocks further N). Frequent services to **Ancud** and **Puerto Montt** by Cruz del Sur and Trans Chiloé. Cruz del Sur also run to Osorno, Valdivia, Temuco, Concepción and Santiago. Bus Nte to Ancud, Puerto Montt, Osorno and Santiago daily; to Punta Arenas, Tur Bus, Ghisoni and Austral.

Local buses: frequent services to Chonchi, choose between buses (Cruz del Sur, Queilén Bus and others), minibuses and collective taxis (from Esmeralda y Chacabuco). Arroyo and Ocean Bus both run to **Cucao**, 1 a day off season, 0945 and 1600 in summer, US$2. To **Dalcahue** frequent services by Gallardo and Arriagada, also collective taxis from San Martín 815. To **Achao** via Dalcahue and Curaco de Vélez, Arriagada, 4 daily, 3 on Sun, last return from Achao 1730. To **Puqueldón** on the island of Lemuy, Gallardo, Mon-Fri 1315, US$2. To **Quemchi**, 2 a day, 1 hrs, US$2.50; to **Quellón**, Regional Sur and Trans Chiloé, frequent; to **Queilén**, Queilén Bus; to **Quemchi**, 2 a day, Queilén Bus.

DALCAHUE

21 km N of Castro, the wooden church dates from 1858, on older foundations. The market is on Sun, from 0700 to 1300;

good quality, but bargaining practically impossible. Tourist kiosk in season. Tenaún, 40 km E of Dalcahue, is an interesting fishing village with a good 18th-century church.

- **Accommodation D/E** *La Feria*, Rodríguez 17, T 641293, without bath, basic; **D/E** *Res Playa*, Rodríguez 9, basic; **E** *Hosp Puteman*, Freire 305, T 330, clean, basic; **E** *Res San Martín*, San Martín 1, T 641207, basic, clean, also meals.

- **Places to eat** *Restaurant La Dalca*, Freire 502, good food and service, rec.

- **Transport** Buses to Castro, hourly, 40 mins, US$1. Also collective taxis.

Quemchi, further N of Dalcahue on the E coast, has extensive beaches. From here you can take the coastal road N towards Ancud, offering coastal views and tanquil rural scenes of the small villages of E Chiloé.

- **Accommodation F** pp *Hosp El Embrujo*, Pedro Montt 431, T 262; **F** pp *Hosp La Tranquera*, Yungay 40, T 250, without bath, basic.

QUINCHAO

On the island of **Quinchao** is **Achao**, a quiet, pretty fishing village. Its wooden church, built in 1730 and saved by a change of wind from a fire which destroyed much of the town in 1784, is a fine example of Chilote Jesuit architecture. The original construction was without use of nails. There is a small museum, entry US$1.

- **Accommodation D** *Plaza*, Plaza de Armas, T 661283, with bath and breakfast, clean, good; **D/E** *Hosp Chilhue*, Zañartu 021, without bath, with breakfast, clean; **D** pp *Hosp Achao*, Serrano 061, 661373, with bath, good, clean; **E** pp *Hosp Sao Paulo*, Serrano 52, basic, poor beds, hot water; **D** pp *Hostería La Nave*, Prat y Aldea, T 661219, with bath, **E** pp without bath, with breakfast, restaurant with fine views over bay.

- **Places to eat** *Arrayan*, Zañartu 19; *Restaurant Central*, Delicias, simple, cheap, good; *Restaurant Mar y Velas*, on waterfront, good fish, cheap, rec.

- **Tourist offices** Serrano y Progreso (Dec-Mar only).

- **Transport** Ferry from Dalcahue, frequent; free for pedestrians and cyclists.

The island of **Mechuque** can be reached by boat from Dalcahue, dep Tues and Thur 1330, return Mon and Wed 1000,

2½ hrs, US$2.50 one way. There is one village on the island which offers splendid walks (accommodation either with the schoolteacher's son or with Sra Dina del Carmen Paillacar, E, good meals, rec).

CHONCHI

25 km S of Castro, this picturesque fishing village has rambling shingled houses painted in many colours and a lively wharf for fishing. The wooden church was built in 1754, remodelled in neo-classical style in 1859 – key from handicraft shop next door. There is another 18th century church at Vilopulli, 5 km N. Tourist information kiosk on main square open Jan-Feb only.

Museums Museo de las Tradiciones Chonchina, Centenario 116, artefacts donated by local families reflecting life in the early 20th century.

- **Accommodation A3** *Posada Antiguo Chalet*, Irrazzával, T 671221, **B** in winter, charming, beautiful location, very good; **B** *Cabañas Amankay*, Centenario 421, T 671367, homely, kitchen facilities, rec; **C** *Hostería Remis*, Irarrazával 27, T 671271, with bath, **E** without, lovely position on waterfront, good food, rec; **D** *Hosp Chonchi*, O'Higgins 379, T 671288, full board available, good value, rec; **D** *Esmeralda By The Sea*, on waterfront 100 m E of Restaurant *La Costanera*, T 671328 (Casilla 79), with breakfast, attractive, welcoming, English spoken, boat trips offered, information, highly rec; **D** *Huildin*, Centenario 102, T 671388, without bath, old fashioned, good beds, also *cabañas*, **A3**, garden with superb views, parking; *Res Los Tres Pisos*, Centenario 330, without bath, basic, overpriced; **D** *Hosp Mirador*, Alvarez 198, with breakfast, friendly, clean, rec; **E** pp Alvarez 891, clean, noisy, friendly, good breakfast; **E** *Res Turismo*, Andrade 299, T 671257, without bath, with breakfast; **E** Baker at Andrade 184, clean, friendly.

- **Places to eat** *La Parada*, Centenario 133, very friendly, good selection of wines, often closes evenings, rec; *El Alerce*, Aguirre 106, excellent value; *El Trebol*, waterfront; *La Quila*, Andrade 183. Cheapest place for lunch is *La Costanera*, on waterfront.

- **Banks & money changers** Nicolás Alvarez, Centenario 429, cash only.

- **Shopping** Handicrafts from *Opdech* (Oficina Promotora del Desarrollo Chilote), on the waterfront, and from the *parroquia*, next to the church (open Oct-March only).

• **Transport** Buses and taxis to Castro, frequent, US$0.75, from main plaza.

A visit to the island of **Lemuy** (*Pop* 4,200) is rec; 90 sq km, quiet, with good walking through undulating pastures and woodland (all roads unpaved). Good walks to Lincay, 5 km, or Lincura, 1-day expedition. Ferry service from Puerto Huicha, 4 km S of Chonchi, approx every 30 mins, foot passengers free, then, once across, 8 km to the main town, Puqueldón. One bus daily from Castro.

• **Accommodation & places to eat** E pp *Restaurant Lemuy* and *Café Amancay*, both clean, without bath, good.

Queilén, 46 km by unpaved road SE of Chonchi, is a pretty fishing village with a long beach and wooden pier.

• **Accommodation & places to eat** F pp *Pensión Chiloé*, without bath, basic; *Restaurant Melinka*, friendly.

• **Transport** Buses to Castro, Queilén Bus, 6 a day, 4 on Sat, 3 on Sun, 2 hrs, US$2.50.

CUCAO

From Chonchi an unpaved road leads W to **Cucao**, 40 km, one of two settlements on the W coast of Chiloé. At Km 12 is Huillinco, a charming village on Lago Huillinco (**E** pp *Res*, good food, or stay at the Post Office). At Cucao there is an immense 15 km beach with thundering Pacific surf and dangerous undercurrents.

• **Accommodation & places to eat** E pp *Hosp Paraíso*, friendly; E pp *Posada Cucao*, with breakfast, hot water, meals, friendly; E pp with full board or *demi-pension* at *Provisiones Pacífico* (friendly, good, clean, candles provided, no hot water), Sra Boreuel or with Sra Luz Vera, next to school, meals and good homemade bread, rec; E pp *Casa Blanca*, with breakfast. **Camping**: several campsites inc *Parador Darwin*, check prices carefully first. *Las Luminarias* sells excellent empanadas de *machas* (*machas* are local shell fish).

• **Transport** For buses from Castro see above; in season as many as 4 buses a day, last departure 1600, reduced service off-season; hitching is very difficult.

CHILOE NATIONAL PARK

The **Chiloé National Park**, which is in 2 sections, includes large areas of forest along the coast N of Cucao. At the entrance to the S sector, 1 km N of Cucao, there is an administration centre (limited information), small museum, guest bungalow for use by visiting scientists (applications to Conaf via your embassy) and a campsite, free firewood, no access by car (there are 2 more campsites on the sandy road that runs N past the park entrance). Park entry US$2.50. A path runs 3 km N from the administration centre to Laguna Huelde (many camp sites) and then N a further 12 km to Cole Cole (*refugio*, key kept at Conaf office at entrance, free camping, dirty) offering great views, best done on horseback (return journey to/from Cucao 9 hrs by horse). The next *refugio* is at Anay, 9 km further N (crossed by ferry, US$10). There are several other walks but signposting is limited. Maps of the park are available from Conaf in Castro (**NB** *refugios* are inaccurately located). Many houses in Cucao rent horses at US$2.50 per hour, US$22 per day. If you hire a guide you pay for his horse too. Horseflies are bad in summer (wear light clothing). The N sector of the park is reached by a path which runs S from Chepu (see page 805).

QUELLON

92 km S of Castro, is the southernmost port on Chiloé; fishing boats are built at the wharf, pleasant beaches. The launch *Puerto Bonito* sails 3 times daily in summer from the pier, US$12.50 to tour the bay passing Punta de Lapa, Isla Laitec and Quellón Viejo (old wooden church). A trip can also be made to Chaiguao, 11 km E where there is a small Sun morning market; horses can be hired US$2.50 per hour. Also kayaks with a guide, US$2.50 per hour; camping US$3.50.

Museums Museo de Nuestros Pasados, Ladrilleros 215, includes reconstructions of traditional Chilote house and mill.

• **Accommodation** A1 *Golfo Corcovado*, Vargas 680, T 681528, F681527, overlooking town, fine views, very comfortable; **D** *Playa*, P Montt 427, T 681278, with breakfast, without bath, clean; **E** pp *Leo-Man*, P Montt 445, T 681298, without bath, pleasant, good value, friendly; **E** pp *Res Estrella del Mar*, García 18, without bath, basic, poor value; **E** pp *El Colono*,

Freire y Ladrillero, without bath; **E** pp *El Chico Leo*, Aguirre Cerda 20,T 681567, without bath, basic; **E** pp *Res Esteban*, Cerda 155; **C/D** *Res El Tráfico*, P Montt 115, with bath, **E** pp without, with breakfast, parking; **E** pp *La Pincoya*, La Paz 422, T 681285; **E** pp *Hosp La Paz*, La Paz 370, with breakfast, hot water; **F** pp *Las Brisas*, P Montt 555, T 681413 without bath, basic; **F** pp *Turino Club Deportes*,La Paz 24, floor space and camping, cold water, kitchen facilities, basic, open Dec-Feb only. *Albergue*, **G** pp locals, **F** pp foreigners; dormitory accommodation. At Punta de Lapa, 7 km W are: *Leo Man*, chalets and *cabañas*; *Cabanas y Camping Las Brisas*.

● **Places to eat** *Rucantú* on waterfront, good food, good value. *El Coral*, 22 de Mayo, good, reasonably priced, superb views; *Fogón Las Quilas*, La Paz 053, T 206, famous for lobster, rec; *Hotel Leo-Man* serves good coffee, pleasant *comedor*; *Nuevo Amanecer*, 22 de Mayo 201, cheap, clean.

● **Banks & money changers** Banco del Estado, US$12 commission on TCs, credit cards not possible, no commision on US$ cash.

● **Tourist offices** Kiosk on the park, open mid-Dec to mid-March. Ask about *hospedajes* not listed in their information leaflet.

● **Transport** Buses to Castro, 2 hrs, frequent, Cruz del Sur, US$4, Trans Chiloé US$3; also services to Ancud and Puerto Montt. **Ferries** In summer only (2 Jan-8 Mar), the Transmarchilay ferry *Pincoya* sails to Chaitén on the mainland, Mon and Wed 1600, return departure Wed and Sat 0900, 5 hrs crossing, US$70-80/car, US$11 pp. The ship continues from Chaitén to Puerto Montt. The *Pincoya* also sails from Quellón to Puerto Chacabuco Sat 1600, all year round, 18 hrs, cars US$110, passengers US$20-27. If you take this ferry when heading S you miss a large section of the Carretera Austral; if you wish to see the Carretera's scenery, take the ferry to Chaitén. From 15 Mar to 29 Dec ferries go only from Pargua to Chaitén and Puerto Chacabuco. **Transmarchilay** office, Pedro Montt 451, Quellón T 681331. Enquire first, either in Santiago or Puerto Montt.

Archipelagic Chile: South from Puerto Montt

THE construction of the Carretera Austral has opened up the impressive landscapes of this wet and windy region of mountains, channels and islands. The main town is Coyhaique. A boat journey, either as a means of access, or for viewing the glacier at Laguna San Rafael gives an equally magnificent, but dif-ferent perspective.

Land and climate

South of Puerto Montt lies a third of Chile, but its land and its climate are such that, until recently, it has been put to little human use: less than 3% of the country's population lives here.

There is no real dry season. On the offshore islands and the western side of the Andes it is frequently wet and windy, particularly S of the Río Baker. North of that river, the summers are drier than the winters, but to the S, summers are windier and marginally wetter. Impenetrable forest covers much of the land, although in many parts there is stark evidence of the felling of trees which began in the 19th century and has accelerated during the last decade. Wood is used for construction, fencing and fuel; in this last respect it is in such demand in population centres like Coyhaique that in winter it costs as much as petrol. It is also increasingly exported, often as woodchips.

It is only the northern part, as far S as Cochrane, and the far S that are inhabited. South of Chiloé, for 1,100 km, there is a maze of islands – the tops of submerged mountains – separated by tortuous fjord-like channels, a veritable topographical hysteria. It is fortunate for shipping that this maze has a more or less connected route through it: down the channel between Chiloé and the mainland, across about 290 km of open sea beyond the southern tip of Chiloé and then down the Moraleda, Mesier, Inocentes and Smyth channels into the Straits of Magellan. In some places along this route the tide levels change by 12m. In one particular place two sharp-cut walls, 900m high, enclose the constricted channel which leads to Puerto Natales; here the waters are deeper than the cliffs are high and slack water lasts for 30 mins only. The Smyth Channel enters the Straits of Magellan at Cape Thamar. Jan and Feb are probably the best months for a trip to this region.

History

The original inhabitants were Tehuelches (Tzónecas, or Patagones), who lived on the pampa hunting guanacos, ñandúes (rheas) and hucmulcs (a large indigenous deer, now almost extinct), and Alacalufes (Kaweshour, or Canoeros), who were coast dwellers living off the sea. The arrival of the Spaniards, who called the region Trapananda, led to little more than exploration of the coast by navigators and missionaries. Inland exploration in the 19th century was greatly helped by Fitzroy's cartographical surveys; George Charles Muster, Enrique Simpson Baeza and Juan Steffen led the main expeditions, travelling up the rivers. Colonization followed the first commercial enterprises (timber extraction, cattle farming) on an E-W axis, from Argentina or the sea, with Puerto Aisén-Coyhaique becoming the most important route.

CARRETERA AUSTRAL

With the opening of the **Carretera Austral** (Southern Highway) in 1988, the Pan-American Highway was extended a further 1,098 km through southern Chile to Puerto Yungay. The highway is divided into three major sections: Puerto Montt-Chaitén (242 km) with 2-3 ferry crossings (see below); Chaitén-Coyhaique (435 km); and Coyhaique-Puerto Yungay (421 km). Unleaded fuel is available as far south as Cochrane.

PUERTO MONTT TO CHAITEN

Before setting out on this section, it is imperative to check when the ferries are running. If travelling by car carry plenty of fuel and spares and protect the windscreen and headlamps. It is essential that motorists make a reservation for the ferries: do this in Puerto Montt, rather than Santiago, at the Transmarchilay office, Angelmó 1666, T 254654.

The road (Ruta 7) heads E out of Puerto Montt, through Pelluco and after an initial rough stretch follows the shore of the beautiful Seno Reloncaví.

PARQUE NACIONAL ALERCE ANDINO

Ruta 7 passes the southern entrance of this national park which contains tall alerce trees, some over 1,000 years old (the oldest is estimated at 4,200 years old), and waterfalls. There are ranger posts at both entrances: 7 km from Correntoso (35 km E of Puerto Montt) at the N end of the park and 7 km E of Lenca at S end. Very little

> "Inside the cold rain forest (Bosque Valdiviano) one can feel and breathe its power – death and birth of the plants in the omnipresent humidity. Great variety of colours from dark green to silver and yellowish, scents of tepa tipo laurel and canelo (the Mapuche sacred tree), occasional sight of a colibri at the edges of the forest. Wear good walking boots for the path is very muddy. Watch out for leeches in the mud." Vladimir Stenek, Santiago.

information at ranger posts; map available from Conaf in Puerto Montt. Good campsite in the Park, 3 km from the S entrance, *refugio* at Laguna Sargazo.

● **Transport** To N entrance: take Fierro bus to Correntoso (or Lago Chapo bus which passes through Correntoso) from where it is a 2-km walk to the Park entrance. To S entrance: take any Fierro buses to Chaica, La Arena Contau and Hornopiren, getting off at Lenca sawmill, from where it is a 7-km walk (signposted).

Further S is the first ferry across the Reloncaví estuary at **La Arena** (Km 46). Allow 1½ hrs to get there from Puerto Montt.

● **Transport** Ferries La Arena-Puelche: 30 mins' crossing, US$4.65 for a car, 7 crossings daily. Ferry leaves Puelche for La Arena 45 mins before it returns from La Arena. Arrive at least 30 mins early to guarantee a place; buses have priority. Roll-on roll-off type operating all year.

58 km S of Puelche is **Río Negro**, also called **Hornopiren** after the volcano above it. Electricity 1900-0100. Río Negro is at the head of a fjord at the mouth of which is **Isla Llancahué**, good for hiking in the forests amid beautiful scenery. *Hotel Termas de Llancahué* charges C pp full board (excellent food), hot spring at the hotel. To get there, make arrangements by phoning 0965-38345. The hotel will send an open boat for you; the 1 hr crossing affords views of dolphins and fur seals. Efforts are under way to preserve areas of ancient emerald araucaria and alerce forest around Volcán Hornopiren, coordinated by Ancient Forest International and Codeff, the Chilean environmental organization.

● **Accommodation** Cabañas at Copec service station; **B** *Perlas del Reloncaví*, clean, pleasant, good restaurant, English and German spoken, highly rec; the cabins are usually taken before the rooms in the two other hotels, the **D** pp *Holiday Country*, on the road to Pichanco, hot shower, restaurant, and the *Hornopiren*, at the water's edge, next to the sawmill, highly rec, T Puerto Montt 255243.

● **Transport** Buses Fierro run daily 0800 and 1500 from Puerto Montt. There are no buses S from Río Negro. **Ferries** Río Negro – Caleta Gonzalo, Transmarchilay, Wed 1600, Thur-Sun 1500, 5 hrs (may be much longer if the ferry cannot dock in rough weather). Going N the ferry leaves Caleta Gonzalo at 0900, Mon, Thur, Fri, Sat, Sun. Fare for

vehicles over 4m US$88, under 4m US$75, passengers US$14, bicycles, US$9. Ferry operates Jan/Feb only and can be very busy; there can be a 2-day wait to get on the ferry. This trip may also use two ferry stages, the first, from Pinchanco up the Fiordo Leptepu, passing a narrow channel in which the German light cruiser *Dresden* hid from the British fleet in 1915. The crew was protected by the local German community. The second stage, after a 10 km stretch of road from Leptepu to Fiordo Largo, crosses the Fiordo Reñihue to Caleta Gonzalo.

South of Caleta Gonzalo there is a steep climb on a coarse gravel surface to Laguna Blanca. Caleta Santa Bárbara, a black sand beach with nice camping and swimming, is at Km 44. (**NB** Do not camp close to the water.) It is a further 12 km to Chaitén.

CHAITEN

The port of **Chaitén** has grown in importance because of the military camp and the new road. The town is quite well-laid out, but is a typical transit place, either full or empty, depending on the movements of the ferries from Puerto Montt and Quellón. Fuel is available (*phone code* 065).

● **Accommodation A2** *Mi Casa*, Av Nte, T 731285 – on a hill – rec, with bath, comfortable, or **E** in youth hostel, negotiable, the owners prefer you to eat in their restaurant (good); **B** *Hostería Schilling*, Av Corcovado 230, T 731295, on waterfront, with bath and heating (hot water is turned on or off on the intuition of the landlady, check your shower before entering), no restaurant; **D** *Continental*, Juan Todesco 18, T 731312, no heating nor private bath, but good meals, very helpful and friendly, rec; **D** *Cordillera*, Todesco y O'Higgins; **D** *Hostería Los Alerces*, Corcovado s/n, F 731266, hot water, clean, restaurant; **D** *Res Astoria*, O'Higgins 442, T 731263, with breakfast, shared bath, clean, bar downstairs; **E** pp *Hosp La Watson*, Ercilla 580, use of kitchen, clean, friendly; **E** pp *Casa Rita*, Rivero y Prat (**F** pp for floor space, **F** pp for camping), use of kitchen, clean, open all year, heating, rec; **E** pp Corcovada 466, family atmosphere, hot shower extra; **E** pp Martín Ruiz, Carretera Austral 1 km N, inc breakfast, friendly, nice views; **E** pp *Hosp Recoba*, Libertad 432, clean, friendly, good meals. *Los Arrayanes* campsite 4 km N, with hot showers and close to sea, good.

● **Places to eat** *Flamengo*, Corcovado, T 314, excellent, popular with travellers; *Mahurori*, Independencia 141.

• **Tour companies & travel agents** *Chaitur*, in bus terminal, friendly and helpful.

• **Transport Air** Flights Puerto Montt-Chaitén-Puerto Montt with Don Carlos, Juan Todesco 42, T 275, 1220 and 1600, Mon-Fri, 1220 on Sat, US$35. Also Aerosur daily except Sun, same fare.

Buses Artetur (Av Costanera) runs microbuses between Chaitén and Coyhaique, once a week (US$30, 12-14 hrs). The service depends very much on demand and in winter especially may not run all the way (ie only to La Junta). On the full service, the bus stops overnight in La Junta in winter but only briefly in summer. Other stops on request, but it is easier to go right through than pick up a bus on route. Similar services by Transportes San Rafael, Mon and Thur 1200, and B and V Tours (Libertad 432) summer only. Hitching the whole route takes about a week, but you must be prepared for a day's wait if you find yourself out of luck.

Ferries Port about 1 km from town. From 2 Jan to early Mar Transmarchilay ferries *Pincoya* and *Mailen* run between Chaitén, Puerto Montt and Quellón on Chiloé: sailings for Puerto Montt are on Mon 2200, Mon 2400, Thur 0900 and Fri 0900, 11 hrs; from Puerto Montt to Chaitén Tues 1200, Tues 1400, Thur 2200 and Fri 2000. Fares to Puerto Montt US$100/car over 4m, US$88 under 4m, US$16/deck passenger, seat US$20, bunk US$31. Sailings to/from Quellón and fares under Quellón. The Navimag ferry *Alejandrina* sails between Chaitén and Puerto Montt, no bunks, no fixed schedule. At other times of the year ferries from Chaitén go only twice a week to Pargua, 9-10 hrs, US$16 foot passengers. Check in advance for exact times; office Av Corcovado 266, T 731272. There is also a ferry to Puerto Montt for trucks, Ro-Ro *Mercedes*, Terminales Marítimos Chilenos, which will also take passengers but with no shelter, standing only, unless someone lets you get in their vehicle, once a week (twice a week Jan-Feb), 12 hrs, US$8. Office is in a hardware store (*ferretería*) on Juan Todesco, T 731333; in Puerto Montt, Chorillos y Pudeto, T 257259.

CHAITEN TO COYHAIQUE

25 km S of Chaitén is **Amarillo** (accommodation in village bar, E, breakfast US$1; meals at *Las Rosas* rec); 5 km E of the village are thermal baths (2 wooden sheds with very hot pool inside, US$3 pp, also outdoor swimming pool), camping possible, and one cabin for hire with woodstove and bath, sleeps 4, **B** (accommodation is being extended).

From the thermal baths it is possible to hike along **the old trail to Futaleufú**, 4-7 days, not for the inexperienced, be prepared for wet feet all the way. The trail follows the Río Michinmawida (passing the volcano of the same name) to Lago Espolón. A sporadic ferry crosses the lake taking cargo only to Futaleufú. Campsite at this end of the lake also has bungalows (see below). There is superb salmon fishing in the rivers, and the local people are very friendly.

Puerto Cardenas, 46 km S of Chaitén, lies on the northern tip of beautiful Lago Yelcho (out of 10 houses and a police post, there are 2 places to stay, inc **C** *Res Yelcho*, clean, full board available). Campsite (US$8 pp) 3 km S of the river crossing, ask the owners in a little white house nr the lake. At Km 60, on the western side of Lago Yelcho, a path leads to the glacier which can be clearly seen from Puente Ventisquero on the road (2 hrs' walk).

At **Villa Santa Lucía** (Km 81), a road branches E to the Argentine frontier at Futaleufú and Palena. Santa Lucía has 30 houses, a military camp, one small shop, bread from a private house, and accommodation on main street at No 7 (Sra Rosalía Cuevas de Ruiz, basic, meals available), No 13 (breakfast extra) and No 16 (not bad), all **F** pp, none has hot water.

The road to the border is single track, gravel, passable in a regular car, but best with a good, strong vehicle; the scenery is beautiful. Accommodation can be found at La Cabaña, Puerto Piedra (*Camping y Cabañas*, T 280) and **Puerto Ramírez** (*Hostería Río Malito* – Sr Soto – nearby, rooms, camping, fishing). At Puerto Ramírez the road divides: the N runs to **Futaleufú** and the southern one to Palena. 6 km before Futaleufú, turn left to Lago Espolón for campsite and cabins, E per bed, US$3.75 for a motorhome; gorgeous lake, warm enough for a quick dip (take care with the current). There is superb rainbow trout fishing in Lago Espolón, ask for the Valebote family's motorboat. The fishing is also excellent in Río Yelcho, Lago Yelcho and Río Futaleufú (the *Isla Monita Lodge* offers packages for anglers and non-anglers on a private island in Lago Yelcho, with fishing in many nearby locations; *Turismo Grant*, PO Box 52311, Santiago, T 639-5524, F 633-7133). See also **Fishing** under **Sport** in Information for Travellers. Aníbal, who owns the campsite, sells meat, bread, beer and soft drinks and will barbecue lamb. The area around Espolón and Futaleufú has a microclimate, 30°C in the day in summer, 5° at night.

● **Accommodation D** *Res Carahue*, O'Higgins 322, T 221; **E** pp *Hotel Continental*, Balmaceda 597, T 222, basic, hot water, clean, rec, cheap restaurant.

● **Transport Air** Aerosur flights from Chaitén Tues and Fri, US$62. **Buses** A microbus runs from Chaitén to Futaleufú on Tues, at least.

FRONTIER WITH ARGENTINA: FUTALEUFU

● **Chilean immigration**
in Futaleufú, 9 km W of the frontier. Allow 1½ hrs for formalities. The border is at the bridge over the Río Grande.

NB only transit visas are issued, which can cause problems. You must either leave within 10 days or renew your entry stamp at an immigration office

● **Entering Chile**
Continue from Futaleufú towards Puerto Ramírez, but outside Ramírez, take the unsigned right turn to Chaitén (left goes to Palena)

● **Exchange**
Change money in Futaleufú (poor rates); nowhere to change at the border.

● **Transport**
From Futaleufú a bus runs to the border, Tues and Fri 1300, 1300 approx, US$3, 30 mins (ask at the small grey store, Kitty, at the school corner on Balmaceda).

FRONTIER WITH ARGENTINA: PALENA

● **Chilean immigration**
At Palena, 8 km W of frontier.

NB Only transit visas are issued (see above under Futaleufú crossing).

● **Accommodation**
Several *pensiones* in Palena.

● **Transport**
Expreso Yelcho bus from Chaitén twice a week, US$12, 5½ hrs.

LA JUNTA

A drab, expensive village at the confluence of Río Rosselot and Río Palena, 151 km from Chaitén, 270 km from Coyhaique. The fishing is good and the walks to Lake Rosselot beautiful. A 74 km road heads E to Lago Verde; at Lago Risopatrón is a Conaf campsite.

● **Accommodation C** *Hostería Valdera*, Varas s/n, T 314105, inc breakfast, with bath, very good value; **E** pp *Copihue*, Varas 611, T 314140, few rooms but clean, without bath, hot water, good meals, changes money at very poor rates; **D** *Café Res Patagonia*, Lynch 331, T 314115, good meals.

● **Banks & money changers** If desperate to change money try the hotels, but bargain hard.

● **Transport** Fuel is available. Buses to Coyhaique, Artetur (Diego Portales 183), US$14.30, twice a week, also Transaustral twice a week US$15.

PUYUGUAPI

Puyuguapi (also spelt Puyuhuapi; *phone code* 068), 196 km S of Chaitén, at the end of the Puyuguapi Canal, is an intriguing town founded by Germans in 1935. The famous carpet factory can be visited. 18 km SW, accessible only by boat, are Termas de Puyuhuapi, several springs with 50°C water filling two pools nr the beach (baths cost US$6.50 pp, children under 12 US$4.40, take food and drink). Sr Alonso runs day-trips from Puyuguapi, US$30.

Parque Nacional Queulat nearby is, according to legend, the place where the rich town of Césares once was. In the park, 24 km S of Puyuguapi, are the beautiful Ventisquero Colgante (hanging glacier), new campsite nearby, US$3.50, and the Salto del Cóndor waterfall. Operation Raleigh opened a number of trails in the park (entry US$1; camping US$3.50). Boat trips on Laguna Tempano; 2 *hospedajes* near the glacier.

● **Accommodation L3-A1** *Hotel Termas de Puyuhuapi* (price depends on season and type of room), inc use of baths and boat to hotel, full board US$35 extra, good restaurant, rec. For reservations: Patagonia Connection, Fidel Oteíza 1921, Oficina 1006, Casilla 16417, Correo 9, Santiago, T 223-5567/225-6489, F (562) 274-8111 (in Puyuguapi T 325103). (See also under Puerto Montt **Shipping**.) Boat schedule from jetty, 2 hrs' walk from town, 0930, 1000, 1200, 1230, 1830, 1900, residents only, US$3 each way, 10 mins crossing. **B** pp *Res Alemana*, Otto Uebel 450, T 325118, a large wooden house on the main road, owned by Sra Ursula Flack Kroschewski, comfortable, highly rec; **C** pp *Hostería Ludwig*, on the road S, T 325131, excellent, often full; **E** pp *Hosp El Pino*, Hamburgo s/n, T 325117, homemade bread, friendly; **E** pp *pensión* of Sra Leontina Fuentes, Llantureo y Circunvalación, clean, hot water, good breakfast for US$1; **E** pp *Res Elizabeth*, Llantureo y Henríquez, inc breakfast, clean; **E** pp *pensión* at Tureo 18. **A3** *Cabañas Fiordo Quelat* (T Coyhaique 233302), rec. There is a dirty campsite by the sea behind the general store. The store is behind the service station, which sells fuel until 1930.

● **Places to eat** *Café Rossbach* with limited menu, not cheap, excellent salmon. There are 2 bars.

● **Transport** Bus transport out of Puyuguapi is very scarce. Artetur (O'Higgins 039, T 325101) to Coyhaique and La Junta twice a week, to Chaitén once a week (Tues), Transaustral twice a week to Coyhaique.

RIO CISNES

59 km S of Puyuguapi a road branches W and follows the Río Cisnes 35 km to **Puerto Cisnes** where you can buy food and find accommodation and petrol.

The Río Cisnes is rec for rafting or canoeing; 160 km of grand scenery, with modest rapids except for the horrendous drop at Piedra del Gato; there is a 150m cliff at Torre Bright Bank. Good camping in the forest.

● **Accommodation B** *Manzúr*, E Dunn 75, T 346453, *cabañas*; **D** pp *Hostal Michay*, Mistral 112, T 346462; **D** pp *Res El Gaucho*, Holmberg 140, T 346483, with breakfast, dinner available, welcoming, hot water; *pensión* at Carlos Condell y Dr Steffen, **D** pp, with breakfast, hot shower, friendly.

● **Transport** Buses Wed and Sun at 1100 to Coyhaique with Litoral, 5½ hrs, US$14, Trans Mañihuales daily US$14, Colectivos Basoli 2 a week, US$12.

Just S of the Río Cisnes is Villa Amengual (provisions, lodging). A few kilometres S, at Cisne Medio (no hotel, restaurant or telephone), 92 km S of Puyuguapi, there is a road, 104 km to La Tapera and to the Argentine border. Chilean immigration is 12 km W of the frontier, open daylight hours only. On the Argentine side the road continues to meet up with Ruta 40. 6 km S of Cisne Medio is the **Parque Nacional Lago Las Torres**, a wonderful lake with good fishing and a small Conaf campsite (free).

At Km 125 a road branches E to El Toqui copper mine. 23 km further S is **Villa Mañihuales**, connected by bus with Coyhaique (Trans Mañihuales, one a day except Sun).

● **Accommodation** There are at least 3 *pensiones*, inc **E** pp *Pensión Bienvenido*, clean, friendly, and restaurant; **E** pp *Villa Mañihuales*, friendly, breakfast, cabañas **A** (both right-hand side of road going S at southern end).

13 km S of Mañihuales the road forks W to Puerto Aisén, E to Coyhaique. At Villa Ortega on the Coyhaique branch, the *Restaurant Farolito* takes guests, **E** pp, rec.

PUERTO AISEN

426 km S of Chaitén, formerly the region's major port, it has been replaced by Puerto Chacabuco, 15 km to the W. They say it rains 370 days a year in **Puerto Aisén** (*Pop* 13,050; *Phone code* 067), quite an attractive town at the meeting of the rivers Aisén and Palos. There are few vestiges of the port left, just some boats high and dry on the river bank when the tide is out and the foundations of buildings by the river, now overgrown with fuchsias and buttercups. To see any maritime activity you have to walk a little way out of town to Puerto Aguas Muertas where the fishing boats come in. There is a good walk to Laguna Los Palos, 2 hrs.

A new bridge over the Aisén and paved road lead to **Puerto Chacabuco**; a regular bus service runs between the two. The harbour is a short way from the town. In season the *Patagonia* sails regularly to Termas de Chiconal, about 1 hr from Puerto Chacabuco, offering a good way to see the fjord, US$20, take own food. Services given below are in Puerto Aisén unless stated otherwise.

Local festival of folklore, 2nd week in November.

● **Accommodation** Hard to find, most is taken up by fishing companies in both ports. **In Puerto Aisén**: **D** *Plaza*, O'Higgins 237,

T 332784, without breakfast; **D** *Res Aisén*, Av Serrano Montaner 37, T 332725, good food, clean, full board available; **D** *Roxy*, Aldea 972, T 332704, friendly, clean, large rooms, highly rec, restaurant; **E** pp unnamed *hospedaje* at Serrano Montaner 471, T 332574, very pleasant and helpful, rec; **E** pp *Yaney Ruca*, Aldea 369, T 332583, clean, friendly. No campsite but free camping nearby. **In Puerto Chacabuco: A2** *Parque Turístico Loberías de Aisén*, Carrera 50, T 351115, F 351188, accommodation over-priced, excellent meals, climb up steps direct from port for drink or meal overlooking boats and mountains before boarding ferry; **D** *Moraleda*, O'Higgins, T 331155. No other places to buy food or other services.

● **Places to eat** *Gastronomía Carrera*, Cochrane 465, large, very good, popular.

● **Banks & money changers** Banco de Crédito, Prat, for Visa; **Banco de Chile**, Plaza de Armas only changes cash, not TCs.

● **Post & telecommunications Post Office**: on other side of bridge from Plaza de Armas. **Telephone Office**: on S side of Plaza de Armas, next to *Café Rucuray*, which posts boat information.

● **Tourist offices** In Municipalidad, Prat y Sgto Aldea, 1 Dec to end-Feb only, helpful.

● **Transport** Buses to **Puerto Chacabuco**, La Cascada on Serrano Montaner, to left of Sgto Aldea (main street) walking away from Plaza de Armas, 6 a day between 0800-1730, 30 mins, US$1; return 0830-1800; colectivo US$1.50 pp. La Cascada to **Coyhaique**, 4 a day between 0830-1900 (Sun and holidays between 0845 and 1930), US$3, 1½ hrs; Transaustral, Sgto Aldea 348, 4 a day; Don Carlos taxi-bus, 8 a day, US$3. Transaustral and La Cascada have daily buses between Coyhaique and Puerto Chacabuco.

Ferries Transmarchilay's *Colono* runs from Puerto Chacabuco via the Canal Moraleda to Puerto Montt, Mon 1600 and Wed 2200, 26 hrs (fares under Puerto Montt); meals are available. This service operates 2 Jan to early Mar only, and in this season the ship also makes an excursion to Laguna San Rafael each Sat at 2100, returning Mon 0800 (fares, inc food, US$105-225 pp, ranging from economy class to cabin). The *Colono's* schedules for the rest of the year on this route are not given in any timetable; enquire locally. Transmarchilay's *Pincoya* sails to Quellón on Chiloé Sun 1600, all year round (fares under Quellón). Navimag's *Evangelistas* sails each Thur and Sun from Puerto Chacabuco to Puerto Montt, taking about 24 hrs (fares under Puerto Montt, the *pionero* seats are quite spacious and comfortable and there is a cafeteria selling burgers, sandwiches, soft drinks, beer, hot beverages, etc); it too diverts from its schedule in

summer to run a 5-day trip to Laguna San Rafael, leaving Sat, from US$250. See under Puerto Montt **Shipping** for *Patagonia Express*. **Shipping Offices**: **Agemar**, Tte Merino 909, T 332716, Puerto Aisén; **Navimag**, Terminal de Transbordadores, Puerto Chacabuco, T 351111, F 351192; **Transmarchilay**, Av O'Higgins s/n, T 351144, Puerto Chacabuco. It is best to make reservations in these companies' offices in Puerto Montt, Coyhaique or Santiago (or, for Transmarchilay, in Chaitén or Ancud). For trips to Laguna San Rafael, see below; out of season, they are very difficult to arrange, but try Edda Espinosa, Sgto Aldea 943, or ask at *Restaurant Yaney Ruca* or *Restaurant Munich*.

The paved road from Puerto Aisén to Coyhaique passes through the **Parque Nacional Río Simpson**, with beautiful waterfalls and good views of the river and very good fly-fishing. There is a campsite near the turning to Santuario San Sebastián.

COYHAIQUE

Coyhaique, 420 km S of Chaitén (*Pop* put at 38,000; *Phone code* 067), the administrative and commercial centre of the region, is located in a large green valley surrounded by mountains. The town provides a good base for hiking and skiing excursions in the area.

Places of interest

There is a good **Museo Regional de la Patagonia Central** in the Casa de Cultura, Baquedano 310 (US$0.75, Tues-Sun 0900-1300, 1500-2000). The museum contains photos of early settlers, history, paleontology, fauna and archaeology. The town's plaza is pentagonal and on it stand the Cathedral, the Intendencia, the Liceo San Felipe Benicio and a handicraft market. When entering Coyhaique from the airport, look left from the bridge over the Río Simpson for the **Piedra del Indio**, a rock outcrop which looks like a face in profile.

Excursions

Excellent views of the Río Simpson valley from the hill, 4 hrs' walk N of town, at **Reserva Forestal Coyhaique**. South to the lakes Elizalde (good salmon fishing), Atravesado, Frío, Castor and Pollux. Skiing at El Fraile, 29 km SE, where there are 5 pistes and 2 lifts, cafeteria, equipment

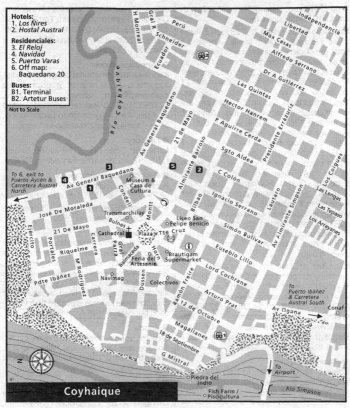

Hotels:
1. Los Ñires
2. Hostal Austral

Residenciales:
3. El Reloj
4. Navidad
5. Puerto Varas
6. Off map:
   Baquedano 20

Buses:
B1. Terminal
B2. Artetur Buses

Not to Scale

Coyhaique

hire (season June to Sept). **Reserva Forestal Mañihuales**, 76 km from Coyhaique, was largely destroyed by forest fires in the 1940s, but the views are good. **Monumento Natural Dos Lagunas**, lakes Toro and Bonito, 21 km on the Coyhaique Alto road, is worth a visit. Entry to all 3 parks about US$1; camping US$4.

Local information
● Accommodation

In summer rooms are in very short supply; the tourist office has a full list of all types of accommodation, but look out for notices in windows since any place with less than 6 beds does not have to register with the authorities (several on Baquedano and Almte Simpson).

A2 *Los Ñires*, Baquedano 315, T 232261, with

breakfast, comfortable, parking; **A2** *Cabañas La Pasarela*, T 234520, Km 1.5 Carretera a Aisén, good atmosphere, *comedor*; **A2** *Cabañas Río Simpson*, T 232183, Km 3 road to Pto Aysén, cabins for 5, or 2, fully-equipped, horse hire, fishing; **A3** *Cabaña Abedules*, 18 de Septiembre 463, F 232396, al Plaza Angol, price/cabin for 5, hot water, heating, kitchen, TV, suitable for families; **A3** *Austral*, Colón 203, T 232522, hot water, clean, English spoken, tours arranged, friendly, rec.

B *Cabaña San Sebastián*, Freire 554, T 231762, with bath and breakfast; **B** *Res El Reloj*, Baquedano 444, T 231108, with restaurant.

C *Licarayen*, Carrera 33A, T 233377 (Santiago T 743-1294) with bath and breakfast, rec; **C** *Res Puerto Varas*, Serrano 168, T 233689, without bath, check which of the bathrooms has hot water, restaurant and bar, basic, tatty.

D pp *El Serrano*, Serrano 91, T 235522, with breakfast, friendly, clean, rec.

E pp *Hosp* at Baquedano 20, T 232520, Patricio y Gedra Guzmán, room in family home (also 3 flats), use of kitchen, breakfast with homemade bread, tent sites with bathroom and laundry facilities down by the river, English spoken, most hospitable, rec; **D** *Hosp* Hermina Mansilla, 21 de Mayo 60, with breakfast, highly rec; **E** pp Manuel Torres, Barroso 957, hot water, use of kitchen, good; **F** pp *Res Navidad*, Baquedano 198, T 235159, without bath or breakfast, comedor, hot showers, use of kitchen, clean; **E** pp *Hosp Pierrot*, Baquedano 130, T 221315 with breakfast, clean, quiet. Several cheap places on Av Simpson, eg **E** *Casa El Fondo*, No 417, clean, friendly; **F** pp at No 649; **E** pp *Los Cuatro Hermanos* Colón 495, T 232647, without breakfast (more with), hot water, clean; **E** pp Baquedano 274, small rooms, very good; **E** pp *Hosp Lautaro*, Lautaro 532, T 231852, clean, comfortable, kitchen facilities, large rooms, rec. Youth hostel in summer at one of the schools (it changes each year), **F** pp with sleeping bag.

Camping: at Baquedano 20, see above. There are many camping sites in Coyhaique and on the road between Coyhaique and Puerto Aisén, eg at Kms 1, 2 (*Camping Alborada*, US$8.50, T 231014, hot shower), 24, 25, 35, 37, 41, 42 (*Camping Río Correntoso*, T 232005, US$15/site, showers, fishing, Automobile Club discount) and 43. Sernatur in Coyhaique has a full list of all sites in XI Región.

● **Places to eat**
Loberías de Chacabuco, Barroso 553, good seafood, slow service; *La Olla*, Prat 176, good, very popular; *Café Oriente*, C 21 de Mayo y Condell 201, good bakery, tea; *Moneda de Oro*, Prat 431, good food, good value; *Café Kalu*, Prat 402, serves set meals, hamburgers; *Café Ricer*, Horn 48, cheap; *Cafetería Alemana*, Condell 119, nice, excellent cakes and coffee; *Lito's*, Lautaro 147, next to Bus Terminal, good food and atmosphere; *Casino de Bomberos*, Gen Parra 365, wide range, cheap. A good bar is *Pub*, 12 de Octubre 361, nice atmosphere and music; around the corner is *Bar West*, Western style.

● **Airline offices**
LanChile, Gen Parra 215, T 231188; Ladeco, Dussen y Prat 188, T 231300; **Don Carlos**, Cruz 63, T 231981.

● **Banks & money changers**
Banco Osorno, Prat 340, T 232214, for cash advance on Visa, and Turismo Prado, 21 de Mayo 417, T/F 231271, both accept TCs. Banco Santander, Condell 100, Mastercard ATM. For dollars TCs and Argentine pesos **Lavaseco** on Gen Parra. **Fincard** (Mastercard), Prat 340, local 1, T 233026, Mon-Fri 0900-1400, 1530-1900, Sat 0930-1330; at same address, oficina 208, *El Libertador*, T 233342.

● **Language schools**
Baquedano International Language School, Baquedano 20, at *Hosp* of Sr Guzmán (see **Accommodation** above), T 212520, F 232500: US$300/week course inc lodging and all meals, 4 hrs a day person-to-person tuition, other activities organized at discount rates.

● **Laundry**
Lavamatic, Bilbao 198; *QL*, Bilbao 160; *Universal*, Gen Parrá 55; *Lottie*, Baquedano 1259.

● **Post & telecommunications**
Post Office: Cochrane 202, open Mon-Fri 0830-1230, 1430-1800, Sat 0830-1200.
Telephone Office: at Barroso 626, open till 2200, opens on Sun about 0900.

● **Shopping**
Feria de Artesanía on the plaza; *Cema-Chile* on plaza, between Montt and Barroso. Large well-stocked supermarkets: *Brautigam*, Horn, Prat y Bilbao; *Central*, Magallanes y Bilbao, open daily till 2230; 2 small ones on Prat, Nos 480 and 533, open Sun. Food, especially fruit and vegetables, is more expensive than in Santiago but cheaper than Argentina.

● **Sports**
Excellent opportunities for fishing on the Río Simpson and Lagos Frío and Pollux, rainbow trout is the main catch. See **Fishing** under **Sport** in Information for travellers.

● **Tour companies & travel agents**
Turismo Prado, address in **Banks & money changers** above; *Expediciones Coyhaique*, Bolívar 94, T/F 232300. Both offer tours of local lakes and other sights, arrange Laguna San Rafael trips, etc; *Prado* does historical tours, while *Expediciones* does fishing trips and excursions down the Río Baker. *Turismo Queulat*, 21 de Mayo 1231, T/F 231441, trips to Queulat glacier, adventure and nature tourism, fishing, etc. *Res Serrano*, C Serrano, organizes trips to Lago Elizalde and Lago Atravesado, US$15 pp. *Aventura*, Bilbao 171, T 234748, offers rafting; *45 Sur*, 12 de Octubre 253, T 234599, horseriding, good value; *Alex Prior*, T 234732, for fly fishing. Tours only operate in season.

● **Tourist offices**
Cochrane 320, T 231752. **Conaf**: office, Ogana 1060. Maps (photocopies of 1:50,000 IGM maps) from Dirección de Vialidad on the square.

● **Transport**
Local Bicycle rental: *Figón*, Simpson y Colón.

Bicycle spares from several shops on Simpson. **Car hire**: **Automóvil Club de Chile**, Bolívar 254, T 231649, rents jeeps and other vehicles. **Budget**, Parra 215; **Traeger-Hertz**, Baquedano 457; **Economy**, Carrera 339, T 233363, cars may be taken across Argentine border, may be returned to a different office; **Automundo AVR**, Bilbao 509. 4WD rec for Carretera Austral. Fuel is available in Coyhaique, several stations. **Taxis**: US$5 to airport (US$1.65 if sharing); fares in town US$1.35. 50% extra after 2100. Colectivos congregate at Prat y Bilbao, average fare US$0.50.

Air Airport about 5 km from town (inc a steep climb up and down to the Río Simpson bridge). Air taxi to visit glaciers, US$350 (5 passengers), also to southern archipelagic region. Don Carlos to Chile Chico (Tues, Thur, Sat), and Cochrane (Wed, Fri, 45 mins, rec only for those who like flying, with strong stomachs, or in a hurry).

Buses Terminal at Lautaro y Magallanes; most buses leave from here, but not all. To/from **Puerto Montt**, via Bariloche, all year, Turibus, Baquedano 1171, T 231333, Tues and Fri 1600, US$28.50, with connections to Osorno, Valdivia, Temuco, Santiago and Castro. To **Puerto Aisén**, Transaustral, Baquedano 1171, T 231333, 4 a day, 5 on Sun, La Cascada (T 231413), 4 daily, and Don Carlos taxi-bus, Subteniente Cruz 63, T 232981, US$3, 8 a day, 3 on Sun; to **Puerto Chacabuco**, Transaustral Thur and Sun, La Cascada 3 times daily, US$3.25. **Puerto Cisnes** daily with Litoral, Baquedo e Independencia, T 232903, Tues and Sat at 1130, US$12.85, or Colectivos Basoli, T 232596, Thur and Sun 1200, same price. There are daily buses to **Mañihuales**, Trans Mañihuales (daily 1700) and Litoral. To **Balmaceda** and **Puerto Ibáñez**, Buses Ruta Sur, T 232788.

To **Puerto Ibáñez** on Lago Carrera, the Chilean section of Lago Buenos Aires colectivos connect with *El Pilchero*, from *El Gran Calafate*, C Prat, 3 hrs, book the day before, US$7; to Bajada Ibáñez, Aerobus from bus terminal, Mon, Wed, Fri 1000, return next day, US$5.45, and Pudú, T 231000/6, Tues and Sat 0815.

Buses on the **Carretera Austral**: N to **Chaitén**, with Artetur, Baquedano 1347, T 233768, F 233367, Wed 0900, US$30, overnight stop in La Junta, extra service on Sun in summer, in winter may go only as far as La Junta, US$14.30. Similar service by Transportes San Rafael, 18 de Sept 469, T 233408, Mon and Thur 0900 in summer, 11 hrs, US$30 and B and V Tours, Simpson 1037. Transaustral goes to La Junta via Puyuguapi, US$15, Tues and Sat. To **Puerto Montt**, Tues and Fri US$35. South to **Cochrane** Pudú, at terminal, T 231008, Don Carlos and Río Baker Taxis (T 231052), all 3 times a week, charging US$23, 10-12 hrs.

To Argentina: options are given below and under Balmaceda, Chile Chico and Cochrane. Many border posts close at weekends. If looking for transport to Argentina it is worth going to the local Radio Santa María, Bilbao y Ignacio Serrano, and leaving a message to be broadcast.

Shipping: Transmarchilay, 21 de Mayo 147, T 231971, Tx 377003 MARCHI CK. **Navimag**, Ibáñez 347, T 233306, F 233386.

FRONTIER WITH ARGENTINA: COYHAIQUE ALTO

On the Argentine side the road leads through Río Mayo to Sarmiento and Comodoro Rivadavia.

● **Chilean immigration**
At Coyhaique Alto, 43 km E of Coyhaique, 6 km W of the frontier, open May-Aug 0800-2100, Sept-April 0700-2300.

● **Transport**
To **Comodoro Rivadavia**, Empresa Giobbi, Coyhaique bus terminal, T 232067, Tues, Thur, Sat 0830, US$30, 12-13 hrs, only twice a week June-Sept.

SOUTH OF COYHAIQUE

The Carretera Austral continues S: at Km 35 is **El Blanco**, a hamlet with *pensión* at *Restaurant El Blanco* (or **F** pp *El Nuevo* – breakfast extra) and shop. At Km 41 a branch road E leads to **Balmaceda** on the Argentine frontier at Paso Huemules (no accommodation). Chilean immigration is open May-July 0800-2100, Sept-April 0700-2100.

● **Transport Air** Balmaceda airport serves Coyhaique. LanChile and Ladeco flights from Santiago via Puerto Montt. Taxi from airport to Coyhaique, 1 hr, US$6, minibus US$4.50. **Buses** Daily to Coyhaique, 0800, US$1.70.

LAGO GENERAL CARRERA

Straddling the frontier, Lago General Carrera (Lago Buenos Aires in Argentina), covers 2,240 sq km. The lake itself is a beautiful azure blue; the Chilean end is predominantly Alpine and the Argentine end dry pampa. The major eruption of Volcán Hudson in 1991, polluted parts of the lake and many rivers, but the waters are now clear. The effects can still be seen in a metre-thick layer of ash on the ground. The region prides itself in having the best climate in Southern Chile with some 300 days of sunshine; much fruit is grown as a result. Rainfall is very low but strong winds are common. The main towns are Puerto Ibáñez, on the N shore, Chile Chico on the S.

Puerto Ibáñez is reached by taking a branch road, 31 km from the Carretera Austral at Km 88. 6 km away are some grand waterfalls on the Río Ibáñez.

● **Accommodation** E pp *Ibañez*, Bertrán Dixon 31, T 423227 clean, warm, hot water; D *Hostería Doña Amalia*, Bajada Río Ibañez. Fuel available at Luis A Bolados 461 (house with 5 laburnum trees outside); it's sold in 5-litre containers.

● **Transport Minibus**: to Coyhaique, 2½ hrs, US$7. There is a road to Perito Moreno, Argentina, but no public transport. **Ferries** The car ferry, *El Pilchero*, sails between Puerto Ibáñez and Chile Chico, 4 times a week. Fares for cars US$33, for passengers US$3.50, 2¾ hr crossing, bicycles US$2.50. Number of passengers limited to 70; reservations possible. Buses and jeeps meet the ferry in Puerto Ibáñez for Coyhaique.

Two alternative routes to Chile Chico are through Argentina, or on the newly-opened long route around the lake.

The Carretera Austral branches off the Coyhaique-Puerto Ibáñez road 97 km S of Coyhaique. It goes through Villa Cerro Castillo (small supermarket, *Res* at Aguirre Cerda 35, D with good meals, two other *residenciales*), named after the fabulous nearby mountain, which looks like a fairytale castle, with pinnacles jutting out of thick snow. This and other peaks in the northern wall of the Río Ibáñez valley, are in the **Reserva Nacional Cerro Castillo** (*guardería* on the Senda Ibáñez, opp Laguna Chinguay, open Nov-Mar, camping US$2.75, picnic entry US$1.15). The Carretera climbs out of the valley, passing the aptly-named Laguna Verde and the Portezuelo Cofré. It descends to the boggy Manso valley, with a good campsite at the bridge over the river, watch out for mosquitoes (this area was seriously affected by the ash from Volcán Hudson). The road then goes on to **Bahía Murta**, 5 km off the Carretera, at Km 198, on the northern tip of the central 'arm' of Lago General Carrera.

● **Accommodation** E pp *Res Patagonia*, Pasaje España; E pp *Hostería Lago Gen Carrera*, Av 5 de Abril, welcoming, excellent meals, also has cabin with own store; free camping by lake, good view of Cerro Castillo.

The road follows the lake's western shore; the colour of the water is an unbelievable blue-green, reflecting the mountains that surround it and the clouds above. At **Río Tranquilo**, Km 223, where the buses stop for lunch fuel is available at the ECA store from a large drum (no sign).

● **Accommodation** D pp *Res Los Pinos*, 2 Ote 41, basic; E pp *Cabañas Jacricalor*, 1 Sur s/n; E pp *Res Carretera Austral*, 1 Sur 223.

At the SW tip of Lago Carrera, at El Maitén, 50 km S of Río Tranquilo, a road branches off E along the S shore of the lake towards Chile Chico. At **Puerto Guadal**, 10 km E, there are shops, a post office and petrol. Bus fare Coyhaique-Puerto Guadal (en route to Cochrane) US$17.

● **Accommodation & places to eat** E pp *Hostería Huemules*, Magnolia 382, T 411212, with breakfast, good views; E pp *Res Maitén*, Las Magnolias. *Restaurant La Frontera*, Los Lirios y Los Pinos.

Further E along the shore are the villages of Mallín Grande and **Fachinal** (no accommodation though people will let you stay for free if you have a sleeping bag). Beyond Fachinal, take care if driving, there are dangerous, unprotected precipices.

CHILE CHICO

A quiet, friendly but dusty town on the lake shore (*Pop* 2,200) has an annual festival at end-January.

● **Accommodation** B *Hostería de la Patagonia*, Camino Internacional s/n, full board, clean, excellent food, English, French and Italian spoken, trekking, horse-riding and whitewater rafting organized (Casilla 91, Chile Chico, XI Region, T 411337, F 411444); rec; E pp *Casa Quinta No me Olvides/Manor House Don't Forget Me*, *hospedaje* and camping, Camino Internacional s/n, clean, cooking facilities, warm, bathrooms, hot showers, honey, eggs, fruit and vegetables for sale, rec, tours arranged to Lago Jeinimeni and Cueva de las Manos; E pp *Plaza*, O'Higgins y Balmaceda, basic, clean, rec;.E pp *Hosp Don Luis*, Balmaceda 175, clean, meals available. **Camping**: free campsite at Bahía Jarra, 15 km E.

● **Places to eat** Apart from *Residenciales*: *Cafetería Elizabeth y Loly* on Plaza serves coffee and delicious icecream and cakes, expensive. Supermarket on B O'Higgins.

● **Banks & money changers** It is very difficult to change dollars (*Café Elizabeth y Loly* changes dollars at bank rate in small amounts); change Argentine pesos in shops and cafés on main street (very poor rates).

● **Tourist offices** On O'Higgins; ask here or at the Municipalidad for help in arranging tours.

● **Transport Minibuses**: are run by 3 companies along the S side of the lake between Chile Chico and Puerto Guadal, up to 3 times a week each, US$9. These connect Puerto Guadal with Pudú service for Cochrane. Minibus to Coyhaique, frequency varies, US$9, 2¾ hrs. Flights to/from Coyhaique (see above).

FRONTIER WITH ARGENTINA: CHILE CHICO

● **Chilean immigration**
open Sept-April 0700-2300, May-Aug 0800-2100.

● **Transport**
Minibuses run from Chile Chico to Los Antiguos on the Argentine side, US$3, ¾ hr inc formalities, ask around for times; from here connections can be made to Perito Moreno, Caleta Oliva and Río Gallegos

Reserva Nacional Lago Jeinimeni

J M Bibby (The Wirral) writes: "60 km S of Chile Chico lies the **Reserva Nacional Lago Jeinimeni**, covering breathtaking snow-capped peaks, impressive cliffs, waterfalls, small glaciers and Lakes Jeinimeni and Verde. The reserve contains huemel deer, pumas and condors. Activities include fishing for salmon and rainbow trout, trekking and rowing. A good map is essential. Entrance fee US$1, camping US$2.75 (take all your requirements). Access only between Nov and Mar owing to high river levels. Lifts may be possible from Chile Chico: try Juan Núñez, Hernán Trizzando 110 for a lift on a timber truck or ask in the Conaf office."

The country to the S and W of Chile Chico, with weird rock formations and dry brush-scrub, provides good walking for the mountaineer. The northern and higher peak of Cerro Pico del Sur (2,168m) can be climbed by the agile from Los Cipres (beware of dogs in farmyard).

You will need a long summer's day and the 1:50,000 map. Follow the horse trail until it peters out, then navigate by compass or sense of direction until the volcano-like summit appears. After breaching the cliff ramparts at an obvious point, there is some scrambling and a 10-ft pitch to the summit: indescribable views of the Lake and Andes. (Brian Spearing).

South of El Maitén the Carretera Austral becomes steeper and more bendy (in winter this stretch, all the way to Cochrane, is icy and dangerous). Just past **Puerto Bertrand**, a good place for fishing (dormitory-style accommodation available – *Casa de Huéspedes*, and **A3** *Hostería Campo Baker*, one small shop), is a sign to the Nacimiento del Río Baker, with the most abundant water of any Chilean river. Note how the colours of the rivers and lakes change in this region. The road climbs up to high moorland, passing the confluence of the Ríos Neff and Baker, before winding into Cochrane. The scenery is splendid all the way; in the main the road is rough but not treacherous. Watch out for cattle on the road and take blind corners slowly.

COCHRANE

Cochrane (*Pop* 2,000), 345 km S of Coyhaique, sits in a hollow a little distance W of Lago Cochrane. It is a simple place, sunny in summer, good for walking and fishing.

Northeast of Cochrane is the **Reserva Nacional Tamango**, administered by Conaf in two sectors (Tamango, 9 km by dirt track, and Húngaro, 4 km, which reaches down to Lago Cochrane). In the Húngaro sector are a few remaining huemules (deer – two radio-tagged); there are also guanaco in the pampa part, foxes, lots of birds including woodpeckers and hummingbirds and lenga forest. It is inaccessible in the four winter months. Ask in the Conaf office on the square (T 422164) about visiting because some access is through private land and tourist facilities are rudimentary, entry US$1. The views from the reserve are superb, over the town, the nearby lakes and to the Campo de Hielo Nte to the W.

● **Accommodation** **B** pp *Hostería Wellmann*, Las Golondrinas 36, T 522171, hot water, comfortable, warm, good meals, rec; **D** pp *Res Rubio*, Tte Merino 04, T 522173, Sra Elva Rubio, very nice, breakfast inc, lunch and dinner extra; **E** pp *Res Austral Sur*, Sra Sonia Salazar, Prat s/n, T 522150, breakfast inc, hot water, also very nice; **D** *Residencia Cero a Cero*, Lago Brown 464, T 522158, with breakfast, welcoming. In summer it is best to book rooms in advance.

● **Places to eat** *Belén*, Esmeralda 301; *Café* at Tte Merino 502.

● **Transport** Bus companies: Pudú *Bottillería Quiaco*, Tte Merino; **Don Carlos**, *Res Austral Sur*; Río Baker Taxis, Río Colonia. All run 3 buses a week to Coyhaique, US$23. Petrol is available, if it hasn't run out, at the Empresa Comercial Agrícola (ECA). Horses can be hired for excursions in the surrounding countryside, ask around, eg at *Hostería Wellmann*. **To Argentina**: 17 km N of Cochrane, a road through Villa Chacabuco and Paso Roballos (78 km), enters Argentina; no public transport, road passable in summer but often flooded in spring. If hitching, allow a week.

The Carretera has been constructed a further 122 km S of Cochrane to Puerto Yungay, with 50 km of the final stretch to Villa O'Higgins completed. En route, it bypasses Tortel, a village built on a hill above the sea. It has no streets, no proper plan, only wooden walkways ('no hay ni una bicicleta'). It trades in wood with Punta Arenas and fishes for shellfish (such as *centolla* and *loco*). Access is by Don Carlos plane, by horse, mountain bike or on foot, several days journey from Cochrane on a good track by the Río Baker (several river crossings by boat), or by kayak down the Río Baker.

PARQUE NACIONAL LAGUNA SAN RAFAEL

Some 150 nautical miles S of Puerto Aisén is the **Laguna San Rafael**, into which flows a glacier, 30m above sea level, and 45 km in length. It calves small icebergs, carried out to sea by wind and tide. The thick vegetation on the shores, with snowy peaks above, is typical of Aisén. The glacier is one of a group of four that flow in all directions from Monte San Valentín.

This icefield is part of the **Parque Nacional Laguna San Rafael** (1.74 million ha), regulated by Conaf.

Park entry fee is US$4.65. At the glacier there is a small ranger station which gives information; a pier and two paths have been built. One path leads to the glacier. The rangers are willing to row you out to the glacier in calm weather, a 3-hr trip.

Robert af Sandeberg (Lidingö, Sweden) describes this journey as follows: "The trip in the rowboat is an awesome venture. At first it is fairly warm and easy to row. Gradually it gets colder when the wind sweeps over the icy glacier (be sure to take warm clothes – a thick sweater, and waterproof jacket are rec – Ed). It gets harder to row as small icebergs hinder the boat. Frequently somebody has to jump onto an icefloe and push the boat through. The glacier itself has a deep blue colour, shimmering and reflecting the light; the same goes for the icebergs, which are an unreal, translucent blue. The glacier is very noisy; there are frequent cracking and banging sounds, resembling a mixture of gun shots and thunder. When a hunk of ice breaks loose, a huge swell is created and the icebergs start rocking in the water. Then great care and effort has to be taken to avoid the boat being crushed by the shifting icebergs; this is a very real danger."

In the national park are puma, pudu pudu (minature deer), foxes, dolphins, occasional sealions and sea otters, and many species of bird. Walking trails are limited (about 10 km in all) but a lookout platform has been constructed, with fine views of the glacier.

● **Transport** The only way there is by plane or by boat: Air Taxi from Coyhaique (Don Carlos), US$110 each if party of 5; some pilots in Puerto Aisén will fly to the glacier for about US$95, but many are unwilling to land on the rough airstrip. The glacier is best seen from the sea: the official cruises are: *Skorpios I* and *II* (see under Puerto Montt); Navimag's *Evangelistas* and Transmarchilay's *Colono* (see under Pto Chacabuco); *Patagonia Express* (see under Puerto Montt); *Pamar*, Pacheco Altamirano 3100, T 256220, Puerto Montt, Sept-Mar only; Compañía Naviera Puerto Montt has 2 vessels: the *Quellón*, with 6-day, 6-night tours to the Laguna from

Puerto Montt via various ports and channels (US$900 not inc flight from Santiago), and *Lago Yelcho*, 2-night trips from Puerto Chacabuco 3 times a week, US$145, in Santiago Av Providencia 199, p 5°, T 274-8150, F 205-2197; Puerto Montt Diego Portales 882, T/F 252547; Puerto Chacabuco T 351106. *Odisea* and *Visun*, motorized sailing boats, Dec to Mar, in Santiago, Alameda B O'Higgins 108, local 120, T 633-0883, in Puerto Aysén, Sgto Aldea 679, T 332908, 6-day trips from Puerto Chacabuco to Laguna San Rafael. Various private yachts can be chartered in Puerto Montt for 6-12 passengers to Laguna San Rafael. Local fishing boats from Chacabuco/Puerto Aisén take about 18-20 hrs each way, charging the same as the tourist boats. Ask for Jorge Prado at the port (he takes a minimum of 7, more expensive than others); Andino Royas, Cochrane 129; Justiniano Aravena, Dr Steffen 703; Rodrigo Azúcar, Agemar office, T 332716; or Sr Ocuña, ask at the port. These unauthorized boats may not have adequate facilities.

NB If you plan to go to Laguna San Rafael by boat, check first with the Gobernación Marítima in Puerto Aisén that the boat is licensed for the trip (very few are).

Chilean Patagonia

THE glacial regions of southern Patagonia and Chilean Tierra del Fuego. Punta Arenas and Puerto Natales are the two main towns, the latter being the gateway to the Torres del Paine and Balmaceda national parks. In summer, a region for climbing, hiking, boats trips and the southernmost crossings to Argentina.

Land and climate

Magallanes (XII Región), which includes the Chilean part of Tierra del Fuego, has 17.5% of Chile's total area, but it is inhabited by under 1% of Chile's population.

In summer the weather is most variable, with temperatures seldom rising above 15°C. In winter snow covers the country, except those parts near the sea, making many roads more or less impassable, except on horseback. Strong, cold, piercing winds blow, particularly during the spring, when they may exceed 100 km an hour. The dry winds parch the ground and prevent the growth of crops, except in sheltered spots and greenhouses. When travelling in this region, protection against the sun's ultraviolet rays is essential.

For much of this century, sheep breeding was the most important industry, before being replaced after 1945 by oil. Although oil production has ceased, large quantities of natural gas are now produced and coal is mined near Punta Arenas. Sheep farming continues to be important: about 50% of all Chilean sheep are in the Magallanes region. Tourism is growing rapidly, making an increasingly important contribution to the area's economy.

PUNTA ARENAS

Punta Arenas (*Pop* 115,000; *Phone code* 061), the most southerly city in Chile, and capi⌐ ⌐f XII Región, 2,140 km S of San-

tiago, lies on the eastern shore of the Brunswick Peninsula facing the Straits of Magellan at almost equal distance from the Pacific and Atlantic oceans. It is the centre of the local sheep farming industry and exports wool, skins, and frozen meat. It is also the home of La Polar, the most southerly brewery in the world. Good roads connect the city with Puerto Natales, 247 km N, and with Río Gallegos in Argentina. Punta Arenas has certain freeport facilities; the Zona Franca is 3½ km N of the centre, on the righthand side of the road to the airport.

Originally founded as a penal colony in the 19⌐ century, its heyday was in the years

Punta Arenas

Hotels:
1. Cabo de Hornos
2. Hostal de la Patagonia
3. Los Navegantes
4. Mercurio
5. Plaza and Residencial París
6. Residencial Sonia Kuscevic
7. Ritz
8. Savoy
Buses:
1 Austral
2 Fernández & Pingüino
3 Sur

Not to Scale

before the opening of the Panama Canal in 1914. The city has expanded rapidly, particularly in recent years, but remains tranquil and pleasant. Several new hotels have been built in response to increased tourism. **NB** Calle Pedro Montt runs E-W, while Calle Jorge Montt runs N-S.

Places of interest

Although there are many architectural styles, it retains a number of interesting buildings from the turn of the century. See especially the interiors of the Museum of Regional History (see below) and of the **Teatro Cervantes** (now a cinema). In the **Plaza de Armas** (Plaza Muñoz Gamero), is a statue of Magellan with a mermaid and 2 Fuegian Indians at his feet. According to local wisdom those who rub the big toe of one of the Indians will return to Punta Arenas. The cemetery, at Av Bulnes 929, is even more fantastic than the one at Castro (Chiloé), with a **statue of Indiecito**, the little Indian (now also an object of reverence, bedecked with flowers, the left knee well-rubbed, NW side of the cemetery), cypress avenues, and many memorials to pioneer families and victims of shipping disasters (open 0800-1800 daily). Walk up C Fagnano to the **Mirador Cerro de La Cruz** for a view over the city. The **British School** on Waldo Seguel, and **St James' Church** next door, are wooden, in colonial style. The **Parque María Behety**, S of town along 21 de Mayo, features a scale model of Fuerte Bulnes and a campsite, popular for Sun picnics.

Museums

There is an excellent modern museum in the **Colegio Salesiano**, 'Mayorino Borgatello', dealing with the Indians, animal and bird life of the region, and other interesting aspects of life in Patagonia and Tierra del Fuego, at Av Bulnes 374, entrance next to church. Open Tues-Sat 1000-1200 and 1500-1800, Sun 1500-1800, hours change frequently (entry US$1.25). **Museo de Historia Regional Braun Menéndez**, C Magallanes 949, off Plaza de Armas, T 244216, is located in a mansion built by one of the early millionaires, recommended. Part is set out as room-by-

room regional history, the rest of the house is furnished (guided tours in Spanish only). Closed Mon, otherwise open 1100-1600 (summer) and 1100-1300 (winter, entry US$1), free booklet in English. The **Instituto de la Patagonia**, Av Bulnes Km 4 N (opp the University), T 244216, outdoor exhibits open Mon-Fri 0800-1800, indoor pavillions: 0830-1115, 1500-1800, has an open air museum with artefacts used by the early settlers, a pioneer home and a naval museum. **Naval and Maritime Museum**, Pedro Montt 981, open Mon-Fri 0930-1230, 1500-1800, Sat 1000-1300, 1500-1800.

Excursions

5 km W of town is the **Reserva Forestal Magallanes**, known locally as Parque Japonés, follow Independencia right through town and up the hill, 3 km from the edge of town is the turnoff for Río de las Minas to the right. The entrance to the reserve is 2 km beyond, there you will find a self-guided nature trail, 1 km, free leaflet. The road continues through the woods for 14 km, passing by several small campgrounds. From the top end of the road a short path leads to a lookout over the Garganta del Diablo (Devil's Throat), a gorge formed by the Río de las Minas, with views over Punta Arenas and Tierra del Fuego. From here a slippery path leads down to the Río de las Minas valley and thence back to Punta Arenas. *Turismo Pali Aike* offers tours to the park, US$ 3.75 pp.

Local information
● **Accommodation**

Most hotels inc breakfast in the room price. Hotel prices are substantially lower during winter months (April-Sept).

L2 *Hotel José Nogueira*, Plaza de Armas, Bories 959 y P Montt, in former Palacio Sara Braun, T 248840, F 248832, beautiful loggia, lovely atmosphere, rec; **L3** *Cabo de Hornos*, Plaza Muñoz Gamero 1025, T/F 242134, rec; **L3** *Finis Terrae*, Colón 766, T 228200, F 248124, modern, some rooms small but all very nice, safe in room, rooftop café/bar with lovely views, parking; **L3** *Isla Rey Jorge*, 21 de Mayo 1243, T 222681, F 248220, modern, pleasant, pub downstairs; **L3** *Los Navegantes*, José Menéndez 647, T 244677, F 247545; **L3** *Tierra del Fuego*, Colón 716, T/F 226200, good

breakfast, parking, rec, *Café 1900* downstairs.
A2 *Hostería Yaganes*, Camino Antiguo Nte Km 7.5, T 211600, F 211948, cabins on the shores of the Straits of Magellan, nice setting; **A1-A2** *Apart Hotel Colonizadores*, Colón 1106, T 243578, F 244499, clean, fully furnished apartments (2 bedrooms **A1**, 1 bedroom **A2**) discounts for long stay; **A3** *Hostal de la Patagonia*, O'Higgins 478, T 241079, with bath (B without), good breakfast, excellent; **A3** *Colonizadores*, 21 de Mayo 1690, T 244144, F 226587, with bath; **A3** *Hostal Carpa Manzano*, Lautaro Navarro 336, T/F 248864, rec; **A3** *Cóndor de Plata*, Colón 556, T 247987, F 241149, very good; **A3** *Mercurio*, Fagnano 595, T/F 242300, bath, TV and phone, good restaurant and service, rec; **A3** *Plaza*, Nogueira 1116 2nd floor, T 241300, F 248613 (B without bath), pleasant, good breakfast.

B *Savoy*, Menéndez 1073, T 241951, F 247979, pleasant rooms but some lack windows, good place to eat; **B** *Ritz*, Pedro Montt 1102, T 224422, old, clean and cosy, rec; **B** *Hotel El Pionero*, Chiloé 1210, T 248851, F 248263, with bath; **C** *Res Central*, No 1 España 247, T 222315, No 2 Sanhueza 185, T 222845, with bath (**D** without), comfortable; **B** *Chalet Chapital*, Sanhueza 974, T 242237, F 225698 (cheaper without bath), good, comfortable, doubles only, welcoming; **B** *Hostal de la Avenida*, Colón 534, T 247532, good breakfast, friendly, safe, rec; **B** *Hostal Del Estrecho*, Menéndez 1048, T/F 241011, with breakfast and bath.

C *Albatros*, Colón 1195, T 223131, without bath, good; **C** *Res París*, Nogueira 1116, p 4, T 223112, rec, heating, some rooms have balconies, others have no windows; **C** *Res Sonia Kuscevic*, Pasaje Darwin 175 (Angamos altura 550), T 248543, popular, IYHA accepted, with bath, breakfast, hot water, heating, parking.

D *Casa Dinka*, Caupolicán 169, T 226056, with breakfast, use of kitchen, noisy, very popular; **D** pp *Res Roca*, Roca 1038, T 243903, without bath, clean; **D** pp *Res Rubio*, España 640, T 226458, with bath, helpful; **D** España y Balmaceda, heaters, shared bath with hot water, pleasant. Accommodation available in many private houses, usually E pp, ask at tourist office; **D** *Hosp Lodging*, Sanhueza 933, T 221035, good value, clean, heating, modern; **D** Sra Carolina Ramírez, Paraguaya 150, T 247687, nice and friendly, hot water, safe motorcycle parking, meals, rec; **D** Mireya Cárcamo, Boliviana 375, use of kitchen, good meals, rec.

E pp Caupolicán 99, T 222436, with breakfast, clean; **E** pp *Casa Deportista*, O'Higgins 1205, T 225205, F 243438, cheap meals, cooking facili-

ties, dormitory style, noisy; **E** pp *Casa Roxas*, Angamos 971, very good, clean, with bath; **E** pp *Hostal Paradiso*, Angamos 1073, T 224212, with bath, breakfast, parking, use of kitchen, rec; **E** pp *Res Internacional*, Arauco 1514 esq Boliviana, T 223677, dormitory beds and private rooms, hot water, popular, owner eccentric; **E** pp *Backpackers' Paradise*, Carrera Pinto 1022, T 222554, F 226863, hot water, popular, large dormitories, cooking facilities, limited bathroom facilities, good meeting place, luggage store, rec; **E** pp Sra Lenka, José Miguel Carrera 1270, heating, clean, use of kitchen, rec; **E** Nena's, Boliviana 366, T 242411, friendly, with breakfast, highly rec; **E** pp Juanita Cofre, Boliviana 533, knowledgeable, helpful; **E** pp, España y Boliviana, T 247422, without bath, clean, friendly, use of kitchen; **E** Sanhueza 750, homely, rec.

F pp *Alojamiento Prat*, Sgto Aldea 0520, clean, rec; **F** pp Boliviana 238, bunk beds, shared bath, basic, use of kitchen; **F** pp Sanhueza 712, T 225127, basic, use of kitchen; **F** pp Bellavista 577, dormitory accommodation, kitchen, hot showers, clean.

Camping: in Reserva Forestal Magallanes, 8 km W of Punta Arenas (no public transport, see **Excursions** above). *Camping Pudú*, 10.5 km N on Route 9, G pp, pleasant, good facilities.

● **Places to eat**
Main hotels: good value set lunches and dinners at *Cabo de Hornos*, excellent restaurants at *Los Navegantes* and *José Nogueira*.

El Mercado, Mejicana 617, open 24 hrs, reasonably-priced set lunch, expensive á la carte; *Centro Español*, Plaza Muñoz Gamero 771, above Teatro Cervantes, large helpings, limited selection, reasonably priced; *El Mesón del Calvo*, Jorge Montt 687, excellent, seafood, lamb, small portions, pricey, rec; seafood at *Sotitos*, O'Higgins 1138, good service and cuisine, excellent, rec; *La Taberna del Silver*, O'Higgins 1037, fast and cheap; *La Mama*, Sanhueza 700 block, little Argentine-style pasta house, rec; *Lucerna*, Bories 624, excellent meat, reasonably priced, good; *Dino's Pizza*, Bories 557, cheap, good, big pizzas; *Café Garogha*, Bories 817, open Sun pm, busy at night, smoky; *Bianco's Pizza*, Bulnes 1306, excellent pizzas, rec; *El Quijote*, Lautaro Navarro 1087, good sandwiches, highly rec; *Asturias*, Lautaro Navarro 967, good food and atmosphere; *Venus*, Pedro Montt 1046, good food, service and atmosphere, reasonable prices; *La Casa de Juan*, O'Higgins 1021, Spanish food; *El Estribo*, Carrera Pinto 762, good grill, also fish; *Yaganes*, Camino Antiguo Nte Km 7.5, beautiful setting, weekend buffet; *Golden Dragon*, Colón 529, Chinese, expensive; *La Terraza*, 21 de Mayo 1288, and *El Porteño*, 21 de Mayo e Independencia, sandwiches, *empanadas* and beer, cheap and good; *La Taberna del Club de la Unión*, Plaza Muñoz Gamero Seguel, for drinks. For economic set lunches several along Chiloé: *Restaurant de Turismo Punta Arenas*, No 1280, good, friendly, rec; *Los Años 60 The Mitchel*, No 1231, also serves beer and 26 varieties of sandwiches, open 24 hours; *Parrilla Apocalipsis*, Chiloé esq Balmaceda; *Carioca*, Menéndez 600 esq Chiloé, *parrilla*, snacks and beer, very friendly. *Lomit's*, Menéndez 722, cheap snacks and drinks, open when the others are closed. *Kiosco Roca* (no sign), Roca 875, early morning coffee. Cheap fish meals available at stalls in the *Cocinerías*, Lautaro Navarro S of the port entrance. Excellent *empanadas*, bread and pastries at *Pancal*, 21 de Mayo 1280; also at *La Espiga*, Errázuriz 632; excellent pastries at *Casa del Pastel*, Carrera Pinto y O'Higgins. Lobster has become more expensive because of a law allowing only lobster pots. *Centolla* (king crab) is caught illegally by some fishermen using dolphin, porpoise and penguin as live bait. There are seasonal bans on *centolla* fishing to protect dwindling stocks, do not purchase *centolla* out of season. At times *centolla* fishing is banned because the crabs can be infected with a disease which is fatal to humans. If this ban refers to the *marea roja* (red tide), it does not affect crabs, only bivalve shellfish. Mussels should not be picked along the shore owing to pollution and the *marea roja*, see page 851.

● **Airline offices**
LanChile, Lautaro Navarro 999, T 241232, F 222366; **Ladeco**, Lautaro Navarro 1155, T/F 241100/223340. **National**, Bories 701, T 221634. **Aerovías DAP**, O'Higgins 891, T 223340, F 221693, open 0900-1230, 1430-1930; **Kaiken**, Magallanes 974, T 242134 ext 106, F 241321.

● **Banks & money changers**
Banks open Mon-Fri 0830-1400. *Casas de cambio* open Mon-Fri 0900-1230, 1500-1900, Sat 0900-1230; outside business hours try *Buses Sur*, Colón y Magallanes, kiosk at *Garogha Café*, Bories 817 and the major hotels (lower rates). **Fincard** (Mastercard), Pedro Montt 837, T 247864, Mon-Fri 0900-1400, 1530-1730. **Banco Concepción**, Magallanes y Menéndez, for Visa. **Banco O'Higgins**, Plaza de Armas, changes Tcs, no commission. Argentine pesos can be bought at *casas de cambio*. Good rates at *Cambio Gasic*, Roca 915, Oficina 8, T 242396, *La Hermandad*, Lautaro Navarro 1099, T 243991, excellent rates, US$ cash for Amex Tcs; *Sur Cambios*, Lautaro Navarro 1001, T 225656 accepts Tcs. *Kiosco Redondito*, Mejicana 613 in the shopping centre, T 247369.

● **Embassies & consulates**
Argentine, 21 de Mayo 1878, T 261912, open 1000-1400; visas take 24 hrs, US$25; **Brazilian**, Arauco 769, T 241093; **Belgian**, Roca 817, Oficina 61, T 241472; **British**, Roca 924, T 247020; **Danish**, Colón 819, Depto 301, T 221488; **Dutch**, Sarmiento 780, T 248100; **German**, Pasaje Korner 1046, T 241082, Casilla 229; **Italian**, 21 de Mayo 1569, T 242497 **Norwegian**, Independencia 830, T 242171; **Spanish**, J Menéndez 910, T 243566; **Swedish**, Errazúriz 891, T 224107. **Finnish**, Independencia 660, T 247385.

● **Entertainment**
Discotheques: discos in the city centre often have a young crowd: *Gallery*, J Menéndez 750, T 247555; *Yordi*, Pedro Montt 937; *Borssalino*, Bories 587. On the outskirts of town, to the S: *Club Boulevard*, Km 5.5, T 265807; *Torreones*, Km 5.5, T 261985; *Salsoteca*, Km 5. To the N: *Drive-In Los Brujos*, Km 7.5, T 212600; *Salsoteca*, Km 6.

Nightlife: *The Queen's Club*, 21 de Mayo 1455. Lots of *Whiskerias*: *Sexywoman*, Av España, and *Tentación*, Av Colón rec.

● **Hospitals & medical services**
Dentists: *Dr Hugo Vera Cárcamo*, España 1518, T 227510, rec; *Rosemary Robertson Stipicic*, 21 de Mayo 1380, T 22931, speaks English.

Hospitals: *Hospital Regional Lautaro Navarro*, Angamos 180, T 244040, public hospital, for emergency room ask for *La Posta*; *Clínica Magallanes*, Bulnes 01448, T 211527, private clinic, medical staff is the same as in the hospital but fancier surroundings and more expensive.

● **Laundry**
Lavasol, the only self-service, O'Higgins 969, T 243067, Mon-Sat 0900-2030, Sun (summer only) 1000-1800, US$6/machine, wash and dry, good but busy; *Lavaseco Josseau*, Carrera Pinto 766, T 228413; *Lavandería Limpec*, 21 de Mayo 1261, T 241669.

● **Post & telecommunications**
Post Office: Bories 911 y J Menéndez, Mon-Fri 0830-1930, Sat 0900-1400.

Telecommunications: for international and national calls and faxes (shop around as prices vary): *CTC*, Nogueira 1106, Plaza de Armas, daily 0800-2200, *CTC*, Roca 886, loc 23, daily 0900-2030; *Entel*, Lautaro Navarro 957, Mon-Fri 0830-2200, Sat-Sun 0900-2200; *Telex-Chile/Chile-Sat*, Bories 911 and Errázuriz 856, daily 0830-2200, also offers telex and telegram service. *VTR*, Bories 801, closed Sat afternoon and Sun. For international calls and faxes at any hour *Hotel Cabo de Hornos*, credit cards accepted, open to non-residents.

● **Shopping**
For leather goods and sheepskin try the Zona Franca; quality of other goods is low and prices little better than elsewhere; Mon-Sat 1030-1230, 1500-2000 (bus E or A from Plaza de Armas; many collectivo taxis; taxi US$3). Handicrafts at *Pingüi*, Bories 404, *Artesanía Ramas*, Independencia 799, *Chile Típico*, Carrera Pinto 1015, *Indoamérica* Colón y Magallanes and outdoor stalls at the bottom of Independencia, by the port entrance. Supermarkets: *Listo*, 21 de Mayo 1133; *Cofrima*, Lautaro Navarro 1293 y Balmaceda, *Cofrima 2*, España 01375; *Marisol*, Zenteno 0164.

Cameras: wide range of cameras but limited range of film, from Zona Franca. *Foto Arno*, Bories 893, for Kodak products. *Foto Sánchez*, Bories 768, for Fuji film and *Fotocentro*, Bories 789, for Agfa: all have same day print-processing service.

Chocolate: hand made chocolate from *Chocolatería Tres Arroyos*, Bories 448, T 241522 and *Chocolatería Regional Norweisser*, José Miguel Carrera 663, both good.

● **Sports**
Golf: 9-hole golf course 5 km S town on road to Fuerte Bulnes.

● **Tour companies & travel agents**
Turismo Lazo, Angamos 1366, T/F 223771, wide range of tours, highly rec; *Turismo Aventour*, J Nogueira 1255, T 241197, English spoken, helpful, good, organize tours to Tierra del Fuego. *Turismo Comapa*, Independencia 840, T 241437, F 247514, tours to Torres del Paine, Tierra del Fuego, also trips to the Falklands/Malvinas, charter boats to Cape Horn and Isla Magdalena; *Turismo Runner*, Lautaro Navarro 1065, T 247050, F 241042, adventure tours; *Arka Patagonia*, Lautaro Navarro 1038, T 248167, F 241504, all types of tours, rafting, fishing, etc; *Turismo Aonikenk*, Magallanes 619, T 228332, rec; *Turismo Pali Aike*, Lautaro Navarro 1129, T 223301; *El Conquistador*, Menéndez 556, T 222896, rec; *Turismo Viento Sur*, Fagnano 565, T/F 225167, for camping equipment; *Turismo Patagonia*, Bories 655 local 2, T 248474, F 247182, specializes in fishing trips. And others. Most organize tours to Torres del Paine, Fuerte Bulnes and *pingüineras* on Otway sound: shop around as prices vary.

● **Tourist offices**
Sernatur, Waldo Seguel 689, Casilla 106-D, T 241330, at the corner with Plaza Muñoz Gamero, 0830-1745, closed Sat and Sun. Helpful, English spoken. Kiosk on Colón between Bories and Magallanes Mon-Fri 0900-1300, 1500-1900 Sat 0900-1200, 1430-1730, Sun (in the summer only) 1000-1230. **Travel Broom,**

Roca 924, T (061) 228312, F 228322. Turistel Guide available from kiosk belonging to *Café Garogha* at Bories 831. **Conaf**, Menéndez 1147, p 2, T 223841, open Mon-Fri.

● **Transport**

NB All transport is heavily booked from Christmas through to March: advance booking strongly advised.

Local Car hire: Hertz, Colón 798 and Carrera Pinto 770, T 248742, F 244729; **Australmag**, Colón 900, T 242174, F 226916. **Autómovil Club**, O'Higgins 931, T 243675, F 243097, and at airport. **Budget**, O'Higgins 964, T 241696. **Internacional**, Sarmiento 790-B, T 228323, F 226334, rec; **Willemsen**, Lautaro Navarro 1038, T 247787, F 241083, highly rec; **Lubac**, Magallanes 970, T/F 242023/247060; **Todoauto**, España 0480, T212492, F 212627. **NB** You need a hire company's authorization to take a car into Argentina. **Car repair**: *Automotores del Sur*, O'Higgins 850, T 224153. **Taxis**: ordinary taxis have yellow roofs. Collective taxis (all black) run on fixed routes, US$0.25 for anywhere on route. Reliable service from *Radio Taxi Austral*, T 247710/244409.

Air Carlos Ibáñez de Campo Airport, 15 km from town. Bus service by Austral Bus, J Menéndez 565, T 247139, T/F 241708, to/from the airport scheduled to meet flights, US$2.50 Lan-Chile, DAP and Ladeco have their own bus services from town, US$2.50; taxi US$10. The airport restaurant is good. To **Santiago**, Lan-Chile, Ladeco, DAP and National daily US$220, via Puerto Montt (sit on right for views), some National flights also stop in Concepción. When no tickets are available, go to the airport and get on the standby waiting list. Aerovías DAP fly to **Porvenir** daily at 0815 and 1730, return 0830 and 1750 (US$20), plus other irregular flights, with Twin-Otter and Cessna aircraft. (Heavily booked with long waiting list so make sure you have your return reservation confirmed.) Military (FACh) flights approx twice a month to Puerto

Montt US$30, information and tickets from airforce base at the airport, Spanish essential, T 213559; need to book well in advance. It is very difficult to get space during the summer as all armed forces personel and their families have priority over civilians.

Services to Argentina: Aerovías DAP to Ushuaia twice a week. To Río Grande, Kaiken 3 a week. Kaiken to Ushuaia in the summer (schedules change frequently). Reserve well in advance from mid-Dec to February.

Buses Company offices: **Pingüino** and **Fernández**, Sanhueza 745, T 242313, F 225984; **Ghisoni**, Lautaro Navarro 975, T 223205; **Pacheco**, Colón 900, T 242174; **Bus Sur**, Colón y Magallanes, T 244464; **Austral Bus**, Menéndez 565, T 247139, T/F 241708. **Los Carlos**, Plaza Munoz Gamero 1039, T 241321. **Turbus**, Errazuriz 932, T/F 225315. Senkovic, Wood 485. Bus timetables are printed daily in *La Prensa Austral*.

Bus services: buses leave from company offices. To **Río Gallegos**, Pinguino daily 1200, return 1300; Ghisoni, daily except Fri, 1000; Mansilla Fri 1000, Magallanes Tour, Tues 1000. Fares US$20-23.50, officially 5 hrs, but can take up to 8, depending on customs, 15 mins on Chilean side, up to 3 hrs on Argentine side, inc 30 mins lunch at Km 160. All customs formalities now undertaken at the border, but ask before departure if this has changed (taxi to Río Gallegos US$130). To **Río Grande**, Hector Pacheco, Mon, Wed, Fri 0715 via Punta Delgada, return Tues, Thur and Sat, 0730, 10 hrs, US$36, heavily booked. To **Ushuaia** via Punta Delgada or Porvenir, Los Carlos, Tues and Sat, 0700, return Mon and Fri, 0300, 14 hrs, US$58, book any return at same time; or take Pacheco to Río Grande with overnight stay in *Hotel Avenida* and next day service with Austral, US$65 inc accommodation. To **Puerto Natales**, 3½ hrs, Fernández, Austral Bus, and Buses Sur, several every day, last departure 1800, US$6. Turbus, Ghisoni and Aus-

tral have services through Argentina to **Osorno**, **Puerto Montt** and **Castro**. Fares: to Puerto Montt or Osorno US$60-75 (cheaper off season) 36 hrs; to Castro US$ 67-83; Turbus continues to **Santiago**, US$95 (cheaper in winter), 46 hrs.

Ferries For services to Porvenir (Tierra del Fuego), see page 838. **Shipping**: Navimag, office at Colón 521, T 244400, F 242003 (confirmation of reservations is advised); Navimag services Puerto Montt – Puerto Natales, see under Puerto Montt; **Comapa** (Compañía Marítima de Punta Arenas), Independencia 830, T 244400, F 247514. Government supply ships are rec for the young and hardy, but take sleeping bag and extra food, and travel pills. For transport on navy supply ships to Puerto Williams, enquire at Tercera Zona Naval, Lautaro Navarro 1150, or ask the captain direct, but be prepared to be frustrated by irregular sailings and inaccurate information. All tickets on ships must be booked in advance Jan-February.

● **To the Falkland Islands/Islas Malvinas**
Punta Arenas is now the main South American link with the islands. Aerovías DAP (address above) fly the following schedule: depart Santiago Wed 1300, arrive Punta Arenas 1600, dep 1700; arrive Mt Pleasant, Falklands/Malvinas 1815; depart Mt Pleasant Thur 1530, arrive Punta Arenas 1700, depart 1800, arrive Santiago 2100, all year. Book well in advance (see under the Falklands/Malvinas for conditions).

● **To Puerto Williams**
For details of sea and air service, see page 840.

To Antarctica

Punta Arenas is a major starting point for Antarctica. Juanita Cofre, Boliviana 533, is frequently recommended as helpful and knowledgeable about transport to the Antarctic, she has good contacts with the Navy. Alternatively try the Navy Office at Navarro 1150. Three naval vessels make regular voyages: the *Piloto Pardo*, an icebreaker, is the largest, US$80-90 pp per day in a 4-berth cabin. The *Yelcho* and *Galvarino* charge US$50 pp per day, women accepted only if ships officers vacate their cabins. All fares include 3 meals a day. Crews very friendly and helpful. For further details, see page 1646.

Overland to Argentina

From Punta Arenas there are 3 routes to Calafate and Río Gallegos: 1) NE via Route 255 and Punta Delgada to the frontier at Kimiri Aike and then along Argen-

tine Route 3 to Río Gallegos. 2) N along Route 9, turning 9 km before Puerto Natales for Dorotea (good road) and then NE via La Esperanza (fuel, basic accommodation). 3) Via Puerto Natales and Cerro Castillo on the road to Torres del Paine joining the road to La Esperanza at Paso Cancha.

Skiing

Cerro Mirador, only 9 km W from Punta Arenas, the most southerly ski resort in the world and one of the few places where one can ski with a sea view. Transtur buses 0900 and 1400 from in front of *Hotel Cabo de Hornos*, US$3, return, taxi US$7. Daily lift-ticket, US$7; equipment rental, US$6 per adult. Mid-way lodge with food, drink and equipment. Season June to Sept, weather permitting. Contact the Club Andino, T 241479, about crosscountry skiing facilities. Also skiing at Tres Morros.

Longer excursions

Within easy reach are Puerto del Hambre and **Fuerte Bulnes**, a replica of the wooden fort erected in 1843 by a Chilean garrison, 56 km S, tours by several agencies, US$12. The trip can be done in a day. 51 km S of Punta Arenas, at the intersection of the roads to Puerto del Hambre and Fuerte Bulnes, is a small marker with a plaque of the Centro Geográfico de Chile, ie the midway point between Arica and the South Pole.

Also S, 53 km from Punta Arenas, is the **Reserva Forestal Laguna Parrillar**, which has older forest than the Magallanes Reserve and sphagnum bogs. There is a 3-hr walk to the tree-line along poorly-marked paths. (No public transport, radio taxi US$60.)

A small colony of Magellanic penguins at **Otway Sound**, 60 km N of Punta Arenas, can be visited (Nov-Mar only); the attentions of some tourists, chasing the birds or trampling over the hatcheries and the illegal use of penguins as bait in fishing for *centolla* (king crab), have led to a decline in the number of penguins. Patience is required to see the penguins since they nest in burrows underground (tread carefully on the soft ground so as not to damage the nests), in the late afternoon they can be seen by the beach where screens have been built to facilitate viewing. Rheas and skunks can also be seen. Tours by several agencies, US$12, entry US$4; taxi US$35 return.

Wildlife Arthur Shapiro (Dept of Zoology, Univ of California, Davis) writes that a good place to photograph rheas (ñandúes) is a few kilometres N of the checkpoint at Kon Aiken, near the turnoff for Otway. Antarctic cormorants can be seen sitting on offshore rocks from the road to Fuerte Bulnes. The local skunk (*chingue*) is apparently very docile and rarely sprays. Also look out for foxes and the Great Horned Owl.

Comapa (address above) charters boats to **Isla Magdalena** (weather permitting). On the island is a penguin colony, deserted apart from the breeding season, Nov-Jan; the island is administered by Conaf. Magdalena is one of a group of three islands (the others are Marta and Isabel), visited by Drake, whose men killed 3,000 penguins for food.

The most interesting excursions are to the Ultima Esperanza region (see below under Puerto Natales) and to the Torres del Paine National Park. Tours to Torres del Paine are offered by several travel agencies in Punta Arenas and Puerto Natales; Sr Mateo Quesada, Chiloé 1375, T 222662, offers local tours in his car, up to 4 passengers.

The fjords and glaciers of Tierra del Fuego (70 km by schooner) are exceptionally beautiful. Comapa runs a once a fortnight 22-hr, 320-km round trip to the fjord d'Agostino, 30 km long, where many glaciers come down to the sea. The luxury cruiser, *Terra Australis*, sails from Punta Arenas on Sat via Ushuaia and Puerto Williams; details from Comapa. Advance booking (advisable) from Cruceros Australis SA, Miraflores 178, p 12, Santiago, T 696-3211, F 331871.

North from Punta Arenas

From Punta Arenas a gravel road runs N to Puerto Natales; beside it, the southbound lane is paved. Fuel is available in Villa Tehuelches, 100 km from Punta Arenas.

● **Accommodation** Along this road are several hotels, inc **B** *Hostal Río Penitente*, Km 138, T 331694, in an old *estancia*, rec; **C** *Hotel Rubens*, Km 183, T 226916, popular for fishing; *Hostería Llanuras de Diana*, Km 215, T 248742, F 244729 (Punta Arenas), T 411540 (Puerto Natales) hidden from road, highly rec; **C** *Hostería Río Verde*, Km 90, E off the highway on Seno Skyring, T 311122, F 241008, private bath, heating.

PUERTO NATALES

Puerto Natales (*Pop* 14,000; *Phone code* 061) is 247 km N of Punta Arenas and close to the Argentine border at Río Turbio. It stands on the Ultima Esperanza gulf amid spectacular scenery, and is the jumping-off place for the magnificent Balmaceda and Torres del Paine national parks. Very quiet in the winter, packed with in tourists in the summer.

Museums
Museo De Agostini, in the Colegio Salesiano at Padre Rossa 1456, 1 room, Tierra del Fuego fauna, free. **Museo Histórico**, Bulnes 285, Tues-Sun 1500-1800.

Excursions
A recommended walk is up to Cerro Dorotea which dominates the town, with superb views of the whole Ultima Esperanza Sound. Take any bus going E and alight at jeep track for summit (Km 9.5). 25 km NW of Puerto Natales the **Monumento Natural Cueva Milodón** (80m wide, 200m deep, 30m high) can be visited. It now contains a plastic model of the prehistoric ground-sloth whose bones were found there in 1895. (Free camping once US$4 entrance fee has been paid.)

● **Transport** Buses J and B regular service US$7.50; taxi US$15 return or check if you can get a ride with a tour, both Adventur and Fernández tour buses to Torres del Paine stop at the cave.

Local information
● **Accommodation**
In season cheaper accommodation fills up quickly after the arrival of the *Puerto Edén* from Puerto Montt. Most prices inc breakfast.

L3 *Eberhard*, Pedro Montt 58, T 411208, F 411209, excellent views, restaurant; **L3** *Costa Australis*, Pedro Montt 262, T 412000, F 411881, new in 1994, modern, good views, popular cafetería.

A1 *Palace*, Ladrilleros 209, T 411134, good food, overpriced; **A2** *Juan Ladrilleros*, Pedro Montt 161, modern, with bath, good restaurant, clean, T 411652, F 412109, rec; **A2** *Glaciares*, Eberhard 104, T 412189, F 411452, new, snack bar; **A2** *Hostal Sir Francis Drake*, Philippi 383, T/F 411553, good views, snack bar, rec; **A3** *Hostal Lady Florence Dixie*, Bulnes 659, T 411158, F 411943, modern, friendly, rec.

B *Blanquita*, Carrera Pinto 409, quiet, rec; **B** *Hostal Melissa*, Blanco Encalada 258, T 411944, private bath; **B** *Natalino*, Eberhard 371, T 411968, clean and very friendly (tours to Milodón Cave arranged), C without bath, parking.

C *Hostal Los Antiguos*, Ladrilleros 195 y Bulnes, T/F 411488, shared bath, pleasant; **C** *Res Carahue*, Bulnes 370, T 411339, hot water, nice; **C** *Bulnes*, C Bulnes 407, T 411307, good, stores luggage; **C** *Hostal Puerto Natales*, Eberhard 250, T 411098, private bath.

D pp *Res Grey*, Bulnes 90, T 411542, hot water, some rooms with heating, very friendly, good dinners; **D** *Res Centro*, Magallanes 258A, T

Travellers
SPECIALIST TOUR OPERATOR FOR CHILE

the great adventure at the end of the world

For off the peg or made to measure arrangements, for individuals or groups, contact us to help organise your visit to this fabulous part of the world.

Fax : + 56 - 65 - 258555
e - mail : gochile@chilepac.net

Avenida Angelmó 2456
P.O. Box/Casilla 854, Ph. + 56 - 65 - 262099
http: //www.chilepac.net/~travellers
Puerto Montt, Chile

411996, private bath; **D** *Austral*, Valdivia 949, T 411593, clean, friendly, good food, without bath, C with bath and breakfast, hot water, cooking and laundry facilties; **D** *Res Sutherland*, Barros Arana 155, with and without bath, welcoming, clean, kitchen facilities.

E pp *Hosp La Chila*, Carrera Pinto 442, use of kitchen, welcoming, luggage store, bakes bread, rec; **E** pp *María José*, Magallanes 646, cooking facilities, helpful; **E** pp *Hostal Famatina*, Ladrilleros 370, T 412067, clean, friendly; *Hosp Milodón*, El Roble 650, T 411420, cooking and laundry facilities, evening meals, tours, clean, highly rec; **E** pp *Los Inmigrantes*, Carrera Pinto 480, good breakfast, clean, kitchen facilities, luggage store, rec; **E** pp *Res El Mundial*, Bories 315, T 412476, large breakfast, use of kitchen, meals, luggage stored; **E** pp *Tierra del Fuego*, Bulnes 29, clean, family of Juan Osorno, will store luggage, good; **E** pp *Casa de familia Bustamente*, Bulnes 317, T 411061, clean, good breakfast, helpful, luggage store, rec; **E** pp *Casa de familia Elsa Millán*, O'Higgins 657, good breakfast, homemade bread, dormitory-style, popular, hot water, warm, friendly, cooking facilities, rec; **E** pp *Casa de familia Dickson*, Bulnes 307, T 411218, good breakfast, clean, helpful, cooking and laundry facilities, rec; **E** pp *Pensión Ritz*, Carrera Pinto 439, full pension available, friendly; **E** pp *Res Temuco*, Ramírez 202 y Bulnes, T 411120, friendly, reasonable, good food; **E** pp *Bories* Bories 206, hostel type, use of kitchen, sleeping bag necessary, good meeting place, friendly; **E** pp Casa Cecilia, Tomás Rogers 54, T/F 411300, clean, cooking and laundry facilities, English and German spoken, rents camping equipment, information on Torres del Paine, rec; **E** pp *Patagonia Adventure*, Tomás Rogers 179, T 411028, dormitory style, and private rooms, friendly, clean, use of kitchen, breakfast, English spoken, camping equipment for hire, book exchange, rec; **E** pp Sra Bruna Mardones, Pasaje Don Bosco 41 (off Philippi), friendly, meals on request; **E** pp *Casa de familia Alicia*, M Rodríguez 283, with breakfast, clean, spacious, luggage stored, helpful, rec; **E** pp *Don Bosco*, Padre Rossa 1430, good meals, use of kitchen, helpful, rec, motorcycle parking, luggage store; **E/F** pp Sra Teresa Ruiz, Esmeralda 463, good value, warm cheap meals, quiet, friendly, rec, tours to Torres del Paine arranged; **F** pp *Res Lago Pingo*, Bulnes 808, T 411026, breakfast extra, clean, hot water, laundry, use of kitchen, will store luggage; similar at O'Higgins 70, 431 and Perito 443; **F** pp private house at Magallanes 1, friendly, cheap meals.

North of Puerto Natales are: **L3-A2** *Cisne de Cuello Negro*, a former guest house for meat buyers at the disused meat packing plant, T 411498, friendly, clean, reasonable, excellent cooking, rec, 5 km from town at Km 275 nr Puerto Bories; **A2** *Patagonia Inn*, Km 26 N, reservations *Hotel Cabo de Hornos*, T/F 242134, Punta Arenas, private bath, restaurant; **C** *Hotel 3 Pasos*, 40 km N, T 228113, simple, beautiful. In Villa Cerro Castillo, 63 km N: **B** *Hostería El Pionero*, T/F 411646, without bath, country house ambience, good service. For accommodation in the Torres del Paine area, see below. **NB** Hotels in the countryside open only in summer months: dates vary.

● **Places to eat**
Nikol's, Barros Arana 160, seafood and salmon very good; *Don Alvarito*, Blanco Encalada 915, hospitable; *El Marítimo*, Pedro Montt 214, seafood and salmon, good views, popular, slow service; *Mari Loli*, Baquedano 615, excellent food, good value; *La Ultima Esperanza*, Eberhard 354, rec for salmon, seafood, enormous portions, not cheap but worth the experience; *La Costanera*, Bories y Ladrilleros, good food, superb views; *Rey Mar*, Baquedano 414, good food; *La Burbuja*, Bulnes 371, huge portions, reasonably priced; *Tierra del Fuego*, Bulnes 29, cheap, good, slow service; *Café Josmar*, Yungay 743, only cafe open every day, packed lunches sold for boat trips; *Melissa*, Blanco Encalada, good cakes; *Centro Español*, Magallanes 247, reasonable; *La Frontera*, Bulnes 819, set meals and à la carte, good value; *La Tranquera*, Bulnes y Blanco Encalada, popular. Cheap meals at *Club Deportivo Natales*, Eberhard 332. *Café Aguila Dorada*, Eberhard 244, T 411982, cheap meals, snacks and ice cream; *Tío Cacho*, Phillipi 553, pizzas and sandwiches. *Delicatessen Pollo Loco*, Baquedano 330, T 411393, good, does packed lunches, rec.

● **Banks & money changers**
Poor rates for TCs, which cannot be changed into US$ cash. **Banco O'Higgins**, Bulnes 633, Mastercard. Casas de cambio on Blanco Encalada 226(Andes Patagónicos) and 266 (Enio América) where Argentine pesos can be changed. **Cambio Stop**, Baquedano 380, good for cash (also arranges tours). Another two at Bulnes 683 and 1087 (good rates; also Argentine pesos); others on Prat. Shop around as some offer very poor rates.

● **Language schools**
Natalis English Centre, Bulnes 1231, T 410316, F 411300, one to one tuition US$4/hr, good.

● **Entertainment**
Discos: El Cielo, Esmeralda y Ramírezl *Milodon*, Blanco Encalada.

● **Laundry**
Lavanderia Papaguayo, Bulnes 518; also *Tienda Milodón*, Bulnes, cheap, or try Sra María Carcamo (at Teresa Ruiz's Hosp at 1000-1200, 1800-2200), good service, more expensive.

● **Post & telecommunications**
Post Office: Eberhard 417, open Mon-Fri 0830-1230, 1430-1745, Sat 0900-1230.

Telephones: CTC, Blanco Encalada 23 y Bulnes, phones and fax.

● **Shopping**
Shoe repairs: *París*, Miraflores between Blanco Encalada and Baquedano.

Supermarket: *Record* on Bulnes 1000 block; 24 hr supermarket Bulnes 300 block; markets good; food prices variable so shop around; cheaper in in Punta Arenas.

● **Sports**
Camping equipment: *Onas*, Bulnes 453, best for camping gear, both sale and hire, helpful; *Luis Díaz*, Encalada 189; *Patagonia Adventures*, see **Hotels** above; *Casa de Familia Elsa Millan*, O'Higgins 657; *Casa Cecilia*, Tomás Rogers 54, German and English spoken, rec. Check all equipment carefully. Average charges, per day: tent US$6, sleeping bag US$3-5, mat US$1.50, raincoat US$0.60, also cooking gear. (**NB** De-

posits required: tent US$200, sleeping bag US$100.) Camping gas is widely available in hardware stores in Puerto Natales.

Fishing: tackle for hire at Andes Patagónicos, Blanco Encalada 226, T 411594, US$3.50/day for rod, reel and spinners; if you prefer fishing with floats, hooks, split shot, etc, take your own. Other companies up to 5 times as expensive.

● **Tour companies & travel agents**
Urbina Tours, Eberhard 554, T 411965; *Onas*, Bulnes 453, T 411098, tours, trekking, climbing, equipment hire, rec; *Turis Ann*, Tomás Rogers 255, T/F 411141, very helpful, accommodation arranged, tours, equipment hire; *San Cayetano*, Eberhard 145, T 411112; *Michay*, Baquedano 388, T 411149/411957 (Pedro Fueyo rec); *Andes Patagónicos*, Blanco Encalada 226, T/F 411594, also horses for hire; *Andescape*, Prat 353, 2°, T 412592; *Knudsen Tours*, Encalada 284, T 411531, rec; *Servitur*, Pratt 353, T411028; *Turismo Zaajh*, Bulnes 459,rec. Patricio Canales, Eberhard 49, rec as a good guide; *Travellers* (agency in Puerto Montt) due to open an office offering similar services to those in Puerto Montt (see under Puerto Montt), address not known. Reports of the reliability of agencies, especially for their trips to Torres del Paine National Park, are very mixed. Several agencies offer tours to the Perito Moreno glacier in Argentina, 1 day, US$70 without food or park entry fee. The agencies are reluctant to let tourists leave the tour in Calafate and continue into Argentina. It is cheaper to book tours direct with agents rather than to go through *Residenciales* in Puerto Natales as the latter add 10% commission.

● **Tourist offices**
Offices in kiosk on waterfront, Av Pedro Montt y Phillipi; maps for US$1 from Eberhard 547. **Conaf**: Carrera Pinto 566.

● **Transport**
Local Bicycle hire: Onas, Bulnes 453, US$10 a day; also try *Hotel Eberhard*. **Bicycle repairs** El Rey de la Bicicleta, Arauco 779, good, helpful. **Car hire**: Andes Patagónicos, Blanco Encalada 226, T 411594, helpful, US$85/day inc insurance and 350 km free; Todoauto, Bulnes 20, T 412837. US$110/day for high clearance vehicle, others US$80/day, or US$85 with driver. Hire agents can arrange permission to drive into Argentina, but this is expensive and takes 24 hrs to arrange. **Mechanic**: Carlos González, Ladrillos entre Bories y Eberhard, rec.

Air Alta from Puerto Montt, fine views, 3 hrs, a rec alternative to the ferry.

Buses To Punta Arenas, several daily, 3½ hrs, US$6. Bus Fernández, Eberhard 555, T 411111, Bus Sur, Baquedano 534, T 411325 and Austral Bus, Baquedano y Valdivia, T 411415. Book in advance. To Coyhaique via Calafate, Urbina Tours, 4 days, US$120 (Nov-March). Out of season the only service to rest of Chile: Austral Bus, Tues to Pto Montt, US$50, book days in advance.

To Argentina: to Río Gallegos direct, Bus Sur, US$22, Tues and Thur 1830 and El Pingüino, Wed and Sun 1200, US20; hourly to **Río Turbio**, Lagoper, Baquedano y Valdivia, and other companies, US$3, 2 hrs (depending on Customs – change bus at border). To **Calafate**, Río Turbio bus from Onas, Bulnes 453, 0630, US$25, otherwise travel agencies run several times a week depending on demand, 7 hrs, US$50, shop around, reserve 1 day ahead.

Shipping See page 800 on services from Puerto Montt. Navimag office: Pedro Montt 380, Terminal Marítimo, T 411421, F 411642.

FRONTIER WITH ARGENTINA

1) Paso Casas Viejas

16 km E of Puerto Natales. On the Argentine side the road continues to a junction, with alternatives S to Río Turbio and N to Esperanza and Río Gallegos.

● **Chilean immigration**
Open all year 0800-2000.

2) Villa Dorotea

16 km NE of Puerto Natales. On the Argentine side this joins the Río Turbio-Esperanza road.

● **Chilean immigration**
Open all year daytime only.

3) Cerro Castillo

65 km N of Puerto Natales on the road to Torres del Paine. On the Argentine side, Paso Canchade Carreras (14 km), the road leads to Esperanza and Río Gallegos.

● **Chilean immigration**
open 0830-1200, 1400-2000, Nov-March or April only.

● **Accommodation**
2 *hospedajes* in Cerro Castillo.

PARQUE NACIONAL BERNARDO O'HIGGINS

At the N end of Ultima Esperanza Sound is the **Parque Nacional Bernardo O'Higgins** (usually referred to as the **Parque Nacional Monte Balmaceda**) which can be reached by sea only. Four boats *21 de Mayo*, *Alberto de Agostini*, *El Explorador* and

Trinidad sail daily from Puerto Natales in summer and on Sun only in winter (minimum 10 passengers), when weather conditions may be better with less cloud and rain, US$38. After a 3-hr journey up the Sound, the boat passes the Balmaceda Glacier which drops from the eastern slopes of Monte Balmaceda (2,035m). The glacier is retreating; in 1986 its foot was at sea level. The boat docks 1 hr further N at Puerto Toro, from where it is a 1-km walk to the base of Serrano Glacier on the N slope of Monte Balmaceda. On the trip dolphins, sea-lions (in season), black-necked swans, flightless steamer ducks and cormorants can be seen.

Bookings through Andes Patagónicos (address above) or other agencies, expensive lunch extra, take own food, drinks available on board. Take warm clothes, hat and gloves. This trip can also be combined with a visit to Torres del Paine. You have to pay full fare on the boat and you need a permit from Conaf. The 35 km walk from Puerto Toro along the Río Serrano to the Torres del Paine administration centre is hard going with no clear path; it is not an authorized route and the *guardaparques* in Torres del Paine discourage its use.

PARQUE NACIONAL TORRES DEL PAINE

145 km NW of Puerto Natales is the **Torres del Paine** National Park, covering 1,630 sq km, a 'must' for its wildlife and spectacular scenery. There are 15 peaks above 2,000m, of which the highest is Cerro Paine Grande (3,248m). Nearby, in the centre of the park are the *Torres* (Towers) and *Cuernos* (Horns) of Paine, oddly shaped peaks of over 2,600m, which fall straight down to the valleys, which are filled by beautiful lakes at 50m to 200m above sea level. In the NW of the Park are the glaciers (*ventisqueros*) Grey, Dickson and Zapata, three of the main ones branching off the huge mass forming the Patagonian icecap. The scenery in the Park is superb, with constantly changing views of fantastic peaks, ice-fields, vividly coloured lakes of turquoise, ultramarine and grey and quiet green valleys. The park enjoys a micro-climate especially favourable to wildlife and plants: there are 105 species of birds including 18 species of waterfowl and 11 birds of prey. Particularly noteworthy are condors, black-necked swans, rheas, kelp geese, ibis, flamingos and austral parrots. There are also 25 species of mammals including *guanaco*, hares, foxes, *huemules* (a species of deer), pumas and skunks. Over 200 species of plants have been identified. The Park is open all year round, although snow may prevent access in the winter: best time is Dec-March.

Torres del Paine has become increasingly popular with foreigners and Chileans alike: in 1994 it received 38,000 visitors, most during the summer. Despite the best efforts to manage this large influx of visitors rationally, their impact is starting to show. Litter has become a problem especially around the *refugios* and camping areas. Please take all your rubbish out of the park and remember that toilet paper is also garbage. Do your share to protect this unique place.

The park is administered by Conaf: the Administration Centre is in the S of the park at the N end of Lago del Toro (open 0830-2000 in summer, 0830-1230, 1400-1830 off season). The Centre provides a good slide show at 2000 on Sat and Sun and there are also exhibitions, but no maps or written information to take away. For information (in Spanish) on weather conditions phone the Administration Centre (T 691931). Six ranger stations (*guarderías*) are staffed by rangers (*guardaparques*) who give help and advice and will also store luggage (except at Laguna Amarga where they have no room). Rangers keep a check on the whereabouts of all visitors: you are required to register and show your passport when entering the park. You are also requested to register at a ranger station before setting off on any hike. There are entrances at Laguna Amarga, Lago Sarmiento, Laguna Azul. Entry for foreigners: US$12 (proceeds are shared between all 35 Chilean National Parks) climbing fees US$800. Allow a week to 10 days to see the park properly.

It is vital not to underestimate the

unpredictability of the weather (which can change in a few minutes), nor the arduousness of some of the stretches on the long hikes (the further W you go, the more likely you are to have precipitation). It is essential to be properly equipped against cold, wind and rain. The only means of rescue are on horseback or by boat; the nearest helicopter is in Punta Arenas and high winds usually prevent its operation in the park.

Hikes

There are about 250 km of well-marked trails. Visitors must keep to the trails: cross-country trekking is not permitted. The most popular hike is a circuit ('El Circuito') starting from either the Laguna Amarga ranger station or from the administration centre, and going past the spectacular Grey Glacier and round the back of the Cuernos and Torres del Paine. Although some people complete the route in less, it normally takes 5-6 days. Lone walkers are not allowed to walk the circuit and camping gear must be carried. The circuit is often closed in winter due to snow. The longest lap is 30 km, between Refugio Laguna Amarga and Refugio Dickson (10 hrs in good weather), but the most difficult section is the steep slippery slope between Paso John Gardner (1,241m) and Campamento Paso. Although most people go anti-clockwise round the circuit, some advise doing it clockwise so that you climb to Paso John Gardner with the wind behind. Footbridges are occasionally washed away.

Several shorter walks are also recommended including: (1) Up the valley of the Río del Francés between (to the W) Cerro Paine Grande and the Ventisquero del Francés and (to the E) the Cuernos del Paine. Allow 2½ hrs from Refugio Lago Pehoé to Campamento Italiano on the shores of the Río Francés, 2½ hrs further to Campamento Británico. The views from a point 20 mins above the Campamento are superb.

(2) To Lago Pingo, S of Ventisquero Zapata (plenty of wildlife, icebergs in the lake), via Refugio Pingo (about halfway) and Refugio Zapata, about 1½ hrs before the Lake.

(3) To the base of the Torres del Paine: from the Park entrance it is 2 hrs to the refugio, campsite and ranger station at Laguna Amarga, then 1½ hrs to an estancia which includes Hostería Las Torres and a campground. From the estancia it is 2 hrs up the valley of the Río Ascensio to Campamento Chileno on the river bank, 1 hr further to Campamento Torres where many climbers make their base camp and 1 hr more to the base of the Torres where there is a lake: the path is well-marked, but the last 30 mins is up the morraine; if you want to see the towers lit by sunrise (spectacular but you must have good weather), it's well worth humping camping gear up to Campamento Torres and spending the night. 1 hr beyond Campamento Torres is the good site at Campamento Japonés.

Equipment

A strong, streamlined, waterproof tent is preferable to the refugios and is essential if doing the complete circuit. Also essential are protective clothing against wind and rain, strong waterproof footwear, compass, good sleeping bag, sleeping mat, camping stove and cooking equipment. In summer take shorts and sun-screen also. Equipment is checked at the entrance. Take your own food: the small shops at the Andescape refugios (see below) and at the Posada Río Serrano are expensive and have a limited selection. Note that rats and mice have become a major problem around camping sites and the free refugios. Do not leave food in your pack (which will be chewed through): the safest solution is to hang food in a bag on wire. Maps (US$3), are obtainable at Conaf offices in Punta Arenas or Puerto Natales. Most maps are unreliable but the one produced by Sociedad Turística Kaonikén, US$5, has been recommended as more accurate than the Conaf map (available at Nandú Artesanía at port end of Bulnes).

Park information

● Accommodation

Hotels: L1 Hotel Explora, new, luxurious and comfortable, at Salto Chico on edge of Lago Pehoé, T 411247, offering spectacular views, pool, gym, tours (reservations: Av Américo Vespucci 80, p 7, Santiago, T 228-8081, F 208-5479); **L3** *Hostería Pehoé*, T 411390, 60 rooms, private facilities, cheaper off season, 5 km S of Pehoé ranger station, 11 km N of park administration, on an island with spectacular view across the Lake to Cerro Paine Grande and Cuernos del Paine, daily boat service to *Refugio Pehoé*, at 1300, good meals (reservations: Turismo Pehoé in Punta Arenas or Nataniel 31, office 68, T 671-8709, F 695572, Tx 240875 PEHOE CL in Santiago); **L3** *Hostería Las Torres*, head office Chiloé 1212, Punta Arenas, T 226054, F 226473, new, modern conveniences, separate restaurant, English spoken at reception, horse-riding, transport from Laguna Amarga ranger station, rec; **L3** *Hostería Lago Grey*, T/F 248220 anexo 29, or Punta Arenas 222681 new, on edge of Lago Grey (reservations through Arka Patagonia or Turismo Runner in Punta Arenas); **A1** *Hostería Estancia Lazo*, on the E edge of the park, 8 cabins beautifully situated on Laguna Verde with spectacular views, very friendly, comfortable, excellent food, very highly rec (reservations: Operatur Patagónia SA, Av Colón 568, T/F 61-221130/240056, Punta Arenas); **A2** pp *Posada Río Serrano*, an old *estancia*, some rooms with bath, some with shared facilities, breakfast extra, nr park administration, with expensive but good restaurant and a shop (reservations advisable: Serco Ltda, Casilla 19-D, Punta Arenas, T 223395 or Zaahy agency in Puerto Natales).

Refugios: **F** pp *Refugio Lago Toro*, nr administration centre, run by CONAF, hot showers, cooking facilities, good meeting place, sleeping bag and mattress essential, no camping, open summer only – in the winter months another more basic (free) *refugio* is open nr adminsitration centre. The following are run by Andescape (addresses under Puerto Natales and Santiago): *Refugio Lago Pehoé*, on the NE arm of Lago Pehoé; *Refugio Grey*, on the eastern shore of Lago Grey; *Refugio Lago Dickson*; all **D** pp,

modern, clean, with dormitory accommodation(sheets not provided) hot showers (US$2 for non-residents) cooking and laundry facilities, meals served, kiosk with basic food and other supplies, rental of camping equipment, campsite (US$3 pp).

In addition there are 6 free refugios: Zapata, Pingo, Laguna Verde, Laguna Amarga and Pudeto. Most have cooking areas (wood stove or fireplace) but Laguna Verde and Pingo do not. These are now in very poor condition and are very crowded in summer (rangers know how many people are on each route and can give you an idea of how busy refugios will be).

Camping: in addition to sites at the Andescape refugios there are the following sites: *Camping Serón* and *Camping Las Torres* (at *Hostería Las Torres*) both run by Estancia Cerro Paine, US$4, hot showers; *Camping Los Perros*, run by Andescape, US$3 pp, shop and hot showers. Free camping and lighting fires are permitted in eight other locations in the park, but nowhere else. (**NB** These restrictions should be observed as forest fires are a serious hazard.) Beware mice, which eat through tents. Equipment hire in Puerto Natales (see above).

● **Boat trips**

From *Hostería Grey* at the S end of Lago Grey to the Grey Glacier, minimum 8 passengers, US$25 inc refreshments, 2-3 hrs, a stunning trip. From *Refugio Lago Pehoé* to *Refugio Pudeto*, US$12 one way daily, from Pudeto 0900, 1300, 1600, from Pehoé 1030, 1430, 1730, 1 hr, in high season reserve in advance at the *refugios* at either end or at Turismo Tzonka in Puerto Natales. Off-season, radio for the boat from *Refugio Pehoé*.

● **Transport**

Car hire: hiring a pick-up from Budget in Punta Arenas is an economical proposition for a group (up to 9 people): US$415 for 4 days. It driving there yourself, the road from Pto Natales is being improved and, in the Park, the roads are narrow,

---

bendy with blind corners, use your horn a lot; it takes about 3½ hrs from Pto Natales to the administration, 3 to Laguna Amarga. Petrol available at Río Serrano, but fill up in case. **Horse hire**: from Baqueano Zamora, T 411594 /411728.

Buses San Cayetano, Servitur and JB Buses (addresses above) run daily bus services to the park from Puerto Natales leaving between 0630 and 0800, returning between 1300 and 1500, 3½ hrs' journey, US$8.75 one way, US$12.50 open return (return tickets are not interchangeable between different companies, buy single ticket), from early Nov to mid March. Buses pass *Guardería Laguna Amarga* at 1030, *Guardería Pehoé* at 1130, arriving at Admin at 1230, leave Admin at 1400 (in high season the buses fill quickly so it is best to board at the Administration). All buses wait at *Refugio Pudeto* until the 1430 boat from *Refugio Lago Pehoé* arrives. Travel between two points within the park (eg Pudeto-Laguna Amarga) US$1.25. At other times services by travel agencies are dependent on demand: arrange return date with driver and try to arrange your return date to coincide with other groups to keep costs down. Luis Díaz has been rec, about US$12 pp, min 3 persons. A new road to the Park from Puerto Natales has been built to the southern entrance, at Lago Toro, although in March 1996, a bridge over the Río Serrano was still missing.

To go from Torres del Paine to Calafate (Argentina) either return to Pto Natales and go to Río Turbio for bus to La Esperanza, or take a bus or hitch from the park to Villa Cerro Castillo border point (106 km S of the administration), cross to Paso Cancha de Carreras and try to link with the Río Turbio-La Esperanza-Río Gallegos bus schedule, or hitch. (See Accommodation **North of Puerto Natales**, above.)

Tours

Several agencies in Puerto Natales including *Servitur, Scott Tours* and *Luis Díaz* offer 1-day tours by minibus, US$37.50 (some travellers report that these are a waste of time as you need to stay overnight to appreciate the park). José Torres of *Sastrería Arbiter* in C Bulnes 731 (T 411637) rec as guide. *Enap* weekend tours in summer cost US$45 including accommodation and meals. *Buses Fernández* offer 2-day tours, US$132 and 3-day tours (which includes trip to the Balmaceda Glacier) US$177. Before booking a tour check carefully on details and get them in writing: increasingly mixed reports of tours. Many companies who claim to visit the Grey Glacier only visit Lago Grey (you

see the Glacier in the distance). Taxi costs US$80 per day, run by Sergio Zaley (Arturo Prat 260), but may be cheaper if you catch him when he's going to the Park anyway. After mid-Mar there is little public transport (ask *San Cayetano*) and trucks are irregular.

Tierra del Fuego is the largest island off the extreme S of South America. It is surrounded by the Magellan Strait to the N, the Atlantic Ocean to the E, the Beagle Channel to the S – which separates it from the southern islands – and by the Whiteside, Gabriel, Magdalena and Cockburn channels etc, which divide it from the islands situated to the W. The western side belongs to Chile and the eastern to Argentina. It produces most of Chile's oil.

Transport to Tierra del Fuego: Ferries There are two ferry crossings to Tierra del Fuego.

1) Between Punta Arenas and Porvenir the *Melinka*, leaving Tres Puentes (5 km N of Punta Arenas, bus A or E from Av Magallanes, US$1; taxi US$3) at 0900 daily (0930 Sun) in season, less frequently off season, depending on tides, 2½ hr crossing (can be rough and cold), US$6 pp, US$5 per bike, US$30 per vehicle. Reservations essential especially in summer, obtainable from Agencia Broom, Bulnes 05075, T 218100, F 212126. Timetable subject to change: check in advance. Return from Porvenir same day at 1400 (1630 Sun). The ferry company accepts no responsibility for damage to vehicles on the crossing.

2) Across the *Primera Angostura* (First Narrows), 170 km NE of Punta Arenas, between Punta Delgada and Bahía Azul, the ferry terminal at Punta Espora. There are several crossings a day; schedules vary with the tides. Price US$1 pp (cycles free) and US$14 per car, one way. The ferry takes about 4 trucks and 20 cars; before 1000 most space is taken by trucks. There is no bus service to or from this crossing. If hitching, this route is preferable as there is more traffic.

● **Accommodation In Punta Delgada**: **E** pp *Hotel El Faro*; **C** *Hostería Tehuelche*, T 061-694433 at Kamiri Aike 17 km from port, with restaurant.

● **Transport Air** From Punta Arenas – weather and bookings permitting, Aerovías DAP, Oficina Foretic, T 80089, Porvenir, fly daily except Sun at 0815 and 1730 to Porvenir, return at 1000 and 1930, US$20. Heavily booked so make sure you have your return reservation confirmed.

PORVENIR

In Chilean Tierra del Fuego the only town is **Porvenir** (*Pop* 4,500, several hundred from former Yugoslavia; *Phone code* 061). There is a small museum, the Fernando Cordero Rusque, Samuel Valdivieso 402, mainly Indian culture.

● **Accommodation Porvenir hotels**: **A2** *Los Flamencos*, Tte Merino, T 580049, best; **C** *Central*, Phillippi 298, T 580077, hot water; **C** *Rosas*, Phillippi, T 580088, with bath, hot water, heating, restaurant and bar, rec; **E** pp *Res Colón*, Damián Riobó 198, T 580108, also full board; **C** *España*, Santos Mardones y Croacia, good restaurant with fixed price lunch; *Res Los Cisnes*, Soto Salas 702, T 580227; **E** pp *Res* at Santos Mardones 366 (**D** with full board), clean, friendly, heaters in rooms, hot water, good; **E** pp *Res Cameron*, Croacia, for shared room, 'friendly folk', good meals, **D** full board, sleep on dining-room floor for US$1; there is a hotel at the Transportes Senkovic office, Croacia y Almeyda; many good *pensiones*, **D**, with full board, but they are often fully occupied by construction workers. **Other hotels on Chilean Tierra del Fuego**: at Cerro Sombrero, 46 km S of Primera Angostura: **E** pp *Hostería Tunkelen*, rec; **F** *Pensión del Señor Alarcón*, good, friendly. *Posada Las Flores*, Km 127 on the road to San Sebastián, reservations via *Hostal de la Patagonia* in Punta Arenas. For accommodation at San Sebastián see below.

● **Places to eat** *Croacia Club*, wholesome and reasonable lunch (about US$5), also *Restaurante Puerto Montt*, Croacia 1169, for seafood, rec. Many lobster fishing camps where fishermen will prepare lobster on the spot.

● **Banks & money changers** At *Estrella del Sur* shop, Santos Mardones.

● **Transport On Tierra del Fuego Buses** 2 a week between Porvenir and Río Grande (Argentina), Tues and Sat 1400, Transportes Senkovic, Croacia y Almeyda, T 580100, US$20 heavily booked, buy ticket in advance, or phone. **Ferries** Terminal at Bahía Chilota, 7 km W, see below for details. From bus terminal to ferry, taxi US$6, bus (if running) US$1.50. **Motorists** All roads are gravel. Fuel is available in Porvenir, Cerro Sombrero and Cullen. **Hitchhiking** Police may help with lifts on trucks from Porvenir to Río Grande; elsewhere is difficult as there is so little traffic.

Cameron, 149 km SE of Porvenir on the opposite side of Bahía Inútil, can be reached by bus from **C** Manuel Señor, Porvenir, Mon and Fri, 1700, US$10; from here a road runs SE to Estancia Vicuña. Before Vicuña is a scenic fishing-ground; beyond Vicuña a horse trail leads across the Darwin Range to Yendegaia. From there you will have to retrace your steps as it seems impossible to get permission to cross the unmanned border to Ushuaia or to get a Chilean exit stamp.

FRONTIER WITH ARGENTINA: SAN SEBASTIAN

The only legal frontier crossing between the Chilean and Argentine parts of Tierra del Fuego is 142 km E of Porvenir. On the Argentine side the road continues to Río Grande.

NB There are two settlements called San Sebastián, one on each side of the frontier but they are 14 km apart; taxis are not allowed to cross.

NB Argentine time is 1 hr hour ahead of Chilean time, March-October.

● **Entering Chile**
No fruit, vegetables, dairy produce or meat permitted.

● **Accommodation**
E pp *Hostería de la Frontera*, in the annex which is 1 km away from the more expensive main building.

● **Transport**
Minibus from Porvenir to San Sebastián, US$14. For transport between Porvenir and Río Grande, see above, between Río Grande and Ushuaia see under Argentina.

PUERTO WILLIAMS

Puerto Williams is a Chilean naval base on Isla Navarino, S of the Beagle Channel. Isla Navarino is totally unspoilt and beautiful, with a chain of rugged snowy peaks, magnificent woods and many animals, including large numbers of beaver which were introduced to the island and have done a lot of damage. Situated about 50 km E of Ushuaia (Argentina) at 54° 55' 41" S, 67° 37'

58" W, Puerto Williams is the most southerly place in the world with a permanent population (about 1,500-1,800; *phone code* 061). It is small, friendly and remote (it suffered a serious fire in 1994).

Excursions

Sights include beaver dams, cascades, the Villa Ukika, 2 km E of town, the place where the last descendants of the Yaghan people live, and the local *media luna* where rodeos are held. For superb views, climb Cerro Bandera (3-4 hrs round trip, steep, take warm clothes). No equipment rental on island; buy food in Punta Arenas.

Museums

'Museo del fin del Mundo' ('End of the World Museum') is full of information about vanished Indian tribes, local wildlife, and voyages including Charles Darwin and Fitzroy of the *Beagle*, a 'must'. Open 1000-1300, 1500-1800 (Mon-Thur); 1500-1800 (Sat-Sun), Friday closed (subject to change). Admission US$1.

Local information
● Accommodation
A3 *Hostería Walla*, on the edge of Lauta bay, T 223571, 2 km out of town (splendid walks), very hospitable, good food; E pp *Res Onashaga* (run by Señor Ortiz – everyone knows him), cold, run down, good meals, helpful, full board available; D pp *Pensión Temuco*, Piloto Pardo 224, also half board, comfortable, hospitable, good food, hot showers, rec; you can also stay at private houses. You can camp nr the *Hostería*: collect drinking water from the kitchen. Aeropetrel will charter a plane, if a sufficiently numerous party is raised, to Cape Horn (US$2,600 for 8-10 people).

● Airline offices
Aerovías DAP, LanChile, Ladeco in the centre of town.

● Post & telecommunications
Post Office: closes 1900
Telephone: CTC, Mon-Sat 0930-2230, Sun 1000-1300, 1600-2200). Telex.

● Tourist offices
Near the museum (Closed in winter). Ask for details on hiking. Maps available.

● Transport
Air From Punta Arenas by air, Aerovías DAP (details under Punta Arenas) on Mon and Fri 1400, Wed 0830, return Mon and Fri 1800, Wed 1000, US$64 single. Book well in advance; 20 seater aircraft and long waiting lists (be persistent). The flight is beautiful, with superb views of Tierra del Fuego, the Cordillera Darwin, the Beagle Channel, and the islands stretching S to Cape Horn. Also army flights available (they are cheaper), but the ticket has to be bought through DAP.

Ferries From Ushuaia (Argentina), the *Tres Marías*, once a week, 3-4 hrs crossing, US$65 pp, take own lunch; there may be no service in winter, and frequent schedule changes (see under Ushuaia, page 231, for other options).

Boats from Punta Arenas: *Ñandú* or *Ultragas* leaves on a fixed schedule every 10 days, about midnight, arrives 1700 each way, reclining chairs, no food, US$45 one way. Enquire at the office, Independencia 865, next to service station. The *Navarino* sails from Punta Arenas in 3rd week of every month, 12 passengers, US$150 pp one way; contact the owner, Carlos Aguilera, 21 de Mayo 1460, Punta Arenas, T 228066, F 248848. A small cargo vessel, the *Beaulieu*, sails from Punta Arenas once a month and carries a few passengers, US$300 return, 6 days. Juanita Cofre, Boliviana 533, Punta Arenas, frequently rec as knowledgeable and helpful in arranging transport to Puerto Williams. Navy and port authorities may deny any knowledge, but everyone else in Puerto Williams knows when a boat is due.

Boat trips: ask at the yacht club on the off chance of hitching a ride on a private yacht. Luxury cruises around Cape Horn are run by Tierra Austral for US$800, 6 days. Captain Ben Garrett offers recommended adventure sailing in his schooner *Victory*, from special trips to Ushuaia to cruises in the canals, Cape Horn, glaciers, Puerto Montt, Antarctica in Dec and January. Write to Victory Cruises, Puerto Williams (slow mail service); Fax No 1, Cable 3, Puerto Williams; phone (call collect) asking for Punta Arenas (Annex No 1 Puerto Williams) and leave message with the Puerto Williams operator.

The Chilean Pacific Islands

TWO national park possessions in the Pacific: Juan Fernández Islands, a little easier to reach (and leave) now than in Robinson Crusoe's time, and the unique Easter Island.

Land

Juan Fernández Islands, some 650 km W of Valparaíso, are named after Fernández, the first European to visit, in 1574. They are now a national park administered by Conaf. One of them was the home (1704-09) of Alexander Selkirk (the original of Defoe's *Robinson Crusoe*), whose cave on the beach of Robinson Crusoe island is shown to visitors. The main island has 550 people housed in simple wood frame houses, who fish for *langosta de Juan Fernández* (a pincerless lobster) which they send to the mainland. The only settlement, the village of San Juan Bautista, located on Bahía Cumberland, has a church, schools, post office, and wireless station. The official names of the three islands are: Robinson Crusoe (previously Más a Tierra), Alejandro Selkirk (previously Más Afuera) and Santa Clara (the smallest island). In summer, a boat goes once a month between Robinson Crusoe and Alejandro Selkirk if the *langosta* catch warrants it, so you can visit either for a few hours or a whole month.

Climate

The climate is mild, the vegetation rich, and there are plenty of wild goats – and some tourists, for the islands are now easily reached by air. There are no beaches to speak of. **Take insect repellent**.

Places of interest

The anvil-shaped El Yunque, 915m, is the highest peak on Robinson Crusoe and it was upon this hill that Selkirk lit his signal fires. A tablet was set in the rock at the look-out point by British naval officers from HMS *Topaze* in 1868, to commemorate Selkirk's solitary stay on the island for 4 years and 4 months. Selkirk, a Scot, was put ashore from HMS *Cinque Ports* and was taken off by a privateer, the *Duke*. The look-out (Mirador de Selkirk) is the only easy pass between the N and S sides of the island. During the WW1, two British destroyers, HMS *Kent* and *Glasgow* cornered the German cruiser, *Dresden*, in Bahía Cumberland. The ship, which was scuttled, is still on the bottom; a monument on shore commemorates the event and, nearby, unexploded shells are embedded in the cliffs.

Each Feb, a yachting regatta visits the islands; it originates in Algarrobo, sails to Robinson Crusoe, thence to Talcahuano and Valparaíso. The bay is full of colourful and impressive craft, and prices in restaurants and shops double for the duration. (Thomas G Lammers, Miami University, Department of Botany).

Local information

● **Accommodation**

C pp *Hotel Selkirk*, clean, good food, full board A pp, rec (T Santiago 531-3772); **A3** *Hostería Robinson Crusoe*, full board, plus 20% tax, about 1 hr walk from the village; **A1** *Daniel Defoe Hotel*, at Aldea Daniel Defoe (T Santiago 531-3772); *Hostería Villa Green*, good. Lodging with villagers is difficult.

● **Banks & money changers**

There are no exchange facilities. Only pesos and US$ cash accepted. No credit cards, no TCs.

● **Transport**

Air Air taxi daily in summer (subject to demand) from Santiago (Los Cerrillos airport, US$395 round trip), by Transportes Aéreas Isla Robinson Crusoe, Monumento 2570, Maipú, Santiago, T 531-4343, F 531-3772, and by Lacsa, Av Larrain 7941, La Reina, Santiago, T 273-4354, F 273-4309; also from Valparaíso. The plane lands on an airstrip in the W of the island; passengers are taken by boat to San Juan Bautista (1½ hrs, US$2 one way).

Sea The boat service, about every 3 weeks from Valparaíso on the *Río Baker* and *Charles Darwin*, is for cargo and passengers, modest accommodation, 36-hr passage; Agentur, Huérfanos 757, oficina 601, T 337118, Santiago. Pesquera Chris, Cueto 622, Santiago, T 681-1543, or Cochrane 445 (near Plaza Sotomayor), Valparaíso, T 216800, 2 week trips to the island (5 days cruising, a week on the island), from US$200 return. No fishing or cargo boats will take passengers.

EASTER ISLAND

Easter Island (Isla de Pascua, Rapa Nui; *phone code* 108) is just S of the Tropic of Capricorn and 3,790 km W of Chile; its nearest neighbour is Pitcairn Island.

Land

It is triangular in shape, 24 km across, with an extinct volcano at each corner. Its original inhabitants called the island Te Pito o te Henua, the navel of the world. The population was stable at 4,000 until the 1850s, when Peruvian slavers, smallpox and emigration to Tahiti (encouraged by plantation-owners) reduced the numbers. Now it is about 2,500, of whom about 500 are from the mainland, mostly living in the village of Hanga Roa. About half the island, of low round hills with groves of eucalyptus, is used for horses and cattle, and nearly one-half constitutes a National Park (entry US$10). The islanders, of Polynesian origin, have preserved their indigenous songs and dances, and are extremely hospitable. Tourism has grown rapidly since the air service began in 1967. Paid work is now more common, but much carving is still done. The islanders have profited greatly from the visits of North Americans: a Canadian medical expedition left a mobile hospital on the island in 1966, and when a US missile-tracking station was abandoned in 1971, vehicles, mobile housing and an electricity generator were left behind. The rainy season is Mar-Oct (wettest in May); the hottest month is Feb, the coldest Aug (15-17°C); the tourist season from Sept to April.

Places of interest

The unique features of the island are the 600 (or so) *moai*, huge stone figures up to 9m in height and broad in proportion. One of them, on Anakena beach, was restored to its (probably) original state with a plaque commemorating Thor Heyerdahl's visit in 1955. Heyerdahl's theories, as expressed in *Aku-Aku, The Art of Easter Island* (New York: Doubleday, 1975), are not as widely accepted as they used to be, and South American influence is now largely discounted (see below). Other *moai* have since been re-erected.

A tour of the main part of the island can be done on foot, but this would need at least 2 days, either camping at Anakena or returning to Hanga Roa and setting out again the next day (but most correspondents agree that this is far too quick). To see more, hire a vehicle. From Hanga Roa, take the road going SE past the airport; at the oil tanks turn right to Vinapu, where there are two *ahu* and a wall whose stones are joined with Inca-like precision. Head back NE along the S coast, past Vaihu (an *ahu* with eight broken *moai*; small harbour); Akahanga (*ahu* with toppled *moai*); Hanga Tetenga (1 toppled *moai*, bones can be seen inside the *ahu*), Ahu Tongariki (once the largest platform, damaged by a tidal wave in 1960, being restored with Japanese aid). Turn left to Rano Raraku (20 km), the volcano where the *moai* were carved. Many statues can be seen. In the crater is a small lake surrounded by reeds (swimming possible beyond the reeds). Good views.

The road heads N past 'the trench of the long-ears' and an excursion can be made to Poike to see the open-mouthed statue that is particularly popular with local carvers (ask farmer for permission to cross his land). On Poike the earth is red; at the NE end is the cave where the virgin was kept before marriage to the victor of ceremonies during the birdman cult (ask directions). The road along the N coast passes Ahu Te Pito Kura, a round stone called the navel of the world and one of largest *moai* ever brought to a platform. It continues to Ovahe. At Ovahe, there is a very attractive beach with pink

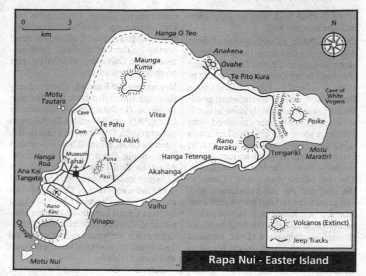

Rapa Nui - Easter Island

sand and some rather recently carved faces and a cave.

From Ovahe, one can return direct to Hanga Roa or continue to Anakena, site of King Hotu Matua's village and Thor Heyerdahl's landing place. From Anakena a coastal path of variable quality passes interesting remains and beautiful cliff scenery. At Hanga o Teo, there appears to be a large village complex, with several round houses, and further on there is a burial place, built like a long ramp with several ditches containing bones. From Hanga o Teo the path goes W then S, inland from the coast, to meet the road N of Hanga Roa.

A 6-hr walk from Hanga Roa on the W coast passes Ahu Tahai (a *moai* with eyes and top knot in place, cave house, just outside town). Two caves are reached, one inland appears to be a ceremonial centre, the other (nearer the sea) has 2 'windows' (take a strong flashlight and be careful near the 'windows'). Further N is Ahu Tepeu (broken *moai*, ruined houses). Beyond here you can join the path mentioned above, or turn right to Te Pahu cave and the seven *moai* at Akivi. Either return to Hanga Roa, or go to Puna Pau crater (2 hrs), where the

topknots were carved (good views from the three crosses at the top).

Rano Kau, S of Hanga Roa, is another important site to visit; one finds the curious Orongo ruins here. The route S out of Hanga Roa passes the two caves of Ana Kai Tangata, one of which has paintings. If on foot you can take a path from the Orongo road, just past the Conaf sign, which is a much shorter route to Rano Kau crater. 200m below is a lake with many reed islands. On the seaward side is Orongo (entrance US$11), where the birdman cult flourished, with many ruined buildings and petroglyphs. Out to sea are the 'bird islets', Motu Nui, Motu Iti and Motu Kao. It is very windy at the summit; good views at sunset, or under a full moon (it is easy to follow the road back to Hanga Roa in the dark).

In Hanga Roa is Ahu Tautira, next to a swimming area marked out with concrete walls and a breakwater (cold water). Music at the 0900 Sun mass is 'enchanting'. Museum near Tahai, US$1, most objects are reproductions because the genuine articles were removed from the island, but it has good descriptions of island life. There is a cultural centre next to the football field, with an exhibition hall and souvenir stall.

David Bulbeck, an anthropologist from Adelaide, proposes one of the main theses about the origins of Easter Island culture: "Far from being the passive recipient of external influences, Easter Island shows the extent of unique development possible for a people left wholly in isolation. It is believed to have been colonized from Polynesia about AD 800: its older altars (*ahu*) are similar to those of (French) Polynesia, and its older statues (*moai*) similar to those of the Marquesas Islands. The very precise stone fitting of some of the *ahu*, and the tall gaunt *moai* with elongated faces and ears for which Easter Island is best known were later developments whose local evolution can be traced through a comparison of the remains. Indigenous Polynesian society, for all its romantic idylls, was competitive, and it seems that the five clans which originally had their own lands demonstrated their strength by erecting these complex monuments. The *moai* were sculpted at the Rano Raraku quarry and transported on wooden rollers over more or less flat paths to their final locations; their red topknots were sculpted at and brought from the inland quarry of Puna Pau; and the rounded pebbles laid out checkerboard fashion at the *ahu* all came from the same beach at Vinapu. The sculptors and engineers were paid out of the surplus food produced by the sponsoring family: Rano Raraku's unfinished *moai* mark the end of the families' ability to pay. Over several centuries from about AD 1400 this stone work slowed down and stopped, owing to the deforestation of the island caused by roller production, and damage to the soils through deforestation and heavy cropping. The birdman cult represented at Orongo is a later development after the islanders had lost their clan territoriality and were concentrated at Hanga Roa, but still needed a non-territorial way to simulate inter-clan rivalry."

Local festivals

Tapati, or *Semana Rapa Nui*, end-Jan/beginning-Feb, lasts one week. Dancing competitions, singing, sports (horse racing, swimming, modified decathlon), body-painting, typical foods (lots of small booths by the football field), necklace-making, etc. Only essential activities carry on outside the festival.

Recommended Reading There is a very thorough illustrated book by J Douglas Porteous, *The Modernization of Easter Island* (1981), available from Department of Geography, University of Victoria, BC, Canada, US$6. See also Thor Heyerdahl's work, details above; *Easter Island, Earth Island*, by Paul Bahn and John Flenley (Thames and Hudson, 1992) for a comprehensive appraisal of the island's archaeology. *Islas Oceánicas Chilenas*, edited by Juan Carlos Castillo (Ediciones Universidad Católica de Chile, 1987), contains much information on the natural history and geography of Juan Fernández and Easter Islands.

Anyone continuing into Polynesia or Melanesia from Easter Island will find David Stanley's *South Pacific Handbook* (Moon Publications Inc, PO Box 3040, Chico, CA 95927, USA, F 1-916-345-6751) a useful guidebook.

Local information

Time zone: Easter Island is always 2 hrs behind the Chilean mainland, summer and winter time.

● **Accommodation**

The airport information desk displays a list of accommodation. In practice this only covers the more expensive places. Flights are met by large numbers of hotel and *residencial* representatives but it is cheaper to look for yourself. Accommodation ranges from US$10-200. Note that room rates, especially in *residenciales* can be much cheaper out of season and if you do not take full board.

L3 *Hanga Roa*, Av Pont, inc all meals (120 beds), no credit cards, breakfast inc, T 223299 (Santiago 633-9130, F 639-5334); **L3** *Iorana Hotel*, Ana Magara promontory, 5 mins from airport, T 223312 (Santiago 633-2650), friendly, excellent food, convenient for visiting Ana Kai Targata caves.

A1 *Easter Island*, Policarpo Toro, Hanga Roa, breakfast and dinner (excellent restaurant), good service, nice garden, T 223294, or Santiago 211-6747; **A1** *Otai*, Te Pilo Te Henua, T 223250, comfortable, friendly, family run, rec; **A1** *Victoria*, Av Pont, T 223272, friendly, helpful owner arranges tours; **A1** *Topo Ra'a*, Atamu Kekena, T 223223, 5 mins from Hanga Roa, very good, helpful, excellent restaurant; **A3** *Poike*, Petero Atamu, T 223283, homely, hot water.

Homes offering accommodation and tours (rates ranging from US$18 to US$35, inc meals): **A1** *Res Pedro Atán*, T 223329, full board, Policarpo Toro; **A1** *Res Apina Nui*, Hetereki, T 223292 (C low season, but bargain), good food, helpful, English spoken; Yolanda Ika's **A2** *Res Taire Ngo Oho*, T 223259, with breakfast, rec, modern; Krenia Tucki's **A2** *Res Kai Poo*, Av Pont, small, clean, friendly with hot water; **A2** *Res Hanga Roa Reka*, T 223276, full board, good, friendly, camping US$5; María Georgina Hucke, of Tiki Tours, **B** with half board, rec; *Res El Tauke*, Tepito Te Henua s/n, T 223253, same rates as *Hanga Roa Reka*, excellent, airport transfers, tours arranged; *Res Taheta One One*, T 223257, same rates, motorbike rental; **B** *Res Tahai*, Simón Paoa s/n, T 223338, with breakfast, A2 full board, nice garden, rec; **B** pp *Res Holiday Inn*, T 223337, half board, excellent food, hot water, rec; **C** Anita and Martín Pate's guesthouse, opp hospital in Hanga Roa, half board in high season, less low season, clean, good food; **D** pp *Res Taniera*, T 223290, also camping, horses; **D** pp María Cecilia Cardinale, nr Tahai Moai, half board, speaks English and French, excellent food, camping US$5; **D** María Goretti, rooms with breakfast, camping US$6; **D** pp *Ana Rapu*, C Apina, T 223540, F 223318, inc breakfast, evening meal US$7, camping US$5, comfortable, family-run, hot water (except when demand is heavy), English spoken; **C** pp *Res Viaka Pua*, Simón Paoa, Hanga Roa, T 223377, full board, comfortable, friendly, rec. **A3** Emilio and Milagrosa Paoa, with full board, rec accommodation and tours. Unless it is a particularly busy season there is no need to book in advance; mainland agencies make exorbitant booking charges.

Camping: free in eucalyptus groves nr the Ranger's house at Rano Raraku (with water tank), and at Anakena, no water, make sure your tent is ant-proof. Officially, camping is not allowed anywhere else, but this is not apparently strictly enforced. Many people also offer campsites in their gardens, US$5-10 pp (Ana Rapu rec), check availability of water first; some families also provide food. Several habitable caves around the coast: eg between Anakena beach and Ovahe. If you must leave anything behind in a cave, leave only what may be of use to other campers, candles, oil, etc, certainly not rubbish. **NB** There is no camping equipment for hire on the island.

● **Places to eat**
Mama Sabina, Av Policarpo Toro, clean, welcoming; another opp municipal market (which does not sell food). *Pizzeria*, opp post office, moderately priced. Several others. Most *residenciales* offer full board. Coffee is always instant. Beware of extras such as US$3 charge for hot water.

● **Banks & money changers**
Best done in Santiago. Bank next to Entel, open 0900-1200 daily for exchange. Bank charges US$12 commission on changing TCs, but you can change as many TCs for this fee as you like (and they can be in different names). Cash can be exchanged in shops, hotels, etc, at about 3% less than Santiago. Prices are quoted in dollars, but bills can be paid in pesos and many items, such as food, are priced in pesos. Amex credit cards are accepted on the island, but credit cards cannot be used to obtain cash. While most places accept TCs, cash dollars are expected. Best rates of exchange at Sunoco service station, also accepts Amex TCs and gives cash on Amex cards. Kia-Koe Land Operator, *Hanga Roa Hotel*, changes Amex cheques.

● **Entertainment**
Discotheques: there are 3 in Hanga Roa: *Maitiki* (open daily), E side of town, with pool table; *Toroko*, nr harbour (open Thur-Sat), US$1.25, and *Piditi*, nr airport (open Thur-Sat). Also *Maitaka* at Tararaina, only one open Wed. Action begins after 0100. Drinks are expensive: a bottle of pisco costs US$9, canned beer US$2.

● **Hospitals & medical services**
There are a 20-bed hospital, 2 resident doctors, a trained nurse and 2 dentists on the island.

● **Post & telecommunications**
Post Office: 0900-1700.

Telephones: Phone calls from the Chilean mainland are subsidized, at US$0.35/minute. Calls to Europe cost US$10 for 3 mins, cheap rate after 1400.

● **Shopping**
On Av Policarpo Toro, the main street, there are lots of small shops and market stalls (which may close during rain) and a couple of supermarkets, cheapest *Kai Nene* or *Tumukai*. Local produce which can be found free (but ask) inc wild guava fruit, fish, 'hierba luisa' tea, and wild chicken. Food, wine and beer are expensive because of freight charges, but local fish, vegetables, fruit and bread are cheap. Average prices: coffee/tea US$0.50, meals about US$7.50, snacks US$1, bread US$2/kg, beer/cola US$1.50 in most bars and restaurants. Bring all you can from the mainland, but not fruit. Vegetarians will have no problems on the island.

Handicrafts: wood carvings, stone moais, best bought from the craftsmen themselves, such as Antonio Tepano Tucki, Juan Acka, Hipolito Tucki and his son (who are knowledgeable about the old culture). The municipal market, left of church, will give you a good view of what is available – no compunction to buy. The airport shop is expensive. Good pieces cost between US$30 and 150. Souvenirs at *Hotu Matuu's Favorite Shoppe* have been described as 'top dollar and she will not bargain', but she does have the best T-shirts. There is a *mercado artesanal* next to the church and people sell handicrafts at Tahai, Vaihu, Rano Raraku and Anakena. Bargaining is only possible if you pay cash.

● **Sports**

Hiking: allow at least a day to walk the length of the island, one way, taking in all the sites. It is 5 easy hours from Hanga Roa to Rano Raraku (camp at ranger station); 5 hrs to Anakena (camp at ranger station, but ask first). You can hitch back to Hanga Roa, especially at weekends though there are few cars at other times. Anyone wishing to spend time exploring the island would be well-advised to speak to Conaf first (T 223236); they also give good advice on special interests (biology, archaeology, handicrafts, etc). **Horseback**: the best way to see the island, provided you are fit, is on horseback: horses, US$20-25 a day. A guide is useful. Try Emilio Arakie Tepane, who also leads horseback tours of the island (Spanish only) T 504.

● **Tour companies & travel agents**

Mahinatur Ltda, vehicle reservations in advance. Their guide, Christian Walter, is rec; *Kia-Koe*, at *Hanga Roa Hotel; Schmidt Osterinsel Reisen*, office in Hanga Roa Hotel, T 223600, F 223532, English, French and German spoken, offers tours around the island and to caves, both US$15. Maps are sold on Av Policarpo Toro for US$15-18, or at the ranger station at Orongo for US$10. LanChile office on Av Policarpo Toro provides tours of the island (inc during stopovers). Many agencies, *residenciales* and locals arrange excursions around the island, eg: *Aku-Aku Tours*, Krenia Tucki of *Res Kai Poo*, Michel Fage, Fernando and Marcelo León (Pai Tepano Rano, rec), Hugo Teave (good English, well-informed, polite), Charles Wilkins, *Agencia de Viajes Mahinatur Ltda*, T 20, English-born guide, rec, as is Victoriano Giralde, *Kia-Koe Tours*. Some go in jeeps, others will accompany tourists in hired vehicles (eg US$130 for 8), prices up to US$30 pp/day. The English of other tour guides is often poor.

● **Transport**

Local There is one taxi and in summer a bus goes from Hanga Roa to Anakena on Sun at 1300, returning 1400 (perhaps). **Vehicle rental**: a high-clearance vehicle is better-suited to the roads than a normal vehicle. If you are hiring a car, do the sites from S to N since travel agencies tend to start their tours in the N. Jeep hire at **Sunoco service station**, Vaihu, T 223325 or 223239, on airport road, US$10/1 hr, US$20/4 hrs, US$50/day. **Hertz**, opp airport, US$50 a day. Many other vehicle hire agencies on the main street. Chilean or international driving licence essential. There is no insurance available, drive at your own risk (be careful at night, many vehicles drive without lights). **Motorbike rental**: about US$35 a day inc gasoline (Suzuki or Honda 250 rec because of rough roads). Rentals from Av Policarpo Toro, T 223326. **Bicycles**: some in poor condition, are available for rent for US$15 on main street or from *residenciales*, or you can buy a robust one in Santiago (LanChile transports bikes free up to a limit of 20 kg) and sell it on the island after 4 days.

Transport to Easter Island Air LanChile fly 4 days a week in high season (Sat, Sun, Tues, Thur), 2 days a week low season (Sun, Thur) 3 hrs 5 mins. Return to Santiago is Mon, Tues, Fri and Sat (Mon, Fri out of season). Most flights continue to Papeete, Tahiti. LanChile's office on Av Policarpo Toro, T 223279, reconfirm flights here – imperative; do not fly to Easter Island unless you have a confirmed flight out (planes are more crowded to Tahiti, to which LanChile's flights continue, than back to Santiago) and reconfirm your booking on arrival on the Island. For details of LanChile's air passes which inc Easter Island and which must be purchased outside Chile, see **Information for travellers**. The fare in April 1996 was US$812 return. Special deals may be available on flights originating outside Chile. Get to airport early and be prepared for a scramble for seats. Students studying in Chile eligible for 30% discount. If flying to, or from Tahiti, check if you can stay over till another flight or even if there is time for sightseeing before the flight continues – US$10 stop-over sightseeing tours can be arranged (in either case it won't be long enough to take it all in properly). Don't take pesos to Tahiti, they are worthless in French Polynesia. The airport runway has been improved to provide emergency landing for US space shuttles. **Airport tax**: flying from Santiago to Easter Island incurs the domestic tax of US$5; if flying to Tahiti without stopping on Easter Island you pay the international departure tax of US$12.50. The airport tax for international flights from Easter Island to Tahiti is US$5.

Sea There are no passenger services to Easter Island. Freight is brought by sea 3 times a year.

Information for travellers

BEFORE YOU GO

ENTRY REQUIREMENTS

● **Documents**

Passport (valid for at least 6 months) and tourist card only are required for entry by all foreigners except citizens of New Zealand, Guyana, Haiti, Kuwait, African countries, Cuba and some ex-Communist countries, who require visas. It is imperative to check visa requirements before travel. These details were correct in May 1996 according to the Chilean Consul in London, but regulations change. National identity cards are sufficient for entry by citizens of Argentina, Brazil, Colombia, Paraguay, and Uruguay. Tourist cards are valid for 90 days (except for nationals of Greece, Indonesia and Peru where their validity is 60 days); they can be obtained from immigration offices at major land frontiers and Chilean airports; you must surrender your tourist card on departure and it is essential that you keep it safe. If you wish to stay longer than 180 days (as a tourist), it is easier to make a day-trip to Argentina and return with a new tourist card, rather than to apply for a visa, which involves a great deal of paperwork. An onward ticket is officially required but is seldom asked for. 90-day extensions (US$8) are obtained from any local Gobernación office, which will require proof of funds, then you have to go to Investigaciones for an international record check. Tourist card holders are not allowed to change their status to enable them to stay on in employment or as students: to do this you need a visa, obtained from a Chilean consulate. On arrival you will be asked where you are staying in Chile. For some nationalities a visa will be granted within 24 hrs upon production of an onward ticket, for others (eg Guyana), authorization must be obtained from Chile. For visitors from New Zealand, single or multiple entry visa costs US$45. For other nationalities who need a visa, a charge is made, but it varies from country to country. Note that to travel overland to or from Tierra del Fuego a multiple entry visa is essential since the Argentine-Chilean border is crossed more than once (it is advisable to get a multiple entry visa before arriving, rather than trying to change a single entry visa once in Chile). A student card is sometimes useful for obtaining discounts on buses, etc. Student cards can be obtained from Providencia 2594, Local 421 and cost US$8, photo and proof of status required.

● **Tourist information**

The national secretariat of tourism, *Sernatur*, has offices throughout the country (addresses are given in the text). City offices provide town maps, leaflets and much useful information. A rec guide book is *Turistel*, published annually in three parts, *Norte*, *Centro*, and *Sur*, sponsored by the CTC telephone company, with information and a wealth of maps covering the whole country and neighbouring tourist centres in Argentina (eg Mendoza, San Martín de los Andes, Bariloche), in Spanish only. Each volume costs between US$11-15, depending where you buy it, but buying the whole set is better value; they can be found in CTC offices, bookshops, but best of all in the news stands in the centre of Santiago. Turistel also publishes a *Mapa rutero* annually, US$4 from news stands and a guide to camping US$9. The publisher is Impresora y Comercial Publiguías SA. **Conaf** (the Corporacíon Nacional Forestal see page 692) publishes a series of illustrated booklets in Spanish/English on Chilean trees, shrubs and flowers, rec, as well as **Juventud, Turismo y Naturaleza**, which lists National Parks, their facilities and the flora and fauna of each. Ancient Forest International, Box 1850, Redway, CA 95560, T/F 707-323-3015, USA, can be contacted regarding Chilean forests. Bird-lovers will appreciate *Guía de Campo de Las Aves de Chile*, by B Araya and G Millie.

WHEN TO GO

● **Best time to visit**

The best time for a visit to Santiago is between Oct and April when fine weather is almost assured, but business visits can be made any time during the year. During the holiday season, between mid Dec and early March, it is sometimes difficult to make appointments.

HEALTH

Tap water is fairly safe to drink in the main cities but bottled water is safer away from the larger centres. Hotels and restaurants are usually clean. Inoculation against hepatitis and typhoid is a wise precaution. Hepatitis type **B** inoculation is unavailable.

Tampons are available but expensive.

MONEY

● **Currency**

The unit is the peso, its sign is $. Notes are for 500, 1,000, 5,000 and 10,000 pesos and coins for 1, 5, 10, 50 and 100 pesos. There is a shortage of change so keep a supply of small denomination coins.

● **Cost of living**

Shops throughout Chile are well stocked and there is a seasonal supply of all the usual fruits and vegetables. Milk in pasteurized, evaporated, or dried form is obtainable. Chilean tinned food is dear. Food is reasonable, but food prices vary tremendously. Santiago tends to be more expensive for food and accommodation than other parts of Chile. Slide film is very expensive, much cheaper in Bolivia.

In 1995-96 the average cost for a traveller on an economical budget was about US$250/week. Cheap accommodation in Santiago costs over US$10 pp while N and S of the capital rates are US$6-10 pp. Breakfast in hotels, if not inc in price, is about US$2 (instant coffee, roll with ham or cheese, and jam). *Alojamiento* in private houses (bed, breakfast and often use of kitchen) costs US$7-10 pp (bargaining may be possible). Southern Chile is more expensive

between 15 Dec and 15 March.

Stop Press Since the calculations for prices in this chapter were made, the peso has continued to appreciate against the dollar. Unless government policy alters the exchange rate, travellers will find that Chile will become more expensive for those carrying dollars.

● **Banks & money changers**

Travellers' cheques are accepted at reasonable rates if exchanging them for pesos, though rates are better in Santiago than in most other places and this has become more difficult in most towns apart from Arica, Antofagasta and Puerto Montt. TCs can be changed into dollars in Santiago, but is much more difficult elsewhere: check if a commission is charged as this practice seems to vary. Even slightly damaged US dollar notes may be rejected for exchange. Exchange shops (*casas de cambio*) are open longer hours and often give slightly better rates than banks. It is always worth shopping around. Rates tend to get worse as you go N from Santiago. Official rates are quoted in *El Economista* and *El Mercurio*.

Prices may be quoted in US dollars; check if something seems ridiculously cheap. Remember that foreigners who pay with US dollars cash or TCs are not liable for VAT.

The easiest way to obtain cash is by using ATMs (in major cities) which operate under the sign Redbank; they take Cirrus, Visa and Mastercard and permit transactions up to US$250. Diners' Club, Visa and Mastercard are common in Chile (Bancard, the local card, is affliated to the last two), offices can be found in most cities and will give cash against the cards: Fincard handles Mastercard and Banco Concepción takes Visa, but American Express is less useful (use in American Express banks does not incur commission). US dollars cash are very rarely given against cards or cheques. For Western Union, T (02) 696-8807.

GETTING THERE

BY AIR

● **From Europe**

To Santiago: British Airways from London via Rio or São Paulo (three times a week); Air France from Paris (3 per week); from Madrid LanChile and Iberia (4 a week each); KLM from Amsterdam (3), Lufthansa (3) and LanChile from Frankfurt (4 a week), Alitalia from Rome (2) and Aeroflot from Moscow (2). Connections from Europe can be in Buenos Aires.

● **From North America**

American Airlines fly daily from Miami, once direct, once via Buenos Aires. LanChile also has daily flights from Miami. Also from Miami,

United flies daily. Also from Miami, Lacsa with connections in San José. From New York, United and Lan Chile. From Los Angeles there are flights with LanChile via Mexico City and Lima, and Lacsa via Mexico City, San José and Lima. From Dallas with American. From other US cities, connect with LanChile flights in Miami, New York or Los Angeles. CP Air have 2 flights per week from Toronto (changing planes in São Paulo).

● **Transpacific routes**
LanChile flies once or twice a week, depending on season, between Tahiti (making connections from Japan, Australia and New Zealand) and Santiago; they stop over at Easter Island. For excursion fares between Australia/New Zealand and Chile, the stopovers at Easter Island now carry a surcharge of about US$125.

● **Within Latin America**
To/from Buenos Aires (about 75/week) by Lan-Chile, Aerolíneas Argentinas, Air France, Alitalia, KLM, Swissair, American, or Avianca (many depart at the same time, check carefully); from Mendoza by Aerolíneas Argentinas or National. From Montevideo (8 per week) by LanChile and Pluna; from Asunción 6 times a week by National, 5 days a week with Lapsa; from Rio de Janeiro with British Airways (once) and Iberia direct (4 a week), Lan Chile, or Varig via São Paulo; from São Paulo non-stop by LanChile, Varig, British Airways; from La Paz 5 per week by Lloyd Aéreo Boliviano (LAB) and daily with LanChile (LAB also from Cochabamba twice a week and Santa Cruz 2 a week, LanChile 3 a week from Santa Cruz); from Caracas, LanChile and Viasa; from Lima (20/week) by Aeroperú, Lacsa, United and LanChile; from Bogotá by Avianca and Lan Chile; from Ecuador, Tame and Saeta non-stop from Guayaquil, all flights start in Quito.

To Arica and Iquique, from La Paz and Santa Cruz by LAB and LanChile. National flies from Arequipa to Arica and Iquique, also to Iquique from Asunción.

● **Overland From Neighbouring Countries**
By land: Roads connect Santiago with Mendoza, and Osorno and Puerto Montt with Bariloche, in Argentina. Less good road connections N and S of Santiago are described in the main text. The main route connecting northern Chile with Bolivia (Arica-La Paz) is paved on the Chilean side. Other routes are poor. Note that any of the passes across the Andes to Argentina can be blocked by snow from April onwards. In 1995, the possibility of all Chile/Argentina land borders being open 24 hrs a day was under study.

Three international railways link Chile with its neighbours. There are two railways to Bolivia:

between Arica and La Paz (448 km), and from Antofagasta via Calama to La Paz. Between Chile and Argentina there is only one line now in operation, between Antofagasta and Salta, in the Argentine NW. There is no international passenger service on this line.

CUSTOMS

● **Duty free allowance**
500 cigarettes, 100 cigars, 500 grams of tobacco, 3 bottles of liquor, camera, and all articles of personal use. Fruit, vegetables, meat, flowers and milk products may not be imported. It has been reported that bringing a video recorder into Chile involves a great deal of paperwork.

NB There are internal customs checks for all travellers going S on leaving the First Region (ie for duty-free goods from the Zofri free zone in Iquique).

WHEN YOU ARRIVE

● **Entry tax**
A US$20 entry tax is charged on all US citizens, valid until expiry of passport.

● **Clothing**
Warm sunny days and cool nights are usual during most of the year except in the far S where the climate is like that of Scotland. Ordinary European medium-weight clothing can be worn during the winter (June to mid-Sept). Light clothing is best for summer (Dec to Mar), but men do not wear white tropical suits. Chileans are very fashion-conscious. Dress well though conservatively: practical travel clothing makes you stick out as a foreigner.

● **Hours of business**
Banks: 0900-1400, but closed on Sat. Government offices: 1000-1230 (the public is admitted for a few hrs only). Business houses: 0830-1230, 1400-1800 (Mon to Fri). Shops (Santiago): 1030-1930, but 0930-1330 Sat.

● **Law enforcement**
Officers are Caribineros (brown military uniforms), who handle all tasks except immigration. Investigaciones, in civilian dress, are the detective police who deal with everything except traffic. Policia Internacional, a division of Investigaciones, handle immigration.

● **Official time**
GMT minus 4 hrs; minus 3 hrs in summer. Clocks change from mid-Sept or Oct to early March.

● **Shopping**
There is an excellent variety of handicrafts: woodwork, pottery, copperware, leatherwork, Indian woven goods inc rugs and ponchos in the S. VAT is 18%.

● **Tipping**
10% in restaurants and a few pesos in bars and soda fountains. Railway and airport porters: US$0.10 a piece of luggage. Cloakroom attendants and cinema usherettes: US$0.05. Taxi-drivers are not tipped.

● **Voltage**
220 volts AC, 50 cycles.

● **Weights & measures**
The **metric** system is obligatory but the quintal of 46 kilos (101.4 lb) is used.

ON DEPARTURE

● **Airport & other taxes**
7,500 pesos, or US$18.25 for international flights; US$8 for domestic flights. There is a tourist tax on single air fares of 2%, and 1% on return fares beginning or ending in Chile; also a sales tax of 5% on all transport within Chile.

WHERE TO STAY

● **Accommodation**
On hotel bills service charges are usually 10%, and VAT on bills is 18%. Prices increase in January. **If you pay in dollars cash or TCs, you do not have to pay VAT.** Dollar rates posted in hotels should not include VAT; peso rates should by law.Whether or not the 18% is added to bills in hotel restaurants that are signed and charged to the hotel bill depends on the policy of the establishment. When booking in make certain whether meals are included in the price or only breakfast or nothing at all, and don't rely on the posted sheet in the bedroom for any prices. It is often worth asking for a discount, especially out of season. Particularly in North and Central Chile breakfast is likely to be coffee and bread or toast. In more popular tourist destinations, especially in the S, large numbers of families offer accommodation: these are usually advertised by a sign in the window; people often meet buses to offer accommodation. If you are looking for a motel, ask for a *motel turístico*; most motels are short stay.

● **Camping**
Camping is easy but no longer cheap at official sites. A common practice is to charge US$10 for up to 5 people, with no reductions for fewer than 5. 'Camping Gaz International' stoves are rec, since green replaceable cylinders are available in Santiago (white gas – *benzina blanca* – is available in hardware shops; for good value try the *Sodimac* chain of DIY stores). Copec run a network of 33 'Rutacentros' along Ruta 5 which have showers, cafeterias and offer free camping. Free camping is also available at many filling stations.

● **Youth hostels**
There are youth hostels throughout Chile; average cost about US$5-8 pp. Although some hostels are open only from Jan to the end of Feb, many operate all year round. The IYHA card is usually readily accepted. In summer they are usually crowded and noisy, with only floor space available. Chilean YHA card costs US$4. An additional stamp costing US$4 enables you to use the card in Argentina, Uruguay and Brazil. IYHA card costs US$15. These can be obtained from the Asociación Chilena de Albergues Turísticos Juveniles, Providencia 2594, oficina 420-421, Providencia, Santiago, T 233-3226; together with a useful guidebook of all Youth Hostels in Chile, *Guía Turística de los Albergues Juveniles*. In summer there are makeshift hostels in many Chilean towns, usually in the main schools.

FOOD AND DRINK

FOOD

A very typical Chilean dish is *cazuela de ave*, a nutritious stew containing large pieces of chicken, potatoes, rice, and maybe onions, and green peppers; best if served on the second day. *Valdiviano* is another stew, common in the S, consisting of beef, onion, sliced potatoes and eggs. Another popular Chilean dish is *empanadas de pino*, which are turnovers filled with a mixture of raisins, olives, meat, onions and peppers chopped up together. *Pastel de choclo* is a casserole of meat and onions with olives, topped with a maize-meal mash, baked in an earthenware bowl. *Humitas* are mashed sweet-corn mixed with butter and spices and baked in sweetcorn leaves. *Prieta* is a blood sausage stuffed with cabbage leaves. A normal *parrillada* or *asado* is a giant mixed grill served from a charcoal brazier. The *pichanga* is similar but smaller and without the brazier. *Bistek a lo pobre* (a poor man's steak) can be just the opposite: it is a steak topped by a fried egg, mashed potatoes, onions and salad.

What gives Chilean food its personality is the seafood. The delicious *congrio* fish is a national dish, and *caldillo de congrio* (a soup served with a massive piece of conger, onions and potato balls) is excellent. A *paila* can take many forms (the *paila* is simply a kind of dish), but the commonest are made of eggs or seafood. *Paila Chonchi* is a kind of bouillabaisse, but has more flavour, more body, more ingredients. *Parrillada de mariscos* is a dish of grilled mixed seafood, brought to the table piping hot on a charcoal brazier. Other excellent local fish are the *cojinoa*, the *albacora* (swordfish) and the *corvina*. Some shellfish, such as *loco* (known to Australians as abalone) and mussels may be periodically banned because they carry the disease *marea roja* (which is fatal in humans). *Cochayuyo* is seaweed, bound into bundles, described as 'hard, leathery thongs'. The *erizo*, or sea-urchin, is also commonly eaten. *Luche* is dried seaweed, sold as a black cake, like 'flakey bread pudding' to be added to soups and stews.

Avocado pears, or *paltas*, are excellent, and play an important role in recipes. Make sure whether vegetables are included in the price for the main dish; menus often don't make this clear. Always best, if being economical, to stick to fixed-price *table d'hôte* meals or try the local markets. A *barros jarpa* is a grilled cheese and ham sandwich and a *barras luco* is a grilled cheese and beef sandwich. *Sopaipillas* are cakes made of a mixture which includes pumpkin, served in syrup (traditionally made in wet weather). Ice cream is very good; *lúcuma* and *chirimoya* are highly rec flavours.

Lunch is about 1300 and dinner not before 2030. *Onces* (Elevenses) is tea taken at 1700, often accompanied by a snack. The cocktail hour starts at 1900. Waiters are known as *garzón* – never as *mozo*. Good, cheap meals can usually be found in Centros Españoles or Casinos de Bomberos. By law restaurants have to serve a cheaper set meal at lunchtime; it is called *colación* and may not be included on the menu.

Coffee is generally instant except in expresso bars including popular chains of cafés such as *Café Haiti*, *Café Brasil* and *Dino*, found in major cities. Elsewhere specify *café-café*, *expresso*. The soluble tea should be avoided, but tea-bags are widely available. If you order '*café*, or *té*, *con leche*', it will come with all milk; to have just a little milk in either, you must specify that. After a meal, instead of coffee, try an *agüita* – hot water in which herbs such as mint, or aromatics such as lemon peel, have been steeped. There is a wide variety, available in sachets, and they are very refreshing.

DRINK

The local wines are very good; the best are from the central areas. Among the good *bodegas* are Cousiño Macul, Santa Carolina, Undurraga, Concha y Toro, Tocornal, San Pedro and Santa Helena. Santa Elena (no H) is less good. The bottled wines are graded, in increasing excellence, as *gran vino*, *vino especial* and *vino reservado*. Champagne-style wines are also cheap and acceptable. A small deposit, US$0.30, is charged on most wine bottles. Beer is quite good and cheap (about US$0.75, plus US$0.75 deposit in shops); the draught lager known as Schop is good; also try Cristal Pilsener or Royal Guard in the central regions and Escudo and

Polar in the S. Malta, a brown ale, is rec for those wanting a British-type beer.

Good gin is made in Chile. Reasonably good brandy, *anís* and crème de menthe are all bottled in Chile. *Pisco* is worth sampling, especially as a 'Pisco Sour' with grapefruit or lemon juice. *Manzanilla* is a local liqueur, made from *licor de oro* (like Galliano); *crema de cacao*, especially Mitjans, has been rec. Two popular drinks are *vaina*, a mixture of sherry, egg and sugar and *cola de mono*, a mixture of *aguardiente*, coffee, milk and vanilla served very cold at Christmas. *Chicha* is any form of alcoholic drink made from fruit; *chicha cocida* is 3-day-old fermented grape juice boiled to reduce its volume and then bottled with a tablespoonful of honey. Cider (*chicha de manzana*) is popular in the S. *Chicha fresca* is plain apple juice. *Mote con huesillo*, made from wheat hominy and dried peaches, is very refreshing in summer.

GETTING AROUND

AIR TRANSPORT

Most flights of LanChile, Ladeco and National, between Santiago and major towns and cities, are given in the text. A new airline, Alta, flies Beechcraft 1900-C planes the length of the country, linking smaller cities. Try to sit on the left flying S, on the right flying N to get the best views of the Andes.

LanChile and Ladeco offer a 21-day 'Visit Chile' ticket; 5 prices: US$300, valid for Santiago and northern Chile, or Santiago and southern Chile; US$550 for all mainland Chile; Pacific 1, US$812, Santiago-Easter Island-Santiago; Pacific 2, US$1080, valid for a trip to Easter Island and either northern Chile, or southern Chile; Pacific 3, US$1,290 for all mainland Chile and Eastern Island. It must be purchased abroad in conjunction with an international ticket and reservations made well ahead since many flights are fully booked in advance. Rerouting charges US$30. Booked destinations can be left out so it is worth including as many destinations as possible. The airpass is not interchangeable between airlines. It is also possible for the route Santiago – Antofagasta – Arica – Santiago to take a coupon ticket which allows greater flexibility. **NB** Book well in advance (several months) for flights to Easter Island in Jan-February. Check with the airlines for matrimonial, student and other discounts. Both LanChile and Ladeco sell out-eXpress tickets (up to 50% off) either as part of special promotions or to stand-by passengers (though the availability of standby fares is often denied). Note that with some fares it is as cheap to fly long distance as take a *salón cama* bus, especially with National, whose fares are usually considerably lower than LanChile or Ladeco. **NB** You have to confirm domestic flights at least 24 hrs before departure.

LAND TRANSPORT

● Train

There are 4,470 km of line, of which most are state owned. Most of the privately owned 2,130 km of line are in the desert N, where the northern terminal is Iquique. The main gauge on the Valparaíso and southern lines is 5-ft 6 in (1.676m). Passenger services in the S go as far as Puerto Montt. Passenger services N of the Valparaíso area have ceased except for the international routes to La Paz. The Ferrocarriles del Estado publish an annual *Guía Turística*, available in various languages from the larger stations.

Trains in Chile are moderately priced, and not as slow as in other Andean countries, but dining car food is expensive. Student discounts are given on *económico* and *salón* fares, but not on sleepers. There is a railway information office at O'Higgins 853 (at end of arcade), Santiago, for all lines except the Antofagasta-Bolivia (Ahumada 11, Oficina 602, T 698-5536). English spoken.

● Roads

About one-half of the 79,593 km of roads can be used the year round, though a large proportion of them is unimproved and about 11,145 km are paved. The region round the capital and the Central Valley are the best served.

The Pan-American (Longitudinal) Highway, Ruta 5, from Arica through Santiago to Puerto Montt and recently extended by the Carretera Austral beyond Cochrane to within 30 km of its terminus, is vital to the Chilean economy and is paved to Puerto Montt.

● Bus

Buses are frequent and on the whole good. Apart from holiday times, there is little problem getting a seat on a long-distance bus. *Salón-cama* services run between main cities (TurBus and Tramaca highly rec). Generally avoid back seats near toilet due to smell and disruption of passing passengers. *Salón-cama* means 25 seats, *semi-cama* means 34 and *Salón-ejecutivo* means 44 seats. Stops are infrequent. Prices are highest between Dec-Mar and fares from Santiago double during the Independence celebrations in September. Since there is lots of competition between bus companies, fares may be bargained lower, particularly just before departure. Students and holders of IYHA cards may get discounts, amount varies, but not usually in high season. Most bus companies will carry bicycles, but may ask for payment (on TurBus payment is mandatory).

● Motoring

Car drivers require a *Relaciones de pasajeros* document, available at borders, and must present the original registration document of their vehicle, as must motor cyclists. Insurance is obligatory and can be bought at borders. See also **Motoring** in **Introduction and Hints**. The Carta Caminera from the Dirección de Vialidad is the most detailed road map (series of 26) but is only available at Vialidad, Marsende y Alameda, Santiago. Reasonable road maps may also be obtained from the Automóvil Club de Chile, Av Vitacura 8620, Santiago; or other regional offices. You will find several individual maps provide much greater detail than the Club's road atlas. Members of foreign motoring organizations may join the Automóvil Club de Chile (US$58/3months), and obtain discounts at hotels. Town maps from the Automóvil Club and Copec service stations. Shell publish a *Guía caminera y turística de Chile*. The *Turistel* Guides are very useful for roads and town plans, but note that not all distances are exact and that the description 'ripio' (gravel) usually requires high clearance; 'buen ripio' should be OK for ordinary cars. Hydrographic maps from Instituto Hidrográfico, Malgarejo 59, Valparaíso. Gasoline (sold in litres) costs the equivalent of US$2.40 a gallon; it becomes more expensive the further N and further S you go. Unleaded fuel, 93 octane, is available at many service stations, but less frequently outside Santiago and not in the Atacama region. Unleaded 95 and 97 octane are less common. Diesel fuel is widely available. Service stations are frequently reluctant to accept credit cards. Often when they advertise that they accept credit cards, they refuse to do so: always ask beforehand. In Santiago car parts available from many shops on C 10 de Julio. For car and motorcycle tyres try Serranos 32, reported to be the best stock in South America.

Carabineros are strict about speed limits: Turistel maps mark police posts, make sure you are not speeding when you pass them. Car drivers should have all their papers in order and to hand since there are frequent checks, but fewer in the S. When driving in the S (on the Carretera Austral particularly), and in the desert N, always top up your fuel tank and carry spare petrol/gasoline. Car hire companies may not have fuel cans. These are obtainable from some supermarkets but not from service stations. Tyres need to be hard-wearing (avoid steel belt); it is rec to carry more than one spare and additional inner tubes.

For motorcyclists the following shops in Santiago have been rec: *Calvín y Calvín*, Av Las Condes 8038, T 224-3434, run by Winston Calvín, friendly, helpful, speaks English, knows about necessary paperwork for buying bikes,

Honda and Yamaha parts and service; *Solo Moto*, Vitacura 2760, T 2311178, English spoken, service and parts for Honda and Yamaha; *Moto Service*, Vitacura 2715, new and second-hand Honda and Yamaha dealer; *Guillermo de Freitas Rojas* (Willy), C Félix Mendelson, 4740-Santiago, T 521-1853, excellent BMW mechanic; *Miebacc*, Doble Almeda 1040, Nunoa, T 2237533, for BMW parts and service. Mechanics, etc outside Santiago are given in the text.

● **Car hire**
Many agencies, both local and international, operate in Chile. Vehicles may be rented by the day, the week or the month, with or without unlimited mileage. Rates quoted do not normally include insurance or 18% VAT. Make sure you know what the insurance covers, in particular third-party insurance. Often this is only likely to cover small bumps and scratches. Ask about extra cover for a further premium. If you are in a major accident and your insurance is inadequate, your stay in Chile may well be prolonged beyond its intended end. A small car, with unlimited mileage costs about US$500 a week in high season, a pick-up much more. In some areas rates are much lower off-season. (At peak holiday times, eg Independence celebrations, car hire is very difficult.) Shop around, there is much competition. Note that the Automóvil Club de Chile has a car hire agency (with discounts for members or affiliates) and that the office may not be at the same place as the Club's regional delegation. **NB** If intending to leave the country in a hired car, you must obtain an authorization from the hire company, otherwise you will be turned back at the frontier. When leaving Chile this is exchanged for a quadruple form, one part of which is surrendered at each border control. (If you plan to leave more than once you will need to photocopy the authorization.)

● **Taxis**
Taxis have meters, but agree beforehand on fares for long journeys out of city centres or special excursions. A 50% surcharge is applied after 2100 and on Sun. Taxi drivers rarely know the location of any streets away from the centre. There is no need to tip unless some extra service, like the carrying of luggage, is given. Collective taxis are often little more expensive than buses.

● **Hitchhiking**
Hitchhiking is easy and safe, but in some regions traffic is sparse.

● **Skiing**
Bradt Publications' *South America Ski Guide*, 1992, gives thorough coverage of all Chile's ski areas.

BOAT
Shipping information is given in the text under Santiago and all the relevant southern ports. Local newspapers are useful for all transport schedules.

COMMUNICATIONS

● **Language**
The local pronunciation of Spanish, very quick and lilting, with final syllables cut off, can present difficulties to the foreigner.

● **Postal services**
Airmail takes 3-4 days from the UK. Seamail takes 8-12 weeks. There is a daily airmail service to Europe with connections to the UK. Poste restante only holds mail for 30 days, then returns it to sender. Lista de Correo in Santiago, Central Post Office, is good and efficiently organized. Rates: letters to Europe/North America US$1.20, aerogrammes US$0.75. To register a letter costs US$0.75. Surface mail rates for parcels to Europe: Less than 1 kg US$14; 1-3 kg US$18; 10 kg US$30.

● **Telephone services**
National and international calls have been opened up for competition. In May 1996 there were eight main companies (*portadores* carriers) offering competing rates (widely advertised). Callers choose companies by dialling an access code before the city code. Access codes: Entel 123; CTC Mundo 188, CNT (Telefónica del Sur – in Regions X and XI) 121: VTR 120; Chilesat 171; Bell South Chile 181; Iusatel Chile 155; Transam Comunicaciones 113. For international calls you dial the company code, then 0, then the country code. International calls are cheap. Ask which carrier has the best links with the country you wish to call (eg for making collect calls); for instance CTC is good for phoning Germany.

Telephone boxes can be used to make local and long-distance calls, for making collect calls and receiving calls. Although it is possible to make international calls from these phones, in practice it may be easier to go to a company office. Telephone boxes have been programmed to direct calls via one carrier: to make a local call, simply dial the number you require and pay the rate charged by the carrier who owns the booth, US$0.20-0.30/minute. To make an inter-urban call, dial '0' plus the area code (DDD) and the number; if you wish to select a carrier, dial its code, then the area code (leaving out '0'), then the number. The area codes given in the text include '0'; omit this if selecting a carrier. To make an international call from a carrier's booth without choosing a different company, dial '00' before the country code. Yellow phones accept only 50 peso coins. Blue phones accept pre-paid phone cards costing 5,000 pesos (*tarjeta telefónica*); available from kiosks. On phone cards, only the time of the call is charged rather than the normal 3 min minimum. There are special phones for long-distance domestic calls which accept credit cards (Mastercard and Visa). Entel has strategically-placed, self-dialling phones, which are white. Users press a button and are instantly connected with the operator from their own country.

To send a fax abroad costs US$4-5, depending on the company. There is also a charge for receiving a fax. VTR also operate telex services. Amex Card holders can often use telex facilities at Amex offices free of charge.

MEDIA

● **Newspapers**

Santiago daily papers *El Mercurio*, *La Nación* (state-owned), *La Epoca* (liberal/left), *La Segunda*, *La Tercera* and *La Quarta*. *Las Ultimas Noticias*. *The Latest Daily News* is an English language paper, published daily except Mon, in Santiago, with international news and tourism details.*Condor*, weekly in German.

Weekly magazines; *Hoy*, *Qué Pasa*, *Ercilla*. Monthly: *Rutas* (official organ, Automobile Association).

● **Television**

TV channels include TVUC (Universidad Católica) on Channel 13, the leading station; TVN (government operated) on Channel 7; Megavisión (private) on Channel 9 and La Red (private) on Channel 4.

SPORT

Sernatur will give all the necessary information about sport.

Skiing Season from June to Sept/Oct, weather depending. For information write to: La Federación de Ski de Chile, Casilla 9902, Santiago.

Horse racing is popular and meetings are held every Sun and on certain feast days at Viña del Mar, Santiago and Concepción throughout the year; horse riding and rodeo are also popular.

Fishing Santiago and Valparaíso residents fish at the mountain resort of Río Blanco. Some of the world's best fishing is in the Lake District, but this region is very popular. Better still, and relatively less-heavily fished, are the lakes and rivers S of Puerto Montt: Lago Yelcho, Río Futaleufú, Río Yelcho, the rivers and lakes S of Chaitén to La Junta, around Coyhaique and around Cochrane. The licence required can be got from the local police or such angling associations as the Asociación de Pesca y Caza, which gives information on local conditions, or Sernap, San Antonio 427, p 8, Santiago, open Mon-Fri 0900-1400, US$2 a year. Check with Sernatur on closed seasons. Outside Chile, all information can be obtained from Sport Elite Ltd, Woodwalls House, Corscombe, Dorchester, Dorset, UK, DT2 0NT, T 093589-1477, F 093589-1797 (Major J A Valdes-Scott).

Other popular sports are football and basketball. Viña del Mar has a cricket ground; on Sat there are polo matches at Santiago.

HOLIDAYS AND FESTIVALS

1 Jan, New Year's Day; Holy Week (2 days); 1 May, Labour Day; 21 May, Navy Day; 15 Aug, Assumption; 18, 19 Sept, Independence Days; 12 Oct, Discovery of America; 1 Nov, All Saints Day; 8 Dec, Immaculate Conception; 25 Dec, Christmas Day.

FURTHER READING

British business visitors are advised to obtain 'Hints for Exporters: Chile' from the DTI Export Publications, PO Box 55, Stratford-upon-Avon, Warwickshire, CV37 9GE.

ACKNOWLEDGEMENTS

For updating this chapter, our warmest thanks are due to Charlie Nurse, who visited Chile in early 1996. He would like to thank Carlos Grady (Chonchi) for his assistance. We are most grateful to Adrian Turner (Puerto Montt) and Patricio Guzmán (Coyhaique) for their assistance in the preparation of this chapter.

Colombia

HORIZONS

Colombia is the fourth largest country in South America. It has coast lines upon both the Caribbean (1,600 km) and the Pacific (1,306 km). Nearly 55% of the area is almost uninhabited lowland with only 4% of the population; the other 96% are concentrated in the remaining 45%, living for the most part in narrow valleys or isolated intermont basins, or in the broad Caribbean lowlands. The population is infinitely varied, ranging from white, Indian, and black to mixtures of all three.

THE LAND

The 620,000 sq km of almost uninhabited land in Colombia lie E of the Eastern Cordillera. Near the foot of the Cordillera the plains are used for cattle ranching, but beyond is jungle. Islands of settlement in it are connected with the rest of the country by air and river, for there are no railways and very few roads.

In the populous western 45% of the country four ranges of the Andes run from S to N. Between the ranges run deep longitudinal valleys. Of the 14 main groups of population in the country, no less than 11 are in the mountain basins or in the longi-

tudinal valleys; the other three are in the lowlands of the Caribbean.

THE PACIFIC COAST

The first 320 km along the Pacific coast N from the frontier with Ecuador to the port of Buenaventura is a wide, marshy, and sparsely inhabited coastal lowland. Along the coast N of Buenaventura runs the Serranía de Baudó. East of this range the forested lowlands narrow into a low trough of land; E of the trough again rise the slopes of the Western Cordillera. The trough (the Department of the Chocó) is drained southwards into the Pacific by the Río San Juan, navigable for 200 km, and northwards into the Caribbean by the Río Atrato, navigable for 550 km. The climate is hot and torrential rain falls daily. The inhabitants are mostly black.

THE CORDILLERAS

From the borders of Ecuador two ranges of mountains, the Western Cordillera and the Central Cordillera, run N for 800 km to the Caribbean lowlands. Five peaks in the Western Cordillera are over 4,000m but none reaches the snowline. The Central Cordillera, 50-65 km wide, is much higher; six of its peaks, snow clad, rise above 5,000m and its highest, the volcano cone of Huila, is 5,439m. Apart from the peaks, mostly inactive volcanoes, there are large areas of high undulating plateaux dissected by deep river gorges giving spectacular scenery. There are narrow ribbons of soil along some of the rivers.

Between the two ranges, as they emerge from Ecuador, lies a valley filled in the S to a height of 2,500m by ash from the volcanoes. Further N between these two ranges lies the Cauca valley; in its northern 190 km, roughly from Popayán N past Cali to Cartago, there is an important agricultural region based on a deep

Colombia

1 Bogotá
2 Bogotá to Cucutá
3 The North Coast and Islands
4 Up the Magdalena River
5 The Central Cordillera: Medellín and Manizales
6 The Cauca Valley
7 Popayán, Tierradentro and San Agustín
8 The Llanos and Leticia
9 Southern Colombia

bed of black alluvial soil which yields as many as five crops a year. This valley, which is at a height of about 1,000m and up to 50 km wide, is drained northwards by the Río Cauca. Cali, the second city, is the business centre of the valley, and a road and railway run from Cali over a low pass of less than 1,500m in the Western Cordillera to Buenaventura. Sugar cane was the great crop of this valley in colonial times, but has now been varied with tobacco, soya, cotton, pineapple, and every other kind of tropical fruit. There is still some cattle raising. Coffee is grown on the Cordillera slopes above 600m.

At Cartago the two Cordilleras close in and the Cauca valley becomes a deep gorge which runs all the way to the Caribbean flatlands. In the Cordillera Central, at an altitude of 1,540m, is the third largest city and industrial centre in Colombia: Medellín. Much of the coffee and 75% of the gold comes from this area. North of Medellín the Cordillera Central splits into three ranges, separated by streams flowing into the Caribbean.

Near Latitude 2°N, or about 320 km N of the Ecuadorean border, the Eastern Cordillera, the longest of all, rises and swings N and then NE towards Venezuela. About Latitude 7°N it divides; one branch becomes the western rim of the Maracaibo basin and the other runs E into Venezuela, to the S of the Maracaibo basin.

Between this Eastern Cordillera and the Central Cordillera runs the 1,600 km long Río Magdalena, with the Caribbean port of Barranquilla at its mouth. There are more intermont basins in the Eastern Cordillera than in the others. Some of its peaks rise above the snow line. In the Sierra Nevada del Cocuy (just before the Cordillera divides) there is a group of snowy peaks, all over 5,200m; the highest, Ritacuba Blanca, reaches 5,493m. The basins are mostly high, at an altitude of from 2,500 to 2,750m. In the Lower Magdalena region the river banks are comparatively deserted, though there are a few clearings made by the descendants of black slaves who settled along the Magdalena after their emancipation. There are oilfields in the valley, particularly at Barrancabermeja.

In a high basin of the Eastern Cordillera, 160 km E of the Río Magdalena, the Spaniards in 1538 founded the city of Bogotá, now the national capital. The great rural activity here is the growing of food: cattle, wheat, barley, maize and potatoes.

Roads run N from Bogotá to the basins of Chiquinquirá and Sogamoso, over 160 km away. Both are in the Department of Boyacá, with Tunja, on a mountain between the two, as capital. Both basins, like that of Bogotá, produce food, and there are emerald mines at Muzo, near Chiquinquirá.

There are other basins in the N of the Eastern Cordillera: in the Departments of Santander and Norte de Santander at Bucaramanga and Cúcuta, and a small one at Ocaña. Movement into these basins by Europeans and *mestizos* did not take place until the 19th century, when chinchona bark (for quinine) rose into high demand. By 1885 this trade was dead, but by that time coffee was beginning to be planted. In Bucaramanga coffee is now the main crop, but it has been diversified by cacao, cotton and tobacco, all grown below the altitude suitable for coffee.

There is one more mountain group in Colombia, the Sierra Nevada de Santa Marta, standing isolated from the other ranges on the shores of the Caribbean. This is the highest range of all: its snow-capped peaks rise to 5,800m within 50 km of the coast.

THE CARIBBEAN LOWLANDS

To the W of this Sierra, and N of where the Central and Western Cordilleras come to an end, lies a great lowland which has three groups of population on its Caribbean shores; at Cartagena, Barranquilla and Santa Marta. The rivers draining this lowland (the Magdalena, Sinú, Cauca, San Jorge and César) run so slowly that much of the area is a network of swamps and lagoons with very little land that can be cultivated. Indeed the whole area E of the channel of the Magdalena is under water at most times of the year. When the floods come, large areas of the land W of the Magdalena – the plains of Bolívar – are covered too, but during the dry season from Oct to Mar great herds of cattle are grazed there.

NATIONAL PARKS

Colombia established its first National Park in 1969 (Tayrona on the Caribbean coast) and now has 43 National Nature Parks (RNN) and Flora and Fauna Sanctuaries (SFF) open throughout the country. They vary in size from the tiny island of Corota in the Laguna de la Cocha near the border with Ecuador to large areas of forest in the eastern lowlands. All the significant mountain areas are National Parks including the Sierra Nevada de Santa Marta, El Cocuy, El Nevado de Huila, Los Nevados (Tolima and Ruíz) and Puracé. There are 14 on or near the Caribbean and Pacific coasts.

All except the smallest parks have one or more centres staffed with rangers (guardaparques) which often offer information and guidance for visitors. Most, however, are remote with difficult access and few facilities. Unlike some Latin American countries, National Parks in Colombia are virtually free of 'tourism' and are thus of particular interest to those looking for unspoilt natural surroundings. Admission charges are high and are based on high and low seasons. High season is: weekends, June-July, Dec-Jan, public holidays, Semana Santa.

Until 1995, the National Parks were administered by Inderena in which various government ministries were involved. Inderena has now been disbanded and the service is the responsibility of the Unidad Administrativa Especial del Sistema de Parques Nacionales Naturales (UAE) at the Ministerio del Medio Ambiente (Ministry of the Environment) referred to in this guide as 'MMA'.

Their main office for information is in the Caja Agraria building at Cra 10, No 20-30, p 8, Bogotá, T 283-0964, F 341-5331. They publish a National Parks guide, attractive and informative, US$10 (pay in Tesorería on the 7th floor, collect book on the 2nd floor). Information on individual parks and the entry charges is available on the 8th floor. Permits to visit the parks are obtainable here and at the many MMA offices near the parks themselves (see text). If you intend to visit the parks, this is a good place to start and ask for up-to-date details. Information is also available here on possibilities to work as volunteer rangers, minimum 30 days.

Other useful address: Ecotourism office on 8th floor of MMA until Oct 1996; thereafter Cra 13, No 93-40, T 623-3508. *Fundción FES*, C5, No 6-05, Cali, or C19, No 22-64 (María Cristina Benevides), Pasto, T (92) 884-5933, F 884-4706 (Cali) for information on private reserves in Nariño. *Red de Reservas Naturales de la Sociedad Civil*, C23N, No 6AN-43, p 3 (Amparo Casasfranco, coordinadora administrativa), Cali, T 661-2581, F 660-6133, e-mail: resnatur@mafalda.univalle.edu.co, also for private reserves around the country. *Organización Nacional de Indígenas de Colombia* (ONIC), C13, No 4-38, Bogotá, T 284-2168, very helpful on indigenous peoples and access to their communities. *Instituto Colombiano de Antropología* (ICAN, C8, No 8-87, T 333-0535, Mon-Thur 0830-1630, Fri 0830-1230, also very helpful.

HISTORY

Before the coming of the Spaniards the country was occupied by Indians, most of whom were primitive hunters or nomad agriculturists, but one part of the country, the high basins of the Eastern Cordillera, was densely occupied by Chibcha Indians who had become sedentary farmers. Their staple foods were maize and the potato, and they had no domestic animal save the dog; the use they could make of the land was therefore limited. Other cultures present in Colombia in the precolumbian era were the Tairona, Quimbaya, Sinú and Calima. Exhibits of their and the Chibcha (Muisca) Indians' gold-work can be seen at the Gold Museum in Bogotá (see page 873).

SPANISH COLONIZATION

The Spaniards sailed along the northern coast as far as Panama as early as 1500. The first permanent settlement was by Rodrigo de Bastidas at Santa Marta in 1525. Cartagena was founded in 1533. In 1536, Gonzalo Jiménez de Quesada (who wrote a full account of his adventures) pushed up the Río Magdalena to discover its source; mounting the Eastern Cordillera in 1536, he discovered the Chibchas, conquered them, and founded Santa Fe de Bogotá in 1538. In the meantime other Spanish forces were approaching the same region: Pizarro's lieutenant, Sebastián de Belalcázar, had pushed down the Cauca valley from Ecuador and founded Pasto, Popayán and Cali in 1536. Nicolás de Federmann, acting on behalf of the Welser financiers of Germany, who had been granted a colonial concession by Charles V, approached from Venezuela. Belalcázar reached Bogotá in 1538 and Federmann got there in 1539. As in Peru, the initial period of settlement was one of strife between contending *conquistadores*. The royal Audiencia de Santa Fe set up in 1550 gave the area a legislative, judicial and administrative entity. In 1564 this was followed by a presidency of the kingdom of Nueva Granada controlling the whole country and Panama, except Belalcázar's province of Popayán. The Presidency was replaced in 1718 by a viceroyalty at Bogotá which controlled the provinces now known as Venezuela as well; it was independent of the Viceroyalty of Peru, to which this vast area had previously been subject.

INDEPENDENCE FROM SPAIN

The movement towards independence from Spain was set going in 1794 by a translation into Spanish by the *criollo* Antonio Nariño of the French Declaration of the Rights of Man. The movement was given point and force when, in 1808, Napoleon replaced Ferdinand VII of Spain with his own brother Joseph. The New World refused to recognize this: there were several revolts in Nueva Granada, culminating in a revolt at Bogotá and the setting up of a *junta* on 20 July 1810. Other local *juntas* were established: Cartagena bound itself to a *junta* set up at Tunja. Late in 1812 the young Bolívar, driven out of Venezuela, landed at Cartagena. In a brilliant campaign in 1813 he pushed up the Magdalena to Ocaña, and from there to Cúcuta, and obtained permission from the *junta* at Tunja to advance into Venezuela. In 90 days he marched the 1,200 km to Caracas over mountain country, fighting six battles, but he was unable to hold Caracas and withdrew to Cartagena in 1814.

Napoleon fell in 1815, and the Spanish Government immediately set about reconquering, with some success, Venezuela and New Granada. Gen Pablo Morillo took Cartagena after a bitter siege of 106 days (Bolívar had withdrawn to Jamaica) and was later "pacifying" Bogotá with a "Reign of Terror" by May 1816.

Bolívar had by now assembled an army of Llaneros, fortified by a British legion recruited from ex-servicemen of the Peninsular wars, in Venezuela at Angostura (now Ciudad Bolívar). In the face of incredible difficulties he made a forced march across the Andes in 1819. After joining up with Francisco de Paulo Santander's Nueva Granada army, he defeated the royalists at the battle of the Swamps of Vargas in July and again at Boyacá on 7 August. He entered Bogotá three days later.

GRAN COLOMBIA

Bolívar reported his success to the revolutionary congress sitting at Angostura, and that body, on 17 December 1819, proclaimed the Republic of Gran Colombia, embracing in one the present republics of Venezuela, Colombia, and Ecuador. A general congress was held at Cúcuta on 1 January 1821, and here it was that two opposing views which were to sow such dissension in Colombia first became apparent. Bolívar and Nariño were for centralization; Santander, a realist, for a federation of sovereign states. Bolívar succeeded in enforcing his view for the time being, but Gran Colombia was not to last long; Venezuela broke away in 1829 and Ecuador in 1830. The remaining provinces were named Nueva Granada; it was not till 1863 that the name Colombia was restored.

COLOMBIA'S CIVIL WARS

Almost from its inception the new country became the scene of strife between the centralizing pro-clerical Conservatives and the federalizing anti-clerical Liberals. The Conservative president Tomás Cipriano de Mosquera (1845) encouraged education, began building roads, adopted the metric system, and put steamers on the Magdalena. The Liberals were dominant from 1849 for the next 30 years of insurrections and civil wars. In 1885 the Conservatives imposed a highly centralized constitution which was not modified for over 100 years. A Liberal revolt in 1899 turned into a civil war, "the War of the Thousand Days". The Liberals were finally defeated in 1902 after 100,000 people had died. It was in 1903 that Panama declared its independence from Colombia, following US pressure.

After 40 years of comparative peace, the strife between Conservatives and Liberals was reignited in a little-publicized but dreadfully bloody civil war known as *La Violencia* from 1948 to 1957 (some 300,000 people were killed). This was ended by a unique political truce. It was decided by plebiscite in 1957 that the two political parties would support a single presidential candidate, divide all political offices equally between them, and thus maintain political stability for sixteen years. In 1978 the agreement was ended, though some elements of the coalition (representation of the main opposition party in the Cabinet, for instance) were allowed to continue until 1986. Sr Belisario Betancur, the Conservative president from 1982-86, offered a general amnesty to guerrilla movements in an attempt to end violence in the country. Following an initial general acceptance of the offer, only one of the four main guerrilla groups, the FARC, upheld the truce in 1985-7. In May 1986, when the Liberal candidate, Sr Virgilio Barco, won the presidential elections, FARC's newly-formed political party, the Unión Patriótica, won 10 seats in congress; the Liberal party took the majority. Right-wing groups refused to accept the Unión Patriótica and by the beginning of 1990, 1,040 party members had been killed since the UP was formed in 1985. During the campaign for the 1990 presidential and congressional elections violence brought the assassination of the Liberal Party and the UP presidential candidates, Luis Carlos Galán and Bernardo Jaramillo.

Violence erupted again in 1992/93. Having begun in June 1991, peace talks between the government and the Coordinadora Guerrillera (CG, an umbrella group representing all the insurgent factions) collapsed. This was followed by several indecisive, but destructive offensives on the part of both the guerrillas and the armed forces.

THE NARCOTICS TRADE

In Medellín and Cali, two cartels transformed Colombia's drugs industry into a major force in worldwide business and crime. Their methods were very different: Medellín being ostentatious and violent, Cali much more low-key. In 1986, President Barco pledged to crack down on the drugs barons and an international effort was launched to bring them to justice, but opposition to extradition of suspects to the USA stymied progress. Pablo Escobar, the alleged leader of the Medellín drugs cartel, who had surrendered under secret terms in 1991, escaped from custody in July 1992. Despite a multi-million dollar reward offered for his recapture and renewed conditional offers of surrender, he remained at large until his death in Dec 1993. Drug trafficking from Cali continued unabated.

Having won the presidential elections held on 27 May, 1990, César Gaviria Trujillo (Liberal), took up the candidacy of the murdered Luis Carlos Galán, appointed a coalition government made up of Liberals from rival factions, Conservatives and the M-19 leader. His government was unable to stem violence, whether perpetrated by drug traffickers, guerrillas or common criminals. Not surprisingly, this was one of the issues in the 1994 election campaign. The two main candidates, Ernesto Samper (Liberal) and Andrés Pastrana (Conservative), supported Gaviria's policy of offering reduced prison sentences for drugs dealers who surrender. Although serious efforts continued in 1995 to eradicate drug plantations and stocks, little progress was made in establishing alternative crops. This left many rural communities without means of support. Much of the current unrest can be traced to this problem.

RECENT DEVELOPMENTS

A plebiscite held concurrently with the 1990 presidential elections showed clear support for reform of the 1886 constitution. In Dec 1990, therefore, a 73-member Constituent Assembly was elected, to reform the constitution by 5 July 1991. There was broad agreement that the electoral system, Congress and the judiciary needed modernizing and democratizing. As a result, general elections were held in Oct 1991 (although not due until 1994), and the Liberals retained a majority in the Senate and the House of Representatives. Voter turnout was low, but many small parties, including M-19 and the indigenous National Indian Organization gained representation in Congress.

The Liberal party retained its dominance of Congress in the year that Ernesto Samper won the presidency (1994). The main thrust of Samper's programme was that Colombia's current economic strength should provide resources to tackle the social deprivation which causes drug use and insurgency. He placed much emphasis on bringing the FARC and ELN guerrillas to the negotiating table and on public spending on social welfare. Much impetus was lost in 1995, though, after revelations that Samper's election campaign had received about US$6mn from the Cali cartel. Amid ministerial resignations, the chief ques-

tion became whether Samper was aware of the funding. The debate lasted until June 1996, almost overshadowing the capture or surrender of most of the leading Cali drug lords. That Congress voted to absolve Samper of all knowledge of the money may have eased the domestic political crisis, but it created new problems. The USA having decided in Mar 1996 to remove Colombia from its list of countries making progress against drugs trafficking, dismissed Congress' ruling and denied Samper the right to a US visa. Meanwhile, the level of violence around the country remained high, with FARC and ELN still active.

CULTURE

PEOPLE

The regions vary greatly in their racial make-up: Antioquia and Caldas are largely of European descent, Pasto is Indian, the Cauca Valley are African or *mulato*. No colour bar is legally recognized but it does exist in certain centres. Population figures of cities and towns in the text refer to the 1993 census; except where stated figures are for cities, not municipalities.

The birth and death rates vary greatly from one area to the other, but in general infant mortality is high. Hospitals and clinics are few in relation to the population. About 66% of the doctors are in the departmental capitals, which contain about half of the population, though all doctors have to spend a year in the country before they can get their final diploma. Deplorable *barrios clandestinos* (shanty-towns) have sprung up around Cali, Barranquilla, Cartagena and Buenaventura.

An estimated 400,000 tribal peoples, from 60 ethnic groups, live in Colombia. Groups include the Wayun (in the Guajira), the Kogi and Arhauco (Sierra Nevada de Santa Marta), Amazonian indians such as the Witoto, the nomadic Nukak and the Ticuna, Andean indians and groups of the Llanos and in the Pacific Coast rain forest. The diversity and importance of indigenous peoples was recognized in the 1991 constitutional reforms when indians were granted the right to two senate seats; the National Colombian Indian Organization (ONIC) won a third seat in the Oct 1991 ballot. State recognition and the right to bilingual education has not, however, solved major problems of land rights, training and education, and justice.

EDUCATION

Education is free, and since 1927 theoretically compulsory, but many children, especially in rural areas, do not attend. There are high standards of secondary and university education, when it is available.

MUSIC AND DANCE

No South American country has a greater variety of music than Colombia, strategically placed where the Andes meet the Caribbean. The four major musical areas are (a) the mountain heartland, (b) the Pacific coast, (c) the Caribbean coast and (d) the Llanos or eastern plains.

The mountain heartland

The heartland covers the Andean highlands and intervening valleys of the Cauca and Magdalena and includes the country's three largest cities, Bogotá, Cali and Medellín. It is relatively gentle and sentimental music, accompanied largely by string instruments, with an occasional flute and a *chucho* or *carángano* shaker to lay down the rhythm. The preferred instrument of the highlands and by extension Colombia's national instrument, is the *tiple*, a small 12-stringed guitar, most of which are manufactured at Chiquinquirá in Boyacá. The national dance is the Bambuco, whose lilting sounds are said to have inspired Colombian troops at the Battle of Ayacucho in 1824. It is to be found throughout the country's heartland for dancing, singing and instrumentalizing and has long transcended its folk origins. The choreography is complex, including many figures, such as la Invitación, Los Ochos, Los Codos, Los Coqueteos, La Perseguida and La Arrodilla. Other related dances are the Torbellino, where the

woman whirls like a top, the more stately Guabina, the Pasillo, Bunde, Sanjuanero and the picaresque Rajaleña. Particularly celebrated melodies are the "Guabina Chiquinquireña" and the "Bunde Tolimense". The following fiestas, among others, provide a good opportunity of seeing the music and dance:- La Fiesta del Campesino, ubiquitous on the first Sun in June, the Fiesta del Bambuco in Neiva and Festival Folklórico Colombiano in Ibagué later in the month, the Fiesta Nacional de la Guabina y el Tiple, held in Velez in early Aug, the Desfile de Silleteros in Medellín in the same month and Las Fiestas de Pubenza in Popayán just after the New Year, where the Conjuntos de Chirimía process through the streets.

The Pacific coast

On Colombia's tropical Pacific coast (and extending down into Esmeraldas, Ecuador) is to be found some of the most African sounding black music in all South America. The Currulao and its variants, the Berejú and Patacoré, are extremely energetic recreational dances and the vocals are typically African-style call- and-response. This is the home of the *marimba* and the music is very percussion driven, including the upright *cununo* drum plus *bombos* and *redoblantes*. Wakes are important in this region and at these the Bundes, Arrullos and Alabaos are sung. Best known is the "Bunde de San Antonio". The Jota Chocoana is a fine example of a Spanish dance taken by black people and tuned into a satirical weapon against their masters. The regional fiestas are the Festival Folklórico del Litoral at Buenaventura in July and San Francisco de Asís at Quibdó on 4 August. Quibdó also features a "Fiesta de los Indios" at Easter.

The Caribbean coast

The music of Colombia's Caribbean lowlands became popular for dancing throughout Latin America more than 30 years ago under the name of "Música Tropical" and has much more recently become an integral part of the Salsa repertory. It can be very roughly divided into "Cumbia" and "Vallenato". The Cumbia is a heavily black influenced dance form for several couples, the men forming an outer circle and the women an inner one. The men hold aloft a bottle of rum and the women a bundle of slim candles called "espermas". The dance probably originated in what is now Panama, moved E into Cartagena, where it is now centred and quite recently further E to Barranquilla and Santa Marta. The most celebrated Cumbias are those of Ciénaga, Mompós, Sampués, San Jacinto and Sincelejo. The instrumental accompaniment consists of *gaitas* or *flautas de caña de millo*, backed by drums. The *gaitas* ("male" and "female") are vertical cactus flutes with beeswax heads, while the *cañas de millo* are smaller transverse flutes. The most famous conjuntos are the Gaiteros de San Jacinto, the Cumbia Soledeña and the Indios Selectos. Variants of the Cumbia are the Porro, Gaita, Puya, Bullerengue and Mapalé, these last two being much faster and more energetic. Lately Cumbia has also become very much part of the Vallenato repertoire and is therefore often played on the accordion. Vallenato music comes from Valledupar in the Department of Cesar and is of relatively recent origin. It is built around one instrument, the accordion, albeit backed by *guacharaco* rasps and *caja* drums. The most popular rhythms are the Paseo and the Merengue, the latter having arrived from the Dominican Republic, where it is the national dance. Perhaps the first virtuoso accordionist was the legendary "Francisco El Hombre", playing around the turn of the century. Today's best known names are those of Rafael Escalona, Alejandro Durán and Calixto Ochoa. In April the Festival de la Leyenda Vallenata is held in Valledupar and attended by thousands. Barranquilla is the scene of South America's second most celebrated Carnival, after that of Rio de Janeiro, with innumerable traditional masked groups, such as the Congos, Toros, Diablos and Caimanes. The Garabato is a dance in which death is defeated. Barranquilla's carnival is less commercialized and more traditional than that of Rio and should be a "must" for anyone with the opportunity to attend. Other important festivals in the region are the Corralejas de Sincelejo with its bullfights in Jan, La Candelaria in Cartagena on 2 Feb, the Festival de la Cumbia in El Banco in June, Fiesta del Caiman in Ciénaga in Jan and Festival del Porro in San Pelayo (Córdoba). To complete the music of the Caribbean region, the Colombian islands of San Andrés and Providencia, off the coast of Nicaragua, have a fascinating mix of mainland Colombian and Jamaican island music, with the Calypso naturally a prominent feature.

The Llanos

The fourth musical region is that of the great eastern plains, the so-called Llanos Orientales between the Ríos Arauca and Guaviare, a region where there is really no musical frontier between the two republics of Colombia and Venezuela. Here the Joropo reigns supreme as a dance, with its close relatives the Galerón, the slower and more romantic Pasaje and the breathlessly fast Corrido and Zumba que Zumba. These are dances for couples, with a lot of heel tapping, the arms hanging down loosely to the sides. Arnulfo Briceño and Pentagrama Llancra are the big names and the harp is the only instrument that matters, although normally backed by *cuatro*, guitar, *tiple* and *maracas*. Where to see and hear it all is at the Festival Nacional del Joropo at Villavicencio in Dec.

THE ECONOMY

Structure of production Colombia has varied natural resources and an economic structure which is no longer dependent on any one commodity. Agriculture is the major employer, providing about 15% of gdp and over half of total legal exports. The traditional crops are coffee, flowers, sugar cane, bananas, rice, maize and cotton. Colombia is the leading producer of mild Arabica coffee and second to Brazil in world production. Diversification since 1984 and disease have reduced output, but exports of coffee still amount to about a fifth of total exports, depending on world prices. About 1 million ha are planted to coffee in the central Andes and production

Colombia: Fact File

Geographic

Land area	1,141,568 sq km
forested	48.1%
pastures	39.1%
cultivated	5.3%

Demographic

Population (1995)	35,099,000
annual growth rate (1990-95)	1.7%
urban	70.3%
rural	29.7%
density	30.7 per sq km
Religious affiliation	
Roman Catholic	93.1%
Birth rate per 1,000 (1990-95)	24.0
	(world av 25.0)

Education and Health

Life expectancy at birth,	
male	69.3 years
female	72.3 years
Infant mortality rate	
per 1,000 live births (1990-95)	37.0
Physicians (1992)	1 per 1,078 persons
Hospital beds (1989)	1 per 693 persons
Calorie intake as %	
of FAO requirement	115%
Population age 25 and over	
with no formal schooling	15.3%
Literate males (over 15)	87.5%
Literate females (over 15)	85.9%

Economic

GNP (1993 market prices)	
	US$50,119mn
GNP per capita	US$1,350
Public external debt (1993)	
	US$12,861mn
Tourism receipts (1992)	US$705mn
Inflation (annual av 1989-94)	26.6%
Radio	1 per 6.4 persons
Television	1 per 6.3 persons
Telephone	1 per 8.9 persons

Employment

Population economically active (1985)	
	9,558,000
Unemployment rate	4.3%
% of labour force in	
agriculture	28.5
mining	0.6
manufacturing	13.4
construction	2.9
Military forces	146,400

Source *Encyclopaedia Britannica*

is around 12-13 million bags a year. Flowers, mostly grown near Bogotá because of ease of access to the airport, are exported mainly to the USA. Expansion has been so successful that Colombia is the second largest exporter of cut flowers in the world. Bananas are grown on the tropical lowlands, about 56 million boxes from around Urabá and 30 million around Santa Marta, while sugar cane is grown in the Cauca valley.

Manufacturing contributes 19% of gdp, with farming activities such as food processing, drink and tobacco accounting for about a third of the sector's value added. Textiles and clothing are also important and provide an outlet for home-grown cotton. Other major industries include chemicals, transport equipment, cement, metalworking and paper.

The most dynamic sector of the economy in the 1980s was mining, with average annual growth rates of 18%, although rates in the 1990s have declined. Mining (coal, nickel, emeralds, gold and platinum) now accounts for about 16% of total exports. Coal reserves are the largest in Latin America, which partial surveys have put at 16.5 billion tonnes. The largest deposits are in the Cerrejón region, where a huge project mines and exports steam coal from a purpose built port at Bahía de Portete. A mine at La Loma (César Department) and deposits in the Chocó are also being developed with railways and ports for export markets. With the exception of a few major projects, mining of precious metals is concentrated in the hands of small scale producers with little technology or organization. Much of their output remains outside the formal economy. Colombia is a major producer of gold, platinum and emeralds, which have traditionally dominated the sector. Mining of precious metals, including silver, is primarily in the Department of Antioquia and El Chocó; huge gold deposits have also been discovered on the borders of the Departments of Cauca and Valle, while others have been found in the Guainía, Vaupés and Guaviare regions near the Brazilian border.

By 1990 oil had replaced coffee as the top export earner. Traditionally, oil pro-

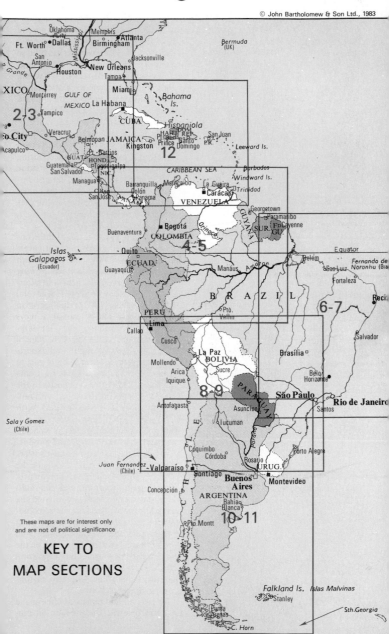

①

© John Bartholomew & Son Ltd., 1983

These maps are for interest only
and are not of political significance

KEY TO
MAP SECTIONS

CARIBBEAN SEA

Pta Gallinas
Uribia
Riohacha
Maicao
Sta Marta
Ciénaga
Barranquilla
Cartagena
Valledupar
S. Jacinto
El Banco
Sincelejo
Magangué
Montería
Caucasia
Yarumal
Quibdó
Itagüí
MEDELLÍN
Manizales
Pereira
Cartago
Armenia
Tuluá
Ibagué
Buga
Buenaventura
Palmira
CALI
Santander
Popayán
Neiva
Pitalito
Florencia
Tumaco
El Diviso
S. Lorenzo
Pasto
Belén
Esmeraldas
Ipiales
Mocoa
Ibarra
Tulcán
Pto Asis
Cojimies
Otavalo
Lago Agrio
Jama
QUITO
Coca
Napo
Manta
Chone
Tena
San Lorenzo
Ambato
Jipijapa
ECUADOR
Guaranda
Chimborazo
GUAYAQUIL
Babahoyo
Riobamba
La Libertad
Milagro
Macas
Playas
I. Puná
CUENCA
Azogues
G. de Guayaquil
Gualaceo
Tumbes
Machala
Zaruma
Loja
Zamora
Talara
Negritos
Sullana
Paita
Chulucanas
Piura
Huancabamba
Catacaos
Pta Aguja
Jaén
Yurimaguas
Lambayeque
Ferreñafe
Moyobamba
Chiclayo
Chachapoyas
Tarapoto
Chepén
Juanjui
Pacasmayo
Cajamarca
Cajabamba
Huamachuco
Otusco
Uchiza
Pomabamba
Trujillo
Huallanca
Tingo María
Pucallpa
Chimbote
Huaraz
Huánuco
Casma
La Unión
Huascarán
Oxapampa
Huarmey
Cerro de Pasco
Pativilca
La Merced
Barranca
Huacho
Tarma
Ancón
La Oroya
Jauja
Acobamba
Callao
Huancayo
LIMA
Huancavelica

FOR GALAPAGOS ISLANDS
SEE PAGE 2

PANAMA
Colón
Panamá
La Chorrera
David
Santiago
Chitré
G. de Panamá
Pen. de Azuero
Pta Mariato
I. Coiba

COLOMBIA

ECUADOR

PERU

ACRE

Maracaibo
Cabimas
Coro
Riecito
Cd Ojeda
Valencia
Barquisim
Machiques
Trujillo
Acarigua
Mérida
Valera
Barinas
Guanare
Cúcuta
San Cristóbal
Pamplona
Bucaramanga
Arauca
Málaga
Tame
Sogamoso
Tunja
Chocontá
BOGOTÁ
Girardot
Villavicencio
Granada
Orocué
Calamar

Cruzeiro do Sul
Feijó
Tarauacá
Río Branco
Brasiléia
Cobija
Porve
Sena
Madureira
Purus

⑦

1:16M

Tropic of Capricorn

400 miles

600 km.

SERGIPE
Lagarto
Estância
Aracaju
Penedo
Arapiraca

BAHIA
Jacobina
Uibiranã
Feira de S.
Cachoeira
Salvador (Bahia)
Alagoinhas
Serrinha
Santo Amaro
R. de Jacuípe
N. Azaré
Valença
Jequié
Itabuna
Ilhéus
Canavieiras
Belmonte
Pôrto Seguro

Chapada
Diamantina

Barreiras
Bom Jesus da Lapa
Januária
Montes Claros
Vitória da Conquista
Caetité
Itapetinga
Caravelas
Itamaraju
São Mateus

ESPÍRITO SANTO
Linhares
Colatina
Vitória
Vila Velha
Cachoeiro de Itapemirim

Diamantina
Teófilo Otóni
Nanuque
Araçuaí
Gov. Valadares
Caratinga
Manhuaçu
Cariacica
Ipatinga

MINAS GERAIS
Belo Horizonte
Itabira
Curvelo
Sete Lagoas
Divinópolis
Ponte Nova
Itapemirim
Barbacena
Ubá
Muriaé
Cataguases
São João del Rei
Pirapora
João Pinheiro
Patos de Minas
Araxá
Lavras
Itaúna
Poços de Caldas
Formiga
Passos
Ribeirão Prêto
São João
Franca
Pedro Leopoldo

GOIÁS
Brasília
Formosa
Anápolis
Pirenópolis
Goiânia
Ceres
Jaraguá
Itumbiara
Catalão
Uberlândia
Uberaba
Ituiutaba
Rio Verde
Jataí
Mineiros
Goiás
Aruanã
Iporá
Aragarças

MATO GROSSO
Cuiabá
Diamantino
Rondonópolis
Caiabis

MATO GROSSO DO SUL
Campo Grande
Três Lagoas
Pres. Prudente
Dourados
Ponta Porã

RIO DE JANEIRO
Rio de Janeiro
Niterói
Campos
Nova Friburgo
Macaé
São João da Barra
Magé
Nova Iguaçu
Barra Mansa
Volta Redonda
Resende
Petrópolis
Cabo Frio
São João de Meriti

SÃO PAULO
São Paulo
Santos
São Vicente
Santo André
Guarujá
Campinas
Jundiaí
Sorocaba
São Carlos
São José do Rio Prêto
Araraquara
Bauru
Marília
Presidente Prudente
Araçatuba
Piracicaba
Limeira
Americana
Itapetininga
Jacareí
São José dos Campos
Taubaté
Itanhaém
Barretos
Catanduva
Jaú
Franca

PARANÁ
Curitiba
Londrina
Maringá
Ponta Grossa
Paranaguá
Guarapuava
Foz do Iguaçu
Cascavel
Toledo
União da Vitória

Ciudad del Este
Col Oviedo

PACIFIC OCEAN

Tropic of Capricorn

1:16M

| 0 | 100 | 200 | 300 | 400 miles |
| 0 | 200 | 400 | | 600 km. |

Islas Juan Fernández
(Chile)

Alejandro Selkirk
Robinson Crusoe
Sta Clara

ON THE SAME SCALE

San Felix   San Ambrosio
(Chile)

Chimbote
Huaraz   Huallanca   Tingo María   Ucayali   Madureira   Abunã
Casma   Huánuco   Río Branco   Guajará-M
Huarmey   Oxapampa   Brasiléia   Riberalta   RO
Pativilca   Cerro de Pasco   La Merced   Cobija   Porvenir   Pto Heath
Barranca   La Oroya   Tarma   Madre de Dios   L. Rogaguado
Huacho   Jauja   Acobamba   Pto Maldonado   Santa Ana
Ancón   Huancayo   Quillabamba   Rurrenabaque   Trini
Callao   Lima   Huancavelica   Cuzco   MACHU PICCHU
Huancavelica   Ayacucho   Abancay   Quince Mil   Huanay
Chincha Alta   Andahuaylas   Sicuani   Titicaca   Coroico   Chulumani
Pisco   Ica   Ayaviri   Ancohuma   La Paz
Pen. de Paracas   Nazca   Juliaca   7014   BOLIVIA
Coropuna   Puno   Juli   Guaqui
Chala   6425   Arequipa   Misti   Quillacollo   Cochabam
Camana   Majes   5822   Moquegua   Oruro   Santa
Matarani   Mollendo   Desaguadero   Sajama   Aiquile
Ilo   Pta Coles   6520   Poopó   Huanuni
Tacna   Sabaya   S. de   Río   Sucre
Arica   Coipasa   Mulatos   Potosí
Iquique   Salar   Uyuni   Cotagaita
de Uyuni   Tupiza
Viña   Vol. Ollagüe   5870   Quiaca   Bermej
Tocopilla   Ollagüe   Loa   Tocorpuri   Abra Pampa   Orá
Pedro de   Chuquicamata   5833   La   Iturbe
Valdivia   Calama   Jujuy   Emt
Mejillones   Salar de   Tilcara   S.M
Antofagasta   Atacama   S.Salvador   Fu
Llullaillaco   de Jujuy   Salta   Salt
6723   S. de   Salta
Taltal   Arizaro   Puna   Cachi   Metán
Catalina   de   Catayate
Chañaral   Atacama   Tucumán
Potrerillos   S.M
Caldera   Ojos del Salado   Fu
Huasco   6104   Pissis   Catamarca   Santi
Copiapó   6858   Londres   del Es
Vallenar   G.n Manuel   Chilecito   Catan
Cabo   Belgrano   La Rioja
Bascuñán   6250   Co. del Toro   Chilecito   La Rioja
6380   S. Agustín   Cruz
La Serena   Rivadavia   Jáchal   Ejé
Coquimbo   5292   San Juan   Córd
Olivares   S. Agustín   V. Dol
Ovalle   Pampa
Punitaqui   de las
Illapel   Salinas
S. Juan   San
Los Vilos   Mercedario   Luis
S.   6770
Quillota   Aconcagua   Mendoza
Viña del Mar   S. Felipe   6960   San
Valparaíso   Lago   Tupungato   Mercedes   Luis
S.Antonio   Santiago   Vol.Maipú   V.Huic
S. Bernardo   5250
Rancagua   S. Rafael
Pichilemu   S. Fernando

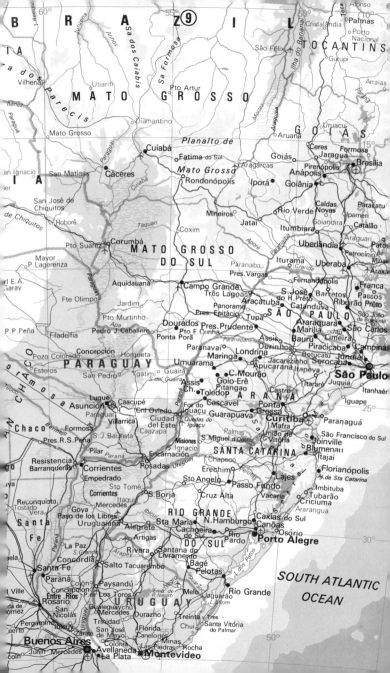

⑪

A T L A N T I C

O C E A N

1:16M

ON THE SAME SCALE

| 0 | 100 | 200 | 300 | 400 miles |
| 0 | 200 | 400 | 600 km. |

South Georia

Shag Rocks

C. Alexandra ○Grytviken

C. Disappointment

FALKLAND ISLANDS
ISLAS MALVINAS

Jason Is ˙˙˙

West Falkland   C. Dolphin   Stanley
                 East Falkland

Weddell   Beauchene Is

Falklan Sd

Golfo
San Matías
Pto Piramides
Pto. Madryn○ Punta Delgada
Rawson

Golfo   Camarones
San Jorge   C. Dos Bahias

Comocoro Rivadavia

Caleta   C. Tres Puntas
Olivia○Perito
Colonia Las Heras   Deseado

Pta Médanosa
Deseado

C H U B U T

Las Plumas Gaiman○ Trelew
Sdo.R.
Chico   Penguino

Madryhuac
○Norquinco
Esquel   Gastre

Pto Lobos

S. Carlos de
Bariloche

Pto Varas
Puerto Montt○   El Bolsón
Ancud   ○Epuyén
I. de Chiloé   ○Cholila
Castro Sacho

Archipiélago
de las
Chones

G. Corovado

Pen. de
Taitao
Melimoyu
● 2400

Pto Aisén
Coihaique
Balmaceda

L. Fontana

L.C. Huapi
L. Muster   Sarmiento

L. Buenos Aires
L. Pueyrredón

C. Valentín
4058   Perito
Moreno

San Cristóbal   L. Cochrane
                 L. San Martín

Gobernador Gregores

S. Julián

Sta Cruz

Bahia Grande

L. Cardiel
L. Argentino   Rio Gallegos

S A N T A   C R U Z

Calafate
Rio
Turbio

L.O Higgins
Lautaro
3600●
Muelion

L. Viedma
O'Higgins
L. Piedra

Pto Natales

Es. de Magallanes

Punta Arenas

C. San Diego
Rio Grande
Isla Grande Tierra del
de Tierra del   Fuego
Fuego
Ushuaia

I. de los Estados

Golfo de
Penas

Campana
Esmeralda
Madre de Dios
Hanover

Wellington

G. de Penas

Arch. de la
Reina Adelaida

Desolación
Santa Inés

Pen. de
Brunswick

Estrecho Magallanes

Dawson

Navarino
Hoste
Londonderry
Is Wollaston
C. de Hornos

⑫

TRINIDAD 1:4M
Toco
Arima
Princes Town
Port of Spain
San Fernando
Guayaguayare
Gulf of Paria
Bonasse

TOBAGO 1:4M
Charlotteville
Plymouth
Scarborough

JAMAICA 1:4M
Montego Bay
Falmouth
St Ann's Bay
Brown's Town
Annotto Bay
Port Mtn Pk. 2256m
Port Antonio
Port Morant
Kingston
Spanish Town
May Pen
Mandeville
Savanna la Mar
Black River
Mt. Denham 986m
Blue Mtn. Pk.
Portland Point

ATLANTIC OCEAN

THE BAHAMAS
Nassau
Eleuthera I.
Cat I.
Andros Is.
Long I.
Acklins I.
Caicos Is.
Turks Is.
Straits of Florida
Gt. Inagua I.

La Habana
Pinar del Río
Matanzas
Saqua la Grande
Santa Clara
Cienfuegos
Sancti Spíritus
Camagüey
Holguín
Bayamo
Turquino 2005m
Santiago de Cuba
C. Cruz
Montego Bay
Savanna la Mar
Spanish Town
Kingston
JAMAICA
Cayman Is.
I. de Juventude (I. de Pinos)

Guantánamo
Windward Passage
Cap-Haïtien
Gonaïves
HAITI
Port au Prince
Les Cayes

Hispaniola
Santiago
DOMINICAN REPUBLIC
La Romana
Santo Domingo
Azua

San Juan
Ponce
Mayagüez
PUERTO RICO
Mona Passage

Virgin Is.
Anguilla
St. Martin
St. Croix
St. Kitts
Nevis
Montserrat
Barbuda
ANTIGUA
Guadeloupe
Point-à-Pitre
DOMINICA
Roseau
Martinique
Fort-de-France
ST. LUCIA
Castries
ST. VINCENT
Kingstown
GRENADA
St. Georges
BARBADOS
Bridgetown

Leeward Islands
Windward Islands
LESSER ANTILLES

GREATER ANTILLES

CARIBBEAN SEA

NETHERLAND ANTILLES
Aruba
Curaçao
Bonaire
Pto. Fijo
Willemstad
Coro
Uribia
G. de Venezuela
Pta Gallinas
La Tortuga
La Margarita
La Asunción
TRINIDAD AND TOBAGO
Port of Spain
Tobago

Riohacha
Santa Marta

HONDURAS
L. de Caratasca
C. Gracias a Dios
Puerto Cabezas
Prinzapolca
Bluefields
NICARAGUA

1:16M

0   100   200   300   400 miles
0   200   400   600 km.

duction came from the Magdalena basin, but these are older fields which are running down. The discovery of the Caño Limón field near Arauca raised output to around 450,000 b/d. The Cusiana and Cupiagua fields, in the Llanos, came into full production in 1995 and average output in 1996 was about 580,000 b/d. Cusiana also has substantial reserves of gas. Investment is taking place to double oil output, build refineries, petrochemical plants and pipelines, although guerrilla attacks and high taxes make operating in Colombia costly for foreign oil companies.

Despite abundant hydrocarbons, some 78% of installed generating capacity is hydroelectric. Three quarters of the nation's hydroelectric potential is in the central zone, where 80% of the population live, giving hydroelectricity a natural advantage over thermal power, but after a severe drought in 1992 the Government encouraged the construction of several thermal plants, due to come on stream in 1998-99. Rationing may have to be reimposed in 1997 if there is not sufficient rainfall. Demand is forecast to grow annually by over 6% and there are plans to increase total capacity from 10,380MW to 13,000MW by 2000. Ten power stations, which generate 3,445MW, are to be privatized under a 1994 law. Two use coal, four gas and four hydro-power. With privatization and new private sector power plants, up to two thirds of generating capacity could be privately owned by the end of the 1990s.

Recent trends Current account surpluses in the late 1970s during a coffee price boom were turned into large deficits in the first half of the 1980s because of lower export receipts and rapidly rising imports. However, Colombia was able to avoid having to reschedule its foreign debt and took steps to adjust its external accounts. The devaluation of the peso was speeded up, reinforced by import restrictions and export incentives. The fiscal accounts were also turned around and the public sector deficit was reduced while economic growth remained positive throughout and per capita income increased. The World Bank and the IMF endorsed the Colombian economic strategy and commercial banks continued to lend to the country to refinance loans falling due. The Gaviria Government accelerated the economic opening of the country and liberalized financial, investment, foreign exchange and tax legislation. High real interest rates encouraged capital inflows and economic stability encouraged foreign investors.

President Samper's 1995-98 development plan emphasized spending on the social sector and productive infrastructure (with private sector involvement) to help combat poverty. The means of achieving this included decentralization; departmental and municipal governments received a larger slice of current revenue, most of which was spent on health, education and sanitation. However, the transfer of responsibilities to the regions, as ordered by the 1991 Constitution, has lagged behind the transfer of revenues, resulting in a growing fiscal imbalance and inflationary pressures. In 1996 uncertainties over the fate of the president were expected to cause delays in investment projects. The USA removed Colombia from its list of countries making progress against drugs trafficking (Colombia is a major producer of cocaine, heroine and marijuana), cutting all US aid and US approval of new multilateral loans.

GOVERNMENT

Senators and Representatives are elected by popular vote. The Senate has 102 members, and the Chamber of Representatives has 161. The President, who appoints his 13 ministers, is elected by direct vote for a term of four years, but cannot succeed himself in the next term. Every citizen over 18 can vote. Reform of the 1886 Constitution was undertaken by a Constituent Assembly in 1991 (see above, **History**).

Administratively the country is divided into 23 Departments, 4 Intendencias, 5 Comisarias, and the Special District of Bogotá.

Liberty of speech and the freedom of the press are in theory absolute but in practice more limited. The language of the country is Spanish. Its religion is Roman Catholicism. There is complete freedom for all other creeds not contravening Christian morals or the law.

COMMUNICATIONS

The three Cordilleras, separated by valleys often no more than 1,500m above sea-level, make internal communications extremely difficult. Originally, there were over 3,000 km of railways, but most lines have been closed. At present there is only a tourist service N of Bogotá and an intermittant connection between Medellín and Barrancabermeja. The 106,220 km of roads have eastern and western systems, with inter-communicating laterals (see maps and text). Only about 10% of the road system is paved. Given these difficulties it is natural that Colombia, which ran the first airline in South America, has taken ardently to the air.

Bogotá

THE capital, with its wealth of museums and historic buildings, and nearby towns for a weekend excursion out of the city.

The full name of the capital of the Republic is Santafé de Bogotá. It is on a plateau of sloping land.

BASICS *Pop* 6.3mn, 1993; *Alt* 2,650m; *Area* 1,587 sq km; *Av temp* 14°C (58°F); *Phone code* 01.

Visitors should not be too active for the first 24 hrs. Some people get dizzy at Bogotá's altitude. Be careful with food and alcoholic drinks for the first day also.

The Calles (abbreviated 'Cll', or 'C') run at right angles across the Carreras ('Cra' or 'K'). It is easy enough to find a place once the address system, which is used throughout Colombia, is understood. The address Calle 13, No 12-45 would be the building on Calle 13 between Carreras 12 and 13 at 45 paces from Carrera 12; however transversals and diagonals (numbers with letters appended) can complicate the system. The Avenidas, broad and important streets, may be either Calles (like 19) or Carreras (like 14). Av Jiménez de Quesada, one of Bogotá's most important streets, owes its lack of straightness to having been built over a river-bed. Part of Carrera 7, one of the main shopping streets, is now closed to motor traffic on Sun and holidays when cycles, roller skates and skateboards take over.

CENTRAL BOGOTÁ

The central part of the city is full of character and contrasts: La Candelaria is the historic centre, occupying the area to the S of Av Jiménez de Quesada and N of Cra 10. There is some modern infill but many of the houses are well preserved in colonial style, of one or two storeys with tiled roofs, projecting eaves, wrought ironwork and carved balconies. Few are brightly painted. The churches, museums and palaces are concentrated around and above the Plaza Bolívar. There are also many intriguing cobbled streets further out from this nucleus. Some hotels are found in this part, more along the margins, eg Av Jiménez de Quesada. The streets are relatively uncrowded and safe; care should be exercised after dark. South of Cra 10 is seedier; the streets accommodate market stalls.

Downtown Bogotá, the old commercial centre with shops, offices and banks, runs in a band northwards from Av Jiménez de Quesada. It is very patchy, with a thorough mix of styles including modern towers and run down colonial and later buildings, together with a few notable ones. This commercial hub narrows to a thin band of secondary shops extending between Cra 7 and Av Caracas to around C 60. The streets are full of life; they are also paralyzed by traffic and laden with fumes much of the time. The pavements can be very congested too, particularly C 7 and Av 19. Many of the budget hotels and some of the better ones are found in this area, which is rated as low to moderate risk.

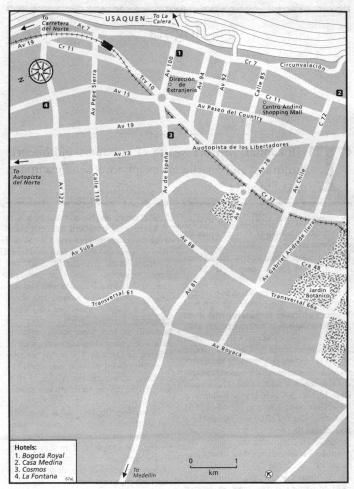

USAQUEN

To La Calera

To Carretera del Norte

Av 7

Av 19

Cr 11

Trv 10

Av Pepe Sierra

Av 15

Av 19

Av 13

Calle 110

Av 127

To Autopista del Norte

Av Suba

Transversal 61

Cr 11

Cr 7

Circunvalación

1

Dirección de Extranjería

Av 100

Av 94

Av 92

Calle 85

Av Paseo del Country

Centro Andino Shopping Mall

C 72

2

3

Auotopista de los Libertadores

Av España

Av 78

Av Chile

Cr 37

Av 81

Av Gabriel Andrade Ilera

Cra 48

Jardín Botánico

Transversal 66a

Av 68

Av 81

Av Boyacá

To Medellín

4

Hotels:
1. *Bogotá Royal*
2. *Casa Medina*
3. *Cosmos*
4. *La Fontana*

67aL

0   1
km

The area in which to exercise most caution is generally SW of Av Caracas. Away from the centre, the whole of the S of the city should be avoided unless there were specific reasons for a visit.

MONSERRATE

There is a very good view of the city from the top of **Monserrate** (3210m), the lower of the two peaks rising sharply to the E. It is reached by a funicular railway and a cable car. The new convent at the top is a popular shrine. At the summit, near the church, a platform gives a bird's-eye view of the city's tiled roofs and of the plains beyond stretching to the rim of the Sabana. Also at the top are several restaurants and a snack bar (good *tamales*, US$1), and the Calle del Candelero, a reconstruction of a Bogotá street of 1887. Behind the church

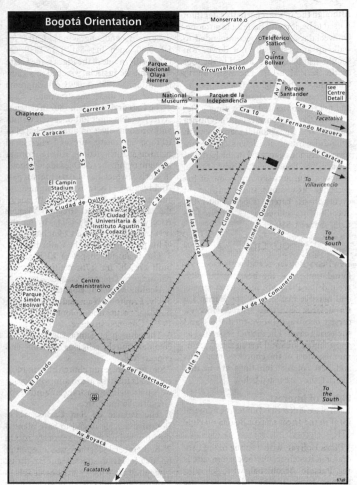

Bogotá Orientation

Monserrate

Teleférico Station

Quinta Bolívar

Parque Nacional Olaya Herrera

Circunvalación

see Centre Detail

National Museums

Parque de la Independencia

Parque Santander

Cra 7

Chapinero

Carrera 7

Cra 10

Av Fernando Mazuera

To Facatativá

Av Caracas

C 45

C 34

Av J E Gaitán

Av Caracas

C 63

C 53

Av 20

To Villavicencio

El Campín Stadium

Av Ciudad de Quito

C 26

Ciudad Universitaria & Instituto Agustín Codazzi

Av de las Américas

Av Ciudad de Lima

Av Jiménez Quesada

Av 30

To the South

Centro Administrativo

Av El Dorado

Parque Simón Bolívar

Diag

Cra 66a

Av de los Comuneros

Av El Dorado

Calle 13

Av del Espectador

To the South

Av Boyacá

To Facatativá

67a8

are popular picnic grounds. The fare up to Monserrate is US$3.20 adult return (US$1.60 child). The funicular works only on Sun and holidays (expect to have to queue for an hour if you want to go up before about 1400, and for coming down); the cable car operates 0600-2400 daily.

A good time to walk up is Sat or Sun about 0500, before the crowds arrive. There are enough people then to make it quite

safe and the view of Bogotá at sunrise is spectacular. The path is dressed stone and comfortably graded all the way up with refreshment stalls at weekends every few metres. It takes about 1¼ hrs up (if you don't stop). Sunset is also spectacular from the top. On no account walk down in the dark; also, take a taxi from the bottom station into town. There are usually taxis waiting by the footbridge across the road.

Although the area is reportedly safer than it used to be, it is still best not to go alone. On weekdays, it is not recommended to walk up and especially not down. You should also take a bus or taxi to the foot of the hill Mon-Fri. The walk up to Guadalupe, the higher peak opposite Monserrate, is said to be more dangerous and not recommended at any time.

At the foot of Monserrate is the **Quinta de Bolívar**, a fine colonial mansion, with splendid gardens and lawns. There are several cannons captured at the battle of Boyacá. The house, once Bolívar's home, is now a museum showing some of his personal possessions and paintings of events in his career. (Open 0900-1700, Tues-Sun; its address is C 20, No 3-23 Este; charge US$0.50.)

OLD CITY

The Plaza Bolívar, coeval with the city's foundation, is at the heart of the city; around the Plaza are the narrow streets and massive mansions of the **Barrio La Candelaria**, with their barred windows, carved doorways, brown-tiled roofs and sheltering eaves. The district is popular as a residential area and has an artists' community. Most of the churches, mansions and best colonial buildings are in this district, they are listed below.

Places of interest

Each place is described under the numeral for it in the street map of Bogotá on page 871.

1 **Plaza Bolívar**, with a statue of the Liberator at its centre. On the eastern side is the **Palacio Arzobispal**, with splendid bronze doors. To one side of it is the colonial **Plazuela de Rufino Cuervo**. Here is the house of Manuela Sáenz, the mistress of Bolívar. On the other side is the house in which Antonio Nariño printed in 1794 his translation of "The Rights of Man" which triggered off the movement for independence.

See the **Casa del Florero** or Museo 20 de Julio in a colonial house on the corner of Plaza Bolívar with C 11. It houses the famous flower vase that featured in the 1810 revolution and shows collections of the Independence War period, including documents and engravings. Entry fee US$0.40, open Tues-Sat, 0915-1830. On the northern side of the Plaza is the **Corte Suprema de Justicia**, wrecked in a guerrilla attack in 1985. A new Corte Suprema de Justicia is under construction.

2 The **Catedral**, rebuilt in 1807 in classical style. Notable choir loft of carved walnut and wrought silver on altar of Chapel of El Topo. Several treasures and relics; small paintings attributed to Ribera; banner brought by Jiménez de Quesada to Bogotá, in sacristy, which has also portraits of past Archbishops. There is a monument to Jiménez inside the Cathedral. In one of the chapels is buried Gregorio Vásquez Arce y Ceballos (1638-1711), by far the best painter in colonial Colombia. Many of his paintings are in the Cathedral.

3 The beautiful chapel of **El Sagrario**, built end of the 17th century. Several paintings by Gregorio Vásquez Arce.

4 **Alcaldía Mayor de Bogotá**.

5 The **Capitolio Nacional**, an imposing building with fine colonnades (1847-1925). Congress sits here.

6 The church of **Santa Clara**, another colonial church; religious museum and concert hall.

7 **San Ignacio**, Jesuit church built in 1605. Emeralds from the Muzo mines in Boyacá were used in the monstrance. Paintings by Gregorio Vásquez Arce.

8 The **Palacio de San Carlos**, where Bolívar lived. He is said to have planted the huge walnut tree in the courtyard. On 25 September 1828, there was an attempt on his life. His mistress, Manuela, thrust him out of the window and he was able to hide for 2 hrs under the stone arches of the bridge across the Río San Agustín. Santander, suspected of complicity, was arrested and banished.

The **Museo de Arte Colonial**, across from the Palacio de San Carlos (Carrera 6, No 9-77) is one of the finest colonial buildings in Colombia. It belonged originally to the Society of Jesus, and was once the seat of the oldest University in Colombia and of the National Library. It has a splendid collection of colonial art and paintings by Gregorio Vásquez Arce, all kinds of utensils, and 2 charming patios. Open Tues to Fri 1000-1700; Sat and Sun 1100-1700. Entry fee US$0.40 for adults; students US$0.20.

9 Church of **María del Carmen**, with ex-

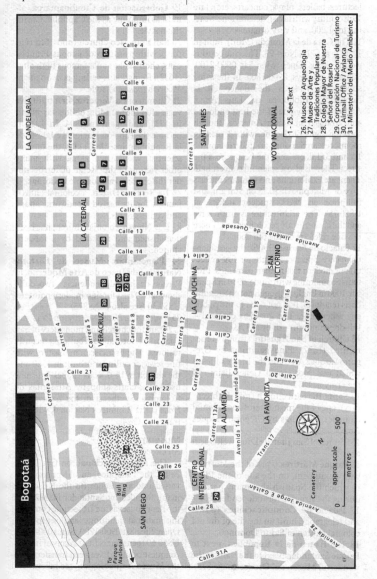

1 - 25. See Text
26. Museo de Arqueología
27. Museo de Arte y Tradiciones Populares
28. Colegio Mayor de Nuestra Señora del Rosario
29. Corporación Nacional de Turismo
30. Airmail Office / Avianca
31. Ministerio del Medio Ambiente

Bogotá

cellent stained glass and walls in bands of red and white.

10 **Teatro Colón**, C 10, No 5-32 (operas, lectures, ballets, plays, concerts, etc), late 19th century with lavish decorations. Seating for 1,200, and very ornate.

11 The **Casa de la Moneda** (Mint), built in 1720, is at C 11, No 4-93. The courtyard is worth seeing. Open Mon-Sat 0900-2100, Sun and holidays, 0900-1800. In the same street, No 4-14, is the Banco de la República's Biblioteca de Luis Angel Arango formerly one of the best endowed and arranged in South America, though showing signs of decline, with 3 reading rooms, research rooms, art galleries on the 1st and 3rd floors and, the best, across the street. There is also a splendid concert hall. There are exhibitions and regular concerts (free on Mon pm, US$0.75 on Sun am, and full-price on Wed, student tickets at US$0.75). The architecture is impressive and the lavatories are recommended. There is a fine cafeteria on the 6th floor.

12 **Palacio de Nariño** (1906), the presidential palace. Spectacular interior, fine collection of modern Colombian paintings. Free tours Sat morning with guide, 0930 in Spanish, 1000 in English, though not on a regular basis (enquire). It is not open to the public any other time. The guard is changed – full-dress uniform – daily at 1700.

13 Church of **San Agustín**, strongly ornamented (1637). Fine paintings by Gregorio Vásquez Arce and the Image of Jesus which was proclaimed Generalísimo of the army in 1812.

14 **Santa Bárbara** church (mid-16th century), one of the most interesting colonial churches. Paintings by Gregorio Vásquez Arce.

15 Church of **San Juan de Dios**, well worth a visit.

16 **Parque Mártires** (Park of the Martyrs) with monument, on the site of the Plaza in which the Spanish shot many patriots during the struggle for independence.

17 **Palacio de Comunicaciones** (postal and telegraph), built on the site of the old colonial church of Santo Domingo.

18 The **Banco de la República**, next to Parque Santander. Next to the Bank is the wonderful **Museo del Oro** (see page 873).

In Parque Santander there is a bronze statue of Santander, who helped Bolívar to free Colombia and was later its President.

19 **Gobernación de Cundinamarca**, almost as imposing as the Capitolio. Corinthian style.

20 **San Francisco** church (mid-16th century), with paintings of famous Franciscans, choir stalls, and a famous high altar (1622). Remarkable ceiling is in Spanish-Moorish (*mudéjar*) style.

21 Church of **La Veracruz**, first built five years after the founding of Bogotá, rebuilt in 1731, and again in 1904. In 1910 it became the Panteón Nacional e Iglesia de la República. José de Caldas, the famous scientist, was buried along with many other victims of the "Reign of Terror" under the church. Fashionable weddings.

22 **La Tercera Orden**, a colonial church famous for its carved woodwork, altars, and confessionals.

23 **Las Nieves**, colonial church, has been demolished and replaced by a modern church.

24 **Planetarium**, **Museo de Historia Natural** and **Museo de Arte Moderno**, in Parque de la Independencia. Two daily showings of best foreign modern painters, US$0.30 (see also page 873).

25 *Tequendama Hotel*. Nearby (on Cra 7 and C 26) are the church and monastery of San Diego, a picturesque old building recently restored. The Franciscan monastery with fine *mudéjar* ceiling was built in 1560 and the church in 1607 as its chapel. It is now used as a crafts shop by Artesanías de Colombia. Southeast of the *Tequendama Hotel* is the Biblioteca Nacional, with entrance on C 24.

Museums

All closed on Mon.

The **Museo Nacional**, on Cra 7, No 28-66, the Panóptico, an old prison converted into a museum (to the NE of the map), founded by Santander in 1823. Its top floor houses a fine art section, comprising national paintings and sculptures. Open Tues-Sat 0900-1700, Sun 1000-1600, US$0.60 (pensioners free). Many of its pre-conquest exhibits have been transferred to the **Museo Arqueológico**, see below.

See map: 8 for **Museo de Arte Colonial**, under 1 for **Museo 20 de Julio** and 11 for the Banco de la República's Luis Angel Arango library (US$0.20, half price for students).

The **Museo de Arte Moderno**, C 24, No 6-00, entry US$0.60, half price for students (open Tues-Sat 1000-1900, Sun 1200-1800), good café. If you want to photograph in the museum you must obtain permission from the office. The **Planetarium** and **Museo de Historia Natural**, C 26 y Cra 7, open Tues-Sun, and holidays, 1000-1700 (see map, No 24). Planetarium, 1100-1630.

The **Museo Mercedes de Pérez**, formerly the Hacienda de El Chicó, a fine example of colonial architecture, is at Cra 7, No 94-17. It contains a world-wide collection of mostly 18th century porcelain, furniture, paintings, etc. Open Tues-Sun, 0930-1230, 1430-1700.

The **Museo de Arte y Tradiciones Populares** is at Cra 8, No 7-21 in an old monastery and exhibits local arts and crafts. It has a shop, selling handicrafts at higher prices than Artesanías de Colombia, and a reasonably-priced bar and restaurant (dishes typical of different regions of Colombia served in colonial setting, usually with regional traditional music). Open 0830-1730, Mon-Sat. Entry fee US$0.50.

Museo Siglo XIX, Cra 8, No 7-93, founded by the Banco Cafetero, has a collection of 19th-century painting, clothes and furniture. Open: Tues-Sat 0830-1730. US$0.30.

The **Museo Arqueológico** (belonging to the Banco Popular) is a fine and extensive collection of precolumbian pottery, assembled in the restored mansion of the Marqués de San Jorge, Cra 6, No 7-43. The house itself is a beautiful example of 17th century Spanish colonial architecture. US$0.60 entry. Open: Tues-Sat 0900-1230, 1315-1700.

Museo Militar, C 10, No 4-92, history of Colombian armed forces and good collection of weapons, T 281-3086, Tues-Sat 0900-1600, US$0.30.

Quinta de Bolívar (Simon Bolívar museum), see page 870.

Casa-Museo Jorge Eliécer Gaitán, C 42, No 15-52, is former residence of the populist leader whose assassination in April 1948 triggered the infamous "Bogotazo", at the outset of La Violencia.

Instituto Nacional de Investigaciones Geológico-Mineras has a library and pleasant museum at Diagonal 53, No 34-53. Entrance US$0.10.

Museo de los Niños, Cra 48, No 63-97, natural sciences explained for children, created by Sra Ximena Rosas with funding from industry, Tues-Fri 0830-1600, Sat, Sun, holidays 0900-1600.

Museo Colsubsidio, C 26, No 25-42, exhibitions of contemporary artists.

Museo del Oro (the Gold Museum), is in splendid premises at the Parque de Santander (Cra 6, No 15-82, see No 18 on map). This collection is a "must", for it is unique. No less than 30,000 pieces of precolumbian gold work are shown. Open: Tues to Sat 0900-1630; Sun and holidays, 0900-1200 (people in shorts not allowed). Charge, US$1.85 (US$1.25 on Sat and Sun). There are tours and films in Spanish and English, enquire for times. Do not miss the Salón Dorado, a glittering display inside an inner vault.

The ancient gold objects discovered in Colombia were not made by the primitive technique of simple hammering alone, but show the use of virtually every technique known to modern goldsmiths.

Casa de Poesía Silva, C 14, No 3-41, T 286-7510, museum, bookshop and audio room/library with readings of almost every Spanish-speaking author.

NORTH BOGOTA

North of C 60 and E of Cra 13 (the extension of Av Caracas which eventually becomes the Autopista del Norte) is an expanding band of wealthy suburbs, shopping malls and classy restaurants. The best hotels are scattered through this area, which is regarded as relatively safe.

Places of interest

The **Universidad Nacional** (about 13,000 students) is housed in the Ciudad Universitaria shown on the orientation map. The oldest centres of learning are in the old centre: oldest of all is the Colegio Nacional de San Bartolomé (C 10, No 6-57), in the same block as the Chapel of El Sagrario (3 on map), founded 1573. The second oldest, founded on 18 December 1653, is the Colegio Mayor de Nuestra Señora del Rosario (C 14, No 6-25); its beautiful colonial building is well worth a look (you can buy a good cheap lunch at the cafeteria; it is not far from the Gold Museum).

There is an interesting and well organized **Jardín Botánico**, José Celestino Mutis, Cra 66, No 56-84. It has a collection of over 5,000 orchids, plus roses, gladioli and trees from all over the country (see map).

Short excursions from Bogotá

If you have a car, drive round the Av Circunvalación for splendid views.

To the E of Bogotá is **Choachi**, an attractive village set in a valley, where there are hot springs (good food at *El Colonial*, 1½ blocks from main square). Flota Macarena bus, several a day. A turnoff from the Choachi road brings one to the Santuario de San Francisco, with better views of Bogotá than one can get from Monserrate.

For longer excursions, see the end of this section.

LOCAL INFORMATION

Security Any 'officials' in uniform asking to register your money are almost certainly thieves.

The Judicial Unit for Tourism (Tourist police) offers 24-hr service for tourists at Cra 7, No 27-42, T 283-4930 or 334-2501. If you are robbed of documents, contact police at C 46 y Cra 14, of valuables, police at C 40, No 8-09.

NB Potholes can be very deep; avoid them, especially when it is wet.

● **Accommodation**

Book hotels in advance whenever possible. IVA tax of 14% is additional to the bill.

Hotel prices

L1	over US$200	L2	US$151-200
L3	US$101-150	A1	US$81-100
A2	US$61-80	A3	US$46-60
B	US$31-45	C	US$21-30
D	US$12-20	E	US$7-11
F	US$4-6	G	up to US$3

Hotels in North Bogotá, Calles 76 and upwards: **L1** *Bogotá Royal*, Av 100, No 8A-01,

T 218-9911, F 218-3362, excellent; **L1** *Bogotá Plaza*, C 100, No 18A-30, T 621-7088, F 218-4050, good restaurant, *Atrium*; **L1** *Charleston*, Cra 13, No 85-46, T 257-1100, F 218-0605, handsome building, close to restaurants and clubs; **L1** *Victoria Regia*, Cra 13, No 85-80, T 616-0202, F 610-3516, PO Box 250-718, superior rooms and suites, all services, pool, restaurant; **L1** *La Fontana*, Av 127, No 21-10, T 274-7868, F 216-0449, distinctive, very good (*Los Arcos* restaurant in hotel, superb, elegant); **L2** *La Bohème*, C 82, No 12-35, T 617-1177, F 618-0003, well-equipped rooms, attractive, good location; **L1** *Hacienda Royal*, C 114, No 6A-02, T 612-1666, F 620-0958, CCH Santa Bárbara, very well-appointed; **L2** *El Belvedere*, Tr 18, No 100-16, T 257-7700, F 257-0331, modern, very good value, excellent restaurant *Balmoral*; **L2** *Cosmos 100*, C 100, No 21 A-41, friendly staff, great view, good breakfasts, T 257-4000, F 257-1035, rec; **L1** *Los Urapanes*, Cra 13, No 83-19, T 218-1188, F 218-9242, very pleasant, smart, smaller hotel; **L2** *Meliá Santafé*, C 116 (Av Pepe Sierra), No 17-64, T 629-0029, F 629-0039, new.

L3 *Dann Carlton*, Av 15, No 103-60, T 635-0010, F 635-2824, new 1996; **L3** *Portón 84*, C 84, No 7-65, T 616-4006, F 616-3905, very good, excellent restaurant; **L3** *Richmond Suites*, C 93, No 18-81, T 616-7121, convenient, quiet, excellent rooms.

A2 *Rincón del Chicó*, C101, No 13-32, T 214-7371, hot water, clean, safe, family atmosphere, TV, helpful, good restaurant; **A1** *Apartamentos 82*, Cra 14, No 81-34, T 256-6751, self catering flatlets, good service, pleasant, safe, rec; **A3** *Chicó 93*, C 93, No 15-73, T 236-2012, F 616-0385, Apdo 094 805, aparthotel with kitchenette.

C *Hostal Residencias Moreno*, Transversal 33 No 95-28, T 218-1226, inc two meals, two house taxi drivers, nearby frequent bus service to centre, very friendly, safe for left luggage, quiet, comfortable, hot water, highly rec.

Between Calles 31 and 75: L1 *Casa Medina*, Cra 7, 69A-22, T 217-0288, F 212-6668, nice interior, chic; **L2** *Orquidea Royal* Cra 7, No 32-16, T 287-0788, F 287-7480, restaurant, pool; **A1** *Centro Internacional*, Cra 13A, No 38-97, T 288-5566, F 288-0850, popular, good location; **A2** *Fiesta Avenida*, Av Caracas, No 47-28, T 285-3407, clean, friendly, safe, restaurant, TV, rec; **A2** *Las Terrazas*, C 54A, No 3-12, 2-star, T 255-5777, very clean, "rustic charm", pleasant, nice view of city; **B** *Hostal Linden*, C 36, No 14-39, T 287-4239, central, small, 2 rooms with kitchenette, credit cards accepted; **C** *Casa Berlinesa*, C 45A, No 21-40, T 232-8504, German and English spoken, full breakfast available; **D** *La Cabaña*, C 58, No 9-55, safe, good value; **D** *Hospedaje Turístico 61*, C 61, No 10-18, T 217-0383, clean, friendly, discounts for stays over 3 days, also has short-stay section.

In Old Bogotá (up to Calle 31): **L1** *Tequendama*, Cra 10, No 26-21, T 286-1111, F 282-2860, restaurant serves excellent *ajiaco*, good for breakfast; **L3** *Bacatá*, C 19, No 5-20, T 283-8300, F 281-7249, downtown on busy street, cheaper at weekends, worth asking at other times, restaurant not rec; **L3** *Dann*, C 19, No 5-72, T 284-0100, F 282-3108, very helpful; **A1** *Nueva Granada*, Av Jiménez, No 4-77, T 286-5877, F 284-5465, relaxed atmosphere; **L3** *Del Parque*, C 24, No 4-93, T 284-2200, F 283-2315, good commercial hotel; **B** *Quiratama*, C 17, No 12-44, T 282-4515, F 341-3246, very nice rooms, TV, telephone, good service, restaurant; **B** *Regina*, Cra 5, No 15-16, with private bath, TV, phone, friendly, good; **A3** *Del Duc*, C 23, No 9-38, T 334-0080, friendly, clean, good French restaurant; **A3** *Virrey*, C 18, No 5-56, T 334-1150, modern, with hot shower, TV, good value restaurant, friendly, rec.

On C 14 near Cra 4 are: **A1** *Dann Colonial*, No 4-21, T 341-1680, F 334-9982, safe parking, friendly; opposite is **D** *Santa Fe*, No 4-48, shower, good service, quiet, clean, friendly, safe, good restaurant, popular with locals, best value in the Candelaria area, warmly rec; **E** *Residencia Aragón*, Cra 3, No 14-13, T 342-5239/284-8325, clean and safe, friendly and honest, hot water, will store luggage, parking facilities, warmly rec; **E** *El Dorado*, Cra 4, C 15, hot water, safe, clean, noisy, upstairs rooms better (cheap taxi to airport can be arranged).

A3 *Santa Mónica*, Cra 3, No 24-11, T 242-8080, a/c, cable TV, comfortable, good location, rec; **A3** *San Diego*, Cra 13 y C 24, T 284-2100, friendly, clean, large rooms, good value, accepts credit cards but not Amex TCs; **B** *Los Cerros*, C19, No 9-18, T 283-8458, pleasant, good restaurant; **C** *La Hostería de la Candelaria*, C 9, No 3-11, T 342-1727, Aptdo Aéreo 15978, highly rec for comfort, atmosphere and service, charming patio, no heat, **A3** suite available with lovely view of old Bogotá, dinner available if ordered in am (good for longer stays); **C** *Bogotá Internacional*, Cra 7, No 21-20, T 342-9428, very central, comfortable, noisy, restaurant and bar, a little run down but very helpful; **C** *La Sabana*, C 23, No 5-23, T 284-4830, F 284-6552, central, quiet, clean, English spoken, small restaurant, Visa accepted; **C** *Príncipe de Viena*, C 19, No 15-35, T 342-0090, big old rooms, with bath, TV, restaurant.

D *Zaratoga*, Av Jiménez de Quesada, No 4-56 (opp *El Turista*, not rec), with bath, no hot

water, quite nice; **D** *Residencia Dorantes*, C 13, No 5-07, very clean (cheaper without bath), hot water, rooms on Cra 5 side noisy, reasonable, safe, rec; **D** *Residencias Ambala*, Cra 5, No 13-46, T 241-2376, cheap, clean, friendly and central; **D-C** *Avenida Jiménez*, Av Jiménez, No 4-71, T 243-6685, helpful, friendly, sauna, safe; **D** *Lima*, Cra 4 y C 16, with bath, clean, secure, TV, phone, hot water, good views from upstairs rooms.

E *Hollywood*, C 18, No 8-68, clean but small rooms with bath; **E** *Italia*, Cra 7, No 20-40, convenient, safe, T 334-6629, hot water, TV lounge, friendly, laundry, safe, rec; **E** *Panamericana*, C 15, No 12-70, T 242-1802, good, with bath, helpful; **E** *Platypus*, C 16, No 2-43, T 341-2874, clean, pleasant, kitchen facilities, hot water, free coffee, friendly informative owner, excellent travellers guest house, highly rec; **E** *Regis*, C 18, No 6-09 (also known as *Residencias María*), C with shower, sometimes hot water, old-fashioned, run down but safe, clean, safe parking for car or motorcycle; **E** *Virgen del Camino*, C 18A, No 14-33, friendly, clean, quiet, safe, T 282-4450; **E** *Internacional*, Cra 5, No 14-45, friendly, hot water, good value, T 341-8731, safe deposit (care, taxi drivers may take you to the *Bogotá Internacional* if you do not specify the address).

F *María Luisa*, Cra 14, between Cs 15 and 16, hot water, very reasonable and food is good; **F** *Asturias*, C 16, No 15-36, T 242-0931, safe, good value but no hot water; **F** *Francés*, C 22, No 15-83, T 282-7492, room with shower, clean, safe; **F** *Residencia Bucamaranga*, C 15, No 16-68, with bath, cold water, basic; **F** *Residencias Americana*, C 13 and Cra 16, clean, safe, but only cold water; **F** *Residencias Avenida Fénix*, Cra 15, No 15-74, T 341-6237, with bath, friendly, family atmosphere, clean; many other cheap hotels in the C 15, Cra 10 area, which is dangerous especially for women alone.

There are a number of small, unregistered *hostales* in the N of the city, ask at tourist offices at airport or in the centre. From C 12 southwards, Cra 13 westwards is not salubrious. visitors are therefore advised to pick hotels in streets NE of C 12, with higher numbers. There are certainly many hotels between Cs 13 and 17 and Cras 15 and 17, many of which are cheap, some of which are clean. Private vehicles should be parked in lockable, guarded parqueaderos.

Youth Hostel Association Alcom, Apdo Aéreo 3220, Cra 7, No 6-10, behind Presidential Palace, safe area, T 280-3041/280-3202, F 280-3460; IYHA member, has a full list of 16 hostels around the country. There is a hostel at this address with 90 beds, US$4.50 pp members, US$5 non-members per night. Ask for full information at Alcom. Reservations for all hostels must be made through Prosocial, Bogotá 16, No 33-29, T 285-9296/285-9351, 0800-2000.

● **Places to eat**

14% value-added tax may be charged. For hotel restaurants, see above.

Recommended restaurants in North Bogotá (C 76 and above) include: *El Arko de los Olivos*, Tr 22, C 122-13, new, rustic style, excellent cooking; *La Fragata*, C 100, No 8A-55, 12th floor of World Center, revolving; also at Cra 13, No 27-98 and Diag 127A, No 30-26, L1, expensive, excellent fish; *La Academia de Golf*, Cra 15, No 85-42, and Cra 15, No 102-20, international, very good; *La Bodega Marina*, Cra 11A, No 93A-46, Cra 9, No 81-49, and 2 other branches, superb; *Le Petit Bistrot*, C 76, No 10-28, excellent French cuisine; *Il Giardino*, C 93, No 18-25, Italian; *Il Piccolo Caffe*, Cra 15, No 96-55, pasta etc, very good quality; *Las Tapas*, Av 19, No 114-13, Spanish bar-restaurant; *Zeukadi*, C 82, corner of Cra 11, fire lit at 2200, candlelight, rec. *Na Zdarovia*, Cra 14, No 80-71, Russian, very good, same owners, *Tandoor*, Cra 11, No 84-53, good Indian; *Viva Villa*, C 82, No 12-70, Mexican, good food, rec; *Casa de Cultura de México*, Cra 14, No 80-44, good Mexican food on second floor; *El Mondongo y Algo Más*, Cra 11, No 97A-38, local food; *El Buque*, Cra 18 y C 101, seafood, excellent; *Fulanitos*, C 81, No 9-13, good Valle Cauca food, friendly atmosphere; *Fridays*, C 82, No 12-18, US$10-12, superb value, rec; *Le Bilbouquet*, C 83, No 12-19, excellent French, nice atmosphere, rec; *L'Epicurien*, Cra 30, No 89-56, French chef, 1960 décor, very good, rec; *Il Pomeriggio*, Cra 11 y C82 in Centro Andino, popular, good atmosphere; *Welcome*, Cra 14, No 80-65, Japanese, good cooking supervised by perfectionist owner; *Hatsuhana*, Cra 13, No 93A-27, Japanese; *Casa Brava*, Km 4.5, Vía La Calera, steak house, superb view, very good food. In these restaurants meals cost from US$20/25 to US$40.

Tony Roma's, C 93, No 13-85, good quality food and excellent service. *Café Libre*, Cra 15, near Universidad Católica, bar with live music, also serves lunches; *Café Oma*, several locations, inc Cra 15, No 82-58, Av 19, No 118-78, Cra 15, No 14-71, and airport Muelle Nacional local 2-33, good food and coffee, nice atmosphere but relatively expensive, open till 0100; *Café y Crepes*, Cra 16, No 82-17, T 236-2905, good food, good atmosphere, climbers meet here; *Shamua*, Av 19, No 114-70, good cocktails, small selection of well prepared food, US style.

Central Bogotá (note that in the colonial centre very little is open after 2000 any day of the week): *Refugio Alpino*, C 23, No 7-49, is

an excellent international restaurant; *Casa San Isidro*, on Monserrate, good, not cheap; *Casa Vieja*, Av Jiménez 3-73, traditional Bogotá food, live music, also at C 116, No 20-50 in North Bogotá and 2 other branches; *Eduardo*, C13, No 8-66, T 243-0118, good business restaurant upstairs, more popular downstairs; *Doña Herta*, C 19, No 8-61, the best goulash in town, friendly, Swiss owned; *Donde Canta la Rana*, Cra 24C, No 20-10 Sur, a few km from centre, is refreshingly local and unspoilt, open 1400-1900; *Tierra Colombiana*, Cra 10, No 27-27, good, expensive food, evening floor show; *Cafetería Romana*, Av Jiménez, No 6-65, all meals, very clean, reasonable pasta, but excellent, expensive breakfast menu; its sister restaurants *Sorrento* (round the corner from *Romana*) and *Salerno*, Cra 7, No 19-43, good value; *Pizzería El Sol de Napolés*, C 69, No 11-58, T 249-2186, small, cozy, excellent antipasto; *Chalet Suizo*, Av 22, No 39A-48, delicious fondues and good steaks. For excellent, inexpensive Arab food, *Ramses*, Cra 7, No 18-64. *Bambú*, Cra 7 y C 61/62, good Chinese, reasonable prices.

Punta Roja, Cra 7 y C 22, good 3-course meal for US$2, open 24 hrs; *Punto Rápido*, Cra 7, No 19-49, self service, good meals, reasonable, friendly, 24 hrs service; *Salón Fontana*, C 14, No 5-98, busy, good, inexpensive; *La Tienda de Don Zoilo*, Cra 4, No 19-56, student pub, good food, friendly, rec; *Crepes y Waffeles*, restaurant chain, good value; also *La Boliche*, C 27, No 5-64, Italian and good crepes; *Empanadas La 19*, Av 19, No 8-56, good, cheap meals and snacks. A cheap two-course meal can be had in the cafeteria of the Ley and Tía supermarkets. For the traveller on a budget, *bandeja* (the local *plato del día*) can cost US$1.50-2 for a 2-course meal at the right places.

Vegetarian: *La Berenjena*, C 19, No 34-37, highly rec, lunch US$2.50; *Loto Azul*, Cra 5A, No 14-00, also good, same price; *El Champiñon*, Cra 8, No 16-36, 2 other branches, good vegetarian lunches; *Lotus Azul*, C 15, Cra 6, good quality and good value; vegetarian food excellent at Cra 8, No 11-19, near Plaza Bolívar; *Govindas*, Cra 8, No 20-56, set (vegetarian) meal US$1, good quality; *Samovares*, Cra 11, No 69-89 (T 249-4549 – lunch only, fixed menu, nice atmosphere), also Cra 11, No 67-63 (T 249-6515) and Av Caracas No 32-64 (T 285-6095). *El Integral Natural*, Cra 11, No 95-10, health food shop with a few tables at street level, restaurant downstairs, fixed menu US$1.50.

Tea rooms: (Pastelerías) *Benalcázar*, near Plaza de las Nieves on Cra 8, No 20-25, excellent pastries; *La Suiza*, C 25, No 9-41, excellent pastries; *Panadería Florida*, Cra 7, No 20-82, also has good pastries; *La Espiga*, Cra 15 esq C 82, and other locations, excellent bread and pastries.

● **Airline offices**

The **Avianca** office is at Cra 7, No 16-36, T 295-4611/243-1613, airport 413-8295. **Satena**, Centro Tequendama, Cra 10 y C 27, T 286-2701, airport 413-8158, military airline, not best for comfort and delays. **SAM**, Cra 10, No 27-91, T 286-8402, airport 413-8868. Most airlines, local and international, have offices in both Central and North Bogotá. Many international airline offices are closed on Sat and Sun. See page 988 for procedure to obtain refunds on unused tickets.

● **Banks & money changers**

Banks: everywhere in Bogotá where there is commercial activity. Many head offices are grouped around the Avianca building at the corner of Plaza San Francisco. **Banco Anglo Colombiano**, Cra 8, No 15-46/60, and 18 local agencies, will cash Thomas Cook and Amex TCs (US$100 min, 0900-1300, passport will be stamped) and will give advances against Visa, good rates. **Banco Unión Colombiana** (Cra 10, No 26-55 – after 1000, take passport, not a copy) and other banks (eg **Banco Popular**, **Banco del Occidente**) will in theory change TCs, but obtaining cash against a credit card is best (your passport will be photocopied). **Credibanco**, Visa, C 72, No 6-12, T 312-4400; **Banco Industrial de Colombia** (BIC), Cra 7, No 24-89, p 43, T 284-1656, Mastercard agency, gives good rates for TCs. See **Hours of Business** and **Currency** in **Information for travellers**.

Money changers: American Express, Tierra Mar Aire Ltda, edif Bavaria Torre B, Local 126, Cra 10, No 27-91, T 283-2955, does not change TCs, but will direct you to those who do, eg Banco Unión. Also very helpful in replacing lost Amex TCs provided you have full details and preferably proof of purchase. Other offices at C 92, No 15-63, T 218-5666 and Cra 8 y C 15 are reported as helpful. **International Money Exchange**, Cra 7, No 32-29, open Mon to Fri till 1600, check all transactions carefully; opp at *Hotel Orquidea Real*, you can exchange on Sat. Also exchange at Av 19, No 15-35. **Exprinter** on Av Jiménez and Cra 6. Inside you can only get pesos and no TCs are exchanged, but the black market operates on the pavement outside, or try the kiosk right there; Peruvian and Ecuadorean currencies available (rates generally little different from official rates). **Orotur**, Cra 10, No 26-05 (very small, below *Hotel Tequendama*) is quick and efficient, cash only; **Money Point**, Cra 10, No 27, in Centro Internacional, unit 161, good rates, take passport photocopy.

Other *cambios* on Av Jiménez de Quesada, between Cras 6 and 11, and in the N of the city. On Sun exchange is virtually impossible except at the airport.

● **Cultural centres**

British Council, C 87, No 12-79, T 236-3976 has a good library and British newspapers. **Anglo-Colombian School**, Transversal 30, No 152-38; postal address: Apdo Aéreo 52969, Bogotá 2. **English School**, C 170, No 31-98 (T 254-1318 or 254-8874), Apdo Aéreo 51284, Bogotá. **American School**, Colegio Nueva Granada, Cra 2E, No 70-20, T 212-3511. **Centro Colombo Americano**, C 109A, No 17-10, T 215-6697, Spanish courses similar to those below, but only if enough students, rec. **Goethe Institut**, Cra 7, No 81-57, T 255-1843. **Biblioteca Luis Angel Arango**, C 11, No 4-14, see under No 11 on map.

● **Embassies & consulates**

Venezuelan Consulate, Av 13, No 103-16, T 256-3015, hrs of business 0900-1230, 1300-1500, visas cost US$30, but allow 3 days (they will tell you to get your visa at the border, which may not be easy; it is hard to persuade them to give visas to overland travellers). **Ecuadorean Embassy**, C 89, No 13-07, T 236-1048; **Brazilian Embassy**, C 93, No 14-20, T 218-0800; **Peruvian Consulate**, C 90, No 14-26, T 257-3147. **Bolivian Embassy**, Tr 12, No 119-95, Apto 101, T 215-3274. **Panamanian Consulate**, C 92, No 7-70, T 257-4452; Mon-Fri, 0900-1300. **Costa Rican Consulate**, Cra 15, No 80-87, Mon-Fri 0900-1300, T 236-1098. **Guatemalan Consulate**, Transversal 29A, No 139A-41, T 258-0746, Mon-Fri, 0900-1200, visa takes 48 hrs, US$10 (cash only), one photo, one airline ticket (not have to be return), tourist visa free for Canadians; takes 48 hrs. **Mexican Embassy**, C 82, No 9-25, T 610-4070. **El Salvador Embassy**, Cra 9, No 80-15, T 212-5932.

US Embassy, C 38, No 8-61 (mailing address: Apdo Aéreo 3831, Bogotá 1, DE), T 232-7749. **Canadian Embassy**, C 76, No 11-52, T 217-5555, open 0800-1630 (mailing address: Apdo Aéreo 53531, Bogotá 2, DE).

British Embassy, C 98, No 9-03, p 4, T 218-5111, postal address: Apdo Aéreo 4508. **German Embassy**, Cra 4, No 72-35, p 6, T 212-0511. **French Embassy**, Cra 11, No 93-12, T 618-0511. **French Consulate**, Cra 7, No 38-99, T 285-4311. **Belgian Embassy**, C 26, No 4A-45, p 7, T 282-8901. **Dutch Embassy**, Cra 9, No 74-08, p 6, T 211-9600. **Finnish Consulate**, Cra 7, No 35-33, p 7, T 212-6111. **Norwegian Consulate**, Cra 13, No 50-78, Oficina 506, T 235-5419. **Swedish Embassy**, C 72, No 5-83, T 255-3777. **Danish Consulate General**, Cra 10, No 96-29, of 611, T 610-0887, 0900-

1300 Mon-Thur, 0900-1200 Fri. **Swiss Embassy**, Cra 9, No 74-08, oficina 1101, T 255-5280, open Mon-Fri 0900-1200. **Italian Consulate**, C 70, No 10-25 (Apdo Aéreo 50901), T 235-4300. **Israeli Embassy**, Edif Caxdac, C 35, No 7-25, p 14, T 287-7783/808/962. **Japanese Embassy**, Cra 9A, No 99-02, p 6, T 618-2800.

● **Entertainment**
Cinema: *Cinemateca Distrital*, Cra 7, No 22-79. The *Museo de Arte Moderno* shows different films every day, all day. Foreign films old and new are shown on weekend mornings at 1030 in commercial cinemas and there are many small screening rooms which run the occasional feature. Consult *El Espectador* or *La Prensa*, and handbills all over town for what is on; frequent programme changes. Admission, US$3.

Nightlife: there are many popular bars, discos etc in the Cra 15, C 82 region, known as the Zona Rosa. Also many popular bars and dancing places on Cra 5 with C 25, relatively safe area. Try *El Viejo Almacén*, Cra 5 y C 13-14, run by an aged Argentine lady who plays 78 tango records and sells reasonably priced beer and *aguardiente* (on Fri and Sat only). *Disco del Teatro de Candelaria*, C 15 between Cras 4 and 5, good atmosphere especially Fri and Sat.

Gay bars: *Adonis*, C 33 y Cra 13A; *Alex*, C 22 y Cra 7, and three bars on Cra 7 between C 17 y 18, all no cover, expensive drinks.

Sauna: Los Andes, Cra 4, No 16-29, good service, open daily 1000-2200. Sauna San Diego, Cra 7 nr C 25, massage, turkish bath and sauna rec.

Theatre: many of the theatres are in the Candelaria area. *Teatro Colón* details on page 872. *Teatro Libre de Bogotá*, C 62, No 10-65, T 217-1988; *Nacional*, C 71, No 10-25, T 235-8069; *La Candelaria*, C 12, No 2-59, T 281-4814; *Teatro Popular de Bogotá*, C 5, No 14-71, T 342-1675.

● **Hospitals & medical services**
Cruz Roja Nacional, Av 68, No 66-31, T 250-661/231-9027/231-9008, open 0830-1800. *Instituto Nacional de Salud*, Av El Dorado y Cra 50, for vaccinations, T 222-0577. *Centro Médico La Salud*, Cra 10, No 21-36, 2nd floor, T 243-1381/282-4021. *Walter Röthlisberger y Cía Ltda*, C 26, No 13-37, T 283-6200, imports medicines, inc Vivotif for typhoid and gamma globulin, and stores them correctly; trade prices. Embassies will advise on doctors, dentists, etc. *Profamilia*, C 34, No 14-46, for contraceptives. *Clínica Marly*, C 50, No 9-67, T 287-1020 (bus runs along Cra 4-14) and *Clínica del Country*, Cra 15, No 84-13, T 257-3100, are well-equipped private hospitals. Dr

Arturo Corchuelo at C 89, No 12-21, T 218-8710, recommended for orthopaedic problems. *Clínica Barraqer*, Av 100, No 18A-51, internationally known eye clinic.
For ambulances, T 115.

● **Language courses**
Pontificia Universidad Javeriana, Centro Latino Americano de Relaciones Humanas e Interculturales, Cra 10, No 65-48, T 212-3009, recommended for full Spanish language and cultural courses; short, one-month courses in June, July and Aug, and mid-Nov to mid-Dec, US$150. At other times of the year courses last 3 months, 2 hrs a day. Accommodation with local families can be arranged, but this is cheaper through the small ads section of *El Tiempo*. All other schools in Yellow Pages offer one-to-one private tuition at US$10/hr.

● **Laundry**
Ask in your hotel, or locally. *Burbujas*, Edif Procoil, Av 19, No 3A-37, open Mon-Sat 0730-1930, 24-hr service, manager speaks English.

● **Post & telecommunications**
Post: main airmail office and foreign *poste restante* in basement of Ed Avianca, Cra 7, No 16-36, open 0730-1900 Mon to Sat, closed Sun and holidays (*poste restante* 0730-1800, Mon-Sat, letters kept for only a month, bureaucratic, US$0.40 for each letter retrieved). At weekends the Post Office only franks letters; stamps for postcards are not sold. Pharmacies and newsagents in Bogotá have an airmail collection. Parcels by air, contact Avianca. To send film abroad pay for recorded delivery, use regulation envelope and get glue from counter 15.

International telephone calls: from several Telecom offices in centre of Bogotá (eg C 12 y Cra 8, C 23, No 13-49, in the *Tequendama Hotel*/Centro Internacional complex); all close within 1/2 hr of 2000.

● **Shopping**
14% value-added tax on all purchases. *Artesanías de Colombia* (state-owned), Almacén San Diego, in the old San Diego church, Cra 10, No 26-50, Claustro de Las Aguas, next to the Iglesia de las Aguas, Cra 3A, No 18-60, has good selection of folk art and crafts, at fair prices. There is a shop in the **Museo de Artes y Tradiciones Populares**, which is recommended. A street market on Av Jiménez and Cra 14 (Av Caracas) sells cheaper *ruanas*, blankets, leatherware, etc. Woollen *ruanas* at *Galerías Nariño* (Mercado La Victoria), or *Almacén Fascinación*, local J36-38, T 281-0239. Mercado de Pulgas (fleamarket) on Cra 3, from C 19, N, on Sun afternoons and holidays. It is a popular place and bar at the N end sells cheap beer and has a reggae band playing all afternoon (on no

account wander around here other than on Sun). Another, also only Sun, Cra 7 y C 19.

Galerías Cano, Ed Bavaria, Cra 13, No 27-98 (Torre B, Int 1-19B), Unicentro, Loc 218, Airport, sell textiles, pottery as well as gold and gold-plated replicas of some of the jewellery on display in the Gold Museum. *Galería Alfred Wild*, C 82, No 12-35, has excellent but pricey drawings and paintings.

The pavements and cafés along Av Jiménez, below Cra 7, Parque de los Periodistas, and C 16 and Cra 3, are used on weekdays by emerald dealers. Great expertise is needed in buying: bargains are to be had, but synthetics and for-geries abound. *La Casa de la Esmeralda*, C 30, No 16-18, wide range of stones; *Joyas Verdes Ltda*, Cra 15, No 39-15 also. Other jewellery shops in the *Hotel Tequendama*. See *H Stern's* jewellery stores at the International Airport, and *Tequendama Hotel*. Modern textiles and knit-wear can be bought at low prices at *Unicentro*, a large shopping centre on Cra 15, No 123-30 (take "Unicentro" bus from centre, going N on Cra 10 – takes about 1 hr). *Centro Granahor-rar*, Av Chile (C 72) No 10 34, is another good shopping centre; also *Metropolis*, Av 68, No 75A-50 (with *Exito* supermarket opposite), *Ha-cienda Santa Bárbara*, Cra 7 y C 116, and *Bulevar Niza*, Cra 52, No 125A-59. *Centro Comercial Andino*, Cra 12 entre C 82 y C 83 (near *Hotel La Bohème*) is a fine, new centre.

Heavy duty plastic for covering rucksacks etc, is available at several shops around C 16 and Av Caracas; some have heat sealing machines to make bags to size.

Bookshops: *Librería Aldina*, Cra 7, No 70-80, most helpful on books and Bogotá alike; excel-lent stock of English-language books inc this *Handbook*, open 0930-1930, Sat 0930-1700. *Oma*, Cra 15, No 82-58 (and other branches), good art and literature books, international newspapers, also sells this *Handbook*, open late inc Sun. *Librería Nacional*, Cra 7, No 17-51 (has small selection of English novels). *Librería Francesa*, Cra 8, No 63-45, also imports English books. Similarly *Libros y Discos*, Cra 15, No 82-58. *Librería Lerner*, No 13-13 (Chapinero), (specializes in 'libros colombianos'). *Librería Buchholz*, Cra 7, No 27-68 (opp *Hotel Tequen-dama*), also at C 59, No 13-13 (Chapinero), most books in Spanish; useful advice in a number of languages. *Sociedad Colombiana de Ar-quitectos*, Cra 6, No 28-85, good bookstore on ground floor; *Ateneo*, C 82, No 13-19, in the N of the city, good selection of Colombian titles, knowledgeable staff; *Librería Tercer Mundo*, Cra 7, No 16-91, knowledgeable; *Librería Cul-tural Colombiana*, C 72, No 16-15; *Casa de Libro*, C 18 between Cras 7 and 6. *Panameri-*

cana, Cra 7, No 14-09, disorganized, but has some guidebooks and maps. Books in Colombia are generally expensive.

Maps: the best current map of Bogotá is by Cartur, scale 1:25,000, 1994, and of Colombia, Mapa Vial de Colombia by Rodríguez, scale 1:2,000,000, also 1994, about US$4 each. You may have to try several bookshops. Hiking, topographical and general maps, also a good new road atlas of the country from Instituto Geográfico Agustín Codazzi, Av Ciudad de Quito y C 45, T 368-3666, F 368-0998 (topog-raphical details are generally accurate, but trails and minor roads less so). Esso road maps from service stations, US$0.40.

Photography: *Foto Japón*, branches all over the city, gives free film, branch at Cra 7, No 50-10, develops slides in 1 hr. *Poder Fotográfico*, Cra 5, No 20-70, T 342-4130, for good developing in 2-3 hrs. Film tends to be cheaper in Colombia than in Ecuador and Peru.

● **Sports**

Bull fighting: on Sat and Sun during the season, and every 2-3 weeks for the rest of the year, at the municipally owned Plaza de Santamaria, nr Parque Independencia. In season, the bulls weigh over 335 kg; out of season they are "comparatively small and unprofessional". (Lo-cal bullfight museum at bullring, door No 6.) **Boxing matches** are held here too.

Football: tickets for matches at El Campín sta-dium can be bought in advance at *Cigarrería Bucana*, C 18, No 5-92. It is not normally neces-sary to book in advance, except for the local Santa Fe-Millonarios derby. Take a cushion; matches Sun at 1545, Weds at 2000.

Hiking: Sal Si Puedes hiking group arranges walks every weekend and sometimes midweek on trails in Cundinamarca; very friendly, welcomes visitors. Hikes are graded for every ability, from 3 km to 4-day excursions of 70 km, camping overnight. Reservations must be made and paid for a week in advance at Cra 7 No 17-01, offices 640 and 641, T 283-3765 or contact Justo Alfonso Gamboa, Diagonal 123, No 50-30, Bogotá, T 283-9980 office, 253-6228 home.

Horse races: at Hipódromo los Andes, on Autopista Norte, races at 1400 (entrance US$1 and US$0.35), and at the Hipódromo del Techo, in the SW, on Sat, Sun and public holidays. Nearby is the Municipal Stadium, which can hold 50,000 spectators. **Football matches** are played here.

● **Tour companies & travel agents**
Recommended: *Tierra Mar Aire*, Cra 10, No 27-91, is Amex agent; does city tours from *Hotel Tequendama* (T 286-1111). Similar tours of the City (4 hrs) can be arranged from *Hotel Nueva*

Granada. Expedición Colombia, Edif KLM, p 9, C 26, No 4A-45, T 284-8284/8456, runs tours to the Llanos by private, chartered plane. *Interamerican Tours*, C 17, No 6-57 very helpful arranging flights to Central America via San Andrés. *Viajes Chapinero*, Av 7, 124-15, T 612-7716, F 215-9099, with branches at C63, No 13-37, Chapinero, and Cra 40C, No 57-08, bloque A1, manager David Krech, helpful with information in English. *Sierra Adventure* (Mauricio Guevara), C 118, No 32-38, Apto 201, T/F 612-5652, cellular 93-333-9050 (home address, office is to be moved, trekking, climbing, bungee jumping, parapenting, rec (also sells climbing gear, Cra 24, No 72-75, T 225-0827, F 231-8145); *Eco Guías*, Cra 8, No 63-27, T/F 212-7450, Luis Enrique La Rotta and Nadia Diamond, specialize in ecotourism, climbing, trekking, riding, swimming and tourism on coffee *fincas*, rec.

● **Tourist offices**
Corporación Nacional de Turismo (CNT), C 28, No 13A-59, admin offices at C 28, No 13A-15, T 413-8202/9830, Ed Centro de Comercio Internacional (the name at the top of the building is Bancafé), Mon-Fri, 0830-1300, 1400-1700, closed Sat and Sun, take passport; they will tell you which parts of the country are unsafe, good maps of major cities available; at Eldorado Airport (also open Sat, Sun and holidays, 0700-1430) and new bus terminal (both helpful, will book hotel rooms). Tourist police kiosk outside *Hotel Tequendama*, nr bridge on Cra 7. Municipal tourist office, **Instituto Distrital de Cultura y Turismo**, C 10, No 3-61, T 286-6555 (also at airport, Mon-Fri 0700-2100, Sat 0800-1700, and bus terminal, T 295-4460). **Alcaldía Mayor**, C 14 y Cra 3, helpful, sells booklets, posters, T-shirts etc. **Corporación de Cultura y Turismo de Cundinamarca**, C 16, No 7-76, T 242-8587, for details of towns around Bogotá. The **Coordinadora de Turismo de Bogotá** (Cra 13, No 27-95) has daily tours of the city with interpreters. For information on 24-hr chemists (pharmacies), events, attractions, etc, T 282-0000.

MMA, the **National Parks Office** (formerly Inderena): full details given in **Introduction, National Parks**. Regional office for Amazonia and Orinoquia, Cra 10, No 20-30, T 283-3009, F 243-3091.

Thefts: most hotels charge US$0.25 a night for insurance against theft. If you have something stolen go to the Corporación Nacional del Turismo for help and collect the insurance; this will probably take a few days of strenuous effort, but it has been known to work.

● **Useful addresses**
DAS Immigration office, Cra 27, No 17-85, open 0730-1530; Dirección de Extranjería (for renewing entry permits), C 100, No 11B-27, open Mon-Thur 0730-1600, Fri 0730-1530. T 610-7371 (División de Extranjería) or 277-6666 (emergency). DAS will not authorize photocopies of passports; look in Yellow Pages for notaries, who will.

● **Transport**
Travel in Bogotá Local Bus: stops in centre by red and yellow "Paradero" boards; otherwise flag buses down. Bus fares are from US$0.20 up, depending on length of route and time of day. Most buses have day/night tariff advertised in the window. *Busetas* charge a little more. There are some "super-executive" routes with plush seats and videos, at US$0.40 (if traffic is heavy you might see the whole film). Fares are a bit higher at night and on holidays. Urban buses are not good for sightseeing because you will be standing as likely as not. A metro is planned. **Car rental**: **Dollar Rent-a-Car**, airport and Diag 109, No 14-61, T 612-8295; **Hertz**, at airport, and at Cra 10, No 26-35, T 284-1445; **Avis**, C 99, No 11-26, T 610-4455, and at airport. **Taxis**: have meters; insist that they are used. If the driver tries to charge more than the meter reading (eg from airport to hotel), tell the driver to wait, take your luggage into the hotel and ask hotel representative to deal with the driver. Starting charge, US$0.40, plus US$0.07 for every 90m, minimum charge US$0.85. Additional charge of US$0.40 after 2000 and on public holidays and Sun (a list of legal charges should be posted in the taxi). At busy times, empty taxis flagged down on the street may refuse to take you to less popular destinations. Tan and green tourist taxis can be rented by the hour or the day from major hotels, most of the drivers speak English and are very helpful (T 284-0856). Radio taxis are rec for safety and reliability; when you call the dispatcher gives you a cab number, confirm this when it arrives (eg Proturismo T 223-2111; Taxis Libres, T 2311-1111). Taxis are relatively cheap, so it is worthwhile taking one if you are carrying valuables, or at night. Tipping is not customary, but is appreciated. If you are going to an address out of the city centre, it is helpful to know the section you are going to as well as the street address, eg Chicó, Chapinero (ask at your hotel). See also under **Airport** and **Buses** below.

Air The airport at El Dorado has the world's second largest landing field. There are two terminals, the Puente Aéreo terminal (T 413-8103) being 1 km before the main terminal (T 413-9500) on Av El Dorado. Frequent buses run between the two. Avianca international flights use both terminals (usually Miami and New York). Puente Aéreo is more comfortable but there is not as much duty-free shopping (there is a 100 pesos tax payable at this terminal). **You must check which terminal your flight will use.** "Tourist Guide" policemen have white armbands. For **Tourist offices**, see above. The main terminal is being slowly modernized. The departure areas with the usual duty-free shops are of a high standard and comfortable. The entrance foyer is run down and crowded. Free Colombian coffee inside the customs area, between gates 2 and 3. Many snack bars and restaurants on first floor. International calls can be made from Telecom on 1st floor, credit cards accepted; post office in main arrivals lounge. Hotel reservations can be made at the airport but their hotel rates are often out of date. The cheapest is in our Category D. Exchange rates are marginally lower than in the city, but pesos cannot be changed back into dollars at the airport without receipts. Airport bank changes TCs, but is not open at holiday times. When closed, ask airport police where to change money. Allow 1½ hrs for checking in and security. There is no baggage deposit.

The taxi fare from airport to city is a fixed charge, by zones. Ask for a fare slip from the taxi office by your airport exit. The cost is usually about US$5 (30% more at night and early am). Make sure you get a registered taxi, normally yellow, found at right (from inside) side of main terminal or Avianca terminal (drivers try to overcharge all the same). Unofficial taxis not advisable. Use only uniformed porters. There are colectivos (US$0.75 plus luggage pp) from airport to centre; also buses in the daytime, US$0.15 (not easy with bulky luggage and they may refuse to take you). You have to cross eight busy lanes of traffic to get a bus into town, and negotiate two drainage ditches. In the city centre buses and colectivos can be picked up on Av 19, anywhere between Cras 3 and 10 at which they turn right for the airport; colectivos can also be taken from the corner of C 13 (Av Jiménez de Quesada) and Av 14 (Av Caracas); buses marked "Aeropuerto" or "Universitaria Dorado"; colectivos marked "Aeropuerto". Watch belongings inside and outside airport, especially at night.

For internal flights, which serve all parts of the country, see page 992. For domestic shuttle flights to Medellín/Montería, Cali/Pasto, and Barranquilla, go to Puente Aéreo terminal. As a rule, all flights are overbooked, so check in well in advance.

Train There are no passenger services at present from Bogotá station at C 13 y Cra 20. Long distance services were suspended in 1992. A tourist steam train runs on Sun and holidays starting at present at Usaquén, C 110, Transversal 10, in the N of the city (see map), due to substantial roadworks toward the city centre. The train departs at 0930 from Usaquén to Nemocón (1212), returning at 1500 and back in Bogotá at 1740. Cost: adult US$12.50, child up to 10, US$7.50. Information, Turistrén Ltda, Transversal 17 A, No 98-17, T 257-1459, or travel agents.

Bus There is a long-distance bus terminal, Terminal de Transportes, near Av Boyacá (Cra 72) between El Dorado (Av 26) and Av Centenario (C 13). There is also access from Cra 68. Exact address C 33 B, No 69-59, T 295-1100. The terminal is divided into modules serving the 4 points of the compass; each module has several bus companies serving similar destinations. If possible, buy tickets at the ticket office before travelling to avoid overcharging. **Fares and journey times are given under destinations below.** If you are travelling N, enquire if the bus company has a pick-up point on the Autopista del Norte around C 160. Velotax busetas are slightly quicker and more expensive than ordinary buses, as are colectivos, which go to several long-distance destinations. To get to the terminal take bus marked "Terminal" from "Terminal Transportes" bus stop at corner of Av Jiménez de Quesada and Cra 15, or *buseta* on Cra 10 before *Hotel Tequendama*. At night take a colectivo taxi from Av 13 y Av Caracas, US$0.35 (no buses). To get into town take Route No 1 or No 3 "Centro" at the terminal: the bus goes through the S of the city, then N on C 13, turning right on Cra 14, closest to the centre (from this junction "Germania" bus goes to the centre). A *buseta* (US$0.05) runs from Cra 68 to the terminal and back. Taxi around US$3, depending on destination, surcharge at night, passengers are given a computer slip showing the cab's registration number and the exact fare (avoid the unofficial taxis, normally touting for particular hotels). The terminal is well-organized and comfortable, but, as usual, watch out for thieves who are also well organized — we have an increasing number of reports of baggage thefts. Free self-service luggage trolleys are provided. There are shops and restaurants. There are showers at the terminal (between Nos 3 and 4), US$0.40, soap and towel provided.

Bus to Venezuela It is better not to buy a through ticket to Caracas with Exp Berlinas as this does not guarantee a seat and is only valid for 2 Venezuelan companies; moreover no refunds are given in Cúcuta. Ideally, if you have time make the journey to Cúcuta in two stages to enjoy the scenery to the full. Bus connections from San Antonio de Táchira in Venezuela to Caracas are good.

EXCURSIONS SOUTHWEST FROM BOGOTA

The Simón Bolívar Highway runs from Bogotá to Girardot (see page 935); this 132-km stretch is extremely picturesque, running down the mountains.

Salto de Tequendama

Take the exit from the Highway marked El Colegio to **Salto de Tequendama** (5 km), where the water of the Río Bogotá or Funza falls 132m over the lip of the Sabana; the water is dirty with sewage but the falls are still a spectacular sight though the smell can be most unpleasant. The site is in an amphitheatre of forest-clad hill sloping to the edge of a rock-walled gorge. There is a good bus service from Bogotá (31 km).

FUSAGASUGA

After the Tequendama Falls turning is **Fusagasugá** (*Pop* 58,215; *Alt* 1,740m) which lies in a rich wooded valley famous for its fruits, its good climate and Sun market. Splendid orchids can be seen in the Jardín Luxemburgo (best flowering Nov-Feb but it is a long walk out of town) and in the Jardín Clarisa; pleasant garden also at the Casa de la Cultura. There are bathing spots on the Río Sumapaz.

● **Accommodation** E *Castillo*, rec; F *La Scala*, rec. There are many luxury hotels on the road to Melgar. Near Fusagasugá is C *Hotel Miramonti*, Italian-run family place, very quiet.

● **Buses** From Bogotá, Autos Fusa and Cootransfusa, US$1.20.

Down the main road from Fusagasugá is El Boquerón, below which is a spectacular rock overhang known as El Nariz del Diablo (Devil's Nose), near which is a side road left to **San Bernardo**, a pretty little town. The cemetery has a macabre attraction; looking through a window near the central "altar" you see mummified figures, including a woman and child, assembled in the dimly lit cellar, entry US$0.25. Off this road go right about 10 km to **Pandi** where there is a park with ancient stones. Nearby, on the road to Icononzo, is a famous natural bridge in a spectacular and very deep gorge through which runs the Río Sumapaz. This can also be reached from the road to San Bernardo (above) by turning right 3 km short of the village. Bus: from Fusagasugá to San Bernardo, 1½ hrs.

MELGAR

A popular weekending place, near Girardot, for Bogotanos who like a little warmth. There are three tolls between Bogotá and Melgar (not always manned). For those driving S towards Neiva there is a new bypass avoiding Girardot.

● **Accommodation** There are lots of hotels in the area most of which have swimming pools; it is best to try whichever you like the look of and move on to another if it is full; there are also camping sites and the state-subsidized Cafam vacation centre, best visited in mid-week. There are good places to stop for snacks and meals, often with good family facilities, eg *Parador Las Villas*, near the Girardot bypass.

EXCURSIONS NORTHWEST FROM BOGOTA

The Sabana de Bogotá is dotted with white farms and groves of eucalyptus. The road passes through two small towns, Fontibón and Madrid. **Fontibón**, 10 km from Bogotá, has a good colonial church, and about 3 km outside the town are stones with Indian pictographs; nearby, on the road from the old Techo airport to Bogotá, there are replicas of San Agustín statues.

Facatativá (*pop* 61,590) is 40 km from Bogotá. Some 3 km from Facatativá, on the road to the W, is the park of Piedras de Tunja, a natural rock amphitheatre with enormous stones, numerous Indian pictographs and an artificial lake. A road goes SW from Facatativá to Girardot through **Tocaima** (*pop* 8,520), a small, attractive holiday town (several hotels; **D** *Bella Vista*, clean, friendly, good simple food, swimming pool, no hot water). A road runs through beautiful mountain country, via La Mesa, to Mosquera on the road between Madrid and Fontibón. This is a good alternative to the Simón Bolívar highway from Girardot to Bogotá.

VILLETA

71 km from Facatativá **Villeta** (*pop* 12,465) is a popular weekend resort for Bogotanos. Not far away are the waterfalls of Que-

brada Cune. Hotels: *Pacífico* and *Mediter-ráneo* (both have swimming pools and are expensive); less expensive is the *Colonial Plaza*, Cra 4, No 6-07 (corner of main square), good restaurant, with swimmimg pool, pleasant. On the road to Bogotá is *Balneario El Descanso*, swimming pool, safe parking. Near the centre is *Llamarade* restaurant, good value; many good ice cream parlours around the square. The road continues to Honda (see page 933).

Midway between Villeta and Honda is **Guaduas**; in the main square is a statue of the liberator Policarpa Sala Varrieta, and a delightful colonial hotel. Public swimming pool; Sun market. Best local dish is *quesillos*. Bus to Honda, US$1.45, 1 hr. The surrounding countryside is beautiful, including waterfalls at Versalles (10 km). Hotels: **B** *Tacuara*, swimming pool, riding, *cabanas*; *Cacique*, 1 km outside village, and *Real Agrada*, in resort area.

NORTH

Interesting day trips can be made to the attractive rolling antiplano, leaving Bogotá on the Autopista del Norte (extension of Av 13), or on the parallel Carretera del Norte (the old road, extension of Av 7). On the latter, once out of Bogotá, there are many old fincas and good typical restaurants, eg *El Pórtico*, a converted *hacienda*. The two roads join at Km 24 at La Caro where a road leaves left (W) to Chía and Zipaquirá. At this junction is the 'castle' of Rodríguez Gacha with a sinister history connected to this drug baron. By contrast, there is opposite the graceful colonial bridge over the Río Bogotá, now preserved and bypassed by the road to Chía

CHIA

Typical Sun market (bus from Av Caracas, Bogotá US$0.30). Near Chía is Terijo, whose metalworks are famous. On the way there you pass through Fonqueta, where tapestries are made. Walk, or take a bus to La Barbanera church on a hill overlooking the Sabana de Bogotá. Good restaurant just outside Chía, *Andrés Carne de Res*, good music, good atmosphere, good food from 1600.

ZIPAQUIRA

From Chía (via Cájica, *pop* 15,315, pleasant town with good shopping for ponchos and carpets) to **Zipaquirá** (*pop* 62,130), centre of a rich cattle farming district, and famous for its rock salt mine, which has enough salt to last the world 100 years, though it has been exploited for centuries. The church in the attractive central Plaza is also worth a visit for its stonework (despite its external appearance, it has a modern interior).

An underground cathedral, constructed by miners inside the huge main salt mine, was dedicated in 1954 to Nuestra Señora del Rosario (patron saint of miners). Continuing deterioration made the whole cave unsafe and it was closed. A new salt cathedral was opened on 16 December 1995 (entry US$7, car park US$1); it is 500m, and 58m below, the old salt cathedral, open Tues-Sun 1000-1600, Sun mass at 1200, admission by ticket. The entrance to the cave is in hills about 20 mins' walk W of the town.

- **Accommodation C-D** *Hostería del Libertador*, Vía Catedral de Sal, T 852-6846, F 852-6851, restored colonial mansion, nr the mine, good food; **E** *Hotel Colonial*, C 3, No 6-57, T 852-2690, showers, clean and friendly. Restaurants on main square, *El Mesón del Zipa*, good, cheap food, US$1.50-2.00; *Los Pijaos*, pleasant.

- **Buses** Many from Av Caracas, Bogotá, marked 'Zipa', Flota Alianza, or others, US$0.70 each way, 1¼ hrs. The Zipaquirá bus station is 15 mins' walk from the mines and cathedral. Zipaquirá can also be reached from Tunja (see page 886), by taking a Bogotá-bound bus and getting off at La Caro for connection to Zipaquirá, US$2.40. Leave plenty of time for the return journey as it can be difficult to stop Bogotá-Tunja buses at La Caro. It can also be difficult to get on a bus from Zipaquirá going N towards Villa de Leiva.

Not far from Zipaquirá, at **Nemocón**, there are salt mines and a church, but the mines are sometimes closed to visitors, following accidents. Restaurant, *El Colonial*, 100m from the station. A side (dirt) road connects with the Bogotá-Cúcuta highway.

A steam-hauled *tren turístico* runs on Sun and holidays from Usaquén in N

Bogotá to Zipaquirá and Nemocón. See under Bogotá, **Train**.

Ubaté is 48 km by road to the N. Sun market; it is the cheese-making centre of the Sabana. Good restaurant, *La Rueda* in Plaza Catedral, trout from local lakes a speciality. A spur from the road to Lenguazaque branches left to Guachetá, 21 km from Ubaté, near which is the **Laguna de Fúquene** (Devil's Lake), about 4,850 ha of water with four cultivated islands.

CHIQUINQUIRA

134 km by road from Bogotá, **Chiquinquirá** (*pop* 32,585; *alt* 2,550m) is on the W bank of the Río Suárez. It is a busy commercial centre and the focus of a large coffee and cattle region. In Dec thousands of pilgrims honour a painting of the Virgin whose fading colours were restored by the prayers of a woman. In 1816, when the town had enjoyed six years of independence and was besieged by the Royalists, this painting was carried through the streets by Dominican priests from the famous monastery, to rally the people. The town fell, all the same.

• **Accommodation** F *Moyba*, Cra 9, No 17-53, facing square, with bath (cheaper without); F *Residencias San Martín*, Cra 9, No 19-84, basic; G *Residencias Viajero*, opposite Banco de Colombia, good, cheap meals. Many others.

• **Places to eat** *El Escorial*, good but expensive.

• **Shopping** The shops display the toys made by local Indians: some ceramics painted in gay colours and others white and porous as they come from the kiln; tops and teetotums and other little things carved from tagua nuts; orange-wood balls to catch on a stick; the most durable tambourines in the world; shining, brightly coloured gourds; diminutive nine-stringed guitars on which children try the first measures of the *bambuca*; many scapularies and a good place for raw emeralds; but better than anything else, the little pottery horses from Ráquira, or, by the same Indian craftsmen, little birds that whistle, hens with their chicks, and enchanting little couples dancing to an orchestra of guitars and mandolins.

• **Buses** From Chiquinquirá to **Villa de Leiva** takes 1¾ hr, US$2.70 (see page 886). To **Tunja**, 3 hrs, US$4; to **Zipaquirá**, US$3.30; to **Bogotá**, 2½ hrs, US$3.60 (last returns at 1730); all from bus station.

MUZO AND RAQUIRA

A poor road, dangerous in the rainy season, runs 105 km SW to **Muzo** (*pop* 5,000; *alt* 600m), on the banks of the Río Carare. **Accommodation** E *Colonial*; E *El Castillo*; F *Hospedaje El Occidente*, all fair. 16 km away a famous open-cast emerald mine has been worked since 1567, and long before that by the Muzo tribe of Indians. You can visit the mine; check at your hotel.

There are roads from Chiquinquirá to Villa de Leiva and Tunja, and to Barbosa. All are described below. On the Tunja road a short branch right at Tinjacá leads to **Ráquira**, where Indians make the pottery described above (sold in about 10 shops on the main street). There are two good hotels, E *Nequeteba*, converted colonial house, pool, restaurant, craft shop, helpful owner, and E *Norteño*, nice and clean (both on plaza). At weekends it is possible to eat at the Museo de Arte y Tradiciones Populares. Market day Sun.

1½ hrs' walk along a very rough road is a beautiful 16th-century monastery, the Convento de la Candelaria, with anonymous 17th-century paintings of the life of San Agustín; they sell honey to finance the monastery (visiting times 1400-1700). C *Parador La Candelaria*, adjoining monastery, picturesque, good food.

• **Buses** Ráquira is best reached from Tunja although there are direct buses from Bogotá (Rápido El Carmen, 0545, 0715, US$3, 6 hrs, returning 1300) on an appalling road. Last bus to Tunja 1330. If stuck after 1330, walk 5 km to Tres Esquinas on Villa de Leiva-Chiquinquirá road, where buses pass between 1530-1630, mostly going E. There are 2 direct buses to and from Villa de Leiva daily.

Bogotá to Cúcuta

THE main road route from Bogotá to Venezuela has some beautiful stretches. It passes through, or near, several colonial towns and gives access to the Sierra Nevada del Cocuy, excellent climbing and hiking country.

A 618-km road runs NE from Bogotá to Cúcuta, near the Venezuelan border, through Tunja, Moniquirá, Barbosa, Socorro, San Gil, Bucaramanga and Pamplona. It is good most of the way. The road out of Bogotá is the *autopista* to La Caro (see page 883), then follow Tunja signs.

From La Caro, the road goes through rich agricultural country with many crops including fruit and flowers. At Km 32.5 is the Alpina Yogurt factory and the Parque Puerto de Sopó with artificial lake. 30 km E into the Sabana is **Sopó** where there is an image of the Saviour which has appeared in an eroded stone; the paintings of angels in the church are very strange and worth seeing (ask at the Casa Cural for entry to church – give a tip). Continuing N from Puerto de Sopó is the large Jaime Dugue amusement park created by one of Colombia's pioneer pilots. A replica of the first Avianca aircraft is the centrepiece. 2 km E of the main road is **Sesquilé**, several restaurants, no accommodation. On your right beyond the town is the large Tominé lake and dam. There is a campsite on the lakeside. 17 km from Sesquilé, overlooking the lake is:

GUATAVITA

The modern town of **Guatavita Nueva**, 75 km from Bogotá, was built in colonial style when the old town of Guatavita was submerged by the reservoir. The original inhabitants were unwilling to stay in the new town, so it is now a week-end haunt for Bogotanos and tourists. Cathedral, artisan workshops and small bull-ring for apprentices to practise Sun afternoons; two small museums, one devoted to the Muisca Indians and the other to relics of the old Guatavita church, including a delightful Debain harmonium (Paris 1867). Sun market best in morning, before Bogotanos get there. Bus from Bogotá (Flota Valle de Tenza, Cra 25, No 15-72, rec; Flota Aguila, Cra 15 No 14-59), US$1.45, 2-3 hrs, departures 0730, 0800 and 0930; last return bus at 1730. Julio A Martínez at the tourist information booth can find accommodation for visitors; he speaks English.

Laguna de Guatavita (also called Lago de Amor by locals) is where the legend of El Dorado originated. The lake is a quiet, beautiful place; you can walk right round it close to the water level, 1½ hrs, or climb to the rim of the crater in several places. Opinions differ on whether the crater is volcanic or a meteorite impact, but from the rim at 3100m there are extensive views over the varied countryside.

● **Access** You can walk (2-3 hrs) or ride (US$7/horse) from Guatavita Nueva to the lake. An easier approach is from a point on the Sesquilé-Guatavita Nueva road (the bus driver will let you off at the right place) where there is a sign "via Lago Guatavita". Nearby, on the main road, are good places to eat at weekends. There is a good campsite nearby. From the main road to the lakeside the road is paved as far as a school, about half way. Follow the signs. This road and subsequent track can be driven in a good car to within 300m of the lake where there is a car park and good restaurant, *Hostería Caminos a El Dorado*, open at weekends.

Beyond Sesquilé, the main road goes through Chocontá (*pop* 13,650), 88 km from Bogotá, the route is across the western slopes of the Eastern Cordillera to Tunja, 137 km from Bogotá.

BOYACA DEPARTMENT

TUNJA

Capital of Boyacá Department, **Tunja** (*pop* 113,945; *alt* 2,820m) stands in an arid mountainous area. The climate is cold; mean temperature, 12°C. One of the oldest cities in Colombia, it was refounded as a Spanish city by Gonzalo Suárez Rendón in 1539. It was then the seat of the Zipa, one of the two Chibcha kings. The city formed an independent Junta in 1811, and Bolívar fought under its aegis during the campaign of the Magdalena in 1812. Six years later he fought the decisive battle of Boyacá, nearby (see below).

Places of interest

Churches Of the many colonial buildings the most remarkable is the church of **Santo Domingo**, a masterpiece begun in 1594; the interior is covered with wood most richly carved. Another is the **Santa Clara chapel** (1580), now the hospital of San Rafael, with some fine wood carving. The church of **Santa Bárbara** is full of colonial woodwork, and in the nearby parish house are some notable religious objects, including silk embroidery from the 18th century. Also impressive is the church of **San Ignacio**.

Museums The **house of Don Juan de Vargas** has been restored as a museum of colonial Tunja, entry US$0.25 includes guided tour in several languages, open 0800-1200, 1300-1800. The **Casa del Fun-** dador **Suárez Rendón**, Plaza Bolívar, is one of the few extant mansions of a Spanish *conquistador* in Colombia (1540-43); museum open Wed-Sun; see the unique series of plateresque paintings on the ceilings. There are some fine colonial buildings on Plaza Bolívar opposite the Cathedral. In **Parque Bosque de la República** is the adobe wall against which three martyrs of the Independence were shot in 1816. Ask the tourist police guarding these buildings for information; they are helpful and often knowledgeable.

Excursions

The battle of Boyacá was fought about 16 km S of Tunja, on the road to Bogotá. On the bridge at Boyacá is a large monument to Bolívar. Bolívar took Tunja on 6 August 1819, and next day his troops, fortified by a British Legion, the only professional soldiers among them, fought the Spaniards on the banks of the swollen Río Boyacá. With the loss of only 13 killed and 53 wounded they captured 1,600 men and 39 officers. Only 50 men escaped, and when these told their tale in Bogotá the Viceroy Samao fled in such haste that he left behind him half a million pesos of the royal funds. There is now a huge modern restaurant overlooking the site.

On a hillside outside Tunja is the carved rock throne of the Chibcha king, the Zipa; ask for directions from the Tourist Office.

About 7 km along the road to Duitama

The Gilded Man

The basis of the El Dorado (Gilded Man) story is established fact. It was the custom of the Chibcha king to be coated annually with resin, on which gold dust was stuck, and then to be taken out on the lake on a ceremonial raft. He then plunged into the lake and emerged with the resin and gold dust washed off. The lake was also the repository of precious objects thrown in as offerings; there have been several attempts to drain it (the first, by the Spaniards in colonial times, was the origin of the sharp cut in the crater rim) and many items have been recovered over the years. The factual basis of the El Dorado story was confirmed by the discovery of a miniature raft with ceremonial figures on it, made from gold wire, which is now one of the most prized treasures of the Museo de Oro in Bogotá. Part of the raft is missing; the story is that the gold from it ended up in one of the finder's teeth! (Read John Hemming's *The Search for El Dorado* on the subject.)

there is a huge bronze statue called 'El Pantano de Vargas', which appears on the back of the 1,000 peso note. At **Paipa**, between Tunja and Duitama, there are popular municipal thermal baths, US$1.75 (disappointing), 15 mins bus ride from Tunja, US$1.20, then 30 mins' walk from plaza (taxi from plaza US$0.70, from hotel US$1 – taxi drivers are likely to take you to a hotel of their recommendation, not yours). Many places to stay; seven restaurants.

Local festivals

During the week before Christmas, there is a lively festival with local music, traditional dancing and fireworks.

Local information

● **Accommodation**

D *Hostería San Carlos*, Cra 11, No 20-12, T 423716, colonial style, good restaurant, highly rec; **D** *San Francisco*, Cra 9, No 18-90, T 426645, on Plaza Bolívar, near cathedral, clean, friendly; **D/E** *Lord*, C 19, No 10-64, small rooms but hot water, friendly; *Res Dux*, near *Res Lord*, nice old hotel, good rooms, cold water, good value.

E *Conquistador*, C 20, No 8-92, on the corner of Plaza Bolívar, hot water, safe, clean, but many rooms don't have outside window; **E** *Saboy*, C 19, No 10-40, clean, friendly, family run; **E** *Americano*, Cra 11, No 18-70, friendly, hot water, attractive lobby.

F *Príncipe*, limited hot water, small rooms but clean, near bus station, 5 mins from Plaza Bolívar, rec.

G *Colonial*, Cra 8, No 20-40, clean, safe, friendly; **G** *Imperial*, C 19, No 7-43, clean, basic, use of kitchen; **G** *Bolívar*, opp bus station, clean, basic. Area around bus station said not to be safe at night.

● **Places to eat**

San Ricardo, C 19, No 8-38, good; *Surtipan*, C 20, No 12-58, good cakes and coffee; *Estar de Hunzahúa*, C 20, No 11-20 (2nd floor), good value, rec; *Pollo Listo* Cra 11, No 19-30, good; *Santo Domingo*, Cra 11, No 19-66, good; *Bodegón de los Frayles*, beside the church of San Ignacio, one block from the Plaza Bolívar, good.

● **Shopping**

Market, near Plaza de Toros on outskirts of town, open every day (good for *ruanas* and blankets). Fri is main market day.

● **Tourist offices**

In Casa del Fundador, Plaza Bolívar, helpful but not always accurate. Guide for the town: Carlos Julio, will take you to major monuments. Ask at the Tourist Office.

● **Buses**

Bus station is a steep 500m down from city centre; from **Bogotá** 2½-4½ hrs, US$5, Villa de Leiva, colectivos, 1 hr, US$2, **Duitama**, Cotrans, and others. To **Bucaramanga**, hourly, 7½ hrs, US$14.50.

VILLA DE LEIVA

The colonial town of **Villa de Leiva** (also spelt Leyva, *pop* 3,310) dates back, like Tunja, to the early days of Spanish rule, but unlike Tunja, it has been declared a national monument so will not be modernized. The first president of Nueva Granada (see page 859), Miguel Venero de Leiva, lived in the town.

Places of interest

There are **two colonial houses** which are worth a visit: the house in which Antonio Nariño lived (Cra 9, No 10-39, open Tues-Sun 0900-1230, 1400-1800) – he translated the *Rights of Man* into Spanish – and the building in which the first Convention of the United Provinces of New Granada was held, C 13 y Cra 9, on corner of plaza. Also worth a visit is the restored birthplace of the independence hero Antonio Ricaurte (Cra 8 y C 5). A **palaeontological museum** has been opened 15 mins walk N of the town on Cra 9, interesting and well displayed, entrance US$0.55. On the Plaza Mayor is the **Casa-Museo Luis Alberto Acuña**, housing fascinating examples of Acuña's work (recommended, entry US$0.70, extra to take photographs). The **Monasterio de las Carmelitas** has one of the best museums of religious art in Colombia, open Sat and Sun 1400-1700.

Excursions

The mountains around Villa de Leiva abound in fossils. 5 km along the road to Santa Sofía can be seen the complete fossil of a dinosaur now housed in a room, entry US$0.50, there are road signs to it, ask for **El Fósil** (open 0800-1200, 1300-1600, Thur only 1300-1600). 2 km from El Fósil along this road is the turning for (1 km) the

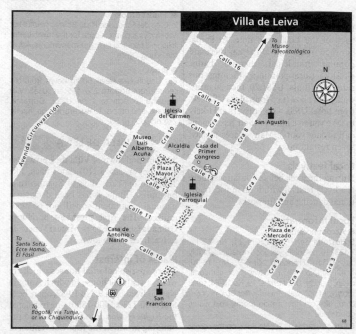

Villa de Leiva

archaeological site of **El Infiernito**, where there are several huge carved stones believed to be giant phalli and a solar calendar (0900-1200, 1400-1700, closed Mon, admission US$0.50). 6 km after the Infiernito turning is the **Monastery of Ecce-Homo** (founded 1620); note the fossils on the floor at the entrance. There are buses from Villa de Leiva at 0645, 0930 and 1345, going to Santa Sofía, US$0.50; it's ½ hr to the crossing, then a 2 km walk to the monastery. Beyond Santa Sofía is La Cueva de Hayal, a cave set in beautiful scenery. A tour including most of these attractions leaves the plaza at 0930, Sat/Sun, US$6, rec.

20 km from Villa de Leiva, there is a left turn for the **Iguaque National Park** (3 km) run by MMA, which is the site of interesting oak woods, flora, fauna and several lakes. Entrance US$0.70 students US$0.55, cars US$1.35. There is a tourist centre with accommodation for 60 and a restaurant with good food at reasonable prices. There are guided paths and a marked trail to Lake Iguaque, a walk of 2½ hrs. The most likely day for a lift is Sat, market day, but there is a daily bus at 0700 from Villa de Leiva to the turn off to the Park. It returns at 1300. (Camping is allowed, safe.)

Local festivals

A festival of light is held every year in mid-Dec which attracts many visitors.

Local information

NB The town tends to be full of visitors at weekends and bank holidays and is generally expensive. It is better not to visit Villa de Leiva on Mon or Tues as many places are closed. Also there are few services in Villa de Leiva, buy fuel etc in Tunja. The houses are closed Mon-Fri out of season, but the trip is worth while just for the views. In any event, the town and surrounding hills are excellent for long, peaceful walks.

● **Accommodation**

A3 *El Molino la Mesopotamia*, C del Silencio, T 320235, a beautifully restored colonial mill, 10% rebate for booking 10 days ahead (closed during the first weeks of Jan), swimming pool, home cooking, excellent food with good *menú*, beautiful gardens, rec; **B** *Mesón de la Plaza Mayor*, Cra 9, No 13-51, T 218-7441 (Bogotá), beautifully restored *hospedaría*, owner, Mauricio Ordóñez, speaks English, helpful; **B** *Hospedaje El Mesón de Los Virreyes*, Cra 9, No 14-51, T 320252, with bath, good restaurant.

C *Hospedaje El Sol de la Villa*, Cra 8, No 12-28, T 320-224, safe, clean, hot shower, very good breakfast, cooking facilities, rec; **C** *Molino del Balcón*, Cra 12, No 11-51, colonial building, garden, friendly.

D *Los Llanitos*, C 9, No 12-31, T 256-1643 (Bogotá), 5 mins' walk from main plaza, quiet, hot water, very friendly, good food; **E/D** *Hostería La Roca*, C 13, No 9-54, clean and pleasant, with some rooms overlooking main square and reasonable breakfast, attractive tiled courtyard and garden, noisy at night because of bar music; **E** *Hospedería Colonial*, C 12, one block from main plaza, with bath. Accommodation with **E** Familia Fitata, C 12, No 7-31, breakfast extra, friendly, clean, safe. **E** *Hospedaje La Villa*, Cra 6 just off main plaza, shared bath, rooms with balcony, upstairs rooms best, can be noisy. The telephone connection from Bogotá is poor and most hotels have reservation numbers in Bogotá. Booking essential during holidays, and advisable at weekends (try bargaining Mon-Thur).

Camping: MMA's *Vivero*, 15 mins walk N of plaza on road to Arcabuco (just before palaeontological museum), nice place with bathroom, warm shower, ask for Juan; also Los Olivares near village of Sáchica, 4 km from Villa de Leiva (no services). Ask for advice on other sites at the Tourist office.

● **Places to eat**
Nueva Granada, Cra 9, No 13-69, good value, friendly, owner Jorge Rodríguez, plays classical music; *El Parrilón de los Caciques*, W side of town on Cra 9, No 9-05, warmly rec, good value; *El Estar de la Villa*, C 13, No 8-89, good; *Donna Mia*, C 9, No 11-102, good pizzas and crêpes, good helpings, Swedish owners, very knowledgeable; *El Rincón Bachue*, Cra 9, C 15, interesting decoration with a china factory behind; *Giorgio*, C 12 between Cra 8 and 9, Italian, good atmosphere, reasonable prices; *La Dicha Buena*, near the Plaza, good vegetarian place, cakes, good breakfasts; *Ricos Pizzería*, Cra 9 y C 14, good pizzas, reasonable prices; *Bar del Pastor*, Cra 9 y C 9, good meeting place, pleasant owners.

● **Post & telecommunications**
Post Office: in Telecom building, C 13, No 8-26.

● **Shopping**
The shops in the plaza have an excellent selection of Colombian handicrafts, while the Sat market, not yet geared to the tourist trade, still offers many bargains.

● **Tourist offices**
Cra 9 y C 13 on plaza; local maps US$0.25. At the bus station; gives advice on cheaper accommodation.

● **Buses**
Station in 8th block of Cra 9. It is rec to book the return journey on arrival. Buses to Leiva from Tunja, 1 hr, US$2 with Flota Reina or Valle de Tenza company. (From Bogotá to Villa de Leiva, via Tunja, takes 4 hrs, US$5, several companies, and via Zipaquirá and Chiquinquirá, US$5.70.) Colectivo taxis leave the bus station in Tunja for Villa de Leiva every hour, US$1.20, and return from the main plaza. Bus at 1000 from Leiva to Moniquirá (see page 891) connects with bus to Bucamaranga, thus avoiding Tunja.

ROUTES Coming from Bogotá, turning left (W) at the Boyacá monument, via Samacá to the Tunja-Chiquinquirá road; turn left (W) then right (N) at Sáchica. From Tunja also go via Sáchica. Alternatively, from the N, turn off the Bucamaranga-Tunja highway at Arcabuco. (Toll at Arcabuco, US$0.40.) Although the surface is not good, the drive affords some beautiful views.

From Tunja there are two possible routes to Cúcuta; the main road, almost entirely paved, goes via Bucaramanga, but the other heading NE via Duitama and Málaga, rejoining the main road at Pamplona, is also interesting, though there are few filling stations N of Duitama.

NORTHEAST OF TUNJA

In **Duitama** there is the interesting tourist complex Punta Larga. (**E** *Isobel*, Cra 18, No 18-60, clean, quiet; many others nearby). About 7 km from Duitama, on the road E to Belencito, there is the **B** *Hostería San Luis de Ucuenga*, in an old *hacienda*. Bus Duitama to Bucaramanga at 0900, 9 hrs, US$9; to Málaga at 0800, sit on right side for best views, 6 hrs.

SOGAMOSO AND LAGO DE TOTA

At Duitama turn right for **Sogamoso**. This was an important Chibcha settlement; destroyed by the Spaniards, but it has been reconstructed on site. Their arts of mummification, statuary, and gold working are shown in the good museum (closed Mon). It is possible to camp in the museum grounds if you ask permission. A museum of religious art is open on the road from Duitama to Sogamoso. East of Sogamoso the churches of **Mongua** (a pleasant colonial town, 20 km) and **Tópaga** are worth a visit.

● **Accommodation** Many hotels near bus station eg **G** *Hostal Aranjuez*, basic, safe, very helpful, **F** *Residencia Embajador*, clean, friendly, rec; **G** *Residencia El Terminal*, basic, clean, safe.

● **Bus** Bogotá-Sogamoso, 4 hrs.

The mountain-ringed **Lago de Tota** (*alt* 3,015m) is S of Sogamoso. **Aquitania**, a cold, expensive town on the lake, is a centre of onion growing. It is reached by bus from Sogamoso, US$0.90, 1 hr; bus from Bogotá (Rápido Duitama), via Tunja and Sogamoso, goes round the lake to Aquitania, passing Cuitiva, Tota and the *Rocas Lindas* and *Pozo Azul* hotels. Above the town is a hill (El Cumbre) with beautiful views. On the opposite side of the lake from Aquitania is the colonial town of **Iza** with several hotels.

● **Accommodation On lakeside: C** *Refugio el Pozo Azul*, T 257-6586 (Bogotá), also has cabins for up to 7 people; good food, fresh trout caught in the lake, suitable for children, friendly atmosphere. Boats and fishing tackle for hire; good walking and bird-watching; rec to book in advance. Also *Las Rocas Lindas*, with bath and hot water, 2 cabins for 7, one for 8 at Playa Blanca campground across the lake, boats for hire, dining room, bar, fireplaces, rec, friendly. **In Aquitania: F** *Residencia Venecia*, C 8, No 144, with restaurant *Lucho* below, reasonable.

Just before the descent to the Lago de Tota, a road branches left, leading in 4 hrs to **Yopal** (*pop* 10,000), capital of the Intendencia of Casanare in the Llanos. The road passes through *páramo* and virgin cloud forest. Direct buses from Sogamoso and Bogotá (US$13).

The road NE of Duitama to Málaga passes **Belén** and **Soatá** (*Residencias Colonial*, excellent, good restaurant; **D** *Hotel Turístico*, swimming pool) before descending to the very dry, spectacular valley of the Río Chicomocha.

SIERRA NEVADA DEL COCUY

By the bridge over the Río Chicomocha at **Capitanejo** is the turning to the very attractive **Sierra Nevada del Cocuy** in the Eastern Cordillera. The Sierra extends in a half circle for 30 km, offering peaks of rare beauty, lakes and waterfalls. The flora is particularly interesting. Everyone wears ponchos, rides horses and is very friendly. The area is good for trekking and probably the best range in Colombia for rock climbers. The most beautiful peaks are Cocuy (5,100m), Ritacuba Negro (5,200m), Ritacuba Blanco (5,330m) and El Castillo (5,100m). The main towns are to the W of the Sierra. See page 989 for security advice and ask locally before going into the mountains.

In Capitanejo are several hotels where the bus stops: **F** *Residencias El Oasis*, **G** *Residencia El Córdobes*, *Residencia El Dorado* and *Villa Del Mar*, and more on the *parque* on block below bus stop, all are basic.

The centre for climbing the main peaks is **Guicán**, a friendly place about 50 km E of Capitanejo. There are three hotels, **F** *Hotel La Sierra*, good, owner "Profe" (Orlando Corea) has good maps of the region, informative visitors' book for trekkers, meals available; **F** *Las Montañas*, basic, but pleasant, meals available, laundry facilities, overlooks main plaza, thin walls; **F** *Del Norte*, on opposite corner. At *Las Montañas*, Teresa Cristancho or Jorge Ibáñez can arrange a stay in *Cabinas Kanwara* at 3,920 m, about 1,000m above Guicán, **E**, restaurant, 9 beds, well furnished, open fires, electrically-heated showers; or camping (US$1.25), horse rental (US$4.55/day) and guide service included, with Dionisio and Berthilda López at the last house before the Nevado on Ritacuba Blanco, highly rec. From here it is 3 strenuous hrs' walk on a clear trail to the snowline on Ritacuba Blanco. Rope and crampons recommended for the final section above 4,800m. This would also be the best base for the 2-3 day walk round the N end of the Sierra and into Ratoncito valley, which is surrounded by snow-capped mountains. A milk truck ("el lechero") leaves Guicán between 0600 and 0700 via Cocuy for La Cruz, 1 hrs' walk below the cabins, arriving 1100, getting back to Guicán around 1230, a rough but interesting ride. Guicán is 1-1½ hrs' drive by jeep from the mountains, so it is recommended to stay higher up (jeep hire about US$17 from José Riaño or "Profe" in Guicán).

The other main town is **Cocuy** (tourist office on Cra 3, No 8-06, very helpful, run by Pedro Moreno; **E** *Gutiérrez*, friendly, hot water, meals, laundry facilities; **F** *Residencia Cocuy*, cold water, meals, laundry).

Above Cocuy there is no formal accommodation, although you can sleep at the unoccupied Hacienda La Esperanza (8 hrs from Guicán) and may be able to get food at the house below La Esperanza. It is best to camp and take your own food. La Esperanza is the base for climbing to the Laguna Grande de la Sierra (7 hrs round trip), a large sheet of glacier-fed water surrounded by 5 snow-capped peaks, and also for the 2-day walk to the Laguna de la Plaza on the E side of the Sierra, reached through awesome, rugged scenery. Between Cocuy and La Esperanza is Alto de la Cuera where you can stay at El Himat meterological station for US$5, basic, including 2 meals. There is a fine walk from here to Lagunillas, a string of lakes near the S end of the range (5 hrs there and back). Permission to camp can easily be obtained from the friendly people. Sketch maps available in Cocuy from the tourist office. It takes 8-10 days to trek from one end to the other through a central rift, but equipment (crampons, ice axe, rope etc) is necessary. Be prepared for unstable slopes and rockfalls, few flat campsites and treacherous weather. The perpendicular rock mountains overlooking the Llanos are for professionals only. The best weather is from Dec to April.

● **Buses** Six buses a day Bogotá-Cocuy, 2 with Tricolor, 2 with Paz de Río, 1 Libertadores and 1 Gacela, either 0300 or 0400 or between 1000-1800, 13 hrs, US$12; Paz de Río or Libertadores Capitanejo-Cocuy at 0400 and 1200, US$2.15, to **Guicán**, 3-4 hrs, US$2.75, Libertadores Tunja-Cocuy/Guicán 0730, 10 hrs, US$9.75. From Guicán buses leave at 0400, 1600 and 1800 for **Capitanejo**, **Duitama** (US$6.15), **Paipa** (9 hrs, US$6.65) and points N. For points N, or to get

to this area from the N, change at Capitanejo. From Capitanejo 3 buses a day to Bucaramanga, 4 to Cúcuta.

MALAGA

The area around **Málaga** (Santander Department), 35 km N of Capitanejo, is very picturesque: pretty red-tiled villages, riders in ponchos and cowboy hats, and mountains (some covered in flowering trees). The roads are twisty but spectacular.

● **Accommodation** **E** *Santander*, friendly, good value; **E** *Arizona Plaza*, with bath, modern, clean, friendly; **E** *Brasilia*, reasonable; **F** *Príncipe*, near main square, shared bathroom, clean, friendly, good meals, rec, and restaurants, eg *La Riviera*, Cra 8, No 13-61, good food; nearby, *La Esperanza*, good Colombian food.

● **Buses** Good services to Duitama (6 hrs), Bucaramanga (6-7 hrs, US$6) and Pamplona.

ROUTES From Málaga to Pamplona is a beautiful, but hard journey. To Bucaramanga is another spectacular trip through the mountains, but the road is not good and is very tortuous.

<hr>

SANTANDER DEPARTMENT

The main road from Tunja goes N to **Moniquirá** (64 km) 1650m (still in Boyaca Department), a pleasant place to stay. Hotels (all on central plaza) **D** *Mansión*, good; **E** *Clara Luz*, OK; **E** *Casablanca*, with swimming pool; **F** *Tairona*, clean, friendly. 10 km beyond is **Barbosa** in the Department of Santander (**E** *Hotel Príncipe*, clean rooms with private bath; youth hostel at *Parador Turístico Barbosa*; *El Palacio del Pollo*, good, simple roadside restaurant).

A road runs NW from Barbosa to the Magdalena at Puerto Olaya, opposite Puerto Berrío. 18 km from Barbosa is **Vélez**, a charming little town where horses and mules are raised.

SOCORRO

The road (toll at Santana, US$0.40) goes NE for 84 km to **Socorro** (*pop* 23,020), with steep streets and single storey houses set among graceful palms. It has a singularly large and odd stone church. Daily market.

At Socorro, in 1781, began the peasant *comuneros*, revolt against poverty. It was led at first by a woman, Manuela Beltrán, and then, when other towns joined, by Juan Francisco Berbeo. They marched as far as Zipaquirá; rebel terms were accepted by the Spaniards, and sworn to by the Bishop of Bogotá, but when they had returned home troops were sent from Cartagena and there were savage reprisals. Another woman from Socorro, Antonia Santos, led guerrillas fighting for independence and was captured and executed by the Spaniards in 1819; her statue is in the main square. The Casa de Cultura museum (opening hours vary according to season) has disappointingly little information on these local heroines, but is still worth a visit.

● **Accommodation** C *Tamacara*, C 14, No 14-15, T 273517, swimming pool; E *Colonial*, Cra 15, good, TV; F *Venezia*, shower, dining room, nice old rooms, good value.

● **Places to eat** *Panadería Imperial*, C 14 y Cra 13, very good, simple; *La Gran Parrilla*, C 9, Cra 15, good steaks.

BARICHARA

From Socorro, a road leads N and W to Barrancabermeja (see page 932). 21 km along, there is a dirt track off to **Barichara** (*pop* 7,175; *alt* 1,336m), a beautiful colonial town founded in 1714 and designated as a national monument. A better road connects Barichara to San Gil. Among Barichara's places of historical interest, is the house of the former president Aquiles Parra (the woman next door has the key). An interesting excursion is to **Guane**, 9 km away by road, or 1½ hrs delightful walk by trail, where there are many colonial houses and an archaeological museum in the priest's house, collection of coins and a mummified woman (admission, US$0.25). The valley abounds with fossils. There are buses from Barichara, but not every day. Another interesting trip is to the waterfall Salto de Mica, a 30 min walk along a trail following the line of cliffs near Barichara.

● **Accommodation** D *Santa Barbara*, C 5, No 9-12, T 7163, old colonial house, quiet, clean showers in rooms, pool, all meals available; D *Corata*, Cra 7, No 4-02, with private bath, charming courtyard, restaurant and lovely cathedral views, rec; F *Posada Real*, Cra 7, No 4-78, restaurant. You can make reservations in Bogotá, at Cra 16A, No 79-61, T 610-3425. Ask at the Casa de Cultura about staying in private homes.

● **Places to eat** *La Casona*, C 6, Cras 5-6, cheap, good food, friendly; *Bahía Chala*, nr the central plaza, goat-meat speciality.

Another 20 km N of Barichara is **Zapatoca**, a town which at one time controlled the traffic between highland Santander and the Magdalena. Local products include juicy sweets (*cocadas*) and *pauche*, a balsa type wood painted and carved into many forms. There is also a small museum. Local excursions to the Cuevas del Nitro and to a natural swimming pool with waterfall, Pozo del Ahogado. There are buses to Bucaramanga, 2 hrs, US$4.20.

SAN GIL

About 21 km beyond Socorro, NE on the main road to Bucaramanga, is **San Gil**, a colonial town with a good climate, which has El Gallineral, a riverside spot whose beautiful trees are covered with moss-like tillandsia. (Entrance US$0.50.) Good view from La Gruta, the shrine overlooking the town (look for the cross). The town has become a truck stop on the Bogotá-Bucaramanga road, and accommodation facing the main road is noisy.

Excursions

1 hr S of San Gil on the road to Duitama, is **Charalá**, which has a beautiful plaza with a statue of José Antonio Golán, leader of the 1781 Comunero revolt. Also an interesting church and Casa de la Cultura; very attractive lush scenery. E *Hotel El Refugio*, with private bath, clean, safe. Bus San Gil-Charalá, US$1.

● **Accommodation** B *Cabañas Mesón de Cuchicute*, on road to Bogotá nr Pinchote, swimming pool, restaurant; E *Alcantuz*, Cra 11, No 10-15, T 3160, clean, free coffee, good location, pleasant; E *Residencia Abril*, Cra 10, C 8, T 3381, secure parking, relatively quiet; E *Residencias Señorial*, C 10, No 8-14, T 4442, pleasant, quiet; F *Victoria*, near bus terminal, with bath; G *San Gil*, C 11, or F with bath, clean, friendly, upstairs rooms are preferable, basic. Between Socorro and San Gil, there is a *Balneario Campestre El Raízon*, swimming pool, showers, restaurant, car campers allowed and a few small rooms.

● **Places to eat** *Central*, C 10, No 10-70,

good and cheap; *La Mama*, Cra 9, good vegetarian; *Antojos*, Cra 9, No 11-19, good juices; *La Palma*, across from *Residencias Abril*, rec; *Bambi*, Cra 10 – at night it is a discotheque, open air restaurant in Parque Gallineral, good in evening, music at weekends; *Aphrodite*, a nightclub built inside a cave with a lake and waterfall outside.

● **Transport** Bus station 5 mins out of town by taxi on road to Tunja. Bus to **Bogotá**, US$7.20; to **Bucaramanga**, US$2.30, 2½ hrs; to **Barichara** from C 12, US$1, 1 hr. Flights to Bogotá.

ROUTES   A road runs E from San Gil to Onzaga (bus), through Mogotes and San Joaquín, dropping from high mountain ridges to tropical valleys. From Onzaga it is 20 km to Soatá (see page 890); no regular public transport.

12 km from San Gil on the main road N to Bucaramanga is Curití noted for handicrafts in fique (agave sisal). About 28 km N of San Gil, a little off the road, is the picturesque village of **Aratoca**, with a colonial church. 10 km further on, the descent from the heights along the side of a steep cliff into the dry Río Chicamocha canyon, with spectacular rock colours, is one of the most dramatic experiences of the trip to Cúcuta, but, if driving, this is a demanding and dangerous stretch.

BUCARAMANGA

Bucaramanga (*pop* 464,585), 420 km from Bogotá, is the capital of Santander Department. It stands on an uneven plateau sharply delimited by eroded slopes to the N and W, hills to the E and a ravine to the S. The city was founded in 1622 but was little more than a village until the latter half of the 19th century. The city's great problem is space for expansion. Erosion in the lower, western side topples buildings over the edge after heavy rain. The fingers of erosion, deeply ravined between, are spectacular. The metropolitan area has grown rapidly because of the success of coffee, tobacco and staple crops.

BASICS   *Pop* 464,585; pop of metropolitan area 782,345; *Alt* 1,018m; *Av max temp* 30°C; *Av min temp* 19.4°C. *Rainfall* is about 760 mm, and *humidity* is high (68% to 90%). *Phone code:* 07.

Places of interest

The **Parque Santander** is the heart of the modern city, while the **Parque García Rovira** is the centre of the colonial area. Just off Parque García Rovira is the **Casa de Cultura**. **Casa Perú de la Croix**, C 37, No 11-18, is a beautiful colonial mansion (closed, temporarily it is hoped, since 1989). The **Club Campestre** is one of the most beautifully set in Latin America. There is an amusement park, **Parque El Lago**, in the suburb of Lagos I, SW of the city on the way to Floridablanca. On the way out of the city NE (towards Pamplona) is the **Parque Morrorico**, well-maintained with a fine view. There is a sculptured Saviour overlooking the park, a point of pilgrimage on Good Friday.

Museums

Museo de Arte Moderno, C 37, Cra 26, US$0.20. Also **Casa de Bolívar**, C 37, No 12-15, an interesting museum (0900-1200, 1400-1700, entry US$0.15, closed Sat and Sun).

Excursions

The suburb of **Floridablanca**, 8 km SW, has the famous El Paragüitas gardens (also known as the Jardín Botánico), belonging to the national tobacco agency. The gardens have been recently reconstructed and open at weekends 0800-1100 and 1400-1700. Entrance US$0.25. There are plenty of buses: take the Cotandra bus (US$0.30) from Cra 22, Bucaramanga, either Florida Villabel which goes by El Paragüitas, or Florida Autopista (continuation of Cra 33) which goes direct to the square in Florida and you have to walk about a km. Toll on road to Floridablanca, US$0.20.

Lebrija (*pop* 19,130), 17 km to the W, is in an attractive plain. Rionegro (*pop* 28,415) is a coffee town 20 km to the N with, close by, the Laguna de Gálago and waterfalls. One fine waterfall is ½ hr by bus from Rionegro to Los Llanos de Palma followed by a 2 hr walk through citrus groves towards Bocas. Complete the walk along a railway to the Bucamaranga-Rionegro road. **Girón** (*pop* 75,155) a tobacco centre 9 km SW of Bucaramanga on the Río de Oro, is a quiet and attractive colonial town, filled with Bumangueses at weekends, with a beautiful church. The buildings are well preserved and the town unspoilt by modernization. By the river are *tejo* courts and popular open air restaurants with *cumbia* and *salsa* bands; in the square at weekends, sweets and *raspados* (crushed ice delights) are sold. (Hotels: **B** *San Juan de Girón*, outside town on road from Bucaramanga, T 466430, swimming pool, restaurant uninspired; **F** *Río de Oro*, in centre, but make sure you get a lock for the door. Restaurants: *Mansión del Fraile* on the square, in a beautiful colonial house, good food – Bolívar slept here on one occasion, ask to see the bed; *La Casona*, C 28, No 27-47, friendly, rec, try their 'fritanga gironesa'. Take the bus from Cra 15 or 22 in Bucaramanga, US$1.75. In **Piedecuesta**, 18 km SE of Bucaramanga (bus from Cra 22, US$0.45, 45 mins, Hotel: **F** *Piedecuesta*, good, safe, clean). Here you can see cigars being hand-made, furniture carving and jute weaving – cheap, hand-decorated *fique* rugs can be bought. There are frequent buses to all these dormitory towns for the city; a taxi costs US$6. Corpus Christi processions in these towns in June are interesting.

Local festivals

The annual international piano festival is held here in mid-Sept in the Auditorio Luis A Calvo at the Universidad Industrial de Santander, one of the finest concert halls in Colombia. The university is worth a visit for beautiful grounds and a lake full of exotic plants and alligators.

Local information

● **Accommodation**

A2 *Chicamocha*, C 34, No 31-24, luxury, a/c, clean, swimming pool (non guests US$1.50); **A2** *Bucarica*, C 35 y Cra 19, T 301592, F 301594, spacious, on main plaza, with bath, telephone, good restaurant and snack bar; **D** *El Pilar*, C 34, No 24-09, T 453147, clean, hot water, quiet, good service and food, rec; **D** *D'León*, C 56, No 21-49, T 436998, parking, TV, friendly; **E** *Tamana*, Cra 18, No 30-31, with bath, F without, clean, friendly, rec.

Wide variety of hotels on C 31, between Cras 18-21. **E** *Las Bahamas*, S of the Central Plaza, opp Copetran terminal, friendly, good value;

E *Residencias San Diego*, Cra 18, No 15-71, T 434273, quiet, good; **F** *Las Islas*, nearby, clean, good value; **E** *Nutibara*, C 55, No 21-42, shower, fan; **F** *Residencias Solo Suite*, C33, No 24-43, clean, friendly; **F** *Residencias Tonchala*, C 56, No 21-23, with bath, good; **F** *Residencias Amparo*, C 31, No 20-29, clean, with bath; **F** *Hostal Doral*, C 32, No 21-65, rooms with bath F, family business, clean, safe, several nice tiny rooms but varying reports. **NB** Since Bucaramanga is the site for numerous national conventions, it is sometimes hard to find a room.

Camping: ½ hr drive S of Bucaramanga, on left of dual carriageway, with swimming pool and waterside restaurant.

● **Places to eat**

Di Marco, C 48, Cra 29 esquina, excellent meat; *La Casa de Spagheti*, Cra 27, No 51-18, cheap and good; *La Tranquera*, Cra 33, C 40, good Baby Beef; pizzas at: *Piz Pan Pum*, Cra 33, No 31-107 (next to Cinema Rivera); *Tropical*, C 33, No 17-81; *Los Notables*, Cra 18, C 34/35, pleasant, good breakfast; *Fonda*, C 33, No 34-42, good, cheap, vegetarian; *Zirus*, C No 30-88, friendly, owner speaks a little English; *Super Pizza*, Centro Comercial Cabecera (pizza by the slice, hamburgers, etc).

Good **snack bars**: inc *Mucho Pinchos* (C 54, No 31-07). Oriental: *Tokio*, Cra 18 between C 33 and 34; *Oriental*, same street.

Vegetarian: *Maranatha*, Cra 24, No 36-20, good lunches and dinners, reasonable prices; *El Toronjil*, Cra 33, No 52-123, a bit dear; *Govinda*, Indian vegetarian, Cra 20, C 35/36, excellent lunch; *Berna*, C 35, No 18-30, best pastries in town. Try the *hormigas calonas* (large black ants), a local delicacy mainly eaten during Holy Week (sold in shops, not restaurants).

● **Banks & money changers**

Banco Anglo Colombiano, Cra 19 No 36-43, and 4 agencies. Banco Industrial Colombiano, by Parque Santander, will cash Thomas Cook and Amex TCs. Long queues (cheques and passports have to be photocopied). Many other banks. Cash changed at *Distinguidos*, C36, No 17-52 local 1A33.

● **Entertainment**

Discotheques: several on road to Girón and on Cra 33. Worth taking a look at: *Barbaroja*, Cra 27, No 28, a *salsa* and *son* bar set in a renovated red and white, gothic-style mansion, happy hour 1700-1800.

● **Shopping**

Camping equipment: *Acampemos*, C 48, No 26-30, last place in Colombia to get camping gas cartridges before Venezuela.

Handicrafts: in Girón (expensive – see below)

and typical clothing upstairs in the food market, C 34 y Cras 15-16. Similar articles (*ruanas*, hats) in San Andresito. *Feria de artesanías* in first 2 weeks of Sept, usually near the Puerta del Sol.

● **Tourist office**

On main plaza in *Hotel Bucarica* building, C 35, No 18-70A, friendly and knowledgeable, T 338461 (closed 1200-1400). City maps free. MMA, Cra 29, No 41-25, T 458309, Dr Armando Rodríguez Ochoa.

● **Transport**

Local Most taxis have meters; beware of overcharging from bus terminals. Buses charge US$0.35.

Air Palonegro, on three flattened hilltops on other side of ravine S of city. Spectacular views on take-off and landing. At least 3 Avianca flights a day to **Bogotá**, regularly overbooked; also daily to **Cúcuta**. Daily flights to **Medellín**. Taxi, US$4; colectivo, US$1. Buses are scarce despite the fact that some bus boards say "Aeropuerto" (direction "Girón/Lebrija" from Diagonal 15). Avianca, C 37, No 15-03, T 27534.

Road To the Magdalena at Barrancabermeja, 174 km; to Cúcuta, 198 km; to Bogotá, 420 km; to Medellín, 1,010 km; to Santa Marta, 550 km, all paved. **Bus**: the terminal is on the Girón road, with cafés and showers. Taxi to centre, US$1.20; bus US$0.35. To **Bogotá**, 8-11 hrs, US$18 (Pullman) with Berlinas del Fonce, Cra 18, No 31-06 (this journey is uncomfortable, there are no relief stops, and it starts off hot and ends cold in the mountains, be prepared); Copetran, C 55, No 17B-57, recommended for advance bus reservations, has 3 classes of bus to Bogotá inc Pullman, 10 hrs, and to Cartagena, leaving at 1930 daily; Expreso Brasilia, C 31, Cra 18-19, T 422152, runs to Bogotá but they sell tickets only ½ hr before departure. **Tunja**, 7½ hrs, US$14.50; **Valledupar**, 8 hrs, US$20; **Barranquilla**, 9 hrs US$18 first class with Copetran); to **Pamplona**, Copetran, 3 a day, US$3.25 (Pullman), US$2.75 (*corriente*), **Cúcuta**, 6 hrs, US$5 (Pullman), Berlinas buses often arrive full from Bogotá, Copetran US$6 and colectivo US$7.20. The trip to Cúcuta is spectacular in the region of Berlín (see below). **Santa Marta**, 9 hrs, maybe more according to season, US$20 with Copetran; **Barrancabermeja**, 3 hrs, US$2.30, a scenic ride with one rest stop permitted; this road is paved. To **El Banco** on the Río Magdalena, US$15, several companies, direct or change at Aguachica. Hourly buses to **San Gil**, US$2.30. To **Berlín**, US$1.20. Other companies with local services to nearby villages on back roads, eg the colourful folk-art buses of Flota Cáchira (C 32, Cra 33-34) which go N and E.

The road (paved but narrow) runs E to Berlín, and then NE (a very scenic run over the Eastern Cordillera) to Pamplona, about 130 km from Bucaramanga.

BERLÍN

Berlín is an ideal place to appreciate the grandeur of the Eastern Cordillera and the hardiness of the people who live on the *páramo*. The village lies in a valley at 3,100m, the peaks surrounding it rise to 4,350m and the temperature is constantly around 10°C, although on the infrequent sunny days it may seem much warmer. There is a tourist complex with cabins and there are several basic eating places. Camping (challenging but rewarding) is possible with permission. At the highest point on the road between Bucaramanga and Berlín, 3,400m, is a café where you can camp on the covered porch. They have a friendly woolly dog.

NORTE DE SANTANDER DEPARTMENT

PAMPLONA

(*Pop* 43,645; *Alt* 2,200m) Few modern buildings have as yet broken the colonial harmony of this city. Founded in the mountains in 1548, it became important as a mining town but is now better known for its university.

Places of interest

Cathedral in the spacious central plaza. The earthquake of 1875 played havoc with the monasteries and some of the churches: there is now a hotel on the site of the former San Agustín monastery, but it may still be possible to visit the ex-monasteries of San Francisco and Santo Domingo. The **Iglesia del Humilladero**, adjoining the cemetery, is very picturesque and allows a fine view of the city.

Museums

Museum of **religious art** at C 5 y Cra 5. **Casa Colonial** archaeological museum, C 6, No 2-56, open Tues-Sat, 0900-1200, 1400-1800; Sun, 0900-1200, "a little gem". **Casa Anzoátegui**, Cra 6, No 7-48, is where one of Bolívar's generals, José Antonio Anzoátegui, died in 1819, at the age of 30, after the battle of Boyacá. The state in NE Venezuela is named after him. The restored colonial house is now a museum covering the Independence period.

Local festival

The town's Easter celebrations are famous throughout Colombia.

Local information

● **Accommodation**

C *Cariongo*, Cra 5, C 9, T 682645, very good, excellent restaurant, US satellite TV (locked parking available); **E** *Residencia Doran*, Cra 6, No 7-21, with bath (F without), large rooms, good meals; **E** *Imperial*, Cra 5, No 5-36, T 682571, on main plaza (cheaper without carpet), large sparse rooms, noisy; **F** *Orsua*, on main plaza, clean, friendly, cheap, good food also available (good, cheap restaurant also to left of hotel); **F** *Llanos*, C 9 y Cra 7, shared bath, cold water, motorcycle parking, rec. Hotel accommodation may be hard to find at weekends, when Venezuelans visit the town.

● **Places to eat**

El Maribel, C 5, No 4-17, cheap lunch; *La Casona*, C 6, No 6-57, limited but good menu; *Las Brazas*, next door, cheap; *La Garza de Oro*, C 6, No 5-46, good; *El Gran Duque*, on main plaza, student-run, good music; *El Rincón Paisa*, also on main plaza, good; *Portal Alemán*, C 7 y Cra 6, good meals, especially breakfasts; *El Trigal de Oro*, near *Hotel Cariongo*, good breakfast; *Angelitas*, C 7 y Cra 7, good coffee; *Piero's Pizza*, C 9 y Cra 5, good.

● **Banks & money changers**

At banks, or try the store at C 6, No 4-37, where "Don Dolar" will change cash and TCs; **Banco de Bogotá**, on the main plaza, gives Visa cash advances.

● **Post & telecommunications**

Post Office: Cra 6 y C 6, in pedestrian passage. **Telecom**: C 7 y Cra 5A.

● **Shopping**

Pamplona is a good place to buy *ruanas*. Good indoor market.

● **Tourist offices**

C 5 y Cra 6, on main plaza. Maps available at Instituto Geográfico, Banco de la República building on the main street.

● **Buses**

To **Bogotá**, US$18, 13-16 hrs; to **Cúcuta**, US$3, 2½ hrs; to **Bucaramanga**, US$3.45, 4 hrs, great views; to **Málaga** from main plaza, 5 a day from 0800, 6 hrs, US$3.75; to **Tunja**, US$10.75, 12 hrs (leaving at 0600). To **Berlín**, US$2.10.

CUCUTA

It is a run of 72 km from Pamplona through sparsely populated country, descending to **Cúcuta** (*pop* 525,465; *alt* 215m; *phone code* 070), capital of the Department of Norte de Santander, and only 16 km from the Venezuelan frontier. It was founded 1734, destroyed by earthquake 1875, and then rebuilt, elegantly, with the streets shaded by trees, and they are needed for it is hot: the mean temperature is 29°C. Coffee is the great crop in the area, followed by tobacco. There are also large herds of cattle. The **cathedral**, Av 5 between C 10 and 11, is worth a visit. Note the oil paintings by Salvador Moreno. The **international bridge** between Colombia and Venezuela is a few km from El Rosario de Cúcuta; just beyond it is San Antonio del Táchira, the first Venezuelan town, and 55 km on is San Cristóbal.

Local information

● **Accommodation**

A3 *Tonchalá*, C 10, Av 0, T 712005, good restaurant, swimming pool, a/c, airline booking office in hall.

C *Casa Blanca*, Av 6, No 14-55, T 721455, good, reasonable meals, rec; **C** *Lord*, Av 7, No 10-58, T 713609, a/c, nice rooms, good restaurant and service, safe.

D *Cacique*, Av 7, No 9-66, a/c, cold showers only, reasonable; **D** *Tundaya*, C 10, No 6-21, T 716161, 1-star, clean, safe, very good restaurant, breakfast $10.

E *Amaruc*, Av 5, No 9-37, T 717625, with fan, private bath, no hot water.

F *Flamingo*, near Venezuelan Consulate, bath, fan, clean, with bath, noisy; **F** *Imperial*, Av 7, No 6-28, with bath, clean, secure, highly rec; **F** *Residencia Leo*, Av 6A, No 0-24 N, Barrio La Merced, T 41984, run by family Mogollón de Soto, with bath, clothes washing, free coffee all day, rec; **F** *Residencia Los Rosales*, near bus station, C 2, 8-39, fan, with bath, good.

G *Residencias Nohra*, C 7, No 7-52, shared bath, quiet; **G** *Residencia Zambrano*, C 4, No 11E-87, breakfast, laundry facilities, family run by Cecilia Zambrano Mariño.

Youth Hostel at El Rosario de Cúcuta in *Hotel El Saman*, T 700411, with bar, restaurant, disco and pools. Details from Alcom in Bogotá.

● **Places to eat**

La Brasa, Av 5, C 7, good *churrascos*, modest prices; *Don Pancho*, Av 3, No 9-21, local menus,

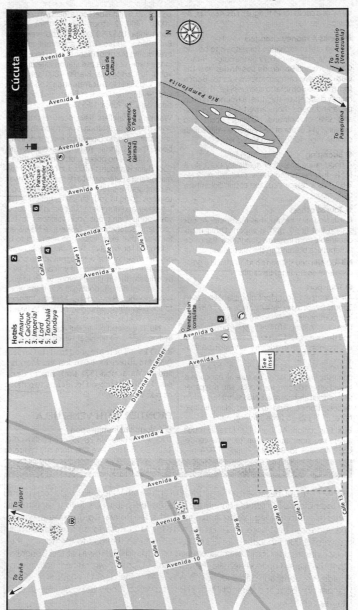

Cúcuta

Hotels
1. Amaruc
2. Cacique
3. Imperial
4. Lord
5. Tonchalá
6. Tundaya

Parque Colón

Avenida 3

Casa de Cultura

Avenida 4

Governor's
Palace

Avenida 5

Parque
Santander

Avanca
(airmail)

Avenida 6

Avenida 7

Calle 13

Avenida 8

Calle 10
Calle 11
Calle 12

N

Río Pamplonita

To San Antonio
(Venezuela)

To Pamplona

See
inset

Venezuelan
consulate

Avenida 0

Avenida 1

Diagonal Santander

Avenida 4

Avenida 6

Avenida 8

Avenida 10

Calle 2
Calle 4
Calle 6
Calle 8
Calle 10
Calle 11
Calle 13

To Airport

To Ocaña

try *lengua criolla* (beef tongue); *Las Acacias*, Av 5, rec.

● **Banks & money changers**
A good rate of exchange for pesos is to be had in Cúcuta, at the airport, or on the border. **Banco Ganadero** and **Banco de Los Andes** near the plaza will give cash against Visa cards. **Banco Industrial Colombiano** changes TCs. There are money changers on the street all round the main plaza and many shops advertise the purchase and sale of bolívares. Change pesos into bolívares in Cúcuta or San Antonio – difficult to change them further into Venezuela.

● **Shopping**
A good range of leather goods: try C 10, Av 8 for leather boots and shoes. *Cuchitril*, Av 3 No 9-89, has a selection of the better Colombian craft work.

● **Tourist offices**
C 10, No 0-30, helpful, has maps, etc. At bus station (1st floor), and at airport. Other maps obtainable from Instituto Geográfico, Banco de la República building, in the main plaza.

NB Cúcuta and the surrounding area is a great centre for smuggling. Be careful.

● **Transport**
Air Airport at Cúcuta for Colombian services to Bogotá (twice a day with Avianca; also SAM and Intercontinental de Aviación) and other Colombian cities. Airport 10 mins by taxi from the town and the border, US$2. It is cheaper to buy tickets in Colombia than in advance in Venezuela. Avianca, C 13, No 5-09, T 277758. Also at San Antonio, Venezuela (30 mins) for Venezuelan domestic lines. At latter, be sure all baggage is sealed after customs inspection and the paper seals signed and stamped. **NB** Do not buy airline 'tickets' from Cúcuta to Venezuelan destinations, all flights go from San Antonio.

Bus Bus station: Av 7 and C O (a really rough area). Taxi from bus station to town centre, US$2.40. Bus to **Bogotá**, hourly, 17-24 hrs,

US$21.40, Berlinas del Fonce (has own terminal) 1000, 1400, 2 stops, inc 15 mins in Bucaramanga (US$2.50 extra for *cochecama*), or Bolivariano, 20 hrs. There are frequent buses, even during the night (if the bus you take arrives in the dark, sit in the bus station café until it is light). To **Cartagena**, Brasilia 1800 and 1930, 18 hrs, US$35. To **Bucaramanga**, US$5, 6 hrs, with Berlinas del Fonce Pullman, several departures daily. To **Tunja**, US$11.

Warning Travellers have been reporting for years that the bus station is overrun with thieves and conmen, who have tried every trick in the book. This is still true. You must take great care, there is little or no police protection. On the 1st floor there is a tourist office for help and information and a café/snack bar where you can wait in comparative safety. Alternatively, go straight to a bus going in your direction, get on it, pay the driver and don't let your belongings out of your sight. Don't put your valuables in bus company 'safety boxes'. Make sure tickets are for buses that exist; tickets do not need to be "stamped for validity". For San Cristóbal, only pay the driver of the vehicle, not at the offices upstairs in the bus station. If you are told, even by officials, that it is dangerous to go to your chosen destination, double check. If the worst happens, the victimized should report the theft to the DAS office, who may be able to help to recover what has been stolen.

    NB The exception to the above is the new Berlinas del Fonce terminal, which is much safer.

ROUTES There are good roads to Caracas (933 km direct or 1,046 km via Mérida), and to Maracaibo (571 km). Bus to Caracas, 14 hrs, Expreso Occidente, two daily, or taxi colectivo.

FRONTIER WITH VENEZUELA

● **Colombian immigration**
DAS, Av Primera, No 28-55, open 0800-1200, 1400-2000 daily. Take bus from city centre to

---

Cúcuta and the Road to Independence

Cúcuta, because it is the gateway of entry from Venezuela, was a focal point in the history of Colombia during the wars for independence. Bolívar captured it after his lightning Magdalena campaign in 1813. The **Bolívar Column** stands where he addressed his troops on 28 February 1813. At **El Rosario de Cúcuta**, a small town of 8,000 inhabitants 14½ km from Cúcuta on the road to the frontier, the First Congress of Gran Colombia opened on 6 May 1821. It was at this Congress that the plan to unite Venezuela, Ecuador, and Colombia was ratified; Bolívar was made President, and Santander (who was against the plan) Vice-President. (Santander was born at a *hacienda* near El Rosario which is now being developed as a tourist centre.)

Barrio San Rafael. Shared taxi from border US$1,
will wait for formalities, then US$0.80 to bus
station. Women should not visit this office alone.

DAS also at airport, which will deal with land
travellers.

Exit and entry formalities handled at DAS
office before international border bridge.

NB If you do not obtain an exit stamp, you will
be turned back by Venezuelan officials and the
next time you enter Colombia, you will be fined
US$7.50.

Entering Colombia You must obtain both a
Venezuelan exit stamp and a Colombian entry
stamp (passport and/or tourist card) at the border. Without the former you will be sent back;
without the latter you will have problems with
police checks, banks and leaving the country.
You can also be fined.

Air travellers All Colombian formalities can be
undertaken at the airport.

● **Colombian customs**
Aduana office on the road to the airport (small
sign); has a restaurant.

● **Leaving Colombia by private vehicle**
Passport must be stamped at DAS in town and
car papers must be stamped at Aduana on the
road to the airport. The same applies for those
entering Colombia.

● **Venezuelan consulate**
Av 0, C 8, Cúcuta, T 713983/712107, open
0800-1300, Mon-Fri. All visitors to Venezuela
need a visa and tourist card, obtainable from
here or the Venezuelan Embassy in Bogotá
(which may send you to Cúcuta). Requirements:
2 passport photographs; proof of transportation
out of Venezuela, with date (not always asked
for in Cúcuta); proof of adequate funds sometimes requested. In Cúcuta (1994), pay US$30
in pesos for visa at a bank, eg Banco Comercial
Antioqueño, Av 6 (open to 1100), then take
receipt to consulate. Apply for visa at 0800 to
get it by 1400. If you know when you will be
arriving at the frontier, get your visa in your home
country.

● **Transport**
From Cúcuta: bus to **Caracas**; **San Cristóbal**,
US$1.20 (Bolivariano), colectivo US$2.40; **San
Antonio**, taxi US$7.20, bus and colectivo from
C 7, Av 4, US$1.

On any form of transport which is crossing the
border, make sure that the driver knows that you
need to stop to obtain exit/entry stamps etc. You
may be asked to pay extra, or alight and flag
down a later colectivo.

Just to visit San Antonio de Táchira, no documents are needed.

The North Coast and the Islands

CARIBBEAN Colombia, very different in spirit from the highlands: the coast stretches from the Darién Gap, through banana planta-tions, swamplands and palm plantations to the arid Guajira. The main resorts are Cartagena, which is also steeped in colonial history, and Santa Marta, near which is the Tairona national park with precolombian remains and the unique Sierra Nevada de Santa Marta coastal range.

Climate
The climate is much the same for the whole area: the heat is great – ranging from 26° to 36°C and there is a difference of only 2° between the hottest and coolest month. From Nov to Mar the heat is moderated by trade winds.

People
Character, like climate, seems to change in Colombia with the altitude. The *costeños* (the people of the coast) are gayer and more light-hearted than the more sober people of the highlands. The coastal peo-ple talk very fast, slurring their words and dropping the final s's.

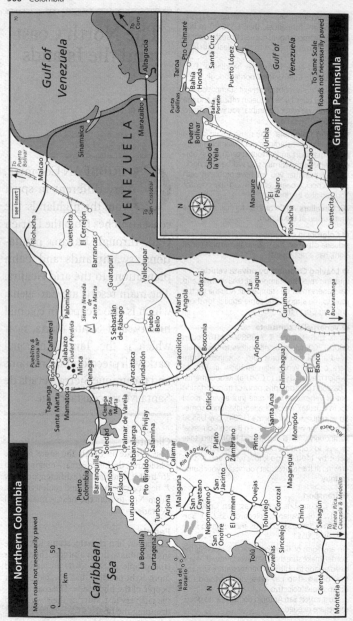

Northern Colombia

Main roads not necessarily paved

km
0   50

Caribbean Sea

Gulf of Venezuela

VENEZUELA

see Insert

Guajira Peninsula

Gulf of Venezuela

To Same Scale
Roads not necessarily paved

CARTAGENA

Cartagena (*pop* 661,830; *phone code* 053), steeped in history, is one of the most interesting towns in South America. An arm of the river, 145 km long, canalized in 1650 by Spain – the Canal del Dique – from Calamar to Cartagena allows free access for ships from the up-river ports.

History

Cartagena was founded by Pedro de Heredia on 13 January 1533. There were then two approaches to it, Bocagrande, at the northern end of Tierra Bomba island – this was a direct entry from the Caribbean – and Boca Chica, a narrow channel at the S leading to the great bay of Cartagena, 15 km long and 5 km wide. (Bocagrande was blocked after Admiral Vernon's attack in 1741 – see below.) The old walled city lies at the N end of the Bahía de Cartagena. To the W is the Caribbean Sea and to the N and E are lakes and lagoons.

Fortifications Cartagena was one of the storage points for merchandise sent out from Spain and for treasure collected from the Americas to be sent back to Spain. A series of forts protecting the approaches from the sea, and the formidable walls built around the city, made it almost impregnable.

Entering Boca Chica by sea, the island of Tierra Bomba is to the left. At the tip of a spit of land is the fortress of **San Fernando** (entrance, US$0.60; guide, US$1.50 for one to five people; if closed, ask around for the key; boat trips to it 1 hr, last one back is at 1830). Opposite it, right on the tip of Barú island, is the **Fuerte San José**. The two forts were once linked by heavy chains to prevent surprise attacks by pirates. North of Barú island stretches Manga island, much larger and now an important suburb. At its northern end a bridge, **Puente Román**, connects it with the old city. This approach was defended by three forts: **San Sebastián del Pastelillo** built between 1558 and 1567 (the Club de Pesca has it now) at the northwestern tip of Manga Island; the fortress of **San Lorenzo** near the city itself; and the very powerful **Castillo San Felipe de Barajas** inland on San Lázaro hill, 41m above sea-level, to the E of the city. Building began in 1639 and it was finished by 1657. Under the huge structure are tunnels lined with living rooms and offices. Some are open and lighted; visitors pass through these and on to the top of the fortress. Baron de Pointis, the French pirate, stormed and took it, but Admiral Vernon failed to reach it (see box). Entrance fee US$5 (half price for students and Colombians). Guide US$1.50 for one to five people. Open daily 0800-1800.

Yet another fort, **La Tenaza**, protected the walled city from a direct attack from the open sea. The huge encircling walls were started early in the 17th century and finished by 1735. They were on average 12m high and 17m thick, with 6 gates. They contained, besides barracks, a water reservoir.

Independence Cartagena declared its independence from Spain in 1811. A year later Bolívar used the city as a jumping-off point for his Magdalena campaign. After a heroic resistance, Cartagena was retaken by the royalists under Pablo Morillo in 1815. The patriots finally freed it in 1821.

Places of interest

The old walled city was in two sections, inner and outer. Much of the wall between the two was razed some years ago. Nearly all the houses are of one or two storeys. The houses in **El Centro** were occupied by the high officials and nobility. **San Diego** (the northern end of the inner town) was where the middle classes lived: the clerks, merchants, priests and military. The artisan classes lived in the one-storey houses of **Getsemaní** in the outer city. Today, the streets of the inner city are relatively uncrowded; budget hotels and restaurants are sprinkled thinly throughout the area. Immediately adjoining is the downtown sector, known as **La Matuna**, where vendors crowd the pavements and the alleys between the modern commercial buildings. Several middle range hotels are in this district, between Avs Venezuela and

The Sacking of Cartagena

In spite of its daunting outer forts and encircling walls Cartagena was challenged again and again by enemies. Sir Francis Drake, with 1,300 men, broke in successfully in 1586, leading to a major reconstruction of the ramparts we see today. Nevertheless the Frenchmen Baron de Pointis and Ducasse, with 10,000 men, beat down the defences and sacked the city in 1697. But the strongest attack of all, by Sir Edward Vernon with 27,000 men and 3,000 pieces of artillery, failed in 1741 after besieging the city for 56 days; it was defended by the one-eyed, one-armed and one-legged hero Blas de Lezo, whose statue is at the entrance to the San Felipe fortress.

Urdaneta Arbeláez. South of the latter is Getsemaní, where many colonial buildings survive; the greatest concentration of budget hotels and restaurants is here. Just under a kilometre from the old city, along an ocean boulevard, **Bocagrande** is a spit of land crowded with hotel and apartment towers. Thousands of visitors flock to the beach with its accompanying resort atmosphere, fast food outlets, shops and dirty seawater.

The old city streets are narrow. Each block has a different name, a source of confusion, but don't worry: the thing to do is to wander aimlessly, savouring the street scenes, and allow the great sights to catch you by surprise. Our map is marked with numerals for the places of outstanding interest. The most attractive streets have been given a star (*). Most of the "great houses" can be visited. Churches generally open to the public at 1800.

The numbers stand for the following places:

1 The **Puente Román**, the bridge which leads from the island of Manga into Getsemaní, with its *casas bajas* or low houses.

2 The chapel of **San Roque** (early 17th century), near the hospital of Espíritu Santo.

3 In an interesting plaza, the church of **Santísima Trinidad**, built 1643 but not consecrated till 1839. North of the church, at number 10, lived Pedro Romero, who set the revolution of 1811 going by coming out into the street shouting "Long Live Liberty".

4 The monastery and church of **San Francisco**. The church was built in 1590 after the pirate Martin Côte had destroyed an earlier church built in 1559. The first Inquisitors lodged at the monastery. From its courtyard a crowd surged into the streets claiming independence from Spain on 11 November 1811. The Iglesia de la Tercera Orden is now the **Teatro Colón**.

Immediately to the N is **Plaza de la Independencia**, with the landscaped **Parque del Centenario** just off it. At right angles to the Plaza runs the **Paseo de los Mártires**, flanked by the busts of nine patriots executed in the square on 24 February 1816 by the royalist Morillo when he retook the city. At its western end is a tall clock tower. Passing through the tower's arches (the main entrance to the inner walled city) we get to

5 The **Plaza de los Coches**. Around almost all the plazas of Cartagena arcades offer refuge from the tropical sun. On the W side of this plaza is the famous **Portal de los Dulces**, a favourite meeting place.

6 **Plaza de la Aduana**, with a statue of Columbus and the **Palacio Municipal**.

7 Church of **San Pedro Claver** and Monastery, built by Jesuits in 1603 and later dedicated to San Pedro Claver, a monk in the monastery, who was canonized 235 years after his death in 1654. He was called the Slave of the Slaves (El Apostol de los negros): he used to beg from door to door for money to give to the black slaves brought to the city. His body is in a glass coffin on the high altar, and his cell and the balcony from which he sighted slave ships are shown to visitors. Entry, US$0.60. Guides charge US$2. Open daily 0800-1800.

8 **Plaza de Bolívar** (the old Plaza Inquisi-

ción), modest, and with a statue of Bolívar. On its W side is

9 The **Palacio de la Inquisición**, established in 1610, but the building dates from 1706. The stone entrance with its coats of arms

and well preserved and ornate wooden door is very notable. The whole building, with its balconies, cloisters and patios, is a fine example of colonial baroque. There is a modest historical museum at the

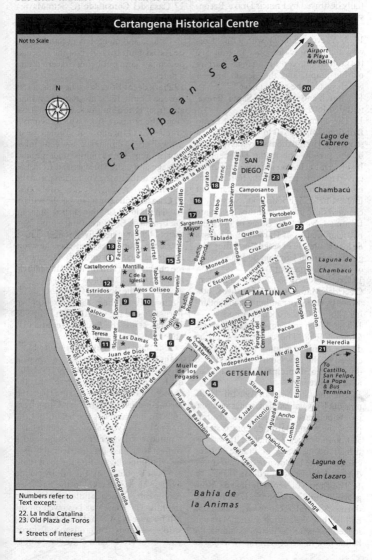

Cartangena Historical Centre

Not to Scale

Caribbean Sea

To Airport & Playa Marbella

Lago de Cabrero

Chambacú

SAN DIEGO

Camposanto

Laguna de Chambacú

LA MATUNA

Parque del Centenario

GETSEMANI

Muelle de los Pegasos

Pl de la Independencia

To Castillo, San Felipe, La Popa & Bus Terminals

P Heredia

To Bocagrande

Bahía de la Animas

Laguna de San Lazaro

Numbers refer to Text except:
22. La India Catalina
23. Old Plaza de Toros

* Streets of Interest

Palacio, and a library. Entry charge US$0.75; good historical books on sale. Open Mon-Fri, 0800-1130, 1400-1700.

10 The **Cathedral**, in the NE corner of Plaza de Bolívar, begun in 1575 and partially destroyed by Francis Drake. Reconstruction was finished by 1612. Great alterations were made between 1912 and 1923. A severe exterior, with a fine doorway, and a simply decorated interior. See the guilded 18th century altar, the Carrara marble pulpit, and the elegant arcades which sustain the central nave.

11 Church and convent of **Santa Teresa**, founded 1609.

12 The church and monastery of **Santo Domingo**, built 1570 to 1579 and now a seminary. The old monastery was replaced by the present one in the 17th century. Inside, a miracle-making image of Christ, carved towards the end of the 16th century, is set on a baroque 19th century altar. Most interesting neighbourhood, very little changed since the 16th century. In C Santo Domingo, No 33-29, is one of the great patrician houses of Cartagena, the **Casa de los Condes de Pestagua**, now the Colegio del Sagrado Corazón de Jesús. North of Santo Domingo, at

13 C de la Factoria 36-57 is the magnificent **Casa del Marqués de Valdehoyos**, now owned by the tourist authority and containing a Tourist Office; open to visitors.

14 The church and convent of **La Merced**, founded 1618. The convent – a prison during Morillo's reign of terror – was occupied by the Law Courts and its church is the **Teatro Municipal**, but now appears to be in disrepair.

15 The monastery of **San Agustín** (1580), now the Universidad de Cartagena. From its chapel, now occupied by a printing press, the pirate Baron de Pointis stole a 500-pound silver sepulchre. It was returned by the King of France but the citizens melted it down to pay their troops during the siege by Morillo in 1815.

16 The church of **Santo Toribio de Mongrovejo**. Building began in 1729. In 1741, during Admiral Vernon's siege, a cannon ball fell into the church during Mass and lodged in one of the central columns; the ball is now in a recess in the W wall. The font of Carrara marble in the Sacristy is a masterpiece. There is a beautiful carved ceiling (*mudéjar* style) above the main altar. Opens for Mass at 0600 and 1800, closed at other times.

17 **Casa del Consulado** (C Sgto Mayor) was one of the great houses but has now become a teachers' college.

18 Church and monastery of **Santa Clara de Assisi**, built 1617-21, now the Hospital de Santa Clara, but being converted into a hotel.

19 **Plaza de las Bóvedas**. The walls of Las Bóvedas, built 1799, are some 12m high and from 15 to 18m thick. Cars can drive along the rampart, from which there is a grand view of the harbour. At the base of the wall are 23 dungeons, now containing tourist shops. Both a lighted underground passage and a drawbridge lead from Las Bóvedas to the fortress of La Tenaza on the sea shore.

20 **Casa de Núñez**, just outside the walls of La Tenaza in El Cabrero district opposite the Ermita de El Cabrero and 5 mins from the old bullring; here lived Rafael Núñez, president (four times) and poet (he wrote Colombia's national anthem). His grandiose marble tomb is in the adjoining church. Mon-Fri 0800-1200, 1400-1800.

Three of the sights of Cartagena are off our map. Two of them, the Fortress of San Fernando and the Castillo San Felipe de Barajas, across the **Puente Heredia** (21) have been described above.

The third is **La Popa** hill, nearly 150m high, from which there is a fine view of the harbour and the city (entry US$1.10); open daily 0800-1745. Here are the church and monastery of Santa Cruz and restored ruins of the convent dating from 1608. In the church is the beautiful little image of the Virgin of La Candelaria, reputed a deliverer from plague and a protector against pirates. Her day is 2 Feb. For nine days before the feast thousands of people go up the hill by car, on foot, or on horseback. On the day itself people carry lighted candles as they go up the hill. The name was bestowed on the hill because of an imagined likeness to a ship's poop. It is dangerous to walk up on your own; either take a guided tour, or take a public bus to Teatro Miramar at the foot of the hill (US$0.50), then bargain for a taxi up, about US$2.50.

Museums

On the opposite side of the Plaza de Bolívar to the Palacio de la Inquisición, the **Museo del Oro y Arqueológico** has been installed in an old building. Gold and pottery, very well displayed. Entrance US$1, but closed on Sun. There is a **Naval Museum** with maps, models and display of armaments a short way towards the city wall along C Baloco, entry US$0.75.

Art Gallery and Museum Contemporary Latin American paintings, Banco Ganadero, Plaza de la Aduana. Nearby is the **Museo de Arte Moderno** (open Mon-Fri, 0900-1200, 1500-1800, Sat, 1000-1200), opposite the San Pedro Claver church.

Beaches

Take bus from Plaza de la Independencia to Bocagrande, whose beaches can be dirty and often crowded. Marbella beach, just N of Las Bóvedas (the locals' beach, and therefore quieter than Bocagrande) is good for swimming, though subject at times to dangerous currents. The Boca Chica beach is dirty. Boats leave from Muelle Turístico (departure point is the 2-storey glass building half-way along, which is also the tourist office). The round trip can take up to 2 hrs each way. *Ferry Dancing*, about half the price of the faster, luxury boats, carries dancing passengers. Boats taking in Boca Chica and San Fernando include *Alcatraz*, which runs a daily trip from the Muelle Turístico. Boats to the Islas del Rosario (see below) may stop at the San Fernando fortress and Playa Blanca on the Isla de Baru for 1 hr (bargain with boatman to leave you, camp on the beach, and continue on a later cruise, take a hammock, food and water since these are expensive on the island, if at all). Playa Blanca is crowded am, but peaceful after the tour boats have left). There are several restaurants on the beach, the best *La Sirena* run by Carmen (La Española), good food, hammocks for hire US$2.50. Another is run by a French/Colombian couple. You can also reach Playa Blanca by taking the bus to Puerto Caballo, crossing the Canal de Dique by canoe and thence by truck to the beach; if walking, 2½ hrs in all. If staying the night at Playa Blanca in cabañas or tents, beware of ferocious sandflies. **NB** Pay for boat trips on board if possible, and be certain that you and the operator understand what you are paying for.

Local festivals

The other great feast, apart from Candlemas, is on in the second week of Nov to celebrate the independence of Cartagena. Men and women in masks and fancy dress roam the streets, dancing to the sound of *maracas* and drums. There are beauty contests and battles of flowers and general gaiety. This festival tends to be wild and can be dangerous. **Caribbean Music Festival** for 5 days in March, groups from all over the Caribbean region and beyond perform salsa, reggae, etc; loud and fun. There is a **film festival** in either Mar or April. Avianca offices everywhere have details of festival dates.

Local information

● Warnings

Carry your passport, or a notarized photocopy, at all times. Failure to present it on police request can result in imprisonment and fines. Generally, the central areas are reported safe and friendly (although Getsemaní is less secure), but should you require the police, there is a station in Barrio Manga.

Beware of drug pushers on the beaches, pickpockets in crowded areas and bag/camera snatchers on quiet Sun mornings. At the bus station, do not be pressurized into a hotel recommendation different from your own choice. On the street, do not be tempted by offers of jobs or passages aboard ship: jobs should have full documentation from the Seamen's Union office; passages should only be bought at a recognized shipping agency.

● Accommodation

On Bocagrande beach, 10 mins by bus from city: at the extreme tip is **L1-2** *Cartagena-Hilton*, El Laguito, T 665-0666, F 665-0661 (Apto Aéreo 1774, best equipped); **L2** *Hotel del Caribe*, Cra 1, No 2-87, T 665-0155, F 665-3707, colonial style with newer annexes, comfortable, a/c, stylish, nice grounds, swimming pool in the (expensive) restaurant; **L3** *Capilla del Mar*, C 8, Cra 1, T 665-1140, F 665-5145, resort hotel, excellent French restaurant, swimming pool on top floor, no connection with restaurant of same name ½ km away; **L3** *Cartagena Real*, Av del Malecón, T 665-5590, F 665-4163, all suites, highrise.

A2-3 range: *Decamerón*, Cra 1, No 10-10, T 665-4400, F 665-3738, all-inclusive resort; *Barlovento*, Cra 3, No 6-23, T 665-3965, smaller scale, 400m from beach; *Las Velas*, Av de las Velas 1-60, T 665-0590, F 665-0530, 3 nights min, holiday resort, good restaurant; *Casa Grande*, Av 1A, No 9-126, pleasant small hotel on beach, restaurant, owner speaks English, a/c, cheaper with fan only; *Costa del Sol*, Av 1 y C 9A, T 665-0866, tower with rooftop pool, very comfortable.

C *India Catalina*, Cra 2, No 7-115, T 665-5392, very good, a/c, safe, clean (acts as youth hostel); **C** *Playa*, Av 2, No 4-87, T 665-0552, all rooms with bath, a/c, very clean, open air bar, restaurant, swimming pool, noisy disco next door; **C** *Residencias Internacional*, Av San Martín 4110, T 665-0675 (D in low season), small rooms, small bath, a/c, cold water, TV, uncomfortable beds, convenient location, friendly; opp at No 5-86 is **B** *Flamingo* (D in low season), T 665-0301, with bath and a/c, clean, helpful, pleasant, eat on the terrace, highly rec; **D** *Leonela*, Cra 3, 7-142, T 665-4761, quiet, comfortable; **D** *La Giralda*, Cra 3, No 7-166, T 665-4507, clean, friendly, with bath, fan, a/c dearer; **E** *Residencia Punta Canda*, C 7 between Cras 2 and 3, reasonable; **F** *La Sultana*, Av San Martín, No 7-44, clean, pleasant atmosphere. On Cra 3, there are plenty of small, pleasant **D** *residencias*, for instance *Mary*, No 6-52, T 665-2822, small, respectable, and No 5-29, cheaper in low season, clean and friendly.

In La Matuna: **C** *Del Lago*, C 34, No 11-15, T 665-3819, more for a/c, phone, no singles, reasonable restaurant, laundry, credit cards accepted, no parking; **D** *Montecarlo*, C 34, No 10-16, T 664-5835, more with a/c, good value, good laundry next door, fair restaurant; **D** *San Felipe*, Cra 9, No 13-72, T 664-5439, central, close to old city, big café.

In Old City: **D** *Hostal Baluarte*, Media Luna No 10-81, T 664-2208, with bath and fan, converted colonial house, family run, helpful, will arrange day trips, well-priced restaurant; **D** *Hostal Santo Domingo*, C Santo Domingo, No 33-46, basic but clean and quiet, well located, rec; **D** *Veracruz*, C San Agustín, No 6-15, opp San Agustín church (more with a/c), clean, safe, helpful but noisy disco on ground floor; **E** *Doral*, Media Luna, No 10-46, nice, fan, large rooms, safe courtyard where you can park cycles/motorbikes, noisy at night and bad water problems; **E** *Holiday*, Media Luna, No 10-47, T 664-0948, clean, fan, friendly, quiet, pleasant courtyard, luggage store, hot water, rec; **E** *Hotel Familiar*, C del Guerrero, No 29-65, near Media Luna, T 664-8374, clean, friendly, safe, fan, space for bike or motorcycle, use of kitchen; **F** *Lina*, San Andrés y Tripita, clean with restaurant; **F** *Viena*, San Andrés, No 30-53, T 664-6242, run

by Patrick Vercoutere, Belgian, clean, safe, cooking facilities, washing machine, book exchange, excellent value, rec, restaurant *Algo Diferente* nearby under same management, profits help street children; **F** *Media Luna*, Media Luna y Centenario, without bath, clean, good value; **F** *Monterrey*, Camellón de los Mártires (opp the clocktower "prison cell"), clean, friendly, central, good Colombian meals in restaurant; **F** *Residencias Venecia*, C del Guerrero No 29-108, friendly, some rooms with fan, garden, washing facilities, clean and secure; **F** *Tropicana*, Plaza Independencia, run down but friendly, helpful and clean. The following are used frequently, but recently none has received good reports (ie insecure, poor value); **F** *El Refugio*, C Media Luna, No 10-35, clean, friendly; **F** *Hostal Valle*, C Media Luna, No 10-15, some rooms with private bath, friendly, free coffee, discounts for long stay, check the room before paying. Many cheap hotels on C Media Luna are brothels; area not advisable for women on their own. *Turístico Margie*, Av 2A, 63-175, Crespo district, convenient for airport, walking distance to old city (or bus), family-run, clean, modern. On the road to the airport are several hotels and *pensiones*, particularly at Marbella beach, eg **D** *Bellavista*, Av Santander, clean, fans, nice patio, English-speaking owner, Enrique Sedó, secure, nice atmosphere, rec for longer stays; right behind is **F** *Mirador del Lago*, clean, large rooms, fan, friendly owner.

NB Hotel prices rise for high season, 1 Nov-31 Mar, and June-July. From 15 Dec to 31 Jan they rise by as much as 50% (ie increase Bocagrande hotels by at least a letter in our range at this time; in town nothing is below E, but price increases are not so steep); hotels tend to be heavily booked right through to March. For hotel insurance, add 5%, plus US$0.05 pp per day.

Camping: on the beach is not secure. Vehicle parking overnight possible at the Costa Norte Beach Club, 2 km NE on coast beyond the airport, US$4 per night.

● **Places to eat**
Bocagrande: *Nautilus*, Cra 3, good, seafood, other branches, facing the statue of La India Catalina and on road to airport in Marbella; *Capilla del Mar*, rec, seafood. On Av San Martín, *Fontana di Trevi*, Italian; *Italia*, Av San Martín 7-55, good Italian, excellent ice creams and sorbets; *Palacio de las Frutas*, Av San Martín y C 6, good *comida corrida*; *La Fonda Antioqueña*, Cra 2, No 6-161, traditional Colombian, nice atmosphere; *La Piragua*, Cra 2, an open-air bar with live music, dancing, pleasant. Good reasonably priced food in the chain restaurants: *Crepes y Waffles*, *Pizza por Metro* and *La Loca*.
Away from Bocagrande: *Pacos*, good bar/res-

taurant on Plaza Santo Domingo; *El Zorba*, Plaza Fernández, small, cosy, good music. On C Quero, close to *Zorba*, *La Tablada*, arty, usually good music, basic; *Mesón Taurino*, No 9-23, good, cheap. *Dalmacia*, C Santo Domingo, just off square, charming, run by a Croatian, rec, closes 2000. *La Crepería*, Plaza de Bolívar 3-110, excellent salads, fruit drinks, crêpes, gets busy around 1230; *Nuevo Mundo*, C 30, No 8B-62 serves typical menu, cheap, good value; *Café-Galería Abaloa*, C Espíritu Santo, No 29-200, Gatsemaní, quiet, cultural ambience, books, music etc, drinks, breakfasts, also has 3 cheap rooms; *El Koral*, next to *Hotel Doral*, Media Luna, good, cheap; *El Ganadero*, also on Media Luna, good value; *Bucarest*, Marbella, next to *Hotel Bellavista*, for seafood and juices. Many restaurants around Plaza Independencia have good value meals, eg *Fonda El Socorro*, C Larga on Plaza Independencia. Several Chinese restaurants in the old city, eg *Wing-Wah*, C Ayos, rec, *Dragón de Oro*, C Venezuela, good, inexpensive; *El Diamante*, C de la Soledad, T 664-4121, large helpings, good; *Jumbo*, C Tabaco, good Chinese and local food, *churrasco*, large portions, reasonable prices. Vegetarian restaurant and health food shop, *Santísimo*, C Quero, lunch under US$1; *Tienda Naturista*, C Quero 9-09, good cheap vegetarian; *Govinda*, C del Estanco del Aguardiente, No 5-90, also vegetarian, mixed reports. *Panadería La Mejor*, Av Arbeláez, good for breakfast, fine wholemeal bread, coffee, yoghurt, expensive.

At cafés try the *palacón*, a biscuit made of green banana, mashed and baked; also in Parque del Centenario in early morning. At restaurants ask for *sancocho* a local soup of the day of vegetables and fish or meat. Also try *obleas* for a snack, biscuits with jam, cream cheese, or caramel fudge, and *buñuelos*, deep-fried cheese dough balls.

● **Banks & money changers**
Banco Unión Colombiana, Av Venezuela (C 35), No 10-26, La Matuna, changes American Express TCs up to a maximum of US$300, without commission. **Banco Industrial**, good rates for TCs; **Bancafé**, gives money on Visa cards, both on Av Venezuela. **Banco Sudameis**, opposite conference centre at harbour, for Visa cash advances. There are many *cambios*; many in the arcade at Torre Reloj and adjoining streets change Amex TCs; also *Caja de Cambio Caldas*, Av San Martín, No 4-118, Bocagrande, and on the corner of Plaza de los Coches, downtown. Be sure to count the pesos yourself before handing over your dollars. Never change money on the street. **American Express** (Tierra Mar Aire), Bocagrande, Cra 4, No 7-196, is a travel agency downstairs, and gives cash against credit cards upstairs. TCs can be changed Sat am (arrive early) at **Joyería Mora**, Román 5-39,

and at El Portal nearby, in the old city.

● **Embassies & consulates**
Venezuelan, C 5A, No 10-106, open to 1500, possible to get a visa the same day (US$30): you need onward ticket, two photos, but ensure you get a full visa not a 72 hrs' transit unless that is all you need. **Canadian Honorary Consul** (for emergencies only), C de la Inquisición con Santo Domingo, esq, No 33-08, Apto 201. **Danish**, Cra 10, No 5-68. **Finnish**, Av San Martín, Centro Comercial Bocagrande, p 3, 308, T 665-7672. **Norwegian Consulate**, Edif Banco Central Hipolecario, La Matuna, T 665-4639. **Panamanian Consulate**, C 69, No 4-97, T 666-2079.

● **Entertainment**
Discos: good discos in Bocagrande eg *La Escollera*, also in Old City, Parque La Marina, upmarket, in stately building. Bar *La Muralla* on the city wall W of Plaza Bolívar, open at night only, live music at weekends, romantic, but drinks expensive; for salsa, *Quiebra Canto*, C Media Luna at Parque Centenario, nice atmosphere.

● **Language schools**
Enysys, Plaza Fernández de Madrid, No 36-123, p 2, T 664-3951, rec.

● **Places of worship**
Anglican Church, C Ricuarte, services in English can be arranged.

● **Post & telecommunications**
Post Office: beside Avianca office between Avs Venezuela and Urdaneta Arbeláez.
Telecom: Av Urdaneta Arbeláez nr corner of C 34; long distance phones behind this building; long distance also in Bocagrande.

● **Shopping**
A good selection of *artesanías* at *Compendium* on Plaza Bolívar, but in general (except for leather goods) shopping is much better in Bogotá. Handicraft shops in the Plaza de las Bóvedas. Woollen *blusas* are good value; try the *Tropicano* in Pierino Gallo building in Bocagrande. Also in this building are reputable jewellery shops. *H Stern* has a jewellery shop in the Pierino Gallo shopping centre and at the *Hilton Hotel*. Comercial Centro Getsemaní, C Larga between San Juan and Plaza de la Independencia, a large new shopping centre has many establishments. *Magali París*, Av Venezuela y C del Boquete, is an a/c supermarket, with cafetería. Good badges for backpacks from the shops along the wall of the old prison.

Markets: there is a new market out of town, which is disappointing; bus from Av Urdaneta Arbeláez. The fish market is in the SE suburbs of the old city.

● **Sports**
Bullfights and cockfights: the former take

place mainly in Jan and Feb in the new Plaza de Toros on Av Pedro de Heredia away from the centre; the old, wooden Plaza de Toros (no 27 on the map) is a fine structure, but is no longer in use. Cockfights are held throughout the year on Sat, Sun and holidays. On Sat and Mon at 1500 cockfighting takes place at the Gallerita Popular de la Quinta and on Sun at 1600 at Club Gallístico Pedro Rhenals in El Bosque.

Watersports: fishing; yachting. Windsurf rental, Bocagrande, US$6.50/hr. **Diving**: *Catagena Divers*, Marina Todomar, Cra 2 No 15-346, Bocagrande, T 665-4493, 2 dives inc all equipment US$60, also snack and drinks; *La Tortuga Dive Shop*, Edif Marina del Rey, 2-23 Av del Retorno, Bocagrande, T 665-6995, 2 dives US$70, faster boat, same price at Hotel Caribe Dive Shop. Recompression chamber at the naval hospital, Bocagrande.

● **Tourist offices**
Empresa Promotora de Turismo de Cartagena, Av Blas de Lezo, Ed Muelle de los Pegasos, T 665-1843; also in Parque Flanagan, Bocagrande, T 665-4987, and at the airport, who will call cheaper hotels (all 3 open 0700-1900 daily, allegedly). There is also a hotel reservations office at the airport but you will only be given information on the more expensive hotels. Town plan for US$0.20. CNT, Calle de la Factoría, Casa del Marqués de Valdehoyos, Cra 3, No 36-57, T 664-7015/9, open daily till 1730, US$0.25 to tour the house. For information T 113. Recommended guide, Fernando Vargas Osorio, C de Magdalena, No 7-52.

DAS: just beyond Castillo San Felipe, behind the church (ask), Plaza de la Ermita (Pie de la Popa), T 666-4649, helpful. DAS passport office is in C Castelbondo, near Plaza de la Artillería.

● **Transport**
Local Bus: within the city large buses (with no glass in windows) cost US$0.10, short-wheel-base type (with glass windows), US$0.25. **Car rental**: National and Hertz at airport; Avis at *Hilton Hotel*. **Taxis**: from Bocagrande to the centre should be less than US$1.50; for airport, see below. Try to fix price before committing yourself. A horse-drawn carriage can be hired for US$10, opp *Hotel El Dorado*, Av San Martín, in Bocagrande, to ride into town at night (romantic but rather short ride).

Air Crespo, 1½ km from the city, reached by local buses from Blas de Lezo, SW corner of inner wall. Bus from airport to Plaza San Francisco US$0.25. Taxi to Bocagrande US$2.45, to town US$1.55 (official prices). Tourist information desk gives list of taxi prices. Good self-service restaurant. No exchange facilities. Commuter flights to Barranquilla. SAM and Avianca (T 664-

4446) offices both in Plaza de la Aduana. From Dec to Mar all flights are overbooked – even reconfirming and turning up 2 hrs early doesn't guarantee a seat; don't book a seat on the last plane of the day.

Bus A new bus terminal opened in 1995, 30 mins from town, taxi US$1.50, or take city buses 'Terminal de Transportes', or 'Puzón'. Pullman bus from Cartagena to **Medellín** 665 km, US$30 (Brasilia, or Rápidos Ochoa, slightly cheaper, rec). Several buses a day, but book early (2 days in advance at holiday times), takes 13-16 hrs. The road is now paved throughout, but in poor condition. To **Santa Marta**, US$9.10 (with Brasilia, C 32, No 20D-55), 4 hrs, also cheaper lines, US$7.20. To **Barranquilla** US$2.75 with Transportes Cartagena, 3 hrs, or US$5 with Expreso Brasilia pullman or La Costeña, US$3.10, 2 hrs. To/from **Bogotá** via Barranquilla and Bucaramanga with Expreso Brasilia pullman or Copetran, eight a day, US$48, may take 21-28 hrs, depending on number of check-points. To **Magangué** on the Magdalena US$8.50, 4 hrs with Brasilia; to **Mompós**, Unitransco, 0530, 12 hrs inc ferry crossing from Magangué, US$9.50. To **Valledupar** with Expreso Brasilia, pullman US$10 (with a ½ hr stop in Barranquilla), for Sierra Nevada and Pueblo Bello. To **Riohacha**, US$12. Bus to **Maicao** on Venezuelan frontier US$16.75 (with Expreso Auto Pullman, Expreso Brasilia at 2000, or Unitrasco), 12 hrs; the road is in good condition, except for 30 km.

Shipping: there are modern wharves. It is possible to ship a car from Cartagena to Panama. For the new ferry service to Panama, see page 911. Two other companies which will ship vehicles to Panama: Hermann Schwyn, Edif Concasa, 10th floor, T 664-7450, and Mundinaves, Cra 53, No 64-72, of 301, T 645-4691. There are boats leaving most days for points S along the coast, for example to Turbo cargo boats take 24 hrs, all in cost about US$15 pp, and up the Ríor Sinú to Montería, and the Atrato as far as Quibdó. For the trip to Quibdó see page 947.

Environs of Cartagena

The little fishing village of **La Boquilla**, NE of Cartagena, is near the end of a sandy promontory between the Ciénaga de Tesca and the Caribbean, about 20 mins past the airport. A luxury hotel has been built nearby. Also **E** *Los Morros* (clean, good food) and campsite, good, clean, showers, restaurant and small market, tents rented with matresses. On Sat and Sun nights people dance the local dances. Go there by taxi, US$3 (there is a reasonable bus service. Visit the mangrove swamps nearby to see the birds.

Golf courses are under development here. On the coast, 50 km NE is Galera Zamba, no accommodation but good local food. Nearby are the clay baths of Volcán del Totumo, in beautiful surroundings.

ISLAS DEL ROSARIO

The National Park of **Corales del Rosario** embraces the archipelago of Rosario (a group of 30 coral islets 45 km SW of the Bay of Cartagena) and the mangrove coast of the long island of Baru to its furthest tip. Isla Grande and some of the smaller islets are easily accessible by day trippers and those who wish to stay in one of the hotels. Permits are needed for the rest, US$10. The islands represent part of a coral reef, low-lying, densely vegetated and with narrow strips of fine sand beaches. Rosario (the largest and best conserved) and Tesoro both have small lakes, some of which connect to the sea. There is an incredible profusion of aquatic and bird life. An Aquarium in the sea is worth visiting, US$3, not included in boat fares. Many of the smaller islets are privately owned.

Travel agencies and the hotels offer launch excursions from the Muelle Turístico, leaving 0800-0900 and returning 1600-1700, costing from US$10 to US$25, lunch included; free if staying at one of the hotels. Book in advance. Rec are Excursiones Roberto Lemaitre, C 8, No 4-66, Bocagrande, T 665-2872 (owner of *Club Isla del Pirata*). They have the best boats and are near the top end of the price range. *Yates Alcatraz* are more economical; enquire at the quay. Apart from fish and coconuts, everything is imported from the mainland, fresh water included. *Hotel del Caribe* in Bocagrande has scuba lessons in its pool followed by diving at Islas del Rosario, US$230 and up. Diving permit from MMA costs US$31.

● **Accommodation A2** *Club Isla del Pirata*, mainland booking office at C 8, No 4-66, Bocagrande, T 665-2873, F 665-2862, complex occupies a tiny islet in the archipelago. Room price pp inc meals, add 14% tax. **L3** *San Pedro de Majagua*, mainland office at Cra 5, No 8-59, Bocagrande, T 665-2745, F 665-2745, inside *Restaurant Capilla del Mar*, under the same ownership. Complex occupies part of Isla

Grande, in the Rosario archipelago. Price pp, inc meals. *Casa Blanca*, white with arched windows, former family home, converted to luxury 5-star hotel.

SOUTH OF CARTAGENA

The highway S towards Medellín goes through **Turbaco** (24 km; Botanical Garden, 1½ km before village on the left, student guides), **Malagana** (60 km; **G** *Res Margarita*, friendly, fan, basic) and **San Jacinto** (102 km; bus from Cartagena US$2.45), where local craft work, eg hand woven hammocks is made.

SINCELEJO

The capital of Sucre Department is a cattle centre 193 km S of Cartagena (*pop* 148,420). The town is hot, dusty and power cuts are common.

Beach excursions 20 mins from Sincelejo, on the coast is **Tolú** (several friendly *residencias*, D-F, and many fish stalls along the beach) for beaches, ask to be let off the bus. A good trip is by boat 3 hrs to Múcura island in the Islas de San Bernardo. If camping, take your own supplies. Trips to the mangrove lagoons also rec. There are better beaches at **Coveñas**, 20 mins further SW. (Accommodation: several *cabañas* on the beach and hotels.) W of Coveñas are beautiful beaches at Porvenir, no food available, afternoon buses infrequent. Tolú and Coveñas can be reached by turning off the main road at Ovejas, 40 km N of Sincelejo.

Local festivals The dangerous bull-ring game in Jan is similar to the San Fermín festivities in Pamplona, Spain, in which bulls and men chase each other. At Eastertime there is the 'Fiesta del Burro' where they dress up donkeys and prizes go to the best and the funniest. A big party for three days.

● **Accommodation B** *Marsella*, C 21, No 23-59, T 820729; **D** *Majestic*, Cra 20, No 21-25, T 821872; **D** *Ancor*, Cra 25, No 20A-45, T 821125; **E** *Panorama*, Cra 25, 23-108, a/c; **E** *Santander*, corner of Plaza Santander, with bath, balconies, good restaurant, *La Olla*, opp.

SOUTH OF SINCELEJO

The main road from Sincelejo passes **Planeta Rica** (127 km) and **Caucasia** (194 km), a convenient stopping place between Cartagena and Medellín. Visit the Jardín Botánico (entry US$0.25).

● **Accommodation** 11 km before Caucasia is *Parador Chambacú* (T 226946), with campsite; next door is the **C** *Mesón del Gitano* (T 94-328-1882); **F** *Residencia Bonaire*, good, quiet, clean, TV in lounge. **In Caucasia**: *Auto Hotel*, Cra 2, No 22-43, T 226355, best, quiet, heavily booked; **D** *Colonial*, Cra 2, No 20-68, T/F 822-7461, clean, pleasant, a/c, cheaper with fan, good view of river, rec for value; **E** *Residencias San Francisco*, Cra 49 y C 45, with bath, good value; **F** *Del Río*, with bath, clean, close to bus station, free morning coffee but avoid front rooms on street; **F** *Residencia El Viajero*, Cra 2, No 23-39, near centre, quiet, clean, ceiling fan; **G** *San Martín*, close to market.

● **Buses** To Medellín US$8.50, 7 hrs; to Cartagena US$16 (Brasilia), US$15 (Rápido Ochoa), US$10 (2nd class, 17 hrs).

50 km S of Caucasia is **Taraza** (**G** *Residencia Magdalena*, friendly, fan, basic but noisy bar). About half way between Caucasia and Medellín is **Valdivia** with a spectacular bridge over the Cauca. The road continues to Yarumal (see page 943).

MONTERIA

Montería (*municipal pop* 266,850), capital of Córdoba Department, on the E bank of the Río Sinú, can be reached from Cartagena by air, by river boat, or from the main highway to Medellín. (Bus from Cartagena – dual carriageway almost completed, US$11, 5 hrs, with Brasilia, has own terminal in Montería, or colectivo, US$10, also 5 hrs.) It is the centre of a cattle and agricultural area turning out tobacco, cacao, cotton and sugar. It has one fine church, picturesque street life and extremely friendly people. Average temperature: 28°C.

● **Accommodation A3** *Sinú*, Cra 3, C 31 y 32, T 823355, F 823980, a/c, swimming pool, TV, restaurant; **D** *Alcázar*, Cra 2, No 32-17, T 824900, comfortable, friendly, restaurant; **F** *Brasilia*, clean, friendly, good value; **F** *Residencias Imperial*, Cra 2; many cheap dives around.

ARBOLETES

67 km W of Montería, on the coast, is **Arboletes** a small quiet town with nearby mud lake of volcanic origins. You can 'swim' in the mud lake, then wash off in the ocean, 100m away.

● **Accommodation E** *Ganadero*, fan, bath, good beds; **E** *Aristi*, very clean but small windows; **F** *Julia*, on the main square, no private bathrooms. Other accommodation along the beach.

● **Places to eat** *Guido's* restaurant is probably the best.

● **Buses** 4 a day to Turbo, 5-6 hrs, US$5.40, 10 a day to Montería, 3 hrs, US$2.40.

An unmade road continues to Turbo (see below), **Chigorodó** (**F** *Residencial Tobi*, fan), **Dabeiba**, 186 km S of Turbo (**F** *Residencia Diana*, on main street, simple, clean, helpful), **Cañasgordas** (**G** *Doña Concha*, private bath, modern, good value), Antioquia (see page 943) and Medellín. Scenic, but a long, bumpy ride.

(see page 943)

COLOMBIA TO PANAMA

TURBO

On the Gulf of Urabá is the port of **Turbo**, now a centre of banana cultivation, which is booming. It is a rough frontier community, not too law-abiding.

● **Accommodation D** *Castillo de Oro*, best, reliable water and electricity, good restaurant; **D** *Playa Mar*, good, but somewhat run down; **D** *Sausa*, running water in early morning only, helpful owners, pleasant dining room; **F** *Residencia Sandra*, good; **F** *Residencia Turbo*, friendly, good; **F** *Residencia Marcela*, friendly, quiet, secure, best value; **G** *Residencia El Golfo*, friendly, good; in Playa district: *Miramar*, *Rotitom*, both **D**.

● **Banks & money changers** No banks are open for exchange of TCs on Mon or Tues; try exchanging money in stores.

● **Transport** Turbo may be reached from Cartagena and from Medellín (6 buses a day, a gruelling 17 hrs, US$12; to Montería, 8 hrs, US$9, bad road, several army checkpoints). Boats are available to Cartagena and up the Río Atrato to Quibdó, but you need plenty of time; services are intermittent and unreliable.

FRONTIER WITH PANAMA

There are various routes involving sea and

land crossings around or through the **Darién Gap**, which still lacks a road connection linking the Panamanian Isthmus and South America. Detailed descriptions of these routes are given in the *Mexico and Central American Handbook* (although in the direction Panama-Colombia). While maps of the region are available, there is no substitute for seeking informed local advice. In all cases, it is essential to be able to speak Spanish. See also **Notes and Cautions** below.

● **Colombian immigration**
DAS Office: at the Postadero Naval, Cra 13 between Cs 101 and 102, Turbo, open 0800-1630. If going from Colombia to Panama via Turbo you should get an exit stamp from the DAS office. There is also a DAS office in Capurganá (see below), opp *Hotel Uvita*, and a Panamanian consultate, but best not to leave it that late. If leaving Colombia, check the facts at any DAS office.

NB Colombian pesos are impossible to change at fair rates in Panama.

● **Entering Colombia**
Arriving from Panama, go to the DAS in Turbo for your entry stamp. Panamanian immigration at Puerto Obaldia is sometimes obstructive (all baggage will be checked for drugs, adequate funds for your stay may have to be shown – US$400, TCs or credit card; a ticket out of Panama is required, although a ticket from another Central American country may do).

NB If travelling from Panama to Colombia by coastal boat or land, we strongly advise you to aim for Turbo (or Buenaventura) and obtain your entry stamp from the DAS office there. Travellers who have requested entry stamps at other DAS offices have been fined or accused of illegal entry. A police stamp is no substitute.

● **Transport Colombia to Panama**
The simplest way is to fly from Barranquilla, Bogotá, Cali, Cartagena, Medellín or San Andrés. **Sea**: there is a ferry service from Cartagena (Terminal Marítimo on Manga Island, beyond the Muelle Turístico) to Colón (Cristóbal). The ship, the *Crucero Express* is operated by Promotora de Navegación SA of Panama City, subsidiary of Flota Mercante Grancolombiana. Sailings from Cartagena are Tues, Thur and Sun 1630 arriving the following morning at 1030. From Colón, Mon, Wed and Fri, same times. Prices are: US$75 pp for 4 people in a quadruple cabin (US$80 pp for 3), US$95 pp, 2 travellers, one way (one person min, US$135), inc cabin, 5-course dinner and breakfast, US$195 pp for a suite. Motor cycles US$50, cars US$125, with trailer US$180; bicycles free. Visa

and Mastercards accepted. This is a ro-ro ferry with disco, casino, jacuzzi, duty free etc, capacity for 1600 passengers and 400m of vehicle deck space (which could be over 200 cars but commercial vehicles and freight will also be carried). Latest information is that, so far, the passenger service is operating, but conditions for the transport of wheeled traffic have not been formally agreed by the two governments. Some cars and larger vehicles (eg campers) are being transported from Panama to Colombia. On arrival in Colombia, entry is straightforward, car registration, fumigation and customs no problem. Permit for 90 days granted if requested, no *carnet* or bond asked for, only passport and car ownership certificate. Also rec to stock up with film on board at US$4 for 36 exposures. For further information: T 286-3050 (Bogotá), reservations: T 342-1330, F 336-2714 (Bogotá), or T 660-7722 for information in Cartagena, or any major travel agent. In Panama City, reservations T 633322, F 633326.

On reputable cargo boats, arrange with the captain the price and destination before departure. Small, irregular boats may well be contraband or arms runners; if a passenger on one you will be in trouble if stopped and, even if not stopped, will have difficulty in obtaining the necessary entry stamp from DAS. Boats may be stopped outside Turbo for medical checks: yellow fever innoculations will be given (free) to all without a certificate.

CROSSING DARIEN: CARIBBEAN SIDE

On the Caribbean side, the starting point is Turbo from where boats sail to Acandí, 3 hrs, Capurganá and Zapzurro (all in Colombia) and Puerto Obaldía (Panama). **Acandí** (*pop* about 7,000), has several *residencias*, eg **F** *Central*, clean, safe; **G** *Pilar*, clean; **F** *Acandí*, OK. Most have their own electricity generators. A little further N is **Capurganá**, now a small tourist resort with several hotels: **B** *Calipso*, a/c, good facilities; **D** *Náutico*, cabins, clean and friendly; **E** *Uvita*, with bath, clean and safe, by harbour; and cheaper accommodation. Across the Panamanian border, **E** *Residencial Cande* in Pto Obaldía is good, with meals.

● **Transport** Boats normally leave Turbo at 0900 daily, US$25, via Capurganá. Enquire for the best passage. There are also cargo boats from Cartagena to Capurganá which take passengers, 30-50 rough hrs, US$25-30, take hammock. From Puerto Obaldía (see above on immigration), boats go to Colón, planes to Panama City (daily except Sun).

Overland from Puerto Obaldía This involves a 4 hr walk to the foot of the Darién range (guide essential, US$10), crossing the hills to the Río Tuquesa (3 hrs) and following the river downstream with a great many crossings and one night camping out, to Maranganti (immigration post). From here a dugout can be taken to B Vigía; walk to the next village, Villa Calleta (take care with directions on this stretch). From Villa Calleta you walk along the Río Chucucanaque to join the Yaviza-Panama City road near La Pinita. Note that locals on this route are very wary of foreigners (much illegal immigration).

Overland from Turbo Two main alternative routes cross the central Gap to Paya, from where there is a well-trodden route to Yaviza: Paya-Pucuro, 6 hrs on foot; Púcuro-Boca de Cupe, by dugout,

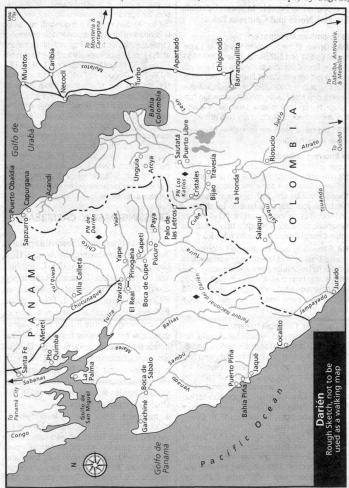

Darién
Rough Sketch, not to be used as a walking map

US$20-50; Boca de Cupe-Pinogana, also by dugout, US$15 pp, plus a walk, 2 hrs in all; Pinogana-Yaviza, walk and ferries/dugouts. From Yaviza (one hotel, **E** *Tres Américas*, basic) buses can be caught to Panama City, US$15, 10-14 hrs, road subject to wash-outs.

One route to Paya: take a boat from Turbo across the Gulf of Urabá into the Río Tarena to **Unguía**, **F** *Residencias Viajero*, with bath; **G** *Doña Julia*, also with bath. Also basic restaurants. From here it is 3-4 hrs to the frontier, then 3 hrs to the Río Paya. You then hike down the Río Paya through dense jungle to Paya itself (about 12 hrs). Do not attempt the Unguía-Paya route without a guide.

The other main route to Paya: motorboat from Turbo across the Bahía de Colombia, through the Great Atrato Swamp and up the Río Atrato, with much birdlife to be seen (US$10 if scheduled, US$130 to hire a boat). At Travesía, also called Puente América, at the confluence of the Río Cacarica, you can buy limited provisions. There is a restaurant and rooms to stay in Travesía. From Travesía you go by another boat to Bijao (3 hrs, up to US$120). **NB** Both Travesía and Bijao are very expensive places to buy supplies, but worse still they have become anti-gringo (1994); we have been told of robbery by officials. From Bijao you have to get by boat to Cristales in the Los Katios National Park; the Inderena rangers may take you for up to US$100 per boat. At Cristales there is an Inderena hut; 7-8 hrs through the Park on foot is Palo de las Letras, the frontier stone, from where it is 4-6 hrs to Paya. A guide is strongly recommended. It is best to take two days for this section. You can approach this route from Quibdó down the Río Atrato to Travesía (see Section 6). Get your Panamanian entry stamp in Boca de Cupe, Púcuro or Yaviza (enquire: it can be very difficult to get an entry stamp anywhere before Panama City on this route; try at every opportunity as hikers have been detained in the capital for not having an entry stamp. It may help to prove you have adequate funds for your stay). Between Travesía and Yaviza there are some walking alternatives to taking river boats, detailed in the *Mexico and Central America Handbook*.

LOS KATIOS NATIONAL PARK

To visit the park, go first to the MMA office in Turbo, where all necessary information is available. The office is 1 km along the road to Medellín. Because of violence and guerrilla activity in the region, MMA discourages entry; if you insist you must sign a disclaimer.

The Katios National Park, extending in Colombia to the Panamanian border, contains several waterfalls: Tilupo, 125m high; the water cascades down a series of rock staircases, surrounded by orchids and fantastic plants. This is 6 hrs return trip. A 5 hr trip passing through splendid jungle is required for two other fine waterfalls, the Salto de La Tigra and Salto de La Tendal. A full day's hike is recommended to Alto de Limón for a fine view of primary forest. You can stay overnight in a hut. Also in the park are the Alto de la Guillermina, a mountain behind which is a strange forest of palms called "mil pesos", and the Ciénagas de Tumaradó, with red monkeys, waterfowl and alligators.

- **Park information** The National Park can be reached by boat from Turbo most days, charging US$8. The boats, normally going up the Atrato to Riosucio, or beyond, will leave you at the MMA headquarters of the Park in Sautatá. Ask in Turbo harbour when they are leaving. You should have a permit from MMA in Turbo for the Park, or you can pay in the park. Arrange your return trip Sautatá – Turbo with the park guide at Sautatá beforehand. Boats do not normally stop. The Park can be visited with mules from the MMA headquarters in Sautatá (cabins US$5.50 pp, or rangers may offer free space for your hammock, very friendly). Food can be ordered half a day in advance.

CROSSING DARIEN: PACIFIC SIDE

On the Pacific side, crossing into Panama involves travel by both boat and on foot, the quantity of each depending on the route chosen.

- **Transport** One sea route is from Bahía Solanó (see page 949) or Juradó in Chocó Department. Canoes go from both towns to Jaqué, 50 km N of the Colombian border (Juradó-Jaqué

1½ hrs, US$20), from where you can take a boat to Panamá City, US$12, 12 hrs, or fly, US$37 or fly to La Palma, capital of Darién in Panama (one *pensión* F, English spoken). Launches and dugouts go from La Palma to Puerto Lardo on the Río Sabanas, from where it is a 2 hr walk (or hitch on a truck) to Santa Fe on the Panamá-Yaviza road. (Bus Santa Fe-Panamá 6-8 hrs; flight with Parsa, T Panamá 26-3883/3808, La Palma – Panama City 3 times a week). Alternatively from La Palma take a boat to Puerto Quimba, then transport to Metetí, from where a bus can be taken to Panama City.

Juradó can be reached by plane from Turbo, or overland from Riosucio by the Trans-Isthmus route, using both boat and walking (30-36 hrs in all). Serious advance planning is essential, although the Trans-Isthmus route is well-trodden by local traders (legal or otherwise). The Embera and Wounan Indians encountered en route are wary, but hospitable. Besides the boat Jurado-Jaqué, there is an overland route involving at least one night camping between Santa Teresita (Wounan village, Colombia) and Mamey (Embera, Panama), detailed local instructions are essential. Transport out of Jaqué is frustrating; you must obtain a DAS stamp in either Turbo or Buenaventura, without it you will have problems in Jaqué or Panama City.

Notes and cautions

We have heard of a number of routes successfully attempted across the land frontier. Well-equipped groups using local paths and information, armed with compass and machete, can more-or-less make their own way. However, accident or illness could be very serious, much of the area is sparsely inhabited, and getting lost is usually fatal.

Anyone considering crossing the Darién Gap overland should bear in mind that the area is becoming less safe because of drug trafficking, banditry and guerrilla activity on both sides of the border, but especially in Colombia (as far into the country as Turbo). The New Tribes Mission, after the kidnap of 3 missionaries, has withdrawn its staff from the area, thus removing one of a travellers' main sources of assistance. Follow these points of advice: 1) travel only in the dry season; 2) travel with a reliable companion or two; 3) hire at least one Indian guide, but do it through the village *corregidor*, whose involvement may add to the reliability of the guide he selects (budget up to US$12/day per guide and his food); 4) travel light and move fast.

Dr Richard Dawood, author of *Travellers' Health: How to Stay Healthy Abroad*, and photographer Anthony Dawton, crossed the Darien Gap at the end of the wet season (Nov). We include an abbreviated version of Dr Dawood's health recommendations for such a journey: **Heat** Acclimatization to a hot climate usually takes around 3 weeks. It is more difficult in humid climates than in dry ones, since sweat cannot evaporate easily, and when high humidity persists through the night as well, the body has no respite. Requirements for salt and water increase dramatically under such conditions. We had to drink 12 litres per day to keep pace with our own fluid loss on some parts of the trip.

In hot countries it is always essential to drink beyond the point of thirst quenching, and to drink sufficient water to ensure that the urine is consistently pale in colour.

Salt losses also need to be replaced. Deficiency of salt, water, or both, is referred to as heat exhaustion; lethargy, fatigue, and headache are typical features, eventually leading to coma and death. Prevention is the best approach: add salt to all fluids, one quarter of a level teaspoon (approx 1 gram) per pint – to produce a solution that is just below the taste threshold. Salt tablets, however, are poorly absorbed, irritate the stomach and may cause vomiting.

Sun Overcast conditions in the tropics can be misleading. The sun's rays can be fierce, and it is important to make sure that all exposed skin is constantly protected with a high factor sun screen – preferably waterproof for humid conditions. A hat is also essential.

Food and water Much caution is needed with food hygiene to prevent diarrhoea. Carry your own supplies and prepare them carefully. In the villages, oranges, bananas and coconuts were available. The freshly baked bread is safe, as is the rice.

Purify water with 2 per cent tincture of iodine carried in a small plastic dropping bottle, 4 drops to each litre – more when the water is very turbid – wait 20 mins before drinking. This method is safe and effective. Alternatively, use a water purifying pump based on a ceramic filter. There are several on the market, eg Katadyn. It takes about a minute to purify a litre of water. When water is cloudy, eg after rain, pumps are less effective and harder work. It is worth travelling with a suitable antidiarrhoeal medication such as Arret.

Malaria Drug resistant malaria is present in the Darien area, and antimalarial medication is essential. Free advice on antimalarial medication for all destinations is available from the Malaria Reference Laboratory, T 0891-600-350 in the UK. An insect repellent is essential, and so are precautions to avoid insect bites.

Insects Beside malaria and yellow fever, other insect-borne diseases such as dengue fever and leishmaniasis may pose a risk. The old fashioned mosquito net is ideal if you have to sleep outdoors, or in a room that is not mosquito-proof. An insecticide spray is valuable for clearing your room of flying insects before you go to sleep, and mosquito coils that burn through the night giving off an insecticidal vapour, are also valuable.

Ticks The currently favoured method of removing ticks is to ease the head gently away from the skin with tweezers.

Vaccinations A yellow fever vaccination certificate is required from all travellers arriving from infected areas, and vaccination is advised for personal protection.

Immunization against hepatitis A (with gammaglobulin) and typhoid are strongly advised.

Attacks by dogs are relatively common: the new rabies vaccine is safe and effective, and carrying a machete for the extra purpose of discouraging animals (and warding off snakes) is advised.

In addition, all travellers should be protected against tetanus, diptheria and polio.

You can get some food along the way, but take enough for at least 5 days. Do take, though, a torch/flashlight, and a bottle of rum, or present of equal worth for the ranger at Cristales.

Wet season travel is not impossible, but with heavy rain every afternoon, the rivers are full and dangerous, and there is mud beyond belief making progress painfully slow.

NORTHEAST FROM CARTAGENA

The main Cartagena-Barranquilla road goes via Sabanalarga (50 km before Barranquilla) and Baranoa. From here a branch road runs to Usicurí (72 km from Barranquilla), known for its medicinal waters and for the grave of the popular Colombian poet, Julio Flores. A spectacular new bridge over the Río Magdalena gives a fine view of Barranquilla and the river.

BARRANQUILLA

Barranquilla (*pop* 1.09 million; *phone code* 058), is Colombia's fourth city. It lies on the western bank of the Río Magdalena, about 18 km from its mouth, which, through deepening and the clearing of silted sandbars, makes it a seaport (though less busy than Cartagena or Santa Marta) as well as a river port.

Places of interest

Barranquilla is a modern industrial city with a dirty, colourful, polluted central area near the river, and a good residential area in the NW, beyond C 53. The principal boulevard is **Paseo Bolívar**; there is a handsome church, **San Nicolás**, formerly the Cathedral, in Plaza San Nicolás, the central square, and before it stands a small statue of Columbus. The new **Catedral Metropolitana** is at Cra 45, No 53-120, opposite Plaza de la Paz. There is an impressive statue of Christ inside by the Colombian sculptor, Arenas Betancourt. The commercial and shopping districts are round the Paseo Bolívar, a few blocks N of the old Cathedral, and in C Murillo. The colourful and vivid **market** is between Paseo Bolívar and the river, the so-called Zona Negra on a side channel of the Magdalena. Good parks in the northern areas include **Parque Tomás Suri Salcedo** on C 72. Stretching back into the northwestern heights overlooking the city are the modern suburbs of El Prado, Altos del Prado, Golf and Ciudad Jardín, with *El Prado Hotel*. There are five stadia in the city, a big covered coliseum for sports, two for football and the others cater for basketball and baseball. The metropolitan stadium is on Av Murillo, outside the city.

Museum

Small **archaeological** collection, C 68 No 53-45 (Mon-Fri 0900-1200, 1400-1700), with big physical relief map on front lawn. Also, **Museo Romántico**, Cra 54, No 59-199, history of Barranquilla.

Zoo

There is a well-maintained zoo with some animals not often seen in zoos, but many are in small cages, C 77, Cra 68 (bus "Boston/Boston" or "Caldes/Recreo"), entrance US$0.60, 0830-1200, 1400-1800. All the trees are labelled.

Excursions

Regular buses from Paseo Bolívar and the church at C 33 y Cra 41 to the attractive bathing resort of **Puerto Colombia**, 19 km (US$0.60, ½ hr). Beach clean and sandy, water a bit muddy. South along the Magdalena to the little town of Palmar de Varela. On this road, 5 km from the city, is the old colonial town of **Soledad** (*pop* 16,000). The cathedral and the old narrow streets round it are worth seeing.

Local festivals

Carnival, lasting four days, parades, floats, street dancing and beauty contests.

Local information

● **Accommodation**

L2 *El Prado*, best, the social centre, swimming pool and tennis courts, good restaurant, sauna, original 1920s building is national monument, new annex behind, some distance from the centre (Cra 54, No 70-10, T 456533, F 450095); **L3** *Dann Barranquilla*, Cra 51B, No 79-246, T 560731, F 455079, highrise, in smart residential Altos del Prado; **L3** *Puerta del Sol*, C 75, NO 41D-79, T 456144, F 455550, totally refurbished.

B *Royal*, Cra 54, No 68-124, T 453058, good service, with swimming pool, modern; **B** *Apartotel*, Cra 44, No 70-242, T 561213, a/c, parking, large rooms.

C *Capricornio*, Cra 44B, No 70-201, T 340244/565045, very clean, good service, with bath, a/c.

D *Canadiense*, C 45, No 36-142, fan, shower, noisy but convenient for bus station 2 blocks away; **D** *Villa Venecia*, C 61, No 46-41, T 414107, clean, TV, a little noisy but rec.

E *Victoria*, C 35, No 43-140, downtown, large, scruffy rooms with fan; **E** *Diplomático*, Cra 38, No 42-60, with private bath, fan, TV room, washing facilities, cafeteria.

F *Horizonte*, C 45 y Cra 44, with bath, clean, quiet, fan; **F** *California*, C 32 y Cra 44, pleasant but about to fall down, enjoy the chickens. **NB** Hotel prices may be much higher during Carnival. Watch for thieves in downtown hotels.

● **Places to eat**

La Puerta de Oro, C 35, No 41-100, central, a/c good for meals (inc breakfast); *El Huerto*, Cra 52, No 70-139, good vegetarian; *Jardines de Confucio*, Cra 54, No 75-44, good Chinese food, nice atmosphere; various Lebanese with belly-dancers; several Chinese and *pizzerias*. Many places, for all tastes and budgets, on C 70 from *Hotel El Prado* towards Cra 42; at C 70 y 44B are several *estaderos*, bars with snacks and verandas.

● **Banks & money changers**

Banco Anglo Colombiano, C 34, No 44-43, and 3 agencies; Banco Internacional de Colombia, cash against Mastercard. *Casa de cambio* El Cacique, C 34, No 43-108, T 326392, reliable.

● **Embassies & consulates**

Venezuelan, C 70, No 53-74 (Centro Financiero El Prado, 4° piso), T 580048/582832, 0800-1500 (take "Caldas/Recreo" or "Boston/Boston" bus), visa issued same day, but you must be there by 0915 with photo and US$30 cash; onward ticket may not be requested; US, Centro Comercial Mayorista, C 77, No 68-15, opposite zoo (Apdo Aéreo 51565), T 457088 or 457181 (visas obtainable only in Bogotá); British, Cra 44, No 45-57, T 326936; German, C 80, near Vía 40 (ask for Herr Schnabel); Norwegian, C 72, No 57-33, T 581043; Dutch, Cra 42H, No 85-33, T 341282; Spanish, C 51, No 37-64, T 313694; Finnish, Vía 40 de las Flores, Cementos del Caribe, T 350080.

● **Post & telecommunications**

Post Office: in Plaza Bolívar.

● **Shopping**

Bookshop: *Librería Nacional*, Cra 53, No 75-129, English, French and German books. Maps from Instituto Agustín Codazzi, C 36, No 45-101.

Market: San Andrecito, or "Tourist Market", Vía

40, is where smuggled goods are sold at very competitive prices; a good place to buy film: Picturesque and reasonably safe. Any taxi driver will take you there.

● **Tour companies & travel agents**
Tierra Mar Aire, AMEX agent, C 74, No 52-34, very helpful for flights to Central America.

● **Tourist offices**
Tourist information at main hotels and at C 72, No 57-43, of 401, T 454458 or 336658. CNT is at Cra 54, No 75-45, T 454458.

● **Useful addresses**
DAS: C 54, Cra 43.
Police: (for declarations of theft, etc), Policia F2, C 47 y Cra 43.

● **Transport**
Local Taxis: within the town cost US$1.25 (eg downtown to northern suburbs).

Air Ernesto Cortissoz airport is 10 km from the city. City bus from airport to town, US$0.15 (US$0.20 on Sun). Taxi to town, US$4.50 (taxis do not have meters, fix fare in advance). To town, take only buses marked "*centro*" from 200m to right when leaving airport; the bus to the airport (marked Malambo) leaves from Cra 44 up C 32 to Cra 38, then up C 30 to Airport. Taxi to Cartagena, US$40. Avianca (C 72, No 57-79, T 454355).

Warnings When leaving by air for the USA, you may be searched by drug squad police; they are very civil, but acquisitive – check your belongings afterwards.

Ship See Warning under Cartagena (page 905) regarding jobs and passages aboard ship. If shipping a car into Barranquilla allow 2 days to complete all paperwork to retrieve your car from the port, unless you have a *carnet de passages*, which opens all doors and dispenses with all other paperwork.

Bus Most bus companies operate from C 34 and Cra 45 (Brasilia and Copetran at C 45 y Cra 35: Brasilia links all N coast towns and S as far as Bogotá, rec a/c buses). To **Santa Marta**, US$3.25, Pullman (less in non-a/c, Coolibertador), about 2 hrs, also direct to Santa Marta's Rodadero beach; to **Valledupar**, 4½ hrs, US$6; to **Montería**, US$11, 8 hrs; to **Medellín** by Pullman, 16 hrs; to **Bucaramanga**, US$18 with Copetran, a/c, first class, departures at 1130 most days, 9 hrs; to **Bogotá**, 20-24 hrs, US$25 direct; to **Caucasia**, US$10.75, 11 hrs. To **Maicao**, US$7.80, 5 hrs (with Brasilia, every ½ hr from 0100-1200); to **Cartagena**, 3 grades of bus, 3 hrs (US$2.75 with Transportes Cartagena, US$5 with Expreso Brasilia, by Brasilia Van Tours mini-bus, from their downtown offices as well as the bus terminals), 2 hrs by colectivo, US$3.10.

SANTA MARTA

Santa Marta (*municipal pop* 279,960) is the capital of Magdalena Department. The third Caribbean port, it is 96 km E of Barranquilla, at the mouth of the Río Manzanares. It is best reached from Barranquilla by the paved road along the coast, which passes salt pans and skirts an extensive and most interesting lagoon, the Ciénaga de Santa Marta (see below). There is a paved road S to Bucaramanga (see page 893) and Bogotá.

Santa Marta lies on a deep bay with high shelving cliffs. The climate ranges seasonally from hot and trying to hot but pleasant in Feb and Mar; occasionally one can see snow-clad peaks of the Sierra Nevada to the E, less than 50 km away and 5,800m high. The city's promenade offers good views of the bay and is lined with restaurants, accommodation and nightlife, not of very high quality. The main shops and banks are on Cra 5.

History

Santa Marta was the first town founded (1525) by the *conquistadores* in Colombia. Founder: Rodrigo de Bastidas. Most of the famous sea-dogs – the brothers Côte, Drake and Hawkins – sacked the city in spite of the two forts built on a small island at the entrance to the bay. It was here that Simón Bolívar, his dream of Gran Colombia shattered, came to die. Almost penniless he was given hospitality at the *hacienda* of San Pedro Alejandrino, see below. He died on 17 December 1830, at the age of 47, and was buried in the Cathedral, but his body was taken to the Pantheon at Caracas 12 years later.

Beaches

Sandy beaches stretch from the Simón Bolívar airport to Punta Aguja across the Rodadero de Gaira and the little fishing villages of Villa Concha, surrounded by meadows and shady trees, and Taganga (see below). A jutting rock – the Punta de Betín – rises from the sea in front of the city and is topped by a lighthouse. Rugged Isla del Moro, 3 km off Santa Marta, completes the panorama. Playa El Rodadero is the most fashionable and tourist-ori-

Santa Marta

Main Streets Only

0   150
metres

Punta
de Betin

Isla
El Morro

Bahía de
Santa Marta

Terminal
Maritimo

To
Taganga

Calle 5

Cra 5

Cra 9

Cra 10

Cra 11

Calle 7

Cra 1

Cra 3

Calle 8

Calle 9

Customs

Casa de la
Aduana
Museum

Cra 2

Calle 11

Parque
Bolívar

Convento de
Santo Domingo
& Tourist Office

Avianca

Cathedral

Cra 7

(M)

(S)

Calle 14

Calle 15

Parque
Santander

Calle 18

Parque San
Miguel

Cra 8

Calle 20

Calle 22

Cra 12

Av de Bastidas

N

Calle 24

To
Rodadero,
Airport &
Ciénaga

Av Bavaria

To
Riohacha &
PN Tairona

Hotels:
1. Andrea Doria
2. Residencias Miramar
3. Sompallón
4. Yuldama

ented part of Santa Marta, though it lies some distance W of the city (local bus service, taxi, US$1.80). Many of the buses coming from Barranquilla and Cartagena stop at Rodadero on the way to Santa Marta. There is also a dirty, unsafe beach with a seaside promenade close to the centre of town.

Museums

Casa de la Aduana, C 14 y Cra 2, displays an excellent archaeological collection, including a large number of precolombian gold artefacts; visit strongly recommended before going to Ciudad Perdida. Open Tues-Sat, 0800-1200, 1400-1800, Sun 0800-1200, during the tourist season, Mon-Fri, 0800-1200, 1400-1800, the rest of the year; entry US$1.

Quinta de San Pedro Alejandrino, 5 km SE of the city: the simple room in which Simón Bolívar died with a few of his belongings can be seen, and other paintings and memorabilia of the period are on display. Entrance US$2.50, open daily 0900-1700; take a bus or colectivo from the waterfront, Cra 1 C, to Mamatoca and ask to be dropped off at the Quinta, US$0.25.

Tours

Tours in air-conditioned jeeps run by Airline travel agency at centre. Launches leave Rodadero beach every hour for the Aquarium, modest, not as good as the one at Islas del Rosario, US$3 return (includes admission). From the Aquarium, one can walk (10 mins) to the Playa Blanca where one can swim in less crowded conditions than elsewhere – food available at the beach. Small

Indian figures are sculptured at José Pertuz, C 38, up the hill beyond Cra 17. They cut stone with traditional instruments and will chisel animals etc to order. They are sold on Rodadero beach. Punta Betín, behind harbour, marine eco-system research centre run by Colombian and German universities. Ask for details at the Tourist Office.

Local information
● **Warning**

The N end of town, beyond the railway station, and areas near, especially S of, Rodadero beach are very dangerous and travellers are advised not to go there alone. If you arrive by bus, beware taxi drivers who take you to a hotel of their choice, not yours. Also beware of 'jungle tours', or 'boat trips to the islands' sold by street touts.

● **Accommodation**

In town. Av Rodrigo de Bastidas (Cra 1) has several seaside holiday hotels while Cra 2 and connecting Cras have many budget *residencias* in our E range. **B** *Yuldama*, Cra 1, No 12-19, T 210063, clean, probably best in the city, a/c, reasonable food.

D *Bermuz*, C 13, No 5-16, T 210004. F 213625, good, clean, also good vegetarian restaurant; **D** *Costa Azul*, C 17, No 2-09, T 232036, with bath and shower, some rooms with a/c, clean, fan, windows into courtyard, very friendly, rec; **D** *Saratoga*, C 11, No 2-29, T 210644, a/c, less with fan, average, plain; **D** *Sompallón*, Cra 1, No 1 B-57, T 237195, modern, with *pizzería* and *casa de cambio*; **D** *Hostal Yuldama*, C 12, No 2-70, T 230057, a/c, cheaper without, modern, plain, safe deposit, clean, rec; **D** *Tairona*, Cra 1, No 11-41, T 32408, with fan, bath, friendly, no frills, not too secure

E *Residencia Park Hotel*, Cra 1C, No 18-67, T 37215, on sea front, with shower, fan, reasonable, friendly, phone, popular with young Colombians; **E** *Residencial Familiar*, C 10 C No 2-14, bath, very friendly, clean family-run, good breakfast, cooking facility, highly rec; **E** *Hotel Residencias Yarimar*, Cra 1A, No 26-37, clean, fan, noisy; **E** *Residencia Nueva Granada*, C 12, No 3-19, clean, large courtyard, quiet; **E** *Residencias Altamar*, C 10C, No 1C-68, friendly, safe; **E** *Andrea Doria*, C 18, No 1C-90, T 234329, clean, friendly with bath and fan; **E** *Residencias Bahía Blanca*, Cra 1, No 11-13, T 234439, private shower, friendly, clean, will store luggage; **E** *Residencia Jomar*, Cra 2, No 18-22, fan, quiet, will store luggage, clean.

F *Miramar*, C 10C, No 1C-59, "gringo hotel", tends to be crowded, robberies have often been reported, and be warned this is a dump, its popularity only because it is cheap, motorbike parking, restaurant, 2 blocks from railway station and beach, can arrange trips (not to be confused with **D** *Hotel Residencias Miramar*, Cra 1C, No 18-23, a/c, clean, tidy, holiday hotel opp is *Altamar*, cheap, safe, no drugs, nice atmosphere.

Youth Hostel: *Hotel Nabusimake*, details from Alcom in Bogotá.

At Rodadero Bay: **L2** *Irotama*, Km 14, between airport and Rodadero Bay, T 218021, all inclusive, has bungalows; **A2** *Arhuaco*, Cra 2, No 6-49, T 227234, 200m from beach, quiet, pool, bar; **A2** *Santamar* (Travelodge), 8 km from Rodadero towards airport, price is pp all inclusive (about half the price low season), T 218486, or 1-800-255-3050 toll free; **A2** *Tamacá*, Cra 2, No 11A-98, T 227015, direct access to beach, fair rooms, good service, fine pool.

C *La Riviera*, Cra 2, No 5-42, Apdo Aéreo 50-69, small, clean, safe, a/c; **C** *Residencias Edmar*, Cra 3, No 5-188, T 227874, a/c, clean, cafetería, welcoming; **D** *Valladolid*, Cra 2, No 5-67, T 227465, good value, large clean rooms, helpful, rec.

● **Motels**

D *El Rodadero*, C 11, No 1-29, T 227262, swimming pool, English-speaking manageress, very helpful.

● **Places to eat**

Yarimar, Cra 1A, No 26-37, next to hotel of same name, good seafood; *El Gran Wah Yuen*, C 14, No 3-74, good Chinese *à la carte* and *comida corriente*, plenty of fresh vegetables. *Cafetería del Calle*, Cra 3A, No 16-26, good *empanadas*. Restaurant opposite Telecom (C 13, Cra 5), good menu and vegetarian dishes.

At Rodadero there are a number of good restaurants, some pricey, some good value; there are also very good juice kiosks along the sea-front.

● **Banks & money changers**

Change money at **Banco de Occidente**, good rates for Mastercard. **Banco Industrial Colombiano**, C 13 y Cra 5 for Amex TC exchange, but in am only. **Amex** office Tierra del Mar, C 15, No 2-60, T 33497. Casas de cambio in 3rd block of C 14, many others on this street. In Rodadero, Apto 201, Cra 1, No 9-23. Santa Marta is a good place to change pesos with Venezuelan bolívares.

● **Laundry**

Lavandería Paraíso, C 14, No 8C-47.

● **Sports**

Diving: diving shops operate at Rodadero: *Buceo y Salvamento*, Edif Libertador, Cra 2 y C8

local 13, 2nd floor, T 228179, 2 dives US$44 inc equipment; *Tienda de Buceo*, C10 y Cra 2, Ed Playa Blanca, local 3, sells good equipment, but for trips sends you to *Pro-Buzos de Colombia*, C14 No 9-170, Santa Marta, T 236383, 2 dives US$55, PADI certification US$150. There are many dive shops in Taganga: *Scuba Sport*, Apdo 1275, T 217228, English and German spoken, offers bed and breakfast, 2 dives US$50; *Oceano Scuba Club*, Frente a la Playa, T 230325 (also at Carrera 44 No 70-56, Barranquilla, T 340857); *Centro de Buceo*, C 12, No 232422, 2 dives US$45, English spoken. You must check that a fully qualified dive master is present.

● **Tourist offices**

Tourist office in the former Convent of Santo Domingo, now Casa de Cultura, Cra 2, No 16-44, T 35773, open office hours Mon-Fri (has library and art exhibitions). There is also an office at Rodadero, C 10, No 3-10. **MMA** office, C 12, No 16D-05, T 203116, F 204506, Urb Riascos, and at the Quinta de San Pedro Alejandrino. **Turcol** which arranges trips (details in text) also at Cra 1, No 22-77. **DAS Office**, corner of C 27 y Cra 8.

● **Transport**

Air Simón Bolívar, 20 km from city; bus, US$0.25, taxi from Santa Marta US$8.50, from Rodadero, US$3. During the tourist season, get to the airport early and book well ahead. Avianca, Cra 3A, No 17-09, T 34958.

Bus Terminal S of the city, towards Rodadero, taxi US$1.50 to centre, minibus US$0.30. To/from **Bogotá**, 22 hrs, US$41.50, 4 a day; coming from the capital check that if the bus is continuing to Barranquilla, you will be dropped in Santa Marta, not short of it. Copetran to **Bucaramanga** about 9 hrs (US$18). Journey time will be affected by the number of police checks. There is a good meal stop at Los Límites. Buses to **Barranquilla**, 2 hrs (US$3.25); to **Cartagena**, 4 hrs (US$7.20, or US$9.10, Brasilia). To Riohacha US$3.45, 3 hrs to **Maicao**, US$9 a/c at 0500, also cheaper non a/c, 4-5 hrs. There are 3 buses a day (Brasilia) direct to **Rodadero Beach** from Barranquilla, taking 2 hrs and costing US$1.80. They return to Barranquilla at 1300, 1530 and 1730.

Port Without a *carnet de passages*, it can take up to 4 working days to get a car out of the port, but it is usually well guarded and it is unlikely that anything will be stolen. (See also under **Motorcycles** in **Information for travellers**.)

CIENAGA DE SANTA MARTA

All types of water birds, plants and animals may be seen in this large lagoon. Cutting off the egress to the sea to build the coast road caused an ecological disaster. A National Environment Programme, funded with the help of IDB, is working to reopen the canals and restore the area's fish and vegetation. On the E shore of the lagoon is **Ciénaga** (*pop* 75,000 – see **Music and Dance** for festival). Cotton, bananas, tobacco and cacao are grown in the area. Hotels in Ciénaga: *Tobiexe*; *Naval*.

Aracataca, 60 km S of Ciénaga and 7 km before Fundación, is the birthplace of Gabriel García Márquez, fictionalized as Macondo in some of his stories (notably *Cien años de soledad*). His home, called a museum, may be seen in the backyard of La Familia Iriarte Ahumada; ask for directions. There are *residencias* (**G**), but it is better to stay in **Fundación**. Banana growing in the area has now been replaced almost entirely by African palm plantations.

● **Accommodation** *Caroli*, Cra 8, No 5-30, best; **F** *Fundación* (E with a/c); **E** *Centro del Viajero*, with a/c, good value; others in this price range.

● **Buses** Ciénaga-Fundación, US$1; Fundación-Aracataca, US$0.20; an all weather road W from Fundación goes to Salmina on the Río Magdalena, ferry to Puerto Giraldo 0500-1800, then road to Sabanalarga, bus Fundación-Barranquilla, US$4.20.

TAGANGA

Close to Santa Marta (minibus US$0.30, taxi US$2.50, 10 mins) is the fishing village and beach of **Taganga**. Swimming good, especially on Playa Grande, 25 mins' walk round coast, but thieving is common there. Taganga is quiet during week, but trippers from Santa Marta pour in on Sun.

● **Accommodation** **A3** *La Ballena Azul*, most attractive, friendly, comfortable, clean, restaurant, also run boat tours to secluded beaches, ask Mauricio about tours, horses for hire (postal address Apartado Aéreo 799, Santa Marta, Telex 38886 CCSMT CO, or Bogotá T 2178606). **B** *Bahía*, C 2, No 1-35, T 217620, overlooking bay, breakfast served on balcony, clean, friendly; **D** *Playa Brava*, fan or a/c, quiet, basic beds; **E** *El Delfín*, fan, basic. Joselito Guerra on the beach, **G** for hammock space, may charge for use of kitchen, secure for luggage; rent houses on beach (not secure). Restaurants expensive, but a good one is *Tibisay*, seafood.

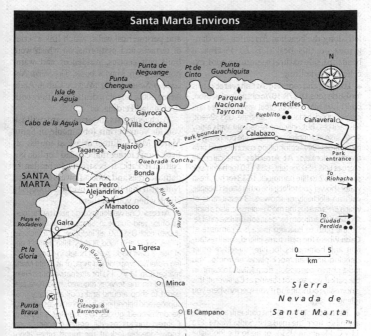

Santa Marta Environs

TAYRONA NATIONAL PARK

The park extends from N of Taganga for some 85 km along the coast. The wild coastal woodland is beautiful and mostly unspoilt. You will see monkeys, iguanas and maybe snakes. In the wet, the paths arc very slippery. **NB** Tayrona park was closed for part of 1995 because of water shortages. Check with MMA in Santa Marta before visiting.

The entrance is at the E end of the park, 35 km from Santa Marta, it opens at 0800 (entry US$10). If you arrive earlier, you may be able to pay at the car park just before **Cañaveral**, 1 hr's walk into the park from the gate. 40 mins W of Cañaveral on foot is **Arrecifes**, from where it is 15 mins' walk to Rancho Viejo, then 1½ hrs on a clear path to the archaeological site of **Pueblito**. A guided tour around the site is free, every Sat or as arranged, with a park guard. Other Tayrona relics abound. At Pueblito there are Indians; do not photograph them. From Pueblito you can either return to

Cañaveral, or continue for 2 hrs to Calabazo on the Santa Marta-Riohacha road. A circuit Santa Marta, Cañaveral, Arrecifes, Pueblito, Calabazo, Santa Marta in one day is arduous, needing a 0700 start at least.

It is advisable to inform park guards when walking in the park. Wear hiking boots and beware of bloodsucking insects. Take your own food and water, but no valuables as robbery is common. You may be able to hire donkeys for the Arrecifes-Pueblito stretch, US$5 each way, but watch them as these animals eat everything. Generally, there is litter everywhere along the main trails and around the campsites.

Beaches

Bathing is not recommended near Cañaveral as there is often heavy pounding surf and the tides are treacherous, but the beach is less crowded and cleaner than Rodadero. 5 km E of Cañaveral are splendid, deserted sandy beaches; you have to walk there, but take care as the park borders drug-growing areas. 15-20 mins' walk left along the beach at Arrecifes (sea dangerous on this beach) is La Piscina, a beautiful, safe natural swimming pool, excellent snorkelling.

● **Lodging and camping At Cañaveral**: cabins for 4-6 persons, US$78-107/night pp (high season, 65-91 low, MMA price), great views over sea and jungle, good restaurant. Campsite US$39/tent; has facilities, but only one restaurant with a tiny store, take all supplies; attractive site but plenty of mosquitoes. Beware of falling coconuts and omniverous donkeys. **At Arrecifes**: one campsite charges US$2.50 for tent, US$1.50 for hammock space, US$2 to hire hammock, US$3 for hut, fresh water shower and toilets; the other site is cheaper, with no electricity or showers. 3 restaurants of which *El Paraíso* is the most expensive; also a basic shop and guardroom for gear, soft drinks available. On the path to Pueblito there is a campsite at **Cabo** where the path turns inland, small restaurant and hammocks for hire; there are other camping and hammock places en route. You must obtain permission from MMA to camp in the park if you are not staying at Cañaveral; this is normally forthcoming if you specify where you intend to stay.

● **Transport** To get to the park entrance, take a minibus from the market in Santa Marta, Cra 11 y C 11, about US$1, or go to the Riohacha road police checkpoint (taxi US$1 or bus to Mamatoca) and catch a bus there. Tourist bus from *Hotel Miramar* in Santa Marta daily at 1030, US$12 inc park entrance but not food. This hotel also arranges tours for US$80-100, very interesting but little care is taken over waste disposal. Other hotels help in arranging tours, but there is no need to take guides (who charge US$20 or more pp for a day trip). A boat can be hired in Taganga to go to Arrecifes, about 2 hrs along the scenic coast, US$80 for 8.

Beyond Cañaveral, along the coast, is **Palomino**. Tours can be arranged from there to Indian villages taking up to 6 days, cost around US$32/day. Enquire at Turcol in Santa Marta.

CIUDAD PERDIDA

Ciudad Perdida, discovered in 1975, was founded near the Río Buritaca between 500 and 700 AD and was surely the most important centre of the Tayrona culture. It stands at 1,100m on the steep slopes of Cerro Corea, which lies in the northern part of the Sierra Nevada de Santa Marta. The site covers 400 ha and consists of a complex system of buildings, paved footpaths, flights of steps and perimetrical walls, which link a series of terraces and platforms, on which were built cult centres, residences and warehouses. Juan Mayr's book, *The Sierra Nevada of Santa Marta* (Mayr y Cabal, Apdo Aéreo 5000, Bogotá), deals beautifully with the Ciudad Perdida.

Archaeologists and army guards will ask you for your permit (obtainable in Santa Marta, MMA, Turcol or ask at tourist office). Don't forget that Ciudad Perdida is a National Park: it is strictly forbidden to damage trees and collect flowers or insects. Note also that there are over 1,200 steps to climb when you get there.

● **Access** One week trips organized by the tourist office and Turcol in Santa Marta (addresses above) cost US$250 all inclusive: price includes mules, guide and food, 3 days' hike there, 1 day at site, 3 days back. Ask at hotels in Santa Marta (eg *Hotel Miramar*) or Taganga, or at Santa Marta market (Cra 11 y C 11) for alternative tours. Prices depend on the services required. If you are prepared to shop around and cook and carry your supplies and belongings, a tour could cost you less. Recommended guides: Frankie Rey, known to German tourists as 'die graue Eminenz', very knowledgeable (ask at the tourist office about him), Donaldo, Wilson Montero, Edilberto Rey and Jairo García, who lives at the *Residencia Miramar*, in Santa Marta. There are many unscrupulous guides about, checking with the Tourist Office is recommended. If you want to see rainforest on the trek, insist on going via La Tagua (more beautiful, but more strenuous).

A circuitous route to the site can be arranged through *Hotel La Ballena Azul* (above). It costs about US$250 pp for the 6-day round trip, all inclusive. Its advantage is that it avoids all settlements, especially in the drug-growing lower valleys and Kogi villages which may not welcome foreigners.

Toyota jeeps go up to La Tagua (about 3 hrs), where it is possible to rent mules and pay local guides (but see above). You need to take a tent or a hammock and mosquito net (probably supplied by the guide), a good repellent, sleeping bag, warm clothing for the night, torch, plastic bags to keep everything dry, and strong, quick drying footwear. Check conditions, especially information on river crossings, and ensure you have adequate food, water bottle and water purifying tablets before you start. Try to leave no rubbish behind and encourage the guides to ensure no one else does.

You can reach Ciudad Perdida by helicopter from Santa Marta in about 20 mins. Ask at Helicol, at the airport, at Tourist Office in Santa Marta, or at Aviatur, Edif Centro Ejecutivo, p 2, Santa Marta, T 213840, 15 days advance booking may be required. Price: about US$350 there and back with a 3 hr stay.

RIOHACHA

Riohacha (*pop* 79,600), capital of Guajira Department, 160 km E of Santa Marta, is a port at the mouth of the Río César: low white houses, concrete streets, no trees or hills. It was founded in 1545 by Nicolás Federmann, and in early years its pearling industry was large enough to tempt Drake to sack it (1596). Pearling almost ceased during the 18th century and the town was all but abandoned. (It is best to travel from Riohacha in a luxury bus, early am as these buses are less likely to be stopped and searched for contraband.)

Local information
● **Accommodation**

B *Arimaca*, C 1 y Cra 9, T 273481, clean and friendly.

D *Gimaura* (state-owned), Av La Playa, T 272234, inc breakfast, helpful, rec, they allow camping in their grounds, with outside shower.

E *Hostal Ota*, opp the bus station, fan, clean, friendly, expensive food; **E** *Hostal Plaza*, clean, friendly, one block from sea and central plaza, two from Venezuelan consulate.

F *International*, Cra 7, No 12A-35, friendly, patio, free iced water, rec; **F** *Residencia Yatoonia*, Cra 7, No 11-26, T 73487, private bath, clean, safe, helpful, half way between beach and bus station.

● **Places to eat**

Glennpy, Av La Marina, S end, good, especially for fish. Many small restaurants along sea-front.

● **Embassies & consulates**

Venezuelan: C 7, No 3-08 (hours 0900-1300, and closed from 1500 Fri to 0900 Mon). With two passport photographs, photocopy of passport and an exit ticket with date most can get a visa on the same day, if you get there early, but be prepared for an interview with the consul himself; visas cost US$30 and should not be a transit visa, valid for 72 hrs only. Travellers report it is easier to get a Venezuelan visa in Barranquilla.

● **Services**

There are an airport, a cinema, and a bank, which changes dollars cash, but not if you're in your beachwear. At the weekend, Riohacha fills up, and bars and music spring up all over the place. The sea is clean, despite the red silt stirred up by the waves.

● **Shopping**

Good hammocks sold in the market. The best place for buying mantas and other local items is *La Casa de la Manta Guajira*, Cra 6, No 9-35, be prepared to bargain.

● **Tourist office**

There is a Tourist Office at Cra 7, No 1-38.

● **Useful addresses**

DAS Office (immigration) C 1 y Cra 6, T 72407.

Going S from Riohacha on an alternative road to Maicao and the Venezuelan frontier, you come to **Cuestecita** (*Hotel Turismo*; *Restaurant La Fogata*), where you can turn SW to **Barrancas**. Here a large coal mine (one of the largest in the world – El Cerrejón) came into operation in 1986. A good dirt road and an industrial railway (no passengers) have been built between the mine and the new Puerto Bolívar in the Bahía Portete, many millions of tons of coal are being exported annually. Visitors are apparently welcome, but it would probably be best to make arrangements first at the El Cerrejón main office in Barranquilla.

VALLEDUPAR

Continuing on this road, which takes you either round the Sierra Nevada to Barranquilla and Santa Marta via Fundación (see above) or S to Bucaramanga, you come to **Valledupar**, capital of César Department (*municipal pop* 247,940). Valledupar claims to be the home of the *vallenato* music (see **Music and dance**). You can change money at *casas de cambio* on C 16.

Local information
● **Accommodation**

A3 *Vajamar*, Cra 7, No 16A-30, T 725121, pool, expensive food; **A3** *Sicarare*, two-star, Cra 9, No 16-04, T 722137; cheaper 2-star hotel is **B** *Kurakata*, C 19C, No 7-96, T 724425; **F** *Residencia El Triunfo*, C 19, No 9-31, with bath, fan, clean, good; next door is *Hotel/Restaurant Nutibara*, excellent cheap meals and breakfast, excellent fruit juices; several other hotels in this street.

● **Transport**

Air To Bogotá and Riohacha.

Bus From Santa Marta, 6 hrs, from Cartagena, US$10 (with Expreso Brasilia); to Barranquilla, 4½ hrs, US$6; to Bucaramanga, 8 hrs US$20: a paved road runs S through Codazzi to the Santa Marta-Bucaramanga highway, Curumaní (*Hotel Himalaya*) and Aguachica.

THE SIERRA NEVADA DE SANTA MARTA

The Sierra Nevada, covering a triangular area of 16,000 sq km, rises abruptly from the sea, or from lowlands which nowhere reach over 300m above sea-level. "Indeed, the N slope is one of the most striking anywhere, lifting from the Caribbean to 5,800-metre snow peaks in about 45 km, a gradient comparable with the S face of the Himalaya, and unequalled along the world's coasts. The interior is made up of some eight E-W ranges with their intervening valleys. The lower parts of these interior valleys are flanked by forests – the homes of Indians as well as of pumas, jaguars, and a variety of snakes and birds – but for the most part the Sierra is almost lunar in its sterile grandeur, bleak *páramos* leading to naked crag and scree and glacier, where only an occasional questing condor moves. In the rocky heart of the area are a large number of small, beautiful lakes, many in cirques." – Frank F Cunningham, in an excellent illustrated article on exploring the Sierra in *The Geographical Magazine*. Hikes in the Sierra go through villages, valleys alive with butterflies, flowers and waterfalls, and to the lakes and the snowfields and summit of Pico Colón at 5,800m. The rainy season in these mountains ends Nov; Jan is best month for a visit.

The Indians of the Sierra do not take kindly to being photographed without permission. (Do not leave litter or disrespect the Indians' sacred grounds; stay on paths and do not stray on to private land.) They like to be given sea-shells which can be ground into powder and mixed with coca leaves. Learning a few words of their language can work wonders.

● **Access** Before leaving for the Sierra Nevada, check with MMA, ONIC and ICAN in Bogotá (see page 858), the Fundación Pro-Sierra Nevada, Edif Los Bancos 502, Santa Marta, T 214697, F 214737, for information and guidance on what permits are required. It is necessary to obtain a safe-conduct pass from Dra Eva Alonso at the Casa Indígena (45 mins out of town) in Valledupar if you are going further than San Sebastián.

● **Transport & Lodging** From Valledupar one route is along the Guatepurí valley. Another route is by jeep from Valledupar, Cra 7A, C 18, Nos 37-55, to Pueblo Bello, 2 hrs US$2 (less, 1 hr, from turn off main road to Pueblo Bello). In **Pueblo Bello** (F *Hotel El Encanto*, good meals US$1, friendly, but poor beds, hot, small, dark; F *El Ensueño*, friendly, clean; F *El Hogar de Mercedes*), enquire for jeeps to **San Sebastián de Rábago** (also called **Nabusimake**), the central village of one of the four tribes of Indians living in the Sierra, the Arhuacos (jeeps leave 0700-0800, 2-2½ hrs, US$5, dreadful road). It is set in beautiful surroundings and is the epitome of an Indian village. Ask for El Salto, a 2 hr walk, guide US$4.50 (not really needed). Jeep drivers may be able to arrange for you to stay on a farm; Doña Inés recommended, F, clean, friendly, good food. Also recommended is Ñoco, a mestizo who has lived in the valley for over 30 years; he has floor space, free camping (cold). Camping is also permitted in the valley.

● **Trekking** Very limited as the Arhuacos will not allow access deep into the Sierra. Climbing is not permitted (1996). Ñoco (see above) can arrange mules for trips (US$8.50 per mule inc guide, per day). Ñoco himself occasionally acts as guide if he is free (he runs a grocery store); he is very knowledgeable. Also recommended is Ricardo Olarté, C 22, No 16-61 Santa Marta, T 203413, who will arrange transport, food, accommodation for treks in the Sierra Nevada region and has a very good relationship with the local Indians.

Before hiking in the Sierra, visitors must get permission from the Arhuaco chief in San Sebastián (at the police HQ); a charge may be made for whatever walk you are allowed to do, this ranges from US$7 to US$15. **NB** The Sierra Nevada is a marijuana-growing area – take care.

There is plenty of drinking water, but Pueblo Bello is the only place to stock up with food. A tent is necessary for trekking. The best place for maps is Bogotá. It is also possible to hike on the coastal side of the Sierra, but it is absolutely essential to take a guide through the marijuana districts. Trekking tours to the Nevada de Santa Marta can also be arranged in Santa Marta, check with the Tourist Office.

GUAJIRA PENINSULA

Beyond Riohacha to the E is the arid and sparsely inhabited **Guajira Peninsula**.

The Indians here collect dividivi, tend goats, and fish. They are Guajiros, and of special interest are the coloured robes worn by the women. Sunsets in the Guajira are magnificent.

To visit a small part of the Peninsula take a bus from Riohacha (twice a day from the Indian market) to Manaure, US$2.40, 3 uncomfortable hours through fields of cactus but offering fine views of flamingoes and other brightly coloured birds. From **Manaure**, which is known for its salt flats, there are *busetas* to **Uribia** (US$1) and thence to Maicao. In Uribia you can buy handicrafts intended for local, not tourist, use by asking around. You can get *busetas* from Uribia to Puerto Bolívar (from where the coal is exported) and from there transport to **Cabo de Vela**, where the lagoons shelter vast flocks of flamingoes, herons and sandpipers. It costs about US$3 from Uribia to Cabo de Vela. There are fine beaches.

● **Accommodation In Manaure**: G *Hotel Flamingo*; *Uribia*, one basic *residencia*, no running water. **In Cabo de Vela**: a basic but friendly, Indian-run hotel, *El Mesón* (rooms, hammock veranda, showers, good meals – excellent fried fish), or sling a hammock at *El Caracol* where there is an expensive restaurant (better value next door at *La Tropicana* if you order food in advance). Also Conchita will hire out a large hut, hammocks for up to 5, cook food with prior request, along the coast, ask anyone.

MACUIRA NATIONAL PARK

Towards the NE tip of the Guajira peninsula is the Serranía de Macuira, a range of hills over 500m which create an oasis of tropical forest in the semi-desert. Moisture comes mainly from clouds which form in the evening and disperse in the early morning. Its remoteness gives it interesting flora and fauna and Indian settlements little affected by outsiders. To reach the area, you must travel NE from Uribia either round the coast past Bahía Portete, or direct across the semi-desert to Nazareth on the E side of the park. There are no tourist facilities anywhere nearby. You may be able to arrange a trip in Riohacha.

NB The Guajira peninsular is not a place to travel alone, parties of 3 or more are recommended. If going in your own

transport, check on safety before setting out. Also remember it is hot, it is easy to get lost, there is little cover and very little water. Locals, including police, are very helpful in giving lifts.

MAICAO

The Caribbean coastal highway, now paved, runs direct from Santa Marta along the coast to Riohacha, and the Riohacha-Maicao road (also paved) has been greatly improved. Now that there are no flights from Barranquilla to Maracaibo, taxi or bus to Maicao, and colectivo to Maracaibo is the most practical route.

Maicao is full of Venezuelan contraband, and is still at the centre of the narcotics trade. Its streets are unmade; most commercial premises close before 1600 and after 1700 the streets are unsafe.

Local information
● **Accommodation**
D *Maicao Juan Hotel*, Cra 10, C 12, T 8184, the only safe one; several others on Cra 10 (*El Dorado*, No 12-45; *Medanos*, No 11-25) and elsewhere; no reports.

● **Buses**
To **Riohacha**, US$1.35; **Santa Marta** (Expreso Occidente), US$9; **Barranquilla**, last one at 1600, US$10.75. **Cartagena**, US$16.75. Colectivos, known as "por puestos" in Venezuela, Maicao-Maracaibo, US$5 pp, or infrequent microbus, US$3.30, very few buses to Venezuela after midday. Brasilia bus company has its own security compound: non-passengers are not allowed in (you can change money, buy bus tickets and food before journey). *Por puestos* wait here for passengers to Maracaibo; very easy transfer.

FRONTIER WITH VENEZUELA
● **Colombian immigration**
At the border. Entering Colombia by *por puesto* make sure the driver stops at the Colombian entry post. If not you will have to return later to complete formalities.

With all the right papers, border crossing is easy.

● **Venezuelan consulate**
There is now no Venezuelan Consul in Maicao. You must get a visa in Barranquilla, Cartagena or Riohacha. Entering Venezuela, everyone travelling overland should have a visa; a transit visa will only suffice if you have a confirmed ticket to a third country within 3 days.

SAN ANDRES AND PROVIDENCIA

Colombia's Caribbean islands of the San Andrés and Providencia archipelago are 480 km N of the South American coast, 400 km SW of Jamaica, and 180 km E of Nicaragua. This proximity has led Nicaragua to claim them from Colombia in the past. They are small and attractive, but very expensive by South American standards. Nevertheless, with their surrounding islets and cays, they are a popular holiday and shopping resort.

Being a customs-free zone, San Andrés is very crowded with Colombian shoppers looking for foreign-made bargains. Although alcoholic drinks are cheap, essential goods are extremely costly, and electronic goods are more expensive than in the UK.

The People

The original inhabitants, mostly black, speak some English, but the population has swollen with unrestricted immigration from Colombia. There are also Chinese and Middle Eastern communities. The population in 1992 was about 41,580 and is now estimated at 65,000.

Culture and festivals

20 July: independence celebrations on San Andrés with various events. Providencia holds its carnival in June.

San Andrés and Providencia are famous in Colombia for their music, whose styles include the local form of calypso, soca, reggae and church music. A number of good local groups perform on the islands and in Colombia. Concerts are held at the Old Coliseum (every Sat at 2100 in the high season); the Green Moon Festival is held in May. There is a cultural centre at Punta Hansa in San Andrés town (T 25518).

SAN ANDRES

San Andrés is of coral, some 11 km long, rising at its highest to 104m. The town, commercial centre, major hotel sector and airport are at the northern end. A picturesque road circles the island. Places to see, besides the beautiful cays and beaches on the eastern side, are the Hoyo Soplador (South End), a geyser-like hole through which the sea spouts into the air most surprisingly when the wind is in the right direction. The W side is less spoilt, but there are no beaches on this side. Instead there is The Cove, the island's deepest anchorage, and Morgan's Cave (Cueva de Morgan, reputed hiding place for the pirate's treasure) which is penetrated by the sea through an underwater passage. At The Cove, the road either continues round the coast, or crosses the centre of the island back to town over La Loma, on which is a Baptist Church, built in 1847.

Marine life and watersports

Diving off San Andrés is very good; depth varies from 10 to 100 feet, visibility from 30 to 100 feet. There are 3 types of site: walls of sea-weed and minor coral reefs, large groups of different types of coral, and underwater plateaux with much marine life. 70% of the insular platform is divable.

Diving trips to the reef cost US$60 with Pedro Montoya at Aquarium diving shop, Punta Hansa, T 26649; also Buzos del Caribe, Centro Comercial Dann, T 23712; both offer diving courses and equipment hire.

For the less-adventurous, take a morning boat (20 mins, none in the afternoon) to the so-called Aquarium (US$3 return), off Haynes Key, where, using a mask and wearing sandals as protection against sea-urchins, you can see colourful fish. Snorkelling equipment can be hired on San Andrés for US$4-5, but it is better and cheaper on the shore than on the island.

Pedalos can be rented for US$4/hour. Windsurfing and sunfish sailing rental and lessons are available from Bar Boat, road to San Luis (opp the naval base), 1000-1800 daily (also has floating bar, English and German spoken), and Windsurf Spot, *Hotel Isleño*, T 23990; water-skiing at Water Spot, *Hotel Aquarium*, T 23117, and Jet Sky. From Tominos Marina there are boat trips around the island. Bay trips for 2 hrs cost US$8.75, for 4 hrs US$17.50, inc 3 free rum-and-cokes.

Beaches and cays

Boats go in the morning from San Andrés to Johnny Key with a white beach and parties all day Sun (US$3 return, you can go in one boat and return in another). Apart from those already mentioned, other cays and islets in the archipelago are Bolívar, Albuquerque, Algodón/Cotton (included in the Sunrise Park development in San Andrés), Rocky, the Grunt, Serrana, Serranilla and Quitasueño.

On San Andrés the beaches are in town and on the eastern coast. Perhaps the best is at San Luis and Bahía Sonora/Sound Bay.

Local information
● **Accommodation**

NB Some hotels raise their prices by 20-30% on 15 Dec. **A1** *Aquarium*, Av Colombia 1-19, T 23120, F 26174, all suites; **A1** *Casablanca*, Av Colombia y Costa Rica, T 25950, central, food; **A1** *Casa Dorada*, Av Las Américas, T 24008, salt water washing, reasonable food; *Decamerón*, road to San Luis Km 15, book through *Decamerón Cartagena*, T 655-4400, F 653-738, all-inclusive resort, pool, a/c, TV, good restaurant, rec; **A2** *Cacique Toné*, Av Colombia, No 5-02, T 24251, deluxe, a/c, pool, on sea-front; **A2** *El Isleño*, Av de la Playa 3-59, T 23990, F 23126, 2 blocks from airport, in palm grove, good sea views; **A2** *Royal Abacoa*, Av Colombia No 2-41, T 24043, good restaurant; **A3** *Bahía Sardinas*, Av Colombia No 4-24, T 23793, across the street from the beach, a/c, TV, fridge, good service, comfortable, clean, no swimming pool; **A3** *El Dorado*, Av Colombia No 1A-25, T 24057, a/c, restaurant, casino, swimming pool; **A3** *Verde Mar*, Av 20 de Julio, T 25525, quiet and friendly, a/c, rec.

B *Capri*, Av Costa Rica No 1A-64, T 24315, with bath and a/c, good value.

C *Mediterráneo*, Av Los Libertadores, T 26722, clean, friendly, poor water supply; **C** *Nueva Aurora*, Av de las Américas No 3-46, T 23811, fan and private bath, pool, restaurant.

D *Coliseo*, Av Colombia No 1-59, T 23330, friendly, noisy, good restaurant; **D** *Residencias Hernando Henry*, Av de las Américas 4-84, T 26416, restaurant, fan, clean, good value, often full, on road from airport; also nr the airport, **D** *Olga and Federico Archibold*, C de la Bodega Marlboro, No 91-18, T 25781, have 3 self-contained apartments, modern, clean, friendly; *Residencia Restrepo*, 'gringo hotel', Av 8 nr airport, noisy ('share a room with a Boeing 727'—till midnight), much cheaper than

others, E, or less for a hammock in the porch, but you get what you pay for, the accommodation is in a poor state and the grounds are a junkyard, not rec. Opposite *Restrepo* is a tobacco/paper shop whose owner rents a/c apartments with kitchen, etc, **D**.

● **Places to eat**

Oasis (good), Av Colombia No 4-09; *El Pimentón*, Av de las Américas, good *menú*, cheap; *El Zaguán de los Arrieros*, Av 20 de Julio (50m after cinema), good food and value; *Fonda Antioqueña Nos 1 and 2*, on Av Colombia nr the main beach, and Av Colombia at Av Nicaragua, best value for fish; *Sea Food House*, Av 20 de Julio, at Parque Bolívar, good cooking, not expensive, second floor terrace; excellent fruit juices at *Nueva China*, next to *Restrepo*, reasonable Chinese; *Fisherman's Place*, in the fishing cooperative at N end of main beach, very good, simple. Cheap fish meals can be bought at San Luis beach.

● **Banks & money changers**

Banco Industrial Colombiano, Av Costa Rica; **Banco de Bogotá** will advance pesos on a Visa card. **Banco Occidente** for Mastercard. Aerodisco shop at airport will change dollars cash anytime at rates slightly worse than banks, or try the Photo Shop on Av Costa Rica. Many shops will change US$ cash; it is impossible to change TCs at weekends.

● **Tourist offices**

Av Colombia No 5-117, English spoken, maps.

● **Transport**

Local Bus: buses cover the eastern side of the island all day (15 mins intervals), US$0.25 (more at night and on holidays). **Taxis**: round the island, US$8; to airport, US$3.50; in town, US$0.60; *colectivo* to airport, US$0.50. **Train**: a 'tourist train' (suitably converted tractor and carriages) tours the island in 3 hrs for US$3. **Vehicle rental**: bicycles are a popular way of getting around the island and are easy to hire, eg opp *El Dorado Hotel* – usually in poor condition, choose your own bike and check all parts thoroughly (US$1.10/hour, US$6/day); motorbikes also easy to hire, US$3.50/hour. Cars can be hired for US$15 for 2 hrs, with US$6 for every extra hour.

Air The airport is 15 mins' walk to town (US$3 pp taxi). All airline offices in town, except Aces at airport. SAM offers hotel packages as well as the airfare, but booking a hotel and meal plan outside San Andrés through a travel agent is not always a satisfactory arrangement. It is best to see the hotel for yourself. Flights to most major Colombian cities with Avianca, Aces, Intercontinental de Aviación, Aerorepública and SAM (you can arrange a stop-over in Cartagena, which is good value). SAM also flies to Guatemala City, San José (also Aero Costa Rica) and Panama City (also Intercontinental). Note that Panama, Costa Rica and Honduras all require onward tickets which cannot be bought on San Andrés, can be in Cartagena. (There are Panamanian and Costa Rican consulates in San Andrés.) For advice on purchasing tickets to Colombia via San Andrés, see page 990. The SAM office in San Andrés will not issue officially one way tickets to Central America. You buy a return, and SAM office on the mainland will refund once you show an onward ticket. The refund (less 15%) may not be immediate. However travellers report that you can purchase a one-way ticket at the SAM desk at the airport. Sun flights are always heavily booked, similarly July-Aug, Dec-Jan. If waitlisted, don't give up hope.

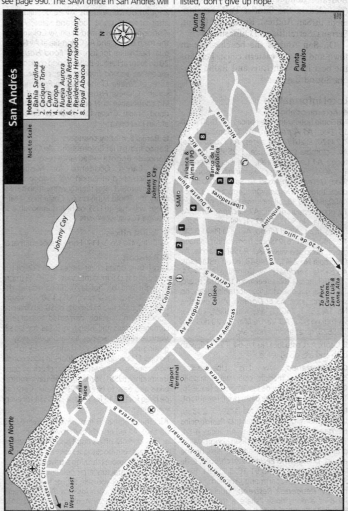

San Andrés

Not to Scale

Hotels:
1. Bahía Sardinas
2. Cacique Toné
3. Capri
4. Europa
5. Nueva Aurora
6. Residencia Restrepo
7. Residencias Hernando Henry
8. Royal Abacoa

Ship Cruise ships and tours go to San Andrés; there are no other, official passenger services by sea. Cargo ships are not supposed to carry passengers to the mainland, but many do. If you want to leave by sea, speak only to the ship's captain. (Any other offer of tickets on ships to/from San Andrés, or of a job on a ship, may be a con trick.) The sea crossing takes 3-4 days, depending on the weather. In Cartagena, ships leave from the Embarcadero San Andrés, opposite the Plaza de la Aduana.

Boat Cooperativa de Lancheros, opp *Hotel Abacoa*.

PROVIDENCIA

Providencia, commonly called Old Providence (4,500 inhabitants), 80 km back to the N-NE from San Andrés, is 7 km long and is more mountainous than San Andrés, rising to 610m. There are waterfalls, and the land drops steeply into the sea in places. Superb views can be had by climbing from Casabaja/Bottom House or Aguamansa/Smooth Water to the peak. There are relics of the fortifications built on the island during its disputed ownership. Horse riding is available, and boat trips can be made to neighbouring islands such as **Santa Catalina** (an old pirate lair separated from Providencia by a channel cut for their better defence), and to the NE, Cayo Cangrejo/Crab Cay (beautiful swimming and snorkelling) and Cayos Hermanos/Brothers Cay. Trips from 1000-1500 cost about US$7 pp. Santa Catalina is joined to the main island by a wooden bridge. On the W side of Santa Catalina is a rock formation called Morgan's Head; seen from the side it looks like a man's profile.

On Providencia the three main beaches are Bahía Manzanillo/ Manchincal Bay, the largest, most attractive and least developed, Bahía del Suroeste/South West Bay and Bahía Agua Dulce/ Freshwater Bay, all in the SW.

Like San Andrés, it is an expensive island. There is no bank, best to take sufficient pesos with you, exchange rates from shops and hotels are poor. Alternatively, use credit cards. The sea food is good, water and fresh milk are generally a problem. English is widely spoken. Day tours are arranged by the Providencia office in San Andrés, costing US$30 in-clusive. SAM flies from San Andrés, US$35, 25 mins, 6 times a day, bookable only in San Andrés. Satena flies twice a day from San Andrés. (Return flight has to be confirmed at the airport, where there is a tourist office.) Boat trips from San Andrés take 8 hrs, but are not regular.

Local information
● **Accommodation**
Most of the accommodation is at Freshwater (Playa Agua Dulce): **B** *Cabañas El Recreo* (Captain Brian's, T 48010); **A1** *Cabañas El Paraíso* (T 26330, a/c, TV, fridge); **B** *Cabañas Aguadulce Miss Elma's*, T 481600, rec for cheap food; also *Morgan's Bar* for fish meals and a good breakfast. On Santa Catalina is the German-owned *Cabañas Santa Catalina*, friendly, use of small kitchen. Several houses take in guests. Camping is possible at Freshwater Bay. Truck drivers who provide transport on the island may be able to advise on accommodation.

Up the Río Magdalena

THE old waterway from the Caribbean, now superseded by road and air, leads from Barranquilla to the limit of navigation at Girardot. The route passes snow-capped volcanoes and *tierra caliente* weekend resorts before climbing to the river's upper reaches entering Huila Department.

THE LOWER MAGDALENA

The Magdalena is wide but shallow and difficult to navigate because of surface eddies, and there are little whirlpools over submerged rocks. Away to the NE, in the morning, one can see the high snow-capped peaks of the Sierra Nevada de Santa Marta. Passenger travel by the lofty paddle boats on the river has come to an end, though the adventurous traveller may still find an occasional passage by cargo paddle boat. In general the only way of getting from one place to the other along the river is by motor launch (*chalupa*). The river trip from the N coast (bus to Magangué) to Puerto Berrío or Puerto Boyacá and thence by bus to Bogotá can be completed in about 4 days (1994).

Insect repellents should be taken, for mosquitoes are a nuisance. Guerrilla activity has been reported in the Magdalena valley away from the river and the main roads. The upper reaches of the Magdalena, beyond Neiva, are dealt with in Section 7.

South of Calamar, the terminus of the Canal del Dique, is Tenerife, where Bolívar had his first victory in the Magdalena campaign. At **Zambrano** (96 km; *pop* 8,210), a cattle and tobacco centre, there is a road W to the N-S Cartagena-Medellín road.

MOMPOS

Near Pinto the river divides: the eastern branch, silted and difficult, leads to **Mompós** (*pop* 10,810): cattle farming and tobacco, and the scene of another victory for Bolívar: "At Mompós", he said, "my glory was born." Mompós was founded in 1537 and, thanks to its comparative isolation, preserves its colonial character.

Places of interest

Old buildings are the Casa de Gobierno, once a home of the Jesuits, and the Colegio de Pinillos. There are 7 churches and the Easter celebrations are said to be among the best in Colombia. The cemetery has considerable historical interest. The town is well known in Colombia for hand-worked gold jewellery.

Local information

● **Caution**

Malaria is endemic in the surrounding countryside. If staying overnight, mosquito nets and/or coils are a must. Drinking fruit juices is not recommended near the river, glasses may be washed in river water.

● **Accommodation**

C *Hostal Doña Manuela*, C Real del Medío, 17-41, T 55620, a converted colonial house, quiet and peaceful, restaurant is the best in town.

D *Residencias Aurora*, shower, fan, good meals, nice and friendly, bargaining possible; **D** *Residencias Unión*, C 18, No 3-43, with bath and fan.

E *Residencias Villas de Mompós*, 500m E of Plaza Tamarindo, family run, friendly, free coffee; **E** *Posada de Vinney*, opp *Doña Manuela*, shared bath, modern, clean, above medical practice.

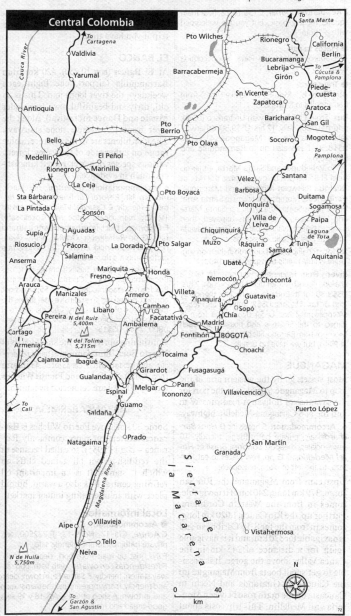

Central Colombia

To Cartagena

Cauca River

Valdivia

Yarumal

Antioquia

Bello

Medellín

Rionegro

El Peñol

Marinilla

La Ceja

Sta Bárbara

La Pintada

Sonsón

Supía

Aguadas

Riosucio

Pácora

Anserma

Salamina

Arauca

Mariquita

Fresno

Manizales

Líbano

Pereira

N del Ruiz 5,400m

Ambalema

Cartago

N del Tolima 5,215m

Armenia

Cajamarca

Ibagué

Gualanday

To Cali

Espinal

Guamo

Saldaña

Natagaima

Prado

Aipe

Villavieja

N de Huila 5,750m

Tello

Neiva

To Garzón & San Agustín

Pto Wilches

Rionegro

California

Berlín

Bucaramanga

Lebrija

Girón

Piede-cuesta

To Cúcuta & Pamplona

Barrancabermeja

Sn Vicente

Zapatoca

Aratoca

Baricharaa

San Gil

Pto Berrío

Pto Olaya

Socorro

Mogotes

To Pamplona

Pto Boyacá

Santana

Vélez

Barbosa

Monquirá

Duitama

Villa de Leiva

Sogamosa

Paipa

Chiquinquirá

Muzo

Ráquira

Laguna de Tota

La Dorada

Pto Salgar

Samacá

Tunja

Aquitania

Ubaté

Honda

Nemocón

Chocontá

Villeta

Zipaquirá

Guatavita

Cambao

Facatativá

Sopó

Chía

Madrid

Fontibón

BOGOTÁ

Choachí

Tocaima

Fusagasugá

Girardot

Pandi

Melgar

Icononzo

Villavicencio

Puerto López

S i e r r a   d e   l a   M a c a r e n a

Magdalena River

Granada

San Martín

0   40

km

Vistahermosa

N

F *Residencias Solmar*, C Cra 18-22, near main square, friendly, basic, but you are welcomed with a "tinto".

● **Places to eat**

El Galileo, next to the Plaza, good *comida corriente*.

● **Transport**

Air There is a Mon-Fri air service (Aces) from Barranquilla to Mompós.

Bus From **Cartagena** with Unitransco (0530, returns 0700), daily, 12 hrs, US$9.50, otherwise take Brasilia bus to **Magangué** 4½ hrs, US$8.50. Buses also go to **Barranquilla** and **Sincelejo**.

To **Valledupar** and **Santa Marta**, either go from El Banco (see below), or cross the river at **Talaigua** (between Mompós and Magangué, *carritos* leave Mompós early am) to **Santa Ana**. Buses leave Santa Ana 0700 for Santa Marta and Valledupar, first 2½ hrs unpaved, then paved; US$8 to Valledupar. For Sierra Nevada alight at Pueblo Bello crossroads.

NB Most *chalupas* and buses run in the morning. There is little public transport after 1400.

River From Magangué you have to take a *chalupa* (launch) either direct to Mompós, 2 hrs, US$3.30, or to Bodega, ¾ hr, and thence by jeep or taxi 1½ hrs, US$2. You can also reach Mompós in 2 hrs, US$4 by *chalupa* from El Banco to the SE. It is also possible to reach Mompós from Barranquilla by *chalupa* changing at Plato, but we have no details.

MAGANGUE

Most vessels go by the western arm of the loop to **Magangué** (*pop* 61,265), the port for the savannas of Bolívar. A road runs W to join the N-S Cartagena-Medellín highway.

● **Accommodation** 5 hotels inc **D** *Hans Burchardt*, a/c, private bath, fridge, friendly; 10 *residenciales*, cheapest *Londres*, *Brasil* or *Hotel Medellín*, all **G** pp. Few places to eat, *Terraza*, to the left of plaza, reasonable.

Upstream from Magangué, the Río San Jorge, 379 km long, 240 km of it navigable, comes in from the Western Cordillera. Further up, the Río Cauca, 1,020 km long, comes in from the far S. Its Caribbean end is navigable for 370 km, and it is navigable again for a distance of 245 km in the Cauca Valley above the gorge. It is possible to get small boats from Magangué up the Cauca, via Guaranda and Nechi to Caucasia on the main road between Montería and Medellín. This trip costs about

US$20 and takes 2 days allowing for unforseen breakdowns etc. A very attractive trip if you have time.

EL BANCO

At **El Banco** (*pop* 10,250), 420 km from Barranquilla (airport, one flight each weekday), the river loops join. This is an old, dirty and beautiful town (see under **Music and Dance** for festival). Along the river front are massive stone stairways. The Cordilleras are in the distance, a blue range on either side of the valley. Egrets, various species of heron, ringed kingfishers much in evidence.

● **Accommodation D** *Central*, nr church, modern, fan; **E** *Hotel Continental*, nr jeep terminal, friendly; **E** *Casa del Viajero*, C 8, colour TV, fan, bath, clean, fridge with Cokes, safe; **F** *Colonial*, 1 block from harbour, with bath and fan; **G** pp *Residencia Ocaña*, basic, clean, noisy; **G** *Residencia Edén*, C 9, friendly, free coffee; about a dozen others.

● **Transport** Daily buses from El Banco to Bucaramanga, US$15, Cúcuta and Valledupar. Bus from Cartagena 0800, US$7.55. Don't get conned into taking an expensive boat across the river instead of the bus ferry. *Chalupa* service El Banco-Barrancabermeja with Cootransfluviales, 0800, 7 hrs, US$15.

Continuing upriver are the small towns of **Puerto Boca**, **Tamalameque** (basic *residencia* and restaurant), La Gloria, **Gamarra** (*pop* 3,700), San Pablo and **Puerto Wilches** (*pop* 5,600). All are connected by launch.

BARRANCABERMEJA

Some 30 km above Puerto Wilches is **Barrancabermeja** (or more commonly Barranca – *pop* 135,955), so called because of the reddish-brown oil-stained cliffs on which it stands. It is an important oil refining centre. It is also a warm, humid place with an interesting indoor market.

Local information
● **Accommodation**

C *Achue*, Cra 17, No 9-12, T 222500, a/c, private bath, restaurant, friendly, safe.

F *Iris*, just up road from port, clean, friendly; **F** *Residencias Ferroviario*, with bath, opp railway station, friendly; **F** *Santa Fe*, in town, clean and friendly; many more around the train station and in town. A shop at C 19, Avs 18 y 19 sells good bread and muesli.

● **Banks & money changers**
Banco de Bogotá will change TCs.

● **Transport**
Air 10 mins by taxi from centre, 2 daily flights to Bogotá, Aces.

Train To Medellín, daily 0500, US$6.60, 15 hrs.

Bus Bucaramanga, 3 hrs, US$2.30; Medellín, 1045, US$17.

River Boat: *Chalupa* to Puerto Boyacá, 0845, 6 hrs, US$12. Several daily to El Banco, 7 hrs, US$15.

PUERTO BERRIO

Puerto Berrío (*pop* 25,200) is on the W bank 100 km above Barrancabermeja and 756 km from Barranquilla. It is the river port for Medellín and Antioquia Department. A railway from Medellín runs down the slopes of the Cordillera Central and over a low pass to Puerto Berrío, where it connects with the Bogotá-Santa Marta line.

● **Accommodation** E *Hotel Magdalena*, pleasant, on a hilltop nr river; F *Residencias El Ganadero*, with bath, clean, modern, with ceiling fans. Many others.

● **Places to eat** *La Buena Mesa*, good big meals; *Heladeria Joi*, good ice cream and sundaes.

● **Transport** Train to **Santa Marta** and **Medellín**, check if trains are running at **Grecia** station, 4 km from the town (taxi service only). There is an airport.

PUERTO BOYACA

75 km upriver from Puerto Berrío is **Puerto Boyacá** (several *residencias*). There has been guerrilla activity in the area.

● **Transport Bus** Rápido Tolima has regular buses to Honda (3 hrs, US$2.70) on the Medellín-Bogotá highway. **River** To Puerto Berrío US$4.10.

LA DORADA

It is 151 km up river from Puerto Berrío to **La Dorada** (*pop* 56,220) on the W bank. The Medellín-Bogotá highway crosses the Magdalena by a bridge from **Puerto Salgar,** on the E bank.

● **Accommodation La Dorada:** F *Rosita*, C 17, No 3-28, T 72301, with bath, friendly, pleasant, rec; on highway to Honda, *Magdalena Motel*; others near railway station; youth hostel at *Centro Vacacional La Mag-*

dalena, 3 km from La Dorada – details from Alcom in Bogotá – *Parador Turístico* next door.
Puerto Salgar: *Salgar*, G *Residencia Antioquia*, with fan.

● **Bus** To Bogotá via Honda (see next section), 5 hrs, US$8.50; to Medellín US$9.

The Lower Río Magdalena navigation stops at La Dorada as there are rapids above, as far as Honda. Currently (1995) there are no passenger services S of Puerto Boyacá. The Upper Magdalena is navigable as far as Girardot (see below).

THE UPPER MAGDALENA

HONDA

Honda (*pop* 25,481; *av temp* 29°C; *alt* 230m) on the W bank of the river, is 32 km upstream from La Dorada (149 km from Bogotá).

Places of interest It is a pleasant old town with many colonial houses. It has an interesting indoor market and a small museum. The streets are narrow and picturesque, and the town is surrounded by hills. El Salto de Honda (the rapids which separate the Lower from the Upper Magdalena) are just below the town. Several bridges span the Ríos Magdalena and the Guali, at whose junction the town lies. In Feb the Magdalena rises and fishing is unusually good. People come from all over the region for the fishing and the festival of the Subienda, as the season is called.

● **Accommodation** C *Campestre El Molino*, 5 km from Honda on Mariquita road, T 3130, swimming pools, fans in rooms, friendly; **C** *Ondama*, C 17 y 13A, T 3565, swimming pool; **D** *Club Piscina*, Cra 12, No 19-139, T 3273, fan, swimming pool, clean, friendly, arranges safe parking at reasonable rates with neighbours, rec; **E** *Residencias Las Mercedes*, with bath, clean and friendly.

● **Places to eat** *La Cascada*, overlooking river, good. There is a row of good cheap restaurants across the Río Magdalena bridge in Puerto Bogotá.

● **Bus** From Bogotá by Velotax US$4.80, and Rápido Tolima, US$3, 4 hrs. **Manizales**, US$3.60. Rápido Tolima run half-hourly buses to **La Dorada** (1 hr), and beyond, to **Puerto Boyacá** (3 hrs), US$2.70. The new Bogotá-Medellín highway passes round the town.

MARIQUITA

West from Honda a paved road goes to **Mariquita** (21 km; *pop* 13,000), the centre of a fruit-growing country, and **Fresno** (a further 30 km), the heart of a coffee growing area. The road continues up the slopes of the Central Cordillera to Manizales (83 km) with bus services (Rápido Tolima).

Mariquita (founded 1551) has several old houses and buildings: a mint, the viceroy's house, the parish church. Here José Celestino Mutis lived for 8 years during his famous Botanic Expedition towards the end of the 18th century (when he and his helpers accumulated a herbarium of 20,000 plants, a vast library, and a rich collection of botanical plates and paintings of native fauna). The collection was sent to Madrid, where it remains.

Between Mariquita and Fresno are the clean and pleasant bathing pool of El Diamante; the Club Deportivo: private, but visitors are welcome to its swimming pool. There is another, El Virrey, in Mariquita.

● **Accommodation** C *Las Acacias*, on Armero road, T 522016; D *San Felipe*, 8 km from Mariquita on Armero road, good, pool, restaurant with slow service; *Hotel Bocaneme* and others; campsites.

● **Bus** From Honda, Rápido Tolima, every 30 mins, US$0.35, 30 mins.

From Mariquita the road turns S to (32 km) **Armero**, which used to be a cotton growing centre until it and surrounding villages were devastated by the eruption of the Nevado del Ruiz volcano (see page 951) in Nov 1985. Over 25,000 people were killed as approximately 10% of the ice core melted, causing landslides and mudflows. (Armero can be reached by colectivo from Honda; no lodging in Armero, nearest at **Lérida**, 12 km S; no drinks available in Armero; there are lots of mosquitoes, though.) A branch road runs 23 km E to Camboa on the Río Magdalena; the road continues to the highway for Bogotá.

IBAGUE

The main road from Armero goes direct for 88 km to **Ibagué**, capital of Tolima

Department. It is a large city (*pop* 386,425; *alt* 1,250m), lying at the foot of the Quindío mountains. It is cooler here (22°C) than in the valley.

Places of interest

Parts of the town are old: the Colegio de San Simón is worth seeing, and so is the market. The Parque Centenario is pleasant. The city specializes in hand-made leather goods (there are many good, cheap shoe shops) and a local drink called *mistela*. There is an excellent Conservatory of Music.

Local festivals

The National Folklore Festival is held during the third week of June. The Departments of Tolima and Huila commemorate San Juan (24 June) and SS Pedro y Pablo (29 June) with bullfights, fireworks, and music.

Local information
● **Accommodation**

A3 *Ambala*, C 11, No 2-60, T 610982, F 633490, with bath, TV, pool, restaurant.

D *Ambeima*, Cra 3, No 13-32, T 634300; **D** *Farallones*, C 16, No 2-88, good, fan, clean and opp **D** *Cordillera*, also good.

E *Bolívar*, C 17 y Cra 4, good, clean, TV; **E** *Bram*, C 17 y Cra 4, convenient, secure, insect-free, cold water; **E** *Residencia Puracé*, opposite Tolima bus station; nearby **F** *La Paz*, C 18, No 3-119, friendly, tinto free in the morning.

F pp *Montserrat*, C 18, Cra 1 y 2, clean, quiet, rec; **F** *Boston*, nr bus station clean, basic.

● **Places to eat**

24-hr restaurants inc *Punto Rojo*, in the shopping precinct on Cra 3, good lunch; *El Espacio*, Cra 4, No 18-14, large helpings, good value. Vegetarian, *Govinda*, Cra 2 y C 13.

● **Tourist offices**

Cra 3, between Cs 10 and 11; helpful; closed Sat and Sun. The Instituto Geográfico Agustín Codazzi has an office at C 14A, No 3-14, 3rd Floor, for maps.

● **Buses**

Terminal is between Cras 1-2 and C 19-20. Tourist police at terminal helpful. To **Bogotá**, US$8 Expreso Palmira 0915, 4 hrs; also buses to **Pereira**, **Cali** and **Popayán**. To **Neiva**, US$7.

NEVADO DEL TOLIMA

Just outside, on the Armenia road, a dirt road leads to the slopes of the **Nevado del**

Tolima, southernmost 'nevado' in the **Parque Nacional Los Nevados**. Gerhard Drekonia of Vienna writes: For climbing the Nevado del Tolima (5,215m) go from Ibagué to Juntas and El Silencio (2 hrs by train if running). From there ½ hr walk to the fabulous natural thermal waters of El Rancho (simple sleeping accommodation and food available). The climb starts from El Rancho. It takes 8 to 10 hrs to the top; equipment (crampons and pica) indispensable. The final climb has to be done at sunrise because clouds and mist invariably rise around 0800. From the top is a breathtaking view across the other snow-capped mountains of the Cordillera Central.

● **Information and guides** Admission US$10, car US$4, camping US$32 (US$25 low season). For information contact Cruz Roja Colombiana in Ibagué, Zona Industrial El Papayo, near the E entrance to the city, T 646014, who can put you in touch with a climbing group, Asociación Tolimense de Montañistas y Escaladores. Helpful guides are: Claus Schlief, who speaks German and English; Manolo Barrios, who has some Himalayan experience and is well rec, ask for information at the Cruz Roja; Fernando Reyes, Cra 11, No 1-21, Barrio Alaska, Ibagué, T 639027, who will take you rock or ice climbing on Tolima at about US$15/day. He can also arrange accommodation and make and repair backpacks.

The Quindío Pass, 3,350m, is on the road to Armenia, 105 km W of Ibagué across the Cordillera central. At night, fog, reckless drivers and stray animals make the pass hazardous. On the E side of the Pass is **Cajamarca**, a friendly town in a beautiful setting (**G** *Residencia Central*; *Nevado*, both on same street, friendly and clean). Interesting market on Sun.

GIRARDOT

79 km E of Ibagué is **Girardot** (*pop* 80,040; *alt* 326m), on the Upper Magdalena. The road from Ibagué runs through **Gualanday** (accommodation; restaurants), joining the highway from Bogotá at **Espinal**, an important agro-industrial town (*pop* 42,780; **B** *Hotel Yuma*, T 4323; **F** *Hotel Bucaros*, central, clean, with bath, restaurant). From Ibagué it is 1 hr by bus to Espinal, whence buses run N and S. Toll

between Ibagué and Espinal US$0.50; between Espinal and Girardot US$0.40.

At Girardot, the climate is hot and there are heavy rains. Bogotanos come down here at weekends to warm up. Here the navigation of the Upper Magdalena ends, although in dry weather boats cannot get this far. Walk across the fine steel bridge to see merchandise being loaded and unloaded – coffee and hides are the main items. Large cattle fairs are held on 5-10 June and 5-10 Dec. Launch rides on the river start from underneath the bridge. A 1-hr trip to Isla del Sol is rec (US$5).

● **Accommodation A2** *El Peñón*, on site of former *hacienda* just outside town, Cra 16, No 79-31, T 26981, fashionable bungalow complex, casino, huge pool, lake, price per bungalow; **B** *Bachué*, Cra 8, No 18-04, T 26791, modern, large cooled pool, excellent, rooms a/c with bath and TV, restaurant; **D** *Nuevo Río*, Cra 10, No 16-31, TV, fan, restaurant, laundry, friendly, English and German spoken; **D** *Los Angeles*, on main plaza, clean, friendly, rec; **E** *Miami*, Cra 7, No 13-57, large rooms, clean, fan, good, central location safe.

Opp new bus terminal, **F** *El Cid*, with fan and **F** *Maroti*; **F** *Rincón*, on main street, C 19, No 10-68, balcony, fan; **F** *Colonial*, Cra 11, 16, showers, bath.

● **Shopping** There is a two-storey market, at its best in early morning but nevertheless good all day, and another good market on Sun mornings.

● **Buses** To Bogotá, 132 km, costs US$7, about 3½ hrs; bus to **Neiva**, US$3, 3½ hrs. To Fusagasugá, US$2.

South of Girardot the highway and the Río Magdalena continue to Neiva. Coffee and tobacco are grown on the slopes, and cattle are raised in the valley. 35 km S of Girardot is **Guamo** (*pop* 13,340). Just before Guamo is a marked turn off to **La Chamba**, where internationally famous pottery is made and sold. 8 km beyond Guamo is **Saldaña**, where there are irrigation works that have made 15,000 ha available for rice, sorghum, sesame and cotton.

A pretty spot is the reservoir located near **Prado**, Tolima, 25 km E of Saldaña; it is well signposted. There is a dirt road for the last 12 km past Purificación, where you cross the Magdalena. Buses can be caught in Bogotá, Ibagué and all intermediate towns. The pretty part of the lake is hidden from the end of the road and must be seen from a boat. Take an official boat trip from the mooring-point down the slope at the end of the road (food is available here). Swimming is good and the water is warm, but wading is not advisable because of the fresh-water stingray.

● **Accommodation** At Guamo: *Lemayá*, Cra 8 y C 9, T 270230, modern, swimming pool, best in region. At **Saldaña**: *Hotel Saldaña*, not too good. At **Prado**: cheap hotels; basic restaurants. At **the Lake**: government hotel, **B** in cabin, **D** in room, pleasant; free camping on shore.

37 km before Neiva you can turn left, cross a fence, and see the **Piedra Pintada de Aipe**, a stone not in fact painted but carved by precolumbian Indians with designs akin to the shapes of some of the pieces in the Museo del Oro at Bogotá.

About 50 km N of Neiva is a small area (300 sq km) of scrub and arid eroded red soil known as the **Tatacoa** desert, with large cacti, isolated mesas and unusual wildlife. Bus from Neiva to Villaviejo, near the Río Magdalena, and the Neiva-Bogotá highway at Aipe daily 1030, 1½ hrs, US$2. Contact Nelson Martínez Olaya, an official tourist guide at the *Restaurant La Tatacoa*, Villaviejo, Cra 4, No 7-32, for 4/5 hr walks through the desert. There is also a museum showing prehistoric finds in the area. You can cross the Magdalena by motorized canoe near Villaviejo for US$0.75.

NEIVA

The capital of Huila Department, **Neiva** (*pop* 248,000; *alt* 470m) was first founded in 1539, when Belalcázar came across the Cordillera Central from Popayán in quest of El Dorado. It was soon after destroyed by the Indians and refounded in 1612. It is now a pleasant, modern city on the E bank of the Río Magdalena.

Places of interest

There is an interesting monument to the struggles for independence by the riverside. There are rich coffee plantations around Neiva, for here the valley bottom is high enough to be in the coffee zone. The cathedral was destroyed by earthquake in 1967. There is a large and colourful market every day. Tourist information is given at the cultural centre with museum and gallery on the main square.

Excursions

To **Rivera**, a ½ hr drive S, with thermal springs and swimming pools to cool off, entrance US$1.25; also S to the Betania dam project with boat trips on the lake formed by the dam, from the village of Yaguará.

Local festivals

18 to 28 June, when the Bambuco Queen is elected: folklore, dances and feasting.

Local information
● **Accommodation**
B *Tumburagua*, C 5A, No 5-40, T 729165, rec; **B** *Sulicam*, Cra 3, No 5-51, T 713062, F 710159, restaurant; **B** *Anayaco*, C 8, No 3-26, T 713044, a/c, TV.

C *Hostería Matamundo*, in old *hacienda* 3 km from centre, on road to Garzón and San Agustín, T 727778, a/c, swimming pool, restaurant, disco.

D *Americano*, Cra 5, No 8-67, T 729240, clean, swimming pool; **D** *Plaza*, C 7, No 4-62, T 723980, swimming pool, fan, pleasant, restaurant, disco.

E *Central*, Cra 3 No 7-82, meals, near market, good value, rec; **F** *Residencias Astoria*, C 6, No 1-41, shared bath, clean, big rooms; **F** *Residencia Magdalena*, C 1A Sur, No 8A-57, T 733586, close to new bus station, restaurant.

● **Places to eat**
Hostería Los Cerros, C 11, No 32-39; *El Caimo*, C 8, No 7A-22; *Los Gauchos*, Cra 15, No 5-12; *Neiva Viejo*, C 9, No 6-49; *Heladería La Pampa*, Pasaje Camacho 8, excellent juices.

● **Tourist office**
Inderena, C 10, No 6-61, T 722580 (Sra María Cristina Sánchez).

● **Transport**
Air La Marguita, 1½ km from city. Aires, Intercontinental and Satena fly from **Bogotá** (Aires to Bogotá daily); to **Medellín**, 3 a week. Satena and Aires fly to **Leguizamo**, via Florencia 3 a week each. Taxi to bus terminal about US$0.85 (overcharging probable).

Bus New bus station out of town; bus from the centre leaves from the old terminal (Cra 2, Cs 5 y 6). To **Bogotá** (331 km, paved road), 5½ hrs,

US$10.50. Regular bus service with Autobuses Unidos del Sur, Cootranshuila (0600) and Coomotor to **San Agustín**, US$6, 5½ hrs (US$5.40 by colectivo). To **Garzón**, US$3.60; to **Pitalito**, US$5. To **La Plata**, for Tierradentro. To **Espinal**, 3 hrs, US$2.40, good road except for stretch between Aipe and Nataguima. To **Pasto**, US$10.75; to **Popayán**, US$9.25, ordinary bus at 0330, 1000, 1930, to **Florencia**, US$7.80. To Ibagué at 1200, US$7.

Warning At the bus stations, both off and on buses, in Neiva, Garzón and especially Pitalito, theft is rife.

South of Neiva lie the plains of Huila Department, arid, but still capable of supporting cattle, dominated by the snow-capped Nevado del Huila to the NW (see page 965).

The Central Cordillera: Medellín and Manizales

MEDELLÍN and Manizales are both busy, industrial centres yet, for all the commerce and coffee, the surrounding countryside is green, mountainous and pleasant. From the Cordillera Central to the Pacific stretches Chocó Department, thickly wooded, mountainous and undeveloped, but rewarding to explore.

The Central Cordillera lies W of the Río Magdalena. In it are two of the most important cities in Colombia: Medellín, the second largest city in the country, and Manizales. Medellín can be reached from Bogotá by road three ways: see **Main roads from Medellín**, below. Manizales can be reached from the capital by a road (309 km) passing through Facatativá and Honda; or through Girardot to Ibagué, then over the high crest of the Quindío pass via Armenia.

HISTORY AND SETTLEMENT

The town of Antioquia was founded in 1541, but the Spaniards, eager for gold, were not interested in the hinterland, which was then very sparsely inhabited by nomadic Indians who made very poor agricultural labourers. But during the 17th century a new wave of settlers came to Colombia from Spain; many of them were Jewish refugees who were deliberately seeking isolation, and found it in the little valley of the Río Aburrá, where they founded the city of Medellín in 1616. Rather than *conquistadores*, they were farmers with their families, intermarrying very little with either Indian or black. They divided the land into small farms which they worked themselves, living on the food they themselves produced. Their only exports were a little gold and silver from their streams.

In the early 19th century the settlement began to expand, particularly to the S. The settlers occupied all the cultivable land on the western side of the Central Cordillera and Manizales, 120 km S, was founded in 1848.

It was coffee, introduced in the Magdalena valley about 1865, that brought stability to this expansion. They were slow to adopt it, none being exported from Antioquia before the end of the century. The 1914-18 war suddenly gave a fillip to the industry: within 20 years the Departments of Antioquia and Caldas were producing half the coffee of Colombia, and they are by far the most important producers today. The industrialization of Medellín followed the coffee boom. There has been little immigration since the original settlement, but the natural growth in population has been extraordinary. Antioquia is considered by many to be the cultural heartland of Colombia. Its residents, referred to as Paisas, are renowned for their distinctive accent and customs.

MEDELLÍN

Medellín (*pop* 1.7mn; *alt* 1,487m; *phone code* 04), capital of Antioquia Department, could hardly be less advantageously placed, for it faces forbidding mountain barriers in nearly all directions. Its climate alone, that of an English summer day

(21°C), is in its favour, despite a certain amount of smog. Yet Medellín is one of the main industrial cities of Colombia, and seethes with energy. The first looms arrived in 1902. Today the city produces more than 80% of the textile output of the country, and textiles account for only half its industrial activity.

Places of interest

Excellent views from **Cerro Salvador** (statue on top), SE of the city, and from **Cerro Nutibara**, S of the city, where there are an outdoor stage for open air concerts, sculpture park, miniature village (known as Pueblito Paisa), souvenir shops and restaurants.

Medellín is a well-laid-out industrial city. There are four universities, together with other higher educational institutions. The old colonial buildings have nearly all disappeared, but there are still some 17th century churches left: the old Cathedral on Parque Berrío and the churches of **San Benito**, **La Veracruz**, and **San José**. The new **Cathedral of Villanueva** (Catedral Metropolitana), built between 1868 and 1931, one of the largest brick buildings in the world, is on Parque Bolívar, an attractive place with a statue of Bolívar. Three churches of the 18th century survive: **San Ignacio**, in Plaza San Ignacio, **San Juan de Dios**, and **San Antonio**. The city's commercial centre, **Villanueva**, is interesting for its blend of old and modern architecture, including many skyscrapers. There is a fine sculpture, **Monumento a la Vida**, next to the Edif Seguros Suramericana on C 50, where exhibitions of work by leading South American artists are held on the ground floor. Cattle auctions are held on Tues and Thur in specially built cattle yards on the outskirts.

Botanical and Zoological Gardens

Joaquín Antonio Uribe gardens, Cra 52, No 73-298, near the campus of the University of Antioquia, which include an orchid garden, are open daily, 0900-1730, US$0.50 entrance (some of the plants are named); there is a restaurant, pleasant but not cheap. The **Zoológico Santa Fe**, at

Medellín

0 | 250
metres

1. Parque Berrío
2. Parque Bolívar
3. Cerro Nutibara
4. Old Cathedral
5. Catedral Metropolitana
6. San Benito
7. La Veracruz
8. San José
9. San Ignacio
10. San Juan de Dios
11. San Antonio
12. Museo Etnográfico Miguel Angel Bulnes
13. Museo de Arte Moderno
14. Museo de Antioquia
15. Casa Museo Pedro Nel Gómez
16. Museo de Antropología at Universidad de Antioquia
17. Museo Filatélico
18. Botanical Gardens Joaquín Antonio Uribe
19. La Macarena bull ring
20. Turantioquia

To Cartagena

C 80
Car 64C
Cra 65
T 78

Río Medellín

Cra 51A
15
18

Parque Norte

Cra 52
Cra 49
To Bogotá

Cerro Volador

16
C 67
C 66

Cra 55
Cra 51
Cra 48

12
Cra 80

Universidad Nacional

Av Echeverri
20
C 58

Av Colombia
13
Cra 57
6

Cra 70
C 47
Cra 50
10

Av La Playa

C 49

Cra 65
Calle 44
19
11

To Airport, & Rionegro

Av Alfonso López
C 41

Av J E Gaitán
Cra 50
Av San Diego

Cra 65
Av Bolivariana
Calle 33
3
C 37

C 16

N

26

23

Hotels:
21. Amarú
22. Ambassador
23. El Balcón
24. Eupacla
25. Europa Normandie
26. Intercontinental
27. Nutibara
28. Veracruz

Cra 53
Cra 52
Cra 51D
Perú
Cra 50
Cra 49
Argentina
5
C 38

Av de Greif
21
22
28
2
Bolivia
Cra 57
C 56

24
27
25
Caracas
Maracaibo
Av Jorge Eliécer Gaitán
C 54
Cra 45
Cra 44

14
L 52
7
Boyacá
Cra 49
Cra 47
C 54

1
4
C 50
Av 1 de Mayo
Cra 46
C 53

17
Junín
Ayacucho
Pichincha
Maturín
C 48
Av Oriental
8
C 50
C 49

9

0 | 50
metres

To El Poblado & Envigado

To Cali

Centre

C 77 y Cra 68, is mainly of South American animals and birds (admission US$0.80). In the zoo grounds is the **Museo Santa Fe** (closed Mon and Tues), an extra US$0.20 to enter. Also visit **El Ranchito**, an orchid farm between the towns of Itagüí and La Estrella (entry US$0.50; April to June is the best time to visit).

Museums

Museo Etnográfico Miguel Angel Builes, Cra 81, No 52B-120, has an extensive collection of artefacts housed in a beautiful new building. The **Museo de la Madre Laura**, Cra 92, No 33B-21, has a good collection of indigenous costumes and crafts from Colombia, Ecuador and Guatemala. **Museo El Castillo**, C 9 Sur, No 32-260, formerly a landowner's home, has interesting objects and beautiful grounds; entry US$1.20; take bus to Loma de los Balsos, El Poblado (US$0.07), then walk 1 km up the hill until you see the road lined with pine trees to the right. Open 1300-1700, closed Sun. The **Museo de Antioquia**, Cra 53 y C 52, opp main post office, shows contemporary pictures and sculptures, including works by Fernando Botero, Colombia's leading contemporary artist (now living in USA), US$1 (guides free). **Museo de Arte Moderno**, Cra 64B, No 51-64, small collection, open Tues-Fri, 0900-1300, 1500-1800 (foreign films 2-3 a week). **Casa Museo Maestro Pedro Nel Gómez**, Cra 51B, No 85-24, T 233-2633, house of the contemporary painter and sculptor (closed during school holidays). **Museo Antropológico** at University of Antioquia, C 67, No 53-108 (new campus), also has exhibitions of modern art, free. **Museo Filatélico**, on 4th floor of Banco de la República building. Most museums are closed on Mon. **Biblioteca Pública Piloto para América Latina**, Cra 64, No 52-32, T 230-2382, art and photo exhibitions, authors reading their own work, foreign films.

Local festival

Flower fair (Feria de las Flores/Desfile de Silleteros) is held annually in the first week of Aug, with parades and music. The flowers are grown at Santa Elena in the Parque Ecológico de Piedras Blancas, 14 km from Medellín (bus from Plaza Las Flores).

Local information

● **Caution**

Travellers should take the same safety precautions as they would in any large city, particularly at night, but remember that Medellín has been the centre of narcotics, and anti-narcotics operations. It is, nevertheless, a friendly place.

● **Accommodation**

L2 *Intercontinental*, C 16, No 28-51, Variante Las Palmas, T 266-0680, the best, some distance from the centre, excellent; **L2** *Poblado Plaza*, Cra 43A, No 4 Sur, T 268-5555, F 268-6949, also excellent; **L3** *Nutibara* (casino and swimming pool), C 52A, No 50-46, T 231-9111, F 231-3713, best in centre; *Residencias Nutibara*, an annex facing hotel of same name, slightly cheaper with all the same facilities.

A2 *Amaru*, Cra 50A, No 53-45, T 511-2155, F 231-0321, central, quiet, good, expensive restaurant with excellent service; **A2** *Arod*, C 44, No 69-80, T 260-1427, small, secure, clean, friendly, 1½ km from centre; **A2** *El Balcón*, Cra 25, No 2-370, near *Intercontinental*, in Transversal Superior, T 268-2511, beautiful view of the city, good meals; **A2** *Ambassador*, Cra 50, No 54-50, T 511-5311, F 231-5312, in connection with **A2** *Veracruz*, Cra 50, No 54-18, T 511-5511, F 231-0542, with bath, swimming pool, very good, restaurant on 11th floor gives fine view over city.

B *Eupacla*, Cra 50, No 53-16, T 231-1765, central, helpful staff; **B** *Europa Normandie*, C 53, No 49-100, T 241-9920, restaurant, cafeteria, sauna, disco, central.

C *Horizonte*, Cra 47 No 49A-24, T 511-6188, good and popular restaurant.

D *Cannes*, Cra 50, No 56-17, T 242-7329, clean, well run; **D** *Linton*, Cra 45, No 47-74, with bath, very clean, TV, safe parking nearby US$0.50 per night, central.

E *Casa Blanca*, Cra 45, No 46-09, clean, small restaurant, safe but noisy; **E** *Mariscal*, Cra 45, No 46-49, T 251-5433, hot shower, good service, clean; **E** *Comercial*, C 48, No 53-94, friendly, clean, hot water available in some rooms, the best of which are on the top floor, doors barred to all but residents after 1800, good meals; **E** *Holiday*, Cra 45, No 50-25, T 231-2415, with bath, clean, safe for bicycles, 5 mins walk from centre; **E** *Residencias Doris*, Cra 45, No 46-23, family run, clean sheets every day, laundry facilities, locked night and day, good value, rec; **E** *Samaritana*, Cra 45, No 45-25, T 251-8011, clean and friendly, but noisy.

F *Gómez Córdoba*, Av Oriental between Cs 50 y 51, good value, renovated, safe, clean, central; **F** *Romania*, Av Echeverri, C 58, No 50-46, with bath, clean, a bit noisy. Many *residencias* on Cras 54 and 55, but this is not a safe area, take a taxi, especially after dark; a safer area for accommodation is around Cra 43.

● **Places to eat**
In El Poblado *Frutos del Mar*, Cra 43B, No 11-51, good seafood; *La Crèperie*, opposite (No 11-88), French; on Av Poblado (Av 43A): *Café Le Gris*, Centro Comercial Oviedo, No 65-15, good upmarket dishes; *Piemonte* (No 5A-170); *La Bella Epoca*, C 4 Sur, No 43A-9, very good and expensive, on road to Envigado, *Aguacatala*, Cra 43A, No 7 Sur-130 (an old country house with patio and wandering musical trio, *comida típica*, quiet surroundings), *La Posada de la Montaña*, Cra 43-B, No 16-22, good, Colombian food. *Asados La 80*, Cra 81, No 30-7, very good, large steaks. *Carbón*, Variante a las Palmas, Km 1, T 262-5425, good grills, good view over city, live music at weekends; *Frutas de mi Tierra*, also Variante a las Palmas, extraordinary fruit salads. Many vegetarian restaurants, eg *Govinda*, C 51 No 52-17; *Crepes y Waffles*, Cra 36, No 10-54, good. There are several round-the-clock cafés in the vicinity of Cra Junín between Maturín and Amador which serve cheap meals. *El Viejo Vapor*, Cra 43, No 53-19, café, bar, artist clientèle, good meeting place, set lunch US$3. Good local food at *Don Edoardo*, Cra 45, No 48-57, central, modest prices. Many good, cheap restaurants on Cra 49 (eg *La Estancia*, No 54-15). Excellent pastries at *Salón de Té Astor*, Cra 49, No 53-39.

● **Banks & money changers**
Banco Anglo Colombiano, C 50, No 51-06; 3 agencies; Banco Industrial de Colombia, in Poblada, cash against Mastercard, Amex, good rates for TCs and cash; and various other Colombian banks. Main hotels will cash TCs for residents when banks are closed, but at less favourable rates.

● **Embassies & consulates**
British, Cra 49, 46A, Sur-103, T 331-8625, F 331-0046, very helpful, take a taxi and phone for directions as it's hard to find. Danish, C 51, No 42-61, T 239-7696. German, C 52, No 47-28. Addresses of others in the phone book. **NB** The Venezuelan consul will not issue visas.

● **Entertainment**
Cinema Free foreign films daily at Universidad de Medellín or Universidad de Antioquia.

Discotheques: in central hotels, and in El Poblado. Many discos and popular dance halls on C 50, between Cras 65 and 75, and Cra 70, between Cs 36 and 44, also in Envigado, nr Plaza

Envigado. For a dark, underground and lively young place, try *Puf* or *Bar Tolomé* next to each other on autopista Palmas, Km 5. Couples only allowed in to many discos. *Bar Berlin 1930*, C 10, No 41-65, attractive, low level music, snooker table.

Music: monthly concerts by the Antioquia Symphony Orchestra. Band concerts and other entertainments in the Parque Bolívar every Sun. Universidad de Medellín theatre has monthly tango shows. Tango also at *Vos...Tango-Show*, C 34, No 66A-13, diagonal al Super Ley de Unicentro, T 265-9352, US$10.

● **Hospitals & medical services**
There is a clinic with free consultations and basic treatment in the airport buildings.

● **Post & telecommunications**
Post Office: main airmail office in Avianca building, Cra 52, No 51A-01, Mon-Sat, 0700-2200, has *poste restante*.

Telecommunications: Pasaje Junín and on corner of C 49 and Cra 50.

● **Shopping**
Poor selection of handicraft shops in the city, but there are *artesanía* shops on the top of Cerro Nutibara and there is a small handicrafts market at C 52 near Cra 46 with many hippy stalls. Mercado San Alejo, Parque Bolívar, open on the first Sat of every month except Jan, and before Christmas it is there Sat and Sun (handicrafts on sale at good prices). Good shopping generally around Parque Bolívar. Many of the textile mills have discount clothing departments attached where good bargains can be had; ask at your hotel. *Aluzia Correas y Cinturones*, Oviedo Shopping Center, Poblado, Unicentro Medellín, also in Bogotá, for an incredible selection of belts, US$15-40. *La Piel*, at C 53, No 49-131, has an excellent selection of leather goods at very reasonable prices. *Supermarket Exito* (Cra 66, No 49-01, C 10, No 43E-135, Poblado) is reasonable for cheap leather bags. There are several shopping centres.

Bookshop: *Librería Continental*, Cra 50 y C 52; *Librería Científica*, C 51, No 49-52, T 231-4974, large selection, some foreign books. *La Anticuaria*, C 49, No 47-46, T 511-4969, antique and secondhand books, inc in English, helpful.

Photography: for developing, *Almacenes Duperly* (several branches, eg C 52, No 46-28), good quality. Camera repairs: *Clínica de Cámaras*, Centro Coltejer, Local 120.

● **Sports**
Bullfights: at the bull-ring of La Macarena, C 44 and Cra 63, in Feb; cheapest US$14, usually fully booked.

● **Tour companies & travel agents**
Marco Polo, C 48, No 65-94, T 230-5944, very helpful, owner speaks some English. *Tierra Mar Aire* (American Express agents), C 52, No 43-124, T 513-0414, helpful. *Terra Nova*, C 5A, No 39-107, T 266-5000, who run an excursion by train to Cisneros, 3 hrs journey, with 3-4 hrs for a picnic and swim.

● **Tourist offices**
C 57 No 45-129, T 254-0800, in bus station (some English spoken, helpful), and in airport (will book hotel rooms), free maps, and Turantioquia, Cra 48, No 58-11, T 254-3864, good information on Antioquia and owns 5 good hotels in the Department. For a cheap tour of the city take any "Circular" bus, for US$0.15.
MMA: Cra 76, No 49-92, T 234-3661, Dr Francisco Giraldo Lotero.

● **Useful addresses**
DAS, T 341-5900, also at C 19, No 80A-40 in Belén la Nubia section, T 34-1451; **Tourist Police** at airport, T 287-2053; police T 112; general information T 113.

● **Transport**
Local Metro 2 lines: A from Niquía to Itagüí, B from San Javier to San Antonio, where they intersect, 1 stop NE of Parque Berrío, one journey US$0.30, two US$0.50. **Taxis**: they have meters, make sure they are used.

Air José María Córdoba, 28 km from Medellín by new highway, and 13 km from Rionegro; *Presto* restaurant, shops, Telecom, Fax service, no left luggage, but Turantioquia may oblige. Taxi to town US$14, colectivo US$3.60, *buseta* to centre, US$2.40, frequent service, about 1 hr journey, sit on right going to town (catch *buseta* or colectivo in small road behind *Hotel Nutibara* to go to airport). To Rionegro, bus US$0.20, taxi US$10.20. By air to **Bogotá**, 45 mins with Avianca (Cra 52, No 51A-23, T 511-3099), SAM, Aces, Satena or Intercontinental, several daily. Also to many other Colombian cities. There is also a small municipal airport, Olaya Herrera, non-jets only 10 mins by taxi with flights to Quibdó (3 flights daily, US$33), Bahía Solano etc.

Train For long-distance travel to Barrancabermeja (running 1996, US$6.60, 15 hrs), Bogotá and Santa Marta (neither running), check. For the tourist train from and to Cisneros, see above under Travel Agents.

Bus The terminal for long-distance buses going N is at Cra 64 (Autopista del Norte) y Transversal 78, about 3 km NW of the centre, with shops, cafeterias, left luggage (US$0.50 per day) and other facilities. Quite safe. Bus service to city centre, US$0.15, buses to station from C 50, marked: "Terminal de Transporte" via A Echeverría and Jorge Eliécer Gaitán. To/from

Bogotá, 9-12 hrs, US$15.50, every 40 mins or so, with 5 companies; to **La Dorada**, US$5.10. To **Caucasia**, US$8.50, 7 hrs. To **Cartagena**, Brasilia, 17-20 hrs, or 12 hrs, by Pullman bus, US$30 (take food with you, the stops tend to be at expensive restaurants); road paved throughout but poor. To **Barranquilla**, 16 hrs by Pullman. To **Sincelejo**, 9½ hrs. To **Turbo**, US$12 with Gómez (the best), 17 hrs.

A new bus terminal for buses going S was opened in June 1995, Terminal del Sur, Cra 65, C 10, alongside the Olaya Herrera airport. To **San Agustín**, Rápidos Tolima, 0600, US$21.50. Frequent buses for **Cali**, Flota Magdalena US$17, 10-12 hrs. Frequent buses to **Manizales**, 6 hrs (US$9 1st class, 5.40 2nd, by Empresa Arauca). To **Cartago**, 7 hrs, Flota Magdalena, US$9. To **Pereira**, 8 hrs, US$9.50 by Flota Occidental Pullman. To **Popayán**, US$19.50, 12 hrs, Flota Magadalena at 1400 and 1800. To **Ipiales**, US$36, 22 hrs, Expreso Bolivariano (takes Visa). To **Quibdó**, 11-13 hrs, US$13.

MAIN ROADS FROM MEDELLIN

SOUTHEAST TO BOGOTA

The new Medellín-Bogotá highway is totally paved, but between Medellín and Honda there are potholes, waterfalls and landslides in wet weather. See pages 933 for services between Puerto Boyacá and Honda. At **Guarne** is the Hipódromo Los Comuneros, with horse races on Sat and Sun, US$1, great atmosphere. At **Marinilla**, 46 km from Medellín, a road N goes to **El Peñol**, a precipitous, bullet-shaped rock which towers above the surrounding hills and the Embalse del Peñol reservoir. It has been eroded smooth, but a spiral staircase has been built into a crack from the base to the summit (entry US$1). At the summit is a snackbar with fine views (meals at holiday times only). There is bungee jumping here. Bus to the rock and to the pretty town of Guatapé with Cía Fco López, US$1.45; bus back to Medellín may have to be caught in the town of Peñol (colectivo from the rock).

The old road to Bogotá (478 km), via Rionegro, is paved to La Unión, from where it is unpaved for 207 km to La Dorada.

RIONEGRO

39 km SE of Medellín is the town of **Rione-**

gro, in a delightful valley of gardens and orchards. Here was born one of Bolívar's generals, José María Córdoba, the hero of the battle of Ayacucho. The **Casa de Convención** (where the 1863 Convention took place) is now an archive museum, entry US$0.20. The cathedral, with its gold and silver altar, deserves a visit. A museum of religious artefacts is behind the altar (entry US$0.20); it includes a virgin's robe with 300,000 pearls, not to be missed, and you can climb up behind the Virgin donated by Philip II to look down into the cathedral. There are processions in Easter Week. Many interesting pottery and ceramics factories in Rionegro area, hardly mechanized, as well as leather working; they welcome visitors and explain the processes. Prices of leather goods are high. 10 km from Rionegro (15 mins by colectivo, leave when full from plaza, US$0.60; buses every 2 hrs, US$0.20) is **Carmen de Viboral**, well-known for its pottery; there are several factories just N of the market place.

● **Accommodation** D Oasis, Cra 50, No 46-23, T 271 0531, with restaurant, bar, laundry, TV in rooms; E Dinastia, Cra 50, clean, good value; E Gutier, Cra 49, No 50-32, T 271-0106, central, with restaurant, nr market.

● **Places to eat** Good restaurant above the bakery in central plaza.

● **Transport** A day trip can cost US$15, but the Medellín-Rionegro rápido taxi service is very cheap. Bus to Rionegro, from Cra 42 y C40, US$1, one hr; bus back to Medellín from plaza every ½ hr. To El Peñol from Rionegro, take a colectivo to Marinilla from nr market, US$0.50.

Near Rionegro: on the road to El Retiro is **Fizebad**, an old estate house, restored with original furniture and artefacts, and a display of flowering orchids (entry US$2.50). Many roadside stalls sell typical Colombian snacks: clotted cream, strawberries, arequipe, fruits and juices. In **El Retiro** itself has a small colonial church and an even older chapel which is seldom open; ask for the caretaker. (To Fizebad by bus, catch a La Ceja or El Retiro bus.) The scenery is splendid and one can see typical Antioquian life.

The Bogotá road continues to **La Ceja**, 16 km from Rionegro; any of the surrounding hills affords an excellent view of the area. (Hotels; youth hostel at Centro Vacacional La Montaña, details from Alcom in Bogotá.) At **Sonsón**, 121 km from Medellín, the Casa de los Abuelos is an old house with many historical objects, including a printing press which produces a weekly newspaper (F Tahami, very good value, and Imperio).

ROADS NORTH

To Cartagena, 665 km: 6½ km N is **Bello** (pop 260,360), where a hut in which Marcos Fidel Suárez, president 1918-1922, was born, is covered in glass for its preservation. **Yarumal** (132 km; pop 23,515) is a friendly town in a cold mountain climate (fine views from Parroquia La Merced; many hosterías, eg E Residencias Horizontes, hot shower, welcoming). The road goes on to Caucasia.

To Turbo on the Gulf of Urabá, 383 km through Antioquia.

ANTIOQUIA

Santa Fé de **Antioquia** (to give it its full name, pop 11,000) lies just W of the Río Cauca; it was founded as a gold mining town by the Spaniards in 1541, the first in the area, and still retains its colonial atmosphere, with interesting Christmas/New Year fiestas. Until 1826 it was the capital of the Department. The fine old Cathedral is worth seeing, as is the church of Santa Bárbara. There are two small museums close to the church. There is an interesting wooden bridge, 300m long, 3 km downstream from the steel bridge which the buses use – ask for directions or take a taxi. It is 80 km from Medellín, the road giving a good idea of the beautiful countryside. Halfway between Medellín and Antioquia is **San Jerónimo** with several places to stay.

● **Accommodation** C Mariscal Robledo, Cra 58A, No 29-39, T 235-2250, swimming pool, good; D Hostería Real, 2 km from town, T 61048, full board, good food, pool; F Hostal del Viejo Conde, C Mocha 10-56, T 82-61091, friendly, good food; Del Río, also outside, San Pedro in resort area, or you can stay en famille with Marta Merizalde de Roldán, Cra 11, No 9-39, very friendly and informative, pretty garden. There is good food in the main square.

● **Buses** From Medellín US$1.80 (Flota Urbara or Transporte Sierra), 2½ hrs.

SOUTHWEST

The towns of Fredonia, Jericó, Jardín and Venecia are all in the coffee-growing district and are worth a visit. All have basic inns. The scenery is beautiful.

To Quibdó This road, via Amagá, goes through coffee, tobacco and pineapple plantations. About half way along is **Bolívar**, in the centre of this coffee region where the evening's entertainment is to watch the local horsemen and women showing off their riding skills around the plaza. **E** *Residencias Bahía*, the best available; *Grillo's* restaurant nearby, good.

SOUTH TO MANIZALES

At **Envigado**, 10 km S of Medellín, craftsmen have for generations turned out the traditional *antioqueño* pouch called *carriel*, carried by the men. Now used for money, its original use was for coffee samples. Envigado is the site of the "maximum security prison" which failed to hold Pablo Escobar.

There are two routes to Manizales, either providing an alternative route to Bogotá. 57 km S of Medellín on the main road is **Santa Bárbara** (*alt* 1,857m), on a green hill top, providing stunning views in every direction of coffee, banana and sugar plantations, orange-tiled roofs and folds of hills. (**F** *Hotel Palomares*, on main plaza, clean, good; restaurants and cafés on main plaza, as is the large church; bus to Medellín, US$1.20.) A further 26 km is **La Pintada** (camping; hotels **D** *Mi Rey*, T 274008, OK; **G** *Residencia Cosina*, basic, clean, fan, mosquitos, restaurant). Here the road crosses the Río Cauca, then splits. To the left an unpaved road runs through Aguadas, Pácora and **Salamina** (**F** *Res Puerto Nuevo*, opp bus office, clean, good meals), all perched on mountain ridges. At Aranzazu, paving begins for the 51 remaining km to Manizales. A longer route, all paved, goes through **Supia**, a pleasant town 140 km S of Medellín (**F** *Hotel Mis Ninietas*, nr plaza, unsigned, with bath, clean). 13 km further is **Riosucio**, another delightful town with fine

views and a large colonial church (many restaurants, bars and shops). At Anserma the road turns E to Manizales via Arauca.

Manizales (*pop* 378,890; *alt* 2,153m; *phone code* 068) is dominated by its enormous (still unfinished) concrete Cathedral and the Nevado del Ruiz volcano, which erupted so catastrophically in Nov 1985.

The city rides its mountain saddle uncompromisingly, the houses falling away sharply from the centre of the city into the adjacent valleys. The climate is extremely humid (average temperature is 17°C, and the annual rainfall is 3,560 mm), encouraging prodigious growth in the flowers that line the highways to the suburbs N and S. Frequently the city is covered in cloud. The best months of the year are from mid-Dec through to early March. The city looks down on the small town of Villa María, "the village of flowers", now almost a suburb.

Places of interest

Several earthquakes and fires have destroyed parts of the city over the years, so the architecture is predominantly modern with high-rise office and apartment blocks. Traditional architectural styles are still seen in the suburbs and the older sections of the city. The departmental government building, the Gobernación, opposite the Cathedral in the Parque Bolívar, is an imposing example of neo-colonial architecture; the bull-ring built 25 years ago is an impressive copy of the traditional Moorish style. Chipre, a recreational park, provides a good view of the city (well-visited on Sun); El Tanque, near Chipre, is another vantage point.

Museums

Banco de la República, Cra 23, No 23-06, gold and anthropology museum open during banking hours, classical music every afternoon in the Bank. **Universidad de Caldas**, natural history museum with good selection of butterflies, moths and birds; open every day from 0800 to 1200 and 1400 to 1800 (take a "Fátima" bus to the University). **La Galería del Arte**, Av

Santander at C 55, exhibitions of work by local artists, pictures can be bought.

Excursion

The small Department of Caldas, of which Manizales is capital, until 1965 contained what are now the Departments of Quindío and Risaralda. The old Department, now known as Viejo Caldas, produces about 30% of all Colombian coffee and picturesque coffee farms abound. To see the full process of coffee growing, apply to the Comité Departmental de Cafeteros de Caldas, Cra 22, No 18-21, T 41706; rec. You can arrange to stay in a coffee finca with full board for 2 for about US$50/day.

Local festival

Early in Jan the Fair and Coffee Festival is held, with bullfights, beauty parades and folk dancing.

Local information
● **Accommodation**

NB In Jan, during the fiesta, hotel prices are grossly inflated. **A2** *El Carretero*, C 36, No 22-22, T 840225, good but slow restaurant, business clientele, comfortable; **A2** *Las Colinas*, Cra 22, No 20-20, T 842009, three-star, two bars, good restaurant, very comfortable.

C *Villa Kempis*, Cra 23, No 19-22, T 830187, on road to Pereira, about 2 km past bull-ring, old religious retreat house, beautiful view over the valley, very quiet, hot water am only, restaurant and bar, good food at moderate prices.

D *Europa*, Av Centenario, No 25-98, T 822253, near the bull-ring, restaurant for breakfast only, comfortable and clean; **D** *Rokasol*, C 21, No 19-16, T 823307, near bus station so noisy, hot water, clean, with bath, good restaurant.

E *Tamá Internacional*, C 23, No 22-43, T 832594, next to Cathedral, with bath, meals, clean and cheap, but noisy.

F *Consol No 4*, Cra 20, No 21-10, clean, friendly, large rooms; **F** *Residencias Avenida No 2*, C 21, No 20-07, T 835251, E with bath, clean, safe; **F** *Residencias Avenida No 3*, C 19, No 16-35, T 844130, opp bus terminal, bath, clean, quiet, safe, friendly, rec (next door is **E** *California*, No 16-37, T 824217, modern, clean); **F** *Residencias Caldas*, Cra 19, No 22-45, near bus station, US$1 surcharge on holidays, hot water, quiet, but not too clean; **F** *Residencias Margarita*, C 17 between Cras 22 and 23, quiet, good, safe, private parking opposite US$0.75 per night; **F** *Residencias Nueva York*, C 20, No 20-17, extremely clean, hot water,

clothes-washing facilities, some bar noise in front but rec; several **F** range hotels around C 18, Cra 22-23; **F** *Marana*, C 18, No 17-34, T 843872, 1 min from bus station, bath, hot water only am, clean, friendly.

● **Places to eat**

Las Redes, Cra 23, No 75-97, predominantly sea food, good but pricey; *Las Brasas*, Cra 23, No 75A-65, good grill and *comida típica*; *Fonda Paisa*, Cra 23, No 72-130, nice local dishes with local Andean music; *Casa Kena*, Cra 23, No 72-49, good Italian, fresh pasta daily, Caruso recordings; *La Suiza*, Cra 23, No 26-57, good fruit juices and cakes; unnamed restaurant with pink façade on Cra 23 nr C 31, economical, huge portions, highly rec; *Caballo Loco*, Cra 61, No 23-07, good; another with the same name at C 21, No 23-40 is mainly a bar but serves expensive pizzas; *El Ruiz*, Cra 19, No 22-25, filling 3-course meal.

● **Banks & money changers**

Banco Anglo Colombiano, Cra 22, No 17-04, and other banks. Exchange not possible Sat and Sun.

● **Entertainment**

Theatre: Teatro de los Fundadores is a modern cinema-theatre auditorium. Interesting wood-carved mural by local artist, Fernando Botero, who also has murals in the entrance hall of the Club Manizales and Hotel Las Colinas. Events held here and at other locations during Theatre Festival in first two weeks of Sept. Free films at the Universidad de Caldar on Wed at 1700. Good way to meet students.

● **Tourist offices**

Parque Bolívar, opp Cathedral, good, helpful.

DAS Office: Cra 23 y C 24.

● **Transport**

Air Manizales has a small airport, La Nubia; Aces flies to Bogotá (also Avianca), Medellín, and Cali.

Bus New terminal with good restaurant, C 19 between Cras 15 and 17. Buses to **Medellín**: Autolegal via Neira and Aguadas, 6 hrs, US$5.40; Empresa Arauca via Anserma, 10 hrs, 1st class US$8, ordinary US$5.40; colectivo to Medellín, US$10.25. Bus to **Bogotá**, Expreso Bolivariano Pullman, US$12, 9 hrs; 7 1/2 hrs by Flota El Ruiz *buseta*, US$13.50. To **Honda**, US$3.60 (Expreso Bolivariano). **Cali** by bus Expreso Palmira, 7 hrs, US$10 ordinary; Pullman 6 hrs, US$12. To **Cartago**, 4 hrs, every 20 mins, US$1.50; **Pereira**, Expreso Palmira, Expreso Trejos, half-hourly, 1 1/2 hrs, excellent road, beautiful scenery, US$1.80 ordinary. **Armenia**, Expreso Palmira, 3 hrs, US$2.40. To **Quibdó**, Transportes Arauca, via Pereira, La Virginia, Pueblo Rico and Tadó, Mon, Wed, Fri, Sat 0600, 14-17 hrs, US$14.

Roads To Medellín, see above. Manizales-Honda-Bogotá: all paved but in poor condition. The road climbs to 3,000m, with most superb scenery and little traffic. First accommodation is in Padua, then Fresno (cheap hotels), Mariquita and Honda (see page 24).

LOS NEVADOS

Parque Nacional Los Nevados: The park comprises 38,000 ha and straddles the departments of Caldas, Quindío, Risaralda, and Tolima. You must check in advance if entry to the park is permitted. For information in Manizales contact MMA, C 20A, No 21-45, 2nd floor, T 848457 (not too helpful); or the tourist office, which organizes day trips to Nevado del Ruiz at weekends (expensive; a rec guide is Javier Echeverría, T Manizales 857239). See under Pereira, page 951, for access from that city and under Ibagué, page 935, for **Nevado de Tolima**. For those planning an independent visit to Nevado del Ruiz (5,399m) with a vehicle, either take the Bogotá road from Manizales, then a branch road to a viewpoint (22 km). La Esperanza is the point to leave the main road for excursions towards the volcano. An alternative route follows the road to Villa María for 6 km, turning left to Barrio La Enea and continuing on an unpaved road for 22 km to Termales del Ruiz at 3,500m (**B** *Hotel Termales del Ruiz*, comfortable, with restaurant and thermal pools on premises). Five km further on, this road meets the road coming from La Esperanza. Turning right, and continuing 2 km brings you to Las Brisas (**D** *Hotel Restaurant Brisas del Cumanday*, very cold, best to have your own sleeping bag, basic, but beautiful surroundings and the only accommodation near the park entrance).

Past Las Brisas the road forks. To the left it continues over enormous landslides caused by the 1985 Nevado del Ruiz eruption to the village of Ventanas (a very scenic drive) and on to Murillo in the department of Tolima. To the right it climbs steeply for 1 km to reach the park entrance and visitors center at 4,050m. 5 km from the entrance is a new chalet at 4,400m run by Carlos Alberto, D, food, hot showers, friendly. The turnoff (left) to Nevado del Ruiz is 10 km beyond the park entrance and one can drive to within 2 km of the snow line (if the road is open). On foot from 4,050m to the summit takes 11 hrs. Near the foundations of a large shelter (destroyed by fire before the eruption), there is a basic hut, no water, no beds nor any facilities, ask at the entrance if it is open. A guide is recommended if you wish to climb to the crater. Another excellent climb nearby is La Olleta (4,850m), the ash cone of an extinct volcano. You can descend into the crater, but note your route well as fog can obliterate landmarks very quickly. The principal road continues (S) below the Nevados del Cisne and de Santa Isabel between which you can visit the Laguna Verde. You can stay at the *Refugio El Cisne*, a small farm at 4,200m, where a farmer lives with his family. He lets you sleep in his warehouse (very cold, but less so than outside) for US$2.50 and offers you milk and coffee. His son will guide you to Laguna Verde. 20 km further along the road and 39 km beyond the turnoff to Nevado del Ruiz is Laguna del Otún at the southern end of the park, trout fishing and camping with permission of MMA.

If you do not have a car, it is still possible to reach Las Brisas and the park entrance with a milk truck that leaves the Celema dairy in Manizales, Cra 22, No 71-97, between 0600 and 0700 daily, returning in the early afternoon, or the Rápido Tolima bus at 1430 from the Terminal in Manizales to Murillo goes through Las Brisas, US$2.50, 2 hrs. One can also walk from Las Brisas down to Manizales in a day, stopping along the way at the Termales del Ruiz, ask about short cuts.

Visitors to the park should come prepared for cold damp weather, and remember to give themselves time to acclimatize to the altitude. Maps of the area are available at the Instituto Geográfico in Manizales, just behind the Club Manizales on Carrera 24.

CHOCO

Stretching like a ribbon between the Cordillera Occidental and the Pacific Coast, from Panama to Valle del Cauca, Chocó is one of Colombia's least developed and